THE CANADIAN ENCYCLOPEDIA

SECOND EDITION

VOLUME I
A – Edu

Hurtig Publishers
Edmonton

Hurtig Publishers Ltd.
10560 – 105 Street
Edmonton, Alberta
Canada T5H 2W7

Every attempt has been made to identify and credit sources for
photographs. The publisher would appreciate receiving
information as to any inaccuracies in the credits for
subsequent editions.

Canadian Cataloguing in Publication Data

Main entry under title:
The Canadian Encyclopedia

Editor in Chief: James H. Marsh.

ISBN 0-88830-326-2 (set) –ISBN 0-88830-327-0
(v. 1). –ISBN 0-88830-328-9 (v. 2). –ISBN
0-88830-329-7 (v. 3). –ISBN 0-88830-330-0 (v.4)

1. Canada–Dictionaries and encyclopedias.
I. Marsh, James H.
FCwe.C36 1985   971'.003'21   C84-091250-1
F1006.C36 1985

Designed, typeset and manufactured
in Canada

SPECIAL ACKNOWLEDGEMENT

Publication of *The Canadian Encyclopedia* would not
have been possible without the generosity and
foresight of the Government of Alberta

To commemorate the 75th anniversary of Alberta's
entry into Confederation, the Province donated
four million dollars towards the research and
development of the first edition of this comprehensive reference
work on modern Canada and its people. The
generous assistance financed five years of
intensive research, writing, editing and verification.
It was the Alberta Government's faith in the project
that made possible this vivid new portrait
of our country.

Special thanks are due to the Honourable
Peter Lougheed, former Premier of Alberta, the Honourable
Mary LeMessurier, the Honourable Horst Schmid
and the Honourable Robert Dowling, for their
enthusiastic support.

Hurtig Publishers
gratefully acknowledges
a major gift from

NOVA Corporation of Alberta

whose financial support made possible the
acquisition of the cartography, artwork and illustrations
which appear throughout these volumes.
Without NOVA's generous assistance
the inclusion of so many colour illustrations and maps
in *The Canadian Encyclopedia* would not have been possible.

Hurtig Publishers
gratefully acknowledges the generous
support and co-operation of

THE UNIVERSITY OF ALBERTA

faculty and staff, whose enthusiastic assistance and
encouragement have continued to play an indispensable support role
in the preparation of *The Canadian Encyclopedia*.
The co-operation provided by the university
community continues to exceed anything the publisher could
reasonably expect and is a reflection of the
University of Alberta's commitment to research,
scholarship and education.

FOREWORD TO THE SECOND EDITION

The great success of the first edition of *The Canadian Encyclopedia* has made this substantially expanded, updated, second edition possible. The response from Canadians to the 1985 edition was remarkable. If we had any doubts about the need for a reliable, comprehensive, readily accessible reference source about Canada, these doubts quickly vanished when the reviews appeared and the first edition virtually sold out in less than 3 months.

I would like to pay tribute again to some of the key people who were responsible for the evolution of the encyclopedia from a decade-long dream to a reality. All of the following made truly vital contributions: Frank McGuire, Harry Gunning, Bob Blair, Dianne Hall, Peter Lougheed, Mary LeMessurier, John S. O'Neill, Myer Horowitz, John Patrick Gillese, David Shaw, Sharon Burton, Jan Steckly, Barry Hicks and Peter Freeman. It would take many pages to simply list the names of all the key individuals who worked together for years to bring *The Canadian Encyclopedia* to publication. Some 5000 Canadians from the 10 provinces and the territories were involved over the 5-year period from the first editorial work to the final packaging and shipping of the first edition. The University of Alberta, from the beginning, has played a very significant role. The administration, academic staff and many others at the U of A have continually provided excellent support, cooperation, enthusiasm and encouragement.

The second edition has been 4 years in the making. Special thanks are due the Government of Alberta, Nova Corporation of Alberta, the Canada Council, the Department of Communications, the Canadian Studies Program of the Secretary of State, the Medical Research Council of Canada, the Social Sciences and Humanities Research Council of Canada and the National Sciences and Engineering Research Council of Canada for valuable financial assistance to help support the research and editorial preparation, and the Bank of Montreal for providing the loan financing for the actual publication.

It is difficult to adequately describe and sufficiently praise the splendid efforts of our Editor in Chief, James Marsh. This encyclopedia is a lasting tribute to his abilities. The high editorial quality of the first edition was frequently praised by reviewers and this accomplishment was achieved in spite of enormous complexities and numerous unforeseen difficulties.

Special thanks for their efforts in relation to this second edition are due Tim Porteous, Kevin Hanson, Bob Young, David Durnan, Ian Cameron, Georgina Garner, Ronalds Printing, and particularly the encyclopedia staff: Sheila Birmingham, David Evans, Nancy Brown Foulds, Micaela Gates, Robyn Ross and Carol Woo and the many researchers who worked so hard to improve the encyclopedia and bring it up to date.

There will be no new edition of *The Canadian Encyclopedia* until 1992 at the earliest. We are now investigating the possibility of publishing an updated supplementary volume yearly or biennially. It is virtually certain that sometime in the 1990s the encyclopedia will be available via electronic means as well, perhaps with immediate updates, via your television set, home, school or office computer, telephone lines or on optical discs.

As I said in the Foreword to the first edition, our intent from the very beginning was to produce a first-class Canadian encyclopedia that would go on sale to the public at a low price so that Canadian families could afford to purchase the set for their own homes. From the thousands of generous letters we have received from across Canada it is clear that we achieved that goal and fulfilled our aspiration that Canada's new national encyclopedia would make an important contribution to our understanding of one another and to our pride in our country. For many years there has been discussion and debate about the so-called "Canadian identity." There is indeed a clearly definable "Canadian identity" and it is readily described in the pages of these 4 volumes.

Mel Hurtig

Mel Hurtig
Publisher
Edmonton, Jan 1988

PREFACE TO THE SECOND EDITION

An encyclopedia must undergo revision if it is to remain current and if it is to hold its place as a reference point amid the rapid proliferation of knowledge. The second edition of *The Canadian Encyclopedia* is more than an "update." It is a continuation of the 5 years of intense activity that produced the first edition and reflects the many helpful comments that we have received since publication. We have taken the opportunity to increase the encyclopedia's coverage, its visual appeal, its accuracy and consistency, and its stylistic uniformity. In order to provide quicker access to information we have greatly expanded the index and have added more tables, cross-references and chronological guides. We have, naturally, taken account of recent events, but we have tried to maintain perspective on what is of lasting interest and significance. We were fortunate in having many of the results of the 1986 census and have incorporated them wherever possible, keeping in mind that statistics are only useful in context or in comparison. The present edition has been paged electronically, which allowed us to make changes right up to press time. Nevertheless, these volumes will go to press at least 6 months before they are distributed. They obviously cannot be as "up to date" as a daily newspaper; the value of a reference work is not in such currency. We have added over 500 new photographs, numerous new graphs and maps and 50 new pieces of original artwork.

Since the publication of the first edition, we have received thousands of helpful suggestions from readers all across Canada. Canadians not only know more about their country than is commonly acknowledged but also care greatly about the accuracy and fairness with which it is presented. We have added over 1700 new entries, making the list of articles more comprehensive, more regionally balanced, more interesting and more representative of men and women who have made important contributions. Nevertheless, we have guarded the objectivity and careful judgement on which the first edition was based and on which we hope to build a lasting acceptance.

We have researched thousands of questions raised by readers, and have made changes where appropriate. We have added words, phrases and paragraphs to clarify or to enrich with pertinent detail. We commissioned special reports from subject experts, read the text critically and sought help in verification from town clerks, company officials, government departments, librarians, sports organizations, university administrations and many others. Most of the authors were asked to reread their entries and provide us with updates and additional information.

Surveying the events of the past 3 years with a view to updating the encyclopedia has emphasized to us the dramatic changes that are taking place in our time. We have experienced major electoral upheavals and economic reversals. Political, sports, business and artistic careers have ended or begun. One of the longest-governing regimes of any Western nation fell as the Conservatives lost power in Ontario. A seeming Liberal hegemony at the federal level was broken as we went to press with the first edition. The Constitution, which was patriated in 1982, has undergone profound change as a result of the Meech Lake Accord, and court challenges based on the Canadian Charter of Rights and Freedoms are radically altering the nature of our political culture. We sadly noted the deaths of such outstanding Canadians as E.L.M. Burns, Tommy Douglas, Claude Jutra, Margaret Laurence, Walter Gordon, Jacques Ferron, René Lévesque and Davidson Dunton. Another Canadian received the Nobel Prize and others were rumoured to be in the running as more Canadians gained world recognition. Important issues, such as free trade and tax reform, entered public debate. Mayor Jean Drapeau resigned, and Ben Johnson became the fastest man in the world.

For those of us who were involved in the intense pressures of delivering the first edition, the second edition has allowed us perspective to recognize what a grand co-operative venture the encyclopedia has been. We relied heavily on other large projects, such as the Dictionary of Canadian Biography and the Encyclopedia of Music in Canada, not only for their research, which was invaluable, but also for their expert advice, always generously given. We have continued to receive help and co-operation from the university community, particularly at the University of Alberta, and from many government departments and agencies, including Energy, Mines and Resources for maps and satellite images; the Directorate of History of the Department of National Defence; the Directorate of History of the Department of External Affairs; the Department of Communications; the Canada Council; Transport Canada; provincial archives across Canada; and many others. We are especially grateful to Statistics Canada, where Linda Wiebe, Lynn Brochu and others provided us with expert help. Joy Houston, Jim Burant and their staff at the National Archives of Canada have continued to help us mine their priceless store of images. No publishing project is more demanding on the production process than an encyclopedia, not only in sheer volume but also in the constant revision of proofs and pressure of time. We have benefited greatly from the commitment of all those who have helped produce these 4 volumes, particularly the staff of Printing Services, U of A. We have also enjoyed the consistent support of the library community. We benefited from the production of the French edition, under the direction of Louise Loiselle, in presenting a more complete representation of Québec. Above all, we wish to express our gratitude to the contributors who responded generously to innumerable queries raised about their entries; the encyclopedia remains their work and its standards are a tribute to their care.

A number of consultants and readers were closely associated with the staff in preparing the second edition, among whom special mention must be made of Carlotta Lemieux, whose scrupulous reading led to many improvements. Among those who acted as consultants or readers on particular subjects for the second edition are the following: Irving Abella, Anna Altmann, Alan Artibise, Michael Asch, Desmond H. Brown, Robert Fraser, Gerry Gall, David Goa, Piers Handling, Norman Hillmer, Roger C. Hutchinson, Susan Jackel, J.A. Kraulis, Daniel Latouche, Robert F. Legget, Paul-André Linteau, Martin Lynch, U.F. Matthews, Eric L. Mills, W.R. Morrison, Arthur Porter, Donald Phillipson, Alan Rayburn, Joan Powers Rickerd, Patricia Roy, N.W. Rutter, Pierre Savard, Stephen Scobie, Alan Seager, Michel Thériault, Dixon Thompson, Norman Ward and Bruce Wilkinson. Finally, special recognition must be made of the accomplishment of the staff of the first edition, particularly the senior editors, Adriana Davies, Patricia Finlay, Mary McDougall Maude, James Ogilvy and Rosemary Shipton; for this is a continuation of the work that they began.

James H. Marsh
Editor in Chief
Edmonton, Jan 1988

INTRODUCTION TO THE FIRST EDITION

The production of an encyclopedia is an undertaking with a long and noble tradition stretching back to ancient Greece. Though the grand "circle of knowledge," from which the word *encyclopedia* is derived, has expanded beyond the scope of any single enterprise, the attempt to draw together the overwhelming accumulation of human knowledge remains a worthy goal that tempts each generation. *The Canadian Encyclopedia* differs greatly from the last encyclopedic work of Canada, published a generation ago. It portrays a country more mature in its literature and arts, more aware of its regional and ethnic diversity, more sophisticated in its politics and foreign policy, and yet still a nation in the making, searching for new solutions to its economic, social and linguistic problems and still struggling to realize the potential of a land of unimaginable size, variety and resources. The entries in *The Canadian Encyclopedia* provide an intricate sketch of Canada, drawn by its finest scholars and writers, that will provide not only an invaluable reference tool and repository for information but also a portrait of its time that will continue to be interpreted by future generations.

The development of a list of articles is the central act in the planning of an encyclopedia. The editors sought to provide coverage of all aspects of life in Canada, of all regions, over a vast time scale from the geological formation of the ancient rocks of the Shield to the most recent political events. Because there exists no cohesive framework that would easily encompass all provinces of knowledge, the process of identifying topics and assigning them weight in relation to the boundless variety of other subjects was one of constant revision. The master article list continued to grow as the editors received reports from the project's consultants and advisers, as new topics were uncovered in the course of editing and as events changed Canada over the 4 years of the editorial process. The lists included all major subjects that a reader would expect to find in a Canadian encyclopedia, such as populated places, the provinces and territories, leading cultural and political figures, political themes such as federalism, Canada's flora and fauna, its ethnic groups and its artistic endeavours. The final list of over 8000 entries also includes numerous topics of particular Canadian character, such as the voyageur, birchbark canoe, ice hockey, Northwest Coast Indian art and Inuit sculpture, as well as many unusual subjects that illuminate lesser-known aspects of Canada, such as ice worms, duels, birchbark biting, cemeteries, La Corriveau and Zouaves. Entries on a representative sample of Canadian literary works, such as *The Apprenticeship of Duddy Kravitz* and *Kamouraska,* are provided in the hope that they will introduce readers to good Canadian books. Some 3500 biographies were chosen to provide information on people from all periods, regions and subject areas, while emphasizing those who, including contemporary Canadians, have made lasting contributions to (or impressions on) Canadian society. Based on advice from consultants, criteria for inclusion varied according to what was appropriate to the area under consideration. For instance, in the case of contemporary painters, limited space required that an age criterion be imposed. In all areas the biographies are representative of a far greater number worthy of inclusion. Emphasis has been placed on including innovators, creators, pathbreakers and discoverers. An effort has been made to include the results of current research, for example, in native and women's studies. In all subject areas, contributors were asked to stress the Canadian aspect of their subject. In discussing topics in the sciences and social sciences, some background information was required to provide a context for Canadian research and accomplishment, but limitations of space prevented extensive treatment of material more appropriate to general reference works or textbooks.

The editors decided early in the planning that the encyclopedia would be written by specialists who were best able to explain their subjects and who could impart to the encyclopedia a feeling of commitment to each topic. This approach places great demands on editors to mold the writing of thousands of contributors into a coherent reference work, but it rewards the reader with expert writing, a broad scope and some sparks of individuality. We were very fortunate in attracting some 2500 authorities from all major Canadian universities, federal and provincial public services, scientific institutions, museums, galleries, newspapers, magazines and private industry, as well as numerous free lances. Many of these contributors did original research on subjects as diverse as snowshoeing and Sikhism. Many entries, such as those on theatre, sculpture, printmaking, the printing industry, philosophy and cartography, are the first reliable syntheses of their subject in Canada.

All articles were evaluated by consultants and expert readers to ensure that controversial issues were treated fairly, that interpretations were based on sound research and that different views of important questions had been explained. The signed entries of the encyclopedia reflect the diversity of the people who have created it. The readers, editors and researchers endeavoured to check every statement for accuracy, to ensure reasonable conformity to the compact style of a reference work, and to make every entry as readable and as current as possible.

The humanist and scholar Dr. Samuel Johnson wrote, in reference to his great dictionary, that "the world is little solicitous to know whence proceeded the faults of that which it condemns." An encyclopedia is a difficult undertaking because of its magnitude and because expectations are so great that it will fulfil so many contrasting demands. *The Canadian Encyclopedia* is delivered in the spirit in which it has been created by its staff, contributors, advisers, consultants, cartographers, photographers, artists, and technical staff, who have sought to bring to Canadians a deeper knowledge about themselves and their diverse country. I express our gratitude to the many Canadians from every part of Canada who have generously given us their time and their support for a project they believed to be of great importance to our nation. My final acknowledgement is to Mel Hurtig, who set us all on the greatest enterprise of our lives. He believed that all Canadians would be drawn together in this national project, and his faith in Canada is reflected in these pages.

James H. Marsh
Editor in Chief
Edmonton, Sept 1985

USING THE ENCYCLOPEDIA

Organization The content of the encyclopedia has been organized in entries which are listed alphabetically. The entry titles, which appear in boldface type (eg, **Humorous Writing in English**), have been chosen to aid the reader in the search for information on particular subjects. This system has the advantage of providing quick access to information and a convenient means of dealing with topics that students or general readers might encounter in their daily readings. Such an arrangement tends to scatter information throughout the alphabet, but through cross-references the editors have tried to maintain the connections between entries and to lead the reader quickly to related articles, as from the biography of J.S. Woodsworth to entries on Social Gospel, Co-operative Commonwealth Federation, etc. Readers should look first among the article titles for the topic they seek, and, if there is not a separate entry, then among the 140 000 subjects listed in the Index at the end of Volume IV. The cross-references within the entries themselves (marked in small capitals, eg, IRON ORE) are provided when they might lead to greater understanding of the main subject of the entry and are not always exactly in the form of the article to which they refer; for example, "Department of EXTERNAL AFFAIRS leads the reader to the article **External Affairs, Department of**, and the cross-references AGRICULTURE or NATIVE PEOPLE may lead to several entries which begin with that title.

The major subject areas have generally been broken down into several types of entries to meet the varying needs of the reader. For example, the field of architecture is dealt with in the overview article with the same title, in an entry describing the profession (**Architectural Practice**), in a historical essay (**Architectural Development**) and in a series of articles on types of architecture (**Government Building** or **Religious Building**), styles, issues (**Heritage Conservation**) and specific buildings (**Massey College**); in addition, biographies of important architects (**Erickson, Arthur**) are presented. The entries have been designed to present basic facts, to explain central concepts and, space permitting, to describe their subjects in greater detail. Through this organization and this variety of approaches the editors hope to have satisfied the different demands that are placed on an encyclopedia.

Alphabetical Arrangement The entries of the encyclopedia have been alphabetized using the "word-by-word system," in which headings are arranged according to the letters of the first word. Second and subsequent words are used for determining the order of the entries only when two or more headings begin with the same word. Hence, entries beginning with a short word appear before entries with the same short word forming the opening letters of a longer word; for example, **Ice Cap** appears before **Icebreakers**, and **Forteau** and **Fortification** follow **Fort Smith**, **Fort Steele** and **Fort Walsh**. For the sake of convenience, all the names beginning with "Mac" and "Mc" have been sorted as though they were spelled "Mac"; and those beginning with "Saint," "Sainte," "St" or "Ste" as though they were spelled "Saint." Numbers are listed as if they were spelled out; for example, **4-H Clubs** is listed as if it were "Four-H Clubs."

Personal Names In the interest of convenience it was decided to enter biographies under the name by which a person is commonly known. Thus, in the case of French compound names or titles, a biography will be found under the name a person used; for example, Louis de Buade, Comte de Frontenac, is placed under **Frontenac**; René-Robert Cavelier de La Salle, under **La Salle**. However, Guy Carleton, First Baron Dorchester, is found under **Carleton** and John Buchan, First Baron Tweedsmuir, under **Buchan**, since that is how they are best known to posterity. Writers are placed under their own name rather than their pen name; for example, Ralph Connor is listed under **Gordon, Charles William**. Indians of the historical period have been entered under their English name, for example, **Poundmaker**. Nuns are generally found under their name in religion, for example, **Marie de l'Incarnation**. Le, La, Du, Des, but generally not de, are considered part of French names and are capitalized.

Place-names Most entries on specific physical features, such as **Saguenay River** or **Helmcken Falls**, follow the style and spelling of the *Gazetteer of Canada* in inverting generic terms that precede the formal name; for example, entries on Lake Erie and Mount Logan are listed under **Erie, Lake** and **Logan, Mount**. Populated places are not inverted under their formal names, for example, the town of **Lake Louise**. The encyclopedia has also adopted the policy of the *Gazetteer of Canada* in using the form of geographic names used within each province; hence, **Trois-Rivières**, **La Grande Rivière** and **Montréal** are used in preference to Three Rivers, Grand River and Montreal.

Readings Lists of readings that should be easily accessible in libraries are included at the end of many entries for those readers who want to pursue a subject in greater depth. It was often not possible to include readings for short entries, but many will be found at the end of the longer overview articles. Those wishing further information on 17th-, 18th- and 19th-century biographical subjects should consult published volumes of the *Dictionary of Canadian Biography*.

Currency The primary function of an encyclopedia is to provide information that will be of enduring value. Nevertheless, the contributors and editors have used the most recent and most reliable information and statistics available to them, and have drawn heavily on the results of the 1986 census. Census information was not available at the time of publication for religious groups and there were only preliminary estimates for ethnic groups; as well, some ethnic and religious groups are no longer included in the census. Every attempt has been made to provide consistent data for comparison; for example, population figures of cities and towns are given for both the 1981 and 1986 census. The results of the 1984 federal election and provincial elections until Nov 1987 have been incorporated and an attempt has been made in the case of biographies to include up-to-date information to December 1987.

SECOND EDITION STAFF

Publisher
Mel Hurtig

Editor in Chief
James H. Marsh

Vice-President, Finance/Production
Barry Hicks

Editors
David Evans
Nancy Brown Foulds

Consulting Editor
Carlotta Lemieux

Project Co-ordinator
Sheila Birmingham

Assistant to the Editor in Chief/Illustrations Editor
Carol J. Woo

Office Manager/Editorial Assistant
Micaela A. Gates

Editorial Assistant
Robyn Ross

Researchers
Glenn B. Foulds
Stanley B. Gordon
Gail E. Kudelik
Debra MacGregor
Kathryn Chase Merrett
David J. Reeves
Shari Lee Saunders
Robert A. Steele
Peter Wons

Proofreaders
Vincent P. Ambrock
Patsy J. Cotterill
Barbara J. Demers
Sandra J. Duane

Data Entry
Susan L. Lang

Translator
Penny Williams

Indexing
Gardner Indexing Service, Edmonton

PRODUCTION

Typesetting and Page Make-Up
Printing Services, University of Alberta
Len Young, *Director*
Earl Olsen, *Manager*
Claire Burke, *Supervisor and Page Make-up*
Douglas J. Martin, *Programmer Analyst*
Nimmi Dua, *Data Entry*
Herbert Lewis, *Page Make-up*

Design Consultant
Robert Young

Endpapers
Michael J. Lee

Computing
Computing Services, University of Alberta

Cartography
Hosford Publishing, Edmonton
Rick Checkland, Consultant

Printing
Ronalds Printing, Montréal, division of BCE Publitech Inc

Binding
T.H. Best, Toronto
Bryant Press

FIRST EDITION STAFF

Managing Director
Frank O. McGuire

Senior Editors
Adriana Albi Davies, *Sciences*
Patricia Finlay, *Social Sciences*
Mary McDougall Maude, *Biography*
James A. Ogilvy, *Humanities*
Rosemary Shipton, *Arts*

Book Design
David Shaw

Fulford, Robert
Writer
Toronto

Gadacz, René Robert
Dept of Anthropology
University of Alberta

Gagnon, François-Marc
Professeur d'histoire de l'art
canadien
Université de Montréal

Gall, Gerald L.
Professor of Law
University of Alberta

Gander, Lois
Director, Legal Resource Centre
Faculty of Extension
University of Alberta

Gendron, Pierre R. (deceased)
Consultant
Hudson, Qué

Gillott, Cedric
Professor of Biology
University of Saskatchewan

Gingras, Yves
Professeur de sociologie
Université du Québec à Montréal

Gnarowski, Michael
Professor of English
Carleton University

Goa, David J.
Curator of Folk Life
Provincial Museum of Alberta
Edmonton

Godard, Barbara Thompson
Associate Professor of English
York University

Govier, George W.
President
Govier Consulting Services Ltd
Calgary

Graham, John Finlayson
Professor of Economics
Dalhousie University

Granatstein, J.L.
Professor of History
York University

Grant, John Webster
Professor Emeritus of Church History
Emmanuel College
Victoria University, Toronto

Grant, Peter S.
Partner, McCarthy & McCarthy
Barristers & Solicitors, Toronto

Gregg, Robert J.
Professor Emeritus of Linguistics
University of British Columbia

Griffiths, Anthony J.F.
Professor of Genetics
University of British Columbia

Gruchy, Charles G.
Assistant Director
Collections & Research
National Museum of Natural Sciences
Ottawa

Haber, Erich
Assistant Curator of Vascular Plants
National Museum of Natural Sciences
Ottawa

Hall, Frederick A.
Associate Professor of Music
McMaster University

Hamelin, Jean
Professeur d'histoire
Université Laval

Handling, Piers
Writer, Toronto

Harker, W. John
Professor of Education
University of Victoria

Harris, Walter E.
Professor Emeritus of Chemistry
University of Alberta

Havens, Betty
Provincial Gerontologist
Winnipeg

Hayne, David M.
Professor Emeritus of French
University of Toronto

Heron, Craig
Associate Professor of Social
Science & History
York University

Heyman, Richard D.
Professor of Sociology of Education
University of Calgary

Hiller, Harry H.
Professor & Head of Sociology
University of Calgary

Hillmer, Norman
Senior Historian
Directorate of History
Dept of National Defence, Ottawa

Hogg, Helen Sawyer
Professor Emeritus of Astronomy
University of Toronto

Hutchinson, Roger C.
Associate Professor, Church & Society
Emmanuel College
University of Toronto

Jackel, David
Professor of English
University of Alberta

Jackel, Susan
Associate Professor of
Canadian Studies
University of Alberta

Jackson, Harold
Professor of Food Microbiology
University of Alberta

Jackson, John N.
Professor of Applied Geography
Brock University

Jarrell, Richard A.
Associate Professor of Natural
Science
Atkinson College, York University

Jewett, Pauline
Member of Parliament
New Westminster-Coquitlam, BC

Joffe, Anatole
Centre de recherche
mathématiques appliquées
Université de Montréal

Johnstone, Rose M.
Professor of Biochemistry
McGill University

Juteau-Lee, Danielle
Professeure agrégée de sociologie
Université de Montréal

Kalbach, Warren E.
Professor of Sociology
University of Toronto

Kallmann, Helmut
Chief, Music Division (retired)
National Library of Canada, Ottawa

Kalman, Harold D.
Principal
Commonwealth Historic Resource
Management Limited, Ottawa

Kapelos, George Thomas
President, Society for the Study of
Architecture in Canada
Toronto

Kealey, Gregory Sean
Professor of History
Memorial University of Newfoundland

Kennedy, Dorothy & Randy Bouchard
British Columbia Indian Language
Project, Victoria

Klymasz, Robert B.
Curator
Slavic & East European Programme
Canadian Centre for Folk Culture Studies
Canadian Museum of Civilization
Ottawa

Kula, Sam
Director, National Film,
Television & Sound Archives
National Archives of Canada, Ottawa

Kupsch, Walter O.
Professor Emeritus of Geology
University of Saskatchewan

Lacroix, Laurier
Professeur d'histoire de l'art
Université Concordia

Laine, Mabel H.
Administrator
Encyclopedia of Music in Canada
Toronto

Lambert, James H.
Rédacteur-Historien
Dictionary of Canadian Biography
Québec

Land, R. Brian
Executive Director
Ontario Legislative Library;
Professor of Library &
Information Science
University of Toronto

Larin, Gilles-N.
Professeur agrégé d'économique
Université de Sherbrooke

LaSalle, Pierre
Energie et Ressources, Québec

Latouche, Daniel
Professeur de science politique
Institut national de la recherche
scientifique

Laycock, Arleigh H.
Professor of Geography;
Director, Water Resources Centre
University of Alberta

Legget, Robert F.
Consultant, Ottawa

Lemieux, Vincent
Professeur de science politique
Université Laval

Lessard, Claude
Professeur agrégé des sciences de
l'education
Université de Montréal

Levin, Malcolm A.
Associate Professor of Education
Ontario Institute for Studies
in Education, Toronto

Levy, Julia G.
Professor of Microbiology
University of British Columbia

Linteau, Paul-André
Professeur d'histoire
Université du Québec à Montréal

Lithwick, N.H.
Professor of Economics & Public
Administration
Carleton University

Lord, Guy
Professeur titulaire de droit
Université de Montréal

McBryde, W.A.E.
Professor of Chemistry
University of Waterloo

McCardle, Bennett
Writer, Ottawa

McCue, H.A.
Director, Education Services
Cree School Board, Chisasibi, Qué

McFadyen Clark, A.
Chief, Canadian Ethnology Service
Canadian Museum of Civilization
Ottawa

McGillivray, Donald G.
National Economics Editor
Southam News, Ottawa

McKenna, Sister Mary Olga
Professor of Education
Mount Saint Vincent University

Mackie, George O.
Professor of Biology
University of Victoria

McKillop, A.B.
Professor of History
Carleton University

McLeod, Lionel E.
President, Alberta Heritage
Foundation for Medical Research
Edmonton

McMillan, Barclay
Broadcaster & writer, Ottawa

MacMillan, Keith
Professor of Music
University of Ottawa

McMordie, Michael
Professor of Architecture
University of Calgary

McNicholl, Martin K.
Executive Director
Long Point Bird Observatory
Port Rowan, Ont

McNulty, Jean
Ontario Ministry of Culture
& Communications, Toronto

Mailhot, Laurent
Professeur de littérature
Université de Montréal

Major, Jean-Louis
Professeur titulaire des lettres
françaises;
Coordonnateur associé
Corpus d'éditions critiques
Université d'Ottawa

Mann, Kenneth H.
Dept of Fisheries & Oceans
Bedford Institute of Oceanography
Dartmouth, NS

Marr, William
Professor of Economics
Wilfrid Laurier University

Martin, Gérard-B
Doyen, Faculté des sciences de
l'agriculture et de l'alimentation
Université Laval

Martin, Sandra
Writer, Toronto

Melody, William H.
Professor of Communication
Simon Fraser University

Miller, Mark
Journalist, Toronto

Mills, Eric L.
Professor of Oceanography
Dalhousie University

Moir, John S.
Professor of History
University of Toronto

Morrison, Alexander
Assistant Deputy Minister
Health Protection Branch
Dept of National Health & Welfare
Ottawa

Morrison, William R.
Professor of History
Brandon University

Murray, Joan
Director
The Robert McLaughlin Gallery
Oshawa, Ont

Naldrett, Anthony J.
Professor of Geology
University of Toronto

Nelles, Henry Vivian
Professor of History
York University

Nelson, Joseph S.
Professor of Zoology
University of Alberta

Nielsen, N. Ole
Dean, Ontario Veterinary College
University of Guelph

Nitecki, André
Professor of Library Science
University of Alberta

Noble, William C.
Professor of Anthropology
McMaster University

Nursall, J. Ralph
Professor of Zoology
University of Alberta

Officer, Jillian M.
Assistant Professor of Dance
University of Waterloo

Ogilvie, John R.
Director, School of Engineering
University of Guelph

Orpwood, Graham W.F.
Science Adviser
Science Council of Canada, Ottawa

Ostiguy, Jean-René
Conservateur chargé de recherches
Galerie nationale du Canada, Ottawa

Ouellet, Henri
Curator, Ornithology Section
National Museum of Natural Sciences
Ottawa

Owram, D.R.
Professor of History
University of Alberta

Palmer, Howard
Professor of History
University of Calgary

Panitch, Leo Victor
Professor of Political Science
York University

Parsons, John
Dept of Social Studies
Booth Memorial Regional High School
St. John's

Pawluk, Steven
Professor of Soil Science
University of Alberta

Percy, Mike
Associate Professor of Economics
University of Alberta

Perks, William T.
Professor of Urbanism & Planning
University of Calgary

Phillips, Ruth B.
Assistant Professor of Art History
Carleton University

Phillipson, Donald J.C.
Historian of Science, Ottawa

Pickard, George L.
Professor Emeritus of Oceanography
University of British Columbia

Plant, Richard L.
Associate Professor of Drama
Queen's University

Porter, Arthur
Professor Emeritus of Industrial
Engineering
University of Toronto

Powrie, T.
Professor of Economics
University of Alberta
Preston, Richard J.
Professor of Anthropology
McMaster University

Quarterman, C. David
President, Alexander Bay Associates
Ottawa

Rea, J.E.
Professor of History
University of Manitoba
Redmond, Gerald
Professor of Physical Education
& Recreation
University of Alberta
Reed, F. L. C.
NSERC Professor of Forest Policy
University of British Columbia
Reid Dennis
Art Gallery of Ontario, Toronto
Reid, John G.
Associate Professor of History
Saint Mary's University
Reid, Robert G.B.
Professor of Biology
University of Victoria
Richardson, Douglas
Associate Professor of History of Art
University of Toronto
Riley, Barbara
Curator, History Division
Canadian Museum of Civilization,
Ottawa
Robertson, Ian Ross
Associate Professor of History
University of Toronto
Robinson, J. Lewis
Professor Emeritus of Geography
University of British Columbia
Rocher, Guy
Professeur de sociologie
Université de Montréal
Rodriguez, E.
Ottawa
Rodway, Margaret R.
Professor of Social Welfare
University of Calgary
Roland, Charles G.
Professor of the History of Medicine
McMaster University
Rose, Phyllis
Graduate Student
University of Toronto
Rouillard, Jacques
Professeur d'histoire
Université de Montréal
Rousseau, Louis
Professeur d'histoire religieuse
Université du Québec à Montréal
Routledge, Marie
Research & Documentation Co-ordinator
Inuit Art Section
Indian & Northern Affairs Canada
Ottawa
Roy, Patricia E.
Associate Professor of History
University of Victoria
Ruppenthal, Karl M.
UPS Foundation Professor;
Director
The Centre for Transportation Studies
University of British Columbia
Rutter, Nathaniel W.
Professor & Chairman of Geology
University of Alberta

Saddlemyer, Ann
Professor of English & Drama
University of Toronto
Sales, Arnaud
Professeur titulaire
Université de Montréal
Scobie, Stephen A.C.
Professor of English
University of Victoria
Scott, Anthony
Professor of Economics
University of British Columbia
Seager, Allen
Associate Professor of History
Simon Fraser University
Sebert, Louis M.
Canada Lands Surveyor, Ottawa
Shadbolt, Doris
Curator Emeritus
Vancouver Art Gallery
North Burnaby, BC
Shaw, Robert F.
Consultant, Monenco Consultants
Limited
Montréal
Shebeski, Leonard H.
Dean Emeritus
University of Manitoba
Shortt, Samuel E.D.
Associate Professor of Family Medicine;
Associate Professor of History
Queen's University
Simeon, Richard
Professor of Public Administration &
Political Studies
Queen's University
Simpson, Kieran
Editor, Canadian Who's Who
University of Toronto Press
Toronto
Sinclair-Faulkner, Tom
Professor of Comparative Religion
Dalhousie University
Sirois, Antoine
Professeur de littérature
Université de Sherbrooke
Slater, Peter
Dean of Divinity, Trinity College;
Professor of Theology
Toronto School of Theology:
Centre for Religious Studies
University of Toronto
Slaymaker, Olav
Professor of Geography
University of British Columbia
Smith, Derek G.
Associate Professor of Sociology &
Anthropology
Carleton University
Smith, Donald B.
Associate Professor of History
University of Calgary
Smith, Peter J.
Professor of Geography
University of Alberta
Stairs, Denis
Professor of Political Science
Dalhousie University
Stamp, Robert M.
Historian, Toronto
Stanbury, W.T.
UPS Foundation Professor of Regulation
& Competition Policy
University of British Columbia
Steeves, Taylor A.
Professor of Biology
University of Saskatchewan
Stelck, Charles R.
Professor Emeritus of Geology
University of Alberta

Stevenson, John T.
Associate Professor of Philosophy
University of Toronto
Stewart, Wilson N.
Professor Emeritus of Botany
University of Alberta
Strate, Grant
Director, Centre for the Arts
Simon Fraser University
Strong-Boag, Veronica
Associate Professor of History
& Women's Studies
Simon Fraser University
Studnicki-Gizbert, Konrad W.
Economist, Chelsea, Qué
Sutherland, Stuart R.J.
Toronto
Swinton, George
Professor Emeritus
Carleton University
Artist & author, Winnipeg

Tartar, John
Professor of Computing Science
University of Alberta
Taylor, C.J.
Historian, National Historic Parks
& Sites Branch
Parks Canada, Ottawa
Taylor, William E., Jr.
President
Social Sciences & Humanities Research
Council of Canada, Ottawa
Tepperman, Lorne
Professor of Sociology
University of Toronto
Thomas, Morley K.
Former Director General
Canadian Climate Centre
Downsview, Ont
Thompson, Dixon A.R.
Professor of Environmental Science
University of Calgary
Tupper, Allan
Professor of Political Science
University of Alberta
Tweedie, Katherine
Assistant Professor of Photography
Concordia University

Vachon, Auguste
Heraldry Archivist, Documentary
Art & Photography Division
National Archives of Canada, Ottawa
Vallee, Frank G.
Professor Emeritus of Anthropology &
Sociology
Carleton University
van Zyll de Jong, Constantinus G.
Curator, Mammalogy Section
National Museum of Natural Sciences
Ottawa
Véronneau, Pierre
Historien
Cinémathèque québécoise/Musée du
cinéma, Montréal
Vézina, Claude
Directeur adjoint
Institut Armand-Frappier
Laval, Qué
Von Borstel, R.C.
Professor of Genetics
University of Alberta

Wagner, Anton
Director of Research
World Encyclopedia of
Contemporary Theatre
York University

Waite, P.B.
Professor of History
Dalhousie University
Ward, Norman
Professor Emeritus of Economics &
Political Science
University of Saskatchewan
Watson, William
Associate Professor of Economics
McGill University
Webster, Donald B.
Curator, Canadian Decorative Arts
Royal Ontario Museum, Toronto
Weinrich, Peter H.
Executive Director
Canadian Crafts Council, Ottawa
West, J. Thomas
Manager, Winter Olympic Hall of Fame
Calgary
Whitaker, Reginald
Professor of Political Science
York University
Whyte, Donald R.
Professor of Sociology & Anthropology
Carleton University
Wilkin, Karen
Independent curator & critic
Toronto & New York
Wilkinson, Bruce W.
Professor of Economics
University of Alberta
Wilkinson, Paul F.
Associate Professor of Environmental
Studies & Geography
York University
Williams, William M.
Birks Professor of Metallurgy
McGill University
Williamson, Mary F.
Fine Arts Bibliographer
York University
Wilson, J. Donald
Professor of History of Education
University of British Columbia
Wise, S.F.
Professor of History;
Dean of Graduate Studies & Research
Carleton University
Wolfe, Morris
Ontario College of Art, Toronto
Wolfe, Roy I.
Professor of Geography (retired)
York University
Wonders, William C.
University Professor &
Professor of Geography
University of Alberta
Woodcock, George
Writer, Vancouver
Wyczynski, Paul
Titulaire de recherche des
lettres françaises
Université d'Ottawa
Wyman, Max
Author & critic, Vancouver

Young, Walter D.
Professor of Political Science
University of Victoria

Zeller, Suzanne E.
Assistant Professor of History
Wilfrid Laurier University

CONTRIBUTORS

Abbott, Caroline Louise
Writer & photographer, Montréal

Abella, Irving
Professor of History
Glendon College
York University

Abler, Thomas S.
Associate Professor of Anthropology
University of Waterloo

Abley, Mark
Writer, Montréal

Abu-Laban, Baha
Professor of Sociology
University of Alberta

Acton, Donald
Agriculture Canada, Saskatoon

Adams, Peter
Professor of Geography
Watershed Ecosystems Program
Trent University

Adell, Jacqueline
Architectural History Division
Parks Canada, Ottawa

Adie, Peter A.
Former Head, Biomedical Section
Defence Research Establishment
Suffield, Alta

Ahearn, Catherine
Author & Poet Laureate of Ottawa
(1982-84), Ottawa

Aiken, David E.
Research Scientist
Dept of Fisheries & Oceans
St Andrews, NB

Albert, Jim
Associate Professor of Social Work
Carleton University

Aldrich, Frederick A.
Professor of Biology & Dean of
Graduate Studies
Memorial University of Newfoundland

Allaire, Gratien
Professeur d'histoire
Faculté Saint-Jean
University of Alberta

Allard, Jacques
Professeur de littérature
Université du Québec à Montréal

Allen, A. Richard
Member of the Ontario Legislative
Assembly;
Professor of History
McMaster University

Allen, Karyn Elizabeth
Curator of Art
The Nickle Arts Museum, Calgary

Allen, Max
Curator
The Museum for Textiles, Toronto

Allen, Robert S.
Deputy Chief
Treaties & Historical Research Centre
Indian & Northern Affairs, Canada

Allen, Willard F.
Professor Emeritus of Chemistry
University of Alberta

Alt, Marlene
Writer, Ottawa

Amatt, John
President
One Step Beyond Adventure Group
Canmore, Alta

Anctil, Pierre
Researcher
Institut québécois de recherche sur
la culture, Montréal

Anderson, Donald W.
General Secretary
Canadian Council of Churches, Toronto

Anderson, Doris H.
Past President
National Action Committee on the Status
of Women, Toronto

Anderson, Duncan M.
Associate Professor of Geography
Carleton University

Anderson, Frank W.
Historian, Saskatoon

Anderson, Grace M.
Professor of Sociology & Anthropology
Wilfrid Laurier University

Anderson, Peter S.
Research Associate of Communication
Simon Fraser University

Andreae, Christopher A.
Historica Research Limited
London, Ont

Andrès, Bernard
Professeur d'études littéraires
Université du Québec à Montréal

Andrew, Sheila
Graduate Student
University of New Brunswick

Andrews, Florence
Associate Professor of Sociology
Carleton University

Andrus, Donald F.P.
Associate Professor of Art History
Concordia University

Anisef, Paul
Associate Professor of Sociology
York University

Anstey, Thomas H.
Agrologist, Ottawa

Applebaum, Louis
Composer & conductor;
Chairman, Federal Cultural Policy
Review Committee (1980-82), Toronto

Archer, Christon I.
Professor of History
University of Calgary

Archer, David J.W
Archaeologist, Vancouver

Archibald, Clinton
Professor of Administration
University of Ottawa

Archibald, Mary
Writer
Shelburne, NS

Arima, Eugene
Ethnologist, Ottawa

Arlett, Allan
Executive Director
The Canadian Centre for Philanthropy
Toronto

Armour, Leslie
Professor of Philosophy
University of Ottawa

Armstrong, Pat
Associate Professor of Sociology
York University

Arnason, John T.
Associate Professor of Biology
University of Ottawa

Arsenault, Georges
Visiting Professor in Acadian
Studies
University of Prince Edward Island

Arseneault, Céline
Botaniste (Bibliothécaire), Jardin
botanique de la Ville de Montréal

Arthur, Eric R. (deceased)
Architect & writer, Toronto

Artibise, Alan F.J.
School of Community & Regional
Planning
University of British Columbia

Asch, Michael I.
Professor of Anthropology
University of Alberta

Asimakopulos, Athanasios
Professor of Economics
McGill University

Asselin, Alain
Professeur de phytopathologie
Université Laval

Asselstine, Alan J.
Farm Machinery Economist
Agriculture Canada

Atchison, John
Senior Lecturer in History
Armidale College of Advanced
Education
Armidale, NSW, Australia

Atwood, Margaret
Writer, Toronto

Aubrey, Irene E.
Chief, Children's Literature Service
National Library of Canada, Ottawa

Augusteijn, Eleanor
Historian, Caledon East, Ont

Aun, Karl
Professor Emeritus of Political
Science
Wilfrid Laurier University

Austin-Smith, Peter J.
Manager, Wildlife Resources, Non-game
Dept of Lands & Forests, Nova Scotia

Austman, Helgi H.
Agricultural consultant
Gimli, Man

Avery, Donald H.
Associate Professor of History
University of Western Ontario

Axworthy, Thomas
Vice-President
The CRB Foundation

Ayer, William A.
Professor of Chemistry
University of Alberta

Ayers, Hugh D.
School of Engineering
University of Guelph

Ayles, G. Burton
Director, Freshwater Institute
Winnipeg

Ayre, John
Writer, Guelph

Aytenfisu, Maureen
Student, Edmonton

Babcock, Douglas R.
Historian, Edmonton

Babcock, Robert H.
Professor of History
University of Maine

Babe, Robert E.
Associate Professor of Communication
University of Ottawa

Bachynski, Morrel P.
President, MPB Technologies Inc
Dorval, Qué

Baerwaldt, Margaret
Regina

Baglole, Harry
Director, Institute of Island Studies
University of Prince Edward Island

Bagnell, Kenneth
Toronto

Bai, David H.
Associate Professor of Anthropology
University of Alberta

Baigent, Margaret J.
Associate Professor of Nutrition
University of Toronto

Baird, David M.
Director
Tyrrell Museum of Palaeontology
Drumheller, Alta

Baird, Patricia A.
Professor of Medical Genetics
University of British Columbia

Baker, Allan J.
Curator-in-charge
Dept of Ornithology
Royal Ontario Museum;
Associate Professor of Zoology
University of Toronto

Baker, G. Blaine
Associate Professor of Law
McGill University

Baker, Melvin
Archivist & Historian
Memorial University

Baker, R.T.
Crop Development Centre
University of Saskachewan

Baker, William M.
Professor of History
University of Lethbridge

Baldwin, Douglas O.
Professor of History
Acadia University

Baldwin, John R.
Former Deputy Minister, Transport
Former President, Air Canada

Bale, Gordon
Professor of Law
Queen's University

Ball, Georgiana G.
Historian, Victoria

Ball, Norman R.
Historian of Engineering, Ottawa

Bandoni, Robert J.
Professor of Botany
University of British Columbia

Banfield, Paul A.
Archival Consultant, Kingston

Banting, Keith Gordon
Professor of Political Studies
Queen's University

Baragar, Alvin
Edmonton

Barber, Marilyn J.
Associate Professor of History
Carleton University

Barbour, Douglas F.
Professor of English
University of Alberta

Barker, Clifford A.V.
Professor Emeritus
University of Guelph

Barlow, Jon C.
Curator of Ornithology
Royal Ontario Museum;
Professor of Zoology
University of Toronto

Barman, Jean
Assistant Professor of Social &
Educational Studies
University of British Columbia

Barnard, David T.
Associate Professor of Computing &
Information Science;
Director of Computing Services
Queen's University

Barnes, John
Research Consultant, Law Reform
Commission of Canada;
Visiting Professor, University of Ottawa
& Carleton University

Barnes, R.G.
Canadian Waterski Association, Ottawa

Barr, Elinor
Writer & researcher
Thunder Bay, Ont

Barr, John J.
Director of Public Affairs
Syncrude Canada Ltd, Edmonton

Barradas, Remigio Germano
Professor of Chemistry
Carleton University

Barratt, Robert F.
Editor, Food in Canada magazine
Toronto

Barrett, Tony
Investment banker & environmentalist
Toronto

Barrie, H.J.
Schomberg, Ont

Barrington-Leigh, John
Associate Professor (Hon) of
Immunology
University of Alberta

Barris, Ted
Author, Toronto

Barry, George S.
Energy, Mines & Resources Canada
Ottawa

Bartlett, David W.
Manotick, Ontario

Bartlett, Donald R.
Professor of English
Memorial University of Newfoundland

Basinger, James F.
Associate Professor of Geology
University of Saskatchewan

Baskerville, Peter A.
Associate Professor of History
University of Victoria

Baszczynski, Marilyn J.
Dept of French
University of Western Ontario

Batten, Alan H.
Senior Research Officer
Dominion Astrophysical Observatory
Victoria
Herzberg Institute of Astrophysics
Baudouin, Jean-Louis
Professeur de droit
Université de Montréal
Baum, Carol
Canadiana Dept
Royal Ontario Museum, Toronto
Bayfield, John
Penetanguishene, Ont
Bazin, Jules
Historien d'art, Montréal
Beal, Bob
Journalist, Edmonton
Bean, Gladys
Sports historian, Montréal
Bearcroft, Norma
Salmon Arm, BC
Beard, William R.
Lecturer in Film Studies
University of Alberta
Beaton, Belinda A.
Writer, Toronto
Beattie, Owen B.
Associate Professor of Anthropology
University of Alberta
Beaudoin-Ross, Jacqueline
Curator of Costumes & Textiles
McCord Museum
McGill University
Beaudoin, Gérald-A.
De l'Académie canadienne-française
Professeur de droit constitutionnel
Université d'Ottawa
Beaudoin, Réjean
Assistant Professor
University of British Columbia
Beaudry, Louise
Historienne de l'art, Montréal
Beauregard, France
Université d'Ottawa
Beaven, Brian P.N.
Research Associate
University of Western Ontario
Bechtel, Brian R.
Executive Director
Edmonton's Food Bank, Edmonton
Beck, J. Murray
Professor Emeritus of Political
Science
Dalhousie University
Beckman, Margaret
Chief Librarian
University of Guelph
Beckwith, John
Composer, Toronto
Bédard, Roger
Professeur d'horticulture
Université Laval
Beeby, Dean
Canadian Press, Ottawa
Beer, Don
Senior Lecturer in History
University of New England
Armidale, NSW, Australia
Behiels, Michael D.
Associate Professor of History
University of Ottawa
Béland, Madeleine
Centre d'études sur la langue,
les arts et les traditions populaires
(CÉLAT)
Université Laval
Béland, Mario
Conservateur de l'art ancien
Musée du Québec, Québec
Bélanger, Guy
Historien, Québec
Bélanger, Réal
Professeur d'histoire
Université Laval
Bélanger, René
Historien
Sillery, Qué
Bélisle, Jean
Professor of Visual Arts
Concordia University
Bell, D.G.
Historian, Fredericton
Bell, Norman
Chief of Research
National Museum of Science &
Technology, Ottawa
Bell, Norman W.
Professor of Sociology
University of Toronto
Bellan, Ruben C.
Professor of Economics
University of Manitoba

Belleau, André
Professeur de littérature
Université du Québec à Montréal
Belzile, René J.
Professeur d'alimentation animale
Université Laval
Bendell, Beverley
Librarian, Alpine Club of Canada
Bennett, Gerry
Writer
Woodbridge, Ont
Bennett, John
Writer, Ottawa
Bensley, Edward Horton
Professor Emeritus of Medicine;
Honorary Osler Librarian
McGill University
Bentley, D.M.R.
Professor of English
University of Western Ontario
Bercuson, David J.
Professor of History
University of Calgary
Bergen, John J.
Professor Emeritus of Educational
Administration
University of Alberta
Berger, Jeniva
Theatre Journalist, Toronto
Berger, Thomas R.
Barrister & Solicitor, Vancouver
Bergeron, Claude
Professeur d'histoire d'architecture
Université Laval
Bergerud, A.T.
Honorary Professor of Biology
University of Victoria
Berkowitz, Norbert
Professor of Fuel Science
University of Alberta
Bernard, André
Professeur de science politique
Université du Québec à Montréal
Bernard, Frank R.
Fisheries & Oceans
Pacific Biological Station
Nanaimo, BC
Bernard, Jean-Paul
Professeur d'histoire
Université du Québec à Montréal
Bernard, Jean-Thomas
Département d'économique
Université Laval
Bernier, Jacques
Professeur agrégé d'histoire
Université Laval
Bernier, Marc
Directeur des relations publiques
Université de Sherbrooke
Bernshaw, Nicole
Ste Thérèse, Qué
Berry, Jonathan
Writer
Chess Federation of Canada
Berry, Michael J.
Director, Geophysics Division
Geological Survey of Canada, Ottawa
Berry, Ralph
Professor of English
University of Ottawa
Berton, Pierre
Writer & broadcaster, Toronto
Besner, Neil
Assistant Professor of English
University of Winnipeg
Bessai, Diane E.
Professor of English
University of Alberta
Betke, Carl
Chief of Research
Historic Sites Service
Alberta Culture & Multiculturalism
Edmonton
Bewers, John Michael
Bedford Institute of Oceanography
Dartmouth, NS
Beylerian, Onnig
Montréal, Qué
Bezeau, M. Vincent
Director of Ceremonial
Dept of National Defence, Ottawa
Bibby, Reginald W.
Associate Professor of Sociology
University of Lethbridge
Bibeau, Gilles
Professeur d'anthropologie médicale
Université de Montréal
Bickell, Ivan B.
Vice-President & Marketing Manager
Gillis Quarries Ltd, Winnipeg

Bigauskas, Julius
Energy, Mines & Resources Canada
Ottawa
Bilaniuk, Petro B.T.
Professor of Theology
University of St Michael's College;
Professor of Religious Studies
University of Toronto
Billings, Robert (deceased)
The League of Canadian Poets, Toronto
Bilson, Geoffrey (deceased)
Professor of History
University of Saskatchewan
Bird, Carolyn J.
Research Officer
National Research Council of Canada
Halifax
Bird, Michael S.
Associate Professor of Religious
Studies & Fine Arts
Renison College & University of
Waterloo
Bird, Richard M.
Professor of Economics
University of Toronto
Birrell, Andrew
Director General
Informatics & Records Services
National Archives of Canada
Bishop, Carol Anne
Writer, Toronto
Bishop, Charles A.
Professor of Anthropology
State University of New York
Oswego, NY
Bishop, Mary F.
Honorary Lecturer of Health Care &
Epidemiology
University of British Columbia;
Historian, Vancouver
Bissett-Johnson, Alastair
Professor of Law
Dalhousie University
Black, Conrad M.
Chairman
Argus Corporation Limited, Toronto
Black, Joseph Laurence
Professor of History
Carleton University;
Director, Institute of Soviet Studies
Black, M. Jean
Assistant Professor
University of North Carolina
Chapel Hill, NC
Black, Naomi
Professor of Political Science
York University
Blackadar, Robert G.
Director
Geological Information Division
Geological Survey of Canada, Ottawa
Blackburn, Robert H.
Librarian Emeritus
University of Toronto
Blackwell, John D.
Instructor of History
Queen's University
Blain, Eleanor M.
Graduate Student of Linguistics
University of Manitoba
Blair, Alex M.
Associate Professor of Geography
York University
Blair, Robert
Professor of Animal Science
University of British Columbia
Blais, André
Professeur de science politique
Université de Montréal
Blakeley, Phyllis (deceased)
Provincial Archivist for Nova Scotia
Public Archives of Nova Scotia
Halifax
Bleakney, J. Sherman
Professor of Biology
Acadia University
Blevis, Bertram C.
Research Manager, Space Technology
Ottawa
Bliss, L.C.
Professor of Botany
University of Washington
Bliss, Michael
Historian, Toronto
Blodgett, E.D.
Professor of Comparative Literature
University of Alberta
Blodgett, Jean
Adjunct Professor of Art History
Carleton University

Blue, Arthur W.
Professor of Native Studies
Brandon University
Boadway, Robin W.
Professor of Economics
Queen's University
Boag, David A.
Professor of Zoology
University of Alberta
Bocking, Douglas H.
Associate Provincial Archivist
Saskatchewan Archives Board
University of Saskatchewan
Boddington, J.
By-Law Officer, Edmonton
Boddy, Trevor
Lecturer, School of Architecture
University of British Columbia
Bodner, John M.
All-Breed Teaching Judge;
American Cat Fanciers Association
Winnipeg
Boer, George J.
Chief, Numerical Modelling Division
Canadian Climate Centre
Atmospheric Environment Service
Downsview, Ont
Bogart, James P.
Associate Professor of Zoology
University of Guelph
Boggs, Jean Sutherland
Chairman & Chief Executive Officer
Canada Museums Construction
Corporation Inc, Ottawa
Boileau, Gilles
Département de géographie
Université de Montréal
Boivin, Aurélien
Professionel de recherche
Dictionnaire des oeuvres litteraires
du Québec
Université Laval
Boivin, Bernard
Herbier, Louis-Marie
Université Laval
Boivin, Jean
Professeur de Relations Industrielles
Université Laval
Bokovay, Geoffrey
Energy, Mines & Resources Canada,
Ottawa
Bolduc, André
Conseiller, Vice-présidence
Information
Hydro-Québec, Montréal
Bolduc, Yves
Professeur de littérature québécoise
Université de Moncton
Boles, Glen W.
Waterworks Planner, City of Calgary
Bolger, Francis W.P.
Professor of History
University of Prince Edward Island
Bollinger, Kenneth E.
Professor of Electrical Engineering
University of Alberta
Bonavia, George
Journalist, Ottawa
Bond, Courtney C.J.
Cartographer & historian, Ottawa
Bondurant, Flint
BC Hydro, Vancouver
Bonenfant, Joseph
Faculté des Lettres et Sciences humaines
Département d'études françaises
Université de Sherbrooke
Bonish, Gayle
Graphic Co-ordinator
Imax Systems Corporation, Toronto
Bonisteel, Roy
Broadcaster & journalist
Trenton, Ont
Boonstra, Rudy
Associate Professor of Zoology
University of Toronto
Booth, Rodney M.
Director of Media Resources
The United Church of Canada, Toronto
Boothe, Paul M.
Associate Professor of Economics
University of Alberta
Bothwell, Robert
Professor of History
University of Toronto
Bott, Robert D.
Writer, Calgary
Bouchard, Randy & Dorothy Kennedy
British Columbia Indian Language
Project, Victoria

Boucher, Michel A.
Economiste (mines et métaux)
Secteur de la politique minerale
Energie, Mines et Ressources, Canada,
Ottawa

Boulet, Gilles
Président
Université du Québec

Boulet, Roger H.
Author & curator;
Director, Burnaby Art Gallery
Burnaby, BC

Bourassa, André G.
Professeur de théâtre
Université du Québec à Montréal

Bourbonnais, Nicole
Professeure de lettres françaises
Université d'Ottawa

Bourgault, Pierre L.
Vice-Rector, Administration
University of Ottawa

Bourne, John Brian
Regional Supervisor Problem Wildlife
Vermilion, Alta

Bovey, Patricia E.
Director
Art Gallery of Greater Victoria
Victoria

Bowen, A.J.
Institute of Oceanography
Dalhousie University

Bowen, Lynne E.
Writer, lecturer & historian
Nanaimo, BC

Bowker, Wilbur Fee
Professor Emeritus of Law
University of Alberta

Bowles, Roy T.
Professor of Sociology
Trent University

Bowsfield, Hartwell
Associate Professor of History
York University

Boyanoski, Christine
Assistant Curator of Canadian
Historical Art
Art Gallery of Ontario, Toronto

Boyce, Farrell M.
Research Scientist
Environment Canada
Burlington, Ont

Bradt, Oliver A.
Research Scientist (retired)
Horticulture Research Institute of
Ontario
Vineland Station, Ont

Brady, William J.
Station Manager, CFPL AM & FM
London, Ont

Braiden, Chris
Inspector
Edmonton Police Dept, Edmonton

Brander, F. Gerald (deceased)
President Emeritus
Tourism Industry Association of
Canada, Toronto

Brassard, Guy R.
Associate Dean of Science &
Professor of Biology
Memorial University of Newfoundland

Brasser, Ted
Ethnologist
Canadian Ethnology Service
Canadian Museum of Civilization
Ottawa

Bray, R. Matthew
Professor of History
Laurentian University

Breen, David H.
Professor of History
University of British Columbia

Bregha, François
Energy analyst, Ottawa

Brehaut, Willard
Professeur of History &
Philosophy of Education
Ontario Institute for Studies in
Education, Toronto

Brennan, J. William
Associate Professor of History
University of Regina

Brennan, Paul W.
Senior Milling Technologist
Canadian International Grains
Institute, Winnipeg

Breton, Raymond
Professor of Sociology
University of Toronto

Brideau, Roland
Réprésentant
Office national du film du Canada
Moncton

Bridgman, Harry John
Historian, Montréal

Brierley, John E.C.
Sir William Macdonald Professor;
Dean, Faculty of Law
McGill University

Briggs, Jean L.
Professor of Anthropology
Memorial University of Newfoundland

Brillinger, David R.
Professor of Statistics
University of California at Berkeley

Brink, Jack
Senior Archaeologist
Archaeological Survey of Alberta
Edmonton

Brinkhurst, Ralph O.
Ocean Ecology Laboratory
Institute of Ocean Sciences
Canadian Federal Dept of Fisheries &
Oceans
Sidney, BC;
Adjunct Professor
University of Victoria;
Associate, Royal Ontario Museum
Toronto

Brisebois, Robert
ENAP, Quebec

Brochet, Aldo
Toronto

Brochu, André
Professeur de lettres
Université de Montréal

Brodo, Irwin M.
Curator of Lichens
National Museum of Natural Sciences
National Museums of Canada, Ottawa

Brodribb, Somer
Dept of Sociology in Education
Ontario Institute for Studies in
Education, Toronto

Brookes, Alan A.
Associate Professor of History
University of Guelph

Brookes, Ian A.
York University

Brooks, David B.
Marbek Resource Consultants Ltd
Ottawa

Broughton, Robert S.
Professor of Agricultural Engineering
McGill University

Brousseau, Yves
Geographie
Université Laval

Brown, David
PhD Student of Physical Education &
Sport Studies
University of Alberta

Brown, Desmond H.
Assistant Professor of History
University of Alberta

Brown, Jennifer S.H.
Associate Professor of History
University of Winnipeg

Brown, Richard G.B.
Research Scientist & writer
Canadian Wildlife Service
Dartmouth, NS

Brown, Robert Craig
Professor of History
University of Toronto

Brown, Roy I.
Professor of Educational Psychology
University of Calgary

Brown, Thomas E.
Alberta Culture
Lethbridge, Alta

Brownell, Don
President, Canadian Handball
Association
Winnipeg

Bruce, Lorne D.
Reference Librarian
Social Science Division
University of Guelph Library

Brumley, John H.
President, Ethos Consultants Ltd
Medicine Hat, Alta

Brunger, Alan E.
Professor of Geography
Trent University

Brust, Reinhart A.
Professor of Entomology
University of Manitoba

Bryan, Rorke Bardon
Professor of Geography & Forestry
Scarborough Campus
University of Toronto

Bryant, Giles Bradley
Organist & Master of the Choristers
St James' Cathedral, Toronto

Brzustowski, Thomas A.
Professor of Mechanical Engineering
University of Waterloo

Buchignani, Norman
Associate Professor of Anthropology
University of Lethbridge

Buck, Ruth Matheson
Writer, Regina

Buckner, Phillip A.
Professor of History
University of New Brunswick

Budden, Geoff
Professor of History
Memorial University of Newfoundland

Buggey, Susan
Chief, Historical Services
Environment Canada, Parks
Prairie & Northern Regions, Winnipeg

Buisson, Lise
Montréal

Bullen, John
History Instructor
Labour College of Canada, Ottawa

Bumsted, J.M.
Professor of History
St John's College
University of Manitoba

Burden, Patrick H.
PhD Student
Simon Fraser University

Burant, Jim
Archivist
National Archives of Canada, Ottawa

Burke, Joan
Royal Ontario Museum, Toronto

Burke, Robert D.
Associate Professor of Biology
University of Victoria

Burnet, Jean
Professor Emeritus of Sociology
Glendon College, York University

Burnett, David
Independent curator & writer,
Toronto

Burnett, Marilyn (Schiff)
Researcher & writer, Toronto

Burnham, Dorothy K.
Research Associate, Textile Dept
Royal Ontario Museum, Toronto

Burns, Eedson Louis Millard (deceased)
Adjunct Professor of International
Affairs
Carleton University

Burns, Robert J.
Historian
Environment Canada - Parks, Ottawa

Burns, Robin
Associate Professor of History
Bishop's University

Burton, Ian
Director
Institute for Environmental Studies
University of Toronto

Buteux, Paul
Professor of Political Studies
University of Manitoba

Butler, Frank Taylor
Professor of Physical
Education & Athletics
Memorial University of Newfoundland

Butler, K.J. (Jack)
Painter, Winnipeg

Butschler, Margaret
Curatorial Assistant
Vancouver Aquarium, Vancouver

Butts, Edward
Writer
Mississauga, Ont

Butts, Robert E.
Professor of Philosophy
University of Western Ontario

Cadotte, Marcel
Professeur agrégé de pathologie
Université de Montréal

Callaghan, John C.
Clinical Professor of Surgery;
Former Director, Division of Thoracic &
Cardiovascular Surgery
University of Alberta Hospital

Callahan, John W.
Associate Professor of Paediatrics &
Biochemistry
Research Institute, The Hospital for
Sick Children, Toronto

Camerlain, Lorraine
Cahiers de théâtre Jeu, Montréal

Cameron, Bill
Writer, Saskatoon

Cameron, Christina
Director General
National Historic Parks & Sites
Environment Canada, Parks, Hull

Cameron, Elspeth
Co-ordinator, Canadian Literature &
Language Programme
University of Toronto

Cameron, James M.
Journalist & broadcaster
New Glasgow, NS

Cameron, Wendy
Toronto, Ontario

Campbell, A. Barrie
Agriculture Canada, Research Station
Winnipeg

Campbell, Beverly
Biosystematics Research Institute
Ottawa

Campbell, Douglas F.
Associate Professor of Sociology
Erindale College
University of Toronto

Campbell, Gordon
Professor of Education
University of Lethbridge

Campbell, Ian A.
Professor of Geography
University of Alberta

Campbell, Jack J.R.
Professor Emeritus of Microbiology
University of British Columbia

Campbell, J. Milton
Biosystematics Research Institute
Ottawa

Campbell, Neil John
Director-General, Marine Sciences &
Information Directorate
Dept of Fisheries & Oceans, Ottawa

Campbell, Percy I.
Chief, Water Survey of Canada
Hull, Qué

Campbell, Sandra
National Arts Centre, Ottawa

Campion, Richard
Richard Campion Consultants, Ottawa

Cannon, William T.
Associate Professor of Business
Queen's University

Cantin, Pierre
Professeur
Collège de l'Outaouais, Hull

Caplan, Usher
Editor, Ottawa

Carasco, Emily F.
Associate Professor of Law
University of Windsor

Carbin, Clifton F.
Executive Director, Deaf Children's
Society of British Columbia;
Vice-President
American Society for Deaf Children

Cardy, Patrick R.T.
Associate Professor of Music
Carleton University

Carefoot, Thomas H.
Professor of Zoology
University of British Columbia

Careless, J.M.S.
Professor Emeritus
Massey College
University of Toronto

Carlisle, Jock Alan
Proprietor, Carlisle Consultants
Deep River, Ont

Caron, Laurent G.
Professeur de physique
Université de Sherbrooke

Carpenter, Carole H.
Associate Professor of Humanities
York University

Carpenter, Ken
Associate Professor Visual Arts
York University

Carrière, Gaston (deceased)
Archiviste, Archives Deschâtelets
Ottawa

Carroll, Carman V.
National Archives of Canada, Ottawa

Carroll, Jock
Journalist, Toronto

Carter, Brian G.
Associate Professor of Immunology
University of Manitoba

Carter, George E.
Professor of Economics
Ryerson Polytechnical Institute

Carter, Margaret
Heritage research consultant, Ottawa

Cashin, Richard J.
President, Newfoundland Fishermen,
Food & Allied Workers Union
St John's

Casselman, Ian
Historian, Toronto

Cassidy, Maureen
Historian, Victoria

Cauchon, Michel
Inventaire des biens culturels
Ministère des Affaires culturelles
Québec

Cavers, Paul B.
Professor of Plant Sciences &
Acting Chairman
University of Western Ontario

Chabot, Richard
Professeur d'histoire
Université du Québec à Montréal

Chagnon, Roland
Professeur de sciences religieuses
Université du Québec à Montréal

Chamberland, Roger
Dictionnaire des oeuvres litteraires
du Québec
Université Laval

Chambers, Edward J.
Professor of Economics
University of Alberta

Chambers, Francis J.
Chief Pilot PISCES IV
Institute of Ocean Sciences
Sidney, BC

Chambers, J.K.
Professor of Linguistics
University of Toronto

Chambers, Robert D.
Professor of English Literature
Trent University

Champ, D.H.
Nyon, Switzerland

Champagne, Guy
Coordonnateur scientifique
Centre de recherche en littérature
québécoise
Université Laval

Champagne, Michel
Musée du Québec, Québec

Chapman, James K.
Professor of History
University of New Brunswick

Chapman, John D.
Professor of Geography
University of British Columbia

Charbonneau, Louis
Professeur de mathématiques
Université du Québec à Montréal

Charles, John
Arts Writer, Edmonton

Charlton, Murray N.
National Water Research Institute
Environment Canada
Burlington, Ont

Chartrand, L. Margaret
Novice historical researcher
Winnipeg

Chartrand, Luc
Journaliste, Radio-Canada
Montréal

Chartrand, René
Senior Military Advisor/Curator
Parks Canada, Ottawa

Chatterton, Brian D.E.
Professor of Geology
University of Alberta

Chaussé, Gilles
Professeur d'histoire religieuse
Université de Montréal

Cheff, Michel Vincent
Galerie Nationale du Canada, Ottawa

Chenier, Nancy Miller
Ottawa

Chiasson, Anselme
Centre d'études acadiennes
Université de Moncton

Chiasson, Zénon
Professeur de littérature
Université de Moncton

Childers, Walter R.
Agriculture Canada (retired)
Ottawa

Chimbos, Peter D.
Associate Professor of Sociology
Brescia College
University of Western Ontario

Ching, Blair
Instructor, R.F. Staples School
Westlock, Alta

Chisholm, Alexander J.
Director, Atmospheric Processes
Research Branch
Environment Canada
Downsview, Ont

Chisholm, Elspeth
Freelance writer & broadcaster
Port Hope, Ont

Choquette, Robert
Full Professor
University of Ottawa

Chorniawy, Catherine D.
Historian, Kitchener

Chown, Diana
Edmonton

Christian, Timothy J.
Dean of Law
University of Alberta

Christian, William E.
Associate Professor of Political
Studies
University of Guelph

Christie, Carl A.
Senior Research Officer, Directorate of
History
Dept of National Defence, Ottawa

Christie, Innis
Dean & Professor of Law
Dalhousie University

Chubey, B. Bert
Research Scientist
Agriculture Canada
Morden, Man

Churcher, Charles Stephen
Professor of Zoology
University of Toronto;
Research Associate
Royal Ontario Museum, Toronto

Chute, Janet
Graduate Student, Doctoral Program
McMaster University

Chutter, S. Donald C.
Ottawa Bureau Chief
Revay & Associates Limited, Ottawa

Cinq-Mars, Jacques
Commission archéologique du Canada
Musée national des civilizations, Ottawa

Clague, John J.
Geological Survey of Canada
Vancouver

Clandinin, Michael Thomas
Professor of Nutrition
University of Alberta

Clark, Howard C.
President
Dalhousie University

Clark, Lovell
Senior Scholar in History
University of Manitoba

Clark, Robert H.
Professional engineer, Ottawa

Clark, T. Alan
Professor of Physics
University of Calgary

Clark, Thomas H.
Professor Emeritus of Geological
Sciences
McGill University

Clark, Wesley J.
Executive Director, Ringette Canada
Vanier, Ont

Clarke, R. Allyn
Physical Oceanographer
Bedford Institute of Oceanography
Dartmouth, NS

Clarkson, Stephen
Professor of Political Economy
University of Toronto

Clement, Wallace
Professor of Sociology
Carleton University

Clerk, Nathalie
Analyste en architecture
Parcs Canada
Hull, Qué

Clermont, Norman
Département d'anthropologie
Université de Montréal

Clermont, Yves W.
Professor of Histology
McGill University

Clifford, Howard
Consultant on Day Care
Health & Welfare Canada, Ottawa

Clink, William L.
Chief, Technology Support Division
Atmospheric Environment Service
Toronto

Clippingdale, Richard
Director, Canadian Studies
Carleton University

Cloutier, Nicole
Curator of Early Canadian Art
Montréal Museum of Fine Arts

Clowes, Gigi
Graduate Student of Physical Education
University of British Columbia

Coad, Brian W.
Curator of Fishes
National Museum of Natural Sciences
Ottawa

Coakley, John P.
National Water Research Institute
Burlington, Ont

Coates, Donna
English Instructor
Mount Royal College, Calgary;
Athabasca University

Coates, Kenneth S.
Assistant Professor of History
University of Victoria

Cochran, Bente Roed
University of Alberta

Cody, William James
Curator, Vascular Plant Herbarium
Biosystematics Research Institute
Agriculture Canada, Ottawa

Cogswell, Dale R.
Government Records Archivist
Provincial Archives of New
Brunswick, Fredericton

Cogswell, Fred
Professor Emeritus of English
Literature
University of New Brunswick

Cohen, Stanley A.
Counsel, Human Rights Law
Dept of Justice, Ottawa

Cole, Susan G.
Writer, Toronto

Coleman, James
Vancouver

Coleman, Patricia H.
Nutritional Sciences
Research Officer
University of Toronto

Collard, Elizabeth
Consultant on Ceramics
Canadian Museum of Civilization;
Honorary Curator of Ceramics
McCord Museum, McGill University

Collet, Paulette
Professor of French
University of Toronto

Collins, Malcolm M.C.
Assistant Director
Division of Electrical Engineering
National Research Council, Ottawa

Collinson, Helen Fabia
Curator, Art Collections
University of Alberta

Colombo, John Robert
Writer, Toronto

Conboy, Alan
Transportation Consultant, Ottawa

Condemine, Odette
Professor of French
Carleton University

Conn, David R.
Librarian, Vancouver

Connelly, M. Patricia
Professor of Sociology
Saint Mary's University

Connor, James T.H.
Curator, Medical Museum
University Hospital, London

Conolly, Leonard W.
Professor of Drama
University of Guelph

Conover, Robert J.
Research Scientist
Bedford Institute of Oceanography
Dartmouth, NS

Conrad, Margaret
Associate Professor of History
Acadia University

Conron, A. Brandon
Professor Emeritus
University of Western Ontario

Conway, Brian E.
Professor of Chemistry;
Killam Research Fellow (1984)
University of Ottawa

Cooch, F. Graham
Senior Research Science Advisor
Canadian Wildlife Service, Ottawa

Cook, Eung-Do
Professor & Head of Linguistics
University of Calgary

Cook, Francis R.
Curator, Herpetology Section
National Museum of Natural Sciences
Ottawa

Cooke, O.A.
Senior Archival Officer
Directorate of History
Dept of National Defence, Ottawa

Cope, Gordon William
Professional Geologist
Calgary

Copeland, Murray J.
Geological Survey of Canada, Ottawa

Copley, John R.D.
Research Scientist
National Bureau of Standards
Gaithersburg, MD

Corbeil, Pierre
Professeur d'histoire
CEGEP de Drummondville, Qué

Corcoran, Frank
Assistant Director
Public Programming
Canadian Museum of Civilization

Cormier, J. Clement
Founding President (1963-67);
Chancellor (1973-78)
University of Moncton

Cornell, Paul Grant
Waterloo, Ontario

Cornell, Peter M.
Economic Consultant
Ottawa

Cosentino, Frank
Professor of Physical Education &
Athletics
York University

Cosper, Ronald L.
Professor of Sociology
Saint Mary's University

Côté, Françoise
Montréal

Côté, Jean G.
Edmonton

Cote, Mark
Toronto

Cotnam, Jacques
Professeur de littérature québécois
York University

Coulter, Rebecca Priegert
Co-ordinator of Women's Studies
Athabasca University

Coupland, Robert T.
Professor Emeritus of Plant Ecology
University of Saskatchewan

Courchene, Thomas J.
Professor of Economics
University of Western Ontario

Courtney, John C.
Professor of Political Science
University of Saskatchewan

Coutts, Sally
Architectural historian
Environment Canada, Parks

Cove, John J.
Associate Professor of Anthropology
Carleton University

Cowan, Jeff G.
Barrister & Solicitor
Weir & Foulds
Toronto

Coward, Harold G.
Professor of Religious Studies
University of Calgary

Cox, Bruce
Associate Professor of Anthropology
Carleton University

Cox, Diane W.
Professor of Paediatrics & Medical
Genetics
The Hospital for Sick Children
University of Toronto

Crabb, Michael F.
CBC
Toronto

Cragg, Laurence Harold
President & Professor Emeritus of
Chemistry
Mount Allison University

Craig, Mary M.
La Fédération des Coopératives du
Nouveau-Québec, Montréal

Craig, Terrence L.
Assistant Professor of English
Mount Allison University

Crain, Ian K.
Canada Land Data Systems
Environment Canada, Ottawa

Crane, Brian A.
Barrister & Solicitor
Gowling & Henderson, Ottawa

Crane, David
Economics Writer
The Toronto Star

Cranmer-Byng, John L.
Professor Emeritus of History
University of Toronto
Cranstone, Donald A.
Energy, Mines & Resources Canada
Ottawa
Craven, David L.
Associate Professor of Art History
State University of New York
College at Cortland, NY
Crawford, Roy D.
Professor of Animal & Poultry
Genetics
University of Saskatchewan
Crawley, Judy (deceased)
Ottawa
Creery, Tim
Journalist, Ottawa
Crine, Philippe
Professeur de biochimie
Université de Montréal
Crookell, Harold
Professor of Business
University of Western Ontario
Cross, Michael, S.
Professor of History
Dalhousie University
Crossley, Diane
Victoria, BC
Crossman, E.J.
Curator
Dept of Ichthyology & Herpetology
Royal Ontario Museum, Toronto;
Professor of Zoology
University of Toronto
Croteau, Omer
Professeur titulaire de sciences
comptable
École des hautes études commerciales
Montréal
Crowe, A. David
Head, Tree Fruits Program
Agriculture Canada
Kentville, NS
Crowe, Jean Margaret
Freelance Journalist, Toronto
Crowe, Keith Jeffray
Consultant
Dept of Indian & Northern Affairs
Ottawa
Crowe, Ronald B.
Climatologist
Canadian Climate Centre
Downsview, Ont
Cruden, David M.
Professor of Civil Engineering &
of Geology
University of Alberta
Cruickshank, David A.
Professor of Law
University of Calgary
Cruikshank, Ken
Toronto
Crunican, Paul
Professor of History
University of Western Ontario
Čuješ, Rudolf P.
Professor of Sociology
St Francis Xavier University
Cumming, Bruce Gordon
Professor of Biology
University of New Brunswick
Cumming, Carman W.
Professor of Journalism
Carleton University
Cumming, Leslie Merrill
Research Scientist
Geological Survey of Canada, Ottawa
Currie, Philip J.
Assistant Director (Curatorial)
Tyrrell Museum of Palaeontology
Drumheller, Alta
Currie, Raymond F.
Associate Professor of Sociology
University of Manitoba
Curtis, Christopher G.
Historian
Parks Canada, Ottawa
Curtis, James E.
Associate Professor of Sociology
University of Waterloo
Cusack, Leonard J.
History Teacher
Kinkora Regional High School, PEI
Cutler, Maurice
Director, Public Affairs
Office of the Auditor General of
Canada, Ottawa
Cybulski, Jerome S.
Curator of Physical Anthropology
Canadian Museum of Civilization
Ottawa

Czuboka, Michael
Historian, author & Superintendent of
Schools
Beausejour, Man
Czypionka, Joachim B.
Historian & writer, Edmonton

d'Agincourt, Lorraine G.
Writer, California
D'Allaire, Micheline
Professeur agrégé d'histoire
Université d'Ottawa
Dagg, Anne Innis
Academic Director
Independent Studies Program
University of Waterloo
Dahl, Edward H.
Early Cartography Specialist
National Archives of Canada, Ottawa
Dahlie, Hallvard
Professor of English
University of Calgary
Dahms, Moshie E.
Reference Librarian
Humanities Division
University of Guelph Library
Dale, Hugh Monro
Professor of Botany
University of Guelph
Dale, Ralph
Librarian, Central Region Libraries
Grand Falls, Nfld
Dales, John H.
Toronto
Daly, Eric W.
Vice-President, Planning & Development
Trilon Financial Corporation, Toronto
Dansereau, Pierre
Professeur d'écologie
Université du Québec à Montréal
Danys, Ruth
Freelance writer, Toronto
Darnell, Regna
Professor of Anthropology
University of Alberta
Daubeny, Hugh A.
Research Scientist
Agriculture Canada, Vancouver
Davenport, Paul
Associate Professor
McGill University
Davey, Frank
Professor of English
York University
David, Gilbert
Ecrivain, Montréal
David, Hélène
Chercheure
Institut de recherche appliquée sur
le travail, Montréal
David, Peter P.
Professeur titulaire de géologie
Université de Montréal
Davidson, William A.B.
Editor (retired)
Canadian Textile Journal, Montréal
Davies, Gwendolyn
Associate Professor of English;
Associate of the Centre for Canadian
Studies
Mount Allison University
Davies, John A.
Professor of Geography
McMaster University
Davis, Ann
Freelance curator
London, Ont
Davis, Chuck
Writer & broadcaster, Vancouver
Davis, Richard C.
Dept of English;
Arctic Institute of North America
University of Calgary
Davis, Vicki L.
Librarian, Ottawa
Davison, James D.
President, Wolfville Historical Society
Wolfville, NS
Dawe, Michael J.
Archivist
Red Deer & District Archives
Red Deer, Alta
Day, John M.
Management Consultant, Vancouver
Day, Lawrence
Writer, Toronto
de Jong, Nicolas J.
Provincial Archivist of Prince Edward
Island, Charlottetown
de Pencier, Honor
Research Associate
Royal Ontario Museum, Toronto

Dearden, Philip
Associate Professor of Geography
University of Victoria
DeBresson, Chris
Assistant Research Professor
Centre for Research of the Development of
Industry & Technology Economics
Concordia University
Decarie, Malcolm Graeme
Associate Professor of History
Concordia University
Deeg, Bart F.
Recreation Planning Consultant
Bart Deeg & Associates, Edmonton
Deeprose, Ronald K.
Director
Technical Services Division
Alberta Environment, Edmonton
DeFelice, James V.
Professor of Drama
University of Alberta
Del Buono, Vincent M.
Senior Counsel
Dept of Justice, Ottawa
Delarue, Norman C.
Emeritus Professor of Surgery
University of Toronto
Delorme, L. Denis
National Water Research Institute
Environment Canada
Burlington, Ont
Dempsey, Hugh A.
Assistant Director (Collections)
Glenbow Museum, Calgary
Dempsey, L. James
Calgary
den Otter, A.A.
Associate Professor of History
Memorial University of Newfoundland
Dence, Michael R.
Executive Director
Royal Society of Canada, Ottawa
Dendy, David
East Kelowna, BC
Dennison, John D.
Professor of Administrative,
Adult & Higher Education
University of British Columbia
Derome, Jacques F.
Professor of Meteorology
McGill University
Derry, Duncan R. (deceased)
Consulting geologist
Derry, Michener, Booth & Wahl
Toronto
Derry, Ramsay (deceased)
Editor, Toronto
des Rivières, Marie-José
Dictionnaire des oeuvres
littéraires du Québec
Université Laval
Desbarats, Peter
Dean, Graduate School of Journalism
University of Western Ontario
Deschênes, Donald
Ethnomusicologue
Moncton, NB
DesGranges, Jean-Luc
Chercheur scientifique
Service canadien de la faune
Région du Québec
Désilets, Andrée
Professeur d'histoire
Université de Sherbrooke
Desloges, Yvon
Agent de recherche
Parcs Canada, Québec
DeSorcy, G. J.
Chairman
Energy Resources Conservation Board
Calgary
Dewan, Philip M.
Director of Policy
Office of the Premier of Ontario, Toronto
Dewhirst, John
Anthropologist, Victoria
Dick, Lyle
Historian, Parks Canada
Winnipeg
Dickie, Lloyd Merlin
Research Scientist
Bedford Institute of Oceanography
Dickin McGinnis, Janice
Lawyer & writer, Calgary
Dickinson, John A.
Professeur d'histoire
Université de Montréal
Dickinson, William Trevor
Professor of Water Resource Engineering
University of Guelph

Dimić, Milan V.
Professor of Comparative Literature
University of Alberta
Dion, Gérard
Professeur de relations industrielles
Université Laval
Dionne, Raoul
Professeur d'histoire
Université de Moncton
Dionne, René
Professeur titulaire de lettres
françaises
Université d'Ottawa
Dirks, Gerald E.
Associate Professor of Politics
Brock University
Dirks, Patricia G.
Assistant Professor of History
Brock University
Diubaldo, Richard J.
Associate Professor of History;
Director, Centre for Mature Students
Concordia University
Dobbin, Murray
Writer, Saskatoon
Dobell, Rodney
Professor of Public Administration
University of Victoria
Dodd, Dianne
PhD Candidate
Carleton University
Dodman, Donald A.
Parish Priest, St Albert, Alta
Doerr, Audrey D.
Indian & Northern Affairs, Ottawa
Dohler, G.C.
Ottawa
Doiron, Allen
Archiviste
Archives provinciales du
Nouveau-Brunswick, Fredericton
Dolman, Claude Ernest
Professor Emeritus of Microbiology
University of British Columbia
Dompierre, Louise
Associate Director/Chief Curator
The Power Plant, Toronto
Donaldson, Mairi
Victoria
Donaldson, Sue Anne
Associate Professor of Environmental
Design, University of Calgary
Donnelly, Margaret Mary
Barrister & Solicitor, Edmonton
Donner, John
Brampton, Ont
Donneur, André
Professeur de science politique
Université du Québec à Montréal
Doob, Penelope B.R.
Associate Professor of English
& Multidisciplinary Studies
York University
Doody, Peter K.
Barrister & Solicitor, Ottawa
Doolittle, Joyce
Professor of Drama
University of Calgary
Dorcey, Anthony H.J.
Assistant Director
Westwater Research Centre
University of British Columbia
Dore, Yvon
Sports Writer
Radio Canada, Montréal
Dorion, Gilles
Professeur titulaire littérature Québécoise
Université Laval
Dossetor, John B.
Professor of Medicine
University of Alberta
Dotto, Lydia
Science writer, Toronto
Doucet, Roger A.
Agronome, Ministère de l'Agriculture
des Pecheries et de l'Alimentation du
Québec
Doucette, Leonard E.
Professor of French
Scarborough College
University of Toronto
Dougall, Charles
Dictionary of Canadian Biography
Toronto
Dougan, Jane L.
Research Assistant
University of Guelph
Douglas, W.A.B.
Director, Directorate of History
Dept of National Defence, Ottawa

Dow, Marguerite R.
  Professor Emerita
  University of Western Ontario
Dowbiggin, William F.
  Executive Sport Publications Ltd;
  Publisher, Edmonton
Downey, R. Keith
  Principal Research Scientist
  Agriculture Canada Research Station
  Saskatoon
Doyle, Arthur T.
  Political historian, Fredericton
Doyle, Denzil J.
  President, Doyletech Corporation
  Ottawa
Doyle, James
  Professor of English
  Wilfrid Laurier University
Doyle, Richard
  Senator, Ottawa
Doyon, Pierre
  Professeur d'histoire de l'art
  Université de Montréal
Drache, Sharon
  Writer, Ottawa
Drager, Derek C.
  Writer, Edmonton
Drainie, Bronwyn
  Writer & Broadcaster
  Toronto
Drake, W.M.
  Toronto
Draper, James A.
  Dept of Adult Education
  Ontario Institute for Studies in
  Education, Toronto
Draper, Wayne
  Environment Canada, Ottawa
Dreisziger, Nandor Fred
  Associate Professor of History
  Royal Military College of Canada
Driedger, Leo
  Professor of Sociology
  University of Manitoba
Drinkwater, Kenneth F.
  Bedford Institute of Oceanography
  Dartmouth, NS
Driscoll, Bernadette
  Curator & writer, Inuit Art
  Washington, DC
Drolet, Jean-Paul
  Mining engineer, Ottawa
Drover, Glenn
  Professor of Social Work
  University of British Columbia
Drummond, Ian M.
  Professor of Economics
  University of Toronto
Drummond, R. Norman
  Associate Professor of Geography
  McGill University
Dryden, Jean E.
  Provincial Archives of Alberta
  Edmonton
Drysdale, Patrick D.
  Lexicographer
  Toronto & Abingdon, England
Dubois, Jean-Marie M.
  Professeur de géographie
  Université de Sherbrooke
Dubro, James R.
  Investigative Journalist
  Norfolk Research Unit, Toronto
Ducharme, Léo
  Professeur, Faculté de droit
  Section de droit civil
  Université d'Ottawa
Duchesne, Raymond
  Professeur d'histoire des sciences
  Télé-université, Université du Québec
Duchesneau, François
  Professeur titulaire de philosophie
  Université de Montréal
Duciaume, Jean-Marcel
  Professeur de littérature et
  civilisation québécoise
  University of Alberta
Ducrocq-Poirier, Madeleine
  Docteur d'Etat es lettres
  (littérature québécois)
  Université de Paris - Sorbonne
  Centre national de la recherche
  scientifique, France
Duffy, Dennis
  Professor of English
  Innis College
  University of Toronto
Duley, Walter W.
  Professor of Physics
  York University

Dulong, Gaston
  Professeur titulaire de linguistique
  Université Laval
Dumont, François
  Centre de recherches en littérature
  Québécoise
  Université Laval
Dumont, Micheline
  Professeure d'histoire
  Université de Sherbrooke
Dunbar, M.J.
  Professor Emeritus of Oceanography
  McGill University
Duncan, Graham W.
  Secretary, Canadian Billiards &
  Snooker Referees' Association
  Willowdale, Ontario
Duncan, Neil J.
  Special Lecturer in Mining
  Engineering
  University of Alberta
Dunham, Robert H.
  Associate Professor of English
  Simon Fraser University
Dunlop, Marilyn E.
  Medical writer, Toronto Star
  Toronto
Dunnigan, Brian Leigh
  Executive Director
  Old Fort Niagara Association
Dunton, Davidson (deceased)
  Fellow, Institute of Canadian Studies
  Carleton University
Duperreault, Jean R.
  School of Human Kinetics
  University of Ottawa
Dupont, Jean-Claude
  Professeur d'ethnologie
  Université Laval
Durflinger, Serge Marc
  Historian, Montréal
Durocher, René
  Professeur d'histoire
  Université de Montréal
Dussault, Gabriel
  Professeur agrégé de sociologie
  Université Laval
Dwivedi, O.P.
  Professor & Chairman of Political
  Studies
  University of Guelph
Dyck, Noel
  Associate Professor of Anthropology
  Simon Fraser University
Dyer, Charles C.
  Associate Professor of Astronomy
  University of Toronto
Dykes, James
  Toronto

Eagle, John A.
  Associate Professor of History
  University of Alberta
Eakins, Peter R.
  Associate Professor of Geology
  McGill University
Eaman, Ross A.
  Assistant Professor of Journalism
  Carleton University
Eastman, Harry C.
  Professor of Economics
  University of Toronto
Eatock, Colin
  Toronto
Eber, Dorothy Harley
  Writer, Montréal
Eccles, William John
  Professor Emeritus
  University of Toronto
Eddie, Christine
  Chercheure en communications, Québec
Edinborough, Arnold
  President & Chief Executive Officer
  The Council for Business and the Arts in
  Canada, Toronto
Edwards, Oliver Edward
  Chemistry Division
  National Research Council of Canada
  Ottawa
Edwards, Peggy
  Fitness consultant, Ottawa
Ehrhardt, Roger B.
  Canadian International Development
  Agency
Eichler, Margrit
  Professor of Sociology
  Ontario Institute for Studies in
  Education, Toronto
Einarson, Neil
  Manitoba Culture
  Heritage & Recreation, Winnipeg

Elder, R. Bruce
  Lightworks, Toronto
Elford, Jean
  Writer, Sarnia
Elias, Peter Douglas
  Prince Albert, Sask
Eliot, C.W.J.
  President & Professor of Classics
  University of Prince Edward Island
Elliott, Bruce S.
  Ottawa
Elliott, David R.
  Historical contractor
  Nanoose Bay, BC
Elliott, James A.
  Research Scientist
  Bedford Institute of Oceanography
  Dartmouth, NS
Elliott, Marie
  Victoria
Ellis, David
  President, Omnia Communications Inc.
  Toronto
Elson, John A.
  Professor of Geological Sciences
  McGill University
Emery, George
  Associate Professor of History
  University of Western Ontario
Emmerson, Donald W.
  Consultant, Ottawa
Emmons, Douglas B.
  Food Research Centre
  Agriculture Canada, Ottawa
Emond, Maurice
  Professeur titulaire de littérature
  Université Laval
Empey, William F.
  President, Applied Economics
  Toronto
English, John R.
  Professor of History
  University of Waterloo
Enkin, Murray W.
  Professor of Obstetrics & Gynecology,
  Clinical Epidemiology & Biostatistics
  McMaster University
Enros, Philip C.
  Science Adviser
  Science Council of Canada
Epp, Frank H. (deceased)
  Professor of History
  Conrad Grebel College
  University of Waterloo
Erb, Robert Bruce
  Executive Vice-President
  Canadian Automobile Association
  Ottawa
Erskine, Anthony J.
  Canadian Wildlife Service
  Sackville, NB
Evans, Brian L.
  Professor of History
  University of Alberta
Evans, D.K.
  Research Scientist
  Atomic Energy of Canada Ltd
  Chalk River, Ont
Evans, W.F.J.
  Chief, Experimental Studies Division
  Atmospheric Environment Service
  Winnipeg

Fahey, Curtis
  Editor, James Lorimer & Company
  Toronto
Fall, Valerie J.
  Executive Director
  The Catholic Women's League of
  Canada, Winnipeg
Fallis, A. Murray
  Professor Emeritus of Parasitology
  University of Toronto
Fankboner, Peter V.
  Associate Professor of Biology
  Simon Fraser University
Farr, D.M.L.
  Professor Emeritus of History
  Carleton University
Farr, Dorothy M.
  Curator
  Agnes Etherington Art Centre
  Queen's University
Farrell, Fred
  Archivist
  Provincial Archives of New Brunswick
Fawcett, George D.
  Transport Canada, Ottawa
Feder, Alison
  Professor of English
  Memorial University of Newfoundland

Fedoroff, Sergey
  Professor & Head of Anatomy
  College of Medicine
  University of Saskatchewan
Fee, Margery
  Assistant Professor of English;
  Director of the Strathy Language Unit
  Queen's University
Fehr, Kevin O'Brien
  Pharmacologist
  Addiction Research Foundation
  Toronto
Feindel, William
  Director Emeritus
  Montreal Neurological Institute
  Montréal
Feldman, Seth R.
  Associate Professor of Film Studies
  York University
Fenna, Donald
  Professor of Applied Sciences in
  Medicine
  University of Alberta
Fennell, William O.
  Professor Emeritus
  Emmanuel College, Toronto
Fenton, M. Brock
  Professor of Biology
  York University
Fenton, Terry L.
  Curator & critic, Edmonton
Ferguson, Bob
  Author, Who's Who in Canadian
  Sport; Sports Writer,
  Ottawa Citizen, Ottawa
Ferguson, Howard L.
  Assistant Deputy Minister
  Atmospheric Environment Service
  Environment Canada
  Downsview, Ont
Ferron, Jean
  Professeur de biologie
  Université du Québec à Rimouski
Fetherling, Doug
  Author, Toronto
Field, George
  Institute of Law Research & Reform
  University of Alberta
Field, John L.
  Research historian
  Niagara-on-the-Lake, Ont
Field, Richard Henning
  Independent curator & writer
  Halifax, NS
Findlay, Leonard M.
  Professor of English
  University of Saskatchewan
Fingard, Judith
  Professor of History
  Dalhousie University
Fink, Howard R.
  Professor of English
  Concordia University
Finkel, Alvin
  Professor of History
  Athabasca University
Finklestein, Maxwell
  Parks Canada, Ottawa
Finlayson, Douglas A.
  Graduate Studies in Geography
  University of Alberta
Finley, Gerald
  Professor of the History of Art
  Queen's University
Finn, Gérard
  Historien, Ottawa
Firth, Christine
  Historian, Soaring Association of
  Canada
Fisher, Richard S.
  Moncrieff Management Ltd, Montréal
Fisher, Robin
  Professor of History
  Simon Fraser University
Fisher, Stan C.
  Canadian Handball Association
  Sherwood Park, Alta
Fitsell, John Walter (Bill)
  Historian, International Hockey Hall
  of Fame & Museum
  Kingston, Ont
Fitzgerald, Patrick J.
  Professor of Law
  Carleton University
Flaherty, David H.
  Professor of History & Law
  University of Western Ontario
Flanagan, Thomas
  Professor of Political Science
  University of Calgary
Fleming, Elizabeth A.
  Remote Sensing Specialist, Ottawa

Fleming, R.B.
Biographer, Argyle, Ont
Fleming, Robert J.
Development Consultant, Toronto
Flemming, David B.
Director, Maritime Museum of the Atlantic, Halifax
Flitton, Marilyn G.
Researcher, Vancouver
Fong, David G.
Mineral Economist
Mineral Policy Sector
Energy, Mines & Resources Canada
Ottawa
Foran, Max
Priddis, Alta
Forbes, Ernest R.
Professor of History
University of New Brunswick
Forbes, R.E.
Project Director, Westarc Group Inc
Brandon, Man
Forbes, William B.
Executive Editor
Canadian Printer & Publisher,
Electronic Publishing, Printing
Product Guide
Toronto
Forbis, Richard G.
Professor of Archaeology
University of Calgary
Forcese, Dennis P.
Professor of Sociology &
Anthropology;
Dean, Faculty of Social Sciences
Carleton University
Ford, Anne Rochon
Policy & Program Advisor: Women's
Health
Women's College Hospital, Toronto
Ford, Clifford
Executive Secretary
Canadian Musical Heritage Society
Ottawa
Ford, Derek C.
Professor of Geography
McMaster University
Ford, Gillian
Devonian Botanic Garden
University of Alberta
Ford, Susan
Ballenford Architectural Books
Toronto
Forest, Bertrand
Agricultural Consultant
Roche Associés Ltée, Québec
Forrester, Ronald W.
President
Canadian Jiu-jitsu Association
Oakville, Ont
Forrester, Warren D.
Oceanographic consultant, Ottawa
Forsey, Eugene Alfred
Retired senator, professor &
trade union official, Ottawa
Forsyth, Frank R.
Plant Physiologist;
Retired Research Scientist, Agriculture
Canada
Berwick, NS
Forsyth, Peter A.
Professor Emeritus of Physics
University of Western Ontario
Fortin, Claire-Andrée
Études québécoises
Université du Québec à Trois-Rivières
Fortin, Gérald
Professeur, INRS-Urbanization
Institut national de la recherche
scientifique
Université du Québec
Forward, Charles N.
Professor of Geography
University of Victoria
Forward, William F.
Research Associate
Science Council of Canada, Ottawa
Foss, Brian F.
London, England
Foster, Franklin
Kingston, Ont
Foster, J. Bristol
Ecological consultant, Victoria
Foster, John Bellamy
Assistant Professor of Sociology
University of Oregon
Foster, John E.
Professor of History
University of Alberta

Foster, Michael K.
Iroquoian Ethnologist
Canadian Ethnology Service
Canadian Museum of Civilization
Ottawa
Foulds, Glenn B.
Edmonton
Fowke, Edith M.
Professor of English
York University
Fowler, Marian
Writer
Shelburne, Ont
Fox, Paul W.
Chairman
Ontario Council on University Affairs
Toronto
Fox, Richard C.
Professor of Geology & Zoology
University of Alberta
Fox, Rosemary J.
Director
Canadian Nature Federation
Smithers, BC
Francis, Daniel
Writer, Vancouver
Francis, Diane
The Toronto Star, Toronto
Frank, David
Associate Professor of History
University of New Brunswick
Frank, Julius F.
Animal health consultant
Manotick, Ont
Franklin, Colin Athol
Director General
Applications Program
Dept of Communications, Ottawa
Franks, C.E.S.
Associate Professor of Political
Studies
Queen's University
Fransen, David
Policy Analyst
Solicitor General, Ottawa
Franson, Robert T.
Associate Professor of Law
University of British Columbia
Frappier, Armand
Retired director & consultant
Institut Armand-Frappier
Laval-des-Rapides, Qué
Fraser, David
National Archives of Canada
Ottawa
Fraser, Kathleen D.J.
Doctoral Student
University of Western Ontario
Fraser, Robert Lochiel
Senior Manuscript Editor
Dictionary of Canadian Biography
Toronto
Fréchette, Pierre
Professeur d'économique
Université Laval
Fredeen, Howard Townley
Adjunct Professor, Animal Breeding
University of Alberta
Freedman, Benjamin
Associate Professor
McGill Centre for Medicine, Ethics & Law
McGill University
Freeman, Gordon Russel
Professor of Chemistry
University of Alberta
Freeman, Mac
Professor of Education
Queen's University
Freeman, Milton M.R.
Henry Marshall Tory Professor
University of Alberta
Freeman, Minnie Aodla
Writer, Edmonton
Freeman, Roger D.
Clinical Professor of Psychiatry
University of British Columbia;
Psychiatric Consultant
Western Institute for the Deaf
Freitag, Walter H.P.
Professor of the Church in Historic
Witness & Biblical Interpretation
Lutheran Theological Seminary
Saskatoon
French, Carey
The Globe and Mail, Toronto
French, Hugh M.
Professor of Geography & Geology
University of Ottawa
Frideres, James S.
Professor of Sociology
University of Calgary

Friesen, Gerald
Associate Professor of History
University of Manitoba
Friesen, James D.
Professor of Medical Genetics
University of Toronto
Friesen, Jean M.
Associate Professor of History
University of Manitoba
Frost, Stanley Brice
Director, History of McGill Project
McGill University
Fuerstenberg, Adam G.
Professor of English
Ryerson Polytechnic Institute
Toronto
Fulford, Robert
Writer, Toronto
Fuller, Anthony (Tony) M.
Professor of Rural Development
University of Guelph
Fuller, George R.
Professor of Interior Design
University of Manitoba
Fuller, William A.
Professor Emeritus of Zoology
University of Alberta
Fullerton, Carol W.
Calgary
Fullerton, Douglas H.
Retired Chairman
National Capital Commission;
Consultant & writer, Ottawa
Furniss, Ian F.
Economist, Ottawa
Fyfe, Richard
Environment Canada
Canadian Wildlife Service
Edmonton
Fyfe, William S.
Dean, Faculty of Science
University of Western Ontario

Gadacz, René Robert
Department of Anthropology
University of Alberta
Gaffield, Chad
Associate Professor of History
University of Ottawa
Gagan, David
Professor of History
McMaster University
Gagnon, François-Marc
Professeur d'histoire de l'art
Université de Montréal
Gaizauskas, Victor
Herzberg Institute of Astrophysics
National Research Council of Canada
Ottawa
Galarneau, Claude
Professeur d'histoire
Université Laval
Gale, Peggy
Independent curator, Toronto
Gall, Gerald L.
Professor of Law
University of Alberta
Gallacher, Daniel T.
Chief, Human History
British Columbia Provincial Museum
Victoria
Gallagher, Paul
President
Vancouver Community College
Galloway, Strome
Writer, Ottawa
Galt, John Alexander
Dominion Radio Astrophysical
Observatory
National Research Council
Penticton, BC
Ganapathy, Natarajan
Metric Commission Canada, Ottawa
Ganzevoort, Herman
Associate Professor of History
University of Calgary
Gardner, David E.
Actor, director & theatre historian
Toronto
Gardner, Norman
President
CPCI - Canadian Productivity
Consultants Inc, Ottawa
Garrett, Christopher J.R.
Professor of Oceanography
Dalhousie University
Garrett, John F.
Institute of Ocean Sciences
Sidney, BC
Gaskell, Jane
Associate Professor of Education
University of British Columbia

Gauvin, Lise
Professeur de littérature
Université de Montréal
Gauvin, M.J.
Nonferrous Commodities Division
Minerals & Metals Strategy Branch
Energy, Mines & Resources Canada
Ottawa
Gayler, Hugh J.
Associate Professor of Geography
Brock University
Geekie, Douglas A.
Director of Communications
Canadian Medical Association, Ottawa
Geiger, John Grigsby
Writer, Edmonton
Geist, Valerius
Professor of Environmental Sciences
University of Calgary
Gellner, John
Magazine editor & writer, Toronto
Gendreau, Paul
Regional Co-ordinating Psychologist
Ontario Ministry of Correctional
Services, Toronto
Gendron, Ghislain
Professeur de phytologie
Université Laval
Gersovitz, Julia
Architect;
Auxiliary Professor
McGill University
Gessler, Trisha
Curator
Queen Charlotte Islands Museum
Queen Charlotte City, BC
Getty, Ian A.L.
Research Director
Nakoda Institute, Stoney Tribe
Morley, Alta
Ghostkeeper, Elmer N.
President
Alberta Federation of Métis
Settlement Associations, Edmonton
Giard, Jacques R.
Associate Professor of Industrial
Design
Carleton University
Gibb, Richard A.
Research Scientist
Geological Survey of Canada, Ottawa
Gibb, Sandra
Head, Exhibition Development
Canadian Museum of Civilization
Ottawa
Gibbons, Kenneth M.
Assistant Professor of Political
Science
University of Winnipeg
Gibson, James A.
President Emeritus
Brock University
Gibson, Lee
Winnipeg
Gibson, William C.
Chairman, Universities Council of BC
Vancouver
Giffen, Perry James
Professor of Sociology
University of Toronto
Giffen, Peter
Don Mills, Ont
Gignac, Elizabeth Hollingsworth
Former Head of Communications
Canadian Museums Association, Ottawa
Giguère, Richard
Professeur de littérature
Université de Sherbrooke
Gilchrist, C.W.
Former Managing Director
Roads & Transportation Association
of Canada
Gillese, John Patrick
Freelance writer, Edmonton
Gillespie, Beryl
Iowa City, Iowa
Gillespie, Bill
Journalist, St John's
Gillespie, Laurence, J.P.
Winnipeg
Gillett, John M.
Curator Emeritus
National Museums of Canada, Ottawa
Gillett, Margaret
Macdonald Professor of Education
McGill University
Gillis, Robert Peter
Historian, Ottawa
Gilliss, Geraldine
Director, Research & Information
Services
Canadian Teachers' Federation, Ottawa

Gilmore, Norbert
  Montréal
Gillmor, Alan M.
  Professor of Music
  Carleton University
Gillott, Cedric
  Professor of Biology
  University of Saskatchewan
Gilson, J.C.
  Professor, Agricultural Economics
  University of Manitoba
Gingras, Yves
  Professeur de sociologie
  Université du Québec à Montréal
Girouard, André
  Dept de français (retired)
  Université Laurentienne
Glendenning, Burton
  Coordinator, Historical Division
  Provincial Archives of New Brunswick
Gnarowski, Michael
  Professor of English
  Carleton University
Goa, David J.
  Curator of Folk Life
  Provincial Museum of Alberta
  Edmonton
Godard, Barbara J.T.
  Associate Professor of English
  York University
Godby, Ensley A.
  Former Director General
  Canada Centre for Remote Sensing
  Ottawa
Godfrey, W. Earl
  Curator Emeritus of Ornithology
  National Museum of Natural Sciences
  Ottawa
Godfrey, William G.
  Professor of History & Dean of Arts
  Mount Allison University
Godwin, R. Bruce
  Executive Director
  Prairie Provinces Water Board, Regina
Gonick, Cy
  Professor of Economics
  University of Manitoba
Gonzales, Cecilia A.
  Associate Professor of Clothing &
  Textiles
  University of Manitoba
Gooch, Bryan N.S.
  Pianist;
  Professor of English
  University of Victoria
Gooding, S. James
  Director, Museum Restoration Service
  Bloomfield, Ont
Goodis, Jerry
  Toronto
Goodman, John T.
  Director, Dept of Psychology
  Children's Hospital of Eastern
  Ontario;
  Professor of Psychology
  University of Ottawa
Gordon, Donald C., Jr.
  Research Scientist
  Bedford Institute of Oceanography
  Dartmouth, NS
Gordon, Glenn
  Co-ordinator of Marketing & Public
  Relations
  Mackenzie Art Gallery
  University of Regina
Gordon, Stanley
  Historian, Edmonton
Gordon, Walter L. (deceased)
  Chairman
  Canadian Institute for Economic
  Policy, Toronto
Gorham, Deborah
  Associate Professor of History
  Carleton University
Gorham, Harriet R.
  Writer, Ottawa
Gorham, Stanley W.
  Honorary Research Associate
  Central New Brunswick Woodmen's
  Museum
  Boiestown, NB
Gotlieb, Calvin Carl
  Professor of Computer Science;
  Faculty of Library & Information
  Science
  University of Toronto
Gottesman, Daniel H.
  Thalassa Research Associates
  Victoria
Gough, Barry Morton
  Professor of History
  Wilfrid Laurier University

Gough, Joseph B.
  Writer, Ottawa
Gouin, Judy
  Artist, Toronto
Gould, Allan M.
  Writer, Toronto
Goulet, Henri
  Research Scientist
  Biosystematics Research Institute
  Ottawa
Gourd, Benoît-Beaudry
  Historien
  Les Productions Abitibi-Témiscamingue
  Inc, Rouyn, Qué
Gow, James Iain
  Professeur de science politique
  Université de Montréal
Gowans, Alan
  Professor of History in Art
  University of Victoria
Graham, J. Wesley
  Dean of Computing & Communications
  University of Waterloo
Graham, Jane E.
  Associate Editor
  Dictionary of Canadian Biography
  Toronto
Graham, John F.
  Professor of Economics
  Dalhousie University
Graham, Katherine A.
  Assistant Professor of Public
  Administration
  Carleton University
Graham, Roger
  Professor Emeritus of History
  Queen's University
Grainger, E.H.
  Arctic Biological Station
  Ste-Anne-de-Bellevue, Qué
Granatstein, J.L.
  Professor of History
  York University
Granger, Alix
  Vice-President, Pemberton-Houston,
  Willoughby Bell Gouinlock Inc
  Vancouver, BC
Granger, Luc
  Professeur titulaire de psychologie
  Université de Montréal
Grant, John A.G.
  Chief Economist
  Wood Gundy Inc, Toronto
Grant, John Webster
  Professor Emeritus of Church History
  Emmanuel College
  Victoria University, Toronto
Grant, Peter
  Writer, Victoria
Gray, Carolyn Elizabeth
  McMaster University
Gray, David
  Professor of Astronomy
  University of Western Ontario
Gray, David Robert
  Associate Curator, Ethology
  National Museum of Natural Sciences
  Ottawa
Gray, Earle
  Writer
  Woodville, Ont
Gray, G. Ronald
  General Manager
  Technical Manpower Development
  Syncrude Canada Ltd, Edmonton
Gray, James
  Professor of Geography
  University of Montréal
Gray, Stephen
  Dept of History
  Simon Fraser University
Greaves, D'Arcy M.
  Classical guitarist, Edmonton
Green, J. Paul
  Professor of Music Education
  University of Western Ontario
Green, Leslie C.
  Professor of Political Science
  University of Alberta
Green, Mel
  Barrister, Toronto
Green, Richard
  Writer
  Bramalea, Ont
Greenberg, Reesa
  Associate Professor of Art History
  Concordia University
Greene, John P.
  Teacher, St John's

Greenfield, Thomas B.
  Professor
  Ontario Institute for Studies in
  Education, Toronto
Greenhill, Pauline
  Assistant Professor of Canadian Studies
  University of Waterloo
Greenhous, Brereton
  Historian, Directorate of History
  Dept of National Defence, Ottawa
Greenshields, John Edward Ross
  (deceased)
  Director
  Canada Agriculture Research Station
  Saskatoon
Greenwood, Hugh J.
  Professor of Geological Sciences
  University of British Columbia
Greer, Allan
  Associate Professor of History
  University of Toronto
Gregg, Arthur E.
  Writer, Sidney, BC
Gregory, E. David
  Associate Professor of History/
  Humanities
  Athabasca University
Gregory, Patrick T.
  Associate Professor of Biology
  University of Victoria
Gregory, Robert W.
  President
  RW Gregory Resources Ltd., Calgary
Grey, Julius H.
  Associate Professor of Law
  McGill University
Gridgeman, Norman T.
  Science writer, Vancouver Island
Griezic, Foster J.K.
  Associate Professor of History &
  Chairman, Labour Studies
  Carleton University
Griffin, Herbert Lawrence
  Research Professor (retired)
  Ottawa
Griffin, John D.M.
  Former General Director
  Canadian Mental Health Association
  Toronto
Griffiths, Anthony J.F.
  Professor of Genetics
  University of British Columbia
Griffiths, Graham C.D.
  Honorary Research Associate of
  Entomology
  University of Alberta
Griffiths, Naomi E.S.
  Dean, Faculty of Arts
  Carleton University
Grinstein, Sergio
  Research Institute
  The Hospital for Sick Children
  Toronto
Grisé, Yolande
  Directrice, Centre de recherche en
  civilisation canadienne-française
  Université d'Ottawa
Groetzinger, Deanna
  Multiple Sclerosis Society of Canada
  Toronto
Grove, Jack W.
  Professor Emeritus of Political Studies
  Queen's University
Grubel, Herbert G.
  Professor of Economics
  Simon Fraser University
Gruber, Patrick D.
  Midland, Ont
Gruen, Hans E.
  Professor of Biology
  University of Saskatchewan
Guernsey, Terry
  Ottawa
Guest, Dennis
  Associate Professor of Social Work
  University of British Columbia
Guest, Hal J.
  Historical resource consultant
  Winnipeg
Guidotti, Tee Lamont
  Professor of Occupational Medicine
  University of Alberta
Guilmette, Armand
  Professeur de lettres
  Université du Québec à Trois-Rivières
Guilmette, Bernadette
  Chargée de cours (lettres)
  Université du Québec à Trois-Rivières
Gundy, H. Pearson
  Professor Emeritus of English
  Language & Literature
  Queen's University

Gunnars, Kristjana
  Writer, Winnipeg
Gunner, S.W.
  Health Protection Branch
  Health & Welfare Canada, Ottawa
Gunning, Harry Emmet
  Killam Professor of Chemistry
  (retired)
  University of Alberta
Guy, Allan
  Professor of Educational
  Administration
  University of Saskatchewan
Gwyn, Julian
  Professor of History
  University of Ottawa
Gwyn, Richard J.
  The Toronto Star
  Ottawa Columnist

Haanappel, Peter P.C.
  Associate Professor of Law
  McGill University
Haber, Erich
  Assistant Curator of Vascular Plants
  National Museums of Canada, Ottawa
Hacker, Carlotta
  Author of The Indomitable Lady
  Doctors
  London, Ont
Hackler, Jim
  Professor of Sociology
  University of Alberta
Haddad, Yvonne Y.
  Professor of History
  University of Massachusetts, Amherst
Hadley, Michael L.
  Professor of Germanic Studies
  University of Victoria
Haehling von Lanzenauer, Christoph
  Professor of Management Science
  University of Western Ontario
Hage, Keith D.
  Professor Emeritus of Geography
  University of Alberta
Haliburton, G. Brenton
  Freelance writer
  Dartmouth, NS
Hall, Anthony J.
  Assistant Professor of Native Studies
  University of Sudbury in
  federation with Laurentian
  University
Hall, David J.
  Professor of History
  University of Alberta
Hall, Frederick A.
  Associate Professor of Music
  McMaster University
Hall, John W.
  Agrologist, Winnipeg
Hall, Roger
  Dept of History
  University of Western Ontario
Hallett, Mary E. (deceased)
  Associate Professor of History
  University of Saskatchewan
Halliday, Hugh A.
  Canadian War Museum, Ottawa
Halliday, Ian
  Herzberg Institute of Astrophysics
  National Research Council of Canada
  Ottawa
Halloran, Mary
  Toronto
Hallowell, Gerald
  Editor, University of Toronto Press
  Toronto
Hallworth, Beryl M.
  Herbarium, Dept of Biology
  University of Calgary
Halpenny, Francess G.
  Professor Emeritus of Library &
  Information Science
  University of Toronto
Halpin, Marjorie M.
  Associate Professor of Anthropology;
  Curator of Ethnology
  University of British Columbia
Hamacher, Vincent Carl
  Professor of Electrical Engineering &
  Computer Science
  University of Toronto
Hamelin, Louis-Edmond
  Géographe, Professeur émérite
  Université Laval
Hamilton, Donald G.
  Director-General (retired)
  Research Branch, Agriculture Canada
  Ottawa
Hamilton, Sally A.
  Mineral Policy Sector, Ottawa

Hamilton, S.W.
Associate Dean of Commerce &
Business Administration
University of British Columbia
Hamilton, William B.
Winthrop Pickard Bell Professor of
Maritime Studies
Mount Allison University
Hampson, Michael C.
Research Manager
Agriculture Canada, St John's
Hamre, Brent M.
General Manager, Canadian Farm &
Industrial Equipment Institute
Burlington, Ont
Hancock, Geoffrey
Editor-in-Chief
Canadian Fiction Magazine, Toronto
Handling, Piers
Writer, Toronto
Hanrahan, James
President, St Thomas More College
University of Saskatchewan
Hansen, Asbjorn T.
Senior Research Officer
National Research Council of Canada
Ottawa
Harbron, John D.
Foreign Affairs Analyst
Thomson Newspapers, Toronto
Harcourt, Peter
Professor of Film Studies
Carleton University
Hardwick, David F.
Research Associate
Biosystematics Research Institute
Ottawa
Hardy, Jean-Pierre
Historien, Musée national des
civilisations, Ottawa
Hardy, René
Professeur d'histoire
Université du Québec à Trois-Rivières
Hare, F. Kenneth
University Professor Emeritus in
Geography
University of Toronto
Hargittay, Clara
Writer, Art Gallery of Ontario
Hargreaves, J. Anthony
Professor & Director
Graduate Studies & Research;
Faculty of Dentistry
University of Alberta
Harland, Gordon
Professor of Religion
University of Manitoba
Harper, Alex M.
Senior Research Scientist
Agriculture Canada Research Station
Lethbridge, Alta
Harper, J. Russell (deceased)
Writer;
Professor of Canadian Art History
Concordia University
Harris, Gretchen L.H.
Associate Professor of Physics
University of Waterloo
Harris, James A.
Board of Directors
The Stephen Leacock Associates
Orillia, Ont
Harris, Peter
Research Scientist
Agriculture Canada, Regina
Harris, R. Cole
Professor of Geography
University of British Columbia
Harris, Stephen
Historian, Directorate of History
Dept of National Defence, Ottawa
Harris, Stuart A.
Professor of Geography
University of Calgary
Harris, Walter E.
Professor Emeritus of Chemistry
University of Alberta
Harris, William E.
Professor of Physics
McMaster University
Harrison, Lionel G.
Professor of Chemistry
University of British Columbia
Harrison, Paul J.
Professor of Oceanography & Botany
University of British Columbia
Harte, Peter J.
Privacy Project
University of Western Ontario
Harvey, David D.
Writer, Ottawa

Hatch, Fred J.
Aviation Historian
Directorate of History
Dept of National Defence, Ottawa
Haufe, Wilbert O.
Head, Animal Parasitology Section
Research Section
Lethbridge, Alta
Hauser, Jo
Physician, Health & Welfare Canada
Ottawa
Haycock, Ronald G.
Associate Professor of History
Royal Military College of Canada
Hayden, Michael
Professor of History
University of Saskatchewan
Hayes, Florence C.
Music Research Assistant
National Library of Canada, Ottawa
Hayne, David M.
Professor of French
University of Toronto
Haynes, Robert H.
Distinguished Research
Professor of Biology
York University
Hayter, Carol
Fine Arts Dealer
Movements In Time Ltd, Toronto
Heald, Henry F.
Writer
Nepean, Ont
Heaver, Trevor D.
UPS Foundation Professor of
Transportation
University of British Columbia
Hebb, Harvey D.
Edmonton
Hebda, Richard J.
Curator of Botany
British Columbia Provincial Museum
Victoria
Hébert, Gérard
Professeur titulaire
Université de Montréal
Hedlin, Robert A.
Professor of Soil Science (retired)
University of Manitoba
Heidenreich, Conrad E.
Professor of Geography
York University
Helleiner, Frederick M.
Professor of Geography
Trent University
Helling, Rudolph (deceased)
Professor of Sociology
University of Windsor
Helm, June
Professor of Anthropology
University of Iowa
Heming, Bruce S.
Professor of Entomology
University of Alberta
Hénault, Odile
Architecte et critique
d'architecture, Montréal
Henderson, William B.
Barrister & Solicitor, Toronto
Hendry, Tom
Writer, Toronto
Hennessy, Ralph L.
Executive Director (retired)
Standards Council of Canada
Henripin, Jacques
Professeur de démographie
Université de Montréal
Henry, A.S.
Nepean, Ont
Henry, Michael M.
Chief of Ophthalmology
North York Branson Hospital
Toronto
Henteleff, Yude M.
Barrister & Solicitor
Buchwald Asper Henteleff, Winnipeg
Herbert-Copley, Brent
Research Officer
North-South Institute, Ottawa
Herbert, Frank A.
Professor of Respiratory Medicine
University of Alberta
Herman, Alex
Research Scientist
Bedford Institute of Oceanography
Dartmouth, NS
Herman, Harry Vjekoslav
Anthropologist, Toronto

Heron, Craig
Associate Professor of Social Science
& History
York University
Herperger, Don J.
Saskatchewan Archives Board, Regina
Herrero, Stephen M.
Professor of Environmental Science
& Biology
University of Calgary
Hesketh, Robert
News Commentator
CFRB, Toronto
Hessel, Ingo
Ottawa
Hewett, Phillip
Minister
Unitarian Church of Vancouver
Vancouver
Hexham, Irving
Assistant Professor of Religion
University of Manitoba
Heydenkorn, Benedykt
Vice-Director & Editor
Canadian Polish Research Institute
Toronto
Hickcox, Edward S.
Associate Professor of Educational
Administration
The Ontario Institute for Studies in
Education, Toronto
Hickman, Michael
Professor of Botany
University of Alberta
Higgins, Donald
Professor of Political Science
Saint Mary's University
Higgs, David
Professor of History
University of Toronto
Higley, Dahn D.
Chief Superintendent (retired)
Ontario Provincial Police,
Peterborough, Ont
Hildebrandt, Walter
Historical Research
Parks Canada, Winnipeg
Hill, Charles Christie
Curator of Canadian Art
National Gallery of Canada
Hill, Harry M.
Director General
Prairie Farm Rehabilitation
Administration
Agriculture Canada, Regina
Hill, Tom
Woodland Indian Cultural Centre
Brantford, Ont
Hiller, James K.
Associate Professor of History
Memorial University of Newfoundland
Hillmer, Anne Trowell
Dept of External Affairs, Ottawa
Hillmer, Norman
Senior Historian
Directorate of History
Dept of National Defence, Ottawa
Hindsgaul, Ole
Assistant Professor of Chemistry
University of Alberta
Hirose, Akira
Professor of Physics
University of Saskatchewan
Hlus, Carolyn
Writer, Edmonton
Hobbs, Helen
Graduate student, Vancouver
Hobbs, R. Gerald
Associate Professor of Church History
Vancouver School of Theology
Vancouver
Hodgetts, John Edwin
Professor Emeritus
University of Toronto
Hodgins, Bruce W.
Professor of History
Trent University
Hodgins, J.W. (deceased)
Professor Emeritus of Engineering
Memorial University of Newfoundland
Hoeniger, Judith F.M. (deceased)
Associate Professor of Microbiology
University of Toronto
Hogan, J.J.
Ottawa
Hogg, Helen Sawyer
Professor Emeritus of Astronomy
University of Toronto
Holdsworth, Gerald
Environment Canada, Calgary

Hollihan, K. Tony
Historian, St. John's
Holman, H.T.
Historian & archivist, Ottawa
Holmes, C. Janet
Royal Ontario Museum, Toronto
Holmes, Jeffrey
Director of Information
Social Sciences & Humanities
Research Council of Canada, Ottawa
Holmes, John W.
Counsellor
Canadian Institute of International
Affairs, Toronto
Holmgren, Eric J.
Historian, Edmonton
Hong, Alvin George
Executive Director
Canadian 5-Pin Bowlers Association
Ottawa
Hopwood, Peter
Ottawa
Horn, Michiel
Professor of History
Glendon College, York University
Horrall, Stan
Royal Canadian Mounted Police, Ottawa
Hourston, Alan S.
Fisheries Biologist
Nanaimo, BC
Houston, C. Stuart
University of Saskatchewan
Houston, James
Author & designer
Stonington, Conn
Howard, Ross K.
National Reporter, The Toronto Star
Toronto
Howard, Victor M.
Professor of English
Michigan State University at East
Lansing
Howell, Colin D.
Associate Professor of History
Saint Mary's University
Hube, Douglas P.
Professor of Physics & Astronomy
University of Alberta
Hudon, Raymond
Professeur de science politique
Université Laval
Hudson, Douglas R.
Instructor of Anthropology
Fraser Valley College
Abbotsford, BC
Huel, Raymond J.A.
Associate Professor of History
University of Lethbridge
Hughes, Richard David
Public Services Librarian
Cariboo College
Kamloops, BC
Hulchanski, J. David
Assistant Professor of Community &
Regional Planning
University of British Columbia
Hulse, Elizabeth
Dictionary of Canadian Biography
University of Toronto
Humber, William
Chairman, Continuing Education
Seneca College, Toronto
Hume, Stephen
General Manager, The Edmonton
Journal
Edmonton
Hummel, Monte
Executive Director
World Wildlife Fund (Canada), Toronto
Humphries, Charles W.
Associate Professor of History
University of British Columbia
Humphrys, Edward William
Consultant, Ottawa
Hunka, Robert F.
Los Angeles, Calif
Hunt, Geoffrey
Architectural Historian, New York
Hunt, John R.
Research Scientist
Agriculture Canada, Research Station
Agassiz, BC
Hunter, Kenneth E.
President, Conestoga College of
Applied Arts & Technology
Kitchener, Ont
Hunter, Robert
Architectural Historian
Environment Canada - Parks

Huston, Mervyn J.
Professor Emeritus
University of Alberta
Hutcheon, Linda
Professor of English
McMaster University
Hutchinson, Gerald M.
Minister, United Church of Canada
Thorsby, Alta
Hutchinson, Roger C.
Associate Professor, Church & Society
Emmanuel College
University of Toronto
Huyda, Richard J.
Director General, Public Programs
National Archives of Canada
Hyatt, A.M.J.
Professor of History
University of Western Ontario

Indra, Doreen Marie
Dept of Anthropology
University of Lethbridge
Ingolfsrud, Elizabeth
Author & consultant, Toronto
Isaacs, Avrom
Director & art dealer
The Isaacs Gallery, Toronto
Isaacs, Colin F.W.
The Pollution Probe Foundation
Toronto

Jackel, David
Professor of English
University of Alberta
Jackel, Susan
Associate Professor of Canadian
Studies
University of Alberta
Jackman, Sydney W.
Professor of History
University of Victoria
Jackson, Bernard S.
Curator, The Memorial University
Botanical Garden at Oxen Pond
Memorial University of Newfoundland
Jackson, Graham
Toronto
Jackson, Harold
Professor of Food Microbiology
University of Alberta
Jackson, John D.
Professor of Sociology
Concordia University
Jackson, John James
Associate Vice-President, Research
University of Victoria
Jackson, John N.
Professor of Applied Geography
Brock University
Jackson Jr, Lionel E.
Geological Survey of Canada;
Institute for Quarternary Research
Simon Fraser University
Jackson, Robert J.
Professor of Political Science
Carleton University
Jackson, Roger C.
Professor & Dean of Physical
Education
University of Calgary
Jackson, Stephen O.
Social Studies Teacher
Booth Memorial Regional High School
St John's
Jaenen, Cornelius J.
Professor of History
University of Ottawa
James, Donna
Writer
Kingston, Ont
James, Ellen
Associate Professor of Art History
Concordia University
James, Ross D.
Associate Curator of Ornithology
Royal Ontario Museum, Toronto
Jameson, Sheilagh S.
Writer & archivist emeritus
Glenbow Museum, Calgary
Jamieson, Margie
Ta Ta Creek, BC
Jamieson, Stuart M.
Professor Emeritus of Economics
University of British Columbia
Janisch, Hudson N.
Professor of Law
University of Toronto
Janssen, Christian T.L.
Professor of Business
University of Alberta

Janus, Lorraine L.
Research Assistant to the Senior Scientist
Canada Centre for Inland Waters
Burlington, Ont
Jarrell, Richard A.
Associate Professor of Natural
Science
Atkinson College, York University
Jean, Marguerite, s.c.i.m.
Secrétaire générale
Congrégation des Soeurs du
Bon-Pasteur de Québec;
Historienne et docteur en droit
canonique
Jeanes, Dennis W.
The Arthritis Society, Toronto
Jeeves, Alan H.
Professor of History
Queen's University
Jekyll, Robert
Artist, Toronto
Jenkin, Michael
Science Adviser
Science Council of Canada, Ottawa
Jensen, Phyllis Marie
Researcher, Toronto
Jensen, Vickie D.
Curriculum designer, Vancouver
Jenson, Jane
Associate Professor of Political
Science
Carleton University
Jerry, L. Martin
Director
Tom Baker Cancer Centre & Southern
Alberta Cancer Program;
Clinical Professor of Medicine
University of Calgary
Jessop, Alan M.
Geological Survey of Canada, Calgary
Jobb, Dean
Reporter & Editor
Halifax Herald, Halifax
Jofriet, Jan C.
Professor of Engineering
University of Guelph, Ont
Johansen, Peter
Associate Professor of Journalism
Carleton University
Johns, Timothy
Assistant Professor of Human Nutrition
McGill University
Johns, Walter H. (deceased)
Professor Emeritus & former
President, University of Alberta
Johnson, Dennis
Associate Professor of Geography
University of Alberta
Johnson, J.K.
Professor of History
Carleton University
Johnson, Peter Wade
Director, Agriculture Canada
Research Branch, Research Station
Delhi, Ont
Johnson, Robert E.
Physiologist
Montpelier, Vt
Johnston, Alex
Historian, Lethbridge, Alta
Johnston, C. Fred
Associate Professor of Education
Queen's University;
Canadian Canoe Association
Johnston, Charles M.
Professor of History
McMaster University
Johnston, Frances E.M.
President & Chief Executive
Officer
The Museum of Promotional Arts,
Toronto
Johnston, Hugh
Professor of History
Simon Fraser University
Johnston, Richard
Associate Professor of Political
Science
University of British Columbia
Johnston, W. Stafford
RR2, Mitchell, Ont
Johnston, William
Directorate of History
Dept of National Defence, Ottawa
Jones, Brian
Curator, Paleontological Collections
University of Alberta
Jones, David C.
Professor of History
University of Calgary

Jones, David Phillip
Professor of Law
University of Alberta
Jones, Elwood Hugh
Professor of History
Trent University
Jones, Gaynor G.
Faculty of Music
University of Toronto
Jones, Laura
Writer & photographer, Toronto
Jones, Raymond E.
Assistant Professor of English
University of Alberta
Jones, Richard A.
Professeur d'histoire
Université Laval
Jopling, Alan V.
Professor Emeritus
University of Toronto
Jose, Colin
Soccer historian
Hamilton, Ont
Jotham, Neal R.
Co-ordinator Humane Trapping
Program
Canadian Wildlife Service
Environment Canada, Ottawa
Jull, Peter
Ottawa

Kach, Nick
Professor of Educational Foundations
University of Alberta
Kadulski, Richard
Past Chairman
Solar Energy Society of Canada Inc
Vancouver
Kage, Joseph
Consultant
Outremont, Qué
Kahil, A.A.
President, CANTECK Consulting Ltd.
Calgary
Kaiser, Patricia
Freelance journalist, Toronto
Kalbach, Warren E.
Professor of Sociology
University of Toronto
Kaliski, Stephan Felix
Professor of Economics
Queen's University
Kallmann, Helmut
Chief, Music Division (retired)
National Library of Canada, Ottawa
Kallweit, Karen Danelle
Faculty of Architecture
Technical University of Nova Scotia
Kalman, Harold D.
Principal
Commonwealth Historic Resource
Management Limited, Ottawa
Kamal, A.N.
Professor of Physics
University of Alberta
Kanuka, Joseph W.
Barrister & Solicitor, Regina
Kapelos, George
City Planner, Toronto
Kaplan, William
Faculty of Law
University of Ottawa
Kaprielian, Isabel
Ontario Institute for Studies in
Education, Toronto
Kareda, Urjo
Artistic Director
Tarragon Theatre, Toronto
Karsten, Peter
Executive Director, Calgary Zoo,
Botanical Garden & Prehistoric Park
Calgary
Kartzmark, Elinor Mary
Professor of Chemistry
University of Manitoba
Kattan, Naim
Head, Writing & Publication Section
Canada Council, Ottawa
Kaufmann, Martin L.
Head, Plant Breeding, Pathology &
Forage Section
Agriculture Canada Research Station
Lacombe, Alta
Kawamura, Leslie S.
Professor & Head of Religious Studies
University of Calgary
Kealey, Gregory S.
Professor of History
Memorial University of Newfoundland
Keane, David R.
Historian, Hamilton, Ont

Kearns, King S.
Winnipeg
Keen, Michael J.
Geological Survey of Canada
Bedford Institute of Oceanography
Dartmouth, NS
Keenlyside, David L.
Atlantic Provinces Archaeologist
Canadian Museum of Civilization
Ottawa
Keillor, Elaine
Associate Professor of Music
Carleton University
Keith, W.J.
Professor of English
University of Toronto
Keizer, William Stirling
Ordained Missionary
Presbyterian Church in Canada
North Tryon, PEI
Kelley, Frances C.
Director of Communications
The Shoe Manufacturers' Association
of Canada, Montréal
Kelly, Louis Gerard
Professor of Linguistics
University of Ottawa
Kemp, David D.
Associate Professor of Geography
Lakehead University
Kemp, Walter H.
Professor of Music
Dalhousie University
Kendall, Kay
Director of Communications
Association of Canadian Distillers
Ottawa
Kendle, John Edward
Professor of History
University of Manitoba
Kennedy, J.E.
Professor Emeritus
University of Saskatchewan
Kennedy, John L.
Assistant TV Program Director
CBC-Toronto
Kennedy, Mark D.B.
Information Specialist, Toronto
Kennell, Elizabeth H.
Assistant to the Head of Extension
Services
Montreal Museum of Fine Arts
Kent, Stephen A.
Assistant Professor of Sociology
University of Alberta
Kentfield, John A.C.
Professor of Engineering
University of Calgary
Kenyon, John P.B.
Associate Professor of History
Scarborough Campus
University of Toronto
Kenyon, Walter A. (deceased)
Archaeological & historical
consultant, Toronto
Kernaghan, Kenneth
Professor of Politics &
Administration
Brock University
Kernaghan, Lois Kathleen
Historical researcher & editor
Boutilier's Point, NS
Kerr, Adam J.
Regional Director
Canadian Hydrographic Service
(Atlantic)
Fisheries & Oceans, Dartmouth
Kerr, Gordon R.
Regional Director
Canadian Wildlife Service, Edmonton
Kerr, Robert B.
Professor Emeritus of Medicine
University of British Columbia
Kerr, Stephen R.
Research Scientist
Bedford Institute of Oceanography
Dartmouth, NS
Kestelman, Paula
Researcher, Montréal
Kesteman, Jean-Pierre
Professeur d'histoire
Université de Sherbrooke
Kesterton, Wilfred H.
Professor Emeritus of Journalism
Carleton University
Ketchen, Keith S.
Senior Scientist (retired)
Pacific Biological Station
Nanaimo, BC
Kevan, Douglas Keith McEwan
Professor Emeritus of Entomology
McGill University

Kevan, Peter G.
*Associate Professor of Environmental
Biology
University of Guelph*
Kew, J.E. Michael
*Associate Professor of Anthropology
University of British Columbia*
Keyes, John
Historian, Québec
Kidd, Bruce
*Associate Professor of Physical
Education
University of Toronto*
Kierans, Thomas W.
*Professional Engineer & President
Atlantic Progress Ltd, St John's*
Killan, Gerald
*Professor of History
King's College
University of Western Ontario*
King, Bill J.
*Senior writer, Communications Unit
PFRA, Regina*
Kingsmith, Ray A.
Calgary
Kirk, Colin
*Executive Director
Canadian Orienteering Federation
Ottawa*
Kirschbaum, Stanislav J.
*Associate Professor of Political
Science
Glendon College, York University*
Kirton, John James
*Associate Professor of Political
Science
University of Toronto*
Klaassen, Walter
*Research Professor
Conrad Grebel College
University of Waterloo*
Klamkin, Murray S.
*Professor of Mathematics
University of Alberta*
Klar, Lewis N.
*Professor of Law
University of Alberta*
Klinck, Harold R.
*Professor of Agronomy
McGill University*
Klymasz, Robert B.
*Curator
Slavic & East European Programme
Canadian Centre for Folk Culture
Studies
Canadian Museum of Civilization
Ottawa*
Knapton, Richard W.
*Assistant Professor of Biological
Sciences
Brock University*
Knelman, Judith
Writer, Toronto
Knight, Alan R.
*Dept of English
University of Alberta*
Knight, David B.
*Professor of Geography
Carleton University*
Knowles, Robert Hugh
*Professor Emeritus
University of Alberta*
Knowles, Stephen T.
Canada West Hockey, Edmonton
Knudsen, Brian M.
Dept of Natural Resources, Winnipeg
Koch, Eric
Author, Toronto
Koennecke, Franz M.
Morriston, Ont
Koepke, Wray E.
*Energy, Mines & Resources Canada
Ottawa*
Koltun, Lilly
*Assistant Director
Documentary Art & Photography
National Archives of Canada*
Koroscil, Paul M.
*Associate Professor of Geography
Simon Fraser University*
Koslow, J. Anthony
*Assistant Professor of Oceanography
Dalhousie University*
Kostash, Myrna Anne
Writer, Edmonton
Krajina, Vladimir J.
*Professor Emeritus & Honorary
University of British Columbia*

Kranck, Kate
*Research Scientist
Dept of Fisheries & Oceans
Bedford Institute of Oceanography
Dartmouth, NS*
Krasnick, Cheryl
*Doctoral Candidate of History
Queen's University*
Krats, Peter V.
*PhD Candidate
University of Western Ontario*
Krebs, Charles J.
*Professor of Zoology
University of British Columbia*
Krenz, F. Henry
*Director, Abrico Energy Management
Services Ltd
Lakefield, Ont*
Kreutzweiser, Erwin E.
Writer, Toronto
Kristof, Andrea
Architect, Toronto
Kroker, Arthur
*Professor of Political Science
Concordia University*
Kröller, Eva-Marie
*Associate Professor of English
University of British Columbia*
Krossel, Martin
*Freelance writer
Toronto*
Krotki, Karol J.
*University Professor of Sociology
University of Alberta*
Kulisek, Larry L.
*Associate Professor of History
University of Windsor*
Kupsch, Walter O.
*Professor Emeritus of Geology
University of Saskatchewan*
Kushner, Eva M.
*President
Victoria University, Toronto*
Kuyt, Ernie
*Wildlife Biologist
Canadian Wildlife Service, Edmonton*
Kwavnick, David
Ottawa
Kyer, C. Ian
*Lawyer
Fasken & Calvin, Toronto*

La Roi, George H.
*Professor of Botany
University of Alberta*
Labelle, Micheline
*Professeur de sociologie
Université du Québec à Montréal*
Laberge, Danielle
*Professeur de sociologie
Université du Québec à Montréal*
Lacombe, Michèle
*Assistant Professor of English
Laurentian University*
Lacoursière, Estelle
*Professeur de biologie
Université du Québec à Trois-Rivières*
Lacroix, Laurier
*Professeur d'histoire de l'art
Université Concordia*
Laferrière, Michel (deceased)
*Associate Professor of Education
McGill University*
Lafrance, Guy
*Professeur de philosophie
Université d'Ottawa*
Lahey, Raymond J.
*Bishop of St George's
Corner Brook, Nfld*
Laidlaw, William G.
*Professor of Chemistry
University of Calgary*
Laine, Mabel H.
*Administrator
Encyclopedia of Music in Canada
Toronto*
Laing, Gertrude M.
*Ex-Commissioner
Royal Commission on Bilingualism &
Biculturalism*
Lajeunesse, Claude
*Director of Targeted &
University-Industry Programs
Natural Sciences and Engineering
Research Council of Canada, Ottawa*
Laliberté, G-Raymond
*Professeur de sciences politiques
Université Laval*
Lalonde, André
*Professor of History
University of Regina*

Lalonde, Gérard L.
*Canadian Aerospace Industries
Association of Canada, Ottawa*
Lamb, W. Kaye
*Former Dominion Archivist
National Archives of Canada*
Lambert, Geoffrey
*Associate Professor of Political
Studies
University of Manitoba*
Lambert, James H.
*Rédacteur-Historien
Dictionnaire biographique du Canada
Québec*
Lammers, George E.
*Curator of Geology
Manitoba Museum of Man & Nature
Winnipeg*
Lamonde, Yvan
*Professeur d'histoire
McGill University*
Lancaster, Peter
*Professor of Mathematics
University of Calgary*
Land, R. Brian
*Executive Director
Ontario Legislative Library;
Professor of Library & Information
Science
University of Toronto*
Landreville, Pierre
*Professeur de criminologie
Université de Montréal*
Landry, Kenneth
*Professionnel de recherche
Université Laval*
Landstreet, John D.
*Professor of Astronomy
University of Western Ontario*
Lane, E. David
*Aquaculture & Fisheries
Malaspina College
Nanaimo, BC*
Lane, Robert B.
Anthropologist, Victoria
Langlands, Robert P.
*Professor of Mathematics
The Institute for Advanced Study*
Langlois, Carmen
Journaliste culturelle, Montréal
Lapins, Karlis O.
*Research Scientist (retired)
Agriculture Canada, Research Station
Summerland, BC*
Lapointe, Pierre Louis
*Historian
Hull, Qué*
Laquian, Eleanor R.
Researcher & writer, Ottawa
Larkin, Peter Anthony
*Vice-President, Research
University of British Columbia*
Larmour, Jean B.D.
Historical researcher, Regina
LaRocque, Emma D.
*Lecturer of Native Studies
University of Manitoba*
Larose, Serge
*Centre de recherches Caraïbes
Université de Montréal*
Larouche, Jeannette
*Historienne
Chicoutimi, Qué*
Larter, Edward N.
*Professor of Plant Science
University of Manitoba*
LaSalle, Pierre
Energie et Ressources, Québec
Latouche, Daniel
*Professeur de science politique
Institut national de la recherche
scientifique*
Launay, Viviane F.
*Executive Director
Canadian Federation for the
Humanities, Ottawa*
Laurence, Gérard
*Professeur d'histoire des
communications de masse
Université Laval*
Laurence, Karen
Free-lance writer, Toronto
Laurendeau, Marc
*Political columnist, La Presse;
Broadcaster on radio & television
Montréal*
Lauzon, Michael
*Editor, Corpus Chemical Report
Toronto*
Lavallée, Omer
*Corporate historian & archivist
Canadian Pacific Limited, Montréal*

Laverty, Kathleen
*Owner, Kathleen Laverty Gallery Ltd
Edmonton*
Lavery, Kenneth R.
Ottawa
Lavigne, Marie
Historian, Québec
Lavigueur, Patricia Johnston
*Consultant, Canadian Federation of
Independent Business (CFIB), Montréal*
Lavkulich, Leslie M.
*Professor of Soil Science
University of British Columbia*
Lavoie, Pierre
*Théâtrotèque
Université de Montréal*
Law-West, Don G.
*Minerals & Metals Strategy Branch
Mineral Policy Sector
Energy, Mines & Resources Canada
Ottawa*
Law, Charles
*General Manager
CHEM info Services Inc*
Laxer, Jim
*Associate Professor of Political
Science
Atkinson College, York University*
Laycock, Arleigh H.
*Professor of Geography;
Director, Water Resources Centre
University of Alberta*
Laycock, David H.
*Assistant Professor of Political
Science
University of Saskatchewan*
Layne, Richard E.C.
*Research Scientist
Tree Fruit Breeding
Agriculture Canada
Harrow Research Station, Ont*
Lazerson, Marvin
*Dean, Graduate School of Education
University of Pennsylvania*
Lazier, John R.N.
*Bedford Institute of Oceanography
Dartmouth, NS*
Le Roy, Donald J. (deceased)
Science Council of Canada, Ottawa
LeBlanc, Hugues
*Agronome
l'Assumption, Qué*
Leblond, C.P.
*Professor of Anatomy
McGill University*
LeBlond, Paul H.
*Professor of Oceanography
University of British Columbia*
LeBlond, Sylvio
*Professor Emeritus of Clinical
Medicine & History of Medicine
Laval University*
Lechasseur, Antonio
*Historien
Rimouski, Qué*
Lecraw, Donald J.
*Professor of Business Administration
University of Western Ontario*
Ledoux, Johanne
Montréal
Leduc-Park, Renée
Hamilton, Ontario
LeDuc, Lawrence
*Professor of Political Science
University of Toronto*
Lee, David
*Historian
Parks Canada, Hull*
Lee, John Alan
*Associate Professor of Sociology
University of Toronto*
Leech, Robin
*Research Associate of Entomology
University of Alberta*
Leefe, John G.
Minister of Fisheries, Nova Scotia
Legault, Marthe
Rédactrice biographique, Montréal
Legendre, Camille
*Professeur de sociologie
Université de Montréal*
Legge, Russel D.
*Associate Professor in Religious
Studies
University of Waterloo*
Legget, Robert F.
Consultant, Ottawa
Leier, J. Mark
Memorial University
Leiper, Jean M.
*Professor of Physical Education
University of Calgary*

Lemaire, Michel
Professeur de littérature
Université d'Ottawa

Lemay, J-P
Professeur de zootechnie
Université Laval

Lemelin, Clément
Professeur de science économique
Université du Québec à Montréal

Lemelin, Maurice
Professeur titulaire de relations du travail
hautes études commerciales
Université de Montréal

Lemieux, Pierre H.
Professeur de littérature
Université d'Ottawa

Lemieux, Raymond U.
University Professor
University of Alberta

Lemieux, Vincent
Professeur de science politique
Université Laval

Lemire, Guy
Professeur de criminologie
Université de Montréal

Lemire, Maurice
Professeur de littérature québécoise
Université Laval

Lemire, Robert
Centre Canadien d'Architecture
Montréal

Lenarcic, Dorothy A.
Communications Co-ordinator
Canadian Jewellers Association

Lennards, Jos L.
Associate Professor of Sociology/ Education
York University

Lennox, John
Associate Professor of English
York University

Leonard, David W.
Senior Archivist
Provincial Archives of Alberta
Edmonton

Lepage, Yvan G.
Professeur de littérature française
Université d'Ottawa

LeRoy, Rodney L.
Electrolyser Inc
Pointe-Claire, Qué

Leslie, Peter M.
Director, Institute of Intergovernmental Relations
Queen's University

Lessard, Claude
Professeur agrégé et vice-doyen aux études des sciences de l'éducation
Université de Montréal

Lesser, Barry
Professor of Biochemistry
University of Calgary

Letheren, Carol Anne
Partner, Mathieu, Williams, Letheren
Toronto

Levant, Victor
Professor of Humanities
John Abbott College, Montréal

Levere, Trevor H.
Professor of History of Science
University of Toronto

Levett, Bruce D.
Writer, Toronto

Levin, Malcolm A.
Associate Professor of Education
Ontario Institute for Studies in Education, Toronto

Levine, Allan E.
Librarian & historian, Ottawa

Levine, Gilbert
Research Director
Canadian Union of Public Employees
Ottawa

Levitt, Joseph
Professor Emeritus of History
University of Ottawa

Levitt, Sheldon J.
Architect, Toronto

Lewis, Brian S.
British Columbia Sports Hall of Fame & Museum, Vancouver

Lewis, Douglas L.
Registrar/Career Counsellor
Athol Murray College of Notre Dame
Wilcox, Sask

Lewis, John B.
Professor of Biology
McGill University

Lewis, Joyce C.
Administrative Assistant
The Ontario Historical Society
Toronto

Lewis, Laurie
Manager, Campus Printing & Design Office
University of Toronto Press

Lewis, Walter
Historian, Acton, Ont

Lexchin, Joel
Physician, Toronto

Leyton, Elliott H.
Professor of Applied Anthropology
Memorial University

Lightbody, James W.
Associate Professor of Political Science
University of Alberta

Lightstone, Jack N.
Associate Professor of Religion
Concordia University

Lindberg, Garry M.
Executive Director, Space Division
National Research Council of Canada
Ottawa

Lindquist, Evert E.
Senior Research Scientist
Biosystematics Research Centre
Agriculture Canada, Ottawa

Lindsay, Peter L.
Professor of Physical Education & Sport Studies
University of Alberta

Lindsey, Joseph D.
Toronto

Linteau, Paul-André
Professeur d'histoire
Université du Québec à Montréal

Lipkin, Mary-Jane
Communications Officer
Canadian Advisory Council on the Status of Women, Ottawa

Lister, Marilyn
Ottawa

Lister, Rota Herzberg
Associate Professor of English
University of Waterloo

Lit, John
Professor of Physics
Wilfrid Laurier University;
Professor of Electrical Engineering
University of Waterloo

Litman, Moe M.
Associate Professor of Law
University of Alberta

Livingstone, Donna
Glenbow Museum, Calgary

Lochhead, Douglas G.
Canadian Studies
Mount Allison University

Lochnan, Carl J.
Consultant & writer, Ottawa

Lock, Anthony R.
Canadian Wildlife Service
Bedford Institute of Oceanography
Dartmouth, NS

Locke, Jack L.
Astronomer, Ottawa

Loken, Gulbrand
Associate Professor of Educational Administration
University of Calgary

Loney, D. Edwards
Professor Emeritus
Queen's University

Lord, Kathleen
Secondary Teacher, Wemindji
James Bay, Qué

Lorimer, James
Publisher
James Lorimer & Company Ltd, Toronto

Lortie, Marcel
Professeur de foresterie
Université Laval

Loughton, Arthur
Director
Horticultural Experiment Station
Ontario Ministry of Agriculture & Food
Simcoe, Ont

Lovick, Laurence Dale
Instructor of English & Canadian Studies
Malaspina College
Nanaimo, BC

Lowes, Raymond Nicholson
Honorary President
Bruce Trail Association
Hamilton, Ont

Lown, Peter J.M.
Professor of Law
University of Alberta

Lowry, W. Mark
Executive Director
Canadian Amateur Diving Association
Ottawa

Lozowski, Edward P.
Professor of Meteorology
University of Alberta

Lumsden, David Paul
Master of Norman Bethune College
York University

Lumsden, Harry G.
Research Scientist, Ontario Ministry of Natural Resources
Maple, Ont

Lumsden, Ian Gordon
Director, Beaverbrook Art Gallery
Fredericton

Lund, John
Professor of Metallurgical Engineering
University of British Columbia

Lupul, Manoly R.
Professor of Canadian Educational History
University of Alberta

Lussier, Réal
Historien de l'art, Montréal

Lynch, Gerald
Assistant Professor of English
University of Ottawa

Lynch, Wayne
Freelance Writer & Wildlife Photographer
Calgary

Lyon, Deborah Maryth
Researcher & writer, Winnipeg

Lyon, John-David
Consultant, Aviation
Director, EER Technologies Inc, Ottawa

Macadam, William I.
Executive Producer
Norfolk Research Unit
Norfolk Productions Ltd, Toronto

McAfee, R. Ann
Housing Planner, City of Vancouver

McAllister, Don E.
Curator, Ichthyology Section
National Museum of Natural Sciences
Ottawa

McAndrew, William J.
Historian, Directorate of History
Dept of National Defence, Ottawa

Macartney, J. Malcolm
University of Victoria

Macartney-Filgate, Terence
Film & television producer, Toronto

McBean, D.S.
Research Station (retired)
Agriculture Canada
Swift Current, Sask

McBryde, W.A.E.
Professor of Chemistry
University of Waterloo

McCall, Christina
Writer, Toronto

McCalla, Douglas
Professor of History
Trent University

MacCallum, Hugh
Professor of English
University of Toronto

MacCallum, Ian
Geographer, St John's

McCallum, Margaret Elizabeth
University of Toronto

McCann, Lawrence D.
Davidson Professor of Canadian Studies
Mount Allison University

McCann, S.B.
Professor of Geography
McMaster University

McCardle, Bennett
Archivist
National Archives of Canada, Ottawa

McCart, Peter J.
Aquatic Environments Limited, Calgary

McClellan, Catharine
Professor Emeritus
University of Wisconsin

McConnell, W.H.
Professor of Law
University of Saskatchewan

McCormack, A. Ross
Vice-President (Academic)
University of Winnipeg

McCracken, Jane
Alberta Culture & Multiculturalism
Historic Sites Service, Edmonton

McCue, H.A.
Director, Education Services
Cree School Board
Chisasibi, Qué

McCulloch, James A.W.
Director General
Central Services Directorate
Atmospheric Environment Service

McCullough, A.B.
Parks Canada, Hull

McDermott, Linda
Physician
New Liskeard, Ont

Macdonald, Cathy
Sport historian, Edmonton

MacDonald, G. Edward
Curator of History
Prince Edward Island Museum & Heritage Foundation,
Charlottetown

MacDonald, Heather
Historical researcher, Halifax

MacDonald, Les
Social Sciences & Humanities Research Council of Canada, Ottawa

MacDonald, Martha
Associate Professor of Economics
Saint Mary's University

McDonald, Michael
Associate Professor of Philosophy
University of Waterloo

Macdonald, R.H.
Author & journalist
Victoria

Macdonald, R.St.J.
Professor of International Law
Dalhousie University

Macdonald, Roderick A.
Professor of Law
McGill University

MacDonald, Stewart D.
Curator, Vertebrate Ethology
National Museum of Natural Sciences
Ottawa

Macdonald, Valerie Isabel
Western Regional Coordinator
National Association of Underwater Instructors, Vancouver

MacDonell, Margaret
St Francis Xavier University

McDougall, Allan K.
Associate Professor of Political Science
University of Western Ontario

McDougall, Anne
Art Historian, Ottawa

MacDougall, April J.
The Rubber Association of Canada
Mississauga, Ont

MacDougall, Heather
Assistant Professor of History
University of Toronto

McDougall, John N.
Professor of Political Science
University of Western Ontario

McDougall, Robert L.
Professor Emeritus of English
Carleton University

McDowall, Duncan
Senior Research Associate
The Conference Board of Canada
Ottawa

MacDowell, Laurel Sefton
Associate Professor of History
University of Toronto

Mace, Thomas F.
Homemaker, Victoria

MacEwan, Grant
Writer, Calgary

McEwen, Alec C.
Commissioner
International Boundary Commission
Ottawa

McEwen, Freeman L.
Dean, Ontario Agricultural College
University of Guelph

McFadden, K.D.
Professor of Anatomy
University of Alberta

McFadyen, Clark A.
Chief, Canadian Ethnology Service
Canadian Museum of Civilization
Ottawa

McFall, Jean
York Pioneer & Historical Society
Toronto

McFeat, Tom
Professor of Anthropology
Scarborough Campus
University of Toronto

McGahan, Elizabeth W.
Honorary Research Associate
University of New Brunswick

McGee, Harold Franklin, Jr.
Professor of Anthropology
Saint Mary's University
McGee, Timothy J.
Associate Professor of Music
University of Toronto
McGhee, Robert
Canadian Museum of Civilization
Ottawa
McGill, William B.
Professor of Soil Science
University of Alberta
McGillivray, Donald G.
National Economics Editor
Southam News, Ottawa
MacGillivray, Royce
Associate Professor of History
University of Waterloo
McGinn, Roderick Alan
Assistant Professor of Geography
Brandon University
MacGregor, James G.
Writer, Edmonton
McGregor, Margaret
Executive Director
Canadian Water Ski Association
Ottawa
McGuigan, Peter T.
Writer & Researcher, Toronto
McGuinness, Eric
Environment Canada
Canada Centre for Inland Waters
Burlington, Ont
MacInnis, J.B.
Undersea Research Limited
Toronto
McIntosh, Dave
Writer, Ottawa
McIntyre, W. John
Teaching Master
Seneca College of Applied Arts &
Technology, Toronto
McKay, Alexander G.
Professor of Classics
McMaster University
Mackay, Daniel S.C.
Geographer, The National Atlas
of Canada
McKay, Gordon A.
Meteorologist
Thornhill, Ont
McKeague, J. Alex
Soil Scientist
Agriculture Canada, Ottawa
McKee, Jon
Artist, Toronto
McKendry, Ruth
Writer
Elginburg, Ont
McKenna, Barbara A.
Historian
Aylmer, Ont
McKenna, Brian
Writer-producer
Montréal
MacKenzie, David C.
Toronto
Mackenzie, Hector M.
(Post-Doctoral) Research Fellow in
History
University of Toronto
MacKenzie, Robert C.
MacKenzie Environmental Consultants
Edmonton
MacKenzie, Ross G.
Associate Professor of Anatomy
(retired)
University of Toronto
McKenzie, Ruth
Writer, Ottawa
MacKenzie, William C.
Consultant, Ottawa
Mackey, William Francis
CIRB Research Professor
Laval University
Mackie, George O.
Professor of Biology
University of Victoria
McKillop, A.B.
Professor of History
Carleton University
Mackinnon, C.S.
Associate Professor of History
University of Alberta
MacKinnon, Frank
Professor of Political Science
University of Calgary
MacKinnon, William R.
Archivist
Provincial Archives of New Brunswick

MacLachlan, Bruce B.
Anthropologist
St Louis, Mo
McLachlan, J.
National Research Council, Halifax
McLaren, Angus
Professor of History
University of Victoria
McLaren, Ian A.
Professor of Biology
Dalhousie University
MacLaren, The Hon Roy
President, CB Media Ltd.
McLaughlin, Kenneth
Associate Professor of History
University of Waterloo
McLay, Catherine M.
Associate Professor of English
University of Calgary
MacLean, Colin
Canadian Broadcasting Corporation
Edmonton
MacLean, Raymond A.
Professor of History
St Francis Xavier University
McLellan, A. Anne
Associate Professor of Law
University of Alberta
MacLennan, Gordon W.
Professor of Celtic Studies
University of Ottawa
McLeod, Cam
Writer, Toronto
MacLeod, Kenneth Ogilvie
National Advertising Manager
Henry Birks & Sons, Montréal
MacLeod, Malcolm
Associate Professor of History
Memorial University of Newfoundland
Macleod, Roderick C.
Professor of History
University of Alberta
McLuhan, Elizabeth
Curator, National Exhibition Centre &
Centre for Indian Art
Thunder Bay, Ont
McMaster, Gerald R.
Curator of Contemporary Indian Art
Canadian Museum of Civilization
McMillan, Barclay
Broadcaster & writer, Ottawa
MacMillan, Carrie
Associate Professor of English
Mount Allison University
Macmillan, David, S.
Professor of History
Trent University
McMillan, Donald Burley
Professor of Zoology
University of Western Ontario
MacMillan, Keith
Professor of Music
University of Ottawa
MacMillan, Stuart R.
Supervisor, Sales Promotion
Cominco Fertilizers, Calgary
McMordie, Michael
Professor of Architecture
University of Calgary
McMullen, Lorraine
Professor of English Literature
University of Ottawa
McMullin, Stanley E.
Associate Professor of Canadian
Studies
University of Waterloo
McMurray, William C.
Professor & Chairman of Biochemistry
University of Western Ontario
McNabb, Debra A.
MA Graduate Student of Geography
University of British Columbia
McNamara, Anne
Writer, Calgary
McNaught, Kenneth
Professor of History
University of Toronto
McNicholl, Martin K.
Naturalist
Port Rowan, Ont
McNulty, Jean
Ontario Ministry of Culture &
Communications, Toronto
Macpherson, Andrew H.
Regional Director-General
Environment Canada, Edmonton
McPherson, Hugo A.
Grierson Professor of Communications
Dept of English
McGill University

MacPherson, Ian
Professor of History
University of Victoria
Macpherson, Kay
Past President, Voice of Women
Canada, Toronto
Macqueen, Roger W.
Geological Survey of Canada, Calgary
MacRae, Donald A.
Professor of Astronomy
David Dunlap Observatory
University of Toronto
McRae, Sandra F.
Institute for the History &
Philosophy of Science & Technology
University of Toronto
McShane, King G.
Adjunct Professor of Law
Carleton University
McTaggart-Cowan, Ian
Biologist, Victoria
McVetty, Peter B.E.
Assistant Professor of Plant Breeding
& Genetics
University of Manitoba
McWhinney, Edward Watson
Professor of Constitutional &
International Law
Simon Fraser University
McWhinney, Ian
Professor of Family Medicine
University of Western Ontario
Madill, Dennis Frank Keith
Research Advisor
Indian & Northern Affairs Canada, Hull
Magnin, Anthony A.
Assistant Director-Research Project
Management
Connaught Research Institute
Willowdale, Ont
Magnuson, Roger
Professor of Education
McGill University
Magnusson, Warren
Associate Professor of Political
Science
University of Victoria
Mailhiot, Gilles-D.
Président, Collège dominicain de
philosophie et de théologie
Ottawa
Mailhot, Laurent
Professeur de littérature
Université de Montréal
Mailhot, Pierre
Institut d'aménagement
Université de Sherbrooke
Maini, J.S.
Director General, Policy Directorate
Corporate Planning Group
Environment Canada, Ottawa
Maisonneuve, Lise
Université de Montréal
Major, Jean-Louis
Professeur titulaire des lettres
françaises
Université d'Ottawa
Major, Robert
Département des lettres françaises
Université d'Ottawa
Malkin, Peter
Art historian, Vancouver
Malloch, David
Professor of Botany
University of Toronto
Mann, Cedric R.
Director-General
Institute of Ocean Sciences
Dept of Fisheries & Oceans
Sidney, BC
Mann, Kenneth H.
Dept of Fisheries & Oceans
Bedford Institute of Oceanography
Dartmouth, NS
Mann, Martha
Designer (ADC), Toronto
Mannion, John J.
Professor of Geography
Memorial University
Mansell, Kate L.
Development Officer
Lester B. Pearson College of the Pacific
Victoria
Marchand, J.R.
Ministry of State for Science &
Technology, Ottawa
Mardiros, Anthony (deceased)
Professor Emeritus of Philosophy
University of Alberta

Margolis, Leo
Research Scientist
Pacific Biological Station
Dept of Fisheries & Oceans
Nanaimo, BC
Mark, Shew-Kuey
Professor & Chairman of Physics
McGill University
Markham, Philip de Lacey
Professional engineer, Ottawa
Markham, W.E.
Ice Branch, Atmospheric Environment
Service
Downsview, Ont
Marr, William
Professor of Economics
Wilfrid Laurier University
Marsh, John S.
Professor of Geography
Trent University
Marshall, Douglas
Toronto
Marshall, J. Stewart
Professor Emeritus of Physics &
Meteorology
McGill University
Marshall, Victor W.
Professor of Behavioural Science
University of Alberta
Martin, Horst
Professor of Germanic Studies
University of British Columbia
Martin, J. Douglas
Director General, Office of Public
Information
Baha'i World Centre, Haifa
Martin, Jean-Claude
President
Canadian Hospital Association
Ottawa
Martin, John E.H.
Manager, Canadian National Collection
(Zoology)
Biosystematics Research Institute
Research Branch, Agriculture Canada
Ottawa
Martin, Kathy M.
Boreal Ecologist
University of Alberta
Martin, Sandra
Writer, Toronto
Martineau, André
Chief, Public Relations
National Archives of Canada, Ottawa
Maskow, May L.
Director, Open College
CJRT-FM, Toronto
Maslove, Allan M.
Professor, School of Public
Administration
Carleton University
Masswohl, R.W.
St Catharines, Ont
Masters, Donald C.
Professor Emeritus
University of Guelph
Matheson, the Hon John Ross
Judge
Perth, Ont
Matheson, R. Neil
Journalist, Toronto
Matheson, William A.
Vice-President
Brock University
Mathews, Robin
Professor of English
Carleton University
Mathewson, William G.
Associate Professor of Animal Science
Nova Scotia Agricultural College
Mathien, Thomas
Transitional Year Programme
University of Toronto
Mathieson, J.R. (John)
Regional Director, Pacific Region
Atmospheric Environment Service
Vancouver
Mathieu, Jacques
Professeur d'histoire
Université Laval
Matthews, Keith
Professor of History;
Chairman, Maritime History Group
Memorial University of Newfoundland
Matthiasson, John S.
Professor of Anthropology
University of Manitoba
Mattison, David
Archivist, Provincial Archives of
British Columbia
Victoria

Maule, Christopher J.
Professor of Economics &
International Affairs
Carleton University

Maurer, A.R.
Research Scientist
Agriculture Canada, Research Station
Agassiz, BC

Maybank, John
Principal Research Scientist
Saskatchewan Research Council
Saskatoon

Maycock, Paul F.
Professor of Botany
Erindale College
University of Toronto

Maze, Jack
Professor of Botany
University of British Columbia

Mealing, Stanley R.
Professor of History
Carleton University

Medjuck, Sheva
Associate Professor of Sociology
Mount Saint Vincent University

Medovy, Harry
Professor Emeritus of Pediatrics
University of Manitoba

Meen, Sharon P.
Social historian, Vancouver

Melançon, Benoît
Université de Montréal

Melody, William H.
Professor of Communication
Simon Fraser University

Melvin, James R.
Dept of Economics
University of Western Ontario

Melvin, Joan S.
Writer, Deep River, Ont

Meredith, Don H.
Writer, Duffield, Alta

Merilees, Philip E.
Canadian Climate Centre
Environment Canada, Toronto

Messenger, Ann
Professor of English
Simon Fraser University

Metcalf, George
Associate Professor of History
University of Western Ontario

Metcalfe, David R.
Agriculture Canada, Research Station
Winnipeg

Mežaks, Jānis (John)
Archivist, Archives of Ontario
Toronto

Michael, T.H. Glynn
Consultant, Ottawa

Michon, Jacques
Professeur titulaire d'études
françaises
Université de Sherbrooke

Middlebro', Tom
Associate Professor of English
Literature
Carleton University

Millar, James Francis Verchere
Professor of Archaeology
University of Saskatchewan

Miller, Carman
Associate Professor of History
McGill University

Miller, Elizabeth
Associate Professor of English
Memorial University of Newfoundland

Miller, J.R.
Professor of History
University of Saskatchewan

Miller, John A.
Canadian Music Centre, Toronto

Miller, Judith N.
Policy Development & Planning Officer
Medical Research Council of Canada
Ottawa

Miller, Mark
Writer, Toronto

Miller, Mary Jane
Associate Professor of Fine Arts
Brock University

Miller, Orlo
Writer
London, Ont

Millin, Leslie
Gondolin Consulting Services
Vancouver

Millman, Peter M.
Researcher Emeritus
National Research Council of Canada
Ottawa

Millman, Thomas R.
Former Archivist
Anglican Church of Canada, Toronto

Mills, Charles A.
Quality assurance specialist
Hamilton, Ont

Mills, David
Associate Professor of History
University of Alberta

Mills, Eric L.
Professor of Oceanography & Biology
Dalhousie University

Mills, Isabelle Margaret
Professor of Music
University of Saskatchewan

Milne, David A.
Professor of Political Studies
University of Prince Edward Island

Milne, William J.
Professor of Engineering
Memorial University of Newfoundland

Milner, Marc
University of New Brunswick

Milton, David G.
Executive Director
Canadian Institute of Treated Wood
Ottawa

Milton, Janice
Research assistant, Halifax

Minnes, Gordon
Executive Vice-President
Canadian Pulp & Paper Association
Montréal

Miquelon, Dale
Professor of History
University of Saskatchewan

Mitchell, Edward
Research Scientist
Dept of Fisheries & Oceans
Arctic Biological Station
Ste-Anne-de-Bellevue, Qué

Mitchell, K.R.
Professor of English
University of Regina

Mitchell, Thomas H.
Senior Research Associate
The Conference Board of Canada
Ottawa

Mitchinson, Wendy
Associate Professor of History
University of Waterloo

Modry, Dennis L.
Divisional Director, (Acting)
Cardiovascular & Thoracic Surgery
University of Alberta

Mohr, Johann W.
Professor of Law & Sociology
York University

Moir, John S.
Professor of History
University of Toronto

Molnar, George Dempster
Professor of Medicine;
Director, Muttart Diabetes Research &
Training Centre
University of Alberta

Moncrieff, Patrick M.
Senior Manager, Agriculture
Bank of Montreal, Toronto

Monet, Jacques, s.j.
President, Regis College
Toronto

Montagnes, Ian
Assistant Director & Editor-in-Chief
University of Toronto Press, Toronto

Moodie, D. Wayne
Professor of Geography
University of Manitoba

Moody, Barry M.
Associate Professor of History
Acadia University

Moogk, Peter N.
Associate Professor of History
University of British Columbia

Mooney, Kathleen A.
Assistant Professor of Anthropology
University of Victoria

Moore, Christopher
Historian, Toronto

Moore, James G.G.
Dept of Language & Literature
Booth Memorial Regional High School
St John's

Moore, Keith L.
Professor & Chairman of Anatomy;
Associate Dean of Basic Sciences
University of Toronto

Moore, Teresa
Public Relations Co-ordinator
Canadian Figure Skating Association
Ottawa

Moppett, George
Saskatoon

Morash, Gordon
Staff Writer, The Edmonton Journal
Edmonton

Morgan, Kenneth
Dept of Epidemiology & Biostatistics
McGill University

Moriarity, Andrew J.
Medi-Edit Ltd, Toronto

Morinis, E. Alan
Anthropologist, Vancouver

Morisset, Pierre
Professeur de biologie
Université Laval

Morissette, Yves-Marie
Associate Dean, Faculty of Law
McGill University

Morlan, Richard E.
Curator, Plains Archaeology
Archaeological Survey of Canada
Canadian Museum of Civilization
Ottawa

Morley, J. Terence
Associate Professor of Political
Science
University of Victoria

Morley, Patricia A.
Professor of English & Canadian
Studies
Concordia University

Morris, Cerise
Professor of Social Service
Dawson College, Montréal

Morris, Peter
Professor of Film Studies
Queen's University

Morrison, David A.
Canadian Museum of Civilization
Ottawa

Morrison, George R.
Teacher (retired)
Espanola, Ont

Morrison, Jack W.
Director General, Research
Agriculture Canada, Ottawa

Morrison, Jean
Supervisor, Library & Research Services
Old Fort William
Thunder Bay, Ont

Morrison, Kenneth L.
Historical writer
Thunder Bay, Ont

Morrison, Rod
Administrator, Victoria

Morrison, W. Douglas
Professor of Animal & Poultry Science
University of Guelph

Morrison, William R.
Professor of History
Brandon University

Morrow, Don
Associate Professor of Physical
Education
University of Western Ontario

Morrow, Patrick A.
Adventure Photographer
Canmore, Alta

Morton, Desmond
Principal, Erindale College
University of Toronto

Morton, John K.
Professor of Biology
University of Waterloo

Moscovitch, Allan
Associate Professor of Social Work
Carleton University

Moss, John
Professor of English
University of Ottawa

Mossman, Mary Jane
Associate Professor
Osgoode Hall Law School
York University

Motut, Roger
Professor Emeritus
University of Alberta

Mount, Graeme S.
Professor of History
Laurentian University

Mowat, Farley
Writer, Port Hope, Ont

Mowat, Susanne
Ottawa

Moyer, David S.
Associate Professor of Anthropology
University of Victoria

Moyles, R. Gordon
Professor of English
University of Alberta

Muehlen, Maria
Curator, Inuit Art Section
Indian & Northern Affairs Canada
Ottawa

Muise, Del
Associate Professor of History
Carleton University

Muldoon, The Hon Francis C.
Federal Court, Ottawa

Mummery, Robert M.
Photographer, Edmonton

Munawar, Mohiuddin
Research Scientist
Great Lakes Fisheries Research Branch
Fisheries & Oceans
Canadian Centre for Inland Waters
Burlington, Ont

Munn, R.E.
Institute for Environmental Studies
University of Toronto

Munro, J. Ian
Professor of Computer Science
University of Waterloo

Murray, Joan
Director
The Robert McLaughlin Gallery
Oshawa, Ont

Murray, Robert G.E.
Professor of Microbiology &
Immunology
University of Western Ontario

Mutimer, Brian T.P.
Associate Professor of Physical
Education
St Francis Xavier University

Mycio, Luba
Canadian Wildlife Federation
Ottawa

Myles, John
Professor of Sociology
Carleton University

Nadeau, Robert
Professeur de philosophie
Université du Québec à Montréal

Nadeau, Vincent
Professeur de littérature
Université Laval

Naidoo, Josephine C.
Associate Professor of Psychology
Wilfrid Laurier University

Nasgaard, Roald
Chief Curator
Art Gallery of Ontario, Toronto

Nason, Roger
Bicentennial Co-ordinator
City Hall, Fredericton

Nattrass, Susan M.
Director, Interuniversity Athletics
University of Alberta

Navin, Francis P.D.
Professor of Civil Engineering
University of British Columbia

Neal, Margaret
Co-ordinator
Standardbred Canada Library
Canadian Trotting Association
Toronto

Neary, Peter
Professor of History
University of Western Ontario

Neatby, H. Blair
Professor of History
Carleton University

Neatby, L.H.
Author;
Professor of Classics (retired)
Saskatoon

Neave, Edwin H.
Professor of Finance
Queen's University

Needler, A.W.H.
St Andrews, NB

Needler, George T.
Director
Atlantic Oceanographic Laboratory
Ocean Science & Surveys Atlantic
Dept of Fisheries & Oceans
Bedford Institute of Oceanography
Dartmouth, NS

Neelin, James M.
Professor of Biology & Biochemistry
Carleton University

Neill, Robin F.
Associate Professor of Economics
Carleton University

Neimanis, V.P.
Senior Research Officer
Environment Canada, Ottawa

Nelles, H. Vivian
Professor of History
York University

Nelson, A.E.
Sechelt, BC
Nelson, Joseph S.
Professor of Zoology
University of Alberta
Nepveu, Pierre
Professeur de littérature
Université de Montréal
Nettleship, David N.
Research Scientist
Seabird Research Unit
Canadian Wildlife Service
Bedford Institute of Oceanography
Dartmouth, NS
Neufeld, Edward Peter
Senior Vice-President & Chief
Economist
The Royal Bank of Canada, Montréal
Neufeldt, Ronald W.
Associate Professor of Religious
Studies
University of Calgary
Neuman, Shirley
Professor of English
University of Alberta
New, William H.
Professor of English;
Editor, Canadian Literature
University of British Columbia
Newark, Michael J.
Meteorologist
Environment Canada, Toronto
Newell, Dianne
Associate Professor of History
University of British Columbia
Newlands, David L.
Museum Studies Program
University of Toronto
Newman, Peter C.
Author & editor
Cordova Bay, BC
Nicholson, Norman L. (deceased)
Professor of Geography
University of Western Ontario
Nicks, John
Reynolds Alberta Museum
Wetaskiwin, Alta
Nicolson, Murray William
Historian
Newmarket, Ont
Nielsen, N. Ole
Dean, Ontario Veterinary College
University of Guelph
Niosi, Jorge E.
Professeur de sociologie
Université du Québec à Montréal
Nkemdirim, Lawrence C.
Professor of Geography
University of Calgary
Noble, William C.
Professor of Anthropology
McMaster University
Nonnecke, Ib L.
Professor of Horticultural Science
University of Guelph
Noonan, James
Associate Professor of English
Carleton University
Norman, David G.
Editor, PR Strategies
Scarborough, Ont
Norrie, Kenneth H.
Professor of Economics
University of Alberta
Novak, Barbara
Writer
London, Ont
Nursall, J. Ralph
Professor of Zoology
University of Alberta
Nutt, Jim Sutcliffe
Retired Diplomat, Ottawa
Nuttall, V. Walter
Agriculture research
scientist (retired), Winnipeg

O'Brien, Allan
Professor Emeritus
University of Western Ontario
Occhietti, Serge
Professeur de géographie physique
Université du Québec à Montréal
O'Clery, Jean
Pacific Press Ltd, Vancouver
O'Dea, Shane
Associate Professor of English
Memorial University of Newfoundland
O'Dor, Ronald K.
Professor of Biology
Dalhousie University

Officer, Jillian M.
Assistant Professor of Dance
University of Waterloo
O'Grady, Jean
Collected Works of John Stuart Mill
University of Toronto Press
Oke, Timothy R.
Professor of Geography
University of British Columbia
O'Leary, Kim Patrick
Editor, Vancouver
Oliphant, John J.
Writer & photographer
Vancouver
O'Neill, Daniel
Former Acting Curator
Historical Photograph Section
Vancouver Public Library
O'Neill, Patrick
Associate Professor of Drama
Mount Saint Vincent University
Onyszchuk, Mario
Professor & Chairman of Chemistry
McGill University
O'Quinn, L.D.
Ottawa
Orford, Robert R.
Deputy Minister
Community & Occupational Health
Government of Alberta
Orkin, Mark M.
Lawyer & writer, Toronto
Orlikow, Lionel
Consultant, Winnipeg
Ormsby, Margaret A.
Professor Emerita
Vernon, BC
Osborne, Brian Stuart
Professor of Geography
Queen's University
Ouellet, Fernand
Professeur d'histoire
Université d'Ottawa
Ouellet, Henri
Curator, Ornithology Section
National Museum of Natural Sciences
Ottawa
Ouellet, Réal
Département de littérature
Université Laval
Owens, John N.
Professor of Biology
University of Victoria
Owram, D.R.
Professor of History
University of Alberta

Packer, John G.
Professor of Botany
University of Alberta
Page, Donald M.
Historian, Dept of External Affairs
Ottawa
Page, Garnet T.
Consultant, Calgary
Page, James E.
Canadian Studies Program
Secretary of State
Hull, Qué
Page, Malcolm
Professor of English
Simon Fraser University
Paikin, Lee (deceased)
Visiting Assistant Professor of Law
University of British Columbia
Paikowsky, Sandra
Associate Professor of Art History;
Curator, Concordia Art Gallery
Concordia University
Pain, Howard
Writer, Toronto
Painter, Michael F.
Consultant forester, Vancouver
Palardy, Jean
Historien
Fondation Macdonald-Stewart
Montréal
Palay, Murray S.
Barrister & solicitor, Winnipeg
Palmer, Bryan D.
Professor of History
Queen's University
Palmer, Howard
Professor of History
University of Calgary
Palmer, Tamara Jeppson
Assistant Professor of General Studies
University of Calgary
Paltiel, Khayyam Zev
Professor of Political Science
Carleton University

Panitch, Leo
Professor of Political Science
York University
Pannekoek, Frits
Alberta Culture & Multiculturalism
Edmonton
Panting, Gerald Ernest
Professor of History
Memorial University of Newfoundland
Paradis, Jean-Marc
Professeur d'histoire
Université du Québec à Trois-Rivières
Pariseau, Jean
Historien en chef
Service historique de la défense
nationale, Ottawa
Parker, George L.
Professor of English
Royal Military College of Canada
Parker, Graham
Professor of Law
Osgoode Hall Law School
York University
Parker, James M.
Director
University Archives & Collections
University of Alberta
Parry, Keith
Associate Professor of Anthropology
University of Lethbridge
Parsons, John
Dept of Social Studies
Booth Memorial Regional High School
St John's
Parsons, Timothy R.
Professor of Oceanography
University of British Columbia
Pastore, Ralph T.
Associate Professor of History
Memorial University of Newfoundland
Patching, Thomas H.
Professor Emeritus of Mineral
Engineering
University of Alberta
Paterson, Donald G.
Professor of Economics
University of British Columbia
Paterson, W. Stan B.
Quadra Island, BC
Patterson, E.P.
Associate Professor of History
University of Waterloo
Patterson, G. James
Professor of Anthropology
Eastern Oregon State College at
La Grande
Patterson, Graeme H.
Associate Professor of History
University of Toronto
Patterson, Robert S.
Professor of Educational Foundations
University of Alberta
Payment, Diane Paulette
Historian, Parks Canada
Winnipeg
Peacey, John G.
Head, Dept of Chemical Engineering
Noranda Research Centre
Pointe Claire, Qué
Peacock, Gordon B.
Professor Emeritus of Drama
University of Alberta
Peake, Frank A.
Professor of History (retired)
Laurentian University
Pease, Jane H.
Professor of History
University of Maine at Orono
Pease, William H.
Professor of History
University of Maine at Orono
Pedersen, Diana
Doctoral Candidate of History
Carleton University
Pedwell, Susan
Writer, Toronto
Peel, Bruce
Chief Librarian Emeritus
University of Alberta
Peers, Frank W.
Professor of Political Science
University of Toronto
Pelletier, Gérard
Chairman of the Board of Trustees
National Museums of Canada, Ottawa
Pelletier, Jacques
Professeur de littérature québécoise
Université du Québec à Montréal
Pelletier, Réjean
Professeur titulaire de science politique
Université Laval

Peltier, W. Richard
Professor of Physics
University of Toronto
Penelhum, Terence
Professor of Religious Studies
University of Calgary
Penner, Norman
Professor of Political Science
York University
Penton, M. James
Professor of History
University of Lethbridge
Percy, Michael B.
Associate Professor of Economics
University of Alberta
Perks, William T.
Professor of Urbanism & Planning
University of Calgary
Perla, R.
Research Scientist
National Hydrology Research Institute
Canmore, Alta
Persaud, Trivedi V.N.
Professor & Head of Anatomy
University of Manitoba
Person, Clayton O.
Professor Emeritus of Botany
University of British Columbia
Peters, Erik J.
Galerie Bernard Desroches
Montréal
Peters, Robert Henry
Professor of Biology
McGill University
Peterson, Jeannie
Contract researcher
Dartmouth, NS
Peterson, R.L.
Curator, Mammalogy
Royal Ontario Museum
Toronto
Peterson, Thomas E.
Associate Professor of Political
Studies
University of Manitoba
Petryshyn, Jaroslav
Instructor of History
Grande Prairie Regional College
Phaneuf, Louis-Philippe
Professeur
Université de Montréal
Phelan, P.P.
National Defence Headquarters
Directorate of Cadets, Ottawa
Phelps, Edward
Librarian, Regional Collection
University of Western Ontario Library
Phillips, Carol
Director
Norman Mackenzie Art Gallery
University of Regina
Phillips, David W.
Climatologist, Environment Canada
Downsview, Ont
Phillips, Paul
Professor of Economics
University of Manitoba
Phillips, Roy A.
Former President & Executive Director
The Canadian Manufacturers'
Association, Toronto
Phillips, Ruth Bliss
Assistant Professor of Art History
Carleton University
Phillips, Truman P.
Associate Professor of Agricultural
Economics & Extension Education
University of Guelph
Phillipson, Donald J.C.
Historian, Ottawa
Picard, Ellen I.
Professor of Law
University of Alberta
Piché, Victor
Professeur de démographie;
Directeur du Centre de Recherches
Caraïbes
Université de Montréal
Pickard, George L.
Professor Emeritus of Oceanography
University of British Columbia
Pierce, Richard A.
Professor Emeritus of History
Queen's University
Pierce, Thomas W.
Lands Directorate
Environment Canada, Hull
Pierre-Deschênes, Claudine
Historienne, Montréal

Pierson, Ruth Roach
Associate Professor of History &
Philosophy; & Sociology in Education
Ontario Institute for Studies in
Education, Toronto
Pill, Juri
General Manager, Planning
Toronto Transit Commission
Pirozynski, K.A.
Palaeomycologist
National Museums of Canada, Ottawa
Pitt, David G.
Professor Emeritus of English Language
& Literature
Memorial University of Newfoundland
Pitt, Janet Miller
Dept of Rural, Agricultural & Northern
Development
Government of Newfoundland &
Labrador
Pitt, Robert D.
Dept of English
Memorial University of Newfoundland
Pivato, Joseph
Professor of Humanities & English
Athabasca University
Plamondon, Réjean
Directeur des communications
Université de Montréal
Plant, Richard L.
Associate Professor of Drama
Queen's University
Ploeg, Jozinus
Director
Division of Mechanical Engineering
National Research Council, Ottawa
Plouffe, Hélène
Rédactrice & recherchiste, Montréal
Plunkett, T.J.
Professor of Public Administration
Queen's University
Poiker, Thomas K.
Professor of Geography & Computing
Science
Simon Fraser University
Polèse, Mario
INRS-Urbanization
Université du Québec
Polnaszek, Frank
Hartford, Conn
Ponting, J. Rick
Professor of Sociology
University of Calgary
Pool, Annelies M.
Writer
Yellowknife, NWT
Pope, Carol Ann
Burnaby, BC
Porteous, Hugh A.
Manager, Issues Coordination
Corporate Planning
Via Rail Canada Inc, Montréal
Porter, Arthur
Professor Emeritus
University of Toronto
Porter, John R.
Professeur d'histoire de l'art
Université Laval
Porter, Marion
Researcher, Ottawa
Posgate, Bruce D.
Toronto
Posluns, Michael
Hoople, Posluns & Associates
Ottawa
Pothier, Bernard
Canadian War Museum, Ottawa
Potvin, Gilles C.M.
Historian, Montréal
Poulin, Gabrielle
Ecrivain, Ottawa
Powell, Deborah J.
Woodstock, Ont
Powell, Jay (James V.)
Associate Professor of Anthropology
University of British Columbia
Prang, Margaret E.
Professor Emerita of History
University of British Columbia
Pratt, Larry
Professor of Political Science
University of Alberta
Pressman, Norman E.P.
Associate Professor of Urban &
Regional Planning
University of Waterloo
Preston-Thomas, Hugh
Associate Director
Division of Physics
National Research Council, Ottawa

Preston, Richard A.
Professor Emeritus of History
Duke University at Durham, NC
Preston, Richard J.
Professor of Anthropology
McMaster University
Price, John A.
Professor of Anthropology
York University
Pringle, Alexander D.
Barrister & Solicitor, Edmonton
Pritchard, Gordon
Professor of Biology
University of Calgary
Pritchard, James
Associate Professor of History
Queen's University
Pritchard, John
Research Director
Haisla Aboriginal Rights Program
Victoria
Proctor, John T.A.
Professor of Horticultural Science
University of Guelph
Pross, A. Paul
Director, School of Public Administration
Dalhousie University
Pugh, Garth Charles
Research Officer II
Dept of Culture & Recreation, Regina
Punch, Terrence M.
Vice-President
Royal NS Historical Society;
Chairman, Genealogical Association
of NS, Halifax
Purdon, Arnold L.
Welland, Ont
Putt, Eric D.
Professional Agrologist
Creston, BC
Pylyshyn, Zenon W.
Professor of Psychology & Computer
Science
University of Western Ontario

Qualter, Terence H.
Professor of Political Science
University of Waterloo
Quamme, Harvey A.
Agriculture Canada Research Station
Summerland, BC
Quayle, D.B.
Marine zoologist
Nanaimo, BC
Quinn, Frank
Ottawa

Radforth, Ian
Assistant Professor of History
University of Toronto
Ralston, H. Keith
Historical consultant, Vancouver
Ramraj, Victor J.
Professor of English
University of Calgary
Ramsay, Donald A.
Principal Research Officer
National Research Council, Ottawa
Ramsden, Peter G.
Associate Professor of Anthropology
McMaster University
Raney, R. Keith
Deputy Director
RADARSAT Project Office
Canada Centre for Remote Sensing
Ottawa
Rapp, Egon
Professor Emeritus of Agricultural
Engineering
University of Alberta
Rasmussen, John B.
Historian & writer, Edmonton
Rasmussen, Mark A.
Historical geographer, Edmonton
Rasporich, Anthony W.
Professor of History
University of Calgary
Rasporich, Beverly J.
Associate Professor of General Studies
University of Calgary
Rawlyk, George A.
Professor of History
Queen's University
Ray, Arthur
Professor of History
University of British Columbia
Rayburn, Alan
Geographer, Ottawa
Raynor, David R.
Assistant Professor of Philosophy
University of Ottawa

Rea, J.Edgar
Professor of History
University of Manitoba
Read, John H.
Professor of Community Health
Sciences & Pediatrics
University of Calgary
Redekop, Magdalene
Associate Professor of English
University of Toronto
Redmond, Gerald
Professor of Physical Education &
Recreation
University of Alberta
Reed, Austin
Canadian Wildlife Service
Ste-Foy, Qué
Reed, F. Leslie C.
Professor of Forestry
University of British Columbia
Reeves, Randall R.
Arctic Biological Station
Ste-Anne-de-Bellevue, Qué
Regan, Ellen M.
Associate Professor
The Ontario Institute for Studies in
Education, Toronto
Regehr, T.D.
Professor of History
University of Saskatchewan
Reid, Alison M.
Consulting biologist
Victoria
Reid, David
Associate Professor of Surgery
(orthopaedic);
Consultant in Sports Medicine
University of Alberta
Reid, Ian A.
Special Surveys Engineer (retired)
Water Survey of Canada, Ottawa
Reid, John G.
Associate Professor of History
Saint Mary's University
Reid, M.H. (Lefty)
Head Curator
Hockey Hall of Fame & Museum
Toronto
Reid, Monty
Tyrrell Museum of Palaeontology
Drumheller, Alta
Reid, Richard
Associate Professor of History
University of Guelph
Reid, Robert G.B.
Professor of Biology
University of Victoria
Reilly, Nolan
Assistant Professor of History
University of Winnipeg
Reilly, Sharon
Curator of History & Technology
Manitoba Museum of Man & Nature
Winnipeg
Reiswig, Henry M.
Associate Professor of Biology
McGill University
Rémillard, Gil
Professeur titulaire de droit
constitutionnel
Rennie, Donald Andrews
Dean of Agriculture
University of Saskatchewan
Rennie, Jim
Publisher
Jim Rennie's Sports Letter
Collingwood, Ont
Ricard, François
Professeur agrégé de littérature
Université McGill
Richards, John
Assistant Professor
Simon Fraser University
Richards, William D.
Assistant Professor of Communication
Laboratory for Computer &
Communication Research
Simon Fraser University
Richardson, Eric Harvey
Principal Research Officer
National Research Council of Canada
Dominion Astrophysical Observatory
Victoria
Richardson, Keith W.
Chief, Education
Cultural & Educational Resources
Secretary of State, Ottawa
Richardson, W. George
Associate Professor of History of
Engineering
Queen's University

Richman, Alex
Professor of Psychiatry;
Community Health & Epidemiology
Dalhousie University
Rickwood, Roger R.
City Solicitor's Dept, City Hall
Hamilton, Ont
Ricou, Laurie
Associate Professor of English
University of British Columbia
Riddell, W. Craig
Professor of Economics
University of British Columbia
Rider, Peter E.
Atlantic Provinces Historian
Canadian Museum of Civilization
Ottawa
Ridington, Robin
Associate Professor of Anthropology
University of British Columbia
Riedel, Walter E.
Associate Professor of German
University of Victoria
Riegert, Paul W.
Professor of Biology
University of Regina
Riendeau, Roger E.
Innis College
University of Toronto
Riggs, Bert
Writer, St John's
Riis, Nelson A.
Geographer & Member of Parliament
Ottawa
Ritchie, J.C.
Professor of Botany
Scarborough Campus
University of Toronto
Robb, S. Andrew
Assistant Professor of History &
Canadian Studies
University of Prince Edward Island
Robert, Guy
Doctor in Aesthetics
Art Writer & Consultant, Montréal
Robert, Jean-Claude
Professeur d'histoire
Université du Québec à Montréal
Robert, Lucie
Professeure de littérature
Université du Québec à Montréal
Robert, Véronique
Journaliste culturelle, Montréal
Roberto, Eugène
Professeur de lettres françaises
Université d'Ottawa
Robertson, Ian Ross
Associate Professor of History
University of Toronto
Robertson, J.A.L.
Consulting scientist
Deep River, Ont
Robertson, Marion
Historian, Shelburne, NS
Robertson, Raleigh John
Professor of Biology
Queen's University
Robidoux, Réjean
Professeur titulaire de littérature
Université d'Ottawa
Robillard, Denise
Conseil canadien des Eglises, Toronto
Robinson, Bart T.
Writer, Equinox magazine
Camden East, Ont
Robinson, J. Lewis
Professor Emeritus of Geography
University of British Columbia
Robinson, Sinclair
Associate Professor of French
Carleton University
Robson, Tom W.
Director of Development
University of Winnipeg
Roby, Yves
Professeur d'histoire
Université Laval
Roche, Douglas
Ambassador for Disarmament
Dept of External Affairs
Rocher, Guy
Professeur de sociologie
Université de Montréal
Rodney, William
Professor of History & Dean of Arts
Royal Roads Military College
Victoria
Rodrigo, Russell G.A.
Professor of Chemistry
Wilfrid Laurier University
Rodriguez, Juan
Writer, Montréal

Roeder, Robert C.
Lazenby Professor of Physics
Southwestern University at
Georgetown, Tex
Rogers, Jacob
Priest
Goulds, Nfld
Rogerson, Robert J.
Professor of Geography
Memorial University of Newfoundland
Roland, Charles G.
Professor of the History of Medicine
McMaster University
Romaniuk, Eugene W.
Professor of Educational Psychology
University of Alberta
Romanow, Joseph R.
President, Machinery & Equipment
Manufacturers' Association of Canada
Ottawa
Romanowski, Barbara
Sexually Transmitted Disease Control
Edmonton
Rome, David
Dept of Religion
Concordia University
Romney, Paul
Historian, Baltimore, Md
Ronald, Keith
Professor of Zoology
University of Guelph
Ronish, Donna Yavorsky
Historian, Greenfield Park
Rooke, Constance
Associate Professor of English
University of Victoria
Rose, Albert
Professor Emeritus of Social Work
University of Toronto
Rose, Phyllis
Graduate Student
University of Toronto
Rosen, Earl
Executive Director
Canadian Independent Record
Production Association, Toronto
Rosenberg, Ann C.
Instructor of Fine Arts
Capilano College, North Vancouver
Ross, Alexander
Editorial Director
CB Media Ltd., Toronto
Ross, Alexander M.
Professor (retired)
University of Guelph
Ross, Catherine Sheldrick
Associate Professor of Library &
Information Science
University of Western Ontario
Ross, David I.
Director of Operations
NORDCO Limited (Newfoundland
Oceans Research & Development
Corporation)
St John's
Ross, David P.
Social economic consultant, Ottawa
Ross, Henry U.
Professor Emeritus of Metallurgical
Engineering
University of Toronto
Rostoker, Gordon
Professor of Physics
University of Alberta
Rothney, Gordon Oliver
Honorary Fellow, St John's College
University of Manitoba
Rothrock, George A.
Professor of History
University of Alberta
Rothstein, Samuel
Professor Emeritus of Librarianship
University of British Columbia
Rotstein, Abraham
Professor of Economics
University of Toronto
Roueche, Leonard R.
Manager, Research
British Columbia Ferry Corporation
Victoria
Rouillard, Jacques
Professeur d'histoire
Université de Montréal
Rousseau, Guildo
Professeur de littérature
Centre de recherche en études québecoises
Université du Québec à Trois-Rivières
Rousseau, Henri-Paul
V-président et Économiste en chef
Banque Nationale du Canada
Montréal

Routledge, Marie
Research & Documentation Co-ordinator
Inuit Art Section
Indian & Northern Affairs Canada
Ottawa
Rowat, Donald Cameron
Professor of Political Science
Carleton University
Rowberry, R. Geoffrey
Professor (retired)
Sidney, BC
Rowe, Frederick W.
Senator
Rowe, John Stanley
Professor Emeritus of Plant Ecology
University of Saskatchewan
Rowe, Kenneth
Fellow of the Royal Philatelic
Society of Canada, Toronto
Rowe, Percy A.
Contributing Editor, Travel
Toronto Sun, Toronto
Rowland, Gordon G.
Senior Research Scientist
Crop Development Centre
University of Saskatchewan
Rowley, Diana
Editor, Ottawa
Rowsell, Harry C.
Professor of Pathology;
Executive Director, Canadian Council
of Animal Care, Ottawa
Roy, David J.
Director, Centre for Bioethics
Clinical Research Institute of
Montréal
Roy, Fernande
Professeur d'histoire
Université du Québec à Montréal
Roy, Muriel K.
Centre d'études acadiennes
Université de Moncton
Roy, Patricia E.
Associate Professor of History
University of Victoria
Roy, Reginald H.
Professor of Military & Strategic
Studies
University of Victoria
Rozee, Kenneth Roy
Professor of Microbiology
Dalhousie University
Rubenstein, Lorne
Journalist, Toronto
Rubin, Ken
Public interest researcher &
consultant, Ottawa
Rubin, Leon J.
Professor of Food Engineering
University of Toronto
Rubio, Gerald J.
Assistant Professor of English
University of Guelph
Rubio, Mary H.
Co-Editor
Canadian Children's Literature
Dept of English
University of Guelph
Ruddel, David-Thiery
Historian
Canadian Museum of Civilization
Ottawa
Ruff, Norman J.
Assistant Professor of Political
Science
University of Victoria
Ruiz, Wilson
Journalist & broadcaster, Toronto
Rukavina, Norman A.
Geologist
National Water Research Institute
Burlington, Ont
Runnalls, Oliver John Clyve
Chairman, Centre for Nuclear
Engineering;
Professor of Energy Studies
University of Toronto
Rupert, Robert John
Associate Professor of Journalism
Carleton University
Ruppenthal, Karl M.
UPS Foundation Professor;
Director, the Centre for
Transportation Studies
University of British Columbia
Rushdy, Roger
Agronome
Station de Recherche Deschambault
Deschambault, Qué

Russell, Dale A.
Curator of Fossil Vertebrates
National Museum of Natural Sciences
Ottawa
Russell, Hilary
Parks Canada, Hull
Russell, Loris S.
Curator Emeritus
Royal Ontario Museum, Toronto
Russell, Peter A.
Resident Tutor, Fircroft College
Birmingham, England
Russell, Victor L.
Manager, City of Toronto Archives
Rutherford, Paul Frederic William
Professor of History
University of Toronto
Rutter, Nathaniel W.
Professor & Chairman of Geology
University of Alberta
Ryan, Douglas E.
McLeod Professor of Chemistry
Dalhousie University
Ryan, James T.
Professor of Chemical Engineering
University of Alberta
Ryan, Joseph
Directorate of History
Dept of National Defence, Ottawa
Ryan, John
Professor of Geography
University of Winnipeg
Ryan, Judith Hoegg
Writer
Caribou Island, NS & Toronto
Ryan, Shannon
Associate Professor of History
Memorial University of Newfoundland
Ryder, June M.
Geologist, Vancouver
Ryerson, Robert A.
Canada Centre for Remote Sensing
Energy, Mines & Resources, Canada

Saarinen, Oiva W.
Associate Professor of Geography
Laurentian University
Sabina, Ann P.
Mineralogist
Geological Survey of Canada, Ottawa
Sager, Eric W.
Assistant Professor of History
University of Victoria
St-Hilaire, Marc
Centre interuniversitaire de recherches
sur les populations
Chicoutimi, Qué
Saint-Jacques, Bernard
Professor of Linguistics
University of British Columbia
St-Laurent, Gaston J.
Professeur de nutrition animale
Université Laval
Saladin-d'Anglure, B.
Professor of Anthropology
Université Laval
Sales, Arnaud
Professeur titulaire
Université de Montréal
Salisbury, Richard F.
Professor of Anthropology
McGill University
Sallot, Jeff
Ottawa Bureau Chief
The Globe and Mail, Ottawa
Salter, Liora
Associate Professor & Chairman of
Communication
Simon Fraser University
Sameoto, Douglas D.
Research Scientist
Bedford Institute of Oceanography
Dartmouth, NS
Sanderson, Marie E.
Professor of Geography
University of Windsor
Sandison, Margaret J.
Executive Director
Saskatchewan Sports Hall of Fame
Regina
Sangster, Joan
Lecturer
Trent University
Santink, Joy L.
Historian, Toronto
Sarfati, Sonia
Journaliste, Montréal
Sarjeant, A. Margaret
Librarian, Saskatoon
Sarjeant, William A.S.
Professor of Geological Sciences
University of Saskatchewan

Sarty, Roger
Historian, Directorate of History
Dept of National Defence, Ottawa
Sauchyn, David J.
Assistant Professor of Geography
University of Regina
Saul, John S.
Professor of Social Science
Atkinson College, York University
Sauriol, Pierre
Agronome
Ministère de l'agriculture du Québec
St-Rémi, Qué
Savard, Pierre
Professeur d'histoire
Université d'Ottawa
Savile, D.B.O.
Research Associate Emeritus
Biosystematics Research Centre
Ottawa
Savishinsky, Joel S.
Professor of Anthropology
Ithaca College, NY
Savitt, Ronald
Professor of Marketing
Michigan State University at
East Lansing
Sawatsky, Rodney J.
Associate Professor of Religious
Studies & History
Conrad Grebel College
University of Waterloo
Sawatsky, Ronald G.
Centre for Religious Studies
University of Toronto
Sawula, Lorne William
National Volleyball Coach (Women)
Regina
Sawyer, Deborah C.
Information Plus Inc, Toronto
Saywell, John T.
University Professor
York University
Scarfe, Christopher M.
Professor of Geology
University of Alberta
Scargill, M.H.
Professor Emeritus of Linguistics
University of Victoria
Schaefer, Otto
Director
Northern Medical Research Unit
Medical Services
Health & Welfare Canada, Edmonton
Schau, Barbara Ann
Sessional Lecturer
Carleton University
Scheffel, David
Cariboo College, Kamloops, BC
Schiff, Harold I.
University Professor
York University
Schipper, Sidney S.
Dean, Fashion Technology Division
George Brown College;
Adjunct Professor of Fashion
Ryerson Polytechnical Institute
Toronto
Schledermann, Peter
Adjunct Associate Professor of
Anthropology
University of Victoria
Schlesinger, Benjamin
Professor of Social Work
University of Toronto
Schmitz, Nancy
Professeur d'anthropologie
Université Laval
Schoenauer, Norbert
Macdonald Professor of Architecture
McGill University
Schrodt, Barbara
Associate Professor of Physical
Education (Sport History)
University of British Columbia
Schultz, George A.
Professor of History
University of Manitoba
Schwartz, Joan M.
Documentary Art & Photography
National Archives of Canada, Ottawa
Schweizer, Elizabeth J.
Editorial Assistant
Studies in History & Politics
Bishop's University
Schweizer, Karl W.
Associate Professor of History
Bishop's University
Schwier, Charles
Research Associate, Canadian
Institute of Guided Ground Transport
Queen's University

Scobie, Stephen
Professor of English
University of Victoria

Scott, David S.
Executive Director
Institute for Hydrogen Systems
Mississauga, Ont

Scott, John
Ottawa

Scott, MaryLynn
Dept of English
University of Alberta

Scott, Peter J.
Associate Professor of Biology
Memorial University of Newfoundland

Scott, Stephen A.
Professor of Law
McGill University

Scott, W. Beverly
Senior Scientist
Huntsman Marine Laboratory
St Andrews, NB;
Professor Emeritus of Zoology
University of Toronto

Scudder, Geoffrey G.E.
Professor & Head of Zoology
University of British Columbia

Seager, Allen
Associate Professor of History
Simon Fraser University

Sealey, D. Bruce
Professor of Education
University of Manitoba

Sealey, Gary
Director, Visitor Activities Branch
National Parks, Ottawa

Sealy, Spencer G.
Professor of Zoology
University of Manitoba

Sebert, Louis M.
Canada Lands Surveyor, Ottawa

Sedgwick, Kent
Assistant Planner
City of Prince George

Segall, Harold N.
Assistant Professor of Medicine
McGill University

Segger, Martin
Director
Maltwood Art Museum & Gallery
University of Victoria

Séguin, Normand
Professeur d'histoire
Université du Québec à Trois-Rivières

Sehon, Alec H.
Professor of Immunology
University of Manitoba

Selwood, H. John
Associate Professor of Geography
University of Winnipeg

Semple, Neil A.
Assistant Archivist
United Church of Canada
Victoria University, Toronto

Senda, Yoshio
National Coach;
Technical Director, Judo Alberta

Senior, Elinor Kyte
Visiting Assistant Professor
St Francis Xavier University

Senior, Hereward
Professor of History
McGill University

Serne, Robert Allan
Regional Manager
Canadian Portland Cement Association
Prairie Provinces Region, Edmonton

Sewell, John
Former Mayor of Toronto;
Journalist, Toronto

Seymour, Christopher M.
Executive Secretary
Canadian Tobacco Manufacturers'
Council, Montréal

Seymour, Patrick D.
Director, Devonian Botanic Garden
University of Alberta

Shadbolt, Doris
Curator Emeritus
Vancouver Art Gallery
North Burnaby, BC

Shadbolt, Douglas
Professor of Architecture
University of British Columbia

Shaffer, Ed
Professor of Economics
University of Alberta

Shaker, Fouad E.
Writer, historian, TV commentator &
international correspondent
Greenfield Park, Qué

Shannon, Elizabeth E.
Associate Professor of Clothing &
Textiles
University of Manitoba

Shapiro, Bernard J.
Director & Professor of Education
Ontario Institute for Studies in
Education, Toronto

Shaver, Frances M.
Sociologist
Concordia University

Shaw, Gordon C.
Professor of Administrative Studies
York University

Shaw, Murray C.
General Manager, Prairie &
Northern Regions
Export Development Corporation
Calgary

Shearing, Clifford D.
Associate Professor of Criminology &
Sociology
University of Toronto

Sheehan, Carol
Ethnologist & art historian
Calgary

Sheehan, Nancy M.
Dean, Faculty of Education
University of British Columbia

Sheffer, Harry
Former Vice-Chairman
Defence Research Board, Ottawa

Sheffield, Edward (Ottawa)
Professor Emeritus of Higher
Education
University of Toronto

Sheinin, Rose
Vice-Dean, School of Graduate Studies
University of Toronto

Shelest, Jaroslaw
Historian, Kitchener, Ont

Shephard, Roy J.
Director, School of Physical & Health
Education;
Professor of Applied Physiology
University of Toronto

Sheppard, R. Ronald
Director of Gaming, Winnipeg

Sheppard, Robert
Correspondent, The Globe and Mail
Toronto

Shifrin, Ellen
Dance researcher, Toronto

Shih, Chang-tai
Curator of Crustaceans
National Museum of Natural Sciences
Ottawa

Shoyama, Thomas K.
Visiting Professor
University of Victoria

Shugg, Orville J.W.
Ottawa

Shultz, Ken R.
Scientific Adviser
Atomic Energy Control Board, Ottawa

Shuter, William L.H.
Professor of Physics
University of British Columbia

Sibbald, Patricia A.
Director, Public/Professional Education
Institute for the Prevention of
Child Abuse, Toronto

Sidor, Nicholas
Dept of Communications, Ottawa

Siegel, Arthur
Professor of Social Science
York University

Silcox, David P.
Writer, Toronto

Sillanpaa, Lennard
Orleans, Ont

Silver, A.I.
Associate Professor of History
University of Toronto

Silverman, Eliane Leslau
Assistant Professor of Women's
Studies
University of Calgary

Silversides, C. Ross
Forestry consultant
Prescott, Ont

Simeon, Richard
Professor of Public Administration &
Political Studies
Queen's University

Simpson, C.J.
Associate Director of Public Affairs
University of Alberta

Sinclair-Faulkner, Tom
Professor of Comparative Religion
Dalhousie University

Sirois, Antoine
Professeur de littérature
Université de Sherbrooke

Sisler, Rebecca
Sculptor, Toronto

Sitwell, O.F.G.
Associate Professor of Geography
University of Alberta

Skeoch, Alan Edward
Head of History
Parkdale Collegiate Institute
Toronto

Skogstad, Grace
Associate Professor
University of Toronto

Slater, Peter
Dean of Divinity, Trinity College;
Professor of Theology
Toronto School of Theology &
Centre for Religious Studies
University of Toronto

Slavutych, Yar
Professor of Slavic Languages
University of Alberta

Slaymaker, H. Olav
Professor of Geography
University of British Columbia

Slinkard, Alfred E.
Senior Research Scientist
Crop Development Centre
University of Saskatchewan

Sloan, W.A.
Instructor, Canadian History
Selkirk College
Castlegar, BC

Slocombe, D. Scott
Graduate Student of Planning
University of British Columbia

Slonecker, Charles E.
Professor of Anatomy
University of British Columbia

Sly, Peter Gerent
National Water Research Institute
Dept of the Environment
Burlington, Ont

Smart, Patricia
Professor of French & Canadian Studies
Carleton University

Smith, Al
Secretary
Nova Scotia Sport Heritage Centre
Halifax

Smith, André
Associate Professor of French
McGill University

Smith, Andrea Barbara
Dept of History
Vancouver Community College, Langara
Campus

Smith, Barry L.
Chief, Regulatory Affairs
Food Directorate
Health Protection Branch, Ottawa

Smith, David B.
Professor of Biochemistry
University of Western Ontario

Smith, David E.
Professor of Political Studies
University of Saskatchewan

Smith, Denis
Dean of Social Science
University of Western Ontario

Smith, Derek G.
Associate Professor of Sociology &
Anthropology
Carleton University

Smith, Donald A.
Associate Professor of Biology
Carleton University

Smith, Donald B.
Associate Professor of History
University of Calgary

Smith, Douglas A.
Associate Professor of Economics
Carleton University

Smith, Frances K.
Curator Emeritus
Agnes Etherington Art Centre
Queen's University

Smith, James G.E.
Curator of North American Ethnology
Museum of the American Indian
Heye Foundation, New York City

Smith, James N.M.
Associate Professor of Zoology
University of British Columbia

Smith, Kenneth V.
Honorary Secretary
Commonwealth Games Association of
Canada

Smith, Maurice V.
Adjunct Professor of Environmental
Biology
University of Guelph

Smith, Peter C.
Research Scientist
Atlantic Oceanographic Laboratory
Bedford Institute of Oceanography
Dartmouth, NS

Smith, Peter J.
Professor of Geography
University of Alberta

Smith, Shirlee Anne
Keeper
Hudson's Bay Company Archives

Smith, T. Bradbrooke
Burritt's Rapids, Ont

Smith, William Young, Jr.
Historian, Fredericton

Snider, D. Laureen
Associate Professor of Sociology
Queen's University

Snow, Dean R.
Professor of Anthropology
University at Albany, SUNY

Snowdon, James D.
Sessional Lecturer of History
Acadia University

Socknat, Thomas P.
Assistant Professor of History
University of Toronto

Solandt, Omond M.
Consultant
Bolton, Ont

Somerville, Margaret A.
Director, McGill Centre for Medicine,
Ethics & Law
Montréal

Soper, James Herbert
Curator Emeritus, Botany Division
National Museum of Natural Sciences
Ottawa

Sorfleet, John R.
Associate Professor
Concordia University

Sormany, Pierre
Sillery, Qué

Southcott, Mary E.
Art historian
Mississauga, Ont

Souther, Jack G.
Research Scientist
Geological Survey of Canada

Spalding, David A.E.
Vice-President, Kanata Heritage
Research & Presentation Corporation
Edmonton

Spaulding, William Bray
Professor of Medicine
McMaster University

Speisman, Stephen A.
Director, Toronto Jewish Congress &
Canadian Jewish Congress
Ontario Region Archives

Spencer, Andrew N.
Associate Professor of Zoology
University of Alberta

Spencer, Deirdre
Craft contractor, Calgary

Spencer, Don
Assistant Archivist/Registrar
The Seagram Museum
Waterloo, Ont

Spencer, Frank
Professor of Biology
University of London, England

Spencer, John F.T.
Research Associate of Biology
Goldsmiths' College
University of London;
School of Biological Sciences
Thames Polytechnic
London, England

Spencer, John H.
Professor & Head of Biochemistry
Queen's University

Spettigue, Douglas O.
Professor of English
Queen's University

Spragge, Godfrey L.
Associate Professor of Urban &
Regional Planning
Queen's University

Sprague, D.N.
Associate Professor of History
University of Manitoba

Spray, William A.
Vice-President (Academic)
St Thomas University

Sprenger, Eric A.
Mechanical Engineer
Fire Apparatus Historian
(Seagrave make)
Prescott, Ont

Spry, Irene M.
Professor Emeritus of Economics
University of Ottawa

Stacey, C.P.
University Professor Emeritus
University of Toronto

Stacey, Robert
Writer, editor & exhibition curator
Toronto

Stafford, David A.T.
Executive Director
Canadian Institute of International
Affairs, Toronto

Stager, John K.
Professor of Geography
University of British Columbia

Stagg, Ronald J.
Professor of History
Ryerson Polytechnic Institute
Toronto

Stahl, Elvira
Director, Biomedical Editorial &
Translation Services
Montréal

Stairs, Denis
Professor of Political Science
Dalhousie University

Stairs, Douglas G.
Professor of Physics
McGill University

Stamp, Robert M.
Historian, Toronto

Stanbury, W.T.
UPS Foundation Professor of
Regulation & Competition Policy
University of British Columbia

Stanley, David M., s.j.
Professor of New Testament Studies
Regis College, Toronto

Stanley, Della M.M.
Historian, Halifax;
Part-time History Professor
Saint Mary's University

Stanley, George F.G.
Professor Emeritus
Royal Military College of Canada; &
Mount Allison University

Stanley, Laurie C.C.
Instructor of History
Queen's University

Stanton, Charles R.
Writer, Ottawa

Starr, Gail
Professor of Law
University of Calgary

Staveley, Michael
Dean of Arts & Professor of Geography
Memorial University of Newfoundland

Stayner, Margaret M.
Education Consultant
Social Hygiene Services, Edmonton

Stead, Gordon W.
Vancouver

Steele, James
Associate Professor of English
Carleton University

Steeves, Taylor A.
Professor of Biology
University of Saskatchewan

Stefansson, Baldur R.
Professor Emeritus
University of Manitoba

Stein, Janet R.
Professor Emeritus of Botany
University of British Columbia

Stein, Michael B.
Professor of Political Science
McMaster University

Stelter, Gilbert A.
Professor of History
University of Guelph

Stenning, Philip C.
Senior Research Associate
Centre of Criminology
University of Toronto

Stepney, Philip H.R.
Assistant Director (Natural History)
Provincial Museum of Alberta
Edmonton

Steppler, Howard A.
Professor of Agronomy
Macdonald College of McGill
University
Ste-Anne-de-Bellevue, Qué

Sterling, Theodor D.
Professor of Computer Science
Simon Fraser University

Stern, H.H.
Professor Emeritus
Ontario Institute for Studies in
Education, Toronto

Stevens, Gail
Calligrapher, Calgary

Stevens, Peter
Professor of English
University of Windsor

Stevenson, Charlotte
Toronto

Stevenson, Garth
Professor of Politics
Brock University

Stevenson, John T.
Associate Professor of Philosophy
University of Toronto

Stewart, J. Douglas
Professor of Art History
Queen's University

Stewart, John B.
Professor of Political Science
St Francis Xavier University

Stewart, John R.
Assistant Archivist
Kamloops Museum & Archives, BC

Stewart, Kenneth W.
Professor of Zoology
University of Manitoba

Stewart, Lillian D.
Area Superintendent
Environment Canada, Parks
Churchill, Man

Stiles, Michael E.
Food Microbiologist
University of Alberta

Stocking, John R.
Associate Professor of Art History
University of Calgary

Stoddart, Jennifer
Director of Research
Canadian Advisory Council on the
Status of Women, Ottawa

Stoicheff, Boris Peter
University Professor &
Professor of Physics
University of Toronto

Stoker, Henry R.
Retired Development Banker, Victoria

Stone, Kay F.
Associate Professor of Folklore
University of Winnipeg

Stonehouse, Donald H.
Energy, Mines & Resources Canada
Ottawa

Storgaard, Anna K.
Professor of Plant Science
University of Manitoba

Stortz, Gerald J.
Assistant Professor of History
Saint Jerome's College
University of Waterloo

Story, George Morley
Professor of English
Memorial University of Newfoundland

Stossel, Dennis L.
Superintendent, Arctic Operations
Atmospheric Environment Service
Winnipeg

Stott, Jon C.
Professor of English
University of Alberta

Strate, Grant
Director, Centre for the Arts
Simon Fraser University

Strausz, Otto P.
Professor of Chemistry
University of Alberta

Stringham, Elwood W.
Professor Emeritus of Animal Science
University of Manitoba

Strong-Boag, Veronica
Associate Professor of History &
Women's Studies
Simon Fraser University

Struthers, J.R. (Tim)
Assistant Professor of English
University of Guelph

Struthers, James
Associate Professor of Canadian
Studies
Trent University

Struzik, Edward
Journalist

Stuart, Richard
Regional Historian, Parks Canada
Calgary

Stuart, Ross
Associate Professor of Theatre
York University

Studnicki-Gizbert, Konrad W.
Economist,
Chelsea, Qué

Sturino, Franc
Assistant Professor of History
Atkinson College
York University

Stursberg, Peter
Writer & Broadcaster, Vancouver

Stursberg, Richard
Director General
Dept of Communications, Ottawa

Sullivan, Brian E.
Edmonton

Sullivan, Kevin
Dept of Philosophy
University of Ottawa

Summers, William F.
Professor of Geography
Memorial University of Newfoundland

Sunahara, M. Ann
Historian & Lawyer, Edmonton

Sung, Shan-Ching
Professor
Division of Neurological Sciences
University of British Columbia

Sutherland, David A.
Associate Professor of History
Dalhousie University

Sutherland, Maxwell
Chief, Historical Research Division
Parks Canada, Hull

Sutherland, Neil
Professor of Social & Educational
Studies
University of British Columbia

Sutherland, Sharon L.
Professor of Public Administration
Carleton University

Sutherland, Stuart R.J.
Toronto

Sutnik, Maia-Mari
Photographic Co-ordinator
Art Gallery of Ontario, Toronto

Suzuki, David Takayoshi
Professor of Zoology
University of British Columbia

Swainson, Donald
Professor of History
Queen's University

Swainson, Neil A.
Professor Emeritus
University of Victoria

Swanson, Robert H.
Edmonton

Sward, Robert S.
English Dept
Monteray Peninsula College, Calif

Sweeny, Alastair
Writer, Ottawa

Swinton, George
Professor Emeritus
Carleton University;
Artist & author, Winnipeg

Swinton, Katherine E.
Associate Professor of Law
University of Toronto

Swinton, William Elgin
Professor Emeritus
Massey College
University of Toronto

Switzer, Jan D.
Museologist
Fort Edmonton Park, Edmonton

Swyripa, Frances
Historian, Edmonton

Sylvain, Philippe
Professeur émérite d'histoire
Université Laval

Sylvestre, Guy
Honorary Librarian
Royal Society of Canada, Ottawa

Symington, Rodney
Professor of German
University of Victoria

Syms, E. Leigh
Curator of Archaeology
Manitoba Museum of Man & Nature
Winnipeg

Szathmary, Emöke J.E.
Professor of Anthropology
McMaster University

Talman, James J.
Professor Emeritus
University of Western Ontario

Tanner, Adrian
Professor of Anthropology
Memorial University of Newfoundland

Tarnopolsky, Walter Surma
Justice, Ontario Court of Appeal

Tarr, Leslie K.
Senior Editor, Faith Today
Toronto

Taschereau, Sylvie
Chercheur en histoire
Université du Québec à Montréal

Tatum, Jeremy B.
Professor of Astronomy
University of Victoria

Tausky, Thomas E.
Associate Professor of English
University of Western Ontario

Taylor, C.J.
Historian, National Historic Parks &
Sites Branch
Parks Canada, Hull

Taylor, Charles
Writer, Toronto

Taylor, Christopher Edward
Director, Policy Dept
Immigration Group, Canada
Employment & Immigration Commission
Ottawa

Taylor, J. Garth
Arctic Ethnologist
Canadian Museum of Civilization
Ottawa

Taylor, J. Mary
Director
Cleveland Museum of Natural History

Taylor, James A.
Editor, Wood Lake Books Inc.
Don Mills, Ont

Taylor, Jeff
PhD Candidate of History
University of Manitoba

Taylor, John H.
Associate Professor of History
Carleton University, Ottawa

Taylor, John Leonard
Writer & consultant, Ottawa

Taylor, M. Brook
Willowdale, Ont

Taylor, Philip S.
Habitat Biologist
Canadian Wildlife Service, Saskatoon

Taylor, Roy Lewis
President, Chicago Horticultural Society
Glencoe, Illinois

Taylor, Sylvia
Botanical Garden
University of British Columbia

Taylor, William Clyne
Professor of Pediatrics
University of Alberta

Taylor, William E. (Jr)
President
Social Sciences & Humanities
Research Council of Canada, Ottawa

Tehrani, Ghassem
Horticultural Research Institute
Vineland Station, Ont

Telewiak, Robert
Mineral Economist
Energy, Mines & Resources Canada
Ottawa

Templin, R. John
Head
Low Speed Aerodynamics Laboratory
National Research Council of Canada
Ottawa

Tennant, Paul
Associate Professor of Political Science
University of British Columbia

Tennyson, Brian D.
Professor of History
University College of Cape Breton

Tepperman, Lorne
Professor of Sociology
University of Toronto

Terasmae, Jaan
Professor of Geology
Brock University

Théberge, Pierre
Chief Curator
Montréal Museum of Fine Arts

Thériault, Léon
Directeur du département d'histoire et de
géographie
Université de Moncton

Thériault, Michel
Assistant Professor of Canon Law
Saint Paul University, Ottawa

Thesen, Sharon
Writer, Vancouver

Thibault, J. Laurent
President
The Canadian Manufacturers'
Association, Toronto

Thiessen, George J.
Distinguished Visiting Scientist
National Research Council, Ottawa

Thiesson, Stuart A.
Executive Secretary
National Farmers Union

Thivierge, Marîse
Historienne
Institut québécois de recherche sur
la culture

Thivierge, Nicole
Professeur d'histoire
Université du Québec à Rimouski

Thomas, Ann
Assistant Curator of Photographs
National Gallery of Canada, Ottawa

Thomas, Clara
Professor of English
York University

Thomas, Eileen Mitchell
Barrister & Solicitor
Ottawa

Thomas, Gerald Arthur
Graduate Student of History
University of New Brunswick

Thomas, Gregory
Historic Park Planner
Parks Canada, Winnipeg

Thomas, Morley K.
Climatologist, Toronto;
Director General (retired)
Canadian Climate Centre
Downsview, Ont

Thomas, Paul G.
Associate Professor of Political
Studies
University of Manitoba

Thompson, Andrew Royden
Professor of Law;
Director, Westwater Research Centre
University of British Columbia

Thompson, Dixon A.R.
Professor of Environmental Science
University of Calgary

Thompson, John Herd
Professor of History
McGill University

Thompson, John R.
Editor
Athabasca University

Thompson, Margaret W.
Professor of Medical Genetics
University of Toronto;
Senior Staff Geneticist
Hospital for Sick Children, Toronto

Thompson, Teresa
General Synod Archivist
Anglican Church of Canada, Toronto

Thompson, William Paul
Associate Professor of Architecture
University of Manitoba

Thomson, Alex J.
Senior Financial Economist
The Royal Bank of Canada, Montréal

Thomson, Colin A.
Professor of History of Education
University of Lethbridge

Thomson, Duane
Chairman of History
Okanagan College, Kelowna, BC

Thomson, Malcolm M.
(Retired), Ottawa

Thomson, Reginald George
Dean, Atlantic Veterinary College
University of Prince Edward Island

Thomson, Stanley
Professor Emeritus of Civil Engineering
University of Alberta

Thorburn, Hugh G.
Professor of Political Science
Queen's University

Thorpe, Frederick J.
Director of Research, History Exhibition
Canadian Museum of Civilization
Ottawa

Thuro, Catherine M.V.
Lighting Historian, Toronto

Tiedje, John L.
Manager, Research Dept (retired)
Esso Petroleum Canada
Sarnia, Ont

Tiessen, Herman
Professor of Vegetable Physiology
University of Guelph

Tinic, Seha M.
Professor of Finance
University of Alberta

Tippett, Maria
John P. Robarts Professor of Canadian
Studies
York University

Tivy, Mary
Assistant Director
Museum & Archives of Games
Waterloo, Ont

Todd, Ewen C.D.
Food-borne Disease Reporting Centre
Health & Welfare Canada, Ottawa

Toguri, James M.
Professor of Metallurgy
University of Toronto

Tomkins, George S. (deceased)
Professor of Education
University of British Columbia

Tomović, Vladislav A.
Associate Professor of Sociology
Brock University

Toner, Peter M.
Associate Professor of History
University of New Brunswick

Tousignant, Pierre
Professeur agrégé d'histoire
Université de Montréal

Town, Harold B.
Artist, Toronto

Townsend-Gault, Charlotte
Writer & anthropologist
Halifax

Townsend, Joan B.
Professor of Anthropology
University of Manitoba

Townsend, Richard G.
Associate Professor of Educational
Administration
Ontario Institute for Studies in
Education, Toronto

Trainor, Lynn E.H.
Professor of Physics & Medicine
University of Toronto

Travill, Anthony A.
Professor of Anatomy
Queen's University

Tremblay, Gaëtan
Professeur de communications
Université du Québec à Montréal

Tremblay, Jean-Noël
Attaché culturel du
gouverneur général

Tremblay, Jean-Yves
Director
Industrial Minerals Division
Energy, Mines & Resources Canada
Ottawa

Tremblay, Marc-Adélard
Professeur d'anthropologie
Université Laval

Trépanier, Cécyle
Professeur de géographie
Université Laval

Trépanier, Pierre
Professeur agrégé d'histoire
Université de Montréal

Triggs, Stanley G.
Curator, Notman Photographic Archives
McCord Museum, Montréal

Trofimenkoff, Susan Mann
Professor of History
University of Ottawa

Troper, Harold
Professor of History
The Ontario Institute for Studies in
Education, Toronto

Trott, Elizabeth A.
Assistant Professor of Philosophy
University of Toronto

Truax, Barry D.
Associate Professor of Communication;
Centre for the Arts
Simon Fraser University

Trudel, Marc J.
Professeur d'horticulture
Université Laval

Trudel, Marcel
Professeur émérite
Université d'Ottawa

Trueman, Mark E.H.
Atmospheric Environment Service
Downsview, Ont

Tuck, James A.
Professor of Archaeology
Memorial University of Newfoundland

Tucker, Albert V.
Professor of History
Glendon College, York University

Tuinman, Jaap
Professor & Dean of Education
Simon Fraser University

Tulchinsky, Gerald J.J.
Professor of History
Queen's University

Tulloch, Judith E.
Historian, Halifax

Tunnicliffe, Verena J.
Assistant Professor of Biology
University of Victoria

Tuomi, Archie L.W.
Consultant, Ottawa

Tupper, Allan
Professor of Political Science
University of Alberta

Turner, H.E.
Associate Professor of History
McMaster University

Turner, M.A.H.
Deputy Commissioner
Canadian Coast Guard, Ottawa

Turner, Nancy J.
Research Associate, Botany Unit
British Columbia Provincial Museum
Victoria

Turnock, William J.
Research Scientist
Agriculture Canada, Winnipeg

Tweedie, Katherine
Assistant Professor of Photography
Concordia University

Tyler, Christopher D.
Author, potter & craft administrator
Halifax

Tyrchniewicz, Edward W.
Director, Transport Institute
University of Manitoba

Urquhart, M.C.
Professor of Economics (retired)
Queen's University

Vachon, Auguste
Heraldry Archivist, Documentary Art
& Photography Division
National Archives of Canada
Ottawa

Vagt, G. Oliver
Mineral Economist
Energy, Mines & Resources Canada
Ottawa

Valaskakis, Gail C.
Associate Professor of Communication
Studies
Concordia University

Vallee, Frank G.
Professor Emeritus of Sociology &
Anthropology
Carleton University

Vallières, Marc
Professeur d'histoire
Université Laval

van Everdingen, Robert O.
National Hydrology Research
Institute, Calgary

van Ginkel, Blanche Lemco
Professor of Architecture
University of Toronto

Van Leeuwen, Hans
Chief, Training Coordination Division
Atmospheric Environment Service
Environment Canada, Downsview, Onte

Van Roey-Roux, Françoise
Professeur de français
Collège de Maisonneuve, Montréal

Van Wagner, Charles E.
Research Scientist, Forest Fire
Canadian Forestry Service
Chalk River, Ont

Van Wart, Alice
Vancouver

van Zwamen, Christine
Canadian Nature Federation, Ottawa

van Zyll de Jong, Constantinus G.
Curator, Mammalogy Section
National Museum of Natural Sciences
Ottawa

Vanasse, André
Professeur titulaire d'études
littéraires
Université du Québec à Montréal

Vanderburgh, Rosamond M.
Associate Professor of Anthropology
University of Toronto

Vanderwolf, Cornelius H.
Professor of Psychology
University of Western Ontario

Varley, Christopher
Toronto

Vastokas, Joan M.
Professor of Anthropology
Trent University

Vaughan, Frederick
Professor of Political Science
University of Guelph

Vaz, Edmund W.
Professor of Sociology
University of Waterloo

Veatch, Richard
Professor of Political Science
University of Winnipeg

Veeman, Michele M.
Professor of Agricultural Economics
University of Alberta

Veeman, Terrence S.
Professor of Economics & Agriculture
Economics
University of Alberta

Verdier, P. Susan
Program Coordinator
Canadian Ski Association - Freestyle
Ottawa

Vermeirre, André
Professeur d'histoire
Université de Montréal

Véronneau, Pierre
Responsable publications et recherches
Cinémathèque québécoise

Vézina, Claude
Assistant Director
Institut Armand-Frappier
Laval-des-Rapides, Qué

Vézina, Raymond
Professeur d'histoire du design
Université du Québec à Montréal

Vick, Roger
Curator, Devonian Botanic Garden
University of Alberta

Vigod, Bernard L.
Professor of History
University of New Brunswick

Villeneuve, Gisèle
Writer, Calgary

Vincent, Aubrey R.
Teacher, St John's

Vincent, Thomas B.
Professor of English
Royal Military College of Canada

Visentin, Louis P.
Dean of Science
Memorial University of Newfoundland

Vita, Kati
Critic, Montréal

Vladykov, Vadim D. (deceased)
Professor Emeritus of Biology
University of Ottawa

Voice, Douglas
Associate Professor of Music
University of Ottawa

Voisine, Nive
Professeur titulaire d'histoire
Université Laval

Volkoff, George M.
Dean Emeritus, Faculty of Science
University of British Columbia

Vollmer, Michael
Yacht designer
Burlington, Ont

von Baeyer, Edwinna
Landscape Historian, Ottawa

Voyer, Roger D.
Principal
Nordicity Group Ltd, Ottawa

Wachna, Pamela S.
Associate Curator
Market Gallery of the City of Toronto
Archives, Toronto

Waddams, Stephen M.
Professor of Law
University of Toronto

Wagg, Susan
Art historian, Montréal

Wagner, Anton
Director of Research
World Encyclopedia of
Contemporary Theatre
York University

Wainwright, J.A.
Associate Professor of English Literature
Dalhousie University

Waiser, W.A.
Associate Professor of History
University of Saskatchewan

Waite, P.B.
Professor of History
Dalhousie University

Wakeling, Thomas W.
Lawyer, Milner & Steer
Edmonton

Walcroft, Michael John
Assistant Vice-President, New Product
Development
Connaught Laboratories Limited
Willowdale, Ont

Walden, David B.
Professor
University of Western Ontario

Walker, Deward E., Jr
Dept of Anthropology
University of Colorado at Boulder

Walker, James W. St. G.
Associate Professor of History
University of Waterloo

Walker, John P.
*Professor of Animal & Poultry Science
(retired)
University of Guelph*

Walker, Karen
*Director, People Against Impaired
Drivers
Edmonton*

Walker, Roger G.
*Professor of Geology
McMaster University*

Walker, Susan
*Publisher
Quill & Quire, Toronto*

Walkom, Tom
Ottawa

Wallace, Birgitta Linderoth
*Staff Archaeologist, Parks Canada
Atlantic Region, Halifax*

Wallace, Carl M.
*Associate Professor of History
Laurentian University, Sudbury*

Wallace, Hugh N.
*Associate Professor of History
Mount Saint Vincent University*

Wallace, P.R.
*Professor Emeritus of Physics
McGill University;
Principal, Science College
Concordia University*

Wallot, Jean-Pierre
*Archiviste Fédéral
Archives National du Canada*

Walsh, Susan
Vancouver

Wanzel, J. Grant
*Professor of Architecture
Technical University of Nova Scotia*

Ward, Norman
*Professor Emeritus of Economics &
Political Science
University of Saskatchewan*

Ward, Philip R.
Conservator, Ottawa

Ward, W. Peter
*Associate Professor of History
University of British Columbia*

Ware, Tracy
*Lecturer
University of Western Ontario*

Wark, Wesley K.
*Assistant Professor of History
University of Toronto*

Warkentin, John
*Professor of Geography
York University*

Warner, John Anson
Long Beach, Calif

Warwick, Peter D.A.
St Catharines, Ont

Wasserman, Jerry
*Associate Professor of English
University of British Columbia*

Waterman, A.M.C.
*Professor of Economics
University of Manitoba*

Waters, Janice
Ottawa

Waterston, Elizabeth
*Professor of English
University of Guelph*

Watkins, Mel
*Professor of Economics
University of Toronto*

Watson, D. Scott
Curator, Vancouver

Watson, Lorne
*Professor of Piano
Brandon University;
Artistic Director, Eckhardt-Gramatté
National Competition for the
Performance of Canadian Music*

Watson, William G.
*Associate Professor of Economics
McGill University*

Watt, Robert D.
*Director
The Vancouver Museum, Vancouver*

Waugh, Douglas
*Executive Director (retired)
Association of Canadian Medical
Colleges, Ottawa*

Waugh, Earle H.
*Associate Professor of Religious
Studies
University of Alberta*

Wayman, Morris
*Professor of Chemical Engineering &
Forestry
University of Toronto*

Weait, Christopher
*Co-principal bassoonist
The Toronto Symphony, Toronto*

Weaver, John C.
*Professor of History
McMaster University*

Webb, James L.
*Endocrinology Laboratory
St Mary's Hospital;
Dept of Pathology
McGill University*

Webster, D.B.
*Curator, Canadian Dept
Royal Ontario Museum, Toronto*

Webster, Douglas R.
*Professor of Developmental Planning
University of Calgary*

Webster, Gloria Cranmer
*Curator, U'mista Cultural Centre
Alert Bay, BC*

Webster, Helen R.
*Mineral Policy Sector
Energy, Mines & Resources Canada
Ottawa*

Wegenast, William G.
*Associate Professor of Engineering
Memorial University of Newfoundland*

Weinrich, Peter H.
*Executive Director
Canadian Crafts Council, Ottawa*

Weir, Thomas R.
*Professor of Geography
University of Manitoba*

Weisbord, Merrily
Writer, Montréal

Wellburn, G. Vernon
*Manager, Western Division
Forest Engineering Institute of
Canada, Vancouver*

Welsh, Harry L.
*Professor Emeritus of Physics
University of Toronto*

Wenaas, Carl J.
Writer, Winnipeg

Werner, Leo H.
*Executive Director
International Maple Syrup Institute*

Wertheimer, Douglas
Newspaper Publisher, Calgary

Weseloh, D.V. Chip
*Canadian Wildlife Service
Burlington, Ont*

West, J. Thomas
*Manager, Winter Olympic Hall of Fame
Calgary*

West, Roxroy
Writer, Winnipeg

Westlake, D.W.
*Professor of Microbiology
University of Alberta*

Weston, Marla L.
*Paleobiology Division
National Museum of Natural Sciences
Ottawa*

Wetherell, Donald G.
Historian, Edmonton

Whalen, Linda D.
Writer, St John's

Wheatcroft, Bruce A.
Organist & historian, Edmonton

Whebell, C.F.J.
*Associate Professor of Geography
University of Western Ontario*

Wheeler, John O.
*Geological Survey of Canada
Vancouver*

Whitaker, Reginald
*Professor of Political Science
York University*

White, Clinton Oliver
*Associate Professor of History
Campion College, University of Regina*

White, M. Lillian
Calgary, Alberta

Whitehead, Margaret Mary
Historian, Victoria

Whitehorn, Alan
*Associate Professor of Politics
Royal Military College of Canada*

Whiteson, Leon
*Architecture critic & author
Toronto*

Whiteway, James R.
*Research Analyst
Ontario Hydro, Toronto*

Whitmore, Gordon Francis
*Professor of Medical Biophysics
University of Toronto;
Head, Physics Division
Ontario Cancer Institute, Toronto*

Whyte, Donald
*Professor of Sociology & Anthropology
Carleton University*

Wickberg, Edgar
*Professor of History
University of British Columbia*

Wien, Thomas
*PhD Candidate
McGill University*

Wiggins, Ernest J.
Consultant, Edmonton

Wight, Darlene
Inuit art consultant, Ottawa

Wilcox, Betty
Victoria, BC

Wilimovsky, Norman J.
*Professor & Curator of Fisheries
University of British Columbia*

Wilkin, Karen
*Independent curator & critic
New York & Toronto*

Wilkinson, Bruce William
*Professor of Economics
University of Alberta*

Willey, Robert C.
*Editor, Canadian Numismatic
Journal
Espanola, Ont*

Williams, David Ricardo
*Adjunct Professor of Law
University of Victoria*

Williams, Glyndwr
*Professor of History
Queen Mary College
University of London, England*

Williams, Maureen C.
*Lecturer in Celtic Studies
St Francis Xavier University*

Williams, Patricia Lynn
Archivist & historian, Saskatoon

Williams, Richard M.
*Uranium & Nuclear Energy Branch
Energy, Mines & Resources Canada
Ottawa*

Williams, Sydney B.
*President, Hays & Williams Ltd
Calgary*

Williams, W.M.
*Birks Professor of Metallurgy
McGill University*

Williamson, Mary F.
*Fine Arts Bibliographer
York University*

Williamson, Moncrieff
*Director Emeritus of Confederation
Centre Art Gallery & Museum
Charlottetown*

Willis, Christopher J.
*Professor of Chemistry
University of Western Ontario*

Willis, Norman M.
*Curator, National Medal Collection
National Archives of Canada, Ottawa*

Willmot, Rod
*Chargé de cours
Université de Sherbrooke*

Wilson, Bruce G.
*Public Programs Branch
National Archives of Canada
Ottawa*

Wilson, Donald R.
*Professor Emeritus
University of Toronto*

Wilson, Harold E.
*Associate Professor of History
University of Alberta*

Wilson, Ian E.
*Archivist of Ontario
Archives of Ontario, Toronto*

Wilson, J. Donald
*Professor of History of Education
University of British Columbia*

Wilson, J. Tuzo
*Professor Emeritus of Physics
University of Toronto*

Wilson, Jean
Editor, Vancouver

Windreich, Leland
Vancouver

Windwick, Brent
*Health Law Project
University of Alberta*

Winks, Robin W.
*Professor of History
Yale University*

Wirick, Gregory
Consultant & Writer, Ottawa

Wirick, Ronald G.
*Professor of Economics
University of Western Ontario*

Wise, S.F.
*Professor of History;
Dean of Graduate Studies & Research
Carleton University*

Withrow, William J.
*Director, Art Gallery of Ontario
Toronto*

Wittenberg, Henry
*President, Canadian Toy Manufacturers
Association*

Wolfe, Leonhard S.
*Professor of Neurology & Neurosurgery
Montréal Neurological Institute
McGill University*

Wonders, William C.
*University Professor & Professor of
Geography
University of Alberta*

Wons, Peter
*Writer & researcher
Edmonton*

Wood, Bernard
*Director
North-South Institute, Ottawa*

Woodcock, George
Writer, Vancouver

Woodruff, M. Emerson
*Professor of Optometry
University of Waterloo*

Woods, Robert James
*Professor of Chemistry
University of Saskatchewan*

Wright, Glenn
National Archives of Canada, Ottawa

Wright, Harold E.
*Partridge Island Research Project
Saint John, NB*

Wright, J.F.C.
*Alberta Consumer & Corporate Affairs
Edmonton*

Wright, J.V.
*Archaeological Survey of Canada
Canadian Museum of Civilization
Ottawa*

Wright, Janet
Parks Canada, Hull

Wright, Kenneth O.
*Former Director
Dominion Astrophysical Observatory
National Research Council of Canada
Victoria*

Wright, Roy A.
Ethnohistorian, Ottawa

Wyczynski, Paul
*Titulaire de recherche
Université d'Ottawa*

Wyman, Max
Author & critic, Vancouver

Wynn, Graeme
*Associate Professor of Geography
University of British Columbia*

Yaffe, Leo
*Emeritus Professor of Chemistry
McGill University*

Yalden, Maxwell F.
Canadian Ambassador to Belgium

York, Derek
*Professor of Physics
University of Toronto*

Young, A.J. (Sandy)
*Professor of Physical Education
Dalhousie University*

Young, Bill
Ottawa

Young, C. Maureen
*MA Graduate Student of History
University of Victoria*

Young, David A.
*Head of Museum Advisory Services
Royal Ontario Museum, Toronto*

Young, Gayle
*Composer & writer
Grimsby, Ont*

Young, Jane
Toronto

Young, Jeffery D.
Queen's University

Young, John H.
*Clergy
Harrowsmith, Ont*

Young, Roland S.
*Consulting Chemical Engineer
Victoria*

Young, Walter D. (deceased)
*Professor of Political Science
University of Victoria*

Zack, Manuel
*Assistant to the President
McMaster University*

Zavitz, R. Perry
Automobile Historian
London, Ont
Zeller, Suzanne E.
Assistant Professor of History
Wilfrid Laurier University
Zeman, Jarold K.
Professor of Church History
Acadia University

Zemans, Joyce
Dean, Faculty of Fine Arts
York University
Zepp, Norman W.
Director, Thunder Bay Art Gallery
Ziegel, Jacob S.
Professor of Law
University of Toronto

Ziff, Bruce
Associate Professor of Law
University of Alberta
Zingrone, Frank D.
Associate Professor of Communication
York University

Zoltai, Stephen C.
Research Scientist
Canadian Forestry Service, Edmonton
Zuk, Louise
St Albert, Alta
Zussman, David
Associate Professor of Public Policy
Faculty of Administration
University of Ottawa

ABBREVIATIONS

" inch
μ micron
a are (unit of metric land measure)
A/C/M Air Chief Marshal
A/M Air Marshal
A/V/M Air Vice-Marshal
AAA Amateur Athletic Association
Adm Admiral
aka also known as
Ala Alabama
alt altitude
Alta Alberta
approx approximately
Apr April
ARC Alberta Resource Council
Ariz Arizona
Ark Arkansas
Assn, assn Association, association
Asst Assistant
Atty Gen Attorney General
Aug August
B Bay
b born
BA Bachelor of Arts
bap baptized
Batt Battalion
BBC British Broadcasting Corporation
BC British Columbia
BComm Bachelor of Commerce
Bdy, bdy Boundary, boundary
BEd Bachelor of Education
BLitt Bachelor of Literature
Blvd Boulevard
BMus Bachelor of Music
BNA British North America
Bor Borough
Brig-Gen Brigadier-General
BSc Bachelor of Science
BSW Bachelor of Social Work
Btu British thermal unit
bu bushels
C City
c census
c circa
cA census adjusted
CA Chartered Accountant
CAF Canadian Armed Forces, Canadian Air Force
Calif California
CAPAC Composers, Authors and Publishers Association of Canada
Capt Captain
CAUT Canadian Association of University Teachers
CBC Canadian Broadcasting Corporation
CBE Companion of the Order of the British Empire
CCCL Canadian Catholic Confederation of Labour
CCF Co-operative Commonwealth Federation
CCL Canadian Congress of Labour
Cdn Canadian
CDPT Collège dominicain de philosophie et théologie
Cdr Commander
CEF Canadian Expeditionary Force
CEGEP Collège d'enseignement général et professionel
CFB Canadian Forces Base
CFDC Canadian Film Development Corporation
CFL Canadian Football League
CGA Certified General Accountant
Chan Channel
chap chapter, chapters
cm centimetre
CMA Census Metropolitan Area
  ACMA CMA adjusted
CMG Companion of the Order of St Michael and St George
CNR Canadian National Railways
CNTU Confederation of National Trade Unions
Co, co Company, company

Col Colonel
Coll College
Colo Colorado
Comm Community
comp compiler, compiled by, compilation
Conn Connecticut
Const constable
Corp, corp Corporation, corporation
COTC Canadian Officer Training Corps
CPCGN Canadian Permanent Committee on Geographical Names
Cpl Corporal
CPR Canadian Pacific Railway
CRBC Canadian Radio Broadcasting Commission
CRTC Canadian Radio-television and Telecommunications Commission
CTC Canadian Transport Commission
Czech Czechoslovakia
Cy County
d died
Dak Dakota
Dan Danish
db decibel
Dec December
Del Delaware
Den Denmark
Dept, dept Department, department
DEW Distant Early Warning
DFC Distinguished Flying Cross
DIAND Dept of Indian Affairs and Northern Development
Dir, dir Director, director
Dist, dist District, district
Div Division
DM District Municipality
DMus Doctor of Music
DSC Distinguished Service Cross
DSO Distinguished Service Order
DSW Doctor of Social Work
dwt deadweight, deadweight tons
E east
e estimate
ed editor, edited by, edition
eds editors
EEC European Economic Community
eg (*exempli gratia*) for example
elev elevation
EMR Dept of Energy, Mines and Resources
Eng England
est established
et al (*et alii*) and others
etc (*et cetera*) and so forth
F/O Flying Officer
fd founded
Feb February
ff folios
fl (*floriat*) flourished
Fla Florida
Flt Lt Flight Lieutenant
Flt Off Flight Officer
Flt Sgt Flight Sergeant
Fr Father
Fri Friday
FRSC Fellow of the Royal Society of Canada
Ft Fort
g gram
Ga Georgia
GATT General Agreement on Tariffs and Trade
GDP Gross Domestic Product
Gen General
gen ed general editor
Ger German, Germany
GHz gigahertz
Gk Greek
GNP Gross National Product
Gov Gen, gov gen Governor General, governor general
govt government
GSC Geological Survey of Canada
GW gigawatt
h hour; hecto
ha hectare

Ham Hamlet
HBC Hudson's Bay Company
hg hectogram
hL hectolitre
hm hectometre
HMCS Her Majesty's Canadian Ship
hp horsepower
hr hour
Hz hertz (one cycle per second)
I, Is Island, Islands
ie (*id est*) that is
Ill Illinois
Inc Incorporated
Ind Indiana
Insp Inspector
Inst, inst Institution, institution
Int, int International, international
intro introduction
IR Indian Reserve
Ire Ireland
Jan January
k kilo
Kans Kansas
KB Knight of the Bath
KC King's Counsel
KCMG Knight Commander of St Michael and St George
kg kilogram
kHz kilohertz
kL kilolitre
km kilometre
km/h kilometres per hour
kPa kilopascal
kW kilowatt
kWh kilowatt-hour
kW/m kilowatts/metre
Ky Kentucky
L litre
La Louisiana
Lab Labrador
Lat Latin
lat latitude
LC Lower Canada
LID Local Improvement District
LLD Doctor of Laws
Lk, lk, Lks, lks Lake, lake, Lakes, lakes
long longitude
LRCP Licentiate of the Royal College of Physicians
Lt Lieutenant
Lt-Gov Lieutenant-Governor
Ltd Limited
Ltée Limitée
m metre
m/s metres per second
MA Master of Arts
Maj Major
Man Manitoba
Mar March
Mass Massachusetts
MBE Member of the Order of the British Empire
Md Maryland
MD Doctor of Medicine
Me Maine
MEng Master of Engineering
mg milligram
Mgr Monseigneur
mHz megahertz
Mich Michigan
MIL Military Reserve
min minute
Minn Minnesota
Miss Mississippi
mj megajoule
mL millilitre
MLA Member of Legislative Assembly
mm millimetre
MNA Member of National Assembly
Mo Missouri
Mont Montana
MP Member of Parliament
MPP Member of Provincial Parliament
MRCS Member of the Royal College of Surgeons

MSc Master of Science
MSW Master of Social Work
Mt Mount
Mt A Mount Allison University
Mtn, mtn, Mts, mts Mountain, mountain, Mountains, mountains
MW megawatt
N north
N Dak North Dakota
N Mex New Mexico
NAC National Archives of Canada
NB New Brunswick
NC North Carolina
nd no date
NDHQ National Defence Headquarters
NDP New Democratic Party
NEB National Energy Board
Nebr Nebraska
NEP National Energy Policy
Nev Nevada
NFB National Film Board
Nfld Newfoundland
NH New Hampshire
NHL National Hockey League
NJ New Jersey
No, no Number, number
Nor Norwegian, Norway
NORAD North American Air Defence
Nov November
NRC National Research Council
NRCC National Research Council of Canada
NS Nova Scotia
NSAC Nova Scotia Agricultural College
NSCAD Nova Scotia College of Art and Design
NTS National Topographic Survey
NWC North West Company
NWMP North-West Mounted Police
NWT North-West Territories (before 1905) Northwest Territories (since 1905)
NY New York
OAC Ontario Agricultural College
OBE Order of the British Empire
Oct October
OECD Organization for Economic Co-operation and Development
Okla Oklahoma
OMI Oblates of Mary Immaculate
Ont Ontario
OPEC Organization of Petroleum Exporting Countries
Oreg Oregon
Pa Pennsylvania
PAC Public Archives of Canada
PC Progressive Conservative
PCO Privy Council Office
PEI Prince Edward Island
Pen, pen Peninsula, peninsula
pH hydrogen-ion concentration
PhD Doctor of Philosophy

PM Prime Minister
PMO Prime Minister's Office
PO Petty Officer; Post Office
pop population
POW Prisoner of War
PQ Parti Québécois
Prem Premier
Pres President
prod produced
pseud pseudonym
Pt Point, Port
publ published
QC Queen's Counsel
Qué Québec
R & D Research and Development
R River
RAF Royal Air Force
RCAF Royal Canadian Air Force
RCN Royal Canadian Navy
RD Rural District
Rear-Adm Rear-Admiral
Reg Regiment
repr reprinted
rev revised
RFC Royal Flying Corps
RI Rhode Island
RIA Registered Industrial and Cost Accountant
RM Rural Municipality
RMC Royal Military College of Canada
RN Registered Nurse
RSC Royal Society of Canada
Ry Railway
Ryerson Ryerson Polytechnical Institute
S South
s second; section (in reference to Criminal Code)
S Dak South Dakota
Sask Saskatchewan
SC South Carolina
Scot Scotland
Sen Senator
Sept September
SFU Simon Fraser University
Sgt Sergeant
SI Système International des Unités
SJ, sj Society of Jesus
Soc, soc Society, society
Sol Gen Solicitor General
Span Spanish
Sqn Cdr Squadron Commander
Sqn Ldr Squadron Leader
SS Ship Title (Steamship)
St Saint
St FX St Francis Xavier University
Staff-Sgt Staff-Sergeant
Ste Sainte
Str Strait
Supt Superintendent
Switz Switzerland
T Town

t tonne
TCA Trans-Canada Airlines
Tenn Tennessee
Terr, terr Territory, territory
Tex Texas
TLC Trades and Labor Congress
trans, tr translated, translation
TV Television
TWh terawatt hours
Twp Township
U University
U de M Université de Montréal
U Leth University of Lethbridge
U Man University of Manitoba
U of A University of Alberta
U of C University of Calgary
U of O University of Ottawa
U of T University of Toronto
U Vic University of Victoria
U Wpg University of Winnipeg
UBC University of British Columbia
UC Upper Canada
UCC United Church of Canada
UCCB University College of Cape Breton
UK United Kingdom
UK£ United Kingdom pound
UMWA International Union, United Mine Workers of America
UN United Nations
UNB University of New Brunswick
UNESCO United Nations Educational, Scientific and Cultural Organization
unpubl unpublished
UP Unincorporated Place
UPEI University of Prince Edward Island
UQ Université du Québec
UQAC Université du Québec à Chicoutimi
UQAM Université du Québec à Montréal
UQAR Université du Québec à Rimouski
UQTR Université du Québec à Trois-Rivières
US United States of America
USSR Union of Soviet Socialist Republics
Va Virginia
Vl Village
vol, vols volume, volumes
VP Vice-President
Vt Vermont
W West
Wash Washington
Wis Wisconsin
WLU Wilfrid Laurier University
WO Warrant Officer
WWI World War I
WWII World War II
Wyo Wyoming
YMCA Young Men's Christian Association
YT Yukon Territory
YWCA Young Women's Christian Association

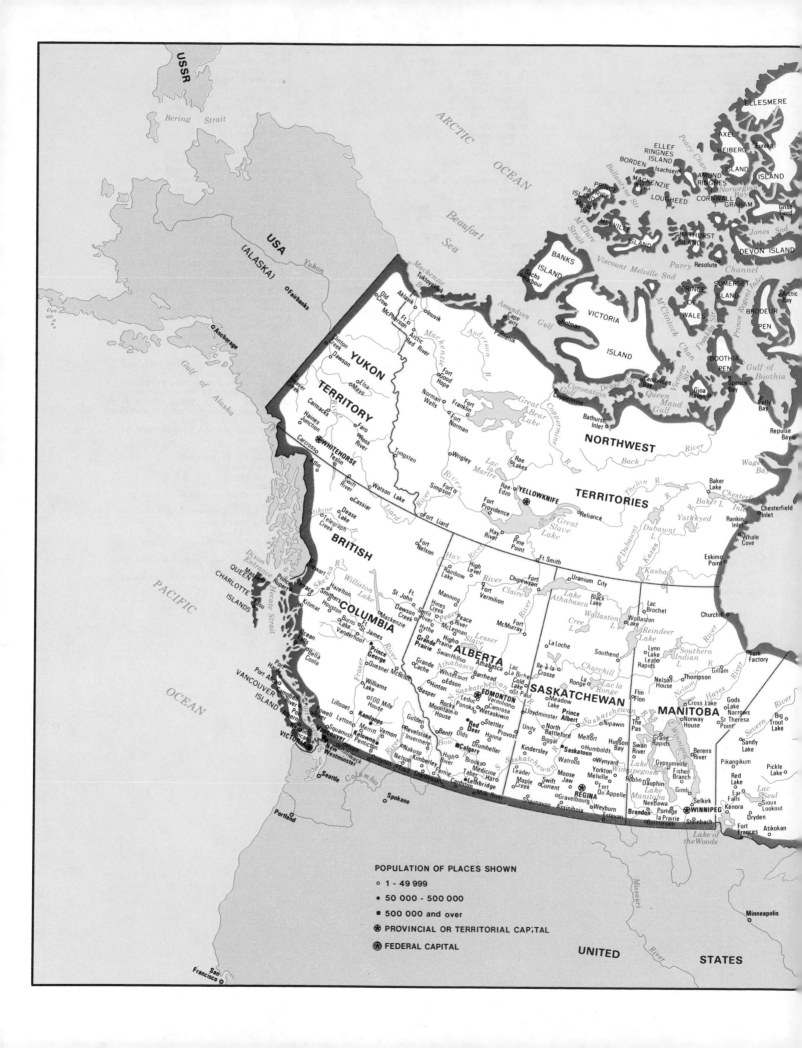

POPULATION OF PLACES SHOWN

○ 1 - 49 999

● 50 000 - 500 000

■ 500 000 and over

⊛ PROVINCIAL OR TERRITORIAL CAPITAL

⊛ FEDERAL CAPITAL

CANADA

0 150 300 600Km

1 : 19 108 300

THE CANADIAN ENCYCLOPEDIA

A Mari usque ad Mare ("From Sea to Sea"), Canada's motto, was derived from Psalm 72:8, which reads in Latin "Et dominabitur a mari usque ad mare, et a flumine usque ad terminos terrae," and in the King James version, "He shall have dominion also from sea to sea, and from the river unto the ends of the earth." Attention was first directed to the verse when, apparently at the suggestion of Samuel Leonard TILLEY, the term "dominion" was chosen to represent Canada as a whole when the British North America Act was drafted. "From sea to sea" could not apply to Canada until 1871, when BC joined Confederation and the Dominion extended from Atlantic to Pacific. In 1872 Rev George Monro GRANT crossed the country as secretary to Sandford FLEMING, who was then in charge of the Pacific railway surveys. The next year he published *Ocean to Ocean*, his journal describing the journey. The title is akin to "from sea to sea" and strong tradition insists that thereafter Grant preached in many centres using Psalm 72:8 as his text and advocating the adoption of "from sea to sea" as Canada's motto. The first official use came in 1906, when the phrase was engraved on the head of the mace of the Legislative Assembly of the new Province of Saskatchewan. This would be known to Joseph POPE, undersecretary of state at the time, and the phrase evidently impressed him. In 1919 Pope was named to a 4-member committee appointed by the federal government to recommend a new design for the Arms of Canada. No motto was included in the old design, but one was to be includ-

ed in the new arms. A draft design, which included the motto, was approved by Cabinet in Apr 1921 and by King George V in May. Maj-Gen W.G. Gwatkin, one of the committee members, had proposed that the motto be *In memoriam in spem* ("In memory, in hope"), but Pope's counterproposal was adopted. On 29 Sept 1921, after viewing the final design, he wrote in his diary: "Our Arms are very handsome ... everything that can be desired. The motto 'A Mari usque ad Mare,' which is an original suggestion of my own, I regard as very appropriate." *See also* EMBLEMS OF CANADA; HERALDRY. W. KAYE LAMB

Abalone (*Haliotis*), genus of primitive, marine, gastropod MOLLUSCS with over 70 species worldwide. The single Canadian species (*Haliotis kamtschatkana*) is called the Japanese, pinto or northern ear shell, depending on locale. This large (up to 12 cm), limpetlike snail prefers semiprotected waters between the low intertidal zone and 18 m depth. The abalone uses its powerful foot to fasten itself to rock surfaces. *H. kamtschatkana* is a gregarious species which grazes on drift and surface algae. Its ear-shaped shell has a wavy texture and bears, on its outer whorl, 4-5 respiratory pores which also act as exit ports for spawn and excreta. The shell's outer surface is mottled red-green. The blue-green iridescence of its inner pearly surface has made it popular with Northwest Coast Indians as material for jewellery and inlays. The abalone's soft, muscular parts (tenderized and grilled as steak or ground up for bisque) are a choice gourmet food. Its only other predators are sea stars and, occasionally, sea otters. PETER V. FANKBONER

Abbotsford, BC, District Municipality, pop 14 496 (1986c), 12 745 (1981c), area 13 856 ha, inc 1972 from amalgamation of the District of Sumas and village of Abbotsford, is located on the S bank of the FRASER R between MATSQUI and CHILLIWACK. The area's traditional agricultural economy has declined, while there has been a marked increase in industrial activity as firms have moved from VANCOUVER seeking less congested areas. The manufacturing sector includes feed and food products, brick and tile. The former village of Abbotsford (likely named after Henry Abbott, CPR superintendent) serves as a retail trade and service centre for the surrounding districts; commercial development has now moved into the adjacent district of Matsqui. Continued growth as an industrial and residential suburb of Vancouver is assured. Abbotsford is served by a newspaper, the *Express*. Each year the famous Abbotsford Air Show brings thousands of visitors to the area from all over the Pacific Northwest. ALAN F.J. ARTIBISE

Abbott, Sir John Joseph Caldwell, lawyer, professor, politician, prime minister (b at St Andrews East [St-André-Est], Lower Canada 12 Mar 1821; d at Montréal 30 Oct 1893). A graduate of McGill College, he was admitted to the bar 1847 and taught at McGill from 1853, serving as dean of the law faculty 1855-80. Although he signed the Annexation Manifesto in 1849, he quickly recanted and during the TRENT AFFAIR of 1861 he raised and commanded a militia force to

Abalone (*Haliotis kamtschatkana*) is a mollusc which has been used by Northwest Coast Indians for jewellery and as a choice gourmet food (*photo by Hälle Flygare*).

The Armorial Bearing of Canada (*courtesy National Archives of Canada/artwork by Karen E. Bailey*).

**Sir John Joseph Caldwell Abbott
Third Prime Minister of Canada**

Birth: 12 Mar 1821, St Andrews East, LC
Father/Mother: Joseph/Harriet Bradford
Father's Occupation: Clergyman
Education: McGill College, Royal Institute for the
    Advancement of Learning
Religious Affiliation: Anglican
First Occupation: Lawyer
Last Private Occupation: Professor/lawyer
Political Party: Liberal-Conservative
Period as PM: 16 June 1891 - 24 Nov 1892
Ridings: Argenteuil, Qué, 1867-74; 1880-87
Other Ministries: Solicitor General 1862
Marriage: 26 July 1849 to Mary Bethune
    (1823-98)
Children: 8
Died: 30 Oct 1893 in Montréal
Cause of Death at Age: Cancer at 72
Burial Place: Montréal
Other Information: First PM born in Canada; first
        senator to become PM; senator,
        1887; KCMG, 1892.
*(photo courtesy National Archives of Canada/PA-
33933).*

patrol the border with the US. He sat in the legislative assembly, and later in the House of Commons from 1860 until he was appointed to the Senate in 1887, except for the period 1874-80. Solicitor general for Canada East in the short-lived administration of J.S. MACDONALD and L.V. SICOTTE 1862-63, he entered the federal Cabinet in 1887 as government leader in the Senate and minister without portfolio. (He was also mayor of Montréal 1887-89.) In 1891 he succeeded Sir John A. MACDONALD as PM. His was largely a caretaking administration and in 1892 he turned over the government to Sir John S.D. THOMPSON.   CARMAN MILLER

Reading: C. Ondaatje and D. Swainson, *The Prime Ministers of Canada 1867-1968* (1968).

Abbott, Maude Elizabeth Seymour, pathologist (b at St Andrews East [St-André-Est], Qué 18 Mar 1869; d at Montréal 2 Sept 1940). Though she graduated in arts from McGill (1890), she was barred from medicine because of her sex, so she earned Bishop's CM, MD (1894); ironically McGill awarded her MD, CM (honoris causa, 1910) also LLD (1936). As asst curator, McGill Medical Museum (1898) and curator (1901), she introduced the use of the museum in teaching pathology. A disciple of William OSLER, she contributed to his text *Modern Medicine* (1908) the

chapter on "Congenital Heart Disease," which he declared the best thing he had ever read on the subject. Apart from 2 years, her whole career was at McGill where, though world famous, she was never promoted beyond the rank of assistant professor. She served as permanent international secretary of the International Association of Medical Museums and editor of its journal (1907-1938), and published many papers on pathology as well as histories of medicine and nursing. A trifle eccentric in later life, she was generous, active, always involved and sometimes known as "The Beneficent Tornado."   MARGARET GILLETT

Reading: Margaret Gillett, *We Walked Very Warily: A History of Women at McGill* (1981).

Abduction, literally leading away, historically meant the seizure of a wife from her husband, or a female infant or heiress from her parent or lawful guardian, for marriage, concubinage or prostitution. From Edward I's time abduction was a criminal offence, and the husband or guardian was entitled to monetary damages for the woman abducted. Under the Canadian Criminal Code abduction occurs when, without her consent, a female of any age is taken out of the possession of her parent or guardian for marriage or illicit sexual intercourse with anyone; or a girl under 16 is unlawfully taken away from anyone with lawful authority over her. In the case of unlawful sexual intercourse with a girl under 16 the accused may be acquitted if there is evidence that she was more to blame than he, or if he can convince the court that he honestly believed she was over 16, but no such defence exists with abduction. Nor does her consent provide her abductor with a defence. It is also abduction to take away a child under 14 years of age with intent to deprive a parent or other lawful guardian of possession of that child, or with intent to steal anything on or about the person of such a child. *See also* KIDNAPPING.   L.C. GREEN

Abenaki take their name from a word in their own language meaning "dawn land people" or "easterners." In 1600 the Eastern Abenaki occupied what is now the state of Maine, except for its northern and easternmost portions. The Western Abenaki lived in the rest of northern New England, from New Hampshire to Lk Champlain. The Western and Eastern Abenaki spoke closely related AL-GONQUIAN languages, each having various local dialects. Eastern Abenaki had at least 4 such dialects, Pequawket (Pigwacket), Arosaguntacook, Kennebec and Penobscot. All Abenaki were part of the Eastern Algonquian cultures and were separated from other Algonquians to the W and N by an intrusion of Iroquoian-speaking cultures over 2000 years ago.

Around 1600, there were nearly 14 000 Eastern Abenaki and 12 000 Western Abenaki, but Old World diseases, particularly measles and smallpox, reduced these numbers by 78% and 98%, respectively, within a few decades. Surviving Western Abenaki, often called Sokoki or Penacook, withdrew into refugee communities and many eventually moved to the villages of Bécancour and St Francis in Québec. The Eastern Abenaki were not as devastated by warfare and disease, and over 800 Penobscot survive on a reservation near Old Town, Maine; many Pequawket, Arosaguntacook and Kennebec people moved to Québec settlements during the colonial period.

The Abenaki are prominent in the journals of CHAMPLAIN and other explorers and missionaries. They survived the colonial wars of the following 200 years by balancing contending French and English interests, and remained politically important even though reduced in number. The fall of NEW FRANCE left the Abenaki with little defence against English expansion after 1760, forcing them

into a weak alliance with other tribes formerly allied with the French. The American Revolution split the Eastern Abenaki from the Western Abenaki, who were by this time living in Québec. The Penobscot sided with the Passamaquoddy of eastern Maine in holding the frontier of New England for the Americans. The Abenaki remained divided in their loyalties through the WAR OF 1812.

In 1600 all Abenaki were hunters, fishermen and gatherers. Attempts to adopt agriculture did not succeed until after the FUR TRADE developed. Consequently, the population density of the Abenaki was only about a tenth that of agricultural Algonquians in New England. They adapted quickly to the fur trade and a world economy. They traditionally lived in villages near falls on major rivers during the seasons when migratory fish could be harvested. During other seasons they dispersed in family groups to the coast or to small camps on interior tributaries. These camps became the bases of trapping territories during the heyday of the fur trade. When the trade declined, many turned to the lumbering industry, CANOE manufacture and basketry. Today, most Abenaki are engaged in the mainstream occupations of Québec and New England. They continue to be known for the quality of their split basketry and their lively folkore. The culture hero Gluskabe (GLOOSCAP) figures importantly in Abenaki tales. However, the stories are now told in English or French, for Abenaki dialects are nearly extinct. *See also* NATIVE PEOPLES: EASTERN WOODLANDS.   DEAN SNOW

Reading: F. Speck, *Penobscot Man* (1970); B.G. Trigger, ed, *Handbook of North American Indians*, vol 15: *Northeast* (1978).

Abercromby, James, army officer (b at Banffshire, Scot 1706; d at Glassaugh, Scot 23 Apr 1781). A career soldier, he came to N America in 1756 and was appointed commander in chief of British forces. He led an army of about 15 000 men up Lk Champlain, and by early July 1758 approached Ft Carillon, where French commander MONTCALM was hastily entrenching with a much smaller army. After a series of futile assaults on July 8 and the loss of nearly 2000 men, Abercromby retreated hastily. Recalled immediately, he was succeeded by Jeffery AMHERST.   STUART R.J. SUTHERLAND

Aberdeen and Temair, Ishbel Maria Gordon, Marchioness of, née Marjoribanks (b at London, Eng 15 Mar 1857; d at Aberdeen, Scot

Lady Aberdeen was active in Canadian social and political life in the 1890s *(courtesy National Archives of Canada/ C-22760).*

18 Apr 1939). Married to the earl of ABERDEEN in 1877, she accompanied him to Ireland when he was lord lieutenant, and to Canada, where he was governor general 1893-98. Lady Aberdeen was deeply involved in the political crises involving the governor general from 1894 to 1896. Far more important, however, was her work with women's organizations. A staunch Presbyterian and Gladstonian Liberal, a woman of great poise and boundless energy, she was an aristocrat-democrat with a strong social conscience. She believed that women represented an enormous, unused capacity in Canada, and that they would be a civilizing force in an untamed country. She was instrumental in forming the Canadian branch of the NATIONAL COUNCIL OF WOMEN. Despite fierce opposition from the medical establishment, she created the VICTORIAN ORDER OF NURSES. The social family compact in Ottawa, Montréal and Toronto opposed and ridiculed her projects. Her attempts to use Rideau Hall to cool the racial and religious passions of the 1890s and to break down social barriers did not endear her to the local establishment.

JOHN SAYWELL

Reading: J.T. Saywell, ed, *The Canadian Journal of Lady Aberdeen* (1960).

Aberdeen and Temair, John Campbell Gordon, 1st Marquess of, GOVERNOR GENERAL of Canada 1893-98 (b at Edinburgh, Scot 3 Aug 1847; d at Tarland, Scot 7 Mar 1934). John Campbell was educated at St Andrews U and University Coll, Oxford. A Liberal, he entered the House of Lords in 1870 upon the death of his elder brother. Made lord lieutenant of Aberdeenshire in 1880, he served as lord lieutenant of Ireland briefly in 1886 and again 1905-15. Aberdeen had visited Canada twice before becoming its governor general in 1893. A social crusader of great zeal and piety, he and Lady ABERDEEN, his irrepressible wife, devoted much of their vice-regal time in Canada to good works. Their sympathies for Liberals in Britain and Canada, however, made relations with Conservative governments in Canada difficult. Aberdeen's refusal to accept appointments made by Sir Charles TUPPER, following his electoral defeat in 1896, produced great controversy. A section of the Aberdeens' reminiscences, *We Twa,* 2 vols (1925) is devoted to their Canadian experiences.

CARMAN MILLER

Aberdeen Lake, 1101 km², elev 80 m, max length 91 km, is located in the NWT, 213 km S of the Arctic Circle. It is part of a closely linked chain (W to E: Lks Beverly, Aberdeen and Schultz) of elongated lakes that, together with Baker Lk, form a 2849 km² drainage basin for the THELON R before it empties into Hudson Bay via the 160 km long CHESTERFIELD INLET. BAKER LAKE, the only community within close proximity (106 km E) is the sole inland settlement of the Inuit in the NWT. Aberdeen Lk was named for Gov Gen Lord Aberdeen (1893-98) by geologist J.B. TYRRELL.

DAVID EVANS

Aberhart, William, "Bible Bill," radio evangelist, premier of Alberta, 1935-43 (b in Hibbert Twp, Perth County, Ont 30 Dec 1878; d at Vancouver 23 May 1943). An important influence in religious sectarianism in western Canada, Aberhart headed the world's first SOCIAL CREDIT government in 1935. He was trained as a school teacher at Mitchell Model School and the Normal School in Hamilton, Ont. Wanting to become a Presbyterian minister, he began studying for an extramural BA from Queen's (completed 1911, after he had moved to Alberta) while he was principal of Central Public School in Brantford. In Ontario he became an active lay preacher and Bible-class teacher and was highly influenced by the *Scofield*

William "Bible Bill" Aberhart. As Alberta premier from 1935 until his death in 1943, he was leader of Canada's first Social Credit government (*courtesy National Archives of Canada/C-16477*).

Reference Bible and its dispensational system of interpretation.

In 1910 Aberhart moved to Calgary to become a school principal. His popular Bible class at Grace Presbyterian Church was transferred to Wesley Methodist Church in 1912 after he was embroiled in a dispute which probably involved both his theology and his personality. In 1915 he became the unofficial minister of Westbourne Baptist Church. In spite of attempts by Baptist leaders to remove Aberhart from the church, his congregation remained loyal. After a brief association with a Pentecostal minister in 1920, Aberhart began introducing "charismatic" practices and doctrines into the church, much to the consternation of the local Baptist ministers. He identified with the fundamentalist movement and became increasingly antagonistic to mainstream denominations.

Aberhart opened a school to train ministers and missionaries for the furtherance of fundamentalism. As early as 1923 he was teaching night-school classes in theology in the basement of Westbourne Baptist Church. He also realized the possibilities of radio and began broadcasting Sunday afternoon services in 1925. Needing a larger facility to house the Bible school and the crowds which were attracted to his meetings, he opened the Calgary Prophetic Bible Institute in 1927 and taught many of its classes, administered the church and conducted the radio broadcasts while being employed as the principal of Crescent Heights High School. In 1929 Aberhart founded his own sect, the Bible Institute Baptist Church, after most of the Westbourne congregation had split from him. By 1939 over 9000 children were enrolled in his Radio Sunday School.

The GREAT DEPRESSION was devastating for the farm-based western economy and misery was widespread. The inability of political parties to find solutions to the problem of "poverty in the midst of plenty" drove Albertans to seek alternative remedies, and they were attracted to the ideas of Aberhart. Previously non-political, in 1932 Aberhart became interested in the monetary-reform doctrines of a British engineer, Maj C.H. Douglas, who believed that conventional capitalism would founder because private control of credit would lead to a chronic insufficiency of mass purchasing power. The solution, he believed, was state supervision of credit and the issuance of consumer discounts to balance consumption with full production. Aberhart modified and popularized this doctrine into a proposal that each citizen be given a $25-a-month

"basic dividend" to purchase necessities. Aberhart built a grass-roots movement, the Alberta Social Credit League, to promote his ideas. When the existing political parties showed little interest, he took the league into the political arena. In Sept 1935, Social Credit took 56 of 63 seats in the Alberta legislature and swept the United Farmers of Alberta from office.

After becoming premier, Aberhart found he could not fulfil his pre-election promises. His moratorium on debt collections saved some farms and homes, but his concept of Social Credit was never realized. In 1937, after a major crisis in his caucus, he was forced to accept assistance from Major Douglas's emissaries from England. The monetary legislation they introduced was quickly disallowed by the federal government and precipitated the Rowell-Sirois Commission on Dominion-Provincial Relations.

Aberhart died in office in 1943. He was succeeded by Ernest C. MANNING, the first graduate of the Calgary Prophetic Bible Institute.

DAVID R. ELLIOTT

Reading: J.A. Irving, *The Social Credit Movement in Alberta* (1959); L.P.V. Johnson and Ola J. MacNutt, *Aberhart of Alberta* (1970); L.H. Thomas, *William Aberhart and Social Credit in Alberta* (1977); D.R. Elliott and I. Miller, "Aberhart and the Calgary Prophetic Bible Institute," *Prairie Forum* vol 9, no 1 (1984).

Abitibi, Lake, 932 km², straddles the Québec-Ontario border about 280 km S of James Bay. Irregularly shaped and about 75 km long, it is actually 2 lakes joined by a narrows. It drains W and N through the Abitibi R and Moose R to the bottom of James Bay. The region is heavily forested and supports a pulp-and-paper industry centered at IROQUOIS FALLS, W of the lake. Gold mining has been important and the wild natural setting attracts a growing number of tourists. The lake was a fur-trade centre from 1686 when the Chevalier de TROYES established a post as he passed on his way overland from Québec to attack forts on the bottom of the bay. The name comes from an Algonquin and Cree expression meaning "halfway water." It was first noted in the JESUIT RELATIONS in 1640 to describe an Indian band which lived near Lake Abitibi, halfway between trading posts on James Bay and those on the Ottawa River.

DANIEL FRANCIS

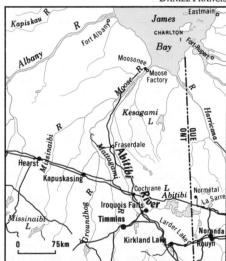

Abitibi-Price Inc is the world's largest producer of newsprint. The company was incorporated as Abitibi Power & Paper Co Ltd in 1914 to acquire Abitibi Pulp & Paper Company, Ltd (fd 1912). It acquired extensive timber, waterpower and mineral rights and became Abitibi Paper Co Ltd in 1965. It adopted its present name in 1979 after acquiring controlling interest in The Price Co Ltd in 1974. In addition to newsprint, the company produces groundwood papers, fine papers, kraft pulp, building products and lumber and also has paper converting operations and a major distribution network for printing papers, industrial paper products and information processing supplies in Canada and the US. Net sales for 1986 were nearly $2.8 billion and assets were $2.2 billion. The major shareholder is Gulf Canada Resources Ltd (83%), and head offices are in Toronto.   DEBORAH C. SAWYER

Aboriginal Rights in Canada are said to derive from the historic use and occupation of land by aboriginal peoples prior to European colonization and/or the original sovereignty of these people. They are conceived as rights to ownership of land and resources, cultural rights, legal recognition of customary law and the inherent right to self-government.

Section 35 of the CONSTITUTION ACT, 1982, recognizes and affirms the existing aboriginal rights of the INDIAN, INUIT and MÉTIS peoples of Canada. In addition, a series of constitutional conferences occurred between 1983 and 1987 to clarify and entrench aboriginal rights, but this goal was not achieved. The courts have traditionally been reluctant to deal with the basic definition of aboriginal rights and this has resulted in uncertain recognition and virtually no enforcement, despite constitutional affirmation.

Sources of Aboriginal Rights Aboriginal peoples have traditionally pointed to 3 principal arguments to establish aboriginal rights: international law, the ROYAL PROCLAMATION OF 1763 and the common law as defined in Canadian courts. Only the last argument has met with any success in the courts, although native groups continue to participate internationally in UN working groups concerned with indigenous populations and minority rights; and the Proclamation of 1763 is now considered to be a historic expression of the common law rather than a source of legal rights.

The courts now look for proof of traditional occupancy of specific land, or recognition of other legal rights by customary law, in order to establish an aboriginal right. This was the approach adopted in cases such as *Calder* (1973), *Baker Lake* (1980) and *Bear Island* (1984). There is, however, concern that the historical date sometimes used for this purpose – the date when Great Britain asserted its sovereignty over the specific territory – may make proof impossible for societies which rely on oral tradition rather than written records. Even so, it may be easier to establish an aboriginal right than it is to maintain its legal force over time in the face of white settlement and legislation.

Content of Aboriginal Rights Canadian courts have not ascribed much value to aboriginal rights, once proven. While aboriginal peoples equate their rights to full ownership, the current trend is to limit rights to historical uses of land and resources. In *Bear Island*, for example, the Ontario High Court found the content of aboriginal rights to be so minimal that they enabled only bare survival with nothing approaching ownership of the land, its mineral or timber resources. That case is under appeal.

Extinguishment of Aboriginal Rights This issue is important because aboriginal rights have proven to be legally fragile, and also because they must be shown to exist as of 1982 in order to attract constitutional protection. Historically, extinguishment has been affected by way of treaty or LAND-CLAIMS settlement rather than by legislation. The *Calder* case considered extinguishing Nishga title to BC land prior to Confederation by enacting laws inconsistent with the rights of the Indians to their territory in the Nass R valley. The Supreme Court of Canada divided on the question of extinguishment by laws that were merely inconsistent with aboriginal rights, but recognized that express legislation could have that effect: 3 judges said there must be a specific law clearly defeating aboriginal rights; 3 judges said that extinguishment could be implied from historical circumstances; the 7th judge rejected the claim solely on procedural grounds.

After Confederation, the issue becomes more confused. All courts recognize the power of Parliament to extinguish aboriginal rights up to 1982, but this was never expressly done. Rights to hunt and fish, however, have been defeated by federal legislation which is merely inconsistent with aboriginal rights. Only in *Bear Island* has a court held that provincial laws can operate the same way and have the same effect, and this ruling raises a re-examination of s92 (24) of the CONSTITUTION ACT, 1867, which gives Parliament apparently exclusive jurisdiction over "Indians and Lands reserved for the Indians." In *Bear Island* it was also held that delay in bringing a court action was sufficient to defeat the claim to aboriginal rights to the land-claim territory. This alone, if correct in law, would be sufficient to defeat almost every land claim that is brought to court. In theory, however, an aboriginal right recognized as still existing in 1982, cannot be extinguished after that date by Parliament or any provincial legislature.

Summary Both legal and political processes have failed to come to grips with the concept, content and priority of aboriginal rights, even though the Constitution assumes the legal existence of such rights and mandates their protection. This may change with developments in the political process and as more cases work their way to the Supreme Court of Canada, which has yet to decide conclusively the issues raised above. Until such change occurs, aboriginal rights remain the most undefined, uncertain and fragile rights known to our law.   WILLIAM B. HENDERSON

Reading: M. Asch, *Home and Native Land: Aboriginal Rights and the Canadian Constitution* (1984); P. Cumming and N. Mickenburg, *Native Rights in Canada* (2nd ed, 1972); K. Lysyk, "The Indian Title Question in Canada: An Appraisal in Light of Calder," *Canadian Bar Review* 51 (1973); D. Sanders, "The Rights of the Aboriginal Peoples of Canada," *Canadian Bar Review* 61 (1983); B. Slattery, *Ancestral Lands, Alien Laws: Judicial Perspectives on Aboriginal Title* (1983); M. Boldt and J.A. Long, eds, *The Quest for Justice* (1985); B. Morse, ed, *Aboriginal Peoples and The Law: Indian, Inuit and Metis Rights in Canada* (1985).

Abortion, termination of pregnancy, especially if deliberately induced. Abortion has been widely practised throughout history as a means of birth control. Abortion after "quickening" (approximately 14 weeks after conception) may have traditionally been a common-law offence, but only in 1803 was abortion before quickening made a statutory offence in England. This and subsequent laws were aimed at abortionists and made abortion a capital crime only if it was performed by someone other than the mother, although theoretically the laws permitted prosecution of the mother herself as "aid or and abettor." There are no reported Canadian cases which considered this question; however, the Offences Against the Person Act (1861) made it a crime in Britain for a woman to perform an abortion on herself. Canadian legislation on the same point predated the English, eg, the 1849 New Brunswick Statute Act to Consolidate . . . the Criminal Law and the 1851 Nova Scotia Law of Offences Against the Person. The Canadian legislation was probably based upon an 1845 New York statute. Growing concern over a falling birthrate among English Canadians at the turn of the century and anxiety over "race suicide" linked opposition to abortion with all forms of birth control and gave rise to further legislation making it an indictable offence to sell or advertise drugs or articles "intended or represented as a means of preventing conception or causing abortion" (s179, Criminal Code, 1892). Nevertheless, significant numbers of women continued to seek abortions from doctors or quacks or to self-abort using dangerous folk methods. The issue was brought to public attention in 1908 in a Toronto newspaper article entitled "Race Suicide," which charged that some doctors were growing rich performing abortions. Several doctors were subsequently charged, but the extent of the practice is unknown because cases usually only came to public attention when something went wrong. The medical profession continued to support the notion that abortion was morally as well as legally wrong.

Pressure to legalize abortion on some or all grounds intensified in various parts of the world after WWII. Impetus was gained by broadening support for women's rights as well as growing concern about the personal and social consequences of unwanted children and the high maternal death rates associated with illegal abortion. By the mid-1960s, restrictions lessened in many parts of the world, particularly in Japan, Eastern Europe, Scandinavia and Great Britain. In 1973 the US Supreme Court ruled that even in the second trimester of pregnancy abortion is a private matter between a woman and her physician. Until 1988, under the Canadian Criminal Code, an attempt to induce an abortion by any means was a crime, whether committed by the woman herself, or by another. Because intervention and intent constituted the crime, it could be committed even if the attempt was unsuccessful, or if the woman was not pregnant. The maximum penalty was life imprisonment, unless the woman herself was convicted, in which case it was 2 years. The law, which was liberalized in 1969 with an amendment to the Criminal Code allowing that abortions were legal if performed by a doctor in an accredited or approved hospital after a therapeutic abortion committee certified that "the continuation of the pregnancy of such female person would or would be likely to endanger her life or health," was interpreted in a widely divergent manner by various hospital committees. One approach was to apply a defence of necessity, which excuses an otherwise unlawful act where the harm avoided by doing the act exceeds the harm which it inflicts, and in which there is no other reasonably available course of conduct. This defence was used in the MORGENTALER case, in which the Supreme Court of Canada concluded that "it is manifestly difficult to be categorical and state that there is a law of necessity, paramount over other laws. . . . If it does exist it can go no further than to justify noncompliance in urgent situations of clear and imminent peril when compliance with the law is demonstrably impossible." The Supreme Court in 1975 overturned the 1973 jury finding in favour of Morgentaler, and he was forced to serve his prison term. However, in Québec, the Liberal government that prosecuted Morgentaler was replaced by a Parti Québécois government which decided not to press further charges and later extended this immunity from prosecution to the publicly financed health clinics in Québec.

The abortion law was not been applied uniformly throughout Canada. Many hospitals did not establish therapeutic abortion committees, and because the law did not define "life" or "health," each committee made its own rules. Furthermore, committees were placed in the questionable position of granting "sick" women legal abortions, while "healthy" women were refused. Case by case, it was impossible to predict how much a woman would suffer if she was compelled to remain unwillingly pregnant. The earlier an abortion, the safer; Canadian law had no limit on the gestation period after which an abortion is illegal, but in practice most physicians and hospitals will not, except in rare cases, perform abortions after 20 weeks' gestation. The national (1985) total was 60 956, or 16.2 abortions per 100 live births, ranging from 26.1 abortions for each 100 live births in BC to 0.5 per 100 in PEI.

Abortion remains a controversial and divisive issue in contemporary society. It is still condemned by some religious groups as contrary to church law and teachings. Roman Catholic canon law condemns abortion except when it results indirectly from a medical procedure intended for another purpose, eg, removal of a cancerous uterus. On the other hand, the United Church of Canada supports the position of freedom of choice. A diverse group bases its opposition to the trend to liberalize abortion law on the rights of the unborn. For opposing groups, the issue centers on a woman's right to choose whether or not to terminate a pregnancy, and is based on the premise that abortion is a moral issue to be decided by individuals, not the state. The issue of abortion raises complex medical and legal questions. The law was criticized by the Canadian Medical Assn and the Canadian Bar Assn because it had on occasion caused hospital-board elections to become political and thus, by allowing the board decisions to be influenced by the preconceived notions of those elected, subverted the Criminal Code provisions.

Challenges to the law have come from both anti-abortion and pro-choice groups. In 1983 the 1969 amendment was challenged before the Saskatchewan Court of Queen's Bench on the grounds that a fetus, from conception, deserves protection under section 7 of the CANADIAN CHARTER OF RIGHTS AND FREEDOMS, which states that "everyone has the right to life," but the court of first instance held that the Charter does not conflict with s251 of the Criminal Code. A leave to appeal this judgement to the Supreme Court was granted July 1987. However, forces seeking further liberalization of the law also invoked the Charter on the grounds of a woman's right to the security of her person, and in a momentous decision the Supreme Court struck down the law on this basis in early 1988. The judgement held that "forcing a woman, by threat of criminal sanction, to carry a fetus to term... is a profound interference with a woman's body and thus an infringement of security of the person." The Court also found that this right was breached by the delays resulting from the therapeutic abortion committee procedures.

Reading: A. McLaren and A.T. McLaren The Bedroom and the State (1986).

Academic Freedom commonly means the freedom of professors to teach, research and publish, to criticize and help determine the policies of their institutions, and to address public issues as citizens without fear of institutional penalties. Other meanings include the autonomy of the university in running its internal affairs, and the freedom of students to function within the academic programs they have chosen. The Canadian Association of University Teachers (CAUT) argues that "the common good depends upon the search for truth and its free exposition. Academic freedom is essential to these purposes." Demands for academic freedom in primary and secondary education have had little success.

In none of its meanings is academic freedom absolute. The freedom to teach, for example, is normally subject to approval of courses by academic bodies; the freedom to carry on research is often dependent on funding by universities or other groups. Hence academic freedom is generally linked to the idea of academic self-government, in the hope that limits will not be imposed arbitrarily and improperly.

Serious threats to academic freedom have come from those who hold the purse strings – wealthy benefactors, church bodies or provincial governments. Governing boards and academic administrators have transmitted such threats, the strongest being the loss of employment, to individuals, or have themselves originated threats. The alleged disloyalty of a professor to the president of an institution or to the ideals it was held to embody has been at the basis of several controversies. Threats to the freedom of professors have also come from colleagues or students unwilling to tolerate ideological or methodological diversity. Notable incidents in the history of academic freedom during the last century include George Workman's difficulties at Victoria University, Toronto, in 1891 and his dismissal from Wesleyan Theological College, Montréal, in 1907, in both cases because of his religious modernism. Salem BLAND lost his teaching position at Wesley College, Winnipeg, in 1917, allegedly because some board members were hostile to his social radicalism. A similar charge was heard when John King GORDON lost his position at United Theological College, Montréal, in 1933. In both instances the need to reduce the college budget may have been more important. Three senior professors were dismissed from the University of Saskatchewan in 1919 because they were held to be disloyal to the President. Three years later the firing of W.G. Smith, Wesley College's vice-principal, had much the same cause. The unsuccessful attempt to fire Frank UNDERHILL from University of Toronto in 1941 resulted from hostility among board members to the historian's provocative and outspoken views about politics. The attempt failed on Underhill's behalf. Such pressure was hard to ignore in wartime; university autonomy has never been more fully compromised than during the Second World War. The dismissal in 1958 of Harry Crowe from United College, Winnipeg, a case in which an individual's attitude to his institution loomed large, led CAUT (fd 1951) to address issues of academic freedom for the first time. Since 1959 CAUT's Academic Freedom and Tenure Committee has investigated and helped resolve many cases across Canada. None was more complicated than the summary dismissal of several social scientists from Simon Fraser University in 1969, rooted in a disagreement between them and the governing board as to how the university should be organized and run. CAUT's ultimate sanction, if negotiations fail, is to urge academics not to take employment at the censured institution.

Silence on controversial subjects largely characterized the years before 1960. Since then, increasing freedom for professors has been due partly to the development of academic TENURE into tenure during good behaviour rather than during pleasure of the governing board, which is what several judgements in the first quarter of this century held it to be. Professors generally cannot be dismissed except for just cause, to be demonstrated before an impartial tribunal. Faculty unionization has tended to transform tenure into a seniority system; its relation to academic freedom is thus becoming less clear at a time when financial constraint is endangering that freedom in all its meanings. MICHIEL HORN

Reading: Michiel Horn, "Professors in the Public Eye," History of Education Quarterly 20 (1980).

Académie canadienne-française Founded 9 Dec 1944 by a group of writers led by Victor Barbeau, its goal was to serve and defend French language and culture in Canada. Its founding members were Victor Barbeau, Robert CHARBONNEAU, Robert CHOQUETTE, Marie-Claire Daveluy, Léo-Paul DESROSIERS, Guy FREGAULT, Alain GRANDBOIS, Philippe PANNETON (Ringuet), Robert RUMILLY, Marius BARBEAU, Roger Brien and Louis LACHANCE. To further its objectives the Academy each year awards a medal to a writer for the body of his or her work (1984, Anne Hébert; 1985, Luc Lacoursière). Each year also, it joins with Molson's Brewery to award a prize for novel of the year ($5000). As a way of reaching Québec authors and the general public, it organizes each fall a writers' conference on a variety of topics: eg, 1983 – Ruptures et continuitès [Continuity and Discontinuity]; and 1984 – Québec/USA; 1986 – Le Québec et la francophonie. The Académie canadienne-française has 24 seats and, since 1982, two membership categories: honorary members (after age 65) and active members. MARTHE LEGAULT

Acadia, name given to the first permanent French colony in N America. The name originated with Giovanni da VERRAZZANO, an Italian explorer serving the king of France. In 1524 Verrazzano made his first trip to the New World and gave the name Arcadie to a region stretching along the Atlantic coast near Delaware, explaining the choice in his diary with a reference to "the beauty of its trees." In ancient Greece this name referred to a Peloponnesian plain which was thought of as a sort of earthly paradise. Sixteenth-century cartographers mistakenly gave the name Arcadia to the region of the Maritime provinces of Canada. The letter "r" eventually disappeared, leaving the present name of Acadia.

History of Acadia

The French Régime (1534-1763) Although it had been visited before the 17th century, notably by Jacques CARTIER in 1534, the first French colonists did not arrive until 1604, under the leadership of Pierre du Gua de MONTS and Samuel de CHAMPLAIN. De Monts settled the 80-odd colonists on Île Sainte-Croix, on the ST CROIX RIVER, but scurvy killed 36 of them during the winter of 1604-05. The next year the colony looked for a new site and chose PORT-ROYAL. When some French privateers (shipowners) challenged his commercial monopoly, de Monts took everyone back to France in 1607; French colonists did not return to Port-Royal and Acadia until 1610. But the territory was also being claimed by England. In 1613 Samuel Argall, an adventurer from Virginia, seized Acadia and chased out most of its settlers. In 1621 the English government changed Acadia's name to Nova Scotia and moved in Scottish settlers in 1629. It was not until 1632 that France, through the Treaty of SAINT-GERMAIN-en-Laye, regained Acadia.

Renewed settlement took place under Governor Isaac de Razilly, who moved the capital from Port-Royal to La Hève, on the south shore of present-day Nova Scotia. He arrived in 1632, with "300 gentlemen of quality." Razilly died in 1635, leaving Charles de MENOU D'AULNAY and Charles LA TOUR to quarrel over his succession. The colonists were brought back to Port-Royal, which once again became the capital. The first official census, held in 1671, registered an Acadian population of more than 400 people. In 1701 there were c1400; in 1750, over 10 000; in 1755, over 13 000 (Louisbourg excluded).

French-English enmity once again affected Acadia's fate, causing it to pass to the English in

1654 and back to France through the Treaty of BREDA (1667). It was taken by the New England adventurer Sir William PHIPS in 1690 and returned to France again through the Treaty of RYSWICK (1697).

In both 1670 and 1680, colonists left Port-Royal to found other centres, the most important being Beaubassin (Amherst, NS) and Grand-Pré (near Wolfville, NS). The population, which numbered some 2500 people around 1711, were primarily descended from natives of the south of the Loire in France, especially Poitou. Most of these French colonists arrived in the 1630s, 1640s and 1670s. These highly self-reliant Acadians farmed and raised livestock, and hunted, fished and trapped as well; they even had commercial ties with the English colonists in America, usually against the wishes of the French authorities.

During the WAR OF THE SPANISH SUCCESSION (1701-13), Acadia passed several more times into the hands of the English, definitively in 1713. Through the Treaty of UTRECHT, the territory which was ceded consisted of "Acadia according to its ancient boundaries," but France and England failed to agree on a definition of those boundaries. For the French, the territory included only the present peninsular Nova Scotia, but the English claimed, in addition, what is today New Brunswick, the Gaspé and Maine.

Following the loss of "ancient Acadia," France concentrated on developing Île Saint-Jean (Prince Edward Island) and Île Royale (Cape Breton), 2 largely ignored regions until that time. On Île Saint-Jean, France tried to establish agricultural centres, fishing in particular, while it gave Île Royale a military role. With the construction of the fortress of LOUISBOURG in 1713, France attempted to protect the entranceway to New France.

England did not make any great effort to establish a presence in "ancient Acadia," once again known as Nova Scotia. It kept a garrison at Port-Royal (renamed Annapolis Royal), but made virtually no other attempt at colonization, with the result that Acadians were in the majority until 1749. England demanded of its conquered subjects an oath of unconditional loyalty, but the Acadians agreed only to an oath of neutrality, promising that they would take up arms against neither France nor England. Unable to impose the unconditional oath, Governor Richard PHILIPPS in 1729-30 gave his verbal agreement to this semi-allegiance. He has been accused of not having informed the authorities of this compromise.

In 1745 Louisbourg fell to an English expeditionary force, whose land army was largely composed of New England colonists. However, France regained the fortress through the Treaty of Aix-la-Chapelle in 1748, to the great displeasure of the English colonies. It was in this context that England decided to make the Nova Scotian territory British. In 1749 the capital was moved from Annapolis Royal to HALIFAX, which was a better seaport and was far from the Acadian population centres. At the same time, Halifax was closer both to Europe and to Boston. Finally, England took steps to bring British colonists into the colony. They came primarily from New England and from German territories with British connections (Hanover, Brunswick, etc). From 1750 to 1760, an estimated 7000 British colonists arrived to settle in Nova Scotia.

The French authorities reacted by building FORT BEAUSÉJOUR in 1750 (near Sackville, NB) to keep the English from crossing the Isthmus of Chignectou which separates the present provinces of New Brunswick and Nova Scotia. The English that same year began building Fort Lawrence less than 3 km east of Beauséjour. Finally, in 1755, England decided to settle the problem once and for

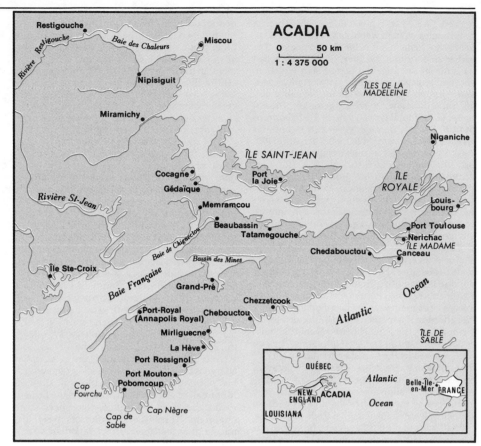

all: under the pretext of a new refusal by the Acadians to swear an oath of unconditional loyalty, British authorities decided to deport them. English troops first took Fort Beauséjour – in peacetime, but England claimed this land as well – and undertook to make prisoners of the entire Acadian population from Fort Beauséjour to Annapolis Royal. These Acadians were thus the first to be uprooted in a process which lasted until 1762. The settlers were put into ships and deported to English colonies and to England. Others managed to flee to Québec.

In 1756 the SEVEN YEARS' WAR broke out between France and England. The 2 French colonies, Île Royale and Île Saint-Jean, fell in 1758 and their settlers were repatriated to France. It is estimated that three-quarters of the total Acadian population of some 13 000 were deported; the rest avoided this fate through flight. An unknown number of Acadians perished from hunger, disease and misery; a few ships full of exiles sank on the high seas with their human cargo. Through the Treaty of PARIS (1763), France ceded to England the entire region of the Maritimes and all of New France.

A New Upheaval (1763-1880) After 1763 the Maritimes took on a decidedly English face. English names replaced French or Micmac ones almost everywhere. The English at first reorganized the territory into a single province, Nova Scotia. In 1769, however, they detached the former Île Saint-Jean, which became a separate province under the name of Saint John's Island; it received its present name of Prince Edward Island in 1799. In 1784 present-day New Brunswick was in turn separated from Nova Scotia, following the arrival of thousands of American LOYALISTS who demanded their own colonial administration.

As for the Acadians, they began the long and painful process of resettling themselves in their native land. England gave them permission once they finally agreed to take the contentious oath of allegiance. Some returned from exile, but the re-

settlement was largely the work of fugitives who had escaped deportation and of the prisoners of Beauséjour, Pigiguit, Port-Royal and Halifax who were finally set free. They headed for Cape Breton, the tips of the Nova Scotian peninsula and of PEI, along the eastern and northern shores of New Brunswick up to Madawaska and along the Saint John R. Basically, the geography of 20th century Acadia is that of the early 19th century, minus the hinterland that was settled subsequently.

The English authorities sought to scatter the Acadians in small groups along the shores of the Atlantic and the Gulf of St Lawrence. These Acadians found themselves on infertile land and so these former farmers became fishermen, cultivating their land only for subsistence. As fishermen, they were exploited and subjected to great dependence and poverty, especially by companies from the Isle of Jersey. It was only with the arrival of the CO-OPERATIVE MOVEMENT in the 1930s that the Acadian fishermen became less economically disadvantaged.

These Acadians were first stripped of civil and political rights; because they were Catholics, they could neither vote nor be members of the legislature. From 1758 to 1763, they could not even legally own land. Nova Scotian Acadians gained the right to vote in 1789; those in New Brunswick in 1810; in Prince Edward Island in 1830. After 1830 Acadians of all three colonies could sit in the legislature.

In general, Acadians at the start of the 19th century aspired only to immediate and basic objectives. Their only ambition was survival: their lifestyle was one of subsistence. They had virtually no institutions of their own: the Catholic clergy came either from Québec or France, and the Church was the only French institution in all the Maritimes. There were few francophone schools and the teachers, for the most part, were simple "travelling masters," who spread their knowledge from village to village. There was no French newspaper. Nor were there any lawyers or doctors. In fact, there was as yet no Acadian middle class and, overall, it is highly probable that the people were much poorer than they had been during the French régime. Yet, whether they were conscious of it or not, these Acadians sowed the seeds of a new Acadia in the soil, without any help from the state.

At the start of the 19th century, there were 4000 Acadians in Nova Scotia, 700 in PEI and 3800 in New Brunswick. Their establishment and growth during that century was remarkable: they counted some 87 000 at the time of Confederation in 1867, 140 000 at the turn of the century and continued to grow for the first half of the 20th century. In 1961 there were 331 000 in the Maritime provinces. The 251 000 New Brunswick Acadians of 1981 comprised 36% of the population of the province; in PEI, the 15 000 Acadians formed 12.5% of the Island population.

The Acadians began to express themselves as a people during the 1830s. They elected their first member to the legislature of Nova Scotia and the 2 other provinces in the 1840s and 1850s. The poem EVANGELINE (1846) of American poet H.W. Longfellow went through several French translations and had undeniable impact. In France, historian Edmé Rameau de Saint-Père brought out in 1859 the first French-language historical study which dealt with Acadians. Moreover, Rameau carried on a voluminous correspondence with the Acadian leaders of the day. In Acadia itself, a pastor born in Québec, Abbé F.X. Lafrance, in 1854 opened the first French-language institution of higher learning, the Saint-Thomas seminary, in Saint-Joseph; it was directed from 1864 on by Québec priests of the congregation of the Holy Cross. Then, in 1867, another Québécois, Israel Landry, started the first French-language paper in the Maritimes, called *Le Moniteur Acadien*, in Shédiac (NB).

The Nationalist Age (1881-1955) As of the 1860s, an Acadian middle class had begun to take shape. Its leadership emerged from Collège Saint-Joseph and began to organize, from 1881 on, huge meetings to discuss the future of Acadians. They founded a Société nationale des Acadiens whose purpose was to promote the French fact. National symbols were chosen: a flag (the French tricolour with a yellow star in the blue stripe), a national holiday (the Feast of the Assumption, celebrated on Aug 15), a slogan ("L'union fait la force") and a national anthem (*Ave Maris Stella*). Programs of action were set up: the promotion of French schooling; the battle against emigration to the US; more attention to agriculture and settling the land; the founding of new papers and colleges; the Acadianizing of the Catholic hierarchy. An Acadian priest became bishop in 1912. Acadian priests and laymen worked closely together through all these steps.

The themes identified during the 1880s remained virtually unchanged until about 1955. But as of the 1920s and 30s, individual characteristics began to appear in the Acadian communities of each of the Maritime provinces. The New Brunswick Acadians, thanks to their numbers and confidence, took the lead in speaking for Acadians as a whole. They could elect one-third the members of the provincial legislature. They had the best cultural and French-language infrastructure. In fact, the province today has a network of schools through the secondary level; a university (UNIVERSITÉ DE MONCTON); hospitals; 2 daily papers; several weeklies; 3 radio stations and one TV station. The Acadian communities of PEI and Nova Scotia have French schools (though some have English-language texts) and one French weekly each. These communities receive radio and TV programming from the Radio-Canada station in Moncton.

The Société nationale des Acadiens is the body which looks after the common interests of Acadians in all 3 Maritime provinces. But each province has its own pressure group: the Société Saint-Thomas-d'Aquin (PEI), the Fédération acadienne de la Nouvelle-Écosse and the Société des acadiens du Nouveau-Brunswick. All belong to the Fédération des francophones hors Québec, founded in 1975. All are financed largely by the federal government and each has a secretariat with a permanent staff.

Contemporary Acadia All Acadians benefit from the federal OFFICIAL LANGUAGES ACT passed in 1969, but only in areas of federal jurisdiction. At the provincial level, Acadians in New Brunswick enjoy double legal protection: an official languages act, passed in 1969, certain of whose sections have been incorporated into the Canadian Charter of Rights and Freedoms, and another, passed in 1981, which guarantees equal status to the English and French communities of the province. Under the 1981 Act, each group has the right to its own institutions in certain fields, education in particular. As of 1986, there is no outline law concerning Acadians in the 2 other provinces, although the governments there do maintain French schools.

The integration of part of the francophone population into primarily anglophone milieux brings with it the phenomenon of linguistic assimilation which in turn weakens the Acadian community. Since the 1960s, there has been an increasing gap between the number of people of French origin and those who speak French, suggesting a loss of French in earlier generations, and another gap between those whose mother tongue is French and those who can use it daily, suggesting it is being abandoned by the present generation.

The 1982 figures are eloquent on the subject:

	Fr Origin	Fr M Tongue	Fr Lang of Use
NB	251 070	234 030	216 410
NS	71 350	36 030	24 450
PEI	14 770	6090	2360

New Brunswick Acadians benefit most from sheer numbers, demographic strength and degree of institutional organization, which explains their lower degree of assimilation. The prognosis for the maintenance of French in the 2 other Maritime provinces, as in the Canadian provinces west of Québec, however, is disturbing and efforts made to counter assimilation do not always give the desired results.

In matters of religion, in 1850 there was a single priest of Acadian origins in all the Maritime provinces. Today, in New Brunswick, and in general in the 2 other provinces, each Acadian parish has its Acadian curé. In the religious hierarchy, the bishops of Edmundston and of Bathurst in NB, of Yarmouth in NS and the archbishop of the ecclesiastical province of NB are all Acadian.

On the other hand, agriculture no longer plays a dominant role in the contemporary life of Acadians, except in northwestern New Brunswick, where there is intensive potato farming. There are still small farms and some cattle, but farm costs, the infertility of the soil, the low yield of the lands and the lack of machinery have all contributed to a significant decline in agriculture. The small dairy industries typically have remained at the family level.

In the past, fishing granted a scanty living to many Acadians who lived near the ocean. The co-operative movement, born in Antigonish in the 1930s, freed fishermen from the economic grasp of the companies. Thanks to this movement, the price of fish rose substantially, fishermen acquired modern boats and equipment and their trade became relatively profitable, putting some fishermen in the ranks of the richest Acadians in the Maritimes. Small and medium-sized fish treatment plants expanded considerably after 1950, which gave a significant amount of seasonal employment to the men and women of the Acadian region. The forest industry plays an important role, under the control of the big corporations for which the Acadians work. But growing mechanization and truck transport mean less manpower is required. Many Acadians work in the paper mills of New Brunswick and Nova Scotia. The coal mines of Minto (NB) provided a great deal of work in the past; those of Cape Breton still operate. Today, the copper and zinc mines and the PEAT industry of County Gloucester (NB) provide work for many Acadians. But they too often lack the professional training needed to make them eligible for the most skilled and remunerative positions.

Acadians have made a great deal of progress since the early 20th century. An Acadian life assurance company, Assomption Compagnie mutuelle d'assurance-vie, was founded in 1903 with headquarters in Moncton. In 1986 it had assets of $186 million. The combination of a fish factory, a co-operative store and a CAISSE POPULAIRE has helped many Acadian parishes boost their economies. In New Brunswick alone, there are 88 caisses and a federation of these with 1986 assets of $581 million and 184 500 members.

Today, a great many Acadians make their presence known in business and commerce, in provincial and federal political life, and in the professions: doctors, oculists, dentists, lawyers, architects, university professors, etc.

Culture and Cultural Activities

The social context of poverty and regional isolation which lasted until the 20th century, and the lack of institutions of higher education until 1864, prevented Acadians from showing their tastes and artistic talents to the larger public. They contented themselves with loving concern for their folklore, the only artistic expression open to them. With the arrival of higher education and access to the larger world, Acadian culture knew a virtual explosion from the mid-20th century on. Acadians now have a strong presence in handcrafts, painting, sculpture, song, dance, theatre, cinema and literature.

Folklore Until the end of the 19th century, Acadians lived in isolated groups, with little contact with the exterior. As a result, they faithfully preserved the traditions of their ancestors, their manner of speech brought from Poitou in the 17th century, the dishes, celebrations, and passed on from generation to generation their beliefs, songs, stories and legends.

At the turn of the century, songs were composed reflecting the national awakening of the Acadians: "L'Evangéline," "Le Réveil de l'exile," "Le Pècheur acadien," "La Fleur du souvenir," etc. The traditional songs were still popular with the people, but the intellectuals seemed blind to their value. It was not until 1939 that the journalist Thomas LeBlanc began a column in the paper *L'Evangéline* about Acadian songs. Fathers Anselme Chiasson and Daniel Boudreau published 3 volumes of *Chansons d'Acadie* between 1942 and 1956. This column and these collections increased respect for Acadian folklore. Then, the researchers arrived: Luc Lacourcière, Mgr Félix-Antoine Savard and Roger Matton from Québec; Carmen Roy, from Ottawa; and Geneviève Massignon from France. Then Acadians themselves began collecting folklore material and put together important collections. Université Laval has a vast ethnological documentation of Acadian material thanks to its researchers and its students. The U of Moncton has been teaching folklore since 1966 and its Centre d'Études acadiennes in 1970 opened a section devoted to folklore, holding thousands of songs, tales, legends and traditions.

Singers and choral groups in Québec and Acadia have rediscovered the traditional songs and sing them in their concerts, on radio and TV. Edith BUTLER and Angèle Arsenault began their brilliant careers with these songs.

This rediscovery of Acadian folklore has given rise to the explosion of an entire literature: books of stories, legends, songs, traditions, recipes and even novels. The many books by world-famous Acadian author Antonine MAILLET are all inspired by folklore.

Music It is said that Acadians are born with songs in their veins and music in the tips of their fingers. Former generations gave instrumental as well as vocal proof of the saying, and today's generation is no different.

Arthur LeBlanc, after studying in Québec and Paris, quickly became a world-famous violinist. Unfortunately illness brought an untimely end to his career. Eugène Lapierre and Benoît Poirier, both from PEI, made their careers as organists in Montréal. Poirier composed many pieces for organ. Roger Lord, a talented young pianist, has already won many competitions.

In the area of popular music, Nova Scotia has given us pianist Paul Saulnier, violinists Johnny Comeau and Kenneth Saulnier, and the instrumental and vocal duo, Wendell and Phillipe D'Eon. Two violin virtuosos in the folklore field, Johnny Aucoin from Cape Breton and Elio LeBlanc from Memramcook, have set many feet in motion. Folklorists Charlotte Cormier and Donald Deschênes interpret rural songs and find some of their most eager audiences in Acadian schools.

Acadia is also known for its classical singers, its chansonniers, its groups of singers and its chorales. Anna Malenfant was one of the first Acadians to distinguish herself on the national and international scene. Laura Gaudet popularized Acadian songs through Acadia and the US in recitals and on the radio. Robert Savoie was a baritone for several years at Covent Garden in London.

The quality of the voices of Gloria Richard and the sisters Marie-Germaine and Marguerite LeBlanc won them renown in national competitions. Today, Claudette LeBlanc from Shédiac, Roland Richard from Rogersville and Rose-Marie Landry from Caraquet all win applause at home and abroad.

Among interpreters and composers of popular song, Edith Butler enjoys great success here and in France. Angèle Arsenault is also famous at the national level. Calixte Duguay and Donat Lacroix are known for their magnificent songs on Acadian topics. The list would be long indeed were it to mention all Acadian singers of renown today, such as Denis Losier, Raymond Breau, Georges Langford, Lorraine Diotte, Ronald Bourgeois, Lina Boudreau, Jac Gautreau.

Young Acadian singers continue the tradition of winning song competitions in Québec and France. Groups of singing musicians, such as Beausoleil-Broussard and 1755, have delighted audiences in Canada and France where they have won, each in turn, the prize for the young French song. Les Tymeux de la Baie represented Acadians at Expo 86, as did the PEI group Panou at the music festival held in conjunction with the Canada Games in St John's in 1985.

Not long ago, most Acadian parishes had a good church choir. One of the loveliest, the choral group Lafrance de Tracadie (director Armand Lavoie), is still well known far beyond the walls of the church and parish. In Bathurst, the Voidunor (Sr Berthe LeBlanc) and in Memramcook, La Fleur du Souvenir (Charles LeBlanc) were also award-winners for Acadian choral societies.

In the former boys' colleges, Saint-Joseph and Sacré-Coeur in NB, Sainte-Anne in NS, brass bands long enjoyed the greatest popularity, but from the 1950s on, choral groups in the colleges and convents stole the limelight. Those from Saint-Joseph and Sacré-Coeur, from Collège Notre-Dame d'Acadie in Moncton and more recently from Université de Moncton have often won top honours in provincial, national and international competitions. Since 1962 the Lincoln Trophy has been won 8 times by one or another of these Acadian groups. The first to make itself known both here and overseas was that of the University of Saint-Joseph, established by Père Léandre Brault in 1946. Neil Michaud took over its direction in 1955; in 1963 it became the choral group of the Université de Moncton.

In some Acadian schools as well, singing has great importance and youth choirs compete at annual music festivals. This is how the choral group of École Beauséjour of Moncton, later known under the name of Les jeunes chanteurs d'Acadie (Sr Lorette Gallent) has since 1957 won honours on national and international stages.

Some of these choral societies have made high-quality records. The list includes those already mentioned, and also the Chanteurs du Mascaret (Neil Michaud), les Alinos (Aline OBriet), the La-Mi-Champlain (Sr Blanche Dupuis) and others. The strong position of Acadian chorale groups in the musical world drew to Acadia, in 1979, the Choralies internationales, a major event in the musical history of the region.

Acadia is also the site of a major baroque music festival. Founded by harpsichordist Mathieu Duguay, this festival has taken place each year since 1975 on the little island of Lamèque in northeastern New Brunswick and draws well-known musicians.

In Nova Scotia, more particularly in the region of Baie-Sainte-Marie near the Université Sainte-Anne, musicians abound and cultural events take place all year long. One of the great instigators of all this activity is Père Maurice LeBlanc, a choral society director and long an energetic promoter of cultural life in the region.

One must also note the huge contribution made by male and female religious communities, who have awakened young people's taste for music. Throughout Acadia, they have developed their talents and put them on the stage so that they may make known one of the most beautiful aspects of Acadian culture.

Painting and Sculpture Professional painting and sculpture are relatively new to Acadia. The first organized teaching of these disciplines, namely the creation at the Université de Moncton of a department of visual arts, occurred barely a generation ago. Some works of talented Acadians from earlier generations survive. Several women studied design and painting abroad: Philomène Belliveau from Memramcook and Caroline Léger from Paquetville in the 19th century, and later Jeanne Léger from Sainte-Marie-de-Kent and Alma Buote from Tignish, who have left evidence of their talent.

In Madawaska, a Québécois doctor settled in Edmundston at the turn of the century and spent 40 years teaching young people the art of wood sculpture. Two names stand out among the talents which blossomed under his instruction: Claude Picard and Claude Roussel. It is Roussel who, while artist and painter in residence at the Université de Moncton, set up its department of visual arts. Picard and Roussel produced sculptures which put them firmly in the ranks of professional artists. Both were recently invited to contribute bas-reliefs and tableaux illustrating the Acadian odyssey to the Église-Souvenir in Grand-Pré. Imposing sculptures by Sr Marie-Hélène Allain are on display in several public buildings in Canada.

A number of painters have received their training elsewhere and then followed their artistic careers in New Brunswick, including Sr Gertrude Godbout, Sr Eulalie Boudreau, René Hébert, Georges Goguen, Roméo Savoie, Hilda Lavoie-Franchon and Claude Gauvin. One of Gauvin's paintings decorates the exterior of a federal building on Sparks Street in Ottawa and a huge mural of his went to Expo 86 in Vancouver.

Edouart Gautreau from Saint-Paul-de-Kent and Claude Picard created large religious paintings for some Acadian churches. New Brunswick has declared the church in Sainte-Anne-de-Kent a provincial heritage because of the Gautreau paintings. In Nova Scotia, Nelson Surette has gained a reputation as a painter through his illustrations of Acadian daily life. In PEI, Adrien Arsenault has shown himself to be a remarkable artist and drawer. In Québec, an Acadian originally from northeast NB, Néré DeGrâce, has seen one of his drawings figure on a Canadian commemorative stamp; his large artistic output on folkloric themes goes to owners far beyond Acadia itself. Léo B. LeBlanc, a self-taught native painter, has exhibited internationally.

A whole new generation of artists – painters, sculptors, drawers, photographers – trained both in Acadian universities and elsewhere, constitute an important body of people who explore and open up new horizons while still following the tradition of excellence handed down by their predecessors. Some of them, such as the multi-talented Herménégilde Chiasson, have already made names for themselves.

Theatre The play by Germaine Comeau was put on by the Théâtre Amateur de Moncton (1969-80), a troupe founded by Laurie Henri. Le TAM knew its best moments in its presentation of the Antonine Maillet play, *Les Crasseux*, mounted by Jean-Claude Marcus at the Lefèbvre monument in Memramcook in 1977. Since then, theatre activity in Acadia has been largely the work of professional troupes, such as the Théâtre Populaire d'Acadia, in Caraquet, and the Escaouette theatre co-operative in Moncton. The 2 troupes have given several new Acadian playwrights a place to develop and express their talents.

In Caraquet, the TPA gave prominence to Jules Boudreau by regularly producing his plays. The best known was *Louis Mailloux* (1975), a musical drama written in collaboration with Calixte Duguay, which brought to life the glorious story of a young Acadian hero who died defending his culture. Boudreau dramatized another piece of Acadian history, the aftermath of the deportation, in his play *Cochu et le Soleil* (1977). In his other plays, Boudreau explores various facets of fantasy and humour in contemporary themes. The TPA has also produced one of the first plays by Herménégilde Chiasson, *L'Amer à boire* (1977), an adaptation of the novel by Régis Brun, *La Marie Como* (1980), a show for children, *Rosîne et Renixou* (1983) by Roseline Blancard and René Cormier, and *Zélica à Cochon Vert* (1986) by Laurier Melanson.

In Moncton, the Escaouette theatre co-operative has concentrated on the dramatic works of Herménégilde Chiasson. Her plays are distinguished by their eclecticism. Hitting every note from the most serious gravity to the brightest comedy, her theatre explores three main themes: revisionist history in *Histoire et histoire* (1980) and *Renaissances* (1984); humour, burlesque and farce in *Au plus fort la poche* (1977), *Cogne Fou*

(1981) and *Y'a pas que des maringouins dans les campings* (1986); fantasy, the dreamworld and marvels in *Becquer Bobo* (1976), *Mine de Rien* (1980), *L'Etoile de Mine de Rien* (1982), this one in collaboration with Roger LeBlanc and *Atarelle et les Pakmaniens* (1983), which in 1985 went on tour in New Brunswick and Europe. Two of these plays, *Au plus fort la poche* and *Becquer Bobo*, were created in the department of dramatic arts at the Université de Moncton rather than in Escaouette.

Other original plays have been presented by Escaouette for school audiences: *Le Pêcheur ensorcelé* (1979) by Marie Pauline and *le Gros ti-gars* (1985) by Gracia Couturier. All these plays explore in some degree or another the dreamworld and the daily experiences of children and adolescents. *Le Gros ti-gars* shows a sure technique, a mastery of text and scenic style which has certainly not yet exhausted all its resources. Gracia Couturier had previously put her name to 4 plays for the Théâtre de Saisons in Shippegan.

Other authors have chosen the theatre as a way to express some aspect of Acadian life. Among them are Raymond LeBlanc (*As-tu vu ma balloune*, 1979, and *Fonds de culottes*, 1981), Clarence Comeau (*Au pays des côtes*, 1978, and *Premières neiges d'automne*), Gérald LeBlanc (*Les Sentiers de l'espoir*, 1983), and Marcel Thériault (*J'avais dix ans*, 1983). In the rather more difficult context of Nova Scotia and PEI, theatrical activity keeps itself going thanks to people such as Jules Chiasson (Chéticamp), Jean-Douglas Comeau (Pointe-de-l'Église) and Paul Gallant (PEI), whose *La cuisine à Mémé* has delighted many spectators at summer theatres in the Acadian region of the Island. Some authors have benefits from this theatrical activity: Claude Saint-Germain and Léonie Poirier, among others. Pierre Gérin has also published some plays, including *Opération Médusa* (1974), but his plays have not been produced. He is the exception which proves the rule that theatre is an art of the stage and not of the book, for in Acadia, apart from the work of Antonine Maillet which is published by Leméac, the repertory of published plays amounts to 8 titles divided among the Éditions d'Acadie, Mionel Henry écriteur and the Imprimerie L'escarbot. All the other plays remain unpublished, but they have all been produced.

The Acadian theatre still gives signs of an encouraging vitality. Antonine Maillet continues a splendid national and international career with *Carrochés en Paradis*, her play created at the Théâtre du Rideau Vert in Oct 1986. A new company was born in 1986, the Compagnie Viola Léger, whose first production, *Harold et Maude*, was very successful: some 50 performances for more than 10 000 spectators.

Cinema Acadian cinema began in 1974 when the NATIONAL FILM BOARD decentralized its French production by opening an office in Moncton; it took the name of Régionalisation/Acadie of the NFB. Acadians now have a structure through which to develop their own cinema and the talents of Acadian filmmakers. Twelve films were made under the direction of Paul-Eugène LeBlanc, the first producer for Régionalisation/Acadie: *Une simple journée* (Charles Thériault), *La nuit de 9* (a collective effort), *Y'a du bois dans ma cour* (Luc Albert), *Abandounée* (Anna Girouard), *La Confession* (Claude Renaud), *La Cabane* and *Les Gossipeuses* (Phil Comeau), *Au Boutte de quai* (Robert Haché), *Kouchibouguac* (collective effort), *Le Frolic, cé pour ayder* (Laurent Comeau, Suzanne Dussault, Marc Paulin), *Armand Plourde, une idée qui fait son chemin* (Denis Godin), and *Souvenir d'un écolier* (Claude Renaud). Producer Rhéal Drisdelle made 2 films in 1980 and 1981: *Arbres de Noel à vendre* (Denis Morisset) and *J'avions 375 ans* (Phil Comeau).

In 1981, Régionalisation/Acadie changed its

The Deportation of the Acadians, Grand-Pré, 1755, painting by George Craig, 1893 (*courtesy Musée acadien, U de Moncton*).

status to become a production studio under the name of Production française/Acadie of the NFB. Under director Eric Michel, 7 more films were made from 1982 to 1986: *Massabielle* (Jacques Savoie), *Une sagesse ordinaire* (Claudette Lajoie-Chiasson), *De l'autre côté de la glace* and *Sorry Pete* (Serge Morin), *Bateau bleu, maison verte* (Betty Arsenault), *Une faim qui vient de loin* (Claudette Lajoie-Chiasson), *Toutes les photos finissent par se ressembler* (Herménégilde Chiasson).

In this account of the evolution of Acadian life, one must also mention the first script writer, Léonard Forest, for his films, *Les Aboiteaux*, in collaboration (1955); *Les Acadiens de la dispersion*, by the NFB, produced in Moncton (1967); *Un Soleil pas comme ailleurs* (1972). Léonard Forest made his career in film with the NFB and was one of the founders of Régionalisation/Acadie.

The film *L'Éloge du Chiac* (Michel Brault), made in 1969, studies the problem of the French spoken in Acadia, a problem which still exists. Other films made by Acadians in the private sector include *C'est nice de parler les deux manières* (1978, Denis Godin), *La Musique nous explique* (1980, Phil Comeau), *La Traîne à M. Lude* (1983, Rodolphe Caron), distributed by Coop Cinémarévie, Edmundston; and *Cap Lumière* (1986, Herménégilde Chiasson), distributed by Ciné Est en Action/Carota Films, Shédiac; and the English-language film of Acadian director Clay Borris, *Rose's House* (1977), NFB.

Literature The revitalization of the 1970s made Acadian literature famous. However, despite a difficult history and difficult conditions, Acadian literary life can be divided into 4 periods.

Up to the Deportation (1604-1755) Originally a commercial post in a strategic position, Acadia was always coveted by both France and England. Thus it never knew the settlement and the institutions of New France, nor the body of writings. Yet that is where Marc LESCARBOT edited the first literary texts of French America in 1606. Those who stayed there later on (Biard, Leclercq, Denys, Dièreville, Maillard, Bourg) described its geography, its settlers, its flora and its fauna.

From the Deportation to the Return (1755-1881) The reconstitution of the Acadians collectively took place very slowly from just after the dispersal to the first national conventions. There was no written literature, at first, but an enrichment of tales, legends and songs. This was an era when their cultural riches became truly Acadian.

Slowly a school system began to take shape. In 1854 the first college was founded (and reorganized in 1864). Some eminent men emerged from it and played active roles in the future of their collectivity. With the clergy, they organized what would be the first important phenomenon of Acadian thought: the nationalist debate, which took place through the first national conventions.

The Age of the Nationalist Debate (1881-1966) For 80 years, the nationalist debate dominated Acadian thought and writing. Rooted in the works of Rameau de Saint-Père, spread through Acadia by the clergy from Québec where the French historian was equally prominent, and carried in the discussions and sermons published in the newspapers (*Le Moniteur, L'Evangéline*), this national debate was entirely devoted to the rebirth of the Acadian people. The trauma of the deportation served first as an identification and then as an identity. This debate brought together politics, economics, demography and culture. In rewriting history, it redefined the traits of the Acadian collectivity.

With an ethnocentrism normal under the circumstances, the nationalist debate dominated literary activity. History played the biggest role, but anecdotal history also had its part (biographies, parish or regional monographs). Genealogical (Placide Gaudet) and linguistic (Pascal Poirier) studies were undertaken. Literary genres conformed to the theme: poetry (F.-Moise Lanteigne, Napoléon-P. Landry) was patriotic and religious; novels (Antoine-J. Léger, Hector Carbonneau, J.-Alphonse Deveau) concentrated on the deportation, making it live again, identifying those responsible for it and showing its aftermath and traumas; theatre also chanted the patriotic song (Alexandre Braud, Jean-Baptiste Jégo) but focused as well on the educational battles of the age (James Branch).

Two phenomena marked the decline of the nationalist debate from its omnipresent position in the world of thought. First, authors turned away from it. Antonine Maillet, in 1958, was more interested in the life of a small Acadian village (*Pointe-aux-Coques*). Donat Coste, an Acadian living in Montréal, wrote *L'Enfant noir* in 1957 to denounce the hypocrisy of society. Ronald Després, musician, poet, translator, also living outside New Brunswick, published poems and a novel in 1962, *Le Scalpel ininterrompu*, a tragicomic fable of the modern world.

This literary withdrawal from the nationalist debate was joined by an even greater one – the young generation challenging it. In 1966 the Rassemblement des jeunes questioned the debate, emblems, symbols, historical viewpoints –

the traditional portrait of the Acadian. And the times were sympathetic to their approach. The Liberal government of Louis J. ROBICHAUD (the first Acadian premier of NB) inaugurated his program of equal opportunity for all. Québec society was renewing itself and its action served as a stimulus and a model. Finally, the radical movement of the 1960s had its impact here as elsewhere.

The Age of Literature (1966-86) Many other factors joined the social revival and the ideological challenge already mentioned: student grievances and their social and legal consequences; the "nuits de poésie" (poetry nights – the term used in the sense of active creation of poetry) where a new sensibility was born, consisting of daring, high spirits and impatience on the part of youth; the enormous success of *La Sagouine* by Antonine Maillet; the chansonniers; the few but increasingly numerous books by young authors for whom the creation of Éditions d'Acadie meant finally a place to be published.

Poetry came first. The first publications had various themes and styles. But given the circumstances, one theme stood out: Acadia. It meant challenge and a search for identity, rebellion and attachment both: these contradictory moods aroused by a homeland both beloved and detested. The context for the theme is the almost political desire to create a country (Raymond LeBlanc), in the violent and sorrowful denunciation of a collective living death (Herménégilde Chiasson). Yet some of the works of these 2 poets, freed from any political stand, celebrate love and the daily routine. That was the starting point for Guy Arsenault and a language of studied naivety, which appears to stroke lightly yet probes deeply into the way Acadia is stealthily being deprived of its very being (freedom, voice, identity). In a more general way, Ulysse Landry denounces the way the individual is nullified by today's society, which ravages people's intimate lives. All these collections, published between 1973 and 1976, combined the language of daily life with the individual stylistic explorations of each author.

Soon, even if some topics remained important (the difficulty of life, for example), poetry changed its tone. Roméo Savoie moved toward philosophy. Gérald LeBlanc, who opened up his poetry to other circumstances and other words, introduced a new cosmopolitan inspiration into Acadian literature. Léonard Forest shares this same sense of opening up toward others and developed a distinctive musical style in which the use of archaic words and restrained emotions gave his work an almost ritualistic allure. A kind of natural surrealism pervades the work of Rose Després and Dyane Léger. The former frees herself from the past in order to find the right gesture and word; the latter gives herself over to a magic universe of words, to the spell of the dream world of literature. Finally, others (Huguette Legaré, Clarence Comeau, Daniel Dugas, Huguette Bourgeois, Robert Pichette, Melvin Gallant) explore, poem by poem, the registers of sentiment and of emotion which shake the heart.

The Acadian novel is dominated by the works of Antonine Maillet, whose boundless energy takes pleasure in mixing the epic with the daily routine by calling on all the resources of the fabulous and of the oral tradition of storytellers. But other voices also make themselves heard. Louis Haché uses his knowledge of the documentation to retrace the life of the Acadians of the northeast, early in history or at the start of the 20th century. Régis Brun takes a revisionist historical perspective by finding his heroes among the ordinary people who have shown their hunger for freedom and their delight in life. Claude Lebouthillier rewrites history through utopian literature which gives back to Acadians their lost homeland.

Jeannine Landry Thériault and Laurier Melanson evoke village life, either through the secret dramas of adults, the hopes and disillusionments of youth, or through truculent lives, bawdy tales and satire. Others (Anne Lévesque, Germaine Comeau, Melvin Gallant) focus on the fates of individuals. Jacques Savoie does so as well in his distinctively spontaneous and lively writings, where he creates a new romanesque structure. France Daigle, in a minimalist and elliptical style, offers a modern, practically abstract, vision of the world of sentiments. Michel Roy's *perdue* is an impassioned and impassioning book which he then buttressed with an historical study; Jean-Paul Hautecoeur produced a brilliant sociological study about *L'Acadie du discours*; Léon Thériault analysed politics in his *La Question du pouvoir en Acadie*. Among the reminiscences and biographies one finds the outstanding *Mémoires d'un nationaliste acadien* by Calixte Savoie. His exemplary commitment makes it a book of the first rank.

Paris is the metropolis of French literature; Montréal, of Québec literature. Acadian literature has no metropolis. Its centre is the admirable, stubborn will of Acadians themselves. Geographic Acadia is lost, but the world of literature now offers a spiritual Acadia to replace it.

PÈRE ANSELME CHIASSON

with the collaboration of Yves Bolduc (*literature*), Roland Brideau (*film*), Zenon Chiasson and Léonard E. Doucette (*theatre*), Raoul Dionne (*economics*), Muriel K. Roy (*demography*), Léon Thériault (*history*) and Muriel K. Roy (*painting and sculpture*).

Reading: Jean Daigle, *Les Acadiens des Maritimes* (1980); Marguerite Maillet, *Histoire de la littérature acadienne* (1983); *Québec français*, no 60 (1985), pp 29-50.

Acadia University, Wolfville, NS. In 1828, the Baptist Education Society of Nova Scotia founded Horton Academy in Horton [Wolfville], NS. Ten years later (1838) the BAPTISTS established Queen's College, sharing the Horton facilities. Contrary to prevailing practices, no religious tests were imposed on either faculty or students. The colonial government chartered the new institution, but reluctantly, since it felt there were already more colleges than it could support. Even the name raised objections, as Queen Victoria declined having a Dissenters' college named after her. "Acadia College" finally received its charter in 1841, and became Acadia U in 1891. Classes began in early 1839 and the first class graduated in 1843, numbering 4.

A theology department was soon added, although Acadia continued to emphasize liberal arts. The Associated Alumni of Acadia College, est 1860, provided crucial early financial support. Still very active, it is one of the oldest alumni organizations in Canada. In the 1860s a Ladies' Seminary was established; by 1880 women were attending college classes, although informally. In 1884 Acadia's first woman graduate received her degree. Other areas of concentration have been

Seminary house constructed in 1879, which now serves as a co-ed residence (*photo by Bruce Cohoon, Acadia U*).

Enrolment: Acadia University, 1985-86
(Source: Statistics Canada)

Full-time Undergrad	Full-time Graduate	Part-time Undergrad	Part-time Graduate
3166	86	608	101

added to the liberal-arts program. Besides the faculties of arts and science, there are schools of computer science, home economics, business administration, music, recreation and physical education, applied science, education, secretarial science and graduate studies. In 1966 the Baptists relinquished control, although retaining a strong presence on the board of governors. The affiliated Divinity College, established 1968, serves that denomination's theological needs.

BARRY M. MOODY

Acadian Trail, a 117 km long-distance coastal trail following the breathtaking W coast of CAPE BRETON I in Nova Scotia. It is hoped that this trail will continue inland through NS, connect with the Fundy Trail in New Brunswick, and eventually join the 3200 km long Appalachian Trail that begins in Maine. The trail traverses the rugged coast across the Cape Breton Highlands, passing over beaches, grasslands, spruce forests and wilderness sections.   BART DEEG

Access to Information Act, enacted by Parliament in 1982 and took effect in July of 1983. This federal Act entitles an individual to examine information concerning the conduct of government, including information in connection with the formulation of federal government policy. This so-called "freedom-of-information" law provides an opportunity for an individual to request information from government and provides for the speedy provision of the information at a reasonable cost. It establishes an Information Commissioner to assist the individual and provides for certain exemptions under which some or all of the information may be withheld. At present, an applicant may apply to the Trial Division of the Federal Court of Canada for a review, in camera, of a decision by government to invoke an exemption and withhold information. Also, at present, there is a section of the Act which excludes Cabinet documents from the ambit of the entire statute. A major review of the experience under the new legislation was conducted by a Parliamentary Committee in 1986 and 1987, culminating in the spring of 1987 with a series of recommendations for improvements in the legislation. Furthermore, the government has proposed amendments to the Act which would allow requests for information to be disregarded where officials consider them "frivolous or vexatious."

G. GALL

Accommodation, first successful steamboat built entirely in N America. It was launched 19 Aug 1809 at Montréal, its engines having been constructed at the FORGES SAINT-MAURICE, Trois-Rivières. The ship was propelled by 2 open-side paddle wheels, though a sail could be raised if the engine failed. John MOLSON and partners paid £2000 for the *Accommodation* but by 1810 losses of £4000 had accrued and it was scrapped. Nothing remains of the pioneering ship, though it signalled a new age. By 1819, 7 steam packets plied the St Lawrence R. *See also* STEAMBOATS AND PADDLEWHEELERS.   JAMES MARSH

Accounting is the process of measuring and reporting on the financial activities of organizations. Accountants must select from a large number of events those which affect an organization and can be measured financially; the events selected and measured are then presented in financial reports. Users of accounting reports include managers within an organization as well as outsiders who are interested in what the organization has achieved, eg, shareholders, creditors, governments and investors.

Accounting can be divided in 2 subdisciplines (correlated to user category). Financial accounting is more widely known because it produces balance sheets, income statements and statements of changes in financial position, which are generally disseminated both within and outside an organization or firm. Managerial accounting, on the other hand, is more concerned with the information needs of internal management and is used to formulate, execute, and evaluate plans and policies. While both financial and managerial accounting require technicians for systematic record keeping and data collection, the more complex part of the work is usually done by professional accountants. In financial accounting, the annual and interim reports are designed and prepared by specialists, and are reviewed and attested by auditors or public professional accountants. For managerial purposes, the selection of relevant information and the determination of measurement rules are normally the responsibility of highly qualified accountants.

Accounting is centuries old and has evolved from a strict custodianship function to one concerned with taxation, auditing, information systems, economics, etc. However, although record keeping can be traced back to Babylon, and double-entry bookkeeping was used as early as 1494, the accounting professions in N America are fairly recent. The first known official meeting of N American accountants was held in Montréal in June 1879, for the purpose of establishing a society to promote the profession. Three large associations now exist in Canada. The oldest, established in 1902 as the Dominion Association of Chartered Accountants, is now called the Canadian Institute of Chartered Accountants; members of the institute are designated as CAs. The Society of Management Accountants (RIAs) was originally formed in 1920 under the name of the Canadian Society of Cost Accountants. The Canadian Certified General Accountants Association (CGAs) was incorporated in 1913 as the General Accounting Association. Each association has a national organization but, since education is under provincial jurisdiction, each has provincial organizations (known as institutes, orders, associations or societies) to establish and control education and entry requirements.

Each association imposes professional examinations and practical experience requirements. The chartered accountants were the first, in 1970, to require a university degree of their members. In addition to a degree, candidates must complete a program of advanced professional study, pass a nationwide final exam and complete a 2- or 3-year term of service with an approved public accounting firm. The certified general accountant candidates can complete their university degrees before or after the professional examinations and must have practical experience in a business firm or in government. Although it is possible to become an RIA with a high-school education, a very large proportion of candidates take university courses. All major Canadian universities offer courses that prepare candidates for the professional examinations.

Private accounting offers a variety of job opportunities, ranging from the technical aspects of bookkeeping to the more complex processes of administrative planning. Private accountants work for specific organizations, eg, governments, hospitals and universities. In medium-sized as well as in large business corporations, important financial positions (eg, controller, chief accountant, treasurer, internal auditor) are usually held by professional accountants.

The effects of acidic gases on the environment. When they rise in the atmosphere, acidic gases are oxidized and carried by the wind many kilometres before falling back to earth as acid rain. Acidity releases toxic metals such as mercury and aluminum from rocks and soil into lakes and rivers. Thus, the environment is under attack from above and below (*courtesy National Research Council*).

Public accounting includes activities such as auditing, management consulting, reporting on other financial information for creditors or governments, and perhaps serving as trustees in bankruptcy cases. Auditing is related to the attest function – the expression of an opinion about the fairness of accounting reports, which is a legal requirement for public corporations. Auditing is reserved, in some provinces, for chartered accountants. Consulting on accounting, taxation, information systems and finance, etc, has expanded rapidly in the last few decades and will probably continue to do so.

The 3 major accounting associations each publish a journal: the *CA Magazine, Cost and Management* and the *CGA Magazine*. O. CROTEAU

Reading: R. Skinner, *Accounting Principles* (1972).

Acid Rain, the wet or dry deposition of acidic substances and their precursors on the Earth's surface. Wet deposition refers to rain, snow, hail, drizzle and other familiar forms of visible precipitation. Dry deposition, mostly invisible, occurs through gravitational settling of large particles and uptake of gases and small particles at the Earth's surface. Rain and other precipitation may be defined as acidic or alkaline depending on chemical composition. The degree of acidity is usually measured on the pH scale, a logarithmic measure of the concentration of hydrogen ions (H^+) in precipitation. On the pH scale, 7 represents a neutral solution. Acidic solutions have values below 7 and alkaline solutions have values above 7. For each change of one pH unit, the hydrogen ion content changes by a factor of 10. A clean water sample in equilibrium with atmospheric carbon dioxide will have a value of 5.6 and this is often used as a definition of "clean" rain. When values are different from this, it means that other substances, either natural or manmade, are present in the rain.

Current annual measurements of the average pH of precipitation in the Northern Hemisphere range from about 4.0 to 7.0. The lower, highly acidic values occur primarily over and immediately downwind of industrialized areas in northeastern N America and Europe. Higher pH values are found over less industrialized regions where the atmosphere contains larger amounts of alkaline dust. The primary cause of low pH in precipitation over northeastern N America is sulphuric acid (H_2SO_4) resulting from industrial and urban emissions of sulphur dioxide (SO_2). Nitric acid (HNO_3) generated from emissions of nitrogen oxides (NO_x) is a significant contributing factor in this region. Current annual emissions of SO_2 amount to about 23 million t in the US and about 4 million t in Canada. Coal-fired thermal electric power plants produce about 70% of US emissions and about 20% of Canadian emissions. Nonferrous smelters, producing such metals as nickel and copper, account for about 45% of Canada's SO_2 emissions. The acid rain precursors, SO_2 and NO_x, can be transported thousands of kilometres through the atmosphere, returning to earth as dry deposition or in wet acid form.

When acid rain reaches the Earth's surface it can cause damage to aquatic ecosystems and buildings. Acid rain and the associated pollutants (SO_2, NO_x, SO_4 particles and ozone) can also damage forests and crops, and there is evidence of adverse human health effects. The degree of effects depends on the acid-reduction capability of the receiving surfaces (eg, vegetation, soils and rock structures). In areas where this buffering capacity is low (eg, the Canadian Shield), acidic deposition over several years had led to increased acidity of rivers and lakes and to accelerated leaching of aluminum from soils. The aluminum can be in a form which is toxic to aquatic organisms. As the pH of surface waters falls below about 5.5, the diversity of aquatic life such as vegetation, zooplankton, amphibians and fish is reduced. Most fish populations are eradicated when the average pH of a lake drops to about 4.5. Thousands of lakes in eastern N America and Scandinavia are devoid of fish because of water acidification; hundreds of thousands more are threatened. Rivers, too, have shown adverse effects such as the marked decline of Atlantic salmon in the Maritimes and in Scandinavia. Birds and other fish predators may decrease in numbers because of reduced food supply.

The effects of acid rain, and the associated pollutants, on forests and agriculture, are not as well documented but are potentially serious. These include direct damage to plant foliage, seed germination failure, retardation of growth particularly at early life stages, deterioration of plant roots associated with the leaching of soil constituents and, possibly, increased susceptibility to insects

ACID RAIN

Areas having Sulphur Dioxide emissions greater than 100 kilotonnes per year

Areas most sensitive to acid precipitation

Prevailing winds

and diseases. Since the Canadian forest industry is valued at $20 billion annually, even a small reduction in productivity is significant.

There are several potential effects of acid rain on human health. Acidified drinking water supplies may become contaminated by leaching of copper, lead and other metals from delivery pipes. Increased concentrations of heavy metals in fish in acidified rivers and lakes can pose a problem for populations consuming quantities of these fish.

Available control methods include the use of low-sulphur coal and oil, removal of sulphur from fuel and feeder ore, the use of flue-gas desulphurization techniques, energy conservation and the use of alternative energy sources. North American techniques for controlling acid rain precursors have been aimed primarily at reducing near-source air concentrations to levels necessary to avoid immediate and short-term impacts on human health (*see* AIR POLLUTION). The installation of pollution control devices and the building of taller emission stacks were effective in achieving the goal of improved air quality in North American cities. However, the result of taller stacks was to disperse SO_2 and NO_x emissions over large regions and the emission standards for the short-term protection of human health are inadequate for the protection of impacted regional environments and longer-term human health.

Emissions of SO_2 in both Canada and the US decreased between the early 1970s and the early 1980s as a result of increased use of pollution control devices, the use of more low-sulphur fuels, the introduction of some nuclear power plants and a slowdown in economic activity. These decreases in SO_2 emissions resulted in partial recovery of some ecosystems in specific locations in eastern Canada, thereby illustrating the potential effectiveness of further control actions. In the absence of such new controls it is anticipated that SO_2 emissions will begin to rise again, and even at current levels the cumulative acidification effects on regional environments remains a serious problem. In addition, NO_x emissions over N America are continuing to increase.

As a first step in controlling the effects of acid rain on surface waters, Canada has adopted a target loading of 20 kg of wet sulphate per hectare

per year. It is estimated that a reduction of current deposition rates to this value would protect moderately sensitive LAKE ecosystems and could be achieved over N America by reducing SO_2 emissions by about 50%. The eastern Canadian provinces and the federal government have agreed to reduce emissions by 50% by 1994; several formal federal-provincial agreements were signed in 1987.

About one half of the sulphate deposition in eastern Canada comes from sources of SO_2 in the US. Therefore, control action in the US is needed for Canada to achieve its target loading goal.

An international agreement developed by the United Nations Economic Commission for Europe (ECE) commits signatory countries to reduce their emissions of sulphur compounds (or their export to other countries via the atmosphere) by 30% by 1993. Canada is a member of the "30% Club" and hosted an international conference in March 1984 when the first 10 countries signed the agreement. Acid rain is but one manifestation of the increasing effects of man-made chemicals on the composition of the global atmosphere. Other anthropogenic effects associated with growing industrialization and the "chemical society" include arctic haze, climate warming and the depletion of the stratospheric OZONE LAYER. These changes in regional and global environments and their socio-economic impacts are attracting increasing international attention. *See also* ENDANGERED ANIMALS.   H.L FERGUSON

Reading: National Research Council of Canada, Report M18475, *Acidification in the Canadian Aquatic Environment* (1981); H.C. Martin, ed, *Acidic Precipitation* (1987).

Acorn, Milton, poet (b at Charlottetown 30 Mar 1923; d there 20 Aug 1986). A carpenter by trade, Acorn supported himself on a disability pension from an injury sustained during WWII. A radical personality with strong left-wing views and working-class sentiments, he translated these elements into an aggressive and polemical quality in his writing which, in his own words, "without apology or embarrassment (made) use of Marxist and existentialist ideas." He began to publish in *New Frontiers* in 1952. His first collection of verse, *In Love and Anger* (1956) was privately issued in Montréal, where he later co-edited the little mag-

azine *Moment* (7 issues, Feb 1960 to June 1962), first with A.W. PURDY and later with Gwendolyn MACEWEN whom he married in 1962. In 1963 Contact Press published a small collection of his verse called *Jawbreakers* and *The Fiddlehead* devoted its spring issue to Acorn's poetry. This, combined with a chapbook, *The Brain's the Target* (1960), with Ryerson Press, and a broadside, *Against a League of Liars* (1961), helped to give him wider recognition. He moved to Vancouver in the middle 1960s where he became well known as a passionate and argumentative member of the literary and journalistic underground. Passed over for the Governor General's Award for his first major collection, *I've Tasted My Blood* (1969), Acorn was honoured by fellow poets with a specially created People's Poet Award which recognized his ability as a writer as well as his nationalist and activist stance. Vocal, restless and angry he had migrated from Montréal to Toronto, then to Vancouver and back to Toronto where he settled for a time and, finally, Charlottetown. In 1971 he published *I Shout Love* and *On Shaving off his Beard*, a 2-poem sequence of private reflection and political invective which was not widely distributed, and in 1972, *More Poems for People* which he dedicated to Dorothy LIVESAY. In 1975 his collection of poems, *The Island Means Minago*, won the Governor General's Award, and Acorn settled into his role of established *enfant terrible* of Canadian poetry. *Jackpine Sonnets* came out in 1977, and *Captain Neal MacDougal & the Naked Goddess* subtitled, "A Demi-Prophetic Work as a Sonnet-Series" in 1982. *Dig up my Heart: Selected Poems 1952-1983*, appeared in 1983 and is the most complete and representative collection of Acorn's poetry. Although given to radical causes, and frequently caught up in their sentiment and jargon, Acorn retained an unalterable Island core that supplied him with his best poetic moments. Subtle in his emotions, his power and directness come from images drawn from everyday Island life. Dedicated to the class struggle, Acorn peopled his poems with working men and women of the visage of Canada, and paid unceasing tribute to their suffering, their humble crafts and their utter reliability. Thwarted in his search for happiness and denied true peace of mind, he was a troubled man at the end of his life.

MICHAEL GNAROWSKI

Acoustics is the science of sound and factors affecting hearing. It can be divided into various subfields, including physical acoustics, practical acoustics, architectural acoustics, musical acoustics, physiological and psychological acoustics. Physical acoustics studies airborne, audible sound, infrasound (below audible frequencies or 16 Hz) and ultrasound (above audible frequencies or 16 000 Hz). It examines propagation and absorption of all frequencies in air and other gases, liquids, semisolids and solids. In gases, only longitudinal waves (ie, those with perpendicular displacement) are important; in liquids and, especially, in solids, shear waves (which cause changes in shape but not in volume) and surface waves occur. Thus, seismic waves (whether on the Earth or the moon) are a legitimate part of acoustics. The large field of sound production, recording and reproduction, with all attendant electronic elements and measuring instruments, is an important part of practical or engineering acoustics. Knowledge of the physical principles of acoustics has further practical application in planning recreational and other developments to reduce the adverse effects of noise. Sound production, by one or more live players, vocalists or lecturers, whether assisted by loudspeakers or not, is greatly affected by the character of the room in which it takes place. Architectural acoustics aims to maximize the acceptability of music or intelligibility of speech in concert or lecture halls. Musical acoustics considers the workings of physical and electronic musical instruments. Since the ear is such an important detector and modifier of audible sounds, its operation is studied in physiological acoustics. Psychological acoustics studies the brain's signal-processing function, which is necessary for a sound to be heard or interpreted. A practical application of this branch would be the study of the elements important to achieving a stereophonic effect. Because of its importance as a modern environmental health problem, noise and its control are treated as a separate subdivision of acoustics. Bioacoustics studies all aspects of acoustic behaviour in animals.

In Canada acoustics research takes place in government laboratories (eg, NATIONAL RESEARCH COUNCIL), the universities (eg, Concordia, McMaster, Toronto) and industry. Canadian research into the transmission of sound in the atmosphere has been extensive; areas studied include the effect of temperature gradient, turbulence, obstruction, ground reflections and ground impedance. This research has applications in architecture, for designing buildings to meet noise-reduction provisions of building codes; in urban and regional planning, for siting of buildings, expressways, airports, sound barriers, etc; in industrial health, for designing provisions of codes relating to noise in the workplace. More esoteric work, such as measuring the velocity and absorption of high ultrasonic sound in various liquids to deduce the detailed architecture of their constituent molecules and the energy needed to change their structure, has application in various fields of engineering. Such work is related to the use of sonar and radar techniques to determine the structure of media (water and air) and the position of objects in them, to seismic techniques used in petroleum exploration and to the use of ultrasound in medicine. The effect of the complex shape of the outer ear on transmission of sound has been studied by segments of the record player, radio and television receiver industry concerned with the development of high-fidelity earphones. Industrial work has also been done on the effect of room shape and furnishings on music reproduced through loudspeakers. Means have been developed for assessing loudspeakers subjectively in normal rooms and correlating the results with standard, objective anechoic-chamber (ie, echofree) measurements. *See also* CONCERT HALLS AND OPERA HOUSES.   G.J. THIESSEN

Act (Statute), law passed by Parliament or a provincial legislature (*see* PROVINCIAL GOVERNMENT). A federal Act must pass 3 readings in the HOUSE OF COMMONS and 3 readings in the SENATE, and must receive royal assent. Assent is given by the SOVEREIGN (rarely), or, in the sovereign's name, by the GOVERNOR GENERAL or (usually) his deputy (a judge of the SUPREME COURT OF CANADA), in the Senate Chamber. A provincial Act must pass 3 readings in the legislature and receive the LIEUTENANT-GOVERNOR'S assent. Royal assent has never been refused to a Dominion bill, but lieutenant-governors have refused assent 28 times, the last time in 1945.   EUGENE A. FORSEY

Act of Union, Act of the British Parliament, passed July 1840 and proclaimed 10 Feb 1841, uniting UPPER CANADA and LOWER CANADA under one government. The reunification was a recommendation of the 1839 DURHAM REPORT, and the necessary legislation to establish the new PROVINCE OF CANADA was introduced in the British Commons in May 1839. In Sept, Charles Poulett Thomson (later Lord SYDENHAM) was sent as governor general to acquire Canadian consent, which he obtained from Lower Canada in Nov and from Upper Canada in Dec. The resolutions of

both Canadian legislative bodies were fused by Lower Canada Chief Justice James Stuart early in 1840. After passage in the British Parliament, July 1840, the Act of Union was proclaimed on 10 Feb 1841 in Montréal.

Its main provisions were the establishment of a single parliament with equal representation from each constituent section; consolidation of debt; a permanent Civil List; banishment of the French language from official government use; and suspension of specific French Canadian institutions relating to education and civil law. The Act naturally aroused considerable opposition. In Upper Canada, the FAMILY COMPACT opposed union, and in Lower Canada religious and political leaders reacted against its anti-French measures. In fact, the Act was unfair to Lower Canada with its larger population and smaller debt. However, both Canadas agreed to work within the Act, especially under the liberal influence of the united Reform party led by Louis LAFONTAINE and Robert BALDWIN. Within 15 years many unjust clauses had been repealed, and prosperity and responsible government had modified many of the Act's financial and constitutional provisions.

JACQUES MONET, S.J.

Action française, L', a monthly magazine published 1917-28 in Montréal. It was the voice of a group of priests and nationalists who comprised the Ligue des droits du français, an organization formed in 1913 to protect the French language. In 1920 Abbé Lionel GROULX became the group's leader, and in 1921 it became the Ligue d'Action française. In 1922 the magazine flirted with the idea of political independence but by 1927 had come out in favour of greater respect for the rights of the French Canadian minority within Canadian confederation. League members deplored the economic weakness of their compatriots and the growth of American investments in Québec; but, worried by the social changes wrought by industrialization and urbanization, most of them argued that agriculture was the way to promote the economic independence of French Canadians. The group published the annual *Almanach de la langue française,* intended for a broader public, and ran a publishing house and a bookstore.

FERNANDE ROY

Reading: Susan Mann Trofimenkoff, *Action française* (1975).

Action libérale nationale Founded in 1934 by discontented Liberals under Paul GOUIN, this third party in Québec politics quickly gained the support of radical FRENCH CANADIAN NATIONALISTS such as Philippe Hamel and Ernest Grégoire. Its program, based on social, economic and political reform, generated wide popular interest. In a nearly successful bid to upset the incumbent Liberal government of Louis-Alexandre TASCHEREAU in the 1935 provincial election, the ALN joined forces with the Conservatives, led by Maurice DUPLESSIS, to form the UNION NATIONALE. In the following months, Duplessis maneuvered to ensure his leadership of the coalition. After the UN's striking victory in the 1936 election, most of the well-known nationalists formerly linked to the ALN broke with Duplessis, whom they accused of refusing to implement the party's program. Paul Gouin, who had not even been a candidate in 1936, unsuccessfully attempted to revive the ALN in the 1939 election, but he was not successful.

RICHARD JONES

Action nationale, L', founded in 1933 by economist Esdras Minville as the voice of the Ligue d'Action nationale, is the oldest journal of opinion in Québec. As a continuation of *L'Action française* (1917-28) and *L'Action canadienne-française* (1928) which represented the "Québec-

first" nationalist doctrine of Lionel GROULX, *L'Action nationale* has always fought for autonomy, against the centralizing thrust of the federal government into fiscal matters (Rowell-Sirois Commission) and culture (Massey Commission). In the 1930s to 1950s it attracted nationalist youth, including editor André LAURENDEAU (1937-42, 1948-54), and in the 1960s progressively radicalized its stand on constitutional matters from one of provincial autonomy to associate-state to outright independence. Directed by Minville and François-Albert Angers, the magazine stressed economics, the continuity of French language and culture, the Catholic church and Laurentian history. It criticized certain reforms of the QUIET REVOLUTION, especially in education. Though it has declined in influence, the magazine has avoided partisan ties and pursues the same objective for which it was founded: free and energetic intellectual effort on behalf of a people and their culture.   PIERRE TRÉPANIER

ACTRA Awards The Alliance of Canadian Cinema, Television and Radio Artists, better known as ACTRA, is the organization that negotiates and administers collective agreements and sets minimum rates and basic conditions governing the English-language radio, television and film industry. ACTRA includes 3 guilds: writers, performers, and broadcast journalists and researchers. The origins of ACTRA were in the 1940s when radio artists in Toronto organized a union to improve their financial compensation and working conditions. There was similar activity in Winnipeg, Vancouver and Montréal. In 1943 the Association of Radio Artists was formed, and this evolved into the Association of Canadian Television and Radio Artists in 1963. ACTRA was restructured in 1984 and given its present name. Some of ACTRA's activities include administering health-insurance and retirement plans for its 9000 members, lobbying for Canadian content and a strong Canadian production industry, and the promotion and celebration of Canadian talent – through such publications as *Face to Face with Talent* and the *Actra Writers Guild Directory* – and the sponsoring of the annual ACTRA Awards. First presented in 1970, the ACTRA Awards honour Canadian writers, broadcast journalists and performers. Until 1986 the award was symbolized by the "Nellie," and other important categories included the Andrew Allan Award for Best Radio Actor, the Jane Mallett Award for Best Radio Actress, the Earle Grey Awards for Best Television Acting, and the Foster Hewitt Award for Excellence in Sports Broadcasting.

JAMES DeFELICE

Actualité, L', a French-language monthly magazine published in Montréal, was founded in 1909 as *Bulletin paroissial* and edited until 1945 by the Jesuit Armand Proulx. The review changed its name many times: to *L'Action paroissiale* (1932), *Ma paroisse* (1949), *L'Actualité* (1960) and *L'Actualité magazine* (1967). Monthly circulation was 140 000 in 1958, 107 000 in 1965 and 267 000 in 1987. Traditionally, the magazine supported the ideas of the UNION NATIONALE PARTY, and featured the work of many leading Québec writers and journalists. Jean-Louis Brouillé (the editor, 1960-72) endeavoured to make it the foremost Québec publication, reflecting the interests of the typical French Canadian Catholic family. Following a serious financial crisis in 1972, which resulted in major changes in staff and content, the magazine was sold in 1976 to MACLEAN HUNTER as part of a merger between *L'Actualité* and the French edition of MACLEAN'S (founded 1961). Former *Maclean's* editor Jean Paré has edited *L'Actualité* since 1976. The magazine presents a variety of news and feature stories in a glossy and colourful design, and appeals to an affluent and well-educated readership.

ANDRÉ DONNEUR AND ONNIG BEYLERIAN

Adam, Graeme Mercer, publisher, editor, author (b at Loanhead, Midlothian, Scot 25 May 1839; d at New York City 30 Oct 1912). During his career in Canada, Adam was a tireless supporter of Canadian letters. He emigrated to Toronto in 1858, where he established a publishing firm known eventually as Adam, Stevenson and Company (1867-76). His firm published the *British American Magazine devoted to Literature, Science and Art* (1863-64). Adam joined Goldwin SMITH in founding the influential *Canadian Monthly and National Review* (1872-78), editing it and its successor *Rose-Belford's Canadian Monthly* (1878-82) for 7 years, and helping to develop a market for Canadian literature. In 1892 Adam moved to the US where he was the editor of *Self-Culture* (1895-1902) in Akron, Ohio.

CAROL W. FULLERTON

Adams, Bryan, singer, songwriter, guitarist (b at Kingston, Ont 5 Nov 1959). Adams lived in England, Portugal and other countries before his family settled in Vancouver at age 15. At 16 he was playing small Vancouver clubs and at age 17 formed a songwriting partnership with Jim Vallance and began writing songs which were recorded by bands such as Bachman-Turner Overdrive and PRISM. In 1979 his first single "Let Me Take You Dancing" was released by A&M records and became a minor hit, resulting in the release of Adams's first album on the label in Feb 1980. Managed by Bruce Allen and supported by an international tour, his third album, *Cuts Like A Knife*, firmly established Adams as a major international singer. The single "Straight From the Heart," reached the top 10 on the Billboard Singles Chart in the US. Adams's fourth album, *Reckless*, was also a smash hit with a number of top-selling singles, including "Run To You." Adams has continued to write songs for other artists such as Tina Turner and Joe Cocker, and in 1985 co-wrote "Tears Are Not Enough," which was recorded by Northern Lights, with profits going toward famine relief in Africa. Adams first won a Juno Award in 1982 as Male Vocalist of the Year and he swept the awards in 1983-84, including top male vocalist, album of the year and producer of the year. He won 2 more Junos in 1987.

JOHN GEIGER

David Adams and Lois Smith in rehearsal in the early days of the National Ballet (*photo by John deVisser*).

Adams, David, ballet dancer (b at Winnipeg 16 Nov 1928). Known primarily as the NATIONAL BALLET OF CANADA's first principal male dancer, he played an important role in establishing the company. He began his training and performing career with Gweneth LLOYD's Winnipeg Ballet (later ROYAL WINNIPEG BALLET) and matured as a fine classical dancer in England and Canada. He performed as lead soloist in both countries, notably with the National Ballet of Canada 1951-61, the London Festival Ballet 1961-69 and the Royal Ballet 1970-76, excelling in the great classical male roles. He returned to Canada as ballet master to the Alberta Ballet 1977-79 and he taught at the Edmonton School of Ballet 1984-86. In 1985 he also became coach and choreographer of Ballet North, a company of young dancers.

JILLIAN M. OFFICER

Adams, Frank Dawson, geologist (b at Montréal 17 Sept 1859; d there 26 Dec 1942). A member of the GEOLOGICAL SURVEY OF CANADA 1880-89, Logan Professor of Geology at McGill 1892-1922, dean of applied science at McGill 1905-19, and acting principal and VP there 1919-22, Adams was Canada's most eminent geologist of the first half of the 20th century. Applying petrographic techniques learned at Heidelberg, where he obtained his PhD, he laid the foundations of modern igneous and metamorphic petrography in Canada. His experimental work on the flow of brittle rocks proved as revolutionary in geology as the work in physics of his colleague Ernest RUTHERFORD, establishing him as the founder of modern structural geology.

A prominent educator, Adams strongly promoted development of graduate studies in Canada. In 1918, as a lt-col overseas, he became deputy director of KHAKI UNIVERSITY, an innovative Canadian plan to further the education of troops awaiting demobilization. After retiring in 1922 he produced the first geological map of Ceylon [Sri Lanka] and published his definitive history, *The Birth and Development of the Geological Sciences* (1938).

P.R. EAKINS

Adams, Thomas, town planner (b near Edinburgh, Scot 10 Sept 1871; d in Sussex, Eng 24 Mar 1940). A leading British planning pioneer, Adams subsequently became one of the founders of the Canadian planning movement. Adams became acquainted with Patrick Geddes and the Garden City movement headed by Ebenezer Howard and was one of the founders and first president of the British Town Planning Inst. In 1914 he became planning adviser to the COMMISSION OF CONSERVATION, established in Canada in 1909. Adams provided great impetus to Canadian planning and promoted the creation of comprehensive legislative, institutional and professional structures. He wrote extensively in *Town Planning and Conservation of Life* and in 1917 published *Rural Planning and Development*. He founded the Civic Improvement League in 1915 and the Town Planning Inst of Canada in 1919. His achievements include planning the town of Kipawa (now Témiscaming), Qué, and drafting an urban-renewal scheme for Halifax following the famous HALIFAX EXPLOSION in 1917 which destroyed many residential districts. This scheme provided Adams with a unique opportunity to use his professional expertise to fashion innovations in town planning and public housing. Adams's influence declined following the demise of the Commission of Conservation in 1921. From 1921 to 1923 he was occupied with projects for the National Parks Division and between 1923 and 1930 was director of the regional plan for New York C and environs. Between 1914 and 1930 Adams was undoubtedly the leading planning figure in Canada, if not the

world. Despite his noteworthy sojourn in Canada, however, he did not succeed in fashioning a uniquely Canadian style of planning. *See also* URBAN AND REGIONAL PLANNING.

O.W. SAARINEN

Reading: Michael Simpson, *Thomas Adams and the Modern Planning Movement... 1900-1940* (1985).

Adaskin, Harry, musician, educator, broadcaster (b at Riga, Latvia 6 Oct 1901), elder brother of Murray and John ADASKIN. An orchestral and chamber violinist, he formed a duo in 1923 with his future wife, pianist Frances Marr, which toured widely in Canada and abroad, often premiering Canadian compositions. From 1928 to 1938 he served as second violin of the HART HOUSE STRING QUARTET. Adaskin established the music program of UBC in 1946, teaching there until 1973. An excellent raconteur whose musical insights were enriched by a knowledge of painting and literature, he was host of several CBC Radio series. In 1975 he was made an Officer of the Order of Canada.

BARCLAY MCMILLAN

Adaskin, John, musician, radio producer, administrator (b at Toronto 4 June 1908; d there 4 Mar 1964), younger brother of Harry and Murray ADASKIN. He was an enthusiastic supporter of young musicians and Canadian composition, and his CBC Radio productions, "Opportunity Knocks" and "Singing Stars of Tomorrow" (in which he also performed as conductor), helped many aspiring artists establish careers. Appointed executive secretary of the Canadian Music Centre in 1961, Adaskin promoted the use of Canadian music in the schools by commissioning composers to write music suitable for student performers. The John Adaskin Project continues this promotion of Canadian music.

BARCLAY MCMILLAN

Adaskin, Murray, composer, educator, violinist, conductor (b at Toronto 28 Mar 1906), brother of Harry and John ADASKIN. An orchestral and chamber musician, he turned to composition in the mid-1940s after studies with John WEINZWEIG. His compositions for a wide variety of performance media, including opera, employ a highly personal neoclassical idiom, frequently using Canadian folk material. In 1952 he became head of music at U Sask. He was conductor of the Saskatoon Symphony Orchestra 1957-60. A most effective spokesman for Canadian music, Adaskin was named an Officer of the Order of Canada in 1981.

BARCLAY MCMILLAN

Reading: G. Lazarevich, *The Musical World of Frances James and Murray Adaskin* (1987).

Administrative Law is one of the 3 basic areas of public law dealing with the relationship between government and its citizens, the other 2 being CONSTITUTIONAL LAW and CRIMINAL LAW. The major purpose of administrative law is to ensure that the activities of government are authorized by Parliament or by provincial legislatures, and that laws are implemented and administered in a fair and reasonable manner. Administrative law is based on the principle that government action, whatever form it takes, must (strictly speaking) be legal, and that citizens who are affected by unlawful acts of government officials must have effective remedies if the Canadian system of public administration is to be accepted and maintained.

The complex nature of the modern state is such that elected representatives are not capable of passing laws to govern every situation. Many of their lawmaking powers, as well as the power to administer and implement the laws, are therefore delegated to administrative agencies. These agencies are involved in virtually every area of government activity and affect ordinary citizens in many ways, whether these citizens be homeowners needing a building permit to erect a new room, injured employees seeking workers' compensation, farmers selling their produce, or owners of a trucking company wishing to transport goods between Vancouver and Montréal.

Government activity is controlled in various ways. First, according to the Canadian Constitution, elected politicians may pass any laws they please, provided such laws do not infringe upon the rights and liberties guaranteed by the CANADIAN CHARTER OF RIGHTS AND FREEDOMS and do not attempt to regulate legislative activity reserved for another level of government. Administrative authorities, as inferior bodies to whom the power to interpret and implement such laws is delegated, are also subject to these constitutional limitations. Second, delegating legislation defines the powers to be allocated to the agency (or minister) and sets forth the requirements to be met before the authority may act. For example, if entitlement to a government benefit depends upon the establishment of certain disputed facts or the interpretation of an ambiguous statute, the applicable legislation will sometimes provide for a hearing before another group of officials (constituted as a "board" or "tribunal") who will make the final decision. In some cases, a decision of the board or ADMINISTRATIVE TRIBUNAL can be appealed to the courts if there is an error of law or a more serious error of fact. Third, certain COMMON LAW principles, derived originally from the courts of England and subsequently developed by Canadian courts, impose limits or obligations upon tribunals. The best example is the principle that administrative authorities must act in accordance with "natural justice," which imposes certain procedural obligations that an authority must meet in exercising power. Common-law doctrine only operates where no statutory legislation covers the matters at issue.

If citizens feel that an administrative authority has made a decision affecting them that violates a constitutional, statutory or common-law principle, they may ask a court of law to review the actions of the authority. Canadian courts will only exercise their control over administrative authorities if the authority exceeds its jurisdiction, if it commits an error of law, or if it follows improper or unfair procedures.

According to the concept of jurisdiction, government bodies must act within the scope of the powers delegated to them by their enabling legislation. If these bodies take action without legal authority, they are said to have exceeded their jurisdiction and their action may be reversed by the courts. It is the role of the courts to interpret the enabling legislation and to determine whether it permits the action which the tribunal proposes.

In some cases, the power granted to administrative authorities is subject to express limits found in the enabling legislation. For example, the power given to a tribunal to regulate rents in apartment buildings of 10 units or more does not give it jurisdiction to regulate rents in buildings with only 4 units. A further example deals with the delegation of power by authorities. Courts have required that powers be exercised only by those to whom they are entrusted. Thus, members of a tribunal empowered to grant liquor licences to restaurants may not delegate this power to a staff member or an outside person.

In other cases, the legislation contains no defined limits on an authority's power; the courts will imply limits to prevent what is termed the "abuse of power" or to ensure that the power can be properly exercised. For example, in the case of the rent tribunal, a court will not permit the tribunal, as part of its power to regulate rents, to require the landlord to supply certain appliances. On the other hand, where ministers have the power to issue visas to foreign visitors, the vast number of applications and the nature of the task implies that subordinate officials may perform this duty in place of the minister.

The concept of jurisdiction does not address the merits of the decision made by government officials. Generally, it is not the function of the courts to intervene in the conduct of government. However, courts may intervene where an authority has abused its power. There are several examples of this. A decision must be made on the basis of relevant considerations; reliance upon irrelevant considerations or the failure to consider relevant ones will enable a court to review the decision. Further, an authority cannot exercise its power for a purpose other than the purpose for which the power was intended. For example, if a minister had the power to close a hospital only for sanitary or safety reasons, he could not use this power for financial and budgetary reasons. A tribunal may not bind itself or limit its discretion by making general rules that apply to every case. Each case must be decided on its own merits. In addition, there must be some evidence before a tribunal to justify decisions of fact. Finally a decision cannot be unreasonable to the extent that it is one which no reasonable person in the position of the decision maker would have made.

The third ground of judicial review of administrative action deals with procedure. Administrative agencies must follow proper procedure in arriving at their decisions. The various procedures stem from the basic requirement of the "right to be heard." In some cases, a statute or regulation will set out the basic procedures that govern the process of decision making, such as what notice must be given of a hearing and to whom, the right to have counsel, the right to call evidence and to cross-examine witnesses. Where a statute establishes no procedures, administrative law will enforce certain common-law principles to ensure that all persons subjected to government action are treated fairly. These are the previously mentioned principles of "natural justice." They have 2 basic objectives: that no person shall be condemned without a hearing, and that any decision must be made by a person or tribunal who is impartial and not biased.

What constitutes procedural fairness will depend upon the nature of the power being exercised, the party affected, the consequences of the intended action, and the practicalities of requiring time-consuming procedures. In serious cases affecting individuals, such as revoking a doctor's licence to practise medicine, procedures similar to those found in a court of law will be imposed. In other cases, such as the decision to terminate a lease in a public-subsidized apartment building, the courts have held that there is only a "duty to act fairly," which is satisfied if the tenant is informed of the complaints made against him or her and is provided with an opportunity to answer or to remedy them. In a few cases, such as a Cabinet decision on a petition from a tribunal that awarded a rate increase to a large private utility, the courts have held there is no duty of fairness to be followed because the decision maker, the Cabinet, was performing a legislative function of a political nature.

The ability of the citizen to challenge administrative decisions in court depends upon the availability of an appeal or judicial review and the status of the individual who comes before the court. As far as the former is concerned, rights of appeal to the courts are often provided by legislation. In other situations, the historic and constitutional ability of the "superior" courts of law to review the actions of "inferior" administrative bodies must be relied upon. In the past, the procedure invoked to seek judicial review was by way of historic "prerogative" remedies, each with its own technical legal requirements. Today, in some provinces, statutory reforms have simplified these procedures into the single remedy of "judicial review," which encompasses all of the historical remedies yet provides the courts with the discretion not to intervene in administrative activity if relief is not justified. The superior courts in each province are responsible for granting these remedies where provincial administrative action is challenged. The decisions or actions of a federal administrative agency are reviewed by the Federal Court of Canada.

The second factor affecting the ability of individuals to obtain judicial review of administrative action is related to the status of the individual to sue. In many cases, the individual is directly affected by a particular decision, such as the termination of a disability pension, and this does not present a problem. In other cases, individuals challenging the constitutionality of legislation may seek to represent a broader public interest. Nevertheless the courts have generally permitted such citizens to proceed where they can show that a serious doubt exists about the validity of the legislation and where there is no other reasonable or effective means of bringing the issue before the courts.

In most cases, a citizen's remedy is restricted to having an administrative decision reversed. The court will, in some instances, grant the relief requested (eg, granting a licence where one is refused) or, as is more likely, will send the matter back to the administrative agency to be decided upon by a proper interpretation of a statute or of proper and relevant facts. In rare cases, eg, when the administrative action was not only illegal but was taken in bad faith, damages will be awarded. In RONCARELLI V DUPLESSIS the Supreme Court of Canada held the premier of Québec liable for $25 000 for wrongfully cancelling a liquor licence because he did not approve of the religious activity of the licence-holder.

In some situations, a statute will provide that the decision of the tribunal cannot be appealed to or reviewed by the courts. Often this occurs in fields of specialized expertise, such as labour relations, where it is felt the courts do not possess the experience or understanding necessary for making final decisions. Such restrictions on appeals have not prevented the courts from reviewing the decisions of these tribunals where there is an excess of jurisdiction. However, the courts have recognized that these tribunals may make decisions that the court, if it were deciding the issue, would not make, either because of its interpretation of the relevant statute or because of its view of the facts. In such cases, the Supreme Court of Canada has stated that the tribunal has acted outside its jurisdiction only if it has reached a decision that is "patently unreasonable." Even where administrative agencies are not protected by such clauses, the courts have tended not to interfere in areas of specialized or technical expertise, such as health professions, securities, urban planning and nuclear energy.   J.G. COWAN

Reading: D.P. Jones and A.S. de Villars, Principles of Administrative Law (1985).

Administrative Tribunals exercise powers delegated by Parliament or a provincial legislature. Examples include the National Energy Board, the Alberta Liquor Control Board, the CANADIAN RADIO-TELEVISION AND TELECOMMUNICATIONS COMMISSION, the Immigration Appeal Board and the Ontario Municipal Board. Usually permanent, tribunals deal with a specialized subject and are frequently established in such a way that their activities are beyond partisan politics or direct government control. Because tribunal members generally are not judges, they do not enjoy total judicial immunity and their activities are subject to judicial review (*see* ADMINISTRATIVE LAW). Only the legislative branch can amend or repeal legislation establishing the tribunal or its terms of reference. Frequently, no appeal on the substantive merits of a tribunal decision is permitted, but when there is such an appeal it may have to be made to another administrative tribunal. Parliament need not make provision for appeals to the courts (although the legislative branch may specifically create such an appeal), but the superior courts always retain their constitutional right to determine whether the tribunal's actions lie within the latter's jurisdiction. DAVID P. JONES

Admiralty (short for Board of Admiralty), a British government department which, between its inception in the early 18th century and its amalgamation into the Ministry of Defence in 1964, was responsible for the conduct of naval affairs. In all matters concerning colonial defence, including the defence of Canada, the Admiralty was a necessary participant because of its role in transporting supplies and ensuring maritime security. *See also* COLONIAL OFFICE.
STUART R.J. SUTHERLAND

Adoption, the legal process severing ties between a child and its biological parents (or "birth parents" as they are called today) who are unable or unwilling to care for it, and creating new ties between a child and people who are not its natural parents.

Adoption, which is governed by provincial law, was introduced into Canadian common law (*see* FAMILY LAW) beginning in New Brunswick in 1873 to save "illegitimate" children from the stigma of illegitimacy and place them with couples unable to have their own children (though some provinces, eg, Ontario, have recently amended their laws to remove the status of "illegitimacy"). Because more unwed mothers now keep their own children, those adopted are often older, sometimes physically or mentally handicapped and sometimes from disadvantaged groups, although increasing numbers of legitimate children are being adopted from families that ended in divorce. There are usually different stages in the adoption process, for example the applicants are screened by welfare authorities before a child is placed, although the restrictions formerly employed to restrict joint applications to adopt to married persons may infringe the equality provisions of the CANADIAN CHARTER OF RIGHTS AND FREEDOMS. In some provinces independent adoptions are possible, provided no payment is involved. The restrictions on advertising or payment of money in return for a child are difficult to enforce given the lack of children available for adoption. There then follows a probationary placement in the adoptive parents' home and finally a court hearing to determine whether an adoption order should be made. If an adoption order is made, the adoptive parents become the legal parents of the child, who acquires succession rights and the family name of the adoptive family, although in some provinces the child may retain rights against his natural family under provincial succession laws. The adoption process normally requires the consent of the natural parents, though that of the father of an illegitimate child is not always necessary. In some provinces the consent of the natural father is normally required and in most provinces he can seek custody of the child in order to defeat the custody application. The court has power to dispense with the need for such consent in specified circumstances. If the child is of a specified age (often 12 years) its consent is also necessary. Since 1982 in Québec the Civil Code has governed adoption with much the same effect as does

the common law in the rest of Canada. Earlier laws had attempted to make it impossible for children to be adopted outside their religion at birth, and this was a manifestation of the strong clerical influence on Québec society.

Adoption is a social as well as a legal process. The practice of adoption has changed in response to changing social attitudes and needs, but the legal process has not kept pace with these changes. There is now mounting pressure from adopted persons for contact with their birth parents to be made possible, and vice versa. Some provinces, such as Ontario, operate a system (the Voluntary Disclosure Registry) to facilitate voluntary disclosure, where adopted persons, having attained the age of majority, can indicate to the registry that they would like to contact their birth parents, and if the birth parents have registered the same request the connection will be made. Before adopted persons reach the age of majority the adoptive parents can veto contact with the birth parents. Other current issues include the debate over the child's right to consent to adoption (at present in Ontario, for example, a child 7 years of age or older must consent); the possibility of subsidized adoptions to facilitate adoption by parents who otherwise could not financially support a child; and the consideration, in recent years, of the concept of open adoption in which birth parents and adoptive parents would co-operate constructively in the adoption process.
ALASTAIR BISSETT-JOHNSON AND JULIUS GREY

Adult Education in Canada is both a field of practice and (since the 1960s) a field of study. According to UNESCO, as a field of practice adult education denotes the entire body of organized educational processes, whatever the content, level or method, whether formal or informal, and whether the processes prolong or replace initial education in schools, colleges, universities or apprenticeship systems. The term "adult" usually means someone beyond the legal school-leaving age. Other than that, there is no upper age limit for learning.

Adult education as a field of study was originally interdisciplinary, borrowing from psychology, sociology, history, philosophy and the medical sciences. Like other fields of study, it has a particular body of knowledge and areas of specialization. University academic programs in adult education are concerned with teaching as well as research. At present, 8 universities in Canada offer a master's degree in adult education, and 3 (the universities of BC, Montréal and Toronto) offer a doctorate. These courses and programs prepare people as instructors, counsellors, community workers, administrators, evaluators, trainers and as professional development co-ordinators. Adult education is therefore really a generic term, variously used to mean a program, a movement, a subject matter, and sometimes a method. In particular, it reflects a specific philosophy about learning and teaching based on the assumption that adults can and want to learn, that they are able and willing to take responsibility for that learning, and that the learning itself should respond to their needs.

Origins Adults have always been engaged in learning, whether for survival, creativity, communal and individual interaction, or personal growth. In the 1800s the MECHANICS' INSTITUTES in Ontario, Québec and Nova Scotia provided information and learning opportunities to workers. Before Confederation, 1867, Queen's University was involved in extramural or extension work by offering public lectures, and the YMCA offered night classes for adults and educational programs for the military. Farmers' Institutes were established, and by the late 1800s the National Council of Women had been founded; home and school associations had expanded; public lectures were being given in many communities; Women's Institutes had been established, and educational programs were being organized by religious and other groups. All these programs were developed in response to adult needs and interests.

Where organizations offering appropriate programs did not already exist, new organizations were created or existing ones changed their mandate of responsibility. An important related development was the establishment of and the rapid increase in publicly supported libraries.

In 1899 Frontier College was established by Alfred Fitzpatrick to extend learning opportunities to those adults (mostly men) who lived and worked in remote communities, such as logging, mining and railway camps (*see* LITERACY). Much later, Frontier College and other organizations extended educational services to people in prisons, factories and farm kitchens, and to fishermen, rural people and immigrants.

From 1900 to 1925 programs for adults continued to expand. KHAKI UNIVERSITY was organized in England for Canadian military personnel returning to Canada after WWI. During this time the Workers' Education Association, which provided opportunities for working people, was introduced to Canada from the UK. With the development of the West, universities extended their educational services to rural and remote communities by means of lectures, debating competitions, musical concerts and motion pictures. Indeed, U of A and U Sask were originally set up to offer extension courses. In the mid-1920s U of A used radio for EDUCATIONAL BROADCASTING and in the early 1930s established the BANFF CENTRE. The efforts of ST FRANCIS XAVIER UNIVERSITY in Antigonish, NS, were especially effective in helping people stricken by the Great Depression, culminating in the establishment of an extensive co-operative movement (*see* ANTIGONISH MOVEMENT). Later the International Coady Institute was established to conduct training courses in the philosophy and practice of co-operation for representatives from developing countries.

Experimental work in public broadcasting, the formation of the Canadian Institute on Public Affairs (*see* COUCHICHING CONFERENCE), the founding of the NATIONAL FILM BOARD (1939), and 2 national radio forums in the 1940s – Citizen's Forum (1943) and FARM RADIO FORUM (1944) – all made use of media technology for learning and educating. Later developments included the use of satellite and television.

In 1935, the Canadian Association for Adult Education was established, with E.A. CORBETT as its first executive director. Prior to taking up this position, Corbett was director of U of Alberta's extension division and was the person responsible for Citizen's Forum, Farm Radio Forum as well as the Banff Centre.

In 1958 the establishment of the Quetico Residential Conference and Training Centre in northwestern Ontario provided adults with further opportunities for learning. From the 1930s to the 1960s, educational programs were initiated by the Canadian Chamber of Commerce; the Labour College of Canada was established in Montréal (1962); and there was increased government support for training and education, eg, the Technical and Vocational Training Assistance Act in 1960 and the Agricultural Rehabilitation and Development Act in 1961 (*see* EDUCATION, HIGHER; EDUCATION, TECHNICAL).

Internationally, Canadians contributed to the development of adult education through such organizations as the International Congress of University Continuing Education, and UNESCO.

With support of participants from the UNESCO conference in Tokyo (1972), and under the leadership of a Canadian adult educator, Dr J. Roby KIDD, the International Council for Adult Education (ICAE) was established in 1973. After Dr Kidd died in 1982, the ICAE established an annual Roby Kidd Award for significant and innovative work in Adult Education. *Convergence,* the journal of the ICAE (begun in 1968), is now published in 4 languages and circulated to 76 countries from its Toronto headquarters.

Four major national adult-education associations have been founded in Canada: the Canadian Association for Adult Education (CAAE, 1935); the Institut canadien d'education des adultes (ICEA, 1952), which primarily serves the French-language sectors of adult education in Canada; the Canadian Association for University Continuing Education (CAUCE, 1954); and the Canadian Association for the Study of Adult Education (CASAE, 1981).

Structures and Agencies Continuing education has become a way of life for many adults in Canada. Organized nonformal learning exists at all levels of government and within trade unions, co-operatives, industrial and commercial enterprises, hospitals, prisons, religious as well as cultural organizations, and health and fitness programs. Adult education takes place in factories, offices, gymnasiums, lecture halls, classrooms, libraries, museums, residential centres and churches, through a wide variety of teaching and learning methods.

Adult education also takes place in formal settings, as part of credited programs within schools, colleges and universities. Such agencies also engage in adult education nonformally through their departments of continuing education and extension. For example, the rapid expansion of the COMMUNITY COLLEGE and CEGEP systems in the 1960s and 1970s added greatly to the educational resources available to adults. Usually the structure of adult education is the responsibility of an instructor or a planner, or in the case of industry and government, a person in charge of professional development. Increasingly, these persons are seeing themselves as adult educators.

Participation The first national survey of adult education in Canada (1934) revealed the wide variety of activities and the large numbers of people that were involved in some kind of purposeful learning. Research by TVOntario indicated that 75% or more of the adults surveyed were or wished to be involved in further learning. A 1982 Gallup study for CAAE and ICEA of Canadians 18 years and over revealed that 34% were involved in some kind of formal or nonformal educational program. A 1985 national survey gave comparable figures on participation. However, most surveys document the participation of adult learners in visible and publicly supported institutions such as schools and colleges, but a large number of adults are involved in some form of purposeful learning outside these institutions. Nevertheless, many adult Canadians do not participate in any available education programs. The implications of this are especially important to Canada, which has one of the highest levels of functionally illiterate adults of any industrialized country. Greater efforts are being made to extend the educational opportunities of this groups of adults.

Issues and Implications The attempts to develop government and institutional legislation that will economically support adult education parallel the increasing involvement of adults in educational programs. Also, many barriers, such as geographical distances and physical handicaps, prevent certain groups (eg, the handicapped, the isolated, the elderly, the undereducated, certain cultural groups, and women with small children)

from participating in these programs (*see* DISTANCE LEARNING).

As adult education develops as a field of practice and a medium for research and study, participation and support will also have to increase. Within the context of adult education itself, the varied ways of learning that have been developed have blurred the formerly rigid roles of teacher and student, a fact that has been held up as proof that all adults, whether teachers or students, have something to teach (from life experience or from training) as well as something to learn from each other. Adult education as a field of practice and study has made an indelible contribution to society through its expression of respect for adults as responsible learners, as instigators of their own learning processes, and as valuable resources.

JAMES A. DRAPER

Reading: D.H. Brundage and D. MacKeracher, *Adult Learning Principles and Their Application to Program Planning* (1980); J.R. Kidd, *How Adults Learn* (1976); Secretary of State and Statistics Canada, *One in Every Five: A Survey of Adult Education in Canada* (1985).

Advertising, the paid use of selected space or time in a communications medium by an identified organization or individual to present a message, is essentially a 20th-century development. Advertisers want to persuade people that certain goods or services are worth buying, to enhance the advertiser's image or to present a viewpoint. Advertising and the communications media have developed together; as technology and communications have progressed, the forms and uses of advertising have changed. In style and content, advertising provides an index of the political, social, economic and artistic climate of the times.

The first formal advertisement in Canada was an offer of butter for sale that appeared in 1752 in an official government publication, the *Halifax Gazette.* In 1764 the *Quebec Gazette* (later renamed the *Chronicle-Telegraph*) was founded, as much to carry news of merchandise as events. To reach Canada's 5 million people in 1900, advertisers could choose among 4 print media: 112 daily newspapers serving 570 000 subscribers; general-interest magazines; special-interest magazines; and street posters, which delivered inexpensive and graphic messages, often at or near retail stores. The most effective vehicle for fostering a national market was the mail-order catalogue, especially Eaton's. Not an advertising medium in the strict sense (because space was not for sale), the seasonal catalogues reached millions of farm and town people with advertising for a wide range of merchandise.

By 1889 newspapers were carrying enough advertising to encourage Anson McKim to open an office in Montréal to arrange the placement of advertisements in Ontario newspapers. He created a completely new type of business. Because the papers paid him a commission, his company became Canada's first advertising agency. He

Percentage of Net Advertising Revenue by Media	
Electronic Media	
Radio	9.1%
Television	16.6%
Print Media	
Newspapers:	
Dailies	22.7%
Weekend supplements	0.7%
Weeklies	5.6%
Business papers	2.9%
Farm papers	0.4%
General magazines	4.3%
Directories	6.3%
Catalogue, direct mail	23.7%
Outdoor	7.3%
Other	0.4%

The 15 Largest Buyers of Advertising Space and Time in 1986		
		$millions
1.	Government of Canada	63.7
2.	Procter & Gamble	51.1
3.	John Labatt	37.5
4.	Molson Cos	32.0
5.	General Motors	27.3
6.	Unilever	27.1
7.	Ontario Government	26.0
8.	The Thomson Group	24.0
9.	McDonald's Restaurants	21.0
10.	Bell Canada Enterprises	20.1
11.	Ford Motor Co	19.4
12.	Coca-Cola	18.7
13.	Dart & Kraft	18.5
14.	Rothmans	18.4
15.	General Foods	18.4

Figures compiled by Media Measurement Services, Inc, Toronto.

brought some order to the newspaper advertising business and deflated newspapers' exaggerated circulation claims by publishing the *Canadian Newspaper Directory.* Another early agency was McConnell Advertising, launched in London, Ont, about 1900.

In 1919 Canada issued its first radio-transmitting licence to Marconi's experimental wireless telephony station in Montréal (XWA, which later became CFCF), and by 1928 more than 60 radio stations had been licensed to operate. Radio became an extremely successful advertising medium; by the end of the 1920s Canadians were complaining of too much broadcast advertising. In 1932 the federal government, deciding that broadcasting should not be left entirely to private enterprise, created the Canadian Radio Broadcasting Commission, later renamed the Canadian Broadcasting Corporation, with authority to own stations in major cities and a monopoly to operate radio networks. In 1953 the government stopped collecting the annual licence fee, funding the CBC directly from public funds and by the mid-1970s advertising had been dropped entirely from CBC radio stations.

Soon after WWII, TV signals started flowing into Canada from US border cities. Alarmed at the number of Canadian antennae tuned to US stations, CBC opened TV stations in Toronto and Montréal in 1952 and licensed privately owned stations for other centres. TV's persuasive blend of sight, sound and motion (and later colour) made it a powerful advertising medium. Within 8 years, advertisers were spending $50 million a year in TV. Canadians' appetite for TV led to the construction of huge cable TV systems in the 1970s, multiplying the number of channels available in millions of homes. Advertisers wanting to reach a mass audience must now spread their expenditures among many stations. Cable networks may have a powerful impact; 2-way TV, for instance, could allow viewers to order a product by pushing a button on a home control unit. Pay TV, which relies on direct charges to the viewer rather than on advertising or government funding, also altered the advertising patterns for broadcasting.

In 1986 advertisers spent about $6.7 billion in the various media, up from nearly $4.3 billion in 1981. Most items sold in supermarkets are packaged goods; by means of media advertising, manufacturers try to influence shoppers in their selection of products from the shelves. Two of the largest companies, Procter & Gamble and John Labatt, spent $89 million on advertising in Canada in 1986. Big spenders are food and alcohol manufacturers, automobile and oil companies, banks and fast-food chains.

Advertisers are classified as either national or local. National advertisers sell their products or services in more than one market, usually in the major markets across the country. The local advertiser, typically a retailer, serves one market only and restricts advertising to that audience. A fast-growing segment of advertising aimed to promote ideas is "advocacy advertising," undertaken by corporations, professional associations, special-interest groups or labour unions that want to communicate their viewpoints in space where they have control of the message, rather than relying on the news media to interpret and carry their views.

Elections are advocacy advertising campaigns, but politicians already in power also use advertising to explain their programs and policies. Governments have become big advertisers; the various departments of the federal government were Canada's largest advertiser in 1986, spending $64 million; the Ontario and Québec governments spent $37 million. Advertising by other provinces and by crown corporations added several more millions of dollars.

Major Advertising Media There are 115 daily NEWSPAPERS in Canada, with total circulations of 5.7 million; a 1986 readership survey indicated that 66% of adults read newspapers Monday to Friday. Daily newspapers receive 22.7% of the dollars spent on advertising and direct mail and catalogues receive 23.7% of the dollars. Direct mail and catalogues have dramatically increased their share: in 1976 it was 19.4% as compared to 29.5% for daily newspapers. In 1986 total advertising revenues for all daily newspapers in Canada reached $1.5 billion, a gain of more than 45% in 7 years. National advertising accounted for 19% of the total and local advertising for 54%; classified ads made up the rest. TELEVISION is by far the largest advertising medium. Canadians are avid TV viewers and advertisers channel 61% of their total spending into TV. Advertising expenditures have been climbing faster for TV than for any other medium: up 114% from 1976 to 1981 and up another 58% 1981-86. A 30-second commercial on the CTV network's 16 stations could cost, depending on the show and the seasonal rate period, from $950 to $13 500.

Radio was forced to redefine its strengths with the advent of TV. Today, it is again successful as an advertising medium. Comparatively inexpensive, it is useful to advertisers who want to repeat their messages frequently. Used creatively, it can invoke the listener's own imagination. Canada's 346 private radio stations earned $610 million in advertising revenues in 1986, 76% of that from local advertisers. In fact, commercials provide most of the revenue of private radio stations.

General MAGAZINES in Canada, aimed at general and leisure interests rather than business or professional interests, are also very important to advertisers. Consumer magazines have 2 methods of distribution: paid circulation magazines are those available only to a paying audience; controlled-circulation magazines are provided free to selected audiences whom the publishers believe to be valuable to advertisers. Although controlled circulation has been common among business publications, it was only in the 1970s that the technique was adopted for many consumer magazines. The later 1970s saw the advent of local TV and entertainment magazines produced by daily newspapers as part of their weekend packages. Net advertising revenues for general magazines rose from $198 million in 1981 to $287 million in 1986.

Community newspapers are usually published once or twice a week. They have changed their role since the 1950s, when most were owned by local printing plants. Now, many are group owned and serve population segments within or surrounding cities. One such newspaper, *Mississauga News*, has an average circulation of 71 000.

Except for English weeklies in Québec, community newspapers have grown in number, size and stature as a result of citizen participation and of economies afforded by computerized typesetting and offset-printing techniques. Advertising revenues of $55.6 million in 1971 climbed to a total of $374 million by 1986. Most of this advertising ($345 million) is local and the rest ($29 million) is national.

Canada has more than 500 business publications, with circulations ranging from a few thousand to more than 100 000. They carry advertising and editorial content of interest to people in business or the professions. The majority of business publications are produced by a half-dozen publishing houses, the 2 largest being MACLEAN HUNTER LIMITED and SOUTHAM Business Publications. Many magazines offer their advertisers other services and activities, such as trade shows and seminars. Revenues have increased from $55 million in 1975 to $196 million in 1986.

In the 1970s the outdoor advertising industry faced a challenge to its existence, when Canadians became increasingly concerned to protect all aspects of the environment. In self-defence, the companies and the advertising industry turned to strict self-regulation. They eliminated some signs, restricted others to commercial thoroughfares, declared a 0.4 km setback from highways and improved design.

Most Canadians now seem to accept outdoor advertising. The industry has expanded in other directions: advertising in bus shelters and on shopping-mall posters, and spectacular displays with moving parts and elaborate lighting. Outdoor advertising is an economical medium. The advertiser can make a prominent statement at low cost, often to supplement advertising in other media, but the sales message must be effective even when seen for only a moment. Transit advertising, located inside and outside of vehicles and in subway, bus and commuter stations, is widespread. Point-of-purchase communication includes both sign and package advertising. Not an advertising medium in the usual sense, it offers a reminder message in or near the retail outlet, in the form of window or shelf stickers and special display cases. Total outdoor advertising revenues increased from $280 million in 1981 to $484 million by 1986.

Advertising Agencies Though many of the largest advertisers have advertising departments within their companies, and a few even have their own in-house agency operations and place advertising themselves, most national advertising is prepared and placed by ad agencies. Some of the largest local advertisers also employ agencies. Agencies are complex organizations that offer clients a range of services: media planning and placement, account management, graphic design and copy writing, production and research to study audience reaction and response. A number of major research organizations have been set up by agencies, advertisers and media to provide objective audience data. The Bureau of Broadcast Measurement, for example, provides regular studies of radio and TV audiences. These surveys estimate how many people of each sex in different age categories listen to or watch various programs. The Print Measurement Bureau analyses the readership of a number of consumer magazines and provides demographic information on readers' age, education, income, marital status, occupation and product usage. Other research companies specialize in measuring the degree to which people remember advertising they have watched, heard or read.

Advertising Regulation Advertising in Canada is highly regulated. The practice of advertising law has become a profitable legal specialty. The provinces regulate liquor, pharmaceutical, business and professional advertising; the federal government regulates every area that comes under its jurisdiction, such as food and drugs. Because government licences are required for all radio and TV stations, broadcasting is regulated more than the print media. The CRTC requires preclearance of all commercials for beer, wine, cider, food, drugs, cosmetics, medical devices and children's products. In 1986, for example, it held hearings in order to review progress made in the broadcasting and advertising industries in eliminating sex-role stereotyping. Beer and wine advertising is examined by Health and Welfare Canada and by provincial liquor boards. Food commercials are studied by the Dept of Consumer and Corporate Affairs. Health and Welfare looks at commercials for drugs, cosmetics and medical devices. Children's commercials are checked by an Advertising Standards Council that includes representatives of the Consumers' Assn of Canada, advertisers, agencies, media and the CRTC. The CBC has its own commercial acceptance process and the CTV, Global and Atlantic TV networks are similarly served by a Telecaster Committee. Beyond these clearly regulated areas is a misty region of taste, sense and judgement. Here there are self-regulatory codes prepared by the Canadian Advertising Advisory Board (CAAB) in conjunction with governments and manufacturers. Through its Advertising Standards Council, CAAB previews advertising on request and bans any advertising in breach of its codes. One issue that has developed in the mid-to-late 1980s is whether tobacco advertising should be banned.

Careers in Advertising Advertising includes business, show business, science and art. The industry offers a range of work, in agencies, advertising departments of large companies and among the media and suppliers. No single course of education covers them all. Employers often require university, or at least community-college, education. They want commerce and business administration graduates for account-management work, art-college training for art directors and illustrators, sociology and psychology majors for market research, journalism or English literature backgrounds for copy writing. Several industry associations offer night courses in advertising. The Institute of Canadian Advertising, an association of advertising agencies, sponsors a 3-year night course leading to designation as a certified advertising agency practitioner, open to those with at least one year's practical experience.

JERRY GOODIS

Aeolian Landform, a feature of the Earth's surface produced by either erosive or constructive action of the wind. The word derives from Aeolus, the Greek god of the winds. Wind erosion processes consist of abrasion, ie, the scouring of exposed surfaces by the sand-blasting action of wind-borne material; and deflation, ie, the re-

Large active dune area advancing into William R on right and into forest in foreground. South side of Lake Athabasca (*courtesy P.P. David*).

moval of sand-sized and smaller particles by the wind. Sand is transported short distances to form dunes; finer silt is transported farther to form loess. Wind transportation causes attrition of the moving particles, which rub one another and develop characteristic surface frosting and pitting. Wind abrasion produces faceted pebbles (ventifacts) found in certain parts of Canada; furrowed bedrock surfaces common in N Saskatchewan; and yardangs (sharp-crested ridges carved from soft but coherent deposits) found mainly in desert regions. Deflation produces wind pits, deflation depressions and basins, all common in dune areas in Canada. Large-scale wind erosion contributed to the formation of valleys or coulees in S Alberta. The process of winnowing through deflation, whereby the smaller grains are carried off by the wind, leaves behind a layer of pebbles and boulders called lag gravel or reg which protects the ground surface from further erosion. These layers are common in some dune areas in Canada, the most spectacular ones occurring S of Lk Athabasca.

Sand dunes are not limited to desert regions, since aeolian features that were once active and are now stabilized are widespread in many temperate and cold zones. Sand-dune areas cover about 26 000 km² or approximately 0.27% of the total area of Canada: Alberta has 45%; Saskatchewan, 36%; Manitoba, 10%. The concentration of dune areas on the prairies results from the availability of suitable sandy deposits left behind by glaciers, the frequent occurrence of dry, westerly winds and the openness of the region. The dry, westerly winds produced the easterly oriented dunes. Elsewhere in Canada, less effective dry winds produced local dune areas. In the ice ages, the ice sheet controlled the distribution of air masses and produced northwesterly oriented dunes in N Saskatchewan and Alberta and southwesterly oriented dunes in the St Lawrence Lowlands, Qué. Most of Canada's dune areas are stabilized by vegetation; relatively few are active, except in the area S of Lk Athabasca. This region contains 385 km² of barren sand surfaces, recognizable on satellite photos, with beautiful, active sand dunes producing breathtaking scenery. This large-scale aeolian activity is not climatically controlled but is due to the prevailing local groundwater conditions. In Canada only about 2.5% of the total dune area is active; 95% of that total occurs in the above-mentioned region.

One common feature of almost all sand dunes in Canada, which distinguishes them from desert dunes, is that they show some parabolic form, concave upwindward. This form develops if moisture is present in the dunes. Individual dunes may have simple or complex forms, depending on the mode and duration of their development. The dune areas of Canada have been grouped into a series of regional zones according to differences in dune form. Each zone has distinct environmental characteristics. In every dune area, local aeolian activity began as soon as sandy surfaces became exposed to the air after the disappearance of the ice. In more humid regions, activity lasted for only a short time. Dry winds blowing from one direction or another amassed the sand to form either transverse or parabolic dunes. Transverse dunes persisted as long as the sand in them remained dry. When moistened by rainfall, they broke up into parabolic dunes. In one region in central Alberta, dunes showing stages of this transformation have been preserved by stabilization. In drier regions where activity continued and dunes migrated downwind, vegetation invaded the interdune areas. When the climate became humid, the dunes were gradually stabilized by vegetation, and soils developed on them. This process occurred in the southern prairies only af-

ter a few thousand years of activity. Later, periodic climate fluctuations caused many of the dunes to become partly active from time to time, and buried parts of their stabilized surfaces and soils. Radiocarbon dating of organic material extracted from buried soils has helped to show that more than 10 periods of renewed aeolian activity have occurred in the last 5000 years. These periods correlate well with other climate-sensitive phenomena such as tree-ring development. In Canada, loess deposits are generally small in area and usually occur downwind from dune areas. They represent the silt-sized portions of aeolian transportation. Other, still less extensive aeolian deposits include the so-called cliff-top deposits formed by sediments that were deflated from barren, cliffy slopes exposed to the winds. Occurrences of these on the southern prairies have been the sites of past volcanic-ash deposition.

P.P. DAVID

Aerodynamics is the branch of ENGINEERING concerned with gaseous fluids (usually air) in motion and, in particular, with the effects of this motion on rigid or flexible bodies. The forces acting on the surface of a body moving through air, or (what is the same thing) the pressure exerted by air flowing past a body at rest, are affected mainly by the shape and size of the body, the relative speed of the flow, and the density, viscosity and compressibility of the gas. Viscosity is the ability of a flowing liquid or gas to develop internal shear stresses that resist flow. In air, viscous forces are generally small in comparison with inertia forces, a condition which leads to flow instability and turbulence. Thus, WINDS near the rough surface of Earth are generally turbulent, as is the flow in the thin boundary layer next to the skin of an airplane in flight. The problem of turbulence has never been completely resolved although, for most engineering purposes, its effects are reasonably predictable.

The compressibility of air determines the speed of sound or the speed at which pressure changes are transmitted through the flow field. The speed of sound is about 340 metres per second at sea level, 296 m/s in the stratosphere. If the speed of a body exceeds the speed of sound, the pattern of flow changes drastically and pressure waves tend to pile up into shock waves. The Mach number is the ratio of the body speed to the speed of sound. The design of efficient aircraft shapes for flight at transonic and supersonic speeds (Mach number near or greater than 1) remains one of the most challenging problems in aerodynamics.

Viscosity and compressibility are the most troublesome factors in theoretical aerodynamics and the steady development of aerodynamics during this century has been possible only through a close association between experimental and theoretical research. The main laboratory tool of the aerodynamicist, the wind tunnel, is a specially designed tube or duct in which air is made to flow under precisely controlled conditions. Many of the engineering departments in Canadian universities have small or medium-sized tunnels that are used for various research purposes. Large, general-purpose wind tunnels (suitable for investigation of aerodynamic design problems of aircraft and road vehicles, and the testing of large-scale models of engineering structures) typically cost tens of millions of dollars to design and build, and are comparatively rare. The largest tunnels in Canada are at the NATIONAL RESEARCH COUNCIL, Ottawa: one is capable of speeds up to about 55 m/s and has a test section 9 metres square; another, with a 1.5 metres square test section, is capable of speeds up to 4 times the speed of sound. The design of large wind tunnels is a highly specialized field in which one Canadian consulting engineer-

ing firm, DSMA International, has developed a worldwide reputation. DSMA's engineers have designed and supervised construction of many tunnels for automotive research and high- and low-speed aircraft development in N America, Europe and Asia.

The needs of aircraft design have prompted many advances in aerodynamics. For example, DE HAVILLAND AIRCRAFT OF CANADA LTD have designed a famous line of STOL (short-takeoff-and-landing aircraft): the DE HAVILLAND BEAVER, OTTER Twin Otter, DASH 7 and Dash 8. De Havilland's success has resulted, in part, from the company's steady progress in design of high-lift wing flap systems and of means of maintaining precise control at unusually low flying speeds. However, the applications of aerodynamics extend far beyond the needs of aeronautics. For example, the University of Western Ontario pioneered development of a specialized wind tunnel, with a very long test section, to model the turbulent characteristics of natural winds over Earth's surface. It has been used to check the design of large structures, including some of the tallest buildings in the world. The universities of British Columbia and Moncton and a private consulting firm, Morrison Hershfield Ltd, in Guelph and Edmonton, all have tunnels of this type for the investigation of such problems as bird flight, pesticide-spray diffusion and snow drifting. NRC's large tunnels have been used to measure pressures and aerodynamic forces on downhill skiers, cars, high-rise buildings, model ships and trains, a flexible stadium roof, an offshore oil platform, snowmobiles, motorcycles and parachutes, as well as on nearly all the aircraft designed in Canada. NRC aerodynamicists have also revived a forgotten French invention: the vertical-axis wind turbine (VAWT), which looks like a large egg-beater. *See also* WIND ENERGY.

R.J. TEMPLIN

Aerospace Industry has specialized capabilities for the design, research, development, production, marketing, repair and overhaul of aircraft, aero engines, aircraft and engine subsystems and components, space-related equipment, and air- and ground-based avionic systems and components. It is economically impractical for the Canadian industry to meet the diverse commercial and defence aerospace-product needs of the Canadian market. Through selective specialization, the industry has developed products in response mainly to export-market demands; 70-80% of its sales are in export markets. Approximately 100 companies are engaged in significant manufacturing. The main centres of production are Montréal, Toronto and Winnipeg. Employment in 1986 was 45 000, sales $4.5 billion.

History CANADAIR LTD, the principal aircraft-manufacturing company, started in the 1920s as the Aircraft Division of Canadian Vickers Ltd in east Montréal. Canadair designed and manufactured a series of airplanes, starting with the Vedette, the first Canadian flying-boat design. The company was relocated at the Cartierville airport in the Montréal suburb of St Laurent during WWII and, under Canadian government ownership, was an important centre of military aircraft production for amphibious Canso aircraft. In 1947 the government sold Canadair to the US Electric Boat Co, only to repurchase the company in 1976 and then to resell it to BOMBARDIER in 1986. Canadair has become an important source of executive jet aircraft, represented by the Challenger aircraft series.

Another major aircraft manufacturer, DE HAVILLAND, has been active in Canada since 1928. Originally, as a subsidiary of the de Havilland Aircraft Co of England, it sold and serviced aircraft designed in the UK. Manufacturing came later, culminating in large-scale production of Anson, Mosquito and Tiger Moth aircraft during WWII. The first serious design venture of the Canadian engineering team was the Chipmunk trainer, followed in 1947 by the famous DE HAVILLAND BEAVER light aircraft. The Beaver initiated a sequence of short-takeoff-and-landing aircraft (STOL): the DE HAVILLAND OTTER, CARIBOU, Buffalo, DASH 7, Dash 8 and Twin Otter. In 1974 the government purchased de Havilland to secure the development and production of the Dash 7 aircraft and the continued operation of the company as an aircraft manufacturer in Canada. In 1985 de Havilland was sold to the Boeing Commercial Aircraft Co.

The first modern aero-engine design unit in Canada was started in Toronto. Acting on the recommendations of a government technical mission, the National Research Council of Canada (NRC) established Turbo Research Ltd in 1944 in Leaside, a suburb of Toronto. A specification for a turbojet was drawn up and work then began on the design of the TR 4 engine, (Chinook).

In 1945 A.V. Roe, Canada, was formed to provide a domestic aircraft- and engine-design manufacturing capability, particularly for defence. The new company took over the assets of Victory Aircraft Ltd, at Malton, Toronto, which had produced Lancaster bombers during WWII. The Turbo Research team joined the group at Malton a year later. In the summer of 1946 the Royal Canadian Air Force requested the design and development of a turbojet engine, the Orenda, with a thrust equal to that of any contemporary engine under design abroad. By 1951 the team of engineers and technicians had expanded and a new manufacturing plant was constructed; it was opened in 1952. Within 17 months some 1000 Orendas had been delivered to the RCAF and production eventually reached 3824.

A.V. Roe began work on the design and development of a supersonic engine, later called the Iroquois, in 1953. This engine was chosen to power the AVRO ARROW (CF-105) supersonic all-weather fighter. On 20 Feb 1959, just a few weeks before the first Iroquois-engined Arrow was to take to the air, the government cancelled the aircraft and engine programs. The termination of the Arrow was a watershed in the history of the Canadian aerospace industry, and of A.V. Roe in particular. Over one weekend the work force at A.V. Roe shrank from 5000 to 1000 workers, with a total of 14 000 workers losing employment throughout the industry. Since that time Canada has not sought to be self-sufficient in aerospace weapon systems. The Malton aircraft facilities of A.V. Roe continued under de Havilland direction until 1963, when the Douglas Aircraft Co assumed ownership to produce wings for its DC-9 commercial jet aircraft. Later the Douglas parent company was taken over by the McDonnell (US) Co and the Malton facility became McDonnell Douglas Canada Ltd. The Canadian entity has developed into an important manufacturer of wings for the MD-80, the DC-10 and the KC-10 aircraft.

The largest company in the Canadian aerospace industry is Pratt and Whitney Aircraft of Canada (PWC), designers and manufacturers of a highly successful series of jet and propjet aero engines with over 50% of the world market for civil turbine engines. Pratt and Whitney established the Canadian company in 1929 as a parts and overhaul facility for Wasp radial engines. During WWII the business grew, owing to the substantial use of Pratt and Whitney engines by the military. Studies during the mid-1950s indicated that the piston-engine business would decline, and it was decided that PWC would organize a team to design and develop gas turbine

Canadair Challenger business jet, which is also in service in personnel transport, flight calibration and inspection, electronic support and air ambulance roles (*courtesy Canadair*).

engines for the general aviation market. An engine specification for a propjet of about 500-shaft horsepower and designated the PT-6 was developed. The engine has since become pre-eminent in its class. Later engines have included the JT-15 fan-jet and the A-50 series used for the de Havilland Dash 7 and other aircraft. By 1978 there were 50 models of the PT-6 and the JT-15D in production and both engine families had set the standard for general aviation engines around the world. The company currently manufactures the PW100 series of engines that power the majority of the world's regional commuter airliners and it is also developing new generations of engines for the helicopter and small executive jet markets.

This historical view of the industry would be incomplete without reference to the development of Canadian Aircraft Electronics. CAE has grown from a fledgling company in Montréal in 1945 to a corporation with subsidiary aerospace companies across Canada engaged in the design and manufacture of aircraft simulators, avionics (aviation electronic equipment), and aircraft components and subsystems.

In space-related activities, Canada's industry is modest by comparison with the US, Russian and European industries, but it is first-rate in special fields. The industry originated in the 1920s with ground-based research projects for the study of the Earth's upper atmosphere conducted by scientists from U of Saskatchewan. An extension of these researches, using high-altitude balloons, was initiated in the 1950s by DRB, and led to work with sounding rockets, developed by Bristol Aerospace, Winnipeg, using the Black Brant rocket. In 1954 the army conducted the first series of rocket firings at Fort Churchill, Man.

At the end of 1958 the US National Aeronautics and Space Administration (NASA) accepted a DRB proposal to create jointly a sounding satellite, the Alouette I, which was supported by a network of Canadian ground stations at Ottawa, Prince Albert and Resolute Bay and 10 other stations around the world. The satellite was launched in 1962 and was a significant technological success. This entry into the field of space technology aroused considerable interest in using the technology for communications satellites. In Sept 1969 Telesat Canada was formed to provide domestic communications services by satellite throughout the country. Hughes Aircraft Corp (US), with Northern Electric and Spar Aerospace, designed and developed the Anik I, II and III satellites, launched in Nov 1972, April 1973 and May 1975 respectively. Canada became the first country in the world to own and operate a domestic SATELLITE COMMUNICATIONS system.

In order to develop the capabilities of its space industry, Canada undertook in the mid-1970s to provide a Remote Manipulator Arm (CANADARM) for the US space shuttle. The arm was successfully deployed during the second flight of the space

shuttle Columbia in 1981, and gained world recognition for the technological capability of Spar Aerospace and the NRC.

The Modern Industry has a hierarchy of 3 tiers of capabilities and products. In the first tier are the principal companies with integrated design and production capability for complete aircraft and engines. The second-tier companies manufacture components and subsystems for the principal companies in Canada and abroad. The third tier comprises machine shops, heat treatment shops, foundries, forges and other companies whose business is predominantly the aerospace industry. All aerospace companies must ensure a very high quality and reliability of products, and as a result the companies have a high cost structure specific to aerospace. They tend not to serve general markets, other than nuclear engineering, which has somewhat similar quality and reliability demands.

The 3 tiers are not integrated; rather, the companies are interdependent with other N American aerospace companies. This interdependence results from the international nature of the world airline business, from the US as the principal trading partner, from foreign ownership (mainly US) of many of the companies, and particularly from a defence-sharing agreement between Canada and the US. Although Canadian military sales had declined as a proportion of total sales from 66% in 1963 to 30% in 1986, the Canada-US Defence Production Sharing Agreement (DPSA) and its associated Canadian financial-assistance program, the Defence Industries Productivity Program for industry and market development, have been very significant in shaping the industry's development since the demise of the Arrow program. The DIPP has helped to finance both defence projects and civilian projects handled by the defence industry. The Dash 7 aircraft and the civilian PT-6 and JT-15 aero engines were partially funded by DIPP. The Defence Industry Productivity Program is Canada's way of financing its aerospace industry as opposed to captive government procurement used in most other countries. In 1985 $104 million in DIPP Funds were applied for research and development, for establishment of Canadian industrial sources and for modernization with advanced production equipment. Government support for the Canadian aerospace industry tends to be much lower than assistance given by many other nations.

For the 20-year period ending in 1981, there was a rough balance between the imports and exports of commercial and defence aerospace products. This balance was assured for military products by adoption of a government policy to seek industrial-benefit offsets for the Canadian industry against major procurements. However, since 1981 Canada experienced a cumulative trade deficit of $2 billion in military aerospace products. Until the 1980s commercial aircraft imports were also, in part, kept in balance through industrial-benefit arrangements with Boeing, Lockheed and McDonnell. However, a Civil Aircraft Agreement of 1980 under the General Agreement on Tariffs and Trade, to which Canada is a signatory, now forbids including offset requirements as a part of a civil aircraft transaction, although it does not prevent negotiating offsets as long as the sale is not conditional upon these offsets. The same agreement removed all tariffs on commercial aircraft trade, and the DPSA referred to earlier has effectively eliminated tariffs on defence trade. The industry now operates with a nonprotected status. This has the twin effect of causing the industry to remain competitive in world terms but leaving it vulnerable against foreign industries, which receive some protection through receiving directed defence procurements.

Aerospace products, such as complete aircraft, aero engines and the electrical, electronic and mechanical subsystems, represent a complex and highly demanding application of advanced technology. The requirement for maximum safety and performance, with minimum weight, is a major reason why aerospace continues to emphasize the use of new and improved materials and new design and production technologies. The industry is a leader in the application of computer-integrated design and manufacturing technologies. The skill rating of engineers, technologists and production workers reflects the high design and quality standards of this industry. One disturbing feature is a pattern of cyclical employment caused by changing personnel requirements at succeeding phases of the relatively few major Canadian aerospace projects. As a result, immigration of engineers has frequently been relied upon to meet intensive demands, and more Canadian universities offer aerospace-related courses. The larger companies in the industry are unionized and labour relations are generally satisfactory. The main unions are the Canadian Auto Workers and the International Association of Machinists and Aerospace Workers.

Institutions and Societies The aerospace industry is represented nationally by the Aerospace Industries Assn of Canada which represents the interests of the industry to the federal government. It has also sponsored valuable co-operative projects for productivity improvement and for the enhancement of labour relations and training arrangements with unions, academic establishments and provincial and federal government departments. The technical society for the industry is the Canadian Aeronautics and Space Institute (CASI).

NORMAN GARDNER AND GÉRARD L. LALONDE

Reading: G.A. Fuller, J.A. Griffin and K.M. Molson, *125 Years of Canadian Aeronautics* (1983); K.M. Molson, *Canadian Aircraft Since 1909* (1982); R.D. Page, *Avro Canuck CF-100* (1982); D. Watson et al, *Avro Arrow* (1980).

Affaires, Les, the main French-language business newspaper in Canada, was founded in 1928. A weekly full-colour tabloid, it has a circulation of about 86 000, mainly in Québec. It is published by Publications Les Affairs Inc. The president and publisher of *Les Affaires* is Claude Beauchamp (1987); Jean-Paul Gagné is editor in chief. *Les Affaires* is noted for its coverage of large Canadian corporations, medium and small Québec companies, Canadian economics and public affairs. It devotes half of its content to personal finances and investment, with a wide variety of specialized pages, tables and graphs. *Les Affaires* gives expert advice to readers and is written in everyday language. In addition to its weekly regular editions, *Les Affaires* publishes over 40 special reports on a wide range of subjects and industrial sectors every week.   D. McGILLIVRAY

Affleck, Raymond Tait, architect (b at Penticton, BC 20 Nov 1922). Educated at McGill and in Zurich, Switz, he began independent practice in 1953 and in 1955 joined in forming the firm of Affleck, Desbarats, Dimakopoulos, Michaud, Lebensold, Sise, from 1958-70 Affleck, Desbarats, Dimakopoulis, Lebensold, Sise, and from 1970 called Arcop Associates, Architects and Planners. While his firm participated in many important projects from St John's (Arts and Culture Centre, 1967) to Vancouver (Queen Elizabeth Theatre, 1955) Affleck is particularly associated with the Montréal developments Place Bonaventure (1964-68), PLACE VILLE MARIE (1956-65), and the Maison Alcan (1983, awarded the Prix d'excellence in 1984); Affleck's concern for the quality of life in a northern climate is expressed in

Place Bonaventure and other projects that interweave many different strands of urban activity with indoor pedestrian streets and atria. The Maison Alcan joins a restored historic hotel and greystone houses on Sherbrooke St to the reticent but entirely modern glass and aluminum clad headquarters behind by means of a glazed atrium. Market Square (Saint John, 1983) is another important architectural conservation and infill project, and provides further evidence of Affleck's urban sympathies.   MICHAEL McMORDIE

AFL-CIO The American Federation of Labor (est 1886) consisted of skilled craft unions that disagreed with the reform policies and organization of the KNIGHTS OF LABOR. The AFL involved Canadian workers from the beginning, and between 1898 and 1902 the first Canadian organizer, John FLETT, chartered over 700 locals. Most Canadian unions were affiliated with the TRADES AND LABOR CONGRESS OF CANADA, which was associated with, and dominated by, the AFL. During the 1920s the AFL hewed to craft union interests, ignoring unskilled workers in the new mass-production industries (steel, auto, electrical). In Nov 1935, these workers set up The Committee for Industrial Organization (later known as the Congress of Industrial Organizations, 1937) organizing by industry rather than by craft. The CIO won several spectacular strikes in Canada (*see* OSHAWA STRIKE), openly engaged in politics and bickered with the AFL. In 1939 the AFL successfully pressured the TLC to oust unions from its ranks. New challenges such as automation after WWII persuaded labour leaders in the US to settle their differences and merge in 1955; their Canadian affiliates merged a year later. The AFL-CIO's decline in recent years has reflected the industrial weakness of the traditional blue-collar strongholds of American unionism. Compared to the less than 20% of the American workforce that is organized today, Canadian unionism, embracing over 35% of the total workforce, looks healthy indeed. In 1986, 1.2 million Canadian unionists were affiliated with the AFL-CIO (or 32.6%).

ROBERT H. BABCOCK

Africans The term "African" includes indigenous Negroid-Blacks of West, East and Southern Africa, the Hamito-Semites of Ethiopia, and people of other ethnocultural origins who view Africa as home by virtue of several generations of settlement on the African continent. Chief among these latter groups are Europeans of British, Portuguese, Afrikaner-Dutch and Jewish ethnocultural origins, people of mixed descent, and Asian Indians of Muslim, Hindu and Goan Christian religious-cultural background.

The vast continent of Africa and its complex array of peoples has not had a close relationship with Canada. Black Africans, in particular, comprise a very small, scattered and almost unknown group of newcomers to Canada, although Africans of European and Asian ancestry have a clearer presence. However, little formal documentation exists on any of these groups.

Historically, Canadian IMMIGRATION POLICY has not favoured immigration by Asians and Africans. From 1946 to 1950 Africans comprised only 0.3% of new immigrants to Canada, a figure that rose to an average of only 1-2% over the next 20 years. With the 1966 White Paper on Immigration and the attempt to introduce a nondiscriminatory screening process the proportion of African immigrants rose to an average of approximately 2% from 1968 to 1970, indicating that while the new system was more objective, it was highly selective. It also favoured certain countries, including the black countries of Nigeria and Ghana. In 1972-73, with Canada's acceptance of some 7000 Ugandan Asians, the proportion of

immigrants rose from 6.8% of total immigration, and it remained at an average of about 5.2% from 1975 to 1978, corresponding to the movement of Portuguese and British settlers to Canada after Angola and Mozambique (1975) and Zimbabwe (1980) achieved independence. From 1973 to 1983, some 16 000 South Africans, mainly of non-black ethnic origins, entered Canada. In 1984, a further 321 entered Canada. The steady, relatively high immigration from Tanzania and Kenya, too, reflects Asian Indian rather than black African migration.

The introduction of the Green Paper on Immigration (1976) had the effect of restricting the entry of potential landed immigrants in the "independent" class. This regulation seriously curtailed movement of people from black African countries, and it is aggravated by the fact that there are just 3 Canadian Employment and Immigration offices in Africa. The office located in Abidjan, capital of the Ivory Coast, serves 23 widely dispersed neighbouring countries; that in Nairobi, capital of Kenya, serves 19 equally dispersed countries in the northeastern part of the continent. By contrast, the office located in Pretoria, the administrative capital of the Republic of South Africa, serves just 5 countries at Africa's southern tip.

The 1976 Immigration Act, however, has had the positive consequence of allowing Canadian citizens to sponsor close relatives. This stipulation has been especially beneficial for landed immigrants from the Republic of South Africa and from Tanzania, Kenya, Uganda, Angola, Zimbabwe, and, to a lesser degree, Nigeria and Ghana. In 1984, 3552 people (comprising about 4% of Canada's total immigration) immigrated to Canada from Africa. Most of the immigrants from this group in the "independent class" came from the Republic of South Africa and the Malagasy Republic. At the present time Canada is looking for entrepreneurs and self-employed immigrants with the funds to establish business operations capable of employing Canadian citizens. Such entrepreneurs are more likely to emerge from the affluent European-Asian African groups than from black African groups. Overall, most Africans in any of the ethnocultural groups are drawn from the former English-speaking colonies of Africa; a smaller number originate in the former French-speaking colonies of Africa, chiefly from Mali, Senegal, Zaire, Malagasy Republic and the Ivory Coast.

It is estimated that only about 10% of people classified as REFUGEES in Africa would be classified as such according to the UN definition of the term, but all groups may count among their numbers self-exiled persons, or persons seeking greater personal freedom for themselves and their families. These subgroups are difficult to identify except where offical data exist on immigrant refugee status, eg, with Ugandan Asian Indians and the Ethiopians of Eritrea. The 1976 Immigration Act established a new "refugee class," and in 1984, for example, Canada accepted 684 refugees from Ethiopia. Most of these people were sponsored by the federal government, but some were privately funded.

According to the 1981 census (the last year for which figures are available) there were 45 215 persons of African origin in Canada, comprising a mere 0.19% of the total population. Most Africans settled in Ontario, followed by Québec, Alberta, Nova Scotia and BC. Approximately 1500 people speak African languages, eg, Ashanti (Ghana), Hausa, Yoruba and Ibo (Nigeria), Kru (Liberia-Sierra Leone), Amharic (Ethiopia), Tigrinya (Eritrea), Sotho, Tswana and Zulu (South Africa), Bamhara, Malnike (Mali-Ivory Coast), Wolof and Dyola (Senegal), in their home settings, but all Africans who come to Canada have a good working knowledge of either English or French.

Social and Cultural Life

Black Africans From 1963 to 1967, Africans immigrated from Ethiopia (641), Ghana (113), Kenya (548), Nigeria (175), Rhodesia (641), Republic of South Africa (3512), Tanzania (242), Uganda (153), Zaire (18), Zambia (424). Many African countries attained independence about that time: Zambia (1964), Tanzania (1962) and Uganda (1961), Kenya and Nigeria (1960). White Rhodesia unilaterally declared its independence from Britain in 1965, and South Africa declared itself a republic and withdrew from the Commonwealth in 1961. Given these changes it is difficult to judge the ethnic mix that entered Canada at the time. Many newcomers may have been European settlers emigrating from a changing Africa, but it seems certain that black Africans as well began to settle in Canada in the 1960s.

Ethiopian refugees accepted into Canada in recent years comprise a linguistic-cultural group distinct from other Africans with whom they tend to have only peripheral contact. Refugees from the secessionist Red Sea province of Eritrea tend to be well educated and skilled. Many speak Italian as a consequence of the WWII Italian occupation of Ethiopia. An interesting but tiny Ethiopian subgroup (of some 10 000-12 000 people) are the Falashas ("Black Jews"), who come from the northwest provinces of Ethiopia. They practise an ancient form of Judaism, but they have no knowledge of Hebrew and their priests use Ge'ez, the Semitic-Sabaean script originating in the 4th century AD, as their liturgical language. Most Africans in Canada are Christian or Muslim.

As a group black Africans generally share only one area of common experience – that of PREJUDICE AND DISCRIMINATION and RACISM in the host country. Contrary to liberal credo held in Western societies, discrimination does not necessarily disappear in boom periods of the economy. White attitudes regarding racial issues are mostly independent of traditional sociodemographic variables such as age, education and income.

Ugandans and Other Asians In 1972, with the so-called "Africanization" of Uganda, approximately 50 000 Ugandan Asians were expelled. Approximately 7000 were invited to settle in Canada. Given the variety of skills and professional background they brought with them, coupled with their initiative and enterprising attitudes, most Ugandan Asians have made steady socioeconomic progress in Canada. They have settled primarily in Ontario (40% in Toronto), BC and Québec.

The largest group of Ugandan Asians in Canada are the Ismailiyah (Ismailis), a sect of the Shiah branch of Islam. A smaller Islamic sect in Canada are the Ithna-Ashariyah. The Ismailis, and to a lesser degree the Ithna Asheri, have developed strong ethnocultural and religious groups that have contributed to their sociopsychological integrity and their economic progress.

The Gujarati Hindus, traditionally a business caste in India and East Africa, have been successful in business and professional occupations in Canada. They tend to be a conservative people, practising the Hindu-Gandhian teachings of Ahimsa (nonviolence), asceticism and respect for all life. They are mostly vegetarian; marriages are endogamous within similar castes and are frequently arranged by parents.

The Goan Indians originated in the Portuguese-dominated province of Goa on the Malabar Coast, 402 km south of Bombay. Many contemporary Goans have some Portuguese background, have Portuguese names, and are Roman Catholic. When ousted by Idi Amin in 1972, many came to Canada, settling mainly in Toronto. They have their own organizations, apart from people coming directly from Goa, and apart from the large Portuguese community in Toronto. Today they are uniformly English speaking.

All the Asian Indian subgroups have more bonds of kinship with people from India and Pakistan and with the religions and cultures of those countries than with black Africans.

Angola-Mozambique Portuguese In 1976-77, 2100 "returnees" (white and coloured Portuguese) from the newly independent territories of Angola and Mozambique were admitted into Canada, even though they did not qualify as genuine refugees since they held Portuguese passports. The Portuguese settlers in Africa had remained Portuguese citizens. Two factors contributed to this "humanitarian" gesture by Canada: pressure from the Portuguese Canadian community and requests from the Portuguese ambassador to Canada to help ease the burden of returning white colonials. Most returnees entered Canada in 1978-79 under contract as skilled workers to firms in Canada. These returnees have prospered, and do not seem to rely on the support of Portuguese aid societies. They are viewed as having integrated well into the larger society, possibly because of their fluency in English.

South Africa and Zimbabwe By far the largest number of people that have entered Canada from any sub-Saharan country have been those originating in the Republic of South Africa. Between 1964 and 1984, 36 145 immigrants, including a large number of English-speaking, British and Jewish people, and small groups of Afrikaners (Dutch-French Huguenot), coloureds (mixed descent), Asian Indians and a handful of black Africans, left South Africa for Canada. Professionals of all types, eg, university professors, medical doctors, school teachers, writers, artists and some skilled artisans, are to be found in all the groups.

The political climate of South Africa is characterized by tension and uncertainty. The white elite leave the country at a steady rate of about 1500 per year. Former white Rhodesians as well have found a wintry haven in Canada. Most white South Africans in Canada are liberal minded, but the barriers to intergroup communication imposed by apartheid seem to continue in the host country. Each racial group has at least some loose bonding within its own group, but little across groups, even where people originate from the same cities and towns.

Only a sprinkling of well-educated black Africans have any chance of enjoying the climate of political and personal freedom afforded by Canada. Even blacks who seek refugee status in Canada must prove they would be persecuted if they returned to South Africa. Living under apartheid does not qualify an individual as a refugee. *See also* BLACKS. JOSEPHINE C. NAIDOO

Agar, Carlyle Clare, helicopter pioneer (b at Lion's Head, Ont 28 Nov 1901; d at Victoria 27 Jan 1968). In 1905 Agar moved to Edmonton, where he was educated and where he learned to fly. He joined the RCAF in 1940 and was awarded an Air Force Cross for contributions as a flight teacher. He attempted to set up an air service in Penticton and Kelowna, BC, and in 1947 flew the first commercial helicopter into Canada, spraying orchards with insecticide. He perfected helicopter flying in mountainous terrain and carried out aerial surveys. In 1949 he airlifted construction material, equipment and personnel to the mountainside Palisade Lk Dam. In 1951 he performed a similar task for the Aluminium Co of Canada's giant smelter complex at Kitimat, BC. His company, Okanagan Air Service, became one of the largest commercial helicopter operations in the world. He was awarded the MCKEE TROPHY in 1950. JAMES MARSH

LAKE AGASSIZ

Agassiz, Lake The largest glacial lake in N America formed 11 500 years ago in front of the northeastwardly retreating Laurentide Ice Sheet, which acted as a dam. The lake covered much of Manitoba, NW Ontario, parts of eastern Saskatchewan and North Dakota, and NW Minnesota. At its largest, Lake Agassiz was about 1500 km long, over 1100 km wide and about 210 m deep. Its history is complicated by the behaviour of the ice sheet, which at times readvanced and affected lake levels and drainage systems. Several outlet channels and about 35 beach ridges at different elevations have been identified. Some of these, such as the prominent Campbell Beach Ridge, can be traced for hundreds of kilometres. For the first 500 years, drainage was southward through the Minnesota R Valley. As glacial retreat continued into NW Ontario, the lake lowered and drainage shifted eastward into Lk Superior via various channels in the Lk Nipigon basin area. About 9900 years ago, a readvance blocked the eastern outlet, raising the lake to earlier levels. Between 9500 and 9200 years ago, the ice sheet rapidly disintegrated and eastern outlets were once again opened. As deglaciation continued, lower lake levels were established until the drainage shifted N into Hudson Bay. The final drainage of the lake occurred about 7700 years ago. Only remnants, eg, Lk WINNIPEG, remain today. The former lake basin and sediments have provided valuable agricultural land. *See also* GLACIER; GLACIATION. N.W. RUTTER

Agawa Bay is located 90 km NW of Sault Ste Marie, Ont, on the N shore of Lk Superior. The area was sacred to the OJIBWA and the name is Indian for "sacred place." The magnificent beach is strewn with innumerable pebbles, worn smooth by the waves. Nearby bands of rock, some 1 billion, some 2.5 billion years old, lie twisted in layers like hardened candy. The famous PICTOGRAPHS are on the sheer rock face above. Located by Selwyn Dewdney in 1959, the red ochre and grease paintings are thought to celebrate a safe passage across the lake, or possibly a war victory of a great chief, some 200 years ago. Among the images are a fabulous panther, a serpent and a rider and galloping horse. JAMES MARSH

Aging for individuals is a continual biological, psychological and social process from infancy to old age. Conventionally, the term narrowly refers to the transition from adulthood to old age. Population aging refers to a decline in relative numbers of young people and an increase in relative numbers of old people. With brief interruptions, the Canadian population has been aging from its inception.

Historical Context The social character of old age has undergone a remarkable transformation in the 20th century. In the past, the elders of the community were defined less by chronological age than by institutional seniority, particularly within the family. To be old meant to hold a particular position within a system of generations – having adult children and grandchildren – rather than to be a member of an age group defined by its date of birth. Therefore, the age at which individuals were actually recognized as being old varied. The contemporary practice of designating all those above age 65 as old is historically unique and derives from another unique 20th-century practice of retiring elderly workers at a fixed age without regard to physical ability or mental capacity. Until well into this century, most people continued to work until death or the onset of extreme DISABILITY. Retirement was a privilege of the wealthy. In 1921, 60% of all males over the age of 65 were actively engaged in the LABOUR FORCE. By 1951, this figure had declined to 40% and by 1986 to 12%. Retirement as a general principle of labour-force management was made possible through the development of a system of retirement wages, eg, OLD-AGE PENSIONS, both public and private. The transition into old age is now defined primarily by the individual's relation to the economy; only in this context is it possible to understand the contemporary conventional practice of defining the elderly as all those who are above 65 years of age.

Social Composition of the Elderly In 1986 there were 2 725 000 persons aged 65 and over in Canada, 58% of whom were women. By 1961, elderly women began to outnumber elderly men, and this trend has continued as a result of the changing sex composition of international migration to Canada and changes in life expectancy. In the early part of this century, more men than women immigrated to Canada, but between 1931 and 1948 more women than men arrived, many joining husbands and families. By the 1960s men and women were immigrating to Canada in approximately equal numbers. As these migrants age, females in the older age groups will become even more marked, because although increases in life expectancy have benefited both men and women, the gap in life expectancy between the sexes has widened. At the beginning of the 1980s the average life expectancy of a 65-year-old male was 15 years; for a female it was 19 years.

Sexual differences in longevity imply that the social experience of aging differs greatly for men and women. Most men live out their lives in a family, with a wife; most women become widows. In 1986, 76% of elderly men were married but only 44% of elderly women; in contrast, only 14% of elderly men were widowed, compared to 48% of elderly women. About 66% of all elderly household heads now live in their own homes. The remaining 34% is composed of renters, lodgers and those in institutions for the elderly. There is no consensus about the proportion of Canada's institutionalized elderly population; estimates range between 5.8% and 10%.

Over time there has been a trend among the widowed, divorced and single elderly to live on their own rather than with family or friends, a trend that is usually interpreted as the result of a rising standard of living. Both residential patterns and surveys indicate that most elderly persons wish to live close to, but not with, their children.

Economic Status of the Elderly While the real standard of living of the elderly has reflected the rising standard of living in Canada as a whole, the relative economic position of Canada's elderly remains low, reflected in the number of elderly persons who qualify for support under the federal government's Guaranteed Income Supplement. The widespread coverage under this program also indicates the prevalence of poverty among the elderly. In 1984, 43% (compared to 53% in 1979) of all elderly couples received such benefits, and among the unattached, most of whom are women, 65% were receiving benefits. In the decades following WWII, the relative economic position of the elderly deteriorated. During the fifties and sixties the percentage of the elderly in the bottom 2 income quintiles increased while the percentage in the highest quintile declined. Such a trend would be expected if rising levels of retirement were not met by compensating increases in retirement benefits to offset the loss of labour force income. This trend was reversed in the seventies as the pension reforms of the late sixties came into effect. In 1965, prior to the reforms, 49% of the elderly were in the lowest income quintile and 5% in the highest quintile. In 1983 35% were in the lowest quintile and 5.7% in the highest quintile. The poverty rate among elderly couples declined from 41.4% in 1969 to 11.1% in 1983. Despite this reversal in the trend, however, the elderly remain highly concentrated at the bottom of the Canadian income distribution. The economic problems of elderly women are particularly acute: 51% of widowed, single and divorced women were below the poverty line in 1985.

It is now commonly agreed that Canada's retirement income system is inadequate for both current and future retirees (*see* SOCIAL SECURITY). Two outstanding problems remain: providing a level of income security that allows the elderly to maintain basic continuity in living standards after retirement and the high incidence of poverty among elderly women. Public pension programs were designed on the premise that government should provide a basic minimum of income security, beyond which additional income needs in retirement would be met through private sector pension plans negotiated between employers and employees. This additional coverage was not, and is unlikely to be, forthcoming. Recent trends in pension legislation have been designed to improve the quality of private pensions for those already covered who make up less than half the labour force and only 35% of women in the labour force. The result will be a growing division between those elderly with both public and private benefits and those who rely exclusively on public pension programs.

Health and Health Services The elderly tend to suffer from more illnesses, both physical and mental, and make greater use of health-care practitioners and facilities than do younger age groups. Unlike the young, however, the elderly tend to suffer primarily from such chronic conditions as heart disease, arthritis and physical impairments of various types. Although 75% of the elderly population suffer from at least one chronic condition, 80% are functionally capable of independent living. Traditional medical practice, which has focused on the acute, short-term conditions typically experienced by the young, cannot be applied appropriately to the health needs of the growing numbers of the elderly. While many of the elderly require temporary hospitalization, health care is primarily a matter of providing ongoing services and assistance to minimize the consequences of long-term or permanent disability. In the absence of sufficient community-based, home-care services, many elderly persons are required to seek access to institutional care prematurely. Consequently, provincial governments during the last decade have emphasized the provision of homemaker, handyman and home-meal services, adult day-care centres and other services not traditionally considered part of health care.

Adaptation to Aging Discovering the secret of a "happy old age" has preoccupied men and women throughout history, but it remains a secret. Popular perceptions to the contrary, considerable research has indicated that retirement does not noticeably affect the well-being of the elderly. If retirement is accompanied by sufficient income to prevent a significant decline in living standards, it is experienced by many as liberation from tedious and debilitating working conditions. Indeed, what most distinguishes the contemporary character of old age is the fact that it is no longer necessary for elderly men and women to work until they fall ill or die. As with the young, however, the morale and well-being of the elderly is jeopardized by poor health, inadequate income and the loss of loved ones through death. What makes old age distinctive is the increased risk of all three conditions and the absence of adequate support from the larger community when these conditions occur. And for reasons already noted, all three conditions are much more likely to strike elderly women than elderly men.

Population Aging In 1851, 65 000 persons in Canada were age 65 or older, comprising less than 3% of the population. In 1986 nearly 11% of the population was old by this conventional definition, and this figure may rise to 20% by 2031. According to the 1986 census the median age of Canadians was 31.5 years, the highest level yet. Population aging began to occur as early as the 19th century in countries such as France and Sweden and since 1900 has become characteristic of all highly industrialized nations. Increased longevity has had only a marginal impact on this development. The major factor contributing to population aging is the supply of young people. The 2 principal sources of the supply of young people are migration and fertility.

International migrants tend to be young adults seeking to improve their economic situation. Any increase in immigration to Canada will considerably alter the projected size of Canada's elderly population in the next century. The exceptionally high level of fertility after WWII accounts for the relatively large numbers of old people expected in the next century. The BABY-BOOM generation, born in the 1950s and early 1960s, is like a bubble moving through the age pyramid. By the year 2030, the last of this generation will have reached age 65.

As a result of unusually high postwar levels of immigration and fertility, the process of population aging has advanced more slowly in Canada. In countries such as Sweden, Austria and Germany, the elderly already constitute more than 16% of the population. Within the industrialized world, only Japan has a significantly younger population than that of Canada. The problems frequently imputed to an aging society in the popular media and in academic circles are both social and economic. The increased costs of supporting an elderly population, the effects on productivity and the blocked mobility channels for younger workers, it is argued, will serve to generate new social conflicts between the old and young. The experience of European nations where this process is already quite advanced, however, does not substantiate this view. Sweden, Austria and Germany were among the most successful countries in surviving the severe economic recession of the past decade and were also among those countries least likely to experience growing popular resistance to rising social expenditures, even though national old-age pension systems in these countries tend to be considerably more generous than those in Canada. These countries have also adapted with relative ease to a large elderly population because, while the elderly population has been increasing, the size of the youthful population below working age has been declining. As a result, the ratio of the nonworking to the working-age population has also declined, so that expenditures on the old have been offset by declining expenditures on the young. A similar trend is projected for Canada. In 2031 the ratio of those over age 65 and under 18 to the working-age population may reach 70%. This is somewhat higher than the 1986 figure of 61% but considerably lower than the 87% of 1961.

Old age has long been a source of private troubles for men and women. In the late 20th century it has also become a public issue. National and social institutions, generally designed to serve a youthful population, will have to adjust to the needs of an aging population. But history has not come to an end and it would be presumptuous to assume that the character and experience of old age will mean the same thing in the next century as it does in this one. The social, legal and political constituency we now call the elderly was created by social, political and economic forces, and it can be dramatically altered by these same forces.

J. MYLES

Reading: Victor Marshall, *Aging in Canada: Social Perspectives,* 2nd ed (1987).

Agnew, John Lyons, mine executive (b at Pittsburgh, Pa 28 July 1884; d at Copper Cliff, Ont 9 July 1931). Agnew attended Pittsburgh schools and worked as a labourer in the steel mills before joining International Nickel's Canadian operations at Copper Cliff in 1904. As general superintendent in WWI, he was closely connected with rapid increases in the company's nickel production for allied armament manufacturers. During the 1920s, first as president of the International Nickel Co of Canada (INCO), a subsidiary of the American parent firm, and later as VP when the Canadian company became the senior enterprise, Agnew was instrumental in promoting nickel for peacetime products, directing the construction of new smelting and refining plants and developing the Frood Mine, later one of the world's largest nickel producers. He was president of the Canadian Institute of Mining and Metallurgy and a director of several corporations.

J. LINDSEY

Agribusiness With the farm as the centre, agribusiness is that sector of the economy that includes all firms, agencies and institutions that provide inputs to the farm and procure commodities from the farm for processing and distribution to the consumer. Traditionally, agribusiness focused on farm inputs (ie, supplies such as farm machinery, feed, pesticides) and services (eg, financial institutions). The modern definition includes firms that buy raw farm commodities (eg, milk, hogs, grain, oilseeds) and process and distribute the wide range of resulting products through numerous channels to domestic and foreign consumers. Examples include firms involved in meat packing, flour and canning companies and retail food stores. Agribusiness differs from other sectors of the economy because of the seasonality of crop and livestock production and, of course, weather. Many specialized institutions, such as AGRICULTURAL MARKETING BOARDS and specialized government agencies (eg, Canadian Livestock Feed Board), play a role in controlling and directing the system. The many transactions surrounding the world's precarious food balance

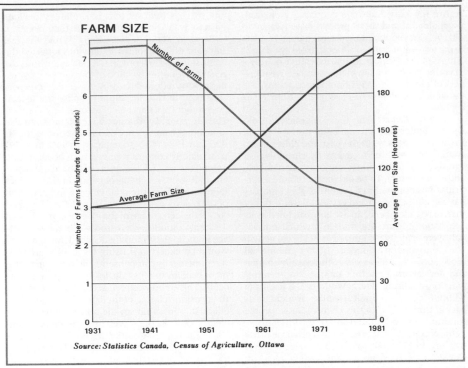

FARM SIZE

Source: Statistics Canada, Census of Agriculture, Ottawa

make it likely that the agribusiness sector of the AGRICULTURE AND FOOD system will continue to expand. *See also* AGRICULTURAL ECONOMICS.

P.M. MONCRIEFF

Agricultural Aid, the provision of agricultural products or technology by one nation to another, normally by developed to developing countries. Aid will continue to be required because in many developing countries 4 out of 10 persons are malnourished; developing countries now grow only 87% of their own food needs and may be able to produce only 74% by the year 2000; and their deficits of wheat, rice and coarse grains are expected to be over 77 million t by 1988.

Agricultural aid is just one component of FOREIGN AID. Canadian agricultural aid is disbursed primarily by the CANADIAN INTERNATIONAL DEVELOPMENT AGENCY (CIDA) and the INTERNATIONAL DEVELOPMENT RESEARCH CENTRE (IDRC). Estimated 1987-88 disbursements by these 2 institutions will be $2.096 billion, ie, 79% of Canadian Official Development Assistance (ODA) and 0.5% of the Gross Domestic Product. Canada is the 7th-highest donor among members of the Organization for Economic Cooperation and Development. In 1985-86 Canada disbursed approximately $580 million of food and agricultural aid through the following 4 channels (the first 3 are CIDA items).

Bilateral Aid is provided to specific countries or groups of countries. In 1985-86 bilateral agricultural and food aid amounted to $290.5 million.

Multilateral Aid is channelled through international financial, research and development institutions. In 1985-86 Canada contributed $73 million to the International Fund for Agricultural Development and close to $13.5 million to the Consultative Group on International Research in support of 14 international research centres. In addition, Canada contributed $150.3 million in food aid through multilateral institutions, primarily the World Food Program. Ninety-five percent of the food was in the form of cereals. The remainder was made up of vegetable oil, pulses, skim milk powder and fish.

Special Programs Aid refers to monies given to nongovernmental organizations (NGOs). The $28.15-million food-aid budgets of the NGOs, in 1985-86, were handled primarily by the NGO Skim Milk Powder Program, the Canadian Food-

grains Bank and the International Committee of the Red Cross.

International Development Research Centre IDRC's contribution to agricultural aid differs from CIDA's to the extent that IDRC promotes the development of a scientific and technical base which developing countries can use to improve their agricultural output. IDRC's agricultural aid is concentrated in 2 divisions: the Agricultural, Food and Nutrition Science Division, with a 1985-86 budget of $21.8 million; and the section of the Social Science Division dealing with Economics and Rural Modernization, with a budget of approximately $2 million.

Other Contributions Canada's agricultural aid includes the assignment of advisers abroad and the training of students from developing countries in Canada. In the year 1985-86 CIDA fully or partially supported more than 360 agricultural and fisheries long-term advisers (over 6 months) and 560 short-term advisers. Sixty-four percent of the long-term advisers were on assignment to Africa. Canadian universities and colleges also contribute to Canada's agricultural aid program. In 1985-86 the 8 university faculties or colleges of agriculture or veterinary medicine undertook $4.5 million worth of new international projects. In addition, these institutions provided training in the areas of agriculture and fisheries for more than 460 students from developing countries. These students were fully or partially supported by CIDA.

TRUMAN P. PHILLIPS

Agricultural Economics, is a field of study related to the application of ECONOMICS theory to problems and issues surrounding the production, processing, distribution and consumption of agricultural food and fibre products. Agricultural economics differs from the study of crop science or animal science primarily because of its relation to human behaviour. In Canada the discipline probably had its origin in the application of economic thinking to problems of physical agriculture in courses taught in the agricultural colleges. Farm management and marketing courses were among the first courses taught that related strictly to agricultural economics. In 1926 a Department of Farm Economics, headed by J.E. Lattimer, was established at Macdonald College, McGill U. The Ontario Agricultural College at Guelph offered

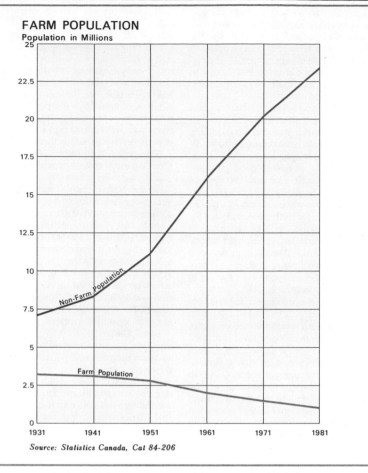

FARM POPULATION
Population in Millions

Non-Farm Population

Farm Population

1931   1941   1951   1961   1971   1981

Source: Statistics Canada, Cat 84-206

undergraduate courses in the discipline; graduate programs were offered with the help of the Department of Political Economy at the U of T. U of T had appointed its first professor of Rural Economics, T. Jackman, in 1921. At the federal level, establishment in 1929 of the Economics Branch of the then Dept of Agriculture was a response to the need for research into pressing agricultural problems, problems which worsened with the GREAT DEPRESSION. Although an agricultural economics department did not then exist at UBC, courses in the field were being offered as early as 1920. The U of Manitoba established a Department of Farm Management and Co-operative Marketing in 1915; U Man's Department of Agricultural Economics had a 4-year agricultural-business program and awarded the first master's degree in the field in 1932. In 1987, degrees in agricultural economics were offered at the bachelor level at Nova Scotia Agricultural College, and at the bachelor and postgraduate levels at Laval, McGill, Guelph, Manitoba, Saskatchewan, Alberta and British Columbia. Various agricultural colleges also offer courses for training in agricultural economics.

Teaching practice, theory and research in the field were influenced by American universities (eg, Cornell, Wisconsin, Minnesota). Course content was originally concerned with production at the individual farm level. Thus, agricultural economics was essentially problem-oriented. Agricultural economists have also made contributions to general economics theory. The most outstanding example, former Harvard professor John Kenneth GALBRAITH, was trained at Guelph as an agricultural economist and developed the theory of "countervailing powers," ie, that competition is less a restraint on corporations than are interest groups on the opposite side of the market. Agricultural economics as a field of study is divided into various subfields, each concerned with a specific major problem area. Common to all activities of the agricultural economist is the need for progressive improvement in the state of agriculture and rural living.

Farm Production Economics Historically the first major problem area addressed was farm-production economics. In this subfield, significant questions pertain to how a greater farm net income may be attained; how production costs may be reduced; which combination of farm inputs is best; and which product or commodity should be produced. These general questions may be translated into very practical terms: Should I plant wheat, corn or barley this year? Would I be better off feeding calves to slaughter weight or buying heavy feeders?

In the past, agricultural economists used 2 perspectives to answer farm-production questions: the farm-management approach and a conceptual approach based on theoretical models. In the first approach, farm surveys were used to determine production costs among groups of similar farms to gain an appreciation of which type of farm was most successful. Recommendations could then be made to all farmers to change their practices to match more closely those of successful farmers. The conceptual approach was based on the application of existing economic theory to agriculture. Economists using the conceptual approach developed farm models to serve as theoretical ideals for comparison with real situations. The major criticism of this type of analysis is that results are too theoretical and too far removed from the practicalities of farming.

Farm-Welfare Economics Farm-welfare economics is concerned both with the needs of farmers and with those of society as they are influenced by developments in agriculture or by the decisions of individual farmers. At one time, Canadian farmers were largely self-sufficient, producing food and fibre for their own families with little surplus for sale. As educational opportunities grew, many farm children gained an education and left the farm for urban areas. At the same time, new technologies were being adopted, eg, use of high-yield, disease-resistant, quick-growing seed and of tractors instead of horses, which allowed one farmer to work a much larger acreage. Specialization also occurred as some farmers became experts at grain production while others raised poultry or hogs. These changes were not accidental; farmers pursued them in an effort to reduce costs and increase sales and gross revenue. Success or failure depended on management capability as well as on differences in basic farm resources (eg, soil productivity). Hence, some areas of Canada have not progressed as much as others and it has been increasingly difficult for smaller farms to achieve incomes above the POVERTY line.

Agricultural economists have attempted to understand the reasons for this evolution and to develop alternative policies and programs that ease the adjustment of those leaving agriculture and strengthen the agricultural capability of rural areas (*see* RURAL SOCIETY).

Agricultural economists have been involved in the design and evaluation of programs to encourage the further processing of farm products and to establish distinctive agriculture and food systems in rural areas. For example, the Canada/Alberta Nutritive Processing Program provides special grants to firms that establish food-processing operations in the province. Provinces such as PEI and Newfoundland have attempted to produce more foodstuffs locally, thereby reducing the flow of funds out of their provinces. Many programs are devoted to building necessary infrastructures such as improved roads, storage facilities, veterinary clinics, etc. In Ontario, emphasis has been placed on improving FARM DRAINAGE to enhance soil productivity.

Agricultural economists have also been involved in international development work, especially through the CANADIAN INTERNATIONAL DEVELOPMENT AGENCY (CIDA) and the World Bank. The World Bank has a detailed program analysis process that specifies beforehand the overall benefits to a country's national economy and the financial benefits to farmers and other participants that may be expected from an agricultural and rural-development program; eg, one of the larger foreign-aid programs is the Canadian wheat program, which introduced large-scale mechanized grain farming to Tanzania in eastern Africa.

Agriculture Policy The agricultural sector is constantly undergoing change as a result of new technology, shifting demands, international agreements and disagreements and changing pressure groups. These changing conditions necessitate the periodic re-evaluation of farm policies. The task of objectively analysing alternative policies frequently requires the expertise of agricultural economists. These policies and programs have taken many forms, from direct subsidies on commodities to control over production and prices. Agricultural economists have been very influential in prescribing the workings of each scheme as well as in the ongoing management of the systems established.

Agricultural Marketing Much of economic theory is based on the concept of the free market; however, farmers usually have found themselves competing to sell their commodities to one or, at best, a few buyers. Agricultural-economics studies have focused on the means by which markets and participants can be judged to be performing marketing tasks efficiently. Such information, combined with farmers' perceptions that their bargaining power is weak against industries such as grain companies and meat-packers, has fostered the development of farmer co-operatives, boards and associations to redress alleged faults in the marketing process (*see* CO-OPERATIVE MOVEMENT). Agricultural economists have also played a role in defining standard grades of products; for example, Canadian hog- and cattle-grading systems serve as world-recognized models (*see* COMMODITY INSPECTION AND GRADING).

One of the basic assumptions underlying the operation of a free market is perfect information. Many farm commodities are marketed outside of a rigidly controlled process; thus the provision of market information for such commodities as CORN, WHEAT, HOGS, cattle and OILSEEDS is important. An area of specialization has developed within agricultural economics to provide market outlooks and analyses. Such specialists study past cyclical trends, current weather behaviour in key producing countries, general demand conditions and government policies in order to make projections on prices in coming months.

Land Resource Economics The applied nature of agricultural economics is nowhere more evident than in the subfield of land economics, a specialized area of production economics that focuses on land, the major factor in farm production. In most instances farmland cannot generate sufficient return to warrant the price paid, because the market price of land is usually higher than its productive value. This discrepancy results from expectations about future increase in value. The balance between personal and public rights over property has long been in debate. For example, does the Crown have the right to expropriate farmland for airports, urban expansion or recreational purposes and, if so, what price should be paid? Intermingled in these issues are public concerns over land use, eg, zoning of agricultural land for food production and laws regarding weed-control or SOIL-CONSERVATION practices. Many agriculturists believe that farmers are custodians of the land, holding it for future generations. Unfortunately, high interest rates and low farm-commodity prices have led some farmers to exploit their land to the fullest to survive. This exploitation has resulted in charges that they are mining the soil of its nutrients to the detriment of the land resource. The impact of economics and public taxation measures on these problems are frequent subjects for study by agricultural economists.

Agricultural economists have also studied the sometimes conflicting needs of farmers, wildlife species, foresters and outdoor recreationists. A complicating factor in the resolution of problems related to land use is the lack of definition regarding the ownership of natural resources. Wildlife eat hay and other crops belonging to farmers, but the wildlife may belong to the Crown or society at large. Land may be privately held, but hunters may pursue wildlife in season. Management of conflicts and of common-use natural resources is yet another area of agricultural-economic endeavour. Benefit-cost analysis has developed from natural-resource economics and the need to quantify decisions. This methodological tool has played an important part in analysing public-sector questions and in ranking projects in which governments can invest. *See also* FARM LAW.

P.M. MONCRIEFF

Agricultural Education in Canada occurs formally at at least 4 levels: school system, diploma (sub-degree) level, university bachelor-degree level, and postgraduate-degree level (master's and doctoral). In addition, another informal level (ie, extension activities) operates as the link between scientific findings, technological developments and the farmer. Agricultural education in

primary and secondary schools generally consists of a course designed to acquaint the student with the complexities of modern agriculture. Usually taught in high school, it is aimed at developing an awareness of the role of agriculture in society. Formal post-secondary education and extension activities constitute Canada's most significant agricultural-education efforts.

Agricultural education began in New France in 1670 at the Petit Séminaire at St-Joachim, an "industrial" school which provided some training in agriculture. This training was most probably directed to practical experience on the school farm, which was described as having good pastures, woods, an area of tillable land and 150 head of cattle. This program, begun by Bishop LAVAL, continued until 1715. Two additional schools, initiated in Québec early in the 19th century, lasted for only one year. In 1859 the School of Agriculture of Sainte-Anne-de-la-Pocatière, sponsored by Abbé Pilote, opened with Émile Dumais as professor of agriculture. It offered a diploma and later a degree program. In 1962 it became part of the Faculty of Agriculture of Laval University.

The first English-language agricultural school was established at Guelph, Ont, in 1874. It began with a 1-year, practical, work-oriented program. In 1880 a 2-year diploma program was instituted and the school underwent a name change, from Ontario School of Agriculture to Ontario Agricultural College and Experimental Farm (OAC). In 1887 a third year was added to the program, and in 1888 the OAC was affiliated with University of Toronto, thus achieving degree-granting status. A fourth year was added to the program in 1902. In 1964 OAC became part of the University of Guelph.

In 1885 a school of agriculture was established at Truro, NS, followed 8 years later (1893) by a school of horticulture at Wolfville. Both were absorbed by the Nova Scotia Agricultural College (NSAC), which officially opened at Truro in Feb 1905, gaining degree-granting status in 1980.

The last agricultural school established in the 19th century was the School of Agriculture of Oka, founded in 1893 by the Trappist Fathers of the abbey of Oka, Qué. In 1908 it affiliated with Laval and changed its name to the Agricultural Institute of Oka. In 1962 it became a part of Laval's new Faculty of Agriculture.

Contemporary Degree-Granting Institutions

Schools of agriculture differ markedly in their affiliation and sponsors. There is no Canadian equivalent of the US Land Grant Act, which established land-grant agricultural colleges throughout that country. Early Québec schools were sponsored by religious groups, while McGill's Macdonald College was endowed by Sir William MACDONALD. NSAC, OAC and the Manitoba Agricultural College (MAC) were established by their respective provincial ministries of agriculture, while the faculties of agriculture of Saskatchewan, Alberta and BC are part of provincial universities. Those schools established as integral faculties of a university did not provide instruction in many of the basic arts and science subjects (eg, literature, chemistry, physics, mathematics); students instead took service courses offered in the arts and science faculties. The MAC and OAC initially provided these basic courses, relinquishing them when the university moved onto the agriculture campus in Manitoba in the former case, and when a university was established on the OAC campus in the latter. Macdonald College, while always a part of McGill, has, by reason of physical separation of the 2 campuses, provided instruction in the basic sciences by its own specialized staff.

The subject areas deemed appropriate to agriculture have changed significantly. The early schools all offered courses in crop and animal production. SOIL SCIENCE, agricultural engineering and AGRICULTURAL ECONOMICS were also a part of many early curricula. The development of AGRICULTURAL RESEARCH and its associated disciplines has broadened the offerings of all faculties. Most faculties now address the processing of agricultural products as well as primary production, and some include WILDLIFE and FORESTRY as a part of natural-resource management training.

Nova Scotia Agricultural College operates as an interprovincial college providing agricultural education to students from NS, NB, PEI and Nfld. In 1980 the NSAC received approval to offer a 4-year program leading to a BSc in Agriculture (in plant science, animal science, agricultural economics and plant protection). Before 1980 the college had offered a 2-year university-level program which prepared students for the final year of a degree program at the OAC, Macdonald or University of Maine; it still offers 2-year programs which permit students to enter areas of specialization available at these institutions but not at NSAC. The NSAC does not offer a program leading to postgraduate degrees.

Laval University The Faculty of Agriculture and Food Sciences currently offers an 8-trimester (4-year) program following the CEGEP (COLLÈGE D'ENSEIGNEMENT GÉNÉRAL ET PROFESSIONNEL, ie, senior matriculation). Students receive a BScA degree with specialization in agro-economy; bio-agronomy with concentration in soil/plant, animal science or agricultural MICROBIOLOGY; agricultural engineering; or food science. Through the School of Graduate Studies, MSc degrees are available in DIETETICS, rural economy and agricultural engineering; MSc and PhD degrees in plant science, agricultural microbiology, soils, food science and animal science; and a PhD in nutrition.

Macdonald College, McGill University, located at Ste-Anne-de-Bellevue, Qué, was built, endowed and staffed through the benefaction of Sir William Macdonald. Construction began in 1905, the first students enrolling in the fall of 1907. An earlier McGill agriculture program was begun by Principal J.W. DAWSON, who in 1864 published *First Lessons in Scientific Agriculture for Schools*. Macdonald is unique among faculties of agriculture in N America in being part of a largely privately endowed university. The faculty currently offers 3 undergraduate degrees through 3-year (6-term) programs following completion of the CEGEP diploma. The areas of specialization for the BSc (Agr) are agricultural chemistry, agricultural economics, animal science, general agriculture, plant science (with emphasis on agronomy, horticulture or plant protection), soil science, environmental BIOLOGY, microbiology, ENTOMOLOGY, community resource development, land planning and CONSERVATION of environmental and wildlife resources. Areas of specialization for the BSc in Food Science are consumer services, nutrition, food administration, dietetics and food science. A BSc in Agricultural Engineering is also awarded. The faculty co-operates with the Faculty of Education to offer the BEd degree in HOME ECONOMICS and with the Faculty of Management to give a BComm in food services administration.

All departments offer MSc and PhD degrees through the Faculty of Graduate Studies and Research. Programs of study and directed research are given in agricultural chemistry and physics, agricultural engineering, animal science (including animal GENETICS, animal physiology and nutrition), entomology, microbiology, plant science (including agronomy, plant breeding, horticulture, plant genetics and plant pathology), soil science and wildlife biology.

Ontario Agricultural College From 1888 until 1964 the OAC degree of BSA was awarded by U of Toronto. Since 1964 the degree has been awarded by U of Guelph. The OAC currently offers a 4-year, post-senior-matriculation program leading to the BSA degree.

All OAC students take the same courses in their first year, after which they may specialize in agricultural business, agricultural economics, agricultural mechanization, animal and poultry science, applied microbiology, crop science, dairy science, entomology-apiculture, environmental biology, horticultural science, plant protection, resource economics and rural development, RESOURCE MANAGEMENT or soil science.

MSc degrees are offered in agricultural business, extension education and rural development. A Master of LANDSCAPE ARCHITECTURE degree is also offered. Programs of study and directed research leading to MSc and PhD degrees are offered in agricultural economics, agrometeorology, animal and poultry science, crop science, dairy science, earth science and geology, engineering, entomology-apiculture, food science, horticulture science, microbiology, plant protection and pathology, resource economics, resources management and soil science.

Manitoba Agricultural College In 1906 the MAC was established as an outgrowth of a dairy school operated by the Manitoba Department of Agriculture since 1894. In 1924 MAC was transferred from the Dept of Agriculture to the Board of Governors of University of Manitoba. The various BSA programs of the university's Faculty of Agriculture require 4 years of study following senior matriculation. All students take common courses in the first year. In years 2-4 they may specialize in agricultural economics and farm management, agricultural engineering (students preparing for the professional association register for the agricultural engineering program in the Faculty of Engineering), agricultural sciences, animal science, entomology, food science, plant science or soil science. MSc and PhD programs are offered in agricultural economics and farm management, animal science, entomology, food science, plant science and soil science.

University of Saskatchewan The Faculty of Agriculture of Saskatchewan was established in concert with the university. The university's location within Saskatoon was, in fact, determined by its suitability for an agricultural college (ie, it had adequate land for a farm and experimental field work). University of Saskatchewan's first agriculture classes were held in 1912. The faculty offers a BSc in Agriculture. All programs consist of 4 years following Saskatchewan Division IV or grade 12. In the first year all students follow a common curriculum. Later they may specialize in agricultural biology, agricultural chemistry, agricultural economics, agricultural mechanics, agricultural microbiology, agronomy, animal science, crop science, dairy and food science, horticultural science, plant ecology, parks and recreation, poultry science or soil science. The College of Graduate Studies and Research offers various graduate degrees: the MAgr, a nonthesis degree, in animal and poultry science and agricultural economics; an MSc in agricultural economics; MSc and PhD programs in animal science, poultry science, crop science, dairy and food science, plant ecology and soil science. In addition, the degrees of MEng, MSc and PhD in agricultural engineering are offered in the College of Engineering.

University of Alberta The Faculty of Agriculture of University of Alberta began instruction in 1915; this program, like Saskatchewan's, was an integral part of the new university. In 1970 a FORESTRY program was added and the faculty's name was changed to the Faculty of Agriculture and Forestry. Two other Alberta institutions, the Vermilion and Olds schools of agriculture, were established in 1913.

The faculty currently has a 4-year post-senior-matriculation program leading to a BSc in Agriculture. A modified first year is also offered at University of Calgary, University of Lethbridge and at affiliated junior colleges. Students specialize after the first year in general agriculture, rural economics (agricultural economics and rural sociology), agronomy, livestock science, poultry science, grazing management, plant protection, plant science or soil science. The faculty also cooperates with the Faculty of Engineering to offer a program leading to a BSc in Agricultural Engineering and with the Faculty of Home Economics to offer a BSc in Food Science. A nonthesis Master of Agriculture is given in agricultural engineering, animal science, food science, soil science and rural economy. A Master of Engineering is offered in agricultural engineering and in food science. A thesis MSc is offered in agricultural engineering and in home economics; MSc and PhD programs are offered in animal science, entomology, food science, forest science, plant science, soil science and rural economy.

University of British Columbia The Faculty of Agriculture received its first students in 1915 and was assisted in its development by Professor L.S. Klinck of Macdonald College. The faculty requires 4 years of study following senior matriculation. The degree of BSc (Agr) is offered in agricultural economics, bio-resource engineering (through the Faculty of Applied Science), agricultural mechanics, animal science, plant science, poultry science and soil science. The degree of Bachelor of Landscape Architecture is also offered. At the graduate level the MSc degree is offered in agricultural economics, agricultural extension and agricultural mechanics. Both MSc and PhD degrees are offered in animal science, food science, plant science, poultry science, resource management (interdisciplinary) and soil science.

Non-Degree-Granting Institutions

At least 4 schools which evolved from practical, non-degree programs are still operating, namely the diploma programs of NSAC, Macdonald College, OAC and University of Manitoba's Faculty of Agriculture. There are 21 institutions offering post-secondary work in agriculture. Of these, 5 offer programs in French (one in NB, 3 in Qué, one in Ont); the remaining 16 offer programs in English (one each in NS, Qué, Man and Sask; 2 in BC; 4 in Alta; and 6 in Ont). All but 5 of the schools are independent of their provincial university faculties of agriculture. These are the diploma schools of NSAC, Macdonald College, OAC and the faculties of agriculture of University of Manitoba and University of Saskatchewan. All these schools offer production-oriented courses to prepare farmers for modern farming. In addition, many offer programs to prepare graduates for jobs as technicians in various agricultural industries. Most programs are of 2-year duration, although some offer a third year.

Subject matter mirrors the changes that have taken place in agriculture. Production courses, which previously emphasized instruction on plowing or home slaughtering of beef or poultry, may now provide information on agricultural chemicals for pest control, farm accounting and use of computers in feed formulation, and adjustment and management of highly complex farm machinery.

Agricultural Extension

The process of transferring new developments in technology and farming techniques from researchers to farmers is called "extension." Those responsible for this process in Canada are called agricultural representatives (agrologists) or, in Québec, agronomes. The need to engage in extension activity has long been recognized. The former Manitoba Agricultural College organized special "Better Farming Trains" which toured the province with demonstrations, lectures, exhibits and staff consultants. A similar technique was used by Macdonald College, which in addition appointed graduates as "demonstrators" and stationed them in rural areas. This function was later taken over by the provincial extension service.

Extension educational and advisory activity is a major responsibility of provincial ministries of agriculture. The educational role is fulfilled by organizing and, in many cases, conducting short courses, workshops, etc, and by the preparation of interpretative bulletins, press releases, etc, for farmer use. Extension services are staffed by agricultural professionals and by specialists in various agricultural production problems. The agricultural representative can play a key role in identifying problems at the local level and in relaying these problems to the research scientist. In many instances the representative co-operates with the research scientist in the conduct of "local" tests of new technology.

HOWARD A. STEPPLER

Agricultural Exhibitions probably began as bazaars or fairs. Through the centuries these gatherings diverged somewhat from their original function and became primarily competitive showplaces for livestock and produce and settings for the display of new agricultural technology, as well as social events. Canadian agricultural exhibitions derive much of their character from the agricultural fairs of England and Scotland. North America's first such fair was held in NS in 1765. Fairs continue to make important contributions to Canada's rural society by providing social and educational opportunities, and to all Canadians by helping to improve agriculture through competition.

Contemporary agricultural exhibitions vary greatly: the majority are country "fairs" lasting one or 2 days and featuring a cross section of agricultural products and local crafts. Regional exhibitions, lasting 3-4 days, are less common, encompass areas served by several local fairs and satisfy the desire for larger events featuring greater competition. A third type of fair, the provincial exhibition, draws exhibits from a still larger geographic area and tends to be more "commercial" in that dealers in farm machinery and other farm technologies display their wares. On the interprovincial or national level, Toronto's Royal Winter Fair, probably Canada's best-known agricultural exhibition, serves a great cross section of the industry. Other well-known exhibitions are the Royal Manitoba Winter Fair at Brandon and the CALGARY STAMPEDE. Most recently, large specialized shows have appeared. For example, well over 1000 head of cattle are exhibited at the annual Agribition in Saskatchewan and Ag-Ex in Manitoba. The Annual Farm Progress Show in Regina represents another type of specialization: agricultural equipment worth millions of dollars and representing the most modern agricultural technology is exhibited.

The main agricultural product exhibited in most of the regional, interprovincial or national exhibitions is livestock, although grain, fruit, poultry, pets, vegetables, flowers and crafts are important features. The spirit of competition of these events has contributed to improvements in livestock breeds. The horse show is an important livestock exhibit because of its entertainment value and the quality of product displayed. Exhibition activities have been largely responsible for the development of keen national and international equestrian competition. Standards of desirability in the appearance of commercial livestock (eg, cattle, sheep, hogs) change as consumer diet preferences change. Swine, for example, have been bred over a period of many years to be long and lean rather than short and fat, as consumers opt for less fat in their diets. Similarly, size and breed of beef cattle have changed to reflect perceived production efficiencies assumed to be inherent in the more rapid weight increase of larger breeds.

Exhibitions have played a special role in personal development through the promotion of 4-H CLUB programs. The 4-H movement really started when, early in the century, exhibitions began sponsoring livestock competitions for youth. Exhibitions continue to change along with the public's desire to observe new developments in the agriculture and food system, to remain current in standards of excellence and to enjoy the opportunity to socialize with people from a cross section of the community at large. *See also* CANADIAN NATIONAL EXHIBITION; AGRICULTURAL EDUCATION.

R.E. FORBES

Agricultural Implements Canadian agriculture changed rapidly between 1850 and 1900, and changes in agricultural implements both caused and reflected changes in other sectors.

In addition to the spade, hoe and rake familiar to modern gardeners, early hand tools used in farming included the seeder, a perforated wooden trough carried by means of a strap around the neck and used in broadcast seeding; the sickle and the scythe, one- and 2-handed knives, respectively, used for cutting field crops and hay; the flail, 2 wooden rods attached by a strap and used to thresh out the kernels of grain; the winnowing tray, a 2-handled, half-moon-shaped receptacle used to cast flailed grain into the air so that the chaff could be blown away; the fork, used for pitching hay or shovelling manure; the wooden grain shovel; the hay knife and hay hook; and the grafting froe, a knife used to split branches in grafting. Most of these implements were superseded; others (eg, the plow) underwent substantial modification.

Plow From wooden-moldboard, single-handled, home-made machines, plows became chilled-steel, mass-produced, scientifically designed 2-handled walking plows; then single-moldboard riding plows, double-moldboard riding plows, and finally giant machines with up to 16 moldboards. These alterations occurred as the source of power changed from oxen (best for root-strewn pioneer farms) to teams of HORSES, then to multiple teams of horses (up to 16 to a hitch), to steam-driven traction engines with the power of 50 or more horses, and finally to lighter, more versatile but equally powerful gasoline tractors.

Threshing Machinery underwent the most dramatic and expensive changes. In 1850 most farmers cut their grain with cradle scythes, and the few short weeks of the harvest dictated the amount grown. In winter, cut grain was threshed on the BARN floor, by beating with flails or treading with horses' hooves until the kernel fell free of the straw and was scooped up and winnowed, by the wind or by an artificial wind created by a fanning mill. More efficient machines (eg, the generation of reapers triggered by the inventions of Cyrus McCormick and Obed Hussey in the US and Patrick Bell in England) allowed farmers to harvest larger and larger amounts of grain. Larger threshing machines, initially powered by one- or 2-horse treadmills, and later by immense steam-

Frost & Wood No 3 binder, built 1902-06.

Cockshutt No 2 cultivator, *c*1921.

Frost & Wood No 8 mower, built 1897-1908.

Frost & Wood "Simplex" reaper, *c*1918.

Frost & Wood Scotch diamond harrows, *c*1918.

Cockshutt manure spreader, *c*1921.

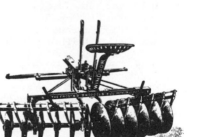

Frost & Wood Windsor disc harrow, *c*1921.

Cockshutt Ontario footlift sulky plow, *c*1918.

Frost & Wood No 9 one-horse mower, built 1909 & after.

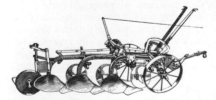

Cockshutt 10″ and 12″ light tractor plows, 2 & 3 furrow, *c*1921.

Frost & Wood "Climax" cultivator, built 1899-1915.

Cockshutt Maple Leaf gang plow, *c*1921.

(From catalogues of company price lists, Alan Skeoch Coll/ Mississauga.)

Horse-drawn mowing machine, c1859 (*courtesy National Library of Canada/Rare Books Div*).

driven traction engines, began to appear. Mechanical threshers were manufactured by Waterloo, Sawyer-Massey, Hergott, Lobsinger, Moody and other Canadian manufacturers.

Seed Drills changed from primitive, arm-held broadcast seeders to precisely engineered 11, 13 and 15 run, horse-drawn grain drills that punched seeds into nicely tilled ground at precise depths and intervals.

Tillage Machinery was also improved. Harrows made from tree branches, with iron spikes driven into them, were replaced by various steel-spring harrows that were able to tear freshly turned sod into a weed-free seedbed in much less time.

The Industry

Rapid change provided opportunities for industrialists. The tiny local blacksmith's shops of Canadian villages began to increase in size as the demand for iron increased, particularly after the railway boom of the 1850s, which allowed cheap iron to move more easily from England and the US. The demand for iron for engines, rolling stock and track led to the establishment of a sophisticated iron industry in Hamilton, Ont. Earlier ironmakers (eg, the Van Normans) had relied on poor-grade bog iron. In the 1850s higher-quality iron stimulated the growth of local foundries.

Iron began to replace wood in farm implements. Implement makers grew in number, particularly around the western end of Lk Ontario, where MASSEY, Verity, Patterson, Wilkinson, Sawyer, Cockshutt, Wisner, HARRIS and others established their factories, making plows, cutting boxes, fanning mills, seed drills, reapers, mowers, threshing machines and steam engines. Because it was cheap and plentiful, wood was used wherever possible. Iron, however, was essential for cutting and moving parts in general. Larger- and larger-scale implement makers seemed to sprout up overnight; some of these companies, eg, those that were conservative or undercapitalized, disappeared as quickly; others thrived and continue to dominate the farm machinery industry into the late 20th century.

As one machine was rendered obsolete by the invention of an improvement (eg, the wire binder replacing the sail-reaper and itself replaced by the twine binder), the pace of competition accelerated. A few Canadian companies, eg, the plow maker William H. Verity, specialized in one implement; however, most of the big implement makers produced full lines of farm equipment. The Massey Manufacturing Co (originally established at Bond Head and later relocated at Newcastle, then Toronto, because of the need for a railway supply and delivery system) only made about 50-odd implements in 1847. In 1860 it was making 2 classes of implements: simple machines of Canadian design (eg, straw cutters, harrows, wheelbarrows, fanning mills) and more compli-

cated machines copied from American patents (eg, Manny's Combined Reaper and Mower, Wood's New Self-Raking Reaper, Pitt's Horse Power, Ketchum's Patent Mower). The manufacture of American machines in Canada was a matter of considerable pride and the absence of a patent law, until 1869, encouraged Canadian implement makers to make annual trips to the US in search of new ideas and special rights to manufacture new American inventions.

Ontario Markets were strongest in western Ontario, where the rural majority in the 1850s had been able to set aside capital from the high grain prices caused by the Crimean War. In eastern Ontario the number of manufacturers was smaller but still significant, the most prominent being Frost and Wood of Smiths Falls, which survived the period of intense competition in the 1890s. Herring of Napanee, which marketed fanning mills and reapers, eventually folded, as Massey-Harris machines moved into a wider and wider market area after 1891. Not all implement makers stayed in that line of production; eg, the Gibbard Co of Napanee initially made fanning mills and coffins, then began making fine furniture, eventually dropping implement manufacturing completely.

The Maritimes Machine makers in the Maritimes also had a period of growth; however, the market was small and was eventually dominated by the larger Ontario manufacturers, who spread their wares eastward following Confederation. Connell Brothers (Woodstock, NB) and Harris and Allen (Saint John) were successful manufacturers in the Loyalist farming centres. Others could be found in PEI and NS.

Québec implement makers were more influenced by European machine patterns and the medieval 2-wheeled plow remained a common sight on Québec farms throughout the 19th century. Since many French Canadians were at least partially agricultural throughout the 19th century, implement makers had many opportunities. Doré et Fils (La Prairie) and Mathew Moody and Sons (Terrebonne) were successful makers of stationary threshing machines and horsepower treadmills in the 20th century; some examples of their machines can still be found in eastern Canada.

Western Canada The growth of prairie agriculture was a 20th-century phenomenon and, although Winnipeg did attract some implement makers, by the time the prairie market opened up, the eastern implement makers (protected by the high tariffs of the National Policy) were ready to provide the latest open-end binders pioneered by the Harris, Massey and Toronto Reaper companies. The popularity of self-propelled steam traction engines after 1900 demanded a high level of technological sophistication, and American companies (eg, Case, Deere, International Harvester) competed stiffly with Ontario manufacturers. These companies were quick to design and construct bigger and bigger steam-engine tractors for the rich prairie grainfields. The threshing-machine industry expanded to meet the increased power provided by these steam-engine tractors. Again Ontario implement makers, with their head start in implement TECHNOLOGY, were able to capture most of the new western market and Waterloo, Lobsinger, Sawyer-Massey, Hergott and Bell were soon shipping larger and larger pórtable threshing machines to the West. Although wooden bodied to begin with, these new dinosaurs of the western prairies soon were made with galvanized metal, and thus were better able to withstand the ravages of time. Many can still be seen abandoned on prairie farms, while their offspring, the combine harvesters, chew their way across the ripening fields of wheat.

ALAN SKEOCH

Agricultural Implements Industry comprises establishments involved in manufacturing a range of farm machinery, including combines, cultivators, harrows, harvesters, threshing machines, etc. Canada's farm equipment industry had its beginnings in the mid-19th century, when the establishment of local iron foundries stimulated development of farm implement manufactories. Some of the earliest of these companies (including Massey, Harris, Cockshutt, etc) were established in the Lk Ontario district. Many early manufacturers failed or were absorbed into larger companies, while other new companies opened. In the 1980s literally hundreds of manufacturers and distributors of farm equipment market their products in Canada. These enterprises range from large, multinational companies that produce a broad range of machinery and implements to smaller, specialty-line manufacturers.

In 1984 there were 231 manufacturers of agricultural implements in Canada, employing over 10 500 workers. Only 2 establishments employed more than 1000 workers; 90% of establishments employed fewer than 100 workers. For the larger, "full-line" manufacturers, the Canadian operations are part of their worldwide production network. Most of the innovative, smaller establishments, which specialize in a small range of equipment (ie, "short-line" manufacturers), are Canadian owned. Many of these are found in the Prairie region. A small number of these short-line manufacturers are branch plants of European companies. Value of shipments in 1984 was $1.04 million and in 1986 was $0.77 billion.

Canada's farmers buy over $2-billion worth of machinery and implements annually, including an average of some 19 000 tractors, 3500 swathers, 4000 grain combines and a host of balers, plows, diskers and other harvesting and tillage tools. A large portion of the farm machinery purchased for Canadian farms, including combines, are imported. The main sources of these imports are the US, the EEC and Japan. The Canadian manufacturing sector, with a base of short-line manufacturers and major manufacturing facilities of some multinationals, exports about 60% of its production. On average Canada has a $1 billion deficit in the farm machinery trade. The industry is represented by the Canadian Farm and Industrial Equipment Institute, Burlington, Ont, the Prairie Implements Manufacturers Assn, Regina, and the Association of Agricultural Equipment Manufacturers of Québec, Montréal.

Farm equipment markets in N America have always been cyclical in nature, with predictable 5- to 7-year cycles. However, with the economic downturn which began in the early 1980s, farm equipment sales began a downward spiral that continues in 1987 and has proven to be particularly severe. For example, in 1979, sales of farm tractors in the 2-wheel drive category, 40 hp and over, totalled 23 383 units; in 1986, 12 584 units

Modern combine in operation near Edmonton (*photo by Earl Olsen*).

were sold, a drop of 45%. Similarly, some 5000 large, self-propelled combine harvesters were sold in 1979; this figure fell to 2818 in 1986. Most other lines of farm equipment have suffered similar sales reductions in the same period. As we enter the 6th year of these low sales, the industry has adjusted by lowering break-even points and closing factories on the assumption that 1986 sales levels are the normal level. Although all manufacturers and distributors suffered, some of the large companies, such as MASSEY-FERGUSON LTD (now Varity Corp), Versatile, International Harvester, the White Farm Equipment organization and others, found themselves in particularly severe financial difficulties. International, White, Versatile and others have been purchased by competitors and Massey-Ferguson was totally restructured, with unprofitable divisions sold off or simply disbanded.

Other changes in the farm equipment industry in N America have been the result of the economic depression in AGRIBUSINESS. Many full-line companies that had produced a broad range of agricultural machines and implements are now concentrating on manufacturing a limited line of key products. Many companies are also "jobbing out" specialty lines previously built in-house, thus freeing capital, reducing overheads and providing better inventory planning. The result is that there are fewer and leaner manufacturers to meet the decreased machinery demand of the late 1980s.

Products

In the last 50 years, the number of people engaged in farming has declined radically and hectarages farmed have increased slightly. These changes have been made possible by developments in farm machinery that permit Canadian farmers to till, seed and harvest ever-larger hectarages with less expenditure of time and labour.

Tillage Equipment In the past, farmlands were continually cultivated and many passes were made across the field to prepare the ground for seeding. Modern tillage practices seek to minimize disturbance of the soil surface to conserve vital topsoil and its nutrients (*see* SOIL CONSERVATION). Tilling implements have been designed to prepare seedbeds with little disturbance of the surface. Thus, while the moldboard plow continues to be used in farming in the moist conditions of eastern Canada, the modern chisel plow, which features a series of cultivating chisel points for preparing a seedbed while disturbing the ground surface only minimally, is popular in the Prairies. The industry has also developed tillage implements that leave stubble from previous crops in place, thus retaining the nutrients that such residues provide and helping to control EROSION.

Seeding Equipment To complement changing tillage practices and equipment, modern seeding implements have been developed for a wide range of seedbed conditions from sod to well prepared seedbeds. Air seeders have only recently entered the marketplace and have already proven to be efficient in seeding through previous crop stubble, particularly in dry-land farming areas in western Canada. A sod seeder will allow farmers to plant a crop with no seedbed preparation. The same equipment can also be used in the precision application of fertilizer and pesticides.

Hay and Forage Equipment Farmers managing large dairy or beef feedlot operations operate highly mechanized businesses. Traditional baling machines which produced a compact, rectangular bale of hay weighing about 45 kg have given way to machines that produce large, round bales of up to 680 kg. This new technology provides for

Potato harvesting, New Haven, PEI (*photo by Wayne R. Barrett/Masterfile*).

better storage capability and improved drying and curing of harvested forage materials. Similarly, FORAGE CROPS may be cut and conditioned using highly efficient forage harvesters. Grinder mixers, machines that prepare silage for proper consistency and exact portioning, as well as adding vitamins, etc, are also available.

Grain Harvesting Equipment Modern combine harvesters are capable of harvesting a broad range of crops, including wheat, barley, corn, soybeans, etc. They can cut and harvest a swath as wide as 10 m in a single pass, thus allowing the farmer to harvest hundreds of hectares per day. Technological advances include computerized monitoring systems to provide the operator with information on grain loss, damage and rate of speed for optimum performance.

Swathers or windrowers, machines designed to cut grain and leave it in lines ready for pickup, are widely used in areas where ripened grain requires some drying prior to harvesting (as in western Canada). When farmers judge the time is appropriate, they harvest the precut crop with a special combine pickup table and the final harvesting steps take place.

Tractors Technological advances in tractor manufacturing during the last 20 years have been dramatic. The typical modern farm tractor is diesel powered (over 90% of all self-propelled farm machines have diesel engines), with a rating of about 90 hp, although models ranging from small 9 hp units up to large 4-wheel-drive units of over 400 hp are being marketed. Many of these provide a wide range of computerized operating features, eg, digital gauges that report wheel slippage, recommended gear settings and information regarding fuel efficiency and productivity. Tractors with front wheel assist and front-mounted 3-point hitches and PTO (European innovations) are expanding their market share, particularly in eastern Canada.

BRENT M. HAMRE AND ALAN ASSELSTINE

Agricultural Marketing Board, a statutory body which acts as a compulsory marketing agent, performing or controlling one or more of the functions of marketing on behalf of producers of specific agricultural commodities. Boards may be established and operated under legislation passed by either provincial or federal governments, depending on whether the products they market or regulate are produced and sold within a province (intraprovincially) or are sold interprovincially or to export markets. Some boards are subject to the jurisdiction of both levels of government. In 1987 there were 121 agricultural marketing boards in Canada. Marketing boards

operate in every province and regulate a wide variety of agricultural products.

The first boards developed from farmers' efforts to gain market power through joint action and as a reaction to unstable farm prices and incomes. Efforts early in this century to organize co-operative agricultural marketing ventures grew into attempts by some producers' groups to achieve compulsory, centralized marketing through boards. Disruption of marketing channels during and after WWI led to centralized GRAIN HANDLING AND MARKETING by temporary government agencies from 1917 to 1920. However, the first Canadian producer-controlled agricultural marketing boards were introduced in BC in the late 1920s. In 1931 the Supreme Court of Canada found that the legislation under which these early producer marketing boards were established infringed upon the authority of the federal government in interprovincial trade, and that the boards themselves constituted an indirect tax. Pressure for national legislation permitting establishment of marketing boards increased as farm prices and incomes fell during the GREAT DEPRESSION of the 1930s. Federal legislation for this purpose was passed in 1934, but was also found to be unconstitutional because it interfered with the authority of the provinces in intraprovincial trade. Subsequent provincial and federal legislation recognized the respective jurisdictions of the 2 levels of government.

Provincial marketing Acts generally establish supervisory boards or councils which develop provincial commodity marketing plans and oversee the introduction and operation of boards and commissions which administer these plans. Directors of commodity commissions are generally government appointed, but board directors are commonly elected by producers. Commodity marketing plans are implemented following a favourable vote by producers of the commodity. Under the Agricultural Products Marketing Act of 1949, the federal government can authorize boards established under provincial marketing Acts to regulate interprovincial and export sales.

Conflicts arising from efforts by some provincial supply-management boards to control the inflow of products from other provinces contributed to passage of the Farm Products Marketing Agencies Act in 1972. This Act provided for the establishment of the supervisory National Farm Products Marketing Council, for the development of national or regional marketing plans, and for the establishment and operation of national marketing agencies or boards. By 1978 there were national boards for eggs, turkeys and broiler chickens, operating in conjunction with the provincial boards for these commodities. National agricultural marketing institutions acting under separate legislation include the CANADIAN WHEAT BOARD (CWB), marketing agency for major prairie grains, which has been in operation since 1935; and the Canadian Dairy Commission, which was established in 1966 and which, together with provincial milk boards, administers the national dairy program for industrial milk and cream.

There is substantial variation in the legislatively sanctioned powers held and exercised by boards and considerable difference in the activities they undertake in pursuit of their objectives. The major objectives of marketing boards are to enhance producers' prices and incomes and to reduce variability in them. Some boards are also concerned that access to market opportunities be shared equitably among producers and that there be standardized terms of sale for the product which they regulate. Boards are empowered to enforce compliance with the marketing regulations they administer and may have power to license processors and handlers of the product they regulate. Boards usually have powers to conduct or sponsor research, information or product-promotion activities and most are empowered to purchase and sell the product they regulate. Some are specified as the sole buyer from producers and the sole seller on their behalf. For example, the CWB is the sole seller in export markets of prairie WHEAT, BARLEY and OATS. Some boards are empowered to pool producer prices or market returns by grade of product (eg, the CWB, many of the HOG boards and some VEGETABLE boards). Some boards have the power to schedule producers' deliveries to the marketing system through delivery quotas. The CWB performs this activity and also regulates shipments of grain through the transportation system to terminal grain elevators or mills. Some marketing boards negotiate prices and other terms of sale with processors or handlers, eg, some hog boards and some of the boards for FRUITS.

The strongest marketing powers held by boards are those to determine prices, when enforced by the power to apply supply-controlling quotas. Such quotas involve control over the entry of new producers and over the amount of the product produced or marketed. The use of these pricing- and supply-control mechanisms by provincial and national boards for POULTRY and DAIRY products is controversial. Advocates note that these programs have reduced variability in farm prices and increased producers' incomes; critics say the programs have contributed to increased food prices and higher consumer expenditures and that the method of administration has created economic inefficiencies in production and marketing. Boards which do not possess or exercise these supply-control powers have given rise to much less controversy and are more widely accepted.   M.M. AND T.S. VEEMAN

Reading: Sidney Hoos, ed, *Agricultural Marketing Boards: An International Perspective* (1979).

Agricultural Products Board, established under the authority of the Agricultural Products Board Act. It is made up of the same members as the Agricultural Stabilization Board. Its broad authority is to buy, sell or import agricultural products. It generally deals with matters ancillary to price-support operations, but not coming specifically under the authority of the Agricultural Stabilization Act. The Agricultural Products Board Act has also been used to provide purchase and resale price support for a number of agricultural commodities, such as sweet cherries, apples, grape juice, grape concentrate, potatoes, peaches, pears, sour cherries, prune-plums; peas, turkeys, sweet corn and whole tomatoes. Because the board has the facility to act quickly during or just prior to the marketing season to remove surplus product from the market, the cost to the taxpayer is usually much less than a general stabilization program provided after the marketing season. Through past programs, the board has supplied the World Food Program with canned turkey, dehydrated potatoes, canned beef loaf and canned whole egg powder. Funds for the board's purchase operations are provided through specific appropriations for this purpose, with revenue from sales of products being credited directly to the Consolidated Revenue Fund. The board reports to the minister of agriculture.

Agricultural Research and Development
The Canadian agri-food industry has become an effective producer and processor of food and feed as the result of the work of innovative, hardworking farmers, good land-resources management, and the application of the technology derived from agricultural research and development or

operational research work. Canadian agriculture is a complex of many independent farms which differ in size and types of production. Farmers operate on a rather small scale, under differing climate, soil and other conditions. They cannot afford to finance, organize and conduct research; thus, because such work is in the public interest, most farming and food research is financed directly or indirectly by governments.

The greatest challenge to agricultural research lies in the primary production of food. However, the AGRICULTURE AND FOOD system also includes those industries involved in the food-processing, supply and agricultural-marketing sectors. Because agricultural products must meet human nutritional needs, food research complements conventional agricultural production research to provide abundant yields of a wide variety of high-quality foods.

The need for agricultural research in Canada was recognized more than 100 years ago. The first step in the organization of research took place in 1874 with the establishment of the Ontario School of Agriculture, later the Ontario Agricultural College and Experimental Farm, at Guelph. While the research conducted at the school was useful, Canada's varied soil and climatic conditions limited its applicability. A decade later, agricultural methods were proving inadequate and resulting in soil impoverishment and poor crop yields. The prevailing agricultural depression brought home the need for agricultural research and, in 1886, Parliament passed a bill establishing 5 experimental farms.

The RESEARCH STATION and experimental farm system has expanded to include over 40 research establishments from coast to coast. Provincial research bodies have been established, and university and industrial research programs have proliferated. During a century of research, plant varieties and animal strains have been improved; good SOIL CONSERVATION practices have been implemented; losses by INSECT PESTS, PLANT DISEASES, animal disease, DROUGHT and frost have been reduced or overcome; economical methods of storage and food preservation have been discovered; and better means of using food CROPS and animal products have been developed. These types of research serve to make Canadian farmers more secure in their undertakings and provide consumers with better products.

Responsibility for Research

In Canada, both provincial and federal governments may legally undertake research. Responsibility for overall adequacy rests with federal authorities, while the provinces have jurisdiction over agricultural teaching and extension. The research function is shared among Agriculture Canada and other federal agencies, provincial departments of agriculture, provincial research councils, university faculties of agriculture and VETERINARY MEDICINE and private industry. The respective roles of these organizations were considered and defined by representatives of the institutions and departments involved at a series of meetings held in 1964. Representatives agreed that all agencies engaging in agricultural research must be at liberty to undertake any or all types of investigation falling within their competence. There are 3632 researchers engaged in research work, full time or part time.

Two major national committees made up of representatives of provincial and federal governments, universities and other organizations involved in research are responsible for the co-ordination of agricultural research. The Canadian Agricultural Services Co-ordinating Committee (est 1932, reorganized 1964) co-ordinates re-

search, extension and education services, and is responsible for assessing immediate and future research needs and developing appropriate proposals. Provincial and regional committees assess and make recommendations regarding agricultural research and education within provinces. The Canadian Agricultural Research Council (est 1974) is the primary adviser to the government on the state of agricultural research in Canada.

Agriculture Canada, the largest of the public research agencies, has assumed the major share of responsibility for agricultural research, directly conducting over 50% of all agricultural research in Canada. The program is largely concentrated in the Research Branch, but funds are also provided for research at universities and other public and private institutions. The Research Branch was formed in 1959 by integrating 2 research services of the Canada Dept of Agriculture, ie, the Experimental Farms Service and the Science Service. Agriculture Canada employs nearly 950 scientists at its various research institutions.

Provincial Departments of agriculture play a vital role in intraprovincial research. Because of their close contacts with farmers, especially through their extension personnel, provinces can readily identify research needs. They also participate in research advisory committees at provincial and national levels. Agricultural research activities vary from province to province as a result of historical development in Canada, including differences in the economic importance and nature of agricultural products in the various provinces. In the West the provinces do relatively little research, instead relying to a greater or lesser extent on universities and federal agricultural research stations. In Ontario and Québec provincial departments sponsor research services, farms and stations and also support agricultural research at the university level. The Atlantic provinces, with only one degree-granting agricultural institution, rely more heavily on federal research programs than do other regions of Canada. Alberta, Ontario and Québec have provincial agricultural research councils to identify research needs, plan and co-ordinate their research programs and make research grants.

Universities across Canada conduct agricultural research programs necessary in the training of research scientists, and act as research institutions for federal and provincial governments to a greater or lesser extent. University researchers (at 11 faculties of agriculture and veterinary medicine) comprise the second-largest single group of agricultural scientists in Canada.

Successes and Goals

Review and adjustment of agricultural research policy is a continuous process. Changes in the structure and organization of research must keep pace with changes in agriculture. Success in agricultural research results in part from linkages between scientific discovery, technological development and application. Results of research are usually disseminated through agricultural extension services of provincial departments of agriculture, although results which can be incorporated immediately into farming practice are sometimes disseminated by the organization which conducted the research.

Canadian successes in plant breeding, disease control, ANIMAL BREEDING, etc, have won international renown. Among the most significant of these achievements are the various developments in WHEAT, from Red Fife (1840s) to Marquis (*c*1903) and beyond to rust-resistant forms (eg, Selkirk). Rust research is undertaken at the Dominion Rust Research Laboratory, Winnipeg (est 1925). The creation of CANOLA as a source of VEG-

ETABLE OIL and oil cake that are safe for human and animal consumption, respectively, was a major success of the postwar period. Researchers at University of Manitoba were largely responsible for the production of an entirely new, man-made cereal crop, TRITICALE, a fertile cross between 2 different genera of cereals, wheat and RYE. Less dramatic but economically very important developments include improvements in SOYBEANS, SUNFLOWERS, TOBACCO, and various FRUIT and VEGETABLE crops to increase both the area in which the crop may be successfully grown and the yield. Perhaps the best-known success in animal breeding is the development of the Lacombe HOG at the Agriculture Canada experimental farm at Lacombe, Alta. Work is also proceeding on POULTRY (for meat and egg yield), BEEF and DAIRY cattle, etc. Such work involves important research into genetic and congenital defects of animals, which may have applicability to the study of human genetic disease.

Agricultural methods have changed, but the responsibility of the Canadian agriculture and food system is still to provide the population with an adequate supply of nutritious and wholesome food. The growing awareness of food quality control has focused attention on agricultural research needs. Emphasis must also be placed on use and conservation of RESOURCES (especially soils) and on developing new sources of ENERGY. *See also* AGRICULTURAL AID.   BERTRAND FOREST

Agricultural Soil Practices

Agricultural Soil Practices Development and management of SOIL RESOURCES for agricultural production requires consideration of land-clearing methods, SOIL and CROP practices (including EROSION control) and environmental impact.

Development of land for agriculture frequently requires the clearing of brush-covered or forested land. Such clearing aims to remove unwanted material efficiently and economically, to minimize topsoil displacement and degradation, and to leave a seedbed sufficiently well cleared and graded to allow use of cultivating, planting and harvesting equipment. Methods selected for surface clearing depend on the nature, density and extent of the cover VEGETATION. Harvesting of marketable timber, if present, constitutes the first stage and may involve individual trees or a stand. Logs may be cut, stripped and piled with tree harvesters; trees may be knocked down, lifted and moved with tree-dozers. Stumpers are often preferred to bulldozers for removing stumps and large stones as they minimize the effect on topsoil. Heavy-duty bar mowers, rotary brush mowers and brush beaters are used to cut, chop and shred brush. When such a device produces a mulch, trash disposal is eliminated. Selective herbicides are used to remove specific plant species; nonselective or contact herbicides, for defoliation. Plants with deep root systems are removed with an undercutting or root-cutting and clearing implement. Soil is cleared to below plowing and cultivation depths. Root rakes and similar specialized equipment allow thorough combing of surface-cleared areas to remove roots, stump fragments, small brush and undergrowth. Final finishing is done with heavy disc plows and harrows; land levellers are used where grading is required for improved drainage.

Soil and Crop Practices

Establishment of an agricultural program requires careful selection of soil and crop management practices to optimize long-term yields, while minimizing soil loss, compaction and degradation. Throughout Canada the erosion of topsoil and subsoil is increasing. Cropping practices dependent on continuous cultivation of a single crop have also precipitated soil degradation across the country.

Spraying tomatoes (*courtesy Agriculture Canada*).

Water Erosion Sheet and rill erosion occur in fields as a result of improper soil and crop management, erodible soil conditions, and excessive surface drainage and field runoff. Spring snowmelt and summer convective storms in western Canada cause most damage. Upland cultivated soils across Canada are subject to soil loss by sheet, rill and gully erosion. Conservation tillage and cropping systems provide the most cost-effective remedial measures. Terraces can be used to form a series of diversions down a slope or to change a steep slope to a series of gentler slopes.

Grassed waterways can be developed on sloping cultivated areas where surface runoff concentrates or where it has produced severe rill damage. These waterways may also be used as outlets for contour strips or contour diversions. Concentrated surface flows can lead to gully formation; water seepage out of the developed banks often aggravates this problem. Small gullies can be regraded and revegetated, but larger ones may require installation of surface diversions (to divert runoff laterally from the slope), check dams (to slow velocity of concentrated flow) or drop structures (eg, rock chutes, subsurface drop inlets, surface drops). Seepage drains can be installed in banks to control sloughing and bank mining (*see* FARM DRAINAGE).

Wind Erosion results in serious soil loss where inappropriate soil and crop management systems are used, where fields are exposed to an extensive wind run, or where topographic features are vulnerable. Late winter and early spring are critical seasons in western Canada, where as much as 30% of cultivated land is left fallow and, thus, is subject to wind erosion. Land-management systems for SOIL CONSERVATION include keeping the surface of soils in a rough condition (eg, by minimizing tillage operations); keeping vegetation, residue and trash on the surface; using manures, green manures and crop rotations; cropping and strip-cropping at right angles to the prevailing wind; and providing wind barriers (eg, tree shelterbelts, grass strips, fence rows).

Streambank and Ditchbank Erosion can be caused by water running over the surface of the bank on its way to the drainageway or stream, by soil instability resulting from subsurface seepage or other locally high soil-water conditions, by shear stresses imposed on the bank by the stream flow, and by land-management activities (eg, pasturing animals on banks, cultivating land immediately adjacent to banks). In a recent inventory of agricultural watersheds in Ontario, erosion is shown as occurring on 37% of the banks and rotational slumping on 25%. Such problems can be controlled with revegetation, runoff diversions, vegetated buffer strips and drop structures. Soil stability problems can be alleviated with regrading and revegetation, bank drainage, limiting animal access and constructing retaining walls.

Problems linked to high stream velocities or localized turbulence can be controlled with vegetative and rock riprap linings; more serious problems require gabions, or asphalt linings.

Accelerated soil erosion on fields and banks causes damage not only in the immediate area but also downstream, as the transported soil particles clog stream channels, silt ponds and reservoirs, or cover fish-spawning beds. Where the capacity of a channel is reduced by sedimentation, flood waters may be forced to reroute overland. Agricultural sediments can be transport agents for potential contaminants (eg, phosphorus, heavy metals, herbicides). Suspended solids can be controlled at the erosion source or in the flow system. Sediment traps at field drainage outlets or in waterways are used to intercept sediment-laden surface runoff.   W.T. DICKINSON

Agricultural Stabilization Board, established under the federal Agricultural Stabilization Act of 1958, is intended to provide income support to producers in periods of depressed market returns. Funds for board operations come from an annual appropriation through the budget of the federal minister of agriculture. The board has 2 means of stabilizing the prices of designated agricultural products: it may offer to purchase any commodity deemed to be in excess supply; or it may make a deficiency payment to producers of a product the market price of which is below some designated minimum support price. The board may be, under the terms of the legislation, assisted in its work by an advisory committee of farmers or representatives of farm organizations, all of whom are appointed by the federal minister of agriculture. Under the original Agricultural Stabilization Act (which replaced the 1944 Agricultural Prices Support Act), the support price for designated commodities was set at 80% of the average price for the preceding 10 years. The Act was amended in 1975 to provide a guaranteed price of 90% of the 5-year average weighted price for cattle, hogs, sheep, industrial milk and cream, corn and soybeans, and for oats and barley produced outside the CANADIAN WHEAT BOARD designated area of the Prairies. In 1985 the Act was amended to allow the Minister of Agriculture to enter into tripartite agreements with provinces and producers for price stabilization programs.   J.C. GILSON

Agriculture, Department of Originally the Bureau of Agriculture (est 1852), it was established by an Act of Parliament in 1868 to concentrate on the urgent need of the time to control livestock diseases and prevent their entry into Canada. The department is responsible for federal policies relating to agriculture and food, including grading and inspection, seed certification, regulations on pesticides and fertilizers, market development programs, scientific research and dissemination of information. The minister is responsible for initiating and administering all federal legislation relating to AGRICULTURE and for operations of the AGRICULTURAL PRODUCTS BOARD, Canadian Dairy Commission, Canadian Grain Commission, CANADIAN LIVESTOCK FEED BOARD and National Farm Products Marketing Council. The Research Branch, located on the Central Experimental Farm in Ottawa, is the principal research organization serving Canadian agriculture. The branch has 35 other establishments across Canada to serve areas of varied soil and climatic conditions. The department's 1987-88 operating budget was $1.742 billion.

Agriculture, Federal Task Force on, est 1967 to advise the federal minister of agriculture on problems of Canadian agriculture and to recommend policies. Surplus production and lagging incomes in the wheat and dairy industries had

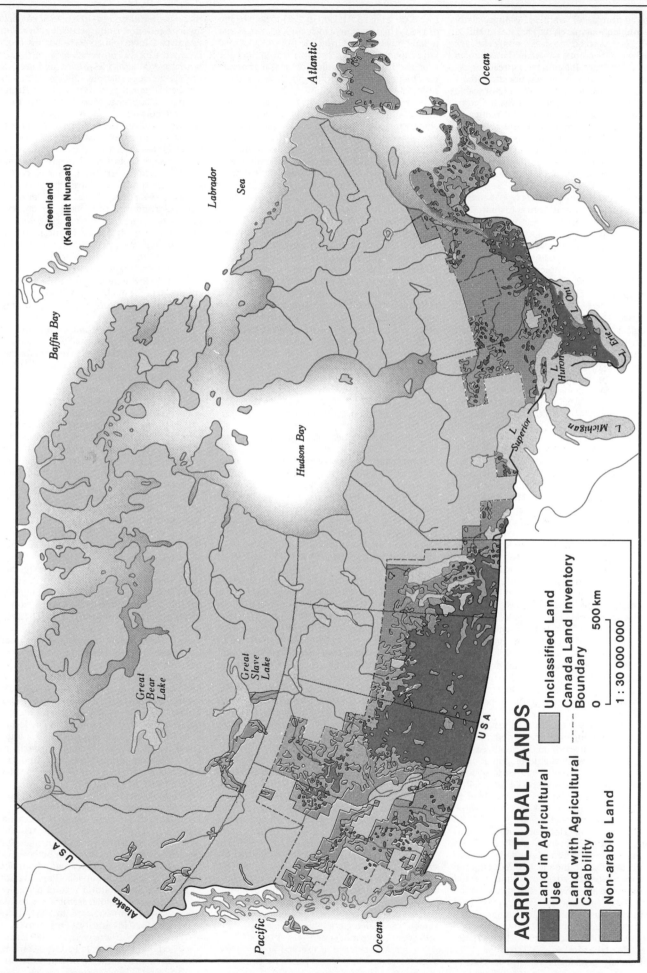

AGRICULTURAL LANDS

Greenland
(Kalaallit Nunaat)

Atlantic

Ocean

Labrador Sea

Baffin Bay

L. Ont

L. Erie

Hudson Bay

L. Huron

L. Superior

L. Michigan

USA

Great
Bear
Lake

Great
Slave
Lake

USA

Alaska

Pacific

Ocean

Land in Agricultural Use

Land with Agricultural Capability

Non-arable Land

Unclassified Land

Canada Land Inventory Boundary

0   500 km

1 : 30 000 000

precipitated threats of a strike by angry dairy farmers and led to a march on Parliament Hill in May 1967 (*see* NATIONAL FARMERS UNION). The task force delivered its report, *Canadian Agriculture in the Seventies*, in 1969. It found widespread dissatisfaction with low farm incomes, uncertain markets and prices, overproduction, small nonviable farms and diminishing export markets. It recommended that the government should reduce its direct involvement in agriculture and phase out subsidies and price supports; that the farm population should be reduced; and that younger low-income farmers should leave farming while older nonviable farmers should be assisted to achieve a better standard of living. Convinced that the surpluses of wheat and dairy products would continue in the 1970s, the commissioners recommended that farmers shift to producing other commodities. The major AGRICULTURE AND FOOD POLICIES of the 1970s that grew out of this report were ironically characterized by greater interdependence between government and agriculture rather than by the looser ties the task force has recommended. GRACE SKOGSTAD

Agriculture and Food Many structural and technological changes have occurred in Canadian farming in the period since 1951 and, although national trends are discernible, significant regional differences exist. In the following profiles of Canadian farming between the 1950s and the 1980s the principal farming regions described are the Atlantic region (Nfld, PEI, NS, NB). Québec, Ontario, the Prairie region (Man, Sask, Alta) and British Columbia. Data for the territories are included when relevant.

Since WWII Canada has changed from a semirural society to a largely industrialized and urban one. As industrialization proceeded, the rural sector rapidly declined in proportion, but it appears that the population engaged in farming has stabilized. The process of agricultural industrialization has been accompanied by important changes in the farming sector, including larger farms, greater capital investment and more sophisticated business management. In many ways the rural sector has almost disappeared as a social entity.

The most popular changes in farming have been economic and social in nature. For example, mixed farming has declined as farmers increasingly specialize in a single CROP or type of livestock. This specialization has led to increased market risk for farmers as evidenced by the higher rates of farm business failures in the 1980s. Such structural changes have taxed existing marketing and financial institutions and have contributed to increased stress for the farming community. Other kinds of changes have been more modest: the crops which farmers grow and the livestock they raise have changed only slightly. Perhaps the most notable changes in crop production in the period included the expansion of grain-corn production in eastern Canada and, in the west, the development of an edible OILSEED CROP — CANOLA. In ANIMAL AGRICULTURE, highly concentrated and specialized poultry, meat and egg production became the norm and, in beef production, leaner animals have become the preferred consumer product.

Stage of Development Under the impetus of allied wartime demands for food and fibre and as a consequence of the reduced labour supply, Canadian farms rapidly became mechanized, larger in size and more specialized in operation, a trend which continued after the war. During the period 1951 to 1981, the amount of improved land farmed in Canada (principally land in crops, improved pasture and summer fallow) increased 18%, from 39 million ha to 46 million ha (the latter figure remained the same to 1986). The real (1971 constant dollar) investment in farm machinery

rose 80%, from $3.8 billion in 1951 to $6.9 billion in 1981. This investment increased, relative to that in land buildings and livestock, from 15% of total farm capital in 1951 to 20% in 1981. In the latter year the machinery portion of total investment was highest in the Atlantic and Québec regions (24-25%) and lowest in BC (12%). Canadian farms became more intensively cultivated, with the real (1971 constant dollar) investment in machinery increasing from $96/ha of improved farmland in 1951 to $151 in 1981. The most rapid increase in the machinery/land ratio was in Québec; the least rapid, in BC. The greater amount of machinery on Canadian farms has resulted in a smaller farm labour force operating larger farms. Total farm size increased by 83%, from an average of 113 ha in 1951 to 207 ha in 1981 (the 1951-86 increase was 104%, to 231 ha). To 1986 the increase in average farm size was greatest in Manitoba (107%) and least in Ontario (38%).

Subsistence farming in Canada largely disappeared in the postwar years and was replaced by the new phenomenon of increased remunerative work by farmers and farm-family members off their own farms. This off-farm work included work for other farmers and nonagricultural employment (eg. operating a school bus). By 1986, 39% of all farm operators in Canada were engaged in some form of paid employment off their own farms for an average of 173 days a year. The highest proportion of farmers doing off-farm work was in BC (51%); the lowest, in Québec (31%). Overall, 12% of the off-farm work by Canadian farmers in 1986 consisted of work for other farmers, but the largest proportion, 88%, was in nonagricultural employment. These proportions were generally consistent in all regions.

Farm Capital The total capital value of Canadian farms in 1986 was $110 billion in current (nominal) dollars, down $20 billion from the amount just 5 years earlier and over 11 times the level of 1951. Average capital value was $374 000 per farm in 1986, compared with $409 000 in 1981 and only $15 000 in 1951. The highest regional average value per farm in 1986 was in the Prairie region ($456 000); the lowest, in the Atlantic region ($227 000). Much of the nominal increase in capital value was in real-estate values: from 1951 to 1981 across Canada the value of farm real estate rose from almost $260/ha in 1951 to over $375/ha in 1981 and to $1181/ha in 1986. From 1951-76 the largest increases were in Ontario but from 1976-81 the highest rate of increase occurred on the Prairies. Average capital value per farm on the Prairies declined during the period 1981-86, from $508 000 to $456 000.

Farming Inputs Modern farming includes the increased use of technical inputs such as chemical fertilizers. The average application rate of the primary fertilizer nutrients (nitrogen, phosphate for phosphorus, and potash for potassium) increased almost 5 times between 1960-61 and 1980-81, from 14 kg/ha to 67 kg/ha for Canada as a whole (and to 175 kg/ha in 1985). Regional differences in fertilizer application reflect differing SOILS, CLIMATES and crops. The highest rates of fertilizer uses are in the more humid eastern Canadian regions; the lowest, in the generally drier Prairie region. Farmers reporting use of fertilizers increased from 38% of all farmers in 1971 to 59% in 1980 and 66% in 1985, with the most rapid increase occurring in the Prairie region. From 1951 to 1985, land area which was treated with commercial fertilizers increased from 16% of all improved farmland to 34%. The Canadian fertilizer market is now relatively mature and increases in rates of use in all regions, although over twice the 1951 level, have moderated since 1980.

Trends in incidence of use and areas treated with PESTICIDES have been generally similar to

those for fertilizers. In 1970, 45% of Canadian farmers reported using pesticides; by 1980 this figure had increased to 53% but by 1985 had dropped to 21% (however, 59% of farmers reported using herbicides). Farmland area treated with pesticides rose from 12% in 1970 to 23% in 1980 and then dropped to 7% in 1985. Regionally the highest incidence of pesticide use in 1985 was in Saskatchewan (17%); the lowest, in BC (2%). As with fertilizer use, regional differences reflect differences in crops grown, intensity of cultivation and the severity of INSECT PEST infestations.

The use of sophisticated electronic computers has increased in farming in the past decade, although no statistical information is available to measure the extent of use. Many farmers have adopted computer technology to obtain daily price information on crops and livestock and to prepare cost analyses and financial summaries. Governments and private institutions have developed programs to encourage the use of computer technology, perhaps the most well-known being the CANFARM system, which allowed farmers to submit data for analysis. CANFARM began as a federal-provincial-university program but is now privately operated.

Tenure and Business Organization Owner-operated farms were the principal form of land tenure in 1951 (79%); although still dominant in 1981, they had fallen to 63% of all farms. In 1981 Québec had the highest proportion of owner-operated farms (80%); the Prairie region, the lowest (54%). The proportion of Canadian farms operated by tenants has remained almost unchanged, 7% in 1951 and 6% in 1981. Part-owner, part-tenant farms increased from 14% of all farms in 1951 to 31% in 1981. Regardless of land tenure, however, family-operated farms in all regions remain the overwhelming practice of farm business organization (99.3% of all farms in 1981).

Farm Population Canada's total population climbed from 14 million in 1951 to 24 million in 1981 (and to $25.3 million in 1986). Farm population, however, fell from 3 million in 1951 (about 21% of the total) to just over one million in 1981 (4% of the total). The greatest regional declines in the farm share of the total population in the 30-year period occurred in the Atlantic region and Québec; the least, in BC. The Prairie region continued to have the highest proportion (11%) of its population on farms in 1981 (compared with 38% in 1951).

Area and Condition of Farmland The total area of Canada is nearly 1 billion ha. Farms occupied less than 7% of this area in 1986 (67.8 million ha). The rest is forest, lakes, mountains, swamps and arctic tundra (*see* SOIL CLASSIFICATION). Improved farmland area in 1986 was even less (46 million ha or over 4%) of Canada's total area. While the 1986 total area in farms has declined by over 3% from 70 million ha in 1951, improved farmland has increased by 7 million ha since then. Thus the proportion of improved land in farms increased from almost 56% of all farmland in 1951 to 68% in 1986.

Changes between 1951 and 1981 in area and condition of farmland differ by region. In eastern Canada, both total and improved area has decreased in all 3 regions, especially in Atlantic Canada. In the West, however, both total and improved-farm areas increased in both regions. In BC improved farmland area more than doubled in the 30-year period. Canada's Prairie region, the largest single agricultural region, accounted for 81% of the national total area in 1986 and 83% of the improved farmland area. In 1951, the region accounted for 71% and 74%, respectively.

Types of Farms There were 293 089 farms of all sizes and types in Canada in 1986, compared to 623 000 in 1951 and 318 000 in 1981. In 1986 about 51% were in the Prairie region; 30 years earlier the region had held 40%. The Atlantic region had fewest farms, 4% of the 1986 total. Since WWII total farm numbers declined more slowly in BC than elsewhere: the province had 4% of all farms in 1951; 6% by 1986. The most rapid 30-year decline in farm numbers occurred in the Atlantic region, almost 82%.

There are 4 main types of farm: livestock (including DAIRY), field crop, FRUIT and VEGETABLES, and combinations of types or specialty farms. Between 1951 and 1981 the principal change in these categories has been a decrease in the relative numbers of livestock farms and an increase in the proportions of field-crop and fruit and vegetable farms. Regionally the dominant farm types in 1981 were distributed as follows: Atlantic – dairy (27%), cattle and HOGS (32%); Québec – dairy (50%), cattle and hogs (22%); Ontario – dairy (19%), cattle and hogs (36%), small grains, including WHEAT (21%); Prairie region – cattle and hogs (22%), small grains, including wheat (63%); BC – cattle and hogs (36%), fruit and vegetables (21%).

Regionally the most important shifts in farm types since 1951 occurred in Ontario and BC. In Ontario small-grain farms were relatively few in 1951, but increased to over one-fifth of all types in 1981 primarily because of increased CORN production. In BC, dairy farms were dominant in 1951; by 1981 they accounted for fewer than 10% of all farm types as dairy operations increased their size of business and became more specialized.

Crops and Livestock There are 7 crops grown in Canada which, together with summer fallow, have accounted for about 82% of all improved farmland throughout the 1961-86 period: wheat, oats, barley, corn, canola, potatoes and tame hay. The principal national changes included increases in areas of wheat, corn, barley, canola and tame hay; the area in oats decreased sharply.

Although there has been a general trend towards larger areas planted to crops in this period, wide variations have occurred. In the Atlantic region the area of oats and tame hay declined, while the potato area increased. In Québec the oats area declined but corn increased. In Ontario the area under corn for grain and silage increased sharply. In the Prairie region the wheat area increased, as did barley, tame hay and canola, the latter from 2000 ha in 1951 to 2.6 million ha in 1986. In BC, areas planted to barley and tame hay were much greater in 1986 than in 1951.

Areas of Selected Principal Field Crops (thousand ha)
(Source: Statistics Canada, *Census of Canada: Agriculture*) [1]

Crop	1961	1971	1981	1986
Wheat	10 245	7 854	12 453	14 230
Oats for grain	3 457	2 765	1 542	1 158
Barley	2 238	5 658	5 457	4 835
Corn for grain	162	571	1 142	994
Canola/Rapeseed	287	2 147	1 405	2 629
Potatoes	124	108	110	112
Tame hay	4 949	4 878	5 116	5 254
Summer fallow	11 275	10 613	9 702	8 499
Total	32 737	34 594	36 927	37 711

[1] Newfoundland data are included as of 1981 but not in years before.

As the population grew, per capita incomes generally rose, as did the demand for most meat and livestock products. Livestock numbers varied over the review period depending on the stage of the beef and hog cycles; however, in 1986 there were 60% more cattle and calves, hogs had doubled and poultry increased by 44%. In the Atlantic region and Ontario hog and poultry numbers increased sharply; in Québec they more than

Aerial view of market gardening near Niagara Falls, Ont (*courtesy SSC Photocentre/photo by Bob Anderson*).

tripled; in BC hog numbers increased fivefold and poultry numbers almost fourfold. In the Prairies the numbers of cattle and calves doubled. Sheep and lamb numbers were down by 48% nationally, as Canadians generally preferred other meats and lamb producers faced strong competition in the small Canadian market from lower-cost Australian and New Zealand producers.

Sources of Farm Income Cash receipts of Canadian farmers from farming operations totalled $20.6 billion in 1986, 7.5 times greater than the amount earned in 1951. About two-thirds of this increase resulted from higher prices; one-third, from greater quantities being marketed.

The relative importance of income from crops rose from 42% of the total in 1951 to 46% in 1986; that from the sale of livestock and products fell from 56% to 50%. In the same interval, payments made by governments to farmers under various price and income stabilization and other programs increased from 2% of total cash receipts in 1951 to 4% in 1986 (*see* AGRICULTURAL MARKETING). With respect to particular commoditites, the proportion of total cash receipts derived from wheat sales decreased; that from canola increased from virtually zero to over 3% of the total. The shares of cattle and dairy products were relatively unchanged, but the proportion contributed to total cash receipts by hogs, poultry and eggs declined on a national basis.

In the Atlantic region, potatoes, dairy products, poultry, eggs, hogs, cattle, calves, fruits and vegetables accounted for 80% of farm cash receipts in 1951 and 85% in 1986. Potatoes, fruits and vegetables doubled in relative shares; cattle and calves dropped by half. Total cash receipts from all sources rose 6.5 times, but some of the increase was a result of greater quantities marketed. In Québec about 80% of farm cash receipts in 1951 and 1986 were derived from dairy products, hogs, poultry, eggs, cattle and calves, but the relative importance of cattle and calves has decreased. Total cash receipts from all sources rose 8.5 times; some of the increase occurred because more of the product was being marketed. The 80% share of Ontario farmers' total cash receipts came from a diverse range of products, with cattle and calves accounting for the largest share (about one-quarter) in both 1951 and 1986. Grain corn and SOYBEANS increased in importance; hogs, poultry and eggs declined. Cash receipts from all sources increased sevenfold; some of the increase was attributable to increased output.

In the Prairie region, wheat sales accounted for nearly half of total cash receipts in 1986. The proportion of total receipts attributable to canola increased from virtually zero in 1951 to nearly 7% in 1986; the share from cattle and calves also rose, but that from hogs fell. Of the 3 Prairie provinces, Manitoba remained the most diversified in 1986. Total cash receipts in the Prairie region from all sources increased over sevenfold 1951-86; much of the increase resulted from greater production.

In BC 84% of total farm cash receipts were derived from dairy products, fruits, vegetables, cattle, calves, poultry, eggs, floriculture, nursery stock and hogs. Dairy products, floriculture, nursery stock and hogs increased in relative shares; cattle and calves decreased. Total farm cash receipts from all sources were up over ninefold between 1951 and 1986; some of the increase resulted from greater output. *See also* AGRIBUSINESS; BANKRUPTCY; FARM LAW; FOOD AND BEVERAGE INDUSTRIES; RURAL SOCIETY.   IAN F. FURNISS

Agriculture and Food Policy Federal agricultural policy is intended to serve national economic and political goals as well as the interests of those directly involved in and affected by Canadian agriculture — primarily producers, food processors, distributors, retailers and consumers. The Task Force Report on AGRICULTURE, official publications such as *Canadian Agriculture in the Seventies* (1969); *A Food Strategy for Canada* (1977); and the 4-volume *Orientation of Canadian Agriculture* (1977) identify the national goals as economic development, rising and stable incomes, full employment and harmonious international and federal-provincial relations. Specific agricultural goals include stable and fair producer returns, adequate supplies of high-quality nutritious food at stable and reasonable prices, and rural development and resource conservation. Over the next decade the focus will be on increased food production and processing and the promotion and expansion of agricultural exports.

From Confederation until the late 1950s, federal agricultural policy was designed to secure Canada's control over the West and to produce food for Canada, its trading partners and war allies. In the years following Confederation, agricultural expansion was encouraged by immigration and settlement of the West and the Department of Agriculture began its existing program of scientific research and development and experimental farms. Governments encouraged the production and export of grain. The freight rates at which grain grown on the prairies moved to export markets were fixed as early as 1897 in the CROW'S NEST PASS AGREEMENT. But the lack of competition in the marketing of grain and the monopolistic trading practices of the private grain and elevator companies troubled farmers. Their calls for regulation of the grain-handling system — including government inspection and standards, public ownership and operation of elevators, and a government marketing agency – were gradually heeded, leading to the contemporary system of grain handling and marketing. During WWI, in order to prevent speculation on wheat prices, the government established the Board of Grain Supervisors to market the 1917 and 1918 crops. It was succeeded by the CANADIAN WHEAT BOARD which handled the 1919 crop. When the Board was subsequently terminated, producers established their own cooperative pools to handle and sell prairie grain (*see* CO-OPERATIVE MOVEMENT). The collapse of these pools in 1930 led to the permanent creation of the Canadian Wheat Board in 1935. It was given monopoly authority over the marketing of prairie wheat in 1943, and between 1949 and 1973, over oats and barley.

The GREAT DEPRESSION forced governments to consider problems of agriculture itself, particularly low and unstable incomes. Severe drought and crop failures, in conjunction with depressed farm prices, led to the federal Prairie Farm Rehabilitation Act (PFRA, 1935) and the Prairie Farm Assistance Act (PFAA, 1939). Under the PFRA, federal and provincial governments co-operated in programs to rehabilitate agricultural land, develop farm water supplies, provide community pastures, and resettle individuals from drought-stricken lands to more arable sites. The first three aspects of the PFRA continue today. The PFAA provided minimal payments to marginal farmers experiencing below normal crop yields.

During WWII, agriculture again became important for its contribution to national objectives. The needs of the agricultural community and producers' concerns were of secondary importance; the emphasis was on pursuing Canada's war effort by filling the food requirements of Canada's wartime allies and curbing domestic inflation of consumer prices. Even so, a number of programs inaugurated during this period remain in effect today, including the Feed Grain Freight Assistance program (1941), the Farm Improvement Loans Act (1944), and the concept of government subsidies to support commodity prices and producer incomes. The Feed Grain Freight Assistance program stimulated livestock production by subsidizing the transportation and storage of feed grains from the prairie provinces to eastern Canada and British Columbia. Subsidies and price supports were used to encourage the production of essential commodities and to offset the price ceilings that held down product prices in spite of rising costs. The government's recognition of agriculture's contribution to the war effort led it to provide some guarantee of income protection in the postwar period. The Agricultural Prices Support Board (1944) was authorized to prescribe prices, to purchase and sell products, and to pay producers the difference between the prescribed and selling prices. And finally, the Farm Improvement Loans Act (1944) made intermediate and short-term loans available to farmers.

Agricultural policy in the 1950s and 1960s was oriented to increasing the productivity and efficiency of agriculture, and thereby, ostensibly raising and stabilizing commodity prices. The Farm Credit Act (1959) made credit available and encouraged the mechanization and growth in size of farms. The Agricultural Stabilization Board (1958), the successor to the Agricultural Prices Support Board, gave farmers a measure of protection from the fluctuating competitive marketing system by guaranteeing a base price for selected farm commodities. Federal expenditures to support and stabilize prices of dairy products expanded significantly in the 1970s, accounting for 80% of federal price and income maintenance payments, and became permanent with the creation of the Canadian Dairy Commission in 1966 (*see* NATIONAL FARMERS UNION). A joint provincial-federal crop insurance program begun in 1959 reduced the financial impact of natural disasters. Federal-provincial co-operation in the Agriculture Rehabilitation and Development Act (1961), later renamed the Agricultural and Rural Development Act (1960), and the Fund for Rural Economic Development (1966) was targetted at enhancing the viability of rural communities through improved resource use and retraining to facilitate the exit of marginal farmers to other jobs. And the Prairie Grain Advance Payments Act (1957) authorized the Canadian Wheat Board to make advance payments to producers on a portion of their farm-stored grain.

Federal programs prior to the 1970s interfered as little as possible with the competitive market system of pricing. Farmers received market prices; the stabilization programs shored up farm incomes when prices fell below average, but did so at levels that minimally distorted the operation of the market system. While the Canadian Wheat Board instituted order in grain marketing and equity in pricing, grain prices themselves were established by changing world market factors. Provincial governments had allowed producers to pool their products and sell them through provincial marketing boards or co-operatives which could negotiate higher prices. When the federal legislation to permit national marketing boards was declared unconstitutional (the *Natural Products Marketing Reference*, 1937), the federal government passed the Agricultural Products Marketing Act (1949). Provincial boards could be delegated federal authority to regulate the outward movement of commodities into export and interprovincial trade but could not restrict the inflow of commodities from other provinces or countries, and were thus unable to control completely the supply, and, therefore, the price of the regulated commodity.

The unusually turbulent markets and a serious cost-price squeeze for many farmers in the 1970s led provincial governments to initiate and the federal government to extend income maintenance programs. Québec, BC and Ontario passed comprehensive stabilization legislation and several other provinces undertook to protect hog and cattle producers from unstable markets and depressed prices. The federal government amended the Agricultural Stabilization Act in 1975 and passed the Western Grain Stabilization Act in 1976. The former guaranteed government support of the prices of industrial milk and cream, corn, soybeans, slaughter cattle, hogs, sheep and oats and barley raised outside the Canadian Wheat Board region, at 90% of the previous 5-year average. The latter stabilized the net profit from the sale of oats, barley, wheat, canola, flaxseed and rye. Along with the crop insurance program, these income protection measures consumed almost 50% of federal agricultural spending and meant that most commodities were protected.

The most innovative policy in the 1970s allowed producers to fix and determine the price of commodities (*see* COMMODITY TRADING). The Farm Products Marketing Agencies Act (1972) authorized 3 national marketing agencies – the Canadian Egg Marketing Agency (1972), the Canadian Turkey Marketing Agency (1973) and the Canadian Chicken Marketing Agency (1979) – to control supply nationally and to administer prices. Supply management had been implemented earlier in the dairy industry. Between 1970 and 1972, a market-sharing quota system was created that attempted to balance industrial milk and cream supplies with domestic demand; in conjunction with import controls (in place since 1951) and federal subsidies, it has significantly raised and stabilized dairy farmers' incomes. Other long-standing policies which continue include the scientific research program, about 50% of which is funded by Agriculture Canada, and the Feed Freight Assistance Act, amended in 1976 to place a ceiling price on feed grain for eastern Canadian buyers.

High interest rates and depressed commodity prices resulted in an unusual number of bankruptcies in the early 1980s. Inclement prairie weather, including droughts and wet harvesting seasons, in conjunctions with the international grain subsidy war between the European Community and the US, and a reduced world demand for grain, caused international and domestic grain prices to plummet. Governments responded with a new emphasis on market promotion and income protection. The Liberal government created Canagrex, a Canadian agricultural exporting agency, in 1983. A crown corporation, Canagrex was designed to help offset Canada's net trade deficit in nongrain agricultural products and to negotiate with the many countries that prefer state owned trading associations to private traders. However, upon their election in 1984, the Conservative government ceased funding Canagrex. Instead, they emphasized federal-provincial co-operation, provided Canada's grain farmers with a $1 billion deficiency payment in 1986-87 to offset US and European Community subsidies, and pursued the goal of more liberalized trade under the GATT (*see* GENERAL AGREEMENT ON TARIFFS AND TRADE) umbrella and with the US as measures to stimulate agricultural exports and raise farm incomes.

Policy Formation and Implementation Despite shared federal and provincial jurisdiction over agriculture, federal legislation is paramount in the event of conflict. Authority over marketing is divided; the federal government regulates export and interprovincial marketing, while the provincial governments legislate marketing within their borders. Provincial agriculture and food policy is almost entirely the work of provincial departments of agriculture. However, there are a number of programs in which federal and provincial officials co-operate financially and administratively, including crop insurance and economic regional development agreements for agriculture.

While Agriculture Canada initiates most agricultural legislation and is primarily responsible for serving producers' interests, a number of federal departments and agencies make and affect agricultural and food policy. The minister of agriculture supervises several agricultural agencies that carry out agricultural policies, including the National Farm Products Marketing Council (an umbrella agency whose primary responsibility is to advise the minister of the formation and operation of national marketing boards), the Canadian Livestock Feed Board (which has administered the feed freight and storage assistance program since 1966), the Canadian Dairy Commission, the Farm Credit Corporation and the Agricultural Stabilization Board. The agriculture minister shares with the minister of consumer and corporate affairs the task of representing consumer interests in food policy. The minister of transport supervises grain transportation by rail and water, as well as government grain elevators, and administers grain freight-rate subsidies to the railways. The Department of Industry, Trade and Commerce negotiates tariffs, promotes trade in foodstuffs and assists the food processing and manufacturing industries.

Critique of Policy A repeated complaint since the early 1970s is that Canada does not have a food policy, only an agricultural policy preoccupied with producers' concerns. Consumers and others feel they have no say in food policy since they are not guaranteed representation, for example, on the marketing boards which determine prices of dairy and poultry products. The Food Prices Review Board, established to monitor food prices between 1973 and 1975, recommended a long-term national food policy. In response, the federal government issued *A Food Strategy for Canada* (1977), and convened a National Food Policy Conference in the same year to which all interested groups were invited. However, these discussions failed to produce a consensus, and the criticism remains that Canada lacks a long-term national food policy, that agricultural policy is ad hoc and often contradictory, and that consumer food concerns are ignored.

The dairy- and poultry-marketing boards with supply-management powers are criticized as monopolistic agencies which have allowed farmers to be inefficient, barred young farmers from entering the poultry and dairy industry by inflating quota values and thus raising the cost of farming operations, and increased food costs to consumers. Interprovincial tensions have developed as provinces with growing populations seek to increase their share of the available market while provinces with stagnant or declining populations resist decreases in their share. The tendency to protect local consumer markets for local producers distresses some provinces and the federal government, which advocate the geographical distribution of production on the basis of natural comparative advantage.

In western Canada and Québec, the issue of whether producers or the railways should receive the grain freight subsidies that replaced the Crow's Nest freight rates in 1983 continues to be outstanding. Finally, agricultural policy is criticized for its failure to provide a long-term solution to the farm debt problem; its inattention to land-use planning, soil quality and other environmental considerations; and its ineffectiveness in restricting concentration in the food-processing and retail industries. Problems of rural poverty, and income instability and market uncertainty, especially in sectors without supply management protection, remain to be solved. Government failure to redress consumer and producer grievances periodically stimulates the formation of pressure groups, such as the National Farmers Union in 1969 and the Canadian Farmers Survival Association in the 1980s, and the high salience of domestic and international trade policy has heightened the political role of farm organizations generally and western Canadian cattle and grains commodity groups in particular.

GRACE SKOGSTAD

Agriculture, History of Canadian agriculture has experienced a markedly distinct evolution in each region. A varied CLIMATE and geography have been largely responsible, but, in addition, each region has been settled at a different period in Canada's economic and political development, with a range of national and international forces being exerted. The principal unifying factor has been the role of government: from the colonial era to the present, agriculture has been largely state directed and subordinate to other interests.

Before 1000 BC, Indians of the lower Great Lakes and St Lawrence regions received horticulture from the S or W. IROQUOIS and related cultures practised slash-and-burn farming, but no group depended on agriculture totally for subsistence. They planted 2 types of maize (Indian CORN), SQUASH and BEANS in row hills. The Indians practised seed selection and elementary principles of forcing but were not aware of the value of manuring. Long before the appearance of French traders, agricultural Indians traded maize for skins and meat obtained by woodland hunters. After the advent of the FUR TRADE, Algonquian middlemen traded maize with more distant bands for prime northern pelts, and traded furs, in turn, with the French. Indian agriculture was important in provisioning the fur trade until the late 18th century.

Maritimes Maritime agriculture dates from the establishment of PORT-ROYAL by the French in 1605. ACADIAN settlers diked the saltwater marshes in the Annapolis basin and used them for growing wheat, flax, vegetables and pasturage. After the signing of the Treaty of UTRECHT (1713),

Engraving of *Canada Farmer* logo, 1869, a monthly journal of horticultural and rural affairs, vol I, no 7 (*courtesy Alan Skeoch Coll/Mississauga*).

France withdrew to Plaisance, Nfld; Île Royale [Cape Breton I]; and Île St-Jean [PEI]. They intended that Île St-Jean would serve as a source of grain and livestock for their naval and fishing base on Cape Breton. Few Acadians moved from their homeland to Île St-Jean before the 1750s. By midcentury the predominantly fishing population in Île Royale was cultivating small clearings with wheat and vegetables, and possessed a variety of livestock.

After acquiring Acadia in 1713, Britain promoted Maritime agriculture in pursuit of objectives of defence and MERCANTILISM. Provisions were needed to support Nova Scotia's role as a strategic bulwark against the French. Britain also promoted agriculture to supply provisions for the West Indies trade, and hemp for its navy and merchant marine. Financial incentives were offered to Halifax settlers to clear and fence their land, but the lack of major markets kept the area in a state of self-sufficiency. The Acadians continued to supply produce to the French on Île Royale, an act which contributed to their expulsion by the British in 1755. Some Acadians were later asked, however, to instruct the British in marshland farming. The influx of LOYALIST settlers in the 1780s increased demand for marshland produce. Since the American states provided stiff competition in flour and grains, the Fundy marshlands were largely turned to pasture and hay for cattle production. On PEI the British government attempted to promote agricultural settlement by granting 66 lots of 8094 ha to private individuals.

Between 1783 and 1850 agriculture was dominant in PEI, but subordinate to the cod FISHERY and the trade with the West Indies in NS, and secondary to the TIMBER TRADE and shipbuilding in NB. With British and Loyalist immigration, the area of agricultural settlement in the Maritimes expanded from the marshlands to include the shores of rivers, especially the SAINT JOHN. Although the new areas were suited to cereal production, settlers tended to engage in mixed farming for cultural, agricultural and marketing reasons. Most full-time farmers concentrated on livestock raising, which required less manpower than did cereal growing. Before 1850 both NS and NB remained net importers of foodstuffs from the US. PEI alone achieved an agricultural surplus, exporting WHEAT to England as early as 1831.

Agricultural development in the early 19th century was limited by the skills post-Loyalist immigrants possessed. Most of these settlers were Highland SCOTS who were ill-prepared for clearing virgin forest, and the standard of agricultural practice was low. In 1818 John YOUNG, a Halifax merchant using the name "Agricola," began agitating for improved farming methods. As a result, agricultural societies were formed with a government-sponsored central organization in Halifax. Young's efforts had virtually no impact, however, since merchants were not involved in local farming. Hence there was little economic incentive for farmers to produce a surplus for sale. Nonetheless, agricultural lands and output grew gradual-

ly, and by mid-century the farming community was a political force, demanding transportation improvements and agricultural protection.

After 1850 Maritime agriculture was affected by 2 principal developments: the transition throughout the capitalist world from general to specialized agricultural production and, especially after 1896, the integration of the Maritime economy into the Canadian ECONOMY. The last 2 decades of the 19th century witnessed an increase in the production of factory cheese and creamery butter and a rapid increase in the export of APPLES, especially to Britain (*see* FRUIT AND VEGETABLE INDUSTRY). After 1896 the boom associated with Prairie settlement opened the Canadian market to fruit (especially apples) and POTATOES. By the 1920s the British market for NS apples was threatened by American, Australian and BC competition, notwithstanding improvements introduced by Nova Scotia producers to increase efficiency. The Canadian market for potatoes was supplemented by markets in Cuba and the US. Although Cuba moved to self-sufficiency after 1928, PEI retained some of the market by providing seed stock.

Those sectors of Maritime agriculture dependent on local markets began to suffer in the 1920s. Difficulties in the forest industries contributed to the disappearance of markets, and the introduction of the internal combustion engine diminished the demand for horses and hay. Meat from other parts of Canada supplanted local production. In the 1930s the potato export market suffered as American and Cuban markets became less accessible. These factors, coupled with problems in the silver fox industry (*see* FUR FARMING), were catastrophic for PEI; its agricultural income dropped from $9.8 million in 1927 to $2.3 million in 1932. Only the apple export market remained stable, a result of British preferential tariff on apples from the empire. In response to various difficulties during the 1930s, many farmers turned to more diversified self-sufficient agriculture, a change reflected in increased dairy, poultry and egg production.

Newfoundland In Newfoundland agriculture was never more than marginally viable. Nonetheless, fishermen practised subsistence agriculture along the creeks and harbours of the East Coast, and commercial farming developed on the Avalon Peninsula and on parts of Bonavista, and Notre Dame and Trinity bays. Newfoundland's agricultural history really began with the food shortages associated with the American Revolution, when 3100 ha were prepared for agriculture in the St John's, Harbour Grace and Carbonear areas. In the early 19th century a number of factors combined to give an impetus to agriculture: the arrival of Irish immigrants with agricultural skills, the growth of St John's as a market for vegetables, a road-building program, and in an 1813 authorization allowing the governor to issue title to land for commercial use.

In the late 19th and early 20th centuries the government intensified its efforts to interest the people in agriculture. By 1900, 298 km² were un-

M. Seagart's farmhouse, Alta; family and binder are seen in foreground (*courtesy Provincial Archives of Alberta/ E. Brown Coll/B219*).

Discing with 7 horses *c* 1920 (*courtesy Provincial Archives of Alberta/H. Pollard Coll/P624*).

Breaking prairie with oxen near present-day Lloydminster c1900 (courtesy Provincial Archives of Alberta/H. Pollard Coll/P451).

Shackleton's outfit on the job threshing, 1898 (courtesy Provincial Archives of Alberta/E. Brown Coll/B273).

der cultivation and there were some 120 000 horses, cattle and sheep in the colony. Through the Newfoundland Agricultural Board (formed 1907) the government established agricultural societies (91 in 1913) which provided assistance in such things as land clearing and the acquisition of seed and farm implements. In the 1920s the government imported purebred animals to improve the native stock. In the 1930s, in order to mitigate the hardship of the economic depression, the government responded to the urgings of the Land Development association, a private group, by providing free seed potatoes in an effort to promote "garden" cultivation. Upon joining Confederation in 1949, Newfoundland took advantage of federal government funding to establish agricultural measures such as a loan program, a land-clearing program, and the stimulation of egg and hog production. Since WWII, in keeping with the general Canadian trend, the number of Newfoundland farms has decreased while the average farm size has increased.

Québec In 1617 Louis HÉBERT began to raise cattle and to clear a small plot for cultivation. Small-scale clearing ensued as settlers planted cereal grains, peas and Indian corn, but only 6 ha were under cultivation by 1625. Beginning in 1612 the French Crown granted fur monopolies to a succession of companies in exchange for commitments to establish settlers. The charter companies brought some settlers, who used oxen, asses and later horses to clear land, but agricultural self-sufficiency was realized only in the 1640s and marketing agricultural produce was always difficult during the French regime. In 1663 Louis XIV reasserted royal control and with his minister Colbert promoted settlement by families. Intendant Jean TALON reserved lots for agricultural experimentation and demonstration, introduced crops such as hops and hemp, raised several types of livestock and advised settlers on agricultural methods. By 1721 farmers in New France were producing 99 600 hL of wheat and smaller amounts of other crops annually, and owned about 30 000 cattle, swine, sheep and horses (*see* SEIGNEURIAL SYSTEM).

After 1763 and the arrival of British traders, new markets opened for Canadian farm produce within Britain's mercantile system. Francophone HABITANTS predominated in the raising of crops, but they were joined by anglophone settlers. British subjects purchased some seigneuries, which they settled with Scottish, Irish and American immigrants. New Englanders also settled the Eastern Townships and other areas. Anglo-Canadians promoted some new techniques of wheat and potato culture through the press and in 1792 formed an agricultural society at Québec. While the focus of the government's promotional activity was in Upper Canada [Ontario] and the Maritimes, Lower Canada [Québec] enjoyed a modest growth of wheat exports before 1800. Nevertheless, Lower Canadian wheat production lagged far behind that of Upper Canada in the first half of the 19th century.

The failure of Lower Canadian agriculture has been blamed by some on the relative unsuitability of the region's climate and soils for growing wheat, the only crop with significant export potential; soil exhaustion; and the growth of the province's population at a faster rate than its agricultural production in this period. Because there was little surplus for reinvestment in capital stock, Lower Canada was slow to develop an inland road system, and transport costs remained relatively high.

By the 1830s Lower Canada had ceased to be self-sufficient in wheat and flour, and increasingly began importing from Upper Canada. The mid-century gross agricultural production of Canada East [Québec] totalled $21 million – only about 60% of Canada West's [Ontario's] production. Both modernizing and traditional farms contained more children than they could adequately support, and widespread poverty induced thousands of habitants to migrate to Québec's cities and to New England (*see* FRANCO-AMERICANS). As well, spurred by religious colonizers, settlement pushed N of Trois-Rivières, S of Lac Saint-Jean and S along the Chaudière R. However, little commercial agriculture was practised.

Later 19th-century Québec agriculture was marked by increases in cultivated area and productivity, and a shift from wheat production to dairying and stock raising. From the 1860s government agents worked to educate farmers to the commercial possibilities of dairying, and agronomists such as Edouard BARNARD organized an agricultural press and instituted government inspection of dairy products. Commercial dairies, cheese factories and butteries developed around the towns and railways, most notably in the Montréal plain and the Eastern Townships. By 1900 dairying was the leading agricultural sector in Québec. It was becoming mechanized in field and factory and increasingly male-oriented as processing shifted from the farm to factories. By the end of the century 3.6 million kg of Québec cheese were being produced, an 8-fold increase since 1851.

By the 1920s, however, agriculture accounted for only one-third of Québec's total economic output. WWI had artificially stimulated production, and new mining, forestry and hydroelectric ventures opened up new markets; but they also contributed to and symbolized the shift from agricultural to industrial enterprises in the Québec economy. By the 1920s Québec soil was again becoming exhausted due to a lack of fertilizer which stemmed from a lack of credit. Farmers' political organizations, such as the Union catholique des cultivateurs (fd 1924), addressed the problem of lack of credit and other issues.

Like their counterparts elsewhere in Canada, Québec farmers suffered during the 1930s. In areas removed from urban markets there was a return to noncommercial agriculture, with a consequent increase in the number of farms. During the decade farm income decreased more drastically than did urban wages. WWII marked a return to widespread commercial agriculture, and postwar trends included a decrease in the number of farm units and in farm population, and an increase in the average size of farm holdings.

Ontario American independence in 1783 both created a potential security threat on British North America's southern border and cut off Britain's principal agricultural base in N America. The British channelled Loyalists into the lower Great Lakes region, where Gov SIMCOE suggested settling soldiers along the waterfront for defence, with other settlers filling in the land behind. The authorities initially promoted hemp culture as an export staple to stimulate British manufacturing and contribute to defence. However, scarcity of

labour in relation to land inhibited its production. Between 1783 and 1815 settlement filled in along the lake shores and the St Lawrence, where some cereal grains and vegetables were grown, chiefly for subsistence.

Agriculture in what is now Ontario was dominated 1800-60 by wheat production. Wheat was the crop most easily grown and marketed and was an important source of cash for settlers. Apart from limited internal demand from such sources as British garrisons, canal construction crews and lumber camps, the principal markets were Britain and Lower Canada. Between 1817 and 1825 Upper Canadian farmers shipped an average of 57 800 hL to Montréal. Dependence on wheat culture was reflected in a boom-and-bust economy. The application of the CORN LAW restrictions in 1820 effectively shut BNA wheat out of British markets, causing a disastrous drop in wheat prices and land values. With the fixing of preferential duties for BNA wheat in 1825, prices and export volumes rallied but the market collapsed in 1834-35. Crop failures in the late 1830s resulted in near starvation in many newly settled areas. Despite the American tariff, similar failures in the US created a temporary market for surplus Upper Canadian wheat. Meanwhile, transportation improvements facilitated shipments out of the region. As a result of these improvements, favourable climate conditions and growth in markets, wheat exports increased from 1 million hL in 1840 to 2.25 million in 1850.

After 1850 Canada West's agriculture became increasingly diversified. Repeal of the Corn Laws in 1846 removed the preferential Status of BNA wheat and thus promoted price instability, but higher American prices after the discovery of California gold helped producers overcome trade barriers to livestock, wool, butter and coarse grains. Favourable trading conditions continued with the RECIPROCITY Treaty, 1854-66. Moreover, a price depression in 1857 and crop destruction by the midge in 1858 hastened the switch to livestock. In 1864 factory cheesemaking was introduced, and by 1900 Canadian cheddar cheese, largely from Ontario, had captured 60% of the English market. At the organizational level, both the Grange (after 1872) and the Patrons of Industry (after 1889) reflected a developing producer consciousness among Ontario farmers.

Technological developments assisted both the grain and livestock sectors in the 19th century. Field tillage was improved by the introduction of copies of American cast-iron plows after 1815. To control weeds biennial naked summerfallow was generally practised between about 1830 and 1850, when crop rotation became prevalent. Government authorities also promoted the British technology of covered drains to reclaim extensive tracts of swampy or bottom land, averting the use of furrow and ditch drainage that impeded mechanization. The reaper diffused rapidly in the 1860s, permitting increased grain production. Widespread use of the cream separator by

Prairie homestead c1920 (*courtesy Provincial Archives of Alberta/H. Pollard Coll/P592*).

Harvesting on the Sadison farm at Brandon, Man; Massey-Harris binders, 1892 (*courtesy National Archives of Canada/PA-31489/photo by J.A. Breck & Co*).

1900 promoted butter production, while refrigeration was a catalyst to the beef and pork industry.

In the late 19th and early 20th centuries urbanization expanded the demand for market gardening around cities and more specialized crops in different regions. These included orchard farming in Niagara Peninsula, Prince Edward and Elgin counties, and tobacco in Essex and Kent counties. Dairying developed on the fringes of cities and cash crop acreages declined in favour of feed grains and fodder, while beef producers were unable to meet the domestic demand. Throughout rural Ontario there were farm-initiated associations of stockbreeders, dairy people, grain growers, fruit growers, etc, as well as the government-initiated Farmers' Institutes and Women's Institutes. The associations reflected a faith in farm life in the face of rural depopulation and an industrializing society. Various farmer-initiated groups worked in the UNITED FARMERS OF ONTARIO movement which formed the provincial government in 1919 under E.C. DRURY.

During the 1920s Ontario farmers experienced a taste of prosperity as prices increased on various agricultural commodities. One result of this prosperity was a decline in the drift to the cities. By 1931, however, Ontario farm receipts had decreased 50% from 1926. Although Ontario escaped the drought conditions of the Prairies, farmers were unable to market much of their produce, and surplus meat, cheese, vegetable and apples were shipped west. The government responded to the crisis with regulation, with dairying the most important example. The Ontario Marketing Board was formed in 1931 with a 5-year plan instituted in 1932. In return for government loans, producers improved their herds and modernized their barns. By WWII Ontario agriculture was diversifed for an urban market, with both AGRICULTURAL MARKETING BOARDS and farmer-owned co-operatives playing important roles.

The Prairies In western BNA, Scottish settlers practised river-lot agriculture at RED RIVER COLONY after their arrival in 1812. While the survey system was French Canadian, agricultural practices followed the Scottish pattern. Land adjacent to the river was cultivated in strips in the manner of the Scottish "infield," with pasturage reserved for the "outfield" behind. The MÉTIS alternated agriculture with the seasonal activities of the BUFFALO HUNT and freighting. Red River came to assume a role in provisioning the fur trade alongside Indian and company agriculture.

Confederation was the spur to the agricultural development of the PRAIRIE WEST. In the mid-19th century central Canadian businessmen were seeking investment opportunities to complement central Canada's industrial development. The prospect of agricultural expansion in the western interior was very appealing. Canada proceeded to purchase the Hudson's Bay Company's RUPERT'S LAND (1870), repress Métis resistance (1869-70 and 1885), displace the Indian population, and survey the land for disposal to agricultural settlers

(*see* DOMINION LANDS POLICY). Wheat quickly established its economic importance. However, continuing low world prices, culminating in a worldwide depression in the early 1890s, halted development until 1900. Western Canada's dry climate and short growing season were the most serious stumbling blocks. Genetic experimentation, leading to the development of Marquis wheat in 1907, in combination with the Dominion government's promotion of summer-fallowing to conserve soil moisture and control weeds, helped remove the technical barriers to continued agricultural expansion. Large-scale RANCHING on leased land began in what is now southern Alberta and Saskatchewan in the 1870s and 1880s. The area's dry climate was practically overcome by small-scale irrigation from the 1870s on and by the introduction of a Dominion irrigation policy in 1894. Western agriculture received the necessary economic stimulus from an overall decline in transportation costs (*see* CROW'S NEST PASS AGREEMENT) and a relative rise in the price of wheat in the late 1890s.

Under Clifford SIFTON's great immigration schemes, the Dominion effectively completed the agricultural settlement of the Prairies. Mechanization of the wheat economy with steam, gas tractors, gang plows and threshing machines contributed to huge production surpluses. An unprecedented boom in wheat prices during WWI promoted cultivation of new lands. Price depressions in 1913 and after WWI precipitated many bankruptcies by overcapitalized farmers. Nevertheless, between 1901 and 1931 the amount of land under field crop on the Prairies jumped from 1.5 to 16.4 million ha.

The collapse of wheat prices after WWI had serious consequences for Prairie farmers. Many operators who had purchased implements and more land at high prices during the war defaulted and lost their farms. Throughout the 1920s and 1930s operators of farms on poorer soils consistently lost money, as did farmers in the dry belt of SW Saskatchewan and SE Alberta. Drought, grasshoppers and crop disease further worsened conditions for farmers in the 1930s; the government responded with the PRAIRIE FARM REHABILITATION ADMINISTRATION. Technological advances such as the development of the combine harvester resulted in both more efficient agriculture and the forcing off the land of farmers lacking sufficient capital to purchase the new technology. The mechanization process in Prairie agriculture as a whole was essentially halted during the 1930s, to be dramatically resumed after WWII.

From the early settlement era western farmers depended on central Canadian business to provide their production inputs and to finance, purchase and transport their grain. In order to gain some control over the economic forces which controlled them, organizations were formed to advance their interests. Early agrarian movements in Manitoba and the North-West Territories espoused the virtues of co-operation and criticized Dominion tariff policy, freight rates and federal disallowance of railway charters to the CPR's rivals. After forcing the government in 1899 to ensure better service from the railways, farmers formed GRAIN GROWERS' ASSOCIATIONS in the Territories in 1901-02 and in Manitoba in 1903. These organizations carried on educational work among farmers, promoted provincial ownership of inland elevators and, ultimately, campaigned for the co-operative marketing of grain. This latter objective was achieved in 1906 with the formation of the Grain Growers' Grain Co (now the United Grain Growers).

The Grain Growers' Grain Co is representative of the first phase of Prairie co-operative grain marketing. In the context of heightened farmer

and worker consciousness after WWI it came under criticism for having become too business-oriented. A radical wing developed in the Prairie farm movement, led by H.W. Wood of the UNITED FARMERS OF ALBERTA. In 1923-24 farmers organized compulsory pools – a new form of co-operative marketing – in the 3 Prairie provinces (eg, *see* SASKATCHEWAN WHEAT POOL). Pools were successful throughout the 1920s, but collapsed after the Depression struck in 1929. Although the federal government moved to save the pools and stabilize the wheat market, it did so by appointing a manager from the private grain trade. Thus the original co-operative design of the pools was undermined. As a further attempt to stabilize the market the government in 1935 introduced the CANADIAN WHEAT BOARD, which farmers had been demanding since their wheat board experience of 1919-20. Again, however, this board was dominated by the private grain trade and reflected its interests as much as those of farmers. In 1943 the wheat board was made compulsory for the marketing of western wheat, and in 1949 the board's authority was extended to western barley and oats.

The agrarian movement in western Canada was more than an economic phenomenon. People in the pools, the grain growers' associations and farm political parties intervened and were influential in Prairie culture, society and politics, as well as in economics. Farm-movement women, for example, were active in the TEMPERANCE crusade, the WOMEN'S SUFFRAGE movement, child welfare and rural education, as well as in the economic and political struggles they shared with farm men. Political protest movements which developed in the 1920s around the pooling crusade, such as the Farmers' Union of Canada, eventually entered the CO-OPERATIVE COMMONWEALTH FEDERATION as an important component of the Canadian socialist tradition.

British Columbia Agriculture in British Columbia was first developed to provision the fur trade. In 1811 Daniel Harmon of the North West Co started a garden at Stuart Lake, and later HBC factors planted small gardens on Vancouver I, at Ft St James, Ft Fraser and Ft George. The HBC also helped establish the Puget's Sound Agricultural Co to assist in provisioning. Commercial demand for agricultural products was spurred by GOLD RUSHES after 1858. However, while ranching was established in the interior along the Thompson and Nicola valleys and some farming settlement occurred, newcomers were more attracted to the lure of gold than to agricultural opportunities. Production lagged far behind demand.

Railway production camps in the early 1880s provided a domestic market for agricultural products, but the establishment of Canadian rail linkages destroyed the early wheat industry, which could not compete with Prairie wheat, either in quality or in price. In the 1890s the establishment of the Boundary and Kootenay mining industries created new markets. Lumbering and fish-packing industries also stimulated agriculture although producers dependent on local industry suffered when lumber camps moved on or mines or canneries closed. Large-scale farming continued in districts such as the Cariboo and Similkameen, while smaller-scale specialized agriculture developed in the Okanagan and Fraser valleys. By the 1880s the Okanagan Valley had developed a specialized fruit industry while market gardening and dairying flourished in the lower Fraser Valley as urban markets increased.

The British Columbia Fruit-Growers' Assn, fd 1889, was the first formal organization of producers in the province. Its objectives were to investigate potential markets on the Prairies and methods of controlling fruit marketing. In 1913 economic difficulties obliged Okanagan fruit growers to set up a co-operative marketing and distribution agency, financed largely by the provincial government. The agency helped eliminate eastern Canadian and American competition on the Prairies. The depression of 1921-22, however, signalled the beginning of an 18-year search for more permanent stability. A 1923 plan called on fruit growers to agree to sell for a 5-year period through a central agency. Only 80% of producers supported the plan and competition among shippers kept prices low. Various government and private schemes were tried without success between 1927 and 1937. In 1938 the provincial government established the Tree Fruit Board to be the sole agency for apple marketing. The following year producers set up Tree Fruits Ltd as a producer-owned central selling agency. In 1939-40 farmers' co-operatives in BC (of which Tree Fruits Ltd was the most important) did a combined business of nearly $11 million. Although there were some difficulties for BC agriculture in WWII, with the export market being cut, a combination of government assistance and improved purchasing power on the Prairies contributed to the creation of a seller's market by 1944.

The North Agriculture N of 60° N lat began with European contact, since the region was beyond the range of native cultivation techniques. Following Peter POND's 1778 experiment in gardening near Lake Athabasca, the HBC established crops and livestock along the Mackenzie R at Ft Simpson, Ft Norman and Ft Good Hope, and at Ft Selkirk at the junction of the Pelly and Yukon rivers. Missionaries developed livestock, gardens and crops at a number of missions in the late 19th and early 20th centuries. During the KLONDIKE GOLD RUSH, some miners grew their own vegetables in the relatively fertile Dawson City soil, but most supplies were imported. The pattern that emerged from the gold rush period and came to characterize northern agriculture in the 20th century was one of small market gardens and part-time farming, subordinate to mining. In the Yukon, ranches developed on the Pelly River and along the Whitehorse-Dawson trail. The mining area around Mayo provided a demand for market gardening. In Mackenzie District the significant agricultural activity was undertaken by Oblate missionaries at Ft Smith, Ft Resolution and Ft Providence. During the 20th century the federal government studied the agricultural potential of the North through co-operative experimental work with selected farmers (such as the Oblate missionaries) and, after WWII, in their own substations. The consensus which developed was that agriculture was not commercially viable. Transportation improvements have allowed southern produce to undercut potential northern production and climate has been a continuing impediment.   LYLE DICK AND JEFF TAYLOR

Reading: D.H. Akenson, ed, *Canadian Papers in Rural History*, 3 vols (1978-82); C. Chatillon, *L'Histoire de l'agriculture au Québec* (1976); V.C. Fowke, *Canadian Agricultural Policy* (1946) and *The National Policy and the Wheat Economy* (1957); R.L. Jones, *History of Agriculture in Ontario, 1613-1880* (1946); J. McCallum, *Unequal Beginnings* (1980); I. MacPherson, *Each for All* (1979); G.E. Reamon, *A History of Agriculture in Ontario*, vol 1 (1970); N. Séguin, *Agriculture et colonisation au Québec* (1980); L.A. Wood, *A History of Farmers' Movements in Canada* (1924; reproduced with new materials, 1975).

Ah-Chee-Wun, Coast Salish Lemalchi Indian chief (b ?; d at Victoria 4 July 1863). The Lemalchi tribe of Kuper Island, BC, was known for warlikeness, and their chief, Ah-Chee-Wun, was said to have killed 11 whitemen and many Indians. In 1863 some Lemalchis killed a settler and his daughter on Saturna Island. Public outcry prompted Governor Sir James DOUGLAS to send a gunboat to apprehend the murderers. At the Lemalchi village the Indians refused to surrender anyone and fired on the gunboat, killing one seaman. The gunboat destroyed the village, whose inhabitants dispersed to neighbouring villages. A large naval force eventually captured Ah-Chee-Wun and 17 other Lemalchis. Two were found guilty of murdering the settlers, and Ah-Chee-Wun was found responsible for the death of the seaman. All 3 Lemalchis were hanged. The Ah-Chee-Wun incident destroyed the Lemalchis as a tribe and appears to have ended native resistance by force to settlers in the Gulf Islands of BC.   JOHN DEWHIRST

Ahearn, Thomas, electrical engineer, businessman (b at Ottawa 24 June 1855; d there 28 June 1938). A telegraph operator at 14, by 25 Ahearn was Ottawa branch manager of the telegraph and telephone companies. In 1882, with W.Y. Soper, he started an electrical contracting business that grew into a network of companies controlling electricity supply, streetcars and streetlights in Ottawa. Ahearn reputedly invented the electric cooking range, installed in the Windsor Hotel. In 1899 he drove the first automobile (electric) in Ottawa. Rich by 1900, Ahearn became a director of the Bank of Canada and other leading institutions and a prominent local philanthropist. Chairman of the Ottawa Improvement Commission (later the NATIONAL CAPITAL COMMISSION) from 1926 to 1932, he established Ottawa's parkway system and personally financed the Champlain Bridge over the Ottawa R in 1928. That same year he was appointed to the Privy Council.
                    DONALD J.C. PHILLIPSON

Ahenakew, Edward, Anglican clergyman (b at Sandy Lake IR, Sask; buried there July 1961). A gifted speaker and writer in Cree and English, Ahenakew stirred his people to a sense of their worth as Indians. Through almost 50 years he travelled from one reserve to another in the Saskatchewan diocese and to church synods across Canada. He collaborated in the publication of a Cree-English dictionary and edited a monthly newsletter in Cree syllabics. During the 1920s he was active in efforts to form a national league of Indians. His "Cree Trickster Tales" appeared in *American Folklore* in 1925. After his death, other articles from his unfinished manuscripts were edited for *Saskatchewan History* and *The Beaver;* and in 1974 *Voices of the Plains Cree,* a collection of his writings, was published. He died en route to Dauphin, Man, to help in a summer school for Indian lay readers.   RUTH M. BUCK

Ahousaht, the largest NOOTKA Indian tribe on the W coast of Vancouver I, BC. Originally the Ahousaht were a small tribe on the outer coast of Vargas I and adjacent Vancouver I. In the late 18th century, the Ahousaht, with firearms obtained from Mowachaht kinsmen, conquered the much larger Otsosaht tribe and took their territories of Flores Island, Millar Channel and Herbert Inlet. The Ahousaht have intermarried extensively with 2 neighbouring tribes, the Manhousaht of Sydney Inlet and Shelter Inlet, and the Kelsemaht of the E coast of Vargas Island and Bedwell Sd. These tribes have formally amalgamated with the Ahousaht Band in the 20th century. Today, the Ahousaht live in the village of Mahktosis, also known as "Ahousat." Many band members also live in Port Alberni and in Victoria.   JOHN DEWHIRST

Aid to (or of) the Civil Power, the calling out of military troops by the civil authorities to help maintain or restore public order. ACP is not to be confused with martial law (military takeover of government), the WAR MEASURES ACT (restrictions of civil liberties imposed by Parliament in times of emergency), military assistance to civil authorities in case of disasters, or assistance to ROYAL CANADIAN MOUNTED POLICE, penitentiaries, customs, etc. It is now considered part of Internal Security Operations, a broader term which comprises RCMP surveillance of enemy agents on Canadian soil and related activity.

In England, a 1360 statute authorized justices of the peace to restrain, arrest and imprison rioters. The first modern Riot Act was proclaimed in 1714. Until 1829, parish constables were responsible for maintaining public order, but they were so few and so poorly trained that army troops had to be called out to repress serious riots. The London Metropolitan Police was created in 1829 to help prevent, rather than repress, public disorders, and in 1856 the Police Act was passed, with specific military functions distinguished from those of the police and of the magistrates.

Following the acquisition of ACADIA in 1713 and Canada in 1760, the British army garrison troops in BNA replied to requests for ACP in accordance with their military regulations. In 1868 Canadian laws concerning the police, illegal assembly and riots were enacted, and the MILITIA ACT authorized calling out Canadian troops in ACP. British practice generally remained the model. Regulations and Orders for the Canadian Militia replaced the British ones in 1870. In 1924 the power of calling out troops was moved from local authorities to provincial attorneys general.

From 1796 to 1870 British troops, occasionally helped by local militiamen, provided ACP roughly 100 times. Since then Canadian troops have helped maintain or restore public order 140 times and have helped repress penitentiary riots 20 times. Half the former occurred before 1900, usually because of absence, shortage or improper training of police. Since 1933, troops have not been involved in strikebreaking except under the War Measures Act, and all callouts except one have taken place in Ontario and Québec, which are the only provinces not policed by the RCMP. Over half the penitentiary callouts have occurred since 1962, and in most cases the army did not have to use force. Recent research has helped to prove that Canadian history has witnessed violence; at the same time, military interventions have not usually resulted in the use of undue force. *See also* ARMED FORCES: MILITIA AND ARMY; OCTOBER CRISIS.   JEAN PARISEAU

Aide-Créquy, Jean-Antoine, priest, painter (b at Québec City 5 Apr 1749; d there 6 Dec 1780). The first Canadian-born painter, he was the son of a master mason. He was ordained in 1773 and became parish priest at Baie-St-Paul. In June 1780, because of delicate health, he went to Québec's Hôtel-Dieu hospital, where he died several months later. His artistic training is unknown, but he learned by studying the work of Frère LUC in local churches and the European works found in the seminary and religious communities of Québec City. His paintings showed these influences, yet bore his own personal stamp. Most of his paintings were for churches, including those at L'Islet, St-Roch-des-Aulnaies, St-Joachim and Île-aux-Coudres (today in the bishopric of Chicoutimi). Aide-Créquy followed the French tradition already established in Canada and his works are representative of the era following 1763.   RAL LUSSIER

AIDS (Acquired Immunodeficiency Syndrome) is a fatal disease due to infection by a virus which damages the immune system, resulting in loss of protection against many infectious diseases and some cancers. This retrovirus is termed human immunodeficiency virus or HIV (formerly known as T-lymphotrophic virus type III, lymphadenopathy-associated virus, or AIDS-related virus). It only infects man and chimpanzees, and this has severely limited its study. Target cells, which this virus infects, are T-lymphocytes (which it can kill) and macrophages. Destruction of these T-lymphocytes and macrophages produces the AIDS immunodeficiency.

Illnesses this infection can produce include a transient disease, developing within several months of exposure. It is characterized by rash, fever, malaise, joint pains and lymphadenopathy (swollen lymph nodes). A later illness, termed AIDS-related complex (ARC), is characterized by malaise, fevers, nightsweats, weight loss, diarrhea, and sometimes fungal infection of the pharynx (thrush). ARC occurs in over 25% of infected persons and is associated with some damage to the immune system. Profound immune system damage is a late manifestation of this infection. More than 5 years may elapse before this immunodeficiency develops, and more than 20% of infected persons may develop this. The opportunistic infections of unusual malignancies which result from this immunodeficiency define this as AIDS. *Pneumocystis carinii* pneumonia occurs in over 60% of persons with AIDS; a cancer, Kaposi's sarcoma, occurs in approximately 20%; among other illnesses are infections by *Toxoplasma gondii, Cryptosporidium, Mycobacterium avium-intracellulare* and rare lymphomas. Retrovirus infection of the brain also occurs. This is a slowly progressive infection, possibly of macrophage-type cells in the brain. It is poorly characterized but manifestations include subacute encephalitis, dementia and a variety of neurological illnesses.

The virus is transmitted through direct inoculation into the body through injection of blood or blood products or transplantation of tissues; through sexual activity with an infected person or by artificial insemination; or through pregnancy to infants of infected mothers. Transmission has not been documented by other potential ways of spread, such as aerosolization, insect bites or nonsexual contact. Infection has been documented worldwide with major sites in the US, Haiti and central Africa. Epidemiology of this infection differs between industrialized and less developed areas. In North America, Europe and Australia, men are the major group infected, most of whom have engaged in homosexual activity; in Africa equal proportions of men and women have been infected. Transmission in Africa and Haiti remains unexplained, but may now reflect heterosexual activity with an infected person. The number of infected persons worldwide is unknown. In some central African cities 15% or more of adults and 65% of prostitutes have been infected. Over 1.5 million Americans may have been infected. In some American cities over 60% of gay men, 80% of persons who

abuse drugs intravenously, and 75% of persons with hemophilia, who regularly receive blood product transfusions, have been infected. Anal receptive intercourse appears to be the most efficient mode of sexual transmission.

Over 20 000 cases of AIDS have been reported in the US and over 600 cases in Canada by 1986. The number of cases has doubled annually. The American government estimates that there will be over 250 000 cases of AIDS in the US in the 10 years since the first cases were recognized (June 1981). How persons have been infected and developed AIDS are similar in most industrialized countries. In Canada, men engaging in homosexual activity represent 81% of reported AIDS cases (*see* HOMOSEXUALITY); intravenous drug abusers represent 17% of cases in the US but only 0.3% in Canada; heterosexual partners of infected persons represent 2.2%; persons receiving blood or blood products represent 5.5%; and children represent 2.9%. Persons who have come from areas where this infection is widespread (eg, Haiti or central Africa) account for 8.3% of Canadian cases. In less than 3% of cases is information insufficient to classify cases into risk categories.

Seventy to 90% of infected persons develop serum antibodies to this virus. These antibodies are used to identify potentially infectious blood donations and to determine if someone has been infected. The virus can be cultured from blood, tissues and body fluids, and can be recovered from most persons who have antibodies, whether or not they are ill. So, anyone who is likely to have become infected is considered *potentially* infectious, whether or not they have antibodies or are ill. This includes anyone who has engaged in homosexual activity since 1978; had sexual activity with someone who is infected, or likely to be infected; abused drugs intravenously; or come from an area where this infection is considered endemic (eg, central Africa). Anyone who could be infected should ensure that their body fluids do not enter another person's body. This means that they must not donate blood, or sperm for artificial insemination; should use condoms during sexual activity and avoid exchange of saliva; and should not share needles or syringes if they abuse drugs.

What determines outcome following infection is unknown. Whether or not an infected person will develop disease, or what diseases may result cannot be predicted now. Also, there is no way to stop this infection once someone has been infected, to limit the damage this infection may produce, or to repair the damaged immune system once this occurs. Meanwhile, therapy is directed at treating opportunistic infections or malignancies which result from this immunodeficiency. Intensive research is directed at developing a vaccine which would protect people from becoming infected, and antiviral drugs that would stop the infection once this has occurred. AIDS is costly. Control is directed at preventing infection. Intensive efforts are underway to educate the public how infection can be prevented. Community-based support groups, hospices and hospital programs are also being developed so that care is available to anyone who is infected, or who has AIDS. All blood donations are now being screened to prevent transmission by blood or blood products. *See also* SEXUALLY TRANSMITTED DISEASE.   NORBERT GILMORE

Aikins, Sir James Albert Manning, lawyer, politician, lt-gov of Manitoba (b at Richview, Peel County, UC 10 Dec 1851; d at Winnipeg 1 Mar 1929). The son of James Cox Aikins, senator, Dominion Cabinet minister (1869-73 and 1878-82) and lt-gov of Manitoba (1882-88),

Aikins was called to the bar of Ontario in 1878 and of Manitoba in 1879. While maintaining a large and influential practice in Winnipeg, where he was western solicitor for the CPR (1881-1911), he was also prominent in local, provincial and national affairs. He served on several royal commissions, was Conservative MP for Brandon (1911-15), leader of the provincial Conservative Party (1915-16), and lt-gov of Manitoba (1916-26). Created QC in 1884 and knighted in 1914, he was president (1910-16) of the Manitoba Bar Assn and a founder and first president (1914-29) of the Canadian Bar Assn.   D.H. BROWN

Aikins, William Thomas, surgeon, educator (b at Toronto Township, Upper Canada 4 June 1827; d at Toronto 25 May 1897). The son of Protestant Irish immigrants, he studied at John ROLPH's Toronto School of Medicine and Jefferson Medical Coll, Philadelphia. Graduating in 1850, he became anatomy instructor in Rolph's school. In 1856 the staff wrested control of the school from the overbearing Rolph; Aikins, then professor of surgery, became president, remaining so until 1887 when, through his efforts, the TSM became the U of T medical faculty. Aikins served as dean until 1893. A superb surgeon and early exponent of Lister's antiseptic methods, he was an inspiring teacher and able administrator under whose direction the TSM and university's medical school acquired national reputations. Moreover, as a leading member of the Council of the Ontario Coll of Physicians and Surgeons, he helped raise the provincial standards for medical education.   DAVID R. KEANE

Ailleboust de Coulonge et d'Argentenay, Louis d', governor of New France 1648-51 (b at Ancy-le-Franc, France 1612?; d at Montréal May 1660). He was a nobleman and military engineer who sailed in 1643 to play a leading role in the newly established Catholic outpost of Ville-Marie [Montréal]. Named governor of all Canada in 1648, he was powerless to prevent the dominant Iroquois from annihilating all but a few of his Huron allies. After 1651, d'Ailleboust remained in New France, serving as acting governor 1657-58.   ALLAN GREER

Air Canada was incorporated by an Act of Parliament 10 April 1937, to provide a publicly owned air transportation service. Stock was vested in Canadian National Railways. Scheduled operations commenced on 1 Sept 1937 when passenger and mail service was inaugurated between Vancouver, BC, and Seattle, Washington. Transcontinental passenger and mail service was introduced 1 April 1939 from Montréal/Toronto to Vancouver via Ottawa, North Bay, Kapuskasing, Winnipeg, Regina and Lethbridge, and Edmonton routes with the fleet of Lockheed L10As and 14.08s. The name of the airline was changed by Act of Parliament from TRANS-CANADA AIRLINES to Air Canada 1 Jan 1965. Under the Air Canada Act 1977, the airline's charter was brought up to date. The common shares passed from CNR to the Crown and the company was made subject to the jurisdiction of the Canadian Transport Commission. In 1987 the airline operated internal trunk services, and routes across the Atlantic to Glasgow, Manchester, London, Paris, Zurich, Düsseldorf, München, Geneva and Frankfurt, Bombay and Singapore and cargo flights to Shannon and Brussels. Air Canada also extensively served the US and the Caribbean. The operational fleet was 113 aircraft, including 5 Boeing 747, 16 L-1011, 36 Boeing 727 and 14 Boeing 767. In 1986 Air Canada's investment in other companies included GPA Group Ltd (22.7%), Innotech Aviation Ltd (30%), MATAC

Cargo Ltd (50%) and Global Travel Corporate Holdings Ltd (86.5%). Air Canada purchased Nordair in 1979 and sold it May 1984. Like most other airlines, Air Canada expanded dramatically in the 1960s and 1970s, but amid rising fuel costs and price wars recession hit in the mid-1970s. Before restrictions were removed for CP Air, Air Canada had 77.8% of domestic traffic. However, passengers and cargo declined drastically in the early 1980s. The company responded with pay cuts and sale of equipment. In 1983 the airline suffered three incidents: a DC-9 skidded off an icy runway at Regina, on June 2, 23 passengers were killed in a fire of a DC-9 at Cincinnati, and a B-767 ran out of fuel and was guided by its pilot, with luck and skill, to a safe landing at Gimli. In 1986 Air Canada had sales and assets of nearly $3 billion each; employees numbered 22 200. Headquarters are at Montréal.

Reading: Philip Smith, It Seems Like Only Yesterday: Air Canada the First 50 Years (1986).

Air Force, *see* ARMED FORCES: AIR FORCE.

Air Law and Space Law are separate and distinct branches of law, although they are occasionally treated as one ("Aerospace Law"). Air law, the older of the 2, is the body of public and private law, both national and international, that regulates aeronautical activities and other uses of airspace. Space law, on the other hand, regulates activities of states in outer space, primarily the use of satellites. The essential difference between air law and space law stems from the legal status of airspace and of outer space. Whereas airspace, except over the high seas and Antarctica, is under the sovereignty of subjacent states, outer space is governed by the regime of freedom. The question of boundaries between outer space and airspace is awaiting international agreement; it is virtually certain, however, that the boundary will not be placed higher than 100 km above sea level.

Space Law The origin of space law can be traced to the launching on 4 Oct 1957 of Sputnik I, the first artificial Earth satellite. Since that time the legal regulation of outer-space activities has been largely centered in the UN Committee on the Peaceful Uses of Outer Space. The bulk of space law consists of norms incorporated in 5 multilateral treaties. The most important is the 1967 Treaty on Principles Governing the Activities of States in the Exploration and Use of Outer Space, including the Moon and Other Celestial Bodies (also known as the Outer Space Treaty). The major principles of the treaty are freedom of access to, and use of, outer space; prohibition against national claims to sovereignty in any part of outer space; and a ban on the placing of weapons of mass destruction anywhere in outer space.

Air Law In Canada legal regulation of air navigation is the exclusive competence of Parliament. The major, relevant legislation includes the Aeronautics Act (the cornerstone of the Canadian civil aviation regulatory system); the National Transportation Act (setting up the Canadian Transport Commission as the principal organ for the economic regulation of air transport); the Carriage by Air Act (governing the liability of air carriers relating to international carriage by air); and the Air Canada Act (establishing a crown corporation to operate air transport services).

Because much air navigation takes place internationally, many legal norms governing the technical aspects of air navigation have been developed internationally and are implemented by national legislation. The International Civil Aviation Organization (ICAO), headquartered in Montréal, was established pursuant to the Convention on International Civil Aviation (Chicago, Ill, 1944). ICAO has a membership of 152 states.

The exchange of commercial rights in international air transport is regulated mainly by hundreds of bilateral agreements, along with the multilateral International Air Services Transit Agreement of 1944 and certain provisions of the Chicago Convention.

The Warsaw Convention of 1929, amended by the Hague Protocol of 1955, is widely accepted and governs the liability of air carriers with respect to the international carriage by air of passengers, baggage and cargo. Canada is a party to the amended convention and has implemented it through the Carriage by Air Act. The rules of Canadian domestic law govern air carriers' liability relating to carriage by air in Canada not covered by the Carriage by Air Act and claims for damage to third parties caused, for example, through aerial collisions, excessive noise, and aerial spraying.

Another important aspect of air law is concerned with offences and certain other acts committed on board aircraft (the Tokyo Convention of 1963), the suppression of unlawful seizure of aircraft (the Hague Convention of 1970) and the suppression of unlawful acts against the safety of civil aviation (the Montréal Convention of 1971). Each of these conventions has been accepted by many states, including Canada.

The 1 Sept 1983 destruction, off the Sea of Japan, by a Soviet military aircraft of a Korean civil airliner, with heavy loss of life, led to the adoption in May 1984 by ICAO member states of an amendment to the Chicago Convention designed to prevent similar attacks on civil aircraft straying into foreign airspace without authorization. In Canada, McGill University in Montréal operates the Institute of Air and Space Law, a unique academic institution for advanced research and study in air and space law.

Air Pollution Air pollutants are substances that, when present in the atmosphere in sufficient quantities, may adversely affect people, animals, vegetation or inanimate materials. The sources of air pollution include industry, vehicles, domestic activities (eg, heating, cooking), agriculture (slash burning, blowing dust, farm odours) and natural events (forest fires, VOLCANOES, dust storms, salt from sea spray, pollen). Water vapour released from combustion of natural gas may cause ice FOG in winter in such northern cities as Edmonton, and thus might be considered a pollutant in those circumstances. Air pollutants occur in minute quantities, mostly measured in parts per million or parts per trillion parts of air. Some chemicals causing highly objectionable odours occur at such low concentrations that they cannot be measured.

Types of Pollutants Pollutants include total suspended particulate matter (TSP), sulphur dioxide (SO_2), oxides of nitrogen (NO_2 and NO), ozone (O_3), carbon monoxide (CO), hydrogen sulphide (H_2S), hydrogen fluoride (HF1) and LEAD (Pb). Many of these result from the burning of fossil fuels (eg, coal, oil, gasoline). There are also a few highly toxic pollutants such as PESTICIDES, MERCURY and PCBs (polychlorinated biphenyls). Occupational and indoor pollutants include factory dust and cigarette smoke. Other pollutants of concern are the sulphate and nitrate fractions of TSP (*see* ACID RAIN), carbon dioxide, chlorofluoromethanes and ionizing radiation.

Air Pollution Pathways The initial behaviour of a pollutant depends on the nature of its source, which may be a chimney releasing gases at high temperature and exit velocity, or the tail pipe of a moving vehicle. Subsequently, the pollutant moves with the wind and is diluted by wind eddies. In some cases, chemical transformations into new forms of pollutants may take place, eg, SO_2

Inco's stack at Sudbury, Ont, a primary source of sulphur dioxide emissions (*photo by J.A. Kraulis*).

may change to sulphates. Pollution is often carried long distances by the wind but is finally removed by wet and dry deposition. Scientists have predicted that, if all man-made pollution sources were turned off suddenly, the atmosphere would return to a pristine state within a few days. Despite the atmosphere's seemingly limitless capacity to accept and dilute the waste products of society, meteorological conditions occasionally lead to serious air-pollution episodes. For ground-level sources, these episodes are associated with light winds and temperature inversions (ie, temperature increasing with height, a condition reducing wind gusts and pollutant dilution rates), which result in smog. For emissions from tall chimneys, pollution episodes are associated with strong, steady winds and also with fumigations (inversions aloft and vigorous mixing near the ground caused by surface heating). The most serious recorded air-pollution episode in Canada is the "Grey Cup smog" of Nov 1962, which lasted 5 days. It caused increased hospital admissions throughout southern Ontario and postponement of the football game in Toronto because of poor visibility.

Effects of Air Pollutants Adverse effects to human and animal health include respiratory ailments (silicosis, pneumonia, asthma, emphysema, bronchitis and hay fever) caused by particles (SO_2, NO_2, O_3, pollens); carboxylhemoglobin, a condition that interferes with the ability of hemoglobin to combine with oxygen, resulting from carbon monoxide uptake by the bloodstream; eye watering and skin irritation caused by ozone; damage to internal organs from lead, mercury, pesticides, etc. It is suspected that lung CANCER and other chronic diseases may be caused or exacerbated by air pollution. Direct damage to vegetation includes necrosis (tissue death), chlorosis (whitening of leaves) and premature aging; indirect damage may result from soil acidification by acid rain. Metal corrosion, caused mainly by SO_2 and sea spray, takes the form of increased rust and metal fatigue. Damage to fabrics, paint and rubber, caused mainly by NO_2, O_3 and H_2S, results in shortened life span, discoloration, cracking and peeling. Soiling of materials, caused by soot, necessitates increased washing, dry cleaning and painting. Climatic effects of pollution can be regional and immediate (eg, ice fogs in Edmonton, large-scale regional hazes) or global and long-term. The main trace substances involved are water vapour, sulphate particles, CO_2, TSP and chlorofluoromethanes.

Air-Resource Management and Pollution Control

Strategies used to control air pollution are varied. Emissions can be reduced by means of burning less or cleaner fuel (eg, gas instead of coal), more efficient burning of fuel (ie, at higher temperatures or with oxygen added) and installation of pollution-control devices. The use of tall chimneys, such as the "superstack" erected by Inco Ltd at Sudbury, Ont, may solve local problems but tends to enlarge the affected area. Meteorological episode control involves reduction of emissions (eg, switching to low-sulphur fuels) when atmospheric dispersal is poor. Other strategies include regional land-use planning, development of pollutant-resistant strains of vegetation, and development of paint, metals, etc, with increased life expectancies in polluted environments. Emission control is of primary importance, but some sources may be technologically or economically difficult to manage. Most air-resource programs, therefore, use a combination of strategies.

Most Canadian provinces and the federal government have Clean Air Acts that specify emission standards (maximum permissible rates of release of designated pollutants from particular types of sources) and ambient air-quality standards (maximum permissible concentrations of designated pollutants in the outdoor environment). Under the Canadian Constitution, health is a provincial responsibility, with air-pollution control undertaken largely by the provinces. However, the federal government has jurisdiction over pollution from trains and ships, regulates lead content of gasoline, and can intervene when air pollution crosses the US-Canada border. The Atomic Energy Control Board regulates ionizing radiation. The federal government also plays an important co-ordinating role, through federal-provincial committees and task forces, in setting standards, and monitoring criteria, research and engineering programs. Indoor pollutants are regulated mostly by industrial hygiene authorities. Some cities broadcast smog alerts and pollution indices. *See also* ENVIRONMENTAL LAW; POLLUTION.

R.E. MUNN

Reading: D.V. Bates, *A Citizen's Guide to Air Pollution* (1973); A.F. Friedlaender, ed, *Approaches to Controlling Air Pollution* (1978).

Air Profile Recorder (APR), a narrow-beam recording RADAR altimeter designed to provide topographic profiles for use in the mapping of wilderness areas. The instrument employs a 3.2 cm pulse transmitter that feeds a parabolic radiator, mounted below the aircraft. This antenna directs the radiation vertically downward, and the height of the aircraft is measured by the electronic timing of the pulse echo time. The height data is presented in the form of a continuous graph, and when the aircraft is held at a constant height above sea level, as indicated by a continuous barometric altimeter recording, the graphic record becomes a profile of the ground beneath the plane. A reference level is established by including one or more points of known elevation (lakes, wide rivers, etc) in the flight path.

The APR was a development of the electronic Terrain Clearance Indicator, a radar alarm system developed early in WWII to warn aircraft pilots when they had descended below some pre-select-

ed height above ground. The use of such a device, after the addition of an appropriate measuring and recording capability, was suggested by John Carroll of the Department of Mines and Resources in May 1943. The development work was done at the NATIONAL RESEARCH COUNCIL OF CANADA by Brian F. Cooper assisted by Sidney Jowett of the Department of Mines and Resources. Test trials were conducted in 1947, and the device went into commercial production shortly after. It has been used for medium scale mapping (ie, in the 1:200 000 to 1:600 000 range) in Canada and many other countries.

L.M. SEBERT

Air Traffic Control (ATC) is the service provided to pilots to assist them in operating their aircraft in a safe, orderly and efficient manner. In Canada the air traffic controllers of the Air Traffic Services Branch, Transport Canada, are responsible for providing vertical and horizontal separation (known as a "block of protected airspace") between each aircraft being flown in controlled airspace using Instrument Flight Rules (IFR). Canadian airspace extends from the Canada-US border to the North Pole and from the Pacific Ocean to halfway across the North Atlantic.

Most flying in Canada is done under what is called Visual Flight Rules (VFR), in which the pilot navigates the aircraft by visual reference to the ground and is responsible for seeing and avoiding other aircraft. Only near busy airports which have a control tower will the pilot's VFR flight come under the direction or guidance of Air Traffic Control. The other type of flight operations are conducted under IFR, in which the pilot uses navigational aids, either ground based or on board the aircraft, to fly from one location to another. All scheduled airlines operate IFR and thus it is the type of flight most people experience as passengers. Under IFR and in controlled airspace, Air Traffic Control is responsible for separating flights and providing them with a moving block of protected airspace to prevent collision.

In VFR conditions the pilots can, to a very large extent, separate themselves from other aircraft including those operating IFR. The IFR flight may be operated regardless of weather conditions such as clouds that do not permit the pilots to see and avoid other aircraft; responsibility for these flights is shifted to the air traffic controllers.

There are several closely interrelated air traffic controller positions, probably the best known of which are the control tower operators. Two types of functions are performed from the control tower. The ground controller issues radio instructions to all aircraft and service vehicles moving on or near the runways and the airport controller mon-

Air traffic controllers in Toronto Area Control Centre (*courtesy Transport Canada*).

itors (visually or on RADAR) all aircraft landing, taking off or flying within the airport control zone. When aircraft get too close to each other, the airport controller gives one or both planes a new course or altitude to avoid a "confliction."

Using radar and providing control by radio as required, the terminal controller guides and directs all IFR aircraft operating within 65 km of major airports. Near the airport but outside the control zone the terminal controller may also provide radar services and flight advisories to VFR aircraft.

The area controller guides aircraft that are flying "on instruments" along the airways which link most airports across the country or lead to tracks taking the aircraft to international destinations. This controller also co-ordinates with towers, terminals, other centres and flight service stations as necessary.

Finally, the oceanic controller monitors aircraft flying through Canadian airspace over the North Atlantic. Most of these flights are controlled by the Gander Oceanic Area Control Centre. The pilots issue position reports which allow the oceanic controller to estimate the actual time that each aircraft is expected to cross each 10 meridians of longitude. In this way, ATC safely "shepherds" the flight to its destination.

In addition to these various types of air traffic controllers the pilot is also aided by flight service specialists who provide a wide range of services mostly at airports with a low density of traffic. These include airport and vehicle advisories, flight information, alerting and emergency services, and pre-flight briefings.

After a pilot files an IFR flight plan, the flight comes under ATC supervision. The flight plan consists of the "airways" that are to be used, the highways in the skies formed by radio navigational aids located on the ground. It also includes the cruising altitude, the estimated time enroute and other information such as aircraft type and speed. After checking the flight plan for accuracy the details are entered into the ATC system. The pilot then boards the aircraft and establishes radio contact with the ground controller to receive taxi instructions: which taxiways should be used to safely enter the runway, the exact time and current altimeter setting plus the present wind direction and speed, and an Air Traffic Control clearance. ATC clearance authorizes the pilot to fly, under specified conditions, from one airport to another.

Control of the aircraft then passes to the airport controller who, when it is safe, clears the aircraft onto the runway and for the takeoff, fitting the flight into the sequence of arriving and departing aircraft at the airport. At most major airports, before takeoff, the controller instructs the pilot to make a Standard Instrument Departure, which takes the flight to a predetermined heading and altitude before moving to the enroute airways.

The terminal controller then follows the flight's progress on radar until the limit of his or her responsibility is reached (about 65 km from the terminal), after which an area or enroute controller has charge of the flight until it crosses into the adjoining area. The aircraft continues to be "handed-off" from area controller to area controller until it reaches the vicinity of its destination and the process is reversed.

Throughout the whole process, from filing the flight plan to landing at the final destination, Air Traffic Control monitors the aircraft's progress and directs the pilots as necessary, and provides current weather, the status of navigational aids or other information important for flight safety. All this makes the controller's job one of extreme responsibility.

In Canada there are 61 control towers handling in peak months over 500 000 landings and take-offs. Vancouver International Airport and Toronto-Lester B. Pearson International Airport are the busiest in the country, with peak days exceeding 1000 operations. In addition to the control towers there are 7 Area Control Centres (ACC), 8 stand-alone Terminal Control Units (TCU) and over 100 Flight Service Stations.

The basic training for air traffic controllers is provided in a residential college environment at the Transport Canada Training Institute (TCTI) in Cornwall, Ont. To qualify, applicants must be at least 18 years old and have successfully completed secondary school. Excellent diction and hearing is required in addition to passing a rigid medical exam. In the Québec region knowledge of both official languages is essential while in the rest of Canada English is essential. The overall training program offered in English and bilingual formats normally takes one to two years depending on the assigned control specialty. The formal training covers both radar and procedural control functions including the control of aircraft flying under VFR and IFR. Through classroom instruction and practical exercises using various simulators, the curriculum includes regulations, aircraft operating characteristics, navigation, radio communications and weather. J-D LYON

Air Transport Industry As would be expected in a large, thinly populated country, air transport is a very important part of the Canadian ECONOMY. In 1985 Canadian commercial air carriers (ie, excluding private and governmental fleets) numbered 604, employed 43 330 on average, and recorded operating revenues of $5.6 billion. Worldwide statistics published by the International Civil Aviation Organization (based in Montréal) show that Canada ranks well behind large, more heavily populated countries such as the US and the USSR in the amount of domestic air traffic, but well ahead of countries such as W Germany and Italy which have more than twice the population but are smaller geographically. Although only 4.6% of all Canadian intercity passenger trips were carried out by air in 1984 and the proportion of freight moving by air is also relatively small, these figures reflect the heavy use of the automobile for comparatively short passenger trips between cities, the economies in freight transportation from very large loads carried in ship and train transportation, the door-to-door convenience of truck transportation and the relatively high energy cost of air transportation.

Air transport occupies a special niche. Any trip of over 500 km taken by a person who travels alone and who places a high value on his or her time is likely to be by air. Distance and the value placed on time are also important factors in air freight eg, perishable food shipped to isolated communities. For the hinterland and for population centres separated by large bodies of water, the high costs per unit of building roads or railways serving very small populations, or of providing ferry services, often mean that the choice is clear; air is the only way to go (*see* BUSH FLYING).

The federal government is an important part of the air transport industry. It builds and operates nearly all of the AIRPORTS serving scheduled flights; designs and operates the system of rules, communications equipment and electronic monitoring devices that form Canada's "airways"; takes partial responsibility for air safety by, for example, operating licensing systems for aircraft, pilots, mechanics, etc; and regulates the activities of air carriers by controlling when an airline can start or stop a service, and the prices charged and qualities of service provided.

The users of airports and airways enjoy benefits much greater than the benefits accruing to taxpayers in general. Under such circumstances, pressures often develop to introduce charges on users for services rendered, thus reducing the burden on the general taxpayer. In 1987-88 the federal air transportation program was expected to incur expenses of $1.3 billion, while revenues from users were estimated at almost $.9 billion, from such things as space rentals, concession and landing fees, charges for licences and the air transportation tax. (This tax is by far the largest single source of Transport Canada's revenues – an estimated $431.5 million in 1987-88.)

Consonant with trends elsewhere in the world during the 1980s, the federal government took a number of initiatives to diminish its role in air transport. For example, on 9 Apr 1987, the Hon John C. CROSBIE announced a new policy for airport management in Canada in which local authorities could take over ownership, operation or partial operation of federal airports. Another large area of government disengagement is in the field of economic regulation. Prior to the 1980s, Canada applied a 2-tiered regulatory system. As one tier, the government selected a carrier or carriers and defined roles for the carrier or carriers to perform. In the early years, TRANS-CANADA AIRLINES was the designated international and transcontinental carrier; gradually, other air carriers were assigned specific roles in specific parts of the country. A second tier of economic regulation was a licensing authority (named the CANADIAN TRANSPORT COMMISSION after the National Transportation Act of 1967) which had quasi-judicial powers, and was obliged to find that a proposed air service was required for the "public convenience and necessity" before it issued a licence.

In 1984, following a period of drastic deregulation in the US, the Canadian minister of transport instructed the CTC to "give much greater weight to the benefits of increased competition in judging the requirements of public convenience and necessity." The succeeding minister carried these changes a step further and spelled out a new, much freer regulatory regime for air transport in a new National Transportation Act (Bill C-18), which makes issuance of a licence virtually automatic, as long as the applicant is at least 75% Canadian owned or controlled, has sufficient liability insurance and can meet Transport Canada's safety requirements.

The effects of deregulation, in the form of mergers resulting in sharp reductions in the number of competitors, has proceeded much more rapidly in Canada than in the US. Canadians now face the prospect of having 3 carriers competing on long-haul transcontinental routes (Air Canada, Canadian Airlines International Ltd and WARDAIR), with only Air Canada and CAIL in sight for other, moderately dense routes. There will probably be but one source of service for a large number of thin markets between small centres and in the hinterland.

The two largest carriers have created alliances, involving partial or complete ownership, with smaller carriers feeding traffic from smaller aircraft to jets at the major centres. In 1987 Air Canada owned 49% of Air Nova, 100% of Air BC, and, through a holding company, 75% of Air Ontario and Austin Airways; CAIL owned 46.5% of Time Air, 30% of Norcanair, 20% of Air Atlantic, 100% of Air Maritime, 100% of Nordair which, in turn, owned 35% of Nordair-Metro (which owned 100% of Quebecair), and was in the process of creating a new Ontario feeder carrier. Virtually all of the large and medium-sized scheduled carriers are now members of one of the two large air carrier groups, with Wardair being the largest exception.

The trend toward deregulation has been most evident for domestic air service, but increasing flexibility is a feature of international regulation, too. International air services are governed by air bilateral agreements between Canada and other countries. Canada is a party to over 40 such agreements, and roughly 12 negotiations are now carried out each year, with half of them resulting in revised agreements.

The long border between Canada and the US and strong north-south ties have resulted in air bilateral agreements between the two countries allowing services between many more points than is the case for Canadian bilateral agreements with any other country. About every 10 years, a new, enlarged Canada/US agreement has been put in place. Recently the two sides have been at an impasse. Canada has proposed a free regime for carriers wishing to provide transborder services, as long as this policy is accompanied by rights to provide "cabotage" services as extensions to transborder services (eg, Air Canada could serve Chicago to Los Angeles traffic on a Toronto-Chicago-Los Angeles flight). The cabotage proposal has met with opposition from US negotiators.

Most Canadian air carriers are members of the Air Transport Association of Canada, based in Ottawa, and airlines providing international scheduled services also belong to the International Air Transport Association, based in Montréal.

ALAN CONBOY

Aird, Sir John, banker (b at Longueuil, Canada E 15 Nov 1855; d at Toronto 30 Nov 1938). Aird, the president of the Canadian Bank of Commerce, is best known for his role as chairman of the Royal Commission on Radio Broadcasting that reported in 1929. He joined the bank in 1878 and rose to become president in 1924. Mackenzie KING's government put him at the head of the broadcasting royal commission in 1928, and Aird's report recommended that a public body regulate private broadcasters and air its own programs. The Canadian Radio Broadcasting Commission, the forerunner of the CBC, came into existence in 1932 as a result. J.L. GRANATSTEIN

Aird, John Black, lawyer, senator, corporate director and lt-gov (b at Toronto 5 May 1923). Following graduation from Osgoode Hall Law School, Aird joined a Toronto law firm which currently bears his name. He was appointed a Liberal senator from Toronto in Nov 1964 and resigned from the Senate in 1974 to become the chairman of the Institute of Research on Public Policy (1974-80). He also chaired the Canadian section of the Canada-US Joint Board on Defence (1971-79). In 1980 he was appointed lt-gov of Ontario. As the viceregal representative, Aird made the job more than ceremonial and he took a keen interest in the disabled, naming this work "civic humanism," and becoming an increasingly active advocate on their behalf. It is, however, his overseeing of the transfer of power to the Liberal Party following the 1985 NDP-Liberal Accord that brought Aird into the public eye. In this task Aird ensured that his actions upheld the nonpartisan character of the lt-gov's office. He resigned his Queen's Park position in Sept 1985 and in July 1986 he succeeded George Ignatieff as chancellor of U of T, having previously served as chancellor at Wilfrid Laurier U (1977-85). WILLIAM KAPLAN

Airdrie, Alta, City, pop 10 390 (1986c), inc 1985. Located 10 km N of Calgary's city limits, Airdrie straddles Highway 2. Originally a railway station on the Calgary & Edmonton Ry completed in 1891, it became a post office in 1900 to serve the growing farm population beginning to occupy the grazing leases which had dominated the area for 20 years. By 1909 Airdrie was an incorporated village with 32 houses. Following 60 years of slow growth, in the 1960s the community began to provide residential sites for people employed in nearby Calgary. This trend accelerated to such a degree that between 1976 and 1981 the population increased almost 500%, and Airdrie was dubbed Canada's fastest growing town. While a majority of Airdrie's work force commutes to Calgary, much local employment is provided in the city's East Lake Industrial Park.

DOUGLAS BABCOCK

Airport An aerodrome is any area of land, water (including frozen surfaces) or other supporting surface used for the arrival, departure, movement or servicing of aircraft, together with any ancillary buildings and other installations. In Canada, an airport is an aerodrome that has been certified by the federal minister of transport to be operated according to the conditions stated in the airport certification document. There are estimated to be more than 6000 aerodromes in Canada, of which 1255 were certified airports in 1985. Over 10% of these airports are operated by Transport Canada, 22% by municipalities and the remainder by private corporations or individuals. An airport may be a large busy international port of entry, such as Vancouver International, which covers approximately 1440 hectares of area, or a small heliport requiring as little as 346 square metres.

Airport Classification An airport supports 2 types of aviation activity: commercial and private. Commercial aviation activities are those which use an aircraft for hire or reward. Activities range from international and domestic air passenger and freight transportation, carried out by the major airlines, to specialty functions such as flight training, crop dusting or aerial photography. The aircraft used in commercial activities can be as large as a Boeing 747 or a Hercules freighter or as small as a Piper Cub. Private aviation, on the other hand, includes aircraft operations that are for the direct benefit of organizations or individuals using their own aircraft which are not offered for hire to others. The aircraft used in private activities range from corporate jets the size of airliners to ultra-light motorized hang gliders.

For statistical and administrative purposes, the federal government has divided the Canadian airport system into 5 major classes of airports: international, national, regional, local commercial and local. This structure groups airports together according to the presence of commercial air services and the number and type of unit-toll route networks connected to the airport. Unit toll is defined as the public transportation of persons, mail or goods by aircraft. Air carriers are awarded a licence which allows them to use a certain class size of aircraft to conduct specified unit-toll services on stated routes between communities.

The international and national classes of airports form the backbone of the Canadian unit-toll air carrier system. There are 22 airports so classified and these airports support all scheduled international travel and most interprovincial domestic travel. For the most part, these airports are located in major urban areas of Canada and in all provincial and territorial capitals. The international airports are so named because they act as gateways or points of access for aircraft arriving from or departing for other airports outside Canada and beyond the continental US. Flights to and from the continental US are called "transborder." Although a subset of international flights for statistical purposes, these flights are not considered to be pure international flights for the purpose of classifying Canadian airports. The regional class airports act as hubs, collecting localized unit-toll services from smaller airports and

Aerial view of Terminal 2 at Toronto-Lester B. Pearson International Airport. Canada's most active airport, it handles 13.7 million passengers a year (*courtesy SSC-Photocentre*).

providing direct access to the larger international or national airports. A local commercial airport supports the most localized unit-toll service. These airports most likely will have fixed-base operators such as crop dusters, flying schools and small charter outfitters, and may support corporate aircraft. A local airport is one that is not a fixed base or point of call for commercial activity.

Current Statistics In 1985, Canadian airports processed 46.7 million enplaned/deplaned air passengers. The table displays selected statistics for Canada's 25 busiest airports, based on the number of enplaned/deplaned (E/D) revenue air passengers accommodated at that airport. An enplaned revenue passenger is defined as a person who purchased a ticket and boards an aircraft at an airport and a deplaned passenger is one who purchased a ticket and gets off an aircraft at an airport. Toronto-Lester B. Pearson International was Canada's busiest airport in 1985, handling 13.7 million enplaned/deplaned revenue air passengers or 29.3% of the national total. There were 284 000 aircraft movements (counted whenever an aircraft takes off or lands at an airport), making it the busiest airport in aircraft movements. It is interesting to note that while Canadian airports accommodated approximately 5 million aircraft movements in 1985, the air carriers, which transport air passengers and goods, accounted for just over 1 million or 22% of the total. The values in the table for enplaned/deplaned cargo volumes do not include mail placed on or off the aircraft at that airport.

Major Components and Activities People who use an airport do not always realize the complexity of functions carried out there and the impact that the airport can have on the community. Airports represent a large capital investment; from initially assembling land, to the actual building of facilities. Once operational an airport can generate major employment in the community. A large international airport can employ as many as 20 000 people, including government officials, airline personnel, clerks behind the car rental booths, restaurant personnel, etc. Its presence also supports many off-airport employment opportunities in service industries such as taxi companies, delivery companies, and aviation supply companies all serving related airport functions.

Any typical unit-toll land airport, regardless of the level of demand, has 3 major components: the groundside; the air passenger terminal building (ATB); and the airside. The individual facilities found within each of these major components must have the capability and capacity to accommodate the specific demand for which they have been designed. The groundside component is the area directly accessible to the public outside the ATB. It includes most ground transportation facilities such as the access/egress roadways leading to the ATB, the service roads to specific airport functional areas (such as air cargo terminals, maintenance garages, firehall), vehicular parking facilities (both surface lots and structures), and the processing curbs in front of the ATB. To accommodate the vehicular demand these facilities sometimes have to be very extensive. For example, at Toronto-Lester B. Pearson International there are approximately 7600 public parking spaces available on the airport property. In a normal day as many as 84 000 surface vehicular trips will be generated to and from the airport involving private automobiles, buses, taxis and cargo vehicles. The groundside also includes related support functions such as hangars, fuel-storage areas and general aviation facilities that require airside access. At large airports, administration complexes and other commercial facilities such as hotels can be situated on the groundside.

The ATB is the transfer point between the aircraft and surface travel for passengers. The functional design and requirements of the building take into account factors such as the design aircraft to be accommodated, airline operational schedules, types of air service provided and the level of service that the airport operator wishes to provide. These factors have an impact on the type of functional areas required and more importantly on the amount of floor space required for each functional area. Again, taking Toronto-Lester B. Pearson as an example, 40-60 000 air passengers daily must be accommodated by the two terminals during the busiest 14- to 16-hour period of operation, as well as twice that many greeters and well-wishers.

The final design of an ATB can take many different forms. It can be centralized with fingers (corridors leading to the parked aircraft such as exist at Calgary International); it can be linear (a long narrow building with the aircraft parked at doorways called gates on one side of the ATB for the loading/unloading of passengers, as at Terminal 2 at Toronto); or it can be transporter, with special passenger transfer vehicles for transporting air passengers to/from remote aircraft parking aprons. Montréal International Airport (Mirabel) is an example of this concept. Each concept performs functionally better for certain types of air service. The linear type is a good design for pure international travel with minimum air passenger connections required between flights. A centralized concept is more functionally suited to a mix of domestic and international services where there is a high percentage of connecting air passengers.

The airside component consists of the part of the airport that is not accessible to the public without proper authorization. It includes the runways where the aircraft take off and land, the taxiways used for the movement of aircraft between the runway and the gate areas adjacent to the ATB, and air cargo terminals where the aircraft load and unload passengers and cargo and are serviced. The airside component is designed according to the type and mix of aircraft expected to use the site, the topographical and environmental factors affecting that location and the amount of traffic expected annually.

Development of Canadian Airports The first flight in Canada took place at Baddeck, NS, by J.A. MC-CURDY in 1909. The first Canadian airport was located at Long Branch, Toronto, in 1915. It was operated by the Curtiss Flying School, part of Curtiss Aeroplanes and Motors Ltd, with the primary purpose of training pilots for the war effort. After the war, with many aircraft available, entrepreneurs felt that civil air transport could be used to provide transportation services to the public. When the Canadian Pacific Railway requested legislation to extend its charter to include the operation of aircraft, Parliament passed the Air Board Act in 1919 to administer and control civil aviation. Part of the board's mandate was to make regulations with respect to licensing, inspection and regulation of all aerodromes and airstations. It was also given the responsibility for constructing and maintaining all government aerodromes and military airstrips.

In the 1920s and 1930s, development of airports lagged behind the technological advances of the aircraft. In 1928 the government decided to construct the Trans-Canada Airway and to provide financial assistance to local flying clubs to upgrade existing airstrips. The purpose of this assistance was to develop a chain of airports operated by municipalities or cities across the country along the airway to cater to commercial aviation. In 1937 Parliament created TRANS-CANADA AIR-LINES, the forerunner of AIR CANADA. The federal government, in the interest of safety, decided to construct intermediate aerodromes at approximately 160 km intervals between municipal airports across the country. The new Department of Transport undertook the cost of this development as well as airport development at those municipalities that were unwilling to upgrade their existing airstrips. WWII necessitated the construction of 148 new military airfields and forced the federal government to assume control of 59 municipal airports in support of Canada's war effort. After the war most of these airports were handed back to the local municipalities or taken over by the federal Department of Transport.

The general economic prosperity and growth experienced in the country during the late 1950s and all through the 60s created a greater propensity to travel. The new jet technology, which allows larger passenger aircraft, longer flying range and greater fuel efficiency, reduced the cost of travelling by air. Coupled with greater consumer discretionary spending ability, the demand for air travel increased dramatically. Existing airport fa-

Selected Canadian Airports 1985 Statistics

Site	Total E/D Revenue Passengers (000s)	Total E/D Cargo (in tonnes) (000s)	Total Aircraft Movements (000s)
Toronto-Lester B. Pearson Intl	13 655.9	218.4	284.0
Vancouver Intl	6046.6	83.1	236.0
Montréal (Dorval)	5489.0	30.6	153.0
Calgary Intl	3681.0	31.4	192.0
Winnipeg Intl	2066.1	18.8	148.0
Ottawa	1980.2	4.4	165.0
Edmonton Intl	1840.2	35.2	80.0
Halifax Intl	1775.5	18.6	66.0
Montréal (Mirabel)	1324.8	79.9	53.0
Edmonton Municipal	760.7	1.8	132.0
Regina	591.5	1.6	77.0
Saskatoon	563.3	1.6	100.0
Québec	535.9	1.5	116.0
St John's	528.8	6.9	47.0
Thunder Bay	415.8	1.1	102.0
Kelowna	396.0	1.0	44.0
Victoria Intl	305.3	0.7	159.0
Windsor	231.9	0.4	47.0
Moncton	228.1	1.1	72.0
Prince George	224.2	0.9	53.0
Saint John	204.5	0.8	32.0
Fredericton	191.4	0.5	48.0

cilities required frequent upgrading and expansion to meet this increasing demand for the movement of passengers and goods and to support the ever-increasing number and size of aircraft. Most local municipalities did not have the expertise or the finances to assume responsibility for the continual need for improvements. Thus, the federal government assumed responsibility for the development and operation of most major airports in order to maintain a safe and efficient national system. These airports comprise the international, national and most regional airports.

Security at Canadian Airports At each major airport there are airport security committees, emergency plans, personal identification systems and passes, airport safety plans and restricted access zones within airport boundaries in order to secure and protect anyone making use of the airport, as well as to protect airport property. The most visible aspects are the RCMP officers stationed at the airport and the passenger and carry-on baggage security checks located between terminal waiting areas and the air passenger holdrooms where the passengers obtain their boarding passes. These security check stations are equipped to detect the presence of metallic objects or explosive devices. Security measures were first introduced at major Canadian airports in 1973 and have since been implemented at all unit-toll airports across the country. These measures were necessary because of the increasing number of aircraft hijackings occurring at airports in the world. In the 1970s and 1980s, organized terrorist groups have used aircraft hijackings as a means of obtaining global news coverage of their cause. Such actions have resulted in threats to aircraft passengers. New measures include security devices that can detect the presence of concentrations of chemicals found in explosive devices and the baggage/passenger match system for international flights. This match system is designed to ensure that all baggage on the aircraft belongs to the passengers of that flight. When a bag cannot be matched to a passenger it will be removed before the aircraft takes off.   G. FAWCETT

Airport Architecture The Aeronautics Act of 1919 made provision for the construction of air-

ports (or "air harbours"), but for many years airplanes used landing fields equipped with few facilities. In 1927 the federal government provided incentives for private flying clubs to develop airports with hangars and workshops. Winnipeg's Stevenson Field, for example, which opened in 1928, had been the aerodrome of the Winnipeg Flying Club. The principal building was a simple rectangular structure; within a few years it was replaced by a larger wide-span hangar with a low-arched roof and a shed to the side for the waiting room and offices, the typical airport design of the early 1930s.

A new wave of construction was inspired by the formation of the Department of Transport in 1937 and the inauguration of TRANS-CANADA AIRLINES (now AIR CANADA) in 1937. Calgary's McCall Field, built by the city in 1938, and Dorval Airport near Montréal (1940) represented the new breed of airports. The passenger terminal, now separate from the hangar, featured a ticket lobby and general waiting area, not unlike the familiar arrangement of a RAILWAY STATION.

The Dept of Transport introduced the severe international style in its airports of the 1950s. Two of the most distinguished were Ottawa International Airport (architect W.A. Ramsay, 1955-60), with passenger handling areas located to either side of a central waiting area and a control tower above, and the larger Winnipeg International Airport (Green, Blankstein and Russell, with W.A. Ramsay, 1960). The new Montréal International Airport – Dorval (Illsley, Templeton, Archibald, and Larose and Larose, 1960) – had, in addition to "fingers" against which the airplanes docked, a remote quay linked to the main terminal by an underground moving sidewalk.

After 1960 there were several experiments in improving passenger convenience. Toronto-Lester B. Pearson International Airport's Terminal 1 (John B. Parkin Associates, with W.A. Ramsay, 1962) is circular in plan to provide the maximum perimeter space for aircraft while offering a short walk for passengers; a large parking garage is situated over the Aeroquay, and the administration building and control tower (both John B. Parkin Associates, with W.A. Ramsay, 1962) are separate structures. Mirabel Airport, near Montréal (Papineau, Gérin-Lajoie, LeBlanc, Edwards, 1975) is shallow in plan so that passengers need walk only a short distance to the departure gate, whence they board wheeled passenger vehicles that transport them to the airplanes. Calgary International Airport (Stevenson, Raines, Barret, Hutton, Seton and Partners, 1977) has a more conventional plan with a 3-storey central terminal area leading to fingers at either side. The new terminals incorporate security barriers, remote lounges and loading bridges, features which have been added to many earlier airports and have obscured the clarity of their design.

In the 1970s Canada exported airport design; a number of Canadian firms designed facilities abroad, eg, the airports at Kabul, Afghanistan, and the island of Saint Kitts. The 1980s saw significant additions to existing terminals. At Ottawa International Airport (Murray and Murray, Griffiths and Rankin, 1984-87) the architects imposed an assertive new design, whereas at Winnipeg International Airport (The IKOY Partnership, 1985-87), the new work carefully respected the original international style design.

HAROLD D. KALMAN

Aitken, Robert Morris, flutist, composer (b at Kentville, NS 28 Aug 1939). After several orchestral appointments – most remarkably with the Vancouver Symphony Orchestra where, at age 19, he was its youngest-ever principal flute – Aitken left orchestral work in 1971 to concentrate

Max Aitken (Lord Beaverbrook). He began selling bonds in 1900 and was a millionaire before he was 30 (*courtesy National Archives of Canada/PA-6467*).

on solo performance and chamber music. He appeared frequently with harpsichordist Greta Kraus and with the Lyric Arts Trio, which he founded in 1964. Widely sought after as a soloist by orchestras in N America, Europe and Asia, he has often given premiere performances of contemporary Canadian works. To his own compositions Aitken brings the virtuoso performer's delight in sound, experimenting adventurously with instrumental timbre, electroacoustical colour and oriental techniques to produce music of high originality. In 1985 he was appointed director of advanced studies in music at the Banff Centre. He premiered and later recorded Murray Schafer's *Concerto for flute and Orchestra* and in 1987 was artistic director of New Music concerts in Toronto.   BARCLAY MCMILLAN

Aitken, William Maxwell, 1st Baron Beaverbrook, financier, politician, author, publisher (b at Maple, Ont 25 May 1879; d at Cherkley, Mickleham, Eng 9 June 1964). The son of a Presbyterian minister, Beaverbrook later claimed that his religion lay at the root of his worldly success. In 1880 his family moved to Newcastle, NB. A clever if mischievous boy, "Max" displayed a passion for moneymaking. He dabbled in journalism and sold insurance before becoming a clerk in a Chatham, NB, law office. There he began his lifelong friendships with R.B. BENNETT and James DUNN. In 1897 he abandoned law school to follow them to Edmonton, where he operated a bowling alley before returning to the Maritimes. In 1900 he began selling bonds, particularly those of expanding industries and Canadian-based utilities. He joined the Royal Securities Corp as manager in 1902 and within 5 years was a millionaire. He moved to Montréal and concentrated on promoting new companies and merging old ones, his most notable creations being Stelco and Canada Cement.

In 1910 he moved to London, Eng, where he pursued his business interests and entered politics. Guided by Andrew Bonar LAW, Aitken won a seat for the Conservatives in the second general election of 1910. He championed tariffs and imperial unity and was knighted in 1911. During WWI he represented the Canadian government at the front and wrote *Canada in Flanders*. His aptitude for political tactics was revealed by his part in Lloyd George's accession as PM. In 1917 he

was made a peer, taking the title Beaverbrook after a stream near his Canadian home. He became minister of information in 1918.

After the war, Beaverbrook left politics and established a chain of British newspapers. He bought the *Daily Express* and the *Evening Standard* and created the *Sunday Express*. He also wrote books on his wartime experiences. In 1929 he spearheaded the Empire Free Trade movement, though the idea found little support in the protectionist climate of the 1930s.

As minister of aircraft production in Churchill's wartime government, Beaverbrook galvanized the aircraft industry. Other wartime appointments followed, but despite his bullish determination Beaverbrook lacked the temperament for lasting political success and left politics in 1945. After the war, he supervised his newspapers and wrote memoirs and biographies of his influential friends.   DUNCAN MCDOWALL

Reading: A.J.P. Taylor, *Beaverbrook* (1972).

Ajax, Ont (1986 OMD), pop 36 550 (1986c), est 1941, incorporated as an improvement district in 1950 and as a town in 1955. Ajax became part of the Regional Municipality of Durham in Oct 1973 and in Jan 1974 expanded to include Pickering village and part of Pickering Township. The centre was named for one of the British "Leander" class cruisers which cornered the German pocket battleship *Graf Spee* in 1939. It was established to service a munitions plant built on a 1200 ha site. It is located 37 km E of Toronto on Highway 401. After WWII, 3000 returned servicemen took courses offered in Ajax by U of T. After their departure in 1949, Central Mortgage and Housing Corporation announced that Ajax would be the first fully planned industrial and residential centre. Ajax is a light industrial centre and also functions as a bedroom community for Metropolitan Toronto.   GERALD STORTZ

Akeeaktashuk, sea hunter, sculptor, storyteller (b at Hudson Bay, near Inukjuak River, Qué 1898; d at Craig Harbour, NWT 1954). Akeeaktashuk was a jolly, robust and outgoing man with an astonishing talent for observing and keenly portraying humans, animals and birds in stone and ivory. He often used these 2 natural materials in combination. In search of a more abundant hunting area, Akeeaktashuk journeyed north with his wife and children, and a number of other hunters and their families from Inukjuak accompanied them. They travelled north aboard the federal government icebreaker *C.D. Howe*, with their skin kayaks, sleds and dogs, and arrived at Craig Harbour on south Ellesmere I in Aug 1951, later moving to GRISE FIORD. Akeeaktashuk died out on the moving ice in search of walrus in 1954. Thus, Canada lost one of its most famous Inuit carvers whose early work was the first to gain worldwide recognition in the postwar era of Inuit sculpture.   JAMES HOUSTON

Aklavik, NWT, Hamlet, pop 763 (1986c), 721 (1981c), is located near the mouth of the MACKENZIE R, 1143 air km NW of YELLOWKNIFE. The name, of Inuvialuit origin, means "where there are bears." It was a major centre of the Mackenzie Delta region in the 1950s, but owing to serious flooding most facilities were relocated to the nearby INUVIK site in 1961. The community is called "the town that wouldn't die" by the Inuvialuit and Loucheux DENE, who refused to relocate. In 1931-32 it was a base for the pursuit of the "Mad Trapper of Rat River," Albert JOHNSON. Most residents subsist on hunting, trapping and fishing.   ANNELIES POOL

Alabama, Confederate warship constructed in Britain during the AMERICAN CIVIL WAR. The US

sought to have the ship detained in Britain, but it escaped. Until it was sunk in June 1864, it attacked Union (Northern) shipping, inflicting great losses. American claims for compensation from Britain, submitted to arbitration in 1871, were omitted from negotiations for the Treaty of WASHINGTON, despite an American suggestion that compensation might be made by cession of some Canadian territory. In 1872 a Geneva tribunal awarded $15.5 million in gold to the US.
                                    ROBIN W. WINKS

Alarie, Pierrette, soprano, teacher (b at Montréal 9 Nov 1921). She studied with Jeanne Maubourg, Albert Roberval and Elisabeth Schumann, and in the studio of Salvator Issaurel. In 1945 she won the Met's Auditions of the Air and made her debut with the Metropolitan Opera 8 Dec 1945. As a soloist, and with her husband Léopold SIMONEAU, she sang on the great European and N American stages and was commended for her crystalline voice and command of the light and lyric repertoire. She and her husband received the 1959 Prix de musique Calixa-Lavallée and the diploma of honour from the Canadian Conference of the Arts (1983), and their record of *Mozart Concert Arias and Duets* won the Grand Prix du disque from the Académie Charles-Cros in Paris in 1961. Among her recorded roles were Leila in Bizet's *Pêcheurs de perles* and Juliette in Gounod's *Romeo and Juliette*. Her farewell concert (with Simoneau) was in Handel's *Messiah* in Montréal 24 Nov 1970. Together she and Simoneau founded the Canada Opera Piccola (1978) and the Advanced Training Opera Centre (1982). She was made an Officer of the Order of Canada in 1967.   HÉLÈNE PLOUFFE

Alaska Boundary Dispute, between Canada and the US over the boundary of the Alaska Panhandle running S to latitude 54°40′ N on the coast of BC. When the US purchased Alaska from Russia in 1867, it inherited the Russian position on the boundary, first defined in the 1825 Anglo-Russian treaty. The US claimed a continuous stretch of coastline, unbroken by the deep fiords of the region. Canada demanded control of the heads of certain fiords, especially the Lynn Canal, which gave access to the Yukon. The KLONDIKE GOLD RUSH, which got underway in the autumn of 1897, brought the smouldering dispute to a head. When direct negotiations in the Joint High Commission of 1898-99 failed, the problem was referred in 1903 to an international tribunal, whose 3 American and 2 Canadian members (A.B. Aylesworth and Sir Louis Jetté) were frankly partisan. The sixth, Lord Alverstone, Lord Chief Justice of England, supported the American claim for a boundary running behind the heads of the inlets, but agreed to the equal distribution of 4 islands at the mouth of Portland Canal. In protest the Canadian judges refused to sign the award, issued 20 Oct 1903, and violent anti-British feeling erupted in Canada.

Irritated at the decision, PM Sir Wilfrid Laurier asserted that Canada's lack of TREATY-MAKING POWER made it difficult to maintain its rights internationally, but he took no immediate action. Canadian anger gradually subsided, although suspicions of the US provoked by the award may have contributed to Canada's rejection of FREE TRADE in the 1911 "reciprocity election." Nevertheless, the Alaska settlement promoted better understanding between the US and Britain that worked to Canada's advantage in WWI.

                                    D.M.L. FARR

Alaska Highway, constructed 1942-43 from Dawson Creek, BC, to Fairbanks, Alaska. In the face of a serious threat of a Japanese invasion, a preliminary road was rammed through forest

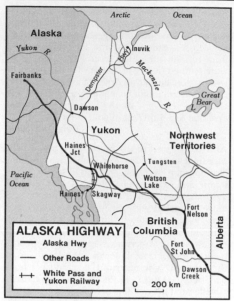

ALASKA HIGHWAY
— Alaska Hwy
— Other Roads
+—+ White Pass and
      Yukon Railway

0   200 km

wilderness and 5 mountain ranges in only 8 months. Called the Alcan Military Hwy, it ran 2333 km from Dawson Creek to Big Delta, Alaska. Groups of US Army engineers working from several starting points built up to 13 km a day. The following year it became a permanent, all-weather, gravel-surfaced road, 7 to 8 m wide, 2451 km long, from Dawson Creek, BC, to Fairbanks, Alaska – the result of the labour of 11 000 soldiers and some 16 000 Canadian and American civilians. There were 133 bridges 6 m or longer and several thousand culverts. The US invested $147.8 million in the project for men, materials and equipment. Canada provided the right of way and on 3 April 1946 took over the 1954-km portion of the road from Dawson Creek to the Alaska border. Canada paid the US $108 million to cover airfields and flight strips, buildings, telephone systems and other assets, but not construction of the highway itself. Opened to unrestricted travel in 1947, the road was regraded and widened by Canadian army engineers during the next 17 years, until it was turned over (1964) to the federal dept of public works, which has continued to improve it. Some of the road has been paved, but hundreds of kilometres are bituminous surface-treated to carry the traffic, which ranges from 220 vehicles a day in isolated areas to 1700 a day near Whitehorse. Maintenance is a continual battle against nature: floods and landslides in spring, blizzards and extreme cold in winter, when temperatures of -48°C can cause bulldozer blades to crack like glass. Although originally built for military purposes, the highway has helped the forestry, oil, mining, tourist and trucking industries. It provided an important impetus to the development of Edmonton as a supply centre and, as an enduring link to northern BC and the Yukon, has had the psychological benefit of ending the isolation of the North.

C.W. GILCHRIST

Albanel, Charles, Jesuit priest, missionary and explorer (b in Auvergne, France c1616; d at Sault Ste Marie 11 Jan 1696). After joining the Jesuit missions in Canada in 1649, Albanel was stationed at TADOUSSAC, from which he made numerous expeditions into the surrounding wilderness with the local Indians. During 1671-72 he was sent by Intendant Jean TALON to explore northward to Hudson Bay to verify rumours of the presence there of French-speaking Europeans (who were, in fact, RADISSON and GROSEILLIERS, then in the service of the Hudson's Bay Co). In June 1672 he reached the bay, probably the first European to

do so overland. In 1673 he was sent back to try to persuade Groseilliers to return to French service. He was detained by the English, and did not return to Canada until 1676. Thereafter, he served in the missions of the western interior.

STANLEY GORDON

Albani, Dame Emma, stage name of Marie-Louise-Cécile-Emma Lajeunesse, soprano (b at Chambly, Canada E 1 Nov 1847; d at London, Eng 3 Apr 1930). Her parents were her teachers in Chambly, Plattsburgh and Montréal, where she gave her first concert in 1856. She was to become the first Canadian-born artist to distinguish herself in the international world of opera, oratorio and concert singing. After studies in Paris and Milan, she made her opera debut at Messina, Italy, as Oscar in *Un Ballo in maschera* (1869), but her first real triumph came soon after, as Amina in *La Sonnambula*. This was to be her debut role in London (1872), Paris (1872) and New York (1874). Though attached to Covent Garden, London, she steadily pursued her international career in many countries. In 1891-1892 she sang at the Metropolitan Opera in New York. By the time she retired from the opera stage in 1896, she had sung 43 leading roles. She made about a dozen enthusiastically received Canadian tours, 1883-1906. Her remarkable voice has been preserved on a Rococo 5255 record, on which she sings 8 titles, including turn-of-the-century songs and three Handel arias.

GILLES POTVIN

Albanians Canadian Albanians have their roots in Albania, although the country of their birth could be Yugoslavia, Greece or Albania itself. Albania is a small nation of some 2 million people in southeastern Europe on the W coast of the Balkan peninsula. There are, however, more than 1.3 million ethnic Albanians in Yugoslavia — "Shqipetare" (Sons of the Eagle) — and another 250 000 Albanians live in Greece. Albanians from Albania are divided into 2 main dialect-groups: the Ghegs from the northern half of the country, and the Tosks from the southern half of Albania. About 70% of Albanians are Muslims; 20% are Orthodox Christians and 10% are Roman Catholics.

Migration and Settlement The first Albanians arrived in Canada at the beginning of the century, following internal prewar revolutionary upheavals. Few immigrated to Canada after WWII. Most of the postwar Albanian immigrants settled in either Montréal or Toronto. Some found jobs in Calgary and a few in small communities in Ontario (eg, Peterborough).

Some Albanians from Yugoslavia developed a kind of dual ethno-civic loyalty. They are part of Canadian-Yugoslav organizations in Toronto such as Bratstvo-Jedinstvo and the Montenegrin cultural association Crna Gora. However, they continue to appreciate their ethnic heritage and their Albanian national history, although their ancestors may have left Albania several centuries ago. Those Albanians from Albania proper are active in their business and social organizations. They are frequently found in the food service industry (eg, restaurants, soda-bars, etc).

Social and Cultural Life According to the census of 1981 (the most recent year for which figures are available) there are 1265 Albanians in Canada, of which 885 lived in Toronto. This is not a true figure by any means because it has been shown that 2nd and 3rd generation Canadians of Albanian origin avoid naming their ethnic background. Therefore, the real number of Albanians in Canada remains undetermined and their sociocultural activities and festivals represent for the most part small groups of families.

VLADISLAV A. TOMOVIĆ

Dame Emma Albani was the first Canadian-born singer to be acclaimed in the international world of opera (*courtesy National Archives of Canada/C-49491*).

Albany River, 982 km long, issues from Lk St Joseph, NW Ontario, and flows E to Eby Falls, where it drops over the rocky ledge of the Canadian SHIELD onto the clay lowlands and into JAMES BAY near Ft Albany (est 1684). It has a DRAINAGE BASIN of 134 000 km² and a mean discharge of 1420 m³/sec. Named for the duke of Albany, later King James II, it was an active FUR-TRADE ROUTE, though less favoured than the HAYES R because of its poorer links to other river systems. Main tributaries are the Ogoki and Kenogami rivers.

JAMES MARSH

Alberta, the westernmost of Canada's 3 Prairie provinces, shares many physical features with its neighbours to the E, SASKATCHEWAN and MANITOBA. The Rocky Mts form the southern portion of Alberta's western boundary with BRITISH COLUMBIA. Alberta's western location places it at considerable distance from the traditional economic and political power centres of Canada; however, the province possesses the country's largest deposits of oil and natural gas, and expansion of the petroleum industry from 1947 to 1982 made it the fastest-growing province in that period, producing a westward shift of economic power in Canada.

Alberta was named after Princess Louise Caroline Alberta, 4th daughter of Queen Victoria. Alberta then was one of 4 provisional districts of the North-West Territories, and included only that part of the present province S of 55° N lat and W of 111° long. Alberta's current boundaries were determined in 1905 when it became a province. Though appearing quite homogeneous, Alberta may be divided into 2 distinct sociocultural regions – southern Alberta, with Calgary as its focal point; and central and northern Alberta, with Edmonton as the metropolitan centre. This division has deep historic roots. Southern Alberta was once the domain of the Blackfoot nation; farther north the Cree and various woodland tribes held sway. In the early days of white settlement, the south welcomed the rancher, while the grain farmer opened the central agricultural region.

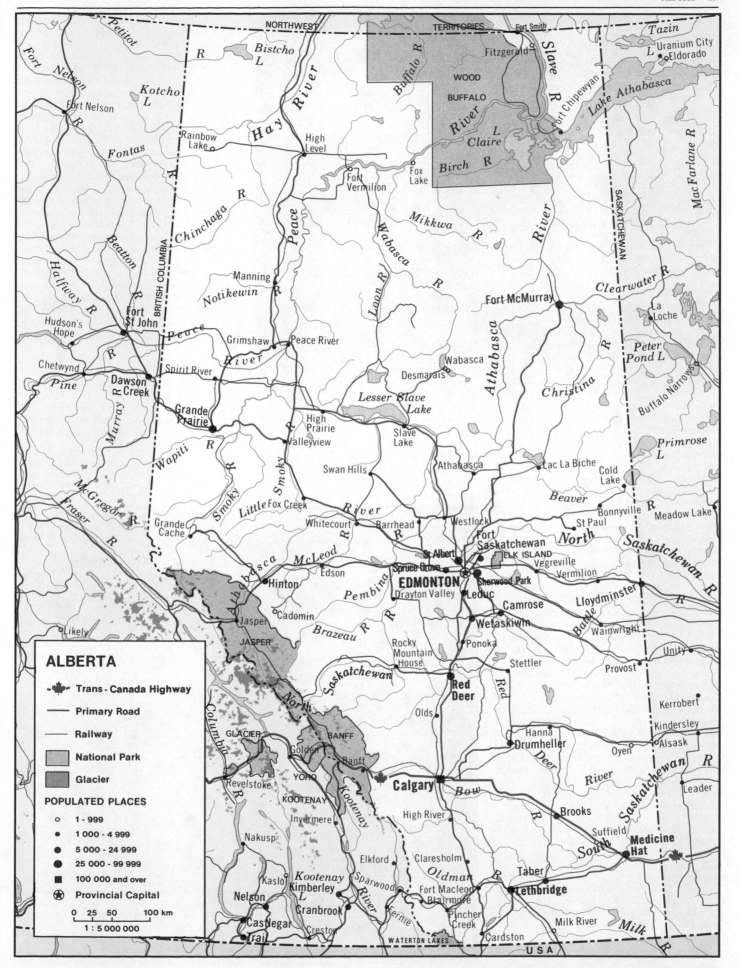

NORTHWEST TERRITORIES

Petitot R

Fort Nelson R

Bistcho L

Buffalo R

Fort Smith

Slave R

Tazin L

Fitzgerald

Uranium City
Eldorado

WOOD BUFFALO

Kotcho L

Hay River

Fontas R

Fort Nelson

Rainbow Lake

High Level

Fort Chipewyan

Lake Athabasca

MacFarlane R

Chinchaga R

Fort Vermilion

Fox Lake

River

L Claire

Birch R

Mikkwa R

Beatton

BRITISH COLUMBIA

SASKATCHEWAN

Halfway R

Peace River

Manning

Notikewin

Wabasca R

Loon R

River

Clearwater R

Fort McMurray

La Loche

Hudson's Hope

Fort St John

Grimshaw

Peace River

Peace River

Wabasca

Athabasca

Christina

Peter Pond L

Chetwynd

Pine

Dawson Creek

Spirit River

Desmarais

Buffalo Narrows

Murray R

Grande Prairie

Lesser Slave Lake

Primrose L

Wapiti R

Smoky R

High Prairie

Valleyview

Slave Lake

Athabasca

Lac La Biche

Cold Lake

Beaver

Bonnyville

Meadow Lake

McGregor R

Fraser R

Grande Cache

Swan Hills

River

North

St Paul

Saskatchewan R

Little Fox Creek

Fox Creek

Whitecourt

Barrhead

Westlock

Fort Saskatchewan

ELK ISLAND

Vegreville

Vermilion

Athabasca

McLeod

Edson

Hinton

Pembina R

St Albert

Spruce Grove

EDMONTON

Sherwood Park

Lloydminster

Columbia R

Jasper

JASPER

Cadomin

Brazeau R

Drayton Valley

Leduc

Camrose

Wetaskiwin

Battle R

Wainwright

Unity

Likely

Rocky Mountain House

Ponoka

Stettler

Provost

ALBERTA

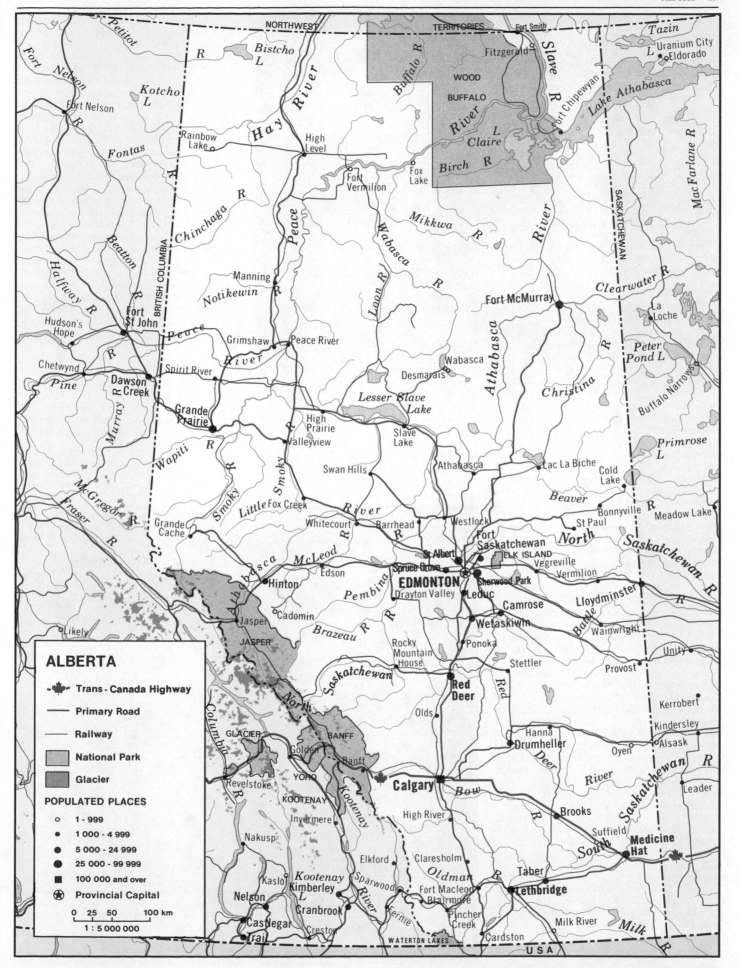 Trans - Canada Highway

—— Primary Road

— Railway

National Park

Glacier

Olds

Red Deer

Red

Kerrobert

Kindersley

GLACIER

BANFF

Hanna

Drumheller

Deer

Alsask

Oyen

Golden

Banff

Revelstoke

YOHO

KOOTENAY

Kootenay R

Calgary

Bow R

River

South

Saskatchewan R

Brooks

Invermere

High River

Leader

POPULATED PLACES

○ 1 - 999

• 1 000 - 4 999

● 5 000 - 24 999

⬤ 25 000 - 99 999

■ 100 000 and over

✪ Provincial Capital

Nakusp

Suffield

Medicine Hat

Elkford

Claresholm

Oldman R

Taber

0 25 50   100 km

1 : 5 000 000

Kaslo

Kimberley

Kootenay River

Sparwood

Fort Macleod
Blairmore

Lethbridge

Nelson

Cranbrook

Fernie

Pincher Creek

Milk River

Milk R

Castlegar
Trail

Creston

WATERTON LAKES

Cardston

USA

Alberta

Capital: Edmonton
Motto: Fortis et Liber ("Strong and free")
Flower: Wild rose (also known as prickly rose)
Largest Cities: Edmonton, Calgary, Lethbridge, Red Deer, Medicine Hat, St Albert, Fort McMurray
Population: 2 365 825 (1986c); rank: fourth; 9.3% of Canada; 79.4% urban; 3.7 per km² density;
     5.7% increase 1981-86
Languages: 81% English; 2.1% French; 13.3% other; 3.6% English plus 1 or more languages
Entered Confederation: 1 Sept 1905
Government: Provincial — Lieutenant-Governor, Executive Council, Legislative Assembly of
     83 members; Federal — 6 senators, 21 members of the House of Commons
Area: 661 185 km²; including 16 796 km² of inland water; 6.66% of Canada
Elevation: Highest point — Mount Columbia (3747 m); lowest point — shores of Lake Athabasca
     and Slave River
Gross Domestic Product: $56.5 billion (1985)
Farm Cash Receipts: $3.85 billion (1986)
Electric Power Produced: 33 253 GWh (1985)
Sales Tax: None

Calgary and southern Alberta were first linked to the east by the Canadian Pacific Railway, Edmonton and the north by the Grand Trunk Pacific and Canadian Northern railways. Later, Calgary became the administrative and financial headquarters for the province's petroleum industry, Edmonton its exploration and production centre. Politically, both regions have consistently supported conservative parties since the 1920s, first through the Social Credit Party and then the Conservative Party; recently opposition in the north has tended to coalesce around the New Democratic Party provincially, while in the south it gravitates to right-of-centre candidates.

Land and Resources

Physiography, climate, soil and vegetation combine to delineate 4 biophysical regions within Alberta. The prairie region includes most of southern Alberta, more precisely the land S and E of an arc stretching from Waterton in the SW corner to a point along the Saskatchewan border E of Red Deer. This gently rolling grassland is relatively dry and mostly treeless. The terrain varies locally, in places broken by deep river valleys, and rising from less than 300 m in the NE to 1200 m in the CYPRESS HILLS in the SE. The parkland region predominates in central Alberta, forming a crescent to the W and N of the prairie region and including most of the N SASKATCHEWAN R drainage basin. This area varies from the flatland of old lake bottoms to rolling landscape with numerous lakes and depressions. It contains both treed and grassy terrain, with soil and climatic factors favourable to agriculture. The boreal-forest region covers the northern half of the province. Here great rivers and lakes dominate the landscape, draining northward to the Arctic Ocean. Soil and climatic factors militate against agriculture, except in the PEACE R region of the NW, where parkland conditions create the world's most northerly grain-growing area. West of the plains an area of FOOTHILL ridges rise to the ROCKY MTS W of Grande Prairie and along the southern portion of Alberta's western boundary with BC. Here is

found some of Canada's most spectacular natural scenery, with several peaks rising above 3600 m.

Geology Alberta's oldest surface landscape is its extreme northeastern part, E of the Slave and lower Athabasca rivers, where crystalline rocks formed during the Precambrian era (3800 to 570 million years ago) appear at the surface. This

small outcrop of the Canadian SHIELD does not end in the NE, for its rocks form a basement under the rest of the province, sloping down to 6000 m in the SW. During the Paleozoic era (570 to 245 million years ago) Alberta alternated between dry land and sea, and life evolved from simple plants and animals to vertebrates and dry-land vegetation. The decay of this plant and animal life, especially during the Devonian period (408 to 360 million years ago), formed the basis of most of the province's oil and natural-gas deposits. The Mesozoic era (245 to 66.4 million years ago) also subjected Alberta to alternating upraisings of the land and infloodings of ocean waters. This was the era of the dinosaurs, the period that bequeathed the BADLAND formations of the Red Deer R valley, and laid down most of the province's coal resources. The Cenozoic era (66.4 million years ago to the present) saw the uplifting of the Rocky Mts and the establishment of the province's physiographic framework. About 25 000 years ago the last advance of continental ice scoured the terrain and virtually covered the entire province. Only the highest parts of the Rockies, the Cypress Hills and the Porcupine Hills escaped. The final retreat of the ice age, beginning about 13 000 years ago, created the current river systems and soils.

Surface The prairie region of southern Alberta includes both short-grass and mixed-grass characteristics. The short-grass area of the SE corner features short, drought-resistant grasses, such as blue grama, growing on light brown SOIL deficient in nitrogen and phosphorus, and about 12 cm deep. Annual water deficiency and wind ero-

This remote-sensing image of southern Alberta shows agricultural activity and pivot irrigation. The blue-green area on the right is rangeland (*courtesy Canada Centre of Remote Sensing, Energy, Mines, & Resources Canada*).

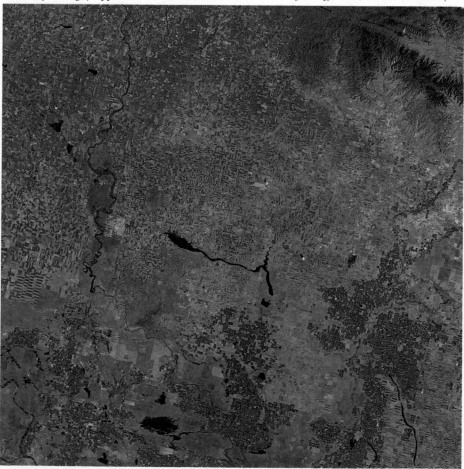

sion cause considerable soil drifting. The mixed-grass area, forming an arc to the W and N of the short-grass region, contains more fertile, dark brown soil, while western wheat grass and other taller grasses provide the natural vegetation. The parkland regions of central Alberta and the Peace R country are characterized by a natural vegetation cover of tall grasses and aspen trees. The central parkland contains fertile black soils, while the dark grey and grey soils of the Peace R area are slightly less fertile. The boreal region of northern Alberta contains forest vegetation varying from predominant aspen and white birch in the S to white spruce, tamarack and black spruce farther N. Balsam fir and jack pine are also found in eastern areas, with alpine fir and lodgepole pine in the W. Nutrient-deficient grey soils underlie the forest cover. Alpine fir, white spruce and lodgepole pine dominate the lower elevations of the Rocky Mts. At higher elevations, scattered stands of black spruce and alpine larch are interspersed with lichens and alpine flowers in picturesque alpine meadows. Rock, permanent snow cover and glacial ice dominate the very highest elevations.

Water The small MILK R basin in SE Alberta drains through the Missouri and Mississippi rivers S to the Gulf of Mexico. The rest of southern Alberta is drained by the S and N Saskatchewan river basins E to Hudson Bay via the Nelson R system. These rivers carry 75% of the water that flows E. Northern Alberta is dominated by the Athabasca, Hay and Peace river basins, which drain N through the Mackenzie R to the Arctic Ocean. Low annual precipitation, high evaporation rates and fast runoff produce chronic water deficits in southern Alberta, varying from a moderate deficiency in the parkland region to a severe shortage in the short-grass prairie area. Irrigation has been used in the latter area since the late 19th century; approximately 450 000 ha are part of formal irrigation systems. Yet the amount of water available for irrigation is itself limited by the water flow in the S Saskatchewan R basin. There have been recurrent proposals to divert water southward from the Peace and Athabasca rivers.

Lk Claire and Lesser Slave Lk are the 2 largest lakes entirely within Alberta.

Climate Alberta's northerly latitude, stretching between 49° N and 60° N, puts the province in the northern cool-temperate zone. Thus cold winters and relatively short, cool summers are to be expected. Yet the most important factors in determining both temperatures and precipitation are the height and width of the Rocky Mts and the direction of the prevailing winds. The mountain ranges intercept air moving in from the Pacific and drain it of moisture. Thus the Rockies' eastern slopes are in a rain shadow, and Alberta's skies are predominantly clear. Precipitation is generally low, ranging from about 30 cm annually in the SE to 40-45 cm in the N except for the foothills region where accumulations reach 55-60 cm annually. The dry clear air provides Albertans with plenty of sunshine, ranging from 1900 annual hours in the N to 2300 in the Lethbridge area in the S. Air funnelling through the Rockies also produces the warm, dry CHINOOK winds, especially strong and prevalent in SW Alberta. Chinooks can raise temperatures dramatically within hours, melting snow and exposing grass, and providing welcome respite during the long, cold winter.

The influence of the Pacific air mass weakens in eastern Alberta, giving way to continental air masses originating in the Arctic and mid-western US. These air masses bring Jan mean temperatures ranging from -8°C in the S to -24°C in the N, and July mean temperatures ranging from 20°C in the S to 16°C in the N. The growing season lasts

Byzantine church near Wasel, Alberta (*photo by Pat Morrow*).

about 120 days in southern Alberta, decreasing to 60 days in the N. In the N the shorter season is offset by longer days and lower altitudes and wheat is grown as far N as the Peace R.

Resources Alberta is Canada's foremost energy-resource province. Proven remaining recoverable reserves were estimated in 1986 as follows: conventional crude, 600 million m³; synthetic crude, 4.2 billion m³; natural gas, 1768 billion m³; and liquid natural gas, 316 million m³. Life indexes for conventional crude have been estimated at about 12 years and 25 years for natural gas. COAL has even longer-term potential. About 70% of Canada's proven remaining coal reserves lie within Alberta, estimated at 21.7 billion t in 1986, with a life index of 790 years at current levels of production. The province's total potential of hydroelectric energy is estimated at 28 000 gigawatt hours/year.

The province possesses an estimated 2.661 million ha of land suitable for agriculture. Alberta's forests total 330 830 km², and have a potential annual yield of 15 million m³ (coniferous) and 13 million m³ (deciduous). Traditional fur and fisheries resources of northern Alberta have declined in recent years, while recreational resources have increased in importance with population growth and urbanization. Within Alberta approximately 54 000 km² of land are reserved as national parks, 4700 km² as provincial parks and recreation areas and 560 000 ha as provincial wilderness areas.

Conservation The Environmental Council of Alberta (formerly the Environment Conservation Authority) was established by provincial legislation (1970) to review government policies and programs on environmental matters, and to hold inquiries and public hearings at the request of Cabinet or upon public representations. The council has subsequently addressed questions of resource exploitation, environmental impact of commercial development, environmental education, water, air and noise pollution, and water and hazardous-waste management. Because its role is advisory rather than regulatory, its recommendations are not always acted upon by government, to the displeasure of environmental groups.

Two of Alberta's national parks began as wildlife sanctuaries. ELK ISLAND (E of Edmonton) and WOOD BUFFALO (44 840 km² straddling the border with the NWT) were created to help the species whose names they bear, but in both cases the most spectacular success has been in preserving the bison of the plains. A number of provincial parks and wilderness areas function as wildlife reserves, including Cypress Hills Park in the SE, Sir Winston Churchill Park on Lac La Biche and Willmore Wilderness Park N of Jasper.

People

Agricultural settlement of Alberta took place primarily in the 1896-1914 period. By 1901 the population of the future province was 73 022; in 1911 it reached 373 943. Settlers arrived from eastern Canada, the US, Great Britain and continental Europe. The rate of growth declined in subsequent years, with total population reaching 584 454 in 1921, 796 169 in 1941 and 1 331 944 in 1961. Growth was slowest during the GREAT DEPRESSION of the 1930s. The rate increased after WWII, through immigration from overseas and the movement of people from other parts of Canada to a visibly prosperous Alberta. The oil boom of the 1970s furthered this trend and the province experienced rapid growth, from 1 768 500 in 1973 to 2 367 400 in 1984. Since then Alberta's population has stabilized. Minimal natural increase has off-set a net out-migration of people. As of the 1986 census, Alberta had reached 2 365 825 in population.

Cowboys round up white-faced Hereford cattle for branding, near the Red Deer R in southern Alberta (*photo by Richard Harrington*).

Urban Centres Alberta's population is classified as 77.3% urban, 14% rural nonfarm and 8.7% farm. Rural population reached its peak in the late 1930s, with 530 000 people accounting for two-thirds of the provincial total. The trend to urbanization quickened during WWII and sharply accelerated in the postwar boom years. By 1951 the rural figure had fallen to 490 000 and the proportion to 61%. The most notable feature of urban growth is concentration in 2 metropolitan centres. In 1946, 27% of Alberta's population lived in EDMONTON and CALGARY; by 1986 this had increased to 56.5%. Edmonton, the provincial capital and administrative centre, had a census metropolitan population of 785 465 in 1986; Calgary, the petroleum and financial centre, had a population of 671 326. Calgary's immediate wholesale and retail hinterland includes all of the province S of Red Deer, plus a portion of southeastern BC. Edmonton's hinterland includes the rest of Alberta and parts of the Peace R region of northeastern BC. Alberta's secondary urban centres have been affected by the metropolitan growth of Edmonton and Calgary. LETHBRIDGE, RED DEER and MEDICINE HAT in the S have been able to preserve their trading areas only at the expense of smaller communities. ST ALBERT, Sherwood Park, LEDUC and FT SASKATCHEWAN are virtually satellite towns within Edmonton's orbit. Only FORT MCMURRAY in the NE and GRANDE PRAIRIE in the NW, because of distance and regional resource development, have escaped the direct metropolitan influences of the 2 largest cities.

Labour Force The number of persons employed in Alberta in April 1987 was 1 167 000. The province's unemployment rate in Oct 1987 was 7.7%. For many years Alberta had Canada's lowest unemployment rate, but in 1982 the province had the second lowest, behind Saskatchewan, with 7.5%; its rate reached 10% in 1983-84. Significant trends in the provincial labour force include growth in the service industries (a 50% increase from 1980 to 1987) and an expanding female-participation rate (up from 56.0% of total work force in 1980 to 63.0% in 1987). The distribution of the labour force, by industry, in April 1987 was recorded as follows: service 35.1%, trade 17.6%, agriculture 7.4%, transportation 7.3%, construction 6.5%, manufacturing 7.5%, other primary industries 5.8% and finance 5.3%. Over the previous 5-year period, service (+118 000), public administration (+11 000), agriculture (+14 000) and trade (+20 000) showed the greatest growth; construction (-39 000), manufacturing (-10 000) and finance (-6000) showed the only declines. The average weekly earnings in Feb 1987 were $447, down 3.8% from 1983, third only to Ont and BC and $8 above the national average.

Ethnicity, Language, Religion Alberta's population is characterized by diversity of ethnic group, language and religion. Native peoples predominated until the 1880s, but were quickly outnumbered by the first influx of English-speaking Protestants and French-speaking Catholics from eastern Canada. The greatest diversity in population dates from the 1896-1914 wave of immigration, which drew from northern, central and eastern Europe tens of thousands of settlers, speaking a variety of languages and representing many religious groups. The major ethnic groups represented in 1981 were British 962 790 or 43.5%; German 233 175 or 10.5%; Ukrainian 136 710 or 6.2%; Scandinavian 78 560 or 3.5%; French 111 870 or 5%; Dutch 65 060 or 2.9%; native peoples 60 005 or 2.7%; Polish 37 660 or 1.7%. Other groups include Austrian, Chinese, Czech, Finnish, Hungarian, Italian, Japanese, Jewish, Russian, Slovak and West Indian. The population by mother tongue in 1986 was overwhelmingly

English: 1 914 450 or 81%. Yet other tongues persisted as earlier non-British immigration was supplemented by post-WWII arrivals. German was the mother tongue of 75 725 or 3.2% of the total population; Ukrainian 48 350 or 2.0%; French 48 685 or 2.1%.

The largest religious group in Alberta in 1981 was the Roman Catholic Church with 573 645 members or 25.9% of the total population. Churches next in order were United with 525 480 or 23.7%; Anglican with 202 265 or 9.1%; Lutheran 144 675 or 6.5%; Baptist 66 370 or 2.9%; Presbyterian 63 895 or 2.8%; Eastern Orthodox 49 270 or 2.2%; Ukrainian Catholic 40 280 or 1.8%. Minor religious groups of greater prominence in Alberta than elsewhere in Canada include the MORMONS (42 980 or 1.9%), MENNONITES (20 545 or 0.9%) and the HUTTERITES (7395).

This diversity has affected popular attitudes and public policies in education and multiculturalism. The split between French Catholics and English Protestants in the years prior to provincehood in 1905 led to the formation of publicly funded, local separate school boards for the Catholic (or sometimes Protestant) religious minority. In later years religious groups such as Hutterites, Mennonites and the Christian Reformed Church gained their own educational privileges, either within the framework of public education or through self-supported private schools. While English has remained the predominant language of instruction in Alberta schools, both provincial and local jurisdictions have tolerated, even encouraged, the use of French, German, Ukrainian and Indian languages as teaching languages.

The high percentage (51.5% in 1981) of people of neither British nor French origin in the province gave rise to criticism of the federal government's English-French bilingual and bicultural policies of the 1960s and 1970s, and a preference for multicultural policies.

Economy

Alberta's economy has followed a pattern of primary-resource exploitation and dependence on external markets, with prices and revenues largely determined by outside economic and political forces. This pattern was established with the FUR TRADE of the 18th century and continued in the 19th century with ranching and then grain growing. The completion of the CPR in 1885 provided market routes for Alberta grain, as well as aiding the penetration of eastern Canadian manufactured goods. Agriculture remained the dominant economic activity until the discovery of oil in the Leduc field in 1947 and has since been surpassed in net product value by mining and manufacturing as well.

A rapid rise in the world price of oil in the early 1970s drove the Alberta economy to unprecedented and frantic growth. After a decade of financial boom, spurred almost entirely by profits created through the petroleum industry, the nationwide economic recession of 1982-83 was particularly severe in Alberta, as construction slowed, retail sales dropped and unemployment rose from 4% to over 10%. Investment and

Gross Domestic Product of Alberta, 1985		
	Amount	Percentage
Mining (including oil & gas)	$16.8 billion	27.0%
Finance (including insurance & real estate)	$13.0 billion	21.0%
Service	$8.6 billion	13.9%
Retail & wholesale trade	$5.0 billion	8.1%
Transportation	$4.0 billion	6.5%
Manufacturing	$3.9 billion	6.4%
Construction	$3.1 billion	5.0%
Agriculture	$2.1 billion	3.4%

Massive bucket wheel extracting bitumen from the Athabasca tar sands. It is estimated that the tar sands contain more oil than the Gulf of Arabia (*courtesy Suncor Inc Oil Sands Group*).

spending declined dramatically in 1982 and 1983 and have since stabilized at levels much lower than those reached during the boom. After several years of little or no economic growth, 1986 brought massive declines in world oil and grain prices. Despite repeated provincial government promises in the 1970s and 1980s to use the enormous royalty revenues generated from oil and gas sales to diversify the economy, Alberta continues to be dependent upon fossil-fuel extraction and the export of its grain harvests, continuing its susceptibility to external market factors. As world prices stay low for Alberta's exports of oil and wheat, the Alberta economy will probably continue to struggle.

Agriculture Alberta's agricultural industry remains of major importance to the province, the nation and – in grain exports – to the world. Between 1975 and 1980 the value of farm cash receipts increased by 65% and has since levelled off. Most of the overall increase came through the sale of livestock (chiefly cattle) and their products, which by 1986 amounted to $1.825 billion, slightly less than half the total farm cash receipts of $3.850 billion. Cereal crops – led by WHEAT, CANOLA and BARLEY – totalled $1.74 billion in receipts, a decrease of 8.5% from 1982, due primarily to the weakening of the international export market for wheat. Other crops, such as sugar beets, potatoes and vegetables, make up the remainder.

Around the metropolitan areas of Edmonton and Calgary, and in the corridor between the 2 cities, are dairy and poultry operations, cattle, and hog and sheep farms. Wheat and small grain farmers are located particularly in the Peace R region, the Edmonton, Camrose and Lloydminster areas, and in a belt from Red Deer SE to the US boundary. Mixed enterprises are again found in the crescent sweeping NW from Lethbridge to Calgary and Red Deer, then NE to Camrose and Lloydminster, plus the counties N of Edmonton. The black and brown soils of the mixed-grass prairie and parkland regions provide the environment with the greatest potential for mixed farming. Away from this fertile crescent, especially in the SE, lie the more specialized ranching and wheat operations, which compensate for their marginal soils with larger size. Irrigated farming, centered in Lethbridge, produces sugar beets, potatoes and vegetables.

Industry Manufacturers in Alberta tend either to process local raw materials (petroleum, agricultural, wood or nonmetallic mineral commodities) or to engage in custom manufacture and fabrication for the resource-development and construction sectors. During the 1970s the most rapidly expanding manufacturing area was the PETROCHEMICAL INDUSTRY, notably ethylene at Joffre and vinyl chloride monomer, ethylene and chloralkali at Ft Saskatchewan.

Construction was one of the most important industrial activities between 1955 and the early 1980s, with the oil and gas industry accounting for a consistently large proportion of this expansion. The recession of the mid-1980s, however, has had a serious negative impact on the industry. The estimated total value of construction work in Alberta in 1986 was $11.8 billion, down almost 12% from 1983. Engineering construction increased by 23.4%, while total building construction was down 16.5% (a 143% decrease in nonresidential construction and a 19.5% decline in residential construction). Edmonton and Calgary, as Canada's fastest-growing cities, were the centres of commercial and residential construction during the 1970s. However, after 1982 the engineering and petroleum servicing industries, facing severe economic restraints, curtailed their expansion. The downturn in construction is one of the primary reasons for Alberta's large increase in unemployment and has resulted in a serious weakening of the province's building trades unions, as contractors seek to cut costs by hiring non-union, lower salaried tradesmen. This has fueled labour unrest in the province and has forced the government's re-evaluation of the provincial labour code.

Tourism is the third major sector of Alberta's industrial economy, contributing over $2 billion to the provincial economy in 1986, over half of which was spent by non-Albertans. This influx of tourists annually supports over 74 000 full-time equivalent jobs throughout the province. The spectacular scenery and year-round recreational facilities of the Rocky Mts – particularly in BANFF and JASPER national parks – draw hundreds of thousands of tourists annually from all over the world. In addition to the parks, many local attractions draw large numbers of tourists to the province, in particular the world-famous CALGARY STAMPEDE. As well, special events such as Edmonton's hosting of the Commonwealth Games in 1978 and the World University Games in 1983, and the hosting of the Winter Olympics in Calgary in 1988 draw thousands of visitors.

Mining The estimated total value of minerals produced in Alberta during 1985 was $27.34 billion, amounting to 60.8% of the Canadian total. The value of fuels, by far the major component of mineral production (96.2% in 1985), reached $26.2 billion, or 83.6% of total national value. Between 1975 and 1985 the crude oil produced in Alberta decreased overall, while the volume of natural gas produced annually increased.

The volume of coal produced in Alberta rose by 67% between 1975 and 1980 to reach 20.1 million t, and has risen another 37% to 27.6 million t in 1985. Coal formed the basis of Alberta's first mining endeavour, in the Lethbridge region in 1872. By the time of WWI, coal mining was a major economic activity in the Lethbridge, Crowsnest Pass and Drumheller areas. Following an initial decline in the 1920s, and a drastic loss of domestic consumers in the 1950s, Alberta's coal industry reached its lowest point in the early 1960s. Since then a slight increase in the domestic market, plus the negotiation of long-term leases to supply the Japanese steel industry and new technologies for coal-liquefaction have pumped new life into the industry. Alberta produces limited quantities of salt, sodium sulphate and peat moss, plus a number of minerals used in the construction industry, such as limestone, sand and clay. The province is the world's largest producer of elemental sulphur from hydrocarbon sources. Small amounts of gold are mined, and the province possesses deposits of low-grade iron ore and uranium in the Lk Athabasca region which have not yet been developed.

Waterton Lakes National Park, southwestern Alberta. The area was once a Blackfoot stronghold and was discovered by Europeans in the 1850s. Situated 276 km SW of Calgary, the park was united with Montana's Glacier National Park in 1932 to form the world's first international peace park (*photo by Richard Vroom*).

Forestry Although nearly one-half of Alberta is covered by forest, a combination of low provincial demand and low-quality timber (compared, for example, with neighbouring BC) results in only a small fraction of the forest potential being exploited. In 1985 forestry accounted for just 0.1% ($66 million) of the province's gross domestic product. Timber quotas and other aspects of forest management are controlled by the Alberta Forest Service, a government agency. The production of sawn lumber, chiefly spruce, totals about 2.4 million m³ (560 million board feet) annually. Pulp mills are located at Hinton and Grande Prairie.

Fisheries The commercial fishing catch (about half of it whitefish) in Alberta's northern lakes averaged 2 million kg in the mid-1970s, with an annual value of about $800 000. In 1986-87 the catch was 2.9 million kg, with a market value of $5.2 million.

Finance The expansion of the petroleum industry after WWII, particularly during the 1970s, produced a westward shift of financial power within Canada, with Alberta the major beneficiary. During the 1970s, Calgary consolidated its position as the major provincial financial centre and emerged as a contending national centre. Between 1978 and 1986 the Calgary-based Alberta Stock Exchange increased its number of company listings by nearly 400, reaching 491, the vast majority of new members being small oil and gas companies. Dollar volumes traded on the exchange grew from $95 million to $480 million during the same period. By 1980 Calgary housed offices of 22 foreign banks (this had dropped to 17 by 1987), and had become the third-largest head-office location for major Canadian companies, behind only Toronto and Montréal. The Bank of Alberta, headquartered in Edmonton, is now the only bank based in Alberta. The province's financial institutions were devastated by the recession of the early 1980s. In 1985 the CANADIAN COMMERCIAL BANK and the Northland Bank collapsed within weeks of each other. Numerous trust and mortgage companies, beginning with Dial Mortgage in 1981 and culminating in the Principal

Group in 1987, succumbed. In 1984 the Alberta government had to guarantee $2.4 billion in deposits in Alberta credit unions and in 1987 forced 8 of them to amalgamate.

Transportation While river transportation provided the communication network for the fur trade in the 18th and early 19th century, it was rail transportation that opened Alberta to extensive settlement in the late 19th century, and tied the region's economy into that of the nation. Southern Alberta is served chiefly by the CPR, central Alberta by the CNR, and northern regions by the Alberta Resources Ry, the Northern Alberta Ry and the Great Slave Ry. CPR and CNR lines transport virtually all of Alberta's grain crop E and W to international markets. So important are these routes to the province's economic well being that railway issues, such as abandoning branch lines, the CROW'S NEST PASS AGREEMENT, and the upgrading of main lines and terminal facilities, are important political as well as economic concerns.

The importance of Alberta's highways to the movement of both people and goods has increased since the end of WWII. The most heavily travelled route is the multi-lane Highway 2 between Edmonton and Calgary. Important interprovincial routes include Highway 1, the TRANS-CANADA HIGHWAY, through Medicine Hat, Calgary, and Banff; Highway 16, the Yellowhead Highway, through Lloydminster, Edmonton, and Jasper; and the Mackenzie Highway running N from the Peace R country to the NWT. Calgary is the headquarters of Greyhound Lines, the largest intercity bus system in Canada, with a network of over 22 500 km.

Alberta's 2 international airports, located at Calgary and Edmonton, experienced the largest annual increases in passenger traffic among all major Canadian airports during the 1970s. Regular passenger service to other parts of the country and abroad is provided by Air Canada, Canadian Airlines International (formed by Pacific Western Airlines' takeover of Canadian Pacific Airlines), plus a number of American and European carriers. Wardair of Edmonton (now headquartered in Toronto) is Canada's largest charter airline, providing both national and international services. Air travel within the province is dominated by Canadian Airlines International and Time Air.

Alberta has over 200 000 km of PIPELINES carrying oil (42 313 km) and gas (165 012 km) to both internal and external markets. Oil moves E through the Interprovincial line (completed from Alberta to Lk Superior in 1953, later to Montréal)

and W through the Trans-Mountain line to the Pacific. NOVA CORPORATION built the pipelines that deliver gas to Alberta's boundaries, where it enters interprovincial or American lines. Nova is the principal partner in the Foothills Pipe Line consortium, formed to deliver Alaskan natural gas to the continental US, although only the southern portion has been completed.

Energy The oil industry in Alberta began with the discovery of the Turner Valley field in 1914. However, apart from a brief flurry of activity in the late 1930s, the industry remained small until the discovery of the Leduc field in 1947, followed by the opening of the Woodbend, Redwater and Pembina fields. The more than 17 000 producing wells are distributed over most of the province. Alberta production, as a proportion of the Canadian total, increased from about 79% in 1972 to 88% in 1985. In 1985, 27.3% was exported to the US, 50.1% to other provinces, while only about 22.7% was consumed within the province. The natural-gas industry is older than oil, dating from 1883 discoveries near Medicine Hat. Alberta produced the bulk of Canada's natural gas through the 1970s, varying from 83% in 1973 to 88.1% in 1985. Provincial markets use 23.4% of production, with 34% exported to the US in 1985, and 39.9% consumed elsewhere in Canada. Within the province, natural gas is used to generate electricity and as fuel for industrial, commercial and residential purposes. Natural gas is also the feedstock on which the petrochemical industry is based. Alberta also possesses reserves of heavy crude (in the Lloydminster and Cold Lake areas) and the vast tar sands of the Ft McMurray region. Only since the 1960s did rising prices for oil make the tar sands a commercially viable operation. The first 2 plants to exploit the tar sands for conversion into synthetic crude oil were Great Canadian Oil Sands (now Suncor) and Syncrude. The development of further MEGAPROJECTS was delayed by the economic recession of the early 1980s. Although the huge Husky Heavy Oil development at Lloydminster was announced in 1984, construction had still not begun in 1987.

Since 1947 the petroleum industry has brought prosperity to both the public and private sectors, transforming Alberta from a "have-not" to a "have" province. While Edmonton became the centre for petroleum servicing, production and transmission, Calgary remained the exploration, administrative and financial centre, owing in part to its proximity to the original Turner Valley field. Royalties from petroleum production swelled provincial coffers, allowing the Social Credit government of the 1950s and 1960s and the Conservatives of the 1970s and 1980s to keep taxes low. Yet disputes over petroleum pricing and export levels have led to acrimonious debates between Alberta and the federal government, and have fueled strong provincial-rights and even quasi-separatist political movements. By the mid-1980s, while most disputes had been at least temporarily resolved, the reduction in the world oil price had a severe impact on the Alberta-based petroleum industry.

Government and Politics

Legislative power is vested in a LIEUTENANT-GOVERNOR (appointed by the governor general on the advice of the prime minister and representing the Crown) and an 83-member, single-chamber, elected Legislative Assembly. However, the traditional powers of the lieutenant-governor have in practice lapsed. Executive power is exercised by a Cabinet of responsible ministers selected by the PREMIER, the leader of the political party commanding a majority in the Legislative Assembly. Each minister presides over one or more depart-

Premiers of Alberta 1905-1987

	Party	Term
Alexander Cameron Rutherford	Liberal	1905-10
Arthur Lewis Sifton	Liberal	1910-17
Charles Stewart	Liberal	1917-21
Herbert Greenfield	United Farmers of Alberta	1921-25
John Edward Brownlee	United Farmers of Alberta	1925-34
Richard Gavin Reid	United Farmers of Alberta	1934-35
William Aberhart	Social Credit	1935-43
Ernest Charles Manning	Social Credit	1943-68
Harry Edwin Strom	Social Credit	1968-71
Peter Lougheed	Conservative	1971-86
Donald Ross Getty	Conservative	1986-

ments of government. The senior division of the judiciary is the Court of Queen's Bench, whose justices are appointed by the federal government. The Trial Division of the Queen's Bench hears both civil and criminal cases, usually the more severe ones, while the Appeals Division hears appeals from both the Queen's Bench and the Provincial Court. This Provincial Court, with its judges appointed by the province, hears the great majority of both civil and criminal cases in the first instance.

Local Government Local municipal authority is derived from the province and based on various municipal acts. MUNICIPALITIES provide local services such as police and fire protection, garbage and sewage disposal, water and other utilities, road maintenance and public transportation, and parks and recreational services. Urban municipalities include cities, towns, "new towns" (with special borrowing powers), villages and "summer villages" (resort areas). Rural authorities include municipal districts (averaging 30 TOWNSHIPS) and COUNTIES (averaging 40 townships). The difference between these 2 forms of rural municipality lies in the responsibility for public education. In municipal districts, public school boards are discrete entities, whereas in counties the public schools are administered by a committee of the county council. A third type of rural municipality is the improvement district – outlying areas which do not elect their own councils but are directly administered by Alberta Municipal Affairs, except for the townsites located within the 5 national parks, which are administered by the federal government.

Federal Representation Alberta has 6 seats in the Senate (a fixed number, constitutionally determined) and 21 seats in the House of Commons in 1987 (a flexible number, subject to REDISTRIBUTION after each decennial census). The Liberal Party won the majority of Alberta's seats in the first 2 federal elections following provincehood, in 1908 and 1911. Conservatives won the province in the 1917 federal election, Progressives from 1921 to 1930, and Social Credit from 1935 to 1957. Beginning with John Diefenbaker's sweep of 1958, Alberta has voted overwhelmingly Conservative. The elections of 1972, 1974, 1979,

Lieutenant-Governors of Alberta 1905-1987

	Term
George Hedley Vicars Bulyea	1905-15
Robert George Brett	1915-25
William Egbert	1925-31
William Legh Walsh	1931-36
Philip Carteret Hill Primrose	1936-37
John Campbell Bowen	1937-50
John James Bowlen	1950-59
John Percy Page	1959-65
John Walter Grant MacEwan	1965-74
Ralph Garvin Steinhauer	1974-79
Frank C. Lynch-Staunton	1979-85
Helen Hunley	1985-

1980 and 1984 saw the Conservatives take every Alberta seat, with the popular vote ranging from 58% to 69%. Such bloc support for the Conservatives, while the majority of Canada returned Liberal governments, had, until 1984, left Alberta MPs on the Opposition side in the House of Commons since 1963, except during the short-lived Conservative government of Alberta native Joe CLARK, 1979-80, and during the 2 years (1977-79) Jack HORNER sat as a Liberal Cabinet minister after leaving the Conservative Party.

Public Finance Residents of Alberta pay among the lowest income taxes in Canada and pay no retail-sales taxes. The province depends instead on various fees, rentals and royalties from oil, natural gas, coal and other mineral companies; this income once accounted for 45% (1981-82) of total government revenue, but by 1987 it had declined to about 20%. Before 1976 all revenue became part of the general budgetary fund used to finance the total range of government expenditures. Following the energy-pricing crisis of the mid-1970s, however, revenues increased dramatically and the government was faced with vast potential surpluses. The result was the creation in 1976 of the ALBERTA HERITAGE SAVINGS TRUST FUND, into which 30% (reduced to 15% in 1982 and 0% in 1987) of the nonrenewable resource revenue was set aside. The Heritage Fund is intended primarily to earn a maximum return on equity, to provide financial resources for periods when resource income declines, to strengthen and diversify the provincial economy, and to undertake special capital projects, such as healthcare facilities, irrigation and recreation projects, and the development of oil-sands technology. Use of the fund has become the key domestic issue in provincial politics in the 1980s.

Health In July 1969 Alberta entered the federal medicare scheme and operates the universal Alberta Health Care Insurance Plan. Negotiations between the province and the medical profession over fee schedules under this plan have at times been heated, with a number of practitioners opting for "balanced billing" or "extra billing." In compliance with the Federal Health Act of 1984, this practice was stopped in 1986. Alberta has now taken nonessential services, such as eye exams, out of public health care. Welfare services within the province include public assistance to the aged, disabled and handicapped, with an increasing emphasis on preventive social services. Heritage Fund money has financed medical research through the $300 million endowment fund, Alberta Heritage Foundation for Medical Reseach, and increased the stock of hospital beds. The 2 largest capital projects are the new Walter C. Mackenzie Health Sciences Centre in Edmonton and the enlarged Alberta Children's Hospital in Calgary. There is a variety of health-care institutions in the province, including large general hospitals in the major urban centres, smaller rural hospitals, auxiliary hospitals specializing in extended-care treatment, provincial mental and psychiatric hospitals, and nursing homes for senior citizens.

Politics Alberta provincial politics is characterized by governing parties commanding huge majorities in the legislature, remaining in power for lengthy periods, and then being decisively beaten and virtually eliminated by a new political force. This pattern was established by the Liberals under Alberta's first premier, Alexander C. RUTHERFORD, who took 22 of 25 seats, with 57.5% of the popular vote, in the first provincial election in 1905. Similar Liberal victories were recorded in 1909, 1913 and 1917 under Rutherford and his successors, A.L. SIFTON and Charles STEWART. The UNITED FARMERS OF ALBERTA, fueled by agrarian unrest at the end of WWI, swept to power in the 1921 provincial election with 38 (all rural) of 61 seats despite gaining only 28.9% of the popular vote. Under premier John BROWNLEE, they repeated this pattern in 1926 and 1930. But in 1935 yet another new provincial force, the SOCIAL CREDIT League under William ABERHART, took 56 of 63 seats with 54% of the popular vote. Under Aberhart and his successors, Ernest MANNING and Harry STROM, Social Credit governed for 36 years, not to be swept aside until the victory of Peter LOUGHEED and the Conservatives in 1971, with 49 of 75 seats and 46% of the popular vote. Lougheed and the Conservatives crushed all opposition in 1975, 1979 and 1982. In 1986, under Don GETTY, the Conservative vote dropped to 51% and they held 61 of 83 seats. The NDP with 29% of the vote, captured 16 seats, 11 of them in Edmonton. The Liberals took 4 seats and the Representative Party 2 seats. Since the United Farmers of the 1920s, successful provincial political parties in Alberta have often opposed policies of the federal government, particularly on issues of taxation, natural resources and the nature of the Canadian confederation.

Education

The first schools in Alberta were founded by Catholic and Protestant missionaries in the mid-19th century. The North-West Territories School Ordinance of 1884 established a dual confessional system of Catholic and Protestant schooling based on the Québec model. Subsequent Protestant settlement and the determination of territorial political leader F.W.G. HAULTAIN saw the gradual weakening of religious duality in education. Alberta entered Confederation in 1905 with a system based on the Ontario model – one provincial educational system, allowing local provision for the dissenting religious minority, known as separate schools, but excluding province-wide duality. Ontario also provided the initial model for programs of study, course content and grade structures, a model that lasted until the 1930s. That decade, however, was a particularly innovative one in education, and saw the introduction of social studies, the junior high school and the large unit of rural school administration, plus expansion in adult education and steps towards the economic and professional betterment of teachers.

Administration Public education in Alberta is a shared responsibility of the provincial government and local public and separate school boards. The provincial Department of Education (Alberta Education) has overall jurisdiction in areas such as curriculum and teacher certification, while local boards employ teachers and operate schools at the elementary (grades 1-6), junior high (7-9) and senior high (10-12) levels. Funding is provided by a combination of provincial grants and local property taxes. In 1985-86, 418 900 students were enrolled in grades 1-12. Pre-grade 1 education is available, though not compulsory, through Alberta Early Childhood Services (ECS), a unique interdepartmental, holistic approach to child development, in partnership with local school board or community ECS operators.

Institutions Post-secondary education is under the jurisdiction of Alberta Advanced Education and Manpower. Provincial grants account for approximately 78% of funding, the balance coming from tuition fees and private grants. The province's 4 universities – Alberta, Calgary, Lethbridge and Athabasca (a unique DISTANCE-LEARNING institution) – are all public, nondenominational institutions, enrolling a total of 51 912 graduate and undergraduate students in 1985-86. Other components of the public, post-secondary sector include Northern Alberta Institute of Technology in Edmonton and Westerra Institute of Technology in Stony Plain and Southern

Alberta Institute of Technology in Calgary (8848 full-time students combined in 1985-86) and 11 public colleges (17 490 full-time equivalent and 10 131 part-time in 1985-86). The colleges offer a variety of university transfer, vocational and high-school upgrading courses.

Cultural Life

Cultural life in Alberta has had to combat 2 major negative forces: the persistence of a "frontier ethos" that emphasizes economic materialism and rugged individualism; and a cultural dependency on external metropolitan centres such as New York, London, Toronto and Los Angeles. Yet it has had advantages: a rich physical landscape that has influenced both painters and writers; a diverse population that perpetuates various ethnic cultures; plus periodic governmental, corporate and private affluence, which has benefited the cultural sector.

The Arts Until the 1960s, visual arts in Alberta were centered in Calgary around the Provincial Institute of Technology and Art (now the Alberta College of Art), and dominated by a British-inspired school of landscape painters. From W.J. PHILLIPS through H.G. GLYDE, W.L. Stevenson and Illingworth KERR, they painted the prairie, foothills and mountain countryside. Calgarians Maxwell BATES (also an architect) and Marion Nicol were 2 modernist exceptions. During the 1960s, abstract expressionist painting of the New York school began to influence Alberta painters through the Edmonton Art Gallery, which also became the national leader in presenting and developing modern metal sculptors. The leading public galleries are the Edmonton Art Gallery and the Glenbow-Alberta Institute in Calgary. Provincial government support for the visual arts includes the Alberta Art Foundation, which purchases works for its permanent collection, and the Alberta Foundation for the Performing Arts which provides grants to artists and various performing arts companies.

The professional performing arts are centered in Edmonton and Calgary, with most critics giving the artistic edge to the capital city. Edmonton hosts a major summer folk festival and "Jazz City," a critically acclaimed international jazz festival. The EDMONTON SYMPHONY and the Calgary Philharmonic dominate orchestral music; there are 2 opera companies, the Edmonton Opera Association and Calgary's Southern Alberta Opera Association; and 2 ballet companies, the ALBERTA BALLET COMPANY and the Alberta Contemporary Dance Theatre, both of Edmonton. Dramatic groups include the CITADEL THEATRE in Edmonton and Theatre Calgary. As well, Edmonton annually plays host to the Fringe theatre event, a weeklong summertime festival of new and old plays at open-air venues and traditional playhouse settings. Many Alberta playwrights (including nationally acclaimed John Murrell and Sharon Pollock) have worked with Alberta Theatre Projects, a Calgary company that has encouraged local writers and indigenous themes. Major facilities for the performing arts include the twin Jubilee auditoriums in Edmonton and Calgary (built for the 50th anniversary of provincehood in 1955), Edmonton's Citadel Theatre and Calgary's new civic-built Centre for the Performing Arts. The BANFF CENTRE School for Continuing Education has emerged as a nationally and internationally renowned training centre for young professionals in the performing arts.

A number of commercially successful and critically acclaimed writers of both fiction and nonfiction are based in Alberta, including novelists Robert KROETSCH (whose works take an irreverent, surrealistic look at 20th-century Alberta life),

W.O. MITCHELL, and Rudy WIEBE (who has explored the ethnic diversity of prairie life). Younger talents have been encouraged by the provincial government's annual Search-for-a-New-Alberta-Novelist competition. Nonfiction writing is dominated by regional historians who appeal to both the academic and the popular reader; these include Grant MACEWAN, James GRAY and Hugh Dempsey of Calgary, and James MacGregor and A.W. Cashman of Edmonton. The University of Calgary library houses one of Canada's best collections of contemporary writers' papers; Mitchell and Wiebe are represented, as well as many out-of-province writers.

Communications Daily newspaper publishing in Alberta is dominated by chain ownership; 6 of the 9 dailies are parts of Toronto-based national chains. These are the Edmonton *Journal,* Calgary *Herald,* and Medicine Hat *News* (Southam newspaper group); the Edmonton *Sun* and Calgary *Sun* (owned by Maclean Hunter); and the Lethbridge *Herald* (part of the Thomson newspaper empire). Bowes Publishers Ltd, a regional chain, publishes the Grande Prairie *Daily Herald-Tribune* and Fort McMurray *Today.* The Red Deer *Advocate,* though independent of Canadian chains, is Canada's only foreign-owned daily newspaper; it is controlled by the Liverpool Post and Echo group in Britain. There are 134 weekly or community newspapers serving metropolitan, suburban and rural areas of Alberta. Among the magazines published in the province are the neoconservative, provincial-rights oriented *Alberta Report* and the arts-oriented *NeWest Review* (both independently owned and published in Edmonton), the leisure- and life-style-oriented *Calgary* and *Edmonton* magazines (owned by Pacific West Press of Vancouver). There are also a number of trade journals serving the petroleum and other industries.

The 12 television stations in Alberta include a mixture of national and local ownership. The CBC has network stations in Calgary and 2 in Edmonton (one of which is a French-language affiliate, CBXFT), and affiliated stations in Red Deer, Lloydminster and Medicine Hat. CTV has affiliated stations in Calgary, Edmonton, Lethbridge and Lloydminster. Independent stations are CFAC Calgary and CITV Edmonton. Most of urban Alberta is also served by cable TV systems, which offer additional American and local channels to subscribers. Alberta Independent Pay Television of Edmonton is the regional pay-TV licensee for the province. The 33 AM and 16 FM radio stations in the province are all privately owned, except the CBC network stations in Calgary and Edmonton, the U of A Students' Union station, CJSR, and the provincially owned CKUA, part of the ACCESS network that utilizes both radio and television primarily for educational broadcasting.

Historic Sites Historic sites in the province are concentrated around early exploration, furtrade, missionary, mounted police and settlement activity. The provincially funded Alberta Historical Resources Foundation assists local groups in heritage-preservation activities, such as the live-

Traders leaving Athabasca Landing for the North (*courtesy Provincial Archives of Alberta/E. Brown Coll/B2863*).

Rockyford, Alta, grain elevators, 1920 (*courtesy Provincial Archives of Alberta/H. Pollard Coll/P658*).

history Ukrainian Cultural Heritage Village E of Edmonton. The major museums are the GLENBOW MUSEUM in Calgary, the Provincial Museum of Alberta in Edmonton, the TYRRELL MUSEUM OF PALAEONTOLOGY at Drumheller and the new Head-Smashed-In Buffalo Jump Interpretive Centre NW of Ft Macleod. The major historical archives are found at the Provincial Museum in Edmonton and the Glenbow-Alberta Institute, Calgary. The Historical Society of Alberta has active chapters in Calgary, Edmonton and Lethbridge.

History

In the late 18th century southern Alberta was occupied by the BLACKFOOT, BLOOD, PEIGAN and Gros Ventre. The Kootenay and other trans-mountain peoples made regular buffalo-hunting expeditions into the area, while more southerly tribes came on warring raids. Along the N Saskatchewan R were the SARCEE, though there is some question whether they existed there before the fur trade; farther N were the BEAVER, and beyond them the SLAVEY. These Indians felt the effects of European culture long before they saw their first Europeans. Metal tools and weapons brought by the HUDSON'S BAY COMPANY were traded and retraded westwards across the Prairies; similarly the horse moved N from Spanish Mexico in the early 1700s. Gradually tribes close to Hudson Bay became dependent on trade goods and began to penetrate westwards in search of furs to use as barter. The Cree and Assiniboine (including the Stoney) moved up the N Saskatchewan R in the 18th century, forcing the Sarcee and Blackfoot tribes S and the Beaver N. The Chipewyan entered the NE corner of Alberta, pushing the Beaver back towards the mountains. By the early 1800s, the Gros Ventre had moved S into the US.

Exploration The first European known to have reached present-day Alberta was Anthony HENDAY, an HBC employee who, accompanied by a band of Cree, travelled through the Red Deer area and likely spent the latter months of the winter near the present site of Edmonton in 1754-55. Competition between the HBC and the Montréal-based NORTH WEST COMPANY dominated the region in the late 18th and early 19th centuries. In 1778 Peter POND, an aggressive Nor'Wester, travelled down the Athabasca R and established the first fur-trading post in the province. Ft Chipewyan on Lk Athabasca was founded in 1788 and served as the jumping-off point for Alexander MACKENZIE's trip down the Mackenzie R in 1789, and his journey up the Peace R and through the Rocky Mts to the Pacific 4 years later. The Hudson's Bay Company countered by sending Peter FIDLER and David THOMPSON to explore and map the Athabasca and Saskatchewan rivers in the 1790s and early 1800s. The 2 companies built competing posts throughout northern and central Alberta until 1821, when the rival companies merged.

By the middle of the 19th century, Christian missionaries in search of Indian souls had begun to challenge the fur traders for possession of the territory. Methodist Robert RUNDLE in 1840 became the first resident cleric in what is now Alberta, followed 2 years later by the Roman Catholic Father Jean-Baptiste Thibault. Missionary activity peaked in the third quarter of the century, with such illustrious names as Albert LACOMBE among the Catholics and the Methodist father-and-son team of George and John MCDOUGALL. The persistent advance of the European frontier challenged the HBC's continued control over the territory. Anticipating the termination of the company's licence and curious about the suitability of the territory for general settlement, both the British and Canadian governments commissioned expeditions in 1857 to explore and report on the Prairies. Capt John PALLISER headed the British expedition, while the moving spirit of the Canadian party was Henry Youle HIND, whose optimistic reports balanced the less enthusiastic findings of Palliser and ultimately influenced Britain to refuse renewal of the HBC licence.

Settlement On 23 June 1870 the Canadian government took possession of the entire HBC territory, including all of the future province of Alberta. The following year the region between the new province of Manitoba and the Rocky Mts was organized as the North-West Territories of Canada, with its administrative centre first at Winnipeg, then at Battleford, and finally at Regina. The DOMINION LANDS ACT of 1872 laid the basis for the quarter-section homestead survey. Two years later the NORTH-WEST MOUNTED POLICE established their first Alberta post at Ft Macleod. The North-West Territories Act of 1875 provided for a lieutenant-governor and legislature (first an appointed council, gradually replaced by an elected assembly). A series of treaties was subsequently signed with Indian groups: Treaty No 6 in 1876 covered the Cree lands of central Alberta; Treaty No 7 in 1877 brought in the Blackfoot, Sarcee and Stoney of southern Alberta; Treaty No 8 in 1899 covered most of northern Alberta (*see* LAND CLAIMS).

Settlement was still slow to materialize during the 1880s, despite the arrival of the CPR in Calgary in 1883 and its transcontinental completion 2 years later. By 1881 only some 1000 non-native settlers resided within the boundaries of the present province of Alberta; 10 years later it was just 17 500. The great influx of settlement at the end of the century followed the development of fast-maturing varieties of hard spring wheat, the exhaustion of good available land in the American West, the easing of the 22-year economic depression that had gripped N America, and the vigorous immigration policy of the federal government under the direction of Clifford SIFTON. From 1896 to WWI, Alberta and other parts of the Canadian Prairies were the beneficiaries of one of the most important and dramatic population migrations in modern N American history. Settlers poured onto the open prairie farmlands and into its bustling towns and cities. Many came from Ontario and other parts of eastern Canada, others from the US and Great Britain, and others from continental Europe; the great variety of linguistic and religious backgrounds imposed an indelible, multicultural stamp on Alberta life. Alberta's population rose from 73 022 in 1901 to 373 943 in 1911 and 584 454 in 1921.

Development The creation of the province of Alberta on 1 Sept 1905 was the logical result of the great immigration boom, and an answer to the political campaign for autonomy that had developed in the North-West Territories. Political controversies at the time of provincehood centred

"Edmonton – This very moment is the capital & Alberta a province in reality" (*by permission of the British Library*).

on the rights of the Roman Catholic minority to publicly funded separate schools, the boundary with the new sister province of Saskatchewan (Albertans sought 107° W long but had to settle for 110°), and Edmonton's victory over Calgary for the site of the new provincial capital. While these issues left a legacy of bitterness towards perceived federal interference in local matters, none was as contentious as Ottawa's decision to retain control of crown lands and natural resources. Not till 1930 were these responsibilities transferred to provincial control.

Fortune smiled on the new province of Alberta during its first decade. Immigration accelerated; grain harvests were bountiful; new communities sprang up, and a network of railway lines rapidly expanded. Yet resentment grew among farmers, who believed that their status as independent entrepreneurs was being jeopardized by the railways, banks and grain-elevator companies. The rise of the United Farmers of Alberta as a political party, and their victory over the Liberals in the 1921 provincial election were in part a manifestation of this unrest. Yet the UFA government had to cope with a provincial economy in the 1920s and early 1930s that was much weaker than the pre-1914 boom years. Grain prices fluctuated and the once-important coal-mining industry declined. The worldwide depression of the 1930s, accompanied by prairie drought, soil drifting and grasshopper plagues, accelerated an economic decline that had begun a year earlier. The Social Credit League won the 1935 provincial election by promising to fight the Depression (and the perceived eastern control of Alberta's economy) with a mixture of religious fundamentalism and radical monetary theory.

The discovery of oil at Leduc in Feb 1947 began the process of transforming Alberta's economic base from agriculture to petroleum. The resulting exploitation of oil and natural-gas resources produced an ever-accelerating flow of royalties to augment provincial revenues, brought prosperity to most segments of the population, and transformed the cities of Edmonton and Calgary into prosperous metropolitan centres. The 1973 worldwide oil-pricing crisis brought an even greater prosperity that lasted until the general economic recession of the early 1980s and the oil and grain price crashes of 1986.

ROBERT M. STAMP

Reading: B.M. Barr and P.J. Smith, eds, *Geographical Dimension of Settlement and Livelihood in Alberta* (1983); John Barr, *The Dynasty: The Rise and Fall of Social Credit in Alberta* (1974); Carlo Cardarola, ed, *Society and Politics in Alberta* (1979); W.G. Hardy, ed, *Alberta: A Natural History* (1967); John Irving, *The Social Credit Movement in Alberta* (1959); James G. MacGregor, *A History of Alberta* (1981); C.B. Macpherson, *Democracy in Alberta: Social Credit and the Party System* (1953); W.E. Mann, *Sect, Cult, and Church in Alberta* (1955); University of Alberta, *Atlas of Alberta* (1969); Rudy Wiebe, *Alberta, A Celebration*.

Alberta Ballet Company, an Edmonton ballet company founded in the late 1950s by Ruth CARSE as a small performing group. From this came the

Edmonton Ballet Co (incorporated 1961), reconstituted as a professional classical ensemble, the Alberta Ballet Co, in 1966. Brydon Paige, who became artistic director of the company (12-14 dancers) in 1976, has choreographed *The Nutcracker, The Firebird* and *Cinderella*. The repertoire also includes the modern works *Promenade, A Soldier's Tale* and *Sundances* by Lambros Lambrou, resident choreographer since 1979.

SUSAN PEDWELL

Alberta Energy Company Ltd was established in 1974 as a CROWN CORPORATION by the Alberta government under the Alberta Energy Company Act. After an offering of public shares in 1975 (including an Alberta Priority Period of 2 weeks to allow Albertans to invest first in the company), AEC became a public company, wholly Canadian owned, with more than 50 000 shareholders. AEC participates in exploration and development of Canada's gas and oil, pipelines, forest products and coal industries. AEC also has direct investments in international oil and gas activities.

Alberta Heritage Savings Trust Fund, est in 1976 by an Act of Legislature with initial resources of $1.5 billion in cash and assets from the General Revenue Fund. Its purpose is to save and invest revenues from Alberta's oil and gas. From 1976 to 1982-83 its funds were derived from an annual transfer of 30% of Alberta's nonrenewable resource revenues and retention of the fund's investment earnings. From 1983-84 to 1986-87 the transfer of resource revenue was reduced to 15% and, effective Apr 1987, the transfer of resource revenue has been suspended. In 1985-86, the fund received 15% of these revenues, totalling $685 million. Since mid-1982, the fund's investment income has been transferred to the province's budget. During 1985-86, $1.67 billion was transferred, providing support equal to 2 months out of 12 of budgetary expenditures. Money from the fund has been invested in capital projects to provide long-term benefits to Alberta, eg, Alberta Oil Sands Technology and Research Authority ($351 million to 1985-86), the Walter C. Mackenzie Health Sciences Centre ($356 million), Kananaskis Country Recreation Development ($212 million) and major irrigation projects ($438 million). Other investments include the debentures of provincial crown corporations, such as the Alberta Opportunity Company ($162 million to 1985-86), Alberta Agricultural Development Corporation ($1041 million), and Alberta Mortgage and Housing Corporation ($3387 million). Investments in development projects include participation in the Syncrude project ($459 million) and loans for the Prince Rupert Grain Terminal ($134 million). Prior to 1982-83, the fund also provided loans to other Canadian provinces ($1.9 billion in debentures were held at the end of 1985-86). As of 31 Mar 1986, the Heritage Fund had $12.7 billion of financial assets and $2.4 billion of deemed assets, for a total of $15.1 billion.

Alberta Oil Sands Technology and Research Authority, an Alberta CROWN CORPORATION funded by the ALBERTA HERITAGE SAVINGS TRUST FUND, was established in 1975 to promote the development and use of new technology for oil-sands and heavy-oil production, with emphasis on reduced costs, increased recovery and environmental acceptability. Enhanced recovery of conventional crude oil was added to AOSTRA's mandate in 1979. AOSTRA reports to the minister of energy. Projects are selected by a government-appointed board consisting of up to 9 members with experience in PETROLEUM development and technology management. AOSTRA operates primarily through projects, the costs of which are shared with industry; the resultant technology is available to any user at fair market value. AOSTRA also supports research at Canadian universities and research institutions, provides grants to inventors, funds the operation of a technical information system and promotes international co-operation in oil sands development.

Educational assistance is provided through scholarships and fellowships. AOSTRA expects to spend more than $600 million over the life of the program, with comparable expenditures by industry. This expenditure makes AOSTRA one of the largest single-purpose research and development programs in Canada. AOSTRA's head office and information centre is in Edmonton; a second office is in Calgary.

E.J. WIGGINS

Alberta Opportunity Company, founded in 1972, is a CROWN CORPORATION with an independent board of directors reporting to the Alberta legislature through the minister of economic development and trade. The company provides financial and management assistance to qualified small- and medium-sized Alberta businesses which are unable to obtain reasonable terms and conditions from the private sector. Loans may be used for a number of purposes, including land or equipment, or refinancing existing loans. Management assistance includes counselling its customers in areas such as accounting, construction, finance, marketing and production. AOC is not involved in such areas as primary agricultural production or residential housing. Since 1972 it has approved over 4000 loans, exceeding $450 million in value, and has provided management assistance to some 600 companies in many other sectors, including student-operated summer businesses. AOC has 11 branch offices and its head office and main branch are in Ponoka. The board of directors is composed of a chairman, a managing director, a representative from the Dept of Economic Development and Trade, and 12 private-sector business people who represent different regions of the province and different business backgrounds.

Alberta Press Act Reference (1938) also called Reference Re Alberta Statutes, concerned an Alberta bill which would have compelled each newspaper in the province, when called upon to do so by a government official, to publish the government's rebuttal of criticism of the government that had appeared in the newspaper. The Supreme Court of Canada judged that the bill was ULTRA VIRES of the province, ie, that it exceeded the power of the provincial legislature. Five of the 6 judges gave as their primary reason that the bill was ancillary to and dependent upon another, invalid legislation, *The Alberta Social Credit Act*. Two judges, however, added that free political discussion was too important to Canada as a whole to be treated as a local and private matter, and one other judge argued that legislation affecting freedom of the press in discussing public affairs was within the CRIMINAL LAW power of Parliament. As our Constitution is declared in its preamble to be similar in principle to that of the UK, 3 declared that free public discussion is the breath of life for our parliamentary institution derived from Great Britain.

GÉRALD A. BEAUDOIN

Alberta Research Council (ARC), the oldest and best-funded provincial research organization, was established by order-in-council as the Scientific and Industrial Research Council of Alberta in 1921. Instrumental in founding the organization were J.-L. CÔTÉ, provincial secretary, and H.M. TORY, president of UNIVERSITY OF ALBERTA. In 1930 a provincial Act formalized the council's mandate to inventory and promote development of natural resources. The government could not fund ARC during the GREAT DEPRESSION, and the council was governed by University of Alberta from 1933 to 1942. In 1951 a revised Act formally established it as independent of the university and appointed its first research director, Nathaniel GRACE. Research facilities were built on the university campus in 1954-55; laboratory and office space has been established in Nisku, Devon, Red Deer, Calgary, Lethbridge and Edmonton. ARC is recognized for expertise in COAL LIQUEFACTION, oil-sands geology and chemistry and other resource-extraction technologies. Research is planned in the areas of computer technology and BIOTECHNOLOGY. ARC is a CROWN CORPORATION, responsible for advising the government, providing technical advice to industry and promoting economic and social development through research. The president, appointed by provincial executive council, presides over about 500 staff. The council now consists of 15 members from business, university and government, and is chaired by a member of the provincial legislature. Funding is primarily through provincial grants and contracts, with smaller business and federal input. *See also* ALBERTA OIL SANDS TECHNOLOGY AND RESEARCH AUTHORITY.

MARTIN K. MCNICHOLL

Alberta Wheat Pool, with head offices in Calgary, is an agricultural CO-OPERATIVE formed in 1923 when the open-market system of selling wheat began to weaken in response to a recession in prices. All original members of the Alberta Wheat Pool contributed $1 per share; when legislation governing the pool was enacted, this money was refunded and the pool became a service association with ownership resting with the operating grain farmers. Today the Alberta Wheat Pool handles seed and fertilizer distribution, and the interests of its grain-producing members come before profits. In 1986 its sales amounted to $1 billion, (including grain purchased for and delivered to the CANADIAN WHEAT BOARD); its assets were $474 million, and it had 1621 employees. The shares are held by co-operative members.

DEBORAH C. SAWYER

Alberton, PEI, Town pop 1103 (1986c), 1020 (1981c), situated in Prince County, 136 km NW of Charlottetown. In 1820, 40 families came to the Cascumpec Bay area. With the development of a shipbuilding industry at Northport and with the production of surplus crops by the settlers, traffic increased on the crossroads near the bay, and traders began locating there in the late 1830s. By 1833 Alberton was known as "Stump Town" because hundreds of stumps were left after the clearing of a forest. Owing to its crossroads location, Alberton was later known as the "Cross." On 27 June 1862, the community was renamed in honour of Albert Edward, the Prince of Wales. Alberton is still a small commercial centre servicing 5000 rural residents.

W.S. KEIZER

Albion Mines Railway, Pictou County, NS, was the second steam railway in Canada and the first to use a standard gauge and split-switch, movable rail. Built by the General Mining Association, 4 km of track were opened with great celebration on 19 Sept 1839; when fully operational in May 1840, the line covered 9.5 km, 123 m from Albion Mines (STELLARTON) to a deep-water terminus at Dunbar's Point (Abercrombie). Three Hackworth locomotives, *Samson, Hercules* and *John Buddle*, serviced the line; their reliability and efficiency marked the Albion Rail Road as the first really effective steam operation in Canada. The line became redundant in 1886 and was torn up in 1889, although about 1.5 km remained and was used for hauling coal until June 1961.

LOIS KERNAGHAN

Albright, William Donald, journalist, agriculturalist (b at South Cayuga, Ont 5 Aug 1881; d at Haney, BC 29 Apr 1946). A graduate of the Ontario Agricultural College (1903), Albright was assistant editor of the *Maritime Farmer* (1903-05) and associate editor of the *Farmer's Advocate* (1905-13) before he homesteaded in the Beaverlodge Valley of NW Alberta in 1913. His successful experiments with crops thought unlikely to mature in the region came to the attention of the Dept of Agriculture, and led to the establishment of an experimental substation on his farm in 1916. Thereafter, as director of the station (1919-45), he worked to demonstrate that attractive homes and good living conditions could be maintained in the PEACE RIVER LOWLAND, testing potentially profitable forage and cereal crops and encouraging the planting of gardens as well as small fruit and ornamental trees and bushes.

STANLEY GORDON

Reading: E.C. Stacey, *Peace Country Heritage* (1974).

Alcan Aluminium Limited, with head offices in Montréal, is a multinational enterprise engaged, through subsidiary and related companies, in all major segments of the ALUMINUM business, including bauxite mining, alumina refining and aluminum smelting and fabricating. In 1902 the Northern Aluminium Company was incorporated in Shawinigan Falls, Qué, as a Canadian subsidiary of the Aluminum Company of America. In 1925 it became the Aluminium Company of Canada, Ltd. In 1928 it became a corporation by acquiring all outstanding stock from its parent, and eventually emerged as a major competitor to the Aluminum Company of America. The present name was adopted in 1966.

Alcan is one of the largest aluminum producers in the non-communist world. In Canada, where the bulk of its aluminum smelting capacity is located, the company generates a significant share of its electricity requirements from its own hydroelectric facilities. This relatively low cost energy source enables Alcan to rank as one of the lowest cost aluminum producers in the Western world. In 1985, Alcan had sales of $8.2 billion (converted from US$), assets of $9.8 billion and 67 000 employees. Shares are broadly held and foreign ownership stands at 57%.

DEBORAH C. SAWYER

Alcoholism is a behaviour pattern characterized by uncontrolled drinking of alcoholic beverages to the extent of impairing health and social functioning. Alcoholism is thus one extreme in a range of drinking patterns that vary among individuals in degree of dependency and tolerance, and in a host of other ways, eg, timing, beverage choice. Groups and countries also differ in drinking patterns, norms and standards, and forms of regulation and control. The term "problem drinker" is used to refer to persons not necessarily physically addicted to alcohol but experiencing (or causing) health, social or other problems.

History of the Use of Alcohol The process of fermenting sugar-containing liquids to make alcohol has been known since the beginning of recorded history and is today practised by many preliterate people around the world. The ancient Egyptians drank both wines and beers, as did earlier peoples elsewhere in the Middle East. Of 139 societies around the world, at least 121 apparently consume alcohol in some beverage form. Stronger drinks, produced by distilling fermented liquids, likely first appeared during the Middle Ages in the Middle East or South Asia (*see* DISTILLING INDUSTRY).

Sociologists have found that the amount of drinking differs among the societies of the world, and that this variation can be explained by tech-

nological complexity and other factors. Although more advanced societies are more likely to use alcohol, drunkenness is more widespread among less complex societies, apparently because of anxiety induced by the uncertainties and other hazards of subsistence. The introduction of distilled beverages from Europe has also tended to disrupt traditional drinking practices in non-Western societies. More controlled drinking is associated with tighter social organization, particularly where alcohol use is incorporated symbolically into collective ceremonies. In industrial societies, the greater personal freedom and wealth people enjoy, together with the requirement for more organized and tightly scheduled work activity, has led to pressure to regulate and limit alcohol use.

Scientific Perspectives on Alcohol Use Ethanol, popularly known as "alcohol," is actually one of a class of organic compounds consisting of a hydroxyl group attached to a carbon atom. Ethyl alcohol (CH_3CH_2OH) is the principal pharmacological ingredient of alcoholic beverages. Other alcohols and related substances are present in small quantities, and these may contribute to the physiological and psychological effects of alcohol, including the "hangover." One ingredient, thujone, a component of wormwood oil, is a potent intoxicant present in absinthe and in lesser quantities in vermouth. In wines, yeast acts on natural sugars to produce ethanol; wines are made not only from grapes, but from many other fruits as well, and have a maximum alcohol content of about 14%, as this is the concentration at which yeast is killed (*see* WINE INDUSTRY). Fortification, in which a portion of the must is distilled and then returned to the original liquid, can increase the alcohol content of wine, as in the production of sherry. Beers are typically lower in alcohol content and are produced from starchy plants by first breaking down, with the help of an enzyme, the complex carbohydrates into simpler sugars. Finally, beverages containing up to 95% alcohol can be produced by distillation, ie, the heating of a fermented liquid to the point that the portion containing ethanol will evaporate and condense back to a liquid state. Popular distilled beverages in Canada include rum, made from sugar cane, and whisky, produced from barley and other grains.

An alcoholic beverage is absorbed rapidly into the bloodstream through the stomach wall and the small intestine because it does not undergo any digestive processes. The rate of absorption can be modified by, among other factors, the type and amount of food present in the stomach. Recent ingestion of a fatty meal substantially slows absorption of alcohol. From the blood, alcohol is distributed to all parts of the body and absorbed until an equilibrium is achieved between the alcohol in the blood and that in various organs. Alcohol is eliminated slightly (10%) through expiration, perspiration and urination, but most of it is metabolized in the liver, ultimately producing water, carbon dioxide and energy.

The degree of intoxication produced by ethanol reflects the concentration of alcohol in the blood, which is primarily a function of the amount ingested, the volume of blood in the body, rates of absorption and metabolism, and time since ingestion. Depending on body weight, an adult male could have a blood alcohol concentration of 0.06% after 3 typical drinks of an alcoholic beverage. Findings on physiological and psychological correlations of these small doses of ethanol are inconsistent, but at larger doses there is no doubt that alcohol becomes a central nervous-system depressant. The evidence suggests that a blood alcohol level of 0.1% affects some of the motor areas of the brain, eg, speech, balance and manual dexterity. An alcohol concentration of 0.2% de-

presses all the motor centres and that area concerned with emotions. At 0.45% the entire area concerned with perception is depressed and coma results. At 0.7% the centres controlling heartbeat and breathing are depressed and the person dies.

In general, the findings of psychological studies of the effects of ethanol, particularly at lower doses, on complex behaviour (eg, aggression, sex) are difficult to interpret. Research on the effects of alcohol on emotions and "moods" are likewise inconclusive. Many laboratory studies have ignored the situational variables, eg, the presence of others, social relationships with these people, and so forth, that set the context for drinking in everyday life. There is also evidence that a person's expectations of the effects of alcohol play a large part in the quality of the drinking experience.

Studies of national drinking patterns and cross-cultural research on alcohol use have revealed considerable societal variation in behavioural responses to alcohol. The definitions held by a group or a society about the functions, uses and effects of alcohol almost certainly significantly affect the responses of persons to dietary alcohol. In some societies, eg, Italy, where alcohol is defined largely as a food, wine is consumed with meals and seems to have little disruptive effect on behaviour. In Scandinavia, especially Finland, alcoholic beverages are traditionally defined as intoxicants, and the consumption of distilled beverages, largely apart from meals, can lead to explosive or violent episodes. In beer-drinking countries of Europe and N America, alcohol is largely defined as a facilitator of social interaction. However, it would be premature to conclude that the strength or type of beverage is the direct or indirect cause of behavioural response. Among certain rural Bolivians, for instance, the normal beverage contains 95% alcohol, and yet the response to gross intoxication in social situations to this unusually strong drink is passiveness, and disruptive behaviour is extremely rare.

Alcoholism and Alcohol Abuse Researchers approach the problem of alcoholism from a variety of perspectives: biological (how alcohol affects the body), psychological (how it affects the mind) and sociological (how alcohol is provided and consumed in society). It is clear that some persons develop a tolerance for alcohol, ie, increasing amounts are required to achieve the same degree of perceived intoxication. Some people also become dependent on alcohol; a change occurs in their body cells, which have become adapted to alcohol. Withdrawal symptoms include craving, shakiness and increased anxiety (the hangover can be considered a mild form of withdrawal). More extreme reactions to cessation of long periods of heavy drinking can include nausea, vomiting and seizures. Delerium tremens ("DTs"), which combines several of these withdrawal symptoms, can include hallucinations and other unpleasant sensations.

Some chronic problems resulting from prolonged heavy drinking are considered manifestations of alcoholism; these include nutritional deficiencies, digestive problems, inflammation of the liver and pancreas, anemia, impotence, neurological dysfunctions and the newly discovered fetal alcohol syndrome. Other problems related to heavy drinking include motor vehicle crashes, other forms of accidental death and injury, suicide and crime (*see* IMPAIRED DRIVING).

Despite much research, the causes of alcoholism remain obscure. Alcoholism, in fact, is better conceived as a set of related problems, each of which differs somewhat in characteristics, causes, prognosis and treatment. Cultural factors, eg, religion, attitudes toward alcohol, and drinking problems, are related to rates of alcoholism. Social phenomena, such as the practices of family and friends and the nature and strength of punishments and rewards for drinking, also affect alcohol use and abuse. Limitations or inducements regarding the availability of alcohol, such as income and regulations on manufacture, distribution and sales, appear in some studies to influence the extent of drinking and alcohol problems. Individuals also differ in their predisposition to alcohol intoxication and dependence, and for this reason much psychological and physiological research has been conducted. There is little evidence, however, that certain personality types are predisposed to alcoholism.

Drinking in Canada About 80% of Canadian adults consume alcoholic beverages at least occasionally. Canada has been classified internationally as a beer-drinking country, as beer and ale account for 51% of the consumption of absolute alcohol. Another 32% represents use of distilled spirits. Although in countries such as Turkey, Poland and Israel the majority of alcohol consumed is in the form of spirits, in absolute terms Canadians are among the world's leaders in spirits consumption also, since many of the countries specializing in spirits have relatively low levels of alcohol consumption overall. Canadians on average drink only 11 litres of wine apiece annually, compared with 84 in Portugal and 88 in France. In general, however, the drinking patterns of the countries of the world are becoming more similar to one another; in Canada this means that consumption of beer has been declining and that of wine increasing. Canada is generally similar to northwestern European industrial countries in alcohol consumption levels.

Canadians drank 10 litres of absolute alcohol per adult in 1986, a slight decrease from previous years, although in 1950 the figure was less than 7 litres per capita. Nevertheless, alcohol use in most countries, including Canada, is relatively moderate today compared with that of the 18th and 19th centuries. It is difficult to obtain figures on early drinking in Canada. In the 1870s provinces officially recorded only about 5 litres per year, but this statistic does not include home-manufactured cider and beer, which in a largely rural, agrarian country could have accounted for a major proportion of consumption. Moreover, in other countries, such as Sweden and the US, the growth of the TEMPERANCE MOVEMENT in the 19th century coincided with a trend of falling alchohol intake. Earlier, in the 1830s in a typical district of Upper Canada (Bathurst), there were 6 distilleries serving the area. Each of these produced about 60 gallons a day of whiskey and other spirits, which would yield a per capita consumption of 13.4 litres of ethanol for people over age 15. This figure is half the official American consumption of 26.9 litres in 1830, but the Canadian (Bathurst) figure does not include beer, cider or wine. Thus, although alcohol consumption has increased since the end of prohibition, it has levelled off and is probably far less than the high levels of consumption prior to the beginning of the temperance movement. Moreover, the types of beverages consumed have been changing, reflecting a long-term trend away from distilled and toward milder beverages.

It has been estimated that there are approximately 600 000 alcoholics in Canada (about 4% of adult drinkers), a figure calculated from the known incidence of mortality caused by cirrhosis of the liver, and therefore probably a conservative estimate. International comparisons of alcoholism generally rely on data on cirrhosis of the liver (the "Jellinek formula"), and it is known that cirrhosis rates are highly correlated with overall consumption levels. Therefore, rates of alcoholism for the countries of the world generally reflect consumption levels, so alcoholism in Canada is about average for Western countries. About 2400 persons annually die in Canada from cirrhosis of the liver, which is equivalent to a death rate per year of 9.5 per 100 000 population. A few hundred more die of other alcohol-related conditions (poisoning, automobile accidents, etc). Rates of death caused by cirrhosis of the liver increase markedly with age and are higher in urban areas and in the West and North, the areas with the highest levels of alcohol consumption in Canada.

Canada is a complex and varied country and it manifests considerable variation in drinking practices. Canadians say they have about 6 drinks per week on the average, although this is undoubtedly an underestimation. Men, however, drink 3 times as much alcohol on the average as do women. In the more traditional Atlantic region the sexes differ by a factor of 4, whereas in BC the sex difference in drinking is less. These reported sex differences in consumption must be treated cautiously, but death rates for cirrhosis are also twice as high for males. English-speaking Canadians drink more than linguistic minorities. For males, alcohol consumption peaks in the fifth and sixth decades of life, whereas the amount of drinking declines steadily with age for women. Married people drink less than the single, divorced or separated.

Other factors appear to influence alcohol use, in particular social class and religion. For women, increases in the level of education, income and occupational skill lead to a greater use of alcohol, although studies suggest that a higher proportion of female heavy drinkers are found in the low-income population. Men in the intermediate levels of occupation and education have the highest levels of alcohol consumption. Jews are the least likely to abstain from alcohol of any religious group, but they also have the lowest rates of alcoholism. This immunity to addiction seems to result from the ritual uses that alcohol is put to in orthodox religious practice. Persons with no religious affiliations are the heaviest drinkers. For men, recent illness is more common among heavier drinkers, whereas the reverse is true for women; this difference probably merely reflects, however, the increase in illness with age and the different effects of aging on alcohol use for men in contrast to women.

Responses to Alcohol Problems Prior to the 19th century in Canada, the use of alcohol was largely taken for granted, and cider, beer and wine were consumed every day. Addiction to alcohol was ignored, since regular use of beverage alcohol was the accepted norm. The exception to this generalization was the early attempts (by both French and British authorities) to regulate the drinking of native people. The drinking of distilled spirits had become more common by the turn of the 19th century, and temperance movements in Britain and the US advocated moderation in the use of alcoholic beverages. The churches, particularly the Baptists and Methodists, became active in the temperance cause, which eventually advocated total abstention from alcohol and the legal prohibition of the "liquor traffic." At this point, conflict between social groups (eg, religious, ethnic and political) began to affect the debate, and plebiscites for prohibition revealed large interprovincial differences in support of the measure. Québec was overwhelmingly opposed to prohibition, while PEI and NS were heavily in favour. Prohibition of spirits became national policy during WWI, although much illicit manufacture and evasion occurred.

Shortly after WWI the provinces began replacing prohibitory legislation with a system of government-controlled distribution and licensing. The ostensible purpose of this role for government was maintenance of public health and order, but the actual function today is largely one of raising revenue and dispensing political patronage. Research does show, however, that the pricing policies and the control of the hours and days of sale do have some impact on alcohol consumption and problems.

Treatment of Alcoholism A variety of programs to treat alcohol-related problems exists in Canada. Some programs treat alcoholics directly, while others offer referrals to treatment facilities, provide counselling for families of alcoholics or provide programs on alcoholism prevention, drinking and driving, etc. Alcoholics Anonymous (AA) and a variety of government-sponsored programs (some affiliated with health-care institutions, others existing only to treat alcoholism) are directly concerned with providing assistance to alcoholics. Government programs have been classified as, first, detoxification, ie, inpatient care for 2 or 3 days; second, short-term residential, ie, inpatient treatment or rehabilitation for a few days or weeks; third, long-term residential; and fourth, outpatient clinics. Outpatient clinics account for over 33% of facilities; 30% of programs are long-term residential and include halfway houses and rural retreats. Nationally, there are about 350 such programs, which admit about 200 new cases per facility annually. About 10% of Canada's addicted population is treated annually by one or another of the alcoholism programs. Males are 6 times as likely as females to be admitted and the mean age of admission is 44 years.

The costs and benefits of a commodity such as beverage alcohol can be analyzed in economic and non-economic terms. Through its monopolies on sales, the governments of Canada earn in excess of $3 billion a year in profits, about two thirds going to the provinces. Some revenues also accrue to farmers growing fruits and grains, as well as to brewers, vintners and distillers, and to the beverage service industry. Workers in alcohol production earn a half-billion dollars in wages and salaries, and alcohol advertising is a big business. Exports of Canadian spirits, particularly whiskey, and more recently beer, have earned valuable foreign exchange. On the negative side, costs to the Canadian health-care system that are directly or indirectly attributable to alcohol have been estimated at $2 billion. Alcohol abuse has also been blamed for excessive costs in other areas such as law enforcement, social welfare and traffic accidents. Lost production in industry due to alcohol probably costs more than $1 billion a year. Many costs and benefits are more difficult to quantify. Wine is indispensable to religious ceremonies in some groups, but is considered anathema by others. Social and psychological benefits of alcohol use are obvious, as is the harm caused by excessive and intemperate use. Moderate drinkers are less liable to suffer heart problems than abstainers and they appear to be healthier and live longer on the average. Heavy drinkers suffer many health problems and have a shorter life expectancy.

Types of Therapy Therapies for alcoholism include drugs (eg, Antabuse), which cause unpleasant reactions in the drinker; individual psychotherapy; behavioural techniques (eg, learned aversion); and group therapy. The efficacy of these therapies is controversial.

Typically, about a third of alcoholics appear to recover or improve after treatment, but estimates may only reflect the fact that the severity of a drinking problem tends to fluctuate and individuals generally seek treatment during acute phases of their condition. There is really not even a consensus on what constitutes "improvement." Although some researchers claim that alcoholics can tolerate "social" drinking, this notion runs counter to the ideology of AA, a widespread and reportedly successful self-help organization for alcoholics. Among its tenets is a firm emphasis on helping other alcoholics, which contributes to morale and solidarity among AA members.

RONALD L. COSPER

Reading: J. Royce, *Alcohol Problems and Alcoholism* (1981); W. Schmidt, R. Smart and A.C. Ogbourne, *Northern Spirits. Drinking in Canada Then and Now* (1986).

Speckled alder (*Alnus rugosa*), with male flowers (left), female flowers (centre) and cones on the right (*artwork by Claire Tremblay*).

Alder, TREE or shrub of genus *Alnus* of BIRCH family. The 30 known species are found mainly in the Northern Hemisphere; 3 are native to Canada. Speckled alder (*A. rugosa*) is a transcontinental shrub and the most common Canadian alder. Red alder (*A. rubra*) is a small, short-lived tree of western BC and Green alder (*A. crispa*) is a transcontinental northern shrub. The Sitka alder (*A. crispa* ssp. *sinuata*) is found in BC mountains, and is considered by some to be a distinct species (*A. sinuata*). The genus displays birchlike characteristics, eg, shallow roots, horizontal bark markings (lenticels) and elongated spring catkins (cylindrical reproductive structures). Alders occupy moist sites and have nitrogen-fixing root nodules. They are distinguished by stalked buds, twig cores somewhat triangular in cross section, and fruiting bodies resembling miniature cones. Healers, artisans and warriors used alders. The bark has been used as a throat medicine; the wood for cabinets and for bridge foundations because of endurance under water; and the charcoal as a constituent of gunpowder. ROGER VICK

Alderdice, Frederick Charles, businessman, politician (b at Belfast, Ire 10 Nov 1872: d at St John's 26 Feb 1936). He was twice prime minister of Newfoundland, Aug-Nov 1928 and June 1932-Feb 1934, and the last person to hold that office before confederation with Canada. A prominent St John's businessman, he entered the Legislative Council in 1924 and assumed the Liberal-Conservative party leadership and the prime ministership on the retirement of Walter MONROE in 1928. Alderdice was defeated by Richard SQUIRES in the ensuing general election but remained leader of the opposition United Newfoundland Party. Newfoundland had been in financial difficulties since WWI and by 1932 international credit had all but disappeared. On 5 Apr 1932, in a climate of unemployment, widespread distress and accusations of government misconduct, there was rioting in St John's outside

the legislature. The House was subsequently prorogued, and in the June elections Alderdice's party defeated Squires 25 seats to 2. With Newfoundland facing imminent bankruptcy, Alderdice appealed to Britain for financial aid and the appointment of a royal commission to consider Newfoundland's future. The resulting Amulree Report of 1933 recommended the temporary suspension of responsible government. The Newfoundland legislature agreed, and on 16 Feb 1934 a COMMISSION OF GOVERNMENT was instituted and continued for 15 years composed of 3 Newfoundlanders, 3 Britishers and the governor. Alderdice was appointed a commissioner. ROBERT D. PITT

Alderfly, small, dark, soft-bodied INSECT of order Megaloptera, family Sialidae, found in freshwater habitats bordered by ALDER. It is characterized by 2 pairs of veined, membranous wings, chewing mouthparts, large eyes and long, many-segmented antennae. Adults may not feed and are short-lived. Alderflies are most active at midday. They deposit 200-500 dark brown eggs in rows forming large masses on branches or other objects near water. Larvae hatch in 10-14 days and drop or make their way to water. Larvae are aquatic, preferring muddy bottoms. They have chewing mouthparts and are predaceous. The larval stage may require 2-3 years to complete. Fully grown larvae pupate in a cell in soil, moss, under stones, etc, usually near water. About one month is spent in the pupal period. Adults appear in early summer and are feeble fliers. Of the 10 species found in Canada, *Sialis velata* is the most widely distributed (BC to Qué). Larvae and adults are food for many freshwater fish and provide bait for anglers. J.E.H. MARTIN

Alert, NWT, Canadian military base located at the N end of ELLESMERE I on rugged terrain surrounded by hills and valleys. The shoreline is composed of slate and shale while the offshore is covered with pack ice throughout the summer months. The site was first visited by Sir George NARES, who commanded HMS *Alert* in 1875-76, the first vessel to land on the shores of northern Ellesmere I. In 1950, the Canadian government established a weather station at Alert. It was taken over by the military in 1958. The military continues to use the base year-round, but does not reveal the number of men or the technology present at the site for reasons of security. Access to Alert is restricted to military personnel.

EDWARD STRUZIK

The Nares Expedition (1875) at lat 79°39′ N, in Dobbin Bay [NWT]. HMS *Alert* was the first vessel to land on the shores of northern Ellesmere I (*courtesy National Archives of Canada/C-52521*).

Alert Bay, BC, Village, pop 679 (1986c), 626 (1981c), inc 1946, is located on Cormorant I, off Vancouver I, 288 km N of VANCOUVER. Its sheltered bay first attracted KWAKIUTL Indians who used the area as a winter dwelling; the village has a striking collection of TOTEM POLES, including the tallest in the world. It is one of the most important fishing areas in BC and is also supported by logging, mining and tourism. ALAN F.J. ARTIBISE

Alexander, Harold Rupert Leofric George, 1st Earl Alexander of Tunis, army officer, governor general (b at London, Eng 10 Dec 1891; d at Slough, Eng 16 June 1969). The last British governor general of Canada (1946-52) was born into the Irish aristocracy. A regimental officer in the Irish Guards during WWI, he had once hoped to be a professional artist, but the war made him a committed soldier. By 1937 he was the youngest major-general in the British army. He led the 1st Division in France in 1940 and the rearguard at Dunkirk, directed the British-Chinese army's retreat from the Japanese invasion of Burma (1942), and from Aug 1942 was senior army commander in the Mediterranean. He was slated to become chief of the Imperial General Staff after the war, but British PM Winston Churchill claimed that "Canada is a much more important post." Handsome, athletic, elegant, and assisted by a popular wife, Lady Margaret, Alexander made a strong public impression as governor general. At ease in an essentially ceremonial role, he travelled widely and led a relaxed life, with ample time to ski, fish and paint. On his return to England he was unenthusiastic minister of defence in the Churchill government, 1952-54.

O.A. COOKE AND NORMAN HILLMER

Alexander, Lincoln MacCauley, lawyer, parliamentarian, public servant, lieutenant-governor of Ont (b at Toronto 21 Jan 1922). Born of West Indian immigrant parents, Alexander grew up in an Ontario in which exceptional blacks could occasionally leap the barriers set by discrimination. When he joined the RCAF, for example, in 1942, that service still had a formal provision restricting non-whites. With a BA from McMaster and a law degree from Osgoode Hall, Alexander practised law and entered politics as Conservative MP for Hamilton West in 1968, becoming the first black Canadian to sit in the House of Commons. He later became minister of labour in the Clark government in 1979. In 1980 he left elected office to become chairman of the Ontario Workers' Compensation Board, a post he held until appointed lieutenant-governor of Ontario in 1985. As lieutenant-governor, he has been better able to take a more active role in the multicultural affairs of Ontario. JAMES W. ST.G. WALKER

Alexander, William, Earl of Stirling, poet, courtier, colonizer (b at Menstrie, Scot *c* 1577; d at London, Eng 1640). Although he never visited N America, he is remembered for his nationalistic foresight, and for providing Nova Scotia with its name, flag and coat of arms. Sir William envisaged colonization as an answer to Scottish expansion, comparable to the contemporary, successful English ventures. Enjoying the support of both James I and Charles I, he was granted territory (1621), necessary funding through the sale of knight-baronetcies (1624), and armorial bearings for the province (1625). Financial problems, the reluctance of Scots to emigrate and French territorial claims all hampered development. Although Sir William's son established 2 brief settlements, in Cape Breton and at PORT-ROYAL (Annapolis Royal), the entire grant was sacrificed to the French in 1632 in return for full payment of Charles I's marriage settlement. LOIS KERNAGHAN

Reading: John G. Reid, *Acadia, Maine and New Scotland* (1981).

Alexandria, Ont, Town, pop 3246 (1986c), 3271 (1981c), inc 1903, located midway on the CNR rail line between Montréal and Ottawa. Father Alexander Macdonell, later bishop of Upper Canada, began the town (first known as Priest's Mills) as a mill site a few years after the War of 1812. In 1890 it became the seat of the Roman Catholic diocese of Alexandria (later relocated at

Cornwall). Around that time it showed much promise in carriage manufacturing. After economic setbacks in the Great Depression and earlier, Alexandria since WWII has regained a considerable degree of prosperity with a concentration on textiles, footwear, milk processing and trucking. It continues its early role as a merchandising and service centre for the surrounding farm community. About two-thirds of the population are French Canadian, but both English and French are spoken. St Finnan's Cathedral, the Bishop's Palace and the Monastery of the Precious Blood are of architectural interest.

ROYCE MACGILLIVRAY

Reading: Royce MacGillivray and Ewan Ross, *A History of Glengarry* (1979).

Alfalfa, or lucerne (genus *Medicago*), herbaceous perennial belonging to the LEGUME family and grown as a FORAGE CROP. It evolved in central Asia, an area with cold winters and hot, dry summers, and spread to Europe, East Asia, Africa and the New World. The major commercial species are *M. sativa* and *M. falcata.* Alfalfa flowers range from purple to yellow and are borne on a long raceme (ie, structure composed of short stalks spaced equally along a central axis). The seed pods are spiral shaped; small, kidney-shaped seeds are produced. The trifoliate leaves are arranged alternately on the stem. The root system is characterized by a deep taproot which, under favourable drainage conditions, may penetrate 7.5 m. The erect stems usually grow 60-90 cm high; regrowth after cutting is very rapid, even in hot summers. When alfalfa is cut for silage or hay, at the later flower-bud stage, the protein content may vary from 10% to 20%. Since 1950, many improved cultivars have been bred to increase alfalfa use in Canada. The yellow-flowered *M. falcata* has been developed for dry-land prairie; blue-flowered *M. sativa* has been made disease and insect resistant to maintain hectarages in areas of Canada with favourable temperature, drainage and soil acidity. Yield varies greatly with temperature and moisture conditions: eg, in the Edmonton area, 2 cuts yield 5136 kg/ha; in Winnipeg, 6787 kg/ha; in Guelph, 3 cuts yield 13 619 kg/ha. Alfalfa will continue to be the most important forage for DAIRY cattle. (Alfalfa sprouts have also become a popular addition to salads and sandwiches.) W.R. CHILDERS

Algae, aquatic organisms that manufacture food by photosynthesis and have relatively simple morphology and unprotected reproductive structures. When conducting tissue is present, it does not contain lignin (compound typical of cell walls of woody plants). The algae, a heterogeneous group, were once included entirely in the PLANT kingdom; however, the present-day 5-kingdom division categorizes BLUE-GREEN ALGAE as monerans, others as protistans. Most researchers still consider certain algae to be properly classed as plants.

Classification

Algae are classified primarily on the basis of biochemical and cytological (cell) differences, which show that some algae are not related as closely to one another as to other organisms. Features used include pigments present (in addition to chlorophyll *a*; storage reserves; nature of cell covering; and presence and location of organelles (cell parts analogous to organs). The generally accepted classification scheme recognizes 4 divisions, primarily based on the presence of specific cell organelles. Within each division, classification is based on biochemical features and cell details. Not all phycologists [Gk, *phykos,* "seaweed"; *logos,* "discourse"] accept this system; there is a

Fucus, a brown algae, commonly called rockweed (*courtesy National Museums of Canada/National Museum of Natural Sciences, artwork by Linda Gowens-Crane*).

tendency to recognize more divisions (7-12), each with fewer classes. The lack of membrane-bound organelles distinguishes the blue-green algae. Rhodophyta are characterized by the complete absence of flagella (organelles for motility). Chromophyta and Chlorophyta are differentiated by pigmentation. The traditional divisions, each containing several classes, are discussed below.

Rhodophyta [Gk, *rhodo,* "red"] occur mostly in marine habitats, often dominating lower intertidal and subtidal regions. Most red algae consist of rows of intertwining cells, linked in a series end to end (as filaments). Cells have a characteristic appearance as cell walls are very thick and swell at death. Individual cells appear to be interconnected by thin strands penetrating the cell walls. Sexual reproduction is common for most species with a complex life history. Cell walls contain agar and carrageenan, used in various industries to stabilize emulsions, coat various materials, etc. Carrageenan is harvested from coastal areas in PEI and NS. The NATIONAL RESEARCH COUNCIL has actively encouraged the establishment of SEAWEED farming of IRISH MOSS. Coralline red algae, an integral component of living CORAL reefs, deposit calcium carbonate in their cell walls. In the Orient one red alga, *nori,* is a prized food. An attempt has been made to provide high-quality *nori* from BC for Japanese markets.

Chromophyta [Gk, *chroma,* "colour"] have a yellow-brown colour resulting from the dominant pigments, including certain carotenoids and chlorophyll c_2. All Chromophyta have complex flagella. The number, form and insertion of these flagella are used to distinguish classes. In some classes, sexual reproduction is unknown. Most classes are primarily unicellular, and are an important component of phytoplankton (small, drifting aquatic plants). Bacillariophyceae (diatoms) occur not only as PLANKTON, but also as benthic (bottom-dwelling) forms. Cell walls contain silica; massive amounts of diatom walls form deposits of diatomaceous earth, used for grinding and polishing or as insulating material. One member of class Xanthophyceae, mustard alga, is known to swimming-pool owners. Another well-known organism, *Euglena* (Euglenophyceae), with both animallike and plantlike features (motility and photosynthesis, respectively), has been variously classified as Chromophyta, Chlorophyta or Euglenophyta.

The Phaeophyceae [Gk, *phaios,* "dusky"] or brown algae, largest group of Chromophyta, dominate cold coastal waters. The intertidal and subtidal Canadian waters abound with representatives of this class; 2 orders are particularly obvious, Laminariales (kelps) and Fucales (rockweeds). Various marine animals live in the large

kelp beds. In arctic and subarctic regions, kelps and rockweeds predominate. The largest and most structurally complex algae belong to these classes; specialized conducting and reproductive cells are present. Sexual reproduction occurs commonly and the life history is usually plantlike, showing alternation of generations or phases. Cell walls contain algin, especially in the kelps abundant along BC coasts. The BC government is studying the possibility of commercial harvesting. In China and Japan kelps (*kombu* and *wakame*) are used as food.

Chlorophyta [G *chloros,* "green"] contain most genera and show most diversity. They may be divided into several classes, separated primarily by morphological and cytological features. Green algae in freshwater and terrestrial habitats are generally microscopic and morphologically simpler than those growing in marine habitats. Masses of green algae form pond scums. Commonly, the algal component of LICHENS is a member of class Chlorophyceae. The life history of the freshwater green algae involves extensive asexual reproduction; the zygote is often only a resistant stage, able to last through periods unfavourable for growth and reproduction. Most marine green algae have either the typical plantlike or animallike life history and lack the resistant zygote.

Charophyceae (stoneworts) occur in the FOSSIL record as calcified remains of female reproductive structures. Stoneworts are restricted to freshwater and some estuarine habitats and are generally microscopic. They are probably similar to the progenitors of vascular plants. As a class, the Charophyceae might be expanded to include some of the Chlorophyceae that have cell features more similar to vascular plants than to the majority of green algae.

Cyanophyta, or blue-green algae, are monerans, ie, prokaryotic cells lacking membrane-bound nuclei. Many researchers consider them to be a special class of bacteria.

Structure and Function

Algal cells may be covered by rigid walls, series of plates, strips or scales. The basic wall consists of carbohydrates, often combined with proteins. Wall composition may involve inorganic materials (eg, silicon, calcium). Certain compounds, phycocolloids [Gk *kollodes,* "glue"], abundant in cells of red and brown algae, are commercially marketed (ie, agar, algin, carrageenan). Storage reserves are also usually carbohydrates (eg, glucose, starch). Fats, oils and proteins may be present but less is known about them.

Chlorophyll *a* is the principal photosynthetic pigment, but accessory pigments allow absorption of light energy at different wavelengths; such energy is transferred to chlorophyll *a* for photosynthesis. Accessory pigments may be soluble in water or organic compounds (eg, alcohol). Water-soluble pigments, the phycobiliproteins [Lat *bilis,* "bile"], are restricted in occurrence; organic-soluble pigments occur in all algae.

Cytological variation among algae includes presence and nature of flagella on some cells. Reproductive cells commonly are flagellated, as are some vegetative cells. A flagellum may be smooth or may have tubular hairs along most of its length. The way the flagella are inserted on the cell is also important in classification.

Many algae reproduce primarily by asexual means, often producing great numbers of organisms in a relatively short time. Such occurrences are termed blooms. Many algae have sexual reproduction as a normal part of their life history. Cells producing reproductive cells have no protective covering of sterile tissue and vegetative cells often become reproductive. Gametes (sex

Algae, Pacific Rim National Park, BC (*photo by J.A. Kraulis*).

cells) may be identical in appearance or different enough to be considered male and female. In the latter instance the smaller, often motile gamete is male. Gametes are normally dispersed freely in water; the zygote is unprotected by parent cells. Some algae, primarily those growing in marine environments, produce 2 multicellular generations, as do terrestrial plants. Other algae produce only one recognizable stage. Some of these have a life history similar to that of most animals, in which gametes are produced by meiosis or reduction division (ie, cells have half of the genetic makeup of the parent cell); hence, fertilization is necessary. Still other algae, primarily those in freshwater habitats, produce gametes by mitosis; the resultant complete single cell of the zygote has the same genetic makeup as the parent cell.

Distribution

Algae have worldwide distribution, growing wherever light and water are present. Their most obvious occurrences are on rocky coasts of all continents (except Antarctica) and as scums of lakes and ponds. Canada's Pacific coast has a richer algal flora than the Atlantic coast, which generally has fewer and smaller species. Distribution on the inner coast differs from that of the open coast, primarily because of differences in salinity. Subarctic and arctic marine algae are more restricted in all ways; there is little growth in unprotected areas. In Canadian marine areas, summer is characterized by the presence of large numbers of algae, the increase being especially noteworthy wherever ice masses occur in winter. The depths to which algae grow depend on light penetration. In coastal estuaries, algae have reduced reproductive potential and are morphologically different from those of open waters.

Open waters, marine or fresh, contain forms too small to be seen without a microscope. Usually unicellular and known as phytoplankton [Gk *phyton*, "plant"; *planktos*, "wandering"], they are primary food producers for ZOOPLANKTON [Gk *zoe*, "life"]. Phytoplankton are usually not present in large masses and must be concentrated to be studied. Members of the Chromophyta are the most common phytoplankton, Dinophyceae and Bacillariophyceae predominating. Phytoplankton can form blooms, eg, red tides composed primarily of Dinophyceae. In inshore waters, such as some BC coastal inlets, the Bay of Fundy or St Lawrence estuary, dinoflagellate blooms produce a toxin which may be concentrated by shellfish feeding on them. Eating the shellfish can cause paralysis and death to seabirds and mammals (including humans).

Canada contains more than 25% of the Earth's fresh water, mainly in lakes and rivers. Phytoplankton in lakes generally are limited to open water, unless the shoreline slopes gradually and contains areas of sediment where rooted aquatic plants can grow. Generally, the larger the ratio of sediment surface to water volume, the more productive the water body. Productivity refers to the number of organisms present and to their physiological activities of growth and reproduction. As phytoplankton are food for zooplankton, which in turn are eaten by fish, attempts to increase phytoplankton production have been undertaken in lakes where commercially important fish live or reproduce.

Studies done in BC and Ontario show that increases in fish size and numbers occur when nursery lakes are fertilized with nitrogen and phosphorus (*see* AQUACULTURE). Rocky or sandy lake shores provide few nutrients for algal growth. The cool, acidic waters of sphagnum bogs are relatively rich in certain of the Chlorophyceae, Chrysophyceae and Xanthophyceae (*see* SWAMP, MARSH AND BOG). In general, large rivers are poor habitats for algae, except in backwater areas or along shores. Slower-moving rivers may have some phytoplankton and some algal growth along shores if sediment is sufficiently stable. Fast-moving mountain streams usually have a specific algal flora, although large populations are rarely present.

Algae can also live in habitats where water occurs only as condensation, eg, dry soil, desert areas, rocks. In moist areas, some algae grow on trees and shrubs, stone, concrete and man-made objects. Some algae grow in hot mineral SPRINGS; some unicellular Chlorophyceae grow in ice and snow, eg, red snow seen in summer in old, melting snowbanks in the mountains of BC and Alberta. A few grow in high concentrations of various chemicals (eg, sodium, magnesium, chlorine, sulphur) as in prairie water bodies that lose water only by evaporation. A few algae live on or in other organisms. *See also* VEGETATION REGIONS.　　JANET STEIN

Reading: F.E. Round, *Ecology of Algae* (1981).

Algoma Central Railway was chartered in 1899 by F.H. CLERGUE as a "feeder line" to his industrial-resource empire at Sault Ste Marie. Originally intended to haul ore, pulp and logs a distance of 260 km from the Michipicoten area of Lk Superior, the ACR fell victim to the bankruptcy of Clergue's Consolidated Lake Superior Corp in 1903. Transferred to the control of an English financial group, the line was gradually extended northward through rocky wilderness to junctions with the CPR and the CNR, ending in 1914 at Hearst, a distance of 470 km from the Soo. Three financial reorganizations were required before heavy initial debts were finally cleared in 1959. Since then, the ACR has become viable through diversification, its haulage of freight supplemented by shipping on the Great Lakes, regular tourist trips into the Agawa Canyon, the ownership and management of extensive forest reserves, and by revenue from real estate in the downtown core of Sault Ste Marie.　　ALBERT TUCKER

Algoma Steel Corporation Limited Algoma started producing steel in SAULT STE MARIE, Ont, to make rails for Canada's transcontinental railways. On 18 Feb 1902 the first steel was tapped and several months later the first rails rolled in Canada were produced. The plant then consisted of a 550 tpd (tonnes per day) Bessemer steel converter and a 900 tpd rail mill. Rails now account for less than 10% of the company's annual steel shipments. Algoma, a fully integrated steel producer, has 5 BOSFs (basic oxygen steelmaking furnaces) and Canada's largest blast furnace, which is over 30 storeys high and has a production capacity of over 5000 tpd of pig iron. Algoma's modern rolling facilities include a 422 cm wide plate mill, the widest in Canada, and over half its steel is sold as plate and sheet. Algoma is a long-established producer of structural shapes for the domestic CONSTRUCTION INDUSTRY. Its 1986 sales amounted to just over $1 billion and assets were $1.5 billion. It is 54% owned by Canadian Pacific. *See also* IRON AND STEEL INDUSTRY.
　　JOHN G. PEACEY

Algonquin (Algonkin) are a group of communities of Algonquian-speaking people living in western Québec and adjacent Ontario, centering on the OTTAWA R and its tributaries. They call themselves *Anissinapek* (*Anishinabeg*) or by the name of their local community. The Algonquin have been known to Europeans since 1603, when they were allies of the French and of the MONTAGNAIS-NASKAPI and HURON against the IROQUOIS. This conflict, which had its origins in the competition over the European FUR TRADE, lasted throughout much of the historic period.

Algonquin has been classified as a dialect of Ojibwa, one of the languages of the Algonquian family. As the dialects of Ojibwa merge one into another, it is not possible to establish a definite linguistic boundary between other Ojibwa dialects and Algonquin. However, the Algonquin are politically distinct from the OJIBWA. Neighbours of the Algonquin include CREE, OTTAWA, Huron and Iroquois. Since Algonquin bands or local communities were largely independent of one another, relations between an individual Algonquin band and other groups depended largely on local conditions. Marriages took place between Algonquin and other groups and generally relations between neighbouring bands were tempered by kinship ties regardless of language or tribal designations. Relationships with the Iroquois fluctuated, with hostilities most pronounced during the 17th and 18th centuries; however, some Algonquin resided alongside Catholic Iroquois at Oka, a mission reservation near Montréal.

The Algonquin were hunters who lived in bands consisting of related families. The bands were egalitarian, with leadership provided by respected individuals and heads of families. In the southern portion of their area where both climate and soils permitted, some bands practised gardening. During the historic period they became involved in the fur trade. Summer encampments near trading posts became larger and, as time spent trapping for furs increased, some necessities were purchased from the traders to supplement hunting and fishing. Their skills have led to employment in forestry and other industries in recent years. During the 19th century, modern INDIAN RESERVES and communities emerged, often near the former trading posts. Hostilities with Iroquoians ceased as Algonquin and Iroquois worked together for the betterment of conditions for Indians as a whole. More recently the Algonquin have joined with the Cree and others to strive for mutual goals as various development projects threaten their traditional way of life. A calculated estimate places the contemporary Algonquin population at about 3258. *See also* NATIVE PEOPLE: EASTERN WOODLANDS and general articles under NATIVE PEOPLE.　　MEREDITH JEAN BLACK

Reading: B.G. Trigger, ed, *The Handbook of North American Indians*, vol 15: *Northeast* (1978).

Algonquin Provincial Park, Ont, established in 1893 (*courtesy Ontario Ministry of Natural Resources*).

Algonquin Provincial Park (est 1893, 7600 km²), the oldest provincial park in Ontario, is located 210 km N of Toronto. The area, which lies across the southern edge of the Canadian SHIELD between Georgian Bay and the Ottawa R, consists mainly of Precambrian granites, smoothed and gouged by ice sheets that receded 10 000 years ago. The rolling topography is dissected by numerous rivers and some 2500 lakes, which provide access by boat to the interior. Poor soils, a harsh climate and fires have produced a varied and changing second-growth forest, including pine, fir, birch and poplar. The PARK is famous for its wolves, and other species (eg, deer, moose, bear, raccoon) are common. About 240 bird species have been recorded, including the gray jay, spruce grouse, brown thrasher, scarlet tanager and loon. The cold, deep, nutrient-poor lakes are especially suited to trout, and smallmouthed bass; pike, muskellunge and walleye are also found. Extensive logging, especially for white PINE, began in the 19th century; today 75% of the park is still subject to controlled logging. Recently, land-use pressures and park planning have led to considerable public debate regarding the appropriate use and designation of the park. Much research has occurred in Algonquin. An astronomical observatory situated in the park was closed in 1987. Facilities include a museum and pioneer logging exhibit, lodges, campgrounds, scenic drives, trails and 1600 km of lake and river canoe routes.   JOHN S. MARSH

Alien Question The earliest settlers of UPPER CANADA were normally AMERICAN immigrants, free to take up land and enjoy the privileges of British subjects upon giving an oath of allegiance to the Crown. Following the WAR OF 1812, further immigration of Americans was discouraged by Gov Frances GORE, who refused to administer the oath of allegiance. Subsequently, the COLONIAL OFFICE ruled that anyone might claim full naturalization by swearing loyalty after 7 years' residency on British soil. By implication those who had not gone through these proceedings were "alien," and exposed to dispossession, disenfranchisement and disqualification from office even though approximately half of the population fell into this category.

The confused status of the citizenship of American-born residents of UC reached a crisis in 1820-21 when Barnabas BIDWELL and his son, Marshall Spring Bidwell, sought election to the provincial assembly and faced opponents who claimed they were ineligible to hold office because of American citizenship. If the Bidwells were aliens, so also were the majority of the province. The controversy was settled in 1828 when the government acquiesced to a new instruction from the Colonial Office retroactively correcting any defects in the citizenship of all UC office holders and landowners who arrived before 1820.   D.N. SPRAGUE

Alikomiak and **Tátimagana** Inuit hunters from the central Arctic, were the first of their race to be condemned and executed (1 Feb 1924) under Canadian law. They had murdered 4 Inuit at Coronation Gulf in Aug 1921 in a dispute over women, and Alikomiak, while under arrest at Tree River, had shot and killed W.A. Doak of the RCMP and Otto Binder of the Hudson's Bay Co. A judicial party travelled from Edmonton to Herschel I in the summer of 1923, and the 2 men were convicted of murder and sentenced to death. It was decided that the earlier policy of leniency had not sufficiently impressed the Inuit with the seriousness of such offences; thus, despite appeals in the press, for the first time in such a case the sentences were not commuted, and the men were hanged in the transport shed of the RCMP detachment at Herschel I.   W.R. MORRISON

Alimony was a term that referred to the right of one spouse to receive financial support from the other during marriage. Under the Divorce Act 1985 a right to financial provision after divorce is termed "support" – either child support or spousal support. Historically, only a wife was able to obtain alimony and this right was dependent on her proving to a superior court that her husband had been guilty of matrimonial misconduct, eg, adultery, physical cruelty or desertion. However, even if misconduct could be proven, the wife might be disentitled where it could be demonstrated that she had also been guilty of specified misconduct or had connived at or condoned her husband's action, or where some other defence was available. Alimony could also be awarded by a court as an additional remedy where, for example, the wife received a court order for judicial separation.

Many of these original concepts have been reformed and there is considerable diversity regarding alimony among the provinces. Alberta, Newfoundland, Saskatchewan, NS and the NWT have retained vestiges of the old fault-based approach, and in the latter 3 jurisdictions certain rights to receive alimony remain available only to the wife. The modern trend, adopted in the other Canadian jurisdictions, is to place the husband and wife on equal terms and to replace the requirement of matrimonial misconduct with a simpler notion of a duty to provide support in cases of financial need.

The provision of maintenance or support involves a money payment, paid either in a lump sum or periodically. The amount ordered depends on a variety of factors, including financial needs, means and the standard of living of the spouses. Under the Divorce Act 1985 and recent provincial legislation there is an increasing trend toward support orders aimed at promoting self-sufficiency by the recipient spouse and to grant orders for limited periods of time to promote that end. These objectives pose problems for older wives who married when society had different values towards marriage and for wives living in parts of the country where unemployment is high. Reallocation of property ownership cannot be ordered as alimony, although all provinces possess separate statutory provisions which permit such orders (*see also* FAMILY LAW; PROPERTY LAW).   BRUCE ZIFF

All-Canadian Congress of Labour This national trade union federation was formed in 1926 as a rival to the TRADES AND LABOR CONGRESS, which was dominated by Canadian affiliates of American craft unions. It was headed by A.R. MOSHER, president of the Canadian Brotherhood of Railway Employees, the largest organization within the 40 000-member ACCL, which also included the remnants of the ONE BIG UNION as well as several communist-controlled unions such as the Mine Workers' Union of Canada. The ACCL denounced American interference in Canadian union affairs and pledged to organize Canadian-controlled unions of industrial workers and to reject the elitist, craft form of organization favoured by the TLC. But it made little headway in this regard. In 1929 the communist unions abandoned the ACCL to form the WORKERS' UNITY LEAGUE, and in 1940, the ACCL itself disbanded by merging with the fledgling CIO unions – all of which had American affiliations – to form the CANADIAN CONGRESS OF LABOUR.   ALVIN FINKEL

Allan, Andrew Edward Fairbairn, radio-drama producer, actor, writer (b at Arbroath, Scot 11 Aug 1907; d at Toronto 15 Jan 1974). Seeing radio as the national theatre of Canada, through his taste, judgement and intelligence he brought the art of radio drama to new heights during his long career with the CBC, and set standards internationally. Allan came to Canada at age 17 and graduated from U of T, where he edited the *Varsity*. His first radio job was with CFRB Toronto. He was working for the BBC in England when war broke out in 1939 and was returning to Canada with his father on the *Athenia* when it was torpedoed and sunk. His father was killed. Allan joined the CBC in Vancouver 1942, and produced the Stage series of over 400 dramas in Toronto 1944-56. It included some classics and some newly created works by writers such as Lister Sinclair, Ted Allan, Len Petersen, Tommy Tweed, Mavor MOORE and many others who wrote scripts for emerging stars Lorne GREENE, Lloyd Bochner, Budd Knapp, Jane Mallett and John Drainie. Robert FULFORD has observed that Allan's CBC Stage "gave many of us ... our first hint that there were Canadian writers who had something interesting to say." He retired in 1962, unable to transfer his great talents to TV. He was the first artistic director of the SHAW FESTIVAL at Niagara-on-the-Lake, Ont, 1963-65, and continued writing, acting and directing for TV and radio until his death in 1974.   JOHN L. KENNEDY

Reading: A. Allan, *A Self Portrait* (1974).

Allan, Sir Hugh, shipping magnate, railway promoter, financier (b at Strathclyde, Scot 29 Sept 1810; d at Edinburgh 9 Dec 1882, buried at Montréal). Allan immigrated to Montréal (1826) and obtained employment through relatives as a clerk in a general merchandising firm. Ten years later, Allan became a partner, and with financing from his father and brothers in Scotland, bought steamers and sailing ships to extend the firm's shipping business. As president of the Montreal Board of Trade (1851-54), Allan persuaded the Canadian government to use mail contracts to subsidize regular steamship lines between Montréal and Britain (1853). Allan, with technologically advanced ships built in Clyde, Scot, and the help of Conservative political friends, was able to wrest the contract from competitors in 1856. By the 1870s, Allan's company, the Montreal Ocean Steamship Co (popularly known as the ALLAN LINE), also obtained government contracts to carry passage-assisted immigrants. Taking advantage of the Québec government's subsidies for colonization railways, Allan expanded into railway building. An Allan-organized syndicate, including some Americans, obtained the contract to build the railway to British Columbia that was promised that province when it joined Confederation. Meanwhile, Allan had contributed some $350 000 to $360 000 to the Conservative election fund. Suspicions that Allan had bought the railway contract led to the PACIFIC SCANDAL and Sir John A. MACDONALD's only period as federal Leader of the Opposition. Allan's interests included new communications technology, manufacturing and mining. He was a director of 2 American telegraph companies, president of the Montreal Telegraph Co (1852) and an early participant in the Canadian telephone industry, selling the Montreal Telegraph Co's "telephone plant" to the newly established Bell Telephone Co for $75 000. Allan owned coal mines on mainland Nova Scotia, and factories for textiles, shoes, iron and steel, tobacco and paper in central Canada. He used his banking and insurance interests to secure favourable press coverage through generous loans to editors. Although a Presbyterian, he successfully cultivated the leading French Canadian clergy, and once had a priest relieved of his parish duties to participate in a campaign to obtain municipal subsidies for an Allan railway. Allan was knighted by Queen Victoria in 1871. *See also* RAILWAY HISTORY; SHIPPING INDUSTRY.

MARGARET E. McCALLUM

Allan, Sir Hugh Andrew Montagu, banker, shipowner, sportsman (b at Montréal 13 Oct 1860; d there 26 Sept 1951), second son of Sir Hugh ALLAN. To avoid confusion with his cousin Hugh Andrew Allan (1857-1938), he changed his name to Hugh Montagu in 1878. His business career began when at age 21 he entered the firm of Hugh and Andrew Allan, shipbrokers and builders. He was chairman of the ALLAN LINE of steamships, 1909-12, but his principal interest was in banking. He served as the last president of the Merchants' Bank of Canada, 1902-22. In 1921 it had 400 branches and assets of $190 million, but its loans were overextended and, to avoid its collapse, Allan arranged for its amalgamation into the Bank of Montreal. He was also president or director of numerous financial and manufacturing companies. Allan was an enthusiastic sportsman, president of the Montreal Jockey Club for many years, his horses winning the QUEEN'S PLATE, the Montreal Hunt Cup and other trophies. He donated the ALLAN CUP, for competition in amateur hockey, in 1910. He was honorary lieutenant-colonel of the Black Watch (Royal Highland Regiment) of Canada, and was knighted in 1904. Of his 4 children, his son was killed in WWI and 2 daughters drowned in the *Lusitania* sinking, 1915. The surviving daughter, Marguerite Martha Allan (1895-1942), founded the Montreal Repertory Theatre, an influential amateur dramatic group between the wars.

D.M.L. FARR

Allan, William, businessman, politician (b near Huntly, Scot 1770; d at Toronto 11 July 1853). Between 1795 and 1822 Allan established himself as a prosperous merchant in York [Toronto], as a government officeholder and as a land speculator. From 1822 to 1835 he was the first president of the BANK OF UPPER CANADA, an institution so successful that it was attacked both politically as the too-powerful tool of the FAMILY COMPACT and commercially for its banking monopoly in Upper Canada. Allan served on the board of the Welland Canal Co, was co-commissioner of the Canada Co 1829-41, and governor of the British America Fire and Life Assurance Co 1836-53. As well, Allan served on the Legislative Council 1824-41 and on the Executive Council 1836-41. His reputation was made in business, however, and rests on his contribution to Ontario banking.

WENDY CAMERON

Allan Cup, trophy emblematic of the senior amateur hockey championship of Canada. It was donated by Sir H. Montagu ALLAN shortly after the STANLEY CUP became the trophy of professional hockey. After the organization of the NATIONAL HOCKEY LEAGUE, senior players who did not turn professional generally retired from the game. The Allan Cup was presented at this time to encourage

amateurs to keep playing. It was made a challenge trophy open to any senior amateur club which had won the championship of its league that year. The cup was presented to the Victoria Hockey Club of Montreal, to be defended by the champion of its league that year. Interest mounted to the point that challenges became too numerous, so the trustees arranged regional elimination. In 1914 a meeting to form a governing body resulted in the CANADIAN AMATEUR HOCKEY ASSOCIATION. In 1928 the Allan Cup was donated outright to the CAHA. In 1920 and 1924 the trustees financed the cost of sending a team to compete in the Olympic Games, and through the 1950s Allan Cup-winning teams such as the Trail Smoke Eaters, Oshawa Generals and Penticton Vs represented Canada at world championship events. *See also* HOCKEY, ICE.

JAMES MARSH

Allan Line was a Scottish-Canadian shipping company founded by Capt Alexander Allan (1780-1854) with his newly purchased brigantine, *Jean,* which sailed from Greenock, Scot, to Québec in 1819. In 1826 his second son, Hugh ALLAN, came to Montréal and developed a successful shipping business there; in 1839 Hugh was joined by a younger brother, Andrew. Two other brothers established offices in Greenock and Liverpool. In 1854 the Allan consortium incorporated the Montreal Ocean Steamship Company, which in 1856 won the government mail contract from Montréal to Liverpool. With innovative engineering and design the Allan ships prospered on the Atlantic and other trade routes. The first steel liner to sail the Atlantic was the Allan Line's *Buenos Ayrean* in 1880. After the turn of the century the company had difficulty financing new ships and was sold to CANADIAN PACIFIC Steamships Ltd in 1909. *See* SHIPPING HISTORY; MARITIME SHIPPING HISTORY.

PETER HOPWOOD

Reading: Thomas E. Appleton, *Ravenscrag* (1974).

Copy of a brochure advertising Allan Line Royal Mail Steamships sailings for summer season, 1881 (*courtesy National Archives of Canada/C-4127/R. Inness Coll*).

Allard, Charles Alexander, businessman, medical doctor (b at Edmonton 19 Nov 1919). Allard graduated in medicine from U of A in 1943. From 1955 until 1969 he was a surgeon and then chief surgeon at the General Hospital in Edmon-

ton. He began his career as an entrepreneur when he constructed a clinic to house his own practice in 1947. He established Allarcom Developments, one of the largest REAL-ESTATE companies in Canada, and was its president and chairman of the board until he sold it to Carma Developers of Calgary for $130 million in 1980. He has been active in finance (North West Trust), life assurance (Seaboard Life Insurance) and the media (Allarcom Broadcasting, which in 1987, owned Edmonton's CITV station and western Canada's Super-Channel) and is a member of the board of directors of Allarco Developments.

JORGE NIOSI

Allard, Jean Victor, soldier (b at Saint-Monique de Nicolet, Qué 12 June 1913). He was commissioned in the Non-Permanent Active Militia in 1933, served during WWII at the Canadian Army Staff College, Kingston, and in England, Italy, (Royal 22e Régiment), Belgium, the Netherlands and Germany (6th Infantry Brigade), finishing with the rank of brigadier. From 1945 to 1948 he was military attaché in Moscow; in 1953 he commanded the 25th Infantry Brigade in Korea and represented Canada at the armistice signing in Panmunjom. He commanded the 4th Division of the British Army of the Rhine (BAOR) from 1961 to 1963, a singular event for a Canadian, and was the first commander of Mobile Command; in July 1966 he was promoted to general and appointed chief of defence staff, the first French Canadian to be thus recognized. He returned in 1969 and published his memoirs in 1985.

JEAN PARISEAU

Allen, Ralph, journalist, editor, novelist (b at Winnipeg 25 Aug 1913; d at Toronto 2 Dec 1966). One of the best-loved and most influential editors of his day, Allen was justly famous for his work at *Maclean's* (1946-60) and the *Toronto Star* (1964-66). Reared in Oxbow, Sask, he began his career with the Winnipeg *Tribune* and was a distinguished war correspondent for the Toronto *Globe and Mail*. He also wrote 5 novels, of which *The Chartered Libertine* (1954), a satirical look at the CBC, is best known, and a popular history of Canada, *Ordeal by Fire* (1961). He is credited with implementing many editorial techniques and procedures which are still in use today.

DOUGLAS FETHERLING

Allergies In a biological sense, the term "immunity" refers to the capability of individuals to resist or overcome infection. The protective response of an individual's system to a foreign agent consists of the production either of selective antibodies (blood proteins), also called "immunoglobulins," or of cells that can recognize and subsequently neutralize the offending agent, or both. The foreign agent that triggers the immune response is referred to as an "antigen." The term "allergy" refers to an altered immunological reactivity of the host to a foreign substance that leads to diverse harmful effects on re-exposure to that substance; more precisely, allergies include those reactions in which immunoglobulin E, a protein produced in white blood cells, is involved. The foreign substance responsible for a given allergy is called an "allergen."

The immunoglobulins, or antibodies, comprise a heterogeneous family of proteins, classified as IgM, IgD, IgG, IgA or IgE. The IgE antibodies are responsible for allergies of the immediate type, eg, allergies to the constituents of various pollens, house dusts, foods, animal danders and hairs, parasites, insect venoms, various pharmaceutical preparations (eg, penicillin) and some industrial chemicals.

IgE antibodies are unique in that they bind with very high affinity to white blood cells (basophilic leukocytes) and to mast cells found in a variety of tissues. Thus, basophils and mast cells (abundant in respiratory and gastrointestinal tracts) in a person who has produced IgE antibodies become coated with these molecules, which are oriented on the cell membrane in such a way that they can still combine with the inciting allergen. Subsequent exposure of such allergic individuals to the allergen results in its combination with the IgE antibodies on the cell surface and the subsequent release from the basophils and mast cells of inflammatory compounds, eg, histamine and leukotriene, which can profoundly affect smooth muscles and blood vessels (causing constriction or dilation leading to abnormal heart rate), mucous secretion and breathing. Allergic reactions of the immediate hypersensitivity type can range in severity from a local skin wheal with reddening of the surrounding area to systemic effects involving a profound drop in blood pressure, swelling, choking and anaphylactic shock. For example, a significant number of people die each year from the systemic effects of drugs such as penicillin, or of the constituents of honeybee venom present in a sting.

It is possible that the capacity to produce IgE reflects a protective function of this immunoglobulin; however, to the sufferers from hay-fever and rhinitis the production of IgE results in disease. Normal persons also produce IgE antibodies, but only some of these individuals develop IgE-mediated immediate-type allergies. Therefore, a person who is allergic may be distinguished from one who is not by the sensitivity of their respective systems, ie, the amount of IgE produced, and not the production itself. The release of histamine and leukotrienes from mast cells and basophils in an allergic person causes a quantitatively different effect from that in normal individuals, allergic persons being extremely sensitive to minute quantities of allergen.

A second type of allergic reaction, qualitatively different from that mediated by IgE antibodies, is typified by the response to POISON IVY and poison oak. If a cellular response has caused a harmful rather than a beneficial reaction, the allergic manifestations seen in, for example, allergic contact dermatitis, can follow direct skin contact with the offending allergen. Drugs such as ampicillin and ordinary industrial chemicals such as formaldehyde and trimellytic anhydride fall into this category. Potentially allergenic compounds may also be found in topical skin creams.

Allergic disorders are widespread in N America, although the actual distribution of disorders varies with the nature of the allergic response. Allergic diseases such as hay fever and extrinsic asthma afflict about 17% of the Canadian population. Clearly, the distribution of allergies caused by environmental allergens such as RAGWEED pollen, house dust or pet animal dander is determined by the distribution of the allergen itself. Allergies to ragweed pollen occur mainly in the eastern provinces; those to grass pollens throughout Canada; and those to western red cedar in BC. Allergies to dietary components occur throughout the country.

In those cases in which the offending allergen can be identified, the obvious treatment is avoidance. If the allergen cannot be avoided, two basic strategies of therapy are currently employed. One attempts to induce, through a series of hyposensitizing injections of the offending allergen, the production of the protective immunoglobulin of the IgG class and the concomitant reduction in IgE antibodies. The other involves the administration of drugs, such as antihistaminics, which ameliorate the symptoms of allergy without, however, curing the disease.

Efforts to improve the effectiveness of allergy treatment have met with little success over the last 70 years. It is only since 1966, when the husband and wife team of Kimishige and Teruko Ishizaka (then working in Denver) discovered the class of IgE antibodies, that real progress has been achieved in the understanding of the molecular and cellular mechanisms underlying immediate hypersensitivity. It is anticipated that through intensified research more effective cures for allergic diseases will be discovered in the foreseeable future. In Canada, research on the various facets of allergic diseases is being conducted at most medical schools, primarily with the financial support of the Medical Research Council of Canada. In particular, in recognition of the specialized expertise available in related biomedical sciences among researchers in the Department of Immunology at University of Manitoba, the MRC established in 1973 a Group for Allergy Research, consisting of a co-ordinated team of 6 senior investigators, their assistants and trainees, all working toward the elucidation of the chemical nature of some of the common pollen allergens and of the basic mechanisms responsible for the regulation of IgE antibody production. The group has recently shown that allergens can be modified chemically to products which are tolerated better by patients than the standard allergenic extracts used for hyposensitization therapy. Recent clinical trials in Scandinavia with honeybee venom, which had been modified according to the procedures developed in Winnipeg, have demonstrated that the patients treated with the modified allergens could tolerate the intravenous injection of a dose of venom equivalent to that delivered by a bee without any untoward effect. Clearly, as with all other diseases, progress in allergy treatment can be achieved only on the basis of a better understanding of the fundamental mechanisms responsible for the disease.

B.G. CARTER AND A. SEHON

Alleyn, Edmund, painter (b at Québec City 9 June 1931). After studying at the École des beaux-arts de Québec, he went to France in 1955 where he lived and exhibited his work until 1971. Upon his return to Québec, he settled in Montréal and has taught visual arts since 1972 at the U of Ottawa. His evolution as a painter is all the more amazing in that his virtuosity and originality have been apparent in each of his successive periods. Beginning with stylized figuration, Alleyn showed much elegance and fluidity in his tachist, or action, works in the period 1952-62, then made a side excursion into works inspired by native mythology before committing himself to a series of schematic pictures, infused with science fiction, dehumanized medicine and other terrifying "zooms, conditionings or aggressions." Both a critic and a part of accelerated technological change, he condensed his research and reflection into *Introscaphe*, a tight synthesis combining the senses and the electronic, a work exhibited to much acclaim at the Musée d'art moderne de Paris in 1970. His impressive show, Une belle fin de journée, held in fall 1974 in Québec C and Montréal, showed again his exceptional talents as an original artist. After a period of inactivity, he began painting again in the mid-1980s.

GUY ROBERT

Alline, Henry, evangelist, hymnist, theologian (b at Newport, Rhode I 14 June 1748; d at N Hampton, NH 2 Feb 1784). An itinerant evangelical preacher in the Maritimes, Alline wrote hymns, religious tracts and a *Life and Journal*. He began his career as a saddlebag preacher in Falmouth, NS, and spent most of his life touring NS and NB. Although self-educated, he was a prolific writer and speaker committed to music as a part of religious worship. He worked unceasingly from 1776 to 1783 to create and sustain a religious revival known as the "New Light" movement. His followers, who were based mainly in NS, were referred to as "Allinites." Alline, despite the uneasiness he aroused in established church communities, was a persuasive preacher. He succeeded in his self-appointed mission to awaken many settlers to religion and is looked upon as a major influence in the establishment of the BAPTIST Church in the Maritimes. Besides his *Life and Journal* (1806) and *Hymns and Spiritual Songs* (1786), he published 5 religious pamphlets and his major theological work, *Two Mites on Some of the Most Important and Much Disputed Points of Divinity* (1781). In this latter work he expresses his personal beliefs on many religious points, including his strong anti-Calvinist stand. *See* GREAT AWAKENING. DOUGLAS LOCHHEAD

Reading: J.M. Bumsted, *Henry Alline* (1971).

Allison Pass, elev 1352 m, is located at kilometre 60, highest point on the Hope-Princeton Hwy (opened 1949) through the CASCADE MTS of southern BC. It was named for John Fall Allison, commissioned by Gov J. DOUGLAS about 1860 to inspect gold strikes on the Similkameen R. He returned to report finding a new, low pass between the Skagit and Similkameen rivers. Allison mined near HOPE and was later a pioneer rancher in the Princeton area. Manning Prov Pk headquarters is situated 9 km E of the pass.

GLEN BOLES

Allotment of Time, rules of the House of Commons, Standing Orders 115, 116 and 117, often confused by the media with the CLOSURE rule, S.O. 57. Since 1968 most bills pass the committee stage in the standing COMMITTEES and may be amended at the report stage, but S.O. 57 applies only in the House and in committees of the whole House and works inefficiently when there are several distinct motions at a stage. The standing orders were passed by the House on 24 July 1969 amid great controversy, which was terminated by the use of closure. The new rules established procedures by which the House may set a time schedule for a bill at one or more stages of the legislative process. S.O. 115 applies when all party house leaders agree, and 116 when the Government house leader has the support of a majority of the parties; 117 allows the Government to propose, and the House to determine, after a 2-hour debate, the reasonable time to be allotted for a bill at a stage, eg, the second-reading stage. When the fixed time (eg, 2 days) elapses, divisions are called; consequently, allotment of time is often called "guillotine closure." *See also* FILIBUSTER.

JOHN B. STEWART

Alma, Qué, City, pop 25 923 (1986c), 26 322 (1981c), inc 1979, located at the head of the SAGUENAY R near Lac SAINT-JEAN, 230 km N of Québec City. County seat of Lac Saint-Jean Est, headquarters of the judicial district of the same name, the present city contains 5 former municipalities: Alma, Riverbend, Isle-Maligne, Naudville and the parish of Alma. Born of the lumber industry in 1860, Alma quickly became a prosperous agricultural parish. It burst into the industrial age in 1923 with the start of construction of the Isle-Maligne hydro station on the Grande Décharge. When completed in 1926, the station supplied power for the Arvida aluminum works and the Price paper mill in Alma. Population multiplied fivefold 1921-31. During WWII ALCAN built an

aluminum plant there that was expanded during the 1950s. In that same era Alma became a tertiary centre for the Lac Saint-Jean area (commerce, professional services, hospital, college). Geographic centre of the Saguenay-Lac Saint-Jean region, it is the site of various regional organizations. Alma is also the departure point for Lac Saint-Jean cruises. MARC ST-HILAIRE

Almanacs, annual compilations in sheet or book form which included a calendar, with saints' days and other significant dates, and astronomical phenomena, such as eclipses, phases of the moon and transits of the planets, were a well-established tradition in Britain and the American colonies by the mid-18th century. Canada's first printers brought this tradition with them, adapting it to the French, English or Indian market. The almanac was a local publication since astronomical tables were calculated according to the longitude and latitude of a particular geographical area. Other information of local interest, such as lists of church and civic officials, postal and customs regulations, and stagecoach and ferry services, was also frequently included. Cheap, practical and annually in demand, the almanac was a "bestseller" for early printers and an important source of revenue.

Many of the earliest almanacs printed in Canada no longer survive. The Brown and Gilmore office in Québec City is known to have issued a sheet almanac each year from at least 1765 and an almanac for the Indian trade from the following year, but most of these early wall calendars are known only from the printers' records. There had been a printing office in Halifax as early as 1751, but it is not known if an almanac was produced there. Brown and his successor, John Neilson, later published the popular *Almanach de Québec* for over 60 years beginning in 1780. Anthony Henry of Halifax printed Canada's oldest surviving almanac, *The Nova-Scotia Calendar* for 1770. In 1788 Henry began the publication of a second almanac, *Der Neu-Schottländische Calender*, for German-speaking settlers of the colony. It is believed to be the first German-language publication printed in Canada. Christopher Sower printed New Brunswick's first almanac (1786); and the oldest surviving almanac printed in Ontario is *Tiffany's Upper-Canada Almanac, for the year 1802*, published by Silvester Tiffany at Niagara (Niagara-on-the-Lake). The King's Printers at York (Toronto) published almanacs with increasing regularity in the early years of the 19th century. Of particular interest today are those issued by Charles Fothergill in the 1820s because of the "Sketch of the Present State of Canada" included each year. Few almanacs seem to have been produced in the Prairie provinces, perhaps because of the relatively late arrival of printing there. Some almanacs published in the American northwest included information about Vancouver I and the mainland, but *The British Columbia Almanac*, which was published in Victoria (1895-98), is the only one known to have been produced in the province.

The use of the almanac as a vehicle for political opinion has a long history in English-speaking countries. A Canadian example is William L. MACKENZIE's *Caroline Almanack* for 1840, published while the rebel leader was in exile in Rochester, NY. Special-interest groups – religious, political, professional, labour and commercial – used the almanac to sell their ideas. Particularly prolific in the late 19th and early 20th centuries were the almanacs issued by patent-medicine manufacturers, in which the calendar itself is lost in a sea of advertisements and testimonials. Canada's oldest continually published almanac, *The Canadian Almanac & Directory*, first issued by Hugh Scobie of Toronto for 1848, still retains a small calendar and astronomical section. As quick reference sources for information about all aspects of Canadian life, this directory is still consulted, as are similar works such as the *Corpus Almanac & Canadian Sourcebook*. ELIZABETH HULSE

Almighty Voice, or Kah-kee-say-mane-too-wayo, meaning Voice of the Great Spirit, also known as Jean-Baptiste, Cree, outlaw (b near Batoche, Sask 1874; d there 30/31 May 1897). Almighty Voice's tragic confrontation with the NWMP resulted in the last battle between whites and Indians in N America. He grew up on the One Arrow Reserve near Batoche. In Oct 1895 he was arrested for illegally butchering a cow. Stories conflict, but shortly after his arrest Almighty Voice escaped from the Duck Lk jail and shot and killed NWMP Sgt Colin Colebrook. For 19 months he evaded police but he was finally cornered with 2 young relatives in a poplar bluff. For 2 days the fugitives fought a force of 100 police and civilian volunteers, killing Cpl C.H.S. Hockin and Const J.R. Kerr of the NWMP, and Ernest Grundy, Duck Lk postmaster. The bluff was bombarded with cannonfire, resulting in the 3 Indians' deaths. EDWARD BUTTS

Almond, Paul, filmmaker (b at Montréal 26 Apr 1931). Educated at McGill and Oxford, Paul Almond joined the CBC in 1954. He directed numerous dramas, "The Hill" (1954), "Under Milk Wood" (1959) and "Point of Departure" (1960). All won Ohio awards. In 1968 he made his first feature, *Isabel* (1968), which starred his wife, Geneviève BUJOLD. Two films also starring Bujold followed, *The Act of the Heart* (1970) and *Journey* (1972). The unique trilogy, displaying Almond's interest in the irrational and mystical, constitute his best work and a distinctive contribution to Canadian film. In 1980 he was called in to direct the ill-fated *Final Assignment* (1980). He then produced and directed *Ups and Downs* (1983) and directed *Fate of a Hunter* (1986). PIERS HANDLING

Almonte, Ont, Town, pop 4122 (1986c), 3855 (1981c), inc 1871, is located on the Mississippi R, 54 km SW of Ottawa. The site was granted to David Shepherd for a gristmill and sawmill (1819) and like most pioneer towns was given several names, including Shipman's Mills, after Daniel Shipman, who is regarded as the town's founder. The name Almonte was chosen (1856) in honour of the Mexican general Juan Almonte, whose championing of Mexican independence in the face of American aggression appealed to the citizens of the town. In 1827 Almonte was made administrative centre for IRISH immigrants, but its chief subsequent importance was for woolen textiles. Power was drawn from the scenic falls within the town. Today, it is an agricultural-supply, electronics, flour-milling and ice cream manufacturing centre. It is the birthplace of R. Tait MCKENZIE, surgeon and sculptor, who restored an old gristmill (c1830) outside the town and used it as a studio; the mill survives as Mill of Kintail Museum and contains 70 of McKenzie's works. Robert Young House (c1835) was the boyhood home of James NAISMITH, inventor of basketball. The weekly newspaper is the *Gazette*. K.L. MORRISON

Alpine Club of Canada, national, nonprofit, nongovernmental MOUNTAINEERING organization founded in 1906 in Banff, Alta. The first president was A.O. WHEELER. The ACC was unlike its British counterpart because it permitted women to become members. Now governed by a board of directors with a permanent office in Banff, the ACC has expanded across Canada with 3000 members. The club's objectives include the encouragement and practice of mountaineering, the exploration of alpine and glacial regions and the preservation of mountain fauna and flora. Activities include summer mountaineering camps and winter ski camps. The *Canadian Alpine Journal* has been published annually since 1907; *The Gazette*, begun in 1921 as a less-formal publication, was replaced in 1986 with a quarterly newsletter. A reference library is maintained in Banff's Whyte Museum of the Canadian Rockies. From 1909 until its destruction in 1973 a clubhouse in Banff served as a centre for mountaineers; a new clubhouse was built in 1980 near Canmore. The ACC has built many huts since 1927 when Fay Hut was constructed in Kootenay National Park. Currently, attention is being focused on an upgraded and expanded system of huts and on the Lake Louise Hostel and Recreation Resource Centre. BEVERLEY BENDELL

Althouse, John George, educator (b at Ailsa Craig, Ont 10 Apr 1889; d at Temagami, Ont 2 Aug 1956). Educated at U of T, he was appointed headmaster of U of T Schools 1923, dean of the Ontario Coll of Education 1934 and chief director of education for Ontario 1944. Though a supporter of moderate progressivist influences during the 1930s, he became the principal agent for Premier George DREW's conservative shift in Ontario education in the 1940s. President of the Canadian Education Assn 1948-49, he was the author of *The Ontario Teacher: An Historical Sketch of Progress, 1800-1910* (1929). ROBERT M. STAMP

Altona, Man, Town, pop 2958 (1986c), 2757 (1981c), inc as a village in 1946 and as a town in 1956, located 96 km S of Winnipeg and 13 km N of the Canada-US border. It was built on local initiative to emerge from Mennonite agricultural settlement in the fertile Pembina Triangle into a diversified regional centre. The townsite was established in 1895 on a Canadian Pacific Ry spur near the agricultural village of Altona, settled in 1880 as part of a reserve W of the Red River for MENNONITES from Russia. Altona gradually surpassed nearby Gretna, expanding its service role to foster the region's CO-OPERATIVE MOVEMENT in the 1930s and 1940s and indigenous economic endeavours such as oilseed processing; printing/publishing; paperbox, clothing and other manufacturing; a broadcasting station; and retailing complex. Altona's development reflected transformation of the hinterland from grain and livestock farming to more intensive production of oilseeds, specialty crops and poultry, enabling smaller farms and relatively dense settlement. Altona's population initially was more cosmopolitan than the hinterland; nonetheless, its sociocultural development reflected the tensions of the Mennonite experience in Manitoba in its adaptation to, or disaffection with, secularization and modernization. D. M. LYON

Altschul, Rudolf, professor of anatomy, scientist, author (b at Prague [Czech] 24 Feb 1901; d at Saskatoon 4 Nov 1963). He received his medical degree in Prague and did postgraduate work in Paris and in Rome. In 1928 he began the practice of neuropsychiatry in Prague, but in 1939 he and his wife fled the Nazi occupation and made their way to Canada and U Sask where he was first an instructor and, by 1955, head of the department of anatomy. Altschul was a man of broad culture: photographer, linguist, connoisseur of the arts, a born raconteur and superb teacher. He was the author of 103 scientific papers dealing with a wide variety of subjects, including the pathology of the nervous system, skeletal muscle degeneration, cell division and, in particular, arterial degeneration, the subject of his books: *Selected Studies on Arteriosclerosis* (1950), and *Endothelium – Its Development, Morphology, Function and Pathology*

(1954). His later research led to niacin therapy for lowering blood-serum cholesterol and in 1964 to the publication of *Niacin in Vascular Disorders and Hyperlipemia.*   S. FEDOROFF

Aluminum (Al), silvery, ductile metal which acquires a dull lustre on exposure to air, caused by the formation of a film of aluminum oxide that adds corrosion resistance. Aluminum is light (its density about one-third that of copper), non-magnetic and melts at 660°C. It is a good conductor of heat and electricity. The element was isolated in 1825 by the Danish physicist and chemist, Hans Christian Oersted, but an economic method of commercial production was discovered only in 1886 by Charles M. Hall of the US and Paul-Louis Tossaint Hérault of France. Both men had been working independently at the time of their discoveries. Abundant hydroelectric power enables Canada to produce primary aluminum from 6 smelters in Québec and one at KITIMAT, BC, the main producer being ALCAN ALUMINIUM LIMITED. Refined metal is fabricated by casting, rolling and extrusion. Manufactured products include doors, windows, house siding, beverage cans, foil, cooking utensils, electrical wiring, etc. Pure aluminum is soft but may be hardened by mechanical working and by the addition of alloys such as copper, magnesium, manganese and zinc.

Canada produced 1 291 566 t of primary aluminum in 1985, about 8.3% of world output. In 1984 the aluminum rolling, casting and extruding industries shipped over $1.4 billion worth of aluminum products. Since Canada consumes only about a quarter of its production, a large amount is exported as primary metal, mostly to the US. Aluminum is the most abundant metal in the Earth's crust but does not occur uncombined. The principal source of the metal, bauxite, contains about 50-60% alumina (aluminum oxide, Al_2O_3) and forms by the weathering of aluminum-rich rocks under tropical conditions. Bauxite is imported principally from Brazil, Guinea and Guyana. Aluminum is produced by separating pure alumina from bauxite in a refinery, then treating the alumina by electrolysis. An electric current flowing through a molten electrolyte, in which alumina has been dissolved, divides the aluminum oxide into oxygen, which collects on carbon anodes immersed in the electrolyte, and aluminum metal, which collects on the bottom of the carbon-lined cell (cathode). The word aluminum was suggested by Sir Humphry Davy in the early 1800s. It has been retained in N America, but has been modified to aluminium in other parts of the world. *See also* METALLURGY.
                                    G. BOKOVAY

Amadjuak Lake, 3116 km², is one of 2 lakes situated in the Great Plain of the Koukdjuak, in S-central BAFFIN I. This lower-lying area has emerged only recently from beneath the waters of FOXE BASIN. Amadjuak Lk is the fourth-largest in the NWT. High inland cliffs are unusual in the Arctic and the lake is noted for the 30 m high limestone cliffs that overlook it. They mark the scarp edge of the cuesta plain and are steepened and swept clear of debris by the action of the lake's waves.   DOUGLAS FINLAYSON

Ambassadors and Embassies When representation is established by one independent state in the capital city of another independent state, the senior representative is usually an ambassador. On occasion the senior representative could be a chargé d'affaires, *ad interim* if pending the arrival of an ambassador (or, later, during his absence from the country), or *en pied* if the chargé is to be in charge indefinitely. In times past the senior representative could have been a minister, where a legation rather than an embassy was the level of representation. After WWII, with the general acceptance of the legal equality of all independent states, the usual practice of accrediting ministers and establishing legations gave way to the accreditation of ambassadors and the establishment of embassies.

Between independent COMMONWEALTH countries, the designation for the senior representative is high commissioner and his establishment, the office of the high commissioner or, now commonly, the high commission. While an ambassador is accredited to a head of state (a monarch or a president), a high commissioner is accredited to a government. Generally speaking, ambassadors and high commissioners are regarded as equivalent in status and function.

The status of ambassadors is governed by the Vienna Convention on Diplomatic Relations (1961), to which Canada is a party. The appointment of an ambassador, while initiated by the sending government, is subject to the approval (*agrément*) of the receiving government. An ambassador must continue to be acceptable (*persona grata*) to the receiving government throughout the appointment otherwise, if unacceptable (*persona non grata*), the receiving government may require withdrawal.

The term ambassadress has been used to describe a female ambassador. In Canadian practice ambassador applies to both sexes. The term ambassadress has also been employed as a style of address of an ambassador's wife, but it is not the practice to do so in Canada.

An ambassador's task is to represent the sending government in its dealings with the receiving government and includes negotiating as may be required. Ambassadors are responsible for safeguarding the property and persons of their nationals from discriminatory treatment in the country of their accreditation. They promote and clarify their government's interests and policies. They provide an informed perspective to their own government on the policies and interests of the receiving government and they report on important and relevant developments in the foreign country.

An ambassador's staff and his residence and offices form the embassy. In practice, the offices are called the "chancery." The same term applies to the offices of high commissioners. Under INTERNATIONAL LAW and custom the physical premises of an embassy are not subject to the jurisdiction of the state wherein the embassy is located. Also, the ambassador and his diplomatic entourage are immune from the jurisdiction of the foreign state unless, in specific cases, the sending state waives their immunity. The purpose of immunity is to protect the embassy from undue harassment; this is not to say the ambassador and his entourage are not expected to abide by the laws of the receiving state.

The designation ambassador may also be accorded to representatives to international organizations, eg, the UNITED NATIONS, NATO; to representatives for a specific international event, eg, EXPO 86; a particular negotiation, eg, the 1987 trade negotiations between Canada and the US; a particular continuing function, eg, disarmament, multilateral trade negotiations of the GATT; or for more general, sometimes itinerant, international undertakings, eg, ambassador-at-large. It is the practice in many countries that the designation ambassador, once bestowed, is carried for life, eg, in the US.

Canada has had representatives abroad for various purposes, particularly immigration and trade promotion, since Confederation in 1867. In 1869 Sir John ROSE, a former minister of finance, was appointed to a senior liaison capacity with the government of the UK and later designated financial commissioner. In 1880 Sir Alexander GALT was appointed to London as the first high commissioner, arguably Canada's first diplomat. In fact, neither he nor the agent general appointed to Paris in 1882 had diplomatic status. Furthermore, although the Department of EXTERNAL AFFAIRS was established in 1909, the Paris and London offices were not placed under the jurisdiction of that department until 1913 and 1921 respectively. It was not until after the Imperial Conference of 1926, which acknowledged the equality of the Dominions with Great Britain, that Canada accredited diplomatic representatives abroad, although the Canadian representatives in London and Paris and, beginning in 1925, the Canadian advisory officer to the LEAGUE OF NATIONS in Geneva, were essentially carrying out the tasks of diplomats.

During and immediately after WWI the question of the appointment of a Canadian representative to Washington had frequently been raised. Finally, in 1926 (later the Rt Hon) Vincent MASSEY was appointed to Washington as Canada's first minister, opening Canada's first legation in 1927 with a staff of 4 officers. (in 1986 the ambassador in Washington had a staff of 60 officers and there were 13 consulates general throughout the US with a combined staff of 122 officers.) This first appointment of a Canadian representative abroad with full diplomatic status was followed in 1928 by the appointment of Phillipe ROY, commissioner general in Paris since 1911, as minister. In 1929, (later Sir) Herbert Marler was appointed minister in Tokyo.

These appointments, in Washington and Tokyo, being "firsts," led to the establishment of further Canadian landmarks abroad. CANADA HOUSE in Trafalgar Square, meant to bring together all departmental representatives in London, had been purchased and christened in 1924. It is still very much a Canadian place in London. The new legation in Washington – both office and residence of the new minister – occupied one of the fine mansions on Massachusetts Avenue, popularly known as "Embassy Row." Since 1947 it has housed only offices and these are soon to be moved to a new Canadian building on a unique site midway between the White House and the Capitol on Pennsylvania Avenue. In Tokyo new offices and an adjacent magnificent residence were built in an auspicious location across from one of the royal palaces. The Canadian buildings in Tokyo survived the fire-bombings of WWII, partly thanks to the efforts of Japanese caretakers. Canada House in London, by good fortune, escaped damage during the air raids on that city.

In 1928 the first British high commissioner arrived in Ottawa to represent the UK government. Until then the GOVERNOR GENERAL had had that role. As well, in 1928, the Commonwealth high commissioners in London (the Canadian was the Hon P.C. LARKIN) were recognized as having equivalent status to ambassadors. At the same time Canada's advisory officer to the League of Nations was regarded as having equivalent status to ambassador. It was not, however, until Nov 1943 that Canada's first ambassador, as such, appeared on the scene, when Canada and the US elevated their legations to embassies. The Canadian minister, the Hon Leighton McCarthy, became Canada's first foreign ambassador and the American minister, the Hon Ray Atherton, became the first foreign ambassador to serve in Ottawa. In Dec 1943 the elevation to ambassador of the Canadian ministers in the USSR, China and Brazil was announced. Thereafter, additional existing legations were raised to embassy status and gradually the practice of exchanging ambassadors, rather than ministers, became the rule. (The last Canadian legation was raised to embassy in Czechoslovakia in 1962.)

WWII brought a rapid expansion of Canada's representation abroad. By the end of the war Canadian diplomatic representatives were accredited to 20 countries and so-called European "governments-in-exile" in London. The expansion continued apace in the postwar period. By 1986, there were 87 Canadian ambassadors and high commissioners accredited abroad: 59 ambassadors accredited to 110 separate countries and, as well, ambassadors to the Holy See and to the European Economic Community; 18 high commissioners accredited to 47 Commonwealth governments and, in addition, 3 commissioners representing Canada in 3 crown colonies; finally, 8 ambassadors accredited solely to international organizations. The apparent inconsistency in the statistics arises from the fact that many ambassadors and high commissioners have multiple accreditations, ie, they represent Canada in more than one country or organization.

Representation in cities other than capital cities, where the task relates to promotion and protection of Canadian interests locally, particularly with the private sector (eg, trade and travel promotion) and with local governments (eg, protection of Canadian citizens), is achieved through the establishment of consulates. These in turn may be substantial establishments under a consul general or simply a single honorary consul or commercial agent working out of his own quarters. Canada's first consulate general was established in New York in 1943. There had previously been, over the years, representation abroad, primarily to promote trade and immigration. A trade commissioner's service was well established by the beginning of WWII. Indeed, the first trade commissioner had been posted in Sydney, Australia, in 1894. Consular affairs had continued to be handled by the British consulates, in the absence of qualified and duly authorized Canadian representatives, well after WWII. Progressively, however, Canadian offices (embassies, high commissions and consulates) were established to manage the bulk of Canadian responsibilities abroad. In 1986 there were 26 Canadian consulates general in 9 countries and 34 honorary representatives in 28 countries.

In total, exclusive of the honorary representatives, there are over 100 heads of post (ambassadors, high commissioners and consuls general) serving Canada abroad.

In the Canadian foreign service, ambassadors, high commissioners and consuls general are interchangeable subject, generally, to their own foreign-service rank (which is distinct from their diplomatic or consular rank) and the classification of the post. Posts are assessed according to the level of responsibility and activity.

Appointments are initially submitted by the prime minister for consideration by Cabinet and are confirmed by order-in-council. Commissions are issued to appointees by authority of the governor general in the name of the Queen. The title Excellency is accorded ambassadors and high commissioners in foreign countries, and foreign ambassadors and Commonwealth high commissioners in Canada are entitled to be so addressed. A Canadian citizen addresses a Canadian ambassador or high commissioner formally, Sir, and informally, Mr Ambassador/High Commissioner.

Originally Canadian high commissioners to London were so-called political appointees, as indeed were Canada's first ministers and ambassadors. The practice of appointing career officers as heads of mission began with the appointments to head the advisory office to the League of Nations in Geneva of W.A RIDDELL in 1925 and of Hume WRONG in 1937. With the expansion of representation abroad which occurred at the begin-

ning of WWII, more career officers were appointed heads of mission: at that time as ministers at legations. The first career member of the Dept of External Affairs to be appointed ambassador was Jean Désy, Canadian minister to Brazil, who was elevated to ambassador in 1943. At the same time Dana WILGRESS, deputy minister of trade and commerce and formerly a senior trade commissioner, was elevated to ambassador in Moscow, where he had been Canada's first minister in 1942. The first career ambassador in Washington was Lester PEARSON who was elevated to that rank, from minister, in 1945.

With the rapid expansion of Canadian representation abroad during and after WWII, the practice favoured appointment of career officers as ambassador, high commissioner and consul general. Appointees came from the ranks of the Dept of External Affairs, the Trade Commissioner Service and occasionally other departments. In later years career appointments were also drawn from the Immigration Service and from the Canadian International Development Agency. All of these specialties are still represented in the ranks of career appointees to ambassador, high commissioner and consul general, who are now members of the same department, External Affairs. Up to 1986 there continued to be a fluctuating, though relatively small, percentage of noncareer appointees. The Rt Hon Ed Schreyer has been Canadian High Commissioner to Australia since 1984; Hon Roy McMurtry Canadian High Commissioner in Britain since 1985; Stephen Lewis Canadian ambassador to the UN since 1984; and Dennis McDermott Canadian ambassador to Ireland since 1986.
                                          JIM S. NUTT

Ambridge, Douglas White, engineer, businessman (b at Mexico City, Mexico 5 Jan 1898; d at Toronto 16 Nov 1976). Educated at Lower Canada College and McGill, Ambridge held various positions in the pulp and paper industry in the 1920s and 1930s and helped construct Ontario Paper Co's plant at Baie-Comeau, Qué, 1937. In WWII, as a member of the Production Board and director general of the Naval Shipbuilding Branch in Ottawa, he played a major role in industrial mobilization. He directed the construction of crown-owned Polymer Corp's synthetic rubber plant in Sarnia, Ont, and was, successively, its VP, president and chairman. In 1946 he was created CBE. He became president of Abitibi Power and Paper 1946, and presided over its recovery and expansion, retiring from the presidency 1963 and from the chairmanship 1967. He was appointed chairman of the Ontario Deposit Insurance Corp in 1967.
                                          J. LINDSEY

Ambrose, Tommy, pop singer, composer (b at Toronto 19 Oct 1939). The creator of many of Canada's most successful advertising jingles, Ambrose is also well known as a club performer and broadcaster. He began his career at age 5 with gospel-singing appearances at Toronto Youth for Christ rallies and on local radio. Primarily a singer of popular music since 1957, he has been host of several CBC TV series: "While We're Young" (1960-61), "The Tommy Ambrose Show" (1961-63) and the gospel music show "Celebration" (1975-76), which first appeared on CBC Radio (1971-74). Ambrose also has made several records.
                                          BARCLAY MCMILLAN

American Civil War, 1861-65, sectional conflict between the Northern US states (Union) and the Southern states that seceded and formed the Confederacy. It was important in the development of a separate Canadian identity. Canadian opinion was generally anti-Northern, and the Washington government, aware of this, was hostile to both Britain and British North America.

Britons and Canadians, predicting a Southern victory, anticipated an attack on Canada by the Northern army, which many thought would seek territory in compensation. Resulting tension along the border led to numerous minor incidents, much misunderstanding and 4 significant crises, including the ALABAMA, TRENT and *Chesapeake* incidents. The fourth, raids on St Albans, Vt, in fall 1864 by Confederates based in Montréal, brought pursuing Northern troops onto Canadian soil. Confederates hoped to draw the North into violating British neutrality in Canada, with a view to inciting Britain to declare war on the North, but the attempt failed. Immediately after the war a series of FENIAN raids heightened tensions along the border; they likely would not have been tolerated by the Americans had there not been a legacy of hostility left between Canada and the Union, notwithstanding the enlistment of many Canadians in the Northern armies. This hostility led to the American abrogation of the 1854 RECIPROCITY Treaty at the earliest possible opportunity, in Mar 1866.

In analysing the causes of the war John A. Macdonald blamed the excessive power given to the states under the American Constitution, and he determined that the BNA Act would not repeat this flaw. He also established a border patrol, forerunner to the NORTH-WEST MOUNTED POLICE. Perhaps most important, the threat of American invasion, made explicit by the aftermath of the ST ALBANS RAID, led the British to favour CONFEDERATION of the BNA colonies for more effective defence. Thus the war contributed directly to both the timing and the form of Confederation.
                                          ROBIN W. WINKS

Reading: Robin W. Winks, *Canada and the United States* (1971).

American Revolution (also known as American War of Independence), 1775-83, struggle by which the Thirteen Colonies won independence from Britain. Disputes over taxes, administration and the territorial provisions of the ROYAL PROCLAMATION OF 1763 and the QUEBEC ACT, simmering since the Treaty of PARIS, 1763, broke into open war at Lexington, Mass, 18 Apr 1775. Prominent American colonists signed the Declaration of Independence on 4 July 1776.

An effective propaganda campaign conducted by the Americans succeeded in eliciting some support, particularly in Montréal, where there was some pro-American activity. The French Canadian clergy, seigneurs and leading citizens adopted a policy of support for the British, but most of the common people remained neutral and reluctant to become involved. Bishop Briand issued an episcopal mandate denouncing the rebels and urging the people to more active support, but Gov Sir Guy CARLETON (Lord Dorchester) had little success raising the militia. In Sept 1775 Gen Richard Montgomery led American forces northward, seizing Ticonderoga, CROWN POINT and FORT CHAMBLY. When Ft Saint-Jean capitulated in Oct, Carleton abandoned Montréal and the Americans took possession Nov 13/14. Meanwhile, Gen Benedict ARNOLD managed, despite hardships and desertions, to bring some 700 men via the Kennebec and Chaudière rivers to Québec. Montgomery joined him in early Dec with another 300 men and during a snowstorm on 31 Dec 1775 launched a desperate assault. Arnold and his men penetrated some distance into Lower Town but surrendered under counterattack. Montgomery and his leading officers were killed in their attack from the other side of Lower Town. The remaining Americans kept up their desperate siege through the winter, but were easily routed when the spring thaw brought British reinforcements. They abandoned Montréal May 9.

The failure of the American invasion left bitter memories among Canadians and drove many sympathizers into exile. However, there had been little active support for the Americans: clergy and seigneurs remained staunchly loyal and, after some equivocation, so did the merchants. Most HABITANTS remained determinedly neutral, in defiance of Bishop Briand and Carleton. Gen John BURGOYNE led a British counterinvasion southward via Lake Champlain, but he overextended himself and, in the first great victory for the Americans, he surrendered at Saratoga 17 Oct 1777.

As in previous conflicts, Nova Scotia remained an uncertain battleground during the Revolution. The provincial Assembly voted addresses of loyalty, but illegal town meetings gave secret support to New England. Nearly every important outpost outside Halifax suffered from American PRIVATEERING. In 1775 rebels seized Partridge I in Halifax harbour and they made a futile attack on Ft Cumberland (FORT BEAUSÉJOUR) in 1776, but by 1779 the British had cleared the Bay of Fundy of privateers.

After a protracted struggle, British forces surrendered in Oct 1781, and the Treaty of PARIS, 1783, formally recognized the United States of America. The failure of the American invasion and the influx of some 40 000 LOYALIST refugees into Nova Scotia and Québec determined that the development of the remaining British colonies would differ profoundly from their southern neighbours.
D.N. SPRAGUE

Reading: J.B. Brebner, *The Neutral Yankees of Nova Scotia* (1937); M. Jensen, *The Founding of a Nation* (1968); G. Lanctôt, *Canada and the American Revolution* (trans 1967); G.F.G. Stanley, *Canada Invaded, 1775-1776* (1973).

Americans Migration between the US and Canada has usually been treated as a natural event – diffusion through a semipermeable border. But any act of migration is an adventure and the adventuring spirit has at times characterized even the American migrant. The interpenetration of the Canadian and American peoples has been such that no Canadian can have escaped its influence. That only 1.3% of the total population in 1981 (the most recent figure available) was American born is deceptive, for the American is one of the oldest and – for all its fluctuations – one of the most enduring stocks in Canada. Perhaps 3 million Americans have immigrated to Canada, beginning with the LOYALISTS of the late 18th century. Two million (about 20% of all immigrants) arrived in the 20th century.

Proximity has made migration and remigration relatively easy, but the transience of the American immigrant has been overstated. The return flow to the US was greatest between 1910 and 1914, when the flow of Americans to Canada was also greatest. But the pre-war period was characterized by high mobility among all immigrants – eg, nearly 60% of American immigrants of the first decade appear to have died or remigrated by 1911, 46% of immigrants from sources other than the US. After the war, and until the 1970s, US citizens were less likely than other foreign nationals to seek Canadian citizenship, but this was not so before WWI. One-tenth of all American immigrants during the century have become Canadian citizens, making up only 7% of all aliens who did so. Yet the alien percentage of the American-born has averaged only 34% over the century, not far from the overall foreign-born norm of 41%. This evidence suggests, then, both a high degree of transience among US immigrants, and a relatively high degree of commitment to Canada on the part of the US-born who have stayed on in Canada.

American immigration has been mainly of individuals seeking land or alternative resources or opportunities, a movement heterogeneous and polyglot, yet with certain distinguishing characteristics (such as an unusually high agricultural element before WWI, and an unusually high professional element after WWII) and including certain notable group movements, such as Loyalists, fugitive BLACKS, draft dodgers, and a few religious groups, such as QUAKERS and HUTTERITES.

Americans have emigrated from all regions of the US (but particularly from the border states) and from all ethnic groups (but especially British and northern European). Canada has traditionally welcomed Americans who emigrate with property and who possess technical skills, a welcome reflected in IMMIGRATION POLICY. However, not all Americans have been considered ideal immigrants; since the late 1800s immigration policy has managed to exclude most American blacks, alleged subversives and the urban poor.

Migration Between 1898 and 1915, after the railways were well established in the West and as good, cheap land diminished in the US, American farmers poured into Canada, making up nearly as many western settlers as those from the British Isles, who were less likely to farm. This is both the midpoint and the apex of American migration so far, and some of its effects are still to be seen, say, in the relatively high US-born presence in Alberta and Saskatchewan, or in the proportion of farmers among the US-born (while British-born workers as a whole have been 3 times US-born workers since WWII, at each census the number of US-born farmers has been on a par with those British-born).

But Americans had all along sought and found land in Canada (eg, clearing the Queen's Bush in Ontario; following the Red River's contours into Manitoba), bringing their experience to bear on land that was only dimly sensed to be foreign. The political distinction of Canada grew, for the potential American immigrant, with the WAR OF 1812 and then with the REBELLIONS OF 1837 and was formalized by the Act of Union in 1840. By that time there were few Americans in Canadian classrooms and in the Protestant pulpits, but skilled workers and entrepreneurs trickled in through the century, especially into Ontario, playing important roles in certain industries, such as the manufacture of iron goods.

American settlers have been involved in many of the significant Canadian adventures – the early FUR TRADE, EXPLORATION, resource discovery and exploitation, early industrialism, railway and bridge building and modern scientific research. Proximity, again, has helped alert these immigrants to opportunity, and they have come with the advantages of a comparatively complex and advanced technology. There have been certain areas in which American immigrant participation has been minimal, however, such as Canadian banking, law and labour management. American settlers were notable among the leaders of western agrarian protest (*see* POPULISM), but Britain has been a much more important source of social and economic radicalism.

American settlers have until recently scattered more widely in Canada than other immigrants: they have been found traditionally in relatively high concentrations in certain border areas, such as the Niagara Pen, but also they are less likely than other foreign-born to congregate in cities. The natural amenities of a locale and region, such as those found on either coast, have been increasingly attractive; by 1981, when the US-born were 8% of all foreign-born in Canada, they were 10% of all foreign-born in BC and 31% in the Atlantic provinces. Yet the traditional tendency to spread is particularly pronounced in the coastal regions, eg, in BC they have for several censuses exceeded their proportion of the national population in virtually all census districts, with no great proportional variance in any one district.

Economic Life American immigrants in this century are wealthier than the immigrant norm. Between 1964 and 1972 they brought into Canada 3 times the money brought by the average immigrant per head, and, while in Canada, they tend to attain greater wealth than the foreign-born norm – eg, in 1926 they were 43% of all foreign-born in the prairies with land holdings greater than 961 acres, and in 1970 the American-born had a higher representation in the top salary range than any other natal group.

An assessment in 1961 of the economic contribution of American immigrants described them as "our technicians and managers, doing a tour of garrison duty in this northern hinterland before returning home." This exaggeration was pertinent, though, only from the 1920s through the 1950s. The character of the American migration changed dramatically in the mid-1960s with a remarkable influx of professional workers, especially university teachers and artists, who frequently reported motives for migration that extended beyond the economic (many describing alienation from the US especially aggravated by the VIETNAM WAR).

American settlers, nevertheless, have traditionally included a disproportionate managerial and proprietary element, who tend to concentrate in industries and in geographic areas where US direct investment is highest, as in oil and gas exploration and extraction in Alberta (*see* FOREIGN INVESTMENT). Resource exploitation has attracted the greatest amount of investment and apparently the most immigrants of the managerial class, though this emphasis began to shift in the 1960s to other areas, such as finance and computers. American entrepreneurs have been prominent in manufacturing in both centuries, but especially in those closely tied to resource exploitation, such as pulp and paper or the development of hydroelectric power. These resources have often been exploited by American-owned firms to satisfy an essentially American market, as in the manufacture of newsprint (per capita consumption in the US soaring from 8 pounds in 1890 to 62 pounds in 1929). American "branch plants" – owned and controlled from head offices in the US – became conspicuous in Canada in the 1890s and continue to thrive, but they are less likely now to involve resident American managers. Many of these, and former American managers of independent Canadian firms, have put in much more than a "tour of garrison duty," founding establishments of note and even towns (such as Walkerville, Ont, and Hull, Qué), and contributing otherwise to Canadian society.

But the proportion of managers among American immigrants began to decline soon after WWII, and by the 1960s the American immigrant labour force was conspicuously professional. Between 1962 and 1980, 44% of all American immigrants intending to join the Canadian labour force described themselves as professional workers (as opposed to 31% of British working immigrants and 24% of all immigrant workers). The distribution of these workers among the professions was distinctive, nearly the obverse of the distribution of British professionals, who were much more likely to be engineers and doctors, much less likely to be religious workers, social workers or university teachers.

The 3 best known and most respected names of individual American immigrant-settlers are probably those of William VAN HORNE, C.D. HOWE and Wilder PENFIELD. The legacies of each are conspicuous in Canada, in the Canadian Pacific Railway, in aspects of modern liberalism at the federal level, and in the mapping of the human brain. Conspicuous too was their identification with Canada, though the absence of this quality in, as well as the transience of, the American immigrant has probably been overstressed. "Building that railroad," Van Horne said, "would have made a Canadian out of the German Emperor."

DAVID HARVEY

Amérique française, magazine fd 1941 by former Collège Jean-de-Brébeuf students led by Pierre Baillargeon, following Collège publications by François Hertel and his colleagues. The magazine accurately reflected the artistic ideals of a certain Québec intellectual elite. Its contributors, worried about the future of letters and culture in Québec, worked for the recognition of French culture in America. The magazine covered the various arts, but favoured literature. Its goal was to promote the growing French Canadian writing movement.

The magazine lost some of its dynamism in 1945, when Gérard Dagenais, the new director, broadened its scope to include social and economic issues. The result lacked a coherent guiding philosophy and attracted few readers. In 1947 Hertel left the magazine to Corine Dupuis-Maillet, who tried unsuccessfully to turn *Amérique française* into a prestigious literary review. Her daughter, Andrée Maillet, took over in 1951 and devoted the magazine almost entirely to new writing until its demise in 1955. It had published 4-12 issues every year since 1941. A number of authors made their first appearance in its pages, including Jacques FERRON and Anne HÉBERT. In 1963 Maillet relaunched the magazine, but only one issue appeared. *See also* LITERARY PERIODICALS IN FRENCH.

LISE MAISONNEUVE

Ames, Alfred Ernest, investment dealer (b at Lambeth, CW 3 Sept 1866; d at Toronto 20 Sept 1934). He worked as a bank clerk, then moved to Toronto and established A.E. Ames Co, investment dealers, 1889, the same year he married Mary Cox, daughter of financier and senator George COX. He was president of the Toronto Stock Exchange 1897-98 and the Toronto Board of Trade 1901-02, chairman of the Temiskaming and Northern Ontario Ry Commission 1902-04, and president of the Bond Dealers' Assn of Canada 1917. He was a director of many companies, including the Home and Foreign Securities Co, F.N. Burt Co, Sterling Coal Co, Canada Life Assurance Co, Wm. A. Rogers Ltd, Moore Corp, Kelvinator of Canada, and International Milling Co. An important member of the Toronto business community, he built one of the oldest and most prominent investment houses in Canada.

JORGE NIOSI

Ames, Sir Herbert Brown, businessman, civic reformer, politician (b at Montréal 27 June 1863; d there 31 Mar 1954). Ames was a successful businessman who wrote books about, and worked for civic reform, and who also worked in the interests of imperial trade and international peace. Employed in his father's firm of Ames, Holden and Co, he was elected a Montréal alderman in 1898 and worked for reform, particularly in health and education. He served as a Conservative MP 1904-20. From 1919 until 1926 he was financial director of the secretariat of the League of Nations in Geneva, and he also held other posts with the league. His book, *The City Below the Hill* (1897), is one of the earliest sociological descriptions of the working-class districts of Montréal.

T.D. REGEHR

Amherst, NS, Town, pop 9671 (1986c), 9684 (1981c), inc 1889, is located near the border with New Brunswick, 15 km E of SACKVILLE, NB. Settlement began in the 1830s, but it was not until shortly before WWI that Amherst became an important regional centre. It boasted a railway-car factory with 2000 workers and an engineering company with an international reputation, as well as factories making woollen goods, enamel products, footwear and pianos. Its population was almost as large in 1914 as it is today. After WWI, the town's economy collapsed along with that of many Maritime centres, as a result of economic policies that favoured central Canada. In the 1920s thousands of Amherst residents left in search of work in New England and western Canada. The town has never really recovered from this crisis. Today, it survives as a service centre for the surrounding agricultural community and supports some light industry. Tourism is important and Amherst residents always have a warm welcome for the many visitors who take advantage of its location as a gateway to Nova Scotia.

NOLAN REILLY

Amherst, Jeffery, 1st Baron Amherst, British army officer (b near Sevenoaks, Eng 29 Jan 1717; d near Sevenoaks 3 Aug 1797). Less recognized than James WOLFE, Amherst was the ultimate conqueror of Canada in the SEVEN YEARS' WAR. Influential patrons gained Amherst command of an expedition against LOUISBOURG in 1758. He obtained the town's surrender on July 27 by a careful but slow siege by his overwhelming forces. Made commander in chief in N America, he undertook a methodical but cautious advance up Lk Champlain in 1759, which had little effect on French efforts to halt Wolfe's operations and ended abruptly after the fall of Québec City in Sept. But in 1760 Amherst planned a campaign that saw 3 armies grind down French resistance in converging on Montréal. The capitulation of Montréal on Sept 8 marked the end of French rule in Canada. Amherst left N America in Nov 1763 for England, where his handling of the earlier PONTIAC uprising provoked criticism. Knighted in 1761 and ennobled in 1776, he twice served as commander in chief of the British army before retiring in 1796 as a field marshal. A formal and taciturn man, Amherst made his reputation in N America, and he owed much of his later advancement to this success.

STUART SUTHERLAND

Amherst, William Pitt, Earl Amherst of Arakan, diplomat and governor general 1835 (b in Eng Jan 1773; d there 1857). The son of Lt-Gen William Amherst and nephew and heir to Lord Jeffery AMHERST, self-styled first governor general of British North America, he served as British envoy to Naples (1809-11) and to Peking (1816-17) before being appointed governor general of India in 1823. Retiring from that post in 1828, he was gazetted governor general of Canada 1 Apr 1835 on the nomination of British PM Sir Robert Peel; but on the resignation of Peel's ministry on Apr 8 he immediately gave up the appointment, ending a term in that office distinguished only by its brevity.

STANLEY GORDON

Amherstburg, Ont, Town, pop 8413 (1986c), 5685 (1981c), inc 1878, located on Detroit R near Lk Erie. First settled 1784, it became the new base for the British after they evacuated Detroit. In 1796, Ft Malden was established, and LOYALIST refugees laid out a townsite. General BROCK used the fort as a base to capture Detroit (1812), but it was under American occupation 1813-15. In 1837-38 Amherstburg was attacked 4 times by Rebel supporters of William Lyon MACKENZIE and was bombarded by the schooner *Anne*, which later ran aground and was captured. The British garrison remained until 1851. Today secondary industries in the town include chemical products and automotive parts and it is the centre for marine salvage. At Ft Malden Historical Pk, original earthworks, stone buildings and a blockhouse have been restored. Christ Church dates from 1818, and Bellevue, a beautiful Georgian mansion (*c* 1819).

JAMES MARSH

Ami, Henri-Marc, paleontologist, prehistorian (b at Belle-Rivière, Qué 23 Nov 1858; d at Menton, France 4 Jan 1931). The son of a Swiss pastor, Ami studied science at McGill, notably under John William DAWSON. He worked for the GEOLOGICAL SURVEY OF CANADA 1882-1911. Ami is best known for his work on geological formations in Québec and the Maritimes. His bibliography contains over 200 titles. He was editor of the *Ottawa Naturalist* 1895-1900. In 1900 he was elected to the RSC, and the Geological Soc of London honoured him with the Bigsby Medal 1905. His comfortable financial situation and marriage to Clarissa Burland, from a prominent Montréal family, allowed Ami to resign from the Geological Survey in 1911 to concentrate on prehistorical studies. After moving to France, he founded the École canadienne de préhistoire, an institution jointly funded by the French government and the RSC.

RAYMOND DUCHESNE

Reading: Morris Zaslow, *Reading the Rocks* (1975).

Amiens, Battle of took place 8-11 Aug 1918, W of Amiens, France. A co-ordinated assault, spearheaded by the Australian and Canadian Corps, involving aircraft, tanks, artillery, cavalry and infantry, it was subsequently characterized by the German Gen Erich Ludendorff as "the black day of the German army." The Allied forces won a major victory. The 4 Canadian divisions defeated parts of 15 German divisions, routing 4, at a cost of some 9000 casualties. Their success initiated the "hundred days" which saw the Germans repeatedly driven back all along the Western Front, and which culminated in the armistice of 11 Nov 1918. *See* WORLD WAR I.

BRERETON GREENHOUS

Amnesty Act, 1 Feb 1849, offered a pardon to all those involved in the 1837-38 REBELLIONS. It originated Mar 1838, when a conditional pardon was extended to minor participants. In 1843, with Colonial Office authority, Gov Gen Metcalfe issued a special pardon to any exiled rebels who petitioned. By early 1844 all 58 rebels who wanted to end their exile had received pardons, and in Jan 1845 they began returning to Canada from Australia and Bermuda. That year Louis-Joseph PAPINEAU, in exile in France since 1839, also returned. Four years later, the Baldwin-LaFontaine ministry introduced its amnesty bill. Only William Lyon MACKENZIE, the one rebel who had not been given a special pardon in 1843, returned to Canada under the Act.

CURTIS FAHEY

Amos, Qué, Town, pop 9261 (1986c), 9421 (1981c), inc 1925, is located 75 km NE of Rouyn-Noranda in northwestern Québec. It owes its existence to its favourable location in the heart of the Abitibi region at the junction of the Transcontinental Railway and the Rivière Harricana, one of the region's major waterways. The area used to be called Harricana, an Algonquin expression meaning "place where bark dishes are obtained for cooking." Founded in 1914, Amos became in the mid-1920s the most important town in Abitibi and the county town of this newly settled region of Québec. It took its name from Alice Amos, the wife of Sir Lomer Gouin, premier of Québec. Amos assumed a leading role in the region because of its many sawmills and the surrounding rich agricultural lands lying among the Harricana. It is also the site of a new papermill belonging to Donahue-Normick Inc. A short distance from Amos, the Abitibiwini ("people of the high ground," an Algonquin band) live in the Indian village of Pikogan. BENOÎT-BEAUDRY GOURD

Amphibian, member of a class of VERTEBRATE animals derived from fish and ancestral to REPTILES. Amphibians are represented by 3 living orders: Anura (FROGS), Caudata (SALAMANDERS) and Gymnophiona (caecilians, tropical, none in Canada). Frogs have one extinct and 23 living families; salamanders, 5 extinct and 8 living families; and caecilians, 4 living families. Amphibians are tetrapod (4-legged) or, in the case of some limbless salamanders and caecilians, derived from tetrapod ancestors. They have a moist, glandular skin without epidermal scales, feathers or hair. Frogs lack a true tail as adults and have disproportionately long hind legs and exaggerated mouths. Most salamanders have a more typical vertebrate body, with elongated bodies and tail and relatively even-sized front and hind legs. Although easily identified by their lack of scales, salamanders are sometimes mistaken for lizards. All frogs and most salamanders have 4 toes on the forefeet, 5 on the hind feet; some salamanders have fewer toes or lack limbs entirely. Caecilians are limbless and have little or no tail. They usually have folds or grooves which give the body a segmented, wormlike appearance.

Modern amphibians are small: the largest salamanders attain 160 cm; caecilians, 120 cm; and frogs, 30 cm. Typically, living amphibians have 2 lungs, although the left lung is reduced in caecilians and members of one salamander family (Plethodontidae) are lungless. The heart has 2 atria and one (sometimes partly divided) ventrical. Poison glands are often abundant in the skin; the poison is distasteful but rarely fatal to predators.

Most species breeding in aquatic situations form large aggregations in spring or after heavy rains. Most male frogs have distinctive breeding calls; those defending calling sites may also have territorial calls. In contrast, salamanders make little sound but have evolved elaborate courtship behaviour. Eggs are fertilized externally in most frogs; many salamanders deposit small packets of sperm which are taken up by the female through her vent and held for internal fertilization. Most amphibians deposit eggs in water or in moist, terrestrial sites; eggs are rarely retained in the female until hatching. Most terrestrial eggs hatch only after the larval stage has been passed within them, but the typical amphibian life history features a gill-breathing, aquatic larva metamorphosing into the lung-breathing adult. Hence, the name of the group [Gk *amphi*, "both"; *bios* "life"]. Striking differences in larval development between groups show their long, divergent evolution. Larval salamanders have forelegs appearing first, hind ones later, and are similar to adults in form and in being carnivorous. Some salamanders remain aquatic, retaining gills throughout their lives. Frog metamorphosis, from aquatic larva to terrestrial adult, is more dramatic. Larval frogs hatch with external gills and without legs. The tadpole intestine is long and coiled. The gills soon become internal; the body becomes globular, with no discernible neck; a small mouth with rasping teeth and beak appears for grazing on vegetation. Later hind legs appear as buds and complete their development externally by the time the forelegs, developed internally, push through the body wall; the intestine shortens for

Green frog (*Rana clamitans*) shown in pond environment with water star grass, tuberous water lily and (lower left) frog egg mass (*artwork by Claire Tremblay*).

a carnivorous diet; the tadpole mouth divides; gills and tail are absorbed. The mouth enlarges for gulping whole animals and the lungs take over respiration.

Amphibians are ectothermic, ie, have a relatively low metabolic rate insufficient to generate enough heat for life processes and thus depend on heat from the environment. Amphibians often function better at lower temperatures than do most reptiles, but are more vulnerable to desiccation throughout the life cycle. Their eggs lack both protective shell and embryonic membranes, being covered only by a layer of jelly. Amphibians breathe, as larvae and adults, through their skin as well as their lungs and must keep moist. They are very adaptable, being able to withstand freezing (eg, wood frog) and to survive losing nearly half their body weight in moisture (spadefoot toads).

Amphibians have lost much of their ancestral diversity and size and have survived by accepting a small predator's role, largely in moist or aquatic habitats. Only tadpoles are plant eaters. Frogs occur on all major landmasses except Greenland and Antarctica. Salamanders, largely restricted to the north temperate zone, are most diverse in Eurasia and N America, but one family (Plethodontidae) has successfully radiated to the tropics of Central and S America. Caecilians are entirely tropical.

Canada has 40 species of native amphibians: 21 frogs and 19 salamanders. None are unique to Canada and most have more extensive ranges in the US. None occur in the northern tundra, but several are abundant in the boreal forest. The deciduous forests of SW Ontario, the coastal rain forest and interior valley grasslands of BC and the central plains of Saskatchewan and Alberta contain many species that barely range into Canada. No amphibians survived GLACIATION in Canada; therefore, this fauna has been here less than 18 000 years. Amphibians are of minimal direct economic importance. Some frogs are caught for food, particularly the bullfrog native to southern parts of eastern Canada and introduced in BC. Small frogs are used for fishing bait. The largest use may be of bullfrogs, leopard frogs and mudpuppies in university and high-school dissection and experimental physiology. Amphibians are, however, a vital part of the ecosystem, forming a significant part of the terrestrial, aquatic and semiaquatic biomass and acting as a biological control on invertebrate members. They have recently been found useful as indicators of the effects of ACID RAIN.

Classification

The class Amphibia is divided, according to differences in the structure of the vertebrae, into 3 subclasses, 2 known only from FOSSILS.

Labyrinthodontia is a diverse group containing 3 orders. The order Ichthyostegalia (3 families, 5 genera) contains the earliest fossils classified as

amphibians, from the Upper Devonian of Greenland and N America (374-360 million years ago). They probably derived from lobe-finned fishes. The order Temnospondyli (3 suborders, 26 families, 128 genera), the most diverse of ancient amphibian groups, occurred from the Mississippian to the end of the Triassic (360-208 million years ago). Temnospondyls were the dominant vertebrates during the Permian (286-245 million years ago). The order Anthracosauria (12 families, 39 genera) appeared in the Mississippian and vanished late in the Permian. The family Dradectidae probably contained the first terrestrial plant eaters. The family Seymouriidae led to the reptiles, and has a combination of amphibian and reptile skull and skeletal characteristics.

Lepospondyli were small, aquatic amphibians of the Carboniferous to early Permian (360-258 million years ago). Many were limbless and eellike. Three orders have been identified: Nectridia (3 families, 13 genera), Aistopida (2 families, 3 genera) and Microsauria (6 families, 21 genera). Salamanders and caecilians may have derived from this subclass, but the most popular classification system links all modern forms.

Lissamphibia is the subclass containing all surviving amphibian orders and one extinct order, Proanura, known from *Triadobatrachus* (also called *Protobatrachus*) of the Lower Triassic of Madagascar. Some authorities consider this fossil intermediate between early amphibians and modern frogs; others suggest it was a metamorphosing tadpole. Fossil frogs and salamanders are first known from the Jurassic (208-144 million years ago). F.R. COOK

Reading: F.R. Cook, *An Introduction to Canadian Amphibians and Reptiles* (1984).

Amund Ringnes Island, 5255 km², located between Ellef Ringnes and Axel Heiberg islands in the ARCTIC ARCHIPELAGO. It is flat (highest point about 610 m) and windswept; in winter its coasts are virtually indistinguishable from the surrounding ice. It was discovered 20 April 1900 by Gunerius Isachsen, a member of the Norwegian SVERDRUP expedition, and named for a member of the brewery that financed the expedition. It was surveyed 1916 by V. STEFANSSON, who found coal and gypsum on the island. JAMES MARSH

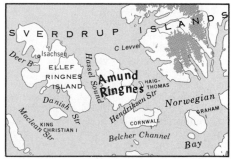

Amundsen, Roald, arctic explorer (b at Sarpsborg, Norway 16 July 1872; d between Norway and Spitsbergen 18 June 1928). Amundsen went to sea as a young man. Determined to navigate the NORTHWEST PASSAGE, he purchased the *Gjoa*, readied it for arctic waters and embarked in 1903. After 2 icebound winters, *Gjoa* emerged in the Beaufort Sea, the first ship to cross the top of N America. In 1911 Amundsen reached the S Pole and in 1920 he sailed through the Northeast Passage. Then he turned his attention to air exploration and in 1926 flew over the N Pole in an airship piloted by Umberto Nobile. Amundsen disappeared in 1928 on his way to search for Nobile, missing on another arctic flight.

DANIEL FRANCIS

Reading: R. Amundsen, *My Life as an Explorer* (1927).

Capt Roald Amundsen, Norwegian explorer who was the first man to sail through the Northwest Passage (1903-06). In 1911 he became the first man to reach the South Pole, photo 1906 (*by permission of the British Library*).

Amyot, Francis, Frank, paddler (b at Thornhill, Ont 14 Sept 1904; d at Ottawa 21 Nov 1962). His father, Dr John A. Amyot, was federal deputy minister of health. In Ottawa Amyot canoed at the Rideau Aquatic Club and the Britannia Boating Club. A large man at 188 cm and 84 kg, he required a custom-made racing shell and paddle to accommodate his long, powerful body stroke. He won 6 national senior single-blade singles championships between 1924 and 1935. In 1936 he was coach, manager and a member of the first Canadian Olympic canoeing team and at Berlin won a gold medal in the 1000 m Canadian Singles. He served in the RCN during WWII and later was an organizer of the Rideau Canoe Club.

C. FRED JOHNSTON

Anabaptists, religious and social dissenters in 16th-century Europe. In Switzerland Anabaptists arose out of the humanistically oriented Reformation in Zürich in 1525; in south and central Germany, out of joint streams of medieval mysticism and apocalypticism (the expectation that the end of the world is imminent) in 1526; in the Netherlands, out of sacramentarianism (the belief that the sacraments are merely outward symbols) and apocalyptic perfectionism in 1530. Major leaders in Switzerland were Conrad Grebel, Michael Sattler and Balthasar Hubmaier; in Germany, Hans Denck, Hans Hut, Jacob Hutter (*see* HUTTERITES) and Pilgram Marpeck; in the Netherlands, Melchior Hoffman, Bernhard Rothmann, Dirk Philips, Menno Simons (*see* MENNONITES) and David Joris. The movement was relatively small in numbers, but it appeared in most German-speaking areas of Europe as well as in France, England, Poland, Moravia and Italy. It quickly came under intense pressure everywhere because of its radical departure from traditional beliefs and polity, and it was regarded as socially and politically dangerous. At least 6000 Anabaptists were executed by 1578.

Although not organizationally linked, the 3 originating groups shared characteristics. The first was emancipation from the tutelages of the past and an insistence upon the freedom of laymen to make their own spiritual choices. The authority of papal and academic hierarchies was rejected in favour of the exclusive authority of Scripture, and scriptural interpretation became the prerogative and obligation of the congregation. Every function of civil government in the congregation was rejected. Anabaptists insisted upon religious liberty and most eschewed participation in government and military service (*see* PACIFISM). All adopted a congregational structure with voluntary internal discipline. The church was seen as the continuing presence and activity of Christ in the world.

The second major shared characteristic was rejection of the LUTHERAN doctrine of salvation by God's grace alone, and an insistence that the believer's faith must be proven and supplemented by deeds: man must bear the cross of discipleship, thus participating in the atonement. Infants were not baptized because they could not make their own commitment to Christian discipleship. Conscious, deliberate human participation in the process of salvation was symbolized in adult ("believer's") baptism; hence the name "anabaptism" [Gk *anabaptizein,* "to baptize again"]. The emphasis on good works produced a strong strain of perfectionism. Christ, who was to return soon, was to find his bride (the church) without spot or wrinkle. Perfectionism led to frequent schisms, such as the Amish schism of 1693 in which the main issue was church discipline.

In 1981 (the last year for which figures are available) some 236 000 Canadians were members of groups that arose within the Anabaptist tradition: Mennonites, Hutterites, BRETHREN IN CHRIST (Tunkers) and The Missionary Church. *See also* EVANGELICAL AND FUNDAMENTALIST MOVEMENTS.

WALTER KLAASSEN

Reading: H.S. Bender, ed, *The Mennonite Encyclopedia,* 4 vols (1955-59); G.H. Williams, *The Radical Reformation* (1962); Walter Klaassen, *Anabaptism in Outline* (1981).

Anahareo, or Gertrude Bernard, conservationist (b at Mattawa, Ont 18 June 1906; d at Kamloops, BC 17 June 1986). More than any other individual Anahareo played an important role in converting Grey Owl [Archibald BELANEY], a trapper, into a dedicated conservationist. In *Pilgrims of the Wild* (1934), Grey Owl recounts how his young Iroquois wife, by saving the lives of 2 beaver kits, led him to change his whole way of life and to work for the protection of wildlife. They had a daughter, Dawn, in 1932 and the couple split up in 1936. Anahareo continued to champion the rights of wild animals. She was admitted into the Order of Nature of the Paris-based International League of Animal Rights in 1979. She is the author of an autobiography, *Devil in Deerskins* (1972).

DONALD B. SMITH

Anansi, House of, *see* HOUSE OF ANANSI.

Anarchism, the political doctrine which teaches that government is evil and unnecessary and that society should be recognized on the basis of voluntary mutual-aid associations. In Canada it has never generated much support, although small groups of activists have existed sporadically in larger cities and anarchist ideas have lightly influenced a number of writers. The movement's most famous theoretician, Peter Kropotkin, visited Canada in 1897; it was on his recommendation that Tolstoy and others decided to settle the DOUKHOBORS on the Canadian Prairies, 1898-99. Anarchist Emma Goldman, after a militant career in the US and USSR, died in Toronto in 1940. Among Canadian anarchists is activist-writer George WOODCOCK, who in 1962 published *Anarchism,* a history of the movement.

Anatomy of Criticism: Four Essays, by Northrop FRYE (Princeton, 1957), has had a powerful international influence on modern critical theory. Frye is a learned and eloquent spokesman for the view that literature constitutes an autonomous system, an order of works and words to be studied through a systematic and classificatory approach, as articulated in the essays comprising the "anatomy." Following his formidable "polemical introduction," Frye sets out 4 critical approaches and their corollary theories, upon which he constructs an elaborate typology: "Historical Criticism: Theory of Modes"; "Ethical Criticism: Theory of Symbols"; "Archetypal Criticism: Theory of Myths"; and "Rhetorical Criticism: Theory of Genres." Frye's work has been attacked by critics who see in his approach a dangerous tendency to dehistoricize both literature and criticism; and it has been praised by those who see his as the most powerful arguments to locate "human desire" at the centre of the literary universe. Frye's long-held view that the Bible stands as the originating document or masterwork of Western literature informs *The Great Code* (1982) which, with its projected companion volume, may in time supersede *Anatomy of Criticism* as Frye's major work. *Anatomy of Criticism* has been translated into French as *Anatomie de la critique* (Paris, 1969) and into German and Italian.

NEIL BESNER

Anciens canadiens, Les (1863), a Canadian classic combining the appeal of historical romance and local realism, was written by Philippe AUBERT DE GASPÉ, Sr, in his seventies in response to the call by the journal *Les* SOIRÉES CANADIENNES for the preservation of the past. Set in rural Québec at the time of the CONQUEST, the action juxtaposes the lives of 2 friends doomed to fight each other: Jules d'Haberville, future seigneur at St-Jean-Port-Joli, and Archibald Cameron of Locheill, an exiled Highlander in love with Jules's sister Blanche. Walter Scott's novels merge with French Canadian folklore in Gaspé's fictionalized memoir; his anecdotal style blends historical materials with legends, such as the story of La CORRIVEAU, in a nostalgic, ultimately heroic portrait of New France. The definitive tenth French edition was published by Fides in 1975; Georgina Pennée's translation (1864) is surpassed by Charles G.D. Roberts's *The Canadians of Old* (1890).

MICHÈLE LACOMBE

Anderson, David, Church of England bishop (b at London, Eng 10 Feb 1814; d at Clifton, near Bristol, Eng 5 Nov 1885). Grandson of a Presbyterian minister and son of an East India Co surgeon he was educated at Edinburgh and Oxford (BA 1836, MA 1839, DD 1849). At school he met Archibald Campbell Tait, later bishop of London and archbishop of Canterbury, and partly through his influence decided to seek orders in the Church of England. After curacies in Liverpool he was on the staff of St Bees Theological College until 1846, then served briefly as perpetual curate of All Saints', Derby. Largely through the influence of members of the Clapham Sect, he was nominated first bishop of the diocese of RUPERT'S LAND. Consecrated in May 1849 he proceeded to his new diocese centered at the RED RIVER COLONY, accompanied by his sister and 3 sons, his wife having died 2 years before. He was bishop and HBC chaplain until 1864, during which time the church's missionary work was extended towards James B and into the Mackenzie and Yukon valleys.

F.A. PEAKE

Anderson, Frank Ross, international chess master (b at Edmonton, Alta 3 Jan 1938; d at San Diego, Calif 18 Sept 1980). Bedridden for 5 years with arthritis, he discovered CHESS at age 15. His first steps outside led to the chess club. Anderson won the Canadian championship 1953 and 1958, but his greatest success was at the Chess Olympics. In 1954 at Amsterdam and again in 1958 at Munich he won the gold medal on 2nd board. He would have gained the grandmaster title in Munich, but reaction to an incorrect prescription prevented him from appearing for the

final game. In the late 1960s he moved to San Diego, where he ran a tax consulting business.
JONATHAN BERRY

Anderson, James Thomas Milton, educator, author, premier of Saskatchewan (b at Fairbanks, Ont 23 July 1878; d at Saskatoon 29 Dec 1946). After teaching in the Yorkton district, Anderson was appointed inspector of schools in 1911 and director of education among new Canadians in 1918 – the year he published *The Education of the New Canadian.* In 1924 he became leader of the Conservative Party and in 1925 was elected MLA for Saskatoon City. Following the defeat of J.G.GARDINER's ministry on 6 Sept 1929, Anderson formed the Co-operative government, a coalition of Conservatives, Progressives and Independents. The controversy surrounding the 1930-31 amendments to the School Act obscured his administration's legislative record. Two years after his government's crushing defeat in 1934, Anderson retired from politics and managed an insurance company before being appointed acting superintendent of the School for the Deaf, Saskatoon, in 1944.
RAYMOND J.A. HUEL

Anderson, John Murray, theatrical entrepreneur, director, author, lyricist (b at St John's 20 Sept 1886; d at New York 30 Jan 1954). Known as "Uncle Broadway" and "the King of Revues," he produced and staged 34 major musical comedies and revues (29 on Broadway, 5 in the West End), 7 circuses for Ringling Bros, 4 Aquacades for Billy Rose, 11 pageants, 61 movie-house stage shows and 24 elaborate nightclub shows. He immigrated to the US in 1910 and began in New York as a ballroom dancer, marrying his partner Genevieve Lyon in 1914. His first Broadway success, *The Greenwich Village Follies* (1919), pioneered a genre of productions noted for their artistry and sophistication.
DAVID GARDNER

Anderson, Patrick, poet, writer, educator (b at Ashtead, Surrey, Eng 4 Aug 1915). A graduate of Oxford and Columbia, Anderson came to Canada in 1940. He taught at a Montréal private school 1940-46, during which time he made probably his foremost contribution to Canadian arts by cofounding PREVIEW (1942) and NORTHERN REVIEW (1945), both literary magazines. Anderson was an assistant professor at McGill for 2 years until he left Canada in 1950, not to revisit until 1971. During his Montréal years he wrote 3 poetry collections: *A Tent for April* (1945), *The White Centre* (1946) and *The Colour as Naked* (1953). In subsequent years, when working primarily in teaching positions in Malaysia and Britain, he wrote numerous travel books and biographies and 2 autobiographical works. A revival of Canadian interest in his work sparked 2 further volumes of a Canadian context: *A Visiting Distance* (1976) and *Return to Canada: Selected Poems* (1977).
MARLENE ALT

Anderson, Rudolph Martin, zoologist, explorer, conservationist (b near Decorah, Iowa 30 June 1876; d at Ottawa 22 June 1961). He participated in explorations of Alaska with the American Museum of Natural History, then served as second in command to Vilhjalmur STEFANSSON in the Canadian Arctic Expedition from Alaska to Bathurst Inlet (1913-16), leading its southern party and editing its 16-volume findings. His conservation efforts started then, when he pointed out declines of caribou and muskoxen in the North. In 1916 he was in Ottawa as part of a government advisory board that drafted the Migratory Birds Convention Act. As head of the biology division of the National Museum 1920-46, he published an important catalogue of Canadian mammals and a guide to collecting and preserving vertebrates still in wide use. He was also associate editor of the *Canadian Field-Naturalist* 1918-55.
MARTIN K. McNICHOLL

St Joseph's Oratory, constructed 1924-55 on the site of a small chapel built by Brother André on the slopes of Mount Royal. The basilica is the only major urban shrine in Canada and is visited by half a million pilgrims a year (*photo by Perry Mastrovito/Réflexion*).

Anderson River, 692 km long, originates in a group of lakes N of GREAT BEAR LK in the NWT and meanders N and W to empty into Liverpool Bay, an arm of the Beaufort Sea, just E of the Mackenzie Delta. Its lower reaches were originally inhabited by Inuit who were decimated by an epidemic of scarlet fever in 1865. During the 1860s the HBC operated a trading post at its mouth, where the modern settlement of Stanton is located. It is named after James Anderson, an HBC factor formerly in charge of the district.
DANIEL FRANCIS

André, Brother, né Alfred Bessette, faith healer, religious counsellor (b at St-Grégoire-d'Iberville, LC 9 Aug 1845; d at Montréal 6 Jan 1937). Although he was functionally illiterate, unimposing in speech and stature, and never advanced beyond the most lowly positions within his religious order, the Congregation of the Holy Cross (CSC), Brother André became the most popular religious figure in Québec in the 20th century. Tens of thousands attributed their miraculous healings to André's intervention with his patron, St Joseph, the husband of the Virgin Mary. His work scandalized many priests, physicians and sophisticated Catholics; but in 1904 his admirers, many from blue-collar families, helped him to build a small oratory in honour of Joseph on the slopes of Mount Royal. Some years later the church hierarchy became involved. A basilica, still Montréal's most imposing landmark, was constructed 1924-55. The church organized pilgrimages and the oratory became the liturgical centre for the Catholic trade-union movement of Québec. Half a million visitors still come to the oratory every year – the only major urban shrine in Canada.

Despite his reputation as a faith healer, Brother André's primary concern was to promote the worship of the suffering Christ through the patronage of St Joseph. Afflicted by poor health throughout his life, André encouraged his closest followers to accept their suffering rather than to seek healing, since suffering brings one closer to Jesus on the Cross. He was declared "venerable" in 1978 and formally beatified on 23 May 1982.
TOM SINCLAIR-FAULKNER

Reading: Henri-Paul Bergeron, *Brother André, Apostle of Saint Joseph* (1958).

Andre, Harvie, politician (b at Edmonton 27 July 1940). Educated at the California Inst of Technology and U of A (PhD 1963), Andre taught chemical engineering at U of Calgary 1966-72. Elected to the House of Commons for Calgary in 1972, he was a key supporter of Joe CLARK's successful bid for the PC leadership in 1976. A trusted Clark adviser thereafter, Andre was a vocal opponent of PETRO-CANADA and the NATIONAL ENERGY PROGRAM. He also developed an expertise on defence questions, pushing as Opposition defence critic for a stronger, better-equipped Canadian Armed Forces. He served as minister of supply and services in the MULRONEY government in 1984-85 and was associate minister of defence 1985-86. A tough but relentlessly cheerful government spokesman, he was appointed minister of consumer and corporate affairs in 1986 as well as minister responsible for Canada Post Corp in 1987.
NORMAN HILLMER

Andrews, Sybil, printmaker (b at Bury St Edmunds, Eng 1891). Before her arrival at Campbell R, BC, in 1947, Andrews studied in England with Claude Flight, a proponent of futurism, a radical art form of the early 1900s. Her themes have continuously been nonpolitical, everyday scenes of industry, sports and urban life. Linocuts, which were the chief medium of Flight's students, dictated the style and form of the art. Economy of line and shape and an emphasis on the positive/negative in colour and shape, combined with the futurist's aim to portray speed and movement, give Andrews's work an enduring art deco look. Her lifelong commitment to her themes and her ability to combine these ideas with her craft have enabled her to interpret everyday aspects of Canadian life.
KATHLEEN LAVERTY

Anemone, or wind flower, perennial, herbaceous PLANT of genus *Anemone,* family Ranunculaceae. The genus contains 120-150 species, most found in temperate and subarctic regions. The usually single, goblet-shaped flower lacks petals but has 5-20 petallike sepals. Colours range from white through purple to red. Anemones have a dry, one-seeded fruit (achene). Of the 20 N American species, 11 are native to Canada. The white-blossomed Canada anemone (*A. canadensis*), the most widespread species in moist locations, is found throughout Canada, excluding Newfoundland. *A. patens,* Manitoba's PROVINCIAL FLORAL EMBLEM since 1906, is commonly but incorrectly known as the prairie crocus. Its purple-tinged sepals are a beautiful sight on the Prairies early in spring. The most familiar cultivated forms are the fall-blooming Japanese anemone (*A. hupehensis*) and the spring-blooming florist's anemone (*A. coronaria*). Anemones require well-drained soil and partial shade. They are grown from seed or propagated by division.
CÉLINE ARSENEAULT

Prairie crocus (*Anemone patens*), Manitoba's floral emblem (*photo by Julie O. Hrapko*).

Angéline de Montbrun (1882), novel by Laure Conan (pseudonym of Félicité ANGERS), is French Canada's first psychological novel and one of its first novels by a woman. In it Angers adapts epistolary fiction, religious meditations and the private lady's journal to narrate the tragedy of a young girl, raised by her godlike father in the isolated village of Valriant, who cannot, after his death, transfer her affections to her fiancé Maurice. Her beauty having been symbolically disfigured in a fall, Angéline renounces the world and her lover. In contrast to her friend Mina, a *mondaine* ("worldly woman") turned Ursuline nun, she struggles in a private agony and ecstasy of regret, eagerly awaiting death and the joys of afterlife. Angers transmutes autobiographical details into a powerful psychological study of the role played by religion in 19th-century family life. *Angéline* was serialized in *La Revue canadienne* (June 1881 - Aug 1882), published in book form in 1884 and reissued several times. It was translated into English by Yves Brunelle in 1974.

MICHÈLE LACOMBE

Angers, Félicité, pen name Laure Conan, writer (b at La Malbaie, Qué 9 Jan 1845; d at Québec C 6 June 1924). A witness to her times and the first French Canadian female novelist, Conan's writings followed the triple imperative of family, nation and religion. *Un Amour vrai* (1878-79) is only a long story, but ANGÉLINE DE MONTBRUN (serialized 1881-82) is an original novel: its form and structure (correspondence, narrative, diary) respond to personal needs and the characters are more than traditional stereotypes. Its first critics called it pious, some modern ones call it unhealthy, others note its fine psychological analysis and daring form. The heroines of *La Vaine foi* (1921) and *L'Obscure souffrance* (1919), both in domestic service, give deeper expression to the sorrow and faith of Angéline de Montbrun. Carried along by the literary current of the day and influenced by François-Xavier GARNEAU's *Histoire du Canada,* Conan wrote 3 historical novels. In *À l'oeuvre et à l'épreuve* (1891), the Christian hero, Garnier, renounces his youthful love to become a Jesuit and dies a martyr's death. In *L'Oublié* (1900), Closse is obedient to familial duty but still dies a hero's death for the homeland. *La Sève immortelle* (1925) demonstrates the courage of 2 young people who give up their foreign loves to marry each other and better serve their country.

GABRIELLE POULIN

Anglicanism is that tradition in CHRISTIANITY whose members are in full communion with the see of Canterbury, Eng. Originally confined to the British Isles, the Church of England has spread to almost every corner of the world, with some 2.4 million adherents in Canada (1981c; latest figures available). Anglicanism considers itself to stand within the primitive catholic tradition, preserving a solid scriptural basis; a ministry of bishops, priests and deacons in unbroken succession from the time of the Apostles; a sacramental order; and a recognition of church tradition which is nevertheless freed from medieval excesses and superstitions. Anglicanism is both catholic in this sense and a product of the 16th-century Reformation. The word "Protestant" is sometimes applied to it, but this is confusing because the same word is also applied to the nonepiscopal bodies that appeared at the time of the Reformation. In Scotland, the US and elsewhere, Anglicans are also known as Episcopalians.

Anglicanism stands within the Greco-Gallican (theological and liturgical) tradition; its nature is to emphasize community and loving relationship as distinct from the legal conformity emphasized by the Latin (Roman Catholic) tradition. It has been concerned with reunifying the Christian

St Anne's Anglican Church, Toronto. The church is a scaled-down model of the Byzantine masterpiece Hagia Sophia in Istanbul. In 1923 J.E.H. MacDonald was hired to direct the beautification and many of the panels were executed by Group of Seven members (*courtesy St Anne's Anglican Church, photo by Tibor Roder*).

faith and has a long history of what are now known as ecumenical encounters. In Canada, discussion among various Protestant bodies in the late 19th century were precursors to the formation of the UNITED CHURCH OF CANADA in 1925. Anglicans took no part in these early negotiations, but began discussions with the United Church in the 1940s and from 1969 included the CHRISTIAN CHURCH (DISCIPLES OF CHRIST). The resulting "Plan of Union" proposed that the Protestant bodies accept the episcopal church structure, and attempts were made to deal with differences in theology. Limited practical co-operation included sanctioning a joint calendar and a common hymn book. But by the early 1970s enthusiasm had cooled, and in 1975 the Anglican Church formally withdrew from negotiations on the grounds that the nonepiscopal bodies had failed to realize that they were not dealing with another Protestant group.

There has been a greater possibility of understanding between Anglicanism and the Church of Rome, although it has been hindered by doctrinal differences and, since the first Vatican Council (1870), by the refusal of Rome to recognize Anglican ordinations. The Anglican-Roman Catholic International Commission (ARCIC) issued a report on the first stage of its deliberations in 1981. This indicated the possibility of agreement on the Eucharist, ordination and the nature of authority in the church. The talks continued in 1987 on the remaining differences and practical ways of bringing a reconciliation.

In its modern form Anglicanism has been a religion of 2 books: the Bible and the Book of Common Prayer. It understands the Bible as *fons et origo* of Christian truth but also as subject to interpretation by the church; tradition plays an important part in its understanding. Anglican scholars have been in the forefront of biblical studies. Anglicanism is also liturgical in its worship. The first prayer book, which appeared in 1549 and was largely the work of Archbishop Thomas Cranmer, was a compilation of ancient biblical and Catholic worship. Current revisions used throughout the world still reflect Cranmer's influence. The Book of Common Prayer has been described as the Bible arranged for worship. The Liturgical Movement of the 20th century has had far-reaching effects on Anglicanism as on all other liturgical churches. In Canada, as in some other branches of the Anglican communion, the Prayer Book has been supplemented by a *Book of Alternative Services*

which, it is anticipated, will contribute to the pattern of a future Book of Common Prayer. Anglicanism emphasizes a ministry of Word and Sacrament. The Eucharist, in theory and increasingly in practice, is the principal Sunday service. There has been some tension between scriptural and sacramental emphasis, the evangelical (low-church) position emphasizing the ministry of the Word and personal religious experience, the catholic (high-church) position seeing the church as a divine society, the Body of Christ, administering the grace of God through the sacraments.

There has always been flexibility in Anglican theology, and hence Anglicanism has not always seemed to present the same face to the world. But because wide differences of interpretation and practice are possible within Anglicanism, schisms have been rare. In "Old Dissent" the principal examples, CONGREGATIONALISTS (or Separatists) and ANABAPTISTS (who originally included those later called BAPTISTS), represent not so much a dissent from Anglicanism itself as a doctrinal divergence from catholicism in general. The outstanding example of "New Dissent" was METHODISM, in which the differences were less doctrinal than practical and behavioural, and the schism was due to misunderstanding and intransigence on both sides.

More recently the only schisms of note have been those of the Reformed Episcopal movement in the 19th century and the Anglo-Catholic group in the 20th. The Reformed Episcopal Church, fd 1843 in the US to protest against "ritualism," appeared in England the following year as the Free Church of England, and in Canada, chiefly in Ontario and BC, about the same time. It was distinctively evangelical and strongly opposed to what it considered to be romanizing tendencies. It has virtually disappeared in the 20th century. The Anglican Catholic Church, which gained a small following in Canada, was born of a reaction against what was regarded as liberalization in the Episcopal Church of the US in the 1970s. Particular objection was taken to proposed revisions of the prayer book and to the admission of women to holy orders. This has been one of the significant changes in modern Anglicanism. Women were admitted to synods in the 1950s and to ordination in 1976. In 1987 there were 176 women clergy. No women have yet been elected to the episcopate.

Anglicans have always been interested in education and have been active in the establishment and support of schools and colleges. Many Canadian universities were originally either Anglican foundations or have been strongly supported by Anglicans.

History in Canada The first known service in what is now Canada was performed by Robert Wolfall, a chaplain in Sir Martin FROBISHER'S expedition, in Frobisher Bay [Iqaluit] on 2 Sept 1578. Thereafter Anglicanism spread through immigration from the British Isles and the coming of LOYALISTS, many of whom were Anglicans, after the American Revolution. In the British colonies it was tacitly assumed that, without special legislation, the Church of England was the established, or "official," church, with the same status and limitations as in the mother country. This was not always understood by the people, particularly non-Anglicans, or by the authorities. Establishment was a thorny issue, hotly debated throughout early Canadian history (*see* CLERGY RESERVES). The purpose of 18th-century Nova Scotia legislation was not to "establish" the C of E, since that was taken for granted, but to assure Protestants of freedom of worship and to exclude Roman Catholics. Establishment imposed certain responsibilities in the conduct and registration of baptisms, marriages, and burials, important in the days before state registration of vital statistics. It did not imply that the church had coercive powers to compel support, nor that it derived financial advantage from the state.

In early Canada there was no local church organization. C of E clergy had been sent by the missionary societies or were military chaplains. In keeping with the principle of establishment, the governor was the ordinary (chief ecclesiastical officer) and made necessary organizational decisions which might include appointments to parishes and the issue of marriage licences; he had no sacramental or ecclesiastical powers.

Missions were the work of the Society for the Propagation of the Gospel (SPG), fd 1701, an extension of the Society for Promoting Christian Knowledge (SPCK), fd 1698; the Church Missionary Society (CMS), fd 1799; and the Colonial and Continental Church Society (CCCS or "Col. & Con."), fd 1838. The 2 former societies undertook the whole of Anglican missionary work among native peoples in BNA until the 1905 formation of the Missionary Society of the Church in Canada, and continued to support a large part until the 1940s. CCCS was an evangelical society which concentrated on ministering to settlers. Beyond that, its greatest single work was maintaining Emmanuel College, Saskatoon, for the training of clergy, 1914-54.

The first Anglican bishopric in BNA was that of Nova Scotia, established in 1787 with Loyalist Charles INGLIS as bishop. Although he was styled bishop of Nova Scotia, his jurisdiction included Newfoundland, Bermuda, PEI, and Lower and Upper Canada. His load was lightened in 1793 with the creation of the Diocese of Quebec with Jacob MOUNTAIN as bishop. The diocese of Québec was further subdivided in 1839 when John STRACHAN became the first bishop. Strachan was a colourful and sometimes controversial figure who contributed greatly to the ecclesiastical, political and educational life of his times. In a real sense he was the founder of University of Toronto and of the University of Trinity College, Toronto. During his episcopate the see was subdivided to form the dioceses of Huron and Ontario. In 1860 the 6 dioceses – Nova Scotia, Quebec, Toronto, Fredericton, Montreal and Huron – had com-

bined to form the Provincial Synod of the Church of England and Ireland in Canada.

The General Synod of the Church of England in Canada was formed in 1893 with the first sessions at Trinity College, Toronto, in September. The General Synod is a legislative and administrative body with clerical and lay representatives from each diocese. Its presiding bishop was accorded the title Primate of All Canada.

The Provincial Synod of RUPERT'S LAND was formed in 1875. The diocese of Rupert's Land had been created in 1849 with David ANDERSON as the first bishop. In the time of his successor, Robert Machray, the see was subdivided by the formation of the dioceses of Moosonee in 1872, with John Horden as the first bishop, and Saskatchewan and Athabasca with John McLean and William Carpenter BOMPAS, respectively, in 1874. A bishop was elected in each province to act as presiding bishop, or metropolitan, and in 1893 it was decided they should be styled "archbishop."

In 1912, the 5 dioceses in the civil province of Ontario (Toronto, Huron, Ontario, Niagara, Ottawa and Algoma), were separated from the province of Canada to form the ecclesiastical province of Ontario. Similarly, in 1914 the dioceses of BC, previously without any provincial organization, combined in the ecclesiastical province of British Columbia. The modern Anglican Church of Canada (the name was changed in 1955) is made up of 30 dioceses, distributed in 4 provinces each with a metropolitan archbishop. The flag of the church is the red St George's cross with a green maple leaf in each quarter.

In the 19th century, Anglican missionaries often failed to distinguish between evangelization and acculturation, tacitly assuming that to be Anglican was to be English. This led to difficulties in later years. In the 20th century, there has been tension between the claims of spirituality and those of social welfare. The church has always been concerned for the needy (in England it was for many years the only agency for the relief of the poor). In 1908 a committee on Moral and Social Reform (later the Council of Social Service) was set up by the Canadian General Synod. It laboured long to awaken and inform the social conscience of Canadian Anglicans. Organizational structures at the national level have changed, but the church continues to be actively involved in social issues such as ABORTION and BIRTH CONTROL, social and economic problems, the PEACE MOVEMENT and native rights. Although there is considerable support for such activities, some members fear that the church's mission is in danger of being distorted and misunderstood: economic well-being does not necessarily imply membership in the Kingdom of God. F.A. PEAKE

Reading: T.C.B. Boon, *The Anglican Church from the Bay to the Rockies* (1962); B. Cuthbertson, *The First Bishop* (1987); J.L.H. Henderson, *John Strachan* (1969); T.R. Millman, *Jacob Mountain* (1947) and *Atlantic Canada to 1900* (1983); F.A. Peake, *The Anglican Church in British Columbia* (1959).

Anglin, Margaret, actress (b at Ottawa 3 Apr 1876; d at Toronto 7 Jan 1958). Daughter of Timothy W. ANGLIN, Speaker of the House of Commons, she was born in the Speaker's Chambers. She made her professional debut in 1894 in *Shenandoah* in New York and was an early success as Roxanne in *Cyrano de Bergerac* (1898), in the title role in *Mrs. Dane's Defence* and in *The Great Divide* (1906). She had her own classical company in 1913, playing Shakespeare's Viola, Rosalind and Cleopatra. In Greek tragedy she was dynamic as Antigone, Medea, Electra and Iphigenia. She retired after *Watch on the Rhine* (1943). She toured once to Australia and frequently performed in Canada. DAVID GARDNER

Anglin, Timothy Warren, journalist, politician (b at Clonakilty, County Cork, Ire 31 Aug 1822; d at Toronto 3 May 1896). Shaped by his IRISH, Catholic, middle-class upbringing he emigrated in 1849 following the Great Famine. In Saint John, NB, he established the *Freeman* newspaper, through which he represented, promoted and defended the interests of Irish Catholics for over 3 decades. Elected to the NB Assembly in 1861, he waged a well-argued and initially successful campaign against CONFEDERATION and became a Cabinet member in the NB Anticonfederate government in 1865. Confederates attacked Anglin in a disreputable but effective campaign in which they accused him and his supporters of disloyalty. Nonetheless, Anglin acquiesced in the new political order after Confederation and from 1867 to 1882 was an elected MP in Ottawa and a prominent member of the Reform (Liberal) Party. During Alexander Mackenzie's administration (1873-78), Anglin was Speaker of the House of Commons. His political interests ranged widely but especially involved religious/ethnic matters such as the New Brunswick schools question of the 1870s. Moving to Toronto in 1883 he continued his lifelong activities in journalism and politics, though in a less prominent fashion. Anglin raised an accomplished family, including Frank, who became Chief Justice of the Canadian Supreme Court, and Margaret, the internationally acclaimed actress. As an articulate but feisty leader of Irish Catholics, Anglin provided an important mechanism for accommodating that group within Canadian society.

WILLIAM M. BAKER

Reading: William M. Baker, *Timothy Warren Anglin 1822-96: Irish Catholic Canadian* (1977).

Anguhadluq, Luke, Inuit artist (b at Chantrey Inlet, NWT 1895; d at Baker Lk, NWT 8 Feb 1982). A powerful camp leader of the Utkuhikhalingmiut people, Anguhadluq had 2 adult sons to hunt beside him, a rare good fortune during the years of starvation among the inland CARIBOU INUIT. When he moved into Baker Lk at age 73, too old to hunt, he turned to drawing as a source of income. His drawings depict a world view unique to hunting peoples and reminiscent of prehistoric art. When Anguhadluq made drawings of the drum dance, he made the skin drum enormous and yellow like the sun, dominating the centre of the picture. Small, static Inuit men and women spiral around the drum like rays emanating from their shamanic source. When drawing, he laid the paper between his outstretched legs and turned the drawing as he worked, conceiving his image like a map, looking down on his subject, with one continuous horizon line formed by the edges of the paper. K.J. BUTLER

Angus, Henry Forbes, educator, public servant (b at Victoria 19 Apr 1891). A professor of economics at UBC, 1919-56, Angus was a key member of the Royal Commission on DOMINION-PROVINCIAL RELATIONS, 1937-40, and an official in the Dept of External Affairs 1940-45. He worked for full rights for JAPANESE Canadians in the interwar years and vigorously opposed their internment during WWII. He also championed international co-operation, particularly among peoples and nations bordering on the Pacific. *Canada and Her Great Neighbor: Sociological Surveys of Opinions and Attitudes in Canada Concerning the United States* (1938) and *Canada and the Far East, 1940-1953* (1953) are his best-known publications.

NORMAN HILLMER

Angus, Richard Bladworth, banker (b at Bathgate, Scot 28 May 1831; d at Senneville, Qué 17 Sept 1922). Trained in a Manchester bank, he immigrated to Québec in 1857 and joined the

BANK OF MONTREAL and became its general manager in 1869. He then served as vice-president of the St Paul Minneapolis and Manitoba Railroad, 1879-83. A business associate of George STEPHEN, he was one of the founding directors of the CANADIAN PACIFIC RY and a member of its executive committee, 1881-1922. He played an active role in CPR affairs and acted as an important link with the Bank of Montreal, of which he was president 1910-15.   JOHN A. EAGLE

Anhalt, István, composer, educator (b at Budapest, Hungary 12 Apr 1919). One of Canada's most individual composers, whose work is strongly influenced by his study of the psychology of speech, Anhalt combines traditional instruments, electronics and the human voice in the textures and sonorities of a highly complex musical language. He came to Montréal in 1949 and joined McGill's music theory department. He founded and directed its Electronic Music Studio 1964-71, and then went to Kingston as head of Queens's music department, where he has been professor emeritus since 1984. Representative of his works are *Symphony No. 1* (1958), *Symphony of Modules*, for orchestra and tape (1967), *Foci* (1969) and *La Tourangelle* (1975), a musical based on the life of the 17th-century Ursuline MARIE DE L'INCARNATION.   BARCLAY MCMILLAN

Animal Animals are many-celled, responsive heterotrophs (eaters of various things). Herbivores eat plants; carnivores eat flesh; omnivores, such as man, eat nearly everything. Parasites inhabit and subsist in other organisms. The shape of animals, the way they move, how they sense and seize and swallow food suggest that the need to find an organic food source is the most important characteristic of their lives. The EVOLUTION of animal structure has resulted in a vast number of adaptations, so that there are now more kinds of animals than of all other living things combined. It is impossible to keep track of all species that have been formally described, but there are more than a million. Two thousand to 4000 new species are found annually, usually small and inconspicuous, often from remote places (eg, Canada's ARCTIC ARCHIPELAGO).

The animal kingdom is divided into 33 groups (phyla), each one of which has characteristics setting it apart from all others. The FOSSIL record shows that animals have existed for more than 600 million years. Although their origins are obscure, they undoubtedly evolved from animallike PROTISTA. Patterns of structure link the members of each phylum. Species within a phylum differ by individual modifications which have evolved to serve different modes of life. During the history of life, perhaps 10 times as many forms as now exist have arisen. Most species of animals persist for millions of years but, invariably, each is supplanted by another, better adapted to the conditions within which it lives.

Animal distribution depends on geography, climate and historical events. Each continental mass has a unique fauna which has evolved largely independently. Within each continent are distinctive associations isolated by features such as mountains, deserts or forests. Events of the past, such as GLACIATION or the shifting of land (*see* PLATE TECTONICS), have strongly influenced the adaptations of animals. Thus, there are more kinds of animals in the tropics than in the high latitudes, because of more equable climatic conditions, and because conditions have been stable for longer periods, allowing for more complete exploitation of available habitats. The fauna of Canada, like its PHYSIOGRAPHIC REGIONS and VEGETATION, reflects its N American association, and the effects of the GLACIERS which only 10 000 years ago covered about 97% of Canada's surface.

Some animals are found nearly everywhere in Canada, eg, northern pike, walleye, whitefish, Canada goose, mallard, ruffed grouse, beaver, muskrat, moose, black bear, weasel. Others are restricted, and almost unique to Canada, eg, muskoxen in the Arctic Lowlands; mountain goats in the Cordillera; pronghorns in the Interior Plains; lake trout around the Shield; snow geese across the Shield and eastern Arctic. The rich assemblage of animals in the St Lawrence Lowlands, a northern extension of southern forms, includes bowfins among the fish, more amphibians and reptiles than anywhere else in Canada, the opossum and many birds.

Canada's animals have influenced its history through their effects on the FUR TRADE, FISHERIES and settlement, as well as story and song. Canada's heritage includes tales of fierce mosquitoes and black flies, vast herds of bison, calls of loon and coyote, busyness of beavers and friendliness of whiskey jacks. The fear inspired by grizzly bear and timber wolf, the sight of killer whale and sea otter, the skill needed to catch Atlantic salmon and the pleasure of dining on Winnipeg goldeye are legendary. It is a rich heritage that must be preserved.

Reading: C.P. Hickman et al, *Integrated Principles of Zoology* (1984).

Animal Agriculture Domesticated animals are those of which the maintenance and reproduction are, to some degree, controlled by humans. Certain behavioural traits are needed if an animal is to be adapted to domestication, including the ability to live in groups, reasonably rapid reproduction rates and the ability to thrive on available food. Modern BEEF and DAIRY cattle, HOGS, HORSES, GOATS, SHEEP and POULTRY are the results of breeding programs extending over centuries (goats were domesticated as early as 7000 BC). Thus, even within poultry (*Gallus domesticus*), the ability to produce large quantities of eggs is carried by certain breeds, while rapid growth (for meat) is carried by others.

Besides being important sources of various foods, animals also supply mankind with many other items. About 40% of the live ruminant, 60% of the live hog and 70% of live poultry are used as human food. The average Canadian dairy cow produces about 5600 kg of milk annually; the average chicken lays about 260 eggs per year. Animals also provide wool, LEATHER and feathers. By-products include INSULIN, bone meal and glycerol.

Since the 1970s Canadian food consumption patterns have changed markedly: beef, pork and poultry consumption has increased substantially, and fruit, vegetable and sugar consumption has also gone up; consumption of dairy products and eggs has decreased, as has that of wheat flour and, to a slight degree, potatoes. The figures indicate only the amount of product purchased; actual consumption is difficult to determine, as a good deal of wastage occurs after purchase. In 1985, the most recent year for which figures are available, per-capita consumption of animal products is as follows: beef, 39 kg; pork, 28 kg; poultry, 25 kg; milk solids, 25 kg; eggs, 12 kg. Total animal products consumption approximates 135 kg per person per year. Canadians eat very little veal, lamb or mutton; per capita totals do not normally exceed 3-4 kg.

Livestock Census In 1986 livestock and products accounted for 50% of farm income in Canada, ie, $10.2 billion. An estimated 13.4 million cattle and calves were held on Canadian farms, including 2.2 million milk cows and dairy heifers and 4.7 million beef cows and heifers. Over 9.8 million pigs and 761 000 sheep and lambs were kept. The estimated poultry population in 1986 included 87.9 million hens and chickens, over 7.7 mil-

lion turkeys and over 2.3 million other poultry. Over 443 million dozen eggs were produced. In the Atlantic region, livestock and livestock products contributed $482.6 million or 66% of total farm cash receipts; in Québec, $2.38 billion or 74%; in Ontario, $3.37 billion or 61%; in the Prairie region, $3.34 billion or 33%; in BC, $629 million or 62%.

Livestock and Food It is often argued that animals produced for food compete with humans for available food and should, therefore, be reduced or eliminated as the world population continues to increase. Some competition for food does occur; for example, domestic animals consume cereal grains, some of which would be suitable for humans. However, ruminants are able to utilize materials not useful to humans and even non-ruminants can use some forage-type material. Much of the world's agricultural land is unsuitable for intensive crop production. In Canada, about 18 million ha is classified as unsuitable for any agricultural use, beyond the production of perennial FORAGE CROPS, because of its topography, climate, soil type, etc. This land can be harvested only by grazing and animals raised on such land do not compete with humans but, rather, contribute greatly to the human diet.

Furthermore, animals can convert poor-quality protein into high-quality protein, which is of particular significance to the diet of small children. The use of cereal and legume by-products for animal foods is an integral part of Canadian agriculture. Economic competition for these products determines the degree to which they are and will be used for animal feed. Waste is a feature of all phases of food production. For example, about 30% of wheat milled is by-products, eg, middlings, shorts and bran. The extraction of oil from soybeans and rapeseed yields vast amounts of by-products, useful primarily as protein sources for livestock. When corn, wheat, oats or barley are harvested for grain, the remaining stalk or straw can be used as an energy source for ruminants. Residues from vegetable and fruit crops, low-quality fruit, vegetables and grain, and many other items, including garbage, can also be used.

Livestock and Soil Conservation Specialization of production has been a continuing trend in Canadian agriculture for many years. Factors contributing to the trend include the development of skills in crop production, housing of animals and applications of technology, combined with the availability of vast amounts of power and access to large markets. Specialization in plant growing has led to increased destruction of soil because one or 2 particular crops are grown year after year on the same land, and because of increased dependence on purchased fertilizers and chemicals, large fields and large equipment. The presence of livestock allows greater variety in crop production and the application of manure, an important fertilizer, to the land. No substitute for such procedures, suitable for maintaining the integrity of the soil, has been found. Thus, livestock production contributes to the long-term integrity of the agricultural system.

Other Uses Animals kept for pleasure include common pets, recreational animals, such as HORSES, and even some food-producing animals. All are important to Canada's society and economy. The racing, riding and workhorse industries alone employ thousands of people and are worth billions of dollars. It is estimated that there are half as many horses in Canada now as when they were used as a primary power source; their main use now is for pleasure. In some parts of Canada, notably Waterloo County, Ont, horses still serve as a power source for farmers, eg, for tilling and transportation. In western Canada the horse is a key factor in efficient RANCHING. Horses consume large amounts of forages and by-product materials and some cereals. The cat- and dog-food business is also of great economic significance as are VETERINARY services, grooming materials, etc. Cats and dogs compete with humans for food to some degree, but many are fed scraps and table wastes.

W.D. MORRISON

Animal Management

Animal management involves integrating the proper feeding, breeding, health care, housing and handling of domestic animals to optimize their productivity. The animal manager requires knowledge and skill to operate within the limits imposed by the available resources of land, labour and capital.

Feeding Farm livestock includes ruminant mammals (cattle, sheep, goats), nonruminant mammals (horses, hogs, furbearers) and poultry. With the help of its microbial "partners" the ruminant is able to digest considerable portions of fibrous materials such as hay, straw and silage, feeds which are unsuitable for pigs or poultry. (The horse, while a nonruminant, possesses a microbial population in the hindgut that permits digestion of fibre to a comparable degree.) The microbes are also able to synthesize the right kind of amino acids (components of protein) from dietary protein in which such acids are missing (or present in inadequate amounts) or, to a limited extent, from nonprotein nitrogen in the diet. They are also able to synthesize some vitamins, notably those of the B group. Nonruminants do not have these capabilities; thus, nonruminant rations must provide all essential vitamins, minerals and amino acids. This consideration also applies in the feeding of calves, lambs and kids, since the young of ruminant species do not possess a developed rumen until they are some months old.

In Canada, feeds are normally classified as roughages (pasture, hay, straw, silage), basal feeds (grain, grain by-products) and protein supplements (mainly residues of OILSEED crops and products of animal origin, eg, fish meal). Roughages are normally the cheapest feeds and, therefore, form the basis of all ruminant and horse diets. Production of quality hay requires early cutting and, in some parts of Canada, the use of a barn drier to eliminate excess moisture. Successful and profitable feeding of farm livestock involves the provision of foodstuffs that supply the requisite nutrients in the cheapest possible form, in amounts permitting the animal to produce up to their genetic potential but without wasting feed by oversupply. The major advances in COMPUTER technology applied to animal operations simplify efficient feeding as well as other processes.

Health and Handling Managers of any animal enterprise must know in what circumstances to take appropriate action and when to call for skilled veterinary help. One of the most characteristic features of modern livestock farming is intensification, especially in the aspect of housing. Intensification increases the inherent health hazard; thus, in designing buildings for livestock, strict attention must be paid to sanitation, ventilation and temperature control, as well as cost and operational ease.

Effective disease control requires avoidance of stress, quarantine of new additions and sick animals, preventive vaccination against some bacteria (eg, those of genus *Clostridium,* which cause tetanus, blackleg, etc) and strict sanitization of such equipment as milking machines. Many potential pathogens (eg, intestinal worms, coccidia) normally live within farm livestock at a level of host-parasite balance. Only when stress or some other factor renders the host weakened or vulnerable does the parasite multiply, often very rapidly,

producing symptoms of illness in the host. Thus, to minimize stress, livestock should always be handled quietly with the aid of such facilities (eg, corrals, chutes, headgates, etc) as will make matters easy for both operator and stock. Agriculture Canada is responsible for legislation to protect Canada's livestock from diseases identified by law as reportable. Scrupulous adherence to such legislation and good management have made Canadian livestock breeders and farmers among the most successful in the world and Canadian livestock (both breeding stock and that intended for human consumption) much sought after.

Marketing

Production of many commodities (eg, milk, eggs, pork, chicken) is controlled by national or provincial regulatory boards, which may set requirements for health and nutrient content and may also regulate output (*see* COMMODITY INSPECTION AND GRADING; FOOD LEGISLATION). For example, milk for sale must be produced on premises meeting strict sanitary standards. It is priced according to its butterfat content and produced according to a quota system, with a differential pricing structure to discourage oversupply or undersupply. Similarly, hogs are marketed at a standard weight (100 kg live weight) and overweight or overfat hogs suffer discount pricing. Among farm livestock, beef cattle, hogs, sheep, goats, horses and fur animals can now be produced in Canada without imposed restrictions of output. Here too, however, the effective manager must keep in mind current market conditions and strive to foresee coming changes to modify production accordingly. Good management must therefore include a responsible and co-operative attitude toward the inspection of products and premises as well as strict observance of such matters as drug use and drug-withdrawal periods.

W.G. MATHEWSON

Animal Breeding The science of animal breeding belongs entirely to the 20th century but the art and practice were ushered in by those who first attempted domestication of wild species. Initial attempts to develop captive herds capable of supporting permanent settlements occurred in the Neolithic era (about 25 000 years ago) and marked the beginning of human intervention in the natural EVOLUTION of animal species.

Amenability to handling was undoubtedly the first selection criterion but, judging from cave paintings that have survived, attention was also paid to hair colour, horn size, hair length, etc. In the absence of written records, there is no certain knowledge of the evolution of animal breeding practices but written documents dating back more than 4000 years indicate that humans appreciated the significance of family resemblances in animal mating schemes, recognized inbreeding hazards and enforced their selection decisions by castrating males not desired for breeding. One consequence of this process was the development of diverse types (breeds) within each domesticated species. In addition, a wide geographical redistribution of species occurred as invading armies, migrating peoples and traders transported livestock into new lands.

The Englishman Robert Bakewell, who lived in the 18th century, was the first to introduce progeny testing to determine the breeding worth of young males, and vigorously promoted such concepts as "like begets like," "inbreeding produces prepotency" and "breed the best to the best." His successes attracted imitators, who established diverse British breeds of BEEF and DAIRY cattle, SHEEP and HOGS, and initiated breed societies and pedigree herd books. Most modern breeds originated from 1790 to 1860.

Animal Breeding in Canada Important early crossbreeding studies were performed at University of Saskatchewan before 1930, under the direction of J.W. Grant MACEWAN and L.M. Winters. Since 1940, the major research centres have been the Agriculture Canada RESEARCH STATIONS at Lacombe, Alta, Brandon, Man, and Ottawa; the major educational centres, the universities of Alberta, Manitoba, Guelph and McGill. The relative scarcity of scientists and research centres in this area reflects the high cost of breeding research on large animals.

Notable crossbreeding studies have included the investigations of Roy Berg (U of A) and Howard FREDEEN and associates (Lacombe Research Station). Inbreeding studies with pigs ended at Lacombe in 1960 but continue with laboratory species (mice) at several locations. Canadian studies on quantitative genetics were initiated by Jack Stothart (1934). He and his successors have used field data to augment and extend the theory and practice of livestock population genetics. Stothart was also the first to evaluate this theory empirically through controlled selection experiments with pigs. His results, since augmented by studies with poultry by Robert Gowe (Ottawa), beef cattle by Jack Newman (Lacombe) and John Lawson (Lethbridge, Alta), and beef cattle and pigs by Gunther Rahnefeld (Brandon) and Howard Fredeen (Lacombe), were in full accord with theoretical expectations. Practical application of population genetics theory by Stothart and Fredeen led to development of the Lacombe breed of pigs, the first livestock breed developed in Canada, and now propagated in 24 countries. Other applications of their theoretical and applied research have been the national performance testing programs for pigs and beef cattle, and practical performance selection programs for the livestock industry.

Show-ring standards, once considered authoritative criteria for potential breeding merit, have given way to performance tests that objectively measure the differences among contemporary animals or progeny groups for quantitative traits such as growth rate and production of eggs, milk, wool and meat. Livestock exhibitions now serve primarily to promote and sell animals that have met performance test criteria (*see* AGRICULTURAL EXHIBITIONS).

Quantitative genetic variability is gradually decreased and selection effectiveness diminished in animal populations subjected to prolonged, intense selection. This fact does not impose an insurmountable barrier to continued genetic improvement; research has demonstrated that genetic variability can be restored by a period of relaxed selection or by the crossing of plateaued lines. A potential barrier, however, is the presence of genes or gene complements that enhance performance for one desired trait but have detrimental effects on others; eg, the single major gene (or linkage group) that causes muscular hypertrophy and simultaneously increases susceptibility to stress. Muscular hypertrophy is desirable because it enhances the shape and muscle content of specific carcass cuts; however, associated stress susceptibility diminishes reproductive rate, increases incidence of death through cardiovascular failure, and promotes undesired postmortem biochemical changes in muscle tissue.

GENETIC ENGINEERING techniques are being applied in research at the Veterinary Infectious Disease Organization (VIDO), U of Sask campus, to create new vaccines for livestock diseases. There is optimism that application of this technology to large animals will clarify the multiple effects caused by specific genes and, with pigs, for example, permit development of stock possessing muscular hypertrophy without stress susceptibility.

Animal breeding research in Canada proceeds on several fronts. Work at McGill emphasizes the genetics of congenital defects in MAMMALS, particularly humans (*see* GENETIC DISEASE). Guelph has specialized in refinement of mathematical techniques for predicting potential breeding worth. Work at other research centres, notably the western universities and units of the Research Branch, embraces both theoretical and applied aspects of population genetics in studies of mating systems, performance selection techniques and the biological interpretation of genotypic and phenotypic variance. Results are published in numerous international journals, including the *Canadian Journal of Animal Science* and the *Canadian Journal of Genetics and Cytology*.   HOWARD FREDEEN

Animal Issues The close relationship between man and animals has persisted since prehistoric times but societies for the protection of animals have been in existence for only about 100 years in the Western World. During the Victorian era, the antivivisection movement developed to oppose science's use of animals in biomedical research. The battle between vivisectionists and antivivisectionists resulted in the UK's Cruelty to Animals Act of 1876. This legislation heralded a clear victory for the antivivisection movement and imposed upon Britain's medical scientists a system of licensing, inspection and bureaucratic practices which is still under debate.

After WWII, biomedical research escalated tremendously. New drugs, treatments and techniques were discovered at a pace that permitted the health sciences to prevent and treat conditions previously thought to be incurable, to prolong life and relieve suffering. In Canada since 1968, surveillance of the ethical use of the 2 million experimental animals used annually in biomedical research has been the responsibility of the Canadian Council on Animal Care. The CCAC pioneered the requirement of local institutional animal-care committees, a concept recently adopted in the US and Australia. Approximately 20 million animals are used annually for research in the US and 4.3 million in the UK. However, numbers are decreasing because of high cost and development of alternative techniques, such as tissue culture and computer simulation. Although animal experiments have resulted in medical and surgical advances for humans and for animals themselves, criticism of the use of animals remains. In 1975, clinical psychologist Richard Ryder coined the term "speciesism," ie, a bias favouring one's own species. This bias has been criticized by philosophers who opposed the Judeo-Christian concept of man's "dominion" over animals and held that animals had rights similar to those of humans (eg, living without suffering and use inflicted by the human animal). Peter Singer, James Mason and others extended the discussion of animal liberation to include a "new ethics" for the treatment of animals. They widened their fields of concern to domesticated animals raised under new, intensive livestock-management practices; those in entertainment such as RODEOS, circuses and ZOOS; and those hunted for sport or for their skins. Animal activist groups have conducted acts of vandalism against scientists, research laboratories and "factory farms." Butchers' windows have been labelled "Meat is Murder." Protests have often culminated in violent acts and arrests which in many instances have given to the perpetrators a sense of martyrdom and accomplishment.

HUMANE SOCIETIES and other less militant animal-welfare groups have been willing to discuss differences in a rational, nonpolarized manner. Some consider the efforts of the activists "misdirected humaneness." Of the 34 organizations devoted to animal welfare in Canada, the Canadian Federation of Humane Societies (CFHS) has the largest membership (200 000, including affiliates). Unfortunately, the proliferation of special-interest groups (eg, "Save Our Seals") has diluted the overall objectives of the animal-welfare community. This splintering effect has sometimes hindered those who take a moderate stand in their attempts to protect animals and eliminate cruel practices. No one, as yet, has defined "humaneness," but the question has been addressed by philosophy professor Bernard E. Rollin in his book *Animal Rights and Human Morality* (1981).

Many symposia have sought to define the problems associated with pet animals. Discussions have focused on disease, dog bites, the fouling of parks, lawns and gardens, animal control and euthanasia of surplus animals. Despite symposia, books, spay-neuter clinics and public education on responsible pet ownership, pounds and humane societies are still obliged to kill excessive numbers of surplus dogs and cats. In Canada, approximately 500 000 unwanted companion animals are destroyed annually. The livestock industry, in developing modern methods of animal production to produce a profit for the farmer and an economical product for the consumer, has developed some intensive livestock-management practices which are being questioned by those concerned about animal welfare (*see* ANIMAL AGRICULTURE). Although legislation covering these practices is not forthcoming, the federal government, aided by the animal-welfare movement, industry, animal scientists and veterinarians has developed a number of codes of practice for handling the various domestic animals.

The dilemma associated with man's relationship to animals is discussed in the book by Oxford biologist Marion Stamp Dawkins, *Animal Suffering: The Science of Animal Welfare* (1980). It provides an outline of the biological approach to animal welfare. Unfortunately, we lack much knowledge about what constitutes pain or distress and about how to recognize latent or masked suffering. To understand the suffering of animals it is necessary to understand better their ethological or behavioural needs, awareness and perception. The closer examination of man's relationship to and use of animals has resulted in the development of scientific recognition of the human-companion animal bond. A prominent international organization, the Delta Society, was established in 1981 to promote animal-human interaction. As of 1987 a Canadian affiliate was being discussed. Researchers studying the bonds between humans and companion animals have suggested that such humans benefit from reduced stress, lower blood pressure and enhanced socialization. The use of dogs to assist the handicapped (eg, blind and hearing impaired) is already familiar. New knowledge acquired through biomedical research, or through man's understanding of and responsibility toward animals themselves, can only lead to an improvement in the health and well-being of both man and animals.

H.C. ROWSELL

Reading: Canadian Council on Animal Welfare, *Guide to the Care and Use of Experimental Animals* (1980); W.J. Dodds and F.B. Orlans, eds, *Scientific Perspectives on Animal Welfare* (1983); J. Mason and P. Singer, *Animal Factories* (1980); R.D. Ryder, *Victims of Science: Use of Animals in Research* (1975).

Animals in Winter In the Canadian temperate zone, cold-blooded (poikilothermic) animals, those incapable of regulating body temperatures internally, become dormant in winter. A period of arrested growth and development (diapause) characterizes the life cycle of most INSECTS that

Ptarmigan in winter (*photo by Harry Savage*).

overwinter in egg, larval, pupal or, uncommonly, adult stages. Some insects produce organic compounds (antifreeze) to protect cells and tissues. To escape sub-zero temperatures AMPHIBIANS lie dormant in swamp and pond mud, in soil or under debris. SNAKES enter rock dens or burrows where, alone or in clusters, they slip into a cold stupor. Warm-blooded (homeothermic) animals survive cold and food-short seasons by adjusting metabolic rates, varying insulation and blood circulation, and modifying behaviour. Winter dormancy in animals (hibernation), during which metabolism may be only 1-5% of normal, is marked by very low body temperatures (hypothermia). Respiration and heart rates drop to low levels and become irregular. Hibernators, eg, jumping mice, nonmigratory bats and ground squirrels (including woodchucks and marmots), accumulate body fat for insulation and to survive dormant periods up to 6 months or longer. Energy-rich brown fat is used by hibernants for internal heat production (thermogenesis) during frequent intervals of arousal. Black bears are deep sleepers because their temperatures remain nearly normal, although respiration and heart rates decrease sharply. Bears, raccoons, skunks and chipmunks awaken on mild, midwinter days to seek food or change dens. MAMMALS and BIRDS rely on heavy, efficient insulating coats and thick fat deposits to meet the stresses of northern winters. They respond to cold by fluffing out fur or feathers (piloerection) to capture air between outer coat surface and skin. Air trapped in the fur of beaver, muskrat, mink and river otter increases tolerance to cold water. White winter coats of ptarmigan, weasels and hares also serve as concealing coloration (camouflage). Physiological reactions of animals to chilling include raising heat production (metabolism), reducing blood flow to skin (vasoconstriction), and producing heat by muscle tremors (shivering). Some animals have complex vascular networks in limbs to move heat from warmer arteries to cooler veins for return to deeper tissues.

Animals use snow as a travel surface and insulating blanket. Thickly feathered feet of ptarmigan and wide, densely furred paws of snowshoe hare and lynx are adaptations for moving over snow. Fringed toes of grouse enable them to grip snow-covered branches firmly. Grouse, ptarmigan and some small birds burrow into snow to reduce heat losses. Other birds conserve heat at night by roosting together under eaves, conifer boughs or in tree cavities. In deep snow, deer and moose gather in areas of softwood shelter and hardwood browse. In mountains, herds of mule deer and elk seek less severe conditions by moving down south-facing slopes. Much winter activity of shrews and small rodents, including breeding, occurs under the snow (subnivean), which offers a stable, windless microclimate with less extreme temperatures than those prevailing above. Runways and tunnels, trampled through ground litter and granular snow, connect food caches with nests of dead grasses where animals curl up (alone or together) to conserve heat. Few small mammals could survive winter above the snow since energy costs of doing so are 15-50% greater than those of remaining below. Yet they sometimes emerge briefly, above that protective cover, exposing themselves to predators while moving from one area to another.

P.J. AUSTIN-SMITH

Anka, Paul Albert, singer, songwriter (b at Ottawa 30 July 1941). Of Lebanese Canadian origins, Anka became famous in his teens with such songs as "Diana" (the second-highest-selling record in history), "You Are My Destiny," "Puppy Love" and "Lonely Boy." He has written over 400 songs, displaying an uncanny ability to create hit songs, including Frank Sinatra's "My Way," "She's a Lady" for Tom Jones and the theme for the "The Tonight Show" on television. Frequent appearances in concert and on TV continue to prove his talent. In 1987 he was president of Park Industries.

ALLAN M. GOULD

Anna Wyman Dance Theatre was launched professionally as the Anna Wyman Dancers with a series of performances at the Vancouver Art Gallery in 1971, and took its current name in 1973. AWDT is considered one of Canada's principal modern-dance companies. It grew from an amateur demonstration and performing troupe created by the Austrian dancer, choreographer, and teacher, Anna WYMAN, after she settled in Vancouver in 1967. The repertoire has consisted exclusively of Wyman choreography. Her style, evolved from lengthy ballet training and modern-dance training in Austria and England, is abstract and highly theatrical, often relying heavily on technical effect. The company, which has received operational support from the Canada Council since 1973, has toured extensively. In 1973 it took part in the International Young Choreographers' Competition in Cologne, Germany, where Wyman's *Here at the Eye of the Hurricane* (music: Karlheinz Stockhausen) was named one of the 3 most outstanding entries. AWDT has toured extensively in Canada and represented BC at the Montréal Cultural Olympics. Its rigorous touring schedule has included performances in China (1980), Europe and Mexico (1983), West Germany (1984), the US (1985, 1986) and India (1987).

MAX WYMAN

Annand, William, politician, publisher, premier of NS 1867-75 (b at Halifax 10 Apr 1808; d at London, Eng 12 Oct 1887). Elected to the NS House of Assembly in 1836, Annand supported the Reform movement. Defeated in 1843, he bought and edited Joseph HOWE's *Novascotian*, then began the *Morning Chronicle* the next year, while continuing the *Novascotian*. Re-elected in 1851, Annand held his seat until 1867, despite rumours of self-aggrandizement. His vacillation on the Confederation issue weakened his role, and leadership of the anticonfederates passed to Howe. After his defeat, Annand was appointed to the Legislative Council and maneuvered to become premier. Weak and indecisive, he was replaced in 1875 by Philip Carteret HILL. Annand spent his remaining years in London, first as Canada's agent general, then as agent for Nova Scotia. LOIS KERNAGHAN

Annapolis Lowlands, situated in Digby, Annapolis and King's counties, NS, extends 155 km from the E shore of St Marys Bay eastward to the W shore of MINAS BASIN. Geologically founded upon weak, mainly red, sedimentary rocks of Triassic age (about 245-208 million years old), its elevation ranges from sea level at its western and eastern ends to about 35 m in the centre, rising to about 60 m on N and S flanks. It is overlooked on the N by the basalt escarpment of North Mtn, which rises to 180-240 m, and on the S by the granite upland of South Mtn, rising to 150-210 m. Following the retreat of glacial ice, about 13 000 years ago, the lowlands were nearly completely flooded by the sea to a height of 30 m. Subsequent isostatic uplift caused withdrawal of the sea, but in the last 6000 years sea-level rise has led to the growth of extensive salt marshes at each end of the lowlands, through which the Annapolis and Cornwallis rivers flow in broad meanders. These marshes were the focal area of ACADIAN French settlement from the founding of PORT-ROYAL (1605) to the mid-18th century. Dikes were built by Acadians to regulate tidal flooding of the marshes and to permit their drainage for use as rich hayfields. Towards the centre of the lowlands, well-drained, stone-free soils on undulating topography free of spring frosts form the basis of apple orchards and dairy farming. Principal towns include KENTVILLE, home of an Agriculture Canada experimental station; DIGBY, terminal for ferries to SAINT JOHN, NB, and a fishing port; and WOLFVILLE, home of Acadia U. The name derives from ANNAPOLIS ROYAL (for England's Queen Anne), the renamed settlement of Port-Royal.

I.A. BROOKES

Annapolis Royal, NS, Town, pop 631 (1986c), 631 (1981c), inc 1893, is located on the south side of the Annapolis R, about 10 km from its mouth near the western shore of Nova Scotia. The entire basin was named PORT-ROYAL by Champlain and de Monts when they discovered the area in 1604. The site was amenable for settlement, offering a temperate climate and arable land, and was perfect for military purposes, protected by surrounding hills. BIENCOURT de Poutrincourt established a small group of farmers there in 1606 and Acadian settlement spread slowly along the basin and river. The habitation was destroyed in 1613 by Samuel Argall and the English erected a fort nearby in 1628-29. In 1632 the French returned and about 1636 MENOU D'AULNAY built a small fort at the present site of Ft Anne. It was captured by Sedgwick in 1654 and reoccupied by the French in 1670. Ft Anne was begun in 1687 and after its completion was strong enough to stave off 2 invasions from New England colonials in 1704 and 1707. Francis NICHOLSON changed the name to Annapolis in honour of Queen Anne when he captured the fort in 1710, and the fort was garrisoned until 1854. The settlement was the capital of Nova Scotia until the founding of Halifax in 1749. After the deportation of the ACADIANS, the area was resettled by New Englanders and LOYALISTS. The old and new names gradually merged to become the official name, Annapolis Royal. Shipping became an important industry in the 19th century, with timber an important export, and an ironworks was established. Ft Anne was restored and in 1917 became Fort Anne National Historic Park, Canada's first national historic park. Much of the downtown area is a restoration of the mid-1700s period and the Historic Botanical Gardens and live theatre during the summer months are further attractions for some 100 000 visitors each year.

HEATHER MacDONALD

Anne of Green Gables, novel by Lucy Maud MONTGOMERY, published in Boston, 1908; its first Canadian edition appeared in Toronto, 1943. The first of 8 novels about Anne, this has remained Montgomery's most popular work. Its appeal lies in Anne's development as a volubly imaginative, overarticulate, spontaneous but sensitive child-heroine. Rescued from an orphanage, she finds ample "scope for the imagination" at Green Gables, where she wins the hearts of Matthew and Marilla Cuthbert, and in Avonlea, where she wins the community's affection. Anne's bright passage from childhood into adolescence has won for the novel international acclaim; it has gone through numerous editions, has been translated into at least 15 languages and has twice been made into a film. A musical version of the story has played annually in Charlottetown, PEI, since 1965, and in 1986 and 1987 widely acclaimed film adaptations were televised.

NEIL BESNER

Annelida, phylum of segmented worms with a true body cavity (coelom) separating gut from body wall. Annelids probably evolved from unsegmented coelomates which became segmented to allow continuous, active burrowing. In turn they gave rise to ARTHROPODS. The phylum is divided into 3 classes: Polychaeta (mainly marine worms); Oligochaeta (EARTHWORMS and many freshwater worms); and Hirudinea (LEECHES). More than 9000 annelid species are known worldwide. In Canada, more than 150 marine and freshwater oligochaete species and 20 earth-

Annapolis Royal, NS. French settlement in the area dates from the early 17th century; today the town is the shipping centre for the Annapolis Valley's apple industry (*photo by John deVisser*).

worm species are known, although many must remain to be described. There are probably 600 polychaete species and 45 species of leech in Canada and the adjacent US.

Annelids are mostly vermiform (worm-shaped), with an anterior (frontal) mouth preceded only by the prostomium, bearing sensory organs; anus is posterior. Most have bristles (chaetae or setae), usually arranged in 4 groups on each segment. Frontal brain has 2 major connections running around the esophagus to the first of a long series of segmental ganglia (nerve masses) along lower side of worm. In earthworms the ventral nerve cord has 3 special, large fibres that allow emergency messages to pass quickly from one end of the worm to the other along the otherwise rather slow conducting system. These fast pathways enable worms to make quick escape movements, eg, if bitten. Worms were the first animals to evolve closed blood vessels, some of which have become enlarged to act as pumps or simple hearts. Very simple eyes and some tentacles may form a head. Some worms bear gills on various body parts, but most breathe through moist skin. There are few internal organs. Worms excrete through the body surface and by tubular nephridia (kidneylike organs). Their simple guts may have a few special organs, and there may be areas for storage (crop) and for breaking up food (gizzard). Only leeches have teeth, used to chew live prey or pierce skin for bloodsucking. Although annelids mate, oligochaetes, leeches and many polychaetes are hermaphroditic.

Some polychaetes [Gk *poly*, "many"; *chaetes*, "bristles"] have jaws or teeth of cuticle. These may be on the end of a pharynx that can be rapidly pushed out to seize or bite prey (eg, blood worm, *Glycera*). Many tube-dwelling polychaetes have elaborate tentacles for capturing food particles. Polychaetes are nearly all found in the sea or in estuaries; a very few, including the Canadian *Maniyunkia*, are found in fresh water. Worms with fewer bristles, oligochaetes [Gk *oligo*, "few"], live mainly on land in moist burrows. These include earthworms (Lumbricidae family and allies) with 8 setae per segment. Other similar but smaller oligochaetes have up to 120 bristles per segment; fewer (about 24), arranged in 4 bundles, are usual. These forms may live in the deep sea, along shorelines, in rivers and lakes, in moist soils, in water trapped in plants or on glaciers (ICE-WORMS). Small, white enchytraeids are familiar denizens of compost heaps, and are raised commercially as fish food. Oligochaete food ranges from bacteria in soil to algae, vegetable matter and some animal remains; one species eats live prey. Leeches (Hirudinea) always have 34 segments but no bristles. They move about using 2 suckers. They live in fresh or salt water, or on land in the tropics. Many are external parasites of vertebrates; some eat snails and worms.   R.O. BRINKHURST

Annexation Association, fd 1849 to promote Canada-US political union. In Oct and Dec it published 2 versions of the "Annexation Manifesto." Most of those who signed it were from the powerful English-speaking business community in Montréal and Québec and the French Canadian radical nationalist movement led by Louis-Joseph PAPINEAU. The businessmen were disappointed at Britain's abolition of preferential duties on Canadian lumber, wheat and flour products and by its decision to consent to the REBELLION LOSSES BILL; the nationalists were republicans who preferred American political institutions. Strongly opposed by the British American League and by followers of Louis-Hippolyte LAFONTAINE, the movement died out after the 1854 RECIPROCITY Treaty was signed.

JACQUES MONET, S.J.

Anorexia Nervosa, misnamed "anorexia" ("loss of appetite"), is a disease that has been on medical records since 1689. It appears to have multiple causes, for example, a desire for self-control or mastery over the body; feelings of being unprepared to meet the demands of adolescence and adulthood; and family conflicts. Typical victims tend to be self-critical and compliant and often come from families where one or more parent is overprotective.

A puzzling and potentially dangerous emotional disorder, anorexia nervosa is increasingly prevalent among teenage girls and women (only one in 15 sufferers is male). The disease is characterized by an obsession with dieting (indicative of psychological problems) to the point of emaciation, which then triggers hormonal changes in the body that further distort mood and behaviour. Clinical symptoms or anorexia nervosa are similar to those seen in human starvation and include preoccupation with food, constipation, insomnia, hair loss and dry skin. Psychological changes may include depression, withdrawal, anxiety, irritability, loss of sensitivity to other people. Two Toronto researchers, authors of *Anorexia Nervosa: A Multi-dimensional Perspective,* found that, of all diagnosed anorexics, 45% recovered fully after treatment, eg, psychological counselling; 20% did not improve; 28% replaced anorexic behaviour with social anxieties or serious neuroses; and 9% died (3% from suicide; 3% largely as a result of body-chemistry disturbances; 3% through starvation).   M.T. CLANDININ

Anson Northup, the first of many steamers to navigate the RED R from Minnesota to the RED RIVER COLONY. Shortly after its arrival in Ft Garry in June 1859, the *Anson Northup* was purchased by the Hudson's Bay Company and entrepreneur J.C. Burbank, who renamed it the *Pioneer.* It went into general service, according preferred rates to the HBC. STEAMBOATS on the Red R heralded the end of HBC dominance in the North-West: bulk cargoes could now be transported into and out of the region, and the region's agricultural and commercial potential was seen in a much more favourable light by Canada, which after 1867 moved quickly to acquire the area.   J.E. REA

Ant, common name for small, mostly ground-dwelling, social INSECTS of family Formicidae, order Hymenoptera. Ants are the most numerous insects. An estimated 12 000 species occur worldwide, about 186 in Canada. They are black, red, brown or yellow; smooth, hairy or spined; and characterized by a slender waist at the base of the abdomen, bearing 1 or 2 beadlike enlargements. Heads are large with elbowed antennae and usually, well-developed mouthparts. Workers are wingless; reproductives are usually winged, mating in flight. After mating, the queen sheds her wings and excavates a chamber where she lays eggs. The first larvae are tended by the queen; later broods, by workers. Ants are the most diverse and specialized social insects. They occur from the tropics to the arctic tundra, and on most islands. Nests of some primitive ants may never contain more than 12 individuals, while those of highly social species may comprise millions. Ants prey on other insects, eat seeds, tend aphids for honeydew excretions or cultivate fungus gardens. Some ants raid nests of other species, capturing slaves which they carry back to work in their own nests. Certain species are specialized social parasites, existing only in nests of other ants.

M.V. SMITH

Antelope, *see* PRONGHORN.

Anthony Island Provincial Park situated on one of the most southerly of the Queen Charlotte Is, BC, holds the remaining fragments of a rich culture. Ninstints, a village of the Kunghit HAIDA, reveals a 2000-year history to archaeologists. The inhabitants of Ninstints were encountered in the late 18th century by European explorers interested in trade. The 2 groups traded peacefully in the 1780s, but bitter conflicts erupted in 1791 and 1795. Smallpox, rather than war, however, took the lives of most of the inhabitants, and the population was reduced from 300 to 30. The village was finally abandoned in the late 1800s.

The overgrowth of lush vegetation has been cleared away from the remains of Ninstints's longhouses and TOTEM POLES, which pay silent homage to their creators. Complex conservation programs to protect the remaining structures will attempt to prolong the future of this UNESCO World Heritage Site, although the remaining artifacts remain exposed to the elements. *See also* NORTHWEST COAST INDIAN ART.   LILLIAN STEWART

Reading: G.F. MacDonald, *Ninstints, Haida World Heritage Site* (1983).

Anthropology is the comparative study of past and contemporary cultures, focusing on the ways of life and customs of all peoples of the world. Specialty subdisciplines have developed within anthropology, owing to the amount of information collected and the variety of methods and techniques used in anthropological research. These subdisciplines are physical anthropology, archaeology, linguistic anthropology, ethnology (which is also called social or cultural anthropology) and theoretical anthropology, and applied anthropology.

Physical anthropology is the study of the evolution and physical varieties of humankind. It includes the physical measurement of skeletal remains and of living people (anthropometry); the study of human genetics, with comparisons to the genetic makeup of other primates; the study of primate behaviour for a detailed description of their social behaviour and comparative generalizations about primate social organization. Research of this kind indicates how the social behaviour of early human groups might have been organized (*see* ANTHROPOLOGY, PHYSICAL).

ARCHAEOLOGY studies the prehistory, and some of the history of mankind through digging up and analysing the remains of past cultures. Archaeology also dates the origins of human occupations in various parts of the world, the origins of tools, other artifacts, art and structures that have developed over the ages. Archaeologists seek to reconstruct the development and total cultures of past peoples.

Linguistic anthropology, or ethnolinguistics, is the study of the organization of language, including the identification and analysis of units of speech, from the simplest units of sound to the complex and various combinations of sound and meaning that are used in the thousands of languages spoken in the world today. Historical and comparative study also makes it possible to reconstruct languages that are no longer spoken, and to establish the relationships among languages. The linguistic anthropologist may also study nonverbal forms of communication and the rules for the proper use of speech (pragmatics) (*see* ANTHROPOLOGY, LINGUISTICS).

Ethnology and theoretical anthropology are the scientific core of anthropology and are described in detail in this entry. Anthropology evolved partly from the specialties mentioned above, and partly from the description of particular, living cultures (ethnography). As our knowledge of prehistory, history and the present varieties of culture increased, anthropology developed as a science that aimed at elaborating comprehensive explanations of social life (theoretical anthropology). Through the comparative analysis of individual behaviour and culture patterns, the science has tried to formulate generalizations and universal tendencies (ethnology). This development followed from improvements in research tools and practical models from which to describe reality. Ethnography is associated with exploration and descriptive work, often among distinctive, non-European tribes, whereas theoretical anthropology employs abstract hypotheses and perspectives from other disciplines, as well as more abstract tools of observation and analysis. Ethnology puts the 2 together, using theoretical models and a wide empirical knowledge of different cultures to allow for comparisons and the formulation of general cultural norms.

Applied anthropology is the use of anthropological knowledge for solving practical problems of human groups. This application has been tried mostly in small communities struggling with problems of poverty, or of rapid cultural, technological or economic change. It is also concerned with the development of new forms of education to help people cope with rapid change, or with more effective ways of improving the health of the community.

Anthropology is a young science with high ambitions to describe, understand and explain the origins, varieties and purposes of mankind's customs, beliefs, languages, institutions and lifeways; to find general cultural norms; and to provide practical guidance for humankind.

Historical Development of Anthropology Curiosity about the lifeways and customs of different peoples is probably as old as humankind. People everywhere learn to recognize as relatives or friends those whose actions, language and dress are familiar. We learn to notice cultural differences, because these differences of speech, appearance and activities define for us what it is to be a "stranger." An enduring record of different customs has been made as far back as the earliest known written records, in ancient Greece, Mesopotamia, China and other centres of civilization. Travellers and philosophers in many parts of the world speculated about the origins of humanity, the use of fire, language, the rise of cities and kingdoms, laws, religion, metals, war, art, agriculture, music and so on. The European age of discovery brought a renewal of interest in the "strange" peoples and customs that were observed by explorers, traders and missionaries.

Anthropology as a profession, as a study by people dedicated to the science of culture, arose during the late 1800s, with the main theoretical interest being cultural evolution, or the determination of when and where human civilization appeared for the first time and how civilizations spread and developed. Cultures, according to this outmoded and now discredited view, are natural systems, developing in organization and content according to natural laws and progressing gradually towards "high" culture – ie, technical, intellectual and moral excellence. Each individual and society was thought to be engaged in this progressive change, but at different rates. Those at the slowest rates remained at the level of savagery, those at medium rates had entered the stage of barbarism (typically as horticulturalists or pastoralists), and those progressing at the fastest rates achieved literacy and finally an industrial economy. This concept of culture was thought to be universal, applying to all humankind. The force behind this progress was thought to be absolute, inevitable and irreversible, sometimes called "the psychic unity of mankind" or human nature.

This view was superseded by an interest in developing a more careful examination of the historical development of cultures. The interest was called historicism. Where evolution held that all cultures necessarily passed through the same stages towards the same goal, the culture historians thought this scheme too simple and uniform to fit the reality of human variations. These historians set out to identify, for each culture, what was invented and what was borrowed (diffusion), a distinction which raised a number of questions requiring researched and documented answers. How were the various hunting tools developed? How did the different pastoral economies form? How did agricultural practices in different parts of the world come about? How did the development of villages with permanent occupation aid the growth of a complex agricultural economy? When did the ability to make metal tools appear? Specific questions were asked about particular cultures and the answers were brought together to give a composite picture of the development of cultural traditions. Each composite was viewed as an emergent system – a system developing according to its own circumstances and with its own direction, integrating items that were borrowed over the years from neighbouring cultures or even from distant cultures. People did not repeatedly reinvent their ways of life, but rather learned their cultures automatically, as a part of what we call "received tradition" – those things that people of a society have known to be useful, true or good. Anthropological historicists, or ethnohistorians, have continued to contribute to our understanding of cultures by reconstructing particular histories.

Another basic interest in theoretical anthropology, strong in the period between the world wars, was the search for universal functions (useful, integrating relationships) that exist in all cultures. The focus of attention is the process by which groups adapt themselves to their natural environment and promote collective activities that ensure the fulfilment of human needs. Basic survival needs are those related to metabolism, reproduction, bodily comforts, safety, movement and health. Secondary needs arise from the ways that people in groups deal with the basic needs, establishing institutions that will function to fulfil economic, kinship, political and other needs by regulating the norms of behaviour and the selection of members for these activities. Symbolic needs are satisfied through communication norms, religious beliefs and ceremonies, and expressions of art, including myths and tales. These anthropologists, termed "functionalists," try to understand how each culture met these needs and what kinds of social institutions were customarily used to meet the various needs.

Similar to the functionalists' interest in universal human needs, the interest of the culture and personality theorists centered on the old controversy of the relation of nature to nurture, with special attention to the cultural foundations of personality. The characteristics of child rearing and temperament were found to vary a great deal from one culture to another. Some cultures, for instance, were remarkably permissive; others were restrictive. Some were characterized by a strong show of emotions and others by little emotional expression. Some showed great consistency in the way that children were treated while others showed little predictability in response to children's behaviour. The various combinations of these norms for child rearing were found to lead to different adult characteristics, and to contribute to the norms of adult behaviour (such as aggressive, placid, friendly, suspicious) for each culture. The ways that persons in each culture mature from infancy through old age is of great interest to many anthropologists today. More recent work in cognitive anthropology has emphasized variability of individual responses to cultural socialization.

By comparison, structural anthropology looks for universal rules of human thought, usually far from our normal awareness, in unconsciously learned (and used) regularities in the mind. The example of language is helpful; we make sentences as we talk with each other, and our sentences always follow rules of grammar, yet we are scarcely aware of the rules we use. We don't think to ourselves, "first the noun, then the verb" as we talk to each other. Much of our behaviour is similarly guided by rules in our deep unconscious, which we use intuitively and easily. In this way we organize our social relations, enjoy the meaning in a book or story, and sense the "rightness" of a ritual such as a wedding, a funeral or a church service. Structural anthropologists believe that all rules of this sort are variations on a few universal "deep" rules, which they are trying to discover. Once again, the interest is in defining human nature or psychic unity.

In Neo-Marxism, or historical materialism, the emphasis is placed on economic systems, modes of production and exchange of goods. Neo-Marxists believe that these economic, production and exchange factors are the products of confrontations between various elements of the social system. They investigate how in the capitalist mode of production, labourers are exploited by the interests of capital, and that as a result they benefit only in small measure from their efforts at production.

A more recent approach to social analysis is cognitive anthropology, the study of units of thought and their combinations. Cognitive anthropologists seek the rules by which different cultures organize their knowledge in their own distinctive styles. The point is to understand cultural features as they are understood by the people within the particular culture and to explain these features to a wider audience outside that culture.

Early anthropologists investigated communities of people in isolated places cut off from the modern world. Since WWII the isolation of these small groups has ended. The study of stability and change has concentrated on cultural contacts, urbanization, industrialization, the effect of media and schools, and other dynamic factors that are transforming even the most remote peoples of the world. There is a renewed interest in cross-cultural studies, using the comparative method to derive general norms and universals of culture, whether in child rearing, mental health or religion. The emphasis is no longer on single items of culture as they are distributed around the world but on the relationships among many items, or clusters of cultural traits and their dynamic interdependency.

Concept of Culture The classic definition of culture, still widely accepted, was published over 100 years ago by E.B. Tylor. It is "that complex whole which includes knowledge, belief, art, morals, law, custom, and any other capabilities and habits acquired by man as a member of society." From an anthropological perspective, virtually every mature human being is thoroughly endowed with his or her culture. Everyone knows a language; knows how to act towards relatives, friends or strangers; how to take a place in society; how to use many of the basic tools; how to make an exchange of goods or services; how to regard the persons who have political power or social prestige; when to evaluate things, actions or ideas as good or bad; and how one's particular world is arranged in size, shape and purpose. People know these things, and they have a sense of what is excellent in each of these aspects of their culture; perhaps a sense of what an ideal person should be. But what is ideal to an 18th-century Montréal gentleman is a far cry from the ideal for a Vancouver artist or a prairie farmer, a Maritime fisherman or an Inuit mother. In order to deal with these differences, the concept of culture is divided into major segments such as technology, economics, kinship and social organization, value systems and ideology.

Technology refers to the things manufactured and the knowledge and skills required to make them. Technology is responsive to the physical environment and to the level of social size and complexity, so that a northern hunting culture, for example, will be different from a tropical farming culture.

Economics is often thought to refer to the production and exchange of goods, but in anthropology is also thought of in terms of the exchange of services, and less tangible exchanges of rights and privileges. This trade may be within a community or among different groups. Often the trade is more than simple exchange, giving a stable and dependable bond, or alliance, to the group.

Kinship and social organization refer to the relations among the people of a group, and include the way an individual knows how to act and what to expect in his relationships to others, as well as whom he may or may not marry, from whom he may inherit property or other rights, and to whom he should will his estate and responsibilities.

Value systems and religious belief and behaviour are the aspects of culture that are closest to the human significance or meanings of events, beyond the events themselves. Birth, reaching adulthood, marriage and death are charged, in the minds of most people, with special value, and often with spiritual meaning. This is also true of the aspects of life that are most closely linked with getting a living, such as rituals of hunting, agriculture or pastoralism. Ideologies, world view and cultural imperatives provide people with their sense of the way the world is constituted or arranged, and how the persons must act to be in harmony with the world, rather than at risk of harm through being in conflict with the natural order. Ideologies are maps or images of what the arrangement of society should become, a statement of the ideal toward which the group should strive.

Each of these major segments of culture has attracted many studies, both at the level of describing how that segment is defined for particular cultures and also how similar or different it may be when viewed cross-culturally. Information about particular cultures, and for cross-cultural comparisons, arises from the basic anthropological activity – field studies.

Field Research was once left to the travellers, traders and missionaries who cared to write about peoples and their cultures. The first anthropologists were social philosophers and intellectuals who understood cultures through the "armchair studies" of historical and travel documents. Only in the last decades of the 1800s did anthropology become a discipline based upon fieldwork and the accumulation of firsthand observations. Training in field methods of observation is an important part of anthropological apprenticeship. Data are usually gathered through systematic observation of daily events, and participant observation in events and situations that are of special importance to the people (such as economic activities, social relationships and ritual acts). The anthropologist seeks out and interviews people who possess special and relevant knowledge and who communicate with accurate detail and completeness (key informants). Every field-worker develops a method for recording and classifying his data so that he can draw upon accurate and appropriate information in writing up his scientific reports. Anthropologists often stay in the field for a year or more, in order to establish good relations

with the people they are studying and to be thorough and accurate in making a record of what people say and do. This kind of field research requires special human skills as well as skill in anthropological theories, concepts, methods and techniques. The observer must also explain who he is, what he is doing, the reasons for doing his research, the use that he will make of the information he collects, how long he will stay, and other questions that are a part of honesty and courtesy towards one's hosts. He must not only abide by the ethical principles of his profession, but also by the ethical principles of the people he is living with and then writing about.

Anthropology in Canada The fathers of Canadian ethnology were the missionaries who lived in French Canada in the 1600s. These men, such as Fathers LeClercq, LE JEUNE and Sagard, were deeply interested in knowing the lifeways and beliefs of the native people they lived among, and they provided the detailed descriptions that were used by professional anthropologists, from the early "armchair" social philosophers to the historically oriented anthropologists of today. Canadian anthropology grew from records written by dedicated individuals whose profession was religion (Jesuits and other missionaries), or who were explorer-traders such as LESCARBOT, or 2 centuries later teachers in our early universities, such as Sir Daniel WILSON at Toronto or John William DAWSON at McGill (in the mid-1880s). Government employees, in particular with the GEOLOGICAL SURVEY OF CANADA, made important records of their travels, including details about the native people they met and observed in the course of their work. The most important of these men is George Mercer DAWSON, who was employed by the Geological Survey from 1875 and rose to be its director in 1895. It was his sustained support more than that of any other one person that resulted in the establishment of a professional basis for Canadian anthropology, though he died before it was given formal recognition.

In 1910 PM Wilfrid Laurier established a Division of Anthropology within the Geological Survey, marking the beginning of professional anthropology in Canada. Offices were in the Victoria Memorial Museum in Ottawa, and professionally trained men were recruited from England and the US. From Professor BOAS came Edward SAPIR, who had just completed his doctorate and was embarking on a brilliant career in anthropology. From Oxford's Professors Tylor and Marett came Charles Marius BARBEAU, a Rhodes scholar born in rural Québec. Barbeau's work at the NATIONAL MUSEUM (as it became known) was only one part of his contribution to Canadian anthropology. Les Archives de folklore at U Laval originated in his great collections of French Canadian material culture, songs, stories and tales, and in his students', especially Luc Lacourcière's, work to establish the archives (1944). Barbeau also recruited to the museum a fellow student from Oxford, Diamond JENNESS. Sapir and Barbeau both made ethnographic studies and collections of the cultures of the Indians of the Northwest Coast, following George Mercer Dawson and Boas in this area. Jenness is best known for his research in the Arctic among the COPPER INUIT. But each also worked in many other areas of Canada, recording traditions and songs, studying native languages, and collecting artifacts for the museum. William WINTEMBERG and Harlan Smith worked archaeological sites to build the collections of prehistoric artifacts. These men, with a very few others, had nearly sole responsibility for the development of the profession in Canada from 1910 until 1925, when Sapir left Canada and Thomas MCILWRAITH took the first academic position in anthropology at a Canadian universi-

ty. Five years later, McIlwraith was still the sole member of his department, and the very slow growth of anthropology is shown by the fact that the next universities to hire anthropologists, UBC and McGill, did so only in 1947. The first doctoral dissertation that is distinctly anthropological was appropriately based upon the Jesuit records and other documents on the subject, "The Conflict of European and Eastern Algonkian Cultures, 1504-1700: A Study in Canadian Civilization." The author, Alfred G. BAILEY, received his degree in history because in 1934 there was no anthropology doctoral program. The first PhD in anthropology was granted in 1956, with only a few more being granted until the late 1960s. The 1970s brought a boom in university development and in professional anthropology, and by 1980 about 400 people with doctorates in anthropology were employed in Canada, and many more with a master's degree. Harry Hawthorne built the department at UBC and set a standard for the use of anthropological research as a guide to policy in his classic report to the federal government, coauthored by M.-A. Tremblay, *A Survey of the Contemporary Indians of Canada* (1966, 1967).

Common trends dominate the development of anthropology in Canada, in spite of differences in language or distances between the various universities and museums. Part of the reason for this uniformity is the widespread influence of the ideas of Boas and his students. Moreover, anthropology in English Canada is built on an interest in the native people of Canada, who lived in small, isolated communities. This fact led to anthropological emphasis on the empirical field-study tradition, with participant observation and interviews with key informants, and resulted in reports that described the technology, economics, social organization, values and world view of each particular community. In many of these communities, people were conscious of their past history, sometimes from a sense of discontent with their present situation and with a concern that the past was slipping away from them without a satisfactory or secure new way of life to replace the old. The anthropologist's interest in traditions could then be an occasion to record the past before it was forgotten. Since the early studies by Boas, Jenness and others of small, tradition-oriented communities in the Arctic, and since the studies by Boas, Barbeau, Sapir and others of Northwest Coast Indian communities, the empirical study of small and isolated communities has continued to occupy the interests of many Canadian anthropologists.

In French Canada anthropology has built upon rural and small-town studies of the Québec region and its people, again emphasizing the study of small and relatively isolated groups. The development of anthropology in Québec is based upon the classic studies of French Canadians by early sociologists. The most important figure is Leon GERIN, whose "L'Habitant de St-Justin" illustrated how, in rural Québec, the old European patriarchal system continued in organizing the community's lifeways. The American Everett C. Hughes also influenced Québec anthropology with his *French Canada in Transition* (1943), a study of the process of industrialization in the town of Drummondville. Another American, Horace Miner, wrote *St-Denis: A French Canadian Parish* (1939), which became a model for community studies in Québec. Miner, an anthropologist, and the sociologists Gerin and Hughes all made extensive use of participant observation and key-informant interviewing during their field research. K.O.L. Burridge and C.S. Belshaw at UBC, and R.F. Salisbury at McGill, did internationally admired research in Melanesia on the religion and other beliefs and the economics of the colonized native people of the area. Research in Africa has been undertaken by nearly 100 anthropologists, of which the work of R.B. Lee of U of T on the political economy of the bushmen is probably the best known.

Anthropology expands by learning about people, and the particular people that anthropologists study have an important influence upon the general and theoretical ideas that are developed. In English Canada the development of anthropology was guided by the studies of small communities of native people, with research in other areas of Canada and the world gradually increasing during the 1960s and 1970s. This wider horizon gives a valuable broadening of empirical and theoretical materials to Canadian anthropology, while the original interests in native peoples continues to develop as well. In Québec the studies of rural and small-town communities added to the cultural "mapping" of more isolated areas that continued through the 1960s, especially at U de Montréal and at Laval. The anglophone McGill U supported this research, but also developed a research program on social change among the James Bay Cree. In the 1970s the regional studies continued, but with more defined focus upon socioeconomic disparities and Marxist interpretations. Laval and Montréal also became interested in the James Bay Cree, and McGill sponsored research in Africa and Latin America. Applied anthropology has grown partly in response to the needs of native people and organizations during the 1970s.

During the 1970s and 1980s increasing specialization within anthropology has provided more refined methods and precision in research, but this specialization has meant that some topics have not received the attention they deserve. In both English Canada and Québec, the study of urban centres is barely begun, and their size and complexity will continue to challenge anthropologists to develop method and theory. Many of the less densely settled areas of Canada still remain to be studied. The emphasis on economic and ecological aspects of culture has resulted in too little emphasis on the family, on male-female relationships, the social and value aspects of work, beliefs and ideology, and the organization of industrial, professional and bureaucratic groups. The feminist perspective may provide a critical and corrective effect on research in all regions, and in all aspects of study. Canada has developed excellent resources for training professional anthropologists who may do this work. As of 1980 there were graduate programs leading to the PhD in anthropology at 9 universities across Canada: Alberta, British Columbia, Laval, McGill, McMaster, Manitoba, Montréal, Simon Fraser and Toronto. There were at least 14 professional organizations in Canada representing anthropologists, of which the Canadian Ethnology Society, founded in 1973 and publisher of the journal *Culture*, is the most broadly representative. There are over 20 other journals or monograph series.

Anthropology is a young discipline, although it is one of humankind's oldest interests. In the past century, the study of human variety and of the universal human qualities that underlie the variety has developed successfully in Canada and in other areas of the world. Much has been done; much remains to be done. If we are to understand human nature, we must be able to understand the many ways that this nature is expressed, and the new ways that will develop in the future. When our knowledge has the accuracy and completeness that a science of humankind works to provide, this understanding can give reliable guidance for efforts to improve the condition of all people. Anthropologists study humanity and serve human interests and values.

R.J. PRESTON AND M.-A. TREMBLAY

Anthropology, Applied, the use of knowledge of other cultures to achieve practical results, was informally used throughout the early period of Canadian anthropology by missionaries, explorers and traders. Later, trained anthropologists such as Franz BOAS and Edward SAPIR (director of the National Museum, 1910-25) were sometimes asked to comment on Indian policy issues. Sapir's successor, Diamond JENNESS, was more actively concerned with policy, and his 4-volume work, *Eskimo Administration*, comparing Alaskan, Danish and Canadian practice is a classic study. The hiring of anthropologists, outside universities and museums, for practical action began only after WWII in Canada. By 1960 the Dept of Citizenship and Immigration (Indian Affairs Branch) had commissioned community action programs for Nova Scotia Indians at St Francis Xavier U, and a survey of the Indians of British Columbia by H.B. HAWTHORN and C.S. Belshaw. The Dept of Northern Affairs and Natural Resources had an active research program in its Northern Co-ordination and Research Centre, directed by V.F. Valentine. It produced studies such as that by F.G. Vallee on emerging Inuit co-operatives. In Saskatchewan the provincial government had earlier employed Valentine in its community development program.

In the 1960s the rapid expansion of universities induced governments to commission more studies. *A Survey of the Contemporary Indians of Canada* (1967) was commissioned, under the direction of Hawthorne and M.-A. TREMBLAY, to recommend improvements to Indian policy, though many of its recommendations were ignored in the White Paper of 1969 (*see* INDIAN ACT). The Dept of Forestry and Rural Development commissioned many studies under its Agricultural Rehabilitation Development Act Program. In Québec a McGill group under N.A. Chance studied Cree involvement in wage employment; in Québec the Bureau de l'Aménagement de l'Est du Québec (BAEQ) hired anthropologists to prepare plans for solving farm poverty. The BAEQ used its field research to stimulate rural groups to organize, through what was termed *animation sociale*. This has now become a common practice in applied anthropology.

The use of anthropological knowledge in the service of small or disadvantaged communities grew in the 1970s. Many young anthropologists put their skills to use in CUSO and other untrained volunteers returned to study and became anthropologists. Within Canada the push to settle Indian LAND CLAIMS led many anthropologists to work for Indian groups, documenting their claims or advising them during negotiations. The first comprehensive claim settlement, the James Bay and Northern Québec Agreement (1975), involved a team from McGill (R.F. Salisbury, H.A. Feit, I. Larusic and others). Other anthropologists worked with the Berger Commission on the MACKENZIE VALLEY PIPELINE and the Lysyk Inquiry in the Yukon.

Groups other than Indians also became a focus for applied work. After the Royal Commission on BILINGUALISM AND BICULTURALISM commissioned studies of "third countries," many anthropologists began work for ethnic groups. In Newfoundland the Institute of Social and Economic Research of Memorial U documented problems of fishing and mining communities, and of NEWFOUNDLAND RESETTLEMENT. The delivery of health services, particularly to disadvantaged or immigrant groups, has involved many medical anthropologists. Anthropologists are being hired by management consulting firms, and anthropological consulting firms have been formed in Montréal, Edmonton, Ottawa, Calgary and Toronto. In 1981 the Society for Applied Anthropology in

Canada was formed. The Society's 1987 project was to approve standards for possible certification of applied anthropologists. RICHARD F. SALISBURY

Anthropology, Linguistic In Canada LINGUISTICS exists as a fully autonomous discipline, represented by about 12 independent programs, as well as by linguistic research within departments of English, various other language areas, education, philosophy, psychology, sociology and anthropology. In spite of this disciplinary diversity, linguistics within anthropology concentrates particularly on the study of American Indian languages. Within N American anthropology, linguistics has been included traditionally as one of the subdisciplines, along with ANTHROPOLOGY, PHYSICAL; ARCHAEOLOGY; socio-cultural ANTHROPOLOGY, and applied anthropology. In the early 1980s 26 Canadian university departments of anthropology had at least one linguist on staff. Eight of the 9 PhD programs offered studies in linguistics and 6 museums were actively engaged in linguistic research.

There are historical precedents for the Canadian study of American Indian languages. Edward SAPIR, the foremost linguist among the students of Franz BOAS, served as director of anthropological research in Ottawa from 1910 to 1925, under the auspices of the Geological Survey, Dept of Mines. This program is now the Canadian Ethnology Service of the CANADIAN MUSEUM OF CIVILIZATION and retains Sapir's linguistic interests. During his tenure, Sapir encouraged detailed fieldwork on particular languages, stressing phonology (sound system) and morphology (word structure). Not content with description, Sapir classified N American Indian languages into a small number of stocks of related families comparable in time depth to Indo-European. Five of Sapir's 6 basic N American stocks — Eskimo-Aleut, Na-Dene (including Athapascan, Haida and Tlingit), Algonquian-Wakashan, Penutian and Hokan-Siouan — are spoken in Canada. Moreover, Sapir pioneered in reconstruction of cultural history from linguistic evidence, demonstrating, for example, the Alaskan and northwestern Canadian origin of the Navajo and Apache tribes of the American SW.

More recent Amerindian studies have continued to focus on descriptive linguistics and language classification. Linguists have become more specialized in method and theory, although many have remained within anthropology. The traditional study of phonology and morphology has expanded to include syntax (sentence structure) and semantics (meaning). A few anthropological linguists have moved from the study of meaning to the socio-cultural context of language use within a particular culture.

Applied linguistics has focused on the development of writing systems for Indian languages, some based on the Roman alphabet and others on syllabics (combinations of consonant and vowel which function together in the construction of words). Much of this work has been carried out in collaboration with Canadian native communities concerned with the maintenance and preservation of their languages.

Linguistics within anthropology remains an essential part of the training of anthropologists and of their potential contribution to the communities they study, particularly in native-language teaching. Simultaneously, anthropological linguistics has maintained its ties to general linguistics, which it enriches by its understanding of less familiar languages spoken today by many native Canadians (*see* NATIVE PEOPLE, LANGUAGES).

REGNA DARNELL

Anthropology, Physical, has no single definition acceptable to all its practitioners, but most agree that the major focus of the field is on problems of human evolution and variation. The foundations of modern physical anthropology, like those of modern biology, rest on Neo-Darwinian evolutionary theory, which provides the common background for a diverse discipline that lacks a common set of methods. Physical anthropologists recognize that interaction between human culture and human biology has shaped and maintained our species, and that full understanding of the processes responsible requires consideration of both biology and culture. Reflecting this interdisciplinary concern, most physical anthropologists work in university departments of anthropology. Many, however, are employed in departments of anatomy, dentistry, human kinetics, and zoology.

Human biological history is most directly told by the fossil record. Although hominid remains (fossils in the human line) are not found in the Western Hemisphere, Canadians have contributed to PALEONTOLOGY. Foremost among them was Davidson BLACK, who named and studied the fossils that were called "Peking Man" (*Sinanthropus pekinensis* = *Homo erectus pekinensis*). Studies on nonhuman primates (prosimians, monkeys, apes) have ranged from the earliest fossils to the living. Though research in primate behaviour is valuable in itself, these works are also used to provide inferences about behaviours that may have been present in the forms from which nonhuman primates and humans are descended.

The greatest contribution of Canadians over the period since 1871 has been in human osteology. Descriptions of the size and shape of skeletons of archaic and prehistoric Inuit and Indian peoples have been superseded by analyses of past population distributions, assessments of group composition by age and sex, and determination of contemporary and earlier population relationships. The effects of nutrition, diseases, climate, culture and genetics on past populations are routinely investigated with techniques borrowed from biochemistry, pathology, epidemiology, demography, radiology and statistics. Tools such as the scanning electron microscope are used to discern age-associated changes in the bone. The U of Toronto has led osteological research; strong contributions are also being made at the universities of Manitoba, Winnipeg, Queen's, Guelph, McMaster, and the Canadian Museum of Civilization.

Studies of living peoples have included assessment of cold adaptation in indigenous groups, determination of adult body composition, and study of the growth and development of children. The U of Montréal is preeminent in research on human morphologic and genetic variation. The impact that specific microevolutionary forces (genetic drift, gene flow) and social factors (marriage patterns) have on the genetic features of populations have been examined in groups as diverse as subarctic Indians and Caribbean island isolates. The effect of gene flow on genetic relationships within Amerindians and the demonstration of genetic linkages between Siberian and N American populations have received emphasis at McMaster. Demographic studies of religious isolates and hunting-gathering groups are increasing in the search to document the action of microevolutionary forces on human groups.

Canadian universities offering a doctoral program in physical anthropology are Simon Fraser, Alberta, Toronto and Montréal. In addition to universities already mentioned, Victoria, Calgary, Saskatchewan and Memorial each has training and research centres. The professional organization is the Canadian Assn for Physical Anthropology. EMÖKE J.E. SZATHMÁRY

Anticosti, Île d', 8000 km², 225 km long and 56 km at widest point, is located in the Gulf of LAWRENCE, athwart the entrance to the St Lawrence R. The name likely derives from the Indian word *natiscosti*, meaning "where bears are hunted." There is logic in the suggestion that it comes from the Spanish *ante* (before) and *costa* (coast), but no real evidence. Though considerably larger than PEI, its population is only about 300. Most of the coastline is dominated by steep limestone cliffs, and several of its rivers cut through deep canyons. The eastern end is an enormous bog. Most of the inhabitants trace their ancestry to Newfoundland, Saint-Pierre and Miquelon, and the Îles de la Madeleine. Entirely French speaking, they have made their living as fishermen, trappers, farmers, lumberjacks and lighthouse keepers. In 1909 over 800 ha were under cultivation, but no farms remain. The lighthouses are now all automatic.

Discovered by Jacques CARTIER in 1534 (he took it for a peninsula), the island was granted as a seigneury 1680 to Louis JOLLIET in recognition of his exploration of the Mississippi R. After the fall of New France, it was annexed to Newfoundland, but in 1774 returned to Canada. In 1872 a Montréal land company was bankrupted trying to colonize the island, and in 1884 it was sold at auction for $101 000 to Francis Stockwell, an English businessman, who also went bankrupt trying to develop it. In 1895 Henri Menier, a millionaire French chocolate manufacturer, bought the island to develop as a private sports preserve. It was sold again 1926 to Consolidated Bathurst Inc, and a pulpwood industry flourished, more or less, particularly in the late 1920s, when the population rose to 3000. These operations were shut down 1972 because of transportation costs and forest fires. The first permanent village was located at Baie-Ste-Claire. Menier developed it as a model town, but it was abandoned in the 1920s for Port-Menier, or Baie Ellis, the only settlement on the island today. Outside Port-Menier lie the ruins of the island's once-famous landmark, Château Menier, a luxurious villa. It was deliberately burned down in 1953.

The island has a rich variety of wildlife, the most notable being the more than 100 000 Virginia white-tailed deer – the progeny of 220 brought by Menier in 1896. Deer hunting is a main attraction. Thousands of ships pass the island each year, and its treacherous reefs have given it the nickname "Graveyard of the Gulf." It is estimated that some 400 ships have foundered on the reefs, most in the 18th and 19th centuries, before the establishment of lighthouses. Ships still run aground occasionally despite navigational aids.

A controversy broke out in 1937, when a group of Germans took out an option to buy the island and develop the forest industry. However, pressure from the federal and Québec governments aborted the attempt. JAMES MARSH

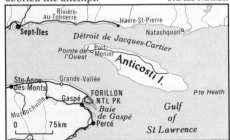

Antigonish, NS, Town, pop 5291 (1986c), 5205 (1981c), inc 1889, is situated on a small plain about 1.6 km from Antigonish harbour. Located midway between HALIFAX and SYDNEY, it is a quiet university and residential community. With no major industry, Antigonish relies on being the market centre for surrounding communities. In 1785 a group of British soldiers first settled the area, then known as Dorchester. Population increased during the NAPOLEONIC WARS, when Antigonish supplied much-needed timber to Britain. From 1821 onward the town was known as Antigonish. The name derives from the Micmac *Nalegitkoonechk* ("where branches are torn off"). In 1855 ST FRANCIS XAVIER U was opened. In the 20th century the university led in the founding of the ANTIGONISH MOVEMENT, a program of ADULT EDUCATION and self-help; the Coady International Institute, which provides education for Third World leaders; and the CO-OPERATIVE MOVEMENT in NS. Antigonish is also home to the HIGHLAND GAMES, the oldest celebration of Scottish dance and sports in N America.

HEATHER MACDONALD

Antigonish Movement, a social and economic movement sponsored by the Extension Dept of ST FRANCIS XAVIER UNIVERSITY, Antigonish, NS. During the 1920s, following several decades of adversity in fishing, mining and agriculture in eastern Nova Scotia, St FX became involved in a series of social and economic programs, and in 1928 it established the Extension Dept. The department was under the direction of Father Moses COADY, but it relied heavily on the inspiration of Father J.J. "Jimmy" TOMPKINS and on the organizing zeal of Coady's assistant, A.B. MACDONALD.

The "Antigonish Movement" was unusual – a liberal Catholic movement at a time when conservatism was dominant in the Roman Catholic Church (*see* CATHOLICISM; CATHOLIC ACTION). It focused on ADULT EDUCATION as a means towards social improvement and economic organization. Typically, one of the movement's organizers would enter a community, use whatever contacts could be found and call a public meeting to assess the community's strengths and difficulties. A study club would be created and a program for a series of meetings developed. Usually, at the end of these meetings, one or more co-operatives would be established to help overcome the difficulties that had been discussed. The CREDIT UNION was most common, but the movement also organized co-operatives for selling fish, retailing consumer goods, building homes and marketing agricultural produce.

During the 1930s the Antigonish Movement spread to, or was imitated in, many areas of ATLANTIC PROVINCES. It also became well known in other parts of Canada and in the US, publicized by its own leaders, the churches and the credit union movement. During the 1940s a series of articles and books made the movement known in Europe, Latin America and Asia. In the 1950s adult educators and social activists began coming to study the movement in Antigonish, and in 1959 the Coady International Institute was established. The institute, a training centre for adult education and social action, soon attracted students for courses on the Antigonish method. Thousands of community organizers have studied in Antigonish. Upon returning to Asia, Latin America and Africa they have attempted, with differing degrees of success, to duplicate the movement's early accomplishments in Nova Scotia. In recent years the movement has played an important role in Canada's FOREIGN AID programs.

Locally the Antigonish Movement has found its study club approach difficult to sustain since the 1950s. The arrival of television, road improvements and a gradually increasing standard of living have made it difficult to assemble groups for sustained study and community activism. The movement has been forced to embrace new media, such as television, and to face current issues, most of which are not resolved through co-operatives, in order to maintain its momentum. The success of these efforts is not as easily demonstrable as were the very concrete accomplishments of the 1930s and 1940s. *See also* DISTANCE LEARNING; CO-OPERATIVE MOVEMENT. IAN MACPHERSON

Reading: G. Baum, Catholics and Canadian Socialism (1980); M.M. Coady, Masters of Their Own Destiny (1963); A.F. Laidlaw, ed, The Man from Margaree (1971).

Anti-Inflation Act Reference (1976), temporary and extraordinary measure instituted by the Trudeau government to control high unemployment and inflation. The Supreme Court of Canada upheld the validity of the federal Anti-Inflation Act (1975), and therefore of certain peacetime emergency powers designed to control profits, prices, dividends and salaries and to combat INFLATION, on the basis of the implicit emergency power (defined by Mr Justice Beetz as a concurrent and paramount power over matters normally under provincial jurisdiction) recognized in, eg, the FORT FRANCES decision. The court held by a majority that Parliament need not make a ritual statement that a state of emergency exists.
GÉRALD-A. BEAUDOIN

Anti-Inflation Board, established by Act of Parliament in late 1975 to administer a wage-and-price-control program. Although the program was phased out during 1978, the AIB did not cease all operations until 1979. Because of its examination of company profits, close to $323.1 million was returned to the marketplace by hundreds of companies. The wide-ranging mandate of the board was highly controversial; it examined auto, fuel-oil and gas prices, Bell Canada employee wages, insurance premiums, beef prices, etc. The board's consequent recommendations resulted in rebates, wage rollbacks and price increases. Amendments were made to the Anti-Inflation Act to ensure that prices and wages did not automatically jump when the control period (and therefore the AIB's recommendations) came to an end.

Antimony (Sb), silvery white, brittle, lustrous metallic element, with a melting point of 630°C. It is a poor conductor of heat and electricity. The most important source of antimony is the MINERAL stibnite. Stibnite and antimony metal have been used since 4000 BC, for example, stibnite as eyebrow pigment. Antimony is used in alloys, especially to impart hardness and strength to lead. Lead-acid batteries are a major but diminishing use; newer, maintenance-free batteries use cadmium-lead instead. Other uses of lead-antimony alloys include cable sheathing, bearing alloys and type metals. Antimony compounds are used in flame retardants, paints, ceramics, enamels and glass. Most antimony ores are upgraded by flotation. Antimony is extracted from concentrates by roasting and reduced to metal by addition of scrap iron and salt. Some antimony is recovered from complex ores by leaching and electrolysis. Antimony is recovered from LEAD ores as antimonial lead (*see* METALLURGY). The major antimony producing countries have been China, Bolivia, the USSR, Thailand, Turkey and Yugoslavia. Antimony minerals are common in the Cordilleran and Appalachian regions of Canada, where antimony is recovered as a lead by-product. In 1986 Canada's antimony production was estimated to be 3900 kg with a value of $24 million.
J.J. HOGAN

Anti-Reciprocity Movement A number of organizations were formed to oppose the RECIPROCITY agreement of Jan 1911 between Canada and the US. Most prominent was the Canadian National League, headed by Toronto lawyer Zebulon LASH. Others were the Canadian Home Market Assn, a branch of the Canadian Manufacturers' Assn which was active in distributing propaganda literature and in raising funds for the campaign; and the Anti-Reciprocity League, established in Montréal in late Feb. Claiming to be politically nonpartisan, this league launched a door-to-door petition campaign and held rallies throughout the country. A leading figure in the anti-reciprocity agitation was Clifford SIFTON, formerly minister of the interior in the Liberal government. CURTIS FAHEY

Anti-Semitism in Canada was from the beginning never restricted only to the cranks of society. Rather it has always been part of the mainstream, shared to varying degrees by all elements of the nation, from the top to the bottom. Until the 1950s it had respectability; no one apologized for being anti-Jewish — no one asked them to. It was heard in halls of Parliament, read in the press, taught in the schools and absorbed in most churches. It existed in Canada 100 years ago, when there were scarcely any JEWS living here.

The earliest manifestation of anti-Jewish sentiment was the expulsion in 1808 of Ezekiel Hart from the Québec legislature, though this may have been more the result of his politics than his religion. But the major exponent of anti-semitism in the 19th century was the prominent writer and critic Goldwin SMITH. A pathological anti-semite, Smith disseminated his hate in dozens of books, articles and letters. Jews, he charged, were "parasites," "dangerous" to their host country and "enemies of civilization." His bilious anti-Jewish tirades helped set the tone of a still unmolded Canadian society and had a profound impact on such young Canadians as Mackenzie King, Henry Bourassa and scores of others. Indeed in 1905 in the most vituperative anti-Jewish speech in the history of the House of Commons, borrowing heavily from Smith, Bourassa urged Canada to keep its gates shut to Jewish immigrants.

Anti-semitism was particularly acute in Québec where the Church associated Jews with modernism, liberalism and a host of other "dangerous" doctrines. From 1880 through to the 1940s such Catholic journals as *La Vérité, La Semaine réligieuse* and *L'Action sociale* denounced the Jew. And led by people such as J.P. TARDIVEL a scurrilous anti-Jewish literature spread throughout the province. There was even some violence against Jews, the most notorious incident occurring in Québec City in 1910 when, following a particularly inflammatory address by a well-known anti-semite, Joseph Plamondon, some of the audience attacked Jewish store-keepers and damaged their businesses. The aggrieved Jews launched a civil action against Plamondon. Four years later the courts finally awarded them minimal costs; but the onslaught continued.

Leading the attack from the 1920s on was the respected French-Canadian intellectual, Abbé Lionel GROULX. In many ways what Goldwin Smith was to English Canada in the 19th century, Groulx was to French Canada in the 20th. His savage denunciations of the Jews influenced the province's elite — its clerics, politicians, teachers and journalists. Not only were Jews denounced in the Catholic press but popular newspapers also joined in the assault. Out of this was created the "Achat Chez Nous" movement, an attempt by Church and nationalist leaders to institute a boycott of all Jewish businesses in the province, thus forcing the Jews to leave. As well, since in the view of the Catholic and Protestant clergy Québec

was a Christian society, Jews were barred for years from various school boards. What is most surprising about this concerted campaign against the Jews was that they made up only 1% of Québec's population.

But anti-semitism was not the preserve of only one province; it existed — indeed thrived — elsewhere in Canada. In English Canada such organizations as the Social Credit Party, the Orange Order and the Native Sons of Canada were rife with anti-Jewish feeling. For Canadian Jews in the 1920s and 1930s, quotas and restrictions were a way of life. Many industries did not hire Jews; educational institutions such as universities and professional schools discriminated against them. Jewish doctors could not get hospital appointments. There were no Jewish judges, and Jewish lawyers were excluded from most firms. There were scarcely any Jewish teachers and — most notably — no professors. Jewish nurses, engineers and architects had to hide their identity to find jobs in their fields.

Furthermore, there were restrictive covenants on various properties preventing them from being sold to Jews. As well, many clubs, resorts and beaches were barred to Jews. Signs warning "No Jews or Dogs Allowed" or "Christians Only!" could be found on Halifax golf courses, outside hotels in the Laurentians and throughout the cottage areas of Ontario, the lake country of Manitoba and the vacation lands of BC.

Worst of all, at least from the point of those Jews desperate to get out of Nazi-infested Europe, anti-semitism had permeated into the upper levels of the Canadian government. While PM King was worrying that allowing in Jews would "pollute" Canada's bloodstream, his government was ensuring that no more would be coming. It is perhaps no surprise therefore that Canada had by far the worst record of any Western or immigration country in providing sanctuary to the Jews of Europe in the 1930s and 1940s.

Why was Canada so anti-semitic? Some hated Jews for religious reasons — after all they had "killed Christ" and had refused to repent or convert. To others the Jew was the symbol of the millions of aliens who had entered Canada since 1900. They hated Jews because they were the most visible element of this "mongrelization" of Canada. To the Canadian elite — its leaders, teachers and intellectuals — the Jew did not fit their concept of what a Canadian should be. Theirs was to be a country of farmers and homesteaders, and they believed Jews could not become successful agriculturalists. They saw Jews as city people in a country that wished to build up its rural base.

Since WWII anti-semitism has been on the decline in Canada. New ideas — and leaders — replaced the old order; attitudes, old habits and traditions were slowly transformed. The creation of the state of Israel changed stereotypes about the Jew. In Canada, following the Holocaust, overt anti-semitism became the preserve of the crank. In the House of Commons, there was still an occasional outburst from several Social Credit members from Alberta, and from a tiny handful of Parliamentarians from Québec. But for the most part vocal attacks against Jews had been banished from the public arena — though not necessarily from board rooms and private clubs.

By the 1970s and 1980s most of the earlier barriers had been removed. Human Rights Commissions, the CANADIAN CHARTER OF RIGHTS AND FREEDOMS and scores of statutes and judicial decisions guaranteed that the discrimination once so rampant in Canada against Jews — and others — would never reappear. Jews were now playing an increasingly crucial role in all sectors of Canadian society — in politics, law, medicine, arts and business.

Though polls taken in 1986 indicate that only 6% of all Canadians consider themselves anti-semites, they indicate that at least another 20% to 25% harbour some anti-Jewish feelings. And the recent appearance in Canadian society of a new breed of hatemonger claiming that Jews invented the Holocaust so that they could gain support for the state of Israel, as well as the resurgence of anti-semitic activity in the right wing of some ethnic communities, should act as warning lights. Clearly though anti-semitism is not the force in Canada it once was, neither has it entirely disappeared. *See also* PREJUDICE AND DISCRIMINATION.   IRVING ABELLA

Anyox, BC, was a town situated on Granby Bay, 60 km N of Prince Rupert. The Tsimshian word means "hidden water." The area was first visited by Capt George VANCOUVER in 1793, but was not settled until Granby Consolidated Mining, Smelting and Power Co Ltd began mining a copper deposit there in 1912. At the peak of operation it was one of the largest producing copper mines and smelters in the British Empire. Total recovery was approximately 140 000 ounces of gold, 8 million ounces of silver, and 760 million pounds of copper. Population was 2500 to 3000, but dwindled soon after the mine closed in July 1935 because of depressed prices for copper and depletion of the ore body. The post office was closed in 1939, and a forest fire destroyed most of the wooden structures in 1942. A book about Anyox (by P. Loudon) called it *The Town That Got Lost*.   MARIE ELLIOTT

Aphid, or plant louse, small, soft-bodied INSECT that sucks plant sap. Aphids belong to order Hemiptera, suborder Homoptera, and may be red, pink, brown, yellow, green, purple or black. Over 3900 species are known worldwide; over 600 in Canada. Aphids appear to have originated about 280 million years ago. In Canada, a fossil aphid over 78 million years old has been found preserved in amber. Aphids can migrate great distances (up to 1300 km) and are very prolific. In autumn, fertilized females lay overwintering eggs. The following spring these eggs hatch into wingless females that reproduce without mating, giving birth to live female offspring. Throughout the summer, several generations of unfertilized, daughter-producing females may occur. In late summer winged males and females are produced. These mate, producing fertilized, overwintering eggs. Often the asexual generations live on a different host plant from the sexually reproducing generation. In warm climates, aphids do not usually produce males, sexual females or eggs. Aphids may be polymorphic with winged and wingless forms in the same species. They are major INSECT PESTS which stunt or kill plants, cause plant galls, reduce yield and vigour, contaminate edible parts, and transmit plant viruses. They are controlled by climatic factors, land and water barriers, predaceous insects, fungus diseases, aphid-resistant plants, irrigation, modification of time of planting or harvest, and insecticides.
A.M. HARPER

Appeal, judicial process by which a party complains to a higher court that a decision against him or her by a lower court was wrong and should be reversed. The availability of an appeal depends on the type of case involved, the level of court making original determination and the nature of that determination. Each province has its own appeal court and the FEDERAL COURT of Appeal hears certain matters of federal jurisdiction; decisions from these courts can be appealed only to the SUPREME COURT of Canada. Appeal courts in Canada almost always sit in panels of odd numbers of judges to ensure a majority decision in favour of one party or another.   LEE PAIKIN

Apple (*Malus domestica*), the orchard apple, a cultivated species of the ROSE family, is Canada's most important FRUIT crop. It resulted from centuries of selection from wild species (eg, *M. sylvestris, M. prunifolia, M. pumila*), with interspecies hybridization. Over 75 wild species have been recognized, but many are hybrids among 17 or more true species (3 of which are native to Canada). Probably originating in the Caucasus, cultivated varieties were recognized in the 3rd century BC. Apple growing was brought to France and Britain by the Romans and from there to the New World, where there were no wild apple trees indigenous. The apple, in the form of fresh fruit and cider, was a highly important source of nutrition. It is possible that the French attempted to plant the apple at Port Royal as early as 1606, and it is certain that improved varieties were growing near Annapolis Royal around 1633-35. From then on, apples were extensively grown by Acadians – a census reported 1584 apple trees at Port Royal alone in 1698. Most of the apples produced in early times were used in making cider. Early records show apple trees growing at LaHave, ACADIA, by 1635. The Fameuse cultivar, grown in Québec for over 150 years, arose from seed or possibly a young seedling brought from France in this early period. The showy flowers are borne in terminal clusters, chiefly on short, lateral, woody shoots (spurs) on spreading trees of modest size. Trees may reach 12 m by 6 m in spread and height, although smaller trees are preferred. Tree size is controlled by choice of rootstock, cultivar (commercial variety), site and soil, and by management practices (eg, pruning). Fruit development depends upon cross fertilization. Cultivars must be propagated by vegetative methods (eg, grafting); however, many fruiting trees have been grown from seed and provide a rich source of new cultivars. Of the thousands of cultivars named, only a few hundred can now be found and only about a dozen are important. McIntosh, Red Delicious, Spy, Spartan, Cortland, Golden Delicious, Idared, Newtown, Winesap and Gravenstein are important in Canada. Spy, Cortland and Gravenstein are not important in BC; Newton and Winesap are grown only in BC. Granny Smith is imported in large volumes. Apples are the preferred fruit of Canadians and are used fresh, cooked or in large volumes of juice; lesser quantities are converted into fermented products and vinegar. After juice extraction, the remains (pomace) may serve as a source of pectin or may be fed to livestock.

Adapted to temperate zones, apple trees must have a dormant period of about 1000 hours below 5°C but do not survive winter temperatures below −40°C. Sites near water are preferred. In Canada, the growing regions are in NS, southern NB and Québec, near Lakes Ontario and Erie in Ontario, and in the southern valleys of BC. After planting, several years of care are necessary before production of break-even crops. Care includes pruning, spraying, providing bees for POLLINATION, irrigation and controlling rodents and deer. Most apples are carefully hand picked. Maturity is important and sprays to control maturation and preharvest drop may be necessary. Harvested fruit is cooled promptly and control of storage atmosphere helps maintain quality. Apples are sold by variety and, for marketing, are graded by size and quality. Below-grade fruit is usually used for juice. In 1985, 478 605 t, valued at $115 598 million, were produced in Canada, of which Ontario accounted for nearly $44.3 million, BC for over $35.4 million, Québec for almost $24.1 million, Nova Scotia over $9.1 million and New Brunswick over $2.7 million.   A.D. CROWE

Applebaum, Louis, composer, conductor, administrator (b at Toronto 3 Apr 1918). After stud-

Louis Applebaum (left), one of Canada's most prodigious composers, has written and conducted scores for film, theatre, and radio and TV drama (*courtesy National Archives of Canada/PA-122729/W.A. Curtin*).

ies at the Toronto Conservatory of Music and U of T with Boris Berlin, Healey WILLAN and Sir Ernest MACMILLAN, Applebaum went to New York to study composition. By the mid-1940s he had moved to Hollywood, where his film scores were in great demand, but in 1949 he returned to Canada. One of Canada's most prodigious composers, he has written and conducted hundreds of scores for film, theatre, and radio and TV drama. His concert pieces, ballets and fanfares, frequently commissioned, are always admired as strong and appropriate, qualities that reflect his awareness of the need for the artist to be pragmatic and conscious of developments in his art. In addition to his busy career as a working composer, Applebaum's administrative skills have made him a consultant for organizations, including the National Film Board, the Canada Council and the CBC. He has served on numerous committees, such as CAPAC-Canadian Association of Broadcasters, for the promotion of Canadian music, and as an adviser on the formation of music faculties, opera and ballet companies. He established the music wing of the STRATFORD FESTIVAL and in 1965 he chaired a government-commissioned committee whose report led to the formation of the National Arts Centre Orchestra. He was executive director of the Ontario Arts Council 1970-79, when he became co-chairman, with Jacques HÉBERT, of the FEDERAL CULTURAL POLICY REVIEW COMMITTEE, which reported in 1982. Applebaum became vice-president of Composers, Authors and Publishers Assn in 1985.   MABEL H. LAINE

Appleyard, Peter, jazz musician (b at Cleethorpes, Eng 26 Aug 1928). A versatile nightclub-studio musician and TV personality in Toronto, Appleyard moved from Bermuda to Canada in 1951 and soon turned from drumming to the vibraphone. His Toronto TV shows included "Mallets and Brass" (1969, with Guido Basso) and "Peter Appleyard Presents" (1977-80); among his recordings are the hit instrumental *The Lincolnshire Poacher* and several pop-music albums, including *Swing Fever* (1982). Appleyard, who has conducted his Canadian career with a keen instinct for popular tastes, also worked in the early 1970s with Benny Goodman.
MARK MILLER

Apprenticeship, as a form of instruction in which a novice learns from a master of a craft or art, has existed for thousands of years. The craft guilds of western Europe, which developed in the 7th and 8th centuries, formalized the apprenticeship system and retained control of it until the 16th century. Until the late 19th century, apprenticeship was the sole means for people to acquire the skills for almost all occupations.

In early 19th-century Canada, apprenticeship training was carried on by the skilled tradesmen who immigrated from Europe. The training was sporadic and it varied even within a particular trade, but as long as a supply of skilled people was readily available through immigration, the lack of training presented no urgent problem; but as Canada became industrialized, it was necessary to develop a Canadian apprenticeship program. As a result of strong pressures from the building trades, led by Joseph Piggott, Ontario passed the first Apprenticeship Act in 1928, providing for regulation and support of apprenticeship. BC (1935) and Nova Scotia (1936) passed Apprenticeship Acts modelled on the Ontario legislation.

In 1944, under the Vocational Training Co-ordination Act, the federal government arranged to enter into an agreement with any province to provide financial assistance for apprentice training. As a result, the majority of provinces enacted legislation establishing apprenticeship programs. Generally provincial legislation provides for the regulation of apprentice training, the establishment of trade-advisory committees and the appointment of a director of apprenticeship.

The apprenticeship system is now being practised in several hundred trades. The provinces have established a co-operative Interprovincial Standards Program to provide for acceptance of certification in all provinces for apprentices who meet the interprovincial standard.

Apprenticeship is founded on a contractual relationship between an employee and an employer, in which the employer agrees to provide opportunities for the employee-apprentice to learn the skills required for a trade under the supervision of someone already qualified in that trade. The period of training is usually from 3 to 5 years and follows a structured training program or curriculum. Up to 90% of the training occurs in the workplace; some of the concomitant theoretical knowledge is taught at an institution, generally a COMMUNITY COLLEGE or institute of technology. The apprentice's progress is monitored by the director of apprenticeship in each province, who also certifies the successful completion of the training by issuing a certificate of qualification.

Apprentices are generally paid a percentage of the certified journeyman's wage, which increases throughout the apprenticeship period. The costs of the in-school portion of the training are paid by the federal government, which also provides apprentices with a living allowance or unemployment-insurance payments. Employers receive a return from the apprentices' labour. In certain trades that are considered critical to the Canadian economy, the federal government provides substantial subsidies to employers of apprentices. The subsidies for women apprentices have been increased to encourage the training of women in nontraditional occupations.

Under the apprenticeship system, a fixed number of hours must be devoted to the practical and theoretical aspects of the curriculum, on the grounds that an employer can thus recover part of the costs of training by having an apprentice with some of the skills of a journeyman for a period of time at less cost than the full journeyman rate. It is also contended, particularly by unions, that competence is best achieved by allowing apprentices to practise their skills in a work setting over a period of time. Recently, however, the adoption of a competency-based system has been proposed, ie, a system under which apprentices could be certified at whatever point in the training they could demonstrate competency.

The regulation of apprentice wage rates as a percentage of a journeyman's wages has been criticized as a barrier to the entry of young people into apprenticeships. It is argued that the rates are too high or too inflexible for current labour market conditions. Various alternatives have been proposed, including complete deregulation (which would permit apprentice wage rates to be set by collective bargaining in unionized industries or by labour-market forces) and a system of using the minimum wage as a base and of raising wages by percentage through the period of apprenticeship.

Another major issue concerns the current requirement for comprehensive training. Many smaller companies cannot offer instruction in all the necessary skills of a trade. In some cases therefore apprentices are contracted to associations of employers who move the apprentices from company to company to learn the full range of skills. Another strategy – the modular curriculum system – is used widely and successfully in the mining industry and is being extended to industrial trades. The modules outline training in discrete packages. Apprentices are credited for the completion of each module and on completing all modules receive a certificate of qualification. The critics of the modular approach have expressed fears that its widespread use will lead to fragmentation of the trades into narrow specialities.

It is well documented that there are many more well-qualified young people in Canada who wish to enter apprenticeship than there are available openings, and that the major barrier to apprenticeship is the unwillingness of employers to offer such training. KENNETH E. HUNTER

Apprenticeship in Early Canada Until the mid-19th century, apprenticeship was a system of training that enabled young men or, more rarely, women to acquire the skills of a particular trade or profession. The 3 major means of access to apprenticeship were through institutions, the family or an agreement with a craftsman or professional, ratified by a notarial deed. Although the last form is that most often mentioned in historical accounts, the training of one family member by another appears to have been at least as widespread and was preferred by merchants and the professions (eg, doctors, lawyers, notaries). Very few apprentices were trained in institutions. In the formal and family systems, training was essentially practical and was given in the craftsman's workshop or the professional's office.

European and Canadian System From the Middle Ages or earlier, many trades in France and other European countries organized themselves into communities which came to be known as corporations or guilds. The guild system was characterized by the creation among craftsmen of a hierarchy comprising apprentices, journeymen and masters. The masters headed the guilds and elected juries responsible for drawing up and implementing regulations. Among these regulations were those governing apprenticeship and access to mastership: a long training period and an often rigorous entry procedure were imposed on apprentices; journeymen wishing to become masters had to pay a large fee and produce an original work of superior quality, ie, a masterpiece.

When the first French craftsmen arrived in NEW FRANCE in the 17th century, they soon discovered that it was impossible to carry on their strict guild traditions and regulations. There was too much to be done in the new country for them to concentrate solely on their own trade; their time was divided among exercising their craft, clearing the land, fishing and trading furs. When the first villages sprang up and the training of a core group of craftsmen became necessary, the French system was no longer suitable, because 17th- and 18th-century Canada lacked specialized manpower. Guilds, as they had existed in France, were abandoned; however, the hierarchy and system of practical training were maintained. Members of the professions enjoyed better conditions: already favoured by a higher social rank, they came to Canada in fewer numbers and were able to devote most of their time to their professional duties.

Certain characteristics of the apprenticeship system in England, France, the US, Québec and the Maritimes bear striking resemblances, particularly the age of apprentices and the duration of apprenticeship. With the exception of many anglophone masters, who hired their apprentices at a younger age and for a longer period, most masters hired apprentices around the age of 16 for a 3-year period. Training was generally completed around the age of 21 but there were some exceptions, notably in the case of apprentices who were orphans. Authorities used official apprenticeship as a means of placing orphans in families and ensuring that they received training in a particular trade. Orphans generally began their training at a much younger age and worked for longer periods than other apprentices. The age of apprentices in the professions was essentially the same as that of craft apprentices, but the length of the training differed considerably. For example, legislation established the training period of lawyers and notaries at 5 years.

Working conditions reveal the characteristics of apprenticeship and the marked differences between craftsmen and professionals. Among 17th- and 18th-century craftsmen, the traditional organization of production and work dominated. With the exception of items produced at the FORGES SAINT-MAURICE and a few large workshops, each piece was the work of one craftsman, master or journeyman, sometimes assisted by an apprentice. Craftsmen generally worked in small workshops (often attached to their homes) and owned all their tools. Work was usually done to order and division of labour was almost nonexistent. The major sources of energy were still muscle power and water; raw materials were processed mainly by hand tools.

Under this system, working relations were not defined solely on the basis of labour supply and demand as today but also in terms of rights, obligations, and personal relationships which were often very authoritarian in nature. Contracts stipulated that the apprentice obey the master, work on his behalf and strive to learn his trade. In return, the master agreed to reveal all the secrets of his craft and provide accommodation, food, clothing and a small annual salary, paid either in cash or in kind. The apprentice worked 6 days a week, his hours varying depending on the trade and whether it was practised indoors or outdoors. Working days were generally from 5 AM to 8 or 9 PM, with a minimum of 2 hours for lunch and dinner. Apprentices worked 12-14 hours a day, a little longer than the journeyman or master, since they had to prepare the others' work before the shop opened and had to clean up after closing. Some apprentices in the 17th and 18th centuries received religious and academic as well as technical training.

Once the apprenticeship period was over, young workers might work for a few years as journeymen and then open their own shop when they had enough money; others inherited their father's shop. The journeyman's salary was 4-6 times greater than that of the apprentice. At this intermediate stage, the journeyman entered the job market and made products of his own. Some journeymen trained apprentices or were responsible for the internal operation of the workshop in the master's absence. The working conditions of apprentices to merchants or in the professions were very different from those of craft apprentices. Apprentices to the professions usually came from wealthier families, worked fewer hours, received some education before beginning their apprenticeship and were not required to perform domestic duties.

Changes in the Nineteenth Century The economic boom of the early 19th century, certain British influences and the process of urbanization provoked irreversible changes in MANUFACTURING, work organization and conditions of apprenticeship. In order to meet the competition from imported products in the expanding local market, many master craftsmen also acted as merchants and manufacturers and modified their production methods. They used machine tools, grouped several craftsmen together under the same roof, shared tasks and were thus able to hire unskilled labour to make products on a large scale. This development marked the transition from individual artisan to workshop and, subsequently, to factory production in urban centres. The transition was a long and complex process spread over nearly the entire 19th century and craftsmen's workshops and factories co-existed for a long time. These major changes affected the role of traditional apprenticeship in the work force and society. Apprentices gradually became a source of cheap manpower and were hired more for their labour than for training purposes. They were hired at increasingly younger ages and their contracts were prolonged and expanded to embrace several tasks so that they could be used as cheap labour for longer periods. The traditional responsibilities of masters (support and moral and religious education) were replaced by a cash payment. Some masters failed to teach apprentices "the secrets of the trade"; others mistreated them. Apprentices often ran away, since they had difficulty breaking their contracts. If caught, they were prosecuted.

While the traditional apprenticeship system deteriorated, other institutions increased in importance. At the beginning of the 19th century, evening schools began to replace the education previously given by the master and his wife. In order to have more control over the education of apprentices and young journeymen, masters and merchants followed the example of their counterparts in Great Britain and established technical institutes in the major cities of eastern Canada (Halifax, Québec City and Montréal). These institutes were viewed by the authorities as training centres where workers could learn respect for the establishment, discipline in the workplace and proper social behaviour. Sunday schools and temperance groups, established during the first half of the 19th century, supported the institutes in the pursuit of a common goal: to teach workers how to use their leisure time so that they would put more effort into their work. During the second half of the 19th century, technical institutes partly replaced workshops as the place in which training was provided.

The founding of the first unions in the 1830s and professional corporations in the late 1840s resulted, in part, from a desire to control access to occupations and to protect their members. With the exception of the construction trades and the professions, which succeeded in limiting the number of apprentices, trades (eg, shoe making, coopering, tinsmithing) were threatened by technological change. Schools gradually took over responsibility for training professionals; hence, the creation of professional associations (eg, of doctors and notaries) gave professionals an opportunity to control not only the quality of education but also the number of graduates (*see* EDUCATION HISTORY). Although government authorities first feared giving so much power to doctors and notaries, these 2 professional groups were granted such powers (in 1845 and 1847) after applying considerable pressure.

JEAN-PIERRE HARDY AND DAVID-THIERY RUDDEL

Apprenticeship of Duddy Kravitz, The, by Mordecai RICHLER, was published in London and Boston, 1959, and Toronto, 1969. Duddy Kravitz is a brash Jewish Montréal kid determined to make it – whatever "it" is, whatever "it" takes. Acting on his grandfather's maxim that a man is nothing without land, Duddy schemes and dreams to develop his first brainstorm, a lakeshore property in the Laurentians. Duddy is an attractive figure, bursting with chutzpah, but he is also driven to exploit others in his drive to succeed. Richler frames Duddy's initiation within a pungently satiric sendup of Jewish and Wasp middle-class gentility as seen from the sharp-eyed, tough-minded St-Urbain Street perspective that has become one of Richler's trademarks. Duddy's eventual triumph is also his downfall, costing him more in lost love than he will ever realize in money. Richler's most popular novel, *The Apprenticeship of Duddy Kravitz* has been translated into French as *L'Apprentissage de Duddy Kravitz* (Elisabeth Gille-Nemirovsky, Paris, 1960; Jean Simard, Montréal, 1976). A movie was made in 1974 and Duddy made his stage debut in Edmonton in 1984.   NEIL BESNER

Apps, Charles Joseph Sylvanus, Syl, hockey player (b at Paris, Ont 18 Jan 1915). He excelled at football and represented Canada in pole vaulting in the 1934 British Empire Games (gold medal) and at the 1936 Berlin Olympics. He played centre for Toronto Maple Leafs 1936-43 and 1945-48, winning the CALDER TROPHY (1937) and scoring 201 goals and 231 assists in 423 games and a further 25 goals and 28 assists in 69 playoff games. A fast, graceful skater and superb playmaker, he was honoured for his team play and leadership. He was elected MPP for Kingston in 1963 and was a member of Cabinet in the Ontario legislature. He retired in 1974.

JAMES MARSH

Aqjangajuk Shaa, *Figure with Ulu* (c1967), green stone (*by permission of the West Baffin Eskimo Co-operative, Cape Dorset/Art Gallery of Ontario/gift of Klamer family, 1978*).

Apricot, common name for certain members of genus *Prunus* of the ROSE family, which produce sweet, round or oblong, nearly smooth FRUIT (resembling a small PEACH), with a large, flat stone. The 6 or more wild species are distributed throughout Asia, Asia Minor and southeastern Europe, mostly in dry areas. Most cultivars (commercial varieties) originated from the common apricot, *P. armeniaca*. Apricots were brought to Greece and Italy in the 4th century AD and to the American continent in the early 18th century. Apricot trees are large and spreading; leaves are large, heart shaped and dark green; flowers are white. The kernels are poisonous in some cultivars; in others they are sweet. Apricots are cultivated mainly for their fruit, though some species are grown as ORNAMENTALS. In Canada apricots are grown primarily in the dry, warm southern interior of BC. Factors that limit successful cultivation include sensitivity of blossoms to spring frosts, susceptibility of trees and fruit to diseases in humid climates, and high temperature requirements in summer. Canadian plantings total 150 ha. Principal cultivars are Wenatchee, Tilton and Blenheim. Apricot fruit is rich in minerals and in vitamins A and B. The fruit is used dried and as a canned product and, to a lesser extent, fresh.

K.O. LAPINS

Aqjangajuk Shaa (Axangayu), artist (b at Shartoweetuk camp near Cape Dorset, NWT 17 Mar 1937). Aqjangajuk, who began carving in stone in the 1950s, does not do a great deal of detailing; instead he works for a total effect, concentrating on spatial interaction, expressive qualities and overall form. While some of his carvings of human and animal subjects are compact, robust, solid and static, others are more open, outwardly thrusting, dynamic forms. His only print, *Wounded Caribou* (1961), is a very effective portrayal of an animal stricken by a hunter's arrow.

JEAN BLODGETT

Aquaculture is the human-controlled cultivation and harvest of freshwater and marine plants and animals. Synonyms include aquiculture, fish farming, fish culture, mariculture, fish breeding and ocean ranching. Throughout the world, aquaculture operations constitute an integral part of FISHERIES and aquatic RESOURCE MANAGEMENT. Organisms as varied as trout, carp and tuna (ie, finfish), shrimps and oysters (ie, shellfish) and seaweed are grown, using ponds, tanks or nets, in salt, brackish and fresh waters.

In 1983 total worldwide aquaculture production amounted to about 10.2 million tonnes, ie, roughly 12% of the total world fish production. Of aquaculture production, 43.6% was finfish; 31.8% molluscs (eg, oysters, mussels); 23.4% seaweeds (eg, kelp); and about 1.2% crustaceans (eg, lobsters, shrimp). Almost every country has some form of aquaculture. The world's major producers are China, India and Japan (56% of the total). From 1971-80, there was a 73% increase in total production. In the 1980s the rate of increase slowed down but the production is still expected to double by the year 2000. This will substantially reduce the projected demands a growing population will place on the world's natural fish stocks, many of which are already overfished.

In the major aquaculture regions of the world, the emphasis has been on species that find wide acceptance among all social groups, eg, trout and salmon in N America and northern Europe, carp in eastern Europe and Israel, mussels in France and Spain, prawns and milkfish in the Philippines, Asian species of carp in SE Asia, and seaweeds in Japan and Korea. In some areas, there has been some emphasis on luxury products, eg, freshwater prawns, for specific markets or export, but the total production of such items remains low.

The origins of aquaculture go back thousands of years. Oysters in Japan and fish in Egypt were cultured before 2000 BC. In China, domestication of carp, the most commonly cultured fish, began 5 centuries earlier than in Europe. The first book on fish culture was reportedly written by a Chinese scholar, Fan Li, in the 5th century BC. Carp were introduced to Europe from the Danube R by the Romans in the 1st to 4th centuries AD. Culture techniques were refined by monks during the 14th to 16th centuries. Trout were first raised in a hatchery in Germany in 1741, and the first attempts at commercial trout culture were made as early as 1853 in the US. Rainbow trout, once found only in N America, are now cultured throughout the world.

The originator of Canadian aquaculture was Samuel WILMOT, who developed techniques for salmon and trout in the 1860s and 1870s that were so successful that nearly a century elapsed before significant changes were made in Canadian trout hatcheries. Most Canadian aquaculture operations have been operated by government. Starting in the 1960s, the value of nongovernment production rose, and it is now higher than government production. Between 1972 and 1985, finfish production has almost tripled. Government production of finfish (now less than 40% of the total) has involved, almost exclusively, the hatching and rearing of young fish in hatcheries for release in the wild for commercial and sport fisheries. Private or commercial aquaculture production is for direct sale as food and for private sportfishing.

Aquaculture practices may be categorized by the degree of human control over production. The following arrangement is in order of increasing control.

Release of Young into the Wild A well-known practice, the stocking of lakes and streams with young trout, is commonly used by federal and provincial hatcheries, and involves rearing the fish in a hatchery from a few weeks to over a year. Once stocked, the fish are exposed to all the hazards of nature, such as predatory fish and birds.

Raft Culture of Molluscs and Seaweed In this type of culture, ropes or nets are suspended from floating rafts. The animals or plants become attached to the ropes or nets and obtain food and nutrients from the water. The organisms are not fed, but they are protected from bottom-dwelling predators and are not as subject to crowding as they would be in nature.

Cage Culture of Finfish Significant advantages can be obtained by growing fish in floating cages. For example, in Norway, Atlantic salmon are confined in large (20 m x 20 m), nylon-mesh cages. The cages, held in specially chosen areas of the fjords, are supplied daily with specially prepared foods. Safe from birds and other fish, the salmon grow rapidly and most survive to a marketable size.

Pond Culture of Fish By growing fish in man-made earthen ponds, even greater control can be maintained. Trout, carp, catfish and numerous other species are supplied with food, either prepared diets or natural food produced by fertilizing the pond waters. The fishes' environment can be improved by adding or aerating water, or treating it with chemicals.

Intensive Tank Culture While most federal and provincial hatcheries produce fish for stocking, virtually the same techniques are used to grow fish from eggs to market size. In the most intensive systems, as many aspects of the environment are controlled as is technically possible. Pumps supply a constant flow of water at controlled temperatures. Food is given at specified times from automatic feeders. Specially bred, disease-free stocks of fish are used.

The types of aquaculture operations in Canada vary considerably from region to region. On the West Coast, there has been a large increase in the rearing and stocking of Pacific salmon, as part of the Canada-BC Salmonid Enhancement Program. The goal of this program is to double commercial and sport harvest of salmon. Private cage-culture operations for growing salmon for market have also been established and the numbers are expanding greatly. As well, preliminary cage culture of other fish (eg, sable fish) is being attempted. BC is also a significant producer of cultured Pacific oysters while the possibilities of mussel culture and scallop culture are being considered. On the Prairies, several thousand farmers regularly stock small prairie pothole lakes with rainbow trout fingerlings in spring and harvest pan-size fish in fall. The production is mainly for private use, but increasing numbers are being marketed commercially. Cage rearing of trout is also being attempted and there are small-scale projects growing Arctic char in tanks. Significant numbers of walleye and whitefish fry are stocked from government hatcheries into large lakes in attempts to enhance and rehabilitate important commercial fisheries. In Ontario and Québec, rainbow and brook trout are reared in ponds and tanks, and recently cage rearing has been attempted. The major production of fish, for direct sale to stores and restaurants, is in these 2 provinces, but there is also significant production of trout for stocking of private fishing ponds. The Ontario government has been stocking Pacific salmon and various species of trout in the Great Lakes in order to rehabilitate the fisheries there. In the Atlantic provinces, the federal government has been stocking hatchery-reared Atlantic salmon and trout since the 1880s. Recently, cage culture of Atlantic salmon and rainbow trout has been established in the Bras d'Or Lakes and the S coasts of NS and NB. Production of Atlantic salmon in cages rose from 78 t in 1981 to 297 t in 1986 – a tenfold increase in 5 years. Another East Coast success has been the culture of blue mussels. In 1981 there was virtually no culture of mussels. By 1986, production rose to 1777 t valued at over $2.7 million. The much larger tuna (350-650 kg) are harvested and shipped directly to Japanese markets. MOLLUSC culture is primarily of oysters, although there is some mussel production in the Atlantic provinces. Operations are gradually introducing new techniques such as the culture of shellfish on suspended ropes and traps.

In the mid-1980s federal and provincial governments in Canada began actions to clarify legislation and regulations related to aquaculture and to co-ordinate government and industry action leading to aquaculture developments. The success of aquaculture operations in Canada will depend on the availability of land, water and capital, on technologies employed, market acceptance and the technical and business competence of the entrepreneur. G. BURTON AYLES

Aquarium, an organization devoted to the public exhibition of both freshwater and marine aquatic life. Exhibit species may include not only fish but also other aquatic animals, including invertebrates, amphibians, reptiles, aquatic birds and marine mammals such as sea otters, seals, dolphins and whales. Identification labels typically identify the species on display. In Canada, aquarium live-animal collections range from 12 to over 500 species. Major aquarium displays in Canada are the Aquarium de Montréal, Qué; Marineland of Canada at Niagara Falls, Ont; Pacific Undersea Gardens, Victoria, BC; Quebec Aquarium, Ste-Foy, Qué; Sealand of the Pacific, Victoria, BC; and Vancouver Public Aquarium, BC. Display emphasis and exhibit philosophy in these aquariums varies from those primarily aimed at family recreation and entertainment to those of a more conservational and biological nature. It is estimated that some 2 million people per year visit aquariums in Canada.

The first public aquarium in Canada was the Vancouver Aquarium, which opened in June 1956. It was built as a result of the 1951 Massey Commission which recommended that a National Aquarium be developed to illustrate the importance of fisheries to Canada. Operated by the Vancouver Aquarium Assn, a private nonprofit society, the Vancouver Aquarium is completely self-supporting and is open every day of the year. The Vancouver Aquarium displays over 8000 specimens of over 535 species. In addition to its live collections it has extensive education programs for school-age children from kindergarten through high school, a continuing education program for adults, a fully staffed research department and a regular publications program. It was the first aquarium in North America to receive full accreditation status from the American Assn of Zoological Parks and Aquariums. While the Vancouver Aquarium presents aquatic life from all over the world, the greatest emphasis by far is on the indigenous marine life of the eastern North Pacific (Canada's West Coast) with ecologically correct exhibits ranging from invertebrates to killer whales. MARGARET BUTSCHLER

Killer whale in the Vancouver Aquarium (*photo by Jeffrey Philips, North Vancouver, BC*).

Aquin, Hubert, novelist (b at Montréal 24 Oct 1929; d there 15 Mar 1977). Best known for his 4 complex modernist novels, Aquin also influenced contemporary Québec culture as political activist, essayist, filmmaker and editor. Brilliant, tormented and deeply committed to a Québec whose contradictions he seemed to embody, Aquin had a flair for drama and public gesture; he once declared: "It is my life that will turn out to have been my super-masterpiece."

Aquin received a licentiate in philosophy from U de M in 1951. From 1951 to 1954 he studied at the Institut d'études politiques in Paris and on his return to Montréal worked for Radio-Canada (1955-59). From 1960 to 1968 he was a colourful and influential figure in the growing movement for Québec independence. While supporting himself by work at the Montreal Stock Exchange (1960-64) and the National Film Board (1959-63), he was an executive member of the first independentist political party, the Rassemblement pour l'indépendance nationale (RIN), 1960-69. During the same period, as an editor of LIBERTÉ, he engaged in debate with Pierre TRUDEAU on the question of Québec independence. In 1964 he declared in a press release that he was going "underground" to work for independence through terrorism; he was arrested shortly afterwards and detained 4 months in a psychiatric institute, where he wrote his first novel, PROCHAIN ÉPISODE (1965), the story of an imprisoned revolutionary. In Dec 1964 he was acquitted of illegal possession of a firearm.

The publication of *Prochain épisode* established Aquin as perhaps the most important cultural figure in Québec of his generation, but he continued to assert his inability to compromise with any established order. In 1966 he was expelled from Switzerland and wrote that the expulsion was due to RCMP influence. In 1969 he became the first Québec writer to refuse the GOVERNOR GENERAL'S AWARD, offered to him for *Trou de mémoire* (1968). In the same year he denounced Pierre BOURGAULT's decision to merge the RIN with René LEVESQUE's Mouvement pour la souveraineté-association and resigned from the party.

The following years seem to have been marked by a growing despair linked to Aquin's sense of separation from the political centre of his beloved Québec. In 1969 he published *L'Antiphonaire*, which unlike his previous 2 novels has no explicit political content. In 1971 he resigned from the editorial board of *Liberté*, claiming that its reliance on CANADA COUNCIL support had kept it silent on the events of the OCTOBER CRISIS of the previous year. In 1974 appeared Aquin's final novel, *Neige noire*, a modern version of Hamlet integrating film, music and painting techniques into its sustained philosophical reflection on time, love, death and the sacred. In Mar 1975 he became literary director of Éditions La Presse, a position which because of its links with POWER CORPORATION was seen by some as a contradiction of his earlier "revolutionary" stance. But Aquin had always claimed he became a revolutionary because as a Québecois he was denied the opportunity of being a banker, and his time at Éditions La Presse was marked by conflicts over money he wanted to invest in "unprofitable" Québec literary ventures. In Aug 1976 he resigned, accusing his superior Roger LEMELIN of "colonizing Québec from the interior," and entered a period of financial insecurity and severe depression which ended in his suicide.   PATRICIA SMART

Arabs, or more specifically, Syrian-Lebanese immigrants, began to arrive in Canada in small numbers in 1882. Their immigration was relatively limited until 1945, after which time it increased progressively, particularly in the 1960s and 1970s. In 1988 nearly 7 out of every 1000 Canadians were Arabic in origin, for a total of 160 000 to 170 000. At present, the label "Arab Canadian" does not refer to one religious affiliation, country of origin or distance from the immigrant generation but to the mixture of characteristics, beliefs, etc, that some 125 000 Canadians of Arab origin have inherited from the past or acquired in Canada.

Origins The Arab world extends from the Arabian Gulf through N Africa to the shores of the Atlantic Ocean. It is a region diverse in physical geography, climate and natural resources, but its inhabitants share cultural traditions and the Arabic language.

The early wave of Arab immigrants originated from Syria and what is now known as Lebanon. More than 90% were Christians seeking freedom from poverty and the Ottoman (Turkish) colonial regime. The post-WWII wave of Arab immigrants comprised a broader mixture of Christian groups and a substantial number of Muslims and Druzes who were motivated by the desire to escape unfavourable social, economic and political conditions in their homelands.

The 2 waves of immigrants came from markedly different social and political contexts – the early immigrants from an economically less-developed Arab world, colonized by the Ottoman Turks, the postwar immigrants from a decolonized Arab world undergoing rapid socioeconomic development. These differences are expressed through different world views, attitudes and behaviour.

Migration By 1901 Canada had about 2000 Syrian immigrants, by 1911 about 7000. For the next 40 years relatively few Syrian immigrants were admitted to Canada because of severe restrictions on the admission of immigrants from Asia (*see* PREJUDICE AND DISCRIMINATION), but between 1946 and 1984 (inclusive), 86 180 immigrants arrived, particularly from Lebanon (36 126), Egypt (23 633), Morocco (10 380), Syria (5838), Iraq (2418), Jordan (1768), Tunisia (1205) and Algeria (1172). Others came from Saudi Arabia, Kuwait, Libya, Sudan, Bahrain, Qatar, United Arab Emirates, Somalia, Mauretania, Arab Republic of Yemen, People's Democratic Republic of Yemen and Oman. Many of these more recent Arab immigrants arrived as highly educated married couples with children. At present, about one half of the Arab ethnic group in Canada are of Lebanese-Syrian origin; one-

fourth are of Egyptian origin and the remainder are from other Arab states. The number of Christians exceeds that of Muslims by a ratio of 3 to 1.

Settlement Patterns Canadians of Arab origin always tended to settle in urban areas but not in neighbourhood concentrations. Since the turn of the century, Québec and Ontario have consistently attracted the majority of Arab immigrants; 80% of Arab Canadians are about equally divided between these 2 provinces. In Québec the heaviest concentration of Arab Canadians is in metropolitan Montréal; in Ontario, they are to be found largely in Toronto and vicinity, but also in Ottawa, Windsor, London and Hamilton. The Arab communities of Alberta and Nova Scotia rank third and fourth in size, but are much smaller than those of Québec and Ontario.

Economic Life Many of the early Syrian immigrants entered the labour force through pedlary, an independent but relatively low status occupation. Through hard work, frugality and reciprocal support, the economic fortunes of pedlars often rose and they expanded their entrepreneurial activities. The postwar immigrants, however, arrived with higher average educational and occupational qualifications, the majority of them planning to follow professional and other white-collar careers.

Religion and Community Life Both the early and postwar immigrants were involved in institution building, particularly religious institutions. At the beginning of this century, several Eastern Christian churches were founded: Antiochian Orthodox, Melkite (Catholic) and Maronite (Catholic). The Coptic Orthodox Church was established in 1965, following the arrival of large numbers of Coptic immigrants from Egypt.

Muslim institutions developed more slowly, because of the small size and dispersal of this religious group. The first mosque in Canada, Al Rashid Mosque, was built in Edmonton in 1938. Since the 1950s mosques have been established in virtually all major urban centres.

Secular associations were also established by both the early pioneers and later immigrants to serve social, cultural, charitable and political needs. Memberships are usually mixed; in a few cases they are confined to youth, women, university students or professionals. Some national groups, eg, Lebanese, Syrians, Palestinians, Egyptians, have established their own distinct associations. Only the Canadian Arab Federation is national in scope and membership. Several Arab Canadian associations have sponsored the publication of multilanguage (Arabic, English and French) periodicals; some newspapers are published by individual Canadian Arabs.

Education Arab immigrants value education highly, both for themselves and for their children. Except for "Saturday" Arabic-language schools they have not established their own community-based schools. The educational attainment of Arab Canadians is comparable to the Canadian average; they are to be found at all levels of the occupational hierarchy and some have achieved renown in their respective fields.

Politics No particular political ideology or political party is dominant among Arab Canadians. They are involved in the political process at the municipal, provincial and federal levels. Arab ethnicity has not been a prominent feature of their political involvement in Canada, except in pressure-group politics involving Canada's Middle East policy.

Group Maintenance Arab immigrants have had to learn a new language, establish new social networks, integrate themselves into the economic system, learn new cultural norms and values and discard some of the ways of the country of origin. The Canadian-born generations have naturally

been even further assimilated into Canadian society. At the same time, however, a moderate degree of institutional development within the Arab ethnic group reflects a tendency towards preserving ethnic traditions. Maintaining the Arabic language, for example, is important, and the family and the community language school helped this process with varying degrees of success. Whether or not an Arab Canadian knows Arabic, links with the ancestral heritage can be, and have been, maintained through Arabic food, music, dances, mass-media exposure, visits to the "Old Country" and correspondence with friends and relatives left behind. Generally, the immigrant generation was more likely to maintain links with the cultural heritage than its Canadian-born counterpart, but although many Canadians of Arabic origin have probably lost contact with the past the majority are aware and proud of their ethnic origins. *See also* ISLAM.   BAHA ABU-LABAN

Reading: Baha Abu-Laban, *An Olive Branch on the Family Tree: The Arabs in Canada* (1980); N.W. and J.G. Jabbra, *Voyageurs to a Rocky Shore: The Lebanese and Syrians of Nova Scotia* (1985).

Arachnida, large class of chelicerate arthropods (segmented, jointed-limbed animals) including orders Araneae (SPIDERS), Scorpiones (SCORPIONS), Opiliones (harvestmen), Pseudoscorpiones (pseudoscorpions), Solifugae (wind scorpions) and Acari (MITES and TICKS). Second only to insects in species numbers, an estimated 300 000 arachnid species may occur worldwide, about 12 000 in Canada. The great majority are mites; spiders are next most common. Characteristically, arachnids have 4 pairs of legs, two pairs of mouth parts, and, if present, simple eyes on the body above the first 2 pairs of legs. Arachnids are an ancient lineage: the earliest known fossils are of 420 million-year-old scorpions. All major living groups had originated by at least 300 million years ago. Mites and spiders occur throughout Canada, including the Arctic. Ticks, pseudoscorpions and harvestmen are transcontinental, excluding arctic regions. Scorpions and wind scorpions live only in southernmost, western Canadian desert areas. Most arachnids are predators of other arthropods, although some harvestmen feed on dead organic matter; ticks are parasites of vertebrates, and mites have diverse feeding habits.   EVERT E. LINDQUIST

Arbitration is a process of legal decision making, usually under a contract, in which the people affected have agreed who will act as judge by naming a person or agreeing upon a means of selecting an individual or tribunal. Arbitrators, who are usually but not necessarily lawyers, are paid by the people who choose them. In every province there is an Arbitration Act or other statutory instrument (eg, Labour Relations Act) that regulates the process to some extent and provides for review by the ordinary courts or another superior tribunal in the event of serious errors by the arbitrators. Labour arbitration is more common than all other kinds together perhaps because grievance arbitration is required by most Canadian labour-relations statutes. In the public sector, interest arbitration may be substituted for the right to strike. *See also* STRIKES AND LOCKOUTS; LABOUR LAW.   INNIS CHRISTIE

Arboretum [Lat *arbor*, "tree"], special garden or part of a BOTANICAL GARDEN devoted to growing TREES and other woody perennials. Specimens are usually planted in groups reflecting botanical relationships or habitat preferences, in a manner producing a pleasing, parklike landscape. There may be only a few woody plants or up to several thousand different kinds, some in special plantings such as rose gardens, lilac dells, azalea and

Siberian firs in the arboretum of the Agriculture Canada Research Centre, Ottawa (*courtesy Agriculture Canada*).

rhododendron beds, hedge gardens, shrub borders and displays of woody climbers. Representative specimens are usually labelled with their common and scientific names; family name and the country of origin may appear as well. The parents of hybrids may be indicated. Educational programs are often developed in conjunction with local schools and regional horticultural societies. A well-equipped arboretum has a library, HERBARIUM and facilities for research. Alternatively, a relationship may be established with a nearby university or RESEARCH STATION which has these facilities. The main functions of an arboretum are to grow and to display effectively as large a selection of named woody plants as possible. Basic research involves discovering and recording characteristics, correct name, botanical relationships, origin, distribution, habitat requirements, economic importance and cultural uses of each kind of plant. Practical research includes testing for hardiness, studying methods of propagation, examining seed production and viability and carrying out breeding experiments to produce new and better varieties. Introduction of plants brought back from expeditions to other parts of the world or obtained by exchange of seeds and propagating stock is an important function. Research programs and publications centre around the collections. Arboretums serve as information centres and to train students in HORTICULTURE. The preservation of diverse plants as living specimens and worldwide exchange of seeds guarantee a material basis for the continuing search for new sources of fuel, food and medicine. Research results provide information to foresters, fruit growers, nurserymen, landscape architects, urban planners, park administrators, and professional and amateur botanists and gardeners.

The Dominion Arboretum and Botanic Gardens, on the Central Experimental Farm, Ottawa, dates from 1887; in 1889 the first planting of trees was made by the Department of Agriculture. Other botanical gardens and arboretums appeared more recently in Canada. The Jardin Botanique, Montréal, and the Royal Botanical Gardens, Hamilton (est 1931 and 1941, respectively) both include arboretums. Morgan Arboretum, Macdonald College, Québec, containing woody plant species, is essentially a project in forest conservation and SILVICULTURE. Québec also has a network of 21 arboretums established since 1969 by its Ministère des terres et forêts. Several universities maintain arboretums on or near campus, eg, Guelph, Western Ontario, Laurentian, Alberta and BC. Other arboretums include Ross Arboretum, Indian Head, Sask; Niagara Parks Commission Apprentice School for Gardeners, Niagara Falls, Ont; Agricultural Research Station, Morden, Man; Van Dusen Botanical Garden, Queen Elizabeth Park, Vancouver, BC; Metropolitan Toronto Zoo; and a number of forest nursery stations in various provinces. JAMES H. SOPER

Arcand, Adrian, journalist, demagogue and fascist (b at Québec C 1899; d at Montréal 1 Aug 1967). A fanatical and shrill-voiced follower of Adolf Hitler, Arcand edited several newspapers and founded and led a series of far-right Québec-based political parties. The Ordre patriotique des Goglus (fd 1929) actively promoted ANTI-SEMITISM. The Parti national social chrétien (est 1934) had as its emblem a swastika surrounded by maple leaves with a Canadian beaver appearing at the crown. This party advocated anti-communism and French Canadian nationalism and it also continued Arcand's campaign against Canadian Jews, demanding that they be resettled near Hudson Bay. At the start of WWII Arcand, the self-proclaimed Canadian Fuhrer, boasted that he and his recently founded National Unity Party would soon take over the country. Instead, he was interned in NB by the federal government for the duration and his party was declared illegal. Arcand returned in 1945 to a Québec that was largely uninterested in either him or his views. An unrepentant Nazi, however, he never stopped promoting anti-semitism, fighting real and imagined communists and plotting a fascist future for Canada. *See also* FASCISM. WILLIAM KAPLAN

Arcand, Denys, filmmaker (b at Deschambault, Qué 25 June 1941). One of Québec's most politically aware filmmakers, he worked for PARTI PRIS before studying history at Université de Montréal, where he co-directed *Seul ou avec d'autres* (1962) with Denis HEROUX and Stéphane Venne. He joined the NFB 1963, where his feature-length documentary on the textile industry, *On est au coton* (1970), was so controversial it was suppressed for 6 years. He made another documentary, *Québec: Duplessis et après...* (1971), before leaving the NFB for the private sector. *La Maudite Galette* (1972), *Réjeanne Padovani* (1973) and *Gina* (1974) were distinctive views of Québec society, original and provocative. He then moved to TV, scripting the "Duplessis" series for Radio-Canada and directing 3 episodes of "Empire Inc." He returned to the NFB to make a feature documentary on the 1980 referendum, *Le Confort et l'indifférence* (1982), which won the Québec Critics Prize. He returned to making theatrical films with the commercial *Le Crime d'Ovide Plouffe* (1984), before achieving major international success with the scathing comedy about sexual mores, *Le* DÉCLIN DE L'EMPIRE AMÉRICAIN (1986), a film that has won numerous festival prizes, including the prestigious Critic's Prize at the Cannes Film Festival. The New York Film Critics voted it Best Foreign Film in 1986 and it won Best Picture, Best Director and Best Original Screenplay at the 1987 Genie Awards. PIERS HANDLING

Archaeological Survey of Canada, established in 1971, is the component of the CANADIAN MUSEUM OF CIVILIZATION that deals with the archaeological heritage of Canada. Its major goals are the preservation of archaeological sites, research into the PREHISTORY of Canadian aboriginal peoples and informing the public of the results of archaeological research through publications and exhibitions. As the lead federal agency involved in the management of archaeological resources, it co-ordinates the protection and rescue of threatened sites on federal lands. Its Mercury Series of monographs is the main outlet for reporting of archaeological research in the country. Its exhibitions, both in the Canadian Museum of Civilization and smaller exhibits which travel across the country, are designed to contribute to public understanding of the prehistory and traditions of the native peoples of the country. ROBERT McGHEE

Archaeology represents the study of past human cultures; the past can be separated into 2 broad periods: the historic and the prehistoric. The historic period is characterized by the availability of written documents, whereas the prehistoric spans some 2 million years from the time man first became a tool-maker. In Canada, the known prehistoric record extends back about 30 000 years (*see* PREHISTORY); the historic begins about 1000 years ago with the NORSE VOYAGES but more concertedly begins with the appearance of European fishermen, explorers and traders on the E and W coasts after 1500 AD. Often, European material items, particularly ironware, penetrated far inland through native traders to distant Indians who had not yet seen the Europeans. Archaeologically, this is known as the protohistoric, a transitional period between the late prehistoric and the historic when direct contacts were continually made between the NATIVE PEOPLES and Europeans.

Archaeology strives to reconstruct the past lifeways of mankind, largely through material remains found preserved on former sites. Such remains are often limited to relatively imperishable artifacts made of stone, antler or fired clay, but sometimes remarkable cases of preservation occur in dry caves, bogs or PERMAFROST. Post-mold patterns, rock alignments, hearths, rock paintings and petroglyphs can furnish important details about past camp sites, villages, and ceremonial-religious features. Burials yield information not only about mortuary practices, but often provide direct biological facts about the past people themselves. Dietary practices can be reconstructed from preserved faunal and floral remains, and some archaeologists even attempt to determine past economic, social, religious and political life of ancient populations.

An archaeological site constitutes any locality that exhibits the material remains of a former people. Site sizes can range from a single artifact, to kill-spots, tipi rings, and more complex cemetery and habitation settlements such as hamlets, villages, towns and FORTIFICATIONS. In Canada, our largest aboriginal sites and monuments include some of the RAINY RIVER BURIAL MOUNDS, the drive lanes for the HEAD-SMASHED-IN BUFFALO JUMP, and certain of the late Ontario Iroquois and historic BC settlements that measure up to 6 ha.

Initially, one of the field archaeologist's main problems lies in determining the nature of a given site. Was it used only once (ie, a single component), or was the site recurrently occupied by the same or a different series of peoples (ie, multicomponent)? Determining contemporaneity of houses or other features on a site, let alone contemporaneity of several sites, also poses important problems for the archaeologist. Throughout Canada, known historic and prehistoric archaeological sites are usually locally named, but since 1952 they also have been nationally recorded according to Charles E. Borden's Uniform Site Designation scheme. The Borden system enumerates Canadian archaeological sites according to their latitude-longitude position within the country.

Contemporary Canadian Archaeology

Archaeologists interested in reconstructing past lifeways work in conjunction with scholars in many fields. They collaborate with geologists, geographers, biologists, physical anthropologists, palaeontologists, chemists, astronomers, mathematicians, physicists, historians, sociologists and anthropologists. The association of archaeologists with social scientists is of long standing, and many Canadian archaeologists affiliated with museums and universities still consider their field to be a specialty discipline within the wider context of ANTHROPOLOGY. Indeed, archaeology is usually taught within anthropology departments across Canada.

Canadian professional archaeology has its origins within the late 19th-century museum movement and is associated in particular with David BOYLE in Ontario. Nevertheless, it was only in 1938 at U of T, Dept of Anthropology, that a trained archaeologist, Philleo J. Nash, began teaching formal courses in the subject. His pioneering endeavours were continued after WWII by the 30-year tradition of J. Norman EMERSON. In the West, Borden initiated the first archaeology courses at UBC in 1949. The first separate department of archaeology established in N America was founded by Richard S. MacNeish and Richard G. Forbis at U of Calgary in 1964; SFU opened the second department in Canada and inaugurated a doctoral program in 1971.

Four types of professional archaeologists practise today in Canada. The first 2 represent the traditional, academic research scientists and educators associated with the nation's major universities and museums. Since 1972, 2 additional areas have had a phenomenal growth: the personnel hired by provincial government agencies to undertake cultural resource management and conservation programs made necessary by new heritage, antiquities, and cultural resource legislation; and archaeologists affiliated with business consulting firms vying for government and industrial contracts. Basically, the new consulting and managerial archaeologists represent applied archaeology as opposed to the traditional research-academic archaeology in Canada.

History of Canadian Archaeology

The Origins of Canadian archaeology lie in early 19th-century antiquarianism as practised in central to eastern Canada. The pre-Confederation era of relic hunting for exotic art objects and valued metal wares saw destruction of many native burial grounds on properties newly cleared by Euro-Canadian settlers. Ontario's NIAGARA PENINSULA stands out, for it was here that historic NEUTRAL cemeteries were dug into as early as 1828, and some of the sites attained international fame. Such was the case for the Dwyer ossuaries N of Hamilton. Opened prior to 1836, Dwyer attracted many men of letters including Sir Daniel WILSON. Their individual interests ranged from relic collecting and preservation of native culture to specific artifact interpretation.

In 1842 Sir William E. LOGAN founded the GEOLOGICAL SURVEY OF CANADA in Montréal. This Survey later produced many famous scientist-explorers who traversed the vast expanse of Canada making invaluable observations on archaeological remains, historic forts, native traditions and other natural history.

From 1867 to 1914 considerable archaeological interest developed across Canada, except in the sparsely populated Saskatchewan, Alberta and northern territories. The E and W coasts attracted collectors to the large shell middens, while southern Manitoba and Ontario had conspicuous burial mounds that evoked interpretations about a vanished race of "Mound Builders" with recognizable ties to the elaborate mounds of the Mississippi and Ohio drainages. In southern Ontario, desecration of HURON burial pits became common Sunday afternoon sport for looters, despite reasoned pleas from concerned intelligentsia. In Québec, concerted attention was paid to identifying HISTORIC SITES, particularly HOCHELAGA at Montréal by Sir John W. DAWSON, and in New Brunswick Loring W. BAILEY and William F. Ganong synthesized known prehistoric and historic sites.

The post-Confederation era was one of intensive archaeological and ethnographic collecting for new museums and universities. Photographic

Prehistoric turtle effigy at Minton, Sask (*photo by Richard Vroom*).

collecting also made a debut. Local naturalist, historic and scientific societies flourished and from them provincial governments were stimulated to establish museums and other educational programs promoting archaeology. NS opened the first provincial museum in 1868 at Halifax, while Ontario and BC sponsored formal museums in 1886. It was primarily from these museum and university milieus that the first generation of professional Canadian archaeologists began doing field work, initiating research, and generally setting standards.

Notables such as T.G.B. Lloyd, William Gossip, Bernard Gilpin, Harry Piers, Spencer Baird, George Matthew, Henry Montgomery, George Laidlaw, Andrew Hunter, Frederick Waugh, Marvin Schultz, George Bryce, Charles HILL-TOUT and James TEIT all contributed to a new archaeological excellence, but paramount among them was Ontario's David Boyle. Once a blacksmith and public-school teacher, Boyle rose to become provincial archaeologist in 1886, a post he held until his death in 1911. He established the first journal in Canada expressly devoted to archaeology and ethnography in 1886, the *Annual Archaeological Reports of Ontario*, and this series continued until 1928. Internationally renowned in Britain and the US, Boyle was an indefatigable worker widely revered as the leading figure in Canadian archaeology and museology.

The Modern Era Of the second generation of professional archaeologists in Canada, 2 individuals became most prominent: Harlan I. Smith and William J. WINTEMBERG. Smith began a distinguished career in BC as a member of the 1898 Jessup North Pacific Expedition organized in New York by Franz BOAS. Wintemberg commenced his researches in southern Ontario as a protégé of Boyle in 1900. In 1911-12 both Smith and Wintemberg joined the Victoria Memorial Museum in Ottawa. This Geological Survey of Canada museum, later renamed the National Museum of Canada in 1927, opened in 1911 with a newly created Anthropological Division headed by linguist, poet and administrator, Edward SAPIR. Shortly after, Diamond JENNESS, Canada's most distinguished anthropologist, joined the museum as did C. Marius BARBEAU. Smith and Wintemberg worked together on various sites across the country and initiated exploratory surveys. As of 1912, Ottawa became the primary centre for Canada-wide archaeological research.

Commencing in 1913, concerned research was directed towards far northern Canada as a result of the interdisciplinary Canadian Arctic Expedition of 1913-18. Vilhjalmur STEFANSSON became interested in prehistoric and modern commerce among the arctic coast Inuit, while Jenness developed the first detailed information about the Coronation Gulf Copper Eskimos (*see* COPPER INUIT), and their material culture. The Stefansson-Anderson Arctic Expedition also recovered various harpoons and darts that were analysed in 1919 by Clark Wissler. In the eastern Arctic, professional archaeological ground was first broken by Therkel Mathiassen, dedicated archaeologist with the Danish Fifth Thule Expedition, 1921-24, organized by Knud Rasmussen, who travelled Canada's entire northern mainland from Greenland to Alaska.

Questions about Inuit origins proved popular during this time, and Kaj Birket-Smith proposed his now defunct hypothesis of an inland origin for Inuit culture in north-central Canada. He and others were unsuccessful with such ideas because they attempted to solve an essentially archaeological problem with the data and techniques of ethnology. In 1925, Jenness made a major breakthrough with this analysis and definition of the prehistoric DORSET Eskimo culture. Its dating was contested by Henry B. Collins until 1948, when Collins found stratigraphic proof that Dorset predated THULE Eskimo at the Crystal II site, Frobisher Bay, Baffin I. This find confirmed many of Jenness's early claims.

In southern Canada, Smith and Wintemberg worked together in 1913-14 in NS; Frank G. SPECK discovered the TADOUSSAC site in 1915; and in Ontario, the Provincial Museum was renamed the ROYAL ONTARIO MUSEUM in 1914 with quarters in a new building. Rowland B. Orr became the second and last provincial archaeologist for Ontario from 1911 until his death in 1933. Also in Toronto, Canada's first archaeological society for professionals and laypersons, the Ontario Archaeological Assn, was founded in 1919 but survived for only a decade. In 1926 Thomas F. MCILWRAITH formed the first department of anthropology in Canada, at U of T. Specializing in Canadian studies, this department maintained close ties with the ROM, where it had its main offices from 1926 until 1961.

In the West, second-generation professional archaeology was alive but not as vibrant or expansionist as within the Toronto and Ottawa centres. Manitoba saw extensive excavation of burial mounds by William B. Nickerson in 1914, but afterwards, archaeological interest generally waned. The same was true for Saskatchewan and Alberta, although interested individuals did form the early Saskatchewan Archaeological Society in 1935 under William J. Orchard. West of the mountains, the main concern was with collecting art objects, particularly TOTEM POLES and their motifs. Some petroglyphs were also studied in 1912-35 (*see* PICTOGRAPHS AND PETROGLYPHS).

1945-60 The immediate postwar era of Canadian archaeology, 1946-55, is characterized by formal training of students, new dating methods, new analytical techniques, increased public awareness and involvement in archaeology, and the development of a personal, closely-knit group of professionals across the country. Of this third generation of Canadian archaeologists, Ontario's Emerson largely led the way in the East, along with Kenneth E. Kidd, while in the West Borden stands out. For northern Canada, Henry B. Collins of the Smithsonian Institution maintained an active program between 1948 and 1955 that introduced various students to arctic archaeology, including William E. Taylor, Jr. Taylor became director of the new National Museum of Man in 1967 and together with James V. Wright established the ARCHAEOLOGICAL SURVEY OF CANADA in 1971.

The growing cadre of trained individuals and nonprofessional archaeologists during the 1950s included Elmer Harp in Newfoundland; Edward S. Rogers in Québec; J. Douglas Leechman of the National Museum as well as Thomas E. Lee and MacNeish; Wilfrid Jury, James F. Pendergast, Clyde C. Kennedy, Richard B. Johnston, Frank Ridley in Ontario; and Taylor in the Arctic. Emerson's students, James V. Wright, Walter A. Kenyon, Kenneth C.A. Dawson and Helen E. Devereux, were beginning to staff new programs. All were instrumental in bringing new research concerns and character to the archaeology of northeastern Canada.

Five large-scale archaeological projects in Ontario illustrate the new directions, techniques and training in Canadian archaeology during this third generation. The excavations at the Jesuit site of STE MARIE AMONG THE HURONS, first by K.E. Kidd in 1941 and later by Jury in 1948, saw concerted effort to recover and restore one of Canada's early historic missions. Thomas Lee's 1951-53 excavation at the Sheguiandah site, MANITOULIN I, revealed one of the largest Paleoindian quarry sites known anywhere in N America, and Emerson's 1956-57 work along the route of the impending ST LAWRENCE SEAWAY marked the first major salvage archaeology in eastern Canada. From 1955 to 1960 the ROM fielded a party under Johnston that provided the first detailed knowledge about a burial mound in Canada, in this case the famed SERPENT MOUND near Peterborough. Kenyon also cut new ground with his near total excavation of the Miller Pickering village in 1958-59. Such advances marked different types of archaeological firsts in Canada.

In the Arctic, something of a "golden era" fluoresced during this third generation of Canadian archaeology. New Paleoeskimo cultures were discovered, and new refinements were geographically added concerning Dorset, Thule and SADLERMIUT INUIT. To these ends the work of Henry B. Collins, Taylor, Jørgen Meldgaard and Moreau S. Maxwell stands particularly paramount. In the adjacent Barren Lands and northern forests of the Yukon and the NWT, MacNeish and Harp undertook pioneering reconnaissances and archaeological excavations that are still useful. Canada's far northern archaeologists have never been numerous, but the use of aircraft has greatly enhanced access to this vast, difficult but beautiful tract of Canada.

Western Canada also experienced exciting new archaeological developments during the years 1946-60. In Manitoba, MacNeish undertook ex-

Archaeological dig at the Dufferin Terrace, Québec City, 1986 (*courtesy Environment Canada/photo by Michel Élie*).

cavations that provided a chronological scheme that augmented the local endeavours of Chris Vickers and Walter M. Hlady. Thomas and Alice B. Kehoe investigated south-central Saskatchewan, while Boyd N. Wettlaufer surveyed portions of southern Saskatchewan and Alberta. The year 1955 saw new directions in Alberta archaeology with the establishment of the Glenbow Foundation directed by Leechman. He introduced various professionals for formal archaeological surveys throughout the province, including H. Marie Wormington, William Mulloy, E. Mott Davis and Richard G. Forbis. Significantly, the Glenbow Foundation, established by Eric L. HARVIE, represented the first private institution to sponsor archaeology in Canada (*see* GLENBOW MUSEUM).

In BC, Borden began his dedicated career with that province's archaeology in 1945, digging the Point Grey site. His later work at Marpole on the lower Fraser R, 1948-57, is most significant, as was the salvage archaeology within Tweedsmuir Park, 1951-52. This work, done in the face of the Kemano power station and flooding of the Nechako reservoir (near KITIMAT), marks Canada's earliest salvage archaeology projects. Roy L. Carlson and Wilson DUFF were trained during this period, and 1960 saw passage of a provincial Archaeological and Historic Sites Protection Act in BC.

Expansionism: 1960-75 The pace of Canadian archaeology significantly changed after 1960. This fourth period was characterized by attempts to define regional sequences, increased interdisciplinary and specialty analyses, expansion of university programs, the development of archaeological field schools, wide-ranging canoe surveys through the boreal forest, and a time when problems of culture history and past peoples motivated considerable research. New funding sources opened, including the CANADA COUNCIL, which began supporting archaeology in 1961, followed by the SOCIAL SCIENCES AND HUMANITIES RESEARCH COUNCIL OF CANADA. This was also the period when Québec archaeology came into its own, with the 1962 establishment of the Société d'archéologie du Québec. Parks Canada also undertook new programs in both prehistoric and historic archae-

ology. The mid- to late 1960s proved most dynamic on all archaeological fronts in Canada.

Expansionism occurred at the NATIONAL MUSEUMS OF CANADA and in universities, paralleling a greater public interest in Canada's national heritage following CENTENNIAL YEAR. To the group of Taylor, Wright, George F. MacDonald, and William N. Irving at the National Museum in Ottawa were added Donald G. MacLeod, Roscoe Wilmeth, Robert McGhee, Donald W. Clark, David Sanger, Richard E. Morlan, William J. Byrne, Roger Marois, Bryan H. Gordon and David L. Keenlyside. In extreme eastern Canada James A. Tuck, Devereux, William W. Fitzhugh, Urve Linnamae, John S. Erskine, David Sanger, MacDonald, Christopher Turnbull and Richard N. Pearson contributed significantly to our archaeological knowledge of that region. In Québec Jacques Cinq-Mars, Charles A. Martijn, René Ribes and Gilles Tassé initiated new dimensions to the discipline. Ontario saw a steady stream of students produced by Emerson that included MacDonald, Romas Vastokas, Donald G. MacLeod, Michael W. Spence, Morgan J. Tamplin, McGhee, William C. Noble, William A. Russell, Alan E. Tyyska, Peter G. Ramsden and William D. Finlayson. Also in Ontario, Kenyon pursued investigations along Rainy R, as well as at historic Ft Albany.

In the West, expansionism was also apparent. The U of Manitoba established an archaeological MA program under William J. Mayer-Oakes. Eugene M. Gryba, E. Leigh Syms, Jack Steinbring, Gary A. Dickson, Leo F. Pettipas and Ronald J. Nash became noteworthy contributors, while in Saskatchewan Ian G. Dyck, George Arthur and James F.V. Millar established important archaeological centres at Regina and Saskatoon, respectively. The U of Calgary became a major archaeological focus with its specialized department, and graduated its first archaeology PhDs in 1968 including Albertan resident Barney O.K. Reeves. At Edmonton, Ruth Gruhn undertook local excavations as did Robert Kidd and Clifford Hickey. In BC, James J. Hester, Philip M. Hobler, Donald Mitchell, Carlson, Sanger, Turnbull and Knut Fladmark all represent prominent contributors during this fourth period of Canadian archaeological development.

The northern sectors of Canada received almost continuous attention during the 1960-75 period.

Wright undertook numerous surveys and excavations through Ontario westward to Alberta and the District of Keewatin that required a stamina reminiscent of the 19th-century GSC scientist-explorers. Guy Mary-Rousselière opened new ground in the Canadian Arctic, as did McGhee, while Noble, Clark, Morlan and Gordon investigated the northern forests and margins.

Archaeology in Canada attained some measure of maturity during this period. Not only did the number of practising archaeologists rise from a mere dozen to nearly 100, but an interested public helped stimulate formation of the nationwide Canadian Archaeological Assn in 1968. This organization has become the official watchdog and forum for archaeology in Canada, and it initiated a *Bulletin* publication series in 1969. This series was later transformed into a major Canadian archaeological serial under the editorship of McGhee, and retitled the *Canadian Journal of Archaeology* in 1977. In 1978, the CAA established the prestigious Smith-Wintemberg Medal, which was awarded to C.E. Borden and J.N. Emerson in 1978, and R.G. Forbis in 1984.

The Archaeological Survey of Canada also inaugurated its archaeological Mercury Series in 1972, thereby superseding the National Museum of Man *Bulletin* series, the *Contributions to Anthropology* and their *Anthropological Papers*. Parks Canada introduced a series on the Canadian Historic Sites Service that included reports on Louisbourg, Lower FORT GARRY and ROCKY MOUNTAIN HOUSE. Clearly, the discipline of archaeology had become firmly established in most parts of Canada during this innovative period.

The Legal Era: 1975-Present The year 1975 signals a significant turning-point in Canadian archaeology. Legalities and legislation, which are initiated in most cases by professional archaeologists, changed the conduct and responsibilities for archaeology in most of Canada's provinces. While legislation concerning archaeological sites existed in Ontario as early as 1952 and in BC in 1960, it was not until after 1975 that forceful legalities came into effect. Not only were licensing procedures introduced, but comprehensive archaeological reporting measures became mandatory. Most provincial governments, activating constitutional powers, assumed a new responsibility for ownership, conservation and disposition of archaeological and other heritage resources. They also developed their own individual systems to manage such matters. By so doing, the role of the Canadian Museum of Civilization became increasingly restricted to archaeology within federal jurisdictions such as the northern territories, National Parks, airports and harbours.

Since 1975 the new legislation has required that lands to be developed, inundated or otherwise disturbed must first be investigated for their archaeological potential. This could lead to mitigation followed by salvage or rescue excavations. In large, the new Canada-wide forms of provincial heritage legislation has resulted in the emergence of new applied archaeologists, a surge in site inventorying, and a plethora of reports. Unfortunately, many of the new reports are unavailable and are often written as impact studies without wider integration with current research syntheses.

The future directions of Canadian archaeology cannot be precisely forecast, but already it is apparent that the number of new applied archaeologists far exceeds the traditional teaching/research specialists. Indeed, there are simply too many to name individually here. It is to be hoped, however, that the various factions of the fifth-generation Canadian archaeologists will recognize specific merits in each other, and not lose sight of the ultimate goals of archaeology, namely, the study of Canada's past peoples. Much of Canada still remains only spot checked from an archaeological perspective, and no comprehensive, authoritative volume has been written detailing Canadian archaeology as a whole.

R.G. FORBIS AND W.C. NOBLE

Reading: D. Jenness, "Fifty Years of Archaeology in Canada" in *Royal Society of Canada, Anniversary Volume 1882-1932* (1932); G. Killan, *David Boyle: From Artisan to Archaeologist* (1983); W.C. Noble, "One Hundred and Twenty-Five Years of Archaeology in the Canadian Provinces" in *Canadian Archaeological Association Bulletin*, 4 (1972).

Archaeology in Québec really took off during the sociocultural movement of 1960 to 1970 known as the Quiet Revolution. This was the time when Québécois created their first official structures to facilitate training (university programs), management (Service d'archéologie of the Québec government), action (numerous archaeological societies) and popularization (Musée de Trois-Rivières, Cahier d'Archéologie Québécoise).

There had previously been occasional digs, private collections and individuals interested in the archaeological riches of the province, but it was only during the Quiet Revolution that the discipline acquired continuity, growth and professionalism. At that time there was much to do and few resources with which to do it. In practice, it was a decade of apprenticeship and enumeration. One of the most important events of this period was the creation of the Société d'archéologie préhistorique du Québec (SAPQ). It brought together a dynamic group of volunteers, moved by their desire to give Québec archaeology the highest possible standards. One must also acknowledge the extensive work done by J. Pendergast and the pioneering activities of M. Gaumont, R. Ribes, C. Martijn, R. Lévesque and C. Kennedy.

This impetus continued through the decade 1970-80, when specific training programs in Québec archaeology were created, when the law about cultural properties was passed, when U de Montréal set up its field school and an association of Québec archaeologists was formed. These are also the years when firms of consultants set up shop and huge projects were initiated in the James Bay region, Ungava, in the Gaspé and in the Montréal region. Many digs were also carried out elsewhere, and major work was done at Place-Royale in Québec and in the FORGES SAINT-MAURICE. It was a time of disciplined activities which led sometimes to severe criticism of amateur efforts but which also produced a considerable quantity of important data. It became clear that prehistoric and historic Québec contained such riches that efforts made to date amounted only to the first scratching of the surface. So archaeology was transformed from a cultural novelty to an integral part of Québec intellectual activity.

Since 1980 several large field projects have ended and the discipline has felt the general austerity as well as the inadequacy of its analytical and field structures. The result is some disillusionment, but not inaction. There are more publications and reports than ever, and work continues in both prehistoric archaeology and historic archaeology. The U du Québec has opened another field school on a prehistoric site, and U Laval has its own in historic archaeology. The creation of a bone archive in Montréal provides a valuable tool for analysis, but its permanent existence is not yet assured.

Prehistoric archaeology allows a better understanding of the population movements which affected the tundra, the Bouclier forest and the Laurentian lowlands over thousands of years. It provides the first substantial documentation of the ancient division of land among the 3 native groups who occupied it at the time of the Europeans' arrival: the Inuit, the Algonquin and the Iroquois. It shows their similarities to and differences from neighbouring populations. It interacts with ethnohistory, ethnoarchaeology and various sciences which share its desire to understand the past.

Historic archaeology – more visible, spectacular, closer to major population centres – has also known its triumphs and while the only interpretative centre for prehistoric archaeology is the one at Pointe-du-Buisson, 50 km from downtown Montréal, thousands of tourists stroll Place-Royale in Québec, visit the Forges immediately upstream from Trois-Rivières, Fort Chambly on the Richelieu, etc.

Twenty-five years ago, archaeology often simply took place on traditional native lands. Now, it increasingly takes place with native co-operation. In the south, municipalities and county regional municipalities are more aware of the archaeological inventory, the impact of major projects and the development of their heritage. This action and productivity are essentially francophone. While it may impede more widespread appreciation, it is necessary for the creation of a Québec tradition.

In sum, in 25 years, Québec archaeology has carried out a first chapter of prehistory and history across a terrain as large as France, Spain, Italy and Greece combined.

NORMAN CLERMONT

Archaeology, Industrial A type of interdisciplinary history that promotes understanding of the industrial era by focusing on physical remains, whether above ground or below, and by combining the insights of fieldwork and historical research. The name is recent in origin but already is well established throughout the world. Industrial archaeology originated in Great Britain, birthplace of the Industrial Revolution, in the late 1950s as a response to the alarming rate at which the nation's industrial and engineering heritage was being destroyed, and as a celebration of the lives and works of industrialists, engineers and inventors of the early industrial period. N Americans formed the Society for Industrial Archeology in 1971 and, while there is no separate Canadian organization, Canada is represented on the International Committee for the Conservation of the Industrial Heritage, created in 1978. The Ontario Society for Industrial Archaeology was organized in 1981. A similar association in Québec will be incorporated legally in the spring of 1988.

The field everywhere is interdisciplinary and focuses on a wide range of industrial objects, structures and sites. However, the industrial experience and contemporary social, economic and political priorities within various countries naturally have shaped the work of industrial archaeologists along individual national lines. In European countries and the US, for example, sites and structures of importance to the Industrial Revolution have received the most attention. These include power sources and transmission systems, canals and railways, and sites devoted to the textile industry and iron and steel production. In addition to the strictly industrial and engineering structures, European practitioners pay considerable attention to industrial villages and workers' housing. In Canada and in Scandinavian countries the early industrial era was more closely associated with staple resource extraction and primary processing. Thus, sites devoted to mining, forestry, fisheries, iron making, brewing and distilling are favoured for study. In Europe, where there is interest in teaching industrial archaeology, the field attracts mostly academic historians of technology or architecture; in N

America work is carried on mainly by museum and HISTORIC-SITES personnel, or historic preservationists, including historians, curators, architects, archaeologists, planners, photographers and teachers.

With such diversity in practice and practitioners, the field has yet to develop a coherent methodology and theoretical framework. In general the research involves fieldwork, comprising recording through photography and measured drawings, oral interviews and site plans. So much tangible evidence of early industry and industrial technology remains above the surface that actual excavation is seldom necessary. The insights of fieldwork are then combined with historical research to provide a record and understanding of what the Industrial Revolution entailed, more complete than that provided by written documents alone. When the subject matter is particularly threatened by loss or destruction, fieldwork resembles salvage archaeology. Threats arise because industrial and engineering structures frequently become functionally obsolete; sometimes they are found in unattractive surroundings or in poor condition; many are even seen in a negative light as symbolic of human misery and exploitation. Thus the goal may be simply to preserve knowledge of the site or structure for posterity. In Canada, there has been less interest in projects devoted to recording and inventorying or in developing industrial archaeology as an academic discipline. Instead, work on industrial museums and historic industrial sites has been of much more importance. There are over 690 industrial and 100 transportation and communication museums alone. However, in 1986-87 the BC Heritage Trust funded a large-scale archival and aerial photo reconnaissance survey of the historic salmon canneries in the province. Numerous industrial archaeological sites are administered by the various levels of government, the most significant being the historic national park of the FORGES SAINT-MAURICE. Located just N of Trois-Rivières, Qué, it is the site of Canada's oldest industrial complex. DIANNE NEWELL

Archaeology, Mediterranean Although Canada did not have its own schools nor Canadian universities their own excavations in the Mediterranean until recently, Canadian scholars have nevertheless long contributed to Egyptian, Greek and Roman archaeological studies; eg, Charles T. Currelly, first director of the ROYAL ONTARIO MUSEUM (ROM), excavated at Abydos [Abdu, Egypt] and Homer A. Thompson spent over 50 years working in the Agora at Athens, Greece. In 1961 the CANADA COUNCIL began to support archaeological research, and in 1969 extended that support to full funding, a policy continued by the SOCIAL SCIENCES AND HUMANITIES RESEARCH COUNCIL OF CANADA. Substantial funding has allowed a burgeoning of exploration organized by Canadian academics.

In Italy, University of Alberta took a lead in both the study and excavation of ancient remains, particularly through a series of research projects, first in the late 1960s at Gravina di Puglia (near Bari) in association with the British School at Rome, then in the early 1970s at Monte Irsi (near Irsina) in collaboration with Marie O. Jentel and Edith M. Wightman. At San Giovanni di Ruoti in the Apennine hills, an excavation was begun in 1977, directed by Alastair M. Small and Robert J. Buck, participants in the earlier projects. The excavations have revealed a large, prosperous, rural villa rebuilt many times between the 1st and 5th centuries AD. Because bones, shell and carbonized seeds are well preserved, much information has been recovered about Roman farming practices over 6 centuries. Another project initiated in

1977 was a surface survey of the lower Liri Valley, South Latium, by Alexander G. McKay and Edith M. Wightman, sponsored by McMaster University. Here too the results will lead to a great increase in data on land use in various periods of Roman history and to a detailed occupational history of the region. From the preliminary excavation in 1976 until 1987, Maurizio Gualtieri has studied the cemetery and "pseudo-urban" settlement of a pre-Roman population at Roccagloriosa, near Salerno.

In Greece, the first excavation permit awarded a Canadian team went to Joseph W. Shaw, sponsored by U of T and the ROM. In 1976 Shaw began investigations at Kommos on the S coast of Crete under the auspices of the American School of Classical Studies at Athens. Work on this Minoan harbour town, linked by road with Phaistos, has led to remarkable discoveries: well-preserved houses of the second millennium BC and a unique Greek sanctuary in use from early Protogeometric through early Roman times, below which are monumental buildings of late Minoan date. The stratigraphy on the site is excellent and valuable ceramic series have been established. A second Canadian team, led by John M. Fossey, professor at McGill and first director of the Canadian Archaeological Institute at Athens (CAIA), surveyed the site of Khostia in Boeotia in 1979, and the following year returned for a season of exploration of the town and its surrounding territory. Here the main emphasis was on recovering the history of Khostia, not only in classical but also in prehistoric times, with concern for natural resources and climate. In 1982 E. Hector Williams of UBC obtained a permit to survey Stymphalos in the Peloponnese. This led to the first complete plan of the remains, and the discovery that Stymphalos was established in the 4th century BC with a street plan organized around a regular grid. From 1983 until 1987, Dr Williams has also led excavations at Mytilene, on the island of Lesbos.

Three Canadian teams have been working in Egypt. Donald Redford of U of T, closely involved in reassembling the temples erected by Pharaoh Akhenaten (c 1375-58 BC) at Karnak from a computerized study of some 40 000 pieces of sculptured reliefs, began excavations in 1975 in E Karnak. Here he identified the foundation of one temple, and ascertained that after its destruction the area was abandoned for 500 years, then reoccupied for domestic and industrial purposes from the 8th to 4th centuries BC, and thereafter abandoned permanently. John S. Holladay, Jr, also of U of T, has been directing since 1979 a multidisciplinary regional study of the transit corridor linking Egypt and Asia, the Wadi Tumilat region of the eastern Nile Delta, with special emphasis on Tell el-Maskhuta, which appears to have been founded in the 7th century BC and survived until the 2nd AD. One important result has been the construction of a stratigraphically dated body of Egyptian pottery for the period c609 BC-135 AD. The third team, led by Anthony J. Mills of ROM, in 1978 began a systematic survey of the Dakhleh Oasis, at over 3000 km² the largest in the Egyptian Sahara. By 1983 the field survey was complete, with over 400 sites recorded; and there have been geomorphological studies as well as floral, faunal and palynological sampling. The results should provide a history of the oasis's settlement and its external connections and an understanding of the environmental factors associated with an oasis and of the effects that man and the area have had on each other.

Intense Canadian involvement in the archaeology of Italy, Greece and Egypt has been very recent and a consequence of the support offered archaeological research by the Canada Council and SSHRC. This activity and support led

to the establishment of CAIA and the Canadian Academic Centre in Italy, both in 1978, and the Canadian Institute in Egypt in 1980, all now united under the aegis of the Canadian Mediterranean Institute. It is to be hoped that with these institutions our links with the Mediterranean past will be strengthened and our indebtedness better acknowledged. C.W.J. ELIOT

Reading: Reports on the Roman and Greek excavations can be found in *Classical News and Views,* or its successor *Classical Views,* publ by the Classical Assn of Canada; and on Egyptian projects in *Archaeological Newsletter,* publ by ROM.

Archaic culture is characterized by archaeologists as the seasonal selective exploitation of forest and woodland resources preceding or paralleling the establishment of horticulture. Though the culture is universal across N America, dating between about 6000 BC and 500 AD, and follows the earlier PALEOINDIAN stage, artifact styles are not identical wherever it is found. In technology, the Archaic stage is typified by specialized varieties of woodworking implements such as axes, gouges and knives. Pottery is found in some areas; formalized burial sites occur in others, but there is little evidence of any housing. The cultivation and domestication of maize, the grain eventually cultivated by all N American tribes, took place during the Archaic in the Mexican highlands. *See also* PREHISTORY.

RENÉ R. GADACZ

Archambault, Gilles, novelist (b at Montréal 19 Sept 1933). He received his BA (1955) from Collège Sainte-Marie and his LL (1957) from U de Montréal. He worked for Radio-Canada (1959-63) before becoming a radio producer. In 1963 he published his first novel, *Une Suprême Discrétion,* in which the disillusioned hero solves his problems through suicide. Next came *La Vie à trois* (1963), in which the novelist developed the same themes: the difficulties of living with a partner, lack of dialogue, the solitude; then *Le Tendre Matin* (1969). Six novels followed, exploring these themes, *Parlons de moi* (1970), *La Fleur aux dents* (1971), filmed by the NFB in a treatment by Pierre Turgeon (1975), *La Fuite immobile* (1974), *Les Pins parasols* (1976), *Le Voyageur distrait* (1981) and *À Voix basse* (1983). He has also published *Enfances lointaines* (1972), a collection of short stories, *Le Tricycle* and *Bud Cole Blues* (1974), 2 radio plays, then 2 prose works: *Stupeurs* (1979), and *Les Plaisirs de la mélancolie* (1980). In 1984 he published *Le Regard oblique,* a selection of texts in which he takes a humorous "oblique look" at the pitfalls of the writer's trade. In 1981 he won the Prix David for his work as a whole.

AURÉLIEN BOIVIN

Archambault, Joseph-Papin, Jesuit priest, (b at Montréal 1880; d there Oct 1966). He received his classical education at Collège Sainte-Marie in Montréal. He was ordained in 1912. While teaching at Collège Saint-Marie, 1904-09, he developed French Canada's first system of closed retreats to promote moral regeneration first at Villa Saint-Martin in l'Abord-à-Plouffe and then Villa Manrèse in Quèbec City. Inspired by the social catholicism of Pope Leo XIII, he helped found, in Jan 1911, the École Sociale Populaire (dir 1929-59), to popularize and disseminate the social teachings of the Catholic Church. In 1921 he created and directed for 40 years Les SEMAINES SOCIALES DU CANADA, a biannual conference aimed at raising the consciousness of the clerical and petit-bourgeoise elites. Following the Congrès de la langue française in Montréal 1912, which had sparked his concern over the abysmal lack of French in the business community of Montréal, he helped found the Ligue des droits du français in March 1913, followed by the Ligue d'Action française in 1917. The latter was responsible for a militant nationalist periodical *l'Action française*, directed by his close friend Abbé Lionel GROULX, 1922-27. In 1933 Archambault helped to launch the Ligue d'Action nationale and its periodical *L'*ACTION NATIONALE. During the 1930s and 1940s, he waged an incessant campaign against communism and socialism, especially the CCF, while promoting the spiritual and material benefits of a Catholic-inspired social corporatism.

MICHAEL D. BEHIELS

Archambault, Louis, sculptor (b at Montréal 4 Apr 1915). He studied at the École des beaux-arts in Montréal, receiving the prestigious Prix du Ministre 1939. In 1948 he joined with others, including Alfred PELLAN, to sign the manifesto *Prisme d'Yeux*. From 1955 to 1968 he received numerous awards, including the Royal Architectural Institute of Canada's medal of honour (1958) and the Centennial Medal (1967). He created major pieces for the Canadian pavilions at the Brussels (1958) and Montréal (1967) international expositions, and has done commissioned works for Place des Arts, Montréal, the Ottawa and Toronto airports and the Ottawa city hall. His work is found in many Canadian and foreign museums, and has been seen in many one-man and group shows. His contribution to the growth and renewal of sculpture in Canada makes him the greatest Canadian sculptor of his generation.

MICHEL CHAMPAGNE

Archer, Violet, composer, educator (b at Montréal 24 Apr 1913). A composer of marked individuality, widely recognized for her command of both traditional and contemporary techniques, she studied composition with Claude CHAMPAGNE and Douglas CLARKE in Montréal and in New York with Béla Bartók and Paul Hindemith. Archer has produced a large body of music embracing most of the vocal and instrumental performance media, including a comic opera, *Sganarelle* (1973), and a documentary-film score (*Someone Cares*). Her *Piano Concerto no 1* (1956), which demands great virtuosity from soloist and orchestra alike, is considered one of the finest concertos composed by a Canadian. After appointments at universities in the US (1950-61), where she also adjudicated state and national young-composer competitions, Archer returned to Canada and taught theory and composition at U of A from 1962 until retirement in 1978, though she continued composing. In 1984 she received the Order of Canada and was also named composer of the year by the Canadian Music Council. She was awarded an honorary doctorate in music by U Windsor in 1987.

BARCLAY MCMILLAN

Archery As a fighting and hunting weapon, the bow and arrow was widely used in prehistoric times and throughout the Middle Ages. Archery became a recreational sport in England in the 15th and 16th centuries, after the decline of the bow and arrow as a military weapon. There are 2 general types of longbow: the ordinary, straight-ended bow and the recurved bow. The latter (made of laminated wood, plastic and fibreglass) is most commonly used in archery competition, of which the most popular forms are target archery (shooting at a standard-size target) and field archery (shooting at targets at random distances in the field).

In Canada, archery clubs were formed in the mid-1800s. In 1864, in Ontario, the Yorkville Archery Club staged a tournament, the first record of archery as a sport in Canada. Little is known about organized competition until 1927, when the Canadian Archery Assn (later Federation of Canadian Archers) was formed. The first

Canadian championships were held in 1931. Ontario was the principal archery province for some years, and it was not until 1951 that the CAA became truly national. Canadians have done well in international competition. A team was first entered in the 1963 world championships, and the Canadians placed 5th in 1967. Dorothy Lidstone became the first Canadian to earn a world title – the 1969 women's world target archery championship; the Canadian women's team placed 2nd that year. In 1971 the men's team was 3rd in the world and Emmanuel Boucher set a world record for the double 30-m distance. At the 1973 Championships of the Americas, Les Anderson and Wayne Pullen were gold-medal winners in field archery, and Anderson placed 2nd overall. Lucille Lessard won the 1974 women's field archery world title and the 1975 Championships of the Americas field archery event, and placed 5th in the 1976 Olympics. Canadian men's and women's teams were 2nd in the 1979 Pan-American Games and the 1980 target Championships of the Americas. The 1982 Championships of the Americas were held in Canada for the first time, in Joliette, Québec. Lisa Buscombe, of Brampton, Ont, became world field champion in Aug 1984 in Finland, and on 28 July 1985 won the gold in a field archery event at the World Games in London, Eng. Canada won a silver medal in individual competition and a team bronze in the 1987 Pan-Am Games.

BARBARA SCHRODT

Archibald, Sir Adams George, lawyer, politician, lt-gov of Man and NS (b at Truro, NS 18 May 1814; d there 14 Dec 1892). After serving as solicitor general (1856-60) and attorney general (1860-63) in the Nova Scotia Assembly, he succeeded Joseph HOWE as provincial Liberal leader in 1863. A strong supporter of Confederation, he attended the 3 conferences at Charlottetown, Québec and London, and publicly defended the scheme against the attacks of Howe and William ANNAND in 1866. In 1867 he entered the federal Cabinet as secretary of state and in 1870 was named lieutenant-governor of Manitoba and the North-West Territories. During his brief term (1870-72), he laid the foundation of the civil institutions of the West, and negotiated the first 2 treaties with western Indians. In 1873 he became lt-gov of NS, retiring in 1883.

STANLEY GORDON

Archibald, Edgar Spinney, agriculturalist (b at Yarmouth, NS 12 May 1885; d at Ottawa 23 Jan 1968). Archibald's greatest contribution to Canadian agriculture was his dedicated and active support of scientists in the Experimental Farms Service, of which he was director 1919-51. Although his training was in livestock, he recognized the importance of all disciplines contributing to food production. He chaired the Tobacco Enquiry Committee (1928), the program committee for the World Grain Exhibition and Conference at Regina (1933), and helped form the Prairie Farm Rehabilitation Administration, which developed successful soil-conservation practices between 1935 and 1951. He received 3 honorary degrees and several fellowships and other honours, including Companion of the Order of Canada. A mountain in the Yukon is named after him.

T.H. ANSTEY

Archibald, Edith Jessie, née Archibald, socialite, feminist, author (b in Newfoundland 1854; d at Halifax 1936). Educated in New York and London, Eng, Archibald married in 1874 Charles Archibald, mining engineer and later president of the Bank of NS. She was president of Maritime WOMAN'S CHRISTIAN TEMPERANCE UNION from 1892 to 1896, president of the Halifax Local Council of Women from 1896 to 1906, president of the Halifax VON from 1897 to 1901, and, as

vice-president of the NS Red Cross in 1914, chaired the department responsible for Canadian prisoners of war overseas. An ardent suffragist, Archibald advised a shift from confrontation to more subtle maternal feminist tactics after the defeat of the suffragist campaign in the early 1890s. She led the suffrage delegation to the legislature in 1917 and later chaired the Halifax Conservative Women's Auxiliary. An eloquent speaker, with a fine writing style, she published articles, pamphlets, songs, plays and several books, including one about her father, *Life and Letters of Sir Edward Mortimer Archibald* (1924), and *The Token* (1930).

ERNEST R. FORBES

Archibald, Edward William, surgeon, scientist, educator (b at Montréal 5 Aug 1872; d there 17 Dec 1945). Archibald was a gifted surgeon who recognized that advance in surgery must come through scientific research, and he changed the character of surgical education at McGill and elsewhere from the purely clinical to the scientific. Part of his early schooling was in Grenoble, where he became bilingual and laid the foundation of lifelong ties with France. A McGill medical graduate, he became associated with the Royal Victoria Hospital in Montréal shortly after its opening. Eventually, he became surgeon in chief of the hospital and professor of surgery at McGill. Archibald had his faults; they included an almost incredible degree of absentmindedness, with an inability to keep track of time. But even his faults seemed merely to increase the affection of his colleagues. One of them wrote, "O Edward you would be sublime/If only you could be on time."

EDWARD BENSLEY

Archibald, John Smith, architect (b at Inverness, Scot 14 Dec 1872; d at Montréal 2 Mar 1934). He came to Canada in 1893 and was employed as supervising architect in the office of Edward MAXWELL in Montréal. From 1897 to 1915 he practised in partnership, and thereafter under his own name. He was known for his administrative ability and expertise in construction methods. He tried to promote economy in relation to architecture through a series of articles distributed across Canada. During the 1920s the CNR commissioned him to design large hotels across Canada from Halifax to Vancouver. In his best works in Montréal – Emmanuel Congregational Church, Montréal Technical School, Masonic Memorial Temple – Archibald adhered to the classical tradition of symmetry and monumental grandeur. He was president of the Royal Architectural Institute of Canada 1924-25 and was elected a fellow in 1930.

ROBERT LEMIRE

Architectural Competitions have been used successfully for many years to select architects or designs for major projects of regional or national importance. Qualified architects are invited to submit designs, based on a fixed program of requirements and a specified set of procedures, which are then assessed by a jury of distinguished architects and representatives of the sponsor. The competition may be used to select an architect or design; to provide an opportunity for participation to architects who might not otherwise be considered; to obtain the best talent available in a given locale, region or nation; or to make an architectural statement.

A competition can take several forms. In open competitions, invitations to participate are extended to all qualified architects within a specified locale, region or nation, or even internationally. Closed competitions are limited by the sponsor to specially qualified or selected architects. In 2-stage competitions the first stage is open, and used to obtain concepts for the design of a project, discover new talent, or to select architects who have credentials appropriate to the project; the second stage is used to obtain a final design for the project.

Architectural competitions are run by architects' professional organizations, such as the Royal Architectural Institute of Canada (RAIC) and the provincial associations. The rules of a competition govern the basis and terms of participation, the fee structure, the eligibility and qualifications of candidates, and the process to be followed should the project not proceed or should a partnership or joint venture be required. The first prize usually consists of the award of a contract to implement the winning design. The PARLIAMENT BUILDINGS in Ottawa, and many other important heritage buildings, were designed in competition. However the history of competitions is fraught with controversy, with many examples of winning designs that are so radical or experimental that the sponsor decided not to proceed.

Vincent Massey, chairman of the Royal Commission on NATIONAL DEVELOPMENT IN THE ARTS, LETTERS AND SCIENCES, recommended in 1951 that all major public buildings in Canada be designed through architectural competition. In 1952 the federal government held a national competition for the NATIONAL GALLERY OF CANADA, an example followed by several other major projects, including Toronto City Hall and Winnipeg City Hall (both international), Winnipeg Art Gallery (national), Massey College, U of T (closed), Simon Fraser U (master plan, local), the Mendel Art Gallery, Saskatoon (national), and, more recently, for the city halls of Edmonton, Calgary and Mississauga.

In 1953 the Massey Foundation sponsored a series of prestigious design awards. Initially, 1 gold and 19 silver medals were awarded but this format was changed to 20 silver medals. These Massey medals, which were awarded 8 times, had a major impact on the quality of architecture in Canada by virtue of the intense competition they generated. Since 1982 they have been superseded by the Governor General's Medals for Architecture, administered by the RAIC and offered every second or third year. The Canadian Housing Design Council introduced a design award competition to stimulate the quality of HOUSING design in Canada and, in addition, several building materials manufacturers have sponsored similar design award programs. *See also* ARCHITECTURAL PRACTICE.   DOUGLAS SHADBOLT

Architectural Practice An architect designs and superintends the construction of buildings. The process by which buildings are constructed and put into use can be divided into 9 stages, each requiring specific approvals and funding commitments. The stages are as follows: *opportunity identification,* in which the purpose, nature and scope of the facility is determined and the general location is established; *feasibility,* in which various options are examined and evaluated, and a site is determined; *project definition,* in which the requirements of the facility are determined in detail; *design development,* in which the conceptual design is prepared and further processed into a detailed design; *working documents,* during which the detailed contract drawings, specifications, and other contract documents are completed; *tendering and procurement,* in which the contract documents are used to obtain bids from contractors to construct or provide the facility; *construction,* in which the facility is built; *commissioning,* in which the facility is turned over from the contractors to the owner's organization, and put into use; *operation and maintenance,* in which the owner operates the facility throughout its useful life. The process will vary in complexity and in the length of

time it takes to complete the facility. The project may be divided into a number of sub-projects, but each of these will roughly follow the stages outlined above. The knowledge and expertise required at each stage also varies. For example, for a small single-family house, one person, such as the architect, can provide almost everything required to complete or co-ordinate each task at each stage. At another scale, a complex facility, such as a large hospital building, would require several hundred experts at various stages, a multidisciplinary team with careful, highly skilled, specialized management and co-ordination.

Buildings are initiated by individual clients or by a group representing a public or private institution or corporate entity. The architect is selected by the client for his skills and capability to lead and manage the implementation and for his ability as a designer and specialist in design quality control. Architectural firms are able to provide specialized services demanded by clients for particular building types, such as schools, hospitals, office buildings, commercial facilities, recreational facilities and churches.

A typical small architectural practice will have 1 or 2 registered architects, with up to 10 or more assistants who may or may not be fully qualified architects. The principal architects are usually generalists with the experience, knowledge and personal capability to handle all stages of small and medium-sized projects. A large architectural practice will be based on one or more principals, with several senior associates or junior partners, all registered architects. The practice may employ 50-200 architects, technologists or draftsmen. Frequently, large practices will include or organize teams with other professional disciplines, such as structural, mechanical, electrical or civil engineers. They are then able to provide the expertise required for large, complex projects.

The practice of architecture in Canada is controlled by the profession under the terms of provincial legislation. Each province has an association or institute of architects which monitors and regulates practice by controlling the licensing of individual architects through admission requirements and procedures, and by disciplining members who transgress the rules of practice. Only members of the provincial association or institute are allowed to call themselves architects or to practise architecture. The association may prosecute other persons who do so. Individual members of a provincial association may join the Royal Architectural Institute of Canada (RAIC). Educational requirements consist of a professional degree of Bachelor of Architecture (or equivalent), followed by supplementary coursework provided by the professional association prior to a pre-registration examination. A candidate may also meet those requirements by completing the RAIC Minimum Syllabus program, which is predominantly a self-study program allowing the candidate to qualify while employed in an architect's office. The RAIC Certification Board screens and approves the education status of all candidates. Architecture schools in Canada have been established at the following universities: British Columbia, Calgary, Manitoba, Carleton, Laval, McGill, Montréal, Toronto, Waterloo, and at the Technical University of Nova Scotia in Halifax. In addition to the educational requirements, a candidate for admission to the profession must have completed 2 or 3 years of practical experience in an architect's office acceptable to the provincial association with which the candidate wishes to register. On completion of these requirements, and with established residency, the candidate will be accepted and registered.

Mobility for registered architects is provided for by arrangements for reciprocal recognition of cre-

dentials, which may include provisions for special examination (eg, where language or legal systems differ) or proof of residence. Mobility for students who may wish to reside in another province or country to complete their professional qualifications is provided in Canada by the national purview of the RAIC Certification Board, and internationally by the recognition of different schools of architecture by bodies such as the Commonwealth Association of Architects, and the Royal Institute of British Architects.
                                 DOUGLAS SHADBOLT

Architectural Styles are a conscious aesthetic response to the challenge of building. They imply academic knowledge on the part of the designer — be he architect, engineer or builder. The succession of architectural styles that have touched Canada reflects the complex political, social and economic influences that have shaped the country. Historically, building design in Canada grew out of western European culture: the early French tradition was supplanted in the 19th century by British and later by American fashions. In the 20th century, however, the influence has become international.

The *French baroque* style reached Canada late in the 17th century and held sway — at least for RELIGIOUS BUILDING and GOVERNMENT BUILDING — for almost a century. The Archbishop's Palace in Québec City (1693-97, demolished) by architect Claude BAILLIF, and the Château de Vaudreuil in Montréal (1723-27, demolished) by engineer Gaspard CHAUSSEGROS DE LÉRY, though reduced in scale and grandeur when compared to their prototypes in France, captured the essential characteristics of baroque taste in the outpost of NEW FRANCE: classical vocabulary including columns, pilasters, domes and pediments from the Italian Renaissance masters, steep roofs alive with tiny round dormer windows and tall chimneys, sweeping double staircases and enclosed courtyards called *cours d'honneur.*

In the second half of the 18th century the influx of British immigrants and LOYALISTS from the American colonies implanted a more discreet and sober version of classical taste, influenced by Italian architect Andrea Palladio. Imbued with a sense of balance and harmonious proportions, the *Palladian* style in Canada, often called the Georgian style, can be identified by such features as a central pediment, rusticated (where the edges of the stones are bevelled to make the joints conspicuous) ground storey, lateral wings, accentuated second storey, and the characteristic Venetian or flanked window. Best illustrated by PROVINCE HOUSE, Halifax (1811-18), Palladianism thrived in the Atlantic provinces and Québec, and to a lesser extent in Ontario, until about 1820.

Neoclassicism, inspired by archaeological discoveries in Greece and Italy, implied a re-evaluation of classical taste and called for strict accuracy in the imitation of original classical structures. Reaching Canada through British and American

An old courthouse in Nova Scotia displaying neoclassical style (*courtesy SSC Photocentre/photo by S. Homer*).

Colonial Building, St John's, Nfld, one of the best-preserved neoclassical buildings in Canada, was built 1847-50. The architect was James Purcell of Ireland, and the building has an affinity with certain Dublin monuments (*courtesy Environment Canada, Parks/Heritage Recording Services*).

architectural publications, and through a new generation of British-trained architects such as George BROWNE, William Footner and John OSTELL, the *neoclassical* style modified the delicate refinement of the Palladian idiom to create smoother, starker forms featuring baseless colonnades or pilasters springing from ground level, and a Greek revival repertoire of scrolls, flat-headed flanked windows, and squat Doric columns. KINGSTON CITY HALL (1842-44) by George Browne and Laval U in Québec City (1854-57) by Charles BAILLAIRGÉ illustrate the varied facets of neoclassicism in Canada.

The *Gothic revival* style was inspired by buildings from medieval Europe. Initially introduced in Canada by Irish architect James O'Donnell at NOTRE-DAME de Montréal (1823-29), Gothic revival persisted across Canada for over a century, especially in religious architecture. Identified by features such as the pointed or ogival arch for door and window openings, buttresses and pinnacles, the style evolved through various stages: the rational phase promoted by a group of British theologians known as the Ecclesiologists is best illustrated by CHRIST CHURCH CATHEDRAL, Fredericton (1846-53), by architects Frank Wills and William Butterfield. The High Victorian Gothic phase, which sanctioned polychromy, asymmetry, texture and picturesque effects, finds expression in the Library of Parliament in Ottawa (1859-76) by Fuller and Jones (*see* PARLIAMENT BUILDINGS). The beaux-arts phase, which witnessed a return to symmetry and monumentality, is exemplified by early U of Saskatchewan buildings (about 1912-20) by architects David K. Brown and Hugh Vallance.

Superimposed upon these distinct styles in the first half of the 19th century was the *picturesque* movement, an 18th-century British taste which had an impact particularly on domestic architecture in Québec, Ontario and the Atlantic

The Ontario Legislative Buildings, Toronto, are a prime example of the Romanesque revival style of the 1890s (*courtesy Environment Canada, Parks/Heritage Recording Services*).

provinces. Not a style in itself, architecture of the picturesque typically enhanced and took account of informal landscape settings. Cottages and villas such as Colborne Lodge in High Park, Toronto (1836), by architect John George HOWARD, had characteristic features of the picturesque: careful siting to explore the vistas, asymmetrical placement on the building lot, broken rooflines with raised towers or tall chimneys, bow, bay or French windows, and a verandah with exotic treillage or delicate posts.

By mid-century the traditional stylistic categories gave way to eclecticism and variety. New sources of inspiration were sought and several fashions coexisted simultaneously. For example, the *Italianate* style made popular in the 1850s and 1860s by the American architectural pattern books, appeared in several guises: BANKS and government buildings such as the Kingston Customs House (1856-57) and Post Office (1856-59), both designed by the Montréal firm of Hopkins, Lawford and Nelson, featured heavy rusticated ground storeys, nearly flat roofs, and semicircular headed openings; Italianate houses such as the rectory of St Mark's Church in Niagara-on-the-Lake (about 1858) acquired irregular plans, tall square towers, overhanging eaves with paired brackets and groups of semicircular windows; and a select group of buildings like the Don Jail in Toronto (1858-65) and the Halifax County Court House (1858-60), both by William THOMAS and Sons, added tortuous forms and vermiculated stonework to the other Italianate features.

Pinehurst, Victoria, BC, an example of the eclecticism of the Queen Anne revival style (*courtesy Environment Canada, Parks/Heritage Recording Services*).

With an increasing taste for pompous and imposing forms in the second half of the 19th century, Italianate gave way to Second Empire influence, a style that began in France during the reign of Emperor Napoleon III (1852-70) and flowered in the US. The *Second Empire* style is a modification of the Italianate style, made more massive through the addition of pavilions, towers and mansard roofs. Adopted by the federal Dept of Public Works in the 1870s, this style was disseminated across the country in public buildings like the Saint John Customs House (1877-81) by supervising architects McKean and Fairweather, and the Toronto Post Office (1871-73) by supervising architect Henry Langley. Though well suited for the houses of the bourgeoisie who deemed the bombastic forms to be appropriate expressions of their wealth, conservative values and social standing, Second Empire fell out of fashion by the end of the 1880s.

In their quest for novelty, architects in the late 19th century turned to unexploited historical periods for inspiration, leading to the brief flowering of styles such as Romanesque revival, Château and Queen Anne revival. Drawn from the work of American architect H.H. Richardson, the *Romanesque revival* appeared in Canada in the 1890s, well illustrated by the old Toronto City

Château Frontenac, Québec City, designed by American architect Bruce Price, and built 1892. It was the first of the numerous steep-roofed palaces that came to symbolize Canadian railway hotels (*courtesy Environment Canada, Parks/Heritage Recording Services*).

Hall (1890) designed by E.J. Lennox, with its rugged wall surfaces, squat columns, massive semicircular arches, round and square towers, and carved foliage and gargoyles. The *Château* style, an adaptation of French 16th-century castles in the Loire Valley, also reached Canada from the US, this time at Québec City where American architect Bruce Price created the Château Frontenac (1892), the first of the smooth-surfaced, steep-roofed and round-towered palaces that came to symbolize Canadian railway hotels (*see* HOTEL). The *Queen Anne revival* style, though theoretically modelled on late 17th-century English buildings, was typical of its period in its asymmetrical composition and profusion of detail. Especially popular for domestic architecture in all regions of Canada, this style encouraged the use of materials such as brick, stone and shingle for their polychromatic and textural contrasts, and the eclectic agglomeration of heterogeneous details from all periods of design, including Flemish gables, Venetian windows, Tudor mullions, Gothic revival ribbed chimney stacks and corner towers.

In contrast to these fussy historical revivals, the *beaux-arts* movement, named for the École des beaux-arts in Paris, offered a refreshing alternative. Important public buildings in Canada in the early 20th century, such as the Union Station in Toronto (1915-20) by architects Ross & Macdonald, Hugh Jones and John M. Lyle, demonstrated well-articulated and rigorously symmetrical facades, axial planning of interior space, and imposing monumentality. CHRISTINA CAMERON

Art deco, or *Art moderne* (both names drawn from the 1925 Paris *Exposition internationale des arts décoratifs et industriels modernes*), brought simplified, more geometric, versions of traditional historic ornament as well as some that were purely abstract, without historic reference, and with bold, often jarring colours. At its extreme, this brash and (for its time) startling style, most evident in interior design, created a suitable setting

Colborne Lodge, High Park, Toronto, constructed 1836 by architect J.G. Howard, displayed characteristic features of the picturesque style (*courtesy Environment Canada, Parks/Heritage Recording Services*).

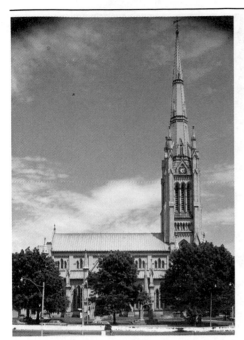

St James Anglican Cathedral, Toronto, constructed 1849-53 in the Gothic revival style (*courtesy Environment Canada, Parks Heritage Recording Services*).

for the frenetic gaiety of the Jazz Age. The Marine Building, Vancouver (McCarter and Nairne, 1929-30), especially the main entrance and lobby, is the supreme public work, while Ernest CORMIER's own house in Montréal (1931) is a sensitive and subtle domestic example.

Influencing transitional styles, through the 1930s and early 1940s, was the superficial application of "streamlining," the sleek rounded forms of the advanced aircraft of the period, to a variety of objects from automobiles to furniture. The result, sometimes called *moderne*, further propagated rounded corners and horizontal stripes. A fine, sedate example is Page and Steele's Garden Court Apartments, Toronto (1939). The epitome of the mixture appeared in the movie theatres, justifying the term Odeon style; its characteristics were flowing curves, grooves and stripes, indirect lighting and pastel colours.

Behind these superficial fashions was a profound revolution in design which, from the turn of the century, began to produce an increasing number of fully realized "modern" buildings. The term "modern," indicating "of the present" or "contemporary," makes no precise reference to style but has generally meant design and construction that adheres closely and obviously to the requirements of utility and efficiency. These objectives inspired early Canadian modernists Peter Thornton, R.A.D. Berwick and C.E. Pratt on the West Coast, and Marcel Parizeau and Robert Blatter in Québec in the 1930s. An even earlier modernist, Francis C. Sullivan of Ottawa, associate of the great US innovator Frank Lloyd Wright, exemplified in his buildings as did Wright in his Banff Pavilion (1913, demolished 1939) the style of the US *Prairie School*, influential especially on later Canadian West Coast architects such as Ron Thom.

Despite the wide variety of forms and approaches called "modern," the version which became most closely identified with the modern movement in architecture was named the *international style* by H.R. Hitchcock and Philip Johnson in their 1932 book of that name. It was characterized by generally cubic forms, unadorned white surfaces, large often horizontal windows, and asymmetrical massing in response to the "functional" arrangement of interior volumes. Not only was there little or no decorative relief but any visual reference to historic style was avoided.

As the architects associated with the international style came to design larger buildings after WWII, particularly commercial offices and apartments, a modern version of the late 19th-century office tower emerged which emphasized the regular repetitive structure and the impersonality of the process by which it was produced and inhabited. The result is exemplified at its most distinguished by the Toronto Dominion Centre in Toronto (Mies van der Rohe, consultant, John B. PARKIN Associates and BREGMAN AND HAMANN, const 1964-68). Variations on this ubiquitous and usually anonymous "international modern" style became characteristic of downtown business districts as they expanded from the 1950s to the 1980s.

By the mid-1960s a significant broadening of international modern had begun, together with the first signs of direct reaction to its abstraction and austerity. First to come were bolder forms earlier associated with European expressionism, especially the pursuit of personal or symbolic expression through sculptural modelling, as in the works of Douglas CARDINAL, Clifford WIENS, Étienne GABOURY, P.M. Côté and Roger D'Astous (eg, Château Champlain, Montréal). Then followed a revived interest in the form and detail of earlier buildings. *Post-modernism,* more a catch-all tag for a mood or attitude than an identifiable style, covers this change of direction. It includes the renewed use of identifiable historic elements from classical Greek or Roman orders to the decorative features of ordinary 19th-century rural houses (as in Peter Rose's Bradley House, North Hatley, Qué, 1977), especially the search for local or regional inspiration. By the later 1980s the prevailing style was an evolved modernism that continued the emphasis on simple forms arranged to satisfy functional requirements, with some ornamental features based on simplified historic and regional motifs. The more adventurous extremes of style include abstract compositions of geometric elements often arranged so as to seem to penetrate one another, or to fly apart as though exploded. At another extreme there are internal attempts to build in the styles of earlier periods. An example which combines something of both tendencies is the condominium addition to the Sylvia Hotel, Vancouver, designed by Richard Henriquez. A renewed interest in the Beaux-arts style is exemplified in Peter Rose's Canadian Centre for Architecture, Montréal (scheduled to open 1988).

MICHAEL McMORDIE

Architecture The transfer of European architectural traditions to Canada began with the arrival of French settlers in the early 1600s. The buildings of Inuit and Indians had little effect on European structures, because native construction proceeded from an entirely different matrix (*see* HOUSE); its symbolic mimetic shapes meant nothing to white settlers, and its technology was too primitive to be usefully borrowed. Even the simplest techniques employed by N America's first European settlers turn out upon investigation to be European in origin rather than indigenously borrowed; indeed, N American architecture has within the last decade or so provided evidence for survivals in Europe of early techniques previously believed to have been lost long before settlement of N America began.

What appeared in NEW FRANCE was a typically colonial architecture. Composed almost totally of medieval and baroque forms and techniques familiar from the homeland, which thus served as instruments to transplant that culture to the New World, this architecture only gradually and to a

Up to the 1950s, anglophone Canadians generally tended to find their identity, as distinct from Americans, in belonging to the British Empire. That feeling climaxed in the 1900-20 period, and to that time belong major Canadian buildings in revived Roman style, such as the Alberta Legislature Building in Edmonton (*courtesy Public Affairs Bureau, Government of Alberta*).

surprisingly small degree adapted to the new land's particular climatic conditions, which were far more severe than France. The typical Québecois house was the farmhouse of Normandy, Maine or Anjou, the provinces of origin of most of New France's earliest settlers. Examples are the Heureux house at Charlesbourg, the Athanase Denis house at Neuville, or the Marcotte house at Cap Santé. Church and palace architecture, eg, the Basilica or Jesuit Church in Québec City or the Château de Vaudreuil in Montréal (now gone or totally altered, but known from photos and drawings), was only minimally adapted to the New World, and more by necessity than choice, in that ornament was less elegant and abundant, symmetry less rigorous and scale smaller, corresponding to the colony's generally limited resources.

Only 2 basic building types from the Old Regime in New France survived the Conquest of 1759-60: the parish church and the peasant homestead. Associations from the Old Regime attaching to these forms made them visual metaphors of, and instruments to promote, Québecois *survivance* in the face of successive waves of English-speaking immigrants. Thus, a standardized type of church loosely modelled on the parish churches of Bishop Laval's 17th-century seigneuries gave visual and social focus to over 30 communities in the Montréal area from 1800 to 1840, stamping them as "French." A corresponding number appeared in the Québec City area; as refined and developed in the French classical tradition by Thomas BAILLAIRGÉ, protégé of Jérôme DEMERS, vicar-general of Québec, they came to

The British element in Canadian life was represented in the first half of the 19th century by elaborate edifices in a rather old-fashioned British style. Victoria Hall in Cobourg, Ont, was dedicated by the Prince of Wales (the future Edward VII) in 1860 (*courtesy Environment Canada, Parks/Heritage Recording Services*).

represent one of the great lasting accomplishments of Canadian arts. The church-type so established in the early 19th century continued to serve as an instrument promoting French survival in variant but readily recognizable forms well into the 20th century, not only in Québec but wherever French-speaking Canadians went, in northern Ontario, Manitoba, Saskatchewan, northern NB and northern Québec (*see* RELIGIOUS BUILDING).

The Québecois house-type continued to be built, generation after generation, in ever-increasing numbers for an ever-increasing population. Its materials varied from stone to timber; it sometimes had a porch and sometimes not; it could be small (the Laurier "birthplace" at St-Lin) or large (Symmes Inn, Aylmer), but its basic proportions and distinctive shapes remained recognizable. Later house-types, such as the flat-topped duplex with outside staircases lining Montréal and Québec City streets and reproduced extensively in expansion towns of the 1890-1920 period in St-Jérôme or Joliette, never entirely displaced it. Today, the popular/commercial "Maison du patriote" continues the tradition.

Following the change in administration in 1763, a number of British administrators, officers and merchant-adventurers settled in the colony, followed 20 years later by streams of dispossessed LOYALISTS from the newly independent American colonies. In the depressed post-Waterloo decades wave upon wave of Britons arrived to populate the English-speaking provinces of Upper Canada and NB, to complete the anglicization of NS and PEI, and create à large English minority in Lower Canada. As French Canadian culture stressed its French and Catholic origins, English Canada manifested an admiration for British institutions – a dependence clearly revealed in architecture.

Immigrants from the old British colonies in N America brought with them the Georgian style of 18th-century America, an architecture influenced by the classical tradition. NIAGARA-ON-THE-LAKE and Queenston show plentiful examples built in wood or stone, as does the old Bath road from Cataraqui to Picton; older Canadian cities have isolated examples, eg, the Campbell house in Toronto or the McMartin house in Perth. Newer immigrants who began arriving directly from Britain in the 1820s built in the Georgian style of their homeland, commonly in stone, with heavier proportions that gave old Loyalist towns (Kingston, Prescott, Brockville, Halifax) distinctive streets of cutstone Georgian façades. Local builders quickly fused the 2 types. This style, marked by symmetry and order, can be seen in PROVINCE HOUSE, Halifax, and the Colonial Building, St John's; courthouses in Napanee and Brockville, Kingston and Saint John; city halls in Perth, Kingston and Sandwich (*see* KINGSTON CITY HALL); and in commercial complexes like the ST LAWRENCE HALL in Toronto, Bonsecours Market in Montréal and Victoria Hall in Cobourg. In contrast to the US, where public and commercial buildings in Georgian style had acquired distasteful connotations of colonialism and had been superseded by Roman and Greek classical temple-styles, in English Canada in 1850 the symbolism of Georgian was still valid and the style alive. Vestigial traces of this "First British Empire" style can be discovered in houses and public buildings of the Canadian West as late as the 1920s, as in the Court House at Nicola, BC.

Revivals of Gothic and other medieval styles (Elizabethan, Tudor) began to appear in Canada early in the 19th century. Broadly speaking, the connotations of this style were continuity of traditions (church, state), as contrasted to revolutionary breaks with the past fostered by the French and American revolutions and proclaimed in French and American classical revivals. In

The concourse of Union Station, Toronto (Ross & Macdonald, Hugh Jones and John M. Lyle, 1915-20), shows the beaux-arts adaptation by Lyle of the vaulted hall of a Roman bath for a 20th-century gathering place (*photo* © *1984 Hartill Art Associates, London, Ont*).

Britain, castles built in Gothic to proclaim hereditary family roots appeared from the 1770s on; Windsor Castle was refurbished after 1815 as a memorial to Waterloo and the concomitant survival of the British monarchy; in the 1830s London's Westminster New Palace (Houses of Parliament) was swathed in Gothic forms which imaged the historical authentication and vindication of English parliamentary government. It was the Gothic revival in France that came first to Canada, in the form of the 1823-29 rebuilding of NOTRE-DAME, the original (1722) parish church of Montréal. Why Gothic was chosen for this huge church (for long the largest Gothic church in N America) has been much disputed; but certainly a major factor was the contemporary revival of Gothic in France to proclaim the restoration of French traditions of monarchy and Catholicism, exemplified by the restored Bourbons' tombs and completion of Ste-Croix Cathedral (1230, destroyed 1568, rebuilding began 1601, completed 1823-29) in Orléans. In English Canada the Gothic revival appeared in houses such as Chief Justice Boulton's "Holland House" in Toronto, which proclaimed British loyalties via a central section emulating Windsor Castle's huge crenellated keep-tower, a tradition climaxed in 1911 by Sir Henry PELLATT's evocation of Balmoral in Casa Loma (Toronto). In the PARLIAMENT BUILDINGS in Ottawa, the picturesque spires, pinnacles, pointed arches and textured walls of the Gothic revival style proclaimed the continuity of British institutions from medieval to modern times, in Canada as in Britain. No other provincial parliament building followed the Ottawa example (in striking contrast to the US where almost all 50 state capitols are recognizable variants of the federal capitol in Washington), perhaps a metaphor of FEDERAL-PROVINCIAL RELATIONS in Canada. After the mid-19th century, Gothic per se was often mixed with elements of other picturesque styles, a process initiated in the remarkable main building of U of T (UNIVERSITY COLLEGE) and perpetuated in many customs houses and post offices sporting French Second Empire mansards, Italianate pediments or Tudor half-timberings.

Distinctively Canadian too are the patterned brick Ontario farmhouses and their row-house counterparts in Ontario cities built from the 1860s into the 1880s; though not consistently Gothic revival in detail (many round-headed windows, Italianate pediments, Second French Empire mansards), they were fundamentally Gothic revival in spirit, revealing continuity with the Old Country (especially Scotland and Ulster) in their verticality, textural variety and assymmetry. Variants of the type, most commonly in wood, appear in other English-speaking provinces. Towards the end of the 19th century these house-styles were superseded in popularity by a picturesque Tudor style favoured for suburban building, 1900-30; Westmount, Montréal; Rosedale, Toronto; Shaughnessy, Vancouver; and Mount Royal, Calgary, all have fine examples, but the finest appear in Oak Bay, Victoria, created by Samuel MACLURE. In due course medieval styles filtered down to middle- and lower-class levels, and they survive in popular/commercial speculative building.

Gothic revival churches flourished in Canada's 19th-century cultural climate, and each major denomination developed distinctive variants. Anglican churches expressed British ties either by ostentatious correctness (the strict ecclesiological cathedrals in St John's and Fredericton, *see* CHRIST CHURCH CATHEDRAL) or "British atmosphere" (from the brass-plaque-studded walls of St James's Cathedral, Toronto, or Christ Church, Montréal, to the tiny "rustic Gothic" churches of the Gulf Islands or Prairies, to the inventive wooden Gothic of the Maritimes). Also to be noted is the distinctive Gothic style introduced by the Presbyterian Church in Canada. This denomination was often, in Ontario at least, the biggest in town and built bold, inventively designed exteriors (Centre Presbyterian, Brockville) and interiors with dramatic space mouldings, curving balconies and pews, and unique abstract geometric windows, thereby belying the popular association of Scottish Presbyterianism with an austere indifference to aesthetic concerns.

Canada's famous chateau-style hotels were basically Gothic revival in spirit and frequently in specific forms as well, as in the dining room and library of the Empress Hotel in Victoria. Their Gothic was polished with academic allusions both to Scottish castles and to French châteaux on the Loire, eg, the Château Frontenac in Québec City, the Château Laurier in Ottawa, the Fort Garry in Winnipeg and the Bessborough in Saskatoon (*see* HOTEL).

Between 1890 and 1914 the British Empire became more self-consciously imperial than before – a development which tended to be exaggerated in Canada because it was as members of the British Empire that English-speaking Canadians identified themselves vis-à-vis Americans. Visible manifestation of this self-consciousness came in an academic (ie, correct) revival of Imperial Roman (2nd-4th centuries AD) architectural style; patriotic Britons thought of themselves as latter-day Romans gone forth to civilize the natives of rude regions of the Earth, as Rome had civilized Gaul, Spain and Britain. A similar sense of mission, though with a lesser element of self-identification, possessed Americans and British at this time; grandiose buildings in Imperial Roman (or beaux-arts, CITY BEAUTIFUL – there are many names) rose everywhere in Anglo-American cities. Canada's principal representatives of this style are the legislature buildings of the Prairie provinces (mainly first decade 20th century, *see* GOVERNMENT BUILDING); Toronto's and Vancouver's RAILWAY STATIONS from the century's second decade (they belong to the "Columbian Exposition" family of Roman-bath city monuments that included stations in Washington, New York, Philadelphia, St Louis); BANKS in the classical temple-style introduced early in the 19th century in the US, now built in a much grander and archaeologically more correct manner (eg, Bank of Montreal at Portage and Main in Winnipeg, by the premier American firm of McKim, Mead & White, 1913; Bank of Nova Scotia on Sparks St in Ottawa, 1924; Bank of Nova Scotia in Halifax by John LYLE, 1929, a pioneer in introducing Canadian ornament to architecture); and that plethora of monuments to the Great War of 1914-18, most of them in recognizable vestiges of "Imperial Bombast" style (as academic Roman has been well called in such contexts), which are one of the most melancholy yet distinctive features of Canadian cityscapes ("died for the Empire" is their most common inscription).

These many different expressions were overwhelmed by the wave of modernism that swept across Western architecture after 1945, to remain unchallenged until the late 1970s. Modernism being by definition not a style but a way of building that is universally and eternally valid, it tended to obliterate regional and national traditions. What distinguished modernism in Canada was a utopianism more unrestrained than elsewhere. Without carrying much of the burden of its own defence, and freer of economic problems than most other countries, Canada provided ideal nourishment for the utopianism that was everywhere latent in modernism. Utopian faith in universities as agents to promote human perfectibility has rarely been so effectively imaged as in BC's SIMON FRASER U (Arthur ERICKSON) or Toronto's Scarborough College (John Andrews), both designs winning international awards. Nor has the idea of culture being something you can create through art ever been more effectively expressed than in the veritable efflorescence of theatre complexes in Canada of the 1960s, the GRAND THÉÂTRE in Québec City, Confederation Centre in Charlottetown, or the NATIONAL ARTS CENTRE in Ottawa.

Not the least interesting aspect of modernism in Canada is the way its formal evolution has followed a general pattern set in the US and Europe at about a 10-year lag. International-style Bauhaus modernism, introduced in the US in the late 1930s, appeared first in Canadian architecture schools (U of T) in the late 1940s, brought back from Harvard by Toronto students including John C. PARKIN; thence it spread across Canada in the early 1950s. Plastic and brute styles of modernism

appearing in Europe in the late 1950s (eg, Corbusier's Ronchamp, reviving Mendelsohn's 1920s molded concrete) became popular in Canada in the late 1960s (eg, Douglas CARDINAL's ST MARY'S CHURCH in Red Deer, Alta, 1968; Moshe Safdie's "Habitat" at EXPO 67). The multiple glass box popular in the US in the early 1960s had its notable Canadian realizations in the 1970s (eg, Erickson's Bank of Canada headquarters in Ottawa, 1979, and Robson Square Law Courts in Vancouver, 1979). The stark technocratic style of the late 1960s in Europe appeared in Canada in the 1970s (eg, McMaster Health Science Centre, Hamilton, by ZEIDLER Partnership, 1972). Obviously this pattern is a cultural expression, reflecting the national psyche. The dominant and controlling element in Canadian society has from the beginning been cautious and nonexperimental when confronted with new ideas – whether those ideas were early 19th-century British conservatism, late 19th-century British liberalism, or 20th-century European modernism. If one had to cite a single area of modern architecture of consistently high quality it would have to be churches. Some modern churches in Canada have received wide publicity, eg, Étienne GABOURY's Precious Blood Church in St-Boniface, Man (1967), but at least equally satisfactory is his parish church of St Claude in Manitoba (1961) that is rarely mentioned. There are literally dozens of churches that deserve far more attention than they get, such as the cathédrale/presbytère/évêché complex in Nicolet, Qué (Gérard Malouin, 1961). *See also* ARCHITECTURAL STYLES; ARCHITECTURE, DEVELOPMENT.

ALAN GOWANS

Reading: C. Ede, *Canadian Architecture 1960-1970* (1971); Alan Gowans, *Building Canada* (1966); L. Whiteson, *Modern Canadian Architecture* (1983).

Architecture, Development of ARCHITECTURE, a consciously intellectual and aesthetic activity, and utilitarian building are both shaped by the materials, technology, money and time available to the designer; the particular activities to be housed; the climate to be tempered; the organization of design and construction; and the ideas about appropriate form held at the time. All these factors have varied significantly through the nearly 4 centuries of European settlement in Canada.

1000-1600 The earliest European buildings so far traced in Canada are simple, crude constructions similar in technique to the stone, earth and timber dwellings of some NATIVE PEOPLES (*see* HOUSE). It is generally accepted that the remains at L'ANSE AUX MEADOWS in Newfoundland are those of an early 11th-century settlement by a small group of Norse adventurers who lived a communal, nearly tribal life crowded together in a few great houses. The buildings were roughly built of logs and stone, with roofs thatched with branches and reeds. Open fires on the beaten earth floors of the houses gave what heat there was, the smoke finding its way out through the textured thatch. In the wake of the Vikings came BASQUES and British seamen who regularly crossed the Atlantic to fish the Grand Banks, and who established homes and villages on the Newfoundland coast. No buildings survive from these settlements, but contemporary illustrations of French settlements in the Atlantic region show low structures built of sod and of upright posts planted in the ground.

New France In the early 17th century French navigators, merchants and missionaries, following Samuel de CHAMPLAIN, established 2 permanent spheres of influence in Canada: on lands known as Acadia on the Bay of Fundy, and on the St Lawrence in the settlements that became Montréal and Québec City. Champlain's first buildings in Québec were gable-roofed timber

Ste-Famille, Île d'Orléans, Qué (1743-49, clochers added in 1809 and 1843). It is more monumental than earlier parish churches, with towers and niches for sculpture (*photo by John deVisser*).

constructions, joined by a gallery at the second level, and protected by a moat and a wall with pointed bastions where cannon were placed. The habitation at PORT-ROYAL was similar.

The French were the first Europeans to plant their culture in Canada, a transatlantic extension of metropolitan France that comprised social organization, economy, religion, art and architecture. The establishment of a full panoply of governmental and religious institutions in Québec City and, to a lesser extent, Montréal meant that occasionally high-style buildings, such as the Archbishop's Palace (Claude BAILLIF, 1693-97) or Notre-Dame Cathedral (Claude Baillif, 1684-97) in Québec City, were erected in a simplified version of the currently popular French baroque taste. The palace was built in rendered stone with a curved baroque gable to the chapel. The reredos, described by a contemporary, Bacqueville de La Potherie, as a simplified version of that at Val-de-Grace Church in Paris, rivalled the beauty of palaces in France. The vast majority of the population was agricultural, settled along the St Lawrence on narrow, long strips of land; the settlers required simple utilitarian structures to shelter them from the harsh climate (*see* SEIGNEURIAL SYSTEM). Plain rural churches were built of rubble masonry, with perhaps cut-stone trim around doors and windows, and protected from moisture by a white stucco rendering called *crépi* (St François Church, Île d'Orléans). Farmhouses, though sometimes built of stone, most often were made from wood, either solid log or heavy wooden frame filled with stone called *colombage pierroté* and increasingly of wood-filled frame. Like their counterparts in France, these early farmhouses had low walls, steep roofs (covered with shingles, boards or thatch), small casement windows, and few interior partitions (eg, maison Girardin, Beauport). The problems of survival imposed by the severe climate in NEW FRANCE left little opportunity for elaborate decoration.

Severed politically from France by the British Conquest of 1759-60, and isolated from European revolutionary upheavals, the original New France culture flourished. The remarkably conservative building traditions of New France – where methods and styles brought from the mother country were repeated with only slight modifications – endured until the end of the 18th century. Though British and US developments began to make inroads in the 19th century, French Canadian traditions persisted into the 20th century in 3 characteristically Québécois architectural types: the church, seigneurial manor

1653 Rue Duke, St-Hubert, Qué (*courtesy Environment Canada, Parks/Heritage Recording Services*).

and rural house (*see* RELIGIOUS BUILDING). Québec churches retained their vaguely Louis XVI design and decorative schemes until well into the century. The house form gradually adapted itself to the Québec climate until it became, by mid-19th century, the distinctive *maison québecoise*. Changes included the raised ground storey (to allow for snow accumulations), multiple chimneys and dormers, and the extension of the bell-cast eaves (intended to keep moisture off the walls) to become the roof of the cantilevered, picturesquely carved verandah.

British and Loyalist Building British colonization of the Canadian territories began on the Atlantic coast in the 17th century. Settlers came from both England and the American colonies, followed, after 1776, by LOYALISTS from the East Coast through Québec into present-day Ontario. In the early 19th century UPPER CANADA became the recipient of large numbers of US immigrants. The British immigrants brought their direct experience of Georgian, then, later, Victorian architecture from the British Isles, while those arriving in Canada from the US brought their version of the adapted Georgian or "federal" architecture.

Both groups had a desire to reproduce familiar surroundings in what was often, particularly for the European immigrants, a harsh and unfamiliar setting. Their neat, rectangular buildings of stone, timber or brick had at least a superficial symmetry and the carefully proportioned sash windows of the Georgian originals. Depending on the availability of money, skills and materials, structures such as the Matheson House (Perth, Ont, 1840), PROVINCE HOUSE (Halifax, John Merrick?, 1811-18), and St Paul's Church (Halifax, 1750) carried the classical detail of the prototypes – the columns or pilasters, decorative friezes, Palladian windows and other trimmings whose origins went back from Georgian England to the Florentine Renaissance and beyond to the architecture of ancient Greece and Rome.

In Halifax, Georgian England had a direct presence, even to the Palladian-influenced country estate the duke of Kent laid out at Bedford Basin at the end of the 18th century. Its only surviving structure is the tidy, circular, white, classically ordered rotunda with its simple Tuscan columns. In Québec the new English presence was established within the matrix of French building by structures such as Holy Trinity Anglican Cathedral of Québec City (by military engineers Robe and Hall, 1800-04, roof raised about 1816). The cathedral's austere Ionic pilasters and blind arches outside, vaulted ceiling and galleries raised on Ionic columns inside, must have seemed an intrusion set among the very different buildings of the Québecois tradition.

Much of the building from this early period of British settlement has gone, decayed, been demolished or, in the case of towns with flammable wooden buildings built side by side, burned in the fires that were a recurrent feature of older, timber

settlements. Some of the buildings, such as the Barnum House (Grafton, Ont, about 1817) featuring a central pedimented block with flanking wings, and some of the quality of the towns – houses, streets, trees and gardens – survive. NIAGARA-ON-THE-LAKE in Ontario, eg, retains traces of the early 19th-century townscape (houses on Queen St, early 1820s). Some buildings from this period have been reassembled in museum villages such as UPPER CANADA VILLAGE in Ontario or KINGS LANDING in NB.

In Britain architecture became greatly enriched in the early Victorian period, when lively irregularity became more fashionable than regular and restrained Georgian. The early 19th century is the period of the picturesque, of Gothic revival and neoclassicism as well as a variety of other ARCHITECTURAL STYLES retrieved from the remote corners of architectural history and geography. Both Gothic revival and neoclassical were important styles in Canada through the mid-19th century. The classical vocabulary was now represented by direct recreation of ancient Greek and Roman features, on the Kingston City Hall (George Browne, 1842-44) and the simpler, baseless Doric order of St Andrew's Presbyterian Church, Niagara-on-the-Lake (James Cooper, 1831).

Competing with classicism, particularly in the Ottawa PARLIAMENT BUILDINGS and the Anglican churches for which it had become the preferred style in England, was revived Gothic: the architecture of pointed arches, ribbed vaults and flying buttresses that seized the imagination of some theorists of church architecture. Examples are CHRIST CHURCH CATHEDRAL of Fredericton, NB (William Butterfield and Frank Wills, 1846-53) and the Cathedral of St John the Baptist in St John's, Nfld (George Gilbert Scott, from 1846), both designed by leading English architects. Along with this elaborated Gothic inspired by the great cathedrals and parish churches of medieval England came a renewed interest in the more modest traditional architecture of the English countryside, from which came the steep-pitched gables and the decorated bargeboards which could be found both in elaborate public buildings and in ordinary town and country houses.

As the 19th century advanced, these changes in the taste and style of building were encouraged and propagated by even more profound social changes: increased population, improved agriculture and industry, in both Europe and the New World. The harnessing of steam power, and the new and sophisticated exploitation of such old materials as cast and wrought iron, accelerated the changes in the way people lived. Steam-powered transportation on land and at sea encouraged the concentration of people and industry, and began to make practicable extensive factories, cities and even large-scale agriculture. In Canada these developments were exemplified by Montréal, Toronto and Hamilton, with industrial complexes like the Massey-Harris agricultural machinery factories in Toronto (from 1879). Cast-iron building components became commonplace. Developments in iron-framed construction reached their symbolic culmination in the Crystal Palace in London (1851), which spawned a generation of crystal palaces around the world, including Toronto and Montréal (the Toronto example was designed by Sir Sandford FLEMING and Sir Collingwood SCHREIBER, 1858; then altered and moved to Exhibition Park, 1879). In the 1850s New York entrepreneurs created and distributed prefabricated cast-iron storefronts, one of which still stands on Granville St, Halifax. In Victoria, BC, mid and late 19th-century cast-iron façades survive from both San Francisco and local iron foundries.

1867-1918 As industrialization advanced, new

kinds of buildings appeared to serve the industrial and commercial economies – factory buildings and warehouses, RAILWAY STATIONS, HOTELS, office buildings. The most spectacular development was the high office building. Its first Canadian appearance in Montréal and Toronto depended on newly developed solutions to the problems of tall construction, vertical transportation and fire protection. High buildings in masonry (in brick or stone) required immensely thick supporting walls at the lower levels as the superimposed load of the high structure increased. The street level, however, was the most desirable for commercial purposes and commanded the highest rents. Stronger, and yet more slender, metal-frame structures offered obvious advantages, but the iron that had been used through the middle of the century was brittle and unsuitable for structures that had to give with slight movements induced by wind and settling. Cast-iron columns and beams had to be cast to final shape before erection and could not be adjusted on the building site. Both these problems were eliminated as structural steel became available through the 1860s. Strong in bending as well as under compression, steel had the necessary elasticity and could be altered to accommodate changes or errors in the building design. The Temple Building (Bay and Richmond Sts, designed by George W. Gouinlock, 1895) was one of the last tall office buildings in Toronto to have a cast-iron frame. Iron and steel, however, were both vulnerable to the heat of building fires. The answer was found with the enclosure of the exposed steel structure within thick masonry or a surface of plaster, to insulate the steel long enough to permit the fire in a burning building to be controlled. An early example with a structural steel skeleton was the old Board of Trade Building (Yonge and Front Sts, Toronto, designed by James and James of New York, 1889).

Finally, with the invention of the Otis elevator (1856), buildings could exceed the walk-up height limit of 4-6 storeys. The New York Life Insurance Co Building on the Place d'Armes, Mont-

Holy Trinity Anglican Cathedral, Québec City (Hall and Robe, 1800-04). The first Anglican cathedral built outside the British Isles, it was designed in a simplified Palladian style (*photo* © *Hartill Art Associates, London, Ont*).

Notre-Dame de Montréal, built 1823-29, was long the largest Gothic revival church in N America (*courtesy Environment Canada, Parks/Heritage Recording Services*).

réal (Babb, Cook and Willard, 1887), 8 storeys, was described as the first Montréal skyscraper. Equity Chambers (Adelaide and Victoria Streets, Toronto, 1878, demolished 1960s), 5 storeys, was described as "the first business block in the city to introduce the elevator." These developments were combined in such early fireproofed steel-framed buildings as the Robert Simpson Co store on Yonge St in Toronto, a rebuilding in 1895 of the store opened in 1894 and destroyed by fire. The second time the steel columns and beams were encased in concrete, and fire-resistant floor construction was used. Another early fireproofed steel frame was used for the Federal Building in Vancouver, 1905-10 (701 West Hastings St), designed by the Dept of Public Works. Similarly, reinforced concrete became a useful material for large-scale buildings from the end of the century (60 Front St W, about 1900, was said to be the first in Toronto), not only for framed structures but also for dams and for buildings with structural walls such as silos. Grain elevators in Montréal, Toronto, Port Arthur and Calgary were an inspiration to the Europeans Walter Gropius and Le Corbusier.

At the same time, the technological revolution in the construction of ordinary wood buildings affected the fabric of every town, village and large urban centre. Traditional construction of preindustrial buildings was either completely in timber frame or a combination of load-bearing brick or stone with heavy timber beams. Two inventions of the early 19th century, economical machine-made nails and light machine-sawn timbers, revolutionized building in wood, and led to a system called "balloon framing." It was fast, economical, flexible and extremely efficient, providing great strength with economy of material. The strength came from the combination of frame with the wood sheathing that covered it. Cladding could be wood, brick or stone, though these were no longer a necessary part of the building structure but merely an exterior surface resisting the weather and giving an attractive appearance. This industrially based framing replaced the older braced timber frame of the eastern settlements as the ordinary construction of late 19th- and 20th-century Canada. It spread across the West, leaving expensive and prestigious solid stone and brick construction for the more elaborate buildings.

In contrast to the long architectural tradition in eastern and central Canada, the architecture of the West was just beginning as the 19th century closed. The exceptions were the forts and trading posts of the FUR TRADE and the first planted settlements on Vancouver I and the RED RIVER COLONY. Usually built in horizontal logs or the so-called Red River Frame (vertical posts grooved to receive tongued horizontal logs, an earlier Québec technique, and occasionally in stone, examples can be seen at Lower FORT GARRY, nucleus of the settlement (1830s-50s). Otherwise the settlement and the architecture of the West belong to the industrial era. This is particularly true of the ordinary buildings of the farms, towns and cities, where machine-sawn lumber, prefabricated ornament and decoration chosen from the mail-order catalogues offered the cheapest and often the best way to build.

A recurrent theme of western Canadian architecture is the contrast between local buildings, modest and relatively unsophisticated, and those of eastern interests, the branch BANKS and branch stores (the Hudson's Bay Co or Birks) designed usually by Toronto or Montréal architects according to prevailing international standards. The most striking example was the château-style railway hotels, originating with the Banff Springs Hotel designed by the CPR's Boston architect, Bruce Price (1888). They are variously described as medieval French, Québecois, Edwardian, Scottish and beaux-arts classical in inspiration, but all are capped by the steeply pitched roofs, often with multiple dormers that suggest a romantic retreat. The effect is most successful at Banff in its wild mountain setting, and most fully developed at Château Frontenac at Québec City (1892-1920).

Another feature of western Canadian architecture was its variety, arising from the diversity of the population. Whereas settlement in the East up to Confederation had been mainly British or French in origin, the open territory of the West attracted settlers from northern Europe, Russia, Ukraine, Germany, Scandinavia, Iceland and China. Each group brought its distinctive traditions, tastes and skills, expressed in buildings ranging from the thatched and stuccoed Ukrainian houses to the striking domed and towered churches of the Orthodox religious traditions (ELK ISLAND NATIONAL PARK and Ukrainian Cultural Heritage Village, Alberta) to the detail and ornament of Chinatown buildings everywhere (especially in downtown Vancouver).

The formation of the province of Manitoba in 1870, the extension of Confederation to include BC in 1871, and the establishment of new provinces in Saskatchewan and Alberta in 1905 created occasions for the most elaborate early buildings of the West, the provincial parliament buildings (*see* GOVERNMENT BUILDING). The BC legislature building was designed by Francis Mawson RATTENBURY in what he called a "free classical style" (1893-97, 1912-16), while the Saskatchewan building is an American beaux-arts version of English baroque by the Montréal firm Edward and William S. Maxwell (completion 1908-12).

In the 1890s outstanding American architects had an impact on the design of the central structures in the growing cities of Canada. H.H. Richardson influenced E.J. Lennox's design of the Toronto City Hall (1890), and Louis Sullivan and the "Chicago School" the early skyscrapers, the Grain Exchange, Calgary (1909), and the Tegler building, Edmonton (H.A. Magoon, 1911). As well, the influence of the British arts and crafts movement inspired architects across the country from Eden Smith in Toronto to Samuel MACLURE in Victoria. By WWI, however, the example of such outstanding original figures as

The entrance arch and elevator lobby of McCarter and Nairne's Marine Building, Vancouver (1929-30), displays the rich form and colour possible with terra-cotta decoration in the art-deco style (*photo by M. McMordie*).

Frank Lloyd Wright (US), Charles Rennie Macintosh (Scotland) and Peter Behrens (Germany) had made little impact on Canadian architecture. Wright's close associate, Francis C. Sullivan, followed his lead with a few innovative buildings around Ottawa, and in the Montréal suburb of Maisonneuve.

Many important commissions in Canada were won by American architects or by immigrant Britons. This competition became an incentive to Canadians to institute more formal and sophisticated arrangements for the education of architects (the first professorship was created in the School of Practical Science in Toronto in 1890 and the first full department at McGill in 1896) and to organize the profession with legislative authority. The Ontario Assn of Architects was established in 1889 and the Province of Quebec Assn of Architects in 1890, followed by other provincial associations. In 1907 these associations formed a national organization which in 1909 became the Royal Architectural Institute of Canada (*see* ARCHITECTURAL PRACTICE).

1919-39 In architecture, the period between the wars was one of experiment and innovation as designers in Europe and America responded to the challenge of new building technology and to the sense of living in a new age of machinery, electricity, rapid travel and communication. Walter Gropius's Bauhaus buildings in Dessau, Germany (1925-26), and Le Corbusier's Villa Savoie in France (1929-30) became the touchstones of the new international style. The core of both Chicago and New York underwent an amazing high-rise development. The new design style, art deco, and technological "streamlining" began popular fashions in decoration. In Canada, however, clients and the profession remained generally conservative in their tastes. The Toronto architect John LYLE modified the classical forms of established beaux-arts architecture to create more up-to-date art deco ornament in such buildings as his Bank of Nova Scotia branch in Calgary (1929-30) and, in response to growing national pride, incorporated decorative motifs drawn from the region: ranchers and cattle, wheat and the derricks of the oil industry. Percy NOBBS, who came from Britain to head McGill's architecture school in 1903, worked across the country with fine buildings from Montréal to Edmonton (campus plan, early buildings for U of Alberta), as did many other Montréal architects. Darling and Pearson's head office building for the Canadian Bank of Commerce in Toronto (1929-31) was the finest of the skyscrapers and for several decades the tallest building in the Commonwealth. Its symmetrical, stepped back tower contrasted plain limestone surfaces with rich Romanesque detail. The Marine Building in Vancouver (McCarter and Nairne, 1929-30) was a splendidly decorated exercise in art deco, built in brick and stone with terra cotta reliefs of contemporary transportation. A major practitioner, the Paris-trained Montréal architect Ernest CORMIER, designed the main block at U de Montréal (1924-42) and the Supreme Court, Ottawa (1938-39, the château-style roof at PM Mackenzie King's insistence). Perhaps the finest example of art deco is Cormier's own home, with boldly abstract forms in stone terrazzo and plaster (1418 Pine Avenue, Montréal, 1930-31).

The first signs of a wholehearted move in Canada to adopt European and US modernism in architecture came with slow economic recovery from the mid-1930s and particularly in the years after WWII. Swiss immigrant Robert Blatter and Québec-born Marcel Parizeau designed the first international-style houses. In the late 1930s Peter Thornton, Robert Berwick and C.E. Pratt (later THOMPSON, BERWICK, PRATT AND PARTNERS) set up practices in Vancouver, and John B. PARKIN (later joined by the younger, unrelated, John C. PARKIN) in Toronto. These architects were significant as representatives of a new generation who contributed to the gradual eclipse of design based on historical styles in favour of an architecture of abstract form, exposed structure and plain materials (often glass, steel or aluminum, concrete, sometimes stone, tile or wood) used without decorative enrichment and with a stern simplicity of treatment.

1940-1980s The war years saw a significant demand for utilitarian buildings, economical and efficient construction, and so promoted the ideals and technology in which the mainstream of modern architecture was based. In Canada, it was in industrial buildings that the new technology was first employed, and the need for the rapid erection of a large number of structures, eg, aircraft hangars, encouraged an innovative approach to design and construction. A government agency, Wartime Housing Corp, constructed a distinctive, simple, standardized housing for workers in defence-related industries.

After 1945 Canada began to respond to the new architecture of the 1920s and 1930s. The return of service people and a surge in the formation of new families created great opportunities for architectural development. Housing was needed and Wartime Housing Corp was replaced by Central Mortgage and Housing Corporation (*see* CANADA MORTGAGE AND HOUSING CORPORATION) in 1946. As the children of the postwar BABY BOOM reached school age they created a demand for schools that followed through in successive waves of building elementary schools, secondary schools, technical colleges, community colleges and universities.

While traditional historical architecture continued to be designed and built, particularly by older architects before the war, a new generation of younger architects (Parkin, Berwick, Pratt, Thornton) believed that the appropriate way to build was in the directions established by the leaders of modernism. These Canadian innovators were increasingly successful in persuading school boards, government departments, industrialists and other important clients to trust their

B.C. Binning designed a number of houses, including his own (above), built in West Vancouver *c*1940 (*photo by M. McMordie*).

vision of architecture as simple, efficient, advanced in construction and services, and free of all historical styles. This vision was to be supported with a new level of technical competence. One of the leading architectural firms, John B. Parkin Associates, sought to bring all the skills and technical knowledge together under one roof as part of a comprehensive, corporate design firm which could offer everything from structural and mechanical engineering, architectural design, detailing and supervision through to design of interiors, landscape and the design of the signs required for a new building (Aeroquay, Toronto-Lester B. Pearson International Airport, Toronto, 1957-65). This view of design as a comprehensive professional service which covered every aspect of the building, its setting and its furnishing, was pursued by many other firms in collaboration with sympathetic consultants.

New architects rose to prominence and some older firms gained new vigour. In Vancouver the leaders were Thompson, Berwick and Pratt; Gardiner and Thornton; and McCarter, Nairne. In Winnipeg a distinguished group included Moody, Moore and Partners; Green, Blankstein and Russell; and Smith, Carter and Searle. In Toronto, among a number of others, the Parkin firm achieved the greatest prominence nationally and internationally. John BLAND, for many years head of McGill University School of Architecture, also distinguished himself in practice in Montréal, as did a younger group, AFFLECK, Desbarats, DIMAKOPOULOS, LEBENSOLD, Sise. A host of younger, smaller firms followed and architects such as Barry DOWNS in Vancouver, Douglas CARDINAL in Edmonton, Clifford WIENS in Regina, Étienne GABOURY in Winnipeg, and Roger D'Astous in Montréal established themselves as outstanding figures. The 1950s and 1960s became a period of great architectural excitement.

International Recognition The postwar growth of architecture in Canada was marked by the building of a number of major structures, many the result of ARCHITECTURAL COMPETITIONS and awards. Among the early triumphs of modern design was the choice of the John B. Parkin firm to

Toronto City Hall from below (*photo by J.A. Kraulis*).

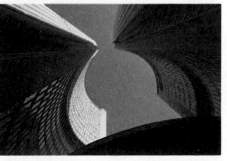

design the new headquarters building for the Ontario Assn of Architects (1954). Other milestone structures included the Ottawa City Hall by Rother, Bland and Trudeau (1958); the BC Electric Building (now BC Hydro) in Vancouver by Thompson, Berwick and Pratt (1955-57); and the new TORONTO CITY HALL designed by the Finnish architect, Viljo Revell, and carried out in association with the Parkin firm (opened 1965). Arthur ERICKSON and Geoffrey Massey won the commission for the new SIMON FRASER U in Burnaby, BC (1963-65). Ron THOM, after a distinguished career in Vancouver, moved to Toronto, establishing an independent practice with such buildings as MASSEY COLLEGE at U of T (1963), Shaw Festival Theatre, Niagara-on-the-Lake (1973), and TRENT U, Peterborough (1963-71). Through the 1950s and 1960s many Canadian architects began to gain commissions that carried their work overseas.

EXPO 67 merits particular attention for its architecture. The contribution of Canadian architects was multiple and significant; individually or in groups they designed or supervised the construction of the national and corporate pavilions but made their mark most obviously with the design of the facilities for the Canadian government. Affleck, Desbarats, Dimakopoulos, Lebensold and Sise were responsible for several remarkable theme pavilions based on massive tetrahedral space frames carried out in exposed structural steel. Erickson designed the Man and Health and Man and Community pavilions, lighter and more delicate in atmosphere, with carefully planned landscaping and interior lighting. John Andrews was responsible for a lively and attractive cluster of spaces designed to house displays by a number of developing countries. Expo 86, held in Vancouver, was less successful in taking advantage of the best current ideas in architecture. Notable exceptions were Peter Cardew's modernist structure for CN, and the playful and colourful Alberta Pavilion by Andrishak and Sturgess.

Architectural Education Through this same postwar period there was an expansion of Canadian architectural education. In 1987 architectural degree programs were offered in 10 Canadian universities (there were just 5 in 1945), and a variety of programs in architectural technology and drafting was available at technical institutes and colleges across the country.

The pattern of architectural education has changed. The system established before WWII at McGill, Toronto and Manitoba was a 5-year undergraduate program leading to the BArch degree. These programs held a traditional view of architectural education that emphasized the design studio (perhaps half of a 26- or 28-hour week) and a series of technical subjects, including materials and methods of construction, structures, acoustics, illumination, heating and air conditioning, as well as varying amounts of architectural theory and history. Through the 1960s this emphasis on technical and professional education, on formal architectural design, came to seem inadequate. There was increasing concern with the response of users to the buildings that were designed for them, and with a variety of social and political issues. At U of T under Peter Prangnell and at UBC under Henry Elder, both English-trained architects (though Prangnell also studied at Harvard), architectural programs were altered to become much broader in their direction, both in giving students choice of subjects and in a strong emphasis on social issues and personal responses rather than on formal and technical content. Following US precedents, U of Manitoba created a new Bachelor of Environmental Studies degree, common to students of architecture, INTERIOR DESIGN and LANDSCAPE ARCHITECTURE,

Toronto Dominion Centre, Toronto (Mies van der Rohe, consultant, with John B. Parkin Associates and Bregman and Hamann, 1964-68). The success of the international modern style — severe, impersonal, highly disciplined — depends largely on proportion and detail (*photo by M. McMordie*).

to be followed for the architects by the professional MArch degree. Admission to the UBC architecture program was changed to require first a bachelor's degree, followed by a 3-year BArch degree. The Faculty of Environmental Design at U of Calgary, which admitted its first students in 1971, also required a first degree for admission, followed by interdisciplinary work bringing together students in architecture, urban planning and environmental science (and, more recently, IN-DUSTRIAL DESIGN), as well as more purely architectural work (*see* URBAN DESIGN; ZONING). The consequence of all these changes was, by the 1970s, a much more varied, experimental educational program.

Changing Patterns of Practice Along with divergent trends in design and education throughout the 1960s and 1970s came increasing variety in the ways architecture was practised and the actual design and construction of building projects. Costs, time and quality control became issues of prime importance during a period of increasing inflation and greater complexity of building functions. Traditionally an architect prepared a design which, when approved, was developed into a full set of working drawings and specifications; then a contractor was selected, often by competitive tendering, to construct the building under the architect's overall supervision. New alternatives included "package deals," "fast tracking" of construction, and project management systems. In package deals, the building user is offered the design and construction of new facilities for a fixed sum or under some lease arrangement by an entrepreneur who might be a building contractor or simply a broker who arranges finance, site acquisition, design and construction. In fast tracking, the project designers and building contractor are selected together or in close succession at the inception of a project and construction begins on the basis of a sequential design process in which the rapid overall preliminary design of a building is followed by detailed design from the lower levels up; excavation and construction of foundations proceeds before design of the upper levels is

complete. Project management involves the placing of design and construction under the overall supervision of a new group of professionals — management experts, cost accountants, professional engineers, and, in some cases, architects who undertake on behalf of the client to control the cost and scheduling of the project from beginning to end (*see* CONSTRUCTION INDUSTRY). These developments were interpreted by many architects as a challenge to their professional competence. Architects' professional associations now require further training prior to professional certification, through monitored practical experience, short courses and professional practice examinations.

Diversity in forms of practice paralleled these developments. There remained a preponderance of small firms and individual architects who continued to offer services of the traditional sort to clients who wished to alter or build private houses, smaller schools and institutional buildings, or small- to medium-sized commercial structures. Some architectural firms began to specialize, eg, in highly complex and demanding building types, particularly hospitals and health-care facilities. A small number of firms incorporated within their own organization all the design competence required to offer a comprehensive service. Most architects, however, continued to employ a variety of independent consultants, to avoid a high degree of specialization in a few types of buildings, and to work in smaller groups which allowed the senior members of the firm a greater degree of involvement in each of the firm's projects. Even within these firms, however, architects and architectural technicians emerged with specialized roles in design, drawings and specifications, project supervision, legal contracts, or management.

Present Trends Widespread allegiance to an international modern style of architecture continues, particularly for commercial buildings which are remarkably similar from country to country, regardless of distinctive historical traditions, climate, landscape and society. As well, a much greater diversity of approaches became evident in the 1960s. This variety affected the designs of new buildings and encouraged the study and conservation of older ones. Place Bonaventure, Montréal (Affleck, Desbarats, Dimakopoulos, Lebensold, Sise, 1964-68) signalled a new emphasis on buildings combining many different uses under one roof. The organization of the building around a large internal "atrium" space became a feature of these and other buildings, eg, EATON CENTRE, Toronto (ZEIDLER Partnership, 1977); Metro Toronto Library (Raymond MORIYAMA, 1977). Climate-protected pedestrian systems began to appear in Canadian cities, either below ground, as in Toronto and Montréal, or above ground, as in Calgary's Plus 15. Some architects are best known for their association with particular developments. Colin Bent of Toronto is recognized for his innovative designs for Arctic conditions (Polaris Mine Project, Little Cornwallis I, NWT, 1981). Webb, Zerafa, Menkes, Housden, based in Toronto but with offices across the country and internationally, has become the country's largest practice through the design of office and retail complexes, including the golden glazed Royal Bank Plaza, Toronto (1976) and the triangular Calgary Municipal Building (completed 1985). Zeidler Partnership, also of Toronto, again a general practice, has specialized in high technology health-science work (McMaster Health Science Centre, Hamilton, 1972; Walter C. Mackenzie Health Sciences Centre, Edmonton, 1982).

A new emphasis on regional and national culture in traditional architecture resulted in Canada in the restoration and conservation of the architecture of New France and Acadia, of British, Loyalist and American settlers, and of Ukrainians and

The grand multilevel daylit interior space, as at the Eaton Centre, Toronto, revives a 19th-century building form and adapts it to the northern climate (*photo by M. McMordie*).

similar groups. On the national level the federal government, through Parks Canada, initiated the Canadian Inventory of Historic Building in 1970 to survey and study architecture across the country, in order to support the work of the Historic Sites and Monuments Board of Canada. A high degree of sophistication in the actual technical documentation and preservation of buildings was established. HERITAGE CANADA FOUNDATION, established in 1973 as a publicly endowed but independent national society, promotes interest, knowledge and preservation of Canada's architectural and urban heritage especially through its magazines, *Canadian Heritage* and *Continuité*. New national associations, like the Society for the Study of Architecture in Canada, ICOMOS Canada and the Association for Preservation Technology emerged to provide a forum and stimulus for the efforts of academics, professionals and laymen. Provincial and, in some cases, local governments moved to enact legislation and bylaws to promote HERITAGE CONSERVATION. In Montréal, the Canadian Centre for Architecture, an institution of international scope and quality devoted to the study of architecture, was founded in 1979 by architect and conservationist Phyllis Lambert. Numerous local and regional societies were reinvigorated or newly formed to promote the conservation, preservation and rehabilitation of Canada's architectural heritage, both public and private.

In design, the influence of this new wave of historical interest can be seen in the work of younger architects such as Peter Rose of Montréal, whose buildings explicitly draw upon regional traditions in design and on occasion employ elements from historical styles. There is a renewed emphasis on traditional forms, a feeling that setback and detached towers like the TD Centre in Toronto or the BC Electric Building in Vancouver represent a tendency that threatens to destroy the coherence of a closely knit, low-rise city of continuous street façades contrasted with more open city squares. Both these concerns were addressed in the program written for a competition for a new city hall for Mississauga, Ont, by George Baird of U of T (1982) and evidenced in the winning scheme by

J. Michael Kirkland and Edward Jones. Norman Hotson's Granville I, Vancouver (1979), combines lively urban design and imaginative conservation in the transformation of an old industrial area into a mixed-use commercial and recreational district.

Present-day trends include the revival of older traditions and their integration into an evolving modernism as exemplified in the work of the Toronto architect A.J. Diamond (Toronto YMCA, 1986; University of Toronto Earth Science Centre, with Bregman & Hamann, scheduled completion 1988) and the Vancouver architect Richard Henriquez (Sylvia Hotel extension, 1986; Sinclair Centre, with Toby, Russell, Buckwell Partners, 1986).

CHRISTINA CAMERON AND MICHAEL MCMORDIE

Reading: M. Archibald, *By Federal Design* (1983); E. Arthur, *Iron: The Story of Cast and Wrought Iron in Canada from the Seventeenth Century to the Present* (1982) and *Toronto No Mean City* (1974); A. Barratt and R. Liscombe, *Francis Rattenbury and British Columbia: Architecture and Challenge in the Imperial Age* (1983); T. Boddy, ed, *Prairie Architecture* (1980); *Canadian Architect*, 1-(1955-); M. Brosseau, *Gothic Revival in Canadian Architecture* (1980); C. Cameron and M. Trépanier *Vieux-Québec: son architecture intérieure* (1986); C. Cameron and J. Wright, *Second Empire Style in Canadian Architecture* (1980); *Canadian Architect and Builder*, 1-22 (1888-1908); *Canadian Heritage*, 1- (1975-); M. Carter, ed, *Early Canadian Court Houses* (1983); R. Cawker and W. Bernstein, *Building with Words: Canadian Architects on Architecture* (1981) and *Contemporary Canadian Architecture* (1982); *Construction*, 1-27 (1907-34); N. Clerk, *Palladian Style in Canadian Architecture* (1984); B. Downs, *Sacred Places: British Columbia's Early Churches* (1980); A. Duffus et al, *Thy Dwellings Fair: Churches of Nova Scotia 1750-1830* (1982); C.M. Ede, *Canadian Architecture 1960/70* (1971); F. Gagnon-Pratte, *L'Architecture et la nature à Québec au dix-neuvième siècle: les villas* (1980); A. Gowans, *Building Canada* (1966) and *Church Architecture in New France* (1955); R. Greenhill, K. Macpherson and D. Richardson, *Ontario Towns* (1974); H.D. Kalman, *The Railway Hotels and the Development of the Château Style in Canada* (1968), *Exploring Ottawa* (1983) and *Exploring Vancouver* (1974); M. Lessard and H. Marquis, *Encyclopédie de la maison québécoise* (1972); M. MacRae and A. Adamson, *The Ancestral Roof: Domestic Architecture of Upper Canada* (1963), *Cornerstones of Order: Courthouses and Town Halls of Ontario 1784-1914* (1983) and *Hallowed Walls: Church Architecture in Upper Canada* (1975); L. Maitland, *Neoclassical Architecture in Canada* (1984); J.C. Marsan, *Montreal in Evolution* (1981); Newfoundland Historic Trust, *Ten Historic Towns: Heritage Architecture of Newfoundland* (1978) and *A Gift of Heritage: Selections from the Architectural Heritage of St. John's, Newfoundland* (1975); L. Noppen, *Les Églises du Québec (1600-1850)* (1977); Noppen, C. Paulette and M. Tremblay, *Québec: trois siècles d'architecture* (1979); J.I. Rempel, *Building with Wood and Other Aspects of Nineteenth-Century Building in Central Canada* (1980); A.J.H. Richardson et al, *Quebec City: Architects, Artisans and Builders* (1984); T. Ritchie, *Canada Builds 1867-1967* (1967); I.L. Rogers, *Charlottetown: The Life in its Buildings* (1983); Royal Architectural Institute of Canada, *Architecture Canada*, 1-50 (1924-73); M. Segger and D. Franklin, *Victoria: A Primer for Regional History in Architecture* (1979); Society for Study of Architecture in Canada, *Selected Papers from the Society of Architecture in Canada* (1976-84); D. Stewart and I.E. Wilson, *Heritage Kingston* (1973); J. Veillette and G. White, *Early Indian Village Churches: Wooden Frontier Architecture in British Columbia* (1977); L. Whiteson, *Modern Canadian Architecture* (1983); J. Wright, *Architecture of the Picturesque in Canada* (1984).

Archives are usually defined as the permanent records. In this sense, archives constitute that coherent body of recorded information created or received by a government, corporate body or organization in the course of its business, or by an individual in his activities, and which is then maintained, preferably in continuous authorized custody, as a record of that business or activity. Given the myriad forms in which information can now be recorded, archives grow correspondingly complex. Archives today range in physical format

from traditional paper files, minute books, ledgers, diaries, letters and reports, to microfilm, photographic images, cartographic materials, architectural drawings, motion-picture film, sound recordings, videotape and machine-readable data files. It follows, too, from this definition, that the archival record is not constant but is continually created and augmented. In any modern administrative body, whether a large government or a local voluntary association, information is recorded for some administrative purpose. It may then be kept for reference or for audit and legal reasons. When it is no longer current, the designated archivist of that administrative body selects records of enduring value for preservation. Larger governments, institutions and corporations maintain their own archives. The archives of smaller bodies are often deposited under formal agreement with an appropriate public archives, federal, provincial, municipal, or university. Similarly, individuals in any walk of life may create records of permanent value to society. In Canada, such personal collections are treated as archival, complementing the official record and documenting the diversity of Canadian society. Most of the public archives as well as some universities and libraries actively seek out such private materials related to their areas of interest.

"Archives" has yet a second meaning. It refers to the institutions or organizational units responsible for maintaining the archival record. An archive in this sense has 4 functions. First, it appraises recorded information for its value, selects that which is permanent, and acquires this portion through formal transfer. Second, the archive conserves the record, by preserving intrinsically valuable documents in their original physical form or by transferring the information to a permanent documentary form. Third, an archive arranges and describes the records in its keeping. The archival principles of arrangement, "provenance" and "respect des fonds," recognize that the archival record is most appropriately kept in its original order, reflecting the manner and context in which it came into being. The tools of archival description are collectively and appropriately termed "finding aids" and include main entry card catalogues, indices, file and shelf lists, inventories, institutional guides and, in Canada, the *Union List of Manuscripts in Canadian Repositories* (2 vols, 1975 and supplements) and the *Guide to Canadian Photographic Archives* (1984). Finally, a functioning archive endeavours to make its records publicly accessible. On occasion, access to archives may be limited by terms, usually of defined duration, imposed to protect recent confidential information, by regulations respecting the protection of personal privacy, or by copyright considerations. However, for the most part, Canadian archives are open to all, encouraging those seriously interested in research to draw on their resources. Most Canadian archives respond to written inquiries and provide copies of their records at cost to assist research. Some are able to provide extended research hours or engage in exhibition, adult education and publication programs.

Archives are an essential aspect of contemporary society for several reasons. The ancient role of archives remains: documenting the rights of governments, corporate bodies and individuals within society. Proof of personal property rights, or eligibility for pension benefits as much as international boundary disputes have rested on the integrity of the archival record. Government, in all its forms, has played a substantial role in the life of every citizen. From the broad development of public policy, to taxation and spending, to government decisions on immigration, conscription, social assistance, development grants, municipal

zoning, and a host of other matters affecting individuals, official records show how the government has fulfilled the public trust. In a democratic society, there exists a basic right to have such records appropriately preserved and to have public access to the government's archives. Archives, when linked to records management programs, perform a valuable administrative function. By applying a systematic approach to handling often bulky administrative information, government and corporate archives have reduced the need for office space and records storage equipment, while simplifying reference to previous decisions or policies. Finally, archives form a basic cultural resource. They preserve in the most direct way possible the thoughts of previous generations. Ideally, an archive mirrors the organization or community on which it is based. Its collections attempt to reflect all aspects of the complex past. Like any memory, it can be drawn upon in diverse ways, providing the foundation for virtually all historical activity.

The Canadian archival tradition derives from the dual administrative and cultural roles of archives in society. The natural concern of government to preserve essential records for administrative and legal purposes can be traced to NEW FRANCE, with a proposal for the appointment of a custodian of the archives in 1724 and a suggestion by the intendant, Gilles Hocquart, for a special archive building in 1731. The Legislative Council of Quebec passed an ordinance in 1790 "For the Better Preservation and due Distribution of the Ancient French Records" to gather records concerning property and "to give cheap and easy access to them." Such initiatives were sporadic and isolated. At Confederation, the Dept of the Secretary of State was assigned the chancellery responsibility "to keep all State records and papers." An official, Henry J. Morgan, was duly appointed to this Records Branch, and served from 1875 to 1883.

The LITERARY AND HISTORICAL SOCIETY OF QUEBEC was formed in 1824 and began an active program of research and publication, assisted in 1832 by the first of a series of grants from the Legislative Assembly of Lower Canada. Members of the society visited Paris, London and New York in their efforts to locate and transcribe historical documents relating to Canada. During the 1850s, the Library of Parliament became closely involved in these efforts, extending the search to include pioneer reminiscences of Upper Canada and the WAR OF 1812.

Canada was not the only province interested in archival matters prior to Confederation. The NS legislature approved a motion by Joseph HOWE, leading to the appointment of T.B. Akins as records commissioner in 1857.

Four years after Confederation, the Quebec Literary and Historical Society again took the initiative by petitioning the new federal government to establish an archive to assist "authors and literary inquirers." In 1872 the government responded. An Archives Branch was formed in the Dept of Agriculture and a journalist, Douglas Brymner, was appointed. Brymner, regarded as Canada's first Dominion Archivist, brought extraordinary enthusiasm and zeal to the task. Until his death in 1902, Brymner pursued his "noble dream," seeking to "obtain from all sources private as well as public, such documents as may throw light on social, commercial, municipal, as well as purely political history." With the limited resources available to him, the archivist obtained a major series of War Office records and acquired or located records, papers and pamphlets. Brymner extended earlier sporadic efforts with a program to transcribe, by hand, the records of Canada's colonial past in the British Museum, the Public Record Office and the Archives nationales. Calendars of

Types of documents held at the National Archives of Canada, Ottawa, c1986 (*courtesy National Archives of Canada/PPB/K-0000004*).

many of these institutions were published in the archive's annual reports. As students and scholars took up the study of Canadian history they found a significant resource in the growing archives and a willing colleague in Brymner.

The National Archives of Canada Following the recommendations of a federal commission concerned about the state of government records, the 2 archival programs, the Records Branch of the Dept of the Secretary of State and the Archives Branch of the Dept of Agriculture, merged in 1903. Arthur G. DOUGHTY was appointed in 1904 as both Dominion Archivist and keeper of the records, with a mandate as inclusive as Brymner's "noble dream."

Over the next 31 years, under Doughty's lively leadership, the Archives expanded in size, scope and staff. The program was recognized by statute in 1912, giving the NATIONAL ARCHIVES OF CANADA (called Public Archives of Canada until 1987) full departmental status. A fireproof archive building, opened in 1906 and expanded in 1926, quickly filled. The overseas copying program grew more systematic and the search for Canadian materials expanded to other European repositories. The descendants, French and English, of colonial governors, administrators and generals responded generously to Doughty's fervent appeals for historical records. Within Canada, the Archives established offices for a time in Montréal, Québec City, Trois-Rivières, Saint John, Halifax and Winnipeg, locating, copying or acquiring archival materials. Maps, pictures of all kinds, and even nonarchival museum objects formed part of Doughty's "storehouse" of Canadian history.

Government records began being transferred to the National Archives in quantity. A royal commission in 1912 recommended a more formal records program for the federal government, but the outbreak of war in 1914 postponed the construction of a suitable records storage building. Despite repeated efforts, a formal records program eluded the Archives until the 1950s.

Even so, the growing collection had its impact on the teaching and writing of Canadian history. The advice of historians was sought through the Historical Manuscripts Commission (formed 1907) and in editing a new series of documentary publications. One of Doughty's own dreams for a new approach to Canadian HISTORIOGRAPHY was realized in 1913-17 with the publication of the ambitious 23-volume series CANADA AND ITS PROVINCES. From 1911 to 1920 scholarships were offered to senior university students to spend the summer at the Archives studying original sources. This was followed in the next 2 decades by a graduate course in Canadian history held at the Archives. For the generation of historical scholars after WWI, the Archives became their summer meeting place, to research, exchange ideas, organize the profession, plan new publica-

tions, and renew enthusiasm before returning to their winter vigils teaching Canadian history, often alone, at scattered universities.

The Archives' programs slowed with the Great Depression. Doughty retired in 1935, honoured by a knighthood; and, at his death, by a statue. His successor, Gustave Lanctôt, shifted the Archives' acquisition focus slightly to emphasize post-Confederation materials and introduced new documentary media with motion-picture film and sound recordings.

Supported by the obvious magnitude of the postwar proliferation of records and by the strong recommendations of the Massey Commission (1951), a new dynamic Dominion Archivist, W. Kaye LAMB, succeeded in giving the archives a central role in a modern records management system for the federal government. The opening of a federal records centre in Ottawa (1956), followed in recent decades by similar regional records centres across Canada, marked a new era for the Archives. The merging of a multimedia cultural archives and a government record office, begun in 1903, became reality. The Archives, under Dr Lamb, his successor Wilfred I. Smith, and their increasingly numerous and professional staff, flourished. Canada's CENTENNIAL YEAR provided the occasion for a long-awaited move to an elegant new building, shared with the NATIONAL LIBRARY OF CANADA. Traditional programs were given new life, as the acquisition of private manuscripts, records and documentary art was placed on a more systematic basis. Earlier efforts were formalized as the National Map Collection, the National Photography Collection, the National Film, Television and Sound Archives, architectural archives, ethnocultural archives, and conservation services assumed greater importance. In 1987 the National Archives of Canada Act changed the name of the institution but provided a solid legal foundation for its traditional roles. New technologies were adapted to archival service. In the 1950s microphotography enabled the Paris and London offices to obtain complete and accurate copies of records series in place of the selective and fallible handwritten copies so painstakingly produced since 1880. Microfilm also provided an economical means of duplicating unique records for security or for consultation across the country. More recently, the establishment of a Machine Readable Archives and experiments in applying digitized laser disc recording to preserving information have made the National Archives a world leader in the archival implications of new technology.

The Archival System The early example of the PAC was not lost upon the provinces. Indeed, its achievements and emphases provided a pattern followed by many of our provincial, municipal and institutional archives. NS's pre-Confederation archival initiatives were reconfirmed by a statute in 1929 and the opening of an archive building in 1931. Ontario established a provincial archive in 1903 and reinforced its program with an archives Act in 1923. The Bureau des archives du Québec (now the Archives nationales du Québec) was established in 1920 and embarked on an impressive program of acquisitions and publications. In other provinces – BC, Alberta, Saskatchewan, Manitoba, PEI and NB – archival activity began in their legislative libraries through the more or less formal interest of their librarians. The BC archives emerged as an identifiable unit in 1908, but for the others, archival activity was rudimentary through the 1920s and 1930s.

The explosion of administrative records both in volume and in physical form, which provided the impetus for the federal archives' growth after WWII, has been equally noticeable in provinces,

municipalities, businesses, universities and, indeed, in all administrative agencies. To cope with this growth, many organizations have established archives and records management programs. Where earlier archives may have grown from cultural inspiration, administrative necessity has loomed large in the proliferation of archives in recent years.

Archival legislation in Saskatchewan in 1945 and 1955 provided a model for others in dealing with provincial records. Ontario, particularly in the decade 1965-75, developed an excellent records management program. By 1968, each of the provinces had established archives and, since that date, each has obtained new or renovated facilities with suitable environmental and security controls (*see* CONSERVATION OF MOVABLE CULTURAL PROPERTY). Significant legislative advances have been achieved with the passage of new archives Acts in NB (1977), Québec (1983) and Newfoundland (1983). Only BC remains without archival legislation. The provincial archives have been joined by archives in the Yukon (1972) and the NWT (1979). Indeed, the last 2 decades have witnessed a considerable expansion of archival activity. The Archives nationales du Québec has established 8 regional offices in the province. Several larger cities now have significant archives programs (Toronto, Vancouver, Edmonton, Calgary, Ottawa). Most universities have archives to preserve their own records while a number, either through their archives or libraries, have developed major research collections: FOLKLORE archives have been gathered at Memorial, Laval and Laurentian; literary papers at Queen's, McMaster and Calgary; and regional collections have evolved at Université de Moncton, Queen's, Western Ontario, Manitoba, Brandon and UBC. Churches, banks, insurance corporations and oil companies have formed their own corporate archives, while a number of museums, historical societies and libraries have endeavoured to provide archival service to their communities.

A report, *Canadian Archives,* published by the SOCIAL SCIENCES AND HUMANITIES RESEARCH COUNCIL OF CANADA in 1980, highlighted the widening interest in archives and the importance of archives to CANADIAN STUDIES. While archival activity has increased, so have both the complexity and volume of the archival record and the research demands placed on the system. The traditional scholarly archival clientele is now outnumbered by the genealogists, local historians, heritage activists, teachers, radio and television producers and journalists, all of whom archivists have encouraged. To cope, the 1980 report recommended the formation of provincial networks of archives to share reference information and specialized facilities, supported by various federal services co-ordinated by the National Archives. The Canadian Council of Archives (1985) and recently established provincial councils have begun co-operative projects designed to improve archival services across the country.

The proliferation of archives in recent years has been accompanied by the emergence of an archival profession. An Archives Section was formed within the CANADIAN HISTORICAL ASSN in 1956. It encouraged the development of an archives course at Carleton U and began publication of *The Canadian Archivist*. In 1967 the Assn des archivistes du Québec was formed, bringing professional and amateur archivists together in a vigorous association with its own publication, *Archives*. The Archives Section evolved into the Assn of Canadian Archivists (1975), and its journal, *Archivaria,* has grown in scope and content. Both associations, loosely joined in the Bureau of Canadian Archivists, and the emerging provincial archival associations have devoted considerable attention to basic problems: education, training, descriptive standards, copyright, freedom of information and government policies as they affect archives. For entry into the profession, a Master of Archival Studies program has developed at UBC and various courses and diploma courses are available in library schools, universities and colleges.   IAN E. WILSON

Reading: Archives, Libraries and the Canadian Heritage: Essays in Honour of W. Kaye Lamb, Archivaria 15 (winter 1982-83); Archives: Mirror of Canada's Past, intro by W.I. Smith (1972); Canadian Archives, Report to the Social Sciences and Humanities Research Council of Canada, by the Consultative Group on Canadians Archives (1980); C. Couture and J-Y. Rousseau, Les Archives au XXe siècle. Une réponse aux besoins de l'administration et de la recherche (1982).

Arctic Animals are animals that have adapted, physically and behaviourally, to the particular conditions of life in the most northerly region of Earth. The Arctic can be defined in various ways. Geographically, it is that part of the world lying N of the ARCTIC CIRCLE (66° 32' N lat) beyond which there is at least one day in the year in which the sun never sets and one in which it never rises. Ecological definitions invoke the major discontinuities: on land, the major break is the TREELINE; in the sea, it is where the characteristically low-salinity arctic waters meet Atlantic and Pacific waters in zones of upwelling and mixing. Typically, the lives of terrestrial and aquatic members of the arctic fauna are closely linked. The sea provides a food source for land birds (from snow buntings to whistling swans) that forage in spring on seaweed windrows on storm beaches; winter ice provides access to marine life for arctic foxes, wolves and polar bears. Conversely, many marine animals (from murres to walrus) use parts of the land for mating and raising young; others, such as the ringed seal and the ivory gull, can raise their young on ice and can thus be independent of the terrestrial environment.

The arctic land fauna resembles more familiar faunas of the northern temperate zones; fewer species are present, but they are generally of the same orders and families as those farther south. The deficiencies arise for several reasons. On land, mean annual temperatures are below freezing and the ground remains frozen at depth; therefore, no warm layer persists near the surface through the winter. Hence, reptiles and most hibernating mammals are not found N of the line of continuous permafrost. Because trees are absent, certain boreal-zone insects, rodents, carnivores and birds that depend on them for food and shelter disappear. Open water is scarce in the Arctic throughout most of the year. Except where rapids and tide-rips occur, solid ice or dense pack generally forbids access to the aquatic environment. Animals wintering on the arctic TUNDRA must quench their thirst with snow. Fish-eating birds and mammals typically migrate for the winter to areas providing better access to prey; the remainder concentrate at the scattered polynyas (ice-free refuges).

The characteristic that most restricts opportunities for animal life may be the brevity of the arctic growing season. The land VEGETATION produced in the few, but long, days of the arctic summer must sustain life over an extended, harsh and demanding winter. It is hardly surprising that the most mobile animals pass the winter elsewhere: birds on ocean coasts farther S and in interior plains and forest lands; and many barren-ground caribou on lichen pastures of the open BOREAL FOREST. The short growing season tends to squeeze certain species out of arctic ecosystems entirely. Beyond the edge of the barrens, it is rare to encounter the plagues of blackflies inevitable

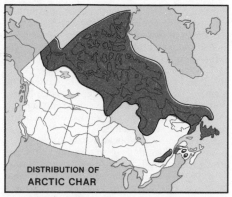

DISTRIBUTION OF
ARCTIC CHAR

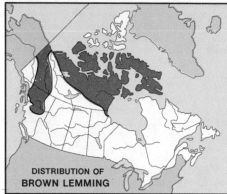

DISTRIBUTION OF
BROWN LEMMING

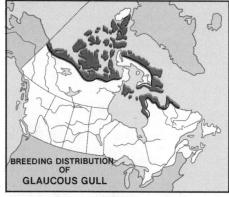

BREEDING DISTRIBUTION
OF
GLAUCOUS GULL

DISTRIBUTION OF
POLAR BEAR

in the boreal forest. The absence of bats and swallows might be attributed to the very short period in which flying insects are available as food.

Another serious constraint is the dangerous heat loss caused by low winter temperature and high windchill. This factor imposes on warm-blooded animals the need for a thick, dense, insulating coat, which means that surface-wintering arctic animals must generally be large. The larger the animal, the greater the body-mass to skin-surface ratio and the smaller the relative heat loss. Northern ravens and arctic foxes are the smallest animals found above the snow surface during the arctic winter. Hard-packed snow denies the use of

drifts for shelter to groups, from grouse to ungulates, which use the softer drifts of the boreal zone for that purpose. Animals using the solid arctic snow drifts for shelter include the collared or varying lemming, which grows special winter claws for the purpose, and the polar bear, which burrows in for its winter and maternity dens. The ringed seal is unique in constructing its maternity den in snow on the surface of land-fast sea ice.

Although food sources may be few, sparse and evanescent, combinations of many provide livings for several successful arctic animals. Most arctic species are quite opportunistic. To the south, insects typically feed on one plant species only and birds and mammals have relatively fixed diets; in the Arctic, exploitation of broader food resources (ie, trophic niches) is common. The polar bear provides one example. Bears are typically omnivorous. Polar bears are amphibious and able to subsist on very diverse and meagre resources, both terrestrial and aquatic, for long periods each year. Among birds, the long-tailed jaeger is equally well adapted, being for the brief arctic summer an eater of terrestrial arthropods (especially spiders and midges), a bird hunter (particularly of nestlings), a lemming catcher, a sea-food gatherer of the tidal flats and a carrion seeker.

The modern Canadian arctic land fauna may be traced back to the Pleistocene epoch (*see* ICE AGE). A few thousand years ago, during the last continental GLACIATION, thick sheets of ice covered most of Canada and much of the northern US. Arctic animals have descended from species that occupied land that was revegetating after the retreat of the ice. At least 2 sources of origin are evident: the west, where ice-free land extended from the YT and Alaska, under what is now the Bering Sea; and the south, which can be visualized as a zone, like that near the foot of a modern glacier, subject to cycles of improvement and deterioration. Presumably, the brown lemming, grizzly bear and barren-ground caribou came from the west; the tundra vole, red fox and moose from the south. A few species, including the Peary caribou, which may resemble more closely the Svalbard reindeer than other N American caribou; and the large, upright-hopping arctic hares of the Queen Elizabeth Is and northern and eastern Greenland, seem likely to have come from a third, high-arctic source area. Polar bears and arctic foxes are so at home on sea ice that they live wherever the ice pack has reached the shore.

Compared to the land, sea and lake waters remain within a narrow temperature range year-round. However, the seasonal fall in temperature affects the aquatic environment profoundly by causing surface water to freeze to a depth of 2 m or more. Ice, particularly when covered with snow, impedes penetration into water of the solar radiation necessary for photosynthesis. Furthermore, bottom freezing and scouring by drifting ice floes greatly reduces the productivity of arctic intertidal and near-shore marine zones. Marine productivity is comparatively low, limited by temperature and the availability of nutrients and light. Because of limited winter productivity, several populations of marine mammals winter in more productive open seas.

Marine vegetation includes benthic and planktonic algae (ie, seafloor and free-floating forms) and algae that live within the lower levels and coat the submerged surfaces of floating ice. This living material feeds the zooplankton preyed upon by arctic and polar cod, by birds such as murres and guillemots, and by marine mammals such as the ringed seal. Algae also feed the molluscs, which sustain the walrus. The predators highest in the food chains of the arctic seas are polar bears and killer whales; important scavengers include glaucous gulls, amphipod crustaceans (which attack fish and seal carcasses left too long in nets) and Greenland shark (lethargic fish attaining lengths of about 3 m). The arctic char, the most important arctic food fish, lives its first year in lakes but, where passage exists, takes up an anadromous habit in later life: ie, it migrates to coastal waters for the summer to feed voraciously on crustaceans and other small marine animals, and returns to spawn in lakes in autumn.

The arctic fauna forms the basis for local subsistence economies and, being partly migratory, supports food, trade and recreation elsewhere in the world. Snow gccsc hatched in the Canadian Arctic are hunted as far S as the rice fields of Texas; harp seal populations, which summer in arctic waters, are harvested in the Gulf of St Lawrence. The earliest known arctic peoples used small stone blades and points suitable for killing thin-skinned game, eg, caribou and birds. Later cultures depended on sea mammals, particularly the bowhead or Greenland whale. This, the largest arctic species, was greatly reduced by American and Scottish WHALING in the late 1800s, and is now the only truly endangered arctic mammal. The Inuit of the historical era have largely been dependent on sea mammals, particularly the ringed seal, which stays in the frozen arctic bays and straits all winter, scratching breathing holes through the ice. The hunter would wait at a hole and harpoon the animal as it rose to the surface. Seals provided fuel (seal oil), skins (used for summer boots and tents) and meat. Warm clothing has always been essential in the Arctic; the bearskin winter trousers of the Greenland hunter have been as distinctive as the guardsman's busby. Caribou killed in Aug, when the hair is still short and fine, provided the most popular clothing skins. Muskox robes and skins of caribou killed in winter were used for bedding. The trade in arctic fox furs began in earnest in the early 1900s. Because both the fox populations and the value of the furs fluctuate so greatly from year to year, trapping in the Arctic yields an uncertain return.

With social and industrial development, CONSERVATION of arctic fauna has demanded increased attention. Recent developments include restrictions by the US on the import of sea-mammal products; imposition by the International Whaling Commission of quotas on the take of bowheads by Alaskan Eskimos; signing of an international convention on the conservation of the polar bear (particularly on the high seas) by the US, Norway, Denmark, the USSR and Canada; and the development of means in Canada to involve northerners more directly in the conservation of the barren-ground caribou vital to their lives. The economies of active villages dependent on cash from sales of wild furs are increasingly menaced by international "animal rights" lobby groups, though some of these now recognize that rights cannot be conferred but only reallocated, in this case from fellow human societies to animal populations, or vice versa. However, the growing interest in oil exploration and production, offshore drilling and year-round shipping is of the greatest concern to environmentalists and native groups. Other threats to arctic animals may include the impact of pollutants, industrial and military, from the south on more fragile ecosystems, and more harvesting pressure as human populations grow. *See also* ANIMALS IN WINTER.

A.H. MACPHERSON

Reading: F. Bruemmer, *Encounters with Arctic Animals* (1972).

Arctic Archipelago Lying N of mainland Canada, these islands, the largest group in the world, cover 1.3 million km² with their intervening wa-

Bache Peninsula on the east coast of Ellesmere Island, NWT, 3rd-largest island in Canada and most northerly in the Arctic Archipelago (*photo by Stephen J. Krasemann/ DRK Photo*).

ters. They contain 6 of the world's 30 largest islands, including BAFFIN I, the fifth largest. They are separated by "channels," some of which would qualify as seas elsewhere in the world. PARRY CHANNEL which runs from LANCASTER SOUND to M'Clure Str and divides the northern QUEEN ELIZABETH ISLANDS from the rest, is an important part of the NORTHWEST PASSAGE. The main islands, and groups of islands, are BANKS, VICTORIA, PRINCE OF WALES, SOMERSET and Baffin islands and the Queen Elizabeth group including the SVERDRUP and PARRY islands and ELLESMERE I.

Some of the islands, especially those towards the E, are mountainous, with peaks over 2000 m. The higher land on these islands is commonly occupied by ice caps that contain most of Canada's glacier ice and from which flow Canada's largest GLACIERS. The southeastern archipelago consists of north-thrusting prongs of the Canadian SHIELD, separated by fairly flat-lying Paleozoic rocks. The northern part, including most of the Queen Elizabeth Is, consists of younger, heavily folded sedimentary rocks, producing mountains on islands such as AXEL HEIBERG and parts of DEVON and Ellesmere in the centre and E. This geological variety produces spectacular variations in scenery, with rugged "old" and "new" mountains and high and low plains of various ages and rock types. Perhaps it is the sedimentary rocks that make this area of Canada so distinctive; elsewhere most of arctic and subarctic Canada is dominated by the Shield. The sedimentary rocks contain few metallic minerals, but may well contain huge deposits of oil and natural gas as well as the coal discovered by early explorers.

Apart from Greenland, which is almost entirely ice covered (and geologically an extension of the archipelago), the Canadian Arctic Archipelago forms the world's largest high-arctic land area. By any measure, this is a truly polar environment. In the northern islands, night lasts 3 or 4 months in winter and day lasts the same period in summer. The Queen Elizabeth Is are a polar desert, with often much less than 13 cm of precipitation a year. The average annual temperature may be as low as -20°C in the N and -6°C in southern Baffin I, with extreme low temperatures in the order of -50°C. Summer temperatures may rise above freezing for one or 2 months. The PERMAFROST exceeds 550 m in thickness and may in places reach 1000 m.

The vegetation is formed largely of low sedges, mosses and grasses, with occasional dwarf wil-

lows. At some favoured locations plant life can be lush and in the short flowering season the vegetation is quite beautiful. Only 17 species of land mammals live in the archipelago, generally in small numbers restricted to certain areas. The island CARIBOU – the special Peary Caribou that are smaller and whiter than the mainland variety – live in small herds and do not migrate like their mainland cousins. Other large animals in the archipelago are the MUSKOX, arctic fox, WOLF, LEMMING and white arctic hare. Only 64 species of birds spend the summer in the high-arctic islands and only 6 species overwinter there. The surrounding seas are home to the polar bear, the walrus and various types of seal and whale, including the NARWHAL and the beluga.

The High Arctic has been occupied by the INUIT and their predecessors for thousands of years, and today they live in settlements scattered throughout the islands, generally on the sea. Ancient links with the Greenlandic people are still maintained. Evidence has been found of contact between the Vikings, who lived in Greenland during the Middle Ages, and the islands (*see* NORSE VOYAGES). The non-Inuit population is made up of government and military personnel in settlements such as IQALUIT, RESOLUTE and ALERT. PETER ADAMS

Arctic Archipelago Channels

The seawaters of the Arctic Archipelago were first sighted by William BAFFIN, who sailed into Smith Sound and northern BAFFIN BAY in 1616 and who first recorded Jones Sound and Lancaster Sound, which is the eastern entrance to the NORTHWEST PASSAGE. In 1819 Sir William PARRY sailed through the W as far as M'Clure Str, where he was stopped by ice. The Northwest Passage was finally sailed by Roald AMUNDSEN 1903-06 and again by Sgt LARSEN of the RCMP 1940-42 (W-E) and 1944 (E-W). The waters N of Baffin Bay, now known as Nares Str, were explored from 1852 on. Very little scientific OCEANOGRAPHY was done in the Arctic Islands until after WWII, although an excellent pioneer expedition under Otto SVERDRUP 1898-1902 produced important geological and biological results. Danish expeditions and US Coastguard *Marion* in 1928 made oceanographic studies in Smith, Jones and Lancaster sounds.

The depths of the channels range from less than 200 m to about 800 m in eastern Lancaster Sound. The most important sill (minimum) depths, related to water transport, are 140 m in Barrow Str and 250 m in Nares Str. The Continental Shelf varies from over 550 m in depth in the W and N to 200 m in the E. In spite of low tidal ranges, which decrease from E to W, tidal currents can be strong in certain narrow passages, such as Bellot Str, Fury and Hecla Str and Hell Gate. The dominant water flow through the islands is from the Arctic Ocean southward through Nares Str and eastward through Lancaster Sound and Fury and Hecla Str. The first 2 currents flow into Baffin Bay and the latter into Foxe Basin, Hudson Bay and Hudson Str. The most recent estimate of the total transport of Arctic Ocean water through the islands is 2.1 million m³/s, but there is probably considerable annual variation. The depth and extent of the channels offer commercial possibilities (for submarine tankers) as well as some strategic concern (as an avenue of approach for submarines).

Ice cover, with an average thickness from 1.6 m to 2 m, is complete in winter throughout the archipelago, with the exception of several recurring polynyas (areas of open water surrounded by sea ice), the largest of which are in northern Baffin Bay and in the southeastern BEAUFORT SEA. These polynyas, which freeze late and thaw early, are a focus for marine and bird life and there is evidence of early human habitation, by the THULE and DORSET peoples, on the landmasses adjoining them. Biologically the waters of the archipelago are rich in mammals and birds (in summer) and poor in fishes. The plankton is typical of that of the upper 250 m of the Arctic Ocean.   M.J. DUNBAR

Arctic Bay, NWT, Hamlet (1976), pop 477 (1986c), is located on the N shore of Adams Sound, off Admiralty Inlet, northern Baffin Island, 1674 air km NE of Yellowknife. Situated on a low gravel beach surrounded on 3 sides by high hills, this community has been occupied by nomadic Inuit hunters during several stages over the past 5000 years. The Inuit call it Ikpiarjuk, which translates into "bag" or "pocket" and is a reference to the sheltered location of the community. The English name is derived from the whaling ship *Arctic* which visited the site in 1872. In 1938, Rev Paul Schulte conducted the first arctic mercy flight when he flew here to rescue a sick missionary. A Department of Transport weather station operated here between 1942 and 1952 and provided year-round employment for the Inuit. This was an incentive for them to settle in one place. A lead-zinc mine nearby, at NANISIVIK, has transformed the community into a predominately wage-employed society.   EDWARD STRUZIK

Arctic Circle, a parallel of latitude 66° 32′ N; similarly, the Antarctic Circle is the parallel of latitude 66° 32′ S. Between these circles the SUN rises and sets daily. N of the Arctic Circle the sun remains above the horizon at midnight at midsummer and never rises at midwinter. Since light rays are bent by the Earth's atmosphere, the sun can be seen when it is slightly below the horizon. Thus, the midwinter sun can be seen at places slightly N of the circle. The number of days the sun stays above (or below) the horizon increases the farther N one goes until, at the pole, the sun never sets for 6 months and never rises during the other 6. These effects occur because the Earth's axis of rotation is tilted relative to the plane of its orbit around the sun. During the northern winter, when the Northern Hemisphere is tilted away from the sun, the Earth's curvature creates an area of permanent shadow centered on the North Pole. This area starts to form at the fall equinox (Sept 22), grows to a maximum at midwinter,

HMS *Assistance* and HMS *Pioneer*, engaged in the search for Franklin under the command of Sir Edward Belcher, shown in winter quarters, Devon I, 1853. The Franklin search led to a great expansion of knowledge of the Arctic (*courtesy National Archives of Canada/C-41305*).

then decreases, vanishing by the spring equinox (Mar 21). For the remainder of the year, when the Northern Hemisphere is tilted towards the sun, an area of permanent sunlight centres on the pole. Because the tilt of the Earth's axis is about 23.5°, the Arctic and Antarctic circles lie at latitudes of about 66.5°. The Arctic Circle is not a climatic boundary. Trees grow N of it in the Mackenzie Delta; in Nouveau-Québec the TREELINE is 1000 km farther S. INUVIK, NWT, is the only moderately large Canadian settlement lying N of the circle.
W.S.B. PATERSON

Arctic Exploration began in the Elizabethan era when English seamen sought a shortcut to the Spice Is of the Far East by the seas north of America – the so-called NORTHWEST PASSAGE. Martin FROBISHER in 3 voyages (1576, 1577 and 1578) found the way blocked by Baffin I. Seeking to round this obstacle, John DAVIS (1585, 1586 and 1587) explored Cumberland Gulf (now Sound) and found the entrance to Hudson Str, which was to conduct Henry HUDSON (1610) into his bay. In 1616 Robert BYLOT and William BAFFIN explored Baffin Bay, sighting the westward-leading channels of Jones and Lancaster sounds. Owing to ice-covered seas and mirage, they mistakenly judged them to be closed bays, a common error among arctic explorers. The arctic littoral of N America remained unexplored for the next 2 centuries. Samuel HEARNE (1771) by the Coppermine R, and Alexander MACKENZIE (1789) by the Mackenzie R, barely reached arctic tidewater and learned nothing of adjoining coasts. Of the vast ARCTIC ARCHIPELAGO to the N, only isolated stretches of Baffin I's E shore had come to light.

In 1818 the British ADMIRALTY renewed its search for the NW Passage. That year John ROSS rounded Baffin Bay but, like Baffin, believed that Lancaster Sound was just a bay. In 1819-20 W.E. PARRY proved the sound to be the gateway to unknown western seas. Hampered by ice, he sailed 800 km along Parry Channel (Lancaster Sound, Barrow Str and Viscount Melville Sound) to Melville I, where he wintered. Across the ice-choked Viscount Melville Sound he obtained a distant view of Banks I. On a later voyage he entered Prince Regent Inlet, where he lost a ship in the ice. The summers were very short, and it was found that a sailing ship could stay at sea for barely 2 months before being immobilized by ice.

To the S, between 1819 and 1839, canoe and boat parties under John FRANKLIN and later Thomas Simpson explored a channel along the

continental shore from Bering Str to Boothia Isthmus. In 1845 Franklin sailed from England to link this channel with Parry Channel, intending thus to complete the NW Passage. His 2 ships never returned, and were for several years unreported. Numerous rescue parties were sent (1848-54) by Britain and the US. The search for the missing crews could not be done thoroughly by ships icebound for most of the year. Small parties hauling equipment and supplies on sledges sought evidence. Although unsuccessful in their assigned task, these parties mapped much of the Canadian archipelago.

John RAE and Richard Collinson explored and mapped the island coasts nearest the continental shore, while 4 crews of Capt Horatio Austin's squadron (1850-51) did the same on both sides of Parry Channel. Other expeditions mapped parts of Somerset and Victoria islands, and gave shape to the S coasts of Devon, Bathurst and Melville islands. Sir Edward BELCHER explored (1852-54) the N shores of the latter 3. The great sledge traveller Leopold MCCLINTOCK, helped by G.F. Mecham, discovered Eglinton and Prince Patrick islands in a return journey of over 2100 km.

The most dramatic voyage in polar history was made by the rescue ship *Investigator*. Having sailed from Plymouth, Eng, on 20 Jan 1850, it rounded S America and entered the Arctic Ocean by way of Bering Str. Its captain, Robert MCCLURE, discovered Prince of Wales Str and travelled through it to the NE angle of Parry's Banks I – thus completing the NW Passage. McClure had, by an alternate route, accomplished what Franklin had died attempting: he had connected Parry's voyage of penetration from the E with Franklin's coastal survey from the W. However, he rashly put his ship into the heavy ice pack, which had stopped Parry. His ship was repeatedly thrown over on its side by gale-driven ice masses. In Sept 1851 he found refuge in the Bay of Mercy on Banks I's N shore, where the *Investigator* was frozen in for 18 months. Its crew was reduced to extreme want, and would have perished but for the timely arrival of a detachment of Belcher's squadron under Capt Henry KELLETT.

This and other strenuous endeavours continued the search for Franklin. Rae (1851) and

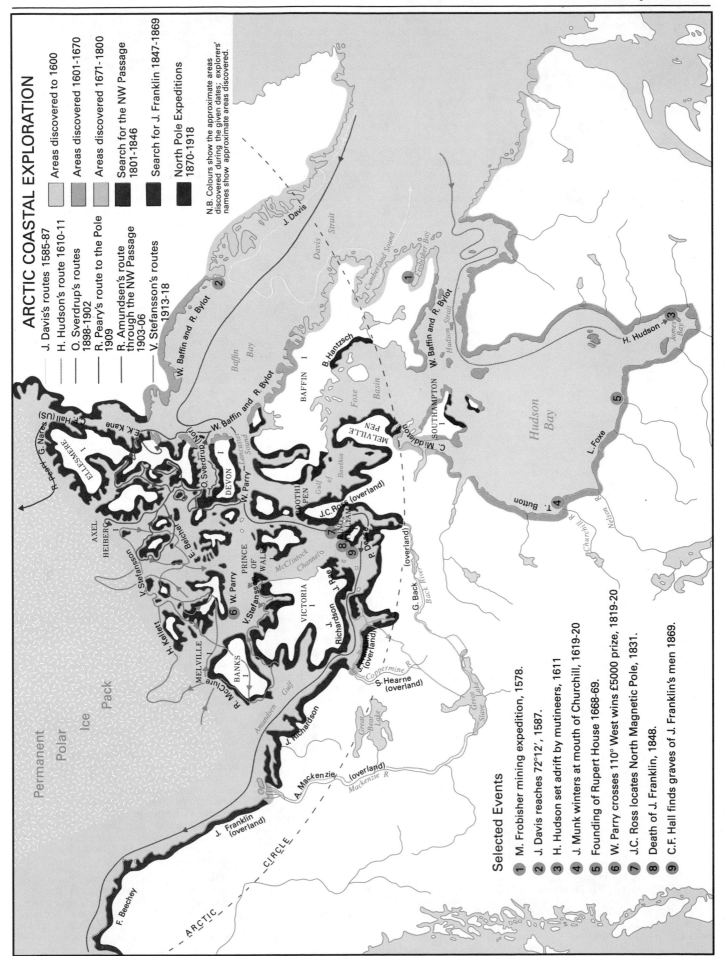

ARCTIC COASTAL EXPLORATION

Areas discovered to 1600

Areas discovered 1601-1670

Areas discovered 1671-1800

Search for the NW Passage
1801-1846

Search for J. Franklin 1847-1869

North Pole Expeditions
1870-1918

J. Davis's routes 1585-87

H. Hudson's route 1610-11

O. Sverdrup's routes
1898-1902

R. Peary's route to the Pole
1909

R. Amundsen's route
through the NW Passage
1903-06

V. Stefansson's routes
1913-18

N.B. Colours show the approximate areas
discovered during the given dates; explorers'
names show approximate areas discovered.

Selected Events

1 M. Frobisher mining expedition, 1578.
2 J. Davis reaches 72°12′, 1587.
3 H. Hudson set adrift by mutineers, 1611.
4 J. Munk winters at mouth of Churchill, 1619-20.
5 Founding of Rupert House 1668-69.
6 W. Parry crosses 110° West wins £5000 prize, 1819-20.
7 J.C. Ross locates North Magnetic Pole, 1831.
8 Death of J. Franklin, 1848.
9 C.F. Hall finds graves of J. Franklin's men 1869.

Skirmish with Eskimos by John White, who accompanied Martin Frobisher to the Arctic in 1577. White's paintings are now recognized as masterpieces of their kind (*courtesy Trustees of the British Museum*).

Collinson (1853) had come near success but had turned back at the approach of winter. In 1854 Rae learned from Inuit that years previously many Europeans had died on western King William I and on the adjacent mainland. In 1859 McClintock reached the island by ship and sledge and ascertained that Franklin's vessels had been frozen in in that region. The crews had perished of hunger and scurvy while trekking for the mainland. McClintock also filled in certain gaps in his predecessors' maps, tracing almost completely the coasts in the archipelago up to 77° N.

Discovery farther N was largely the work of Americans and Scandinavians. Englishman E.A. Inglefield and Americans E.K. KANE, I. Hayes and C.F. HALL opened up the channel between Greenland and Ellesmere I, and the survey of Ellesmere's E shore was completed by the 1875-76 British polar expedition under G.S. NARES. In 1876 P. Aldrich rounded the top of Ellesmere and named the northernmost point of what is now Canadian territory Cape Columbia. Norwegian Otto SVERDRUP explored the W shore of Ellesmere I (1898-1902) except for a gap filled in by American Robert Peary in 1906. Norwegians in separate groups also surveyed the entire coast of Axel Heiberg I, and to the W discovered and mapped the 2 Ringnes islands and King Christian I, the latter a promising source of natural gas in the 1980s. Sverdrup had accomplished a vast amount with a minimum of mishap or danger. The Norwegians' use of skis and their familiarity with the northern climate gave them a great advantage over their British predecessors. This was illustrated in the 1913-18 journeys of Vilhjalmur STEFANSSON, which opened to Europeans the last lands in the Canadian North previously unknown to them. In the employ of the Canadian government he took his ship through Bering Str, where it was crushed in the ice. With ready adaptability he organized a foot party and crossed the hazardous moving ice of the Beaufort Sea to Banks I. Taking to the ice again he put the finishing touch to McClintock's survey of Prince Patrick I, and went NE to discover Brock and Borden islands. The latter was afterwards found to be 2 islands: Borden and Mackenzie King. With the discovery of Meighen I in 1916 Stefansson made the last substantial addition to Canadian territory.

The NW Passage had been traced but its navigation was long deferred, as no sailing ship could hope to get through, nor could a steamer stow enough coal to wrestle its way through the ice pack that was certain to be encountered. From 1903 to 1906 the Norwegian explorer Roald AMUNDSEN, when engaged in a magnetic survey, made use of the internal combustion engine to propel his 80-ton *Gjoa* from ocean to ocean. The voyage of US tanker *Manhattan* in 1969 made it plain that the most nearly usable NW Passage is by way of Parry Channel and Prince of Wales Str.

These explorations have done more for general science than for material interests. There has been little success in extracting seemingly abundant fossil fuels from the northern islands, but the attraction of petroleum and mineral deposits has provided a fresh impetus, and aerial photographs and more detailed maps improved tools, for a new phase of exploration on this Canadian frontier. *See also* EXPLORATION.   LESLIE H. NEATBY

Reading: A. Cooke and C. Holland, *The Exploration of Northern Canada 500-1920* (1978); D. Francis, *Discovery of the North* (1985); S. Milligan and W. Kupsch, *Living Explorers of the Canadian Arctic* (1985); Leslie H. Neatby, *In Quest of the North West Passage* (1958), *Conquest of the Last Frontier* (1966) and *The Search for Franklin* (1970).

Arctic Oceanography The study of OCEANOGRAPHY reveals information about the origin, composition and movements of marine waters; OCEAN basins; interactions with the atmosphere; and the living organisms of the sea, ie, the plants and successive levels of animals that feed on them (*see* MARINE ECOLOGY). The seas of the Canadian Arctic (here defined as reaching from the LABRADOR SEA in the E to the BEAUFORT SEA in the W) are covered by ice for more than half the year. Cold, arctic surface water, originating in the upper 200-300 m of the Arctic Ocean, flows out of the Arctic basin through the Canadian ARCTIC ARCHIPELAGO and between Canada and Greenland towards the Atlantic Ocean. In Baffin Bay, Davis Strait and neighbouring regions, it mixes with warmer water from the Atlantic to form subarctic water. The Subarctic covers a relatively large area in eastern Canada; its western counterpart, formed where Pacific and Arctic waters meet and mix, is restricted to a narrow band along the shore of the Beaufort Sea (*see* COASTAL WATERS). Oceanographic information is obtained from the Arctic for many users, including navigators, hunters and fishermen, petroleum and mine developers, traders and climatologists.

Danish scientists aboard the vessel *Godthaab* and Americans on the *Marion* began oceanographic investigation of waters bordering the eastern Canadian Arctic long before comparable Canadian efforts were launched. In 1930 the Hudson Bay Fisheries Expedition (under H.B. HACHEY), supported by the federal government, provided the first extensive account of circulation and general Physical OCEANOGRAPHY of the Canadian Arctic. In 1948 the Canadian government responded to a need for expanded Canadian oceanographic effort in the Arctic with establishment of the Eastern Arctic Investigations (now the Arctic Biological Station, Ste-Anne-de-Bellevue, Qué). The 15 m research vessel *Calanus* was built in NS in 1948, and a program, mainly of Biological OCEANOGRAPHY, was begun in the eastern Arctic. M.J. DUNBAR was in charge of the survey. In the western Arctic, G.L. PICKARD in 1949 participated in a program in the Bering and Chukchi seas with the US Naval Electronics Laboratory. Co-operative research with US oceanographers began in the early 1950s in the Beaufort Sea. W.M. Maxwell, of the Defence Research Board, played a significant role in this research and survey work. In 1954 HMCS *Labrador* completed a cruise that linked the eastern and western Arctic through the NORTHWEST PASSAGE, culminating in a circumnavigation of N America; a series of eastern arctic cruises followed.

The Polar Continental Shelf Project began in 1959, supporting a wide variety of arctic research projects, including oceanography; this organization continues to provide valuable service. In the same decade, Canadians joined American oceanographers on Ice Island T-3 in the Arctic Ocean. In the 1960s the Frozen Sea Research Group began work; the group was based at the Institute of Ocean Sciences, Victoria. The BEDFORD INSTITUTE OF OCEANOGRAPHY participated in oceanographic surveys in the eastern and central Arctic during the early 1960s, and in 1969-70 continued with the more spectacular *Hudson* cruise around the Americas. A portion of that cruise was spent in the Beaufort Sea. *Hudson* (built 1963) was the first Canadian vessel specially built for oceanographic research. More recently, multidisciplinary ship-based studies have been carried out by the Bedford Institute in the eastern Arctic.

The 1970s saw the beginning of a period of oceanographic study encouraged, at least partly, by questions of possible effects of OIL AND NATURAL GAS exploration on the environment. Studies were concerned with the effects of ocean currents, ocean waves and SEA ICE on vessels and fixed installations, and conversely with the impact of vessels and drill sites on the environment (eg, consequences of oil spills on the biota of arctic seas). The period marked appearance of a high level of nongovernment funding of oceanographic research and the growth of private consultants in a field largely occupied until that time by government-sponsored researchers. The first major study of the new era was the Beaufort Sea Project, jointly sponsored by government and the PETROLEUM INDUSTRY and comprising some 40 projects dealing with all major divisions of oceanography. Other studies followed, including the Eastern Arctic Marine Environmental Studies program (EAMES) in Baffin Bay and Davis Strait, the Offshore Labrador Biological Studies program (OLABS) and the Baffin Island Oil Spill project (BIOS).

In recent years, Canadian oceanographers have participated in a number of arctic studies outside Canadian waters, most of them being international co-operative undertakings. Among them are AIDJEX (Arctic Ice Dynamics Joint Experiment), a Canada-US oceanographic program in the Beaufort Sea; LOREX (Lomonosov Ridge Experiment), FRAM (a series of studies named after the vessel of arctic explorer Fridtjof Nansen), EUBEX (Eurasian Basin Survey) and CESAR, all located in the Arctic Basin; and MIZEX (Marginal Ice Zone Experiment), involving several countries off the East Greenland and Alaskan coasts.   E.H. GRAINGER

Arctic Red River, NWT, Settlement, pop 108 (1986c), 120 (1981c), is situated at the confluence of the Arctic Red and MACKENZIE rivers, 1011 air km NW of YELLOWKNIFE. This tiny community is on a site that was probably a seasonal fishing camp for Loucheux DENE many centuries before European contact. The settlement remained isolated until the late 1970s when construction of the Dempster Hwy gave its residents seasonal access to larger centres. It is the site of the Dempster Hwy ferry across the Mackenzie R. Trapping, hunting and fishing are the occupations of most of its residents.   ANNELIES POOL

Arctic Sovereignty A country's claim to SOVEREIGNTY over land or sea depends on the complexities of INTERNATIONAL LAW. Among generally accepted proofs of sovereignty are discovery, cession, conquest and administration. Central to the idea of European sovereignty over N American territory has been the idea that native people have no legal title to the land they live in – they do

Bernier Expedition tablet left on Parry's Rock, Winter Harbour, NWT, 1 July 1909, by Captain J.E. Bernier (*courtesy National Archives of Canada/C-29604*).

not "own" it – but merely have ABORIGINAL RIGHTS, particularly "usufructuary," or the rights to use the land and its products.

Canada's claim to its North rests first on the charter granted to the Hudson's Bay Co by Charles II in 1670, giving the company title to Rupert's Land (the watershed of Hudson Bay, or about half of present-day Canada). To this in 1821 was added the rest of the present-day NWT south of the arctic coast. Thus when in June 1870 the HBC transferred title to its lands to Canada, the new Dominion acquired sovereignty over all of the present-day NWT except for the arctic islands. This sovereignty has never been questioned.

Where doubt has risen over Canada's claims to arctic sovereignty is in the islands north of the Canadian mainland. Some of the early explorers here were British (Martin FROBISHER, 1576, John DAVIS, 1585 and 1587, and others) but many of these islands were discovered and explored by Scandinavians or Americans. In July 1880 the British government transferred to Canada the rest of its possessions in the Arctic, including "all Islands adjacent to any such Territories" whether discovered or not – a feeble basis for a claim of sovereignty, since the British had a dubious right to give Canada islands which had not yet been discovered, or which had been discovered by foreigners. The Colonial Boundaries Act of 1895 attempted to alleviate these doubts, but still contained a vague definition of the territory claimed.

Meanwhile, although Americans made no formal claims, they were particularly active around Ellesmere I. Lt A. Greely led a scientific expedition in 1881-84 and in 1909 Robert Peary reached the North Pole from his base on northern Ellesmere. The greatest danger to Canada's claims came from the expedition of Otto SVERDRUP, who between 1898 and 1902 discovered Axel Heiberg, Ellef Rignes and Amund Rignes islands – the first man (including among the Inuit) to set foot on them. All his discoveries, about 275 000 km^2, he claimed for Norway. Other large arctic islands were also discovered by non-British explorers.

Beginning in the 1880s the Canadian government sponsored periodic voyages to the Eastern Arctic in order to establish a presence there in support of its claims. Beginning in 1897 a series of arctic patrols was begun, as Capt W. Wakeham raised the flag on Kekerton I, claiming "Baffin's Land" for the Dominion. In 1904 A.P. LOW sailed up to Cape Herschel on Ellesmere I, which he mapped and claimed for Canada. Capt J. E. BERNIER carried out numerous voyages between 1904 and 1925. Perhaps the most important was that of 1909, when he set up a plaque on Melville I claiming the Arctic Archipelago for Canada, from the mainland to the North Pole. In the western Arctic from 1913 to 1918, Vilhjalmur STEFANSSON discovered the last of the arctic islands and claimed them for Canada. But these symbolic acts of raising flags and erecting plaques carried

little weight in international law since they were not accompanied by effective occupation or administration.

The first vigorous assertion of Canadian sovereignty in the Arctic came with the establishment of a Mounted Police post at Herschel I in 1903; set up to control the activities of American whalers in the Western Arctic, it enforced Canadian laws and showed the flag in the region, making Canada's sovereignty there unquestionable.

After WWI the Americans and Danes showed signs of ignoring Canada's claims to the High Arctic, particularly to Ellesmere I which the Danish government stated in 1919 was a no-man's land. This was a direct challenge to Canada's arctic sovereignty, and was met by a plan for effective occupation of Ellesmere and other islands. In 1922 an RCMP post was established at Craig Harbour, at the south end of the island, and the Inlet on Baffin I. In 1923 another detachment was placed at Pangnirtung, and in 1924 at Dundas Harbour, on Devon I. In 1926 the Bache Peninsula detachment was established on the east coast of Ellesmere I, at 79° N latitude.

Though there were no Canadians living within hundreds of kilometres of Bache peninsula, the RCMP operated a post there (mail delivery was once a year), because operation of a post office was an internationally recognized proof of sovereignty. The RCMP also continued its extensive patrols; on Ellesmere I, where there was no population, these were exploratory. In 1921, S/Sgt A.H. Joly was sent to establish a post on Baffin I. In the next few years other detachments were placed at Craig Harbour on Ellesmere I and on Devon and Cornwallis Is. In 1929 a patrol commanded by (now Inspector) Joly covered 3000 km by dog team. Some new land was discovered: eg, in 1928 Constable T.C. Makinson discovered the large inlet off Smith Sound which now bears his name. On Baffin I the police visited each Inuit camp annually, took the census, explained the law and reported to Ottawa on local conditions – all demonstrations of sovereignty. Where necessary they enforced the criminal law, as in the murder of the Newfoundland trader Robert Janes near Pond Inlet in 1920. This activity further strengthened Canada's claims to the Arctic. In 1930 Norway formally abandoned its claim to the Sverdrup Is and Ottawa paid Sverdrup $67 000 for the records of his expeditions. This made Canada's formal claim secure.

Present-day controversy over arctic sovereignty arises from 2 causes. First, though Canada's claim to its arctic land area is now secure, the fact that large areas are uninhabited and virtually undefended raises the possibility that it may not be secure forever. Second, and more important, is that there is international consensus only about the land area; the channels and straits – particularly the NORTHWEST PASSAGE – are not universally recognized as Canadian.

Canada regards the channels and straits as internal waters, through which foreign vessels must request permission to pass. With the prospect of bringing home oil from arctic discoveries off Alaska, the US has increasingly seen them as international waters, open to all, and has demonstrated this belief by sending oil tankers (1969) and the *Polar Sea* (1985) into Canada's Arctic without permission. There is a legal case to be made on both sides, and Canada has offered to submit the matter to the World Court.

The outcry in Canada over these 2 voyages might be taken to indicate that Canadians care deeply about the Arctic. More likely it is a manifestation of Canadian nationalism (or anti-Americanism) that basically has little to do with an active interest in the region, for as soon as the danger passes, Canadians return to their habit of

ignoring the North. As a result of the 1985 voyage of the *Polar Sea*, External Affairs minister Joe Clark put forward plans for a new $500 million icebreaker. In 1987 the government also announced that it would build and station nuclear-powered submarines in arctic waters, but this has as much to do with Canada's role in continental defence as with sovereignty. Some of the strong emotions stirred up the issue result from a genuine concern for the fragile arctic environment, but they may also contain an element of guilt; Canadians, while promising to stand on guard for the "True North, strong and free," have been reluctant to display a real commitment to the region.   W.R. MORRISON

Arctic Winter Games, biennial games initiated 1970 to provide northern athletes with opportunities for training and competition and to promote cultural and social interchange among northern peoples. The first games drew 710 participants from Alaska, the YT and the NWT to Yellowknife. Athletes from northern Québec and observers from the Soviet Union and Greenland joined the 1972 games. Subsequent events were held in Anchorage, Alaska, 1974; Schefferville, Qué, 1976; Hay River and Pine Point, NWT, 1978; Whitehorse, YT, 1980; Fairbanks, Alaska, 1982; Yellowknife, NWT, 1984; Whitehorse, 1986; and Fairbanks, 1988. Events include badminton, cross-country skiing, curling, figure skating, hockey, indoor soccer, shooting, snowshoeing, speedskating, triathlon and volleyball. The most unusual events are traditional arctic sports, developed over the years by Inuit to test stamina, strength and endurance (for example the high kick in which athletes leap into the air with one foot or both feet).

The high kick, one of the Arctic Winter Games' unique events (*photo by Jim Merrithew*).

Arenas and Stadiums The word, "arena," is defined as "an enclosed area for entertainment." Its Latin root means "a sandy place," conjuring up visions of the blood stained sands of Rome's gladiatorial contests. A "stadium" is a structure that involves tiers of seats built around a field for sports events. In Canada, both have evolved from being relatively simple structures designed to house sports contests to elaborate and costly facilities which have multipurpose uses. Arenas are homes, most of the time, for hockey and ice skating. Generally they enclose an ice surface which can be removed for box lacrosse, public meetings and, in the case of the larger arenas, concerts.

Stadiums developed in Canada as a place to stage football games. Over the years large facilities of this type have been built to accommodate major international sports events such as the Olympics and the Commonwealth Games. Following these events the facility is available for professional football and baseball and many other activities not necessarily related to sports.

The first covered ice rink in Canada was built in Québec City, in 1852, a full decade before others were built elsewhere in the country. The next 20

Exhibition Building Rink, Halifax, NS, c1885 (*courtesy Public Archives of Nova Scotia/from W. Notman Studio*).

years saw others opened across Canada. The most famous of all of these early arenas was Montréal's Victoria Rink. Built in 1862, it was declared, at that time, to be the largest and the best in the world. The peak of its roof rose 15.8 m above the ice surface. Gaslit lamps provided light for its capacity 2000 spectators. It also was prominent in the origin of HOCKEY; the first game played under rules similar to those used today took place there on 3 Mar 1875. The size of its ice surface, 200 feet long by 85 feet wide (60 m x 25 m), is still the regulation size for NATIONAL HOCKEY LEAGUE rinks.

The first arenas built specifically for hockey were raised in Ottawa and Kingston in 1895. They had boards that were only 30 cm high. All of these arenas used natural ice. The first arena with an artificial ice surface was built in 1911 in Victoria, BC, by Frank and Lester PATRICK.

Since 1917, the establishment of the NHL has seen the construction of Canada's most famous arenas. The Montreal Forum was built in 1924. Maple Leaf Gardens, in Toronto, was built in the depths of the Depression in 1931. Other NHL arenas in Canada are the Saddledome in Calgary, the Northlands Coliseum in Edmonton, the Pacific Coliseum in Vancouver, the Winnipeg Arena in Winnipeg and the Colisée de Québec in Québec City. The Saddledome is the most recently constructed of these. Having a capacity of 17 500 spectators, it was opened in 1983 after a cost of $38 million and served as a major facility for the 1988 Calgary Winter Olympic Games. In Nov 1985, the city of Hamilton, Ont, opened the Victor Copps Coliseum after having spent $43 million. It too holds 17 500 spectators and since the city lacks an NHL franchise, it has been used for the world junior hockey championships, tractor and monster truck shows and other diverse attractions.

Historically, Canada's stadiums evolved out of a growing interest in intercollegiate football. For example, temporary facilities were constructed at the U of T in 1893, in the attempt to take advantage of the interest in the annual contest against Queen's by charging a first time admission fee of 25 cents. Three years later a temporary 3-tiered structure was erected to accommodate 5000 spectators for another contest against Queen's. It was not until 30 Sept 1911 that Varsity Stadium opened its gates in Toronto. Its capacity was 11 000 spectators; by 1930 it was increased to 19 000. Varsity Stadium became the home to Toronto's professional football team, the Argonauts and served as the facility for many Grey Cup games as well. In 1959 the Argonauts moved to the larger quarters in Exhibition Stadium, a facility that was expanded in 1976 at a cost of $17.8 million to permit its use for professional baseball. It can seat 45 000 people for baseball and 54 000 for football. In 1987 work had begun in Toronto on a larger facility at a projected cost of $300 million. It will be a covered stadium but will have a retractable roof so that 91% of the stadium will

be open under fair-weather conditions. To be known as the Skydome, it will hold 56 000 spectators for baseball games and an additional 2000 people for football. Its opening is projected for early 1989.

In the early 1970s more and more stadiums installed artificial grass surfaces. While this initially extended the use of these facilities, it also made possible the construction of completely covered stadia, the first one being built in Vancouver. BC PLACE opened in June 1983 and was built at a cost of $126 million. The first Grey Cup game to take place under a roof was played in Nov 1984. The first stadium to offer both an open and covered field is Montréal's OLYMPIC STADIUM. This giant elliptical structure was built for the 1976 Summer Olympic Games. Its designer planned for a 150 m tower above the stadium which would support a 18 500 square metre membrane which could be dropped over the roof opening in inclement weather. This, however, was completed only in the spring of 1987. The Olympic Stadium built at an estimated $1 billion cost will long remain as Canada's most expensive facility of this type.

Other stadiums have been constructed to accommodate international sports contests. Hamilton built a new stadium in 1930 for the British Empire Games. Empire Stadium in Vancouver was built for the 1954 British Commonwealth Games. Both accommodated between 20 000 and 25 000 spectators. Edmonton's Commonwealth Stadium, an open stadium seating over 42 000 people, was built at a cost of $23 million for the 1978 Commonwealth Games.

The development of arenas and stadia in Canada has occurred with the rise of organized sport along with the growing urbanization and industrialization of the country. Technological innovations such as electric lights, artificial ice and grass have not only lengthened playing seasons but have also made such facilities available for other uses beyond the realm of sport.

J. THOMAS WEST

Argenson, Pierre de Voyer d', governor of New France 1658-61 (bap in France 19 Nov 1625; d there 1709?). There was an Iroquois attack the day following Gov d'Argenson's arrival at Québec, and negotiations with and defence against these powerful enemies were his major preoccupations. He devoted almost as much energy to his public quarrels with Bishop Laval and the Jesuits. Also concerned about the fragility of the Canadian economy, he urged a monopoly control over the fur trade and an increased agrarian population, but his advice was not heeded.

ALLAN GREER

Argentia, Nfld, UP, pop 50, (1986c), 93 (1981c), is located on the W coast of the AVALON PENINSULA. Formerly the fishing community of Little Placentia (*Petit Plaisance*) founded by the French in the late 1600s, it was the site of English merchant premises by the 1700s. A small silver-lead mine, opened near the community in the 1880s, operated sporadically until 1925; consequently Little Placentia was renamed Argentia around 1900. In 1940 the US leased most of the small peninsula for a naval base. Argentia residents were resettled in nearby communities. The base served the largest US task force in the Atlantic, 12 403 personnel in 1943. Near this base, in Placentia B, US Pres Roosevelt and British PM Churchill met aboard the USS *Augusta* to negotiate the historic Atlantic Charter in 1941. The construction of the base created work for up to 15 000 Newfoundlanders, but it was phased down in 1969; in 1947 the air station was abandoned and in 1975 the naval station was closed. A small Canadian and American oceanographic facility remains.

J.E.M. PITT AND R.D. PITT

Argentia, Nfld, founded in the late 1600s. A US navy base here served the largest US task force in the Atlantic in WWII (*photo by Janet Green/Masterfile*).

Argue, Hazen Robert, politician (b at Moose Jaw, Sask 6 Jan 1921). The Argue family came to Ottawa from Ireland in 1821 and has had many prominent members over 9 generations, including Dr Thomas Herbert Argue, country doctor and inventor, Dr Andrew William Argue, former chancellor of U Sask, and Fletcher Argue, for whom the Arts and Science Building of U Man was named. Hazen was MP from 1945 to 1963 for Assiniboia (formerly Wood Mountain), Sask, and was Parliament's youngest member when he entered. Argue was the only opposition member from Saskatchewan to survive the DIEFENBAKER sweep in 1958. He became House leader of the 8-member CO-OPERATIVE COMMONWEALTH FEDERATION caucus that year. In 1960 he was elected national leader of the CCF. When the CCF and the Canadian Labour Congress formed the NEW DEMOCRATIC PARTY in 1961, T.C. DOUGLAS easily defeated Argue for the leadership. Six months later, Argue shocked the NDP by resigning, charging that its structure gave too much power to the unions. He was re-elected to the Commons in 1962 as a Liberal but was defeated in 1963. Over the objections of some Saskatchewan Liberals of longer standing, Argue was named to the Senate in 1966. He was minister of state responsible for the CANADIAN WHEAT BOARD, 1980-82.   BILL CAMERON

Argus Corporation Ltd, with head offices in Toronto, is a specialized investment and holding company, incorporated in 1945. Attracting little interest to itself or its activities for much of its history, Argus was thrust into the spotlight in 1978 when members of the Black family acquired majority control through the acquisition of 2 blocks of Ravelston shares from the estates of J.A. (Bud) MCDOUGALD and Eric PHILLIPS. Hollinger Inc, a holding company itself with substantial interests in the newspaper publishing business, is now Argus's only company. Ravelston Corp Ltd holds 100% of Argus shares; Ravelston itself is controlled by Conrad M. BLACK. As of 30 June 1987 Argus's assets were valued at $297 million and it had 20 employees.   DEBORAH C. SAWYER

Arluk, George, artist (b in the Keewatin region, NWT 5 May 1949). An Inuit sculptor now living in Baker Lake, NWT, Arluk began to teach himself how to carve soapstone at age 9. In the 1960s he was influenced by sculptors TIKTAK and KAVIK and John PANGNARK. By the mid-1970s he had developed a unique style of semiabstraction. His subjects sometimes include spirits and arctic animals, but his main theme is the human figure. He depicts single figures such as hunters and mothers with babies in their hoods. Most often he groups figures together to form abstracted compositions of gently curving forms that undulate rhythmically. His sculptures often have antler parts added that protrude in complex patterns from the stone.

DARLENE WIGHT

Armaments, fighting tools, including devices for surveillance and reconnaissance. The first armaments were probably jagged pieces of rock (missile weapons) and crude wooden clubs (shock weapons), both instinctive adaptations of food-gathering implements. Eventually a combination created a battle-axe or spear, which like most weapons could be used either offensively or defensively. Wood or leather in the form of shield or body armour was purely defensive and of little value by itself.

The variety of defensive armaments now ranges from spaced and layered steel and ceramic armour on tanks to airborne warning and command systems (AWACS). Offensive weapons have become more complex and deadly, with greater range, accuracy and hitting power. Modern missile weapon systems can be conveniently broken down into 3 components: a transportation and launching platform, a delivery mechanism and the missile itself. They range from the foot soldier bearing an automatic rifle to the nuclear-powered submersible carrying submarine-launched ballistic missiles (SLBMs) holding multiple, independently targeted re-entry vehicles (MIRVs) with atomic warheads, remote piloted vehicles (RPVs) and aircraft loaded with napalm, bombs or target-seeking missiles. The high-technology aspect of some current armaments, such as satellite reconnaissance and computerized laser range-finding and communications, makes it extremely difficult to distinguish in some instances between armaments and industrial tools. Space may become a battlefield of the future involving nuclear-powered lasers and other exotic devices as part of the Soviet and American "strategic defense initiatives" (SDIs).

Archaeological evidence suggests that prehistoric armaments in N America developed in the same sequence as in other parts of the world. The earliest written evidence comes from the 14th-century *Greenlanders' Saga*, which recounts that NORSE adventurers armed with axes, exploring the N Atlantic coast about 1000 AD, fought with "skraelings" (perhaps BEOTHUKS) who used bows and arrows. These were still the dominant weapons when Europeans began to infiltrate the continent again in the 16th century, bringing with them the age of gunpowder. Jacques CARTIER used primitive hand guns ("fire lances") to impress Indians in the Baie des Chaleurs during the summer of 1534, and mounted cannon on the ramparts of his Québec fort in the winter of 1535. In 1609 Samuel de CHAMPLAIN, allying himself with Huron and Algonquin warriors, killed 2 Iroquois with his harquebus (a matchlock musket), thus initiating a long-lived enmity. Pehr KALM, a Swedish traveller, reported 140 years later that there was scarcely a French Canadian "who was not a clever marksman and who did not own a rifle." He also noted the production of cannon and mortars at the FORGES SAINT-MAURICE near Trois-Rivières. Some Indians were armed with muskets by that time, although the bow and tomahawk remained more popular.

As the indigenous inhabitants were subdued, driven farther west or killed, fighting in N America between people of European descent relied increasingly upon more sophisticated missile weapons, and the limited Canadian production of armaments ceased. In the early 19th century the flintlock musket gave way to the breech-loading rifle, while an ever smaller proportion of people possessed weapons. Some magazine rifles from the US were used by the Canadian Militia to repel the FENIANS in 1866 and 1870, and an American Gatling machine gun was used in suppressing the NORTH-WEST REBELLION of 1885. However, the militia continued to rely upon British rifles and artillery. The DOMINION ARSENAL began to produce

small-arms ammunition in 1882, but the first Canadian-built, breech-loading, magazine rifle issued to the militia was the Ross (a variation on the Austrian Mannlicher), which first went into production in 1903. An excellent sporting rifle, it proved unsatisfactory under the rigours of active service in 1915, and production ceased in Mar 1917. In the CANADIAN EXPEDITIONARY FORCE it was replaced with the British Lee-Enfield rifle. Militiamen were again issued ROSS RIFLES for home defence during WORLD WAR II.

For that war Canada manufactured a wide range of armaments, including combat aircraft such as the de Havilland Mosquito and Avro Lancaster bombers, armoured vehicles, artillery and naval guns, landing craft, convoy escorts, radios, RADAR, SONAR, small arms and enormous quantities of ammunition, explosives and pyrotechnics. Few, however, were of Canadian design, nor were Canadian forces necessarily equipped with them. One of the rare Canadian design initiatives, the Ram tank, was not a success and was never used in action; Ram hulls, however, with the turrets removed, were used in NW Europe in 1944 as the first armoured personnel carriers (APCs).

Since WWII Canada has continued to rely largely upon armament designs of its allies, sometimes modified to meet Canadian needs, for major weapon systems (*see* BOMARC MISSILE CRISIS). For example, the British Centurion tank served as Canada's main battle tank for 25 years, 1952-77. Exceptions have been the AVRO CF-100 fighter aircraft and the various classes of small warships in the naval service, most notably the "Tribal" Class destroyers and "St Laurent" Class destroyer escorts. Advanced and complex projects such as the *Bobcat* APC, the AVRO ARROW fighter and the *Bras d'Or* hydrofoil have had to be abandoned because of restricted marketing possibilities and excessive design costs. Canada has had more success in producing high-technology components for American weapon systems. NATO allies employ the Canadian-designed CRV-7 air-to-ground rockets, "Elsie" antipersonnel mines and the extended-range, full-bore (ERFB) artillery rounds. Canadian forces depend heavily upon the Hornet fighter and Twin Huey, Kiowa and Sea King helicopters (all American) and the Leopard C 1 tank (W German), armed with a variety of appropriate missiles, for their tactical launching platforms. Small arms currently carried by the Canadian infantryman (who rides in American-designed, Canadian-built APCs) include Belgian rifles and light machine guns, American heavy machine guns and antitank and antiaircraft missile launchers.

As part of the NORAD agreement, nuclear-tipped air-to-air missiles under American control were held in Canada to be used by Canadian aircraft in case of need. With the adoption of the CF-18 Hornet during the 1980s, these have been phased out of service. Canadian forces in Europe are also backed by American nuclear-weapon systems, but Canada has renounced nuclear armaments of her own, a decision that in 1970 removed the Honest John missile, acquired 1961, from the Canadian weapon inventory. Meanwhile, arguments over the offensive or defensive nature of weapons systems such as the Cruise missile and the Stealth bomber rage fruitlessly, since — as in prehistoric times — their use is largely a function of the intentions of those who wield them. The "quality or quantity" debate is now receiving much attention within the terms of Lanchester's N-Square Law: for the odds to be equal, the effectiveness of the numerically weaker side has to be raised by the square of the ratio of the numbers involved; ie, against twice as many the weaker side needs to be 4 times as good in order for it to stand an even chance. Should weapon systems be

simplified at the cost of effectiveness in order that more may be available? Among the superpowers the US has consistently favoured effectiveness while the USSR has emphasized numbers. *See also* DISARMAMENT.   BRERETON GREENHOUS

Armed Forces, the combined land, naval and air forces prepared to engage in a nation's defence or in warfare. Canada's indigenous armed forces have evolved from the earliest militia through the establishment of the regular army, navy and air force to the modern Canadian Armed Forces.

Militia and Army

Militias, part-time forces organized for defence, date from the early Middle Ages – in England from the Anglo-Saxon *fyrd* (the national militia before the Norman Conquest). By the 18th century the few *milices* left in France were almost exclusively ceremonial, but in New France the system was revitalized to meet the Indian and English menaces. In Canada the name "militia" covered both part-time and regular forces until WWII. In the 1950s the militia became the part-time RESERVE FORCE. From about 1883 to 1940 the regulars were called the Permanent Force, or Permanent Militia. Thereafter, until unification in 1968, they were the Canadian Army.

In 1669 Louis XIV, expanding on earlier experience with militia training in Québec, Montréal and Trois-Rivières, advised that the militia system should be adopted throughout New France. Gov FRONTENAC later appointed a captain of militia in each parish, and required all males 16-60 to train for 1 or 2 months annually. The honorary *capitaines de milice* were highly respected by the habitants, and were leaders in both military and civil spheres. New France's militia was more effective than those in the English colonies, since it was skilled in the *petite guerre:* swift movement through the forest and surprise attack – tactics borrowed from the Indians. It made some notorious raids on New England settlements. Along with the TROUPES DE LA MARINE, or colonial regular troops, the militia protected the colony until the SEVEN YEARS' WAR brought regular regiments from both England and France. The militia also provided CORVÉE labour to build roads, bridges and FORTIFICATIONS. When Gen James WOLFE threatened Québec in 1759 the militia was called out in a *levée en masse,* and several thousand militiamen were incorporated into the regular army that Montcalm had brought from France. After the capitulation of Montréal in 1760, the British used the militia captains in the administration of the country. They called up Canadian militia for service during PONTIAC's rebellion of 1763 and when the Americans invaded in 1775.

In Nova Scotia captains of militia were appointed as early as 1710, and there was a militia in Hal-

Grizzly armoured personnel carrier, part of a family of vehicles developed and owned by a Swiss company, MOWAG, and built in Canada by its licensee, General Motors (*courtesy National Defence Headquarters*).

ifax in 1749. But the chief sources of support for the British garrisons in the Maritimes during the AMERICAN REVOLUTION were regiments raised for local defence, or fencibles enlisted for service anywhere in N America.

In 1793 provincial regiments were raised in Montréal and Québec. Disbanded in 1802, these Lower Canadian units were replaced in 1803 by the training of 1200 militiamen in service battalions. In 1791 Upper Canadian Lt-Gov John Graves SIMCOE raised a permanent corps of veterans, the Queen's Rangers, for defence and public works. It was disbanded in 1802 and replaced in 1811 by a fencible regiment. Simcoe had also attempted to establish a compulsory militia based on counties, but there was no provision for training it until 1808. During the WAR OF 1812 Canadian militia were assigned transport and labour duties. Volunteers fought alongside British regulars and provincial regiments. Canada was saved by British regulars, but the militia played an important role and Canadian legend later gave it credit for the victory. (*See* VOLTIGEURS.)

Militia volunteers aided in suppressing the 1837 REBELLIONS, and some companies were kept together for several years. With the unification of the Canadas in 1841 the British government raised the Royal Canadian Rifles, a regiment of veterans, for garrison duties. Cavalry raised by Toronto's Denison family, the Montréal Fire Brigade (which doubled as an infantry battalion), the Halifax Militia Artillery and the "Uniform" Companies of Artillery in New Brunswick trained in peacetime at little cost to the government. In 1855 the MILITIA ACTS retained the principle of compulsory enrolment in the Sedentary Militia, but also authorized paid volunteer units. Thus the voluntary principle was accepted as the basis of Canadian defence. It proved so popular that it led to the formation of many historic units, but compulsory enrolment remained the theory, though not the practice, for 2 more decades.

When the AMERICAN CIVIL WAR raised fears of an American attack on Canada, an attempt to introduce compulsory training failed. In 1863 the volunteer militia that could be paid was increased to 10 000 and the number that could be trained but not paid was to be 35 000. None were trained in the Canadas before the war ended, but 34 800 men trained for 5 days in the Maritimes, and officers' schools were established. In 1865, 1100 Canadian officers attended a 3-week camp at La Prairie, Qué. In 1866, 20 000 volunteers faced FENIAN raiders and some fought them at RIDGEWAY. Militia infantry attended camps of instruction at Thorold (Ont), where they were brigaded with the British regulars. Cavalry and artillery camped at Toronto.

After Confederation the militia system continued. Forty thousand volunteers in cavalry, infantry, rifle and artillery units were to train annually for 8 to 17 days. In 1870, 2 militia battalions accompanied British regulars sent to suppress the RED RIVER REBELLION. In 1871 artillery schools opened at Kingston and Québec. A British general officer commanding (GOC) was appointed to the militia in 1874, and the Military College was opened in 1876 at Kingston. From 1883 the staffs of 3 artillery schools (another was in Victoria, BC), a cavalry school at Québec, infantry schools at Fredericton, St-Jean, Toronto, and later at London, and a mounted-infantry school at Winnipeg were the beginnings of the Permanent Force (PF). Under a British GOC, Frederick MIDDLETON, almost 8000 Canadian troops helped to suppress the NORTH-WEST REBELLION in 1885. Shortcomings revealed in training, equipment and organization had been caused by the government's failure to make adequate provision for defence except in times of crisis, such as the Russian scare of 1878,

when the threat of war between Britain and Russia suggested the possibility of Russian attacks on Canadian ports.

Maj-Gen Ivor Herbert, GOC 1890-95, secured approval of much-needed reform. Headquarters staff was expanded, officers were sent to England for training and, at the time of the 1895 Venezuela crisis (when the US threatened war with Britain over the determination of Venezuela's boundary with British Guiana), the PF infantry received a new rifle, the long Lee-Enfield. This was the last occasion on which fear of an American attack led to military preparations in Canada. In 1898, 200 PF volunteers went to the Yukon to help police and customs officers maintain order during the KLONDIKE GOLD RUSH. Before the YUKON FIELD FORCE returned in 1900, English Canadians induced PM Sir Wilfrid Laurier to send 1000 men to the SOUTH AFRICAN WAR. Militia volunteers, their numbers stiffened by regulars, formed a special service battalion of Royal Canadians under PF officer Lt-Col W.D. OTTER. A second contingent drew heavily on the permanent staff of the cavalry school and on the NORTH-WEST MOUNTED POLICE. Canada also raised an infantry battalion to relieve the British garrison in Halifax for war service.

The Canadian Militia was riddled with political patronage. Three reforming GOCs, Herbert, E.T.H. HUTTON and the earl of Dundonald, fought against it and ended their Canadian tours of duty abruptly. Nevertheless, Sir Frederick BORDEN, minister of militia and defence 1896-1911, was sincerely anxious for reform. In 1904 the British GOC was replaced by a Militia Council and the way was cleared for a Canadian chief of the general staff. The first was Otter in 1908. Ancillary corps were added: Medical, Army Service Corps, Ordnance, the Canadian Corps of Guides (for intelligence), Engineers and Signals. The infantry was re-equipped with a Canadian-made rifle, the Ross. In 1909 Canada agreed at an imperial (defence) conference to standardize organization and equipment on British models and to accept imperial general staff officers. By 1914 Canada's PF numbered 3000 and there were almost 60 000 partially trained militia. A mobilization plan had already been prepared. But instead of using this during WORLD WAR I, Minister of Militia Sir Samuel HUGHES created the CANADIAN EXPEDITIONARY FORCE (CEF) by appealing for volunteers.

By the end of the war Canada had organized 5 divisions for overseas service. The Canadian Corps was commanded by a Canadian, Lt-Gen Sir Arthur CURRIE, and it was staffed by Canadians in all but a few key positions. After the war the number of PF infantry regiments was raised from 1 to 3, and the total PF establishment was 10 000. Actual strength remained around 4000 and Canada had no tanks or modern guns. Militia units were largely self-financed and self-equipped. At the height of the Depression only a few more than 2000 men went to camp, and then for only 4 days. The deteriorating international situation brought reorganization in 1936. Non-Permanent Active Militia (NPAM) establishment was reduced from a paper figure of 134 000 in 15 divisions to 86 557 in 7. Some cavalry units were mechanized, and by 1939 the number of artillery units had been increased from 97 to 155. The militia began to get new uniforms and equipment to replace WWI issue, and for the first time the men received service boots.

In WORLD WAR II Canada fielded an army of 3 infantry and 2 armoured divisions, and raised 3 divisions for home defence. Nearly three-quarters of a million men and women served. In June 1940 the NATIONAL RESOURCES MOBILIZATION ACT authorized the government to requisition Canadians' services for home defence. After the NRMA

was amended in Nov 1944 to permit CONSCRIPTION for overseas service, some 2500 conscripts actually went into operational units during the last months of the war.

The Canadian Army establishment was fixed in 1946 at 25 000. In 1951 Canada sent troops to support the UNITED NATIONS forces in the KOREAN WAR, and almost 22 000 eventually served there. In 1952 the Canadian Army establishment was raised to 52 000 to meet Canada's obligations to NATO. In the 1950s the militia of 6 divisions was renamed the Reserve Force, but its assignment to security duties and civil defence, along with the disbandment of some ancient units, weakened morale. By 1987 it numbered only 16 000, reflecting only a slight increase from the 1977 strength. *See also* REGIMENTS.   RICHARD A. PRESTON

Navy

Indigenous naval forces in N America can be traced to the colonial period. Until the late 19th century, armed flotillas met specific colonial, provincial or national needs, both on the coasts and on the Great Lakes (*see* PROVINCIAL MARINE). Anglo-German naval rivalry nourished the idea that the fisheries-protection vessels of the Dept of Marine and Fisheries should become a separate organization, and on 29 Mar 1909 Parliament approved expenditure on a Canadian naval service to co-operate with Britain's Royal Navy. On 4 May 1910 the NAVAL SERVICE ACT brought the Royal Canadian Navy (RCN) into being. The navy was a major political issue, and it suffered severe setbacks under Conservative rule between 1911 and 1914. Divided between Halifax, NS, and Esquimalt, BC, it was directed from a distant headquarters in Ottawa. L.P. Brodeur, the first minister, George J. Desbarats, deputy minister, and Rear-Adm Charles E. KINGSMILL, RN (retired), director, were transferred from the Dept of Marine and Fisheries; they understood the navy's problems, but the naval staff sometimes failed to appreciate the fleet's needs, and often it could not explain them to government. After WWI, Conservative and Liberal administrations alike starved the navy. Commodore Walter HOSE, director of the naval service 1921-28 and chief of the naval staff (CNS) 1928-34, had to resist efforts by the militia to subordinate and even disband it. Forced to close Royal Naval College of Canada in 1922, Hose established the ROYAL CANADIAN NAVAL VOLUNTEER RESERVE in 1923. Rear-Adm Percy NELLES, CNS 1934-44, built on this foundation when international tension in the late 1930s at last, and almost too late, aroused Ottawa to the need for an effective navy.

In both world wars, U-BOAT threats in the western Atlantic led to the unexpected growth of the RCN. In 1917-18 this simply meant diverting to Canada's East Coast resources previously allocated to the Royal Navy. In 1941 it meant creating a major oceanic fleet through a massive program of shipbuilding and recruiting. Anticipated commitments in the Pacific compounded the problem in 1943. The RCN grew from 13 warships and about 3000 men in 1939 to some 365 warships and 100 000 personnel in 1945. At first expansion diluted efficiency, especially in the navy's main function, convoy escort. When in 1943 the naval staff lost touch with changing operational requirements in the fleet, Angus L. MACDONALD, minister of national defence for naval services 1940-45, replaced Nelles with Rear-Adm G.C. JONES. Partly because Naval Service Headquarters mounted skilful shore-based control of shipping, radio-intercept and intelligence operations, and partly because Canada provided half the escorts on the N Atlantic routes (*see* ATLANTIC, BATTLE OF THE), Britain and the US agreed to establish a new theatre of operations, the Canadian Northwest

Atlantic. On 1 May 1943 Rear-Adm L.W. MURRAY, who with other Canadian officers resented subordination in that region to the US Navy, became the theatre's commander in chief, an appointment unique in Canadian history. From 1943 to 1945 the RCN became the third-largest navy among the Allies, and satisfactorily carried out a wide variety of operations in many theatres.

Canadians often saw the RCN as a pale imitation of the RN; PM Mackenzie KING suspected that the Canadian service was a mere instrument of the British ADMIRALTY. Nevertheless, to preserve a continuing oceanic fleet, in 1945 his government approved a small permanent navy of 2 aircraft carriers, 2 cruisers and 12 destroyers. However, there was no rush to join the regular navy and it was necessary to extend the service of some reserve personnel who had joined during the war. Relations between officers and men soured under the pressures of adjustment to peacetime, which for many old hands meant resuming the merely routine prewar activities. After 3 mutinies in 1949, Rear-Adm E. Rollo MAINGUY presided over a commission that eloquently urged casting off certain inappropriate British customs. Its report, which was received with mixed feelings by the naval profession, became the RCN's Magna Carta.

In the Korean War, 1950-53, the RCN kept a highly professional force of 3 destroyers in Korean waters. By 1964, fed by COLD WAR tensions, the navy had grown to 1 aircraft carrier (the BONAVENTURE), 22 Canadian-designed and Canadian-built destroyers, 17 ocean escorts of WWII vintage, 10 coastal minesweepers and 21 500 personnel, committed for the most part to antisubmarine operations in NATO. Unification followed in 1968. Bitter opposition came from naval officers, many of whom resigned; Rear-Adm W.M. LANDYMORE was so vocal and indiscreet that he was dismissed. Greatly reduced in size and capability in the 1970s, and less readily identified than the RCN with its British progenitor, Maritime Command of the Canadian Armed Forces still derives much professional knowledge from the RN. The Defence White Paper of 1987 calls for construction of nuclear submarines to enable Maritime Command to play a greater role beneath the arctic ice cap.   W.A.B. DOUGLAS

Air Force

The Royal Canadian Air Force came into existence on 1 Apr 1924, and lost its distinct identity with the unification of the Canadian Armed Forces in 1968. Before 1914 military aviation in Canada did not exist; it was a matter for greater world powers. J.A.D. MCCURDY and F.W. "Casey" BALDWIN, members of Alexander Graham BELL's Aerial Experiment Association, carried out flight trials of the SILVER DART and *Baddeck I* in Aug 1909 at Petawawa, Ont, but aroused little interest in the Dept of Militia and Defence. Military and naval aviation underwent extraordinary development after WWI began, but the reluctance of the Canadian government to develop a distinct air force persisted until late in the war. Over 20 000 Canadians served as pilots, observers and ground support staff in the British ROYAL FLYING CORPS, the ROYAL NAVAL AIR SERVICE and, after 1 Apr 1918, the Royal Air Force, in every theatre of the war. The publicity given to Canadian participation in the air war, and especially to the exploits of such outstanding fighter pilots as W.A. BISHOP, W.G. BARKER, Raymond COLLISHAW and D.R. MACLAREN, helped to build pressure for the establishment of a distinctly Canadian service. So did the fact that German long-range submarines were a threat to shipping on Canada's East Coast. The Borden government accordingly authorized the creation of 2 small forces: the ROYAL CANADIAN NAVAL AIR

Technicians servicing a CF-18 fighter plane (*Canadian Forces photo by WO Vic Johnson*).

SERVICE, for coastal defence, and the Canadian Air Force, which was intended to work with the Canadian Expeditionary Force on the Western Front. Both organizations were short-lived, the RCNAS being disbanded in Dec 1918 and the CAF in mid-1919.

Before the fledgling CAF was dissolved, steps had already been taken to formulate a national aviation policy. An air board, chaired by Minister of Customs A.L. SIFTON, was appointed in June 1919 and given the task of advising government on future aviation policy. This board laid the foundation for the development and regulation of civil aviation and, on the assumption that military aviation strength really depended upon a strong commercial sector, envisaged the formation of only a small, temporary military air force. The Canadian Air Force was thus established in Apr 1920, but it was soon clear that something more permanent was required. Under the National Defence Act of 1922 the Air Board was absorbed by the new Department of NATIONAL DEFENCE, and its civil and military air arms were united under the director, CAF, who reported to the army chief of staff (later chief of the general staff). The CAF was now a permanent force. Not until Nov 1938 did the air force's senior officer become chief of the air staff, directly responsible to the minister of national defence. In 1923 the CAF was designated "Royal," and on 1 Apr 1924, when the King's Regulations and Orders for the Royal Canadian Air Force came into effect, it adopted the RAF ensign, motto, UNIFORMS and rank structure, and even the same official birthdate.

Despite these colonial trappings, the RCAF was a Canadian service in personnel and function. Until the early 1930s about half the RCAF's manpower performed civil air operations. Forest spraying and fire patrol, fisheries and customs surveillance on both coasts, mercy flights and aerial photography (which contributed greatly to the mapping and geological survey of remote areas) were the bulk of the RCAF's duties. Its aircraft, such as the Canadian Vickers Vedette flying boat, were designed for such missions. In 1928 the force purchased a few Siskin fighters and Atlas army co-operation aircraft from Britain to replace its long-retired military aircraft. No further important purchases were made during the Great Depression. For the first half of the interwar period, therefore, Canada had a military flying service in name only, although connections with the RAF, through exchanges, a liaison staff and the posting of Canadian officers to British staff schools, ensured a degree of professionalism and some acquaintance with air doctrine.

When WWII began in 1939, the RCAF had no first-class aircraft or other equipment, with the exception of some Hawker Hurricanes. Nevertheless, a framework for future expansion had been established. Western and Eastern Air Commands were responsible for coastal air defence, and Training Command was centered at Trenton,

Ont. Eight Permanent Active Air Force squadrons and 12 Auxiliary Active Air Force squadrons had been organized.

The key to wartime expansion was the BRITISH COMMONWEALTH AIR TRAINING PLAN. This vast program graduated 131 553 aircrew by its close, of whom 72 835 were Canadian. Despite the Canadian government's commitment to training Commonwealth aircrew, it did not accord the RCAF an independent status commensurate with that of the Canadian Army during the war. Although the BCATP Agreement contained a British undertaking that Commonwealth aircrew "shall ... be identified with their respective Dominions," the Canadian government failed to provide financially for the ground crew needed to support Canadian aircrew overseas, or for full financing of Canadian aircrew serving abroad, or even for the support of Canadian air units overseas. As a result, Canadian pilots, navigators, air gunners and other aircrew found themselves dispersed throughout the RAF, rather than being concentrated in RCAF groupings. Minister for National Defence for Air C.G. POWER, with the assistance of the RCAF senior officers, prevailed upon the RAF to permit the formation of more RCAF squadrons as the war progressed.

Of 250 000 men and women in the wartime RCAF, 94 000 served overseas. Most airmen flew with the RAF, but 48 separate Canadian squadrons took part in operations around the globe, from No 1 (later 401) Squadron's participation in the Battle of BRITAIN to 435 and 436 (Transport) Squadrons' missions in India and Burma during the final days of the conflict with Japan. 417 Squadron and 331 Wing fought in N Africa, and the former went on into Italy. Canadian squadrons played a part in all RAF operational home commands. They formed a group of their own, 6 Group (RCAF) in Bomber Command, and contributed half the strength of the RAF's 83 Composite Group in the Second Tactical Air Force. Airmen such as Air Vice-Marshals C.M. "Black Mike" MCEWEN and G.E. Brookes, Group Capts W.R. MacBrien and G.R. McGregor and Wing Cdrs George Keefer and Stan Turner became noted air leaders. Wallace McLeod, "Buck" McNair and George "Buzz" BEURLING carried on the tradition of Bishop, Barker, Collishaw and MacLaren.

From the beginning, the RCAF was deeply involved in the Battle of the Atlantic. Squadrons from East Coast bases carried out convoy duties and antisubmarine patrols, flying Lockheed Hudsons and Venturas, Catalinas, Cansos and Liberators. RCAF squadrons participated with American forces in the defence of Alaska against Japanese incursions. In addition, the RCAF flew on antisubmarine duties in the Far East.

Bomber Command was the largest RAF operational command. Into it were poured thousands of Canadian BCATP graduates to take part in the massive area-bombing campaign. Canadians were involved from the start, but the first Canadian unit was 405 Squadron, which was operational in mid-1941 and was part of the elite Pathfinder group. In Jan 1943, 6 Group became operational, commanded first by Brookes and then by McEwen. (These were the highest operational commands held by Canadian airmen in WWII.) Wing Cdr J.E. FAUQUIER was the leading Canadian bomber pilot. Casualties were heavy; of the more than 17 000 fatal casualties suffered by the RCAF during WWII, nearly 10 000 were sustained in Bomber Command.

By late 1946 RCAF numbers had dwindled to 13 000 all ranks. The permanent force resumed such duties as transport, search and rescue, and survey patrols. Jet flight did not enter the service until 1948, when some British Vampires were purchased. In the Korean War, Canada's official air contribution was limited to the transport duties of 426 Squadron, although some RCAF pilots flew with the US Air Force. It was the Cold War threat that reversed the trend towards reducing the RCAF's size. In Feb 1951 the Canadian government committed an air division of 12 fighter squadrons to Europe as part of its NATO involvement. In 1958 Canada and the US joined in the formation of the North American Air Defence Command (NORAD): in addition to substantial home defence commitments, this new orientation in Canadian defence policy meant that a Canadian became deputy commander. The first to serve was Air Marshal C.R. SLEMON.

Canadian air defence in the post-1945 period relied heavily upon foreign-produced aircraft, a policy underlined by the cancellation of the AVRO ARROW in 1959. The tendency to respond to outside initiatives, a long-term characteristic of the RCAF, did not end with the disappearance of the force when the armed services were unified in 1968. In today's Canadian Armed Forces, signs of the RCAF remain, as in its numbered squadrons and in the less tangible, but no less real, air force spirit.   S.F. WISE

Unification and After

The Canadian Forces Reorganization Bill, proclaimed 1 Feb 1968, abolished the RCN, the Canadian Army and the RCAF, and created a single service, the Canadian Armed Forces, with regular and reserve components and the potential for a special force to meet NATO, United Nations or other external commitments. The experiment of unification was unique to Canada and was not imitated by other countries. Within a decade the 3 service identities had to some degree re-emerged.

Integration had been a recurrent policy since the establishment of a single National Defence Headquarters in 1922. Under Brooke CLAXTON, minister of national defence 1946-54, Canada's MILITARY COLLEGES and systems of military law had been unified, as had other aspects of military administration. During the years of John Diefenbaker's Conservative government (1957-63), medical, legal and chaplains' services were integrated. The armed forces expected major changes when the Liberals returned to power in 1963. Military leaders could not escape some responsibility for the indecision and confusion in defence policies which had helped bring down the Diefenbaker government. The Glassco Royal Commission (1963) was highly critical of inefficiency and triplication of administration. It seemed reasonable to blame administrative waste for part of the rapid decline of capital spending in the defence budget, from 42.4% in 1954 to 18.9% in 1962. In Opposition, the Liberals had dropped their earlier arguments against nuclear warheads, but promised a searching review of defence policy and an easing out of alliance roles involving nuclear arms.

Toronto businessman Paul HELLYER had been defence critic in Opposition, and as minister of defence he first undertook the promised policy review. When his report appeared in March 1964, adjectives such as "mobile," "flexible" and "imaginative" and an emphasis on PM Lester Pearson's favourite accomplishment, PEACEKEEPING, did not conceal a continuing commitment to NATO, to continental air defence and to domestic security. Almost overlooked was the one-line promise of "a single unified defence force."

Unification had not been Hellyer's policy initially. The idea grew on him as he tried to deal with 3 service chiefs, each struggling for his own service. The Glassco Commission had found over

One of the Spitfires of No 126 Wing, RCAF, that helped destroy 12 enemy aircraft over Normandy 7 June 1944 (*courtesy Canadian Forces/PCN 3519/National Defence Headquarters*).

200 interservice committees, few of them collaborating. In future, Hellyer believed, the services would have to work closely together. His first step, approved by Parliament on 7 July 1964, was full integration of National Defence Headquarters under a single chief of the defence staff. Staff functions were divided among 4 branches: operations, personnel, logistics and finance. There was little criticism. Even the services welcomed a streamlined headquarters if it would fulfil the promise of badly needed new equipment. On 7 June 1965, navy, army and air force commands were replaced by 6 functional commands, most of them with regional responsibilities. Maritime Command took over the RCN's ships and the RCAF's antisubmarine squadrons on both coasts. Mobile Command at St-Hubert, Qué, was to control the army's brigade groups and militia and the RCAF's ground-support squadrons. Training Command and Material Command integrated tri-service functions, while Air Defence and Air Transport Commands passed unaltered from the RCAF. Communications Command was added later; Canada's ground and air forces in Europe reported directly to Ottawa. On 1 May 1966 camps, stations and the navy's land-based "ships" became 39 Canadian Forces Bases. Unified training schools and a single pay system took shape.

Many senior officers now expected a breathing space, but Hellyer's commitment to unification was undiluted. Institutional changes had gone far to make unification natural. When senior officers protested, Hellyer regarded their opposition as verging on a challenge to civil supremacy over the military. Politicians, editors and cartoonists often ridiculed the officers' objections. The public was reminded that several who resigned in protest enjoyed generous pensions. By appointing Gen Jean-Victor ALLARD as chief of the defence staff, Hellyer secured an enthusiast for unification and for eliminating many British features of the forces. Although debate over the Reorganization Bill was prolonged and sometimes rancorous, the legislation passed the Commons with NDP and Social Credit support. Within a year, members of the Canadian forces had begun to appear in new green uniforms modelled on those of the US Air Force, with rank badges recognizable to American as well as Canadian personnel.

The public spectacle of integration and unification overshadowed government efforts to find new roles and equipment for its revamped military organization. Instead of reducing interna-

tional roles to fit reduced strength, the government committed major forces to peacekeeping in Cyprus in 1964 – a "brief" task which had not ended by 1984. The search for a nonnuclear role in NATO led to a promise to send forces to Norway if NATO's northern (and nonnuclear) flank was threatened. The ill-equipped Canadian brigade group in Germany did not receive armoured personnel carriers until 1967 or modern tanks until 1977. When air force advisers asked for American-built F-4 Phantoms, the government chose the CF-5, a cheaper, less sophisticated aircraft. A navy program of 8 general-purpose frigates was cancelled and replaced by construction of 4 helicopter-equipped destroyers for antisubmarine work and a costly refit of the single aircraft carrier, the *Bonaventure*.

Well aware that public opinion and most colleagues favoured defence cuts, Hellyer had negotiated a fixed budget of $1.5 billion a year for his department. His drastic reorganization, with the accompanying drop in personnel, was a trade-off for modernization. Inflation ate up most of the savings. A destroyer worth $20 million in 1960 cost $50 million by 1967. Canadian apathy regarding defence spending grew with the decade and with criticism of American involvement in Vietnam. Domestic concerns, inflation, unemployment and Québec SEPARATISM preoccupied Canadians.

On 26 June 1968, Canadian voters gave their confidence to a new Liberal leader, P.E. Trudeau, who promised systematic policymaking and a cure for the "strategist's cramp" that had bound Canadian defence since WWII. On 3 Apr 1969 the new prime minister proclaimed new defence priorities: surveillance of Canadian territory and coastlines (protection of sovereignty); defence of N America in co-operation with the US; fulfilment of NATO commitments; and performance of any international peacekeeping roles Canada might assume. The list turned Hellyer's 1964 priorities upside down. Peacekeeping, the justification for Hellyer's unification, was lowest; "surveillance" was now on top. Hellyer's successor as minister of national defence, Léo Cadieux, went to Brussels to warn of drastic cuts in Canada's NATO force. In Aug 1969 Canada's NATO contingent of 10 000 was halved and the remaining ground forces were transferred from British to American command. In Parliament, Cadieux announced that Armed Forces strength would fall from 110 000 to 80-85 000. *Bonaventure*, newly refitted, was scrapped. Five regular regiments vanished from the active list. Most CF-5 fighters went into storage. The new policies were costly and military leaders took the blame. Disposal of the costly aircraft carrier, the mothballing of an experimental hydrofoil and delivery of the now-inappropriate new destroyers made Maritime Command look foolish. One consequence of criticism was a 1972 policy of "civilianization" in NDHQ.

The government's policies, summarized in *Defence in the Seventies* (1970), elaborated the military role in ensuring Canadian sovereignty, not merely in the Arctic and on the oceans but in AID TO THE CIVIL POWER. This last was a historic but half-forgotten role for Canadian forces, but urban violence in the US and potential peacekeeping roles had justified planning and training. In Oct 1969 troops were rushed to Montréal when rioting accompanied a police strike. A much more massive intervention occurred during the OCTOBER CRISIS: on 14 Oct 1970 troops were ordered to Ottawa to protect public buildings and prominent figures. On Oct 16 the prime minister proclaimed the WAR MEASURES ACT, and more than 10 000 troops in battle order were soon deployed in Montréal, Québec and Ottawa. It was a dramatic and dangerous exercise of power. Some officers recognized that such activity posed great danger for the Armed Forces as an institution. The troops were fortunate that they could withdraw as early as Nov 12 without suffering or inflicting casualties.

The October Crisis heightened awareness of the importance of making the Canadian forces more representative of an essentially bicultural nation. The Royal Commission on BILINGUALISM AND BICULTURALISM had demonstrated that the Armed Forces remained typical of federal institutions which frustrated French-speaking Canadians. Outside of a few army units, the forces had operated almost entirely in English. Few French Canadians had ever reached the highest ranks. In 2 world wars, unilingualism of the forces had contributed to bitterly divisive conscription crises. The Trudeau government was determined to make federal agencies effectively bilingual, and the Armed Forces were an obvious place to start.

New policies included expansion of language training, recruiting and promotion policy to achieve proportional representation through the rank structure, separate training for French-speaking personnel covering most of the 300 specialist trades, and French-language ships, flying squadrons and ground-force units. The program, coinciding with sharp reductions in overall strength, a weak budget and allegations of political interference, was acutely unpopular with the English-speaking majority. The French-language units often made the Armed Forces look as divided as the country they served. Time, patience and new generations of personnel would gradually make bilingualism, like unification, seem more natural.

Both experiments had been easier because it was unclear how Canadian forces could be used in a world that seemed to be moving towards détente. But in the 1970s the world began to appear more dangerous. The creation of the Organization of Petroleum Exporting Countries and its power to raise oil prices revealed unexpected vulnerability among Western industrialized countries. The growth of a powerful Soviet fleet with a potential global reach added to a threat hitherto limited to massive armoured forces and powerful missile batteries. The Canadian government, seeking to improve commercial relations with Europe, discovered the cost of the 1969 decision to halve the NATO contingent: not only could the remnant not be removed, but its obsolete tanks and aircraft had to be replaced to assuage the anger of NATO partners. Despite painful and costly delays, Canada began re-equipping (*see* ARMAMENTS). During the 7-year process of choosing a maritime patrol plane, the price rose from $300 million to more than $1 billion. The search for a new fighter airplane led to the McDonnell

Douglas F-18D, essentially an unproven aircraft. The decisive consideration was the amount of business the deal would distribute to Québec and Ontario industries. While the aging ships and aircraft of Maritime Command spent long periods in harbour awaiting repairs, delivery dates for 6 patrol frigates receded into the late 1980s and the 1990s.

The reluctant commitment to re-equip reflected a belated realization that Canada's influence in the world was not improved by the debilitated state of its Armed Forces. Purchases of German Leopard tanks and American aircraft served as much a diplomatic as a military purpose. Even domestic opinion appeared to support a modest strengthening of the forces. Before the 1979 election, the Trudeau government promised to add 4700 men and women to a uniformed strength that had fallen to 78 000 and to add a capital-spending program equal to at least 20% of the defence budget. The commitment was endorsed by Joe Clark's Conservative government, which won the election. Clark's government also established a task force to report on the possible unscrambling of unification.

The task force reported to a renewed Liberal government. Unification was not to be undone. Its original rigour had already begun to fade. The functional commands had been modified by 1975 to restore a shadow of the original 3 services: Maritime Command, Mobile Command and Air Command. Officers in charge, isolated in Halifax, St-Hubert and Winnipeg, were granted improved access to NDHQ. Distinctions developed in the training and career planning of members of each command, but it took the 1984 victory of the Conservatives and a new minister, Robert Coates, to revive 3 separate service uniforms though with common badges and rank insignia.

When Coates resigned in 1985, his interim successor, Erik Nielsen, was preoccupied by government cost-cutting. Only in the summer of 1986 did National Defence receive an effective full-time minister, Perrin BEATTY. In June 1987, he delivered the Conservatives' long-promised white paper on defence.

For the most part, the paper reflected trends in DEFENCE POLICY developed through the 1980s. Like many of their European allies, many Canadian leaders regarded the aggressive, confrontational style of Ronald Reagan's White House with some alarm. Yet it had been apparent to Liberals and Conservatives alike that Canada had to renovate its conventional military strength in order to influence Washington and show solidarity with the Europeans. Reagan's first visit to Ottawa in Mar 1981 was the occasion for the third renewal of the NORAD agreement; his first lengthy meeting with Brian Mulroney, at Québec in Mar 1985, occasioned announcement of a substantially improved and modernized North Warning System which would be capable of tracking the new threat of Cruise missiles.

The Beatty white paper of 1987 reiterated Canada's commitment to both its military alliances and its traditional search for peace. After a 1986 exercise confirmed that it was impractical, Canada abandoned its commitment to share in the defence of Norway but promised the same forces – a brigade of infantry and 2 fighter squadrons – to NATO's Central Front where Canadians had served since 1951.

The main thrust of the new policy, however, was a renewed emphasis on the defence of Canada and particularly northern air space and sea lanes. Beatty's proposal to modernize the Canadian navy with a dozen nuclear-powered submarines, capable of operating under arctic ice, was a bold bid to move Canada's fleet from the 1950s to the 1990s. The audacity of the proposal

and its projected cost provoked opposition.

Canada's armed forces consist of 85 000 men and women in full-time service and about 22 000 in the reserves, though the latter total will rise if the 1987 policy proposals are carried out. Canada's operational fleet of 23 overage destroyers and frigates, many with helicopter-carrying capacity, and 3 submarines will be reinforced and partly replaced by patrol frigates in the 1990s and possibly by the powerful submarine force promised in the white paper. Three mechanized brigade groups, including 1 stationed in Europe, and an airborne regiment are also being re-equipped and modernized. The backbone of Canadian air strength at home and in Europe is 138 state-of-the-art CF-18 fighters, while maritime surveillance is provided by a modern but overworked force of 18 Lockheed Aurora patrol aircraft.

If Canada's armed forces are no longer embarrassingly outdated, except at sea, they remain tiny by the standard of its allies. Less than 1% of the Canadian work force is in uniform compared to 2.8% among its NATO allies. Canada's defence spending is lower per capita than any of the wealthier NATO members. However, military force has never been a major component in Canada's search for security. Instead, Ottawa has concentrated on encouraging its powerful, suspicious superpower neighbours to live in peace. Canada has also sought to develop alliances both as a source of security and a means of avoiding isolation. Self-defence, at least in peacetime, has never been seriously contemplated. Even the 1987 white paper acknowledges that a home-based effort is designed to preserve sovereignty in what, in any case, would be a continental strategy. Since the Ogdensburg agreement of 1940, nothing much has changed in the fundamentals of Canadian strategy even if the world and its weapons have changed out of recognition.

DESMOND MORTON

Reading: James Boutilier, ed, *The RCN in Retrospect 1910-1968* (1981); Canada, Army Headquarters, Historical Section, *The Regiments and Corps of the Canadian Army* (1964); B. Cuthbertson, *Canadian Military Independence in the Age of the Superpowers* (1977); W.A.B. Douglas, *Creation of a National Air Force* (Official History of the Royal Canadian Air Force, II, 1986); James Eayrs, *In Defence of Canada*, 5 vols (1964-83); D.J. Goodspeed, *The Armed Forces of Canada* (1967); S. Kostenuk and J. Griffin, *RCAF Squadron Histories and Aircraft, 1924-1968* (1977); K. Macpherson and J. Burgess, *The Ships of Canada's Naval Forces, 1910-1981* (1981); Desmond Morton, *A Military History of Canada* (1985); Leslie Roberts, *There Shall Be Wings* (1959); G.F.G Stanley, *Canada's Soldiers: The Military History of an Unmilitary People* (1974); G.N. Tucker, *The Naval Service of Canada*, 2 vols (1951); S.F. Wise, *Canadian Airmen and the First World War* (Official History of the Royal Canadian Air Force, I, 1980).

Armenians The Armenian Soviet Socialist Republic, the only Armenian political unit in existence today, comprises only a portion of historic Armenia, which also includes territories in present-day Turkey. Most of the Armenian students and factory recruits who started the chain of Armenian migration to Canada in the 1880s were born in territories occupied by Turkey. By 1915 approximately 1000 Armenians had settled in Canada, primarily in southern Ontario. Most were sojourning men of the peasant class from Anatolia. From 1915 to 1922 more than 1.5 million Armenians perished as a result of the Turkish government's policy of genocide. The remnants sought refuge in neighbouring countries. Canadian immigration restrictions passed in 1909 effectively barred all but 1500 survivors of the Genocide from entering Canada after 1919. Among these immigrants was a group of approximately 100 orphan boys who were brought out in the 1920s by the Armenian Relief Association of

Canada to live on a farm near Georgetown, Ont. A year after the United Church of Canada took over in 1928, the farm was closed down and the "Georgetown Boys" were dispersed among Ontario farmers, either as foster children or as contracted farm labourers. During the 1920s, the Armenian Relief Association also brought out a group of about 40 young girls as domestics.

Destabilization in the Middle East, liberalization of Canada's immigration regulations, and removal of the classification of Armenians as Asiatics in the 1950s and 1960s have led to an influx of Armenian immigrants, almost exclusively from Middle Eastern and Mediterranean countries. Because Armenians have been displaced twice in 50 years, there is a far-reaching desire among many of Armenian background to regain their homeland. Recently, new and clandestine groups have used political violence to draw attention to and articulate legitimate Armenian claims.

Most Armenians in Canada are entrepreneurs or professionals. About 60% live in metropolitan Montréal, 35% in the Toronto-Hamilton area, and the remainder in other urban centres. It is estimated that there are about 50 000 people of Armenian descent in Canada today.

The majority of Armenians belong to the Armenian National Apostolic Church; others adhere to the Armenian Catholic or Protestant churches. In addition to administering to the religious needs of the community, the churches also engaged in social and cultural functions.

The Armenian National Committee of Canada, affiliated with the Armenian Revolutionary Federation, has been, for more than 80 years, the major nationalist party in Canada. The Democratic Liberal (Ramgavar) and the Social Democrat Hnchagian parties also have followers. Along with the Armenian General Benevolent Union, the parties and their affiliates organize cultural, social, charitable, athletic and scout and guide activities. The Armenian language press, including a large number of bulletins and newsletters, and the weeklies *Horizon* and *Abaka,* play an important role in linguistic and cultural maintenance.

The Genocide and the fear of ultimate national extinction have spurred Armenians to strenuous efforts to preserve their ethnic heritage, especially through Armenian schools. Approximately 2000 children in Montréal and Toronto attend 4 full-time elementary and secondary day schools based on a trilingual curriculum.

ISABEL KAPRIELIAN

Armour, Leslie, philosopher (b at New Westminster, BC 6 Mar 1931). Armour, with a BA from UBC (1952) and a PhD from U of London (1956), taught PHILOSOPHY first in the US, then at Waterloo and now at U of O (since 1977). Like many Canadians foremost in their fields, his work (7 books and more than 45 articles and book chapters) is better known abroad than at home. He is a pioneer in publishing early Canadian philosophy and has philosophical publications in metaphysics, religion, law, politics and community. His first 3 books, *The Rational and the Real* (1962), *The Concept of Truth* (1969) and *Logic and Reality* (1972), attempt to extend the idealist tradition. The idea of Canada has sparked his lifelong, often tumultuous, pursuit of just causes, stemming from his time as a student editor, newspaper journalist and contributor to Canadian and British news services. Much of his work, eg, *The Idea of Canada and the Crisis of Community* (1981) and "The Metaphysics of Community" (forthcoming), reflects Canada's unique political and philosophical federalism and expresses his undaunted commitment to Canada.

ELIZABETH A. TROTT

Armstrong, BC, City, pop 2706 (1986), inc 1913, is the business centre of a farm and forest economy of the Spallumcheen municipality. It is at the N end of the OKANAGAN VALLEY 23 km N of VERNON and 13 km S of ENDERBY. Spallumcheen, a Salish word, has been variously interpreted as meaning "beautiful valley," "flat meadow," "meeting of the waters" and "prairie-banked river." The district was first settled in 1866 by A.L. Fortune and J.B. Burns in Landsdowne, the original townsite. When the Shuswap and Okanagan Railway extended its line to Okanagan Landing (1891-92) the townsite moved to its present location. The town was named for London financier W.C. Heaton-Armstrong, who raised the bonds for the railway project. Catherine Schubert (1837-1918), the only woman member of the OVERLANDERS OF 1862, lived in the area from 1881. Armstrong, once known as "Celery City," has since diversified from grain, livestock and dairy products (from 1938 it has been home of the famous "Armstrong" cheese) to light manufacturing and, since a forest company constructed a mill near town in 1975, lumber and plywood. The Armstrong fall fair, started in 1900, became western Canada's largest grade B livestock exposition.

PETER GRANT

Armstrong, Ernest Howard, journalist, lawyer, politician, premier of NS (b at Kingston, NS 27 July 1864; d at Bridgewater, NS 15 Feb 1946). Educated at Acadia and Dalhousie (LLB, 1888), Armstrong edited the Weymouth *Free Press* from 1889 to 1892, and later moved to Yarmouth where he held various administrative posts. He was MLA for Yarmouth County (1906-20) and held the public works and mines portfolio in the Liberal government of Premier G.H. MURRAY 1911-23. A hardworking but unimaginative politician, Armstrong sought retirement to the bench when, as senior Cabinet member, he succeeded to the premiership (1923-25). Although the Liberals' rout in the June 1925 election was basically the result of regional depression, Armstrong's misreading of the MARITIME RIGHTS movement and mishandling of labour problems in the coal mines contributed to the Conservative landslide.

ERNEST R. FORBES

Armstrong, James Sherrard, lawyer, author, judge (b at Sorel, LC 27 Apr 1821; d there 23 Nov 1888). An able but undistinguished Québec advocate, Armstrong was given an unprecedented promotion in 1871 when he was appointed chief justice of St Lucia in the West Indies. On its cession to Britain in 1803, the island had retained its prerevolutionary language and law. With the appointment of British judges trained in the common law, who could neither speak nor read French, the legal system and laws became increasingly confused. Selected for the appointment by the COLONIAL OFFICE because he was bilingual and trained in civil law, Armstrong not only performed his judicial duties but also codified the laws of St Lucia, using the civil and procedural codes of Québec as his models. Hence Québec became, and remains, a prime source of jurisprudence for St Lucia. Resigning in 1881, Armstrong returned to Canada where he was later appointed chairman of the Royal Commission on Capital and Labour, one of the most important government investigations in the 19th century.

D.H. BROWN

Armstrong, John, printer, labour leader (d at Toronto 22 Nov 1910). The major Conservative labour spokesman in Toronto in the 1880s, Armstrong was active in the Toronto Trades and Labor Council and in the TRADES AND LABOR CONGRESS OF CANADA. Fired from the Toronto *Mail* after the unsuccessful 1884 strike, Armstrong helped lead Toronto workers away from the Tories briefly. Sir John A. MACDONALD's timely intervention allowed Armstrong to arrange a truce between the printers and the *Mail.* Appointed to the Royal Commission on the Relations of Labour and Capital, he led a pro-labour faction which issued a separate report. When the Conservatives came to power in Ontario, Armstrong was named secretary of the Ontario Bureau of Labour.

G.S. KEALEY

Armstrong, John Archibald, business executive (b at Dauphin, Man 24 Mar 1917). A geologist, he graduated from University of Manitoba and worked 42 years for Imperial Oil, Canada's largest oil company, including 4 as president and 8 as chairman of the board, before retiring 1982. His tenure as president and chairman was a difficult time for Canada's oil industry and for Imperial. After nearly 30 years of rapid growth, the industry had entered a period of declining supplies, production rates and consumer demand, with sharply higher prices and national controversy over revenue sharing between the oil companies, oil-producing provinces and the federal government. Under Armstrong's administration, Imperial appeared to cope with these difficulties with comparative success.

EARLE GRAY

Armstrong, William, civil engineer, artist, photographer (b at Dublin, Ire 28 July 1822; d at Toronto 8 June 1914). He immigrated to Toronto in 1851, and his work as a railway engineer gave him opportunities to indulge his hobby of painting in not yet settled parts of the country. He painted native life in the style of Paul KANE and his sketches of troops in the RED RIVER REBELLION (1870) appeared in the *Canadian Illustrated News.* He was a competent watercolourist and in works such as *The Arrival of the Prince of Wales at Toronto* (1860) he has left a valuable record. He was much admired in his day and, as drawing master at the Toronto Normal School for 26 years, had a lasting influence. He was associate member of the Royal Canadian Academy at its founding. Armstrong was also one of the earliest collodion wet-plate practitioners, but few of his photographs have survived.

JAMES MARSH

Army, *see* ARMED FORCES: MILITIA AND ARMY.

Army Benevolent Fund Board, est under the Army Benevolent Fund Act (1947) to administer funds in special accounts existing in the Consolidated Revenue Fund. The board comprises 5 members, nominated from each of the National Council of Veterans Associations in Canada and from the ROYAL CANADIAN LEGION. The funds represent a source of relief for WWII veterans and their dependants when help is not available from other veterans' programs or social programs. Educational assistance is also provided. The board reports to Parliament through the minister of veterans affairs.

Arnold, Benedict, soldier (b at Norwich, Conn 14 Jan 1741/42; d at London, Eng 14 June 1801). He apprenticed as an apothecary but ran away to join a New York company serving in the SEVEN YEARS' WAR. He later established a trading business in New Haven. Reacting to news of the Battle of Lexington at the onset of the AMERICAN REVOLUTION he mustered the local militia and launched a successful attack on Ticonderoga, 10 May 1775. As part of the campaign to invade Canada led by Richard Montgomery, Arnold led an expedition along the Kennebec, Dead and Chaudière rivers, arriving before Québec with only 700 of his original troop of 1100 men. He assumed command when Montgomery was killed on the ill-fated attack on Dec 30-31 and remained camped before Québec until he was transferred to Montréal in

April. He was in full retreat by June and saw further action on Lake Champlain and in the Saratoga campaign, each time distinguishing himself with conspicuous bravery. Though he pleaded that he was unsympathetic with the revolutionary cause, his treason was motivated by disappointment at being passed over for promotion, by a reprimand for using his office for personal gain, and by money. He defected in 1780 and was rewarded with £6315 and a generous pension. He moved to England in 1781 and to Saint John in 1786, departing in 1791 amid further controversy, resentment and legal entanglements. In 1798 he was awarded a large grant of land in Upper Canada but never took up residence there. An arrogant, ambitious man, Arnold's military accomplishments have largely been obscured by his controversy and his name remains synonymous in American lore with treason and infamy.

JAMES MARSH

Arnprior, Ont, Town, pop 6022 (1986c), 5828 (1981c), inc 1892, located at the confluence of the Madawaska and OTTAWA rivers, 56 km W of Ottawa. The community was founded by the despotic Scots laird Archibald MCNAB in 1823, and the site was named after the ancestral home (Arnpryor) of his Buchanan kinsmen. McNab lost his settlement rights in 1840, and the site was deserted until 1851, when Daniel McLachlin began large-scale lumbering operations on the Madawaska. Lumber and textiles dominated the economy for a long time. Now helicopters and tourism are important, and the Canadian Civil Defence College is located here. Memorabilia of McNab's days, including the original deed of land and the petition by which his compatriots had him removed, are displayed at the Arnprior and District Museum; his summer home, Waba Lodge, is recreated 10 km SW. K.L. MORRISON

Aroostook War, a point of crisis in the Maine-New Brunswick boundary dispute which in early 1839 saw both sides send troops into the valley of the Aroostook, a tributary of the SAINT JOHN R. By the Treaty of PARIS, 1783, the boundary was supposed to run N from the ST CROIX R to an undetermined height of land. At stake were the Acadian settlements of Madawaska, communication between the British provinces, and rich timber resources. Serious conflict was avoided through compromise and the dispute was resolved by the ASHBURTON-WEBSTER TREATY of 1842.

ERNEST R. FORBES

Arpent, a French measure of length and area. Numerous regional variants of the arpent coexisted in 17th-century France; of these, the *arpent de Paris* came into use in Canada before 1636 as part of a system of measures. The *arpent de superficie,* or square arpent (equivalent to 0.342 ha), remained the standard measure of land area in the old seigneurial districts of Québec until supplanted by the metric system in the late 1970s.

TOM WIEN

French Unit	English Equivalent	Metric Equivalent
pied	1.066 ft	.325 m
toise (6 pieds)	6.40 ft	1.95 m
perche (3 toises)	19.18 ft	5.85 m
arpent (10 perches)	191.8 ft	58.5 m
lieue (84 arpents)	16 111.2 ft (3.051 mi)	4.91 km

Arsenault, Angèle, singer, songwriter (b at Abrams, PEI 1 Oct 1943). A collector and singer of Acadian folk songs, she was encouraged by her impresario Lise Aubut to write and sing her own songs in English and French (1973-74). She was cofounder (1974) of the Société de production et de programmation de spectacles (SPPS). Her long-playing record *Libre* won the 1979 ADISQ

Gala Award for best-selling album. She changed her image to a more natural style in the early 1980s, but her rhythmic songs are still the vehicle for her own special brand of humour.

HÉLÈNE PLOUFFE

Arsenault, Aubin-Edmond, lawyer, politician, premier of PEI (b at Abrams Village, PEI 28 July 1870; d at Charlottetown 29 Apr 1968). In 1917 Arsenault became premier of the Island, the first Acadian premier of any Canadian province. Son of Joseph-Octave Arsenault, a longtime provincial member and the first and only PEI Acadian named to the Senate, Aubin-Edmond sat in the PEI assembly 1908-21. He was successively minister without portfolio, premier and attorney general and 1919-21 leader of the opposition. From 1921 to 1946, Arsenault served as judge of the Supreme Court of PEI. GEORGES ARSENAULT

Art The native people of Canada excelled in all forms of art (*see* INDIAN ART; INUIT ART; NORTHWEST COAST INDIAN ART; PREHISTORY), but their great achievements are beyond the scope of this article. Early Canadian art in the European tradition cannot be separated from European artistic production of the same period. From the time they arrived in Canada, French colonists attempted to reproduce an architectural environment that reminded them of their motherland (*see also* ARCHITECTURE). Before launching more ambitious projects, they erected a system of protection used in Europe since the late Middle Ages: the fortified manor. Early construction at PORT-ROYAL; Champlain's residence in Québec City (1608); and Maisonneuve's Pointe-à-Callières fort in Montréal (1642) were built on these lines, though in materials such as wood which were available and easily worked. Construction methods borrowed nothing from indigenous habitations.

Objects of curiosity as well as of conquest, the native people of the New World were first depicted on maps by illustrators who had no direct knowledge of their subject. They reflected more the traditional preconceptions about peoples who were supposed to inhabit the far reaches of the known world than the actual accounts of the discoverers, who themselves were not without prejudice. Books about Canada were more accurate. *The Works of Samuel de Champlain,* for instance, were illustrated by a few engravings based on Champlain's drawings, which gave a relatively good view of some aspects of Huron life, such as hunting, healing rituals and funerary practices. The portraits of Inuit painted by John White during Martin FROBISHER'S expedition are astonishingly accurate. Drawings by the Jesuit Louis Nicolas, now known as the *Codex canadensis,* took their inspiration from François Du Creux's *Historia Canadensis...* (1664), but they added so many details to their models that they contribute immensely to knowledge of the first inhabitants of Canada, particularly the Algonquin.

Population growth, while much slower than in New England during the same period, soon made it necessary to construct more permanent dwellings. Towns began to flourish. QUÉBEC CITY had taken shape by the end of the 17th century, its major buildings already in locations they occupied during the French regime (to 1760). Cathedrals, convents and the headquarters of the governor and the intendant occupied the best land on Cap Diamond or, as it was then called, "la haute ville." The commercial Lower Town developed around the small Notre-Dame-des-Victoires Chapel (1688), in front of which a bust of the king graced a small square. Built according to plans drawn up by engineers Claude Baillif, Levasseur de Néré and Chaussegros de Léry, if not by professional architects, these buildings were solid con-

Ex voto of marquis de Tracy (1666). Mercantilism made the development of indigenous painting virtually impossible during the French regime. Ex voto painting was among the few exceptions (*courtesy Basilique Ste-Anne-de-Beaupré*).

structions in stone, recalling the style of provincial France of the same period.

Founded a little later, MONTRÉAL followed a similar development. Maisonneuve's old fort was abandoned, and the city spread out along the St Lawrence R between the parish church, almost where Notre-Dame is today, and the Bonsecours Chapel, construction of which began in 1657. A fortified wall was built in an attempt to establish the town boundaries. A striking example of 18th-century military architecture, the massive fortress of LOUISBOURG on Cape Breton I was designed by Jean-François de VERVILLE to follow Sébastien Le Prestre de Vauban's system of FORTIFICATIONS and proved extremely costly to build. After 1960 it was rebuilt by Parks Canada in meticulous detail.

At the same time as this urban development was taking place, the SEIGNEURIAL SYSTEM was creating rural habitations along the river. Villages, the centre of which was always the parish church, were slow to develop. By the 18th century the countryside was dotted with churches that imitated the splendid town churches, which in turn were reminiscent of French provincial churches. Québec's Notre-Dame and the churches of the Jesuits and Récollets had a determining influence on these rural churches. Houses around Québec, in contrast, resembled those on Norman farms, and houses elsewhere recalled those found in Maine, Perche or Anjou, the native regions of most of the colonists. In contrast to New England architecture, stone and wood were used frequently, but brick was never employed.

By the late 17th century, sculptors were commissioned to adorn the churches with high altars in carved and gilded wood. Unlike church paintings, which were created on canvas and could be rolled up and transported by ship, the more cumbersome sculptures were produced locally by tradesmen who passed their knowledge down through the generations from master to apprentice. The most famous were the LEVASSEURS and BAILLAIRGÉS of Québec, Philippe Liébert and, later, Louis QUÉVILLON of Montréal. In style these sculptors were catching up to the prevalent trends in France – Louis XV, rococo, neoclassical – though with some delay owing to the difficulties in communication between the metropolis and the colony (*see also* SCULPTURE).

France's MERCANTILISM made it more difficult for PAINTING to develop. With the exception of ex-voto paintings (*see* VOTIVE PAINTING) and a few portraits of nuns (especially posthumous portraits) and officers done in New France, paintings dating from the French regime were imported. Frère LUC might be considered an exception, but he spent only 15 months in Canada. On one level these difficult conditions contributed to the quality of early painting in Canada, for they have a spontaneity and naïvety which are not always found in sculpture.

The British Conquest in 1760 did not immediately alter the face of architecture. Buildings damaged during the war were reconstructed and churches were built according to traditional plans, now slightly more formalized under the influence of Abbé Conefroy's plan for the Boucherville Church (1801). Later, under the influence of Jérôme Demers, a professor of architecture at the seminary in Québec, architects such as his pupil Thomas Baillairgé became receptive to French neoclassicism. Demers was a devoted follower of French architects like Vignole and Blondel.

The arrival of the British in N America had an immediate effect on painting. English officers trained at the Military Academy in Woolwich showed their enthusiasm for the Canadian landscape by producing many TOPOGRAPHIC PAINTINGS and ornamental landscapes which were often engraved in London. Thomas Davies was one of the earliest and the most famous of these English watercolour artists. His works have a freshness that is not found in those of Richard Short or James Patterson Cockburn, which are of a more documentary nature.

New waves of colonists had a profound influence on the arts. Like the French before them, the British tended to prefer the style which they knew best, Georgian, which for a long time thereafter symbolized allegiance to the British Crown. The LOYALISTS brought art objects and ideas with them from the US, including silver, engravings and paintings, as well as the memories of the architecture of various regions. By 1800 an expanding economy favoured growth of a middle class and several garrison communities. Portraits of merchants and their families, of soldiers, government officials and the clergy were in demand. After spending 14 years as a portrait artist in the US, Robert Field lived for 8 years in Halifax, where he continued in this genre; his English background and training made him a polished painter, familiar with the styles and techniques fashionable during this period.

The turn of the century saw the beginning of what is sometimes called the Golden Age of Québec painting. New stimuli became available; Québec artists went to Europe to study, and European artists continued to arrive in Canada. François Beaucourt, Antoine PLAMONDON and Théophile HAMEL belonged to the former group, William BERCZY and Cornelius KRIEGHOFF to the latter. Joseph LÉGARÉ, however, never set foot in Europe; his interest in art and collecting developed parallel to his pictorial records of landscapes, dramatic events in the history of Québec and occasional bursts of pictorial fantasy.

Stylistically, European influence in Canada remained strong, but subject matter in painting broadened. In small precise paintings Peter RINDISBACHER showed what it meant to a young Swiss to sail into Hudson Bay and settle in the Red River Colony. Working out of Upper Canada, Paul KANE can really be called an artist/adventurer; in 1845 he was inspired by the American George Catlin to make a journey across Canada,

recording Indians, the portages and the scenery in many sketches and paintings, still small in format and stylistically dense.

As in the US during the first half of the 19th century, Canada too was sensitive to a variety of architectural styles. British architects such as John Wells (Bank of Montreal, 1848) and John OSTELL (Notre-Dame-de-Grace, 1851) used a neoclassical style in their buildings in Montréal, whereas James O'Donnell and his patrons favoured the neogothic for the Church of NOTRE-DAME (1829) in the same city. Both stylistic tendencies were also employed in Halifax, Kingston and Toronto.

In 1796 York (named Toronto in 1834) became the capital of Upper Canada. Growing prosperity attracted portrait painters such as G.T. BERTHON, landscape painters such as Robert R. Whale, and explorers and genre painters such as William HIND, whose sketches are as interesting as his paintings. All were precursors of the more important Lucius O'BRIEN, John A. FRASER and Allan EDSON, who, like American painters of the same period, favoured a romantic approach to landscape, with richer brushwork and subtler use of colour. These men were the first to attempt to convey on canvas the majesty of the Rocky Mts or the atmospheric effects of the Atlantic Coast.

With Confederation in 1867, the urge to express a new sense of Canada as a unified country was felt in the arts. The Parliament Buildings in Ottawa were completed in 1866; Robert HARRIS was commissioned to paint his famous group portrait, *The Fathers of Confederation*, in 1883. The Royal Canadian Academy of Arts and the NATIONAL GALLERY OF CANADA were created in 1880 by the marquis of Lorne (*see* ARTISTS' ORGANIZATIONS).

Following a brief slowdown caused by the economic crisis in 1873, Canadian architecture grew at an unprecedented rate and, in the East at least, reflected the evolution from an essentially rural to an industrial economy. The period 1873-1914 witnessed a new taste for historicism, as if each architect felt the need to compete with his colleague in his ability to quote some architectural elements of the past: Gothic spires or windows were linked to French mansards, Italianate elements with Tudor styles. Public buildings (churches, RAILWAY STATIONS such as Windsor Station in Montréal, "château"-style HOTELS such as the Frontenac in Québec City and the Empress in Victoria) as well as domestic architecture, particularly in rural Ontario, showed this eclecticism. In the midst of this "revival" frenzy a new feeling for modern architectural space, and innovative materials such as cast iron, glass and, later, cement appeared, leading to basic structural changes in Canadian architecture.   At the turn of the century, painting was marked by such major figures as James Wilson MORRICE, the father of Canadian modernism; Ozias LEDUC, who divided his time between ambitious church decorations and exquisite still lifes and landscapes of St-Hilaire; Homer WATSON, who presented a more intimate vision of the Canadian landscape; and George REID and Paul PEEL, who were closer to the academic tradition. Nevertheless, with the exception of Morrice, who was an avid admirer of Matisse as early as 1908, and perhaps William BRYMNER, the influence of the *école de Paris* was not felt until later.

In the meantime, sculpture, which up to then had simply continued along traditional lines, began to change. New materials were explored, wood being replaced by bronze and plaster. New needs were answered: historical monuments in town squares, particularly war monuments in many towns and cities following WWI; ornamentation of the façades of new buildings, such as Louis-Philippe HÉBERT'S project for the legislature building in Québec City; elaborate TOMBSTONES in cemeteries. New subjects and figures from folk-

lore and Canadian history were attempted. As in the past, new styles appeared emulating European trends: academism, art nouveau, symbolism (Alfred LALIBERTÉ) and later, art deco. Sculpture became public (*see* PUBLIC ART) and, in Québec, less exclusively religious.

The early 1920s were great years for Canadian painting. The Toronto-based GROUP OF SEVEN, completely committed to the task of giving Canada a truly national form of painting, sought in the Canadian landscape their source of inspiration. They responded to its grandeur and captured it in decorative patterning and bold colours, without falling into the naturalism of the previous generation. Despite his short career, Tom THOMSON left behind a remarkable group of paintings and oil sketches. Concurrently with this Canadian "coast to coast" movement, a regionalist painting style developed in Québec. It was less a reflection of nature than of the French Canadians' 3-century attachment to the land. On the West Coast, Emily CARR expressed her unique response to both Northwest Coast Indian art and the BC landscape. Influenced by Fauvism and the mysticism of Lawren HARRIS, she made a contribution of her own and was the first woman artist to achieve eminence in Canadian art.

John LYMAN, a great admirer of Morrice, attempted after his return from Europe in the early 1930s to realign the art movement with the *école de Paris*. In 1939 he created the CONTEMPORARY ARTS SOCIETY and organized the modernist offensive in Canadian painting. WWII coincided with unprecedented growth in painting in Québec. In 1940 Alfred PELLAN returned from Paris and soon exhibited the strong influence that Cubism and especially Picasso had made on him. Paul-Émile BORDUAS gathered a number of young painters, including Jean-Paul RIOPELLE and Fernand LEDUC, and formed the AUTOMATISTES. Their 1948 manifesto, REFUS GLOBAL, had considerable ideological repercussions even beyond Québec's artistic world. After this breakthrough, one movement followed another in Québec, where painting tended to be more theoretically defined than in the other provinces. In reaction to automatism, the PLASTICIENS, Guido MOLINARI and Claude TOUSIGNANT, freed painting from its surrealistic attachments and directed it toward formal research. From then on, painters became concerned with structural and colour problems. Similar concerns were surfacing in Toronto. PAINTERS ELEVEN, of whom the most famous were Harold TOWN and Jack BUSH, moved from the abstract expressionism practised in New York to formalism. In general, the problem of contemporary Canadian painting is to maintain its originality in the face of strong American influences. Michael SNOW, with his remarkable original contributions to contemporary cinema, and the London, Ont, group with Greg CURNOE and Jack CHAMBERS, were particularly successful in differentiating their work from American art of the 1960s. The same concern has haunted young Canadian sculptors such as Armand VAILLANCOURT, Robert ROUSSIL and Robert MURRAY.

At first sight, modern architecture in Canada may look more international in style than do painting or sculpture. Climate and tradition, however, have led architects to achieve a style with a specific Canadian character. Foreigners are more thrilled than Canadians by the extent of Canadian subterranean architecture in cities like Montréal or Toronto, where it is possible to go from hotel to shopping centre to living quarters without stepping outside into the cold. Arthur ERICKSON at Simon Fraser University in Vancouver and John Andrews at Scarborough College, University of Toronto, have achieved buildings of great elegance and distinction.

The Amphitheatre of Lutetia (1953), oil on canvas, 81 x 106.4 cm, by Paul-Émile Borduas. Borduas gathered together a number of young painters and formed a group called Automatistes *(courtesy National Gallery of Canada/ gift of the Douglas M. Duncan Coll).*

What, then, is distinctive about Canadian art? From the beginning, artists in Canada have refused to operate in a vacuum, to cut themselves off from their European roots, whether French, English, Scottish, Irish or Ukrainian. At the same time, freed from a heavy weight of traditions, they display a certain inventiveness, imposed by isolation, by adaptation to difficult physical conditions. In many respects the Canadian experience in art may seem to parallel the American one, but the French influence, completely lacking in the US, is too overwhelming in Canadian art not to maintain an essential distinction between the art forms of the 2 countries. This quality is true not only for Québec and French Canadian artists, but for all Canadian artists. Moreover, federal institutions like the CANADA COUNCIL, the Art Bank and the National Gallery have succeeded in creating among contemporary Canadian artists a sense of community that goes beyond the language barrier and seeks a specific Canadian answer to the problems of art in our day.

FRANÇOIS-MARC GAGNON

Reading: D. Burnett and M. Schiff, *Contemporary Canadian Art* (1983); A. Gowans, *Building Canada* (1966); J. Russell Harper, *Painting in Canada* (1977); D. Reid, *A Concise History of Canadian Painting* (1973); L. Whiteson, *Modern Canadian Architecture* (1983).

Art Conservation and Restoration, *see* CONSERVATION OF MOVABLE CULTURAL PROPERTY.

Art, Contemporary Trends Contemporary art in Canada, as elsewhere, is marked by a questioning of the nature of art – what art has been about historically, what it ought to be about and who its intended audience is to be. This questioning has been accompanied by experimentation and innovation. The resulting work varies in content from the intensely personal to the public investigation of social and political issues; it ranges in form from the intellectually disciplined to the free and intuitive; and differs in production from the solitary to the collective.

As traditional art forms were discarded, contemporary art tested its limits as seldom before: it explored the link between means and ends, reset the boundaries between art and "reality," and redefined the art object in its aesthetic, social and economic contexts. The art processes have gained momentum and direction from forces as varied and contradictory as developments in computer and communications technology, oriental mysticism, and new thinking in the social and behavioural sciences, in philosophy and linguistics, including the work of Marshall MC-LUHAN; and from the international flow of ideas about art, coming during this period largely from the US – but, as modernism has given way to post-modernism, increasingly coming again from Europe. The need to experiment has been met by the new materials and tools made available by technological advance – plastics, computers, lasers, holograms, and the communications media – which by their nature suggested alternative contexts for art and access to a wider audience.

In Canada the diversity of contemporary trends has been compounded by the distance between centres of art activity and by their different histories, resources and responses to outside influences. This isolation has been offset by official support for alternative spaces and by the growing number of avant-garde art magazines with a national circulation: *Vanguard, Parachute, Canadian Magazine* and *Parallelogramme*, the organ of the artist-run centres.

Both Fusion des Arts in Montréal (fd 1964) and Intermedia in Vancouver (fd 1967) grew out of this climate. They were loose groupings of artists working in different media (film, music, dance, poetry) and in the traditional categories of painting and sculpture, which were perceived by many to be pointlessly restricting when isolated. Glenn Lewis, Glenn Toppings, Dennis Vance, Dallas Sellman, Gary Lee Nova, Evelyn Roth, Gerry Gilbert and many others were associated with Intermedia, although they often worked cooperatively or anonymously through pseudonyms. The artists of Fusion, whose founders were Richard Lacroix, François Soucy, François Rousseau and Yves Robillard, also pooled resources and shared ideas. The resulting happenings and performances – works combining touch and sound, vision and movement to experiment with sensory awareness, located as often outside

as in an art gallery – exuded a sense of optimism about the anticipated social benefits to be gained from the arts now that they were speaking a common and comprehensible language.

In forming the N.E. Thing Co (1966, incorporated 1969), Iain and Ingrid (formerly Elaine) BAXTER, who were among the founding members of Intermedia, demonstrated multimedia and interdisciplinary principles by setting up categories of their own, departments of their company which would deal with its multifarious products – the vacuum-formed still lifes, the inflatable plastic landscapes, works transmitted by telex, photographs of found images bearing the N.E. Thing Co's ACT (Aesthetically Claimed Thing) or ART (Aesthetically Rejected Thing) seals, and all of it to stimulate the GNG (Gross National Good), which was far more important than the GNP (Gross National Product). A company button proclaimed the message "Art is all over" – meaning that art can literally be anything at all, or else nothing special. It was a logical extension of the gesture, newly influential in the 1960s, made in 1913 by French artist Marcel Duchamp when he mounted a bicycle wheel on a stool and displayed it in an art gallery along with other "Readymades." In demonstrating that art could be a business with a product (Visual Sensitivity Information) the N.E. Thing Co was trying to demystify art, to link it to the real world, to show, as Duchamp had done, that art is in the eye of the beholder.

Despite its mimicry of capitalist business practices, the N.E. Thing Co shared the conviction of many progressive artists of the time that art should not be understood primarily as a marketable commodity. Among numerous suggestions Les Levine has made since the late 1960s, as to how else art might be understood, were his Disposibles (1968-69). These brightly coloured, vacuum-formed plastic modules were intended to be disposable, had no inherent value as objects, and could be arranged and rearranged at the whim of their owners. Levine's idea was the art; how it looked was up to anyone else. Michael SNOW, like Levine, was living in New York at this time. In their different ways they were responsible for channelling the ideas of conceptual art into Canada, though by its nature it easily travelled through the mail, the magazines and word of mouth.

Conceptual Art maintained that if the traditional forms of painting and sculpture were bankrupt and abstraction merely an irrelevant attenuation, then the object in making art was to isolate some essential "artness" which existed independently of any form it might take. The main result of conceptual art in Canada has been a way of thinking about art rather than any notable works, though the most memorable ideas were those that were given some kind of form and, therefore, were not properly conceptual. Snow has centered his work on an internally consistent exploration of the camera's potential, a process which has resulted in films and works both on and off the wall, of great poetry and coherence. Snow's work, which has an international following, has been an inspiration for many other artists, especially those for whom art stands or falls on the basis of the strength of its idea or concept.

In the early 1970s the NOVA SCOTIA COLLEGE OF ART AND DESIGN in Halifax was the focus for conceptual art in Canada. Characteristic of work by influential staff at NSCAD was Eric Cameron's *Camera Inserted in my Mouth* (1973-76), in which the camera lens, inserted into the artist's mouth for the duration of a standard 30-minute tape, with the only visible record on an otherwise black monitor being the shadowy trickle of sali-

Rita McKeough's *Defunct* (1981), mixed media installation and performance. McKeough installed replicas of old Calgary houses in the gallery of the Alberta Coll of Art, and in the evenings she destroyed them, bit by bit, acting out her strong feelings about the destruction of the urban environment (*courtesy Rita McKeough/photo by Charlie Fox*).

va, used the medium to clarify an idea about the ultimately self-reflexive nature of art.

In *One Million Pennies* (1980) Gerald Ferguson gave vivid realization to the critical notion that art and money might be synonymous, no other way having been devised to indicate value, in a work that consisted of a heap of one million pennies, newly minted, on a gallery floor. The paintings of Garry Neill Kennedy are also typical of a later development of conceptual art. Intending a comment on the irreducible nature of paintings as art objects, Kennedy perversely located it in format and pigment. He systematically analysed the colours and sizes of 32 paintings from the permanent collection of the Art Gallery of Ontario. The result was a parallel and entirely schematic series of drawings, *Canadian Contemporary Collection - The Average Size - The Average Colour* (1978), the thirty-third item representing the average of the total.

Body Art While conceptual art remained concentrated in eastern Canada, body art, in which the artist's person is interpreted as both the source of all ideas about art and the ultimate tool in their realization, was the related form which gained the widest following. In Vancouver it became part of the aesthetic of anarchic satire and expressive indulgence which characterized the work of Al Neil and the artists of the Western Front; in Toronto it served to release the interest of many artists in the exploration and expression of the individual. Everywhere it was used to further the feminist cause. Montréal artist Sorel Cohen gave graphic summation to the physical activities (bed making, window cleaning) and social role (organizer and homemaker) traditionally expected of women. In accord with the pared-down sensibilities of minimal and conceptual art, Cohen's photographic sequences reproduced the physical experience directly, without poetry or drama.

In *Smile*, a videotape made by Albert McNamara in 1971 while a student at NSCAD, the particularity of an individual's smile is lost in a half-hour-long contemplation of a generalized cliché about the body and its expressiveness. Video, with its unique blend of privacy in the making and infinite publicity for the product, adapted

well to the concerns of body art. In *Birthday Suit*, Lisa Steele scrutinized the scars and defects of her body while recounting their history. Vincent Trasov, whose work for 5 years consisted of disguising his body as a peanut, ran, as Mr Peanut, for mayor of Vancouver in 1974; his campaign – an artist/politician encased in his image in the public arena – put in a nutshell the predicament of art and the artist in taking meaningful roles in society.

Environmental Art Awareness of the person is extended in environmental art into the person's awareness of the environment. Reality "out there" is thought to have more presence, more potency, than any representation in paint or other traditional medium. The artist intervenes only to appropriate the existing qualities. Since the late 1960s this very durable strategy has been employed to very different ends. For a number of years, Irene Whittome has been installing in galleries objects and colours that she has made to be metaphors for her feelings about a particular place, room or city, so that the original atmosphere is recreated.

In 1971 Bill Vazan's *World Line*, which was realized with the help of a civil engineer and many people in 25 different locations around the world, cast an imaginary, zigzag line around the globe. Its only visible form was 25 angles in black tape on 25 floors, the arms of each leading geodetically on to the next point on the line. *World Line* invited us to consider (as did another work of Vazan's which put Canada in parentheses, with brackets drawn on beaches in PEI and Vancouver I) some of our strongest preconceptions about an environment that we are hardly able to conceive. In *Defunct* (1981), Rita McKeough installed in the gallery of the Alberta College of Art replicas which she had built of old houses of Calgary. In the evenings she came into the gallery to destroy them, acting out her strong feelings about the wanton destruction of our urban environment. In *Destruck* (1983) the houses have evolved arms with which to defend themselves, but the ensuing fight with the bulldozers only prolongs the death throes. The architectural environment also concerns Melvin CHARNEY, Montréal architect/artist, who, in the street gallery, recreates versions of the vernacular architecture which he feels we overlook and destroy at our peril; when we lose the past which is written on our buildings, however humble, we risk losing our identity in the present. In 1976 Charney orchestrated "Corridart," in which Sherbrooke St, Montréal's main processional axis, was transformed by responses to the street and its history from many of the city's artists. In a vivid demonstration of the power of art, Mayor Drapeau, within a week of its installation and before the Olympic visitors arrived, ordered the destruction of what was perceived as a threat.

Krzystof Wodiczko's "Public Projections" reveal that we see a building or locale as a myth in an interplay with changing social and cultural circumstances. Using slide projectors, he temporarily projects images of this myth on the physical structures themselves. The images he threw onto the façade of the Art Gallery of Ontario in 1981 suggested the collusion of art, business and cultural bureaucracy. The myth which we construct around mountains, and the very different ones around nuclear weapons, together with the announcement of the planned testing of the US Cruise missile in Alberta, led to the projection of the image of that missile on a rock face near Banff.

Correspondence Art, art that uses the postal system for its distribution, provides another method of circumventing the confines of art object and art gallery. Chuck Stake (Don Mabie), who has been mailing out of Calgary for 10 years, and Anna Banana are 2 of Canada's most prolific links in a

global network of those who make and share art for the price of postage.

Collage, the random assemblage of found images in such a way that the whole has impact and meaning that is greater than the sum of its parts, has complex roots in Duchamp, dada and the early surrealists. It fits a contemporary notion that we have no grounds for discriminating between one object or image and another, or between one interpretation and another, since all have a part to play in the way we construct our view of the world.

This idea is also a component of structuralism, an approach to knowledge made widely accessible through the writings of the French anthropologist Claude Levi-Strauss. His remark, "The decision that everything must be taken into account facilitates the creation of an image bank," provoked Michael Morris and Vincent Trasov to initiate Image Bank in Vancouver – a flow of images and requests for images which circulated around an international network of visual artists, poets, writers and musicians, thereby extending the chance of random relationships and juxtapositions in a scheme of things where everything was worth something. These same ideas inspired Glenn Lewis to initiate the *Great Wall of 1984* (1973). He invited 165 people to contribute the contents of 365 plexiglass boxes, which were stacked along the wall, forming a huge co-operative collage which intrigued passersby at the National Science Library in Ottawa.

The re-emergence of collage has been followed by the return of imagery and, with it, illusion, drama and narrative. In these pluralist circumstances, which were prevailing by the late 1970s, one response has been analysis. An intellectual and highly self-aware analysis of how contemporary art can proceed and claim meaning and status for itself, echoing similar procedures elsewhere, is offered in the work of 2 Vancouver artists, Jeff Wall and Ian Wallace. They use photography to scrutinize the value of images, their own and those of the mass media, and to ask how the "art" version of them is distinguishable from any other version.

Performance Art, and the often related installations, has been one of the most significant of the hybrid art forms, variously betraying its origins in the political urgency of agitprop, the high spirits of dada cabaret, the spontaneity of the happening and, in a concern with the processes through which images and ideas acquire meaning or have their meaning eroded, in its relationship with conceptual art. Bruce Barber, in carefully didactic performances, offers a reproof to both senders and receivers of the implicit sociopolitical content offered in the mass media. Elizabeth Chitty shows how we can meet the essentially sensory blandishments of those same media, while Marcella Bienvenue in her performances re-enacts the philosophical confusion into which the individual must inevitably be thrown by the barrage. In these instances, and many others, performance has been an effective vehicle, though by no means the only one, for the concerns of feminism.

An outrageous parody of this society and its promotional styles has been evolved through an ongoing series of performances, videotapes, installations and more by General Idea, the alias of 3 Toronto artists, A.A. Bronson, Felix Partz and Jorge Zontal: all art needs some kind of promotion and must make or find for itself a context if it is not to be socially meaningless.

Native Art Edward Poitras in his mixed-media installation *Stars in Sand* (1982) conveyed the wry poetry that results from the ambivalence of Indian artists towards their ancestry and the art forms of their ancestors. Many native artists from all parts of the country, wishing to communicate with society at large, are searching for forms that combine elements from traditional arts and mythology with

Bill Vazan's *World Line* was realized with the help of a civil engineer and people in 25 locations around the world, casting an imaginary zigzag line around the globe (*courtesy Bill Vazan*).

their own responses to the present. They are often in the company of those other artists who take the risk of creating a personal mythology. Gathie FALK's *tableaux vivants*, similar to her work in other media, show that it is possible to communicate effectively through a set of highly idiosyncratic symbols.

"Political Art" The personal poetry found in recent performance works by Bruce Parsons is used to point up a message of the widest relevance: the imbalance between man's use and abuse of the natural world in advanced industrial societies. Among the growing number of artists who are prepared to appropriate any means, including the so-called "revival" of painting, to make uncompromising response to a troubled world, 2 should be mentioned: Jamelie Hassam, who, in *Desaparecidos* (1981), recreated in all its desperate anguish the protest of the grandmothers of the "disappeared ones" of Argentina, and Ron Benner, whose works deal with the plunder of nature by man, of one society by another.

How artists can operate at all in the compromised role allowed by their historically privileged position is the question that Carol Condé and Karl Beveridge have attempted to answer in photographic installations, which deal with specific social issues such as the personal consequences of strike action and the role of women in the workplace. For Brian Dyson, who founded Syntax (Calgary International Artists' Contact Centre) in 1980, and his colleague Paul Woodrow, the only solution to the predicament of art, the only way to meet their social responsibilities, has been to stop making art and devote their energies to animating broadly based cultural activities in their local Calgary community of Hillhurst-Sunnyside. They believe that today direct social action is the only effective way for artists to give form to their ideas and perceptions. Other artists, particularly in Toronto, among them Janice Gurney and Ian Carr-Harris, chose to deal with this predicament by insisting that a valid art practice can only be founded on theory – the articulation of ideas and prescriptions gathered by various intellectual disciplines, which are reflected in, or implied in, the work. Art theory, in this sense, is yet another descendant of Conceptual Art. *See also* PAINTING; VIDEO ART.   CHARLOTTE TOWNSEND-GAULT

Reading: R. Bringhurst et al, eds, *Visions: Contemporary Art in Canada* (1983); D. Burnett and M. Schiff, *Contemporary Canadian Art* (1983); J. Murray, *The Best Contemporary Canadian Art* (1987).

Art Dealers in Canada have served as art dealers everywhere, not only as sellers of art but as tastemakers. Since they act as a link between the work of art and the art-buying public, they have an important role in the identification of who is important in Canadian art. By their sales, they help determine how much fame the artist will have, at least in the marketplace. In recent years, many of the more prominent members of the profession, such as G. Blair Laing in Toronto and Walter Klinkhoff in Montréal, Kenneth G. Heffel in Vancouver, the Masters Gallery in Calgary, as well as Geoffrey Joyner and Sotheby's in Toronto and Woltjen-Udell in Edmonton, significantly affected the field through their connoisseurship. To be successful, a dealer must act responsibly, not only towards the field but also towards the artist and the public. The Professional Art Dealers Assn (fd 1966) maintains basic guidelines and ethical standards for the operation of commercial art galleries.

Until the mid-19th century, dealers in Canada were forced to diversify their stock so that they carried art along with other salable items. James Spooner in Toronto, for instance, ran a small picture gallery with works by Daniel FOWLER, John FRASER, Paul PEEL and Homer WATSON in the rear of his tobacco shop on King St East. William Scott and Son, founded in 1859, sold mainly Barbizon School paintings but from 1901 were the dealer for M.A. SUZOR-COTÉ as well as handling the work of Cornelius KRIEGHOFF. In 1897 William R. Watson inherited John Ogilvy's in Montréal, an art business begun by Ogilvy as a hobby. By the 1930s several important galleries had been established – Leroy Zwicker in Halifax; Robertson and Wells in Ottawa; Mellors Fine Art, Laing and Roberts in Toronto. All these galleries sold mostly 19th-century English and European paintings. The taste of the public and the Depression made sales of Canadian paintings difficult. Some art dealers, however, played a significant role as pioneers in supporting young Canadian artists, eg, Watson who sold the paintings of Maurice CULLEN from 1908 until Cullen's death in 1934, Douglas Duncan who opened the Picture Loan Society in Toronto in 1936, and in the 1950s Agnes Lefort and Denyse Delrue in Montréal and Dorothy Cameron in Toronto (her Here and Now Art Gallery opened in 1959), David Mirvish for 15 years from the time his gallery opened in 1963. Success did not come easily. PAINTERS ELEVEN, with the help of Jack BUSH who showed with Roberts Gallery in Toronto, managed to have 2 shows there in 1954 and 1955. Though critics were interested and, by the second show, there was considerable public attention, sales were few. Avrom Isaacs in Toronto opened the Greenwich Gallery as a framing shop in 1955. By 1959 he had changed the name to the Isaacs Gallery and begun to foster a group of young artists that included Michael SNOW and Graham COUGHTRY who are now part of Canadian art history.

In the 1960s, with the growing enthusiasm for Canadian art and increasing affluence, there was a proliferation of art dealers, particularly in Toronto. The audience by now counted among its ranks the corporate sector. Businesses such as CIL, the Toronto Dominion Bank, and various oil companies, particularly Imperial Oil, began collections. The CANADA COUNCIL Art Bank program, established in 1972 with a budget of $1 million a year, and the program of the Department of Public Works (1964-78), in which 1% of the cost of all government buildings had to be spent on art, added substantially to the funds available (*see* PUBLIC ART). Today, possibly 50% of sales in the marketplace consists of those to corporate collections. At the same time, since public galleries are acutely unfunded, they rely more and more on gifts from the corporate and private sector.

The 1960s also saw the emergence of a new kind of dealer, the co-operative gallery or "alternate" space. A Space in Toronto, SAW in Ottawa, and other artist-run centres in a network across the country operate art galleries dedicated to promoting contemporary artists and sales, with no stigma of "commercialism." They meet a need created by a more diversified art scene – art that involves performance, VIDEO ART or large installations. Many contemporary dealers, eg, Ydessa Handeles in Toronto who opened her business in 1980, have gone along with the new trend. They consider their role more one of finding sponsors than of actively selling, though selling, particularly to the NATIONAL GALLERY OF CANADA, is important too. (*See* ART, CONTEMPORARY TRENDS.)

Dealers have had a significant role in influencing public taste and promoting the unusual. Private galleries across Canada have been largely responsible for the promotion and sale of the art of native people. Max Stern's Dominion Gallery in Montréal and G. Blair Laing introduced the sculpture of Henry Moore to Canada. Stern was also the first gallery to give contracts to artists, beginning with Goodridge ROBERTS in 1949. Mirvish guaranteed income as well as made purchases from many living artists, starting with Jules Olitski in 1964. His relationship with American artists provided an impetus to the changing role between artists and dealers in America. In addition, his gallery participated in the introduction of artists such as Jack Bush, Frank Stella, Kenneth Noland and Anthony Caro, among others, who have now become world famous. Many painters, curators and collectors in Canada and America today recall his gallery as their classroom. He brought Canadians into a new relationship with the international scene.

The commercial relationship between artist and dealer is usually based on commission (usually 40% or even 50% to the gallery, though it may be as low as 30% for established artists) and most work is sold on consignment. Some dealers, such as Walter Moos in Toronto, may buy an artist's production for several years and market it accordingly. Sales by commission are difficult for the unknown artist, who often must help pay for the opening and associated expenses. The dealer may advance money months before exhibitions, as well as providing exhibition space and sometimes a modest catalogue or flyer as well as the cost of framing and advertising. (These costs may be shared.) Some dealers show remarkable intuition for the future market value of an artist's work. They may hold works of art until an artist dies and then dictate market value. Max Stern bought many works by the unrecognized Emily CARR. Walter Klinkhoff, who started dealing art in 1949, recalls that he could once mount shows of work by Jackson, Lismer, Goodridge Roberts and Henri Masson, paintings he had bought to prevent others from getting them, but these stocks have all been exhausted.

By 1986 the market had taken an upsurge after a depression lasting from 1981. Auctions began to dominate public and private collecting. In 1986 the highest price achieved for a single work of art was at an auction – $450 000 for a Lawren Harris canvas (hammer price). The most successful auction ever held in Canada was that of Fraser Bros in Montréal in 1986, which realized $3.7 million (hammer price) for 128 works of art.

JOAN MURRAY

Reading: A. Jamis, ed, *Douglas Duncan: A Memorial Portrait*, (1974); G. Blair Laing, *Memoirs of an Art Dealer* (2 vols 1979, 1983); Georges Loranger, *Private and Public Collecting in Canada: The Tip of the Canadian Icejam* (1985); J. Morris, *Adrift on Course* (1979); W.R. Watson, *Retrospective: Recollections of a Montreal Art Dealer* (1974).

Art Education and the training of artists in Canada are directly related to the changing status of art in our society. Art education, whether for personal or professional purposes, corresponds to the development of psychological and pedagogical knowledge and to the current definition of a work of art. The development of creativity has only recently been defined as a separate activity and is part of that larger debate over whether an artist is born or trained. The role of the art school – whether it should simply teach the techniques which allow innate talent to develop or should actively redefine the nature of a work of art – remains an open question. Early art education in Canada was based mostly on the APPRENTICESHIP system. The myth that Bishop Laval established Canada's first school of arts and crafts at St Joachim in 1685 has been discredited. Most early artists received their training before they arrived – Frère LUC, Louis Dulongpré, William BERCZY – though some colonists, such as Mother Marie Madeleine Maufils de St Louis, received individual tutoring from artists who were passing through. In the apprenticeship system a master artist would train a young apprentice in exchange for assistance. Apprenticeship first appeared in the woodcraft and decorative art fields – woodworking, cabinetmaking, tinsmithing, ironmongery, silversmithing – fields for which the demand was greatest and which helped meet the need for repair work on imported objects. Apprenticeship is intrinsically a conservative system in which knowledge and methods in the arts and crafts are passed on relatively unchanged through several generations. While these artists/craftsmen were rarely innovative, there was some response to new techniques, stylistic influences and competition, mostly from abroad.

The apprenticeship system served a purpose: it established traditions of local practice and culture which survived over several generations. Some of the most important early centres of creativity owed their existence to the apprenticeship system, especially in SCULPTURE and ARCHITECTURE. The LEVASSEUR and BAILLAIRGÉ family dynasties dominated art activity in Québec and passed on a tradition of high achievement clearly based on French models and subject matter, but with its own characteristics of technical sophistication, human warmth and simplicity. In silversmithing in Québec there is a connection from Laurent Amyot to François Sasseville and Pierre Lespérance; in Nova Scotia a preference for English or American styles can be seen in works by Peter Norbeck, Michael Septimus Brown and Thomas Brown. In painting the most prestigious of these lineages is that which runs from Joseph LÉGARÉ to Louis-Philippe HÉBERT, via Antoine PLAMONDON, Théophile HAMEL and Napoléon BOURASSA. The indigenous art production of the 19th century is indebted to this system.

Apprenticeship played a relatively small role in the fine arts, developing only at the end of the 18th century in a combination school and workshop where the training was adapted to small groups. François Baillairgé's studio was functioning like a school when it offered courses in drawing, painting and sculpture; Louis QUÉVILLON used his workshop in the same way to train woodworkers and sculptors, complementing art lessons with academic studies. The type of education proposed by Baillairgé was basic and generalized, and its aim was less the formation of artists than of technicians and amateurs appreciative of the arts. In this sense, art education moved further away from the ideal of a school modelled on the European academies.

A system of private art instruction developed throughout the 19th century as the number of itinerant artists declined and many immigrant artists settled in the colony. Most of the art teachers who advertised in the papers prior to 1850 stressed their teaching abilities, and instruction was an important source of revenue for people such as William Eagar in Halifax and George Theodore BERTHON in Toronto. Despite the frequency and quantity of the courses, we have little information about their content, style and clientele. It seems that most students were young, cultured and socially privileged ladies. Instruction was specialized by medium (crayon, watercolours, pen and ink, oils), genre (landscape, still life) or style (learning to paint like a known artist). Drawing was basic, and the students learned to copy various themes and fragments of artistic works. Imitation was considered a way to transmit artistic knowledge. Students learned to reproduce the pictorial conventions found in certain works and transmitted either by engravings or by examples provided by the art master.

Private educational establishments (colleges, universities, convents) also offered courses by local artists. Charles Mondelet, in his well-known *Letters of Elementary and Practical Education* (1841), made no mention of art instruction in his plan for public and normal schools; such courses had to wait another decade. Art education, which until then had been available only to the privileged classes, underwent a process of democratization and simplification. Education officials in Upper and Lower Canada established art-education programs in the schools, based on the principle that instruction in drawing is as essential as instruction in reading and writing and should be taught to all children. This recognition of the fundamental importance of drawing led to the creation of exercises intended to stimulate the child's visual vocabulary. The *Dominion Drawing Books* appeared, systematizing both the methods and the materials to be used.

In the 19th century the Industrial Revolution brought a new awareness of the relationship between form and function in manufactured objects (*see* INDUSTRIAL DESIGN). In England and Europe this development led not only to the creation of schools of art and design with industrial application, but also to a rejuvenation of arts and crafts. This influence spread to Canada in the 1860s and, in succeeding years, various schools of applied art and technology were established, eg, the Conseil des arts et manufactures, and Joseph Chabert's Institution nationale, founded in Montréal in 1870. Such colleges offered a complete program that included freehand drawing and technical drawing (mechanical, architectural), decorative painting, lithography, modelling and wood sculpture; since these programs were aimed at specialized workers, they sensitized a new social group to artistic techniques and the application of aesthetic principles to the environment. The courses, however, emphasized technical qualities (correct drawing, harmonious colours, balanced composition) rather than expression and formal research, and increased the conceptual gulf between applied art and fine art. Consistent efforts were made well into the 20th century, as at École du meuble founded in 1937, or by Donald Buchanan at the National Industrial Design Council after 1946, to keep strong ties between design and fine arts, and today numerous schools and university departments, one of which is the NOVA SCOTIA COLLEGE OF ART AND DESIGN, offer both programs.

Apprenticeship and private art schools were replaced in the late 19th century by schools founded and directed by societies of artists and amateurs which had come into being about 25 years earlier. The Ontario Society of Artists, the Art Assn of Montreal and the Royal Canadian Academy established courses which tended to be adaptations of academic European models (*see* ARTISTS' ORGANIZATIONS). Their methods taught respect for tradition, the hierarchy of different media and genres and the supremacy of drawing. Art colleges and the Toronto Normal School under Egerton Ryerson collected plaster castings, photographs and engravings of European works. Some European-trained teachers taught in and led their schools for more than 30 years, and so influenced several generations of students. William Brymner at the Art Assn of Montreal school, George Reid at the Ontario College of Art, John Hammond at the Owens Art Institute of both Saint John and Sackville, NB, were particularly well known. Art studies often led to a stay abroad, in the US or Europe. It was essential to see, study and copy the masterpieces and to meet foreign colleagues in the hope of winning professional recognition for careers in Canada.

The basic structure of the professional art schools remained unchanged until the mid-20th century, despite internal developments (eg, the Ontario College of Art after 1912) and proliferation (eg, the École des beaux-arts in Québec City, 1920, and in Montréal, 1923). The relationship between fine arts and applied arts continued. Young Canadian artists preparing for a career turned increasingly to the US because the range of courses was broader and instruction more specialized. Many students continued to be wealthy young women whose training was seen as a complement to their general education, though the status of female artists developed more quickly in English Canada. The Beaver Hall Hill Group, which consisted mainly of graduates of the Art Assn of Montreal school, helped pioneer recognition of female artists in 1920-21.

In the 1940s there was a major reform in the specialized schools. The structures which had been put in place 70 years earlier gave way to a variety of methods of instruction. The dissolving of the link between art and industry, the downgrading of the importance of art from the past in favour of the development of the artist's own values, and the predominant role of colour and gesture to express individuality, all characterized post-WWII art and affected the kinds of courses being offered. Two major reactions followed. One was to return to individualized training, with exchanges between artists of different ages and statures. This system took various forms such as workshops, symposiums and seminars, as at Emma Lake or the BANFF CENTRE School of Fine Arts, where professionals share their beliefs and experience with younger people.

The other major reaction, as the university took responsibility for the training of a large number of artists in the humanist tradition, was to expand the student's awareness in areas other than his immediate interests. Since the first Bachelor of Fine Arts was awarded in 1939 at Mount Allison U in Sackville, NB, many institutions of higher learning across the country have established their own programs, offering a rich academic structure with great social and aesthetic value as well.

Art education as a SOCIAL SCIENCE, a system based on the psychological development of the child, was also developed in the 1940s. Arthur LISMER is considered the pioneer of this form of art education in Canada. He put the principles into practice at the Art Gallery of Toronto after 1919 and in the Musée des beaux-arts de Montréal (Montréal Museum of Fine Arts) after 1941. For Lismer, art education meant placing individuals in a situation in which their natural creativity could blossom. The needs, resources and limits of each person were considered, and the role of the educator was to facilitate the creativity. This approach, developed in Europe, had considerable success and was integrated into art education in the public schools. In Montréal, Irène Senécal introduced this method at the École des beaux-arts.

Historical, theoretical and practical reflection on art education, begun by C.D. Gaitskell in his book *Arts and Crafts in the Schools of Ontario* (1948) and continued by various royal commissions on the status of the arts in Canada (eg, Rioux Report; NATIONAL DEVELOPMENT IN THE ARTS, LETTERS AND SCIENCES, ROYAL COMMISSION ON), has been the concern of relevant university research departments. Based on the most recent psychological, aesthetic and pedagogical information, they try to expand the range and quality of artistic experiences offered to the student, making innovative use of museums and galleries and other art activities available outside the classroom. LAURIER LACROIX

Reading: F.W. Rowe, *Education and Culture in Newfoundland* (1976); J.D. Wilson, *Canadian Education* (1970).

Art Galleries and Museums are institutions that collect, preserve, study and present permanent collections of heritage objects to the public.

Although authentic documentation of the early history of Canadian museums is meagre, it is known that 18th-century religious institutions in Québec and the Maritimes had natural history collections that were used by the priests-educators. These same church schools accumulated religious relics, curiosities and VOTIVE PAINTINGS, which marked the beginnings of immigrant art in Canada. What was later U Laval had mineralogical collections as early as the 1790s, followed soon after by other universities, but museums as formally organized institutions were unknown. In the early 1800s MECHANICS' INSTITUTES in the Maritimes accumulated collections for teaching purposes; in addition, models that illustrated physical phenomena and the means by which machinery functioned were constructed. Also during this time, miscellaneous collections were garnered from exhibitions, teaching collections or personal "cabinets of curiosities" and assembled in LIBRARIES or government buildings for temporary show or special events.

The first museum in Canada seems to have been opened by Thomas Barnett, who advertised his personal museum of local and foreign specimens at NIAGARA FALLS in 1831. Soon after, a less commercial museum opened at Niagara-on-the-Lake, and Dr Abraham GESNER founded his museum at Saint John, NB, in 1842. Museums were formally established at U Laval and the Canadian Institute in Toronto in 1852, followed by one at McGill U in 1856. Nova Scotia opened the first provincial museum in 1868 in Halifax, based on collections assembled in a local mechanics' institute, and BC and Ontario sponsored formal museums in 1886 and 1887, respectively.

It was not until after Confederation, 1867, however, that the museum movement swept across Canada, becoming a hallmark of the late 19th century. An outline of the early history of the National Museum of Canada illustrates the blend of private initiative, government support and opportune circumstances that marked the development of museums. In 1842 William LOGAN had become geologist of the Province of Canada, and by 1845 he had amassed and catalogued a large comparative collection of specimens. After the collection was exhibited in London in 1851, Logan and the government were encouraged to found a permanent geological museum. By midcentury, developers and the government recognized the value of national collections in encouraging exploration and resource development. In 1853 Logan wrote a report to Parliament that eventually generated a grant of $28 000 for the maintenance of the collection and for publications. In 1881 Logan's museum was moved to Ottawa to be a part of the research collection and

museum of the GEOLOGICAL SURVEY OF CANADA. A long period of underfunding and lack of organization followed, though in 1911 the museum moved into the new Victoria Memorial Museum Building. In 1927 the museum was formally recognized as the National Museum of Canada. The NATIONAL GALLERY OF CANADA was established in 1880 (*see also* NATIONAL MUSEUMS OF CANADA).

It was in the first half of the 20th century that small community museums and the remaining provincial museums were founded (*see* ART GALLERY OF ONTARIO; GLENBOW MUSEUM; ROYAL ONTARIO MUSEUM). The earliest museums were situated in eastern Canada, but as immigrant settlers moved to the West, pride in the varied ethnic origins gave birth to many collections that eventually became community or regional museums. The growth of museums was slow and 2 major reports, the Miers-Markham Report of 1932 and the Massey Report of 1951, showed little development over a 20-year period.

CENTENNIAL YEAR in 1967 and several provincial and metropolitan birthdays in the 1960s gave a marked impetus to museum development. Provinces and communities alike chose to commemorate their heritage by starting new museums or modernizing old ones. A second reason for the expansion of museums was the secretary of state's announcement in 1972 of massive aid to the cultural sector, primarily to "decentralize and democratize" our national heritage in museums. This influx of money allowed museums to reach new audiences with new programs, and brought about a growing cultural awareness. By 1987, according to the Canadian Museums Assn, there were approximately 2000 museums, art galleries and related institutions in Canada.

Although federal funding policy is under review, museums continue to be funded with tax dollars in the form of a budget, if a part of a larger governing body, or by grants if funding is from outside the direct line of responsibility. Some 21 major museums receive substantial direct federal funding through the Dept of Communications and all other permanent, nonprofit, public museums are eligible to receive grants under the Museum Assistance Programs (whose operating budget in 1987 was $8.5 million). Consequently, the source of museum funding may be federal, provincial, municipal or self-generated, and occasionally private. Frequently, contributions may be derived from several of these sources. Museums are also confronted with the responsibility of raising a large part of their money through fund raising or marketing the unique services a museum can offer. See ARTS FUNDING; MUSEUM POLICY.

GEORGE LAMMERS

Reading: B. Dixon et al, *The Museum and the Canadian Public* (1974); A.F. Key, *Beyond Four Walls: The Origins and Development of Canadian Museums* (1973); T. Poulos, ed, *Conference Proceedings for 2001: The Museum and the Canadian Public* (1977).

Art Gallery of Ontario, founded in 1900 as the Art Museum of Toronto, became the Art Gallery of Toronto in 1919 and in 1966 – reflecting an expanded role in the province – the Art Gallery of Ontario. The 10 000 paintings, sculptures, prints and drawings of the permanent collection include examples from the Old Master traditions, the Impressionists and early 20th-century movements – paintings by such masters as Rembrandt, Hals, Poussin, Chardin, Delacroix, Renoir and Picasso, and sculptures by Rodin, Degas and Matisse. The gallery's Henry Moore Sculpture Centre holds the largest and most comprehensive public collection of Moore works anywhere. More than half the permanent collection is the work of Canadian artists dating from the 18th century to the present day. The gallery averages about 40 special exhibi-

tions each year. Major international shows in recent years have included "Treasures of Tutankhamun" and, organized by the gallery, collections of works by J.M.W. Turner, Vincent van Gogh, William Blake, Lawren HARRIS, Alex COLVILLE and Gershon ISKOWITZ. Other exhibitions have explored 20th-century international sculpture, from Paul Gauguin to Henry Moore, and the northern landscape painting in Europe and N America, with a focus on the Canadian tradition.

Lectures, films, tours and concerts are regularly scheduled. In the Activity Centre, children and adults enjoy art-related activities or take classes in the Gallery School. The Edward P. Taylor Reference Library and the Audio-Visual Centre are invaluable information centres for researchers, art historians and students. The original gallery home, The GRANGE, is a restored Georgian mansion and a museum of life in Upper Canada in the 1830s. Reaching into communities across Ontario and Canada, Extension Services offer touring exhibitions, studio programs, and advisory services to community centres and contribute to the Ontario Ministry of Citizenship and Culture Festival Program.

The gallery's collection, facilities and programs have attracted a strong membership of 28 000, the largest per capita in N America. By 1987, annual attendance at the gallery averaged 412 000 visitors. The gallery receives about 60% of its annual operating costs from the province of Ontario, supplemented by grants from federal and municipal governments. The remainder of the budget is earned from membership support, program fees, retail shops, a restaurant, and by private gifts and corporate donations. All works of art in the collection have either been donated or have been purchased with income from donations.

WILLIAM WITHROW

Art Ross Trophy is awarded annually to the player who leads the NATIONAL HOCKEY LEAGUE in scoring points during the regular season. If there is a tie at the end of the season, the trophy is awarded to the player with the most goals. It was first presented in 1947 by Arthur Howie Ross, former manager of Boston Bruins. Gordie HOWE won it 6 times, Phil ESPOSITO 5, Stan MIKITA 4, Guy LAFLEUR 3 and Wayne GRETZKY in 7 of his first 8 seasons.

JAMES MARSH

Art Writing and Criticism dates for the most part from the 1950s. A distinction must be made between art criticism, which is a qualitative judgement of works of art, and the philosophy of art, which is concerned with interpreting works, with discovering the nature, significance and symbolism of art in general. There is, however, a reciprocity in the relationship of art criticism and the philosophy of art: every evaluation of quality always includes an explicit or implicit interpretation of the meaning of the work, and every interpretation implies a previously formulated qualitative judgement.

Art criticism can address various aspects of the visual arts such as qualitative judgement in public and private collecting, architecture, the decorative arts, patronage of artists, art dealings, conservation of art and organization of exhibitions. Much Canadian art criticism has been of a fairly practical nature. The vast increase in the number of artists, public and commercial galleries, and art patrons since WWII reveals an expansion of artistic discernment. Written art criticism has increased at a comparable rate.

The first art writing and criticism in Canada was published as short articles in daily and weekly newspapers or general interest periodicals. The earliest of these periodicals included the short-lived *L'Abeille canadienne*, a Montréal fortnightly published 1818-19, the *Halifax Monthly Magazine* of 1830 and the Upper Canadian *Canadian Literary Magazine* of 1833. Later *La Revue canadienne, The Week, Foyer domestique* and the *Canadian Home Journal* devoted regular columns to art. These articles usually examined current exhibitions, discussing the works in fashionably flowery language in relation to Victorian ideals rather than pictorial qualities. By the end of the 19th century, longer studies, such as Sherwood's chapter in Hopkins's *Canada: An Encyclopaedia of the Country*, made an appearance. However, it was only in the 1920s that books devoted exclusively to art were published, including those by Georges Bellerive and Newton MacTavish. Despite this interest, neither authors nor critics could make a living on art writing alone.

In the early 20th century this economic factor continued to affect the types of authors who published. A considerable number of authors were artists, some were curators employed at public galleries and a few were professional critics. Practising artists such as Arthur LISMER, Lawren S. HARRIS and C.W. JEFFERYS produced important articles; Eric Brown, director of the National Gallery of Canada, added writing to his many duties, a practice continued by Donald W. Buchanan, a coeditor of *Canadian Art* and later staff member of the National Gallery. Robert Ayre furthered the tradition of spare-time writer; while fulfilling his duties with the CNR Public Relations Department, he wrote for the *Montreal Standard* and subsequently the *Montreal Star*. Some professional art journalists did exist. One of the earliest of note was Hector Charlesworth, who wrote on many subjects, including art. In the post-WWI period Jean Chauvin contributed perceptive pieces in the French press, as did Pearl McCarthy in the 1950s and early 1960s at the Toronto *Globe and Mail*. Journalists such as Newton MacTavish and F.B. Housser wrote some of the few early books on Canadian painting. Little effort was made at dispassionate, rational criticism, with the notable exception of those, such as Ayre and McCarthy, who wrote regular columns.

The first changes, evident in the 1950s, occurred as a result of the expansion of public galleries (*see* PAINTING). At that time these institutions experienced a considerable growth in number, staff and programs. A greater interest developed in historic overviews, especially in book form, through the influence of research-oriented curators such as R.H. Hubbard, Gérard Morisset and J. Russell HARPER. Their books on the history of Canadian art were characterized by the use of extensive primary materials; they revolutionized the field, opening it to serious study. Within a decade other surveys and specialized studies appeared, such as Alan Gowans's *Looking at Architecture in Canada*, F.M. Gagnon's *Premiers peintres de la Nouvelle France* and Jean Palardy's *The Early Furniture of French Canada*. Themes were enlarged to include more thorough studies of the arts of the native peoples of Canada. Marius BARBEAU's and Diamond JENNESS's pioneer works on Canadian Indians were expanded by scholars such as Wilson Duff. The art of the Inuit, having been seriously neglected, was first promoted by James HOUSTON and then analysed by George Swinton. After 1960 contemporary art began to have its advocates, too many to be listed; approaches tended to be formalist, sometimes Maoist. These studies, however, are only the beginning, for many areas remain untouched; we lack informative studies of Canadian sculpture, Maritime architecture, patrons, dealers and critics, and most of the decorative arts.

The second dynamic expansion in gallery activity, occurring in the mid-1970s and caused by an injection of federal funds, garnered an increased public and stimulated art writing. Galleries themselves were becoming more numerous and more specialized. Viewers could attend public or commercial art galleries and artist-run spaces, all producing exhibitions and, potentially, catalogues (*see* ART, CONTEMPORARY TRENDS). These new shows in turn provoked reviews and articles in newspapers, general periodicals and specialized art journals. In the popular press, the amount of space devoted to the visual arts remained relatively small and the level of reportage remained descriptive. Museum newsletters became more numerous, influential and diverse. *ArtsAtlantic* (1977) introduced the concept of co-operative sponsorship, for the publication is supported by 11 Maritime galleries and museums. The Vancouver Art Gallery's *Vanguard* began in 1972 as a tabloid newspaper, but in 1979 changed its format to a magazine style and extended its scope to the national scene.

The increasing exhibition activity was reflected in the expanding number of specialized art journals, which, since WWII, have added important dimensions to the art field. *Canadian Art*, initiated in 1943 and renamed *artscanada* in 1967, was followed by *Vie des arts* in 1956; both publications concentrated on contemporary issues. In 1983 financial problems precipitated the demise of *artscanada* and *artmagazine* (fd 1969), but the next year, 2 new periodicals, *C Magazine* and *Canadian Art*, went to press. Only with the National Gallery's *Bulletin* and the 1974 creation of *RACAR* and the *Journal of Canadian Art History* have historical issues received continuing attention. Recently, numerous magazines have appeared written and published by artists. Many of these emanate from artist-run galleries, including the *Only Paper Today* from Toronto's A Space, *Centrefold* from Calgary's Parachute Centre, and *Virus* published by Montréal's Véhicule. Others come from art groups, such as General Idea's *File*. Some are broadly based, including *Parachute*, a magazine devoted to fine contemporary criticism. Specialized and more commercial publications such as *Video Guide, Canadian Architect* and *Photo Canada* are addressed to a restricted readership.

With this considerable increase in art writing came a change in the types of writers who published. The artist was still an important contributor, acting both as commentator and critic; the professional art critic, though often working part-time, became more prominent; and the university-trained art historian, a new generation of specialist, added considerably to the dialogue.

As catalogues became more common, they also became more varied and complex. Introductions gradually shifted from being straightforward biographical information to more probing analytic appraisals, complemented by an increasing number of reproductions. The approaches used are as diverse as the material covered. Alvin Balkind's soft-cover catalogue *17 Canadian Artists: A Protean View* accomplished its educational aim through the use of many illustrations and an evocative text. Working with a more defined subject – David MILNE's prints – Rosemarie Tovell effectively led the reader through the development of this important aspect of Milne's art (1980) while the authors of *Joyce Wieland* (1987) expanded the scope to consider the full range of this artist's creativity. Unfortunately, in this the largest area of art writing, distribution remains a major problem; some galleries are experimenting with co-publishing certain catalogues as trade books through established publishers.

In books the trends are somewhat different. Biographies are favoured. These, including F.M. Gagnon's impressive *Borduas*, contain much solid research. But the greatest proportion of books published are of the coffee-table variety, a format eminently suited to lavish and large colour illustrations and a moderate amount of popular text. Recently this trend has been pushed further to the production of limited editions, collector volumes selling for thousands of dollars and dealing with well-known artists such as Christopher PRATT and KENOJUAK. Writers are drawn from the same pool that produces most of the catalogues and articles, although academics are gradually becoming more involved.

Along with the increased amount of art writing and criticism being done in Canada, there is a new professionalism and an expanded range of approach. This is due, in part, to the recent attention universities and galleries have accorded Canadian art history. The erstwhile norm – nonevaluative, first-person documents and biographical data – is gradually being expanded to produce interpretive or critical catalogues and journal articles. While one single philosophy of art has not become dominant in Canada, imported concepts, such as American critic Clement Greenberg's formalist approach, have attracted adherents. Yet there is increasing recognition of the politico-cultural nature of art and the global dimension of the contemporary artist's environment. Writers are acknowledging these individual and cultural values in particular works rather than seeking values through the application of rules formulated in advance; they are more conscious too of current literary theories. On the whole, Canadian art writing is becoming more analytic and more critical, seeking both new interpretations and better methods of evaluation.   ANN DAVIS

Reading: K. McKenzie and M.F. Williamson, eds, *The Art and Pictorial Press in Canada* (1979).

Arthabaska, Qué, Town, pop 7244 (1986c), 6827 (1981c), inc 1903, is located on the Rivière Nicolet in the uplands of the Appalachian region, 5 km SE of VICTORIAVILLE and halfway between Québec City and Sherbrooke. The name is derived from the Cree word *Ayabaskaw*, meaning "place of the bulrushes and reeds." The founder, Charles Beauchesne, who arrived in 1834, was impressed by the size of the trees and quality of the soil. The first industries were potash and maple-sugar production. Establishment of the Arthabaska Convent (1870), the Arthabaska Commercial College (1872) and Collège St-Joseph (1905) made the town a popular centre of culture and education. Sir Wilfrid LAURIER began his law career here in 1867. His summer home has been converted into a museum. By 1882 cigar manufacturing, tanneries, flour mills and sawmills had been established. Furniture manufacturing was introduced around 1948. Located in the heart of a dairy and lumber-manufacturing region, Arthabaska is known as the "Capitale des Bois-Francs." Mont St-Michel, called "Monte Cristo" by the first settlers, dominates the town.
                JEAN-MARIE DUBOIS AND PIERRE MAILHOT

Arthritis, from the Greek *arthron* ["joint"] and *itis* ["inflammation"]. The word encompasses a wide range of disorders involving the various joints of the body, but always signifies the existence of varying degrees of inflammation which, if left unchecked, or if persisting over sufficient time, causes pain and ultimate destruction of the joint surfaces. Rheumatism, from the Greek *rheumatismos* ["flowing condition"], is used by the public (but rarely by medical practitioners) to describe any acute or chronic aching or stiffness of muscles, tendons, ligaments and joints, including arthritis and painful muscle conditions.

The rheumatic diseases are important both clinically and economically. About one in 50 Canadians by the age of 75 years (in a female to male ratio of 65.4% to 34.6%) will have suffered some form of rheumatic complaint. Although between 7% and 10% of visits to doctors' offices relate to musculoskeletal problems (ranking only behind circulatory, respiratory and endocrine disorders), this percentage does not reflect the prevalence of the disease, because as many as 75% of individuals with rheumatic complaints do not seek medical attention.

The campaign against rheumatic disease is conducted by professional societies, voluntary health organizations and official governmental agencies. The International League Against Rheumatism was founded in 1927. The Pan-American League is one of its subdivisions, and in Canada The ARTHRITIS SOCIETY co-ordinates and supports much of the work and research at all levels.

Osteoarthritis and rheumatoid arthritis are the most prevalent forms of arthritis. Osteoarthritis is characterized by morning stiffness, pain proportional to activity, swelling and grating of the joints with movement, and a gradual loss of motion. The articular surface gradually thins and the joint becomes mechanically unsound. It is most common with the elderly, but it is unclear if it is simply a manifestation of aging. It is usually classed as a degenerative condition and occurs mainly in the chief weight-bearing joints, eg, hips and knees. Treatment can include the use of anti-inflammatory medications (eg, aspirin), physiotherapy and walking aids. Total replacement of a joint, particularly the hip, by an artifical joint is possible.

Rheumatoid arthritis is a chronic inflammatory disorder of unknown cause, although it may be related to the body's immune system. It affects approximately 1% of the N American population over the age of 15 years with an overall female-to-male ratio of 3 to one. Although rheumatoid arthritis affects the joints, it is a systemic illness and affects most other tissues of the body to varying extents. This disease, which usually starts with swelling, warmth, pain and stiffness in one or more joints, is classically symmetrical, ie, it affects the small joints of the hands, wrists and feet but tends, except in its severe, progressive forms, to spare the hips and spine. Treatment can include anti-inflammatory medications, such as gold therapy, rest, splints, walking aids and physiotherapy. Artificial joints made of a combination of metal and various plastics and silastic materials can also be implanted.

Of the less common forms of arthritis a particularly virulent type, juvenile rheumatoid arthritis, commonly affects children (male and female) between the ages of one to 5 years. Characterized by a high fever, a rash, joint pains and sometimes heart trouble, the disease may destroy many of the joints.

Other arthritides include ankylosing spondylitis, psoriatic arthritis and Reiter's syndrome. Ankylosing spondylitis, a genetic disease to which native peoples seem particularly vulnerable, primarily affects young men, particularly their spines and large pelvic joints. Psoriatic arthritis, an inflammatory arthritis, is associated with the skin disease psoriasis. Reiter's syndrome is associated with infections of the urinary tract or bowel.

Gout, in which the body's inefficiency to handle certain chemicals allows the precipitation of crystals of uric acid (monosodium urate) in and around joints, is the best-known metabolic cause of arthritis. Other crystals identified as causing arthritis include calcium pyrophosphate, which leads to a disease called "pseudogout" because of the similarity of the symptoms to gout. Gouty infections affecting joints lead to rapid destruction of the articular surface because of the enzymes liberated by the body's white blood cells. These enzymes digest the substance of the joint surface, depriving it of its mechanical properties.

DAVID C. REID

Arthritis Society is the only registered nonprofit agency in Canada devoted solely to funding and promoting ARTHRITIS research, patient care and public education about arthritis. The Canadian Arthritis and Rheumatism Society, as the society was called until 1977, was founded on 14 Oct 1947. Its first volunteer president was Dr Wallace Graham. In 1949 Edward A. Dunlop, the society's first executive director, helped create "Arthritis – Plan for Attack," a keystone document that would be the first in a series of 5-year plans which called for the establishment of Rheumatic Disease Units (RDUs) in each of Canada's 16 university medical schools, as well as the funding of scholarships and professional bursaries in order to attract and educate the necessary medical manpower to cope with arthritis in Canada. The groundwork was also laid for programs that would financially support clinical and basic-science research projects. The society launched the first of its annual fund-raising campaigns in 1949, eventually declaring September as National Arthritis Month in Canada.

The society has since played a major part in increasing the number of arthritis specialists, called rheumatologists, from 4 in 1949 to more than 200 by the 1980s. RDUs are now operating in all Canadian university medical schools, which serve as focal points for a nationwide network for patient care and education, as well as ongoing clinical and scientific research. The Arthritis Society now has a national administrative office in Toronto, division offices in each province and nearly 1000 community branches throughout Canada. It has allocated more than $35 million in public donations to its research, medical manpower and public-education programs.

DENNIS JEANES

Arthropoda, phylum of bilaterally symmetrical animals having external skeletons (exoskeletons), multisegmented bodies and paired, jointed appendages. Including SPIDERS, MITES, CRUSTACEANS, CENTIPEDES and INSECTS, they are practically ubiquitous and comprise 75% of known animal species (over 923 000 species worldwide; over 33 670 in Canada).

Structure Arthropods are distinguished by a cuticular exoskeleton, secreted by an underlying layer of epidermal cells. The exoskeleton consists of protein and chitin (a substance similar to cellulose) and has 2 layers: an outer epicuticle, often containing wax which reduces water loss, and an inner procuticle. The exoskeleton consists of plates (sclerites) and cylinders of hard cuticle linked by flexible regions (articular membranes). In sclerites the outer procuticle is hard exocuticle; the remainder is softer endocuticle. Because exocuticle is absent from joints, arthropods can move appendages and flex one body segment on another. Movement results from contraction and relaxation of striated muscle fibres. Most arthropods use their appendages for movement, for example, as paddles in aquatic species or as legs in terrestrial ones. Young arthropods grow by periodically shedding and replacing their exoskeleton (molting), a process controlled by hormones (principally ecdysterone). The body cavity is filled with blood, and a weakly developed heart moves the blood through one or more arteries. Arthropod blood is usually colourless because it lacks the respiratory pigments of vertebrate blood.

Aquatic arthropods breathe using gills borne on appendages or body segments; terrestrial forms, by book lungs (membranes arranged like leaves of a book) or tracheal tubes. Exoskeletal sense organs include hairs sensitive to sound, touch, odour, taste, humidity or temperature, and often 2 compound eyes and one or more simple eyes. Sensory information is processed in a

central nervous system consisting of a brain connected to a ventral (lower surface) nerve cord of paired ganglia (nerve masses) linked, longitudinally, by paired connectives.

Arthropods feed on living or dead organic matter or may parasitize other animals. The structure of gut and mouthparts varies with diet. Organs of excretion are gills, antennal glands, coxal glands or Malpighian tubules.

Reproduction and Development Most arthropods have separate sexes. Sperm are usually passed to the female in a sealed package (spermatophore); the process is often preceded by elaborate behaviour. Newly hatched juveniles are smaller than and often differ from parents in form, food and habit. Such juveniles become adults through hormone-controlled metamorphosis.

Limits to Size The size of arthropods is limited by surface-volume relationships. The surface area of an arthropod varies with the square of its linear dimensions; its weight varies with the cube. Thus, large arthropods are relatively heavier than smaller ones and small arthropods have a relatively larger surface area. Small, terrestrial forms must occupy humid microhabitats to avoid drying out. Because the power of muscle fibres is proportional to their cross-sectional area, large arthropods are relatively weaker. Large forms are too heavy and weak to move quickly and also have trouble breathing, since gas exchange is mostly by simple diffusion. Therefore, size and habitat are somewhat restricted among terrestrial forms. Being supported by water, marine arthropods can be very large (body length up to 60 cm).

Evolution and Phylogeny Arthropods probably evolved in Precambrian seas, over 570 million years ago, from the same ancestor or ancestors as polychaete ANNELIDS (worms with many hairlike appendages). The oldest known FOSSILS (lower Cambrian, 570-540 million years old) are diverse and many belong to groups still in existence. These facts suggest that splitting of lineages occurred much earlier. It is uncertain whether arthropods evolved from a common ancestor or from several, unrelated ancestors. Arthropods are classified into 4 subphyla, described below.

Trilobitmorpha TRILOBITES, now extinct, predominated in Paleozoic seas, 570-245 million years ago.

Chelicerata Chelicerates are the only arthropods lacking antennae. The body consists of cephalothorax (fused head and thorax) and opisthosoma (abdomen), and bears a pair of pincerlike feeding appendages, a pair of pedipalps and 4 pairs of walking legs. The group includes horseshoe crabs, sea spiders and ARACHNIDS, with over 64 550 species described (3225 in Canada).

Crustacea Crustaceans, with over 31 300 known species, are mainly marine with some freshwater and terrestrial forms. The head bears 2 pairs of antennae, a pair of stalked or unstalked compound eyes, 2 mandibles and 2 pairs of maxillae. Segmentation and appendages of thorax and abdomen vary with species and lifestyle. Appendages are biramous (2-branched) and adapted for filter feeding, respiration, swimming, burrowing, brooding young and mating. The subphylum includes WATER FLEAS, copepods, BARNACLES, CRABS, LOBSTERS, CRAYFISH, SHRIMPS, etc.

Uniramia Subphylum includes the myriapods (centipedes, MILLIPEDES, symphylans and pauropods) and insects. About 760 000 species are known (some 30 580 from Canada) – the vast majority being insects. Some scientists link uniramians with crustaceans in the subphylum Mandibulata because of similar head structure. Most uniramians possess a pair of antennae and mandibles, and one or 2 pairs of maxillae (often fused on the midline). Insects have 3 pairs of unbranched legs; myriapods have more. Most adult insects have one or 2 pairs of wings. Body segments are grouped into compound body sections (2 for myriapods, 3 for insects).

Related Groups Three other phyla are frequently considered with arthropods because of similar structure. Onychophorans comprise 70 known species of terrestrial, caterpillarlike animals of the tropics and Southern Hemisphere. The body is soft, covered with flexible cuticle and adapted for squeezing into confined spaces. Onychophorans possess a pair of antennae, a pair of clawlike mandibles, many pairs of ventral, unjointed limbs and internal organs having both annelid and arthropod characteristics.

Tardigrades (water bears) are small (0.3-1.2 mm), 8-legged animals that live in the water film on moss, in soil or in fresh or salt water, and feed on plants cells, detritus or other animals. They share characteristics with both gastrotrichs (phylum of aquatic, somewhat wormlike organisms) and arthropods. About 400 species are known (48 in Canada).

Pentastomids comprise about 90 species (2 in Canada) of highly specialized tongue worms which infest lungs of vertebrates, mostly reptiles. It has been suggested that they have arachnid, myriapod or crustacean affinities. B.S. HEMING

Reading: Sybil P. Parker, ed, *Synopsis and Classification of Living Organisms* (1982).

Arthur, Eric Ross, architect, author (b at Dunedin, New Zealand 1 July 1898; d at Toronto 1 Nov 1982). Educated in England, Arthur came to Canada in 1923 to become an associate professor of architecture, U of T. Throughout his career, he was concerned with the preservation of Toronto's architectural heritage. He was a founder of the Architectural Conservancy of Ontario (1932) and was thereafter actively involved in numerous restoration projects in Toronto, including the ST LAWRENCE HALL (1967). He was author and coauthor of several books on architecture. His best known, *Toronto: No Mean City* (1964), is a standard reference on the city and its architectural past. He was named a Companion of the Order of Canada in 1968. *See also* BARNS; TOMBSTONES. SUSAN FORD

Arthur, Sir George, soldier, colonial administrator (b at Plymouth, Eng 21 June 1784; d at London, Eng 19 Sept 1854). After an undistinguished military career and 2 minor colonial appointments, he became lieutenant-governor of Upper Canada in 1838. An early decision to execute 2 prisoners taken in the REBELLIONS OF 1837 made him seem a bloodthirsty Tory. More lenient in reality than his advisers and the Assembly, he remained a moderate even after the border was set aflame by American raids, restraining Upper Canadians from retaliation. Though sympathetic to the FAMILY COMPACT, he introduced important administrative reforms. After the arrival of Gov Gen C.E.P. Thomson (SYDENHAM) in 1839, he became largely a figurehead. He returned to England in 1841 and served as governor of Bombay 1842-46. P.A. BUCKNER

Reading: A.G.L. Shaw, *Sir George Arthur* (1980).

Artificial Intelligence (AI) Long before the first computers were built, many scientists were convinced that certain kinds of artifacts could be made to exhibit intelligent behaviour. So it was natural that as soon as electronic computers became available, researchers began to program them to do things that had been considered the sole prerogative of the human mind, such as solving non-numerical problems, understanding the English sentence, or playing chess.

Despite some impressive initial successes, the main result of early AI research was the development of basic programming tools (eg, list-processing languages and time sharing came out of AI laboratories). Researchers also learned to appreciate the limitations of "brute-force" techniques, such as exhaustive search and statistical learning methods, and began to understand the importance of being able to encode large amounts of specialized knowledge and of being able to draw relevant inferences from this knowledge.

The 1970s brought the first commercial applications of machines that could reason from a base of knowledge meticulously gleaned from human experts. Such "expert systems" now serve as automated consultants for certain narrow areas of expertise, including specialized medical diagnosis, chemical analysis, circuit design and mineral prospecting (the best-known prospecting system was designed in California in collaboration with a Canadian mining expert). Programs also exist that "understand" a limited range of spoken or typewritten language, and they can visually examine layouts (such as metal castings or integrated circuit chips on an assembly line) or X-ray photographs.

In the early 1980s Japan, followed closely by Britain and the EEC, announced major national programs to develop what are sometimes called "fifth-generation" AI computer systems. In Canada there are a small number of university research groups specializing in AI. The main areas of specialization have been in image analysis, especially as applied to satellite and medical images (*see* REMOTE SENSING), and in fundamental research into techniques for knowledge representation and reasoning. Perhaps because of our bilingual heritage, Canadians have also had a tradition of research in machine translation. For example, in the mid-1970s a group at the U de Montréal developed what is probably still the only fully automatic, high-quality translation system in continuous daily use. This system, which translates rather stereotyped weather forecasts at Dorval airport, is a far cry from the more sophisticated system later developed by the same group for translating aircraft maintenance manuals. Even though the quality of translation was considered high, government funding for this project was abandoned in 1981 because the cost of post-editing and dictionary updates made the system uneconomical to use.

Canada's special geopolitical status requires that we keep on the forefront of "knowledge-based" industries, including communications, language processing, office automation, remote medical treatment, education and resource management. We can only function effectively in these areas if we can bring the most advanced AI computer technology to bear on those problems. The importance of AI research to Canada's future has been recognized by a number of private groups and government departments. For example, in 1982 the Canadian Institute for Advanced Research, a private group dedicated to promoting basic research in strategically important areas, selected Artificial Intelligence and ROBOTICS as its first area of concentration, and has managed to put together an internationally recognized team of researchers located at 9 universities across the country. Other similar research groups specializing in AI have also been formed in several provinces (notably Alta, BC, Ont and Qué). More recently, a group of several dozen Canadian companies (including not only small high-technology industries but also large steel and mining companies, and public utilities) formed a consortium (Precarn Associates) to promote precompetitive, long-term applied research into AI technologies. Because of the high cost and strategic importance of such research, consortia of this kind are becoming common in most countries. ZENON W. PYLYSHYN

Reading: S.C. Shapiro, ed, *The Encyclopedia of Artificial Intelligence* (1987); Science Council of Canada, "A Workshop on Artificial Intelligence" (1983) and "The Uneasy Eighties" (1985).

Artists' Organizations The history of visual artists' groups in Canada is filled with short-lived societies which have had a major influence on both professional and amateur artists. All kinds of associations have existed at one time or another, with artists grouped by age, region, aesthetic idea, medium, profession or even by gender. Artists' organizations have often been founded to meet specific needs (to form pressure groups, organize exhibitions, improve representation in the market) and are generally the product of one person's labour, someone who leads the group as its president or secretary.

The mixed associations created before the 1840s paid little attention to the visual arts, but through their meetings artists were integrated into a network of intellectual exchanges. The Halifax Chess, Pencil and Brush Club (1787-1817) is considered the first artists' organization in what is now Canada, though its mandate extended beyond art to polite pursuits. The Society for the Encouragement of Art and Science in Canada (Québec, 1827) joined with the LITERARY AND HISTORICAL SOCIETY OF QUEBEC in 1829 and was composed mainly of military personnel and members of the clergy and liberal professions with scientific, historical and literary interests. The artists in this group were mostly amateurs or young professionals, as in the Society of Artists and Amateurs of Toronto (1834). At irregular intervals, the Toronto Society of Arts (1847) and the Montreal Society of Artists (1847) brought artists together with a public that could give them entry to the wealthiest circles, those few who were commissioning works.

The Montréal association was revived in 1860 as the Art Assn of Montreal, but its artists became increasingly inactive. Collectors dominated the association and rented space once a year to show their collections and the works of the few member artists and guests, most of them part of the ephemeral Society of Canadian Artists (1867). In 1879 the art association acquired permanent premises, which enabled it to hold annual exhibitions based on the model of the Paris salons, to host the Royal Canadian Academy exhibits, and to use some artists as instructors and members of committees. Artists benefited from these activities, but when the art association became a museum, its values changed for many artists. Nevertheless, the school continued to have good teachers; it attracted many promising students, and was an important forum for art educators (*see* ART EDUCATION).

The founding of the ROYAL CANADIAN ACADEMY OF ARTS (RCA) in 1880, under the impetus and patronage of Governor General the marquis of Lorne and Princess Louise, marked an important stage in the recognition of the artist's status in Canadian society. The Academy adopted several regulations from the European and British academies, for example, the election of members by nomination and the artists' donation of admission work; these works became the core of the collection of the NATIONAL GALLERY OF CANADA. The RCA continued to play a most important role in the history of Canadian art. It became the arbiter of taste in established art circles; its annual exhibitions, held in a few towns throughout the country, became national events; its competitions promoted the development of PUBLIC ART; it was responsible for showing Canadian art abroad at British Empire exhibitions and world fairs; and all the while it sponsored courses as a means of improving the quality of artwork in Canada.

The RCA was less effective in meeting the specific needs of artists in various regions. While its members were selected on a national basis, their representativeness was questionable. It had limited means and a structure constantly hampered by large distances and administration. From its foundation the RCA was challenged by artists who questioned its hold on the aesthetic standards of the nation. Other societies became important to Canadian painters, sculptors, graphic artists and architects.

The Ontario Society of Artists (OSA), founded in 1872, was always dynamic. It created its own collection, had annual exhibitions and founded the Art Union of Canada to encourage collectors to acquire its members' works. In co-operation with the Ministry of Education, the OSA founded a school of art known today as the ONTARIO COLLEGE OF ART; OSA members planned the curriculum and taught at this school.

As the number of trained and professional artists increased in a society that was expanding both demographically and economically, new artists' organizations appeared, most of which tended to be more specialized. Toronto had many such organizations, less prestigious than the RCA or the OSA, but different goals attracted people who wanted to share their specialities with others of the same mind. The Toronto Art Students' League, founded in 1886, was not only a school but a setting where members met to draw, discuss, comment on each other's work and create projects together. Most of its members were illustrators, as in the Pen and Pencil Club of Montréal. The Art Students' League gave rise to the Graphics Art Club, which played an important role in the development of graphic art, even before becoming the Canadian Society of Graphic Art in 1933.

Specialized groups were established whose membership included only professionals, people interested in one medium. The short-lived Assn of Canadian Etchers (1885) was revived on a more solid basis in 1916 as the Society of Canadian Painter-Etchers and Engravers. The Toronto Camera Club (1891) and the Montréal Sketching Club (1899) had premises for meetings and exhibitions and published texts and catalogues. The large number and membership of these associations indicate how strongly artists felt the need to meet with their colleagues (*see also* PHOTOGRAPHY; PRINTMAKING).

In contrast to highly structured groups like the RCA or the Women's Art Assn of Toronto (1890), there were clubs such as the Arts and Letters Club of Toronto (1908), the Mahlstick Club (1899), l'Arche and the Arts Club of Montréal (1912). Members were usually friends who met together when they felt like it, came from the same social class and had the same tastes. Meetings were pleasant; people discussed freely, each in turn presenting his works for friendly criticism. Resources were pooled in order to organize private or public shows, dinners, excursions or exhibitions. The Canadian Art Club (1907) in Toronto was simply a group of well-known artists, some of them members of the RCA, whose sole purpose was to organize exhibitions of members' works and thus to lobby collectors more effectively.

At the turn of the century, artists' groups appeared in the West. The Winnipeg Art Society (1902), the British Columbia Society of Artists (1909) and the British Columbia Art League (1920) were evidence of the country's growth and of the desire of artists and amateurs in these regions to stimulate each other and enliven their activities. In the years after WWI new groups were added to the network: the Manitoba Society of Artists (1925), the Women Painters of Western Canada and the Alberta Society of Artists (1931).

The Maritimes were also active, with associations multiplying there as well. The Maritime Art Assn, founded in 1935, drew on the experience of earlier Maritime groups (eg, the Nova Scotia Society of Artists, Newcastle Art Club, Moncton Arts Society, Art Society of Prince Edward Island). In 1940 the Maritime group was unified and strengthened by the publication *Maritime Art*, which helped to spread news of artists' work. The magazine unexpectedly developed into a national magazine, *Canadian Art*, coedited by some curators from the National Gallery of Canada and finally became the independent Toronto publication *artscanada*.

New national groups were established in the spirit of their predecessors. The Canadian Society of Painters in Water Colour (1925) focused on and renewed interest in watercolours, a medium already very popular in the 19th century. The Council of the Guild of Sculptors (1896) was revived and transformed to become the Sculptors' Society of Canada (1928).

The GROUP OF SEVEN (1920-33) was typical of other associations formed later in the century, in that it was organized by several artists who shared an aesthetic ideal. Together they searched for a Canadian iconography based on landscape, yet individually each artist sought to distinguish himself from the group. The Seven were succeeded by the Canadian Group of Painters (1933), which drew its members from across Canada; it was open to men and women and was concerned with modernism and figure painting as well as the landscape, with "the right of Canadian artists to find beauty and character in all things."

Many artists resented the "national institution" the Group of Seven had become, and in the ensuing climate of protest several new groups were formed, particularly in Québec. The Beaver Hall Hill Group (1920-24) in Montréal, mainly women painters from the Art Assn school, explored contemporary art trends, and psychological and formal aspects were of utmost importance in their compositions. The Eastern Group of Painters (1938) included 7 active Montréal artists whose common interest was painting, not a nationalist theory. The CONTEMPORARY ARTS SOCIETY (1939-48) was founded in Montréal by John Lyman to defend modern art. The society was composed of artists and a few intellectuals who did not necessarily share the same style or thinking but who wished to show their support of nonacademic art. In 1948 both the AUTOMATISTE and the Prisme d'yeux movements published manifestos which adopted opposing attitudes to artistic creation and caused the demise of Lyman's group (*see* REFUS GLOBAL).

Nonfigurative art was established across Canada by the Calgary Group (around 1947), the PLASTICIENS (manifesto published in 1955), the Association des artistes non-figuratifs de Montréal (1956-61), PAINTERS ELEVEN (1953-60) in Toronto and the REGINA FIVE (early 1960s). These groups did not attempt to define a new artistic current. Rather, by concentrating on a particular element of their work, from the creative process (individuality of gesture, spontaneity) to the enhancement of certain formal and pictorial elements (surface, space, light, line, colour), artists gave a new perspective to art, while at the same time participating in an international movement. The groups provided a forum for debate among artists concerned with the common issues of the role of art and its meaning in a post industrial civilization (*see also* PAINTING).

The militancy of Western society in the 1960s and early 1970s was reflected in the types of artists' organizations established. The 1960-80 period saw the consolidation of existing societies and the creation of new groups that attempted to increase governmental and public awareness of the artist's role and needs. Artists became more politically and socially involved through their associations, seeking to become part of current debates while affirming the professional aspect of their careers. Groups of artists appeared, such as General Idea in Toronto and N.E. Thing Co in Vancouver, which were stimulated by the development of a common aesthetic and art (*see* ART, CONTEMPORARY TRENDS). Existing groups generally tried to become more cohesive and more effective in action. The Society of Canadian Painter-Etchers and Engravers, for example, joined with the Canadian Society of Graphic Art to form the Print and Drawing Council of Canada in 1976.

The need for an increasingly international and competitive market led artists to analyse more objectively their associations' goals and the means at their disposal. The Society of Cooperative Artists (1957), which in 1967 became the Society of Canadian Artists, began publishing *artmagazine* in 1969 in order to give the public better information on its members' work and the activities of other institutions and associations. Supersocieties were formed on a national scale to represent visual artists throughout Canada on terms different from those of the RCA. The Professional Artists of Canada (PAC) was created in 1969 as an association of associations, comprising 7 existing societies that wished to join together to make themselves heard by the public, whose opinion they were increasingly seeking.

PAC's founding was a reaction by existing associations to the establishment, at the end of 1967, of a more demanding group, the Canadian Artists Representation/Front des artistes canadiens (CAR/FAC). Created through the initiative of Jack CHAMBERS, CAR/FAC was a decentralized structure from the outset which attempted to unite its members on the basis of professional demands, such as royalty payments to artists for the reproduction of their works and a schedule of rates for works hung in exhibitions. In 1957 the Canadian Conference of the Arts had raised the issues of copyright, tax reform and social security for visual artists who had no agents or regular incomes. With the exception of copyright, these problems remain unsolved, and it appears that artists as a group are not strong enough to ensure that their most elementary demands are met.

Recent formations such as Western Front in Vancouver or Art Metropole in Toronto, although socially aware, exist primarily to provide members and their guests with an organization similar to many "parallel galleries" and artist-run centres across Canada. They give artists facilities and space in which to realize and show their experimental and often unmarketable work.

Québec artists have always remained a separate group within the umbrella associations, though in the 1970s they formed specialized artist groups. Sculptors and engravers have been particularly active (Association des sculpteurs du Québec, 1961-76; Conseil de la sculpture, 1978; Association des graveurs du Québec, 1971; Conseil de la gravure, 1978, which prepared a code of ethics for its members). As within the other Canadian associations, efforts for the long-term unification of Québec artists (Société des artistes professionels du Québec, 1966) have had mixed results because of the lack of general interest and solidarity on the part of the artists as a group.

The most constructive and active groups in the history of art in Canada appear to have been the small, organic ones in which natural affinities have appeared and artists have put the elements of a common aesthetic ideal into practice. These natural associations enable the artist to compare his opinions and works with those of a few colleagues and friends, through direct and informal exchanges, thus helping him face the hesitations and isolation of the studio with more assurance and confidence. LAURIER LACROIX

Reading: D. Reid, *A Concise History of Canadian Painting* (1973).

Arts Funding Artistic ventures in Canada receive funding from 3 main sources: governments at all levels; the private sector including individuals, corporations and foundations; and self-generated earnings through the sale of tickets, works of art, memberships, broadcast services and other operations. Some have argued that artists themselves have been prime funders through "their unpaid and underpaid labour."

Government involvement in arts support is not a recent development since ART GALLERIES AND MUSEUMS have been maintained by one level of government or another for over 100 years. In contrast, orchestral and theatrical companies active before WWI sustained their operations without government help, through box-office earnings and assistance from private benefactors. Orchestras, mainly amateur, functioned in Montréal, Halifax and Hamilton before the turn of the century and the Société (now Orchestre) symphonique de Québec can trace its history back to 1903. In Toronto, beginning in 1908, concerts were performed by a semiprofessional ensemble supported by a group of businessman.

The absence of appropriate theatres and CONCERT HALLS inhibited growth of most performing groups. A donation of a building to the community made by a wealthy patron often stimulated professional artistic ventures, as was the case with MASSEY HALL in Toronto.

Individual and Corporate Donations In recent years, corporate and private donations to the arts have traditionally been encouraged by government tax policies. In 1917, the federal government's Income War Tax Act allowed deductions, without limit, for private donations to activities that could help the war effort. In 1929 and again in the 1948 Income Tax Act, a ceiling of 10% of income was placed on allowable deductions when applied to churches, hospitals, universities and educational institutions, with "educational" donations often including arts and cultural activities. In 1957, an optional automatic deduction of $100 was introduced and in 1972 the ceiling for charitable deductions was raised to 20%. This higher ceiling had little effect on the flow of funds since only rarely did such charitable donations reach even the earlier 10% ceiling.

Of the total of donations for all charitable purposes, only about one-twentieth reaches the arts community. Nevertheless, there has been a substantial rise in the amount of private funding directed to the arts. In 1946, the total was $73.4 million, of which $62.5 million came from individuals and $10.9 million from corporations. In 1979, $884.8 million was donated by individuals and $171 million by corporations. Of the 419 835 corporations operating in Canada in 1979, fewer than 4% (15 619) claimed charitable deductions of any kind; nearly all of these gifts were directed primarily (95%) to welfare, health, religion and education.

Some companies offer supplies and personal services as supplements or alternatives to donations in cash. An increasing amount of corporate funding has lately been assigned to the sponsorship of specific events or performances, since these can provide visible, public identification of the sponsor, thus justifying expenditures from marketing or operational budgets. New buildings and other capital projects have appealed to many donors since they represent tangible, lasting manifestations of the gifts. The Council for Business and the Arts, founded in 1974, has successfully

The commissioners of the Royal Commission on National Development in the Arts, Letters and Sciences (from left to right) Arthur Surveyer, Rev Georges-Henri Lévesque, Rt Hon Vincent Massey, Hilda Neatby, Norman A.M. MacKenzie (*courtesy National Archives of Canada/Canadian Assn for Adult Education*).

stimulated an increase in corporate arts donations and sponsorships. It provides research, information, advice and expertise to about 125 of the largest corporate donors which, between them, provide over three-quarters of the funds flowing to the arts from the business world.

Priorities for giving within a single corporation shift with changing times and interests, and since corporate donations are affected by annual profits, nonprofit arts companies can find corporations as a source of income somewhat unstable and unreliable. Currently, corporations allocate their giving in the following order of priorities: symphonic music, museums and galleries, theatre, dance, opera, choral music, libraries, ethnic groups, archives. They also face the need to reconcile conflicting demands from well-established and new ventures, from large and small operations, from professional and amateur activities, from national, regional or local programs and from individual artists and arts organizations.

Government Support Governments participate in arts funding in both direct and indirect ways. Direct support includes grants, loans and subsidies, information services and the proprietorship of galleries, museums, libraries, archive parks, historic sites, and sometimes performing arts centres. Federal support was for many years centered in the Dept of the Secretary of State but the Arts and Culture Branch was shifted to the Dept of Communications in 1980. Most arts agencies now report through that ministry and the department itself operates a number of support programs. In addition to these 2 ministries, several other departments participate directly or have great influence on the functioning of the arts sector. These include the Departments of Indian Affairs and Northern Development, Employment and Immigration, External Affairs, Environment, Supply and Services, Consumer and Corporate Affairs, Regional Industrial Expansion, Finance and the Central Agencies located in the Office of the Prime Minister.

Some federal agencies are, in fact, operators of arts programs. Among these are the CANADIAN BROADCASTING CORPORATION, the NATIONAL ARTS CENTRE, the NATIONAL FILM BOARD, the NATIONAL LIBRARY, the Public Archives (now the National Archives of Canada) and the 4 national museums and galleries located in the capital region. Some federal agencies have been created to provide grants, subsidies, investments and scholarships: the CANADA COUNCIL, the CANADIAN FILM DEVELOPMENT CORPORATION (now called Telefilm Canada) and, until 1987 when it was discontinued, the National Museums Corp, whose granting functions were taken over by the Dept of Communications itself.

Though some provincial governments provide aid to the arts directly through their ministries,

others (Newfoundland, Ontario, Manitoba, Saskatchewan) have created independent granting councils or boards. The largest of these, the Ontario Arts Council (founded in 1963), had a budget of over $26 million in 1988. On a per capita basis, provincial cultural expenditures in 1984 averaged $40, with Alberta and Québec registering $51, Manitoba and PEI close to the average and the others, including Ontario, in the $31-34 range. However, in dollars, Ontario and Québec account for about two-thirds of all provincial expenditures in the arts. Income from lotteries has provided substantial funding to the arts especially in those provinces where certain lottery earnings are directed specifically towards arts functions and development.

Another form of support is provided through the purchase of services which are then offered free to the public. These include concerts, books for library distribution and works of art to enhance buildings and offices. Through contracts worth hundreds of millions of dollars each year, governments build, furnish and decorate office buildings, courthouses, council chambers, embassies and post offices. The impact on the architectural, industrial design and artistic communities through these government projects can be substantial.

Indirect support is provided mostly through foregone taxes and deductions from taxes of the value of gifts of art objects to the Crown. Internal subsidies, such as those provided by the Dept of Communications to the post office to reduce the cost of mailing books, magazines and newspapers, are also a factor. Government regulations can dramatically change the artistic climate for some cultural industries, like broadcasting, for example. An important regulator, the CRTC, effectively stimulated production and creation in the recording industry when it ruled that radio broadcasters must play a minimum amount of Canadian-originated recordings. The recording industry received a further boost in 1986 when the federal government established a 5-year, $25 million Sound Recording Development Program, designed to increase record production by Canadian companies. The film industry is assisted by regulations, direct funding and the activities of the National Film Board. Canadian-content regulations, imposed by the CRTC on TV and pay-TV broadcasters, are of great import to film and TV production companies and the artists performing in those media. Telefilm Canada, in 1984, was assigned a new Broadcast Program Development Fund which increased that agency's target, resulting in a 1986 appropriation of $75.7 million. The government had tried to promote film production in the late 1970s by permitting a 100% capital cost write-off in one year for investment in Canadian film productions, but this led to a serious abuse of the goals by those more interested in a tax shelter than in film production. The new fund, aimed at stimulating the production of TV shows, is a selective granting and investment program in the hands of Telefilm Canada. Some provinces have also established programs to aid the arts industries. Both levels of government are considering other regulatory and support mechanisms in support of broadcasting, film, recording and publishing activities within their jurisdictions.

A major review of arts funding was undertaken in 1986 by the federal government through a 3-member task force. The principal recommendation, among the 60 contained in its report, *Funding the Arts in Canada to the Year 2000,* called for an annual increase of 5% in constant dollars, from all sources, over the remainder of this century. Since this would use only one-tenth of 1% of gross domestic product, the group considered the sum sufficiently modest to be widely accepted.

Canada Council In 1949 the federal government formed a Royal Commission on NATIONAL DEVELOPMENT IN THE ARTS, LETTERS AND SCIENCES, naming Vincent MASSEY as chairman. Its report, published in 1951, had a marked effect on government attitudes and several of its programs. It brought the federal government into direct support of universities and generated the establishment of the National Library in 1953 and the Canada Council for the Arts, Humanities and Social Sciences in 1957. The council's mandate was "to foster and promote the study and enjoyment of, and the production of works in the arts."

The council at first had an income of under $2.4 million (1957-58) earned from a $50-million endowment fund created by the government. In 1965, its insufficient funding base led the Canada Council to request and receive its first governmental appropriation, $10 million, which covered a period of 3 years. For 1987, the council's total revenue was over $98 million, including its earnings and a parliamentary allocation of $88.4 million.

In 1978 the Humanities and Social Sciences division was separated from the original council, becoming an independent SOCIAL SCIENCES AND HUMANITIES RESEARCH COUNCIL, primarily concerned with research within the academic community. Meantime, grants by the Canada Council have become vital to the continued good health and aspirations of professional arts companies and to creative artists. Most grants are made on the advice of peer groups and juries of experts in the various disciplines. The council's 1987 grant allocations of over $82 million break down as follows: theatre, 20.9%; music, including opera, 19%; writing and publishing, including a new Public Lending Right fund, 15.3%; dance, 12.3%; visual arts, including the Art Bank and media arts, 12.2%; touring, 4.9%; Explorations, a miscellaneous regional program, 3.1%; and other multidisciplinary projects, 2.3%. The remaining 10% goes to Arts Awards, which are grants to individual artists.

The budget of the Canada Council represents only a small part (4.6%) of the federal government's allocations in support of the arts and culture which, in turn, comes to about 2% of all federal expenditures. About two-thirds of the arts and culture expenditures in 1983-84 went to the CBC. The provinces, either through departmental programs or arm's-length agencies, support similar activities, though their goals and clientele may be somewhat different. They, and local governments, often provide financial assistance to amateur and ethnic groups, for example. Municipal granting decisions are most often made by governing councils, only occasionally with the help of independent citizen groups or juries of experts. In some cities, especially in the West, locally based and funded general foundations have emerged with some of their revenue reaching their local arts activities. Though arts funding by municipalities is still generally meagre, the level seems to be rising steadily. Together with the provincial and federal governments, they form a funding triumvirate that has become an essential ingredient in the maintenance of arts services.

Dealing with the many and particular funding sources has become a complex process, often leaving arts companies hard pressed to find and pay for appropriate staff and expertise. Though administrative life might be easier if funding came from a single patron or government, most arts organizations support the present system of multiple-source funding. They feel that they are thus assured a greater degree of freedom in artistic planning and development, which they value more than a reduced administrative load. The report of the Federal Cultural Policy Review

Federal Gross Expenditures[1] on Culture, 1985-86 (in Millions$)	
Canada Council	75.5
CBC	1083.1
Telefilm Canada	77.7
CRTC	21.4
National Arts Centre	30.8
National Film Board	76.7
National Library of Canada	31.9
National Museums Corporation	74.9
National Archives of Canada	41.8
Social Sciences and Humanities Research Council	63.2
Arts & Culture Branch, Dept of Communications	99.9
Secretary of State for Multiculturalism	22.7
Official Language Minorities	5.5
Federal and Provincial Parks	288.5
Others, for cultural programs	319.0
Total	$2312.6
Cultural net costs as percentage of government net costs	2.0%

[1]Included are gross expenditures of federal departments and agencies. Excluded are expenditures not requiring a cash outlay.

Committee (1982) endorsed that principle and also recommended that the federal government continue to regard the Canada Council as its primary instrument for the support of the arts.
LOUIS APPLEBAUM

Arvida Strike began 24 July 1941, when some 700 workers in the Aluminium Co of Canada (Alcan) in Arvida, Qué, spontaneously walked off the job. The next day the strike spread to 4500 workers, who decided to occupy the plant. Since the industry had been classified as essential to the war effort, the strike was illegal under federal law. A commotion resulted when Minister of Munitions and Supply C.D. HOWE told the press that 300 men had seized the factory and enemy sabotage was suspected. Consequently, two companies of soldiers were sent to Arvida to protect the factory.

Work resumed 4 days later and negotiations began, with the union as intermediary, assisted by federal conciliators. A subsequent royal commission rejected the sabotage theory, concluding that the strike had been the result of workers' frustration over their long struggle for better salaries and working conditions. The immediate catalysts to the strike had been deductions from the July 23 pay envelopes and a stifling heat wave. The company made amends several days later by giving a slight increase in salaries and in cost-of-living bonuses.
JACQUES ROUILLARD

As For Me and My House, novel by Sinclair ROSS (New York, 1941; Toronto, 1957), explores the spiritual, social and natural forces which threaten to crack a strained marriage. Philip Bentley, a thwarted artist turned minister, and his wife have just moved to Horizon, a small Saskatchewan town struggling through the 1930s. Their story is told in diary form by Mrs Bentley, whose descriptions of Horizon's false-fronted stores become increasingly suggestive of the Bentley's false-fronted lives. She also records the bleak oppression of a pretentious and puritanical social ambience, and of a constantly threatening natural environment which assaults the town's flimsy structures with seasonal cycles of heat and cold, dust and snow. The novel closes with the Bentleys adopting Philip's illegitimate child, determined to make a new life beyond Horizon. Ross depicts the trials of small-town life on the Prairies with a starkly repetitive style and beautiful clarity.
NEIL BESNER

Asbestos, generic term normally used to describe 6 MINERALS, some of which are asbestiform, ie, separable into long, silky, flexible fibres. The 3 main minerals are chrysotile, amosite and crocidolite. Of these, chrysotile is by far the most important commercially and is the only type produced in Canada. Asbestos is valuable because of its fibrous structure, high tensile strength and resistance to high temperature and chemical attack. The Romans used asbestos cloth for wrapping the dead for cremation over 2000 years ago. Asbestos was first discovered in N America in 1860, in the Des Plantes R region of Québec. Canadian production began in 1878 at THETFORD-MINES, Qué. Subsequent discovery of large reserves in the Eastern Townships led to establishment of 5 mining towns, making up the present Québec asbestos region. Asbestos is used in over 3000 products serving the CONSTRUCTION, TRANSPORTATION, ELECTRICAL APPLIANCE, equipment and other industries. Asbestos-cement pipe and sheet account for about 60% of world consumption; other uses include flooring and roofing products, friction products (brake linings and clutch facings), coatings and compounds, special papers and insulation. The asbestos content of products ranges from 10-90%.

Canada, the world's second-largest producer of asbestos, accounted in 1985 for about 18.7% of estimated world production of 4.1 million t. The USSR accounted for about 60%. About 5% of Canadian production is used by manufacturing plants, mainly in Québec and Ontario; the remainder is exported. Asbestos-fibre shipments in 1986 were valued at $300.6 million or 0.06% of GNP; Québec accounted for 81% of Canada's 1986 production of 640 000 t; BC for about 12%; and Newfoundland for about 7%. In Canada a mechanical dry-milling process separates fibres from rock by repetitive breaking and return of nondisintegrated rock, drying, separation of fibres from rock by suction at each step, cleaning, grading and packaging. The Canadian grading system divides mine products into crude asbestos; hand-selected, cross-vein material, which may comprise up to 10% or more of the rock; and milled asbestos, all grades produced by mechanical treatment of ore.
G.O. VAGT

Asbestos-Related Health Effects

Medical researchers suspected as long ago as 1898 that serious health effects could result from the inhalation of asbestos dust. It was not until a series of studies beginning in the 1950s that exposure at levels then common in the workplace was shown to cause a variety of OCCUPATIONAL

Asbestos mine, Advocate Mines Ltd, Nfld (*photo by J.A. Wilkinson/Valan*).

DISEASES, the major ones being asbestosis, mesothelioma and lung cancer. Asbestosis develops over years of exposure to relatively high levels of asbestos dust and results in extensive scar formation in the lung, causing breathing abnormalities, inadequate oxygenation of the blood, and a high risk of developing cancer later. These effects often cause disability and sometimes death. Malignant mesothelioma is a cancer of the membranous lining of either the chest or the abdomen. Usually fatal, malignant mesothelioma is very rare except among persons exposed to asbestos, among whom it usually develops 30 years or more after moderate to high exposure. Lung cancer may develop 20 years or more after the first exposure to asbestos even in the absence of asbestosis or other visible effects. Cigarette smoking greatly increases a person's risk of lung cancer after exposure to asbestos but plays little or no role in the other disorders mentioned. Some evidence suggests that chrysotile is less dangerous than amosite and crocidolite, but all forms of asbestos should be considered hazardous. Canadian researchers, particularly those associated with institutions in Québec, were among the world leaders in establishing the risks of exposure to asbestos. The safety of replacement materials, such as man-made mineral fibres, is still under study. Occupational exposure regulations in all provinces require dust concentrations in the air to be controlled at levels presumed to be safe, and most provinces require periodic medical examinations of workers handling asbestos. Because of such regulations, improved technology to control dust levels, industry awareness and education among workers, exposure to asbestos in the workplace is much less of a problem today in Canada than in past decades. TEE L. GUIDOTTI

Asbestos, Qué, Town, pop 6961 (1986c), 7967 (1981c), inc 1937, is located in the Lower Appalachian plateau 63 km N of Sherbrooke and 55 km SE of Drummondville. Charles Webb discovered an ASBESTOS deposit in 1881 on the present site, which has been mined and expanded by John Manville Co (1905-83) and JM Asbestos Inc (1983-) ever since. The Jeffrey mine is the largest open-face asbestos mine in the Western world, measuring 350 m in depth and 2000 m in diameter. The mill has an annual capacity of 650 million t of fibre and its current (1987) rate is 225 000 t. The region has also been the site of copper, iron and slate mines, the latter having been used in the manufacture of school blackboards. On 14 Feb 1949 a strike of asbestos-industry workers began that involved 5000 miners, lasted for 120 working days and became a turning point in Québec's social history (see ASBESTOS STRIKE.) The mine's steady growth has transformed the town's landscape; some streets and homes were eliminated in 1975 to allow further industrial development. The added presence of wood-product and electrical-equipment manufacturers has enabled Asbestos to become the major economic centre of Richmond County. The town has a mineralogy and mining history museum.
JEAN-MARIE DUBOIS AND PIERRE MAILHOT

Asbestos Strike began 14 Feb 1949 and for the next 4 months paralysed major asbestos mines in Québec, the most important of which were American owned. From the start, this strike of 5000 workers affiliated with the CCCL (later

Jean Marchand (left), secretary of the Canadian Catholic Confederation of Labour (later CNTU), talks to workers during the strike at Asbestos, Qué, April 1949 (*courtesy National Archives of Canada/PA-128762/photo by Glay Sperling*).

CONFEDERATION OF NATIONAL TRADE UNIONS) presented a challenge to the entire union movement, to the anglophone management in Québec, the province's political system and the Roman Catholic Church, and disrupted their former relationships. It began illegally, and thus broke with the CCCL's long tradition of co-operation with management. The asbestos fight also produced unprecedented inter-union solidarity. Unions had previously formed a common front to battle an anti-union bill of the UNION NATIONALE government, and now the CCCL, the Fédération provinciale du travail du Québec (FPTQ, later part of QFL) and unions affiliated with the CCL and CIO organized strike-support meetings throughout Québec. The church also backed the strikers. This put the bishop's office in direct conflict with Prem Maurice DUPLESSIS, whose police, based in mining-company offices, were in conflict with the strikers. The strike became a historical and political event of symbolic import that introduced Québec to an era of embittered labour conflict and presaged the QUIET REVOLUTION. HÉLÈNE DAVID

Ash (*Fraxinus*), genus of TREES or SHRUBS of olive family (Oleaceae). About 60 species occur worldwide, primarily in cold temperate regions; 4 are native to Canada. Native ashes (white, red, blue and black) grow in the East; some forms of red ash reach southeastern Alberta. Trees are of medium height with generally straight, slender trunks. The large compound leaves, consisting of 5-11 leaflets, occur in pairs on the twig. The small, dark flowers are grouped in clusters. Ashes produce

White Ash (*Fraxinus americana*), one of the four species of ash native to Canada, with male flowers and fruit (*artwork by Claire Tremblay*).

large amounts of fruit in the form of winged seeds, which remain on the tree well into winter and are an important food source for birds and squirrels. Ashes prefer the rich, moist soils of swamps and riverways. Except in black ash, the wood is heavy, hard, tough and strong and widely used for sporting goods, tool handles and furniture. *See* PLANTS, NATIVE USES.
ESTELLE LACOURSIÈRE

Ashburton-Webster Treaty (Treaty of Washington), 9 Aug 1842, negotiated by Alexander Baring, First Lord Ashburton, for Britain, and US Secretary of State Daniel Webster. Several sources of friction between the 2 countries were removed, especially regarding those boundaries between BNA and the US which remained in doubt following the Treaty of GHENT. A particular problem had been the 12 000 square miles (approx 31 000 km²) disputed between NB and Maine, 5000 square miles (approx 13 000 km²) of which went to NB. The treaty also provided for the surveying, mapping, and marking of the agreed NB-Maine boundary, completed June 1847. It made some minor adjustments along the northern boundaries of Vermont and New York, and described for the first time the boundary from Lake Huron to Lake of the Woods.
N.L. NICHOLSON

Ashcroft, BC, Village, pop 1914 (1986c), 2156 (1981c), is situated on a flat bench above the THOMPSON R in the interior of southern BC, about 90 km W of Kamloops. Ashcroft was named after Ashcroft Manor, the estate of Clement and Henry Cornwall, who came from England in 1862. They were ranchers on a large scale who built a stopping house on their property when the CARIBOO ROAD was built in 1863. Clement became a member of both provincial and federal parliaments, was a senator and served as BC's lieutenant-governor 1881-87. In 1883 a townsite was surveyed on the property of 2 founding fathers of Ashcroft, J.C. Barnes and E.W. Brink. Ashcroft's history began with the coming of the Canadian Pacific Ry in 1884. A bridge was built over the Thompson R and Ashcroft became the railhead for the north and mile "0" for the Cariboo Road. Once a road was built to link the railway to the old Cariboo Road, Ashcroft quickly replaced Yale as the gateway to the Cariboo and for the next 30 years it served as a major supply centre for the goldfields in the north. The famous pioneering stage and mail company, B.C. Express, carried supplies to Barkerville with heavy freight wagons drawn by 4 to 8 teams of oxen, mules or horses, and stagecoaches carried mail and passengers north and gold on the return trip. When the Cariboo Road was upgraded to accommodate mechanized transportation, and the Pacific Great Eastern Ry (now BC Ry) pushed through from Vancouver to the Cariboo about 1914, Ashcroft lost its position as the main supply centre for the north. The area turned to agriculture and a tomato cannery was opened in 1925 which helped to sustain the town through the Depression years and WWII. Mining breathed new life into the economy in the 1960s, and now Ashcroft mainly acts as a supply centre for nearby open-pit copper mines.
JOHN R. STEWART

Asparagus (*Asparagus officinalis*), perennial VEGETABLE of the LILY family. Of Eurasian origin, asparagus was grown for food and medicinal purposes over 2000 years ago. Some medicinal benefits attributed to asparagus are that when eaten before dinner it refreshes and opens the liver, spleen and kidneys and helps those afflicted with the gravel, or who are scorbatic or dropsical. It is also of singular efficacy in disorder of the eyes and is salutory in many disorders of the breast.

The crop spread throughout Europe and later to N America. The spears, cut when 15-18 cm high, are relished as a cooked or raw vegetable. The crop is established from one-year-old crowns (grown from seed in a nursery), set out in spring in a 15 cm deep furrow, and covered with 5 cm of soil. The emerging spears of a newly established field are harvested for about 2 weeks in the spring of the third year; the full cutting season (6-8 weeks) is achieved the fifth year. An established field can produce for 15-20 years; one commercial field in BC is over 50 years old. After harvest, spears are permitted to grow into ferns (1.5-2.5 m high) for the manufacture of carbohydrates, which are stored in the fleshy roots and used to produce new growth in spring. The fern, killed by frost, is left to trap snow and insulate roots. Asparagus beetles in eastern Canada and aphids in the OKANAGAN VALLEY, BC, are the principal INSECT PESTS. The major disease is *Fusarium* wilt; asparagus rust is a problem in humid regions of eastern Canada. Asparagus varieties include Mary and Martha Washington, Viking, Beacon, Jersey Centennial and the all-male hybrids Lucullus and Jersey Giant. The main growing areas in Canada are Ontario, 1722 ha in 1986; BC, 218 ha; Québec, 450 ha; and Manitoba, 32 ha. In 1985, 3070 t of asparagus were produced.   H. TIESSEN

Aspens, Kananaskis Range, Alta (*photo by J.A. Kraulis*).

Aspen, deciduous, hardwood TREE in genus *Populus* of WILLOW family. Trembling (quaking) aspen (*P. tremuloides*) and largetooth aspen (*P. grandidentata*) are native to Canada; the former, found

Aspens are the most widely distributed tree in N America (*photo by Tim Fitzharris*).

Trembling aspen (*Populus tremuloides*), with male flowers, left, and female flowers, right (*artwork by Claire Tremblay*).

from the TREELINE to northern Mexico, is the most widely distributed tree in N America. Trembling aspen grows on most soils, doing best on well-drained, moist, sandy or gravelly loams. It is shade-intolerant and short-lived (about 60 years). A "pioneer" tree, it colonizes areas disturbed by logging or fire, propagating by root suckers rather than seeds. It also acts as "nurse tree" to softwood or hardwood forest taking over a site. On the Prairies, it may be the only tree. Leaves are nearly circular, with a short tip; the flattened stalk makes them tremble in the wind. Twigs are slender, shiny and brownish grey, the bark smooth, waxy and pale green to chalky white in colour. Trees reach 12-18 m in height. Open grown specimens have a profusely branched, globular crown; forest trees have long, cylindrical trunks with short, rounded crowns.

Assembly of First Nations is the national political organization representing Canada's status Indians (*see* INDIAN). The AFN is the culmination of efforts to form a national Indian organization which go back as far as the 1920s. It succeeds both the National Indian Advisory Council (fd 1961, *see* NATIVE COUNCIL OF CANADA) and the National Indian Brotherhood, which was active in representing Indian interests throughout the 1960s and 1970s under leaders Walter DEITER, George MANUEL and Noel Starblanket. In the late 1970s the increase of power at the local level of Indian government, the need to react to federal constitutional proposals, and the ideology of "Indian nationhood" led to calls for reform. Thus the Assembly of First Nations was founded by chiefs representing a majority of bands during a meeting in Ottawa in 1980. The chiefs declared their assembly the one and only voice of the First Nationals of Canada, referred to as Indian bands in the INDIAN ACT. The AFN replaced the National Indian Brotherhood (which had been based on an executive chosen from the provincial Indian organizations) with a new structure based on the common vote of individual Indian local governments. The NIB corporate structure was retained for legal transactions. The chiefs outlined their objectives for the new organization in the Declaration of First Nations.

Although the AFN does not have a formal constitution, it agreed in Apr 1982 to elect a national chief for a 3-year term to manage the assembly's ongoing work. The chief is assisted by 6 regionally elected vice-chiefs. A Confederacy of Nations meets from time to time as an interim executive

committee, and the chiefs meet at least once a year to determine policy and direction.

The new organization immediately faced formidable challenges. It was recognized by the federal government as the organization to represent Indian people in the First Ministers' conferences held to identify and define ABORIGINAL RIGHTS in Canada's patriated constitution. Disputes in Mar 1983 over what the official position would be, and whether the AFN should even participate, caused the withdrawal of a number of chiefs who constituted themselves as the Coalition of First Nations. Further disagreements resulted in the creation in 1985 of the Prairie Treaty Nations Alliance whose founders saw the constitutional position of their own people as sufficiently unique to justify a special organization not under the umbrella of the AFN.

The main thrust of the AFN has been the entrenchment of the right of Indian self-government in Canada's constitution and recognition of aboriginal title and rights. It has made representations on these subjects to UN commissions. When a Parliamentary Task Force on Indian Self-Government was struck in 1982, the AFN was invited to have an ex-officio member work with the committee with all privileges except that of voting. In Ottawa, AFN officials lobby MPs and ministers of government to make sure its positions are considered in the formulation of government policy. Secretariats in such areas as education, health, social services and economic development carry on consultations, develop policy and assist individual First Nations. In 1987 the first ministers constitutional conferences on aboriginal rights ended in failure. At the final meeting, the AFN issued *A Joint Proposal for Aboriginal Self-government* together with the Native Council of Canada, the Métis National Council and the Inuit Committee on National Issues. Within a month of the breakdown of negotiation on aboriginal rights, the first ministers met privately at Meech Lake where they agreed to describe Québec in the Canadian Constitution as a "distinct society." George Erasmus, national chief of the AFN, was among many aboriginal spokespeople to express bitterness at the discrepancy between the first ministers' successful accommodation of Québec and the breakdown of negotiations on native self-government. *See also* LAND CLAIMS; NATIVE PEOPLE, POLITICAL ORGANIZATION AND ACTIVISM.

MICHAEL POSLUNS AND ANTHONY J. HALL

Assiniboia, a name derived from the ASSINIBOINE Indians, applied to 2 political units in the 19th century, and still in use. The first territory in RUPERT'S LAND delimited for governmental purposes, as distinct from trading districts, was the 1811 HBC grant of 116 000 square miles (*c*300 000 km²) to Lord SELKIRK. This District of Assiniboia (RED RIVER COLONY) was supervised by a governor and council until Nov 1869, when Louis RIEL's resistance effectively ended its life. The second provisional government of the Red River resistance, convened 9 Mar 1870, named itself the Legislative Assembly of Assiniboia and, in its third List of Rights to Ottawa, requested that "Assiniboia" become Canada's fifth province. However, without consulting the assembly, Riel suggested to Ottawa the name Manitoba to avoid confusion. To ensure Manitoba's smooth transition to Canadian authority, Col Garnet WOLSELEY persuaded Donald SMITH, HBC representative, to revive the original council and greet Lt-Gov A.G. ARCHIBALD formally on 6 Sept 1870. The first Assiniboia then ceased to have an official existence.

On 8 May 1882 the federal government created 4 "provisional districts" in the North-West Territories: Alberta, Assiniboia, Athabasca and Saskatchewan. Assiniboia was the southern district, present-day southern SASKATCHEWAN. The districts, designed "for the convenience of settlers and for postal purposes," were roughly equal in size and natural-resource distribution. Along the CPR, Assiniboia developed rapidly. With the 1886 grant of 2 seats in the federal Parliament and the use of the district boundaries to determine representation in the Territorial Assembly, a district consciousness developed. When provincial status and new boundaries were being considered in 1904-05, Assiniboia and Saskatchewan were potential names. Minister of the Interior Clifford SIFTON preferred Assiniboia but, when residents of the northern district asked that their choice be used, he acquiesced.

Today the name applies to a rural municipality and provincial constituency in Manitoba, and to a town and federal constituency in Saskatchewan. This riding was prominent in 1919, when an independent farmers' candidate defeated a former provincial Liberal Cabinet minister, and again in 1935 when it sent former premier James G. GARDINER to Ottawa to become federal minister of agriculture.   GERALD FRIESEN

Assiniboia, Sask, Town, pop 3001 (1986c), 2924 (1981c), inc 1913, is located on the CPR Weyburn-Lethbridge line, 105 km S of Moose Jaw. Founded on arrival of the railway (1912), it was named after the former District of ASSINIBOIA, which in turn was named for the ASSINIBOINE who lived in the area. Situated on the brown soil of the short-grass prairie in the heart of Palliser's Triangle, it developed as a retail service centre for an agricultural community growing mainly wheat. Its selection by Dominion Electric Power (1928) as the site for a generating station to provide power to one of Saskatchewan's first transmission lines led to Assiniboia supplying power to various southwestern communities for over 20 years. During WWII it was also a training base for allied airmen. Though disastrously affected by the 1930s Depression, wartime developments and recovery of the farm economy enabled Assiniboia to reassert itself and thereafter gradually expand. It possesses a weekly newspaper and provides judicial and limited health services to the adjacent areas.   C.O. WHITE

Assiniboine received their name from an OJIBWA word for their practice of boiling food by dropping heated rocks into water. They were first described in the *Jesuit Relations* as having split off from the Yanktonai Sioux sometime prior to 1640. From a homeland around the Mississippi headwaters, they moved northwestwards, to the Lake of the Woods and towards Lk Winnipeg. At the peak of their power their territory ranged from the Saskatchewan and Assiniboine river valleys in Canada to the region N of the Milk and Missouri rivers in the US. Linguistically they belong to the Siouan family, speaking a dialect of Dakota.

Trading with the HUDSON'S BAY COMPANY from the late 17th century, they were noted for their PEMMICAN production and their role as middlemen, trading European goods to the distant Plains tribes. Through the 19th century they were closely allied with the CREE, while intermittently in conflict with the BLACKFOOT, the Gros Ventres, and their Siouan relatives to the S. They suffered greatly from European diseases, especially smallpox. From an estimated population of 10 000 in the late 18th century, their numbers declined to 2600 by 1890. Numbers began to increase only in the 1920s, owing to improved health and living conditions.

Assiniboine culture exhibited most of the classic Plains Indian traits. They were noted for their expertise in constructing buffalo pounds, and made a greater use of dogs, having fewer horses than other Plains tribes. Their image among white

A settler's home near Carberry, Assiniboia. Painting by Edward Roper (*courtesy National Archives of Canada/ C-11030*).

traders and settlers was generally positive, with frequent reports of their hospitality.

In Canada the White Bear and Carry the Kettle bands were signators to Treaty No 4 (1874), and the Mosquito-Grizzly Bear's Head bands were signators to Treaty No 6 (1876), while those bands residing south of the international border signed the Judith R Treaty (1855). In Canada they are now located on 3 Saskatchewan reserves: Carry the Kettle (shared with a Sioux group); Mosquito-Grizzly Bear's Head; and White Bear (shared with Ojibwa and Cree). In 1986 the total population of Assiniboine in Canada was 1850. Those found in Alberta are known as STONEY. In the US Assiniboine reside on the Ft Belknap and Ft Peck reservations. *See also* NATIVE PEOPLE: PLAINS and general articles under NATIVE PEOPLE.

IAN A.L. GETTY

Reading: E.T. Denig, *Five Indian Tribes of the Upper Missouri* (1961); D. Kennedy (Ochankugahe), *Recollections of an Assiniboine Chief*, ed J.R. Stevens (1972); R.H. Lowie, "The Assiniboine," American Museum of Natural History, *Anthropological Papers* 4, Pt 1 (1909).

Assiniboine, Mount, elev 3618 m, the highest mountain between the Trans-Canada Hwy and the US border in the ROCKY MTS, is often called "The Matterhorn of the Canadian Rockies." Situated on the Continental Divide, 35 km S of Banff, its western slopes are in Mt Assiniboine Prov Pk, the eastern slopes in Banff National Pk. It was named in 1885 after the Stoney Indians by Dr G.M. DAWSON of the Geological Survey of Canada. Father de Smet and his guides were probably the first white men to see the peak in 1845. After several other attempts to climb the peak, Sir James Outram, with Swiss guides, made the first ascent in 1901. It is an easy ascent by today's standards,

Mt Assiniboine, in the Rocky Mts, is often called the "Canadian Matterhorn" for its similarity to the famous Swiss mountain (*photo by J.A. Kraulis*).

but numerous accidents have occurred on the mountain.   GLEN BOLES

Assiniboine River, 1070 km long, rises in SE Saskatchewan. Fed by the Etomami and Whitesand rivers, it swells into Lake of the Prairies and flows SE across the Manitoba border, where it is joined by the QU'APPELLE R and, 30 km SE of BRANDON, the SOURIS R. Joining the RED R at the "forks" in Winnipeg, it cuts a wide, scenic valley through the Manitoba Escarpment, and drains a broad, fertile plain that is one of Canada's prime wheat-growing areas. LA VÉRENDRYE built Fort La Reine (1738) on the river near present-day PORTAGE LA PRAIRIE. Its route was well travelled by fur traders, and after 1850 settlement crept westward from the forks, where light, dry soil offered excellent farming prospects. The river is navigable for some 500 km, and before the railway came, 7 sternwheelers plied its course from Winnipeg to Fort Ellice. The name, meaning "those who cook by placing hot stones in water," was taken from the ASSINIBOINE who inhabited the area.

JAMES MARSH

Association for Canadian Studies, fd 1973, has grown into a distinctive LEARNED SOCIETY with over 150 institutional and 500 individual members. Its formal emphasis is to encourage teaching, research and publication about Canada, and it has attempted to translate into reality T.H.B. SYMONS's study, *To Know Ourselves* (2 vols, 1975). The association views Canadian studies as an interdisciplinary exploration of all aspects of Canada's social, cultural and physical environment, its economic system and its place in the world; it generally supports thematic studies of Canada as an entity, rather than discipline-based scholarship or regional studies (*see* CANADIAN STUDIES). ACS has organized conferences on national themes (the Canadian North, Canada and the Sea), supported projects on ethnohistory, multiculturalism and film, and promoted archival development. James E. Page, formerly of Seneca College, Willowdale, Ont, was the driving force until 1982, and through ACS he was able to initiate the International Council for Canadian Studies. Recently, priority has been given to an active student and faculty exchange program, granting awards and developing a stronger presence in western and Atlantic Canada.

PAUL GALLAGHER

Association of Universities and Colleges of Canada (AUCC) dates from 1911 and assumed its present name in 1965. Most of the universities and some university-level colleges are members, as are the 2 provincial and 2 regional associations of universities. A voluntary organization with a secretariat in Ottawa, the AUCC promotes co-operation among universities, co-ordinates some of their activities (eg, collective relations with governments), assists in their international relations, administers central services such as scholarship programs, and serves as a clearing house of information on Canadian higher education. Its publications include a monthly newsmagazine, *University Affairs*, and a biennial *Directory of Canadian Universities.* EDWARD SHEFFIELD

Associations are voluntary, nongovernmental, nonprofit organizations composed of personal or institutional members, with or without federal or provincial incorporation, formed for some particular purpose or to advance a common cause, especially of a public nature. Related terms include foundation, society, institute, federation, alliance, club and union. The freedom of association is one of the fundamental freedoms guaranteed by the Canadian Charter of Rights and Freedoms. It is estimated that individual Canadians on average are associated with 3.6 organizations such as business, trade and professional associations, chambers of commerce and boards of trade, labour organizations and unions, health and welfare groups, religious organizations, athletic associations, political organizations, learned societies, cultural groups, fraternal organizations and service clubs, and community and neighbourhood groups.

In 1987 there were approximately 6850 active nonprofit organizations incorporated at the federal level, many of which were associations, and about 1200 boards of trade and chambers of commerce incorporated federally. In addition, thousands of associations are incorporated under provincial law. Ontario, for example, reported about 21 500 active nonshare corporations, including associations, in 1987. There are also hundreds of associations operating without federal or provincial incorporation.

Historical Background The history of associations in Canada dates from when Samuel de Champlain founded the ORDRE DE BON TEMPS for the promotion of recreation and relaxation at Port-Royal. A few Canadian associations still in existence can trace their origins back to the 18th century. For example, the Halifax Board of Trade was founded in 1750; the Grand Lodge of Upper Canada of the Ancient Free and Accepted Masons was established in 1792; and the Law Society of Upper Canada was organized in 1797. (Most dates given in this article are formation dates, not incorporation dates.)

Associations formed before Confederation include the Montreal Board of Trade (1822); the Nova Scotia Barristers' Society (1825); the Toronto Board of Trade (1845); the Barristers' Society of New Brunswick (1846); Le Collège des Médecins et Chirurgiens de la Province de Québec (1847); the Royal Canadian Institute (1849); Le Barreau du Québec (1849); the Medical Society of Nova Scotia (1854); the Nova Scotia Board of Insurance Underwriters (1857); the Ontario Fruit Growers' Assn (1859); the Ontario Educational Assn (1861); the Nova Scotian Institute of Natural Science (1862); the Law Society of British Columbia (1863); the Nova Scotia Fruit Growers' Assn (1863); the Entomological Society of Canada (1863), the first national association formed in the sciences; the College of Physicians and Surgeons of Ontario (1866); the CANADIAN MEDICAL ASSN and the Ontario Dental Assn (1867).

From 1867 to 1900 many new associations were established at both the national and provincial level. Examples of national associations formed during this period and still in existence are the CANADIAN MANUFACTURERS' ASSN (1871); the ROYAL SOCIETY OF CANADA (1882); the Canadian Institute of Surveying (1882, as the Assn of Domin-

ion Land Surveyors); the Engineering Institute of Canada (1887, as the Canadian Society of Civil Engineers); the Canadian Electrical Assn (1889); the Royal Astronomical Society of Canada (1890, as the Astronomical and Physical Society of Toronto); the Canadian Bankers' Assn (1891); the Canadian Education Assn (1892); and the Canadian Institute of Mining and Metallurgy (1898). From 1900 to the end of WWII there was a steady increase in the number of associations. The period of greatest growth coincided with the economic prosperity of the 1960s. More than one third of the 1500 nonprofit corporations incorporated under federal legislation from 1900 to 1970 were incorporated in the 5-year period 1966-70.

The headquarters of national associations are concentrated heavily in the vicinities of Toronto (about 38%), Ottawa (about 27%) and Montréal (about 11%). The Vancouver, Edmonton and Winnipeg areas have smaller concentrations of association headquarters.

Origins and Growth A number of Canadian associations owe their origins to foreign parents, particularly American or British. When Canadian membership in foreign associations has increased to a significant number, members have withdrawn to form their own associations with headquarters in Canada. There are still scores of foreign associations with Canadian chapters or divisions, such as the American Society of Mechanical Engineers, New York, and the Royal Commonwealth Society, London. In addition, several international associations such as the International Air Transport Assn have their headquarters in Canada. Many Canadian labour unions are affiliated with international unions headquartered in the US. By 1986, however, the percentage of total union membership affiliated with international unions had declined to less than 41%, a drop of 10% in 10 years, as new national unions and independent local organizations were organized in Canada.

The proliferation of associations is a result of the growth in population, the expansion and diversification of the economy, and greatly increased government activity, especially in health care and social services, as well as the desire for communication with others who share common interests.

Types There have been various attempts to classify associations into types according to purpose, function and structure. No classification has been satisfactory because of the diversity in membership, objectives, structure, methods of operation and concerns. One classification makes a distinction between those associations that function primarily for the benefit of the public (charitable organizations) and those that carry on their activities primarily for the benefit of their members (membership organizations). Another distinguishes between corporate-type and federation-type organizations. The latter may bring together associations devoted to the same subject, or to several different subjects. It is also possible to classify associations according to their principal activity. *The Directory of Associations in Canada* uses more than 1050 subject classifications ranging from accounting to zoology to describe the activities of the 15 000 associations listed.

Incorporation is often advantageous or necessary for nonprofit corporations to carry out certain of their activities. The principal advantages of incorporation as a nonprofit corporation without share capital are that it provides greater continuity and permanency for the organization, frees members from liability for the debts and obligations of the corporation, and facilitates certain activities such as the holding of real estate. Such corporations must be conducted without pecuniary gain for the members.

Federal nonprofit corporations in Canada include many of the large charitable and membership organizations and virtually all the boards of trade and chambers of commerce incorporated under the Boards of Trade Act. For associations carrying on activities within a single locality or province, provincial incorporation as a nonprofit corporation is sufficient. Each province has its own requirements and procedures for incorporation.

Organization and Operation The board of directors of an incorporated nonprofit corporation manages its business and affairs. The board is legally responsible for holding the constitution and bylaws, for making policy to further the attainment of its stated goals and objectives, and for appointing the chief executive officer. A small group of board members, including the officers, constitutes the executive committee, which sits between board meetings to make decisions on behalf of the board.

The usual officers of an association are the president, vice-president, treasurer and secretary. The officers may be selected by the membership or appointed by the board, and their duties are set out in the bylaws or established by the board. The chief executive officer or executive director (the title may vary) performs duties assigned by the board of directors. This officer executes policies as prescribed by the board, selects employees for the operation of the association office, prepares budgets, approves expenditures and attends all meetings of the board and its executive committee.

The committee structure of associations usually reflects its goals and objectives. Typical committee responsibilities include membership, nominations, education, research, publishing, public and government relations. Officers and directors are expected to render a periodic account of their stewardship, usually in the form of an annual report. The requirements for membership are usually stated in the bylaws of the association and there may be several classes of membership, such as member, associate, student and honorary member. Some associations admit anyone interested in its activities; others, such as professional associations, have specific requirements for membership. In general, charitable organizations rely for their income on grants from government and on donations from business and the general public, whereas membership organizations obtain most of their income from fees and dues.

Contribution to Society Associations registered federally as charitable organizations are legally obligated to provide services beneficial to the community at large. Although membership associations have the advancement of the interests of their members as their primary aim, they too may respond to changing conditions in society by engaging in programs and activities in the public interest. Associations have an important role in building consensus in society by providing the mechanism for their members to reach agreement on social values, on objectives to be pursued and on the means to achieve objectives. Through interaction with government, associations participate in shaping public policy. National associations, many of which are bilingual, can contribute to the strengthening of national unity by improving communications and understanding among the different peoples and regions of Canada. Associations are also important as sources of information about hundreds of specialized activities in our society. By helping those in need, supporting and publishing worthwhile research, educating members of the public, contributing to the personal development of citizens and pressing for just and humanitarian causes, associations are making a significant contribution to Canadian society. *See also* FOUNDATIONS. R. BRIAN LAND

Aster [Lat, "star"], the common name applied mainly to 2 herbaceous genera (*Aster* and *Callistephus*) of flowering PLANTS in family Compositae or Asteraceae. Over 250 species of true *Aster* are known worldwide. Of 52 *Aster* species native to Canada, about 40 have been brought under cultivation. *A. alpinus* and *A. campestris* of the Rocky Mts are most popular for alpine gardens. Canadian species are mostly perennial, late-season flowering and are usually blue, purple, pink or white. Plants have alternate, simple leaves and large clusters of showy flower heads, usually comprising a central disc surrounded by showy rays. Wild asters are found in prairie, forest and desert areas. Some species are woody at base. China aster (*Callistephus chinensis*), introduced from China in 1731, is now among the most popular of cut flowers, being diverse in form and providing blue shades, rare in the related chrysanthemum. Infusions of *Aster* roots were used by some Canadian Indians as remedies for cuts, heart ailments or eye problems. *See also* ORNAMENTALS; PLANTS, NATIVE USES.   ROGER VICK

New England Aster (*Aster novae-angliae L.*) (artwork by Claire Tremblay).

Astman, Barbara, photographer, multi-media artist (b at Rochester, NY 12 July 1950). Astman is a graduate of Rochester Institute of Technology (1970) and Ontario College of Art (1973). Her camera works and sculptural installations are a mixture of various traditional art forms — drawing, painting, photography, sculpture — which are redefined by a contemporary sensibility. A fascination with current technological developments has resulted in images of remarkable colour, texture and scale. Her "red" series (1980) represented a breakthrough on several levels — symbolism, content and form. The artist is posed frontally amidst a carefully balanced composition of objects, each spray-painted red, which because of their redness assume a variety of implications at once playful and vaguely threatening. In the

From Barbara Astman's "red" series, ektacolour mural of woman reading a book and holding a mug (*courtesy Barbara Astman/Sable Castelli Gallery Ltd*).

Places series (1982) she explored the traditional dimension of sculptural assemblage — mixed-media construction of linoleum, wood and plastics. *Settings for Situations* (1984) consist of formal sculptural wood constructions mounted on the wall and placed on the floor. Astman's use of material and technology place her in the forefront of post-modern activity. Her work is not only technically and aesthetically exquisite but also reaches for the deepest mysteries of the self.

KARYN ELIZABETH ALLEN

Astronaut [from Gk *astron*, "star"; *nautikos*, "sailor"], or cosmonaut, individual involved in flight beyond Earth's atmosphere. Both the US and the USSR have well-established spaceflight programs. American astronaut trainees were initially test pilots selected from the military services. In the US the National Aeronautics and Space Administration (NASA, est 1958) is in charge of manned flights; in the USSR, the Academy of Sciences. Manned spaceflight became possible only after a series of unmanned flights, the first being that of the Earth-orbiting SATELLITE Sputnik I, launched by the USSR on 4 Oct 1957. Yuri Gagarin piloted the first manned Earth-orbiting spacecraft, Vostok I, launched on 12 Apr 1961 from Kazakhstan, USSR. The first American to orbit Earth was John Glenn, in Friendship 7, on 20 Feb 1962.

Although Canada has been involved in the development of SPACE TECHNOLOGY since the early 1960s (the US launched the Canadian-built scientific satellite Alouette I on 29 Sept 1962), its direct participation in manned flight is very recent. In 1983, as a result of Canada's contributions to the American space program (eg, development of the CANADARM), NASA offered to fly Canadian astronauts as "payload specialists" aboard the space shuttle. In June 1983, the NATIONAL RESEARCH COUNCIL OF CANADA began a 6-month, nationwide hunt to fill 6 positions in a program to train Canada's first astronauts. The 5-member screening committee was made up of representatives from the NRC, the Department of National Defence and the Ministry of State for Science and Technology. Almost 4300 people applied; 68 applicants were interviewed between 18 Oct and 9 Nov 1983. The 19 finalists were interviewed again in Ottawa, participated in orientation sessions and technical briefings, and underwent medical examinations. The final selection was made in the first week of Dec 1983. The 6 candidates selected were chosen on the basis of their academic background, technical expertise and physical fitness. They began astronaut training in

Feb 1984, working with the NRC as staff, as staff seconded from the DND, or on contract.

Brief biographies of members of the Canadian Astronaut Program follow. Ken Money (b 1935 at Toronto, grew up Noranda, Qué), a physiologist with the Defence and Civil Institute of Environmental Medicine, Dept of National Defence, Toronto, is an expert on space motion sickness. He was involved in shuttle experiments with US scientists and was co-designer of the Canadian motion sickness and disorientation experiments. Money is a former Olympic athlete and a jet pilot who has flown search and rescue missions. Roberta Bondar (b 1945 at Sault Ste Marie, Ont), a neurologist at McMaster University's medical centre, was an assistant professor and director of the Multiple Sclerosis Clinic when selected. She is a pilot and has been active in the Canadian Society for Aviation Medicine. Marc GARNEAU (b 1949 at Québec City), an electronics expert, worked with the DND as head of the Communications and Electronic Warfare section. He attended the Royal Military College, Kingston, Ont, and received his PhD in electrical engineering from University of London in England. When chosen, Steven MacLean (b 1954 at Ottawa) had just received his PhD in physics from York University. He was a postdoctoral student at Stanford University in California, working under Nobel Prize winner Arthur Schawlow on laser research that will be applicable to his work on Canadian shuttle experiments. Robert Thirsk (b 1953 at New Westminster, BC) was a medical doctor at Montréal's Queen Elizabeth Hospital and has a degree in mechanical engineering (biomedical) from the Massachusetts Institute of Technology. Bjarni Tryggvason was a research officer with the NRC, specializing in aerodynamics and meteorology. Born in Iceland (1945), Tryggvason grew up in BC and is a Canadian citizen. He did graduate work in engineering at University of Western Ontario. He is a pilot and flying instructor. In Mar 1984 Marc Garneau and Robert Thirsk were chosen as prime and backup crew for the Oct 1984 shuttle flight. Garneau became the first Canadian to cross the "last frontier" when the US space shuttle Challenger took off from the Kennedy Space Center, Florida. Various space sickness and space vision experiments were successfully completed by Garneau in the 8-day mission, during which Challenger circled the earth 132 times. Future space shuttle missions were cancelled after the Challenger disaster of 1986.

LYDIA DOTTO AND ADRIANA A. DAVIES

Astronomy, science that studies the SUN, the solar system, the remote stars, distant GALAXIES and all other detectable bodies in the universe. Its major subdisciplines include astrophysics, the closely related field of SPECTROSCOPY and COSMOLOGY. Astronomy is often regarded as the oldest SCIENCE, since more than 5000 years ago motions in the sky were used to predict events such as the annual flood on the Nile. During the era of modern exploration, astronomy had practical applications in navigation, SURVEYING and timekeeping. Modern astronomy, however, is more concerned with the physical and chemical nature of matter beyond Earth, where conditions of temperature and pressure, and gravitational and magnetic fields allow astronomers to observe matter under extremes unattainable in terrestrial laboratories. Astronomy is also closely related to PHYSICS, CHEMISTRY, MATHEMATICS, GEOLOGY, ENGINEERING and COMPUTER SCIENCE.

History in Canada

The earliest astronomical observations in what is now Canada were scattered observations made as early as 1612 by arctic explorers and occasional sightings of COMETS and eclipses recorded by French missionaries, as early as 1618. Jesuit missionaries recorded an eclipse 27 Oct 1632. There may be some disagreement about the earliest astronomical OBSERVATORY, depending on the definition adopted. One of the earliest observatories in N America was that built by the marquis de Chabert 1750-51 at LOUISBOURG. Chabert produced maps and astronomical observations as well as a report, *Voyage fait par ordre du Roi en 1750 et 1751 dans l'Amerique septentrionale.* Unfortunately, nothing remains of this observatory. There is evidence that Joseph Frederick Wallet DESBARRES built a small observatory in 1765 at Castle Frederick, NS, for testing his surveying instruments. The building probably also housed astronomical telescopes. Nothing remains of this structure. The Toronto Magnetic Observatory began observations in 1840, but the astronomical instruments intended for it were never received. In 1850 an observatory was constructed on the Citadel at Québec City to support the requirements of marine navigation, but neither the original structure nor its successor, built on the Plains of Abraham in 1874, survives today. An astronomical observatory was built in 1851 on the campus of University of New Brunswick and an official plaque, unveiled in 1955, identifies this building as the "First Astronomical Observatory in Canada." A public observatory was built in Kingston in 1856; an observatory for TIME determination followed in Montréal in 1862; and modest telescopes were erected in other towns and cities in the next 3 decades. The federal government became involved in 1885 because of the urgent need to survey lands adjacent to the transcontinental railway, since astronomical techniques were required in mountainous regions.

The determination of longitude (relative to the meridian of a city in western Europe) for a ship at sea, a recently discovered island or a colony in the Americas, was a major problem during the voyages of discovery. The invention and perfection of the marine chronometer by John Harrison in 1761 solved the practical problem. Before this, however, various astronomical methods were used in attempts to determine longitude: in New France the Jesuits and others had observed more than a dozen eclipses between 1632 and 1694; 5 lunar eclipses observed at Québec City or at STE MARIE AMONG THE HURONS (Midland, Ont) were also observed in Europe, and some useful longitudes were derived. Although some solar eclipses were observed quite well, the theory of the time was inadequate to derive accurate longitudes from the observations.

By the 19th century, interest in eclipses had shifted from the determination of longitudes to the study of the sun; therefore, total solar eclipses became the events of interest. Eclipse expeditions involve careful planning and frequently difficult journeys to remote locations, such as that made by an American expedition to northern Manitoba to observe the total eclipse of 17 July 1860. The party, which included Simon Newcomb, an American astronomer born in NS, suffered the fate common to later expeditions: clouds on the crucial day. The 20th century has produced 8 total solar eclipses in Canada, which have been studied by ground parties and, since 1945, from aircraft and even rockets. The most significant Canadian expedition, however, remains the one led by C.A. CHANT to Australia in 1922, during which observations were made of the displacement of stars near the eclipsed sun. These measurements helped provide observational support for the theory of relativity.

Few stories in the history of astronomy can rival those associated with early observations of the transits of Venus. On the rare occasions when Venus is directly between Earth and the sun, it is seen to cross the solar disc over the course of several hours. It was realized in the 17th century that accurate timing of such transits (which come in pairs, 8 years apart, once every 122 years) could be used to establish the scale of the solar system. Immense efforts were made to observe the transit of 1769, including an arduous expedition to the area of CHURCHILL, Man, by the astronomer William Wales and another English observer, Joseph Dymond. After a frightening winter, they made successful observations of the transit. An attempted observation from Île aux Coudres, 100 km downstream from Québec City, was incomplete because of clouds. In 1882 there were plans to observe the transit from more settled areas of Canada, including substantial observatories in Woodstock, Ont (which was clouded out at crucial times), and Kingston, Ont (where useful observations were made). These international campaigns were moderately successful, but observational problems limited the accuracy of the final result.

Canadian astronomy shows a pattern of parallel development in universities and federal government agencies. The provinces have been involved indirectly through their general support of university development. The federal government made its first provision for astrophysical research with the establishment of the Dominion Observatory in Ottawa (1905), a facility that was equipped with a refracting telescope and a reflecting solar telescope, in addition to transit instruments for positional astronomy. Government research facilities expanded in 1918, when the Dominion Astrophysical Observatory near Victoria, BC, was opened. Its 1.88 m (72-inch) telescope was the world's largest at the time of its installation (1918). Facilities at Victoria have been upgraded with the addition of a second telescope and continuous modernization of detecting equipment. Major observatories for radio astronomy have been built near Penticton, BC, and in ALGONQUIN PROVINCIAL PARK, Ont. In recent years the most important instrument for Canadian optical astronomers has been the Canada-France-Hawaii Telescope on Mauna Kea in Hawaii, opened in 1979. All government astronomical research programs were placed under the aegis of the NATIONAL RESEARCH COUNCIL in 1970. The NRC's Herzberg Institute of Astrophysics was formed in 1975, adding programs in laboratory astrophysics and space science.

The first Canadian department of astronomy was established at U of T in 1904 and, in 1933, through the efforts of Dr Chant, the university acquired the David Dunlap Observatory. In 1971, U of T inaugurated the first Canadian telescope operating in the Southern Hemisphere, at Las Campanas, Chile. Early in 1987, a Canadian astronomer, Ian Shelton, discovered a supernova outburst in the Large Magellanic Cloud with this telescope, a major astronomical event with far-reaching implications in astronomical research. The University of Western Ontario, Queen's University, York University, University of Calgary, University of Alberta and University of Victoria also have their own observatory facilities. The Université de Montréal and Laval share facilities at Mont Mégantic, Qué. Undergraduate training only is available from the following universities: McGill, Laurentian, Laval, Lethbridge, Manitoba, Saskatchewan and Simon Fraser. The universities of Alberta, British Columbia, Guelph, Lakehead, Montréal, Queen's, Saint Mary's, Toronto, Victoria, Waterloo, Western Ontario and York offer both undergraduate and graduate training.

The first major planetarium in Canada was the Queen Elizabeth Planetarium, opened in Edmonton in 1962. Several cities in Canada now have planetariums which offer the public visual instruction in astronomy for a moderate fee.

Despite its small size, the Canadian astronomical community has included many eminent scientists renowned for their contributions to international astronomy, among the most prominent being C.S. BEALS, Sidney VAN DEN BERGH, C.A. Chant, Arthur COVINGTON, J. Donald Fernie, W.E. HARPER, Frank Hogg, Helen HOGG, W.F. KING, J.L. LOCKE, Donald C. Morton, Andrew MCKELLAR, Peter MILLMAN, Joseph PEARCE, R.M. PETRIE, J.S. PLASKETT, R.M. STEWART and R.K. YOUNG.

Societies and Journals Active astronomical societies, the members of which are professional astronomers or amateur enthusiasts, flourish today at local, national and international levels. The earliest Canadian astronomical society was the Toronto Astronomical Club, formed in 1868 through the initiative of Andrew Elvins. The club was an outgrowth of the Canadian Institute and, after 2 decades of variable vitality, became the Astronomical and Physical Society of Toronto in 1890. The name was changed to the Royal Astronomical Society of Canada (RASC) in 1903, and local centres have joined until at present there are 20 centres in major cities across Canada. The membership of nearly 3000 includes both professional and nonprofessional members. Each centre operates its own program of lectures and many have constructed fine observing facilities. An annual general assembly attracts members from throughout Canada and from abroad for a 3-day meeting held in different parts of the country to exchange ideas and reports on achievements. Not all local astronomy clubs are part of the RASC. Several autonomous clubs exist in various cities and towns and there is an association of French-language clubs in Québec, l'Association des groupes d'astronomes amateurs (AGAA). More than a dozen clubs belong to the AGAA, including the 2 French-speaking centres of the RASC; total membership is about 1000. The Canadian Astronomical Society (CAS) was formed in 1970 as the society of professional astronomers in Canada and has nearly 300 members. The society conducts an annual meeting for the presentation of research results and represents astronomers in matters of national concern.

Astronomical papers appeared as early as the 1850s in *The Canadian Journal,* published by the Canadian Institute. The first *Transactions of the Astronomical and Physical Society of Toronto* were published in 1891; this annual publication was superseded by the *Journal of the Royal Astronomical Society of Canada* in 1907. The journal has published at least 6 issues per year since then. The periodical is designed to be of interest to both amateurs and professionals and has a substantial circulation abroad. The society also publishes annually the *Observer's Handbook,* a compendium of forthcoming sky events and astronomical data. The RASC, many of its individual centres, the AGAA, the CAS and other clubs also publish newsletters on a regular basis.   IAN HALLIDAY

Reading: Donald Fernie, *The Whisper and the Vision: The Voyages of the Astronomers* (1976); Helen S. Hogg, *The Stars Belong to Everyone: How to Enjoy Astronomy* (1976).

Astrophysics is the study of the physical makeup and behaviour of celestial objects. Astrophysics and ASTRONOMY are not sharply distinguished. If the term astronomy is used to mean the whole science of celestial bodies, then the term astrophysics would apply to that portion of astronomy dealing with the application of physical laws. Alternatively, if astronomy means the older astronomy of positions and motions of astronomical objects, then the term astrophysics could be applied to most of modern astronomy. By the first definition, which will be followed here, astrophysics is largely concerned with studying the composition and physical characteristics of STARS, including main sequence stars such as our SUN, double or binary stars and star clusters. Astrophysical research also includes studies of GALAXIES, QUASARS and the expanding universe.

Astrophysicists use many branches of PHYSICS: nuclear physics to study power generation in stars; atomic physics to understand the spectra of stars and gaseous nebulae; gas laws and magnetic theory to probe starspots and flares on star surfaces. Other sciences also make important contributions; for example, CHEMISTRY is needed to study atomic and molecular reactions in interstellar space; GEOLOGY, geophysics and METEOROLOGY contribute to studies of PLANETS. Technical skills in optics, ELECTRONICS and COMPUTERS are needed to collect astrophysical data and compare it to theory. When an astrophysically important law is studied in a laboratory, the work may be called laboratory astrophysics.

Radiation Information about astronomical objects arrives in the form of electromagnetic radiation, ie, light waves or photons. The most energetic form is gamma radiation, followed by X-rays, ultraviolet radiation, visible light (violet through red), infrared light, millimetre waves and radio waves. Optical, X-ray, radio and other telescopes are required to measure the full range of radiation. Photometry, polarimetry and SPECTROSCOPY are techniques for analysing light.

Photometry measures brightness. Hotter stars emit more blue than red light, compared to cooler stars. Starlight collected with a telescope is measured by a light detector; the relative amount of light in different colours is established by placing colour filters in front of the detector. The DDO (*David Dunlap Observatory*) colour system, designed by R.D. McClure and S. VAN DEN BERGH, both of the Dominion Astrophysical Observatory (DAO), has been widely used. X-ray photometry can be used to study the outermost parts of a star. Stellar eclipses and pulsation are also studied by photometry.

Polarimetry measures the orientation of light. In natural-source radiation, waves are seen in all possible orientations and the light is unpolarized. If a magnetic field exists in the material emitting the light, the orientation becomes ordered and the light is polarized. The polarization of visible light is detected by placing a polaroid or Nichol prism in the light beam. Polarized radio waves are detected at the focus of a dish antenna. In many cases, astronomical sources show only partial polarization (under 10%) if any. Magnetic fields are known to be strong in some types of galaxies because of the strongly polarized light they emit.

Spectroscopy measures the detailed features in the electromagnetic spectrum. In astrophysical studies, spectrographic analysis can give information about the chemical composition, temperature, pressure, and velocities of approach or recession of the object under study, etc. Canadian researchers have done pioneering work in stellar motions, mass loss, rotation and magnetism, using spectroscopy. DAVID F. GRAY

Atchison, John D., architect (b at Monmouth, Ill 1870; d after 1930). Atchison was the most prominent member of the "Chicago School" of architects who practised in Winnipeg. He worked in Chicago for William Le Baron Jenney and had his own firm there 1894-1904. He then moved to Winnipeg, remaining there until 1922 when he left for California. During this Manitoba period he designed nearly 100 buildings in styles varying from the progressive Wardlaw Block (1905) to the historically eclectic Great-

West Life Assurance Building (1911). A professional of high competence, Atchison brought Winnipeg a connection with the most progressive architectural centre in N America at that time, and helped building there advance technically and stylistically. WILLIAM P. THOMPSON

Athabasca, Alta, Town, pop 1970 (1986c), 1731 (1981c), is located on the Athabasca R, 150 km N of Edmonton. It was known until 1904 as ATHABASCA LANDING. Athabasca Landing reached its zenith during the Klondike era and was incorporated as a town in 1911, changing its name to Athabasca in 1913. However, the CNR reached Athabasca in 1912, and with the completion of the Alberta and Great Waterways Ry and the Edmonton Dunvegan and BC Ry in 1919, the town's importance waned. It became a local agricultural service centre, and is today the home of ATHABASCA U. FRITS PANNEKOEK

Athabasca, Lake, 7936 km², elev 213 m; located in NE Alberta and NW Saskatchewan, at the edge of the Precambrian SHIELD, fourth-largest lake entirely in Canada. It is fed by the ATHABASCA and PEACE rivers, and drains N via the SLAVE R into GREAT SLAVE LAKE. The lake was a pivotal point in the fur-trade system, being as far W as canoes could go and still return before the ice. Northern brigades returned from the Arctic via the Mackenzie and Slave rivers, and western brigades from the Pacific via the Peace or Athabasca. Ft Chipewyan (est 1788) was the meeting point, and is still a centre of trade. Camsell Portage, URANIUM CITY and Eldorado are on or near the northern shore. The lake was discovered by Samuel HEARNE (1771). Its name is of Cree origin and might mean "where there are reeds" or "meeting place of many waters." The lake has a good stock of whitefish, which was used in earlier days to feed the fur traders. JAMES MARSH

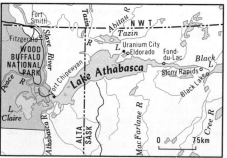

Athabasca Landing, at the site of the present town of ATHABASCA, Alta, was from 1876 until 1913 an important trading centre linking the Prairies with the far Northwest. Known locally as "the gateway to the North," the Landing was also used by the Anglican Church as headquarters for its missionary activity in the Northwest, and from 1895 to 1916 served as the seat of the extensive diocesan see of Athabasca. Its commercial development began in 1876 when the Hudson's Bay Co, seeking a better fur-trade route to the PEACE RIVER region, completed construction of the ATHABASCA LANDING TRAIL from Edmonton. The small HBC post at Athabasca Landing, est 1877, expanded during the 1880s when the company made it the headquarters of a new network of

STEAMBOAT transportation on the North Saskatchewan, Athabasca, Slave and Mackenzie rivers, and the home-port of the SS *Athabasca* (launched 1888). During 1897-98 a tent-city at the Landing was the effective starting-out point for adventurers following the all-Canadian water route to the Yukon goldfields, and both the KLONDIKE GOLD RUSH and a lengthy visit by the Indian Treaty and Scrip Commission in 1899 stimulated the growth of a village around the HBC post. In the mid-1900s the HBC monopoly of the local fur and carrying trade was challenged successfully by rival businesses while the number of steamboats built, docked and serviced at the Landing increased dramatically. The expanding river traffic, the arrival of thousands of homesteaders, a speculative real-estate boom and railway fever brought rapid economic and demographic growth from 1909 to 1913. In 1911 Athabasca Landing was incorporated as a town, and by Aug 1913, when its name was changed to Athabasca, the new municipality had a population approaching 2000. However, by 1919 railways had bypassed Athabasca and destroyed its raison d'être as an inland port.
DAVID GREGORY

Reading: David Gregory et al, *Athabasca Landing: An Illustrated History* (1986).

Athabasca Landing Trail was est 1875 by HBC between Edmonton and ATHABASCA LANDING to improve and expand northern transportation. This 161 km portage, which links the N Saskatchewan R with the Mackenzie R system, played a vital role in the development of northern Alberta, the YT and the NWT. Surveyed in 1879, the trail was Canada's busiest northern route for 40 years, during the transformation of the area from fur-trade monopoly to a modern, diversified economy; the settlement of western Canada; and the evolution of modern transportation. The development of railways (Athabasca, 1912; Grande Prairie, 1916; and Ft McMurray, 1917) diminished the importance of the trail. The trail experienced a brief revival with the building of the ALASKA HIGHWAY during WWII, but modern highways now bypass most of the historic route. What remains of the trail today begins at Gibbons, Alta. J.B. CZYPIONKA

Athabasca Pass, elev 1748 m, a solitary spot now visited rarely by hikers and mountaineers, is situated on the extreme SW boundary of JASPER NATIONAL PK, on the BC-Alberta border. It is reached from the E by gentle slopes from the Whirlpool R, an Athabasca R tributary. Its W side drops steeply down Pacific Cr to Wood R, a Columbia R tributary. Its first recorded crossing was by David THOMPSON and his party in 1811. Thereafter the pass was used for several years as a main fur-trade route across the ROCKY MTS, though heavy snow caused voyageurs some hardship during late spring crossings. A small lake at its summit was named the Committee's Punch Bowl after the governing body of the HBC.
GLEN BOLES

Athabasca River, 1231 km long, rises in the COLUMBIA ICEFIELD, flows N through Jasper National Park, then NE past FT MCMURRAY, Alta, to Lk ATHABASCA; it is the southernmost headstream of the MACKENZIE R, and its chief tributaries are the Pembina, Lesser Slave and McLeod rivers. In NE Alberta, it passes through huge deposits of oil sands containing BITUMEN. Near the river, the oil sands are close to the surface, and outcrops can be seen on its escarpment. Peter POND wintered on the river 1778; and the first freight route to the Rockies followed the Athabasca to Jasper and then by pack horses over ATHABASCA PASS. Goods were later moved by horse N from Edmonton to Athabasca Landing and then by barge along the river. This

Athabasca River, Jasper National Park, Alta, the southernmost headstream of the Mackenzie R system (*photo by Hälle Flygare*).

route fell into disuse when the railway was built from Edmonton to Waterways (1917).

JAMES MARSH

Athabasca University, Athabasca, Alta, was established 1972 in Edmonton to provide DISTANCE LEARNING at the university level. Athabasca's mandate is to make university education accessible to adults seeking the benefits of an open education, not campus-based. Home study, supplemented by tutor support, is central to most courses. Athabasca provides courses in administrative studies, social sciences, natural sciences and humanities, and undergraduate degrees in administration, arts and general studies. The university was moved to new facilities in Athabasca in 1984.

B. BEATON

Enrolment: Athabasca University, 1985-86 (Source: Statistics Canada)			
Full-time Undergrad	Full-time Graduate	Part-time Undergrad	Part-time Graduate
—	—	6779	—

Athans, George, Jr, water-skier (b at Kelowna, BC 6 July 1952). Athans began competitive waterskiing at age 12, and at 15 won his first Canadian slalom title. Before his career was ended in 1975 by a knee injury, he was 10 times Canadian champion 1965-74 and set 5 Canadian records. He won the world overall title at Banolas, Spain, in 1971 and again in 1973 at Bogota, Colombia. In 1973 he became the first non-US skier to win the coveted US Masters title. He has been Canadian amateur, BC and Québec athlete of the year and in 1974 he was awarded the Order of Canada.

REG BARNES

Atheism and Agnosticism An atheist believes there is no God. An agnostic believes we are unable to know whether or not there is a God. Although the word "agnosticism" was invented by T.H. Huxley (1825-95), the position is very old, going back to the Greek Sceptics. Since in practice the agnostic cannot commit himself to religious belief any more than the atheist can, believers seldom distinguish between them. Both views are widespread today, for 3 main reasons. First, the enormous growth of scientific knowl-

edge has required no use of the idea of God: there is no Christian physics or chemistry. Since claims about God cannot be tested by science, atheists reject them, and agnostics say we cannot decide about them. Second, the power of technology has reduced the human sense of dependence on outside forces, and so lowered the psychological barriers to scepticism. Third, the study of religion itself by science and history has suggested that it, too, can be understood without assuming the reality of God.

In Huxley's time, the atheist or agnostic was probably someone brought up as a Christian, who would retain a deep interest in religion even after rejecting it. This is less commonly true today, and religious thinkers have now to speak to a world where doubt and denial are combined with widespread indifference. One academic expression of this is the philosophical position popularly known as positivism, which argues that claims about God are not merely beyond knowledge, but cannot even be stated clearly. In Canada the decline of RELIGION may have been held back by the thinness of population and by ethnic loyalties; but while religion remains a potent force, scepticism is a widespread view. *See also* PHILOSOPHY.

TERENCE PENELHUM

Athlone, Alexander Augustus Frederick William Alfred George Cambridge, Earl of, soldier, governor general of Canada 1940-46 (b at Kensington Palace, London, Eng 14 Apr 1874; d at London 16 Jan 1957). Athlone was the second member of the royal family (after the duke of CONNAUGHT) to be governor general of Canada. His wife, the Princess Alice, was a granddaughter of Queen Victoria. Retiring from his career as a soldier after WWI, Athlone took an interest in education and medical research, and was governor general of S Africa, 1923-30. He was to have been appointed governor general of Canada in 1914, but requested that his name be withdrawn because of WWI. Although thinking himself too old when asked again during WWII, he served more than a full term. He and PM Mackenzie KING were fellow fussbudgets and got along well, the more so because Athlone was unfailingly discreet, cautious and without affectation. Even so, King found it difficult to share the spotlight with a head of state "not belonging to one's own country."

NORMAN HILLMER

Athol Murray College of Notre Dame, located in Wilcox, Sask, was founded in 1927 by

Father Athol Murray under the patronage of Notre Dame ("Our Lady"). The college is a Roman Catholic school with a strong ecumenical tradition. It is a coeducational, residential college offering a fully accredited university preparatory curriculum (grades 9-12). Under the motto *Luctor et Emergo* ("we struggle and emerge"), the college's aim is the spiritual, physical, emotional and intellectual growth of the individual through its academic, religious, cultural and social programs; with special emphasis on athletics, particularly HOCKEY. Notre Dame has received national acclaim for the game by winning the Air Canada Cup in 1980 and 1986. The physical framework of the college is developed around a church, classrooms, dining hall, 2 boys' residences, one girls' residence, a lounge, and in 1985 a new multi-use centre which houses an arena, classrooms, gymnasium, computer centre and library. The college had 407 full-time students in 1986-87.

DOUG LEWIS

Atikokan, Ont, UP, pop 4345 (1986c), 4389 (1981c), in northern Ontario on the Atikokan R, 220 km W of Thunder Bay. The name derives from an Ojibwa word for caribou bone. It was a small bush settlement until the 1940s, when huge iron-ore deposits were opened on nearby Steep Rock Lk. After WWII it was one of several prosperous communities on Ontario's mining frontier, although the late 1970s brought a decline in mining activity. It is at the centre of a popular wilderness recreation area and is a jumping-off spot for nearby Quetico Provincial Pk.

DANIEL FRANCIS

Atlantic, Battle of the, phrase used 6 Mar 1941 by British PM Winston Churchill to describe efforts to defeat attacks by the German navy on Allied shipping between America and Europe during WORLD WAR II. By that time German forces had sunk some 61.2 million tons, of which only a third could be replaced. In May 1941 British cryptographers solved the German naval Enigma code, giving Britain the advantage in the E Atlantic. After June, Allied naval escorts provided continual convoy protection, and in Sept American forces were committed to the task. Terrible losses continued, but by Nov 1942 ship construction overtook sinkings. Tactical skill and air cover eventually drove U-boats into mid-Atlantic, beyond the range of shore-based aircraft. Further cryptographic breakthroughs in Dec 1942 and Mar 1943, roving support groups, and very long-range and carrier-borne aircraft closed the gap. In the first 3 weeks of May 1943 escorts sank 31 U-boats, forcing Germany to abandon the N Atlantic convoy routes; an attempted comeback in Sept failed.

Depth charges explode astern a frigate, 1944, near Halifax, NS (*courtesy National Archives of Canada/PA-133246/Lawrence/DND*).

Canada provided about half the naval escorts in the Newfoundland (later Mid Ocean) and Western Local Escort Forces, most land-based air coverage from Newfoundland and the Maritimes, and 7 RCAF squadrons used elsewhere by Britain's Coastal Command. Desperately short of equipment and training, Canadian forces eventually reached adequate operational standards, winning responsibility for the new Canadian Northwest Atlantic theatre. By war's end 25 421 convoyed merchant ships had crossed the Atlantic successfully, and the RCN and RCAF received credit for 47 of the 788 U-boats and 2 Italian submarines that had been destroyed. *See also* U-BOAT OPERATIONS.   W.A.B. DOUGLAS

Atlantic Provinces NOVA SCOTIA, PRINCE EDWARD ISLAND, NEW BRUNSWICK and NEWFOUNDLAND constitute the Atlantic provinces. The 3 MARITIME PROVINCES (NS, PEI and NB) have much in common; among other things they share a historical and cultural heritage, and their residents have remarkably similar attitudes towards Canada, the US and Britain. Newfoundland development and Newfoundlanders have been shaped by quite different forces and personalities. Until 1949 most Newfoundland residents had few emotional and economic ties with the Maritimes in particular and Canada in general. Throughout the 18th and 19th centuries Newfoundland, unlike the Maritime provinces, was not an integral part of the economic, cultural and political system of N America. Rather, it was the western vantage point of a British way of life, providing a powerful undercurrent for Newfoundland's unique brand of local patriotism. CONFEDERATION in 1949 began the difficult process of transforming Newfoundlanders into Canadians.

Since 1949 many attempts have been made to draw the Atlantic provinces closer. Possibly most important was the 1954 establishment of the Atlantic Provinces Economic Council. APEC was to have united economic thinking in Atlantic Canada and projected a positive regional image. But despite APEC and many similar organizations, few residents of the Atlantic provinces see themselves as parts of such a region. In the Maritimes there has been strong support for Maritime Union, but there has been little enthusiasm, as the Task Force on Canadian Unity discovered in 1978, for Atlantic Union. Newfoundland has never been interested in Atlantic Union and the discovery of the Hibernian oil field off its E shore has merely strengthened its resolve to remain apart.   GEORGE A. RAWLYK

Atlantic Salmon (*Salmo salar*), probably the best-known member of the Salmonidae family, occurs on both sides of the Atlantic Ocean. In Canada, Atlantic SALMON are found in some 300 rivers from Ungava Bay southward along the Labrador coast to Québec and the Maritimes, notably the RESTIGOUCHE R and MIRAMICHI R (NB), HUMBER R and GANDER R (Nfld), Matane and Bonaventure rivers (Qué) and the Eagle and Forteau rivers (Lab). Until the late 1800s, they were abundant in Lk Ontario; their decline there was a result of dam building to provide water power for mills, which prevented access to spawning grounds. They still occur, landlocked, in lakes in Eastern Canada. Atlantic salmon have a streamlined body, soft-rayed fins and an adipose (fatty) fin. Specimens may attain weights of over 27 kg, but fish over 13.5 kg are uncommon. Commercially caught fish average about 4.5 kg. Atlantic salmon are renowned for leaping in their attempts to ascend falls to reach spawning grounds. A very high percentage of salmon return to their natal streams to spawn. Spawning occurs in autumn and the large eggs overwinter. Young spend 1-3 years in the river before going to sea as

"smolts." Salmon returning to the river after one year at sea are called grilse and may weigh about 2.2 kg; salmon at sea for 2 years will weigh 4.5-6.7 kg. Not all Atlantic salmon die after spawning and some spawn more than once. *See also* TROUT.   W.B. SCOTT

Atlin, BC, UP, pop 456 (1986c), elev 671 m, is situated on ATLIN LAKE in the lake district of the NW corner of the province, 182 km SE of Whitehorse. In 1898 Fritz Miller and Kenneth McLaren found gold in Pine Creek, which flows into Atlin Lake, giving rise to an influx of thousands of gold seekers diverted from the Klondike and the town at Pine Creek mouth. Both placer and hydraulic mining have continued on Atlin Lake tributaries since then. The area is noted for its alpine scenery and such tourist attractions as big-game hunting and fishing.   GEORGIANA BALL

Atlin Lake, 774 km^2, is a long, narrow lake in northwestern BC touching the Yukon border. The source of the YUKON R, it was inundated by prospectors during the KLONDIKE GOLD RUSH 1898-99. The town of ATLIN is on the E shore. Once isolated behind high mountain ranges, it is now linked to Whitehorse by highway, and is the centre of an extensive mining and hunting region. The name corresponds to an Indian word (Tlingit, *aht-lah*) meaning "big" or "stormy water."   DANIEL FRANCIS

Atomic Energy Control Board, est 1946 under the Atomic Energy Control Act, with the declaration that NUCLEAR ENERGY is essential to the national interest (and therefore under the exclusive jurisdiction of the federal government). The Act gives broad powers of regulation and sets out AECB's form as a departmental corporation. The 5-member board controls and supervises the development, application and use of nuclear energy in Canada through regulations and control programs, and participates on behalf of Canada in international measures of control. The AECB achieves its control through a comprehensive licensing system administered with the co-operation of other federal and provincial government departments in such areas as health, environment, transport and labour. Control also extends to the export and import of prescribed substances and equipment and involves Canadian participation in the activities of the International Atomic Energy Agency and compliance with the requirements of the Treaty on the Non-Proliferation of Nuclear Weapons. Current regulations require that a licence be obtained from the AECB before any person or organization is allowed to produce, mine, refine, process, sell, export or use prescribed substances and devices or equipment containing prescribed radioactive substances or to operate a nuclear facility for the production of deuterium oxide (heavy water) or nuclear energy in Canada. In order to exercise its regulatory role, the AECB defines standards that must be met, assesses the potential licensee's capabilities to meet and maintain them and, once a licence is issued, carries out inspections to ensure that its requirements are being met. The AECB is responsible also for the administration of the Nuclear Liability Act, as amended, including the designation of nuclear installations and the prescription of basic insurance to be carried by the operators of such nuclear installations. The AECB is designated as a CROWN CORPORATION and reports to Parliament through the minister of ENERGY, MINES AND RESOURCES.   KEN SHULTZ

Atomic Energy of Canada Ltd was incorporated as a crown agency in 1952 under the Atomic Energy Control Act to take over the Chalk River project from the National Research Council. Reporting to Parliament through the minister of EN-

ERGY, MINES AND RESOURCES, the company is involved in heavy-water production and most applications of NUCLEAR ENERGY in Canada. AECL undertakes more than 90% of nuclear-energy research and development in Canada to support the design, development and construction of CANDU (Canadian Deuterium Uranium) nuclear power stations. It has subsidiaries operating under the names AEC Radiochemical Co (Commercial Products), AEC Engineering Co and AEC Chemical Co.

Attawapiskat River, 748 km long, formed by the confluence of the Pineimuta, Trading and Otoskwin rivers at Attawapiskat Lk, in NE Ontario, flows E, jogs N and runs E to the flatland by JAMES BAY. Its drainage area is 50 200 km^2 and its mean discharge 626 m^3/s. Its mouth, mired in bog and marsh, is a migratory stopover for great numbers of ducks and geese. The whole course is largely uninhabited except for a few trading posts and the small Cree settlement of Attawapiskat at the river mouth. The name, from the Indian word (Algonquian, *atawabiskat*) meaning "rock bottom," refers to its limestone bed, once the bottom of an ancient sea.   JAMES MARSH

Attikamek (Tête-de-Boule) Around 1972 the CREE-speaking Indians in the Bouclier region of the upper St-Maurice R in Québec decided to readopt the name Attikamek (White Fish) used by their predecessors in the 17th century, and to abandon the name Tête-de-Boule, of uncertain origin, which had been applied to them since 1697. This name change does not necessarily imply a close ethnic relationship between the Attikamek of the 17th century and those of today. Following various social upheavals linked to epidemics at the time of contact and during the violent IROQUOIS WARS in the mid-17th century in these regions, a complete reorganization took place among nomadic hunters in Québec, and various groups, hitherto distinct, began to band together. It is known that ethnic boundaries remained relatively flexible over the years and that today's Attikamek have discovered genealogical links with several neighbouring groups. Although these people numbered 500-550 in the mid-17th century, by 1850 there were only about 150 scattered over 7000 km^2 and divided into 2 major bands, the Kikendatch and the Weymontachingue. The Manouane band appeared a little later (around 1865-75) as an offshoot of the Weymontachingue.

Over the centuries, the Attikamek of the St-Maurice region have led a hard life of hunting, fishing, trapping and wild-berry picking around trading posts established in their region in the late 18th and early 19th centuries. They placed a high value on maintaining the autonomy of each nuclear family, but families combined into small winter co-operative or hunting groups, each with an experienced leader. Their economic activities were a compromise between traditional, seasonal activities and economic dependence upon the FUR TRADE.

Despite a long history of involvement in the fur trade, continuous contact with missionaries did not begin until about 1837. After 1830 Attikamek ancestral lands were actively coveted by lumber merchants. In 1910 the railway reached Weymontachingue and the harnessing of the St-Maurice and Manouane rivers added to environmental and social pressures. A wage-earning class appeared during WWII, along with various social-security benefits. In 1986 the 3208 Attikamek of the St-Maurice region were fighting to preserve their traditional cultural autonomy and a role in society equal to the non-Indian Québec culture. Since 1975, they have joined with the MONTAGNAIS-NASKAPI to form the Attikamek-

Montagnais Council. *See also* NATIVE PEOPLE: SUB-ARCTIC and general articles under NATIVE PEOPLE.
NORMAN CLERMONT

Reading: Norman Clermont, *La Culture matérielle des indiens de Weymontachie* (1982) and "Qui étaient les Atikamèques?" in *Anthropologica* 16, 1 (1974); J. Helm, ed, *Handbook of North American Indians*, vol 6: *Subarctic* (1981).

Attorney, someone appointed to represent another or to act in his place. Power of attorney is the legal document appointing this representative. Before 1574 attorneys-at-law were persons permitted to practise in the superior courts of English common law as representatives of suitors who did not appear. After 1873 the term attorney was replaced by "Solicitor of the Supreme Court of Judicature." In N America attorney and attorney-at-law have become synonymous with lawyer. The federal minister of justice is ATTORNEY GENERAL for the Queen in Canada. K.G. McSHANE

Attorney General The office of attorney general is essentially that of the chief law officer of the Crown. In that capacity, the attorney general is responsible for the conduct of prosecutions of offences on behalf of the Crown and serves as solicitor to the Crown in respect of any civil matters. The bulk of prosecutions conducted in Canada are done under the auspices of a provincial attorney general. In that capacity, the attorney general has the discretion, based on the evidence presented to him or to his agent, to prosecute or not to prosecute in a given instance. With respect to certain offences, such as the hate propaganda provisions of the CRIMINAL CODE, the direct consent of the attorney general is necessary before his office can commence a prosecution. Some prosecutions are conducted by the office of or through an agent of the attorney general of Canada (in particular, drug, tax and combines prosecutions). Recently, there have been several constitutional cases involving this division of prosecutorial responsibility between federal and provincial authorities.

Regarding the attorney general's function as solicitor to the Crown, any communication between the office of the attorney general and other offices of government is privileged under the solicitor-client privilege at common law.

In all provinces, the office of the attorney general is established under the authority of s92(14) of the Constitution Act, 1867, which gives the provincial legislatures authority over "the administration of justice." However, the attorney general of a province may be formally designated as the attorney general or as the provincial minister of justice (as in Québec, for example) or both. Federally the attorney general is both the attorney general of Canada and the minister of justice of Canada. In some provinces, the attorney general's office may incorporate the functions of the office of the SOLICITOR GENERAL; in other provinces, the 2 offices may be separate and distinct with a division of responsibilities. Federally the 2 offices are separate.

Recently, some cases have arisen under the CANADIAN CHARTER OF RIGHTS AND FREEDOMS which test the independence of provincial court judges and justices of the peace, given their legal attachment to the office of the attorney general and their constitutional requirement of independence under the new entrenched Charter. G. GALL

Atwood, Margaret Eleanor, "Peggy," poet, novelist, critic (b at Ottawa 18 Nov 1939). A varied and prolific writer, Atwood is one of Canada's major contemporary authors. She studied at Victoria Coll, U of T, 1957-61, where the influence of Jay MacPherson and Northrop FRYE directed her early poetry towards myth and archetype as exemplified by *Double Persephone* (1961). Her poetic reputation was established

Margaret Atwood's writings have captured the issues of her time in the satirical, self-reflexive mode of the contemporary novel (*photo by Graeme Gibson*).

when *The Circle Game* (1966) was awarded the Gov Gen's Award. In 1969 she published *The Edible Woman*, a novel in which themes of women's alienation echo those in her poetry. In *Procedures for Underground* (1970) and *The Journals of Susanna Moodie* (1970), her next books of poetry, personae have difficulty accepting the irrational. The inadequacy of language to come to terms with experience is extended in *Power Politics* (1971) to sexual politics where words are a refuge of weak women against male force. In the 1970s Atwood was involved with nationalist cultural concerns as an editor of House of Anansi Press 1971-73 and as an editor and political cartoonist for *This Magazine*. She published SURVIVAL: A THEMATIC GUIDE TO CANADIAN LITERATURE in 1972, the same year as SURFACING, her best-known novel, in which the technology-nature conflict is cast in political terms, Americans against Canadians. As in her other novels, the Atwood protagonist goes through an archetypal retreat to the wilderness, the irrational, before reintegrating into society.

Continued critical success marked her publication of *You are Happy* (1974) which includes a reworking of *The Odyssey* from Circe's perspective and her third novel *Lady Oracle* (1976), a parody of fairy tales and gothic romances. In these years Atwood also worked less successfully in new genres, writing several TV scripts and screenplays. She published a history, *Days of the Rebels: 1815-1840* (1977) and short stories, *Dancing Girls* (1977) and *Bluebeard's Egg* (1983). Two books followed in 1978: *Two-Headed Poems*, which continued to explore the duplicity of language, and *Up in the Tree*, a children's book, which introduced Atwood the artist. *Life before Man* (1979) is a more traditional novel than most of her fiction, developing a series of love triangles through exposition rather than image.

In 1980 Atwood became vice-chairman of the WRITERS' UNION OF CANADA. She worked on a TV drama, *Snowbird* (CBC, 1981), and published another children's book *Anna's Pet* (1980) adapted for stage by the Mermaid Theatre (1986). Always interested in civil rights, she was active over several years in Amnesty International, and this activity had an impact on *True Stories*, a book of poetry, and *Bodily Harm*, a novel appearing in 1981. In

both works she "bears witness," breaking down distinctions she herself makes between poetry (at the heart of her relationship with language) and fiction (her moral vision of the world). More recently, she has continued to fight for literary censorship as president of PEN International's Anglo-Canadian branch (1984-86). Her collected criticism, *Second Words* (1982), contained some of the earliest feminist criticism written in Canada. Her involvement with the revised *Oxford Book of Canadian Poetry* (1982), which she edited, marked her central position among Canadian poets of her generation. Her eminence as a prose writer was confirmed in her co-editing *The Oxford Book of Canadian Short Stories in English* (1986). *Murder in the Dark* (1983), experimental, post-modern prose poems and short fictions, excited critical attention in new circles. She continued to alternate prose with poetry, *Interlunar* (1984) and *Selected Poems II: Poems Selected & New, 1976-1986* (1986). However, the phenomenal international critical and popular success of *The Handmaid's Tale* (1985) — Gov Gen Award, *Los Angeles Times* Prize, runner-up Booker Prize and Ritz-Paris-Hemingway Prize — a dystopia set in a right-wing monotheocracy located in a nuclear wasteland once known as Boston, which practises censorship and state control of reproduction, has won Atwood greater renown as a novelist. Her international readership has been swelled by audiences and students of her many readings, creative writing and Canadian studies courses in such varied places as the universities of Alabama, New York and Berlin. 1987 has brought success in new literary ventures, the script for *Road to Heaven*, a film about the Barnardo children in Canada, and *The Festival of Missed Crass*, a fantastic and satiric children's story transformed into a musical for the Young People's Theatre. In all her writing her careful craftsmanship and precision of language, which give a sense of inevitability and a resonance to her words, are recognized. In her fiction, Atwood has explored the issues of our time, capturing them in the satirical, self-reflexive mode of the contemporary novel. Atwood has had continued critical success since the mid-1960s; her many honours include the MOLSON PRIZE in 1981, the Philips Information Systems Literary Prize (1986), Toronto Arts Award (1986), Ms Magazine's Woman of the Year for 1986, the Ida Nudel Humanitarian Award from the Canadian Jewish Congress (1986), and the American Humanist of the Year Award (1987). BARBARA GODARD

Reading: J. Castro and K. Van Spanckeren, eds, *Margaret Atwood: Vision and Forms* (1988); A.E. Davidson and C.N. Davidson, eds, *The Art of Margaret Atwood* (1981); S. Grace, *Violent Duality* (1980); Grace and L. Weir, eds, *Margaret Atwood: Language, Text, System* (1983).

Aubert de Gaspé, Philippe-Ignace-François, journalist (b at Québec City 8 Apr 1814; d at Halifax 7 Mar 1841). He wrote the first French Canadian novel. After attending the Séminaire de Nicolet, Aubert de Gaspé became a stenographer and journalist. In November 1835 he was imprisoned for a month following an altercation with a member of the Assembly, and he avenged himself by planting a stinkpot in the vestibule of the Québec House of Assembly. Obliged to take refuge at St-Jean-Port-Joli, he amused himself by composing a novel, *L'Influence d'un livre* (1837). One chapter at least (chap 5) appears to have been contributed by his father, Philippe-Joseph AUBERT DE GASPÉ, who later wrote *Les Anciens Canadiens* (1863). Young Aubert de Gaspé defended his novel against charges of sensationalism and lack of realism, but when the book was republished posthumously in 1864 as *Le Chercheur de trésors*, Abbé Henri-Raymond CASGRAIN toned down many passages and deleted others.

DAVID M. HAYNE

Philippe-Joseph Aubert de Gaspé. In B. Sulte, *Histoire des canadiens-français*, Vol VI, 1882 (*courtesy National Archives of Canada IC-14256*).

Aubert de Gaspé, Philippe-Joseph, novelist (b at Québec City 30 Oct 1786; d there 29 Jan 1871). Scion of an old seigneurial family, Aubert de Gaspé studied law under Jonathan SEWELL and was admitted to the bar in 1811. That year he married Susanne Allison, by whom he subsequently had 13 children, and began to practise law. In 1816 he was named sheriff of Québec City, but was removed from office in 1822 for faulty accounts. He retired to the ancestral manor house at St-Jean-Port-Joli, and was later imprisoned for debt (1838-41), being released by a special Act of Parliament. While he was in prison, his son, Philippe-Ignace-François AUBERT DE GASPÉ, died at Halifax. After his release Aubert de Gaspé spent the summers on his estate and winters in Québec City, participating in the capital's social and literary life and frequenting Octave CRÉMAZIE's bookstore, — a meeting place of writers. In 1863 he published his historical romance *Les ANCIENS CANADIENS*. It was an immediate success and is considered the first classic of French Canadian fiction. Three years later Aubert de Gaspé published his *Mémoires*, containing recollections of early 19th-century French Canadian life; a further collection, *Divers* (1893), appeared posthumously.

DAVID M. HAYNE

Aubut, Françoise, married name Pratte, organist, educator (b at St-Jérôme, Qué 5 Sept 1922; d at Montréal 8 Oct 1984). She was one of the first performers to play the works of Marcel Dupré and Olivier Messiaen widely in Canada. She studied at the Conservatoire national in Montréal with Eugène Lapierre and Antonio Létourneau, at the New England Conservatory (Boston) and at the Paris Conservatory with Dupré and Messiaen. In 1945 she returned to Canada, having won the Grand Premier Prix, awarded for the first time to a N American. As well as giving numerous recitals, she taught at U de M, the Conservatoire de musique du Québec à Montréal and at the École Vincent-d'Indy. Her repertoire included the works of Canadian composers Jean PAPINEAU-COUTURE and Roger Matton. She received the 1961 Prix de musique Calixa-Lavallée.

HÉLÈNE PLOUFFE

Auditor General of Canada, Office of, est 1878 to audit the accounts of the federal government's departments, agencies and many of its CROWN CORPORATIONS. The auditor general is independent of the government and reports results of annual examinations of government financial statements to the House of Commons. The office also conducts comprehensive audits of individual departments and agencies and government-wide issues such as management of human resources, contracting and the use of computers. The Audit Office operates under the Auditor General Act of 1977, which requires the auditor general to examine and report on whether public funds have been spent economically and efficiently and whether audited organizations are in a position to measure whether the funded programs are effective.

MAURICE CUTLER

Auditory Impairment (or hearing impairment) is more common in Canada than is generally realized. According to Health and Welfare estimates in 1976 (based on US rates) some 1.5 million Canadians had trouble hearing in one or both ears, but even this is not a true measure of the impact of auditory impairment, which often results in impairment of speech as well. Approximately 745 000 Canadians (or 3.2%) suffer significant bilateral impairment. Those who are deaf (cannot hear or understand speech) number almost 300 000. This figure includes those who lost their hearing before age 19 (some 47 000) and those who were deaf before age 2 or 3 (some 23 000). The more severe the hearing loss and the earlier the onset, the more speech development will be affected. Even in adult life the onset of deafness is likely to produce some speech defect.

Auditory impairment may be caused by infections, drugs, heredity, injuries, tumours and NOISE. Readings of sound are made in decibels (db). For example, a conversation is 60 db, ordinary city traffic is 80 db. Hearing damage (after sustained exposure) begins at 85 db (lawnmowers, garbage trucks, motorcycles are all above this level). A typical rock band emits 110 db of sound, which after 15 minutes can harm unprotected ears. The pain threshold (125 db) is exceeded by the discharge of shotguns and jet engines.

For practical purposes, those termed "deaf" demonstrate severe or profound losses on hearing tests, while those termed "hard-of-hearing" do not suffer the same severity of impairment. Methods of instructing the deaf have been disputed from the time that Alexander Graham BELL, who like his father Alexander Melville BELL taught the hearing impaired, debated the preferable method of instructing the deaf – the oral or sign language – with Edward Miner Gallaudet, founding president of Gallaudet U in Washington, DC. Deaf people considered Bell's ideas on oral teaching questionable. Gallaudet was a strong advocate of sign language.

The majority of deaf Canadians who lost their hearing before age 2 are so severely impaired in hearing and speech that they prefer sign language for comfortable communication. American Sign Language is the major sign language used in Canada; French Canadian Sign Language (Langue des Signes québécois) is related to it, with some significant differences. Both languages differ from spoken language in many ways. Although sign language or some form of signing has always existed in schools for deaf children, its officially permitted use has only become widespread since the relatively recent debunking of the idea that it would impair speech development. There has been a major shift to the inclusion of "signing" in US programs for deaf children, but Canada has followed this development unevenly.

Deaf people have their own cultural interests, eg, theatre, mime, jokes and sports, while sharing many of the interests of hearing Canadians. Official organizations for the deaf include the Canadian Association of the Deaf (1940), Canadian Cultural Society of the Deaf (1970) and the Federation of Silent Sports of Canada (1959), renamed the Canadian Deaf Sports Association in 1985. The Canadian Co-ordinating Council on Deafness was founded in 1975; 50% of its board members are hearing impaired.

The first school for the deaf in Canada was opened in Champlain, Qué, in 1831 and functioned for about 5 years. The earliest continuing Canadian schools for the deaf were established in Montréal for French Catholic deaf boys in 1848 and for French Catholic deaf girls in 1851. Other provincial schools followed in later years. Those founded by deaf persons were the Halifax School for the Deaf in 1856 (replaced by the Atlantic Provinces Resource Centre for the Hearing Handicapped in 1963 at Amherst, NS) by 2 English immigrants, George Tait and William Gray; The Protestant Institution for Deaf-Mutes (1870) in Montréal (now Mackay Center for Deaf and Crippled Children) by Thomas Widd from Scotland; The New Brunswick Deaf and Dumb Institution (1873-84) in Saint John by Alfred H. Abell, an alumnus of the Halifax School for the Deaf; The Saskatchewan School for the Deaf (1930) in Saskatoon (renamed The R.J.D. Williams Provincial School for the Deaf in 1982) by Rupert J.D. Williams, an alumnus of the Manitoba School for the Deaf. Recent educational changes include early intervention programs (*see* EDUCATION, SPECIAL), integration into ordinary schools, better amplification, the use of sign language and the inclusion of deaf studies in the school curriculum.

Technical aids are now highly developed for deaf people. For wake-up alarms, an ordinary clock radio or electronic alarm is adapted to flash one or more lights or to activate a small vibrator under a mattress or pillow. An electronic doorbell button, a knock on the door, a baby-cry device with a microphone and other alerting devices such as smoke and burglar alarms can be connected with lights that flash on and off at a recognizably different rate within the same building. Closed-captioned decoders display captions on the bottom of the television screen. Deaf people are able to communicate with each other by TDD (Telecommunication Device for the Deaf), which converts typed letters, numbers and punctuation marks into a tone signal sent through the ordinary telephone handset and phone lines and decoded by a compatible TDD at the receiving end. The display is similar to that of an electronic calculator. Since the early 1980s, TDDs have been installed in police stations, hospitals, crisis centres, government offices, department stores, schools for deaf children, airline offices, hotels and in credit card and rail travel offices throughout N America. The Western Institute for the Deaf in Vancouver and BC Tel introduced N America's first 24 hour/7 days a week Message Relay Centre in 1984 to enable deaf TDD users to call hearing people who do not have a TDD, and vice versa.

Unique contributions to the Canadian cultural mosaic by deaf persons are currently being documented. A few examples follow: Edward T. Payne became the first licensed deaf male pilot in the world in 1931; Donald J. Kidd became Canada's first deaf person ever to receive a Doctor of Philosophy degree (U of T) in 1951; Jo-Anne Robinson broke several swim records at the World Games for the Deaf in 1965 and 1969; although Archibald and Duncan MacLellan were the first 2 deaf solicitors in the 1860s, Henry Vlug was the first to hold both titles of barrister and solicitor, as well as the first to be called to the bar (1986). A chair of deaf studies at the Western Canadian Centre of Specialization in Deafness

(U of Alberta) in 1987 was named after David Peikoff, a famed deaf Canadian who fought for better educational opportunities on behalf of the deaf many years ago.

R.D. FREEMAN AND C.F. CARBIN

Auger de Subercase, Daniel d', military officer and French colonial governor (b at Orthez, France 12 Feb 1661; d at Cannes-L'Ecluse, France 20 Nov 1732). Subercase arrived at Québec in 1687 as a captain in the Marine. He was noted for his energetic approach and served with distinction in several campaigns against the English and Indians. In 1702 he became governor at Placentia, Nfld, where he launched, in 1705, an ambitious but unsuccessful attack upon St John's. He brought a measure of stability to the foundering colony, and in 1706 was rewarded with the governorship of ACADIA. Subercase attempted to strengthen the French presence there but was defeated by low morale, official neglect and repeated attacks from the English. PORT-ROYAL was besieged twice, unsuccessfully in 1707, and again in 1710, when the garrison of less than 300 capitulated to a landing force of 2000. The surrender was permanent; the colony became British, and Subercase, the last governor of French Acadia, retired to France and obscurity.

LOIS KERNAGHAN

Augustines de la Miséricorde de Jésus, female religious congregation formed in 1957 by the federation of 14 Canadian convents (plus 3 foreign missions) of the Augustines hospitalières, which until then had been autonomous. The first convent founded in Canada was HÔTEL-DIEU in Québec City, 1639; its members were all drawn from the convent in Dieppe, France, which had existed prior to 1285 and perhaps even 1155. These Augustines were the hospitalières in N America and, along with the URSULINES, the first nuns in Canada. Since 1946 a federation has also existed in France, with its generalate (mother house) in Rennes. In 1986 there were 515 sisters and 17 convents. The generalate is in Sillery, Qué. *See also* CHRISTIAN RELIGIOUS COMMUNITIES.

MICHEL THÉRIAULT

Augustus, or Tattanoeuck, Inuk hunter, interpreter (b N of Churchill, NWT early 1800s; d near Rivière-à-Jean Feb or Mar 1834). Noted for his loyalty, integrity and outstanding capabilities as an interpreter, Augustus accompanied FRANKLIN and BACK on their early northern explorations. He was employed as a hunter for the HBC at Ft Churchill from 1816 until Jan 1821 when he joined Franklin's first land expedition, travelling with him until May 1822. On Franklin's second expedition, Augustus averted almost certain disaster by venturing alone to speak with 40 hostile Inuit who had pillaged Franklin's boats. So impressed were the Inuit by Augustus's bravery and loyalty to his officers that no harm came to the party. In 1834 Augustus disappeared enroute to meet Back at Ft Reliance; it is not known how he died.

HARRIET GORHAM

Augustyn, Frank, ballet dancer (b at Hamilton, Ont 27 Jan 1953). Widely praised as a classical dancer and greatly admired for his elegant bearing, Augustyn trained at the NATIONAL BALLET SCHOOL, joined the NATIONAL BALLET OF CANADA in 1970 and swiftly became a soloist in 1971 and principal dancer in 1972. He and frequent partner Karen KAIN won the award for best *pas de deux* at the 1973 Moscow International Ballet Competition, and more recently the 2 have starred in several Norman CAMPBELL films, have performed *Giselle* at Moscow's Bolshoi Theatre and have toured widely. In 1979 Augustyn was invested as Officer of the Order of Canada. In 1980 he joined the Berlin Opera Ballet, returning to the National

Ballet in 1982. In 1985 he suffered a serious knee injury, but after lengthy recuperation he made a comeback, dancing at a Toronto gala with Rudolf Nureyev and others in *Songs of a Wayfarer*.

PENELOPE DOOB

Auk (Alcidae), family of highly specialized SEABIRDS that contains auks (including the now extinct GREAT AUK), auklets, MURRES, murrelets, RAZORBILLS, dovekies, guillemots and PUFFINS. The 23 species of this ancient and diverse group occupy a special niche in nearshore and offshore northern polar and temperate waters. Alcids are diving birds which pursue small fish and invertebrates by "flying" underwater. They have a chunky appearance and are 15-65 cm long. Plumage is typically black or dark brown above, white underneath. Wings are short. Alcids come ashore only during breeding season. Most species are colonial and breed at a few coastal sites (often islands) which are free of predators and near an adequate food supply. They are long-lived, breed first at 4-5 years, and normally lay only one egg annually. Depending on the species, eggs are laid on exposed ledges on steep sea cliffs, in rock crevices or between large boulders, or in burrows. Both parents incubate eggs and rear young; incubation and chick-rearing usually last a total of 10 weeks. Of the 21 species breeding in N America, 11 breed in Canada. The common and thick-billed murres (*Uria aalge* and *U. lomvia*) breed in Atlantic and Pacific oceans; razorbills (*Alca torda*), black guillemots (*Cepphus grylle*) and Atlantic puffins (*Fratercula arctica*) in the Atlantic and parts of the Arctic Ocean; pigeon guillemots (*Cepphus columba*), marbled and ancient murrelets (*Brachyramphus marmoratus, Synthliboramphus antiquus*), Cassin's and rhinoceros auklets (*Ptychoramphus aleuticus, Cerorhinca monocerata*), and tufted puffin (*Lunda cirrhata*) breed in the Pacific. Four other species are nonbreeding visitors: dovekie (*Alle alle*), horned puffin (*F. corniculata*), Xantus' murrelet (*Endomychura hypoleuca*) and parakeet auklet (*Cyclorrhynchus psittacula*).

D.N. NETTLESHIP

Aurora, Ont (1985 OMD), pop 20 905 (1986c), located in York County, 30 km N of Toronto. Incorporated as a village in 1863 and as a town in 1888, Aurora became part of the Regional Municipality of York in Oct 1970 and the next year annexed portions of King and Whitchurch Twps. Originally called Machell's Corners after a local merchant, the name was changed by postmaster Charles Doan in 1853 for Aurora, the Greek goddess of dawn. The same year, the *Toronto*, the first locomotive to run in Ontario arrived in Aurora, thus heralding an era of prosperity connected with the railway and agriculturally based industry. In the 19th century, the Aurora area was a strong centre of Quakerism. Aurora now functions as an educational centre, being the home of De La Salle and Saint Andrew's colleges and 2 private institutions, a light industrial centre and a bedroom community for Metropolitan Toronto.

GERALD STORTZ

Australia, *see* CANADA AND AUSTRALIA.

Austrians come from the Federal Republic of Austria (Österreich), a neutral democratic state located in the alpine region of central Europe. The official language of Austria is German and the predominant religious denomination is Roman Catholicism.

Prior to 1918 the present Austria was part of a much larger multinational state, called the Austro-Hungarian Empire, of which Vienna was the capital. Austro-Hungary's territory also included present-day Hungary and Czechoslovakia, as well as parts of Yugoslavia, Romania, Poland, the Soviet Union and Italy. Ethnic Germans from the

non-German countries of the former empire are sometimes called Old Austrians (Altösterreicher). In 1918 Austria-Hungary disintegrated into a number of successor nations. The Republic of Austria was proclaimed, but its development was hampered by economic difficulties and political dissension. It was occupied in 1938 by German forces, but was re-established after WWII.

Since the final decades of the 19th century, Austrians have arrived in Canada in a number of distinct waves. Like other immigrants, they left their homes for economic or political reasons, to seek freedom, opportunity or land in Canada. In the 2 decades prior to WWI, a large number of German-speaking families of Austro-Hungarian origin were attracted to the Prairies. They came from Ukraine, the Bukovina, Hungary, Transylvania, Burgenland and Lower Austria. The Saskatchewan communities of Claybank, Edenwold, Fort Qu'Appelle, Indian Head, Kendal, Kennell-Craven, Mariahilf-Grayson, Markinch, Silton, Spring Valley and Vibank were among the destinations of this wave of agricultural immigrants. The 1921 census showed 57 535 Austrians in Canada. A second phase of Austrian immigration brought about 5000 people to Canada between 1926 and 1933. This group was more urban and tended to settle in the larger population centres to a greater extent.

After Austria's annexation by Germany a number of refugees and prominent émigrés of Austrian origin came to Canada. While their political views were divergent, these Austrians initiated a number of organized activities toward the re-establishment of an independent Austria. Finally, the most numerous influx of immigrants from Austria took place after WWII, from 1946 until the early 1970s. During this period, 67 000 people – giving Austria as the country of their last permanent residence – arrived in Canada. In 1981, the last year for which census figures are available, 40 630 persons were listed as being of Austrian origin. More than one-third of this total reside in Ontario where the biggest concentration exists in the Toronto-Hamilton urban areas.

Austrians are widely dispersed among the general population of Canada. They have been able to adapt quickly, culturally as well as economically, to the Canadian way of life. Many have been successful in business and industry, the arts and professions. Austrian societies and clubs exist in many major cities in Canada. The focus of these organizations tends to be social, cultural and sentimental, rather than nationalistic. For this reason, Austrians in Canada often affiliate with German and Swiss Canadians with whom they are most akin culturally. German-language newspapers and ethnic broadcasts usually accommodate the ethnic spectrum of these 3 German-speaking groups in Canada.

R.W. MASSWOHL

Authors and Their Milieu Only a handful of professional authors in Canada survive on the royalties from their books, a situation documented in the first survey of writers undertaken by Statistics Canada in 1979. Of 1045 writers sampled (representing the 4479 writers who were then members of writers' unions), 71% lived in Ontario and Québec; 24% earned over $20 000 annually and 42% under $5000; and only 311 were employed full-time as writers. Authors are not motivated by profits alone, yet the payment they receive for their intellectual labours encourages them to contribute to our cultural life, and payment is determined by their relations with publishers, the state, their audiences in schools and the public at large.

Commercially successful or not, professional writers must be devoted to their craft, for a manuscript can take a year or longer to finish.

Then follows the lengthy process of finding a publisher (a literary agent may be hired to do this). If the publisher's readers respond favourably to the manuscript, the publisher determines the retail price of a book by estimating expenses for editing, design, printing, binding and distribution. Distribution costs include a 20-50% discount to jobbers and retailers. Sometimes these expenses are shared with another publisher when foreign publication is arranged. The author, whose royalty may be 5-15% of the retail price, is usually the last to profit from such ventures but is paid for every copy sold. Publishers normally expect to break even when about 70-80% of an edition is sold.

Because the survival of our national literature cannot be left to the vagaries of the marketplace, it is generally accepted that authors' incomes need to be supplemented. In the absence of private patronage and writers with private means of support, the obligation to fund writers has fallen to agencies of the federal and provincial governments. This situation evolved because historically Canada's geography and economy, along with foreign competition, made the market for local books and magazines precarious. Distribution is costly because Canada's small population is stretched along a 6500 km ribbon. British and American publishers, who recoup their distribution costs here through their larger markets, gained control of Canada's market in the late 19th century by establishing branches in Toronto, the centre of English-language publishing. In so doing, they effectively denied Canadian publishers direct access to their markets, and they retained the lucrative world and subsidiary rights to Canadian and other authors. Much original publishing in Canada was possible only because books were issued jointly with a foreign house – a common international practice. Sometimes the decision to publish a Canadian author in Canada was made in another country. However, even authors who publish both at home and abroad do not necessarily make a living from book sales.

Writers' fortunes are affected by those of their publishers. The Toronto book trade prospered in the 1950s and 1960s, but since 1970 inflation and recession have severely shaken the major locally owned houses. Ryerson and Gage were sold to American firms (Gage was repatriated in 1978); Macmillan changed owners twice; others went into receivership or verged on bankruptcy. Government investigations of foreign control of publishing and distribution caused both Ontario and Québec to give financial aid to their publishing industries. Federally, foreign takeovers were slowed down with the establishment of the FOREIGN INVESTMENT REVIEW AGENCY (1974), which was reorganized in the mid-1980s as Investment Canada. Meanwhile, production and distribution costs climbed, and retail prices skyrocketed. Provincial textbook budgets were cut, public and college libraries reduced their purchases, and new products vied for consumers' money.

These circumstances would have been far harder on authors had it not been for the 1951 Royal Commission on NATIONAL DEVELOPMENT IN THE ARTS, LETTERS AND SCIENCES (Massey Commission), which recommended government support for publishing and authorship. As a result, the CANADA COUNCIL was created in 1957, and similar arts councils were later established in all the provinces. Although government aid is welcomed by authors and publishers, it has meant some regulation and intervention in creative matters by the vast bureaucracies that administer the programs. In the early 1970s the federal government began to assist in the promotion of Canadian books abroad, and in 1979 it established the Canadian Book Publishing Development Program to provide direct grants to the publishing industry. In recent years most federal funds have come from the Dept of COMMUNICATIONS, as direct subventions to publishers for individual titles or as grants for the subsistence of writers. The Canada Council also sponsors the annual national Book Festival for the promotion of books and reading, and it administers the Governor General's Awards. The provincial arts councils operate in a similar way. The councils, as well as some cities, universities and publishers, also offer LITERARY PRIZES, which can stimulate sales of individual authors' books.

However, in the 1980s both the Liberals and the Conservatives re-examined their involvement with the arts community. The report of the Federal Cultural Policy Review Committee (1982), chaired by Louis APPLEBAUM and Jacques HÉBERT, recommended increased government patronage in support of publishers and writers, while reaffirming writers' freedom from political control. After 1984 the Conservatives' desire for free trade with the US often clashed with their policy on cultural sovereignty, especially as the Americans questioned the nature of the subsidies given to our cultural industries. The minister of communications, Marcel MASSE, tried to replace the inefficient Canadian Book Publishing Development Program, and both he and his successor Flora MACDONALD witnessed the failure of Investment Canada to affect their book industry patriation policy. In 1986 the temporary but unfortunate 10% duty on English-language books as a retaliation for the American duty on Canadian shakes and shingles was universally condemned by the book trade. But Masse implemented the long-awaited Public Lending Right in 1986, a program administered by the Canada Council to reimburse about 6000 Canadian authors for the use of their works in public libraries.

In the early 1980s the government began to prepare a comprehensive new copyright Act (to replace the 1921 Act), consulting with the book trade, authors and librarians on such questions as international copyright, the free flow of books across international borders, unauthorized photocopying and electronic publishing. A white paper on COPYRIGHT LAW appeared in 1984.

Copyright problems inspired the establishment of the Canadian Society of Authors (1899) and the CANADIAN AUTHORS ASSOCIATION (1921). Besides copyright, more recent organizations such as the League of Canadian Poets (1966) and the WRITERS' UNION OF CANADA (1973) and the Union des écrivains québécois have lobbied for more domestic ownership of publishing and distribution, more funds for literary translation, income-tax adjustments and the Public Lending Right. In 1975 the Writers' Union protested when the large retail chains, Coles and W.H. Smith, sold remaindered American editions of Canadian authors whose own Canadian editions were still in print. Such importing was possible because court injunctions were slow and penalties for infringement of copyright were minimal.

The grim economic circumstances surrounding the major publishers and the disappearance of well-paying outlets like the *Star Weekly*, *Family Herald* and *Weekend Magazine* were offset by the greatest flourishing of regional publishing since Confederation. SMALL PRESSES were established from coast to coast in the 1960s and the 1970s. They awakened a new interest in regional literature, and in spite of harsh economic conditions, many of them managed to survive and grow.

Canadian writers have received critical and popular acclaim at home and abroad, especially since WWII. Canadian literature courses have become more numerous in schools and universities, facilitated by reprint series and anthologies, and by index tapes and records of authors discussing and reading from their works. Many colleges offer writer-in-residence programs that are supported by the institutions and by various arts councils. Literary and intellectual research flourishes in LITERARY PERIODICALS; bibliographies, biographies, collections of letters and surveys all help to locate our writers in the panorama of Canadian life, a situation which hardly existed before 1960. Authorship has been a central topic at the Canadian Writers' Conference (Queen's University, 1955), the State of English Language Publishing in Canada (Trent University, 1975), the Conference on the Canadian Novel (University of Calgary, 1978) and similar gatherings. Since 1970 the popularity of public readings by authors has made us far more sympathetic to contemporary writing.

Although the writer's situation is subject to many economic variables, the growing recognition of Canadian writing and its creators is an encouraging sign, with both intellectual and economic benefits for writers, that our society is beginning to acknowledge their importance in its culture. *See also* BOOK PUBLISHING; LITERATURE IN ENGLISH; LITERATURE IN FRENCH.   GEORGE L. PARKER

Reading: Paul Audley, *Canada's Cultural Industries* (1983); W.J. Keith and B.Z. Shek, eds, *The Arts in Canada* (1980).

Autobiographical Writing in English Letters, journals, diaries, memoirs and autobiographies are all ways of saying to the reader, "I was there." Although differing in many ways, these forms are alike in having an authoritative "I" who recounts events and impressions experienced amid a specific social context, and a "there" that can be readily located in time and space. Because they speak in such personal tones, these records and narratives are rich in human interest. Social and intellectual historians find them especially valuable sources, and they are sometimes studied by literary historians and critics as well.

The circumstances of colonial life particularly favoured the writing of journals, diaries and letters. Explorers, fur traders, missionaries, surveyors, government officials and army and law-enforcement officers were all obliged by their superiors to keep daily records of their work (*see* EXPLORATION AND TRAVEL LITERATURE). Emigrants and travellers, especially women, wrote long letters home to their families and friends, and many kept diaries and journals. Although seldom written with publication in mind, these documents occasionally reached print because they contained information and commentary of use or interest to a wider readership. Written on the spot, they are a treasure trove for historians seeking to reconstruct the daily lives of private individuals. Literary scholars recognize in them a means by which newcomers to Canada practised putting into words whatever they found new and noteworthy in the landscape, climate, inhabitants, institutions, customs or speech of British North America. Although all 3 forms are now almost lost arts, the journals, diaries and letters of earlier generations of Canadians are becoming increasingly available in modern editions and reprints.

By contrast, memoirs and autobiographies continue to appear regularly. Unlike letters and diaries, they view events in retrospect and are often written with publication and posterity in mind. These works are more limited in historical reliability – the writer will have forgotten or suppressed a good deal – but the author has greater opportunities for achieving a shaped and finished narrative. Memoirs are more loosely constructed than autobiographies, and reveal more of external circumstances than of inner development. Often appearing under the simple title *Memoirs* or a variant (*Recollections, Reminiscences, Forty Years in ...*), they are characteristically anecdotal and episodic, with the focus dispersed among the many interesting people and places the writer has known. Autobiography, on the other hand, downplays the context and highlights the unfolding drama of self-knowledge and growth, thus drawing in the literary critic, who analyses the autobiography's projection of a narrative persona, the deployment of dramatic, descriptive and narrative skills, and the achievement of structure, pattern or design in the whole.

A cluster of books describing Upper Canada [Ontario] before 1850 shows all these forms in their characteristic 19th-century guises. Elizabeth SIMCOE, wife of Lt-Gov John Graves Simcoe, kept a diary from 1791 to 1796 that was published in 1911 and then re-edited in 1956 by Mary Quayle Innis as *Mrs. Simcoe's Diary*. Describing life in official circles at York [Toronto], it is at a far remove from *Our Forest Home* (1889), based on the letters and journals of Irish emigrant Frances Stewart, who settled in the 1820s on the Otonabee R near Peterborough. Among Stewart's neighbours were Samuel Strickland, author of *Twenty-Seven Years in Canada West* (1853), and his more famous sisters, Catharine Parr TRAILL and Susanna MOODIE. Traill's letters to her family in England were published as *The Backwoods of Canada* in 1836 for the information of intended middle-class British emigrants; it is now one of the classics of Canadian literature. Moodie wrote autobiographically of her years of *Roughing It in the Bush* (1852) and her later *Life in the Clearings* (1853). The British author and feminist Anna JAMESON visited her attorney general husband in York and then used her journals as the basis for *Winter Studies and Summer Rambles in Canada* (1838), giving the observations and opinions of a sophisticated and adventurous visitor.

Other times and places yield their quota of firsthand accounts. Labrador is the scene for journals by Capt George Cartwright (1911), recollections by Lambert de Boileau (1861) and Capt Nicholas Smith (1937), and autobiographies by Sir Wilfred GRENFELL (*A Labrador Doctor*, 1919; *Forty Years for Labrador*, 1932) and Elizabeth Goudie (*Woman of Labrador*, 1973). Col William Baird recorded his *Seventy Years of New Brunswick Life* (1890) but was overtopped by New Brunswick Baptist minister Joshua N. Barnes in *Lights and Shadows of Eighty Years* (1911). Sir Andrew MACPHAIL's *The Master's Wife* (1939) is a polished and memorable vignette of Prince Edward Island life in the later part of the 19th century.

Travel and adventure in the North and West have likewise proved fertile themes. Accounts by fur traders include John MCLEAN's *Notes of a Twenty-five Years' Service* (1849) and P.H. Godsell's *Arctic Trader* (1934). Missionary work lies behind the letters and journal of Charlotte Selina Bompas, edited in 1929 by S.A. Archer as *A Heroine of the North*, and memoirs in 5 volumes by Methodist John C. MCDOUGALL, including *Pathfinding on Plain and Prairie* (1898) and *In the Days of the Red River Rebellion* (1903). Early Mounted Policemen of a reminiscent bent include John G. Donkin (*Trooper and Redskin in the Far Northwest*, 1889) and Col Sam STEELE, who wrote his Mountie days and much else in *Forty Years in Canada* (1915). Of many Klondike books, 2 that stand out are Martha Louise Black's *My Ninety Years* (1976; first published in 1938 as *My Seventy Years*) and Laura B. Berton's *I Married the Klondike* (1954).

HOMESTEADING on the Prairies generated dozens of first-person settlers' accounts and memoirs. Mary Georgina Hall wrote letters home describing *A Lady's Life on a Farm in Manitoba* (1884), and E.A. Gill told of his days as *A Manitoba Chore Boy* (1912). *Wheat and Woman* (1914) is Georgina Binnie-Clark's self-portrait as a woman grain farmer in Saskatchewan. In his *Northwest of 16*

(1958) J.G. MacGregor describes growing up on the Alberta frontier; the journals and letters of Sarah Ellen Roberts, whose family also homesteaded in Alberta, were edited for publication by Latham Roberts under 2 titles, *Of Us and the Oxen* (1968, Canadian ed) and *Alberta Homestead* (1971, US ed). An unusual and striking story is contained in the letters of Hilda Rose, written from near Fort Vermilion, Alta, first published in the *Atlantic Monthly* in 1927 and issued as *The Stump Farm* a year later. *Homesteader* (1972), the title James M. Minifie chose for his recollections of a Saskatchewan boyhood, speaks for an entire genre.

Although the majority of autobiographers and memoirists have some other, previously established, claim to fame, a few have written in the role of spokespersons for the unknown and unsung. G.H. Westbury published *Misadventures of a Working Hobo in Canada* in 1930, just as the Great Depression began to make hoboes of many men. *Saints, Devils, and Ordinary Seamen* (1946) were the subjects of memoirs by Lt W.H. Pugsley, while Norman B. James made his mark in history with his *Autobiography of a Nobody* (1947). Phyllis Knight, through tape recording and editing by her son Rolf, has shown us the extraordinary dimensions of *A Very Ordinary Life* (1974). Maria CAMPBELL's moving story in *Halfbreed* (1973) represents a side of Canadian life too little known or understood.

Prime ministers occasionally write memoirs, but seldom autobiographies; their private letters and diaries are often useful correctives to the "official" selves that appear in state papers. Two volumes of Robert BORDEN's *Memoirs* were published in 1938; John G. DIEFENBAKER's *One Canada* appeared in 1975. Lester B. PEARSON's *Mike* (3 vols, 1972-75) is autobiographical, although the last 2 volumes were ghostwritten after his death. *Affectionately Yours* (1969), edited by J.K. Johnson, is an attractive little collection of letters by, and occasionally to, Sir John A. MACDONALD. The diaries of PM Mackenzie KING, running to many volumes, have raised more questions than they answer. But the "inside story" provided by slightly lesser lights in politics and public life can entertain and inform, witness Judy LAMARSH's *Memoirs of a Bird in a Gilded Cage* (1968), and Humphrey Carver's *Compassionate Landscape* (1975). Meanwhile, Charles RITCHIE continues to prove that superb diarists are not altogether extinct: *The Siren Years: A Canadian Diplomat Abroad* was published in 1974, to be followed by *An Appetite for Life* (1977), *Diplomatic Passport* (1981), and *Storm Signals* (1983).

Literate and shapely autobiographies often rest on long years of practice in prose writing. Journalists such as James M. Minifie and Grattan O'LEARY (*Recollections of People, Press, and Politics*, 1977) have the fluency and wit of professionals. Florence Bird is another longtime journalist and public figure with an important story to tell; the fact that she tells it under the title *Anne Francis, An Autobiography* (1974) will confuse some younger Canadians until they read her book. Full-fledged men and women of letters having until recently been rare in Canada, we have few accounts of a literary life, but those few are worth seeking out, especially John GLASSCO's *Memoirs of Montparnasse* (1970), a *tour de force*; Lovat DICKSON's 2 autobiographical volumes, *The Ante-Room* (1959) and *The House of Words* (1963); and George WOODCOCK's *Letter to the Past* (1982). Scholars read and write a good deal, but like prime ministers they are generally too discreet to lay bare their inmost thoughts and feelings in autobiography. Notable exceptions are historian Arthur Lower, with *My First Seventy-Five Years* (1967) and Victoria College's Kathleen Coburn, who, while disclaiming

autobiographical intent, nevertheless charts a fascinating course in *In Pursuit of Coleridge* (1977). Emily CARR was a painter before she turned to writing, and her style in both art forms is distinctively her own. Carr's sketches in *The Book of Small* (1942), her autobiography *Growing Pains* (1946) and her journals, *Hundreds and Thousands* (1966), are the work of a major talent.

It is generally assumed that autobiographers, having chosen to tell their life stories, may write selectively and with some dramatic colouring, but will not deliberately mislead the reader as to essential facts. Thus it was something of a literary scandal when noted naturalist and conservationist Grey Owl, whose autobiographical *Pilgrims of the Wild* appeared in 1935 (2nd ed, 1968), was revealed at his death in 1938 as English-born Archie BELANEY. Much the same excitement attended Douglas Spettigue's unmasking of novelist Frederick Philip GROVE, a development that put large parts of Grove's much-admired autobiography *In Search of Myself* (1946) into the category of fiction.

There are several once-popular Canadian authors who have written autobiographies that seem more durable than their poetry and fiction. James Oliver Curwood and Ralph Connor (Charles W. GORDON) sold millions of copies of their novels in the early 20th century; Curwood's *Son of the Forests* was published in 1930, Gordon's *Postscript to Adventure* in 1938, shortly after his death. Nellie MCCLUNG, although now best known for her early feminist activism, first made her name as a writer of stories. Her 2 volumes of autobiography, *Clearing in the West* (1935) and *The Stream Runs Fast* (1945) convey a warm and attractive personality. Laura Goodman Salverson was an Icelandic-born novelist who won a Governor General's Award for her 1939 autobiography *Confessions of an Immigrant's Daughter,* and Frederick NIVEN's reflections on his life in *Coloured Spectacles* (1938) have more artistry and interest than his long historical novels. It seems probable, however, that Stephen LEACOCK's *The Boy I Left Behind Me* (1946) will always rank below his satiric sketches, and poet Robert SERVICE added nothing to his fast-dimming lustre in *Ploughman of the Moon* (1945) and *Harper of Heaven* (1948). Whether Mazo DE LA ROCHE will be remembered for her novels, her autobiography *Ringing the Changes* (1957), both, or neither, is for posterity to decide. These authors and hundreds more Canadians have put it on record that, like Edith Tyrrell in 1938, *I Was There,* and in so doing they have added imaginative texture and depth to Canadian prose writing. SUSAN JACKEL

Reading: Jay Macpherson, "Autobiography," in Carl F. Klinck, ed, *Literary History of Canada* (2nd ed, 1976), 616-23.

Autobiographical Writing in French The golden age of personal literature (*littérature intime*) in the Western world occurred in the late 18th and early 19th centuries. Examples of the genre are not found in Québec before the mid-19th century. Québec writers, timid about self-revelation, were extremely discreet about their personal lives. Their characteristic reserve, which led writers to speak more comfortably of others than of themselves, was typical of the literature until the late 1950s.

Those diaries which were not straightforwardly external in orientation revolved around the dominant theme that had provoked their existence in the first place. The subject was war for Octave CRÉMAZIE's *Journal du siège de Paris* (1870-71) and for Simone Routier's *Adieu, Paris!* (1940). It was the stifling effect of prison life, 1948-51, for Marcel Lavallé's *Journal d'un prisonnier* (published posthumously, 1978). Clear-eyed introspection marked this book, as it did the typical adolescent diary, Fadette's *Journal d'Henriette Dessaulles, 1874-80* (published posthumously, 1971). Poet Saint-Denys GARNEAU offered an analysis tinged with mysticism in his *Journal* of the period 1935-39 (published posthumously, 1954; trans *The Journal of Saint-Denys Garneau*, 1962), and the analysis in *Notes pour une autre fois* (1983) by Jean-Ernest Racine was coloured by the imminence of death.

Memoirs are an older genre in French Canada, though their intimacy is sometimes debatable. They concentrate on career development and are often avowedly didactic. There are numerous political memoirs, though not one of a really prominent person. Most such memoirs are partisan pleadings that completely ignore the subject's private life. The truly autobiographical and literary qualities of the *Mémoires* (3 vols, 1969-73) by Georges-Émile LAPALME are in striking contrast to the banality prevalent in the field. These disillusioned memoirs of the unfortunate adversary of the all-powerful Maurice DUPLESSIS help to illuminate the *Chronique des années perdues* (1976) of Lapalme's close collaborator, Guy Frégault. The actor Palmieri (J. Sergius Archambault) used pleasant little anecdotes to evoke theatrical life in *Mes souvenirs de théâtre* (1944); sculptor Alfred LALIBERTÉ (1878-1953) illuminated the plastic arts with his more revealing *Mes souvenirs* (published posthumously, 1978). Intellectual life was represented in the *Souvenirs* (1944-55) of Édouard Montpetit and the impressive *Mes mémoires* (4 vols, 1970-74) of Lionel GROULX, who described almost a century of evolution in Québec society. Finally, the aristocratic style of life evoked in the 19th-century *Mémoires* (1866) of Philippe AUBERT DE GASPÉ, Sr, found its 20th-century echo in the *Testament de mon enfance* (1952; tr *Testament of My Childhood*, 1964) and *Quartier Saint-Louis* (1966) by Robert de Roquebrune.

Like memoirs, volumes of remembrances were intended to keep the national heritage alive and to instruct future generations. They developed themes already familiar in journals: war, whether through civilian eyes (Marcel Dugas, *Pots de fer*, 1941) or military ones (Joseph-Damase Chartrand, *Expéditions autour de ma tente*, 1887); a humourous account of prison life by Jules Fournier (*Souvenirs de prison*, 1910); the profession of writing discussed in the singularly unconfiding *Confidences* (1959) of Olivier Maurault and of Ringuet (Philippe PANNETON, 1965). Authors also described their traditional Québec childhoods. These "collective" remembrances painted an idyllic picture of the past and of rural family life: best known were *Les Rapaillages* (1916) by Lionel Groulx and *Chez nous, chez nos gens* (1924) by Adjutor Rivard. Though there were happy exceptions to the rule, eg, Louis-Honoré FRÉCHETTE's *Mémoires intimes* (treating the period 1839-1903 and published posthumously, 1961), the earlier of these childhood remembrances usually followed this model, whereas later ones built new stereotypes around city life.

Since true autobiography requires the author to centre his account on his own evolution, the genre was practically nonexistent in Québec until 1960. The celebrated trilogy by Claude Jasmin, *La Petite Patrie* (1972), *Pointe-Calumet, Boogie-Woogie* (1973) and *Sainte-Adèle, la vaisselle* (1974), combined autobiography with collective remembrances. The various writings of Paul Toupin gathered together in *De face et de profil* (1977) dealt strictly with his personal life and his writing career; both the *Souvenirs en lignes brisées* (1969) by J.E. Racine and the *Journal dénoué* (1974) by Fernand OUELLETTE dug into the author's personality in a painful search for a deeper level of the self. This kind of search can veer from its original in-

tent to produce an activist work such as *Nègres blancs d'Amérique* (1968; tr *White Niggers of America*, 1971) by Pierre Vallières or an awakening to the feminine condition, such as *La Vie défigurée* (1979) by Paule Saint-Onge. In more popular autobiographies, self-revelation is a pretext for denunciation of social injustice.

An overview of Québec personal literature would be incomplete without examples of private correspondence. Three poets are included among those whose letters were posthumously accorded the honour of publication: Octave Crémazie, Nérée Beauchemin and Saint-Denys Garneau. If to this list is added *Lettres d'un artiste canadien Napoléon Bourassa* (1929), one has the only virtually complete published editions of private correspondence: the most personal writing of all.

Québec society was long turned in on itself. It gave its writers no privileged status and demanded that they exercise the greatest possible discretion about their private lives. However, writers of the 1980s, now at the height of their powers, seem determined to live more openly and so to join the international literary mainstream.

FRANÇOISE VAN ROEY-ROUX

Autobiographies, Political Canadian politicians, federal and provincial, have never been particularly literate, their skills running more to the mastery of stump orations and the management of patronage than to writing literate accounts of their political lives. While this was particularly true for the early years of the country, this comment stands unchallenged to the middle of the 20th century, too. Not until the ready availability of ghostwriters and the advent of the taped interview that could be transformed into prose did politicians rush into print, often aided by large advances from publishers. Even then the numbers stayed surprisingly small.

Among the earliest memoirists was Sir Francis HINCKS whose *Reminiscences of His Public Life* (1884) covered a long career that ran from the Rebellions of 1837 through the 1850s in the Canadas and then into the imperial service. Hincks's book was not very revealing, stuffed full of speeches and public correspondence. It was in every way a model for what was to come. Sir Charles TUPPER's *Recollections of Sixty Years in Canada* (1914), the first account by a Dominion prime minister, was also anodyne, although Sir Richard CARTWRIGHT, a free trader who was always difficult in the Liberal caucus, put more bite into his *Reminiscences* (1912) which unfortunately ended in 1896, before his years in the Laurier Cabinet. George W. ROSS's memoir (*Getting Into Parliament and After*, 1913) covered 11 years in Ottawa and almost a quarter-century at Queen's Park, Toronto, including service as premier. But there is nothing by Laurier, Mowat, Mercier and other major figures.

Sir Robert BORDEN's *Memoirs* (2 vols, 1938) are unreflective and dry as dust, a barebones chronicle out of which all life has been squeezed. E.M. Macdonald, a lacklustre Maritime politician who served as Mackenzie KING's minister of national defence, left an unrevealing account (nd), and so too did Armand Lavergne (1934), a fiery *nationaliste* of a conservative bent. E.C. DRURY, the *Farmer Premier* (1966) who led the UNITED FARMERS OF ONTARIO to victory and defeat, revealed little of how he had managed this. Senator Raoul Dandurand (1967) could have added something to our understanding of 1920s foreign policy, but his book was riddled with errors, despite its being edited by an academic and published long after his death. Another politician-diplomat of the period, Vincent MASSEY, also left a bland account in *What's Past is Prologue* (1963). Dr R.J. "Fighting Bob" MANION's *Life is an Adventure* (1936), written be-

fore he became Conservative leader in 1938, demonstrated the dangers of rushing into fine print. His comments about the CONSCRIPTION crisis of 1917 hurt him in Québec in the 1940 election. The winner of that contest (and many others), Mackenzie King, died before he could write one word of his story, but his massive diary is, literally, among the great ones of our time. Chubby Power, the able and engaging Québec Liberal who first won election in 1917, wrote, with the assistance of Norman Ward, a very helpful (and humorous) account of his distinguished career, notable for its shrewd comments on Québec Liberal organization (1966). From Alberta, there is Alf Hooke's *30 + 5: I Know I Was There* (1971), the story of a Social Credit MLA and Cabinet minister from 1935 to 1968 who makes it all sound as simple as A+B. And Tim BUCK, the engaging little man who led Canada's communists legally and underground, left a party-line account (1977).

Joey SMALLWOOD's immodestly titled *I Chose Canada* (1973) was a rich tale of the life of Newfoundland's Father of Confederation, a book that could be paired with those by his friend and political ally J.W. PICKERSGILL, *My Years With Louis St. Laurent* (1975) and *The Road Back* (1986). Pickersgill's volumes follow the course of parliamentary debate closely from 1948 through to the first months of the Pearson government. John DIEFENBAKER's *One Canada* (3 vols, 1975-77) a ghostwritten work, nonetheless conveys the flavour of the prairie populist who led the Conservatives to the heights in 1957 and 1958 and then to disaster in 1963. His great opponent, Lester B. PEARSON, had already published 3 volumes of his own (*Mike,* vol 1, 1972), the last 2 of which (1973, 1975) were put together after his death by Diefenbaker's ghostwriter. Pearson could laugh at himself, he could keep the facts straight, and he won the battle of the memoirs just as he won the political struggles.

Donald FLEMING, Diefenbaker's minister of finance, left a huge account (2 vols, 1985) that, while tedious and self-serving, contains immensely useful information and a ringing denunciation of Diefenbaker. Pierre SÉVIGNY's story (1965) is very discreet. Judy LAMARSH's *Memoirs of a Bird in a Gilded Cage* (1968) had the best title of any Canadian political memoir and was feisty, especially in its attacks on Pearson, while Walter GORDON's *A Political Memoir* (1977) spoke sparely of the hurt his break with Pearson caused. Paul MARTIN, the longtime MP and Cabinet minister from Windsor, Ont, produced 2 well-written volumes (1983-85) that are historically accurate and often self-revelatory. The only autobiography in English that compares in quality is Dalton CAMP's *Gentlemen, Players and Politicians* (1970), a book that ends well before his battles with Diefenbaker. Other stories by Tories include those of Jack HORNER (*My Own Brand*, 1980) and Sean Sullivan (*Both My Houses*, 1986).

On the left, there is Thérèse CASGRAIN's autobiography available in French (1971) and English (1972), chronicling the career of that most unlikely of mid-century species – a female, French Canadian socialist. David LEWIS wrote of *The Good Fight* (1981), an occasionally moving account of one of the men who was the heart and soul of the CCF and NDP. Sadly, all we have of the remarkable Tommy DOUGLAS is *The Making of a Socialist* (1982), based on interviews done in 1958.

Québec politicians who have gone into print include Jean CHRÉTIEN, whose *Straight From the Heart* (1985) sold extraordinarily well, and more on the basis of style than content; René LÉVESQUE (*Memoirs*, 1986) who had the embarrassment of correcting errors in public after his book was released; and the lesser known and very sober Georges-Émile LAPALME (1969-73) who led the

Liberals in the dark days under Duplessis, and another *rouge* of the same era, Lionel Bertrand (1972). Much the best memoir by a Québécois was that of Gérard PELLETIER, Pierre TRUDEAU's longtime friend and colleague. His account – in French (1983-86) and English (1984-87) – was perceptive and beautifully written.

The end of the Trudeau regime produced a flood of autobiography, some of which verged on campaign literature. James Jerome (1985), Donald Johnston (1986), Eugene Whelan (1986), Roy MacLaren (1986) and Keith Davey (1986) all offered their interpretations of Trudeau's years; Trudeau himself said little and wrote less.

Most Canadian political autobiographies unfortunately are little more than ephemera, written for self-serving purposes or to promote a cause. The few that are reflective and relatively honest – Camp's, Martin's and Pelletier's, for example – stand out like beacons on a wasteland.

J.L. GRANATSTEIN

Automatistes, Les The painter Paul-Émile BORDUAS, inspired by the stream-of-consciousness writing (*écriture automatique*) of French poet André Breton, transposed this idea onto canvas, PAINTING spontaneously and without preconception. The Automatiste movement was born when Borduas showed 45 of these gouaches at the Ermitage Theatre in Montréal from 25 Apr to 2 May 1942. He gained a few followers from among his students at the École du Meuble, including Marcel BARBEAU, Jean-Paul RIOPELLE and Roger Fauteux; others, such as Pierre GAUVREAU and Fernand LEDUC, came from the École des beaux-arts in Montréal, and Jean-Paul MOUSSEAU came from the Collège Notre-Dame. The group met in Borduas's studio to discuss Marxism, surrealism and psychoanalysis, all subjects looked down on by the church. The Automatistes held a number of exhibitions, notably in New York in 1946 and in Paris in 1947. Their first Montréal exhibition was on Amherst St in Apr 1946, and they were designated as "Automatistes" at their second Montréal showing, on Sherbrooke St in February 1947. What had begun as a dissident student group was now an important cultural movement.

In 1948 Borduas released the manifesto REFUS GLOBAL, which served as a preface for a series of texts by Claude GAUVREAU (poet and brother of Pierre), Françoise Sullivan (a dancer), Bruno Cormier and Fernand Leduc, and expressed the views of the Automatistes. It extended the movement's aesthetic intuitions into the political field, "resplendent anarchy" being the mirror of the spontaneous painting encouraged by the group. The group dispersed after the manifesto was published, for Riopelle and Leduc had already left for Paris. Their last show – "La Matière Chante" organized by Claude Gauvreau – took place in 1954.

FRANÇOIS-MARC GAGNON

Reading: D. Burnett and M. Schiff, *Contemporary Canadian Art* (1983); François-Marc Gagnon, *Paul-Émile Borduas. Biographie critique et analyse de l'oeuvre* (1978); J. Russell Harper, *Painting in Canada* (1977); D. Reid, *A Concise History of Canadian Painting* (1973).

Automobile Few inventions have had as great an impact on the world as the automobile. The first Canadian automobile, built in 1867 by Henry Seth Taylor, was regarded as a novelty, as were the single-cylinder vehicles that were imported from the US in 1898. In 1904 Canada's AUTOMOTIVE INDUSTRY began with the establishment of Ford Motor Co of Canada, Ltd. By 1913 there were some 50 000 motor vehicles in Canada; by 1985 the number had increased to nearly 15 million. With the world's second-highest ratio of automobiles to inhabitants, Canada is often regarded as automobile dependent. Today the automobile is used for 78% of all

The Canadian Highway on Vancouver Island. Thomas W. Wilby en route to Alberni, BC, *c*1912 (*courtesy National Archives of Canada/PA-29916*).

"journey-to-work" trips, 86% of all overnight travel and 88% of all uses combined. Canadian vehicles travel some 15 billion km per year on some one million km of highways, roads and streets.

The number of vehicles in each province generally reflects provincial population, with Ontario having the most vehicles (over 5 million in 1985) and PEI (76 000) the fewest.

Early automobiles were used by the wealthy for racing and amusement. Although these vehicles had engines, they truly were "horseless carriages" – little more than lightweight buggies with motive power. They were unreliable, expensive and sometimes dangerous. The earliest automobiles were hand made and sometimes built to order. Ransom Olds conceived the idea of interchangeable components, which made assembly-line production possible. By thus reducing costs, the automobile was made available to many customers for whom the price had previously been too high. As automobile sales increased, so did production. Detroit, Mich, which became the automotive centre of the world and nearby Windsor, Ont, prospered. Automobiles made it easier for people to travel, enabled salesmen to cover more territory and encouraged travel. They allowed people to live farther from work and consequently had a profound effect on URBAN DESIGN. Automobiles created the demand for more streets, highways and freeways. They soon spawned service stations, garages, insurance underwriters and numerous other types of services.

Today the automobile, together with its suppliers, infrastructure and supporting industries, represents an important component of the economy, notably the CONSTRUCTION INDUSTRY. Transport consumes about half of all the petroleum used in Canada, and automobiles take half of that quantity – as much as all of the other modes of transport combined.

The enormous impact of the automobile has not been without costs. Roads, highways and freeways require land that might otherwise be used for housing, parks or agriculture. Concern over the loss of land to the automobile has led to pressures by environmental groups. Their pressures resulted in the cancellation of plans to build the Spadina Freeway in Toronto and plans to expand highways in national parks in the West.

Auto-related Accidents, Deaths and Injuries 1965-85			
Year	Accidents	Fatalities	Injuries
1965	398 127	4 902	150 612
1970	498 839	5 080	178 501
1980	184 302	5 461	262 977
1981	183 643	5 383	260 658
1982	160 376	4 169	225 717
1985	183 352	4 360	258 808

Each year Canadian cars produce millions of tonnes of carbon dioxide, carbon monoxide, various particulants and other types of gas. They contribute to the smog that plagues many Canadian communities (*see* AIR POLLUTION; POLLUTION). Auto-emission standards are more lax in Canada than in the US. Many of the vehicles sold in Canada do not meet the minimum requirements of the US Environmental Protection Agency. Far more Canadians are injured in automobiles than by any other mode of transport. Young persons are the victims: in 1985, for example, 52% of all persons killed in auto-related accidents were between the ages of 15 and 34. Before 1980 the accident statistics included all automobile accidents that were reported; after that date the statistics gathered by the provincial governments included only those accidents that resulted in death or personal injury. In 1985 the YT had the fewest number of fatalities per 100 million vehicle kilometres and PEI the highest.

In recent years, all provinces have passed legislation that makes the use of seat belts compulsory. Safety experts believe that their use has reduced auto-related deaths and the severity of injuries sustained. Since focus on the value of seat belts has intensified, increasing numbers of drivers have used them.

Today, most Canadian automobiles are gasoline powered; a smaller number use diesel engines. Some vehicles (principally taxicabs and fleet vehicles) are powered by propane, liquified natural gas and other petroleum products. While alcohol can be used as vehicle fuel, it is generally more expensive than gasoline. Proponents of electric-powered vehicles see a great future for them, but thus far their use has been limited, because of their cost, the weight of their batteries and their restricted range. *See also* AUTOMOBILE ASSOCIATIONS.

K.M. RUPPENTHAL

Automobile Associations The first touring clubs and associations were for people travelling by cycle, train or on foot. Automobile clubs were formed later when the automobile became more widely used and distributed. The clubs were mainly social in nature, and almost entirely confined to Europe until the end of the 19th century. At the beginning of the 20th century, the owners of automobiles throughout Europe and N America felt the need to meet and discuss their problems: laws that restricted their activities, the organization of races, the development of the motor car as a practical means of conveyance, the encouragement of technical progress, and their defence against a hostile public. In Canada, the establishment of automobile clubs began in 1903 with the founding of the Hamilton and Toronto Automobile clubs when there were fewer than 178 automobiles in the country. By 1913, a dozen small nonprofit provincial and regional motor clubs united to establish the not-for-profit Canadian Automobile Association (CAA) with a mandate to promote a better understanding of the automobile and to improve roads and motoring conditions in general. Today, there are 19 constituent clubs comprising the CAA which span from coast to coast and boast a total membership of more than 2.5 million motorists. The CAA is a major club in a worldwide network of about 200 motoring and touring associations and clubs, all with the common bond of promoting travel and tourism and the protection and preservation of motorists' rights and privileges. Each of these individual organizations consists of many component clubs and branch offices located in every community where there are motor vehicles and tourists. The main purpose of such an affiliated network, comprising thousands of offices in over 100 countries, is to ensure that members of the various clubs have access to club services and assistance wherever they travel.   ROBERT ERB

Automobile Racing in Canada can be said to have originated during the last 3 decades of the 19th century with the great popularity of CYCLING. The tremendous interest in developing an alternative mode of personal transportation to that provided by the horse led to the rapid evolution of technological innovations. Such inventions as the pneumatic tire and the drive shaft, which appeared on early bicycles, eventually found their place on the automobile. Also, the early supporters of cycling formed clubs, engaged in tours and races, and campaigned for good roads. Many carried this enthusiasm into the 20th century with the arrival of the automobile.

The earliest automobile racing took the form of speed trials and tours. In 1900, F.S. Evans set a record of 3 hrs, 20 min, driving an automobile the 60 km between Toronto and Hamilton. Both Toronto and Winnipeg witnessed many tours and "runs" by the automobile owners of their cities during this time, but the first automobile race took place in the latter city. There, in 1901, the driver of a 12-horsepower Ford won the first automobile race in Canada. Four years later, the Winnipeg Automobile Club was holding regular night races for passenger and light touring cars. In Toronto, automobile racing appears to have found its earliest home at the CANADIAN NATIONAL EXHIBITION. In 1913, a form of automobile polo was staged at the CNE's grandstand, and the following year races and hurdling in automobiles were added to increase the popularity of the show. In 1917, Gaston Chevrolet raced successfully in an automobile against an airplane flown by Ruth Law, a noted aircraft pilot of the time. In 1919, Ralph De Palma was invited to drive the world's fastest car in a time test on the CNE's track. From 1920 to 1928, a series of races were held with prizes totalling $9000.

Despite its early start, automobile racing has not been a premier sporting event in Canada. Only in the past decade, with the advent of the Can-Am series of races and the annually staged Canadian Grand Prix for Formula One cars, has the sport aroused broader interest. For many years it was confined to a number of quarter- and eighth-of-a-mile oval tracks of asphalt or dirt construction. The cars used were greatly modified passenger vehicles known as "stock" cars. Competition was localized and there was little success at establishing national races, let alone international events like those occurring in many other sports. This form of racing continues to this day. More recently, stock-car races, sanctioned by the US Automobile Club (USAC), have been held at the better-established race tracks in Canada, and a few Canadians have tried to find success on the very popular US Grand National Circuit organized by NASCAR. Another form of US racing which enjoyed great popularity in the 1950s and 1960s in Canada is drag racing. Two drivers race their cars against each other and the clock from a standing start over a quarter-mile straight track. By 1965, there existed a dozen sanctioned Canadian drag tracks.

The real impetus to involve Canada and Canadian drivers in international racing has come from road racing, which takes place on closed circuits featuring a variety of turns and straightaways. A wide variety of cars, divided into different classes, from small sedans and sports cars to the more exotic open-wheeled formula racers, are raced on these tracks. The roots of this form of racing can be found in the interest that developed in N America after WWII in the small sports cars brought back from Europe by returning servicemen. The availability of abandoned air strips provided the facilities to race these automobiles. In fact, the first road race in Canada took place on the Abbotsfield Airfield in BC in 1949. One of the first tracks in Ontario was created in Edenvale, near Stayner, Ont. In Winnipeg, the old Netley Airport was the scene of racing activity, starting in 1955. Although similar racing spread across the West, the centre of Canadian road racing was southern Ontario. These early years of racing on airport strips were without much organization. In 1951, the Canadian Automobile Sports Club was formed as a federation of auto sports clubs across Canada.

By 1959, a growing disagreement between those who raced for fun and those who believed the sport could only be developed through competitions between well-known drivers lured by substantial cash prizes led to the formation of the Canadian Racing Drivers Assn. In May 1956 the British Empire Motor Club opened Harewood Raceway near Jarvis, Ont. Here many of Canada's top drivers of the 1960s got their start. A major development, however, was the construction of Mosport, a 2.46-mile (4 km) road-racing circuit N of Bowmanville, Ont. On 24 June 1961 a crowd of 40 000 spectators gathered to watch Britain's Stirling Moss defeat an international field in the first Player's 200 race. Further efforts were made to develop the sport. Edmonton International Speedway and LeCircuit at St-Jovite, Qué, were opened in the years that followed. In 1963, Don Hunt of Toronto developed the concept of a Canadian-American challenge series for unrestricted sports cars and, 3 years later, the first Can-Am race was held. Each year a series of races is held over a number of road courses in Canada and the US. Although American drivers have won most of the races, in 1968 John Cannon of Montréal won the last Can-Am race prior to the complete domination of the event until 1974 by the McLaren team of Britain.

On 27 Aug 1967, the first Canadian Grand Prix for Formula One cars was held at Mosport Park. The race has been a highlight of the automobile racing season since. In 1978, it was moved to Montréal, where it was won for the first time by a Canadian, Gilles VILLENEUVE – for whom the course is now named. The first Canadian to compete at the Formula One level was Peter Ryan of Mont-Tremblant, Qué. A highly promising young driver, his career ended tragically on 2 July 1962 when he was killed while racing in Europe. In 1969 and 1970, George Eaton of Toronto drove for the BRM team in N America and in selected European events. By far the most successful Canadian driver was Gilles Villeneuve. After a brilliant career in N America, he joined the Ferrari racing team in 1977. From then until his death in 1982, he won 6 world-championship races, including, in 1981, the crown jewel of the sport, the Monaco Grand Prix. Other successful Canadian drivers include Earl Ross, who was NASCAR's rookie of the year in 1974, and Gary BECK of Edmonton, who won the 1974 world drag-racing championship. Nierop Kees won the Rothman's Porsche challenge in 1986, in addition to a number of other European races. Richard Spenard won the Player's Challenge (1986), the Formula 2000 Series (1986) and the Rothman's Porsche (1987). In 1986 Stephane Proulx won the Formula 2000 Series and Scott Goodyear won the Eastern Zone Formula Atlantic, and in 1987 Peter Lockart won the Player's Challenge.

In spite of these successes, Canadian automobile racing remains at the periphery of the sport worldwide – perhaps reflecting Canada's relation to the automobile industry, based in the US, Europe and Japan.   J. THOMAS WEST

Reading: Len Coates, *Challenge: The Story of Canadian Road Racing* (1970).

Automotive Industry in 1986 comprised some 500 establishments, producing almost $37 billion in vehicles and parts; it ranked first among Canada's manufacturing industries. The first horseless carriage in Canada was built by Henry Seth Taylor in 1867 in Stanstead, Qué. Taylor's steam pleasure carriage was considered a novelty, but as other pioneers built steam, electric and gasoline engines in the late 19th century, the automobile began to find a place in personal and goods TRANSPORTATION. The automotive industry began in Canada when a group of young businessmen in Windsor, Ont, led by Gordon M. McGregor, formed the Ford Motor Co of Canada, Ltd (1904), only a year after Henry Ford, the promotor and inventor, had begun production in Detroit. Cars were assembled in the works of the Walkerville Wagon Co, Ltd, as parts were ferried by wagonload across the Detroit R. Canadian Fords were soon being shipped to most parts of the far-flung British Empire. Col R.S. MCLAUGHLIN, Canada's pioneer in the industry, converted the family's thriving carriage and sleigh production in Oshawa, Ont, to the new horseless carriage with its noisy internal-combustion engine. In 1908 McLaughlin arranged with William C. Durant, the financial wizard who formed General Motors, to use David Buick's engines. Buick engines with McLaughlin-designed bodies gained world renown. Later, Durant offered McLaughlin the Canadian rights to the Chevrolet "Classic Six," a 5-passenger touring car designed by racing-car driver Louis Chevrolet. General Motors of Canada Ltd was formed in 1918, under the presidency of McLaughlin, when McLaughlin Motor Co Ltd and Chevrolet Motor Co of Canada Ltd merged. Detroit, just across the Detroit R from WINDSOR, became the world centre for automotive production at the beginning of the century. The reasons for Detroit's predominance seem to have been based on its well-established carriage, bicycle and boat-engine industries and the excellent road system in the surrounding region. Windsor became the Canadian extension of Detroit because of 2 inducements: a 35% tariff on carriages of all kinds entering Canada and a preferential tariff entry to British countries.

The development work in automotive technology was done in Europe; even the name "automobile" is French. A French army captain, Nicholas Cugnot, built a steam-artillery tractor, the first self-propelled land vehicle, and another Frenchman, Jean-Joseph-Étienne Lenoir, first used a gas engine in a vehicle to drive on a highway. Steam and electric vehicles offered many advantages, but the internal-combustion engine has dominated. Nicolaus A. Otto, a German engineer, developed the 4-stroke engine, the foundation of the industry which has produced the 400 million cars and trucks on the roads of the world today. Gottlieb Daimler and Wilhelm Maybach worked together at the end of the 19th century to produce a practical, Otto-cycle automobile engine. Emile Levassor, of Panhard and Levassor, conceived the central frame structure suited to carrying an engine. By adding pneumatic tires, most of the obstacles to the beginning of motoring had been removed. It was the master mechanics of Detroit who turned the luxury plaything into a mass-produced, low-priced, reliable convenience for common use. Ransom E. Olds was the first successful mass producer in the US, with his rakish, curved-dash "merry" Oldsmobile. Important contributions were made by Ford, Charles and Frank Duryea, Henry Leland, Walter Chrysler, Charles Nash and Charles "Boss" Kettering, who invented the self-starter which made motoring less dangerous and more reliable.

In the early years, thousands of automobiles were introduced but few survived. In Canada

A spare tire being placed in a car trunk on the assembly line by a semi-automatic arm at the Ford plant, Oakville, Ont (*courtesy SSC Photocentre*).

these included the LeRoy, the popular Russell, the Tudhope, the Thomas, the Galt and many others. But no independent Canadian automobile company survived; Canada did not have enough people to support a native industry. The motor vehicle industry, however, burgeoned because of the demands of the first mechanized war. As a result, from 1918 to 1923 Canada was the second-largest vehicle producer in the world and a major exporter. Those Canadian manufacturers who succeeded were allied to successful American companies.

The form and size of today's automotive industry was shaped by the first "Canadian-content" legislation in 1926, the Tariff Board hearings of the mid-1930s, the Royal Commission on the Automotive Industry of 1960, the subsequent CANADA-US AUTOMOTIVE PRODUCTS TRADE AGREEMENT (APTA or Autopact) of 1965, and the Iranian oil crisis of 1979 which ushered in the automotive depression of the early 1980s. The recovery has seen the entrenchment of Asian companies in N America, both through direct exports and investment. These companies operate outside the Autopact. One result of the Autopact is continental, conditional free trade in motor vehicles and original equipment parts. The agreement contains safeguards requiring that APTA producers in Canada maintain levels of assembly related to the value of their sales here. At present, over 80% of the vehicles produced in Canada are exported.

In the 1980s the automotive industry accounted for about 14% of total direct manufacturing employment in Canada and 10% of the value of total manufacturing shipments. The industry consumed 14% of iron foundry production, 11% of rubber products, 7% of machine-shop products, 9% of wire goods, 14% of processed aluminum, 6% of carpeting and fabrics and 9% of glass products. The Canadian automotive industry is the final destination of over 20% of all domestic steel shipments, representing over 10 000 jobs in the Canadian steel industry. There are soon to be more than 10 producers of cars and trucks in Canada, and Canada is the sixth-largest producer in the world. These vehicle assemblers also produce nearly half of the value of parts and components going into vehicle production. A further 40% of these original equipment parts is produced by some 450 Canadian-owned parts companies, and the balance is produced by the 12 largest, independent multinational parts compa-

nies. Ontario continues to be the centre for vehicle assembly with 83%; about 12% of assembly is in Québec; and smaller facilities are maintained in BC, Manitoba and NS. Original equipment-parts plants are also concentrated in Ontario (80%) and Québec (10%). After-market parts production, which is about one-quarter that of original equipment parts, is located in Ontario (68%), with 16% each in Québec and Western Canada. The automotive industry also includes a distribution system of about 3500 dealers employing almost 80 000 persons.

Canada's automotive industry is not independent but is a fully integrated N American industry bound by the Autopact. The effects have been generally positive for Canada, creating more jobs, higher wages and lower car prices for Canadians. The Canadian industry has also grown more efficient since the agreement and Canadian plants are competitive with those in the US. However, several developments of the 1970s put the N American industry in a crisis. The most visible sign of change was the growing sales of Japanese, Korean and European cars, as Canadian consumers turned to smaller, more fuel-efficient cars. Nevertheless, while the Japanese have implemented self-imposed restrictions on cars exported to Canada, recent models from General Motors, Ford and Chrysler have begun to regain the confidence of consumers as well as car enthusiasts. The issue of import restraints has been controversial, with the 1983 Federal Task Force on the Canadian Automotive Industry claiming that they are necessary to protect jobs and consumer groups claiming that they restrict choice and cause an overall rise in car prices.

In Canada over $12 billion was committed to new plants and equipment between 1980 and 1986. Huge sums went into single projects; eg, about $3 billion to renovate and expand GM's transmission plant in Windsor, over $900 million on Ford's new engine plant, $500 million spent by Chrysler to renovate production in the continent's most robotized assembly plant, and $764 million by American Motors in Brampton. Management methods and organization, as well as relationships with labour and suppliers have been revamped in attempts to promote greater productivity and quality. Governments are also involved in the automotive industry. The federal government is using its impressive $25-million test track and facilities at Blainville, Qué, and Ontario has established 6 technology centres, an Automotive Parts Technol-

ogy Centre in St Catharines, and a Robotics Technology Centre in Peterborough. In future years there will be more innovations in this revitalized, restructured industry.   JAMES G. DYKES

Autonomy Bills, 1905, became the Acts creating the provinces of Alberta and Saskatchewan. The federal government refused to accept the scheme proposed by the North-West Territories Prem F.W.G. HAULTAIN, which envisaged a single province controlling its own lands, resources and educational policy, and instead created 2 provinces. The legislation defined the boundaries of the provinces, granted them the same status as other provinces (except that public lands and resources remained under federal control until 1930), provided for representation in the federal Parliament and for local RESPONSIBLE GOVERNMENT, spelled out federal subsidies, and ensured the continuation of Catholic and Protestant schools originally provided for in the NORTH-WEST TERRITORIES ACT of 1875. The bills proved so controversial that they occupied almost 10 weeks of debate between Feb and July 1905 and led to the climax of the NORTH-WEST SCHOOLS QUESTION and to continuing resentment of an allegedly semicolonial status for the Prairie provinces within Confederation.

DAVID J. HALL

Autopact, *see* CANADA-US AUTOMOTIVE PRODUCTS AGREEMENT.

Autumn Colours Vibrant colours are one of the delights of autumn in Canada. The transformation from green to yellow, amber, crimson and purple is caused by a fascinating chemical process. Within all leaves there is a blend of colourful substances; temperature, rainfall and length of day determine which of these will dominate in the different seasons.

In spring and summer the most abundant substance in leaves is chlorophyll, which gives them their green colour. Chlorophyll is essential for photosynthesis, the process which converts the energy of sunlight into sugar. Sunlight is also necessary for the synthesis of chlorophyll itself. During summer when the days are long and sunlight is plentiful, chlorophyll is synthesized in a steady, abundant supply, so that throughout the season the leaves remain green. But as autumn ap-

Aerial view of fall colours at Lake Fortune, Gatineau Park, Qué (*courtesy SSC Photocentre/photo by A. Holbrook*).

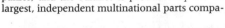

Leading Canadian Automobile Manufacturers, 1986				
Company	Sales	Rank among Cdn companies	Employees	Foreign company ownership
General Motors	$18.5 b	1	45 994	100%
Ford	$14.3 b	3	27 500	94%
Chrysler	$7.4 b	8	12 093	100%

Maples leaves, Muskoka Lakes region, Ont (*photo by J.A. Kraulis*).

proaches and the hours of daylight diminish, the production of chlorophyll slows down. Also, cool autumn temperatures slow the passage of nutrients into the leaves and this further decreases the synthesis of chlorophyll. As the amount of chlorophyll in the leaf decreases, other colourful substances that were always present but had been masked by the green become visible.

One group of substances that shows up once the amount of chlorophyll diminishes is the carotenoids. These colourful yellow pigments confer the Midas touch to aspens and to many other trees such as birch, cottonwood, alder, hickory, maple, sycamore and black cherry. Carotenoids are common in many other living things, imparting the characteristic colour to canaries, corn and carrots, as well as buttercups, bananas and egg yolks. Carotenoids, unlike chlorophyll, do not require sunlight for their synthesis, so they are unaffected by the shortening days of autumn and their colour dominates with the disappearance of chlorophyll. An example of how carotenoids do not need sunlight is seen in the yellow colour of grass that has been temporarily shaded from the sun by a piece of wood or a rock.

One of the most colourful habitats in Canada is the bog. A bog is a type of wetland in which sphagnum moss is the principal plant cover (*see* SWAMP, MARSH AND BOG). The water in bogs is highly acidic and low in oxygen, characteristics not suited to many plants. Two groups of plants, in addition to sphagnum moss, do thrive in bogs however, the heath and the larches, both of which sport vibrant colours in autumn. The heath family, which includes blueberries and other woody shrubs such as leatherleaf, bog rosemary, Labrador tea and sheep laurel, turn a vivid crimson in autumn. The tamarack, which belongs to the LARCH group of coniferous trees, turns from light green to rich, translucent gold. The long, slender needles of the tamarack give its branches a delicate, feathery appearance. Unlike other coniferous trees, the tamarack sheds its needles in autumn.

Yellow autumn foliage is common in the temperate latitudes worldwide, but the vibrant reds occur only in N America, Japan, N and S Korea and northern China. The N American red maple has been introduced into many countries, and selective cultivation has yielded many domestic varieties with such enticing names as October Glory, Red Sunset and Autumn Flame.

The reds and purples of autumn foliage result from the presence of another group of pigments called anthocyanins. These red substances are not present throughout the growing season as are the yellow carotenoids, and only develop in late summer as a result of a change in the metabolic breakdown of sugar. Anthocyanins are responsible for the resplendent reds of maples, oaks, sumac, dogwood, heaths and black gum. They also give the familiar colour to such common fruits as cranber-

ries, plums, grapes, apples, cherries and strawberries. These same pigments frequently combine with the yellow carotenoid pigments to produce the bronze and deep orange hues of other hardwood trees.

Some autumns are not as colourful as others. Drought conditions will cause leaves to fade, turn brown and fall with only a trace of colour. Heavy rains also inhibit the best autumn colour. When hard rains combine with wind, the trees may be stripped of their leaves before they reach their peak. The best conditions are warm, sunny days and cool nights without frost, which contrary to common belief are not necessary for the colour transition and may cause leaves to fall prematurely. Although clear, bright days and cool nights emphasize the reds, these conditions seem to have little effect on the brilliance of the yellows.

Trees shed their leaves in autumn because it is the most economical way for them to survive the winter. While on the tree, leaves continually lose water through surface pores which remain open to absorb carbon dioxide for photosynthesis. Once the temperature becomes too cold for photosynthesis, if the tree retains its leaves, it continues to lose moisture with no benefit. Once the ground freezes the tree cannot extract water from the soil to replenish these losses. Also, if leaves were retained they would become heavy in winter with a burden of ice and snow and would probably break off, taking with them important nutrients essential for the welfare of the tree. As it is, deciduous trees drain the minerals and other nutrients from their leaves before they are lost and store them for the next growing season. Coniferous trees do not need to shed their needles in autumn because they are better protected against water loss. Their needles are covered with a thick coating of wax, and their pores can close completely so that no moisture is lost.

The fate of autumn leaves is determined weeks before they are finally snapped from the tree. At the end of the growing season in late summer, a corky layer of cells begins to form at the base of the leaf stem. These cells prevent the passage of minerals, water and other nutrients from flowing out to the leaf. This layer gradually weakens the attachment of the leaf, and eventually the wind snaps the leaf free. A waxy, waterproof substance seals the leaf scar. Over winter the fallen leaves become packed down by rain and snow. In spring

they are slowly decomposed by bacteria, fungi, insects and worms and converted into nutrients which can be absorbed again by the tree and so contribute to another glorious autumn harvest of colours.   WAYNE LYNCH

Auyuittuq National Park (est 1972), located on the Cumberland Pen of BAFFIN I, is Canada's first national PARK located N of the Arctic Circle. It is a harsh land of barren TUNDRA, jagged mountain peaks, deep FJORDS and ice. The Penny Ice Cap covers over 25% of the park's 21 500 km². Vegetation is sparse, although in the brief arctic summer flowers such as white mountain avens, yellow arctic poppy and purple saxifrage colour the sand. Wildlife is not abundant; herbivores, including arctic hare, lemming and a few barren-ground caribou, are preyed upon by wolves, arctic fox and weasel. The coast is home for millions of SEABIRDS. Glaucous gulls, fulmars and black guillemots nest on sheer cliffs. Polar bears, seals, walrus, beluga and narwhals patrol the icy coastal waters. Stone-age DORSET people lived here over 2500 years ago. Norse explorers visited but did not linger. In the 12th century ancestors of the present Inuit arrived. These Thule people hunted whales and caribou. English explorers arrived in 1585, but contact with European culture was not established until the mid-1800s, when whalers set up shore stations on the coast of Baffin I. From April to July, the park provides wilderness camping, hiking and mountaineering challenges for enthusiasts.   LILLIAN STEWART

av Paul, Annette, ballet dancer (b at Stockholm, Sweden 11 Feb 1944). Trained at the Royal Swedish Ballet School, she was chosen from among company apprentices to dance the lead in *The Stone Flower* in 1962. For 10 years she remained with the Royal Swedish Ballet as principal dancer and danced as guest ballerina with the ROYAL WINNIPEG BALLET, Harkness Ballet, Norwegian Ballet and other companies before joining Les GRANDS BALLETS CANADIENS in 1973. She brought beauty, vast experience and artistic maturity to the many roles created for her, including those by her husband, choreographer Brian MACDONALD. She retired from performance in 1984 and in 1986 became the founding artistic director of Ballet British Columbia.   JILLIAN M. OFFICER

Auyuittuq National Park, Baffin I (*courtesy Environment Canada, Parks/Prairie and Northern Region*).

Avalanche, rapid, downslope movement of snow, ice, water, rock, soil, vegetation, etc, mixed in various proportions. The term is used most often when snow or ice is the major component (as in a LANDSLIDE or ROCKSLIDE). Numerous avalanches fall annually in the mountains of Alberta, BC, NWT and the YT. They are less frequent in the rounded mountains and hills of the East; however, a fatal avalanche burial within the Toronto city limits shows the vulnerability of any place where snow and a suitable slope occur. In Canada avalanches kill an average of 7 people annually (usually mountaineers or skiers). Occasionally, avalanches cause major DISASTERS: 60 killed near Dyea, BC-Alaska, 3 Apr 1898; perhaps 62 near Rogers Pass, BC, 5 Mar 1910; 57 in rock and snow avalanches near Britannia Mine, BC, 27 Mar 1915; and 26 near Granduc Mine, BC, 18 Feb 1965.

The order-of-magnitude estimates of avalanche size and corresponding effects are as follows: a large avalanche which could destroy a village or forest would fall about 1000 m (up to 5000 m in extreme cases, as on Mts Logan or St Elias), deliver over 100 000 m³ of snow, ice, etc, and impact with pressures exceeding 100 kPa; a medium-sized avalanche which would be capable of destroying a house or car would fall about 100 m, deliver about 1000-10 000 m³ and impact at about 10 kPa; a small avalanche which could bury, injure or kill a human could descend less than 100 m, with volumes of 10-100 m³ and impact at about 1 kPa.

Avalanche paths consist of 3 zones: starting, track and runout deposition. Most starting zones of large avalanche paths are high-angle bowls, cirques and open slopes, oriented to prevailing winds to trap and accumulate blowing snow. A starting zone would normally include at least one section where slope steepness exceeds 25°, although slush avalanches may release on more gentle slopes (5-10°). Ice avalanches typically start at the snout of a GLACIER or tributary ice stream, advancing or retreating over a cliff face. Snow or ice released from the starting zone pours into the track (an open slope or, more often, a gully confining and directing the flowing mass). As the avalanche accelerates, additional snow, ice, water, rock, soil, vegetation, etc, may be entrained into the flow. Maximum avalanche speed depends on steepness, length, shape and roughness of track; flow height; properties of flowing material; and other factors. The NATIONAL RESEARCH COUNCIL has measured maximum speeds of about 50 m/sec for large, dry-snow avalanches at Rogers Pass. A fast-moving, dry-snow avalanche is characterized by a spectacular "powder cloud" and "wind blasts" causing damage in front and to the sides of moving snow. Wet snow and slush avalanches normally flow at slower speeds and do not have powder clouds or wind blasts.

The runout-deposition zone occurs where the avalanche decelerates because of decreasing steepness, because of widening or termination of a gully onto an open slope or alluvial fan, or because of a zone of increased surface roughness. In the Alps, avalanches sometimes outrun historically recorded boundaries, destroying buildings that have been standing for centuries. By contrast, most damage in Canada occurs at relatively new constructions (buildings, powerlines, bridges, railways) placed in the runout zone of avalanche paths for which little or no historic information is available. Economic consequences of avalanches are especially felt in BC where, in addition to causing damage and fatalities, avalanches block highway and railway traffic.

Snow avalanches begin in either of 2 ways. A small volume (less than 1 m³) of loose snow can

Powder avalanche crosses the highway in Kootenay National Park, BC. The path of a previous avalanche can be seen in the background (*photo by Jim Davies, Banff*).

slip out from the snow surface in the starting zone. As this initial mass descends it entrains an ever-widening, triangular area of snow, giving the impression from a distance that the avalanche started at the upper vertex point of the triangle; hence, this type of avalanche is sometimes called a point avalanche. Conversely, a cohesive snow slab can release almost instantaneously over a relatively wide area of shear weakness (100-100 000 m²). Slabs could be as little as 0.1 m thick, or could involve the entire snowpack (5 m thick in extreme cases). Slab avalanches are particularly hazardous because a large amount of snow is set in motion almost simultaneously. After slab failure, sharply defined fracture surfaces remain at the starting zone.

A snow slab fails when the slab's load exceeds the shear strength of supporting layers. Such failure of snow is most common during or immediately after heavy snowstorms when potentially weak layers cannot strengthen fast enough through crystal-to-crystal bond formation (sintering) to keep up with the increasing load of new snow. Slabs also release when thaw and creep deformation lower the strength of a weaker layer. A weakness may originate as the snow recrystallizes deep within the pack. One weakness, depth hoar, is a layer of weak, coarse grains recrystallized in the presence of strong temperature gradients. Another, surface hoar, develops when atmospheric water vapour deposits directly onto the snow surface, growing cohesionless, feathery crystals. Slab instability occurs when a heavy layer of new snow is added to a snowpack weakened by an existing layer of depth or surface hoar. Slab avalanches tend to release on ice crusts or smooth grassy slopes, especially when bonds are weakened by a thaw.

Snow-slope instability is evaluated from observations of weak layers and from meteorological data (snowfall, WIND, temperature). At Rogers Pass, avalanche forecasters operate several mountain meteorological and snow-study stations. New snow loading is observed during critical periods and the shear strength of potentially weak layers is evaluated with shear frames, ram penetrometers, and by simulating shear failure on

miniature inclined planes. Observers also record avalanche activity because often, once avalanches start to run on certain slopes (test slopes), the activity will continue and possibly intensify. If snow-slope instability is suspected, authorities may restrict public access and then artificially release avalanches by explosive blasting of the starting zone. Avalanche defences (eg, concrete sheds and wedges, earth mounds and dams) are sometimes placed in the runout-deposition zone.

About 50% of victims buried in avalanche debris suffocate in the first half-hour. On the other hand, victims buried favourably (within air pockets) have survived lengthy burials (even days). Thus, rescue is attempted whenever possible by trained teams using probe poles and avalanche dogs. A victim equipped with a transmitting device (audio-induction field, Rf field, magnetic field) can be located relatively quickly by search parties equipped with a compatible receiver. In the winter of 1986-87, avalanches resulted in 14 casualties.   R.I. PERLA

Reading: C. Fraser, *Avalanches and Snow Safety* (1978).

Avalon Peninsula, 10 360 km², is a spreading peninsula thrust out into the rich fishing grounds of the N Atlantic, forming the SE corner of insular Newfoundland. The orientation of the land tends to be NE, following folds in the peninsula's Precambrian, Cambrian and Ordovician structures. The Isthmus of Avalon, less than 5 km at its narrowest, joins the peninsula to the rest of the island. From Grates Pt in the N to Cape Freels-Cape Pine in the S, the peninsula stretches 180 km and spans nearly 100 km E-W. The peninsula is, and has been since the settling of the island, its most populous region. By the early 1800s it was home to more than three-quarters of the colony's population and today about 40% of Newfoundlanders live here, more than half in the ST JOHN'S metropolitan area.

The peninsula's rugged coastline was the earliest settled in the province and its 4 major bays, TRINITY, CONCEPTION, ST. MARY'S and PLACENTIA, were among the earliest fished. Newfoundland's first formal colony was begun at CUPIDS, Conception B, in 1610, followed by several other chartered "plantations" around the Avalon. Sir George CALVERT was granted a portion of the peninsula 1623 and lived there 1627-29, with his headquarters at FERRYLAND on the "Southern Shore." It was his holding, called Avalon after the legendary site where Christianity was introduced to Eng-

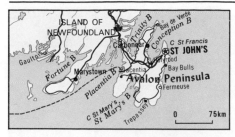

land, for which the peninsula was named. During the 1600s and 1700s the peninsula saw conflicts between the French and English with France establishing PLACENTIA on the SW coast as its capital in the 1660s. Today, in addition to being the principal commercial and administrative region of the province, the peninsula is the location of many historic sites, 3 national historic parks, several provincial parks, a nature park near Salmonier, a spectacular seabird sanctuary at CAPE ST MARY'S, and a 862 km² wilderness area in its SE quadrant.

ROBERT D. PITT

Reading: J.J. Manion, ed, *The Peopling of Newfoundland* (1977).

Aviation, the art and science of flying, has been a practical reality only since the early 20th century. Canadians have participated in its development almost from its inception. Significant early research was initiated by Rupert TURNBULL, who built the first wind tunnel in Canada in 1902, and by the farsighted Alexander Graham BELL, who founded the Aerial Experiment Assn in 1907 and recruited 2 U of T graduates, John MCCURDY and F.W. BALDWIN, as well as 2 Americans, Glenn Curtiss and Tom Selfridge. Working from laboratories in Hammondsport, NY, near Curtiss's engine factory, and BADDECK, NS, just W of Sydney, the team developed several aircraft. The *Red Wing*, designed by Selfridge and completed in 1908, made 2 successful flights, piloted by Baldwin, at Hammondsport before crashing. Baldwin thus became the first Canadian to fly, albeit in the US. Next the *White Wing*, also piloted by Baldwin, took to the air. Curtiss's *June Bug* was third, and this craft became the first to remain airborne for a full 1000 m. Finally, after an initial attempt at Hammondsport, McCurdy's SILVER DART was shipped to Baddeck, and on 23 Feb 1909 he made the first powered, heavier-than-air flight in Canada.

In Aug 1909, in an attempt to find additional financing, McCurdy flew both the *Silver Dart* and the *Baddeck I* (the first aircraft to be made in Canada) before an assembly of militia officers at Camp Petawawa, Ont. Though both aircraft performed well in the air, neither survived its encounter with the rough landing field. Despite this setback, interest in aviation survived, and more experimental craft were built. In 1911 McCurdy flew from Key West to Havana, the longest overwater flight to that date. John Porte was preparing to fly from Newfoundland to Ireland in 1914, but the attempt was cancelled by the onset of war.

Commercial Aviation The first commercial cargo flight in Canada took place in Oct 1913, when Montréal newspapers were carried from Montréal to Ottawa. Unfortunately the aircraft crashed on the return takeoff. In 1919 the CANADIAN PACIFIC RAILWAY requested parliamentary approval to amend its charter to include air transportation. The government extended regulation to cover the fledgling industry by passing the Aeronautics Act (1919), which created the Air Board to consider such requests.

The first commercial passenger flight took place in 1920, when 2 bush pilots flew a fur buyer north to The Pas, Man, from Winnipeg. One month later, the first regular services were initiat-

ed when Imperial Oil chartered several Junkers aircraft to ferry men and supplies from Edmonton to the newly discovered oil fields at Ft Norman, NWT.

From 1920 to 1937 air transport expanded rapidly, although it was still composed of a large number of small carriers, operating predominately north-south routes, feeding traffic from the railroads to the interior (*see* BUSH FLYING). Although long-distance airmail services were tested as early as 1920, it was not until 1927 that the Post Office authorized air delivery in cases where surface transportation was interrupted by the onset of winter.

In 1936 Parliament transferred control of civil aviation from DND to the newly created Dept of Transport, then under the aegis of C.D. HOWE. Faced with applications from US investors who wished to open a transcontinental passenger air route, and pressure from several Commonwealth countries that wanted the same system established as part of a more grandiose all-British, round-the-world network, Howe approached the 2 major railways and Canadian Airways, requesting that they participate in a nonprofit, government-guaranteed national carrier. CPR and Canadian Airways backed away over the issue of government representation on the board of directors, and Howe's preference shifted to the establishment of an all-government carrier. Thus, Trans-Canada Airlines was formed in 1937 as a wholly owned subsidiary of the CNR. In 1964 the name was changed to Air Canada, and in 1977 the Air Canada Act transferred share ownership from CN to the Crown. Air Canada is now Canada's largest airline, and the government by 1987 was considering its sale to private investors or its employees.

CPR acquired 11 aircraft operating companies during 1941 and continued operations under the name United Air Services Ltd. The name was changed 24 Mar 1942 to Canadian Pacific Airlines Ltd. In 1944 it applied for transcontinental status, which it was not granted until 1958 when it was allowed to operate a single daily service. The terms were gradually extended and in 1979 it was given the transcontinental route without restriction. Hampered by government in its attempt to fly domestically, CP Air expanded internationally from its Vancouver base, appropriating routes that Air Canada, which had the right of first refusal on all external services, did not visualize as being profitable. Flights were inaugurated to Australia, Japan and Hong Kong (1949); to South America (1953); and to Europe (1955), pioneering the transpolar Vancouver-Amsterdam route. In order to expand quickly enough to compete effectively with Air Canada under a deregulated environment, CP Air purchased Eastern Provincial Airways in 1984, and Nordair in 1985. CP Air was in turn taken over by Pacific Western Airlines in 1987, and the merged carrier was renamed Canadian Airlines International Ltd.

The original 5 regional airlines have now all been absorbed into CAIL. These were Pacific Western (BC/Prairies), Transair (Manitoba), Nordair (Ontario, Northern Québec), Québecair (Québec), and Eastern Provincial (Atlantic Provinces).

Since 1985, domestic air transport has been effectively deregulated, and major structural changes are now underway, leading perhaps to the establishment of 2 "mega-carriers" (Air Canada and CAIL) in place of the 3-tiered structure (national, regional and local airlines) which, with very few changes, lasted from just after the war until very recently. Both major airlines are now either purchasing feeder carriers outright, or establishing them themselves, to maximize traffic feed. At present, their equity participation in-

Dominion Skyways Ltd main base of operation, Rouyn, Qué, winter 1935 (*courtesy National Aviation Museum*).

cludes Air Canada (Air BC, Air Ontario, Austin Airways, Air Nova) CAIL (NorCanair, Air Atlantic, Nordair Metro, Québecair, Time Air). It remains to be seen how the situation will finally develop. WARDAIR, a charter airline with headquarters in Edmonton, was formed in 1953 as a bush charter company and started the overseas charter business in 1962. It operates a number of wide-bodied jets on international charter services, and its revenue equals that of any of the regionals. Under deregulation, Wardair began scheduling domestic and international services in 1986.

General Aviation General aviation has become a major force in Canada. In late 1986 there were 26 898 civil aircraft registered in Canada, or one for every thousand persons. Of this total, only about 200 were owned by major airlines. The total number, which more than doubled over the previous decade, breaks down into 24 690 airplanes, 1276 HELICOPTERS and about 932 miscellaneous craft such as gliders, gyroplanes and BALLOONS. About 21 000 registrations (78%) were for private use only, 5600 (21%) were for commercial use and the remainder were either for experimental craft or were operated by government agencies. Corporations owned and operated about 1000 private aircraft for executive transportation. The other 20 000 private planes were used for both business and recreational purposes, generally owner-operated. Canada had about 61 000 licensed pilots in 1986, a 50% increase over the previous decade. However, as a result of the rapidly increasing costs of recreational flying, the number of student pilot permits is currently at less than half the 1980 level.

Commercial general aviation is a major industry in Canada. In 1985 this sector, exclusive of the major airlines, comprised 1055 licensed Canadian operators. In 1983 Transport Canada estimated that over 2.4 million hours were flown. The major categories of use included charter flights, flying training, nonprofit flying clubs, and unit toll services. Other categories included crop spraying, fire fighting, construction, aerial photography and sightseeing.

Government Regulation Most countries, including Canada, consider that aviation has sufficient inherent risks to warrant government controls to ensure that minimum standards of safety are met and minimum levels of proficiency demonstrated (*see* TRANSPORTATION REGULATION). The government has also determined that commercial aviation is in effect a public utility and that the public interest must therefore be protected. In a Supreme Court decision in 1932, aviation was deemed to be wholly within federal jurisdiction; consequently, provincial regulation is minimal.

The arrival of Col Robert Leckie and Maj Basil Hobbs at Rivière-du-Loup, Qué, in darkness and a driving rain, using a Curtiss HS-2L (*courtesy National Aviation Museum*).

Responsibility for air safety is exercised by TRANSPORT CANADA through one of its agencies, the Canadian Air Transportation Administration. In addition to providing and maintaining airports, air navigation facilities and air traffic control services, CATA is charged with the licensing of personnel (pilots, mechanics, controllers) and equipment, registration of aircraft, and accident investigation.

Economic regulation is carried out by the Air Transport Committee, part of the CANADIAN TRANSPORT COMMISSION, which grants licences for the provision of commercial air services, including scheduled and charter carriage of passengers, freight and mail, as well as specialty services such as pilot training, crop spraying and fire control. However, as part of a movement towards reduced economic regulations, the minister of transport in 1985 proposed that the CTC be replaced by a new regulatory agency with a revised organizational structure. An Act to create the new agency, called the National Transportation Agency of Canada, was passed in 1987.

The Future When Canada's newest international airport, MIRABEL, was being planned during the late 1960s, air traffic in Canada had been growing at the rate of about 15% per year and was expected to increase indefinitely. Provision was made in the design to handle such expected improvements as the supersonic transport (SST) and the 800-passenger stretched double-deck jumbo jet. In 1986 long-term projections of traffic growth had fallen to about 4% per year; the super jumbo was still on the drawing boards; and the SST was losing money. Aircraft designs and airline operations are being developed to suit reduced traffic expectations, and the emphasis is on fuel economy and operational efficiency through improved aerodynamics, engine design, structural weight and operational control procedures. Cost will be the primary consideration in the future.   RICHARD FISHER

Reading: F. Ellis, *Canada's Flying Heritage* (1954, rev 1968); G.A. Fuller, J.A. Griffin and K.M. Molson, *125 Years of Canadian Aeronautics* (1983); L. Milberry, *Aviation in Canada* (1979); K.M. Molson, *Pioneering in Canadian Air Transport* (1974); Molson and H.A. Taylor, *Canadian Aircraft Since 1909* (1982).

Aviation, Military Military aviation began with the use of balloons for observation as early as 1794, during the French revolutionary wars. In 1883 Capt H. Elsdale of the Royal Engineers took aerial photos of the Halifax Citadel using a clock-operated camera hung beneath a balloon. Italy used aircraft for reconnaissance and to attack ground targets in Libya (1910-11) and the Balkans (1912-13). Aircraft engaged in air-to-air combat for the first time in WWI. When the war started each major belligerent possessed a few primitive aircraft; before it ended large fleets of fighters, general-purpose machines, torpedo carriers, large flying boats, heavy bombers and cigar-shaped dirigibles were in use. Despite some pre-war urging from aviation pioneers J.A.D. MCCURDY and F.W. BALDWIN, Canada had no air service when it went to war; nevertheless, about 22 000 Canadians flew with British squadrons overseas in WWI. At home Canadian Aeroplanes, Ltd (Toronto) produced 1200 training planes for the Royal Air Force and 30 Felixstowe flying boats for the US. No other combat aircraft were built in Canada until 1938. In 1919 Britain gave Canada about 100 aircraft: an assortment of trainers, fighters, bombers and flying boats. Another 12 flying boats were received from the US. These were the first planes flown by the Canadian Air Force, an interim force (1920-23) preceding the Royal Canadian Air Force (1924). In creating the RCAF, the government adopted the view that military aviation could be justified only if it served peaceful purposes. Consequently, most early flying by the RCAF consisted of such activities as topographical surveys, forest and fishery patrols, and anti-smuggling operations. In 1934, when war again threatened, the RCAF had 166 aircraft, only 28 of which were military types. In a belated attempt to rearm, the government found that the only military aircraft available were obsolete planes about to be discarded by the British. Out of necessity some of these were purchased, and others were manufactured in Canada even though they were outdated. On the eve of war, apart from 19 Hawker Hurricanes obtained from the UK in 1939, Canada's operational aircraft consisted of outmoded biplanes.

Canadian AVIATION industry burgeoned during WWII, producing about 15 000 military planes — two-thirds of which were trainers for the BRITISH COMMONWEALTH AIR TRAINING PLAN. The others

were operational types of British or American design: Bristol Bolingbrokes, Consolidated Cansos, Curtiss Helldivers, Handley Page Hampdens, de Havilland Mosquitoes, Avro Lancasters and Hurricanes. The 48 Canadian squadrons operating overseas were equipped with aircraft supplied by the British Air Ministry. RCAF squadrons flew in the Northwest Europe, Mediterranean and Southeast Asia theatres of war and also played major roles in the DIEPPE RAID, the Battle of the ATLANTIC and the combined bomber offensive over Germany. During the war, the RCAF became the third-largest air force of the Western Allies.

Since 1948 Canadian military aviation has had several distinct roles: to deter aggression, to assist UN PEACEKEEPING operations and to support ground and naval forces in defence exercises, and to assist in search and rescue missions. In 1948, compelled by East-West tension to upgrade its air defences at home, Canada equipped 6 squadrons with its first operational jet fighter, the British-made Vampire. For the defence of Europe the RCAF contributed 12 squadrons of F-86 Sabres, the only Allied aircraft equal to the Soviet MiG-15. The RCAF Sabres, and also those flown by the air forces of Great Britain, Greece, Turkey and Italy, were manufactured under licence by CANADAIR LTD of Montréal. Two Sabre versions, V and VI, powered by the Canadian-designed and manufactured Orenda engine, gave outstanding performance. The AVRO CF-100 CANUCK, a long-range, all-weather plane equipped with 2 Orenda engines, was the first military aircraft wholly designed and built in Canada. It made its appearance in 1953, replacing the Vampires in N American defence; in addition 4 CF-100 squadrons were assigned to Europe to meet the need for all-weather fighters. In the 1950s Canadian and American air-defence organizations were integrated under the NORAD Agreement and the completion of a continental radar defence network. Previously, the Canadians and Americans had foreseen the requirement for an aircraft of advanced design that could effectively exploit the advantages of this system. The RCAF was depending on the AVRO ARROW, but owing to prohibitive costs of development and political considerations the Arrow was abandoned in the experimental stage. The cancellation was considered a disaster for the military aviation industry in Canada and practically ensured that future aircraft would have to be purchased abroad.

In the next decade, 3 American fighters were procured: CF-104 Starfighters (1961) and CF-5 Freedom Fighters (1968) for deployment in Europe and CF-101 Voodoos as replacements for the CF-100s in 1961. The CF-104s and CF-5s were manufactured under licence by Canadair. Both types reflected the tremendous impact of modern technology. The CF-104s, for example, then the fastest combat planes in the world, had comput-

A Canadian Forces CF-18 fighter from 409 Tactical Fighter Squadron, CFB Baden-Soellingen, flies a routine training mission over southern Germany (*Canadian Forces photo by WO Vic Johnson*).

CHRONOLOGY OF CANADIAN AVIATION

Date	Facts
10 Aug 1840	Louis Anselm Lauriat of Boston, Mass, ascended from Barrack Square, Saint John, NB, in his balloon
28 Dec 1905	Alexander Graham Bell's tetrahedral cell kite lifted Neil MacDermid into the air at Baddeck, NS.
12 Mar 1908	The first flight of a powered heavier-than-air machine piloted by a Canadian was made by F.W. Baldwin in the *Red Wing* at Hammondsport, NY.
6 Dec 1908	J.A.D. McCurdy made first flights in *Silver Dart* at Hammondsport, NY.
23 Feb 1909	The first flight in Canada, made by J.A.D. McCurdy in the *Silver Dart* at Baddeck, NS.
8 Sept 1910	First Canadian aircraft engine was tested. William Gibson of Victoria, BC, made a short test flight in an aircraft powered with an engine of Gibson's own design.
24 May 1912	The first parachute jump in Canada made at Vancouver by Charles Saunders.
6 July 1912	The first seaplane flight in Canada was made by Fred G. Eells at Hanlan's Point in Toronto Harbour.
31 July 1913	The first airplane flight by a woman pilot in Canada was made by Alys McKey Bryant at Vancouver.
6 Aug 1913	The first fatal airplane accident in Canada. John M. Bryant was fatally injured in a crash at Victoria.
8 Oct 1913	First commercial intercity flight in Canada was made by W. Robinson from Montréal to Ottawa.
16 Sept 1914	The first Canadian military air service, the Canadian Aviation Corps, was formed by Sir Sam Hughes.
14 July 1915	The first aircraft to go into production in Canada, the Curtiss JN-3, was test flown near Toronto.
14 Dec 1915	The first Canadian to be credited with bringing down an enemy aircraft was Flight Sub-Lt Arthur Strachan Ince, RNAS, off the Belgian coast.
2 June 1917	Capt Billy Bishop attacked a German aerodrome and shot down 3 enemy aircraft; he was later awarded the Victoria Cross for this action.
21 Apr 1918	Capt Arthur Roy Brown, was credited with shooting down Baron von Richthofen, the "Red Baron."
20 Nov 1918	First Canadian squadrons formed, at Upper Heyford, Eng, with all-Canadian personnel.
15 June 1919	First nonstop transatlantic flight completed by Capt John Alcock and Lt Arthur Whitton Brown from St. John's to Clifton, Ireland.
Aug 1919	First aerial survey – a timber survey carried out in Labrador.
30 Aug 1919	W.R. "Wop" May flew Det J. Campbell from Edmonton to Coal Branch, Alta, in pursuit of a murderer.
7-17 Oct 1920	First trans-Canada flight, from Halifax to Vancouver, 49 hrs 7 mins.
1 Apr 1924	Royal Canadian Air Force formed.
23 May 1924	The first Canadian scheduled air service began, between Angliers, Lake Fortune and Rouyn, Qué.
Sept 1924	The first Canadian regular air-mail service began, between Haileybury, Ont, and Rouyn, Qué.
29 June 1927	First flight test of the W.R. Turnbull variable pitch propeller.
Mar 1928	de Havilland Aircraft of Canada Ltd was incorporated at Toronto.
28 Aug 1928	C.H. "Punch" Dickins left Winnipeg, Man, with Lt-Col C.D.H. MacAlpine
	on long inspection trip in northern Canada, including a flight across the Barren Lands for the first time.
1 July 1929	Canada's western arctic coast was reached by air for the first time. "Punch" Dickins landed at Aklavik, NWT.
1 Aug 1930	British dirigible R-100 arrived at St-Hubert Airport, Montréal, the only occasion that a large dirigible visited Canada.
9-10 Oct 1930	J. Erroll Boyd became first Canadian to fly across the Atlantic.
10 Apr 1937	Creation of Trans-Canada Airlines (later Air Canada).
19 Nov 1938	The RCAF achieved equal status with the RCN and Canadian Army.
17 Dec 1939	The British Commonwealth Air Training Plan set up in Canada for the training of aircrew.
24 Mar 1942	Canadian Pacific Airlines Ltd was formed.
27 July 1942	Sgt G.F. "Buzz" Beurling destroyed 4 enemy aircraft over Malta.
22 July 1943	First regular Canadian transatlantic air service inaugurated by TCA.
31 Mar 1945	The British Commonwealth Air Training Plan was terminated; 131 553 aircrew had been trained.
9 Aug 1945	Lt R.H. Gray, sank a Japanese destroyer at Onagawa Bay, Japan; he was awarded a posthumous VC.
1 Dec 1945	Avro Canada Ltd was formed.
16 Aug 1947	The DHC-2 Beaver prototype was test flown at Downsview, Ont.
17 Mar 1948	The first Canadian jet engine, the Avro Chinook, was tested at Malton, Ont.
14-15 Jan 1949	The first nonstop trans-Canada flight was made by F/O J.A.F. Jolicoeur, from Vancouver to Halifax.
10 Aug 1949	The world's second jet transport, the Avro C-102 Jetliner, was test flown at Malton, Ont.
19 Jan 1950	The prototype Avro Canada CF-100 Canuck was test flown at Malton.
31 July 1951	A CP Air DC-4 crashed between Vancouver and Alaska, killing 36.
18 Dec 1952	An Avro CF-100 exceeded Mach 1, the first straight-winged aircraft to do so without rocket power.
5 May 1955	Agreement concluded between the US and Canada for construction of DEW radar defence line.
30 June 1957	The aerial surveying of Canada, begun in the 1920s, was completed.
11 Aug 1957	A TCA DC-4 crashed near Issoudun, Qué. All 79 people aboard died.
25 Mar 1958	The Avro Arrow (CF-105) prototype was test flown at Malton, Ont; the project was cancelled 2 years later.
4 Dec 1958	The last Avro CF-100 was rolled from the production line; 692 were built.
28 Mar 1961	The first CF-104 Starfighters, built by Canadair, were delivered.
1 Feb 1968	Unification of Canadian Forces.
Oct 1984	Marc Garneau became the first Canadian in space.
23 June 1985	Air India Flight 182 from Toronto crashed, likely a result of a terrorist bomb, in the N Atlantic off the coast of Ireland, killing all 329 aboard, including 280 Canadians.
12 Dec 1985	A DC-8 carrying 256 passengers (248 US soldiers) crashed after take-off from Gander, NFLD. All were killed.
Apr 1987	PWA acquired CP Air; new company is named Canadian Airlines International.

erized navigation and firing-control systems that required only monitoring by the pilot. However, the single-engined aircraft had a dismal record, suffering numerous crashes.

All these machines were replaced in 1982 by the McDonnell Douglas CF-18, a versatile, twin-engined fighter with a maximum speed of Mach 1.8 (almost twice the speed of sound) and a built-in capability for subsequent additions in avionics and armaments. Heavily computerized and armed with a cannon as well as missiles, the CF-18 is a complex weapon which, despite serious teething problems, is likely to remain in the first rank of combat aircraft for years to come.   FRED HATCH

Avison, John Henry Patrick, conductor, pianist (b at Vancouver 25 Apr 1915; d there 30 Nov 1983). After beginning a career as a solo pianist and accompanist, Avison accepted appointment as first conductor of the CBC Vancouver Chamber Orchestra in 1938. During 42 years under his versatile direction, this proficient orchestra performed works of all periods, specializing in the 18th-century repertoire and premiere performances of new Canadian works.

BARCLAY MCMILLAN

Avison, Margaret, poet, librarian, social worker (b in Galt [Cambridge], Ont 23 Apr 1918). Educated at Victoria College, U of T, Avison began her career as a writer with a poem in the *Canadian Poetry Magazine* in 1939. She was a Guggenheim fellow in 1956, and won the Governor General's Award with her first collection of poetry, *Winter Sun* (1960), in which she established herself as a difficult and introspective poet given to private images and subtle shadings of emotion that challenge and frustrate the reader. These complexities in her writing conceal a deeply religious and vulnerable sensibility. In 1966 Avison published *The Dumbfounding,* a more accessible record of spiritual discovery, and a more revealing account of the unmasked, narrative "I." This was further developed in *Sunblue* (1978), a combination of social concern and moral values fused by religious conviction and a continuing restatement of personal faith. Avison has taught at Scarborough College, and has done social work at the Presbyterian Church Mission in Toronto. She studied creative writing at the universities of Indiana and Chicago, and has been writer in residence at UWO. Among her other works are *History of Ontario* (1951) intended for young people, and a collaboration in translation from the Hungarian of *The Plough and the Pen: Writings from Hungary 1930-1956* (1963).   MICHAEL GNAROWSKI

Reading: E. Redekop, *Margaret Avison* (1970).

Avocet (order Charadriiformes, family Recurvirostridae), large, long-legged SHOREBIRD, about 50 cm long, with striking white-and-black plumage. The 4 species (one in each of N and S America, Eurasia and Australia) breed in small, loose colonies in coastal saltmarshes and shallow, alkaline inland lakes. Avocets feed on small crustaceans, worms and other benthic animals. Their long, slender, upward-curving bills are well adapted to their hunting technique. The birds wade slowly through shallow water, sweeping their bills from side to side just above the muddy bottom and seizing whatever prey is stirred up. Avocet numbers have declined with reclamation of their marshy habitats. However, their re-establishment in Britain, since the 1940s, is a classic example of successful conservation of an ENDANGERED ANIMAL through habitat management. The American avocet (*Recurvirostrata americana*), with a yellow neck and bright blue legs, breeds in southern Alta, Sask and Man, and south to California and Texas, wintering in Texas, California and Central America.   R.G.B. BROWN

Avro Arrow (CF-105), an advanced, supersonic, twin-engined, all-weather interceptor jet aircraft developed by A.V. Roe of Canada from 1949 until the government's controversial cancellation of the project in 1959. Encouraged by A.V. Roe's success in developing the AVRO CF-100 CANUCK and recognizing the need for an aircraft to counter the threat of Soviet bombers over the demanding Canadian North, enthusiastic RCAF officers, defence scientists and defence-industry officials had persuaded the Liberal government by Dec 1953 to authorize 2 prototype airframes in anticipation of a production run of up to 600 aircraft costing $2 million apiece. Canada was also forced to develop the Arrow's engine, and fire-control and missile systems, and estimated costs rose to $12.5 million per aircraft. Test flights indicated that, with the proper engines the plane could well be the world's fastest and most advanced interceptor. However, doubts mounted as the government's order shrank to 100 and unit costs rose. In Oct 1958, to cut costs, the new Conservative government terminated Canadian fire-control and missile development, and renewed efforts to sell the aircraft to the US, just when the US was promoting BOMARC MISSILES and the USSR's launch of an ICBM missile was raising doubts about the priority of the Soviet bomber threat.

After export efforts again failed, the project was cancelled on 20 Feb 1959. A.V. Roe bitterly fired 14 000 employees; the government ordered all plans and prototypes destroyed; and many Canadians bemoaned the devastation of Canada's aircraft industry, the resulting flight of scientists and engineers to the US, and Canada's renewed dependence on the US for interceptor aircraft.

JOHN KIRTON

Avro CF-100 Canuck, first jet fighter designed and built in Canada. After 4 years' development, it first flew Jan 1950, and 692 were built. It became operational April 1953 and served 10 years in NORAD and NATO squadrons. It was not as fast as contemporary fighters, but its good climb rate, excellent radar, twin-engined reliability and all-weather capability made it suitable for defence in the extreme conditions of the Canadian North and in the cloud of W Germany. Fifty-three were sold to Belgium. Two are preserved in the National Aviation Museum, one in Calgary Centennial Planetarium and others in parks and bases across Canada. The name "Canuck" was considered inappropriate for a fighter. JAMES MARSH

Avro Jetliner (C-102), N America's first jet airliner, designed in Canada by James Floyd. It first flew on 10 Aug 1949, exceeding 800 km/h, the first flight of a jet transport in N America, second in the world. (The de Havilland Comet flew on 27 July 1949.) In April 1950 it made the first international jet-transport flight in N America, from Toronto to New York. It aroused much interest in the US and was one of the outstanding aeronautical achievements of its day, but it never saw production. TRANS-CANADA AIRLINES lost interest even before the first flight, and in the Cold War atmosphere C.D. HOWE insisted that Avro concentrate on the CF-100 fighter. The RCAF, the first air force to operate jet transports, ordered 2 Comets in November 1951. The Jetliner was sold for scrap in 1956; only the nose section and engines survive in the National Aviation Museum.

JAMES MARSH

Reading: J. Floyd, *The Avro Canada C-102 Jetliner* (1987).

Axel Heiberg Island, 43 178 km², third-largest in the Arctic QUEEN ELIZABETH IS and seventh-largest in Canada, is separated from ELLESMERE I to the E by Eureka and Nansen sounds. Mountains of the Princess Margaret Range rise precipitously

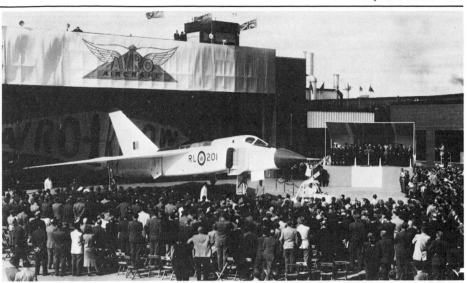

The *Avro Arrow*'s first public appearance at Malton, 1957. Although it was perhaps the world's most advanced interceptor, the project was cancelled 2 years later (*courtesy the* Globe and Mail).

on the W, reaching a height of 2211 m. Ice fields and glaciers cover 14 733 km² of the mountains. The eastern part is hilly, with local plains. Vegetation is scant, but well-vegetated spots occur in the lowlands. Arctic hares are the most common mammals. Muskoxen occur in the lowlands, but caribou are scarce. The island was discovered in 1899 by a Norwegian expedition led by Otto SVERDRUP who named it after the Norwegian consul.

S.C. ZOLTAI

Axelrad, Arthur Aaron, histologist (b at Montréal 30 Dec 1923). Educated at McGill (MD, CM 1949; PhD 1954), Axelrad was professor and head of histology in the anatomy department at U of T from 1966 to 1985. He has achieved international acclaim for his research in hemopoiesis and leukemia. Axelrad's research group is known worldwide for its studies on various aspects of blood cell differentiation, with special reference to the myeloproliferative disorders. The group's work at present is focused on finding regulatory molecules that control the proliferation of hemopoietic stem cells and investigating the genes that code for them. Axelrad has published over 80 scientific papers. He was elected a fellow of the RSC in 1982.

KEITH L. MOORE

Axworthy, Norman Lloyd, politician (b at North Battleford, Sask 21 Dec 1939). He was a Princeton PhD and left-wing political activist. He taught at University of Winnipeg and directed its Institute of Urban Affairs before serving as Manitoba MLA 1973-79. He was elected to the House of Commons for Winnipeg in 1979 and again in 1980. A combative parliamentarian, tough-minded administrator and assiduous constituency politician, Axworthy was the sole elected Cabinet minister from the West in PM P.E. TRUDEAU's last government and served as minister of employment and immigration 1980-83, and minister of transport, 1983-84. He was the only Prairie Liberal to win a parliamentary seat in the 1984 election. In Opposition he was a prominent critic of FREE TRADE and defence policy. NORMAN HILLMER

Axworthy, Thomas Sidney, politician (b at Winnipeg 23 May 1947), the younger brother of Lloyd AXWORTHY. He received a BA (Hons) at U of Winnipeg, and an MA and PhD from Queen's (1979). He joined the LIBERAL PARTY in the early

1960s, and in 1967 he undertook research for, and was strongly influenced by, Walter Gordon's nationalist Task Force on the Structure of Canadian Industry. He joined the PRIME MINISTER'S OFFICE in 1975, actively participating in its politicization under Principal Secretary Jim COUTTS. Axworthy's primary responsibility was for the western provinces and, subsequently, national economic policy. In 1980 he became principal secretary and primary speech writer for PM Pierre Trudeau, and a major strategist for the NATIONAL ENERGY PROGRAM and constitutional patriation. Following the retirement of Trudeau, Axworthy was invited to join the Kennedy School of Government at Harvard and, since mid-1986, has been vice-president of the CRB Foundation (Montréal). As a writer for the Toronto *Star*, as a media commentator and as a well-connected party tactician, his career represents the nationalist, progressive elements in the federal Liberal Party. JAMES LIGHTBODY

Aylmer, Qué, City, pop 28 976 (1986c), 26 695 (1981c), inc 1975, is located on Lac Deschênes in the OTTAWA R, 10 km SW of HULL. Created through a legislative merger of Aylmer (inc 1847 and named to honour Lord Aylmer, governor general of BNA), Lucerne (1965, formerly Hull-Ouest, which dated from 1878) and Deschênes (1920), this suburban municipality is spread over a large territory and is a golfer's paradise (6 golf courses) and the home of the Connaught Race Track. Its oldest built-up area, the original town of Aylmer, was the administrative centre of Hull Township for most of the 19th century. Aylmer is the most bicultural city of the National Capital Region: 59.3% of its citizens have French as their mother tongue, 36.9% English (1981c).

PIERRE LOUIS LAPOINTE

Aylmer, Matthew Whitworth-Aylmer, 5th Baron, colonial administrator (b 24 May 1775; d at London, Eng 23 Feb 1850). After a distinguished military career he was appointed governor general of British N America in 1830, taking office 4 Feb 1831. Despite his efforts to pacify the francophone majority, the Assembly of Lower Canada became increasingly radical and in 1834 passed the 92 Resolutions of grievance, one of them demanding his recall. Embittered, he inclined to the anglophone minority and thus exacerbated ethnic divisions. Blamed for the failure of conciliation, he was dismissed in 1835. Without doubt he was politically inept but much criticism of him was unfair. He cannot be held responsible for the crisis in Lower Canada that led to the REBELLIONS OF 1837. P.A. BUCKNER

Babiche is made from rawhide and has multiple uses. Hide is denuded of hair through a soaking process, stretched until dried, and cut into long narrow strips. Named by the early French traders, these thongs were used for fishing and harpoon lines, lacing for SNOWSHOES, bowstrings, gill nets, tumplines and headbands, rackets and drumheads. Bags of fine workmanship were knit of babiche. Braided babiche was used in making halters and carrying straps. The hides of land and aquatic animals were made into babiche and varied, according to animal, in thinness, colour and strength.   RENÉ R. GADACZ

Baby, François, businessman, militia officer, politician (b at Montréal 4 Oct 1733; d at Québec City 6 Oct 1820). A fur trader from Montréal during the 1750s, Baby was taken prisoner to England in 1760. He returned from France in 1763 to set up as a merchant at Québec. In 1773-74 he travelled to London as an influential defender of the constitutional proposals of Governor CARLETON (Dorchester), eventually adopted as the QUEBEC ACT. His resistance to the American invasion of 1775-76 and his political conduct thereafter earned him appointment to the legislative council in 1778, and he lived the rest of his life on revenues from landed property, life annuities and government salaries. Baby backed Governor HALDIMAND'S opposition to the colonial merchants' demands for an elective assembly, and later opposed attempts by the PARTI CANADIEN to extend the assembly's authority over colonial finances. A bright light in Québec's worldly high society, Baby was nevertheless a devout Roman Catholic, whose conduct secured him the admiration of the censorious Bishop PLESSIS.
                           JAMES H. LAMBERT

Baby, James (bap Jacques), officeholder, politician, militia officer (b at Detroit, Mich 25 Aug 1763; d at York [Toronto] 19 Feb 1833). Son of wealthy Detroit merchant Jacques Baby, *dit* Dupéront, he was an obvious choice when Lord Dorchester recommended adding "one or two Canadians" from Detroit to the lists of executive and legislative councillors for the proposed province of Upper Canada. Appointed to both councils in 1792, he sat for life. Described by John Graves SIMCOE as a "French Gentleman of indisputable loyalty," Baby was regarded as the perfect liaison with the French-speaking, Roman Catholic community in the western extremity of the province. He held a plurality of offices during his lifetime, the most important being inspector general. On his appointment in 1816 he moved to York. Assiduous in his attention to duty, he was of limited abilities. "A man of most Gentlemanly manners tho' rather slow of apprehension" was how John STRACHAN put it. Although not a cipher, Baby was susceptible to Strachan's bullying on important issues. On one famous occasion, noted by William Lyon MACKENZIE, the affable and gentle Baby was reduced to tears by Strachan's tactics.   ROBERT L. FRASER

Baby Boom, a period of increased birthrates lasting from the early 1950s to about 1965. The GREAT DEPRESSION of the 1930s had prolonged the decline in Canada's birthrate (*see* POPULATION) as it had in most Western countries. The low point in Canada was reached in 1937, when the gross birthrate (the annual number of live births per 1000 inhabitants) was 20.1. Improved economic conditions caused a recovery that accelerated during WWII. By 1945 the birthrate had risen to 24.3 per 1000 inhabitants; by 1946 it had jumped to 27.2 per 1000 inhabitants, and it remained between 27 and 28.5 per 1000 until 1959, after which time it gradually fell. The baby boom began (1950-52) with the births of children who had been postponed during

the Depression, but 2 other factors affected it as well. First, a larger proportion of adults married, and those who did had more children. Taking married and single women together, those born in 1911 and 1912 had an average of 2.9 children, whereas those born between 1929 and 1933 had an average of 3.3. This is called "completed fertility." These 2 generations are separated by 20 years and, between the older and the younger, the number of children per woman increased by 0.4 (13%). Second, more than 50% of baby-boom births can be attributed to what demographers call "timing phenomena." More young adults married at a younger age (the median age for a woman's first marriage was 23.2 years in 1940 and 21.1 years in 1965), and between the end of the war and 1965, young couples tended to have their children during the first few years of married life.

Between 1940 and 1965 the number of births in Canada rose from 253 000 in 1940 to 479 000 in 1960 but dropped to 419 000 in 1965. Over a period of 25 years, the baby boom produced 1.57 million more births than would otherwise have occurred (about 8.65 million), an increase of more than 18%. By 1965, however, people were marrying at a later age and were waiting longer to have children, partly because more women were entering the work force and partly because there was general access to better contraceptive measures.
                          JACQUES HENRIPIN

Long Term Effects The end of the baby boom is generally taken to be 1965 as this was the last year with a birth total of more than 400 000. In 1973 the number of births declined to 343 000, a crude birthrate of 15.5. The birthrate has fluctuated slightly since and has occasionally dipped below 15, a situation that has been referred to as the "baby bust."

The effects of the baby boom on Canadian society have been, and will continue to be, significant. As the baby boomers age, they affect the forces of supply and demand. Their requirements for primary, secondary and university education and for employment have already created economic and social pressures. Although their fertility rate is lower than at any time in Canadian history, their sheer numbers have helped to keep the birth totals steady, a phenomenon which has been referred to as the baby boom echo. Their anticipated demand for health care and pension benefits is expected to place a great strain on government resources in the future.

In 1986 the median age of Canada's population reached an historic high of 31.6 years. Unless significant increases in the birthrate occur, by the year 2016 the median age of Canadians will be 40. When the youngest baby boomers reach age 65 in 2031, all the baby boomers will make up almost a quarter of the consumers, as against 10% in 1986, while the producers in society, aged 20-

64, will amount to 58%. In other words, by 2031 there will be 2 producers per 1 old-age consumer, as against 6 producers to the consumer in the 1980s.   KAROL J. KROTKI

Back, Frederic, film-animation artist, graphic designer, teacher (b at Sarrebruick, Territoire de la Sarre, France 8 Apr 1924). Internationally acclaimed for his many animated films for children produced by the French-language division of the CBC, he attended the École des beaux-arts in Rennes, France, and immigrated to Canada in 1948. Hired by the CBC, Montréal, in 1952, he designed graphics and models for various TV series. He was encouraged to develop his animation skills and in 1970 proceeded to create several short, animated films, primarily for young children, usually with a message associated with ecology or conservation or Québec nationalism. He won the Academy Award for *Crac* in 1982. In 1987 he completed *L'Homme qui plantait les arbres,* a 30-minute film.   JOHN L. KENNEDY

Back, Sir George, arctic explorer, naval officer, artist (b at Stockport, Eng 6 Nov 1796; d at London, Eng 23 June 1878). Back made his first voyage N in 1818 and thereafter spent much of his life exploring the Arctic. He was stationed in Halifax in 1814 and accompanied Lt John FRANKLIN to the Coppermine R in 1819. His heroism in saving comrades' lives during this expedition is recorded. He joined Franklin in 1824 and accompanied him overland to Great Bear Lk and the Arctic coast in 1825. On a search mission for John ROSS in 1834, Back found and travelled the Thlew-eechoh R, later named for him. Though his final expedition (1836) was aborted because of severe ice conditions, Back's lifetime accomplishment was honoured with the medal of the Royal Geographical Society and a knighthood (1839).

Back is said to have learned watercolour techniques while a prisoner of war in France (1809-14), and he was the most important Arctic topographer of his day. Using a camera lucida, he sketched forest fires, rapids, rock formations, campsites and native life along the routes. Records of the second Franklin expedition and Back's overland expedition up the Thlew-eechoh R are preserved in the National Archives of Canada.   JAMES MARSH

Back River, 974 km long, rises in Contwoyto Lk, N of GREAT SLAVE LK, NWT, and flows NE across the Barren Lands to Chantrey Inlet, S of King William I. It has a drainage area of 107 000 km² and a mean discharge of 612 m³/sec. The river is turbulent in its upper course, but as it enters a broad plain, it widens to form Lks Pelly, Garry and MacDougall. On its final leg it narrows to cut through another rocky section to the coast. The river is named for Sir George BACK, who first explored the river 1833-35. The original name was *Thlew-eechoh*, likely Inuktituk for "great fish river." He named the lakes after Sir John Henry Pelly and

View of the Arctic Ocean from the mouth of the Coppermine R at midnight, 20 July 1821, by Sir George Back; aquatint (*courtesy National Archives of Canada/C-41288*).

Nicholas Garry, governor and deputy governor of the HBC, and his friend Lt-Col MacDougall of the 79th Highlanders. JAMES MARSH

Backwoods of Canada: Being Letters From the Wife of an Emigrant Officer, Illustrative of the Domestic Economy of British America, The,

by Catharine Parr TRAILL, was published 1836 in London. Traill's letters to her mother in England provide a perennially optimistic account of her day-to-day life in the "backwoods" of UPPER CANADA. The letters describe her month-long voyage to Canada with her husband, and their travels to the "interior" to settle near Peterborough, where Traill lived for over 60 years. The letters, particularly vivid in natural description, give us both a portrait of a persevering, buoyant and resourceful woman adapting to a new life and place, and an encyclopedic cataloguing of the details of her new surroundings. Whether describing Indians, Americans, wildlife, natural scenery, illnesses or Canadian customs, or providing recipes for soft soap, candles, vinegar or pickles, Traill's letters brim with vigour and with her evident pleasure at discovering the nature of her adopted homeland. *Backwoods* was translated into French (Paris, 1843). A selected English edition, edited by Clara Thomas, appeared in Toronto in 1966. NEIL BESNER

Bacteria, microscopic, prokaryotic [Gk, "before nucleus"] cells, capable of rapid growth. As monerans, they are characterized by nucleoplasm (central part of cell, containing genetic material) not bounded by a membrane; small ribosomes (particles active in protein synthesis) uniformly distributed throughout the cell; and the absence of membrane-bounded organelles. Many bacteria exist as single cells of spherical (coccus), rodlike (bacillus) or spiral (spirillum) form. They range in size from 0.01 μm^3, the size of large viruses, to 50 μm^3, the size of some eukaryotic cells (ie, cells having a membrane-bound nucleus). Some bacteria move through the action of flagella (whiplike structures), bundles of flagella or via a gliding action. Growth commonly occurs by binary fission, which yields 2 cells if separation is complete, or filaments if cell separation does not take place. A few bacteria reproduce by budding or by formation of conidia (asexual spores). Aerobic bacilli and anaerobic clostridia form endospores (thick-walled reproductive structures) resistant to heat, drying and disinfectants and capable, under certain conditions, of germinating to produce vegetative cells.

Aerobic (oxygen-dependent) bacteria possess energy-yielding systems based on aerobic oxidation of organic matter, such as occurs in higher life forms. In aerobic oxidation, bacteria using free or atmospheric oxygen convert organic matter into carbon dioxide and water and release energy for growth and reproduction. Some aerobic bacteria are capable of oxidizing sulphur, hydrogen and nitrogen, processes which are unique to bacteria. Because they release oxygen in photosynthesis, certain photosynthetic prokaryotes (ie, BLUE-GREEN ALGAE) are thought to have been responsible for the presence of oxygen in the atmosphere. Anaerobic bacteria grow only in the absence of free oxygen, carrying out fermentative processes, anaerobic photosynthesis and anaerobic respiration for the maintenance of life processes. A third form, facultative bacteria, can grow aerobically or anaerobically, depending on nutritional and environmental conditions. Carbon for cell growth may be obtained from organic matter or carbon dioxide. Because of these diverse physiological processes, bacteria are found everywhere in our environment and in places where higher life forms cannot exist. For example, certain bacteria are found in acid soils and waters; others, in sa-

line environments, high-pressure systems like deep ocean waters, cold arctic waters and soils, thermal hot pools, or anaerobic environments such as swamps, aquatic sediments and the rumen (first stomach) of animals.

Useful Properties Bacteria are involved in cycling elements such as carbon, nitrogen, phosphorus and sulphur, all of which are essential for maintenance of life. In the carbon cycle, carbon dioxide is fixed into organic matter by PLANTS and ALGAE which can be consumed by animals. For photosynthesis to continue, excretory products and plant and ANIMAL remains must be decomposed to release carbon dioxide. Aerobic and anaerobic bacteria play key roles in this mineralization process. Bacteria are the biological agents responsible for recycling nutrients found in man's domestic, agricultural and industrial wastes. Methane gas, an important ENERGY source with domestic and industrial applications, is a byproduct of these processes. Some bacteria are capable of fixing nitrogen while free-living; others require an association with a plant (symbiotic nitrogen fixation). The latter process is widely distributed in LEGUMES and such bacteria are commercially produced and seeded with the legume to enhance the association. Bacteria capable of producing sulphuric acid have been used in MINING copper and uranium; those capable of growing on hydrocarbons are involved in cleaning oil spills. In the FOOD INDUSTRY, bacteria are used in production of cheeses, yogurt, vinegar and flavour-enhancing compounds (eg, glutamic acid, nucleotides). The amino acids methionine and lysine are produced from bacteria and are added to cereals and rice to improve nutritional value. Bacteria are used to produce medically important compounds like vaccines, vitamin B_{12}, antibiotics (eg, polymyxin and bacitracin) and steroids. GENETIC ENGINEERING techniques have made it possible to use the fast-growing *Escherichia coli* for production of insulin, interferon and related eukaryotic materials, not normally produced by bacterial cells. The enzymes used in the cleaning industry and in detergents, and those used in hydrolysis of starch, can also be obtained from bacterial sources. The anaerobic clostridia have been used in the production of industrially important solvents. Bacteria capable of specifically infecting caterpillar larvae have been used for biological control of insect infestations (*see* INSECT PESTS).

Harmful Properties Bacteria are involved in deterioration of building materials, in spoilage of food and in dental caries. Approximately 10% of known species are capable of causing plant or animal DISEASES. Bacterial colonization and production of acids accelerate corrosion of metals and disintegration of concrete. Hundreds of millions of dollars are spent annually on biocides in an attempt to control such activities. Large losses in productivity occur because of bacterial wilt of cultivated plants; other bacteria cause soft rot of vegetables. The 19th-century studies of bacterial diseases associated with humans (eg, typhoid fever, cholera, diphtheria, tuberculosis and plague) led to many cultural techniques used in modern bacteriology. Some bacterial diseases (eg, FOOD POISONING, dysentery) are contracted by ingestion of food or water contaminated by toxins or fecal bacteria. Other bacteria cause venereal diseases (*see* SEXUALLY TRANSMITTED DISEASE) and are transmitted by direct contact; still other bacterial diseases, such as bubonic plague, require animal vectors (eg, rats and fleas). The pasteurization process and improvements in sanitary procedures used in handling water and food supplies and in disposal of human wastes have significantly decreased incidence of bacteria-associated diseases. More virulent bacterial infections have been

brought under control by intensive vaccination programs and by the use of antibiotics. *See also* MICROBIOLOGY. D.W.S. WESTLAKE

Reading: T.D. Brock et al, *Biology of Micro-Organisms* (1984).

Baddeck, NS, UP, pop 995 (1986c), 972 (1981c), is located on the N shore of BRAS D'OR LK, 77 km W of SYDNEY. It is the beginning and end of the Cabot Trail, and was the summer home of inventor Alexander Graham BELL, as well as the site of the first airplane flight in the British Empire (1909). The flight of the SILVER DART and many of Bell's inventions are brought to life in the Alexander Graham Bell Museum. The early settlers of the area were LOYALISTS, although the first land grant was to an English settler in 1819. Nineteenth-century Baddeck supplied the surrounding areas with manufactured goods. There were also gold and gypsum mines, gristmills and a major shipbuilding industry. Modern Baddeck relies heavily on its reputation as a vacation haven. The museum, beautiful scenery and sailing are major attractions. HEATHER MACDONALD

Badger The American badger (*Taxidea taxus*) is the only N American WEASEL specialized for burrowing and capturing prey underground. The body is squat; legs, short and heavily muscled; feet, large with long, heavy claws. Adult males may reach 11.4 kg in weight and 80 cm in length. The head is small, triangular and flattened, with prominent snout and ears. The long, coarse pelage on the body is silvery yellowish, underparts are paler and feet are black. The head is brown with white crescents on the face. A narrow white stripe runs from muzzle to shoulders. Badgers inhabit grassland and open woodland of the southern Prairie provinces and BC, extending southward through the prairies and semideserts of the US and northern Mexico. The badger is primarily nocturnal, resting by day in extensive burrows, usually alone or, if a female, with kits. Food is mostly burrowing rodents. Mating occurs July-Aug. Litters (1-4 young) are born Mar-Apr. Young are independent in 2-3 months and mature early; females may breed at 5 months, males usually not until 7 months. Both sexes hibernate. Overhunting and predator control have reduced the badger to the verge of extinction in Canada. *See also* ENDANGERED ANIMALS.

IAN MCTAGGART-COWAN

Badger (*Taxidea taxus*), squat, muscular weasel specialized for burrowing and capturing prey underground (*photo by Tim Fitzharris*).

Badlands Barren, scoured and eroded by water and etched by weathering and wind-driven sand and rain, badlands are dramatic landforms that develop an intricate network of deeply incised, narrow, winding gullies and occasional fantastically shaped HOODOO ROCKS. Steep, often precipitous and densely rilled slopes, almost devoid of vegetation, are striking evidence of the forces of EROSION. To European settlers, such areas were

Typical badland landscape, in Dinosaur Provincial Park, SE Alberta (*courtesy Provincial Museum of Alberta*).

clearly worthless. Perhaps the term badlands derived from the French *terres* ("lands") *mauvaises* ("bad"), as the French were among the earliest explorers in the interior of western N America. Areas of badlands occur at scattered locations throughout the prairies of western Canada where they stand in stark contrast to the gently rolling landscape of the plains. Badlands are particularly prevalent along the river valleys of southern Alberta, especially along the Red Deer R, where they flank the river for 300 km and culminate in their most impressive display in DINOSAUR PROVINCIAL PARK, where they are associated with the world-famous dinosaur fossils. Badlands form where weak, relatively unconsolidated SEDIMENTARY ROCKS, such as shale, siltstone and poorly cemented sandstone, are exposed to vigorous erosion processes. They tend to occur in arid or semiarid regions such as southern Alberta where rain often falls in short, torrential convectional storms. Rapid runoff on the barren, relatively impermeable, clay-rich rocks quickly cuts rills and gullies, producing rates of erosion of several mm a year. Surface erosion is often accompanied by extensive fracture-controlled subsurface piping or tunnel erosion which frequently leads to the formation of sinkholes and slope failure. Many of the badlands areas of Alberta were initially formed as a result of rapid channel downcutting by glacial meltwater during the retreat of the Wisconsin ice sheet about 14 000 years ago. The steep valley walls, cut into the soft Upper Cretaceous rocks that dominate the geology of southern Alberta, were ideal for the development of badlands.   I.A. CAMPBELL

Badminton is a game played on a rectangular court divided into equal halves by a 5-ft-high (1.5 m) net by 2 players (or 4 players in doubles) whose object is to hit the shuttlecock ("shuttle") with their racquets so that it touches the opponent's side of the court. Very light racquets are used to hit the specially designed shuttlecock with great speed or skilful deception. Top-class play demands a wide range of motor skills, excellent eye-hand co-ordination and superb physical fitness. It is likely that badminton originated about 2000 years ago in China and Siam. Some sources say it was British army officers serving in Poona, India, who adopted the ancient game, possibly bringing it home when on leave during the 1860s. It may have first been played in England at the duke of Beaufort's

country estate, called Badminton House. The game was adopted at several English seaside resorts, and soon after in the London suburbs. The Badminton Assn of England was founded in 1893 and wrote the laws of the game, which have changed very little since.

Military personnel introduced badminton to Vancouver, BC, in the late 1890s. It was slow to spread to other regions, though there is evidence of it being played in Ottawa in 1900 and the first Canadian club was founded in Montréal in 1907. The first open tournament was the BC Championships (1913-14 season). After WWI, the Canadian Badminton Assn (CBA) was founded (1921-22) and the first Canadian Championships were held in Montréal (1922). The tournament was only for Canadians at first, but was opened to the world in 1957, and is now regarded as a major international tournament. The greatest initial stimulation to the game in Canada came in the fall of 1925 when a British team toured the country and provided the impetus to erect specially built halls in many cities. Five years later a similar tour was arranged; both British teams were captained by Sir George Thomas, who donated the Thomas Cup to the International Badminton Federation (IBF) in 1939. During the 1930 tour Jack PURCELL of Guelph, Ont, defeated the 4 best British players and, in 1933, he was world professional champion. Dorothy WALTON dominated Canadian women's play in the 1930s and won the All-England women's singles title in 1939. Canada has been active and successful in the badminton tournaments played at the Commonwealth Games. Jamie Paulson (Calgary) won the gold medal at the 1970 Edinburgh Games and the silver 4 years later in Christchurch, NZ, while Canadians won 2 silver and 2 bronze medals at the 1978 Edmonton games. At the 1982 Commonwealth Games in Brisbane, Canada won the silver medal for the team event and the gold in ladies doubles. Four years later at the games in Edinburgh, Canada won silver medals in the team event and ladies doubles.

There are 30 facilities in Canada built for badminton (1987), though most play occurs in school gymnasia, church halls or community centres. It is estimated that some 1.5 to 2 million Canadians play badminton recreationally. Of these, 60 000 are registered members of the CBA, which continues to promote recreational and elite badminton for the benefit of all interested people.

JOHN J. JACKSON

Reading: Canadian Badminton Association Handbook; Badminton Canada.

Baer, Erich, chemist, educator (b at Berlin, Ger 8 Mar 1901; d at Toronto 23 Sept 1975). He studied at U Berlin under Hermann O.L. Fischer with whom he worked until 1948 (from 1937 at U of T). Baer became a professor in 1951 and professor emeritus in 1969. His work dealt with the synthesis of substances based on glycerol. One of such compounds became known as the Fischer-Baer ester, which plays a central role in the metabolism of carbohydrates. To arrange atoms in molecules in the right order and have them assume the proper configuration in 3-dimensional space, Baer made use of the configuration already available in natural sugar alcohols in a simple and most elegant way. The glycerol derivatives thus obtained were the starting materials for the synthesis of a series of phospholipids, fatlike substances containing a substituted phosphate group. These are essential structural elements of the cell membrane of all living organisms. Baer published well over 100 scientific papers and received many honours and awards. His legacy includes a generation of well-trained scientists.   LEON J. RUBIN

Baffin, William, explorer (b probably at London? 1584?; d 1622). One of the most proficient navigators of his time, he was chief pilot with Capt James Hall on his ill-fated voyage to Greenland in 1612. He was pilot on 2 expeditions to the Spitsbergen region in 1613 and 1614 and made his next voyage under Robert BYLOT aboard the DISCOVERY in 1615 in search of the NORTHWEST PASSAGE. They examined the entrance to Hudson Str, and turned back, because of ice conditions, in sight of land later named Baffin I by W.E. PARRY. On this voyage Baffin obtained the first longitude ever figured at sea by observing an occultation of a star by the moon. Bylot and Baffin undertook another expedition to the Northwest, departing Mar 1616. They sailed north to 77° 45' – the farthest north reached for the next 236 years — mapped Baffin Bay and discovered LANCASTER SOUND, not recognizing it as the entrance to the Northwest Passage. Baffin was killed in action against the Portuguese in the Gulf of Oman. He had been asked to make observations on the castle walls but "received a shot from the Castle into his belly, wherewith he gave three leaps, and died immediately." Baffin was the most skilled navigator who observed Canada's Arctic in the 17th century, although his great discovery of Lancaster Sound was soon forgotten.   JAMES MARSH

Baffin Bay, 689 000 km^2, is a deep body of water located between Greenland and BAFFIN I. Water depths are generally less than 1000 m, but reach a maximum 2400 m near its centre. The bay is connected to the Arctic Ocean in the N through Nares Str, Jones and LANCASTER sounds, and to the LABRADOR SEA in the S by DAVIS STR. Discovered by Robert Bylot in 1616, the bay was named after his chief pilot, William BAFFIN. Circulation is generally anticlockwise; off Greenland, relatively warm, salty water moves N, while along Baffin I, cold,

A dory from CSS *Hudson* passes in front of an iceberg in Baffin Bay (*courtesy Dept of Fisheries and Oceans/Bedford Institute of Oceanography/photo by Roger Bélanger*).

fresher water originating from the Arctic Ocean flows S. Icebergs, formed by calving off the Greenland glaciers, appear year-round, but are most numerous in Aug. Extensive coverage by pack ice occurs seasonally Nov to July. In the N there is a recurring polynya, or area of open water ("north water"), the reason for which is still unknown. Fishing began in the bay as early as 1650 and by 1900 intensive fishing by Europeans and Americans had depleted the bay's large whale population. Exploitation of other mammals (seals, walrus) as well as fish (cod, halibut, haddock, herring) has been very minimal.

ALLYN CLARKE AND KEN DRINKWATER

Baffin Island, NWT, 507 451 km², 1500 km long and 200-700 km wide, is the largest island in Canada and the fifth-largest island in the world. Located in the ARCTIC ARCHIPELAGO, it is separated from Greenland by DAVIS STRAIT and BAFFIN BAY, from Northern Québec by HUDSON STRAIT, and from the Melville Pen by Foxe Basin and the narrow Fury and Hecla Str. The island's immensity and bewildering coastline confused early explorers and concealed its geography until recent times. It was likely here that one of the great ice sheets that covered most of Canada originated some 18 000 years ago, and ice lingered on the island until almost 1500 years ago; vast areas are still sheathed in ice year-round. Geologically, Baffin I is a continuation of the eastern edge of the Canadian SHIELD, which tilts upward in the E to form a mountainous spine, sloping away into plateaus and lowlands in the W. A desolate plateau in the N comprises Brodeur and Borden peninsulas, separated by Admiralty Inlet — thought to be the world's largest FJORD. From S of the Hantzsch R to Foxe Pen is the remarkable Great Plain of the Koukdjuak, consisting of a coastal strip of flat, grassy marshland and a slightly higher plain showing a series of old beaches. The Foxe Pen is rocky in the S and drops over dramatic bluffs to the sea on the W coast. There are numerous freshwater lakes on the island, including NETTILLING (5543 km²) and AMADJUAK (3116 km²). Baffin Bay is the wintering ground for narwhal, walrus, beluga, bowhead whales and bearded and harp seals. The island is the nesting ground for millions of birds: thick-billed murres, kittiwakes and fulmars. A sanctuary at Cape Dorset protects eiders, guillemots, gulls, buntings, water pipits and redpolls.

The Dorset people likely settled around Cumberland Pen about 1500 years ago. In the 12th and 13th centuries the THULE spread over the island (*see* BAFFIN ISLAND INUIT). It was probably visited by NORSE seafarers in the 10th and 11th centuries, and is likely the Helluland of the Viking sagas. Martin FROBISHER reached the island in 1576 and made 2 more voyages (1577 and 1578), carting back loads of worthless ore he thought was gold. John DAVIS led 3 expeditions to the area (1585, 1586, 1587), each taking him to Cumberland Sound; William BAFFIN, for whom the island is named, charted the E coast 1616; and Luke FOX penetrated Foxe Channel 1631. But the island's bays and fjords continued to perplex navigators seeking a NORTHWEST PASSAGE, and Baffin Bay was not rediscovered until 1818. W.E. PARRY explored the W coast 1821-23, followed by Scottish and New England whalers, who established shore stations around Cumberland Sound. Sailors' graves and relics of the WHALING, which lasted until the early 20th century, have been uncovered at Kivitoo on the Davis Coast. German scientists built a meteorological station on Cumberland Sound 1882-83. Franz BOAS wintered at Kekertuk 1884 and was able to sketch a reasonably accurate map of the whole island. J.E. BERNIER wintered at Pond Inlet (1906-07) and Arctic Bay (1910-11), and

from the latter base J.E. Lavoie traced the coastline from Admiralty Inlet to Fury and Hecla Str. The whaling stations at Kekerton and Blackhead I were the first European settlements. The Anglican Church set up missions at the stations and the HBC established its first post on the island at Lake Harbour (1911). Today the largest settlement is IQALUIT [Frobisher Bay] (pop 2947, 1986c). Significant quantities of lead, zinc and silver are mined at Nanisivik and shipped to smelters in southern Canada. The hamlet of Pangnirtung is the southern gateway to AUYUITTUQ NATIONAL PARK (21 500 km²), Canada's first national park N of the Arctic Circle. The park contains some of the island's most spectacular scenery, including Pangnirtung Pass – a 100 km U-shaped trench – glaciers, lakes, waterfalls and the 2200 m peak, Mt Odin.

JAMES MARSH

Baffin Island Inuit occupy BAFFIN I, the largest island in the ARCTIC ARCHIPELAGO, and they display considerable regional diversity in both dialect and culture. Those in the extreme N belong to the IGLULIK INUIT, who also live on the mainland. The remaining groups, often lumped together and referred to as the Inuit of S Baffin Island, are concentrated along the rugged E coast, including Cumberland Sound and Frobisher Bay, and along the N shore of Hudson Strait. The latter share many cultural traits with the LABRADOR INUIT on the other side of Hudson Strait, which was frequently crossed for trading purposes. The Inuit of Baffin I became known to the outside world as early as 1576, when Martin FROBISHER traded with the Inuit and kidnapped one of them in the bay which now bears his name; more conflict ensued on his 1577 expedition. Throughout the 18th and early 19th centuries Inuit along the S coast had occasional trade contacts with European exploration and supply vessels that stopped briefly on their way through to Hudson Bay. Farther N, the Inuit of Davis Strait did not encounter outsiders in any numbers until after 1820, when Scottish and American whalers started making annual visits to Baffin I through the heavy drift ice of western Baffin Bay. Inuit material culture was greatly modified by the increased flow of trade goods, including firearms, and by the large supply of wood provided by frequent shipwrecks. Contact with Europeans increased during the late 19th century when whalers started to establish permanent shore stations. Although the Inuit may have welcomed regular trade and occasional employment,

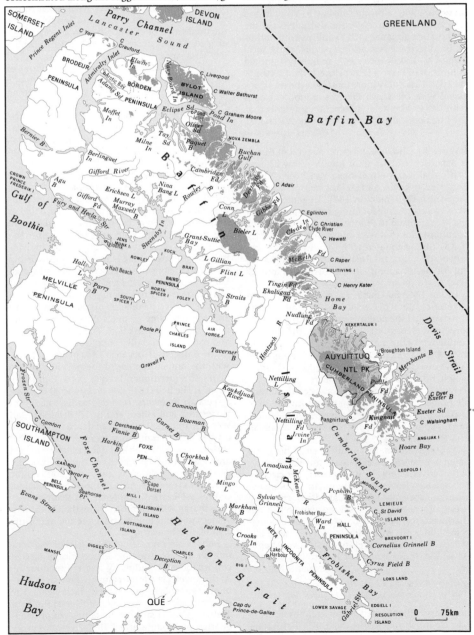

it is thought that their population declined rapidly because of dietary changes and exposure to European diseases.

After the decline of commercial whaling in the early 20th century, the Inuit of Baffin I turned increasingly to fox trapping in order to satisfy their dependence on European manufacturers. Since the 1950s the Inuit have become much more sedentary, moving into modern communities such as IQALUIT [Frobisher Bay], the transportation hub and largest settlement on the island. One of the best-known communities on Baffin Island is CAPE DORSET, now recognized around the world for the outstanding soapstone carvings, prints and drawings of its Inuit artists. *See also* NATIVE PEOPLE: ARCTIC.   J. GARTH TAYLOR

Reading: Peter Pitseolak and Dorothy Eber, *People From Our Side: An Inuit Record of Seekooseelak* (1975).

Baggattaway, *see* LACROSSE.

Bagnall, James, printer, publisher, politician, officeholder (b at Shelburne, NS 1783; d at Bedeque, PEI 20 June 1855). The son of New York LOYALISTS, he moved with his parents to Charlottetown as an infant. Despite limited formal education, he published several early newspapers in PEI and NS between 1805 and 1828 after apprenticing with a brother-in-law in Virginia and the District of Columbia. He also published the Island's first almanac (1815) and, as king's printer, produced the first printed *Journal* of the local assembly (1805) since 1797, and the first printed volume of PEI laws (1817) since 1789. Elected to the Island assembly more than once, he was associated with the Loyal Electors, a group at odds with the local elite and sometimes described as the first political society in what is now Canada.

IAN ROSS ROBERTSON

Bagot, Sir Charles, governor general of British N America 1841-43 (b at Ruguley, Eng 23 Sept 1781; d at Kingston, Canada W 19 May 1843). Educated at Rugby and Oxford, he was elected to the British Parliament in 1807. He served as undersecretary of state for foreign affairs and successively as minister to France and to the US, as well as ambassador to Russia and to The Netherlands. In 1817 he negotiated with the American secretary of state, Richard Rush, an agreement providing for disarmament on the Great Lks and Lk Champlain (RUSH-BAGOT AGREEMENT).

In Jan 1842 Sir Charles arrived in Kingston as governor general of Canada. By September it was apparent that the administration of his predecessor, Lord SYDENHAM, was about to lose the confidence of the majority in the assembly. Bagot invited the French Canadian leader, Louis-Hippolyte LAFONTAINE, to join the Executive Council, which he did along with Robert BALDWIN. Although Bagot had not fully conceded the principle of RESPONSIBLE GOVERNMENT, his invitation to LaFontaine was not fully approved in London, and his policy was repudiated by his successor, Sir Charles METCALFE.

Although for many months before his death Bagot was bedridden and unable to play an active part in government, he was severely criticized by Tory leaders. However, his popularity among Reformers, especially French Canadians, remained strong. It was aided by his fluency in French, his charm as a speaker and his great gift for diplomacy in politics. His wife, Lady Mary Wellesley-Pole, a niece of the duke of Wellington, was very popular in the social circles of Kingston and Québec.   JACQUES MONET, S.J.

Reading: J.M.S. Careless, *The Union of the Canadas* (1967); Jacques Monet, *The Last Cannon Shot* (1969).

Bagshaw, Elizabeth Catherine, physician (b near Cannington, Ont 18 Oct 1881; d at Hamilton, Ont 5 Jan 1982). She had a successful 60-year medical practice after graduating from U of T (MB) in 1905, but is best known for her 30 years as medical director of the Hamilton Birth Control Clinic. Cheerful and courageous, she accepted the post in 1932 despite opposition from medical colleagues and local clergy, and worked with dedicated volunteers to provide Hamilton women with inexpensive and reliable contraceptives. Bagshaw received numerous honours throughout her long life, including an honorary doctorate from McMaster.   DIANNE DODD

Baha'i Faith, a world religion with followers in 340 countries and territories, and with 148 National Spiritual Assemblies. The 1981 census (the most recent data available) showed 7955 Baha'is in Canada. Although its forerunner, the Babi movement, had its roots in Shi'ah (ISLAM) Iran, the Baha'i faith is independent rather than a sect of another religion, and derives its inspiration from its own sacred scriptures. These consist primarily of the writings of the founder, Baha'u'llah (1817-92), who Baha'is believe is the Messenger of God to our age, the most recent in a line stretching back beyond recorded time and including Abraham, Moses, Buddha, Christ and Muhammad. The central teaching of Baha'u'llah is that mankind is one human race, and that the age for the unification of this race in a global society has arrived. Among the principles of justice on which it is based are equality of the sexes, the right of all people to education, the abolition of all forms of prejudice and the need for the establishment of a world government with its own peacekeeping force.

Baha'is believe that all great religions of the past have been stages in the progressive revelation of what Baha'u'llah called "the changeless Faith of God." God himself is unknowable. From age to age he reveals himself through his messengers, whose lives and teachings reflect God's qualities. These successive revelations provide the chief impulse in the evolution of all civilization. Other messengers will follow Baha'u'llah so long as the universe exists, but the challenge of the next thousand years will be to realize Baha'u'llah's vision of world unity. For the individual, the purpose of life is to know and worship God. This lifelong process occurs as the individual learns to serve mankind and in the process develops his own spiritual, moral and intellectual capacities. Prayer, meditation on the creative Word and the discipline of one's physical nature are necessary aids to this effort. The soul is immortal and continues to evolve after death.

The Baha'i Faith began in 1844 in Persia [Iran], with the announcement of the new age by Baha'u'llah's forerunner, known as the Bab ("The Door"). The Bab (1819-50) and some 20 000 early Persian followers, regarded as heretics, were persecuted and killed, and in 1868 Baha'u'llah was exiled to the Turkish penal fortress of Akko, on the bay of Haifa in present-day Israel. The shrines where the Bab and Baha'u'llah lie buried are today the focal points of a vast complex of gardens and institutions. By 1987 over 2000 ethnic groups were represented in the 120 000 Baha'i centres established worldwide. At that time Baha'is in Iran who refused to recant their faith were subject to punishment under the regime of the Ayatollah Khomeini.

Baha'is have no clergy. The affairs of the community are governed by democratically elected councils locally, nationally and internationally. At the lower 2 levels the councils, known as Spiritual Assemblies, are elected each year. The supreme governing body, the Universal House of Justice, whose seat is at the faith's world headquarters on Mount Carmel, Haifa, is elected every 5 years. Because of its beliefs, the Baha'i Faith has placed great importance on co-operation with all efforts toward world unity. The body which represents it in international affairs, the Baha'i International Community, holds consultative status as one of the nongovernmental organizations at the UNITED NATIONS, and it takes an active part in many of the UN's humanitarian and educational activities.

Baha'i Faith in Canada Canada has played an unusually important role in Baha'i history. After a brief visit here in 1912 the founder's son, Abdu'l-Baha, gave US and Canadian believers joint responsibility for expansion of the Baha'i Faith around the world. Canadian Baha'is responded enthusiastically, and today their community shoulders the second-largest burden of responsibilities for international activities. Two Québec architects, Jean-Baptiste Louis Bourgeois and William Sutherland Maxwell, designed the 2 most important of the many shrines and houses of worship erected by Baha'is: the first House of Worship in the Western world, Chicago, Ill, and the Shrine of the Bab on Mt Carmel in Haifa. One of the community's members, W.S. Maxwell's daughter Mary, in 1937 married the great-grandson of the founder of the Baha'i Faith, Shoghi Effendi Rabbani, who served in the central role of Guardianship until his death in 1957.

Canadian Baha'is work in countless community-development projects undertaken by their faith around the world, and their National Assembly collaborates with the CANADIAN INTERNATIONAL DEVELOPMENT AGENCY on a range of such activities. The Canadian community pioneered the concept of an international organization for Baha'i studies to bring together scholars and students in an application of Baha'i principles to various social concerns. The Association for Baha'i Studies, fd 1977, has its headquarters in Ottawa.

The faith has attracted members from all Canadian provinces and territories and from every ethnic group and social class. Some 60 of the faith's 350 elected Local Spiritual Assemblies are on Indian reserves and others, with Inuit members, are in remote Arctic centres. The Canadian National Spiritual Assembly was the first Baha'i institution in the world to be incorporated formally by a special Act of a sovereign parliament, an example since followed in many other countries. The Baha'i National Centre is located in Thornhill, Ont, and the former Maxwell home in Montréal is maintained as a Baha'i place of PILGRIMAGE.

J. DOUGLAS MARTIN

Baie-Comeau, Qué, Town, pop 26 244 (1986c, boundaries adjusted), 12 866 (1981c), inc 1937, is located on the N shore of the St Lawrence R, at the mouth of the Rivière MANICOUAGAN, about 420 km NE of Québec City. At the start of the 20th century, the area was still a huge hunting and fishing land of the MONTAGNAIS-NASKAPI, completely isolated and without transportation routes. Its geographic advantages (deep bay, neighbouring rivers with strong flows, huge forestry resources) led Col Robert R. McCormick, publisher of the Chicago *Tribune*, to build a paper mill and create a town in 1936. It took the name of Napoléon-Alexandre Comeau, a celebrated N-shore naturalist. During the 1950s, Baie-Comeau grew rapidly: the Quebec North Shore Paper Co enlarged and renovated its paper factory, a huge aluminum company (Reynolds) came in 1958 and grain silos (Cargill Grain Co) in 1960. The economic growth of the town and region was stimulated by the 1960 construction of a 448 km highway linking N-shore towns and the 1959-79 harnessing of the hydroelectric potential of the Outardes and Manicouagan rivers. The Manic-Outardes complex built by HYDRO-QUÉBEC supplies

Québec City's electricity. The Daniel Johnson Dam (Manic 5), 210 km N of Baie-Comeau, is one of the world's largest. Baie-Comeau is also endowed with a deepwater sea port. An historical museum houses a collection of native artifacts. Baie-Comeau is the birthplace of Brian MULRONEY, prime minister of Canada.   CLAUDINE PIERRE-DESCHÊNES

Baie des Chaleurs Scandal In 1890-91, when only about 100 km of the 320 km Baie des Chaleurs Railway had been built, serious questions arose about relations between the contractors and the sponsoring governments. The railway had received subsidies from both the federal government and the Québec Liberal government, and on 4 Aug 1891 the Conservatives launched a Senate inquiry. It turned out that the Québec government had been bribed with its own railway subsidy, the money probably having been used to pay off election expenses. A royal commission was established by the province, and the dismissal of Honoré MERCIER's government followed on 16 Dec 1891.   P.B. WAITE

Baie Verte, Nfld, Town, pop 2049 (1986c), inc 1958, located on the Baie Verte Pen on the NE coast of Newfoundland. Although part of the FRENCH SHORE until 1904, the area was used by English settlers from the 1870s. A copper mine opened near the site in the 1850s, and mining and lumbering were the main occupations of the community until the mine closed in 1915. Mining again became important in 1963 when Advocate Mines Ltd began asbestos operations and shortly afterwards Consolidated Rambler began mining copper again. By the late 1970s half the labour force was employed in mining, but in the early 1980s declining prices led to work stoppages; the copper mine closed and the Advocate mine was taken over by Baie Verte Mines Inc. As a consequence of the copper mine closing, the population of the town declined by 20% during the next 5 years, although recent new mineral discoveries in the area have created optimism about the community's future. Baie Verte remains the main service centre on the peninsula.   ROBERT D. PITT

Bailey, Alfred Goldsworthy, historian, poet, man of letters (b at Québec City 18 Mar 1905). Bailey was educated at UNB, U of T and the LSE, and has led a life of scholarship and academic endeavour which took him from the New Brunswick Museum to UNB where he served, variously, as professor of history, dean of arts and vice-president, academic. He is best known for *The Conflict of European and Eastern Algonkian Cultures, 1504-1700: A Study in Canadian Civilization* (1937). Bailey's first collection of verse, *Songs of the Saguenay* (1927), was privately issued at Québec, and shows him, both in this collection and in *Tao* (1930), as a young craftsman of a traditional persuasion. In Fredericton he moved in literary circles and helped to establish the little magazine, *The Fiddlehead.* In 1952 he published, *Border River,* a collection which is more modern in tone and freer in form. His collected poetry, *Miramichi Lightning* (1981), shows the closing of the circle of Bailey's growth and development as a poet. From conservative beginnings that echoed strongly the romantic tones of late 19th-century verse, Bailey has evolved into a contemporary poet whose statement is full of the surrounding reality, whose voice is, at times, deceptively subdued but whose imagination ranges widely and wisely. In 1972 he published a collection of his essays, *Culture and Nationality,* which further confirmed his role of cultural historian. He is a Fellow of the Royal Society of Canada, and an Officer of the Order of Canada.   MICHAEL GNAROWSKI

Bailey, Loring Woart, geologist, educator (b at West Point, NY 28 Sept 1839; d at Fredericton 10 Jan 1925). Son of a professor at the US Military Academy, Bailey was educated at Harvard and Brown and knew many important scientists. At UNB he taught chemistry and natural science 1861-1900 and biology and geology 1900-07. Bailey pursued interests in geology, biology, anthropology and applied physics. In 1863 and 1864, accompanied by G.F. Matthew and C.F. Hartt, he undertook mineralogical and geological surveys of NB. They discovered the Silurian (Cambrian) age of the rock formations, not Precambrian as had been believed, and laid the foundations for elucidating the entire geological region, including New England. From 1868 Bailey contributed summer fieldwork to the Geological Survey of Canada. A RSC charter member (1882), he retired as professor in 1907; then as a member of the Biological Board he continued his earlier researches on Canadian diatoms.   SUZANNE ZELLER

Bailiff, sheriff's deputy employed for the execution of judgements (eg, seizure of judgement debtor's goods, repossession of chattels, and evictions); also, an officer of the court having custody of prisoners under arraignment. Individuals may be appointed to carry on business as bailiffs in counties where they are needed for the public convenience.   K.G. McSHANE

Baillairgé Family, architects, sculptors and painters active in Québec for 5 generations until well into the 20th century, the most prominent of whom are Jean, François, Thomas and Charles.

Baillairgé, Jean, master carpenter, sculptor, joiner, architect (bap at Blanzay, France 31 Oct 1726; d at Québec C and buried 6 Sept 1805). Brought to New France in 1741 by Bishop Pontbriand, Jean Baillairgé possessed technical competence in carpentry and joinery as well as a rudimentary grasp of French academic classicism. For 60 years he executed and occasionally designed woodwork for shops, houses, public and religious buildings. Of particular note was the interior sculpture for churches in and around Québec, especially the pulpit, churchwardens' pew and steeple (1768) and retable (1786-93, with his son) for Notre-Dame cathedral in Québec. A man "stern in matters of religion, duty and authority" but "cheerful in character," he fought in the militia of New France in 1759 and with the British garrison against the American invasion in 1775-76. He fostered a love of the building arts among his contemporaries and founded a dynasty of architects, sculptors and painters.

Baillairgé, François, sculptor, architect, painter, city treasurer (b at Québec C 21 Jan 1759; d there 15 Sept 1830). François Baillairgé surpassed his father Jean in the quality of his craftsmanship, especially ornamental sculpture. At a time when Québec was cut off from the mother country, he renewed contact with the French classical principles of the Louis XVI period. Recognizing François's talents early, Jean and the Séminaire de Québec sent him to study in Paris 1778-81 at the Académie royale de peinture et de sculpture. On his return, François produced altarpieces and retables for many parish churches as well as large religious canvases, ships' figureheads and fanciful works such as the coat of arms for the duke of Kent's carriage. Working first with his father and later with his son, François excelled in the design and execution of richly carved and classically inspired church interiors. Among the best are those at L'Islet (1782-86), St-Ambroise-de-la Jeune-Lorette (1810-16), St-Joachim at Montmorency (begun in 1816) and Baie-St-Paul (1818-28). To François can be attributed the introduction of the baldachin and the Louis XVI domed tabernacle to Québec altarpieces.

His academic training is evident in the classes he offered in painting, sculpture and mathemat-

Le Bon Pasteur, gilded and painted wood sculpture by François Baillairgé, who was one of 5 generations of the Baillairgé family active in the arts (*courtesy Musée du Québec/photo by Patrick Altman*).

ics, as well as his application of theoretical knowledge found in the architectural treatises he had purchased in France. He consciously used principles from the 1568 book by Philibert de L'Orme, that French interpreter of Italian Renaissance taste, in his solutions for the tabernacle of Notre-Dame cathedral in Québec and the façade of the Québec prison (1808-14). With his son Thomas and Abbé Jérôme DEMERS, François Baillairgé set the stage for the full flowering of Québec academic neoclassicism.

Baillairgé, Thomas, architect, sculptor, painter (b at Québec C 20 Dec 1791; d there 9 Feb 1859). Thomas drew on the architectural inheritance of his father François and grandfather Jean to bring architecture of the Québec church to its most perfect form. His practice witnessed the gradual shift from execution to design. He collaborated closely with Abbé Jérôme Demers, who attempted to set down the rules and guidelines for architectural design and practice in his *Précis d'architecture* (1828). This course outline on architecture, supplemented by Thomas's plates and carved models of the classical orders, is the first architectural treatise written in Canada.

Thomas Baillairgé synthesized his Renaissance inheritance with a blend of French and English neoclassicism to produce a series of harmonious and monumental church designs. Both the striking 3-dimensional interior at St-Joachim in Montmorency (1816-29) and the twin-towered churches exemplified by the façade design for Notre-Dame cathedral in Québec (1843), Ste-Geneviève de Pierrefonds (1844) and St-Roch-de Québec (1845) reveal his ability to capture the spirit of classicism by the rigorous integration of all design elements into a unified ensemble.

True to family tradition, he maintained a professional practice, training apprentices in architecture and sculpture and certifying their competency after 3 years' practical work, formal classes and reading in his splendid library. An affable, music-loving bachelor, he often entertained the French Canadian elite at social evenings where discussions ranged from politics to science and history. The greatest church architect of French Canada, he influenced religious architecture for almost a century.

Baillairgé, Charles, architect, civil engineer, surveyor, mathematician, inventor, writer (b at Québec C 29 Sept 1826; d there 10 May 1906). Member of the fourth generation of this architectural dynasty, he broke with the classical tradition of his forebears to become an eclectic designer well versed in the technological changes and stylistic diversity of his own era. Apprenticed to his father's cousin Thomas, Charles qualified as an architect, civil engineer and provincial land surveyor by age 22. The transition from craftsman to designer was then complete, for Charles, unlike the previous Baillairgés, did not execute his own work. An ambitious and intellectually curious individual, he quickly put aside the neoclassicism of his mentor to produce unusual and innovative buildings. Two of the earliest, a Gothic revival chapel with triple balconies for the Sisters of Charity (1850-54) and the Bilodeau shop with 8 m high Doric columns and interior floating mezzanine (1849-50), startled architecturally conservative Québec.

During the 1850s he secured important commissions including the Québec Music Hall (1851-53), U Laval (1854-57), the church at Ste-Marie-de-Beauce (1854-60) and the Québec prison (1860-63). Such was his reputation that he was called to Ottawa in 1863 to supervise the PARLIAMENT BUILDINGS and departmental buildings. His private ambition to transform his appointment as associate architect into the position of chief architect of public works was ruined by the corruption that he encountered at Ottawa. Instructed to prepare evidence against the contractors, Charles was abruptly dismissed so that his testimony could not be heard. He returned to Québec C where he replaced his father as city engineer, a post he occupied 1866-98.

An avid reader, Charles Baillairgé augmented François's and Thomas's architectural library by collecting a wide variety of books from England, France, Belgium and the US. He himself wrote extensively in both English and French on architecture, engineering, language and mathematics. His Stereometrical Tableau, a mathematical formula for measuring volumes, won him international recognition. His love of study and his mechanical bent of mind led him to invent a steam-propelled automobile at age 17, an electro-chromatic rotating fountain and an iron Eiffel Tower for London. Restless and hardworking, Charles Baillairgé designed over 180 buildings, wrote more than 250 books and articles, and fathered 20 children. His son William-Duval succeeded him as city engineer, thereby extending the family's influence on the Québec building scene to the fifth generation.

CHRISTINA CAMERON

Baillie, James Little, ornithologist, naturalist, writer (b at Toronto 4 July 1904; d there 29 May 1970). Employee of the Royal Ontario Museum for 48 years, Baillie's profession and avocation were devoted to the study and interpretation of ornithology. At his death, he was assistant curator of ornithology at the ROM. He had also been registrar, cataloguer and custodian of the museum's ornithological collections. His activities and accomplishments in his field were innumerable. He served on the Council of the American Ornithologists' Union; acted as secretary-treasurer of the Canadian Audubon Soc; was a founding member of the Toronto Ornithological Club; was president of the Toronto Field Naturalists; for 29 years wrote a weekly bird column in the *Toronto Telegram;* and lectured on ornithology at U of T. Baillie wrote many papers on ornithology published by the ROM. He also compiled volumes of data on N American naturalists now at U of T. The Toronto Field Naturalists' Club acquired 36 hectares of land near Uxbridge, Ont, for the Jim Baillie Nature Reserve.   G. BENNETT

Baillie, Thomas, soldier, administrator (b at Hanwell, Eng 4 Oct 1796; d at Boulogne, France 20 May 1863). After a stint in the British infantry, Baillie secured an appointment as commissioner of crown lands and surveyor general of NB in 1824, and for 2 decades he was at the centre of controversy in that province. Required to collect taxes from the expanding TIMBER TRADE, Baillie gave wide powers to loosely controlled subordinates in enforcing what were regarded as tyrannical regulations. Arrogant and ostentatious, he soon antagonized local politicians and timber

traders. He even circumvented the governors and came to be seen as representing all that was wrong with the colonial system. Eventually the united effort of his opponents forced the British to curtail his powers in 1837. Undaunted, Baillie continued to fight for executive control of development. Personal bankruptcy in 1839 should have finished him, but he recovered, was elected to the Assembly in 1846, and became a member of the Executive Council. Compelled to resign in 1848, he remained surveyor general until 1851 when he retired to England.   CARL M. WALLACE

Baillif, Claude, builder/architect (b *c*1635; d in the West Indies 1698 or 1699). The SÉMINAIRE DE QUÉBEC hired Baillif, a Parisian, as a stonecutter for 3 years and he arrived in Canada Sept 1675. After 1678 he was a building contractor for walls, houses, churches, gun batteries, a cathedral tower and the bishop's palace. For colonial craftsmen, versatility was essential for survival. Baillif's designs were guided by books on civil and military architecture. He had 2 partners 1682-83, then worked independently, employing subcontractors and his own journeymen or apprentices. This builder and his wife had only a small home and little in movable effects. He carried 2667 *livres,* however, when he sailed for France Oct 1698. After a shipwreck in the Caribbean, Baillif died on another vessel off St Martin.

PETER N. MOOGK

Bain, Francis, geologist, ornithologist, botanist, author, artist (b at Charlottetown 25 Feb 1842; d at York Point, PEI 23 Nov 1894). Bain, a self-educated farmer, was an authority on PEI rocks, FOSSILS and natural history. He began DINOSAUR collecting in Canada when he found and identified a primitive reptile fossil (*Bathygnathus borealis*) on PEI. He also discovered a species of fossil fern on PEI that Sir William DAWSON subsequently named *Tylodendron baini.* In 1892 Bain was commissioned by the federal government to investigate the feasibility of constructing a submarine tunnel from PEI to NB. Between 1881 and 1893, he published over 20 scientific papers and 2 books, *The Natural History of Prince Edward Island* (1890) and *Birds of Prince Edward Island, Their Habits and Characteristics* (1891). He also wrote more than 50 natural science articles in the *Daily Examiner* and the *Chignecto Post*, including a column "Notes of a Naturalist." Francis Bain's knowledge and understanding of natural science mark him as the first Islander to whom the contemporary term "ecologist" is appropriate.   KATHY MARTIN

Bain, George, journalist, author, educator (b at Toronto 29 Jan 1920). Bain was educated in Toronto and served as a pilot in Bomber Command during WWII. In the mid-1950s, he began the Ottawa column in the Toronto *Globe and Mail.* Bain's serious but witty concern with federal politics led to the acceptance by many editors of a daily Ottawa column as something crucial to the political consciousness of Canadians. He was London correspondent 1957-60 and Washington correspondent 1960-69, when he returned to Ottawa. In 1964, he gradually introduced into the Ottawa column his *Letters from Lilac* (a fictional Saskatchewan town). Pearson's chuckle, Diefenbaker's wagging forefinger, Trudeau's shrug and Canada's political issues were widely disseminated through the fictional *Lilac Advance* and its correspondent Clem Watkins. Bain moved to the *Toronto Star* 1973-81 and was subsequently appointed director of journalism at King's College, Halifax. He retired in 1985. He has authored several books and has been awarded the Stephen Leacock Medal. He returned to the *Globe and Mail* until May 1987. He continues to write as a freelancer.

JEAN MARGARET CROWE

Bait Acts During the early 1880s the Newfoundland salt-fish trade was in trouble as the product's market value declined. A principal cause was increased competition from Norwegian and French fishermen, the latter heavily subsidized by the French government. Although Newfoundland could not affect the Norwegian fishery, the local government felt it could influence the French. The GRAND BANKS fishery was the largest French operation in Newfoundland waters, requiring fresh bait generally purchased from Newfoundland fishermen on the S coast. The government that took office in 1885 decided to use bait as a lever to reduce French competition in foreign markets by prohibiting the sale of bait to French fishermen if subsidization continued. The first Bait Act was introduced in 1886, but Britain refused to give the necessary assent until it was modified in 1887. This Act and subsequent variations did not noticeably curtail the French, who found alternative supplies. During the 1890s and the early 20th century, Newfoundland tried to use Bait Act provisions to control the sale of bait to Canadian and American fishermen. The Acts did not solve Newfoundland's economic problems, and the colony returned to seeking solutions in railway development and industrialization. *See* FISHERIES HISTORY.

SHANNON RYAN

Baker, Carroll, singer, songwriter (b at Bridgewater, NS 4 Mar 1949). Baker's electric performance of Conway Twitty's "I've Never Been This Far Before" on the 1976 Juno Awards telecast established her as a talent to be reckoned with. Performing since age 4, at 16 she moved to Ontario and by the time she was 19 she had started to sing with country bands. After meeting country manager Don Grashey, she started on a professional career, recording first for Grashey's Gaiety label (1971-75) then for RCA Records (1976-82). Throughout the late 1970s she had a string of hit records. She dominated the Big Country Awards and won the Juno in 1976, 1977 and 1978 as top female country singer. In 1983, in an effort to establish her career in the US, she left RCA and signed with Tembo Records.   RICHARD GREEN

Baker, Russell Francis, bush pilot, businessman (b at Winnipeg 31 Jan 1910; d at West Vancouver 15 Nov 1958). After several unhappy years working as a pilot for a number of airlines, including Western Canada Airways and Canadian Pacific, Baker established Central British Columbia Airways in 1946 on the strength of a fire-patrol contract from the BC Forest Service. Subsequent freighting contracts from the Alcan hydroelectric project near Kitimat and the DEW Line and, after 1949, the remorseless absorption by CBCA of its competition in BC and Alberta, advanced Baker toward his goal of building an airline serving every western Canadian community on a regular schedule. In 1953 CBCA changed its name to Pacific Western Airlines, as more appropriate to the dominant western regional air carrier. At the time of his death Baker was making plans to transform his company into a national airline — a feat accomplished subsequently with PWA's purchase of CP Air in 1987.   STANLEY GORDON

Reading: J. Condit, *Wings Over the West* (1984).

Baker Lake, NWT, Hamlet, pop 1009 (1986c), 954 (1981c), is situated 946 km NE of Yellowknife. It is 160 km E of the TREELINE, at the NW end of Baker Lk (1888 km²), and is approximately at the geographic centre of Canada. The only inland Inuit community in the NWT, its people, the CARIBOU INUIT, have evolved a life-style dependent on caribou and fish of the interior rather than on the sea mammals that sustain other Inuit groups. The community developed rapidly after WWII, when it was an advance base for the Canadian Army's

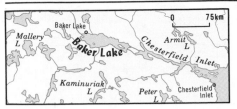

"Operation Muskox" snowmobile expedition. In the late 1970s the hamlet made national headlines in a landmark ABORIGINAL RIGHTS court case, when its residents contested the right of companies to mine URANIUM in the area. Although the majority Inuit population still subsists on traditional hunting and carving activities, today the community has a hotel, arts and crafts centre, general store and airstrip. ANNELIES POOL

Baking Industry The Canadian baking industry consists of companies that manufacture bread, cakes, pastries and similar perishable bakery products. MANUFACTURING of breadlike products goes back to antiquity, but the first known production of leavened bread occurred in Egypt after the process of fermentation was discovered about 4000 years ago. Modern breads only began appearing a little over 100 years ago. In early Canada, bread was produced in the home. As communities appeared, small bakeries were established to supply village needs; some of these bakeries gradually evolved into today's major commercial baking establishments. It has been estimated that in 1900 only 8% of Canadian housewives bought bread; by the early 1960s, more than 95% of homemakers regularly purchased bread and the bulk of their bakery requirements from commercial bakeries.

The Canadian baking industry has a sound reputation for product improvement. For example, during WWII government concern about the lack of iron in the diets of some Canadians led to the decision to add iron to the bread supply. Canada became one of the first countries to adopt this standard. Then, in 1953, the Canadian industry introduced vitamin-enriched bread. This bread proved to be the ideal food to deliver extra, necessary vitamins such as thiamine, riboflavin and niacin to consumers.

During the last 40 years, dramatic changes have occurred in the baking industry. Modern technology has led to increasingly larger and more sophisticated production operations, which in turn have created excess production capacity in many parts of the country. At the same time, road and rail improvements have increased distribution capability. Finally, efficient, new packaging systems and materials have greatly extended the "shelf life" of many bakery products. Thus, a modern wholesale baking company can easily supply many products to markets over 800 km from a central plant base. Consequently, smaller regional plants have been phased out.

As is the case with all other sectors of the FOOD AND BEVERAGE INDUSTRY, the baking sector must comply with a great many federal, provincial and municipal government regulations (see FOOD LEGISLATION). For example, packaging guidelines have been established by Consumer and Corporate Affairs Canada; the Health Protection Branch of Health and Welfare Canada is concerned with plant sanitation and related subjects. At the national level the industry is represented by the Bakery Council of Canada in Toronto. There has been a steady decline in the number of commercial baking operations: in 1939 the number of producing baking plants was reported at 3231; by 1981, 1431.

Published statistics on the baking industry also undergo periodic changes in definition. For example, bakeries baking their own products and selling them over the counter are now classified as retail establishments. The effect of such changes has been to reduce further the number of "bakeries": by 1985 Statistics Canada recognized only 485. Of these, Nfld had 5; PEI, 1; NS, 16; NB, 7; Qué, 176; Ont, 139; Man, 20; Sask, 16; Alta, 38; and BC, 55. In 1973, with 1690 plants in operation, the industry achieved an annual value of factory shipments of about $598.4 million. Materials and supplies for bread and related bakery products cost over $259 million. Cost of fuel and electricity was $11.9 million. At that time the industry employed more than 28 000 workers. By 1985, its sales reached about $1.46 billion. Materials and supplies cost $610 million in that year; fuel and electricity, $51.4 million. Employment had declined to 21 506. ROBERT F. BARRATT

Balaklava Island, 8 km², situated off the N coast of VANCOUVER I, is located between Nigel and Hurst islands, and is flanked by Queen Charlotte Str in the N and Goletas Channel in the S. It is 15 km NW of PORT HARDY, BC. This tiny island has a lighthouse at Scarlett Pt (1905) to aid shipping. It was named after the Battle of Balaklava (CRIMEAN WAR) on its ninth anniversary (25 Oct 1863) by Capt Pender of the *Beaver*. DAVID EVANS

Balance of Payments, or balance of international payments, is an accounting statement of the economic transactions that have taken place between the residents of one country (including its government), and the residents of other countries during a specified time, usually a year or a quarter. The term also refers to the difference between receipts and payments in some category of international transactions, often merchandise trade or the current account, which may be the subject of economic analysis (what explains the state of this balance or what the consequences of such a balance are) and the object of government policy (how to attain what is judged to be a desirable state of this balance).

The balance of payments statement is based on double-entry bookkeeping in which each economic transaction gives rise to a credit and a debit. A credit shows a decrease in assets or an increase in liabilities, a debit the opposite. If residents of 2 countries bartered goods, for example, declining inventory of exported goods would constitute a credit, while an increasing inventory of imported goods would constitute a debit. Residents are likely to be paid for their exports with an increase in a bank balance, an increase in the indebtedness to them of the foreign residents or decline of their own indebtedness to foreigners. The increase in the bank balance and loans to foreign residents or the decrease in liabilities to the foreign residents would be debits that matched the credit created by the exported goods. When transactions without payment occur (eg, exports of personal gifts, unreciprocated foreign aid or remittances by immigrants to relatives at home), the debit side is recorded to maintain the equality of credits and debits. Because all transactions have both a credit and a debit side, a difference between the sum of credits and debits can only occur for some categories of transactions, not for the entire balance of payments. Because some transactions are incorrectly recorded and others are not recorded at all, a difference between recorded credits and debits arises which is offset by an arbitrary balancing entry entitled "statistical discrepancy." In Canadian statistics, credits are receipts (identified with a plus sign), debits are payments with a negative sign.

Transactions in the Canadian balance of international payments comprise the current account, which records international transactions in goods and services and unilateral transfers (see also INTERNATIONAL TRADE) and the capital account, which records international transactions in assets and liabilities and includes international reserves. Official monetary movements, which record changes in the federal government's stock of gold and foreign currencies resulting from its interventions in the market for foreign exchange. The most important current transactions are those for merchandise trade, eg, in 1986 exports accounted for 80.7% of current receipts and imports for 69.8% of current payments. Other current transactions are for services and income from investments abroad. In 1986 Canada's merchandise trade surplus was $10.1 billion. However, the total current account was in deficit of $8.8 billion, because of an $18.9 billion deficit in "invisible" current transactions (nonmerchandise, etc). The principal nonmerchandise current receipts of Canadian residents were for the sale of travel, business services and freight to foreign residents and the earnings from Canadian investments abroad. Canadian residents made payments to foreigners for travel and freight, but the largest nonmerchandise payments, in the form of interest and dividends ($23.9 billion), went to nonresidents for the use of their capital in Canada.

A country's purchases of goods and services from other countries need not equal its sales. Canada usually incurs more current payments than receipts, though it did not do so in the recession of the early 1980s. The current balance is financed by net borrowing or lending or by the purchase or sale of equity (capital that represents ownership). Canadian residents, including governments, are net debtors internationally (and are among the world's highest per capita net debtors). The capital account records the net international transactions in different types of assets. In 1986 there was a net inflow (receipt) of direct investment capital into Canada of $1.557 billion (compared to a net outflow from Canada in 1985 of $8 billion and a net inflow into Canada of $.5 billion in 1980). This net flow resulted from large gross flows in each direction, but the result was that foreign residents reduced their ownership of Canadian enterprises. In 1986 Canadian residents made major net direct investments in foreign countries, of $4.8 billion, 90% of which went to the US. The purchases of enterprises abroad continued, but foreign investors were yet bigger purchasers of enterprises in Canada ($6.4 billion). Total foreign direct investment in Canada still exceeds by a large amount Canadian direct investment abroad, especially considering the relative sizes of the economies. The total receipt of capital exceeded the net outflow from direct investment transactions in that year, chiefly because Canadians also sold bonds to foreign residents ($23.1 billion in 1986). The balance on the entire capital account was a net capital inflow (a credit or receipt) of $13.7 billion in 1986 (compared to $2.6 billion in 1980). In 1986 the surplus on capital account covered the recorded deficit of $8.8 billion on current account. The difference between the estimated current account payment and capital amount receipt ($4.9 billion) could not be identified and appears as a statistical discrepancy. The sums of all credits and debits or all receipts and payments were, as required, equal.

MERCANTILIST policy, dominant until the end of the 18th century, advocated the development of a surplus of receipts over payments in a country's merchandise trade or on current account. Foreign residents paid the surplus with gold or silver and therefore increased the stockpile of precious metals considered the measurement of a nation's wealth. International flows of precious metals were the only kind of capital transaction recognized at the time. This is the origin of the term "favourable" balance of payments to denote a surplus, and "unfavourable" to denote a deficit on merchandise or current account. Other mercantilists believed that a surplus created employment, and advocated policy to create a merchandise surplus for that reason. In 1752 the Scottish philosopher David Hume undermined the theoretical basis of the mercantilist balance-of-payments policy by explaining that a permanent surplus on current account was impossible to achieve, because the inflow of gold and silver necessary to finance it would increase the money supply and so raise domestic prices, with a resulting increase in imports and decrease in exports. The current-account deficit or surplus is basically determined by where people choose to hold their assets; eg, when a country's residents decide to increase their holdings in foreign bonds, the foreign currency needed is obtained by selling more goods and services abroad than are bought, creating a current-account surplus. The currency finances the net accumulation of capital assets from foreign sources – a capital-account deficit. According to modern Keynesian analysis, a current-account surplus stimulates employment because exports add more to earned incomes, and therefore to domestic expenditures, than imports lose abroad. However, if one country attempts to create a surplus, other countries may retaliate. Balance of payments is also viewed as a means of distributing the world's capital resources. Residents in an area of high capital productivity will import more goods and services than they export and use that balance to build up domestic productive capacity.   H.C. EASTMAN

Balcer, Léon, politician (b at Trois-Rivières, Qué 13 Oct 1917). Educated as a lawyer at Laval, Balcer was elected to the House of Commons as a Progressive Conservative in 1949. He became solicitor general in the John DIEFENBAKER government in 1957 and minister of transport in 1960. Re-elected in 1963, Balcer became the French Canadian Conservative spokesman, but his disagreements with Diefenbaker became increasingly evident. Balcer broke ranks with Diefenbaker over the new Canadian flag (*see* FLAG DEBATE) and did not run in the 1965 election. In 1966, running provincially as a Liberal, he was defeated and retired to private life.
ROBERT BOTHWELL

Baldoon, UP, settlement fd 1804 for Highland SCOTS by the earl of SELKIRK on the swampy north shore of Lk St Clair on the Chenail Écarté [The Snye], Upper Canada (near Wallaceburg, Ont). Selkirk chose the site on his 1803-04 tour of UC because of its isolation and its apparently strategic location, and named it after a recently sold family estate in Scotland. He projected a large sheep farm there. The first 102 settlers reached Lachine, Qué, on the *Oughton*, on 19 July 1804, and travelled overland to Baldoon, only to arrive during the annual malaria season. Many soon joined in sickbed members of the advance party led by William Burn (who himself succumbed). Sheriff Alexander C. Macdonell, Selkirk's agent, struggled for years at considerable expense to the earl to make a success of the venture, but found the swampy land and the difficulty of sheep farming to be serious obstacles. Macdonell's problems, combined with the UC authorities' lack of enthusiasm for Selkirk's settlement schemes, encouraged Selkirk to transfer his efforts to the RED RIVER COLONY. Baldoon staggered on until the WAR OF 1812, when the earl's farm was ravaged by the invading American army of Gen Isaac Hull. Although this spelled an end to the settlement, some of the original Highlanders remained in the area.   J.M. BUMSTED

Baldwin, Frederick Walker, "Casey," aviator, inventor (b at Toronto 2 Jan 1882; d at Neareagh, NS 7 Aug 1948). He completed engineering stud-

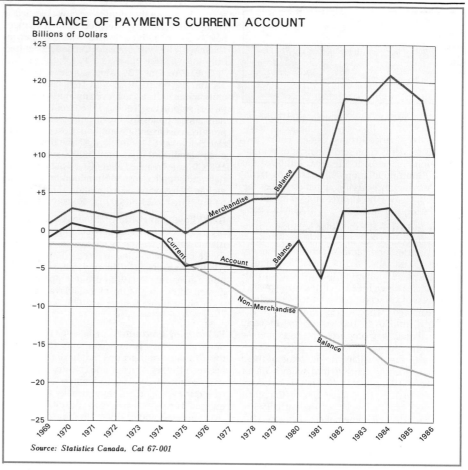

BALANCE OF PAYMENTS CURRENT ACCOUNT
Billions of Dollars

Source: Statistics Canada, Cat 67-001

ies at U of T 1906. In 1907 he became a founding member of the Aerial Experiment Assn with A.G. BELL, J.A.D. MCCURDY and 2 Americans. After working on the design and construction of their first aircraft, on 12 Mar 1908 he became the first British subject to pilot an aircraft, at Hammondsport, NY. He and McCurdy formed the Canadian Aerodrome Co at Baddeck, NS, and constructed 2 more aircraft. He also piloted the SILVER DART on 12 Aug 1909. He developed methods of transmitting sound through water and perfected a hydrofoil. He was elected to the NS Legislature in 1933.
JAMES MARSH

Baldwin, Robert, lawyer, politician, office holder (b at York [Toronto] 12 May 1804; d at Yorkville [Toronto] 9 Dec 1858). The eldest son of William Warren BALDWIN was called to the bar in 1825. Temperamentally and intellectually unlike his gifted father, the shy, introspective Robert entered politics in 1829 as a Reformer, winning a seat in the Assembly in a by-election. Defeated the following year he retired to private life. Melancholic, withdrawn, tortured by doubts and demons, his life and happiness revolved around his family and most especially his wife (they were married in 1827). Her death on 11 Jan 1836 shattered him emotionally and may explain the severe depressive illness that plagued him in later years. Despite his grief and a profound distaste for public life he was impelled to accept office as an executive councillor the following month by his Christian sense of duty.

The resignation in Mar 1836 of Baldwin and the other councillors over Lt-Gov Francis Bond HEAD's refusal to consult them plunged the colony into the gravest political and constitutional crisis prior to the REBELLION OF 1837. Baldwin remained neutral during the uprising. In its aftermath, he and his father met briefly with Lord Durham during Durham's visit to Toronto in July 1838. Bald-

win then submitted to Durham a detailed memorandum, dealing with the principle of RESPONSIBLE GOVERNMENT which probably influenced Durham's adoption of the principle in his famous Report. Baldwin became the rallying figure in rebuilding the postrebellion Reform opposition and forging an alliance with L.H. LAFONTAINE's Lower Canadian Liberals.

Although not a natural politician or a towering intellect, Baldwin commanded respect and exercised moral leadership by reason of his character. In a preindustrial society that revered the code of gentlemen, he embodied the cherished virtues of adherence to honour, duty and principle. Each time he gained office he left it by resignation rather than compromise his principles. Solicitor general in Gov Gen Lord SYDENHAM's ministry and an executive councillor in 1841, Baldwin resigned that June when the governor refused to implement responsible government. In the Assembly, Baldwin and LaFontaine steadily attracted members to the cause of responsible government until they had built a majority. They attained office in 1842-43 and again in 1848-51, the latter the so-called "Great Ministry." The first government was active and successful but a conflict with Gov METCALFE over his refusal to consult them on patronage led to their resignations in Nov 1843. During this, and the subsequent ministry Baldwin served as co-premier and attorney general (Upper Canada).

In the second ministry his great accomplishments were the formal attainment of responsible government and its confirmation during the REBELLION LOSSES crisis of 1849, the establishment of UNIVERSITY OF TORONTO, reform of the Upper Canadian judiciary, and establishment of an adequate system of municipal government in the upper province. Baldwin's hold on power was weakened, however, by a left-wing revolt in the party

Portrait of Robert Baldwin, 1846 (*courtesy Metropolitan Toronto Library*).

(by the CLEAR GRITS), by his own deteriorating health, and by differences over economic policy with Francis HINCKS. Discouraged and wracked by depression Baldwin resigned on 30 June 1851. Later that year he sought re-election but was defeated. The tormented figure withdrew to his home, to give himself over to the rituals of his preoccupation with his dead wife. As a man Baldwin was little understood or loved by contemporaries, or historians. He had failed to preserve the social order he sought to defend, but his reputation is secure as the popularizer of responsible government and one of the first, if not the first, proponents of a bicultural nation.

MICHAEL S. CROSS AND ROBERT L. FRASER

Reading: J.M.S. Careless, ed, *The Pre-Confederation Premiers* (1980); M.S. Cross and R.L. Fraser, "'The Waste that Lies Before Me': The Public and the Private Worlds of Robert Baldwin," *Historical Papers* (1983).

Baldwin, William Warren, doctor, lawyer, politician (b at Knockmore, Ire 25 Apr 1775; d at Toronto 8 Jan 1844). He arrived in Upper Canada in 1799, eventually settling at York [Toronto]. Urbane, talented, and in due course wealthy, Baldwin established a comfortable and distinguished law practice. His enduring reputation derives from his political activity. Although he served only 2 terms as an assemblyman he made a signal contribution to the cause of political reform and organization. Baldwin was an 18th-century man, an Irish whig who supported aristocracy, primogeniture, ministerial responsibility, and the civil and religious liberties of the British constitution. His great cause was RESPONSIBLE GOVERNMENT, that "the English principles of responsibility be applied to our local Executive Council." The fight was carried on by his eldest son Robert BALDWIN, whom he had instilled with a sense of providential mission.

ROBERT L. FRASER

Balfour, St Clair, publisher (b at Hamilton, Ont 30 Apr 1910). Balfour attended Trinity College School and U of T. He served with distinction in the Royal Canadian Navy during WWII, winning a Distinguished Service Cross. In 1955 he became executive vice-president of Southam and was chairman 1975-85. Balfour was instrumental in diversifying the company's interests into radio and TV.   J.L. GRANATSTEIN

Balfour Report, 1926, the conclusions of an Imperial Conference committee under the chairmanship of Lord Balfour, a British Cabinet minister and former prime minister, on relations between the self-governing parts of the empire-COMMONWEALTH, a pivotal document in Canada's evolution to fully self-governing nationhood. The report declared that Britain and the Dominions of Canada, South Africa, Australia, New Zealand and the Irish Free State were "autonomous Communities within the British Empire, equal in status, in no way subordinate one to another in any aspect of their domestic or external affairs, though united by a common allegiance to the Crown, and freely associated as members of the British Commonwealth of Nations." Incorporated verbatim in the conference proceedings, the report led directly to the legislative recognition of Dominion autonomy in the 1931 STATUTE OF WESTMINSTER.

NORMAN HILLMER

Ball Hockey is a fast, skilful sport, with leagues operating in all Canadian provinces. The game traces its ancestry to the simple stick-and-ball games of the Middle Ages. Ball hockey became popular in the 19th century, using some of the techniques of ice HOCKEY but replacing the puck with a tennis ball, and was played informally in streets or back alleys across Canada. With the invention, in 1969, of a hollow, no-bounce, plastic ball, ball hockey developed as a separate sport. The first organized league in Canada was formed in New Westminster, BC, in 1958, and the Canadian Ball Hockey Assn was founded in 1976. All ages participate, and games are played in hockey arenas, lacrosse boxes and gymnasia.

BARBARA SCHRODT

Ballard, Bristow Guy, research engineer (b at Fort Stewart, Ont 19 June 1902; d at Ottawa 22 Sept 1975). Ballard was educated at Queen's and worked for 5 years on Westinghouse high-speed electric locomotives before joining the NATIONAL RESEARCH COUNCIL staff in 1930. He became director of the Radio and Electrical Engineering Division in 1948, VP (scientific) in 1954, and president in 1963. His appointment as president took place in the last days of the DIEFENBAKER government, and Ballard told several friends he had neither wanted nor asked for the post, which he was reluctant to accept since his deafness had inhibited his making himself well known among Ottawa "mandarins." He had a clear aim, to stimulate Canadian ENGINEERING to catch up with Canadian science in its disciplinary development, but his attempts to achieve this were frustrated. In 1955, when he convened a conference of university deans of engineering to offer them the array of research grants and scholarships available to scientists, his proposals were rebuffed. When as NRC president he attempted to reorient the Council towards industrial engineering, he was overborne by the academics who then made up the majority of the Council. Ballard's policies were largely implemented by his successors, W.G. SCHNEIDER and J. Larkin KERWIN.

DONALD J.C. PHILLIPSON

Ballet, in strictest terms, is an artistically stylized form of theatrical dance based on a codified system of movement. Combined with music, sets and costumes it can be used to tell a story, evoke a mood, illustrate a piece of music or, simply, to provide a presentation of theatrical movement that is entertaining or intriguing in dance terms alone. Today, the word ballet is used more loosely to describe not only the classic academic dance with its well-defined technique but also more contemporary, free-ranging forms of theatrical dancing. Ballet, in its traditional form, has evolved from the early court entertainments of Renaissance Italy. These dances were brought to France by Italian masters in the 16th century. The *ballet de cour* (court ballet) developed from social dancing for the aristocracy to become elaborate, spectacular, and highly theatrical presentations used to demonstrate the wealth and power of French monarchs. The most notable was *Le Ballet comique de la Reine Louise*, mounted in Paris (1581) as part of 2 weeks of celebration marking an important royal marriage. The 5-hour performance was remarkable in offering a continuous dramatic narrative. Although these court dances continued, the development of ballet as a theatrical art gained momentum with the emergence of the popular opera-ballet in late 17th-century France. Dance interludes were placed between the vocal scenes. Ballet increasingly became a professional activity for trained dancers. The opera-ballet allowed little room for the independent development of ballet and in the 18th century, dance masters began to create dances which alone would carry a story.

The work of French choreographer and theorist Jean-Georges Noverre (1727-1810) was particularly influential in advancing the cause of the *ballet d'action*. His *Letters on Dancing and Ballets* (1760) rejected the subservient role of dancing within the tradition of the opera-ballet and strongly advocated the more dramatic style. This required a more expressive style of dancing than the rather formal dance movements of the opera-ballet. The *ballet d'action* had as its aim the establishment of dance as a discrete theatrical art. Passages of dancing continued to be included in operas but ballet slowly exerted the right to its own place in the theatre. *La Fille mal gardée* (1789) is among the earliest ballets from this period to have survived into our age.

The first half of the 19th century witnessed important developments in ballet. The Italian dancer, choreographer and teacher Carlo Blasis (1797-1878) wrote extensively about his theories of ballet and published an important codification of its technique. At the same time, European middle-class audiences flocked to see such famous ballerinas as Marie Taglioni, Fanny Elssler and Carlotta Grisi. Indeed, as the century progressed, the art of ballet in France and much of Europe came to be dominated by the ballerina, with male dancers taking a secondary role. Although the intellectual and aesthetic movement

Karen Kain with Frank Augustyn dancing *Romeo and Juliet* (*courtesy National Ballet Archives*).

known as the Romantic Movement was slow to touch ballet, works such as *Les Sylphides* (1832) and *Giselle* (1841) captured the public imagination and remain audience favourites even today. Ballet in France degenerated artistically during the latter part of the 19th century but thrived in Denmark under the brilliant ballet master August Bournonville (1805-79) and in Russia, where the French-born Marius Petipa created, among many others, such enduringly popular ballets as *The Sleeping Beauty* and *Swan Lake*.

A great Russian impresario, Serge Diaghilev, helped to restore the art of ballet in western Europe by bringing groups of Russian dancers to Paris and other leading capitals in the years before WWI. His excellently trained dancers performed exciting new works by such innovative choreographers as Vaslav Nijinsky (also a dancer of legendary gifts) and Mikhail Fokine. After the Russian Revolution of 1917, many important figures of the Russian ballet settled in Europe and N America, doing much to advance ballet wherever they went. Even after Diaghilev's premature death in 1929, groups of Russian dancers continued to make extensive tours of N America until the 1950s. Under Diaghilev's auspices, great artists, writers, composers and choreographers were brought together to create new works in which theme, steps, decor, costumes and music formed an authentic whole. This did much to fortify ballet's right to be considered a true theatrical art form, not just entertainment. Even as Diaghilev was helping to restore and rejuvenate ballet in the West, other very different forms of theatrical dance were being developed in Europe and N America. In large part these forms rejected what was perceived as the rigidity, and therefore artistic limitations, of traditional ballet. What came to be known as modern dance grew from a different set of ideas about movement and produced its own distinct type of dance theatre. In recent years, however, the boundaries that used to separate ballet from modern dance have been eroded. A process of cross-fertilization has seen a partial blending of techniques and styles. Choreographers of ballet now often draw on ideas and movements that find their origin in modern dance.

Until the middle of the 20th century, Canadians were more often spectators than participants in the art of ballet. The French colonization of the St Lawrence Valley from the 17th century onwards had seen the introduction of dance masters to Canada but their activities were directed mostly to teaching children of the rich. The real beginnings of professional ballet in Canada date from the 1930s, when such important teachers as Boris VOLKOFF in Toronto, Gwendolen Osborne in Ottawa, Gérald Crevier in Montréal, and June Roper in Vancouver began to produce dancers equipped to pursue professional careers. Without Canadian companies for them to dance in, however, these talented artists had to find work abroad. Patricia Wilde from Ottawa and Melissa HAYDEN from Toronto are 2 outstanding examples. During the early 1950s both rose to international stardom dancing in American ballet companies. More than a decade later, Lynn SEYMOUR, who was born in Alberta and initially trained in Vancouver, felt it necessary to pursue her career overseas, in England. As a dancer in the Royal Ballet she came to be hailed as one of the century's greatest dramatic dancers.

In 1938, however, 2 English ballet teachers, Gweneth LLOYD and Betty FARRALLY, established what later (1949) was to become Canada's first truly professional company, the Winnipeg Ballet. In Toronto, a distinguished British dancer and choreographer, Celia FRANCA, founded the NATIONAL BALLET OF CANADA (1951); and 7 years later

Ballet dancer Vanessa Harwood, photo by André Kertész, 1981 (*courtesy Jane Corkin Gallery*).

Les GRANDS BALLETS CANADIENS was founded in Montréal by Ludmilla CHIRIAEFF. These 3 major companies provide work for about 130 dancers. Each has developed its own identity. The ROYAL WINNIPEG BALLET has long been considered one of N America's most popular ballet troupes. The works it performs are selected to appeal to audiences without sacrificing artistic integrity. The dancers are notable for their extraordinary energy and obvious desire to perform always to the fullest extent of their capacities. The National Ballet, in contrast, has followed the traditions of the great European classical repertory companies and, although it has a large repertoire of one-act works, is particularly noted for its lavish, full-length productions of such ballets as *Swan Lake* and *The Sleeping Beauty*. Les Grands Ballets Canadiens, like the Royal Winnipeg Ballet, has for the most part avoided costly productions of full-length story ballets with elaborate sets and costumes. The company has been particularly distinguished in recent years by its willingness to experiment with the work of new choreographers (many of them Canadian) and to include a number of works by leading modern-dance choreographers. The NATIONAL BALLET SCHOOL and the schools attached to the Royal Winnipeg Ballet and Les Grands Ballets Canadiens are leaders in the provision of professional training to young dancers. Despite its short history, ballet in Canada has established firm roots. Leading Canadian companies have toured overseas and Canadian dancers such as Karen KAIN and Evelyn HART have won recognition at important international ballet competitions. For many years, concerned observers regretted the apparent lack of good Canadian choreography, a shortage felt by companies around the world. However, Canada has an increasing number of choreographers, such as Brian MACDONALD and, of a younger generation, James KUDELKA who have established international reputations. MICHAEL CRABB

Ballets Jazz de Montréal, Les, is a dynamic dance company devoted to ballet-jazz, based on strong ballet technique and jazz music. The company was formed (1972) by Hungarian-born Eva VON GENCSY, Genevieve Salbaing and Eddy Toussaint, with a nucleus of dancers from the dance school founded by Von Gencsy in Montréal in 1962. Today, that school, together with others in Québec City and Toronto, provides the major financial support for the company. In 1977, Salbaing took over complete artistic direction. Choreographers Brian MACDONALD, Rael Lamb,

Lynne Taylor-Corbett, Buzz Miller, Herb Wilson, Mauricio Wainrot and Vincent Nebrada have created original works for the company, which was also the first group to perform jazz works from the archives of New York's American Dance Machine company. Les Ballets Jazz has received critical acclaim throughout Canada and abroad. In its 15-year history it has performed in 40 countries. CAROL BISHOP

Balloon, vehicle that can rise within Earth's atmosphere because its total weight is less than that of the air it displaces. This principle was first enunciated by Greek mathematician and inventor Archimedes. The necessary lift or buoyancy is obtained by filling an envelope with a gas lighter than air (eg, hydrogen, helium, heated air). The first manned balloon flight was made over Paris on 21 Nov 1783 by François Pilâtre de Rozier and the Marquis d'Arlandes in a gondola beneath a cloth and paper envelope, inflated by air heated by a fire hung below it. The balloon was constructed by the Montgolfier brothers. Ten days later, French scientist J.A.C. Charles and his assistant flew about 43 km suspended beneath a hydrogen-filled silk-and-rubber balloon, returning safely to Earth. This balloon incorporated many features of a modern gas-filled balloon, eg, an open-necked envelope allowing for gas expansion, a top-mounted gas-release valve and a supply of ballast for altitude control. Many significant flights followed, as ballooning developed military, sporting and scientific applications.

Within about 10 years of the first manned flights, tethered balloons were being used as military observation posts, while free balloons were used as somewhat unpredictable delivery systems for passengers, bombs and messages during long sieges. In WWI, bombing of civilian and military targets from airships changed the nature of warfare. Tethered barrage balloons protected strategic targets from low-level aircraft attack during WWII.

In the 20th century, powered airships were used extensively for passenger transportation, until the *Hindenburg* disaster in 1937 demonstrated the danger of using highly flammable and explosive hydrogen as lift gas. Balloons are still used as heavy-lift vehicles in remote, inaccessible areas (eg, logging operations in BC forests). Modern variants of the airship, lifted by the light but inert gas helium, are used as platforms for television cameras at sporting events, spectacular advertising billboards and, more recently, passenger vehicles on tourist flights across major cities. New designs are being tested in Canada as bulk-cargo carriers.

Balloon-flying has always had a sporting component, with rallies, races and long-duration flights catching the public imagination. In the 1960s, development of the modern hot-air balloon, with a strong, light nylon envelope inflated by hot air from a reliable propane burner, led to a resurgence of interest in the sport. The many long flights made in gas-filled balloons culminated in crossings of the Atlantic and Pacific oceans by American teams (1978 and 1981, respectively). So far, attempts to circumnavigate the globe in a free balloon have been unsuccessful.

In science, routine meteorological soundings (atmospheric temperature, moisture content, wind speed and direction) by small instrument packages on rubber balloons are an essential part of modern global WEATHER FORECASTING. The modern scientific balloon is a huge but extremely thin polyethylene envelope, reinforced with nylon tapes and inflated with helium. It can place instruments within the layers of interest for atmospheric studies or above absorbing and turbulent layers for astronomical observations. Balloon-

Launch of a modern scientific balloon and payload from Churchill, Man, 1974, under sponsorship of the National Research Council. Airborne instrumentation has led to advances in many scientific fields (*courtesy T.A. Clark*).

borne instrumentation has led to advances in atmospheric POLLUTION studies, cosmic ray research, X-ray and infrared ASTRONOMY and high-resolution photography of astronomical sources, including the sun. X-ray measurements from smaller balloons during auroral displays have been important in unravelling the complex interactions of the solar wind with Earth's magnetic field, which cause the NORTHERN LIGHTS. In biology, balloons have often provided silent platforms for the observation of wild animals in their undisturbed habitat.

Scientific ballooning is supported by the NATIONAL RESEARCH COUNCIL through its space division. Several universities, particularly Calgary, Saskatchewan, York and Toronto were active in astronomical, atmospheric and aeronomical research from balloons. Several launch sites including Churchill and Gimli, Manitoba were used for these studies.   T.A. CLARK

Balmoral, NB, Village, pop 1969 (1986c), inc 1972, located 12 km SW of Dalhousie, is named for Balmoral castle in Scotland. Following the survey of 1856 some land was taken up by ACADIANS, but the area was not settled to any extent until the Free Grants Act of 1874 brought an influx of English and Scottish immigrants. The new settlers developed an extensive agricultural industry which has given way in recent years to forest industries. The village has a sawmill, but many of its inhabitants work in neighbouring towns in the forest and mining industries.
          BURTON GLENDENNING

Bancroft, Henry Hugh, organist, composer (b at Cleethorpes, Eng 29 Feb 1904). Educated in England, Bancroft arrived in Canada in 1929 to serve as organist-choirmaster at St Matthew's and All Saints' Anglican churches, Winnipeg, and later at Christ Church Cathedral, Vancouver. In 1948 he moved to Sydney, Australia. He returned to Winnipeg in 1953 and then moved to Nassau, Bahamas. In 1958 he became organist-choirmaster at All Saints' Cathedral, Edmonton, retiring in 1980. In 1977 he received the Lambeth degree from the Archbishop of Canterbury and in 1980 was awarded an honorary LLD from University of Alberta.   ERIC J. HOLMGREN

Band is a basic form of local residential group in traditional simple hunting and gathering societies all around the world. Canada had 26 band organized societies: the Inuit, several Athapascan (DENE) societies, several northern Algonquian societies, and the BEOTHUK. The *local bands* were essentially several families, usually from about 20 to 50 people, who lived and worked together in a co-operative and egalitarian way with extensive sharing of food. The size and membership of these local groups fluctuated according to such factors as the local abundance of game and movements related to marriages. In the annual round of hunting, fishing and plant gathering, it was common for several of these local bands to get together once or twice a year for festivals with a few hundred people. These larger groups are called *regional bands*.

Today the Canadian government uses the term "band" to describe the local unit of administration by Indian Affairs, including the dozens of more complex native societies that were traditionally organized not as bands but as tribes or chiefdoms. There are currently 592 of these modern administrative bands, which function as small native municipalities and are managed by elected band councils according to the laws of the Indian Act of Canada. *See also* NATIVE PEOPLE, DEMOGRAPHY.   JOHN A. PRICE

Band, The, internationally popular rock band (1968-76), began *c*1960 as the Hawks, backing "rockabilly" singer Ronnie HAWKINS in southern Ontario, and subsequently (as the Crackers) toured the world (1965-66) with Bob Dylan. The Band, based in the US, was known for musically kaleidoscopic albums and for such hits as "The Weight" and "Up on Cripple Creek." Canadian members were guitarist and songwriter Robbie Robertson, bassist Rick Danko, organist Garth Hudson, pianist Richard Manuel; drummer Levon Helm was born in Arkansas. The Band reunited without Robertson in 1986; Manuel committed suicide in March of that year, while the band was on tour.   MARK MILLER

Banff, Alta, Town, pop 4627 (1986c), 4208 (1981c), is located on the Bow R, 128 km W of Calgary. Founded in 1883 near a proposed CPR railway tunnel site, the first town, 3 km from present-day Banff, was known as "Siding 29." Renamed by Lord Strathcona (Donald SMITH) on 25 Nov 1883 for his hometown in Scotland, and relocated 3 years later, the new townsite grew to

300 residents that first year. Banff's development has always been determined by the federal government, tourism and the railway. In 1885, the Banff Hot Springs Reserve was formed on 10 acres (4 ha) of land around the local hot springs, and in 1887 a major expansion of park land occurred with the formation of the Rocky Mountain Parks Reserve. The park soon began to be centered around Banff, spurring the single-most significant event in the town's history, the opening of the Banff Springs Hotel, 1 June 1888. In 1930, the Rocky Mountain Parks Reserve was renamed Banff National Park. Home to famous Albertans, such as Mary Schaffer Warren, Walter Philips, Earle Birney, Carl Rungius, as well as Dr Brett, lt-gov of Alberta and owner of the Park Sanitarium Hotel, Banff early established itself as one of Alberta's main cultural and recreational centres, with its world-class ski resorts and outdoor facilities. This richness of culture was further evidenced by the establishment of the BANFF CENTRE School of Fine Arts in 1933, and later the Peter Whyte Archives of the Rocky Mountains.
          FRITS PANNEKOEK

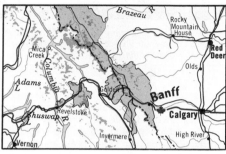

Banff Centre for Continuing Education began in 1933 as a special summer program sponsored by the U of Alberta's Division of Continuing Education and was intended to provide cultural enrichment for beginners and serious amateurs in drama, music and art. It was called the Banff School of Fine Arts from 1933 to 1978 when it was officially renamed the Banff Centre for Continuing Education to emphasize its broader scope. Under the able leadership of the first 2 directors, Donald Cameron and David Leighton, this school had evolved by the 1980s into a leading world centre for continued learning. It served advanced students as well as professionals with a year-round curriculum of depth and variety.

The Banff Centre is located in one of the choicest locations in N America, nestled on the side of Tunnel Mt and overlooking the resort of BANFF and the picturesque Banff Springs Hotel. It provides participants with the advantages of a wilderness setting, combined with highly developed modern facilities in the performing arts, visual arts and music. Over the years, a faculty of internationally recognized fine-arts instructors and a generous scholarship endowment have ensured the enrolment of a student body of well-demonstrated potential and competitive spirit.

Although diplomas are given for successful completion of the various specific programs offered, the basic concept of education at the Banff Centre differs, through insistence on independent research, from that found at most art schools, conservatories or university fine-arts graduate programs. The Centre assumes that the participant has already mastered the fundamentals of technique or craft and is seeking a fresh start as a mature and creative artist in a serene and vitalizing environment.   J.R. STOCKING

Reading: D. Cameron, *Campus in the Clouds* (1956); D. and P. Leighton, *Artists, Builders and Dreamers* (1982).

Banff National Park (6640 km²), Canada's first and most heavily visited national park; its eastern

Banff National Park, showing Bow Valley, Mt Rundle and the Banff townsite viewed from Mt Norquay (*photo by Tom W. Parkin/Pathfinder*).

gate is located 111 km W of Calgary in the Rocky Mts, and stretches 240 km along the eastern slope of the Continental Divide. Originally set aside in 1885 to preserve sulphur hot springs for public use, Banff's blend of towering peaks and flower-strewn meadows makes it among Canada's most exhilarating holiday areas. The GLACIERS still clinging to upper mountain slopes have helped shape the park's landscape, creating numerous lakes, waterfalls and broad, U-shaped valleys. Forests of lodgepole pine, Engelmann spruce and alpine fir soften the flanks of the mountains and are home to many large mammals, including moose, elk, black bear and the awesome grizzly – the park's most formidable resident. Bighorn sheep, mule deer and other wildlife can often be seen alongside park roads. In contrast, the small population of cougar and wolf are rarely seen. Campgrounds, resorts, alpine and cross-country skiing, and 1100 km of hiking trails radiate from BANFF townsite. In 1986-87 there were 3 million visitors. LILLIAN STEWART

Bank Act is the law passed by Parliament to regulate Canada's CHARTERED BANKS. The Act has 4 main goals: the protecting of depositors' funds; insuring the maintenance of cash reserves (see MONETARY POLICY); promoting the efficiency of the financial system through competition; and preserving a range of separate financial institutions.

The Act divides BANKS into 2 groups known as Schedule A and Schedule B banks. Schedule A banks are widely held (no single owner may control more than 10% of the banks' voting stock) and mostly domestically owned. Schedule B banks are closely held and primarily owned by their foreign parent companies. The Act allows the government to control the size of Schedule B banks. The Act also sets out the conditions for entry into the BANKING business. To start, a chartered bank must have $2 million of capital. Banks are required to hold cash reserves equal to about 4% of "reservable" deposits (defined in the Act to be all deposits except term deposits of more than one year to maturity). Secondary reserves, which may be held in the form of interest-bearing treasury bills, must also be held at a level at the discretion of the BANK OF CANADA. Additionally, the Act

specifies the reporting requirements of banks to the inspector general of banks and limits the kind of activities in which a chartered bank may be engaged. For example, chartered banks are currently not allowed to manage TRUSTS, sell insurance or underwrite corporate securities. However, proposed changes in legislation may permit chartered banks to offer a much broader range of financial services.

After passage by Parliament, the Bank Act remains in force for 10 years. This insures that legislators will periodically update the Act in order to keep pace with changes in the Canadian financial system. PAUL BOOTHE

Bank Architecture Institutionalized banking came to British N America in 1820, when the Bank of New Brunswick at Saint John was granted a charter by the provincial government. In 1822 the BANK OF MONTREAL, in operation since 1817, was chartered by the Province of Lower Canada. By year's end, there were 5 chartered banks in the provinces; on the eve of Confederation there was a total of 28 in the provinces of Canada, NS and NB.

Because banks – both family businesses and those under government charter – competed for clients, they recognized the value of an architectural image that would attract customers. They adopted chiefly Greek and Roman architectural forms, which symbolized wealth, integrity, endurance and confidence. In 1818 the Bank of Montreal constructed a stolid 3-storey building on St James St, with a portico consisting of a classical pediment supported by Doric columns. The BANK OF UPPER CANADA on Toronto's Adelaide St (architect W.W. Baldwin, 1830) resembled a respectable London townhouse and featured a Doric portico. As the century progressed, imposing institutional structures, predominantly in the classical revival styles, characterized most big-city banks. Montréal's St James Street was the financial heart of Canada, where stood the Bank of Montreal headquarters (John Wells, 1846-48), Molsons Bank (George Browne, 1866) and the Merchants Bank (Hopkins and Wily, 1870). Smaller cities followed Montréal's lead; the Commercial Bank in London (F. Kortum and William Hay, 1859-61) had a refined Italian Renaissance revival façade.

The opening of impressive bank buildings in Winnipeg early in the 20th century proclaimed that the prairie city had achieved a dominant financial position. A series of imposing banking

structures around Portage and Main streets included the large neoclassical regional centres of the Bank of Montreal (McKim, Mead and White, 1913) and the Canadian Bank of Commerce (Darling and Pearson, 1910), the 10-storey Bank of Hamilton Building (J.D. ATCHISON, 1916), and the smaller but sophisticated Bank of Toronto (H.C. Stone, 1906) and ROYAL BANK OF CANADA (Carrère and Hastings, 1910). All featured superb banking halls as well.

Branch banking had been legalized in 1841, and by 1900 there was a proliferation of branch operations. Many branches were designed from a central office. In order to remain competitive in the rapidly expanding West, the Canadian Bank of Commerce hired the Toronto firm of Darling and Pearson to design prefabricated branches in 3 sizes; between 1906 and 1910 the B.C. Mills Timber and Trading Co produced almost 70 structures which, shipped from Vancouver by rail to their destination, could be erected in a single day. Architect John M. LYLE designed both large and small banks for the BANK OF NOVA SCOTIA in the 1920s and 1930s. The templelike Bank of Nova Scotia (1924) on Sparks St, Ottawa, with its free-standing columns and decorated frieze, represents the height of Lyle's classical bank designs.

After 1945 major changes occurred in the attitude of banks towards their buildings, as reputations established in the preceding decades removed the need to be identified by impressive, symbolic architecture. Efficiency became paramount as the policy of centralized, standardized design intensified. Old branches were judged obsolete and replaced with new ones designed by the banks' architectural staffs. Each bank had its preferred material – the Banks of Commerce and Montreal chose brick, and the Royal Bank black granite. Most were single-storey, plain, rectangular structures. In contrast to the era when banks dominated their surroundings, standing as the symbols of a town's sense of wealth and worth, recent branch banks are frequently understated buildings.

National and regional head offices have continued the tradition of assertive designs. Since the 1960s, a number of banks have occupied large portions of distinguished high-rise towers in the international style. Most noteworthy are the Toronto Dominion Centre in Toronto (L.M. van der Rohe, with John B. PARKIN Associates, and BREGMAN and Hamann, 1964-68), the Royal Bank in Montréal's Place Ville Marie (I.M. Pei and Associates, with AFFLECK, Desbarats, Dimakopoulos, Lebensold and Sise, 1958-65) and Royal Bank Plaza, Toronto (Webb, Zerafa, Menkes, Housden Partnership). The Bank of Canada, the regulator of the nation's money, has enlarged its original neoclassical headquarters (Marani, Lawson, and Morris, with S.G. Davenport, 1937) by wrapping the building with twin 12-storey towers of mirrored glass (Arthur ERICKSON, with Marani, Roun-

Bank of Upper Canada, Toronto, built in 1830 and restored in 1982 (*photo © Hartill Art Associates, London, Ont*).

Royal Bank Plaza, Toronto, designed by Webb, Zerafa, Menkes, Housden Partnership (*photo by J.A. Kraulis*).

thwaite and Dick, 1974-79). The Bank of Montreal in Winnipeg expanded its 1913 building with a slender 22-storey granite-faced tower (Smith Carter Partners, 1982-84) which succeeds in respecting the historic structure. *See also* URBAN DESIGN.   HAROLD D. KALMAN

Bank of British Columbia, a bank chartered in 1966 with headquarters in Vancouver. In 1986 it had 1410 employees and maintained branches in BC and Alberta, as well as offices in the Cayman Is, the US and Hong Kong. Assets in 1986 were $2.7 billion (ranking 27th among banks and financial institutions in Canada); the 1986 revenue was $324 million. The Bank of BC is now 100% owned by the Hongkong Bank of Canada, which is itself wholly owned by Hongkong & Shanghai Banking of Hong Kong.   DEBORAH C. SAWYER

Bank of Canada, wholly owned by the Government of Canada, is Canada's central bank or monetary manager. Established in 1935, it is responsible for issuing paper currency, for acting as fiscal agent and banker for the federal government, for setting the BANK RATE and for implementing and helping to formulate MONETARY POLICY. As banker and fiscal agent the bank manages the issue and redemption of federal government securities and the payment of INTEREST they accrue. It also operates in the foreign exchange market as the government's agent to exert a stabilizing influence on the Canadian dollar EXCHANGE RATE. It does not engage in commercial BANKING activity.

According to the BANK OF CANADA ACT, the essential purpose of money management is to help achieve price, employment and economic growth conditions that are "in the best interests of the economic life of the nation." As monetary manager the bank controls the growth of bank deposits (the main component of MONEY supply), in different ways. Each chartered bank is required to maintain minimum cash (computed as a percentage of its deposits) reserves in the form of notes or deposits with the Bank of Canada. Each bank is also required to maintain secondary reserves in the form of excess cash reserves, treasury bills and day-to-day loans to investment dealers. The Bank of Canada may vary this reserve ratio from 0-12% of deposits. The Bank of Canada can alter chartered-bank cash by buying or selling securities in the

open market. Cash reserves will increase as soon as the cheque in payment of the securities is cleared and deposited in a chartered bank's account with the Bank of Canada. It can similarly manage cash reserves by transferring Government of Canada deposits between the chartered banks and itself. Through its control over cash reserves the bank influences the supply of money and consequently the level of interest rates and availability of credit. As lender of last resort, it can also make advances to some financial institutions (including banks) for temporary periods to relieve unusual financial pressures. On rare occasions the bank has used moral suasion, ie, it has persuaded institutions to act in a certain way. For example, it might indicate to the chartered banks its views on a particular lending activity. These views are taken seriously by the banks.

The Bank of Canada is managed by a senior governor, a senior deputy governor and 12 directors. In addition the deputy minister of finance is a nonvoting member of the board. Directors are appointed by the federal minister of finance, with Cabinet approval, for 3-year terms. In turn the directors appoint the governor and senior deputy governor, again with Cabinet approval, for 7-year terms. The Bank of Canada has had 5 governors: G.F. TOWERS, J.E. COYNE, L. RASMINSKY, G.K. BOUEY and John W. CROW. Although the bank enjoys substantial independence, the Bank of Canada Act gives the finance minister the right to issue a formal, written policy directive to the Bank of Canada if, after consultation, disagreement on policy persists. It was the resignation of Coyne in 1961, over differences with the government, that influenced the introduction of the legal provision clarifying that ultimate responsibility for policy rests with the government.   E.P. NEUFELD AND A.J. THOMSON

Bank of Canada Act, 3 July 1934, created the BANK OF CANADA 1935 in response to the 1933 Royal Commission on Banking and Currency. The Bank of Canada was at first privately owned, but was nationalized by 1938. The Act and associated revisions to the Bank Act also changed the legal framework for Canada's chartered banks, which were now obliged to maintain a specified ratio (not less than 5%, usually 10%) between liabilities to the public (current and savings accounts) and their claims on the national monetary authorities (Bank of Canada paper currency, plus deposits with the Bank of Canada). The banks lost the right to borrow on demand from

the government as had been permitted under the 1914 FINANCE ACT. Instead they could borrow from the Bank of Canada, which would also hold the main accounts of the Dominion and lend to it, while in general managing the national monetary system. It would do this by issuing paper currency, by changing the rate of INTEREST at which it would lend to the chartered banks, by buying and selling bonds in the securities markets so as to affect the supply of credit and the demand for it, or by buying and selling gold and foreign monies so as to affect the demand-supply balance in the foreign-exchange market, where Canadian dollars are exchanged for foreign monies. Through such operations the Bank of Canada can and does affect the cost and availability of credit, but it has never fixed interest rates for the public at large or rationed the supply of credit directly. During WWII it helped the Dominion in financing the war effort. Under later legislation its powers were extended and modified, but not changed in essentials. It also acquired a subsidiary, the Industrial Development Bank, est 1945. The Bank of Canada may be called Canada's central bank, because of its special functions in relation to the chartered banks, the international environment and the federal government.   IAN DRUMMOND

Bank of Montreal, with head offices in Montréal, is Canada's oldest chartered bank. Founded in 1817, the Bank of Montreal participated in many of the developments spurring the growth of Canada: the first CANALS, the TELEGRAPH, the CANADIAN PACIFIC RAILWAY, major hydroelectric projects and the development of Canada's ENERGY and MINING industries. It was the banker in Canada for the Canadian government from 1863 until the founding of the BANK OF CANADA in 1935. It was also the first Canadian bank to establish representation outside the country, with correspondent agencies started in London and New York in 1818. In 1893 it was named the Canadian government fiscal agent in Britain, a function it still performs. Between 1903 and 1962 the Bank of Montreal purchased the assets and business of smaller banks, mainly in Atlantic Canada. Today, it has over 1300 branches in Canada and overseas, and it offers corporate, government, merchant and personal banking services with a variety of commercial and international services. As of 30 Sept 1987 the Bank of Montreal owned 75% of Nesbitt, Thomson, a Canadian investment firm. In Oct 1986, the bank had revenue of $8.3 billion and assets of $87 billion (ranking 2nd among financial institutions in Canada) and 32 988 employees.   DEBORAH C. SAWYER

One-penny coin issued by the Bank of Montreal in 1842 after the union of Upper and Lower Canada (*courtesy Currency Museum, Bank of Canada/Jas Zagon*).

Bank of Nova Scotia, fd 1832 in Halifax, is Canada's second-oldest chartered bank. Its first branches were in the Maritimes, but it expanded into Winnipeg and Minnesota in the 1880s as the CPR was built. Between 1883 and 1919 it amalgamated with smaller banks, beginning with the Union Bank of Prince Edward Island and ending with the Bank of Ottawa. It was the first Canadian bank to operate in the Caribbean, opening a branch in Jamaica in 1889; it also established a branch in London in 1920.

During the 1960s the bank again diversified internationally; it operates over 200 branches and subsidiaries in 45 countries, as well as its more than 1000 branches in Canada. It offers a variety of financial services, including gold and silver trading, mortgage loans, leasing, real-estate and trust services. Now known familiarly as "Scotiabank," it pioneered several financial services to simplify banking for the ordinary consumer. In 1981 it became the first Canadian bank to offer complete branch services in Japan and it also participated in a test of the business applications of satellite communications. Although the general office was moved to Toronto in 1900, the head office is still in Halifax. As of Oct 1986, it had annual revenue of $6.2 billion, assets of $64.0 billion (ranking 4th among financial institutions in Canada) and 26 215 employees.

DEBORAH C. SAWYER

Bank of Upper Canada, chartered 21 Apr 1821, commenced operations at York [Toronto] July 1822. It owed its origins to pressure from the commercial community, to close links with the FAMILY COMPACT, and to the local government's hope that a bank would provide it with sorely needed capital. William ALLAN, president for 12 of the bank's first 13 years, adapted British banking theory to the reality of a capital-starved frontier and provided generally sound leadership. Thomas Gibbs Ridout, cashier (general manager) 1822-61, and William Proudfoot, Allan's successor (1835-61), were less successful. During the REBELLIONS OF 1837, the bank annoyed local commercial interests and, partly as a result, the Commercial Bank of the Midland District expanded more rapidly in the 1840s. During the 1850s, the bank held the government account, provided significant short-term capital for railway development and, in the boom years, recklessly speculated in land and railways. The bank never recovered from the 1857 economic collapse, losing the government account in 1864 and entering trusteeship in Nov 1866. Despite its great contribution to the development of Canadian commerce, it became a casualty of the very process it had helped facilitate: the transition from MERCANTILISM to an industrial economy.

PETER A. BASKERVILLE

Bank Rate, the BANK OF CANADA's minimum interest rate on short-term loans to the chartered banks, to savings banks under the Québec Savings Bank Act, to other members of the Canadian Payments Association that maintain deposits with the Bank, and to investment dealers. The bank rate often indicates the Bank of Canada's preferences concerning the level of short-term interest rates, but it is generally higher than other rates of short-term credit in order to encourage borrowers to obtain funds elsewhere. The rate has been fixed throughout most of its history, but at present it has been set at one-quarter of one percent above the average yield on 91-day Government of Canada treasury bills sold at the latest weekly auction. Hence, the bank influences bank rate indirectly each week through its own tender price for treasury bills (see also BANKING).

E.P. NEUFELD AND A.J. THOMSON

Banking, a financial process carried out by an institution that accepts deposits, lends money and transfers funds. The 2 principal types of banks are central banks and commercial banks, or CHARTERED BANKS as the latter are called in Canada. A central bank such as the BANK OF CANADA operates as an arm of the federal government, carrying out its MONETARY POLICY, acting as a lender of last resort to the commercial banks, holding deposits of governments and chartered banks and issuing notes or money. Chartered banks accept deposits from the public and extend loans for commercial, personal and other purposes. Other financial institutions, known as "near-banks," perform some of these functions, but banks are the only financial institutions that can increase or contract the basic money supply (see MONETARY POLICY).

History of Banking In one of the earliest codes of law, compiled by Hammurabi, king of Babylon from 1792 to 1750 BC, several paragraphs were devoted to banking. By *c*1000 BC in Babylon the transfer of bank deposits to a third party was common, and the palace or temple extended loans from its own assets. The Greeks established private banks, which accepted deposits and acted as agents in the settlement of debts. Pasion of Athens, a famous 4th-century-BC banker, invested his own funds and those of his depositors in commercial ventures. Roman bankers acted as money changers, auctioneers, discounters and creditors; they formed a banking association and maintained something similar to a modern current-accounts system.

"Bank" derives from the Italian word *banco*, the bench on which money changers sat to conduct their business, and from the 5th to the 11th century bankers acted primarily in this capacity. With the advent of the Crusades, the Lombards, N Italian merchants, formed merchant guilds; they accepted deposits, granted advances and made payments, preferring to operate where they were not required to pay taxes. In the 12th century, the Lombards established themselves in London, and Lombard Street remains a symbol of financial power. From the 14th to the 19th century various banks were established in countries such as Italy, Holland, Spain, France, Germany and England. The Bank of Amsterdam was established in 1609 and acted as a guarantor of coinage, since it would accept coins only at what it perceived as their real value. The Bank of Stockholm, founded at about the same time, issued receipts for deposits that were circulated for purchasing goods and as bills of exchange, in effect, the first bank notes. The Bank of England was established in 1694 as a private bank (remaining so until 1946) under a royal charter to raise money for war. Banking history in England is distinguished by the early development and use of the cheque; on the continent the limitations of the non-negotiable cheque precluded extensive use of deposit credit until well into the 19th century.

In 1782 Montréal merchants formed the Canada Banking Company, but because it could not obtain permission to issue bank notes it failed, as did 2 other similar ventures in 1807 and 1808. During the War of 1812 the governor issued "army bills" that bore interest and could be exchanged for cash, government bills of exchange in London or more army bills. In 1817 the BANK OF MONTREAL (a joint-stock operation owned by a handful of men) opened its doors in Canada, but because of delays in the approval of its charter until 1822, 2 other banks – the Bank of New Brunswick in 1820 and the BANK OF UPPER CANADA in 1821 – were granted a head start. The Bank of Upper Canada was controlled by the FAMILY COMPACT and the legislature of the time refused charters to any group unless some of its members belonged to the oligarchy. Another bank, the Bank

of the People, was established by the enterprising Francis HINCKS, who became prime minister of the Province of Canada and later John A. Macdonald's finance minister. He was responsible for ensuring the passage of Canada's first Bank Act (1871) and was later named president of the Consolidated Bank. (He was also brought to trial on various offences and convicted of fraud, although the conviction was reversed on appeal.)

The Bank of Montreal's charter was similar to that of the first Bank of the US, established to be the creature and agency of the national government under the new federal constitution, but Canadian and American banking systems developed quite differently. Canadian banking has been described as "a branch plant of English commercial banking," and, as one historian notes, "it was the model least suited to promoting industrial development in the colony." Regional growth suffered as well. For example, by 1912, in one area of the Maritimes, only 5 cents of every dollar deposited in the bank was loaned locally and 95 cents was transferred to central Canada.

Many of Canada's first bankers, eg, Samuel Zimmerman, who was involved in the Great Southern Railway swindle, were not examples of probity, and until the 1920s banks in Canada were generally unstable. (Between 1867 and 1914 the failure rate of Canadian banks was 36% as opposed to 22.5% in the US, costing Canadian shareholders 31.2 times more than was lost to American shareholders; of the 26 failures in this period, 19 resulted in criminal charges against bank officers or employees.) Under the new French regime, BARTER had generally been the method of trade. The coins and merchandise customarily sent from France returned there for the purchase of imports. One year, when a shipment did not arrive, Intendant François BIGOT issued signed playing cards, redeemable in coins and merchandise (when they arrived), and ordered the colonists to accept them as money. Later he issued due bills redeemable not not in real coins or merchandise but in card money. By 1760 the colony was 80 million livres in debt, much of it in worthless *ordonnances* issued by Bigot. After the CONQUEST the British used Mexican, Spanish, Portuguese, French and German coins to pay their troops, which, with trade goods, became the coin of the realm.

In the US, in contrast, where banking was fiercely competitive and regionally oriented, 2 types of banks developed. Eastern banks favoured stability and gradual expansion, while those burgeoning in the West were more venturesome. The number of banks in Canada was restricted by high capital requirements and vested interests allied to the legislators. Attempts by westerners to form their own bank were vetoed by the Canadian Bankers' Association, officially incorporated in 1901. As a result the Canadian banking system became characterized by the creation of a few dominant banks with many branches, compared to the American practice of encouraging many unit banks and restricting or prohibiting branches. Until 1867 charters were issued by Upper Canada and Québec and subsequently by the federal government. Canadian banks were also regulated by law in considerable detail, eg, the fixing of a minimum paid-up capital ($100 000 in 1871 and $250 000 since 1890). Twenty-eight banks were chartered by 1867 and 38 by 1886. This number changed little until WWI when it declined sharply, until by 1964 only 8 remained, of which 5 were nationally significant. As a result of legislative changes and economic expansion of the West, the number of domestic banks increased to 12 and the number of foreign-owned banks to 59. In contrast, Denmark, with a population of 5 million, has about

40 commercial banks and 200 savings banks as well as a number of foreign banks; Austria has about 38 joint-stock banks, 10 private banks, 165 savings banks, 1279 rural co-operatives, 10 provincial mortgage banks and a postal savings bank; and the US has about 14 700 banks. The Canadian banking system remains basically a banking oligopoly dominated by the "Big Five" (*see* BUSINESS ELITE), banks large not only by Canadian but by world standards. Ranked by assets in 1986, in a list of the largest banks in the free world, the ROYAL BANK ranked 45th; the BANK OF MONTREAL 55th; the CANADIAN IMPERIAL BANK OF COMMERCE, 63rd; the BANK OF NOVA SCOTIA, 78th; and the TORONTO-DOMINION BANK, 87th. The "Big Five" control over 90% of bank assets in Canada.

The development of the ECONOMY also changed banking practices. In the 19th century, the banks issued their own notes, which were used as money, but gradually governments supplanted this privilege until finally only the Bank of Canada could issue legal tender. Lending practices evolved from the primary banking function of making commercial loans that were self-liquidating within a year to making loans on grain secured by warehouse receipts, on proven reserves of oil in the ground and in the form of mortgages on real estate.

Other financial institutions providing some of these banking functions also began appearing early in Canadian history. Mortgage loan companies patterned after building societies in the UK opened in the 1840s and they evolved into "permanent" companies, eg, the Canada Permanent Mortgage Company, selling debentures and investing in mortgages. TRUST COMPANIES were also formed during this time to act as trustees and professionally manage estates and trusts; they gradually assumed banking functions, eg, providing savings and chequing accounts, and became major participants in the mortgage market. Savings banks first appeared in 1846 to collect savings from the public but that form of near-bank is relatively insignificant in the financial system.

The other major type of near-bank is the savings and credit co-operative, called a CREDIT UNION in most of Canada and a CAISSE POPULAIRE in some areas. After a slow start in the first half of the 20th century, credit unions grew rapidly by using deposits to extend loans to their members.

Role of Banks As is true with all financial institutions, the basic function of banks is to channel funds from individuals, organizations and governments with surplus funds to those wishing to use those funds, which is why they are called financial intermediaries. But banks also have a premiere position in this financial intermediation because of their role in providing the payment system while acting as the vehicle for Canadian monetary policy and as the federal government's instrument for some social and political policies. Consequently the actions of the banks have a major impact on the efficiency with which the country's resources are allocated. In addition to these wider roles, the banks also have an obligation to their shareholders to earn an adequate return on their equity and pay sufficient dividends. If these goals are neglected, investors will withdraw their capital from the banking system and force either a contraction of the money supply or government ownership.

The experience of the early 1980s reveals the conflict that can arise among these purposes and goals in the Canadian banking system. The federal government encouraged the banks to extend huge loans to Canadian companies that wished to take over subsidiaries of foreign companies, especially in the oil and gas industry. This was sometimes in defiance of sound banking practice, and it had wider economic implications, such as the misallocation of credit resources, pressure on the Canadian dollar and an inflationary expansion of the money supply. As a result, the domestic loan portfolio of the banks began deteriorating sharply in 1982 to what was certainly its worst condition in the postwar period. Loans to the highly cyclical real-estate industry accounted for about 120% of bank capital; loans to oil and gas companies such as DOME, Sulpetro and Turbo, to forest product companies and to MASSEY-FERGUSON and International Harvester also imperilled the financial strength of the banks.

International lending practices of Canadian banks were equally disastrous. Brisk demand and wide profit margins encouraged the larger Canadian banks to pursue international borrowers vigorously with the result that their foreign assets increased from $21.7 billion in 1973 to $156.7 billion in 1983. Many of these loans were made to governments or government-guaranteed borrowers on the theory, which any student of history knows is incorrect, that governments do not default on loans. By the summer of 1983, over 40 countries had agreed to or had applied for rescheduling of their debt or had accumulated substantial arrears in interest payments. Furthermore, banks began extending new credits to foreign lenders to enable them to pay interest on older loans. This sleight of hand was good for the reported earnings of the banks but did little or nothing to resolve the serious problem of international debt.

Predictably, the result of both the domestic and international lending policies was huge losses for the banks and intensified malaise and costs for Canadians. In an effort to combat the impact on bank earnings, the margin or difference between the prime rate and the cost of funds was pushed to the highest level in many years. In 1980 the banks' prime rate was 15.5% and the rate on bank savings deposits was 12.5%, a "spread" of 3%, but 2 years later, the prime rate was at the same level while the savings account rate had dropped to 11%, a spread of 4.5%. In 1986 the spread dropped slightly to 4%. Borrowers were therefore paying a higher than normal price for money while savings received less than a normal return. In addition to these penalties, the high proportion of bank assets tied up in nonproductive loans restricted the banks' flexibility in accommodating credit-worthy borrowers.

Source of Assets and Liabilities When a bank or other financial institution is incorporated, it begins operations by selling shares to investors and the funds raised in this manner become the shareholders' equity. The bank will then try to attract deposits from the public in the form of demand deposits, which can be withdrawn by cheque at any time and which normally pay no interest; savings accounts, which pay a variable rate of interest and have restrictions on their withdrawal; and deposits with a fixed term of a few days to 5 years, paying a fixed rate of interest. In 1986 the banks held $19.2 billion in demand deposits, $85.3 billion in savings accounts and $83.3 billion in term deposits. All of this deposit money is a liability or debt of the bank, used to acquire assets that can generate profits and pay the interest and operating costs. Public demand and government regulations require that the banks keep some of their assets in the form of cash and investments, eg, treasury bills, which can be quickly converted into cash. Most of the remaining financial resources are invested in securities such as bonds and term-preferred shares and in loans and mortgages. In 1986 Canadian banks held $3.0 billion in cash, $28.3 billion in securities, $132.4 billion in Canadian loans, $47.9 billion in mortgages and $146.9 billion in foreign currency loans.

Banks, trust companies and credit unions have historically concentrated their assets and liabilities in different areas but this has been changing over the past 10 years. The banks monopolized the market for demand accounts because at one time they were the only deposit institution offering bank accounts with chequing privileges; they still control the huge corporate accounts, but the trust companies and credit unions have been taking a larger slice of the market for personal chequing accounts. The market shares for savings accounts have changed little over the past decade. On the liability side, banks are still the predominant lenders to business and government but have also recently grabbed a big share of the consumer credit and mortgage market.

Profits The profits of the Canadian banks rose rapidly between 1972 and 1982 because of a combination of factors. First, the assets of the banking system increased 5.8 times (domestic assets 4.5 times and foreign assets 9.6 times). The increase in foreign assets (from 26% to 43% of total assets) was largely responsible for rising profits because their rate of return rose from 0.58% in 1975 to 0.69% in 1980. In contrast the rate of return on domestic assets fell from 0.68% to 0.42% during the period. Second, the banks increased their assets faster than they increased their shareholders' equity. As a result of this higher leverage, the assets-to-capital ratio rose from 22.3 in 1972 to 29.8 in 1982. This trend increased both the potential for profit and the degree of risk in the banking system. Third, the wider spread between the lending and borrowing rates coupled with increased bank charges for services such as chequing, safety deposit boxes and lending fees became more important in boosting profits towards the end of the decade. Fourth, loan losses had not yet become a significant depressant to profits. The banks stated that their actual loan loss rose from $364.4 million in 1978 to $2.42 billion in 1982, but there is enormous variation in the way different banks account for problem loans. Earnings of the different banks were consequently overstated by 20-45% depending on the problems they encountered. Fifth, the 41% increase in bank profits in 1981 and continued gains in early 1982 created such a public outcry that the federal government attempted to mollify the public by appointing a parliamentary committee to examine bank profits. Not unexpectedly, the committee reported that the apparent excess profit resulted from higher leverage, rapid asset growth and international operations. Profits were not excessive, and the low rate of income tax was largely the result of government policy. The committee also recommended a number of measures to strengthen the banking system, increased disclosure of their financial condition, and the provision of some means for resolving consumer complaints. The inspector general of banking has acted on some of these recommendations, particularly in the areas of loan loss provisions and directives regarding the adequacy of the capital base and the leverage ratios.

Banking Structure and Operation Canadian commercial banks, like other investor-owned organizations, are managed by a board of directors, headed by a chairman, which oversees a president and vice-presidents representing special areas of the bank. These boards of banks are considered the most prestigious appointments of all boards; they are large (35 to 50 members) and their members are generally also members of boards of other major companies. Fifty-six directors of the 5 largest banks sit on the boards of the 16 largest life insurance companies, controlling 83% of that industry. The directors of the Royal Bank and the Bank of Montreal also sit on the boards of 44% of the companies that rank among the 250 largest nonfinancial, nonbanking companies in Canada. Thirteen out of the 16 large insurance companies have 31 "interlocking directorships" with 14 trust companies. At one time, many bank directors were also directors of trust companies, but interlocks between banks and trust companies are now forbidden – a restriction that has had little practical effect in loosening the control of the many by the few.

The structure of Canadian banking is also distinguished by the system of branch banking. Canadians have one of the highest ratios of banking branches to population in the world, with one deposit branch for every 3200 Canadians; but if the branches of the trust companies and credit unions are included, there is one deposit branch for every 1900 Canadians. Fifty-three percent of the branches, however, belong to 5 banks. However, there is a strong trend toward the reduction of branches and the cutting of their personnel.

In the last revision (1980) of the Bank Act, 2 types of banks were defined in Canada: Schedule A banks have wide public ownership and only 10% can be owned by a single foreign or domestic investor and only 25% by all foreign investors. Schedule B banks can be partially or wholly owned by domestic or foreign investors but can, in total, own no more that 16% of total outstanding bank loans to Canadian residents. There are now 58 Schedule B banks in Canada, concentrating and competing heavily in the market for loans to medium- and small-scale business.

Regulation of Banking According to the CONSTITUTION ACT, 1867, banking is regulated by the federal government and property and civil rights are provincial responsibilities. The first BANK ACT, virtually drafted by the Bank of Montreal, put Maritime banks under the control of federal banks. In 1894 the Bankers Association (later the CBA) was founded. A powerful lobby group, it was given the right to determine the fitness of bankers seeking charters, and under the regimes of both Macdonald and Wilfrid Laurier, bankers effectively chose the ministers of finance by threatening to excite financial crises if the candidates suggested by the prime ministers were approved.

In 1964 the Royal Commission on BANKING AND FINANCE (Porter Commission) recommended "a more open and competitive banking system," but most of its suggestions for reform (eg, that banking be legally defined to prevent banks from straying into other areas) were not followed. The 1967 Bank Act revision lifted the 6% per annum interest-rate ceiling banks could charge and allowed banks to enter the mortgage field. As a result, banks increased their mortgage portfolio in 3 years from $825 million to $18.6 billion. The 1967 Act also barred the previously legal practice of collective rate setting by banks and required banks to inform borrowers better about the real cost of loans. In the same year, the federal government also passed an act to establish the Canada Deposit Insurance Corporation to provide $20 000 insurance for deposits in banks and federally chartered near-banks. Provincially chartered trust companies were protected to a similar extent by provincial legislation.

The 1977 Bank Act revisions were delayed until 1980. In 1977 a legislative proposal that would have required banks to provide better disclosure of interest charges was defeated. As a result of changes in the Bank Act of 1980 the Canadian Payments Association was established as the agency responsible for the cheque clearing system; reserve requirements were reduced, increasing bank assets by millions of dollars; the minister of finance became the sole arbiter deciding which new banks could be established; foreign banks were allowed to establish themselves and required to keep reserves but their growth was restricted in various ways; banks were allowed to become involved in the business of leasing large equipment; banks were allowed to become involved in factoring; and banks (but not their subsidiaries) were limited to a 10% holding of residential mortgages. The banks are also regulated by the Bank of Canada under the authority of the Bank of Canada Act. The Bank of Canada regulates principally by controlling its cash reserves – the principal factor determining ability of the chartered banks to expand credit and increase their deposits. The Bank of Canada also uses its moral suasion to persuade banks to pursue certain desired courses of action.

Total Assets of the Canadian Banking System
(Source: Bank of Canada)

	1976 Million$	1986 Millions$	Annual(%) Increase 1976-1986
Banks	126 403	451 006	13.6
Trust and Mortgage Loan Companies	18 335	78 882	15.7
Credit Unions	15 692	44 045	10.9
Savings Banks	1118	3612	12.4
Total	161 548	577 545	13.6

Future of Banking The major structural change in banking, still in its formative stage, is the move towards an electronic funds transfer system. The old paper trail provided by cheques, passbooks and handwritten or hand-entered data is being replaced by computerization of the banking system through automatic teller machines, automatic clearinghouses, preauthorized payments and the automatic depositing of government cheques, payroll and bond interest. For the user of banking services, resulting advantages include multi-branch banking, increased hours of access to the banking system and a wider range of banking services and products. Disadvantages include problems in correcting errors and assigning responsibility for them and for infringements on personal PRIVACY by both banks and governments through easy access to the enormous data banks. Bank customers are also discovering that computerization has enabled banks to assign costs more accurately to individual banking transactions and then charge for these costs.   ALIX GRANGER

Reading: H.H. Binhammer, *Money, Banking and the Canadian Financial System* (1982); D.E. Bond et al, *The Economics of the Canadian Financial System* (1983); Alix Granger, *Don't Bank on It*, 2nd ed (1986); T. Naylor, *The History of Canadian Business*, vol 1 (1975).

Banking and Finance, Royal Commission on (Porter Commission), est 1961 (after the governor of the Bank of Canada, James COYNE, had publicly disagreed with the federal government's economic policies), to examine and to make recommendations for the improvement of "the structure and methods of operations of the Canadian financial system, including the banking and monetary system and the institutions and processes involved in the flow of funds through the capital markets."

The commission, which included several representatives of BANKING institutions, made many recommendations in its 1964 report, including the abolition of the 6% interest rate ceiling on bank loans; disclosure of bank-loan costs; entry of banks into conventional mortgage financing; and legislation to prevent banks from agreeing to set common interest rates, chequing costs and other customer charges. It also recommended that trust companies, finance companies, creditors and other "near-banks" be brought under the authority of the BANK OF CANADA; that the Bank Act be amended so that the government could overrule the central bank on MONETARY POLICY; and that government regulations be established to control mergers between banks and TRUST COMPANIES or bank takeovers of other financial institutions. Some of the recommendations were incorporated into the 1967 Bank Act revisions.

MARTIN KROSSEL

Bankruptcy, a legal process that provides financial relief for debtors and a protection for creditors. When an individual or a corporation goes bankrupt, an accountant (called a trustee) is appointed to take control of the debtor's assets and distribute them among the unpaid creditors. Once this process is completed the debtor is released from any further obligation to pay those debts. The bankruptcy process can be initiated either by the debtor or by one or more creditors. The debtor whose debts become unmanageable may go bankrupt so that he can be released from his debts and get a fresh start.

A debtor commences the process by making an "assignment in bankruptcy," which is essentially an agreement to turn over all of his assets to a trustee for sale and distribution to his creditors. Creditors can also "petition" a debtor into bankruptcy. There are several reasons why they would do this. Debtors are sometimes overoptimistic, spending all their remaining assets in an unrealistic hope of success. Sometimes they try to hide or sell property to keep a personal benefit and defeat creditors' claims. The appointment of a trustee in bankruptcy can prevent this. Creditors can petition the Bankruptcy Court (a division of the Supreme Court or Court of Queen's Bench in the common law provinces and of the Court Superior in Québec) and if they establish the individual or corporation's insolvent status then the court will grant a "receiving order," ie, a court order giving a trustee in bankruptcy control of the bankrupt's assets.

If the bankrupt is an individual, the trustee acquires control of all the assets except those that under the law of the province are exempt from seizure; if the bankrupt is a corporation, the trustee takes control of all its assets. Each province has slightly different exemptions, but most allow a debtor to keep a basic stock of clothing, furniture, tools and sometimes a car or truck and a basic equity in a home. A wage earner who has declared bankruptcy or is petitioned into bankruptcy can continue to work and earn money, but the trustee or the court may require that some payments be made to the trustee for the creditors before the final discharge is granted. The amount will depend on the income of the debtor and his degree of fault in becoming bankrupt. A corporation cannot resume business under its own control until or unless it pays all its debts. A bankruptcy deals only with unsecured debts; secured creditors with mortgages or liens remain free to enforce their security, and the trustee can only take what remains on behalf of the unsecured creditors.

Consumer bankruptcies passed the rate of 3000 per month, for the country as a whole, in Sept 1982; by Dec 1986 the monthly rate was 1666. There is now less stigma attached to bankruptcy in Canadian society. In addition, the recession of the early 1980s meant that, stigma or not, many more people were forced to bankruptcy as a last resort solution to problems of indebtedness. The incidence of bankruptcies tends to follow widespread crop failures, plant closures, mine shutdowns and local or general market collapses. There is also a marked "domino" effect, especially in single-industry towns and in cities heavily dependent on one form of economic activity.

The Bankruptcy Act provides a rehabilitative scheme for consumers short of bankruptcy called the "orderly payment of debts" plan. Under the plan, individuals with nonbusiness debts have their debts frozen. They work out a budget with a counsellor and make one monthly payment which is distributed among the creditors, who receive all their principal but over a longer period, and with interest reduced to a low rate. This plan (or an equivalent), offered through a provincial Consumer Affairs Department, is available in most provinces.

An increasingly used procedure under the Bankruptcy Act is a "proposal." A person or corporation in financial trouble can make a formal proposal to the creditors to pay them less money over a longer period of time in satisfaction of their debts. If the creditors agree, no bankruptcy occurs, leaving the individual in control of his assets. If they disagree or if a default is made in these lesser payments, bankruptcy occurs automatically. This allows some businesses to restructure their debts and continue to operate without going bankrupt. It is still, however, the least popular of the 2 alternatives: in Dec 1986 there were only 74 proposals across Canada but 618 business bankruptcies.   GAIL STARR

Banks, Harold Chamberlain, "Hal," trade-union leader (b at Waterloo, Iowa 28 Feb 1909; d at San Francisco, Calif 24 Sept 1985). A tough and ruthless seamen's leader, Banks was invited to Canada in 1949 by shipping-company interests acting with the support of the federal government and organized labour. They intended him to oust the communist-controlled CANADIAN SEAMEN'S UNION. Within 2 years the Canadian District of the Seafarers' International Union had, under Banks, won control of the collective-bargaining rights of almost all of Canada's sailors. While Banks achieved impressive gains in wages and working conditions for his members, he also ran the SEAFARERS' INTERNATIONAL UNION in a dictatorial manner. His attempt to expand his union's jurisdiction to represent mates and engineers brought him into conflict with other unions and ultimately with the CANADIAN LABOUR CONGRESS. This conflict precipitated bloody battles at Canadian ports and a general disruption in shipping. The federal government appointed a commission of inquiry under BC Court of Appeal Justice T.G. Norris. In

Banks Island, NWT, the 5th-largest island in Canada and the westernmost island of the Arctic Archipelago (*photo by Lyn Hancock*).

his report Norris described Banks as a hoodlum and a bully, and following a conviction for conspiracy to assault, Banks fled the country. Extradition was refused by the American government.
WILLIAM EDWARD KAPLAN

Reading: P. Edward, *Waterfront Warlord* (1987); W. Edward Kaplan, *Everything That Floats* (1987).

Banks Island, 70 028 km², fifth-largest island in Canada, westernmost island of the ARCTIC ARCHIPELAGO. It is bordered on the W by the Beaufort Sea and separated from Melville I on the N by M'Clure Strait and from Victoria I on the E by Prince of Wales Str. The SE coast is marked by dramatic cliffs of yellow, white and red quartzites. The low W coast is characterized by long, sandy offshore bars, rising at the SW tip to the spectacular Nelson Head cliffs (425 m) of Precambrian rock almost 2 billion years old – 325 million years older than any other part of the island. Limestone cliffs rise at Cape M'Clure and Cape Crozier on the N coast. Along the E coast the land slopes up from the beach into mud, sand and gravel cliffs. The highest point is Durham Heights (almost 730 m). The central portion is a level plain, cut by valleys of the larger rivers that rise near the E side. Seams of hard, impure coal underlie the NE plateau, and softer coal has been found around Mercy Bay. On the E side, which was glaciated, lakes are numerous and glacial till covers the hills.

Banks I was first sighted by Lt F.W. BEECHEY, a member of the W.E. PARRY expedition, Aug 1820, and named for Sir Joseph Banks, president of the Royal Society. R.J. MCCLURE landed on the S coast 1850. V. STEFANSSON reached the island across the ice of the Beaufort Sea and established a base near Cape Kellet. The island was inhabited by Inuit at least 500 years ago, but except for an air base at Sachs Harbour, it is now uninhabited except for trappers. There is a large arctic fox population, as well as caribou, polar bears, wolves, muskoxen, arctic hare, lemmings, wolverines, seal and occasionally grizzly bears. White and bowhead whales are common offshore. Numerous species of birds are found, including some 200 000 lesser snow geese, black brant, eiders, whistling swan, snowy owls, rough-legged hawks and ravens. Arctic char have been taken at the mouths of the Sachs, De Salis and Thomsen rivers; whitefish and trout at the Thomsen. The only biting insect is the mosquito.   JAMES MARSH

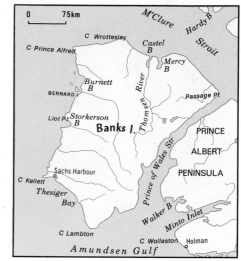

Bannatyne, Andrew Graham Ballenden, businessman, politician (b on South Ronaldsay, Orkney Is 31 Oct 1829; d at St Paul, Minn 18 May 1889). Bannatyne was one of Red River's most prominent businessmen whose concern for the future led him, in 1869-70, to support Louis RIEL and the hope for a multiracial society. He entered the service of the HBC at 14, but left it in 1851 to set up as a free trader with his father-in-law Andrew McDermot. By the late 1860s, Bannatyne and his new partner, Alexander BEGG, were the largest retail and wholesale merchants in Red River. When Riel began his resistance in 1869, Bannatyne supported the demand for a negotiated entry into Canada and tried with some success to act as a liaison between whites and mixed bloods. There were some stormy scenes with the erratic Riel, but Bannatyne brought stability as a member of the provisional government. In 1873-74, he abetted Riel's elections to the House of Commons and, after Riel was declared an outlaw and his seat of Provencher vacated, Bannatyne was elected by acclamation in 1875.

Bannatyne had little interest in federal politics and did not seek re-election. During the 1870s, he sold his business and turned to land speculation, at which he prospered; but his fortunes were shattered when the western land boom collapsed in 1882.   J.E. REA

Bannock [Old English *bannuc*, "morsel"], a form of bread that served as a staple in the diets of early settlers and fur traders. It took the form of a flat round cake or pancake. Ingredients included unleavened flour, lard, salt, water and sometimes baking powder. Bannock derives from the cookery of Scotland and N England.
JOHN ROBERT COLOMBO

Banting, Sir Frederick Grant, co-discoverer of INSULIN (b at Alliston, Ont 14 Nov 1891; d near Musgrave Harbour, Nfld 21 Feb 1941). Youngest of 6 children of a middle-class farm family, Fred Banting persevered through high school, failed first year in arts at U of T and then enrolled in medicine. He graduated in 1916 with above average grades, served as a medical officer in France, where he was wounded in action and decorated for valour, and in 1919-20 completed his training as an orthopedic surgeon. In July 1920 he began the practice of medicine in London, Ont.

On the night of 31 Oct 1920, after reading a routine article in a medical journal, Banting wrote down an idea for research aimed at isolating the long-sought internal secretion of the pancreas. He received support for his proposed research at U of T, where he began work on 17

Sir Frederick Banting, co-discoverer of insulin and recipient of the Nobel Prize (*courtesy National Archives of Canada/PA-123481/Arthur S. Goos*).

May 1921 under the direction of J.J.R. MACLEOD and assisted by C.H. BEST. Banting's and Best's experiments were crudely conducted and did not substantiate Banting's idea, which was physiologically incorrect. But their apparently favourable results encouraged greater efforts, which culminated in the winter of 1921-22 in the discovery of insulin by a team of researchers that included Macleod, Banting, J.B. COLLIP and Best.

Insulin was immediately and spectacularly effective as a lifesaving therapy for DIABETES MELLITUS. Banting was hailed as the principal discoverer of insulin because his idea had launched the research, because of his prominence in the early use of insulin, and because he and his friends carried on a campaign to discredit his senior collaborators, Macleod and Collip, with whom he was temperamentally incompatible. On learning that he was to share the 1923 Nobel Prize for physiology or medicine with Macleod, Banting gave half his prize money to Best. He was awarded a life annuity by the federal government, appointed Canada's first professor of medical research at U of T and knighted in 1934.

Banting supervised important research into silicosis and problems in aviation medicine before his death on a flight to England in 1941 to look into the state of medical research there. But his own research was trivial, for he was not in fact a skilled or well-trained scientist. The burden of his fame weighed heavily on an insecure but determined man, leading to a turbulent personal life and considerable unhappiness. He became an accomplished amateur painter, whose work strongly reflects the influence of his friend and sketching companion, A.Y. JACKSON. He was survived by his second wife and by a son from his first marriage. In several magazine polls during his lifetime, he was judged the most famous living Canadian.
MICHAEL BLISS

Reading: Michael Bliss, *Banting: A Biography* (1984) and *The Discovery of Insulin* (1982).

Baptists, originally ANABAPTISTS ("rebaptized"), persons and groups who, during the 16th-century Protestant Reformation, rejected infant baptism and (re)baptized adult believers upon profession of faith. The 2 terms later came to signify divergent traditions. Baptists accept the Bible as the reliable record of God's revelation to mankind and as the only norm for Christian beliefs and practices. They have produced many confessions of faith, but such statements are not regarded as binding interpretations of the Bible. Ideally, every believer and every congregation has "soul liberty," freedom to interpret the Scriptures and to seek guidance from the Spirit of God on all matters. The local church is seen as a fellowship of believers who have made a commitment to follow Christ, usually in an experience of spiritual rebirth or conversion, have made a public confession of faith, and have submitted to the rite of "believer's baptism." As a rule, only such persons may join a Baptist church. Since the 1640s Baptists have used immersion of the whole body under water as the only form of baptism. The second ordinance (seldom described as a sacrament) is communion, a simple commemoration of Christ's sacrifice on the cross observed by most Baptist churches on the first Sunday of each month.

Ministry is conceived as a service to which all disciples are called in order to make use of their gifts (the priesthood of all believers). The pastor's task is seen as a full-time calling to preach, teach, counsel, train and co-ordinate the ministries exercised by all members. Ordination, to which in many Baptist churches both women and men are admitted, is not a sacrament; it provides for public recognition of the call, gifts and training for ministry. Deacons are lay men and women elected from the local congregation to assist with pastoral care, communion celebration and general administration. Local churches enjoy freedom to make decisions concerning beliefs, practices, calling of ministers, organization, finances and property. Democratic procedures are accepted at all levels of church government. Wider ecclesial structures (never designated as churches but rather as associations, conventions, unions, conferences, federations) do not in any way limit the autonomy of local churches. They facilitate fellowship and co-operative programs. The principle of congregational self-government, as well as theological and ethnic differences, have prevented the formation of one national body. Baptists in Canada remain divided into 5 major and several smaller bodies.

The first English-speaking Baptist church was founded 1609 in Amsterdam, Netherlands, by Puritan refugees from England. The oldest congregation in England was organized 1612 near London, and the first in America at Providence, RI, in 1639. The original Baptist churches in Canada were formed under ministers from Massachusetts, at Sackville, NS (now in NB), in 1763 and Horton (now Wolfville), NS, in 1765 or 1766. Both congregations ceased to exist in the mid-1770s, although the church in Wolfville, re-covenanted in 1778, is the oldest continuing Baptist church in Canada. The GREAT AWAKENING in Nova Scotia, and revivals in the 19th century led to rapid growth in the Maritimes. In New Brunswick Baptists became the largest Protestant denomination. Originally, the majority adhered to the Regular (CALVINIST) theological orientation while a minority endorsed the opposing Free Will (Arminian) position, maintaining the possibility of salvation for all. The 2 groups merged in 1906 to form the United Baptist Convention of the Maritime Provinces. In 1963 "Maritime" was changed to "Atlantic" (UBCAP) to include Newfoundland, where Baptist churches were introduced in the 1950s. Churches organized in the African United Baptist Assn (part of UBCAP) have been important in the large black community in NS. Only in the Atlantic provinces have Canadian Baptists avoided organizational schism.

In Upper and Lower Canada Baptist life was shaped from the beginning by conflicting convictions and traditions among immigrants from the US and Britain. The first churches were planted by American ministers (Caldwell's Manor in the Eastern Townships, LC, in 1794, and a church near Beamsville, UC, in 1796). They excluded non-Baptists from communion. Newcomers from England endorsing "open communion" influenced the development of Baptist churches in Montréal and eastern Ontario. From 1815 on, immigrants from the Scottish Highlands brought the revivalist tradition of James and Robert Haldane to the Ottawa Valley. Controversy over communion practice and other disagreements hindered co-operation in missionary work and education for several decades. In 1888, 2 regional bodies united in the Baptist Convention of Ontario and Quebec (BCOQ). From the 1820s on, slaves escaping from the southern US by the UNDERGROUND RAILROAD established a network of black congregations. In the 1830s, French-speaking immigrants from Switzerland arrived in Québec, and under Henriette Feller (1800-68) initiated Baptist work in Montréal and the Eastern Townships (the Grande Ligne Mission). In 1969 the French churches organized their own Union d'églises baptistes françaises au Canada (UEBFC).

In 1873 Ontario Baptists sent a minister to Winnipeg. The First Baptist Church was established there in 1875, and in 1884 the Baptist Convention of Manitoba and the North-West was organized. Meanwhile, churches were founded on the Pacific coast, in Victoria (1876) and New Westminster (1878). The Convention of Baptist Churches in BC was formed in 1897. Ten years later the churches in the western provinces formed the Baptist Convention of Western Canada, renamed the Baptist Union of Western Canada in 1909. In central and western Canada, Baptist congregations, composed of immigrants, worship in more than 30 different languages. In recent years, the fastest-growing Baptist churches in Canada have been Chinese speaking.

Repeated calls for a national fellowship finally led in 1944 to the Baptist Federation of Canada. The name was changed to Canadian Baptist Federation in 1983. Affiliation with any of the unions or conventions implies membership in CBF. Its primary concerns are national, international and interdenominational. It also facilitates consultation and co-operation in work done by the 4 constituent bodies in such areas as EVANGELISM, Christian education and chaplaincies, and it sponsors an extensive program of relief and development overseas. The only other national agency related to CBF is the Canadian Baptist Overseas Mission Board, fd 1912. It assists churches in 11 countries and supports 120 Canadian missionaries. *See* MISSIONS AND MISSIONARIES.

The Fellowship of Evangelical Baptist Churches in Canada (FEBC), the second-largest Baptist body, dates back to the 1953 merger between the Union of Regular Baptist Churches, fd 1927, and the Fellowship of Independent Baptist Churches, fd 1933. Both groups appeared in the aftermath of the fundamentalist-modernist theological controversy of the mid-1920s, led by Dr Thomas Todhunter SHIELDS, pastor of Jarvis Street Baptist Church in Toronto (*see* EVANGELICAL AND FUNDAMENTALIST MOVEMENTS). About one-seventh of the churches in BCOQ left the convention and formed 2 groups. In 1965 the Convention of Regular Baptists of BC, fd 1927, and the Prairie Regular Baptist Missionary Fellowship, fd 1930, joined FEBC.

In addition to the 2 largest Baptist bodies, CBF and FEBC, with their roots in the Canadian Protestant tradition, there are 3 conventions and several smaller groups which maintain close links with the corresponding Baptist groups in the US even though they now have separate Canadian

Baptists in Canada

Groups	Churches	Members
Canadian Baptist Federation (includes the following groups):	125	136 000
United B Conv of Atlantic Provinces	550	67 000
B Convention of Ont and Québec	390	47 000
Union of French B Churches	25	1000
B Union of Western Canada	160	21 000
Fellowship of Evangelical B Churches	475	56 000
North American Baptist Conference	120	18 000
General Conference of Canada	75	6000
Canadian Convention of Southern B	80	5000
Other B bodies – estimated total	75	4000
Independent B churches – est total	150	5000
Total	2100	230 000

administrations. The North American Baptist Conference is a fellowship of originally German-speaking churches. The oldest such congregation was organized in Bridgeport, Ont, in 1851 but most of the churches today are located in the western provinces and have long since lost ethnic identity. Swedish immigrants founded Baptist churches in Waterville, Qué, Winnipeg and elsewhere in the 1890s. Their descendants continue a separate fellowship known as the Baptist General Conference of Canada. Nearly all of their congregations today are in western Canada. Against the protests of the older indigenous Canadian Baptist bodies, the largest Protestant denomination in the US, the Southern Baptists, expanded work into western and central Canada from the 1950s on. In 1985 the congregations, which were originally associated with the American body, formed the Canadian Convention of Southern Baptists, with affiliated churches in all except the Atlantic provinces. A few Bible Baptist Churches and Seventh-Day Baptist Churches relate to the corresponding bodies in the US.

The Canadian Baptist mosaic has been further enriched by several small groups with distinctive identities. For example, the Alliance of Reformed Baptist Churches, fd 1888 in NB as part of the holiness movement, merged with the Wesleyan Methodist Church in 1966. In 1968 the new body joined the Pilgrim Holiness Church to become the Wesleyan Church. The Primitive Baptist Conference of New Brunswick traces its origin (about 1875) to the leadership of George W. Orser. Recently this conference established links with the National Association of Free-Will Baptists in the US. The Association of Regular Baptist Churches (Canada), organized in 1957, comprises a small cluster of churches led by Toronto's Jarvis Street Baptist Church. There are also many independent Baptist congregations which are not affiliated with any larger group.

Several conventions or conferences co-operate in the Baptist World Alliance. With 125 member conventions in 100 countries, the BWA reports global membership of 34 million adults. Baptists have been divided in their attitudes to ecumenical relations. Many congregations co-operate with other churches in evangelism, joint services and social ministries, and many support the EVANGELICAL FELLOWSHIP OF CANADA. The BUWC and the Baptist General Conference are member bodies of the EFC. CBF was a member of the CANADIAN COUNCIL OF CHURCHES from its founding in 1944. In 1980, however, it terminated its affiliation because of lack of consensus among its 4 constituent conventions. Only BCOQ remains in the CCC. No Canadian Baptist body joined the World Council of Churches.

Baptists were among the earliest advocates of religious freedom and of separation between church and state. They participate in the political, economic and cultural life, and seek to implement the lordship of Christ in all spheres of life.

In the second quarter of the 19th century Bap-
tists fought for equal educational opportunities for all citizens. Acadia College in Wolfville, NS, was the first post-secondary institution in Canada which did not impose denominational tests for students or teachers. In Ontario Baptists gave leadership in the struggle over CLERGY RESERVES and the establishment of a nonsectarian provincial university in Toronto. Baptists founded several colleges: Acadia College (1838), later called ACADIA UNIVERSITY; Canada Baptist College at Montréal (1838-49); Woodstock College, Woodstock, Ont (1857) and Toronto Baptist College (1881), both to be replaced by MCMASTER UNIVERSITY; and Brandon College (1899-1938), now BRANDON UNIVERSITY. All have passed from Baptist control. However, the different Baptist conventions and conferences today operate 2 colleges, 11 seminaries and several BIBLE SCHOOLS and centres for lay training. Among the many Baptist educators and scholars 2 deserve special mention: George P. Gilmour, pres of McMaster U (1950-61), and Watson KIRKCONNELL, pres of Acadia U (1948-64). In politics, several leaders enjoyed close association with the Baptist fellowship: PMs Alexander MACKENZIE, Charles TUPPER and John DIEFENBAKER; and premiers William ABERHART, Ernest MANNING and Thomas DOUGLAS.

Baptist membership statistics as listed in the table do not include children nor adherents who may actively participate in church life but have not joined the church after public profession of faith and baptism. The total constituency as reported by the 1981 census (the last year for which figures are available) was 696 850 persons, a substantial increase from 422 312 in 1921. Nevertheless, Baptists, like other major Protestant denominations, declined as a proportion of the total Canadian population from 4.8% in 1921 to 2.9% in 1981. *J.K. ZEMAN*

Reading: Paul R. Dekar and Murray J.S. Ford, eds, *Celebrating the Canadian Baptist Heritage* (1985); J.E. Harris, *The Baptist Union of Western Canada* (1976); Stuart Ivison and Fred Rosser, *The Baptists in Upper and Lower Canada Before 1820* (1956); George Edward Levy, *The Baptists of the Maritime Provinces 1753-1946* (1946); H. Leon McBeth, *The Baptist Heritage* (1987); Robert G. Torbet, *A History of Baptists*, 3rd ed (1973); J.H. Watt, *The Fellowship Story* (1978); J.K. Zeman, *Baptist Roots and Identity* (1978) and, ed, *Baptists in Canada* (1980).

Barachois Pond Provincial Park (est 1962, 35 km²), one of the largest of over 70 parks in Newfoundland and Labrador, is located at the head of St George's Bay, 70 km S of Corner Brook along the Trans-Canada Highway. It occupies part of the Appalachian Mts, known in the area as the Long Range, formed over 450 million years ago. Subsequent EROSION reduced the peaks to less than 400 m and glaciers gouged out the valley now filled by Barachois Pond. The area is forested, predominantly with spruce, fir, larch and aspen, although stands of black ash and white pine (rare in Newfoundland) occur, as do many ORCHIDS. Mammals include snowshoe hare, beavers, caribou and the elusive pine marten. Over 100 species of birds inhabit the park, including the rare arctic 3-toed woodpecker. For generations the area was used by moose, caribou and rabbit hunters, and by loggers and local residents seeking fuel wood. The area is now dedicated to nature protection and recreation. There is a modern campsite and opportunities for swimming, motorboating, canoeing, fishing and hiking (the trail to Erin Mt offering fine views). In winter, no services are provided but the park is available for skiing, snowshoeing, snowmobiling and ice fishing. *JOHN S. MARSH*

Barbeau, Charles Marius, ethnologist, folklorist, ethnomusicologist (b at Ste-Marie-de-Beauce, Qué 5 Mar 1883; d at Ottawa 27 Feb

Marius Barbeau collected a vast archive of French Canadian and Indian songs, texts and artifacts, and was the founder of professional folklore studies in Canada (*courtesy National Archives of Canada/C-34447*).

1969). Founder of professional FOLKLORE studies in Canada, he worked at the National Museum from 1911 to the late 1960s, collecting a vast archive of traditional songs, texts and artifacts – especially of French Canadian and native peoples. Taught at home by his parents until age 12, he entered training for the priesthood at 14, but then went on to study law at Laval. After law school, he studied as a Rhodes scholar at Oxford, where he became intrigued by anthropology. With his diploma in anthropology he was recommended for a post at the newly formed National Museum in Ottawa. Barbeau made his most enduring contribution as a collector of folk traditions, with nearly 1000 publications and many more thousands of texts and songs now preserved in archives.

His first loyalty was to his homeland in Québec, and he was sure that rural Québec had preserved folk traditions reaching back to medieval times. Nevertheless, he worked in the US and across Canada, in particular with the TSIMSHIAN in BC. Two themes are prominent in his life – homeland and journeys – and the Tsimshian myth of an ancient migration from a distant homeland convinced him that they had journeyed as a tribe from Asia within living memory. While anthropologists no longer accept this hypothesis, it was a powerful motive for Barbeau's activity over the years, aided by Tsimshian William BEYNON, in recording the tribe's traditional lore in order to preserve the legacy of a fading past in the face of the pressures of the industrial age.

Barbeau also founded the Archives de folklore at Laval and several folklore groups, and was especially successful in bringing ethnology and folklore to the Canadian public, through several prizewinning books and tireless lecturing and teaching. He received many honours and awards, including honorary doctorates from Montréal, Laval and Oxford, and was made a Companion of the Order of Canada. *R.J. PRESTON*

Reading: C.M. Barbeau, *The Downfall of Temlaham* (1928) and *Quebec: Where Ancient France Lingers* (1936); Barbeau and Edward Sapir, *Folk Songs of French Canada* (1925).

Barbeau, Jean, dramatist (b at St-Romuald, Qué 10 Feb 1945). He is best known for his humorous but sympathetic treatment of *joual,* the popular idiom of Québec, in such plays as *Manon Lastcall* (1972) and *Joualez-moi d'amour* (1972), the latter a brilliant description arising from Québec's linguistic and cultural dichotomy. *Le Chemin de Lacroix* (1971), *0-71* (1971) and *Ben-Ur* (1971) also deal, in less amusing fashion, with the psychological victims of his province's malaise. Barbeau's more recent works deal with broader themes, as in *Le Jardin de la maison blanche* (1979), a stinging criticism of the materialistic values of contemporary N American society. He is one of the most productive and most popular of current playwrights in Québec.   L.E. DOUCETTE

Barbeau, Marcel, painter, sculptor, filmmaker (b at Montréal 18 Feb 1925). An active member of the AUTOMATISTES led by Paul-Émile BORDUAS, Barbeau is a widely exhibited, innovative artist. His early training was thorough. As well as studying drawing at the École du meuble, Montréal, he worked with Borduas, with architect Marcel Parizeau and art historian Maurice Gagnon. He travelled extensively 1962-74, living and exhibiting in Paris, New York and California, and his style changed, moving from the lyrical abstracts of the Automatiste period towards a more geometric mode. By the 1980s, however, he had returned to the free-form, all-over surface activity that he had favoured before. His sculptures have appeared in shows in Montréal (1984) and Toronto (1986). Barbeau is also a filmmaker, producing *Désirs-mouvements* (1977), and a performance artist.   ANN DAVIS

Barber, Clarence Lyle, economist (b near Wolseley, Sask 5 May 1917). His experience of prairie farm life during the GREAT DEPRESSION gave him a commitment to improving Canadian economic policy, and a concern for the needs of farmers. After study at the universities of Saskatchewan, Clark and Minnesota and 2 years in the RCAF, Barber joined the Dominion Bureau of Statistics in 1945, moving to McMaster in 1948 and in 1949 to the University of Manitoba, until his retirement in 1984. Barber has written many articles and monographs on economic theory and policy in a Canadian context. He directed the research which led to the Greater Winnipeg Floodway, served as UN adviser to the Philippines; and, from 1966 to 1970, conducted a one-man Royal Commission on Farm Machinery. He was a member of the Royal Commission on the ECONOMIC UNION AND DEVELOPMENT PROSPECTS FOR CANADA 1982-85. In 1977 he was elected to the RSC.   A.M.C. WATERMAN

Barber and Barber, Winnipeg's most prolific architectural firm 1876-88. Founded in 1876 by Charles Arnold Barber (b at Irish Creek, near Athens, Canada W *c*1847; d 1916) and joined in 1882 by his brother, Earle William Barber (b 1855; d 1915), the firm designed over 100 buildings in Manitoba in little more than a decade. Apparently neither brother had professional or academic architectural training, and by the mid-1880s their style began to lose favour in competition with better-educated architects. After a scandal over contracting estimates for Winnipeg City Hall, the brothers left town (1887) and set up practice in Duluth, Minn, and Superior, Wis.   WILLIAM P. THOMPSON

Barbour, Douglas, poet, professor, critic, publisher (b at Winnipeg 21 Mar 1940). Minimalist, unmetaphoric, his work since *Land Fall* (1971) aims for precise linguistic equivalence to the poet's relation to what his eye *sees*, a theme worked out most fully in *Visions of My Grandfather* (1977). In *Songbook* (1973), *Shore Lines* (1979) and *The Harbingers* (1984), writing itself becomes the landscape: the poems create meaning largely through phonemic, often contrapuntal, sound patterns.

This phase of Barbour's work finds its most radical development in his collaboration with Stephen SCOBIE in the "homolinguistic translations" of *The Pirates of Pen's Chance* (1981) and in their performance duo *re:sounding*. Concluding his selected poems, *Visible Visions* (1984), "breath ghazals" conjoin sound poetry and colloquialism in a new exploration of lyric. Barbour is an active publisher, a member of NeWest Press (1978) and co-founder (with Shirley Neuman and Stephen SCOBIE) of Longspoon Press (1980-87). He is professor of English at U of A.   SHIRLEY NEUMAN

Barker, William George, "Billy," fighter pilot (b at Dauphin, Man 3 Nov 1894; d at Ottawa 12 Mar 1930). He was credited with 53 aerial victories during WWI, but is mostly remembered for the epic, single-handed combat against some 60 German aircraft that won him the Victoria Cross on 27 Oct 1918. After the war he joined W.A. BISHOP in an ill-conceived commercial aviation venture in Toronto, but in June 1922 he accepted a commission in the Canadian Air Force and briefly became the first director of the RCAF. He was fatally injured when his Fairchild aircraft crashed at Rockcliffe Air Station, Ottawa.   BRERETON GREENHOUS

Barkerville, BC, is a restored gold-rush town in the BC interior. The Fraser R GOLD RUSH, the first of several in BC, reached the area (125 km SE of PRINCE GEORGE) in 1862 when William Barker, a Cornish sailor, made a huge strike there. The CARIBOO ROAD, of which Barkerville was the northern terminus, was completed 1864, and brought large freight wagons and stagecoaches to the town, making it part of the Cariboo district, a long corridor of contiguous development. Barkerville's population soared. In 1863 the gold commissioner estimated the town's population at 10 000, though most of the miners still wintered in Victoria or San Francisco. Its permanent residents included merchants, hoteliers, builders and bankers. As the region's population stabilized, Barkerville began to develop a cultural life. Sunday labour was stopped; the miners unionized for shorter shifts; a Masonic Hall was built (1866); an HBC store set up (1867); resident preachers became prominent in the town; entertainment shifted from horse racing and variety to legitimate plays (1868); and gambling was outlawed. On 16 Sept 1864 most of the town, including the Masonic Hall, was destroyed by fire. Some 100 houses and businesses had been rebuilt by 1869. Government offices were maintained there owing to the occasional mining "excitement" in the district, but by 1900 the town had faded considerably. During the 1930s it became a satellite of

Col Billy Barker, VC, in one of the captured German airplanes against which he fought his last battle (*by permission of the British Library*).

Wells, site of the Cariboo Gold Quartz mine. Barkerville lost its role as an administrative centre in the 1950s, and became a ghost town. In 1958 the provincial government undertook to restore the historic town as part of its centennial celebrations. In 1959 Barkerville was made a provincial historic park.   ALAN F.J. ARTIBISE

Reading: Fred Ludditt, *Barkerville Days* (1969).

Barley, common name for members of genus *Hordeum* of the GRASS family (Gramineae). Many wild and cultivated forms occur and, since all cultivated forms and some of the wild ones are interfertile, they are assumed to belong to one species, *H. vulgare.* Because of its ability to adapt to a wide range of soil and climate conditions, barley is widely grown in many parts of the world and was one of the earliest cultivated CROPS. Although the centre of origin is not known, barley has been gathered or cultivated for thousands of years in the Middle East, Far East, North Africa and east-central Africa.

The barley plant has a cylindrical stem which is hollow, except at the nodes (solid areas from which the leaves arise). The spike or head is composed of spikelets attached to the nodes of a zigzag structure known as a rachis. Each spikelet consists of 2 husks or hulls, enclosing male and female floral parts. The rachis nodes may have either one or 3 spikelets, giving the spike the appearance of having 2 or 6 rows of kernels; hence, the names 2-rowed and 6-rowed barley.

Barley is referred to as having either a spring or a winter habit of growth. Spring-sown types, which mature in 80-90 days, predominate in Canada. Slightly acid, well-drained loams or clay loams are preferred. Barley can be attacked by fungal plant diseases (eg, stem rust, smuts), bacterial blight and virus diseases (eg, yellow dwarf). It is also prone to agronomic problems (eg, weak straw, head shattering). In Canada, plant scientists working to improve barley are producing new strains (cultivars) with genetic resistance to disease, higher yield and improved agronomic features.

Most of the 4.8 million ha devoted to barley production in Canada is located on the PRAIRIES. Approximately 15 million t of barley was produced in 1986: about one-half is marketed through commercial channels; the remainder is kept on the farm for livestock feed or for seed. A large proportion of marketed barley is made into malt for beverages or malt-enriched food products (*see* BREWING INDUSTRY). Barley can also be made into pearled grain for soups, into flour for flatbread or can be eaten as porridge. Canada exports approximately one-half of the barley it markets (currently 3.8 million t annually), representing about one-fifth of world exports. *See also* GRAIN HANDLING AND MARKETING.

D.R. METCALFE

Barnacle, common name for marine INVERTEBRATES of subclass Cirripedia, class Crustacea. Barnacles, the only sessile CRUSTACEANS, have adopted an odd life-style: they stand on their heads and kick food into their mouths. Six appendages (cirri), operating like a miniature net, filter food from the water. The eyes and second antennae are absent and the body reduced; the carapace (shell) is covered with calcareous plates. Acorn barnacles are common on Canadian intertidal rocks; some members of this group are specialized for life attached to whales. The stalked goose barnacle is named for its resemblance to a bird neck and head. Aggregates of some species reproduce simultaneously and, in spring, intertidal rocks are coated with spat (spawn) cementing themselves in place. The cement can withstand enormous pressure. In Canada, the barnacle's main economic importance is as a fouling organism: extensive growth on ship hulls can greatly slow vessels. Barnacles are delicacies in some countries, but are rarely sampled in Canada.

V. TUNNICLIFFE

Goose-necked barnacles, named for their resemblance to a bird neck and head (*photo by Tim Fitzharris*).

Barnard, Édouard-André, agronomist and journalist (b at Trois-Rivières, Qué 30 Sept 1835; d at Varennes, Qué 19 Aug 1898). An important Québec agronomist in the second half of the 19th century, Barnard had abandoned his studies early to go into trade. In 1856 his interests turned to agriculture, however, and for several years he was also involved with the army, organizing 2 companies of volunteers in Trois-Rivières during the TRENT AFFAIR in 1861. He became involved in the ZOUAVES movement and in 1868 went to Rome. He returned to Trois-Rivières and ran *La Semaine agricole* from 1869 to 1872 before settling in Varennes and giving speeches on farming. He then spent a year in Europe, encouraging immigration to Canada and studying European agri-

culture. On his return he held various senior positions in the Dept of Agriculture and in 1877 founded *Le Journal d'agriculture.*

J.-C. ROBERT

Barnard, Sir Frank Stillman, entrepreneur, politician (b at Toronto 16 May 1856; d at Victoria 11 Apr 1936). Barnard moved to BC in 1860. In the early 1880s he succeeded his father, Francis Jones Barnard (Conservative MP, Yale, BC, 1879-86) as general manager and president of the British Columbia Express Co which provided transportation and banking services in the interior of BC. The younger Barnard invested in mining, lumbering, real estate and other transportation enterprises. After serving briefly on Victoria City Council, he was elected Conservative MP for Cariboo, BC in 1888 and sat until 1896. He was lt-gov, 1914-19, and was knighted in 1918. His younger brother, George Henry Barnard, was Conservative MP for Victoria, BC (1908-17) and senator, 1917-45.

PATRICIA E. ROY

Barnes, Howard Turner, physicist (b at Woburn, Mass 21 July 1873; d at Burlington, Vt 4 Oct 1950). Graduating from McGill in 1893 in applied sciences, he was initiated into research work by his physics professor Hugh L. Callendar, an authority in electrical precision measurements. Applying the techniques of his teacher to a peculiarly Canadian problem, Barnes devoted his life work to the study of the physical properties of ice. In 1906 he published *Ice Formation.* In the years following he tackled the applied side of the problem and published his results in *Ice Engineering* (1928), a few years before his retirement in 1933. His ability in precision measurements led to his election to the Royal Soc of London in 1911. He delivered the coveted Tyndall Lectures in 1912 at the Royal Inst in London on his favourite subject "Ice Formation in Canada, Physical and Economic Aspects." A member of the Royal Soc of Canada since 1902, he became president of Section III in 1908. That same year he was named Macdonald Professor of Physics at McGill, succeeding Ernest RUTHERFORD.

YVES GINGRAS

Barns, like certain of our native birds and animals, have joined the ranks of "endangered species." No funds from wealthy societies, heritage trusts or governments are spent on the purchase and preservation of our oldest barns, and their demise can be expected. Changes in agricultural economy have caused many farmers in Canada to go bankrupt and farms to be abandoned. On farms that are still prosperous, new barns have often been built that lack the cultural and architectural interest of barns from earlier years.

Barn design has always been affected by regional inherited customs and by available building materials. Building materials were often timber, brick and stone for exteriors; wood shingles, slate and thatch for roofs. Though slate is rare, thatch in Québec is extinct. It was never as durable and weather resistant as thatch in countries where reeds were used in the composition; Canadian thatch was usually straw. For the barn enthusiast with a camera it is rewarding to find a well-designed old barn built with any of these materials on walls and roof; and nothing is more shocking than to see a barn, perfect in form, covered by a galvanized roof or with walls protected by shining aluminum sheathing. The all-aluminum sheeted barn is now a common sight, and the barn of the future will likely be of metal or other weatherproof, prefabricated material.

In form and function Canadian barns are classified as Pennsylvania, Dutch and English. In all eastern regions, barns that are circular or polygonal are infrequent except in Québec, where many examples abound, immaculately main-

tained and painted in the brightest hues. The connected barn is of ancient origin and few remain in Canada. Of the types mentioned, the Pennsylvania is most common except for the little English barn. The majority are sheeted in timber planks, but there are superb examples in stone and more permanent materials. However, it is not for their construction that they are important, but for their form and function. A typical site is one with a southerly exposure on rising ground. The barn is built with its great doors opening at the upper level onto what is called the threshing floor, which is actually a broad aisle flanked by stout, squared timbers in bays stretching from floor to ceiling. The granary, opening off the threshing floor, is neat, well-built in consideration of its precious contents, and is divided into 6-8 bins separated by a passage. At the close of the season, the threshing floor is filled with farm machinery. During the autumn and winter, hay is lowered by chute to the cattle below.

For the housing of animals, the Pennsylvania barn is outstanding. Usually the upper structure, or mow, is cantilevered as much as 2.4 m, an admirable invention because of the shelter it gives the cattle in the byre behind the barn. Nearly all Canadian Pennsylvania barns are built of pine planks, but in Pennsylvania some of the finest are stone or brick, or combinations of stone or brick gable-ends with timber vertically or horizontally nailed on the projecting mow. The Dutch barn can be seen at its best on each side of the Hudson R, but there are Canadian examples. Its plan can be easily remembered – the only barn type with main doors at the end and not on the side. This barn plan, sometimes called Basilican, has a "nave" or threshing floor and aisles, on one side for cattle and on the other side for horses. Historically, in Holland, women servants slept over the cattle and men over the horses. A fascinating historic feature of the early Dutch barns in Holland was the living space at the "sanctuary" end of the Basilican prototype. There, furniture could be arranged around a centrally placed fire and flanked on 2 sides by bedrooms or built-in beds which would be lowered for sleeping. The farmer could be seated so that he had supervision over the threshing floor, horses and cattle. One barn has been saved for UPPER CANADA VILLAGE, and though it has the central door, the structure has been anglicized by eaves that are higher than the prototypes in Holland or the Hudson R region.

A very curious survival of the ancient plan is a barn built (1906) at Weyburn, Sask. Externally it shows no signs of the traditional type with low eaves and central door, but the family lived under the same roof as their animals; living quarters were 6 m in depth and consisted of 2 storeys, the upper being bedrooms. The ground-floor door and windows overlooked the threshing floor.

The ubiquitous little English barn gets its name from one of identical use and form in Britain. It

Dalziel barn, built in 1809, is an outstanding example of Pennsylvania-German log construction in Ontario (*courtesy Black Creek Pioneer Village*).

Polygonal barn, Arcola, Sask: round barn (to right), windmill (left of centre) and outhouse (centre) (*courtesy Glenbow Archives, Calgary/NA-3597-12*).

has a central threshing floor, with space to the left for threshed grain and on the right for unthreshed grain. This barn, whose measurements were often as little as 16.8 x 7.6 m, flourished at a period when wheat cultivation dominated agriculture. When more room for storage became necessary after a bountiful harvest, the threshing floor was extended by one bay with a loft overhead. To achieve this, a pine beam of awesome dimensions was cut from the kind of tree then to be found in the primeval forest. Square holes show where joists were once fitted to hold the floor and its load. Farmers were reluctant to use part of the barn for cattle during a period of agricultural change, and after the old barn was left to its original uses, a small cattle barn was built at right angles to the old, or with still further need, a third barn for horses would be added to form a 3-sided court. At Carleton Place, Ont, the ultimate was reached with a piggery which filled the gaps and created an inner court, a sheltered place with many uses. At one time the house was attached to the barn. The idea of having the farmer in such an intimate relationship to his animals and storage was good, but fires could be devastating. The only remaining example in Canada is the barn in Weyburn, Sask.

The French Canadians showed much ingenuity and a love of primary colours in barns. Their barns were usually long and low, with a surprising number of circular and polygonal shapes adding variety to the traditional single-storey rectangles. They had tight-tongued and grooved, painted walls. Where wooden barns elsewhere relied for ventilation on shrinkage of boards, the Québécois provided it by cupolas placed on ridges. In clapboard walls on barns outside of Québec City the cracks allowed the free passage of air and permitted a host of pigeons, numerous owls, swallows, mice and cats to enter. The Qué-

English barn, built in 1825 by Daniel Stang. This barn has 2 large grain mows and a double threshing floor (*courtesy Black Creek Pioneer Village*).

bec barn is pre-eminent for decoration in paint, and its plain surfaces give the farmer ample opportunity for the display of colour. In many old barns outside of Québec City, farmers take advantage of flat areas to demonstrate the raison d'être for their operations, and large faded paintings of cows or horses are a rewarding sight. One very spirited painting of horses in motion can be seen at Petit Chocpiele in NB. It is a mural and approaches the standards of fine art rather than the vernacular (*see* FOLK ART).

Carved stone lintels on wooden barns were used for decoration. An excellent example still exists. Lettering in stone has been moved from a barn in Erin Township, Ont, to a stone wall at Rockwood Academy, Rockwood, Ont. The inscription (1863) reads: "When your barn is well filled all snug and secure, Be thankful to God and remember the poor."   ERIC ARTHUR

Reading: Eric Arthur and Dudley Witney, *The Barn* (1972).

Barr, Dave, golfer (b at Kelowna, BC 13 Apr 1952). Barr learned his GOLF while banging balls around a Kelowna schoolyard before joining the Kelowna Golf Club on a junior membership. He later attended Oral Roberts University on a golf scholarship, and turned professional in 1974. Self-taught, he brings to the game a natural and free style that is the envy of many who watch him. His victories include the 1981 Quad Cities Open in Coal Valley, Ill, on the US Tour; the individual championship in the 1983 World Cup in Jakarta; the 1985 Canadian Professional Golfers Assn Championship in Brampton, Ont; the team title in the 1985 World Cup in La Quinta, Calif, with fellow Canadian Dan HALLDORSON, and the 1987 Georgia-Pacific Atlanta golf classic. He also tied for second in the 1985 US Open in Birmingham, Mich, one shot from the lead. That was the best finish ever by a Canadian to that point in a US Open. Barr plays the US tour regularly and competes frequently in Canada, being a strong supporter of Canadian golf.   LORNE RUBENSTEIN

Barr, Murray Llewellyn, anatomist, geneticist (b at Belmont, Ont 20 June 1908). A major contributor to the establishment of the science of human cytogenetics, Barr was educated at Western and was a member of its faculty 1936-73. From 1939 to 1945 he was an RCAF wing commander. In 1949 he and E.G. Bertram co-discovered the sex chromatin, an X-chromosome derivative, the presence of which distinguishes cells of normal females from those of normal males. A simple buccal-smear test, introduced in 1955 with K.L. MOORE and using cells rubbed from the lining of the mouth, identified persons with abnormal numbers of sex-chromosome bodies and therefore errors of the sex chromosome complex. The exact nature of these errors was then established by chromosome studies or karyotyping. This research contributed substantially to understand-

ing the cause of various congenital syndromes. Barr wrote *The Human Nervous System* and *A Century of Medicine at Western.* He is a fellow of the Royal Society of London and has received many other honours. In 1962 he received the Joseph P. Kennedy Jr Foundation Award from US President John F. Kennedy for his work in mental retardation.   W.J. BRADY

Barr Colonists In 1902 the Rev Isaac Barr secured a huge land tract between the present-day Alberta-Saskatchewan border and Maidstone (Sask). In Mar 1903 he brought approximately 2000 colonists from England. Arriving Apr 17 in Saskatoon, they spent 2 weeks bickering and reorganizing before embarking on an easy 270 km wagon trip to the colony. Many discontents left to form their own communities. Tired of continual criticism, Barr resigned, went to Toronto to sort out his money problems, and moved to the US and eventually Australia. Leadership passed to his rival, the Rev George Lloyd, after whom the colony's first town was named LLOYDMINSTER in July 1903. Despite initial setbacks, the Barr colonists opened up the vast area west of Saskatoon. In 1905, the provinces of Alberta and Saskatchewan were created (*see* AUTONOMY BILLS), and the interprovincial boundary passed through Lloydminster. Although the CANADIAN NORTHERN RAILWAY, which arrived that year, placed its station on the less populated Alberta side, the colonists continued to develop the Saskatchewan side. Not until the 1970s oil boom, however, did the western portion match the eastern side.

FRANK W. ANDERSON

Barre du jour, La (*BJ*), magazine fd 1965 by Nicole BROSSARD, Marcel Saint-Pierre, Roger Soublière and Jan Stafford, to stimulate writing through writing and to transform both the production and the reading of literature. In 1977, *BJ* was reorganized as *La Nouvelle Barre du jour* (*NBJ*) by Brossard (who left in 1979), Michel Gay and Jean-Yves Collette. Despite a change of management in Sept 1981 to H. Corriveau, Louise Cotnoir and Lise Guèvremont, the magazine's purpose has remained unchanged. From the start, *BJ* wanted to combine formal research with appreciation for a certain tradition, and so it presented the unpublished works of Charles GILL, Louis-Joseph QUESNEL, Nérée Beauchemin, Saint-Denys GARNEAU, Gaëtane de Montreuil and Émile NELLIGAN. By abandoning the "cult of the soil" as subject matter (*see* NOVEL IN FRENCH) and skirting revolutionary politics, *BJ* distinguished itself from both *Hexagone* and PARTI PRIS. *BJ* favoured articles about theory and formalism; *NBJ* prefers fiction and applied literary theory, and publishes on the theory and practical battles of feminism. There have been various series, dealing with such subjects as literary history and literary theory, and special issues devoted to such genres as fantasy and science fiction. *NBJ* is a laboratory of creation and research, a permanent writing workshop, drawing in contributors as the need arises. It has not merely echoed current literary trends in Québec; it has pioneered their creation. Although it has at times been repetitive in dealing with themes and issues, the publication has played an important part in Québec literature. *See also* LITERARY PERIODICALS IN FRENCH.

JOSEPH BONENFANT

Barrett, David, social worker, politician, premier of BC (b at Vancouver 2 Oct 1930). From a working-class Jewish family, he pursued university studies in the US in philosophy (Seattle U) and social work (St Louis U), returning to BC 1956 to work for the Dept of Corrections. He won a seat for the CCF in the 1960 provincial election, was re-elected for the NEW DEMOCRATIC PARTY

Barr Colonists arrive at Saskatoon (*courtesy National Archives of Canada/PA-38667*).

(1963, 1966 and 1969), and was chosen provincial leader in 1969 when his opponent, Tom BERGER, failed to be re-elected. The NDP won the 1972 election and initiated many reforms, notably a freeze on the conversion of agricultural land, a mineral-royalties tax, the establishment of a powerful labour-relations board and an expanded public sector. Opposition to the government's zealous approach and declining revenues enabled the Social Credit Party to defeat the Barrett administration in 1975. Barrett returned to the Assembly in a 1976 by-election and remained leader of the Opposition. He announced his resignation as leader of the provincial NDP after another general-election defeat in May 1983 and in 1984 became host of a radio talk show in Vancouver. In late 1986 he announced that he would seek a seat in the House of Commons in the next federal election. He is noted for his emotional, entertaining platform style and informal manner.   J. T. MORLEY

Barrett, Silby, labour leader (b at Bishop's Cove, Conception B, Nfld 27 Sept 1884; d at Toronto 9 Aug 1959). Barrett fished with his father and worked in the coal mines in Cape Breton and Ohio before settling in GLACE BAY in 1908. He became president of the United Mine Workers of NS in 1916 and of the Amalgamated Mine Workers of NS in 1917; when the miners affiliated as District 26, UMWA, in 1919, Barrett became international board member, a post he held repeatedly until 1942. Despite his early reputation as a "red," Barrett soon became a staunch ally of international UMWA president John L. Lewis. When District 26 was suspended in 1923, Lewis appointed Barrett the district's provisional president, and in 1936 Lewis appointed Barrett Canadian director of the Steelworkers' Organizing Committee. A founder of the CANADIAN CONGRESS OF LABOUR in 1940, Barrett was elected to the executive annually until 1955. Moving to Toronto in the 1940s, he became director of District 50, UMWA. A strong backer of the CCF, Barrett was famed in labour circles for his political shrewdness and salty wit: whatever he had to confess, he boasted, "I never cast a Liberal nor a Tory vote."

DAVID FRANK

Barrette, Antonio J., politician, premier of Québec 1960 (b at Joliette, Qué 26 May 1899; d at Montréal 15 Dec 1968). He began his political career by winning the Joliette seat for the UNION NATIONALE Party in the 1936 election that brought Maurice DUPLESSIS to power. He was easily re-elected 6 times between 1939 and 1960. Because of his labour experience – as a mechanical engineer and leader of the Conseil régional du travail – he served as minister of labour 1944-60, and was responsible for applying his party's labour policies, including some that were clearly anti-union. Upon Paul SAUVÉ's death in Jan 1960, he was chosen the new party leader and thus became Québec premier, remaining in office only until the June election that year, won by the Liberals. He finished his public career as Canadian ambassador to Greece 1963-66.

DANIEL LATOUCHE

Barrhead, Alta, Town, pop 3991 (1986c) inc 1946, located 90 km NW of Edmonton in the Paddle R valley near the historic fur trade trail (1825) that linked Edmonton and Ft Assinboine, over which hundreds of gold seekers passed during the KLONDIKE GOLD RUSH. Beginning in 1906, settlers reached the valley from diverse origins, chiefly Britain and the US, and cleared land for cereal crops, while numerous sawmills exploited the timber stands. Barrhead originally sprang up around the store, post office and community hall established by the Paddle River and District Cooperative Society (inc 1912) but was resited closer to the Pembina Valley Railway when it arrived in 1927.   DOUGLAS BABCOCK

Barrie, Ont, City, pop 48 287 (1986c), 38 423 (1981c), inc 1959. Located at the head of Kempenfelt Bay on Lk SIMCOE, 70 km N of Toronto, it lay along an important supply route, inaugurated during the War of 1812, linking York (Toronto) on Lk Ontario to British military posts on the upper Great Lakes. The name refers to Commodore Robert Barrie, a British naval officer on Lake Ontario. Settlement began in 1833. Barrie enjoys excellent highway connections with Toronto. Its economy is based on diversified manufacturing – principally automotive, clothing, brewing, electronics and the service industry. In winter it is a favourite spot of ice fishermen. The main campus of Georgian College of Applied Arts and Technology is located here. On 31 May 1985 a TORNADO caused extensive damage to part of the city where it was blamed for 8 deaths.   DANIEL FRANCIS

Barrington, Shelburne County, NS, UP, pop 304 (1986c), located 35 km from Shelburne, on the S Shore, was a thriving ACADIAN settlement before the Expulsion. Completely destroyed by the British, the village was rebuilt (1761) by immigrating Cape Cod and Nantucket fishermen, who named it after Viscount Barrington, Britain's war secretary. Trade and close ties with New England meant this potential "rebels nest" was closely watched by the navy during the American Revolution. Fishing was the primary industry, and after 1800, ships were built for the lumber and fish trade to the W Indies. The Old Meeting House, now a museum, is the oldest extant Nonconformist church in Canada (built 1765). Barrington is the municipal centre for the surrounding district. Five km S, Barrington Passage, the former Acadian settlement of "Passage de Bacareau," is the commercial hub, and junction to the Cape Sable I causeway. Fishing remains the area's staple industry.

JUDITH HOEGG RYAN

Barrister, member of legal profession in England who has exclusive right of audience in high and superior courts. Usually retained by a SOLICITOR, barristers have unique legal status. In Canada the term is used informally to describe lawyers who appear in higher courts, but all Canadian common lawyers are both barristers and solicitors, although some provincial legislation refers to the 2 categories. In Québec CIVIL LAW the distinction is made between "notaires" (NOTARY) and "avocats."   K.G. McSHANE

Barrow, John, football player (b at Delray Beach, Fla 31 Oct 1935). Barrow's stellar 14-year career (1957-70) with the HAMILTON TIGER-CATS included recognition as an Eastern all-star 12 times and all-Canadian 11 times; the SCHENLEY AWARD as outstanding defensive player in 1962 and runner-up in 1959, 1961, 1964, 1965 and 1967; and he was voted the CANADIAN FOOTBALL LEAGUE "lineman of the century" in 1967. Barrow anchored a Tiger-Cat defence renowned for its hard hitting and vicious tackling, and led his team to 9 GREY CUP appearances in 11 years, winning the championship in 1957, 1963, 1965 and 1967. His skills were not, however, confined to defence, as evidenced by 4 additional all-star selections as an offensive tackle in 1957, 1958, 1959 and 1960. After retiring from playing, Barrow was the TORONTO ARGONAUTS general manager from 1971 to 1975. He was inducted into the CANADIAN FOOTBALL HALL OF FAME in 1976.

PETER WONS

Barter is the exchange of one commodity or service for another without the use of money as a medium of exchange. A barter agreement (also called "countertrade") among countries calls for the exchange of stated amounts of goods.

Within Canada bartering has been used by struggling companies. For example, a radio station may offer its weekly commentators a week's holiday, including free flights and hotels. This trip is paid for by a travel agency, which receives a discount on its advertising rates on the station. In the 1960s, because of the growing use of such cashless commerce, the Canadian federal tax authorities began to restrict the practice of barter. Now companies giving individuals cashless benefits must issue a slip stating the value of the goods or services for income tax purposes. If such benefits are not reported as taxable income, the tax burden shifts to other Canadian workers who receive only monetary remuneration.

While increasing taxes and tough economic times have spawned the growth of barter and the so-called UNDERGROUND ECONOMY within Canada, the deteriorating world economy since the early

Timber Slide at Les Chats, Bytown, Upper Canada (c1838), brown wash by William Henry Bartlett, one of the artist's many depictions of Canadians at their daily work (*courtesy National Archives of Canada/C-40331*).

1970s has resulted in an increase in the amount of barter, or countertrade, between nations.

Countertraders accept payment in the form of goods or services. The countertraders must not only sell their own goods, but they must accept and sell someone else's too. Countertrade is therefore also known as "triangulation" because it requires at least 3 parties: buyer, seller and customers. A conservative estimate developed by Business International of New York suggests that 10% of world trade is affected by countertrade, although other estimates range from 1% to 40% ($US 15-900 billion).

Sophisticated dealings are conducted elsewhere in the world by gigantic trading companies such as Mitsubishi in Japan or Phibro-Salomon Corp in New York City, the world's largest trading company. The Royal Bank of Canada became the first Canadian bank to create a division to facilitate cashless transactions. A Canadian company selling computer equipment and programming services may have to accept teak from Thailand in exchange for its commodities. The bank finds a buyer for the teak, and pays the Canadian company cash for its goods and services when they are sent or completed. The bank, in turn, makes a profit by paying the Canadian company slightly less than it obtains for the teak.

Canadian companies have made countertrade transactions in 21 countries. Many large Canadian companies with worldwide operations, eg, Massey-Ferguson Ltd, General Motors of Canada, Noranda Mines Ltd, Bata Shoes and the Potash Corp of Saskatchewan, now employ their own countertrade specialists. In Dec 1984 the Dept of External Affairs established the Trading House and Countertrade Division to formulate policy and assist Canadian exporters competing in the international market. *Countertrade Primer for Canadian Exporters* (1985) defines countertrade agreements and provides useful information on such topics as contracts, world trading houses and the countertrade practices of other countries.   DIANE FRANCIS

Bartlett, Robert Abram, arctic mariner (b at Brigus, Nfld 15 Aug 1875; d at New York C 28 Apr 1946). A sealer and merchant seaman from his youth, Bartlett began his arctic career in 1898, as

commander of the ship *Windward* on the first of Robert Peary's 3 attempts to reach the N Pole. On Peary's last attempt in 1908-09, Bartlett accompanied him to within 250 km of the pole. In 1913 Bartlett commanded KARLUK, supply ship of the CANADIAN ARCTIC EXPEDITION lead by Vilhjalmur STEFANSSON. The ship was wrecked near Wrangel I north of Siberia and Bartlett made a daring sled trip across the ice to the east Siberian port of East Cape, where he took ship for Alaska. Later he commanded the *Effie M. Morrisey* on scientific voyages to the Arctic spanning 2 decades. He published his autobiography, *The Log of Bob Bartlett,* in 1928.   DANIEL FRANCIS

Bartlett, William Henry, artist, author, traveller (b in Kentish Town, Eng 26 Mar 1816; d at sea off Malta 13 Sept 1854). As a boy Bartlett served an apprenticeship (1822-29) under John Britton during which he showed ability as a draftsman and landscape artist. In 1832 he met William Beattie, who remained his lifelong friend and biographer and who arranged for him to make sketches for his travel book, *Switzerland Illustrated* (1836). From this time until his death, Bartlett travelled widely in the Middle East, Europe and America, making hundreds of sketches for engravings in more than 40 books, 12 of which he wrote himself. His popularity owed much to his architectural training which, when combined with his penchant for the picturesque and the sublime, guaranteed that the reader saw scenes he could recognize as charming, impressive and representational.

Bartlett spent several months in Canada in 1838 sketching prominent sights such as the falls at Montmorency and Niagara, the fish market at Toronto, the view over Montréal, and the locks on the Rideau Canal at Ottawa. As well, he showed Canadians at their daily work: clearing the forest, fishing, rafting on the Ottawa, excavating the Long Sault Canal, bringing in nets at Wellington in Prince Edward County, ferrying cattle in the Eastern Townships, and building the esplanade at Québec C. The many engravings that illustrate the 2 volumes of *Canadian Scenery* (1842) constitute an important and attractive documentation of living conditions in the Maritimes and the Canadas in 1838.

ALEXANDER M. ROSS

Reading: Alexander M. Ross, *William Henry Bartlett* (1973).

Baseball is a game played with a bat and ball between 2 teams (of 9 players each), which alter-

nate between being at bat and in the field. The object is to score runs by advancing players counter-clockwise around 4 bases, each 90 feet (27.5 m) apart. Games of bat and ball have their roots in ancient religious rites celebrating spring's return and appear throughout history. The game in N America is a descendant of English rounders. In New England, rounders evolved into a popular regional sport, known as townball, played at public meetings in the early 19th century. From these informal games emerged 2 interpretations of baseball, each with its own written rules and organized teams. These 2 styles competed for popularity until the American Civil War. The "Massachusetts game" was closest in form to townball and allowed 10 to 14 men on the field. A variation of this game was played in Beachville, UC [Ont], on 4 June 1838 at a celebration to mark the previous year's victory by government forces over insurgents. This was the first recorded baseball-type game in Canada and predated by 7 years the establishment by Alexander Cartwright and his team, the New York Knickerbockers, of the "New York game" with 9 men on the field.

The early history of organized baseball in Canada is closely associated with what is now SW Ontario. The first Canadian team was the Young Canadians of Hamilton, formed in April 1854. A local clerk, William Shuttleworth, was instrumental in its development. Other early teams included the Burlingtons of Hamilton (1855), a London team (1856) and a St Thomas team (1858). The Massachusetts game rules were favoured. The New York rules were introduced in 1859 in Hamilton. The popularity of the 9-man game in the US and the beginning of international play in 1860, with Buffalo's victory over the Burlingtons, led to its rapid adoption in Ontario. The Young Canadians of Woodstock awarded themselves a silver ball in 1863 and it became an annual prize for the Canadian champion. Woodstock's lineup included 7 Ontario-born players whose occupations varied. In 1864 they were defeated by the American champions, the Brooklyn Atlantics, at a Rochester, NY, tournament. In 1867 Woodstock, Hamilton and Ingersoll entered the world baseball tournament in Detroit, Mich, and Ingersoll won the junior class team championship. By 1868 large financial rewards induced some teams to move toward a semiprofessional status, with team members sharing tournament prizes. In 1869 the Guelph Maple Leafs replaced Woodstock as Canadian champions. The Guelph team was the first to import American professionals, who together with such Canadians as star pitcher William Smith won the Guelph world semiprofessional baseball championship in 1874 in Watertown, NY.

Guelph's president, George Sleeman, and Harry Gorman formed the first Canadian League in 1876, with members in Kingston, Toronto, Hamilton, Guelph and London. The London Tecumsehs dethroned Guelph as Canadian champions, in no small part through signing one of baseball's first curveball pitchers, Fred Goldsmith, and 5 other American professionals. That same year several large American cities formed an exclusive National League to monopolize the best baseball talent. In 1877 a number of smaller American industrial centres organized the reform-minded International Assn. London and Guelph joined and the Tecumsehs won the first championship with a season-ending victory over the Pittsburgh Alleghenys. London then rejected membership in the National League, owing to the league's restrictions on games with nonleague teams, and was the lone Canadian entry in 1878. Financial difficulties led to the Tecumsehs' mid-season collapse. Organized baseball in Ontario lacked clear direction again until the 1885 forma-

Toronto Blue Jays' outfielder Lloyd Moseby at bat. The Blue Jays joined the American League in 1977 and drew 6 million fans in their first 4 seasons, a major league record (*courtesy Toronto Blue Jays*)

tion of another Canadian League based in the province. Toronto's decision to join an American minor league in 1886 led to the end of professional baseball's independent character in Ontario, since the Ontario teams became subservient to the interests of American major league organizations.

Baseball gained in popularity in other parts of Canada. In 1865 a bylaw was passed in Montréal preventing the playing of baseball in city parks or public places. In a more positive vein, the game spread to the Maritimes from New England and the first Canadian-born major league player, William Phillips of Saint John, NB, played for Cleveland in 1879. In western Canada a crude form of baseball had been played at Red River in the 1840s, but the modern game did not appear until 1874 in Winnipeg. Its growth followed the railway and many of the early promoters were associated with companies anxious to move players and fans along the rails. Rail workers and a future Saskatchewan premier, Walter SCOTT, were among those who enjoyed the amateur game in the 19th century. American professionals contributed to the game's spread as did eastern Canadians such as James Ross, a member of London's champion amateur team of 1877. He took the game west, becoming a rancher and later a member of the Canadian Senate. By 1904 baseball was so popular in the Yukon that a 2-game international championship was played and won by Whitehorse over the Alaskan town of Skagway. In 1907 the Western Canada League, a minor professional organization, was formed in Alberta and 2 years later included teams from Saskatchewan and Manitoba. The league led a financially troubled and brief existence, duplicating the history of other minor professional sports organizations in Canada. The Cape Breton Colliery League, based in coal-mining towns in NS, survived as an official minor league from 1937 to 1939. The Provincial League in Québec, at times an outlaw league outside the control of major league baseball, lasted from 1935 to the early 1960s. Several French Canadian stars such as Roland Gladu and Jean-Pierre Roy were developed in this league.

Toronto and Montréal had teams in the International League, a respected minor league, for periods of 78 and 55 years, respectively. Montréal developed a reputation as a good baseball town and the team's ownership included, at one time or another, Canadian baseball star "Tip" O'NEILL and Charles Trudeau, father of the future Canadian prime minister. In 1946 Jackie Robinson became the first black player in modern "organized" baseball when he played for the Montreal Royals. He was a crowd favourite, leading the Royals to the minor league baseball championship. A new era began in 1969 with the introduction of major league baseball to Montréal. In 1977 the MONTREAL EXPOS moved from the comfortable surroundings of Jarry Park to Olympic Stadium where they have drawn crowds of over 2 million in one season. A second Canadian major league franchise began in 1977 when the TORONTO BLUE JAYS joined the American League. They attracted over 6 million fans in their first 4 seasons, a major league record. In 1987 they set several league attendance records: 2 778 459 fans at home games, 1 959 280 fans at road games, and the overall home/away game attendance record. In 1989 the Blue Jays will move from Exhibition Stadium to the Skydome stadium in downtown Toronto. Each season these teams play an exhibition game for the Pearson Cup, with funds going to Canadian amateur baseball.

The amateur game in Canada is overseen by a hierarchy of local and provincial organizations, such as the Ontario Baseball Assn founded in Hamilton in 1918. At the national level, the Canadian Federation of Amateur Baseball coordinates in such areas as coaching and umpiring programs, Canadian national championships and national amateur teams. There were 238 305 registered amateur players in Canada in 1987 (up from 115 000 in 1981) in the senior, junior, bison, midget and under-midget categories. Québec and Ontario with approximately 65 000 players each and BC with 36 000 lead the provinces. In 1987 there were only 4 Canadians playing in the major leagues. Since 1871, 140 Canadians have made it to major league baseball, including Bob Emslie, George "Mooney" GIBSON and Phil MARCHILDON; of these only 82 were trained in Canada, but their ranks include such contemporary stars as pitcher Ferguson JENKINS and out-

Montreal Expos' Tim Raines. The Expos joined the National League in 1969 and in 1977 moved to Olympic Stadium (*courtesy Montreal Expos*).

fielder Terry Puhl. Baseball remains identified as the national game of the US, but its popularity has spanned many generations in Canada and the 2 very different societies of the 19th and 20th centuries. The Canadian Baseball Hall of Fame opened at Exhibition Place, Toronto, in 1983. Its first inductees were Phil Marchildon, Tip O'Neill and George Selkirk (players); John Ducey and Frank Shaughnessy (builders); and Lester PEARSON (honorary). The following have since been inducted: 1984 – Andy Bilesky, Claude Raymond, Charles Bronfman, Goody Rosen, Jack Graney; 1985 – Dick Fowler, John Hiller, Dr Ron Taylor, Jack Kent Cooke, Carmen Bush; 1986 – Reggie Cleveland, Bob Emslie, Oscar Judd, Bob Prentice; 1987 – Ferguson Jenkins, Mooney Gibson, Russell Ford and Glen Rocky Nelson, the first American player to be inducted.

Softball is a variation of baseball in which a larger ball is delivered in an underhand motion to the batter. Two types of softball are played in Canada: fast pitch, in which the ball is delivered to the batter in a rapid motion; and slow pitch, in which the ball is tossed in an arc. The game began as a form of indoor baseball in the 1890s in the US, but soon came to Canada where it has become a popular summer recreation for men and women. The Ontario Amateur Softball Assn, formed in 1923, was the first such organization anywhere. Softball has since spread throughout the world. Canadians are credited with introducing it into Holland during WWII. In 1949 Tip Top Tailors of Toronto won the N American championship in Little Rock, Ark. In 1972, represented by the Richmond Hill Dynes of Ontario, Canada won the men's world championship in Manila, and in 1976 another Canadian team, Victoria Bate Construction of BC, tied for the men's world title with the US and New Zealand at the tournament in New Zealand. A Canadian team won the gold medal at the 1987 Pan-American Games and qualified to attend the 1988 Olympics. Softball is overseen by local and provincial organizations, and the Canadian Amateur Softball Association acts as a nationwide co-ordinating body responsible for 7 annual national championships. Over 567 000 men and women play organized softball on close to 40 000 teams across Canada.

WILLIAM HUMBER

Reading: L. Cauz, *Baseball's Back in Town: A History of Baseball in Toronto* (1977); William Humber, *Cheering for the Home Team: The Story of Baseball in Canada* (1983); H. Seymour, *Baseball* (vols 1 and 2, 1960, 1971).

Basil, *see* HERBS.

Basile, Jean, né Bezroudnoff, novelist, literary critic, essayist and publisher (b at Paris 1932). After university studies in Paris, he immigrated to Montréal and joined *Le Devoir* in 1962 as a journalist, then as literary critic, before being named director of the literary section, a position he left in 1967. He helped found the magazine *Mainmise* (1970) and at the end of 1973 returned to *Le Devoir* as literary critic. Director of Éditions de l'Aurore (1976-77), he founded his own publishing house, Les Éditions Jean Basile (1979). In 1984 he returned to journalism with the magazine *La Presse Plus*. In 1963 he published *Lorenzo* (1964), the first volume of a romanesque trilogy which he completed with *Le Grand Khan* (1967) and *Les Voyages d'Irkoutsk* (1970). He tried theatre with *Joli Tambour* (1966), a psycho-historical drama and returned to the novel with *Le Piano-trompette* (1983). He also published *L'Écriture radio-télé* followed by *Suggestions de Robert Choquette* (1976), *Coca et cocaine* (1977), an essay on the use of drugs, *La Culture du canabis* (1979) and *Iconostase pour Pier-Paolo Pasolini* (1984).

AURÉLIEN BOIVIN

Basilians, the Basilian Fathers or Congregation of St Basil, founded in France in 1822, now centered in Toronto. They came to Canada in 1850 and in 1852 founded St Michael's College there. They have concentrated on high-school and university education, working in high schools in Toronto, Windsor, Sudbury and Sault Ste Marie in Ontario and in Calgary and Lethbridge, Alberta. They pioneered the federation of Catholic colleges with provincial universities and work with the universities of Toronto, Windsor, Saskatchewan, Alberta and British Columbia, as well as having chaplaincies on other campuses. They conduct the Pontifical Institute of Medieval Studies in Toronto.   REV JAMES HANRAHAN

Basinski, Zbigniew Stanislaw, physicist (b at Wolkowysk, Poland 28 Apr 1928). Recognized as the doyen of Canadian metal PHYSICS, he received the BSc, MA, DPhil and DSci degrees from Oxford, at the same time holding the post of research assistant in the department of metallurgy. From 1954 to 1956 he was a staff member at the Oxygenic Engineering Laboratories, Massachusetts Institute of Technology. He joined the NATIONAL RESEARCH COUNCIL's division of physics in 1956, and since 1974 has headed the Material Physics Section. Sabbaticals have taken him to the Carnegie Institute of Technology in Pittsburgh, Pa, as a Ford distinguished visiting professor of metallurgical engineering; to Oxford as a Commonwealth visiting professor of metallurgy and materials science, and a fellow of Wolfson College, Oxford; and to the Cavendish Laboratory, Cambridge, Eng, as an overseas fellow at Churchill College. For a number of years he has been adjunct professor at Carleton U in Ottawa. Basinski's research in metal physics has earned him national and international acclaim, particularly his work on the mechanics and thermodynamics of plasticity in metals (including work hardening, solution hardening and fatigue) and his contributions to instrumentation and observational techniques (in low-temperature measurements, transmission and scanning electron microscopy). In 1977, he became the first recipient of the Canadian Metal Physics Medal awarded annually for outstanding service to metal physics. He is a fellow of the Royal Society of Canada and the Royal Society of London, and in 1986 was invested as an Officer of the Order of Canada. He is author of more than 70 reviews and original papers.

Basketball is a team sport, invented by Canadian James A. NAISMITH in 1891, which has spread throughout the world. The game had its origin at the YMCA International Training School, now Springfield College, in Springfield, Mass. Naismith, a psychology student at that time and then an instructor at the school, responded to a need for an indoor winter recreational activity that could be easily learned and played in teams. Naismith tried to find a way of using a ball without the football tackle and of throwing it with skill instead of force. The result was a team sport whose object was to score by throwing a large ball into a basket placed horizontally about 3 m above the floor. Having conceived this idea Naismith defined specific rules for orderly play. From the original game, with 13 basic rules, basketball has progressed to a highly skilled sport, with an intricate blend of timing, intuition and co-operation. Records indicate that basketball was played in Canada prior to 1900; and photographs of the Vancouver YMCA basketball team of 1900-01 are on display at the Pacific National Exhibition in Vancouver.

Graduates of the former YMCA School exported the sport throughout the world. By the 1930s it was played in over 50 countries, prompting its

acceptance as an official Olympic competition in 1936. It had already appeared as a demonstration sport at the 1904 St Louis Olympics and, through the EDMONTON GRADS, a women's team, at the 1924, 1928 and 1932 Olympic Games. Canada's team at the Berlin Olympiad, the Windsor Ford V8s, made up of players primarily from Windsor, Ont, and strengthened by players from the West Coast, won the silver medal. Canada's achievements in men's competition in subsequent Olympiads were as follows: XIVth London 1948, 9th place; XVth Helsinki 1952, did not qualify for quarter-finals; XVIth Melbourne 1956, 9th place; XVIIth Rome 1960, did not qualify in pre-Olympic tournament; XVIIIth Tokyo 1964, 14th place; XIXth Mexico City 1968, did not qualify; and XXth Munich 1972, narrowly missed a berth with a 5th place at the pre-Olympic qualifying tournament in Augsburg; XXIst Montréal 1976, the USSR defeated Canada 100 to 72 to win the bronze medal giving Canada a reputable 4th place finish; XXIInd Moscow 1980, Canada boycotted the Games; and XXIIIrd Los Angeles 1984, 4th place. Women's basketball, in 1976, became an official Olympic event and Canada placed 6th, and had a 4th place finish in Los Angeles.

Canada's record in other international competition is highlighted by the achievements of Edmonton Grads under J. Percy PAGE. From 1915 to 1940 they dominated basketball with 4 world championships and a record 502 wins in 522 games, of which 78 were consecutive. Since 1976, Canada's men's national team has consistently placed among the top 6 amateur teams in the world, winning a gold medal in the 1978 Commonwealth Cup and the gold medal in the 1983 World University Games. In 1981 the women's national team was ranked 4th in the world behind USSR, the US and Cuba. At the World Student Games in Tokyo, Canada's men finished with a bronze medal and the women placed fourth. At the 1987 Pan-Am Games, Canada's women's team won a bronze medal; the men's team finished 5th.

The official governing body for basketball in Canada is the Canadian Amateur Basketball Assn, now called Basketball Canada, formed in Dec 1928 in Port Arthur [Thunder Bay], Ont. Its initial main function was to assist with national championships, but its programs, beyond men's and women's national championships, now include men's and women's national team development; technical development with coaching, official and player certification; youth programs; a Hall of Fame; educational services; and promotion and revenue generation. In 1973 Basketball Canada voted to adopt the international playing rules of the International Amateur Basketball Federation (FIBA). With the formation of a National Assn of Basketball Officials (NABO), the transition to international rules has been relatively smooth, although Canadian universities and some high schools have maintained the former rules.   FRANK T. BUTLER

Basques were expert fishermen and sailors from the SE corner of the Bay of Biscay. With the Portuguese, they were early arrivals to Newfoundland's GRAND BANKS. Around 1525 they began WHALING and fishing for COD off Newfoundland, along the N shore of the St Lawrence R from the Str of Belle Isle to the Saguenay R, and in places where similar conditions attracted such northern marine life. The Basques controlled the fishery along *la haute main* (NE coast) for over a century. Every spring until about 1626 they sailed to their N American whaling stations, where they set up scaffolding to dry codfish and built stone ovens to prepare whale oil, a commodity that was highly prized in Europe. Their encounters with natives,

particularly MICMAC, were friendly. In Dec or Jan, when ice conditions began to worsen, the Basques returned home.

Basque activities in the St Lawrence estuary reached a peak in the period 1550-80. In the early 17th century a combination of factors eventually ended their voyages. These included a decrease in the whale population, a weakening of Spain's influence during its war with France, English-Dutch competition in northern waters, increased Inuit hostility and the growing strength of NEW FRANCE.

Samuel de CHAMPLAIN encountered Basque fishermen during his early voyages and he benefited from their knowledge of the N shore of the St Lawrence. He had close ties with those who came from France, in spite of their protests over the founding of Québec. With Marc LESCARBOT, Champlain described the major Basque settlement at Lesquemin (Les Escoumins, Qué); at Tor Bay (NS) he met an experienced Basque fisherman who had come there every year since 1565. He described the Str of Belle Isle as an area frequented by Spanish Basques.

The Basques left many traces of their presence on our shores, including place-names such as Mingan (Qué) and Ingornachoix, Port au Choix and Port au Port (Nfld). French Canadians adopted the Basque word *orignal* for the Canadian MOOSE. Archaeological work at RED BAY, Nfld, has uncovered important evidence of Basque habitation, including an abundance of red roof tiles (used for ballast), pottery, glassware and skeletons. Five Basque shipwrecks have been located in the area; the earliest, the *San Juan*, dates from 1565.   RENÉ BÉLANGER

Reading: Harry Thurston, "The Basque Connection," *Equinox* (Nov-Dec 1983).

Bass, name applied to members of 3 FISH families: temperate bass (Percichthyidae) with 4 species in Canada (white perch, white and striped bass, wreckfish); sunfish (Centrarchidae) with 12 species in Canada (including largemouth, rock and smallmouth basses); and sea bass (Serranidae) with 3 species in Canada (yellowfin bass, black sea bass, snowy grouper). It can be seen that some members of bass families are not called bass. Anglers also use the word for several unrelated species. Temperate basses are found in marine, brackish or fresh waters of eastern Canada, with striped bass occurring along the BC coast as a result of introductions. Like sunfish, temperate basses have teeth in the mouth and spiny fins. They are distinguished by a spine on the gill cover and 2 dorsal fins (the spiny dorsal fin is separate from the soft-rayed dorsal). Temperate basses are occasionally fished commercially and as sport fishes. The white perch has recently become established in Lk Ontario, invading northwards from the US. This species has a high fecundity and tends to become overabundant, with many stunted individuals. Sunfish family members are fresh water fishes found in lakes, ponds and slow-moving, warm streams of southern Canada. They are native to eastern waters but have been introduced

Largemouth bass (*Micropterus salmoides*), an important Canadian game fish (*courtesy National Museums of Canada/National Museum of Natural Sciences*).

into Pacific drainages. They are characterized by having bands of teeth on the roof of the mouth and tongue, as well as on the jaws; by spines in the anal fin and in the continuous dorsal fin; and ctenoid (rough-bordered) scales. They feed on insects, crayfish and other fishes. The large-mouth and smallmouth basses are important game fishes. Sea bass family members are found along the Atlantic coast, but little is known about them in these waters. The yellowfin bass has only recently been reported in Canada.

BRIAN W. COAD

Bassett, Carling Kathrin, tennis player (b at Toronto 9 Oct 1967), daughter of John Basset. In 1981 she won the Canadian junior indoor title and in 1982 was ranked first among world juniors after wins in Tokyo and Taipei. Also in 1982, at age 14, she became the youngest winner of the Canadian closed championship, winning the title again in 1983, the year in which she turned professional, and 1986. By age 16 she had emerged as Canada's premier tennis player, scoring several victories over top international players and winning the Gunze Invitational at Osaka, Japan. She lost to Chris Evert in the final of a World Tennis Assn championship and in 1983 advanced to the quarterfinals of the French Open, Australian Open and Wimbledon. She was a semifinalist in the 1984 US Open, and in 1985 she reached the semifinals of 5 Womens International Tennis Association tournaments. In 1986 Bassett was again a quarterfinalist in the French Open, losing once more to Chris Evert, and in 1987 she won her first Grand Prix tournament – the $75 000 Strasbourg Grand Prix at Strasbourg, France.

JAMES MARSH

Bassett, John White Hughes, broadcasting executive (b at Ottawa 25 Aug 1915). The son of the publisher of the Montréal *Gazette*, Bassett graduated from Bishop's U in 1936 and became a reporter with the Toronto *Globe and Mail*. After wartime service with the Canadian Army in Italy and Europe, Bassett returned to run unsuccessfully as a Conservative candidate in the 1945 general election. He then joined the Toronto *Telegram* as its manager. In 1952 he purchased the *Telegram* and ran it until its demise in 1971. Bassett diversified his interest in journalism by investing in television and sports. He still sits as chairman of BATON BROADCASTING INC, which owns station CFTO in Toronto. He maintains an interest in other newspapers and at various times has been owner of the Toronto Argonauts football club and part owner of Maple Leaf Gardens. In 1962 he again ran unsuccessfully in a federal election, this time in Toronto's Spadina riding. Known for his colourful and outspoken business style, Bassett has since youth been well connected in the social and business circles of Toronto and Montréal. Bassett's son John (d 14 May 1986) was an active businessman and sports promoter; his son Douglas (b 22 June 1940) is president and CEO of Baton; and his granddaughter, Carling BASSETT, is an international tennis star. DUNCAN McDOWALL

Bat, nocturnal MAMMAL of order chiroptera. Bats are the only flying mammals. Two families are known from Canada: Vespertilionidae, smooth-faced bats; Molossidae, free-tailed bats. The 19 Canadian species range in size from the 5 g small-footed bat (*Myotis leibii*) to the 35 g big free-tailed bat (*Tadarida macrotis*). Although all bats can see, most fly and hunt using echolocation or biosonar. Little brown bats use 50-500 calls per second to detect insects smaller than mosquitoes at distances of 1-2 m. Since the difference between the original call and its echo contains the information about the target, an echolocating bat must listen to each outgoing call. Although echolocation is

associated with high frequency (ultrasonic) sound, some bats use lower frequency (less than 20 kHz) calls that are audible to man.

In Canada the biosonar sounds of spotted bats can be heard, but other bats use ultrasonic calls. Most bats produce the orientation sounds in their voice boxes. More intense calls probably provide greater range (up to 15 m) than softer calls. Ears that are sensitive to the ultrasonic sounds alert many moths to the threat of bats. In summer Canadian bats consume daily up to 50% of their body weight in insects. In winter they hibernate or migrate to warmer areas. Bats annually produce one litter of 1-2 (rarely 3-4) young. Most Canadian species mate in autumn; females store sperm over winter. Ovulation and fertilization occur when females leave hibernation in spring; young are born 50-70 days later. Newborn bats are about 25% of their mothers' mass and grow very quickly, feeding on their mothers' milk until they are large enough to fly and hunt insects. Young little brown bats (*M. lucifugus*) may fly by age 3 weeks. Bats may be long-lived; a little brown bat banded in Ontario had survived over 30 years in 1977. Banding studies indicate that some Canadian bats migrate several hundred kilometres to summer roosts. In summer Canadian bats roost in trees, cliffs or buildings; in winter most select caves or old mines as hibernation sites. Only big brown bats (*Eptesicus fuscus*) regularly hibernate in buildings. In Canada bats occur from the US border to the TREELINE, although a vagrant red bat (*Lasiurus borealis*) was reported from Southampton I in the Arctic. In the tropics, many species occur including some that feed on fruit or nectar and pollen and spectacular carnivorous species taking fish, birds, frogs, mice and even other bats. The most infamous bats are the vampires. Three species of these blood-feeders occur in Central and S America. Razor-sharp incisor teeth are used to cut into prey and an anticoagulant in vampire saliva keeps blood from clotting. These bats do not occur in Canada.

M.B. FENTON

Bata, Thomas John, shoe manufacturer (b at Prague, Austria-Hungary [Czech] 17 Sept 1914). Son of Thomas Bata, owner of the world's largest shoe manufacturing companies, he began his career as apprentice in his father's factory at Zlin, Czech, in 1929. In 1935 he went to England as assistant general manager of British Bata Shoe Co. He came to Canada in 1939 and built a new plant at Batawa, Ont. At that time the company was established in more than 30 countries. In 1985 it manufactured in 61 countries, operated 92 plants and 6000 retail stores, and sold through 100 000 merchants in 115 countries. The company makes a million pairs of shoes a day. Bata himself is now chairman of Bata Ltd, an adviser for the UN Centre on Transnational Corporations, chairman of a number of international economic organizations and honorary governor of Trent U.

JORGE NIOSI

Bateman, Robert McLellan, painter (b at Toronto 24 May 1930). Bateman received his early training as a naturalist at Toronto's Royal Ontario Museum and studied painting and drawing with Gordon Payne and Carl SCHAEFER. Bateman's work relates both to traditional wildlife illustrators, such as Fuertes and Allen Brooks, and to the GROUP OF SEVEN and contemporary realist artists. For about 20 years until 1976, he taught high-school geography and art in Toronto and Burlington, Ont, and travelled widely. Throughout the 1950s and early 1960s he painted mainly in abstract and semi-abstract styles, though he continued to sketch plants, birds and mammals. Then, after seeing an Andrew Wyeth exhibition in 1963, he began producing

realistic paintings in which wildlife is the central or incidental subject, often within a richly worked environment. These achieved international success, and there have been major showings of his work in Canada and abroad. RAMSAY DERRY

Reading: Ramsay Derry, *The Art of Robert Bateman* (1981) and *The World of Robert Bateman* (1985); S.G. Shetler, *Portraits of Nature: Paintings of Robert Bateman* (1987).

Bates, John Seaman, chemist, environmentalist (b at Woodstock, Ont 9 June 1888). A graduate of Acadia U, in 1914 Bates obtained the first PhD in chemical engineering granted by Columbia U. In his first career, in the pulp and paper industry, he was one of the first to apply scientific principles to pulp processing. At an age when most have retired, Bates moved to government and consulting work in the water supply and environment field in NB, NS and PEI. Bates is probably best known for his contributions to the establishment of scientific and technical societies such as the Technical Section of the Canadian Pulp and Paper Association and the Chemical Institute of Canada. In 1986 he was awarded an honorary doctorate by Dalhousie. T.H.G. MICHAEL

Bates, Maxwell, artist, architect, author, poet (b at Calgary 14 Dec 1906; d at Victoria 14 Sept 1980). Apprenticed in his father's architectural office in 1924, he attended life classes at the Calgary Art Club and studied painting at the Provincial Institute of Technology and Art 1926-27, identifying strongly with French postimpressionist painters. He lived in London, Eng, 1931-39, exhibiting regularly. His book *A Wilderness of Days* (1978) details his experience of internment in a German prisoner-of-war camp 1940-45. He returned to Calgary in 1946 and joined his father's architectural firm; with partner A.W. Hodges he designed Calgary's St Mary's Cathedral, a unique prairie monument. He was part of the Calgary Group of artists formed by Jock (J.W.G.) MACDONALD and others (1947). Although suffering a severe stroke that left him partially paralysed in 1961, he moved to Victoria and continued to paint landscapes and boldly coloured and expressive figure studies (*Cocktail Party I,* 1965). His poetry collection *Far Away Flags* was published in 1964. JOYCE ZEMANS

Bates, Patricia, née Martin, artist (b at Saint John 25 June 1927). She studied art in Belgium, France and New York, as well as at Mt Allison U, NB. Her principal medium has always been PRINTMAKING, and she is one of the few artists to exploit embossing techniques successfully. Highly innovative, her work includes 2-sided prints meant to hang away from the wall. They are usually perforated, and may employ laminations and embroidery. Her colour, which is limited to black, white and silver, is used symbolically, as is her imagery – geometric compositions inspired by the cosmology of the Islamic Middle East or the Zen Buddhist mandala. She is professor of fine arts at U Victoria and in 1986 a show of her work was held in Vancouver. JUDY GOUIN

Batfish, underwater vehicle designed to carry oceanographic instruments and sensors. It is towed behind a ship in a sawtooth, undulating pattern. The Batfish can dive or ascend by rotating its hydroplanes ("wings") on ship command, and is capable of diving between the surface and approximately 400 m. Control power, used to activate the wings, is derived from an impellor-driven hydraulic pump within the Batfish. The core of the armoured towing cable contains 7 electrical conductors through which electronic information is transmitted to the surface from sensors mounted on the Batfish. The information is transferred to a shipboard computer and stored on magnetic tape. The Batfish was developed at the BEDFORD INSTITUTE OF OCEANOGRAPHY, Dartmouth, NS, and manufactured by Guildline Instruments Ltd, Smiths Falls, Ont. It is equipped with 3 sensors: a conductivity-temperature-depth probe, used to measure physical oceanographic features; a fluorometer (mounted atop the Batfish), measuring chlorophyll *a* fluorescence, the indicator of phytoplankton or plant biomass; and an electronic zooplankton counter (mounted below the Batfish), measuring small marine animals (approximately 0.5-4 mm long) which consume mainly marine plants. Information from the biological sensors is used in fisheries studies of the marine food chain. *See* ECOLOG. ALEX W. HERMAN

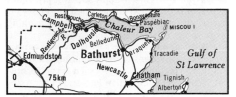

Bathurst, NB, City, pop 14 683 (1986c), 15 705 (1981c), inc 1966, administrative centre of Gloucester County, is located on Bathurst harbour at the mouth of the Nepisiguit R in northern NB. Founded by Nicolas DENYS in 1652, the site was abandoned after his death in 1688. The next settlers were dispossessed ACADIANS (1757) and English traders (1776). First called Nepisiguit, then St Peters, it was renamed Bathurst in 1826 after the colonial secretary, Henry Bathurst, 3rd earl of Bathurst. Lumbering, shipbuilding (begun here in the 1820s) and sawmills dominated the economy until a pulp mill opened in 1914; it was expanded to make paper in 1923 and underwent major renovations in 1983 and 1987. The discovery of sizable base-metal deposits in 1953 in the surrounding region spurred the city's development. The area has 40% of Canada's reserves of silver, lead and zinc; its mine-mills process 10 000 tonnes of ore daily. The community is primarily English and French speaking and besides English and French high schools, has a bilingual trade and technology community college.

BURTON GLENDENNING

Bathurst Inlet, a SE extension of CORONATION GULF, penetrating the arctic shore for some 200 km. The hamlet of Bathurst Inlet is located at the mouth of the Burnside R, which drains Cont-

Bathurst Inlet, NWT, still icebound in mid-July (*photo by Richard Harrington*).

woyto Lk to the SW. The inlet was named by Sir John FRANKLIN in 1821 for Henry Bathurst, 3rd earl of Bathurst, who was then colonial secretary. Some of its numerous islands have rocky cliffs in which peregrine falcons and golden eagles nest.

JAMES MARSH

Bathurst Island, 16 042 km² and over 18 000 km² including its offshore islands, is located in the ARCTIC ARCHIPELAGO, NWT. The present position of the N Magnetic Pole is near its northern end. Its physiography is greatly influenced by a geological structure of relatively undisturbed sedimentary strata. The island's form is a low-relief plateau, sloping to the S and W, with few parts higher than 330 m in elevation. Widespread surface exposure of the shale and siltstone formations supports abundant vegetation for this latitude and has given Bathurst I a prolific wildlife population compared to other arctic islands. Although discovered by PARRY as early as 1819, and later explored by search parties seeking traces of Sir John FRANKLIN, it was only after aerial reconnaissance by the RCAF in 1947 that its final shape was revealed. The "peninsula" forming the western coast was discovered to be in reality a series of islands. Parry named the island for Henry Bathurst, 3rd earl of Bathurst, longtime British secretary of war and the colonies in the early 19th century. DOUG FINLAYSON

Bathurst Island, NWT, discovered in 1819 by Admiral Parry; the final shape of the island was revealed only after aerial reconnaissance by the RCAF in 1947 (*photo by Stephen J. Krasemann/DRK Photo*).

Batoche, national historic site 44 km SW of Prince Albert, Sask; Métis community and scene of a major confrontation, 9-12 May 1885, during the NORTH-WEST REBELLION. Maj-Gen Frederick MIDDLETON with about 900 men attacked less than 300 MÉTIS, Cree and Dakota defenders on 2 fronts: by river, from the HBC steamer *Northcote,* and by land. The strategy failed when the Métis lowered a ferry cable, decapitating the *Northcote*'s smokestack and leaving the steamer to float harmlessly downstream. The Métis also effectively resisted Middleton's land forces from elaborate rifle pits built under the supervision of Gabriel DUMONT. On the morning of May 12, Middleton's forces — two 9-pounders, a Gatling gun and about 130 men — feinted north, drawing the Métis out of their rifle pits around St-Antoine-de-Padoue Church and towards the Gatling gun. A strong wind prevented Lt-Col Van Straubenzie from hearing the guns and co-ordinating his attack on the church with Middleton's action. Shortly after noon Middleton's colonel, impatient with his caution, led a frontal attack on the weakened defenders, who were reduced to firing nails and stones from their rifles. The village was captured and the spirit of the resistance broken. Over 25 men from both sides were killed. Louis RIEL surrendered a few days later, Gabriel Dumont fled to the US, and other participants were captured and held for trial. Batoche is now a national historic site, although the church and rectory are the only buildings standing from 1885. Remains of the Métis rifle pits and Middleton's camp can be seen, and Dumont and other Métis leaders are buried in the cemetery nearby. As well, there is now a visitor reception centre to interpret the events of the battle and the Métis social and economic life.

WALTER HILDEBRANDT

Reading: B. Beal and R. Macleod, *Prairie Fire* (1984); W. Hildebrandt, *The Battle of Batoche* (1985); W. Oppen, *The Riel Rebellions: A Cartographic History* (1980); D. Payment, *Batoche* (1983).

Baton Broadcasting Incorporated, a diversified Canadian communications company, is 52% owned by the EATON family (Eaton's of Canada) through Telegram Corporation Ltd. John W.H. BASSETT is chairman of Baton, and his son Douglas Bassett is president. Baton operates a radio station in Saskatoon (CFQC) and television stations in Saskatoon (CFQC-TV), Regina (CKCK), Yorkton (CKOS/CICC), Prince Albert (CKBI/CIPA) and Toronto (CFTO). The company purchased CJOH-TV in Ottawa in 1987, subject to CRTC approval. Through its subsidiary Glen Warren Productions Ltd, Baton operates facilities in Toronto for the production of television programs, commercials and movies. Other holdings include a broadcast sales company and business forms, graphics and packaging operations. Total assets of Baton as of Aug 1986 were $187 million, with revenues of $188 million. PETER S. ANDERSON

Battle, Helen Irene, zoologist, educator (b at London, Ont 31 Aug 1903). A pioneering Canadian zoologist and much-loved teacher, she has been emeritus professor of zoology at Western since 1972. As one of the first zoologists actively engaged in laboratory (as opposed to field) research in marine biology, she demonstrated that the methods of the histology and physiology laboratories could provide answers to marine problems. Many of her papers are beautifully illustrated with her own ink drawings. One of the first women to enter a field dominated by men, she campaigned to improve the place of women in universities and encouraged many to take up careers in science. She was selected by the National Museum of Natural Sciences in Ottawa as one of 19 outstanding women scientists in Canada and was represented in a travelling exhibit to mark

International Women's Year. Many honours have accrued to her. Her first love was her teaching, which spanned some 50 years. Her students have become leaders in Canadian biology and her influence has been felt worldwide.

DONALD B. McMILLAN

Battleford, Sask, Town, pop 3833 (1986c), 3565 (1981c), inc 1910, is located at the confluence of the N SASKATCHEWAN and Battle rivers, 130 km NW of Saskatoon. It was once among the most important of early settlements in western Canada. While little more than a small fur-trade post and surveyor work camp, the settlement was named capital of the vast North-West Territories in 1876. A large government complex including Government House and a nearby North-West Mounted Police post were then established, as well as a townsite. Its trade and government functions grew rapidly, but in 1882 the capital seat was officially relocated to Regina and the CPR main line, which had been projected for Battleford, went to southern Saskatchewan. During the NORTH-WEST REBELLION (1885), Métis and native problems further damaged settlement prospects for the region.

In 1905 a rail line finally reached the area, but the Canadian Northern Ry had chosen to bypass Battleford, an event that eventually led to the creation of the adjacent community of North Battleford. Battleford prospered as a government centre for land title registration, a judicial district and an Indian Affairs office, but never fulfilled its earlier expectations. The legacy of the days before it was stripped of its "capital" status has been preserved in Fort Battleford, a national historic park, Government House and other historic buildings. Today Battleford and North Battleford, with a combined population of 18 709 (1986c), form a service centre for the surrounding region, which depends largely on agriculture, oil and gas development, manufacturing and tourism.

MARK RASMUSSEN

Reading: A. McPherson, *The Battlefords: A History* (1967).

Battles, *see* AMIENS; ATLANTIC; BATOCHE; BEAVER DAMS; BRITAIN; CHÂTEAUGUAY; CRYSLER'S FARM; CUT KNIFE HILL; DIEPPE; DUCK LAKE; FISH CREEK; FORT BEAUSÉJOUR; FORT DUQUESNE; FORT FRONTENAC; FRENCHMAN'S BUTTE; FREZENBERG RIDGE; HILL 70; HINDENBURG LINE; HONG KONG; KAP'YONG; LELIEFONTEIN; LIBERATION OF HOLLAND; LUNDY'S LANE; MONT SORREL; MORAVIANTOWN; NORMANDY INVASION; ORTONA; PAARDEBERG; PASSCHENDAELE; PLAINS OF ABRAHAM; PLATTSBURGH; PUT-IN-BAY; QUEENSTON HEIGHTS; RESTIGOUCHE; RHINELAND; RIDGEWAY; SAINT-CHARLES; SAINT-DENIS; SAINT-EUSTACHE; STE-FOY; SEVEN OAKS INCIDENT; SOMME; STEELE NARROWS; STONEY CREEK; VIMY RIDGE; WINDMILL; YPRES.

Bauer, Father David William, BASILIAN priest, educator, hockey coach (b at Kitchener, Ont 10 Nov 1925). Father Bauer comes from a large hockey-loving family. His brother Robert (Bobby) was a premier member of the famous "Kraut" line of the NHL Boston Bruins and coached the Kitchener-Waterloo Dutchmen to the Olympics in 1956 and 1960. As a youth he attended St Michael's High School in Toronto, an all-boys school then famous for its junior hockey program. An outstanding left winger, he later returned to coach the St Mike's Junior As, winning the MEMORIAL CUP in 1961. In 1961-62 he was transferred to St Mark's College, UBC. On 26 Aug 1962 the Canadian Amateur Hockey Assn approved Father Bauer's proposal for a national team, which would re-establish Canada in international competition, while providing its players with the opportunity to acquire an education. In 1967 the team won the Centennial Tournament

in Canada and a bronze medal in the 1968 Winter Olympics at Grenoble, France. On 4 Jan 1970 Canada withdrew from international competition because the vast improvement in European teams made it impossible to compete at the highest level without the participation of Canadian professionals. The national team was disbanded, but Father Bauer's dedication to the ideals of amateur sport and his success in promoting athletic skill along with education have inspired respect in Canada and abroad. He has been honoured with a UBC scholarship in his name and in Sept 1986 an Olympic rink in Calgary was dedicated to him. *See also* CANADIAN OLYMPIC HOCKEY TEAM.

GIGI CLOWES

Baumann, Alex, "Sasha," swimmer (b at Prague, Czech 21 Apr 1964). Soon after he arrived with his family at Sudbury at age 9, he began setting age-group records in swimming under coach Jeno Tihanyi. In 1978 he won the 200 m individual medley (IM) at the Darmstadt International meet (butterfly, breaststroke, backstroke, freestyle) and won numerous national and international meets in the 200 IM, 400 IM, freestyle, backstroke and butterfly before setting a Commonwealth record in the 400 m IM 28 July 1981 and a world record in the 200 m IM the next day. Forced out of swimming for 10 months because of a chronic shoulder problem, he returned to lower the Commonwealth record in the 400 m IM and the world record in the 200 m IM at the COMMONWEALTH GAMES in Brisbane, Australia in Oct, 1982. He won the 400 m and 200 m IM events at the WORLD UNIVERSITY GAMES in Edmonton, July 1983, and lowered the 400 m IM world record to 4:17.53 at the Olympic trials. His 2 gold medals at the Los Angeles Olympics (200 m IM, world record 2:01.42; 400 m IM, world record 4:17.41) made him one of only 4 Canadians to win 2 Olympic gold medals (along with George HODGSON, Pĕrcy WILLIAMS and Gaëtan BOUCHER). He continued competitive swimming, winning 2 gold medals (400 m IM, 200 m IM) at the 1986 Commonwealth Games and recording a world best in 1987 (200 m IM), but in Oct 1987 he announced his retirement from competitive swimming. He is an Officer of the Order of Canada.

JAMES MARSH

Alex Baumann with one of his 2 gold medals at the 1984 Los Angeles Olympics (*courtesy Athlete Information Bureau/Service Information-Athlètes*).

Baxter, John Babington Macaulay, lawyer, politician, premier and chief justice of NB (b at Saint John 16 Feb 1868; d there 27 Dec 1946). Baxter played a leading part in the development of the Conservative Party in NB and was a leader in the MARITIME RIGHTS movement of the 1920s. He was a city councillor (1892-1910), attorney general of NB (1915-17), federal minister of customs (1921), premier 1925-31 and chief justice 1935-46. He was the author of *Historical Records of the New Brunswick Regiment, Royal Artillery* (1896), the unit he had commanded from 1907 to 1912.

ARTHUR T. DOYLE

Baxter, Joseph Iain Wilson, artist (b at Middlesbrough, Eng 16 Nov 1936). Brought to Canada by his parents in 1937, Iain Baxter began his artistic career as a painter, but by 1965 he was creating plastic bas-reliefs of such objects as plastic bleach, milk and detergent bottles. *Bagged Place* (1966), a 4-room furnished apartment, every part and item of which was bagged in plastic, contained psychological and sociological overtones. In 1967 he and his wife Elaine (from 1971 she used Ingrid), formed the N.E. Thing Co, which was incorporated and became the N.E. Thing Co Ltd in 1969. The NETCO collaboration continued until 1978 and produced ACTs (Aesthetically Claimed Things), ARTs (Aesthetically Rejected Things), conceptual works that deal with ways of perceiving the environment, construction analogues, works using communication media as extensions of man, and participatory pieces. Since 1978 Baxter has prepared photo works and mixed-media pieces, incorporating polaroid photos, drawings, painting and sometimes objects. An uninhibited attitude towards art and a partiality for common "things" are combined with sureness of line and sometimes sensual colour in works enriched as much with ambiguity, wit and inventive play as by his persistent aesthetic questioning.

Reading: M.L. Fleming, *Baxter²: Any Choice Works* (1982).

Bay Bulls, Nfld, Town, pop 1114 (1986c), 1081 (1981c), is located on the E coast of the AVALON PENINSULA. One of the earliest settlements, it has the earliest-known English place-name in Newfoundland. (The name may have come from the bull or the ice bird.) First used by the French, it was the site of wintering English fishermen by 1635, fortified by Gov David KIRKE 1638 and attacked by Dutch Admiral De Ruyter 1665. The semipermanent fishing settlement was attacked by the French 5 times, 1696-1796, during Anglo-French rivalry over Newfoundland's fishery. A year-round fishing community of mainly Irish immigrants was established by 1800. Resident merchants established thriving fish firms during the 1800s and Bay Bulls became a local business centre. A fisheries research station was established 1931, and during WWII the area was leased to Canada as a naval repair base. Modern Bay Bulls is a fishing and fish-processing centre, and the site of an RCA-Bell Canada microwave satellite station.

JANET E.M. PITT AND ROBERT D. PITT

Bay d'Espoir is a fjordlike arm of Hermitage B on Newfoundland's S coast, entered between West Head and Dawson Point, 3 km NW. More than 50 km from mouth to head, ice-free Bay d'Espoir (French for "hope") has sheer cliffs and steep-sided hills rising 180 to 300 m. The bay divides into 2 principal arms to the N, and NE beyond 14 km long Bois I. Because of the tremendous watershed from a surrounding glacial plateau, the area was chosen as the site of a hydroelectric power development, built 1964-77, at 600 MW the largest in insular Newfoundland. Until 1964 Bay d'Espoir was sparsely settled by Newfoundlanders originating in PLACENTIA B in the 1700s, and by MICMAC who established the Conne River settlement by the mid-1800s. Today fishing, lumbering and construction work are the area's main sources of employment.   JANET E.M. PITT

Bay Roberts, Nfld, Town, pop 4446 (1986c), 4512 (1981c), inc 1951, is located on the W shore of CONCEPTION BAY. Established by the late 1600s by English fishermen, Bay Roberts is probably named for a French family name, Robert. The inshore fishery and later the Labrador fishery and seal hunt contributed to the growth of Bay Roberts as a leading fishing, trading and commercial settlement by the 1800s. With CARBONEAR and HARBOUR GRACE, Bay Roberts became an important service, supply and communications centre with numerous wholesale companies and small-scale industries. Today, it is the largest salt-fish producing centre in Newfoundland, supplying European, Brazilian and Caribbean markets. In the 1970s the original settlement expanded to include several nearby communities.
                    JANET E.M. PITT AND ROBERT D. PITT

Bayefsky, Aba, artist, teacher (b at Toronto 7 Apr 1923). Bayefsky studied at Central Technical School, Toronto, 1937-42, then enlisted in the RCAF. As an official WAR ARTIST he produced a visual record of Belsen concentration camp. He studied in Paris (1948) and later travelled to India (1958) and Japan (1960, 1969, 1982). Besides his well-known watercolour and oil works depicting Toronto market scenes and portraits of friends, Bayefsky has done several large-scale murals and created portfolios of lithographs based on Canadian Indian legends and mythology and Hebrew religious themes. Throughout his career the human figure has been the basis of his work; most recently he completed a large series of paintings depicting tattooed people in Canada and Japan. Since 1957 he has been an instructor at the Ontario College of Art, Toronto. In 1979 he was appointed to the Order of Canada; he has achieved international recognition for his watercolours and graphics.   PAMELA WACHNA

Bayfield, Henry Wolsey, naval officer, hydrographic surveyor (b at Hull, Eng 21 Jan 1795; d at Charlottetown 10 Feb 1885). At age 11, Bayfield joined the Royal Navy. In 1816 he was engaged by Capt W.F. Owen to assist in surveying Lk Ontario. On Owen's recall to England in 1817, the Admiralty instructed Bayfield to survey Lk Erie and then Lks Huron and Superior. After completing these surveys, Bayfield was appointed surveyor of the St Lawrence. Working from Québec City 1827-40, he surveyed and charted the Québec shores of the St Lawrence R and Gulf, part of the Labrador coast, also the E coast of NB; and from Charlottetown, 1841-56, the PEI coastline, most of the NS coast and part of Newfoundland's coast. His surveys included the main river estuaries; the harbours of Montréal, Québec, Halifax and Charlottetown; and Anticosti, Sable and the Magdalen Is. Motivated by a desire to prevent shipwrecks and loss of life, he took pride in the accuracy of his charts. Bayfield was promoted rear-admiral 1856, vice-admiral 1863 and admiral 1867. His sailing directions were published as *The St Lawrence Pilot* (1860) and *The Nova Scotia Pilot* (1856, 1860).   RUTH MCKENZIE

Bazalgette, Ian Willoughby, aviator (b at Calgary 19 Oct 1918; d in France 4 Aug 1944). He joined the Royal Air Force in 1941 and was awarded the Distinguished Flying Cross for gallantry in 1943. He was awarded the VICTORIA CROSS posthumously for a courageous attack on a target at Trossy St-Maxim, France, despite heavy anti-aircraft fire. He managed to land his crippled Lancaster bomber but perished in an explosion.

In 1949 a mountain in Jasper National Park was named in his honour.   JAMES MARSH

BC Hydro Formed by provincial legislation in 1962, BC Hydro and Power Authority, a CROWN CORPORATION, was given a mandate to provide a secure ENERGY future for British Columbia. Today, the company serves more than 90% of the population and is responsible for the overall planning, generation and supply of ELECTRIC POWER for the province. In addition to developing British Columbia's hydroelectric potential, BC Hydro provides a natural-gas distribution system in the lower mainland and distributes propane-air gas in Greater Victoria. BC Hydro also operates a rail freight service on the SW tip of the lower mainland. Until 1980, the utility operated city transit services in Greater Vancouver and Greater Victoria and, before 1979, an interurban bus service on the lower mainland and Vancouver I. BC Hydro employs approximately 6400 people. Its headquarters are in Vancouver.

In 1962 most of the province's 443 000 electric customers were served by the BC Electric Company and the provincially owned BC Power Commission. The provincial government had acquired BC Electric in 1961, and the 2 utilities were amalgamated the following year as BC Hydro. BC Electric began its hydroelectric and electric-railway operations in the late 1890s. The Power Commission was established by the provincial government in 1945 to consolidate the operations of many small utilities outside the BC Electric service areas.

After amalgamation, BC Hydro began developing the hydroelectric potential of the Peace and Columbia rivers. The W.A.C. Bennett Dam on the PEACE R is among the largest earthfill structures in existence, and the project's 2416 megawatt (MW) Gordon M. Shrum Generating Station was the world's largest underground powerhouse when it started operating in 1968. The COLUMBIA RIVER TREATY (signed in 1961, effective 1964) between Canada and the US opened the way for construction in BC of 3 dams, Duncan, Keenleyside and Mica, to regulate the flow of the Columbia R, enabling BC and the US to construct large power plants along the river and its tributaries. Only the Mica project, which has an ultimate capacity of 2604 MW, included generating facilities. The 650 MW Seven Mile project on the Pend d'Oreille R and the 700 MW Peace Canyon project on the Peace R began operations in 1980. The 1843 MW Revelstoke project on the Columbia R, completed 1984, brought BC Hydro's total installed generating capacity to 10.5 million kW.

Most of BC Hydro's generating capacity is produced at 30 hydroelectric-generating plants, which have a total capacity of 9332 MW. The remainder is generated by conventional thermal, gas turbine and stationary diesel plants. BC Hydro's most recent Electric System Plans and Evaluations, for the period 1 Apr 1987 to 31 Mar 1997, indicate that "no major new generation facilities are required (in British Columbia) during the 10-year program period." BC Hydro is, however, investigating the possibility of building a 900 MW project on the Peace R, near Fort St John, to serve a firm export market in the US, starting in the mid-1990s. *See also* ELECTRIC UTILITIES.   FLINT BONDURANT

Beach, *see* COASTAL LANDFORM.

Beals, Carlyle Smith, astronomer (b at Canso, NS 29 June 1899; d at Ottawa 2 July 1979). Astronomer and assistant director of the Dominion Astrophysical Observatory, Victoria, BC, until 1946, Beals was Dominion Astronomer in Ottawa until his retirement in 1964. While at Victoria, he made important contributions to the ob-

servation and interpretation of emission lines in the spectra of certain hot stars, to the understanding of the nature of the gas clouds in interstellar space and to the development of instrumentation for astronomy. As Dominion Astronomer he guided the postwar development of astronomical and geophysical research in Canada. Combining his knowledge of ASTRONOMY and his interest in geophysics, he initiated a highly successful program in the identification and study of meteorite craters in Canada. Recognized internationally as one of the leading astronomers of his day, he was the recipient of many honours, including the Order of Canada. In Sept 1987 minor planet 3314 was named after him.   J.L. LOCKE

Beam, Carl, artist (b West Bay, Manitoulin I, Ont 1943). He graduated from U Vic 1976 and then studied at U of A. Beam works on a large format, canvas or paper, with acrylics. He abstracts realistic details from life and by repetition and juxtaposition of various elements forces the viewer to find meaning. His deep concern is to keep alive traditional Anishnabe (Ojibwa) cultural values. New works were shown in Toronto in 1986.   MARY E. SOUTHCOTT

Bean, Green (*Phaseolus vulgaris*) There are at least 6 classes of green bean, and many cultivars (commercial varieties) are available within each class. Common types include the "snap" bean (green or wax) and kidney beans. The fruit is a pod, round or flat, curved or straight. Plant breeders have perfected a tender, round, fleshy, stringless pod with minimum fibre in the walls. Green beans are either quick-growing bush types or pole types, requiring a long growing season. Bush types are low growing, self-supporting and non-climbing. Pole types, with never-ending stem elongation, must be supported by string or posts. The bean plant is shallow rooted and requires adequate moisture. Bush-bean pods mature in a concentrated manner and successive plantings every 14 days are necessary for continuous podding; given optimum growing conditions, they are harvested 45-65 days after seeding. Pole-bean pods begin maturing 55-75 days after seeding; one planting will give continuous podding. Green beans (especially bush types) grow well throughout temperate parts of Canada. Main areas of commercial production are Québec, Ontario and BC. Yields of 4-6 t/ha are not uncommon for bush beans and pole types give considerably higher yields. The estimated annual worth of green beans grown in Canada exceeds $8-10 million; imports (mostly from southern US) are of about equal value.   I.L. NONNECKE

Bear (family Ursidae), stocky, bob-tailed MAMMAL with 5 clawed toes on each paw. Three species inhabit Canada: POLAR BEAR (*Ursus maritimus*), GRIZZLY BEAR (*U. arctos horribilis*) and black bear (*U. americanus*). Grizzly and black bears are omnivores, eating flesh or vegetable matter in season; polar bears prey mainly on seals. Black bears, the most common and widespread in Canada, may also be brown or cinnamon. Males weigh 80-250 kg; females are 10% lighter. Black and grizzly bears occupy coniferous forest, deciduous forest, swamp and tundra habitats, with polar bears on the arctic coasts and islands. Bears will eat growing grain, vegetables and domestic stock, and will scavenge garbage from camps or dumps. Breeding begins at 3 years, with mating in June-July. Embryos do not develop until Dec because of delayed implantation. In delayed implantation the fertilized egg develops slowly, while floating in the uterus. Eventually it becomes attached to the wall of the uterus and development continues until birth. In Jan-Feb, after 200-225 days gestation, usually 2 (range, 1-3) cubs are born in dens. Cubs become independent after about one year. In winter, bears sleep in dens but do not truly hibernate. Adults are solitary and often dangerous when unafraid of man. Bear skins are used as rugs and covers; their flesh is eaten.

Bears have inhabited N America since Miocene times (less than 23.7 million years ago) and evolved into large massive, small compact and long-legged cursorial forms. During the Pleistocene (1.6 million years ago) a large long-legged short-faced cursorial bear (*Arctodus simus*) existed in N America. This running bear was probably primarily carnivorous and ran down its prey over open country. It is recorded from Alaska, the Old Crow region of the Yukon, and the western US, in association with other extinct mammals, mammoth, bison, schrub-oxen and sabre-toothed cats. The running bear was as big as a polar bear and a formidable predator.   C.S. CHURCHER

Bear, by Marian ENGEL (Toronto, 1976), winner of the Governor-General's Award, has been called the most controversial novel ever written in Canada because of its heroine's erotic relationship with a bear. Lou is a lonely, middle-aged archivist who ekes out a molelike existence in the city, alienated from the natural world. Her summer journey to a wooded island in northern Ontario on a historical research assignment becomes a spiritual awakening for, after her gradual communion with primitive forces in the wilderness, she is profoundly transformed, reborn as a fully integrated person, ready to start a new life in the city. Although Engel's unconventional, imaginative tale has an economical, unpretentious prose style and a deceptively simple plot, the novel achieves its power through the complex symbolic and mythic levels on which it operates.

DONNA COATES

Bear Attacks Infrequent attacks on humans have been made by grizzly, black or polar bears. Bears can run at speeds exceeding 50 km/h, are significantly stronger than people and can inflict serious injury. However, most bears, but especially black bears, are normally tolerant of people. Black bears and, to a lesser extent, GRIZZLY BEARS and POLAR BEARS, use aggressive displays such as charging, but stop short of contact or make loud vocalizations to get people who have come too close to move away. It is hard to predict the behaviour of individuals because bears learn readily and have distinct personalities. Despite these limitations, accurate records of attacks have been used to describe and understand the rare attacks made on people.

One of the most common circumstances associated with a grizzly bear attack is the "sudden encounter," especially with a grizzly bear female and her young. Here, people hiking are typically unaware of the bear until less than 50 m separates them and attack occurs. To decrease chances of such incidents people should avoid areas where grizzly bears are likely to be found or be alert when travelling through them. Warning noise may help prevent incidents, as may "playing dead" if attacked. About half the cases of attacks by grizzlies in the national parks were inflicted by bears that had lost their avoidance of people as a result of having foraged on people's food or garbage, or because of repeated exposure to people. A less frequent correlate of a grizzly bear inflicted injury was the bear being provoked, as by a person's dog, by being shot by a hunter or by a photographer getting too close. About half of all grizzly bear inflicted injuries were serious. Injury rates were low. For example in the 7-year period 1980-86, there were 5 grizzly bear-inflicted injuries in Banff National Park, none in Jasper.

Unlike grizzly bears, black bears almost never attack in "sudden encounters." The typical black bear inflicted injury is minor and occurs in or nearby roadside campgrounds or other areas where black bears are trying to get people's food or garbage and in the process scratch or lightly bite a nearby person. A person should back away from such "attacks," watching the bear. Only 5-10% of black bear-inflicted injuries are serious. These very rare incidents typically occurred in rural or remote areas. In many of these cases black bears have attempted to or have actually preyed on people. Between 1900 and 1986, an exhaustive search revealed records of 27 black bear inflicted-deaths throughout N America.

A detailed, N American-wide search for records of attacks by polar bears revealed only 20 cases, of which 5 were fatal. Male polar bears occasionally stalk and attempt to prey on people. Knowledge of polar bear habitat, constant vigilance and a firearm are essential elements of safety around polar bears.   STEPHEN HERRERO

Bearberry, or kinnickinnick, trailing, evergreen shrub of heather family. Flexible, rooting branches grow up to 2 m long, are covered with reddish, shreddy bark and bear alternate, dark green, oval leaves. Small, waxy, urn-shaped flowers are white or pink, tipped with red. They grow in small clusters at branch ends, in late spring and early summer, and develop into bright red, fleshy fruits. The genus name, *Arctostaphylos*, derives from Greek *arctos*, "bear," *staphylos*, "bunch of grapes"; species name, *uva-ursi*, from Latin *uva*, "bunch of grapes," *ursus*, "bear" — literally "bearberry, berry-bear." Bearberry grows across Canada on dry sandy soils (often called sandberry), but is also found on gravel terraces, sand dunes and in the boreal forest, and is valuable as ground cover for checking erosion on watersheds. It is less common above the TREELINE. Kinnickinnick [Algonquian, "that which is mixed"] leaves were combined with tobacco and smoked by Blackfoot and other Indian groups in religious ceremonies. Bearberry extract has a high content of tannic and gallic acids which make it an astringent. It also contains arbutin, which becomes a germicide in the renal tract. The Thompson Indians of BC used it for kidney diseases, and the Blackfoot made an infusion for sore gums, and salve for skin diseases.   BERYL HALLWORTH

Bearberry (*Arctostaphylos uva-ursi*) grows across Canada on dry, sandy soils (*artwork by Claire Tremblay*).

Beardy, Jackson, artist (b Quentin Pickering Jackson Beardy at Island Lake, Man 24 July 1944; d at Winnipeg 8 Dec 1984). He was educated at a government residential school and studied art at the Winnipeg Technical Vocational High School and U of Man. In his twenties he struggled with episodes of serious illness. His art draws on a deep knowledge of his native Cree tradition gained from a close childhood relationship with his grandmother and from his systematic collection of myths and legends in northern Manitoba during the mid-1960s. In 1972 he joined with ODJIG, MORRISSEAU, RAY, JANVIER, Cobiness and Sanchez to form the "Group of Seven." Although Beardy's early work often narrates specific legends, his mature art expresses fundamental cosmological and spiritual concepts such as balance in nature, regeneration and growth, and the interdependence of all things. His distinctive graphic style is characterized by precisely defined flat areas of warm colour and curving ribbons of paint. From 1982 to 1983 he was senior arts ad-

Calling the Night, painting by Jackson Beardy, whose art drew on a deep knowledge of his native Cree myths and legends (*courtesy Department of Indian and Northern Affairs*).

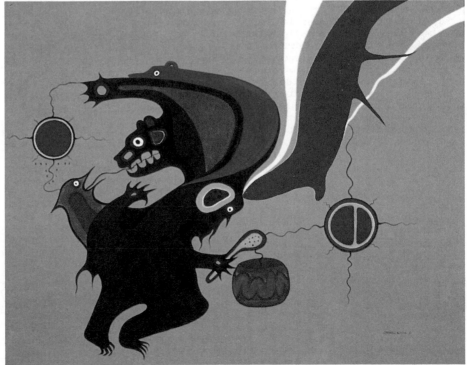

viser to the federal Dept of Indian Affairs and Northern Development. RUTH B. PHILLIPS

Bearlake are Athapaskan-speaking people who live near GREAT BEAR LK in the NWT. Their trading post and settlement is Ft Franklin, at the western end of the lake. The Bearlake were not considered a distinct people by self-designation or by outsiders until the 20th century. Historically, and probably before records exist, Great Bear Lk was exploited by various small bands of HARE, DOGRIB and SLAVEY intercepting the caribou herds and fishing the shores and tributaries. An aboriginal enemy of the Athapaskan peoples were the INUIT, who sometimes approached the NW area of the lake in pursuit of caribou. Occasionally this contact may have produced open hostilities, but mutual fear was generally handled by avoidance, and hostility was gradually reduced during the historical period.

Ft Franklin, on Keith Arm near the entrance of Great Bear R, is close to one of the few fishing sites open all year at this latitude. It was an obvious place for friendly neighbouring peoples to enjoy a dependable resource and to mingle socially. With the coming of the FUR TRADE, and a trading post intermittently active since 1804, there was increased contact among Indian groups. Through the 19th century and into the 20th, these groups gradually began to consider themselves "Bear Lakers" as a larger unit. They also developed their own dialect, incorporating features from Dogrib, Hare and Slavey-Mountain languages. In 1986 the population of the band was only 572. In 1930 uranium and silver were discovered at the eastern end of Great Bear Lk. Uranium mining during the 1940s brought some involvement in the Canadian economy for the Bearlake, but by the 1950s this involvement was minimal. The Bearlake still rely on traditional hunting and fishing activities, with trapping and limited employment providing cash for other necessities. BERYL C. GILLESPIE

Reading: J. Helm, ed, *Handbook of North American Indians,* vol 6: *Subarctic* (1981).

Beatty, Sir Edward Wentworth, lawyer, railway official (b at Thorold, Ont 16 Oct 1877; d at Montréal 23 Mar 1943), son of Henry BEATTY. After studying at Upper Canada College, U of Toronto and Osgoode Hall, Beatty articled with a law firm in Toronto. When A.R. Creelman, a partner in the firm, was appointed CPR general counsel in 1901, he took Beatty to Montréal as his assistant. Beatty's ability impressed CPR President Thomas SHAUGHNESSY and he was appointed general counsel in 1913 and became the first Canadian-born CPR president in 1918. The CPR faced competition from the CNR, particularly in accommodation and construction of prairie branch lines in the 1920s. Beatty strengthened the system, which he had inherited from Shaughnessy, and in 1942 created Canadian Pacific Airlines. He was knighted in 1935. JOHN A. EAGLE

Reading: D.H. Miller-Barstow, *Beatty of the C.P.R.* (1951).

Beatty, Henry, businessman, pioneer transportation official (b at Cootehill, Ire 1 May 1834; d at Toronto 10 Apr 1914). Beatty immigrated with his parents to Thorold, Canada W, when he was 9. In 1857, apprenticing in the hardware business, he travelled widely and, seeking adventure, struck gold in the Cariboo. In 1870 he became a partner in his uncle's steamship firm. Under Beatty's management the firm expanded from one to 5 steamships and extended its operations from Sarnia to Port Arthur, Ont, and Duluth, Minn. In 1882 he was appointed manager of lake transportation for the CPR. One of his first duties was to supervise construction in Scotland of 3 vessels that became the nucleus of CPR

Steamships. A man of unusual executive ability and vision, he served as marine adviser to the CPR after his retirement (1892). JOHN A. EAGLE

Beatty, Henry Perrin, politician (b at Toronto 1 June 1950). After graduating from Toronto's Upper Canada College, Beatty received a general BA at U of Western Ontario in 1971. He was active in Progressive Conservative student groups, worked for the Ontario government, and in 1972 was elected MP for Wellington-Dufferin-Simcoe. He was re-elected in 1974, 1979, 1980 and 1984. Beatty became minister of state for the Treasury Board in 1979 during the Joe Clark administration, becoming the youngest person to enter Cabinet to that time. In early 1984, he headed a panel created by the Opposition Conservatives to hear Canadians' complaints about the tax department, and after the Conservative electoral win of Sept 1984 was appointed minister of national revenue and minister responsible for Canada Post. In August the following year, he was made solicitor general, and in June 1986 became minister of national defence. His White Paper on Defence Policy, delivered June 1987, called for increased spending on military equipment and announced the government's intention to purchase 12 nuclear-powered submarines. DEAN BEEBY

Beatty, Patricia, dancer, choreographer (b at Toronto 13 May 1936). She trained at Bennington College, Vt, and in New York and Connecticut with Martha Graham and Pearl Lang. She then danced with Lang's company 1960-65 before returning to Canada. In 1966 she founded the New Dance Group of Canada, which gave its first performance 1967 with guest artists Peter RANDAZZO and David EARLE, and in 1968 Beatty became co-director with them of the TORONTO DANCE THEATRE. Much of her early choreography focused on the relationship between the sexes. Later dances, such as *Seastill* (1979) and *Skyling* (1980), both designed by Aiko SUZUKI, and *Emerging Ground* (1983), a collaboration with Graham COUGHTRY, have found inspiration in the natural world. GRAHAM JACKSON

Beau, Henri, painter (b at Montréal 27 June 1863; d at Paris, France 15 May 1949). After his first design and painting lessons in Montréal, he left for the US in 1884, ending up in San Francisco where he did coloured engravings. Returning to Montréal in 1886, he went on to Paris, studying at the Académie Julian and the École des beaux-arts. He had his first showings in the 1890s and in 1900 won third prize for painting at the Universal Exhibition. Beau appeared regularly in exhibitions in Europe and America. In Canada the Salon du printemps of the Art Assn and the Royal Canadian Academy frequently hung his works. He was official painter of the Public Archives of Canada 1915-38. An active member of several French art societies, he was made an officer of the French Academy.

With his brother Paul, a fine-arts ironworker, Beau left a definite mark on Canadian art, heralding the coming young generation of painters. Yet, with his French academy training and French tastes, he was one of the last representatives of a dying age. Among his important works are *Les Noces de Cana* (1894) in the Sacré Coeur chapel of NOTRE-DAME de Montréal, *La Dispersion des Acadiens* (1900) at Saint-Joseph's (now part of U de Moncton, NB), and *L'Arrivée de Champlain à Québec* (1908) at the Musée du Québec. MICHEL CHAMPAGNE

Beauchemin, Micheline, tapestry weaver (b at Longueuil, Qué 24 Oct 1930). Beauchemin began her career making stained-glass windows but early turned to the vibrant colours found in skeins of wool to hook, weave and embroider spectacu-

lar wall hangings. She then studied at the École des beaux-arts in Montréal, winning a scholarship to study with Ossip Zadkine in Paris (1953). Travels to N Africa and Greece inspired her to embroidery, a favourite occupation as a child, sending *Visage de Mistra* to Chartres, 1954. Back in Canada in 1957 she used a tumult of wool, acrylic, gold and silver threads, and aluminum, for some 60 tapestries, floating walls, and forms in space, found in Place des Arts (Montréal, 1963), the National Arts Centre (Ottawa), Tokyo, San Francisco and cities across Canada. In 1977, 1978 and 1979 she sold the Oiseau totem curtain, a tapestry, and 30 wings of floating nylon thread to business buildings in Montréal, Shawinigan and Québec City, respectively. Beauchemin has travelled and studied in Japan, China, India, the Canadian Arctic and the Andes, adding depth and mystery to her love of light, water, wings and nets. ANNE MCDOUGALL

Beauchemin, Yves, writer (b at Noranda, Qué 26 June 1941). Before becoming a Radio-Québec researcher, Beauchemin taught and worked in publishing. His first novel, *L'Enfirouapé* (1974), was a burlesque replay of certain events of the 1970 OCTOBER CRISIS. *Le Matou* (1981; tr *The Alley Cat*, 1986) describes the crazy, tragic adventures of a young Montréaler who decides to free himself from the collective history of economic dependence by running a restaurant. That *Le Matou* became the all-time best-selling novel in Québec literature and has been translated into 6 languages is because of its lucid observation of individuals and societies, its sure delineation of colourful personalities, its detached tone, in which humour tempers irony, and its teeming life, conveyed by a quick, exuberant and controlled style. It was made into a film by Jean BEAUDIN (1985). GABRIELLE POULIN

Beauchêne, Robert Chevalier, dit, adventurer, privateer (b at Pointe-aux-Trembles [Montréal] 23 Apr 1686; d at Tours, France Dec 1731). As a young man, Beauchêne served as a VOYAGEUR and on raiding expeditions against the English colonies. In 1707 he joined an Acadian privateer. He later crossed the Atlantic, wandered through western France and was killed in a brawl in Tours. His memoirs, with many exaggerations and inaccuracies, were published in 2 vols by Alain-René Lesage as *Les Aventures de monsieur Robert Chevalier, dit de Beauchêne, capitaine de flibustiers dans la Nouvelle-France* (1732). ALLAN GREER

Beaucours, Josué Dubois Berthelot de, military officer, engineer, governor of Trois-Rivières and Montréal (b in France c 1662; d at Montréal 9 May 1750). Beaucours came to New France 1688 as an infantry officer but is far better known for his work in FORTIFICATIONS: at Trois-Rivières (1690-91), Québec (1692-93, 1710-11 and 1713-14), Chambly (1709-11), Montréal (1702 and 1707-09) and LOUISBOURG (1715-16). Strongly supported by colonial governors and administrators for his practicality, he was less well regarded at Versailles for the technical quality of his work, which remains a subject of debate. His appointments as chief engineer for Canada (1712-14) and Île Royale [Cape Breton I] (1715-16) were brief, but after 1716 he slowly climbed the administrative ladder, becoming governor of Trois-Rivières in 1730 and of Montréal in 1733. He retired from the latter post in 1748. F.J. THORPE

Beaudet, Jean-Marie, conductor, pianist, administrator, organist, teacher (b at Thetford-Mines, Qué 20 Feb 1908; d at Ottawa 19 Mar 1971). As a conductor and administrator, he promoted Canadian music at home and abroad. He held several positions with the CBC 1937-64 and was responsible for giving music a larger role in

CBC programming. During this time he also conducted several concerts for the CBC. After serving as CBC's representative in Paris (1957-59), he returned to Canada as executive secretary of the Canadian Music Centre (1959-61). In 1964 he was appointed music director for the National Arts Centre where he assembled the centre's permanent orchestra, which made its debut in 1968. In 1971, he was awarded, posthumously, the CM Council Medal. HÉLÈNE PLOUFFE

Beaudin, Jean, filmmaker (b at Montréal 6 Feb 1939). After studying at École des beaux-arts, Montréal, and the School of Design, Zurich, Switz, Beaudin joined the NFB 1964. His first experimental feature, *Stop* (1970), was followed by *Le Diable est parmi nous* (1971), which he made in the private sector. He returned to the NFB, making 4 beautiful dramatic shorts, including *Cher Théo* (1975), before directing *J.A. Martin photographe*, a *succès d'estime* for which Monique Mercure won the best actress award at Cannes. The film's success enabled him to make *Cordélia* (1980) for the NFB, a feature film based on a well-known murder case. This was followed by *Mario* (1984) and his adaptation of Yves BEAUCHEMIN's best-selling novel *Le Matou* (1985).
PIERS HANDLING

Beaufort Sea can be taken to include the whole of the clockwise gyre of the Canada Basin of the Arctic Ocean N of Alaska, the Yukon and the Mackenzie Delta coast, bounded on the E by BANKS I and PRINCE PATRICK I. In a more restricted, official sense, it has been defined as that part of the Arctic Ocean lying S and E of a line connecting Point Barrow, Alaska, and Lands End, Prince Patrick I. In this narrower definition it has an area of 450 000 km². The coast is low lying, with barrier islands and sandspits, and is subject to considerable scouring by ice and erosion by storm surges. The inshore waters are shallow (the line of 200 m in depth varying from about 80-200 km from shore), and the shelf is much wider in the Canadian than in the US section. From the edge of the shelf (200 m) the bottom deepens fairly rapidly to 3500 m, the main Canada Basin to the N being close to 4000 m at its deepest.

Tides are predominantly semidiurnal (twice a day), with a small range from 0.3 to 0.5 m. Inshore currents in the ice-free zone in summer are variable and chiefly wind driven, dominated by alternating NW and easterly winds. NW winds, enhanced by the effect of the Earth's rotation, cause the MACKENZIE R discharge, laden with sediment, to turn eastward along with the general easterly flow of seawater. Easterly winds tend to reverse this current. Dominant features in summer are a northwesterly flow of water E of Herschel I and an easterly flow along the Tuktoyaktuk Peninsula. Farther offshore, in the ice-covered region, the general Beaufort Sea Gyre takes over in the form of a westerly flow. The water is typically Arctic Ocean water, low in temperature and salinity, but a Pacific influence is discernible, originating in the Bering Sea and reflected in the fauna, which include Pacific herring and salmon.

The region is rich in seabirds in summer and is an important breeding ground and migration staging area. The general level of biological production is fairly high, subarctic rather than arctic, and seals and whales form an important element in the native economy. Exploration for oil and gas on the Canadian shelf began with seismic tests in the late 1960s, and the first well was drilled in 1973. The promise of the Beaufort Sea for oil and gas production was realized in 1986 with the Amauligak project. In its first year of production, it yielded 50 400 cubic metres of oil, which were marketed in Japan. M.J. DUNBAR

Artificial island used for petroleum exploration in the shallow waters off the Mackenzie Delta in the Beaufort Sea (*courtesy Petroleum Resources Communication Foundation*).

Beauharnois, Charles de Beauharnois de La Boische, Marquis de, governor of New France 1726-47 (b at La Chaussaye, near Orléans, France 12 Oct 1671; d at Paris, France 12 July 1749). Beauharnois brought long experience as a naval officer in the wars of Louis XIV to the difficult task of checking British colonial expansion. With the help of allied Indian nations, he successfully defended strategic points on the Acadian boundary, on Lk Ontario and in the West despite peacetime financial restrictions. The spread of the WAR OF THE AUSTRIAN SUCCESSION to N America in 1744 resulted in a shortage of trading items, which severely strained the French network of alliances with the Indians. After Beauharnois's departure in 1747, several of his recommendations, such as the FORTIFICATION of Québec City and the reinforcement of French might in the West, were approved.
JEANNETTE LAROUCHE

Beauharnois de La Chaussaye, François de, Baron de Beauville, INTENDANT of New France 1702-05 (bap 19 Sept 1665 near Orléans, France; d there 9 Sept 1746). Beauharnois, a protégé of the minister of marine, faced a difficult situation on his arrival in New France. The fur trade was in decline, following a price slump in Europe, and war had broken out between England and France. He tried, with subsidies to the Compagnie de la Colonie, to save the fur trade and also to develop agriculture, but his brief stay gave him no opportunity for significant achievements. His 3 years as intendant were undoubtedly an apprenticeship that put him in line for promotions in France, culminating in his appointment as intendant of the marine at Rochefort. His brother Charles, the marquis de BEAUHARNOIS, served as governor of New France. JEANNETTE LAROUCHE

Beauharnois Scandal became public between June 1931 and Apr 1932 when committees of the House of Commons and Senate investigated allegations that the Beauharnois Light, Heat and Power Co had made substantial contributions to the Liberal Party in return for permission to divert the St Lawrence R 30 km W of Montréal to generate hydroelectricity. Company director R.O. SWEEZEY testified that Liberal senators W.L. McDougald and Andrew Haydon had personally received Beauharnois funds, and that the company had paid approximately $700 000 into the campaign fund of the federal and Québec Liberal parties. Although no connection was established between the donations and the power policy of the Mackenzie King government, McDougald was forced to resign from the Senate and Haydon

was dismissed in disgrace from his role as campaign treasurer. Mackenzie King, then Opposition leader, denied any knowledge of the affair but said in Parliament that the scandal had thrust the Liberals into "the valley of humiliation." The Beauharnois Scandal caused no long-term political damage to the Liberal Party, which won a large majority in the 1935 federal election. Fear of another such scandal prompted the creation in 1932 of the National Liberal Federation, which formally separated fund-raising from the parliamentary leadership. JOHN HERD THOMPSON

Beaulé, Chevalier Pierre, union leader/organizer, public servant (b at Québec City 31 Aug 1872; d there 8 Oct 1957). A shoemaker/machinist by trade, he was a member of the Shoemaker-Machinist Union at Québec and a participant in Cercles d'études ouvrier. A proponent of confessional and national unions, he helped unite Catholic Labour Councils at Québec, becoming its organizer. He was first president-elect of Canadian and Catholic Confederation of Labour (1921-33), now the CONFEDERATION OF NATIONAL TRADE UNIONS, and established service sector, industrial and craft unions. He was first CCCL representative in the Canadian delegation at the International Labour Organization at Geneva and again on 3 subsequent occasions. He served on various committees to assist the unemployed during the 1930s. He was appointed Chevalier de l'Ordre St-Gregoire-de-la-Grande by the Papacy. Two years after resigning from the CCCL presidency Beaulé joined the Québec provincial public service. F.J.K. GRIEZIC

Beaulieu, Michel, writer, literary critic and translator (b at Montréal 31 Oct 1941; d there 10 July 1985). He studied at Collège Jean-de-Bré-beuf then at the arts faculty of U de Montréal. In succession art critic, sub-editor and director of *Quartier latin* (1961-64), he founded *L'Odyssée* (1963), the student paper for the arts faculty, before being elected (1964) director of publications for the Association générale des étudiants. In 1963 he became a journalist at *La Presse* and founded, with Gaston MIRON, Les Éditions Estérel. He was theatre critic for *Le Devoir*, 1971-72, and helped found the Centre d'essai des auteurs dramatiques and the review, *Jeu*. He was simultaneously critic, publisher, journalist and translator, and worked for many periodicals both in Québec and abroad. He published his first collection of poetry in 1964, *Pour chanter dans les chaînes*, and by 1985 had brought out some 20 titles, including 3 novels, as well as some 15 radio plays. But it was in poetry that he distinguished himself primarily. He received the 1973 award from the review *Études françaises* for his collection *Variables*; won the Grand Prix littéraire of the *Journal de Montréal* in 1980 for his retrospective *Desseins*, poems 1961-67; and received a Governor General's Award (1982) for the collection *Visages* and, posthumously, the Prix Gatien Lapointe (1985) for *Kaléidoscope*. ROGER CHAMBERLAND

Beaulieu, Victor-Lévy, journalist, novelist, essayist, playwright, publisher (b at St-Paul-de-la-Croix, Qué 2 Sept 1945). A well-known figure, Beaulieu is important to Québec literature as much as for his various activities as his own respected writing. He has won many literary prizes: Grand prix littéraire de la Ville de Montréal (*Les Grands-pères*, 1971), Gov Gen's Award (*Don Quichotte de la démanche*, 1974), Prix France-Canada (*Monsieur Melville*, 1978; tr 1985) and Prix Jean-Béraud-Molson (*Satan Belhumeur*, 1981). Beaulieu loves to experiment with various literary styles and shatter their usual boundaries. *Blanche forcée* (1976) is a story; *N'évoque plus que le désenchantement de ta ténèbre, mon si pauvre Abel*

(1976), a lamentation: *Sagamo Job J* (1977), a hymn; *La Tête de Monsieur Ferron* (1979), a humorous epic. As an essayist he is interested in his literary ancestors (*Pour saluer Victor Hugo*, 1971; *Jack Kérouac*, 1972) as in forgotten Québec writings (*Manuel de la petite littérature du Québec*, 1974). He has written 2 TV series (*Les As* and *Race de monde*, a fine adaptation of the first novel in the "Vrais Saga des Beauchemin") and several plays (including *Ma Corriveau*, 1976, and *Monsieur Zéro*, 1977). After working for Éditions du jour and Éditions de l'Aurore, he operated his own publishing company, VLB éditeur, 1976-84, and has published poetry, novels, plays and stories, each with equal attention to detail. Constantly evolving, Beaulieu's work testifies to his exploration of a real and literary homeland.

BENOÎT MELANÇON

Reading: G. Bessette, *Trois Romanciers québécois* (1973).

Beaulne, Guy, director (b at Ottawa 23 Dec 1921). His father was artistic director and director of an Ottawa theatre company, Le Groupe Beaulne, as well as director of arts at U Vic. After graduating from U of O, Guy studied drama under Denis d'Inés in Paris while working as a correspondent for Radio-Canada and a theatre critic for *Le Droit*. Returning home, he worked as a radio drama producer for Radio-Canada until 1956, and in TV until 1963. He then joined the Québec Dept of Cultural Affairs where he was executive director of artistic education until 1970; first director of the Grand Théâtre de Québec until 1976; and member of the Délégation générale du Québec in Paris until 1979. Since 1981 he has been director of the Conservatoire d'art dramatique de Montréal. He founded the Association canadienne du théâtre d'amateurs in 1958 and served as its director until 1963. He is credited with the creation of the radio program *La Famille Plouffe*, and followed Jean-Paul Fugère as producer of the TV program of the same name. In the area of experimental drama, he worked on a radio program, "Nouveautés dramatiques," as well as the English-language TV program, "Shoe string theatre."

ANDRÉ G. BOURASSA

Beausejour, Man, Town, inc 1912, pop 2535 (1986c), is located 60 km NE of Winnipeg on the transition between prairie and Canadian Shield. Originally known as Stony Prairie, Beausejour was named in 1877 by Mrs H.W.D. Armstrong, wife of a government railway surveyor, when a telegraph office was installed there to serve settlers along the nearby Brokenhead River. After the railway was completed in 1887, and an influx of East Europeans and Scandinavians in the 1890s, the town consolidated its position as principal service and administrative centre for the surrounding agricultural district. Other significant industries include the processing of peat moss, and the famed Tyndall limestone quarries nearby. Edward SCHREYER, former provincial premier and governor general, hails from the district. Beausejour is also home to the annual Canadian Power Toboggan Championship Races. JOHN SELWOOD

Beausoleil, Claude, professor, writer and literary critic (b at Montréal 16 Nov 1948). After a BA (1970) and MA (1973) in literary studies at the U du Québec à Montréal, he received his certificate in art history and took more courses at the Centre international de linguistique et de sémiotique d'Urbino in Italy (1978). Professor in the dept of French at the Edouard-Montpetit CEGEP, he has also been literary critic for *Mainmise* (1975-77), *Hobo-Québec* (1973-79), *Le Devoir* and the magazine *Spirale*; he has had his manuscripts published in many reviews, including *Lèvres urbaines*, which he founded in 1983. A prolific author, Beausoleil has published more than 25 titles since

his first book, *Intrusion ralentie*, appeared in 1972, and he received the Prix Émile-Nelligan (1980) for his collection *Au milieu du corps l'attraction s'insinue*. Since the early 1970s, Beausoleil has been carrying out formal research into language, using contemporary theories such as structuralism and psychoanalysis. ROGER CHAMBERLAND

Beautiful Losers (Toronto and New York, 1966; London, 1970) is a novel by Leonard CO-HEN. Cohen's scholar-narrator researches the history of Catherine (Kateri) TEKAKWITHA, an Iroquois saint, and broods over his memories of his dead Indian wife, Edith, and his dead male lover, mentor and genius, the mysterious, all-knowing "F." The recreation of Catherine's ascent toward sainthood coalesces with the narrator's contemporary beatification as he descends from F's treehouse, hitchhikes to Montréal and is miraculously transformed in front of gaping crowds on St Lawrence Boulevard. The language of *Beautiful Losers* plays seriously, sensually and poetically over Tekakwitha's history as a saving source of inspiration for the "beautiful loser" who invokes her life as a prayer for his own body and soul. *Beautiful Losers* has been translated into Japanese, German, Dutch, Swedish, Italian, Danish, Norwegian and Spanish, as well as French (*Les Perdants magnifiques*, Paris, 1972, 1973).

NEIL BESNER

Beaven, James, philosopher (b at Westbury, Eng 9 July 1801; d at Niagara, Ont 8 Nov 1875). Educated as an Anglican clergyman, he arrived at King's Coll, Toronto, in 1843. He published the first philosophical work written in English Canada, *Elements of Natural Theology* (1850). Beaven sought a rational basis for belief. His design theory of the universe, emphasizing order in all things, set a trend in Canadian thinking that was continued by his philosophical and literary successors. Although Daniel WILSON, president of U of T at the time, called him a "dry old stick," Beaven's wit was well known in class. His sensitivity to the environment and concern for native peoples are evident in his travel journal, *Recreations of a Long Vacation* (1846).

ELIZABETH A. TROTT

Beaven, Robert, businessman, politician, premier of BC (b at Leigh, Eng 20 Jan 1836; d at Victoria 18 Sept 1920). He was attracted west from Toronto by the gold rushes and went into business in Victoria. During the agitation for BC's union with Canada he was secretary of the Confederation League. Elected in 1871 to the BC legislature, he served in the DE COSMOS and WALKEM Cabinets, and in 1882 succeeded Walkem as premier. On losing the July 1882 election, he clung to office until defeated in the legislature, Jan 1883. Beaven continued to sit in the Assembly until 1894, part of the time as leader of the Opposition. He also served as mayor of Victoria in 1892, 1893 and 1896.

H. KEITH RALSTON AND BETTY WILCOX

Beaver are Athapaskan-speaking people of the PEACE R area of BC and Alberta. They were called Beaver by early explorers, after the name of a local group, the tsa-dunne, and call themselves Dunneza ("our people"). In 1986 there were about 1200 status Indians who spoke Beaver dialects. Before contact there may have been more than 1000 in an area of about 194 250 km². Their neighbours are the Athapaskan SEKANI and SLAVEY to the W and N, and the Algonquian CREE who invaded the eastern part of their territory in historic times. Fur-trading posts were established along the Peace R in the 1790s, and Roman Catholic missionaries won many Beaver converts after 1850.

The Beaver traditionally lived in small nomadic hunting bands of 25-30 people. They came together into larger groups along the Peace R for summer ceremonials, at which they sang, danced and played the hand game, a guessing competition between teams of men. Most food came from hunting large game animals: bison in the prairie country near the Peace R, moose in the muskeg and forests, caribou near the mountains, and bears. Before they obtained firearms from fur traders, hunting was often done by groups of people who surrounded animals or drove them over cliffs (*see* BUFFALO HUNT). These communal hunts were led by religious leaders or prophets known as "Dreamers." Beaver children were sent into the bush on vision quests to gain supernatural power from the animals. The introduction of rifles made individual hunters more efficient and led to a decline in game populations, particularly bison, which became extinct in the area by 1900. The Dreamers tried to help their people understand and anticipate the changes brought about by white people. Although most Beaver are Roman Catholic and some now accept evangelical Protestantism, most also retain their traditional beliefs.

The Beaver signed Treaty No 8 in 1899, 1900 and 1910, formalizing their right to live by hunting and trapping (*see* INDIAN TREATIES). They now live on INDIAN RESERVES in BC and Alberta. Much of their former land is developed for farming and petroleum production, but hunting and trapping are still possible in the northern part of their territory. These activities are important sources of food and income, and help to maintain a sense of identity. *See also* NATIVE PEOPLE: SUBARCTIC and general articles under NATIVE PEOPLE.

ROBIN RIDINGTON

Reading: P. Goddard, *The Beaver Indians* (1917); J. Helm, ed, *Handbook of North American Indians*, vol 6: Subarctic (1981); R. Ridington, *Swan People: A Study of the Dunneza Prophet Dance* (1978).

Beaver (*Castor canadensis*), Canada's largest RODENT (15-35 kg). Its thick-set body is covered with dark, reddish brown fur consisting of coarse guard hairs over dense, soft underfur. The black tail is horizontally flattened, paddle shaped and scaly. Large, webbed hind feet are powerful paddles for swimming. Beavers are superb swimmers, and can stay underwater for 15 minutes. When alarmed, they slap the water with their tails, warning others to take refuge underwater. Beavers inhabit forested regions across Canada and N to the TREELINE, but are infrequent on the prairies. Typically, they occupy slow-flowing streams where they construct dams of sticks, logs, debris and mud. These dams protect their lodges, which are built of the same materials and have entrances below water level and ramps leading up to living quarters above water. Beavers gather their building materials by collecting wood and felling trees and they often build canals for floating logs. The dams maintain a water supply to protect the lodges and also provide greater access to the beaver's major food items: leaves, buds, twigs and bark of deciduous and (rarely) coniferous trees. Beavers also eat herbaceous pond vegetation. They do not hibernate but store branches for food in a submerged mass beside the lodge. Each lodge normally contains an adult pair, newborn kits and yearlings born the previous year, and a colony may consist of a cluster of lodges. Beavers breed in Jan-Feb, have a gestation period of $3\frac{1}{2}$ months, and give birth to 2-4 young. Beaver was once considered the most valuable fur, particularly when felt hats made from the underfur were symbols of prestige. The pursuit of the beaver from the Maritimes to the Mackenzie Valley led to the exploration of vast regions of what became Canada. Although the beaver almost be-

Beaver (*Castor canadensis*), Canada's national emblem. The beaver was trapped almost to extinction during the fur-trade era, but thriving populations now occur across Canada (*photo by Al Williams*).

came extinct at that time, thriving populations now occur across Canada. It is rightly Canada's national emblem and has been immortalized in 1000 place-names across Canada. Though Canada has been the recipient of numerous exotic species, it has occasionally served as the source of a species introduced successfully elsewhere. The beaver was introduced in 1946 to Tierra del Fuego at the tip of S America and is now abundant there. One other species exists, the European beaver (*C. fiber*). *See also* FUR TRADE. R. BOONSTRA

Beaver, wooden paddle steamer – the first steamship on the Northwest Coast. It was launched 2 May 1835 near London, Eng, and sailed to the Columbia R in 204 days, arriving at Vancouver 10 April 1836. The *Beaver* served as a supply ship for the HBC until the Fraser R GOLD RUSH of 1858, when it entered passenger and freight service between Victoria and the mainland. From 1862 to 1874 the HBC trader became Her Majesty's Hired Survey Ship *Beaver*. After the HBC sold the ship in 1874, it was used as a workhorse and tow until 1888, when it was wrecked in the First Narrows in Vancouver harbour. Only a few relics remain. JAMES MARSH

Beaver, The, magazine published by the Hudson's Bay Company, was started in 1920 as a staff magazine. It was published monthly until 1924 when it became a quarterly. Douglas MacKay, editor 1933-38, was responsible for the change of format and content, as he recognized that the magazine was of interest to people outside the Company. The subscription rate was then $1.00 per year. Staff news items were discontinued in 1941. Under dedicated editors, the magazine gradually emerged with well-written and well-illustrated articles on Company history, the history of native peoples and native art. It has been recognized and won awards for its accuracy and meticulous editing. Beginning in 1986, the magazine became a bi-monthly; the masthead has been changed from *The Beaver – A Magazine of the North* to *The Beaver – Exploring Canada's History*. As the masthead indicates, the focus of the magazine is on the history of Canada, with an emphasis on the social aspects. *The Beaver* had a paid circulation of 29 000 in 1987. SHIRLEE ANNE SMITH

Beaver Club, Montréal club, fd in 1785. Admission was restricted to FUR TRADE veterans of the PAYS D'EN HAUT. The club embraced as members wealthy fur merchants, retired traders and well-connected WINTERING PARTNERS (principally, but not exclusively, from the NORTH WEST COMPANY); as honorary members, ships' captains and army officers; and as guests, illustrious persons. It embodied the heart of Montréal society, with winter bacchanalian feasts its principal activity. The club evidently ceased functioning around 1825, to be revived briefly in 1827. Its motto was "Fortitude in Distress." JEAN MORRISON

Beaver Creek, YT, Settlement, pop 113 (1986c), located on the ALASKA HIGHWAY, 457 km NW of Whitehorse. There, on 20 Oct 1942, the 18th US Army Engineers grading the Alaska Highway N from Whitehorse met the 97th Engineers working S from Fairbanks. A small settlement took shape in the 1950s and it received a post office in 1958. Located just E of the Alaska-Yukon border, the settlement has a Canada Customs office, a landing strip, and service industries for travellers on the Alaska Highway. It is Canada's most westerly community. H. GUEST

Beaver Dams, Battle of On 24 June 1813, almost 500 American troops under Lt-Col Charles G. Boerstler were ambushed by a party of Caughnawaga and Mohawk warriors, along an enclosed, wooded section of the trail near Beaver Dams (Thorold, Ont). After the Indians had killed a number of the enemy, Lt James FitzGibbon, who had been warned by Laura SECORD of the American intention to surprise him, convinced Boerstler that his own force of fewer than 50 regulars was simply the vanguard of a larger British contingent lurking behind the trees and that, if the fighting continued, it might be impossible to control the savagery of the Indians. It was later generally accepted that "the Cognawaga Indians fought the battle, the Mohawks or Six Nations got the plunder, and FitzGibbon got the credit." Along with their defeat at STONEY CREEK 3 weeks earlier, the Battle of Beaver Dams convinced the Americans that they could not safely venture from the protected confines of Fort George, and it led directly to the dismissal of Major General Henry Dearborn by US Secretary of War John Armstrong. *See also* WAR OF 1812. CARL A. CHRISTIE

Beaver Pelts were divided into 2 major classifications in the FUR TRADE: coat beaver and parchment. Coat beaver (*castor gras*) pelts were pro-

cessed and worn by the Indians before being traded. The inner sides were scraped and rubbed with animal marrow; the pelts were then sewn into robes. After several months of wear, the long guard hairs fell out, their roots loosened by the scraping, and the skins became oiled and pliable. The under fur or beaver wool (*duvet*), consisting of barbed hairs that could form a durable, luxurious felt, was of prime importance to the European hat industry until the 1830s, when silk hats became fashionable. The wool could easily be removed from the skins, which yielded a useful leather.

Parchment (*castor sec*) pelts were sun dried immediately after skinning. Once in Europe, they required combing to remove the guard hairs. Indians trading to the St Lawrence Valley furnished pelts mostly of this type. In the late 1600s the HBC successfully tapped new supplies of coat beaver from northern Indians, touching off intense English-French rivalry for these desirable furs. Indian-white relations were sometimes strained as traders sought to match their coat and parchment beaver-pelt inventories with changing European market requirements. JENNIFER S.H. BROWN

Bécancour, Qué, City, pop 10 472 (1986c), inc 1855, located almost directly opposite Trois-Rivières on the S shore of the St Lawrence R at its junction with the Bécancour R. Covering a vast expanse of territory recognized for its beauty, Bécancour's traditionally rural and agricultural character began to give way in the 1960s to industrial growth. Near the end of that decade a large industrial park was built to accommodate the iron and steel and other lesser industries. The city is named for Pierre Robineau, Sieur de Bécancour, who led an expedition against the Iroquois in 1696. The first French missionary contact with the local Abenakis occurred in 1669, and a permanent European settlement was established 3 years later. In 1702, a small fort was erected on the site to protect against Iroquois attack. Although overwhelmingly French in origin, the population includes a small Irish community which dates from the 1840s. Several sawmills were built in the 19th century, but these did not survive the Great Depression of the 1930s. Bécancour is served by major highway and rail transportation networks. An imposing, combination neo-Gothic and Romanesque church with a 55 m steeple was built in 1892. SERGE DURFLINGER

Beck, Sir Adam, manufacturer, politician, power-authority commissioner (b at Baden, Canada W 20 June 1857; d at London, Ont 15 Aug 1925). Feared and revered as an empire builder, Beck dominated Ontario politics for a generation as he built and expanded the Hydro-Electric Power Commission of Ontario into the largest publicly owned power authority in the world. Son of a German Lutheran foundryman and miller, Beck made his name as a manufacturer of cigar boxes, outstanding athlete, mayor and MPP in London. As mayor he led a movement of Ontario municipalities and boards of trade to get cheap electric power from NIAGARA FALLS. In 1905 James P. WHITNEY made Beck head of a public inquiry that ultimately recommended creating a municipally owned, provincially financed, cooperative hydroelectric distribution system.

Supported by bipartisan public ownership advocates, the Hydro-Electric Power Commission of Ontario began in a small way in 1910, but through Beck's aggressive promotion of "Power At Cost," thousands of new industrial, retail and household customers soon were gained. By charging initial low rates to induce a large demand, then building huge, efficient generating stations whose low costs permitted further rate reductions, Beck rapidly expanded his system and drove most of his private competitors out of business. He also browbeat balky municipalities, tyrannized provincial governments with his powerful following and abused his regulatory authority to hamper private rivals. Eventually he overreached himself and E.C. DRURY's government cancelled his electric railway scheme; G. Howard FERGUSON also kept Beck and Hydro on a short leash.

As principal founder and guiding genius of ONTARIO HYDRO, Beck helped establish the public enterprise tradition in Canada, though his methods did little to render such enterprises more politically accountable.   H.V. NELLES

Reading: H.V. Nelles, *The Politics of Development* (1974); J. Sturgeon, *Adam Beck* (1982).

Beck, Gary, drag race driver (b at Seattle, Wash 21 Jan 1941). Beck raced stock cars for 12 years before becoming a drag racer, operating from his home in Edmonton, Alta. He was an outstanding competitor in this sport during the 1970s. He won the National Hot Rod Assn championship at Indianapolis, Ind, in 1972, and in 1974, his finest year, he won an unprecedented 3 NHRA and 2 American Hot Rod Assn events, was world champion, and was named *Car Craft* top fuel driver of the year and *Drag News* driver of the year. Beck also won several 1975 events, including the Canadian Open.   GERALD REDMOND

Beck, Tom, conservationist, oil-field environmental and social-management consultant (b at Wishaws, Scot 11 Mar 1932). Beck pioneered environmental protection and management in the Canadian PETROLEUM INDUSTRY. Twenty years in the Alberta oil business led to his appointment in 1970 as environmental co-ordinator for Elf Oil Exploration and Production Ltd and later Aquitaine Co Ltd. From 1980 to 1982 he was director of Environmental and Social Affairs for Petro-Canada. Dedicated to maintenance of natural environments and to sensitive development of natural resources, Beck has had wide influence. He was a founder of the Alberta Wilderness Assn, governor of the Arctic Inst, and chairman of the Canadian Environmental Advisory Council in 1978-87.   IAN McTAGGART-COWAN

Becker, Abigail, née Jackson, "The Heroine of Long Point" (b in Frontenac County, UC 14 Mar 1831; d at Walsingham Centre, Ont 21 Mar 1905). After marrying Jeremiah Becker, a hunter and trapper, in 1848 she settled on the S shore of LONG POINT, a long, narrow peninsula bedeviled by tricky winds and shifting sandbars and stretching out into Lake Erie. During a vicious storm on 24 Nov 1854 the overloaded schooner *Conductor* foundered on a nearby sandbar. The captain and crew clung to the frozen rigging all night, not daring to enter the raging surf. Abigail found the men in peril the following morning and, although unable to swim, she waded shoulder-high into the icy water and persuaded the men to swim towards her. The captain and 6 crew members were coaxed ashore; the cook remained lashed to the rigging until he was rescued the following day. The crew loudly praised Abigail's heroism. She received a purse of $500 collected from the sailors and merchants of Buffalo, NY; a special gold medal struck by the New York Lifesaving Benevolent Assn; a handwritten letter accompanied by £50 from Queen Victoria; a letter of praise from Gov Gen Lord Aberdeen; and a bronze medal from the Royal Humane Society. In later incidents she came to the aid of 6 other shipwrecked sailors who had struggled ashore, and she saved the life of a boy who had fallen down a well. A plaque erected in Port Rowan, Ont, 10 Sept 1958, commemorates her heroism, and the Abigail Becker Conservation area takes in part of what was her

farm. She raised 19 children, of whom 6 were step-children and 2 adopted.   E.E. AUGUSTEIJN

Beckwith, John, composer, educator (b at Victoria 9 Mar 1927). One of the most distinctively English Canadian voices among Canada's composers, Beckwith has created a wealth of music rooted in his sensitive experience of the Canadian environment. Although he has composed much instrumental music, the majority of his important works are for voices, often settings of texts by Canadian writers. Several of Beckwith's most eloquent works have emerged from his long collaboration with poet-playwright James REANEY, among them the operas *Night Blooming Cereus* (1953-58) and *The Shivaree* (1965-78). His *Sharon Fragments* (1966) for unaccompanied choir, commemorating the Children of Peace, a music-loving 19th-century Ontario religious sect, is one of the most frequently performed of his works based on historical themes. Widely read and highly articulate, Beckwith is well known as a writer, lecturer and broadcaster. He has written music criticism for Toronto newpapers and has contributed articles on various aspects of Canadian musical life to periodicals and books of reference. He planned and wrote several music series and documentaries for CBC radio. A member of the faculty of U of T since 1952, he was dean of music 1970-77. In 1984 he was appointed first Jean A. Chalmers Professor of Canadian Music and first director of the Institute for Canadian Music at U of T.   BARCLAY McMILLAN

Reading: Peter Such, *Soundprints* (1972).

Bédard, Pierre Stanislas, politician, judge (b at Charlesbourg Château, Qué 13 Nov 1762; d at Trois-Rivières, LC 26 Apr 1829). Called to the bar in 1790 and first elected to the legislative assembly of Lower Canada for Northumberland in 1792, Bédard quickly became a leader of the forming PARTI CANADIEN and a notable critic of the ruling CHATEAU CLIQUE. In 1806 he assisted in the establishment of *Le Canadien*, a journal intended to broadcast his party's platform among the province's intelligentsia; in 1810 he and other staff of *Le Canadien* were arrested, on order of Governor Sir James CRAIG, as a result of comments published in the paper, and imprisoned. He was later released without being brought to trial, and his appointment to the bench in 1812 was widely seen as an atonement by the administration for his arrest. He remained on the bench, with some interruptions due to ill health, until his death.   STANLEY GORDON

Bedford, NS, Town, pop 8010 (1986c), 6777 (1981c), inc 1980, is situated at the head of Bedford Basin, about 10 km NW of Halifax. MICMAC inhabited the site initially and the French harboured there from the early 17th century. Both the basin and the community were named in honour of John Russell, fourth duke of Bedford (1710-71), who was secretary of state for the colonies when Halifax was founded in 1749. At first called Sackville when established as a fort in 1749 to keep open the overland route to Minas and to protect against Indian raids, it took its present name in 1856 when the Nova Scotia Railway (later the Intercolonial) built a station in the area. With access to Halifax, Bedford grew as a summer resort area and dormitory suburb. Some small industries in the 19th century used local power, including Moirs, the confectioners, but the town's real growth came after 1961 as people sought its suburban location away from built-up Halifax.   L.D. McCANN

Bedford Institute of Oceanography (BIO), located at DARTMOUTH, NS, founded 1962. It is operated by the federal Dept of Fisheries and Oceans

Bedford Institute of Oceanography, Dartmouth, NS, is Canada's principal oceanographic facility, performing research in all fields of marine science (*courtesy Bedford Institute of Oceanography/photo by K. Bentham*).

and includes units of the Environment Canada and the Dept of Energy, Mines and Resources. It is the principal oceanographic institution in Canada, comparable to the Scripps and Woods Hole institutions in the US. BIO performs long-term research in all fields of the marine sciences over a wide geographic area; undertakes shorter-term research in response to national needs; carries out surveys and cartographic work to ensure a supply of navigation charts for the region from Georges Bank to the Northwest Passage; and responds with all relevant expertise to any marine emergency. To this end it is organized into groups devoted to physical, chemical and biological OCEANOGRAPHY, HYDROGRAPHY, FISHERIES as well as marine geology and environmental protection. BIO has one medium and 2 large research vessels, several smaller craft and a central library and computer system. Research results are published in international scientific journals and in the official reports of the various government departments.   K.H. MANN

Bedford Magazine Explosion, 18-19 July 1945, initiated when an ammunition barge blew up at the naval magazine jetty on Bedford Basin, Halifax harbour. Fire spread quickly to adjacent piles of ammunition, which had been temporarily stored outside because of overcrowding in the main compound. A chain reaction of fire, explosion and concussion rocked Halifax for a day. Contingency plans existed for such an accident, and by late July 18, much of Halifax's northern half had been evacuated smoothly. None of the explosions approached the force of the 1917 HALIFAX EXPLOSION, but shattered windows, cracked plaster, occasional minor injuries and one death were reported. The community felt a lingering resentment towards the navy after the VE-DAY RIOTS, but voluntary firefighting by naval personnel at the ammunition depot largely offset this negative feeling.   LOIS KERNAGHAN

Bee, member of INSECT order Hymenoptera characterized by branched hairs on the body, chewing mouthparts (sometimes modified for lapping or sucking), transparent wings with few veins, enlarged hind appendages with stiff hairs for gathering pollen, and a large crop (honey stomach) for storing and carrying nectar. The sting at the tip of the female's abdomen is connected to poison glands. The stings of worker honeybees are barbed and, when removed, usually tear the bee's body, causing death. The queen's sting is used only against other queens. Bees may be solitary (eg, carpenter, plasterer, leafcutting, burrowing), social (bumblebees, stingless bees, honeybees) or parasitic. Most species are adapted for gathering nectar and pollen from blossoms. Of an estimated 20 000 species worldwide, about 1000 occur in Canada. Most bees are solitary in habit. Most short-tongued bees excavate tunnels in soil where they construct nest cells. Leafcutting bees fashion cells from precisely shaped leaf pieces; carpenter bees nest in holes drilled in dead wood. Some members of genus *Anthophora* (mining bees) fashion unique, clay nest cells. Females of all these species provision each cell with pollen and nectar, deposit an egg, and leave offspring to develop independently.

Relatively few species (*c*500) are social, ie, have communal nests, co-operative brood care, and a caste system. Caste structure and behaviour is regulated by external secretions (pheromones), which induce behavioural or developmental responses. Pheromones are used to mark trails to food sources, although honeybees also use "dance" language to communicate direction. The most widely studied social bee is the honeybee (*Apis mellifera*). The precise architecture of the honeycomb, the complex social behaviour of the colony, the honey and beeswax they provide (*see* BEEKEEPING), and their efficiency in POLLINATION of fruit and seed crops, make honeybees among the most fascinating and useful insect friends of man. Honeybees were introduced to N America by European settlers during the 17th century.

Bumblebees, many of which are native to N America, are primitively social bees with annual societies. They are large and well adapted to temperate climates, where they are most numerous. In Canada, 42 free-nesting bumblebee species are found, several above the Arctic Circle. Some stingless bees have large social colonies. These are mostly tropical and semitropical in distribution. In the New World they occur from Mexico through Central and S America. These are the only honey-producing bees native to the western hemisphere, and have been kept for centuries by local beekeepers. They produce relatively little honey compared to honeybees.

Some bees have evolved into parasites of their relatives and have lost the ability to gather food and rear their own offspring, eg, bees of genus *Psithyrus* of the bumblebee family. The *Psithyrus* queen seeks out an established bumblebee nest and either replaces or lives alongside its original queen. She lays eggs which the host workers rear. *Psithyrus* bees produce only reproductives. Some solitary bees, eg, cuckoo bees, are also parasitic, depositing their eggs in nests of other bees.

M.V. SMITH

Beech (*Fagus*), genus of TREES of beech family (Fagaceae). Ten species occur worldwide; one, American beech (*F. grandifolia*), is native to N

American beech (*Fagus grandifolia*), with male flowers (bottom left), female flowers (top left) and nut on bottom right (*artwork by Claire Tremblay*).

America. In Canada, this species is found primarily in the East. American beech has a straight trunk covered with thick, smooth, bluish grey bark and can attain 30m in height. The leaves are alternate, single, long ovals with saw-toothed edges. Leaves of young trees often remain on the twigs throughout winter. The edible beechnut is an important food source for a number of animals, particularly squirrels. American beech is usually found with sugar maples on temperate, well-drained slopes. Its leaves decompose very slowly, forming a thick leaf litter which acidifies soil and makes regeneration of sugar maple increasingly difficult. European beech (*F. sylvatica*) is planted as an ORNAMENTAL in Canada. Varieties include copper beech, weeping forms, variegated leaf forms. The heavy, hard, tough wood is used for tool handles, floor planks and furniture.

ESTELLE LACOURSIÈRE

Beechey, Frederick William, naval officer, artist, explorer (b at London, Eng 17 Feb 1796; d there 29 Nov 1856). Beechey joined the British navy at the age of 10, and saw action at the Battle of New Orleans in 1815. In 1818 he served as second in command of the *Trent*, under (later Sir) John FRANKLIN, in a search for the NORTHWEST PASSAGE. In 1819-20 he served under W.E. PARRY in the *Hecla* on a voyage of discovery to the eastern Arctic, spending the winter in Winter Harbour, Melville I, where he made scientific observations and sketches of the terrain. Prince Regent Inlet, Barrow Strait, Wellington Channel and the Parry Islands were discovered on this expedition. From 1825 to 1827 he commanded a voyage of exploration to the western Arctic. He rose to the rank of rear-admiral and was the president of the Royal Geographical Society. Beechey Lake (on Back R, NWT), Beechey Point (in Alaska) and Cape Beechey (on Ellesmere I) are named for him; Beechey I (NWT) is named for his father.

W.R. MORRISON

Beechey Island is on the N side of LANCASTER SOUND off the SW corner of DEVON I at the entrance to Wellington Channel in the ARCTIC ARCHIPELAGO. At low water it is joined to the larger island by a narrow gravel isthmus and forms the NW side of Erebus Bay. Sir John FRANKLIN's ships are believed to have spent the winter of 1845-46 at the island, and during the subsequent search for Franklin it was used as a supply depot and rendezvous. The island is small, only 2.5 km across, but its steep shores, rising to a flat plateau 244 m high, make it a prominent landmark.

DANIEL FRANCIS

Beecroft, Norma, composer, broadcaster (b at Oshawa, Ont 11 Apr 1934). A composer of the avant-garde, she has created music for a variety of performance media, combining traditional instruments, voice and electronically produced or altered sounds, with appealing individuality. *From Dreams of Brass* for soprano, narrator, choir, orchestra and tape, one of her best-known works, is typical of Beecroft's style. Like *Rasas II* and *The Living Flame of Love*, it uses text written or translated by her sister, poet and painter Jane Beecroft. An enthusiastic promoter of Canadian music, Beecroft has produced programs for CBC radio and became widely known as host of "Music of Today." She has also been active in promoting concert performances of new music. In 1986-87 she was course director of the Music Writing Workshop at York.

BARCLAY McMILLAN

Reading: Peter Such, *Soundprints* (1972).

Beef Cattle Farming Cattle (family Bovidae, genus *Bos*) were first brought to Canada by French settlers. In 1677 there were 3107 in NEW FRANCE; in 1698, 10 209; by the mid-18th century, 50 013. Cattle were valuable as a food source (milk,

cheese, butter, meat) and for their hides, used in LEATHERWORKING. Cattle farming spread across the country with settlement, and RANCHING became particularly important in the rangelands of western Canada. The importance of beef cattle to Canadian agriculture has increased steadily since WWII. In 1986 there were an estimated 13.4 million cattle and calves on Canadian farms, 5.3 million of which were beef cows and heifers. Cattle slaughtered in 1985 totalled 3.6 million.

Most of Canada's veal and young beef comes from a 3-phase system involving the cow-calf enterprise to produce weanling calves, the stocker or holding enterprise and the finishing (usually feedlot) operation. Two or 3 of these operations may be combined on a single farm or ranch. The triple combination, most common where breeding-herd size is small, is often a subsidiary enterprise of a mixed farming operation.

Cow-Calf Enterprise

The cow-calf enterprise involves maintaining a breeding herd to produce the heaviest weight of weaned calves possible. Breeding-herd size varies

The Shorthorn breed originated in Scotland and England and was introduced to Canada in 1832 (*photo by Walt Browarny, Browarny Photographics Ltd*).

Horned Hereford. The Hereford, known for its foraging abilities under difficult conditions, is western Canada's main breed (*courtesy Walt Browarny/Browarny Photographics Ltd*).

Aberdeen Angus, a Scottish breed, has persistently found a place in beef production (*photo by Walt Browarny/Browarny Photographics Ltd*).

considerably, from a few cows on small mixed farms to several hundred in large range herds. The larger units (averaging 38 breeding females) are found in the 4 western provinces, where over two-thirds of Canada's breeding herds are located. However, about one-sixth of Canada's supply of veal and young beef comes from unneeded male and female calves of dairy herds, most of which are located in Ontario and Québec.

The western emphasis on beef production probably stems from the fact that the cow-calf operation is usually based on a low-cost pasture resource, eg, sparsely vegetated areas, nonarable land (12 ha required per cow), or very intensively cultivated and irrigated pastures (0.5 ha per cow). Some of the largest operations are found on predominantly natural pastures requiring 8 ha or more per cow. In such areas, the winter feed supply may be purchased but most often comes from improved native meadows or intensively managed arable land.

The female side of the breeding herd usually consists of cows and heifers of a single breed, or the female crosses of breeds that are likely to produce hybrid vigour in the various maternal characteristics such as milking and mothering ability. Performance-tested, purebred bulls from breeds noted for their post-weaning growth and carcass characteristics make up the male side of the herd (*see* ANIMAL BREEDING).

Shorthorn, originating in NE England and S Scotland, was the first beef breed to be established and the first to arrive in Canada (1832). Its superior growth and fattening propensity (over the nondescript cattle of the day) quickly made it popular. Reds, roans, whites, and red and whites are common colours in purebred herds, reds being the most popular. Mature cows weigh over 600 kg and bulls, 900 kg. A dual purpose or milking Shorthorn strain has frequently been used in beef herds. A polled (hornless) mutant of the breed has become popular.

Hereford, originating in the county of that name, is a well-muscled, hardy breed. Well known for its foraging abilities under difficult range conditions, the breed quickly established itself as western Canada's main commercial breed. Its attractive, predominantly white face, underline and other white markings on a red body became a trademark ("white face" or "baldy") among cattle producers. A polled strain was developed in Canada and the US from mutants.

Aberdeen Angus, a smoothly finished black-coloured Scottish breed, has persistently found a place in beef production. Noted for its ease of calving and the easier delivery of Angus-sired calves, the breed also has other valuable characteristics in crosses (eg, early maturity, marbling quality of meat). A frequently occurring red mutant has now been developed as a separate strain.

Other British breeds, including Galloway (polled and dun, black or white-belted black), Black Welsh, Lincoln Red (of Shorthorn origins), South Devon, Devon and Luing, have appeared over the years but have not been significant in Canadian beef production.

Over the past 3 decades, the emphasis on growth and the hybrid vigour produced by crossing has resulted in considerable interest in continental breeds ("exotics"), especially since new quarantine regulations were adopted to facilitate importation.

Charolais, a very large white or creamy white breed of east-central France, was one of the earliest introduced. Its exceptional growth rate and muscling make it particularly valuable in crossing. Mature bulls average over 1000 kg and cows, 700 kg. A polled strain is being developed.

Limousin, a yellow-brown horned breed about the size of the Hereford, was the second continental breed to arrive in Canada and is valued for its excellent ratio of lean to fat and bone, a characteristic persisting in crosses.

Simmental, one of the most popular European breeds, is a dual-purpose (predominantly dairy) breed. Of Swiss origin, this large red and white breed is known under various names throughout Europe. For beef production, the valuable characteristics are rapid growth and milk production.

Other continental breeds popular in cross-breeding are Maine d'Anjou, a large red and white breed from NW France; Blonde d'Aquitaine, from southern France; 3 white breeds from Italy, ie, Chianina, equal in growth rate and mature size to the Charolais, and its smaller sister breeds Romagnola and Marchigiana; Gelbvieh, a large, red German breed; and Salers, a smaller red breed of central France.

Summer grazing is usually controlled by a good distribution of watering facilities and trace-mineralized salt licks, pasture rotation, or movable electric fences. Calves, "identified" at birth, run with cows. If not naturally polled, they are usually dehorned and vaccinated against common diseases (eg, blackleg) early in the pasture season. Male calves are generally castrated. If range is limited or extra gain is economically warranted, calves may have access to grain.

Breeding takes place in summer, preferably during a 6-week to 2-month period when cows are exposed to fertility tested bulls (approximately one bull to 30 cows). Yearling heifers (approximately 15 months old), if well grown (300 kg), are bred to sires known to produce easily delivered calves. High conception rates are extremely important but seldom exceed 85-90%. Calves are weaned from early Oct to mid-Nov, usually just before winter feeding. At 6 months, calves from British breeds and their crosses usually average 200 kg for males and 185 kg for females. Earlier-born calves or crosses with "exotics" may be 50-100 kg heavier. Male calves and those females not needed for breeding are transferred to stocker operations, as are cows that failed to become pregnant or produced poorer calves.

Wintering requires feeding in most areas, although pasture or cash crop residues may be used, weather permitting. In some areas, eg, the CHINOOK belt, winter grazing of mature herds on specially reserved pastures is normal. Feed is supplied only under severe weather conditions and before calving. The herd is usually broken into 3 or 4 groups so that replacement heifer calves, pregnant yearling heifers and 2-year-olds expecting their first calves can be fed to facilitate growth. In large herds, bulls are usually fed and managed separately. In the smaller herds, they may be allowed to run with the mature and pregnant cows. Winter feed is usually home-grown hay or silage from GRASSES, legumes or CEREAL CROPS. Grain and protein concentrates may augment poor-quality feeds; mineral mixtures and vitamin A supplements are the main purchased feeds. The average cow will consume 2% of its body weight in dry feed (eg, hay) per day; hence, wintering a mature cow normally requires 2 t of feed.

Stocker Operation

The stocker operation is normally attached to the cow-calf or the finishing enterprises, being essentially a period of growth between weaning and the finishing phase for slaughter (6-12 months). It is roughage and pasture based, aimed at getting as much efficient youthful growth of skeleton and muscle as possible. As a single enterprise, it is highly speculative and is usually a "grasser" operation for individuals with ample pasture but no winter feed. These farmers buy wintered steer and heifer calves in spring, and then resell them in late summer or fall to feedlot operators.

Finishing Operation

Finishing, the final step in preparing animals for slaughter, aims to increase body weight and value. While some cow-calf operators may carry out this enterprise after a stocker phase for their own calves, most finishing is now done in specially designed units, holding several hundred or thousands of animals. Some farmers, eg, a few in Ontario, traditionally used the feedlot to enhance the value of their home-grown crops and to provide a winter occupation. Larger units may be equipped with feed-preparation mills and most use mixing and unloading trucks to distribute the feed in long troughs, twice daily. Profits arise from 2 sources: price margin, ie, the difference between the buying and selling price (the original 300 kg weight of a steer purchased for $1.80/kg and sold for $2.00/kg has produced a profit of $60.00 through the $0.20/kg price margin); and feed margin, ie, the difference between the cost of a kilogram of gain and the selling price of that gain. Thus, if it cost $1.90/kg to put on 200 kg in the feedlot and the 500 kg finished steer sold for $2.00/kg, the operator has had a gain of $20.00 through a positive $0.10/kg feed margin.

Astute and fortunate buying and selling may govern price-margin profits, but feed margin is dependent on cattle that are efficient users of feed and on low-cost rations. Calves, 6-8 months old, are the most efficient converters of feed (7-8 units of feed per unit gain) but are the slowest gainers (1.0-1.1 kg/day) and require the longest feeding period. Yearlings are less efficient (8-9 units of feed per unit gain) but gain faster (1.1-1.3 kg/day) and usually require 140 days in the feedlot. Heifers usually gain slightly more slowly in the feedlot and finish at lighter weights.

The key in finishing is high-energy feed (eg, grains of BARLEY, CORN and, to some extent, WHEAT and OATS) fed with bulky roughages (eg, corn silage, hay, straws). In local areas, some refuse or by-products (eg, distillers' slops, brewers' grains, BEET pulp and molasses, milling and canning crop residues) may form the basis of less efficient but profitable feeds. Lower-quality feeds are usually used in the first part of the finishing period. As the animal increases in weight, each new unit of gain requires more or better feed, and higher-energy feed is needed to produce economical gains. In most parts of Canada, finishing cattle on grass alone is not economical, as top grades can seldom be reached because of the yellow colour of the fat in most breeds or the lack of sufficient fat covering in yearling or younger cattle. It is very effective and more economical, especially for yearling heifers, if the last 60 days are spent in dry lot.

In spite of the vagaries of price fluctuations and increasing costs, beef farming has persisted, as beef is the meat preferred by most consumers. Over the long term, it has produced reasonable returns; however, since the annual operating costs are high, because of the large capital involved in land and cattle, many operators cannot withstand years of low returns and high interest rates.   E. STRINGHAM

Beekeeping The art of keeping BEES for honey and beeswax evolved from honey hunting. European and African cave paintings indicate that people raided wild honeybees' nests for their sweet bounty at least 15 000 years ago. Egyptian records show that, as early as 3000 BC, bees were provided with domiciles and kept for honey production. Early Greek and Roman writers mention apiculture. The products of the hive were so sought after that the Romans sometimes levied taxes of honey and beeswax. Many references to bees and honey occur in the Bible. Honeybees were kept in clay pots or cylinders, hollow logs, wicker baskets and straw skeps (hives). However, management for honey production was very limited until the mid-19th century, when the Rev L.L. Langstroth, in the US, invented the movable-frame hive. It was then possible to open the hive, examine it, and remove honey without destroying the combs. This invention increased honey production and made possible the development of the modern beekeeping industry. European settlers, colonizing N and S America, Australia and New Zealand, introduced honeybees from their homelands. The bees did well in the new environments; these areas now have important beekeeping industries. In 1986, an estimated 19 060 Canadian beekeepers kept 702 375 honeybee colonies with a total honey production of 33 million kilograms.

Honey is obtained commercially from 4 species of genus *Apis: A. mellifera,* the most important and widely used honeybee, native to Europe, Asia Minor and Africa; *A. cerana,* the most important Asian species; *A. dorsata* and *A. florea,* also Asian species, which cannot be kept in hives, but wild honey is sometimes harvested from their nests. Several species of stingless bees, mainly of families Meliponidae and Trigonidae, are also used. Stingless bees, which occur only in tropical and semitropical areas, are sometimes kept in log hives or specially designed nest boxes, where they produce limited amounts of honey. All of these bees form perennial societies, and store considerable amounts of honey to help the colony survive periods of dearth. This characteristic makes it possible for the beekeeper to harvest surplus honey. Many other wild bees (eg, bumblebees) feed on nectar but do not store it in excess and are not useful for honey production. In midsummer, a strong honeybee colony will contain one queen, as many as 60 000 to 80 000 workers (undeveloped females) and some hundreds of drones (males). The queen may lay as many as 2000 eggs daily, mostly fertilized eggs which develop into worker bees in 21 days. Under special circumstances, bees can develop a few of the fertilized eggs into queens in 16 days, by rearing them in large peanut-shaped queen cells and feeding the developing larvae on a glandular secretion, royal jelly. A mated queen can withhold fertilization when laying, the unfertilized eggs developing into drones. A drone completes development in 24 days. Although honeybees are kept in hives and

The movable-frame hive, invented in the 19th century, made it possible to open the hive and remove honey without destroying the combs (*artwork by Claire Tremblay*).

are often selected and bred for superior honey-producing characteristics, they cannot be considered domesticated. They retain their wild instincts and can be managed only within limits.

Most Canadian beekeepers winter their bees. In winter, bees cluster together and generate enough heat to keep warm. The beekeeper must ensure that the bees have sufficient food and protection from cold. Most honeybee colonies are wintered outside, but some are moved into unheated cellars (particularly in Québec). Many beekeepers in the western prairies kill their bees in fall and purchase packaged bees (a queen and about 10 000 workers in a screen cage) from the southern US in spring. Interest in the wintering of colonies is increasing in western Canada, despite severe winters.

By seeing that the bees have adequate food and space, are kept healthy and have a productive young queen, the beekeeper tries to bring the colony to its maximum population in time for the "honey flow" – the period (usually during June, July and Aug) when many flowers are in bloom and bees gather and store excess nectar. The stored nectar is converted into honey through the evaporation of water and by the conversion of the sucrose in the nectar to the simple sugars, dextrose and levulose.

Prior to 1900 honey was consumed mainly in the comb. Today, extracted honey commands most of the market. Full combs of honey are taken from the hive, the wax cappings removed, and the combs placed in an extractor where honey is separated from the cells by centrifugal force. Honey that has been heated and strained will remain liquid for several months and is often marketed in this form. Over a period of time, the dextrose in the honey tends to crystallize, forming granulated honey. The granulation process can be controlled by adding a small amount of previously granulated honey to liquid honey and storing it at a lower temperature (14°C). This speeds up the crystallization and results in a smooth, creamy honey. Granulated honey can be returned to the liquid state by heating it (not above 60°C) until the crystals are completely melted. The colour and flavour of honey depends on the blossoms from which it is derived. Honey from clover, alfalfa, rapeseed, fireweed and basswood is white; that from sunflower, goldenrod and aster tends to be golden; buckwheat honey is quite dark. In general, darker honeys tend to be somewhat stronger in flavour, but this does not mean they are inferior in quality. Most honeys are blends, since the bees visit many different plant species in collecting nectar.

Honeybees derive their food almost entirely from flowering plants. Nectar is gathered in minute quantities from each blossom and carried back to the hive in the bee's honey stomach. Pollen is transported as pellets in pollen baskets on the bee's legs. Pollen is not used in making honey but serves as a protein source for the developing larvae and for the adult workers. To obtain the large amounts of nectar and pollen required, bees from each colony visit millions of blossoms in a season. While foraging, they act as agents of POLLINATION and provide a vital service to agriculture, a service estimated to be worth 10-20 times the value of the honey and beeswax harvested by the beekeeper. Because their numbers can be controlled and they can be readily transported, honeybee colonies are often rented and moved to areas where fruit and seed crops are grown commercially. The complex social organization, the biology, and the industrious nature of honeybees have long fascinated people. This may be why an increasing number of Canadians are becoming hobbyist beekeepers. With only a few hives to manage, they have time to observe more closely the behaviour of these most interesting and beneficial social insects.

M.V. SMITH

William George Beers, who promoted lacrosse in Canada by claiming that it "knocks timidity and nervousness out of a young man, training him to temperance, confidence and pluck" (*courtesy Canada's Sports Hall of Fame*).

Beers, William George, lacrosse player, dentist (b at Montréal 5 May 1843; d there 26 Dec 1900). He was the prime mover in organizing and popularizing LACROSSE; he also founded and edited Canada's first dental journal and was dean of Canada's first dental college. Introduced to lacrosse at age 6, he was chosen at 17 to represent Montréal as goalkeeper in the match played before the Prince of Wales. In 1867 he campaigned to have lacrosse accepted as Canada's national game. Though unsuccessful, his efforts helped raise the number of clubs from 6 to 80 that year, as did a national convention he organized in Kingston, Ont. He was elected secretary of the National Lacrosse Assn which originated there. The rules Beers had published in 1860 to help standardize the game were also adopted at this convention. In 1869 he published *Lacrosse: The National Game of Canada.* He played a continuing role in the sport's development, accompanying teams to England in 1876 and 1883.

PETER LINDSAY

Beet (*Beta vulgaris*), biennial herbaceous plant of the Chenopodiaceae family. There are 4 cultivated varieties: red or vegetable beet, fodder beet (mangel-wurzel), chard and sugar beet. Beets originated in the Mediterranean basin where *B. maritima,* forerunner of *B. vulgaris,* still grows wild. All beets are adapted to temperate climates with optimal growing temperatures of 18-28°C and rainfall of 500-700 mm over a 5-7 month growing season. They develop bulbous, sugary roots and many long-stalked leaves during the first year. The roots must be exposed to prolonged periods of frost before the plant flowers in its second year. Fodder beets have been in existence for thousands of years and are used as cattle feed in northern Europe. Red beets have been eaten from time immemorial, either cooked or pickled, and are grown in all temperate and subtropical countries. The root is spherical (up to 10 cm in diameter) and coloured by

betaine, a dark red pigment. Red beets are a popular market garden vegetable throughout Canada.
GHISLAIN GENDRON

Sugar Beets produce a large, succulent, white, cone-shaped root and a rosette of large leaves in the first year. If they overwinter, they produce large, branched seed stalks up to 2 m high the second year. They are pollinated by wind and will cross readily with other members of the species. In 1747 Andreas Margraff, a German chemist, proved that the sugar extracted from beets was identical to that from sugar cane. The first sugar-beet processing plant was built in Silesia in 1802. In 1840 sugar beets supplied 5% of the world's sugar. The first refinery to extract sugar from sugar beets in Canada was established at Farnham, Qué, in 1881. Today, 40% of the sugar used worldwide and 10% of Canadian requirements are produced from them. Sugar beets are adaptable to a wide range of soils and climates. In N America they are grown commercially from Canada (Alta, Man and Qué) to the Mexican border. Specialized machinery is used to plant the seed, apply pesticides, cultivate and harvest beets. Seedling diseases are controlled by treating seeds with fungicide. Other diseases are not an economic problem in Manitoba and Alberta; however, *Cercospora* leaf spot can cause severe damage in Québec. In Canada insect pests include cutworm, wireworm, flea beetle and webworm.

Sugar beets are grown under irrigation in Alberta and under natural rainfall conditions in Manitoba. The yield is 25-60 t per hectare, depending on the growing season and rainfall. An average of 125 kg of granulated white sugar is produced from a tonne of beets. The leaves that remain in the field are fed directly to livestock or worked into the soil as green manure. When dry, beet pulp, the part of the sugar beet remaining after the sugar is extracted, equals about 6% of the weight of the roots; molasses, the dark, heavy, viscous liquid that remains after the sugar is extracted from the beet juice, equals about 5%. Both products are excellent livestock feed. Molasses is also used extensively for yeast production.
J.W. HALL

Swiss Chard (*B. vulgaris* var. *cicla*) is a foliage beet: it develops no edible root but is grown for its large, fleshy leafstalks and very broad leaves. It is one of the best summer potherbs because it is very heat tolerant. Chard plants grow 50-100 cm high. Common types have crumpled green leaves and greenish white stalks. The newer cultivar (commercial variety), Rhubarb, has crimson stalks. In the cultivar Burgundy, the deep red in the stalk, midrib and main veins makes it a suitable ORNAMENTAL in mass border plantings. If harvested frequently, a spring planting is productive until fall frosts; therefore, Swiss chard is a good substitute for spinach. It is a good source of vitamin A. Leafstalks and midribs can be cut and eaten like asparagus; leaves can be frozen or canned like spinach. Commercial production is limited, but Swiss chard is a popular garden crop.
V.W. NUTTALL

Beetle, term referring to the INSECT order Coleoptera [Gk, "sheath wing"], the largest order of living organisms. Beetles occur in a wide variety of terrestrial and aquatic habitats and use many different types of food. It is estimated that of the 3 million insect species worldwide, 30-40% are beetles. In Canada 6750 species are known; an estimated 2400 have not yet been recorded. Familiar beetles include scarabs (sacred symbol of early Egypt), weevils, and tiger, ground, blister, June and leaf beetles. Beetles are well represented as FOSSILS, the earliest known being Upper Permian forms (260-245 million years old). Representatives of all 4 modern suborders occur in Lower Triassic deposits (245-240 million years old).

With so diverse a group a specific description is difficult, but most beetles share the following characteristics. They pass through a complete metamorphosis (ie, have distinct egg, larval, pupal and adult stages). Larvae and adults generally have chewing mouthparts. Adults have 2 pairs of wings; the outer, horny or leathery pair (elytra) cover the inner, membranous flight wings to form a straight line down the back when at rest. The adult body is usually hardened; antennae usually have 11 or fewer segments. The first segment of the thorax is free; the dorsal surface, large and shieldlike. Size ranges from 0.25 mm to over 10 cm. Most Canadian beetles are brown or black, although an extremely wide range of colours and patterns occurs. Colour may be produced by structural modifications to the cuticle (waxy covering), producing metallic greens and blues, etc; or by pigments in the cuticle, producing oranges, reds, yellows, etc.

The number of beetle species becomes markedly reduced approaching higher latitudes: only 300-400 species extend into the Canadian Arctic. Coleoptera probably is not the largest insect order in this country; however, beetles occupy extremely varied habitats and occur throughout Canada except in the northernmost Arctic islands. Since mobility is often somewhat restricted, the habitat of a given species is directly related to its food. Many families are primarily phytophagous, feeding on plant material; many are predacious, feeding on other invertebrates; relatively few are parasitic on vertebrates. Many species are carrion, dung or pollen feeders. Larvae and adults of a species may feed on the same host; or adults may have strikingly different feeding habits from larvae, not feeding at all, or using a different food source.

Beetles are of immense economic importance, since they include many of the most destructive INSECT PESTS known. Many species attack household and stored products (eg, carpet beetles, confused flour beetle, granary weevil). Plant feeders destroy crop foliage, attacking virtually all cultivated crops. Wood borers attack nearly all trees and shrubs (eg, bark beetles, apple bark borers, poplar borers, etc). Others transmit disease: Dutch elm disease is caused by a fungus transmitted by the elm bark beetle. Coleopterids do very little direct damage to humans and domestic animals although, in rare cases, domestic animals (eg, horses) may die from eating hay containing dead blister beetles. Several species give off toxic chemicals which cause blisters on contact with skin. Some beetles are beneficial. Many predatory species feed on destructive insects, eg, ladybird beetles have been introduced to control aphids and scale insects attacking crops. Families such as ground and rove beetles contain hundreds of species that feed on destructive insects and regulate their populations. Some species considered highly beneficial in one stage may cause damage in another (eg, some larval blister beetles feed on grasshopper eggs, but adults are leaf-feeders, attacking only legumes and other plants). Other species are of considerable benefit as pollinators, or in the decomposition of dead and waste organic material. BEVERLY CAMPBELL AND J.M. CAMPBELL

Begbie, Sir Matthew Baillie, judge, first chief justice of BC (b at the Cape of Good Hope 9 May 1819; d at Victoria 11 June 1894). Sent from England in 1858 to be the first judge of the new colony of British Columbia, he quickly established his reputation as a resolute, but fair, upholder of British law and order in the scattered mining camps of the colony, the white population of which was largely American. His efforts and those of Governor James DOUGLAS ensured that the colony remained British, to become part of

Canada. Upon BC entering Confederation in 1871, Begbie became its first chief justice. He guided the judicial system of the province to an era of considerable sophistication, displaying characteristics unexpected of a Victorian judge: espousal of the rights of Chinese and Indians; a lifelong interest in progressive law reforms and a tendency to take the side of the "little man." In later years he was the social lion of the genteel society of Victoria where he lived in bachelor comfort.
DAVID RICARDO WILLIAMS

Reading: David R. Williams, *The Man For a New Country*: *Sir Matthew Baillie Begbie* (1977).

Begg, Alexander, writer, historian (b at Québec City 19 July 1839; d at Victoria 6 Sept 1897). Educated at St John's, Québec C and Aberdeen, Scot, Begg was trading in manufactured goods at the RED RIVER COLONY in 1867. After a brief period in journalism, he worked for the Manitoba government as auditor, deputy treasurer and queen's printer from 1877 to 1884. He became immigration agent of the CPR, but later returned to journalism at Seattle in 1884 and then at Victoria as editor of the *Daily British Colonist* in 1892. Drawing upon his firsthand knowledge of the events of the Red River Rebellion and the creation of the province of Manitoba, Begg published historical works, including *The Creation of Manitoba* (1871), *Ten Years in Winnipeg* (1879), *The Great Canadian North-West* (1881) and *History of the North-West* (1894-95).
DAVID EVANS

Reading: Alexander Begg, *Red River Journal*, ed W.L. Morton (1969).

Bégin, Monique, first Québec woman elected to the House of Commons (b at Rome, Italy 1 Mar 1936). After a teaching certificate (1955), a BA (1958) and a MSoc from the U de Montréal (1961), she pursued doctoral studies in Paris. She distinguished herself as the executive secretary-general of the Royal Commission on the Status of Women. Her political career began when she was elected a Liberal member of the House (1972), and was then re-elected (1974, 1979, 1980) with, in the last 2 cases, the greatest majorities ever recorded. First as minister of national revenue (1976-77), then as minister of national health and welfare (1977-84), she brought about an increase (3 times) in the old-age supplement for needy senior citizens, the child tax credit and a new health law (1984) which strengthened the health-insurance system. She inaugurated the policy of turning over health services to indigenous peoples. She has received honorary doctorates from various universities and was first winner of the Dr Brock Chisholm medal, offered (1984) by the World Health Organization of Geneva. She has held academic positions at Notre Dame University in the US (1984-85) and McGill (1985-86). The U d'Ottawa named her first holder of the Joint Chair in Women's Studies at Carleton U and U d'Ottawa.
MARTHE LEGAULT

Bégon de La Picardière, Michel, INTENDANT of New France 1712-26 (b at Blois, France 21 Mar 1667; d at La Picardière, France 18 Jan 1747). When he arrived, the economy of New France was suffering from depression in the beaver trade and inflation caused by the use of PLAYING-CARD MONEY. His superiors accepted Bégon's proposal to redeem the card money in instalments, at half face value. He failed in attempts to liberalize the fur trade and to establish industries capable of overcoming the colony's deficit. Extensively involved in private trade and suspected of embezzlement, he was recalled to France in 1723.
FRANCE BEAUREGARD

Belaney, Archibald Stansfeld, alias *Grey Owl*, writer, conservationist (b at Hastings, Eng 18 Sept

Conservationist Grey Owl (Archibald Belaney) feeding a baby beaver in Riding Mountain Park, 1931 (*courtesy Archives of Ontario*).

1888; d at Prince Albert, Sask 13 Apr 1938). Raised by 2 maiden aunts and his grandmother, Belaney had an unhappy childhood. As a boy he was fascinated with N American Indians and dreamed of becoming one. At 17 he left for northern Canada where, apart from his war service, he spent the remainder of his life. Through his association with the Ojibwa of northern Ontario he learned about the wilderness. Shortly after his arrival he imaginatively presented himself as the son of a Scot and an Apache and began to use the name Grey Owl. As Grey Owl he published his first book *The Men of the Last Frontier* (1931). ANA-HAREO, his Iroquois wife, convinced him of the need for CONSERVATION, and that became the central theme of his writings. Appointed to Riding Mountain, and later to Prince Albert National Park to look after a beaver conservation program, he wrote 3 books in western Canada: *Pilgrims of the Wild* (1934), *The Adventures of Sajo and her Beaver People* (1935) and *Tales of an Empty Cabin* (1936). His work was extremely popular, especially in Britain, where he made 2 lecture tours. After his death the press discovered his English birth, and in the ensuing uproar his contributions as a conservationist were forgotten. Only a generation later were they again recognized.

DONALD B. SMITH

Reading: Lovat Dickson, *Wilderness Man* (1973).

Belcher, Sir Edward, naval surveyor, explorer (b at Halifax 27 Feb 1799; d at London, Eng 18 Mar 1877). As a surveyor he participated in major British naval expeditions to Bering Str, Africa, the Americas and the Far East. He proved able, though quarrelsome and vindictive. In 1852 he was given charge of 5 ships sailing in search of Sir John FRANKLIN. Belcher's expedition rescued Robert MCCLURE and his men, marooned for 3 winters during their own search, but his ships were icebound and in summer 1854 he ordered 4 abandoned. Back in England he was rebuked but not court-martialled. Belcher spent the rest of his life in literary and scientific pursuits. *See also* BELCHER ISLANDS. DANIEL FRANCIS

Belcher, Jonathan, lawyer, chief justice, lieutenant-governor of NS (b at Boston, Mass 23 July 1710; d at Halifax 30 Mar 1776). Educated at Harvard, Cambridge and the Middle Temple (London, Eng), Belcher served at the English and Irish bars until appointed in 1754 as first chief justice of NS, an office he held until his death. The first formally trained law officer appointed in the province, he established orderly courts, English as opposed to Massachusetts legal precedents,

and solidly drafted legislation. As administrator and lieutenant-governor (Oct 1760-Sept 1763), he found himself in open conflict with the elected House of Assembly over issues affecting its mercantile leaders. His continuance of Governor Charles LAWRENCE's encouragement to New England settlements in NS was fruitful, but he also repeated, in 1762, his predecessor's inhumane expulsion of ACADIANS. Belcher's lack of political judgement and financial ineptitude left him subject to the pervasive power of Joshua MAUGER, who, as the province's agent in London, successfully undermined the lieutenant-governor's credibility with the Board of Trade. Belcher was replaced March 1763. The Board's dissatisfaction with Belcher led to its separation of powers, excluding the chief justice from thereafter assuming the position of provincial administrator. Learned, well-intentioned but pompous, Belcher contributed most significantly as a jurist.

SUSAN BUGGEY

Belcher Islands in southeastern HUDSON BAY, 100 km W of Great Whale R, Québec. The total landmass of about 13 000 km² is composed of a group of long, narrow islands, lying NE/SW along a very extensive coastline. From Henry HUDSON's 1610 logbook, he likely sighted the islands prior to the mutiny of his crew. Hudson reputedly drifted onto the Belchers and was buried there. The Belchers, like all islands in the bay, are part of the NWT, and are said to be named after a HBC employee. The islands became less and less prominent on successive admiralty maps and were virtually rediscovered by explorer R.J. Flaherty in 1915 in his search for iron ore. Flaherty produced the film documentary masterpiece *Nanook of the North* in 1922, based on his contact with the Inuit. Inhabitants of the Belchers are said to be the last Inuit group to enter into contact with other Canadians. In the 1960s a schoolhouse complex was opened, the first teacher being the author of this entry. Later, a nursing station was added. Belcher Is carvings have distinctive eyes, made by rotating the end of a file. MICHAEL C. HAMPSON

Belgians are citizens of Belgium, a European country divided linguistically into those in the N who speak a Dutch dialect (the Flemish) and those in the S who speak a French dialect (the Walloons). There is also a small German-speaking community along the eastern border of the country. Belgian immigration to Canada (with a few individual exceptions) did not really begin until 1880. In 1901 there were 2994 Belgians in Canada; in 1981 (the last figures available) more than 50 000 Canadians of Belgian origin were listed in the census.

Migration and Settlement Belgian immigration was particularly active before WWI and between 1951 and 1961, when some 2500 Belgians immigrated annually. Québec and western Canada were particularly attractive to Belgians at the end of the 19th century. The Québec government, under Premiers Mercier and Gouin, encouraged Belgians to settle in rural areas. In the cities, they became tradesmen, small businessmen, teachers and musicians. Belgian financiers invested in the real estate and paper industries and in the mines.

Most Flemish Belgians went to the West, where they were primarily involved in agriculture. Some largely Belgian communities developed in Saskatchewan, Alberta and Manitoba (eg, St-Boniface). Some 100 Belgian peasants settled in the Vancouver region around 1900; a decade later Belgian investors were attracted to the vineyards of the Okanagan Valley. In Ontario Belgians moved into sugar-beet and tobacco cultivation (eg, in Chatham, Delhi, Wallaceburg). Prior to WWI, some Belgian miners worked in the coal mines of Nova Scotia, New Brunswick and Alberta.

Belgians have distinguished themselves in every aspect of Canadian life – music, painting, higher education, business and municipal politics. There are several Belgian bishops within the Canadian Roman Catholic Church. Belgians established the Redemptorist (1879), Benedictine (1912) and Premonstratensian (1949) orders in Canada; the Belgian Oblates are known for their work in the Far North. Belgians have integrated easily into the Canadian population, probably because they are few in number, widely dispersed and culturally very similar to French and English Canadians. There are Belgian associations in Québec, Ontario and Manitoba; some of the oldest are the Union belge in Montréal (1902), Club belge de St-Boniface (1905) and Société belge de bienfaisance (1921). ANDRÉ VERMEIRRE

Beliveau, Jean, hockey player (b at Trois-Rivières, Qué 31 Aug 1931). He learned to skate in the backyard of his home in Victoriaville and played junior hockey at Québec City. Idolized by fans who packed the Colisée de Québec to watch him play, Beliveau played 2 more years with Québec Aces, despite the entreaties of the Canadiens. He finally joined MONTREAL CANADIENS in 1953, signing the most lucrative contract to that time. By 1956, when he won the NHL scoring championship and HART TROPHY (most valuable player), he had become the dignified leader of the most powerful team in hockey history. In 18 seasons and 1125 games he scored 507 goals and 1219 points. In 162 playoff games he scored 79 goals and his record 176 points stood until broken in 1987 by Wayne Gretzky. He retired 1970-71 and became a VP of the Canadiens.

JAMES MARSH

Alexander Graham Bell arrived in Brantford, Ont, in 1870. He was the inventor of the telephone and was also instrumental in the early development of aviation in Canada (*courtesy National Archives of Canada/C-17335*).

Bell, Alexander Graham, inventor (b at Edinburgh, Scot 3 Mar 1847; d at Baddeck, NS 2 Aug 1922). Generally considered second only to Thomas Alva Edison among 19th- and 20th-century inventors and, through their inventions, originators of social change, Bell came from Scotland with his parents in 1870 to Brantford, Ont. There he and his father worked as speech therapists for the deaf. A scientific approach to their work, an awareness of the electric telegraph, and the invention of a successful microphone led to the invention of the TELEPHONE 1874-76 (*see also* TELECOMMUNICATIONS). By then Bell was teaching at a school for the deaf in Boston, Mass, and spending his summers with the family at Brantford. He patented the telephone and energetically promoted its commercial development in the US, founding the Bell Telephone Co in 1876. Victory in a number of lawsuits over telephone patents made him rich by age 35. By then he had moved to Washington, DC, to watch over his business interests. In 1890 he bought land at Baddeck and later built himself a house there named Beinn Bhreagh ("beautiful mountain" in Gaelic).

Bell spent the rest of his life in scientific research, both in person and by paying for the experiments of others. In the US he collaborated with S.P. Langley, builder of a steam-powered aircraft in the 1890s, and funded the early atomic experiments of A.M. Michelson. Bell himself worked on the photoelectric cell, the iron lung, desalination of seawater, and the phonograph, and attempted to breed a "super race" of sheep at Baddeck. His wife, Mabel Gardiner Hubbard (1857-1923), whom Bell first met owing to her deafness, shared his scientific as well as his philanthropic interests. She was a full member of the Aerial Experiment Assn, undertook her own horticultural experiments, and with their 2 daughters lobbied from at least 1910 for women's right to vote.

The Aerial Experiment Assn was formed by Bell in 1907 in partnership with J.A.D. MCCURDY, F.W. BALDWIN and a few other young engineers, such as Glenn H. Curtiss, an American builder of motorcycle engines. After early experiments with man-lifting kites, the AEA turned to gasoline-powered biplanes (which they called "aerodromes") and built several successful aircraft. The flight of the SILVER DART at Baddeck 23 Feb 1909 is generally accepted as the first manned flight in Canada. The AEA worked simultaneously on "hydrodromes" or hydrofoil boats from 1908. The HD-4, built in 1917, set a world water-speed record of 114.04 km/h in 1919 that was not approached by any other boat for more than a decade.

The HD-4 and other Bell memorabilia have been preserved at the national historic site at Baddeck. There are many biographies of Bell; the basic technical history of the AEA is *Bell and Baldwin* by J.H. PARKIN (1964).   DONALD J.C. PHILLIPSON

Bell, Alexander Melville, educator, founder of the Canadian telephone industry (b at Edinburgh, Scot 1 Mar 1819; d at Washington, DC 7 Aug 1905). He was the father of Alexander Graham BELL. Prior to moving his family to Tutela Heights near Brantford, Ont, in the 1870s, he was professor of elocution at the universities of London and Edinburgh. He invented "visible speech," a written code especially useful to the deaf, which indicates exactly how all human vocal sounds are made, and he authored several texts on this subject. Receiving 75% of the Canadian patents to the telephone in 1877, Bell proceeded to hire agents to solicit telephone rentals; the instruments were to be attached to private lines owned by the lessees. Failing to find a Canadian buyer for the patents, he sold them to National Bell (US) in 1880. In Canada he was professor of elocution at Queen's Coll, Kingston, Ont, before moving to Washington, DC, in 1881.
ROBERT E. BABE

Bell, Alistair Macready, graphic artist (b at Darlington, Eng 21 Oct 1913). He moved to Vancouver in 1929, where he enrolled at the Vancouver School of Art in 1935. A draftsman in a structural steel plant until 1967, he worked in his free time as an artist, becoming a fine draftsman and an adept in the graphic media drypoint, etching, wood engraving and woodcut. His spare, sometimes stark designs express the essence of his favourite subjects – birds and animals, ships, bare landscapes – and elevate them into moving ab-

stractions of form. He has travelled in Europe and N America in search of inspiration, and has exhibited in Europe, Latin America, Canada and the US; his works are in the Victoria and Albert Museum in England, the Museum of Modern Art in New York and the National Gallery in Ottawa. Major retrospectives were held at the Burnaby Art Gallery (drawings and graphics, 1971) and the Art Gallery of Greater Victoria (prints, 1981).
GEORGE WOODCOCK

Bell, John, fur trader, explorer (b on the Isle of Mull, Scot 1799; d at Saugeen, Ont 24 June 1868). John Bell joined the NORTH WEST COMPANY as a clerk in 1818. In 1824, working for the HUDSON'S BAY COMPANY, he was transferred to the Mackenzie District, becoming chief clerk of Ft Good Hope (1825-26), the HBC's most northerly post. On the Company's behalf he explored northwestern British North America, looking for new fur trade routes. In 1840 he opened Peel's River Post (FT MCPHERSON), the most northerly HBC post at the time. In the summer of 1845 he reached the junction of the Yukon and Porcupine rivers, the first European to do so. In 1847-48 he participated in the search for the lost Franklin expedition (*see* FRANKLIN SEARCH). He served in northern postings until 1851. A modest, unassuming man, he was the classic blend of fur trader and explorer.   KENNETH S. COATES

Bell, John Howatt, lawyer, politician, premier of PEI (b at Cape Traverse, PEI Dec 1846; d at Los Angeles, Calif 29 Jan 1929). Member of the PEI Legislative Assembly 1886-98 and MP 1898-1900, Bell, a Liberal, was re-elected provincially in 1915 and was premier 1919-23. The thrust of his government's activity was road building. During his office the provincial vote was extended to women in 1922.   NICOLAS J. DE JONG

Bell, Leslie Richard, choir conductor, arranger (b at Toronto 5 May 1906; d there 19 Jan 1962). A versatile musician with wide-ranging interests, Bell devoted his life to bringing art music to ordinary people. He founded the Leslie Bell Singers, a women's choir, in 1939. Convinced that the best of both art and popular music had much in common, he had the singers perform his own arrangements of music, embracing a diversity of styles from Renaissance madrigals to popular songs of the day – a programming concept highly successful with audiences and widely imitated by choirs elsewhere.   BARCLAY MCMILLAN

Bell, Marilyn, swimmer (b at Toronto 19 Nov 1937). When she was 16 years old, Bell waded into Lk Ontario on the chilly night of 9 Sept 1954 and swam 32 miles (51.5 km) from Youngstown, NY, to a slimy breakwater off Toronto's western shore, a feat that caught the imagination of the country. A war between the *Toronto Star* and the *Toronto Telegram* reporters who covered the event came to real blows while Bell was in the water, fighting lamprey eels and choking on oil spills. Gus Ryder, her coach, was forgiven for refusing to pull her out even when she seemed semiconscious. Later she became the youngest person ever to swim the English Channel and the Str of Juan de Fuca, but nothing could match the euphoria that gripped the waiting crowd in Toronto when she weakly touched the wall 20 hours and 59 minutes after setting out. It was said to be a quintessential Canadian achievement: an individual, grim and steadfast, who was not defeated by the elements. Many people later equalled her exploit and in faster times as marathon swimmers plunged into a mania for lake crossing, but none ever equalled the moment of glory that Bell achieved in what became the high point of the decade. To the joy of the public, who showered gifts and praise on her, she was a model hero –

Marilyn Bell's swimming feats are part of Canada's national sports lore. Her 1954 swim across Lake Ontario in 21 hours captured the admiration of people across Canada (*courtesy Canada's Sports Hall of Fame*).

modest, intelligent, appreciative and charming. She left the spotlight as abruptly as she had entered it, her halo intact.   JUNE CALLWOOD

Bell, George Maxwell, "Max," newspaper publisher, industrialist, sportsman (b at Regina 13 Oct 1912; d at Montréal 19 July 1972). When his father, George Melrose Bell, publisher of the debt-ridden Calgary *Albertan*, died in 1936, Max Bell (at the time the newspaper's business manager) scraped together $35 000 in loans from friends and took over the operation. In 3 years he paid off the loans and the bank and by 1943 became the *Albertan*'s publisher. Successful investments in oil and elsewhere enabled Bell to amass a fortune and to build a newspaper empire. He was at one time the largest individual shareholder in the CPR. In 1959 he came close to buying control of the Hudson's Bay Co, backing out at the last minute only because he realized he lacked retail expertise. Also, in 1959, with Victor Sifton of the *Winnipeg Free Press*, he formed FP Publications. Beginning with 6 newspapers (the Ottawa *Journal, Winnipeg Free Press, Free Press Weekly*, Calgary *Albertan*, Victoria *Times* and Victoria *Daily Colonist*), Bell expanded the chain in 1963 with his purchase of controlling interest in Vancouver's Sun Publishing. FP also took over the *Lethbridge Herald*, the *Montreal Star* and the *Globe and Mail*. By the mid-1960s more Canadians read FP newspapers than any other. Bell gave his papers free rein, saying that he was more interested in their profits than their editorial policies.

A sports enthusiast all his life, Bell played hockey for the Kimberley, BC, Dynamiters for 2 years following his graduation from McGill in 1932. He later invested in the VANCOUVER CANUCKS of the NHL and in racehorses. In 1965 his horse, Meadow Court, won the Irish Derby; another won the Queen's Plate. A lifelong physical fitness advocate, Bell neither drank nor smoked. He would often exercise during business meetings and at the age of 50 astonished a gathering of editors by walking across the room on his hands.

A vigorous, affable and deeply religious man (and one said never to have made an enemy), Bell contributed generously, and often anonymously, to community efforts, with particular support for the Presbyterian Church. He died of brain disease at 59, triggering heartfelt tributes from contemporaries all across the continent and in Europe. He left an estate valued at $22 million.

CHUCK DAVIS

Bell, Robert, geologist, explorer (b at Toronto 3 June 1841; d at Rathwell, Man 19 June 1917). In 1857 Bell was junior assistant to the GEOLOGICAL SURVEY OF CANADA. He obtained a BSc from McGill (1861) and in 1862 was made a member of the prestigious Geological Soc of London in recognition of the Canadian contribution to the London Exhibition. Following George LAWSON, he was interim professor of chemistry and natural science at Queen's 1863-67. In 1869 Bell was employed full-time by the survey, and began a series of northern and western explorations, mapping rivers draining into HUDSON BAY and reconnoitering the route for a transcontinental railway. A GSC assistant director 1877, charter member of the ROYAL SOCIETY OF CANADA (1882) and an MD (McGill) by 1878, Bell in 1884-85 was medical and science officer aboard 2 government expeditions to explore HUDSON STR. He called Hudson Bay "the Mediterranean of N America" and advocated its utilization as a natural highway between western Canada and Europe. In 1889 he was a member of the Royal Commission on the Mineral Resources of Ontario and in 1890 became chief geologist of the GSC. In 1897 he explored BAFFIN I and in 1899 GREAT SLAVE LK.

Despite many honours and his remarkable exploration of many areas of geology, zoology, ethnology, botany and forestry over a vast and previously unknown terrain, Bell never realized his ambition to become GSC director. Appointed acting director 1901, he retired in 1906. After living in Paris 1912-14, Bell and his family moved to the Assiniboine R in Manitoba.   SUZANNE ZELLER

Bell, Robert Edward, nuclear physicist, university educator (b at Ladner, BC 29 Nov 1918). After graduating from UBC (BA 1939, MA 1941), he worked on RADAR development at the NATIONAL RESEARCH COUNCIL during WWII. He resumed his graduate studies at McGill in 1945, and received his PhD in nuclear physics in 1948 while already a member of the research staff of the Canadian Atomic Energy Project at Chalk River. In 1952 he joined the staff of McGill, and was appointed Ernest Rutherford Professor of Physics in 1960, becoming emeritus professor of physics upon retiring in 1983. He held several important positions at McGill, including principal and vice-chancellor (1970-79). In addition to being an internationally renowned nuclear physicist, he was a highly successful university educator.

Bell was best known for his scientific contributions to the study of the nuclear interaction energy between a proton and a neutron, the invention of the direct timing method for measuring nuclear processes down to a fraction of a billionth of a second, and the discovery of proton radioactivity. His accomplishments brought him prestigious fellowships in the American Physical Society (1954), the Royal Society of Canada (1955) and the Royal Society of London (1965). He was the recipient of the 1968 Medal for Achievement in Physics of the Canadian Assn of Physicists (CAP), honorary doctorate degrees from 10 leading Canadian universities, and was made Companion of the Order of Canada (1971). He was president of CAP, 1965-66, and of the Royal Society of Canada, 1978-81. Bell capped his distinguished career with an appointment as director of the Arts, Sciences and Technology Centre in Vancouver (1983-85).   S.K. MARK

Bell Canada Enterprises Inc, is a transnational holding company whose subsidiaries operate primarily in telecommunications carriage, research and equipment manufacturing; international consulting; communications and information services; energy; printing, packaging and publishing; and real estate. On 1986 revenues of $13.9 billion, BCE ranked 9th among Canadian corporations while in 1985 it became the first to surpass $1 billion in annual profit.

Formed in 1983 through a corporate reorganization, BCE became parent to over 80 companies previously known as the Bell Group, of which Bell Canada, the country's largest telephone company, had been head. This reorganization was designed to cast off charter restrictions inhibiting certain corporate acquisitions and investments, and removed from detailed regulatory scrutiny many activities and intercorporate dealings. Since 1983 the federal government has been considering what, if any, legislation is needed to redress the situation.

Bell Canada, a subsidiary telephone company, still accounts for 45% of the holding company's revenues and almost 70% of its net income. Incorporated by federal charter in 1880, Bell attained thereby the right to construct telephone lines alongside all public rights-of-way in Canada, a most valuable privilege. Since 1906 Bell has been regulated by various federal regulatory tribunals, most recently the CANADIAN RADIO-TELEVISION AND TELECOMMUNICATIONS COMMISSION (CRTC). Its service area encompasses most of Ontario and Québec and portions of the NWT.

Other companies in which BCE hold major equity interest include Ronalds Printing, Northern Telecom Ltd (52.3%), North America's second largest telecommunications equipment manufacturer; Bell-Northern Research Ltd (30%), Canada's largest private research and development company; TransCanada PipeLines Ltd (48.5%); Maritime Telegraph and Telephone Co Ltd (32%), Nova Scotia's sole provider of public telephone service; Bruncor Inc (31.2%), parent of New Brunswick Telephone Co, sole provider of telephone service in that province; and NewTel Enterprises Ltd (53%), parent of Newfoundland Telephone Co, largest provider of telephone service in Newfoundland. BCE's telephone subsidiaries and affiliates account collectively for about 60% of the Canadian telephone industry.

ROBERT E. BABE

Bell Island, 34 km², the largest island in CONCEPTION BAY, off Newfoundland's AVALON PENINSULA, is a flat outcropping of Ordovician sandstone and shale interbedded with red hematite, an iron ore. Its high, red-stone cliffs are visible from Portugal Cove to the E from which a ferry runs the 5 km to the island. Off-lying Bell Rock gave the 9 km long, 3 km wide island its name. First settled in the mid-1700s, the island experienced a drastic change in its economy in the 1890s, when iron-ore mining was begun there. The mine site at Wabana in the N became its largest community. Nova Scotia Steel first operated the mine but ownership eventually passed to Dominion Steel Corp and finally to Hawker-Siddeley Canada. Until the beginning of operations in Labrador, the Bell I mine was the largest producer of iron ore in Canada; during its life it was the world's most extensive submarine iron mine. The ore was smelted at SYDNEY, NS, until competition and declining markets led to the cessation of mining on Bell I in 1966. The island suffered economic difficulties and a loss of residents as a result; many of the work force now commute to nearby St John's.   ROBERT D. PITT

Bell-Smith, Frederic Marlett, painter (b at London, Eng 26 Sept 1846; d at Toronto 23 June 1923). Bell-Smith received his early art training in London and came to Montréal in 1867. He worked in photographic firms in Montréal and then in Hamilton, Ont, and Toronto, and exhibited primarily watercolours of sporting subjects. In 1881 he was appointed art director at Alma College in St Thomas, Ont, and in the 1880s sketched in Québec, Maine and the Rocky Mts. From 1888 his income was derived from sales of his work, and he exhibited regularly. His attempts to obtain official government patronage in 1895 and in 1897, on the occasion of Queen Victoria's Jubilee, were unsuccessful. Nevertheless, he did achieve some notoriety in being granted a sitting by the queen in 1895. Bell-Smith was a popular and prolific artist. He was especially known for his landscapes from the Rocky Mts and the Selkirk Range, where he often travelled, as well as for London and Paris street scenes.

ROGER H. BOULET

Reading: Roger H. Boulet, *Frederic Marlett Bell-Smith, 1846-1923* (1977).

Bella Bella, now Heiltsuk, is the language spoken by the older people in the Indian villages of Bella Bella and Klemtu situated on islands along the BC central coast. The present residents of Bella Bella (which had an on- and off-reserve membership of 1513 in 1986) are mostly descendants of 4 separate groups of Indians who amalgamated towards the end of the 19th century. Kitasoo (with an on- and off-reserve population of 309 in 1986) is composed of Indians who have ancestral ties either with a Coast TSIMSHIAN-speaking group from farther N or a Heiltsuk-speaking group from Kynoch Inlet, E of Klemtu.

Heiltsuk is part of the N Wakashan division of the Wakashan language family and is closely related to Oowekyala, the language of the Oweekeno (Owikeno) people of Rivers Inlet, SE from Bella Bella. The Heiltsuk still maintain close cultural and social ties with the Rivers Inlet people (population 157).

Like other peoples of coastal BC, the Heiltsuk and Oweekeno cultures were characterized by elaborate POTLATCHES, cedar plank houses, TOTEM POLES and concern with social ranking. These 2 groups differ from one another in that the Oweekeno live primarily in a freshwater environment, while the Heiltsuk are on the ocean and participate in a sea-life economy.

Information concerning the traditional social system of the Heiltsuk (and of the Oweekeno) is scant, though it seems to have been based on unilineal clans, each composed of a number of family groups or lineages occupying one or more houses. However, influence from the matrilineal clans to the north resulted in the Heiltsuk favouring descent reckoned along the mother's line. There were 4 or more clans, including Raven, Eagle,

Bella Bella deer mask (*courtesy National Museums of Canada/Canadian Museum of Civilization/S82-39*).

Blackfish and Wolf. Each clan owned its own resource-gathering sites and shared in hosting ceremonials. Winter ceremonials were dominated by the Tsaika (SHAMAN's) dance series, which included the Hamatsa or cannibal dances. Some researchers believe the Hamatsa dance, well known throughout Wakashan, Tsimshian and HAIDA areas, originated among the Heiltsuk.

First contacts with non-Indians were in the 1790s. A HUDSON'S BAY CO fur trading post, Ft McLaughlin, operated in Bella Bella territory between 1833 and 1843 and involved the native people in the maritime FUR TRADE. The focus of trade shifted in 1849 with the establishment of Ft Rupert near the northeastern end of Vancouver I. By the 1880s a mission and hospital were located in Bella Bella. The people became successful commercial fishermen in the early 1900s and many of them continue to play an important role in the industry.

Since the early 1970s, the Heiltsuk Cultural Centre has been involved with language and culture programs. Other band projects include the operation of a hotel and a store, and the development of an airport. Progress in economic development, and in the maintenance and teaching of language and culture, has also been made by the Oweekeno under the direction of their band council. *See also* NATIVE PEOPLE: NORTHWEST COAST and general articles under NATIVE PEOPLE.

Reading: R. Olson, "Social Life of the Owikeno Kwakiutl," *Anthropological Record* 14, 3 (1954) and "Notes on the Bella Bella Kwakiutl," *Anthropological Record* 14, 5 (1955).

Bella Coola live in an isolated fishing village on the central West Coast of BC. In 1986 their registered population was 889. The term "Bella Coola" once referred collectively to the Bella Coola, Talio, Kimsquit and some Kwatna who inhabited villages around North Bentinck Arm and the Bella Coola Valley, South Bentinck Arm, Dean Channel and Kwatna Inlet, respectively. By the 1920s they had abandoned all their other village sites and amalgamated on the present reserve at the mouth of the Bella Coola R. Since the late 1970s the Bella Coola have called themselves the "Nuxalk Nation," derived from the native term that in earlier times referred exclusively to the people of the Bella Coola Valley. They speak a Coast Salish language known as Bella Coola that is isolated from the other Salish languages of the coast and forms a linguistic island surrounded by Athapaskan and Wakashan languages. Culturally the Bella Coola are most similar to their Wakashan neighbours, the Heiltsuk (BELLA BELLA).

Villages traditionally consisted of descent groups who traced their lineage to a group of mythical first ancestors. Each group of ancestors, equipped with tools and ceremonial knowledge, descended from a mountaintop and established a village at its base. Through marriage, a network of descent groups developed that linked the villages. Most people chose to live in their fathers' villages. However, they were also related to their mothers' descent groups, if different. The multiple-family cedar-plank dwellings were large enough to house as many as 6 couples and their children. Members of the household, which included elderly relatives, supported one another in potlatching and economic pursuits.

The most prominent characteristic of Bella Coola life was its extremely rich and complex ceremonialism, dominated by the POTLATCH and 2 secret societies, the sisaok and the kusiut. Membership in the sisaok was limited to the children and certain relatives of chiefs. Initiation included a period of seclusion, followed by a public display of a masked figure representing the initiate's crest. They performed at potlatches and funerals and occasionally at less important ceremonials. Bella Coola winter ceremonials were dominated by the kusiut. Each member possessed a special kusiut name and had a supernatural patron whose dance he or she imitated.

Bella Coola was a fishing, hunting and gathering society. Salmon and eulachon ("candlefish") fishing in the Bella Coola R continues to be important (*see* SMELT). Each year, eulachons are netted, rendered into grease and traded. The fish are smoke-dried in the traditional manner (*see* SMOKEHOUSE), canned and frozen. Band administration, a band-operated commercial fish-smoking plant, and salmon-enhancement programs provide employment.

The first recorded encounter with the Bella Coola occurred briefly in the summer of 1793 when Captain George VANCOUVER entered their waters. He was followed only weeks later by an overland exploration team headed by Alexander MACKENZIE. This historic occasion became incorporated into Bella Coola oral tradition and the story of the welcome they gave Mackenzie is still a source of Bella Coola pride. *See also* NATIVE PEOPLE: NORTHWEST COAST and general articles under NATIVE PEOPLE.

DOROTHY KENNEDY AND RANDY BOUCHARD

Reading: T.F. McIlwraith, *The Bella Coola Indians*, (2 vols, 1948).

Bella Coola, BC, UP, pop 241 (1986c) is situated on the N arm of Burke Channel, where Alexander MACKENZIE first sighted the Pacific in 1793. The first white settlers were fur traders, arriving during the 1860s. In 1894-95, some 220 Norwegians, chiefly from Minnesota, settled in the Bella Coola Valley where they and the indigenous BELLA COOLA (Nuxalk) Indians were soon joined by other settlers in the development of a mixed farming and fishing economy. Fish canneries formerly operated here. The community has a diverse economic structure as a logging, sawmilling and mixed-farming centre, and as a commercial and sportfishing base. GEORGIANA BALL

Bellefleur, Léon, painter, engraver (b at Montréal 8 Feb 1910). He took evening classes at the École des beaux-arts de Montréal and, starting in 1942, met artists such as Alfred PELLAN. He was one of the signatories of the "Prisme d'yeux" manifesto in 1948. He was part of exhibitions held abroad such as the cobra movement in Liège, Belgium, in 1951. A teacher in Montréal until 1954, he then lived in France where he studied engraving. Upon his return to Québec, he developed in 1957 his "facetted" style in which nonfigurative compositions were built up with a spatula. In 1958 Bellefleur returned to France, in Provence and soon punctuated his canvasses with spurts and swipes of paint. Bellefleur drew close to André Breton's surrealist group and shuttled between Paris and Montréal until 1968, when a first retrospective of his works appeared in Ottawa, London, Ont, and Montréal. Exhibitions in Canada, England and Denmark followed his return to Québec, and in 1977 he won the Prix Borduas. His drawings, paintings and prints are mainly inspired by an esoteric imaginary world, writhing with burgeoning shapes, lyric pulsations of colour and the revelation of enchanting secrets. GUY ROBERT

Belleville, Ont. The original settlers were fur traders, but the town later became an important sawmilling centre; the photo shows the city hall on the Moira R (*photo by Barbara K. Deans/Masterfile*).

Belleville, Ont, City, pop 36 041 (1986c) 34 881 (1981c), inc 1877, seat of Hastings County, located on the Bay of Quinte, an arm of Lk Ontario about 180 km E of Toronto at the mouth of the Moira R. The original inhabitants were fur traders, but the settlement's founder is considered to be the Loyalist, Capt John Meyers, who built a gristmill beside the river in 1790. The village of Meyer's Creek grew up at the site. In 1816 it was officially surveyed and the name was changed to Belleville after Arabella, wife of Francis Gore, lt-gov of UC. As the forests of the hinterland were logged, Belleville became an important sawmilling centre. The GRAND TRUNK RY passed through in 1855 and the town became a divisional point; the GTR station, dating from the 1850s, is a well-preserved example of the early railway era. Logging died out in the 1870s, but the city developed a thriving cheesemaking industry and in this century an economy based on diversified light manufacturing. The Hastings County Museum and campus of Loyalist College are located here. DANIEL FRANCIS

Bellevue House, built between 1838 and 1840 for businessman Charles Hales, was one of several elegant villas built on the outskirts of Kingston in the mid-19th century. Its spacious landscaped gardens, vista over Lk Ontario, and its slightly exotic Italianate design with an irregular plan, tower, verandahs and decorative eave fringe reflect the picturesque taste both in architecture and landscape design. In 1848-49 Bellevue was leased to John A. MACDONALD, then a member of the Legislative Assembly and receiver general for the Province of Canada. Bellevue was purchased by Parks Canada in 1964 and is now operated as a national historic park. It has been restored to the late 1840s period. JANET WRIGHT

Bellevue House, one of the elegant villas built on the outskirts of Kingston, Ont, in the mid-19th century. It was leased to John A. Macdonald 1848-49 (*photo by Richard Vroom*).

Bellot Strait, at 71°58′ N, separates Somerset I from the Boothia Pen, marking the northernmost point on the mainland of N America. The 2 km wide passage was discovered in 1852 by Capt

William Kennedy, then commanding an expedition searching for Sir John FRANKLIN, and Joseph René Bellot, a French naval officer and arctic explorer who was Kennedy's second-in-command. Bellot died in the Arctic a year later, aged 26. F.L. McClintock wintered in the strait in 1858-59.

STANLEY GORDON

Beluga Whale, or white whale (*Delphinapterus leucas*), grows to a maximum length of about 6 m and is widely distributed in the Arctic, with a few small populations in subarctic areas. Most N American populations are migratory and are identified by their summer grounds, eg, Cook Inlet (Alaska), Bristol Bay, Beaufort Sea, Lancaster Sound (especially Cunningham Inlet), Cumberland Sound, E and W Hudson Bay, Ungava Bay and St Lawrence R. Like the closely related NAR-WHALS, belugas are often found near ice. They have long been hunted by northern natives for meat and oil, and by commercial whalers for hides and oil (*see* WHALE; WHALING). Belugas prey on various marine organisms and some fishermen have considered them serious competitors for salmon and cod. During the 1930s an extermination program carried out in the St Lawrence R by the Québec government included payment of a bounty for each *marsouin blanc* (beluga) killed. Today, the St Lawrence population is severely depleted, as are those in Cumberland Sound, Ungava Bay and SE Hudson Bay. Adults are distinctively white except for margins of flippers and tail flukes. There is no dorsal fin. The high, rounded forehead ends in a short, broad beak. Calves and juveniles are grey to blue, but otherwise resemble adults. Belugas have a remarkably varied vocal repertoire and have been called sea canaries. Their biosonar system, used for echolocation in navigation and hunting, is among the most sophisticated found in nature.

R. REEVES AND E.D. MITCHELL

Belzberg, Samuel, financier (b at Calgary 26 June 1928). Educated at U of A, Belzberg was active in oil and gas investment and all aspects of real-estate development. In 1962 he founded City Savings and Trust in Edmonton in response to the need in western Canada for real-estate development financing. Belzberg moved to Vancouver in 1968 and, with his partners (including brothers Hyman and William), formed Western Realty, an amalgamation of 16 private companies. The sale of Western Realty in 1973 enabled the Belzbergs to buy Far West Financial Corp of California, which brought them national attention. In 1970 First City Financial Corp was formed as parent company to City Savings and by 1986 it was a diversified holding-investment company with assets in excess of $4.5 billion and operations throughout Canada and the US. City Savings and Trust, renamed First City Trust Company in 1978, had grown by 1986 to a $3.1 billion corporation. In 1985 Scovill Inc, a major US manufacturer, was purchased for $523 million. In 1987, Belzburg was chairman of the Simon Fraser U Bridge to the Future Campaign, trustee to the FRASER INSTITUTE and member of the Rockefeller U Council. The Belzbergs, many of whose relatives died during WWII, financed the Simon Wiesenthal Center at Yeshiva U, Los Angeles, which conducts studies of the holocaust and is being expanded to include a Museum of Tolerance. Belzberg also established in 1977 the Dystonia Medical Research Foundation which has joint headquarters in Vancouver and Los Angeles and clinics at UBC, Columbia U and in London, England.

CHUCK DAVIS

Benedictines Various monastic traditions were already in existence in western Europe when Saint Benedict of Nursia founded the Abbey of

Richard Bedford Bennett
Eleventh Prime Minister of Canada

Birth: 3 July 1870, Hopewell Hill, NB
Father/Mother: Henry/Henrietta Stiles
Father's Occupation: Shipbuilder
Education: Dalhousie U, Halifax
Religious Affiliation: Methodist/United
First Occupation: Teacher
Last Private Occupation: Lawyer/businessman
Political Party: Conservative
Period(s) as PM: 7 Aug 1930 - 23 Oct 1935
Ridings: Calgary East, Alta, 1911-17 Calgary West, Alta, 1925-39
Other Ministries: Justice 1921 Finance 1926
Marriage: None
Children: None
Died: 26 June 1947 in Mickleham, Eng
Cause of Death at Age: Heart failure at 76
Burial Place: Dorking, Eng
Other Information: Created Viscount Bennett of Mickleham, Calgary and Hopewell, 1941.
(*photo courtesy National Archives of Canada/C-687.*)

Monte Cassino in Italy in 529. His rule, which quickly replaced all others in Western monasteries, is known for its moderation and flexibility. As a consequence, various branches of the order, each very different from the others and composed of autonomous houses, were formed over the succeeding centuries. Those represented in Canada are, in chronological order, the Congregation of Saint Gertrude the Great (Winnipeg, 1905, female); the American Cassinese Congregation (Muenster, Sask, 1908, male); the Congregation of France (St-Benoît-du-Lac, Qué, 1912, male; Ste-Marthe-sur-le-Lac, Qué, 1937, female); the Benedictine Federation of the Americas (Ladner, BC, 1939, male); the Benedictine Nuns of Mont-Laurier, Qué (became Benedictine in 1949); the Benedictines of Saint Lioba (Vancouver, 1951-68, female); and the Benedictine Nuns of the Precious Blood (Joliette, Qué, who became Benedictines in 1974); the Benedictine Community of Montréal (1977, male).

MICHEL THÉRIAULT

Bengough, John Wilson, political cartoonist (b at Toronto 7 Apr 1851; d there 2 Oct 1923). One of the first substantial figures in editorial cartooning, he started off on George BROWN's *Globe* in 1871 but left to found the satirical weekly *Grip* (1873-94), which established itself by ridiculing PM John A. MACDONALD during the PACIFIC SCANDAL. Indeed, our mental picture of Macdonald,

with his sly posture, witty mouth and whisky nose, owes much to Bengough's treatment. He is also of secondary interest as a 19th-century social radical, to whom communalism, vegetarianism, feminism, antivivisectionism and prohibition combined in one vast utopian ideal. In later life he returned to journalism, and was a much-loved but little-listened-to public scold, frequently honoured in Canada and abroad for his lectures, called "chalk talks," and books. Selections from *A Caricature History of Canadian Politics* (1886) were reprinted in 1974.

DOUG FETHERLING

Bengough, Percy, labour leader (b at London, Eng 1883; d at Vancouver 10 Aug 1972). Bengough came to Canada in 1905, worked at his trade as a machinist and joined the Amalgamated Soc of Engineers. In 1916 he joined the International Assn of Machinists and held many offices in that union. From 1921 to 1942 he was secretary of the Vancouver Trades and Labor Council. He was elected VP of the TRADES AND LABOR CONGRESS in 1931 and president between 1943 and 1954. He actively supported the merger with the Canadian Congress of Labour to create the CANADIAN LABOUR CONGRESS in 1956. In 1949 Bengough helped found the International Confederation of Free Trade Unions and served on its executive board. During the war he served on several government advisory committees, for which he was awarded a CBE.

LAUREL SEFTON MACDOWELL

Bennett, Charles James Fox, merchant, politician, premier of Nfld 1870-74 (b at Shaftesbury, Eng 11 June 1793; d at St John's 5 Dec 1883). Bennett was one of the wealthiest merchants in mid-19th-century Newfoundland. Besides involvement in the fish trade, he started a brewery, a distillery, a foundry and a shipbuilding yard. He commissioned extensive mineral surveys along the coasts, and in the 1860s developed the prosperous copper mine at Tilt Cove (Notre Dame Bay). Bennett was also an important leader of the anticonfederate party in the late 1860s. He was largely responsible for the overwhelmingly successful campaign mounted against the confederates (led by Frederick B.T. CARTER) in 1869. The anticonfederate government of 1870 to 1874 managed the colony's affairs with reasonable efficiency, but the premier could not maintain party unity. Bennett's resignation in Jan 1874 ended his effective political career, although he remained an MLA until 1878.

J.K. HILLER

Bennett, Richard Bedford, Viscount, businessman, lawyer, politician, prime minister (b at Hopewell Hill, NB 3 July 1870; d at Mickleham, Eng 26 June 1947). He led the Conservative Party, 1927-38, and was prime minister of Canada, 7 Aug 1930 to 23 Oct 1935. After graduating from Dalhousie in 1893, Bennett went to Calgary and became the law partner of Senator James A. LOUGHEED. In 1898 he won election as a Conservative to the Assembly of the North-West Territories, but failed in bids to enter federal politics in 1900 and the new Alberta legislature in 1905. Through his associations with Lougheed and Max AITKEN, Bennett prospered, and by 1909, when he was elected in Alberta, he was financially independent. In 1911 he went to Ottawa as the Conservative member for Calgary E. He became discouraged when PM Borden did not appoint him to the Cabinet and, expecting to be appointed to the Senate, he did not stand for re-election in 1917. In 1921 Arthur MEIGHEN, who disliked Bennett but respected his influence, named him minister of justice. Bennett was defeated in the 1921 general election, but won in 1925 in Calgary W. In Meighen's brief 1926 government he was minister of finance.

In 1927 Bennett gained the Conservative leadership at the party's first convention. An excellent parliamentary debater, he strengthened the party, but it was the GREAT DEPRESSION which assured victory in the 1930 election. He promised aggressive action to combat the Depression, but once in office found it difficult to develop a coherent program. His business instincts did not serve his political interests. His major initiative, to persuade the British Empire to adopt preferential tariffs, brought some economic relief to Canada but not enough. His establishment of relief camps for single men lost him much popularity. By 1933, the nadir of the Depression, he seemed indecisive and ineffective. He became the butt of endless jokes. Cars towed by horses because owners could not afford gasoline were dubbed "Bennett buggies." In 1934 he was increasingly isolated and faced major dissent both in the party and the country. Early in 1935 he dramatically announced that he supported "government control and regulation." He called for progressive taxation, unemployment insurance, health insurance, and other major social reforms. Unfortunately for Bennett, Canadians did not find his New Deal as convincing as Americans found Roosevelt's. In Oct 1935 Mackenzie KING's Liberals swept the Conservatives out of office.

Bennett continued ineffectively as opposition leader until 1938, when he bitterly abandoned Canada and bought an estate in Surrey, Eng. His British friends, notably Aitken (Lord Beaverbrook), secured a viscountcy for him in 1941. He never forgave Canada for failing him, and, in ignoring his career, Canadians, it seems, have not forgiven Bennett. *See also* BENNETT'S NEW DEAL.

JOHN ENGLISH

Bennett, William Andrew Cecil, merchant, politician (b at Hastings, NB 6 Sept 1900; d at Kelowna, BC 23 Feb 1979), premier of BC 1952-72, a period of unparalleled economic expansion. Educated in NB schools, in 1930 he bought a Kelowna hardware store which became successful. He was elected Conservative MLA for Okanagan in 1941, sitting as a Coalition backbencher and serving on the Post-War Rehabilitation Council. He crossed the floor in 1951 and sat as an independent, but was re-elected as a SOCIAL CREDIT candidate in the confused June 1952 provincial election and was subsequently chosen caucus leader. The lieutenant-governor called him to form a government 1 Aug 1952.

During 2 decades of prosperity, Bennett's administration took credit for the construction and improvement of highways, the northern extensions of the Pacific Great Eastern Ry and major hydroelectric projects on the Peace and Columbia rivers. Although Bennett espoused free enterprise, he expropriated the province's largest privately owned hydroelectric firm in 1961; took over the Black Ball ferry line and created the BC Ferry Corp in 1958; and attempted to establish the BANK OF BRITISH COLUMBIA with 25% provincial ownership.

From 1953 on, Bennett acted as his own finance minister. Following a "pay as you go" policy that closely watched spending and transferred debts or "contingent liabilities" to agencies such as the Toll Highway and Bridge Authority, Bennett claimed in 1959 that the province was debt free. His administration curbed the power of labour unions, limited social-welfare spending, kept the civil service trim but expanded post-secondary educational facilities. Bennett proclaimed himself a Canadian but had prolonged disputes with the federal government over the COLUMBIA RIVER TREATY, tax sharing and constitutional reform.

In Aug 1972, BC elected an NDP government under David BARRETT. Subsequently, Bennett resigned as MLA and leader of the Social Credit Party and was succeeded by his son, William Richards BENNETT.

PATRICIA E. ROY

Bennett, William John, businessman (b at Schreiber, Ont 3 Nov 1911). A graduate of U of T Bennett became private secretary to C.D. HOWE in 1935 and served as Howe's executive assistant in the Dept of Munitions and Supply during WWII. In 1946 Bennett was appointed VP and general manager of Eldorado Mining and Refining Ltd, a crown corporation responsible for producing uranium. Under Bennett, Eldorado brought its Beaverlodge uranium-ore deposit into production in 1953. As president of both Eldorado and Atomic Energy of Canada Ltd in the 1950s, Bennett directed the development of Canada's NUCLEAR ENERGY industry. He retired from Eldorado and AECL in 1958, becoming VP of the Iron Ore Co in 1960 and president in 1965. He retired in 1977.

J. LINDSEY

Bennett, William Richards, businessman, politician, premier of BC (b at Kelowna, BC 14 Apr 1932), son of W.A.C. BENNETT. After leaving high school, Bennett devoted his efforts to a career in business and with his brother made a success of various real-estate and other speculative ventures. In 1973 he sought and won the SOCIAL CREDIT nomination in the Okanagan South seat left vacant by his father's resignation and shortly after became leader of the party and leader of the opposition. He was able to rebuild the party membership and provided a rallying point for opposition to David BARRETT's NDP government. His party was returned to power late in 1975 and he became premier. He did not enjoy an easy time in office. Before 1983 his government was marred by minor scandals and suggestions that some of his leading ministers were actually in control. In recent years it has been plagued by a stagnant economy. After the May 1983 election, in which Social Credit increased its majority, Bennett responded to the economic situation and rising unemployment by attempting to cut government payroll and by encouraging large scale development projects such as coal mining in the province's northeast, a rapid transit system in Vancouver and a world's fair in Vancouver — EXPO 86. The controversial restraint program was met by large-scale demonstrations mounted by the SOLIDARITY Coalition of trade unions and community organizations. In compromise, late in 1983, the government abandoned a number of the more far-reaching proposals introduced in that summer's budget but continued to reduce public-sector funding, which in turn continued to provoke hostility to government action from many groups. In May 1986, shortly after opening Expo 86, Bennett announced his retirement as premier and was succeeded by William VANDER ZALM in early August.

J.T. MORLEY

Bennett's New Deal In the mid-1930s, at the height of the GREAT DEPRESSION, Prime Minister R.B. BENNETT's political demise seemed inevitable. Seeking to reverse the tide running against his Conservative Party, on 2 Jan 1935 he began a series of live radio speeches outlining a "New Deal" for Canada. It promised a more progressive taxation system, a maximum work week, a minimum wage, closer regulation of working conditions, unemployment insurance, health and accident insurance, a revised old-age pension and agricultural support programs. Nevertheless, Bennett lost the Oct 1935 general election, and in Jan 1937 the JUDICIAL COMMITTEE OF THE PRIVY COUNCIL declared most of the "New Deal" ULTRA VIRES.

JOHN ENGLISH

Benoît, Jacques, writer (b at Lacolle, Qué 1941). In 1967 Benoît published *Jos Carbone*, a short narrative, blending violence with the fantastic, which won the Québec Literary Competition in 1968. Encouraged by this success, Benoît published in rapid succession *Les Voleurs* (1969), *Patience et Firlipon* (1970) and *Les Princes* (1973). He then turned to scriptwriting and produced *La Maudite Galette*, *Réjeanne Padovani* (co-writer; both directed by Denys ARCAND) and *L'Affaire Coffin*. As a journalist with *La* PRESSE, Benoît won the 1976 Judith Jasmin Award for a series of articles entitled "Il était une fois dans l'est" ("Once upon a time in the East"). In 1981 Benoît published *Gisèle et le serpent*, which established him as an undisputed master of the fantasy novel.

ANDRÉ VANASSE

Benoît, Jean, surrealist artist (b at Québec C 1922). He studied at the École des beaux-arts in Montréal where he taught for a time. He became involved in the 1945 "cadavres exquis" experiments with Léon BELLEFLEUR, Albert DUMOUCHEL, Jean Léonard, Mimi Parent and Alfred PELLAN, and in 1948 signed the free-art "Prisme d'yeux" manifesto using the pseudonym "Je Anonyme." He later settled in Paris with Mimi Parent. Benoît became famous for his costume-sculptures, in particular one designed for the 1959 surrealist ceremony, "Executing the Will of the Marquis de Sade." Parts of this costume were exhibited at the 8th international surrealist exhibition held that year. In 1963, he published sketches of costumes for Fernando Arrabal's play *Le Communion solennelle*, in the surrealist review *La Brèche*. One of these costumes, "Le Nécrophile," was created for "L'Écart absolu" exhibition in 1966. His work has been praised on numerous occasions by writer André Breton. The manuscript of *Les Champs magnétiques*, the first surrealist text, written by Breton and Philippe Soupault, is kept in one of Benoît's "objects," a sculptured casket.

ANDRÉ G. BOURASSA

Benoît, Jehane, née Patenaude, food consultant, author, TV and radio commentator (b at Montréal 21 Mar 1904; d at Sutton, Qué 24 Nov 1987). Through her books and TV appearances on CBC's Take 30, Madame Benoit was a pioneer in explaining Canadian CUISINE to Canadians. She studied at the Cordon Bleu in Paris and graduated as a food chemist from the Sorbonne, 1925. In Montréal, she began an English/French cooking school, Fumet de la Vieille France, attracting 8000 students over 4 years. From 1935 to 1940 she operated The Salad Bar, one of the earliest Canadian restaurants to concentrate on vegetarian cuisine. Her 30 books, many of them bestsellers, delineate Canadian and Québécois cooking, and she was an early proponent of microwave cooking with the publication of *Madame Benoit's Microwave Cook Book* (1975). In 1985, she embarked on a 6-volume *Encyclopedia of Microwave Cooking*. In 1973, she was made an Officer of the Order of Canada.

GORDON MORASH

Benson, Clara Cynthia, professor of chemistry (b at Port Hope, Ont 1875; d there 24 Mar 1964). Associated with U of T for 50 years, she was the first woman to graduate in chemistry (1899), optimistic that there would be many openings for women selecting this area. She became one of the first 2 women awarded a PhD at Toronto (1903). Appointed science instructor in the Lillian Massey School of Household Science, she assisted her colleagues in their struggle for academic recognition of this area. A capable teacher, stimulator of research and friend of her students, Benson served as professor and head of the Dept of Food Chemistry, Faculty of Household Science 1926-45. She was honoured by a scholarship in her name. The Benson Building at U of T was named in recognition of her efforts to obtain better athletic facilities for women students.

PATRICIA H. COLEMAN

Bentley, Maxwell Herbert Lloyd, Max, hockey player (b at Delisle, Sask 1 Mar 1920; d at Saskatoon 19 Jan 1984). He played senior hockey at Drumheller, Alta, and Saskatoon and turned professional with Chicago, where he played 5 years as centre of the "Pony Line," with brother Doug on left wing and Bill Mosienko on right. He was traded for 5 players to Toronto in 1947, after winning the scoring title the previous 2 years. He played 6 years for TORONTO MAPLE LEAFS and one for New York Rangers. Bentley was a masterly stickhandler and a quick, darting skater – one of the most skilled players of his era. He retired to operate the family wheat farm in 1954. He scored 245 goals and 544 points in 646 games, and 18 goals, 45 points in 52 playoff games.   JAMES MARSH

Beny, Roloff, photographer (b Wilfred Roy at Medicine Hat, Alta 7 Jan 1924; d at Rome, Italy 16 Mar 1984). Beny took up photography as a child. He also painted and had a watercolour show at age 15. After studying fine arts at U of T and State U of Iowa, he concentrated on painting and printmaking. In the mid-1950s, however, he turned to photography, having his first show in 1955 in London, Eng. After that Beny had many exhibitions and produced over a dozen lavishly illustrated books based on his travels, including *To Everything There Is a Season: Roloff Beny in Canada; Japan in Colour; India; Odyssey: Mirror of the Mediterranean;* and *Forty Countries in Forty Years.* His honours included the gold medal at the 1968 Leipzig International Book Fair. He made his home in Rome for many years.   LOUISE ABBOTT

Beothuk ("the people" or "true people") were the now-extinct inhabitants of Newfoundland. Word lists, transcribed in the 18th or early 19th centuries, have been thought by some to indicate an Algonquian linguistic affiliation; others argue that the language cannot be proven to be related to any native N American language family. At the time of European contact the Beothuk occupied at least the S and NE coasts of Newfoundland. They may have numbered no more than 500 to 1000; their population is difficult to estimate owing to a contraction in their territories in the early contact period and in the absence of surviving documentation.

Archaeological evidence suggests that the Beothuk inhabited Newfoundland long before European colonization and that they may be descended from earlier people who occupied the Island for several thousand years. In prehistoric times, they seem to have been primarily a coastal people organized in small bands throughout the various bays to fish and hunt seals, other sea mammals and birds. They also may have visited interior locations to take caribou at river crossings, but the pattern of a winter-long interior occupation does not seem to have occurred until postcontact times. In both the prehistoric and historic periods the Beothuk dwelt in bark- or skin-covered tents in summer and in semisubterranean houses during the cold months. Bows and arrows, harpoons and spears were used in hunting, which often took place from seaworthy bark canoes with a high prow and stern, and a sheer which rose markedly amidships. However, the most distinctive of Beothuk artifacts are carved bone, antler and ivory pendants intricately decorated with incised patterns. Many of these items were recovered from grave sites in caves or rock shelters in the late 19th and early 20th centuries. Another notable feature of Beothuk culture was the people's lavish use of powdered hematite, or red ochre, with which they

The Woolsey Family (1808-09) by William Berczy; oil on canvas. A masterpiece of early Canadian painting, it is also a valuable representation of the family values and dress of early Canada (*courtesy National Gallery of Canada/ Gift of Major Edgar C. Woolsey, 1952*).

painted their canoes, other artifacts and even their bodies. Since these people were the first N American aborigines encountered by Europeans, it is possible that their custom of using red ochre was responsible for the sobriquet "Red Indians," which was later applied to all native peoples on this continent. As a result of European encroachment, slaughter and diseases to which they had no natural resistance, the Beothuk's numbers diminished rapidly following contact. The last known surviving Beothuk, SHAWNANDITHIT, died of tuberculosis in St John's in June 1829.

JAMES A. TUCK

Reading: J.P. Howley, *The Beothuks or Red Indians* (1915); F.W. Rowe, *Extinction: The Beothuks of Newfoundland* (1977).

Berczy, William, painter, architect, colonizer (b Johann Albrecht Ulrich Moll in Wallerstein [Germany] and bap 10 Dec 1744; d at New York C 5 Feb 1813). He spent his youth in Vienna, studied in Italy and worked in England before leading a group of colonists to New York state in 1792 and, in 1794, to Markham, UC. Thereafter he considered himself a Canadian and, from 1805, relied exclusively on painting for his living, first in York [Toronto] and later in Montréal. He became a popular portraitist, and also did some church decoration and architectural work, including the design of Christ Church in Montréal in 1803. He is best known for 2 portraits in oil: the dramatic full-length portrait of Joseph BRANT (c1805) in colourful costume, and the group portrait *The Woolsey Family* (1808-09), remarkable for composition and architectural detailing and regarded as one of the masterpieces of early Canadian art.

ROSEMARY SHIPTON

Beresford, NB, Town, inc 1984, pop 3826 (1986c), located 9 km north of Bathurst on the Bay of Chaleur, had been incorporated as a village in 1967. It was settled after 1812 and was named for William Carr Beresford, a general in Wellington's army at the Battle of Waterloo. During the late 19th and early 20th centuries it was the site of several sawmills, but today it is primarily a residential community with local service industries.

Most of the work force is employed in mining and forestry or the paper mill in nearby Bathurst. It is located on a good beach and has a large summer community.   BURTON GLENDENNING

Beresford-Howe, Constance, novelist (b at Montréal 10 Nov 1922). The author of 7 novels and various magazine pieces, Beresford-Howe was educated at McGill (BA, 1945, MA, 1946) and at Brown U (PhD, 1965). While a member of the McGill department of English (1949-71), she wrote 4 novels exploring the emotional lives of young women: *The Unreasoning Heart* (1946); *Of This Day's Journey* (1947); *The Invisible Gate* (1949); and *My Lady Greensleeves* (1955). In 1971 Beresford-Howe moved to Toronto, where she has taught English at Ryerson Polytechnical Inst. Four more novels have been published: *The Book of Eve* (1973), *A Population of One* (1977), *The Marriage Bed* (1981) and *Night Studies* (1985). These novels concern the daily lives of contemporary women. *Eve,* a stage adaptation by Larry Fineberg of *The Book of Eve,* premiered at the STRATFORD FESTIVAL 14 July 1976.   JEAN WILSON

Berger, Thomas Rodney, lawyer, judge, humanitarian (b at Victoria 23 Mar 1933). Berger practised law in Vancouver 1957-71. He was NEW DEMOCRATIC PARTY MP for Vancouver-Burrard 1962-63 and MLA and leader of the BC NDP 1966-69. From 1971 to 1983 he served as justice of the Supreme Court of BC, and from 1974 to 1977 as commissioner of the MACKENZIE VALLEY PIPELINE Inquiry. His report, *Northern Frontier, Northern Homeland* (1977), recommended eloquently against a pipeline across the northern Yukon and for a 10-year moratorium on pipeline construction in the Mackenzie Valley to permit prior settlement of native LAND CLAIMS. Berger's 1981 criticism of the federal-provincial constitutional accord for its removal of aboriginal rights and of the Québec veto resulted in 1982 in formal criticism of his "indiscretion" by the Canadian Judicial Council.

In April of 1983 Berger resigned in disagreement with the council's view that judges should not comment on matters of great public concern. From 1983 to 1985 he was head of the Alaska Native Review Commission, a 2-year inquiry sponsored by the Inuit Circumpolar Conference into the effects of the 1971 Alaska Native Claims Settlement Act.   DENIS SMITH

Reading: T.R. Berger, *Fragile Freedoms* (1982); C. Swayze, *Hard Choices: A Life of Tom Berger* (1987).

Bering, Vitus Jonassen, explorer (b at Horsens, Denmark 1680; d on Bering Island 8 Dec 1741). An officer in the Russian navy, Bering was appointed in 1725 by Peter the Great to explore the Siberian coast. After 3 years' delay, Bering sailed from Okhotsk and passed through Bering Str, proving that Asia and America were not joined. On a subsequent expedition in 1741 he sailed from Siberia eastward into the Gulf of Alaska and was the first navigator to sight mainland Alaska. On the return voyage his ship was delayed by storms and had to put in at Bering I, where he died of scurvy. DANIEL FRANCIS

Bering Sea Dispute During the 1880s, while Americans hunted seals on the Pribilof Is, which the US had acquired from Russia in 1867, Canadians conducted SEALING in the open waters. In 1886 US government revenue cutters, claiming to protect "American property," began seizing Canadian sealing vessels. An international tribunal in 1893 upheld the Canadian right to hunt seals in international waters, but imposed certain restrictions. In 1911 an international conference banned pelagic sealing in the Bering Sea but provided handsome compensation to Canada.

N.F. DREISZIGER

Beringia is a landmass including portions of 3 modern nations (Canada, US and USSR) and extending from the Siberian Kolyma R and Kamchatka Pen, through Alaska and YT, to the Mackenzie R in the NWT. Near the centre of the region is Bering Str for which it was named. Today, this strait links the Arctic and Pacific oceans, but in the past lowered sea levels, resulting in part from growth of continental glaciers, exposed portions of the continental shelves to form a broad land bridge between northeast Asia and northwest N America. The importance of Beringia is twofold: it provided a pathway for intercontinental exchanges of plants and animals during glacial periods and for interoceanic exchanges during interglacials; it has been a centre of EVOLUTION and has supported apparently unique plant and animal communities. The history of Beringia is important not only in the evolution of landscapes but also in that of plants and animals.

Beringia is a land of great beauty with the highest mountains in N America overlooking broad plateaus and meandering rivers. It extends from frozen arctic coasts on the N to Pacific coasts warmed by the Japanese Current on the S. The temperatures range from some of the coldest on the Earth in winter to uncomfortably warm in summer. Twenty-four-hour summer days contrast with long periods of winter darkness. Because of its aridity, much of Beringia remained unglaciated during the ice ages. The stratigraphy of long sequences of nonglacial sediment exposed at various sites can be correlated with alpine and continental glacial advances elsewhere. FOSSILS from such sediments are often exceptionally abundant and well preserved. They include pollen grains, plant fossils, invertebrates and vertebrate bones. Studies of fossils and of the sediments in which they occur have permitted tentative reconstructions of paleo-environments in western and eastern Beringia.

Beringia is of special importance in the study of human PREHISTORY since it is most likely the area through which man first entered the Western Hemisphere, presumably following the migrations of large MAMMALS, known from fossil evidence to have roamed eastward across the Bering Land Bridge. Portions of western Beringia (now eastern Siberia) may have been occupied by humans as early as 35 000 years ago. Artifacts of comparable age have been tentatively identified in eastern Beringia on the basis of broken and butchered mammal bones, but the oldest secure evidence of human occupation in Alaska or YT dates to the period 20 000-25 000 years ago. Permanent settlement of Beringia depended upon the invention and perfection of a complex array of cultural and technological skills. Tailored skin clothing, secure dwellings, control of fire, special methods of food procurement and storage and possibly some form of watercraft to cross large, cold-water bodies were prerequisites of human life in these latitudes. Some writers have suggested that the ancient colonization of Beringia represented a technological achievement equivalent to the penetration of such environments as Antarctica, the deep sea and the moon.

RICHARD E. MORLAN

Berkeley, Edith, née Dunington, biologist (b at Tulbagh, S Africa 6 Sept 1875; d at Nanaimo, BC

25 Feb 1963) and **Cyril**, chemist (b at London, Eng 2 Dec 1878; d at Nanaimo, BC, 25 Aug 1973). Edith and Cyril met as undergraduates at London U, married in 1902, and went to Bihar, India, where Cyril studied the culture and processing of indigo. Moving in 1914 to BC, they farmed for 2 years near Vernon; both taught at the new UBC, and in 1919 settled at the Nanaimo Biological Station. Following her lead, they became world authorities on the classification of marine polychaete worms and deeply respected members of the station's scientific community. In recognition of their achievements Cyril was granted an LLD by U of Victoria in 1968. Both were enthusiastic gardeners, collecting rhododendron species and developing new species of irises.

A.W.H. NEEDLER

Berkinshaw, Richard Coulton, company executive (b at Toronto 2 Sept 1891; d there 4 May 1970). Berkinshaw attended Upper Canada College, U of T and Osgoode Hall. After serving in WWI he practised corporate law with a Toronto firm until 1920, when he joined the Goodyear Tire and Rubber Co of Canada. He became general manager and treasurer in 1933. He played a major role in Canada's industrial mobilization during WWII as chairman of the Wartime Industries Control Board, president of Polymer Corp and director general of the Priorities Branch of the Department of MUNITIONS AND SUPPLY. He was created a CBE in 1946. Berkinshaw returned to Goodyear 1945, becoming president 1952 and chairman 1959. He was chancellor of Trinity College, Toronto, and president of the CANADIAN NATIONAL EXHIBITION, the Queen Elizabeth Hospital and the Toronto Board of Trade. J. LINDSEY

Bernardi, Mario, conductor (b at Kirkland Lake, Ont 20 Aug 1930). Considered the leading Canadian-born conductor of his generation, Bernardi has appeared widely in Canada and abroad. A career as pianist and accompanist, begun after study in Italy and Toronto, gradually gave way to conducting, following his CANADIAN OPERA CO debut in 1957. He conducted opera extensively in Canada before becoming a musical director of the Sadler's Wells Opera Co in London (1966-68). First conductor of the National Arts Centre Orchestra, formed in Ottawa (1968), Bernardi created a disciplined, finely balanced ensemble, internationally praised for sensitive playing and transparent sound. Leaving Ottawa in 1982, he became conductor of the CBC Vancouver Orchestra in 1983 and has been the music director of the Calgary Philharmonic Orchestra since 1984. He was named a Companion of the Order of Canada in 1972. BARCLAY McMILLAN

Bernier, Joseph-Elzéar, arctic mariner (b at L'Islet, Qué 1 Jan 1852; d at Lévis, Qué 26 Dec 1934). Captain of the government steamship *Arctic*, Bernier led seagoing expeditions into the Arctic between 1904 and 1911, certifying Canada's claim to the northern archipelago. Bernier left school at age 14 to sail as a cabin boy on his father's ship. Three years later he was captain of his own ship carrying timber from Québec to England. For 25 years he commanded sailing vessels all over the world. In 1895 Bernier became governor of the Québec jail, a position which gave him leisure to pursue his interest in polar navigation. He devised a plan for reaching the N Pole, a feat not yet accomplished, but at the last moment in 1904 he and his ship *Arctic* were pressed into government service patrolling the eastern Arctic. On annual cruises Bernier explored the archipelago and collected customs duties from whalers and traders. In July 1909 he unveiled a plaque on Melville I which officially claimed the Arctic Islands for Canada. After 1911 Bernier carried on

BERINGIA

▨ Extent of land exposed by lowered sea levels

Bernier commanded sailing ships all over the world. In 1904 he and his vessel *Arctic* (shown here leaving Québec City) were pressed into service to patrol the eastern Arctic (*courtesy National Archives of Canada/PA-133369, photo by E. Livernois*).

private trading on Baffin I and during WWI he commanded an Atlantic convoy ship. After the war he returned to the arctic patrol, retiring in 1925. During his career Bernier commanded over 100 ships, crossing the Atlantic 269 times. He knew more about navigating the difficult arctic waters than any contemporary mariner. His 3 *Reports on the Dominion Government Expeditions to the Arctic Islands and Hudson Strait, 1906-1910 (1910-11)* are classics of Canadian arctic literature.

DANIEL FRANCIS

Bernier, Sylvie, diver (b at Québec C 31 Jan 1964). She won a silver medal in the 3 m springboard DIVING event at the 1982 COMMONWEALTH GAMES in Brisbane, Australia (478.83 points), a bronze at the 1983 WORLD UNIVERSITY GAMES (462.48 points) and a bronze at the 1983 PAN-AMERICAN GAMES (473.97 points). She finished first at the Ft Lauderdale International (506.52 points) in May 1984 and continued her rapid improvement to win a gold medal in the 3 m springboard diving event (530.70 points) at the 1984 Los Angeles Olympics – Canada's first gold medal in Olympic diving, and the first Olympic gold medal for a female athlete from Québec. In Dec 1984 she announced her retirement from competitive diving. JAMES MARSH

Bernstein, Harold Joseph, physical chemist (b at Toronto 26 Aug 1914). After graduating (PhD) from U of T (1938), he moved to U of Copenhagen on a scholarship. Picked up by the Nazi invaders of Denmark 1940, he underwent the devastating experience of a 5-year internment in Germany. After the war he joined the NATIONAL RESEARCH COUNCIL in Ottawa 1946, established a molecular SPECTROSCOPY section, opened up a study of nuclear magnetic resonance – with W.G. SCHNEIDER and J.A. Pople he wrote an important text, *High Resolution Nuclear Magnetic Resonance* (1959) – and pioneered a new field called resonance Raman spectroscopy. His long career brought international recognition and many honours and awards have accrued to him. He retired in 1978.

N.T. GRIDGEMAN

Berries, Cultivated The most important small or soft FRUITS produced in Canada are strawberries (*Fragaria ananassa*), red raspberries (*Rubus idaeus*), highbush and lowbush blueberries (*Vaccinium corymbosum* and *V. angustifolium,* respectively) and cranberry (*V. macrocarpon*). Blackberries (various *Rubus* species), also an important N American soft fruit, are not produced commercially in Canada. Within Canada, southwestern BC is the most important production region for all berries except lowbush blueberries.

Strawberries are an important crop in Ontario, Québec and the Maritime provinces, and are produced in localized areas outside urban centres in the Prairie provinces. In recent years, red raspberry production has increased dramatically in BC (making it the leading producing area in the world) but has declined in eastern Canada. Production of highbush blueberries has increased in BC and has remained stable in localized areas of Ontario, Québec and the Maritimes. Lowbush blueberry production, which is restricted almost entirely to the Maritimes, has increased.

Strawberries and red raspberries perform best on fertile, well-drained soils. On heavier soils, growth of both crops can be seriously impaired by root rots. Highbush blueberries flourish on acid soils high in organic matter. Lowbush blueberries do best on acid soils, usually of moderate to low fertility, eg, abandoned or run-out farmland. Cranberries thrive on acid soils in marsh or bog conditions. All the small fruit crops are considered to be perennial; however, some strawberry plantations are replaced every other year, especially where there are disease or insect problems. Plantations of the other crops can continue to produce for 25 or more years. Each of the crops is self-fruitful; however, more and larger fruits are produced by cross-pollination. Thus, there must be enough bees to ensure pollen movement within plantations. Strawberries are harvested by hand. Machine harvesting by various types of shaking mechanisms is common in red raspberries and highbush blueberries. All cranberries are harvested by machines that rake or beat the berries from the vines. Lowbush blueberries are harvested by hand-operated rakes.

Strawberries are grown under one of 2 cultural systems. In the hill-row system, all runner plants are removed; fruit production is entirely from the original mother plants, which are spaced 30-35 cm apart in rows 2.7-3 m apart. In the matted-row system, predetermined numbers of runner plants are allowed to root; thus, both mother and runner plants produce fruit. The original plants are spaced 50-75 cm apart in rows 2.7-3 m apart. Fruit from hill rows usually is larger and goes to fresh-market outlets; the smaller fruit from matted rows goes to processing market outlets.

Red Raspberry plants, which are usually planted in early spring as one-year-old dormant canes, are spaced 75 cm apart in rows 3 m apart. In established plantations as many as 12 canes are left per plant or stool. The spent fruiting canes are removed in winter. In early spring, the current year's fruiting canes are pruned to 1.5 m.

Blueberries Highbush blueberries are spaced 1.5-1.8 m apart in rows 3 m apart. Annual pruning, which removes the older wood and weaker canes, is done in winter. Since most lowbush blueberry plantations are developed from natural stands, there are no spacing recommendations. Pruning is done in late fall or early spring by burning with oil-, propane- or straw-fueled fires.

Cranberries are grown from 7-10 cm long vines and are planted at a rate of 1700-2200 kg/ha. Pruning is not required.

Insects and Diseases

All small fruit crops are attacked by insects and various disease-causing organisms. Strawberries and red raspberries are particularly susceptible to both preharvest and postharvest fruit-rotting FUNGI, which can be at least partially controlled by a combination of chemical sprays and genetic resistance in the plants. Virus diseases, which are transmitted by APHIDS, can seriously affect strawberry production. Some culti-

vars (commercial varieties) are more resistant than others and this resistance, combined with chemical control of aphids, can help to prevent spread of the viruses. Viruses also can affect red raspberry production but resistance has been relatively successful in controlling them. Root problems in both crops can be caused by insects and NEMATODES as well as by fungi. Fungi often are controlled by improving soil drainage and thus increasing aeration in the root region. Insects and nematodes, which attack the roots, usually are controlled by chemical PESTICIDES applied as fumigants or drenches.

Serious fungal diseases of blueberry and cranberry are mummyberry and cottonberry, respectively. In both, infected fruits contain a white cottonball-like mass of fungi mycelia surrounding the seeds. Control is either by chemicals or by sanitary methods, ie, destruction of infected fruits. Blueberries usually are not seriously affected by INSECT PESTS. Insects can be serious pests on cranberries; however, most can be controlled by cultural methods that involve flooding the bogs. In recent years, the high cost of hand labour has made it necessary to use chemical methods of WEED control in all of the crops. Recommendations vary for crop and location.

Prospects

The future of small fruit production seems to be assured in Canada because of a number of interrelated factors including development of more efficient, labour-saving cultural practices (eg, machine harvesting, improved training methods); new products (eg, yogurt, juice); and alternative marketing systems (eg, "U-pick" operations, farmers' markets). Increased production has been stimulated by the desire for more self-sufficiency in fruit production and by the knowledge that small fruit products can be satisfactory nutritional substitutes for products derived from imported fruit. More self-sufficiency means greater need for stable production in recognized and marginal production regions. The demand for increased production should stimulate CROP RESEARCH efforts in all aspects of small fruit culture. HUGH A. DAUBENY

Berries, Wild Over 200 species of small, fleshy, wild FRUITS occur in Canada. Most people consider them all "berries" but, technically, they are classed in different categories, including drupes (eg, cherries, elderberries), pomes (eg, saskatoon berries), true berries (eg, gooseberries, blueberries) and aggregate fruits (eg, raspberries, strawberries). Here "berry" is used in its less technical connotation. Some berries are poisonous; some are of doubtful edibility or unpalatable. No rules exist for distinguishing poisonous from edible types. People wishing to harvest wild berries must familiarize themselves with species in their area and learn how to prepare them. Almost all edible species in Canada were used by native peoples. Many were dried or preserved in water or oil for off-season use. They added variety and, because many were rich in vitamins and minerals, played a vital nutritional role in the traditional diet. European settlers also valued wild berries, using them for desserts, confections, preserves, juices and wines. Canadians still enjoy using them, often preferring their flavour to that of commercial types. The following are favourite Canadian wild berries.

Blackberries (genus *Rubus*, rose family, Rosaceae); over 12 species occur in woods and clearings, mainly in eastern provinces and southern BC. They are choice fruits, raw or cooked, making excellent pies, jams, jellies and wines.

Blueberries, Bilberries, Huckleberries (genus *Vaccinium,* heath family, Ericaceae); some 18

Wild berries found in Canada, clockwise from top left: blueberry (*Vaccinium myrtilloides*), garden gooseberry (*Ribes grossularia*), red raspberry (*Rubus strigosus*), highbush cranberry (*Viburnum trilobum*), buffaloberry (*Shepherdia canadensis*), Saskatoon berry (*Amelanchier alnifolia*), chokecherry (*Prunus virginiana*) and strawberry (*Fragaria vesca*) (*artwork by Claire Tremblay*).

species, including bog cranberries (discussed separately), occur in Canada. All are shrubs, with edible fruits which vary in colour from red through blue to black. Cultivated varieties have been developed from wild species.

Buffaloberries (genus *Shepherdia*, oleaster family, Elaeagnaceae); silver buffaloberry (*S. argentea*) and russet buffaloberry or soapberry (*S. canadensis*) are deciduous shrubs with small, reddish orange fruits. In Canada, the former grows mainly on the prairies, the latter from coast to coast. Fruits are bitter but good in jelly; those of *S. argentea* were used by Indians to flavour buffalo meat. BC Indians whip soapberries with water to make a favourite confection.

Chokecherries (*Prunus virginiana*, rose family, Rosaceae), shrubs or small trees, which occur across southern Canada, northwards to the YT. Fruits, ranging from red to black, grow in long clusters. They have large stones and can be astringent, but are excellent in jellies, juices or syrups. Six other species of *Prunus* (4 cherries and 2 plums) are native.

Cranberries (genus *Vaccinium*, heath family, Ericaceae), low, vinelike perennials growing in muskeg and peat bogs. Three or 4 closely related species are identified, one of which is the forerunner of the cultivated cranberry. Berries are tart but good in sauces and desserts. Lowbush cranberry (*V. vitis-idaea*) is related, but has smaller, clustered berries. Highbush cranberries (*Viburnum opulus*, honeysuckle family, Caprifoliaceae) are tall shrubs with tart, clustered fruits.

Currants (genus *Ribes*, Saxifragaceae family, gooseberry subfamily, Grossularioideae); some 14 species are found in Canada, most of which resemble garden varieties and are used similarly. Fruits range from red to bluish to black. Currants lack spines or prickles and are thus distinguished from gooseberries.

Gooseberries (genus *Ribes*, Saxifragaceae family, gooseberry subfamily, Grossularioideae), spiny or prickly shrubs related to currants. Gooseberries occur almost everywhere in Canada except the Far North. At least 12 species are found. The reddish to dark purple berries are tart and, like their cultivated relatives, are best in jellies and preserves.

Raspberries (*Rubus idaeus* or *strigosus*, rose family, Rosaceae); found in woods and clearings from Newfoundland to BC and in northern territories, wild raspberry was used to develop cultivated varieties. Relatives of raspberry include black raspberry (*R. occidentalis*), blackcap (*R. occidentalis leucodermis*), cloudberry (*R. chamaemorus*), arctic raspberry (*R. arcticus*), thimbleberry (*R. odoratus*, *R. parviflorus*) and salmonberry (*R. spectabilis*).

Salal (*Gaultheria shallon*, heath family, Ericaceae), an evergreen shrub, restricted mainly to coastal BC. Salal has clustered berrylike fruits which, mashed and dried for winter storage, were, and still are, a major Northwest Coast Indian food. Four other species of *Gaultheria* occur in Canada.

Saskatoon berry (*Amelanchier alnifolia*, rose family, Rosaceae), a deciduous shrub that grows from western Ontario to BC and the YT. The city of Saskatoon takes its name from a Cree word for the sweet, fleshy fruits, which were of prime importance to Indians and early settlers. On the prairies, saskatoons were a major constituent of PEMMICAN. They are still enjoyed and plant breeders are developing varieties for commercial production. Some 15 related species, all with edible fruits, occur in Canada.

Strawberries (genus *Fragaria*, rose family, Rosaceae); 3 species are native to Canada, growing in woodlands, meadows, clearings and coast lines. All are herbaceous perennials with leaves in 3 parts, and they closely resemble domesticated strawberries, which were derived from 2 wild species. Despite their softness and small size, their delicate flavour makes wild strawberries a favourite. *See also* BERRIES, CULTIVATED; PLANTS, NATIVE USES. NANCY J. TURNER

Reading: Adam F. Szczawinski and Nancy J. Turner, *Edible Wild Fruits and Nuts of Canada* (1979).

Berthon, George Théodore, portrait painter (b at Vienna, Austria 3 May 1806; d at Toronto 18 Jan 1892). Son of René Théodore Berthon, court painter to Napoleon, George Berthon was a classical European portraitist, trained by his father and influenced by Jacques-Louis David. He worked in England 1827-40, where he taught one of Sir Robert Peel's daughters. Settling in Toronto *c*1841, he had a successful career doing formal portraits of Upper Canada's business and judicial establishment, now hanging in Osgoode Hall and Trinity Coll, Toronto, and the Senate Chamber, Ottawa. His masterpiece is considered the portrait of Chief Justice Sir John Beverley ROBINSON. ANNE McDOUGALL

Berton, Pierre, journalist, historian, media personality (b at Whitehorse, YT 12 July 1920). Berton is arguably Canada's best-known living writer and is particularly well regarded as a serious popularizer of Canadian history. He worked on the Vancouver *News-Herald* (beginning in 1942), the *Vancouver Sun* (1945-47), *Maclean's* (beginning in 1947) and on the Toronto *Star* (1958-62). Since the late 1950s he has been a staple of Canadian TV as host of his own shows or as a panellist. His first important book was *Klondike* (1958), a narrative of the KLONDIKE GOLD RUSH of 1898, an event in whose long shadow Berton had lived for years, being the son of a gold-seeker and having grown up in Dawson amid the debris of the stampede.

But for more than a decade following *Klondike*, Berton's name was represented with books drawn from his enterprising *Star* column and his interview programs and with such polemics as *The Comfortable Pew* (1965) and *The Smug Minority* (1968), which attacked the Anglican Church and the business-political axis, respectively. It was not until the 1970s that he attempted to pick up the serious thread of *Klondike* and resume work as a popular historian. His subject was the building of the CPR, as treated in *The National Dream* (1970) and *The Last Spike* the following year. The subject

was well suited to Berton's strengths: patriotic verve, the marshalling of colourful detail and above all a driving narrative.

The Dionne Years (1977) carried him nearer social history and a smaller canvas. In turning to the WAR OF 1812 in *The Invasion of Canada* (1980) and *Flames Across the Border* (1981) Berton again dealt with events large enough to contain his heroic vision of what the past should be, and the smell of gunpowder quickened his pace without often leading to narrative excesses. Other historical works have included *My Country* (1976) and *The Wild Frontier* (1978), collected sketches of characters and events. *Hollywood's Canada* (1975) examines the way Hollywood films misrepresented Canada. *Drifting Home* (1973) is an unexpected slice of autobiography in the form of an account of a northern rafting trip. More recently Berton has returned to the writing of popular history, with *The Promised Land* (1984), a history of the settling of the Canadian West, and his hugely successful *Vimy* (1986), an examination of the WWI battle in which the Canadian Corps took VIMY RIDGE in Apr 1917. In *Starting Out* (1987), he picked up the autobiographical thread again with a memoir that ends in 1947. Berton has received 3 Gov Gen's Awards, 11 honorary degrees and is a Companion of the Order of Canada.

Bertrand, Jean-Jacques, politician, premier of Québec 1968-70 (b at Ste-Agathe-des-Monts, Qué 20 June 1916; d at Montréal 22 Feb 1973). Elected UNION NATIONALE member for Missisquoi in 1948, and re-elected several times between 1952 and 1970, he was always seen as a leader of the party's progressive wing. Minister of resources 1954-58, and of lands and forests 1958-60, he lost to Daniel JOHNSON in his bid for the party's leadership after the party's defeat in 1960. When his party returned to power in 1966, he became minister of education and was largely responsible for continuing the Liberals' educational reforms. Upon Johnson's death in 1968 he was chosen party leader and so became premier. He had to handle the first symptoms of the language crisis – particularly the school issue in St-Léonard, battleground for supporters and opponents of French schools – proposing BILL 63, which guaranteed parents' right to choose their children's schools. An ardent nationalist and defender of Québec rights, he was one of the main architects of Québec's demands for constitutional reform. His party lost the 1970 election to the Liberal Party of Robert BOURASSA. He continued as leader of the Opposition until 1971.

DANIEL LATOUCHE

Bessborough, Vere Brabazon Ponsonby, 9th Earl of, governor general of Canada 1931-35 (b at London, Eng 27 Oct 1880; d at Stansted, Eng 10 Mar 1956). He was the only prominent British businessman ever to be governor general and as such something of a surprise appointment. Born into the Irish peerage and trained as a lawyer, he was a staff officer in WWI, and an MP in 1910 and again 1913-20, when he went to the House of Lords. In the 1920s he headed the São Paulo Ry and the Margarine Union and was deputy chairman of De Beers. He and his French wife were enthusiastic amateur actors, having built a theatre at their Sussex home. In Canada they inaugurated the DOMINION DRAMA FESTIVAL. The handsome, rich, well-fed and impeccably dressed aristocrat must have been an incongruous sight at the height of the Great Depression, but he showed his sympathy with the plight of Canadians in small ways, and was granted his wish for a 10% cut in salary. NORMAN HILLMER

Bessette, Gérard, novelist, critic (b at Ste-Anne-de-Sabrevois, Qué 25 Feb 1920). Bessette

graduated from the École normale Jacques-Cartier in 1944 and obtained a doctorate in French literature from U de M in 1950. He was already a poet: his poem "Le Coureur" had taken 2nd prize at the Concours littéraires du Québec (1947) and he had been Canada's representative at the 1948 Olympic Games (poetry section). He went on to publish novels about Québec and Montréal society of the 1950s – *La Bagarre* (1958), *Le Libraire* (1960) and *Les Pédagogues* (1961) – in which he denounced the stifling influence of tradition on social and aesthetic standards. Bessette became a pioneer in psychoanalytic literary criticism in Canada with *Une Littérature en ébullition* (1968), *Trois romanciers québécois* (1973) and *Mes romans et moi* (1979). The development of this body of work was substantially influenced by a teaching career that took its author from U of Sask (1946-49) to Duquesne U (1951-58), to RMC, Kingston (1958-60), and then to Queen's, from which he retired in 1979. He was visiting writer at U du Québec à Montréal in 1984. Two works are directly linked to Bessette's teaching career: an anthology, *De Québec à Saint-Boniface: récits et nouvelles du Canada français* (1968) and *Histoire de la littérature canadienne-française* (1968), which he co-authored. Since his novel, *L'Incubation* (1965, Prix du Québec and Gov Gen's Award), critics have more fully recognized the richness and originality of his writing, which experiments in an ironic way with intimist and contemporary forms of expression. These forms are found in Bessette's more recent fiction: *Le Cycle* (1971; Gov Gen's Award 1972; trans 1987), *Les Anthropoïdes* (1977), *Le Semestre* (1979) and *Les Dires d'Omar Marin* (1985). A fellow of the RSC since 1966, Bessette received Québec's most prestigious literary award, the Prix David, in 1980 for the entire corpus of his work. JACQUES ALLARD

Best, Charles Herbert, physiologist, co-discoverer of INSULIN (b at West Pembroke, Maine 27 Feb 1899; d at Toronto 31 Mar 1978). The son of a Canadian-born physician, Charles Best had just completed his BA in physiology and biochemistry at U of T in the spring of 1921, when his summer employer, Professor J.J.R. MACLEOD, assigned him to work on a project devised by Frederick BANTING. Best won a coin toss with one of his classmates to see who would start with Banting; later the other student was not interested in taking Best's place. Banting's and Best's exciting experiments in the summer of 1921 persuaded Macleod to support and expand the research, and by the spring of 1922 a well-trained, well-funded team of researchers, including Macleod, Banting, J.B. COLLIP and Best, had discovered the internal secretion of the pancreas, which they named insulin. As corecipient (with Macleod) of the 1923 Nobel Prize for physiology or medicine for the discovery of

Pierre Berton's mastery of narrative history, infused with colourful detail and patriotic verve, has made him one of the most widely read Canadian authors (*photo courtesy Michael Bedford*).

Charles Herbert Best, who won a coin toss to see who would start work with Frederick Banting on research that led to the discovery of insulin (*courtesy National Archives of Canada/PA-112972*).

insulin, Banting announced that he would share his half of the prize money with Best.

After graduate training in England, Best succeeded Macleod as professor of physiology at U of T in 1929. He was an active researcher and director of students, publishing important studies of choline, heparin and histaminase, as well as much further work on carbohydrate metabolism. He co-authored a widely used physiology textbook and in later life was honoured throughout the world for his contribution to the discovery of insulin. MICHAEL BLISS

Reading: Michael Bliss, *The Discovery of Insulin* (1982).

Best-Sellers in English Canadian books that have maintained high circulation over the years (such as L.M. MONTGOMERY'S ANNE OF GREEN GABLES, 1908) reveal persistent tastes in a wide readership; books with sudden sharp sales show shorter-lived fashions. Some authors, such as Arthur HAILEY, have produced one best-seller after another. Lists of best-sellers, both fiction and nonfiction, first appeared in 1888 in *The Canadian Bookseller*, and have been published since 1970 in the *Toronto Star* and since 1975 in *Maclean's*. The numbers vary widely: in fiction, the same list of best-sellers may include, in the top 10, books that have sold only 3000 copies together with others that have sold 75 000-100 000; the range in nonfiction is more likely to be between 20 000 and 40 000, although a few have reached 100 000 copies. Since publishers, bookstores and authors are sometimes reluctant to furnish exact figures and the research is not strictly scientific, such lists give only a partial record. Nor do they include textbooks, although these are frequently sold in great quantities. Nevertheless, both the current and the long-range lists are important indicators of changing tastes and interests among Canadian readers.

Some Canadian books have not only sold well in Canada but have also reached masses of readers abroad. Canadian authors discovered early that international popularity does not depend on the use of non-Canadian settings. T.C. HALIBURTON'S *The* CLOCKMAKER (1836) quickly found a large readership in Britain and the US. Nova Scotian Margaret Marshall Saunders's *Beautiful Joe* (1894) was carefully set in New England, but other early best-sellers carried images of Canadian places to the world: Gilbert PARKER'S *The Seats of the Mighty* (1896) was set in old Québec City, Ralph Connor's *Black Rock* (1898) in the Rockies, Robert SERVICE'S *Songs of a Sourdough* (1907) in the Yukon, Montgomery's *Anne of Green Gables* in Prince Edward Island and Stephen LEACOCK'S *Sunshine Sketches of a Little Town* (1912) in Ontario.

A successful author's reputation often guarantees large sales for subsequent books. Parker, Connor (pseudonym of C.W. GORDON), Montgomery, Service and Leacock topped best-seller lists year after year until the 1920s, each new book catering to established tastes. Montgomery's *Anne*, for instance, with its imaginative use of language and its central character's free spirit and vivid response to nature, portrayed an idealized Canadian childhood that had worldwide appeal. By 1918 more than 750 000 copies had sold in the US; in Japan and Poland *Anne* is still among the top best-selling books for children.

At the end of WWI R.C. STEAD'S *The Cow Puncher* (1918) was very successful in Canada, though not so well-received abroad. The next worldwide best-seller to come from Canada was Mazo DE LA ROCHE'S *Jalna* (1927), which portrayed a passionate family in an attractive Ontario setting. By the 1980s, De la Roche's Jalna series had sold over 9 million copies. A huge public in the 1920s and 1930s also enjoyed less elegant

Canadian fare: Luke Allan's books, such as *Blue Pete: Half Breed* (1921), Frank Packard's Jimmy Dale stories, and murder stories such as Hulbert Footner's *Easy To Kill* (1931). These books rivalled the sales of quieter rural idylls like Patrick Slater's *The Yellow Briar* (1933) and historical novels like Frederick NIVEN'S *The Flying Years* (1935).

History dominated the lists at the beginning of WWII, in Canada as elsewhere. Canadian offerings included F.D. McDowell's *Champlain Road* (1939), Alan Sullivan's *Three Came to Ville Marie* (1941) and the more sentimental *Thorn-Apple Tree* (1942) by Grace Campbell. No Canadian books had worldwide success after *Jalna*, however, until Gwethalyn Graham's *Earth and High Heaven* (1944), a story of family tensions stirred by ANTI-SEMITISM in wartime Montréal. Ethnic conflicts also form the base of Hugh MACLENNAN'S best-selling novel of 1945, *Two Solitudes*. Both books sold well in the US despite their Canadian settings, and Graham's book was among the top 6 on American lists for the year. Morley CALLAGHAN'S *The Loved and the Lost* (1951), with a Montréal setting and interracial conflict, took advantage of the taste established by Graham and MacLennan.

In the postwar years, war stories came into mass circulation, eg, Lionel Shapiro's *The Sealed Verdict* (1947), Ralph ALLEN'S *Home Made Banners* (1946) and Earle BIRNEY'S *Turvey* (1949). But a social history of the 1950s would also have to note the proliferating sales of romances such as Thomas RADDALL'S *The Nymph and the Lamp* (1952), comic sketches such as Eric NICOL'S *The Roving Eye* (1950) and CHILDREN'S LITERATURE, including W.O. MITCHELL'S *Who Has Seen the Wind* (1947) and Farley MOWAT'S *Lost in the Barrens* (1956).

In 1959 the Canadian fictional best-seller was Mordecai RICHLER'S *The Apprenticeship of Duddy Kravitz*, set in Montréal, whereas in 1960 David WALKER'S *Where the High Winds Blow* showed there was still a market for tales of adventure in Canada's barren North. In the 1960s the reading and buying habits of Canadians changed under the impact of television and a surge in paperback publication. The New Canadian Library, book clubs and authors' reading tours all boosted sales. Between 1960 and 1970 the number of English Canadian books in print increased by about 250%, although no single Canadian book became a worldwide best-seller. In the early 1970s, world best-sellers illustrated shifting attitudes toward violence, feminism, race relations, drugs and family life, and Canadian writers tried plots featuring the new attitudes. But traditional formula fiction also flourished (*see* POPULAR LITERATURE); Canadian novelists turned out HARLEQUIN romances about spunky, beleaguered working girls and their struggles (in exotic settings) toward luxury and married happiness. Publishers faced difficult, inflationary times and rejoiced in clever authors like Richard Rohmer, whose fiction capitalized on current sensations in finance and politics. Nonfiction lists featured Pierre BERTON'S *The National Dream* (1970) and *The Last Spike* (1971), and Peter C. NEWMAN'S *The Canadian Establishment* (1975).

A list of best-sellers since the 1970s would probably include political memoirs and biographies, eg, J.G. DIEFENBAKER'S *One Canada* (1975-77), L.B. PEARSON'S *Mike* (1972-75) and Richard GWYN'S *The Northern Magus* (1980); adventure stories such as William Stevenson's *A Man Called Intrepid* (1976); humour such as Don HARRON'S Charlie Farquharson books; financial guides such as Morton Shulman's "How To Invest" series; novels such as Robertson DAVIES'S Deptford trilogy, especially *Fifth Business* (1970), and Margaret

LAURENCE'S Manawaka novels, especially *A Jest of God* (paperback, 1974; sales were increased by the movie version, *Rachel, Rachel*); Alice MUNRO'S story sequences, especially LIVES OF GIRLS AND WOMEN (1971); and the entertaining tales by Harry BOYLE and Constance BERESFORD-HOWE. Margaret ATWOOD'S cool, honest and acidly funny novels have had wide sales, especially *The Handmaid's Tale* (1985), which outsold all her other books. The best-seller lists reflect Canadian choices, and perhaps Canadian needs: the need for escape, for unavailable pleasures, for information and guidance on urgent questions. Best-seller lists reveal not what Canadians should read, but what they do read. *See also* BEST SELLERS IN FRENCH; POPULAR LITERATURE IN ENGLISH; AUTOBIOGRAPHIES, POLITICAL. ELIZABETH WATERSTON

Reading: Mary Vipond, "Best Sellers in English Canada, 1899-1918," *Journal of Canadian Fiction* 24 (1979).

Best-Sellers in French Although the best-seller in the modern sense of the word is a relatively recent phenomenon in French Canada, there have always been popular novels which reached a wide readership in translation or in European editions. Sales figures are rarely available for the early period, but it is possible to establish a list of the most popular money-makers. In general, the 19th century is characterized by the fashion for historical romance and adventure stories, while in the 20th century this factor is compounded by the role played by translation and especially LITERARY PRIZES such as the GOVERNOR GENERAL'S AWARD in the creation of a best-seller.

Demographic patterns have always obliged the professional writer in French Canada to aim for an international audience, and it is not surprising that 19th-century best-sellers were often written by European immigrants and exiles primarily for foreign consumption. Henri-Émile Chevalier (1828-79) published his "*romans-feuilleton*," or dime novels, in the series Drames de l'Amérique du Nord; the most lucrative of his many adventure tales about pirates, Indians and historical figures was *L'Ile de Sable* (1862), retitled *Trente-neuf Hommes pour une femme: Épisode de la colonisation du Canada*, and widely reprinted in Paris and in an American translation. The popularity of books exploiting N American local colour dates back to Champlain's *Des sauvages* (1603) and survives well into the 20th century. The French writer Maurice Constantin-Weyer (1881-1961) is remembered for his series L'Epopée canadienne, and won the Prix Goncourt 1928 for his "Canadian" novel *Un Homme se penche sur son passé* (1928); more recently, Anne and Serge Golon have achieved tremendous popularity with their juvenile series set in 17th-century New France, notably with *Angélique et le nouveau monde* (1967). The most famous best-selling novel written by a foreigner but considered part of the French Canadian canon is, of course, Louis HÉMON'S *MARIA CHAPDELAINE* (1916); until recently the 1921 translation by William H. Blake offered most English Canadians their only exposure to the fiction and culture of French Canada.

A number of Québécois wrote historical fiction which reached a fairly wide readership in the 19th century; their work tends to be eclipsed today by the more serious "*roman du terroir*" then promoted by the church and now recognized by the critics. These historical romances include the works of Philippe-Joseph AUBERT DE GASPÉ (*Les Anciens Canadiens*, 1863) and Laure Conan (pseudonym of Félicité ANGERS); the latter writer, who lived in retirement in La Malbaie, was one of the first professionals to support herself entirely by her writing income. Rosanna LEPROHON (née Mullins), whose de Villerai trilogy achieved commercial success in French translation but not in the original English version, was enthusiastically adopted by French readers as late as the 1920s; *Le Manoir de Villerai* (installments 1851, book form 1861), frequently reprinted in French, has yet to appear in book form in the original English.

The *roman du terroir*, in ironic or sensationalized versions, experienced a surge of popularity in the 1930s, when its life span was extended by the emergence of radio drama. The most famous and beloved of these was undoubtedly *Un Homme et son péché* (1933) by Claude-Henri GRIGNON; the radio serial gave way to a long-lived television series. Grignon's cousin Germaine GUÈVREMONT scripted her own prize-winning novel *Le SUR-VENANT* (1945) and its sequels for the less popular but equally long-lived radio-television series. The most durable of novels in this tradition is TRENTE ARPENTS (1938) by "Ringuet" (Philippe PAN-NETON), a critical as well as a popular success, and translated into English and German following its reception of the Prix David, Viking and Governor General's awards.

Radio encouraged the popularization of new literary genres during the 1930s and 1940s, assisting Gratien GÉLINAS with the sales of his Fridolin texts and Émile Coderre with the publication of poems by his persona "Jean Narrache." Urban realism emerged with Roger LEMELIN's award-winning novel *Les PLOUFFE* (1948), which launched the successful radio-television series of that name in 1952. Lemelin's success was surpassed only by the popular and critical acclaim of Gabrielle ROY's *Bonheur d'occasion* (1945), translated into many languages following its reception of the Prix Fémina.

The dry period between the war and the Quiet Revolution was spanned by the dime novels of Pierre Daignault, who as "Pierre Sauriol" authored, from 1947 to 1966, over 900 weekly episodes narrating the spying adventures of "Agent IXE-13" in the pages of *Éditions Police-Journal*. Daignault sometimes collaborated with Yves THÉRIAULT, the most prolific of professional writers to establish a reputation during this period; his 2 critically acclaimed novels about native peoples, *Agaguk* (1958) and *Ashini* (1961), are joined by over a thousand stories and novellas in which Thériault explores the darker, primitive drives of sex and violence and their reflection in Québec society.

The regional best-seller finally emerged in full force as a by-product of the cultural nationalism in the late 1960s, as witnessed by the success of Jacques GODBOUT's SALUT GALARNEAU! (1967), Roch CARRIER's LA GUERRE, YES SIR! (1968) and Anne HÉBERT's KAMOURASKA (1970), among others. In the true sense of the word, however, the French Canadian best-seller did not fully emerge until the late 1970s: since the publication of Antonine MAILLET's PÉLAGIE-LA-CHARRETTE (1979) and Yves BEAUCHEMIN's *Le Matou* (1981), local authors can now aspire to reach a wide, international readership by employing their own idiom and by dramatizing material peculiar to French N America. As the first novel by a Canadian to win the Prix Goncourt, *Pélagie* was assured the considerable sale it merited; however, it is Beauchemin who can now claim the distinction of having sold a million copies of a French Canadian novel. *See also* POPULAR LITERATURE IN FRENCH.

MICHÈLE LACOMBE

Bethune, Charles James Stewart, clergyman, entomologist, educator (b in W Flamborough Twp, Upper Canada 11 Aug 1838; d at Toronto 18 Apr 1932). He was a graduate of Toronto's Upper Canada Coll and U of Trinity Coll (BA 1859) and was ordained an Anglican priest in 1862. After serving parishes for 9 years, he was appointed headmaster of Trinity Coll

School, Port Hope, which he turned into one of the most prestigious boys' schools in Canada. As professor and head of the entomology dept at the Ontario Agricultural Coll (now part of University of Guelph) 1906-20, he pioneered the instruction of the science of insects at the university level. Always an ardent collector of insects, he cofounded with William SAUNDERS the Entomological Soc of Canada in 1863, served for 11 years as its president and edited its journal, the *Canadian Entomologist*, for about 30 years. At Guelph he developed the teaching of economic ENTOMOLOGY based on sound scientific principles, promoted the collection and careful identification of insects, and published widely on the lives of insects and on their control.

P.W. RIEGERT

Bethune, Henry Norman, surgeon, inventor, political activist (b at Gravenhurst, Ont 3 Mar 1890; d at Huang Shiko, N China 12 Nov 1939). Bethune's fame in Canada has resulted from his status as a hero in the People's Republic of China and the impact of this on Sino-Canadian relations. Son of the manse, Bethune took up the profession of his surgeon grandfather. He interrupted his medical studies in Toronto to be a labourer-teacher at Frontier Coll (1911-12) and to serve in 1915 as a stretcher-bearer in WWI. Following a stint in the Royal Navy, postgraduate training in Britain and private practice in Detroit, Mich, he was found in 1926 to have contracted pulmonary tuberculosis. After this personal crisis, he devoted himself to other tuberculosis victims and to thoracic surgery in Montréal at the Royal Victoria Hospital and later at the Hôpital du Sacré-Coeur, Cartierville, Qué. Between 1929 and 1936 he invented or redesigned 12 medical and surgical instruments and wrote 14 articles describing his innovations in thoracic technique. He became increasingly disillusioned with surgical treatment and concerned with the socioeconomic aspects of the disease. He challenged his profession and proposed radical reforms of medical care and health services in Canada.

After a visit to the Soviet Union in 1935 Bethune joined the Communist Party. This commitment took him to the Spanish Civil War in 1936 where he organized a mobile blood-transfusion service, the first of its kind, to operate on a 1000 km front. He returned to Canada in 1937 to raise money for the antifascist cause in Spain and

Norman Bethune; a portrait taken in Spain during the Spanish Civil War, in which he organized the first mobile blood-transfusion service (*courtesy National Archives of Canada/PA-114788*).

soon turned his attention to the war being waged by communist forces against the Japanese invaders in China. "Spain and China," he wrote, "are part of the same battle." Bethune left Canada for the last time in 1938 to join the 8th Route Army in the Shanxi-Hobei border region. There, he was a tireless and inventive surgeon, teacher and propagandist, and he adopted the cause and the people as his own. His accidental death from septicemia evoked Mao Zedong's essay "In Memory of Norman Bethune," which urged all communists to emulate his spirit of internationalism, his sense of responsibility and his devotion to others. One of 3 prescribed articles during the Cultural Revolution, the essay made Bethune's name almost synonymous with Canada in China.

HILARY RUSSELL

Reading: T. Allan and S. Gordon, *The Scalpel, the Sword: The Story of Dr. Norman Bethune* (1971); W. MacLeod et al, *Bethune: The Montreal Years* (1978); R. Stewart, *Bethune* (1973) and *The Mind of Norman Bethune* (1977).

Betula Lake, Man, is a freshwater lake and resort area in Whiteshell Provincial Park, 145 km by road NE of Winnipeg. Opened to cottage development in the 1950s, Betula is a popular swimming, waterskiing and fishing area. Its cultural history is especially notable, for located in the area are petroforms — boulder mosaics created by prehistoric peoples. These outlines, made of rocks weighing up to several hundred kg, are laid on open granite tablerock. Turtle and snake effigies predominate, but circles, human effigies and geometric patterns have also been found. The petroforms are thought to stem from the Laurel Culture (500 BC to AD 800). Some may have been used to mark portages, but the more remote sites were likely used for religious ceremonies and rituals. Some alignments correspond to astronomical phenomena. Their creators may have been ancestors of Algonquian-speaking peoples who continued to arrange petroforms after moving W to the High Plains. Systematic study of the Whiteshell mosaics began in the late 1960s.

D.M. LYON

Beurling, George Frederick, "Buzz," fighter pilot (b at Verdun, Qué 6 Dec 1921; d at Rome, Italy 20 May 1948). He destroyed 28 enemy aircraft in 4 months while serving as a sergeant-pilot with 249 Sqdn, RAF, on Malta in 1942 and was commissioned and promoted flying officer. Wounded in 1942, he transferred to the RCAF as a flight lieutenant. Flying with 403 and 412 Sqdns, he was credited with 3 more victories for a total of 32. He rebelled against service discipline and was released in Oct 1944. Lost in a world without air combat — "It's the only thing I can do well; it's the only thing I ever did I really liked" — he joined the Israeli Air Force in 1948, and died when the aircraft he was ferrying to Palestine crashed.

BRERETON GREENHOUS

Beynon, Francis Marion, journalist, feminist social reformer (b at Streetsville, Ont 21 May 1884; d at Winnipeg 5 Oct 1951). The Beynon family moved from Ontario to Manitoba during her childhood, and she worked in advertising and as a journalist in Winnipeg. She was active in the Canadian Women's Press Club and helped to organize the Political Equality League of Manitoba, the province's chief women's suffrage organization. In her column for the GRAIN GROWERS' GUIDE, where she was woman's page editor 1912-17, she took a wide-ranging view of the "Woman Question," discussing, in addition to suffrage, women's work and the structure of marriage and the family. When war broke out, Beynon took a pacifist position. This stand forced her resignation from the *Grain Growers' Guide* in 1917. She then left Winnipeg for the US, where she remained for the rest of her active life. DEBORAH GORHAM

Beynon, William, Nishga hereditary chief, ethnographer (b at Victoria 1888; d 1958). Initially ambiguous about his native heritage, Beynon became increasingly involved in it through research. From 1915 until 1956, he worked as an interpreter and field researcher among the Tsimshian, Nishga and Gitksan of BC. With Marius BARBEAU, he prepared an ethnographic census of those cultures, particularly their social organization and mythology. For brief periods he also assisted Franz BOAS and Philip Drucker. Despite a lack of formal training in anthropology, his field notes supply major data for these cultures.
J.J. COVE

Biard, Pierre, Jesuit missionary (b at Grenoble, France 1567 or 1568; d at Avignon, France 17 Nov 1622). After long preparation for missionary work, Biard left for ACADIA in early 1611. Determined and resourceful as a missionary to the Micmac and Maliseet, Biard nevertheless incurred the enmity of French colonial promoters such as Charles de BIENCOURT, whose methods he criticized as selfish and materialistic. In July 1613, as he was attempting with 3 other Jesuits to set up a religiously based colony on the Maine coast, he was captured by an English raiding party, and subsequently returned to France. Biard's *Relation de la Nouvelle-France* (1616) was a perceptive appraisal of the problems facing early European colonizers. JOHN G. REID

Reading: John G. Reid, *Acadia, Maine and New Scotland* (1981).

Bible Schools, colleges and institutes are mainly sponsored by the EVANGELICAL Protestant churches in Canada although 2 Catholic institutions exist in Alberta. The first 2 Bible schools in N America were begun by the Canadian founder of the Christian and Missionary Alliance Church, A.B. Simpson (Nyack, NY, 1882) and by evangelist D.L. Moody (Moody Bible Institute, Chicago, 1887). Toronto Bible Training School (later Ontario Bible College), est 1894, the first permanent Canadian Bible school and the third in N America, was modelled on Moody's institute. The purpose of Bible schools, institutes and colleges is to prepare students for Christian ministries through biblical and practical training. Most were founded by evangelicals reacting against the "liberalism" of established theological colleges. These church colleges trained ministers at a graduate level, whereas Bible schools and colleges were primarily post-secondary institutions for laity involved in the local church or in foreign and home missionary work. Evangelicals suggest that these institutions represent a resurgence of Protestant spirituality in reaction to secular humanism and agnosticism, and a return to the central concern of Christian education: the implementation of Christ's commission, "Go ye into all the world, and preach the gospel to every creature." Social scientists draw attention to economic and social factors, noting that the great periods for the establishment of Bible schools and colleges (particularly in western Canada) followed the Great Depression and WWII. For instance, William ABERHART, fundamentalist radio preacher and charismatic founder of the Social Credit Party, started the Prophetic Bible Institute in Calgary in 1929.

No single term describes the variety of Bible institutions. All offer Bible-centered day and evening programs, teach evangelical theology, stress Christian service (SUNDAY SCHOOL teaching and personal evangelism), promote overseas and home missions, and encourage personal devotional piety. Bible colleges offer 4-year under-

graduate degrees in theology, whereas Bible schools or institutes generally offer only 3-year diploma programs. The term "Bible training schools" appears to have been applied only to a few schools in the early 20th century. Although many Bible schools or institutes have faculty with baccalaureates, a considerable number have some faculty who are essentially self-taught clergy or returned missionaries without extensive formal education. The colleges, in contrast, require faculty to have bachelor or even postgraduate degrees, and have maintained generally higher academic standards. Since 1959 about 40 Canadian Bible schools and colleges have organized as the Association of Canadian Bible Colleges (ACBC, inc 1968) to foster higher standards of learning. Most Bible schools and colleges offer 4 categories of specialization: General Bible (theological), Christian Education, Missions and Church Music. Some also offer a pastoral program leading to the ministry. This Bible-centered curriculum (the Bible is, in fact, the "textbook") is augmented by structured programs requiring students to participate regularly in Christian service. Also, virtually all of these institutions originally emphasized biblical prophecy from a premillennial and dispensational point of view (*see* MILLENARIANISM).

Since 1894 more than 120 Bible institutions have been established in Canada, including part-time day or evening schools with under 10 students and full-time institutions with enrolments up to 900. It was only after 1920, however, that the movement burgeoned across Canada. In total, 69% of the institutions have been in western Canada, 22% in Ontario and Québec, and 9% in the Maritimes. In 1960, 47 Bible schools and colleges reported 3417 students, and in 1987 the ACBC reported 43 schools belonging to the association, with a total enrolment over 7000.

Most Bible schools and colleges have a direct denominational affiliation, but approximately 15% are interdenominational (operated by an independent board of directors). MENNONITES have the largest number, followed by PENTECOSTALS, HOLINESS CHURCHES, BAPTISTS, Church of Christ, Church of God (Anderson, Indiana), Missionary Church, and Christian and Missionary Alliance. Some of the interdenominational institutions such as Prairie Bible Institute (Three Hills, Alta), Briercrest Bible Institute (Caronport, Sask) and Ontario Bible College (Toronto) have achieved national and international attention, especially through missionary endeavours. Prairie Bible Institute, the largest Bible institution in Canada (with a peak enrolment of 900 in 1949) was also one of the largest and most respected in North America.

Two Roman Catholic Bible institutions opened in Alberta in 1984. The Catholic Bible College of Canada, located in Canmore, was endorsed by the Western Conference of Bishops and provides programs to assist its lay pupils to explore the scripture in the light of the faith and doctrine of the church. John Paul II Bible School, located in Radway, is influenced by the Charismatic movement in the Catholic Church and is, therefore, evangelical in its orientation. *See also* CATHOLICISM.
RONALD G. SAWATSKY

Reading: S.A. Witmer, *The Bible College Story* (1962).

Bic, Île du, uninhabited island, 14 km², is located in the ST LAWRENCE R, 30 km W of Rimouski, Qué. Because of its advantageous position at the mouth of the St Lawrence near the natural harbour of Bic, it played a key military role under the French regime. From the time Québec was captured by the KIRKE brothers in 1629, Île du Bic served as a communications base for vessels operating between the colony's outposts (Gaspé, Ta-

doussac, Québec City) and as a port for fleets during the French-English and Anglo-American wars. Missionaries also used the island as a rallying point. Before and after the Conquest, 1760, several development projects for the Bic harbour were successively devised and abandoned. Because of the many hazards for shipping in the river, during the French regime many sailors became pilots for transatlantic vessels. James MURRAY, the governor of Québec, regulated pilot activities on the river and established a pilotage station on the island. The pilots built several small houses at what came to be called Anse-des-Pilotes. In 1905 the station moved 40 km downstream to Pointe-au-Père. Countless tales are told of this island's enigmatic past and of the many shipwrecks on its reefs. ANTONIO LECHASSEUR

Bickell, John Paris, mining executive (b at Molesworth, Ont 26 Sept 1884; d at New York City, NY 22 Aug 1951). A Toronto broker, Bickell invested in a Porcupine gold property that formed the basis of McIntyre Porcupine Mines Ltd, of which he was president and later chairman. During the 1930s, Bickell championed the interests of Ontario mine owners and made newspaper headlines with his airplanes, fast cars and close friends, including Premier M. HEPBURN. In WWII he served in England's Ministry of Aircraft Production under Lord Beaverbrook (Max AITKEN) and in Canada's Dept of Munitions and Supply, where he was president of Victory Aircraft Ltd. Bickell became the first president of Maple Leaf Gardens (the annual trophy awarded to the outstanding player on the Toronto Maple Leafs is named for him) and helped to establish the Toronto Art Gallery (later Art Gallery of Ontario). He was a senior partner of Thomson, McKinnon, members of the New York Stock Exchange. The J.P. Bickell Foundation, provided for in his will with a capital fund of $13 million, was established chiefly to assist medical and mining research in Ontario.
J. LINDSEY

Bickert, Edward Isaac, jazz guitarist (b at Hochfeld, Man 29 Nov 1932). Canada's best-known jazz guitarist, Bickert began his professional career about 1955 in Toronto, working with Ron COLLIER, Rob MCCONNELL, Don Thompson and, for more than 25 years, Moe KOFFMAN. Developing a unique, understated style of considerable harmonic sophistication, he achieved international prominence through his work 1974-76 with US saxophonist Paul Desmond. His emergence was supported by his own early recordings 1975-78 and by those with McConnell's Boss Brass. Bickert's reticence has kept him in Toronto, where his steadily growing popularity is attributed to his last 3 albums, the latest of which was *Wishes on the Moon* (1986).
MARK MILLER

Biculturalism This neologistic term came into public consciousness with the appointment of the Royal Commission on BILINGUALISM AND BICULTURALISM in 1963. On examining its terms of reference the commission could not find the word in a dictionary. It knew, however, that "biculturalism" had been used as far back as 1929 when Graham SPRY, in a speech to the Canadian Club of Québec, had spoken of the "bi-cultural character of the Canadian nation." The commission concluded that the term referred to the existence in Canada of 2 principal cultures – that associated with the English language and that associated with the French. Its function was to examine the state of each of the 2 cultures, and the opportunity for each to exist and flourish; and also the set of conditions that would enable members of the 2 cultures to co-operate effectively. Commission members did not think the term had an implication about individuals becoming bicultural, which seldom happens. They believed rather that an important factor would be whether both cultures are properly represented in common institutions and whether persons participating in these institutions have the opportunity to conserve and express their own culture.

Members of the commission rejected the notion that culture was determined by ethnic descent. They considered current language and a sense of belonging to be much more important factors. They noted that Canadians whose ancestors came from countries other than the British Isles participated fully in the culture of English-speaking Canada, and that some whose forebears were not from France participated in the culture of French-speaking Canada. They also noted that some groups, bound by ties of common ethnic origin, desire to maintain and foster their particular cultural heritages, in most cases while also taking a full part in the life of the Canadian society around them. The commission wrote extensively about these "cultural groups" and made recommendations about the assistance necessary for them to preserve their languages and to support their cultural activities. These observations gave rise to the federal government's statement about MULTICULTURALISM in 1971.

Though the term is recent, the concept of biculturalism goes back to the origins of modern Canada. After the CONQUEST of 1759-60, the British authorities allowed French Canadians full use of their language and system of civil law, and gave freedom to the Roman Catholic Church, a mainstay of their culture. In 1839 Lord Durham held in his report (*see* DURHAM REPORT) that French Canadians should be assimilated through the joining of Upper and Lower Canada into a single entity. But French Canadians proved thoroughly resistant to assimilation and their politicians, such as LAFONTAINE, ensured that the government of the PROVINCE OF CANADA take account of their partnerships in the legislature. French was soon recognized by the legislature as an official language, and a structure for public education was established that in effect gave full protection for French education in Canada East. A distinct French Canadian culture continued to flourish, and under the CONFEDERATION arrangements of 1867 the Province of Québec, with its large francophone majority, gained full control over education and other matters affecting culture. Basic support for French Canadian culture in that province was henceforth assured. But by the 1960s it was plain that many French-speaking Canadians were dissatisfied with the place of their language within Québec and the position of Québec in Canada. Many thought that French culture was threatened by the dominance of English and English speakers in the industrial and commercial life of Québec; by the obstacles to Francophones working in the federal administration; and by the plight of French-speaking minorities outside Québec, whose language and culture had nothing like the support enjoyed by the anglophone minority in Québec.

Since the 1960s francophone cultural life in Québec has developed vigorously. There have been remarkable achievements in education, literature, theatre, television, radio, films and other fields. And more and more Francophones take their culture as well as their language to work in senior positions in business. Many Francophones have some much-needed forms of support for their culture: French television and radio, newspapers and periodicals, and cultural organizations. However, Québec's 1977 language legislation, BILL 101, diminished the bicultural nature of that province by rendering it officially unilingual. Meanwhile, outside Québec, many groups of

both Anglophones and Francophones now have access to public education in French. It seems evident today that Canada does indeed have 2 principal cultures – that associated with the English language and that associated with the French. It is still debatable whether each has fully equal opportunities for development. *See also* BILINGUALISM; CULTURAL DUALISM.　　A. DAVIDSON DUNTON

Reading: Royal Commission on Bilingualism and Biculturalism, *Report* (prelim, 1965; final, 6 vols, 1967-70).

Bicycling The familiar, 2-wheel, human-powered bicycle and its 3-wheel, tandem, and oddly shaped modern variations represent the design culmination of a largely 19th-century progression from the pedal-less hobby horse and unwieldy "boneshaker," to the improbable high wheel, and eventually the contemporary styled safety. Of these stages, the first to appear in Canada was the usually homemade, 2-wheeled boneshaker, so named because of the uncharitable ride afforded by its heavy wooden or iron form on generally unpaved roads. This machine, distinguished by pedals attached directly to the front wheel, appeared in the Maritimes in 1866 though its popularity awaited a N America-wide craze in 1869. Velocipede rinks were built from Halifax to Toronto and rented bicycles and lessons were provided. There was an exhibition of riding that year in the Mechanics Hall in St John's, Nfld, and cyclists in Victoria, BC, held races in Beacon Hill Park. In the same year the brothers Michael and John Goodwin of Stratford, Ont, started a company which built iron bicycles.

The fad was short-lived and its next manifestation was the display at the 1876 Philadelphia Centennial Exposition of the high wheel, or penny farthing, so named because of the alignment of its 2 wheels, one of upwards to 60 inches (152.4 cm) in diameter and the other a maximum-sized wheel of 18 inches (45.7 cm) usually in the rear for balance. By the 1880s the high wheel and its patrons were a publicly recognized elite whose exploits were recorded in the daily newspapers. The difficulty of riding such a machine, together with a $300 cost, narrowed participation to a largely youthful, male, professionally employed class of riders. The first Canadian Club was formed in Montréal in 1878 and 3 years later a gathering of riders in London, Ont, first discussed a national organization which was eventually constituted as the Canadian Wheelmen's Assn a year later. By 1883 Winnipeg had its own club and at its inauguration in 1892 the Calgary Bicycle Club numbered 22 members though women were accepted only as honorary members.

The last decade of the 19th century witnessed the bicycle's supreme prominence as private transportation. In Canada as elsewhere mass production and the arrival of the bicycle's modern form, together with pneumatic tires, gear and chain systems, opened the sport to men and women from most social classes. Popular history suggests that the bicycle released women from a fashionable inactivity and freed them from restrictive, conventional dress by bringing forth the then startling bloomer costumes. In fact, the bicycle was merely one agent through which larger societal changes, in public roles and in the workplace, occurred.

Enthusiasts included poet Archibald LAMPMAN who sold verses to buy a bicycle for his wife. Kit Coleman, the *Toronto Mail*'s first women's page editor, noted with some disdain that "it is the old girls who are the ardent wheelers."

Semmens, Ghent and Co of Burlington, Ont, had produced nickel-plated bicycles in 1882 and Thomas Fane's company in Toronto produced a machine specially designed for Canadian conditions. By 1898 there were over 25 distinct manu-

facturers in the country and in Toronto alone over 90 bicycle shops operated. The formation of a large American conglomerate that year caused 5 of the leading Canadian companies, Massey-Harris, H.A. Lozier, Welland Vale, Goold, and Gendron to join a year later and form Canada Cycle and Motor Co (CCM). With annual production among the 5 members of around 40 000 bicycles and a total employment roster of 1700, the future looked promising. A general glut in the market by the turn of the century, however, and the arrival of the AUTOMOBILE resulted in a steady decline in bicycle sales until WWI.

The bicycle's utilitarian role was by now well recognized. Incredibly, the machine was adopted by many travellers to the gold fields during the KLONDIKE GOLD RUSH. The 530 km route from Dawson to Whitehorse was the most heavily travelled "bicycle path" and in the late winter of 1901, 250 were on the trail before the spring thaw. When Dawson challenged for hockey's Stanley Cup in 1904, they began their 23-day trek to Ottawa on bicycles.

Bicycle racing, limited in competitive scope in the 1880s, spread to a larger audience in the next decade. Typical of the response was the start of the Dunlop road race in Toronto in 1894, an annual custom lasting until `1926. The world championships were held in Montréal in 1899 and within a few years Canadians were leading performers on the better organized American scene. Archie McEachern from Ontario and Newfoundland's Urban McDonald were killed in separate board track-racing accidents. Burns Pierce, and brothers Tom and Nat Butler, all from Nova Scotia, survived successful racing careers in the US. Nat defeated many of the best European racers during a tour of France and Germany in the winter of 1905-06.

Canadians maintained their competitive position through the next several decades. In 1917 Toronto's Art Spencer won the American cycling title in Newark. A decade later a gangling redhead from Victoria, William "Torchy" PEDEN emerged as an unlikely talent. He was to become the star of the incredibly popular indoor 6-day bicycle races which peaked in the Depression years. A genuinely likable person, his size created a menacing presence on the track and woe to the rider who dealt him an unfair blow. Peden's record total of 38 wins lasted until 1965. It was also in the 1930s that Pierre Gachon of Montréal became the first Canadian to compete in the Tour de France. Symbolic of the sport's appeal was a planned 4300-mile (7166.7 km) race in 1933, starting and ending in Montréal and looping through the American Midwest. Terrible road conditions and underfinancing eventually shortened the event, which Peden won, but its very ambition showed the willingness of N Americans to challenge European leadership in the sport.

Bicycle organization focusing on recreation suffered a serious blow in the first decades of the 20th century when many of its organizers switched to the automobile. Dr Perry Doolittle, an active 19th-century proponent of good roads for bicyclists, became a leader of Ontario's automobile users' movement. The bicycle's proletarian image confined it in many parts of Canada to an activity reserved for children and those with few apparent means. Still, there were some outstanding personalities. Awakened back in 1883 by an American cyclist Lyman Hotchkiss Bagg to the machine's touring possibilities, Canadians on wheel were among the country's first organized tourists. By the 1890s, 70 hotels from the Maritimes to Manitoba advertised special rates for bicyclists. In 1899 Karl Creelman of Truro, NS, left his hometown on a 2-year world journey becoming the first Canadian to accomplish the feat.

Mrs Campbell with bicycle, June 1897. Cycling became the rage of both men and women in the late 19th century (*courtesy National Archives of Canada/PA-130015*).

In WWI young men with the cycling urge were encouraged to join the Canadian Corps Cyclists' Battalion. Over 1000 men eventually did so and their duties ranged from message delivery and map-reading to reconnaissance and actual combat. A battalion publication, the *Cyclone*, served these cycling veterans for over 50 years. After the war organizational enthusiasm was largely regional, with Québec remaining a leading centre up to and beyond WWII. Tours by the Metropole Cycling Club of Montréal to Dorval and St-Eustache sur le Lac in 1943 under the leadership of Romeo Martin, a veteran of 75 000 touring miles (125 000 km), attracted over 300 cyclists. Notable individual achievements of the period included Harold Peterson's 10 000 mile (16 667 km) return tour from Saskatchewan to Texas, sponsored by the Quaker Oats company in the 1930s, and Harrison Randall of Fredericton, dubbed Canada's cycling serenader, who travelled 17 500 miles (29 167 km) through N America during WWII entertaining over 900 communities that supplied the necessary piano.

In the immediate postwar period, bicycling's adolescent character was reinforced by the promotional priority of large manufacturers appealing to the BABY BOOM phenomenon. Only in the late 1960s did a more mature appraisal of the bicycle's role develop, fed by a growing concern for the environment and fitness. By the 1970s it was estimated that over a quarter of all Canadian households contained at least one bicycle, though in the absence of effective nationwide licensing regulations the figures were guesses at best.

Also fueling the increased interest in the bicycle were the racing accomplishments of Jocelyn LOVELL who almost single-handedly inspired other competitors and in the 1970s earned the sport increased financial support from public agencies. After the war the sport had been kept alive by isolated pockets of support from Belgian immigrants in Winnipeg and Delhi, Ont, Italian and British communities throughout Canada and local organizers in BC and Québec.

By the mid-1970s new races like the Gastown Classic in Vancouver and the world and then Olympic championships in Montréal in 1974 and 1976, respectively, were attracting international interest. Lovell was joined by a host of equally ambitious men and women, including Karen Strong, Sylvia BURKA, Gord Singleton and Steve Bauer. In 1978 Strong and Burka placed 3rd and 4th in the women's 3000 m individual pursuit at the world championships. In 1982 Singleton won Canada's first ever world championship in the professional keirin event. In 1984 Steve Bauer's silver medal in the Olympic road race was followed by Curt Harnett's silver in the kilometre time trial. Bauer finished the year with a third in the road race at the professional world championship and continued to startle seasoned European observers with a 10th-place finish in his first Tour de France the next year. In 1986 another Canadian, Alex Stieda, became the first N American ever to wear the leader's yellow jersey in the Tour, though the honour lasted less than a day.

In the past 100 years over 400 Canadian companies have produced items ranging from bicycle parts to complete products. The collapse of CCM in the 1980s indicates that the mass production of bicycles, while the backbone of the industry, remains fraught with economic peril, subject as it is to changing tastes and foreign competition.

Despite its increased use for recreation, Canadians retain a strange ambivalence to the bicycle's place on the road. However, interest among Canada's trend-setting professional and business elite in custom-designed machines, such as the Mariposa, produced by Bicyclesport of Toronto, may augur well for a cultural re-evaluation of the bicycle's social role as significant as that which greeted it 100 years ago.   WILLIAM HUMBER

Reading: W. Humber, *Freewheeling: The Story of Bicycling in Canada* (1986); T. Sandland, *Something About Bicycling in Newfoundland* (1983); H. Watts, *Silent Steeds: Cycling in Nova Scotia to 1900* (1985).

Bidwell, Barnabas, lawyer, teacher, politician (b at Monterey, Mass 23 Aug 1763; d at Kingston, Upper Canada 27 July 1833), and his son, **Marshall Spring Bidwell,** lawyer, politician (b at Stockbridge, Mass 16 Feb 1799; d at New York C, NY 24 Oct 1872). Barnabas Bidwell was an important Massachusetts politician who fled to UC in 1810 when charged with forgery and embezzlement. He actively opposed the Tory elite in Kingston during the Robert GOURLAY agitation and contributed to the latter's *Statistical Account of Upper Canada*. He probably introduced the label "Family Compact," to identify the local elite; it was applied to the provincial administration by his son. He was elected to the UC Assembly for Lennox and Addington in 1821, but was expelled because he was a criminal and an alien (see ALIEN QUESTION). The Tories maintained that Americans who had arrived before 1812 had to be naturalized to secure property and political rights. Marshall Spring, who came to UC in 1811, attempted to replace his father in the Assembly but was declared ineligible as an alien. The younger Bidwell emerged as a reform leader, sitting in the Assembly 1824-36, acting as Speaker in 1828 and 1834. He advocated secularization of the CLERGY RESERVES, abolition of primogeniture, liberalization of marriage laws, abolition of imprisonment for debt, and greater Assembly control of revenues. He rejected the radicalism of William Lyon Mackenzie and after his defeat in 1836 left politics. He played no role in the rebellion, but was advised by Lt-Gov Sir Francis Bond HEAD to leave the province in Dec 1837 because he was "disloyal."   DAVE MILLS

Biéler, André Charles, painter and teacher (b at Lausanne, Switz 8 Oct 1896). He immigrated with his family to Montréal in 1908 and served with the Princess Patricia's Canadian Light Infantry in WWI. He studied 1920-26 at the Art Students League, Woodstock, NY, in Paris and in Switzerland with his artist-uncle Ernest Biéler. From 1927 to 1930 he lived on Île d'Orléans, Qué, painting the life of the Québec habitants with fresh insight. Having established a studio in Montréal in 1930, he survived by teaching and taking commercial art work. Invited to Queen's in 1936, he remained as professor of art until retirement in 1963.

His concern for the position of the artist in Canada led him to organize the first conference of Canadian artists (1941), from which emerged the Federation of Canadian Artists with Biéler as first president. More importantly, it set in motion ideas and actions that led to the establishment of the Canada Council in 1957. He was chiefly responsible for the founding of the Agnes Etherington Art Centre, Kingston, in 1957 and was its first director. Nevertheless, painting has dominated Biéler's life. An energetic and prolific artist, he has drawn his subject matter from life experience. Stylistically, much of Biéler's work relates more to modern French painting, especially of the "School of Paris," than to contemporary Canadian movements. He has made sculpture in various media, and in 1968 invented a unique pneumatic press for printmaking. In later years his painting has been concerned with light and colour as he reinterprets thousands of early sketches.

FRANCES K. SMITH

Reading: Frances K. Smith, *André Biéler: An Artist's Life and Times* (1980).

Biencourt, Charles de, Baron de Saint-Just, colonizer in ACADIA (b in Champagne, France 1591 or 1592; d in Acadia 1623), eldest son of Jean de BIENCOURT DE POUTRINCOURT. He accompanied his father on colonizing expeditions to Acadia in 1606 and 1610, and then took charge on his father's behalf at PORT-ROYAL [Annapolis Royal, NS]. He was given command of the colony in 1615. As a young man, Biencourt was reputedly tactless in dealing with others, and his violent quarrels with Jesuit missionaries undoubtedly harmed the colony. His determination, however, was crucial to the survival of the French presence in Acadia after a disastrous English raid in 1613. He struggled for 10 years thereafter to promote the colony's recovery.   JOHN G. REID

Biencourt de Poutrincourt, Jean de, Baron de Saint-Just, colonizer in Acadia (b 1557; d at Méry-sur-Seine, France 1615). As a young army officer, he fought in the French Wars of Religion, then entered the service of King Henry IV 1593. After Henry's grant of the colony of Acadia to Pierre Du Gua de MONTS 1603, Poutrincourt set sail with de Monts the next year. Their expedition had some success, but the colony was abandoned 1607 after the revocation of its trading monopoly. Poutrincourt, who had received a seigneurial land grant at PORT-ROYAL [Annapolis Royal, NS], was determined to return to Acadia, and finally did so in 1610 with an expedition that included his sons Charles and Jacques. Returning to France 1611 to raise money for the colony, Poutrincourt visited Port-Royal for the last time in 1614, only to find it devastated by English raiders. Nevertheless, a few colonists remained in Acadia with Charles, thus maintaining a continuous French presence there. Poutrincourt was killed during renewed civil strife in France in 1615.

JOHN G. REID

Bienville, Jean-Baptiste Le Moyne de, governor of Louisiana (bap at Montréal 23 Feb 1680; d at Paris, France 7 Mar 1767). Louisiana was New France's offshoot and the Canadian Le Moyne family were its godparents. A naval midshipman under his brother d'IBERVILLE, searching for the Mississippi's mouth in 1698-99, Bienville was left as second-in-command at the Biloxi post and became acting governor in 1701. For the next 40 years, he was frequently Louisiana's senior administrator because the nominal governors were absent or ineffectual. Officially, he was commandant general 1717-25 and royal governor 1732-43. He founded New Orleans in 1718 and secured

Louisiana's frontiers by military prowess, experience, ability to negotiate with Indian allies and diplomacy, keeping a small, sickly French colony caught between the Spanish and British empires alive. He retired voluntarily to France in 1743.
PETER N. MOOGK

Bienville, Lac, 1248 km², elev 427 m, max length 89 km, is located in a sparsely populated region of northern Québec. This elongated lake, dotted with numerous islands, is fed by Lacs La Forest, Louet, Brésolles, Ossant, Roz and De La Noue. It drains W, via the 334 km Grande Rivière de la Baleine (Great Whale R), into Hudson Bay. After the Sieur d'IBERVILLE's successful assault on Ft Nelson in the bay region in 1697, the lake was named for his younger brother, Jean-Baptiste Le Moyne, Sieur de Bienville. DAVID EVANS

Big Bear (Mistahimaskwa), Plains CREE chief (b near Ft Carlton, Sask 1825?; d on the Poundmaker Reserve 17 Jan 1888). By the 1870s Big Bear had emerged as a head man of about 65 lodges. He was concerned with the disappearance of the buffalo, the increasing numbers of European settlers, and impossible treaty conditions that seemed to ensure perpetual poverty and the destruction of his people's way of life. In 1876 he refused to sign Treaty No 6 and maintained that position until 8 Dec 1882, when with the last buffalo gone, starvation was a reality. He wanted to take a reservation near Ft Pitt, but when he saw the poverty of his friends there, he worked to wring further concessions from the federal government. In an attempt to unite the Northern Cree, several meetings were held at Battleford, the largest in 1884 when over 2000 Indians joined in Big Bear's thirst dance at Poundmaker's reserve. The event nearly erupted into violence, but through the efforts of the NWMP and Big Bear peace was maintained.

As a result of the federal government's refusal to negotiate with Big Bear, he lost the support of his more extreme followers. By 1885 they had become dominant and, led by Little Bad Man (Ayimisis) and Wandering Spirit (Kapapamahchakwew), they killed 9 whites at Frog Lake, burned Ft Pitt, and were defeated at Loon Lk. Big Bear, in

Big Bear (Mistahimaskwa), Plains Cree chief who refused to sign Treaty No 6 in 1876 because he believed that the treaty conditions would ensure the destruction of his people's way of life (courtesy National Archives of Canada/C-1873).

the background at these events and always counselling peace, surrendered at Ft Carlton on 2 July 1885. He was tried for treason-felony, found guilty and sentenced to a 3-year sentence at the Stony Mountain Penitentiary. A broken, sick man, Big Bear only served 2 years of the term and was released on 4 Mar 1887. *See also* NORTH-WEST REBELLION. FRITS PANNEKOEK

Big M Drug Mart Case Big M Drug Mart had been accused of selling merchandise on Sunday contrary to the Lord's Day Act. On 24 Apr 1985, the Supreme Court of Canada found that this federal statute conformed to the federal criminal law power as found in s91(27) of the Constitution Act, 1867, but was contrary to the freedom of religion guaranteed in s2 of the CANADIAN CHARTER OF RIGHTS AND FREEDOMS and consequently was inoperative by virtue of s52 of the Constitution Act, 1982. The Lord's Day Act had a religious, not a secular, purpose. It held the population to an ideal of the Christian religion. In the field of freedom of religion, the Lord's Day Act does not constitute a reasonable limit demonstrably justifiable in a free and democratic society and, therefore, it cannot be saved pursuant to s1 of the Charter. This statute furthermore was not in accordance with the maintenance and encouragement of the multicultural heritage of Canadians recognized in s27 of the Charter. GÉRALD-A. BEAUDOIN

Bigelow, Wilfred Gordon, surgeon (b at Brandon, Man 18 June 1913). Dr Bigelow's special contribution to surgery of the heart has been the use of hypothermia to slow tissue metabolism and thus protect the heart and brain from damage. He began this work with tedious but indispensable animal trials and by 1952 he was ready to apply this procedure to patients. At Toronto, the hypothermia research program led to another equally important breakthrough for cardiac surgery – the development of the first implantable cardiac pacemaker. Bigelow's account of these studies is in the book *Cold Hearts* is interwoven with the story of his own development as a surgeon-scientist. The book is a significant contribution to the history of cardiac surgery and for it he was awarded the Jason A. Hannah Medal of the Royal Society of Canada. He is professor emeritus of surgery, U of T. DONALD J.C. PHILLIPSON

Biggar, Sask, Town, pop 2626 (1986c), inc 1911, is located in W-central Saskatchewan, 100 km W of Saskatoon. Established by the Grand Trunk Pacific Railway, it was named for W.H. Biggar, general counsel of the GTPR. The community's initial development was based on the railway's decision to establish a divisional point at that location. It has continued its role as a railway centre and it still serves as the commercial hub of a good grain-farming area. Two large secondary industries process barley for malt and manufacture tractors. Its well-known slogan "New York is Big, but this is Biggar" greets visitors as they enter the town. DON HERPERGER

Biggar, Henry Percival, historian, archivist (b at Carrying Place, Ont 9 Aug 1872; d at Worplesdon, Eng 25 July 1938). Educated at Upper Canada College, U of T and Oxford, he joined the National Archives of Canada and served as chief archivist for Canada in Europe from 1905 until his death. An authority on the history of New France, he wrote *The Early Trading Companies of New France* (1901), and edited *The Precursors of Jacques Cartier* (1911) and *A Collection of Documents relating to Jacques Cartier and the Sieur de Roberval* (1930). He translated and edited *The Voyages of Jacques Cartier* (1924) and was general editor of *The Works of Samuel de Champlain* (1922-36). DAVID EVANS

Bighorn Sheep, *see* MOUNTAIN SHEEP.

Bigot, François, financial commissary of Île Royale 1739-45, intendant of New France 1748-60 (bap at Bordeaux, France 30 Jan 1703; d at Neuchâtel, Switz 12 Jan 1778). Traditionally Bigot has been remembered for administrative fraud so massive as to cause the CONQUEST of New France by the British during the SEVEN YEARS' WAR.

After the British capture of Louisbourg in 1745 Bigot was sent back to Canada in 1748, against his personal wishes, to assume chief responsibility for the civil government of New France. Soon merchants began to complain that only Bigot's friends were receiving contracts to supply the government. Recalled to France in 1754 to answer these charges, his explanations apparently were satisfactory, since he was reassigned to Canada in 1755.

Government spending on Canada during the Seven Years' War rose from just over 6 million *livres* in 1755 to over 30 million in 1759. The French government believed Bigot and his associates (*see* GRANDE SOCIÉTÉ) stole much of the money. Following a show trial in Paris, referred to as the "Affaire du Canada," Bigot was sentenced to "restore" 1.5 million *livres* to the French Crown in 1763. He paid the money and ended his days in relative poverty and disgrace in exile in Switzerland. Ever since historians have debated the degree to which Bigot's dealings were criminal. The recent consensus is that his behaviour was typical of the period and that skyrocketing expenditures resulted from the war and the British blockade. In fact, Bigot was an extremely able administrator. He also presided over magnificent banquets and balls that scandalized the clergy in Canada, and his gambling bouts were notorious. HUGH A. PORTEOUS

Bilingualism is the ability to speak or write fluently in 2 languages. In Canada the term has taken on a more particular meaning: the ability to communicate (or the practice of communicating) in both of Canada's official languages, English and French. It has been formalized in LANGUAGE POLICY, in an attempt by government to respond to a difficult social question: to what extent is it possible to make legal and practical accommodations that will allow the 2 official language communities to preserve their cultural distinctiveness and at the same time pursue common goals? "Institutional bilingualism" refers to the capacity of state institutions to operate in 2 languages and should not be confused with a requirement that everyone be bilingual.

Historically, institutional bilingualism has recognized the facts of Canada's settlement and development. Implicit in the founding of the Canadian federation was the idea that the English- and French-speaking communities should not only coexist but should complement each other. The BRITISH NORTH AMERICA ACT of 1867 established English and French as legislative and judicial languages in federal and Quebec institutions. It also set out the right to denominational schooling, which at that time was closely associated with the anglophone (Protestant) and francophone (Roman Catholic) linguistic and cultural traditions.

The development of the bilingual and bicultural nature of the Canadian federation soon experienced setbacks, partly as a result of the uneven application of principles and partly from a simple lack of linguistic tolerance. Although the BNA Act and the Manitoba Act (1870) accorded the French language official status in Quebec and Manitoba respectively, no such recognition was granted to the substantial French-speaking populations of Ontario and New Brunswick. Furthermore, in the late 19th and early 20th centuries a series of legislative enactments across Canada seriously restricted French-language education and virtually eliminated the use of French in provincial legislatures and courts outside Québec.

Although the effects of these and other measures understandably linger in the minds of many Canadians, Canada has, since WWII, found a new concern for the official status of English and French and the destiny of minority language communities throughout the country. At the same time, demographic patterns, and particularly the tendency of Francophones outside Québec to become assimilated to the English-speaking community, have increased the polarization between the official language groups. This in turn has brought attention to the relationship of linguistic justice and national unity. Increasingly the enhancement of the French language and culture in Canada and a reaffirmation of the rights of the English language and culture in Québec are seen as fundamental to maintaining a reasonable degree of national integrity.

The problems and demands of bilingualism within the national framework were clearly set forth by the Royal Commission on BILINGUALISM AND BICULTURALISM (1963-69). Central to the commission's recommendations was the premise that the English and French minorities throughout Canada, when of reasonable size, should be assured public services in their own language and afforded as much opportunity as possible to use their mother tongue. The commission also urged that French become a normal language of work, together with English, in the federal administration and that government documents and correspondence be generally available in both languages. Moreover the commission stressed that there was room within an officially bilingual state for other forms of linguistic and cultural pluralism, so that bilingualism and MULTICULTURALISM might complement each other.

The commission's work culminated in the adoption of the federal OFFICIAL LANGUAGES ACT (1969), designed to be the cornerstone of institutional bilingualism in Canada. The Act, which declares the "equality of status" of English and French in Parliament and the Canadian public service, applies to all federal departments, judicial and quasi-judicial bodies, and administrative agencies and crown corporations established by federal statute. In addition to prescribing federal reforms and establishing the office of Commissioner of Official Languages to see that they are carried out, the Act has prompted initiatives beyond the federal administration. With encouragement and financial assistance from Ottawa, provincial governments and parts of the parapublic and private sectors have begun to re-examine their linguistic policies, at least in the services they offer, and have made some effort to pursue a policy of institutional bilingualism.

The success of any Canadian policy on bilingualism is closely tied to the co-operation of the provinces. Provincial powers in the fields of justice, public services and education can be influenced only indirectly by federal policies. To complete the picture, numerous administrative, judicial, social and educational services need to be provided by municipal and provincial authorities in regions where there are large minority-language populations.

New Brunswick passed an Official Languages Act in 1969, giving equal status, rights and privileges to English and French; since the early 1970s, Ontario has increased the use of French in its courts and has passed a bill guaranteeing French services in those areas of the province where the majority of Franco-Ontarians live; and Manitoba, as a result of a 1979 Supreme Court ruling, is moving towards the translation of its statutes into French and the transformation of its courts into bilingual institutions. The extent of

Manitoba's compliance with its constitutional requirements has become the focus of a heated political debate both inside and outside the province and in 1985 the Supreme Court of Canada gave the province 3 years to translate its laws.

Québec has recognized French as its sole official language since 1974. Although a number of government services are available in English (usually on request) the province has the peculiarity of being institutionally bilingual at the constitutional and federal levels while giving official recognition only to French at the level of provincial institutions. All provinces, helped to some extent by the federal Official Languages in Education Program, now have minority-language education programs. Furthermore, SECOND-LANGUAGE INSTRUCTION has made remarkable gains across Canada, most conspicuously through the expansion of French-immersion programs in primary schools.

In Apr 1982 the CANADIAN CHARTER OF RIGHTS AND FREEDOMS came into force. The Charter reinforces previous constitutional principles regarding language use in federal courts and the courts of Québec and Manitoba, reaffirms the availability of bilingual services in the federal administration and confirms New Brunswick as the only completely bilingual province. It also breaks new ground by entrenching minority-language education rights in Canada, guaranteeing the right of children of Canadian citizens who find themselves in an official-language minority situation to an education in their own language wherever numbers warrant it. This guarantee represents a recognition that minority language education rights may be the key to the survival of minority language communities across the country.

The Charter defined what was possible at the time of its enactment in the realm of institutional bilingualism, but its provisions may be developed and extended. The leadership of federal and provincial authorities in this respect is essential to achieving the underlying goal of language reform in Canada: the possibility for individuals of either anglophone or francophone background to move from province to province without forgoing their fundamental language rights and cultural identity. *See also* FRANCOPHONE-ANGLOPHONE RELATIONS; CULTURAL DUALISM.

Reading: Canada, Commissioner of Official Languages, Annual Reports; Royal Commission on Bilingualism and Biculturalism, *Report* (6 vols, 1967-70).

Bilingualism and Biculturalism, Royal Commission on, (1963-71), often referred to by the names of its co-chairmen, Laurendeau-Dunton. It was commissioned to examine existing BILINGUALISM and BICULTURALISM, and to recommend ways of ensuring wider recognition of the basic CULTURAL DUALISM of Canada. The commission was established in response to the growing unrest among French Canadians in Québec, who called for the protection of their language and culture and the opportunity to participate fully in political and economic decision making. It had 3 main areas of inquiry: the extent of bilingualism in the federal administration, the role of public and private organizations in promoting better cultural relations and the opportunities for Canadians to become bilingual in English and French. The commissioners used as their guiding principle the concept of "equal partnership" – equal opportunity for Francophones and Anglophones to participate in the institutions affecting their individual and collective lives. The commissioners were also to report on the cultural contribution of other ethnic groups and the means of preserving this contribution. In addition to a preliminary report (1965), a final report in 6 books was published, titled *The Official Languages* (1967), *Educa-*

tion (1968), *The Work World* (Socioeconomic Status, the Federal Administration, the Private Sector, 1969), *The Cultural Contribution of the Other Ethnic Groups* (1969), *The Federal Capital* (1970), and *Voluntary Associations* (1970). Ten commissioners representing Canada's cultural-linguistic composition were chosen. All spoke English and French and commission business was conducted in both languages. Since education is a provincial responsibility, the co-chairmen called on all provincial premiers to obtain their co-operation in that section of the inquiry.

A royal commission to examine Québec's dissatisfaction had first been suggested by the editor in chief of *Le Devoir*, André LAURENDEAU, and it was established later under PM Lester B. Pearson. Laurendeau and A. Davidson DUNTON were appointed co-chairmen of the commission. Laurendeau died in 1968 and his post was assumed by Jean-Louis Gagnon. For many Québécois, the RCBB was a maneuvre to obscure the political issues. For many Anglophones, especially in western Canada, it was an attempt to force the French language on an unwilling population. The enquiry, however, revealed that Francophones did not occupy in the economy, nor in the decision-making ranks of government, the place their numbers warranted; that educational opportunities for the francophone minorities were not commensurate with those provided for the anglophone minority within Québec; and that French-speaking Canadians could neither find employment nor be served adequately in their language in federal-government agencies.

Recommendations to correct these and other serious weaknesses were implemented with unusual alacrity. Educational authorities in all 9 anglophone provinces reformed regulations concerning French minority education and moved to improve the teaching of French as a second language with financial assistance from the federal government. NB declared itself officially bilingual; Ontario did not, but greatly extended its services in French. French-language rights in the legislature and courts of Manitoba, disallowed by statutes passed in Manitoba in 1890, were restored by decision of the Supreme Court of Canada in 1979. A federal department of multiculturalism was established. Institutional bilingualism at the federal level became a fact with the passing of the OFFICIAL LANGUAGES ACT (1969) and the appointment of a Commissioner of Official Languages. Because of lack of time, the commission did not examine constitutional questions, as anticipated in the introduction to the final report, and the movement toward independence in Québec continued. It did, however, lay the foundation for functional bilingualism throughout the country, and for increased acceptance of cultural diversity.   G. LAING

Bill 22, *Loi sur la langue officielle*, sponsored by the Québec Liberal government of Robert BOURASSA and passed by the legislature July 1974. It made French the language of civic administration and services, and of the workplace. Only children who could demonstrate sufficient knowledge of another language of instruction would be exempted from receiving their instruction in French. Increasing social unrest and a rise in nationalist sentiment had led to the repeal of BILL 63 and the introduction of this more comprehensive bill which, in parliamentary committee, attracted 160 written submissions. Nationalist and labour groups thought the law did not go far enough and rejected it. Anglophone and ethnic groups thought the language tests imposed by the law were unjust, and showed their displeasure in the provincial election of November 1976 by denying the Liberal Party their traditional support.   R. HUDON

Bill 63, *Loi pour promouvoir la langue française au Québec* (Nov 1969), required children receiving their education in English to acquire a working knowledge of French and required immigrants to enroll their children in French-language schools. In 1967, the school board of Saint-Léonard (Montréal) had insisted that children of immigrants within its jurisdiction receive unilingual French education. Anglophone opposition caused the UNION NATIONALE government to introduce Bill 85, which never passed the parliamentary committee stage. The Gendron Commission was then established to investigate language problems in Québec, but when a compromise proposed by the Saint-Léonard school board trustees led to violent demonstrations, the government introduced Bill 63 without awaiting the commission's recommendations. Bill 63 aroused unprecedented opposition among Québec's francophone population who believed it was too weak a measure. It was eventually repealed and replaced by the more comprehensive BILL 22.   R. HUDON

Bill 101, *Charte de la langue française* (1977), marked the culmination of a debate that had produced BILL 63 (1969) and BILL 22 (1974). It made French the official language of the state and of the courts in the province of Québec, as well as making it the normal and habitual language of the workplace, of instruction, of communications, of commerce and of business. Education in French became compulsory for immigrants, even those from other Canadian provinces, unless a "reciprocal agreement" existed between Québec and that province. For the PARTI QUÉBÉCOIS government a new language law was a high priority. After publishing a White Paper on the subject (1977), it introduced Bill 1, which was strongly supported by nationalist and union groups among others, and was just as sharply opposed by management circles and the province's anglophone population. The bill was withdrawn because of pressure from the Liberal opposition and reappeared as Bill 101. In 1980 the Supreme Court of Canada supported a judgement of the Québec Superior Court that struck down the section of *Charte* which declared French the language of the legislature and courts, and in 1984 ruled that the CANADIAN CHARTER OF RIGHTS AND FREEDOMS (article 23) limited the bill's power to regulate the language of instruction.   R. HUDON

Bill 101 Case On 26 July 1984, the Supreme Court of Canada declared invalid s72 and s73 of BILL 101 (the Charter of the French Language) concerning English-language schooling in Québec on the grounds that these provisions were incompatible with s23 of the CANADIAN CHARTER OF RIGHTS AND FREEDOMS. Supposing that s1 of the Charter applies to s23, these provisions cannot be legitimized on the basis of s1 of the Charter. Section 73 of Bill 101 is precise and in essence redefines the categories of persons entitled to receive instruction in the language of the anglophone minority. The restrictions authorized by s1 of the Charter cannot have equal value to the derogations allowed under s33 of the Charter, which, whatever the circumstances, does not apply to s23. Only a true constitutional amendment can bring about a redefinition of the categories of s23.

GÉRALD-A. BEAUDOIN

Billiards games have been played for several hundred years and have been popular in N America since the early 1800s. In Canada, snooker is the most popular of these games, with some pool and varieties of billiards also being played. The game of billiards, while using the same equipment of the rectangular table, balls and leather-tipped cue, has developed into several variations. English billiards is usually played by 2 players,

using a set of 3 balls (one red and 2 white). A player scores by pocketing his cue ball after striking another ball, by pocketing another ball by striking it with the cue ball, or by striking both other balls with his cue ball. Canadian Cyrille Dion was world champion in 1873 of a pocketless variation of billiards, in which the scoring is entirely by caroms.

In snooker 22 balls are used: a white (cue) ball, 15 red balls and 6 numbered colours – yellow (2), green (3), brown (4), blue (5), pink (6) and black (7). Two players usually compete. A player must strike a red first and if it is potted (1 point) may then choose one of the "colours" which, if potted, is replaced on the table and another red is attempted. When all the reds have been potted the colours must be played in order of value. The winner has the most points when all the balls have been potted. A match will consist of a number of games. The word "snooker" refers to a position in which a player cannot hit the ball that he is required to play because of the obstruction of another ball. The performance of George CHENIER from the mid-1940s to mid-1960s raised the status of billiards and snooker in Canada. The maximum run (or "break") possible in snooker is 147. The first and youngest Canadian to run 147 was the 17-year-old Vic Kireluk (1926-81) in Oshawa (1944). The first Canadian to run 147 in a competition was Bernie Mikkelsen in 1977. Cliff THORBURN with 26 perfect games has the most by any Canadian. In England in 1983 he scored the first perfect run in World Championship play. Two Canadian women hold records: Natalie Stelmach was the first woman to make a century run (109 in 1977) and Sue LeMaich has the most centuries, 12, with a high run of 128.

Billiard games are played in clubs, private homes and in public "pool halls". There are about 2500 public rooms in Canada and over 250 000 regular players. The social stigma of the pool hall is fading as many rooms are now well furnished, respectable centres of family recreation. The term "pool" includes the more than 60 games played on the American tables and is sometimes loosely applied to snooker. The major pool games are 8-ball, 9-ball and 14-1 (or straight pool). In 8-ball and 9-ball the winner is determined by the first player to pocket the 8 or 9 ball; in 14-1 the winner is the first player to pot the agreed number of balls. The pool games use a set of 15 object balls numbered from 1 to 15 and a white cue ball.

In the 1970s the nationwide organization of games began. The major governing bodies are Canadian Snooker Control Council (formed 1975), Canadian Billiards and Snooker Referees Assn (1974), Canadian Professional Snooker Assn (1979) and Women's Snooker Assn of Canada (1979).   GRAHAM DUNCAN

Billings, Elkanah, paleontologist (b at Gloucester, Upper Canada 5 May 1820; d at Montréal 14 June 1876). Billings's interpretation of fossils belonging to the GEOLOGICAL SURVEY OF CANADA was partly responsible for that organization's early success. He started professional life as a lawyer (1844-52), subsequently devoting himself exclusively to natural history. He contributed articles to the Bytown [Ottawa] *Citizen* and the *Canadian Naturalist and Geologist*, which he founded in 1856. His publications on fossils came to the attention of W.E. LOGAN, director of the GSC, who appointed him survey paleontologist in 1856. The study of fossils collected by the survey occupied him for the rest of his life. His insight into the stratigraphic value of fossils helped to identify the formations visited by GSC field parties, and provided Logan with information upon which he later based his concept of the "great overlap" (first published description of thrust faulting), and

contributed to the success of Logan's monumental work *Geology of Canada* (1863). Of Billings's scientific writings, 2 items stand out: *Figures and Descriptions of Canadian Organic Remains* (1858-59) and *Palaeozoic Fossils* (1865-74).   T.H. CLARK

Billion Dollar Gift, the Canadian government's first comprehensive attempt to help finance Britain's war effort during WORLD WAR II. Canada's war production, and its wartime prosperity, was dependent upon British orders, but Britain lacked gold and dollar reserves. Consequently, Canada gave its ally "munitions of war" worth $1 billion, in an act of unprecedented generosity. The grant, which was announced in Jan 1942 and accompanied by an interest-free loan of $700 million and other assistance, was expected to last approximately 15 months. Instead, it was depleted before the year ended. Emphasis on the gift's monetary value, rather than on the goods produced and provided, distorted its image in the public's eyes. The gift was thus politically unpopular, especially in Québec, where it was depicted as tribute to "perfidious Albion." Nonetheless, it dramatically illustrated the importance of Canada's material contribution to the Allied cause. It was succeeded in May 1943 by MUTUAL AID.

HECTOR M. MACKENZIE

Binning, Bertram Charles, painter (b at Medicine Hat, Alta 10 Feb 1909; d at Vancouver 16 Mar 1976). B.C. Binning, as he signed his work, came of a line of architects, but during years of adolescent illness he turned to drawing. In 1927 he began studying at the Vancouver School of Decorative and Applied Arts (shortly to become the Vancouver School of Art) under F.H. VARLEY. In the 1930s he studied in New York and London, under Mark Gertler, Amédée Ozenfant and Henry Moore. In 1934 Binning was first appointed to the Vancouver School of Art, and in 1949 to the UBC School of Architecture; shortly afterwards he founded the Dept of Fine Arts, which he headed for a quarter century.

Binning built an international reputation as a draftsman before taking to oil painting in 1948; he thought of drawing as "the most revealing expression of the artist" and his drawings, with their disciplined yet joyfully wandering lines, are his most valued work. His first paintings were of boats, and were characterized by gay colour and the use of the painting's flatness as a structural element. His continuing interest in architecture led him to design large mosaic murals for public buildings. His later paintings became stylized seascapes and, by the 1960s, purely abstract forms seeking to express what he called "the great quiet spatial ideas." His late years were shadowed by illness, and he painted little. The 1973 retrospective exhibition in Vancouver was his last. He was one of the first modernist painters in western Canada and a rare classicist among Canadian artists.   GEORGE WOODCOCK

Biochemistry, study of the chemical nature of living material and of the chemical transformations that occur within it. Living things consist of many types of molecules (biomolecules) which, when isolated and examined, have no particular "living" characteristics, but behave in ordinary chemical ways. The properties of some of these molecules, especially large ones, are complex and subtle but are the result of the operation of chemical and physical laws. The special characteristics of living things arise from the ways in which these biomolecules are assembled within the cell. The methodology of biochemistry originated largely in PHYSICS, CHEMISTRY, IMMUNOLOGY AND GENETICS.

Biochemistry began to emerge in Canada and the world during the last decades of the 19th century. Topics in early biochemistry were usually taught in medical schools by chemists. For example, a course in clinical and physiological chemistry was established by R.F. Ruttan and William OSLER at McGill in 1883. The department of biochemistry organized at the University of Toronto under Archibald B. MACALLUM was the first in the country and the second in the British Empire. Maud L. Menten, a student of Macallum's, worked with the German biochemist Leonor Michaelis to clarify the kinetics of enzyme reactions; the basic equation used in enzyme kinetics is called the Michaelis-Menten equation.

During the first 3 decades of the century, biochemistry research was conducted primarily at the universities. In this early period, courses in biochemistry were established at the following universities: Manitoba, 1909 (dept, 1923); Montréal, 1911 (dept, 1951); Queen's, 1914 (dept, 1937); Alberta, 1915 (dept, 1922); Saskatchewan, 1916 (dept, 1946); Western Ontario, 1921; Dalhousie, 1924; British Columbia, 1927 (dept, 1950); Laval, 1928 (dept, 1940). Most Canadian universities now offer courses in biochemistry, through faculties of medicine, science and agriculture. In addition, many of the agricultural colleges offer plant biochemistry programs.

Canadian reseachers have done excellent basic research in all areas of biochemistry, from studies of the proteins in cereal grains to studies of substances that inhibit neural (ie, brain) responses. Medical biochemists have made significant contributions in the study of hormones (endocrinology), blood fractions and the metabolism of chemical elements (eg, zinc and sulphur) and proteins. The outstanding early biochemical event in Canada was the first successful extraction from pancreas tissue of INSULIN and its application to the alleviation of diabetes. F.G. BANTING, C.H. BEST and J.J.R. MACLEOD were involved in the discovery, for which Banting and Macleod received a Nobel Prize in 1923. J.B. COLLIP was largely responsible for the purification procedures which made possible the use of insulin on human patients. Other Canadian research with direct application to medical practice included early studies in toxemias and nausea in pregnancy by V.J. HARDING (McGill, U of T), which led to the use of glucose therapy; research into the production of glandular extracts by E.W. McHenry (Connaught Laboratories, U of T), which led to a procedure for preparing active liver fractions for oral (later intramuscular injection) use in pernicious anemia; studies in steroids by J.S. Browne and Eleanor Venning (McGill) and in protein metabolism in shock victims by Browne; immunological research by J.S. Colter (U of A), A. Sehon (McGill, U Man), L.C. Vining (Dalhousie) and others; and research into malignancies and cancers by J.H. QUASTEL (Montreal-McGill General Hospital Research Inst), J.S. Colter, M.J. Fraser (U Man, Ontario Cancer Inst, McGill) and others. M. Chrétien, Institut de recherches cliniques de Montréal, has done pioneering work on peptide hormones. Some Canadian biochemists have attempted to elucidate the biochemical processes in brain tissue (eg, K.A.C. ELLIOTT, McGill; R.J. Rossiter, U of Western Ontario) and potential biochemical abnormalities associated with epilepsy (eg, E.A. Hosein, McGill) and mental illness (eg, J.H. Quastel). Other medically oriented research conducted in Canada relates to genetics and to GENETIC ENGINEERING. Canadian university researchers have also made major technological innovations; for example, K.A. Evelyn, then a research fellow at McGill, developed a photoelectric calorimeter with filters, manufactured commercially and used until the 1950s.

Beginning in the late 1930s, biochemists working at federal research institutions have made substantial contributions to biochemical knowl-edge, many of which have had immediate, practical effects. Biochemistry research was first undertaken at the NATIONAL RESEARCH COUNCIL OF CANADA after the establishment of biochemical laboratory facilities in 1932. Initially, NRC's research was very practically oriented, dealing, for example, with the processing and preservation of food, the effect of hormones on wheat and, later, the preservation of human blood fractions. Later research dealt with more diverse subjects and the early food-processing orientation became of minor importance. More recently, research has also involved biochemical processes in micro-organisms (eg, relating to lipoproteins, ribosome structure). Atomic Energy of Canada Ltd has facilities for biochemical research into the effects of radiation. Environment Canada has biochemical laboratories in each of its major divisions (eg, Fisheries, Forestry). Health and Welfare Canada maintains extensive facilities across the country to conduct the analyses necessary for enforcement of the Food and Drugs Act. Agriculture Canada has been responsible for much significant research in various areas, including the protein content of grains and the means of enhancing protein content, and the baking properties dependent upon it; the metabolism of plant toxins; pathogenic fungi; fatty acids in oilseeds; synthesis of hormones in animal species; and animal disease. Some biochemical research is carried on by the provincial research organizations; the earliest provincial biochemical research program was established by the ALBERTA RESEARCH COUNCIL (1951).

Various special, largely medically oriented, institutions undertake some biochemical work, eg, Montreal-McGill General Hospital Research Institute, Allan Memorial Institute of Psychiatry (Montréal), Montreal Neurological Institute, Banting Institute (U of T), Hospital for Sick Children Research Institute (Toronto) and National Cancer Institute (research units across Canada).

In industry, biochemistry research has been largely confined to the drug manufacturing companies, eg, Ayerst Laboratories, Frosst, CONNAUGHT LABORATORIES, INSTITUT ARMAND-FRAPPIER, Veterinary Infectious Disease Organization (University of Saskatchewan). Biochemistry has important practical applications in the food and beverage industries; hence, many industries have quality control laboratories and some, notably Canada Packers and Labatt Brewing, also operate research laboratories. Several BIOTECHNOLOGY companies have opened across Canada in the 1980s, and this field will continue to expand.

Research in Canada is largely federally funded. Grants (primarily to individual researchers and to the universities) are co-ordinated principally by the MEDICAL RESEARCH COUNCIL of Canada.

With the exception of the Royal Society of Canada, the first national society with substantial representation among biochemists was the Canadian Physiological Society (est 1934); the Canadian Biochemical Society was an offshoot of this association. In 1957 the Canadian Federation of Biological Sciences was established. Biochemists have also supported and been represented by chemical associations (eg, Chemical Institute of Canada, est 1945) and nutritionists' associations (eg, Nutrition Society of Canada, est 1957). Canadian biochemists contribute to various national and international journals, the principal national journal being the *Canadian Journal of Biochemistry and Cell Biology* (formerly the *Canadian Journal of Biochemistry*). *See also* BIOLOGY.   DAVID B. SMITH

Reading: W.C. McMurray, *A Synopsis of Human Biochemistry* (1982); E. Gordon Young, *Development of Biochemistry in Canada* (1976).

Bioethics, from the Greek word for life (*bios*) and the traditional word for systematic study of right conduct (ethics). Bioethics is one of society's attempts to manage new and far-reaching powers over life, powers coming from quite recent advances in MEDICINE, GENETICS, MOLECULAR BIOLOGY, reproductive BIOLOGY and other specializations in the life sciences. The most extensive developments and applications of these sciences have occurred in pluralistic societies, ie, those composed of a number of communities holding different moralities and philosophies of life. These communities differ on questions of right and wrong and often take conflicting positions on how advances in the life sciences may, should or should not be applied. The conflict may arise from differences about governing beliefs and assumptions concerning human life (ethos), fundamental and dominant values (morality) or the norms and methods to be used in resolving value conflicts (ethics). Such moral and ethical issues may arise in any domain of activity; however, those created by developments in the life sciences have been most prominent in attracting public attention and mobilizing societal reflection over the past 15 years. The principal issues have come from questions about research involving experimentation on human subjects; withholding or withdrawing various forms of life-support treatment from critically ill patients; euthanasia; ABORTION; prenatal diagnosis, genetic screening and selective abortion; sterilization of the mentally handicapped, BIRTH CONTROL, artificial insemination, *in vitro* fertilization and surrogate motherhood; transplantation of organs and implantation of artificial organs; the definition of DEATH; psychosurgical, psychopharmacological and conditioning approaches to the control of human behaviour; recombinant DNA technology (RDT), GENETIC ENGINEERING and genetic therapy; and finally the just distribution of limited resources.

During the late 1960s and early 1970s, a number of ethics institutes, law-reform commissions and public-policy commissions throughout the world have promoted the interdisciplinary study and resolution of these issues. Following the leadership of the Institute of Society, Ethics, and the Life Sciences (Hastings-on-Hudson, NY, est 1969), Kennedy Institute of Ethics (Georgetown University, Washington, DC, 1971) and the Society for the Study of Medical Ethics (London, Eng, 1972), institutes for bioethics have been established in many countries. The principal Canadian organizations that have contributed to the development of bioethics are the Center for Bioethics of the Clinical Research Institute of Montréal (1976), the Protection of Life Project of the Law Reform Commission of Canada (Ottawa, 1976), the Westminster Institute for Ethics and Human Values (London, Ont, 1978) and bioethics research and teaching institutes at Laval (1980), U de M (1981), UQAR (1984), U of C (1984), U Man (1985), McGill (1986) and U of A (1986). A number of professional associations, such as the CANADIAN MEDICAL ASSOCIATION, have established their own bioethics committees and the Canadian Hospital Association has given its support to the concept of ethics committees as an aid to ethical decision making in hospitals and in health-care facilities.

Institutes and committees for bioethics represent a societal effort to mount and maintain systematic reflection on the ethical uncertainties, dilemmas and conflicts raised by advances in biomedical science and technology. Innovations in genetics, human embryology, fetal medicine, geriatrics, gerontology, immunology and the neurosciences, and the appearance of new epidemic diseases such as AIDS, will add new challenges to the agenda of those working in bioethics in the coming decades. The goal of interdisciplinary, international and intercultural research and reflection in bioethics is to clarify the content of policies designed to harmonize individual rights and welfare with the common good of present and future generations. *See also* MEDICAL ETHICS.   DAVID J. ROY

Reading: Warren Reich, ed, *Encyclopedia of Bioethics*, (4 vols, (1978); *SYNAPSE: A Canadian News Service for Biomedical Ethics*, published quarterly by the Center for Bioethics, Clinical Research Institute of Montréal; J.R. Williams, *Biomedical Ethics in Canada* (1986).

Biogeoclimatic Zone, large ecosystem that is geographically limited and controlled by a special ("single") macroclimate. The same predominant soil-forming processes determine the zone's SOIL and, consequently, its vegetation and animal life. Such a zone encompasses a number of smaller, vegetationally and environmentally more uniform ecosystems, which differ in those components that develop in response to conditions which are drier or moister than the zone's mesic (average) environment. The stable community of plants that develops in response to the climatic conditions of mesic sites is the most significant characteristic community of a biogeoclimatic zone. If common enough, edaphic plants, ie, those that develop in response to soil rather than climatic conditions, may also be significant. In Canada, the soils most commonly used for zonal soil characterization are those that have developed since glaciation from glacial drift or its outwash, or from at least several-thousand-year-old lacustrine (lake) alluvial (running water) or aeolian (wind) deposits. Below the zonal level are subzones or their variations; above are higher units, ie, biogeoclimatic regions and formations. Biogeoclimatic zones have been studied in Canada (BC, Alta and the YT), the Hawaiian Is, Japan (Hokkaido I) and Indonesia. V.J. KRAJINA

Biogeography studies all aspects of the adaptations of an organism to its ENVIRONMENT, considering systematically the origins, migrations and associations of living things. Hence, it aims for a synthesis of data from nonbiological and biological disciplines: GEOLOGY, PHYSICAL GEOGRAPHY, GEOMORPHOLOGY, CLIMATOLOGY and METEOROLOGY, on the one hand; BIOLOGY, taxonomy, GENETICS and physiology, on the other. Biogeographical relationships cannot be understood except from an ecological perspective which tries to explain the exchanges between an organism and its environment. Ecology is subdivided into 3 fields of study: autecology (relations of individual species or populations to their milieu), synecology (composition of living communities) and dynecology (processes of change in related communities). Therefore, in its widest compass, biogeography concerns itself with the EVOLUTION of species, with changes in their ranges and with their extinctions. The principal factors influencing evolutionary development are climatic and edaphic (ie, soil-related) constraints, genetic adaptation and social integration.

Ultimately, biogeographic phenomena are explicable only as resolutions of conflicts between heredity and environment. The macroenvironment must contain resources that meet the requirements of individual organisms. Hence, the living population must be viewed as existing in nested environments of increasing magnitude that contain the positive and negative forces that act upon it. From smallest to largest these environments may be designated niche, ecotope, community, ecosystem, landscape and bioclimate. The defining of orders of magnitude in the environment permits the identification of providers of resources and factors of constraint. At its lowest spatial level, the niche, the organism encounters an accumulation of all environmental impacts. Such impacts can usually be traced to larger spatial units and to higher orders of control.

For example, the tiny annual plant *Koenigia islandica* and the summer-breeding Lapland longspur occupy different ecotopes of a Baffin I sedge community, which itself is part of a larger marsh ecosystem (flats that undergo inconstant flooding) in an otherwise varied landscape under the severe stress of a high-arctic bioclimate.

The ultimate explanation of plant and animal behaviour and of the fitness of an individual population to its habitat must be sought at each level. Questions concerning the relative importance of, for example, climate/soil, acidity/alkalinity (of soil), sun/shade, may be irrelevant if not set in a frame that will allow the assessment of cumulative effects. For example, climatic effects are most significant in determining the range limitations of many species. Consequently, present-day climatic limitations and knowledge of past circumstances can provide information about the place of origin of species and the migrations that have resulted in their present position.

The principle that must be kept in sight is that each kind of plant and animal (including man) has an individual ecological strategy that makes it more or less fit to survive in its environment. An estimation of fitness depends on 3 factors: requirements (R), tolerance (T) and efficiency (E). The table lists responses in some Canadian plant, animal and human populations and shows outstanding features of their ecological strategy. Marginal notations give an overall estimation: H (high), L (low), V (variable). The table does not provide an inventory of the living conditions wherein the life cycle of each organism unfolds, but it draws attention to some of the responses that result from R, T and E in each case. Two species having the same requirements and tolerance do not necessarily have the same efficiency. Thus, where sugar maple and beech grow together (eg, in the eastern Canadian forest), the maples seed more regularly and abundantly and usually far outweigh the beeches in the total biomass. Several nesting birds share cattail marshes with the redwinged blackbird, but do not equal its numbers or stability. Inuit populations in contact with southern Canadians rapidly increase their efficiency by applying their ability to learn new technology and move into a storage-exchange economy.

The study of all existing species of plants and animals in a given area (a forest stand, a lake, a region) often reveals the presence of units that have come there from many diverse areas. Thus, some very old geological events have left closely related species very far apart: northeastern Asia and eastern N America have very similar pairs of deciduous trees (eg, birches, maples, beeches, walnuts, tulip trees); the plains and deserts of N and S America harbour similar species long isolated from one another; Argentina and New Zealand have forests and grasslands dominated by closely related units (eg, *Nothofagus, Podocarpus*); the mammals and fishes of northern Europe and Canada show many affinities (eg, moose, pike).

Undoubtedly, the geological episode that has cast its stamp most visibly on Canada's landscape is the Pleistocene ice age, the last million years or so. Several successive vegetation sequences followed the retreat of the ice sheet (from 18 000 years ago to the present). For example, the following table describes the vegetation sequences of the Mt Shefford area of southern Québec. It is especially interesting to note the temporary prevalence of vegetation types (eg, aspen parkland) that no longer exist in contemporary eastern N America.

The living flora of southern Québec contain many species that originated in the Tertiary (from 66.4 million to 1.6 million years ago) eastern deciduous forest (sugar maple, beech, white trilli-

um, bloodroot, woodland frog, ovenbird, white-tailed deer, etc); other species are closely linked to the boreal transcontinental spruce-fir (or Canadian) forest (white spruce, bunchberry, twinflower, feather mosses; brook trout, moose, purple finches, etc). Some have midwestern affinities (creeping ferns, cork elms, mud pickerel, evening grosbeaks, etc). Atlantic coastal-plain elements are rarer (grey birch, candleberry, broom crowberry, etc). Truly arctic-alpine species (eg, purple saxifrage, mountain avens) are generally restricted to higher altitudes. There are, of course, many widespread organisms (aspens, raspberries, crows), and some that have a nearly worldwide range (bracken ferns, reeds, cattails, etc). None of the above include the introduced weeds (eg, dandelion, crabgrass, galinsoga) or pests (eg, starlings, rats) that are completely naturalized (capable of fulfilling their life cycle unaided).

Similar regional units in Canada or elsewhere, if analysed floristically, would also reveal a composite picture reflecting the history of past fluctuations. Plants of the southern prairies belong to several units that witness more or less unresolved conflicts. The tall-grass prairie (big bluestem), mixed-grass prairie (blue grama, wheatgrass) and short-grass prairie (fescue) have repeatedly moved N and S and left traces. The spotty occurrence of N American halophytes (plants that grow in salty soil, eg, samphire, atriplex, greasewood) and of Great Basin desert plants (umbrella plant) also points to fluctuation of drought and high temperatures. Western boreal-forest elements (Murray pine, Alberta spruce, western prince's pine, devil's paintbrush) and eastern ones (twinflower, bunchberry, bearberry) come together in the cooler highlands. Some eastern deciduous forest species (American elm, false Solomon's seal, sweet cicely) migrate far W along the bluffs and floodplains.

The patterns of geographic distribution of plants and animals are, therefore, very revealing of past fluctuations in the displacement of the communities that harboured them, and indeed of whole bioclimatic areas that have shifted across continents. The biogeography of Canada must be seen as a whole, not solely as patterns of key species of plants and animals. This perspective requires the broader framework of world units. Worldwide, 20 bioclimatic formation classes have been identified, based on the 2 more or less independent variables, heat and moisture: tropical rain forest, temperate rain forest, tropical deciduous forest, summer-green deciduous forest, needle-leaved evergreen forest, evergreen hardwood forest, tropical woodland, temperate woodland, tropical savannah, temperate and cold savannah, thornbush, tropical scrub, temperate and cold scrub, tundra, prairie, steppe, meadow, warm desert, cold desert and crust vegetation. These classes are very unevenly distributed on the planet.

An extreme combination of heat and moisture favours the development of tropical rain forest; an extreme combination of heat and drought, warm desert. Extreme cold (almost always very dry as well) allows only snow or bare rock, or at best crust or tundra. The order in which one formation class will replace another is predictable and depends on warming or cooling trends, changes in moisture, or both (*see* CLIMATE). During the last million years, the unglaciated parts of Canada have undergone periodic shifts from summer-green deciduous forest through needle-leaf evergreen forest, temperate woodland, temperate savannah and meadow to tundra and back again, depending on warmth; from needle-leaf evergreen forest through temperate savannah, temperate woodland and prairie to steppe and back again, depending on moisture; and from

	Organism	Requirement	Tolerance	Efficiency
Eastern forest	sugar maple	H moist-cold climate; deep well-aerated soil; constant summer shade	H very cold winters; early and late frosts; insect parasites	H abundant yearly seeding; good growth rate; dominance
Grassland	aspen	L open areas for establishment	H variety of soil types; resistance to fire, insect parasites	H intensive vegetative propagation; rapid growth
Southern cattail marsh	red-winged blackbird	L marshes for nesting; varied landscape for feeding	H fluctuations of water level; changes in marsh dynamics	H territoriality; high reproductive rate; gregariousness
High northern marsh	whooping crane	H narrowly limited marsh area at each end of migration path	L competition with other birds	L vulnerability to habitat change, predators; low reproductive rate
Maritime arctic tundra	Inuit	H extremely high fat and protein diet	H cold; scarcity of vegetable food	L survival requires considerable cultural skills and occasional innovation
Southern industrial town	factory worker	L minimal food and shelter	H substandard living conditions	V survival depends on a patterned, mostly imposed technology

steppe through temperate scrub to warm desert and back, depending on both factors. The extreme north has experienced relatively stable conditions of cold desert and crust during the entire period. Hence, when the temperate rain forests of BC are included, modern Canada contains 12 of the 20 possible bioclimatic formations.

Biogeography operates with broadly based working hypotheses that have been variously tested. It provides an essential background to cultural geography and to human ecology. In earlier stages of its development, it was more concerned with the impact of landscape on man. Fortunately, in recent years the ever-swinging oscillation of physical/cultural anthropology and the emergence of human ecology as an increasingly autonomous discipline have rendered the notions briefly outlined above more relevant to human studies, environmental planning and landscape management. Human activity is proving to be a very significant factor in the distribution of plant and animal species. In Canada the historical regression of many important animal species is well documented, eg, wapiti and mountain lion that were once present in the East, salmon that used to reach Lk Ontario. On the other hand, the white-tailed deer has extended its range greatly; the beaver has made several comebacks. But extinction of the great auk is forever, and there are many endangered species.   PIERRE DANSEREAU

Reading: Pierre Dansereau, Biogeography: An Ecological Perspective (1957) and "Vegetation Zones, World" in McGraw-Hill Encyclopedia of Science and Technology, Vol 14 (1971); I.G. Simmons, Biogeography, Natural and Cultural (1979).

Biography in English, the written record of a person's life. Canada's search for an identity has been long, continuous, sometimes so fervent that it becomes notorious, at its best positive as an effort of understanding. Part of knowing what we are is knowing who we are, and biographical writing in Canada, in its several forms, has taken up this question. Biography has shown itself to be an approach which appeals to readers of differing tastes and experience, partly perhaps because they can satisfy curiosity about the past, even secure light upon the present, through the lives of people who actually existed in a real and pressing world. Answers about who Canadians are are still far from plentiful, but many have been attempted over the last century or so.

Obituaries, eulogies and biographical accounts of essay length and style are forms of biography in brief that began to appear in the 19th century. Obituaries, of some fullness and in which appear the leading facts and some effort at interpretation going beyond the litany of funeral rhetoric, have remained important sources. The most valuable often appear in publications of societies or year books, such as the Proceedings of the Royal Society of Canada. Memorials of book length, some of which provide useful documentary evidence along with the prevailing appreciation, appeared in the mid-19th century, eg, in John Carroll's celebration of Methodist preachers, Case and His Cotemporaries (5 vols, 1867-77), Henry Scadding's The First Bishop of Toronto (1868) for John Strachan, and Fennings Taylor's Thos. D'Arcy McGee (1868).

In the latter half of the 19th century, coinciding with one of the periods when interest in the nature of the Canadian identity was strong, there were a number of efforts to compile collections of short accounts. Henry James Morgan is the revered early name with Sketches of Celebrated Canadians in 1862, the year he also began the first continuing publication of biographical interest, the Canadian Parliamentary Companion. His works include Types of Canadian Women (1901) and the important Canadian Men and Women of the Time (1898; rev ed 1912). This latter work, including only persons alive at the time of publication, was the ancestor of the "Who's Who" that began appearing at the turn of the century. Morgan's Men and Women was, in fact, incorporated into The Canadian Who's Who, first published in 1910. Another pioneer of the short biographical sketch was Fennings Taylor, who collaborated with William Notman to produce Portraits of British Americans (3 vols, 1865-68). To the 1880s belong the works of J.C. DENT, with The Canadian Portrait Gallery (4 vols, 1880-81), and G.M. Rose, ed, A Cyclopaedia of Canadian Biography (2 vols, 1886, 1888). Hundreds of other compilations have appeared, sometimes as part of larger works, and presenting national, regional, local or topical coverage. An example is A Standard Dictionary of Canadian Biography by Sir Charles G.D. ROBERTS and A.L. Tunnell (1934-38). These efforts to bring together brief accounts of men and women continue to be made. They are generally useful, but are not usually literary works.

Since its first appearance in 1926, W. Stewart WALLACE's Dictionary of Canadian Biography, because of its comprehensiveness, has taken pride of place among the collections and has retained it through several revisions. It assumed the title Macmillan Dictionary of Canadian Biography in 1963, a few years before the DICTIONARY OF CANADIAN BIOGRAPHY/DICTIONNAIRE BIOGRAPHIQUE DU CANADA published its first volume, in English and French editions, in 1966. This large project's scholarship and reference strengths are complemented by readability, and a special contribution of its "life and times" account of Canada is the large number of biographies of persons hitherto known only fleetingly and unlikely to command attention on their own from biographers.

Biographical series were another early form of presenting the "doers" of Canada. From 1903 to 1908 appeared the "Makers of Canada" series (20 vols), edited by literary men Duncan Campbell Scott and Pelham Edgar. The "Chronicles of Canada" (1914-16) allotted 13 of 32 volumes to individuals. Lorne PIERCE, pursuing his redoubtable efforts to encourage Canadian writing, set up the "Makers of Canadian Literature" series (12 vols, 1923-26). Activity of this type came again in the 1970s, when a number of series were launched. These include "Canadian Biographical Studies" (UTP), "Canadian Lives" (Oxford), and the National Gallery's "Canadian Artists," all of which make particular use of scholarly research; "The Canadians" (Fitzhenry and Whiteside), designed especially for students; and Lorimer's paperback reprint series "Goodread Biographies." In 1971 the province of Ontario started a major historical studies series including biographies of premiers, 5 of which have appeared to date.

Significant individual volumes of biography began to appear sporadically around the turn of the century: G.E. Fenety's Life and Times of the Hon. Joseph Howe (1896), J.S. Willison's Sir Wilfrid Laurier (2 vols, 1903; rev 1926), C.R.W. Biggar's Sir Oliver Mowat (2 vols, 1905), James Cappon's Roberts and the Influences of His Time (1905), and W.D. LeSueur's Count Frontenac (1906) – all by established writers and dealing with major figures. In the 1920s attention to the genre quickened, with O.D. Skelton's The Life and Times of Sir Alexander Tilloch Galt (1920), V.L.O. Chittick's Thomas Chandler Haliburton (1924); William Kennedy's Lord Elgin (1926); Chester New's Lord Durham (1927); G.P. deT. Glazebrook's Sir Charles Bagot, Lorne Pierce's William Kirby, Carl Y. Connor's Archibald Lampman (1929) and James Cappon's Bliss Carman (1930).

From the 1950s to the 1970s, biographies appeared in numbers that escape easy enumeration. Figures associated with the governance of Canada received major attention from a growing company of Canadian historians using documentary holdings to give reinterpretations and fullscale accounts that went beyond the "life and letters" approach favoured by earlier writers. The magisterial title is Donald CREIGHTON's John A. Macdonald (2 vols, 1952, 1955), which became, and has remained, a landmark. Many important political figures have still not found book-length biographers, but the field has had significant entries that continue to be viewed as "classics" for Canada and additions are steady: C.B. Sissons, Egerton Ryerson (2 vols, 1937, 1947); William Kilbourn, The Firebrand: William Lyon Mackenzie (1956); Kenneth McNaught, A Prophet in Politics: J.S. Woodsworth (1959); W.J. Eccles, Frontenac (1959); Roger Graham, Arthur Meighen (3 vols, 1960-65); J.M.S. Careless, Brown of "The Globe" (2 vols, 1959, 1963); Dale Thomson, Alexander Mackenzie (1960); George F.G. Stanley, Louis Riel (1963); John Morgan Gray, Lord Selkirk of Red River (1963); Margaret Prang, N.W. Rowell (1975); Thomas Flanagan, Louis "David" Riel (1979); Robert Craig Brown, Robert Laird Borden (2 vols, 1975, 1980); and J. Murray Beck, Joseph Howe (2 vols, 1982, 1983); Jeffrey Williams, Byng of Vimy (1983); Patrick Brode, Sir John Beverley Robinson (1984). The extensive source material for William Lyon Mackenzie KING and the enigmas of his long career have attracted an unusual number of biographical approaches, from Bruce Hutchison's popular The Incredible Canadian

(1952) through the 3 "official" volumes of Mac-Gregor Dawson and H. Blair Neatby (1958-76) to a psycho-biographical study by Joy Esberey in 1980 and Heather Robertson's fictional treatments, *Willie: A Romance* (1983) and *Lily: A Rhapsody in Red* (1986).

Entries into biography from academic historians are now rarer, except for the major cross-country efforts elicited by the DCB/DBC. Historical interests change over time, and the newer fields of business history, labour history, women's studies, native studies and ethnic studies have often led to group portraits rather than to those of individuals. Business history is one "new" area, however, which has attracted the attention of a number of biographers. In the 1960s came Ross Harkness's *J.E. Atkinson of the Star* (1963) and Alan Wilson's *John Northway* (1965), early entries in a field that now includes major studies such as Michael Bliss's *A Canadian Millionaire: The Life and Business Times of Sir Joseph Flavelle* (1978). With his *Sir Frederick Banting* (1984), Bliss moved on to science, another growing field of interest for biographers accompanying recent scholarly examinations of the history of science and technology in Canada. Norman BETHUNE's colourful medical career, for instance, has continued to provoke curiosity since Ted Allan and Sydney Gordon published a first study in *The Scalpel and the Sword* (1952, rev 1971); Roderick Stewart followed in 1973 with *Bethune*.

In recent years journalists have been prominent in the field of biography. In 1963 came Peter C. NEWMAN's *Renegade in Power: The Diefenbaker Years*, inaugurating a series on recent leaders that includes Richard GWYN's *Smallwood* (1968; rev 1972) and *The Northern Magus: Pierre Trudeau and the Canadians* (1980) and Geoffrey Stevens's *Stanfield* (1973). Joseph SCHULL has made valuable contributions to biography in his *Laurier* (1965) and *Edward Blake* (2 vols, 1975, 1976). Such accounts fall in with a long-established tradition of popular biography that has embraced writers of other backgrounds on subjects as various as James Fitzgibbon and Laura Secord, "Tiger" Dunlop and D'Arcy McGee, Josiah Henson, Pauline Johnson and L.M. Montgomery, Emily Murphy, Sara Jeannette Duncan, Ernest Thompson Seton, Gabriel Dumont, Gilbert Parker, J.S. Woodsworth and C.D. Howe. The University of British Columbia established a medal for contributions to popular biography in 1951. The list of winners shows that any attempt to draw a line between popular and scholarly biography hardly holds, and the medal is now given simply for "biography."

The literary biography of Canadian writers has been slow to emerge, and the explanation undoubtedly lies in the delayed appearance of serious attention to Canadian literature in the universities. Collections began to appear in the 1960s and 1970s: Guy Sylvestre, Brandon Conron and Carl Klinck, *Canadian Writers/Écrivains canadiens* (1964, 1966), Clara Thomas, *Our Nature – Our Voices* (1972) and Frank Davey, *From There to Here* (1974), are examples. Lengthier treatments have appeared in series already mentioned and in such undertakings as the Twayne World Authors series (from the 1960s onwards), W.H. New's volumes for the *Dictionary of Literary Biography* (vol 1, 1986) or the ECW Press series of "Canadian Writers and Their Works," which provide biographical accounts in support of literary analysis and criticism. Literary biographies, as such, are still not numerous. Contemporary examples are Norman Shrive's *Charles Mair* (1965), Clara Thomas's study of Anna Jameson, *Love and Work Enough* (1967), and Lovat DICKSON's several accounts of Grey Owl. A quickening pace is discernible with Douglas Spettigue's *FPG: The Eu-*ropean Years* (1973), David R. Beasley's account of John Richardson in *Canadian Don Quixote* (1977), Elspeth Cameron's *Hugh MacLennan* (1981) and *Irving Layton* (1985), Usher Caplan's portrait of A.M. Klein, *Like One that Dreamed* (1982), *William Arthur Deacon: A Canadian Literary Life* by Clara Thomas and John Lennox (1982), David Pitt's first volume on *E.J. Pratt* (1984) and John Caldwell Adams's *Sir Charles God Damn* (1986) on G.D. Roberts. Claude BISSELL's 2 volumes on Vincent Massey (1981, 1986) have made much clearer the role of a major figure in the development of Canadian culture. Canadians have also made significant contributions to the biography of writers elsewhere, eg, Lovat Dickson, *H.G. Wells* (1969) and *Radclyffe Hall* (1975); George Woodcock, *The Crystal Spirit* (1966), on George Orwell; Phyllis Grosskurth, *John Addington Symonds* (1964), *Havelock Ellis* (1980) and *Melanie Klein* (1986); and Michael Millgate, *Thomas Hardy* (1982).

The same delayed response, and the same reliance on biographical material as part of something else, has characterized the attention given to artists. Single volumes have, however, appeared, eg, Moncrieff Williamson's *Robert Harris* (1971), Maria Tippett's *Emily Carr* (1979) and J. Russell Harper's *Krieghoff* (1979).

Since the 1960s libraries and archives have rapidly acquired documents and papers relating to Canadian writers and other cultural figures, the majority of whom are still living and working. Indeed, no account of biography, in any field, can ignore the major contribution made to it by the development, particularly since WWII, of library and archival collections in all parts of Canada and the sharing of them made possible by interlibrary loan, microfilm and microfiche. Because of these resources, biography can be sounder and surer in its documentation of the events of a life.

It still remains, however, that biography is a literary art. Any author attempting it is challenged to call upon gifts of understanding and interpretation, of choosing and shaping, of style and colour to give life and truth to the subject. For this reason, the work of biography is never done, and new readings of individuals are inevitable over the years. Biography, one of the "great observed adventures of mankind," as Henry James put it, is not likely to lose its power to attract the talents of writers and the curiosity of readers.

FRANCESS G. HALPENNY

Biography in French Biography is the study of a life. It reveals a personality and an analysis of an individual's work in the context of the age in which it existed. Biography has always been popular in French Canada. For a people with limited education and a limited standard of living until very recently, this literary genre was often, in the most elementary form, the only one which received space in the meagre public and private libraries. Among the cultivated elite in Québec, especially among historians, biography has been both in and out of favour. Its history corresponds to that of ideologies. In its evolution, therefore, one can trace the major trends of more than 2 centuries of French Canadian society. Before taking the path where quality depends on concern for scientific rigour and fidelity to historical accuracy, biography served to showcase virtue, spread a message and support the national cause.

The first biographies of French Canada were "edifying lives," popularized or frankly distorted, and they hold an important place in the history of Québec literature. Until about 1880, biography was closer to medieval hagiography than to true biography. After 1840, the Catholic Church began the rise which brought it control of society for a good century. It sought to consolidate its position on 2 fronts. Internally, it tried to increase its strength and inculcate in the population a value system conforming with its vision of society. Externally, it tried to show its power and credibility with Rome. In this perspective, the recognition, official or not, of the sainthood of various individuals could only reinforce its position. Hence the interest of the clergy in the biography of the founders of the Church in Canada.

It is perhaps not by accident that *La Vie de Mme d'Youville* (1852) by Etienne Michel Faillon appeared just when her beatification was under consideration in Rome. And it was to happen again. Faillon also published the biography of *Soeur Bourgeoys* (1853), of *Jeanne Mance* (1854) and of *Jeanne Le Ber* (1860). In the purest medieval tradition, Faillon's biographies paid much more attention to God and His work in New France than to the subject of the biography and her creative role. Faillon adopted the clergy's view of history, namely that it should immortalize "good" people, people who conformed to the values of society and could serve as role models.

With a little more talent, Henri-Raymond CASGRAIN continued in the same vein as Faillon, and his *Histoire de la Mère Marie de l'Incarnation* (1864) was the greatest bookstore success in French Canada at the end of the 19th century. As for the *Vie de Mgr Laval* (1890), written by Auguste Gosselin, its main purpose was to promote the ULTRAMONTANE cause by stressing the required rights, real or assumed, of the Church in Québec and by insisting on the importance of these ties with Rome from the beginning. It helped to nourish an already conservative school of thought. Even if only a small part of the population had access to these biographies, their influence stretched far beyond their readers. They reached the masses through priests' sermons and schooling, and stimulated the recruitment of clergy and creation of many religious communities. The various biographies of the 19th century were thus an instrument of social control which reached the people through the intermediary of the elites.

The end of the 19th century and the first quarter of the 20th century saw the birth and development of the first true biographies. Now well established, the Québec Church, allied with the bourgeois elite, concerned itself with the preservation of economic, cultural and social strength in French Canada. The idealization of a glorious past, of an exemplary style of life reinforced the ideology of survival. And so along came the national heroes and the biographies of laymen, politicians, explorers and military men, to enrich a literature which already overvalued the historical patrimony. French Canadian history was thus presented as a succession of lives of heroes, illustrious or unknown, who were all living examples of the virtues of the ancestors, all of them outstanding. The first of these biographies was that of *Guillaume Couture, premier colon de la Pointe-Levy* (1884) by Joseph-Edmond Roy. Of "populist" inspiration, this biography of a pioneer exalted the rough life of the homesteader and the purity of rural society. Here we find the 2 themes which Michel BRUNET emphasized a century later: agriculturism and messianism. But the book was also in the avant garde, in the sense that instead of praising submission, it showed that French Canadians could moderate the consequences of the CONQUEST.

It is worth noting that most of the biographies of this period dealt with pre-Conquest figures. Jacques Cartier, Samuel de Champlain, Sieur de Maisonneuve, Louis Jolliet, Jean Talon, Marquis de Montcalm and François Lévis each found his biographer. In each work, we see the classic triptych of Québec at the time: the Cross, the plough and the sword. Recalling a glorious past through these idealized heroes was a way to obscure the real situation of inferiority of French Canadians, all the while justifying the preservation of values handed down by these illustrious men. It was also, in a way, a reply to the DURHAM REPORT: in place of a future, French Canadians had a past. Moreover, the appearance of these biographies often coincided with the building of a monument to their heroes, which also helped to strengthen this belief in the population.

Three authors stand out among all these biographers by the quantity as well as the quality of their work: Henri-Raymond Casgrain with *Marie de l'Incarnation* (1864), Narcisse-Eutrope Dionne with *Samuel de Champlain* (1891-1906), Thomas CHAPAIS with *Jean Talon* (1904) and the *Marquis de Montcalm* (1911). All 3 were ultraconservatives and representatives of the old aristocratic and clericalist rural society. At a time when economic and social changes were under way, their exaltation of the past amounted to a rejection of these changes.

Even if the biographies of this period dwelt on a religious past overlaid with nostalgia for the French régime, some biographers focused their analyses on political matters, the second element of traditional French Canadian thought. It was this myth of the leader that inspired Laurent-Olivier David's biography about the *Patriotes de 1837-1838* (1884) and *Laurier et son temps* (1919), as well as Alfred-Duclos DeCelles's studies of *LaFontaine* (1907), *Cartier* (1913) and *Laurier* (1920). These 2 biographers belonged to opposing ideologies: David incarnated the purified liberal thought of the turn of the century while De-Celles belonged to the conservative nationalism which had reconciled itself to Confederation. But they were united in their admiration for political strong men. They made these men the new heroes, even if abundant archival material compelled less hyperbole and more realism.

After WWI, which coincided with Abbé Lionel GROULX's entry on the historiographical scene, the biography changed its tone. It remained moralizing and romantic, lacking sufficient grounding in historical reality (eg, Groulx wrote in the course of a polemic about Dollard des Ormeaux: "I retain my admiration for and devotion to these 17 young men of Long-Sault whose memory, revived in 1920, has truly exalted a generation and created for it an atmosphere of French pride"). What changed was the subjects of biography and its orientation. The heroes were no longer only pious and valiant men, obedient to God and authority; they were combative warriors who did not passively accept destiny. Dollard des Ormeaux, Madeleine de Verchères, d'Iberville and La Vérendrye are only a few examples. For Groulx and his disciples, it was no longer enough to assure survival; they meant to demand and win back the rights and pride of the French Canadian people, laid low by 150 years of coexistence with the conquerors.

In this spirit, several historians sought to highlight the elements of the constitutional battles of the 19th century. Louis-Hippolyte LaFontaine, George-Étienne Cartier and Honoré Mercier were the subjects of various studies. Here one finds the monumental output of Robert RUMILLY, which included many biographies, the most important being *Honoré Mercier* (1935), *Mgr Laflèche et son temps* (1936), *Henri Bourassa* (1953) and, in particular, *L'Histoire de la Province de Québec*, to which he imparted a biographical flavour by giving each volume the name of the person who had pretty well dominated the short period of time under consideration. This series constituted, in fact, a gallery of individuals, great and small, who were judged by the yardstick of their nationalism and their battles for the rights of Québec.

It is significant that during the years 1920-50 more attention was paid to periods other than the French régime, even if the most notable biographies were still stuck in that era. This is the time when Guy FRÉGAULT, disciple of Groulx and member of the neo-nationalist school, published *Iberville le Conquérant* (1944), *Bigot* (1948) and *Vaudreuil* (1952). These were rigorous biographies, universally praised by the critics, which could have consolidated the genre had they not appeared at the moment when SOCIAL SCIENCES were undergoing a reorientation.

In fact, after WWII, biography in Québec, as in France, went into a period of disfavour, especially in intellectual circles. The new historiographic trends, which emphasized economics and social matters, pushed the individual to the background of history. Moreover, the quantitative approach inspired by American sociology, which thought it unscientific, ridiculous even, to show interest in personalities, profoundly influenced the historiography of Québec and distanced historians of the biographical genre. And the negative view of biography was reinforced by the anti-Duplessis and anticlerical spirit which equated, not without reason, moreover, traditional biography with conservative nationalism and the domination of the Catholic Church.

At the end of the 1960s, however, the genre came resoundingly back into fashion in Québec, as in the entire Western world, but in a different form and with different content. Biography proved that it could be and had become a contribution of major importance to the growth of historical knowledge. Since then, numerous biographies, solid and serious works, have added knowledge and timely analyses, essential for the construction of any synthesis of quality. It is scientific history, but personified, much more revealing than the cold monographs which too often simplify questions along with their answers. In this new biography, not only the subject is revealed; so is the group, class or ideology which he or she represents, plus the times this person helped to create. And the individual belongs to an economic, social and cultural world as much as a religious and political one. The new biography thus comes to the rescue of all-embracing history.

Several names deserve mention here, such as Pierre Savard with *Tardivel* (1967), Henri Masson with *Joseph Masson* (1972), Robert Rumilly with *Duplessis* (1973), Nive Voisine with *Mgr Laflèche* (1981), Brian Young with *George-Étienne Cartier* (1982), Andrée Désilets with *Hector-Louis Langevin* (1969) and *Louis-Rodrigue Masson* (1985), Réal Bélanger with *Albert Sévigny* (1983), Jean-Paul Delagrave with *Fleury Mesplet* (1985) and the many contributors to the DICTIONARY OF CANADIAN BIOGRAPHY/DICTIONNAIRE BIOGRAPHIQUE DU CANADA and *Le Dictionnaire des Oeuvres littéraires du Québec*.

It is evident that after having abandoned the biographical genre for almost a quarter of a century, historians are rediscovering its attractions and real value. The public loves biographies more than ever, whether scientific or romanticized. The amazing success in Québec of televised series about d'Iberville, Riel and Duplessis proves that biography can meet public taste as well as the demands of the professional historian. ANDRÉE DÉSILETS

Biological Product, substance derived from a living organism and used for prevention or treatment of disease. Biologicals are too complex for chemical synthesis. These products include antitoxins, bacterial and viral vaccines, blood fractions and hormone extracts. Organizations active in the production of biologicals in Canada include CONNAUGHT LABORATORIES LTD of Toronto, INSTITUT ARMAND-FRAPPIER of Montréal and the Winnipeg Rh Institute.

Vaccines

Viral Vaccines The original vaccination procedure employed by Edward Jenner made use of a VIRUS that caused a mild form of cowpox. Acquired immunity to this disease also gave protection against smallpox, a far more virulent virus. Such vaccines provided good protection because the body was responding to a replicating virus. Since this early period, knowledge of virus structure and mechanism of action has been gradually acquired; however, until the development of tissue culture, there was no way of growing viruses in the laboratory. Some cells had been grown in culture before 1945, but the principal breakthrough occurred when Dr Raymond Parker at the then Connaught Medical Research Laboratories discovered a defined chemical-nutrient medium in which cells would grow and replicate. Parker's discovery permitted Jonas Salk to develop his polio vaccine. Salk vaccine was produced largely in Toronto for field trial in Canada and the US: virus was grown in monkey kidney cells, then separated from the cells, concentrated and killed with formalin. The success of the new killed-virus vaccine was soon apparent and the annual polio epidemics disappeared. The Sabin polio vaccine, an attenuated vaccine also grown in monkey kidney cells and given orally, was developed a few years later.

In recent years human diploid fibroblast cells (which, in the body, develop into connective tissue) have been grown in culture. The cells are more rigorously defined than monkey kidney cells and have permitted the preparation of more highly purified viral vaccines (eg, Salk and Sabin polio, rabies, measles, mumps, rubella). The first killed rabies vaccines were prepared in neural tissues (eg, mouse brain) and later in duck embryo. The injections are painful and multiple doses are required. The vaccine may be given both prophylactically or after exposure. With the diploid-cell-grown vaccine, fewer doses are required and adverse reactions are decreased.

Other attenuated viral vaccines in use include ERA rabies veterinary strain, developed at Connaught, and the measles and rubella strains currently in favour. Future viral vaccines will be of 2 types: traditional whole virus vaccines, which are highly purified from defined cell substrates; and split or single-antigen vaccines, prepared by GENETIC ENGINEERING (eg, foot and mouth disease vaccine), extraction or chemical synthesis.

Bacterial Vaccines are of 3 basic types: whole organisms or bacterins, including pertussis (whooping cough) and vaccines for veterinary or fish use; single-antigen vaccines prepared by extraction or genetic engineering, eg, a new vaccine for calf scours; and toxoids. Many bacteria, such as those that cause tetanus or diphtheria, release toxins that cause cellular damage. These toxins have been purified and treated to make them inactive, ie, toxoids. When injected, toxoids induce the formation of antibodies against the original toxin. Some other bacterial vaccines produced include typhus, typhoid, cholera, pneumococcal, meningococcal and bacille Calmette-Guérin (BCG, used for the prevention and testing of tuberculosis). Vaccines for veterinary use include those for household pets, farm animals and other cultivated species, such as mink or fish. The vaccination of fish is a new approach necessitated by the crowding of fingerlings in AQUACULTURE operations. Administered by injection, immersion or spray, such vaccines are remarkably effective.

Blood Fractions and Serums

Beginning in the 1930s and stimulated by WWII, blood serum was collected and freeze-dried. When reconstituted, this product was of some use in the treatment of blood loss and shock following trauma. A method of fractionating blood plasma (noncellular fluid) was developed in the US and, subsequently, introduced to Canada, allowing the Canadian Red Cross Transfusion Service to use blood for many purposes. Products prepared from donated blood include red cells, white cells, platelets, albumin, immune serum globulins (including specialist products such as tetanus, Rh and rabies immunoglobulins), and coagulation factor concentrates for the treatment of hemophilias A and B.

Hormones The principal peptide hormone products prepared in Canada are INSULIN and human growth hormone. The latter, extracted in Winnipeg from donated human pituitary glands, is used to prevent dwarfism. The product is in extremely short supply. Insulin was first isolated in Toronto by Frederick G. BANTING and Charles H. BEST in 1921-22 and has been prepared there ever since. It is currently made by extraction of bovine or porcine pancreas. Human, bovine and porcine formulations of each type are available to Canadian diabetics. In recent years genetically engineered human insulin and human growth hormone have been marketed. *See also* ESTROGEN.

A.A. MAGNIN

Biology [Gk *bios* "life," *logos* "discourse" or "reasoning"] is the science of life, embracing all studies of living organisms and, as such, is inherently interdisciplinary. Attempts by some specialists to use the term in a narrow sense are shortsighted and damaging.

Biological studies of individuals and groups of organisms can occur at various levels (eg, molecular, cellular, anatomical, functional, behavioural, ecological and evolutionary). Great strides, notably in BIOCHEMISTRY and electron microscopy, have strongly influenced classification at all taxonomic levels in the last 40 years. Many organisms placed together on the basis of form and structure (gross morphology) are now seen to be unrelated, and it is clear that living beings are better classified as monera, protista, FUNGI, PLANTS or ANIMALS, rather than simply as plants or animals, the classical division. The 5 kingdoms are placed in 2 "super kingdoms": Prokaryota (cells having no membrane-bound nuclei); and Eukaryota (cells having true membrane-bound nuclei). Other distinctions correlate with nuclear structure to make the separation conspicuous and absolute.

Prokaryota include only the kingdom Monera, made up of groups of bacteria (including the so-called BLUE-GREEN ALGAE, better termed cyanobacteria). The lower boundary of Monera is ill-defined because the viruses, which are not cellular in structure, may or may not be included. Some viruses are so simple that they are little more than self-replicating molecules, and cannot yet convincingly be defined as "living." The simplest eukaryotic kingdom is Protista, primarily one-celled organisms with organized nuclei and other organelles which function in photosynthesis, cellular respiration, metabolism, etc. The kingdom is somewhat miscellaneous; however, protists nearly always reproduce by some form of mitotic nuclear division (ie, the nucleus divides to form 2 new nuclei, each having the same number of chromosomes as the parent nucleus). The cells are usually considerably larger than those of prokaryotes.

Protista evolved from Monera by processes not wholly understood. Current theory states that the specialized cell parts (organelles) evolved from separate entities which lived inside the one-celled body of the moneran, in symbiosis with it. This theory of "symbiotic origins" is convincing for chloroplasts (photosynthetic organelles): those

of red algae deriving from cyanobacteria; those of green algae from a green prokaryote like the *Prochloron;* and those of other algal groups from extinct or undiscovered photosynthetic prokaryotes. Although less convincing for other organelles, the theory is more plausible than some proposed alternatives. The protistan level may have been reached more than once from different Monera. Protista is not a convincingly "natural" kingdom but, rather, a convenient repository for organisms at similar evolutionary levels.

The 3 "higher" kingdoms (Animals, Plants, Fungi) arose from different groups of protistans. Defining the boundaries between Protista and the "higher" kingdoms is a major problem. For example, although slime molds (Myxomycetes) seem closer to protozoa than to true fungi, they shed dry spores, form fruiting bodies and have been studied mainly by fungal specialists (mycologists), so that most collections are in mycological HERBARIA. A more contentious case involves the Chytridiomycota (microscopic, aquatic organisms), included in Protista by some theorists, but grading imperceptibly into typical fungi and studied exclusively by mycologists. Such problems demonstrate that classifications are man-made rather than completely natural. Except at their lower limits the 3 higher kingdoms are clearly distinct.

The terms taxonomy and systematics have become nearly synonymous through careless use. "Taxonomy," coined in 1813, covers the bases, principles and rules of classification and nomenclature (naming), including the hierarchic framework, and refers not to a research discipline but to a supporting methodology. Modern "systematics" (the actual arranging, grouping and naming of organisms) began with the work of 18th-century Swedish botanist Carl von Linné (Linnaeus), who developed "binomial" nomenclature (with separate names for genus and species), which both assigns to each organism a unique scientific name (in Latin form) and indicates relationships among organisms. Advances in systematization were slow until the re-emergence of GENETICS and the growth of cytology (study of cell contents). Botanists especially made increasing use of cytogenetic data in their groupings. Through Julian Huxley and others, the "new systematics" sprang into prominence about 1940, and was soon rechristened "biosystematics," defined as the scientific study of kinds and diversity of organisms and of any and all relationships between them. The general approach to systematics for most kinds of organisms uses all appropriate disciplines, although choice varies with organisms involved, eg, cytogenetics, which studies chromosome sets within cells, cannot be used routinely with many fungi whose chromosomes are scarcely detectable.

Although attempts have been made to restrict it, biosystematics is well established as using any discipline that may complement morphology and anatomy, eg, cytology, genetics, biochemistry, ecology, BIOGEOGRAPHY, reproductive biology, host-parasite relationships, ethology (animal behaviour) and, with the advent of computers, mathematical analysis of data. A student taking a higher degree in plant systematics must now complement morphology with one or more subsidiary approaches, and advanced students must usually be familiar with methods of statistical analysis and computer programming. Biosystematics is thus the focal point of all biology, linking all disciplines and demonstrating EVOLUTION in action, although the complexity of biology makes its complete unification very difficult, if not impossible.

Biological exploration began early in Canada, but collectors returned their specimens to Europe

for study. Inevitably, systematics had a late start in Canada, but early in this century the pace increased. The rise of biosystematics found systematists in Canadian universities and research institutions ready to embrace the broadened discipline. Canadian contributions have been perhaps most conspicuous in studies of some groups of flowering plants, insects and fungi.

Disciplines The terms for the study of each of the 5 kingdoms (bacteriology, protistology, mycology, BOTANY and ZOOLOGY) are too sweeping to be considered individual disciplines, except at the introductory level. The following is a list of biological academic disciplines (omitting specifically medical disciplines): anatomy (internal structure of organisms), biochemistry, biogeography, biometry and biostatistics, cytology, cytogenetics, ecology, embryology, ENTOMOLOGY, ethology, evolution, fisheries biology, genetics, GENETIC ENGINEERING, histology (study of cellular tissues), limnology (aquatic biology, especially freshwater), marine biology, microbiology, MOLECULAR BIOLOGY, morphology (forms of whole organisms), PALEONTOLOGY (including micropaleontology and PALYNOLOGY), PARASITOLOGY, pathology (diseases of man, other animals or plants), physiology, taxonomy and systematics, toxicology and pharmacology, and ultrastructure (detailed structure of cell organelles). Some disciplines (eg, ecology, genetics and microbiology) may be variously divided, and others tend to overlap (eg, biogeography with ecology). Many disciplines are applicable to organisms in more than one kingdom. The number of potential fields of study is thus enormous. Evolution, included in the above list because courses are taught under this title, is not a discipline but, rather, a theory which informs all biological disciplines.

Multidisciplinary Successes Almost all organisms are influenced by several fluctuating physical factors, notably light, temperature, humidity, precipitation, wind, soil texture and nutrients, erosion and fire. The total ecology of an organism potentially involves these factors as well as interplay with all other organisms in the community. As a result, most biological problems involve more variables than are usually dealt with in a problem in the physical sciences. All atoms of a chemical element are identical, but all individuals of sexually reproducing organisms are different. Very often only a partial solution of a biological problem is possible; but a biologist alert to the factors involved can usually interpret the phenomena under study.

The rapid growth and increasing complexity of biology favour narrow specialization even among beginning students; but, since many problems require contributions from several biological disciplines and from the physical sciences, some compromise must be made. In advanced studies, the team approach is popular. Several examples of Canadian contributions to multidisciplinary successes are described below.

With the help of a mathematician, a botanist-mycologist having some knowledge of aerodynamics and meteorology gained an understanding of the "splash cup" mechanism found in various plants, which uses falling water to disperse seeds or spores. They found, surprisingly, that a 4-4.5 mm drop, such as falls from foliage, has greater momentum after less than 1 m of fall than a typical 2 mm raindrop at terminal velocity. It was then clear why golden saxifrage (*Chrysosplenium*) flourishes in arctic marshes where fog and drizzle cause drops to fall scarcely 0.5 m from nodding grasses and sedges, and why bird's nest fungi grow beneath the dwarf shrubs of the Peruvian desert where fog is the only precipitation.

Elementary aerodynamics enabled an amateur ornithologist to show that the extinct Jurassic bird, *Archaeopteryx*, was not a powered flier, but surely a good glider. Its wing form and function were shown to be similar to those of most modern passerines. Paleontologists had tried to explain the wings, which had no anchorage for powerful pectoral muscles, as paddles to beat down insects, and the feathers as a shawl to keep the bird warm.

Study of various parasites throws light on plant relationships, and requires combining studies in plant systematics with mycology, entomology or nematology. Rust fungi and their host plants reflect one another's ages of origin because compatible gene complements are most likely to occur in hosts and parasites in the evolutionary youth of each group. This explanation was developed through years of combined studies on the ecology and biogeography of hosts and parasites and finally yielded increased understanding of the relationships and relative ages of many plant groups.

The collared LEMMING usually has a fairly regular 4-year population cycle but, in parts of the High Arctic, the population fluctuates irregularly. Wildlife zoologists, combining microclimatological and ecological studies, found that scanty and irregular snow cover in these regions may keep burrow temperatures so low that the lemmings do not achieve breeding condition.

Arctic botanical studies, which started in early spring when sea ice was still intact and windpacked snow was smooth and very hard and which applied elementary aerodynamic principles, showed that seeds of most arctic plants are easily blown long distances during most of the year even if they lack wings or plumes, and that they tend to accumulate on desirable sites at the foot of banks. Elucidation of this means of dispersal allowed an explanation of the high uniformity of the relatively young arctic flora.

Applied Biology Biology can be classified as basic research, applied research and the applications of research, but the 3 intergrade completely. A good example occurs in WHEAT production. Cultivated wheat has been hybridized from wild species. Further improvements depend on accurate information on wild species that may possess useful characteristics. Such information must be supplied by the systematic botanist. The cereal geneticist must develop techniques to transfer the appropriate genes into a wheat plant. The breeder must secure a balance of desirable characteristics to produce a new variety. Finally, propagators must increase stocks of the new variety for release to farmers. Although much agricultural research is "applied," it may be necessary to revert to basic studies to solve problems, eg, in crop protection, food storage, plant pathology or veterinary medicine. The failure of early attempts to control wheat stem rust (*Puccinia graminis*) led to establishment of the Rust Research Laboratory in Winnipeg, where basic studies led to new understanding of wheat genetics, and the genetics and life history of the pathogen (agent of disease). Further information on the biology of rusts resulted from systematic studies of rusts of native plants. For agricultural crops in general, a botanist, chemist or mycologist may supply data to the geneticist and breeder; after full testing, the improved variety is propagated commercially.

Among other examples of successful interaction are the propagation of leaf-cutter bees to induce seed set in alfalfa, a practice which developed from pollination biology; the growth of the antibiotics industry from many years of laboratory testing and experiment; the field of genetic engineering, which developed from basic studies in microbial genetics and molecular biology – the new techniques developed help both industry and medical research, as in the identification and manipulation of potentially cancer-inducing genes. The fields that involve mainly applied research include ANIMAL BREEDING, animal diseases,

WILDLIFE CONSERVATION AND MANAGEMENT, economic entomology, forest research, plant breeding, the study of PLANT DISEASES, soil survey and testing. Several fields are almost wholly commercial, calling on research only when trouble arises, eg, beekeeping, brewing and winemaking, cheesemaking, farming, fish-hatchery operation, horticulture, industrial fermentation and mushroom cultivation. Other applied fields serve education or research: biological illustration and modelling, specimen cataloguing, commercial specimen preparation, laboratory technical work, maintenance and operation of parks or botanical and zoological gardens, and taxidermy.

Research Organizations Most biological investigation in Canada is centered in university biology departments, in national and provincial museums or institutes, and in the laboratories of Agriculture Canada, Fisheries Research Board, Forestry Service, NATIONAL RESEARCH COUNCIL and Wildlife Service. Research may be published in bulletins, eg, of the National Museum of Natural Sciences or the Wildlife Service, monographs of Agriculture Canada, or a wide range of journals. Some papers are published in foreign or interdisciplinary journals, but the main Canadian journals (not including medical publications) are *Canadian Entomologist, Canadian Field Naturalist, Canadian Jnl of Animal Science, Canadian Jnl of Botany, Canadian Jnl of Forest Research, Genome* (formerly *Canadian Jnl of Genetics and Cytology*), *Canadian Jnl of Microbiology, Canadian Jnl of Plant Pathology, Canadian Jnl of Plant Science, Canadian Jnl of Zoology*, and *Le Naturaliste canadien*.

D.B.O. SAVILE

Reading: L. Margulis, *Symbiosis in Cell Evolution* (1981); E. Mayr, *The Growth of Biological Thought* (1982).

Biomass Energy, or bioenergy, is the ENERGY stored in nonfossil organic materials such as wood, straw, vegetable oils, animal tissues, human and animal excrement, and municipal and mill wastes. Like the energy in fossil fuels, bioenergy is derived from SOLAR ENERGY that has been stored in plants through the process of photosynthesis; the principal difference is that fossil fuels require thousands of years to be converted into usable forms, while properly managed biomass energy can be used in an ongoing, renewable fashion. PEAT is also a form of biomass and continues to have considerable potential as an energy source. After direct solar energy and hydroelectricity, biomass is one of the most important renewable energy forms (wood and dung burning account for about 14% of the world's energy supply) and its use in Canada involves both the oldest and the newest of energy technologies.

Although biomass energy accounted for only 145 PJ (petajoules), its potential use by the year 2000 has been estimated as 264 PJ. Biomass already provides more of Canada's energy supply than nuclear power, accounting for 2% of secondary energy use by the residential sector and 8% of energy use in the industrial sector, mainly in the forest industries. Including lumber and pulp and paper, forestry accounts for 7% of Canada's total energy consumption; the forest industries meet more than one-quarter of this demand themselves with biomass. The forest industries have been increasing their use of wood wastes that otherwise would be burned, buried or left on the forest floor. Principal uses include firing boilers in pulp and paper mills and providing heat for lumber-drying kilns. In some areas (eg, northern Ontario, PEI, NB) forest industries supply wood chips and pellets to nearby industrial, commercial and residential customers. In addition, wood is the principal heating fuel for more than 100 000 Canadian homes and a supplemental (though largely decorative) heating source in

several million others. Most official estimates understate the residential consumption of wood fuel because a large proportion is harvested and used locally and does not appear in tax records or government statistics. The other major sources of biomass are agriculture, food-processing residues, industrial wastes, municipal sewage and household garbage. Energy-from-waste projects include steam production or electricity generation from garbage in Hamilton, Québec City, Montréal and Charlottetown.

Biomass-energy products may be in solid, liquid or gaseous form, permitting a wide range of applications. At present, virtually all of Canada's biomass energy is supplied in solid form (eg, logs, chips, sawdust, pellets, charcoal, garbage), but there is also considerable potential for liquid and gaseous forms. The emphasis of much current research is in the conversion of biomass to alcohol for use as a transport fuel (to extend or replace gasoline and diesel oil). For example, at present the production of alcohol from cellulose is a 2-stage process: converting cellulose into sugars and then the sugars into alcohol through fermentation. A new symbiotic co-culture containing 2 kinds of bacteria performs both functions to make possible a one-step production of alcohol from cellulose. Another Canadian development is the discovery of a yeast with the capacity to convert 5-carbon sugars (pentoses) to alcohol. These sugars cannot be converted to alcohol by ordinary brewer's yeast. The development of special membranes for concentrating dilute solutions by reverse osmosis is another breakthrough. Ethanol concentrations of up to 75% have been achieved and this process can displace conventional energy-intensive distillation processes.

Liquid forms of biomass energy include methanol (wood alcohol), ethanol (grain alcohol) and vegetable oils. When methanol or ethanol is mixed with gasoline, the product is sometimes called "gasohol." Methanol, produced by the distillation of wood and forest wastes, may provide an alternative fuel for transportation and industry at prices competitive with fuels from bitumen and coal liquefaction. Ethanol, although it is also a viable fuel, is more expensive to produce and uses potential food supplies for raw materials. The gaseous form of biomass energy is called biogas, a methane-based gas with a low heating value. It is typically derived from the anaerobic (ie, without the presence of oxygen) digestion of organic material, such as municipal sewage or animal manure. In 1987, energy generated from municipal wastes amounted to 4 PJ but it is estimated that by the year 2000 energy from this source will increase to 32 PJ.

Forest Biomass To meet the goal of 5% of Canada's primary energy requirements (by the year 2000), a 3-stage program of development of forest biomass has been proposed. The first stage would use all logging and mill wastes created by existing forest industries. This material is being increasingly used, generally with considerable savings, as a substitute for fossil fuels. Economics are usually favourable because the material is concentrated and the costs of handling and transport are carried by the primary forest product of which this material is the residue. The second stage would be the use of residues and residuals not currently used in conventional forest-harvesting operations. Residues are tree components left behind after merchantable material (eg, sawtimber, pulpwood) has been removed. Residuals are unmerchantable species of trees as well as defective, dying and dead trees currently unusable. The forest industry might use this material for producing steam or steam-generated electricity for on-site consumption; surplus electricity might be fed to the power grid. The third stage would be based upon extensive unused forest stands, along with serious consideration towards the establishment of energy plantations.

Although conventional forest industries have expressed the concern that increased use of forest biomass for energy might infringe on the production and cost of their raw material, the available supply of forest material for biomass energy has been estimated at 5 times the amount of wood now harvested by all the Canadian forest industries. Harvesting energy from forest biomass could be an economic boon for the forest industries: all cellulosic material now thrown away (ie, branches, bark, boles and stumps, and crooked, diseased, insect-infested, fire-damaged, dying and dead trees) could become valuable energy products. Use of forest biomass for energy also affords the opportunity to liquidate low-grade stands and replace them with productive stands of the more valuable species. In some areas (eg, BC), it has been estimated that forest-industry wastes alone could provide enough solid and liquid fuels to replace much of the current oil consumption.

In other parts of Canada, eg, the Prairie provinces and eastern Canada, energy plantations would be needed to provide enough biomass for significant oil displacement. Marginal and submarginal agricultural land, as well as nonagricultural land (eg, wetlands), could be used for high-yield "forest farming" with rotations of less than 10 years between harvests (*see* SILVICULTURE). The tree species under trial in Canada are primarily poplar hybrids and include larch, green ash, willow, alder and soft maples. By selection of species, provenances and phenotypes, and by cloning, it is possible to increase yields greatly and to develop disease resistance and frost hardiness.

Agricultural Biomass Agricultural biomass includes animal manure, cellulosic crop residues, fruit and vegetable cells and food-processing effluents. Potential energy crops include high-yielding, high-carbohydrate crops such as sweet sorghum, Jerusalem artichoke and fodder beet, vegetable-oil crops such as canola and sunflower, and hydrocarbon plants such as milkweed and gumweed. Agricultural biomass has a much more limited potential than forestry biomass in Canada. Most agricultural residues have alternative uses as animal fodder or soil conditioners and typically have a much lower energy intensity than wood (ie, 1 m^3 of wood contains as much energy as 5-10 m^3 of baled field residues). Agricultural biomass is also usually only available at one time of year, while forests can be harvested year round. The average inventory on forestland is about 20 times the annual yield from cropland. However, agricultural biomass does have a place in farm-scale or localized operations. Biogas from animal manures can be used to heat farm buildings or, if scrubbed and compressed, to power farm vehicles. The use of animal and food-processing wastes can abate pollution and reduce disposal problems as well as produce energy. Straw can be burned in a specially designed furnace to dry grain and heat farm buildings. The use of canola oil in farm diesel engines is undergoing continual development.

The Future Various federal government departments and federal and provincial research organizations have studied proposals to develop the potential of biomass energy. For example, ENFOR, the federal Energy from the Forest Program, received strong backing, and the Dept of Energy, Mines and Resources is in charge of the Biomass Development Program. Since 1981 a distillery in Minnedosa, Man, has produced ethyl alcohol from grain.

The main problems facing expansion of biomass energy are the relatively high costs of new facilities and the need to make the industry truly renewable. The cost barrier may be overcome by government policy and rising prices of conventional energy sources; however, careful attention is also needed for problems of reforestation, land use, water use, soil quality, erosion and pollution. Producing energy, in addition to lumber and paper, could put new stress on the renewability of a forest-resource base that is already endangered by past practices of the forest industries. Biomass energy must be farmed, not mined; otherwise it will merely join coal, oil and natural gas as yet another nonrenewable energy source.

C.R. SILVERSIDES

BIONESS (*B*edford *I*nstitute of *O*ceanography *N*et and *E*nvironmental *S*ampling *S*ystem) is a multiple-net sampler for ZOOPLANKTON and micronekton (pelagic animals 1-10 cm in length). It uses a new design concept, with nets arranged horizontally rather than vertically as in earlier multiple-net samplers. The 10 one metre-square nets open sequentially and are towed from a ship at a speed of 3-6 knots on a conductor cable that transmits and receives information. The sampler supports sensors for temperature, conductivity, depth, illumination, pitch, roll, yaw and net closure, together with internal and external flowmeters and a 35 mm camera with a strobe light. This system can collect biological samples and environmental data simultaneously and can photograph animals in front of the sampler. The sampler can operate to depths of 2500 m. It weighs 782 kg and is best handled from an A-frame or large crane on a ship's stern. The towing wire and depressor attachments can be adjusted so that, at any towing speed up to 4 knots, the mouth is vertical. The sampler's weight, combined with the depressor, makes the depth variation during towing small, 0.2 m up or down in seas with waves of 1-2 m. The mouth area to surface area of the nets is 1:10; the mesh size, normally 243µm. Nets are dark green and all surfaces are painted dark grey to make the sampler as inconspicuous as possible. Catches consist of animals ranging from 0.3 mm copepods to krill, squid and fish up to 20 cm long. Advantages of BIONESS include its ease of handling, its steep towing angle at high speeds and its reduced front profile. Data first collected by this sampler have made it possible to explain the ecological relationships between zooplankton, the micronekton that prey on them and the physical environment. For example, a dense layer of zooplankton at 500 m depth will not be preyed upon by a population of fish at 700 m depth because of the 200 m separation. Older methods of sampling did not reveal this fact. Such information is being used to explain the abundance and distribution of commercial species of fish.

D. SAMEOTO

Biotechnology was defined by the 1981 Federal Task Force on Biotechnology (Brossard Committee) as the "utilization of biological processes, be they microbial, plant, animal cells or their constituents, for the provision of goods and services." In some respects, biotechnological techniques represent elaborations of familiar industrial processes (eg, fermentation). While such processes were used initially to produce potable alcohol, organic acids, solvents and other products (eg, antibiotics, amino acids, vitamins, gums, steroids), recent spectacular advances in MOLECULAR BIOLOGY and GENETIC ENGINEERING have extended their range of application. Throughout the world, programs are being vigorously pursued to develop means of using biotechnology in fuel production; recovery of raw materials; crop fertilization and plant breeding; waste treatment and POLLUTION

control; development of more effective health-care products, new feedstuffs and new sources of industrial chemicals; and pest control. Hence, a number of countries (eg, EEC countries, Japan, Israel) have mounted special long-term, government-financed programs in biotechnology, and the US has a commanding lead in the basic biomedical sciences. Individual Canadian scientists have made major contributions, and there is increasing industrial participation in the commercial opportunities offered by these processes.

Techniques

Biotechnology is strongly interdisciplinary, its current strength based on key techniques spawned by interdisciplinary advances in BIOCHEMISTRY, CHEMISTRY, ENGINEERING, GENETICS, MATHEMATICS, microbiology and PHYSICS. These techniques include genetic engineering, industrial enzymes, cell fusion, plant cell culture, and biological process and systems engineering.

Genetic Engineering, based on recombinant DNA technology, provides the capability to select DNA fragments or genes (from selected organisms or plant and animal cells, or the products of chemical synthesis), join them to other pieces of DNA, and transfer them to an appropriate production host cell. The resultant micro-organisms thereby acquire novel genetic properties that endow them with the ability to create new products or to use and transform new substrates in fermentation-type processes. Present and future areas of application include production of hormones (eg, insulin, human growth hormones), regulators of the immune system (eg, interleukons), growth factors, polypeptide drugs, vaccines and antibiotics. In Canada, research capabilities in this field have now extended beyond the universities and in federal government laboratories. Considerable expertise has been developed but the number of trained researchers remains seriously inadequate. Further, more effective mechanisms for transferring technology from laboratories to industry are rapidly evolving.

Industrial Enzymes are increasingly being used by industry and in health-care applications. Traditionally, enzymes from various natural sources have been used in food production in Japan, the US and Europe; no comparable industry has developed in Canada. Now that enzymes are produced microbiologically and by genetic engineering, "tailor-made" products can be expected. Enzyme immobilization is a crucial part of this technology, and the use of BACTERIA, yeast, FUNGI, and plant and animal cells will provide increasingly sophisticated multi-step, multi-enzyme systems. This includes the use of enzymes in organic media. New and existing products will increasingly be made with enzyme processes. Essential for scale up and automation of such processes are the development of biosensors and optimized computer control of bioreactors and the associated downstream processing equipment.

Cell Fusion techniques have opened up new opportunities in agriculture, forestry and health-care products. In agriculture and forestry, cell fusion can produce hybrid plants exhibiting faster growth, enhanced atmospheric nitrogen-fixing capabilities, and greater resistance to disease, chemical herbicides and climatic factors. Canada's major economic dependence on the agriculture and forest industries should make the application of these techniques a high priority. Other hybrid cell techniques result in the production of monoclonal (ie, derived from a single cell) antibodies, used to produce more specific diagnostic reagents, to treat patients with autoimmune reactions, in the targeting and immunotherapy of cancer and for more effective industrial purification of a variety of products.

Plant Cell Culture Plants have always been a rich source of medicinal agents and the development of techniques for culturing plant cells *in vitro* makes possible the production of a wide variety of pharmaceutical products (*see* PHARMACY). The NRC's Plant Biotechnology Institute in Saskatoon possesses world-class expertise in plant cell culture.

Biological Process and Systems Engineering The very nature of biological or microbiological products and processes requires special handling techniques and procedures. Specialized bioprocess and engineering systems are therefore central to eventual commercialization. Past paucity of large-scale biotechnology exploitation in Canada leads to a serious shortage of process and bio-engineering expertise. The task force stated that development of such expertise is urgent, and the provision of training represents the major activities at the NRC's Biotechnology Inst in Montréal and the Alberta Research Council in Edmonton.

Applications

Five major biotechnology process applications are of particular interest to Canada's resource industries: biological nitrogen fixation, cellulose utilization, waste treatment and use, mineral leaching, and development of new plant and animal strains.

Biological Nitrogen Fixation is increasingly important because of the escalating cost of nitrogen fertilizers. Plant breeding and genetic engineering techniques are expected to produce plants (eg, cereals) capable of symbiosis with nitrogen-fixing bacteria. LEGUMES are the only major family of food plants that naturally possess this ability.

Cellulose Utilization Canada's large agricultural and forestry resource base offers important and novel opportunities for the use of cellulose (ie, for BIOMASS ENERGY). Cellulose pretreatment processes, coupled with microbiological or enzyme hydrolysis, are receiving industrial attention throughout the world. Cellulose is attractive to Canada because of the size of the forestry industry, which makes a net annual contribution of nearly $12 billion to Canada's balance of trade; however, Canada's extensive fossil fuel reserves and consequent relatively low energy prices are expected to provide serious competition to commercial development of cellulose as an energy feedstock for some time.

Waste Treatment and Use Detoxification of effluent and the transformation of waste to useful products is increasingly important in the evolution of an industrial society. Biological processes offer particular advantages in adapting to varying waste compositions and conditions of degradation.

Mineral Leaching Microbiological action on mineral sulphides and conversion to more soluble forms have been known for centuries; these methods have already been adapted to the recovery of copper and uranium and will eventually be used for such metals as nickel and zinc (*see* METALLURGY). The one obvious advantage of biotechnological techniques is their very low energy requirements.

Plant and Animal Breeding Genetic engineering and cell fusion techniques will prove essential for the future economic development of Canada by providing new plant strains capable of fixing atmospheric nitrogen and exhibiting a greater pest resistance with an earlier maturation, a higher nutritional value, and a greater tolerance to a variety of climatic conditions. Also important is the genetic development of farm stock with improved disease resistance and increased fertility and productivity.

Other Uses Some chemicals, at present derived from petroleum or coal, will be supplied by biological processes, including cellulosics, microbial polysaccharides, lignin derivatives, lactic and other organic acids, ethanol, acetone, butanol, vegetable oils for plasticizers, lubricants and RUBBER. In addition, certain FOOD ADDITIVES, proteins, fragrances and monomers for specialty PLASTICS and related substances, may best be produced by biotechnological techniques. It is anticipated that plants and plant cells will eventually be designed to produce predominantly single complex chemicals. Because of the rising cost of petroleum-based insecticides and the adverse effect of many of these on the environment, more highly specific biological control agents will be produced. Use of pathogenic insect viruses is increasingly being explored. The production of new and existing pharmaceuticals by biotechnological techniques has already started in other countries. However, Canadian pharmaceutical industry research and development is still underdeveloped, largely because of present compulsory licensing provisions of the CANADIAN PATENT ACT. Proposed legislation (Bill C22) is designed to encourage increased research and development by the Canadian industry on the basis of extended protection of its propriety of pharmaceutical discoveries.

Because the development of biotechnology is just beginning in Canada and its full economic impact has not yet been realized, the national Biotechnology Development Plan is intended to create a climate appropriate for the establishment and growth of various industries. A National Biotechnology Advisory Committee was organized under the Ministry of State for Science and Technology, with the crucial responsibility of co-ordinating and catalysing a nationwide effort. This committee represents the various sector interests in Canada, and holds regular meetings focusing on problem areas. A number of information networks, with their own newsletters, have been formed in the key sectors and have proved very useful for information exchange and in fostering collaboration. An inventory of biotechnology activities has been published by the Ministry of State for Science and Technology.

The development of biotechnology in Canada is very exciting, paralleling growth in other countries. Biomedical applications, perhaps the most advanced, have already resulted in the organization of a number of new pharmaceutical and diagnostic companies, and in the expansion and extension of university based research and production institutes. Problem areas have been identified, and attempts are being made, at the academic level, to train more fermentation technologists and biotechnology oriented business graduates. Some provinces have organized major efforts, with some provincial research agencies taking on a leading role.

In some respects, biotechnology has been the first and prime beneficiary of the federal government's new high-technology policy. This development seems only appropriate as it has been estimated that 25% of world sales will be biotechnology dependent by the year 2000.

ANDREW J. MORIARITY AND JOHN BARRINGTON-LEE

Birch (*Betula*), genus of TREES and shrubs of birch family (Betulaceae). About 50 species are found in Arctic and N temperate regions worldwide. Ten species are native to Canada: 6 trees and 4 shrubs. Several species, especially the white or paper birch, are widespread throughout the country; other birches are regional (yellow and grey, East; cherry, Ontario; Alaska and water, Northwest). Leaves are alternate, oval to triangular in shape and veined, and have teeth of 2 sizes on the margins. Birches are best known for their paperlike bark. Most species prefer well-drained soils and good lighting. Paper and grey birches are pioneer-

Paper, or "canoe," birch (*Betula papyrifera*), with cones and flowers. Ten species of birch are native to Canada (*artwork by Claire Tremblay*).

ing species in abandoned fields and burned-over areas. European silver or weeping birch is a popular ORNAMENTAL. Canadian Indians used birches, especially paper birch, for CANOES, baskets and kitchen utensils. Today the wood is widely used for furniture and veneers. *See also* PLANTS, NATIVE USES.   ESTELLE LACOURSIÈRE

Birch-Bark Biting is the art of dentally perforating designs on intricately folded sheets of paper-thin bark. The technique is known to have been practised by OJIBWA (or Chippewa), CREE and Algonquian groups who utilized birchbark extensively in fabricating domestic containers, architectural coverings, CANOES and pictographic scrolls. Bark biting was a casual art among Indian women, a means of experimenting with designs that might later be translated into porcupine quill or bead appliqué on bark containers or hide clothing (*see* QUILLWORK). It was a form of recreation or friendly competition. More recently, through the work of Cree artist Angelique Merasty of Beaver Lk, Man, bark biting has achieved the status and market of a fine art. Merasty's own technical virtuosity and visual repertoire have greatly amplified the traditional range of rudimentary geometric designs to include rich curvilinear floral, insect, animal and human figures. *See also* INDIAN ART.   ELIZABETH MCLUHAN

Reading: Elizabeth McLuhan and M. Zoccole, *Wigwas: Birch Biting by Angelique Merasty* (1983).

Birchall, Reginald J., murderer (b at Accrington, Eng 25 May 1866; d at Woodstock, Ont 14 Nov 1890). Birchall, a confidence man, gambler and wastrel, lured 2 young Englishmen, Douglas Pelly and Frederick C. Benwell, into a partnership with him to purchase a farm near Woodstock, Ont. Under the Farm Pupil scheme, a system much abused by dishonest promoters, they agreed to pay Birchall £500 each. Birchall's plan was to kill them and take their money. On 17 Feb 1890, he shot Benwell to death in a swamp. Later he tried unsuccessfully to kill Pelly. Birchall was arrested for the murder by John W. MURRAY, Canada's "Great Detective." Because he was an English gentleman, the son of a clergyman, and educated at Oxford, Birchall's case drew considerable attention in Canada, the US and Europe. He was executed in Woodstock by a hangman whose use of an experimental noose which caused slow death by strangulation was greatly criticized.   EDWARD BUTTS

Birchbark Canoe, *see* CANOE, BIRCHBARK.

Bird, member of a unique group of VERTEBRATES, Class Aves. The FOSSIL record, comparative anatomy and embryology indicate that birds have a common ancestry with REPTILES. Paleontologists believe that, among living reptiles, crocodilians may be the closest relatives of birds. Birds are unique because they possess 2 major anatomical adaptations: feathers, probably evolved from reptilian scales, which provide an insulating coat and give them the ability to maintain a constant body temperature, independent of the temperature of the air surrounding them; and considerably modified forelimbs, from the five-fingered form of their probable reptilian ancestors to a wing covered with specially adapted feathers, which give birds the power of flight. Additional adaptations include modifications to the skeleton that lessened its weight, through the evolution of air-filled, hollow bones; increased its rigidity, through fusion of its parts (eg, sections of the vertebral column); and provided bony projections (processes) to which flight muscles attach, eg, the keel (projecting ridge) on the sternum (breastbone). The lungs evolved a series of associated air sacs, which penetrate into bones and between muscles. This respiratory system both decreases body mass and increases gas exchange efficiency by permitting a continual flow of fresh air over the respiratory surfaces. Body weight was reduced further through the ability of birds to excrete a nitrogenous waste (uric acid) that requires little water for its discharge, making it unnecessary for birds to carry this water. The reproductive system is functional only seasonally, becoming enlarged and heavy during the brief period of reproduction. In females of most species, it is represented by only a single ovary and oviduct that produce the shelled eggs, which allow the young to develop outside the mother's body and also help reduce weight.

These adaptations in form, function and associated behaviour have enabled birds to surmount what were, for other vertebrates, impassable geographic barriers, and to exploit virtually every habitat from arctic tundra and desert wastes to tropical forests and ocean solitudes. In Canada, about 417 species of birds have been recorded as breeding. Throughout most of the country, most species are migratory, arriving in spring to nest and rear their young, and departing for more hospitable climates in autumn. At least a few species are resident throughout the year, even in the Arctic to which such birds as the common raven, glaucous gull and rock ptarmigan have become adapted to exploit the meagre food resources available during the long, dark winters. Farther S in Canada, visitors arrive in late autumn from breeding grounds in the arctic islands, northern tundra and boreal forest to winter along the seacoasts, in the deciduous hardwood forests and on the central plains. Such birds as oldsquaw (ducks), redpolls, pine grosbeaks and snow buntings fall into this category.

Birds usually are most conspicuous during their reproductive cycle. This is the time when most species undertake complex behavioural patterns that involve courtship display and song. The breeding plumage, characteristically striking in breeding males, makes them visually conspicuous as they undertake their ritualized displays. Perhaps the most spectacular example is the courting peacock. Birds are also conspicuous at this time through the sounds they produce, particularly when males of many species are advertising their occupancy of territory by singing. Most birds appear to establish nesting territories, ranging from relatively large areas in which most foraging and nesting occur, as in the American robin, to very small spaces, that encompass only the nest sites, as in colonial species like the ring-

Canada goose (*photo by Bill Brooks/Masterfile*).

billed gull. Territories are defended against trespass by other individuals of the same species and, in some cases, of other closely related species. The nest is built and the clutch of eggs is deposited within the territory. The size of the clutch varies considerably, from one egg in cliff-nesting seabirds like the northern gannet, to about 18 in game birds like the gray partridge. The young hatch from the eggs after periods of incubation varying from about 2 weeks in small songbirds like swallows and sparrows, to about 9 weeks in large birds like albatrosses. The hatchlings require parental attention for some time. For those species (eg, house wrens and American robins) whose young hatch naked and remain in the nest until they make their first flight, both parents bring food during the entire nesting period. For them, food availability is a factor of major importance. Other species (eg, ruffed grouse and Canada geese) produce chicks that are able to feed themselves shortly after hatching. In these forms, the young soon leave the nest, always accompanied by their parent(s). Their ability to avoid predators before they learn to fly is of major importance, as is suggested by the marvellous camouflage created by the colours and patterns of their downy plumage.

Birds have evolved the ability to use a great variety of foods. Some species are largely herbivorous: geese graze on herbaceous plants; grouse browse on the leaves and needles of woody plants; many tropical birds live largely on fruit; and one group, which includes the hummingbirds, uses flower nectar. At the other end of the food spectrum are birds that are largely carnivorous: loons live principally on fish; hawks and owls prey primarily on terrestrial vertebrates such as rodents; and a large group of small birds has evolved to exploit the populations of insects that exist throughout the terrestrial sphere. Among these are such diverse forms as swifts and swallows, which feed on aerial insects, wood warblers, which glean leaves of trees for the arboreal insects they harbour, and dippers, which enter fast streams to feed on aquatic insects living among the bottom sediments. *See also* BIRDS OF PREY; GAME BIRDS; SHORE BIRDS; SEA BIRDS; and individual entries on birds. D.A. BOAG

Bird, Florence Bayard, née Rhein, pen name Anne Francis, senator, journalist, broadcaster, author (b at Philadelphia, Pa 15 Jan 1908). She moved to Canada in 1931 and established herself as a broadcaster and journalist. From 1946 to 1966 Bird was a news commentator for the CBC, also producing documentaries on women's rights and international affairs. In 1967 PM Pearson appointed her chairman of the Royal Commission on the STATUS OF WOMEN IN CANADA. Tabled in 1970, the report of the commission made 167 recommendations to eliminate sexual inequality in Canada and sparked the formation of several women's groups to push for implementation. Bird was appointed to the Senate in 1978. She is the author of *Anne Francis: An Autobiography* (1974) and *Holiday in the Woods* (1976). In 1983, Bird was appointed to the federal government Advisory Council on the Status of Refugees, on which she served a 2-year term that ended in 1985. That same year she won the Gov Gen's Persons Award for her work on behalf of Canadian women. Bird participates as a panel member on the CBC radio program "Morningside." She was made a Companion of the Order of Canada in 1971. CERISE MORRIS

Bird, James Jr, "Jemmy Jock" or "Jimmy Jock," trader, interpreter, native leader (b in Rupert's Land *c*1798; d in Montana 11 Dec 1892). Son of a HUDSON'S BAY CO chief factor and a Cree woman, Bird was an HBC apprentice by about 11 and a clerk by 18. Sent southward in the 1820s by John ROWAND to gain the Blackfoot, Blood and Peigan trade, he became accepted and respected by the Indians. He aided the HBC and American Fur Co in their rivalry for the Plains trade, but each found his loyalty suspect. Bird's most historic role was as "a very intelligent interpreter" of the Blackfoot language in the signing of Treaty No 7 (1877). JENNIFER S.H. BROWN

Bird, William Richard, novelist (b at East Middleton, NS 11 May 1891; d at Sackville, NB 28 Jan 1984). Bird had a diverse career while at the same time publishing almost annually for 4 decades. He homesteaded in Alberta, served with the 42nd Royal Highlanders in WWII, and was a touring lecturer, before settling into a Nova Scotia bureau of information position from 1933 to 1950. He first published in 1928 with the nonfiction *A Century of Chignecto*. Other nonfiction works include books about the Maritimes. Two of his most popular novels, *Here Stays Good Yorkshire* (1945) and *Judgement Glen* (1947), won the Ryerson fiction award. From 1949 to 1950 Bird served as president of the CANADIAN AUTHORS ASSOCIATION. During his long career he was awarded the Queen's

Coronation medal, a DLitt from Mount Allison U (1949), a Canada Council Fellowship (1961-62) and a national award in letters from U of Alberta (1965).   MARLENE ALT

Bird Classification and Evolution *Archaeopteryx,* the oldest BIRD yet discovered, is known from 5 FOSSILS recovered from fine slate deposits in Bavaria. This crow-sized animal lived during the Jurassic period (208-144 million years ago) in a tropical environment. *Archaeopteryx* possessed reptilian features (solid forearm bones, toothed bill, unfused backbone, claws on 3 fingers, etc). It would probably be classified as a reptile or small DINOSAUR but for the feathers (resembling those of modern birds), and fused furcula (wishbone), unique among Jurassic animals. The solid bones and lack of a keel on the breastbone limited its powers of flight, making it more a glider than a powered flyer. The 2 theories of bird origins currently recognized differ in tracing the details of bird evolution. Both agree that pseudo-suchian thecodonts, long-tailed, scaly reptiles of the Triassic period (245-208 million years ago), are ancestral, directly or indirectly. The number of fossil birds is small (about 900 species known to date) because bird bones are fragile and have been preserved only under very favourable conditions. This makes tracing the ancestry and relationships of modern birds difficult. Fossil birds, generally, are so much larger than modern species that they can often be viewed as giant relatives. Less than 30 species are known from the Cretaceous period (144-66.4 million years ago). Most appear to be aquatic, with great similarities to modern grebes, flamingoes, cormorants and loons. The Paleocene period (66.4-57.8 million years ago) has yielded few bird fossils; however, the ancestors of modern families (including perching birds) appeared during this period.

Although bird classification is better known than that of any other animal group, new species are still discovered almost yearly. Current research provides new information permitting scientists to understand better the relationships between species, genera, families and orders. Over 9020 species of recent birds are recognized. These belong to 2045 genera, 160 families and 24 orders. About two-thirds of known species (5274 species in 1104 genera and 60 families) belong to the order Passeriformes (perching birds). The re-

maining 3746 species belong to 23 orders divided into 100 families and 941 genera. The following summary of orders currently recognized by ornithologists indicates the extent of diversity displayed by birds.

Ratites (6 families, 58 species; none Canada). Ostriches, rheas, cassowaries, emus, kiwis, tinamous. Large birds, except kiwis and tinamous; flightless and cursorial (running), except tinamous.

Sphenisciformes (one family, 18 species; none in Canada). Penguins. Medium-sized to large diving birds with flipperlike wings; found in the Southern Hemisphere.

Gaviiformes (one family, 4 species; 4 breeding species in Canada). Loons. Large diving birds with 3 webbed toes and straight, pointed bill; Arctic and Subarctic.

Podicipediformes (one family, 20 species; 5 in Canada). Grebes. Small to large diving birds with lobed feet and straight, pointed bills; worldwide distribution.

Procellariiformes (23 families, 104 species; 2 families, 4 species in Canada). Albatrosses, shearwaters, fulmars, petrels, storm-petrels, diving-petrels. Very small to very large oceanic birds with tubular nostrils; found on all oceans; nest on land.

Pelecaniformes (6 families, 62 species; 3 families, 6 species in Canada). Tropicbirds, pelicans, boobies, gannets, cormorants, snakebirds, frigatebirds. Medium-sized to large aquatic birds with 4 webbed toes, throat pouches, pointed or hooked bills; primarily colonial nesters; worldwide distribution.

Ciconiiformes (5 families, 114 species; 2 families, 8 species in Canada). Herons, bitterns, hammerkops, storks, ibises, egrets, spoonbills. Small to very large wading birds with long legs and necks; bill varies from long and spearlike to broad, flat and shovellike or decurved; all continents except Antarctica.

Phoenicopteriformes (one family, 6 species; none in Canada). Flamingoes. Large wading birds with long legs and necks; bill thick with lamellae and bent sharply downward at midpoint; toes webbed; colonial nesters.

Anseriformes (2 families, 150 species; one family, 38 species in Canada). Screamers, ducks, geese, swan, teals, mergansers and widgeons. Worldwide, medium-sized to very large swimming birds with 3 webbed toes and lamellate bill, except screamers (restricted to S America) which have unwebbed feet, chickenlike bills, wading habits, spurs on wings. The Labrador duck, formerly found in Canada, is extinct.

Falconiformes (5 families, 288 species; 3 families, 19 species in Canada). Vultures, secretary birds, kites, hawks, eagles, osprey, falcons, caracaras. Very small to very large diurnal BIRDS OF PREY; legs short to very long; wing shape highly variable from very pointed to broad and rounded; hunters or carrion feeders; and has a worldwide distribution.

Galliformes (4 families, 269 species; one family, 16 species in Canada). Megapodes, mallee fowl, curassows, guans, chachalacas, grouse, pheasants, quails, peafowls, partridge, turkeys, hoatzins. Small to very large chickenlike birds occurring almost worldwide.

Gruiformes (12 families, 210 species; 2 families, 8 species in Canada). Mesites, button quails, hemipodes, cranes, limpkins, trumpeters, rails, sun-grebes, kagus, cariamas, bustards. Very small to very large birds; structure and habits diverse; worldwide distribution.

Charadriiformes (16 families, 329 species; 6 families, 83 species in Canada). Jaçanas, painted-snipes, crabplovers, oystercatchers, avocets, thick-knees, pratincoles, plovers, sandpipers,

jaegers, skuas, gulls, sheathbills, skimmers, auks. Small to large birds; many species with long legs, cursorial habits; some with webbed feet and aquatic or diving habits; structure and habits diverse; worldwide distribution. Great auk, which nested in Canada, is extinct.

Columbiformes (3 families, 322 species; one family, 4 species in Canada). Sandgrouse, dodos, pigeons, doves. Very small to very large birds; worldwide distribution; solitary to highly gregarious; arboreal or terrestrial. Dodo, native to the Mascarene Is, and passenger pigeon, formerly very common in Canada, are extinct.

Psittaciformes (3 families, 340 species; none in Canada). Parrots, lories, parakeets, budgerigars. Very small to large tropical birds with brightly coloured plumage, strong hooked bill; 2 toes in front, 2 behind. Carolina parakeet, formerly of N America, is extinct.

Cuculiformes (2 families, 147 species; one family, 2 species in Canada). Plantain-eaters, turacos, cuckoos. Small to large birds with long tail; 2 toes in front, 2 behind, or fourth reversible; many species have parasitic nesting habits; mostly arboreal, few terrestrial species; worldwide distribution.

Strigiformes (2 families, 146 species; 2 families, 15 species in Canada). Barn owls and owls. Small to large birds; primarily nocturnal and arboreal; raptorial habits, noiseless flight; large eyes directed forward; worldwide distribution, except Antarctic.

Caprimulgiformes (5 families, 105 species; one family, 4 species in Canada). Oilbirds, frog-mouths, goatsuckers, nightjars, nighthawks, potoos. Small-to medium-sized birds; bill usually with wide mouth surrounded with bristles; small weak feet; nocturnal or crepuscular insect or fruit eaters; worldwide distribution.

Apodiformes (3 families, 428 species; 2 families, 7 species in Canada). Swifts, crested swifts, hummingbirds. Small birds with weak feet. Swifts, distributed worldwide, have long, strong wings; hummingbirds restricted to New World have slender, pointed, long to very long bills, and bright, iridescent plumage.

Coliiformes (one family, 6 species; none in Canada). Colies. Small African birds with long tails; gregarious and arboreal.

Trogoniformes (one family, 37 species; none in Canada). Trogons. Small-to medium-sized tropi-

Yellow-bellied sapsucker, one of 13 species of woodpecker found in Canada (*photo by Tim Fitzharris*).

East coast horned puffin (*Fratercula corniculata*) (*photo by Stephen J. Krasemann/DRK Photo*).

cal birds with long tails, red or yellow underparts and iridescent upperparts; solitary and arboreal.

Coraciiformes (10 families, 200 species; one family, one species in Canada). Kingfishers, todies, motmots, bee-eaters, rollers, hoopoes, hornbills. Small to large birds; usually solitary or in pairs; bill highly variable, from long, straight and pointed to heavy, curved and adorned with casque; some toes fused at base; worldwide distribution.

Piciformes (6 families, 383 species; one family, 13 species in Canada). Jacamars, puffbirds, barbets, honey guides, toucans, woodpeckers, piculets, wrynecks. Small to large birds; most species solitary and arboreal; bill highly variable, from short, straight and pointed to very large; 2 toes in front, 2 behind, some species have only 3 toes; worldwide distribution. Ivory-billed woodpecker, formerly of N America, is extinct.

Passeriformes (60 families, 5274 species; 19 families, 188 species in Canada). Perching birds. Comprises more species than all other orders together; highly diversified; adapted to perching, 3 toes in front, one behind; 9-10 primary wing feathers, 12 tail feathers; small to medium size; contains all songbirds; and has worldwide distribution. HENRI OUELLET

Reading: W. Earl Godfrey, *The Birds of Canada* (1979).

Bird Distribution and Habitat Animals' lives are circumscribed by 2 imperatives: finding food for survival, growth and reproduction; and avoiding becoming prey before reproducing. For an animal to occupy a habitat, it must be able to survive and reproduce within it. Birds have evolved many ways of meeting these challenges. Their feeding structures (feet, bills, gastrointestinal tracts) are adapted to take available foods. Plumage structure, colour and pattern protect them from their physical environment and camouflage them from potential predators and sometimes from potential prey. Their behaviour patterns use these physiological adaptations to meet the 2 imperatives and, at the same time, enable each species to recognize its own kind. For example, the birds of Canada's south-central plains are adapted for the zone's short, sparse vegetation. Their feet are adapted for walking (not hopping). Food, mainly plant parts or invertebrates, is taken with bills adapted to clip vegetation, crush seeds or pick up invertebrates. Many species forage in flocks, thereby enhancing their efficiency in finding food and perhaps increasing their relative safety. Plumage, characteristically dull coloured, often with darker streaks and vermiculations (wavy lines), allows them to blend with their habitat; contrasting colours, usually confined to underparts or flight feathers, become apparent only when the bird is in flight. Most species (eg, long-billed curlew, horned larks and chestnut-collared longspurs) advertise their occupancy of space to prospective mates and competing members of the same species through aerial displays that are unique for each species. These displays, which are accompanied by song, make use of special flight patterns that show off contrasting colours.

The power of flight has enabled birds to overcome barriers to dispersal (eg, deserts, mountains, oceans) and to establish themselves in the breeding fauna of continents and islands throughout the world. Often, they have apparently been aided in colonizing new habitats by accidents, eg, being blown off course by storms during migration or, more recently, by human activities, eg, transport of species into areas where they did not exist previously.

Distribution of any given species is limited by availability of appropriate habitat. The number of species of breeding birds, greatest in the tropics where habitats have had most time to diversify, diminishes towards the poles, mountain tops and islands farthest from continental shores. For example, 1556 species of birds have been recorded breeding in the tropical forests of Colombia (5° N), whereas on Ellesmere I (82° N) breeding species fall to 14. The distribution of birds is constantly changing: some species expand their range; others exhibit an ever-contracting distribution; still others fluctuate, expanding for a while, then declining again. Two major factors influence such changes: human activities and prolonged shifts in climate. Both influence availability of food and protective cover that enable birds to survive and reproduce.

Canada's avifauna now consists largely of species that are believed to have evolved elsewhere and to have subsequently invaded habitats available in northern N America. Wood warblers, blackbirds and flycatchers are among families that apparently evolved in tropical America and spread N, via the Isthmus of Panama and Caribbean Is, to inhabit various habitats across Canada each spring and summer. By contrast many other families (eg, grouse, thrushes and finches), are believed to have originated in Eurasia and then invaded N America via beringia. Many species in these families reside or winter in the more southern parts of Canada. *See also* MIGRATION; and individual entries on birds.

D.A. BOAG

Bird Feathers Feathers are only found on birds. They probably evolved as a temperature-control device from scales, much like those of modern REPTILES. Feathers are complex structures, typically composed of a shaft, vanes, barbs, barbules and, sometimes, an aftershaft (eg, in a spruce GROUSE). They are light but can be extremely rigid, depending on their function and location on the body. Flight feathers (remiges) include primaries (large, outer wing feathers) and secondaries (inner wing feathers). These, together with tail feathers (rectrices), allow control of lift, steering and braking. Contour feathers, including all body feathers, give a bird its shape. Down (particularly abundant in WATERFOWL) and semiplumes are small feathers hidden under contour feathers to increase insulation. Some very specialized feathers, eg, rictal bristles around the bill of species that feed in flight (eg, nighthawks), or powder down feathers of herons, may not resemble feathers at all; they can be very beautiful, eg, the tail feathers of peacocks or the wing feathers of African nighthawks. Feathers grow on specific areas of the body – feather tracts – which vary in form and location and have been used as an aid to BIRD CLASSIFICATION. Birds molt, ie, shed their old feathers and replace them with new ones, at least once annually. Body feathers molt gradually, but in some groups (eg, geese) all flight feathers are shed simultaneously, rendering the bird flightless until new ones grow. Feathers may change colour (eg, in scarlet tanagers) or shape between molts because of wear and abrasion (eg, snowbuntings, starlings). The original colour may fade through exposure to light and weather. In many species, plumage of young birds differs markedly from that of adults (eg, in brownheaded cowbirds) and that of females from males; therefore, feather colour and shape can be used to determine age or sex (eg, in waterfowl). Feather number can vary seasonally, eg, birds living in cold climates, such as the Canadian Arctic or Subarctic, may have more feathers in winter than in summer (eg, in gray jays). Of Canadian species the ruby-throated hummingbird has the fewest feathers, with 940; the tundra swan has the most, 25 216; many small passerines have 1119 to 4607. Large birds have more feathers than small birds; however, in relation to body weight, plumage is lighter in heavier birds. HENRI OUELLET

Bird Flight A bird wing is an airfoil, combining the functions of an aircraft wing and propeller blade to give lift and thrust. It is radically modified from the vertebrate arm for strength and lightness. The upper and forearm bones are elongated, joined by a feather-bearing membrane, and support secondary flight feathers. The wrist and hand bones are fused (some are lost entirely), and support the primary flight feathers. Wing evolution has been affected by the habitats to which birds have adapted (eg, the open ocean, cliff tops or the closed environment of forests) and by the need to reduce drag, or air resistance. Wing shape and size have been modified to reduce drag and to enable the bird to achieve the most advantageous kind of flight in its usual habitat. The relationship between the wingspan and the average width of the wing, called the "aspect ratio," also varies. It is calculated by dividing wingspan (tip to tip) by the average width of wing. The long, narrow wings of oceanic soarers have high aspect ratios, enabling these birds to sustain flight over long distances without flapping, and consequently reducing energy expenditure.

Birds soar (without flapping), hover (with wings beating backward and forward in configurations resembling the figure 8), or achieve fast, level flight (wings beating rhythmically up and down). Wing forms correlate closely with these types of flight and 4 slightly overlapping wing types can be identified.

Elliptical Wing, a slightly asymmetrical curve, gives good maneuverability and nearly even pressure distribution. With minor variations, it is seen in most BATS, perching birds and other birds of closed habitats in which long primary feathers would soon fray. The aspect ratio is usually 4.5-6. The house sparrow has the plan of a WWII Mk5 Spitfire. Such wings have a large alula (thumbwing) forming a midwing slot, and several outer primary feathers forming tip slots, all giving extra lift. The Jurassic bird *Archaeopteryx* had a well-formed but unslotted elliptical wing. It lacked power in flight but was a competent glider. The gray catbird, which favours dense shrubbery, combines very short wings with ample slotting. Moderately fast, flapping wing beat is usual to this wing type.

High-speed Wing is unusually flat, tapering to a narrowly elliptical tip. It has a smooth outline, which blends the trailing edge of the wing into the body, thereby reducing turbulent drag. Its aspect ratio is moderately high (5-9), ie, wings are relatively long and narrow. The high-speed wing has a pronounced sweepback, which reduces drag. This wing type has evolved independently in ducks, falcons, most plovers, swallows, swifts and hummingbirds. Flapping is constant with a rapid beat; specialization allows high flight speed, and relatively low energy expenditure. No wing slots are present.

High Aspect Ratio Wing is best developed in oceanic soarers (notably albatrosses) which are seldom on land except when nesting; they launch from cliffs with little or no beating, and are almost immune to feather damage. This long, slender, pointed wing allows soaring at high speed with low energy expenditure. Wingspan can reach 5 body lengths. The aspect ratio is about 8 in gulls, and up to 15 in albatrosses.

Slotted Soaring or high-lift wing is seen in BIRDS OF PREY. Specialization allows soaring at low speed, and enables the bird to takeoff and land in confined areas. The aspect ratio is about 6-7, as high as nesting and hunting terrain permits. Lift is increased by extensive square-based slots. The lift from wing-tip slots shows in the upcurved primary feathers of a soaring raptor.

Wing Action Most birds have a relatively slow, powered downstroke and a fast, neutral upstroke with the wing partly folded. Swifts and hummingbirds have very rapid wings that supply lift and thrust on the downstroke, thrust on the upstroke or lift if hovering. Short wing bones and a massive tendon anchoring the hand prevent sagging at the wrist. This rigidity distinguishes the flight of a swift from the fluid action of a swallow. In most sandpipers and related waders, there is a normal downstroke; then, by increasing the angle of attack, the spread wing is lifted more slowly, giving lift and saving muscle power at the cost of some added drag. When a wing is pulled forward to its limit, complex changes in form affect its behaviour. Soaring is essentially gliding in an updraft. The main updrafts are mechanical, as when a wind blowing against a ridge forces air aloft; and thermal, as when cylindrical updrafts are formed on sunny days. Thermals are strongest over dark and dry surfaces, eg, ploughed fields. Birds become adept at detecting reduced lift on the outer wing tip, and thus spiral within the thermal. The tail is not a rudder, but a combined landing flap and elevator. It is spread and lowered at landing, the wing being pulled forward to keep the centre of pressure above the centre of gravity. In turning, the bird banks, through unequal lift on the wings, and raises the tail.   D.B.O. SAVILE

Reading: D.B.O. Savile, "Adaptive evolution in the avian wing," *Evolution* 11 (1957), and "Gliding and flight in the vertebrates," *American Zoologist* II (1962).

Bird Sanctuaries and Reserves At the turn of the century with bird populations severely depleted by uncontrolled HUNTING, attempts to protect BIRDS focused on the establishment of bird sanctuaries, areas in which hunting was prohibited at all times of the year. More recently, with hunting under control but with an increasing and industrialized human population encroaching on forests and wetlands, the focus has shifted to include protection of habitats. Protection may be achieved by various means, including land-use zoning, long-term agreements with land-owners and outright acquisition of land by wildlife agencies. Protected land areas may be designated as national wildlife areas, conservation areas, game reserves, etc. Where habitat protection is the main goal, hunting may be permitted or prohibited depending on circumstances at the site. Both types of protection seek the same end – conservation of Canada's heritage of birds and other wildlife. At present, 96 migratory bird sanctuaries are administered by the federal CANADIAN WILDLIFE SERVICE: Nfld has one; PEI, one; NS, 8; NB, 2; Qué, 32; Ont, 12; Sask, 15; Alta, 4; BC, 7; NWT, 14; one straddles the NWT-Ont border; another that of NWT-Qué. Some of the most renowned of these are described below.

Sable I (NS), the only breeding site of the rare Ipswich sparrow, also has important populations of breeding gulls and terns.

Machias Seal I (NB), home of many nesting SEABIRDS including common puffins, arctic terns, razorbills and Leach's storm-petrels.

Bonaventure I (Qué), spectacular concentrations of northern gannets, black-legged kittiwakes, common murres and other cliff-nesting seabirds.

Upper Canada (Ont), stopping-off area for Canada geese.

Last Mountain Lk (Sask), the oldest bird sanctuary in N America, celebrated its 100th birthday in 1987 with a dedication ceremony presided over by Prince Phillip. It hosts many migrating ducks, geese, swans and cranes and is a breeding ground for sharp-tailed grouse, common terns, American avocets, mallards and many others.

George C. Reifel Migratory Bird Sanctuary (BC), now part of a complex of protected sites near the mouth of the Fraser R, harbours many species of WATERFOWL and SHOREBIRDS during migration and

is used by wintering lesser snow geese, American widgeon and American coots.

Bylot I (NWT) Greater snow geese nest on southwestern outwash plain; thick-billed murres, black-legged kittiwakes and other seabirds on its northern and eastern shores.

Most provincial wildlife agencies have also established bird sanctuaries within their own boundaries; of particular importance are Newfoundland's seabird sanctuaries and the pelican and grouse refuges in Manitoba, Saskatchewan and Alberta.

Important migratory bird habitats are protected in the Canadian Wildlife Service's 45 National Wildlife Areas in 8 provinces. They include the following well-known sites.

Tintamarre (NB), area of marsh (Tantramar Marsh) at the head of Bay of Fundy, used by migrating and breeding waterfowl.

Cap Tourmente (Qué), freshwater, tidal marsh and adjacent meadows harbour a high proportion of the world's greater snow geese during their migration.

Long Point (Ont), along the N shore of Lk Erie, part of a complex of sites protected by federal, provincial and private organizations, is an exceptional gathering location for migrating songbirds and waterfowl.

Alaksen (BC), part of the Fraser R complex which includes the Reifel Sanctuary.

Polar Bear Pass (NWT), on Bathurst Island in the home of an impressive array of high arctic wildlife including, during the breeding season, such birds as snow geese, brant, king eiders, rock ptarmigan, jaegers and several species of shore birds.

Provincial wildlife agencies have also set aside several wildlife habitat areas, many chosen specifically for their variety and richness as bird habitats. Several other important bird areas are protected and managed jointly by federal and provincial wildlife departments. For example, in the Creston Valley Wildlife Management Area, BC, provincial and federal governments, in collaboration with private agencies and individuals, protect and manage a rich wetland area important to migrating waterfowl.

Birds and their habitats are protected in Canada's national parks and in most provincial parks. Of special interest is Wood Buffalo National Park (Alta-NWT border), the only known nesting area of the endangered WHOOPING CRANE. Municipalities, private institutions, bird clubs and individuals have also done much to protect important areas, eg, Ile-aux-Basques, a nesting island for eiders, gulls and herons in the St Lawrence estuary, purchased in 1927 by the Provancher Society of Natural History; J.T. MINER's sanctuary near Kingsville, Ont, which has attracted flocks of Canada geese for over 50 years; and Alf Hole's goose sanctuary near Rennie, Man.

Migratory birds regularly travel across national boundaries and must be considered an international heritage. In signing the Ramsar Convention for the Conservation of Wetlands of International Importance as Waterfowl Habitat (1981), Canada pledged to protect several important wetlands, including such sites as Alaksen, Cap Tourmente and the Queen Maud Gulf (NWT), an important breeding ground for Ross's, lesser snow, and Brant geese and many other waterbirds. Although Canada enjoys an enviable reputation for establishing bird sanctuaries and reserves, reason for concern remains. Pollution, disturbance, habitat destruction and hunting continue to threaten bird populations. *See also* ENDANGERED ANIMALS; WILDLIFE CONSERVATION AND MANAGEMENT; WILDLIFE PRESERVE.   AUSTIN REED

Bird Watching, the field observation of BIRDS. The popularity of bird watching has burgeoned,

especially since WWII, probably because of increased leisure, a rich literature of books and periodicals, more organizations and better educational and travel facilities. Few Canadian cities do not have at least one bird club and there are international organizations that cater to all levels of expertise. People watch birds for recreation. Many who become highly efficient at field identification compete with one another, locally and internationally, for highest numbers of species identified in a given period and specified area. However, thousands of dedicated bird watchers produce more useful information. The National Audubon Society's bimonthly *American Birds* is devoted almost entirely to publishing data provided by bird watchers. Each season one issue monitors and summarizes masses of distributional and numerical data gathered by US and Canadian birders. One issue publishes results of breeding censuses and winter censuses in ecologically defined habitats. Another is devoted to the continentwide Christmas Bird Count, begun in 1900, and now the most highly organized event of the bird watcher's year. In the 81st count, 33 802 observers reported on 1358 carefully defined areas. Such long-term records are invaluable sources of information on species distribution, population trends, periodic fluctuations, etc. Such counts quickly alert conservation officials to any species whose numbers are becoming perilously low. The notebooks, field lists, nest-record cards and banding data of bird watchers also contribute a vast body of vital information on migration, life histories, behaviour, food, economic status and ecology. It is often said that more is known about birds than any other class of animal. For this, bird watchers may claim much of the credit.

W. EARL GODFREY

Reading: J.C. Finlay, ed, *Bird-Finding Guide to Canada* (1984); J.H. Hickey, *A Guide to Bird Watching* (1963).

Birds of Prey could be defined as birds that prey on other living animals; however, the term is usually reserved for species with hooked bills and large, strong, sharp talons. These birds include HAWKS, EAGLES, FALCONS and their relatives (order Falconiformes) and OWLS (order Strigiformes). Representatives of both orders are found almost worldwide. Although these groups are distantly related, their behavioural and anatomical similarities appear to result from parallel evolution. Some significant differences result from the diverse strategies required by day-hunting and night-hunting birds.

Fifteen species of owl are found in Canada, including the large, reclusive great gray owl (*Strix nebulosa*) (*photo by Wayne Lankinen/DRK Photo*).

Falconiformes

This order includes 288 species of mostly diurnal hunters. They are grouped into 5 families: the Cathartidae, comprised of the 7 living New World VULTURE and condor species, all principally carrion feeders; the Falconidae, 60 species including the caracaras, forest falcons and falcons; the Sagittaridae, one species of secretary bird; the Pandionidae, one species of osprey; and the Accipitridae, 219 species of kites, eagles, Old World vultures and hawks. Although many of the Falconiformes are superficially alike, each family is highly specialized and individuals vary widely in habitat requirements and food preferences. The birds range in size from the diminutive falconets, barely larger than sparrows, to the giant condors, with wingspans exceeding 3 m. All have keen day vision; many are fierce predators, spotting small animal prey while in flight or perching and then swooping to kill.

The turkey vulture (*Cathartes aura*) is the sole representative of the Cathartidae to breed as far N as Canada. The falcons are well represented in the Northern Hemisphere; 5 species breed in Canada. They are most easily identified in flight by their long, pointed wings and rapid flight. The only pandionid, the osprey, a fish-eating bird, breeds in Canada. The Accipitridae are represented by one species of kite, 2 eagles and 10 "hawks." Hawk is a general name given to several predatory birds that are smaller than eagles. The Canadian hawks can be subdivided into 3 species of forest hawks; 6 buteos, large, soaring hawks; and one harrier, ground-nesting hawks of open fields and marshes. R.W. FYFE

Strigiformes

Strigiformes, the owls, are predominantly nocturnal. This order contains 146 species classified in 2 families, Tytonidae (barn owls and relatives) and Strigidae (typical owls). Owls have superb night vision made possible by enormous pupils and light-efficient retinas. The large eyes do not move in their sockets, but an owl can rotate its head more than 180°. Acute hearing allows an owl to locate its prey by sound, as when a great gray owl plunges through deep snow to catch mice it cannot see. Soft feathers permit almost noiseless flight. C. STUART HOUSTON

Birge, Cyrus Albert, industrialist (b near Oakville, Ont 7 Nov 1847; d at Hamilton, Ont 14 Dec 1929). After early careers as a merchant and an accountant for the Great Western Ry, Birge became manager of the American-owned Canada Screw Co at Dundas, Ont in 1882. Five years later he moved the plant to Hamilton and in 1898 bought out American interests. Meanwhile he allied with other Hamilton businessmen to promote local enterprise. When Canada Screw was absorbed in the new Steel Co of Canada in 1910 he became that corporation's VP. By this point Birge held directorships in insurance and trust companies and eventually in the Canadian Bank of Commerce. He was a leader in the Canadian Manufacturers' Assn and in the Methodist Church, whose Victoria College he supported generously. CRAIG HERON

Birks, Henry, silversmith, founder of Henry Birks and Sons (b at Montréal 30 Nov 1840; d there 16 Apr 1928). He graduated from Montreal High School in 1856 and spent the next winter perfecting his French. In Apr 1857 he joined Savage and Lyman, a large firm of watchmakers and jewellers. On 1 Mar 1879 he opened the first Birks store on St James St in Montréal. Six years later he moved to larger premises on the same street. In 1893, since 3 sons were active in the business, the company name was changed to Henry Birks and Sons. The following year the store was moved to their new building at the corner of St Catherine and Union streets. The Birks building still stands on Phillips Square and houses the organization's head office. Since its founding in 1879, 5 successive generations of the Birks family have been involved in the company. K.O. MACLEOD

Birney, Alfred Earle, poet (b at Calgary 13 May 1904). Beginning with *David and Other Poems* (1942), Birney's poetry has consistently explored the resources of language with passionate and playful curiosity. He was educated at UBC, U of T, Berkeley and U of London, where his primary interests were in Old and Middle English, culminating in a dissertation on Chaucer. Throughout his career he has been an experimental poet, publishing over 20 books of verse that vary as widely in form and voice as they do in subject. His poems reveal his constant concern to render his encyclopedic experience – be it of Canada's geographical or cultural reaches, of nature, of travels, or of the trials of love by time – into a language marvellously dexterous and supple, always seriously at play.

Birney has also had an important career as a teacher of creative writing and literature, and as a playwright, novelist and editor. He taught at several universities, most notably at UBC (1946-65), where he founded and chaired the first Canadian department of creative writing in 1963. But his greatest contribution has been to modern Canadian poetry. In long poems and lyrics, sight poems, sound poems and found poems, whether on the page or in his recent collection of recorded poems with the percussion ensemble Nexus (1982), Birney demonstrates his deep commitment to making language have meaning in every possible and eloquent way. He has won the Gov Gen's Award for poetry twice (for *David*, 1942, and for *Now Is Time*, 1945), the Stephen Leacock Medal for his novel *Turvey* (1949) and the Lorne Pierce Medal for Literature (1953). Recent works include *Copernican Fix* (1985), *Words on Waves* (1985) and *Essays on Chaucerian Irony* (1985). NEIL BESNER

Birth Control Attempts by humans to control their own fertility have included continence, contraception, induced ABORTION and infanticide. "Birth control" is a term coined in 1914, and at that time it meant voluntary control of conception by mechanical or chemical means, or by both. Today, hormonal and "fertility awareness" methods and surgical sterilization are also recognized as techniques of contraception.

Before WWI, a few Canadians advocated birth control as a health measure, but organized groups to foster it did not appear until the 1920s. Like groups in Britain and the US, they argued that every child should be wanted and nurtured. Birth control could free women from debilitating annual pregnancies and reduce the incidence of illegal abortion. It could improve marital relations, maternal and child health, and FAMILY welfare. Canadian advocates did not, however, make the claim that it was the panacea of POVERTY. Supporters were, generally, educated men and women. Some were inspired by the SOCIAL GOSPEL, and some were feminists. Their occupations were varied, and their political biases ranged from socialism to conservatism.

Under the 1892 Criminal Code, birth control was obscene, "tending to corrupt morals." Unless an accused could prove that its advocacy had been "for the public good," he or she was liable to serve a 2-year jail sentence. Contraception was opposed by pronatalist business, religious, and political interest groups. Their attacks on the "birth controllers" were frequent and often defamatory.

Nevertheless, by the 1920s, foreign research in human sexuality was creating interest in Canada, the 1892 law was being questioned, and family size among those in higher socioeconomic brackets was shrinking. Informed couples could limit their fertility by "under-the-counter" purchases of commercially made contraceptives, or with materials for homemade methods. High fertility persisted among the less educated poor, however, and the birth controllers urged that contraception should be free for all who wanted it. Politicians quoted the law to evade the issue, but scattered groups of determined volunteers made referrals to a few courageous physicians or provided information themselves to married women. The first advocacy organization in Canada was formed in Vancouver in 1923, and the first birth-control clinic was started in Hamilton in 1932.

From 1930 onwards a birth control program for low-income women was also provided by a philanthropist, A.R. Kaufman of Kitchener, Ont. From his Parents' Information Bureau (PIB), clients could obtain simple contraceptives by mail order and could get referrals to selected physicians for diaphragms and for contraceptive sterilization. When one of the PIB field workers, Dorothea Palmer, was arrested in 1936 in a predominantly French-speaking, low-income suburb of Ottawa, Kaufman's lawyers won her acquittal, arguing that her work was not for profit but "for the public good." The PIB was soon helping 25 000 clients a year. The landmark verdict reassured other advocacy groups, but until the 1960s they were unable to match the popularity of Kaufman's program.

After WWII and the BABY BOOM, public acceptance of birth control increased rapidly. In 1955 SERENA (Service de régulation des naissances) was started in Lachine, Qué, by Gilles and Rita Breault to teach "natural methods" of birth control. The growth of other volunteer groups was speeded by news stories of the birth-control pill and the plastic IUD (intrauterine device) and by word of the world population "explosion." In 1963 the Canadian birth-control activists, Barbara and George Cadbury, organized a federation of the Vancouver, Winnipeg, Hamilton, Toronto and Ottawa birth-control societies and arranged for its membership in the International Planned Parenthood Federation (IPPF). Its objectives were "responsible parenthood" and population education. New groups in Edmonton, Montréal and Calgary joined, but the PIB and SERENA refused invitations. The Canadian federation was first titled Canadian Federation of Societies for Population Planning, but in 1967 it changed its name to the Family Planning Federation of Canada and in 1975 to Planned Parenthood Federation of Canada (PPFC).

Member groups in Vancouver and Winnipeg won United Way grants. Since 1967 the Québec government has financed instruction for French-speaking trainers and service providers, and has also provided funds to SERENA. Early in 1969, the BC government granted funds to the Family Planning (now Planned Parenthood) Association of BC.

Robert W. Prittie led the cause in Parliament; and with informal support from the Anglican, Presbyterian, United and Unitarian churches, and later the Canadian Home Economics Association and the Salvation Army, the PPFC pressed the Canadian government to remove contraception from the Criminal Code. The Canadian Medical Association and other respected national voluntary organizations joined the campaign. The Canadian Conference of Catholic Bishops stated that it would not oppose the amendment. The law was changed in 1969.

Beginning in 1971, with grants from Health and Welfare Canada, the PPFC also undertook to act as the catalyst for government-funded birth-control information and services across Canada. Its advocacy and service organizations multiplied, and in response, some provincial governments began to offer their own programs. The PPFC also raised money for the IPPF. The Canadian government began to meet Third World requests for help and made grants also to the IPPF and the United Nations Fund for Population Activities. These forms of international birth-control assistance continue. SERENA has developed a network of "fertility awareness" groups both in Canada and abroad.

Since 1976 the federal government's assistance for birth-control services diminished. The FPD was abolished and only small sustaining grants to the PPFC and SERENA remain. Birth-control education and services have become political issues, and a hodgepodge of public and privately owned programs has emerged. Many observers attribute the rise in unplanned pregnancies (especially among teenagers) and in legally induced abortions to the decline in support of education and birth-control services. PPFC members continue to inform all Canadians of the benefits of education for responsible parenthood and the services to implement it. Canada now lags behind many Third World countries in co-operation between governments and nongovernmental agencies for this socially significant health-promotion program. Regrettably, also, AIDS has produced another patchwork of responses. MARY F. BISHOP

Birthing Practices

Birthing Practices in Canada during the past half century have been largely determined by 4 periods of sequential, although overlapping, emphasis. The first concern was the high mortality rate associated with childbirth and the need to make labour and delivery safer for the mother. Obstetrical research and training improved, and birth moved from the home to the hospital. Maternity care also benefited from advances in other medical fields, such as safer blood transfusion and antibiotics. Maternal survival rates rose from 9942.4 per 10 000 births in 1930 to 9999.6 in 1985. The relief of pain in childbirth became a second major concern. Heavy narcosis during labour and general or spinal anesthesia for delivery became the normal practice, but were gradually eliminated because of adverse effects both on mothers and babies. Psychological preparation of the expectant mother during the prenatal period became increasingly popular, as did epidural anesthesia.

The focus of concern then shifted from the mother to the baby and perinatal survival rates increased from 940.1 per 1000 births in 1930 to 991.3 in 1985. Electronic and chemical surveillance of the fetus and intensive care of the premature or sick newborn improved their chances of survival, but this improvement was not achieved without cost. Obstetrical technology and intervention became almost routine. Caesarean section rates rose from 4.8% in 1960 to 20% in 1986 and are still rising. Inevitably, this led to the fourth phase, a resurgence of concern about both the short-term and long-term effects of the psychological factors associated with childbirth.

The medicalization of childbirth has led many individuals, including providers of maternity care, to search for alternatives that may provide psychological satisfaction without sacrifice of physical safety. Interest has been expressed in a revival of midwifery as an independent profession. Although midwifery training for outpost nurses who work in isolated areas of the country is provided in 3 Canadian universities (U of A, Dalhousie and Memorial), birth in Canada can legally be attended only by physicians. Canada remains one of only 8 countries in the World Health Organization that has not officially recognized midwives. Professionals on the whole have strongly opposed any move to out-of-hospital alternatives. Attempts to establish freestanding birth centres in Canada have so far been unsuccessful. Attendance at home births has been forbidden to physicians in one province and is actively discouraged in the others.

The major effect of consumer involvement in childbirth has been a change in hospital policies. Family-centered birth practices have been advocated in many Canadian hospitals, although the degree to which these practices have been implemented varies widely. Almost all hospitals allow fathers in the labour and delivery room, but less than half permit grandparents, and fewer than 10% allow siblings to be present. While most hospitals still move women to a separate delivery room for birth, combined labour and delivery ("birthing") rooms are becoming increasingly available. MURRAY W. ENKIN

Bishop, William Avery, "Billy," fighter pilot (b at Owen Sound, Ont 9 Feb 1894; d at Palm Beach, Fla 10 Sept 1956). He was the top scoring Canadian and Imperial ace of WWI, credited with 72 victories. A fellow pilot accurately described him as "a fantastic shot but a terrible pilot."

A flamboyant extrovert, he was the first Canadian airman to win a VICTORIA CROSS, awarded him for a single-handed dawn attack on a German airfield on 2 June 1917. His last victory came on 19 June 1918 when he claimed 5 enemy aircraft. In Aug he was promoted lt-col and sent to England to help organize an abortive 2-squadron Canadian Air Force. After the war Bishop and W.G. BARKER operated a commercial flying enterprise before Bishop went into sales promotion in England and Canada. During WWII he was an honorary air marshal in the RCAF.

In 1982 a National Film Board of Canada production, Paul Cowan's *The Kid Who Couldn't Miss*, challenged the veracity of many of Bishop's claims, including his own, unsubstantiated, account of the raid which won him his VC. The film caused a furore in Parliament and the media. Investigation by 2 Senate sub-committees exposed a number of minor errors in this apparent "documentary" and confirmed that statements had been wrongly attributed and incidents shifted in time for dramatic effect. However, the senators were unable to demonstrate that Bishop's claims were valid, and consequently recommended only that the film be labelled as "docu-drama." This was done. BRERETON GREENHOUS

Reading: W.A. Bishop, *The Courage of the Early Morning* (1966); H.C. Chadderton, *Hanging a Legend: The NFB's Shameful Attempt To Discredit Billy Bishop, VC* (1986).

Bishop's Falls, Nfld, Town, pop 4213 (1986c), inc 1961, is situated on the Exploits R in central Newfoundland. The falls, for which the community is named, were so designated after they were visited by Bishop John INGLIS in the 1820s. It was settled by 1900 and a pulp mill and an electric-generating station were operating there by 1911. A decade later when the Anglo-Newfoundland Development Co obtained the timber rights for their paper mill in Grand Falls 15 km upstream, a flume was built through which local pulp was pumped (until 1952) to be manufactured into newsprint. From the early 1920s and through the next 5 decades Bishop's Falls was a principal railway depot. ROBERT D. PITT

Bishop's University, Lennoxville, Qué, was founded 1843 under the sponsorship of George Jehoshaphat Mountain, 3rd Anglican bishop of Québec. Bishop's was to provide a liberal education for English-speaking Lower Canada (Eastern Townships), and to train Anglican clergy. In 1853 it received a royal charter to grant degrees. In 1871 a medical faculty was established, which in 1905 merged with MCGILL U Faculty of Medicine. The 1920s saw specialized programs in professional education and natural sciences introduced. In 1947 Bishop's became nondenominational. Since then, extensive campus development has taken place with public support. Bishop's offers undergraduate degrees in arts, sciences and business administration, and graduate diplomas in education and collegial teaching. Now part of a provincially supported system of higher education, Bishop's has shared its campus with Champlain College, a pre-university institution (CEGEP), since 1971. Full-time undergraduate enrolment in 1985-86 was 1186. K. AND E. SCHWEIZER

Bison, hoofed MAMMAL of the cattle family (Bovidae), variously classified by mammalogists in one or 2 species. European bison (*Bison bonasus*) is known as the wisent. The N American species, better known as buffalo, has 2 subspecies: prairie bison (*B. bison bison*) and wood bison (*B. b. athabascae*). Both have curved horns, beard, shoulder humps, short tail and mane of hair around the head and neck. Bulls attain adult size at 6-8 years; cows, at approximately 4 years. Bison can live in excess of 20 years. Canada's most conspicuous

Capt William "Billy" Bishop, VC, had brought down 37 German planes when this photo was taken in Aug 1917 (*courtesy National Archives of Canada/PA-1651/photo by William Rider-Rider*).

The population of prairie bison (*B. bison bison*) is estimated to have been 50-60 million in 1800, but by 1885 they were virtually extinct (*photo by Tim Fitzharris*).

CONSERVATION successes and blunders are associated with bison. The population of prairie bison is estimated to have been 50-60 million in 1800, declining to about 40 million by 1830. Huge herds grazed the prairies and, by their somewhat unpredictable movements, offered periods of feast or famine for their predators. Bulls and cows were segregated; bulls were less mobile, congregating on choice feeding areas, and were more likely to stand against predators. Herds were food for wolves, plains grizzlies and scavengers, as well as for Plains Indians and Métis. They also fed white settlers in the 19th century and sustained a short-lived hide industry. By 1885, prairie bison were virtually extinct, except for some captive individuals and a small herd in Yellowstone National Park (northwestern US). The Canadian government bought specimens to establish a park at Wainwright, Alta.

Wood bison lived in lowland meadows and deltas of the Athabasca, Peace and Slave rivers, several hundred kilometres from the plains bison. Larger than the plains bison, the wood bison also differed in pelage, having no long hair chaps on its front legs, shorter beard, long hairlock hanging from between its horns, shorter head hair and shorter, darker, less extensive robe. Wood bison lived in smaller groups, were notoriously more flighty and apparently lacked major migratory movements. WOOD BUFFALO NATIONAL PARK, Canada's largest national park, was established in 1922 to protect the subspecies, and all went well until some 6673 animals, some of which were diseased, were transferred from Wainwright in 1925, resulting in hybridization that almost destroyed the wood bison as a separate subspecies. Today, the park shelters a hybrid population. In 1957 Dr N.I. Novakowski of the Canadian Wildlife Service discovered a remnant population of apparently pure wood bison in the park. Animals from this herd were transferred to the N shores of Great Slave Lk where a vigorous, expanding population now thrives. Others were transported to ELK ISLAND NATIONAL PARK where a captive population now exists.

The buffalo's excellent meat and superb hide, combined with its winter hardiness and unequalled ability to exist and even gain weight on poor forage, have prompted attempts at domestication and cross-breeding with cattle. Male "cattalo" are sterile, but females make excellent, long-lived, breeding stock. Experimental work on cattalo was unsuccessful, because of male sterility and market requirements for fat carcasses. Today, lean, meaty carcasses are again preferred, and interest in buffalo ranching has increased. Ironically, bison may again become a source of meat for human consumption on the prairies. VALERIUS GEIST

Bissell, Claude Thomas, cultural administrator and author (b at Meaford, Ont 10 Feb 1916). He was educated at Toronto public schools, U of T (BA 1936, MA 1937) and Cornell (PhD 1940). He was president of Carleton U (1956-58), president of U of T (1958-71), and professor in the department of English at U of T, 1973-83. His tenure as president at Toronto coincided with widespread agitation for a more democratic form of administration, and concluded with the adoption of a constitution that incorporated substantial student and staff representation. He placed great emphasis on the development of graduate studies and was largely responsible for the university's decision to build a major research library. He was the chairman of the Canada Council, 1960-62, and the first Mackenzie King professor of Canadian studies at Harvard, 1967-68. He is the author of *The Strength of the University* (1968), *Halfway up Parnassus* (1974), *The Humanities in the University* (1977), and a 2-volume biography of Vincent Massey: *The Young Vincent Massey* (1981) and *The Imperial Canadian* (1986).

bissett, bill, poet, artist, performer, publisher (b at Halifax 23 Nov 1939). James Reaney calls bissett "a one-man civilization," a fitting description of this multimedia explorer of alternate cultural visions. His work is strongly antiestablishment, even in its refusal to obey normal spelling and grammar rules. Today, bissett is internationally recognized as a performing sound poet; he has published almost 50 books of poetry of which *Nobody Owns the Earth* (1971) and *Beyond Even Faithful Legends: Selected Poems* (1980) provide the best introduction to his work; his paintings and drawings are energetically primitive analogues to his poetic vision. By 1987 he had published over 50 books of poetry and completed over 2000 paintings. DOUGLAS BARBOUR

Bitumen is the heaviest, thickest form of PETROLEUM. The 2 largest-known sources of bitumen (in Alberta and Venezuela) each contain more petroleum than the entire proven conventional oil reserves of the Persian Gulf. Synthetic crude oil produced from bitumen accounts for about 13% of Canada's total oil production. Compared to conventional oil (obtained from traditional, easily accessible sources), however, synthetic crude from bitumen is expensive and complicated to produce.

Unlike conventional crude oil, bitumen does not flow freely: it is heavier than water and more viscous than molasses. Most of the hydrocarbons in bitumen are heavier than pentane, and about half are very heavy molecules with a boiling point over 525°C. The light fractions are high in naphthenes (used in making gasoline and PETROCHEMICALS); the heavy fractions are high in asphaltenes (used in making asphalt). Bitumen also contains up to 5% sulphur by weight, and small amounts of oxygen, heavy metals and other contaminants. Most deposits contain mixtures of bitumen (up to 5% sulphur by weight), sand, water, small amounts of heavy metals and other contaminants. In its natural state, bitumen is suitable only for paving roads. Compared to conventional crude oil, bitumen contains too much carbon and too little hydrogen. In making synthetic crude oil, special refining processes are used to remove impurities and correct the carbon-hydrogen imbalance. Most Canadian refineries require this type of feedstock. To deliver bitumen to those refineries equipped to handle heavy crude oil, it must first be diluted with condensate to make it pumpable.

The bitumen reserves occur in 3 major Alberta areas, Athabasca, Cold Lake and Peace River, and are found in oil sand and carbonate sedimentary formations. The 41 000 km³ Wabiskaw-McMurray deposit (historically referred to as the Athabasca deposit) surrounding Fort McMurray is largest and nearest the surface. The ATHABASCA R cuts a channel through the oil sands in places, and Indians used the tarry bitumen to caulk canoes before the first Europeans arrived in the late 18th century. Since the late 19th century, people have schemed to tap the petroleum wealth of the oil sands. Some Edmonton streets were paved with bitumen early in this century. The International Bitumen Co and Abasand Oils Ltd produced asphalt from the Athabasca sands in the 1930s. Until recently, Alberta's bitumen deposits were commonly known as "tar sands," but industry and government now prefer the more descriptive term, oil sands.

In the NE corner of the Athabasca deposit, several ore bodies lie within 80 m of the surface. About 20% of the deposit's approximately 144 billion m³ of bitumen occurs here. About 5.3 billion m³ of bitumen, corresponding to 4.5 billion m³ of synthetic crude and equivalent to more than 50 years of Canadian oil consumption at the 1987 rate, were considered recoverable under economic conditions prevailing in 1985. This area contains the world's only 2 commercial surface mining oil-sands operations; both use the hotwater process, developed by Karl CLARK of the ALBERTA RESEARCH COUNCIL in 1948, for separating bitumen from oil sands. In 1967 Great Canadian Oil Sands Ltd, now part of Suncor Ltd, opened the first modern upgrading plant, and now produces 9000 m³/day of high-quality synthetic crude oil. Syncrude Ltd, which opened in 1978, should see its production level of 20 500 m³/day increase to 26 000 m³/day in 1988 with the completion of its capacity addition project. Syncrude is contemplating a further expansion, costing $4 billion, to 41 000 m³/day by 1993.

A sizable market for heavy oil opened in the northern US in the 1980s and, in response, 5 commercial *in situ* recovery operations started producing bitumen in the years since 1984. The British Petroleum and Petro-Canada Wolf Lake I project produces 1300 m³/d and development of Wolf Lake II, another $200 million phase, was underway in 1987. Esso Resources brought 6 phases on-stream at Cold Lake through 1987, achieving 12 000 m³ of bitumen per day, and work has started on Phases VII-X which should increase production to 22 000 m³/d by the end of the decade at an additional cost of $375 million; another 6-8 phases will likely be added in the 1990s. Murphy Oil mothballed its Lindbergh operation in 1986 because of the collapse in oil prices but brought it back on-line in late 1987, achieving 400 m³/d. Suncor produces 375 m³/d at Fort Kent. These first 4 commercial *in situ* projects are located on the Cold Lake deposit whereas the fifth, belonging to Shell Oil, produces 1600 m³/d from the Peace River deposit.

Esso had originally proposed a large *in situ* project at Cold Lake in the 1970s, but shelved it in 1981 because of uncertainty about inflation, interest rates and world oil prices (*see* ENERGY POLICY). In 1982, for similar reasons, the Alsands consortium dropped its plans for a large

Mining the Athabasca oil sands (*courtesy Alberta Oil Sands Technology and Research Authority*).

surface-mining project near FORT MCMURRAY. Both Esso and Alsands planned 22 000 m³/day operations, with capital costs estimated at $12 billion each. Their proposals, which included upgraders, indicated that the economics of surface and *in situ* extraction are very similar. It is interesting to note that if Esso continues with its projected development schedule, by the 1990s it will be producing enough bitumen to feed an upgrading complex of the size contemplated in its 1979 proposal.

Mining of Oil Sands Because of the contaminants and the high viscosity, the first problem in exploiting bitumen is bringing it to the surface. Both Suncor and Syncrude use open-pit MINING techniques to extract oil sands. However, only about 3% of Alberta's bitumen can be reached by surface mining; the remainder requires *in situ* recovery techniques.

At Suncor and Syncrude the ore bodies are 30-70 m thick and buried at depths of 15-35 m. The overburden consists of varying proportions of Cretaceous silts, clays and shales (Clearwater formations, 65-140 million years old) overlying the Ft McMurray oil sands, and Pleistocene (1.6-0.01 million years old) sands and gravels deposited unconformably on the Clearwater formations. MUSKEG, up to 5 m in thickness, covers about 40% of the terrain. Muskeg-free areas are generally covered by bush.

Areas to be mined are cleared of trees, then drained. The muskeg is removed during winter and stockpiled for reclamation use. At Suncor, overburden is removed by a bucket-wheel excavator which strips the material and loads it into trucks. About 80% is used to construct haulage roads and tailings dikes. At Syncrude, part of the overburden is cast directly into the mined-out area by draglines, but most is removed by two 15 m³ hydraulic shovels, a fleet of 170 t electric trucks, and other earth-moving equipment. Suncor mines the oil sand with 3 huge bucket-wheel excavators operating on benches 20m high. The oil sand is dynamited before excavation to facilitate digging and to prolong the life of digging teeth and buckets. It is transferred to the extraction plant by a system of belt wagons and convey-

ors. Mining at Syncrude is performed by four 61 m³ draglines, 2 moving east, the others west, on 2 faces 4500 m long. The oil sand is piled in windrows behind the draglines, then loaded onto conveyor systems by 4 bucket-wheel reclaimers. Generally speaking, oil sands containing less than 6% (Syncrude) or 8% (Suncor) bitumen are discarded as unprofitable. Direct operating costs of mining (excluding utilities) account for 25-35% of the total direct costs (excluding interest, royalties and taxes).

In Situ Recovery The Athabasca deposit contains an estimated 212 billion m³ of bitumen lying under 0-750 m of overburden; Cold Lake contains 35 billion m³ and Peace River 21 billion m³, each at depths ranging from 300-600 m, for a total of 268 billion m³. Surface mining, currently limited to overburden depths of less than 46 m, might ultimately be feasible up to about 80 m. Successful *in situ* experimentation, notably by Esso at Cold Lake, has demonstrated that a significant portion of the bitumen lying below 300 m can also be recovered.

Esso Resources has been experimenting continuously with *in situ* techniques at Cold Lake since 1964. Pilot plant production, which reached commercial volumes in the early 1980s, had increased to 3100 m³/day by late 1987. Esso's method, called "huff and puff," involves injection of high-pressure steam for 1-2 months to heat the formation. Injection is then discontinued for 4 or more months. The bitumen seeps back to the injection wells, which now become production wells operated by pumping. Cold Lake bitumen is 2-3° API (American Petroleum Institute specific gravity scale) lighter than Athabasca bitumen and this relative lightness facilitates recovery. Initial recovery is about 20% of the in-place reserves, but it is expected that communication between wells will be established eventually, increasing recovery efficiency.

Shell Canada Resources Ltd's Peace River lease is unique in that it contains a 24 m layer of uniform oil sand over a 3 m water layer. Shell's pilot-plant technique has been to inject steam into the water layer and allow the heat and pressure to spread into the oil sands through a series of wells extending upward from the water layer. Following an extensive pressurization period, steam injection is discontinued; the heated bitumen then

flows down the injection wells into the water layer and is recovered by production wells.

At Gregoire Lake, Amoco Canada experimented for many years with a process, referred to as COFCAW (*combination of forward combustion and waterflood*), based on injecting air to heat the formation, followed by water to generate steam and loosen the bitumen. A lengthy test was terminated in 1982 after repeated failures to establish communication between wells.

Mine-Assisted In Situ Production For the substantial Athabasca reserves lying between 80 and 300 m, an alternative form of technology must be developed. Mine-assisted *in situ* production (MAISP) is a promising technique. In this scheme, patterned after one at Yarega, Siberia, horizontal tunnels would be driven under the deposit and closely spaced vertical collector wells drilled upward into it. Low-pressure steam would be injected into the deposit from above to raise the temperature of the heavy oil and lower its viscosity, enabling it to flow into collector wells. The Alberta Oil Sands Technology and Research Authority (AOSTRA) and Chevron are investigating this technique in a pilot project near Mildred Lake. Shafts, 3 m in diameter and 223 m deep, have been drilled into the underlying limestone and 6 horizontal holes have been drilled into the McMurray formation. Steaming commenced in Oct 1987, with the first production expected 2-3 months later.

Bitumen Extraction Oil sand, as mined commercially, contains an average of 10-12% bitumen, 83-85% mineral matter and 4-6% water. Most of the mineral matter is coated by a film of water and this property permits extraction by the hot-water process. The oil sand is put into massive rotating drums and slurried with hot water and steam. Flecks of bitumen separate from the grains of sand and attach themselves to tiny air bubbles. Conditioned slurry is screened and put into large, conical separation vessels where the aerated bitumen is skimmed off as a froth containing about 65% oil, 25% water and 10% solids. The coarse sand settles and is pumped to disposal sites. Some of the smaller bitumen and mineral particles remain in an intermediate water layer, called middlings, which is withdrawn and pumped to secondary flotation cells. Generally, 88-95% of the bitumen is recovered in the process. Coarse sand from the primary separators is used to build dikes, forming the large tailings ponds needed to contain the effluent. In these ponds the fine particles settle slowly, producing clarified water that is reused in the extraction process. The fine particles do not consolidate to their original density, so every cubic metre of oil sand mined creates 1.4 m³ of material for disposal. Removal of the contaminants from the froth stream is achieved through dilution with naphtha followed by 2 stages of centrifugation. Syncrude has recently installed inclined-plate gravity settlers in series with the centrifuges. About 98% recovery is achieved in the froth treatment process. The water needs of a large project like Syncrude are substantial, amounting to about 0.2% of the average flow of the Athabasca R (*see* WATER POLLUTION).

Economic and environmental incentives still exist to improve recovery, reduce heat and water requirements, and shrink or eliminate tailings ponds. Consequently, many alternatives have been investigated over the years, including retorting, solvent extraction, addition of chemicals, spherical agglomeration and the use of oleophilic sieves. Since the hot-water process has been demonstrated successfully on a commercial scale, it has been continually optimized and accounts for only about 10% of the initial capital investment of a total oil-sands project, radical new technologies will probably be introduced only when they demonstrate sufficient advantages.

Bitumen Upgrading Suncor and Syncrude both use coking processes to remove carbon from the heavy fractions of bitumen. Coking involves thermally cracking the heavy fractions (at 468-498°C) to produce lighter fractions (eg, gasoline, fuel gas) and petroleum coke (used as fuel in the coking process or sold). Syncrude's fluid coking process produces less coke and more liquid hydrocarbons than the delayed coking used by Suncor. Fluid coking, however, is a very capital-intensive process and the quality of the distillate is lower. The aborted Cold Lake project planned to use Flexicoking, a modified version of fluid coking, which incorporates a gasification step to convert the net coke to a low-heating-value fuel gas. The sulphur in the coke, instead of being oxidized to sulphur dioxide, is reduced to hydrogen sulphide which can be more readily removed with conventional technology and converted to elemental SULPHUR.

Hydrocracking processes, which add HYDROGEN, offer higher liquid yields, better distillate qualities and lower emission levels of sulphur dioxide. However, short catalyst life from contamination by organometallic compounds, large energy requirements and the need to obtain hydrogen from natural gas penalize the hydrocracking schemes. A continuing surplus of natural gas and lower prices have recently made this technology more attractive and Syncrude has incorporated it in the capacity addition program scheduled for 1988 completion.

To make the primary distillates into synthetic crude, a process called hydrotreating is used to remove additional sulphur, nitrogen and oxygen, and to enhance the hydrocarbon molecular characteristics. Hydrotreating involves costly ancillary processes such as hydrogen-manufacturing plants, sour-gas scrubbing facilities and sulphur-recovery units.

The 2 surface-mining oil sands plants have been quite successful in holding down their direct operating costs (mining, extraction, upgrading, utilities and off-site facilities, subsidized housing, research and development, administration and corporate management). Syncrude's costs, in the order of $125/m³ ($20/barrel) of synthetic crude in 1982, were reduced to less than $94/m³ ($15/barrel) in 1986. With world oil prices expected to be maintained at considerably higher levels than that, the oil sands hold out the promise of continued Canadian self-sufficiency.   G.R. GRAY

Biyiasas, Peter, chess grandmaster (b at Athens, Greece 19 Nov 1950). He moved to Canada as a child, began to play seriously in Vancouver in the late 1960s, and won the BC championship 1968-71. He played as a reserve on the Canadian student team which won a bronze medal in the World University Games at Mayaguez, Puerto Rico, in 1971. In 1972 he won the Canadian Closed Championship in Toronto and repeated as champion in 1975 in Calgary. He received the grandmaster title in 1978 for his results in 3 tournaments: Olympiad (Haifa) 1976, Lone Pine 1978 and New York 1978. He played on Canadian Olympiad teams in 1972, 1974, 1976 and 1978 before immigrating to the US.   LAWRENCE DAY

Bjarnason, Jóhann Magnús, author, poet, teacher (b at Medalnes, Nordur-Mulasysla, Iceland 24 May 1866; d at Elfros, Sask 8 Sept 1945). The greatest and most prolific of Icelandic Canadian novelists, Bjarnason immigrated to Canada in 1875. His childhood years in the Icelandic settlement of Markland, Halifax County, NS, provided the background for his first novel *Eiríkur Hansson* (1899-1903). When the Markland settlement collapsed in 1882, Bjarnason went to Winnipeg and from there to New Iceland in 1889, where he began a teaching career. Bjarnason

taught in several Icelandic communities in Manitoba and N Dakota (except for a stint in Vancouver 1912-15) until 1922. Bjarnason's real claim to fame lies in his extensive writings, particularly his 3 novels, *Eiríkur Hansson, Braziliufararnir* (1905-08) and *Í Raudárdalnum* (1914-22), and his numerous short stories. He also wrote articles, poetry, at least 20 plays and maintained a vigorous correspondence with the leading Icelandic Canadian cultural figures of his day, such as Stephán G. STEPHANSSON. Although romantic tales of adventure were Bjarnason's forte, these usually remained firmly rooted in the Icelandic Canadian immigrant experience.   LAURENCE GILLESPIE

Bjarni Herjolfsson, merchant, trader (*fl* 986). Bjarni was likely the first European to sight the E coast of N America. In the summer of 985 or 986 he headed to Iceland and then Greenland to join his father. Driven off course by stormy weather he sighted land, which he described as wooded and hilly, and continued northward sighting mountainous land and mountains partly covered with snow. Realizing these lands did not fit the description of Greenland, he changed course and eventually reached his father's estate. Scholars generally agree that Bjarni sighted Newfoundland, Labrador and Baffin I, though some argue that he strayed as far S as Maine. A few years later LEIF ERICSSON bought Bjarni's ship and rediscovered the new lands, which he named Helluland, Markland and Vinland.   JOHN PARSONS

Black, Conrad Moffat, financier (b at Montréal 25 Aug 1944). The son of George Montegu Black Jr, an affluent but unconventional businessman from Winnipeg, Black received a BA from Carleton and a law degree from Laval. For his MA at McGill he wrote part of a biography of Maurice DUPLESSIS, later published as *Duplessis* (1977). In 1969, he and a few partners began buying small English-language newspapers, building the Sterling chain. In 1978, after the death of Bud MCDOUGALD, Black, through intricate corporate and financial maneuvres, achieved control of Argus Corporation, a holding company controlling, through minority shareholdings, a large number of Canadian corporations. He gradually sold off traditional Argus investments, bought out most of his partners, and repositioned his company in the newspaper business, buying London's *Daily Telegraph* (1985), one of the world's largest quality newspapers, at a time when the climate of British labour relations was improving. He also bought Québec City's *Le Soleil*, Ottawa's *Le Droit*, over 40 smaller newspapers in the US and, in June 1987, SATURDAY NIGHT magazine. Black has also earned some attention as a commentator on economic and political matters in the *Globe and Mail*.   CHRISTOPHER G. CURTIS

Black, Davidson, anatomist, anthropologist (b at Toronto 25 July 1884; d at Beijing [Peking], China 15 Mar 1934). Professor and head of the department of anatomy, and honorary co-director of the Cenozoic Research Laboratory of Peking Medical Union College, Black identified a new species of ancient human, *Sinanthropus pekinensis*, from fossils found at Chou Kou Tien (Zhoukoudian) near Peking. His research on "Peking Man" formed the basis for contemporary knowledge about human evolution. Internationally acclaimed for his work, he also published extensively on more recent prehistoric human groups in China and on modern anatomy and neuroanatomy. He was little recognized in Canada during his lifetime, but is now honoured by a commemorative plaque at U of T, his alma mater.   JEROME S. CYBULSKI

Black, George, lawyer, politician, commissioner of the Yukon Territory, MP (b at Woodstock,

NB 10 Apr 1873; d at Vancouver 23 Aug 1965). Although less a celebrity than his wife Martha Louise BLACK, whom he married in 1904, Black was an outspoken Conservative politician and a staunch defender of Yukon interests for almost half a century. Educated in Richibucto and Fredericton, he was called to the New Brunswick Bar in 1896. He joined the rush to the KLONDIKE in 1898 and spent 2 years mining on Livingston Creek. Beginning in 1900, he practised law in Dawson and Whitehorse. He was active in politics, representing Klondike in the Yukon Council from 1905 to 1911, and unsuccessfully contesting the Yukon seat in Parliament in 1909. From 1912 to 1918, he served as commissioner of the YT. In 1916 he was instrumental in recruiting the Yukon Infantry Co and held the rank of captain. He was wounded in action in France in 1918.

An unsuccessful candidate in the BC election of 1920, Black won the Yukon seat in Parliament in 1921 and held it until 1935. He was speaker of the Commons during the R.B. Bennett administration and in that office acquired a reputation for eccentric behaviour. When ill health prevented his seeking re-election in 1935, his wife ran and held the seat. He was returned again in 1940 and 1944. Black later came out of retirement to contest the Yukon seat in 1953 but was defeated.
                                    H. GUEST

Reading: D.R. Morrison, *The Politics of the Yukon Territory, 1898-1908* (1968).

Black, Martha Louise, née Munger, naturalist (b at Chicago, Ill 24 Feb 1866; d at Whitehorse, YT 29 Oct 1957). Despite her ladylike veneer, she was remarkably tough. In 1898 she abandoned Chicago society to join the KLONDIKE GOLD RUSH. Fascinated by the North, she returned in 1901 to open a milling business and support her 3 sons by her first marriage. In 1904 she married George BLACK and instantly became a loyal Canadian Conservative. When Black was appointed commissioner of the Yukon (1912-18), Martha reigned as first lady. She followed Black to England during WWI; there she received an OBE for her aid to Yukon servicemen and became a fellow of the Royal Geographical Soc for her work with Yukon flora. When George Black was unable to defend his Commons seat in 1935, Martha ran instead. At 70, she campaigned the vast Yukon constituency – often on foot – to become the second woman ever elected to the Canadian Parliament. Martha Black had style and spirit; northerners appreciated these qualities and made her a legend.   MARGARET CARTER

Reading: M.L. Black, *My Ninety Years,* ed F. Whyard (1976), and *Yukon Flowers* (1936).

Black, Samuel, fur trader, explorer (b at Pitsligo, Scot 3 May 1780; d at Kamloops, New Caledonia [BC] 8 Feb 1841). He joined the XY Co, which was absorbed by the NORTH WEST CO in 1804. A fierce opponent of the HUDSON'S BAY CO, he was one of the few Nor'Westers rejected by it at the 1821 union of the companies. But in 1823 he was admitted as clerk and in 1824 became chief trader. That year he explored the Finlay R, leaving a journal of his findings. Stationed at Kamloops in 1830, he became chief factor over all Thompson R District posts in 1837. Never popular with the Indians, he was eventually murdered by one after a dispute.   ERIC J. HOLMGREN

Black, William, Methodist clergyman (b at Huddersfield, Eng 10 Nov 1760; d at Halifax 8 Sept 1834). Black settled near Amherst, NS, with his family in 1775. In 1779 he became a Methodist and began preaching throughout present-day NS and NB, stressing the Methodist creed of the sinfulness of man and the need for regeneration through faith. By 1784 he had communicated with Methodist leaders in the US who sent missionaries to help him. In 1789 Black was appointed bishop and superintendent for the Maritimes and Newfoundland, a position he held until he retired in 1812. He is considered the founder of Methodism in the Maritimes. When he died, the church numbered some 6000.   DEAN JOBB

Reading: E.A. Betts, *Bishop Black and his Preachers* (1976).

Black Creek Pioneer Village, North York, Ont, depicts life as it was in rural UPPER CANADA [Ontario] before 1867. The nucleus comprises 5 buildings constructed on the site by Daniel Stong, including a 3-room cabin built 1816. The other buildings were moved to the site, including a school, gristmill, church, inn, blacksmith shop and others. The Dalziel Barn Museum, a huge cantilever barn, contains the largest collection of 19th-century toys in Canada.   JAMES MARSH

Black Fly, small insect belonging to order Diptera, family Simuliidae. Black flies are small, 1-5 mm long. Not all species are black; some are yellowish orange or brownish grey. More than 1250 species are known worldwide; at least 110 in Canada. Black flies occur nearly anywhere that rivers and streams are present for juvenile stages, including arctic regions, and are especially abundant in northern, wooded regions. Juveniles (larvae) live in flowing water, gathering food by straining the water with their head fans. Females have biting mouthparts with toothed stylets for cutting skin. Males do not bite and are rarely observed. Both sexes require nectar for flight energy; females use blood for egg development. Eggs (150-600 per female) may be laid on substrates in water or dropped as females fly over water. Larvae attach to rocks or .vegetation and complete development in 3-14 days, depending on water temperatures. Pupae are inactive and do not feed. Adults may emerge from any water depth, floating upward in a bubble of air generated during emergence. They are ready to fly when they break the surface. Average life span is about 3 weeks. In Central America, tropical S America and Africa, black flies frequently transmit nematodes causing river blindness (onchocerciasis) in humans. In Canada, black flies cause human suffering and are a scourge to livestock. In the Athabasca R region of northern Alberta, weight loss in cattle caused by black fly attacks in one outbreak (1971) amounted to 45 kg per animal; 973 animals were killed in one area alone by *Simulium arcticum,* a species whose saliva contains a toxin causing anaphylactic shock and death in cattle. In Saskatchewan, 1100 cattle were killed by this black fly during the outbreak years of 1944-47. Black flies also prevent many human activities in northern Canada during the summer and, together with MOSQUITOES, present a barrier to northern development. For example, forest workers in northern BC and Québec demand black fly control as part of their work contract. *See also* FLY.   R.A. BRUST

Reading: M. Laird, *Black Flies* (1981).

Black Hole The notion of black holes originated with the English physicist John Michell and later with the French mathematician Pierre Simon de Laplace, who realized that if light was composed of particles, a sufficiently compact gravitating astronomical body could have such a high surface gravity that light particles (photons) could not escape from its surface, resulting in a black star. Einstein showed that no material particle could travel faster than the speed of light; therefore, neither light nor matter could escape from Laplace's black star (hence the modern name, black hole). Einstein's General Theory of Relativity is used to

study black holes, since the older Newtonian theory of gravity does not provide an adequate basis for discussing the curved space-time near them. The black hole consists of a spherical surface, called the event horizon, which separates the part of space accessible to an outside observer from the inside of the black hole from which nothing can escape. The radius of this sphere, called the Schwarzchild radius in honour of the German astrophysicist who derived the first black-hole solution to Einstein's equations in 1916, is proportional to the mass of the object that collapsed to form the black hole. For an object with mass equal to that of the sun, this radius is about 3 km.

Werner ISRAEL of University of Alberta conjectured in 1967 that, once formed, a black hole can be described by a very small set of parameters, which have been shown to be total mass, and the charge and angular momentum of any matter that went into it. Kayll Lake of Queen's University and Robert Roeder of South Western U, Texas, have shown that a compact object falling into its own black hole appears as a ring that dims very rapidly.

The existence of black holes outside the realm of theory has not yet been demonstrated. It has been assumed that a sufficiently massive star will not be able to resist its own self-gravitation forever and must eventually become a black hole. Most discoverers of black holes have based their claims on this assumption, including U of T's Thomas Bolton who postulates a black hole in Cygnus x-1. Bolton's is the best candidate so far. Sun Kwok of U of Calgary has shown that, by large-scale mass loss, many massive stars may be able to avoid collapse to a black hole. Work of Crampton, Hutchings and Kormendy, all of the Dominion Astrophysics Observatory, Victoria, BC, and others have suggested the existence of black holes at the centres of a number of galaxies. Again, these demonstrations are based on effects possibly induced by the supposed black holes, in this case, the peculiar structure of the distribution of light near the centre of the galaxy.

In 1974 Stephen Hawking of Cambridge University, UK, demonstrated theoretically that a black hole radiates at a temperature inversely proportional to its mass. For a solar-mass black hole the temperature of radiation is about 10^{-7} Kelvin, much below observable limits, but for a mass the size of a large mountain, the temperature is about 10^{11} K. This theory results in the consideration of such mini black holes as sources for highly energetic cosmic radiation. Primordial black holes, much less massive than these, would probably have had time to evaporate since the beginning of the universe. The size of a primordial black hole is such that the theories of gravitation and of quantum mechanics must both be used in its description, and it is hoped that this work may provide the long-sought link required to unify these theories. *See also* ASTRONOMY; ASTROPHYSICS.   CHARLES C. DYER

Reading: Iain Nicolson, *Gravity, Black Holes and the Universe* (1981).

Blackbird, common name for several species of BIRDS of the New· World subfamily Icterinae (which also includes MEADOWLARKS, ORIOLES, cowbirds and grackles). Blackbirds are medium-sized songbirds, about 20 cm long, with sharply pointed beaks. While black predominates, bright reds and yellows are conspicuous on several species. The red-winged blackbird (*Agelaius phoeniceus*), the most common blackbird in Canada, may be the most abundant bird in N America. Other blackbirds in Canada include yellow-headed, Brewer's and rusty blackbirds (*Xanthocephalus xanthocephalus, Euphagus cyanocephalus, E. carolinus,* respectively). Blackbirds display diverse

Red-winged blackbird (*Agelaius phoeniceus*) on speckled alder (*artwork by Claire Tremblay*).

breeding systems. Red-winged and yellow-headed blackbirds nest in colonies in marsh vegetation or in more widely spaced nests in upland habitats. One male often has a harem of 3-8 females nesting in his territory. The female incubates the 3-5 eggs and feeds the nestlings. Males help feed the young after they leave the nest. Rusty blackbirds are monogamous, solitary nesters in marsh edge or evergreen habitat; Brewer's range from solitary pairs to a few monogamous pairs nesting in a loose colony. In red-winged and yellow-headed blackbirds, males and females differ in form, the brightly coloured male being conspicuously larger than the more neutrally coloured female. Red-winged blackbird populations have expanded in recent decades. In early spring and late summer, tens of thousands of birds may roost together. During the day, they feed in flocks in nearby grain fields, causing economic losses. However, they also eat deleterious insects, weed seeds and waste grain, thereby compensating for damage caused. Grackles and cowbirds are sometimes referred to as blackbirds. The common grackle (*Quiscalus quiscula*), a black bird with iridescent green-blue head, and the brown-headed cowbird (*Molothrus ater*), the male black with a brown head and the female grey, are often found in flocks with red-winged blackbirds and STARLINGS. Cowbirds are brood parasites, depositing their eggs in nests of other species and relying on the host to raise the nestlings.   R.J. ROBERTSON

Blackfoot, the smallest of the 3 tribes that make up the BLACKFOOT NATION. In their own language, they are called *siksikaw,* meaning "black foot" or "black feet." They are of Algonquian linguistic stock and speak the same language as the BLOOD and PEIGAN, with only slight dialectal variations.

Occupying hunting grounds on the Battle R and Red Deer R, the Blackfoot were the most northerly of the 3 tribes making up the nation. As a result, they were the first to be met by fur traders, and it is likely that this caused their tribal name to be applied to the whole nation. Although they ranged as far S as the Missouri R, they were considered to be British Indians and were not usually

Blackfoot prehistoric buffalo effigy (*courtesy Glenbow Archives, Calgary*).

Blackfoot chief, his wife and daughter in transit, their belongings carried on a travois (*courtesy Provincial Archives of Alberta/H. Pollard Coll/P126*).

involved in American trading or treaties. Their population during the nomadic period varied between 2000 and 3000 and was officially registered as 2249 in 1879.

During the nomadic period, the Blackfoot were buffalo hunters and warriors, their main enemies being the CREE and ASSINIBOINE. Their leading chief in the late 1700s was The Swan, who was succeeded by Gros Blanc. By the mid-19th century, Old Swan, Old Sun and Three Suns were the head chiefs, and they in turn were replaced by Old Sun, Jr and CROWFOOT. Crowfoot was destined to become the great leader of the tribe, taking them successfully from a nomadic life to existence on an INDIAN RESERVE.

In 1877 the Blackfoot signed Treaty No 7 and took a reserve at Blackfoot Crossing, E of Calgary. There they settled down to become farmers and ranchers, with some finding employment in their own coal mine. In 1912 and 1918 the Blackfoot gained a unique status when they sold about half their reserve for approximately $1.2 million, making them the richest tribe in western Canada. They obtained new houses, regular interest payments and other services. However, the advantages were only temporary, for by the end of WWII their funds were expended and they had little to show for their wealth except a smaller reserve and some aging houses. Their population in 1986 was about 3500. *See also* NATIVE PEOPLE: PLAINS and general articles under NATIVE PEOPLE.   HUGH A. DEMPSEY

Reading: Hugh A. Dempsey, *Crowfoot, Chief of the Blackfoot* (1972) and *Indian Tribes of Alberta* (1979).

Blackfoot Nation is made up of 3 tribes, the BLOOD, PEIGAN and BLACKFOOT. In addition, both the SARCEE and the Gros Ventre were allied to them in the nomadic period, forming the Blackfoot Confederacy. The term Blackfoot is accepted in Canada, and Blackfeet is common in the US. The Blackfoot nation called itself *soyi-tapix*, meaning "prairie people."

The territory of the Blackfoot Nation from the mid-1700s to the settlement period was roughly from the Battle R in the N to the upper Missouri R, and from the foothills to roughly the Alberta-Saskatchewan border. Thus, the Blackfoot hunting area included the rich buffalo ranges of southern Alberta and northern Montana. Their population varied over this period, ranging as high as 11 200 in 1823 and as low as 6350 after the 1837 smallpox epidemic. By 1986, their population had risen to more than 12 300, almost equally divided between INDIAN RESERVES in Alberta and Montana. Linguistically the Blackfoot are Algonquian and are thus related distantly to the CREE and Gros Ventre. However, their language is distinctive, with only slight variations in dialect among the 3 tribes. The Blackfoot claim a long plains occupancy, a tradition confirmed by archaeological research. Their culture is based entirely upon a buffalo economy.

The Blackfoot felt the influence of the white man before the first explorers met them in the mid-1700s. The horse, which had been brought to the New World by the Spanish, reached them from the S about 1725, at the same time as they received the gun from Cree middlemen. Throughout most of the 18th and 19th centuries, the equestrian Blackfoot dominated their hunting area and were constantly at war with the Cree, ASSINIBOINE, Crow, DAKOTA, Nez Percé, Shoshoni and other enemy tribes. They frequented the HUDSON'S BAY CO and NORTH WEST CO posts on the N Saskatchewan R, but carried on an incessant war with American trappers and free traders in the S until peace was made in 1831. From that time on, the Blackfoot divided their trade between the British and Americans. In 1855 the Blackfoot signed a treaty with the American government and in 1877 Treaty No 7 was signed with the Canadian government. Most of the Peigan settled on a reservation in Montana, and the Blackfoot, Blood and N Peigan tribes each took a reserve in southern Alberta.

Because of the size of their reserves, the Blackfoot tribes were able to retain much of their culture and language, although both have rapidly diminished in the post-WWII era. Today the reserves rely upon ranching and farming as their main industries, with small factories and plants being operated from time to time. *See also* NATIVE PEOPLE: PLAINS and general articles under NATIVE PEOPLE.   HUGH A. DEMPSEY

Reading: Hugh A. Dempsey, *Indian Tribes of Alberta* (1979); J.C. Ewers, *The Blackfoot, Raiders of the Northwestern Plains* (1958).

Blacks have lived in Canada since the beginnings of transatlantic settlement. Africa is the ancestral homeland of all Canada's black population, but very few arrived in Canada from there. The earliest arrivals were slaves brought from New England or the West Indies. Between 1763 and 1865 most blacks migrating to Canada were fleeing slavery in the US. Until the 1960s the majority of blacks had emigrated from the US. Today they constitute about 2% of the Canadian population.

Migration Olivier Le Jeune is the first black to have been transported directly from Africa to Canada. He was sold in 1629 in Canada as a slave, but apparently died a free man. From then until the British Conquest (1759-60) approximately 1000 blacks brought from New England or the West Indies were enslaved in New France. Local records indicate that by 1759 there had been a cumulative total of 3604 slaves in New France, including 1132 blacks. Most of the slaves lived in or near Montréal. SLAVERY, which prospered in economies dependent upon one-crop, mass production and gang labour, did not develop strongly among these colonists, but under British rule it was given new life. The English civil and criminal law which was introduced into Québec in 1763 (and which remained in force until the 1774 Quebec Act restored French civil law) contained no strictures against slavery.

The LOYALISTS brought about 2000 black slaves with them into British N America, but 3500 free blacks, who had won their freedom through allegiance to Britain, emigrated at the same time, settling in Nova Scotia and New Brunswick. Within 2 decades, slavery had virtually disappeared among the Loyalists.

In 1793 Upper Canada became the only colony to legislate for the abolition (though gradual) of slavery. With no prospect of new imports, slavery declined steadily. By 1800 courts in other parts of British N America had effectively limited the expansion of slavery, though as late as 1816 an advertisement for a runaway slave appeared in the *Royal Gazette*. On 28 Aug 1833 the British Parliament passed a law abolishing slavery in all British N American colonies; the law came into effect 1 Aug 1834.

Black migration to British N America included, in 1796, a band of Jamaican Maroons, descendants of black slaves who had escaped from the Spanish before the British conquest of Jamaica and who were feared and respected for their courage. Then, between 1813 and 1816, 2000 slaves who had sought refuge behind British lines during the War of 1812 were taken to Nova Scotia. The largest number of American blacks arrived in Canada independently, using a network of secret routes known as the UNDERGROUND RAILROAD. By the time of the American Civil War it is estimated that around 30 000 slaves had found their way to Canada.

With the end of American slavery in 1865, many thousands of Canadian blacks returned to the US, although in response to American legal inequalities small groups of black Americans continued to move into Canada. From Oklahoma about 1000 blacks moved into Alberta 1909-11. The black population in Canada did not increase substantially, however, until the 1960s, when changes in the Immigration Act removed a bias against nonwhite immigrants and permitted large numbers of qualified WEST INDIANS and AFRICANS to enter Canada. This major influx of black people has greatly outnumbered the original black population in every Canadian region except the Maritimes (between 1950 and 1985 there were about 250 000 immigrants from the West Indies and over 100 000 from Africa – including persons of Asian and European descent).

Settlement Patterns Most of the Loyalist blacks, Maroons and refugee blacks in the Maritimes were located, by government policy, in segregated communities on the outskirts of larger white towns. Many of the slaves of Loyalists were taken to the Eastern Townships of Québec. Halifax, Shelburne, Digby and Guysborough in Nova Scotia and Saint John and Fredericton in New Brunswick had all-black settlements in their immediate neighbourhoods. In Ontario the Underground Railroad fugitives also tended to concentrate in settlements, less as a consequence of government policy than for the sake of mutual support and protection against white Canadian PREJUDICE AND DISCRIMINATION and American kidnappers. Most of Ontario's black settlements were in and around Windsor, Chatham, London, St Catharines and Hamilton. Toronto had a black district, and there were smaller concentrations near Barrie, Owen Sound and Guelph. Migrants to Alberta early in the 20th century established several rural settlements around Edmonton. Un-

A black woodcutter at Shelburne, NS, 1788. About 3500 free blacks immigrated to Nova Scotia during and after the American Revolution (*courtesy National Archives of Canada/C-40162*).

til recently, most of Canada's black population was relatively isolated not only from whites but from other black communities. The pattern began to break down in the 1930s and 1940s as rural blacks migrated to the cities in search of jobs. Many of the original black settlements were abandoned or considerably depopulated. The new black migration from the West Indies and Africa has been overwhelmingly directed towards the cities. Blacks are now among the most urbanized of all Canada's ethnic groups. White Canadian attitudes have been changing in the generation since World War II, and although urban blacks still face discrimination the pressures for segregation no longer apply.

Economic Life The black Loyalists, Maroons and refugees met with numerous obstacles in trying to establish themselves in the Maritimes. The small land grants they received could not permit self-sufficiency through agriculture. Forced to seek occasional labouring jobs in neighbouring white towns, the blacks were vulnerable to exploitation and discrimination in employment and wages. Throughout the Maritimes blacks received smaller allotments of farmland and lower wages than whites. Poverty was thus a basic component in the early black experience.

Partly as a result of poor conditions in their new country, substantial numbers of blacks left Nova Scotia and New Brunswick for Sierra Leone in West Africa. In 1792 almost 1200 black Loyalists sailed from Halifax to found the new settlement of Freetown. Their descendants can still be identified there today. Then in 1800 over 500 Maroons followed the same route to Sierra Leone. Their arrival coincided with a rebellion of the black Loyalist settlers against their British governors. By siding with the colonial authorities, the Maroons ensured the failure of the rebellion. In 1820 some 95 refugee blacks left Halifax for Trinidad. Though encouraged to migrate by West Indian and Nova Scotian officials, and despite poor land, severe winters and the competition of abundant white labour, the vast majority of refugees were determined to survive in Canada. Most present-day blacks in the Maritimes are descendants of these people.

The fugitive blacks who had arrived in Ontario via the Underground Railroad typically arrived destitute, and without government land grants were usually forced to become labourers on the lands of others, although some farmed their own land successfully, and some worked for the Great Western Ry.

Many individual fugitives, particularly those who migrated to Victoria, BC, in the 1850s because of discrimination in California, brought skills or savings which enabled them to establish small businesses. Many also worked on farms or in shops on the new wharf at Esquimalt, BC. Until well into the 20th century, however, most Canadian blacks were employed in the lower-paying service categories or as unskilled labour. Many young blacks are now entering businesses, professions and trades, but in 1980 black Canadians still received lower average wages than white Canadians. Recent West Indian and African immigrants have generally possessed a high level of skills, education and experience, and are found in every occupational category.

Community and Cultural Life In their concentrated settlements the early blacks had the opportunity to retain cultural characteristics and create a distinct community. Styles of worship, music and speech, family structures and group traditions developed in response to the conditions of life in Canada. The chief institutional support was the separate church, usually BAPTIST or Methodist (*see* METHODISM), created when white congregations refused to admit blacks as equal members.

The churches' spiritual influence pervaded daily life and affected the vocabulary, routines and ambitions of their members. Inevitably, they assumed a major social and political role and the clergy became the natural community leaders. The many fraternal organizations, mutual-assistance bands, temperance societies and antislavery groups formed by 19th-century blacks were almost always associated with one of the churches. In the 20th century the churches led the movement for greater educational opportunity and for civil rights.

In slavery black women were forced to work to support themselves, and economic circumstances perpetuated this tradition in Canada. Black women have always played an important economic role in family life and have experienced considerable independence as a result. Raised in a communal fashion, frequently by their grandparents or older neighbours, black children developed fraternal relationships throughout the local community. A strong sense of group identity and mutual reliance, combined with the unique identity provided by the churches, produced an intimate community life and a refuge against white discrimination.

A tradition of intense loyalty to Britain and Canada developed among blacks from the beginning of their settlement in Canada. The black Loyalists fought to maintain British rule in America, and their awareness that an American invasion could mean their re-enslavement prompted them to participate in Canada's military defence. Black militiamen fought against American troops in the War of 1812, were prominent in subduing the Rebellions of 1837 and later helped to repel the Fenian incursions. For a period in the 1860s the largely self-financed Black Pioneer Rifle Corps was the only armed force protecting Vancouver I, although it was later denied the opportunity to participate in the Vancouver Island Volunteer Rifle Corps. During WWI, blacks were initially rejected by recruitment offices, but persistent volunteering finally resulted in the creation of a separate black corps, though it went overseas as a construction battalion rather than a fighting force.

Urbanization and increasing secularization have changed the role of the church and the local community, and the new immigrants are bringing their own Caribbean and African heritages to Canada, though they too are adapting them to the conditions of Canadian life. There is no longer a single black Canadian tradition, but the historic values of a people who sought freedom in Canada continue to influence black institutions and attitudes today.

Education British charitable organizations sponsored schools in most of the Maritime black communities beginning in the 1780s and, during the 19th century, British and American societies established schools for blacks throughout Ontario. In addition the governments of both Nova Scotia and Ontario created legally segregated public schools. Although almost every black community had access to either a charity or a public school, funding was inadequate and education tended to be inferior. When combined with residential isolation and economic deprivation, poor schooling helped to perpetuate a situation of limited opportunity and restricted mobility. In 1965 the last segregated school in Ontario closed.

With urbanization black children were admitted into integrated city schools. Until recently the average black person had a lower educational level than whites, and this is still true in the Maritimes. The new migration is changing this situation dramatically. Blacks in every Canadian region except the Maritimes now have a higher standard of educational achievement than

whites, and though they still tend to receive lower wages this may be a symptom of immigrant adjustment rather than overt prejudice.

Politics The law in Canada, with few major exceptions, has insisted on the legal equality of blacks. Until Confederation this meant English law, and black voters were inclined to support Conservative candidates committed to the preservation of British ties. Since Confederation blacks have been active in every political party and over the past 20 years have been elected as Conservatives, Liberals and New Democrats.

Though blacks have never formed a large enough group to wield direct political influence, several individual blacks have made significant contributions to political affairs. There have been black municipal councillors and school trustees for more than a century, most notably Mifflin Gibbs, who sat on the Victoria City Council in the 1860s and was a delegate to the Yale Convention deliberating BC's entry into Confederation, and William Hubbard, who served as councillor, controller and acting mayor of Toronto 1894-1907. Leonard Braithwaite was the first black in a provincial legislature when he was elected in Ontario in 1963, and Lincoln ALEXANDER from Hamilton became the first black federal member in 1968. Emery Barnes and Rosemary Brown were both elected in the 1970s to the BC legislature. New honours were achieved in the 1980s when Lincoln Alexander became lieutenant-governor of Ontario, Alvin Curley joined the Ontario Cabinet, Ann Cools was appointed to the Senate and Howard McCurdy of Windsor, Ont, was elected to the House of Commons.

Group Maintenance Historically the rural black community served to buffer the effects of discrimination and in its protective atmosphere a distinctive black identity evolved. The co-operative strength of community life enabled continual probings against racial limitations, but because the communities were localized and scattered their efforts were never successful in destroying the barriers entirely.

The diversified origin of today's black population makes a unified group identity less than apparent, yet whatever their background blacks face a typical set of problems. Opinion surveys and provincial human-rights commission reports reveal that racism survives and that blacks still face discrimination in employment, accommodation and public services. This creates the basis of a common experience and encourages a common response. Fostered by black newspapers, magazines and community organizations, and enriched by greater numbers and cultural variety, a new and broader black community is being developed in the modern Canadian city.

JAMES W. ST. G. WALKER

Reading: James W. St. G. Walker, *The Black Loyalists* (1976) and *A History of Blacks in Canada* (1980); Daniel G. Hill, *The Freedom Seekers, Blacks in Early Canada* (1981); C. Kilian, *Go Do Some Great Thing* (1978); H. Palmer, *Peoples of Alberta* (1985); Robin W. Winks, *The Blacks in Canada: A History* (1971).

Blacksmithing Until the mid-18th century, few ironsmiths practised their trade full-time. Those who repaired arms and tools in the forts and trading posts also engaged in the fur trade. During the same period other metalworkers became established in the towns and countryside. These craftsmen included locksmiths, gunsmiths, nailsmiths, cutlers, edge-tool makers and farriers, who shod draught horses and oxen, polished runners, put metal rims on wheels and repaired various objects. All these workers practised a TECHNOLOGY that came from the great French craft tradition; their highly skilled art derived from trade guild knowledge, instruction

Shaping a horseshoe on an anvil, blacksmith shop, Innisfail, Alta, *c*1910 (*courtesy Glenbow Archives, Calgary/ NA-1709-52*).

and scientific treatises. APPRENTICESHIP, usually lasting 3 years, was rigorous and entry to the trade was virtually restricted to the sons of ironsmiths, the descendants of other tradesmen, orphans under religious guardianship and the sons of protected HABITANTS. In English Canada, the first blacksmiths were brought to Canada by the HBC in the 1760s. Young journeymen were brought from England to help build trading posts and to make and repair goods that would be too costly to ship from England.

Metalworkers were important in society and set up business mainly in the major centres, clustering in the same parts of the town. At the end of the 17th century, they incorporated farming and animal husbandry into their trade. Around the mid-18th century, about one-quarter of these artisans changed occupations to become carpenters, masons, merchants or contractors.

The various craftsmen produced work of high aesthetic and technical quality: their products were as remarkable for their symmetry and proportional motifs as for their complex mortice-and-tenon joints, reinforced by dowels and flanges. Their work drew its inspiration from religious symbols or copies of well-known motifs. Their customers were mainly religious communities, factories, administrators, merchants and wealthy families. In the early 19th century, most of the iron trades in rural areas tended to be performed by separate craftsmen. Around 1850 the blacksmith's shop became the new reality: here a single craftsman performed all the varied forms of ironwork that could no longer support those who practised the individual crafts. Although the blacksmith made objects that were less refined than those of his predecessors, he built a unique technology based on knowledge derived from the various iron trades and from skilled habitants, blacksmiths from Ireland, Scotland and England, and artisans who had worked with metal in small American industries (eg, quarries, brickworks). Blacksmiths were particularly important in the new towns that sprang up in the West along the railway lines. They were needed not only for shoeing horses and repairing wagon wheels but for making and repairing parts for the new farm machinery that was revolutionizing farming on the prairie.

The smith's basic means of working the metals were physical and chemical: air from the bellows, fire from the forge, water for tempering and tools operated by hand. Transformation processes were heating, hammering and tempering (mainly with water). Besides shoeing horses and sometimes trading in them as well, the blacksmith made and repaired all the tools needed for agriculture, cattle rearing, fishing, forestry, heating and transportation. He also fashioned objects with decorative motifs (eg, fleur-de-lys, rattail, leaf, heart, cross, sun, rooster). Blacksmiths also practised VETERINARY MEDICINE and, in some areas, doctored humans as well. In rural Québec in the 19th and early 20th centuries, blacksmiths practised a magico-religious medicine based on vaguely scientific notions, combined with folk beliefs and superstitions.

The village smithy was always brimming with activity. It was a meeting place where men held their stag parties, learned to drink, played power and parlour games and discussed politics. The blacksmith indulged in certain popular practices: he was called to re-establish order in the village; he struck the new fire of Holy Saturday in his forge and carried it into the church; he headed the labour group and maintained the fire used in flax crushing; his horses drew the hearse. The blacksmith himself, the theme of tales, legends and songs, held a privileged place in folklore. The end of the 19th century and the first half of the 20th century saw the development of the country blacksmith's role. At that time, there was an average of one blacksmith for every 100 families, 3-5 blacksmiths per village. The blacksmith enabled the community to save money. Inhabitants paid a fixed price for the year and could have their horses shod as often as they wished. Clients used a barter system and paid in kind with farm or forest products. Sometimes the blacksmith lent money at interest; sometimes he resold grains, vegetables, meats and other produce that he received in payment.

When the colony of New France was established, there was a movement to set up associations similar to those found in France; however, the best that could be done was to form societies of artisans that were more symbolic than corporate in nature. These associations had no control over the quality and conditions of work. The masterpiece required for entry to the trade was never a tradition in Québec; in the early days of the colony, the only requirement was an agreement between the master and his apprentice, drafted by a notary. In the 19th and 20th centuries, the terms of engagement were less and less official. By the turn of the century, toolmaking machines had already been in use for a long time and complex implements were produced industrially. Gradually, horses were replaced by traction engines for most draught purposes. Blacksmiths became garage mechanics or wandering smiths, shoeing horses at forest work sites or setting up in an area where race or riding horses were found. In the traditional shop, machine tools had been adopted by the mid-19th century to accelerate production and organize human energy; however, except for a general decline in knowledge of the trade and some diversity in manual tools, the physical nature of the blacksmithing trade changed little up to its final disappearance in the 1950s. The country blacksmith has left behind him the memory of a strongly individualistic, boasting, swearing, noisy man who associated mostly with other men and worked with percussion tools. The urban smith, working first in a shop and then in industry as a worker, belongs to an era characterized by scientific knowledge. If he persisted in his trade, the city smith had to adapt to the evolving industrial process of working with cast IRON AND STEEL.

J.C. DUPONT

Blackwood, David Lloyd, printmaker, painter (b at Wesleyville, Nfld 7 Nov 1941). Although Blackwood lives in Port Hope, Ont, his attachment in his subject matter is to his Newfoundland past, and particularly to Wesleyville, on Bonavista Bay. Around this setting, he has created an almost epic story celebrating the community's 63 skippers and 12 captains. Blackwood sees himself as part of Newfoundland tradition, as a balladeer who tells a story in visual images. Blackwood studied PRINTMAKING, and today he is considered one of Canada's important etchers. Since graduating in 1963 from Toronto's Ontario College of Art, he has taught drawing and painting at Trinity College School in Port Hope. From 1969 to 1975 he was artist in residence at U of T.

JOAN MURRAY

Bladen, Vincent Wheeler, economist (b at Stoke-on-Trent, Eng 14 Aug 1900; d at Toronto 26 Nov 1981). Bladen came from Balliol to U of T in 1921. Teacher, scholar, department head and dean, he was also an adviser to government, and his policy papers were responsible indirectly for the Canadian-American Autopact (1965). His writings treated the auto industry, university financing, Canadian economic affairs, industrial organization and "the literature of political economy," the topic for which generations of undergraduates remember him. As chairman of political economy and then dean of arts, he presided over U of T's expansion in the 1950s and 1960s, taking a special interest in area studies and graduate work, where he favoured Canadian self-reliance. A man of immense energy, he founded the *Canadian Journal of Economics and Political Science*, and found time to interest himself in cooking, horsemanship and the National Ballet of Canada.

IAN DRUMMOND

Blades, Ann, author and illustrator (b at Vancouver 16 Nov 1947). One of the foremost contemporary illustrators of children's stories, Blades received the CLA Book of the Year for Children Award for *Mary of Mile 18* (1971), her first book. Set in northern BC, it is based on the life of a child she taught. *A Boy of Tache* (1973) is also based on northern experiences. Her illustrations for *A Salmon for Simon* (1978), set in a native fishing village, received the Canada Council Children's Literature Prize. *By the Sea: An Alphabet Book* (1985), won the Elizabeth Meazik-Cleaver Award for Illustration. Blades's watercolour illustrations, often called primitive, have been praised for their evocation of landscape and the emotions of young children confronting the problems of their daily lives. JON C. STOTT

Blair, Andrew George, lawyer, politician, premier of NB (b at Fredericton NB 7 Mar 1844; d there 25 Jan 1907). First elected MLA for York in 1878, he became leader of the Opposition in 1879, premier and attorney general in 1883, and molded his coalition into the NB Liberal Party. He formalized election campaigning and party platforms. In 1892 he suffered personal defeat in York over religious education but was re-elected for Queens. He resigned in 1896 to serve as minister of railways and canals in the LAURIER Cabinet, and sat as MP for Queens-Sunbury 1896 and Saint John City 1900. Opposed to Laurier's plan to build the Grand Trunk Pacific Ry, he resigned in 1903; in 1904 he was associated with a political conspiracy to defeat Laurier.

DELLA M.M. STANLEY

Blair, Sidney Robert, Bob, industrialist (b in Trinidad 13 Aug 1929). He rose to national prominence in 1977 when his Alaska Highway pipeline proposal defeated a powerful consortium of large oil and gas companies sponsoring a MACKENZIE VALLEY PIPELINE. A champion of Canadian-owned and western-based industries, Blair traces his nationalistic roots to schooling in the US and 10 years with the Canadian subsidiary of an American gas company. Under his aggressive leadership, NOVA (formerly Alberta Gas Trunk Line) grew rapidly in the 1970s by diversifying into gas marketing, petrochemicals, manufacturing and resource development. In 1985 he was made a Companion of the Order of Canada.

FRANÇOIS BREGHA

Blais, Marie-Claire, author (b at Québec C 5 Oct 1939). One of Québec's finest contemporary writers, Blais grew up in the Québec C working-class district of Limoilou. Educated by Roman Catholic nuns, she became increasingly disillusioned with school as she became absorbed in her early literary endeavours. She decided to quit her academic program and take a year's commercial training. She then worked at a variety of jobs for 3 years before moving in 1958 to the Quartier Latin near U Laval, where she attended lectures on French literature and was befriended by professors Jeanne Lapointe and Father Georges-Henri LÉVESQUE. Her first novel, *La Belle Bête,* published in 1959, was highly acclaimed as well as being criticized for its lack of conventional morality. It was published in France in 1960 and was translated into English (*Mad Shadows*), Spanish and Italian. A second novel, *Tête blanche* (1960) soon followed (English tr 1961). The young novelist then spent a few moody months in Paris and wrote a poetical novel, *The Day is Dark.* Back in Montréal Blais met American critic Edmund Wilson and was awarded 2 Guggenheim fellowships that enabled her to live in New England with friends, painter Mary Meigs and journalist Barbara Deming. Perhaps her best novel, *Une* SAISON DANS LA VIE D'EMMANUEL (1965) was awarded the Prix France-Canada and the prestigious Prix Médicis, and brought her a much wider international audience with translations into 13 languages. Over 2000 books, theses, articles, reviews and interviews have been written on it, and the critical contradictions they express are a tribute to the novel's rich intricacy. Blais moved to Brittany with Meigs in 1972 and, after some years in Europe, settled in Montréal where she continues to write at a steady pace. She has published some 25 books, critical editions, translations, plays, and radio and TV scripts, most recently 2 plays, *Sommeil d'Hiver* (1985) and *Fière* (1985). Her honours include 2 Gov Gen's Awards (*Les Manuscrits de Pauline Archange,* 1968, *Le Sourd dans la ville*, 1979) and Québec's Prix David in 1982. She is a Companion of the Order of Canada. In her novels, drama or poetry, Blais writes about mankind's success or failure, in reality or through fantasy, in redeeming human suffering in a material, moral or spiritual way. VINCENT NADEAU

Blaise, Clark, novelist, short-story writer (b at Fargo, N Dak 10 Apr 1940). A graduate of Denison U (1961) and U of Iowa (1964), he moved to Montréal and, acquiring Canadian citizenship in 1966, taught at Sir George Williams U (now Concordia) and then at York U, Toronto. In 1984 he taught at Skidmore Coll, NY; since then he has taught writing at a number of American universities, and again at Concordia. Blaise's fiction sympathetically explores various conditions of alienation, isolation and displacement. His characters typically find themselves (as he often has) at odds in a foreign culture and place; their keen sense of wonderment at the sharply observed details of their immediate environment – oppressively eccentric or pedestrian, exotic or banal – emphasizes their private disorientation. His first book of stories, *A North American Education* (1973) was followed by *Tribal Justice* in 1974. *Days and Nights in Calcutta,* a fascinating joint au-

tobiographical account of Blaise's year in India written with his wife, novelist Bharati MUKHERJEE, appeared in 1977. He has also written the novels *Lunar Attractions* (1979) and *Lusts* (1983). He describes his most recently published book, the highly praised *Resident Alien* (1986), as an "autobiography in tales and essay." His current work includes the novel *Embassy;* a collection of short stories tentatively entitled *The Love God;* and, co-authored with Bharati Mukherjee, an account of the 1985 Air India crash, *The Sorrow and the Terror.* NEIL BESNER

Blake, Edward, lawyer, politician, premier of Ontario (b in Adelaide Twp, Upper Canada 13 Oct 1833; d at Toronto 1 Mar 1912), son of William Hume BLAKE. Edward was an unhealthy child and received, according to his mother, "a desultory sort of education for some years – and in the morning while dressing [his father] gave him his Latin lesson." A tutor and his mother taught him other subjects. Blake then attended Upper Canada College and U of T, receiving a BA in 1854 and an MA in 1858. He studied law simultaneously and was admitted to the bar in 1856, becoming a successful and wealthy equity lawyer in Toronto. In 1858 he married Margaret Cronyn, daughter of the first Anglican bishop of Huron.

Blake, a Liberal, was recruited to active politics in 1867 by the redoubtable George Brown, proprietor of the Toronto *Globe,* who commented that "Edward Blake is ready and will be a boost. As a lawyer he is admirable – excellent common sense, immense industry and great pluck. Not much of a politician, but anxious to learn and as sharp as a needle." He held South Bruce provincially 1867-72 and sat in the federal House of Commons 1867-91. In 1868 he became leader of the Ontario Liberal Party, and in 1871 ousted Premier John Sandfield MACDONALD to become the second premier of Ontario. He left provincial politics in 1872, but during his brief tenure as premier established the Liberal dynasty that ruled Ontario from 1871 to 1905. In 1873 Blake refused the leadership of the federal Liberal Party, but agreed to join Canada's first Liberal government under Alexander MACKENZIE. Minister without portfolio (1873-74), minister of justice (1875-77) and president of the Privy Council (1877-78), he succeeded Mackenzie as party leader in 1880 but lost the elections of 1882 and 1887, resigning the leadership in 1887 and leaving Canadian politics in 1891. In 1892 he entered the British House of Commons as an Irish Nationalist MP. Blake retired to Canada in 1906 and for many years served U of T as senator and chancellor (from 1873).

The only Liberal leader who never became prime minister, Blake never attained the prominence his abilities warranted. Part of his lack of success was poor luck: as Liberal leader in the federal elections of 1882 and 1887 he was required to face John A. Macdonald, then at the height of his popularity. At the same time, he authored some of his own problems. Blake, as party leader, was excessively dominant in party matters and parliamentary activity. He often gave long speeches – up to 6 hours in length – that left little for his colleagues to say and consequently left them minimal opportunity to display leadership, gain experience or please the electorate. The result was a somewhat alienated Liberal high command, a problem illustrated by the eminent Liberal frontbencher, Sir Richard CARTWRIGHT, who noted in his memoirs that in the House of Commons Blake routinely left "nothing for his supporters to say." Cartwright described this syndrome as a problem which "became almost a positive disease," and described Blake further as a man of great "general ability," but "intensely ambitious," "exceedingly

Edward Blake, second premier of Ontario. He became leader of the federal Liberal Party in 1880 but lost the elections of 1882 and 1887. He resigned the leadership 1887 – the only Liberal leader who never became prime minister (*courtesy National Archives of Canada/PA-27030*).

sarcastic," and "absurdly sensitive to criticism," who "often behaved like a spoilt child." John Charles DENT, perhaps Canada's best 19th-century historian, suggested that Blake possessed "a manner as devoid of warmth as is a flake of December snow, and as devoid of magnetism as is a loaf of unleavened bread." However, Edward Blake did leave his mark, encouraging the CANADA FIRST movement and English Canadian nationalism, and recruiting Oliver MOWAT (his successor as premier of Ontario) and Wilfrid LAURIER (his successor as federal leader), 2 of Canada's most effective and electorally successful politicians.

DONALD SWAINSON

Reading: M.A. Banks, *Edward Blake* (1957); F.H. Underhill, "Edward Blake," in C.T. Bissell, ed, *Our Living Tradition* (1957); Joseph Schull, *Edward Blake* (2 vols, 1975-76).

Blake, Hector, "Toe," hockey player and coach (b at Victoria Mines, NS 21 Aug 1912). He joined MONTREAL CANADIENS in 1936 and won the HART TROPHY (most valuable player) and scoring championship 1938-39. Later he played left wing on the effective "Punch Line," with Maurice RICHARD and Elmer Lach. He broke an ankle in 1948 and retired. He was a tenacious, productive player, with 235 regular season goals and 62 points in 57 playoff games. Part French Canadian, he coached in Valleyfield, Qué, before taking over the Canadiens in 1955. He inherited perhaps the most talented team in history, but he encouraged them to work as a team, and achieved unprecedented results. In his 13 seasons, Montréal finished first 9 times and won the STANLEY CUP 8 times, including 5 straight 1956-60. He was an emotional coach, often abrasive and boisterous, and coaching strained him. He retired in 1968 and was appointed a VP of the team. JAMES MARSH

Blake, William Hume, lawyer, politician, judge (b at Kiltegan, Ire 10 Mar 1809; d at Toronto 15 Nov 1870), father of Edward BLAKE. Though now largely forgotten, Blake, a leading lawyer of his time and a pioneer in LEGAL EDUCATION at King's Coll, Toronto, initiated significant reforms in the Upper Canadian judicial system. Of a devout Anglo-Irish gentry family, Blake attended

Trinity Coll, Dublin, and immigrated to Canada in 1832 with family and friends. After a brief attempt at farming, Blake and his accomplished wife, Catherine Hume, settled in Toronto, where he began legal studies. The spirited and ambitious Blake rose quickly in professional, political and provincial life. In 1848 he was elected to the Legislative Assembly, and as solicitor general West in the tumultuous second government of Robert BALDWIN and L.H. LAFONTAINE, piloted long overdue legislation to reorganize the senior provincial courts. Blake ably served as first chancellor of the reformed Court of Chancery 1849-62, when poor health forced his retirement. He returned briefly to public life in 1864.

JOHN D. BLACKWELL

Reading: John D. Blackwell, "William Hume Blake and the Judicative Acts of 1849: The Process of Legal Reform at Mid-Century in Upper Canada," in D.H. Flaherty, ed, *Essays in the History of Canadian Law* (1981).

Blakeney, Allan Emrys, lawyer, civil servant, politician, premier of Saskatchewan (b at Bridgewater, NS 7 Sept 1925). Blakeney came to politics as an experienced civil servant with a strong commitment to state-led economic development and extensive social-welfare programs. He was born and raised in conservative NS and spent 2 decades in the politically innovative environment of Saskatchewan before becoming premier. Recruited by T.C. DOUGLAS in 1950, the Rhodes scholar became one of the CCF government's most valuable civil servants, first as a legal adviser to the province's embattled crown corporations, then as a senior official in the Treasury Dept. He was minister of education, finance and health in the Douglas and W.S. LLOYD Cabinets, and a key figure in the Opposition 1964-70. He was elected provincial NEW DEMOCRATIC PARTY leader in 1970, and led his party to a decisive victory over Ross THATCHER's Liberals in 1971. Re-elected in 1975 and 1978, the NDP lost badly to the successfully rebuilt Conservative Party in 1982 and 1986.

Blakeney's major achievements were the establishment of a nationally admired provincial administration and the establishment of a state-led economic development strategy featuring crown corporations in the booming oil and potash industries. Blakeney came to be recognized as one of the most capable and intelligent advocates of a more decentralized yet equitable federal system in Canada, and as the political architect of a stronger and more diversified Saskatchewan economy. The Saskatchewan NDP acclaimed him as leader at its annual meeting in July 1987, but one month later Blakeney stepped down.

DAVID LAYCOCK

Blakiston, Thomas Wright, naturalist, magnetic observer and explorer (b at Lymington, Hampshire, Eng 27 Dec 1832; d at San Diego, Calif 15 Oct 1891). In 1857 Blakiston joined the expedition led by John PALLISER. Assisted by botanist Eugene Bourgeau, Blakiston made hourly measurements of the Earth's magnetic force at Fort Carlton on the N Saskatchewan R during the winter of 1857-58. He published observations of 100 bird species collected and 29 others observed near Carlton. Together with Dr John Richardson's observations in the 1820s, knowledge of pre-settlement bird life at Carlton is thereby unsurpassed. In 1858 Blakiston explored passes through the Rocky Mountains near the 49th parallel, naming the Waterton Lakes (after a celebrated naturalist) and mapping Kootenai Pass. Blakiston Brook and Mt Blakiston, the highest peak in Waterton Lakes National Park, bear his name. After exploring the upper reaches of the Yangtze-Kiang R in China, he settled in Japan in 1862 where he collected birds and first recognized the Tsugaru Straits

as an important boundary in animal distribution – Blakiston's Line. C. STUART HOUSTON

Blanchard, Hiram, lawyer, politician, premier of NS (b at West River, NS 17 Jan 1820; d at Halifax 17 Dec 1874). Blanchard began his legal career at Port Hood, moving to Halifax only after election as Reform (Liberal) member for Inverness County in 1859. His support of CONFEDERATION resulted in his appointment as attorney general and government leader (succeeding Sir Charles TUPPER) in the new Cabinet of July 1867. The Reform Party was defeated in the Sept general elections, however, and Blanchard served as Opposition leader 1871-74.

LOIS KERNAGHAN

Blanchet, François, doctor, politician (b at St-Pierre-de-la-Rivière-du-Sud, Qué 3 Apr 1776; d at Québec City 24 June 1830). Blanchet studied in New York and Québec. He practised medicine in Québec and held a variety of posts: superintendent of hospitals for the Lower Canada militia, doctor at the Hôpital des Émigrés, health officer for the port of Québec, and member of the office of medical examiners. He was involved in various public health projects and medical education projects. He helped set up the first medical society in Québec and the first medical journal in Canada. He also was active in politics and was a spokesman for the PARTI CANADIEN in the House of Assembly where he represented Hertford 1809-16 and from 1818 to his death. He fought, among other causes, for the democratization of administrative structures in the colony and the development of education. With P.S. BÉDARD, he was among the Parti canadien supporters imprisoned by Gov CRAIG in 1810. JACQUES BERNIER

Bland, John, architect, town planner, author, educator (b at Lachine, Qué 13 Nov 1911). He graduated as an architect from McGill in 1933, and then studied town planning in London, Eng. In 1941 he became director of McGill's School of Architecture, a position he held until 1972. He reorganized the school to accord with contemporary design-teaching principles and expanded it to accommodate postwar students. Many of his students have become known internationally as architects, educators and researchers. Professor Bland has served on the councils of architects' associations and on several commissions appointed to safeguard Canada's historical and cultural heritage. In private practice and in various partnerships, he has been involved in the design of Ottawa's city hall and several large developments. He has written books on architectural history, housing and community planning and coauthored several major planning reports on Canadian cities. In 1987 he was curator of McGill's Canadian Architecture Collection and continued to publish and lecture on the history of Canadian architecture. NORBERT SCHOENAUER

Bland, Salem Goldworth, Methodist (later United Church) minister, author (b at Lachute, Canada E 25 Aug 1859; d at Toronto 7 Feb 1950). A leading popularizer of liberal theology and the SOCIAL GOSPEL, Bland held a succession of churches in the St Lawrence and Ottawa valleys, then taught at Wesley College, Winnipeg, from 1903 to 1917. When a financial crisis at the college during the war was used as a reason for staff reorganization and for Bland's dismissal, his removal became a cause célèbre across the west. A CHAUTAUQUA lecturer and columnist for the GRAIN GROWERS' GUIDE (1917-19), he returned to the pulpit ministry in Toronto in 1919 and became a regular columnist in the reform *Toronto Star*, under the byline "The Observer."

Always in the reform wing of the church and immensely popular with young people, Bland

mixed temperance, sabbath observance and church-union advocacy with moderately socialist views. He spoke widely in the West. A favourite of the labour movement and farmers' organizations, he was an early advocate of a third party for Canada, helping to form the CO-OPERATIVE COMMONWEALTH FEDERATION in Ontario in the 1930s. He was a founder and mentor of the Fellowship for a Christian Social Order in 1934, a participant in Popular Front organizations in the mid-1930s (a children's home in Spain was named after him), and an ardent supporter of the Allied cause in WWII. He wrote *The New Christianity* (1920) and *James Henderson D.D.* (1926).

RICHARD ALLEN

Blaser, Robin, poet, editor, essayist, translator (b at Denver, Colo 18 May 1925; Canadian citizen 1972). Blaser's poetry and poetics were central to the San Francisco renaissance of the 1950s and 1960s, reclaiming for poetry a voice other than the subjective. He grew up in Idaho and attended Berkeley. In 1966, he joined the faculty of Simon Fraser U in Vancouver and brought important energy and insight to the many influences prominent among Canadian writers at the time. He has edited *The Collected Books of Jack Spicer* (1975), the *Imaginary Letters* of Mary Butts (1979), the *Selected Poems* of George BOWERING (1980), and a collection of conference papers called *Art and Reality* (1987), which he co-edited. His essays have appeared in journals and anthologies in the US and Canada. His work is characterized by passionate commitment to and examination of the experience of beauty. His poems have been published in numerous volumes and broadsides and in anthologies such as *The New American Poetry* (1960), *The Long Poem Anthology* (Michael Ondaatje, ed, 1979) and *The Postmoderns* (1982). SHARON THESEN

Bleus, see PARTI BLEU.

Blewett, George John, philosopher (b at St Thomas, Ont 9 Dec 1873; d at Go Home Bay, Georgian Bay, Ont 15 Aug 1912). English Canada's first native-born philosopher, he turned down job offers from the US, preferring to teach at Victoria College, Toronto (1906-12). His books *The Study of Nature and The Vision of God* (1907) and *The Christian View of the World* (1912) reflect the developing Canadian culture in their emphasis on the concept of community and on nature as a life force in need of protection. His students influenced succeeding generations and his works are still quoted by teachers, clergymen and philosophers. ELIZABETH A. TROTT

Bley, Paul, jazz pianist (b at Montréal 10 Nov 1932). An important and influential participant in New York avant-garde jazz in the 1960s, Bley began working as a teenager in Montréal before commuting 1950-53 to New York's Juilliard School of Music. He was a principal in the Montréal Jazz Workshop in 1953; thereafter he worked in the US. After associations with several great jazz musicians (Ornette Coleman, Charles Mingus, Sonny Rollins) he emerged in 1963 as a personal, introspective improviser. Working largely in trio or solo formats and, after 1968, employing the synthesizer, he has sustained an international following. His music has been documented by more than 35 recordings, the earliest from 1953. MARK MILLER

Blind River, Ont, Town, pop 3553 (1986c), 3444 (1981c), is located at the mouth of the Mississagi R on the North Channel of Lk HURON, 132 km SE of SAULT STE MARIE. Named by early VOYAGEURS because it was difficult to detect from Lk Huron, the site was important for the FUR TRADE from the mid-17th to the mid-19th century. From

1853, when the first sawmill was constructed, until the closure of McFadden Lumber Co in 1969, lumbering was the main economic activity of the community. More recently the town has benefited from the URANIUM mining boom in nearby ELLIOT LAKE, from the establishment of the Eldorado uranium refinery and from the continuing growth of tourism.   MATT BRAY

Blindness and Visual Impairment In Canada, as well as in many other countries, blindness is defined in such a way as to include persons who have some sight. The expression 6/60 (20/200) means that persons considered blind must come within 6 metres (20 feet) of an object in order to see it, while persons considered sighted (ie, 6/6 vision, 20/20) can see that same object from 60 metres. Those with approximately 10% or less of normal vision are therefore considered blind. This definition of blindness provides a practical model for organizations such as social service agencies, educational, medical and government institutions.

In Canada the largest agency serving blind and visually impaired persons is the Canadian National Institute for the Blind (CNIB), which has 9 geographic divisions and one national service division throughout Canada and 51 regional offices. The objectives of the CNIB are to "ameliorate the condition of blind and visually impaired people in Canada, to prevent blindness and to promote sight enhancement services." It operates a variety of rehabilitative, low vision and social programs, as well as prevention of blindness and public-education programs. Other organizations providing services to the blind and the visually impaired include the Canadian Council of the Blind and the Montreal Association for the Blind, which houses an elementary school for the blind. Other schools for the blind exist in Brantford (W. Ross Macdonald School), Montréal (l'Institut Nazareth et Louis Braille) and Halifax (Sir Frederick Fraser School).

Persons who feel that the term blind has certain psychological and social implications that do not apply to them because they retain some residual vision prefer the term visually impaired. Many groups of blind and visually impaired persons, such as the Blind Organization of Ontario with Self-help Tactics (BOOST), the Manitoba Federation of the Visually Handicapped, and the Regroupement de l'association des amblyopes et aveugles du Québec (RAAQ), have played an important role in the awareness of blindness and visual impairment.

Statistics on the number of blind and visually impaired Canadians are kept within a CNIB registry, to which individuals voluntarily give their names. According to this registry, there are about 52 436 blind and visually impaired persons in Canada (1986). CNIB officials estimate that approximately 90% of these persons have some residual vision. The registry's figures are approximate because many blind or visually impaired Canadians may choose not to register with the CNIB.

Causes of Blindness

There are roughly 4 major causes of blindness and visual impairment in Canada: macular degeneration, diabetic retinopathy, glaucoma and cataracts. The remaining causes are from various diseases, genetic predispositions and accidents.
Macular Degeneration The macula is a small spot near the centre of the retina, the light-sensitive innermost coat of the eye. This area is responsible for sharpest vision. If the macula deteriorates, the centre of the person's field of vision becomes blurred, and the ability to read is lost.

Macular degeneration seems to be part of the normal aging process.
Diabetic Retinopathy The retina contains the light-sensitive nerve cells and fibres that transmit images to the brain. It is nourished by a network of blood vessels. In some diabetics, these fine blood vessels become more fragile and likely to bleed, causing loss of sight (*see* DIABETES MELLITUS).
Glaucoma is an eye disease associated with abnormal pressure in the eye causing degeneration of the optic disk and defects in the field of vision.
Cataracts A cataract is a clouding of the crystalline lens of the eye. The purpose of the lens is to bring the light rays entering the eye to a focus on the retina. When the lens becomes cloudy, the light rays cannot get through and the person loses sight. The only treatment for a cataract is surgical removal of the lens (*see* OPHTHALMOLOGY).

There are many new surgical techniques that have been developed to help visually impaired individuals. Children with congenital cataracts are treated with surgery before they are a year old and are fitted with contact lenses. The laser is being used in some cases of diabetic retinopathy, glaucoma and macular degeneration. Many persons with partial sight can make use of various low vision aids.

Blindness and visual impairment should not restrict a person from living a full life. Many blind persons have productive careers, attend school and universities, and participate in recreational activities. On the other hand, there are many blind and visually impaired Canadians who have not been as successful in their adaptation and who require extensive rehabilitation and social services. The attitude of blind or visually impaired individuals towards their handicap is a contributor in determining the sort of life they live.

Blizzard, major snowstorm accompanied by strong WINDS and low visibility. These 2 features determine the severity of the storm more than the amount of fresh snow involved and more than the temperature, which may be only just below freezing. In Canada the official national meteorological service definition of a blizzard is a period of 6 or more hours with winds above 40 km/h, with visibility reduced to below 1 km by blowing or drifting snow, and with windchills over 1600 W/m² (watts per square metre). A blizzard is part of a low-pressure storm system, created as an inflow of mild air from the S is rapidly displaced by a cold front sweeping through from the N or W. The system tends to travel from W to E across the country and may last up to a week. Blizzards may occur in any region of Canada, except the southwestern districts of BC; the Prairie and Maritime provinces are most frequently and severely affected. Blocked highways and rail lines, electrical-power disruption, stranded motorists and lost livestock are the predictable results of large blizzards. *See also* METEOROLOGY; CLIMATE SEVERITY.   J. MAYBANK

Bloc populaire canadien, a Canadian federal and Québec provincial political movement formed Sept 1942 in reaction to the National Resources Mobilization Act, Amendment Act, 1942, which removed the existing ban on CONSCRIPTION for military service overseas. The Act violated promises made specifically to Québec in 1939, and followed a plebiscite in which a majority in every province except Québec had voted in favour of releasing the government from its commitments restricting "the methods of raising men for military service." Inspired by Henri BOURASSA and led by Maxime Raymond, MP, the Bloc included in its basic program Canadian independence and neutrality, provincial autonomy, English-French equality, a co-operative economy and family-based social reforms such as provin-

cial health insurance. By 1944, 5 MPs belonged to the Bloc.

Led provincially by André LAURENDEAU, the Bloc was a distinct third party in the Québec legislature until the 1948 provincial election, which it did not contest. In Ottawa, the Bloc had supported Canadian membership in the United Nations, considering it to be a genuine world organization, but in Mar 1949 its 2 remaining federal members voted against participation in NATO because "it is an armaments race." When Parliament dissolved on 30 Apr 1949, the Bloc populaire canadien ceased to exist. Among its leaders had been René Hamel, later a provincial Liberal Cabinet minister and judge; Roger Duhamel, who became Queen's Printer at Ottawa; Jean Martineau, afterwards chairman of the Canada Council; André LAURENDEAU, later co-chairman of the commission on BILINGUALISM AND BICULTURALISM; and Jean DRAPEAU, the longtime mayor of Montréal.
                        GORDON O. ROTHNEY

Blodgett, Edward Dickinson, poet, literary critic, translator (b at Philadelphia, Pa 26 Feb 1935; Canadian citizen). Ted Blodgett began teaching at U of Alberta in 1966; he served as chairman of the dept of comparative literature (1975-85), where he continues to lecture and write. He has written 5 books of poetry: *take away the names* (1975); *Sounding* (1977); *Beast Gate* (1980); *Arché/Elegies* (1983), a contemplation of the idea of Canada; and *Musical Offering* (1986). For Blodgett, language is the essential material which affords us our humanity, and his verse searches the edges of language and mind with extraordinary craft and delicacy. His speech, with its fine questioning method, is made rich by its resonance with the many languages and literatures, ancient and modern, that he has made it his business to know. His critical essays show him as medievalist and comparatist, and in *Configuration: Essays on the Canadian Literatures* (1982), he seeks to practise an ideologically precise comparative literary theory.
                        ROBERT DUNHAM

Blood, one of 3 tribes which make up the BLACKFOOT NATION. In their own language they are called *Kainai*, which is a corruption of the term *a-kainaw*, meaning "many chiefs." They are of Algonquian linguistic stock and speak the same language as the Blackfoot and PEIGAN, with only slight variations in dialect. The Blood once occupied hunting grounds from the Red Deer R to the Belly R, but by the mid-19th century they had moved farther S to the Pakowki Lk, Belly R and Teton R regions. They often ranged far into Montana and traded as frequently with the American Fur Co as they did with the HUDSON'S BAY CO. They were a nomadic buffalo-hunting tribe (*see* BUFFALO HUNT), with complex religious societies and the reputation for being fierce warriors. Their enemies included the CREE, KOOTENAY, Shoshoni and Crow tribes. The population of the Blood during the nomadic period was from 2500 to 3500, dropping to a low of 1750 people after the 1837 smallpox epidemic.

The leading chief of the tribe in the late 1700s was Bull Back Fat, who was succeeded by 2 descendants bearing the same name. The second Bull Back Fat made peace with the Americans in 1831, permitting them to open trading posts on the upper Missouri R. In 1855 the Blood, under Father of Many Children, Bull Back Fat and Seen From Afar, signed a treaty with the Americans. In 1877 Seen From Afar's nephew, RED CROW, was the tribe's chief signer of Treaty No 7 with the Canadian government and remained leader of the tribe until his death in 1900.

Initially the Blood were given a reserve adjacent to the Blackfoot on the Bow R, but in 1880 they moved to a new site between the St Mary R and Belly R, where they established the largest INDIAN RESERVE in Canada. In the 1890s the Blood launched a successful ranching industry, and after the turn of the century they became large-scale farmers. Over the years, they gained the reputation of being hardworking, proud people who retained many of their cultural values. Like other tribes, they faced the stresses of integration and social breakdown, but have been relatively more successful in dealing with these problems. *See also* NATIVE PEOPLE: PLAINS and general articles under NATIVE PEOPLE.　　　HUGH A. DEMPSEY

Reading: Hugh A. Dempsey, *Indian Tribes of Alberta* (1979); Mike Mountain Horse, *My People the Bloods* (1979).

Bloody Falls, rapids located about 15 km above the mouth of the COPPERMINE R in the central Arctic, is named for the massacre of local INUIT by CHIPEWYAN led by MATONABBEE, accompanying Samuel HEARNE on his exploration of the area in 1771. In later times the area was used as an important summer fishing site by the COPPER INUIT, as well as a stop on the route to the interior in order to obtain native copper and wood from the forests that begin 20 km upstream. Archaeology has discovered traces of Inuit occupation dating to about 1500 AD. The area was also occupied by Paleoeskimos about 1300 BC, and by Indian caribou hunters between roughly 500 BC and 500 AD. For more than 3000 years this site has probably marked a zone of tension between Indian and Inuit cultures.　　　ROBERT McGHEE

Bloore, Ronald, painter (b at Brampton, Ont 29 May 1925). Bloore studied at U of Toronto (BA 1949) and in the US and England. Appointed director of the Norman Mackenzie Art Gallery Regina in 1958, he brought in important, progressive exhibitions, and he introduced his students at the School of Art (Regina College: later U Sask) to the work of the American abstract expressionists. Bloore was instrumental in inviting Barnett Newman to lead the summer workshop at Emma Lake, Sask, in 1959, an event of lasting influence on the Regina art scene. In 1960 Bloore organized an exhibition of a group, including himself, that became known as the REGINA FIVE. The exhibition went on a national tour and was presented to the National Gallery of Canada in 1961. Their work, still influential, was seen as the expression of the new painting emerging in the Canadian West. Bloore

Ronald Bloore, *Painting* (1959), stovepipe enamel on masonite (*courtesy Ronald Bloore/Galerie Dresdnere*).

achieved a remarkable control and resolve in his painting early in his career, confining himself to the limited subject matter of "symbol-like elements" and a severely restricted palette. The paintings come alive by the play of light and shadows on the raised textured surfaces. Bloore has been a professor at York U since 1966. A major show of paintings, drawings, etc, was held in 1987.　　　CLARA HARGITTAY

Blue-green Algae (phylum Cyanophyta) are the only ALGAE characterized by cells which lack a distinct nucleus (prokaryotes). They include unicellular, colonial and filamentous forms. FOSSILS of blue-green algae make up layered formations (stromatolites) 3 billion years old in South Africa, up to 2.5 billion in the Canadian Shield. They were probably the first oxygen-producing organisms and are thought to have been responsible for the early accumulation of oxygen in the atmosphere.

Their cell structure places blue-green algae in the same kingdom (Monera) as bacteria; hence they are called cyanobacteria by some scientists. Unlike most true bacteria, blue-green algae can photosynthesize chemical nutrients. Their photosynthetic machinery, including both chlorophyll and phycobiliprotein pigments, is contained in platelike membranes scattered throughout the cell; hence, they differ from "eukaryotic" algae and higher plants, in which photosynthesis occurs in distinct organelles (chloroplasts). Blue-green algae contain glycogen as a stored carbohydrate. In general, a gelatinous sheath of varying thickness envelops the cell or colony. It can be red or blue depending on whether the species grows in highly acidic or basic conditions, respectively. The cell wall resembles that found in "gram-negative" bacteria (ie, those which are sensitive to penicillin) both in construction and chemistry, and contains amino acids and sugars. Some unicellular species "fix" atmospheric nitrogen, another characteristic they share with bacteria. Gas pockets (vacuoles), visible in many free-living PLANKTONIC forms, act as flotation chambers to aid cell buoyancy. Many filamentous species move when in contact with a solid surface. This movement occurs without evident organs of locomotion. Motile blue-green algae, on submerged sediments, move to the sediment surface in daytime and descend into the upper few millimetres at night (vertical migration rhythm).

Most blue-green algae reproduce by cell division. In certain filamentous forms, specialized fragments of the filament (hormogonia) serve in reproduction. Several unicellular reproductive

agents (eg, akinetes, endospores, exospores and heterocysts) are also formed by many filamentous types. Heterocysts function mainly as the site of nitrogen fixation, but in a few species (eg, *Gloeotrichia ghosei*) they will germinate like spores. Sexual reproduction does not occur, but evidence exists showing that genetic recombination may take place through the joining of 2 cells which then exchange DNA. This "conjugation" is also found in bacteria.

Blue-green algae are very widespread, occurring in waters varying greatly in salinity, nutrient status and temperature; and in planktonic, benthic and aerial communities. In general, they are more abundant in neutral or slightly alkaline habitats. They occur in alkaline hot SPRINGS at temperatures approaching 73-74°C. In nutrient-rich (eutrophic) lakes, several species (eg, *Microcystis aeruginosa, Anabaena flos-aquae, Aphanizomenon flos-aquae*) are members of water "blooms" in late summer. Genetic strains of the first 2 species are responsible for poisonings of various animals. In stagnant waters, excessive growth may also cause noxious odours. Many species form symbiotic relationships with other organisms in which they supply nitrogen. Partners include FUNGI (to form LICHENS), MOSSES, FERNS, SEED PLANTS and animals. *See also* WATER POLLUTION.　　　MICHAEL HICKMAN

Bluebell, common name for several PLANTS with bell-shaped flowers of Campanulaceae and Boraginaceae families. Common bluebells, genus *Campanula* [Lat, "bell"], are perennial, herbaceous plants with milky juice, native to north temperate and arctic regions. More than 230 species are known worldwide; 9 species are native to Canada, 5 others have been introduced as garden escapes. The best-known Canadian species, *C. rotundifolia,* found from the YT to the Atlantic provinces (in PEI, it is an escape), is the "bluebell" of Scotland or "harebell" (contraction of heatherbell). Bluebells grow in stony tundra, rocky crevices, roadsides, rich meadows and woods, from low elevations to alpine habitats. The plants flower June-Aug, and the petals are joined into bell shape. The nodding bells are blue or purple, sometimes white. The mature female element (pistil) resembles a bell clapper. Insect POLLINATION is normal but, if it does not occur, the mature pistil bends backward and self-pollinates from pollen at the base of the bell. The fruit develops pores on the side which open to release many seeds. Lungworts, sometimes also called bluebells, belong to genus *Mertensia,* borage family.

Bluebird (genus *Sialia*), common name for 3 species of THRUSHES occurring in North and Central America. Males have bright blue heads, backs, wings and tails. Females, although similar in size, are much greyer overall, but have blue wings and tails. They breed in open country, one species across SE Canada and all 3 in parts of the West. Nesting in natural and woodpecker cavities or birdhouses, usually at shrub level, they lay 4-5 pale blue eggs, which are incubated about 14 days. Long trails of nest boxes have been established for them, especially in the Prairie provinces. They are primarily insectivorous but eat some small fruits.　　　R.D. JAMES

Bluefish Caves contain the oldest undisturbed archaeological evidence in Canada. Located on a limestone ridge overlooking the upper Bluefish R in the Keele Range of the northern YT, the caves consist of 3 small cavities in which loess accumulated during late Pleistocene time. Buried in these aeolian deposits are the bones of mammoths, horses, bison, caribou, sheep and many other

The famous Nova Scotia schooner *Bluenose*, 1921 (*courtesy Knickle's Studio, Lunenburg*).

mammals, as well as birds and fish. Numerous large mammal bones exhibit butchering marks made by stone tools. Associated with the bones, some of which have been dated to between 12 000 and 18 000 years ago, are the lithic remains of a burin and MICROBLADE technology akin to that found in the American Paleoarctic tradition. The paleoenvironmental reconstruction based on pollen, macrofossil, pedological and micro-mammal evidence is in keeping with that obtained from other eastern Beringian regions for the period of the late Wisconsinan maximum and subsequent millennia. *See also* ARCHAEOLOGY; PRE-HISTORY.   JACQUES CINQ-MARS

Bluenose, The, Canada's most famous ship, was launched at LUNENBURG, NS, in 1921 and named with the common sobriquet first applied by T.C. HALIBURTON to natives of NS. The schooner was designed by William J. Roué to fish the Grand Banks and to race. Skippered by Capt Angus J. WALTERS against the fastest American schooners, it won the International Fisherman's Trophy, emblematic of the sailing championship of the fishing fleets of the N Atlantic, in 1921, 1922 and 1923. Its only defeat was by the Boston schooner *Gertrude L. Thebaud* in the Lipton Cup in 1930, but it outraced the *Thebaud* for the Fisherman's Trophy in 1931 and 1938. The *Bluenose* also held the record for the largest catch of fish brought into Lunenburg. It came to an ignominious end, sold in 1942 to a West Indies trading company and wrecked off Haiti in 1946. A sculptured profile of the *Bluenose* has been reproduced on the Canadian dime since 1937. A replica, *Bluenose II*, was built in the same Smith and Rhuland shipyards in Lunenburg and launched in 1963 amid nostalgia for the lost golden age of sail.   JAMES MARSH

Blumenfeld, Hans, urban and regional planner, educator, author, consultant (b at Osnabrück, Ger 18 Oct 1892). Appointed to the Russian State City Planning Institute from 1930 to 1933, Blumenfeld left the USSR in 1937 for the US where he worked primarily for the Philadelphia Planning Commission. He came to Canada in 1955 as assistant director of the Metropolitan Toronto Planning Board and was instrumental in shaping Toronto and its hinterland. In 1961 he became a private consultant and in 1964 a professor at U of Toronto. He is the author of numerous acclaimed articles and books, including *The Modern Metropolis* (1967) and *Metropolis and Beyond* (1979). His most significant contribution has been his vision of the "metropolis" as a new urban organism whose unique scale and structure require diagnosis and treatment. Acknowledged as one of the leading figures in 20th-century URBAN AND REGIONAL PLANNING, he is a fellow of the Canadian Institute of Planners and is a recipient of the American Institute of Planners Distinguished Service Award. He has had a lifelong involvement in the world peace movement. His autobiography, *Life Begins at 65...*, was published in 1986.   NORMAN PRESSMAN

Blyth Festival in SW Ontario specializes in Canadian plays. Started by director James Roy and board president Keith Roulston in 1975, the festival produces plays aimed first at local audiences and secondarily at visitors, and enjoys strong community support. Theatre Passe Muraille's popular *Farm Show* had been developed around nearby Clinton. Janet Amos, director 1979-84, was a *Farm Show* veteran, as have been many other Blyth Festival artists. Since 1984, under direction of Katherine Kaszas, the festival has developed a national presence. The festival has restored the Memorial Hall, which was built 1919-20 but allowed to fall into disrepair. Many Blyth plays have dealt with local history (eg, *The Blyth Memorial History Show*) or rural issues (eg, Ted Johns's *He Won't Come In From the Barn).* Some have been adapted from the stories of regional writers Harry BOYLE and Alice MUNRO. However, a growing number of Blyth Festival plays have attracted national attention. Peter Colley's often-produced thriller *I'll Be Back For You Before Midnight* premiered there, as did Anne Chislett's award-winning drama *Quiet in the Land.*   ROSS STUART

Boas, Franz, anthropologist, ethnologist, folklorist, linguist (b at Minden, Westphalia 9 July 1858; d at New York City, NY 21 Dec 1942). He developed with his students the professional and intellectual direction of American anthropology, emphasizing the method of empirical culture history. His work stressed the cumulative historical factors that blend to give each society its distinctive character. Boas's first interest was in historical geography, but his pioneering work with the BAFFIN ISLAND INUIT (1883-84) showed him that people's ways are not merely a matter of geography, and that they often act against the constraints of their environment. His field research shifted permanently in 1886 to the Northwest Coast Indians. Their rich art and mythology further convinced him of the need to take into account psychological characteristics as well as geographical environment. These characteristics develop through centuries of borrowing traits from other cultures, modifying them and integrating them within the new culture. Boas's many students were his greatest legacy. His most brilliant student, Edward SAPIR, became the first chief of what is now the CANADIAN MUSEUM OF CIVILIZATION. For many years Boas reigned at the hub of American professional anthropology, and was the mentor of most of the first women in the profession, Ruth Benedict and Margaret Mead among others. He worked effectively and tirelessly to move the public away from its belief in race and towards a scientific conception of culture as the basis for explaining the most significant human differences.   R.J. PRESTON

Reading: Franz Boas, *The Mind of Primitive Man* (1938, rev 1965) and *Race, Language, and Culture* (1940).

Boat People, *see* SOUTHEAST ASIANS.

Boating Canadians are among the most active boaters in the world: over 50% or 13 million people go boating each year in some form of recreational craft. Canadians own 2.3 million boats, ranging from canoes to yachts over 20 m – more than twice the number of boats per capita compared with the US. Each year, boating generates over $2.5 billion of direct expenditure.

Despite the limitations on year-round boating imposed by climate everywhere except on the West Coast, Canada has many natural resources that encourage this activity. Canada has more fresh water than any other nation, dotted in a myriad of lakes and streams across the country; some of the longest rivers in the world, which stretch into the far corners of the land; and sea coasts bordering on 2 large oceans.

Historically, Canadians lived by and travelled on the water. The first inhabitants developed many unique boat designs ranging from skin or bark CANOES to magnificent ocean-going boats capable of extended voyages. The early explorers and traders were quick to realize the usefulness of native craft and adopted them as their own. Each year the Hudson's Bay Co, North West Co and others arranged shipment of their goods by water over vast distances and, by necessity, began to modify the canoe to their needs. The first boat factories utilizing specialized production-line techniques were set up in the late 18th century in Québec to meet the demands for canoes.

By the mid-19th century, boating flourished at all levels of society. While many people enjoyed the pleasures of a canoe or pulling boat, those of more substantial means lavished money on sleek racing craft and on the wagers accompanying them. Clubs catering to these pleasures were formed for all types of boats, and organized competitions for members became common. Not content with local endeavour, Canadians soon became prominent on the world stage. Ned HANLAN won the world champion sculling competition in 1880; Canada challenged twice for the America's Cup, in 1876 and 1881; and in 1896 a yacht appropriately named *Canada* won a trophy on the

Boating off Vancouver (*photo by Al Harvey/Masterfile*).

Great Lakes, emblematic to this day of YACHTING rivalry between Canada and the US.

Boating became mechanized around the turn of the century. Factories were built using sophisticated methods to satisfy the increasing demand for boats, and engines became available to propel craft of all kinds. Though small steamboats had been used for some time, the gas engine revolutionized boating and culminated in the outboard motor we know today. Materials and techniques developed for other uses, particularly fiberglass and aluminum, were adapted to boat construction. In 1950 there were 72 558 licensed boats in Canada. Only those boats with engines over 7.4 kW (10 hp) require a licence, so this figure represents but a portion of the boats. However, by 1987, 1 310 000 licences had been issued. Almost all of these boats have been constructed of either fiberglass or aluminum.

In the 1980s the small outboard was the most popular boat, accounting for about 45% of the total. Easily operated or transported, it provides millions of fishermen, hunters, waterskiers and casual boaters with enjoyment. The canoe comprises 30% of all Canadian boats; it can go almost anywhere and is inexpensive. Rowboats, long in the shadow of powerboats, are finding new interest among fitness devotees. Sailboats, often the most dramatic and visible of all watercraft, total 10% of Canada's fleet. Once the preserve of the wealthy or the working fisherman, sailboats were revolutionized by the use of fiberglass. Thousands of people now have access to sleek, well-designed, economical and durable boats. In this field, in particular, Canadian manufacturers have been quite successful; one of every 2 sailboats built in Canada is exported, generating $60 million each year in foreign sales. Larger powerboats with inboard-outboard or inboard engines make up about 6% of all boats. Various concerns about fuel consumption have led to improvements in hull design, and careful attention to styling and detail have created new demand.

Boaters in Canada operate under the Canada Shipping Act and Small Vessel Regulations. Both of these are administered by the federal Dept of Transport through the CANADIAN COAST GUARD, though in many instances local enforcement is carried out by police forces. These groups, in conjunction with the Dept of National Defence and many volunteers, provide search-and-rescue services across Canada. Working in close conjunction with the government are several associations of boaters often grouped by interests into national bodies. The Canadian Yachting Assn and the Canadian Power and Sail Squadrons cater to sailors and powerboaters from coast to coast and have developed broad courses for teaching seamanship and navigation. Other groups involved in similar activities include the Canadian Boating Federation, which also governs powerboat racing in Canada, the Canadian RED CROSS SOCIETY and the Royal Life Saving Society Canada.

In addition to their interests in teaching boating, several of these groups also administer the sporting aspects of boating. Recent victories by Canadian sailors have put them in the forefront of Olympic and Pan-American competition. Canada challenged for the America's Cup in 1983 and 1987 and had creditable finishes both years. Canadian athletes have seen considerable success in CANOEING and ROWING competitions. In 3 successive years, 1959-61, *Miss Supertest* won the Harmsworth Trophy for hydroplanes.

Canada's geography provides unequalled opportunities for boating, which Canadians have taken up without reservation. MICHAEL VOLLMER

Bobak, Bronislaw Josephus, "Bruno," artist, arts administrator (b at Wawelowska, Poland 28 Dec 1923). Bobak has maintained a lifelong devotion to the figure, landscape and still life while extending the expressionist attitude of the early 20th century. He was Canada's youngest official war artist when commissioned in 1944. His WWII art used an expressive-realist mode, derived from his training with Carl SCHAEFER. After the war he lived in BC (1947-59) where he developed a "surrealist" style in response to the mystical qualities of BC's interior landscape. Following visits to Europe (especially Norway), he settled in NB (after 1960) and joined a passionate response for the art of Edvard Munch and Gustave Vigeland with an admiration for Oskar Kokoschka. The result was a series of powerful oils (*Wheel of Life*, 1966), drawings and woodcuts dealing with the figure and landscape. He has exhibited throughout Canada, the US and Europe. In 1962 he became director of the Art Centre, UNB. D.F. ANDRUS

Bobak, Molly Joan, née Lamb, painter (b at Vancouver 25 Feb 1922), daughter of Harold Mortimer-Lamb. Molly Lamb's early interest in the creative arts, drawing and writing in particular, was largely due to her home environment. She studied at the Vancouver School of Art (1938-41) under Jack L. SHADBOLT, who had a profound influence upon her, and joined the army (1942) becoming the only woman to be appointed a war artist (1945). With her husband Bruno BOBAK she moved to Fredericton in 1960 and began to teach at UNB. The depth of her perceptions and the richness of her imagery are demonstrated as much through her writing and her work on radio and TV as through her painting. She was awarded honorary degrees by UNB (1983) and Mt Allison U (1984). She illustrated the children's book, *Toes in My Nose*, by Sheree Finch (1987). IAN GORDON LUMSDEN

Reading: Molly Lamb Bobak, *Wild Flowers of Canada* (1978).

Bobcat (*Lynx rufus*, family Felidae), medium-sized, carnivorous mammal, also known as wildcat or bay lynx. It is distinguished from the similar Canada LYNX by its relatively small feet, ears tuftless or with very short tufts, and bobbed tail, white below. The coat is of one colour or spotted; fur behind the jaws and elsewhere is shorter than in lynx. Colours, more varied than in lynx, range from light grey to reddish brown. Bobcats vary greatly in size (5-18 kg), males being larger than females. Bobcats have a more southern distribution and occupy a wider range of habitats than lynx. They spread into parts of southern Canada following European settlement. Bobcats and lynx coexist in spruce-pine forests of northern and southwestern Ontario, southern Québec, NB and NS. Their chief prey is hares, but other small mammals, birds and, occasionally, even deer are taken. Bobcats may purr or mew but, unlike lynx, cannot be tamed. Like lynx, bobcats breed late Feb to early Mar, have a 50-day gestation period,

and bear 1-4 young. Newborn kittens weigh 285-370 g, are spotted with strong facial markings, and are cared for by both parents. Bobcat fur is less valuable than lynx. C.S. CHURCHER

Bobsledding Sledding, or tobogganing, was first recorded in the 16th century and modern racing began in Switzerland in the mid-19th century. Three forms of tobogganing developed. A bobsled, or sleigh, has 2 axles and 2 pairs of runners, is steered with a wheel, rope or bungie cord and is operated by teams of 2 or 4 racers. Luge uses a single sled (a 1 or 2 seater) with the rider lying back from a sitting position; in Cresta tobogganing the rider lies on his chest. Tobogganing developed independently in eastern Canada among Indian tribes who used their transportation sleighs for occasional fun. It was refined by groups such as the Montreal Tobogganing Club, the first such club in Canada, formed in 1881. Most sleds could take as many as 4 riders; some accommodated 12. Tobogganing was one of Canada's prime winter sports in the 19th century. The Montmorency Ice Cone, outside Québec City, was a popular site for recreational sledding. When the sport grew less popular in Canada after the 1880s, the original toboggan runs were abandoned. No new runs were built in the 20th century and Canadian competitors were forced to practise in Europe or at Lake Placid, NY.

Bobsled racing started in 1881. Today 31 countries participate. It is a highly technical and physically demanding sport. Pushing the steel and fiberglass sled (the 2-man sled weighs 210 kg and the 4-man, 390 kg, without crew) from a dead start takes great strength, speed and timing. The driver's skill in maneuvering 16 curves over the 1500 m course, while taking the "fastest line," can mean the difference between winning and losing. Speeds can reach up to 150 km/hr, and the crew experiences up to 5 G's of gravitational force. The Canadian Amateur Bobsleigh and Luge Assn was formed in 1957 and the first Canadian team entered international competition in 1959. In 1962, a 4-man team, led by Lamont Gordon, won the Commonwealth bobsled championship. The EMERY brothers, Victor and John, who had formed the Laurentian Bobsledding Assn in 1957, began racing in the world competition in 1959. By 1964, with Douglas Anakin and Peter Kirby, they had gained the experience necessary to challenge the world's best at the Olympic Games at Innsbruck, Austria. Despite few opportunities to practise, they set a record time in their first run and won the gold medal. The Canadian team, again led by Vic Emery, retained its title at the 1965 world championships. In 1986 Grey Haydenluck placed 5th at the World Cup event in Cortina, Italy. Haydenluck, Chris Lori and David Leuty all qualified in 1987 for the 1988 Olympics.

Luge racing began in 1879. Today 33 countries participate in 3 events: men's singles, women's singles and men's doubles. The luger must maintain a prone position while maneuvering hairpin turns over the 1000m (for men) or 750m (women) track at speeds up to 135 km/hr. Although Douglas Conner set a world record in the Cresta run at St Moritz, Switz, in 1954, Canada's first luge team was not formed until 1967, when the first Canadian championships were staged. A luge team entered the 1968 Olympics and Linda Crutchfield won the 1968 N American women's luge championship. Canada finally gained modern facilities in 1976 with a 213 m luge run built in Etobicoke, Ont. In 1977 Carole Keyes and Bjorn Iverson won the N American women's and men's luge singles championships; Larry Arbuthnot won the men's championship in 1978. Czech-born Miroslav Zajonc, racing for Canada, won the world luge championship in 1983. Marie-Claude Doyon ranked 6th in the 1986 overall World Cup standings.

Naturbahn has recently gained acceptance in Canada, with some 3000 participants and 8 tracks, including a world-class facility at Canada Olympic Park, Calgary. The tracks vary from 50 to 1000 m and can be constructed anywhere there is a snow-packed or ice-covered hill; there are no turns. The slider lies down, feet-first, and steers by pulling on a strap. Informal competition speeds start at 30 km/h and can reach 80 km/h.

Calgary has one of the premier combined bobsled/luge runs in the world, in operation since Mar 1986.   BARBARA SCHRODT

Bodega y Quadra, Juan Francisco de la, naval officer, explorer, administrator (bap at Lima, Peru 3 June 1743; d at Mexico City 26 Mar 1794). In 1775 he made a difficult voyage of exploration from San Blas, Mexico, to 58°30′ N and Bucareli Sd, Alaska. In 1779 he commanded the frigate *Favorita* to Alaska in the expedition of Ignacio de Arteaga. Following naval duty, he was given command in 1789 of the naval department of San Blas, which controlled Spanish activities on the NORTHWEST COAST. In 1792, he took charge at the Nootka post and negotiated with Capt George VANCOUVER over implementation of the 1790 Nootka Convention. Bodega y Quadra was polite but firm in defending Spanish sovereignty. He returned to Mexico in 1793, where he died suddenly. *See also* NOOTKA SOUND CONTROVERSY.   CHRISTON I. ARCHER

Bodsworth, Fred, nature writer (b at Port Burwell, Ont 11 Oct 1918). Before turning to book-length fiction Bodsworth was a journeyman journalist, particularly with *Maclean's* and later the Toronto *Star*, and much of the technical expertise of the professional magazine writer is evident in his complex yet simply written wilderness parables. *The Last of the Curlews* (1954), his first and best-known book, centres on the passing of traditional Inuit life. Less well known is *The Atonement of Ashley Morden* (1964), an anti-war novel whose plot revolves around germ warfare experiments. In their subjects both books were ahead of their time. *The Sparrow's Fall* (1967), a tale of survival in the wilderness, brings Bodsworth's concerns with ethics and religion nearer the surface. He has also written nonfiction in the natural history field.

Bois-Brûlé [French, "charred wood" or "burnt wood"], a 19th-century term for a mixed-blood Indian or a MÉTIS, especially the descendant of an Indian and a French Canadian. The expression referred to the brownish skin colour of the Métis.   JOHN ROBERT COLOMBO

Boky, Colette, née Giroux, soprano, professor (b at Montréal 4 June 1935). On the advice of conductor Jean Deslauriers, she began studying singing in 1953. She made her Canadian début (1961) in Mozart's *Marriage of Figaro*, and her European début (1964) in Haydn's *The Apothecary*. In 1962, she won the Prix d'Europe and a second award, as well as a medal in the Geneva international competition. She sang at the Bremen Opera, at the Salzburg Festival, the Munich Festival and the Volksoper in Vienna. Her arrival at the Metropolitan Opera (1967) in the role of the Queen of the Night in *The Magic Flute* was a highlight of her career. Gifted with great sensitivity, a warm voice and an easy stage presence, Boky is a sought-after artist in Europe as well as in Canada. Since the start of the 1980s she has been teaching vocal arts at U du Québec à Montréal. She has received both the Prix de musique Calixa-Lavallée (1971) and· the Prix Denise-Pelletier (1986).   HÉLÈNE PLOUFFE

Bolt, Carol, née Johnson, playwright (b at Winnipeg 25 Aug 1941). A socially committed dramatist, Carol Bolt is known for her political, women's and children's plays. In the tradition of Antonin Artaud's opposition to masterpiece theatre, she rejects the continuing emphasis on international classics in Canadian theatres; nevertheless, her own aesthetic is thoroughly traditional in its insistence upon delightful instruction. Even thrillers like *One Night Stand* (1977) and metatheatre comedies like *Escape Entertainment* (1981) evoke the social malaise of contemporary urban rootlessness while providing laughter and suspense. Allan King's TV version of *One Night Stand* won 3 Canadian Film Awards in 1978. Her contribution to CBC Radio's "Sextet," *Unconscious* (1986) was nominated for the ACTRA Award for best radio drama and her dramatization of Justine Blaney's challenge to all-male hockey, *Ice Time* (1986) was commissioned by Theatre on the Move for tours to high schools in 1987.

Her best-known plays, *Buffalo Jump* (produced 1971, publ 1972), *Red Emma – Queen of the Anarchists* (1974) and *Shelter* (1975), successfully combine the methods of Brechtian epic drama with those of collective creation. She was one of the Canadian writers of CBC's *Fraggle Rock*, in 1984.   ROTA HERZBERG LISTER

Bomarc Missile Crisis In the fall of 1958 PM Diefenbaker's Conservative government announced an agreement with the US to deploy in Canada 2 squadrons of the American ramjet-powered "Bomarc" antiaircraft missile. This controversial defence decision was one of many flowing from the 1957 NORAD agreement with the US. It was argued by some that the surface-to-air guided missile, with a range of 640 km, would be an effective replacement for the manned AVRO ARROW, which was also scrapped. Fifty-six missiles were deployed at North Bay, Ont, and La Macaza, Qué, under the ultimate control of the commander in chief, NORAD. Unfortunately, the Canadian government did not make it clear that the version to be acquired, the Bomarc-B, was to be fitted with nuclear warheads. When this became known in 1960 it gave rise to a dispute as to whether Canada should adopt nuclear weapons. In the end, the government could not bring itself to accept nuclear warheads for the Bomarcs, a reluctance which contributed to poor CANADIAN-AMERICAN RELATIONS in this period. With the Conservatives' fall in 1963 and the Liberals' return to power under PM Pearson, a decision was finally made to accept nuclear warheads for Canadian nuclear-capable forces, and the Bomarc warheads were delivered to their sites on 31 Dec 1963. Nevertheless, the decision was made reluctantly, and in 1969 PM Trudeau's new Liberal government announced that Canada would withdraw its ARMED FORCES from their nuclear roles. As part of this process the Bomarc missile was phased out of service by 1971.   PAUL BUTEUX

Bombardier, J. Armand, inventor of the snowmobile (b at Valcourt, Qué 16 Apr 1907; d at Sherbrooke, Qué 18 Feb 1964). Like many other inventors, Bombardier first tried as a teenager to realize his idea of an all-terrain vehicle, equally reliable on soft ground (eg, muskeg) or snow. The specific invention that made his machine of 1937 a success was the principle of steering by skis in front of a tracked drive. A decade later, based partly on wartime research, he made a 12-passenger machine, for which there was a small market, chiefly military. In 1959 Bombardier's firm offered the Ski-Doo, creating a new type of vehicle, a new sport and a new market. What was different about the Ski-Doo was its size, an analogue of the motorcycle instead of the car or truck, and propulsion by a single track as wide as the whole

machine, behind the steerable skis. Within a decade it transformed the social life of Inuit and arctic communities, creating a demand for gasoline, oil and spare parts. Competing SNOWMOBILE producers threatened to overwhelm the Bombardier family firm in the early 1970s, but it survived and expanded.   DONALD J.C. PHILLIPSON

Bombardier Inc is a Canadian manufacturer with headquarters in Montréal. Bombardier Limited was founded in 1942 by J. Armand BOMBARDIER, inventor of the SNOWMOBILE; in 1975 it purchased majority interest in MLW-Worthington Limited (fd 1902) and, after financial consolidation in 1976, the present name was adopted in 1978. Developing, manufacturing and selling transportation and recreation products worldwide, including Ski-Doo snowmobiles, Bombardier is also involved in heat-transfer products, aerospace components and engines. The company operates plants in Québec, Austria, Iceland and the US. In Jan 1986 it had annual sales of $656.6 million (ranking 142nd in Canada), assets of $420 million (ranking 176th) and 4900 employees. Its major shareholder, Les entreprises de J. Armand Bombardier Limitée, owns 63% of the company. Bombardier was successful in Aug 1986 in taking over CANADAIR LTD, the troubled aircraft company, for $120 million.   DEBORAH C. SAWYER

Bompas, William Carpenter, Church of England missionary, bishop (b at London, Eng 20 Jan 1834; d at Cariboo Crossing [Carcross], YT 9 June 1906). Bompas left England in 1865 and spent the next 40 years in the Canadian North, becoming the first bishop of Athabasca in 1874, first bishop of Mackenzie R in 1884 and first bishop of Selkirk (Yukon) in 1891. In response to his appeals, a detachment of NWMP was sent to the Yukon in 1894. A prolific writer, his works included *The Diocese of Mackenzie River* (1888), *Northern Lights on the Bible* (1892) and *The Symmetry of Scripture* (1896).   H. GUEST

Bonaventure, light fleet aircraft carrier purchased 1952, commissioned 17 Jan 1957 as HMCS *Bonaventure*, the name of an island bird sanctuary in the Gulf of St Lawrence. With the latest equipment, jet fighters, helicopters, and propellor-driven antisubmarine patrol aircraft, it spent its career training air pilots, participating in naval exercises, and patrolling the Canadian coast. In 1964 it ferried a Canadian Army UN PEACEKEEPING contingent to Cyprus. Political controversy arose after a major refit in 1966-67, for which $8 million had been budgeted, cost between $12.5 and $17 million. As an economy measure, the government sold *Bonaventure* for scrap in 1970, although it could have had another 10 years of usefulness. It was not replaced. All Canadian fixed-wing naval aircraft have since operated from shore.   ROGER SARTY

Bonaventure, Île, 5 km², located in the Gulf of St Lawrence, 3 km offshore from Percé, Qué. For centuries, this site has been an object of curiosity and wonder among its explorers and visitors. The most noteworthy feature of the island is a migratory bird population of gannets (*Sula bassana*), approximately 21 000 pairs (1979 estimate), assumed to be the largest colony of this species in the world. Other bird species inhabit the island in smaller numbers.

Despite its minute size, a favourable climate and abundant cod stocks induced French entrepreneurs to establish a seasonal fishery operation there in the 1600s. Simon Denys obtained seigneurial title (1674); his son Pierre had a chapel erected, soon thereafter razed by fire (1690). The population has been noted for its folkloric imagination. Irish and Channel Islanders arrived by the final decade of the 18th century. Jersey merchant families built the cod exportation industry. Peter Du Val (1767-1851), a Jersey-born merchant and privateer, is a prominent figure in the island's mythology. Mountenay William DU VAL and his wife, Matilda, began conservation efforts during a period of the bird population's greatest decline.

The population of the island peaked (at approximately 200) before 1850. Full expropriation by the province of Québec in 1971 decreed depopulation. The site has since been designated a provincial park.   ALDO BROCHET

Reading: Aldo Brochet, "Peter Du Val" in Dictionary of Canadian Biography (Vol 8, 1985); W. Earl Godfrey, *The Birds of Canada* (1985).

Bonavista, Nfld, Town, pop 4605 (1986c), 4460 (1981c), inc 1964, is located on the tip of the Bonavista Pen on the Island's NE coast. Its name may have come from the Italian *O Buon Vista* ("Oh happy sight"), attributed to John CABOT, as it is traditionally thought he made his first landfall in the New World at Cape Bonavista in 1497. The community, one of the oldest in N America, was established on a flat, rocky plain SW of the cape in the late 1500s. Settled by English West Country fish merchants, it was attacked on several occasions by the French; the cape became the northeastern terminus of the FRENCH SHORE. In 1726 the Church of England built in Bonavista what is claimed to be Newfoundland's first school. Bonavista was from its founding the major fishing centre of Bonavista Bay and was later important in the Labrador fishery and seal hunt. In the 20th century it has become a major fish-producing centre. It is the northern terminus of the Bonavista branch of the Newfoundland Ry and the Cabot Hwy. Bonavista has remained a regional social services, transportation and marine services centre, although its importance as a port has declined with the increase in land-based transportation.
                                        JANET E.M. PITT

Bonavista Bay is an inlet on the Atlantic coast of Newfoundland between Cape Freels and Cape Bonavista. Roughly 65 km wide, it contains a large number of densely forested islands that shelter the mainland from northeasterly winds and create hundreds of kilometres of virtually landlocked waters. A portion of this attractive and historic area has been set aside as TERRA NOVA NATIONAL PARK. Several fishing villages, the largest of which is BONAVISTA, lie along the bay's rugged, deeply indented coastline. The Labrador Current sweeps past Cape Freels, regularly filling the outer bay with water cooler than -1°C and occasionally depositing an iceberg. Nonetheless, the protected inner bay warms up sufficiently for propagation of lobsters and supports an important inshore cod fishery. Apart from fishing, lumber and transportation are the major industries of the area. Over the years the waters of the bay have been the scene of scientific investigations of cod distribution relative to temperature and of fishing methodology. Cape Bonavista is the starting point for a series of hydrographic sections (the "Bonavista Triangle") carried out

by the International Ice Patrol to monitor the Labrador Current and to help to forecast iceberg movement.   P.C. SMITH AND R.J. CONOVER

Bond, Sir Robert, politician, premier of Newfoundland 1900-09 (b at St John's 26 Feb 1857; d at Whitbourne, Nfld 16 Mar 1927). Largely educated in England, Bond returned to Newfoundland about 1874, articled with Sir William WHITEWAY but never practised law. He entered the Assembly in 1882. A Newfoundland nationalist, Bond supported construction of the transisland railway, promoted economic ties with the US and Newfoundland's position within the Empire. Appointed colonial secretary in Whiteway's Liberal Cabinet in 1889 he negotiated an abortive reciprocity treaty with the US in 1890 which led to a serious quarrel with the Canadian government. During the colony's financial crisis of 1894-95, he failed to secure agreement on terms for confederation with Canada but arranged a loan in England which saved the colony from bankruptcy. Bond became Liberal leader himself in 1897 and premier in 1900. His main concern as premier was with external affairs. He again failed to achieve a reciprocity treaty. His disappointment led to retaliatory action which precipitated a prolonged dispute with the US and UK over fishery rights. The 1908 election saw a tie between himself and Sir Edward MORRIS's People's Party from which the latter emerged victorious. Bond led the Opposition until 1914 when he retired from political life.   J.K. HILLER

Bond-Blaine Treaty In the 1880s, parts of Newfoundland's government and mercantile community felt that RECIPROCITY with the US would solve growing economic problems by providing new markets for dried cod. In 1890 Robert BOND, a minister in the colonial government, negotiated an agreement with American Secretary of State James Blaine that stipulated lower duties on imports from Newfoundland in return for access by American fishermen to the colony's bait supplies. The treaty was not ratified by Britain because of objections from Canada, which believed any such agreement should be for all British N America, and feared American expansionism. *See also* BAIT ACTS. SHANNON RYAN

Bonet, Jordi, painter, muralist, sculptor (b at Barcelona, Spain 7 May 1932; d at Montréal 25 Dec 1979). Bonet met violence early in life as his native city suffered greatly during the Spanish Civil War. At age 7, he fell from a tree, breaking his right arm which, owing to gangrene, had to be amputated at the shoulder. Art then became his refuge, as his father introduced him to Goya, Gaudi, Picasso and Dali. By 20, he had his own studio and held showings with older Catalan painters. Bonet decided to visit Québec, stayed in Trois-Rivières and settled in Montréal in Dec 1954. Already painting and drawing with virtuosity, he began working in ceramics, dreaming of murals as well. He produced about 100 of them during the 1960s, in ceramics or cement, in aluminum or stained glass, from Halifax to Vancouver, and especially in the US from New York to San Francisco and from Chicago to Dallas. In 1969 he bought the manoir in Saint-Hilaire, which he began restoring while still finishing the monumental triptych for the Grand Théâtre de Québec. In 1973 illness ended his career as a muralist; he returned to drawing and especially aluminum sculpture. He dreamed of more spiritual and sacred art, and then was gone at 47, leaving behind him a large body of truly great works.
                                        GUY ROBERT

Bonheur d'occasion (1945), novel by Gabrielle ROY. Set in the Montréal slum of St-Henri during WWII, it is French Canadian literature's

first example of urban realism. The inhabitants greet the war as a source of salvation, rescuing them from unemployment. Florentine Lacasse, a dime-store waitress, is seduced by Jean Lévesque, a successful but selfish engineer; pregnant, she marries Emmanuel Létourneau, an innocently idealistic soldier. Her mother, Rose-Anna, is a modern *mater dolorosa*, giving birth to yet another child only to lose her husband to the war. Florentine's young brother, Daniel, dying of leukemia in a hospital, experiences material comfort for the first time, helplessly surrounded by new toys. Their dreams about to be shattered, all are presented with sympathy and insight. Roy's talent for describing the sights, smells and sounds of St-Henri is complemented by her skills as an ironist. The novel won the Governor General's and other awards, and has been translated twice as *The Tin Flute*, by Hannah Josephson (1947) and Alan Brown (1981).   MICHÈLE LACOMBE

Bonhomme is the generic term for a figure (*bonhomme de sucre,* "sugar baby"; *bonhomme de neige,* "snowman") used in several combinations in French Canada: *bonhomme carnaval,* the Québec carnival snowman mascot figure; *bonhomme de sable,* "the sandman"; and *bonhomme sept-heures* (from the English "bone-setter"), a frightening figure.   NANCY SCHMITZ

Bonisteel, Roy, broadcast journalist (b at Ameliasburg, Ont 29 May 1930). The youngest of 10 children, he was 16 when he began his career as a newspaper reporter. Shifting to radio he moved up through newsroom ranks to become program manager at CKTB St Catharines, leaving in 1965 to become a radio producer for the UNITED CHURCH OF CANADA. From 1967 to 1970 he was National Radio Coordinator for the Anglican, Roman Catholic and United Churches. Bonisteel has hosted the internationally acclaimed CBC "Man Alive" television series since its inception in 1967. The series has won over 50 international awards and Bonisteel has twice received ACTRA awards for excellence in broadcasting. The integrity and humanity of the series and its host has led to interviews with such notables as Mother Theresa, Jacobo Timmerman, Bishop Desmond Tutu and the Aga Khan. Bonisteel has been awarded 6 honorary degrees and has written 2 best-selling books (*In Search of Man Alive* and *Man Alive*).
                                        RODNEY BOOTH

Bonnycastle, Sir Richard Henry, soldier, author (b in Eng 1791; d at Kingston, Canada W 2 Nov 1847). Educated at the Royal Military Academy, Woolwich, Bonnycastle entered the Royal Engineers as an officer, serving in the WAR OF 1812. Knighted for his service as commander of the Kingston garrison in the REBELLIONS OF 1837, he rose to commander, Royal Engineers, for Upper Canada 1837-39 and later headed the Royal Engineers in Newfoundland, retiring shortly before his death. Like many military men, Bonnycastle was an acute observer of the local scene, and in the last years of his life produced a series of books describing the provinces in which he had served for so many years.   J.M. BUMSTED

Bonnyville, Alta, pop 5470 (1986c), 4454 (1981c) inc 1948, is located 240 km NE of Edmonton in Alberta's lake district and prairie parkland. While the area had been known for its fur trading activity as early as the late 1700s, permanent settlement began with a group of French Canadian pioneers in 1907, with a few farms and a hamlet initially referred to as St Louis de Moose Lake. In 1908, the community was renamed after its first colonizing priest, the well-travelled missionary Rev Father F.S. Bonny. By 1920, the village had a hotel, bank, general store, blacksmith, garage, churches, schools, telegraph and telephone, and electric lighting was being installed, yet it still had to be reached by stage. After considerable negotiations by its citizenry, a CNR line eventually reached Bonnyville in 1928. The rail link allowed for the first time ready shipment of the region's produce in trade for commercial goods from elsewhere. The town continues as a regional service centre for the area's mixed farming activities, as well as the oil and local tourism industries.   MARK RASMUSSEN

Book Clubs Canada's first book club was started in 1928 when the T. EATON CO offered its customers "a selective literary service." A committee of literary authorities made a monthly selection of titles – sold to the membership at an average price of $2.00 – which was announced in advance of publication. Although the Eaton Book Club at one time had 5000 members, it lasted only 4 years.

The Readers Club of Canada, launched by Peter and Carol Martin in 1959, was the only book club in Canada to offer its members an entirely Canadian book selection. When the club got into financial difficulty in 1978, it was sold to New Leaf, the holding company that owned SATURDAY NIGHT magazine. New Leaf president Ed Cowan ran the club for 3 years. Substantial investments in promotion failed to raise the club's membership from 6000 to a target 20 000, and it was eventually closed down by *Saturday Night*'s next owner, Norman WEBSTER.

The Book Club Division of Doubleday Canada first recruited members for its book clubs, including The Literary Guild and the Doubleday Book Club, in 1944. With some 250 000 members in Canada (1987), the club offers a wide selection of titles – 14 times a year – at discounts ranging from 10% to 60% off list price. An average of 125 Canadian titles are selected annually by an international editorial committee. The New York-based Book-of-the-Month Club has served Canadian members since its founding in 1926. It publishes a separate catalogue for Canada and offers Canadian members, numbering about 100 000 in 1987, about 100 Canadian titles in the 14 annual mailings. Scholastic TAB Publications Ltd, also based in the US, operates book clubs for preschoolers up to high-schoolers out of its marketing division, which orchestrates mailings into the classroom and the home. Approximately 15% of their offerings are Canadian titles.

SUSAN WALKER

Book Publishing, English-Language Severe obstacles impeded the growth of a publishing industry in early Canada. A large territory with a small, scattered population made distribution difficult and expensive; unfavourable competition from US publishers not bound by imperial copyright laws often swamped the market with cheap imported editions; successful Canadian authors usually published through established foreign companies and avoided the stigma of a colonial imprimatur; major British and American publishers established branch offices in Canada after 1890 and returned most profits to the parent company; local firms acted as agents for foreign publishers and promoted agency books to the neglect of indigenous, original publishing; finally, Canadian publishers were unable to get international rights and secure profits from subsidiary rights, and were, in effect, forced to operate only inside Canada.

In colonial times there were no clear distinctions between printing and publishing, and pioneer printers performed the roles of editors, publishers, distributors, stationers and booksellers. William Brown and Thomas Gilmore, who set up the first press in Québec City in 1764 and published the province's first newspaper, the *Quebec Gazette/La Gazette de Québec*, also published its first books, including an ABC primer, legal works by F.J. Cugnet, a 180-page catechism, and *Abram's Plains,* a poem by Thomas Cary. Hugh C. Thomson of Kingston went on from newspaper publishing to issue 2 volumes of verse and a 2-volume novel, *St. Ursula's Convent* (1824), by Julia Beckwith HART – the first fiction published by a Canadian-born author. John Neilson of Québec published the *History of Canada; from its First Discovery, to the Peace of 1763* in 1826. Joseph HOWE of Halifax published the first major literary talent in British North America, Thomas C. HALIBURTON, whose *The Clockmaker* (1836) sold rapidly and gained international sales when it was pirated in London, Philadelphia and Paris; Howe claimed he made little profit from the book. By 1851 there were several printer-publishers in Montréal and Toronto, and publishing received impetus from a budding interest in Canadian history. F.X. GARNEAU's 4-volume *Histoire du Canada* appeared in Québec 1845-52, and provoked a Tory response in Robert Christie's 6-volume *History of the Late Province of Lower Canada* (1848-55), published by Thomas Cary, Jr, and John Lovell. John Mercier McMullen of Brockville compiled and published on his own a *History of Canada* (1855), which sold steadily for 2 decades.

John Lovell and Son was the most successful original publisher of the 19th century in Canada. Lovell inaugurated the *Literary Garland* in 1838 and published, among others, William KIRBY, Michel Bibaud, Charles SANGSTER, Rosanna LEPROHON, Catharine Parr TRAILL and translations of F.X. Garneau. His closest counterpart was George Maclean Rose, a printer who, with bookkeeper Robert Hunter, founded Hunter, Rose and Co in Québec City in 1861, moving to Ottawa in 1865 and Toronto in 1871. Rose joined briefly with Alexander Belford, who had made a great success of pirating American authors and flooding the US market with cheap editions of such books as Mark Twain's *Tom Sawyer.* Rose-Belford published *Rose-Belford's Canadian Monthly* (1878-82), a continuation of the *Canadian Monthly* (1872-78), and continued the book piracy. Rose brought out 2 volumes of the *Cyclopaedia of Canadian Biography* 1886-88. In 1891 a new American copyright law and the subsequent Anglo-American Copyright Agreement effectively ended book piracy in the US and Canada.

The most influential Canadian publishing house in the 1890s was the Methodist Book and Publishing House, called the RYERSON PRESS after 1919 in honour of its first book steward, Egerton RYERSON. Established in 1829, it published religious books and some trade books until the Rev William Briggs took over in 1879 and widely expanded the trade publishing, bringing out 37 new titles in 1897 alone. Briggs published numerous important Canadian writers, including Kirby, Traill, Nellie MCCLUNG, Charles G.D. ROBERTS, J.W. BENGOUGH, Charles MAIR, Isabella Valancy CRAWFORD, Robert W. SERVICE and Pauline JOHNSON. The Methodist printing plant produced early Ralph Connor (Charles W. GORDON) novels for the Westminster Press. Although Connor went on to sell in the millions outside Canada, the pattern in which profits derived from selling foreign (agency) books rather than Canadian books was already well established.

Schoolbooks had also become important. The earliest texts were mostly imported from the US, but in 1846, 31 titles were adopted from the Irish National School series. This series was used for decades, but there were Canadian series as well. John Lovell's Series of School Books (1858) contained Canadian texts, and James Campbell's Canadian National Series included locally written as well as British adoptions. When the Ontario Readers began in 1884, the textbook market across the country passed to the control of Thomas Nelson, Edinburgh, William J. Gage and, soon after, Copp Clark. Canadian editions of foreign texts have continued to the present as a significant branch of the publishing industry.

Over a dozen new publishing houses were established between 1876 and 1913 – a period of confident expansion in all areas of Canadian life. Among them were Musson Book Co (1894), G.N. Morang (1897), McLeod & Allen (1901), University of Toronto Press (1901), Oxford University Press (1904), John C. Winston (1904), Macmillan Co of Canada Ltd (1905), McClelland and Goodchild (1906, later MCCLELLAND AND STEWART), Cassell and Co Ltd (1907), J.M. Dent and Sons (1913) and Thomas Nelson and Sons Ltd (1913). Many of the new firms were Canadian branches of US or British houses, and all Canadian publishers were agents for foreign books. This period saw 3 significant enterprises in the publishing of Canadian history and biography: the MAKERS OF CANADA, in 20 vols (Morang 1903 to 1908); the Chronicles of Canada, in 32 vols (Glasgow, Brock and Co 1914-16); and the monumental CANADA AND ITS PROVINCES, in 23 vols (Glasgow, Brock and Co 1914-17).

WWI provided a major impetus to publishing to fill the demand for books on the great events and their participants. Patriotic poems, notably John MCCRAE's *In Flanders Fields* (1919), were popular, as were firsthand accounts such as Billy Bishop's *Winged Warfare* (1918). The 1920s brought a slump from overproduction, but also saw the emergence of 3 important figures in publishing, Lorne PIERCE, Hugh Eayrs and John McClelland. Pierce, who became editor of the Ryerson Press in 1920, believed that the new sense of national identity fostered by Canada's war effort could be channelled into a literary revival. He edited a new anthology and the multivolume Makers of Canadian Literature in 1923 (only 12 appeared), and compiled *An Outline of Canadian Literature* (1927). Eayrs became president of Macmillan (a British firm) in 1921 and also encouraged Canadian literature, notably Mazo DE LA ROCHE and Morley CALLAGHAN. McClelland published more Canadian authors than almost all other publishers combined. The 1920s also saw brief careers for 2 new publishers outside Toronto; Graphic Publishers was started by Ottawa printer Henry C. Miller in 1924 and published perhaps 34 titles before bankruptcy in 1932; Louis Carrier founded his firm in Montréal.

Hard times during the Depression of the 1930s saw salaries cut and original Canadian publishing slump, as popular foreign books were promoted. However, Clarke Irwin and Co was formed in 1930, first as an agency and later as a vigorous publisher, and some new Canadian authors were first published in these years, including Hugh MACLENNAN and Sinclair ROSS. There was a brief recovery late in WWII, but recession in the book industry lasted into the 1950s. A flood of inexpensive British and American paperbacks hit the Canadian market, and more British and US subsidiaries opened branches. Nevertheless the publishing industry experienced dramatic growth in supplying textbooks to a growing student population. McClelland and Stewart was at the centre of a virtual renaissance in Canadian literature, publishing Irving LAYTON, Leonard COHEN, Mordecai RICHLER, Margaret ATWOOD, Al PURDY and others. M & S undertook a new 18-volume history of Canada, the Canadian Centenary Series, and published best-selling authors such as Pierre BERTON and Farley MOWAT. Jack MCCLELLAND succeeded in marketing many indigenous BEST-SELLERS, such as Berton's *Comfortable Pew* (1965), and established the reprint series New Canadian Library (1958) and the Carleton Library series (1963). Most of the publishing industry was centered in Ontario and Québec, notably Toronto, but during the 1960s and 1970s numerous publishers sprang up across the country: Oberon (Ottawa), Harvest House (Montréal), Fiddlehead Books (Fredericton), Douglas & McIntyre (Vancouver), Western Producer Prairie Books (Saskatoon), Breakwater (St John's), Hurtig (Edmonton), Talonbooks (Vancouver), and James Lorimer, Anansi, Lester & Orpen Dennys, New Press, Peter Martin and Women's Press (Toronto) (*see* SMALL PRESSES).

Between 1969 and 1985 the size of the domestic market for books rose from $222 million to $1.4 billion. However, the industry has been widely publicized because of its financial difficulties, some of which are chronic. The market for English-language Canadian books is relatively small and faces powerful competition from American and British books. As costs increase, the chances that a publisher can print and sell 5000 to 10 000 copies of a Canadian book at a profit become less certain. Even in their most independent and lucrative era, most Canadian publishers depended on sales of foreign books to survive. Since the 1950s, more and more of this "agency" business has been removed from Canadian firms as growing numbers of the foreign publishers have established their own subsidiaries or branches in Canada. By 1985 foreign-controlled publishers and distributors accounted for about 60% of the industry's sales revenue. This development unfortunately amounted to a skimming of profits from the industry, with foreign-controlled firms generating profit from imported books while leaving the financially weakened Canadian-owned companies to publish new Canadian titles, incurring greater and greater debt as they did so. Canadian-controlled publishers still produce over 80% of the new titles in Canada (4105 of 5135 in 1985). In 1984 foreign-owned publishers accounted for 60% of overall sales but only 20% of new titles in English. To the extent that foreign-controlled firms have become involved in publishing Canadian books, they have concentrated heavily on the textbook market, which involves somewhat lower risks, and in which many provincial government policies encourage Canadian-authored texts; however, they are also active in trade publishing.

By 1970 the situation of many of the Canadian companies was critical. The venerable Ryerson Press, $2.8 million in debt, was sold to McGraw-Hill (a US firm) in 1970. The Ontario Royal Commission on Book Publishing, chaired by lawyer and author Richard ROHMER, was established to examine the industry. The Ontario government put into place its recommendation of a loan-guarantee system for Canadian publishers, although many other recommendations made by the commission were not acted upon. However, the guarantees failed to save Clarke Irwin in 1983; it went into receivership but was subsequently resurrected by John Irwin.

It is difficult to isolate the problems of foreign control from other generic problems of Canadian publishing, and governments have been uncertain about what, if anything, should be done. There are programs in virtually every province, ranging from modest to generous, to fund book publishing, and most entail eligibility requirements for Canadian ownership, recognizing that foreign-owned firms are committed primarily to selling foreign books and returning maximum profits to the parent company. Many of the provinces insist on Canadian authors, although these authors often publish with American companies.

The federal government has provided support for Canadian publishing through the Canadian Book Publishing Development Program, now the Book Publishing Industry Development Program (est 1979-80 and administered by the Dept of Communications), the CANADA COUNCIL and the SOCIAL SCIENCES AND HUMANITIES RESEARCH COUNCIL. Echoing an earlier concern with Canadian sovereignty in NEWSPAPER and MAGAZINE publishing, the federal government stated as its objective in 1979 that the Canadian-controlled sector of the book-publisher/agent industry should play a dominant role in both language markets in Canada. In 1986-87, $11 million was disbursed to publishers.

Meanwhile the educational market for Canadian texts has become more fragmented than in the past, with Ontario, for example, eliminating its provision of specific funding for textbook purchases, offering more courses with smaller enrolments and approving a greater number of texts for each course. In principle, however, the various provincial governments continue to require that Canadian texts be available for use in their school systems. Canadian-owned firms continue to live a precarious existence because of the policy of allowing returns of virtually unlimited quantities of unsold books, the weakness and foreign control of BOOK CLUBS, mass paperback and wholesale distribution, and the reluctance of Canadian banks to lend money to publishers.

English-speaking Canadians do not lack for books. With some 75 000 books a year published in the US and Great Britain, there is almost an embarrassment of choice. However, the continuing domination of the industry by foreign-controlled firms that devote only a small portion of their profits to publishing Canadian authors casts grave doubts on the future viability of a critical area of Canadian cultural expression. *See also* AUTHORS AND THEIR MILIEU; CULTURAL POLICY.

JAMES MARSH

Reading: P. Audley, *Canada's Cultural Industries* (1983); Dept of Communications, *Summary of briefs and hearings* and *Report of the Federal Cultural Policy Review Committee* (1982)and *Vital Links* (1987); Dept of Secretary of State, *The Publishing Industry in Canada* (1977); J.M. Gray, *Fun Tomorrow* (1978); H. Pearson Gundy, *Book Publishing and Publishers in Canada before 1900* (1965); Ontario Royal Commission on Book Publishing, *Background Papers* (1972) and *Canadian Publishers and Publishing* (1973); G. L. Parker, *The Beginnings of the Book Trade in Canada* (1985); L. Pierce, *House of Ryerson* (1954); State of English-Language Publishing in Canada, special issue of *Journal of Canadian Studies* (May 1975); Statistics Canada, Culture Statistics, *Book Publishing: An Industry Analysis* (catalogue item 87-601), *A Cultural Analysis* (87-602), *Textbooks* (87-603) and *A Financial Analysis* (87-604).

Book Publishing, French-Language It is generally agreed that there was no publishing in New France. William Brown and Thomas Gilmore installed the first presses in Québec City, 1764, and Fleury Mesplet in Montréal in 1776. These presses were used primarily for NEWSPAPERS, but also filled some printing contracts for the government, the army, the clergy and various merchants. Thus the first French-language or bilingual publications were official government texts, pastoral letters from the bishop, religious books, textbooks and advertisements. During the 19th century most books continued to be imported and commerce was largely controlled by the British under terms of the Navigation Acts, which were not finally abolished until 1849.

Few literary works were published in any quantity. Most 19th-century literature appeared in newspapers or MAGAZINES, the exceptions being publications such as *Épitres, satires* by Michel Bibaud (1830), *L'Influence d'un livre* (1837) by Philippe-Ignace-François AUBERT DE GASPÉ, and *Les Fiancés de 1812* (1844) by Joseph DOUTRE. Since authors had to show guaranteed sales before they could get a contract with a publisher, many writers were involved in founding literary magazines; J.O. Letourneux, for instance, established *La Revue canadienne* in 1845, its *L'Album* devoted to literature, and the newspaper *La Minerve* launched *l'Album littéraire et musical de la Minerve* in 1849. James Huston, in *le Répertoire national* (1848-50), published a collection of literature which had appeared first in newspapers, and Henri-Émile Chevalier founded *La Ruche littéraire* in 1853 for the same reason. Then came the great national literary magazines: Les SOIRÉES CANADIENNES (1861), *Le Foyer canadien* (1863) and *la Revue canadienne* (1864) (*see* LITERARY PERIODICALS IN FRENCH).

Expansion of schools and universities after 1860 greatly stimulated book publishing. Beauchemin of Montréal was founded in 1842, but Québec City became the publishing centre. Bookmakers, progressing from mere printer to printer-publisher or publisher-bookseller, no longer merely provided publishing materials, but took charge of the text. Georges-Hippolyte Cherrier, in his preface to *Charles Guérin* (1853), was one of the first to define publishing as a career.

The state gave the church responsibility over education, and the religious communities, as they consolidated their position in the mid-19th century, took over the production and distribution of textbooks. The Frères des écoles chrétiennes founded their bookstore in 1877, followed by the Congrégation de Notre-Dame (1881), the Librairie Saint-Viateur (1887), the Frères de l'instruction chrétienne (1900), and the Frères du Sacré-Coeur (1902). The pattern continued until 1960, making school texts the backbone of Québec publishing until the establishment of the Ministry of Education in 1964. The situation left room for the kinds of abuses named in the Bouchard Report (1964), which described how the publishers of school texts were often the same people who recommended that these texts be included in the official lists of the Comité catholique de l'instruction publique.

Except for a nationalist revival, there were no major changes in Québec publishing in the early 20th century. The founders of various small papers, such as *Le Nationaliste, Le Semeur, La Libre Parole* and, especially, *Le DEVOIR* (1910), all promoted a kind of literature which appealed primarily to the collèges classiques. The zenith of this movement was the founding in 1917 of ACTION FRANÇAISE by Lionel GROULX. The bookstore, Librairie de l'Action française, soon became the outlet for nationalist publications. However, Groulx had to cease his publishing activities when Pope Pius XI denounced the movement in France. In 1926 Albert Lévesque took up the cause and became the main publisher of nationalist works. The movement had its opponents, however, exemplified in the founding of magazines such as *La Relève* in 1934 and *Les Idées*, which was founded in 1934 but its first issue was Jan 1935. That same year, Albert Pelletier started his Editions du Totem, a milestone in the history of Québec publishing. Still, major works including *Les Engagés du Grand Portage* by Léo-Paul DESROSIERS, *Né à Québec* by Alain GRANDBOIS and *TRENTE ARPENTS* by Philippe PANNETON were all published in Paris.

The defeat of France in 1940 was a turning point in Québec publishing. Many writers who fled the Vichy regime to preserve their freedom of expression turned to publishers in New York and São Paulo, but most chose Montréal. Between 1940 and 1946, 21 million books came off the Montréal presses. Though Fides and Éditions Variétés dominated the market, new publishing houses sprang up: l'Arbre-Robert Charbonneau,

Les Éditions du Lévrier, Les Éditions du Lumen, Les Éditions du Mangin, Gérard Parizeau, Société des Éditions Pascal, Jean-Guy Pilon, Victor Serge, Bernard Valiquette. At war's end, however, some French writers denounced the hold exercised by Montréal publishers, a charge answered by Robert CHARBONNEAU in his book, *La France et nous* (1947). Although the postwar years were difficult for Montréal publishers, resulting in several bankruptcies, the experience had been beneficial. Québec publishers had gained experience in their craft and freedom from the control of the clergy and nationalist movements.

With the return of peace, publishing again centered on educational work. General prosperity increased the number of students, who were the main customers, at all levels. Established publishers, eg, Beauchemin, Granger and Fides, were joined by the Centre pédagogique (1940), the Centre de pédagogie et de psychologie (1945), the Centre éducatif et culturel (1959), the Éditions du pélican, the Éditions pédagogiques (1960), and the Presses de l'université Laval (1950).

The success of novelists Gabrielle ROY and Roger LEMELIN proved that Québec publishers could produce books other than school texts. Fides generally avoided fiction, but added Robert Rumilly's *L'Histoire de la province de Québec* and the historical works of Guy Frégault, Marcel Trudel and others to its lists. Pierre Tisseyre founded the Cercle du livre de France, a book club which guaranteed an audience for works of fiction and awarded an annual prize, and launched Françoise LORANGER, André LANGEVIN and others whose works have become classics.

Despite this success, Québec publishing had serious problems. There was no proper distribution system. Bookstores were concentrated in Montréal and Québec City, while some cities of 10 000 inhabitants lacked even a single bookstore. The large firms of Beauchemin, Fides, Librairie Granger Frères, Limitée, and André Dussault and a few newer houses sold more than 70% of their production directly to the educational institutions. Regional bookstores could not survive on the remainder. Moreover, the public library system was in its infancy, and educational institutions tightly controlled their students' reading material. The book market was just too small to support more than strictly pedagogic materials.

Literature continued to move ahead, however, during the 1960s some publishers played a major role in the QUIET REVOLUTION. Gaston MIRON, who founded les Éditions de l'hexagone in 1953, gathered together Québec poets celebrating the fact they belonged to the "land of Québec." The *Écrits du Canada français* brought out, in magazine form, many literary works. The publications of Éditions parti pris took on an anticlerical and anticolonial tone. A number of smaller houses, eg, Éditions Erta and Éditions Orphée, concentrated on poetry; Leméac published theatrical works exclusively. Other publishers explored nonscholastic markets. Les Éditions de l'homme and les Éditions du jour, stressing news and politics, brought literary mass-marketing to Québec. They used agencies to escape the narrow bookstore world and move into tobacco shops, supermarkets, drugstores, train stations. Even so, publishers were still in trouble.

By the end of the 1960s, publishers depended more than ever on government. Their association, founded in the 1940s, had met with the new provincial Ministry of Cultural Affairs in 1961, which responded the following year with a guarantee Act to assist publishing. A Direction des lettres et des arts was established, which led to the formation of a Conseil supérieur du livre, a federation of publishers' and booksellers' associations,

to advise the ministry on publishing issues. The Bouchard Report on the dissemination of culture, tabled in 1964, suggested among other things the creation of a central book organization. A 1965 law setting the framework for bookstore accreditation took the first steps toward creating a government book policy, but was shortsighted in not eliminating wholesalers. Circumstances, however, forced the government to take more effective measures.

After 1960 major French publishers took an interest in the Québec market, which was growing at an annual rate of 12%. In 1968 Hachette, through the intermediary of Messageries internationales (MIL), forced all Québec bookstores to buy their French books from their company, alarming the Conseil supérieur du livre, which feared that French-language publishing and distribution in Québec would fall into foreign hands. Those fears were confirmed when Hachette bought out the Garneau bookstore chain. The Québec government did not act until 1973, when 3 laws were passed obliging establishments receiving Québec-government subsidies to buy their Québec and foreign books from accredited bookstores more than 50%-owned by Québec interests. This second step toward an official book policy reached fruition in the 1976 green paper by Jean-Paul L'Allier, clearly dissecting the main problems of Québec publishing: market penetration by major foreign houses; lack of foreign sales outlets; an inadequate network of public and educational libraries; the high cost of books; the poor protection afforded authors; lack of an appropriate distribution network; the government's unsatisfactory efforts to develop an effective book policy. This analysis was largely repeated in the 1978 white paper, *La Politique québécoise du développement culturel*. A shortage of money prevented the implementation of these recommendations, however, and publishers began looking more to Ottawa than to Québec City.

With the establishment of the CANADA COUNCIL in 1957, the federal government had taken a timid step into the field of culture, hitherto a provincial jurisdiction. At first its budgets were too modest to cause offence, but over time, and especially with the rising separatist movement in Québec, its subsidies grew and became the most accessible source of publishing assistance. Publishers, beneficiaries of 2 sources of income, federal and provincial, expanded their lists enormously during the 1970s. In 1968, 819 titles were published; in 1977, 3997. This increase was not solely due to publishing grants. Since they were taking fewer risks, publishers grew less selective about their titles. Some critics felt quantity had not improved quality, yet the situation probably had more to do with social change than with quality. After 1968, literature took second place to the human and social sciences as the vehicle for ideas, for society's trends and aspirations. The new generation of readers, many of whom were college graduates, worked in educational and cultural fields such as the civil service, radio, television, newspapers and the universities. Specialized books on administrative and political science took their place alongside literary and pedagogic works. University presses (and, later, publisher Gaëtan Morin) took a large part of this market, but other publishers tried to balance their lists with a mixture of theoretical, practical and fictional titles. New houses such as La Presse, HMH, Québec amérique, Les Quinze, Alain Stanké and VLB éditeur still emphasize literature, but publish in a broad range of subject areas.

Despite the protection offered by government policy, large subsidies and growing readership, Québec publishing is still in difficulty, mainly because of its limited market. A recession, such as

that experienced in 1982, can have serious repercussions on many publishers.   MAURICE LEMIRE

Reading: I. Cau, *L'Édition au Québec, de 1960 à 1977* (1981); G. Laberge and A. Vachon, "Book Publishing in Quebec," in Ontario Royal Commission on Book Publishing, *Background Papers* (1972); Y. Lamonde, ed, *L'Imprimé au Québec: Aspects historiques, 18e-20e siècles* (1983); Maurice Lemire, *Introduction à la littérature québécoise (1900-1939)* (1981); A. Pontaut de Bellefeuille et al, *La Bataille du Livre au Québec* (1972).

Books, Antiquarian Interest in collecting old, rare and out-of-print books dates back to late 18th- and early 19th-century British N America, as private collectors and institutional libraries developed extensive collections. Many of these collections were, and continue to be, of a general nature, though in more recent times many collectors and antiquarian book dealers have specialized in such areas as childrens' books, literary classics, military history, Arctica, Canadiana, modern first editions, art books, or they have concentrated on the work of individual authors, illustrators and publishers.

Adjectives such as rare, scarce and antiquarian tend to lack precise definition when applied to out-of-print and used books. The value of an older book may be determined by such factors as age, condition, first edition status, and importance of author or illustrator, though market value depends mostly on supply and demand pressures.

Antiquarian books reach the public market through estate and auction sales, book fairs and charity sales, and via second-hand book stores ranging in nature from the low-price, general stock used bookstore to the higher-price, more specialized antiquarian bookseller. Book fairs with upwards of 30 to 50 dealers are held on a regular basis in Ottawa, Vancouver, Montréal, Toronto and Halifax. Alfred Van Peteghem Books of Montréal is Canada's only specialized antiquarian book auction house.

The Antiquarian Booksellers Association of Canada/Association de la librarie ancienne du Canada (ABAC/ALAC) was founded in 1966 to foster interest in rare books and manuscripts and to maintain standards in the antiquarian book trade. Today it numbers some 50 member dealers, from Halifax to Victoria. In 1980 the Amtmann Circle was founded as a book collectors' club and named in honour of the late Bernard Amtmann, Montréal bookseller and founding president of ABAC/ALAC. Today the Amtmann Circle numbers approximately 100 collector, librarian and bookseller members. It sponsors lectures, publications and grants-in-aid for research on book history and book-collecting topics.

Books in Canada (fd 1971) is a book-review magazine distributed by subscription and sold in bookstores and newsstands throughout English-speaking Canada; it appears 9 times a year. It was founded by its first editor, Val Clery, as the result of a report on the promotion of books in Canada that Clery prepared for the Book Publishers' Council. *Books in Canada* publishes extensive reviews of current books, together with interviews with and profiles of authors, and special columns on first novels, children's books and other topics.   GEORGE WOODCOCK

Bookselling The earliest booksellers in Canada were Jean Seto and Joseph Bargeas, who in the 1840s and 1850s operated out of Montréal, importing books "for the gentry, the merchants, and the garrison: that is, a small middle and upper-middle-class readership." The earliest English-language bookseller was James Rivington of Halifax, who began operating in May 1761. In North America generally, early booksellers also acted as printers and binders. H.H. Cunningham of Montréal was the only colonialist bookseller to aspire to be a publisher. He issued John Perrin's *The Elements of French Conversation* in 1810, and other works, including *The Canadian Review and Magazine* (1824-26). Later, other booksellers also began publishing. The first trade bookseller in Toronto was Thomas Maclear, who came to the city from Blackie & Son of Glasgow in 1842. He bought a retail bookstore and attracted some leading writers to his house, including Susanna Moodie and Catharine Parr Traill. Booksellers in Canada during the 19th century usually purchased their books from 3 sources: directly from British publishers, from American printers of "pirated" British books (often sold at a fraction of the price of the British editions), or from Canadian printers who pirated British works or reproduced them under licence.

Beginning in the 1850s booksellers in Montréal and Toronto began to act as wholesalers (agents) for UK and US publishers, distributing the agency lines to local and country booksellers. By the 1860s some booksellers were also starting their own publishing ventures. The bookstore market was eroded during the latter half of the 19th century by the expansion of the railway and the opening of "railway stalls" where books were sold. And in the 1880s and 1890s several bookstores were driven out of business when the large department stores – Eaton's and Simpson's – began selling books as loss leaders (a development which parallels competition from chain booksellers today).

No official figures exist for the actual number of retail bookstores in English Canada today. According to the *Book Trade in Canada* (1987), there are at least 2000. Of these, about 605 are independently owned, 466 are members of a chain operation, 127 are college or university outlets specializing in texts and scholarly books, 290 are religious bookstores, and approximately 319 are retailers who sell books as a sideline. About 45% of these stores are located in Ontario, by far the largest market for new books in Canada; BC has about 25%, and the Prairie region, perhaps 20%. The remaining 10% of the English-language stores are thinly distributed throughout the Maritimes and Québec. The exact size of the retail book industry is unknown, but it has been estimated as high as $1.3 billion.

The selling of educational books (textbooks and learning aids) is left almost entirely to college and university outlets. Most booksellers are concerned with what are known as "trade books," which are sold by publishers to booksellers in hardcover or paperback format and which cover any subject – novels, biography, cookbooks, self-help, art, etc. Trade books have been categorized as books that people do not have to buy for educational or professional purposes, though some trade books do find their way into the educational market. Specialization is increasing among Canadian bookstores and it is common to find a bookstore devoted entirely to science fiction, cookbooks, theatre books or some other specific subject.

Most Canadian booksellers rely to a great degree on imported – mainly American – books for their sales. About 70% of all books sold in bookstores in English Canada are of US origin; Canadian books account for about 20%, and the rest were mainly British. Canadian books comprise a vital and positive element in bookstore sales, often monopolizing the fall and Christmas bestseller lists and making the difference between annual profit and losses for the book retailers. The great majority of American and British books purchased by Canadian booksellers arrives through exclusive Canadian agencies or the Canadian subsidiaries of foreign publishers. Virtually all US or UK publishers of any size have

either a Canadian office or an agency arrangement, though a few booksellers do buy their foreign titles directly from the US or UK wholesalers.

There are virtually no Canadian wholesalers selling to booksellers except in the mass-market field, where some booksellers prefer to deal with a local wholesale supplier. Canadian titles are bought from the publishers, who either have a Canadian publishing program as well as agency (US, UK) lines or devote themselves entirely to the publishing of Canadian books.

The Canadian Retail Booksellers Assn, founded in 1957, has a healthy and steadily growing membership of about 630 (1987). It also offers associate nonvoting memberships to publishers and agents. Each year in June, a large and lively annual convention takes place, along with a trade fair at which publishers display their new titles in preparation for the major fall and Christmas season. Booksellers from across Canada make many of their buying decisions during the CBA trade fair.

Corporate Concentration

In 1985, when WH Smith bought Classic Bookshops which was in financial difficulty, it left about 50% of the market's purchasing power in the hands of 2 companies. Independent booksellers, which have traditionally been the primary supporters of Canadian-authored titles, fear that the power of the chains will result in even greater disparities in trading terms, with greater margins being awarded to the chains. The greater the margin advantage the chains have, the more they are able to offer discounts to the public which the independents cannot match. If the trend results in fewer independent bookstores, it is expected that the variety of books available to the public will decrease. On the other hand, the 2 large chains have rapidly increased the number of bookstores in Canada and have often provided outlets in communities without bookstores.

Taxation Throughout the history of Canadian bookselling major battles have been fought over taxation or duties on books. Since the 19th century booksellers have opposed a "tax on knowledge." In 1987, a 10% tax on imported books was reinstated during a trade dispute with the US and then eliminated after a media outcry and efforts by the book industry. Today booksellers are concerned that a value-added tax system, which the government wishes to introduce, will apply to books, thereby increasing their cost and limiting their availability to the public.

Sunday Shopping Although legislation prohibiting Sunday shopping has been recently overturned or eliminated in many provinces, booksellers have had to fight these laws for many years. While exceptions to businesses being open on Sunday have grown, bookstores are rarely considered among the exempt groups, unlike theatre, films, etc.

Electronic Ordering In order to preserve Canadian sources of supply for books, the book industry, with the active participation of booksellers, has moved to introduce an electronic ordering system for the trade. The purpose of the system is to ensure that it is more efficient for Canadian booksellers to purchase books from Canadian publishers and Canadian agents of imported books than it is from US-based wholesalers (who do not carry Canadian titles) or directly from US publishers.

Boot and Shoe Workers Union was established in Boston 1895 and incorporated the militant Boot and Shoe Workers International Union (fd 1889), which had led a Toronto shoe-

makers' strike in 1890. The BSWU, led by Guelph-born John Tobin, was committed to resisting mechanization. Hamilton, Toronto and the shoe-producing stronghold of Montréal became centres of BSWU activity. By 1914 the union had abandoned its original radicalism. It had 16 Canadian branches with 1752 members, just over 1% of international union membership. It would remain a small, struggling and reactionary union, precariously clinging to the remnants of an obsolete craft, and challenged by Québec's Catholic unions in the 1920s and INDUSTRIAL UNIONISTS in the 1930s.

BRYAN D. PALMER

Booth, John Rudolphus, lumber manufacturer, railway builder (b near Waterloo, Lower Canada 5 Apr 1827; d at Ottawa 8 Dec 1925). In 1857 Booth took over a small shingle mill in Ottawa, which he gradually expanded until he held the most extensive timber limits in Canada and was the foremost manufacturer of lumber for American and British markets. In 1904 he entered the pulp and paper industry and developed a far-flung transportation network. Booth, William Perley and George Noble completed the Canadian Atlantic Ry after persuading PM John A. MACDONALD of its value to the lumber trade and their value to the Conservative Party. Booth then added the Ottawa, Arnprior and Parry Sound Ry, and a fleet of Great Lakes boats. He avoided politics, although he actively campaigned against the Taft-Fielding RECIPROCITY agreements of 1911. He was co-founder of the Dominion (Canadian) Forestry Association and contributed to various charities.

RICHARD REID

Boothia, Gulf of, NWT, is entered through Prince Regent Inlet. To the E it is bounded by the NW coast of BAFFIN I, and to the W by the Boothia Pen. Depths are generally about 275 m, decreasing southward. The gulf was named after Felix Booth, a wealthy London distiller, who in 1829 sponsored the Sir John ROSS expedition, which first explored the gulf in an ill-fated attempt to find the NORTHWEST PASSAGE. In fact the Boothia Pen bars any passage farther west from the gulf.

DOUG FINLAYSON

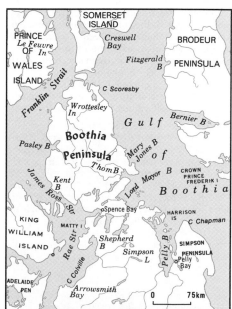

Boothia Peninsula, 32 300 km², northernmost tip of mainland N America, juts some 200 km N into the ARCTIC ARCHIPELAGO, separated from SOMERSET I by BELLOT STR, which is a mere 2 km wide. It is joined to the mainland by a narrow neck almost severed by 2 deep inlets and a chain of large lakes. To the E, across the Gulf of Boothia, is BAFFIN I. PRINCE OF WALES I lies NW, across Franklin Str. The desolate, treeless peninsula is formed on a central spine of Precambrian rock, flanked by flat-bedded limestone lowlands. Discovered in 1829 by John Ross, it was named for Felix Booth, a distiller who had financed the expedition. Imprisoned in the ice for 3 winters, Ross was forced to abandon his ship *Victory* and return on foot. His nephew, James C. ROSS, later confirmed that Boothia is a peninsula and discovered the N magnetic pole near Cape Adelaide. (The pole has since migrated northward.) Roald AMUNDSEN travelled the W coast by sled in 1904, and H.A. LARSEN wintered at Pasley Bay on his successful voyage through the NORTHWEST PASSAGE 1940-42, journeying all around the peninsula by sledge. There is a post and airfield at Spence Bay, on the isthmus, and a mission at Thom Bay.   JAMES MARSH

Borden, PEI, Town, pop 514 (1986c), 485 (1981c), situated 56 km SW of Charlottetown. William Carruthers first settled the area in 1819 and it was then known as Carleton Pt. As a result of its fertile soil and navigable harbour, other Scots soon immigrated to the area. Just 14 km of deep water separate Borden from Cape Tormentine, NB; this feature of geography has influenced its development. In 1851, the first submarine telegraph cable in BNA was laid between the 2 land points. With the federal decision to establish a permanent car ferry before the Great War, Carleton Pt was chosen as the Island terminal. In 1916, the village was renamed in honour of PM Sir Robert Borden. Today, Borden is heavily dependent upon CN Marine for employment.
                                    W. S. KEIZER

Borden, Canadian Forces Base, Ont, 80 km NW of Toronto, was named after Sir Frederick BORDEN, Laurier's militia minister (1896-1911). Camp Borden was created 1916 on 60 km² of sandy plain as a training ground for fliers and soldiers in WWI. This dual role continued for the next 2 decades, with medical, service corps and infantry schools, and the first armoured school established in the 1930s. During WWII more than 185 000 personnel trained here. After 1945 the school role intensified and the camp became more urban with the construction of permanent military and civilian support facilities. Unification of the armed forces gave the camp its present name. Occupying 85 km², it can house 8000 residents although its population is now 3137. Its 15 000 yearly graduates have made the camp Canada's largest training centre for military trades and classifications.   R.G. HAYCOCK

Borden, Sir Frederick William, physician, merchant, politician (b at Upper Canard, NS 14 May 1847; d at Canning, NS 6 Jan 1917). As minister of militia and defence 1896-1911, he reorganized the Canadian Militia. Borden represented King's County as a Liberal 1874-1911, except for 1882-87. A merchant in the carrying trade, Borden also acquired large corporate assets. While he was minister of militia, Canada sent troops to serve in the SOUTH AFRICAN WAR and expanded, reorganized and reformed its militia to create an autonomous, self-contained, decentralized, citizen army capable of contributing to imperial defence.
                                    CARMAN MILLER

Reading: Carman Miller, "Sir Frederick William Borden and Military Reform," *CHR* (1969).

Borden, Henry, businessman, public servant (b at Halifax 25 Sept 1901). Educated at McGill, Dalhousie and Oxford, Borden became one of Toronto's most prominent corporate lawyers. At the outbreak of WWII he was appointed to the War Supply Board in Ottawa and in 1942 was made

chairman of the War Time Industries Control Board. Borden and C.D. HOWE, the minister of munitions and supply, worked well together and became friends. In 1943 Borden returned to his law practice and became chief fund raiser for the Conservative Party. From 1946 until 1963 he was president of Brazilian Traction, Light and Power Co (Brascan); vice-chairman (1947-64) and chairman (1964-68) of the board of governors of U of Toronto. Borden coauthored *Handbook of Canadian Company Law* (1931) and edited 2 books originally drafted by his uncle: Sir Robert BORDEN's *Memoirs* (1938) and *Letters to Limbo* (1971).
                                    ROBERT BOTHWELL

Borden, Sir Robert Laird, lawyer, politician, prime minister of Canada, 1911-20 (b at Grand Pré, NS 26 June 1854; d at Ottawa 10 June 1937). The eighth prime minister of Canada, Borden was a Halifax lawyer, leader of the Liberal-Conservative Party 1901-20, architect of the Conservative victory in the "Reciprocity Election" of 1911, PM during WWI and a leading figure in the achievement of "Dominion Status" and the transition from the British Empire to the British Commonwealth of Nations.

Borden was a self-made man. After a brief formal education, he spent 5 years teaching at private academies in NS and New Jersey. Returning to NS in 1874 to article in law, he was admitted to the bar in 1878 and by 1890 headed a prestigious Halifax law firm. He was elected to Parliament in 1896 and in 1901 was selected by the Conservative caucus to succeed Sir Charles TUPPER as leader of the Liberal-Conservative Party. Over the next decade he worked to rebuild the CONSERVATIVE PARTY and establish a reform policy (the Halifax Platform of 1907). In 1911 he led the opposition to the Reciprocity Agreement negotiated by Sir Wilfrid LAURIER's government with the US and forced a general election. By skilful political management Borden brought together a coalition of anti-Laurier groups (Liberal businessmen opposed to RECIPROCITY, French Canadian *Nationalistes* opposed to the Naval Service Act, Conservative provincial administrations and his own parliamentary party) which defeated the Liberal Party.

Borden's leadership during WWI was remarkable. At home, his wartime government was responsible for the Emergency WAR MEASURES ACT (1914), the first measures of direct taxation by the Ottawa government (the Wartime Business Profits Tax, 1916, and the "temporary" Income Tax, 1917), the nationalization of the Canadian Northern Ry as the first step in the creation of the CNR and, after the collapse of the voluntary recruiting system, the Military Service Act, 1917. Conscription was accompanied by the creation of a UNION GOVERNMENT of pro-conscriptionist Conservatives and Liberals which won the bitterly contested general election of 1917.

Overseas, the Canadian Expeditionary Force grew from one division to a full Canadian Corps commanded after 1917 by a Canadian, Lt-Gen Sir Arthur William CURRIE. Borden believed that the distinguished record of the CEF at Ypres, Vimy Ridge and Passchendaele and in the final 100 days was the ultimate proof of the maturity of Canadian nationhood. Principal author of Resolution IX of the Imperial War Conference of 1917, he argued that Canada and the other dominions deserved recognition "as autonomous nations of an Imperial Commonwealth." As leader of the Canadian delegation at the Paris Peace Conference in 1919, he was primarily responsible for international recognition of the autonomous status of the Dominions. Borden retired as PM in 1920. In his last years he was

**Sir Robert Laird Borden
Eighth Prime Minister of Canada**

Birth: 26 June 1854, Grand Pré, NS
Father/Mother: Andrew/Eunice Laird
Father's Occupation: Stationmaster
Education: Acadia Villa Acad, Horton, NS
Religious Affiliation: Anglican
First Occupation: Teacher
Last Private Occupation: Lawyer
Political Party: Conservative
Period(s) as PM: 10 Oct 1911 - 10 July 1920
Ridings: Halifax, 1896-1904; 1908-17 Carleton,
       Ont, 1905-08 King's County, NS, 1917-20
Marriage: 25 Sept 1889 to Laura Bond (1863-
       1940)
Children: None
Died: 10 June 1937 in Ottawa
Cause of Death at Age: Heart failure at 82
Burial Place: Ottawa
Other Information: GCMG, 1914

(photo courtesy National Archives of Canada/C-81453)

recognized as an international statesman and firm advocate of the League of Nations. He pursued a successful career in business and served as chancellor of Queen's, 1924-30.
                                ROBERT CRAIG BROWN

Reading: H. Borden, ed, *Robert Laird Borden: His Memoirs* (1938) and *Letters to Limbo* (1971); R. Borden, *Canadian Constitutional Studies* (1922) and *Canada in the Commonwealth* (1929); R. Craig Brown, *Robert Laird Borden,* 2 vols (1975, 1980).

Borden Island, 2795 km², is one of the Queen Elizabeth group in the High Arctic. Discovered by Vilhjalmur STEFANSSON in 1916 during the Canadian Arctic Expedition, its NW coast fronts on the Arctic Ocean. A generally low shoreline, cut by several streambeds, rises to a hilly interior. The island, named after Sir Robert BORDEN, prime minister 1911-20, is uninhabited.
                                    DANIEL FRANCIS

Borduas, Paul-Émile, painter (b at St-Hilaire, Qué 1 Nov 1905; d at Paris, France 22 Feb 1960). Leader of the AUTOMATISTES and author of REFUS GLOBAL, he had a profound influence on art in Canada. Ozias LEDUC encouraged young Borduas to study at the École des beaux-arts in Montréal (1923-27) and helped arrange his first stay in Paris (1928-30) at the Ateliers d'art sacré, directed by Maurice Denis. Upon his return to Canada, the economic crisis forced Borduas to abandon his dream of becoming, like "Monsieur Leduc," a church decorator, and to survive he had to settle

Paul-Émile Borduas, *L'Étoile noire* (1957), oil on canvas. At the end of his life, Borduas's painting became simplified to contrasts of black and white, and *L'Étoile noire* is probably his masterpiece (*courtesy Montreal Museum of Fine Arts*).

for teaching drawing in Montréal. In 1937 he obtained a post somewhat closer to his aspirations, that of professor at the École du meuble. Throughout this period, he painted little and destroyed much. His painting was figurative and gradually began showing the influence of Renoir, Pascin, James W. MORRICE and, later, Cézanne. In 1942, under the influence of the surrealism of André Breton, he produced some 60 nonfigurative gouaches, of which 45 were shown at the Théâtre de l'Ermitage in Montréal that year. In 1943 he transferred to oil the discoveries he had made with gouaches and showed the results at the Dominion Gallery in Montréal.

From then on, Borduas had increasing influence on the young, especially his students at the École du Meuble, and became leader of the Mouvement Automatiste which had showings in makeshift galleries in 1946 and 1947. In 1948 he drew up a manifesto called *Refus Global* in which, denouncing the suffocating power of establishment thinking in Québec, he proclaimed the right to total freedom of expression. The authorities responded by removing Borduas from his teaching position. The following year, he unsuccessfully

attempted to defend his views in the autobiographical pamphlet, *Projections libérantes*, but to no avail. He was never to return to teaching. All that remained to him was painting, and he became completely immersed in his work.

Borduas moved to New York and lived there 1953-55. His pictorial goals expanded under the influence of action painting. Always dissatisfied, he left for Paris in 1955. Toward the end of his life, his painting became simplified to contrasts of black and white. *L'Étoile noire* (1957) is probably his masterpiece. Though always successful with Canadian collectors, he had difficulty penetrating the Parisian milieu. Increasingly lonely, he dreamed of returning to Canada but died in Paris in 1960, leaving behind an outstanding life and body of art. The National Gallery of Canada, the Musée d'art contemporain and the Musée des beaux-arts de Montréal contain examples of his work.   FRANÇOIS-MARC GAGNON

Reading: François-Marc Gagnon, *Paul-Émile Borduas* (1978).

Boreal Forest, the northernmost and coldest forest zone in the Northern Hemisphere, forming a continuous belt 1000 km in N-S width across N America, Europe and Asia. It is the most extensive vegetation zone in Canada, with representation in every province and territory. Its forest and woodlands in Canada are usually dominated by needle-leaf evergreen trees, including black and white spruce, jack and lodgepole pine, and bal-

sam fir, by needle-leaf deciduous American larch, or by small-leaf deciduous trees, including paper birch, trembling aspen, and balsam poplar. Bordered to the N by arctic tundra and to the S by temperate forest or grassland, depending on precipitation amounts, the zone includes 3 distinct subzones (Northern Boreal Woodland with widely spaced trees and lichen carpets; Main Boreal Forest with closely spaced trees and feathermoss carpets; and Southern Boreal Forest with occasional temperate trees) and 2 transitional subzones (Hemi-Arctic Forest-Tundra along the N margin; and Hemi-Boreal Aspen Parkland [west] and Conifer-Hardwoods Forest [east] along the S margin), correlated with warmer climates from N to S but embracing a wide E-W range of annual precipitation. In the eastern Appalachian and the western Cordilleran mountain systems, it merges with subalpine forest, which extends southward at climatically similar elevations. Lightning- and man-induced fires burn vast areas of its highly inflammable coniferous forest every year, but most of its plant species are adapted to survive fires or to recolonize burn areas quickly; hence there is a predictable succession of post-fire vegetation, often beginning with fireweed and ending with shade-tolerant spruce-fir forest, which persists until the next fire. Treed and untreed wetland complexes composed of acidic peat bogs, circum-neutral fens, and nutrient-rich marshes underlain by varying amounts of undecomposed organic material cover large areas, especially in flat lowlands where drainage is poor. Important mammals include moose, caribou, black bear, timber wolf, beaver, muskrat, varying hare, red squirrel, deer mouse and red-backed vole; important birds include Canada goose, common loon, great blue heron, numerous hawks, owls and ducks, ruffed and spruce grouse, belted kingfisher, gray jay, robin and other thrushes, black-capped and boreal chickadees, several nuthatches, vireos and grosbeaks, and many species of warblers and sparrows. Justly infamous insects include mosquitoes, black flies and sand flies (no-see-ums). Most of its present range in Canada was covered with glaciers until 12 000 years ago, hence much of its topography and surficial geology results from glaciation, and most of its soils are young compared with those in unglaciated areas.   GEORGE H. LA ROI

Bornstein, Eli, artist, educator (b at Milwaukee, Wis 28 Dec 1922). He was educated at U Wis and in 1950 began teaching at U Sask, becoming head of the art department in 1963. His works of the 1950s started from small, low-form, white reliefs and progressed towards larger, more complex works, with planes projecting further into space and utilizing primary colours. In 1954 he was introduced to the works of Charles Biederman, an experience which reaffirmed his direction and his major influences – Claude Monet/Paul Cézanne and cubism/constructivism. In 1957, when in Europe, Bornstein met Jean Gorin, Joost Baljeu, Anthony Hill, Kenneth and Mary Martin, Victor Pasmore and Georges Vantongerloo and returned to Saskatoon committed to the exploration of form-colour-structure relationships through 3-dimensional works. He began to work with a coloured ground plane and an expanded colour range in the 1960s. In 1966 he made his first double-plane reliefs and then went on to explore multiplane reliefs. Bornstein's structurist works combine elements of both painting and sculpture to develop and extend the landscape tradition. A Canadian citizen since 1972, he founded and edited *The Structurist* (1960), an international art publication.   GEORGE MOPPETT

Borsos, Phillip, film director (b at Hobart, Tasmania 5 May 1953). After a successful career producing and directing theatrical short subjects, he gained international recognition with his first feature film, *The Grey Fox*, the story of train robber Bill Miner. Borsos was named best director and *The Grey Fox* was named best film at the 1983 Canadian Film Awards. He had an early interest in film and acquired a 16 mm movie camera when he was in high school in Maple Ridge, BC. He studied film at the Banff Centre School of Fine Arts and the Vancouver School of Art as well as apprenticing himself at Alpha Cine, a Vancouver film laboratory. In 1976, he formed Mercury Pictures. Three of his early films, *Cooperage* (1976), *Spartree* (1977) and *Nails* (1980) were named Best Theatrical Short at the Canadian Film Awards. In addition, *Nails* received an Academy Award nomination. Borsos's films have been praised for their distinctive visual style and their poetic realism. Other feature films include *The Mean Season* (1985), *One Magic Christmas* (1985) and *Bethune: The Making of a Hero* (1988).   JAMES DEFELICE

Bossy, Michael, hockey player (b at Montréal 22 Jan 1957). A skilful skater and prolific goal scorer, he was (in 1987) the sole player in National Hockey League history with 9 consecutive seasons of more than 50 goals each. He played junior for Laval Nationals. On 24 Jan 1981 he scored his 50th goal during the 50th game of the 1980-81 season, equalling the 26-year-old record established by Maurice RICHARD. At the end of the 1986-87 season he was the 5th highest goal scorer in NHL history, with 573. He has won the Calder Trophy (1978), the Lady Byng Trophy (1983, 1984, 1986) and the Conn Smythe Trophy (1982); was 4 times member of a Stanley Cup winner (New York Islanders) and 5 times the first All-Star right-winger. He is the all-time goalscoring leader in playoffs, with 85. He was sidelined in 1987 with a back injury that threatened his career.   YVON DORE

Bostock, Hewitt, newspaperman, MP, Senator, (b at Walton Heath, Surrey, Eng 31 May 1864; d at Monte Creek, BC 28 Apr 1930). Graduating from Trinity College, Cambridge, he was called to the bar in 1888, but in 1893 left for Canada, becoming a rancher and fruit farmer at Monte Creek, British Columbia. In the 1890s he organized the Kootenay Lumber Co which he later sold. In 1894 he founded *The Province* newspaper as a weekly in Victoria, moving it to Vancouver in 1898 as a daily. After becoming involved in politics, he sold his interest in the paper. In 1896 he was elected to represent Yale-Cariboo in the House of Commons under Laurier. In 1904 he was appointed to the Senate, becoming Liberal Senate leader in 1914. From 1921-22 he was minister of public works in the King government and in 1922 was appointed Speaker of the Senate.   JEAN R. O'CLERY

Botanical Garden A botanical garden is distinguished from a public park or display garden (eg, Butchart Gardens, BC) by having a documented collection of woody or herbaceous PLANTS on which scientific research and teaching are conducted. Arrangement of plants within a botanical garden is often made according to a botanical evolutionary sequence, or by geographic origin, special use or function. Modern botanical gardens typically serve 3 functions: education, research and public information. In Canada, most gardens are federal, provincial or municipal institutions or, most frequently, are associated with a university. If the collection consists primarily of woody plants, it may be called an ARBORETUM. Canadian gardens form part of the American Assn of Botanical Gardens and Arboreta and participate in the International Assn of Botanical Gardens.

The early herbal or physic gardens were created by physicians and students of medicine to grow plants having medicinal or pharmaceutical properties. The first botanical gardens devoted to broader studies of plants, including those of both economic and horticultural significance, were developed in Italy: in Pisa (1543) and Padua (1545). Shortly thereafter, botanical gardens were established in Leipzig, Germany (1580); Leyden, Holland (1587); and Montpellier, France (1593). In the 17th and 18th centuries, many gardens were founded to examine scientifically new plants introduced to Europe. Governments saw the potential of developing these plants as crops. The importance of botanical gardens in the introduction of new crop plants is exemplified by the Royal Botanic Garden, Kew, England (est 1759), which pioneered the development of rubber, banana, tea, pineapple, coffee and cacao. Many botanical gardens continue to introduce new plants, emphasizing both economic and ORNAMENTAL varieties. The tradition of systematic BOTANY (classifying and identifying plants) continues, and recent ecological studies are providing a better understanding of plant resources, particularly of rare and ENDANGERED PLANTS.

Development of Canadian Botanical Gardens

The first botanical garden was established in 1861 by George Lawson at Queen's College (now Queen's University), Kingston, Ont, but it lasted only until the 1870s. In 1886, the Experimental Farms Act of the federal Dept of Agriculture was passed and, one year later, an arboretum and botanical garden was initiated at the Central Experimental Farm, Ottawa. Other research- and display-oriented gardens were later developed by the department at other stations. The second university botanical garden was established at Vancouver by John Davidson in 1916. It continues to thrive as a separate academic service department of UBC. The city of Montréal established the Jardin Botanique before WWII; it is now one of the major world gardens. The Royal Botanical Gardens, Hamilton, were established in 1941. The postwar period saw several new gardens develop as population centres increased. A review of some Canadian botanical gardens follows.

British Columbia UBC Botanical Garden (44.5 ha), including Nitobe Memorial Garden, Lohbrunner Alpine Garden, Asian Garden and BC Native Garden, operates a program of plant introduction to the nursery industry and an active educational research program. Van Dusen Botanical Display Garden (est 1972, 22 ha), operated by Vancouver Board of Parks and Recreation, specializes in displays of ornamental plants and offers educational programs with the Vancouver Botanical Garden Assn.

Alberta Devonian Botanic Garden, University of Alberta, Edmonton (est 1959, 77 ha), devotes special attention to alpine and native plants and conducts research on the hardiness of ornamental perennials and woody plants.

Saskatchewan Ross Arboretum, Indian Head (est 1946, 10 ha), operated by Agriculture Canada, specializes in the development of hardy trees for the Prairie region; planting began in 1902.

Manitoba Morden Research Station Arboretum (est 1930, 254 ha), operated by Agriculture Canada, specializes in selection and introduction of cold-hardy ornamental cultivars of herbaceous perennials, trees and shrubs.

Ontario University of Guelph Arboretum (est 1970, 133.5 ha) houses a research and evaluation collection of conifers and hardwoods, including shrub roses, nut-bearing trees and ornamental shrubs; the collection includes natural woodland.

Central Experimental Farm, Ottawa, part of the annual flower display (*courtesy Agriculture Canada*).

Royal Botanical Gardens, Hamilton (809 ha), comprises a series of attractively landscaped gardens within a larger natural woodland setting, including Katie Osborne Lilac Garden, Iris Garden, Centennial Rose Garden, Rock Garden and Trail Garden of Annuals. The garden includes extensive natural areas and operates active educational and research programs. Erindale College Arboretum, Mississauga (est 1973, 73 ha), specializes in trees, shrubs and woody ornamentals for urban regions; natural woodland forms part of the arboretum. Agriculture Canada Arboretum and Botanic Gardens, Ottawa (est 1887, 55 ha), has some of the oldest cultivated woody specimens in Canada that have been evaluated for hardiness. Rose, hedge and rock garden annual and perennial test gardens are also present. Laurentian University Botanical Garden, Sudbury (est 1972, 7 ha), specializes in native plants of the region. Lakehead University Arboretum, Thunder Bay (est 1975), contains a special collection of woody plants, particularly conifers, junipers and lilacs, which are used as part of the campus landscape.

Québec Jardin Botanique, Montréal (est 1931, 73 ha), operated by Service des Parcs de la Ville de Montréal, includes outstanding conservatory displays, particularly bromeliads, orchids, ferns, gesneriads, aroides, cacti and other succulents, and a tropical rain forest. Extensive outdoor display gardens feature such specialties as taxonomic, economic, aquatic and medicinal gardens. Morgan Arboretum, Macdonald College, Qué (est 1948, 243 ha), contains a collection of native Canadian trees, with special emphasis on birch.

Newfoundland Oxen Pond Botanic Park, Memorial University, St John's (est 1972, 34 ha), contains specialized display gardens, including a garden to attract butterflies, set in a natural woodland setting.   ROY L. TAYLOR

Botany, the study of PLANTS and plant life, is both a descriptive and an experimental science. It began with the collection of medicinal herbs; in the process, herbalists identified many plants not used in healing. In the Middle Ages, plants known to be effective as medicines were cultivated in herb gardens (*see* BOTANICAL GARDENS). Drugs derived from such plants were important articles of long-distance trade. Botany now studies all aspects of plant life, from the biochemistry of plant pigments to the measurement of total plant production for the planet.

Subdivisions The study of plant life is organized in 3 ways, which are also applicable to zoological material.

The first scheme divides botanical material into a hierarchy of plant systems based on progressively larger units: molecules, organelles, cells, tissues, organs, whole plants, populations, communities, ecosystems, landscapes, biomes and the biosphere. Examples of levels of organization are large molecules, eg, DNA or chlorophyll; organelle systems, eg, nucleus or chloroplast; cells;

tissue systems consisting of several types of cell; and whole plants, which may be as different as tiny planktonic plants and lofty Douglas firs. Within the hierarchy, each organizational system contains components, including more basic systems and nonliving features (eg, air spaces, oil vacuoles or space between individual plants). Each level, however, is individually integrated, and an understanding of simpler systems does not imply an understanding of higher ones, eg, the behaviour of a whole plant cannot be predicted from knowledge of its cells. The attributes of life (growth, metabolism, reproduction, movement, responsiveness to environment) are equally obvious at each level.

In the second scheme, botanical material is studied as part of a particular group of plants, eg, GRASSES, LICHENS, MOSSES, FERNS, TREES, WEEDS.

In the third scheme, botanical material belonging to a particular type of system in the hierarchy and to a particular group of plants is studied from one of several perspectives. Each may be examined in its composition, structure, function, heredity, relation to environment, development, history, classification and distribution. At the whole plant level, these divisions are termed, respectively, anatomy, morphology, physiology, genetics, ecology, genesis, evolution, taxonomy and plant geography.

In Canada, interest in plant identification, classification and distribution developed early; however, there are still vast areas for which plant inventories are incomplete. One important historical factor affecting the distribution of plant populations and VEGETATION in Canada is glaciation. Some botanists believe that the 10 000 years since the retreat of the last ice sheet is too short a period for some plants to have recolonized the whole range of available habitats. Mapping the migration of these returning plants, and the movement of alien weeds into open or disturbed habitats, gives a historical perspective, as does analysis of fossil pollen (PALYNOLOGY), which traces sequences of types of vegetation inhabiting different parts of Canada since glacial times. Study of evolutionary changes in pigments, cells and tissues gives a historical view at other levels. The development of a single organism at early stages (embryogenesis) may occur in a few days; at the vegetation level, development (succession) may take place over several hundred years.

The ecological focus, a more recent development, attempts to assess the influence of environmental factors on populations, individuals, cells and organelles. Not only well-known environmental factors (eg, temperature, water, energy as food or radiation, minerals, air and harmful or beneficial animals), but also chemical pollutants (eg, ACID RAIN) must now be included as specific environmental factors that operate in concert to affect development, structure and functioning at the various levels of plant organization.

Plant genetics began early with the selection of crop and ornamental plants for yield, flavour, beauty, perfume or medical value. This remains an active area of research for scientists convinced that the balance between food production and increasing human populations can be achieved through the development of more efficient plants. Plant breeders are at the forefront of the "green revolution." Correct environment, with adequate mineral nutrients and water, also contributes to higher crop yields, while crop protection methods ensure that the output survives for human use.

The study of plant genetics has led to successful plant-breeding programs in crop species. For example, the Canadian range of corn has been extended to areas formerly thought to have too short a growing season, and plant breeders can now tailor a specific variety of corn to a particular geographic area. For many plants, multiplication and propagation are solely vegetative, resulting in a large clone of very uniform genetic material. For example, all important varieties of apple are propagated by grafting or budding, and potatoes are seldom produced from seed. Less welcome results of vegetative propagation can be seen in great overgrowths of pondweeds in waterways (eg, Trent and Rideau systems) and in the Okanagan Valley. These large "nuisance" populations are produced from fragments which separate from parent plants. Although vegetative propagation is common in plants, it is impossible in nature for vertebrate animals in which each individual develops from a fertilized egg.

All life on earth is dependent on green plants storing energy in chemical bonds and producing oxygen, and on nongreen plants making available the minerals that are essential for growth. Nongreen plants (like most other living things) are "heterotrophic" and must get energy for life processes in the form of chemical compounds. Green plants' energy requirements are met through photosynthesis. Examination of the process of energy use by green plants has shown, however, that up to 50% of all energy fixed by at least some green plants "leaks out" again and is lost. Until a clearly defined function for these "escaped" substances is found, the system must be considered inefficient.

An understanding of the development of plant structure contributes to our view of the functions of cells, tissues, plants and vegetation, and may lead to better control of growth. Techniques developed for the electron microscope, in which electrons are either passed through thin tissue sections or bounced off plant material, are used to examine composition, structure and development. Many details of plant structure at the tissue and cell level, formerly hidden because of small size, have been revealed by these methods, and new techniques continue to be developed to display further the elegance of life within cells. All institutions in Canada that research plant structure use both transmission electron microscopes and scanning electron microscopes.

Applications Natural drugs, dyes, flavours and spices produced by plants have been important since ancient times. Recently, many of these have been replaced by synthetic copies. Aspects of agriculture dealing with plants that have botany as a foundation include crop production, horticulture, pasture renovation, market gardening, crop breeding, FORESTRY, flower production, LANDSCAPE ARCHITECTURE and WILDLIFE CONSERVATION AND MANAGEMENT. In addition, many POISONOUS PLANTS must be understood so that their deleterious effects can be reduced. Botany, therefore, contributes in various ways to the health, welfare and happiness of Canadians.

Fields of Work Botanists are employed by federal and provincial governments and as consultants in industry. They also teach in universities, colleges and schools. Their endeavours may be academic ("pure" research) or applied to solving problems of economic or other significance. Frequently, they co-operate with zoologists, meteorologists, soil scientists, oceanographers or other scientists.

Societies Studies undertaken by botanists are diverse and depend upon level of hierarchy, type of plant material and focus of interest. As a result, membership of the several botany-related societies in Canada does not fully reflect the botanical interests of Canadian botanists, who also belong to international societies. If a botanist classifies lichens, he is likely to join a society where he will meet individuals from other countries (eg, Australia or Finland) primarily interested in lichens, rather than joining a Canadian society of less specific focus. The botanist studying population dynamics of algae would have more in common with members of a society dealing with populations (plant and animal) than a society devoted to algae classification. Some Canadian associations that include botanists in their membership are the Canadian Botanical Assn, Royal Soc of Canada, Canadian Soc of Plant Physiologists, Canadian Phytopathological Soc, Assn canadienne-française pour l'avancement des sciences, Agricultural Inst of Canada, Arctic Inst of N America, Canadian Forestry Assn, Canadian Inst of Forestry, Canadian Soc for Cell Biology, Canadian Soc of Cytology, Canadian Soc of Environmental Biologists, Canadian Soc of Microbiologists, Genetics Soc of Canada, Canadian Biochemical Soc, Canadian Soc of Landscape Architects, Canadian Ornamental Plant Foundation, Jeunes biologistes du Québec, and the various provincial institutes of agrologists. There are 80 local or provincial naturalists' clubs. Journals published in Canada include *Canadian Jnl of Botany, Canadian Jnl of Plant Science, Canadian Jnl of Microbiology, Canadian Jnl of Genetics and Cytology* (since 1 Jan 1987, *Genome*), *Canadian Jnl of Plant Pathology, Canadian Jnl of Forest Research, Le Naturaliste canadien, Canadian Field Naturalist, Ontario Field Biologist. See also* ANIMAL; BIOLOGY; FUNGUS. HUGH DALE

Botany History Long before formal study of PLANTS began in Canadian academic institutions, they were studied by explorers and talented amateurs. The vegetation of Canada was first known through descriptive reports of travellers, then through the exporting of seeds and bulbs for cultivation in Europe, and finally through collection and distribution of HERBARIUM specimens. The first references are a few names in vernacular in Icelandic sagas; the Norse are now known to have travelled as far as northern Newfoundland, Labrador and Baffin I. From descriptions and vernacular names in the reports of Jacques CARTIER's voyages, it is possible to recognize 35-40 species of eastern Canadian plants. Cartier also brought back seeds and is known to have introduced white PINE (*Pinus strobus*) and white CEDAR (*Thuja occidentalis*) to European gardens. Further progress was slow, but in 1576 Clusius provided the first formal descriptions of the following Canadian plants: common MILKWEED (*Asclepias syriaca*) and PITCHER PLANT (*Limonio congener*, now known as *Sarracenia purpurea*).

In 1623 a series of 27 Canadian species were given scientific names by C. Bauhin; identification was based on cultivated materials; and specimens are found today in the herbarium at Uppsala, Sweden. The source is stated to be an unnamed apothecary, but circumstantial evidence points to Louis HÉBERT, the first European to cultivate land on the St Lawrence R, who resided in Paris for a few years after his travels in Acadia. About 60 Canadian plants were described, named and illustrated by Jacques Cornuti in his *Canadensium Plantarum Historia* (1635). The descriptions were based on material cultivated in the garden of V. Robin, and brought over by a French navigator (probably CHAMPLAIN, who took with him plants from his garden when he left Québec in 1629). Other plants are occasionally noted in the reports of Gabriel Sagard and other travellers and in the JESUIT RELATIONS. The next principal source is the *Histoire véritable et naturelle...de la Nouvelle-France...*(1664), by Pierre BOUCHER, in which about 50 (mainly woody) plants are discussed. His botany was analysed by Jacques ROUSSEAU in 1964.

Herbaria originated in Europe around 1550, but this research tool was not to play a role in

Canada until a century and a half later. Michel SARRAZIN, appointed Médecin du Roi for New France and correspondent of the French Academy, took his post at Québec in 1697. He collected his first herbarium specimens at Plaisance in southern Newfoundland. Every year Sarrazin sent written observations and specimens to his correspondents at the Paris Academy. From his first shipment, J.P. Tournefort in 1700 described 8 new plant species. Later shipments went to Sébastien Vaillant and B. Jussieu. Some 16 new species were published from 1700 to 1716; otherwise, Sarrazin's botanical work remained largely unpublished. It is now known from a manuscript draft of about 1708, which describes about 225 species, and was annotated and published in 1977. Sarrazin's specimens are in the Muséum d'Histoire Naturelle, Paris.

Sarrazin's contemporary, W. Hay, a ship's surgeon, collected in Newfoundland in 1699; his specimens are at the British Museum, London. The same year, another surgeon, Dièreville, came to Acadia and collected some 25 specimens, one of which is now known as *Diervilla lonicera*, the bush HONEYSUCKLE. The 3-volume *Histoire et description générale de la Nouvelle-France* (1744) by P.F.X. de CHARLEVOIX contains some plant information, including a botanical appendix (largely based on Cornuti) and describes 3 new species contributed by Sarrazin.

The next king's physician, J.F. GAULTIER, arrived in 1742. A few of his botanical discoveries were published by D. DuMonceau but his botany is mostly known through 400 pages of surviving manuscripts. He accompanied Pehr KALM during his 1749 Canadian expedition, which provided C. Linnaeus with most of his Canadian material (about 200 species) included in his *Species Plantarum* (1753). In 1755 the Hôtel-Dieu, Québec City, was destroyed by fire. Losses apparently also included the herbarium of Sarrazin and Gaultier. Duplicate specimens have been found at the Muséum d'histoire naturelle, Paris.

André MICHAUX arrived in N America in 1785, primarily to study TREES, and was responsible for introducing to Europe various native Canadian species. In 1792 he spent 3 summer months collecting plants in Lower Canada and as far N as Lk Mistassini. Returning to France in 1796, Michaux took with him a large herbarium, a manuscript FLORA and a monograph on oaks. The flora contains 1720 species, hundreds of them new and about 520 from Lower Canada and the Illinois country. The Michaux flora, published posthumously in 1803, seems to have evoked little interest in Canada, but in the US it was a pattern-making publication and the source of an intellectual explosion. By providing better coverage of the vegetation and by eliminating all extraneous species, it was more practical than the world floras then in use. Within 11 years, Frederick PURSH came out with a flora of N America containing more than 3000 species. Pursh moved to Canada intending to prepare a flora of Canada, but died in Montréal (1820) without completing it. A.F. Holmes, founder and future dean of the Faculty of Medicine at McGill, collected plants in the Montréal area from 1821 to 1825. His herbarium remained in Canada (McGill). The only earlier surviving herbarium retained in Canada, that of A.M. Percival, is now with Agriculture Canada, Ottawa.

William J. Hooker was a man of encyclopedic botanical knowledge. His personal herbarium (about one million sheets) was acquired by Kew Gardens, London, in 1867. In about 1820, Hooker became interested in the flora of Canada and contacted local amateurs (eg, A.M. Percival, Harriet and William Sheppard and Lady Dalhousie, who collected in NS, starting in 1816, then Qué-

bec in 1820 and later). With the co-operation of the Hudson's Bay Company, he was able to send a number of natural-history explorers to N America, including John Goldie, T. DRUMMOND, D. DOUGLAS and J. RICHARDSON. From this accumulated material, Hooker produced a 2-volume flora in 1840; because of its high cost, it was out of reach of all but the wealthiest amateurs. Léon PROVANCHER's flora was published in 1862; the catalogue of John MACOUN in 1883-1902. Macoun's herbarium, Canada's largest at the time, now forms the basis of the National Herbarium, Ottawa.

Canada's first botanical society, founded at McGill in 1855, was short-lived. The Botanical Society of Canada was founded in Kingston, Ont, in 1860 and in 1861 inaugurated the *Annals of the Botanical Society of Canada*. This society and 2 later ones were also short-lived. In contrast, the Botanical Club of Canada, Halifax, lasted from 1891 to 1910. The Field Botanists of Ontario was founded in the 1890s.

An outstanding characteristic of Canadian botany in the 19th and early 20th centuries is the domination by American botanists (F. Pursh, T. Nuttall, J. Torrey, A. Gray, A. Wood, N.L. Britton, M.L. Fernald, P.A. Rydberg, L. Abrams, etc). Other foreign contributors were also important: a flora of Labrador was published in Germany by E. Meyer; the Yukon was included in a 10-volume flora by E. Hultén, a Swede; Hooker has already been noted; N. Polunin, a British citizen of Russian origin, wrote a flora of the eastern Arctic; I. Hustich, a Finn, compiled a list and physiogeographic study of Labrador.

Canadians were not, however, totally absent from the scene. George LAWSON was appointed professor of chemistry and natural history at Queen's in 1858. He was primarily interested in botany and was instrumental in founding the Botanical Society of Canada before leaving to become professor of chemistry at Dalhousie. H. Reeks compiled a list of the flora of Newfoundland in 1873. In 1893 A.C. Waghorne began publishing a list for Labrador, Newfoundland and Saint-Pierre and Miquelon. J.W. DAWSON, an outstanding paleobotanist, published mainly in the *Proceedings and Transactions of the Royal Society of Canada*. A.W. Lindsay published a list of NS plants in 1875. Various lists and studies of vascular plants of NS were also published, mainly by G.U. Hay and A.H. MacKay. A group of amateurs studied the flora of NB and the results were compiled by W.J. Fowler in lists published in 1878 and 1885. PEI was the last Atlantic province to have its list published (by F. Bain in 1890). Most provinces and territories now have their own flora: southern BC since 1915; a manual for SW Qué, 1931, and a broader and more elaborate flora, 1935; the YT, 1941-50; NS, 1947 and 1966-69; Man, 1957; Alta, 1959; PEI, 1961; the NWT, 1957 and 1979. A flora of the Prairie provinces in 5 parts came out from 1967 to 1981. Two items of national scope should be noted: an *Enumération* published in 1966-67 provides distributions by provinces and extensive bibliographies, while H.J. Scoggan's 4-volume *The Flora of Canada* (1978-79), National Museum of Natural Sciences, supplies keys and synonymy.

Thus, at the turn of the century, Canadian botanists were still primarily concerned with lists and inventories. Not much had been done outside the field of floristics (except for Dawson's work in paleobotany). Another noted 19th-century paleobotanist was D.P. Penhallow of McGill, who also authored papers on botanical history and bibliography. In the early 20th century numerous local centres of activity arose gradually in each province: most in universities, some in museums, and a few in government laboratories. In the late

19th century in Canadian universities, broad scientific disciplines (eg, natural history, natural sciences, physical sciences) began to be divided into more specialized subject areas. Plant studies first came under the auspices of biology departments, which subsequently split, in some universities, into departments of botany and zoology.

In mycology (the study of FUNGI) the main centre has been the Dept of Agriculture (now Agriculture Canada) in Ottawa, recently with D.B.O. SAVILE as principal mycologist (1957-75). For a time, University of Manitoba was also very active. Under A.H. Buller (appointed professor of botany in 1904) and G.R. Bisby much research was carried out and basic surveys of the fungi of Manitoba and Saskatchewan were published. Buller's *Research in Fungi* (7 vols, 1909-34) became a standard authority. An outstanding amateur, John Dearness, of London, Ont, had a herbarium of 50 000 specimens and published taxonomic papers, while participating in the studies of the Winnipeg group. More recently, R. Pomerleau has published a monumental work *Flore des Champignons au Québec*. Bryology (the study of LIVERWORTS and MOSSES) and lichenology (study of LICHENS) have attracted professionals and amateurs. Among the amateurs, Ernest LEPAGE, an outstanding botanical explorer (Labrador to Alaska), contributed to both bryology and lichenology. His herbarium and botanical library were left to Laval. Algology (study of ALGAE) is currently a very active field on both coasts. Desmids were the subject of major contributions by Frère Irénée-Marie, starting in 1939. Cytotaxonomy is practised in many places, especially in Ottawa where H.A. Senn assembled an active team soon after WWII. The outstanding team of A. and D. Löve worked in Winnipeg and then Montréal before moving to the US in 1962. In these and other fields, workers are scattered across Canada in university departments of botany or biology and government laboratories.

Amateurs have also contributed to scientific botany, mainly in the fields of floristics, taxonomy and ecology. J. Dearness and E. Lepage have already been mentioned; others include A.H. Brinkman, a bryologist working in Craigmyle, Alberta; H. Dupret, also a bryologist, in the Montréal area; W.C. McCalla, a schoolteacher, amateur photographer and outstanding plant collector in southern Ontario and Alberta; Frère Rolland-Germain, a keen field botanist and constant companion of Frère MARIE-VICTORIN, whose Québec and Ontario collections are outstanding; N.B. Sanson, a park naturalist in Banff; G.H. Turner, a retired physician in Fort Saskatchewan, Alta. At least 10 others have herbaria of 10 000 or more specimens. Many amateurs eventually became leading professionals, eg, Macoun, A.E. PORSILD and Marie-Victorin. Marie-Victorin's herbarium (65 000 specimens) is now part of the herbarium of the Université de Montréal's Institut Botanique which, with holdings of 500 000 specimens, is the largest outside Ottawa. *See also* BOTANICAL GARDEN; CROP RESEARCH; PLANT BREEDING.　　　　　　　　　　　B. BOIVIN

Botterell, Edmund Harry, neurosurgeon, medical educator (b at Vancouver 28 Feb 1906). Graduation in medicine from U Man was followed by neurosurgical training at U of T and research at Yale. During WWII Botterell served as senior neurosurgeon to No 1 Canadian Neurological Hospital, Basingstoke, Eng. On returning to Toronto, as chief of The Joint Services Neurosurgical Unit, Christie St Hospital, he became committed to the rehabilitation of paraplegic veterans. In 1952 he was appointed chief of neurosurgery at the Toronto General Hospital and he was chairman of U of T's division of neurosurgery 1953-61. Between 1962 and 1971 Botterell served as dean of medicine and then vice principal (health sciences) at Queen's. His personal magnetism and enthusiastic leadership stimulated unprecedented expansion in teaching, research and patient care in Kingston. He was later commissioned to study health-related matters in penitentiaries. His honours include the Order of Canada and an OBE.   A.A. TRAVILL

Botulism, a severe but rare type of acute FOOD POISONING occurring in humans, various mammals and birds. The disease results from the consumption of food containing the potent botulinum toxin. The causative organism is *Clostridium botulinum,* an anaerobic, rod-shaped bacterium that produces heat-resistant spores. The spores are universally distributed, occurring in soils, freshwater and marine sediments and the intestinal tracts of many animals. For an outbreak of botulism to occur, the spores must get into food and germinate. The germinated cells must then multiply and secrete the toxin. After the contaminated food is consumed, the toxin is absorbed from the small intestine. The characteristic symptoms usually develop in 8-72 hours. The toxin is a neurotoxin affecting nerve terminals of the parasympathetic nervous system; accordingly, the symptoms present a type of progressive paralysis. Gastrointestinal symptoms (eg, nausea, vomiting, diarrhea) may be evident before the neurological symptoms appear. Neurological symptoms are weakness, dizziness and vertigo, followed by blurred vision and difficulty in speaking and swallowing. Death may result from asphyxiation caused by paralysis of the diaphragm and chest muscles. The fatality rate has declined from over 60% to about 30%, in part because antitoxin is administered promptly in suspected cases and because mechanical respirators are used.

Control of botulism is based almost entirely on thermal destruction of the spores. Through the establishment and enforcement of strict, standardized time-temperature treatments, the commercial food-canning industry has been so successful in preventing botulism that it has become almost insignificant as a source of the disease. Home canning may lead to botulism because the time-temperature treatment of foods may be insufficient to kill the spores, especially in "low-acid" foods (eg, corn, peppers, green beans, mushrooms). Home canners should use approved pressure-cooker processes for such products. An additional safeguard is boiling these foods for 10-15 minutes before serving; this process will inactivate the botulinum toxin, if present. Some traditional foods of the native peoples of Canada, including whale, seal and walrus meat and salmon eggs, present special problems. The foods *per se* are not hazardous, but when they are preserved in various dried and fermented forms conditions conducive to the growth of *C. botulinum* are created.

H. JACKSON

Botwood, Nfld, Town, pop 3916 (1986c), inc 1960, is located in the Bay of Exploits, a long arm of Notre Dame Bay on the N coast of Newfoundland. It was an anchorage for explorers of the Exploits R and DEMASDUWIT died there in 1820 on board John Buchan's ship while waiting to be returned to Red Indian Lk. Known as Ship Cove when it was settled as a sawmilling centre in the 1870s and 1880s, it was soon after renamed Botwoodville, and later Botwood, for Rev Edward Botwood (1828-1901). In 1910 it became the shipping port for paper carried by rail from Grand Falls and, after 1928, for ore from Buchans. Periodically during the 1920s and 1930s it was a seaplane base for local aviation and a stopover for many transatlantic flights until the opening of Gander airport. Today Botwood is an important

regional service centre and year-round transhipment base for many commodities.

ROBERT D. PITT

Bouchard, Télesphore-Damien, journalist, politician (b at St-Hyacinthe, Qué 20 Dec 1881; d at Montréal 13 Nov 1962). After several years as a journalist, Bouchard became virtually permanent mayor of St-Hyacinthe (1917-44) and, simultaneously, perpetual Liberal MLA (1912-44). He became Speaker of the Québec legislature in 1930 and entered the Taschereau government in 1935. Bouchard became Opposition leader in 1936, entered the government of Joseph-Adélard GODBOUT in 1939, and in 1944 was appointed by PM Mackenzie King to the Senate. Bouchard was best known for his 1944 charges that a French Canadian secret society, the ORDRE DE JACQUES CARTIER, was a danger to Canadian society.

ROBERT BOTHWELL

Boucher, Adélard-Joseph, publisher, choirmaster, organist, conductor, teacher, numismatist (b at Maskinongé, Lower Canada 28 June 1835; d at Outremont, 16 Nov 1912). Thanks to his efforts, the musical works of his period were published in Québec, particularly by A.J. Boucher Co, which he founded in Montréal. The company published the works of Canadian and foreign composers, as well as instrumental pieces, until it closed in 1975. In 1862 Boucher founded the Société de numismatique de Montréal, serving also as its first president.

HÉLÈNE PLOUFFE

Boucher, Frank, hockey player (b at Ottawa 7 Oct 1901; d at Kemptville, Ont 12 Dec 1977). He played for the RCMP, Ottawa and Vancouver before joining New York Rangers in 1926. He was the playmaking centre on the famous line with Bun and Bill COOK. Respected for his clean play, he won the LADY BYNG TROPHY 7 times in 8 seasons; it was finally given to him and another one made.

JAMES MARSH

Boucher, Gaëtan, speed skater (b at Charlesbourg, Qué 10 May 1958). Boucher began SPEED SKATING as an adjunct to hockey. By the time he was 14 he had won his first of many Canadian championships. A ninth place in the 1000 m at the 1976 Innsbruck Winter Olympics established him as a top international competitor. In 1977 he was world indoor speed-skating champion and in 1978, 1980 and 1982 he finished second at the more prestigious World Sprint Speed-skating Championships. At the 1980 Lake Placid Winter Olympics he finished behind American Eric Heiden to win the silver in the 1000 m, one of only 2 Canadian medals that year. The 1984 Sarajevo Olympics saw Boucher return from a broken ankle suffered the previous year to record the greatest performance ever by a Canadian Olympian. With a fine technique developed because of his small stature, he won gold medals at 1000 and 1500 m and a bronze in the 500. He followed this by capturing the 1984 and 1985 World Sprint Speed-skating Championship. He is an Officer of the Order of Canada.

DEREK DRAGER

Boucher, Pierre, interpreter, soldier, seigneur (bap at Mortagne, France 1 Aug 1622; d at Boucherville 19 Apr 1717). He lived in HURONIA 1637-41, assisting the missionaries, living among the Indians and learning their dialects. From 1645, he lived in Trois-Rivières, distinguishing himself in its defence against IROQUOIS raids. He became captain of Trois-Rivières 1649, and governor 1654. Boucher was sent to France 1661 to plead for help, returning with soldiers and supplies and a commitment to make NEW FRANCE a crown colony. He built his seigneury of Boucherville into one of the most prosperous in the colony. His memoirs contain a valuable

record of the fur trade, the Indians, and his remarkable life.

JAMES MARSH

Boucherville, Sir Charles-Eugène Boucher de, doctor, politician, premier of Québec 1874-78 and 1891-92 (b at Montréal 4 May 1822; d there 10 Sept 1915). A Conservative member of the Assembly of the Province of Canada, he was appointed to the Québec Legislative Council in 1867. He was premier of the province from 1874 until Mar 1878 when Liberal Lt-Gov Luc Letellier de Saint-Just, in a move labelled a *coup d'état* by the Conservatives, removed him from office and replaced him with Liberal Henri-Gustave JOLY DE LOTBINIÈRE. Boucherville's administration ushered in electoral reform and in 1875 abolished the Dept of Public Instruction, replacing it with an appointed superintendent of education. In 1891 after MERCIER's government had been tainted by the BAIE DES CHALEURS SCANDAL, Boucherville again became premier but he resigned a year later and was succeeded by L.O. TAILLON.   DANIEL LATOUCHE

Boudreau, Walter, composer, saxophonist (b at Montréal 15 Oct 1947). At age 19 he formed his own jazz band and at 20 led various jazz groups during Expo 67. In 1969 he founded Infonie with Raôul Duguay. Boudreau was associated with this mixed-media ensemble until 1973, giving performances of both avant-garde and classical music arranged as pop numbers. Infonie also made 3 albums, one of which presented Boudreau's own composition *Paix.* Largely self-taught initially, Boudreau studied composition and theory intensively in the 1970s. He won the CBC National Radio Competition for Young Composers in 1973 with *Variations I* for chamber ensemble, derived from one of several earlier film scores. Boudreau's other chamber works include *Les Sept Jours* (1977) for percussion. By 1986-87 he had begun to concentrate again on conducting.

ANN SCHAU

Bouey, Gerald Keith, banker (b at Axford, Sask 2 Apr 1920). He became governor of the BANK OF CANADA in Feb 1973 and guided the country's MONETARY POLICY through the inflationary difficulties of the early 1980s. A quiet man, Bouey emerged from wartime service in the RCAF and from university education at Queen's to join the Bank of Canada in 1948. He succeeded Louis RASMINSKY as governor in 1973, turned the bank's policy in monetarist directions, and struggled to control interest rates at the beginning of the 1980s. Many disagreed with his policy prescriptions, but few doubted his integrity and determination. He became a Companion of the Order of Canada in 1987, the year he retired from the Bank of Canada.   J.L. GRANATSTEIN

Bougainville, Louis-Antoine de Bougainville, Comte de, soldier, sailor (b at Paris, France 12 Nov 1729; d there 20 Aug 1811). After studying law and mathematics, he published a *Traité de calcul intégral* (1754-56) and was elected to the Royal Society (London). Having entered the military in 1750, he was posted to Québec in 1756 as aide-de-camp to MONTCALM. Bougainville was involved in the campaigns of the SEVEN YEARS' WAR leading up to the Battle of the PLAINS OF ABRAHAM. Although he failed to bring reinforcements in time to alter the outcome, some considered Bougainville one of Montcalm's abler officers. In 1758 he wrote a remarkable document recommending reforms that would free New France from the restrictions of MERCANTILISM. In 1763 he entered the French navy and proceeded to found a short-lived colony composed mostly of ACADIANS, on the Falkland Is. His scientific expeditions, 1766-69, were written up in *Voyage autour du monde* (1771; trans *A Voyage Round the World,* 1772), and the tropical vine "bougainvillaea" was named after him. He saw action in the French navy during the American Revolution and, despite his royalist sympathies, survived the subsequent French Revolution and received the patronage of Napoleon.   DAVID EVANS

Boulton, Henry John, lawyer, politician, judge (b at Kensington, Eng 1790; d at Toronto 18 June 1870). Although Boulton was an officeholder in the 1830s, he is remembered chiefly for his controversial role in both Upper Canada and Newfoundland. Coming to Canada around 1800, Boulton studied law in York [Toronto] 1807-11 and continued his education in England until 1816. Returning to Upper Canada, he was welcomed into the governing circles of the FAMILY COMPACT, being appointed solicitor general in 1818 and attorney general in 1829. An "independent," he was elected to the Assembly for Niagara in 1830 and took a leading part in the expulsion of William Lyon MACKENZIE from the assembly in 1831 and 1832. When ordered in 1832 to reinstate Mackenzie, Boulton sharply criticized the Colonial Office, which promptly dismissed him. The following year he was named chief justice of Newfoundland, where he was again controversial and was recalled in 1838. He resumed his law practice in Toronto, was elected to the Assembly in 1841, and by 1847 had moved within the Reform orbit of LAFONTAINE and Robert BALDWIN. An individualist, by 1850 he had broken with the Reformers; he gave up politics in 1851 and retired from his law practice in 1861. His widow, the former Eliza Jones of Brockville, married Goldwin SMITH.   HEREWARD AND ELINOR SENIOR

Boundaries The political boundaries that are of concern to Canada today are the international boundaries primarily with the US and Greenland and, because they are of more than local importance, the boundaries of the provinces and territories. The evolution of both types involved 2 distinct stages. After political decisions were made on the allocation of territory, such territories were delimited and the boundaries described in state documents. Then, usually some time later, the boundaries were surveyed and marked on the ground (the process of demarcation). The beginnings of international and internal boundary delineations can be traced to the Treaty of PARIS (1763), which produced a great rearrangement of boundaries in N America. For this reason the SEVEN YEARS' WAR (1756-63) between Britain and France, which immediately preceded the treaty, is sometimes called the "War of the Boundary Lines." All of eastern N America except SAINT-PIERRE AND MIQUELON became British, and the boundaries of the various colonies were adjusted to accommodate the changed circumstances. Later, as a result of the AMERICAN REVOLUTION, the colonies S of Newfoundland, Nova Scotia and the Province of Quebec, as well as that part of Quebec between the Ohio and Mississippi rivers, were lost to Britain, and thus Canada's present boundaries with the US began to emerge after the Treaty of PARIS (1783).

International Boundaries In 1783 the boundary between the US and BRITISH NORTH AMERICA was described as running from the mouth of the St Croix R on the Bay of Fundy to its source, thence along a line drawn due N to the "northwest angle" of Nova Scotia (today northwestern NB), thence along the watershed between the Atlantic and the St Lawrence to the northwest head of the Connecticut R, from there along that river to 45° N and along this parallel to the St Lawrence R. The boundary continued up the St Lawrence and through Lk Ontario, the Niagara R, Lk Erie, Lk St Clair, Lk Huron and Lk Superior to the Pigeon R, and thence to Lake of the Woods. From the northwest point of that lake the boundary was to run

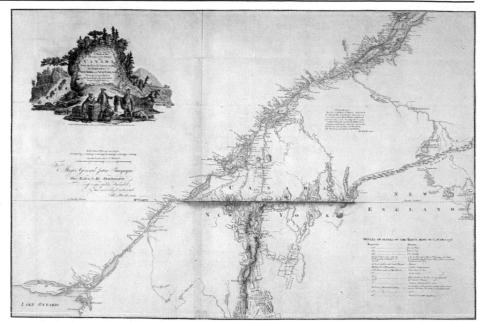

Map published by William Faden in 1777, showing the first survey line of the international boundary between Canada and the US (*courtesy National Archives of Canada/ NMC-24915*).

due W to the Mississippi R. This description, based on a map of N America first published in 1755 by John Mitchell, and inaccurate in many respects, led to at least 9 boundary problems. In 1794 JAY'S TREATY began to clarify these problems.

The first controversy developed over the exact location of the St Croix R because 3 rivers existed where the Mitchell map showed only 2. Arbitrators favoured what is now the Schoodic R, but it had 2 branches, and when the eastern branch was selected, a line drawn N from it almost cut off the Maritime provinces from Lower Canada. Commissions and arbitrations in 1814 and 1831 could not reach an acceptable solution. During the following period of tension, a clash occurred between lumbermen from NB and Maine in the disputed area (*see* AROOSTOOK WAR). The dispute ended only when a compromise was reached through the ASHBURTON-WEBSTER TREATY of 1842.

Another difficulty developed when it was discovered that a line drawn due W from the northwestern point of Lake of the Woods did not encounter the Mississippi R, which rose farther S than was indicated on the Mitchell map. This difficulty was resolved by the CONVENTION OF 1818: the FORTY-NINTH PARALLEL, accepted as the southern boundary of the HUDSON'S BAY COMPANY's territories between Lake of the Woods and the Rocky Mts, very roughly approximates the northern watershed of the Mississippi-Missouri drainage system embraced by Louisiana Territory, which had been acquired by the US from France in 1803.

West of the Rocky Mts the British were unwilling to relinquish control of the Oregon country then in the hands of the HBC. Britain and the US therefore agreed to occupy Oregon jointly for 10 years. In 1827 this compromise was reaffirmed for an indefinite period. However, in the 1840s American settlers in large numbers began to enter the area and demand exclusive US jurisdiction as far N as 54°40' N, the southern limit of Russian territory on the Pacific coast. Although "fifty-four forty or fight" became an American election campaign slogan in 1844, the British proposal to divide the area by extending the boundary along the 49th parallel westward to the coast and then through the Str of Juan de Fuca was incorporated

into the OREGON TREATY 2 years later. This treaty did not precisely describe the water boundary, and further controversy was ultimately resolved by arbitration in 1872 (*see* WASHINGTON, TREATY OF).

The boundary between Russian and British territory was described in 1825, well before the American purchase of Alaska in 1867. The 141st meridian was chosen as the northern part of the boundary, probably because it ran N from Mt St Elias, one of the few outstanding and unmistakable features in a relatively unknown area, and because it separated the maritime interests of the Russians from the land interests of the HBC. South of Mt St Elias to Prince of Wales I, Russian territory extended inland from the coast for 10 marine leagues (about 55.6 km). Difficulties in interpreting the exact location of this boundary arose after the KLONDIKE GOLD RUSH. The crucial question was whether the Anglo-Russian Convention of 1825 called for a boundary drawn around the heads of the coastal inlets (favoured by the US), or one which followed the summits of the mountains paralleling the general trend of the coast and cut across all inlets and fjords (which Canada advocated). The problem was referred to a joint commission and later a tribunal, which described the boundary as it still exists today (*see* ALASKA BOUNDARY DISPUTE). The boundary follows the American contention, so the Alaska Panhandle shuts Canada off from direct access to the Pacific Ocean in the north and is regarded as one of the circumstances limiting the development of mining and hydroelectricity in northwestern BC.

Between 1870 and 1880 Canada's northern limits coincided with those of the former HBC territory. Britain transferred its rights to the arctic islands to the federal government. In 1907 the claim to the sector between 141° W and 60° W was first made, although it was not officially supported until 1925. The dividing line or "line of allocation" between Canada and Greenland from 61° N northward was agreed upon with Denmark in 1974.

Canada's seaward limits embrace the territorial sea, and generally include the marginal seas within 3 nautical miles (5.5 km) of the baselines on the coast. The most notable exceptions are in the Arctic, where Canadian sovereignty includes the waters between islands. Canadian coastal fishing zones extend seaward 200 nautical miles (about 371 km), as do those of many other nations.

Interprovincial and Interterritorial Boundaries The present-day boundaries of NS, PEI and NB

John Rapkin's map of N America (c 1845), beautifully embellished with vignettes representative of the continent, clearly shows Canada's international boundaries (*courtesy National Archives of Canada/NMC-19271*).

resulted from circumstances that were significant only when these regions were created British colonies in the 18th and 19th centuries. After 1763, Nova Scotia included the present provinces of Prince Edward Island and New Brunswick. Prince Edward Island, practically deserted by the French by that time, was resettled, but the inconvenience of having to refer judicial and legal matters to Halifax and the relative inaccessibility of the Island, especially in winter, resulted in a separate government in 1769. After the American Revolution, thousands of LOYALISTS moved into the Saint John R valley and along the N shore of the Bay of Fundy. They also created administrative and judicial problems, and so New Brunswick was created a separate province in 1784 with a southern boundary across the Chignecto Isthmus from Cumberland Arm to Baie Verte.

Almost all of LABRADOR has been under the jurisdiction of Newfoundland since 1763, except from 1774 to 1809 when it was governed from Québec. But its boundaries on the landward side were never precisely delimited, and in 1902, when Newfoundland granted timber-cutting leases in the area between Lk Melville and Grand Falls (now Churchill Falls), Québec maintained that the area was properly under its jurisdiction. The federal government believed that Labrador extended only one mile (1.6 km) inland from the high-water mark along the coast. In 1927 the JUDICIAL COMMITTEE OF THE PRIVY COUNCIL decided that the boundary for the most part followed the watershed of those rivers flowing into the Atlantic Ocean. In the S, however, the boundary runs N from a point just E of Blanc Sablon to 52° N, thence westward to and up the Romaine R to the watershed portion of the boundary. This means that the headwaters of such rivers as the Romaine, Natashquan, Petit Mécatina, St-Augustin and St-Paul which drain through Québec into the Gulf of St Lawrence are in Newfoundland (*see* LABRADOR BOUNDARY DISPUTE).

Québec, like Nova Scotia, became the home of thousands of Loyalist refugees. Most settled along the N shores of the St Lawrence R and Lakes On-

tario and Erie in the area between Montréal and what is now Windsor, Ont. The French SEIGNEURIAL SYSTEM of land tenure was unfamiliar to these newcomers, who were accustomed to holding their land in free and common socage (ie, leasing or renting the land). They also resented the absence of popular government, delays in administration owing to the great distance from Montréal to Windsor, the lack of any connecting road, and the tedious, precarious (and, during the winter, nonexistent) water route linking them. Petitions for their own government were heeded, and in 1791 the province was divided into UPPER CANADA and LOWER CANADA. The boundary between them ran northward from the St Lawrence R, following the westernmost limits of the seigneuries to and up the Ottawa R to Lk Timiskaming, and then due N to HBC property. However, this arrangement was not entirely satisfactory, largely because the trade of both provinces was through the St Lawrence and because the division of revenues caused dissatisfaction. In 1841 the 2 provinces were united into the PROVINCE OF CANADA. Following the passage of the BRITISH NORTH AMERICA ACT of 1867, the Province of Canada was divided into the provinces of Ontario and Québec by the same boundary that had been established in 1791. Their northern limits followed the watershed of the rivers draining into the Great Lakes-St Lawrence system. When RUPERT'S LAND was acquired by the federal government in 1870, and the province of Manitoba was created from part of it, both Manitoba and Ontario claimed the area between Lake of the Woods and what is now Thunder Bay. The controversy was not settled until 1889, when the boundary of Ontario was extended northward generally to follow a series of lakes and waterways and the Albany R to James Bay. Similarly, in 1898 the northern boundary of Québec was extended northward to follow the Eastmain R and a series of smaller waterways to the boundary of Labrador.

The colony of Vancouver's Island was established in 1849. Soon after, GOLD RUSHES on the mainland led to the establishment of the colony of BRITISH COLUMBIA in 1858 and STICKINE TERRITORY in 1862. All 3 were united into British Columbia in 1866 with boundaries as they now exist. The boundaries were intended to embrace all the rivers and creeks from which it was thought that alluvial gold might be obtained, not only to control the mining itself, but so that proper jurisdiction might be exercised over miners. Similar considerations later led to the boundaries of the Yukon Territory, which were first established in 1895. Substantial sections of the eastern boundaries of BC and the Yukon followed the watershed of those rivers draining into the Pacific Ocean.

Meanwhile, the North-West Territories were being peopled and more of the area came to be divided into provisional districts for administrative and postal purposes – the District of Keewatin in 1876; Saskatchewan, Assiniboia, Alberta and Athabaska in 1882; followed by Ungava, Yukon, Mackenzie and Franklin in 1895. Their boundaries were almost invariably straight lines and were expressed in terms of the Dominion Lands Survey system devised to facilitate settlement. By 1905 much of the area was deemed ready for provincial responsibilities. It was felt that the area N of 60° was unfit for agriculture, without which there could be little hope of the "thick and permanent settlement" necessary for stable provincial government, and that the area S of this parallel was too large for a single province when compared with the other provinces. Most of the southern area was therefore divided by the 110° W into 2 provinces of approximately equal size when Alberta and Saskatchewan were established in 1905. The fact that these two provinces

extended 60° N encouraged Manitoba, Ontario and Québec to request northward extensions. Both Manitoba and Ontario claimed the area between the Albany and Churchill rivers. In 1912 the boundary divided this area more or less equally between them, the extensions came into force, and Québec was extended northward to the shores of Hudson Str and Hudson Bay.

The demarcation of Canada's boundaries began in 1771 when the 45th parallel was marked as a boundary between Québec and New York. But the work was crude and the need to resurvey was accentuated by the American Revolution, when this boundary, originally between British provinces, became an international boundary. The demarcation of Canada's international boundaries was largely completed by 1913. The methods varied from region to region. The earliest boundaries in forested areas were merely compass lines marked by blazes on trees or by heaps of stones. In the prairie West they were mounds of sand or grass sod and later iron posts. Where a boundary crossed wooded land, a path or "vista" was usually cut on each side of the surveyed line. Provincial boundaries are marked in a similar way but their demarcation proceeded more slowly, usually only when it was administratively expedient. By 1962 the establishment of boundaries had essentially been completed, except for the Québec-Newfoundland boundary.

N.L. NICHOLSON

Reading: H.G. Classen, *Thrust and Counterthrust* (1965); H. Dorion, *La Frontière Québec-Terre-Neuve* (1963); Energy, Mines and Resources Canada, "Canada Then and Now" in *The National Atlas of Canada* (5th ed, 1982); J.A. Munro, *The Alaska Boundary Dispute* (1970); N.L. Nicholson, *The Boundaries of the Canadian Confederation* (1979).

Boundary Waters Treaty, 11 Jan 1909, between Canada and the US, resulted from a need to settle and prevent disputes regarding the uses and apportionment of waters along the international boundary. The treaty established the INTERNATIONAL JOINT COMMISSION, the first permanent joint organization between Canada and the US, to fix and apply the rules of boundary water resource use. Negotiated for Canada mainly by George C. Gibbons, the treaty also prohibited the diversion of these waters without the commission's approval, proclaimed certain general principles of boundary water resource development, and called for an end to cross-boundary pollution. It failed, however, to impose sanctions against polluters or to prevent the diversion or damming of waters crossing the boundary. N.F. DREISZIGER

Bourassa, Henri, politician, journalist (b at Montréal 1 Sept 1868; d there 31 Aug 1952). His family was one of the most prominent in the province; his father was a well-known painter, and his grandfather, Louis-Joseph PAPINEAU, was a celebrated folk hero of the REBELLIONS OF 1837. Bourassa got an early start in politics when he was elected mayor of the town of Montebello at age 22. Six years later, in 1896, he entered federal politics, where he stayed until 1907. He resigned his seat to enter provincial politics. He was elected to the Québec Assembly in 1908 and served until 1912. Meanwhile, in 1910 he founded *Le DEVOIR*, one of the great and influential Canadian newspapers, and remained its editor until 1932. In 1925 he was again elected from his old federal constituency of Labelle and remained a member until defeated in 1935. Because of his sensitivity to long-term issues fundamental to French Canadian society, his ability to articulate them and his courage in speaking on them, Henry Bourassa inspired the growth of a vigorous nationalist movement in French Canada around 3 main themes: Canada's relationship with Great Britain, the re-

Henri Bourassa, founder of *Le Devoir* and its editor until 1932. He came to prominence opposing Canadian participation in the South African War and inspired the growth of a vigorous nationalist movement in French Canada (*courtesy National Archives of Canada/C-27360/ Henri Bourassa Coll*).

lationship of French to English culture, and the values that should guide economic life.

Bourassa's career coincided with a time when most Anglo-Canadians were strongly emphasizing the British nature of the country (*see* IMPERIALISM). But did this mean that Canada was automatically at war when Great Britain went to war? It was over this issue that Bourassa, a young and promising Liberal MP, came to prominence in Oct 1899 when he resigned his seat to protest the Liberal Cabinet's decision to send Canadian troops to aid the British in the SOUTH AFRICAN WAR without consulting Parliament. By 1900 he was back in the House, having won his by-election by acclamation. There he tried to establish that Parliament was the only authority that could declare war on behalf of Canada. Although his resolution was voted down, the question at issue would be fundamental to Canadian politics for the next 40 years.

In 1910 Bourassa opposed the government's naval bill because it allowed the Cabinet to turn over its proposed Canadian Navy to the British Admiralty without the permission of Parliament. Over this issue he succeeded in the federal election of 1911 in organizing an anti-Liberal campaign effective enough to lead to a considerable depletion of Laurier's electoral strength in Québec.

After some hesitation, Bourassa came to oppose Canadian participation in WWI because the Conservative government under PM Robert BORDEN had announced the Dominion's entry without consulting Parliament. Such action, he feared, would strengthen the claim of both Canadian and British imperialists that Canada should automatically take part in all British wars. Bourassa became notorious in 1917 because both major parties used him as a symbol of extreme FRENCH CANADIAN NATIONALISM for their own political purposes. Liberal leader Wilfrid LAURIER was unwilling to agree to CONSCRIPTION because he was afraid of handing over Québec to Bourassa. Later in their victorious election campaign of that year, Borden's UNION GOVERNMENT warned that if the Liberals led by Laurier were elected, Bourassa would be the real ruler and would take Canada

out of the war. But this was the last time that Bourassa would be a serious factor in Canadian politics. Mackenzie King, who replaced Laurier as leader of the Liberal Party in 1919 and dominated the era between the wars, took up Bourassa's idea that the Canadian Parliament alone could declare war. He kept Canada legally neutral for 7 days after the British went to war against Germany in 1939, thus fulfilling the program first set out by Bourassa at the turn of the century.

Another side of Bourassa's nationalist program was his insistence that Canada ought to be an Anglo-French country. French culture must resist assimilation and have equal rights throughout the country. In 1905 he became publicly identified with what came to be called biculturalism in the 1960s through his unsuccessful campaign for Catholics to control their own schools in the new provinces of Saskatchewan and Alberta. He warned that the equality of cultures was an absolute condition for French Canadians to continue to accept Confederation. Later, after Ontario issued Regulation 17 in 1912 severely limiting the use of French as a language of instruction in elementary schools, Bourassa opposed the measure before English audiences as well as French (*see* ONTARIO SCHOOLS QUESTION). He only called off his campaign in Sept 1916 when the pope counselled moderation in the struggle for Franco-Ontario rights. But it was not until the late 1920s that this offensive regulation was repealed.

In the early 1920s Bourassa found his conception of a Canadian nation, one that would be Anglo-French in nature, under attack by Québec nationalists led by Abbé GROULX. In 1922 Groulx raised, in a tentative and theoretical way, the idea of a separate Laurentian state as a desirable goal for French-speaking Quebeckers. Bourassa vehemently opposed even this vague ideal of a separate state, and his prestige was such that he was virtually able to deny it respectability.

Although his nationalist program had the greatest political impact, Bourassa believed that his most important work was to help his people be a beacon of light for Catholicism in N America. His greatest ambition was to prevent the Americanization of Canada and resist placing the accumulation of wealth above the worship of God as the dominant value of Canadian society. Although he accepted private property as essential to man's liberty, he believed that in economic matters the public good should prevail.

He was much troubled by the coming of big industry. He believed that the profit of a large enterprise was immoral but that of a small firm, comprising perhaps 5 or 10 people, was legitimate. He always considered small businessmen as the social class that by instinct and interest was best prepared to conserve Catholic values. He seems to have thought that the growth of big business was due not to economic efficiency but to greed, and that if Catholic teachings were accepted, this trend might be halted or reversed. Occasionally, he dreamed that society would revert back to one in which the rural sector was all important and the economy was one of small firms. This viewpoint was an important reason for his inability to develop a realistic program to regulate the powerful influence of big business in economic life.

JOSEPH LEVITT

Bourassa, Napoléon, sculptor, architect, author, painter (b at L'Acadie, LC 21 Oct 1827; d at Lachenaie, Qué 27 Aug 1916). One of the finest Canadian artists of the 19th century, as is evident from his drawings, portraits and murals, and his architecture, Bourassa was influenced by the French neoclassicist, Ingres, and by historic painting. His most complete work was for the Notre-Dame de Lourdes Church, Montréal,

though the Montebello Church and the St-Hyacinthe Dominican Convent are also fine examples of his architecture. Other major projects, never completed or now destroyed, included decorative work for the Nazareth Chapel, Montréal, the St-Hyacinthe Cathedral, and the Apothéose de Christophe Colomb. He taught drawing for many years and Louis-Philippe HÉBERT, Olindo Gratton and Édouard Meloche were among his students. His correspondence and lectures are valuable documents deserving publication. He became vice-president of the Canadian Academy of Fine Arts on 6 Mar 1880.

RAYMOND VÉZINA

Bourassa, Robert, politician, premier of Québec (b at Montréal 14 July 1933). Admitted to the Québec Bar in 1957, and a graduate of Oxford (1959), he was successively (1960-66) fiscal adviser to the Dept of National Revenue, a professor at U of Ottawa, Laval and U de M, and research director for the Bélanger Commission on fiscal policy. He was elected MNA for Mercier in the Québec provincial elections of 1966.

Despite his youth, Bourassa was chosen to succeed Jean LESAGE as leader of the Québec Liberal Party in Jan 1970 and became premier after the Liberal victory in April 1970. In 1968 he had been a prime instigator of the party's decision to reject the constitutional proposals of René LÉVESQUE. Immediately after becoming premier he was faced with the OCTOBER CRISIS and the FRONT DE LIBERATION DU QUÉBEC agitations. Although he was re-elected in 1973 with a majority of 102 of 110 seats, his second term saw a weakening of Québec's position within Confederation, caused in part by his refusal to sign the constitutional agreement reached in Victoria in 1971. By 1976 his government was in ruins, amid accusations of scandal and corruption. The party lost the 1976 election to the Parti Québécois; Bourassa himself was defeated. After a long stay abroad, he returned to support the *Non* side during the 1980 REFERENDUM campaign. He was re-elected leader of the Liberals in the fall of 1983, replacing Claude RYAN. Although he personally failed to gain a seat in the riding of Bertrand in the provincial election

Robert Bourassa, premier of Québec, 1970-76. He resigned the leadership after his party's defeat by the PQ but made a remarkable political comeback, becoming leader of the Québec Liberals again in 1983 and premier again in Dec 1986 (*photo by Bernard Brault/Reflexion*).

of 2 Dec 1986, he led his party to a sweeping victory over the Parti Québécois. He was subsequently elected (Jan 20) in the riding of St Laurent. As premier, he was instrumental in negotiating the terms of the MEECH LAKE ACCORD and strongly supported Mulroney's FREE TRADE deal with the US.

DANIEL LATOUCHE

Bourdon, Rosario, né Joseph Charles, conductor, cellist, record-company executive (b at Longueuil, Qué 6 Mar 1885; d at New York City, NY 24 Apr 1961). Bourdon toured Europe as a child prodigy and enjoyed early success as an orchestral cellist and recitalist in Canada and the US. In 1909 he began a versatile career with the Victor Talking Machine Co. As cellist or piano accompanist he appeared on recordings with many famous artists. As Victor's music director until 1931 he conducted its house orchestras and Sousa's band, and in 1923 also became music director for NBC radio.

BARCLAY McMILLAN

Bourgault, Pierre, journalist, politician, professor (b at East-Angus, Qué 23 Jan 1934). After a career as a radio and TV announcer and actor, he joined the Rassemblement pour l'indépendance nationale (RIN), becoming its president in 1964. A formidable orator, he used every avenue to promote and popularize the idea of political independence for Québec. The RIN won almost 6% of the vote in the 1966 elections and in 1968 agreed to merge with the PARTI QUÉBÉCOIS. For a while a member of the PQ's national executive, Bourgault slowly withdrew from active political life. Since 1976 he has been a professor of communications at UQAM.

Bourgeau, Eugène, botanical collector (b at Brizon, France 20 Apr 1813; d at Paris, France Feb 1877). His interest in plants began early and as a young man he attracted the interest of the director of the Botanical Gardens at Lyons, where he learned the rudiments of botany. He collected plants in the Canary Is, Spain, North Africa and Algeria. In 1857 he was appointed collector to the British North American Exploring Expedition under John PALLISER. His enthusiasm and ability to co-operate with others drew praise from Palliser. During the expedition (1857-60) Bourgeau collected some 1200 species from western Canada.

ERIC J. HOLMGREN

Bourgeois, according to an 18th-century writer, were not nobles, ecclesiastics or magistrates, but city dwellers who "nevertheless by their properties, by their riches, by the honorable employments which adorn them and by their commerce are above the artisans and what is called the people." By extension, it meant the owner of a ship, the man who gave artisans work and, in Canadian usage, the fur trader employing hired men. *See also* FUR TRADE.

DALE MIQUELON

Bourgeoys, Marguerite, founder of the Congrégation de Notre-Dame de Montréal (b at Troyes, France 17 Apr 1620; d at Montréal 12 Jan 1700; canonized 31 Oct 1982). In 1640 Marguerite Bourgeoys joined a noncloistered congregation of teachers attached to a Troyes convent directed by the sister of Governor Maisonneuve of VILLE-MARIE (Montréal); she sailed for Canada in 1657 and a year later opened a girls' school in a stable on Pointe St-Charles. Besides chaperoning girls sent from France as brides for settlers (FILLES DU ROI), she recruited French and Canadian girls as teachers, organized a boarding school for girls in Montréal, a school for Indian girls on the Sulpician reserve of La Montagne, and a domestic arts school. Her "sisters" began teaching in rural parishes. Bishop LAVAL refused to permit them to take vows, but his successor Bishop SAINT-VALLIER invited them to open a school on the Île

Marguerite Bourgeoys, founder of the Congrégation de Notre-Dame de Montréal. Already revered as a saint when she died in 1700, she was canonized in 1982 *(courtesy National Archives of Canada/C-12340).*

d'Orléans. Soon they had a domestic arts school and a primary school in Québec City. On 1 July 1698 the secular sisters took simple vows and became a recognized noncloistered religious community. Marguerite Bourgeoys spent her last 2 years in meditation and prayer, already revered as a saint by the colonists when she died. *See also* SAINTS.

CORNELIUS J. JAENEN

Bourget, Ignace, second Roman Catholic bishop of Montréal (b at Lauzon, Qué 30 Oct 1799; d at Sault-au-Récollet, Qué 8 June 1885). Bourget studied theology and taught at the Séminaire de Nicolet for 3 years before being appointed secretary to Bishop Jean-Jacques Lartigue in 1821, who ordained him in 1822. Energetic, a tireless worker and possessing good judgement, Bourget gained the confidence of his superior who placed him in charge of construction of the bishop's palace and St-Jacques Cathedral. Bourget saw both completed by 1825. Lartigue recommended Bourget to Rome and on 25 July 1837 Bourget was installed as his coadjutor with right of succession, which took effect at Lartigue's death on 19 April 1840. His vast diocese covered the area from the American border to James Bay and encompassed the 22 000 Roman Catholics of Montréal, 79 parishes, 34 mission churches and 4 Indian missions; in all a population of 186 244 souls. Faced with a task that would have discouraged anyone else, the new bishop assigned the training of future priests to the Sulpicians and established a newspaper, *Les Mélanges religieux*, to spread "good principles." His greatest achievement lay in persuading French religious orders to come from Europe to help promote the "Christianization" of his diocesans. In addition, he supplemented their efforts with the work of indigenous religious institutions that he either inspired or founded. Under Bourget's leadership, the clerical hold on the population of the Montréal diocese increased over the years. Male and female religious orders were given an increasingly important role in both elementary education and the classical colleges that he personally directed; hospitals and charitable organizations were also administered by religious orders.

The activity inspired by Bourget met with a heated reaction from the sector of the lower middle class that had been converted to the liberal principles of the INSTITUT CANADIEN and the democratic PARTI ROUGE. Two ideological groups struggled to be the dominant influence on French Canadian society. Bourget led the ultramontanes who maintained that the state should be linked to and dominated by the church (*see* ULTRAMONTANISM), while his liberal opponents demanded separation of church and state, and the exclusion of the clergy from politics. After 30 years of struggle, which culminated in the GUIBORD AFFAIR, victory went to Bourget who repeatedly attacked the Institut until it was virtually annihilated by 1885.

No other Canadian bishop of the time was as attentive to the directives from Rome or as fervent a supporter of the papal cult. Bourget's zeal inspired the raising of 507 ZOUAVES, who from 1868 to 1870 were sent from his diocese to defend the papal state. Despite his attachment to Rome, Bourget did not always obtain the support of the religious orders. In addition to his struggle with the Sulpicians over the subdivision of the parish of Notre-Dame, his most significant failure lay in his efforts to obtain an independent university in Montréal. Following pressure from the Séminaire and the archbishop of Québec, Rome agreed only to the establishment of a "satellite" of U Laval. This failure, and the controversy surrounding ultramontane involvement in politics, led to Bourget's resignation as bishop of Montréal in Sept 1876. In poor health, he celebrated his diamond sacerdotal anniversary on 9 Nov 1882 and retired from public life.

The monument erected in Bourget's honour in the centre of the memorial chapel of bishops and archbishops of Montréal is a symbol of the role he played in the history of the diocese. Current historiography is increasingly critical of his religious and political views. But despite his shortcomings, his achievements make him one of the great architects of Québec society.

PHILIPPE SYLVAIN

Bourinot, Sir John George, writer, historian (b at Sydney, NS 24 Oct 1837; d at Ottawa 13 Oct 1902). Bourinot graduated from Toronto's Trinity University in 1857 and then settled in Halifax, where he founded the *Herald* and became its editor. He joined the HANSARD staff in Ottawa in 1868 and in 1873 was appointed assistant clerk to the House of Commons, becoming chief clerk in 1880. One of a number of Canadian intellectuals attracted to Ottawa following Confederation, Bourinot avidly sought to define the character of the new country. He became a leading expert on Canadian government and history, writing a number of books, including *How Canada is Governed* and *Parliamentary Procedure and Practice.* A founder of the ROYAL SOCIETY OF CANADA, he was its president in 1892.

C.J. TAYLOR

Bourinot's Rules *Parliamentary Procedure and Practice with an Introductory Account of the Origin and Growth of Parliamentary Institutions in the Dominion of Canada,* by Sir John George BOURINOT, Clerk of the Canadian House of Commons, was published in 1884, with 3 later editions – 1892, 1903 and 1916. It was the first Canadian book on the subject, and is still the basic authority on PARLIAMENTARY PROCEDURE. Arthur Beauchesne's later work is a handbook for ready reference by MPs. Bourinot also produced (1894) *A Canadian Manual of Procedure at Public Meetings* (2 later eds 1963 and 1977).

EUGENE A. FORSEY

Bourns, Arthur Newcombe, professor of chemistry, university administrator (b at Petitcodiac, NB 8 Dec 1919). Educated at Acadia and McGill (PhD, chemistry), he began teaching at Acadia and Saskatoon and continued at McMaster for 35 years. An inspiring teacher and a researcher internationally known for his contributions to physical organic chemistry, he also showed exceptional administrative skills. He became successively graduate studies dean, department chairman, VP and president (1972-80). In times particularly difficult for university presidents, he gave strong leadership marked by sound judgement, fair-mindedness and breadth of understanding and concern. These qualities brought appointment to scores of important scientific and educational bodies. He has acted as a scientific and educational adviser to governments in Canada and abroad (eg, since 1985 as chairman of the International Advisory Panel – Canada, US, Britain – advising Chinese government and university officials on the development of China's universities). L.H. CRAGG

Bousfield, Edward Lloyd, invertebrate zoologist (b at Penticton, BC 19 Jun 1926). An authority on amphipod crustaceans, marine biogeography and a fellow of the RSC, Bousfield has been at the National Museums of Canada (National Museum of Natural Sciences) since 1950 as invertebrate zoologist, as chief zoologist (1964-74) and since 1974 as senior scientist. Educated at U of T and U of Toronto under A.G. HUNTSMAN and at Harvard (PhD 1954), his early work was on barnacle ecology. Since the early 1950s he has studied the taxonomy and distribution of invertebrates on collecting expeditions all over Canada, in Alaska, on southern US coasts, in the Pacific, and on the HUDSON 70 EXPEDITION. Bousfield has described dozens of new species and made major revisions of amphipod classification. His studies of the taxonomy and distribution of Canadian marine animals are major contributions to knowledge of the country's fauna. In 1985 Bousfield received the government of Canada's Outstanding Achievement Award. ERIC L. MILLS

Boutroue d'Aubigny, Claude de, chevalier, INTENDANT of New France 1668-70 (b at Paris, France 1620; d in France 1680). A Parisian judge and member of the *noblesse de robe,* Boutroue served as intendant of Canada between Jean TALON's first and second terms. He was reported to be assiduous in his duties and attempted to suppress the brandy trade with the Indians. Though he quarrelled with the governor, Rémy de COURCELLE, Boutroue continued to enjoy the patronage of Colbert, the French minister in charge of colonies. ALLAN GREER

Bovell, James, physician, educator, clergyman (b in Barbados 28 Oct 1817; d at Charlestown, Nevis, W Indies 15 Jan 1880). Bovell studied medicine at London, Edinburgh, Glasgow and Dublin. Licensed in 1839 by the Royal Coll of Physicians, London, he immigrated to Toronto in 1848, becoming prominent as a physician-educator, devout high churchman and synodical secretary. In Nov 1850, with Edward Hodder and other prominent physicians, all ardent churchmen, Bovell offered to John STRACHAN, Bishop of Toronto, the recently organized Upper Canada College of Medicine as the medical faculty of the new Trinity College. Bovell was dean of Trinity College's medical school from 1851 until 1856, when the school dissolved following disputes with Bishop Strachan and his council. Bovell then lectured in physiology at the Toronto School of Medicine and (after 1864) at Upper Canada Veterinary Coll. He co-founded a professional journal, published medical articles and religious works, denounced inebriety and cholera-promoting filth. Bovell practised microscopy at Trinity Coll School with warden William Arthur Johnson and William OSLER, head prefect in 1866, whom he profoundly influenced. Returning to the W Indies in 1871, Bovell was ordained in 1871 and served various Anglican parishes before a stroke incapacitated him. C.E. DOLMAN

Bow River, 644 km, rises in Bow Lk, fed by glacial meltwater from the Bow Glacier (Wapta Icefield) in the Waputik Mts in Banff National Park, Alta. It flows S and E from the Rockies through BANFF townsite and CALGARY to join the OLDMAN R, forming 2 main tributaries of the S SASKATCHEWAN R in Alberta. It drains an area of 25 300 km², encompassing a wide variety of physiographic and vegetational regions, from alpine ice fields and tundra, through dense conifer forest and aspen parkland, to semiarid shortgrass prairie. Several dams have been built in its middle and lower reaches for hydroelectric power (325 MW developed), flood control and irrigation. Calgary, the Eastern and Western Irrigation Districts and the Bow R Development are important beneficiaries. The name may derive from a Cree word referring to the good bow-making wood along its banks. IAN A. CAMPBELL

Sir Mackenzie Bowell
Fifth Prime Minister of Canada

Birth: 27 Dec 1823, Rickinghall, Eng
Father/Mother: John/Elizabeth Marshall
Father's Occupation: Carpenter-contractor
Education: Apprenticeship
Religious Affiliation: Methodist
First Occupation: Printer
Last Private Occupation: Editor
Political Party: Conservative
Period(s) as PM: 21 Dec 1894 - 27 Apr 1896
Ridings: North Hastings, Ont, 1867-92
Other Ministries: Customs 1878-91, Militia 1891-92, Trade and Commerce 1892-94
Marriage: 4 Dec 1847 to Harriet Moore (1829-84)
Children: 4 boys, 5 girls
Died: 10 Dec 1917 in Belleville
Cause of Death at Age: Pneumonia at 93
Burial Place: Belleville Cemetery, Belleville, Ont
Other Information: Second senator to become PM; Senator 1892; KCMG, 1895; Grandmaster of Orange Order of BNA 1870-78

(*photo courtesy National Archives of Canada/PA-27161*)

Bowell, Sir Mackenzie, prime minister of Canada, 1894-96 (b at Rickinghall, Eng 27 Dec 1823; d at Belleville, Ont 10 Dec 1917). Editor and owner of the Belleville *Intelligencer* and an active Orangeman, Bowell was first elected as a Conservative to the House of Commons in 1867, representing North Hastings until 1892 when he became a senator, retiring finally in 1906. Bowell held several important Cabinet

portfolios before he became PM in 1894 after the death of Sir John THOMPSON. But dissatisfaction with his leadership, particularly over such issues as the MANITOBA SCHOOLS QUESTION, soon forced his resignation on 27 Apr 1896. He was succeeded by Sir Charles TUPPER, who actually led the Tories to defeat in 1896. Although Bowell was not politically active after his resignation, he led the Opposition in the Senate 1896-1906. J.M. BUMSTED

Bowering, George, poet, fiction writer, editor, critic (b at Penticton, BC 1 Dec 1935). Although recognized as one of the foremost Canadian writers of his generation, Bowering has yet to receive the critical attention his large and varied body of work deserves. After RCAF service, Bowering attended UBC, where with Frank Davey, David Dawson, James Reid, Fred WAH and others he studied the new poetics of Creeley, Duncan and Olson, and founded the poetry newsletter *Tish.* He taught in Calgary, London and Montréal before returning to Vancouver to teach at SFU. He founded *Imago* (1964-74) and is a contributing editor to *Open Letter.* A prolific writer, whose poetry, both lyric and extended, seeks to capture flux in the rhythms of its open structures, and whose fiction seeks to subvert realist conventions through self-conscious textual invention, Bowering has published over 40 books. A witty sense of play animates his vision in them all. His poetry includes *Rocky Mountain Foot* (1969) and *The Gangs of Kosmos* (1969), for which he won his first Gov Gen's Award; *The Catch* (1976), *Selected Poems: Particular Accidents* (1980), *West Window* (1982), *Kerrisdale Elegies* (1984) and *Delayed Mercy and Other Poems* (1987). Of his fiction, *A Short Sad Book* (1977), *Burning Water* (1980), a novel about George VANCOUVER's voyages of discovery, for which he won his second Gov Gen's Award, and *Caprice* (1987) stand out. He has also published 3 collections of critical essays: *A Way with Words* (1982), *The Mask in Place* (1983) and *Craft Slices* (1985). The best introduction to his work is Robin Blaser's essay in *Particular Accidents.* DOUGLAS BARBOUR

Bowling, Indoor, game in which a player attempts to knock down pins by propelling a ball down a wooden lane. Similar games were played as early as 5000 BC in Egypt. The 10-pin version was developed in the US in the 19th century; and 5-pin bowling was invented in Canada in 1908 or 1909 by Thomas F. RYAN. Ryan owned a 10-pin bowling club in downtown Toronto, and tried a number of experiments to regain the interest of his elite patrons, who found the 10-pin ball too heavy and the game too strenuous. Finally, he had his father shave a regulation pin on a lathe, placed 5 of these pins on the 10-pin floor, and introduced the use of a duckpin ball (roughly 2 kg in weight and 13 cm in diameter). Ryan then developed a scoring system in which the pins were numbered from 1 to 5, making it possible to score 15 points if all pins were bowled over in each player's turn (called a frame). The player was allowed 3 balls per turn. In order to add a challenge to the game, Ryan made it obligatory to knock down the left corner pin (4 pin) before the player could be awarded any points. With 3 balls per frame and 10 frames per game, the player aimed at a perfect score of 450 points. Since the pins were very light, they easily flew through the air following contact with the ball, and the game was far noisier than before. In 1912, Ryan solved both problems by adding a thick rubber band to the belly of the pin, a feature still used today. Five-pin bowling soon became one of the most popular sports in Canada and the northern US. The first international competition was held in 1913.

In 1918, Alfred Shrubb bowled the first 400 game, and in 1921, Bill Bromfield became the first player to score a perfect 450. In 1927, 500 bowlers gathered in Toronto's King Edward Hotel to found the Canadian Bowling Assn. Over the next few years, several governing groups were formed throughout the country, but in 1978 they amalgamated to form the Canadian 5-Pin Bowlers' Assn, which now serves over 250 000 members from coast to coast by organizing tournaments, providing instructional aids and granting awards. In 1956, Double Diamond, Ltd, invented a machine to set pins up automatically, thus replacing the "pinboy." The invention of a string pinsetter followed in 1963, reducing mechanical expenses and adding speed and smoothness to the game. The game remains essentially the same, and is played by more than 2 million Canadians in over 700 bowling centres each year. It is easy for children to play, and thousands of men and women participate annually in tournaments and in provincial, national and international championships. Five-pin bowling is Canada's own game and is the number-one participant sport in this country.

Ten-pin bowling has remained popular in Canada and it is now claimed to be the largest participation sport in the world. Several Canadians have excelled in international competition, notably Graydon Robinson of Toronto, who won the world championship in Tokyo, 1969; Ray Mitchell, originally from Alberta, who won the world's master championship in Hamburg, W Ger, 1972; Cathy Townsend of Montréal, who won the women's World Cup in Manila, 1975; and Jean Gordon of Vancouver and Ron Allenby of Ottawa who ranked high in the FIQ world championships in Helsinki in 1987. *See also* LAWN BOWLING.   A.G. HONG

Bowmanville, Ont, located 25 km E of Toronto on Highway 401. Originally called Darlington Mills, it was renamed in the 1820s after Charles Bowman, the principal landowner. Bowmanville was incorporated as a village in 1852 and as a town in 1857. In Jan 1974, Bowmanville became part of the town of NEWCASTLE (pop 34 073, 1986c) in the new Regional Municipality of Durham. Home of diverse manufacturers in the 19th century, the town now serves as a dormitory for Toronto and Oshawa. In WWII a local boys reformatory housed a prisoner-of-war camp. When German prisoners were handcuffed in retaliation for the cuffing of Canadians taken at Dieppe, a riot ensued which is known locally as the Battle of Bowmanville.   GERALD STORTZ

Bowring, Benjamin, silversmith, watchmaker, merchant (b in Devonshire, Eng 1778; d at Liverpool, Eng June 1846). One of a large number of Devonshire tradesmen who immigrated to St John's, Bowring first visited Newfoundland in 1811; in 1815 he sold his shop in Exeter and opened a store in St John's. A careful, prudent man, he avoided the bankruptcies endemic in Newfoundland between 1815 and 1840. By the late 1820s he had entered the general import trade of the colony and was speculating in the seal hunt. When his sons came of age in the 1830s, Bowring moved to the company's new head office in Liverpool. In 1839 he gave up active involvement in the company, which under his sons became known as "Bowring Brothers." His sons made the decisions that resulted in the family's great fortunes, but Benjamin, by moving to St John's and by careful and frugal management, gave them the base from which to start.

KEITH MATTHEWS

Bowser, William John, lawyer, politician, premier of BC (b at Rexton, NB 3 Dec 1867; d at Van-

couver 25 Oct 1933). A graduate of Dalhousie, Bowser moved to Vancouver in 1891 and practised law. First elected to the legislature in 1903 as a Conservative, he remained an MLA until his defeat in 1924. Attorney general from 1907, when he succeeded Sir Richard MCBRIDE as premier on 15 Dec 1915, Bowser inherited a divided party and an unpopular administration, and his government was soundly defeated in the 1916 provincial election. From 1916 to 1924 he led the Opposition. In 1933 he emerged from retirement to lead an independent nonpartisan group but died during the election campaign.

PATRICIA E. ROY

Boxing is a contest between 2 opponents wearing padded gloves who attempt to win by rendering their opponents unable to continue, or by winning a judge's decision at the end of a prearranged number of rounds. Boxers may hit only with their fists and from the waist up. Boxing as a sport was introduced by the Greeks in the OLYMPIC GAMES about 686 BC.

The first bouts in Canada were "bareknuckle" fights. Gloves began appearing regularly around the turn of the century, primarily to protect the fists of the boxer rather than the fighter being hit. It was not unusual for Canadian bouts before 1900 to be scheduled for 40 rounds. The early bouts with gloves were said to be governed by the Marquis of Queensbury rules, though many think that reference was made to the "Marquis" to give the sport respectability. Early Canadian boxing was governed by each province, many of which outlawed its existence. It was frequently claimed that police interfered only when bouts were not going the way the promoters intended. The military, especially in GARRISON TOWNS such as Halifax, could hold bouts; but with rare exceptions, such as the "Gentlemen's Sparring Club of Ottawa" in the 1880s, promoted fights were thought to be "outlaw" events. Canadian boxing began its climb to respectability in the 1890s. Today, despite the controversy that surrounds the sport because of its violence, boxing draws large crowds in many Canadian cities. Most of its competitors have come from less affluent sections of big cities such as Vancouver, Toronto and Montréal and from poorer areas such as the Maritimes. Sam LANGFORD, who was born in Weymouth, NS, has often been listed among the best heavyweights of all time. As a lightweight he beat the renowned Joe Gans of the US. Though weighing only 71 kg, he boxed 15 rounds with 84 kg Jack Johnson but was denied a title fight. Another Halifax fighter, George Dixon, is considered the greatest bantamweight boxer ever. He won the bantamweight title in London in 1890 and the featherweight championship the next year. Tommy BURNS from Hanover, Ont, and Jimmy MCLARNIN from Vancouver have also been world champions. Though never world champion, heavyweight George CHUVALO of Toronto held Canadian and Commonwealth titles and in a career in which he fought most of the great heavyweights was never knocked down. Yvonne Durelle, "the fighting fisherman" from Baie Ste Anne, NB, fought Archie Moore twice for the light-heavyweight championship of the world. Durelle knocked Moore down 4 times in the first fight but lost in 11 rounds.

The Canadian Amateur Boxing Assn oversees 10 provincial boxing associations and one from each of the territories. While most excellent Canadian amateurs eventually turn pro, many retain their amateur standing and aim for specific goals such as the Olympics or world amateur championships. Bert SCHNEIDER (1920) and Lefty GWYNNE (1932) were Olympic gold medal winners. Shawn O'SULLIVAN of Toronto gained

Canada's first world amateur boxing championship in 1981, winning the World Cup Amateur Boxing light-middleweight competition. O'Sullivan and Willie DE WIT, of Grande Prairie, Alta, won silver medals at the 1984 Los Angeles Olympics and went on to pro careers. In 1987 Michael Olajide, Jr, lost a bout that would have given him the World Boxing Assn title. Mathew HILTON of Montréal won the IBF Middleweight Title in Oct 1987, becoming the first Canadian world champion since Jackie Callura of Hamilton in 1943. Professional title bouts are governed by the Canadian Professional Boxing Federation, with local commissions controlling other professional boxing.   A.J. "SANDY" YOUNG

Boyd, Alfred, merchant, politician, premier of Manitoba, 1870-71 (d in Eng 1909). Described as a "native of Canada," Boyd was operating a general store at Red River prior to the troubles of 1869-70. He was elected to the Convention of Forty, which met on 28 Jan 1870 to decide the fate of the RED RIVER COLONY. In Sept 1870 he was appointed provincial secretary by Lt-Gov Adams George Archibald. Elected as MLA for St Andrew's N on 30 Dec 1870, he was appointed minister of public works and agriculture on 10 Jan 1871. He resigned 9 Dec 1871 to make way for a representation of the half-breed population and was succeeded by John NORQUAY. Boyd acquired considerable business and real-estate interests in Winnipeg before he settled in England about 1890.   LOVELL C. CLARK

Boyd, Edwin Alonzo, bank robber (b at Toronto 2 Apr 1914). The son of a Toronto policeman, Boyd hoboed across the country as a youth and had minor scrapes with the law during the Depression of the 1930s. He served with the Canadian Army in WWII but, failing to find adequate employment in the postwar years, he turned to crime. Operating at first as a lone bandit, then later with a gang, Boyd committed several daring bank robberies in the late 1940s and early 1950s, most of them in the Toronto area. His holdups and 2 spectacular escapes from the Don Jail brought him notoriety. On 6 Mar 1952, 2 members of the Boyd Gang, Steve Suchan and Leonard Jackson, killed Edmund Tong, a Toronto police detective, and were later hanged for the murder. Boyd was not involved in the homicide, but for his robberies and jail breaks he was sentenced on 16 Oct 1952 to life imprisonment. He was eventually paroled and retired to private life under a new identity.   EDWARD BUTTS

Reading: M. Lamb and B. Pearson, *The Boyd Gang* (1976).

Boyd, Liona, classical guitarist (b at London, Eng 11 July 1950). After moving to Toronto with her parents in 1958, Boyd began years of study with Eli Kassner, followed by 2 years with Alexandre Lagoya. Her first Canadian album, *The Guitar – Liona Boyd* (1974), sold more than 30 000 copies. She has a rare ability to play both the Segovia and Lagoya methods of fingering and is noted for extremely clean guitar interpretations. Boyd won a Juno Award in 1978. Her 1986 album, *Persona,* broadened her repertoire to "New Age" music.   ALLAN M. GOULD

Boyd, Mossom, lumberman (b in India 1814; d at Bobcaygeon, Ont 23 July 1883). A member of the Anglo-Irish gentry, Mossom Boyd emigrated to the Sturgeon Lk area of Upper Canada in 1834. He became assistant to Thomas Need, owner of the Bobcaygeon sawmill and took over the mill when Need returned to England in 1843. Boyd quickly developed it into a multifaceted lumbering enterprise with sawn-lumber sales in Albany, NY, local retail outlets in the Kawartha region and timber sales in Great Britain. By the 1870s Boyd's enterprise was among the largest in the region. An enthusiastic promoter of local economic development, Boyd was a constant proponent for the Trent Valley canal. After his death in 1883 the family business was run by Mossom Martin Boyd, who extended its operations to Québec and Vancouver I as well as moving into steamboating, stock raising and railway development. Mossom Martin Boyd is included in the Agricultural Hall of Fame for his work in developing the N American strain of polled Hereford beef cattle.

CHRISTOPHER G. CURTIS

Boyd, Rob, alpine skier (b at Vernon, BC 15 Feb 1966). A skier from age 3, he began competing at 11, and entered both national (Fleischmann Cup) and international (Nor-Am) competition at 14. Over the next few years he advanced from overall Fleischmann Cup winner in 1984, to an auspicious 10th-place finish in his first World Cup downhill at Val di Gardena, Italy, in Dec 1985, and a first-place tie in the season's Nor-Am downhill standings. His reputation for aggressive, all-out attack of even the most treacherous terrain was reinforced by a dramatic victory from 26th starting position on his second appearance on the demanding, icy Val di Gardena course in Dec 1986. At age 20, Boyd became the youngest male World Cup winner in over 10 years and a key member of a resurgent Canadian downhill team.

MURRAY SHAW

Boyd, William, pathologist, educator, author (b at Portsoy, Scot 21 June 1885; d at Toronto 10 Mar 1979). Bill Boyd obtained his medical degree in 1908 at Edinburgh and published his first book, *With a Field Ambulance at Ypres*, in 1916. He was professor of pathology at U Manitoba, 1915-37, U of T, 1937-51, and UBC, 1951-54. His first pathology textbook was *Surgical Pathology* (later called *Pathology for the Surgeon*), published in 1925. Later textbooks were *Pathology of Internal Disease* (1931; later called *Pathology for the Physician*), *Textbook of Pathology* (1932) and *An Introduction to Medical Science* (1937). His books were popular with students all over the world for their clarity, fine prose and infectious enthusiasm for the subject matter; translated into many languages, they ran into innumerable editions. He was greatly sought after as a speaker at scientific meetings and social occasions for he could capture his audience with wit and a fine delivery. He was made a Companion of the Order of Canada in 1968.

H.J. BARRIE

Boyd's Cove, in eastern NOTRE DAME BAY, Nfld, has been occupied intermittently for about 2000 years. BEOTHUK pit houses dated late 17th or early 18th century, have yielded diagnostic stone tools in association with European artifacts which have established a link between the Beothuk and their prehistoric ancestors. Faunal analysis indicates a late-winter to fall occupation and a subsistence pattern balanced between marine and land resources. Numerous fur-bearing animal remains and a number of trade beads hint at a fur trade. Other evidence, however, suggests that most European goods were stolen. Retaliation for such theft, and a growing white population, eventually forced the Beothuk away from sites such as Boyd's Cove and into the interior, where, hungry and sick, they became extinct in the early 19th century. *See also* ARCHAEOLOGY. RALPH T. PASTORE

Boyle, David, blacksmith, teacher, archaeologist, museologist, historian (b at Greenock, Scot 1 May 1842; d at Toronto 14 Feb 1911). Although apprenticed as a blacksmith on arriving in Canada in 1856, Boyle became internationally prominent as Canada's premier archaeologist before WWI. Motivated by the artisan self-improvement ethic, he became a rural Ontario teacher in 1865

and a principal in Elora (1871-81). He was a practitioner of the radical child-centered theories and methods of Swiss educator Johann Pestalozzi. Subsequently, Boyle became curator-archaeologist of the Canadian Institute Museum (1884-96) and the Ontario Provincial Museum (1886-1911), laying the groundwork for development of Ontario ARCHAEOLOGY as a systematic and scientific discipline. From 1887 to 1911 he published his *Annual Archaeological Reports for Ontario*, the first Canadian periodical devoted primarily to the study of the archaeological record. Boyle was also an avid history buff and preservationist and the author of a book of nonsense poetry for children.

GERALD KILLAN

Boyle, Harry J., broadcaster, author (b at St Augustine, Ont 7 Oct 1915). He worked alternately as a free-lance writer and radio reporter in southwestern Ontario before joining the CBC in Toronto in 1942. He held various positions, including radio producer and department head, at the CBC until 1968, when he left to take a seat on the CANADIAN RADIO-TELEVISION AND TELECOMMUNICATIONS COMMISSION. He has published several collections of light essays and a number of realistic yet nostalgic novels, such as *The Great Canadian Novel* (1972) and *The Luck of the Irish* (1975).

Boyle, John Bernard, painter (b at London, Ont 23 Sept 1941). Self-taught, Boyle, whose aim in youth was to be a writer, began painting around 1962 with the support of friends Greg CURNOE and Jack CHAMBERS. Boyle favours primary colours and bold handling. His work, which includes heavily painted portraits, often huge, of well-known Canadian figures such as Tom THOMSON, POUNDMAKER and Stephen LEACOCK, express his determined Canadian nationalism. He has also experimented with baked porcelain on steel. His paintings of the male and female nude (often himself or his wife) are as bold as any in contemporary art.

JOAN MURRAY

Boyle, Joseph Whiteside, "Klondike Joe," mining entrepreneur, adventurer (b at Toronto 6 Nov 1867; d at London, Eng 14 Apr 1923). As a youth he spent 3 years at sea as a deckhand. He settled in New York where he started a feed and freighting business, and was married and divorced. He began managing Australian boxer Frank Slavin in 1897, touring Toronto, San Francisco and Victoria. They heard of the KLONDIKE GOLD RUSH while in Juneau, Alaska, and were among the first group of gold seekers to cross WHITE PASS. It was Boyle who opened the trail to Lk Bennet and Lk Tutshi. He and Slavin filed a claim of 8 mi (13.3 km) along the Klondike R, but Boyle immediately realized that success would depend on a large-scale operation. He lobbied in Ottawa for a concession to dredge, finally achieving it in 1900. Meanwhile, he established a profitable sawmill, docks and wharfs. In 1904 he formed the Canadian Klondike Mining Co and by 1910 had massive dredging equipment in operation, as well as a hydroelectric plant (May 1911). He was embroiled in law suits, territorial disputes, local politics and in 1905 he led a team (Klondike Wanderers) to challenge for the STANLEY CUP (they lost).

At the outbreak of WWI Boyle raised his own machine-gun unit and was made an honorary colonel. He left for England in 1916 and, after lobbying to get into the action, was sent to Russia to organize the railway system. After the Bolshevik takeover he was appointed chairman of the All-Russian Food Board, responsible for the collection and distribution of food. After clearing the congestion of 10 000 cars around Moscow, his reputation for extraordinary action spread. He was entrusted with returning the national archive and paper currency (likely not the crown jewels,

as has been claimed) to Roumania and had to run a Russian blockade to achieve it. He was a trusted emissary between Roumania and the Bolsheviks, and succeeding in getting a peace treaty signed. On yet another venture he secured the escape of 54 Roumanian prisoners being kept as hostages at Sevastopol. He was meanwhile supplying intelligence to the British and French, as well as working tirelessly for the relief of the destitute Roumanian people. After the war he worked to rehabilitate the Roumanian oil industry and managed a brief Canadian aid mission. Boyle's efforts made him a national hero in Roumania and he became the confidant, friend and possibly the lover of Queen Marie, who described him succinctly as "frightened of nothing and who, by his extraordinary force of will and fearlessness, gets through everywhere." Boyle left Roumania after 2 years of action that had exhausted him to the point of death. He was awarded the Order of St Anne and the Order of St Vladimir by Russia, the Croix de Guerre by France, DSO by Britain, and the Crown of Roumania, the Star of Roumania and the Grand Cross by Roumania. His remarkable career in eastern Europe went unrecognized in Canada. Like many men of remarkable achievement he was held in suspicion for his independence.

JAMES MARSH

Boyle, Robert William, physicist (b at Carbonear, Nfld 2 Oct 1883; d at London, Eng 18 Apr 1955). The first PhD in physics from McGill (1909), Boyle is best known for his work on the properties of ultrasonic waves and his contribution to the development of an echo method for detecting submarines during WWI. He began research on the radioactivity of RADIUM under Sir Ernest RUTHERFORD at McGill and continued his work in Manchester, Eng, 1909-11. In 1912 he became head of physics at U of A and started research on ultrasonics. During WWII he supervised research on radar at the NATIONAL RESEARCH COUNCIL. He was elected to the RSC in 1921 and awarded the Flavelle Medal in 1940. He was director of physics at the NRC, 1929-48.

YVES GINGRAS

Boys and Girls Clubs of Canada, the national organization representing all Boys and Girls Clubs across Canada. The Canadian movement began in Saint John, NB, in 1900. The organization's main goal is "to enhance the quality of life for youth," especially the socially and economically disadvantaged; there are 119 units operating in 67 communities in the 10 provinces. About 330 professional staff and 7000 volunteers administer club programs involving some 50 000 young Canadians 5-19 years of age. Programs include arts and crafts, sports and fitness, junior leadership training, prevention of alcohol and drug abuse, and after-school and lunch-time latchkey facilities. Funding comes from corporate sponsors, foundations and the federal government; a board of directors provides administration and Gov Gen Jeanne SAUVÉ is the honorary patron.

Bracebridge, Ont, Town, pop 9811 (1986c), located in the DM of Muskoka, on the north branch of the Muskoka R. In 1860 J.S. Dennis brought his survey party by canoe to the vicinity of the falls. The location was advantageous as a convenient crossing (a rough hewn bridge was built close to the falls) and as a source of water-power. The first inhabitants were an advance party working on the Muskoka Rd. In 1864 North Falls, as it was called, was renamed by W.D. LESUEUR, the secretary of the PO, likely from the novel by Washington Irving *Bracebridge Hall* that also gave its name to Gravenhurst. Bracebridge was incorporated as a village in 1875; by 1889, when it acquired town status, the population had risen to 1600 and industries included 2 large tanneries (using local hemlock for tanning hides), a grist mill, a woolen mill, a flour mill and a sawmill – all taking advantage of the ample water power. In 1865-66 the first steamboat, the *Wenonah*, was built, and there was stagecoach service to Parry Sd. The railway first arrived in 1886. Bracebridge's first newspaper was the *Northern Advocate*; the present newspaper, the *Herald Gazette*, dates from 1872. Bracebridge was amalgamated with parts of 3 other townships and annexed parts of 3 others to form the Town of Bracebridge Area Municipality. The town contains the courthouse, registry and administration building for the DM. Present manufacturing industries include agriculture equipment, aluminum foil, cement, lumber and steel products. Bracebridge also shares in the tourist industry of the region.

On 1 Oct 1894, the town took possession of a private electric generator constructed on the Upper Falls in 1892, becoming the first municipality in Ontario to own and operate a water-power electric-generating station. A second plant was opened at the foot of the lower falls in 1902 and with 2 other plants upstream continues to supply the town with power.

Brachiopoda, phylum of bivalved marine INVERTEBRATES, sometimes called lamp shells. Brachiopods attach to the seabed by a stalk and feed on particles caught in currents that are generated by their ciliated crown of tentacles (lophophore). The approximately 260 living species are relicts of some 30 000 FOSSIL forms which inhabited Continental Shelf areas, especially during the Paleozoic era (570-245 million years ago). They are important to geologists in establishing stratigraphic sequences useful in oil exploration and in determining shorelines and depths of ancient seas. The living genus *Lingula* differs little from a Cambrian fossil relative more than 500 million years old. Brachiopodlike forms are represented in the BURGESS SHALE, BC. *See also* GEOLOGY; LOPHOPHORATE; PALEONTOLOGY. J.R. NURSALL

Bracken, John, politician, premier of Man (b at Ellisville, Ont 22 June 1883; d at Ottawa 18 March 1969). A graduate of the Ontario Agricultural College, he worked for federal and provincial governments in the West until 1910, when he became a professor of field husbandry at U Sask. In 1920 he moved to Manitoba Agricultural College, joined the Progressive movement, and at the request of the elected members became premier at the head of a United Farmers of Manitoba government in 1922. For the next 2 decades he led a careful government, dealing as well as anyone could in a province with limited financial resources with the problems of the Great Depression. In 1942, although he had become close to the Liberals, the Conservative Party called on him to be leader, a task he accepted on condition the party add "Progressive" to its name. Bracken's appeal was limited, in part because of a halting speaking manner and his unwise decision to remain out of Parliament for almost 3 years. In 1945 he led the party to defeat and he resigned in 1948. J.L. GRANATSTEIN

Reading: J. Kendle, *John Bracken* (1979).

Brady, James Patrick, prospector, MÉTIS leader (b at Lac St Vincent, Alta 11 Mar 1908; disappeared in the Foster Lks area, Sask, after 7 June 1967). A grandson of one of Riel's soldiers, self-educated in politics and history, Brady became a leader among the Métis of northern Alberta and Saskatchewan. A disciple of the radical politics of the 1930s and a lifelong communist, he directed his political energies on behalf of the Métis,

trying in vain to persuade the CCF in Saskatchewan to implement progressive native policies. He was a major figure in the Association des Métis d'Alberta et des Territoires du Nord-Ouest and a patient and influential political teacher. He disappeared on a prospecting trip. MURRAY DOBBIN

Braithwaite, Max, novelist, story writer, juvenile writer, humorist (b at Nokomis, Sask 7 Dec 1911). One of 8 children, he was raised in Prince Albert and Saskatoon, and educated at U of Saskatchewan. He taught in rural and continuation schools from 1933 to 1940 when he joined the navy and was sent to Toronto with the Royal Canadian Volunteer Services. Discharged in 1945, he remained in Ontario and worked as a free-lance writer. During his 40-year career of steady writing, he has written plays for radio and television, scripts for theatre and film, contributed articles to major Canadian magazines and produced 25 books. Samples of his lighthearted writing are collected in *Max: The Best of Braithwaite* (1983). He is best known for *Why Shoot the Teacher?* (1965), an autobiographical novel which tells, with humour and compassion, of his fledgling teaching experiences in a Saskatchewan one-room school during the Depression. The novel was made into an award-winning film of the same title in 1977, and is part of a trilogy – *Never Sleep Three in a Bed* (1969), and *The Night We Stole the Mountie's Car* (1971), which won the Leacock Memorial Medal for Humour in 1972. In *All the Way Home* (1986), Braithwaite once again explores the coming of age on the poverty-stricken and desolate prairies. Braithwaite is the recipient of an honorary degree from the University of Calgary. DONNA COATES

Brampton, Ont, City, pop 188 498 (1986c), 149 030 (1981c). Located on the Etobicoke R 32 km NW of Toronto, it was established as a crossroads hamlet in the 1830s. It was originally called Buffy's Corners and was renamed for a town in Cumberland, Eng, when it was incorporated as a village in 1853. Economic development was spurred by the arrival of the GRAND TRUNK RY in 1856. Brampton was chosen county seat of Peel County in 1867 and was incorporated as a town in 1873. The horticultural business was begun in 1860 and remains important today, along with a number of manufacturing industries. Brampton is the birthplace and home of longtime Ontario premier, William DAVIS.

Brandon, Man, City, pop 38 708 (1986c), 36 242 (1981c), inc 1882, the province's second-largest city and economic hub of its SW region, is located on the ASSINIBOINE R, 200 km W of Winnipeg. It is governed by a mayor and 10 aldermen.

History From 1793 to 1832, 3 HBC posts – each called Brandon House after the duke of Brandon, an ancestor of Lord Selkirk – were established in the Brandon area. Permanent settlement began in the late 1870s at Grand Valley, 3 km E, and the Brandon Hills. Ontario and Maritime Protestants were among the first arrivals, followed by British and American immigrants. Brandon became a divisional point on the CPR in 1881, and soon was the transportation, distribution, service and trade centre for the surrounding hinterland. Industry also had an early role in the economy as manufactured goods were produced

in the 1880s and 1890s. Brandon was a judicial and regional medical centre and, by the end of the 19th century, had a federal agricultural research station, provincial jail, mental hospital, school of nursing, industrial school for Indians, and Baptist-sponsored Brandon College (post-secondary).

After WWI, labour unrest and unfavourable economic conditions occurred. Both the city and Brandon College faced financial crises. During WWII thousands of armed-forces personnel trained in the city or at nearby Shilo and Commonwealth air schools. Following the war, economic and physical growth was steady. Brandon College became a provincial university in 1967 (*see* BRANDON UNIVERSITY); Assiniboine Community College was established; petrochemical manufacturers set up plants; a regional library, arts centre and museums were developed; and facilities such as the Keystone arena-convention complex were built.

Economy Agriculture, commerce, health care and administration are the economic mainstays of Brandon. Important industries include petrochemicals, processed foods, metal products, woolens, electrical and farm equipment and publishing. Medical and educational institutions, the CPR, CNR and government agencies are among the major employers. Brandon's regional trade population extends to Portage la Prairie, eastern Saskatchewan, the international boundary and Dauphin.

Cityscape Brandon has ready access to some of Manitoba's most attractive natural recreation areas – Spruce Woods Provincial Forest and Park to the E, Turtle Mtn Provincial Park (S), Riding Mtn National Park (N) and Brandon Hills Wildlife Management Area. In 1979 the city hosted the Canada Winter Games. It also is known for its agricultural shows – the Royal Manitoba Winter Fair, the Provincial Exhibition of Manitoba and the Ag-Ex, Manitoba's largest livestock show and sale. Brandon has numerous cultural, social and sports organizations. Musical activity is centered at Brandon U's School of Music. D.M. LYON

Reading: G.F. Barker, *Brandon: A City 1881-1961* (1977); W. Leland Clark, *Brandon's Politics and Politicians* (1981); Mary Hume, ed, *Brandon: Prospect of a City* (1981).

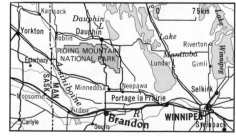

Brandon University, Brandon, Man, was founded in 1967. Brandon College, developed by the Baptist Convention of Manitoba and the North-West in 1898, was affiliated with the UNIVERSITY OF MANITOBA until 1911, and then with MCMASTER UNIVERSITY, 1911-38. It became non-denominational in 1938 and rejoined U of Manitoba until 1967, when it received its own charter. Brandon U offers undergraduate courses in arts, science, education and music, and general studies and a master's degree in music (performance and music education). B. BEATON

Enrolment: Brandon University, 1985-86 (Source: Statistics Canada)			
Full-time Undergrad	*Full-time Graduate*	*Part-time Undergrad*	*Part-time Graduate*
1358	–	1467	4

Brandtner, Fritz, painter (b at Danzig [Gdansk, Poland], Germany 28 July 1896; d at Montréal 7 Nov 1969). Generally considered to have introduced German expressionism to Canada, Brandtner was trained in Berlin and came to Winnipeg in 1928. He worked as a house painter until L.L. FITZGERALD, principal of the Winnipeg School of Art, encouraged him to exhibit his own experimental paintings. In 1934 he moved to Montréal, where he found greater scope for his "modern" approach. He was associated there with John LYMAN and the CONTEMPORARY ARTS SOCIETY and later with the Canadian Group of Painters and with Marian SCOTT, with whom he taught children's art classes. A strong sense of design, exuberant colours and characteristic, slashing black diagonals marked his work in oil, watercolour graphics and linoleum, the latter used for panels for the Queen Elizabeth Hotel and Jasper Park Lodge. Murals by Brandtner are in Saskatoon and Boston.　　　　　ANNE McDOUGALL

Brandy Parliament, an assembly of 20 notables of NEW FRANCE, who on 10 Oct 1678 were asked their opinion of the sale of brandy to the Indians. (The title was bestowed in 1921 by historian W.B. Munro.) The Jesuits, as well as the colony's clergy, saw liquor as the chief obstacle to the success of missionary activity, whereas some colonial administrators were half-hearted when it came to banning the traffic. Colbert, the minister of marine, rejected proposals that might lead to a decline in French exports of brandy and the customs revenue of the Canadian administration. He asked that a meeting of notables be convened, leaving little doubt about the verdict he desired. At the meeting, 15 of the 20 spokesmen favoured retention of the brandy trade. Although a royal edict of 24 May 1679 forbade the sale of liquor to Indians outside the settlements, alcohol continued to flow westward.　　　　　TOM WEIN

Branscombe, Gena, composer, conductor (b at Picton, Ont 4 Nov 1881; d at New York City, NY 26 July 1977). Through a long and vigorous life she composed music for piano, voice, orchestra and choir, winning particular recognition for her music for women's voices. Her choral drama *Pilgrims of Destiny* was acclaimed by the League of American Pen Women in 1928 as the finest work composed by a woman. Though she lived in the US, several of her compositions embrace Canadian themes: eg, the orchestral *Quebec Suite* and the choir piece "Our Canada from Sea to Sea." In 1960 the RCN adopted her hymn "Arms that Have Sheltered Us." She founded the Branscombe Chorale of New York in 1934 and remained its conductor for 20 years.　　　　　BARCLAY McMILLAN

Brant, Joseph, or Thayendanegea, Mohawk war chief, Loyalist, statesman (b at Cayahoga [near Akron, Ohio] *c*Mar 1742/43; d at Burlington Bay, UC 24 Nov 1807), brother of Mary BRANT. Joseph Brant saw limited action during the SEVEN YEARS' WAR and was with Sir William JOHNSON in the expedition against Ft Niagara in 1759. In 1761 Johnson sent him to Moor's Indian and Charity School at Lebanon, Conn, where he stayed for 2 years. In 1765 Brant married an Oneida (who died in 1771) and settled at Canajoharie in the Mohawk Valley. For nearly a decade, he acted as an interpreter for Johnson and his successor in the British Indian Dept, Guy Johnson, aided missionaries in teaching Christianity to the Indians, and helped translate religious materials into Mohawk. With the outbreak of the AMERICAN REVOLUTION, Brant immediately rallied to the royal cause and visited England in 1776 with Guy Johnson. On his return Brant fought throughout the war with an Indian-Loyalist band. He was greatly admired as a soldier and was commis-

Portrait of Joseph Brant by English painter George Romney, *c*1776 (*courtesy National Gallery of Canada*).

sioned a captain by the British in 1780, but fought as a war chief. Beginning in 1783 and through the mid-1790s Brant worked to form a united confederation of Iroquois and western Indians in order to block American expansion westward. His dream ultimately was undermined by factionalist jealousies among the Indian nations, by American opposition, and finally by British betrayal.

About 1779 Brant married Catharine, a Mohawk from a prominent family. In May 1784, following the war, Brant led the Mohawk LOYALISTS and other native peoples to a large tract of land on the Grand R [Ont] granted them in compensation for their losses in the war. Convinced that Indians would have to learn white agriculture to survive and thinking that the tract was too small for hunting, Brant wanted to lease or sell land to whites, which would provide an income as well. A complicated controversy with the government over the nature of Indian land tenure then arose; at the same time there was discontent among some of the Grand R Indians over disposition of the money. In his later years Brant lived quietly in his magnificent house at Burlington Bay in an English style and translated parts of the Bible into Mohawk.　　　　　ROBERT S. ALLEN

Brant, Mary, or Konwatsi'tsiaiénni, meaning "someone lends her a flower," Mohawk, (b *c*1736; d at Kingston 16 Apr 1796). Mary, or Molly Brant as she was generally known, was one of the most important women in N American Indian history. From her influential position as head of a society of Six Nations matrons, she enjoyed a much greater status than her more colourful younger brother, Joseph BRANT. She was consulted by the Indians on all matters of importance. Much of her power also came from her relationship with Sir William JOHNSON, first superintendent of the northern Indians of British N America, whom the Six Nations honoured as a good friend and adviser.

In her late teens Molly became Johnson's consort. The attractive and intelligent woman presided over his household with great ability and managed his estate in the Mohawk Valley, NY, during his frequent absences. After his death (1774), she and her brother Joseph remained staunch LOYALISTS. Molly rendered invaluable assistance to the Crown by encouraging the Six Nations to keep their alliance with England. At the end of the war she moved to Cataraqui [Kingston, Ont].　　　　　DONALD B. SMITH

Brantford, Ont, City, pop 76 146 (1986c), 74 315 (1981c), inc 1877, seat of Brant County, located on the Grand R, 104 km SW of Toronto. Originally inhabited by the NEUTRAL, the surrounding area was part of a large land grant of the British government in 1784 to the Six Nations Indians in gratitude for their loyalty during the American War of Independence and in compensation for the loss of their land in the Mohawk Valley (*see* IROQUOIS). In 1827 the centre of the settlement was named Brant's Ford after Mohawk leader Joseph BRANT. Non-native settlers were welcomed by the Indians, who surrendered title to the townsite in 1830. With the arrival of the railway, it became the distribution centre of a rich agricultural area. In this century manufacturing has flourished. It is the site of the first Protestant church in Ontario, St Paul's, Her Majesty's Chapel of the Mohawks, built 1785 with a grant from George III; Brant's son is buried in the churchyard. Alexander Graham BELL worked on the invention of the telephone at his home nearby and in Aug 1876 made the first long-distance call, from Brantford to Paris, Ont, 11 km away. The Bell Homestead (1858) has been restored, as has Henderson House – the first telephone office in Canada. The Indian Museum and Art Gallery traces the history and culture of the Six Nations.　　　　　DANIEL FRANCIS

Bras d'Or Lake, 1098 km², is an arm of the Atlantic Ocean occupying the centre of CAPE BRETON I that nearly divides the island in 2. On the N it is linked to the ocean by 2 narrow channels down either side of Boularderie I. On the S it is divided from the ocean by a low strip of land that is breached by a ship canal at ST PETERS. The lake is about 70 km long and is circled by high hills. MICMAC were the earliest inhabitants and in 1650 a French trading post was built at St Peters. Late in the 18th century, LOYALISTS settled along its shores, followed by Scottish immigrants. The lake has long been known for good fishing and today is popular for water recreation of all kinds. BADDECK, on the N shore, has been a shipbuilding centre. The name is a corruption of "labrador," a term applied by Portuguese explorers to a large part of Nova Scotia.　　　　　DANIEL FRANCIS

Brascan, Ltd, formerly Brazilian Traction Light and Power Co, Ltd, is a major natural-resources company with substantial consumer product interests and extensive holdings in the financial services of the Canadian, American and Brazilian economies. In 1899 William MACKENZIE and others took over an old mule-drawn tramway in São Paulo and reorganized it as the São Paulo Tramway, Light and Power. In 1904, the same promoters created the Rio de Janeiro Tramway, Light and Power Co. Ownership of these 2 companies was assumed in 1912 by the newly created Brazilian Traction, Light and Power Co, a holding company known to Brazilians as "the Light." Chief among the company's management was Alexander MACKENZIE (no relation to William), who devoted his whole career to the Brazil company. It furnished Brazil's industrial southeast with electric-power, tramway, telephone and gas services until late 1978, when these assets were sold to the Brazilian government. Its early ownership was primarily in European and American hands. By 1954 it was 51% Canadian owned; by 1975, 54%. The company's first major investment in Canada was John Labatt, Ltd. From its Toronto head office it controls assets of $4.3 billion (1986). Its annual sales revenue of $4.4 billion ranked it 16th among Canadian corporations, and it is 85% Canadian owned.　　　　　DUNCAN McDOWALL

Reading: P. Best and A. Shorthill, *The Brass Ring: Power, Influence and the Brascan Empire* (1987).

Brassard, François, composer, ethnomusicologist, organist, critic, teacher, pianist (b at St-Jérôme [Métabetchouan], Qué 6 Oct 1908; d at Québec City 26 Apr 1976). He studied music primarily with Claude CHAMPAGNE and Léo-Pol MORIN. From time to time, 1930-70, he was organist at St-Dominique church in Jonquière. The author of numerous essays, as well as analyses and harmonizations of French Canadian folk songs, Brassard is closely linked with U Laval's Archives de folklore. In 1946 he was appointed to the archives' publications committee and in 1971 joined its research centre. He also wrote articles using the noms de plume Braz Arpiani and Thibaut de Champagne. In 1974 Brassard received the Canadian Music Council Medal. *See also* FOLKLORE. HÉLÈNE PLOUFFE

Brault, Cédia, mezzo-soprano (b at Ste-Martine, Qué 4 Jan 1894; d at Montréal 27 June 1972). She studied voice with Céline Marier and Salvator Issaurel and harmony with Rodolphe MATHIEU. She made her debut as Carmen with tenor Victor Desautels in 1918 and, in 1920, married him. Carmen was also her last role (1939). She performed in the premiere of Guillaume COUTURE's *Jean le Précurseur.* One of the first to perform the works of Ravel, Casella and Milhaud in Canada, she also gave the Canadian premiere of Léo-Pol MORIN's *Chants de sacrifice* and of Debussy's *Proses lyriques.* In 1928, on a visit to Montréal, Ravel praised her interpretation of his *Chansons madécasses.* HÉLÈNE PLOUFFE

Brault, Jacques, writer (b at Montréal 29 Mar 1933). Brault is a major poet of contemporary Québec. He studied at the Collège Sainte-Marie (Montréal), U de Montréal and the Sorbonne (Paris), before becoming a professor at U de M in 1960. He has written for various magazines, notably *Liberté,* and is a literary critic and producer of literary radio programming for Radio-Canada.

Born to a poor family, Brault in all his work has expressed his attachment to the humble realities of life and his search for a simple and basic wisdom. His collection, *Mémoire* (1965 and 1968, Prix de poésie du Québec, 1965, and Prix France-Canada, 1968), containing "Suite fraternelle," made him famous as a poet of contemporary urban life and of a country as yet unbuilt. His poetic works continued in a more philosophical vein with *La Poésie ce matin* (1971), *Poèmes des quatre côtés* (1975), *L'en dessous l'admirable* (1975), *Trois fois passera* (1981) and *Moments fragiles* (1984). Playwright (*Trois partitions,* 1972, including *Quand nous serons heureux,* Governor General's Award, 1971), essayist (*Alain Grandbois,* 1968; *Chemin faisant,* 1975) and novelist (*Agonie,* 1984, Governor General's Award; tr 1987 as *Deathwatch*), he has received the Prix Duvernay (1978) and the Prix Athanase-David (1986) for his work as a whole. MICHEL LEMAIRE

Brault, Michel, filmmaker (b at Montréal 25 June 1928). A professional photographer, Brault filmed the series *Les Petites Médisances* with Jacques Giraldeau in the early 1950s. He joined the NFB as a cameraman in 1956 and worked on the *Candid Eye* series. Quickly moving into film directing, he became a leading figure in direct cinema, using a light, portable camera. Noted for the quality of his cinematography, he went to Europe to work with directors of the *cinéma-vérité* school. Returning to Canada, he worked as director of photography on productions by Québec filmmakers such as Claude JUTRA, Anne Claire POIRIER and Francis MANKIEWICZ. At the same time, as a film director, he collaborated with Pierre Perrault on 3 feature films, including the classic *Pour la suite du monde* (1963). His ability to combine the documentary impact of direct cinema with the

emotional richness of fiction films is demonstrated in *Entre la mer et l'eau douce* (1967) and especially in *Les Ordres* (1974), a documentary dramatization of the 1970 October Crisis that won first prize at Cannes 1975. Since 1976 he has produced and co-directed films with André Gladu for the series *Le Son des français d'Amérique;* he was for many years president of the Syndicat national du cinéma. Brault has been an inspiration to a generation of filmmakers. In 1986 he was awarded the Prix Albert-Tessier. PIERRE VÉRONNEAU

Breadalbane is a ghost ship, a 3-masted barque lying beneath the ice of the NORTHWEST PASSAGE. Sunk in 1853, she is the world's northernmost known shipwreck and the best-preserved wooden ship yet found in the ocean. Built in Scotland in 1843, she was a merchant ship sailing to Europe's great seaports carrying wine, wool and grain. In spring 1853 *Breadalbane* was called into service by the Royal Navy and sent to the Arctic to carry supplies to Sir Edward BELCHER's expedition which, since 1852, had been searching for the ships and men of the FRANKLIN EXPEDITION. Belcher's squadron was the Royal Navy's last and largest search expedition.

Breadalbane was about 40 m long, generously built, a square-rigged ship typical of the hundreds that linked the great oceans during the reign of Queen Victoria. But she was no match for the Arctic. In spite of her sturdy wooden hull and the skill of her crew, she was trapped in the polar ice. On 21 Aug 1853, just after midnight, a slab of ice knifed through her starboard bow. The 21-man crew scrambled over the side to safety. Within 15 minutes *Breadalbane* sank. The crew were picked up by her surviving sister ship, the *Phoenix.* For 127 years she remained hidden below the grinding polar pack, hard on her keel, her broken bowsprit pointing eastward, towards home and England.

Joseph B. MACINNIS's first expedition to find the ship (Aug 1978) was prompted by research by arctic marine historians Stuart Hodgson and Maurice Haycock. Available documents included eyewitness accounts from the archive of the Scott Polar Research Institute, Cambridge, Eng. She was found in 1980 after 3 years of searching the waters S of Beechey I. On 13 Aug *Breadalbane* ghosted onto the screen of the side-scan sonar, her hull intact, 2 of her masts still standing. In 1981 the expedition went back for a more detailed look, supported by the Canadian Coast Guard, the National Geographic Society and other institutions. A remotely piloted submersible was lowered into the lethally cold water. One hundred metres down, with still and video cameras, colour photographs were taken. Her bow, masts, rudder and anchor could be seen; the green copper sheathing that still protected her hull looked like new. In a small cabinet hanging on her deckhouse were her compass and a signal light; nearby was the big wooden wheel that had guided her across the stormy N Atlantic.

Like all historical artifacts, the *Breadalbane* will take time to study, and special problems are raised by her position in the Arctic. She lies under an unpredictable barrier of ice. Marine geologists and sea-ice morphologists, under the guidance of senior scientist Steve Blasco of the BEDFORD INSTITUTE OF OCEANOGRAPHY, wish to study ice formation over the ship and the effects of ice scouring on nearby sediments. This information is of interest to all parties working in northern waters, including oil companies. Yet *Breadalbane* lies far below the depths at which marine archaeologists can work. To unlock her secrets, new DIVING and photographic techniques specific to the Arctic are being developed. The new technology includes the Sea-Otter submersible, a lock-out diving system

and WASP, a physiologically protective diving suit. All are operated by Can-Dive Services, located in Vancouver.

Breadalbane is unique among shipwrecks, being beautifully preserved by arctic waters. For scientists, she is a drowned benchmark, an opportunity to learn more about arctic biology and geology and about the sea ice that floats over her masts. Historically, she is a time capsule: some of her cargo and working tools and personal effects of the crew are still on board. Diving down to her, studying her remains, is an excursion into Canada's past and into our future. JOSEPH B. MACINNIS

Reading: Joseph B. MacInnis, *The Breadalbane Adventure* (1983).

Breadner, Lloyd Samuel, air chief marshal (b at Carleton Place, Ont 14 July 1894; d at Boston, Mass 14 Mar 1952). Commissioned in the Royal Naval Air Service 28 Dec 1915, he won a DSC as a fighter pilot in 1917. He became a squadron leader in the Canadian Air Force in 1920 and held various staff appointments between attending the RAF Staff College and the Imperial Defence College, London. In 1940, as an air vice-marshal, he became chief of the air staff, then in 1943 air officer commander in chief, RCAF Overseas. After retiring in 1945, Breadner was promoted air chief marshal, the first (and only) Canadian to hold that rank. BRERETON GREENHOUS

Breau, Lenny, jazz guitarist (b at Auburn, Maine 5 Aug 1941; d at Los Angeles, Calif 12 Aug 1984). As a boy, he was taken to Winnipeg by his parents, country singers Hal Lone Pine and Betty Cody. His youthful virtuosity, eclecticism and technical innovation drew attention in Toronto as early as 1962, but his career was hampered by personal problems, including a lengthy drug addiction. Early recordings – *Guitar Sounds, The Velvet Touch* – made Breau something of a legend outside Canada, and in 1975 he returned to the US. His career and influence subsequently grew with further recordings in jazz and country contexts. MARK MILLER

Brébeuf, Jean de, Jesuit missionary, author of *Relations des Jésuites,* 1635, 1636 (b at Condé-sur-Vire, France 25 Mar 1593; martyred at St-Ignace in HURONIA 16 Mar 1649; canonized 29 June 1930). Brébeuf came to Canada in 1625 as a missionary to the nomadic MONTAGNAIS. Sent to the HURON near Georgian Bay in 1626, he learned their language and preached there until 1629, when Québec was captured by the KIRKE brothers and the Jesuits were forced to return to France. He returned in 1633 and was among the Huron again in 1634, remaining in charge of the mission (*see* STE MARIE AMONG THE HURONS) for 4 years. Brébeuf, an accomplished linguist, supervised the preparation of a Huron grammar and dictionary. In 1640, following a devastating smallpox epidemic, the Huron attacked him and his companion, beat them and damaged their mission. In 1640-41 he began a mission among the NEUTRAL, but they regarded him as a sorcerer. In 1644 he returned to Huronia, remaining there until 16 Mar 1649 when he was captured by invading IROQUOIS at the St Louis mission, taken to St-Ignace and brutally killed. His bones are buried at the Martyrs' Shrine near Midland, Ont. CORNELIUS J. JAENEN

Brebner, John Bartlet, historian (b at Toronto 19 May 1895; d at New York C, NY 9 Nov 1957). Educated at U of T, Oxford and Columbia U, he taught 1921-25 at U of T and then moved to Columbia U for the rest of his academic life. Here he established his reputation as a historian and teacher; he was also very active in the Carnegie Endowment for International Peace. Brebner's most influential books are *New England's Outpost*

(1927), *The Neutral Yankees of Nova Scotia* (1937), *The North Atlantic Triangle* (1945) and, with M.L. Hansen, *The Mingling of the Canadian and American People* (1940). His explanation for the expulsion of the Acadians in 1755 and the neutrality of Nova Scotia during the American Revolution is still widely regarded as the "classic account."

G.A. RAWLYK

Breda, Treaty of agreements signed 21 July 1667 at Breda, the Netherlands, between England and the Netherlands and between England and France, ending the second Anglo-Dutch War. The former treaty recognized the English conquest of Amsterdam (New York) in 1664. The latter provided for French restoration of the English part of the island of St Christopher's, West Indies, in exchange for ACADIA, captured from the French in 1654 by Britain's New England forces while France and England were allies. The actual handover of territory was delayed until 1670.

STUART R.J. SUTHERLAND

Breeze, Claude Herbert, painter (b at Nelson, BC 9 Oct 1938). Breeze was taught by Ernest LINDNER in Saskatoon (1954-55) and then studied at Regina with Kenneth LOCHHEAD and Arthur MCKAY. After graduating in 1958, he spent a year at the Vancouver School of Art. One of the important West Coast painters, Breeze was the first in Canada to depict the violence shown by the media, especially television. In many ways his work of the early 1960s, particularly his series Lovers in a Landscape, with its probing content and dry handling, anticipates the work of the young contemporary figure painters. Breeze has completed a number of lithographs based on his fascination with aikido, a Japanese martial art. In Apr 1985 a large show of his work was held at Bare-X Gallery in Toronto. He has taught at York U in Toronto since 1976.

JOAN MURRAY

Bregman, Sidney (b at Warsaw, Poland); **Hamann, George Frederick** (b at Toronto 14 June 1928); architects. The partnership, founded in Toronto in 1953, is active across N America primarily in the design and construction of health-care facilities (Mount Sinai Hospital, Toronto, and the Ottawa General Hospital) and of commercial and retail space. Alone or in joint venture, the firm has designed over 2.8 million square metres of office accommodation, much of it in downtown Toronto: the Toronto Dominion Centre with John B. PARKIN Associates; the EATON CENTRE with the ZEIDLER Partnership; Harbour Square; the Simpson Tower; and the 72-storey First Canadian Place.

GRANT WANZEL AND KAREN KALLWEIT

Bren Gun Scandal Before WWII the British government was anxious to acquire new, secure sources for weapons production. The Canadian government was reluctant to co-operate, fearing isolationist opinion, especially in Québec. In 1938, however, the deputy minister and minister of national defence recommended a Canadian appliance manufacturer, John Inglis, and the British and Canadian governments awarded his firm a contract for production of the Bren light machine gun. Impropriety was alleged, and a royal commission was appointed. Although it found no evidence of corruption, it recommended that civilian business advice be sought in future. This report helped lead to civilian control over war production in WWII (*see* MUNITIONS AND SUPPLY, DEPARTMENT OF). Bren gun production was very successful: some 200 000 were made in Canada.

ROBERT BOTHWELL

Brener, Roland, sculptor (b at Johannesburg, S Africa 22 Feb 1942). His sculptural style has been influenced by constructivist theories and by his instructor, Anthony Caro, at St Martin's School of Art, London. This school has taught a nontraditional approach to sculpture since the early 1960s, centering on syntactical construction rather than techniques of modelling. Brener uses prefabricated materials such as pipes and scaffolding in his abstract sculptures, allowing him to build linear sculptures on a large scale. Yet, because of their logical structural order, their visual shape belies their complexity. A major show of Brener's work was held in Regina in 1986. In 1973 he began teaching in the visual arts department, U of Vic.

KATHLEEN LAVERTY

Brethren in Christ (identified as "Tunkers" in Canada in the 19th century) were a group of Christians who shared the ANABAPTIST belief in adult baptism. They trace their origins to 1770 when concerned members of the MENNONITE, LUTHERAN and BAPTIST churches in Lancaster County, Pa, broke with the formalism of their parent churches. The organization of the new group was very loose and various small independent groups emerged, the most important of which were probably the so-called River Brethren. After the American Revolution, many of the Brethren, who had taken a PACIFIST position in that conflict, immigrated to what is now Ontario, where their pacifist convictions were officially recognized and respected in the Militia Act of 1793. Canada's roughly 2500 adult Brethren in Christ participate in the international relief activities of the Mennonite Central Committee, but their church has retained a separate denominational identity in Canada and the US.

T.D. REGEHR

Brett, George Sidney, philosopher (b at Briton Ferry, Wales 5 Aug 1879; d at Toronto 27 Oct 1944). Educated at Oxford and having taught in India, he moved from teaching classics (1908) at Trinity Coll and University Coll, U of T, to the department of philosophy, where he was chairman 1927-44. His 3-volume *A History of Psychology* (1912-21) assesses the philosophy of mind theories; Brett presents psychology as the study of the immediate data of the inner life, distinguishes it from other sciences, and resists the new experimentalist approach. *The Government of Man* (1913) traces political stages in societies. Freedom is seen here to emerge from the relation between man's inner life and changing social orders. Brett's commitment to historical modes of understanding led him to be seen by some as the founder of the "Toronto School of Intellectual History." He guided courses and appointments in Toronto for many years. A fellow of the Royal Soc of Canada, he founded the *Canadian Journal of Religious Thought,* served as an editor for the *Journal of General Psychology* and the *International Journal of Ethics,* and was first editor of the *University of Toronto Quarterly.*

ELIZABETH A. TROTT

Brewing Industry Brewing began in Canada with the first settlers and traders. At first, beer making was a cottage industry, but in 1668 Canada's first commercial brewery was built by the Intendant Jean TALON at Québec City. Its aims were to promote temperance (by offering an alternative to strong imported French liquors), to keep currency from leaving the country for imported beverages and to make use of the abundance of grain available in the New World.

In its early development period the industry consisted of small, independent breweries scattered throughout the country. As a result of modern distribution systems, quality control and rising costs, production became centralized and most local breweries disappeared (although as a result of the "real ale" movement in Europe, small "brew pubs" are beginning to enjoy a re-

naissance). Today, Canada's brewing industry comprises Carling O'Keefe Breweries of Canada Ltd, Labatt Brewing Co Ltd and MOLSON Breweries of Canada Ltd, each of which has plants in 9 of the 10 provinces; and large regional breweries: Pacific Western Brewing Company in BC, Drummond Brewing Company Ltd in Alberta, Northern Breweries Ltd and Amstel Brewery Canada Ltd in Ontario, and Moosehead Breweries Ltd in NS and NB. In 1986 there were 53 brewing plants operating across Canada. In the mid-1980s, smaller microbreweries were established to meet specific local markets: Big Rock Brewery Limited in Calgary; Brick Brewing Company Limited in Waterloo, Ont; Upper Canada Brewing Company in Toronto; Ottawa Valley Brewing Company in Nepean, Ont; Island Breweries Ltd in Charlottetown; and Highland Breweries Limited Partnership in Sydney, NS.

As a result of provincial regulations imposed over the past century, beer cannot be sold competitively unless it is produced within that province. The Canadian brewing industry has therefore developed as a series of small-scale plants across the country, with most beer marketed locally and very little crossing provincial boundaries. This is in sharp contrast with the US, where the industry developed on a national basis, achieving economies of scale and therefore lower production costs. Thus, Canadian breweries would have difficulty competing with US companies shipping into the Canadian market.

Canadians consume about 20.5 million hL of beer annually. Consumption per capita is 82 L. In the early 1970s Canada ranked tenth among the nations of the world in per capita consumption; in 1985, fifteenth. Lager has become the preferred type of beer consumed, accounting for 56% of the market; ale accounts for 34% and light beer for 10%. Twenty years ago the shares of ale and lager were reversed, with ale accounting for 59% of sales. Beer is used as a generic term and includes both lager and ale. The difference between the 2 is that lager is made by fermenting with a type of yeast that drops to the bottom of the fermenting tank and is lighter in taste; whereas more hops are used to brew ale and the yeast usually rises to the top of the tank. Less than 1% of the remainder of beer is sold as stout (heavy-bodied darker and sweeter beer brewed with roasted malt and a higher percentage of hops) and porter (weaker stout). Light beers, containing 4% alcohol by volume, were introduced in Canada in the late 1970s. Brands of this nature are becoming increasingly popular in the 1980s. Regular-strength Canadian beers contain 5% alcohol by volume.

The production, distribution and sale of beer contributed $8.8 billion to Canada's Gross Domestic Product in 1986. This figure represents 1.7% of the GDP and illustrates the impact on the economy of beer consumption. Export volume accounted for 11% of beer production (Canadian beer is particularly popular in the US). Over 98% of the beer consumed in Canada was produced by Canadian brewers. The brewing industry's annual purchases of domestic materials and supplies were substantial ($672 million in 1986). For example, BARLEY malt cost over $137 million; bottles bought in Canada came to over $75 million; and cartons and labels amounted to more than $166 million.

Salaries, wages, commissions and employee security benefits paid by the industry amounted to over $819 million. However, this item is a small part of the wage bill when the total employment arising from the brewing and marketing of beer is considered. There are some 20 000 persons employed directly by the brewing industry; an additional 68 000 are employed in jobs related to distribution and sales. Further indirect employment is generated from brewing and marketing: the earnings of an additional 101 000 persons depend indirectly on the production, distribution and sale of beer. Thus, total employment amounts to 189 000 jobs, accounting for 1.5% of Canada's labour force.

Revenue to all levels of government generated by the brewing and marketing of beer amounted to about $3.3 billion in 1986. About $2 billion came from federal excise duty and sales tax and provincial liquor-board profits and sales taxes; the remainder represented various taxes paid to the different levels of government by the employees and companies involved.

Advertising of alcoholic beverages is strictly controlled by provincial governments (NB and PEI have banned it on radio and television). This restriction, combined with others (eg, uniformity of price, distribution outlets and, until recently, packaging), has caused the industry to seek innovative and distinctive promotional opportunities. The competition among the breweries for a static market also led to the demise of the "stubby" beer bottle, the uniform glass container used by all companies. Marketing pressures to differentiate products, and a desire to project a more up-to-date image, resulted in the introduction of a variety of "private mold" bottles for different companies and brands. Today, breweries sponsor a range of sporting events (eg, cycling, downhill skiing) and Carling O'Keefe, Labatt and Molson own sports teams (eg, Montreal Canadiens, Toronto Argonauts and Quebec Nordiques). *See also* Sir John CARLING; John Sackville LABATT; Eugene O'KEEFE. KEN LAVERY

Brewster, Elizabeth Winifred, writer (b at Chipman, NB 26 Aug 1922). Since 1972 Brewster has taught English at U of Sask, but before that she was a librarian and cataloguer in NB, Ontario, Alberta and BC. She was educated at UNB, Radcliffe Coll, U of T and Indiana U. Winner of several awards and honours, Brewster has written 13 books, most of them poetry collections. Her first book of poetry was *East Coast* (1951) and since then she has produced 8 others, including *Passage of Summer* (1969), *Sunrise North* (1972), *Sometimes I Think of Moving* (1977) and *The Way Home* (1982). As well, she has written 2 novels and 2 story collections. Her most recent work is *Visitation* (1987). JEAN WILSON

Brewster, Harlan Carey, politician, premier of BC (b at Harvey, NB 10 Nov 1870; d at Calgary 1 Mar 1918). Educated in NB and Boston, Mass, and qualified as a printer and deep-sea navigator, Brewster moved to BC about 1893. Successively employed as ship's purser, accountant and salmon cannery manager, he eventually became owner of the Clayoquot Sound Cannery in 1907. In 1909 he was elected Liberal MLA for Alberni. In 1912, as leader of the Opposition, he ran against Premier Richard MCBRIDE in Victoria but, like all other Liberals, was defeated. He returned to the legislature through a Vancouver by-election in 1916 and was re-elected in the general election, serving as premier until his death. His brief administration introduced such reforms as WOMEN'S SUFFRAGE and PROHIBITION and attempted to clean up political corruption, especially surrounding the Pacific Great Eastern Ry. PATRICIA E. ROY

Bricklin American promoter Malcolm Bricklin wanted to build his own US-designed sports car, and, lured by loan guarantees of $2 880 000 plus $500 000 for 51% of the stock, he set up shop in Saint John, NB, and at Minto, NB, where the fibreglass bodies were made. Plagued by technical problems with the "gull-wing" doors and the poor quality of the bodies, production was de-

layed. The company's indebtedness to the provincial government escalated to $23 million, at which point the government refused to grant more aid unless the private sector provided 50%. But the private sector would not, and the company fell into receivership. During 1974 and 1975, 2857 cars were made. All went to the US because Bricklin could not join the CANADA-US AUTOMOTIVE PRODUCTS AGREEMENT. AMC and Ford engines and other parts were imported from the US duty free with the understanding that every Bricklin be sold there. R. PERRY ZAVITZ

Bridge is a card game played by 4 people, 2 in each of 2 partnerships. Contract Bridge evolved from whist through bridge whist and auction bridge. Harold S. Vanderbilt in 1926 proposed changes in the rules which introduced an element of risk into the bidding auction on every hand by awarding the bonus for games and slams only if the declaring side had contracted to take the requisite number of tricks, unlike auction bridge where the award was automatic whenever the required number of tricks were won. In this highly competitive new game, judgement, concentration and stamina (all qualities of a tournament sport) are rewarded.

For many years, the American Contract Bridge League has promoted tournament bridge in N America by sanctioning tournaments. In 1958, the ACBL met with the European Bridge League and the Australian Bridge Council to form the World Bridge Federation with the organization and sponsorship of international tournaments as its principle function. Canadians, notably Eric Murray and Sami Kehela of Toronto, played for ACBL teams. When the World Olympiad was introduced in the 1960s, the time to form an organization to select Canadian representation had come. Murray, with the help of Douglas Cannell of Winnipeg, Henry Smilie of Vancouver, Aaron Goodman of Montréal and others created the Canadian Bridge Federation in 1966-67. Its function has been to represent the interests of the 18 000 Canadians who from time to time play in tournaments. Since 1968, Canada has been represented at every WBF event for which it was eligible. Eric Murray played for the second place NA team in 1962 (with Charles Coon), 1966, 1967 and 1974 (with Sami Kehela), losing in each year to the powerful Italian Blue Team. In pairs Olympiads, Eric Kokish and Peter Nagy of Montréal were second in the Open Pairs in 1978 and Dianna Gordon and George Mittelman of Toronto won the Mixed Pairs in 1982. ALVIN BARAGAR

Reading: The Official Encyclopedia of Bridge (1971).

Bridges have always been important in Canadian TRANSPORTATION, if only because of the many waterways to be crossed by roads and railways. Logs cut from the local forests had to suffice for stream crossings on primitive trails before the advent of truss designs early in the 19th century. In winter the frozen surfaces of rivers and lakes provided safe crossings when ice had gained suffi-

Lion's Gate Bridge, Vancouver, BC, is a fine example of a suspension bridge (*photo by J.A. Kraulis/Masterfile*).

cient thickness. Ice bridges are still used; carefully designed crossings (with ice artificially built up) served, for example, on the long access road to the JAMES BAY PROJECT during the winter of 1971-72 prior to the erection of permanent bridges. More remarkable was the use of an ice bridge across the St Lawrence R in the winters of 1880-81 and 1881-82, from Hochelaga to Longueuil [Montréal], to carry a standard-gauge railway; from Jan to Mar in each of those winters a small train, weighing 60 tons, safely used this unique bridge.

Covered bridges, still to be seen on secondary roads in eastern Canada, were important in early Canadian bridge building. First used in 1805 in Philadelphia, and long known as "kissing bridges" (for the most obvious of reasons), they came into wide use by the end of the century. There were then at least 1000 in Québec and more than 400 in NB. Today, there are probably not more than 200 in either province, and special efforts have been made in NB for their preservation. The covered bridge over the Saint John R at HARTLAND, NB, is 391 m long, renowned as "the longest covered bridge in the world."

Covered bridges were all built of timber, various types of trusses enabling steadily increasing span lengths to be used after the first US patent for trusses was taken out in 1830. Three years earlier, using a European design, John BY had incorporated a 60 m span truss bridge across the Big Kettle of the Chaudière at Bytown [Ottawa] in the Union Bridge across the Ottawa R, the first link between Lower and Upper Canada, built at the start of work on the RIDEAU CANAL. On the associated Ottawa R CANALS, engineer officers of the Royal Staff Corps had used prefabricated timber bridges even before 1827. Timber has continued in use for bridges in Canada to the present day, some of the most notable examples being the great timber trestle bridges used in early railway construction in the West, now generally replaced by steel structures.

It was a common practice to use timber for bridges in early railway building in Canada. An exception was the INTERCOLONIAL RY, completed in 1876. The chief engineer, Sir Sandford FLEMING, insisted on masonry piers for all his bridges and wrought iron for his bridge spans, as in the 2 multispan bridges across the Miramichi R, NB. Steel trusses now replace the original wrought iron spans; the piers, however, are the originals from over a century ago. Even more significant were some of the bridges erected in the 1850s for the GRAND TRUNK RY from Montréal to Toronto, particularly the Victoria Bridge (1860) across the St Lawrence R at Montréal, even today one of the world's great bridges (2742 m long). Its original spans, and those of the bridge carrying the track over the Ottawa R at Ste-Anne-de-Bellevue, were wrought iron rectangular boxes, later replaced by steel trusses.

By the end of the century, steel was used widely. Its capability for bridges is well shown by the

Covered bridges were all built of timber, a system of trussing making possible increasing spans. This bridge over the Gatineau R at Wakefield, Qué, recently burned down (*photo by John deVisser*).

World's first aluminum bridge, near Jonquière, Qué (*photo by J.A. Kraulis*).

Interprovincial Bridge over the Ottawa R at Ottawa, the longest cantilever span in the world when built, still in active use although now for road traffic rather than rail. Downstream, the Jacques Cartier Bridge at Montréal (opened in 1929) is another fine cantilever structure. The Quebec Bridge, farther downstream still, is Canada's most famous bridge. Designed to carry the National Transcontinental Railway across the St Lawrence, it was officially started in 1900 as the longest steel cantilever bridge of the world. It failed, with tragic loss of life, during erection in Aug 1907 and Sept 1916 (*see* QUÉBEC BRIDGE DISASTERS). The finished bridge was opened on 22 Aug 1919. The accident was studied to good effect by an expert royal commission, and its report, a classic of structural engineering, has benefited bridge design around the world.

A suspension bridge for road traffic now parallels the Québec Bridge, one of a small number of such graceful structures found at strategic spots in Canada: across the Lion's Gate at Vancouver; the international section of the St Lawrence; and linking Halifax with Dartmouth across its harbour entrance. So successful was the latter that it has now been duplicated. The first bridge over the Niagara R, below the falls, was an elaborate suspension bridge carrying not only highway traffic but also the GREAT WESTERN RY. It was replaced later by the first of a series of fine steel-arched bridges.

Repair of bridges without disrupting traffic has been a significant part of Canadian bridge engineering. One of the most famous examples was the reinforcing of the steel arched truss bridge over Stoney Cr on the CPR main line through the Rocky Mts. In the 1950s, similar well-planned changes were made to some of the bridges crossing the ST LAWRENCE SEAWAY in order to give adequate clearance beneath them. Equally notable was the replacement of the fixed centre spans of 3 bridges over the Beauharnois power canal with vertical-lift bridges to permit passage of seaway traffic, this feature having been incorporated in the original designs 20 years before.

Reinforced concrete was first used in bridge construction in the early 20th century, eg, the Hurdman Bridge in Ottawa built in 1906. Today, probably the majority of small highway bridges are of reinforced concrete, an increasing number built of prefabricated units. Some quite large bridges have been constructed of this versatile material, as in the multispan, arched Broadway Bridge across the S Saskatchewan R at Saskatoon. The Broadway Bridge and the earlier University Bridge, also multispan arched, add greatly to the distinctive appearance of the central part of this prairie city. Some older bridges can hardly be considered beautiful, but the use of reinforced concrete has had a beneficial effect on bridge aesthetics. The elegant lines of the rigid frame bridges on major Ontario highways, for example, are believed to have influenced similar designs in the US and the UK. *See also* ENGINEERING. ROBERT F. LEGGET

Bridgewater, NS, Town, pop 6617 (1986c), inc 1899, is located at the head of navigation on the LaHave R, 16 km from its mouth. Pierre du Gua de MONTS visited the area in 1604, but settlement began about 1780 when German settlers from nearby LUNENBURG moved into the area. The actual founding of the town dates from *c*1812. As this was the main bridging point of the LaHave, it was called Bridgewater. A pluralistic society slowly took form, growing in response to the demand for the area's timber. The Davison sawmill, one of the largest in Nova Scotia, employed some 350 men late in the 19th century. The lumber and pulpwood industry remains important, but a Michelin tire plant, established in 1972 through grants from DREE, is now the mainstay of the economy. Tourism and the provision of regional services support the local economy. Bridgewater has a weekly newspaper and hosts an annual agricultural fair. A disastrous fire on 12 Jan 1899 destroyed the downtown area, but domestic architecture records New England and Victorian influences. L.D. McCANN

Brier, the abbreviation for one of the most prestigious trophies in Canadian sport. A Dominion championship competition for men's CURLING was inaugurated in 1927, sponsored by the W.D. Macdonald Co for a trophy known as the Macdonald Brier Tankard. This annual event gave curling a significant impetus. It includes one representative rink from each province, plus an extra one from Northern Ontario. In 1975, a rink was entered from the Northwest Territories-Yukon as well, making a total of 12 teams. Each province (or territory) holds provincial and district playoffs to determine the provincial winner. The winner of the Brier represents Canada in the World Curling Championship (Scotch Cup, from 1959 to 1968, then the Silver Broom). In 1949, Ken WATSON (Man) became the first curler to win the Brier 3 times. Matt Baldwin (Alta) also won 3 times in 1954, 1957 and 1958, before Ernie RICHARDSON (Sask) won 4 Briers in 5 years between 1959 and 1963. Ron NORTHCOTT (Alta) was another 3-time winner in 1966, 1968 and 1969. Western provinces have dominated the Brier; from 1927 to 1986 the leaders were Man (22 wins), Alta (14) and Sask (7). In 1980, under the new sponsorship of Labatt's, the format of the competition was changed to include semifinals and a final after the round robin. GERALD REDMOND

Bright, John Dee, football player, teacher (b at Fort Wayne, Ind 11 June 1931; d at Edmonton 14 Dec 1983). He graduated from Drake U (Des Moines, Iowa), where he led all US college ground-gainers, and joined the CALGARY STAMPEDERS in 1952. During the 1954 season he moved to the EDMONTON ESKIMOS. As an outstanding linebacker and powerful fullback with the Eskimos, he won the Schenley Award as Canada's outstanding player in 1959, the first black to win a major football award in Canada. He was Western Football Conference all-star 7 times and Canadian Football League all-star 4 times, and played in 4 Grey Cup games. Bright retired in 1965, having amassed 10 909 yards rushing in 1969 carries, and 71 touchdowns. He was a schoolteacher in Edmonton until his death. FRANK COSENTINO

Brill, Debbie, track and field athlete (b at Mission, BC 10 Mar 1953). Originator of the reverse jumping style, the "Brill bend," she won the high-jump gold in her first international competition, the 1969 Pacific Conference Games, and was the first N American woman to clear the 6-ft (1.83 m) barrier. Brill has been a member of every Olympic team since 1972, finishing out of the medals each time; she won gold medals in the 1970 Commonwealth Games, the 1971 Pan-American Games and the 1979 World Cup, as well as a silver in the 1978 Commonwealth Games. She is a Member of the Order of Canada. Her book *Jump* was published in 1986. TED BARRIS

Brintnell, Wilfred Leigh, pilot, businessman (b at Belleville, Ont 27 Aug 1895; d at Edmonton 22 Jan 1971). Following service as a pilot instructor in WWI, Brintnell worked for the Ontario Provincial Air Service (1924-27) and Western Canada Airways (1927-31) before establishing his own company at Edmonton in 1931. From 1932 to 1940 Mackenzie Air Service successfully provided both regular and unscheduled transport into the NWT; but in 1940 it was sold to Canadian Pacific to be absorbed into CP Airlines. Brintnell shifted his attention to another company, Aircraft Repair, which during WWII overhauled or repaired 856 aircraft and 2672 engines for the RCAF and USAF. In 1945, Aircraft Repair became Northwest Industries Ltd. From 1945 to 1949 that company built 13 Bellanca Senior Skyrocket aircraft under licence in Edmonton before abandoning the unprofitable manufacturing experiment to specialize in overhaul and repair operations. STANLEY GORDON

Brisebois, Ephrem A., soldier, mounted policeman, registrar of land titles (b at South Durham, Qué 7 Mar 1850; d at Minnedosa, Man 13 Feb 1890). He served briefly in the Union Army during the American Civil War, and from 1868-70 with the Canadian Pontifical ZOUAVES in Rome. In 1873 Brisebois was appointed an officer in the newly organized NWMP. Two years later a troop of NWMP under his command was sent to establish a post at the confluence of the Bow and Elbow rivers. In defiance of his superiors, who designated the new post "Fort Calgary," Brisebois persisted in naming it after himself, "Fort Brisebois." Already considered unfit to command his men, his continued insubordination led to his resignation from the NWMP Aug 1876. Well educated, a devout Catholic and an active Conservative Party supporter, Brisebois was registrar of land titles in Minnedosa 1880-89. During the NORTH-WEST REBELLION he served with the 65th Mount Royal Rifles. S.W. HORRALL

Britain, Battle of, 10 July to 31 Oct 1940, the first battle in history to be fought exclusively in the air, resulted in the Royal Air Force's Fighter Command compelling the German Luftwaffe to abandon its attempt to establish air superiority over S and E England. Without that superiority, a German invasion of Britain was impracticable. Only one Canadian unit participated, although many more Canadians serving in the RAF were in the forefront. No. 1 (Fighter) Squadron (later No 401), flying Hawker Hurricanes and commanded by Sqn Ldr E.A. McNab, first met the enemy on Aug 25. When withdrawn on Oct 9 the squadron had been credited with 30 enemy aircraft destroyed and 8 "probables." Three Canadians had been killed and 10 wounded or injured in crash landings. *See also* WORLD WAR II. BRERETON GREENHOUS

British American Land Company, chartered 20 Mar 1834 and promoted by John GALT, CANADA COMPANY founder; Edward ELLICE, Lower Canada's largest absentee landowner; and others. It purchased 343 995 ha of crown land in the Eastern Townships (Qué) for £120 000. Before 1844 its activities satisfied no one: the few settlers who came to the relatively inaccessible holdings complained of high land costs and harsh company policy; local politicians resented the fact that control over the purchase of money went to the executive branch of the government; and British shareholders demanded dividends. After ceding 206 898 ha to the government in 1841 in lieu of overdue payments, the company appointed Alexander T. GALT, John Galt's son, as local commissioner (1844-55). He increased land prices, but allowed a longer payment time. General immigration and local land sales increased. Urged by Galt and his successor, R.W. Heneker, the company invested in railways and industrial pursuits to stimulate sales. Although it operated until the 1950s, most of its land had been sold by 1910.

PETER BASKERVILLE

British Block Cairn and Suffield Tipi Rings, located in the open prairie of southeastern Alberta, consist of a central stone cairn 10 m in diameter and 2 m high surrounded by a 24 m diameter stone circle. Between the central cairn and the surrounding ring is a human figure outlined in stone. In the immediate vicinity are numerous smaller stone circles, or "tipi rings," used by Indians to hold down the edges of their lodges. The site is the largest known example of one type of ceremonial aboriginal structure found rarely throughout the Northern Plains and included in the general category of MEDICINE WHEELS. Although the specific ceremonial function of structures such as the British Block is unknown, research indicates that their construction began about 4000 to 5000 years ago and that they continued to be enlarged and added to intermittently until the early historic period.   JOHN H. BRUMLEY

British Columbia is Canada's most westerly province. It is a mountainous area whose population is mainly clustered in the southwestern corner. It is a land of diversity and contrast within small areas. Coastal landscapes, characterized by high, snow-covered mountains rising above narrow FJORDS and inlets, contrast with the broad forested upland of the central interior and the plains of the NE. People live around the shores of sheltered Georgia Strait in the SW and are dispersed in linear patterns along the N-S valleys in the southern half of the province. With an area of 948 596 km², BC is Canada's third-largest province, after Québec and Ontario. The provincial population of 2 883 365 in 1986 is third in numbers in Canada, after Ontario and Québec. The intense "Britishness" of earlier times is referred to in the province's name, which originated with Queen Victoria and was officially proclaimed in 1858. The province is closely tied to the American Pacific Northwest with which it shares locational continuity.

Land and Resources

Regions British Columbia has 2 main regions, loosely called "the Coast" and "the Interior," with numerous contrasts and variations within each. The so-called "Lower Mainland," dominated by metropolitan Vancouver, contains 50% of the province's population and is its commercial, cultural and industrial centre. A slightly broader region, sometimes called the Georgia Strait region, includes Victoria and the SE coast of Vancouver I; this area holds 70% of the population. The vast interior is dominated by parallel mountain ranges and population is strung north-south along valleys, notably the Okanagan and the Kootenay. Nodes of population are dispersed, as at Kamloops and Prince George in the interior, Prince Rupert and Kitimat on the northern coast and Dawson Creek and Ft St John in the PEACE RIVER LOWLAND, each the centre of a separate subregion and each depending more on world markets than on local markets. Much of the evolution of resource-based economic activity in the province has been concerned with linking together these separate regions into a broader provincial economy. The northern half of the province is virtually uninhab-

ited N of Prince Rupert and is cut off from the Pacific by the Alaska Panhandle. The Peace River Lowland of the NE is actually an extension of the Interior Plains and more closely resembles neighbouring Alberta than the rest of the province.

Landforms, Geology and Drainage The Cordilleran mountain system of western N America covers most of British Columbia, except for the Peace R area of the NE. The ROCKY MOUNTAINS rise abruptly about 1000-1500 m above the foothills of Alberta, and some of their snow- and ice-covered peaks tower more than 3000 m above sea level; the highest peak in the Canadian Rockies, Mt Robson, W of Jasper, Alta, is 3954 m. In the southern Rockies, the sharp, jagged sedimentary-rock peaks of mainly Paleozoic geological age differ from the more rounded, lower peaks of Proterozoic age to the N. The Rocky Mountains terminate S of the LIARD R in northeastern BC and do not extend into the Yukon or Alaska – contrary to some foreign maps and atlases. The western boundary of the Rocky Mountains is the narrow ROCKY MOUNTAIN TRENCH – the longest valley in N America, extending more than 1500 km along the length of BC from Montana to the Yukon. Out of the trench flow the headwaters of the Kootenay, COLUMBIA, FRASER, Parsnip, Finlay, Kechika and Liard rivers, each separated from the others by low drainage divides.

Two other mountain systems lie W of the Rocky Mountain Trench: the COLUMBIA MOUNTAINS to the S and the Cassiar-Omineca Mountains to the N. The Columbia Mountains (a collective name seldom used in BC) consist of 3 parallel, N-S ranges (Purcell, Selkirk, Monashee) which have sharp peaks of 2000-3000 m, separated by long, narrow valleys occupied by Kootenay Lk and the Columbia R. These mountains consist mainly of sedimentary and intrusive rocks of Cretaceous, Triassic and Jurassic ages, and they have been well mineralized. The fourth range of the group, the CARIBOO MOUNTAINS NW of the Thompson R, is composed of sedimentary rocks of Proterozoic age which appear to be less mineralized.

The broad, gently rolling uplands of the Interior Plateau cover central British Columbia. The region

can be considered a basin because it is surrounded by higher mountains. Many of the rocks are lavas of Cretaceous and Tertiary geological ages with apparently little mineralization except around the plateau edges. The Fraser R has cut deeply into the bedrock in the southern part to form the spectacular FRASER RIVER CANYON. Northward the Stikine Plateau is another upland area of mainly Jurassic lava rocks, with some recent volcanoes, containing the headwaters of the Stikine R. Average altitudes of both the Interior and Stikine plateaus are about 1000 m above sea level.

The western section of the Cordillera consists of the COAST MOUNTAINS along the coast and the offshore Insular Mountains. The northern end of the Cascade Mountains of Washington state terminates at the Fraser R, and then the high, snow and ice-covered peaks of the Coast Mountains extend northward along the Alaskan Panhandle into the Yukon. These scenic mountains have peaks up to 3000 m in the southern part, with Mt Waddington, the highest peak entirely in BC, rising to 4019 m. Numerous long, twisting, deep fjords penetrate into the mountain mass along the coast. The rocks are mostly granitic intrusions of Cretaceous and Tertiary ages and there are some recent volcanoes. The lower Coast Mountains (1500-2000 m) near the Skeena R are less of a barrier to the penetration of Pacific air masses, but they increase in altitude to the N. The highest peak in BC, Mt Fairweather (4663 m), straddles the Alaska border in the St Elias Mountains just NW of the Coast Mountains. Only 3 major rivers, the Fraser, Skeena and Stikine, have cut through the barrier of the Coast Mountains; the first 2 of these valleys have become important topographic funnels for the only land-transportation routes reaching the coast from the interior. The offshore Insular Mountains are the partially submerged northern continuation of the Olympic Mountains and Coast Ranges of Washington state. They provide the land mass for both Vancouver I and the Queen Charlotte Is. The highest peak on Vancouver I is GOLDEN HINDE, at 2200 m.

All of British Columbia was under a thick sheet of ice during the Glacial Age. Some coastal areas,

British Columbia

Capital: Victoria
Motto: Splendor Sine Occasu ("Splendour without diminishment")
Flower: Pacific dogwood
Largest Cities: Greater Vancouver, Greater Victoria, Prince George, Kamloops, Kelowna, Nanaimo, Penticton
Population: 2 883 365 (1986c), rank third; 11.4% of Canada; 79.2% urban; 20.8% rural; 3.2 per km² density; 5.1% increase from 1981-86, 16.9% from 1976-86
Languages: 80.9% English; 1.4% French; 14.5% Other; 3.2% English plus one or more other languages
Entered Confederation: 20 July 1871
Government: Provincial — Lieutenant-Governor, Executive Council, Legislative Assembly of 69 members; federal — 6 senators, 28 members of the House of Commons
Area: 948 596 km²; including 18 068 km² of inland water; 9.5% of Canada
Elevation: Highest point — Fairweather Mountain (4663 m); lowest point — sea level along coasts
Gross Domestic Product: $50.8 billion (1986)
Farm Cash Receipts: $1.0 billion (1986)
Value of Fish Landings: $383.6 million (1986e)
Electric Power Generated: 59 126 GWh
Sales Tax: 7% (1987)

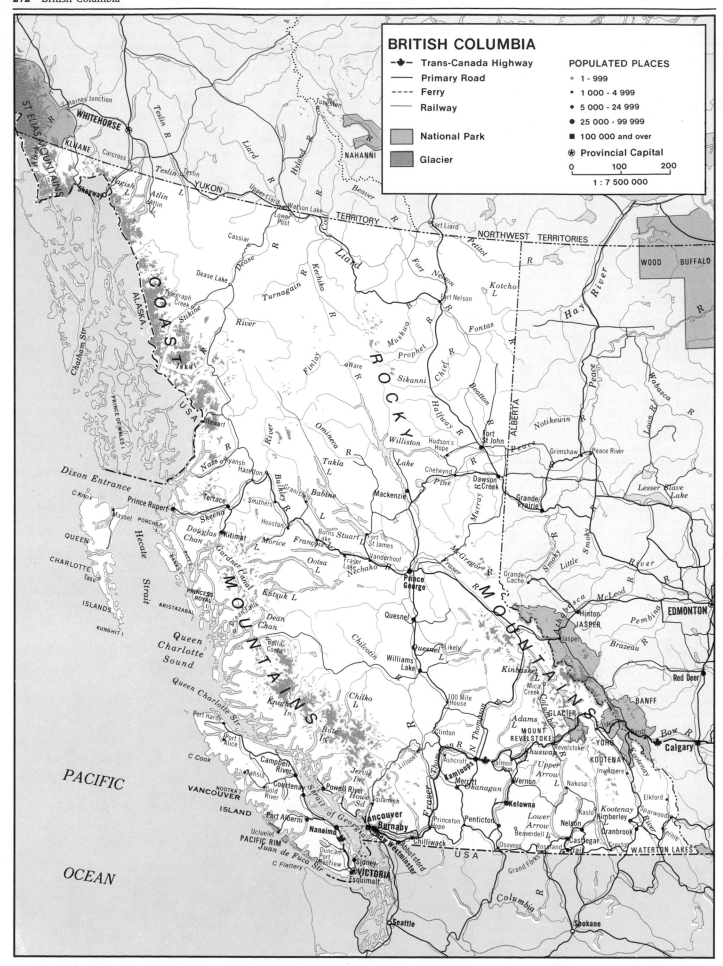

BRITISH COLUMBIA

- ⚜ Trans-Canada Highway
- ── Primary Road
- ─ ─ Ferry
- ≈ Railway

National Park

Glacier

POPULATED PLACES
- ○ 1 - 999
- • 1 000 - 4 999
- ● 5 000 - 24 999
- ● 25 000 - 99 999
- ■ 100 000 and over
- ⊛ Provincial Capital

0   100   200

1 : 7 500 000

PACIFIC

OCEAN

Classic U-shaped valley in the Coast Mountains of the western section of the Cordillera of BC (*photo by Tom W. Parkin/Pathfinder*).

and perhaps interior valleys, became ice free about 12 000-15 000 years ago, and coastal lowlands have been rising, relative to sea level, since that time. The remainder of the province became ice free 7000-13 000 years ago. The results of continental and alpine glaciation are seen everywhere in the province in fjords and cirques in the mountains, ground moraines across the Interior Plateau and terraces and benches along interior rivers.

Soils and Vegetation It is estimated that 3% of British Columbia has soils suitable for agricultural production. As in most mountainous areas, only the narrow floodplains, terraces and deltas of the river valleys have alluvial soils on which crops can grow. Glacial deposition on the middle slopes of the mountains provides sufficient soil to support tree growth.

The coniferous trees of coastal British Columbia are the tallest, broadest trees in Canada. Douglas fir, western cedar, balsam fir, hemlock and Sitka spruce grow very well in the mild, wet climate and are the basis for the province's most valuable primary industry, FORESTRY. Similar trees, plus lodgepole and ponderosa pine and aspen, occupy the middle slopes of the interior mountains and plateaus. Depending on local conditions of slope and exposure, the upper treeline across southern BC is about 2000 m and declines to about 1000 m in the N. In contrast, grassland cover indicates the drier climate E of the Coast Mountains and in the lower valleys of the rivers across the southern third of the province.

Climate There are wide variations in climatic conditions within small areas in British Columbia. The major climate contrast is between the coast and the interior, but there are also significant variations between valleys and uplands, and between the northern and southern parts of the province. Relatively warm air masses from the Pacific Ocean bring mild temperatures to the coast during the winters, while cold water keeps coastal temperatures cool in the summer. The barrier of the Coast Mts hinders these moderating conditions from being carried inland. Average Jan mean temperatures are above 0°C at most coastal stations – the mildest in Canada – and July averages are about 15°C in the N and 18°C in the sheltered Georgia Strait region. In contrast, the interior may be covered in winter by cold air masses pushing S from the Yukon or Alaska, particularly in the northern part of the province. Average daily mean January temperatures are -10°C to -15°C across the central interior and are a cold -20°C or more on the northeastern plains.

The southern interior valleys may heat up during the summer, recording July average monthly temperatures of more than 20°C, but farther N stations at higher altitudes on the central Interior Plateau average about 15°C in midsummer.

The air masses which cross the Pacific bring ample rainfall to the coast, particularly in the autumn and winter. On the lee (eastern) side of the mountains, the interior valleys receive much less precipitation. The west-facing mountains of Vancouver Island receive more than 250 cm of annual precipitation, whereas the east-coast lowland records only about 70 to 100 cm. The western slopes of the Coast Mountains accumulate 100 to 300 cm annually, of which a high percentage is snowfall; but the OKANAGAN VALLEY receives a mere 25 cm of annual precipitation. The frost-free season on the coast is the longest in Canada, averaging more than 200 days; in contrast, the central Interior Plateau is handicapped by a short frost-free season of only 75 to 100 days. In summary, the well-publicized, mild, wet winters and cool, dry summers associated with British Columbia are characteristic only of the southwest; the rest of the province experiences temperature conditions similar to those on the plains of Alberta and Saskatchewan.

Natural Resources About 55% of British Columbia is forested, and as a result of excellent growth conditions for coniferous trees, the province has about 40% of the merchantable wood in Canada on 17% of the forested land.

The geology of most mountainous areas is favourable to mineralization, and BC is no exception. A wide range of metals has been discovered throughout the Cordilleran part of the province, including lead, zinc, gold, silver, molybdenum, copper and iron. The Peace River Lowland, NE of the Rocky Mountains, has a different geological base consisting of younger, sedimentary rocks which have been the sources of petroleum, natural gas and coal. The heavy precipitation, steep mountain slopes and large, interior drainage basins are ideal physical conditions for the production of hydroelectric power, and BC has the second-largest provincial potential for electric-power generation, after Québec; but some of the large interior rivers have not been harnessed because their use would damage the habitat of the PACIFIC SALMON, which spawn in the headwaters of coastal and interior rivers flowing into the Pacific. The physical environment of BC is itself a valuable resource, attracting visitors from throughout the world, as well as giving pleasure to local residents.

Conservation The balance between economic development and preservation of the environment is particularly troublesome in British Columbia, which relies heavily on nonrenewable resources. Many of the resources seemed inexhaustible, but by the 1930s the coast forest was being rapidly depleted. The salmon fishery has been threatened by overfishing and by destruction of marine and river habitats in some places, and some of British Columbia's scarce agricultural land has been lost to roads, housing and industry. There are people who argue that such uses of the land are more productive (of income) than agriculture.

Early provincial governments were primarily concerned with rapid development to promote local employment, but especially since WWII much legislation has been enacted to preserve the environment and natural resources. The success of the REFORESTATION program has been questioned and is interpreted differently by the forestry industry and by critics, but forestry is being managed by the principle of "sustained yield." Fishing is confined to certain places and times, and hydroelectric developments have been delayed indefinitely to protect salmon runs. A freeze was placed on changing the use of agricultural land in 1973, and the British Columbia Ecological Reserves Act (1971) set aside numerous reserves of representative ecosystems.

People

Settlement The coasts and interior valleys of British Columbia were first occupied by NATIVE PEOPLE some time after the last Ice Age. Occupation of some sites in BC has been confirmed at about 6000-8000 years ago by carbon dating. The people of the NORTHWEST COAST lived in a particularly bountiful environment, which provided abundant shellfish, salmon and even whales. The coastal people concentrated along the lower reaches of the major salmon rivers. They were a semisedentary people and developed an elaborate culture, typified by TOTEM POLES and the POTLATCH (*see* TAGISH; TSIMSHIAN; HAIDA; WAKASHAN; TLINGIT; KWAKIUTL; NOOTKA; and NATIVE PEOPLE: NORTHWEST COAST). The interior inhabitants, such

Grasslands in the BC interior (*photo by Tim Fitzharris*).

Osoyoos – lake, valley and town in the southern Okanagan in south-central BC (*courtesy Elliott and Nicole Bernshaw/Bernshaw Photography*).

as the CARRIER, Interior SALISH and KOOTENAY were generally nomadic and depended on hunting.

The first permanent European settlement came with the development of the FUR TRADE in the early 19th century. A flurry of activity followed the discovery of gold on the lower and middle Fraser R, resulting in a system of supply and transportation inland along the Fraser R to the Cariboo Mts. More permanent mining towns began to dot the valleys of the SE area by the 1880s – each supported by local forestry, small farms and complex rail, road and water transport. In contrast, settlement was more urban and commercial on the SW coast. VICTORIA, the capital, was the main administrative and commercial settlement and the supply centre for interior and coastal resource development during the period 1860-90. After VANCOUVER, on Burrard Inlet N of the mouth of the Fraser R, was selected as the site for the western terminal of the CPR in 1886, it soon replaced Victoria as the commercial centre and became the main port through which both coastal and interior products moved to world markets.

Thus, British Columbia developed contrasting coastal and interior settlement patterns, which remained the same throughout the 20th century, although densities increased. Population has always been primarily urban, and in 1986, 79.2% of the population was so classified, 80% of it in the southwestern region. The remaining population is dispersed in linear patterns across the southern half of the province, mainly occupying the N-S valleys or in resource-based settlements along the main transportation lines. The only major groups of farming population live in the Okanagan Valley and dispersed along the highway between Kamloops and Prince George. These linear population clusters are separated from each other by unoccupied mountain ranges. Few people live N of Prince George and Prince Rupert, except for an urban and agricultural cluster in the Peace R area of the NE.

Urban Centres Metropolitan Vancouver is the largest city in the province and ranks third in population among the metropolitan cities of Canada. Victoria is the only other BC metropolitan city larger than 100 000 population. These 2 cities and many nearby municipalities have most of the secondary and consumer-goods manufacturing in the province; the main water, road, rail and air

transportation and transfer facilities; most of the head offices and commercial and financial offices; and most of the cultural and entertainment attractions. These cities and their activities are supported by the largest number of farmers in the province, in the adjoining Lower Fraser Valley and along the E coast of Vancouver I.

Other large cities are resource-based processors and service and supply centres for subregions dispersed throughout the province. They had populations of about 45 000 to 70 000 in 1986 and included PRINCE GEORGE, KAMLOOPS, KELOWNA and NANAIMO. A number of smaller cities with populations of 15 000 to 40 000 include CRANBROOK-KIMBERLEY, TRAIL-CASTLEGAR, PENTICTON, VERNON, DAWSON CREEK-FORT ST JOHN, PRINCE RUPERT and PORT ALBERNI.

Labour Force People in business, finance, trade, service and manufacturing make up around 70% of the work force. Those in primary industries total only about 7%. They include forest workers (but not those in sawmills and pulp and paper mills), fishermen (but not those in fish-processing plants), miners (but not those in mineral processing) and farmers. In the period of expanding economy and rapidly increasing population since 1950, it is not surprising that there have been as many labourers in the construction industries as in the primary, resource-based industries (both about 7% of the labour force). Many people are needed in transportation, both to move people and products within the large cities and to move natural resources in partially processed form to the coastal ports or to central Canadian and American markets. Such workers constitute slightly less than 10% of the work force.

British Columbia is a separate and distinct labour complex and has experienced patterns of industrial conflict sometimes different from the rest of Canada. A much higher percentage of workers belong to unions, and strikes have been frequent and prolonged. Various reasons have been suggested for this, for example, that BC is an

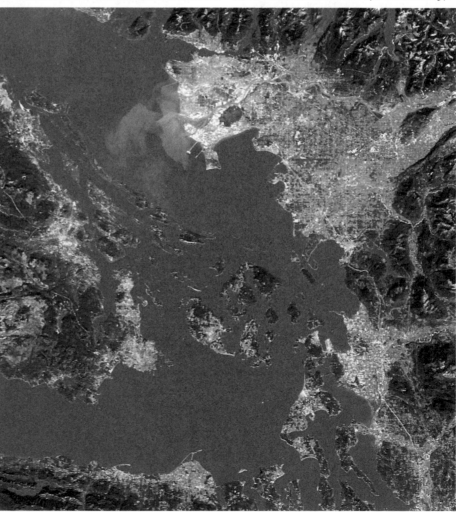

Enhanced natural colour Landsat composite of Vancouver, Victoria and Nanaimo. Most of the population of BC lives in this southwestern corner of the province (© *MacDonald Dettwiler 1986, image courtesy Advanced Satellite Productions and Canada Centre for Remote Sensing*).

The Revelstoke Dam was built after an international agreement to make American downstream power plants more effective. Turbines were installed in the 1970s to produce electric power for Vancouver (*courtesy British Columbia Hydro and Power Authority*).

extension of the Pacific Northwest region of the US – the most unionized area in that country – and the province's workers have been influenced by their more highly paid American neighbours; and that the concentration of economic life in Vancouver has led to centralization of unions and bargaining. Finally, it has been argued that the rapid but erratic pattern of economic growth in the province has led to bitter dispute, particularly in the forest and construction industries, which are already vulnerable to seasonal and cyclical fluctuations.

Languages, Ethnicity and Religion In the early part of this century more than 75% of the residents were of British origin and most of the population spoke English as their first language. In the mid-19th century the only group of non-British settlers were the CHINESE who worked as labourers in the mines of the Cariboo. In the early 1880s many more Chinese were brought to BC as labourers for the building of the CPR. Afterwards many of them settled in Vancouver where they formed the largest Chinese community in Canada. A smaller "Chinatown" also arose in Victoria. Most Chinese worked in service or commercial occupations. JAPANESE also settled in southwestern BC between 1900 and 1940. They were a significant group in the fishing industry, in Fraser Valley farming and in a small commercial core in Vancouver. The native Indian population was recorded as about 82 000 in 1981, many of whom were nonstatus; in 1986 there were 66 585 registered Indians. Most of the status Indians live on reserves dispersed throughout the province. One of the few distinctive social groups that did not settle in southwestern BC was the DOUKHOBORS. In the 1920s and earlier this religious group migrated to south-central BC from the Prairies and settled on small, communal farms in the Kootenay, Slocan, Columbia and Kettle valleys.

As in other parts of Canada, the percentage of people of British origin has declined rapidly since 1950. After 1970 the influx of large numbers of East and SOUTHEAST ASIANS and SOUTH ASIANS particularly affected BC. Some were REFUGEES; others sought better opportunities in service and business occupations. These demographic changes in BC's population are reflected in the cityscapes particularly of Vancouver, in the variety of restaurants and the areas known as "Chinatown," "Little Italy" and the "Greek Village." English as a second language was a major subject in the province's primary schools in the 1970s. The French Canadian share of the population and language is minor in BC.

The figures for ethnic and national origins may be misleading because most of the BC population was born within the province. Most people are therefore at least second- or third-generation residents. In addition to immigrants who have

recognizably distinct cultures and physical characteristics, there were even larger numbers who migrated to BC from other parts of Canada, although by 1986 the net migration was only 1221. The "newness" of BC and its rapid population growth contrast with those of the Atlantic provinces and Québec, most of whose population was born within the eastern region.

Since the majority of people are of British national origin and English speaking, as in other parts of Canada they are predominantly CHRISTIAN within the UNITED, ANGLICAN and Roman CATHOLIC churches. The variety of other cultures and second languages can be seen in the relative significance of other religions such as SIKHISM and ISLAM.

The earlier part of the province's history was marred by RACISM, particularly the anti-Asiatic riots of 1907 and the KOMAGATA MARU incident of 1914. Stirred up by politicians of all parties, fears were rampant that British Columbia's future as a "white province" was threatened. The population of Japanese and Chinese was less than 40 000 in 1921, but their concentration in the Lower Mainland and southern Vancouver I and the restricted forms of employment they could take made them conspicuous. Forced to take lower wages and hardworking, they were considered unfair competition by the unions and the agricultural community. The campaign of the Asiatic Exclusion League (est 1921) and others resulted in the Chinese Immigration Act of 1923, which effectively ended Chinese immigration. Many Japanese were evicted from their coastal fishing villages during WWII and placed in INTERNMENT camps – a bitter episode in their history in Canada. Political discrimination against nonwhites in BC finally ended after WWII when the Chinese and Hindu populations were enfranchised in 1947, with the Japanese following in 1949.

Economy

Resource-based activities have been the basis of BC's economy throughout its modern history. The Indians depended on the animal population of land and sea for their food, clothing and exchange. The first items of trade desired by Europeans were sea-otter pelts from the coast and animal furs from the interior. Settlers of European origin were primarily attracted by mineral resources, notably gold in the central interior and SE, and also coal on Vancouver I, near Nanaimo and Cumberland. By the 1880s the tall, straight coniferous trees of the coast forest were being cut for lumber to supply other Pacific Rim settlements, and salmon were being canned at numerous river-mouth canneries to be shipped throughout the world. In the 19th century the natural resources of BC were utilized to supply markets elsewhere in Anglo-America or in East Asia or Europe. Local manufacturing consisted primarily of some first-stage processing of these resources.

As population increased in the 20th century and concentrated in or near the ports of the SW, consumer-goods manufacturing became possible in the southwestern cities, aided by the high cost of transporting manufactured goods from eastern Canada and the US and by an ample supply of inexpensive hydroelectric power. Agricultural settlement expanded across the lowland and delta of the Lower Fraser R. The management and financial activities concerned with resource developments remained in the coastal cities, mainly Vancouver, maintaining the long-established contrast between the primary activities of the N coast and interior, and the commercial business and assembly activities of the southwestern cities.

Forestry Forestry has been the main component of BC's economy throughout this century.

Forest products rank first in value among provincial primary industries, and BC produces 63% of Canada's sawn lumber, most of its plywood and 25% of its chemical pulp. Commercial logging began in the 1840s on Vancouver I and spread to the Lower Fraser after the gold rush of 1858. Lumber mills were established in the SW after the middle of the 19th century to supply the building needs of the growing settlements and to export to nearby Pacific settlements. Temporary SAWMILLS also operated near all of the scattered mining communities in the interior; some of these mills, located on the 2 main railway lines, were able to export lumber eastward to the growing Prairie towns in the early 20th century. Lumber production expanded rapidly along the coast after WWI, as the newly opened PANAMA CANAL made eastern US and European markets more accessible to West Coast mills. Most lumber companies made operational decisions to extend their logging camps northward along the coast and to transport the logs by a variety of water transport means to large sawmills around the Georgia Strait region. With minor exceptions, such as near Prince Rupert, this pattern of N coast primary cutting and S coast processing and export has been maintained.

Pulp and paper mills were established at a few places around Georgia Strait early in the 20th century, but these mills did not have large consuming markets for newsprint and paper similar to the markets in the eastern US available for eastern Canadian mills at that time. Unlike eastern mills, the pulp and paper mills of BC became integrated into existing sawmill operations and received much of their wood fibre raw material from product residue such as sawdust and chips from adjoining lumber mills. The pulp and paper industry remained coastal until the mid-1960s, when mills were opened in several places across the interior. This interior expansion was part of the general spread of the forest industry into the interior of the province, stimulated by increased foreign markets, improved interior road and rail transport, new government concessions and cutting rights to forested areas, and a concern for possible depletion of the coast forest reserves.

Throughout the 1970s the interior produced about half of the value of provincial forest products. Small sawmills disappeared along the coast early in this century and across the interior after 1950, and were replaced by very large, centrally located sawmills, sometimes with adjoining pulp and paper or paper mills. Although water transport, often in self-dumping log barges, is still the chief means of transporting logs to the mills along the coast, water transport is rarely used in the interior – unlike the river-based log transport system which evolved in eastern Canada, eg, on the Miramichi and Ottawa rivers. Interior logs and finished forest products are all moved by road or rail and therefore all forestry-based settlements are located on the main railways or highways.

Gross Domestic Product of British Columbia, 1986
(millions of dollars)

	Amount	Percent
Commercial, Business and Personal Service	11 383	22.4%
Finance	8052	15.8%
Manufacturing	6765	13.3%
Transportation	6344	12.5%
Wholesale and Retail Trade	5563	10.9%
Public Administration	3260	6.4%
Construction	3257	6.4%
Mining	2101	4.1%
Forestry	1595	3.1%
Utilities	1482	2.9%
Agriculture	747	1.5%
Fishing	225	.4%

In 1978 the BC Legislature passed 3 new Acts dealing with the responsibilities of the Department of Forests in managing, protecting and conserving the forest resource. Pressures on the industry, which is hard pressed in recessionary times, increase as demands grow for preservation of the forests for recreation, wildlife and aesthetic screens, and as a resource for future generations. In 1986-87 the industry, after dramatically increasing its penetration of the US market, was under pressure from US producers for alleged unfair competition (*see* SOFTWOOD LUMBER DISPUTE). *See also* FOREST; FOREST ECONOMICS; FOREST HARVESTING; FOREST REGIONS; and FORESTRY EDUCATION.

Mining Mining and mineral processing employ about 3% of the labour force (1984), but yield nearly 20% of the value of the products of the major industries of BC. Coal and copper account for about one-half of the total and others in order of importance are natural gas, oil, zinc and gold (1986). Mining became important in BC in 1858 with the FRASER GOLD RUSH and later discoveries in the Cariboo region. Between 1890 and 1910 the Kootenay region of southeastern BC became one of the most important mining areas of Canada. The huge smelter-refinery at Trail receives ore from BC, the Yukon and the NWT.

Coal was first mined near Nanaimo on Vancouver I in the mid-19th century. Immense coal deposits in the Fernie-Crowsnest Pass area were used by the Trail smelter and by the railways until they converted to diesel fuel. Both metallurgical and thermal coal are exported from southeastern BC to Japan and elsewhere. The younger, sedimentary rocks of northeastern BC, like those of the interior plains of Alberta, are the sources of coal, petroleum and natural gas. The latter 2 products are transported by pipelines to urban markets in southwestern BC and the adjoining northwestern states of the US.

Metal mines have opened and closed across the southern interior from Grand Forks to Princeton throughout this century. In the early 1980s mining in the area was highlighted by large, open-pit copper mines SW of Kamloops. Other metal mines have produced intermittently across the Interior Plateau from near Williams Lake to Babine Lake in the NW. Mines have also operated intermittently along the coast of BC for more than a century. Base-metal mines opened and closed near Stewart, NE of Prince Rupert, and at several places on Vancouver I. Iron ore and copper, to name just 2 examples, have been exported to Japan from coastal mines. Because nearly all of the mineral production of BC is consumed outside of the province, the fortunes of the mining industry are largely determined outside the province.

Fisheries Commercial fishing and sportfishing in the many large lakes in the interior of the province are minor compared with the rivermouth, alongshore and deep-sea FISHERIES of the coast. The most valuable fishery is for the 5 species of Pacific salmon, which have 2- to 5-year cycles of river spawning, sea migration and return to the same spawning rivers. As the returning fish approach and concentrate off river mouths they are caught by large, modern fishing vessels. Although most coastal rivers produce some salmon, the largest catches are obtained off the mouths of the Fraser and Skeena. Early in this century salmon canneries were dispersed all along the BC coast, close to the catching areas because salmon were perishable. However, the gradual introduction of improved boats, with longer ranges and refrigeration, resulted in the closing of most canneries on the central coast and the concentration of fish processing into a few large plants near Prince Rupert and Vancouver.

Other fish caught along the coast and offshore include HERRING (and a valuable by-product, her-

Steamships on Lake Kootenay, 1908. Steamships played a large role in opening up interior BC (*by permission of the British Library*).

ring roe), halibut and other groundfish such as COD and sole, as well as a large variety of shellfish, particularly oysters which are farmed at various locations along the coast. The physical character of fjorded, submerged coastal BC provides numerous shelters and harbours for fishing vessels, but the province lacks the broad, shallow offshore continental shelf which is a favourable fish habitat off East Coast Canada.

Agriculture In cultivated land as a percentage of total provincial area, BC ranks second lowest in Canada, behind Newfoundland; however, BC still produces 5% of Canada's total agricultural products. Farming began in BC to supply the trading posts in the mid-19th century. The growing cities of Vancouver and Victoria stimulated agricultural expansion in the Fraser Valley and on Vancouver I. In the 1890s fruit and vegetable growing were established in the Okanagan and beef ranching in the Cariboo region.

The largest area of cultivated land is in the Peace R area, which accounts for about 90% of the grain harvested in BC. Aided by the longest frost-free season in Canada, the small farms of the Lower Fraser R produce dairy and livestock products, vegetables, small fruits and specialty crops such as blueberries, cranberries and flower bulbs. In the dry southern interior, agriculture flourishes only where irrigation systems have been established. The narrow benches and terraces above Okanagan Lk comprise one of Canada's 3 main fruit-growing regions and one of 2 grape-growing areas. The small, intensive farms produce apples, pears, peaches, cherries, plums, grapes and apricots. Cattle ranching is carried on across small areas of grassland on the southern Interior Plateau, but not enough meat is produced to supply even the Vancouver market.

Despite the scarcity of high-quality agricultural land in BC, in the period from 1966 to 1971 urban sprawl was consuming over 6000 ha per year of prime agricultural land. About 20% of the prime agricultural land of the Lower Fraser and 30% of the Okanagan had already been converted when in 1973 the Land Commission Act froze the disposition of agricultural land for nonagricultural use, despite the great demand for it for housing, industry, hobby farms and country estates.

Energy British Columbia produces a surplus of energy in the form of electrical power, coal, petroleum and natural gas. The small, accessible coalfields on eastern Vancouver I and in the southwestern Interior Plateau were worked out early in the 20th century. The coalfields in the southern Rocky Mts were developed at the beginning of this century to supply smelters in the Kootenay region. Beginning in the 1960s technological improvements in open-pit mining, unit trains and new port facilities made it possible for both thermal and metallurgical coals to be mined in the SE in larger amounts for export to Japan. In

addition, other coal mines were opened in the 1980s in the Rocky Mountains and foothills of northeastern BC, also for export. Because both areas are far from ocean transport the rail system had to be improved to move such large quantities of coal into world markets.

British Columbia is well endowed with steep and rugged landforms and ample precipitation, which together produce enormous seasonal runoffs in numerous rivers and vast amounts of potential hydroelectric power. Hydroelectric power was first produced at the close of the 19th century from small rivers in the SW for urban consumers in Victoria and Vancouver. The largest single power site in the SW prior to 1940 was developed on Bridge R, just E of the Coast Mountains. The southwestern power sources were sufficient for industrial and residential markets in the Georgia Str region until the 1960s. Around the turn of the century, the Kootenay and other rivers in the SE were dammed to produce electric power for the many local mines and towns. This power was ample until the 1960s. Following international agreement, the Columbia R was dammed at Mica Creek in the "Big Bend" N of Revelstoke in the late 1960s to help even out the flow of the river and make American downstream power plants more efficient (*see* COLUMBIA RIVER TREATY). In the 1970s, turbines were installed in the dam to produce electric power for metropolitan Vancouver.

In the northwest, a special power project was completed in 1954 to supply inexpensive power for a large aluminum smelter at Kitimat. In this project the headwaters of the Nechako R, a fish-spawning tributary of the Fraser R, were dammed and the water diverted through a tunnel in the Coast Mountains to a large subterranean power plant at Kemano on the coast. This has resulted in reduced spawning activity of salmon in the river. The northeastern section of the province was the last to be developed for hydropower. As a result of technological improvements in long-distance transmission facilities, it became possible to dam the Peace R where it spilled out of the Rocky Mountains and to send the power about 1000 km to the growing markets in metropolitan Vancouver. The Peace R development is now the third-largest hydropower producer in Canada with a capacity of over 2000 MW. The Fraser R, occupying the central part of the province, is the greatest potential source of hydroelectric power, but technology has not yet solved the problem of using the river for both fish and power. *See* BC HYDRO.

Transportation Land transportation has been funnelled into the narrow river valleys across the southern half of the province. The 2 transcontinental railways used the Fraser and Skeena valleys to cross through the western mountain barrier to reach the coast. Only 4 passes through the Rocky Mts have been used by the railways and, later, roads to enter BC from the E. From S to N these strategic passes are CROWSNEST, KICKING HORSE, YELLOWHEAD and PINE. The only S-N railway, the BRITISH COLUMBIA RY (originally called the Pacific Great Eastern), is owned by the provincial government. In the 1950s it was extended from Vancouver through Prince George to the Peace R area in the NE; another extension of the railway into the unoccupied area NW of Prince George was halted in the 1970s.

British Columbia lacked an interconnected highway system in the interior until the 1950s. The first paved road entirely across the province, the TRANS-CANADA HIGHWAY, was not completed until 1962. Most roads still follow the valley floors — where people and settlements are — and therefore have a general S-N pattern, with fewer E-W links. The provincial government is responsible for the construction and maintenance of all public roads in unorganized territory and for clas-

Government House and camp, New Westminster, BC, 1860-65 (*courtesy Provincial Archives of British Columbia/ HP-15084*).

sified arterial highways through incorporated areas. Several parts of BC have little or no land transportation lines. There are no roads along the long section of mainland coast between Powell River and Prince Rupert because of extremely high construction costs around the innumerable fjords, plus the lack of permanent settlements. Only one road crosses northwestern BC from Prince Rupert (and Stewart) to Cassiar and the ALASKA HIGHWAY; the latter is the only road across northeastern BC.

Coastal British Columbia is served by an extensive ferry service which moves freight, cars and passengers across the Strait of Georgia. Small coastal boats, tugs and barges move natural resources, supplies and people along the sheltered "Inside Passage" between Vancouver I and the mainland and northward to Prince Rupert, the Queen Charlotte Is and the Alaska Panhandle. Early in this century, shallow-draft lake vessels operated during summer on the long, narrow lakes of the central and SE interior, but they gradually disappeared after all-season highways were built.

All major cities in British Columbia are served by airlines, which, like rail, road and water transportation, further reinforce the dominance of metropolitan Vancouver and the densely occupied southwestern corner of the province.

Tourism and Recreation British Columbia is known internationally for the extent and diversity of its opportunities for outdoor recreation, particularly sportfishing, camping, hiking, boat cruising, driving for pleasure, skiing and hunting. Most tourists come by car, with the heaviest flow via Revelstoke, Kamloops and the Fraser Canyon or S from Salmon Arm down the Okanagan. Much of northern BC still lacks a network of roads and therefore attracts relatively few people. Most of the visitors come from the Prairies – three-quarters of all Canadians visiting BC come from Alberta – with significant traffic from the states of Washington, Oregon and California.

The spectacular mountain scenery and varied local physical environments are most accessible in the many provincial and federal parks. The national parks are mainly in the mountains of eastern BC and include YOHO, KOOTENAY, GLACIER and MOUNT REVELSTOKE. PACIFIC RIM NATIONAL PARK on western Vancouver I has the longest continuous stretch of sand beach in the province. In July of 1987, an agreement was reached to establish a new national park in the South Moresby region of the Queen Charlotte Is. This unique rain forest is one of N America's most diverse plant and animal wildlife habitats and is the ancestral home of the Haida Indians whose ancient sites and totem poles are of significant archaeological value (*see* ANTHONY ISLAND PROVINCIAL PARK). BC had 365 provincial parks and recreation areas in 1986, totalling more than 4.5 million hectares. These are classified into 4 types: 32 recreation areas; 291 class A parks, which are usually campsites and picnic grounds; 4 larger class B parks, which include very large areas such as GARIBALDI, STRATHCONA (BC's first provincial park in 1911) and Tweedsmuir, 37 class C parks which are small local recreation areas and the PURCELL WILDERNESS CONSERVANCY near Kaslo in the Kootenay region.

Government and Politics

British Columbia is governed by a legislative assembly of 69 members (1987) elected from 52 ridings (35 one-person and 17 two-person ridings). Electoral districts are redefined after each major census to maintain representation in proportion to current population distribution. A lieutenant-governor, appointed by Canada's governor general on the advice of the prime minister, is the head of provincial government in title only; power resides with the premier of the province, who is the leader of the political party winning the most seats in the legislature at elections, which must be held at least every 5 years. A cabinet is chosen by the premier from the majority party and government service is provided by a civil service, headed by deputy ministers, with headquarters in Victoria. BC has 6 appointed senators in the federal Senate and 28 elected members in the federal House of Commons in Ottawa. This representation is proportionate to BC's population, which is 11.4% of Canada's total.

The highest court in BC is the Court of Appeal, made up of the chief justice and 10 puisne justices. The Supreme Court is lower than the Court of Appeal; it has a chief justice and 26 puisne justices. There are 7 county courts, although the term "county" is not used to define an administrative unit. Magistrates and justices of the peace may preside over provincial courts, which may deal with family matters and juvenile delinquents. The Governor General-in-Council (the Crown, in effect) appoints all provincial judges. The attorney general is the chief law officer of the province, empowered to act in all litigation in which the province is a party; the ministry is responsible for the administration of justice, policing and the provision of legal services.

Local Government Most people in British Columbia live in communities with local government, but most of the area of the province has no local government, or people, and the resources and lands of this unorganized territory are administered by departments in the provincial government. Less than 1% of the provincial area is incorporated into (in 1986) 35 cities, 47 district municipalities, 13 towns, 48 villages and 28 regional districts with various forms of local government. These incorporated areas include about 80% of the provincial population. In all municipalities, local voters elect a mayor and several aldermen as members of a council. In the 99% of the provincial area classified as Unorganized Territory, there is no specific local government except for the 28 regional districts. Each regional district has a board made up of local elected and nominated members, plus provincial government representation. Regional districts are established by Cabinet partly to assist the joint financing of certain services such as water, sewers, regional parks and transportation among a group of municipalities. These districts may do regional planning but the implementation of the plans is the responsibility of the local municipalities. BC does not have township and county administrative units, as have other parts of Canada.

Public Finance Most of the revenue of the provincial government comes from taxes levied on a wide range of property, sales and incomes of citizens, companies and corporations. For exam-

Premiers of British Columbia 1871-1987

	Party	Term
John Foster McCreight		1871-72
Amor De Cosmos		1872-74
George Anthony Walkem		1874-76
Andrew Charles Elliott		1876-78
George Anthony Walkem		1878-82
Robert Beaven		1882-83
William Smithe		1883-87
Alexander Edmund Batson Davie	Conservative	1887-89
John Robson	Liberal	1889-92
Theodore Davie		1892-95
John Herbert Turner		1895-98
Charles Augustus Semlin	Conservative	1898-1900
Joseph Martin	Liberal	1900
James Dunsmuir	Conservative	1900-02
Edward Gawler Prior	Conservative	1902-03
Richard McBride	Conservative	1903-15
William John Bowser	Conservative	1915-16
Harlan Carey Brewster	Liberal	1916-18
John Oliver	Liberal	1918-27
John Duncan MacLean	Liberal	1927-28
Simon Fraser Tolmie	Conservative	1928-33
Thomas Dufferin Pattullo	Liberal	1933-41
John Hart	Coalition Govt	1941-47
Byron Ingemar Johnson	Coalition Govt	1947-52
William Andrew Cecil Bennett	Social Credit	1952-72
David Barrett	New Democratic Party	1972-75
William Richards Bennett	Social Credit	1975-86
Willam Vander Zalm	Social Credit	1986-

Lieutenant-Governors of British Columbia 1871-1987

	Term
Joseph William Trutch	1871-76
Albert Norton Richards	1876-81
Clement Francis Cornwall	1881-87
Hugh Nelson	1887-92
Edgar Dewdney	1892-97
Thomas Robert McInnes	1897-1900
Henri-Gustave Joly de Lotbinière	1900-06
James Dunsmuir	1906-09
Thomas Wilson Paterson	1909-14
Francis Stillman Barnard	1914-19
Edward Gawler Prior	1919-20
Walter Cameron Nichol	1920-26
Robert Randolph Bruce	1926-31
John William Fordham Johnson	1931-36
Eric Werge Hamber	1936-41
William Culham Woodward	1941-46
Charles Arthur Banks	1946-50
Clarence Wallace	1950-55
Frank MacKenzie Ross	1955-60
George Randolph Pearkes	1960-68
John Robert Nicholson	1968-73
Walter Steward Owen	1973-78
Henry Pybus Bell-Irving	1978-83
Robert Gordon Rogers	1983-

ple, there are taxes on nonmunicipal lands, gasoline, liquor and tobacco, and a general provincial sales tax; provincial licences and permit fees include charges for the right to cut timber on crown land and for the use of other natural resources. The province receives a share of income tax which is collected by the federal government and returned to the province as part of various federal-provincial tax-sharing arrangements. Most of the expenditures of the government go to education, health and social services, the latter including hospitals, medical care, welfare and social-assistance payments. Part of public expenditure pays the salaries of civil servants who administer the government bureaucracy and provide services to citizens. The government also maintains ferries, which are more important in British Columbia than in other provinces, as well as roads and bridges.

Health British Columbia's health services were provided through 16 health districts and 5 municipal health departments in 1986. The provincial government provides all personnel working within the health districts. All permanent residents of the province qualify for benefits under the Hospital Insurance Act, including hospital care and doctors' fees. This medical service is partly paid for by premiums paid by all residents. The Ministry of Health also operates long-term care programs, care for mental patients and a subsidized ambulance service.

Politics The federal party lines of Liberal and Conservative were not introduced to the province until 1903, when Richard MCBRIDE, the first Conservative leader, became premier. The Liberal Party formed its first government in 1916, led by H.C. BREWSTER, and the Conservatives regained power in 1928 under Simon TOLMIE. Many labour leaders had come from Great Britain, bringing experience as organizers, and they gained early success in BC when legislation for improved working conditions and social services was introduced. Various third parties were active. The Labour Party elected members in 1920, 1924, 1928 and 1933. Progressive and Socialist parties emerged with the serious economic difficulties of the GREAT DEPRESSION, and the Conservatives were nearly wiped out in 1933, finishing behind the new CO-OPERATIVE COMMONWEALTH FEDERATION (CCF) who won 7 seats and 31% of the vote and the new Liberal government of Premier T.D. PATTULLO that ruled for the next 8 years. Premiers John HART (1941-47) and Byron I. JOHNSON (1947-52), both Liberals, were called upon to lead COALITION GOVERNMENTS.

In 1952 a new party led by W.A.C. BENNETT broke away from the Conservative Party and called itself SOCIAL CREDIT, after a similar party in Alberta. This party instantly won a minority government in 1952 and then governed the province for 20 years during a period of enormous resource development and growth, particularly in the interior of the province, which was being better interconnected internally and linked to the SW coast by road-building programs and the northern extension of the British Columbia Ry to the Peace River area. The NEW DEMOCRATIC PARTY (formerly CCF) became the official Opposition in the 1960s with the virtual disappearance of the provincial Liberal and Conservative parties. The NDP was elected to government for the first time in 1972, led by David BARRETT. The electorate has tended to polarize in roughly equal numbers around the 2 parties, with Social Credit advocating free enterprise and government restraint, and the NDP advocating moderate socialism and government economic and social involvement. Social Credit regained power in 1975, led by William BENNETT, son of W.A.C. Bennett, was re-elected in 1979, 1983, and again in 1986 under a new leader, William VANDER ZALM.

Emily Carr, *Shoreline* (1936), oil on canvas. One of BC's great artists, Carr was affected both by the province's great natural beauty and its native heritage (*courtesy The McMichael Coll/gift of Mrs H.P. DePencier, 1966*).

Education

Elementary schools were established in Victoria in 1852, a few years after a fort was built there by the HBC, and they were maintained by the colonial government after 1858. The Public School Act of 1872 established a free provincial school system. The first secondary schools (then called high schools) were available in Victoria in 1876 and in Vancouver in 1890. Education is free and compulsory for children from 7 to 15 years of age. Children who live in isolated areas may be taught through correspondence courses provided by the Ministry of Education. Elementary and secondary schools are administered by local boards, made up of elected local citizens, with financial support mainly from the provincial government, in addition to local taxes on property. British Columbia was divided into 75 school districts in 1986. There are a few private schools, modelled on the British system, and some schools supported by religious groups. These schools charge fees for attendance and also receive limited government financial support. The provincial government provided special programs for the hearing impaired in 41 school districts in 1986, and also operated the residential Jericho Hill School for the Deaf in Vancouver. The curricula for school courses and programs are established by the Ministry of Education and are usually similar throughout all schools in the province. This uniformity allows for student transfers from one district to another. Within this structure, however, individual schools and classes may adapt the curriculum for local needs.

Post-secondary education is offered by 4 universities, and an Open Learning Institute which supplies correspondence courses. The original university in the province was UNIVERSITY OF BRITISH COLUMBIA, located on a scenic peninsula adjoining the western edge of Vancouver. Victoria College, affiliated with UBC, supplied the first 2 years of university education to residents of Victoria; it was expanded to university status in 1963 (*see* UNIVERSITY OF VICTORIA). A new university, SIMON FRASER, was built in Burnaby in 1965 to accommodate the greatly increased population of metropolitan Vancouver. A former religious college, Trinity Western, in the Lower Fraser Valley

near Langley, was granted a charter to offer university-level courses through 4 years in 1979. The BC Institute of Technology in Burnaby provides a wide range of technical and vocational courses for post-secondary students and the province operates 4 other vocational schools. Teacher-training programs are offered at each of the 3 large provincial universities. The smaller cities in the rest of the province, and suburban metropolitan Vancouver, are served by a system of 16 COMMUNITY COLLEGES offering first- and second-year university-level courses and vocational and technical programs. Academic courses in the colleges can receive transfer credit to the major provincial universities.

Cultural Life

The culture of the people of BC has evolved from the traditions of the people who migrated to the region. British influences were strong in the 19th century, being brought by settlers and entrepreneurs from England, who came directly to the colonies and the new province. In the 20th century British cultural characteristics were diversified by people from eastern Canada who had second- or third-generation British origins. These eastern influences became more dominant after 1950 when internal migration from eastern Canada rapidly increased BC's population and brought the institutions, societies and cultural events and activities found across the rest of Canada to BC. Many of Canada's finest writers, such as Phyllis WEBB and George BOWERING, are resident in BC. The mix of BC's culture is different from that of the rest of Canada in 2 notable ways. First, the mixture of people from India, Pakistan,

Vancouver's 60 000-seat BC Place stadium, built in 1983, is the home of the BC Lions. It was the first covered football stadium in Canada (*photo by Al Harvey/Masterfile*).

Malaysia, the Philippines, Hong Kong, Japan and China brings distinct forms and activities to West Coast culture. At one time these characteristics were visible in turbans, saris, etc, but distinctive clothing has now virtually disappeared except for special cultural or religious events. "Chinatown" remains an enduring part of the urban landscape of central Vancouver. West Coast Indians, the second distinct culture group, had a highly developed culture (*see* NORTHWEST COAST INDIAN ART). Indian arts and crafts have been revived in recent decades and have left their imprint on the broader society. The province's most famous artist, Emily CARR, was profoundly influenced by Indian art.

The BC government gives financial assistance to cultural and ethnic groups, publishers and community organizations through the BC Cultural Fund (est in 1967). Additional activities are also aided by grants from LOTTERIES.

Major museums, archives and art galleries are located in Vancouver and Victoria and, in addition, local museums are maintained in several smaller cities in the interior. The Centennial Museum and the H.R. MACMILLAN Planetarium, located on the waterfront in the western part of the city, adjoin the City Archives and the distinctive Maritime Museum; the latter, in which the famous RCMP schooner ST. ROCH is preserved, emphasizes the importance of the sea in Vancouver's past and present. The Provincial Museum in Victoria is noted for its lifelike panoramas and displays and for the several floors of material illustrating the natural environment and Indian and early European settlements. The UBC Museum of Anthropology, designed by Arthur ERICKSON, houses an impressive collection of Northwest Coast Indian artifacts.

Numerous theatrical companies perform in Victoria and Vancouver, and some of the productions are taken on tour to coastal and interior cities. The geographical problem of the concentration of cultural, social and athletic events in the southwestern corner of the province and their scarcity elsewhere is a well-known theme in BC. The VANCOUVER CANUCKS have been in the NHL since the 1970-71 season and the BRITISH COLUMBIA LIONS in the CFL since 1954; the latter now play in BC Place – Canada's first covered stadium. The Vancouver Whitecaps were Canada's most successful professional soccer franchise in attracting fans until the demise of the NASL in 1984. As well, Vancouver was host city for the 1954 British Empire Games (*see* COMMONWEALTH GAMES) and EXPO 86.

All of the major cities have daily newspapers and the smaller coastal and interior cities publish weekly newspapers. Similarly, the major television and radio stations are in Vancouver and Victoria, but many smaller communities have their own radio and television stations, which are often fed programs from the main networks. Most of the province's book and magazine publishers are in Vancouver, which is in the peculiar position of being an attractive market for eastern publishers and media but also having just a large enough share of the British Columbia population and income to be a sufficient market for local firms.

HISTORIC SITES include FORT LANGLEY, the first fur-trading post in the Lower Fraser Valley, BARKERVILLE and FORT STEELE. The provincial government has numerous historical signs at scenic pull-off sites along all major highways.

History

British Columbia was one of the last frontiers of discovery in N America. In 1774 Spaniards under Juan PÉREZ HERNÁNDEZ were probably the first Europeans to see the coast of BC. They did not land, but Pérez claimed the region for Spain. Four

Klondikers buying miners' licences at Custom House, Victoria, BC, 21 Feb 1898. Much of the early business done in the colony resulted from gold rushes to the interior (*by permission of the British Library*).

years later James COOK took his 2 British ships into NOOTKA SOUND on the W coast of Vancouver I. Within a few years British traders came by sea and developed a flourishing fur trade with coastal Indians. In 1789 Spain and Britain disputed ownership of West-Coast N America. The Spanish had established a trading post at Nootka Sd and seized British ships there. This NOOTKA SOUND CONTROVERSY was settled by the Nootka Conventions of 1790-92, which gave equal trading rights to both countries but did not determine ownership. British claims were strengthened after 1792 when ships under George VANCOUVER carried out a careful 3-year mapping of the coast from Oregon to Alaska. Vancouver named many of the bays, inlets and coastal landform features. In this period of worldwide European colonialism there was no concern among European governments and businessmen that this area was already occupied by the native peoples.

In 1793 the first European report about the interior of BC was made by the NORTH WEST CO fur trader, Alexander MACKENZIE. He entered the region from the E via the Peace and Upper Fraser rivers, exploring westward across the Chilcotin Plateau and through the Coast Mountains to the long inlet at BELLA COOLA. Two other members of the NWC, Simon FRASER and David THOMPSON, explored other parts of the interior early in the 19th century and opened fur-trade posts supplied from Montréal – the first permanent settlements in the province. In 1808 Fraser reached the mouth of the river which now bears his name, and Thompson found the mouth of the Columbia R in 1811, after exploring the river routes of southeastern BC. For about 50 years, while eastern N America was being occupied and settled by agricultural people and dotted with commercial cities, the mountainous western part of the continent remained little-known territory on the fringes of fur-trade empires controlled from eastern cities.

During the first half of the 19th century, the British-owned HUDSON'S BAY COMPANY controlled the western fur trade, including the area of present-day Washington and Oregon. As American settlers moved into the southern part of this region in the 1830s they refused to recognize the authority of the British company. Conflicting territorial claims (the US claimed N to 54°40') were settled in the 1846 OREGON TREATY, establishing the southern boundary of BC along the 49th parallel, except for Vancouver I. In anticipation of this result, the HBC moved its headquarters to newly established Fort Victoria in 1843.

In 1849 the British government granted Vancouver I to the HBC for colonization, and in 1851 James DOUGLAS, an official of the company, became governor of the colony. In 1856 Douglas established a legislative assembly for Vancouver I (periodically called Vancouver's Island). At mid-

century the only white settlements in what was to become British Columbia were fur-trade posts on the coast, such as Victoria, Nanaimo and Ft Langley, and in the interior, such as Kamloops, Ft (later Prince) George and Ft St James.

Development This quiet period of history ended in 1857 when gold was discovered in the sand bars along the Lower Fraser R. The ensuing GOLD RUSHES brought thousands of fortune hunters, mainly from the California goldfields, but also from other parts of the world. Many came by boat from San Francisco, crowding into inadequate facilities in Victoria to buy supplies and receive permits. Prospecting proceeded upstream along the banks and bars of the Fraser R during 1858. The town of YALE was established as a transshipping centre at the S end of Fraser Canyon and the eastern end of water transport from the Fraser R mouth. Gold seekers walked the tributaries of the Fraser R and major finds were made E of Quesnel. The boomtown of Barkerville arose at the western edge of the Cariboo Mountains as the chief service town for the Cariboo goldfields. At its peak in the early 1860s Barkerville probably held a fluctuating population of about 25 000, making it the largest settlement in western Canada.

In order to establish government and maintain law and order around the goldfields, the British established the mainland colony of British Columbia in 1858 under the authority of James Douglas who remained governor of Vancouver I. The new settlement of NEW WESTMINSTER, located slightly inland on the N bank of the Fraser R delta, was proclaimed capital of the new colony in 1859. This administrative centre controlled river traffic entering the Fraser R en route to the interior. In the early 1860s the amazing feat of building the CARIBOO ROAD along the walls of the Fraser Canyon was accomplished in order to move supplies to interior settlements.

With gold production declining and people leaving, the British government united the 2 colonies in 1866 to reduce administrative costs. New Westminster was the capital of the combined colony for 2 years before protests from the older capital, Victoria, resulted in the seat of government being moved there in 1868. The resulting physical separation of the capital from the majority of the people and economic activity on the mainland created later communication problems for the region. Many government services and offices had to be duplicated on the mainland.

After 1867 the British colony on the West Coast debated whether it should join the new CONFEDERATION of eastern provinces known as Canada. In 1871 the 12 000 white residents of BC agreed to enter the Dominion of Canada on the condition that the federal government build a transcontinental railway to link it with the East. The new province was to wait, rather impatiently at times, for 15 years before the CANADIAN PACIFIC RY reached the SW coast. The union with Canada was an unhappy one at first. The new province ran heavily into debt; the cost of governing a large mountainous area with few people was very high and revenues from resource users were low. More than one-third of the province's white residents lived in or near Victoria. Even by 1881 the white population of 24 000 was less than the estimated 25 000 Indians. The hoped-for expansion of trade with East Asia did not develop immediately with the completion of the CPR in 1885. But the railway did bring people to the port of Vancouver and by 1901 that city had surpassed Victoria in population. Vancouver's population of almost 27 010 in 1901 had been achieved in 15 years, whereas Victoria had only 23 688 people after 58 years of occupation.

Entrepreneurs came to British Columbia around the turn of the century to exploit the province's vast resources. A salmon-cannery industry was established along the coast. Sawmills were in operation all around the shores of Georgia Str and particularly along eastern Vancouver I. The first pulp and paper mill was completed at Powell River in 1912. The major expansion of the forest industry came, however, after WWI when the opening of the Panama Canal gave access to markets around the N Atlantic region. BC attracted a different type of settler from those who settled on the land on the Prairies and across eastern Canada. A need for capital and access to natural resources for export were more important than ownership of farmland.

In the 1890s the major resource development and settlement in interior BC centered on the mining activity in the Kootenay region of the SE. Prospectors, mainly from mining camps in western Montana and Idaho, moved northward along the valleys and discovered gold and base metals in the area W of KOOTENAY LAKE. Mining camps arose in the Slocan Valley, at ROSSLAND, near Grand Forks and elsewhere. NELSON became the main service, supply and administrative centre, with a population of about 4500 in 1911. Railways extended northward into the region from the US, and the CPR built a line westward through the Crowsnest Pass in 1899 to bring coal from FERNIE to smelters in the mining centres. By about 1914, however, many of the mines had closed and some towns were abandoned, although other mines opened in later years. The extension of the Kettle Valley branch of the CPR to the coast during WWI came after the peak of mining activity in the Kootenay region.

Agriculture brought settlers to the S-central interior. At the time of the Cariboo Gold Rush, ranching was established in the grassland valleys and rolling basins across the southern interior plateau. Irrigation was developed early in the century west of Kamloops and in the northern Okanagan Valley. Irrigation for orchards that spread S from Vernon aided settlement projects for returning soldiers after WWI (*see* VETERANS' LAND ACT).

The building of the Grand Trunk Pacific Rwy W from Edmonton through the Upper Fraser, Bulkley and Skeena valleys in 1907-14 was intended to give Canada a second gateway through the mountains to the Pacific coast. Prince George then became a minor sawmill centre, with rail access eastward to the growing housing market in the Prairie provinces. But the port and rail terminal at Prince Rupert never developed the anticipated volume of traffic, partly because there was little need for incoming freight. The small town remained mainly a fisheries centre, with continuing hopes.

Resource-based activities suffered serious economic decline in BC during 1930-45 because of the loss of world markets. After about 1950, however, the improved transportation system did much to integrate the interior resource economies and settlements with coastal collection, processing and management centres. Appropriately, the theme of Expo 86, held in Vancouver, was transportation and communications. Thousands of Canadians migrated to BC, attracted by the mild climate and perceived economic opportunities, joining thousands of other immigrants from Asia. These people were not only labour and management for the growing commercial and service occupations, they were also consumers of goods, services and entertainment.

J. LEWIS ROBINSON

Reading: G.P.V. and H.B. Akrigg, *British Columbia Chronicle, 1847-71* (1977); Mary L. Barker, *Natural Resources of British Columbia and Yukon* (1977); M.L. Cuddy and J. Scott, *British Columbia in Books* (1974); Albert L. Farley, *Atlas of British Columbia* (1979); Robin Fisher, *Contact and Conflict* (1977); Margaret A. Ormsby, *British Columbia* (1958); H.K. Ralston and J. Friesen, eds, *Historical Essays on British Columbia* (1976); J. Lewis Robinson, *British Columbia* (1973); Marie Tippett and Douglas Cole, *From Desolation to Splendour* (1977).

British Columbia Lions, FOOTBALL team. The BC Lions played their first game on 11 Aug 1954 in Vancouver's Empire Stadium. Under coach and general manager Annis Stukus they achieved only one victory in their initial season and did not make the Western Conference playoffs until 1959. In 1963, coached by Dave Skrien and led by the quarterbacking of Joe Kapp, the Lions appeared in their first GREY CUP, losing 21-10 to Hamilton but coming back in 1964 to defeat the Tiger-Cats 34-24. The Lions waited 19 years before they returned to the national final in 1983, losing to Toronto. Under Coach Don Matthews, they posted 3 consecutive first-place finishes (1983-85) while playing in their new 60 000-seat home, BC Place (Canada's first covered stadium). In 1985 the Lions followed the best season in club history (13-3) with a Grey Cup victory versus Hamilton.

DEREK DRAGER

British Columbia Provincial Police had its origin in the police forces established in the colonies of Vancouver I and British Columbia in 1858 to provide law and order following an influx of gold miners and settlers. With the union of the colonies in 1866, the 2 forces were amalgamated under a superintendent of police. It became the Provincial Police following the entry of British Columbia into Confederation in 1871. A civilian, non-uniformed body that policed the province's unorganized territory, it was reorganized in 1923 along lines similar to the RCMP. The province was divided into divisional commands, and semimilitary ranks and a uniform were adopted, the latter resembling that of the RCMP, although khaki in colour with green trimmings. In the 1930s it began to police municipalities under contracts with local authorities. On 15 Aug 1950 the BCPP (492 men) and its duties were taken over by the RCMP.

S.W. HORRALL

British Columbia Railway was incorporated as the Pacific Great Eastern Railway in 1912 to build a line from North Vancouver to Prince George, where it was to link up with the GRAND TRUNK PACIFIC RAILWAY. Initially it was privately owned, but financial difficulties developed quickly and in 1918, after only 283 km of track from the coastal port of Squamish to the head of the inland river transport at Quesnel had been built, the Pacific Great Eastern was taken over by the BC government. The remaining track from North Vancouver to Squamish and from Quesnel to Prince George was not completed until 1956. Two major northern extensions and several branch lines were built after that date. A northeastern extension through the Peace R country reached Ft Nelson in 1971. A proposed northwestern extension to Dease Lk has been abandoned. Significant portions of the line have been electrified to expedite the carriage of coal. The British Columbia Railway serves the resource industries of the northern interior of the province, operating over 2300 km of track, which were built at a cost of more than a billion dollars in public funds.

T.D. REGEHR

British Columbia Research Council, nonprofit society incorporated in 1944 to provide facilities for technological research and industrial development in BC. BC Research, a technical wing of the council, comprises scientific, engineering and technical laboratory facilities. Under its mandate to enable small BC firms to improve their competitive position in Canadian and world markets, BCR attempts to balance short-term contract work for primary industries with longer-term "core" investigations, often in co-operation with university researchers and funded through provincial and federal grants. BCR is recognized internationally for expertise in dual-fuel diesel/ compressed natural gas systems; fish and food processing technologies; aquaculture; waste management and bulk materials handling; occupational health and industrial hygiene; organic and inorganic chemical analyses; and specialty chemical processing technologies. About 140 staff members work in laboratories located at UNIVERSITY OF BRITISH COLUMBIA campus. Research is conducted in 4 divisions. Almost half of BCR income is derived from industry. Co-operative ventures include the provision of free information to business in collaboration with the NATIONAL RESEARCH COUNCIL, and delivery of the federal Industrial Research Assistance Program and provincial Technology Assistance Program to help small companies undertake research and development projects.

MARTIN K. MCNICHOLL

British Columbia Sports Hall of Fame and Museum was founded to pay tribute to those British Columbians who have brought special honour to the province through their sports accomplishments. Opened in 1966, it is one of the largest multi-sport museums in N America, and preserves BC's rich sports heritage. In its displays, photos, scrapbooks, newspaper clippings, memorabilia, trophies and film theatre, visitors can view the development of sports in BC from before the turn of the century and learn about the Hall's honoured members. Located in Vancouver, the hall is also used as a research and education centre for students.

BRIAN S. LEWIS

British Columbia Woodworkers' Strike 15 May - 20 June 1946, the first strike of BC District 1 of the INTERNATIONAL WOODWORKERS OF AMERICA (IWA) after coast-wide bargaining rights were won in 1943. It initiated a nationwide, postwar strike wave of CANADIAN CONGRESS OF LABOUR (CCL) affiliates aimed at readjusting wages to wartime inflation and at consolidating the recent attainment of legislative union recognition by the signing of full union security agreements. Twenty-seven thousand workers in both the coast and interior regions, led by district president Harold Pritchett, struck when demands for a 25-cent hourly increase, a 40-hour week, union shop and mandatory dues check-off were refused by Stuart Research Service, the bargaining agent for 145 coast operators. The strike, coming prior to compulsory conciliation proceedings under the still operable wartime labour regulations, was technically illegal. The federal government intervened with the appointment of BC Chief Justice Gordon Sloan as an industrial disputes inquiry commissioner. His recommendation for a coastal settlement of 15 cents, the statutory 44-hour week and a voluntary revokable check-off was rejected by the IWA but accepted by the operators with the backing of the Coalition provincial government of John HART. The IWA responded with a 3000-strong trek to Victoria, the culmination of the 37-day strike. Sloan's continued mediation efforts resulted on June 12 in a modified offer by the coast operators of a 40-hour week for logging camps during the last half of the contract following 48 in the first half. With the marketing of the Okanagan fruit crop endangered by the shutdown of box factories, the federal government, on June 18, appointed Gordon Bell controller of interior operations engaged in box production and ordered all affected employees back to work with a settlement to be mediated by Sloan. The forced end to the interior strike resulted in quick acceptance of Sloan's modified terms by the coast locals and a return to work on June 20. The greatest

BRITISH COMMONWEALTH AIR TRAINING PLAN
PILOT TRAINING FACILITIES
1940-1945

Reproduced by Mapping and Charting Establishment.

*Compiled and drawn by the Directorate of History.

gains were won by the interior workers. Their mediated settlement provided a first industry-wide contract, reduced the work week from 54 to 44 hours, increased wages 10 cents and awarded the coast check-off clause. Although the IWA failed to win union security, the strike consolidated its position in the industry by attracting 8000 - 10 000 new members to its ranks. The 15-cent increase served other CCL unions as an important standard with which to enter their postwar wage negotiations. STEPHEN GRAY

British Commonwealth Air Training Plan, an agreement of 17 Dec 1939 between Canada, the UK, Australia and New Zealand, making Canada the focus of a British Empire-wide scheme to instruct aircrew. It was a major Canadian contribution to Allied air superiority in

Officers at No 2 Air Observer School, with the original pilots and office staff, 1941 (*courtesy Provincial Archives of Alberta/A. Blyth Coll/BL-3541*).

WORLD WAR II, and lasted until 31 Mar 1945. Called the "Aerodrome of Democracy" by US Pres F.D. Roosevelt, Canada had an abundance of air training space beyond the range of enemy aircraft, excellent climatic conditions for flying, immediate access to American industry, and relative proximity to the UK via the N Atlantic shipping lanes.

Canada had been the home of a major recruiting and training organization in WORLD WAR I, and the British again looked to it for aviators when the international situation worsened in the 1930s. Prime Minister W.L.M. KING's peacetime caution about such schemes evaporated after the declaration of war in 1939: a training program would keep Canadians at home, ward off demands for a large expeditionary force and bury the politically divisive issue of overseas CONSCRIPTION.

Negotiating the agreement was difficult. Canada agreed to accept most of the plan's costs but insisted that the British consent to a public pronouncement that air training would take

precedence over all other aspects of the Canadian war effort. The British expected that the Royal Air Force would absorb Canadian air training graduates without restrictions, as in WWI. The King government demanded that Canadians be identified as members of the RCAF by their shoulder badge. Nevertheless, Article 15 of the agreement, providing for the possible organization of Canadian "units and formations" overseas, was vague and unsatisfactory, the more so because of Ottawa's understandable reluctance to pay both for training and for the maintenance of an operational force abroad. Most RCAF personnel overseas served with the RAF, not with their national air force, and the process of creating distinctly Canadian squadrons was slow and painful.

Canada administered and controlled the plan in accordance with standards and overall policy set by the RAF. The training program was carried out by the RCAF, supported by the Canadian Flying Clubs Assn, commercial aviation companies and the federal Department of Transport. Training began on 29 Apr 1940, but was hampered by a shortage of aircraft, instructors and completed airfields. After the fall of France in June 1940, the plan was accelerated, and the first of a series of transfers of RAF aircrew schools to Canada took place. In 1942, after renewal of the agreement and reorganization of the plan, all British units in Canada were integrated formally into the BCATP.

At the plan's peak, there were 107 schools and 184 ancillary units at 231 sites. The aircraft establishment stood at 10 906 and the ground organization at 104 113 men and women. The Canadian government paid more than $1.6 billion, three-quarters of the total cost. Graduates totalled 131 553 pilots, navigators, bomb aimers, wireless operators, air gunners and flight engineers from the 4 founding partners, other parts of the COMMONWEALTH, the US and countries of occupied Europe. Almost half the total aircrew employed on British and Commonwealth flying operations were products of the BCATP. Canadian graduates numbered 72 835, providing crews for 40 RCAF home defence and 45 overseas RCAF squadrons, as well as constituting about 25% of the overall strength of RAF squadrons. This major commitment to the air war overseas, and particularly to Bomber Command, inevitably exacted a very heavy toll in Canadian casualties, a result very different from Mackenzie King's original aim.

F.J. HATCH AND NORMAN HILLMER

Reading: F.J. Hatch, *Aerodrome of Democracy* (1983).

British North America, the term usually applied to the British colonies and territories in N America after the US became independent in 1783 until CONFEDERATION in 1867. At first it consisted of the provinces of Quebec, NOVA SCOTIA, St John's I [PEI], NEWFOUNDLAND, the HUDSON'S BAY COMPANY territories, and lands belonging directly to the Crown.

The influx of LOYALIST settlers from the US into NS resulted in the creation of NEW BRUNSWICK and CAPE BRETON I as separate colonies in 1784. The division of the PROVINCE OF QUEBEC into UPPER CANADA and LOWER CANADA in 1791 separated the people of predominantly British and American origin in the west from those of mainly French origin in the east. In 1799 St John's I was renamed PRINCE EDWARD ISLAND. In 1820 Cape Breton I was reunited with NS and in 1841 Upper and Lower Canada were united to form the PROVINCE OF CANADA. On the west coast the HBC colony of Vancouver I was established in 1849 and what is now southern British Columbia became another crown colony in 1858. In 1866 the two were united as BRITISH COLUMBIA, a single colony with enlarged boundaries. N.L. NICHOLSON

Reading: N.L. Nicholson, *The Boundaries of the Canadian Confederation* (1979); R.C. Harris and J. Warkentin, *Canada Before Confederation* (1974).

British North America Act, statute enacted 29 Mar 1867 by the British Parliament providing for CONFEDERATION. In Apr 1982 it was renamed the CONSTITUTION ACT, 1867, as part of the movement toward "patriation" of the Constitution.

W.H. McCONNELL

Britnell, George Edwin, political economist, professor (b at London, Eng 9 June 1903; d at Saskatoon 14 Oct 1961). Head of the Dept of Economics and Political Science at U Saskatchewan from 1938 until his death, Britnell also served as university administrator, government adviser and royal commissioner and was Canadian delegate to 3 international economic conferences. For 16 years he was special adviser on transportation to the Saskatchewan government and, with V.C. FOWKE, won retention of the CROW'S NEST PASS AGREEMENT on grain rates. In addition to a distinguished academic publishing career, he was also president of the Canadian Political Science Assn 1956-57, chairman of the Canadian Social Science Research Council 1956-58 and representative to the International Economic Assn. Elected fellow of the Royal Soc of Canada 1950, he was the first Harold Innis Visiting Research Professor of Political Economy at U of T in 1954.

PAUL PHILLIPS

Reading: G.E. Britnell *The Wheat Economy* (1939) and (with V.C. Fowke) *Canadian Agriculture in War and Peace* (1962).

Brittain, Donald, filmmaker (b at Ottawa 10 June 1928). After several years with the *Ottawa Journal,* he joined the NFB in 1955. He soon became one of the most respected Canadian documentary filmmakers. In 1962 he produced the 13-part series, *Canada at War.* Two years later, with John Kemeny, he co-directed *Bethune,* a film that marked the beginning of his approach to portraying controversial figures. In his lively, humorous, original and often biting style he portrayed such personalities as Leonard COHEN, Lord THOMSON of Fleet, Ferguson JENKINS, Malcolm LOWRY and the DIONNE QUINTUPLETS. It was *Volcano: An In-*

quiry into the Life and Death of Malcolm Lowry (1976) that firmly established his international reputation. Perhaps because of his training as a journalist, Brittain selected sensitive, topical subjects. In *The Champions* (1978) he took on the political careers of Pierre TRUDEAU and René LÉVESQUE. He ruffled bureaucratic feathers with *Paperland – The Bureaucrat Observed* (1979), chosen film of the year at the Canadian Film Awards. After the series on Canadian national security *On Guard for Thee* (1981), he described the career of a controversial union leader in *Canada's Sweetheart: The Saga of Hal C. Banks* (1985). In 1974 he directed his first full-length film on the history of Canadian cinema 1895-1939, *Dreamland,* and provided the commentary for a follow-up film entitled *Has Anybody Here Seen Canada?* (1978). He was, in 1987, producing a docudrama on the life of Mackenzie King. The quality and variety of his output has placed Brittain among leading documentary filmmakers. PIERRE VÉRONNEAU

Brittain, Miller Gore, painter (b at Saint John, NB 12 Nov 1912; d there 21 Jan 1968). His early paintings, inspired by life in Saint John, were in the style promoted by the Art Students League, New York, which he attended 1930-32. Depicting labourers at work, local citizens on crowded streetcars or derelicts congregated outside drinking establishments, his paintings earned him the label "the Canadian Brueghel." During WWII Brittain served in the RCAF and worked briefly as a WAR ARTIST. In 1946 he returned to Saint John, and the balance of his life he devoted to painting works with surrealistic overtones: figurative compositions of tortured bodies, pastel landscapes that pictured flowers, heads and bodies set in strange lunar landscapes, and portraits of frenzied religious subjects. J. RUSSELL HARPER

Broadbent, John Edward, political theorist, MP (b at Oshawa, Ont 21 Mar 1936). He was born to a family of auto workers in a company town. After studies at U of T (PhD, 1966) and the London School of Economics, he joined the political science department at York U in 1965. He was elected to the House of Commons in 1968 as NEW DEMOCRATIC PARTY member for Oshawa-Whitby, winning the seat by a tiny margin. In his early years as MP he was identified with the party's left wing. Unsuccessful in his first attempt to win the leadership in 1971, he became a serious contender in 1974 when party leader David LEWIS lost his seat while Broadbent's own majority increased enormously. After some hesitation he again offered himself and was elected July 1975. As leader he emphasized economic issues and helped the party recover from its disastrous 1974 defeat. He was elected a vice-president of the Socialist International in 1978. In 1980-81 Broadbent faced a caucus revolt (centered in Saskatchewan) against his support for the patriation of Canada's Constitution. The party convention in 1981 endorsed his position, but some discontent remained, and at the 1983 convention prairie delegates circulated a manifesto implicitly critical of Broadbent's leadership. Although NDP support appeared to decline prior to the 1984 election campaign, Broadbent waged a brilliant campaign, emphasizing tax reforms, lower interest rates and equality for women. The NDP emerged with 30 seats, only 10 fewer than the Liberals, including 13 seats in Ontario. After the election, Broadbent's popularity in the polls was consistently ahead of Liberal leader John Turner and PM Brian Mulroney. GARTH STEVENSON

Broadcasting, Community is designed to fulfil social and cultural needs by allowing members of the audience to participate in decisions about programming and, in the case of radio, in the owner-

ship of stations. It serves local communities, reflecting the diversity of their views and needs, and provides access to volunteer participants. It is public broadcasting, but it is not operated by a government or a government agency.

In the past 15 years, more than 150 community radio services have been developed. They are supported by donations, advertising, memberships and, particularly in the case of Québec and native broadcasting, with federal and provincial grants. Community radio takes many different forms. In Vancouver and Montréal stations are owned by members of a society or co-operative, and programming includes news, public affairs, music, "live" performances, coverage of public meetings, special interest material and a multilingual service. In several smaller centres, mainly in Québec, community radio stations focus primarily on a single type of programming, such as music or a multilingual service. Student-operated radio is provided on FM to or by closed circuit, often appealing to a wider community with educational programs, unusual music selections, and coverage of university sports and events. Multilingual radio, on FM or transmitted by cable, is community broadcasting, if it is operated on a nonprofit basis.

In northern, rural and remote communities, community radio stations provide programming similar to that of small commercial stations. They are operated by native broadcasting societies, and some broadcast in native languages. Some are supported by the CBC, which also broadcasts native programming as part of its northern service. In 1981 the first 2 native networks were licensed to provide radio and television, using the facilities of Cancom, the Canadian satellite service. Since that time, and with the help of the federally sponsored funding project, the Northern Native Access Program (est 1983), the level of participation from native groups in community broadcasting has increased significantly.

The first community radio stations were licensed on an experimental basis by the Canadian Radio Television Commission (CRTC) in the early 1970s, and commercial advertising was not permitted. In 1975 the CRTC formally recognized community radio with a special licence, and permitted limited advertising. By 1984 commercial broadcasters complained that community radio stations, particularly in Québec, were competing with them unfairly in small communities because community stations received subsidies from the provincial government and carried advertisements. The CRTC conducted a comprehensive review and its policy, issued in 1985, developed regulations for different types of community stations, removing many of the restrictions on advertising.

Cable systems have included a community television service since the early 1970s, and provisions for a community channel on cable were included in the CRTC cable regulations in 1975. Cable operations are required to provide a channel on a priority basis on their basic service, and all but the smallest systems are expected to contribute 10% of their gross revenues to its operation. Community television is intended to be different from commercial television, and to be local in orientation, drawing upon voluntary contributions from its audience. Its programs include "live" coverage of meetings, hearings and special events, consumer service programming and programs for special interest groups. Advertising on the community television channel is prohibited. Revenues come from the licensed cable operators, who are legally responsible for all programming, although most appoint a community advisory committee. A few cable systems also provide a nonprofit multilingual channel, where limited advertising is permitted.

Two organizations represent the community radio broadcasters, the Association des radio diffuseurs communautaires du Québec and the National Campus/Community Radio Organization. The organization of community television broadcasters in Québec is the Regroupment des organization communautaires de communication du Québec.

In urban centres, community broadcasting has attracted small audiences, even though it overcomes some problems with the mass media: the influence of advertiser sponsorship on programs, the lack of coverage of local issues and of diversity in the television portrayal of community life. Its difficulties are its limited funding, the control exerted by the cable licensees, the preoccupation of some community broadcasters with being "representative" of all groups or their avoidance of public controversy, and the emphasis placed on participation at the expense of the quality of programming. Nonetheless, the Canadian effort is extensive, and the CRTC policies establishing community broadcasting are unique. Audience loyalty and public support for community broadcasting compensate for the relatively small size of its audiences.   LIORA SALTER

Broadcasting, Educational, *see* EDUCATIONAL BROADCASTING.

Broadcasting, Radio and Television In a northern land marked by long winters, vast distances and a fragmented population, the communication provided by Canadian radio and TV is crucial. Broadcasting has not only become a principal source of entertainment but also links the citizen to what is going on outside the home and has helped to develop a sense of community. Canada has a more elaborate and advanced physical structure for delivering radio and TV programs than is found in any comparable country in the world. For example, in 1979 the US had 982 transmitters in operation, but Canada, with a tenth of the population, had 1045 (including rebroadcasting transmitters), a number that grew to 1225 in 1981. Canada was a pioneer in SATELLITE COMMUNICATIONS, and was the first to use geostationary satellites in domestic COMMUNICATIONS. The national broadcasting service, the CANADIAN BROADCASTING CORPORATION, distributes most of its programs nationally by satellites, also using them in the assembling of programs. TV services to the Canadian North are almost completely dependent on satellites and Earth stations. As a result of these technical developments, 99% of the population has a choice of 2 TV channels, 91% has 3 channels, and over 50% has 8 or more. The weak element in the broadcasting system lies not in the physical facilities but in the amount of original Canadian programming (*see* RADIO PROGRAMMING; TELEVISION PROGRAMMING; MUSIC BROADCASTING). The CBC produces an impressive number of radio and TV programs in English and French, many of high quality; but the private TV stations broadcasting in English have depended mostly on imported foreign (principally US) programs for prime time. Many of these imported programs have been popular, but such dependency has led to a continuing struggle to devise public policies that would ensure a more distinctively Canadian broadcasting service. For the past 50 years, Canada has employed a combination of public and private enterprise, falling somewhere between the strong state-owned element of the British system and the less regulated private-enterprise system of the US. The stages in this evolution can be related to successive Acts of Parliament and to the regulating bodies set up to license stations and to establish and administer the rules.

The Pioneer Stage (1913-28) Under the Radio-telegraph Act of 1913, a government minister (for

Frank Willis reporting from a mining disaster at Moose R, NS, Apr 1936, in what was the first "on-the-spot" news broadcast in Canada. (*courtesy National Archives of Canada/MISA/14024*).

most of this period, the minister of marine and fisheries) had the power to license radio broadcasting stations and to charge a $1 licence fee on each receiving set. The first licence was issued in 1919 (to XWA, an experimental station in Montréal operated by Canadian Marconi Co) and by 1928 something over 60 stations were in operation, most of them of low power or providing intermittent service. Regulations were minimal.

Emergence of Public Ownership and Regulations (1928-36) By 1936, the present pattern in the ownership and control of broadcasting had emerged. In 1928 the government established a royal commission, under the chairmanship of Sir John AIRD, to advise on the future of broadcasting in Canada. Canadian radio development had been rudimentary, and many listeners were turning to American stations and the newly established US networks. Moreover, Canadian stations were experiencing greater interference from unregulated frequencies in the US.

There were also many complaints about intrusive advertising on the commercial stations in both Canada and the US, and some saw a possible model in the British Broadcasting Corporation. The Aird Commission's report (1929) proposed a publicly owned corporation not unlike the BBC, and its main recommendations were taken up by an active group of citizens organized as the Canadian Radio League. Broadcasting, they argued, should be regarded as a national public service rather than merely as a profit-making industry, and its ownership and operating structure should be organized to recognize this principle. Québec, supported by Ontario, contested the right of the federal government to assume control of broadcasting, and a reference was made to the Supreme Court of Canada with a subsequent appeal to the Judicial Committee of the Privy Council. Its judgement (1932) confirmed federal jurisdiction over radio communication and the content of programs; and a special parliamentary committee was appointed to devise the means for implementing the Aird Commission's recommendations.

An Act creating the Canadian Radio Broadcasting Commission (CRBC) was passed with all-party support on 26 May 1932. The 3-man commission was empowered to regulate, control and carry on broadcasting in Canada; to originate and transmit programs; to lease, purchase or construct stations; and eventually to assume complete ownership of all Canadian broadcasting, if the means were provided. In its term of office, the commission was beset by many difficulties. In the depths of the Depression, the government of R.B. Bennett never gave the commission the money to carry out its programming responsibilities satisfactorily. The CRBC managed to establish outlets in only 5 centres; in most cities privately owned stations distributed the commission's network programs. Thus the mixed system, combining public and private stations in one network, was established. It characterizes CBC radio and TV to the present day.

The CBC as Operator and Regulator (1936-58) The weaknesses of the Radio Commission and growing criticism in Parliament led to a new broadcasting Act when the Liberals under W.L. Mackenzie King took office in 1935. The commission had been regarded as too dependent on government; suspicions were aroused that some of its decisions had been influenced by partisan considerations. The new prime minister, at the urging of the Radio League, determined to revise the legislation to reflect more fully the Aird Report and to bring it up to date.

By 1936, the year the revised Canadian Broadcasting Act was passed, conditions were considerably altered. The number of homes purchasing licences for their radios had increased from one-half million in 1931 to 1 million by the end of 1936. Canadians had become accustomed to receiving their own network programs, in English or French, for at least a few afternoon and evening hours. There was no thought in government of abandoning the national experiment. But the private radio stations had not only survived, they had prospered. Private radio provided music, weather and community information. Most private stations also carried popular American entertainment programs, with which Canadian advertisers were eager to be associated. In Nov 1936 the Canadian Broadcasting Corporation, with a board of 9 governors, replaced the Radio Commission, and it enjoyed much greater autonomy. Financed by an increased licence fee, the CBC took vigorous steps to increase Canadian coverage through high-powered regional transmitters. It also expanded the national program services by broadcasting many more hours each week, incorporating in its schedule some imported programs from the US networks. By 1944 it operated 3 radio networks, 2 in English (Trans-Canada and Dominion) and one in French. The private radio stations were not allowed to form their own national network, although under the rather liberal regulations of the CBC they indeed thrived. There were some complaints about the CBC's alleged monopoly position, but successive parliamentary committees and the Royal Commission on NATIONAL DEVELOPMENT IN THE ARTS, LETTERS AND SCIENCES (Massey Commission) all expressed approval of the governing system and of the contribution of the CBC to Canada's cultural life.

The arrival of TV in 1952 foreshadowed an end to the system under which the CBC was at once the regulatory authority and the principal Canadian programmer. TV began under CBC auspices, as the Massey Commission had recommended, but the twin responsibilities for program production and national distribution were so expensive that the government of Louis St. Laurent decided against construction of CBC outlets in every province. CBC TV could not be self-sufficient as was BBC TV in Britain. Once more, private-station licensees were expected to distribute the national programs provided by the CBC. It must be said that the policy adopted by the government in the mid-1950s, of authorizing only one station, public or private, in the principal Canadian cities, was extraordinarily successful in spreading TV service rapidly across the land. However, appetites for additional TV outlets were so quickly stimulated that a one-station policy for each city could not be maintained, and a Royal Commission on Broadcasting (Fowler Commission) 1955-57 led to new legislation.

Regulation by the BBG (1958-68) The Broadcasting Act of 1958, replacing the legislation of 1936, was introduced by the Conservative government of John Diefenbaker. During the previous decade the Canadian Assn of Broadcasters, representing most private radio and TV stations, had conducted a vigorous campaign to convince the public that it was unjust to have the same public body (the CBC) as operator and as regulator of its private competition. This argument persuaded the Progressive Conservative Party to abandon its support of the 1936 legislation and to proceed with the new Act. It continued to treat all broadcasting in Canada as a single system, with a 15-member Board of Broadcast Governors (BBG) assigned the responsibility of regulating "the activities of public and private broadcasting stations in Canada and the relationship between them" and "ensuring the continued existence and efficient operation of a national broadcasting system." The BBG was to hear applications for new stations and make recommendations to the government minister who issued such licences. Despite the BBG's regulatory authority, the CBC continued to have its own board of directors under the Act, and continued to report directly to Parliament. Under the BBG, the TV system expanded rapidly, and radio became more a local and community service, except for the radio networks of the CBC. A second TV network, CTV, consisting of second stations in the larger Canadian cities, began operations in 1961, and the CBC TV networks in English and French continued to distribute programs, partly commercial and partly unsponsored, through CBC-owned stations and a larger number of private affiliates.

Broadcasting under the CRTC (1968-present) The 1958 legislation had brought about disputes between the 2 public agencies, the BBG and CBC, and in 1968 a new Act was passed to correct some of the ambiguities. The authority to issue licences was delegated to the Canadian Radio-Television Commission, and the new legislation brought CABLE TV, already securely established in a number of cities, under the authority of the new regulatory body, the CRTC (in 1976 renamed the CANADIAN RADIO-TELEVISION AND TELECOMMUNICATIONS COMMISSION, also CRTC). The CRTC has been more active than the BBG in trying to ensure that radio and TV stations and networks (in the words of the Act) "should be effectively owned and controlled by Canadians so as to safeguard, enrich and strengthen the cultural, political, social and economic fabric of Canada," and also that the programming provided should be "of high standard, using predominantly Canadian creative and other resources." The CBC has had no difficulty in meeting or exceeding the Canadian-content quotas imposed by the CRTC, but the private stations and networks have barely met the minimum standards, especially in prime time. Added to the effect of importing American TV by cable, the result of these minimum standards has been that more US than Canadian programs are available to Canadian audiences.

The CRTC clearly did not intend to increase the share of viewing time going to American TV programs, but that has happened. There are several explanations. Most important was the decision, influenced by public demand, to license cable systems in all parts of Canada to import 2, 3 or more US channels, thus making full US network services available almost everywhere. There was also a decision to license a regional Canadian network in the most populous Canadian province, Global Television in Ontario, which did not have the resources to schedule as many attractive Canadian programs as the 2 national networks, CBC and CTV. Moreover, because of the CRTC's loose definition of prime time as the hours from 6 PM to midnight, the private broadcasters were able to cluster their American programming within the peak hours, between 7 and 11 PM. All this has increased the share of audience watching US programs to over 70% for English-language programs. The situation is not as serious in French-speaking Canada, where about 60% of TV programs are Canadian in origin. Even in Québec, however, the share of non-Canadian viewing has been growing.

The CBC continues to distribute a great deal of Canadian programming. It has been said that it produces more original TV and radio programming than any other broadcaster, public or private, anywhere in the world. Also, the CRTC has licensed 3 other public services producing many of their own programs, TVOntario, the Access Network in Alberta and Radio-Québec, each as an educational service financed by the province it serves. Their evening programs attract a substantial general audience. The private TV network in Québec, TVA, with 10 stations, is a very important source of French-language programs and complements the service of the CBC's French network.

Whether broadcasting will help preserve Canada's cultural sovereignty is still unresolved; the question will grow in complexity as technology advances. Canada has built the biggest physical system in the world, but in large part has turned it over to the US entertainment industry. Canadian governments are now searching for a way to establish a national information grid using all the possibilities of a modern TELECOMMUNICATIONS system. As for broadcasting, there is the prospect of several dozen TV channels, or even 100, in place of the 10 or 20 so far employed, and it is not clear how many of these can be programmed in Canada. Another unresolved issue, as technology changes, is how much will be regulated and controlled by a federal authority and how much by the provinces. The provincial governments have sought a larger place in CABLE TELEVISION, PAY TELEVISION, determination of program content, and regulation of common carriers. Whether these claims will be resolved by redefining jurisdictions, or by concurrency or interdelegation is yet to be determined. In 1985 a new Conservative government appointed a Task Force under the co-chairmanship of Gerald CAPLAN and Florian Sauvageau to advise it on changes that should be made in broadcasting policy. Three of the 7 members of the task force were from private broadcasting; one was an independent film and television producer; one was a specialist in communications law; and the 2 co-chairmen had been members of university faculties. Despite their varied backgrounds, they brought in a unanimous report. All broadcasting undertakings, they said, should be part of a composite system, and all licensees regarded as trustees of the Canadian public – a principle established by former bodies such as the Massey and Fowler Commissions. The CBC should have a central role in assuring that Canadians have a truly Canadian broadcasting system; any new statute should continue to recognize it as the national broadcasting service, in both radio and television, in English and in French. Its basis of funding should be secure, for the same period as its station and network licences. CBC television might remain partly commercial, but as soon as possible should phase out its American programming. The CRTC should set conditions of licence to ensure that private stations and networks would in future commit greater resources to Canadian programs. Some degree of state support and protection for the entire private sector should be provided, in return for which each component would contribute to the objectives of the broadcasting system. To assist in redressing the imbalance of American over Canadian programs within the Canadian broadcasting system, Caplan-Sauvageau proposed that a new non-commercial satellite-to-cable television service in the public sector should be established, to be known as TV Canada in English and Télé-Canada in French.

The report of the task force was referred to an all-party committee of the House of Commons which has generally supported its recommendations. However, up to the end of 1987 the minister of Communications had not made clear how much of the report will be acted upon. A new broadcasting act has been promised for 1988.

FRANK W. PEERS

Reading: David Ellis, *Evolution of the Canadian Broadcasting System* (1979); F. W. Peers, *The Public Eye* (1979).

Broadcasting, Royal Commission on (Fowler Commission) established (1955) under Robert FOWLER, shortly after the development of private television in Canada, to consider the problems of financing the Canadian BROADCASTING system and the roles of public and private broadcasters in solving them. It rejected the private broadcasters' arguments that cultural goals should be met primarily by the CBC and suggested the establishment of minimum cultural standards for private broadcasting and the creation of an independent regulatory agency to supervise broadcasting. The 1958 Broadcasting Act, which was based on the report, was replaced (1967-68) by a new Act establishing the CANADIAN RADIO-TELEVISION AND TELECOMMUNICATIONS COMMISSION (CRTC). NICK SIDOR

Broccoli (*Brassica oleracea*, Botrytis Group), annual or biennial VEGETABLE belonging to the Cruciferae family. The species is native to the Mediterranean region. In Europe the term "broccoli" is used for the cold-tolerant overwintering cauliflower and what is known in N America as broccoli is often called "calabrese." Broccoli is cultivated for its tightly packed flowering head and upper stalks, which are consumed when the flowers are in bud. It is becoming an increasingly important vegetable crop in Canada and is particularly well suited to parts of the Maritimes and BC. The crop does not perform well if temperatures are excessively high. Traditional cultivars were harvested July-Sept; European and Japanese cultivars selected in BC have extended the season from June to the first heavy frost. Broccoli is grown for both the fresh and processing markets. In 1986 the Canadian processing crop was worth $1.7 million. A.R. MAURER

Brock, Sir Isaac, military commander, administrator of Upper Canada (b at St Peter Port, Guernsey 6 Oct 1769; d at Queenston Heights, UC 13 Oct 1812). He arrived in Canada in 1802 with his regiment, the 49th Foot. He was promoted maj-gen in 1811, and in the absence of Francis GORE was made provisional administrator of UPPER CANADA. At the outset of the WAR OF 1812, Brock's bold initiatives in ordering the capture of Michilimackinac and in leading attacks on AMHERSTBURG and Detroit raised the confidence of the militia. He was killed by a sharpshooter when leading troops against an American battery on QUEENSTON HEIGHTS. The memory of

Isaac Brock (*courtesy National Archives of Canada/C-36181*).

Brock, the fallen hero and saviour of Upper Canada, remained extraordinarily strong in Ontario history. His body, interred at Ft George, was moved in 1824 to the summit of Queenston Heights under an imposing monument, which was destroyed in 1840, but replaced in 1853 by the stately monument that dominates the battlefield today.   ROBERT S. ALLEN

Brock University was founded in 1964 in St Catharines, Ont. It is named after Maj-Gen Sir Isaac BROCK, who led British forces in the WAR OF 1812 in a battle fought 8 km from the present-day site of the campus. The university offers programs in the arts and sciences, and has specialized schools of administrative studies, physical education, recreation and education. The university's facilities include a science complex, a physical education complex with an Olympic-size pool, and residence accommodation for 650 students. The campus is located on the edge of the Niagara Escarpment overlooking the city.

Enrolment: Brock University, 1985-86
(Source: Statistics Canada)

Full-time Undergrad	Full-time Graduate	Part-time Undergrad	Part-time Graduate
4473	69	3205	521

Brockhouse, Bertram Neville, physicist (b at Lethbridge, Alta 15 July 1918). Brockhouse pioneered the use of thermal neutrons to study structural, dynamical and magnetic aspects of the behaviour of condensed matter systems at an atomic level. After studying at UBC and U of T, he worked at the Chalk River Nuclear Laboratories from 1950 to 1962, and then as professor of physics at McMaster U. At Chalk River he developed sophisticated thermal neutron-scattering equipment and experimental methods: in particular, he invented the triple-axis crystal spectrometer, which is now used in neutron-scattering research laboratories worldwide for detailed investigations of excitations in a very broad range of materials. He performed many pioneering experiments, including measurements of atomic vibrational modes in metals, semiconductors and insulators, frequency spectra in a variety of liquids, and magnetic excitation spectra ("spin waves") in various magnetic compounds. His in-

fluence on the field of condensed matter research has been profound. He has received many awards and honours, and was appointed professor emeritus at McMaster U in 1984.   J.R.D. COPLEY

Brockington, Leonard Walter, first chairman of the CANADIAN BROADCASTING CORP (b at Cardiff, Wales 6 Apr 1888; d at Toronto 15 Sept 1966). He immigrated to Edmonton in 1912 and moved to Calgary shortly after. He was called to the bar in 1919, and was Calgary city solicitor for more than 20 years. His wide interest in the arts led to his appointment as chairman of the CBC 1936-39, an unpaid office. He oversaw the establishment of a national network of high-powered regional transmitters and significant increases in program production. Brockington established for the CBC the principles of nonpartisanship and nonsponsored broadcasts. He felt free speech was best promoted through the free apportionment of time to competent speakers on various sides of controversial issues, as opposed to the sale of time to individuals or commercial concerns. He was a skilled arbitrator, called on to arbitrate disputes between the US government and its employees at the UN, the Toronto Transportation Commission and its employees, the Seafarers' Union and the shipowners, and other disputes. He became special assistant to PM Mackenzie King 1939-42, and was adviser on Commonwealth affairs to the British ministry of information, 1942-43, for which he received the CMG. He was president of Odeon Theatres in Canada, a member of the first Canada Council and rector of Queen's.   ROBERT E. BABE

Brockinton, archaeological site located along the SOURIS R of southwestern Manitoba. It has yielded 3 distinctive occupations: an early bison-butchering pound about 800 AD, a Blackduck culture occupation about 1200 AD, and the first excavated evidence of the Williams culture, about 1600 AD. The Blackduck occupation demonstrated the adaptation of woodland Indians adjusting to seasonal bison hunting. The Williams occupation showed the reliance upon bison by a Plains tribe; it is distinguished by uniquely decorated pottery consisting of small bowls, some with incurved rims, decorated with 2-strand cords impressed in the clay and with zones of punctates made by using hollow tubes such as quills of bird feathers.   E. LEIGH SYMS

Brockville, Ont, City, pop 20 880 (1986c), 19 896 (1981c), inc 1962, located on the St Lawrence R, 80 km E of Kingston. An important transshipment centre in the past, it remains a divisional point on the CNR and, as "gateway to the THOUSAND ISLANDS", a major tourist centre. Founded as a LOYALIST settlement in 1784 by William Buell and Daniel and Charles Jones, it was called Elizabethtown and renamed in 1812 in honour of Maj-Gen Sir Isaac BROCK. The railway encouraged growth, and Canada's oldest railway tunnel was built (1854-56) from the river front one-third of a mile N under the city. For a time foundries and machine shops were active, but these have been replaced by electrical, electronic, pharmaceutical and chemical industries. Many fine old houses survive, and the massive stone Brockville Courthouse (1842-44), designed by John G. HOWARD, is one of Ontario's oldest public buildings. Nearby Blockhouse I was used as a quarantine station during a cholera epidemic (1832). Newspaperman R. Ogle Gowan founded the Grand Lodge of British N America in 1830 (*see* ORANGE ORDER), and the daily *Recorder and Times* has been published since 1821, longer than any newspaper in Ontario. A campus of St Lawrence College of Applied Arts and Technology is located here.   K.L. MORRISON

Broda, Walter, "Turk," hockey player (b at Brandon, Man 15 May 1914; d at Toronto 17 Oct 1972). He was an outstanding goaltender with TORONTO MAPLE LEAFS 1936-52, winning the VEZINA TROPHY in 1941 and 1948, and sharing it with Al Rollins in 1951. He played his best under pressure, allowing only 2.09 goals per game in 101 playoff games. He had 61 shutouts in regular season play, and another 13 in playoffs.
                                           JAMES MARSH

Brodeur, Louis-Philippe, barrister, politician (b at Beloeil, Qué 21 Aug 1862; d at Québec C 1 Jan 1924). He was the son of Toussaint Brodeur, a rebel of 1837. He was educated at the Collège de St-Hyacinthe and Laval and called to the bar in 1884. He entered Parliament as MP for Rouville in 1891, served as Speaker 1901-04, and as minister of inland revenue under Wilfrid Laurier in 1904. He was a staunch advocate of Canadian autonomy, his most important portfolio being marine and fisheries 1906-11; as minister he introduced legislation founding the Royal Canadian Navy. He sat on the Supreme Court of Canada from 1911 until becoming lieutenant-governor of Québec in 1923.   MARC MILNER

Broley, Charles Lavelle, banker, ornithologist (b 7 Dec 1879; d at Delta, Ont 4 May 1959). A banker in Winnipeg, he was also active in ornithology and conservation. In 1939 he "retired" to winters in Florida and summers in Ontario. In Florida he began a raptor-banding study, in 8 years banding 814 bald eagles. Recoveries showed that eagles dispersed northwards after nesting prior to southern migration, the first study to demonstrate this phenomenon with large numbers. Declining hatching success during his study resulted in one of the first alerts to science of the dangers of insecticides. Broley was to assume membership in a special conservation committee on bald eagles when he died fighting a brushfire. He was honoured for his work by a life membership in the Natural History Soc of Manitoba.   MARTIN K. McNICHOLL

Reading: M.J. Broley, *Eagle Man* (1952); J. Gerrard, *Charles Broley, An Extraordinary Naturalist* (1983).

Bromley, Walter, social activist (b at Keelby, Eng 1775; d at South Australia 7 May 1838). After he retired in England from active military service in 1813, Bromley went to Nova Scotia, where he devoted the next 12 years to the education and relief of the Halifax poor and the amelioration of Indians in the Maritimes. He established the Royal Acadian School, maintained a spinning and knitting manufactory, and actively participated in the Halifax Poor Man's Friend Society. In the course of promoting agricultural settlements for the Indians, especially at Shubenacadie, NS, he exposed the colonists' exploitation of the Indians at Sussex Vale, NB, at the expense of the New England Co, an English missionary society. Disappointed with the results of his ventures he returned to England in 1825 and went to work among the aborigines of South Australia in 1836, an enterprise cut short by his accidental drowning.   JUDITH FINGARD

Bronfman Family Descendants of a Russian immigrant tobacco farmer, Ekiel Bronfman, members of the Bronfman family own and control huge financial empires that have been built from the profits of the family liquor business. Until recently the best-known member of the family was **Samuel Bronfman** (b at Soroki, Bessarabia, or en route from Russia 27 Feb 1889; d at Montréal 10 July 1971). In 1924 Sam founded Distillers Corporation Ltd in Montréal, merging it with Joseph E. Seagram and Sons of Waterloo, Ont, in 1928 and building the new company into the world's largest distilling firm. Sam

Samuel and Saidye Bronfman in the early 1930s. Sam Bronfman built his distilling company into the largest in the world (*courtesy Winnipeg Free Press*).

played a leading role in Canadian Jewish affairs and was president of the Canadian Jewish Congress from 1939 to 1962.

Soon after their arrival in 1889, the Bronfman family left their homestead near Wapella, Sask, for Brandon, where Ekiel started a wood-fuel delivery business with sons **Abe** (b in Russia 15 Mar 1882; d at Safety Harbor, Fla 16 Mar 1968), **Harry** (b in Russia 15 Mar 1886; d at Montréal 12 Nov 1963) and Sam. In 1903 the family borrowed money to buy the Anglo-American Hotel in Emerson, Man. The hotel business boomed with railway construction and by the middle of WWI the family was running 3 profitable hotels in Winnipeg. With the coming of PROHIBITION in Canada, the Bronfmans turned their energies to the interprovincial package liquor trade, purchasing stocks of spirits which were sold at a good profit. During the later years of prohibition in the US (1920-33) Sam Bronfman, who was the driving force in Seagrams, developed a large business in export sales to that country. When prohibition ended in 1933, Seagrams was ready with huge amounts of well-aged and carefully blended spirits which were sold bottled to the consumer through a network of distributors, a marketing approach developed by Sam. Success in the US brought huge profits and led to the company's expansion throughout the world. Seven Crown and Seagram's VO became the largest-selling brands of whisky in the world. Under Sam's leadership the company invested in wineries and distilleries and by 1965 reached sales in 119 countries of over $1 billion.

In 1987 the SEAGRAM COMPANY LTD was controlled by Sam's descendants, along with large real estate and financial investments. **Edgar M. Bronfman** (b at Montréal 20 June 1929), Sam's eldest son, was chairman of the board and chief executive officer of the company. He ran the US operations from New York and was president of the World Jewish Congress. Sam's second son **Charles Rosner Bronfman** (b at Montréal 27 June 1931), was co-chairman and directed Seagram's Canadian business. A Canadian nationalist, Charles owned the Montreal Expos baseball club and in 1986 created the CRB Foundation to promote studies on Canadian and Jewish affairs. Sam's daughter, **Phyllis Lambert** (b at Montréal 24 Jan 1927), founded the Canadian Centre for Architecture and in 1987 was building a museum in Montréal to house the centre's substantial collection.

Financiers in their own right were **Edward** (b at Montréal 1 Nov 1927) and **Peter** (b at Montréal 2 Oct 1929), the sons of **Allan Bronfman** (b at Brandon 21 Dec 1895; d at Montréal 26 Mar 1980). Sam excluded his brother Allan's family from Seagrams. However, Edward and Peter have, through Edper Investments, built their own financial empire considered by many to rival that of Sam's heirs. For example, in 1987, Edper indirectly controlled Canada's largest forestry company and largest trust company.

CHRISTOPHER G. CURTIS

Bronson, Erskine Henry, manufacturer, politician (b at Bolton, NY 12 Sept 1844; d at Ottawa 19 Oct 1920). His father Henry Franklin BRONSON moved the family to Bytown [Ottawa] in 1853 during an influx of Americans attracted by cheap waterpower at the Chaudière Falls. In 1867 he entered the Bronsons and Weston Lumber Co, assuming control in 1889 on his father's death. His concern for forestry conservation drew him into provincial politics in 1886, and 3 years later he joined Oliver MOWAT's Reform Cabinet as minister without portfolio, a position he held in the A.S. HARDY Cabinet until 1898.

During the 1890s Bronson diversified his business concerns into a corporate empire based on hydroelectric and traction utilities. He believed that only large corporations with immense capital working in co-operation with government could develop Canada's industry. This philosophy, and his interests in the Ottawa Electric Co (director) and Ottawa Power Co (president), involved him in a 1905 public utilities plebiscite in Ottawa, which he lost. His prestige and influence declined swiftly and he retired in 1910 a frustrated and disillusioned man. RICHARD REID

Bronson, Henry Franklin, lumber manufacturer (b at Moreau Twp, Saratoga County, NY 24 Feb 1817; d at Ottawa 7 Dec 1889). In 1852 Bronson and his partner John Harris moved to Bytown [Ottawa] to exploit the timber reserves of the Ottawa Valley, bringing his family the following year. Utilizing modern mills, they were among the first to ship lumber from Ottawa to American markets. Abijah Weston replaced Harris, and the Bronsons and Weston Lumber Co became one of the largest in Canada. Although Bronson retained his American citizenship, he became a leading Ottawa citizen, a major philanthropist and a supporter of the Reform Party.

RICHARD REID

Brooke, Frances, née Moore, novelist, dramatist, essayist (christened at Claypole, Eng 24 Jan 1724; d at Sleaford, Eng 23 Jan 1789). In London, Frances moved in literary and theatrical circles. She published a weekly *The Old Maid* (Nov 1755-July 1756) and a tragedy *Virginia* in 1756. Turning to fiction, in 1760 she translated a novel of sensibility, 3 years later publishing her own such novel, *The History of Lady Julia Mandeville.* That year she sailed for Québec, where her husband, the Reverend John Brooke, was military chaplain. Here she wrote what may be described as the first Canadian novel, *The History of Emily Montague* (1769), which she enriched with descriptions of landscape and climate, current events and inhabitants of the new colony. Returning to England in 1768, she continued her literary career with 2 translations from the French and several novels. From 1773 she, with tragic actress Mary Ann Yates, managed the Opera House, and she finally achieved theatrical success with her tragedy *The Siege of Sinope* (1781) and 2 comic operas, *Rosena* (1783) and *Marian* (1788). LORRAINE McMULLEN

Brooker, Bertram Richard, artist, novelist, poet, journalist, advertising executive (b at Croydon, Eng 31 Mar 1888; d at Toronto 21 Mar 1955). He immigrated to Portage la Prairie, Man, in 1905 and worked with the Grand Trunk Pacific Ry. He then owned and operated a motion picture theatre in Neepawa, Man, subsequently working on newspapers in Manitoba and Saskatchewan. Brooker moved to Toronto in 1921 as an advertising executive. As an artist – working in oil, watercolour, pencil, ink and print media – he executed both abstracts and realistic works. Brooker became the first Canadian artist to exhibit abstracts in 1927; *Sounds Assembling* (1928) and *Alleluiah* (1929) are early important paintings. As a novelist he won the first Governor General's Award for fiction with *Think of the Earth* (1936). He initiated, introduced and edited *The Yearbook of the Arts in Canada 1928-1929*, and a second volume in 1936. Brooker was an active member of Toronto's cultural life, painting, writing both prose and poetry, and regularly reviewing contemporary art and literature. PATRICIA E. BOVEY

Brooker, Todd, alpine skier (b at Paris, Ont 24 Nov 1959). He began skiing at 4 and by 12 was racing throughout Ontario and Québec. An extremely aggressive skier, he has experienced both spectacular wins and devastating injuries. In 1979, his first year on the elite team, he injured a knee and was sidelined for over a year. In 1982-83, he won 2 World Cup events and ended the season with the number-one Fédération internationale du ski ranking in downhill. He remained one of the world's finest racers through 1986, with a win in Japan (1985) and 8 other top-ten finishes. In 1987 he was forced to retire after a serious knee injury suffered at Kitzbuehel, site of his first World Cup victory. MURRAY SHAW

Brooks, Alta, Town, pop 9464 (1986c), 9421 (1981c), inc 1911, is located 185 km SE of Calgary on the Trans-Canada Hwy. A CPR siding was built on the site (1883), but when a townsite was surveyed in 1907, the population was only 9, including divisional engineer N.E. Brooks, after whom the town is named. In 1914 the CPR built a dam on the BOW R at Bassano (50 km NW), irrigating much of the surrounding country and encouraging settlement. Today a 3 km long canal irrigates more than 40 000 ha of prosperous farmland, the water being carried by a siphon under the CPR tracks. The Provincial Horticultural Research Station is located in the town, and to the S is Kinbrook Island Prov Pk, located on Lk Newell, Alberta's largest artificial lake, which serves as an irrigation reservoir. DINOSAUR PROVINCIAL PARK (40 km NE) has some of the world's most extensive fossil remains. ERIC J. HOLMGREN

Brooks, Allan Cyril, naturalist, artist, soldier (b at Etawah, India 15 Feb 1869; d at Comox, BC 3 Jan 1946). Born to a prominent naturalist family, he received his early education in England. His family moved to Milton, Ont, in 1881, and then to Chilliwack, BC, in 1887. Brooks spent most of his remaining life in the Okanagan Valley and on Vancouver I. Drawings of birds, some of which survive from his fifth year, form his greatest legacy; he was illustrator of TAVERNER's books on Canadian birds and of several American ornithological and popular works. An ardent hunter and collector, he carefully prepared bird skins as taught by T. MCILWRAITH and mounted his own big-game heads, selling many specimens to museums. His scientific publications number about 130 and concentrate on faunistics and taxonomy. He travelled widely, especially in N America, and was known for his boundless enthusiasm. In WWI he quickly rose to the rank of major and received the DSO. MARTIN K. McNICHOLL

Reading: H.M. Laing, *Allan Brooks: Artist Naturalist* (1979).

Brooks, Lela Alene, speed skater (b at Toronto 7 Feb 1908). Encouragement from speedskating parents, strong self-motivation and a fierce competitive instinct enabled Brooks to succeed. Without formal coaching, she learned to leave the starting post quickly and had the stamina to hold her lead. Between 1921 and 1935 she won all the speed skating titles available to women, from provincial to world levels, and set new records at most of these levels. She was named to the 1936 Olympic team but opted instead for marriage and retirement. BOB FERGUSON

Brooman Point Village, archaeological site located at the tip of a long peninsula extending from the eastern coast of BATHURST I in the High Arctic. Although the site shows traces of Paleoeskimo occupations between about 2000 BC and 1 AD, the major prehistoric settlement occurred from about 900-1200 AD. Archaeological excavations have revealed the presence of a late DORSET Paleoeskimo village, the remains of which were almost totally obliterated by early THULE-culture Inuit who built a village on top of the Dorset site and incorporated many Dorset artifacts into the wall-fill of their houses, thus preserving them in permafrost. These artifacts include one of the largest known collections of Dorset carvings in wood, ivory and antler (see INUIT ART). The Thule village is radiocarbon dated to about 1100 AD and consists of 20 winter houses, of which only 4 or 5 were occupied at one time. The bones of at least 20 bowhead whales, used in house construction, indicate that the local Thule people efficiently exploited an environment much richer than that which exists in the area today. *See also* ARCHAEOLOGY; PREHISTORY.
ROBERT MCGHEE

Brossard, Jacques, public servant, writer (b at Montréal 24 Apr 1933). He holds a BA (1952) from Collège Sainte-Marie, a L ès L (1955) from U de Montréal and a social science degree (1957) from Oxford. Admitted to the bar (1956), he joined the foreign service in 1957. He was assigned in turn to the economic affairs section of the Colombo Plan, the Atlantic Alliance, to Bogota (Colombia) as the vice-consul and chargé d'affaires, and to Port-au-Prince (Haiti) as consul. He was then named director of Latin American Affairs and executive assistant to the minister of external affairs. He left the civil service (1964) to become chief researcher at the Centre de recherche en droit public at U de Montréal. In 1969 he became adviser to the Ministry of Intergovernmental Relations in Québec, having specialized in constitutional problems. He published, in order: *L'Immigration – les droits et les pouvoirs du Québec* (1967); *La Cour suprème et la Constitution* (1968), Prix du Québec, 1969; *Le Territoire québécois* (1970), in collaboration; and *L'Accession à la souveraineté et le cas du Québec* (1976). He entered the field of literature with a collection of short stories, *Le Métamorfaux* (1974), which received critical attention, and a novel, *Le Sang du souvenir* (1976). He has also written for several periodicals. He won the Prix Duvernay (1976) for his work as a whole and the medal of the city of Paris (1977). AURÉLIEN BOIVIN

Brossard, Nicole, writer, publisher (b at Montréal 27 Nov 1943). Brossard is a leading exponent of so-called formalist poetry in Québec and a major theoretician and promoter of literary and cultural feminism. In 1965 she founded *La* BARRE DU JOUR, a literary magazine which rebelled against nationalist-inspired poetry. Her poetry, in collections such as *Le Centre blanc* (1970) and *Suite logique* (1970), is abstract and antilyrical, and influenced the young poets of the magazine *Les Herbes rouges*. Brossard has also written novels. Her career took on a feminist dimension with *Mécanique jongleuse suivi de masculin grammaticale*

(1974), which won the Gov Gen's Award for poetry. She founded the feminist paper *Les Têtes de pioche* (1976-79) and the magazine *La Nouvelle Barre du jour* (1977), and has participated in many conferences in Canada and abroad about women's writing or Québec literature. While being an active member of the Union des écrivains québécois and getting involved in publishing, she has since 1980 written important collections of poetry, such as *Double impression* (Gov Gen's Award 1984) and a few novels in which she experiments with new forms of fiction.
PIERRE NEPVEU

Brother Twelve (also, Brother XII), religious leader (b Edward Arthur Wilson at Birmingham, Eng 25 July 1878; d at Neuchatel, Switz 7 Nov 1934?). A mystic and former sea captain, Brother Twelve established an occult society and utopian community called The Aquarian Foundation outside Nanaimo, BC, in 1927. The society claimed more than 2000 members at its height, including many wealthy and prominent individuals. A series of sensational court cases, during which Brother Twelve was accused of misusing foundation funds, advocating free love and claiming to be the reincarnation of the Egyptian god Osiris, led to the break up of the original colony. Brother Twelve formed a new settlement, a "City of Refuge," on nearby Valdes and DeCourcy Is, where he and his disciples believed they would survive the coming Armageddon. Conditions at the colony gradually deteriorated, as Brother Twelve and his sadistic mistress, a woman known as "Madame Z," turned their followers into slaves, subjecting them to the most appalling hardship and privation. They also attempted to murder their enemies, including high-ranking government officials, by black magic. The disciples eventually revolted, bringing a court action against their leader to recover their money. They won their case, but Brother Twelve wrecked the colony in vengeance, and fled with a fortune in gold. His death in Switzerland is unconfirmed. A complex mixture of mystic and charlatan, Brother Twelve ranks as one of Canada's most notorious cult leaders; how sincere he was originally, and how authentic his powers were, is still uncertain. He claimed to be the twelfth Master in an occult Brotherhood said to guide the evolution of the human race; hence the name, Brother Twelve. JOHN OLIPHANT

A rare photograph of the infamous Brother Twelve, wearing a hat, seated among a group of followers under the "Tree of Wisdom" at the colony's headquarters on Vancouver I (*courtesy John Oliphant*).

Brothers of the Christian Schools, a religious congregation founded in Reims, France, by Saint Jean-Baptiste de la Salle for the "Christian education of children" (Common Rules, I, 4). The first schools were founded in 1679. The brothers came to Montréal in 1837 and spread throughout Canada and the US. Their excellent reputation is the result of the quality of their teaching and the respect they receive for the fact they have always given preference to the poor and disadvantaged. Brother MARIE-VICTORIN, the famous Canadian botanist, was a member of this congregation. In 1986 there were 381 brothers in Canada (4% of the world total) in 44 houses.
MICHEL THÉRIAULT

Alexander Brott, conductor and composer. On conducting tours abroad, he is an enthusiastic champion of the music of Canadian composers (*courtesy SSC Photocentre*).

Brott, Alexander, conductor, composer, violinist, educator (b at Montréal 14 Mar 1915). Early success as a violinist led to a teaching appointment at McGill in 1939, where he founded the McGill Chamber Orchestra (1945); he was still conductor of the orchestra in 1987. Concertmaster (1945-58) and at various times (1948-61) assistant conductor of the ORCHESTRE SYMPHONIQUE DE MONTRÉAL, he was artistic director of the Kingston Symphony 1965-81 and has guest conducted most major Canadian orchestras. On frequent conducting tours abroad, he has been an enthusiastic champion of the music of Canadian composers. Brott's own output as composer for a variety of instrumental and vocal media is large. A skilful craftsman with a sure mastery of form, he uses counterpoint as his primary construction technique. Much of Brott's music is distinguished by good humour, elegant wit and satire. BARCLAY MCMILLAN

Brott, Boris, conductor, violinist (b at Montréal 14 Mar 1944), son of Alexander BROTT. After his

debut as a violinist at age 5, youthful conducting studies and award-winning performances in prestigious conducting competitions, Brott became assistant conductor of the TORONTO SYMPHONY (1963-65), then conductor of England's Northern Sinfonia at Newcastle-upon-Tyne (1964-68). He has been artistic director and conductor of the Hamilton Philharmonic Orchestra since 1969; as well he was conductor of the BBC Welsh Orchestra (1972-79) and artistic director of Symphony Nova Scotia (1983-86) and Ontario Place Pops since 1983. He made his Carnegie Hall debut conducting the Orchestra of the Americas in 1987, the year he was made Officer of the Order of Canada. Brott is known for musicianship, artistic flair and innovative programming concepts successful in audience building, not least in the domain of contemporary music.

BARCLAY MCMILLAN

Broughton Island, NWT, Hamlet, pop 439 (1986c), is located off the E coast of BAFFIN I in Davis Strait, on Broughton I, 2373 air km NE of Yellowknife. Situated on a rocky spur several kms from the ocean, the Inuit population and its ancestors had contact with European whalers throughout the early part of the 17th century. Up until 1956-57, the settlement site was located at Kitvoo, 64 km N of the present village. It was here that the Inuit traded with the whalers (*see* WHALING). The Inuit eventually moved to Broughton Island following construction of the Distant Early Warning (DEW) Line station and a federal administrative office in the 1950s. Today the community relies heavily on marine mammal harvesting and the making and selling of handicrafts. Broughton Island is also an important staging centre for tourist-adventure travel through AUYUITTUQ NATIONAL PARK located nearby.

EDWARD STRUZIK

Brown, Arthur Roy, fighter pilot (b at Carleton Place, Ont 23 Dec 1893; d at Stouffville, Ont 9 Mar 1944). A flight commander with 209 Squadron, Brown has often been credited with killing Manfred Freiherr von Richthofen, the famed "Red Baron," on 21 Apr 1918. It is more likely, however, that von Richthofen was killed by ground fire from Australian machine gunners. Credited with 11 victories, Brown survived a serious flying accident in July 1918 and left the RAF a year later. He subsequently engaged in various businesses involved with flying.

BRERETON GREENHOUS

Brown, Daniel Price Erichsen, painter, printmaker (b at Forestville, Ont 21 Aug 1939). D.P. Brown's interest in art was sparked on frequent childhood sketching trips with A.Y. JACKSON and Will OGILVIE near Georgian Bay, and continued on his annual vacation visits to the great art collections of Europe while studying abroad. He was encouraged by Lawren P. HARRIS to return to Canada in 1958 to study at Mount Allison with Alex COLVILLE. After graduating in 1961 Brown moved back to Ontario to paint full-time. The wide variety of his subject matter appears to be the mundane familiarity of his rural surroundings recorded with an almost photographic accuracy. But closer examination reveals the creation of carefully controlled compositions with a larger purpose – hidden juxtapositions, relationships and comparisons of intense philosophical insight and social commentary in the tradition of the finest classical and Renaissance masters he so greatly admires. His major works include images of farmers and city dwellers interacting at a farm auction (*The Auction*, 1975); the nude artist startled by a skeleton hanging in a doctor's office (*Nude and Skeleton*, 1978); a majorette posing too proudly before a draped Canadian flag (*The*

Twirler, 1979); and aging Orangemen parading past a monolithic Catholic church (*Orangemen's Parade*, 1984; *see* ORANGE ORDER). He paints exclusively with egg tempera and prints all his serigraph stencils by hand, creating one composition at a time and producing a total of only 3 or 4 works per year. In 1985 he was the subject of a 6-city retrospective exhibition: "D.P. Brown; Twenty Years."

BOB HUNKA

Brown, Edward Killoran, professor, critic (b at Toronto 15 Aug 1905; d at Chicago, Ill 24 Apr 1951). E.K. Brown was educated at U of T and U of Paris, and he taught at U of T, U of Man, Cornell and U of Chicago. His most important contributions to Canadian criticism were his well-known study *On Canadian Poetry* (1943, rev ed 1944); his annual surveys of Canadian poetry in the UNIVERSITY OF TORONTO QUARTERLY 1936-50; and his edition of Duncan Campbell SCOTT's poems (1951). At home in French and English, Brown was the first modern Canadian critic to establish a context for the study of 19th- and 20th-century Canadian POETRY by identifying Canada's major poets (Archibald LAMPMAN, D.C. Scott and E.J. PRATT), tracing their influences and closely defining the strengths of their verse.

NEIL BESNER

Reading: E.K. Brown, *Responses and Evaluations: Essays on Canada*, ed D. Staines (1977).

Brown, Eldon Leslie, mining engineer, executive (b at Toronto 19 Aug 1900). After working as an engineer for the Mond Nickel Co, Brown joined Sherritt Gordon Mines Ltd in 1927, becoming president and managing director 1946. He also served as manager of God's Lake Gold Mines Ltd, consulting engineer of Madsen Red Lake Gold Mines and VP and general manager of Michipicoten Iron Mines Ltd. A brilliant mine engineer, he played a key role in the discovery and development of Sherritt Gordon's Lynn Lk nickel-cobalt mine, brought into production in the early 1950s, employed airborne geophysical equipment to locate the Fox mine 1960 and encouraged the development of complex chemical and metallurgical extraction processes. He retired as chairman 1968. He served as president of the Canadian Metal Mining Assn in 1950 and received University of Toronto's Engineering Alumni Medal.

J. LINDSEY

Brown, Ernest, photographer (b at Newcastle upon Tyne 8 Sept 1877; d at Edmonton 3 Jan 1951). He arrived in Edmonton in 1904 and recorded the quick growth of the city during the boom years 1904-14. His business collapsed in 1914 and in 1920 he was forced to vacate his premises. Embittered, he ran unsuccessfully as Labour Independent in the 1921 provincial election. Having set up his former assistant Gladys Reeves as a photographer, he spent 8 years in Vegreville photographing, cataloguing his collection and writing a history, "The Birth of the West." He returned to Edmonton in 1929 and operated the Pioneer Days Museum 1933-39, exhibiting his artifacts and photographs. In 1947 the province purchased his museum artifacts and his collection of 50 000 negatives (now housed in the Provincial Archives of Alberta).

ERIC J. HOLMGREN

Brown, George, journalist, politician (b at Alloa, Scot 29 Nov 1818; d at Toronto 9 May 1880). Raised in Edinburgh, he immigrated with his father to New York in 1837. They moved to Toronto in 1843 and began a paper, the *Banner*, for Upper Canadian Presbyterians. The next year George launched the Toronto *Globe* to back Reform efforts for RESPONSIBLE GOVERNMENT. He helped win the Reformers' victory of 1848, and made his *Globe* a vigorous force in Upper Canada. New

issues rising there in church-state relations (notably Catholic demands for state-aided separate schools) led him into the Assembly as member for Kent in 1851. In the then PROVINCE OF CANADA, Brown's pronouncements against church-state ties drew favour within its predominantly Anglo-Protestant Upper Canadian half, but animosity in largely French-Catholic Lower Canada. Moreover, in 1853 he took up the idea of representation by population, which would give the more populous Upper Canada a majority of seats in the legislature. Beset by sectional strains, the Reform regime collapsed in 1854. The Liberal-Conservatives took office, while Brown sought to rebuild the Reform Party.

He won over the CLEAR GRIT radicals, strong in rural Upper Canada, whom he had formerly opposed for their sweeping American-style democracy. In Jan 1857 a reorganized Upper Canadian Reform Party adopted his policies of "rep by pop" and annexation of the Northwest, the fur trade expanse beyond the Great Lakes. This potent combination of Toronto leadership, the *Globe* and agrarian Grit numbers swept the Upper Canada elections of late 1857. In Aug 1858 Brown even formed a government with A.A. DORION, head of the Lower Canada Liberals; but sectional balances were too shaky, and it swiftly fell. The Upper Canada leader then steered a Reform Convention of 1859 in Toronto to the concept of a federal Union of the Canadas as a remedy for sectional division. Yet his concept did not carry Parliament, and in 1861, ill and temporarily defeated, he withdrew to recuperate. In 1863 he returned as member for S Oxford, after a visit to Britain where he married Anne Nelson, daughter of a prominent Edinburgh publisher.

A restored, deeply happy Brown explored more conciliatory means to achieve reform of the Union. In 1864 he chaired an all-party parliamentary committee on that subject, which on June 14 reported in favour of the "federal principle" to overcome the sectionalism which by then had brought political deadlock. When on the same day a last, ineffectual Conservative ministry broke down, Brown offered to support a new

George Brown's initiative in forming a coalition with his Conservative rivals was crucial in achieving Confederation. He was killed by a disgruntled former employee at the *Globe*, which Brown had founded in 1844 (*courtesy National Archives of Canada/C-26415*).

government ready to pursue constitutional changes. In consequence, he joined with his chief Conservative rivals John A. MACDONALD, A.T. GALT and G.É. CARTIER, to form a coalition which would seek a federal union of all the British provinces or, failing that, of the Canadas. Through this strong new coalition, stemming from Brown's crucial initiative, the movement to CONFEDERATION now surged ahead. He played a major role at the CHARLOTTETOWN CONFERENCE and the QUEBEC CONFERENCE which formulated the plan; he was first to carry it to the British government in Dec 1864, and spoke compellingly for it in the 1865 Confederation debates in the Canadian Assembly. In Dec 1865, however, he resigned from the coalition Cabinet over internal dissensions. He continued to support Confederation nonetheless and ran in the first federal elections in fall 1867. Defeated, he then left Parliament. He felt satisfied still that his chief aims had been realized and he retired to the *Globe* office, to his warm family life with wife and 3 children, and to the Bow Park estate near Brantford which he developed as a large-scale cattle-breeding enterprise.

Brown remained a power in Liberal circles as elder statesman and director of a formidable mass-circulation journal. He was active in Ontario party affairs, was a senator from 1874, and was close to Alexander MACKENZIE, his former chief lieutenant, who was federal prime minister 1873-78. Brown's death came in 1880 by tragic accident. A dismissed *Globe* employee, George Bennett (whom he had never known), accosted him in his office and shot him in a sudden struggle. The seemingly minor leg wound grew infected and finally brought his death. *See also* FATHERS OF CONFEDERATION.　　J.M.S. CARELESS

Reading: J.M.S. Careless, *Brown of The Globe*, 2 volumes (1959-63).

Brown, James Sutherland, "Buster," soldier (b at Simcoe, Ont 28 Jun 1881; d at Victoria 13 Apr 1951). Brown joined the militia in 1896, transferred to the Royal Canadian Regiment in 1906, and served in a number of staff appointments overseas during WWI. Of Loyalist stock, the outspoken Brown was deeply suspicious of the US and a champion of Canada's British heritage. In the 1920s, as director of military operations and intelligence, he drafted Defence Scheme No 1, Canada's contingency plan for defence in a war between the British Empire and the US. The scheme was dropped in 1931 by the chief of the general staff, A.G.L. MCNAUGHTON, who knew the Americans would inevitably win such a war. Brown commanded Military District 11 in BC from 1929 to 1933, when he retired following a clash with McNaughton over the administration of the unemployment relief camps managed by the Dept of National Defence. He took refuge in Victoria, running unsuccessfully for office as a Conservative and railing against socialism and other "isms" which he considered disruptive of society.　　STEPHEN HARRIS AND NORMAN HILLMER

Brown, John George, "Kootenai," army officer, prospector, constable, whisky trader, buffalo hunter, wolfer, dispatch rider, guide, scout, driving force in establishing WATERTON LAKES NATL PK (b at Ennistymon, Ire 10 Oct 1839; d at Waterton Lks, Alta 18 July 1916). Through his grandmother's persistence Brown was commissioned in 1857 "without purchase" as an 8th Regiment ensign. After service in India 1858-59, he sold his commission and in 1862 set out for the Cariboo goldfields of BC. There he prospected unsuccessfully, trapped and served briefly as constable at Wild Horse Cr. In 1865 he travelled through the Rocky Mts to Waterton (Kootenay) Lks, which

enchanted him and from which ultimately his nickname was derived.

Continuing across the prairie to Ft Garry, he was wounded by marauding Blackfoot, then traded whisky in the Portage area. Employed briefly by a private company carrying mail for the US Army in the Dakota and Montana territories, Brown remained with the military as a civilian "tripper." Despite capture and near death at the hands of SITTING BULL in 1869, he continued dispatch riding until 1874. Brown then joined his wife's people – he had married a Métis in 1869 – hunting buffalo and wolfing. In 1877, at Ft Benton, Montana, Brown quarrelled with and killed Louis Ell, a celebrated hunter. Acquitted by a territorial jury he settled at Waterton Lks, where he traded and established a reputation as guide and packer. During the 1885 NORTH-WEST REBELLION, he became chief scout for the Rocky Mt Rangers.

Brown early foresaw the need to preserve the Waterton area and campaigned strenuously on its behalf. With the establishment of the Kootenay Forest Reserve in 1895 he became fishery officer and, in 1910, forest ranger. In 1914 his dream of further CONSERVATION was realized when the reserve became Waterton Lks Natl Pk, was enlarged and made contiguous with the international boundary and Glacier Natl Pk in the US.

WILLIAM RODNEY

Brown, William, journalist, printer (b at Nunton, Scot *c*1737; d at Québec C 22 Mar 1789). In partnership with Thomas Gilmore he published the first issue of the *Quebec Gazette/La Gazette de Québec* 21 June 1764. The *Gazette* was the first periodical in the PROVINCE OF QUEBEC and began with the ideal of informing the public with impartiality. However, mention of the revolutionary events in the Thirteen Colonies was censored by Gov Guy CARLETON after 1768 and publication was suspended during the American invasion of 1775-76, resuming thereafter as, in Brown's description, "the most innocent gazette in the British Dominions." Brown and Gilmore also published the first books in Québec, including a catechism, legal works and *Abram's Plains* (1789), a collection of poems by Thomas Cary.

JAMES MARSH

Browne, George, architect (b at Belfast, Ire 5 Nov 1811; d at Montréal 19 Nov 1885). He created some of 19th-century Canada's finest buildings. In the 1830s he designed houses in Québec City and Montréal. With the union of Upper and Lower Canada (1841) and the establishment of the new capital at Kingston, Browne (then a government architect) did considerable work, including many private, commercial and civic buildings. Mostly in local limestone, they show a sophisticated handling of mass and texture. Their style, which might be called "heroic primitive," expresses the triumphant character of a society just emerging from the pioneering stage. The finest example is Kingston City Hall, but the Kingston branch of the Bank of Montreal (1844), which may be the earliest example of a large-scale branch bank building in Canada, also survives (as the Frontenac Apartments). Browne moved with the capital to Montréal in 1844, where his splendid Second-Empire-style Molsons Bank 1864-66 (now Bank of Montreal) survives.

J. DOUGLAS STEWART

Browne, George, Jr, architect (b at Montréal, Canada E 1852 or 1853; d at South Nyack, NY 12 Mar 1919). After study with his father, a prominent Montréal architect, Browne travelled in Europe and went to South Kensington School of Art, London. He returned to Montréal in 1877 and in 1879 went to Manitoba. His design for the Massey Block (1885) in Winnipeg for the implement

company of that name established a unique Manitoba style of commercial buildings by its use of local materials and a primitive Romanesque classicism in style. He also built Wesley Coll (U Winnipeg) in 1895, the finest Richardsonian Romanesque building extant in Winnipeg. Browne left for New York C in 1910.　　W. P. THOMPSON

Brownell, Peleg Franklin, painter, teacher (b at New Bedford, Mass 27 July 1857; d at Ottawa 13 Mar 1946). After studying at the Boston Museum of Fine Arts, he went to Paris to study under Robert-Fleury, Bouguereau and Bonnat. In 1886 he became principal of the Ottawa Art School and subsequently headed the Woman's Art Assn of Ottawa (later Ottawa Art Assn), retiring 1937. He also painted in the West Indies, the US, the Gaspé and the Gatineau. Besides highly keyed landscapes, he produced portraits, flower studies, marine and genre scenes in oil, watercolour and pastel. A founder-member of the Canadian Art Club (1907), he was represented in the exhibitions of several art associations and showed internationally at the 1893 Chicago World's Columbian Exposition; the 1900 Paris World's Fair, at which he won a bronze medal for his RCA diploma work, *The Photographer*, 1896; the Louisiana Purchase Exhibition, St Louis, 1904; and the British Empire Exhibition, 1924-25. His paintings are found in major Canadian collections. Perhaps his best-known canvas is *The Beach, St. Kitts* (1913).　　ROBERT STACEY

Brownlee, John Edward, lawyer, politician, executive, premier of Alberta 1925-34 (b at Port Ryerse, Ont 27 Aug 1883; d at Calgary 15 July 1961). He was one of Alberta's most effective premiers and for 5 decades a major voice in western farmer organizations. Son of a small-town merchant and a devout Methodist teacher, he moved to Calgary in 1909 to pursue a career in the booming West. He became solicitor for the fledgling UNITED FARMERS OF ALBERTA and played an important part in the amalgamation of United Grain Growers in 1917. When the UFA won the 1921 Alberta election, he became attorney general and helped organize the ALBERTA WHEAT POOL. After a well-mannered backstairs revolt, he became premier in Nov 1925, and his most significant achievement was his negotiation of the transfer to Alberta of control over its natural resources, an agreement drafted by him and signed 14 Dec 1929. During the Depression, Albertans became frustrated with his fiscal restraint, cautious assistance programs and political conservatism. A vigorous but lonely voice against the tide of SOCIAL CREDIT, and undermined by accusations of personal scandal orchestrated by his political opponents, he was forced to resign as premier in July 1934. Both he and the UFA saw their political careers brought to a devastating end in the election of Aug 1935. In 1948 he rejoined UGG as president and general manager, modernizing the company's financial structure and rationalizing the elevator system by closing smaller, inefficient operations and concentrating on larger delivery points.　　FRANKLIN L. FOSTER

Bruce, Charles Tory, poet, novelist (b at Port Shoreham, NS 11 May 1906; d at Toronto 19 Dec 1971). Bruce graduated from Mount Allison U in 1927, worked for 8 months as a reporter for the Halifax *Chronicle*, and then joined the Canadian Press. Over the next 35 years he became one of the country's most respected newsmen, and served as CP's general superintendent from 1945 until his retirement in 1963. *News and the Southams*, his history of the Southam newspaper company, appeared in 1968. Bruce's first book of poems, *Wild Apples*, was privately published during his final university year, but he was then taken up by commercial houses, and there followed *Tomorrow's Tide* (1932), *Personal Note* (1941), *Grey Ship Moving* (1945), *The Flowing Summer* (1947) and *The Mulgrave Road* (1951). The latter won him the Governor General's Award and a wide readership. Bruce's best lyrics, which are about the Chedabucto Bay region where he was born and spent his boyhood, rely on simple, concrete imagery, display an original voice, and reveal his basic tenet that, in poetry, "the gleam of truth [is] glimpsed through lived experience." In 1954, his only novel, *The Channel Shore*, was published. Its essential theme of time as "a continuing whole" is conveyed through its compelling characterization and memorable setting. His collection of linked short stories, *The Township of Time* (1959), traces various fictional bloodlines down through 160 years of Channel Shore settlement, emphasizing his firm belief in "continuity...a sense of relationship to past generations, a feeling of kinship to generations still to come."

J.A. WAINWRIGHT

Bruce, Herbert Alexander, surgeon, military officer, politician (b at Blackstock, Ont 28 Sept 1868; d at Toronto 23 June 1963). Founder of Toronto's Wellesley Hospital (1911), he was appointed special inspector-general of the Canadian Army Medical Corps overseas by Sir Sam HUGHES in 1916. His *Report on the Canadian Army Medical Service* recommended a complete reorganization, including segregation of Canadian wounded in Canadian facilities. Although many of his ideas were subsequently implemented, Bruce and his report were disowned by the government. He later published his charges in *Politics and the Canadian Army Medical Corps* (1919). As lieutenant-governor of Ontario, 1932-37, he struggled to maintain his office against Mitch HEPBURN, the Liberal premier elected on a promise to reduce government expenditure. As a Conservative MP, 1940-46, Bruce was an outspoken proponent of wartime CONSCRIPTION. His lively memoirs, *Varied Operations* (1958), recount his medical, military and political careers.

O.A. COOKE

Bruce, William Blair, painter (b at Hamilton, Canada W 10 Oct 1859; d at Stockholm, Sweden 17 Nov 1906). He was Canada's first impressionist painter. His love for genre painting and innate feeling for "sentiment" brought him success in the Paris Salon of the day, particularly with *Temps Passé* (1884) and *The Phantom Hunter* (1888). Bruce's masterpiece, *The Smiths* (1894), was a portrait of workers forging a wheel and may have been intended as a tribute to Hamilton and its tire industry. In 1888 Bruce married the Swedish sculptor Caroline Benedicks and after years of travel settled on the Swedish island of Gotland. Bruce's paintings are divided between Gotland's Fornsal Museum and the Art Gallery of Hamilton.

JOAN MURRAY

Bruce Peninsula, 100 km long, 38 km wide at base, juts NW from OWEN SOUND to Tobermory, thus forming GEORGIAN BAY in Lk HURON, Ontario. Composed of NIAGARA ESCARPMENT strata, it has a gentle tilt from the cliffs on Georgian Bay to the flat sand and clay plains on Lk Huron's shore. Owen Sound and Colpoys Bay form fjordlike harbours on Georgian Bay. Cape Croker, projecting 10 km into the bay, is an Ojibwa IR. Adjacent Hope Bay is famous for its sheer limestone cliffs and sandy beach. At Lion's Head a jagged rock formation, 51 m high, gives the site its name. At Tobermory the clear waters and numerous shipwrecks have produced a diving centre. In July 1987 Bruce National Park was created out of existing provincial parks and federal land in the area. Called "the N American rendezvous of plants," the Bruce is a paradise for botanists, containing northern, transitional and southern tree

species, approximately 49 orchid species and 30 species of ferns. The BRUCE TRAIL follows the rugged wilderness of the Georgian Bay side, much of which was recommended for preservation in the Niagara Escarpment Plan.

RAYMOND N. LOWES

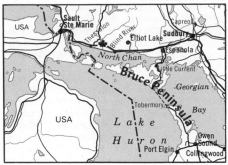

Bruce Trail is a continuous, 720 km footpath on the NIAGARA ESCARPMENT connecting QUEENSTON, near NIAGARA FALLS, with the village of Tobermory in the BRUCE PENINSULA, Ontario. The trail follows the escarpment cliff through the fruit lands of Niagara and the city of HAMILTON, across the Dundas Valley, N through the Caledon Hills to the Blue Mts, then NW across the Beaver Valley to OWEN SOUND and onward, seldom out of sight of Lk Huron's GEORGIAN B, to Tobermory. This opportunity to explore Ontario on foot has been grasped by thousands, making the trail an important tourist attraction for Canada and encouraging the Ontario government to take steps towards preserving the escarpment. Public-spirited landowners gave permission for the trail route to cross their properties; volunteer members of the Bruce Trail Assn built the trail and now maintain it. The idea for a nature trail across Ontario leading to "the Bruce," a paradise for naturalists, was proposed by Ray Lowes, a Stelco metallurgist, in 1960, and from this idea the BTA grew into a dedicated organization that manages the trail and channels the efforts of its members into maintenance, appropriate hiking behaviour, nature appreciation and respect for landowners' property.

RAYMOND N. LOWES

Bruhn, Erik Belton Evers, ballet dancer, choreographer (b at Copenhagen, Denmark 3 Oct 1928; d at Toronto 1 Aug 1986). After WWII he danced for the Royal Danish Ballet Co and moved to England to join the Metropolitan Ballet. There he met and danced with Celia FRANCA, who invited him to Canada soon after the founding of the NATIONAL BALLET OF CANADA. As a dancer Bruhn excelled in roles with many ballet companies, and his many awards included the Nijinsky Prize 1963 and the Diplôme d'honneur of the Canadian Conference of the Arts 1974. After staging *La Sylphide* for the National Ballet of Canada in 1964, Bruhn was closely associated with the company (and its school) as guest artist, choreographer, teacher, resident producer and (from 1983) artistic director. His works for the company, including the controversial psychological *Swan Lake*, were mainstays of the repertoire, and his impeccable classical style and dramatic intelligence influenced numerous Canadian dancers.

PENELOPE DOOB

Brûlé, Étienne, explorer, interpreter (b probably at Champigny-sur-Marne, France *c*1592; d in Huronia *c*June 1633). Brûlé was the first Frenchman to live among the native people. Champlain wrote that Brûlé was sent among the HURON, likely in 1610, in exchange for a young Huron. He became a skilful interpreter and intermediary. Travelling with his adopted people, Brûlé was likely the first European to see Lks Ontario, Huron and Superior and on a mission to the

Susquehannock he roamed as far as Chesapeake Bay. He was captured by the Iroquois and ritually tortured but was released, likely on a promise to promote an alliance with the French. In 1621-22 he travelled northward and reported the rapids at Sault Ste Marie. Unfortunately Brûlé left no account of his career and reports of the missionaries were coloured by their contempt for his native lifestyle. The original COUREUR DE BOIS, he was an independent, adventurous spirit. In 1629 he deserted to the KIRKE brothers when they attacked Québec. Accused of treason by CHAMPLAIN, he returned to Huronia. Despite lurid speculations that he was tortured and eaten, Brûlé was likely murdered for political reasons, possibly because of his dealings with the Seneca or another tribe feared by the Huron.

JAMES MARSH

Brundage, John Herbert, pen name John Herbert, writer and theatre director (b at Toronto 13 Oct 1926). After studying at Toronto's New Play Society School for Drama and the National Ballet School, 1955-60, Brundage founded and ran 3 pioneering alternate theatres in Toronto, including the Garret (1965-70). Under the name John Herbert, he wrote the play for which he is best known, *Fortune and Men's Eyes*, in 1963. An autobiographically based prison drama, it premiered in 1967 off-Broadway and from there went on to international success still unmatched by any other Canadian dramatic work. *Fortune* won the DOMINION DRAMA FESTIVAL'S Massey Award in 1968, which Brundage refused, and the Chalmers Outstanding Play Award in 1975. He has had little success with subsequent plays, but *Fortune* remains one of the few true classics of the Canadian THEATRE.

JERRY WASSERMAN

Brunet, Louis-Ovide, priest, teacher, botanist (b at Québec City 10 Mar 1826; d there 2 Oct 1876). After working as a parish priest for 10 years, Brunet was offered a position as a science teacher at his alma mater, the Séminaire de Québec. In 1862 he succeeded Thomas Sterry HUNT as professor of natural history at Laval. His numerous botanical field trips in Québec and Ontario, as well as 2 years spent in Europe visiting herbaria and attending courses given by experts at the Musée national d'histoire naturelle in Paris, provided him with basic training in botany, which was completed when he developed close contacts with Canadian and American botanists. He published his first original work in 1865. By 1870 Brunet had become an expert botanist and was expected to undertake a study of Canada's flora. Strongly encouraged in this endeavour by the great American scholar Asa Gray, Brunet assembled an extensive set of notes which unfortunately were never published, his promising career having been cut short by illness.

RAYMOND DUCHESNE

Brunette Island, 30 km², is situated at the mouth of Fortune B on Newfoundland's S coast, 18 km S of Connaigre Head. The island, roughly triangular, measures 11 km E-W and 6 km N-S. A steep ridge backs the NW shore, at one point rising to 160 m. From the early 1800s the island supported a fishing community at Mercer's Cove in the SE until the islanders were resettled, with government assistance, in the late 1950s. Brunette I then became a provincial wildlife reserve and the site of experimental colonies of caribou, moose, arctic hare and bison, the latter brought from Alberta in 1964 in a unique but unsuccessful attempt to introduce the animal to Newfoundland.

ROBERT D. PITT

Brussels Sprouts (*Brassica oleracea*, Gemmifera Group), biennial vegetable of the Cruciferae family. Brussels sprouts are native to western Europe. The plant develops small heads or sprouts at the leaf axils along the stem, rather than one large head. A long-season crop, brussels sprouts mature in autumn and early winter. Some cultivars are more cold tolerant than others and can be overwintered in temperate areas. The crop is best suited to the Maritimes and coastal BC, and requires a high level of fertilization and adequate soil moisture throughout the season. Most cultivars grown in Canada are first-generation hybrids developed in Japan or Holland. They are produced for the fresh and processing markets. Although some of the fresh-market crop is still hand harvested, mechanization is developing rapidly. In 1986 the Canadian processing crop was worth $2.6 million, most of which originated in BC. Imports amounted to 4886 t in 1986, valued at $3.8 million.   A.R. MAURER

Brutinel, Brig-Gen Raymond, CB, CMG, DSO, geologist, journalist, soldier and entrepreneur, a pioneer in the field of mechanized warfare (b at Alet, Aude, France 6 Mar 1872; d at Couloume-Mondebat, Gares, France 21 Sept 1964). He immigrated to western Canada 1904, surveyed the route for the GRAND TRUNK RAILWAY and edited *Le Courrier de l'Ouest* (Edmonton), the first French-language newspaper west of Winnipeg. In 1914 he raised a motorized automobile machine-gun unit for service on the Western Front which, by 1918, had grown into a Motor Machine-Gun Brigade that played a significant part in halting the great German offensive of Mar 1918. From Oct 1916 until Mar 1918, Brutinel was Corps MG Officer of the Canadian Corps and, in addition to his decorations, he was 7 times mentioned in despatches. He pioneered the virtues of mobility and concentration of firepower and developed the concept of indirect machine-gun fire. In 1920 he returned to Europe, where he was a Creusot sales representative in the Balkans, but he retained many Canadian ties. Maj-Gen Georges VANIER, Canadian ambassador to France, recorded the "considerable help" Brutinel provided in evacuating embassy staff from Paris, June 1940. In 1961 he became a member of the Canadian Institute of Mines and Metallurgy Fifty-Year Club.   BRERETON GREENHOUS

Bryce, Peter Henderson, physician (b at Mount Pleasant, Canada W 17 Aug 1853; d at sea 15 Jan 1932). He served as first secretary of the Ontario Board of Health (1882-1904) when he joined the federal Dept of Immigration as its chief medical officer. A man of strong opinions, Bryce agitated for health reform, concentrating his attack on tuberculosis. His condemnation of Indian boarding schools as breeding grounds of the disease caused official embarrassment. Retired in 1921, Bryce studied Canadian letters and finished a manuscript on the life of Sir Oliver MOWAT shortly before dying on a voyage to the West Indies.
JANICE DICKIN McGINNIS

Reading: Peter Henderson Bryce, *The Illumination of Joseph Keeler* (1915) and *The Value to Canada of the Continental Immigrant* (1928).

Bryce, Robert Broughton, public servant (b at Toronto 27 Feb 1910). An engineering graduate from U of T, Bryce studied economics at Cambridge (under J.M. Keynes) and at Harvard. He joined the federal Dept of Finance in 1938, and over the next decade his abilities contributed significantly to the department's pre-eminence in Ottawa and to its concentration of power there. He was appointed clerk of the Privy Council and secretary to the Cabinet in 1954. He served there throughout the Diefenbaker government and was remarkable for his ability to win the trust and co-operation of an often difficult PM. In 1963 he became deputy minister of finance, and in 1971 Canadian executive director to the INTERNATIONAL

MONETARY FUND. His last major position was the chairmanship of the Royal Commission on CORPORATE CONCENTRATION. He is the author of *Maturing in Hard Times: Canada's Department of Finance through the Great Depression* (1986).
ROBERT BOTHWELL

Brymner, William, painter, teacher (b at Greenock, Scot 14 Dec 1855; d at Wallasey, Eng 18 June 1925). Brymner's father was the first Dominion archivist. William is remembered as Canada's first great art teacher. His respect for academic training and his own delicate painting skill, combined with a gentle way with others' talent, influenced many men and women studying in Montréal in the early 1900s. Educated at Richmond, Qué, Brymner went to Paris to train for architecture. While there he decided to paint. In 1886 he was appointed director of art classes at the Art Assn of Montreal. The same year he became a full RCA member. He painted the human figure and interiors in a representational style; he also did watercolours on silk, and murals, as found in the old Porteous house on Île d'Orléans. He sketched landscape with J.W. MORRICE and Maurice CULLEN, his 1899 *Early Morning in September* illustrating a fine palette of glowing sensual colour, while the pastoral scene holds a lingering touch of Europe in its settled tranquility.
ANNE McDOUGALL

BTO, Bachman-Turner Overdrive, rock band including Robin Bachman, Randy Bachman, Blair Thornton and Fred Turner. They were internationally popular during the mid-1970s. BTO's third album *Not Fragile*, spawned the million-selling single "You Ain't Seen Nuthin' Yet." By 1977, when Robin Bachman left, 20 million records had been sold worldwide. BTO continued touring and recording. Until 1979 it was one of the most successful Canadian rock bands; it reunited in 1984 and toured Canada.   JOHN GEIGER

Buchan, John, 1st Baron Tweedsmuir, author, governor general of Canada 1935-40 (b at Perth, Scot 26 Aug 1875; d at Montréal 11 Feb 1940). Buchan published 6 books of fiction, poetry and history while an Oxford undergraduate. He was briefly an administrator in S Africa, a political journalist and tax lawyer, and then was chief literary adviser (later a director) of publishers Thomas Nelson and Son 1906-29. This, and the books that he produced at a prodigious rate all his life, including historical biographies, such as *Lord Minto* (1924), and fast-paced thrillers, such as *The Thirty-Nine Steps* (1915), gave him a creative outlet and a comfortable income. There was always a tension in Buchan between his desire to live quietly and his ambition to be a part of bigger things. Despite serious illness, he went to France in WWI as an intelligence officer. He was a popular MP 1927-35 but was too lacking in partisan fervour for a Cabinet post. In Canada Buchan had time to indulge his contemplative side. He loved the variety, beauty and adventure of a big land, and tried to convey a sense of community and unlimited potential on his frequent tours, which included the first by a governor general to the Arctic. Horrified by WWI, he worked with US President Roosevelt and PM Mackenzie KING in their peace initiatives of the late 1930s. Although admiring King more politically than personally, Buchan forged strong links with the PM. King noted the governor general's weaknesses – his self-importance and love of titles – but he deeply appreciated Buchan's "real support...sterling rectitude and disinterested purpose." Buchan's autobiography, *Memory Hold-the-Door* (1940), was completed shortly before his death. He instituted the GOVERNOR GENERAL'S LITERARY AWARDS in 1937.
NORMAN HILLMER

Buchanan, Donald William, (b at Lethbridge, Alta, 9 Apr 1908; d at Ottawa 28 Feb 1966). He was the son of Sen W.A. Buchanan, publisher of the *Lethbridge Herald*, and received a degree in modern history from U of T as well as an Oxford fellowship. Serious illness caused severe hearing loss which perhaps increased his interest in visual communication. In the 1930s, he was one of the founders of the *Ottawa Times*, a spirited weekly challenging staid cultural and political mores. He played a key role in founding the NATIONAL FILM BOARD, persuading W.L.M. King to invite John GRIERSON to Canada. He was founder of the National Film Society (1935; now the Canadian Film Institute), director of talks and public affairs for the Canadian Radio Commission (now CBC) from 1937 to 1940. In 1940 he joined the NFB as director of special projects where he built the most extensive nontheatrical distribution among allied nations. He was director of photo and graphics division, NFB; member of the WARTIME INFORMATION BOARD staff; 1942 editor of *Canadian Art Magazine* (1942); joined the National Gallery staff (1947); and founded the Industrial Design Council where "passion for the enhancement of the quality of life led him to introduce two comparative strangers, the Canadian designer and the Canadian manufacturer." In 1960 he retired as associate director of the national gallery and took up photography, holding successful shows in Canada and abroad. His photographs showed gentle humour and strong dramatic sense. He was killed in a car accident while arranging for the international art exhibit for Expo 67. Though reserved and reflective in manner, he was regarded by many as the most significant Canadian of his time. His personal art collection has been presented to the art gallery in his birthplace, Lethbridge, Alta.   JUDITH CRAWLEY

Buchanan, Isaac, merchant, politician, pamphleteer (b at Glasgow, Scot 21 July 1810; d at Hamilton, Ont 1 Oct 1883). As founder and leading local partner of Upper Canada's largest wholesale firm, he was prominent from 1832 to 1844 in the commerce of Toronto and, after 1851, of Hamilton. Strongly independent in politics, he was MPP for Toronto, 1841-43, and Hamilton, 1857-65. He was an early advocate of a protective tariff, either for Canada alone or for Canada and the US together, which he said would foster Canadian industry. Of his many pamphlets on politics, religion and economics, the best known is a compilation of materials by himself and others titled *The Relations of the Industry of Canada, with the Mother Country and the United States* (1864). His business, and with it his influence, failed in 1867.
DOUGLAS McCALLA

Reading: D. McCalla, *The Upper Canada Trade 1834-1872: A Study of the Buchanans' Business* (1979).

Buchanan, John MacLennan, lawyer, politician, premier of NS (b at Sydney, NS 22 Apr 1931). Elected to the NS Assembly 1967 and appointed to the Cabinet 1969, Buchanan was chosen provincial Conservative leader 1971. He lost the election of 1974, but led his party to victory in 1978, added to its majority in 1981, and won by a landslide in 1984. As premier, his concerns have been revitalizing Sysco, the publicly owned steel plant, controlling domestic energy costs, increasing coal production by opening new mines, developing offshore mineral resources, and proposing, at least tentatively, the transmission of coal-generated power by underwater cable to New England. His government also successfully promoted a pilot tidal project at the head of the Annapolis Basin, the first step towards harnessing Fundy tides. He was awarded an honorary LLD by St Francis Xavier U in 1986.
J. MURRAY BECK

Buck, Gary, singer, songwriter, administrator, record producer (b at Thessalon, Ont 21 Mar 1940). Besides being a successful country music singer-songwriter, his recording of "Happy to Be Unhappy" (1963) was an international hit. Buck managed Capitol Record's Beechwood Music 1970-71 and in 1971 established his own recording and publishing firm, Broadland Music, which handled some of the top names in Canadian music before being taken over by Quality Records in 1976. A director of the Country Music Assn in Nashville 1971-75 and founder of the Canadian country music organization Academy of Country Music Entertainment (ACME) 1976, Buck won Juno Awards 1964-66 and in 1975 won the Big Country Awards for "top male singer" and "top producer." RICHARD GREEN

Buck, Tim, machinist, trade unionist, communist leader (b at Beccles, Eng 6 Jan 1891; d at Cuernavaca, Mexico 11 Mar 1973). Like many skilled British workers, Buck immigrated to Canada in 1910 in search of a better living. He was soon immersed in radical working-class politics in Toronto. Buck later claimed to have been a founding member of the COMMUNIST PARTY OF CANADA, organized in a secret 1921 meeting in a barn near Guelph, and soon became a leading architect of its trade-union policy. After a struggle against a party leader who supported Trotsky's critique of developments in the international communist movement in 1928, and alleged supporters of Nikolai Bukharnin in 1929, Buck emerged as the party's general secretary, a post he held for 32 years. He published many articles, pamphlets and books. He spent over 2 years in jail 1932-34 and 3 years underground during WWII when his party was banned. In 1971 he received the Order of the Great October Revolution from the USSR. CRAIG HERON

Bucke, Richard Maurice, psychiatrist, author (b at Methwold, Eng 18 Mar 1837; d at London, Ont 19 Feb 1902). Brought to Upper Canada when one year old, Bucke was raised and educated on the family farm near Hamilton. Following an adventurous youth in the American West, he graduated in medicine from McGill in 1862, studied abroad for 2 years and then began his practice in Sarnia, Canada W. He was appointed superintendent of the Asylum for the Insane in Hamilton in 1876 and of the London asylum in 1877. He was a founder of the School of Medicine at U of Western Ontario. His theories on the causes and treatment of mental diseases and his advocacy of the "moral restraint" of the insane attracted widespread attention. Bucke corresponded voluminously with Walt Whitman and became Whitman's official biographer and ultimately one of his literary executors. He found in Whitman's poetry a confirmation of his belief that the mystical experience, once the preserve of the few, will become accessible to the many. To this end he published his popular *Cosmic Consciousness* (1901), which attempts to demonstrate that man is on the verge of a psychic revolution. The book has enjoyed a vast readership. Bucke's papers are in the library at Western. JOHN ROBERT COLOMBO

Buckler, Ernest, novelist (b at Dalhousie West, NS 19 July 1908; d at Bridgetown, NS 4 Mar 1984). Buckler showed a remarkable sensitivity to the landscape and human character of his native Annapolis Valley. One of his principal strengths was his lyrical and metaphorical prose style. After studying at Dalhousie and U of Toronto, Buckler worked for 5 years as an actuarial mathematician in Toronto before ill health prompted him to return to NS. He began his writing career by contributing short stories and essays to *Esquire* and *Saturday Night*. His major achievement, however,

The Mountain and the Valley (1952), is a novel about a gifted, ambitious boy who remains so deeply attached to life in rural NS that his creativity becomes stifled. *The Cruelest Month* (1963) explores the unhappy passions of a group of intellectuals. Buckler returned to his youthful community life in *Ox Bells and Fireflies* (1968), a "fictional memoir" (Buckler's term). *Nova Scotia: Window on the Sea* (1973) again uses elements of fiction and lyrical description, this time to accompany Hans Weber's photographs. *The Rebellion of Young David and Other Stories* (1975) is a collection of 1940s and 1950s stories. *Whirligig* (1977), a volume of light verse and prose, won the Leacock Award for Humour (1978). THOMAS E. TAUSKY

Buckley, Kenneth Arthur Haig, economist, professor (b at Aberdeen, Sask 16 July 1918; d at Saskatoon 30 May 1970). After graduating from U of Toronto and London School of Economics, Buckley returned to the dept of economics and political science at U of Saskatchewan 1945. He was a Canadian pioneer in quantitative economic history. His first major work, *Capital Formation in Canada, 1896-1930* (1955), was a study of the impact of the wheat economy on Canadian economic growth, and influenced a generation of economic historians. His later work encompassed a wide range of subjects – from a critique of the STAPLE THESIS to historical estimates of internal migration. He was well known to students for the text *Economics for Canadians*, written with Helen Buckley (1960), and (with M.C. Urquhart) the monumental *Canadian Historical Statistics* (1965). PAUL PHILLIPS

Buckwheat (genus *Fagopyrum*), broad-leaved, erect annual belonging to the buckwheat family (Polygonaceae). The cultivated species, common buckwheat (*F. esculentum*) and tartary buckwheat (*F. tataricum*), are grown as field crops. Wild buckwheat (*Polygonum convolvulus*), a common weed, is distantly related. Buckwheat originated in Asia and was introduced to Europe and N America. The plant consists of a single main stem (smooth, grooved and hollow), several branches and a shallow taproot system. The dark green leaves are heart shaped. Flower clusters (usually white, sometimes pink) are found at branch ends or arise from axils of leaves. The seed, an achene (dry one-seeded fruit), is triangular and varies in colour from brown to grey to black. Buckwheat is grown mainly for human consumption (eg, flour for pancake mixes, bread and ethnic dishes, breakfast cereal) and is also used for livestock and poultry feed, as a green-manure crop, as a smother crop and as a source of buckwheat honey. In Canada it is grown mainly in Manitoba (53%) and in Québec (47%). Its importance as a cash crop has decreased. In 1986, of the 38 000 t produced, 20% was exported and the remainder was consumed in Canada. B.B. CHUBEY

Buctouche, NB, Village, pop 2420 (1986c), 2476 (1981c), is located 40 km N of MONCTON. This Northumberland Str port draws its name from the Micmac word for "big bay." ACADIAN families returning from exile settled here as early as 1784, followed by the English after 1800. The current population is 93% French speaking (1981c, latest figure available). Fishing, lumbering and shipbuilding were the main industries, and construction of a branch railway to Moncton (1888) spurred local commerce until it was abandoned in the 1960s. While the traditional primary industries remain important, future prosperity is seen to lie in the field of high technology. Buctouche is the birthplace of 2 prominent Canadians – Antonine MAILLET, internationally renowned Acadian author, and millionaire industrialist K.C. IRVING. DEAN JOBB

Buddhism, a major world religion encompassing various systems of philosophy and ethics. In 1981, the last year for which figures are available, there were about 52 000 adherents in Canada. It was founded around 500 BC by a prince of the Sakya clan, Siddhartha Gotama, who came to be known as Gotama the Buddha. Though accounts of the founder's life vary, the Northern (Sanskrit) and Southern (Pali) traditions agree that Siddhartha was born in Lumbini Garden (present-day Nepal), attained enlightenment at Bodhgaya (India) began preaching in Benares (Varanasi) and entered *nirvana* (passed away) at Kusinara (Kasia, India).

At the age of 29 Siddhartha turned his back on his life as a prince in order to seek enlightenment. After 6 years as an ascetic he became Buddha (Sanskrit *bodhi*, "enlightened" or "awakened"), and now recognized the principle of relativity (the interdependence of all phenomena), which implied that nothing lasts forever (*anitya*); everything will eventually become dissatisfying (*duhkha*); nothing has a nature of its own (*anatman*); and, when attachment to calculated and established values is extinguished (*nirvana*), bliss (*santi*) is gained. Thus to become a Buddha does not mean that one becomes divine. A Buddha is one who recognizes that nothing, including his soul, has an eternal essence. Wishing to share his insight (*dharma*), Gotama Buddha preached his first sermon on the Middle Path and on the Four Noble Truths: the unsatisfactoriness of life, the origin of that unsatisfactoriness, its cessation and the path leading to its cessation. The 5 monks who attended him were the first Buddhist congregation (*sangha*) in Gotama Buddha's 45 years of preaching.

After his death a schism arose between those determined to emulate the religious practices that led Gotama to enlightenment, and others stressing the experience of enlightenment itself. Gradually 2 distinct traditions appeared. The Theravada system, developed by those holding the former view, bases its philosophy and ethics on the Pali texts compiled by Buddhists in southern India. It spread through Burma, Sri Lanka, Cambodia, Thailand and other SE Asian countries. The latter system, the Mahayana tradition, bases its philosophy and ethics on the Sanskrit texts from northern India. It spread to Korea, Vietnam, Japan and other E Asian countries by way of China and Tibet. As each tradition spread, it changed to accommodate the language, culture, customs and attitudes of the new country. As well, some Buddhist teachings have influenced, or become integral to, various NEW RELIGIOUS MOVEMENTS.

Buddhism in Canada JAPANESE immigrants probably brought Buddhism to Canada during the late 1800s. Because it was identified with a particular ethnic group, this form of Buddhism did not become integrated into the Canadian milieu. More recently, Buddhism has come to Canada with both Asians and non-Asians, and is rooted doctrinally in either the Theravada or Mahayana (including the Vajrayana) tradition. Among new immigrants and their children, Buddhism often takes on an organizational structure holding little religious significance, but designed to fulfil requirements for incorporation under the Societies Act. Membership is normally open, although most Buddhist societies expect commitment to the Buddha, the dharma and the sangha in a manner consistent with each society's understanding of these terms. Buddha is considered to be an understanding celestial being by some, an earthly being by others.

Dharma is law to some, to others a guiding principle. For some, sangha is a community of ordained monks, for others the community of monks and laity. Some societies require the layman's vows of refraining from the 3 physical acts of taking life, taking what has not been given, and sexual excess; the 4 speech-related actions, lying, slandering, foolish talk and harsh talk; and the 3 mental actions, selfishness, malice and seeing wrongly. With increasing intermarriage, the predominantly Asian societies have had to adapt their ways to retain non-Asians as members.

Each society is centered on a leader known by different titles in different groups: *bhikkhu, lama, sensei,* monk, spiritual director, *roshi,* spiritual adviser, teacher, *oya,* minister, *geshe, tulku,* master or reverend. In some groups the leader acts as social worker, foreign-language teacher and family counsellor, while attempting to transmit something about the religion to his or her congregation. Such groups are usually "closed systems," in which the leader is closely aligned with the parent culture.

In other groups, especially those whose members wish to devote their lives to meditation, the leader oversees and supervises the members' spiritual growth. Such members are very dependent, yielding themselves to the leader's charismatic power and establishing a close bond. Groups continuing from Asian parent organizations use English translations of their scriptures in the belief that the younger generations of "hyphenated Canadians" (Japanese-Canadians, TIBETAN Canadians, etc) will thus learn to appreciate their religious and cultural history.

Although Sunday has no ecclesiastical meaning for Buddhists it is set aside for religious observances because in Canada it is difficult to attend services on weekdays. Special religious days are New Year's Day, Nirvana or Parinirvana Day (Feb 18), Wesak (Full Moon, Apr-May) or Hanamatsuri Day (Flower Festival, Apr 8), Founder's Day, Organization Day, Bodhi Day (Dec 8), Special Anniversary Day and New Year's Eve.

Buddhists also celebrate specific times in life: birth, naming, confirmation or ordination, marriage and death. These are considered religiously significant because they are especially conducive to reflecting upon the principle of relativity, or dependent co-arising. Ceremonies associated with the techniques of meditation include those related to daily activities such as eating, shaving and bathing.

The Toronto Mahavihara (Buddhist Centre), est 1978, was the first Theravada temple in Canada. It continues the tradition established at the Mahavihara in Anuradhapura, Sri Lanka, begun in the third century BC. The Sri Lankan government, through its High Commission in Ottawa, donates funds for the basic needs of the resident bhikkhus. Membership is open. There are also the Toronto Buddha Vihara and the Ottawa Buddhist Association that are of Sri Lankan origin. In Vancouver a Theravada Buddhist Society, Dhamma, is devoted to self-development through moral living, Vipassana (insight) Meditation and methodical study of the Abhidhamma philosophy of Buddhist scriptures as handed down in the Pali canon. The Ariya Theravada Society, fd 1981 in Calgary, has expanded into Vancouver. This group, which follows the Pali tradition, promotes Buddhist teaching and practice through meditation and retreats. These last 2 societies are led by occidentals who were trained and ordained in India and Thailand, respectively. Other Theravada Buddhist organizations are the Thai Buddhist Association in Weston, Ont, and the Anagarika Dhamma Society in Halfmoon Bay, BC.

The Ambedkar Mission, fd 1979 in Scarborough, Ont, follows the religious and social philosophy of Dr Ambedkar, who rose from among the untouchables to become one of India's most respected Buddhist leaders. The society promotes social justice, peace and understanding. Member-

ship is open, although the group was originally made up mostly of people of Indian origin.

Within the second tradition, the Mahayana, was developed the doctrine of *bodhisattva,* which includes the belief that the historical Buddha was a brief manifestation of an eternal, absolute Buddha. Mahayana Buddhist organizations in Canada can be categorized according to the parent group's country of origin. Before Tibet became an "autonomous region" of the People's Republic of China, there were 4 major orders of Tibetan Buddhism (Gelugpa, Sakyapa, Nyingmapa and Kagyupa), of which the Kagyupa and the Gelugpa are best represented in Canada. Organized in Canada as the Karma Kargyu Society, the Karma-Kagyupa lineage was headed by His Holiness Rangjung Rigpe Dorje, the 16th Gyalwa Karmapa (1924-81). The Gelugpa, which has no national organization, is headed by His Holiness Tenzin Gyatso, the 14th Dalai Lama (b 1934).

One of the centres that study, practise and promote the teachings of the Kargyu order of Tibetan Buddhism is the Marpa Gompa Meditation Society, fd 1979 in Calgary. It is officially headed by Karma Tinley Rinpoche, founder of Toronto's Mikyo Dorje Institute and Khampo Gangra Drubgyudling meditation centre. Other Kargyu centres are located in St Catharines, Toronto, Montréal and Burnaby. At the Gaden Choling in Toronto, fd 1980, members learn Gelugpa meditation practices, Tibetan language and Madhyamaka philosophy, and occasionally take part in retreats. The Tibetan children are instructed in traditional songs, dances, music and language. Other centres affiliated with the Gaden Choling are in Vancouver and Nelson, BC; and Ottawa and Thunder Bay, Ont. The Temple Bouddhiste Tibetain (Chang Chub Cho Ling) located in Longueuil, Qué, was officially incorporated in 1980 to preserve the Gelugpa tradition. The Victoria Buddhist Society or the Sakya Thubten Kunga Choling carries on the Sakya Lineage. The Sakya Lama, Tashi Namgyal, gives teachings through a translator and holds regular meditation classes and puja ceremonies. Many meditation centres were organized under the late Venerable Chogyam Trungpa (d 1987). His centres, located across the country, are easily identified by the name "Dharmadhatu." They are predominantly Kargyupa in meditative practices, but members may also be introduced to the Nyingmapa tradition.

In China in the 6th century AD, Zen became a separate school of Buddhism when Bodhidharma stressed that Buddhist life should emphasize meditation. Zen Buddhism in N America is usually associated with Japanese culture. However, the Zen Lotus Society (also called Zen Buddhist Temple), a "lay monastery," was incorporated in 1980 under Samu Sunim (Sunim is a title of respect), a Korean Zen monk, who came to Montréal in 1968 and moved to Toronto in 1970. Kwangok Sunim, a Korean nun who immigrated to Canada in 1976, founded the Bulgwang-sa (Buddha Light Temple) in Toronto. The Taegak-sa (Temple of Enlightenment) was founded by P'yongdungsim Posal and Inhwan Sunim in 1979. The current abbot of the temple is Taeung Sunim. Special days observed are Buddha's enlightenment, lunar new-year celebration, *kido* (chanting scriptures for a week), all in Jan; spring equinox; Buddha's birthday; and ancestral day and autumn equinox in Sept. In spring and autumn, captive animals are taken to the countryside and, after a special ceremony, set free to symbolize the intention "not to kill but to cherish all living beings." Zen centres occur throughout Canada.

Soto Zen was transmitted to Japan from China in the 13th century. The Edmonton Buddhist Priory, inc June 1979, has close spiritual bonds with the Soto Zen Church of Japan. A priory of the Or-

der of Buddhist Contemplatives (OBC), established by and for Western followers of Soto Zen, is a Western expression of Zen practice based upon the teachings of Roshi Jiyu-Kennett, founder and spiritual director of Shasta Abbey at Mt Shasta, Calif. The Vancouver Soto Zen Meditation Group is also associated with Shasta Abbey.

There are a growing number of Buddhist societies and groups formed by the Vietnamese, in Brossard, Montréal, Toronto, Vancouver, Calgary and Edmonton.

Basically a Pure Land Buddhist group, the Universal Buddhist Church, est 1986 in Vancouver, comprises an all-Chinese congregation which practises a Buddhism having Pure Land, Zen and Yogacara flavours with strong Confucian and Taoistic tendencies. Among other interests, this group studies meditation and parapsychology. The International Buddhist Society in Richmond is designed in traditional Chinese style and was completed in 1983.

The Tai Bay Buddhist Temple (Toronto) was officially opened in 1985. The temple offers meditation instructions during the week. The Cham Shin Temple (Thornhill, Ont) was completed in 1979 and is the main temple and headquarters of the Buddhist Association of Canada.

The highly organized and progressive Reiyukai (Spiritual Friendship Society) was founded in Japan by Kakutara Kubo (1892-1944). Within 60 years this lay association has established offices throughout the world. The Reiyukai encourages individuals to seek and develop their inner character through *senzo-kuyo* (unselfishly caring for ancestors) and *michibiki* (sharing the personal experience with others unfamiliar with the Reiyukai teaching). The society's office in Canada is the Reiyukai Society of BC, Vancouver.

The Soka Kyoiku Gakkai (Value-Creation Education Society), which became the Soka Gakkai in 1946, was formed to promote peace among mankind by bringing happiness and harmony to individuals. Members of this lay organization propagate by means of *shakubuku* ("break and subdue") the teaching that all individuals are already Buddhas. The method is derived from Nichiren (1222-82), founder of the Nichiren sect of Japanese Buddhism. Nichiren Sho-shu of Canada (NSC) was established in Toronto in 1961.

During WWII the removal from BC and the INTERNMENT of people of Japanese ancestry almost eradicated Japanese Buddhism from Canada. Although adherents had likely resided in BC as early as 1889 when the first Japanese consulate was established, the first recorded assembly of Japanese Buddhism in Canada took place in Vancouver in 1904, when 14 Buddhists met to request a minister from the Honpa Honganji Temple in Kyoto, Japan (mother temple of the Jodo Shinshu sect). In 1905 the first resident minister, Rev Senju Sasaki of the Vancouver Nihon Bukkyo-kai (Japanese Buddhist Association), began preaching, and the Nihon Bukkyo-kai was incorporated in 1909 with about 650 members. By 1926 the mother temple in Kyoto had sent 7 ministers to the Vancouver area. By 1941, 11 ministers were serving 16 temples in BC. Administration for the period 1904-32 was from San Francisco, but in 1932 the Canadian body requested independence, and until the evacuation of 1942 the churches were governed by a ministerial superintendent. The lifting of the War Measures Act in 1949 restored Japanese freedom of movement throughout Canada; some Japanese Buddhists returned to BC and others settled elsewhere.

A national conference of Japanese Buddhists was held in 1955 in Toronto, and from that meeting arose the Buddhist Churches of Canada (BCC). BCC churches follow the interpretation of the Buddha-dharma according to Shinran (1173-

Shrine to the Amida Buddha, Buddha of infinite light, infinite life, at the Raymond Buddhist Church, in Raymond, Alta. Buddhism was likely first brought to Canada by Japanese immigrants in the late 1800s (*courtesy Provincial Museum of Alberta, Folklife Coll*).

1262), the founder of Jodo Shinshu Buddhism, who promoted the principle of dependent co-arising as the basis for individual salvation. Shinran attempted to understand the dharma in view of his own existence and thus derived the *Nembutsu* (recitation of *Namu Amida Butsu*) teaching, which he emphasized as an expression of gratitude and joy in realizing the interrelated nature of human existence. At the conference that created the BCC the question of a national headquarters was an important issue, but that idea has not materialized. In 1956, 6 ministers were serving 18 congregations comprising 3500 members; in 1987 a bishop presided over 11 ministers administering 18 congregations comprising over 3000 active members, most of them in the Vancouver and Toronto areas and southern Alberta. In 1975 the BCC adopted English and parliamentary procedure for meetings so that younger delegates, not proficient in Japanese, could attend national meetings.

Other Buddhist groups include the International Buddhist Foundation, formed in 1982 to encourage scholarly research in studies related to Buddhism. The Toronto Buddhist Federation, fd 1982, resulted from an earlier gathering of Buddhists in Toronto that was preparing to attend a peace conference. Membership, limited to registered Buddhist charitable organizations, includes Buddhists from Burma, Cambodia, Canada, China, India, Japan, Korea, Laos, Sri Lanka, Thailand, Tibet, the US and Vietnam.

LESLIE S. KAWAMURA

Reading: Government of India, *2500 Years of Buddhism* (1956); Emma McCloy Layman, *Buddhism in America* (1976); K.W. Morgan, *The Path of the Buddha* (1956); Walpola Rahula, *What the Buddha Taught* 2nd ed, 1974); R.H. Robinson and W.L. Johnson, *The Buddhist Religion* (1982). The Buddhist Library in Oshawa, Ont, was established in 1979 to provide the public with information on Buddhist philosophy.

Budgetary Process is designed, at all levels of government, to ensure that there is control, accountability and planning. In theory, the preparation by the executive (usually annually) of a budget for presentation to and approval by the legislature makes possible the exercise of popular control over spending. The budget statement must include all the annual revenues and expenditures. As a planning instrument, the budget, again in theory, allows a government to analyse the revenue and expenditure implications of its current and proposed programs and the financial interrelationships among them. Federally, the budgetary process also serves to stabilize the economy.

In the Canadian government there are really 2 budgets (revenue and expenditure) and 2 budgetary processes. The revenue budgetary process culminates with the presentation of the budget speech to Parliament by the minister of finance. In it and in accompanying documentation, the minister reviews the current and projected state of the economy and the government's financial situation, and announces any specific changes in tax rates and tax structures. Following the budget debate, the House of Commons votes to accept or reject the budget. This vote is a matter of confidence. If the revenue budget is rejected by the Commons the government resigns and an election may be called, which happened with the MINORITY GOVERNMENT budgets of May 1974 and Dec 1979.

Considering the crucial importance to the ruling government of a budget speech, the process of budgetary preparation is rather odd. Traditionally, the revenue budget is prepared in strict secrecy by the minister of finance and a relatively small group of his officials. With the possible exception of the prime minister, the rest of Cabinet is seldom informed of its contents until just before the budget speech. The ostensible reason for this secrecy and for the lack of consultation is that prior knowledge of a budget's contents might enable some individuals to profit unfairly at the expense of others. However, in recent years several ministers of finance have acknowledged the desirability of pre-budget consultations and have considered easing the secrecy surrounding the budget's preparation. The preparation of the expenditure budget is much less secret, at least within the government. Tabled in the House each Feb for the fiscal year beginning the following Apr, it is officially called the Estimates, and unofficially the Blue Book. General direction and priority setting in the budget are prepared by the CENTRAL AGENCIES who then negotiate adjustments, reconcile budget submissions of individual departments and prepare the total expenditure budget for submission to Parliament by the president of the Treasury Board.

Prior to 1971 Parliament was asked to approve everything from salaries to supplies to old-age pensions to travel expenses for public servants. The most important determinant of expenditures on most items in one year was the levels of spending on those items in the previous year. The prevailing view among those who participated in or studied the budgetary process was that the expenditure budget did not enable Parliament to exercise meaningful control or allow the Cabinet to plan effectively. In many cases members of Parliament could not see any links between the planned spending of a particular department and the services the department provided. In addition, information was provided only for the fiscal year under consideration, so MPs were unable to gauge the potential expenditure implications of a budget item for subsequent years. The same factors made it difficult for the government and its officials to relate its policy and program planning to its expenditures. It had no satisfactory way of determining the impact on spending of new programs under consideration. The reverse was also true; problems were exacerbated by the inevitable interdependencies among departments, because the spending of one department could reinforce, duplicate or cancel that of another.

Significant reform was attempted in the early 1970s by PM Pierre TRUDEAU's government, which adopted a "scientific" or "rational" budgeting and decision-making process in the form of a Planning-Programming-Budgeting System (PPBS). As its name implies, PPBS was intended to integrate the policy-planning and budgetary processes. Rather than focusing on inputs or objects of expenditure, PPBS focused on outputs, the ultimate effects of government activities on Canadians. Departmental activities were classified into programs and subprograms. A program was defined in relation to a particular aspect of special welfare, eg, health, justice, safety or national security, and all activities with an impact on that area were to be part of that program. In practice, the classification of activities into programs was never clear-cut. Theoretically, under the PPBS system, the Cabinet and the relevant central agencies (principally the PRIVY COUNCIL OFFICE) were to plan and decide priorities as programs. Departments were to submit budget requests within the same framework and to conduct analyses showing how their activities contributed to the objectives of the various programs. Unsatisfactory activities could be altered or eliminated and interrelationships among departments' activities would be taken into account explicitly.

In operation, PPBS never fulfilled its promise, largely because the analysis, integral to the system, required massive quantities of data, including not only financial statistics, which were usually obtainable, but less readily available reliable information on program operations and effects. In many cases the basic social science and other knowledge necessary to evaluate the impact of programs does not exist, eg, it is very difficult to gauge, even conceptually, how expenditures for drug testing, a public medical-care system, the promotion of better nutrition, or health-related education actually affect the population's health, even if a level of health could be measured. PPBS ignored the political realities of the budgetary process. A budget represents a compromise among competing interests and objectives both inside and outside government. Whether more money is spent on national defence or on social programs is fundamentally a question of social values and requires a political decision. Once these decisions are made, it is extremely costly and disruptive to fight all the bureaucratic and political battles anew each year. That is why, traditionally, budgetary processes have concentrated attention on the margins; except in exceptional circumstances, the bulk of government expenditure has remained basically undisturbed and discussion centres on the allocation of new or incremental spending. PPBS, if it had worked as planned, would have involved negotiating the entire budget every year. PPBS did, however, result in some modest improvements in the budgetary process. Analysis of the impacts of programs and activities is now commonplace. The format of the Blue Book presented to Parliament, while far from perfect, is more useful to MPs and fosters more informed debate.

A more recent reform in the federal budgetary process was instituted in 1979 by the Conservatives under PM Joe CLARK and continues in a somewhat altered form today. Introduced as PEMS, Policy and Expenditure Management System, its purpose is the integration of priority-setting and budgeting (as was the case with PPBS), the increase of ministerial control over policy and planning, and the establishment of an adequate schedule in the planning and budgetary processes. To operate PEMS the Cabinet is divided into 6 committees: 2 central committees (Priorities and Planning, and Treasury Board) and 4 policy committees (Economic Development, Social Development, Foreign and Defence Policy, and Government Operations). The Priorities and Planning Committee, chaired by the prime minister, establishes the general policy directions for the government. It approves the fiscal plan prepared by the Department of Finance. The fiscal plan reviews the existing and projected state of the economy and the revenue and expenditure implications of various policy alternatives, and decides the total spending limit of the government for the upcoming and subsequent fiscal years. The fiscal plan is the chief link between the revenue and expenditure budgetary processes (*see* FISCAL POLICY).

All government spending is divided into a number of policy sector resource "envelopes," or sectoral budgets, which are managed by the Priorities and Planning Committee and the 4 policy committees. In setting the fiscal plan, the Priorities and Planning Committee determines how much of the government's total spending will be allocated to each of the resource envelopes. Each policy committee develops plans for its policy sector within the general policy goals established by the government, guides the departments reporting to it in the preparation of their plans and budgets, and manages the envelope(s) for which it is responsible. Only in exceptional circumstances can the total allocation of a sectoral resource envelope be exceeded; if ministers want to increase spending on one program, they may have to pay for it by decreasing spending on other programs in the same envelope. The current budget is meant to strengthen the decision-making power of the elected Cabinet ministers with whom, according to the principles of responsible government, such power should reside. It is intended that the planning and budgeting in PEMS is conducted in 5-year plans which include the current year, the upcoming year for which the expenditure budget is being prepared, and the following 3 years. In practice this multi-year planning framework is not always followed. ALLAN M. MASLOVE

Buffalo, *see* BISON.

Buffalo Hunt, the means by which the primary food resource of the Plains Indians and MÉTIS was harvested. In addition to approaching the BISON herd stealthily, and occasionally using subterfuges such as cloaking themselves in prairie wolf skin or bawling like calves, hunters co-operated in funnelling the herd towards a cliff (buffalo jump) or a strongly built corral (pound), permitting a large kill. The BLOOD, PEIGAN, CREE and SARCEE stampeded the buffalo between 2 barriers (sometimes made of logs interwoven with brush) that led to a cliff ("jump"). Plummeting over the cliff, the buffalo were either killed in the fall or immediately butchered. Deep snows or marshy ground enabled hunters to close with their floundering quarry. With the introduction of the horse, about 1730, the charge and the surround became additional hunting methods. A large number of jump sites have been documented by archaeolo-

gists. Perhaps one of the oldest is HEAD-SMASHED-IN BUFFALO JUMP in southwestern Alberta, now a UNITED NATIONS WORLD HERITAGE SITE.

The hunt was the basis of the Plains Indian way of life, since it provided the essentials: the meat was food, sinew and bone became tools, and hides became clothing and shelter. The hunt and its products gave rise to and supported complex social, political and cultural institutions. The hunt was also essential to the FUR TRADE. Provisioning posts along the Red, Assiniboine and N Saskatchewan rivers acquired dried meat and PEMMICAN, and fresh buffalo meat in season. After the mid-19th century, hides were used to make industrial drive belts.

The increase in the Indian and Métis population, the demands of industrial centres and the incompatibility of free-running herds with agricultural settlement have been cited as explanations of the extinction of the bison. The use of the horse may also have been critical: pedestrian hunters harvested buffalo with little discrimination as to sex and age, but the horse hunters could focus on the favoured heifer or young cow. By the early 1880s the prairie bison were virtually extinct; a few wood bison survived in northern forests. JOHN E. FOSTER

Buffalo Robe Trade In western Canada, the export trade in buffalo robes, hides with the hair left on, was first promoted by the HUDSON'S BAY CO in the 1830s as part of a campaign to keep American traders S of the 49th parallel. There never was a European market but in the 1870s robes became very popular in eastern Canada and the US as sleigh throws. Americans most aggressively exploited the resource. Robes were the key point of interest concerning western Canadian relationships among the HBC, the Canadian government and the Americans in the 1870s, and the trade was the basis for the debilitating alcohol trade in the period. Robes were the first commodity directly exported from the West to eastern Canada. The robe trade was the major factor in the disappearance of the Canadian BISON herds. It collapsed in a market glut in the mid-1870s. BOB BEAL

Buffaloberry, *see* BERRIES, WILD.

Bug, name properly applied to a member of the Hemiptera, the most diverse order of insects having incomplete metamorphosis. Over 55 000 species have been described worldwide; about 3080 species (of a probable 4230), in Canada. Bugs are most closely related to THRIPS and probably shared

a common ancestor in the Carboniferous era (360-286 million years ago). They range from 0.1 to 9 cm long and are classified into 2 suborders: Herteroptera (true bugs) and Homoptera (including cicadas, leafhoppers, APHIDS, SCALE INSECTS and mealy bugs). All have piercing and sucking mouthparts. Most bugs feed on vascular tissues of higher plants but many true bugs eat other insects or take blood from vertebrates, including humans (eg, bedbug, *Cimex lectularius*). Bugs are widely distributed across forested and prairie regions of Canada but few species occur in the Arctic or Subarctic. In a given area, species diversity is usually related to host plant diversity, since most bugs are host specific. Although bugs are generally terrestrial, some (eg, back swimmers and water boatmen) are aquatic. Most semiaquatic bugs (eg, pond skaters and saldids) prey on other small arthropods.

Most adult bugs have 2 pairs of wings, 2 large, compound eyes, and 2 or 3 dorsal ocelli (simple eyes), but a few are wingless or vary in wing length and have their eyes reduced accordingly. Forewings in heteropterans are hemi-elytra: the basal half opaque and stiff, the apex transparent. These are folded flat over the abdomen when not in use. Forewings in homopterans are either transparent or opaque throughout and are folded, rooflike, over the body. True bugs have 5 juvenile stages, homopterans 3-7. Whiteflies and male scale insects have 1 or 2 nonfeeding, "pupal" stages. Female scale insects reproduce while still juvenile. Males lack functional mouthparts and are short-lived. Most bugs have separate sexes and deposit eggs, but some (eg, aphids) are parthenogenetic (eggs develop without fertilization), and viviparous (deposit live young).

In Canada, 112 species of Hemiptera, including plant bugs, aphids, leafhoppers, psyllids, and scale insects, have been recorded as crop pests. Their feeding can kill or deform seedlings, reduce plant vigour, and lower seed set by damaging flowers or seeds. Many aphids and leafhoppers transmit plant diseases. Large populations of aphids and scale insects excrete "honey dew" onto leaves of host plants, providing a substrate for growth of photosynthesis-inhibiting "sooty mold." Many predatory heteropterans are beneficial to man because they feed on INSECT PESTS. B.S. HEMING

Reading: J.A. Slater and R.M. Baranowski, *How to Know the True Bugs* (1978).

Bugnet, Georges-Charles-Jules, pseudonym Henri Doutremont, editor, writer, botanist (b at Chalon-sur-Saône, France 23 Feb 1879; d at St Albert, Alta 11 Jan 1981). A homesteader in Alberta from 1905, Bugnet rarely found favour in the eyes of Québec literary critics. Nevertheless, the range of his writing, as well as its religious intensity, places it among the most important work in French published in Canada in the 1930s. His work in the hybridization of roses earned him the Chevalier de l'ordre des palmes académiques in 1970. Bugnet was founder and president of the Association canadienne-française de l'Alberta, as well as editor of *Union.* This interest in French pioneers in Alberta is reflected primarily in his celebrated novel, *La Forêt* (1935; tr *The Forest*, 1976). His knowledge of, and sympathy for, the Métis is developed in *Nipsya* (1924). After Gabrielle ROY, Bugnet may be considered the major francophone writer of the Canadian West. E.D. BLODGETT

Buhay, Rebecca, "Becky," political activist, educator (b at London, Eng 11 Feb 1896; d at Toronto 16 Dec 1953). She immigrated to Canada in 1912 and became active in Montréal socialist causes during WWI. After studying at the radical

---

A Buffalo Rift (1867), by A.J. Miller, illustrates a method of buffalo hunting used by the Blood, Peigan, Cree and Sarcee (*courtesy National Archives of Canada/C-403*).

Rand School of Social Sciences, New York, she became an organizer in Montréal garment unions. She joined the Workers (Communist) Party of Canada, likely in 1921. In the 1920s and 1930s she toured and lectured, taught at party schools and took a women's delegation to the USSR. During WWII she worked to free interned communists. After the war she resumed her educational work, stressing women's role in the struggle for socialism. She was revered among colleagues for her ability to communicate radical ideas and her loyalty to political friends and the communist movement. JOAN SANGSTER

Buies, Arthur, bap Joseph-Marie-Arthur, journalist, chronicler, essayist (b at Montréal 24 Jan 1840; d at Québec City 29 Jan 1901). A lucid witness to and passionate participant in the late 19th-century ideological battles, Buies left behind a body of exceptional works which are not well known. Buies was educated in Québec and Paris. In 1860 he enrolled in Garibaldi's army and rashly sang its praises upon returning to Montréal in 1862. Buies was the most radical member of the INSTITUT CANADIEN's second generation. He never involved himself in active politics, but participated in all the PARTI ROUGES' intellectual crusades. He handled words with ease and vigour. His *Lettres sur le Canada* (1864, 1867) raised crucial social issues and denounced obscurantism, prejudice, laziness and fanaticism. After another stay in Paris, Buies founded in 1868 *La Lanterne canadienne,* an anticlerical, nationalist and democratic paper which was condemned by Québec's bishops. Gradually he moved beyond polemical writing to a more relaxed, refined and subtle prose style – his 3 collections of *Chroniques* being excellent 19th-century literary works. Humour came to temper his irony and his ideas turned into impressions. After meeting with Antoine Labelle in 1879, Buies became an explorer and geographer and described the regions of Québec then being opened up to settlement. LAURENT MAILHOT

Building Codes and Regulations Under Canadian law the regulation of buildings is a provincial responsibility and is carried out through various laws, Acts, codes and regulations, often administered at the municipal level. Provincial legislation empowers government agencies or departments to regulate different aspects of buildings, depending on the objectives of the specific law or Act. Such legislation permits the establishment of detailed regulations by which the objectives of the law are to be met; or it may refer to other documents. For example, laws protecting the safety and health of building occupants usually refer to building codes for additional requirements. Building codes generally apply to new construction and have traditionally been concerned with fire safety, structural sufficiency and the health of the building's occupants. More recent codes have dealt with accessibility for handicapped persons and with energy conservation.

Zoning and planning legislation play an important role in regulating buildings by restricting the type, size, spacing, setback and use of buildings and by controlling general land use in a community. Its purpose is to maintain certain neighbourhood characteristics and to allow for a community's orderly development. In addition to building codes, there are various miscellaneous Acts aimed at specific building types or at specific services within buildings. Liquor-licensing, hotel, theatre and factory Acts, for example, may affect the construction or use of specific types of buildings. Regulations under such Acts may parallel, or even conflict with, building-code provisions, although the trend is to rely on building codes where practicable. Plumbing, electrical, elevator, and boiler and pressure-vessel codes are exam-

ples of STANDARDS aimed at particular building services and may be enacted separately or combined in a single Act.

Fire-prevention bylaws or fire codes regulate the ongoing safety of existing buildings. They regulate maintenance provisions for the purpose of fire safety, control the handling and storage of flammable materials in buildings, control furnishings (where appropriate) and regulate hazards related to certain industrial processes. While building codes are generally administered by building departments, fire-prevention bylaws and fire codes, which take over where building codes stop, are administered by the fire services.

History Although the regulation of buildings now falls within provincial jurisdiction, past governments delegated this responsibility to municipalities, with the result that building regulations diversified. Since municipal resources varied widely, the quality and efficiency of building regulations also varied; before WWII building regulation was nonexistent in many areas.

To promote uniformity, a model set of requirements, the National Building Code of Canada, was published in 1941 under the auspices of the NATIONAL RESEARCH COUNCIL (NRC). By 1987, 9 editions had been published. From its inception, the National Building Code had a major unifying influence on building-code requirements, although it had no legal status unless adopted by an authority having jurisdiction. By the 1970 edition, an estimated 75-85% of construction in Canada was built in conformity with the National Building Code or an adaptation of it. Provincial authorities took an increased interest in building regulations and began reversing the process of delegating the development of code requirements to municipalities. Mandatory provincial codes were introduced: by 1987 BC, Alta, Man, Ont and Qué and NS had adopted provincial codes based on the National Building Code; Sask and NB did not have provincial codes, but their legislation required that a municipality adopting a building code use the National Building Code. In those provinces without provincial codes, the National Building Code was in general use by the larger municipalities. Local authorities may amend or revise the requirements of the National Building Code to meet local conditions.

The National Fire Code has a shorter historical development. First published in 1963 by the NRC (5th edition, 1985) its general acceptance has lagged behind that of the National Building Code and provincial acceptance has been fairly recent. It has been adopted or has formed the basis of fire prevention requirements in BC, Alta and Man; is referred to in the legislation in several other provinces; and has been adopted by many municipalities.

Development The associate committees responsible for providing the National Building Code and the National Fire Code are appointed by NRC. A number of technical committees operate under their direction with the assistance of the NRC to produce these documents. The Associate Committee, National Building Code, also produces the Canadian Plumbing Code, Canadian Farm Building Code and Measures for Energy Conservation in New Buildings. All are written as model legislation for adoption by authorities having jurisdiction.

A number of standards-writing agencies produce standards on various aspects of building, which are referred to in building codes or in other regulations. The National Building Code, for example, refers to 192 such standards, including standards for construction materials, design, installation, equipment and testing. Provincial Acts also refer to such standards or base their regulations on them. For example, the Canadian

Electrical Code, produced by the Canadian Standards Association, forms the basis for electrical requirements in every province. Other standards-writing bodies in Canada include the Canadian General Standards Board, Underwriters Laboratories of Canada and the Canadian Gas Association. All such bodies are privately financed, except the Canadian General Standards Board, which operates out of the Dept of Supply and Services. The standards produced by these bodies play a major role, along with building codes, in regulating the construction of buildings in Canada. *See* ARCHITECTURE; CONSTRUCTION INDUSTRY, HISTORY OF; HOUSING. A.T. HANSEN

Bujold, Geneviève, actress (b at Montréal 1 July 1942). Since 1965, when she appeared in Alain Resnais's *La Guerre est finie,* Bujold has had an international career, starring in *Le Roi de coeur* (1966), *Anne of a Thousand Days* (1969), *Earthquake* (1974) and *Murder by Decree* (1978). Her first important Canadian role was in Michel BRAULT's *Entre la mer et l'eau douce* (1967) and she starred in *Kamouraska* (1973) by Claude JUTRA. However, it is on 4 of Paul ALMOND's films – *Isabel* (1968), *Act of the Heart* (1970), *Journey* (1972), and *Final Assignment* (1980) – that her personality and presence are imprinted. Her most remarkable successes have been in roles in which her vulnerable feminine appearance is contrasted with powerful passions and impulses. She has continued her career in the US, with leading roles in *Monseignor* (1981), *Tightrope* (1984) and *Trouble in Mind* (1985). PIERRE VÉRONNEAU

Geneviève Bujold at the World Film Festival in 1984 (*courtesy La Presse*).

Bulau, Horst, ski jumper (b at Ottawa 14 Aug 1962). Trained at Camp Fortune, he began skiing at $2\frac{1}{2}$, competing in alpine events at 5. Entering national ski-jumping competition for the first time in Thunder Bay, Ont, in 1975, he won handily, demonstrating outstanding potential with his explosive takeoff. In 1979 he won the world junior ski jumping championship, the first world nordic title for a Canadian. Since that time, he has 13 World Cup wins in 4 years and has been ranked 2nd or 3rd in the world for 3 of those years. Although he became famous in Europe long before his achievements were fully appreciated in Canada, his successes have attracted a great deal of Canadian attention to the sport. He won a silver medal at the Canadian championship in Thunder Bay in 1987. MURRAY SHAW

Bull, Gerald Vincent, scientist (b at North Bay, Ont 9 Mar 1928). Orphaned at 3, Bull displayed scientific brilliance early and earned a PhD in aerodynamics at only 23. He worked for the Defence Research Board at Valcartier, near Québec C, 1950-64, specializing in the development of guns to shoot instrument packages into the upper atmosphere and beyond. (In the early years of space technology, rockets were both unreliable and too expensive for most countries to develop.) Bull's High Altitude Research Project (HARP) was transferred from the DRB to McGill in 1964. Bull installed a giant 16-inch (407 mm) cannon (made of US naval guns fastened end to end) on Barbados and developed production workshops near Atwater, Qué. When Canadian and US government support ended, he formed the Space Research Corp in 1971 to continue HARP, funded by offering scientific services to countries unable to afford national space programs and by selling the products of SRC's special workshops. These products extended to shells for 155 mm artillery. (Bull had earlier designed a cannon shell shape that offered significant advantages over conventional designs.) In 1980 Bull was convicted in US courts of exporting munitions to the Republic of South Africa, contrary to the UN arms embargo, and was sentenced to 6 months in prison. SRC was declared bankrupt and liquidated. After his release in 1981 he moved to Europe, where he re-established the company as a consulting firm.

DONALD J.C. PHILLIPSON

Buller, Annie, married name Guralnick, political activist, union organizer (b in Ukraine 9 Dec 1895; d at Toronto 19 Jan 1973). Her Jewish parents immigrated to Montréal when she was a child. During WWI she became active in the Socialist Youth Movement, and after studying Marxism at the Rand School of Social Sciences, New York, established the Montréal Labour College with Becky BUHAY and Bella GAULD. She joined the COMMUNIST PARTY OF CANADA in 1922 and devoted herself to full-time party organizing and managing party publications. In the early 1920s she went to Cape Breton to organize mine workers. She organized for the communist-led Industrial Needle Trades Workers Union in Toronto and Winnipeg in the early 1930s. Because of her organizing work among coal miners in Estevan, Sask, in 1931, Buller was jailed after a riot in which 3 strikers were killed by the RCMP (*see* ESTEVAN COAL MINERS STRIKE, 1932). While working as a business manager of the *Western Clarion* in 1939, she was again arrested and was interned until 1942. After the war she was business manager of the *Tribune* and *National Affairs* and participated in a consumer campaign to roll back prices. She retired from full-time party work in the late 1950s but remained politically active until her death. JOAN SANGSTER

Bungee (Bungi) was a dialect of English spoken in the Red R valley N of Winnipeg, Man. Its origins are linked to families of mixed Cree and Orkney, Scottish or English descent who moved there early in the 19th century from HBC trading posts. Some Cree elements appear in the sentence patterns and sound structures of Bungee, eg, the interchangeable use of "s" and "sh." The vocabulary includes Cree, Scots, Gaelic and French words and expressions; and the Scots influence is further reflected in the accent and "lilt" of Bungee speech. Some of these features persist in the dialect still spoken by some older residents.

ELEANOR M. BLAIN

Bunkhouse Men The term "bunkhouse men" is typically applied to some 50 000 workers who constituted a labour pool for the booming Canadian economy in the first 3 decades of the 20th century. They lived in frontier work camps and provided unskilled labour in logging, harvesting, mining and construction. Mainly single and "foreign," they experienced brutal exploitation. Partly as a result of this, but primarily because jobs moved around, bunkhouse men were highly mo-

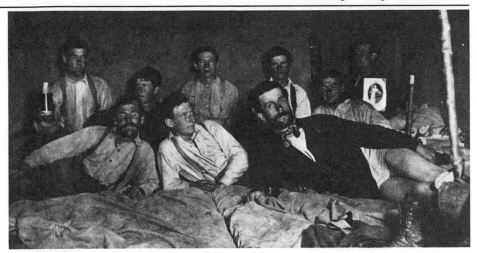

National Transcontinental Railway survey party in bunkhouse, Ont, 1905 (*courtesy Glenbow Archives, Calgary /NA-3553-5*).

bile, tramping within regions and sometimes across the country to find work. They were also often at the forefront of labour radicalism. *See also* REVOLUTIONARY INDUSTRIAL UNIONISM; INDUSTRIAL WORKERS OF THE WORLD. A. ROSS McCORMACK

Bunting, common name for several not particularly closely related members of the SPARROW family (Emberizidae). Four species nest in Canada: indigo bunting (*Passerina cyanea*) in open deciduous forests and parkland from SW Québec, across southern Ontario to southern Manitoba; its western counterpart, lazuli bunting (*P. amoena*), in brush country from southern BC to southern Saskatchewan; lark bunting (*Calamospiza melanocorys*) locally in open grassy prairies of southern Saskatchewan, Alberta and SW Manitoba; and snow bunting (*Plectrophenax nivalis*), a circumpolar species, on tundra, wintering in open country in southern Canada and northern US. Male indigo buntings are blue all over; male lazuli buntings have blue heads and backs, 2 white wing bars and cinnamon breasts shading to white on the abdomen. Female indigo and lazuli buntings have quite similar, dull brown plumage. The female lazuli bunting has 2 wing bars. Both species are around 14 cm long. Hybrids have been discovered where ranges overlap. Both species are migratory, wintering in Mexico and Central America. Male lark buntings are all black with large, white wing patches; females are brown with dark streaks and light wing patches. Their numbers and breeding-range boundaries fluctuate considerably from year to year. Males often sing in flight, holding their wings at an angle above the body and circling slowly back to earth while uttering a long and varied song of whistles, trills and buzzes. Snow bunting males are immaculate in breeding plumage; white with black back and black patches on wings and tail. Females, and males outside the breeding season, are slightly duller. In Canada, snow buntings are among the most northerly of nesting birds, breeding up to northern Ellesmere I. Flocks of snow buntings are a familiar sight in most of southern Canada in winter, usually over weedy fields and stubble.

RICHARD W. KNAPTON

Bunyan, Paul, mythical giant lumberjack. Tales of how Bunyan and his blue ox Babe created the Great Lks, the Rocky Mountains and the tides of the Bay of Fundy are related in E. Shepard, *Paul Bunyan* (1924) and J.D. Robins, *Logging with Paul Bunyan* (1957). The Bunyan mythology first appeared in print in columns of the Detroit *News Tribune* (1910), but a Canadian origin has often been claimed. It may have originated in the French Canadian folk tradition of Ti-Jean or Jean Bonhomme, or possibly from the woods of NB and Maine, where the legendary feats of the hero GLOOSCAP were well known. JAMES MARSH

Buoy, floating object, usually anchored but occasionally allowed to float freely or to be dragged by sea anchor. Buoys are widely used as navigation markers to indicate channels, the presence of shoals, etc. In oceanography, buoys function to protect or mark the position of equipment and as platforms to hold instruments. Instrumented buoys range in size from 10 m diameter, discus-shaped hulls moored to the seafloor and weighing many tens of tonnes to small, 10 cm diameter, free-drifting cylinders weighing a few kilograms. Large hulls, with mast heights of up to 10 m, are used at open-ocean sites such as continental shelves; smaller hulls, of discus, boat, spar or spherical shape, are suitable nearshore or in lakes. Sensors on buoys monitor environmental parameters such as air and water temperature, wind, ocean currents and ocean wave motion. Information can be recorded on board or telemetered to a shore station, directly or through a geostationary satellite. Data from buoys support research, forecasting, monitoring and emergency measures. For example, buoy networks on the East and West coasts monitor sea state to provide wave-climate information. Canada has developed open-ocean "drifters" which use a polar orbiting satellite for tracking and communication. They have circumnavigated Antarctica, drifted across the Pacific and followed the circulation pattern around and across the N Atlantic. Similar drifters track spilled oil, sea ice and icebergs. Nearshore drifters can be tracked using a VHF beacon. J.A. ELLIOTT

Burbidge, George Wheelock, lawyer, jurist, author (b at Cornwallis, NS 6 Feb 1847; d at Ottawa 18 Feb 1908). Hard working and dedicated, Burbidge was a complex individual who typified the 19th-century legalist in being fair and a staunch supporter of the rule of law, but uncompromising and elitist. As deputy minister of justice 1882-87, he blocked the proposed 1884 legislation to bar Canadian-born Chinese from inheriting or purchasing land. In 1885 he was the federal government's chief strategist in the trial of Louis RIEL. His *Digest of the Criminal Law of Canada* successfully collected Canadian penal law in one volume and was superseded only by the Criminal Code of 1892, of which Burbidge was coauthor with Robert SEDGEWICK. When elevated to the bench in 1887 as the first justice of the Exchequer Court, he organized that tribunal and developed much of the procedure it follows today.

D.H. BROWN

Bureau, André, communications administrator (b at Trois-Rivières, Qué 10 Oct 1935). Head of the CANADIAN RADIO-TELEVISION AND TELECOMMUNI-CATIONS COMMISSION, Bureau was trained in law at Université Laval and at Paris's Université de Droit Comparé. He was in private practice in Montréal from 1960 to 1968 and then joined Montréal's *La Presse* as executive vice-president, a post he held until 1972 when he returned to law. In 1976 Bureau became president of Télémedia Communications and, in 1982, president of Canadian Satellite Communications, positions that prepared him for his entry into the federal regulatory world in 1983. He successfully managed the transition from Liberal to Progressive Conservative governments when he became chairman of the CRTC.

J.L. GRANATSTEIN

Bureaucracy may be defined as a formal organizational arrangement characterized by division of labour, specialization of functions, a hierarchy of authority and a system of rules, regulations and record keeping. In common usage, it refers to the administrative branch of government. This definition avoids the derogatory use of the word as synonymous with red tape, ie, with delay, inefficiency and inflexibility. It does, however, reflect the common association of bureaucracy with the growth of government activities and expenditures and with the consequent increase in the number and power of government or public sector employees, also called bureaucrats, public servants or civil servants (*see* PUBLIC SERVICE).

The activities of Canadian governments have expanded rapidly since 1945. Governments are primarily involved in providing service and in regulation. To support these services and regulatory functions they conduct research on matters ranging from new ways of sorting mail to the inspection of food and drugs. From Confederation to WWII growth in the level of government expenditures and the number of government employees was relatively small, but the increasing scale and complexity of government activities (with newer responsibilities such as consumer and environmental protection, medicare and atomic energy research) have resulted in an enormous growth in public expenditures and public sector employment. As a proportion of the Gross Domestic Product (GDP), the total combined expenditures of the federal, provincial and municipal levels of Canadian government increased from 32.5% in 1961 to 45% in 1986. The federal percentage of total expenditures has decreased steadily since 1945, but expenditures by provincial and municipal governments have increased, mainly because of the increased demand for services within the provinces' constitutional jurisdiction, notably in the fields of health, education and transportation.

By 1982, the number of public-sector employees (excluding military personnel) had reached 2.1 million or 17.9% of the labour force. This total included 489 576 federal employees, 476 667 provincial employees, and 332 680 municipal employees as well as 509 000 employees in the education sector and 297 195 hospital employees. By 1986, 2.3 million Canadians in the labour force, again excluding military personnel, were public-sector employees.

Organization of the Bureaucracy To carry out their responsibilities, governments use a variety of administrative organizations, the 2 major forms being departments and nondepartmental bodies. The federal government has about 30 departments, ranging from traditional departments, eg, Agriculture, External Affairs and Justice, to newer ones, eg, Consumer and Corporate Affairs, and Environment. The federal government also has several hundred nondepartmental bodies

known as Crown agencies, including CROWN COR-PORATIONS and various boards, commissions and tribunals, and several important administrative units generally described as CENTRAL AGENCIES which are responsible for co-ordinating the activities of departments and, to a lesser extent, nondepartmental bodies. Similar administrative organizations exist in the provincial and local governments.

Power of the Bureaucracy Because government activities are too large and too complex for all powers to be exercised by elected representatives and the courts, much discretionary power is granted to public employees. Senior bureaucrats are often responsible for the initiation of policy proposals (to which end they frequently work closely with the representatives of powerful PRES-SURE GROUPS) and for the implementation of legislation. The subject matter of many laws is very technical, eg, atomic energy, and very complicated, eg, tax reform. Moreover, the implications of many laws are widespread and their full consequences are unpredictable. Elected representatives are therefore obliged to pass laws written in general and sometimes vague language and to delegate to public employees the authority to interpret and enforce these laws (*see* ADMINISTRATIVE TRIBUNALS). Similarly, judges have neither the time to hear all the cases requiring interpretation of the law nor the knowledge needed to understand and to interpret correctly laws involving very technical matters. Parliament therefore delegates to public employees the power to pass regulations that have the force of law, to enforce these regulations and to penalize those who do not obey them. As a result these employees now exercise powers of a legislative and judicial nature traditionally exercised by the legislatures and the courts (*see* REGULATORY PROCESS). Public employees also have power to influence the content of laws. Since elected politicians do not have as much knowledge as public employees about the subject matter or implications of the many laws proposed, they must rely heavily on the advice of the employees.

Image of the Bureaucracy The negative attitude of many Canadians towards public employees has several causes. Governments, because of their size, their pursuit of political objectives and their focus on service rather than profit, tend to operate less efficiently than business enterprises. Citizens who believe that they receive too few government services for their tax dollars and that there is too much government regulation often blame public employees as well as politicians. There is also a widespread public perception that public employees sometimes misuse their discretionary powers. Control and influence over public employees are exercised by elected politicians, judges, journalists, pressure group representatives, individual citizens, and other public employees, but public employees will continue to exercise a large measure of discretionary power.

KENNETH KERNAGHAN

Reading: K. Kernaghan and David Siegel, eds, *Public Administration in Canada; A Text* (1987).

Bureaucracy and Formal Organization The term BUREAUCRACY is traditionally associated with the administration of government and its various agencies. (The definition of the word *bureaucratie* in the dictionary of the French Academy, 1789 supplement, was "power, influence of the heads and staff of government bureaux.") Bureaucracy is also basic, however, to the operation of private corporations, political parties, unions, churches and any other large modern organization. Its association with routine, paperwork, lengthy procedures, and a centralized and rigid hierarchy has traditionally given the term a pejorative meaning.

Technically, however, in the social sciences, the term generally refers to the development of formal organizations.

Bureaucracy is first of all a form of social organization. The common denominator of bureaucratization lies in the quest for a "rational" model for administration. Mass organizations meet their objectives through an elaborate division of labour which results in compartmentalization and diversification of duties, which in turn leads to specialized functions, ie, implementation, management and special expertise. This multiplicity of functions clearly requires the establishment of a co-ordinated structure, and of regulations, administrative procedures and standards that define the responsibilities of each position and its relation to other positions. Such specialization by function itself increases the need for centralized control and administration, and thus the establishment of a hierarchy that integrates each function in a chain of command. Authority is delegated within specific areas of competence and is subject to a final authority that defines the organization's policies as a whole and monitors, or controls, the material or symbolic results at a central point. This final authority is more political than administrative in nature, and is therefore not purely bureaucratic. Bureaucracy as a whole is organized as a pyramid, as may be seen from the sometimes very complex organization charts used to describe large modern organizations. Within this structure, emphasis is given to vertical channels rather than to horizontal channels of communication between individuals. Similarly, indirect communications are common because individuals must transmit information to the higher levels of organization through a superior. This reduction in personal contacts, which is viewed as an element of efficiency, is also the cause of communication breakdowns and "red tape."

Recruitment in bureaucratic organizations is usually conducted according to recognized rules, eg, the competition system in the PUBLIC SERVICE. While positions involving the most routine tasks are occupied by personnel with relatively few qualifications, the executive, management and specialized positions are occupied by individuals who usually have a university degree. These individuals are sometimes hired or appointed, however, not for their skills but out of political considerations, eg, as PATRONAGE for past favours. In contrast a considerable number of positions in BUSINESS MANAGEMENT are occupied by individuals who do not have a university degree, but are trained by the company. A system of hierarchically organized titles corresponding to the organization chart is used to define the status of the individuals and to project his or her probable "career path."

The modern theory of bureaucracy, which derives largely from the German sociologist Max Weber, sees it as a formal codification of the idea of rational organization and the major element in the rationalization of modern capitalism. In the bureaucracies of private firms as well as government, objectives are set by rational, systematic, standardized techniques, thereby eliminating the effects of interpersonal relationships. Bureaucratic organization thus reflects the belief that maximum efficiency can be achieved through logical planning and calculation.

Considerable doubt is cast on the validity of this belief in contemporary theory. Studies have revealed many malfunctions in bureaucratic systems, including lack of dynamism resulting from their ritualistic behaviour. Problems and conflicts tend to be resolved through the imposition of new controls and rules which ultimately reinforce the bureaucracy (bureaucracies also tend to reproduce themselves, to divert energy into maintaining their own existence rather than fulfilling their original purpose). It is questionable as well whether the technical rationality of bureaucracy, expressed strictly as goals and means, is suitable to all types of organization. Even if it seems to apply easily to companies that espouse the fundamental logic of maximizing profit and to some routine governmental activities, this same rationality becomes inefficient and harmful when applied to government activities that cannot be reduced to pure repetition and controls. It is impossible to administer schools, hospitals, public housing and community service centres bureaucratically and without distortion because these services, which are dependent upon social needs and political decisions, cannot be determined strictly on the basis of rational abstract forecasts.

Bureaucracy cannot exist without bureaucrats; therefore the term denotes not only an organizational structure but a social group. Such a group is found in every large organization, and in the government it ranges from individuals responsible for administrative functions (eg, "paper pushers," who are traditionally assigned generally routine subordinate tasks and whose situation is rapidly changing as a result of computerization) to the "mandarins" in the senior echelons of the public service, who are often held in awe by new ministers. But the heart of any bureaucracy is the executive and middle managers, who represent the true power base.

In Western societies, bureaucracies differ in nature because of the substantial autonomy of individual institutions. Public and private bureaucracies are clearly distinct, notwithstanding their common characteristics and a degree of interpenetration that results from the movement of senior and middle managers from one sector to the other. In Canada there is significantly more movement from private to public than vice versa. Although they participate in the power system, the bureaucracies in Western countries cannot take it over entirely and become a class unto themselves as has happened in the Soviet Union, where political and economic power blend in the name of technical rationality. History has shown the importance of resisting the dynamics of bureaucratic growth and of maintaining heterogeneous bureaucracies to preserve a democratic order and social freedom. ARNAUD SALES

Reading: K. Kernaghan, ed, *Public Administration in Canada* (1982); M. Weber, *Economy and Society* (vol 3, 1968).

Burgeo, Nfld, Town, pop 2582 (1986c), 2504 (1981c), inc 1950, is a principal fishing and fish-processing centre on the SW coast of insular Newfoundland. The name is a corruption of Virgeo ("a thousand virgins" referring to the 11 000 virgins said to be martyred in the 4th or 5th centuries) first applied to the Burgeo Is. The main part of the community is on 2.5 km long Grandy I, connected to the mainland by a causeway. Settled since the late 1700s, the community's only link with the rest of Newfoundland was by sea until 1979, when a road connected Burgeo to the Trans-Canada Hwy. ROBERT D. PITT

Burgess Shale Site in YOHO NATIONAL PARK, BC, shows the beginnings of life in fossil-bearing rock formations. In 1909 Charles Doolittle Walcott, while searching for fossils, accidentally and literally stumbled upon a block of shale bearing the imprints of soft-bodied organisms. Most fossil remains result from the imprint of a hard structure (a shell or a skeleton) being preserved. This site, with its INVERTEBRATE fossil remains, is unique. About 140 species of marine invertebrates have been discovered: sponges, sea worms and tiny "sea monsters" such as the 5-eyed Opabinia and

the Hallucigenia with its 7 pairs of stiltlike spines and 7 tentacles. Many of these species are rare, resembling nothing else so far discovered in fossil sites. The Burgess Shale has been declared a UNITED NATIONS WORLD HERITAGE SITE. *See also* FOSSIL ANIMALS. LILLIAN STEWART

Burglary became a crime under English COMMON LAW in the Middle Ages; it was once punishable by death. Burglary is prohibited by provisions in the Canadian CRIMINAL CODE (s306-308) against "breaking and entering." If convicted, a person is liable to life imprisonment if the burglarized place is a dwelling, or 14 years if it is not. There are 3 major elements to the crime. First, there must be a breaking; someone lawfully entering a place through an open door cannot be liable. Secondly, there must be an entry into the place, an intrusion of some part of the offender's body or an instrument being used by the offender. Finally, the person must either intend to commit a serious (indictable) offence as he is making his intrusion, or actually commit such an offence once inside. Although the crime of burglary once referred specifically to intrusions at night, under present provisions of the Criminal Code this is no longer true. *See also* ROBBERY. LEE PAIKIN

Burgoyne, John, army officer (b in Eng 1722; d at London, Eng 3 Aug 1792). A distinguished cavalry officer and public figure, Burgoyne arrived in Québec in 1776 with large reinforcements, and served during the successful campaign of that year. In summer 1777, he led a force of 9000 soldiers southward along the Lk Champlain-Hudson R route with the objective of severing New England from the other colonies. After a series of costly battles, he was forced to surrender at Saratoga, NY, 17 Oct 1777, an event which led perhaps to the eventual American victory. STUART R.J. SUTHERLAND

Burin, Nfld, Town, pop 2892 (1986c), inc 1950, is located along a protected inlet of Placentia Bay on the SE coast of the Burin Pen. Present-day Burin is an amalgamation of communities along Burin Inlet and adjacent islands, most of which date from the 1700s or 1800s. The name, which appears on early French charts, may have come from the French *burin*, a graver or chisel. Basque and French fishermen were using the area by the second half of the 1600s, and after the Treaty of UTRECHT, 1713, it began to be settled by English fishermen. Throughout the 19th and 20th centuries, it developed as a major port for the Grand Banks and inshore fisheries and as a shipbuilding and dry-dock centre. As the principal harbour on the peninsula it had a school and courthouse before 1800 and a variety of local industries after that date. It continues to be an important fishing, fish-processing and service centre. ROBERT D. PITT

Burka, Petra, figure skater (b at Amsterdam, Netherlands 17 Nov 1946). While competing in the 1962 Canadian figure-skating championships at age 15, Burka became the first woman skater to complete the triple salchow jump in competition. In 1964 she won the Canadian championships and placed 3rd in the Olympics

and the world championships. Burka won the 1965 Canadian, N American and world championships. She received the LOU MARSH TROPHY that year as Canada's top athlete. After a 2nd-place finish in the 1966 world championships, she turned professional and toured with an ice show until 1969. BARBARA SCHRODT

Burka, Sylvia, speed skater, cyclist (b at Winnipeg 4 May 1954). Through hard work and determination, she overcame a visual handicap to become a world-class athlete in 2 sports. Despite losing an eye in a childhood accident, Burka was Canada's national junior SPEED-SKATING champion by age 15. Four years later, in 1973, she won the world junior championship. Ill during the 1976 Winter Olympics, her best result was a 4th in the 1500 m event. However, she recovered to win the world championship 2 weeks later. In 1977 she won the world sprint speed-skating title. Her speed-skating accomplishments also included 2 world records. She has also competed in international cycling competitions, finishing 4th in the individual pursuit event at the 1977 world championships and setting a world record while training in 1982. J. THOMAS WEST

Burke, Johnny, poet, playwright, songwriter (b at St John's 1851; d there Aug 1930). While working at a variety of jobs, Burke moonlighted as a poet, writing hundreds of broadsheet ballads about events in St John's, printing them on his own press and selling them for 2 to 5 cents a copy. He was said to have used an old-fashioned gramophone with a huge horn to attract customers. His first songbook was published in 1901. Some of his most famous songs are "Cod Liver Oil," "The Trinity Cake" and "The Kelligrews Soiree." His musical comedies include *The Battle of Foxtrap, The Topsail Geisha* and *Cotton's Patch*. JAMES G.G. MOORE

Reading: P. Mercer, ed, *The Ballads of Johnny Burke* (1974).

Burlington, Ont, City, pop 116 675 (1986c). Located at the head of Lake ONTARIO, 50 km W of Toronto, Burlington was first incorporated in 1873 as a village encompassing the earlier settlements of Port Nelson and Wellington Square. It achieved the status of a town in 1914 and became a city in 1974. Burlington's first and most distinguished settler was the Mohawk Loyalist Joseph BRANT who received a grant of 3450 acres (almost 1400 ha) on Burlington Bay in 1798. In the 19th century the local economy was built on waterborne commerce, particularly the transshipment through Port Nelson, Wellington Square and Port Flamboro (later Aldershot, now part of Burlington) of wheat, lumber and quarried rock. Commerce was stimulated further by the arrival of the railway in 1854. However, economic growth stalled as timber reserves depleted and as larger steamships bypassed local wharves for the ports of Hamilton and Toronto. Between the 1890s and WWI the shift of local agriculture to market gardening and fruit growing transformed Burlington into the "Garden City" of southern Ontario. Its modern role as a residential area for nearby cities was given impetus by completion of the QUEEN ELIZABETH WAY in 1939 and of the Burlington Skyway Bridge in 1958. Since WWII, Burlington has increasingly developed an economic base of secondary manufacturing and service industries. In 1958, Burlington, Nelson Township and the Aldershot area of East Flamborough were amalgamated to form one municipality (Burlington). Burlington is the home of the world-renowned Royal Botanical Gardens. DAVID GAGAN

Reading: C. Emery and B. Ford, *From Pathway to Skyway* (1967); C.M. Johnston, *The Head of the Lake* (1958).

Burnaby, BC, District Municipality, pop 145 161 (1986c), 136 494 (1981c), area 10 682 ha, inc 1892. It adjoins VANCOUVER on the W, COQUITLAM on the E and NEW WESTMINSTER on the SE. Named after Robert Burnaby, a businessman and legislator of the 1860s, it features Burnaby Mt (365 m), Burnaby Lk, the Fraser R and Burrard Inlet. Burnaby is governed by a mayor and 8 aldermen and is a member of the Greater Vancouver Regional Dist. Originally a sparsely populated rural district – with a population of 400 in 1900 – it developed into a residential community for workers in Vancouver and New Westminster. Industrial development and construction of large wholesale and retail outlets followed, and urbanization has continued in recent years. Burnaby ranks second in the region to Vancouver in industrial diversity, employment and output. Its industries include steel fabrication, manufacturing of trucks and telecommunications equipment, lumber and shingle operations, and commercial fishing and fish processing. Residential and industrial developments have almost eliminated agriculture. Its educational facilities include SIMON FRASER U, and the BC Institute of Technology. Attractions are Burnaby Village Museum (recreating a typical 1890-1925 community), Ismaili Mosque, Barnet Marine Park, the Burnaby Art Gallery and Four Rinks, one of the world's largest indoor skating and hockey complexes.

ALAN F.J. ARTIBISE

Burnford, Sheila, author (b in Scotland 11 May 1918; d at Bucklers Hard, Hampshire, Eng 20 Apr 1984). Educated at private schools in England, France and Germany, Burnford served as a volunteer ambulance driver during WWII before immigrating to Canada and settling in Port Arthur, Ont. Her first novel, *The Incredible Journey* (1961), an immediate international best-seller and a Walt Disney movie (1963), recounts the struggle for survival of 3 friends, a bull terrier, a golden labrador and a siamese cat, who travel over 300 km through the northern Ontario wilderness to return home. Among her other works are *The Fields of Noon* (1964), a book of autobiographical essays; *Mr Noah and the Second Flood* (1973), an ecological parable for children; and the novel *Bel Ria: Dog of War* (1977). MARYLYNN SCOTT

Burns, Eedson Louis Millard, soldier, diplomat, author (b at Westmount, Qué 17 June 1897; d at Manotick, Ont 13 Sept 1985). After graduating from RMC in 1915, Burns fought on the Western Front with the Royal Canadian Engineers, 1916-18. Between the wars he attended the School of Military Engineering, Chatham, Eng, and the Staff College at Quetta, British India, and was an instructor at RMC. From 1931 to 1936 he was in charge of the Geographical Section of the General Staff, where he made a major contribution to the development of Canadian military mapping. In 1939 he was a lt-col attending the Imperial Defence College, London, Eng. After staff appointments in England and Canada, he commanded the 4th Canadian Armoured Brigade and 2nd Canadian Infantry Division in England, and then the 5th Canadian Armoured Division and 1st Canadian Corps in Italy. He led the corps during operations in the Liri Valley (May 1944) leading to the capture of Rome, and in the highly successful attack on the Gothic Line (Aug/Sept 1944). A subtle sense of fun, well disguised beneath a dour exterior, accompanied his formidable intellect. However, he could not win the confidence of his subordi-

nates and a "him or us" ultimatum brought about his relief in Nov 1944.

Burns retired from the army in June 1947 and began a second career as a public servant. He joined the Dept of External Affairs and was loaned to the UN, becoming commander of the UN Emergency Force in the Middle East, 1954-59 (*see* PEACEKEEPING). From 1960 to 1969 he was chief adviser to the Canadian government on DISARMAMENT conferences. He was a professor of strategic studies at Carleton 1972-75. His books include *Manpower and the Canadian Army, 1939-1945* (1956), *General Mud: Memoirs of Two World Wars* (1970), *Between Arab and Israeli* (1962), *Megamurder* (1966) and *A Seat at the Peace Table: The Struggle for Disarmament* (1972). BRERETON GREENHOUS

Burns, Patrick, meat packer, rancher (b at Oshawa, Canada W 6 July 1856; d at Calgary 24 Feb 1937). A farm boy without much formal schooling, Burns joined the vanguard of Ontario farmers moving to Manitoba after the Riel uprising. In 1878 he walked 250 km from Winnipeg to the homestead he had selected near Minnedosa. To earn working capital, Burns began to freight goods from Winnipeg and trail neighbours' cattle to the Winnipeg market. By 1885 Burns was buying cattle full-time and in 1886 he got his first contract to supply beef to a railway construction gang. His business grew with the railway boom and he expanded aggressively into ranching, packing and the retail meat trade. By WWI Burns was established internationally and had become one of Canada's most successful businessmen. In 1928 he sold his packing business for $15 million but retained his vast cattle ranches. He was made a senator in 1931 and is honoured as one of the "Big Four" western cattle kings who started the CALGARY STAMPEDE. DAVID H. BREEN

Reading: Grant MacEwan, *Pat Burns, Cattle King* (1980).

Patrick Burns got his first contract to supply beef to a railway construction gang in 1886 (*courtesy Glenbow Archives/Calgary, NA-1149-1*).

Burns, Tommy, boxer (b Noah Brusso at Hanover, Ont 17 June 1881; d at Vancouver 10 May 1955). Starting as a welterweight in 1900, Burns became, 6 years later, the only Canadian to hold the world heavyweight championship when he beat Marvin Hart. Known as a tenacious boxer and strong hitter, the 170 cm, 79.4 kg French Canadian defended his title 10 times in 33

Tommy Burns, Canada's only world heavyweight champion, lost only 4 of 60 fights and defended his crown 10 times in less than 3 years (*courtesy National Archives of Canada/C-14092*).

months before losing to Jack Johnson in Sydney, Australia, on 25 Dec 1908. His defences included victories over the heavyweight champions of England and Australia. He knocked out the Irish champion, Jem Roche, in 1 min, 28 secs, the shortest title defence ever. The $30 000 he received for fighting Johnson was the beginning of "big" money for boxers. A.J. "SANDY" YOUNG

Burns Lake, BC, Village, inc 1923, pop 1723 (1986c), 2159 (1981c), located on Highway 16 in the centre of the Nechako Plateau, 226 km W of Prince George in central BC. The village serves as the local trading and service centre for agriculture and forest industries in the region. The area was first settled late in the 19th century during construction of the Overland Telegraph line to Alaska and Siberia. The village is named after Michael Byrnes, a surveyor for the Collins Telegraph Co who passed through in 1866. There was little development until after construction of the GRAND TRUNK PACIFIC RY, now the Canadian National Railway, between Jasper and Prince Rupert in 1914. Four major mines, producing molybdenum, copper, gold and silver, were opened in the region in the 1960s and 2 large sawmills were built nearby in the 1970s. Cattle ranching is also important in the district. JOHN STEWART

Burpee, Lawrence Johnston, civil servant, librarian, author (b at Halifax 5 Mar 1873; d at Oxford, Eng 13 Oct 1946). He entered the Canadian civil service in 1890 and served as private secretary to 3 ministers of justice. From 1905 to 1912 Burpee was librarian of the Ottawa Public Library, and from 1912 until his death was Canadian secretary to the INTERNATIONAL JOINT COMMISSION. Burpee was a founder of the CANADIAN HISTORICAL ASSN and honorary secretary 1926-35 and president 1936-37 of the Royal Soc of Canada. A prolific writer, he published many articles and works on Canadian studies. DAVID EVANS

Burt, George, labour leader (b at Toronto 17 Aug 1903). Burt became a journeyman plumber, but during the Depression he moved to Oshawa to work for General Motors. He was the first treasurer of Local 222 United Automobile Workers (UAW), organized just before the historic 1937 OSHAWA STRIKE. In 1939 he was elected Canadian director of the UAW over C.H. MILLARD. Burt was a VP of the Canadian Congress of Labour, a general VP of the Canadian Labour Congress, and was president 1951-53 of the Ontario Federation of Labour. He led the Canadian UAW from its militant infancy until 1968, when it was the second-largest and most socially conscious union in Canada. Burt was involved in labour politics and gained support from communist and CO-OPERATIVE COMMONWEALTH FEDERATION factions in his union at different times. He was a member of the NEW DEMOCRATIC PARTY's founding committee.

LAUREL SEFTON MACDOWELL

Burton, Dennis, painter (b at Lethbridge, Alta 6 Dec 1933). Burton achieved renown in 1965 for his "Garterbeltmania"—large paintings of women in garterbelts. He had become interested in drawing the nude and abstraction at the Ontario College of Art (1952-56) and was influenced by William RONALD's work. In 1960 his images of genitalia first became obvious in *Smokeshop Sex Marauder*. With Joyce WIELAND and Michael SNOW, he represents a rigorous exploration of erotic themes in Canadian art. His paintings, figurative, abstract or "calligraphic," are full of dashing energy.

JOAN MURRAY

Burton, Eli Franklin, physicist (b at Green R, Ont 14 Feb 1879; d at Toronto 6 July 1948). Educated at U of T and Cambridge, Burton spent his whole career at U of T, succeeding J.C. McLennan as head of the physics department in 1932. He was a council member of the NATIONAL RESEARCH COUNCIL 1937-46 and served on the board of Research Enterprises Ltd, the secret wartime radar factory. His most notable achievement was building the first electron microscope in N America, with Cecil Hall, James Hillier and A.F. Prebus at Toronto in the late 1930s. Hillier and Prebus went on to scientific careers in the US, where the electron microscope was manufactured by RCA Ltd.

DONALD J.C. PHILLIPSON

Burwash, Nathanael, Methodist minister, university chancellor (b at St Andrew's, Qué 25 July 1839; d at Toronto 30 Mar 1918). Theologically moderate, he trained a generation of Methodist ministers and undergraduates to pursue enlightened research in theology and the humanities. Raised in Baltimore, Canada W, he was educated at Victoria College, graduated 1859, and was ordained 1864. He began teaching science 1866 at Victoria College. In 1871 he became professor and in 1873 dean of the newly created Faculty of Theology. He became chancellor (president) of Victoria 1887 and oversaw the university's move from Cobourg to Toronto. He retired 1913 but taught theology until his death. While he was not an original scholar, his writings and lectures became the standard for generations of Methodist clergy and laity. Committed to the scientific method and free enquiry, he played a conciliatory role in the debate over EVOLUTION and HIGHER CRITICISM. He was also widely respected in the Canadian intellectual and religious community and was an active supporter of ecumenism. His published books include *Wesley's Doctrinal Standards* (1881); *A Manual of Christian Theology on the Inductive Method* (1900) and *The History of Victoria College* (1927).

NEIL SEMPLE

Bus Transportation The word "bus," short for omnibus, refers to any self-propelled road vehicle capable of carrying more persons than a private automobile. The terms coach and bus are used interchangeably, although, strictly speaking, buses are outfitted for short-distance travel and coaches have more comfortable seating and other amenities for longer journeys. Buses are the most common means of public conveyance within and between cities and towns in Canada and often the only public service. For intercity markets with distances of less than 500 km, the bus provides an attractive combination of low price and frequent departures.

Development of Bus Transportation The earliest bus and coach services in Canada were horse-drawn and began to make their appearances following the Seven Years' War. Prior to 1800, Halifax had a stage service to Windsor. Montréal was linked with Québec City, Albany and St Johns (Saint Jean). Upper Canada had several routes, including one between Newark and Chippawa. Startup dates were later in the West, reflecting the pace of development. The famous BX (Barnard's Express, later BC Express) ran its first stage up the CARIBOO ROAD in 1863, between Lillooet and Soda Creek, BC. As the road network expanded, so did Barnard's route, connecting what was then BC's largest community, Barkerville, with Fraser R steamers at Yale.

The inauguration of the CPR across Canada also spurred the development of stagecoach lines on the Prairies. An early hub was Moosomin, Sask, which had stagecoaches N to Fort Ellice (Qu'Appelle R steamboats), S to the US at Boscurvis and NW to Redpath, Kinbrae and Montreal Colony (now Bredenbury). Moosomin stages played an important transport role at the time of the North-West Rebellion.

Urban, horse-drawn bus lines began to appear as Canadian cities grew. Some of these were livery or station transfer services, such as those in Montréal, Toronto and elsewhere which took people from steamer docks or railway stations to commercial and residential districts, or served as a portage between one water system and another. Others offered a more comprehensive city service as was the case in Victoria during the 1880s. Still others were adjuncts to horse-drawn streetcar networks, either year-round or seasonally. In Montréal, the usual pattern of operation was horse streetcars in the summer and fall, horse buses in the slush of spring, and sleighs in winter. Some companies survived the transition from horse to self propelled buses and exist to this day: Brewster Transport (Alta, BC) and Penetang-Midland (Ont) are two. In other cases, the individuals in charge of a horse operation made the transition to electric street railways and motorbuses, as did Francis Stillman Barnard of Victoria (son of the BX founder).

Following some early experiments, urban motorbus and electric trolleybus services began to appear in earnest after WWI, first as a supplement to streetcar lines, and in most cities subsequently, as a replacement. The rural and intercity bus industry similarly flowered in the late 1920s and 1930s, largely supplementing other modes, subsequently experiencing its major growth from the late 1940s to the late 1960s. The extension of highway networks and the growth of suburban areas have offered new opportunities in subsequent years.

Types of Bus Service Most people are familiar with the scheduled or regular route service: a bus runs according to a fixed timetable, serving set points along specific roads. Anyone may ride, upon payment of a set fare, and packages may be sent on intercity/rural services. Most buses are used for scheduled route service. Charter services represent another common type of bus operation in which people pay as a group for transportation directly to the place and at the time of their choosing. Tour services are a form of bus transportation and may operate on a regular schedule; alternatively the tour may follow a circuit covering a major part of the country, with arrangements for meals and lodging included. Hundreds of bus companies are engaged in the charter and tour fields. Industrial bus systems provide scheduled services for commuters to a particular job location not covered by public transportation, particularly in BC and Alberta. Most commonly these services are paid for by the employer, both to assist the worker and as an alternative to maintaining parking areas. Some industrial fleets have hundreds of buses. In the BC lumber industry there are more buses in industrial service than in the Vancouver urban motor bus fleet.

Airport bus services, similar to the railway "station bus" of an earlier era, link airports with the downtowns of major cities. They may also provide a direct ride to smaller cities nearby.

The yellow school bus is a common sight across Canada. Both public and private ownership is to be found, with funds for operation in either case coming from the education tax base. Over 700 million trips are handled each year on some 36 000 school buses.

Though most regions of Canada have good route coverage, there is one striking omission from networks in both Canada and the US: the virtual absence of short-distance rural routes. In Canada, these movements are handled by special-purpose services: yellow school buses, minibuses for the elderly or the handicapped and industrial contract runs for workers. In Europe these various travel demands are usually handled on one system.

Bus Transportation Companies There are over 1000 companies providing bus service, but most routes are operated by such major carriers as Acadian Lines, Canada Coach, Gray Coach, Grey Goose, Greyhound Lines of Canada, SMT Eastern, Saskatchewan Transportation, Terra Transport (Canadian National) and Voyageur. Five of these companies are privately owned and the remainder are crown corporations. The nature of the territory, frequency of service and growth rate of the economy in the area served determine whether any given company makes a profit.

Technology and Manufacturing Buses come in many types: the standard rear-engine, 2-axle bus, found in every city, and its 2- or 3-axle motorcoach equivalent for intercity service; the school-type bus, employing a truck chassis with the engine out front; the articulated bus, of extra length and hinged for easier cornering; and the doubledecker, used on many sightseeing routes. Electric trolleybuses have been used since the beginning of bus transport, with 4 major cities possessing modern fleets at present.

Historically, many small firms were engaged in bus manufacturing, such as Sunnyside Auto Body Works (Alta), Laurie Wagon (Man), Smith Brothers (Ont), St-Lin Bodies (Qué) and Middle West Pubnico Bus Builders (NS). As time passed, a reduced number of larger companies met Canadian domestic and export needs. For city transport, General Motors Diesel Division, Flyer Ltd, and Ontario Bus Industries dominate. For intercity and rural applications, 2 builders (1987) are noteworthy, each of which has evolved some special feature: Prevost Car (Qué) and Motor Coach Industries (Man). Prevost has developed a cost-effective way of providing large windows that curve up into the roof of a coach, which is of special appeal to tour and charter operators. Motor Coach Industries, through its link with Greyhound Lines of Canada, has developed a coach that can produce 2 or more million kilometres of service at low cost and high reliability, resulting in its widespread use in scheduled service.

Regulation of bus transportation rests with the provincial governments. The Supreme Court of Canada has ruled that the federal government has the right to regulate interprovincial bus transportation, but for practical reasons the individual provinces undertake this function in consultation with each other.

Scheduled services are closely regulated. Most rural routes lack sufficient population to support more than one carrier. Busier city-to-city lines are usually restricted to one carrier, so that profits earned there can supplement service to thinly populated territory. Fares, as well as entry and exit from the marketplace, are controlled. Charter and tour services are also regulated, though in some jurisdictions the restriction on the number of authorized carriers has been eased. For all practical purposes, operating authorities are granted in perpetuity.

Airports usually have insufficient bus-traffic potential to warrant more than one carrier per route, so monopolies are awarded. An important element of competition is introduced every 5 to 10 years, when open bidding is held by airport authorities to choose a carrier for exclusive operation over the subsequent period.

Future Prospects Canada may be a nation of automobile owners, but for surface travel its people have a strong propensity to use public transport. Canadians use scheduled bus lines and railway services more than 3 times as often as their US neighbours. Similar results are found when urban-transit ridership is compared between the 2 countries for cities in comparable population groups. With the widespread network of services and bargain-priced fares, Canadians are likely to continue their support of this safe and energy-efficient form of transport. *See also* STREET RAILWAYS; TRANSPORTATION; URBAN TRANSPORTATION.

BRIAN E. SULLIVAN

Bush, John Hamilton, "Jack," painter (b at Toronto 20 Mar 1909; d there 24 Jan 1977). Internationally acclaimed as Canada's leading abstract painter in the 1960s and 1970s, Bush established his local reputation as a radical in the 1950s as a member of PAINTERS ELEVEN.

He obtained his formal training in Montréal

Bridge Passage (1975) by Jack Bush, acrylic on canvas, displays the artist's remarkable colour orchestration *(courtesy Woltjen-Udell Gallery).*

and Toronto 1926-28. For most of his life he was a successful advertising artist, which he said allowed him great freedom in his own work. His earliest paintings, small landscapes and city scapes, aspired to the manner of the GROUP OF SEVEN, but by the late 1930s he had established a personal figurative style that won him access to Canada's official painting societies. He was a member and frequently an officer of the Canadian Society of Painters in Water Colour, the Ontario Society of Artists, the Royal Canadian Academy and the Canadian Group of Painters (1940-64). In the late 1940s, dissatisfied with his work, he produced a group of stylized, expressionist figure paintings with emotional and religious themes. About this time, too, he became interested in American abstract expressionism. His painting was completely abstract but still expressionist and gestural by the early 1950s, and, with like-minded artists such as William RONALD, Harold TOWN, Oscar CAHÉN, Alexandra LUKE and Jock MACDONALD, Bush found himself in opposition to standard Toronto painting. He exhibited with 6 of these colleagues in "Abstracts at Home" at Simpsons department store in 1953. With some additions, they exhibited as Painters Eleven 1954-60, including a showing at New York's Riverside Museum in 1956. A 1957 visit from American art critic Clement Greenberg to the group confirmed Bush's interest in thinner, simpler painting (and introduced him to a lifelong friend). Despite this support, Bush did not fully explore this mode for several years. His first solo show in New York (1962), however, consisted of "Thrust" pictures which stated themes that would preoccupy him for the rest of his life: thin radiant colour, eccentric shapes and expansive compositions – evidence of his deep admiration for Matisse. In "Flags" and "Sashes" (1962-63) – probably his best-known series – he simplified structure even further, to allow colour more autonomy. His paintings of the later 1960s and 1970s rely increasingly on his remarkable colour sense, culminating in the rich orchestrations of innumerable colour strokes in his last "musical title" series. At the same time, he explored subtle variations in surface in the rollered and sponged ground pictures of the 1970s.

From the mid-1960s on, Bush travelled fairly often to Europe and the US, making friends with many international artists of similar beliefs. Though quick to respond to what he saw, he always remained highly individual. After 1965 he exhibited with these international contemporaries in the new David Mirvish Gallery in Toronto. (As though to indicate his new, nonofficial, nonprovincial status, he had resigned from all societies in 1964.)

Despite his growing international fame, however, Bush remained interested in and accessible to younger artists. His encouragement and his work influenced many of the present generation of Canadian painters and sculptors. He represented Canada at the 1967 São Paulo Bienal and has been included in many prestigious international exhibitions. In 1972 his one-man exhibition opened the new contemporary galleries of the Boston Museum. The Art Gallery of Ontario organized a 1976 retrospective that toured Canada. Bush's awards include a John Simon Guggenheim Foundation fellowship and the Order of Canada.

KAREN WILKIN

Reading: Terry Fenton, *Jack Bush, A Retrospective* (1976); Karen Wilkin, ed, *Jack Bush* (1984).

Bush Flying In Canada, the word "bush" has been used since the 19th century to describe the hostile environment beyond the clearings and settlements. In bush flying it has been used to refer to flying in adverse, if not hostile, conditions in the remote expanses beyond the ribbon of settlement in southern Canada, into the "bush" of the Canadian SHIELD and the barren Arctic. By the end of WWI most of southern Canada had been linked by railways, but the North remained as inaccessible as ever by land. Its innumerable lakes and rivers did, however, provide alighting areas for water-based aircraft in summer and ski-equipped aircraft in winter. Winter flying began in 1917-18 and the first winter bush flying in Canada was undertaken by Fairchild Aerial Surveys (of Canada). In 1926 H.A. "Doc" Oaks flew supplies from Hudson, Ont, to Narrow Lake, Ont, on Dec 27 for Bathurst Mines. Under Oaks's directions, methods of engine heating and maintenance in difficult winter conditions were developed. The Elliot Brothers of Sioux Lookout, Ont, are credited with the development of special skis for landing on snow or ice. Early navigation was basically by recognition as pilots followed the course of rivers.

Bush flying began as aerial reconnaissance for spotting forest fires. Laurentide and other paper companies hired ex-RNAS pilot, Stuart GRAHAM, in 1919 to fly forest-fire patrols over the St Maurice R valley. Using 2 war-surplus Curtiss HS-2L flying boats, Laurentide extended their patrols from Lake-of-the-Woods to James Bay. These early operations were succeeded by a general air service, Laurentide Air Service Ltd, which carried out operations in both Québec and Ontario, including the first regular Canadian airmail, passenger and freight service from Haileybury, Ont, to Rouyn, Qué (1924). Laurentide ceased operation in 1925 and from then to 1927 the major bush-flying organization in Canada was the Ontario Provincial Air Service, established in 1924 and devoted almost entirely to forestry operations.

The usefulness of aircraft in northern mining operations was demonstrated after the gold strike in the Red Lk district of northwestern Ontario (1925). Patricia Airways and Exploration Ltd carried passengers, freight and mail to the remote area. In 1928 Northern Aerial Mineral Exploration began prospecting by air vast areas of Ungava and the Yukon. Western Canada Airways (renamed Canadian Airways 1930) was formed in 1926 by James A. RICHARDSON, a wealthy Winnipeg grain merchant. One of WCA's pilots, Leigh BRINTNELL, set out from Winnipeg in 1929, dropped off prospector Gilbert

Bush pilots at Great Bear Lake, NWT. Bush flying was important in the discovery and exploitation of the radium and uranium in the area. By Jan 1929 there was a regular air service down the Mackenzie R from Ft Mc-Murray (*courtesy City of Edmonton Archives*).

LABINE at Great Bear Lk, flew on to Aklavik, across the Richardson Mts to Whitehorse and Prince George, then to Edmonton and back to Winnipeg – some 15 000 km. (In 1930 LaBine found pitchblende, striking it rich.)

By Jan 1929, WCA had established a regular air service down the Mackenzie R from Ft McMurray. One of the most dramatic events of the late 1920s was the flight of 2 aircraft, led by Lt-Col C.D.H. MacAlpine, N from Churchill, Man. The planes got stranded on Queen Maude Gulf. With the help of local Inuit, the men made their way safely overland to Cambridge Bay. In 1930 an expedition piloted by Walter Gilbert flew up the Boothia Pen and found a cairn containing artifacts of the FRANKLIN EXPEDITION. Bush pilots made major surveys of the proposed route of the Hudson Bay Ry in 1926, and in 1927, 7 aircraft were ferried to Southampton I in the Arctic to gather information on the navigation of Hudson Str.

The use of bush flying in the development of mining continued even through the Great Depression. By the mid-1930s more freight was being moved by air in Canada than in all the rest of the world combined. The scale of bush flying was greatly expanded during the development of iron ore reserves in Québec and Labrador. Hollinger Ungava Transport (HUT) hauled fuel, food, disassembled bulldozers and even cement for dams in the late 1940s. With up to 96 aircraft arrivals per day, HUT carried 170 000 passengers in 10 000 flights before the project ended. In the mid-1950s,

The operations of the St-Maurice Forestry Protective Assn began with the launching of this Curtiss HS-2L from USN Air Station at Halifax, seen here flying it to their Lac-à-La-Tortue base (*courtesy National Aviation Museum*).

Maritime Central Airlines made some 28 000 flights in 29 months during construction of the DEW line across northern Canada. More recently, the James Bay Project depended entirely on bush planes in its early stages, while massive Hercules transports delivered huge loads of food, fuel and equipment.

Bush flying transformed the North. It became possible by the 1930s to charter an aircraft and fly almost anywhere. Aircraft services became available to trappers and missionaries as well as to geologists and surveyors. Moreover, victims of accidents or illness could be brought out quickly for medical attention. The first such incident occurred on 28 Aug 1920, when J.W. Thompson was flown out for a mastoid operation from Moose Factory on James Bay to Cochrane, Ont, by W.R. Maxwell in a Curtiss HS-2L. By the late 1920s and through the 1930s such flights were common; the longest such flight occurred from 27 Nov to 20 Dec 1939, when W.E. Catton flew a Junkers W-34 from Winnipeg to Repulse Bay, NWT, and returned to bring out a man with frozen, gangrenous hands. In the postwar period, air strips have been built in the larger northern settlements, HELICOPTERS have been introduced, and good radio and navigation facilities have been established along with up-to-date weather information services. All this has greatly changed northern Canada and bush flying, but aircraft equipped with floats or skis continue to serve all those who live and work in remote areas. *See also* NOORDUYN NORSEMAN; DE HAVILLAND BEAVER; DE HAVILLAND OTTER.

Bushnell, Ernest Leslie, pioneer broadcast executive (b near Lindsay, Ont 19 Nov 1900; d at Ottawa 30 Apr 1987). He trained as a singer at the Toronto Conservatory but turned to announcing and then station management. He managed CFRB and CKCN in Toronto 1929-33, then started Canada's first advertising agency for radio. With the CBC 1945-58, he became asst general manager 1953 and retired as a vice-president. He was acting president while Joseph-Alphonse OUIMET was absent owing to illness and had to deal with the Montréal producers' strike in 1958. His difficulties with a parliamentary committee after cancellation and reinstatement of "Preview Commentary" after political pressure led to his being pensioned off. In 1960 he founded, in partnership with Stuart Griffiths, CJOH-TV in Ottawa, the second station of the CTV network. In 1983 he was honorary chairman of Bushnell Communications Ltd.

Business Cycles are fluctuations in economic activity that occur in most modern economies. They trace out a wavelike pattern with a length of between 3.5 and 7 years. Since 1945 the duration of periods of above-average economic performance has usually been greater than that of below-average performance with a general rise in the long-term average. The peaks in economic activity are normally higher in successive cycles.

Business cycles are divided into phases which describe economic activity as it moves from a peak to a trough and back. They describe the behaviour of a variety of economic indicators which reflect basic business conditions, although in complex economies the government role in establishing such conditions is necessarily measured at the same time. Important indicators are industrial production, exports, imports, railway freight loadings, construction contracts awarded and bank clearings. Occasionally monetary indicators are also included as descriptive statistics. To achieve precision these data are taken weekly or monthly; together they trace out a reference cycle which maps the congruence of peaks and troughs in an attempt to indicate average business cycle behaviour. Some indicators persistently tend to peak and trough before others and are described as leading (as opposed to lagging) indicators. In Canada, exports and construction contracts are leading indicators because of the export orientation of the economy and the important role played by the construction industry in natural resource development. Although this analysis is normally applied to the economy at large, there is evidence of significant difference in business cycle behaviour between the various regions of Canada in both the timing of cycles and their severity.

Business cycles are a phenomenon of relatively developed and diversified economies. They are thought to originate from the timing of real investment and the adjustment of inventories of goods, particularly those with some manufacturing component. In Canada's open economy these influences are both domestic and foreign. Marxist interpreters hold that business cycles are inherent in the capitalist system and are generated by the method of appropriating surplus value; that they are simply one set of a structure of cycles, some of which are thought to be of very long duration. Non-Marxists view the business cycle as being independent of business ownership and more deeply rooted in investment, in its inevitably lumpy nature, and in the nature of both domestic and international trade. Marxists and non-Marxists agree that the Kuznets cycle of 15 to 25 years duration, evident in the international economy of the late 19th and early 20th centuries, and the business cycle are linked.

Probably the first evidence of a business cycle phenomenon in Canada occurred 1854-59. A peak in economic performance, associated with the demand growth brought about by the CRIMEAN WAR and the RECIPROCITY Treaty with the US, was followed in 1857 by a recession brought about by factors which included a slackening in the pace of railway construction. The recovery phase was brought about by both an increase in domestic investment and a revived export demand. The post-1850 business cycle was the product of growing market integration, which was itself linked to the new transport and communications forms: steamships, railways and telegraphs. The Canadian economy grew in size and scope as a result of this integration, and the first appearance of the business cycle was concomitant with the first major signs of industrial diversification.

Some 19th-century business cycles were almost wholly domestic. The best example is that found in the 1880s which was almost exclusively dominated by the pace of transcontinental railway construction; the cycle peaked in 1885, the last year of major new construction on the CPR. Many business cycles were, in contrast, associated with both booms and crises in the international economy. Prosperity immediately following Confederation was brought to an end by a domestic response to the worldwide financial crisis of 1871-72 and its consequent restriction on the availability of investment capital. A trough in 1889 coincided with a similar but less severe international crisis. Business cycles were also governed by noncrisis international forces such as the peak in British lending to the international capital market in 1913.

All evidence suggests that before 1914 there was a growing coincidence of business cycles in Canada and the US, Canada's major trading partner. However, between the world wars the transmission mechanism weakened. The GREAT DEPRESSION, the most famous of all business cycles, was brought about by more than the usual influences of cyclical motion: the instability of the international structure of both trade and payments mechanisms, inappropriate exchange rate policies, and world instability in certain commodity markets. Since 1945 there has been an increasingly similar pattern of business cycles in Canada and the US. Cycles transmitted from the US with both a shorter lag and an increasingly similar amplitude have been the dominant feature of recent Canadian business cycle history. Business cycles often become associated with particular events: eg, the Korean War expansion and a natural resource boom in Canada in the early 1950s; the Eisenhower recession of 1959; the oil crisis of the early 1970s; and the monetary contraction of the early 1980s. The trough in economic activity in 1982, while part of a wavelike pattern, was accentuated by policies which acted to deepen the business cycle beyond what otherwise might have occurred. Such policies included the high nominal and real interest rates introduced by most Western governments during this period.
DONALD G. PATERSON

Reading: W.L. Marr and Donald G. Paterson, *Canada: An Economic History* (1980).

Business Education In the 1985-86 school year there were 45 543 full-time and 31 707 part-time students enrolled in bachelors programs in business offered by Canadian universities, amounting to 12.0% and 14.4% of undergraduate enrolment respectively. Full-time community college enrolment in business subjects was 65 066, or 29% of total enrolment in these institutions.

A vast variety of continuing-education courses in all areas of business, available through postsecondary institutions, professional bodies (eg, the Institute of Chartered Accountants and the CANADIAN BANKERS' ASSN), management consulting firms and in-house organizatons, are offered to practising managers in the private and public sectors of the economy. In recent years female enrolment in these programs has increased significantly. For example, in the period 1970-71 women represented only 9.5% of total business undergraduate involvement. By 1985-86 this had increased to 62% (up from 39% in 1981). These changes are indicative of the shifts that will occur in the next 20 years in the sex composition of managerial occupations.

In Canada university undergraduate degrees in business administration are generally designated as bachelors of commerce (B Comm). The first B Comm degree in Canada was granted by Queen's University in 1919, 2 years after a commerce program was introduced. Fifty-five Canadian universities now offer undergraduate business de-grees. Undergraduate business education prior to the mid-1960s was heavily, though not exclusively, oriented to training people for ACCOUNTING, particularly those intending to become chartered accountants. While substantial numbers of commerce graduates still aspire to professional accountancy, the design of university business programs changed as a result of two 1959 reports (Gordon-Howell and Pierson, sponsored respectively by the Ford and Carnegie foundations). The reports emphasized that the primary objective of higher education in business should be student development of the requisites for managerial competence. The present curriculum focuses on problem identification and problem solving, and their relationship to managerial decision making. As well, the recognition that many factors external to an organization (eg, fiscal and monetary policies, changes in statutes and new interpretations of constitutional law) will strongly influence the options open to management has revolutionized business education and has resulted in major curriculum reform, a significant increase in the academic qualifications of teaching staff and an increase in research, which had been almost totally lacking.

Students in undergraduate business courses are required to take a program incorporating courses in general education with others more narrowly professional. General education courses, eg, those in the humanities, social sciences (including economics) and in quantitative analysis and analytical reasoning, will typically comprise about 40-60% of the student's program. The core of the curriculum will include the study of behaviour in organizations, the design and structure of organizations, managerial and financial accounting, finance, marketing and production management. A student may major in any one of these areas, or may choose to pursue a general business degree. Courses concerning law, business-government relations and business policy and strategic planning are mandatory. There is also an increasing tendency to regard a course in international business as mandatory.

In the 1985-86 school year, there were 4079 full-time and 4856 part-time students enrolled in MBA programs (12.7% and 15.2% enrolment respectively of all master's programs). Of those in MBA programs, 29% were female. There are now 30 Canadian universities offering MBA programs. This is a professional rather than an academic graduate degree, and is designed for students of differing educational backgrounds, eg, in liberal arts, science, engineering, who wish to pursue a professional career in management. The MBA is a 2-year degree. The first year covers the core foundation and functional areas of managerial training (quantitative reasoning, organizational structure and behaviour, managerial and aggregative economics, accounting, finance and marketing); the second year normally combines required courses in organizational policy formation and execution, and in the impact of public policy upon the business organization, with a number of elective options.

Business Education in the Future Business schools have been praised for producing superb analysts and business theorists (for applying the tools of rational analysis to decision making), but severely criticized for failure to encourage innovative and experimental thinking, to come to grips with the process of making decisions, and in general for failing to recognize that management is also an art. What is likely to emerge in business programs is an effort to reconcile the past Gordon-Howell and Pierson emphasis on rational analysis with the need to remedy these identified deficiencies.
EDWARD J. CHAMBERS

Business Elites The role of business ELITES has never been as straightforward in Canadian society as it has in countries with longer histories and more clearly defined class systems. The Canadian "Establishment" (also known as the Economic Elite, Corporate Elite and Business Elite) constitutes a loosely knit group of contenders for economic, political and cultural power. Although its structure and sources of authority are constantly in flux, the members of the group tightly control the country's decision-making processes.

Economic power in Canada has shifted according to the way money has been made, eg, furs, railways, banking, mining, oil, microchips, fast food and financial services. At the same time, Canada's economic centre of gravity has shifted from Montréal to Toronto, where it largely remains, despite some minor movement westward.

The very existence of an Establishment – a cabal of power brokers bent on what Lord Russell called "the production of intended effects" – runs contrary to the traditional notion of Canada as a land of freely accessible opportunities. To reinforce this notion, even the most outspoken power wielders strenuously disavow any mutual benefits derived from their elitist credentials. In fact, they seldom need to conspire among themselves because their interests so seldom conflict.

Most Canadians tend to view the class system – if they think of it at all – as a reference to ways of life or levels of sophistication. The common misconception that everyone belongs to what George Orwell called "the lower-upper-middle class" – a class that can provide its offspring with the advantages of education but not much in the way of inherited wealth or social position – was not challenged until 1965, when John PORTER published his monumental VERTICAL MOSAIC, a detailed examination of Canada's power structure in the 1950s. Porter revealed dramatic inequalities of income and opportunity among Canadians, demonstrating that only about 10% of Canadian families could actually afford the middle-class life-style then considered average. He argued that the corporate elite (only 6.6% of whom were French Canadian) was rooted in 183 dominant corporations that controlled the majority of economic activities. Power was held by a predominantly Anglo-Saxon economic elite of only a few hundred; ethnic origin was virtually as significant in determining membership in the elite in 1951 as it had been in 1885 and 1910.

Porter also demonstrated that the majority of Canadian political leaders were middle class in origin. He wrote, "The upper class doesn't seem attracted to the turbulence of politics and, in any case, the privileges they enjoy are not threatened by the holders of political power. Nor is there any tradition of working-class participation in politics. I think the real problem with Canada is that its political system is ineffective to cope with national problems. It leaves the definition of major goals – and therefore the power – to the corporate elite...Although it has a class structure peculiar to its own history and geography, Canada is probably not unlike other Western industrial nations in relying heavily on its elite groups to make major decisions and to determine the shape and direction of its development...Power arises because of the general social need for order. Everyone in society has a set of expectations about how others will behave. Among such ordered relationships are those which grant the right to a few people to make decisions on behalf of the group." Porter's original thesis was expanded and brought up to date a decade later by Wallace Clement, who concluded that "Canada has been and remains a society controlled by elites. With increasing economic concentration over the past twenty years, the structure has become increasingly closed, thus making it more difficult for those outside the inner circles of power to break through."

Because they have deliberately set themselves apart from the politicians, members of Canada's business elite exercise a mandate virtually bereft of public accountability. Many of the wealthiest individuals escape to offshore tax havens; others lobby strenuously for the protection of their privileges (*see* PRESSURE GROUPS) and, in fact, their efforts have not been unsuccessful. Canada has one of the lowest corporate tax rates of any industrialized country. Although collectively the corporate elite endow universities, preserve landmarks, donate artworks and raise money for appropriate charities, the impulse toward creative generosity is hardly overwhelming; corporate charitable donations account for only 2% of corporate profits.

Canada's Establishment is composed of overlapping rings of power. While no social compact exists, a confederacy of regional elite groupings – loosely knit yet interlocking – comprises a psychological entity. Its members share habits of thought, values and enemies.

Unlike the power of the political and cultural elites, economic power is usually handed down through the generations. Cradled in an Indian summer of extended adolescence, the children of the rich learn early that established family wealth (with its palace guard of legal retainers, chartered accountants and investment counsellors) is not so much for spending on private fripperies as for influencing positions and events.

By the early 1980s the hereditary pews of the business Establishment were filled with a new breed of ambitious crown princes, symbolized by the death of John Angus "Bud" MCDOUGALD in 1978 and the capture of his ARGUS empire by Conrad BLACK. "Canada is widely assumed to be an egalitarian society, but the extent to which rich men's sons dominated the financial news in the 1970s was absolutely astonishing," Alexander Ross noted in *Canadian Business*. "It was almost as though control of major portions of the Canadian economy were being passed on, like family memberships in the Granite Club."

Like the charter members of every elite, Canada's decision makers disavow the possession of power even if they value its exercise. They are accustomed to running things, promoting those men (and very occasionally those women) recognized as reliable. Much of this process operates through negative sanctions; the overly ambitious or unsuitable interloper is blocked by invisible but unbreachable barriers. This system of sanctions operates through the exclusive clubs, private schools and other elite institutions that close and open their doors according to sets of unspoken values that can be called Canadian mainly because they cannot properly be described as anything else. There are certain people who, no matter how many deals they make with Establishment firms, no matter how often they best their competitors, will never be part of its world. They and many others are the victims of the Establishment's most potent weapon: the power to exclude. This ability to withhold favours is most frequently exercised through the "Big Five" chartered banks – the Royal, the Commerce, the Bank of Montreal, the Toronto Dominion and the Bank of Nova Scotia (*see* BANKING). Even during the depths of the recession of the early 1980s, when their own balance sheets looked shaky, the bankers continued to exercise papal control over the Canadian economy. The executive board meetings of the 5 largest banks represent the greatest source of nongovernmental power in Canada. During these deliberations, personal relationships through which the economic elite consolidates its existence and swells its authority are formed, strengthened and multiplied.

Canada is held together through the influence of a relatively tiny coterie of power wielders, but power is a difficult commodity to isolate in Canadian society. The definition of it as the "ability to compel obedience" is not broad enough to describe how it is exercised in Canada; neither is Max Weber's view of power as "the chance of a man or a group or a number of men to realize their own will in a communal action, even against the resistance of others who are participating in it." C. Wright Mill's "power elite" theory is not really relevant, because Canada has no significant military industrial complex – no group of centurions sliding in and out of a Pentagon, a state department, a White House or the equivalent of a Ford Foundation or Council on Foreign Relations. There is no cabal comparable to the Pittsburgh Mellons strong enough to control any region, although the McCains and Irvings approach that stature in the closed duchy of NB.

The Canadian business elite is also distinguished by the fact that so much important decision making is exercised by surrogates. Two-thirds of Canada's 100 largest corporations are owned outside the country. Even if local managers exercise apparent autonomy, their authority is not final – they answer to outside boards of directors. The chief executive officers who run these companies must act as colonial administrators. Most, though not all, American companies treat Canada as a slightly backward acreage of their northern sales territories, reflecting the comment by Jacques Maisonrouge, head of the IBM World Trade Corporation, that "for business purposes, the boundaries that separate one nation from another are no more real than that of the equator."

Few members of Canada's business elite have resisted Canada's Americanization. In fact, it may be the only national elite in history that has cheerfully participated in its own demise. The attitude of E.P. TAYLOR, one of the most successful Canadian entrepreneurs of his day, was typical: "If it weren't for the racial issue in the US and the political problems they have, I would think that the two countries could come together....I'm against this trend of trying to reduce American ownership in Canadian companies. I think nature has to take its course."

This let's-surrender-with-profit syndrome has prevented Canada's capitalist class from attaining any clear perspective of itself and its long-term role. Northrop FRYE has interpreted this colonial attitude as frostbite on the roots of the Canadian imagination. "Colonialism," he has written, "produces a disease for which I think the best name is prudery. By this I do not mean reticence in sexual matters. I mean the instinct to seek a conventional or commonplace expression of an idea." Frye's description of the prudery of spirit, the snobbish modesty and the reluctance to take risks characterizes Canada's elite. National power grids of enormous corporations have replaced traditional family control of wealth and power (except in the Maritimes). Many of the most influential men in Canadian cities and towns no longer belong to local power clusters but are instead the ambassadors of large multinational or transnational corporations. Their loyalty to Canada is at best ambivalent; their dollars seek the highest rate of return regardless of the implications that this may have for the country.

Because they believe so implicitly in themselves, most members of the corporate elite are seldom able to distinguish between the public interest and their own. However, for an Establishment to flex its muscles freely requires the kind of compliant political authority Canada has not always elected. The private sector's leaders demand that their parliamentary representatives

"maintain investor confidence," ie, laws should be enacted and enforced for the business community's benefit. The business elite believes that the only good government is one willing to grant their efforts unbridled rein. Occasionally this happens – for example, the business-government axis forged during WWII by C.D. HOWE.

By the 1980s, the conflict between government and the private sector was growing bitter. The business community reacted to the initiatives of the TRUDEAU government with self-righteous rage. The federal LIBERAL PARTY, determined to find policy initiatives that might maintain them in their accustomed perch of power, abandoned their traditional stance which in the past had allowed them to strike the most marketable balance between elitism and egalitarianism. Their new mood was reflected in the NATIONAL ENERGY PROGRAM, designed to restore some of the control of Canada's most vital industry to Canadians (*see* ENERGY POLICY). The business elite, interpreting such actions as massive interference in the "free" flow of market forces, reacted with outraged threats of exodus, and under the succeeding Mulroney government, these policies were quickly reversed.

Capitalism is concerned above all with the promotion of economic efficiency, but social democracies are concerned with other objectives as well, eg, a more equitable distribution of wealth. With governments less willing to sponsor indiscriminate corporate handouts and businessmen becoming increasingly opposed to satisfying the demands for the expansion of social services, the 2 value systems continued to drift apart. Under Brian Mulroney the tension between Ottawa and the business community was largely diffused.

PETER C. NEWMAN

Reading: W. Clement, *The Canadian Corporate Elite* (1975); M. Fraser, *Quebec Inc: French Canadian Entrepreneurs and the New Business Elite* (1987); Peter C. Newman, *The Canadian Establishment* (2 vols, 1975, 1981).

Business History, defined as the written record of the activities of individuals and enterprises seeking private profit through the production of goods and services, has deep roots in Canadian history, although it has matured only recently.

The evolution of Canada's business structure – encompassing enterprises, businessmen and business practices – dates from the earliest European contact with the continent. The Atlantic FISHERIES and the FUR TRADE were developed by French and English merchants exercising their metropolitan influence through such companies as the COMPAGNIE DES CENT-ASSOCIÉS (fd 1627) and the HUDSON'S BAY COMPANY (fd 1670). The progressive development of fur, timber and wheat staples provided the backbone of early Canadian business development, eg, large fur trading companies (the NORTH WEST COMPANY, *c*1780-1821), timber companies (Mossom Boyd and Company fd *c*1848) and wheat traders (the Richardson family of Kingston). From these central enterprises, ancillary activities developed. Diversification stimulated the emergence of BANKING (BANK OF MONTREAL, 1817), early manufacturing (Montreal Nail and Spike Works, 1839) and service industries (John Molson's Montréal brewing, banking and steamboat enterprises, *c*1810).

Early Canadian entrepreneurs did not function in an environment of unbridled free enterprise. The state exercised a formative role from the beginning. Mercantilist legislation (the English NAVIGATION ACTS), commercial policy (Galt's 1859 tariff) and financial guarantees (GUARANTEE ACT, 1849) all influenced the businessman's risk-taking. In this light, Confederation may be viewed as the equipping of the federal government with powers to create a transcontinental commercial nation. Tariff increases arising from the NATIONAL

POLICY of 1879 stimulated Canadian manufacturing, both Canadian-owned (Massey, fd 1847) and foreign-owned (Canadian Rand Drill Company, fd 1889). The combination of turn-of-the-century prosperity, new staples such as western wheat and pulp and paper, and the impact of urbanization fostered the creation of new enterprises. HYDROELECTRICITY, for instance, prompted the establishment of Canadian Westinghouse in 1903. The period saw the creation of new companies through mergers (STELCO, 1910).

The 20th century has seen the elaboration of the established pattern of staples exploitation (nickel, iron ore) together with the introduction of new technologies (automobiles, aviation, electronics). Manufacturing has generally remained the preserve of central Canada, where indigenous industry has been overshadowed by FOREIGN INVESTMENT. The state continued to influence business through competition, taxation and labour policies as well as by entering the marketplace itself through crown corporations (TRANS-CANADA AIRLINES, est 1937). Canadian companies have prospered as conglomerates (Power Corporation, GEORGE WESTON LIMITED) or as purveyors of unique technology (BOMBARDIER INC, est 1942) or in specified precincts such as broadcasting and banking.

Historians have interpreted these developments in a variety of ways. The central role of staple trades attracted early attention. D.G. CREIGHTON's *The Commercial Empire of the St. Lawrence* (1937) and H.A. INNIS's 1930 study, *The Fur Trade in Canada*, followed in 1940 by *The Cod Fisheries*, placed businessmen and their aspirations and activities in a broad national framework. Although akin to ECONOMIC HISTORY in their macroeconomic reach, these works contained much detail on Canada's earliest large enterprises. Such thematic treatments have been perpetuated by journalists (Peter NEWMAN, *The Canadian Establishment*, 2 vols, 1975 and 1981), sociologists (Wallace Clement, *The Canadian Corporate Elite*, 1975) and economists (R.T. Naylor, *History of Canadian Business*, 1975), all of whom seek to portray the business community as the tightly knit, all-powerful upper stratum of Canadian society (*see* BUSINESS ELITES).

On a microeconomic level, Canadian business historians have produced a varied collection of company histories and biographies which range from hagiography to credible scholarship. Such company-sponsored histories as William Kilbourn's *The Elements Combined* (1960) on Stelco, E.P. Neufeld's study of MASSEY-FERGUSON (*A Global Corporation*, 1969) and Shirley E. Woods's, *The Molson Saga* (1983) set a high standard. Journalistic company histories, such as those of Merrill Denison (*The People's Power*, 1960) frequently verge on uncritical exercises in public relations. Others appearing at times of corporate crisis (Peter Cook, *Massey at the Brink*, 1981; Peter Foster, *Other People's Money: The Banks, The Government and Dome*, 1983), display competence but often treat historical research as a backdrop to examining present business problems. Few industry studies exist, an exception being O.W. Main's 1955 study, *The Canadian Nickel Industry*. Biographies of Sir Joseph FLAVELLE (Michael Bliss, *A Canadian Millionaire*, 1978) and C.D. HOWE, a businessman in politics (William Kilbourn and Robert Bothwell, *C.D. Howe*, 1980), serve to reverse the past tradition of business biography as puffery. Royal commissions reports (CORPORATE CONCENTRATION, 1978) frequently contain useful sections on business history.

Research in business history has generally been impeded by business suspicion, academic condescension and archival neglect. Furthermore, the writing of business history in Canada has tended to focus too exclusively on the forward and back-ward linkages of the staple trades, ignoring other areas of economic growth (eg, the spread of Canadian banking and electric utilities abroad). Despite the contributions of expatriate Canadians such as N.S.B. Gras (1884-1956) and H.G.J. Aitken (1922-) to the study of business enterprise abroad, Canadian business history lags behind its British and American counterparts. Many gaps exist; studies of business failure, individual companies, business-government relations, the role of foreign investment, the evolution of corporate law and management and labour relations all merit attention.

Innovative work has nonetheless been produced. H.V. Nelles's 1974 study, *The Politics of Development*, on the Ontario hydroelectric industry, and Tom Traves's 1979 examination, *The State and Enterprise*, of the interaction of business and the state after WWI, both break new ground (eg, in analysing the businessman's dynamic role in FEDERAL-PROVINCIAL RELATIONS). Popular business histories such as Philip Smith's *The Treasure-Seekers* (Home Oil, 1978), Donald MacKay's *Empire of Wood* (MacMillan Bloedel, 1982) and Peter C. Newman's *Company of Adventurers*, 1985, and *Caesars of the Wilderness*, 1987 (Hudson's Bay Co) have broadened business history readership. Labour historians frequently touch on business concerns, such as the fractious labour-management relations of the Cape Breton steel industry. Québec business historians have tended to focus on broad themes such as the province's "economic inferiority" (Yves Roby, *Les Québécois et les investissements américains*, 1976, and René Durocher and Paul-André Linteau, *Le "Retard" du Québec et l'infériorité économique des Canadiens français*, 1971). The Montreal Business History Project (est 1976) is the first collective attempt to chronicle the evolution of business in one of Canada's leading commercial centres.

Despite these advances, no journal of business history or dictionary of business biography exists in Canada. Future development will depend on greater interest and co-operation from the business community, the pursuit of academic excellence in the field and, possibly, the growth of business history as "public history" (eg, corporate archives, use of business history as a facet of business administration programs).

DUNCAN MCDOWALL

Reading: Michael Bliss, *Northern Enterprise: Five Centuries of Canadian Business* (1987); D.S. Macmillan, ed, *Canadian Business History: Selected Studies, 1497-1971* (1972); G. Porter and R. Cuff, eds, *Enterprise and National Development* (1973).

Business Management is the problem-solving process of planning, co-ordination and control of a business. A business is an organization that produces and sells products, has assets and liabilities, and must be profitable and liquid in the long run if it is to survive. To do this, it must create value by producing products that have a higher value for its customers than its costs of production. Solving the problems that confront a business in its role as a value-creating organization is the overall task of business management.

Business management is vitally important for the Canadian economy. In 1986, most of Canada's whole labour force of 12 870 000 was employed in the public sector. Businesses accounted for over 85% of nonresidential gross fixed capital formation, and for almost all of Canada's exports and imports. Good business management is also important for the efficient and effective operations of government-owned enterprises such as Air Canada, Canada Post and Petro-Canada and organizations such as schools, universities and hospitals. Without an efficient, competitive business sector, Canada's economy would cease to grow and its standard of living would fall. Yet Canadian business is under increasing competitive pressure from businesses in the US, Europe, the PACIFIC RIM and S America.

Business managers must have knowledge and expertise in the 5 functional areas of business (production, marketing, personnel, finance and accounting), as well as in research and development. Production managers purchase and take inventory of raw materials and semifinished inputs, manage the use of these inputs in the production process, and control final goods inventory and the shipping, transportation and distribution of final products. Marketing managers conduct research to determine which products, at which prices and quantities and with which characteristics will create value for consumers, and manage the advertising, promotion and sales of the firm's products. Personnel managers hire, train, evaluate, promote and chart the careers of the firm's production, administrative and management personnel. Financial managers raise capital for the firm from external sources such as the stock market, banks, individuals and the public-debt market, manage the internal flow of funds within the firm, and evaluate capital expenditures for plant and equipment and research and development. Management accountants collect and evaluate cost data on wages, equipment and materials inputs, and combine them with sales data to calculate the firm's profits or losses and taxes. Research and development managers manage the development of new process technology to increase production efficiency and the development of new product technology to expand the range, quality and performance of the firm's products. One of the most important aspects of business management is to ensure that all employees possess the information, skills, attitudes and motivation to use their full potential in furthering the firm's success.

Crucial to the firm's success is an overall business strategy. Top managers assess the strengths and weaknesses of the firm in relation to its competitors at home and abroad; set the firm's objectives and goals; formulate and implement the firm's strategy; and assess the success of the firm in creating value for its various constituents. Top management influences the corporate management style, the "corporate culture," of interpersonal relationships and values within the firm. Top management is also responsible for the management of the firm's relations with various levels of government and with the general public.

If business management in one area fails, it is difficult for the firm to survive. In the early 1980s, the after-tax profits of Canadian firms were only about 5% of sales; consequently small errors in any area or level of management could easily lead to losses and ultimately to BANKRUPTCY; about 1% of all businesses went bankrupt each year during this period.

Although each aspect of business management is important, the relative emphasis on each within a firm depends on the firm's competitive strategy, the industry and country in which it operates. Business management differs among banks, retail stores, and manufacturing companies, as well as among firms in Canada, the US, Japan, the Soviet Union and China. Business management in Canada has developed unique characteristics because of Canada's geography, economy, and political, social and cultural system and history.

Business Management in Canada Because Canada has a very large geographic area but a small, dispersed population, government has been involved extensively in infrastructure development: roads, railways, electric power – and in industrial development. Government influence is more pervasive at the firm, industry and economy-wide levels in Canada than in the US: the decisions of business managers in Canada are more circumscribed by government regulations, but Canadian business managers are also more likely to seek government assistance than are their American counterparts.

Canada's relatively small, dispersed markets and its proximity to the large, high-income US market may partly explain why Canadian business managers are relatively risk-averse compared to managers in other countries. New products and processes have often been developed and introduced in the US and subsequently transferred to Canada. Research and development expenditures as a percentage of Gross Domestic Product (GDP) in Canada are less than half those of Canada's major trading partners. This relatively low level of technological development, combined with the relatively small-scale firms and plants needed to serve Canada's protected domestic markets, has led to a relatively low level of productivity and productivity growth rate in the manufacturing sector.

Under the NATIONAL POLICY of PM John A. Macdonald, relatively high tariffs were placed around Canada's MANUFACTURING sector to protect it and to promote industrial development. Foreign, especially American, firms invested in Canada to circumvent these tariffs and sell their products in the Canadian market and to gain access to Canada's plentiful natural and agricultural resources (*see* CANADIAN-AMERICAN RELATIONS, ECONOMIC). Consequently, FOREIGN INVESTMENT in Canada's mining and manufacturing sectors is extensive (almost 60% of total assets in the early 1970s, and 40% by the mid-1980s). Foreign ownership of Canadian firms may have had the effect of reducing the scope, independence, authority and flexibility of Canadian business managers in foreign-owned subsidiaries over key decisions for the firm. These decisions are frequently made abroad at the head offices of the multinational enterprise. Some critics of the high level of foreign ownership in Canada have also charged that it has stunted the development of Canadian entrepreneurs and Canadian-owned businesses; foreign-owned firms often hire the "best and the brightest" of Canadian managers and foreign direct investment in Canadian firms has had the effect of reducing investment by Canadians, who feel threatened by the perceived technological, financial and management superiority of foreign-owned subsidiaries.

Compared with Canadian-owned firms, US firms have a larger percentage of managers with university educations and with formal education in business and commerce at the undergraduate and master's levels. In the past, and especially in Canadian-owned firms, promotion to the top ranks of business management in Canada was more often based on experience with the firm and on family background than on educational achievement, performance and initiative (*see* ELITES). This situation has been changing as the number of business-school graduates has increased in Canada. Yet by the mid-1980s Canada still had less than 5% of the number of bachelor's and master's graduates in commerce and business administration that the US had, and only 1% of the doctoral graduates in business administration (*see* BUSINESS EDUCATION).

INDUSTRIAL RELATIONS is another distinctive feature of business management in Canada. Canadian business has a generally poor record of days lost to STRIKES. A relatively high percentage of workers, especially in the public sector, are unionized in Canada, and unions tend to be more militant in Canada than in the US; management tends to be more rigid, formal and confrontational and less progressive in its relations with workers than management in the US, Europe (with the exception of the UK) and Japan. This situation has led not only to a generally higher level of strikes but also to greater rigidity in work rules, overmanning and lower productivity, and to high wage costs in some industries.

Future of Business Management Canada is a trading nation (30% of GDP is exported) and INTERNATIONAL TRADE has become more competitive as transportation and communications costs and tariff and nontariff barriers to trade have fallen and as the production and export capabilities of firms in countries around the world have increased. Canadian business managers must be able to manage their firms so that they can compete worldwide with these firms both in export markets and in the Canadian market, despite higher capital costs, taxes, welfare payments and government intervention, a more difficult labour situation, lower levels of formal business education and technological expertise, and a generally inward-looking manufacturing sector utilizing subscale plants and equipment. This situation will challenge Canadian business management to increase the productivity of capital, labour and raw materials utilization; to introduce and develop an increasing number of new products and processes; to expand plant scale and rationalize operations; and to become more export oriented in their business operations. As well, business management must be able to deal with problems arising out of political, economic, social, technological and international environments that affect the firm's operations and strategy. For example, the CANADIAN MANUFACTURERS' ASSOCIATION has supported the initiative for freer trade with the US in the belief that it would expand their opportunities to compete head to head with foreign firms in markets abroad and in Canada.

DONALD J. LECRAW

Reading: P.F. Drucker, *Managing in Turbulent Times* (1980); R.H. Waterman and T.J. Peters, *In Search of Excellence* (1982); J.A. Humphrey et al, *An Introduction to Business Decision Making* (1981).

Butchart, Robert Pim, industrialist (b at Owen Sound, Canada W 30 Mar 1856; d at Victoria 27 Oct 1943). Educated in Owen Sound, he joined his father's hardware business. In 1888 he began the Owen Sound Portland Cement Co. He moved to BC in 1904, and at Tod Inlet, near Victoria, established the first Portland cement plant in BC. He eventually had interests in several cement mills in Canada, including mills at Calgary and Montréal, and in the US. During WWI he directed the Shipbuilding Dept of the IMPERIAL MUNITIONS BOARD in BC. In 1884 he married Jennie Foster Kennedy of Toronto. She turned the abandoned quarries surrounding her home into Butchart Gardens, now a famous tourist attraction.   PATRICIA E. ROY

Butler, Edith, singer-composer-interpreter (b at Paquetville, near Caraquet, NB 27 July 1942). Through her stormy songs and her expressive warmth, she helps spread Acadian culture. She studied ethnography at Laval (1966-69). Since 1973 she has composed her own music which has evolved from pure folk to a marriage with spirited rock and roll. She sang at the International Exposition at Osaka, Japan (1970), and has toured Europe and taken part in many festivals. She is cofounder of Éditions de l'Acadie, of Acalf (Aide à la création artistique et littéraire de la femme) and of the record publishing company, SPPS (Société de production et de programmation de spectacles). She has won the award of the Académie Charles-Cros in Paris (1984), received the Ordre du Mérite de la culture française from the Canadian Senate (1971), the Order of Canada (1975) and is a knight of the Order de la Pleiade (1978). By 1987 she had issued 11 albums of Acadian material.

HÉLÈNE PLOUFFE

Butler, Sir William Francis, military officer, author (b at Ballyslateen, Suirville, Ireland 31 Oct 1838; d at Bansha Castle, Ireland 7 June 1910). As intelligence officer to the 1870 RED RIVER EXPEDITION, Butler preceded the force to the settlement, then travelled by canoe and YORK BOAT to Ft Frances to meet Sir Garnet WOLSELEY. Commissioned to report on conditions in the Saskatchewan R country, he made a 6000 km trip to Ft Carlton and Rocky Mountain House which he recounted in *The* GREAT LONE LAND (1872). Another trip from Ft Garry to Ft St John, through the Rockies, and down the Fraser R to the Pacific inspired *The Wild North Land* (1873).   O.A. COOKE

45 species of buttercup (*Ranunculus*) occur in Canada (*artwork by Claire Tremblay*).

Buttercup, common name for several herbaceous plants of genus *Ranunculus*, family Ranunculaceae [Lat, "little frog," from wet habitat]. An estimated 600 species occur in north temperate and arctic regions, with a few species in tropical alpine zones. In Canada 45 species occur, of which 7 are introduced Eurasian weeds. Buttercups have alternate, simple or deeply divided, compound leaves, the latter being the source of another common name, crowfoot. A few are aquatic, bearing much-divided leaves. About 40 species are cultivated as ORNAMENTALS, 2 or 3 of these being double-petalled forms. Buttercups are acrid in taste, or even poisonous. Flowers are usually yellow, but may be white or, rarely, red. The shiny petals have a nectar pit or scale at the base. Stamens and pistils are numerous, pistils being arranged spirally on an elongated axis or receptacle. After fertilization, the pistils ripen into hard fruits (achenes). *See also* POISONOUS PLANTS.

J.M. GILLETT

Butterfly, term referring to insects of order Lepidoptera [Gk, "scaly wings"]. The Canadian fauna includes 272 known species, compared to 695 known from N America as a whole, and over 20 000 worldwide. Possibly about 60 species remain to be discovered or recorded in Canada. Butterflies are characterized by having antennae that are knobbed or hooked at the tips. They fly by day and are usually brightly coloured. Species found in Canada are varied in size, wingspans

The Monarch caterpillar, with its brilliant black and yellow stripes (*photo by Bill Ivy*).

The mature Monarch larva hangs inverted from a suitable plant, in the form of a lovely green chrysalis (the pupa) (*photo by Bill Ivy*).

An adult Monarch butterfly emerges from the pupal skin. It takes 10 to 20 minutes for the wings to spread, dry and stiffen (*photo by Bill Ivy*).

ranging from under 2.5 cm to 7.5 cm. Adults have a long, hollow tongue (proboscis) and usually feed on nectar. Larvae of all butterflies in Canada feed on vegetation. The life cycle of a given species may require from a few weeks to 2 years to complete, and it involves a complete metamorphosis through egg, larva (caterpillar) and pupa (chrysalis) to adult. Different families have characteristically shaped and marked eggs, which are usually laid on a host plant, singly or in batches of up to 300. Species differ in ways of overwintering: most pass the winter in the egg, larval or pupal stage, but a few (eg, mourning cloak and Milbert's tortoiseshell) overwinter as adults. Butterflies inhabit all areas of Canada where flowering plants occur. Their numbers diminish northwards, down to about 16 species in the Arctic. Although some species (eg, red admiral and common sulphur) are widely distributed, others are confined to particular habitats or geographical regions. Monarch and painted lady butterflies migrate to Canada from the US.

Butterfly populations are controlled by inclement weather, diseases, parasites, predators and habitat suitability. Cool, sunless summers and mild, damp winters are particularly detrimental. Birds consume many caterpillars and adults, while dragonflies and spiders also take their toll. Diseases can be particularly rife when population densities are high, but the many parasitic flies and wasps that regularly prey on caterpillars probably exert the greatest natural control. Larvae of some species of blues and hairstreaks are tended by ants for the honeydew they secrete, and probably receive some protection from other insects. Natural controls are necessary and probably do not threaten the existence of butterflies. However, destruction of natural habitats, large-scale spraying to control economic pests and, possibly, ACID RAIN are manmade hazards that could have far-reaching, detrimental effects on Canada's butterfly fauna.

Although butterflies are generally harmless to human interests, a few are pests. Larvae of cabbage white butterflies are a widely distributed pest of plants of the cabbage family, while another accidentally introduced butterfly, the European skipper, has become a pest of hayfields. Occasionally, others may become a local nuisance when unusually high population levels develop. Butterflies are useful in plant POLLINATION, in providing food for other creatures, and as indicators of environmental stability. They are a source of scientific and recreational interest, bringing charm and beauty to wherever they live. *See also* MONARCH BUTTERFLY. BERNARD S. JACKSON

Button, Sir Thomas, seaman, explorer (b in Wales; d probably at Worleton, Eng 1634). In 1612 he was chosen to command an expedition to determine the fate of Henry HUDSON, though no mention of this was made in his written instructions, which directed him to search out the NORTHWEST PASSAGE. With the *Resolution* and DISCOVERY he sailed through Hudson Str and across Hudson Bay to a point he called "Hopes Checkt." He wintered at the mouth of a river he named for Robert Nelson, master of the *Resolution*, who among others had perished there. In the spring he examined the W coast of the bay and discovered Mansel I, which he named for a friend. Frustrated in his hope of finding an outlet from the bay, he sailed home. For years Hudson Bay was called Button Bay. Button served ably and with courage throughout his career and was made "Admiral upon the Irish Coast." JAMES MARSH

By, John, lt-col, Royal Engineers (b at Lambeth, Eng and bap 10 Aug 1779; d at Frant, Eng 1 Feb 1836). By was one of the greatest early engineers in Canada. He built the 200 km RIDEAU CANAL

Tiger swallowtail butterfly (*photo by Mary W. Ferguson*).

(1826-32) from Bytown (named for him, now Ottawa) to Kingston, involving construction of about 50 dams and 47 masonry locks. Without the aid of modern construction equipment, it was completed in 5 summer working seasons. By was born into a family of Thames watermen but was admitted in 1797 to the Royal Military Academy, Woolwich. Commissioned in 1799, he served for 2 years at Plymouth before being sent to Canada in 1802. Here he worked on the first small locks on the St Lawrence R and on the FORTIFICATIONS of Québec. Returning to England late in 1811, he served briefly under Wellington in the Peninsular War but early in 1812 was appointed engineer officer for the Royal Gunpowder Mills. Soon after the victory at Waterloo, munitions requirements being minimal, he was retired, but he was recalled in 1826 to build the Rideau Canal. On returning to England in 1832, despite his superb achievement, he was criticized by the Treasury Board for some allegedly unauthorized expenditures. He died, a broken man, 3 years later. R.F. LEGGET

Bye-boat (by-boat), a name applied historically to any small inshore fishing craft, usually an open boat carrying 5-10 men, used in Newfoundland in the bye-boat fishery. Bye-boat operators or keepers were a large and significant factor in the Newfoundland cod fishery from the mid-1600s until the beginning of the 1800s. They usually competed with the larger fish merchant firms, although sometimes a merchant would outfit the operator and buy his catch. The bye-boat keeper and the fishing servants he employed travelled to his "fishing room" in Newfoundland each summer as passengers on a fishing ship. He and his crew would fish for the summer from one or two bye-boats he kept there, usually selling the cured catch to a fishing ship before returning to England in the autumn. A couple of men might be hired to remain in Newfoundland over the winter to protect the boats and room *See also* FISHERIES HISTORY. ROBERT D. PITT

Byelorussians, like RUSSIANS and UKRAINIANS, are an eastern Slavic people. Byelorussia is now a constituent republic of the USSR, although it existed as a separate country from as early as the 13th century. As the Byelorussian Soviet Socialist Republic (BSSR) it encompasses 207 600 km^2 and has a population of some 10 million. According to one source, 3 Byelorussians settled in Canada in 1817. It has also been argued that some of the POLES who served in Canada with the De Watteville regiment were actually Byelorussians. (Byelorussia was part of Poland from 1569 to 1772, and again from 1921 to 1939).

At the beginning of the 20th century, according to Soviet sources, Byelorussians immigrated to Canada in large numbers. The majority of the immigrants were peasants and were considered, officially, as Russians. After WWI, western Byelorussia was temporarily under Polish rule. It may be assumed that Polish immigrants to Canada included, in 1927, 3500 Byelorussians; in 1928, 3800; in 1929, 5100; and in 1930, 4200.

Among the first Byelorussians to immigrate to Canada after WWII were soldiers from the Polish Second Command who were recruited by Canadian agriculturalists as "agricultural workers." Of the 2800 recruited, 2200 were probably Byelorussians; in 1947 some 800 more Byelorussians arrived in Canada. It can be estimated that Byelorussians comprised 60% of Polish immigrants from 1948 to 1956, and it is probable that as many as 48 000 Byelorussians immigrated between 1946 and 1971. The Byelorussians who immigrated in the postwar period varied in age and in socioeconomic, cultural and political background, and many possessed a sense of national consciousness. It was not until 1971 that Byelorussians were listed in the census. There are today some 100 000 Canadians of Byelorussian origin.

Settlement and Economic Life Byelorussians who arrived in Canada before WWI settled primarily in industrial cities, particularly in northern Ontario, where they worked as labourers. Many immigrants who arrived between the wars settled on the Prairies. In 1927 a group cleared land in Saskatchewan; both they and their children spoke pure Byelorussian.

The postwar immigrants (peasants, labourers, skilled workers, technicians and professionals) enjoyed better economic status and were geographically more mobile. Many Byelorussians are represented in medicine, engineering, broadcasting and academia. According to estimates, the majority of Byelorussians are in Ontario, followed by Alberta, BC, Manitoba and Québec.

Religious and Cultural Life The majority of Byelorussians belong to the Roman Catholic or Greek Orthodox churches, but some adhere to the United Church, Anglican and Baptist faiths, among others.

After WWII, nationality-conscious Byelorussians in Canada established various organizations, including the Byelorussian Canadian Alliance (1948) in Toronto, the Byelorussian National Committee (1950) in Winnipeg and the Alliance of Byelorussians (1952) in Montréal, and several monthly newsletters have been published. In 1969 the communal portion of a Byelorussian resort at Lk Manitouwabing, Ont, was opened, and it has become known as a Byelorussian village. "Byelorussian Week," first held in 1974, is now a tradition in Toronto.

Reading: John Sadouski, *A History of the Byelorussians in Canada* (1981).

Bylot, Robert, (*fl* 1610-16), English seaman, was the mate on HENRY HUDSON's ill-fated voyage of 1611. He was deprived of his rank just prior to the marooning of Hudson in James Bay, joined the mutineers, but was later pardoned, likely for his skill in bringing the ship home. In 1612-13 he sailed with Sir Thomas BUTTON to Hudson Bay. In 1615 and 1616, with William BAFFIN as pilot, he made 2 voyages in the DISCOVERY to the eastern Arctic. In the first, the 2 men demonstrated that Hudson Str was not the NORTHWEST PASSAGE. In the second, Smith, Jones and Lancaster sounds were

Glacier on Bylot Island, NWT, located off northeastern Baffin I (*photo by Stephen J. Krasemann/DRK Photo*)

located, and a "farthest north" was reached at 70°45', a record not broken for 236 years. Bylot was a skilled ice-pilot and a capable seaman, but little else is known of his life. KENNETH S. COATES

Bylot Island, 11 067 km², is nestled into the NE corner of BAFFIN I at the entrance to LANCASTER SOUND. Its southern aspect looks across Pond Inlet and Eclipse Sound; on the W it is divided from Baffin I by the narrow Navy Board Inlet. Bold, rugged coasts, glaciers and a high, mountainous interior have not been conducive to habitation. Inuit from Baffin I have visited seasonally and a trading station operated at Button Pt on the SE corner for several years after 1910, but there are no settlements today. To the E the island overlooks a part of BAFFIN BAY, which was much frequented by European whalers in the 19th and early 20th centuries. It was officially claimed as part of Canada by Capt J.E. BERNIER in 1906. The island is named after Robert BYLOT and today is a bird sanctuary for greater snow geese, thick-billed murres and other seabirds. DANIEL FRANCIS

Byng of Vimy, Julian Hedworth George, Viscount, governor general of Canada, 1921-26 (b at Wrotham Park, Eng 11 Sept 1862; d at Thorpe-le-Soken, Eng 6 June 1935). A British aristocrat and cavalry officer, Byng was appointed to command the Canadian Corps in May 1916. He directed it in the attack on VIMY RIDGE in Apr 1917 and was promoted to command the British 3rd Army. In 1921, the first time the Canadian government was formally consulted about the selection of a governor general, Byng was a prominent nominee. But PM Arthur MEIGHEN preferred someone of civilian experience. Byng was finally chosen because he was willing and available. In

Apr 1926 PM Mackenzie KING pronounced Byng the ideal governor; in June, however, Byng refused King's request for a dissolution of Parliament, precipitating the KING-BYNG AFFAIR. Byng had acted honestly and (in the view of most constitutional experts) correctly, but he departed from Canada under a shadow. His last major appointment was as chief commissioner of the London Metropolitan Police, 1928-31. Byng's wife Evelyn wrote movingly about Canada in *Up the Stream of Time* (1945). In 1925 she donated the LADY BYNG TROPHY, the National Hockey League's award for sportsmanship combined with excellence. O.A. COOKE AND NORMAN HILLMER

In 1926 Viscount Byng refused PM King's request for a dissolution of Parliament, precipitating a constitutional crisis (*courtesy National Archives of Canada/PA-1356*).

Cabbage (*Brassica oleracea*, Capitata Group), usually biennial VEGETABLE of the Cruciferae family, which is grown as an annual. The cole crops (BROCCOLI, CAULIFLOWER, BRUSSELS SPROUTS, etc) were developed from wild cabbage, native to southern and western Europe. Garden cabbage, the most universally grown cole crop, is popular because of its adaptability, hardy tolerance of low temperatures (young spring cabbage can tolerate temperatures as low as -10°C) and easy growing requirements. In temperate climates, a very large choice of strains enables cabbages to be grown year round. In Canada, however, summer cabbage is consumed immediately after harvesting; late cabbage, picked in autumn, can be stored for several months. Depending on the variety, cabbage heads may be round, flat or conical in shape; red, white or green in colour; and have smooth or wrinkled leaves (Savoy cabbage). Cabbages may be grown from seed (maturing in 90-120 days) or as transplanted seedlings (maturing in 60-90 days). Although 90% water, cabbage is an excellent source of minerals and of vitamins A, B_1, B_2 and C. In 1985 Canadian cabbage production was 156 202 t; the main areas of cultivation are in Québec and Ontario.   ROGER RUSHDY

Cabbagetown, a district in east-central Toronto, the general boundaries of which are the Don River on the east, Parliament St on the west, Gerrard St on the north, and Queen St on the south. It was settled by working-class immigrants from Ireland and England in the 1860-80 period, who erected cottages and terraced (row) housing with some Victorian and Georgian ornamentation and grew vegetables on the small lots, especially cabbages, which lent the district its name. Cabbagetown deteriorated into a slum between the world wars, but thereafter its character changed with urban renewal and subsidized housing in the 1950s and renovation of many still-standing houses by young professionals from the 1960s to the present. A number of the neighbourhoods were painted by Albert Jacques Franck. Hugh GARNER, born in the district, depicted working-class conditions in his popular novel *Cabbagetown* (1950, 1968). Street signs now identify the district as "Old Cabbagetown."   JOHN ROBERT COLOMBO

Cabinet, "government-of-the-day," political executive that formulates government policies and priorities. It has been described as the "hyphen which joins, a buckle which fastens, the legislative part of the state to the executive part of the state." It is responsible for the introduction and passage of government legislation, the execution and administration of government policies, and the finances of the government. Although its powers are so substantial that some observers refer to "Cabinet dictatorship," for a government institution of such obvious power and potency it has no specific constitutional or statutory basis. In Canada it acts formally as the PRIVY COUNCIL, deriving its legal powers to advise and act in the name of the CROWN from its ability to secure and maintain majority support in the HOUSE OF COMMONS. The governor-in-council is the GOVERNOR GENERAL acting on the advice of the Privy Council (in practice, the Cabinet) through an ORDER-IN-COUNCIL, which has the force of law. Provincial Cabinets are known formally as executive councils and follow the federal model except in certain powers of appointment.

Formed and led by the PRIME MINISTER, the Cabinet comprises members of the legislature invited by the prime minister to head major government departments or ministries of state (*see* CENTRAL AGENCY). With the expansion of government activity Cabinets have increased in size from the original 12 to 40 members (PM Brian MULRONEY's Cabinet, Sept 1987). Choosing a Cabinet in

Canada requires considerable artfulness (if not artistry) on the part of the prime minister, who must try to ensure that it represents the country's regional, linguistic and religious diversity. When a victorious party fails to elect MPs in certain regions, a prime minister often resorts to the Senate to fill out the Cabinet.

Because it has been Canadian practice to include all ministers in the Cabinet, the Cabinet has grown to an unwieldy size, and as a result a secretariat and an elaborate committee system have been developed. The secretariat for full Cabinet and its committees is provided mainly by the PRIVY COUNCIL OFFICE, the staff of co-ordinating ministries of state and Treasury Board Secretariat. The TREASURY BOARD itself is a statutory Cabinet committee created by Parliament. (An unusual feature of Cabinet committees in Canada is that senior nonelected public servants participate, although they are excluded from Cabinet meetings proper.) In his short-lived government of 1979, PM Joe CLARK organized an inner Cabinet of approximately 12 ministers whose functions (establishing government priorities and spending limits) were similar to those of PM Trudeau's main Cabinet committee, the Policies and Priorities Committee, created during his first term of office.

All members of Cabinet are bound for life by the Privy Council oath of secrecy, which protects Cabinet deliberations and organization. Opinions publicly expressed by a minister are those of Cabinet, and ministers may disagree publicly with those opinions only after resigning from Cabinet and then must not reveal details of Cabinet discussions or documents. The OFFICIAL SECRETS ACT, which enjoins all Canadians, but particularly public employees, opposition critics and investigating journalists from possessing, distributing and publicizing information deemed injurious to the state, has also been used to protect Cabinet members, who can choose to pose as privy councillors to the Crown rather than as a government responsible to the Commons, from embarrassment. The secrecy surrounding Cabinet business is defended on the grounds that it is necessary for maintaining Cabinet solidarity, without which Cabinet may lose its hold over the legislature and therefore its right to govern. To dominate the legislature, Cabinet can rely as well on its control over the party. Parliamentary government is party government, and prime ministers have substantial legislative patronage at their disposal to ensure party loyalty, including appointment of Cabinet ministers and parliamentary secretaries and of chairmen of legislative committees. In fact, the control exerted by Cabinet over the legislature through the levers of party discipline has contributed to the outcry against Cabinet power. The traditional capacity of the legislature to bring down the government and therefore the Cabinet through a no-confidence vote appears to be losing force, largely because the Cabinet has the power, through its legislative party majority, to prevent such votes, or at worst to refuse to accept their implications or consequences. The dwindling ability of the legislature to hold the executive accountable has had a debilitating effect on the disciplinary impact of the doctrine of collective and ministerial responsibility to the legislature, a doctrine upon which rests the whole notion of RESPONSIBLE GOVERNMENT.

The imbalance between the legislature and the Cabinet is exacerbated by the increasing use of discretionary powers, conferred by the former on the Cabinet collectively or on ministers individually, to legislate by order-in-council or by ministerial order. When added to the Cabinet's tradi-

Conservative government's Planning and Priorities Cabinet meeting, held at St John's, Aug 1986. PM Brian Mulroney is seated at the centre (*photo by Andrew Clark, Prime Minister's Office*).

tional role of initiating the budget and ensuring its safe passage (*see* BUDGETARY PROCESS) and its preparation and introduction of all major legislative proposals, this development accounts for the growing belief that Parliament is in decline. Many reforms for improving the legislature's ability to scrutinize Cabinet activities have been proposed. It is because the bureaucratic infrastructure for which ministers are expected to be accountable to the Commons has become so enormous that the doctrine of ministerial responsibility has been discounted by the Cabinet as unreasonable. As a result, the problem of Cabinet dictatorship has been transformed into the larger problem of domination of both Cabinet and legislature by nonelected public servants. Any reforms designed to hold the Cabinet accountable will also have to address this related problem.

In addition to reforms to the Commons COMMITTEES, which may increase the surveillance capacities of the legislature, recent measures, in the name of FREEDOM OF INFORMATION, may alter the imbalance between the Cabinet and the legislature. To give better protection of citizen's rights, which are endangered by the exercise of discretionary executive powers, the office of OMBUDSMAN or parliamentary commissioner has been widely adopted by the provinces. Whether any remedy can now stem a tide running so strongly in favour of executive domination is doubtful, but responsible Cabinet government will not survive in Canada without such efforts.   J.E. HODGETTS

Reading: T.A. Hockin, *Government in Canada* (1976).

Cable Television, a technique for transmitting information to and from the home, is revolutionizing many aspects of Canadian COMMUNICATIONS. Although it has been in Canada since 1952 and is technically simple, cable television in the 1980s is transforming Canadian broadcasting and program production, and has far-reaching implications on other aspects of communications as well.

For its first decade, cable TV was only a minor adjunct to the over-the-air television broadcasting system. Primarily a rural phenomenon, cable was concentrated in small communities that lacked a local TV service. Early CATV systems ("community antenna television") consisted of a "head-end" or antenna array placed atop a hill or high tower to trap distant, usually American, signals, and a coaxial cable distribution network to transport these signals to the homes; amplifiers periodically strengthened the signals en route. Even into the mid-1960s the industry remained small and insignificant. By 1964 only 215 000 homes (4% of Canadian households) subscribed.

The industry experienced rapid growth between about 1965 and 1975. Penetration approached 60% of Canadian households and systems were established in all major centres. Two factors help explain cable's popularity in urban communities: the proliferation of high-rise buildings debasing over-the-air reception, and the use of microwave to import distant (US) signals.

By 1985, 5.7 million households subscribed, representing 77% of the homes for which cable was available and 62% of all Canadian homes. Cable is provided on a local monopoly basis, and in 1985, 495 companies provided cable service; nonetheless, the industry is dominated by 3 multisystem companies – ROGERS TELECOMMUNICATIONS LTD, Télécable Videotron Ltée and MACLEAN HUNTER LTD – which together account for over 50% of cable subscriptions (*see* MEDIA OWNERSHIP).

Evidently approaching maximum penetration in the mid-1970s, cable companies began to seek new ways of making money. The larger systems expanded capacity from 12 channels to 24 or more with a view to offering additional programming services, such as PAY TELEVISION and special-

ized channels, for additional fees. Two-way (interactive) capability was also introduced to facilitate nonprogramming services, such as medical alerts, burglar alarms, meter readings, and, prospectively, electronic banking, again at additional fees. Finally, hitherto discrete systems became interconnected by satellite, thereby potentially constituting cable television as a national data TELECOMMUNICATIONS network.

These developments have taken place only under controversy and with bitter disputes. One major obstacle hindering cable's development was the set of restrictions imposed on cable by the telephone industry. The cable industry has always been dependent on telephone companies for access to poles, ducts, easements and rights-of-way; without access to these facilities, few cable systems could even have been constructed. Access was granted, however, only under highly restrictive conditions that were designed to limit service offerings and to neutralize cable's potentially competitive threat. Under the "partial system agreements" offered by the telephone industry, cable companies were precluded from owning coaxial cable; they were required to lease it from the telephone companies after paying for the costs incurred in construction. Moreover, cable companies were prohibited from transmitting signals other than radio or television signals. Frequently proscribed also was all limited network point-to-point and 2-way communication, which meant that many services, including pay television, were excluded. In BELL CANADA ENTERPRISES' territory (Ontario and Québec) these types of restriction were struck down only in 1977 by a decision of the CANADIAN RADIO-TELEVISION AND TELECOMMUNICATIONS COMMISSION (Decision CRTC 77-6) which ordered that cable companies be permitted to own cable, that access charges imposed by Bell be reasonable, and that no restrictions on services be imposed (*see* TELEPHONES).

A second major obstacle slowing cable development was regulatory policy designed to protect over-the-air television broadcasters from a potential financial crisis. Declared to be a component of the broadcasting system by the Broadcasting Act, cable systems (termed "broadcasting receiving undertakings") were placed under the jurisdiction of the newly created CRTC in 1968 (*see* COMMUNICATIONS LAW). Until the late 1970s the commission was most concerned with preventing cable from fragmenting broadcasters' audiences and thereby reducing ADVERTISING revenues to the detriment of the cultural goals set for Canadian broadcasting. In 1969 and 1970, for example, the CRTC announced that cable systems would not be allowed to use microwave to improve the reception of US signals, and that normally only one US commercial and one US noncommercial signal would be authorized for cable rediffusion. Public outcry and the lobbying efforts of the cable industry forced the commission to relent, and in 1971 liberalized policies were announced. First, Canadian signals were to be given priority; paradoxically, this requirement induced many cable systems to expand channel capacity beyond the 12 existing channels in order to carry a full complement of US stations, thereby further fragmenting television audiences. Second, cable systems were "requested" to compensate broadcasters for the use made of their signals; this request was rarely fulfilled, however. Third, cable companies were required to delete US signals during times of program duplication with Canadian stations; however, this obligation served to protect the American content of Canadian stations while it left their Canadian content exposed to the full measure of competition. Finally, while required to offer "community programming," cable companies were nonetheless precluded from

selling advertising time and from distributing program material, such as movies, sports and drama, that was competitive with the programming of the over-the-air broadcasters (*see* TELEVISION PROGRAMMING).

A new stance toward cable became evident in the early 1980s, signalled first by the CRTC's publication of *The 1980's: A Decade of Diversity: Broadcasting, Satellites and Pay-TV* (1980). Noting that some 35 non-network programming services were then being transmitted on US satellites, the document proclaimed that "a new technological universe ... [was] already taking shape at a pace that is inexorable." It therefore recommended that cable systems quickly become interconnected by satellites and that pay television and other new programming services be licensed. In 1982 the commission duly licensed several satellite-to-cable pay television services and in 1984 it similarly licensed several specialty channels (music videos, sports, news, etc). These licensing decisions all signal a reversal from the previous protectionist stance of the regulator in favour of established television broadcasters, and an easing of its restrictions on cable television (*see* SATELLITE COMMUNICATIONS).

Cable TV has also been at the centre of continual federal-provincial jurisdictional disputes. For example, during the mid-1970s, Québec asserted authority to license all cable undertakings in the province; consequently, cable companies for a time required both federal and provincial licences. In Rimouski the conflict came to a head as different companies were licensed by the 2 governments. In the summer of 1975 the provincial licensee, Cablodistribution de l'Est, actually hid its receiving antennae in the surrounding marshlands to prevent it being confiscated by federal authorities. Subscribers complaining about the resulting disruption in service were told that the antennae, on loan from the provincial government to replace an earlier set already confiscated, would be reconnected as soon as the RCMP left the area. In Québec's view, cable should be under provincial jurisdiction because of its local nature and its impact on language, education and culture (*see* COMMUNICATIONS IN QUÉBEC).

The Prairie governments too have asserted provincial jurisdiction, viewing cable as a telecommunications carrier akin to, and indeed potentially competitive with, provincially owned telephone companies. Exclusive federal jurisdiction was confirmed by the Supreme Court in 1977, however. By the *Radio* case of 1932 the radio frequencies are subject to federal authority; consequently, cable television systems (as "broadcasting receiving undertakings") also fall within federal authority since they make use of radio frequencies.

It is apparent that cable television is transforming Canadian broadcasting. Heretofore the number of entities authorized to broadcast in any locality was limited by spectrum scarcity and by the technical necessity of apportioning radio frequencies geographically. Cable television, however, by using wires instead of space (ether) to diffuse television signals to the home, permits a much enlarged channel capacity, dramatically increasing the number of competing services. Furthermore, government policy on broadcasting has traditionally centered on the message, using broadcasting as a means of promoting national unity and safeguarding Canadian culture. These goals, always elusive, have become even more problematic as market forces increase and heighten competition, reducing the ability of government to legislate or administer performance (*see* BROADCASTING, RADIO AND TELEVISION).

Because of the abundance of channels available on cable and because satellite reception covers a broad area, a reorientation is taking place in broadcast programming. Instead of being targeted geographically at particular locations, programs are increasingly being targeted at identifiable audiences (eg, the young, the old, women, blacks, professionals). Cable television in conjunction with satellites will, therefore, largely destroy broadcasting as an instrument for Canadian political and cultural sovereignty.

Cable television is also a factor revolutionizing Canadian telecommunications. Hitherto, cable and telephone systems were distinct, both technologically and in the services offered. Although both industries brought communication to the home by wire on a monopoly basis, cable was one-way for many years while telephone systems were bidirectional. Moreover, telephones possessed full switching capacity and offered point-to-point service, whereas cable was unswitched, offering only a point-to-mass service. Furthermore, telephone companies were interconnected nationally by microwave while cable systems were discrete, local entities. Finally, telephones were optimized at the terminal for one voice channel, while cable systems employed bandwidths of up to several hundred thousand voice channels (50 TV channels). Today, however, telephone and cable systems are converging technologically; consequently their services will increasingly overlap as well, at least in the absence of regulatory or collusive arrangements to divide up the markets. Both telephone and cable companies are experimenting with optical fibre (10 KHz bandwidth), which will give enormous capacity at the terminal for both systems. Modern cable systems are bidirectional, and some are experimenting with switched services and techniques; packet switching will probably make introduction of switching quite feasible. Cable is now interconnected nationally through satellite, another development that points to technological convergence.

Inasmuch as cable is transforming broadcasting and converging with telecommunications, it is also causing broadcasting to converge with telecommunications. Cable is thereby placing a severe strain on policy, since the laws, goals and regulations in these hitherto separate areas have been diametrically opposed. Broadcasting policy has historically focused on the messages and their perceived cultural impact, and rarely upon economic or technological issues such as prices, profits, rates of depreciation, and innovative techniques for relaying messages. Licences to transmit were apportioned on the basis of expected contribution to Canadian social, political and cultural goals. By contrast, in telecommunications, regulation focused on economic factors and the means of transmission, attempting to ensure just and reasonable access for senders and receivers of messages, and largely ignoring the nature of the messages or their cultural impact.

It is apparent that such dichotomous policies can no longer be maintained with the convergence of broadcasting and telecommunications. Fundamental policy questions are raised. Should cable continue to be governed by historic broadcasting concerns – the licensing of message originators on the basis of contributions to culture? Or should cable be treated as a common carrier, with price and profit regulation to ensure equitable access by any and all message originators? Should cable companies be required to pay broadcasters for the programming that is at present being rediffused without compensation? Or should program originators pay cable companies access fees for diffusion over cable facilities? Should cable companies be allowed to select (any of) the programming or to integrate vertically into program production (as has been the practice in television

broadcasting)? Or should cable companies be precluded from exercising any control whatsoever over the messages they diffuse (the principle of the common carrier)? These are some of the difficult issues facing policymakers in the 1980s. *See also* COMMUNICATIONS TECHNOLOGY.   ROBERT E. BABE

Reading: Robert E. Babe, *Cable Television and Telecommunications in Canada* (1975) and *Canadian Television Broadcasting* (1979); Babe and C. Winn, *Broadcasting Policy and Copyright Law* (1984); CRTC, *The 1980's: A Decade of Diversity – Broadcasting, Satellites and Pay-TV* (1980); Dept of Communications, *Towards a New National Broadcasting Policy* (1983); R.B. Woodrow et al, *Conflict over Communications Policy* (1980); Woodrow and K.B. Woodside, eds, *The Introduction of Pay TV in Canada* (1982).

Cabot, John, Anglo-Italian navigator, explorer (b perhaps at Genoa, Italy 1449/50; d probably off the coast of Newfoundland 1498/99). Cabot's voyages of discovery from Bristol, Eng (1497, 1498), were the first recorded landfalls on the N American continent since the Norse voyages. Cabot conceived the idea of reaching Asia by sailing westward across the Atlantic. In 1496 Henry VII authorized him and his 3 sons to search, at their own expense, for unknown lands to the west. Cabot left Bristol on 2 May 1497 with 18 men. On 24 June 1497 he landed somewhere on the N American coast – the actual place of landing most likely being in Labrador, Newfoundland or Cape Breton I. Cabot claimed the land for England and returned to Bristol, arriving in Aug. Early in 1498 Henry VII authorized a second expedition consisting of 5 ships and 300 men. After landing in Greenland, Cabot sailed southward, probably as far as Chesapeake Bay, but failing to find the rich lands he had envisaged and because supplies were running low he turned back towards England. It appears that Cabot perished on this voyage, though one or more of his ships may have returned to Bristol. Most historians maintain that he was probably lost off the coast of Newfoundland. Because the fact that Cabot had found a new continent soon became known in Europe, Cabot made what has been called "the intellectual discovery of America." His voyages provided the basis for England's claim to N America and led to the opening of the rich NW Atlantic fishery.   JOHN PARSONS

Cabot Strait, the passage between SW Newfoundland and CAPE BRETON ISLAND. Named for explorer John CABOT, it is 110 km wide between Cape Ray, Nfld, and Cape North, NS. The principal oceangoing route to the Gulf of ST LAWRENCE,

and hence to much of Eastern Canada, it has been of strategic importance in Canadian military and commercial history. Though sometimes hindered by pack ice from the gulf, steamers between CHANNEL-PORT AUX BASQUES and SYDNEY (later NORTH SYDNEY) connected the Newfoundland railway with the Canadian system after 1898. CN Marine ferries now connecting the 2 provinces carry more than 300 000 people across the strait each year. A submarine telegraph cable was laid across Cabot Str in 1856, eventually joining N America and Europe via the transatlantic cable (1866).   ROBERT D. PITT

Cache Creek, BC, Village inc 1967, pop 1147 (1986c), located in the dry belt of the southern interior of BC at the junction of Hwys 1 and 97, 346 km NE of Vancouver and 85 km W of Kamloops. The name refers to the fur-trade era of the early 1800s, when the site probably served to cache furs and supplies for traders and the native Shuswap. The village originated as a stopping house on the CARIBOO ROAD during the GOLD RUSH of the 1860s. Cattle ranching, still important in the region, began at the same period. The community was little more than a crossroads until upgrading of the Cariboo Highway 97 in the 1950s and the Trans-Canada Highway in the 1960s brought a huge increase in through traffic. That traffic was much reduced after the COQUIHALLA HIGHWAY opened in May 1986 and rerouted traffic between Vancouver and the interior of the province.   JOHN STEWART

Cactus (Cactaceae), family of plants having fleshy, often spined, stems and branches. Cacti are succulents, ie, they store moisture in spongy tissues. Of an estimated 2000 species, fewer than 50 are cold resistant. Four species are known in Canada: 3 belonging to genus *Opuntia;* one, to genus *Coryphantha.* The most northerly growing cactus in the world, the fragile or little prickly pear (*O. fragilis*) is the smallest Canadian cactus. The easily detached pads (2-4 cm long) are as thick as

This left portion of La Cosa's world map of *c* 1500-1508 shows the Caribbean area and the region of North America supposedly explored by John Cabot (*courtesy National Archives of Canada/NMC-26688*).

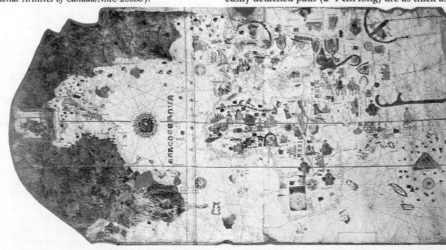

they are wide (1-2 cm); the small spines (1-2 cm long) are savagely barbed. The species occurs singly or in colonies up to one metre across. The most widespread and adaptable of Canadian cacti, the little prickly pear lives in the most diverse environments: the dry belt and Peace River areas of BC; Whiteshell Provincial Park, Man (which experiences the coldest Canadian winters); the granite rocks along Mellon Creek near Kaladar, 150 km SW of Ottawa. The common plains prickly pear (*O. polyacantha*) has larger, more typical pads, 5-10 cm long, 4-10 cm wide, 1 cm thick. It is common only in southern Alberta and Saskatchewan. The high concentration on rangelands is thought to result from overgrazing, which thins out the natural grass and leaves behind noxious weeds. Only deer and a few small rodents can eat it without hurting themselves with the sharp, 5 cm long spines. Eastern prickly pear, *O. compressa* (formerly *O. humifusa*), 10-15 cm long, 8-10 cm wide and 1 cm thick, has pads, and has a few long, sharp spines projecting from the top. The rest of the pad is covered with almost invisible, sliverlike barbs. *O. compressa* occurs in large clumps, some over one metre across. It is limited to Essex County, southern Ontario, eg, Point Pelee National Park. The fragrance-free flowers of Canadian *Opuntias* have vivid yellow, silk-textured, rounded petals and bright red or yellow central filaments.

Coryphantha vivipara, a charming little ball or pincushion, grows as single balls (up to 8 cm diameter) or as a cluster (up to 20 cm) of up to 20 equal-sized balls. Sharp spines (under 1 cm long) surround the ball in tight rosettes. The small flowers (2-3 cm diameter) have pointed, deep magenta petals surrounding the centre of golden-yellow filaments. The blooms usually appear in June. The ball cactus is common throughout the southern prairies.

It has been suggested that cacti came to Canada as a result of dispersal of fruits and seeds by rodents and birds. Barbed species could have spread by sticking to migratory animals. The processes by which cold-resistant cacti survive extreme low temperatures are not completely understood; however, they do dehydrate in the fall, thereby concentrating their sap into an antifreezelike solution. Prickly pears become flabby and lie almost

Ball or pincushion cactus (*Coryphantha vivipara*) in bloom in southern Alberta (*courtesy Elliott and Nicole Bernshaw/Bernshaw Photography*).

flat against the ground. A blanket of protective snow then shields them from the full force of the winter.   NICOLE BERNSHAW

Caddisfly, small, drab insect of order Trichoptera [Gk "hairy wings"]. Adults have long legs and antennae, large, compound eyes, rudimentary mouthparts and 2 pairs of veined, hairy wings. At rest, wings are held rooflike over the body. 546 species are known from Canada; world total may be over 10 000. Larvae are common in most freshwater habitats. Those of the most familiar species live in a portable case of plant fragments or mineral particles held together by silk. They feed principally on leaves. Others spin silken nets, which filter food from water currents, or are free-ranging predators. One to several years are spent as larvae. Larvae transform to adults through a nonfeeding pupal stage, spent in a sealed case in the water. Adults swim to the surface and discard the pupal skin. They are generally nocturnal, with a terrestrial existence lasting a few weeks.   G. PRITCHARD

Caddy, John Herbert, painter and teacher (b at Québec C 28 June 1801; d at Hamilton, Ont 19 March 1887). In 1816 he began military training at Royal Military College, Woolwich, Eng, and was commissioned 2nd lieutenant in the Royal Artillery in 1825. Topographical drawing and painting in watercolour were important and influential aspects of this training. His military career consisted of 2 tours of duty with the RA in the West Indies (1828-38), and in British Honduras (1838-41) where he recorded in drawings and a lively diary an expedition to the Mayan ruins at Palenque. Promoted to captain in 1840, he was posted to London, Canada West, in 1842 and retired on half pay in 1844. He moved to Hamilton about 1851 and worked first as a land surveyor and engineer but gradually concentrated on his career as artist and teacher. Numerous watercolours of Canadian landscapes give evidence of travel from Ft William to Québec, with concentration in the Hamilton-Niagara Falls region. His powers of observation, love of nature and a touch of romanticism, disciplined by training as an engineer, combined to imbue his work with both charm and topographical accuracy.
                                   FRANCES K. SMITH

Cadet, Joseph-Michel, butcher, military provisioner (b at Québec City 24 Dec 1719; d at Paris, France 31 Jan 1781). Born of generations of butchers, Cadet worked first for his uncle, a Québec butcher, and became the Crown's purveyor of meat in 1745. Two wars and the increase in the colony's garrisons expanded his trade and opportunities. In 1749 he received a monopoly as beef retailer at Québec and in 1756 became general contractor for military provisions in Canada. His rise owed much to his shrewdness and willingness to take risks. His business expanded and the ships he bought and hired kept the colony supplied until 1759. In 1760 he left for France where he and others were arrested for embezzling government funds. After paying nearly 4 million *livres* "in restitution," he lived as a country gentleman in France. He is regarded as either the greatest profiteer under Intendant François BIGOT or a luckless scapegoat for the loss of New France.
                                   PETER N. MOOGK

Cadets Public interest in the military training of young Canadians has waxed in time of wars and threat of wars, and waned in peacetime. For more than a century the preparation of young men (and recently, of women) for careers as professional soldiers has been done within the ARMED FORCES, mainly at MILITARY COLLEGES. Less extensive and less specialized training aimed at youth of high-school age has been provided mainly

through the Canadian cadet organizations. Under the National Defence Act, the Department of National Defence is in partnership with the NAVY LEAGUE, the Army Cadet League, and the Air Cadet League in operating and supporting a movement for youth (both male and female) between 12 and 19. In 1987 there were 59 700 cadets, located in 1084 corps across Canada. Training is conducted at corps headquarters during the school year and at more than 30 DND-supported summer camps. About 22 600 cadets participate in cadet training each summer and 200 take part each year in exchange programs with Britain, the US, and various other European countries.   N.F. DREISZIGER AND PETER PHELAN

Cadieux, Jean, legendary French Canadian VOYAGEUR of the 18th century who lived in the Ottawa R region. When his cabin was attacked by Indians, he sent his family down the rapids in his canoe and stayed behind to prevent pursuit. The Virgin Mary is supposed to have guided the canoe through the rapids, which were generally portaged. Pursued by the Indians through the forest, Cadieux gradually weakened; he dug his own grave, erected a cross above it and composed a ballad about his misfortune, which he wrote in blood on birchbark; it was found by those who came to look for him. The ballad is well known in French Canadian tradition.   NANCY SCHMITZ

Cadieux, Marcel, diplomat (b at Montréal 17 June 1915; d at Pompano Beach, Fla 19 Mar 1981). A tough, astute international lawyer and fierce anticommunist, Cadieux served in the Dept of External Affairs 1941-79. As undersecretary of state 1964-70, Cadieux was an efficient administrator and uncompromising federalist, pressing for a department and a foreign policy that would reflect Canada's bicultural origins. He subsequently was ambassador to Washington 1970-75, headed the Canadian Mission to the EEC 1975-77, and was chief negotiator for Canada-US fisheries and boundary disputes 1977-79. He wrote an elegant diplomatic primer, *The Canadian Diplomat* (1963).   ANNE HILLMER

Cadillac, Antoine Laumet, dit de Lamothe, fur-trader, military officer, founder of Detroit (b at Les Laumets, France 5 Mar 1658; d at Castelsarrasin, France 15 Oct 1730). Cadillac succeeded in promoting himself from obscure origins — he gave himself the noble title de Lamothe Cadillac — to wealth and positions of command. In Acadia *c*1683-91 he served with a privateer, and traded and quarrelled with the governor. He moved to Québec in 1691 and was then commissioned in the TROUPES DE LA MARINE. One of FRONTENAC'S protégé's, he was commandant at Michilimackinac 1693-97, where he successfully pursued the fur trade. With the west closed to trade because of the glut in furs, Cadillac established a settlement at Detroit as a way of preventing English expansion and controlling the trade with the western tribes. There 1701-10, he was removed from command when it became clear that he was attempting to create an empire for himself. He again attempted to enrich himself as governor of Louisiana 1710-17 and was soon at odds with officials there, including BIENVILLE. He left the colony in 1718 and finished his life as governor of Castelsarrasin. Regarded as "sharp," a liar and greedy, he also was an articulate, plausible man with a good deal of charm and undoubted energy.
                              MARY MCDOUGALL MAUDE

Cadmium (Cd), soft, ductile, silvery white metal which melts at 320.9°C and is present in the Earth's crust at 0.1-0.5 parts per million. The most common cadmium MINERAL, greenockite (CdS), is generally found in zinc-bearing ores and is recovered as a by-product during processing.

Cadmium is used principally as a protective coating for other metals, eg, for electroplating IRON AND STEEL products to improve appearance and protect against rusting. The second-largest use is in the manufacture of yellow and red pigments. A growing application is in the production of rechargeable nickel-cadmium and silver-cadmium batteries. In 1986 Canada had an estimated production of 1421 kg with a value of over $5.4 million, and was the Western world's third-largest producer of cadmium, following Japan and the US. Cadmium is produced at all 4 Canadian ZINC plants. About 90% of Canadian production is exported, mostly to the US and the UK.

M.J. GAUVIN

Cahén, Oscar, painter, illustrator (b at Copenhagen, Denmark 8 Feb 1916; d at Oakville, Ont 26 Nov 1956). Trained in Europe, he taught in Prague before escaping the Nazi occupation in 1938. Because he held German citizenship, he was interned in England in 1939 and then shipped to Canada in 1940 as an enemy alien and interned at Sherbrooke, Qué. His artistic contacts in Canada secured his release in 1942, and he worked in Montréal before moving to Toronto in 1944. Cahén gained a major reputation as an illustrator working for such magazines as *Maclean's, Chatelaine* and *New Liberty.* In the late 1940s he met Walter Yarwood, Harold TOWN and others involved in avant-garde art in Toronto. Cahén was included in the "Abstracts at Home" exhibition held in 1953 at the Robert Simpson Co, Toronto. He became one of the PAINTERS ELEVEN when the group was formed later that year. Cahén's dark, expressionist paintings of the late 1940s, often on religious subjects, gave way in the early 1950s to brilliantly coloured abstractions. He and his colleagues in Painters Eleven achieved the breakthrough of radical painting in Toronto.

DAVID BURNETT

Reading: David Burnett, *Oscar Cahén* (1983).

Cain, Larry, canoeist (b at Toronto 9 Jan 1963). He finished first in the C-1 canoe over 1000 m (time 4:35.1) and second over 500 m (2:01.7) at the Pan-American Championships in 1980 and in 1981 was the first Canadian canoeist in 46 years to win a world or Olympic event with 2 gold medals at the junior world championships. He competed in numerous international canoeing events through to 1984, in which he finished first in the C-1 1000 m and the C-1 500 m at the Nottinghamshire International Regatta. At the 1984 Los Angeles Olympics he won a gold medal (C-1 500 m, 1:57.01) and a silver (C-1 1000 m, 4:08.67). He remained active in international competition through to 1987.   JAMES MARSH

Larry Cain in action at the 1984 Los Angeles Olympics, where he won a gold medal in canoeing (*courtesy Athlete Information Bureau/ Service Information-Athlètes*).

Caiserman-Roth, Ghitta, painter (b at Montréal 2 Mar 1923), outstanding example of the creativity of women artists that has characterized a century of artistic activity in Montréal. Caiserman-Roth's studies in New York led to work characterized by a strong social orientation and expressionist style (*Backyard,* 1948). In the early 1950s she began exploring domestic and studio interiors, self-portraits and portraits of her child and of anonymous models, handling these subjects with quiet and disturbing intensity. Throughout the years certain themes and images have been repeated – the harlequin, the "Flying Wallendas," the deliberate confusion of interior and exterior space, the human figure imprinted on abandoned clothes, lawn chairs, sheets (*Bedscape with Shadow,* 1978). In 1984 she had her first New York show, at the Dyansen Gallery. She helped establish the Montréal Artists School and has taught at Sir George Williams U and the Saidye Bronfman Centre.

D.F. ANDRUS

Caisse de dépôt et placement du Québec, the investor of various Québec public pension and insurance funds. Investments are made with a view to ensure the profitability of funds under its administration and to support Québec's economic development. To achieve these objectives, the Caisse uses various investment instruments such as bonds, shares and convertible securities, mortgages, real estate and money market investments. The Caisse has investments in Alcan, Bell Canada, Canadian Pacific, Domtar, Provigo and the major Canadian chartered banks. It is one of the largest financial institutions in N America. Its principal place of business is in Montréal. As of 31 Dec 1986, net income generated from investments totalled approximately $3 billion and assets reached $25 billion. The Caisse has some 200 employees.

Caisse populaire, established 1900 as a co-operative savings and loan company with nonfixed capital and limited liability in Lévis, Qué, by Alphonse DESJARDINS, a journalist and French-language stenographer in the House of Commons. Desjardins used European savings and loan companies as models for his enterprise. He encouraged the working classes to save and plan for the future and provided the credit they needed for economic recovery. Desjardins also hoped the caisse would contribute to the economic emancipation of French Canadians. The Caisse populaire de Lévis opened on 23 Jan 1901 in Desjardins's own home; 12 people paid a total of $26.40 as first payment of their share in the partnership. The first savings deposit, made on Feb 7, was for only 5 cents. By 1906, savings amounted to only $9556.53; in the same year, after vigorous lobbying by Desjardins and his friends, the Québec legislature adopted the Act on co-operative CREDIT UNIONS. In 1920, when Desjardins died, 206 caisses populaires had been established, including 23 in Ontario and 9 in French Canadian communities in New England, largely as a result of the clergy's unfailing support of and eager participation in this undertaking. Many caisses were connected to churches through the bond-of-association concept.

Today, what is known as Le Mouvement Desjardins includes 1217 caisses populaires (affiliated to 10 regional caisses populaires) and 147 caisses d'économie (grouped under the Fédération des caisses d'économie which became affiliated to the Mouvement Desjardins in 1979). The federations are grouped under the Confédération des caisses populaires et d'économie Desjardins, which operates a wide range of services to the caisses and federations, from management and personnel counselling through marketing, data processing, credit card accounts management, securities transportation, etc.

The federations jointly own many financial subsidiaries among which are 4 insurance companies, one trust company (the Caisse centrale Desjardins, operating as a financial agent for the benefits of the federations), and Société d'investissement Desjardins which specializes in industrial and commercial lending and financing. As of Dec 1986, the assets of the Mouvement Desjardins exceeded $25 billion and the number of members of the caisses populaires and caisses d'économie exceeded 5 million.   YVES ROBY

Calder, Frank Arthur, politician, businessman (b at Nass Harbour, BC 3 Aug 1915). Calder, a Nishga, was the first Indian member of a Canadian legislature (1949) and second native legislator after Louis RIEL. He graduated from the Anglican Theological Coll, UBC, in 1946 and worked at various times as fish-plant tallyman, trade unionist, machinist and entrepreneur. He served as a British Columbia MLA for 26 years, first with the CCF-NDP and after 1975 with Social Credit. In 1972 he became the first native Canadian Cabinet minister but was dismissed amid controversy in 1973. He was president of the N American Indian Brotherhood in 1944, organizer for the Native Brotherhood of BC, and a founder of the Nishga Tribal Council, now the Nishga Nation (president, 1955-74). Calder's views on Indian economic development, his opposition to the reserve system and his partial endorsement of the 1969 White Paper (*see* NATIVE PEOPLE, GOVERNMENT POLICY) brought him into conflict with others in the Indian movement. His name is widely known through the CALDER CASE, a landmark 1973 Supreme Court decision which dealt with Nishga LAND CLAIMS. *See also* ABORIGINAL RIGHTS.

BENNETT McCARDLE

Calder Case (1973) reviewed the existence of "aboriginal title" claimed over lands historically occupied by the Nishga Indians of northwestern BC. The Supreme Court of Canada by a majority recognized that aboriginal title could exist in common law, but split 3-3 on its validity, half of them declaring the right was never extinguished by statute or treaty. Justice Pigeon tipped the balance against the Nishga on a procedural point – that permission to sue the BC government had not been obtained from the attorney general. Chief CALDER lost his case, but the aboriginal title question was not settled, and the decision led to federal willingness to negotiate native LAND CLAIMS.   DAVID A. CRUICKSHANK

Calder Trophy is awarded annually to the player chosen by hockey writers as being the most proficient in his first year of competition in the NATIONAL HOCKEY LEAGUE. To be eligible, a player cannot have previously played more than 25 games in any major professional league. It was first presented in 1936 by Frank Calder, NHL president, and was renamed Calder Memorial Trophy after his death in 1943. The first winner was Carl Voss. Among players who have won the trophy and gone on to stardom are Terry SAWCHUK, Bernie GEOFFRION, Frank MAHOVLICH, Bobby ORR and Mario Lemieux.   JAMES MARSH

Calèche, French word used in Canada for a light, 2-wheeled carriage, drawn by a single horse, with a folding hood and seats for 2 passengers with another for the driver on the splashboard. Slow-moving calèches are commonly seen in Old Montréal and Québec City where they are used for the conveyance of sightseers.

JOHN ROBERT COLOMBO

Caledon, Ont, Town, located 15 km NW of Metro Toronto, pop 29 666 (1986c), 26 645 (1981c). Created 1974 from townships of Caledon and Albion, part of Chinguacousy, and villages of Bolton and Caledon East, Caledon East was first named Tarbox Corners after a Loyalist family, then Munsie's Corners after an early postmaster. It became a police village 1913 and a village 1957. It is named for James Bolton, an early settler. The area is noted for the scenic beauty around the upper reaches of the Credit and Humber rivers.   K.L. MORRISON

Calgary, second-largest city in Alberta, is situated on the BOW R in the southern part of the province, about 220 km N of the American boundary at the meeting point of the western prairies and mountain foothills. Strategically located on major rail, highway and air corridors, Calgary is an important transportation centre. It is also the financial centre of western Canada and headquarters of Canada's oil and natural-gas industries. With its panoramic backdrop of the Rocky Mountains and its historic association with the ranching frontier, Calgary is one of N America's most identifiable cities.

Population: 636 104 (1986c); 592 808 (1981cA); 671 326 (1986 CMA); 625 966 (1981A CMA)

Rate of Increase (1981-86): (City) 7.3%; (CMA) 7.2%

Rank in Canada: Sixth (by CMA)

Date of Incorporation: Town 1884; City 1893

Land Area: (City) 1189.4 km²; (CMA) 5055.96 km²

Elevation: 1084 m

Climate: Average daily temp, July 16.4°C, Jan -11.8°C; Yearly precip 423.8 mm; Hours of sunshine 2314.4 per year

Settlement The earliest indications of human settlement in the Calgary area, dating back some 12 000 years, consist of spearpoints found in ploughed fields E of the city. This period coincided with the end of the last ice age when glaciers from the Canadian Shield receded from the valley of the Bow R. The successive cycle of nomadic hunting peoples over the next 10 000 years included at least 3 dominant cultures. The last, around the time of Christ, brought the Blackfoot from the eastern woodlands. Among later arrivals were the Sarcee, who came from the N in the 1700s, and still later the Stoney from the Manitoba area. Archaeological evidence of prehistoric peoples is confined mainly to campsites and bison kills. Fireplaces, storage pits and tipi rings date back over 4000 years. Sites depicting religious customs also exist in the form of fieldstone medicine wheels, cairns and effigies, while a pictograph panel can be seen on the Big Rock near Okotoks, S of Calgary.

The westward movement of the fur trade brought the first Europeans to the area in the late 18th century. David THOMPSON, then of the North West Co, wintered near Calgary (1787), and Peter FIDLER of the same company skirted the Calgary region (1792). In the late 1860s buffalo hunters from the US appeared in increasing numbers, joined by illicit-whisky traders who erected a network of fortified posts in southern Alberta from which they sold vile alcholic concoctions to the Indians in return for buffalo robes. One such post was located in the Calgary area near the present-day Glenmore Reservoir. The whisky traders' activities in part led to the formation of the NORTH-WEST MOUNTED POLICE by the federal government (1873). Their second post was established at the confluence of the Bow and Elbow rivers in 1875, and was named Fort Calgary in 1876. (The word Calgary, likely of Gaelic origin, may be translated to mean "Bay Farm.") The railway reached Fort Calgary in 1883 and the CPR subsequently laid out its Calgary townsite W of the Elbow and S of the Bow rivers. Calgary was incorporated in 1884 as the

CALGARY
Employment by Industry, 1986

% of total workers

(bar chart with y-axis "% of total workers" from 0 to 40, categories: Primary Industries; Manufacturing; Construction; Transportation, Communication and Other Utilities; Retail and Wholesale; Finance, Insurance and Real Estate; Services; Public Administration)

Total does not add to 100% because some estimates are not available and some workers are unclassified

Source: Household Surveys Div, Statistics Canada

first town in what is now the province of Alberta, receiving city status in 1893.

Development Calgary's economic growth was closely associated with the development of the livestock industry, and with the city's focal position as the chief transportation centre in Alberta. Before 1906 the open-range cattle industry was dominant and Calgary effected its influence commercially, industrially and socially. The city's first millionaire, Pat BURNS, built up the largest integrated meat business in Canada. The cattle industry, especially following the crippling winter of 1906-07, contributed a volatile element to Calgary's urban development, despite the boosters who continually referred to the city as a thriving cattle town.

The opening of southern Alberta to cash-crop farming in the early 1900s brought rapid growth in Calgary, which increased its population by over 1000% from 1901 to 1911. Rails stretching in all directions solidified the city's position as the prime distributing centre for S-central and southern Alberta. After 1912 Calgary's development slowed along with that of rural Alberta, appreciably so after the end of the immigration boom and the onset of WWI.

A third and most crucial element in Calgary's economic development has been the oil and natural-gas industries. Beginning with the first strike in 1914 at TURNER VALLEY, a few km SW of Calgary, local entrepreneurs such as W.S. Herron, A.W. Dingman and R.A. Brown continually promoted Calgary's future as a major oil centre. Alberta's first oil refinery opened in Calgary (1923). Subsequent important discoveries at Turner Valley (1924, 1936) established Calgary's pre-eminence in Canada's oil and natural-gas industries. When the lid was eventually lifted off western Canada's vast oil reserves at LEDUC in 1947, Calgary stood ready to reap the rewards. The city's subsequent phenomenal growth from an urban expression of southern Alberta to a metropolis of international status is a direct offshoot of its economic development. Another aspect of Calgary's development has been a continuation of a longstanding and

intense rivalry with Edmonton. The 2 Alberta cities have competed keenly at every level, and have produced one of Canada's most identifiable urban rivalries.

Cityscape The Bow R valley forms the main topographical feature of the city. Two smaller streams, the Elbow R and Nose Cr, flow through the city into the Bow, creating a configuration of valleys and bluffs. The placement of railways has also affected spatial growth patterns. The main business section is compressed between the Bow R and the CPR main line. Residential development has tended to follow the river valleys, originally along the Elbow, and more recently along the Bow to the NW and SE. Other influencing factors include University of Calgary and the International Airport to the N, and the Glenmore Reservoir, Sarcee Indian Reserve and Fish Creek Prov Pk to the S. Manufacturing districts are located to the E, in the railway suburbs of Ogden, and in zoned areas along the railways. Formal planning began in 1911 when an English town planner, Thomas Mawson, was commissioned to prepare a comprehensive scheme. His extravagant proposals (1914) were never implemented. A zoning bylaw was instituted in 1934 and a city planning department established in 1950. In 1963 the city adopted its first general plan for controlling future development (rev 1970, 1973). The Alberta Planning Act (1977) directed Calgary to adopt a more regional approach to planning.

Population Calgary's population is predominantly Anglo-Saxon (56%, 1970; 54%, 1981) and Protestant (57.9%, 1970; 54%, 1981). In 1986 English was the mother tongue of 85% in Calgary, the highest of any large Canadian urban centre. The rapid population growth 1900-11 and post-1947 stemmed from extensive immigration. The large migration of young adults has generally kept the city's average age well below the national average. Since the Second World War Calgary has consistently ranked as one of Canada's fastest-growing cities.

Population Growth in Calgary 1891-1986			
Year	Population	Numerical Change	Percent Change
1891	3 876	—	—
1901	4 398	522	13.5
1911	43 704	39 306	893.7
1921	63 305	19 601	44.8
1931	83 761	20 456	32.3
1941	88 904	5 143	6.1
1951	129 060	40 156	45.2
1961	249 641	120 581	93.4
1971	403 319	153 678	61.6
1981	591 857	188 538	46.7
1986	636 104	44 247	7.3

Economy and Labour Force Calgary's economy has historically been associated with commerce and distribution. Its more recent emergence as a world energy and financial centre is reflected in its third-ranking national position in the location of head offices (53, 1986), including those of NOVA, TRANSCANADA PIPELINES, PETRO-CANADA and DOME. The work force therefore shows a heavy orientation towards the professional, management and commercial sectors. "Blue collar" occupations have traditionally been dominated by the building, railway and, more recently, oil-supply trades. Calgary exceeds the national average in per capita income as well as in the percentage of total population in the work force. Yet, in spite of its position as Canada's fastest-growing and most prosperous city in the early 1980s, it remained heavily dependent economically on a single, high-risk industry. It suffered accordingly in the recession in the oil industry in the mid-1980s.

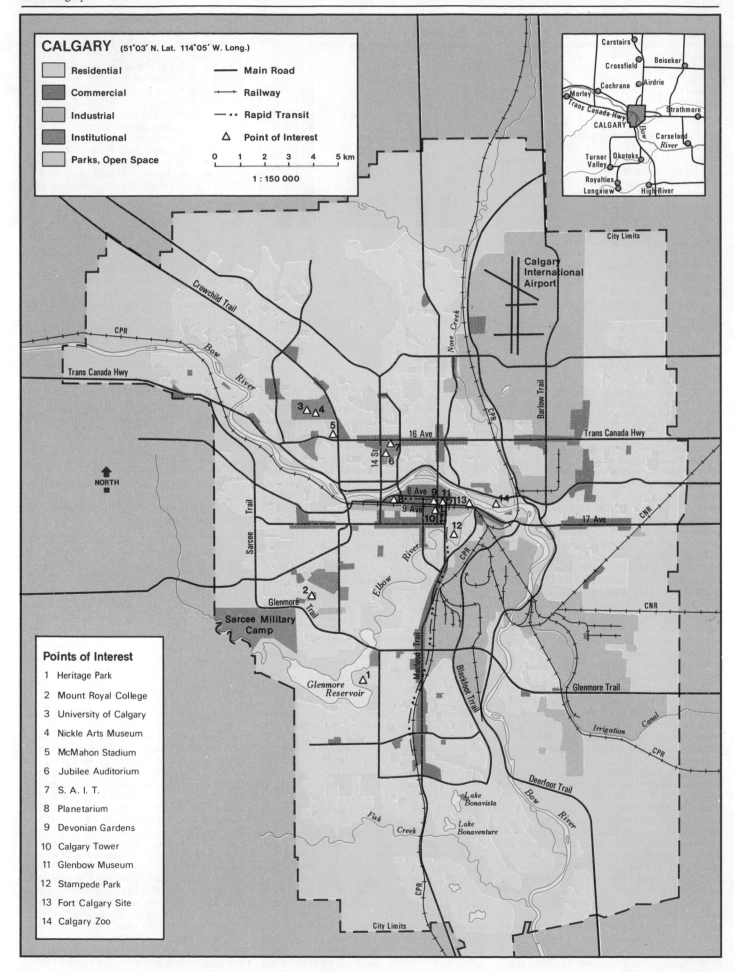

CALGARY (51°03′ N. Lat. 114°05′ W. Long.)

Residential
Commercial
Industrial
Institutional
Parks, Open Space

Main Road
Railway
Rapid Transit
△ Point of Interest

0 1 2 3 4 5 km

1 : 150 000

NORTH

Crowchild Trail

CPR

Trans Canada Hwy

Bow River

Sarcee Trail

Glenmore Trail

Sarcee Military Camp

Glenmore Reservoir

Elbow River

Macleod Trail

Blackfoot Trail

Nose Creek

Calgary International Airport

City Limits

Barlow Trail

Trans Canada Hwy

16 Ave

14 St

6 Ave

9 Ave

17 Ave

CPR

CNR

CNR

Glenmore Trail

Deerfoot Trail

Irrigation Canal

CPR

Lake Bonavista

Lake Bonaventure

Fish Creek

Bow River

City Limits

Points of Interest

1 Heritage Park
2 Mount Royal College
3 University of Calgary
4 Nickle Arts Museum
5 McMahon Stadium
6 Jubilee Auditorium
7 S. A. I. T.
8 Planetarium
9 Devonian Gardens
10 Calgary Tower
11 Glenbow Museum
12 Stampede Park
13 Fort Calgary Site
14 Calgary Zoo

Carstairs
Crossfield
Beiseker
Cochrane
Airdrie
Morley
Trans Canada Hwy
CALGARY
Strathmore
Bow
Carseland River
Turner Valley
Okotoks
Royalties
Longview
High River

Aerial view of Calgary, showing the Saddledome in the foreground. The city was established in 1875 as a North-West Mounted Police post at the confluence of the Bow and Elbow rivers (*courtesy City of Calgary/Jim Hall*).

Transportation Calgary is the centre of CPR rail operations in western Canada, with world-class freight classification yards at Alyth and major repair facilities at Ogden. The CNR has container and intermodal services into its Sarcee yards. Calgary's airport, one of the largest in Canada, features a $130-million terminal (1977). The 12 primary airlines serving Calgary averaged 1155 domestic and 294 international flights weekly in 1986. The city's municipal transportation system consists of motor buses supplemented by a Light Rail Transit (LRT) system.

Government and Politics The government of the city has been conducted under powers originally granted by the North-West Territories and later

Esso Plaza, Calgary. In spite of its position as Canada's fastest-growing city in the early 1980s, Calgary remained dependent on a single, high-risk industry (*Photo by Peter Christopher/Masterfile*).

(1905) by the Government of Alberta, most recently through the Municipal Government Act (1968). Before 1909 civic business was conducted almost entirely by council alone. Since then the system of a council and board of commissioners has been in operation in one form or another. The mayor and council members (representing the city's wards) fill 3-year terms. The board of commissioners consists of the mayor and 4 appointed members. The municipal franchise was reformed to exclude plural voting (1913) and property restrictions (1915). A preferential system of voting was initiated in 1916 and continued until 1958. Since the establishment of a board of public utilities (1916) the provincial government has wielded an ever-tightening control over the scope of local government in Calgary.

Cultural Life Cultural and recreational facilities have reflected Calgary's recent growth. Educationally the city is served by the UNIVERSITY OF CALGARY, Mount Royal Community College, Southern Alberta Institute of Technology, Alberta Vocational Centre and the third-largest public-school system in Canada. Major cultural facilities include the GLENBOW MUSEUM, Fort Calgary Interpretive Centre, Calgary Centennial Planetarium and Heritage Park. The Calgary Centre for Performing Arts, which opened in 1985, is home to the Calgary Philharmonic Orchestra and the city's 2 main professional theatre companies: Alberta Theatre Projects and Theatre Calgary. The centre includes the 1800-seat Jack Singer Concert Hall. Calgary also has a professional opera company, The Calgary Opera Assn. The greatest concentration of enclosed spectator and exhibition facilities is in Stampede Pk, the home of the world-famous CALGARY STAMPEDE. Also the nearby Olympic Saddledome, built in anticipation of the 1988 Winter Olympics, is home to the CALGARY FLAMES of the NHL. The city's other professional sports teams are the CALGARY STAMPEDERS of the CFL and the Calgary Cannons, a Triple A baseball team. Calgary boasts the second-largest zoo in Canada, which includes a prehistoric park. Fish Creek Prov Pk, one of the world's largest urban parks, is located at the city's southern edge. Another attraction is Devonian Gardens, a 7 ha indoor garden in the heart of the downtown area.

MAX L. FORAN

Reading: R.P. Baine, *Calgary: An Urban Study* (1973); B.M. Barr, ed, *Calgary, Metropolitan Structure and Influence* (1975); Max L. Foran, *Calgary, An Illustrated History* (1978); J.W. Grant MacEwan, *Calgary Cavalcade* (1975); Tom Ward, *Cow Town: An Album of Early Calgary* (1975).

Calgary Flames, hockey team. They were originally the Atlanta Flames, part of the 1972 NATIONAL HOCKEY LEAGUE expansion. Vancouver businessman Nelson Skalbania brought the Flames to Calgary in May 1980 and after one year sold his interest in the team to a group of Calgary businessmen, including Byron and Daryl Seaman, Harry Hotchkiss, Norman Green, Ralph Scurfield and Norman Kwong. Under their inaugural and enduring general manager, Cliff Fletcher, the Flames have made the playoffs in all but 2 of their first 15 NHL campaigns, and in the 1985-86 playoffs defeated the EDMONTON OILERS in the Smythe Division playoffs and went on to lose to MONTREAL CANADIENS in the Stanley Cup final. Since 1983 the team has occupied the 16 700-seat Olympic Saddledome.   DEREK DRAGER

Calgary Herald, newspaper, was first published by Andrew Armour and Thomas Braden on 31 Aug 1883 as the *Calgary Herald, Mining and Ranche Advocate and General Advertiser*. It began as a 4-page weekly, produced on a handpress in a tent pitched at the junction of the Bow and Elbow rivers not far from where the *Herald* plant is now. Ownership and editorship changed frequently over the early years until 1908 when control was acquired by SOUTHAM. The *Herald* became a daily in 1885 and since fall 1983 it has been produced 7 days a week. It was an afternoon paper until Apr 1985; since then, it has appeared in the morning. The paper's paid circulation in 1986 was 175 174 (Friday), 134 417 (Mon-Thur, Sat) and 119 395 (Sunday). Operations were moved to a new $70-million plant in 1981. From the early days the *Calgary Herald* was a supporter of the pioneer ranching industry; this support has since expanded to include the area's oil and gas interests. The paper is often at odds with the views expressed in other parts of the country and even with Alberta's other major newspaper, the EDMONTON JOURNAL. National awards have been won in news, photography and production.

Calgary Stampede, whose proper title is Calgary Exhibition and Stampede, is a combined agricultural fair and RODEO. Other presentations such as manufacturing, and home and garden exhibitions occur at the same time, as well as Indian displays, an evening stage show and a large midway with sideshows and rides. Every July the Stampede opens with a parade; the rodeo and other events continue for 10 days.

Billed as the "Greatest Outdoor Show on Earth," the first exhibition took place in 1886 and the world-famous Stampede rodeo began in 1912, instigated by Guy Weadick, an American trick roper who had visited Calgary and judged the emerging town to be a prime location for a big rodeo. The first Stampede was financially underwritten by local businessmen A.E. CROSS, George Lane, A.J. McLean and Patrick BURNS. It was a great success. The parade, combined with the annual Labour Day parade of the Calgary Trade and Labor Council, was enriched by the inclusion of rodeo competitors, the duke and duchess of Connaught and their daughter Princess Patricia, and 2000 Indians in full dress — and some 14 000 spectators. Prizes totalling $16 000 were provided for the rodeo events, which were highlighted by an electrifying bronc ride by Tom Three Persons on the famous Cyclone. In spite of its success, the Stampede was not repeated until after WWI, in August 1919, when a "Great Victory Stampede" was held. In 1923 the annual Agricultural Exhibition joined with a stampede, with Weadick continuing as the Stampede Arena Director. An immediate success, the joint venture has continued to this day. As its fame spread, the Stampede expanded its facilities to include a 16 000 seat grandstand, a large trade centre, the Stampede Corral ice rink, an agricultural complex, a recreated western town and a combined curling, tennis and trade show facility.

The rodeo events include the traditional tests of cowboy versus animal, including bareback bronc riding, saddlebronc riding, bull riding, steer wrestling and calf roping. It is one of the largest rodeos in the world, with some $500 000 prize money. Weadick, the Stampede's first director, first brought CHUCKWAGON RACES, known as the Rangeland Derby, to the show in 1923 and they have become an outstanding spectator event. The wagons are modifications of the food wagons once used to supply meals to cowboys out on the range during roundup. Each wagon is pulled by 4 horses and accompanied by 4 mounted outriders. The race starts with a tight figure-8 maneuvre in the infield before the wagons burst out onto the track for a dash around to the finish. Prize money is over $225 000 for the race. Some 1 million visitors attend the Stampede annually and another 2.5 million attend functions at other times during the year. JEAN LEIPER

Reading: F. Kennedy, *The Calgary Stampede* (1964).

Calgary Stampeders, football team. Prior to WWII Calgary was represented in interprovincial competition by such teams as the Tigers, the Canucks, the Altomahs and the Bronks. The Stampeders were formed in 1945, with prewar Regina star Dean Griffing as coach, and 3 years later the club won its first of 4 western championships to date. Coached by Les Lear, they defeated Ottawa in the 1948 GREY CUP game and the celebrations of their accompanying fans gave birth to the annual festival that has surrounded the game ever since. The team played in the national final again the following year but lost to the Montreal Alouettes and waited 19 years for their next Grey Cup appearance. In 1960 the community-owned Stampeders moved into their present home, McMahon Stadium, and in 1968 and 1970 they returned to the Grey Cup, losing to Ottawa and Montreal, respectively, but capturing the championship a year later against the Toronto Argonauts. The team had limited success on the field in the 1980s and was saved in 1986 only by a special promotional drive. DEREK DRAGER

Callaghan, Morley Edward, novelist, short-story writer, broadcaster (b at Toronto 22 Feb 1903). Educated at University of Toronto and Osgoode Hall Law School, Callaghan published his first stories in Paris in *This Quarter* (1926) and *transition* (1927). His first novel, *Strange Fugitive,* was published in 1928. Ezra Pound bought 2 stories for an issue of *Exile,* and by 1929 Callaghan was publishing in *Atlantic Monthly, Harper's Bazaar, Scribner's* and *The New Yorker,* while also working as a journalist in Toronto and Montréal.

The next 2 novels – *It's Never Over* (1930) and *A Broken Journey* (1932) – concern Callaghan's perception of 2 apparently irreconcilable worlds, the self-seeking empirical jungle and the spiritual realm of trust and faith. In SUCH IS MY BELOVED (1934) the problem is faced directly. The hero, Father Dowling, befriends 2 prostitutes, but is reviled by the world, including his bishop. *They Shall Inherit the Earth* (1935) advances another small step: the hero and heroine reconcile physical and spiritual love. In another fine novel, *More Joy in Heaven* (1937), a reformed bank robber is welcomed by the community as a prodigal son, but pays with his life when he tries to prevent a bank robbery.

Morley Callaghan's masterpiece, *The Loved and the Lost,* received the Gov Gen's Award for 1951. His works have often gained recognition abroad before their recognition in Canada (*photo by Nigel Dickson*).

From 1937 to 1950 Callaghan was silent, except for *Luke Baldwin's Vow* (1948), a children's story, and *The Varsity Story* (1948), about University of Toronto. Then, in 1951, came *The Loved and the Lost,* perhaps Callaghan's masterpiece. Set in Montréal, it is a moving reprise of his temporal and eternal theme. From this intricately plotted and multilayered novel, Callaghan proceeded to *Morley Callaghan's Stories* (1959) and *The Many Coloured Coat* (1960), another novel set in Montréal, with echoes of the ancient story of Joseph and his brethren; and *A Passion in Rome* (1961), in which secular lovers find their physical-spiritual solution on the occasion of the election and installation of a new pope. In these novels, Callaghan maintains his concern with the meaning of spirit in the temporal world.

If Callaghan published relatively little in the 1950s, he was not idle. In broadcasting, he emerged as a "public" personality. In 1960 American critic Edmund Wilson identified him as "unjustly neglected" and compared him to Chekhov and Turgenev. This pronouncement undoubtedly led to many reprints of Callaghan's works, though he had already been published in France, Germany, Italy, Japan, Sweden and China, where his concern for "the little man" attracted popular taste. *That Summer in Paris* (1963), his reminiscences of 1929, is one of the finest memoirs in Canadian literature. In 1975 Callaghan published *A Fine and Private Place,* a novel in which a writer is both the hero and victim of a new generation. Then, in *A Time for Judas* (1983), Callaghan turned to the ultimate question of sanctity and human weakness. Judas is perhaps his ultimate image of the temporal-spiritual conflict. Judas, he believed, experienced a "terrible sense of isolation." "Death," said Callaghan, is mysterious, but "you can make out of life whatever you want to make....This is your truth."

Recipient of numerous awards and prizes, Callaghan received the 1951 Governor General's Award for *The Loved and the Lost.* Possibly because of his speculations about time and eternity, Canadians have not always been friendly to Callaghan, but in the larger world of literature he remains a classic. Besides many honours and citations, he has received the Royal Bank Award and is a Companion of the Order of Canada. HUGO MCPHERSON

Reading: B. Conron, ed, *Morley Callaghan* (1975).

Callière, Louis-Hector de, governor general of New France 1699-1703 (b at Thorigny-sur-Vire, France 12 Nov 1648; d at Québec 26 May 1703). From the Norman nobility and aided by a brother who was private secretary to Louis XIV, Callière impressed his superiors as an able commander at Montréal 1684-98. He was made acting governor of Canada following FRONTENAC's death in Nov 1698 and his appointment was confirmed spring 1699. In 1701 he negotiated a peace treaty between the Iroquois and a number of western tribes allied with the French. Although inflexible and rather high-handed, Callière won respect for his leadership during wars with the English and the Iroquois. ALLAN GREER

Calligraphy Before the advent of type, when all books and documents were hand-written, many different hands were developed over the centuries. With the advent of type, the techniques of writing with the broad-edged pen were lost until British Craft Movement member Edward Johnston rediscovered them. This rediscovered art was brought to Canada by Grace Melvin, who came from Glasgow to set up a design department at the Vancouver School of Art in 1927, and Esme Davis, a student of Johnston's, who moved to Victoria after WWII and taught design and calligraphy there.

Calligraphy as a leisure time activity for enthusiastic hobbyists burgeoned in the mid-1970s, influenced by a revival of interest in both the US and Britain. Leisure time courses taught not just italic, bookhand, uncial and germanic scripts (*see* GERMANIC FRAKTUR AND CALLIGRAPHY), with historical samples as models, but a design approach that turned the written word into works of art.

The resulting numbers of calligraphers, who work for both love and profit, have found it useful to form guilds for support and education. These guilds offer courses to their members both from local talent and by calligraphic artists imported from England, W Germany and the US. A yearly show of members' works is a feature of most Canadian guilds. Calligraphy guilds are located in Montréal, Ottawa, Toronto, Winnipeg, Regina, Calgary, Vancouver and Victoria as well as smaller centres in Ontario, Alberta and BC. The oldest are Victoria's, Vancouver's and Toronto's, all founded in 1976, and the largest is Calgary's with 400 active members. GAIL STEVENS

Callihoo, John, politician, native-rights leader (b at Michel IR, Alta 1882; d at St Albert, Alta 11 Aug 1957). Of Iroquois-Cree extraction and self-educated, he was a freighter and then a farmer, but his leadership capabilities soon made him a rallying point for Indian causes. During the early 1930s he assisted nonstatus relatives in forming a Métis association and in successfully urging the Alberta government to pass the Métis Betterment Act. In 1937 he became president of the League of Alberta Indians and soon gained the nickname of "The Lawyer" from frustrated Indian Dept officials with whom he was often in conflict. In 1939 he reorganized his group as the Indian Assn of Alberta and saw it expand to become a successful province-wide organization. While president he was a delegate to Ottawa and helped to bring about changes in the INDIAN ACT and in provincial legislation affecting Indians. He retired in 1947 but saw the association carry on as one of the most effective native political bodies in Canada. HUGH A. DEMPSEY

Callwood, June, journalist, civil libertarian (b at Chatham, Ont 2 June 1924). A prominent magazine writer in the 1950s, particularly for *Maclean's,* she became in the 1960s an activist for such social causes as homeless youth and drug addicts. She subsequently fought against censorship, and in 1983 she was a member of the council of Amnesty International in Canada. She has continued writing, for the *Globe and Mail* and elsewhere, and besides ghosting the autobiographies of American celebrities, has published various works, including *The Law is Not for Women* (1976), *Portrait of Canada* (1981), *Emotions* (1986) and *Twelve Weeks in Spring* (1986). She became an Officer of the Order of Canada in 1986. She is married to sportswriter Trent FRAYNE.

Calumet, from the Norman-French term for pipe or pipestem in early N American historical records, was a potent item of ritual magic in a Plains MEDICINE BUNDLE and an object of religious symbolism. The calumet was also the focus of tribal solidarity and power. Present among many Eastern Woodland groups, the pipe was used to burn TOBACCO as an offering to the Almighty. Associated with thunder and signifying honour and the sacredness of all life, the calumet was used to ratify alliances, to bring needed rain and to attest contracts and treaties (*see* NATIVE PEOPLE, RELIGION). With the exception of northern and northwestern N America where tobacco and smoking were introduced by European traders, pipe smoking itself was central to the religious thought and behaviour of most native N Americans. There were calumets for commerce and trade, and they were smoked as both peace and war pipes. Descriptions of the calumet usually refer to the entire pipe, including bowl and stem, and not merely the stem. Shafts are often long, made of light wood, painted in different colours and adorned with quills, beads, fur and feathers. Pipe bowls are typically carved from stone or catlinite, a red clay, and were engraved with geometric designs, adorned with bone and stone inlay or were simply polished.   RENÉ R. GADACZ

Calvert, George, 1st Baron Baltimore, English colonizer (b at Kipling, Eng 1579/80; d at London, Eng 15 Apr 1632). In 1621 he established a colony at FERRYLAND on Newfoundland's Avalon Peninsula, which became, by royal charter (1623), the province of Avalon. Calvert visited the colony personally in 1627 and the next year stayed the winter with his family. He was forced to defend his colony against attacks by French privateers, and also encountered difficulties when the Puritans there resented the Roman Catholic priests and settlers he had brought to Newfoundland. In 1629 Calvert left to seek a grant of land in a more hospitable climate. He obtained, under his son Cecil, what became the colony of Maryland.   JOHN PARSONS

Calvinism, Protestant Christian theological system constructed by religious reformer John Calvin (Jean Cauvin, 1509-64) and made more stringent and narrower in focus by his successors. It is considered to have been widely influential in Canadian life. Though educated in law, Calvin published a short manual of religious instruction, *Institutes of the Christian Religion,* in 1536, 2 years after leaving the Roman Catholic Church. Later he enlarged the *Institutes* several times until it became a major theological treatise adopted by most Reformed churches; it also influenced LUTHERAN and ANGLICAN theology. According to Calvin, Scripture gives humankind knowledge of God and of one's duties to God and fellow man. He emphasizes God's sovereignty and humanity's alienation from the Creator because of sinful pride. Since man has lost his free will he cannot avoid sin and is totally dependent on God's love. Salvation (reconciliation) can come only by grace through faith in Christ (receiving God into one's life). Calvin's most controversial teaching concerns election (double predestination): that God has already chosen those to be saved and those to

be damned. In this world, however, people achieve fellowship through groups such as the church and the state, which are separate but partners. Although the state's authority comes from God, a bad government may be deposed by society (not the individual) when all other remedies for justice fail.

Calvin, a French citizen, was invited to "reform" the free city of Geneva. With the city council's support his puritanical plans to improve morals and religious life were enforced, but Calvin also enhanced popular control of city politics and created a welfare system for the poor, sick and handicapped. Elsewhere Calvinism was denounced as a revolutionary attack on government and religion, and its followers were persecuted until eventually restricted to Switzerland, the Netherlands, France, Hungary, Britain and some German states. Calvinism was first introduced into Canada by French HUGUENOTS and it later flourished among Scottish, Irish, Dutch and New England settlers. By the end of the Victorian period the PRESBYTERIAN CHURCH was the largest Protestant denomination in Canada, the second-largest Calvinist group being the BAPTISTS.

Before WWI Calvinism was formative in the program of the SOCIAL GOSPEL movement for religiously based social, moral and political improvements to society. More recently it has influenced Canadian support for humanitarian and democratic developments in the Third World. The so-called "Protestant work ethic" has been credited rather inaccurately to Calvinism, as have Canadian puritanical views on sexual matters, sabbatarianism, TEMPERANCE and individualism, all attitudes shared by most Christian denominations during the Victorian era. A late 19th-century revival of European interest in Calvinism influenced Canadian theological thought by the 1930s through the writings of such "neo-orthodox" thinkers as Karl Barth. Canada has also shared in the Dutch branch of this revival, thanks to the postwar immigration of Dutch Calvinists who have sought to establish Christian-controlled schools and Christian trade unions.

JOHN S. MOIR

Reading: J.T. McNeill, *The History and Character of Calvinism* (1954).

Cambridge, Ont, City, pop 79 920 (1986c), 77 183 (1981c) located 55 km NW of Hamilton near KITCHENER-WATERLOO, was created 1 Jan 1973 when the communities of GALT, Preston and HESPELER were amalgamated. Prior to 1830 Preston was known as Cambridge Mills, after Cambridge, Eng. The economy is based on diversified manufacturing and there is a campus of Conestoga College of Applied Arts and Technology. The annual Can-Amera, held alternately in Cambridge and Saginaw, Mich, attracts about 2000 amateur athletes.   DANIEL FRANCIS

View from the river showing the old post office and warehouses in Cambridge, Ont (*photo © Hartill Art Associates, London, Ont*).

Cambridge Bay, NWT, Hamlet, pop 1002 (1986c), 815 (1981c), is located on the SE coast of VICTORIA I, 866 air km NE of YELLOWKNIFE. The peo-

ple of the area are known as the COPPER INUIT because they fashioned implements from native copper and bartered these to other groups. Few Inuit lived year round at the site before the 1950s. Named for the duke of Cambridge (1774-1850), the settlement began to expand with the construction of a loran navigational beacon in 1947 and a DEW Line site in 1955. The economy is still centered around the traditional Inuit activities of hunting and trapping. The community became a NWT government administrative centre in 1981.

ANNELIES POOL

Cameron, Alexander Thomas, biochemist (b at London, Eng 1882; d at Winnipeg 25 Sept 1947). Educated in chemistry at U of Edinburgh, Cameron came to U Man as lecturer of physiology and remained there (except for WWI service in France) until his death. When biochemistry was separated from physiology in 1923, he became head of the new department. His work on the distribution of iodine in plants and animals led to many contributions in the developing field of endocrinology, especially thyroid and parathyroid gland biochemistry. The award of the DSc in 1925 by the University of Edinburgh recognized his work on iodine biochemistry. He authored a once widely used textbook of biochemistry and other books. His interest in oceanography, stemming from his research on iodine, culminated in his chairmanship of the Fisheries Research Board of Canada (1934-47).   DAVID B. SMITH

Cameron, William Maxwell, physical oceanographer (b at Battleford, Sask 24 July 1914). Educated at UBC, he was a biologist at the Fisheries Research Board, Pacific Biological Station 1938-41, when he moved to the Meteorological Service as a forecaster at Western Air Command Headquarters, Vancouver. In 1944 he joined the RCN and became involved in antisubmarine warfare research. After WWII he studied under Dr H.U. Sverdrup at the Scripps Institution of Oceanography, U of California. He joined the Defence Research Board of Canada (1949) and played a major role in establishing the Institute of Oceanography (now Dept of Oceanography) at UBC in 1949. He carried out extensive arctic research and hydrographic surveys as chief scientist of the Canada/US Joint Beaufort Sea Expeditions 1949-54. He moved to the Dept of Mines and Technical Surveys (later the Dept of Energy, Mines and Resources) 1960 and was director of Marine Sciences Branch 1962 to 1971 when he retired from permanent service. Cameron's initiative in establishing the BEDFORD INSTITUTE OF OCEANOGRAPHY and his theoretical studies of estuarine circulation and ocean modelling are of international significance.   NEIL J. CAMPBELL

Camp, Dalton Kingsley, writer, politician (b at Woodstock, NB 11 Sept 1920). Educated at UNB, Columbia U and London School of Economics, Camp was first engaged in student politics as a Liberal. Disillusioned, he switched to the Conservatives and helped organize Robert STANFIELD's election as premier of NS in 1956. Camp was the PC Party's national president from 1964 to 1969; in that capacity he helped to organize the removal of John DIEFENBAKER as the party's leader. Camp's success in intraparty politics was not matched by personal success in general elections; he was defeated in 1965 and 1968. Thereafter, he advised PC leaders during campaigns, including that of 1984. In 1986 he returned to public life and controversy as a consultant to the Mulroney government. Camp achieved prominence in advertising and as an author and columnist; his books include his graceful and informative memoirs, *Gentlemen, Players and Politicians* (1970).

ROBERT BOTHWELL

Camp X A special training school run by the British near Whitby, Ont, during WWII, Camp X has become a legend. *A Man Called Intrepid* (1977), the best-selling account of the wartime activities of Sir William STEPHENSON, director of the New York-based British Security Co-Ordination (BSC), made several dramatic assertions about its operations, most notably that the Czech secret agents who assassinated SS General Reinhard Heydrich in 1942 were trained there. Most of this is untrue. The camp, whose official title was STS (Special Training School) 103, provided the British Special Operations Executive (SOE) with a preliminary training school for those it recruited in N and S America and with a convenient place to teach espionage to the Americans while the US was still neutral. Neither the agents who assassinated Heydrich nor others recruited in Europe were trained there. Most of the camp's graduates were either Canadians or Americans, many from the American OSS (Office of Strategic Services). SOE provided the training staff, BSC looked after administrative and financial matters, and the Canadian military authorities provided auxiliary services. Exclusively under BSC control was a secondary operation on the same site known as "Hydra," a radio station which handled top-secret British transatlantic intelligence communications. The school opened 9 Dec 1941 and closed 2 years later. *See also* INTELLIGENCE AND ESPIONAGE. DAVID STAFFORD

Reading: David Stafford, *Camp X* (1986).

Campagnolo, Iona, née Hardy, broadcaster, politician (b at Galiano I, BC 18 Oct 1932). She was raised in Prince Rupert, BC, where she worked as a broadcaster 1965-74. Chairman of the Prince Rupert School Board 1966-72, she was elected alderman for Prince Rupert in 1972. She was Liberal MP for Skeena 1974-79, serving as minister of state for fitness and amateur sport 1976-79. In Nov 1982 Campagnolo was elected president of the Liberal Party of Canada, the first woman to hold that position. She was unsuccessful in her bid for a seat in Vancouver in the 1984 federal election and, after guiding the party through its first leadership change in 16 years, retired as president of the Liberal party 27 Nov 1986. HARRIET GORHAM

Campbell, Alan Newton, professor of chemistry (b at Halifax, Eng 29 Oct 1899). After receiving a doctorate from King's Coll, London, Campbell became assistant professor of chemistry at U Man in 1930. When he arrived, the department concentrated on teaching, but Campbell began research and founded a research school. He became head of the department in 1945. For 6 years in the 1950s he served on the National Research Council. He retired as head in 1965 but continued teaching until 1969 when he became professor emeritus. He received the DSc degree, U of Man, in May 1981. Throughout his life he has actively pursued research on the conductance of electrolytic solutions and the thermodynamic properties of solutions. His students, many now eminent chemists, remember him also for his love of literature, music and classical studies. E.M. KARTZMARK

Campbell, Sir Alexander, lawyer, politician (b at Hedon, Eng 9 Mar 1822; d at Toronto 24 May 1892). At age 17, Campbell became John A. MACDONALD's second articled student; he was admitted to the bar in 1843. He practised law initially as Macdonald's partner. Campbell was a successful lawyer and businessman. In 1858 he was elected to the legislative council for Cataraqui district and remained there until 1867 when he was called to the Senate. Campbell held a succession of ministerial posts: commissioner of crown lands (1864-67); postmaster general (1867-73, 1879-80, 1880-81, 1885-87); minister of the interior (1873); receiver general (1878-79); minister of militia (1880); and minister of justice (1881-85). He was leader of the Opposition in the Senate from 1873 to 1878. As a member of the GREAT COALITION (1864-67), Campbell attended the Quebec Conference and was thus a FATHER OF CONFEDERATION. From the 1860s to the 1880s, Campbell was a leader in the Ontario wing of the federal Conservative Party. In 1887 he left the Senate to become lt-gov of Ontario. Campbell was knighted in 1879. DONALD SWAINSON

Campbell, Alexander Bradshaw, lawyer, politician, premier of PEI 1966-78 (b at Summerside, PEI 1 Dec 1933). In 1966 Campbell became one of the youngest (age 33) premiers ever elected. In 1969 his government and Ottawa signed a Comprehensive Development Plan under which large-scale farms, tourism and school consolidation were encouraged; the number of ports designated for government assistance was reduced; and incentives were offered to attract nonresource-based manufacturing. After a decade of substantial expenditure, mounting criticism and few signs of sustained development, Campbell abandoned reform rhetoric and advocated an ecologically balanced, sustainable, CONSERVER SOCIETY. His government also enacted controls over nonresident ownership. In 1978 Campbell was appointed to the PEI Supreme Court. DAVID A. MILNE

Campbell, Sir Archibald, soldier, colonial administrator (b 12 Mar 1769; d in Eng 6 Oct 1843). After a distinguished military career in India, Portugal and Burma he became lt-gov of NB in 1831. Aloof and authoritarian, he was soon at odds with the Reform group in the Assembly. Though criticized for not curbing the unpopular commissioner of crown lands, Thomas BAILLIE, he placed him at the head of the Executive Council in 1833. When instructed to surrender the crown revenues to the legislature in return for a moderate civil list and to make his Executive Council more acceptable to the Assembly, he balked and was recalled in 1837. His departure was lamented only by the few officials he had sought to protect. P.A. BUCKNER

Campbell, Clarence, sport administrator (b at Fleming, Sask 7 Sept 1905; d at Montréal 23 June 1984). As president of the NATIONAL HOCKEY LEAGUE from 1946 to 1977, Campbell's tenure was longer than any executive in any other sport. He graduated from U of Alberta and then attended Oxford as a Rhodes scholar in 1925-26. A lawyer, he became an army major in 1944, commanded the 4th Canadian Armoured Division, and was mentioned in dispatches. His suspension of hockey star Maurice "Rocket" RICHARD in Mar 1955, which touched off a riot in Montréal, was perhaps his most controversial act as NHL president, but he was also instrumental in the inauguration of the all-star game (1947), the NHL pension society (1948), the Hockey Hall of Fame in Toronto (1960) and league expansion to its present size. After retirement, Campbell was found guilty of conspiracy and influence-peddling in the "Sky Shops Affair," but was only sentenced to a "symbolic" day in prison and a fine of $25 000 (paid by the NHL). GERALD REDMOND

Campbell, Sir Colin, soldier, colonial administrator, lt-gov of NS 1834-40 (b in Scot 1776; d at London, Eng 13 June 1847). Scion of a Highland family with a strong military tradition, Campbell ran away from home at age 16, served as a midshipman and then a soldier with his close friend the duke of Wellington in Spain and at the Battle of Waterloo, and rose to the rank of lt-gen. In 1834 he became lt-gov of Nova Scotia. He soon clashed with the Assembly over the control of the crown revenues and with prominent reformers such as Joseph HOWE. In 1839 the Assembly appealed to London, which sent Charles Poulett Thomson (Baron SYDENHAM), then gov gen of British N America, to investigate. Thomson advised Campbell to add more reformers to both the legislative and executive councils, but Campbell refused and in Sept 1840 he was replaced by the more conciliatory Lord Falkland. He went on to be governor of Ceylon 1841-47. Campbell was admired, even by many reformers, for his integrity but he was too conservative to govern Nova Scotia successfully by the 1830s. P.A. BUCKNER

Campbell, Douglas Lloyd, politician, premier of Manitoba 1948-58 (b at Portage la Prairie, Man 27 May 1895). D.L. Campbell won election to the Manitoba legislature in 1922 as a Farmers' candidate in Lakeside riding, which he represented for 47 years. In 1936 he was appointed minister of agriculture in the Liberal Progressive government of John BRACKEN, and in Nov 1948 he replaced Bracken's successor, Stuart GARSON, as premier. In coalition with the Conservatives in 1950, his government was re-elected in 1949 and 1953 but defeated by the Conservatives, led by Duff ROBLIN, in 1958. Apart from extending electric service to rural areas and creating the first independent electoral commission in Canada, his government was cautious and thrifty. Succeeded as party leader in 1961 by Gildas Molgat, and retiring in 1969, he continued to denounce big government, bilingualism and deficits. His career exemplifies the transformation of the farmers' protest of the 1920s into a neo-conservative force in western Canada by the 1970s. THOMAS PETERSON

Reading: M.S. Donnelly, *The Government of Manitoba* (1963).

Campbell, Hugh Lester, air marshal (b at Salisbury, NB 13 July 1908; d at Ottawa 25 May 1987). Commissioned in the RCAF in 1931 after gaining an engineering degree from UNB, Campbell was director of training plans at Air Force Headquarters during the formative stages of the BRITISH COMMONWEALTH AIR TRAINING PLAN in 1939-40. He then served in the UK and Middle East before finishing the war as an air vice-marshal and member of the Air Council, Ottawa. Campbell was the first commander of the Canadian Air Division in Europe 1952-55, a period that saw Canada's European air commitment to NATO rise to 12 squadrons. A dynamic leader who did not suffer fools gladly, he became chief of the air staff in 1957, retiring in 1962 when he was appointed a commissioner of the NWT. NORMAN HILLMER

Campbell, Marjorie Wilkins, author (b at London, Eng 1901; d at Toronto 23 Nov 1986). Campbell's career as a writer of historical fiction reflects her affinity for the early Canadians, developed from childhood after her family immigrated to the Saskatchewan Qu'Appelle Valley in 1904. The recipient of a Guggenheim Fellowship (1959) and a Member of the Order of Canada (1978), she won a Governor General's Award in nonfiction for *The Saskatchewan* (1950), which introduced her favourite subject, the fur trade, and led to 5 more books, of which *The Nor'Westers* (1954) won a Governor General's Award in juvenile literature. Author of 13 novels and biographies, Campbell contributed articles to magazines such as *Saturday Night* and *Maclean's*, edited the *Magazine Digest* and was a consultant to the Ontario government on the restoration of Fort William, a North West Co trading post. MARYLYNN SCOTT

Campbell, Norman Kenneth, composer, television producer and director (b at Los Angeles, Calif 4 Feb 1924). Campbell, who planned a career in meteorology after his graduation from UBC, composed several songs which brought him to the attention of the CBC while he was learning to be a weatherman on Sable I, Nova Scotia. He became a music producer for radio in Vancouver and moved to Toronto in 1952 to work in television. Long a champion for the presentation of classical ballet on TV, Campbell produced CBC's first full-length ballet, *Swan Lake*, in 1956 and his later productions of *Cinderella* and *Sleeping Beauty* earned him Emmy Awards. Campbell composed the music and collaborated with Donald HARRON in writing the lyrics for the musical version of L.M. Montgomery's ANNE OF GREEN GABLES which opened at the Charlottetown Festival in 1965 and had a successful run in England. In 1972 he composed the music and his wife Elaine wrote the lyrics for *The Wonder of it All*, a musical drama based on the life of Emily CARR. He has also produced Gilbert and Sullivan operettas and opera on TV. His important opera productions include Humperdinck's *Hansel and Gretel* with Maureen FORRESTER in 1970 and Puccini's *La Rondine* with Teresa STRATAS in 1972. *Music East, Music West,* Campbell's filmed account of the Toronto Symphony's historic tour through China, was honoured by the Canadian Music Council in 1978. In 1986 he won a Gemini for his 1985 CBC-TV version of the Stratford Festival's *Pirates of Penzance*. In 1986 as well, he produced and directed the CBC's version of the Canadian Opera Co's *Onegin* and the COC's *Dialogue of the Carmelites*.

JAMES DeFELICE

Campbell, Thane Alexander, premier, chief justice of PEI (b at Summerside, PEI 7 July 1895; d at Ottawa 28 Sept 1978). A Rhodes scholar, Campbell became attorney general of PEI in 1930 before being elected to the legislature. He won a seat in 1931 but his party lost power. When the Liberals regained office in 1935, Campbell was renamed attorney general. He assumed the premiership on 14 Jan 1936, serving until 11 May 1943 when he became chief justice. He held that post until 1970 and then was appointed chief commissioner of the Foreign Claims Commission. A Companion of the Order of Canada, he was also active in heritage matters.

PETER E. RIDER

Campbell, William Bennett, teacher, politician, premier of PEI (b at Montague, PEI 27 Aug 1943). Campbell succeeded Alexander CAMPBELL (no relation) as leader of the Liberal Party and premier of the province in 1978, but his caretaker government was defeated by the PCs in the 1979 election. Campbell entered federal politics, winning the seat left vacant by the death of Cardigan MP Daniel MacDonald in 1980 and subsequently took over MacDonald's portfolio as minister of veterans' affairs. He lost his seat in the 1984 Conservative election sweep, and subsequently was defeated in the riding of 3rd Kings in the provincial election of 21 April 1986. On 4 Aug 1986 he was appointed superintendent of insurance and official trustee for the province of PEI.

DAVID A. MILNE

Campbell, William Wilfred, rector, civil servant, novelist, poet (b at Berlin [Kitchener], Canada W 1 June 1858?; d at Ottawa 1 Jan 1918). Although currently less fashionable than the other Confederation poets, Campbell was a versatile, interesting writer, influenced by Burns, the English Romantics, Poe, Emerson, Longfellow, Carlyle and Tennyson. At his best, Campbell controls his influences and expresses his own religious idealism in traditional forms and genres. A lively contributor to the Toronto *Globe* column "At the Mermaid Inn" (1892-93), Campbell wrote 2 prose romances, several closet dramas and, in later years, political poetry and prose setting forth his concept of a "vaster Britain."

TRACY WARE

Reading: C.F. Klinck, *Wilfred Campbell* (1942; repr 1977).

Campbell River, BC, District Municipality, pop 16 986 (1986c), 15 832 (1981c), area 133 km², inc 1964, replacing former village of Campbell R (inc 1947), is located on the E coast of Vancouver I, about halfway between Victoria and Cape Scott, at the northern end of the Strait of Georgia. Capt George VANCOUVER of the Royal Navy surveyed the waters here in the early 1790s when the region was inhabited by the Southern KWAKIUTL tribes. By 1900 European settlers, engaged chiefly in logging, had occupied the area, using the estuary of Campbell R as a booming ground. Forest-related industry has continued to dominate the local economy and employment, along with commercial fishing and tourism. Campbell R is famous for the tyee salmon caught in the waters of nearby Discovery Passage. The region has many good fishing lakes and provides numerous outdoor recreation opportunities – all of which have greatly increased tourism over the years. Its strategic location makes Campbell R an increasingly important service centre for the northern area of Vancouver I.

ALAN F.J. ARTIBISE

Campbellton, NB, City, pop 9073 (1986c), 9218 (1981c), inc 1958, administrative centre of Restigouche County, is located on the Québec border near the mouth of the RESTIGOUCHE R. The population is primarily English and French speaking (49.7%/49.4%, 1986c). The site of 16th- and 17th-century French missions and Scottish fish and lumber trading posts, it was settled by dispossessed ACADIANS in 1757, though most left with the French defeat in the 1760 naval Battle of the Restigouche. Named Pointe-des-Savages, Pointe-Rochelle and Martin's Point (after Cpt Martin who had established a shipbuilding business) earlier, it received its present name (for Lt-Gov Sir Archibald Campbell) after a post-1825 influx of Scots. Its early industries were fishing, shipbuilding and trapping. Lumbering became most important in the late 19th century and remained so until a pulp mill was built at Atholville in 1928. Sugarloaf Mt, 300 m, dominates the skyline and is a provincial park with ski hills. The Restigouche is famous for its AT-LANTIC SALMON sportfishing, and Campbellton holds a salmon festival each summer. Its present major industry is tourism. The Restigouche Gallery is a National Exhibition Centre of Museums Canada and houses the NB Art Bank.

BURTON GLENDENNING

Campeau, Robert, real-estate entrepreneur (b at Sudbury, Ont 3 Aug 1923). In 1949 Campeau began residential construction in Ottawa; in 1953 he incorporated Campeau Construction Co Ltd and in 1969 amalgamated a number of subsidiaries into Campeau Corp Ltd. One of the largest real-estate companies in Canada, Campeau Corp has been operating in the US since 1978. In 1985 Campeau Corp was involved in development projects in Canada and the US that involved a total expenditure of over $1 billion. The following year his successful $5 billion takeover of Allied Stores Corp was the largest foreign takeover in Canadian history. A founding member of the board of governors of Laurentian University, Campeau has been chairman of the finance committee for the Children's Hospital of Eastern Ontario and is a member of the advisory board of Guaranty Trust of Canada.

JORGE NIOSI

Camping may be defined as living in a temporary or mobile shelter in the outdoors, whether a lean-to, tent or camper van. For the native peoples of Canada, camping was usually a way of life in precontact times; for early pioneers, explorers, prospectors, surveyors and trappers, it was often a necessity.

The first recreational campers travelled by canoe, horse transport or on foot, and were limited in mobility by the weight and bulk of the equipment available to them. Military tents of army duck, sheet-iron stoves, folding cots and sheepskin sleeping bags encouraged campers to stay in one spot while they enjoyed HUNTING or SPORTFISHING within close range. In the 1890s the YMCA, followed in later decades by the Boy Scouts, Girl Guides, churches, labour unions and local governments, began sponsoring camps to improve the health and character of the young. The early organized youth camps might have had a few permanent buildings for dining and recreation, but campers generally slept "under canvas." Activities varied from water sports to HIKING and CANOE-ING, but all stressed the development of self-reliance and life skills. From the 1890s, as well, the CPR publicized camping and climbing in the Rockies. In the early 20th century, the nature and wilderness travel books of Ernest Thompson SE-TON were read widely, and the GROUP OF SEVEN helped bring an awareness of canoe camping to the Canadian public.

The increasing use of the AUTOMOBILE and expansion of the road network made car camping popular in the 1920s and 1930s. Camping supply houses opened and a variety of camping outfits, trailers and tents were marketed. Several Canadian companies did business in producing camping equipment, including the Peterborough Canoe Co (Ont) and Chestnut Canoes (NB) for wood and canvas canoes, Jones Leisure Products Ltd of Vancouver for the Trapper Nelson packboard, Woods Canada Ltd of Toronto for tents and sleeping bags, and Coleman for gas stoves and lanterns. Travellers camped by the roadside, and municipal governments began providing free camping grounds, both to attract tourists to their area and to control health standards. Private campgrounds were also established, for which a fee was charged, and which offered increasingly sophisticated facilities such as cabins, electrical and sewage hookups for motorized vehicles, and organized recreation activities. After WWII, as Canadians had more time and money to spend on leisure and as a vast flood of war-surplus equipment hit the market – tents, packs, rucksacks, sleeping bags – there was a tremendous expansion in outdoor camps. Governments released land for campsites in designated areas in national and provincial PARKS and, in 1960, a federal-provincial agreement undertook to develop campgrounds every 160 km along the TRANS-CANADA HWY. These campgrounds had fewer conveniences and lower rates than their private competitors, and proved so popular that authorities had to impose limited stays to allow maximum accessibility to all campers.

In the 1960s the "backpacker boom" hit N America, encouraged by the development of durable, lightweight equipment made from nylon and polyester, dehydrated foods, and a public increasingly concerned with fitness and outdoor skills. Camping became big business, and a number of new Canadian companies (eg, Taiga Works-Wilderness Equipment Ltd, Far West, Canadian Mountaineering Equipment Ltd) emerged to meet the demand. By 1985, Statistics Canada estimated that 26% of Canadian households owned camping equipment, with 1.7 million households having tents, 371 000 having tent trailers, and 224 000 owning truck campers. There were 2966 tent and trailer campgrounds distributed across the country.

In 1987 the Canadian Camping Assn estimated there were approximately 1500 youth camps in Canada, the majority of which were run by agencies and nonprofit organizations. Camps for special groups, such as the handicapped or children with particular health problems, were becoming more common. Private camps, often begun by teachers in their free summer months as an extension of their educational role, were concentrated mainly in southern Ontario and the Montréal area, parts of Alberta and lower mainland BC; these camps may offer a specialty in canoeing, hiking or similar outdoor skills.

Ironically the greatly increased activities of camping and hiking have had a severe impact on fragile wilderness ecosystems. Much-travelled portage trails have become eroded gullies and camping areas have been denuded of vegetation by scores of people searching for firewood. The result in many national and provincial parks is restriction of entry by a system of permits and a host of regulations about where to camp and the kinds of packaged foods that may be brought in by campers. JAMES MARSH

Campobello Island abuts the border with the US in PASSAMAQUODDY BAY, on the S coast of New Brunswick. Sovereignty over the ruggedly picturesque island was early in dispute, but passed to NB by convention in 1817. The first settlers were imported after 1770 by Capt William Owen, whose family owned most of the island for a century. The name is partly a reference to Lord William Campbell, who was governor of NS 1766-73, and partly descriptive of the place. Fishing has been the major activity, though it is most famous as the summer home of American President Franklin Delano Roosevelt. DANIEL FRANCIS

Camrose, Alta, City, pop 12 968 (1986c), 12 570 (1981c), inc 1955, located 95 km SE of Edmonton, is a distributing, medical, government and manufacturing centre for a rich, mixed-farming area. François Adam, a Belgian who came to the Duhamel mission in 1886, was responsible for the founding of the town in 1905. Initially called Sparling, Camrose is named for a town in Wales, but the name may also refer to the wild roses that grow along Stoney Cr, which flows through the town. The area was settled in the early 1900s, mostly by Scandinavians, whose influence remains in the Lutheran College and Canadian Lutheran College, a degree status university. One of Canada's first ski clubs was formed here in 1911. The city is served by both CNR and CPR, has 2 weekly publications, the *Camrose Canadian* and the *Camrose Booster*, and a giant country and western radio station.
ERIC J. HOLMGREN

Camsell, Charles, mining engineer (b at Ft Liard, NWT 8 Feb 1876; d at Ottawa 19 Dec 1958). Son of a Hudson's Bay Co factor, Camsell was appointed geologist with the Geological Survey in 1904, became chief exploration geologist in 1914 and deputy minister of mines in 1920, a post he held until retirement in 1946. Author of many geological papers, Camsell was possibly more important as an organizer, leading his department's methods from the canoe to the aeroplane, initiating laboratory research to complement field exploration, broadening its functions to include publishing and the National Museum (including Indian anthropology and its fossil collections, notably of dinosaurs) and keeping its old esprit de corps alive through the hard times of the Depression. He became a fellow of the Royal Soc of Canada, was a member of the NATIONAL RESEARCH COUNCIL 1921-36 and in 1944 with C.J. MACKENZIE reorganized postwar government science. The Charles Camsell General Hospital in Edmonton is named in his honour.
DONALD J.C. PHILLIPSON

Reading: C. Camsell, *Son of the North* (1954).

Canada, a name derived from the Huron-Iroquois *kanata*, meaning a village or settlement. On 13 Aug 1535, as Jacques CARTIER was nearing Île d'Anticosti, 2 Indian youths he was bringing back from France informed him that the route to Canada ("chemin de Canada") lay to the S of the island. By Canada they meant the village of Stadacona, on the future site of QUÉBEC CITY. Cartier used the word in that sense, but also referred to "the province of Canada," meaning the area subject to DONNACONA, chief at Stadacona. The name was soon applied to a much larger region. The "Harleian" world map of *c*1547, the first to show the discoveries made on Cartier's second voyage, applied it to an area N of the gulf and river St Lawrence, and by 1550 maps were also placing the name S of the river.

Cartier referred to the St Lawrence as the "rivière de Canada" and the name was in general use until the end of the century. But on 10 Aug 1535 he had given the name St-Laurent to a bay north of Île d'Anticosti, and the name spread gradually to the gulf and river. In 1603, on his first voyage to Canada, CHAMPLAIN spoke of the river of Canada, but by 1613 referred to St Laurens for the gulf. The name Canada was used loosely, even in official correspondence, as a synonym for NEW FRANCE, which included all French possessions; but it was always understood, as Father Pierre Biard pointed out in the Jesuit *Relation* for 1616, that "Canada ... is not, properly speaking, all this extent of country which they now call New France; but it is only that part, which extends along the banks of the great River Canada, and the Gulf of St. Lawrence." In 1664 François Du Creux, in his work *Historia Canadensis*, drew the same distinction.

As French explorers and fur traders pushed ever westward and southward, the area to which the name Canada applied increased rapidly, but its extent seems never to have been defined officially. In Mar 1762, after the CONQUEST, Gen Thomas GAGE informed Gen Jeffery AMHERST that the limits between Canada and Louisiana had never been clearly described. He could only state "what were generally believed ... to have been the Boundaries of Canada & give you my own Opinion." He judged "not only the [Great] Lakes, which are Indisputable, but the whole Course of the Mississippi from its Heads to it's Junction with the Illinois" had been considered by the French to be part of Canada. This may be one reason why Britain temporarily abandoned the name and called the colony the Province of Quebec.

Canada came into its own in 1791 when the CONSTITUTIONAL ACT (or Canada Act) divided Québec, then considerably enlarged, into the provinces of UPPER CANADA and LOWER CANADA. In 1841 they were joined to form the PROVINCE OF CANADA. In 1867 the BRITISH NORTH AMERICA ACT united the Province of Canada (divided into Ontario and Québec) with NS and NB to form "One Dominion under the name of Canada." The new area was relatively small, but it expanded rapidly. The purchase of RUPERT'S LAND in 1870 extended it to the Rocky Mts and the Arctic Ocean; the addition of BC in 1871 created a Canada extending from sea to sea; PEI was added in 1873 and Britain handed over title to the arctic islands in 1880. This gave Canada substantially the present boundaries, except for Labrador and Newfoundland which joined the federation in 1949. In a striking comment, the distinguished American historian Samuel Eliot Morison remarked that "never, since the Roman empire, have two local names received such a vast extension as Canada and St. Lawrence." *See also* EXPLORATION; TERRITORIAL EVOLUTION.
W. KAYE LAMB

Canada and Australia are large, highly industrialized and urbanized countries with small populations and with standards of living tied to the export of natural-resource products. Both countries achieved independent Dominion status within the British Empire (Canada in 1867, Australia in 1901) as federations of former British colonies, and their parliamentary structures of federal government are comparable. Their economies have depended on substantial immigration. Both have experienced economic penetration by foreign investors, with a concomitant sense of cultural threat. Their similar interest in matters related to investment by foreign parties is, nevertheless, subordinate to the maintenance of military alliances with countries that are also their trading partners. In 1941 Robert Menzies became the first Australian prime minister to visit Canada; more recently, Pierre Trudeau's 1970 visit to Australia, the first by a Canadian prime minister, led to greater public recognition of mutual interests and common problems and to increasing contact between the countries, especially in trade and technology. In early 1984 former Gov Gen Edward SCHREYER became Canada's high commissioner to Australia.

Early links between the colonies were sporadic and often accidental. Movement was predominantly from Canada to Australia, with London, Eng, as a common base. James COOK's navigational experience in the Gulf of St Lawrence during the SEVEN YEARS' WAR influenced his appointment to HMS *Endeavour* and led to his 1770 survey of Australia's E coast. The first settlement of Sydney Cove in 1788 included officers with experience in N America, mostly in Halifax. Four of the first 6 governors of New South Wales – John Hunter, Philip King, Lachlan Macquarie and Sir Thomas Brisbane – had served in British North America. A fifth, William Bligh, had been on the NORTHWEST COAST with Cook on the latter's third voyage. Later Australian governors Sir George Gipps, Sir Charles FitzRoy and Sir William Denison continued this pattern. The settlement at Sydney was George VANCOUVER's only link with British officials from 1791 to 1794 when he negotiated with the Spaniards at NOOTKA SOUND and surveyed the Northwest Coast.

Expansion westward in Canada and Australia was effected in large part by companies devoted to exploiting the land's capacity to produce staple commodities: the Australian Agricultural Co and the Van Diemen's Land Co produced wool, whereas the NORTH WEST COMPANY and the HUDSON'S BAY COMPANY sought furs. Settlement was conducted in part by COLONIZATION COMPANIES, such as the South Australia Co and the West Australian Co and, in Canada, the BRITISH AMERICAN LAND COMPANY and the CANADA COMPANY. The British settlers' common heritage can be seen in similar PLACE-NAMES, indicating close ancestral ties or the perception by settlers of resemblances between the landscape of the new country and that of the old.

After the Canadian REBELLIONS OF 1837 a number of rebels were sent into exile. Through George Arthur, lieutenant-governor of Upper Canada and previously of Van Diemen's Land [Tasmania], 91 followers of William Lyon MACKENZIE were sent to Van Diemen's Land. A monument in Hobart commemorates their pardon and return. Fifty-eight followers of Louis-Joseph PAPINEAU were transported to New South Wales where France Bay, Exile Bay and Canada Bay in Sydney remain as evidence of their presence there before their pardon.

Notable British North Americans moving to Australia included Henry Samuel Chapman and Francis Forbes. Chapman, who in 1833 founded the first daily newspaper in Canada, the *Montreal Daily Advertiser*, supported demands for an elective legislative council as a step towards RESPONSIBLE GOVERNMENT. Subsequently, as a member of the Victoria Legislative Council, he contributed to the evolution of responsible government in Australia (a constitutional gain indebted to Canadian precedents). Forbes, chief justice of Newfoundland 1816-23, became first chief justice of New South Wales, where he served from 1823 to 1837. During the 1850s, British North Americans, including villagers from Barrington, NS, and Carbonear, Nfld, mined gold in what is now Australia. Canadians Alexander Robertson, John Wagner and William Bradley assisted in the extension and reorganization of Cobb & Co coach services, which revolutionized Australian inland transport. Others built slipways and took Maritime timber entrepreneurship to Tasmania. Cape Breton Highlanders followed Rev Norman MCLEOD to Victoria before moving on to New Zealand. Sir William PARRY and Sir John FRANKLIN were natives of England who made important contributions in both BNA and Australia: both were explorers in what is now the Canadian Arctic; Parry was commissioner, Australian Agricultural Co, 1830-34, and Franklin was lieutenant-governor of Van Diemen's Land, 1836-43.

Between Canadian Confederation and WWII there was increased contact between the countries, especially after the federation of Australia in 1901. The 2 governments were frequently in touch over matters of education, health, transport, communication, immigration restriction and agriculture. Although the countries competed for immigrants from Britain, some settlers from Australia migrated to the Canadian West, and vice versa. Parallel surges of nationalism were evident as well, and were expressed, for example, in the art of Canada's GROUP OF SEVEN and of the Australian Heidelberg School, a group of Melbourne painters of the late 19th and early 20th centuries. A movement of professionals began between the countries; eg, Alfred SELWYN, director of the Geological Survey of Victoria, in 1869 became director of the GEOLOGICAL SURVEY OF CANADA, and Thomas Griffith TAYLOR, first professor of geography at U of Sydney, became professor of geography at U of Toronto in 1935.

Closer international bonds were established during WWII, as 9600 Australian airmen trained in Canada under the BRITISH COMMONWEALTH AIR TRAINING PLAN. After the war, as the promise of mineral resources and concern for defence motivated both national governments to map their large territories, professional links developed in geodetic survey and topographical mapping. Although GEOPOLITICAL priorities influence their foreign policies in different ways, in the 1980s both countries purchased the American F-18 fighter aircraft. Both countries are participating with the US in building and operating Starlab, to be launched on a space shuttle in 1989. Knowledge and experience in high technology, satellite communication, agriculture, transport, land rights

and resource development increase mutual contact. In the early 1980s over 25 Canadian-based oil companies set up joint ventures in Western Australia, creating an economic link which although now modified has continued into the late 1980s. Frequent competition in resource exports includes a British Columbia project, begun in 1983, involving export to Japan of 94 million t of coking coal over 15 years (*see also* PACIFIC RIM).

In 1894 Canada's first agent to New South Wales was posted. By 1909 the Massey-Harris Co had arranged to sell agricultural machinery to western Australian farmers. Australia established a trade commissioner in Toronto in 1929, reinforcing a long-developing association which has grown recently. Trade missions to Australia from Nova Scotia, Québec, Ontario and Alberta were designed specifically to strengthen trade and technology links. Canadian-Australian trade reached Cdn$ 1.2 billion in 1986, operating within the framework of the General Agreement on Tariffs and Trade (GATT) and a 1973 bilateral trade agreement.

Since the 1960s a regular public-service exchange has occurred at the federal level, especially in immigration, and in mapping and personnel-training programs. Higher salaries and landed-immigrant status attracted Australians to Canada in the 1960s. Since then graduate studies and educational exchanges have been continual. Canadian medical and health care systems were prototypes for Australia's Medibank in the 1970s. Canada's diplomatic representation (high commission in Canberra, the Australian capital, and consulates in Sydney, Melbourne and Perth) matches that in W Germany, and is second only to Canadian representation in the US.

Considerable interest in each other's literature is symbolized by the Canada-Australia Literary Award, which was inaugurated in 1976. In journalism, the Canadian Award (est 1975) is allocated for merit in reporting international affairs pertaining to the Pacific region. The formalization of comparative studies, which has been attempted since 1945, was achieved in 1981 with the Canada-Australia Colloquium: Public Policies in Two Federal Countries; with the establishment of the Canadian Visiting Fellowship at Macquarie University; and with the formation of the Australian Association for Canadian Studies. The latter (now the Assn for Canadian Studies in Australia and New Zealand) has held conferences on, eg, theory and practice in comparative studies, and regionalism and national identity. The annual journal *Australian-Canadian Studies* (fd 1983) is published jointly by the faculties of social work at La Trobe U, Melbourne and U Regina.

Although the national governments have worked in co-operation for many years, and exchanges at the scholarly level are becoming more common, there has been relatively little opportunity for the ordinary citizen of one country to learn about the other. It is to be hoped that this situation will improve as Canada and Australia continue to increase contact with each other.

JOHN ATCHISON

Reading: H. Albinski, *Canadian and Australian Politics in Comparative Perspective* (1973); Bruce Hodgins, *Federalism in Canada and Australia* (1978).

Canada and Britain, *see* COMMONWEALTH; COLONIAL OFFICE; various history articles.

Canada and Its Provinces: A History of the Canadian People and Their Institutions (23 vols, Toronto, 1913-17), ed Adam SHORTT and Arthur G. DOUGHTY, was written by "one hundred associates." *Canada and Its Provinces* was the most comprehensive study of Canadian historical and political development to appear before WWI. The first 6 of its 12 sections deal with Canada's evolu-

tion into a Dominion, the next 5 trace the history of the provinces and regions, and the last is a one-volume general index. In its editors' view, the purpose of the work was to prevent "sectionalism" and to promote "a broad national spirit in all parts of the Dominion" as the means to "an enlightened patriotism which vibrates to the sentiment of nationality." Today's reader may find the language dated, but these volumes are still an essential source for Canada's view of itself before 1918.

NEIL BESNER

Canada and the United States "The Americans are our best friends whether we like it or not." That perfect malapropism, uttered in the House of Commons by Robert Thompson, the leader of the Social Credit Party early in the 1960s, captured the essence of Canada's difficult relationship with its nearest neighbour. The Americans *are* our best friends for their wonderful qualities of openness and friendship, their idealism and their generosity. But it is just as well that we are friends, for with their massive military and economic power, the Americans could crush Canada in an instant through deliberate intent or inadvertence.

Instinctively Canadians have always understood the paradoxes in the relationship. When the United Empire LOYALISTS fled the vengeance of the winning side in the American Revolution and came to the raw British colonies north of the line, they brought with them an abiding distaste for what they saw as excesses of democracy, even mobocracy, that had dispossessed them. But at the same time, their intellectual baggage included a host of American attitudes and ideals. The Loyalists wanted no state religion and they sought public education, for example. Their political heirs could design a Confederation bargain that included an appointed Senate to act as a check on the democratic excesses of the elected House of Commons. But the British North America Act, 1867, would also include a concept of FEDERALISM that, while different from the model adopted in the US Constitution, bore strong affinities to it.

American ideas and attitudes, American models and failures, shaped the very nature of Canada. So too did a combination of fear and profit. The RECIPROCITY treaty of 1854 had been demanded by merchants frightened by the loss of hitherto assured markets in the United Kingdom. Reciprocity was popularly believed to have created an economic boom with the access it gave the British N Americans to the great market to the south. But when the terrible Civil War wracked the Republic from 1861 to 1865 and increased tension between the British and American governments, the 1854 treaty was a casualty. Indeed, so great was the ill-feeling between the governments that many in Canada feared that the soon-to-be victorious North might try to reunite its people by staging an invasion of Canada. FENIAN incursions and plots lent credence to the rumours. The result of such factors was increased pressure in the British provinces to unite in the Dominion of Canada. In that way, defence might be easier to manage (if still fundamentally hopeless), and the economies of the colonies might be enhanced in a wider market. The US, in other words, was the godfather at the wedding, just as American pressures would lead to a hurried absorption of Manitoba in 1870.

If Canada now existed as a separate N American colony-nation, the attractions of the US did not wane. Reciprocity remained a sought after goal and Conservative PM Sir John A. MACDONALD craved it just as fervently as the Liberal Alexander MACKENZIE. Macdonald's last great campaign in 1891, an election he won on the cry, "A British subject I was born, a British subject I will die," is the stuff of history books and legend. Almost forgotten is that Macdonald, the creator of the NATIONAL POLICY of high tariff protection that had produced singularly few economic benefits since its implementation in 1879, had sought a trade agreement with the Americans just before the election; only when he was rebuffed once more did the Old Chief wrap himself in the bloody shirt and campaign against the rapacious Yankees. Twenty years later, in 1911, PM Sir Wilfrid LAURIER struck a deal with the US for reciprocity in natural products, but the country, now industrialized to an extent undreamed of in 1891, rejected the great Québec Liberal leader and reciprocity for Robert BORDEN's campaign that called for "No Truck or Trade with the Yankee." The irony of it all was that a mere half dozen years later, the necessities of WWI forced PM Borden to the south to seek economic assistance from President Woodrow Wilson's government. His most telling argument with the President? That Canada was the best friend of the US. More ironic still, the argument worked, and the US extended to Canada assistance it was very wary about giving to its other Allies.

The US clearly also believed that Canada was its best friend. Most Americans knew little about Canada beyond that contained in their books about hunting and fishing and, later, their films about gallant Mounties rescuing fair damsels. But that did not matter at all. Canadians were, while still subservient to the kings of England, they thought, much the same as Americans. And, of course, it was true. Was Canada not the safest place for Americans to invest? Certainly the large corporations thought so as, during and after WWI, they quickly and effortlessly displaced the United Kingdom as the major source of FOREIGN INVESTMENT in Canada. Was the Canadian consumer not exactly the same, if a little less wealthy, than the American? Again, the corporations believed so as they won the same brand loyalty for soaps and chewing gum from a resident of Moose Jaw as they had in Peoria. Did Canadians not watch the same movies and read the same magazines as Americans? The owners of the *Saturday Evening Post* and of the Metro-Goldwyn-Mayer studios certainly considered it so. It was true that Canada and Canadians were similar, and the Americans could be forgiven if they missed the subtle shadings that differentiated the 2 countries. After all, most Canadians could scarcely tell the 2 countries apart – and tens of thousands of Canadians immigrated to the US each decade in search of greater opportunity for themselves and their children.

Greater opportunity. That was the major attractive force of the US. There was certainly prejudice there against blacks, Jews and "foreigners" (although Canadians were never seen as foreigners except for French-speaking "Canucks" in the New England states), but there was also a willingness in the US to accept the idea that people could get ahead through their own talents and hard work. Sometimes that opportunity seemed to be lacking in Canada where the old "family compact" seemed to retain a stranglehold on the economy and social status and where only those of British origin had any claim to prestige and power. Order was the great Canadian good, and order meant not only the upholding of the law but also the maintenance of the status quo. Such an attitude had its virtues – French Canadians as a collectivity were not assimilated, after all, unlike the fate of millions of immigrants absorbed into the great melting pot to the south – but it was undeniable that a greater share of the pie and the honours remained in the hands of a few.

Worse yet, it cost more to be Canadian. Thanks to the high tariff that protected the manufacturers

of Canada, the cost of living was always higher than in the US. A workingman's pay packet did not go as far in the Dominion, and hence necessities were dear and luxuries were fewer. The climate was worse, an inevitable result of geography, and the land generally less fertile and the growing season shorter. People had to pay a price to be and remain Canadian, but pay it they did for manifold reasons. For some, it was inertia; for others, it was loyalty to Crown and Empire; but for many, it was because Canada had escaped the excesses of America and Americanism.

This was particularly evident once the US rose to globalism and superpower status during and after WWII. The idealism of the US, demonstrated, for example, in the Lend-Lease Act that had given the Allies the munitions and supplies to win WWII and the Marshall Plan that had helped so greatly to reconstruct Europe after that war, seemed to have been replaced by a military-industrial complex that pursued unwinnable wars for geopolitical ends. The VIETNAM WAR was the classic example, a war so dreadful in its effects on the American polity that draft-dodgers and military deserters by the thousands sought and found sanctuary in Canada, along with thousands of ordinary men and women looking for a saner life-style. For the first time, the flow of immigration from the south to the north exceeded that of Canada to the US. Canada's smallness and what many Americans perceived as innocence had become virtues as the US seemingly lost its way.

Many of those American immigrants in the late 1960s, however, misunderstood their new home, something that was strikingly apparent when the Trudeau government implemented the War Measures Act in Oct 1970 (*see* OCTOBER CRISIS). Recent arrivals from the US could not understand how it was that Trudeau received overwhelming public support in English Canada for the suspension of civil liberties and the employment of the armed forces in the streets of Montréal and Ottawa. In the US, they said, the people would have been out in the streets in protest while in Canada the only rallies were those in support of the government.

The Vietnam War provided opportunities for Canadian business, the darker side of the new Canadian prosperity that marked the 1960s and after. The Defence Production Sharing Agreement, negotiated by the Diefenbaker government in 1958, created a quasi free-trade agreement in defence materials in an attempt to decrease the trade imbalances that Canada faced because of its military purchases in the US. Bombs and bandages, gunsights and grenades, produced in Canada, were used in the war zone.

To some Canadians, the economic integration with the US symbolized by the DPSA prevented Canada from pursuing an independent foreign policy. That there was economic integration seemed undeniable. Since the signing of the GENERAL AGREEMENT ON TARIFFS AND TRADE in 1947 and subsequent international conferences, tariffs between Canada and the US had been lowered dramatically. American investment in Canada, just 23% of the total in 1914, had risen to 60% in 1939, 70% in 1945, 76% in 1955, 81% in 1967 and 82% in 1982; by 1986 it had fallen to 50%. Whole sectors of Canada's ECONOMY were owned and controlled in the US, and the possibility of Canadians determining their own destiny seemed to be slipping away. The result was a resurgence of NATIONALISM, stronger in central Canada than the East or West, the creation of such organizations as the COMMITTEE FOR AN INDEPENDENT CANADA, and efforts by political figures such as Liberal finance minister Walter GORDON (1963-65) to attempt to control foreign investment. The Trudeau government's establishment of the FOR-

EIGN INVESTMENT REVIEW AGENCY in 1973, even if it turned out to be a paper tiger, was one legislative result of the new nationalism, and while FIRA drew the ire of American investors and the US government, its disappearance under the Mulroney government was not much lamented.

Brian Mulroney's Progressive Conservatives, meanwhile, moved toward a FREE TRADE agreement with the US in 1985. Tariffs, as has been noted, were generally low between the 2 countries, but nontariff barriers (such as those that favour the price of domestic wines over California vintages) were prevalent, subsidies were employed by both to protect weak sectors of their economies, and a host of other issues divided the nations. Although there was, according to opinion polls from 1985 to 1987, substantial although declining support for free trade, there was no doubt that certain sectors might suffer. Even after the agreement was signed in Oct 1987, questions continued. Could the weak cultural industries of Canada survive an open border? Would agriculture sectors such as Ontario and BC fruit survive? How many industrial jobs might be lost? The answers were unclear, but when they became evident then the public's support might increase or decline. The one certainty was that free trade would eliminate a psychological border that had helped to keep Canadians safe in the belief that they were different from their southern cousins (*see* CULTURAL POLICY).

Canada's economic sovereignty had been severely compromised by the flow of American capital to the north. Political sovereignty was similarly threatened by the desire of the Canadian government and people to follow the American lead in the world. Vietnam was the exception that proved the rule, for if Canada did not send troops to the Americans' war, it was only because the nation was represented there on the International Commission for Control and Supervision set up by the Geneva Agreements of 1954. But in NATO and in NORAD Canada did its duty, dragging its feet on occasion, but a good ally all the same. When, as in the CUBAN MISSILE CRISIS of Oct 1962, the Diefenbaker government was slow in bringing the Canadian component of NORAD to alert status, the minister of national defence and the military acted anyway, and the next year American intervention helped to topple Diefenbaker's divided Conservative government. Given geography, Canada has no option but to do its share in defence of N America and the US heartland; abroad, the constellation of forces seemingly requires that we carry our (small) share of the load.

Still, Canadian SOVEREIGNTY over the nation's territory was secure. Or was it? The US had never recognized Canada's sovereignty over the arctic waterways and islands, and during WWII, American military operations in the North, undertaken with the full consent of Ottawa, had blossomed to such an extent that the federal government paid in full for every installation to ensure that the Americans would depart after 1945 (*see* ARCTIC SOVEREIGNTY). The Cold War, however, had brought the US military back to the Arctic, and there were upsetting incidents when Canadian parliamentarians had to secure permission from the Pentagon before being allowed to visit DEW-Line stations. The development of American and Soviet nuclear submarines capable of operating under arctic ice also called Canadian sovereignty in the North into question, as did American insistence in 1968 and 1985 on sending a giant oil tanker and a US Coast Guard vessel through the Northwest Passage without Canada's consent. Even if it had the will to act against those who violated Canadian territory with impunity, Canada lacked the military capacity in the Arctic to do anything. Beyond occasional surveillance flights and token military forces at scattered locations, Canadian occupation of the North, other than the light Inuit and Dene population and oil drillers, was strictly limited.

Best friends or not, the US sometimes acts like the bully on the block. Canadians derive many benefits from their proximity to the US, but they have to pay a price for it, too. How high a price remains negotiable, but economic, cultural and political sovereignty must be protected constantly or else be lost. The Loyalists knew that, the Fathers of Confederation knew it, and so, one hopes, do Canadians and their governments in the late 20th century.   J.L. GRANATSTEIN

Canada Centre for Inland Waters (CCIW), one of the world's leading WATER-research centres, provides Environment Canada and the federal Dept of Fisheries and Oceans with shared facilities for a range of environmental and marine research and surveys. Established by the federal government in 1967, CCIW occupies a large waterfront site in Burlington, Ont, just inside Hamilton Harbour. CCIW houses the headquarters of Environment Canada's National Water Research Institute, National Water Quality Laboratory, Wastewater Technology Centre and the Ontario Region offices of the Inland Waters Directorate. The Dept of Fisheries and Oceans at CCIW is the Bayfield Institute and includes the Great Lakes Laboratory for Fisheries and Aquatic Sciences and the Central and Arctic Region headquarters of the Canadian Hydrographic Service, one of 3 Canadian centres for nautical-chart production.

Since 1974 CCIW has been the World Health Organization's Collaborating Centre for Ground and Surface Water Quality, responsible for establishing and collecting data from a worldwide network of water-quality monitoring stations, part of the United Nations' Global Environmental Monitoring System (GEMS). Scientists at CCIW play a critical role in developing information for the management of the GREAT LAKES, but are also involved with LAKES, RESERVOIRS and RIVERS across the country, dealing with issues such as ACID RAIN, toxic chemicals, ice jams and shore erosion. *See also* WATER POLLUTION.   ERIC McGUINNESS

Canada Committee, a British parliamentary committee established 2 May 1828 to settle political disputes which were paralysing representative government in Lower Canada and creating difficulties in Upper Canada. The committee heard the testimony of several notable Canadians and recommended, among other proposals, that the Houses of Assembly should control public revenues in exchange for a permanent Civil List; that the Legislative Council (upper house) should be more independent and should represent the populace as a whole; and that the CLERGY RESERVES in UC should be sold, the proceeds to be used to benefit all Protestant denominations. The report was an immense boost to the Reform cause, for its recommendations echoed the demands of reformers in both Canadas. Nevertheless, despite attempts to adopt many of the recommendations, political tension failed to ease and culminated in the REBELLIONS OF 1837.   CURTIS FAHEY

Canada Company, brainchild of John GALT, established in late 1824 and chartered in 1825 as a land and COLONIZATION COMPANY in Upper Canada. In 1826 the company purchased from the government about 2.5 million acres (1 million ha) of land for $295 000. Roughly half lay in the Huron Tract (western Ontario) and the rest consisted of scattered crown reserves. The payments, spread over 16 years, went directly to the executive branch of the Upper Canada government, to the

Lands in Upper Canada to be disposed of by the Canada Company, from advertising material printed 1832 (*courtesy National Archives of Canada/C-55033*).

bitter resentment of Reformers in the elected assembly, who also charged that the company failed to provide promised improvements in its structure and treated immigrants dictatorially.

After the ACT OF UNION (1841), the company's connection to the Tory elite lessened and, with the implementation of a leasing system, the company operated more effectively and less conspicuously – though settlement would likely have proceeded as quickly without it. Following the sale of its last holdings in the 1950s, it ceased operation.   PETER A. BASKERVILLE

Canada Corn Act, passed in 1843 by the British Parliament and applying to all grains, allowed Canadian wheat to enter the British market at a nominal duty, and flour manufactured in Canada at a proportionate rate. The latter clause was a victory for those seeking to make the St Lawrence a major conduit for American wheat. By removing barriers to Canadian wheat exports imposed by periods of low prices in Britain, the Act encouraged expansion of wheat acreage and flour-milling capacity in Upper Canada. But the Act was short-lived, since Britain was moving towards free trade, and repealed the CORN LAWS in 1846.   DOUGLAS McCALLA

Canada Council In accordance with the recommendation of the Massey Report, on 28 Mar 1957, the House of Commons adopted a bill which officially created the Canada Council. One month later, the Council held its first meeting. According to its mandate as defined by Parliament, the Council was to encourage the study and enjoyment of the arts, humanities and social sciences, as well as the production of related works. From the start, the federal government intended that the Council should have a large measure of autonomy and therefore put aside $50 million in an endowment fund to finance the Council's programs. During its first year the Council had a budget of $1.5 million for the arts, humanities and social sciences.

A board of 21 members operates the Canada Council. Its members are drawn from all 10 provinces and are named by the federal government, as are the director and associate director. The headquarters is in Ottawa. By 1964 the endowment fund was seen to be insufficient, and the government decided to grant enough addi-

tional money each year to cover the organization's needs. This grant now accounts for about 85% of the Council's budget. In 1986-87 the Council's appropriation from Parliament was $85 311 000. In 1978 a new organization, the SOCIAL SCIENCES AND HUMANITIES RESEARCH COUNCIL OF CANADA, was established, leaving the Canada Council responsible for the arts.

In order to carry out its enormous mandate, the Council tries to keep in touch with its public. Its employees function simultaneously as bureaucrats, administrators, organizers and cultural travelling salesmen. The Council offers assistance both to individual artists and to artistic organizations and professional associations. Demands on funds exceed the money available, and the Council calls on a number of committees, juries and advisers to help allocate grants. An interdisciplinary consultative committee of artists from every region of the country meets periodically to make recommendations on desirable cultural policies. To date, the Council has defined its mandate broadly. It helps everything from children's theatre to publishing houses, across the whole range of cultural activities. Through its Explorations program, it tries to fill the gaps which precisely defined disciplines cannot accommodate.

The Council celebrated its 30th anniversary in 1987. If its achievements seem prestigious, it is because the foundation of the Council coincided with a Canada-wide cultural revolution. This fortunate coincidence has allowed artists' energies to find expression and the public's thirst for its own culture to be satisfied.   NAIM KATTAN

Canada Cup Capitalizing on the public interest aroused by the CANADA-SOVIET HOCKEY SERIES, 1972, Douglas Fisher, of Hockey Canada, and Alan EAGLESON, of the NHL Players' Assn, arranged to bring national teams from Europe to compete against Canada and the US in tournaments which would be staged, every 3 or 4 years, in N American arenas.

The first Canada Cup tournament, in 1976, was won by Canada, which defeated Czechoslovakia in the playoff final. The second tournament was held in 1981 and was won by the Soviet Union, which defeated Canada in the final match.

The third Canada Cup tournament was staged in 1984 and was won by Canada, which defeated Sweden in a 2-game playoff. However, the highlight of that series was Canada's dramatic 3-2 victory over the Soviets in a semifinal match. Mike Bossy deflected Paul Coffey's shot into the Soviet net to score the winning goal after 12 mins and 29 secs of overtime.

The 1987 tournament was won by Canada after a thrilling 3-game playoff with the Soviet Union. The Soviets won the first game, 6-5, after 5 minutes and 33 seconds of overtime. Canada won the second game, 6-5, in 30 minutes and 7 seconds of overtime. After falling behind, 0-3, in the early stages of the final game, Canada came back to win, 6-5, when Mario Lemieux scored the deciding goal at 18.34 of the third period.   JIM COLEMAN

Canada Development Corporation, with headquarters in Toronto, develops and maintains Canadian-controlled and -managed companies in the private sector. Created in 1971 through a special Act of Parliament, the CDC has helped to widen the investment opportunities open to Canadians. Some 31 000 private shareholders have invested in the corporation, and during its first decade CDC was able to acquire diversified assets. Major investments 100% owned by CDC include holdings in petroleum, mines and petrochemicals. In 1986 CDC had sales or operating revenue of $2.6 billion (ranking 34th in Canada), assets of $6.3 billion (ranking 13th) and 7835 employees. Major shareholders include the federal government (14%) and Noranda (12%).

DEBORAH C. SAWYER

Canada East, *see* PROVINCE OF CANADA.

Canada First, nationalist movement fd 1868 by Ontarians George DENISON, Henry Morgan, Charles MAIR and William FOSTER; and Robert Grant Haliburton, a Nova Scotian living in Ottawa. Inspired by the recently assassinated Thomas D'Arcy MCGEE and viewing CONFEDERATION as a political transaction among elites, Canada First sought to promote a sense of national purpose and to lay the intellectual foundations for Canadian nationality. During the 1869-70 Red River Rebellion the group helped provoke the reaction against Métis, Catholics and French which swept Ontario following Thomas SCOTT's execution. It also campaigned for exclusively British immigration, envisaging a vigorous Anglo-Saxon and Protestant "northern" race that would harness the country's great economic potential. In 1871 the group turned to a less inflammatory expression of its nationalism: Canada's relationship with Britain. The Canada Firsters were dedicated to Canadian independence from the US and to the British connection, but after Britain concluded the 1871 Treaty of WASHINGTON with the Americans, Canada First placed greater emphasis on Canadian autonomy and self-reliance, though the aim was some form of imperial federation, not separation from Britain.

Between 1872 and 1874 the founders, whose circle had expanded to embrace the "Twelve Apostles," drifted apart geographically. Leadership passed to a Toronto group primarily interested in launching a new political party, the Canadian National Association, which was founded in 1874. Its weekly organ, the *Nation*, had a healthy circulation, and there was speculation that Edward BLAKE, a prominent Liberal, might lead the party. But political action was not in keeping with Canada First's original intentions, and the movement had limited appeal outside Ontario; in fact, the call for reform had blatantly anti-Catholic overtones. The new leaders were divided, and Blake finally entered PM Mackenzie's Liberal government. The political organization quickly collapsed, leaving Canada First with no institutional basis.

Historians have called Canada First the harbinger of 20th-century political developments: third-party challenges, and Canada's complete independence from Britain. But these were not its original goals. Its real heirs were the later imperialists who called for consolidation of the British Empire, as they sought an instrument to protect and advance "superior" Anglo-Saxon values and institutions, and a vehicle for the definition and assertion of Canadian nationhood. Their implicit rejection of French Canadian nationality produced division and conflict rather than unity of purpose. B.L. VIGOD

Canada Games (Jeux du Canada) The idea of the Canada Games was first suggested in 1924 by Norton Crow, secretary of the Amateur Athletic Union of Canada, but received little support. The idea often resurfaced in the next 25 years but each time met with lukewarm response. In 1962 the chairman of the National Advisory Council on Fitness and Amateur Sports once again suggested a sports festival. A Québec lawyer, André Marceau, took the initiative and, along with other sports authorities in Québec, set up a corporation of the top Canadian winter sports. In 1964 the Canadian Centennial Commission recommended that winter games be held in 1967 and the federal government endorsed the idea. On 30 May 1965 a financial agreement was signed and the

first Canada Winter Games finally came into being. Since then, summer and winter games have been held every 4 years. Their objectives are to provide first-rate sports facilities, to train as many young athletes as possible to international standards, to encourage competition in the provinces and territories, and to develop human resources from judges on up to director general of the games' organizing groups. YVON DORE

Canada Goose, *see* GOOSE.

Canada House, a distinctive symbol of Canadian interests in Britain, located in London's bustling Trafalgar Square. After immigration, financial, and trade promotion had been directed for years from rented quarters, the imposing Union Club premises were purchased in 1923, refurbished by the Hon Peter Larkin, high commissioner, with Canadian materials, and opened by George V in 1925. Successive Canadian high commissioners to Britain used its offices until expansion into Sir John A. Macdonald House. Today Canada House is the headquarters in Britain for promoting Canadian culture and information, and a focal point for travelling Canadians.

D.M. PAGE

Canada Land Inventory (CLI) is a comprehensive federal-provincial survey of LAND capability and use for regional resource and land-use planning established under the Agricultural Rehabilitation and Development Act (ARDA), 1961. In the late 1950s and early 1960s, problems of land-use conflict, competition for land and land misuse were becoming more common. These problems were addressed in a series of conferences, and a major recommendation emerged to classify and map land capabilities across southern Canada.

The inventory, covering roughly 2.6 million km² (25% of Canada), includes assessments of land capability for agriculture, forestry, outdoor recreation and wildlife (waterfowl, ungulates and sportfish) and land use circa 1967. Output from the program has been large and includes 18 000 manuscript maps at 1:50 000, 1200 published maps at scales of 1:250 000 and 1:1 000 000, and numerous reports and analyses. A computerized data bank, the Canada Geographic Information System (*see* GEOGRAPHIC INFORMATION SYSTEMS) was developed to store and analyse this large volume of information. Reports are available describing the classifications and summarizing the results.

The program provides a common reference for professional and lay bodies concerned with land-use planning and has fueled policy development in every province. It has enabled some provinces to enact legislation to protect agricultural land and to identify submarginal farmland. Planners have used it to identify potential PARKS and WILDLIFE RESERVES and to assess areas of recreation and tourism potential. T.W. PIERCE

Canada Mortgage and Housing Corporation is the federal CROWN CORPORATION responsible for administering Canada's National Housing Act. CMHC was created in 1946 as the successor to Wartime Housing Corporation, and until 1979 was called Central Mortgage and Housing. Its mandate was to help improve housing and living conditions in Canada. Since 1946 one-half of all housing built in Canada has been assisted through the National Housing Act. CMHC has helped Canadians house themselves through grants, loans and by insuring mortgage monies borrowed from private lenders. Good housing and community design are encouraged through CMHC's research and design programs.

Immediately after WWII, CMHC concentrated its activities on providing homes for returning war veterans. During the 1950s housing quality

concerns were added to the task of providing for sufficient quantity of housing. Urban renewal programs to redevelop inner cities were funded during the 1960s. In the 1970s neighbourhood improvement programs and a residential rehabilitation assistance program encouraged the maintenance and improvement of existing communities. The CMHC is concerned with providing housing for low-income people and meeting the special needs of the elderly and disabled. The corporation administers programs to encourage provinces, cities, and nonprofit and co-operative societies to provide housing for Canadians who would otherwise be unable to obtain adequate and affordable shelter. CMHC publishes annual housing statistics, reports the results of housing research and produces a number of publications related to housing. ANN MCAFEE

Canada Packers Inc, with head offices in Toronto, is the largest Canadian producer of food products. The original company, established in 1927, was Canada Packers, Ltd, which acquired the capital stock of Gunns Ltd, The Harris Abattoir Co Ltd, the Canadian Packing Co Ltd and William Davies Co, Inc. In 1932 these operations were consolidated and Canada Packers, Ltd, became an operating company. The present name was adopted in 1979. Today the company produces a full line of food products, processing and distributing meat and poultry products, and canning and freezing fruits and vegetables. It also produces and distributes soap, chemical, pharmaceutical, leather, feed and animal health products across Canada. The company has facilities in W Germany, Britain, Australia, Mexico and the US. As of Mar 1986, it had annual sales of $3.2 billion (ranking 28th in Canada), assets of $623 million (ranking 137th) and 13 200 employees. Its shares are widely held, with W.F. Mclean holding 34%.

DEBORAH C. SAWYER

Canada Pension Plan (CPP), introduced in 1965 and in effect in 1966, is an earnings-related public PENSION plan that transfers incomes from workers to the retired. The current contribution (tax) rate of 3.8% on earnings between the maximum pensionable earnings ($25 900 in 1987) and the basic exemption (about 10% of the maximum) is split equally between employers and employees. Retirement pensions (obtainable from 65 years of age) are 25% of average pensionable earnings, calculated in terms of the wage standards existing at the time of retirement. The CPP also provides survivors' benefits (spouses' pensions, orphans' benefits, lump-sum death benefits) and disability benefits. All payments are indexed to the CONSUMER PRICE INDEX and adjusted annually. The initial CPP contribution rates were designed to produce a pension fund of billions of dollars – money invested in provincial bonds at interest rates tied to rates paid by federal bonds. As the number of those eligible for full pensions increases, benefits threaten to exceed the contributions unless contribution rates are increased. The CPP's financial strength ultimately depends on the contribution rates that workers will accept. If the ratio of the elderly to those of working age increases, so will the cost to workers of public pensions. A. ASIMAKOPULOS

Canada Post Corporation, was established by the Canada Post Corporation Act 16 Oct 1981, replacing the previous Post Office Department of the federal government. It is a CROWN CORPORATION, exempt from income taxes. The corporation may make regulations prescribing rates of postage that are fair and reasonable so as to provide revenue sufficient to defray expenses. Despite major increases in postage rates, the corporation continues to be criticized for poor service, generally blamed on outdated equipment and labour disputes. Canada Post is the largest civilian government organization, administering some 8500 post offices across Canada and employing 61 372 full-time and part-time people. It handled about 7.7 billion pieces of mail (delivered to more than 10 million addresses) and its revenues totalled more than $2.7 billion in 1985-86. Its deficit of $306 million in 1983-84 was reduced to $184 million in 1985-86. The corporation operates a museum in Ottawa which contains philatelic material, postal artifacts and a postal library. *See also* POSTAL SYSTEM.

Canada Safeway Ltd is a food retailer with head offices in Winnipeg. Started as Safeway Stores Ltd in 1929, the company adopted its present name in 1947. In 1986, directly or through its subsidiaries, it operated 244 food retail stores from Ontario to BC. It also operates wholesale grocery warehouses, bakeries, canneries and food-processing plants in Canada. As of Jan 1987, it had $3.6 billion in sales or operating revenue (ranking 23rd in Canada), and assets of $1.3 billion (ranking 72nd). The company is 100% owned by Kuhlberg, Kravis, Roberts of New York.   DEBORAH C. SAWYER

Canada Savings Bonds differ from other government bonds in that they can be cashed at any bank for the face value plus accrued interest. They cannot be sold by the original buyer but must be held until cashed or until they mature (usually in 7 years) from the time they were bought. The interest rate has been as high as 19.5% and as low as 2.75%, the rate on the first issue in 1946. Canada Savings Bonds, which can be bought on payroll deduction plans and which range in denomination from $100 to $10 000, grew out of the successful raising of money for the war effort in WWII by Victory Bonds and the sale of War Savings Certificates and stamps, not to traditional investors, but to ordinary citizens and even to school children. From the start there has been a limit on the amount of any one issue that any Canadian – they are not sold outside the country – can buy. This limit has been as low as $15 000 and as high as $75 000 (1986). Canada Savings Bonds are a major source of federal government finance; in late 1987 the federal government had borrowed about $41 billion from the public in this form, out of a total debt of $193 billion.
                                        D. McGILLIVRAY

Canada-Soviet Hockey Series, 1972 Soviet teams had totally dominated international hockey for the previous 10 years, but this was the first time they played the best Canadian professionals. The series began amid great anticipation in Canada and the Soviet Union. The victory of the Soviets in the first game, Sept 2 in Montréal, by 7-3, stunned the Canadian players and shocked the Canadian public. The Soviets displayed speed, skill and a haughty disregard for Canadian confidence. The Canadians regrouped in Toronto 2 days later and won 4-1, but the third game in Winnipeg on Sept 6 was a 4-4 tie and Team Canada lost 5-3 in Vancouver, Sept 7, amid the jeers of the local fans. In Moscow, Sept 22, the Soviets swept to another victory 5-4, but the Canadians fought back to tie the series with victories on Sept 24 (3-2) and Sept 26 (4-3). The last game, on Sept 28, was watched intently by the largest Canadian TV audience on record. It began with 2 quick Soviet goals, the ejection of a Canadian player, and a long delay as Canadians raged over the officiating. The Soviets led 5-3 at the end of the second period, but Phil ESPOSITO and Yvan Cournoyer tied the game. Paul Henderson scored the most famous goal in hockey history, with only 34 seconds remaining, to win the series for

Paul Henderson's winning goal in the first Canada-Soviet hockey series, Moscow, 1972 (*photo by Frank Lennon/Toronto Star*).

Canada. The team played one more match, against Czechoslovakia, a 3-3 tie, before returning home to an outpouring of pride and relief. On the surface, the series was a dramatic sports event – in retrospect won by determined athletes against the odds. But the series affected Canadians more deeply. Their cherished myth of hockey superiority had been shattered.   JAMES MARSH

Canada Steamship Lines, Inc is Canada's largest marine company and the dominant shipping operator on the Great Lakes. Incorporated in 1913, the company is the result of an amalgamation of several shipping companies, including the Richelieu and Ontario Navigation Company whose origin dates back to 1843.

By 1915 Canada Steamship Lines had not only expanded its Great Lakes fleet but had also added 16 oceangoing vessels for the Atlantic freight traffic. However, by 1925 the company withdrew from the ocean trades to concentrate its efforts on the Great Lakes, with a fleet now numbering 115 vessels, including 23 ships.

In 1959 the St Lawrence Seaway was opened, linking the 5 Great Lakes and St Lawrence R with the Atlantic Ocean. This allowed for much larger ships to replace the existing fleet of smaller vessels. By the mid-1960s the days of passenger steamboat travel came to an end and Canada Steamship Lines now carries only general freight and bulk cargoes, primarily grain, coal, ore, salt, gypsum and potash.

In 1981 Paul MARTIN Jr, president of the company, formed a partnership with Federal Commerce and Navigation Ltd to acquire the CSL Group Inc, Canada Steamship Lines' parent company each party owning 50%. Since then, CSL has not only substantially modernized its Great Lakes fleet but has also entered into the coastal and ocean trades and currently operates in Europe, the Caribbean and the US East Coast. It is expected that the company will soon announce a further expansion into South America and Asia. This international de-

mand has arisen because of the marketing by CSL of its state of the art specialized materials handling of marine-transported bulk cargoes. The company is the worldwide leader in the design and operation of self-unloading bulk vessels. Canada Steamship Lines' total fleet consists of 34 lakers and ocean lakers.

Canada Studies Foundation, fd 1970, following revelations of the National History Project (1965-68) that the average Canadian high-school student had an abysmal knowledge of Canada. A.B. Hodgetts, who had perceived through the project, as well, that the study of Canada in schools was itself a divisive force, set out to provide opportunities for people from different levels of education and different parts of Canada to work together on Canada Studies project teams across linguistic, cultural and regional barriers. Walter L. GORDON served as chairman and private-sector fund-raiser for the initial 5 experimental years, with Hodgetts and George S. Tomkins as co-directors of activities; the first year's expenditures were over $500 000. With a solid core of active participants by 1974, the foundation's support was assumed by provincial ministers of education and the federal secretary of state, and by contributions in kind from teachers, schools and local school jurisdictions; the 1975-76 budget was $600 000. From 1978 to 1986 direct support was almost exclusively by the Secretary of State, with yearly expenditures below $300 000. For 15 years the foundation was the sole nonprofit developer of Canadian Studies material. It pioneered new approaches to teaching about Canada. Some 30 000 teachers in Canada received in-service education regarding Canadian Studies. The foundation developed and published some 150 volumes of teachers' manuals, stimulated a new market for Canadian textbooks publishers, established a network of more than 2000 teachers across the country, distributed a widely read bilingual newsletter (*Contact*) and promoted a structured approach to the study of Canada, as described in *Teaching Canada for the 80's* (1978). The foundation surrendered its charter in 1986, its original objectives having been met. *See also* CANADIAN STUDIES.
                                        PAUL GALLAGHER

Canada-Third World Relations The decolonization of the European empires after WWII produced many "new nations" and revealed how little economic and social development the colonial system had permitted its wards. The problem of the "Third World" and its "underdevelopment" was thus placed firmly on the global agenda. In this postwar context, Canada projected an image of genuine concern for the demands and requirements of the Third World, an image which has struck a responsive chord with many Canadians and with many in the underdeveloped world itself. The allocation by the Canadian government of significant sums for foreign aid – a process marked by the launching of the COLOMBO PLAN (1950) and other regionally focused aid programs; by the founding of the External Aid Office (1960) and its transformation into the CANADIAN INTERNATIONAL DEVELOPMENT AGENCY (CIDA) in 1968 – is the most concrete manifestation of this concern (in 1985-86 CIDA dispensed $2.2 billion in aid to more than 50 countries). The "liberal internationalism" vigorously espoused by Lester B. PEARSON – he followed his prime ministership by presiding over an influential international inquiry into the causes of world poverty – and the support for "North-South dialogue" on development advocated by Pierre TRUDEAU have also been noteworthy.

These initiatives must be put in their proper context, however. Many Third World thinkers and activists have criticized their countries' inheritance of a subordinate and dependent position within the international economic system (termed by them "neo-colonialism") and have advocated a radical and structural transformation of the situation, both locally and internationally. In contrast, Canadian policymakers have consistently defended the broad merits of the existing global economy; their goal is primarily one of reform at the margin of the international economic system to allow some amelioration of the condition of the world's poor and to pre-empt more revolutionary demands. Though never quite as extreme as its counterpart in the US, the Canadian government has tended to view radical development strategies proposed by some Third World countries as either unacceptably threatening or as manifestations of an international "communist menace," an interpretation which parallels the American Cold War perspective on the Third World.

There has also been a gap between rhetoric and reality in the Canadian approach. In 1984 the Canadian government pledged to reach an aid target of 0.5% of gross domestic product by 1985; there would be a gradual increase to 0.6% from 1991 to 1995 and to 0.7% by the year 2000. Nevertheless, FOREIGN AID has consistently fallen below levels recommended by the UN. Moreover, foreign-aid programs often emphasize the interests of Canadian suppliers and contractors more than the requirements of the recipient countries themselves; simultaneously, there has been a shift in emphasis away from aiding the poorest of the poor countries and towards aiding those larger and wealthier Third World economies which are also the more attractive potential trading partners. This approach also has marked Canada's participation in international forums such as the General Agreement on Tariffs and Trade (GATT), the United Nations Conference on Trade and Development (UNCTAD), the LAW OF THE SEA conferences, and the various negotiations directed towards redressing inequities in the realm of INTERNATIONAL TRADE and investment that have emerged around the theme of a "New International Economic Order." In such settings, Canada has frequently found itself taking up a far more intransigent and defensive posture than other western "middle powers" such as the Scandinavian countries.

Canada's own economic difficulties in recent years may partly account for these tendencies, but the very close integration of the Canadian business community into the policymaking process in such spheres has been an important factor as well. Canada's relationship to the less developed areas of the world was structured, long before the post-WWII period, by the expansive role of Canadian-based banks, mining and utility companies. By the turn of this century, this was already true of the links Canada was establishing with the Caribbean and Latin America. Such business interests have continued to be one of the dominant determinants of Canada's relationship with the Third World. However, Canada's links to the Third World are not monopolized by government and the business community. There is a large network of church-sponsored groups and agencies, voluntary "nongovernmental (aid) organizations" (of the OXFAM type) and more overtly political Third World support groups. A majority of these groups have supported critical views of present workings of the global economy and the causes of underdevelopment, views that are sensitive to the claims of international equity and the legitimacy of revolutionary action in some settings (eg, South Africa). Often critical of Canadian government and business practices in the Third World, such groups have generally not succeeded in determining Canadian policy to any

major degree, but they have kept alive a sharp debate on the nature of Canada's links to the Third World. JOHN S. SAUL

Canada Trustco Mortgage Company, founded (1864) London, Ont; for many years known as the Huron and Erie Mortgage Corporations. Several branches were opened in the Prairies in the late 1800s to funnel surplus eastern savings in the form of mortgages to western farmers and developers to finance western development. After WWII the company focused on mortgage lending in cities and most recently on lending to corporations investing in plant and equipment. In 1959 it became the first trust company to sponsor a MUTUAL FUND. In addition to its trustee and lending components, the company has been a leader and innovative retailer in the areas of on-line banking, daily interest chequing and service hours. In 1986 it had assets of $24 billion and revenues of $2.7 billion. Employees numbered 10 247 and Imasco owned 99% of the shares. ERIC W. DALY

Canada-US Automotive Products Agreement (Autopact) a conditional free-trade agreement signed by Canada and the US in Jan 1965 to create a single N American market for passenger cars, trucks, buses, tires and automotive parts. In Canada FREE TRADE does not apply to consumer sales; it applies solely to manufacturers who meet certain conditions. Under the agreement, motor-vehicle manufacturers are obliged to maintain the same ratio of production to sales in Canada as existed in the 1964 model year; to maintain Canadian value-added or Canadian content equal to the 1964 model year; and have been required (from 1965 onwards) to increase Canadian value-added by 60% of the growth in the value of passenger cars sold (50% for trucks and 40% for buses). Between 1965 and 1982 Canada had an overall automotive trade deficit of $12.1 billion with the US, with a surplus of about $28 billion in assembled vehicles and a deficit of about $40.5 billion in automotive parts. Canada had overall surpluses in 1970, 1971, 1972 and 1982. Since 1982 Canada has had a continuing surplus with the US. In 1982-86 exports were $135.5 billion and imports were $112.9 billion, for a 5-year surplus of $22.5 billion. The 2 principal purposes of the Autopact were to lower Canadian production costs through more efficient production of fewer lines of motor vehicles and parts, and to lower consumer prices. However, critics note that the industry has remained essentially foreign controlled and that Canadian subsidiaries are less autonomous than they once were. In addition, they note that the industry spends little on research and development in Canada. Automotive industry employment totalled 70 600 in 1965, reached about 125 000 in 1978 before falling to about 99 000 in 1982. Since then employment has recovered to about 140 000. Under the FREE TRADE agreement negotiated with the US in 1987, Canadian safeguards would remain, with N American auto producers losing their right to import parts and vehicles duty-free from other countries unless the safeguards were met. Japanese and other offshore automakers would not be able to join the Autopact. The Canada-US pact can be terminated at any time by 12 months written notice by either government. DAVID CRANE

Canadair Challenger, corporate executive aircraft developed and built in Canada. Exhaustive testing resulted in an advanced wing design, broad body and quiet, efficient engines. It carries up to 19 passengers at a normal cruise speed of 819 km/h. It first flew Nov 1978, but the crash of a prototype and financial troubles at Canadair delayed certification. The original 600 series was replaced by the 601 in 1983 and the 601-3A in

1987. By 1987, 147 Challengers were in service in N America, Europe, the Middle East, the Far East, Africa and Australia.

Canadair CL-215, unique amphibious aircraft designed to fight forest fires with water bombing and chemical fire retardants. It can scoop up a load of over 5000 litres of water in 10 seconds, while skimming over a body of water, and jettison it over a fire in less than 1 second. It first flew Oct 1967, and 91 had been delivered by the end of 1986. The federal government (17), Québec (17), Spain (19), France (15) and Greece (15) have been the main customers.

Canadair CL-215, a unique firefighting aircraft used in Canada and several other countries (*courtesy Canadair*).

Canadair CL-28 Argus, long-range maritime patrol plane built in Canada. Based on the Bristol Britannia, a British passenger aircraft, it carried an operational crew of 15, and was equipped with sophisticated radar and antisubmarine weapons. With a range of over 8100 km, it operated primarily from bases at Greenwood, NS, and Summerside, PEI. The Argus first flew in Mar 1957, and a total of 46 were built in 2 versions. It was replaced by the American-built Lockheed Aurora.

Canadair Ltd, aerospace manufacturers. The company had its origins in the aircraft division of Canadian Vickers Ltd, formed in 1923. It was purchased by Canadians in 1927 and during WWII produced the Canso, a long-range flying boat used for maritime patrol. The company was reorganized in 1944 by the Canadian government, under the name Canadair, and sold to Electric Boat Co of the US in 1946. Electric Boat formed General Dynamics Corp in 1952 and Canadair became a subsidiary. In 1976 Canadair became a CROWN CORPORATION and in Dec 1986 was sold to BOMBARDIER INC.

Since 1944 Canadair has produced over 4000 aircraft, including versions of American-designed

The launch of a Canadair CL-227 Sentinel (*courtesy Canadair*).

fighters Sabre (1949-58), Starfighter (1961-86) and Freedom Fighter. It also produced 2 trainers for the RCAF, the T-33 Silver Star (1952-58) and Tutor (1960-66) and the CANADAIR CL-28 ARGUS, a maritime patrol aircraft. In current production (1987) are the CANADAIR CHALLENGER executive jet, the CANADAIR CL-215 waterbomber and a number of unmanned, airborne surveillance systems. Canadair's production facilities are located at Cartierville and Dorval, Qué. In 1987 the company's work force totalled 5385.   JAMES MARSH

Canadarm, name given to the Shuttle Remote Manipulator System (RMS), Canada's contribution to the US Space Shuttle. Canadarm is a complex, 6-degrees of freedom, remotely controlled manipulator used for cargo deployment and retrieval from and to the shuttle's cargo bay. The 15 m manipulator arm functions in a manner similar to that of a human arm and has 6 rotating joints, 2 at its shoulder (yaw, pitch), one at its elbow (pitch) and 3 at its wrist (pitch, yaw, roll). Its snare-type end effector (or hand) is cylindrical; 3 snare wires grasp a post or grapple fixture on the SATELLITE to be captured. The $110-million Canadarm program was largely carried out by Canadian industry, under the direction of the National Aeronautical Establishment, a division of the NATIONAL RESEARCH COUNCIL OF CANADA. The industrial team, led by SPAR AEROSPACE LIMITED, included CAE Electronics Ltd and DSMA Atcon Ltd. Industrial benefits to date include the sale of 3 additional Canadarm systems to NASA and the establishment of an industrial capability in the HIGH-TECHNOLOGY fields of advanced manipulator systems and ROBOTICS.

While the mechanical arm, mounted in the shuttle's cargo bay, is the most visible part, the system also includes hand controllers for ASTRONAUT operation, a display and control panel and a signal processing-interface box. A TV camera (or eye) located on the wrist — and an optional second TV camera at its elbow — are part of the shuttle's closed-circuit television system that provides visual cues when an astronaut is performing grappling maneuvers. One of the 5 on-board shuttle COMPUTERS provides the "brain" of the arm.

Extensive computer programs enable the arm to be operated automatically or allow the astronaut to operate the arm in several control modes, ranging from complete end-point control (where the astronaut "flies" the end of the arm) to single-joint operation. The arm also has a contingency back-up mode that can be used to complete missions, if the primary control system fails.

The Canadarm is capable of maneuvering payloads of nearly 30 000 kg mass in space at speeds (depending on the payload mass) of up to 60 cm/s. It must be able to place such payloads in any position, with an accuracy of approximately 5 cm. Each joint is powered by an optically commutated, brushless DC motor, driven by a specially designed servo-power amplifier. To obtain the high joint-output torque needed from the relatively low motor torque available, a high-reduction gearbox with an epicyclic/planet system is used for each joint. Gear ratios range from 1842:1 to 739:1 on different joints. All joints are back-drivable and have zero backlash to maintain positioning accuracy and control.

Demanding stiffness and strength requirements, coupled with volume constraints imposed by the shuttle, have dictated extensive use of the latest AEROSPACE materials (eg, TITANIUM, stainless steel, ultra-high modulus graphite epoxy). The harsh environment necessitated special attention to thermal design and lubrication. The arm is entirely covered with a multilayer insulation system, consisting of alternate layers of goldized kapton, dacron scrim cloth and a beta cloth (fibre-

The mechanical Canadarm is capable of picking up satellites from the cargo bay of space vehicles and releasing them precisely in space. It can also retrieve, service and repair satellites (*courtesy National Research Council*).

glass) outer covering. In extremely cold conditions, thermostatically controlled electric heaters protect critical hardware. Canadarm was designed to have a minimum lifetime of 10 years and to be used for up to 100 missions without maintenance. It weighs under 450 kg and cannot support itself in normal gravity; hence, a complex simulation facility (SIMFAC) had to be developed to verify its operation in space and facilitate astronaut training. On Earth, the assembled arm could only be tested in 2 dimensions by using a special air-bearing cradle, operating on a specially designed flat-floor area.

The arm first flew in Nov 1981 on the second Space Shuttle flight and performed well, exceeding all design goals. It was declared operational one year later, after 3 successful test flights. It has since been used to deploy and retrieve free-flying satellites, and to deploy the large Long Duration Exposure Facility (LDEF), and it played a key role in the mission to retrieve, repair and redeploy the Solar Maximum Satellite, the first satellite repaired in space.   GARRY LINDBERG

Canada's Economic Prospects, Royal Commission on (Gordon Commission) The idea for this royal commission was based on a draft article by Walter GORDON in 1955 questioning the validity of a number of the government's economic policies, particularly the question of selling control of Canada's natural resources and business enterprises to foreigners. Gordon was then asked if he would act as chairman.

With the help of Douglas LePan, the commission's director of research, a research staff was assembled, mostly from universities. Thirty-three studies were undertaken, each of which was published separately. This was the first time that any country had attempted such a comprehensive undertaking, and there was a great deal of public interest in the commission's work. A recurrent theme throughout was the concern felt about the acquisition by foreigners, mostly American, of Canadian resources and business enterprises. The commission completed its work within the 18 months it had set for itself, and its conclusions were summarized in a preliminary report of 3 Dec 1956. The final report was not completed until Nov 1957.

In its 2 reports, the commission made some long-term forecasts for the next 25 years about the population growth, the size of the labour force, and the probable development of different sections of the economy. Most of these various estimates were remarkably close to the actual results. The commission also submitted over 50 proposals and suggestions, nearly all of which have since been incorporated in legislation or adopted administratively. The principal exceptions were its proposals with regard to FOREIGN INVESTMENT.   WALTER GORDON

Canada's Food Guide is a daily eating plan designed to help people of all ages choose their food wisely. The Dietary Standard for Canada recommends a daily nutrient intake for Canadians, but because people select food and not nutrients, nutrient recommendations have been translated into food choices. The guide enables many individuals to meet their nutrient needs by following a simple daily food pattern based on 4 food groups, each of which contains a variety of nutrients. Some studies reveal that the pattern will not supply the Recommended Daily Nutrient Intakes (RDNI) for all individuals; women, for instance, may need more iron.

The central principle of Canada's Food Guide is variety. The guide recommends that a specific number of food servings should be chosen every day from the following food groups: milk and milk products (2-4 servings), bread and cereals (3-5 servings), fruit and vegetables (4-5 servings) and meat and alternatives (2 servings).

Each food group offers its own particular pattern of key nutrient strengths. Some people, however, because of allergies or digestive problems, budget limitations, energy requirements (calories), food availability, personal preferences and dislikes, or philosophical or religious beliefs, may not eat a food or foods within a food group. The guide is sufficiently flexible to accommodate these factors.

Both numbers of servings and serving sizes are often expressed in the guide as a range, eg, 4 to 5 servings of fruit and vegetables or 60 to 90 grams of cooked lean meat. Individuals can generally select from within this range the size and number of servings compatible with energy needs and personal preferences. However, with milk and the milk-products group, the recommended number of servings varies because the need for calcium and vitamin D is greater during certain periods of an individual's life.   M.T. CLANDININ

Reading: Health and Welfare Canada, *Canada's Food Guide Handbook; Dietary Standard for Canada* (1975).

Canada's Sports Hall of Fame is Canada's national museum of sport, dedicated to preserving and increasing Canadians' awareness of their sport heritage. Founded in 1955 through the efforts of Harry I. Price, a former assistant athletics commissioner of Ontario, it is located in the centre of Exhibition Place in Toronto, Ont. Its exhibit area covers 900 m² and its displays are viewed by an estimated 300 000 people annually. The Hall of Fame maintains a substantial archives of sport, including nearly 40 000 historical photographs. It also publishes a quarterly newsletter and conducts educational programs for school-age children.

The annual election of honoured members draws the most public attention. Chosen by a selection committee of 12, with representatives from every province, men and women are elected to 2 categories, Athletes or Builders. Normally, athletes are only elected after a 3-year waiting period from their retirement from active competition. As of 1987, 340 Canadians have been so honoured. The Hall of Fame is administered by a small staff responsible to a board of governors and also has representatives from coast to coast. It charges no admission fee, being supported by government grants and public and corporate donations. It is open to the general public throughout the year.   J. THOMAS WEST

Reading: D. Fisher and S.F. Wise, *Canada's Sporting Heroes* (1974), published under the auspices of CSHF.

Canadian Advisory Council on the Status of Women

Canadian Advisory Council on the Status of Women (CACSW) was established in 1973 by the federal government on the recommendation of the Royal Commission on the STATUS OF WOMEN. The CACSW advises the federal government on, and informs and educates the public regarding women's concerns. As an autonomous agency, the CACSW reports to Parliament through the minister responsible for the status of women, while retaining the right to publish its views without ministerial consent. The CACSW is composed of 3 full-time members (a president and 2 vice-presidents), 27 regionally representative part-time members appointed for 3-year terms and an office staff of approximately 30 employees. It has been a leading publisher of research on women and its recommendations have prompted legislative change concerning constitutional reform, pensions, parental benefits, taxation, health care, employment practices, sexual assault, wife battering and human rights.   MARY-JANE LIPKIN

Canadian Airlines International, *see* PACIFIC WESTERN AIRLINES LTD.

Canadian Amateur Hockey Association The first organization dealing with the administration of HOCKEY was the Ontario Hockey Assn, est 1890. A number of other organizations came into being and on 4 Dec 1914 a meeting was held in Ottawa to provide for a governing body. W.F. Taylor of Winnipeg was selected president and the newspaper publisher and venerable sports figure John Ross ROBERTSON was chosen honorary president. The prime purpose of the CAHA in its early years was the promotion of senior hockey and a national championship in this division (*see* ALLAN CUP). It introduced the MEMORIAL CUP in 1919 for junior hockey. In an era of growing professionalism (*see* SPORTS HISTORY), the association maintained a very strict code of amateurism, and it was not until 1935 that the code was liberalized so that players could receive payment for loss of time or could take part in exhibitions against professionals. In 1936 an agreement was reached with the NATIONAL HOCKEY LEAGUE for uniform playing rules and for professional sponsorship of individual amateur clubs. In 1967 sponsorship was eliminated and was replaced by an amateur draft for players reaching a certain age. In 1963 the CAHA authorized the formation of a national team, led by Father BAUER, to represent Canada at the 1964 Olympics, and it continued the program until 1969 when it was turned over to HOCKEY CANADA. Formation of the WORLD HOCKEY ASSOCIATION in 1972 created a crisis for the draft, as the WHA drafted underage players. Today, no formal agreement exists between professional and amateur hockey.   JAMES MARSH

Canadian-American Relations Canada's nationhood is in many ways a by-product of the AMERICAN REVOLUTION, when the victory of the Thirteen Colonies led to the exodus of LOYALIST Americans to BRITISH NORTH AMERICA. Many brought with them a deep distrust of the US and its democratic ways. Many American revolutionaries thought the revolution incomplete while Britain retained any N American outpost. Conflict seemed inevitable, and the Napoleonic Wars spilled over into N America in 1812. The WAR OF 1812 was fought defensively by the British and halfheartedly by the Americans. Both sides welcomed the Treaty of GHENT, which brought some settlement of outstanding problems between BNA and the US. The RUSH-BAGOT AGREEMENT of 1817 limited the presence of armed vessels on the Great Lakes. The CONVENTION OF 1818 provided for continuation of the boundary from Lake of the Woods to the Rocky Mts. In the East,

commissioners appointed under the Treaty of Ghent sorted out boundary problems, except in northern Maine.

In the 1820s and 1830s Upper and Lower Canadians opposed to their governments looked with increasing favour upon American democracy. William Lyon MACKENZIE and Louis-Joseph PAPINEAU sought American support in their REBELLIONS OF 1837. After his defeat Mackenzie fled to the US, where he fomented border troubles for the following year (*see* HUNTERS' LODGES). A British show of military force and American official unwillingness to support the rebels ended the threats to BNA. In 1842 the ASHBURTON-WEBSTER TREATY settled the NE boundary, but problems west of the Rockies were cleared up in the 1846 OREGON TREATY only after war threatened.

In 1854 fears subsided as BNA and the US were linked by a RECIPROCITY treaty, but they returned suddenly with the AMERICAN CIVIL WAR, 1861-65. Northern Americans resented what they felt was Britain's pro-Southern sympathy. BNA and the US managed to avoid military confrontation, but the end of the war led to new tensions, because it was thought that the North might take revenge against Britain, and because FENIANS were organizing to invade BNA. The Fenian Raids of 1866 failed, but spurred BNA towards CONFEDERATION the following year.

Confederation, the subsequent withdrawal of British garrisons, and conflicts in Europe impelled Britain and Canada to seek settlement of outstanding differences with the Americans in the 1871 Treaty of WASHINGTON. PM Sir John A. MACDONALD, a member of the British negotiating team, grumbled about the terms, but the treaty was useful to Canada in that the US, through its signature, acknowledged the new nation to its north. Thereafter, Canada's concern about the American military threat diminished rapidly. There were fears of American interference as Canada established sovereignty over the North-West, but by the late 1890s both nations looked back at 3 decades of remarkably little conflict. In 1898-99 a Joint High Commission, reflecting this spirit as well as the Anglo-American desire for rapprochement, sought to remedy remaining discord. The commission broke down, with only minor matters settled. One question on which agreement was not reached was the ALASKA BOUNDARY DISPUTE, for which another tribunal was established 1903 and which led to Canadian anger, more towards Britain than against the US. It produced a conviction that in the future Canada must rely increasingly on its own resources and less on Britain.

Canada therefore undertook to establish direct institutional links with the US. Best known was the INTERNATIONAL JOINT COMMISSION, established 1909. In 1911 PM Wilfrid LAURIER went farther than most Canadians would go when he proposed a reciprocity agreement with the US. In the 1911 election campaign old animosities reappeared, the Conservatives were elected and reciprocity died. Nevertheless, new PM Robert BORDEN quickly reassured the Americans that he wanted to maintain good relations. Borden's action probably eased tensions when Canada entered WORLD WAR I in 1914 while the US remained neutral. When the US finally entered the war in 1917, the 2 countries recognized their common heritage and interests to an unprecedented extent. Immediately after WWI Canadian politicians fancied themselves interpreters between the US and Britain, eg, at the 1921 Imperial Conference, when PM Arthur MEIGHEN dissuaded Britain from renewing the Anglo-Japanese Alliance because it might bring the British Empire into conflict with the US. With

PM Mackenzie KING's Liberals in power, there was an ever stronger tendency to emphasize Canada's "North American" character and, by implication, its similarity to the US.

In the 1920s and 1930s Canadians and Americans mingled as never before. Canadian defence plans were altered as planners dismissed the possibility of conflict. Economic and cultural linkages strengthened as suspicion of American influence receded. Canada and the US established legations in 1926 and no longer dealt with each other through British offices. More important was the impact of American popular culture through radio, motion pictures and the automobile. The Canadian government tried to regulate BROADCASTING and FILM but largely failed. Other organizations such as the Roman CATHOLIC Church in Québec tried moral suasion and political pressure to prevent Canadians from partaking of the most frivolous aspects of American culture.

Through the new media, Canadians became familiar with US Pres Franklin Roosevelt. In 1938, as another European war loomed, he publicly promised support if Canada was ever threatened. Roosevelt did co-operate closely after WORLD WAR II erupted in Sept 1939. Although the US remained neutral, Roosevelt and King reached 2 important agreements which formalized the American commitment: the Ogdensburg Agreement (1940) established the PERMANENT JOINT BOARD ON DEFENCE, and the Hyde Park Agreement (1941) united the 2 economies for wartime purposes (*see* LEND-LEASE). Both agreements won widespread popular approval.

Canadians' admiration for the US increased after it joined the war in Dec 1941. Public-opinion polls indicated that many Canadians would have liked to join the US. This new affection frightened King, but Canada retained and even expanded defence and other relations with the US after the war. The COLD WAR with the USSR convinced most Canadians that the US was the bulwark defending common values and security. In Aug 1958 Canada and the US signed a plan for joint air defence (NORAD), and the following year agreed to the Canada-US Defence Production Sharing Program. Some deplored the growing links. Vincent MASSEY and Walter GORDON headed royal commissions on culture and economic policy which were critical of American influence in Canada. In Parliament the 1956 PIPELINE DEBATE and the debate on the SUEZ CRISIS indicated that some parliamentarians also feared American influence upon Canada's government and its attitudes.

PM John DIEFENBAKER committed Canada to NORAD and the defence-sharing plan and quickly befriended Pres Dwight Eisenhower. Nevertheless, he lamented Canada's increasing distance from Britain and the extent of American cultural and other influence. This feeling became suspicion of the US itself when John Kennedy became president in 1961. The leaders disliked each other, and policy differences grew rapidly. Diefenbaker refused nuclear arms for Canada (*see* BOMARC MISSILE CRISIS) and hesitated to back Kennedy during the 1962 CUBAN MISSILE CRISIS. The Americans openly accused Diefenbaker of failing to carry out commitments. In the 1963 general election Diefenbaker accused the Americans of gross interference, blaming them for his election loss.

Both countries expected better relations when the Liberals assumed power. By 1965, however, relations had deteriorated significantly as PM Lester PEARSON and Canadians found it difficult to give the US the support it demanded during the Vietnam War. By 1967 the Canadian government openly expressed its disagreement with American policies in SE Asia. Canadians generally became less sympathetic to American influence and foreign policy. A nationalist movement demanded that American influence be significantly reduced. The first major nationalist initiatives occurred in cultural affairs, but those most offensive to Americans, such as the NATIONAL ENERGY PROGRAM, were economic. Relations during the first Reagan administration were strained. It was evident that the government of Pierre TRUDEAU and the administration of Ronald Reagan perceived international events from a different perspective. Canada, nevertheless, did permit Cruise missile testing despite strong domestic opposition. In 1984 the election of Brian MULRONEY's Conservatives signalled a reconciliation with the US, one which led to a weakening of nationalistic legislation and agencies such as FIRA. Canadian public opinion did not reject these initiatives, and polls in 1985 and 1986 even showed strong support for FREE TRADE, though this support declined in 1987. After protracted negotiations, the 2 governments reached a tentative trade agreement on 3 Oct 1987. Although recent Canadian-American relations have not reflected the degree of hostility and suspicion which marked them earlier, neither do they reflect the co-operation of the immediate postwar period. *See also* CANADA AND THE UNITED STATES.   JOHN ENGLISH

Canadian-American Relations, Economic
Economic relations between Canada and the US are of paramount importance to Canada. The US is Canada's most important trading partner (Canada exports 30% of its Gross Domestic Product and almost 70% of Canadian exports are to the US) and the US has provided Canada with much of its investment capital and TECHNOLOGY through FOREIGN INVESTMENT, resulting in a high level of US ownership and control of the Canadian ECONOMY. Canada is also the largest export customer of the US (about 10% of US exports go to Canada, and account for more than 60% of Canadian imports, although the trade in manufactured goods between the 2 countries favours the US) as well as a major source of natural resources for US industry (*see* INTERNATIONAL TRADE).

While access to US markets, investment and technology have benefited Canadians, the resulting commercial arrangements, along with the great disparity in population between the 2 countries, has created serious problems for Canada, including a high level of dependency on and vulnerability to US policies. Recently, US corporate interests have successfully enlisted the support of the US government in widening the Canadian market for US goods and services (eg, banking, data services), in opposing Canadian policies to strengthen Canadian industry (eg, government incentives and grants for Canadian industry, measures to gain Canadian industrial spin-offs for Canadian resource development) and in weakening Canadian measures to control foreign investment (eg, screening of foreign investment, the role of crown corporations, changes to the tax and land regulations to favour Canadian oil and gas companies, and curbs on the role of foreign banks).

The key theme that ran through the first 50 years of Canadian-American economic relations was the issue of FREE TRADE. Historically, Canadians opposed to complete free trade have argued that it would entail the eventual loss of political SOVEREIGNTY, lead to greater integration in economic and industrial policy, and further constrain Canada's ability to adopt independent ECONOMIC POLICIES. Opponents of free trade have contended that even if the US agreed to free trade, the US Congress would use nontariff barriers to hinder any gains that may accrue to Canadians from such arrangements. Supporters argued that only through free trade, and the consequent

unimpeded access to US markets, would Canadian manufacturers be able to become efficient producers with large enough sales volumes to support research and development (*see* INDUSTRIAL RESEARCH AND DEVELOPMENT; INDUSTRIAL STRATEGY). The debate was renewed as free-trade negotiations were assiduously undertaken by the Mulroney government in 1986-87.

In 1866 the US abrogated the Reciprocity Treaty of 1854 in angry response to British aid to the Confederate states. Although negotiations leading to the Treaty of WASHINGTON (1871) failed to restore RECIPROCITY or procure compensation for the damage resulting from FENIAN raids, they did result in US recognition of Canada as a nation in the N American continent. In the 1891 federal election, the Liberals campaigned on a platform of unrestricted free trade, losing by a narrow margin. For its part, the US rebuffed free-trade proposals from Canada and maintained protectionist or high-tariff policies.

Despite the mutual political suspicions, the 2 countries developed from 1875 to 1900 the linkages that determined the pattern for closer economic integration. Americans invested heavily in Canada, establishing "branch plants" and taking over many Canadian-owned enterprises (eg, in 1898 the giant Standard Oil company acquired Canada's largest oil company, Imperial Oil). Trade increased, and business and financial ties were quickly formed, reinforced by transportation, labour and other links. The high-tariff policies of the NATIONAL POLICY attracted enormous amounts of US capital and investment. In 1914, although 72% of nonresident investment in Canada was from the UK, the US supplied twice as much capital for direct investment in mining and manufacturing as the UK. Canadian unions, which burgeoned during this period, were closely affiliated with their US counterparts.

In 1911 President William Howard Taft's administration reversed decades of US protectionism when Taft and PM Wilfrid LAURIER reached an agreement providing for a limited free-trade pact covering tariffs on a significant list of manufactured products. Enabling legislation was passed by the US Congress but was blocked by the Conservative Opposition in Parliament. The Canadian general election of that year was fought largely on the free-trade issue, and Laurier's defeat was partly a result of fears that free trade was the first step to political annexation.

In both the US and Canada the INDUSTRIALIZATION that had begun in the mid-19th century expanded rapidly in the early 20th century. Hundreds of millions of US dollars poured into Canada to create more subsidiaries or branch plants or to take over ownership of promising Canadian companies to serve Canadian and British preferential markets in fast-developing new industries such as motor vehicles, electric appliances, chemicals, machinery and metal processing. With the GREAT DEPRESSION, however, Canadians were made aware of the vulnerable position in which they had been placed by excessive dependence upon the US economy. In 1930 the US Congress passed the Hawley-Smoot Tariff, which raised the duty on US imports to the highest levels in history. Canada responded with new high tariffs of its own while Canadian Prime Minister R.B. BENNETT pledged to "blast a way" into the world markets and reduce Canadian dependence on the US economy. In 1932 his government hosted the Imperial Economic Conference in Ottawa to revise the system of tariffs within the British Commonwealth and Empire.

Trade relations improved following the passage in the US of the Reciprocal Trade Agreements Act in 1934; Canada and the US began negotiations

to lower tariffs and increase trade. In 1935 PM Mackenzie KING concluded the Canada-US trade agreement that had been initiated by the Bennett government. A second and broader Canada-US trade agreement was signed in 1938, leading to further reductions in tariffs. Canadians and Americans collaborated intensively during WWII. In 1940 a meeting between PM King and President Roosevelt near Ogdensburg, NY, led to the creation of the PERMANENT JOINT BOARD ON DEFENCE (PJBD), which also provided the means for close economic and other relations between the 2 countries. Following US entry into the war, the PJBD organized a number of major American-financed activities in Canada, including the ALASKA HIGHWAY and the Canol project, which expanded oil production at Norman Wells, NWT.

Before the official US entry into the war, Canada dramatically expanded its industrial capacity, partly by purchasing vast amounts of machinery and equipment from the US. By early 1941 Canada's foreign exchange reserves of US dollars had plummeted to dangerously low levels and Canada turned to the US for help. King and Roosevelt negotiated the Hyde Park Agreement, which provided for significantly increased US purchases in Canada and allowed British use of US lend-lease funds for American war components imported by Canada for use in British military equipment. Both these measures increased Canadian holdings of US dollars to cover imports from the US.

The postwar demand for consumer goods, the vast influx of immigrants, and the need to convert a wartime industrial machine to civilian needs resulted in a sharp increase in Canadian imports of US consumer goods and industrial machinery. Canada's postwar exports, however, fell sharply. By 1947 Canada was importing twice as much as it was exporting to the US. Because Britain and Europe were devastated by the war and short of foreign exchange, Canada could not, as it had in the past, pay for its US trade deficit from a trade surplus with the rest of the world. By 1950, however, these problems had largely disappeared, and Canada was enjoying an investment boom. In the Cold War atmosphere of the late 1940s and early 1950s, US corporations embarked on a massive program to locate and develop Canadian natural resources, from oil and gas to uranium and nonferrous metals such as copper and iron ore. This program of investment, along with parallel investment in other major industries, helped fuse the Canadian economy even more closely with that of the US. A large and increasing share of Canada's mining, oil and gas and manufacturing industries fell under US corporate ownership and control.   In an attempt to avoid a return to bilateral negotiations with the US, which exposed Canada to the possibility of having to make concessions in one area to obtain US concessions in another, Canadian leaders turned to multilateral arrangements, such as the General Agreement on Tariffs and Trade (GATT) in international economic relations, and the North Atlantic Treaty Organization (*see* NATO) in military relations, believing they offered greater opportunity, through alliances with other countries, to curb the unilateral exercise of power by the US and to reduce the danger of direct Canada-US confrontation.

Nevertheless the process of continental integration continued, with Canada the supplier of raw materials and the US the supplier of industrial capacity and technology. For a number of years the Joint Ministerial Committee on Trade and Economic Affairs, composed of the principal economic Cabinet ministers for each country, met annually to deal with issues such as a US program for the disposal of surplus grains to developing countries, which undercut Canadian commercial grain sales, and the extraterritorial application of

US law to US-owned subsidiaries in Canada, which barred exports by these subsidiaries to China, and later Cuba, and which infringed upon Canadian sovereignty.

In 1957 a new Conservative government under John DIEFENBAKER promised to reduce Canada's economic ties to the US. The Royal Commission on CANADA'S ECONOMIC PROSPECTS, which reported in 1957, warned that Canadians were losing control of their destiny, while other critics voiced concern that Canada's economy was being developed in a distorted manner as a resource supplier for the giant US industrial base. Although in 1965 Canada and the US signed the Autopact agreement, which created, for manufacturers, a conditional free-trade zone for motor vehicle and motor vehicle parts production in Canada, many Canadians had begun to express a desire to reduce foreign ownership and influence in their economy. This desire led to disputes in tax and banking policy and even to diplomatic quarrels over the status of US magazines in Canada. In an attempt to halt the flow of US funds abroad, in 1963 the US government introduced a tax to discourage the outflow of funds, which sparked an immediate crisis in Canadian financial markets, since Canada was highly dependent on access to US capital markets. Canada negotiated an exemption, but only with the understanding that if Canadian borrowing in the US rose above traditional levels the exemption would be reviewed by the US. Canada also had to promise not to increase its foreign-exchange reserves through the proceeds of new US borrowings. Through these constraints, Canada's ability to conduct economic policy was narrowed. In 1968 the US government imposed mandatory guidelines for American multinationals. US subsidiaries were ordered to increase the repatriation of profits from Canada, to carry out more investment in the US than in subsidiaries, and to increase exports for US plants instead of from subsidiaries in Canada or elsewhere. In 1971 President Nixon introduced a series of measures to protect the US balance of payments by imposing a 10% surcharge on those US imports subject to duty. Canada was able to negotiate exemptions to these policies, but the incidents revealed Canada's vulnerability to changes in US policies and led to Canadian efforts to develop a THIRD OPTION designed to increase Canada's economic ties with the rest of the world and to reduce its dependence on the US.

ENERGY POLICY became an issue between Canada and the US during the 1970s. In the late 1960s and the early 1970s, Canada was anxious to increase oil and gas sales to the US, but oil sales were restricted by US import quotas. Canada also attempted unsuccessfully to persuade the US to build an oil pipeline from Alaska to the US through the Canadian North (*see* MACKENZIE VALLEY PIPELINE). Canadian interest in expanding oil and gas exports to the US had cooled by the mid-1970s, following the 1973-74 OPEC crisis and concern over the adequacy of Canadian oil and gas reserves to meet future Canadian needs. During this period the US reacted angrily to increases in Canadian oil export prices to match world oil prices. Energy re-emerged as a source of conflict with Canada's implementation in 1980 of the National Energy Program. One of the NEP's major objectives was that the oil industry be 50% Canadian controlled by 1990. In 1980 the oil and gas industry in Canada accounted for 30% of all nonfinancial industry profits in Canada, and roughly 70% of those profits accrued to foreign-controlled, mainly US, firms. To achieve the Canadianization target, Canada encouraged takeovers by Canadians of foreign-oil subsidiaries, altered the tax system so that government funding of risky oil exploration favoured Canadian compa-

nies, and amended land regulations to require 50% Canadian participation in frontier oil and gas fields. The US vigorously protested these various measures. A second NEP objective was to increase the Canadian share of engineering and other services, and of manufactured equipment used in the oil and gas industry projects. US multinationals had relied heavily on the same engineering and other suppliers as their US parents, so that Canadian industry had not benefited to the extent that it might have from oil and gas development. As a result of US objections, some of these provisions were relaxed.

The broader issue of foreign ownership also affected Canadian-American relations during the 1970s and early 1980s. As a result of widespread concerns in Canada over the regulation of massive US investment in the Canadian economy, the FOREIGN INVESTMENT REVIEW AGENCY (FIRA) was created and began screening new foreign investment plans in 1974. By the early 1980s the US had become a harsh critic of FIRA. The dispute was taken to GATT which in 1983 concluded that, while FIRA was generally acceptable, it should be less vigorous in its efforts to persuade foreign investors to use Canadian goods and services.

While the issue of Canada-US FREE TRADE has been a recurring theme in Canadian history since Confederation, it had laid dormant since 1948, when the Canadian government negotiated, then retreated from a bilateral pact with the US. But in 1983, the government of PM Trudeau embarked on negotiation of sectoral free-trade arrangements with the US. With the election of the Conservatives and PM Mulroney in 1984, Canada sought closer economic ties with the US and in 1985 Mulroney asked the US to negotiate a comprehensive free-trade agreement. In Oct 1987 the 2 countries announced they had an agreement, which has yet to be ratified by the US Congress or implemented by the Canadian Parliament and, where relevant, the provincial governments. Under the proposed agreement, all tariffs between the 2 countries would be eliminated over a 10-year period, starting 1 Jan 1989. In addition, a binational dispute settlement mechanism would be established to review, on points of law, the application of countervail or other penalties of trade-remedy laws of national trade agencies against the other country. If the imposition of a penalty again was not in accordance with US trade law, for example, the binational body could require it be removed. The US could still unilaterally enact harsher trade remedy laws but it would have to notify Canada and mention Canada by name in amendments to its trade laws. A Canada-US Trade Commission, headed by the trade ministries of the 2 countries, would be established to implement and administer the proposed agreement. In other provisions, Canada will largely eliminate its restrictions on US takeovers of Canadian companies, except for those with assets of $150 million or more, and will not in future require US subsidiaries to sell shares to Canadians or force them to promote exports or use Canadian suppliers. US-owned companies will have to be treated in the same way as Canadian-owned companies. On energy, Canada would have to share oil and gas shortages with the US, and will not use its energy, including electricity, to create an advantage for Canadian industry or Canadian consumers through lower prices. The proposed agreement also covers services, including financial services. US banks and other financial institutions would have the same rights in Canada as Canadian financial institutions. Other features of the proposed agreement include the elimination of tariffs and other barriers in agriculture and a 50% North American content rule for duty-free

movement of non-North American motor vehicles between the 2 countries.

While Canadians and Americans share many fundamental values, there are wide differences in economic, cultural and social concerns and policies. The US, for example, champions the cause of free markets and free investment flows, but the Canadian concern is to preserve the capacities of an independent nation. Thus, Canadians are more willing to use government and CROWN CORPORATIONS to develop their own economy and industry to meet Canadian needs. It is hard, as former PM Trudeau once remarked, for a mouse to live next to an elephant. From the Canadian perspective, it is critical that the US understands that Canada has legitimate interests and aspirations that are separate from those of the US. In the future, Canada-US economic relations will be tested by a wide array of issues. The US need for water may even lead to pressures on Canada to supply that resource. Canadian desires for greater Canadian ownership and control of their own economy and US desires for international codes for the free flow of investment dollars and trade in services will continue to generate conflict. US deregulation and changes in technology will have major implications for Canadian airlines, telecommunications services and broadcasting. But there will also be areas of common interest, and the ties that bind will no doubt continue to be as compelling as those that divide. DAVID CRANE

Canadian Arctic Expedition (1913-18), funded by the Canadian government and commanded by the controversial explorer Vilhjalmur STEFANSSON, was a mixture of achievement and disaster. Its accomplishments included the discovery of Lougheed, Borden, Meighen and Brock Is and much valuable scientific work done by the zoologist R.M. Anderson, second in command, and by the ethnographer Diamond JENNESS. But it was plagued by violent internal dissension; its ship, the KARLUK, was caught by ice off Alaska, and eventually 11 men were lost. The expedition strengthened Canada's claims to sovereignty over the Arctic, and established Stefansson's reputation as a genius to his admirers and a charlatan to his enemies. *See also* ARCTIC EXPLORATION; ARCTIC SOVEREIGNTY. KENNETH S. COATES

Canadian Association of College and University Libraries, est 1963, is a division of the Canadian Library Assn. As such, CACUL is not a separate entity but does have the authority to act in the name of CLA on matters such as academic status, which are of concern and interest to librarians and libraries in Canadian institutions of higher education. Its annual meeting serves as a forum for discussion of issues and as an informal means of continuing education. A more formal educational program is conducted through a series of workshops offered in conjunction with the annual meeting. Publication is another important activity. The *CACUL Newsletter,* issued 1963-75, was a major scholarly journal in academic librarianship. At present, accounts of CACUL activities appear quite frequently in *Feliciter* (CLA journal), and some of the workshop proceedings are published as monographs. Membership in CACUL is open to both personal and institutional members and no qualification is required. Its constitutional objective is "to develop high standards of librarianship and to promote these in institutions of post-secondary education." The Community and Technical College Section, a subdivision of CACUL, has been active in producing standards and a directory. SAMUEL ROTHSTEIN

Canadian Authors Association, Canada's first national literary organization, was founded in 1921 to combat proposed changes in COPYRIGHT

LAW; it incorporated both official language groups until the establishment of the Société des écrivains canadiens in 1938. In addition to fighting for writers' control over copyright, the association devoted its early efforts to promoting Canadian writing through the establishment of the annual Canadian Book Week (1921-57). In the 1930s the CAA was responsible for promoting the formation of the Association of Canadian Bookmen (1935-39), establishing *The Canadian Poetry Magazine* (1936-68), and initiating the GOVERNOR GENERAL'S LITERARY AWARDS in 1937 which it administered until 1959. In 1946 the association drew up a standard book contract and secured special income tax privileges for Canadian writers; the following year, it agreed to administer the fledgling Leacock Award for Humour. In 1975, after a lapse of several years, the CAA instituted a new system of literary awards, each of which for the first time carried a cash value of $1000. Its official publication, *The Canadian Author and Bookman* (est 1921), continues to speak for the largest literary organization in Canada.

JOHN LENNOX

Canadian Bar Association was formed in Ottawa in 1914; its prime mover, Sir James AIKINS (CPR counsel in Winnipeg and later lt-gov of Manitoba) was elected president (1914-29). Its objectives were to promote uniformity of legislation across Canada and generally to improve the administration and advance the interests of the profession. As the first objective proved too demanding for the fledgling organization, it fostered the founding of the Uniform Law Commission, an independent body which still functions. Otherwise its goals have remained constant, except that the advancement of LEGAL EDUCATION was added in 1921 when the CBA was incorporated by statute. It has had considerable success in achieving its objectives. The need for a journal was soon recognized, and this caused the merger of the *Canada Law Journal* and the *Canadian Law Times* as the *Canadian Law Review*, which began publication in 1923. With national headquarters in Ottawa and 32 000 members in 1986, the CBA forms a strong lobby and has often been successful in having its views considered at the highest levels and reflected in legislation.

D.H. BROWN

Canadian Bible Society, fd 1904 to publish and distribute biblical scriptures. The British and Foreign Bible Society was founded 1804 in London, Eng, and in 1805 its first overseas publication, the Gospel of John in Mohawk, arrived in Canada. Early NS settlers obtained Bibles from the BFBS, and as early as 1808 collected offerings for its work. Branches sprang up in the Maritimes, and then farther west. After some time the formation of a national Bible society was a logical development, and on 14-15 Sept 1904, in Toronto, the BFBS branches in Canada joined together in the Canadian Bible Society. In 1946 a number of national Bible societies formed the United Bible Societies, a world fellowship. The CBS was a charter member. The CBS limits itself to the Scriptures only, leaving interpretation to the churches. This ecumenical organization works with all Christian denominations. In 1986 it distributed over 12 million Bibles, Testaments, Gospels and Scripture selections in 104 languages in Canada. The Scriptures are now in 1848 languages, and annual world distribution by the various societies is 500 million.

Canadian Bill of Rights, PM John DIEFENBAKER's pathbreaking 1960 HUMAN RIGHTS charter, applied only to federal law because the requisite provincial consent was not obtained. It recognizes the rights of individuals to life, liberty, personal security and enjoyment (not "possession," which is provincial) of property. Deprivation of these is forbidden "except by due process of law." It protects rights to equality before the law and ensures protection of the law; protects the freedoms of religion, speech, assembly and association, and the press; and legal rights such as the rights to counsel and "fair hearing." Laws are to be construed and applied so as not to detract from these rights and freedoms. One of the bill's weaknesses was that many judges regarded it as a mere interpretative aid. Section 2 provides that Parliament can override the mentioned rights by inserting a "notwithstanding" clause in the applicable statute; this has been done only once, during the 1970 OCTOBER CRISIS. To the extent that it is not superseded by the 1982 CANADIAN CHARTER OF RIGHTS AND FREEDOMS, the bill remains in effect. *See also* DRYBONES CASE; LAVELL CASE. W.H. MCCONNELL

Canadian Brass quintet was formed in 1970 as the Canadian Brass Ensemble, consisting of Stuart Laughton and William Phillips, trumpets, Graeme Page, french horn, Eugene Watts, trombone, and Charles Daellenbach, tuba. In 1971 the group became Canadian Brass and Ronald Romm replaced Laughton. The following year Fred Mills replaced Phillips. The ensemble then remained unchanged until 1983 when Martin Hackleman replaced Page. In 1986 Hackleman left and was replaced by David Ohanian. Initially members of the Hamilton Philharmonic Orchestra, the group also became artists-in-residence at the BANFF CENTRE. Their first European tour, in 1972 with the Festival Singers, was assisted by the Canadian government and quickly led to a highly successful international career which has included performances at the Paris Festival, Edinburgh Festival and Kennedy Center, tours of China, England, Europe and the USSR, and many international radio and TV appearances. As well as being superb musicians, the members of the quintet have established reputations for on-stage hilarity which has a broad appeal for young and old. The Canadian Brass has performed with Canada's major symphony orchestras, and has unearthed several little-known works by major composers. Many Canadian composers have been commissioned and premiered by Canadian Brass. The group's long list of recordings is a clear indication of the breadth of its repertoire, versatility and skill. Canadian Brass plays on a matched set of gold-plated instruments made for it by Renold Schilke.

MABEL H. LAINE

Canadian Broadcasting Corporation, one of the world's major public BROADCASTING organizations. It currently operates national mono radio, FM stereo, and colour television networks in English and French; provides regional and local radio and television programming in both official languages; broadcasts locally produced programs in English and native languages for people living in the Far North; runs a multilingual shortwave service for listeners overseas; televises the proceedings of the House of Commons via cable; and provides closed captioning for the deaf. It is funded primarily by federal statutory grants (about 80% of its budget), but also derives revenues from commercial sponsorship and the sale of programs to other countries. While ultimately responsible to Parliament for its overall conduct, it is independent of government control in its day-to-day operations. From its creation in the midst of the Depression to the present day, it has sought to provide Canadians with a broad range of high quality indigenous information and entertainment programming rather than simply to cater to the interests of particular groups.

The establishment of the CBC as a CROWN CORPORATION on 2 Nov 1936, followed 2 earlier experiments with public broadcast ownership in Canada. During the 1920s, Canadian National Railways developed a radio network with stations in Ottawa, Montréal, Toronto, Moncton and Vancouver. Its schedule included concerts, comic opera, school broadcasts and historical drama, though by the end of 1929 it was still providing only 3 hours of programming a week nationally. Together with the example of the British Broadcasting Corporation, however, it helped to make the merits of public ownership more apparent to the Royal Commission on Radio Broadcasting appointed by Mackenzie King on 6 Dec 1928, under the chairmanship of Sir John AIRD. The privately owned Canadian stations were not only beginning to fall into American hands but also seemed quite incapable at the time of providing an adequate Canadian alternative to the programming that was flooding across the border from the US.

The moving force within the Aird Commission was Charles Bowman, editor of the *Ottawa Citizen*, who was convinced that public ownership of broadcasting was necessary to protect Canada against American cultural penetration. After receiving submissions from across the country and visiting other broadcasting systems, the Aird Commission submitted its report on 11 Sept 1929, less than 2 months before the stock market crashed. It recommended the creation of a national broadcasting company with the status and duties of a public utility and a source of public funds to develop a service capable of "fostering a national spirit and interpreting national citizenship." It specifically called for the elimination of the private stations, albeit with compensation. Because of the economic crisis, consideration of the Aird Report was delayed and this enabled some of the more powerful private stations and their principal lobbying agency, the Canadian Association of Broadcasters, to launch a campaign against it. But its basic principles were defended by the Canadian Radio League (CRL), an informal voluntary organization set up in Ottawa by Alan PLAUNT and Graham SPRY in the fall of 1930. They prepared pamphlets stating the case for public ownership; recruited other voluntary organizations as well as representatives from business, banking, trade unions, the farming community and educational institutions; and sent a formal delegation to meet the minister of marine.

The newly elected Conservative government of R.B. BENNETT responded to the appeals of the CRL by passing the Canadian Radio Broadcasting Act (1932). It established a publicly owned Canadian Radio Broadcasting Commission with a mandate to provide programs and extend coverage to all settled parts of the country. The CRBC took over the radio facilities of the CNR and began to broadcast in English and French under the guidance of commissioners Thomas Maher, Hector Charlesworth and Lt Col W. Arthur Steel. The private stations, whose fate was left in the commission's hands, helped the CRBC to get some of its programs aired nationally, but did not co-operate fully. Nonetheless, the CRBC allowed them to continue and even expand and in the end most of them outlived the commission itself.

The CRBC suffered from underfunding, an uncertain mandate, inappropriate administrative arrangements and a series of tactless political broadcasts. But as a result of further lobbying by the CRL, the returned Liberal government of King was persuaded to replace it with a stronger public agency rather than abandon broadcasting to the private sector. A new Canadian Broadcasting Act in 1936 created the CBC with a better organizational structure, more assured funding through the use of a licence fee on receiving sets (initially set at $2.50), and decreased vulnerability to political pressure. The CBC assumed the assets, liabilities and principal functions of the CRBC, including responsibility for regulating the private stations and providing indigenous programs for all Canadians.

From 1936 to 1958, the CBC was headed by a board of governors, initially composed of 9 unsalaried members representing the various sections of Canada. The board was responsible for the formulation of general policy and for regulating the private stations. Its first chairman was Leonard W. BROCKINGTON, a noted lawyer from Winnipeg; in 1939 he was succeeded by René Morin. In 1944 the Broadcasting Act was amended to provide for the appointment of a full-time salaried chairman for a term of 3 years. On 14 Nov 1945, A. Davidson DUNTON, who had previously served as general manager of the WARTIME INFORMATION BOARD, was appointed to the position; he continued to serve as chairman until 1 July 1958. The board was also responsible for appointing a general manager and an assistant general manager to oversee the day-to-day operations of the corporation. The first general manager was Gladstone Murray, a Canadian-born director of public relations for the BBC.

The CBC began operations with 8 stations of its own and 16 privately owned affiliates. A technical survey authorized by the board of governors revealed that this network provided assured coverage for only half of Canada's 11 million inhabitants and mainly for those in urban communities. It also confirmed that residents in major cities suffered from constant interference from high-power American stations. In 1937, therefore, 50 kW transmitters were built in Montréal and Toronto, increasing coverage to about 76% of the population. The same year the CBC helped to organize a N American conference in Havana at which Canada was allocated 6 clear channels for stations with 50 kW or more, 8 clear channels for stations from 0.25 to 50 kW, and shared use of 41 regional and 6 local channels. To reach outlying areas, the CBC added 50-kW transmitters in Saskatchewan and the Maritimes in 1939 and began building low-power relay transmitters in BC, northern Ontario and parts of New Brunswick. After the war, additional 50-kW stations were built in Manitoba and Alberta and the power of CJBC Toronto was increased to the same wattage.

The development of indigenous programming proceeded more slowly than the extension of coverage. Considerable use was made initially of entertainment, serious music and talk programs produced in the US and Britain. But following a program survey to determine the extent and location of Canadian talent, the CBC gradually created its own distinctive service featuring: variety programs such as "The Happy Gang"; regional farm broadcasts and Harry Boyle's national FARM RADIO FORUM for what was still a predominantly rural nation; women's interests programs such as "Femina" together with daily morning talks by a network of women commentators organized by assistant talks supervisor Elizabeth Long; sports broadcasts including NHL hockey on Saturday nights with Foster HEWITT; children's programs such as "Just Mary" with Mary Grannan; and extensive coverage of events such as the coronation of King George VI and Queen Elizabeth in 1937 and the royal tour of Canada in 1939. A separate French-language network was established and program production was decentralized into 5 regions: BC, the Prairie provinces, Ontario, Québec and the Maritimes.

With the outbreak of war, the CBC created an Overseas Service to relay reports of war correspondents such as Matthew HALTON and Marcel Ouimet. On 1 Jan 1941, it ended its reliance on news bulletins prepared by the Canadian Press by inaugurating its own News Service under chief

editor Dan McArthur. Through the objective treatment of news on its national newscast, which was read by Charles Jennings and later by Lorne GREENE (the famous "Voice of Doom"), the CBC News Service quickly established a reputation for impartiality and integrity. During the war, the CBC also established Radio-College in Québec and began its National School Broadcasts (1942). In 1944 its English-language network was divided into the Dominion network (composed of one CBC station and 34 affiliates) and the Trans-Canada network (6 CBC stations and 28 affiliates). At the end of the war, the CBC joined forces with the government to establish a multilingual international service (1945), which later became Radio-Canada International. Programs were transmitted from studios on Crescent Street in Montréal to Sackville, NB, by land-lines and then sent overseas by wireless.

Public affairs programming did not initially receive much emphasis on CBC radio. Shortly before his departure as chairman, Brockington took steps to change this situation by formulating a "White Paper" on political and controversial broadcasting. Adopted by the board of governors in July 1939, it stated that the CBC would seek to present a variety of opinions on controversial issues and would refrain from selling network time for the propagation of personal views. With the outbreak of WWII, however, the CBC found itself under government pressure to curtail the discussion of public affairs on the air. Proposals by the CBC Talks Department for a series of forums on war-related issues were rejected by Murray in favour of BBC rebroadcasts and one-man pep talks intended to inspire the war effort. The CBC general manager eventually approved a discussion program called "Citizens All," but demanded personal approval of speakers and subjects. It was not until Murray was replaced by J.S. Thomson in Aug 1942, that the efforts of the Talks Department to promote serious discussion on matters of public concern began to bear fruit. By the end of Thomson's one-year term, the department had demonstrated the democratic role that public affairs broadcasting could fulfill through the introduction of programs such as "Weekend Review," "National Labour Forum," "CBC Discussion Club," and the popular "Of Things to Come – An Inquiry into the Post-War World." Chaired by author Morley CALLAGHAN, the latter program evolved into the popular "Citizen's Forum," which made use of listening groups and lasted into the television era.

The further expansion of public affairs programming after the war was accompanied by programs on the arts such as "Critically Speaking" and a significant increase in the production of Canadian drama. In 1940 the CBC had introduced "Canadian Theatre of the Air" and in 1944 Andrew ALLAN's greatly admired "Stage" series made its debut. But the heyday of Canadian radio drama came during the early post-war period. A repertory company of young Canadian actors was formed and a major program was launched to train young Canadian writers. During the 1947-48 season, there were 320 radio drama productions in English, 97% of which were by Canadian writers. In addition to Allan, producers such as Esse Ljungh, Rupert Caplan and Fletcher Markle led the way in N America in serious drama programming.

By this time, however, the days of radio drama were already numbered as Canadians began mounting pressure for the introduction of TELEVISION, which had become available in the US after the war. Initially, both the CBC and the government chose to proceed with caution in dealing with the costly new medium. Dr Augustin Frigon, who had served on the Aird Commission and was

head of the French network before replacing Thomson as general manager, advised the 1946 parliamentary Radio Committee that "it would be a mistake to encourage the introduction of television in Canada without sufficient financial support and, therefore, taking the risk that unsatisfactory programs would, at the start, give a poor impression of this new means of communication." But while Frigon refused to be "stampeded into premature action," board chairman Davidson Dunton did discuss with the Canadian Association of Broadcasters the idea of having the staff of the CBC and private broadcasters undertake television training at CBC facilities in Montréal and Toronto.

The major impetus to action from within the CBC came from the Report on Television (1947) for which the corporation's assistant chief engineer, J. Alphonse OUIMET, was largely responsible. Ouimet, who had built and attempted to market his own television system in Montréal in the early 1930s, was appointed co-ordinator of television and later replaced Frigon as general manager. Arguably the single most important figure in the history of Canadian broadcasting, he deserves much of the credit for the rapid introduction and expansion of television in Canada once the government finally decided to go ahead with television and allocated funds from an excise tax on television sets for its development. At the time of its introduction on CBFT Montréal 6 Sept 1952, and 2 nights on CBLT Toronto, television was available only to 26% of the population. But by 1954 this had increased to 60% and Canada ranked second in the world in live television program production. CBC stations had been constructed in Ottawa, Vancouver, Winnipeg and Halifax and private affiliates were already starting to make their appearance in other cities. By 1957 the CBC English and French networks were each broadcasting up to 10 hours a day and their coverage had been extended to 85% of the population through a combination of CBC-owned and -operated stations and privately owned affiliates.

The advent of television created major problems for CBC radio. Its audience share plummeted as creative talent and capital funds were siphoned off by the new medium and both commercial revenues and the supply of American entertainment programs were greatly reduced. Forced to compete against local information and American pop music formats on the private stations, CBC radio became increasingly demoralized and out of touch with Canadian listeners. During the 1960s, a few steps were taken to reclaim audience loyalty: some new current affairs programs were introduced and Canadian-produced drama and serious music was increased. But it was not until the outset of the 1970s that CBC radio underwent the revolution that made it the pride of the corporation.

Following the submission of an exhaustive radio study in 1970, CBC radio made a fundamental shift in its priorities. Substantial program resources were reallocated from the evenings (when television is the main attraction) to the morning and afternoon periods. Local information programs were developed, block programs formats were devised, and national news and current affairs was strengthened through the introduction of programs such as "This Country In The Morning" and "As It Happens." At the same time, the potential of FM radio was finally pursued in earnest after 2 decades of experimentation. In 1975 a stereo FM network was inaugurated and the same year the use of commercials on both AM and FM was eliminated. Eventually, as both AM and FM coverage was extended through the Accelerated Coverage Plan which began in 1974, 2 networks emerged offering distinctive program services. The AM network concentrates on news, information, light entertainment and local community affairs; the FM network focuses on serious music, drama, documentaries and the arts and culture.

CBC television adapted less successfully to its own particular problems in this period. During the 1950s, a new generation of producers responded to the challenge of developing programs for the medium with energy, enthusiasm, and great creativity. Men such as Ross McLean, Norman Campbell, Bob Allen, Jean-Paul Fugere, Sydney Newman and Mario Prizek created an impressive array of information and entertainment programs, including "Tabloid," "G.E. Showcase," "La Famille Plouffe," FRONT PAGE CHALLENGE, "Festival," "Don Messer's Jubilee," "Les Idées en Marche" and "Cross Canada Hit Parade." But the remarkable programming performance of the CBC during the 1950s did not eliminate the desire of Canadians for access to American entertainment programs as well. In addition to producing Canadian programs, the CBC was also expected to relay popular American programs to Canadian viewers, especially in areas where American signals could not be picked up with the aid of rooftop antennae.

Eventually, with the introduction of CABLE and SATELLITES, the need for CBC to rebroadcast American programs was eliminated. By that time, however, CBC television had developed a strong dependency on American programs. This process began in the late 1950s as the era of live television broadcasting gave way to the production of expensive, pre-filmed comedy and drama series which could be shown repeatedly. The CBC was soon caught in a vicious circle insofar as it needed to carry popular American programs in order to acquire the advertising revenues necessary to produce comparable programming. Moreover, with the licensing of the CTV network in 1961, the CBC found that it also had to use American programs to generate audiences for its own programs through the so-called "inheritance factor."

During the 1960s, the CBC developed new television dramas such as "Wojeck" and "Quentin Durgens MP" by Ronald Weyman; exciting information programs such as THIS HOUR HAS SEVEN DAYS, "Man Alive" and "The Nature of Things"; and long-standing children's favourites such as "Mr. Dressup," "The Friendly Giant" and "Chez Hélène." Nonetheless, its continued reliance on a relatively high proportion of American programs made it increasingly vulnerable to accusations that it was not fulfilling its mandate under the Broadcasting Act. Between 1967-68 and 1973-74, therefore, the CBC responded to growing public criticism by increasing its Canadian content on television from about 52% to about 68%. A host of new Canadian programs were added to its schedules, including "Marketplace," "The Beachcombers," "Performance" and "the fifth estate."

During the same period, an attempt was made to improve the balance between network and regional programming and increase efficiency by consolidating the English network, French network and regional broadcasting systems into 2 administrative divisions: the English Services Division with headquarters in Toronto and the French Services Division with headquarters in Montréal. Further consolidation since then has facilitated additional steps towards the Canadianization of the television schedule. Between 1983-84 and 1985-86, for example, Canadian content was increased from 74% to 77% on the English television network of the CBC and from 69% to 79% on its French television network. However, crippling reductions in the CBC's budget in the mid-1980s by the Mulroney govern-

ment have postponed indefinitely the dream of completely eliminating both foreign programs and advertising on CBC TV.

It is arguable that some of the problems confronting the CBC have been compounded by the fact that it no longer performs the regulatory role assigned to it by the 1936 Broadcasting Act. The Royal Commission on NATIONAL DEVELOPMENT IN THE ARTS, LETTERS AND SCIENCES (1949-51) chaired by Vincent Massey was not persuaded by the long-standing argument of the Canadian Association of Broadcasters that the CBC should not be "at one and the same time competitor, regulator, prosecutor, jury and judge." However, the views of the private broadcasters received a more sympathetic hearing at the Royal Commission on Broadcasting chaired by Robert FOWLER in 1955-56. Its recommendation for a separate regulatory agency was given substance with the passage of a new Broadcasting Act by the Conservative government of John Diefenbaker in 1958. The task of regulating the broadcasting system was taken away from the CBC and given to a separate Board of Broadcast Governors (BBG). At the same time, the CBC board of governors was replaced by a 15-person board of directors and the principal responsibility for running the corporation was placed on the shoulders of a president appointed by the government for a 7-year term. The BBG was subsequently replaced by the Canadian Radio and Television Commission (CANADIAN RADIO-TELEVISION AND TELECOMMUNICATIONS COMMISSION) in 1968, but the principle of a separate regulatory authority remained intact.

The removal of regulatory functions from the mandate of the CBC was probably inevitable and did enable the corporation to concentrate on the primary task of providing Canadians with high quality radio and television programming. But it also reduced the ability of the 5 men who have occupied the presidency of the CBC – J. Alphonse Ouimet (1958-67), George Davidson (1968-72), Laurent Picard (1972-75), A.W. (Al) Johnson (1975-82) and Pierre JUNEAU (1982-) – to influence the broadcasting environment in which the CBC must operate. The CBC was unable to prevent the introduction of rival networks devoted to foreign programming; it could do nothing to ensure that funds for Canadian programming were generated by the rapid expansion of cable systems carrying foreign signals; and it could only stand by helplessly as scarce programming resources were siphoned off by PAY TELEVISION for the benefit of the more affluent. Nor could it even secure for itself second channels in English and French so as to increase its audience share, though a CBC all-news channel was approved in 1987.

Despite the steady erosion of faith in the principle of public ownership, there is little evidence that the cultural goals which Canadians have set for their broadcasting system could ever be achieved by the private enterprise system. The CBC has often been criticized for having a top-heavy bureaucracy, but studies have shown that it compares favourably in efficiency and productivity with other public and private broadcasting organizations throughout the world. The most encouraging development for supporters of public broadcasting in recent years was the publication of the report of the Caplan-Sauvageau TASK FORCE ON BROADCASTING POLICY (1986), though the Mulroney government showed no indication of acting on its recommendations. However, even its recommended course of action might further undermine the position and morale of the CBC by forcing it to compete against yet another broadcasting agency. *See also* CULTURAL POLICY; COMMUNICATIONS; RADIO DRAMA; TELEVISION DRAMA.

ROSS EAMAN

Canadian Business, magazine established in 1927, is Canada's leading general interest business monthly magazine. It was owned by the Montreal Chamber of Commerce and published in Montréal, from its inception until 1978 when it was bought by Michael de Pencier, Alexander Ross and Roy MacLaren. MacLaren was later a member of the Trudeau and Turner federal Cabinets. The 1986 average circulation of *Canadian Business* was 95 908. *Canadian Business* covers the gamut of business interests, but it is directed more to executives and small-business readers than to investors and is noted for its profiles of business leaders. The publisher is Roy MacLaren and the editor is Joann Webb (1987). It is now published at Toronto.

D. McGILLIVRAY

Canadian Business Review, established in 1974, is a quarterly published by The Conference Board of Canada from its headquarters in Ottawa. With a circulation of about 8000 it fulfils the same role in Canada as the board's US magazine, *Across the Board,* does in that country. S. Scott Hatfield is editor, assisted by an advisory board including James R. Nininger, president of The Conference Board of Canada, and Jim Frank, the chief economist (1987). The *Canadian Business Review* includes pro-and-con discussions of economic questions, but its most distinctive feature is a quarterly survey of economic forecasts of the major Canadian banks and investment houses. The average of these forecasts, published in the review, is usually taken as the consensus view of Canada's economic future in the next year or so. The *Canadian Business Review* accepts no advertising and is funded mainly by the more than 700 associates (members) of the Conference Board of Canada, a list that includes corporations, government departments and labour unions.

D. McGILLIVRAY

Canadian Cancer Society, fd 1937 and incorporated as a national body in 1938 as a result of action taken by the CANADIAN MEDICAL ASSOCIATION and lay groups in some provinces to provide a lay-medical organization that would help bring CANCER patients into doctors' offices earlier. In 1986 the society had a national office, 10 divisions, 3802 contact points, 350 full-time staff and some 350 000 volunteers. A prime responsibility of the society is public education about the need for early diagnosis and treatment of cancer. In 1986 over $9 million was spent on films, pamphlets, posters, school kits, special meetings and conferences. The services provided to patients have traditionally focused on the nonmedical needs. More recently, services have been expanded to meet the social and psychological needs of patients and their families and a range of special programs, such as provision of dressings or prostheses.

The appeal for funds usually takes place in one annual campaign; additionally, the Terry Fox "Marathon of Hope" provides funding specifically directed by Terry FOX towards research. Research funds are administered by the National Cancer Institute of Canada, a volunteer scientific and professional organization (est 1947), which has representatives from all bodies in Canada concerned with cancer research. The institute coordinates research, trains scientists and compiles and interprets cancer statistics. The Canadian Cancer Society offers fellowships to provide specialized training for clinicians and has provided capital funds for cancer research facilities. Annual expenditures of the society are about $54 million, of which roughly one-half goes to research.

Canadian Charter of Rights and Freedoms, the only Charter of Rights entrenched in the Canadian Constitution, came into force on 17 April 1982. According to section 52 of the CONSTI-

TUTION ACT, 1982, every law that is inconsistent with the Constitution is, to the extent of the inconsistency, of no force and effect. The SUPREME COURT OF CANADA in the *Skapinker* case of May 1984, declared unanimously that the Charter "is a part of the Constitution of a nation ... part of the fabric of Canadian law ... the supreme law of Canada." It also declared that "the Charter is designed and adopted to guide and serve the Canadian community for a long time.... With the Constitution Act, 1982, comes a new dimension, a new yardstick of reconciliation between the individual and the community and their respective rights, a dimension which like the balance of the Constitution remains to be interpreted and applied by the court."

The Canadian Charter of Rights and Freedoms was an important issue in the debate concerning the patriation of the Constitution (*see* CONSTITUTION, PATRIATION OF). The majority of the provinces, while not adverse to a Charter of Rights, had other priorities, particularly the enlargement of some of their powers. In Nov 1981 Prime Minister P.E. TRUDEAU accepted the Alberta-Vancouver formula of amendment endorsed by 8 provinces, and the provinces accepted the Charter of Rights, but not without imposing the exercise at will of a derogatory clause ("notwithstanding" clause of s33) for certain sectors of the Charter: fundamental rights, legal rights and the equality rights. By invoking the derogatory clause, the provinces (and Parliament) can declare any law exempt from the provisions of sections 2 and 7 to 15 of the Canadian Charter. The compromise resulted in the Canada Act, 1982 and the Constitution Act, 1982 (*see* DISTRIBUTION OF POWERS; CONSTITUTIONAL LAW).

Within the Canadian Constitution, the Charter occupies a central place. The courts, which in the past have ruled on the division of powers and have declared ultra vires statutes that violated such division, will now rule also on whether federal and provincial statutes are compatible with the Charter.

A constitutional Charter of Rights always gives rise to a profound debate between 2 philosophies at the time of its entrenchment in a constitution. The first favours entrenchment, so as to ensure that the courts have the last word in the field of liberties; the second holds that Parliament and the legislatures should have the last word. The general tendency in the constitutions since WWII is in favour of the entrenchment of rights.

The object of a Charter of Rights is to protect the citizen against the STATE, and to protect minorities against parliamentary majorities. The Canadian Charter is comprehensive and covers several fields: fundamental rights, democratic rights, mobility rights, legal rights, equality rights and linguistic rights. The equality between men and women is also expressly protected by a particular section of the Charter. Aboriginal rights and freedoms are not affected.

The Canadian Charter of Rights and Freedoms was not adopted by the House of Commons and the Senate in its original form. More than one amendment was brought to the Oct 1980 version. Several individuals and pressure groups appeared before the Special Joint Committee of the Senate and of the House of Commons on the Constitution of Canada. The 1208 submissions and the hearing of 104 witnesses resulted in the April 1981 version, which in the form of a Resolution was passed by both Houses. The April version, after the decision of the Supreme Court on patriation in Sept 1981, was further amended as a result of the 5 Nov 1981 agreement between the federal authority and 9 provinces. Québec has invoked the derogatory clause of s33 of the Charter in respect of all its previous laws dealing with matters

related to sections 2 and 7 to 15 of the Canadian Charter; Québec has done the same since 17 Apr 1982 for its statutes concerning those matters. Québec challenged, without success, the whole process, arguing that it had a right of veto according to a convention of the Constitution. The Supreme Court declared that such a convention does not exist. However, the new government of R. BOURASSA elected on 2 Dec 1985, decided not to use the derogatory clause in a global way.

By 1987, the Supreme Court of Canada had rendered more than 20 decisions on the Charter. Many of them are landmark decisions; eg, the CRUISE MISSILE CASE (Cabinet's decisions subject to Charter), BIG M DRUG MART (the Lord's Day Act violates the freedom of religion), OAKES CASE (presumption of innocence, and, limitation clause in s1 of the Charter), VALENTE CASE (judicial independence), Québec's BILL 101 CASE, *Hunter* v *Southam* (unreasonable seizure), SINGH CASE (fundamental justice). Article 35 (native rights) was amended, article 28 (sexual equality), article 40 (compensation for education and culture) and article 59 (language rights in Québec) were added in Nov 1981, after the constitutional conference, before the Resolution was finally adopted by the federal Houses and sent to the UK as part of the patriation process.   GÉRALD-A. BEAUDOIN

Canadian Coast Guard The CCG was founded as the "Marine Branch" of the Dept of Marine and Fisheries in 1867. In 1936 it came under the jurisdiction of the Dept of Transport, Marine Services, and in 1962 was officially named the Canadian Coast Guard. It currently operates within a total budget of $700 million with 6200 employees. The distinctive red-and-white vessels of the CCG fleet are stationed at the 5 CCG regional offices (Western, Central, Laurentian, Maritimes and Newfoundland with their headquarters at Vancouver, Toronto, Québec City, Dartmouth and St John's) as well as at 11 strategically located bases and 5 subbases. The fleet consists of 56 major vessels as well as 35 helicopters and one fixed-wing aircraft. In addition to the larger ships, there are 74 frontline rescue vessels and 4 hovercraft.

The responsibilities of the CCG under the National Transportation Act and other applicable legislation are icebreaking, search and rescue, aids to navigation and northern resupply. The CCG also has a regulatory responsibility under the Canada Shipping Act with respect to ship inspection and standards. The CCG provides and maintains some 13 000 channel buoys and 10 000 land-based aids of which 266 are major LIGHTHOUSES; 33 coastal radio stations and 15 vessel traffic centres provide navigational hazard and weather advice.

The powerful fleet of ICEBREAKERS aid navigation along the East Coast, across the North and through the Great Lakes-St Lawrence system. In addition to allowing vessels to operate more safely and economically, the icebreaking activity also contributes to flood control and shoreline protection. The 55 permanent and seasonal SAR stations provide year-round search-and-rescue services, staffed by 750 specialists within the CCG assisted by a Coast Guard Auxiliary of volunteers trained in search-and-rescue techniques. Northern resupply activities in the Arctic and along the Mackenzie R ensure the continued existence of remote settlements.

The CCG enforces safety standards and regulations, investigates marine casualties and responds to emergency oil spills. Boating safety personnel offer courtesy inspections and give safety lectures to thousands of yachters and fishermen every year. *See also* SHIPPING.

Reading: T.E. Appleton, *Usque Ad Mare: A History of the Canadian Coast Guard and Marine Services* (1968).

Canadian Commercial Bank (CCB) became Canada's tenth Schedule A bank when chartered as Canadian Commercial and Industrial Bank on 30 July 1975. With corporate offices in Edmonton, the bank officially commenced business on 6 July 1976 in Vancouver and Edmonton on initial share capital of $22 million. By Aug 1984 the bank had become international in scope with 16 deposit and lending offices located across Canada and the western US. Capital had increased to $107 million through public preferred shareholders and private common shareholders composed of leading pension and institutional funds. The present name was adopted 25 April 1981. The bank collapsed in Sept 1985 after a failed rescue attempt by federal and provincial governments and by several other chartered banks. The ESTEY COMMISSION subsequently investigated the failure of the CCB, as well as that of the Northland Bank. The commission heard evidence that both bad management practices and the recession then affecting western Canada were contributing factors in the banks' collapse.

Canadian Congress of Labour, fd fall 1940 as a merger of the All-Canadian Congress of Labour and the Canadian section of the Congress of Industrial Organizations. For 16 years the CCL was in the forefront of Canadian union activity and organization. From an initial membership of some 77 000, it had enrolled some 360 000 workers by 1956 when it joined with the TRADES AND LABOR CONGRESS to form the CANADIAN LABOUR CONGRESS. Its affiliates included the international INDUSTRIAL UNIONS in Canada: packinghouse workers, steelworkers, woodworkers, autoworkers, clothing workers, miners, electrical workers, and the mine, mill and smelter workers, as well as several large national unions led by the Canadian Brotherhood of Railway Employees. The president of this latter union, Aaron MOSHER, also headed the CCL though the real power lay with secretary-treasurer Pat CONROY, a strong nationalist who resigned in 1951 in a dispute with some of the international union leaders.

The CCL was more aggressive than its CRAFT UNION counterpart, the TLC, and organized thousands of unskilled workers whom most labour experts thought were unorganizable. In 1945 the CCL officially allied itself with the CCF and many of its leaders ran in provincial or federal elections. As well, following WWII, the congress took the lead in expelling influential communist-dominated unions from its ranks. As the voice of Canadian industrial unionism, the CCL played an important role in national political and economic affairs.   IRVING ABELLA

Canadian Council of Churches, fd 1944, the national ecumenical fellowship of Canadian churches: Anglican, Armenian Orthodox, Baptist, Canadian Conference of Catholic Bishops, Christian Church (Disciples of Christ), Coptic Orthodox, Ethiopian Orthodox, Evangelical Lutheran Church in Canada, Greek Orthodox, Polish National Catholic Church, Presbyterian, Reformed Church of America – Classis of Ontario, Religious Society of Friends, Salvation Army and United Church. The word "ecumenical" comes from the Gk *oikoumene*, "the whole inhabited earth." The purpose of any ecumenical organization is to seek unity for a divided church and to remind Christians that they share Christ's mission of reconciliation, peace, dignity and justice for the whole community. Within individual member churches, local needs and specifically denominational concerns have, in practice, frequently taken precedence over ecumenical efforts, but all CCC members nevertheless maintain a theological commitment to ecumenism. The council works closely with nonmember Christian churches, as well as with communities of other faiths. It participates in Canadian interchurch coalitions for social justice, the Ecumenical Forum of Canada and local councils of churches.

The Canadian Council, which provides an agency for consultation, planning and common action, was founded to co-ordinate the growing number of Canadian co-operative ventures in social service, religious education, evangelization and overseas mission, and to participate in the international ecumenical movement leading to the 1948 formation of the World Council of Churches, in which Canadians were prominently involved. The council communicates and co-operates with other national councils. It works closely with the WCC, though it neither contributes funds to nor receives financial support from the World Council. The CCC, with headquarters in Toronto, is governed and supported by its members through a semiannual General Board and Triennial Assembly. Three commissions co-ordinate its work: Justice of Peace, Ecumenical Formation, and Faith and Order. *See also* CHRISTIANITY; ECUMENICAL SOCIAL ACTION; EVANGELICAL FELLOWSHIP OF CANADA.   DONALD W. ANDERSON

Canadian Council of Professional Engineers

(Le Conseil canadien des ingénieurs) was est in 1936 as the federation of the provincial and territorial authorities that license engineers and oversee the profession across Canada. The council serves these bodies and the public through a series of programs initiated to ensure a high quality of engineering education, improve the understanding of ENGINEERING as an economic activity, and promote the role and image of the engineer in society.

The council's prime objective is to assist the 12 provincial and territorial authorities in co-ordinating their activities in the areas of licensing and professional ethics, and establishing the qualifications necessary for maintaining standards of excellence. The council reviews and accredits undergraduate engineering programs in Canada, conducts labour-force surveys, provides a central information service for the public and manages an insurance program. The council also addresses itself to research and development and continuing education. The council is headquartered in Ottawa.

Canadian Council on Social Development

(Conseil canadien de développement social), fd 1920 as Canadian Council on Child Welfare. It became the Canadian Welfare Council in 1935; in 1970 the organization took on its present name. A voluntary, nonpartisan, Ottawa-based organization that sought to secure clearly defined but limited objectives in social service and welfare, the CWC worked within existing political and economic structures. It initially concerned itself with the needs of children and their mothers, especially war widows. Under its long-time executive director, Charlotte WHITTON, the CWC expanded its work during the GREAT DEPRESSION to deal with the effects of unemployment. The welfare of military service personnel, war workers and their dependants became a major concern after 1939.

Since WWII the council has examined and made recommendations about old-age security, disability and rehabilitation, unemployment insurance, poverty, and income security, health services, housing, penal reform, daycare and the education of social workers. More recently, the problems of women and native peoples have increasingly gained its attention. The CCSD, which is funded by all levels of government and through agency memberships and publications sales, has been more effective in co-ordinating the activities of private social service and welfare agencies than in lobbying for legislation involving social change.   MICHIEL HORN

Canadian Cystic Fibrosis Foundation

The CCFF is a national, nonprofit, voluntary health agency established 15 July 1960. Cystic fibrosis is a disorder that occurs when a child inherits 2 genes for the condition, one from each parent. An estimated one in 20 Canadians carries the defective "CF gene," and approximately one in 1800 children born in Canada has CF. The CCFF aids persons affected by cystic fibrosis (CF) by raising and allocating funds for medical research to find a cure for CF, promoting improved cure and treatment and increasing public awareness of cystic fibrosis. The CCFF is the world's second largest funder of CF research; it allocated over $28 million to its medical and scientific research and professional training programs, as well as to CF clinics across Canada, between 1960 and 1986. Volunteers working through the foundation's 50 chapters located across Canada raise over 50% of its revenue. Significant support for CF research, since 1964, has also come from Kinsmen and Kinettes and from Shinerama, Canada's largest annual fund-raising event involving post-secondary students. Canada's world leadership in CF treatment and research is reflected in improved life expectancy for those with CF: the median survival age of Canadians with CF has risen from 4 years of age in 1960 to 24 years in 1987. Today in Canada, CF is no longer exclusively a disease of childhood, as 30% of all persons with CF are 18 years of age or older.

Canadian Expatriates in Show Business

The extent to which American popular culture has invaded Canadian movie houses, television screens, magazine stands, and indeed the Canadian consciousness, hardly needs to be reiterated. Moreover the vivid and consistent (if not always truthful) picture of Americans seen in Hollywood movies and network television has to a degree overfaced our own rather diffuse and disadvantaged picture of ourselves in the "show business" field, so that Canadians have been encouraged to enter vicariously into the American cultural pageant while at the same time feeling vaguely excluded from the drama. The awareness of America's complete indifference towards anything Canadian, and especially towards Canadian appreciation for and actual contributions to American show business, merely adds to the sense of exclusion, and arouses the desire to stake some kind of a claim to actual participation, however marginal. Hence the enthusiasm with which we point to the Canadian origins of many famous "American" show-business figures, particularly when Americans seem to assume that any show-business personalities not immediately identifiable as foreign must of course be American. From this point of view it seems highly appropriate that 2 of the most famous movie portrayals of the arch-American cultural icon Abraham Lincoln were undertaken by Canadian-born actors (Walter Huston in 1930 and Raymond MASSEY in 1939), that "America's sweetheart," Mary Pickford, was a Toronto girl, and that *Star Trek*'s Captain Kirk, a mythic embodiment of liberal All-Americanism, was played by a Canadian, William Shatner.

However, there seems to be no meaningful pattern to the life-histories of show business figures who were born in Canada and became famous elsewhere. For those men and women who lived in Canada through their teens or at least long enough to develop professional ambitions, the US of course acted as a magnet because of its vastly larger audiences, salaries, career opportunities and public visibility. But even here, much of the southward emigration appears to be ruled by chance or whim rather than an inevitable economic or cultural undertow – merely

Robert Beatty (*courtesy Phototeque, New York*).

a part of the traditional large-scale movement both ways across the Canada-US border. Many other figures departed this country in childhood when their parents moved for their own reasons, and are not Canadian in any real sense. But naturally we maintain an interest in claiming them, and the number of Canadians who know that Mary Pickford (or even Deanna Durbin) was born in Canada probably exceeds as a percentage that of most other countries whose native sons and daughters have turned the same trick. In any event, the Canadian curiosity as to which luminaries happen to have been born in Canada is close to universal, and the following catalogue of vital statistics and career descriptions contains many of the most famous names.

Beatty, Robert, actor (b at Hamilton 1909). Educated at U of Toronto and trained at the Royal Academy of Dramatic Arts in the UK, he began appearing in theatre and films in Britain in 1938. During the 1940s and 1950s, less frequently afterwards, he appeared in a succession of rugged character and lead roles in Hollywood films.

Blue, Ben, actor, comedian, dancer (b Benjamin Bernstein, at Montréal 1901; d 1975). Vaudeville, film and television comedian, famous for his sad face and pantomimic routines. A vaudeville headliner during the 1920s and 1930s, Blue made films at MGM during the 1940s and appeared sporadically in movies afterwards (a notable late cameo in *It's a Mad, Mad, Mad, Mad World* in 1963), and performed frequently on television during the 1950s in variety shows. His first stage experience was as a 15-year old chorus boy in a Montréal tryout of a George M. Cohan musical comedy, *Irene*.

Raymond Burr (*courtesy Phototeque, New York*).

Yvonne DeCarlo (*courtesy Phototeque, New York*).

Burr, Raymond, actor (b at New Westminster, BC 1917). Educated at Stanford and Columbia, he worked in stage and radio for several years before making his first film in 1946, where he was typecast as a figure of smooth menace. He was mostly confined to small parts (notably as the murderer in *Rear Window*, 1954), where his burly physique and sleek manner nevertheless made him highly effective. In 1957 his big break came when he was cast in the title role of the popular television series "Perry Mason" (1957-66), and it is for this and the subsequent TV series "Ironside" (1967-75), in which he played a wheelchair-bound detective, that he is best known.

Cameron, Rod, actor (b Roderick Cox at Calgary 1910). Sturdy cowboy hero of the 1940s and 1950s, he began as a stunt double and progressed to starring roles in many B-Westerns and serials.

Carson, Jack, actor (b John Elmer Carson at Carmen, Man 1910; d 1963). Educated at Carleton College (Minnesota), he first appeared in films in 1937, and was known mostly for a large

Marie Dressler (*courtesy Phototeque, New York*).

variety of supporting roles in comedies, musicals and dramas. His hefty build and forthright (often loud) manner made him a natural playing crude gladhanders in comedy and bullies in drama, but the apparent simplemindedness of many of the characters he played concealed a good deal of intelligence, subtlety and skill in his performances. He had many fine appearances, but notably *The Male Animal* (1942), *The Hard Way* (1943), *Hollywood Canteen* (1944, playing himself), *Mildred Pierce* (1945) and *A Star is Born* (1954).

Clark, Susan, actress (b at Sarnia, Ont 1940). Trained at the Royal Academy of Dramatic Arts in London, she appeared in films as a leading lady beginning in 1967 before moving to series television ("Webster") in the 1980s. Her impeccable performances have often been enlivened by a fine unspoken hint of irony, though perhaps most people think first of her fiery red hair, startling eyes and willowy charm. Notable appearances were in *Coogan's Bluff* (1968), *Tell Them Willie Boy is Here* (1969), *Night Moves* (1976) and *Murder By Decree* (1979).

DeCarlo, Yvonne, actress (b Peggy Yvonne Middleton at Vancouver 1922). She made her film debut in 1942 and was quickly typecast as an exotic siren or a dance-hall girl in Westerns. She had a prolific career as a leading lady in middling movies through the 1950s, and continued to appear in secondary roles during the 1960s and 1970s, and also in television series (eg, "The Munsters").

Dmytryk, Edward, film director (b at Grand Forks, BC 1908). The son of Ukrainian immigrants, he began in films as a 15-year old messenger boy at Paramount. During the 1930s he was a film editor, and he began directing full-time at the end of the decade. After making some fine *film noir*s (*Murder, My Sweet; Crossfire*) he was convicted in 1949 by the House Un-American Activities Committee as one of the celebrated Hollywood Ten. After a year in jail he continued his career in England and then back in the US, overseeing such films as *The Caine Mutiny* (1954), *Raintree Country* (1957) and *The Carpetbaggers* (1964).

Dressler, Marie, actress (b Leila von Koerber, at Coburg, Ont 1869; d 1934). The daughter of an emigré music teacher, she left home at 14 to act in travelling troupes, eventually arriving on Broadway in 1892. She became enormously popular in vaudeville and later films, and at the end of her life had 4 years as the most popular performer in movies. Large-framed and square-jawed, she turned her ungainly looks to good account in comedy by trading on their incongruity and developing an athletic enthusiasm, a rubber face and an exquisite sense of comic timing. Her most famous movie appearances were in *Min and Bill* (1930, for which she won a Best Actress Oscar), *Anna Christie* (1930), *Tugboat Annie* (1933) and *Dinner at Eight* (1933).

Durbin, Deanna, actress, singer (b Edna Mae Durbin, at Winnipeg 1921). Raised from infancy in California, she became a teenaged singing star at Universal in 1936. She modulated smoothly from bouncy innocence and sweetness to more glamorous maturity in a 12-year career that left her as the highest paid actress in movies at her early retirement in 1948. Notable films include *Three Smart Girls* (1936), *100 Men and a Girl* (1937), *Mad About Music* (1938).

Dwan, Allan, film director (b at Toronto 1885; d 1981). The son of a clothing merchant, he moved to the US before he was 10 and was educated at Notre Dame. Though not a household name, Dwan was an important pioneer in the silent film era first as a technical assistant, then as a writer and editor, and finally (after 1911) as a director. He was at the helm of some large-scale

Glenn Ford (*courtesy Phototeque, New York*).

silent spectaculars, notably *Robin Hood* (1922), and worked extensively with Douglas Fairbanks. He continued to direct at less exalted levels until 1958 and made several well-regarded "programmers." He is listed in the *Guiness Book of Records* as having directed more films than any other person (over 400).

Ford, Glenn, actor (b Gwyllyn Ford at Québec 1916). The son of a railway executive, he moved to California at the age of 7 when his father accepted a job there. After stage experience in high school and with regional stage companies, he signed with Columbia Pictures in 1939 and took leading roles there and on Broadway. Following World War II he achieved great popularity, especially after starring in *Gilda* with Rita Hayworth and in *A Stolen Life* with Bette Davis (both 1946). A versatile performer, he was particularly effective in forceful dramatic roles (eg, *The Big Heat* 1953, *The Blackboard Jungle* 1955, *3:10 to Yuma* 1957), though he was also adept in comedy. In 1958 he was Hollywood's Number One box-office star.

Fox, Michael J., actor (b at Edmonton 1961). As the son of an army dispatcher, he moved amongst various towns until his family settled in Burnaby, BC, in the early 1970s. When he was 15

Michael J. Fox (*courtesy Phototeque, New York*).

he appeared in a brief CBC sitcom ("Leo and Me"), then picked up occasional parts in theatre and TV. In 1979 he moved to Los Angeles to pursue his career, which blossomed in 1982 when he landed the part of Alex Keaton in the hugely popular and long-running TV series "Family Ties." He attained star status in movies in 1985 with two films, *Teen Wolf* and, especially, *Back to the Future*. Diminutive and bursting with friendly charm, he has become one of the most popular of all screen personalities in the US, and has also shown the ability to deal with serious roles, as in *The Light of Day* (1986). He retains Canadian citizenship.

Hall, Monty, television personality (b at Winnipeg 1923). After working as a radio actor as early as 1940, he resided in Canada until 1955, making occasional forays to American network TV as a substitute for host Warren Hull in the CBS game show "Strike It Rich." In 1958 CBS gave him his own show, "Keep Talking," but it wasn't until 1964 that he made his biggest mark as "Television's Big Dealer," hosting "Let's Make a Deal" for NBC (and then from 1968-76, ABC).

Henning, Doug, magician (b at Fort Garry, Man 1947). Raised in Oakville, Ont, he graduated in psychology from McMaster U. He studied MAGIC under Ottawa-born American performer Dai Vernon and in 1973 he appeared in the Toronto magic-and-rock show *Spellbound*. He vaulted to stardom the following year when *The Magic Show* opened on Broadway and became a tremendous hit. His casual appearance (long hair and jeans) began a new style in the profession. He has toured his show worldwide.

Huston, Walter, actor (b Walter Houghston, at Toronto 1884; d 1950). He was the son of a cabinet-maker whose family had moved to Canada from Ireland in 1840. By his late teens he was on the road in touring repertory companies. In 1902 he moved permanently to the US (briefly displaying his considerable skills as a hockey player for a team in Brooklyn in 1902-03), and became a star in vaudeville and stage drama. In 1929 he went to Hollywood and embarked on a distinguished career in movies, occasionally returning to Broadway. Impressive in both physical stature and histrionic presence, his film performances continue to convey a unique authority, even in projects where every other aspect has dated badly. His important movie appearances include those in *Abraham Lincoln* (1930), *American Madness* (1932), *Rain* (1932), *Dodsworth* (1936), *All That Money Can Buy* (1941), and, perhaps best-remembered nowadays, *Treasure of the Sierra Madre* (1948), for which he won an Academy Award under the direction of his son, John Huston.

Ireland, John, actor (b at Vancouver 1914). He moved to New York as a child, and after some stage experience began his movie career in 1946. An intense, dark-browed actor, he moved gradually into secondary roles, mostly as heavies, and by the late 1960s was appearing largely in low-quality films. Earlier, he had performed memorably in *A Walk in the Sun* (1946), *Red River* (1948) and *All the King's Men* (1949, Academy Award), among others.

Jory, Victor, actor (b at Dawson City, YT 1902). Educated at the U of California, he began his acting career in live theatre in 1929, shifted to movies in 1932, and spent most of his career playing character parts. His burning eyes and grim demeanour ensured immediate impact and subsequent recognizability. His career spanned such various roles as Oberon in *A Midsummer Night's Dream* (1934) and smaller parts in *Gone With the Wind*, *The Miracle Worker* (1967) and – his last film – *Papillon* (1973).

Keeler, Ruby, actress, singer, dancer (b at Halifax 1909). Her family moved to New York City when she was 3, and she began dancing in chorus

Mary Pickford (*courtesy Phototeque, New York*).

lines in 1923. Married to Al Jolson in 1928, she remains famous as the sweet, somewhat pallid heroine of several Warner Brothers musicals of the early 1930s, most of them choreographed by the lunatic genius Busby Berkeley. Her best-known films are *42nd Street*, *Gold Diggers of 1933*, *Footlight Parade* (all 1933) and *Dames* (1934).

Knox, Alexander, actor (b at Strathroy, Ont 1907). Educated at the U of Western Ontario, he made his stage debut in Boston in 1929, and after 1938 had a notable career in films, dividing his time between Hollywood and the UK in mostly character roles. His most celebrated appearance was in the presidential title part in *Wilson* (1944), for which he received an Oscar nomination.

Linkletter, Art, television personality (b Arthur Brown at Moose Jaw, Sask 1913). Adopted by John and Mary Linkletter, he moved with the family to Massachusetts as an infant. He was naturalized in 1942. During WWII he began emceeing 2 network radio shows, "People Are Funny" and the long-running "House Party," and in 1950 began appearing in television series. His easy delivery and relaxed manner made him a huge success as an interviewer of "average folks" and children for over a quarter-century. He is also a popular nonfiction author (eg, *Kids Say the Darndest Things*).

Lockhart, Gene, actor (b at London, Ont 1891; d 1957). He made his professional debut at the age of 6 with the Kilties Band of Canada, and at 15 he played in sketches with Beatrice Lillie. Educated in Canada and at Brompton Oratory School in England, he made a career in vaudeville and, after 1916, on Broadway. His movie career began in 1935, and for the next 2 decades he appeared in more than 300 films, usually in strong character parts, as for example in *His Girl Friday* (1940), *The House on 92nd Street* (1945), *Miracle on 34th Street* (1947), *The Inspector General* (1949) and *Carousel* (1956). On Broadway his important appearances included those in *Ah, Wilderness* (1932) and (replacing Lee J. Cobb as Willy Loman) in *Death of a Salesman* (1949). In the latter part of his life he made frequent television appearances. He was also talented as a writer, singer and composer. He was the father of actress June Lockhart, and became an American citizen in 1939.

MacKenzie, Gisèle, singer (b Gisèle La Flèche at Winnipeg 1927). She studied violin at the Royal College of Music 1941-45, but it was as a singer that she made her name, first in Canada (on her own CBC radio show, "Meet Gisèle," 1946-49), and then in the US. Jack Benny introduced her to American radio listeners in 1953, and that year NBC began starring her in the television show

"Your Hit Parade," which ran until 1957. In 1955 she became an American citizen.

Mayer, Louis B., film producer (b Eliezer Mayer at Minsk, Russia 1885; d 1957). His working-class family immigrated to New York when he was a small child, and in 1890 moved to Saint John, NB, where his father became a junk dealer. As a youth he helped with the family business, and in later years liked to recall the crude anti-Semitism he was subjected to while picking through Canadian garbage for useful scrap. In 1899 the now-profitable business modulated into ship salvage, and by 1904 Mayer was travelling through various American cities selling scrap metal. Settling in Boston, he bought a small theatre in 1907 and began showing movies. Later he bought other theatres, and in 1915 he made an enormous profit after securing the regional distribution rights to D.W. Griffith's *Birth of a Nation*. By 1917 he had his own production company as well, and in 1924 achieved the summit when it merged with the Metro and Goldwyn companies to form MGM, of which he remained vice-president and general manager until 1951. During the 1930s and 1940s, Hollywood's "golden era," Mayer was the most powerful man in the business, at least on the production side, and the paradigm of the tyrannical movie mogul.

Nielsen, Leslie, actor (b at Regina 1926). The son of a British-immigrant RCMP constable (and brother of politician Erik NIELSEN), he grew up in Fort Norman, Yukon and, later, in and around Edmonton. After service in the RCAF during WWII he was briefly a radio DJ in Calgary, then trained at the Academy of Radio Arts (Toronto), The Neighborhood Playhouse (New York) and the Actors Studio (New York). After some US radio and television work he moved to Hollywood to become an MGM contract player in 1954. He assumed US citizenship around this time. His career since then, in movies and television and occasionally theatres, has been immensely prolific. Cleancut, durable and versatile, he has appeared in B-movies (*Forbidden Planet*, 1956), disaster films (*The Poseidon Adventure*, 1972), numerous TV series ("The New Breed," "Peyton Place," "Police Squad"), and some Canadian productions (eg, *Riel* for CBC-TV), among many other undertakings. In recent years he has become particularly celebrated as the nun-slapping doctor in *Airplane!* (1980).

Pickford, Mary, actress (b Gladys Smith, at Toronto 1893; d 1979). After the death of her father in 1898 she became a member of the Cummings Stock Company in Toronto at the age of 5, already a breadwinner for her mother and 2 younger siblings. Three years later, the family moved to the US, and Mary (or "Baby Gladys," as she was advertised) worked her way up the theatrical ladder to Broadway, where she appeared in a David Belasco play as a 14-year-old. In 1909 she charmed D.W. Griffith into giving her a job and she appeared in dozens of his 2-reel films, becoming one of the first real movie stars in the process. Her career grew by leaps until, in 1917, she was getting $350 000 a picture for First National and, along with Chaplin, was the most famous movie performer in the world. For many years she was "America's Sweetheart," a golden-curled young girl with a heartwarming innocence and an impish sense of humour. In 1919 along with Griffith, Chaplin and Douglas Fairbanks, she was a founding member of United Artists, and the following year she married Fairbanks, the pair becoming known as "Hollywood's Royal Family." Among her innumerable successful films, those which occasionally still surface include *Stella Maris* (1916), *Daddy Long Legs* (1919) and *Sparrows* (1926). She maintained her box-office appeal until the late 1920s, but could not escape the

William Shatner (*courtesy Phototeque, New York*).

coming of sound and the fact that she had aged out of the parts the public loved to see her in.

Pidgeon, Walter, actor (b at East Saint John, NB 1897; d 1984), educated at the U of New Brunswick and the New England Conservatory of Music (Boston). He made his first films in the late silent period (1926) and established himself during the 1930s as a solid and versatile performer (he appeared in both character and leading roles, and even sang in musicals). His career peaked in the 1940s, especially in John Ford's *How Green Was My Valley* (1941) and William Wyler's *Mrs. Miniver* (1942), the latter opposite Greer Garson, with whom he was paired several times. He created an impression of craggy honesty and steadiness, with his large frame, deep voice and slow delivery. Altogether he appeared in over 100 films through the 1970s, and also acted from time to time on Broadway.

Qualen, John, actor (b John Oleson at Vancouver 1899; d at Los Angeles 12 Sept 1987). His family was Norwegian. After graduating from Northwestern U, he joined a stock company. In 1931 he began his career in films, and over 4 decades he appeared in more than 100 movies, always in character roles. His reedy voice and slight physique made him a natural for weak characters and victims. He was memorable in *His Girl Friday* (1940), *The Grapes of Wrath* (1940) and scores of other movies. Ironically, perhaps, he also played the father of the DIONNE QUINTUPLETS in the movies in which those children appeared during the 1930s.

Robson, Mark, director (b at Montréal 1913; d 1978). Educated at UCLA, his first significant work was as co-editor (uncredited) on *Citizen Kane* (1941). During the mid-1940s he directed horror movies for Val Lewton, and in the late 1950s began producing his own films – many of them ambitious best-seller adaptations such as *Peyton Place* (1957), *From the Terrace* (1960), *Von Ryan's Express* (1965) and *Valley of the Dolls* (1967), ending up with disasters (*Earthquake* 1974, *Avalanche Express* 1979).

Sahl, Mort, comedian, actor (b at Montréal 1926). Raised in California, he is best known as an acerbic socially conscious monologist. His initial fame, never since quite equalled, came in the mid-1950s as a nightclub comedian flaying American politics from a quasi-Beat Generation perspective. On stage, television and records, and in the occasional movie, he has remained a persis-

tent gadfly on the body politic, his cynical deadpan style not concealing an underlying Liberal idealism.

Sarrazin, Michael, actor (b at Québec C 1940). Trained at the New York Actors Studio, he appeared in a few NATIONAL FILM BOARD documentaries before moving to the US to work in television. He broke into feature films in 1967, and especially after *They Shoot Horses, Don't They?* (1969) seemed very much a rising young star. Since then his career has levelled off, but he has remained a very noticeable performer, largely on account of his startling blue eyes and sensitive manner.

Sennett, Mack, director, producer, actor (b Mikall Sinnott at Danville, Qué 1880; d 1960). His parents were working-class Irish immigrants who moved to Connecticut when he was 17. At first he hoped for a career as an opera singer, but he was working as a labourer when a 1902 meeting with Marie Dressler (also Canadian-born) elicited a letter of introduction to theatrical producer David Belasco. That too led nowhere, but he stayed in New York to work as an actor, and in 1908 began appearing in films for the Biograph Studios, many of them directed by D.W. Griffith, and eventually graduated to directing himself. In 1912 he co-founded the Keystone film company, and in the next few years created there a style of wild and rambunctious comedy that made his name a byword for delirious, uninhibited slapstick. The stars of his company included such talents as Mabel Normand, "Fatty" Arbuckle, Chester Conklin, and, for a year, Charlie Chaplin, who made his first screen appearance for Sennett. The lunatic chorus of "Keystone Kops" was another feature of these films, many of which Sennett edited himself with consummate comic skill. After 1917 Sennett formed his own company and continued to produce comedies until the end of the silent era, but his career gradually declined in the 1930s until he was driven into a 4-year retirement to Canada in near-penury in 1935. He returned to Hollywood in 1939 for a series of peripheral appointments, perhaps prompted by a special Academy Award presented to him in 1937.

Shatner, William, actor (b at Montréal 1931). Educated at McGill U, he worked in repertory theatre and appeared at the STRATFORD FESTIVAL before beginning a career in American stage and films in 1958. But his film and Broadway appearances were definitely secondary to his television career, above all as Captain Kirk in the "Star Trek" series, where his air of bland idealism and sturdy authority and integrity made him the perfect straight man in a circus of alien beings and multicultural supporting characters. Never extraordinary as an actor, Shatner, in the person of Captain Kirk, has nevertheless become a culture hero celebrated in stand-up comedy routines and bumper stickers across the continent. More recently, Shatner has appeared in the *Star Trek* movies and in another television series, "T.J. Hooker."

Shearer, Norma, actress (b at Montréal 1900; d 1983). The daughter of a wealthy businessman, she went to New York with her mother during WWI after her father's business failed, hoping to break into show business. She began appearing in New York-based films in 1920 and in 1923 was brought to MGM by her future husband, the powerful producer Irving Thalberg. By 1927 she was a star, and in the early 1930s MGM was calling her "The First Lady of the Screen." She received 5 Academy Award nominations and some of the studio's juiciest parts, but after Thalberg's death in 1936 her career began a slow decline, ending in 1942. A classy and competent actress, though not really an outstanding one, her notable appear-

Fay Wray (*courtesy Phototeque, New York*).

ances include those in *The Divorcee* (1930), *The Barretts of Wimpole Street* (1930), *Romeo and Juliet* (1936) and *The Women* (1939).

Smith, Alexis, actress (b at Penticton, BC 1921). She acted in summer stock theatre in BC as a teenager, and during her attendance at Los Angeles City College she was "discovered" by a Warner Brothers talent scout while appearing in a school production. She made her first film in 1940, and was soon appearing in lead or second-lead roles, which she continued to do through the 1950s. Her cool intelligence and charm made her always a pleasure to watch. At the end of the 1950s she retired, but made a Broadway comeback in the early 1970s and began appearing in films again in 1975.

Steinberg, David, comedian (b at St Boniface, Man 1941). The son of a Romanian rabbi, he performed with the Second City Revue after studies at the U of Chicago. He achieved success as a stage and television stand-up comic and has often performed as a guest-host on comedy and talk shows.

Wiseman, Joseph, actor (b at Montréal 1918). Tall, lean and authoritative, he has made a career largely of formidable master criminals (eg, *Dr No* 1962, *The Valachi Papers* 1972) and patriarchal types of one sort or another. His stage career began in 1936 and during the 1960s he appeared frequently with the Lincoln Centre Repertory Company.

Wray, Fay, actress (b at Medicine Hat, Alta 1907), raised in Los Angeles. Her first really important movie was Erich von Stroheim's *The Wedding March* (1928), and she appeared in a multitude of films until 1958. A slight, big-eyed blonde of competent talents, she remains famous as the screaming heroine carried off by the lovestruck giant ape in the original *King Kong* (1933).

WILLIAM BEARD

Canadian Expeditionary Force, the army raised by Canada for service abroad in WORLD WAR I. In Aug 1914 Canada offered and Britain accepted an expeditionary force whose strength was fixed at first at 25 000. The strength of the first contingent which sailed for England Oct 1914 was in fact over 31 000, many of this number British-born. The size of the mobilized force steadily increased. The 1st Canadian Division went to France early in 1915. A Canadian corps of 2 divisions was formed there later that year, and in 1916 it reached its full strength of 4 divisions. A 5th Division was formed in England, but because of anticipated difficulties in providing reinforcements, it was not sent to the theatre of operations except for its divisional artillery and certain spe-

7 a.m., April 22nd, 1915, depicting members of the CEF in action. Watercolour by A. Nantel (*courtesy Canadian War Museum/CMC/8629*).

cial units. Apart from the Canadian Corps, the CEF included the Canadian Cavalry Brigade, also serving in France, the Canadian Railway Troops, which in addition to working on the Western Front provided a bridging unit for the Middle East, the Canadian Forestry Corps which cut timber in Britain and France, and special units which operated in the Caspian area and in N Russia and eastern Siberia.

The Candian Expeditionary Force was maintained by voluntary enlistment until the MILITARY SERVICE ACT of Aug 1917 introduced conscription. In total 619 636 officers and men served in the CEF, of whom 142 588 were enlisted under the Military Service Act; 424 589 served overseas. The peak strength of the CEF at any one point was 388 038 all ranks in July 1918. Total fatal casualties from all causes, 1914-20, were 59 544 all ranks. (This figure does not include Canadians who died with the RFC, RNAS, RAF or in other Allied forces.)

During the war Canadian authority over the Canadian Expeditionary Force was steadily strengthened. In the beginning the relationship to the British military authorities was vague. After the Canadian MINISTRY OF OVERSEAS MILITARY FORCES was set up in London in 1916, the force's national nature was fully established. Canadian training in England became entirely a Canadian responsibility. In 1917, for the first time, a Canadian officer, Sir Arthur CURRIE, took command of the Canadian Corps. In 1918 it was formally recognized that while the direction of operations in the field remained the province of the British commander-in-chief, the internal organization and administration of the Canadian force were matters for Canadian authorities. By the end of the war the CEF, which in 1914 had been thought of as a colonial contingent serving under the British Army Act, had become in effect a Canadian national army.   C.P. STACEY

Reading: A. Fortescue Duguid, Official History of the Canadian Forces in the Great War 1914-1919 (1938); G.W.L. Nicholson, *Canadian Expeditionary Force 1914-1919* (1964); Desmond Morton, *A Peculiar Kind of Politics* (1982).

Canadian Federation for the Humanities, fd Dec 1943 as the Humanities Research Council of Canada. An elected, nongovernmental organization representing, in 1986-87, 30 academic associations and 58 Canadian universities, CFH is dedicated to promoting scholarship and research in the humanities. Through published reports, surveys and major conferences, it has successfully urged the establishment of a National Library, a federal granting council, increased provincial support for universities, regular sabbatical leave for professors, and the creation of national organizations of university specialists (*see* LEARNED SOCIETIES).

The HRCC was originally funded by American philanthropic foundations. Since the creation of

the CANADA COUNCIL in 1957 it has received a majority of its funds from the federal government, and the balance from universities and learned societies. The formation of the SOCIAL SCIENCES AND HUMANITIES RESEARCH COUNCIL in 1978 resulted in HRCC's incorporation as the Canadian Federation for the Humanities. The federation administers programs subsidizing the publication of Canadian scholarly books, financing and co-ordinating the meetings of learned societies, and lobbying governments and granting agencies on behalf of the humanities.   VIVIANE F. LAUNAY

Canadian Federation of Labour (National Trades and Labor Congress until 1908), fd 1902 as a solely Canadian body dedicated to national organization. Its founding bodies were the KNIGHTS OF LABOR and the national unions of shoemakers, cigar makers, painters and carpenters, which had been ousted from the TRADES AND LABOR CONGRESS in 1902 after the latter, dominated by the American Federation of Labor, rejected dual unionism by refusing to recognize a national union where an international union existed. This decision created bitter divisions in the Canadian trade-union movement.

The CFL remained weak. At its 1911 conference, for example, only 17 unions were represented, and the delegates were mainly from Québec and the Provincial Workmen's Assn of NS. There were many reasons: its conservatism and attitude toward strikes alienated unionists who might otherwise have been more supportive; it faced fierce opposition from the AFL which regarded dual unionism as anathema; and it concentrated on luring members from rival unions instead of promoting unions among unorganized workers. In 1927 the CFL became a founding member of the ALL-CANADIAN CONGRESS OF LABOUR. In 1981, a group of CRAFT UNIONS was suspended by the CANADIAN LABOUR CONGRESS. It united as a new Canadian Federation of Labour on 31 Mar 1982; by 1986 its membership was 208 822, or 5.6% of all unionists in Canada.   C.D. CHORNIAWY

Canadian Federation of University Women was founded in 1919 as a Canadian counterpart to and member organization of the International Federation of University Women, and with the aim of emphasizing women's role in social reconstruction and the prevention of war. In 1987 there were 120 University Women's Clubs in Canada, not necessarily associated with a university, with a total membership of 12 400 women graduates representing all ages and academic disciplines. CFUW promotes the involvement of women individually and collectively in professional, economic and political life, and is concerned to encourage women scholars and to safeguard the rights of women. Local clubs are involved in community-based and charitable activities, and participate in the federation's work of compiling submissions, briefs and resolutions directed to government task forces and commissions on a wide range of issues of interest to women, including microtechnology, pension reform, education, the environment and peace.   SOMER BRODRIBB

Canadian Fiction Magazine, Canada's first literary quarterly devoted to short fiction. The magazine played an important role in developing a high standard for Canadian short fiction. Beginning in 1971 as a student publication at UBC, this LITERARY MAGAZINE has become an independent journal of national scope. Located in Toronto since 1978, it publishes work by both new and established writers in English, and also has a continuing program of fiction in translation from French and other languages. Over 600 stories were published in its first 15 years. The magazine has published entire issues devoted to individual

authors such as Robert HARLOW, Jane RULE, Mavis GALLANT, Leon ROOKE, Keath Fraser and Michel TREMBLAY. Other features include interviews with writers, a series on the "future of fiction" that encourages discussion about the aesthetics of contemporary fiction, and portfolios of literary portraits. Several book-length anthologies of stories and interviews that appeared in CFM have been published. These include *Magic Realism; Illusion: fables, fantasies, and metafictions; Metavisions; Moving off the Map; A Decade of Quebec Fiction; Invisible Fictions; 45 Below; Canadian Writers At Work;* and *Shoes and Shit: stories for pedestrians*. CFM also published the first anthology of contemporary fiction by native people.   GEOFFREY HANCOCK

Canadian Film Development Corporation (Telefilm Canada) was created by an Act of Parliament in 1967 "to foster and promote the development of a feature film industry in Canada." This crown corporation was originally given $10 million to invest in the FILM industry as a loan fund. Under its first executive director, Michael Spencer, it invested in a number of low-budget English and French films of cultural value. Increasing commercial pressures were brought to bear and by 1973 international co-productions were favoured. In 1978 a new executive director, Michael McCabe, accelerated this process, encouraged the use of foreign stars and, under the advantages of the Capital Cost Allowance, increased total Canadian budgets from $19 million in 1977 to $165 million in 1980. This commercial orientation was not completely successful as many films remain unreleased (and by 1986 total Canadian budgets had fallen to $86 million). In 1980 André Lamy replaced McCabe, committing himself to a more indigenous industry. In 1983 the Canadian Broadcast Program Development Fund was created to allocate $175 million over a 5-year period to films that were co-financed by television networks, the private sector and Telefilm Canada. This arrangement guaranteed the films a broadcast playdate, thereby avoiding problems of distribution that had plagued the industry. Peter Pearson was executive director 1985-87. As a result of *Canadian Cinema – A Solid Base* (the report of the Film Industry Task Force, published late 1985), the Feature Film Fund was created with $33 million in additional resources to provide for the production of feature films (22 by 1987) and for distribution of films and their subtitling, etc. In 1987 it was announced that the Broadcast Fund would be given permanent status, beginning in 1988, with an annual budget of $60 million. Other programs supported by Telefilm Canada include the International Marketing Assistance Fund and the Versioning Assistance Fund. Head offices are in Montréal.

PIERS HANDLING

Canadian Fisheries Expedition, 1915 Noteworthy as the first oceanographic study of the Gulf of ST LAWRENCE and Scotian Shelf, the expedition originated with E.E. PRINCE, dominion commissioner of fisheries. Prince, with other members of the Biological Board of Canada, hoped to develop new FISHERIES, especially for HERRING, to offset overfishing of lobster and oyster. Johan Hjort, Norwegian director of fisheries, was chosen to investigate herring stocks and their environment. Arriving in Toronto late in 1914, Hjort first analysed herring collections before beginning a series of oceanographic cruises in May 1915 using the government ships *Princess* and *Acadia* and a Scottish herring drifter. The results, including discussions of the PLANKTON collections, fish catches, temperature and salinity measurements written by several specialists, including Hjort, were published in 1919. They showed the presence of 4 distinct herring stocks, indicated the northern properties of·the waters, and gave quantitative calculations of the currents. The expedition brought sophisticated European analyses of fish populations and mathematical physical OCEANOGRAPHY to Canada for the first time. Nevertheless, it did not lead directly to new fisheries, probably because of economic conditions, and its physical oceanographic results were ignored until H.B. HACHEY's work in the 1930s.   ERIC L. MILLS

Canadian Football Hall of Fame and Museum, *see* FOOTBALL.

Canadian Football League (CFL) began its formal existence in Jan 1958. Previously, it had been known as the Canadian Football Council (CFC), formed in 1956 as a loose merger of the Western Interprovincial Football Union and the Interprovincial Rugby Football Union. Through the CFC, professional FOOTBALL came under its own jurisdiction without outside interference. Ottawa, Hamilton, Toronto and Montréal and the western cities of Winnipeg, Regina, Calgary, Edmonton and Vancouver were represented in the 2 unions. In 1987 teams in the CFL were HAMILTON TIGER-CATS, OTTAWA ROUGH RIDERS, TORONTO ARGONAUTS, WINNIPEG BLUE BOMBERS (eastern division); and SASKATCHEWAN ROUGHRIDERS, CALGARY STAMPEDERS, EDMONTON ESKIMOS and BRITISH COLUMBIA LIONS (western division). The MONTREAL ALOUETTES folded at the beginning of the 1987 season, necessitating the move of Winnipeg to the "eastern" division. Except for Winnipeg, each club in the eastern division is privately owned and operated as a business enterprise. The 4 western teams are community owned and are operated as nonprofit organizations. Regional as well as east-west rivalries have acted as a catalyst for the growth of the league and of the sport, though falling attendance and reduced TV revenues jeopardized the future of teams in Regina, Calgary and elsewhere in 1987.

Until 1961, teams in the 2 divisions played among traditional rivals, each deciding a winner to meet in the GREY CUP game. By 1981, both divisions were playing 16 games and a fully interlocking schedule. In 1987 the play-off system still admits 6 of 8 teams to post-season play, though not necessarily 3 from each of the divisions, ie, a better 4th-place finish in one division will eliminate the 3rd-place team in the other. Usually, the 3rd- and 2nd-place finishers meet in a semifinal match, the winner playing the 1st-place club for the division championship. The winners meet in the Grey Cup game, traditionally in the last week of Nov, at a site determined 2 years in advance. Each year the league honours outstanding players through the SCHENLEY AWARDS. League offices are in Toronto. The CFL's commissioners have included G. Sydney Halter (1956-66), Ted Workman, Allan McEachern, Jake GAUDAUR (1968-84) and Douglas H. Mitchell (1984).   FRANK COSENTINO

Canadian Forces Bases, *see* BORDEN, CANADIAN FORCES BASE; CHATHAM; CHILLIWACK; COLD LAKE; COMOX; CORNWALLIS, CANADIAN FORCES BASE; ESQUIMALT; GAGETOWN, CANADIAN FORCES BASE; HAPPY VALLEY-GOOSE BAY; KINGSTON; MASSET; MILITARY AND STAFF COLLEGES; MOOSE JAW; OROMOCTO; PETAWAWA, CANADIAN FORCES BASE; PORTAGE LA PRAIRIE; ROYAL MILITARY COLLEGE OF CANADA; SHILO, CANADIAN FORCES BASE; SUMMERSIDE; TRENTON, CANADIAN FORCES BASE; and WAINWRIGHT.

Canadian Forum, fd in 1920, is Canada's oldest continually published political periodical. It originated at University of Toronto as the offshoot of a tiny magazine, *The Rebel*, and its first editorial board intended the new publication to be what its name suggested – a forum of political and cultural ideas. From the start, the *Forum* was avowedly nationalist and progressive, and usually on the left of the spectrum on political and cultural questions.

The *Canadian Forum* has always given ample space to poetry, fiction and the best work of Canadian artists. The *Forum* supported the GROUP OF SEVEN painters. Some of Canada's finest writers, a group that includes A.J.M. SMITH, Irving LAYTON, Dorothy LIVESAY, Earle BIRNEY and Margaret ATWOOD, began in its pages and have continued to publish there. On the political front, the *Forum* provided a home for Frank UNDERHILL's mordant wit and slashing prose all through the 1930s and 1940s, for Abe Rotstein and Mel Watkins, the leading economic nationalists of the 1960s, and for such well-known and committed intellectuals as Frank SCOTT, Eugene FORSEY and Ramsay COOK.

The *Forum* was co-operatively owned for most of its history, but for a time in the 1920s and 1930s it was operated by the publisher J.M. Dent and Sons, by Liberals, by Graham SPRY and by the LEAGUE FOR SOCIAL RECONSTRUCTION. Whatever the ownership, however, its editors – including Northrop FRYE, Milton Wilson, Rotstein and Michael Cross – have been remarkably independent. *See also* JOURNALISM; MAGAZINES.

J.L. GRANATSTEIN

Reading: J.L. Granatstein and P. Stevens, eds, *Forum: Canadian Life and Letters 1920-70.*

Canadian General Standards Board, established in 1934 under the National Research Council Act as the Government Purchasing Standards Committee. In 1948 it was renamed the Canadian Government Specifications Board and its present name was adopted in 1980. Answering to the minister of supply and services, its role is to provide voluntary standards for testing, technical practices, and legislation and to support international standardization. It provides standards in both official languages and integrates the efforts of 300 committees and 3000 members representing government, producers, consumers, research agencies, educational institutions and others. It works closely with the Standards Council of Canada and Metric Commission Canada. Its board of directors comprises 8 federal deputy ministers.

Canadian Geographic is the bimonthly magazine of the Royal Canadian Geographical Society. Both were founded in 1929 under stimulus from geologist Charles CAMSELL and explorer Joseph B. TYRRELL, who served as the society's first honorary president. The society's goal was to produce a magazine which "should be popular in character and aim at the general diffusion of information on the geography of the Dominion." The magazine continues to take a wide-ranging approach to every phase of GEOGRAPHY – historical, human, physical and economic. Membership in the society accompanies subscription to the magazine (paid circulation mid-1986 was 157 000). First edited by Lawrence J. BURPEE, the *Canadian Geographic* has served as an outlet for the popular writing and ideas of prominent Canadians, including Marius BARBEAU, Frederick BANTING, E. Cora HIND and Alf E. PORSILD. Since 1959 the society has annually awarded the Massey Medal for "outstanding personal achievement in the exploration, development or description of the geography of Canada." The gold medal, awarded periodically since 1972, recognizes "a particular achievement or event, national or international, in the field of geography." The Ottawa-based society also provides grants for field research in geography.   DUNCAN McDOWALL

Canadian Girls in Training (CGIT) was established in 1915 by the YOUNG WOMEN'S CHRISTIAN ASSN and the major Protestant denominations to promote the Christian education of girls aged 12 to 17. Based on the small group whose members planned activities under the leadership of adult women, the program reflected the influence on

Canadian Protestantism of progressive education, historical criticism of the Bible, the SOCIAL GOSPEL, and Canadian NATIONALISM. CGIT provided leadership training for many young women. Membership declined after WWII but the organization continued to flourish in numerous congregations. After 1947 the movement was under the direction of the Dept of Christian Education, CANADIAN COUNCIL OF CHURCHES. In 1976 the organization became an independent ecumenical body. Membership in 1987 was 4000.   MARGARET E. PRANG

Canadian Government Railways was the descriptive name of all federally owned railways in Canada from about the 1880s until 1918 when its operations were combined with the recently nationalized CANADIAN NORTHERN RAILWAY; in the following year the CANADIAN NATIONAL RAILWAYS were incorporated to operate both companies. The Canadian Government Railways, entrusted to the CN for operation in 1923, still exists as a component of the CN and has 4 principal constituents: the Intercolonial, National Transcontinental, Prince Edward Island, and Hudson Bay railways.

In 1867 the Government of Canada organized the INTERCOLONIAL RAILWAY to fulfil a Confederation promise of linking the Maritime provinces by rail to Ontario and Québec and assuming ownership of provincially owned railways in NS and NB. In 1879 the Intercolonial purchased the GRAND TRUNK RAILWAY line from Rivière-du-Loup to Point Lévis, opposite Québec City. In 1873, when PEI joined Canada, one condition of union was that the Dominion government assume operation of the expensive island railway system. This network was operated separately from the Intercolonial Railway. Gradually the titles Intercolonial Railway and Prince Edward Island Railway were dropped in favour of the term Canadian Government Railways.

At the turn of the century, the government constructed a new transcontinental railway in conjunction with the Grand Trunk Railway. A Grand Trunk subsidiary, the GRAND TRUNK PACIFIC, completed the western section while the government built the section from Moncton to Winnipeg under the name National Transcontinental Railway. Operation of the National Transcontinental was assumed by Canadian Government Railways in 1915. The final component of Canadian Government Railways was the HUDSON BAY RAILWAY from The Pas to Churchill, Man. This line had been championed by western farmers as an alternative way of exporting grain from western Canada. However, the limited traffic prospects of a Hudson Bay railway deterred private ownership. Consequently, the Canadian Government Railways completed the line in 1929.   C. ANDREAE

Canadian Historical Association, founded in 1922 when the Historic Landmarks Assn, est 1907 by the ROYAL SOCIETY, was renamed and reconstituted. The CHA is the professional association of all historians in Canada and was incorporated in 1970. It is the largest and one of the oldest of the LEARNED SOCIETIES; its paid membership (from Canada and worldwide) includes over 400 institutions and 2100 general and student members. The CHA sponsors the National Archival Appraisal Board and acts as an umbrella organization for many local and provincial HISTORICAL SOCIETIES. The association has maintained a broad program of publications in both English and French, including the CHA *Annual Report* (now *Historical Papers*), published since 1922, and a series of historical booklets published since the early 1950s. Through these publications, awards and annual meetings, the CHA actively encourages historical research, particularly in the history of Canada, and promotes the preservation of the nation's heritage.   JACQUES MONET, S.J.

Canadian Historical Review, fd in Toronto in 1920 and published by U of T Press, was the continuation of an earlier Toronto publication dating from 1896. For many years the CHR was edited from the U of T's history department, and many of Canada's most prominent historians, eg, George WRONG, George Brown, G.P. de T. Glazebrook, Donald CREIGHTON, John Saywell, Ramsay COOK and Craig Brown, took turns as editors. At times there was an editorial committee coupled with an advisory board drawn from across Canada. The function of the CHR was to publish articles on Canadian history and events, as well as reviews of important historical works on non-Canadian subjects. Over time, it became more historical and less contemporary, and concentrated its space exclusively on Canadian history, including reviews. Since the 1970s other Canadian historical periodicals have competed with the CHR for articles, but it remains Canada's most prominent historical journal. Average total circulation in 1986 was 2643.   ROBERT BOTHWELL

Canadian Human Rights Commission, est 1977 by the Canadian Human Rights Act to deal with discriminatory practices. It consists of 2 full-time members, the chief commissioner (Gordon Fairweather 1977-87, and Max Yalden as of 1 Nov 1987) and 3 to 6 other members, and reports to Parliament through the minister of justice. The commission may appoint an investigator to examine a complaint of discrimination and may appoint a conciliator to effect a settlement. One member, designated by the minister of justice, investigates complaints regarding the misuse of information in a federal information bank. *See also* CANADIAN CHARTER OF RIGHTS AND FREEDOMS.

Canadian Imperial Bank of Commerce is a chartered bank with head offices in Toronto. One of CIBC's 2 predecessors was the Bank of Canada (incorporated 1858), which became the Canadian Bank of Commerce in 1867. It absorbed smaller banks, beginning with the Gore Bank in 1869 and ending with the Standard Bank of Canada in 1928. CIBC's second predecessor, the Imperial Bank of Canada (incorporated 1875), also absorbed other banks between 1875 and 1956, ending with Barclays Bank (Canada). The present name was adopted in 1961 on the merger of the Bank of Commerce and the Imperial Bank of Canada. The CIBC provides commercial and personal banking services in 1630 branches in Canada and operates agencies and branches overseas, including 56 of the latter in the West Indies alone. With changes in the Bank Act during the 1970s, the CIBC, like other Canadian banks, began to promote itself more actively, engaging Canadian entertainer Anne MURRAY as its spokesperson. As of Oct 1986, it had an annual revenue of $7.9 billion, assets of $80.8 billion (ranking third among financial institutions in Canada) and 33 914 employees.

DEBORAH C. SAWYER

Canadian Institute for Economic Policy, privately funded, independent institute, established in 1979 with a 5-year mandate to study Canadian fiscal, industrial and other public-policy issues. Its 30 monographs included studies critical of the BANK OF CANADA's monetarism and of the extent of FOREIGN INVESTMENT in Canadian industry; its studies of CANADIAN-AMERICAN RELATIONS and the failure of Canada to develop an industrial policy received wide attention. Former Liberal finance minister, Walter L. GORDON, was chairman and chief benefactor of the institute. It closed in 1984.   W.F. FORWARD

Canadian Institute of International Affairs (CIIA), an offspring of the British (later Royal) Institute of International Affairs launched in 1928 by such prominent Canadians as Sir Robert BORDEN, Sir Arthur CURRIE, John W. DAFOE, John Nelson and Sir Joseph FLAVELLE. They believed that in coming decades governments would increasingly rely on the support of their citizens in the conduct of world affairs. If Canada was to play an important role, an informed public opinion must be created through the dissemination of information and expert opinion. Branches were established in major cities to host speakers and study the current issues. Its Toronto headquarters initiated research projects and study trips, and published scholarly books and journals on Canadian foreign affairs and international relations. Although it has never been large, its members are found among Canada's leading experts on international affairs in academic, business and government circles.

D.M. PAGE

Canadian International Development Agency (CIDA), formed in 1968 to give prominence to the Canadian government's development assistance to needy nations. Such assistance had begun in 1950 with the COLOMBO PLAN, but the government's mechanism both at home and abroad for co-ordinating the flow of wheat, capital, and technology to the underdeveloped world was inadequate. An External Aid Office, est 1960, managed these diverse activities but it took CIDA's first president, Maurice STRONG, and his successors to define long-term strategies. Disbursements, restricted to countries where they would be of most benefit, became more important than Canadian contributions to multilateral programs administered by the United Nations or the World Bank. Nongovernment projects were also partially funded by CIDA in over 100 countries. Canadian industry provides most of the materials for capital projects, and Canadian professionals share their skills in engineering, social development, medicine, agriculture and education. Additional emergency relief is available for victims of famines, earthquakes or political disturbances. By 1987-88 CIDA assistance had risen to about $2.1 billion.   D.M. PAGE

Canadian Journal of Economics and Political Science was the academic journal of the Canadian Political Science Assn, whose membership originally covered all the social sciences. It was published by University of Toronto Press from 1935 to 1967, when, having earlier spun off a separate journal for sociology and anthropology, it was succeeded by the *Canadian Journal of Economics* and the *Canadian Journal of Political Science*, the latter now published by Wilfrid Laurier U. The *Journal* contained academic articles and book reviews in the fields of economics, political science, geography, sociology and anthropology, although there were few papers or reviews on the last 3 topics. It also contained a Bibliography of Economics which, until the elaboration of the National Library bibliographic services in the mid-1950s, was an essential guide to the subject. Its articles and book reviews, many of them on Canadian topics, were intelligible to the general reader.   IAN M. DRUMMOND

Canadian Labor Union Founded in 1873 on the initiative of the Toronto Trades Assembly, the Canadian Labor Union represented organized labour's first attempt at a national federation. Moderate in ideology and practice, the CLU would only extend support to striking members who had sought arbitration first. The establishment of favourable legislation for workers and growth in trade-union membership comprised the CLU's 2 primary concerns. At annual conventions held between 1873 and 1877, the CLU passed resolutions in support of universal manhood suffrage, direct labour representation in parliament, the establishment of a labour department, stricter regulation of the apprenticeship system, and shorter hours of work. The CLU opposed government-assisted immigration, child labour, and the use of prison labour in competition with free labour. CLU lobbying resulted in amendments to the Criminal Law Amendment Act, the Mechanics' Lien Act and the Master and Servant Act. Despite its claim of being a national body, the CLU never contained more than a small minority of Canadian unionists and remained Ontario dominated throughout its existence. A lingering depression led to its demise in 1878.   JOHN BULLEN

Canadian Labour Congress, a national UNION CENTRAL fd 23 Apr 1956 from the merger of the CANADIAN CONGRESS OF LABOUR and the TRADES AND LABOR CONGRESS OF CANADA. The ONE BIG UNION was absorbed into the CLC, but Québec's Catholic unions chose to remain apart (*see* CONFEDERATION OF NATIONAL TRADE UNIONS). In 1961 CLC and CO-OPERATIVE COMMONWEALTH FEDERATION leaders joined to form the NEW DEMOCRATIC PARTY, a link that has been maintained ever since. In 1986 there were 2.2 million trade unionists affiliated with the CLC through 92 international and national unions. The 3 largest are PUBLIC-SERVICE UNIONS; the fourth largest is the United Steelworkers of America. Economic and legislative questions of national importance constitute a major focus of the CLC. Provincial and territorial federations of labour and municipal labour councils co-ordinate comparable programs of CLC affiliates. Every second year some 2500 delegates from affiliated unions convene to set policy for the central body. Between conventions, policy decisions are made by the 38-member executive council. CLC headquarters are in Ottawa.

Canadian League of Composers/La Ligue canadienne de compositeurs was founded in Toronto in 1951 to increase contact between professional composers, to advance common interests, and to stimulate public awareness of Canadian music. Membership has grown from nearly 20 composers in 1951 to approximately 180 in 1987 and includes composers of concert, film and broadcast music. The league promoted some 40 concerts, mainly of Canadian music, in its first 18 years. Many of these were organized in Montréal and Toronto with the help of 2 concert committees run by nonmembers, the Canadian Music Associates (Ontario) and La Société de musique canadienne (Québec). The league conceived the plan for the CANADIAN MUSIC CENTRE, organized the International Conference of Composers at Stratford, Ont, in 1960, and established a scholarship for young composers in 1967. The principal founder and longest-serving president was John WEINZWEIG. By lobbying on behalf of composers' economic and legal interests and by promoting the appreciation of Canadian music at home and abroad, the league has raised the status of the composer in the cultural fabric of Canada and has encouraged individual composers to develop their creativity. The papers of the league are deposited in the NATIONAL LIBRARY OF CANADA.   HELMUT KALLMANN

Reading: Helmut Kallmann et al, eds, *Encyclopedia of Music in Canada* (1981); *The Canada Music Book* 2 (1971).

Canadian Library Association is a nonprofit voluntary organization founded by Elizabeth Homer Morton, and established in Hamilton in 1946 to develop high standards of librarianship and of library and information services. The first president was Freda Waldon. In Mar 1987 CLA consisted of approximately 3500 personal and 800 institutional members. There are 5 divisions representing the various interests of public, special, college and university and school libraries, as well as library trustees. In 1968 CLA became a unilingual association, leaving representation of francophone librarians to ASTED (Association pour l'avancement des sciences et des techniques de la documentation). CLA membership is open to anyone with an interest in libraries and is governed by an elected council and board of directors. Council is composed, in part, of representatives from provincial library associations. CLA maintains an active publication, seminar/workshop program, and it speaks for librarian's concerns at the national level by making representation to government and official commissions. *See also* LIBRARIES; LIBRARY SCIENCES.

Canadian Literature (fd 1959) was the first quarterly concerned entirely with the discussion of Canadian writing. Published by UBC, it was edited by George WOODCOCK 1959-77, and since then by W.H. New. A variety of critical approaches has been encouraged; poets and novelists have been invited to write about their own arts and discuss the works of their fellows. In recent years poems have been published regularly. Many important Canadian critics have appeared in *Canadian Literature*, as have creative writers as varied as Hugh MACLENNAN, Margaret ATWOOD, Irving LAYTON, Timothy FINDLEY, Dorothy LIVESAY, F.R. SCOTT, A.J.M. SMITH, P.K. PAGE and Audrey THOMAS.

Canadian Liver Foundation, the first organization in the world to devote itself exclusively to providing support into the causes and treatment of diseases of the liver. It was founded, as the Canadian Hepatic Foundation, in 1970, and the present name was adopted in 1979. There are over 100 known liver diseases which can affect all ages and which can be fatal; one in 20 Canadians suffers from some form of liver disease. Because much liver disease is preventable, the CLF promotes earlier and better diagnosis and increased general awareness. It has organized 5 international symposia which allow scientific and medical communities worldwide to share research progress and findings through published proceedings. It supports the Liver Pathology Reference Centre and provides research grants and fellowships. In 1981 the CLF Epidemiology Unit at U of T was established to study liver disease patterns and to promote early detection. Headquarters are in Toronto; financial support is derived from corporate sources (38%), special projects (18%), individual and other sources.

Canadian Lung Association, Canada's first national voluntary health organization, was founded in 1900. Its roots were in the former Canadian Tuberculosis Association. Initially its aim was to provide facilities for the care of TUBERCULOSIS patients through sanatoria and diagnostic and treatment clinics (at the beginning of the century, TB was the main cause of death in Canada). Since 1927 Christmas Seals have been used to raise the necessary funds; the annual Christmas Seal Campaign is the chief method of support for lung associations across Canada. The Canadian Lung Association now directs its efforts towards public-awareness campaigns designed to prevent or reduce the effects of SMOKING-induced illness and other lung diseases caused by the environment. Educational and awareness programs are conducted for children and adults with asthma, emphysema or chronic bronchitis. Special interest groups within the association are the Canadian Thoracic Society, the Canadian Nurses' Respiratory Society and the Physiotherapy Section. A research grants and fellowships program was established in 1959 to promote research into any field of acute or chronic lung disease.

Canadian Manufacturers' Association, fd 1871, incorporated by Act of Parliament 1902, "to promote Canadian industries and to further the interests of Canadian manufacturers and exporters." The CMA operated the forerunner of the present Canadian Trade Commissioner Service, helped create the Board of Railway Commissioners (which became the Board of Transport Commissioners, the CANADIAN TRANSPORT COMMISSION and, in 1987, the National Transportation Agency) and the Canadian National Exhibition, and conducted studies basic to the drafting of Ontario's Workmen's Compensation Act. To be a member, a company must manufacture in Canada and employ at least 5 persons. Most companies (75%) have fewer than 100 employees. The association provides members with information important to the manufacturing industry, and submits its views to all levels of government on matters affecting manufacturers' interests. The CMA employs full-time staff across the country to help members solve problems relating to customs and excise, environmental standards, export and import procedures, energy, labour relations, research and development, taxation, technical standards, telecommunications and transportation. The association is structured nationally, provincially and locally. In addition to its Toronto head office it maintains 7 divisional offices and an Ottawa office.

J. LAURENT THIBAULT

Canadian Medical Association, est 1867 by 167 doctors in Québec City. It is a voluntary federation of 10 autonomous provincial medical associations united at the national level and now represents more than 46 000 English- and French-speaking physicians across Canada. Dr Charles TUPPER was its first president.

CMA policies are arrived at after careful study by one of 3 councils, 4 statutory boards, a number of special committees and the board of directors. A final debate on major issues normally follows the General Council (called the "Parliament of Canadian Medicine") comprising over 225 elected physicians. Wholly owned subsidiaries of the association – MD Management Ltd, MD Investment Service and Lancet Insurance Agency Ltd – operate a number of membership services programs, including a retirement savings plan, investment portfolios and a variety of professional development training programs.

Over 40 organizations representing various fields of medical specialization from sports medicine to neurology and family medicine are affiliated with the CMA. In addition, more than 30 societies, such as the Canadian Cancer Society (founded by the CMA in 1937) are associated members. The *CMA Journal,* published bimonthly, is the association's official publication.

DOUGLAS GEEKIE

Canadian Museum of Civilization (formerly National Museum of Man) traces its origins to 1841, when Queen Victoria granted £1500 for the "creation of the Geological and Natural History Survey of the Province of Canada" (*see* GEOLOGICAL SURVEY OF CANADA). The Survey was located in Montréal and scholars spread out across Canada collecting geological, archaeological and biological material. In 1877 an Act of Parliament ensured the continued existence of the Survey, which had broadened the collection base to include botanical, zoological and ethnographic specimens and artifacts. Four years later the Survey moved to the Clarendon Hotel in Ottawa. The fieldwork continued and the national collections grew. In 1911 the Survey occupied the new Victoria Memorial Museum building, an imposing piece of Gothic architecture usually called "the castle."

In 1910 a new Anthropology Division was established, under the direction of Edward SAPIR, which included 2 sections in charge of archaeological and ethnological fieldwork. Since 1911 the museum has been a centre for research in Canadian anthropology. When fire destroyed most of the PARLIAMENT BUILDINGS in 1916, however, the Parliament of Canada was housed in the museum building and the collections put in storage until 1920. In 1927 an Act of Parliament created the National Museum of Canada, although it was not until 1950 that its operational links were finally severed from the Geological Survey.

In 1942 the Canadian War Museum, established in 1880 but in storage since 1897, was formally inaugurated in the War Trophies Building. The CWM became a division of the National Museum of Canada in 1958, and expanded significantly when it took over the old Public Archives of Canada building in 1967.

The NATIONAL MUSEUMS OF CANADA Corporation was established in 1968, comprising the NATIONAL GALLERY, National Museum of Man (including the Canadian War Museum), NATIONAL MUSEUM OF NATURAL SCIENCES and NATIONAL MUSEUM OF SCIENCE AND TECHNOLOGY (and its National Aeronautical Collection). The name of the National Museum of Man was changed to Canadian Museum of Civilization in 1987.

By the 1980s the CMC had grown to be one of the largest museums in the world. There are 5 scientific divisions: ARCHAEOLOGICAL SURVEY OF CANADA, Canadian Ethnological Service, Canadian Centre for Folk Culture Studies (*see* FOLKLORE), Canadian War Museum, and the History Division. The CMC carries out the usual museum activities in the areas for which it is responsible: collection of artifacts and data; conservation and preservation; scientific research; and exhibition and publication. Monographic series are published in archaeology, physical anthropology, ethnology, linguistics, folk culture studies and history, including military history. In the decade 1976-86 approximately 200 travelling exhibitions were circulated within Canada and to the US, Europe, Africa, New Zealand and Japan. Museum kits for schools, fact sheets and catalogues, and film and video programs are also produced.

In 1984 construction began on a new CMC building in Hull, Qué, designed by Douglas CARDINAL. The grand opening is scheduled for 1989 and growth is expected to continue well into the 1990s.

FRANK CORCORAN

Canadian Museums Association has seen dramatic change since its modest beginnings in 1947. Fewer than 2 dozen members, representing 20 ART GALLERIES AND MUSEUMS, were present at the association's first meeting at the Musée du Québec. The founding members interpreted museums in the broadest sense and aimed to promote the public understanding of the function of museums and the service they could render to research, education and recreation. The young association struggled with problems stemming from its small but diverse membership scattered across great distances. By 1987, following the growth in the number of museums in Canada, the CMA's membership of individuals and institutions had reached 1900.

The association operates a full-time secretariat in Ottawa and offers a variety of services. Members receive *museogramme,* a monthly newsletter, as well as a quarterly journal with news and issues of interest to the museum community. A Museum Documentation Centre (library), open to all members, is maintained in Ottawa and bibliographies and a biennial *Directory of Canadian Museums* are published. A book-sales program offers substantial discounts to members. For professional development, the CMA offers a correspondence course as an introduction to museum philosophy and operations, operates a bursary program to assist museum personnel in upgrading their museological training through workshops, seminars, study tours and internships, and has an individual professional accreditation program. An awards program recognizes special contributions of members to CMA projects or museums. The annual conference provides a forum for information exchange.

The governing body of the CMA is an elected council of 15 members. Standing committees of council are as follows: Finance, Government and Public Policy, Research and Editorial, Professional Development and Standards, Nominations and Membership.   ELIZABETH GIGNAC

Canadian Music Centre, founded in 1959, is an arts service organization supporting about 250 of Canada's serious or concert composers. Composers become CMC associates after being selected by a committee of their peers. The national office and library of the centre is in Toronto; regional centres are in Vancouver, Calgary, Toronto and Montréal. By collecting, freely distributing and promoting the associates' music, the CMC aims to encourage the study, performance and appreciation of these compositions. It offers the public and music groups both in Canada and overseas information on the associates, publications on the 7000 scores in its libraries and inexpensive reproductions of the music itself. Centrediscs, the CMC's record label, produces and distributes quality discs of associates' works performed by Canadian concert artists.

The CMC is funded by a number of government agencies – federal, provincial and municipal – and by performing rights organizations, foundations, industries and the donations of its lay members.   JOHN A. MILLER

Canadian National Exhibition, world's largest annual exhibition, held in Toronto in late Aug and early Sept. The CNE, or "Ex" as it is popularly called, originated in an agricultural fair that circulated among the towns of Canada West in the 1840s (*see* AGRICULTURAL EXHIBITIONS). In 1878 the city of Toronto leased 20 ha of land on the lakefront as a permanent fairground and held its own exhibition the following year. Called the Toronto Industrial Exhibition, all but one of the 23 wooden buildings – the Crystal Palace – were devoted to agriculture. In 1882 the fairgrounds became the first to be lit by electricity, and Torontonian J.J. Wright introduced the electric railway there in 1883. The Crystal Palace was destroyed by fire in 1906 and replaced by the Horticultural Building, an additional imposing structure of brick and stone. The fair was officially renamed the Canadian National Exhibition in 1912.

The CNE continued to grow and to reflect the changes in Canadian society as emphasis shifted from agriculture to industry. By 1912 the fairgrounds covered 141 ha and included one of the finest amusement parks and permanent exhibition facilities in the world. Elaborate grandstand shows were presented, usually on Canadian themes and, during both world wars, on effort, loyalty and victory. Marathon swims across the lake, such as that of Marilyn BELL, who in 1954 became the first person to swim Lk Ontario, and special events, such as an exhibition of the first television broadcast in Canada, proved popular. A growing American influence was evident, particularly in the performers selected for the grandstand shows. By the 1960s the Ex had evolved into a vast consumer market, displaying the latest automobiles, electrical appliances, computers and the like. The CNE has not been without critics and was cast in a shadow in 1967 by EXPO 67. Nevertheless, in 1987, 2 124 816 people visited the CNE; along with Ontario Place, the Ex remains part of an extensive recreational development on the revitalized Toronto lakefront.   JAMES MARSH

Poster for the Canadian National Exhibition, 1937, by Eric Aldwinkle (*courtesy Canadian National Exhibition Archives*).

Reading: J. Lorimer, *The Ex: A Picture History of the Canadian National Exhibition* (1973); G. Wall and N. Zalkind, "The Canadian National Exhibition: Mirror of Canadian Society," in G. Wall and J.S. Marsh, eds, *Recreational Land Use* (1982).

Canadian National Institute for the Blind, *see* BLINDNESS AND VISUAL IMPAIRMENT.

Canadian National Railways incorporated 6 June 1919, is the longest railway system in N America, controlling more than 50 000 km of track in Canada and the US. Now called Canadian National, the CROWN CORPORATION's holdings have expanded since the 1920s to include marine operations, hotels, TELECOMMUNICATIONS and resource industries, but the core of CN still lies with its railway system (now called CN Rail), which had its origins in the amalgamation of 5 financially troubled railways during the years 1917-23: the GRAND TRUNK and its subsidiary the GRAND TRUNK PACIFIC; the INTERCOLONIAL; the CANADIAN NORTHERN; and the NATIONAL TRANSCONTINENTAL. The Grand Trunk was itself an amalgamation of various smaller lines, including the 23.2 km CHAMPLAIN AND ST LAWRENCE RAILROAD (1836) which connected Montréal with boat traffic to Lk Champlain and the port of New York; the GREAT WESTERN RAILWAY linking Niagara, Hamilton and Toronto with Windsor and Sarnia; and the ST LAWRENCE AND ATLANTIC RAILROAD, which gave Montréal access to the year-round port facilities of Portland, Maine. The Grand Trunk became the dominant long-distance railway in central Canada, but its English shareholders would not agree to the expense of building from Québec City to Halifax over Canadian soil, nor to construction westward over the 1600 km of the Laurentian Shield. Those challenges were faced after Confederation by the government-owned Intercolonial from Halifax to Québec City and by the heavily subsidized CANADIAN PACIFIC RAILWAY.

Although Canada by the 1890s was traversed from sea to sea by the CPR, the issues of monopoly in the West and of partisan politics federally led to further transcontinental ventures. The Canadian Northern, founded by William MACKENZIE and

Donald MANN, was begun with small Manitoba lines in 1895. In 1903 Sir Wilfrid LAURIER's Liberal government authorized the building of the Grand Trunk Pacific, from Winnipeg west to Prince Rupert, and the National Transcontinental, from Winnipeg east to Moncton. All of these lines were financed by heavy borrowing and, when WWI diverted the credit of English banks, the debt loads of these railways had to be absorbed through government nationalization.

Completion of government ownership in the early 1920s led to the appointment of Sir Henry THORNTON as CN's first president. Despite an inherited debt of $1.3 billion, gross earnings that barely covered operating expenses, and the difficulty of keeping the government at arm's length, Thornton gradually established annual surpluses while drawing remarkable personal support from among the 99 000 employees of CN. He promoted community service, supporting branch lines and introducing school cars and Red Cross units to serve children and the sick in regions remote from urban centres. Between 1923 and 1932 he was responsible for using CN facilities to develop a network of radio stations, which inaugurated programs such as "Hockey Night in Canada" and led to the formation of the CANADIAN BROADCASTING CORPORATION (*see* BROADCASTING, RADIO AND TELEVISION). Unfortunately, partisan politics forced Thornton's resignation in 1932.

Economic depression in the 1930s reduced traffic volume, leading to cuts in wages and dismissal of employees. At the same time, highway and air travel diverted traffic away from the railway. In 1937, however, under C.D. HOWE as minister of transport, CN organized formation of TRANS-CANADA AIRLINES (now AIR CANADA), and in1938 the federal government cancelled more

Canadian National Railways - Chronology

20 Dec 1918	Name Canadian National Railways authorized
6 June 1919	Canadian National Railways Company incorporated to consolidate Canadian Northern and Canadian Government Rys
20 Jan 1923	Management of Canadian Northern Ry and Canadian Government Rys entrusted to the CNR Co, along with the Intercolonial Ry, National Transcontinental Ry, Hudson Bay Ry, etc
30 Jan 1923	The Grand Trunk Railway was amalgamated with the CNR under the latter name
25 June 1926	Hudson Bay Ry was terminated and construction by CNR was authorized
7 Aug 1929	Acquisition of Kent Northern Ry Co; Inverness Ry and Coal Co; Québec, Montreal and Southern Ry Co; Quebec Oriental Ry; Atlantic, Quebec and Western Ry, and, Saint John and Quebec Ry
23 May 1933	Canadian National-Canadian Pacific Act was passed, directing the two companies to agree to co-operate in effecting economies
4 July 1952	CNR Capital Revision Act became law. It released the CNR from 50% of its debt ($736 million) and lessened interest payments for 10 years
13 May 1954	Amalgamation of 6 companies with the CNR, the largest of which is the National Transcontinental Ry Branch Lines Co
17 May 1956	Amalgamation of 17 companies with the CNR, including the Canadian Northern Ry, Canadian Northern Ontario Ry, Canadian Northern Consolidated Rys and Grand Trunk Pacific Ry

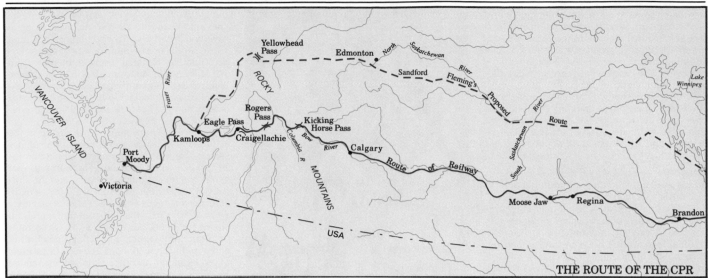

THE ROUTE OF THE CPR

than $1 billion of its inherited debt. As a result, before WWII, CN was able to purchase and to finish and service in its own huge shops at Pointe St-Charles, Montréal, a large number of Canadian-built steam locomotives, in particular the 4-8-4 Northern type, which hauled millions of tons of freight and thousands of troops during the war.

In the 1950s and 1960s, CN was modernized under the dynamic presidency of Donald GORDON, who rationalized 80 subsidiary companies down to 30, one of which, CN Marine, operates all ferry service in the Atlantic provinces. Gordon also directed the conversion to diesel locomotives and electronic signalling while adding to CN assets the Queen Elizabeth Hotel (1958) and a new head office in Montréal.

By the end of the 1970s CN had merged its own system of telecommunications with that of CP, and completed construction in Toronto of the CN TOWER. CN Real Estate redeveloped company-owned downtown properties in several cities, including the Toronto Convention Centre Complex. In 1981 CN Exploration was formed to develop CN-owned mineral rights in western Canada. On the highway, Canadian National amalgamated all its trucking subsidiaries into CNX/CN Trucking, their trailers carried over long distances on piggy-back rail cars. In early 1988 CN announced plans to sell off its many hotels.

Two problems remain characteristic of CN as a huge crown corporation with profits in 1985 of $75 million. Financially, it has until recently depended on federal subsidies to compensate for statutory freight rates in the long-distance haulage of Prairie grain (*see* CROW'S NEST PASS AGREEMENT). Politically, ownership by the federal government has often influenced high-level appointments with at least as much respect for partisan interest as for "hands off" direction. *See also* RAILWAY HISTORY.   ALBERT TUCKER

Reading: J. Schull, *The Great Scot: Biography of Donald Gordon* (1979); G.R. Stevens, *History of the Canadian National Railway* (1973).

Canadian Nature Federation, a national, nongovernmental, charitable CONSERVATION organization, created from the Canadian Audubon Society in 1971. The CNF is aided in its work by a coast-to-coast network of naturalist societies and by its membership in national and international protection groups, including the Committee on the Status of Endangered Wildlife in Canada (COSEWIC), the Canadian Coalition on Acid Rain, the International Union for the Conservation of Nature and Natural Resources (IUCN) and the Arctic International Wildlife Range Society.

Through its magazine, *Nature Canada*, and its bookshop, nature sanctuary, nature art scholarship program and conservation directory, the CNF endeavours to foster a greater understanding and appreciation of Canada's wildlife and wilderness heritage. The CNF's environmental action program presents briefs, speeches and reports to government review boards, conferences and environmental protection agencies to ensure that members' concerns are considered when critical decisions affecting the environment are made. This organization is headquartered in Ottawa and is supported by membership fees, bookshop revenues and donations.

CHRISTINE VAN ZWAMEN

Canadian Northern Railway was incorporated (1899) as a result of the amalgamation of 2 small Manitoba branch lines. It was built up over the next 20 years by its principal promoters, William MACKENZIE and Donald MANN, to become a 16 093 km transcontinental railway system. The promoters depended heavily on land grants and on the sale of government guaranteed bonds of their company. They built a strong Prairie system, but came to face stiff competition from their transcontinental rivals, the CANADIAN PACIFIC RAILWAY, the GRAND TRUNK RAILWAY and the GRAND TRUNK PACIFIC RAILWAY. To meet that competition, a transcontinental expansion program was undertaken. The last spike was driven in Jan 1915 and in Oct of that year an excursion train carried parliamentarians and journalists to Vancouver and on to Victoria. That expansion, however, proved crippling, and severe financial exigencies during WWI repeatedly forced the promoters to seek government assistance. In return for aid given, the federal government ultimately demanded all the shares of the company. Mackenzie and Mann were forced out of the company, which then became one of the first major components of what would soon become the publicly owned CANADIAN NATIONAL RAILWAYS. The corporate identity of the Canadian Northern Ry was retained until 1956, but its existence as an independent company ended with nationalization in 1918.   T.D. REGEHR

Reading: T.D. Regehr, *The Canadian Northern Railway* (1976).

Canadian Olympic Hockey Team Prior to the 1964 Winter OLYMPIC GAMES, Canada, represented by club teams, had appeared in 9 Olympic hockey tournaments, winning 6 gold medals, 2 silver medals and one bronze. After the most recent gold (awarded to the Edmonton Mercurys at the

1952 Olympics in Oslo, Norway), it had become increasingly difficult to find clubs that were able to compete effectively for Canada in the Olympics against such countries as the Soviet Union and Czechoslovakia, whose rapidly improving teams were the products of carefully conceived national programs. In 1962 Father David BAUER gained the approval of the CANADIAN AMATEUR HOCKEY ASSOCIATION for the concept of a Canadian Olympic hockey team. Bauer had coached the St Michael's (Toronto) Majors to the 1961 Memorial Cup championship. In Sept 1963 a group of university players began training under his direction at UBC in Vancouver. This team suffered only 2 narrow defeats, to the Soviet Union and Czechoslovakia, at the 1964 Olympics in Innsbruck, Austria, but placed fourth. In 1965 a permanent national team was established in Winnipeg. Coached by Jackie MacLeod and managed by Father Bauer, it won the bronze medal in the 1968 Olympics at Grenoble, France. As a result of disagreements with the International Ice Hockey Federation over the use of professionals at world championships, Canada withdrew from international amateur hockey entirely and did not send a team to the 1972 and 1976 Winter Olympics. Father Bauer participated in the revival of the Canadian team for the 1980 Olympics at Lake Placid, New York, where they were defeated by the Soviet Union, Finland and Czechoslovakia to finish out of the medals. At Sarajevo, Yugoslavia, in 1984, the Canadian team coached by Dave King lost to Sweden in the bronze medal game. King was also named coach of the team which represented Canada in Calgary in 1988.

DEREK DRAGER AND GIGI CLOWES

Canadian Open, an annual event run by the Royal Canadian Golf Assn for professionals and amateurs who qualify. It is the fourth-oldest national GOLF championship in the world, having first been played in 1904 at the Royal Montreal Golf Club. Until 1980 the tournament moved around Canada each year, but that year the RCGA-owned Glen Abbey Golf Club in Oakville, Ont, became the permanent site. Some people feel that as a national championship it should still go from course to course; but Glen Abbey was designed to give golf fans excellent views and is recognized as one of the finest courses in the world upon which to hold a tournament, particularly one that draws up to 100 000 spectators. The tournament has had such winners as top players Byron Nelson, Sam Snead, Arnold Palmer, Lee Trevino and Curtis Strange, while through 1985 Glen Abbey course designer Jack Nicklaus had finished second 7 times. The professionals play

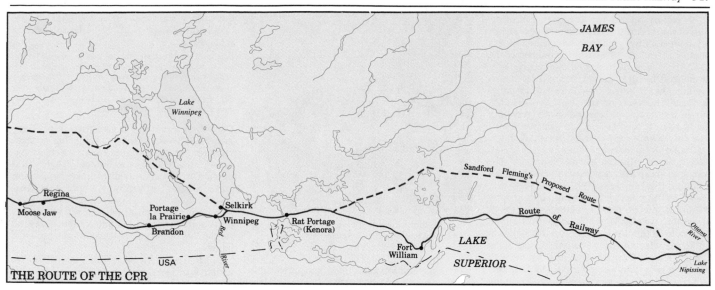

Lake Winnipeg

JAMES BAY

Regina

Moose Jaw

Portage la Prairie

Brandon

Selkirk

Winnipeg

Red River

Rat Portage (Kenora)

Fort William

Sandford Fleming's Proposed Route

Route of Railway

LAKE SUPERIOR

Ottawa River

Lake Nipissing

USA

THE ROUTE OF THE CPR

for a purse which in 1987 reached $850 000. It is expected to continue to grow to keep pace with other events in the golf world. LORNE RUBENSTEIN

Canadian Opera Co, Canada's leading producer of OPERA, evolved from the Opera Festival of the Royal Conservatory Opera Co. Incorporated in 1950, its name changed from Opera Festival Assn to Company (1954) to COC (1958). Under Herman Geiger-Torel, stage director 1950-56, artistic director 1956-59 and general director 1959-76, the COC forged a strong tradition using Canadian talent and made extensive tours. General director from 1976, Lotfi Mansouri, while building the company's international stature, has introduced the *stagione* system, increased the number of annual productions to seven and augmented the repertoire. Since 1980 through the COC Ensemble, Mansouri has the nucleus of a permanent company ready for a new opera house (1993).
GAYNOR G. JONES

Canadian Pacific Railway Commencement of a transcontinental railway within 2 years and completion within 10 years were conditions of British Columbia's entry into Confederation in 1871 (*see* RAILWAY HISTORY). Competition for the lucrative contract for the railway was bitter, and disclosure of methods used by Sir Hugh ALLAN to secure the charter led to the defeat of Sir John A. MACDONALD's government in 1873 (*see* PACIFIC SCANDAL). Macdonald returned to power in 1878, with the completion of the railway as one facet of his National Policy, and the contract was finally awarded to interests led by Donald A. SMITH, J.J. Hill and George STEPHEN. The Canadian Pacific Railway was incorporated 15 Feb 1881. The difficulties of construction and demand for early completion of the line ensured generous provisions to the company, including $25 million in cash, 25 million acres (about 10 million ha) of land in a belt along the railway, the cost of surveys totalling $37 million, monopoly over transportation S to the US for 20 years, etc. These terms were loudly denounced by opposing interests at the time and remained contentious with the development of the PRAIRIE WEST. However, in the face of American expansion westward, Macdonald and the federal Conservatives considered completion of the railway a national imperative.

Under the management of W.C. VAN HORNE, construction was rapidly pressed across the plains. Sandford FLEMING had recommended a route through the YELLOWHEAD PASS but a more southerly route through KICKING HORSE PASS was decided upon late in 1881. Construction through the rock and muskeg of the Canadian SHIELD al-

most equalled in difficulty the ENGINEERING feats of construction through the mountains of BC. Extreme difficulties in obtaining an adequate work force in BC led to the controversial importation of thousands of Chinese. At the height of the building activity on the Yale to Kamloops Lake section more than two-thirds, or approximately 9000 workers, were Chinese. The line through to the Pacific coast was completed with the driving of the "Last Spike" at CRAIGELLACHIE in EAGLE PASS, BC, on 7 Nov 1885. The section from Callander to Port Arthur [Thunder Bay], Ont, was used to move troops westward during the NORTH-WEST REBELLION, though it was not quite complete. The first through passenger train left Montréal 28 June 1886 and arrived at Port Moody, BC, July 4.

During construction the CPR became involved in the sale and settlement of land (1881), acquisition of the Dominion Express Co (1882) and the acceptance of commercial TELEGRAPH messages (1882). The company provided its own sleeping and dining cars on trains and constructed tourist hotels (eg, at Lake Louise, Alta) and dining halls along the route in the western mountains. This foothold on the tourist industry benefited the CPR later in its international development of hotels, steamships and airlines (*see* HOTEL; TOURISM).

Following construction, the greatest challenge facing the CPR was to develop business to make the line self-sustaining. Though settlement proceeded rapidly in the wake of the rail lines, population in western Canada was insufficient to sus-

tain the line fully for many years. To increase business, the corporation became very active in promoting trade on the Pacific. Within days of the arrival of the first train on the West Coast in 1886, sailing vessels chartered by the CPR began to arrive from Japan, bringing tea, silk and curios. By 1891 the company had secured a contract from the British government to carry the imperial mails from Hong Kong to Britain via Canada. The result was the purchase of 3 ocean passenger-cargo vessels, forerunners of the present-day fleet.

By 1900 the mountain hotel system had expanded into the major cities, led by the Hotel Vancouver (1887), Québec's Château Frontenac (1893) and Montréal's Place Viger (1898). Other services expanded simultaneously. A line was opened (1889) across northern Maine from Montréal to Saint John giving the CPR direct access to an all-weather Atlantic port. Attempts to capture traffic from the western American states were made with construction of a line to North Dakota (1893), and control (which remains today) of what is now the Soo Line Railroad Co in the US. Branch lines were greatly extended to feed traffic to the E-W main line. Rapid settlement followed construction of branches to southern Manitoba, from Regina to Prince Albert (1890) and from Calgary N to Strathcona [Edmonton] in

Construction of a snowshed through the Rogers Pass on the CPR line in the 1880s (*courtesy Provincial Archives of Alberta/E. Brown Coll*).

1891. Expansion into the Kootenay mining region of southern BC (1898) involved the acquisition of a railway charter which included a smelter at Trail, BC. This was the nucleus of the CPR's involvement in MINING and METALLURGY, formalized by the formation of what is now Cominco Ltd (1906), a CP-controlled company. The Pacific fleet was improved and, in 1903, CPR purchased the Beaver Line and opened service in the N Atlantic. In 1914-15, after the 1909 purchase of the long-established ALLAN LINE, Canadian Pacific Ocean Services (after 1921 Canadian Pacific Steamships Ltd) was organized. The widespread expansion of the company, much of it under the presidency of T.G. SHAUGHNESSY (1899-1918), placed a heavy drain on company resources, but continuance of the NATIONAL POLICY, with its substantial tariffs, meant continuing high rates in the West. Attacks on these rates in 1896 had helped to bring about the defeat of the Conservatives. The Liberals reduced rates with the CROW'S NEST PASS AGREEMENT in 1897 and certain grievances were removed by passing of the Manitoba Grain Act in 1900. Finally, charters were granted to the CANADIAN NORTHERN RY to develop the huge area of northern Prairie left vacant by the CPR. Between 1899 and 1913, the CPR increased its trackage from approximately 11 200 km to 17 600 km. More than half of the new track was in the Prairie provinces and it was intended both to provide branch lines into areas of need and to ensure that the CPR would remain competitive in relation to the developing transcontinental lines or the Canadian Northern Ry and the Grand Trunk Pacific Ry.

Consolidation and expansion in the 1920s and the Depression in the 1930s were major challenges, as was competition from CANADIAN NATIONAL RAILWAY, formed by the government of Canada between 1917 and 1923. The CNR consolidated the failing Grand Trunk Pacific, Canadian Northern, Intercolonial and Canadian Government Railways, and competed with the CPR in hotels, telegraphs, steamships and express services as well as railway services. Despite this massive, government-supported competition, CPR survived as a commercial enterprise. In WWII it provided not only transportation, but also the production in its own main shops of armaments and materiel. During the conflict, much of its merchant fleet was commandeered for military transport purposes, resulting in the loss of 12 vessels.

Canadian Pacific Air Lines (later CP Air) was organized in 1942 with the purchase of Grant MCCONACHIE's Yukon Southern Air Transport and numerous other flying concerns. Under McConachie's leadership after 1947, CPA developed into an international carrier serving the Far East, Australasia, most of S America and several European countries (see AVIATION). In 1987 CP Air was acquired by Pacific Western; the 2 companies began operations as Canadian Airlines International.

Until the late 1950s CP's diverse interests were looked upon as ancillary to the rail system. Beginning at this time, management embraced a policy of full diversification by making each operation fully self-supporting. Thus, operations which had been handled traditionally by specific departments in the railway corporate structure were set up as enterprises in their own right, eg, Marathon Realty Co Ltd (1963), which took over the administration of real estate other than that required for railway use; CP Hotels Ltd (1965); and CP Oil & Gas Ltd [now PanCanadian Petroleum Ltd] (1958). Concurrently the nontransportation interests were vested in a holding company, now Canadian Pacific Enterprises Ltd, fd 1962, leaving the railway, air, ship and high-

CPR train in the Crowsnest Pass, SW Alberta (*courtesy Elliott and Nicole Bernshaw/Bernshaw Photography*).

way transportation fields under the jurisdiction of the parent company. In 1968 a new corporate identity program gave the names CP Rail, CP Ships, CP Transport and CP Air to the various transportation modes. In 1971, to reflect the new and broader orientation of the company, its original name was altered to Canadian Pacific Ltd. In 1967 the communications wing was integrated, along with CN's parallel organization, into a new, jointly owned company known as CNCP Telecommunications Ltd. In 1986 Canadian Pacific Ltd ranked second among Canadian corporations with gross revenue of $15 billion, it ranked fourth by assets ($17.7 billion) and had 93 800 employees. Foreign ownership of

Canadian Pacific Railway — Chronology

1871	July 20	BC formally admitted to Confederation, with the promise of a railway
1872	April	Fleming settles on Yellowhead Pass as route through Rockies
	July 26	Sir Hugh Allan assured by Macdonald that influence will be used to establish him as president of CPR
	Aug 26	Macdonald's telegram to Allan: "I must have another ten thousand"
1873	July	Newspapers publish revelations re "Pacific Scandal"
	Nov 5	Macdonald government resigns
1874	Jan 22	Liberals under Mackenzie elected
1875	June 1	Construction begins on main CPR line at Ft William, Ont
1877	Oct 9	*Countess of Dufferin*, first locomotive on prairies, arrives at Winnipeg
1878	Sept 17	Conservatives returned to power
1880	Apr 22	A. Onderdonk commences construction at Yale, BC
1881	Feb 16	Canadian Pacific Ry Co incorporated
	Dec 13	W.C. Van Horne arrives in Winnipeg as general manager
1882	June 17	Line between Ft William and Selkirk, Man, completed
	July 24	Rogers finds pass through Selkirks
	Aug 23	First train arrives at Regina
1883	Aug 20	Official party arrives in Calgary
1884	Feb 28	CPR Relief Bill passes House
1885	Mar 19	Riel sets up provisional Métis government in Saskatchewan
	Apr 5	First Canadian troops reach Winnipeg
	May 15	Riel surrenders
	May 16	Last rail on Lk Superior line
	June 10	CPR Aid Bill passes House
	July 29	Onderdonk completes line from Port Moody, BC, to Savona's Ferry
	Sept 30	Onderdonk completes line between Savona's Ferry and Eagle Pass, BC
	Nov 7	Last spike driven at Craigellachie

the shares stands at 30%; shareholders are widely distributed. OMER LAVALLÉE

Reading: P. Berton, *The National Dream* (1970) and *The Last Spike* (1971); J.M. Gibbon, *Steel of Empire: The Romantic History of the Canadian Pacific, the Northwest Passage of Today* (1935); H.A. Innis, *A History of The Canadian Pacific Railway* (1923); W. Kaye Lamb, *History of the Canadian Pacific Railway* (1977); J.L. McDougall, *Canadian Pacific: A Brief History* (1968).

Canadian Permanent Committee on Geographical Names In 1897 Canadian government resource scientists and mapmakers, recognizing a need to standardize geographical naming in Canada, to discourage duplication and to simplify orthography, founded the Geographic Board of Canada. During its early years the board published its decisions in annual reports and sponsored the publication of several studies on the origin and use of geographical names.

In 1948, when the board was renamed the Canadian Board on Geographical Names, a program to publish the *Gazetteer of Canada* series by province and territory was started. In 1961 the board was reorganized as the Canadian Permanent Committee on Geographical Names to clarify federal and provincial authority regarding the adoption of geographical names. In 1979 the federal government recognized that the provinces have authority to name features in lands under their jurisdiction, while sharing responsibility for naming in federal crown lands in the provinces.

The committee has 21 members, one from each province and 11 other members representing federal mapping agencies, territorial administration, archives and translation services. The committee is supported by 4 advisory committees on undersea feature names, glaciological and alpine nomenclature, toponymy research and names outside Canada. A very active role has been played by the committee in the international standardization of geographical names. The federal Dept of ENERGY, MINES AND RESOURCES provides the committee with its chairman and secretariat. Some provinces (Alberta, Newfoundland, Ontario, Québec and Sask) have their own boards, which undertake a variety of toponymic studies. *See also* PLACE-NAMES. A. RAYBURN

Canadian Physicians for the Prevention of Nuclear War (originally Physicians for Social Responsibility-Canada) is a voluntary nonprofit organization dedicated to the prevention of nuclear war. It came into being largely as the result of the efforts of the founding president, Dr Frank Sommers. The American PSR first began in Boston in 1961, compiling the information that was crucial in building public pressure for the Limited Test Ban Agreement of 1963. PSR was revived in 1978 in the wake of the accident at the Three Mile Island nuclear reactor in Pennsylvania. In Dec 1980 in Geneva, 3 Harvard doctors met with 3 Soviet doctors to lay the foundations for the International Physicians for the Prevention of Nuclear War (IPPNW).

The first World Congress of IPPNW was held near Washington, DC, in Mar 1981. There were 73 doctors from 12 countries, including Donald Bates, Paul Duchastel, Etienne LeBel and Frank Sommers from Canada. Since then there have been 6 other congresses. IPPNW now has affiliated groups in over 50 nations, representing a total of more than 160 000 physicians worldwide. In recognition of its efforts to inform the public, IPPNW was awarded the 1986 Nobel Peace Prize. Drs Bernard Lown and Evgueni Chazov as cofounders accepted the prize jointly.

Within Canada, local initiatives have included major conferences to educate both the profession and the general public about the potential disastrous consequences of a nuclear war. Nationally, the efforts of CPPNW have been recognized and endorsed by the Canadian Medical Assn and the Canadian Public Health Assn. CPPNW is also part of a rapidly expanding network of organizations that are uniting to bring about the elimination of nuclear weapons. Public campaigns have dramatized the dangers of relying on technology to defend against nuclear attack and the waste of global resources in perpetuating the arms race. "The True North Strong and Free?" conference in Edmonton 1986, cosponsored by CPPNW and the COUNCIL OF CANADIANS, was attended by 5000 people from across Canada.

CPPNW has 25 chapters across Canada and a membership of more than 4000. The 8th International Congress of IPPNW, with the theme "Healing our Planet – A Global Prescription," will be held in Montréal in 1988.   LINDA McDERMOTT

Canadian Political Science Association was founded in 1913. It lost its membership to WWI, but was reconstituted in 1929 and has operated continuously since. It was incorporated under the Canada Corporations Act in 1971. Among the association's objectives are to encourage and develop POLITICAL SCIENCE and its relationship with other disciplines and to publish journals, newspapers, books and monographs relating to political science. In Jan 1986 the association had 1200 members, representing 51 Canadian university departments of political science, as well as provincial governments, the federal government and the private sector. It functions in both French and English and carries out joint activities with La Société québécoise de science politique. The association has a permanent secretariat housed at U of Ottawa. In 1935 the association began publishing the prestigious CANADIAN JOURNAL OF ECONOMICS AND POLITICAL SCIENCE. In 1967 the economists formed their own association and the publication continued as *The Canadian Journal of Political Science*. Funds are derived by membership fees and subscriptions to the journal; major support is received from the Social Sciences and Humanities Research Council of Canada. CPSA is a member of the Social Sciences Federation of Canada, the International Political Science Assn and UNESCO, and it is associated with other political science organizations around the world. Among its distinguished presidents have been Stephen LEACOCK, O.D. SKELTON and Eugene FORSEY.

Canadian Press (CP), Canada's principal news agency, is owned co-operatively by 109 daily newspapers and operates as a nonprofit organization. In addition to providing members with a continual supply of domestic and foreign news, CP sells its service to private broadcasters through Broadcast News Ltd and provides news to CBC through another subsidiary, Press News Ltd. It also sells a computerized data file to non-media organizations and offers a photo service. CP's output in 1987 was approximately 250 000 words per day. A French-language service was inaugurated in 1951. CP was founded in 1917, partly to provide for an exchange of news among newspapers. Today, two-fifths of its domestic coverage is from member papers, who are obliged to provide swiftly any local news of potential interest to other papers. The remaining Canadian news is written by CP reporters. A news staff of nearly 330 is situated in 13 cities across Canada; the head office is in Toronto. CP maintains bureaus in NY, Washington and London, but most international copy comes from 3 agencies: Associated Press (US), Reuters (England) and Agence France-Presse (France).   PETER JOHANSEN

Canadian Public Policy/Analyse de politique was established in 1974 by the Canadian Economics Association with the co-operation of the Canadian Political Science Association and scholarly associations in the areas of political science, sociology, anthropology, law, geography, public administration and others. A quarterly journal, it occasionally publishes a fifth issue devoted to some particular question of public policy. It is funded primarily by subscriptions, but also receives a grant from the Social Sciences and Humanities Research Council of Canada. Its first home was at U of Guelph (where the business office is still located), but its editorial offices have been housed at UBC under editor Anthony Scott and at the U of Alberta under Kenneth Norrie. *Canadian Public Policy/Analyse de politique* is an interdisciplinary, academic journal devoted to stimulating research and discussion of public-policy issues in Canada. It publishes articles which are deemed to be of a high intellectual standard but are written so as to be accessible to a wide readership.   D. McGILLIVRAY

Canadian Radio-television and Telecommunications Commission The Broadcasting Act, 1967-68, established the Canadian Radio-Television Commission to regulate and supervise all aspects of the Canadian BROADCASTING system. These functions had been carried out since 1958 by the Board of Broadcast Governors, and before that by the Board of Governors of the CANADIAN BROADCASTING CORPORATION. In 1976 Parliament transferred to the CRTC jurisdiction over federally regulated TELECOMMUNICATIONS companies, formerly exercised by the Canadian Transport Commission, and changed the name to the Canadian Radio-television and Telecommunications Commission. The CRTC decides on the issuance and renewal of licences for all broadcasting undertakings, including networks and cable systems. It may attach conditions to licences and makes regulations respecting BROADCASTING. It may also revoke any licence, except one issued to the CBC. The governor-in-council may set aside the granting of any licence or ask that it be reconsidered. The chief function of the Commission in the telecommunications field is in approving rates or tolls to be charged to the public by companies not under provincial jurisdiction. Decisions in this area are also subject to Cabinet review. The legislation provides for a chairman, 2 vice-chairmen and 6 other full-time members, all of whom are normally appointed for 7-year terms and who form the executive committee. There is also provision for 10 part-time members regularly resident in different parts of the country but who take an active part in the work of the Commission. The executive committee has power to make decisions on all broadcast licensing matters except revocations, after consulting with part-time members, and it alone rules on telecommunications matters. The full Commission makes decisions involving the revocation of licences, general broadcasting policies, and regulations and rules of procedure. Public consultation, either through written notice and comment or through public hearings, is a general practice. In 1986-87, for example, the Commission received 3079 applications, and held 36 public hearings across the country. In the same year it issued 1174 decisions in broadcasting matters. Among the important early decisions of the CRTC were a provision for a minimum of Canadian music on the air; rules respecting Canadian content in TV schedules; licensing of third TV networks in Ontario and Québec; and the wide licensing of cable systems that would carry American programming directly to areas well beyond the range of US stations.

The staff of some 400 work in a building on the Promenade du Portage in Hull, Qué. The organization is divided into 5 major sectors: secretariat,

Pierre Juneau, the first chairman of the CRTC (*photo by Ron Watts/First Light*).

broadcasting, telecommunications, legal and corporate management. The first chairman was Pierre JUNEAU who held office until he resigned in 1975. Harry BOYLE, a veteran member who was then vice-chairman, became acting chairman for a time, and then was appointed to the office in Jan 1976 for a term to end the following year. He was succeeded by Pierre Camu who resigned after a 2-year period. In Dec 1979 John MEISEL, a social sciences professor at Queen's, was named as chairman. He was replaced in Nov 1983 by Québec lawyer André BUREAU. In 1981 the Commission licensed a SATELLITE distribution system to provide radio and TV service to remote and underserved areas. After some years of study and lengthy public hearings, the Commission now has licensed 3 national and 4 regional PAY-TELEVISION systems. In late 1987, 23 proposals for new specialty TV services, such as an ethnic or a French-language service, were being considered and an all-news service was awarded to the CBC in 1987.   A. DAVIDSON DUNTON

Canadian Seaman's Union, established 1936 to improve the archaic working conditions and wages for ordinary commercial seamen. Affiliated to the TRADES AND LABOR CONGRESS, this effective, well-supported, nationalist, communist-led, industrial union contributed handsomely to Canada's WWII effort despite the leadership's flip-flops. It gained concessions, was recognized as collective-bargaining agent for ordinary seamen, and fought unsuccessfully to retain Canada's merchant fleet, the Western world's fourth largest. Using the red scare (although most members were not communist) and an ill-timed strike in 1949, some shipping companies, including the federal government's, in collusion with the government and Canadian union leaders pressured by US international unionists, imported a known criminal, Hal BANKS of the SEAFARERS' INTERNATIONAL UNION, who violently broke the CSU. The SIU (Canadian branch) a quasi-company union, was stripped of its union status and disaffiliated by the TLC in 1950. National unionism lost, temporarily.   F.J.K. GRIEZIC

Canadian Security Intelligence Service (CSIS) was created by Act of Parliament in 1984 as an agency of the Dept of the Solicitor General. The agency's first director was Thomas D'Arcy Finn (1984-87), a lawyer and career public servant. The CSIS's purpose is to conduct security investigations within Canada related to suspected subversion, TERRORISM and foreign espionage and sabotage. In its first years of existence, its priority was the investigation of terrorist groups because of a number of violent crimes with political overtones, including the bombing of an Air India jet on a flight from Montréal and the armed takeover of the Turkish embassy in Ottawa. The CSIS also conducts background investigations of public servants whose positions require them to hold a high-level security clearance because they have access to sensitive national security information.

The CSIS replaced the security service of the ROYAL CANADIAN MOUNTED POLICE. Many of its first members transferred directly to the civilian agency from the federal police force. Although CSIS members are not police officers, the agency can obtain judicial warrants to conduct searches and electronic surveillance, such as telephone wiretapping. The CSIS does not conduct regular intelligence operations in foreign countries, but its members share intelligence and work closely with sister security services in the West under various agreements. The CSIS was the result of a reform of the RCMP after officers in the force were discovered to have used illegal investigative techniques, such as mail-opening operations and break-ins. A federal royal commission (the McDonald Commission) recommended the creation of a new civilian agency. In an effort to prevent similar abuses by the new agency, Parliament set up 2 review mechanisms. The 5-member Security Intelligence Review Committee (SIRC) and the CSIS inspector general can examine all aspects of the CSIS's operations and can report any irregularities directly to the solicitor general, who is a minister in the federal Cabinet. The SIRC also presents an annual report to Parliament. Nevertheless, in late 1987 director T.O. Finn resigned over allegations of improper activities. CSIS was accused of violating civil liberties and spying on the labour movement, and the government announced a major reorganization.

CSIS maintains headquarters in Ottawa, has field offices in major Canadian cities and posts liaison officers to the capitals of allied countries. The exact number of CSIS members is kept secret for security reasons, but the size of its budget suggests that it employs about 2000 people. The agency recruits its members from other areas of the public service and from the general population. Lawyer Ron Atkey was the first chairman, Richard Grosse the first inspector general. New members are given extensive specialized secret training at Camp Borden, Ont. JEFFREY SALLOT

Canadian Ski Marathon In 1967, several hundred cross-country skiers celebrated the Centennial year by skiing 100 miles (160 km) from Montréal to Ottawa. Their 3-day expedition has since evolved into the Canadian Ski Marathon, the longest ski event in N America. The CSM has become a 2-day tour annually attracting almost 3000 skiers from Canada, the US and as many as 10 foreign countries. The course runs from Lachute, Qué, through the forests and farms of the Outaouais region to finish in the National Capital Region at the climax of the "Winterlude" festival in mid-Feb. Its many categories cater to skiers of all ages and abilities, from 4-year-olds skiing 10 miles (16 km) a day to Gold Coureur de Bois carrying 10 kg packs over the entire distance and camping out overnight. The marathon is organized by a small office staff and approximately 600 volunteers. MURRAY SHAW

Canadian Studies The use of the phrase "Canadian studies" to designate a distinctive interdisciplinary approach to research and teaching about Canada owes much to the evolution of Canadian NATIONALISM in the 1960s and 1970s. In 1968, inspired by the Centennial celebrations, A.B. Hodgetts published *What Culture? What Heritage?* Hodgetts examined the teaching of Canada in hundreds of schools and concluded, "We are teaching a bland, unrealistic consensus version of our past; a dry-as-dust chronological story of uninterrupted political and economic progress told without the controversy that is an inherent part of history." This analysis was followed in 1969 by a report – *The Struggle for Canadian Universities*, by R. Mathews and J. Steele – on the large numbers of non-Canadians teaching in the country's universities, and in 1972 by a decision of the Association of Universities and Colleges of Canada (AUCC) to commission T.H.B. SYMONS to "study, report, and make recommendations upon the state of teaching and research in various fields of study relating to Canada." The Symons Report, *To Know Ourselves*, released in 1976, advocated a wide variety of activities in universities and within government agencies, professional associations and private and public organizations. Symons's initial study was followed by changes at all educational levels, by new government programs, and by numerous further studies, commissions and reports. Hodgetts, Symons and others raised issues concerning not only education, but also the BOOK PUBLISHING industry, science and technology, archives, international relations, etc.

The public debate over the concept of a "Canadian identity" had its most dramatic impact on education, however, and contributed to the creation of several new agencies and organizations devoted to the promotion of "Canadian studies." In 1970 the CANADA STUDIES FOUNDATION, an independent, nonprofit organization, was created with the support of the Ontario Institute for Studies in Education to suggest ways of improving the quality of Canadian studies in the country's elementary and secondary schools. Among its many achievements was the publication in 1978 of a design for curriculum entitled *Teaching Canada for the 80's*. The CSF, faced with declining public funding and little outside support, closed down in 1986. At the college level, similar initiatives were undertaken in the early 1970s by the Association of Canadian Community Colleges through a Canadian Studies Project. Funded at first by the Kellogg Foundation and later by the federal government, this project was established to increase the level of Canadian content in COMMUNITY COLLEGE courses and to increase the number of interdisciplinary programs. Through CURRICULUM DEVELOPMENT grants, travel awards for students, faculty and administrators, and through publications and other initiatives, this project achieved considerable success. At the university level, faculty interested in Canadian studies created, in the 1970s, the ASSOCIATION FOR CANADIAN STUDIES, an interdisciplinary organization devoted to encouraging teaching, publication and research about Canada at the post-secondary level through various national and regional programs (by 1987, more than 35 Canadian universities offered various Canadian studies programs). It also directed some of its programs and publications to the general public, including a newsletter, published quarterly. By 1987, ACS had over 600 members, and offices in Ottawa and Montréal.

In 1981 the INTERNATIONAL COUNCIL FOR CANADIAN STUDIES (ICCS) was formed, partly to provide a means of exchanging information among a growing number of national or multinational associations for Canadian studies abroad. By 1987 its membership included the Association for Canadian Studies (in Canada), the British Association for Canadian Studies, the Association for Canadian Studies in the US, the Association for Canadian Studies in German-Speaking Countries, the Japanese Association for Canadian Studies, the Australian and New Zealand Association for Canadian Studies, the Association of Canadian Studies in Ireland, the French Association for Canadian Studies, the Italian Association for Canadian Studies, and the Nordic Association for Canadian Studies. The ICCS also has affiliate members, eg, Canadian studies centres in Thailand, Belgium, Israel and India.

Financial support for Canadian studies in Canada and abroad comes from a variety of sources, including membership fees, foundations (private and public), granting agencies, and, most notably, from the federal Department of External Affairs and the secretary of state. By the mid-1980s, however, formal interest in Canadian studies by government funding agencies was beginning to wane. In the period 1981-84, for example, the National Program of Support for Canadian Studies of the secretary of state had provided $3.8 million to aid major organizations in the field and some 60 independent projects across Canada. In the period 1984-87, the secretary of state for Canada had announced approval to spend $11.7 million to support Canadian studies. In Nov 1985, however, a Task Force on Program Review, in reporting to the federal Conservative government, recommended that the Canadian Studies Program should be abolished. While the program was funded in 1986 and 1987, its future is still uncertain.

Formal Canadian studies has made great strides during the past 2 decades. When Professor Symons (in collaboration with J.E. Page) published the third and final volume of his report on Canadian studies in 1984, it could be reported that much had happened in the preceding decade, both in the creation or expansion of teaching programs and in the research, publication, collection and preservation of Canadian materials. The challenge for formal Canadian studies in the future will be to discover new and innovative approaches to financing Canadian studies programs. Accordingly many university and academic organizations have begun to approach the private sector for support. *See also* CULTURAL POLICY. S. McMULLIN

Reading: Directory to Canadian/Québec Regional Studies in Canada (1984).

Canadian Tax Foundation, a nonprofit research and publishing organization that sponsors studies and conferences on taxation and public-finance issues. Founded in 1945 and headquartered in Toronto, it was instituted (but not supported) by the Canadian Bar Association and the Canadian Institute of Chartered Accountants. Many members of these 2 organizations are also members of the foundation. Corporations and other individuals may also become members. In addition to a wide range of special studies, the foundation publishes annually *The National Finances*, a review of federal spending and revenues, and *The Conference Report*, a collection of the papers delivered at its annual national conference. It also publishes the *Canadian Tax Journal* and *Provincial and Municipal Finances*. DAVID CRANE

Canadian Tire Corporation Limited, with headquarters in Toronto, is a wholesaler and merchandiser of automotive products. It started in Sept 1922 as the Hamilton Garage and Rubber Company, founded by brothers John W. and Alfred J. Billes. The brothers capitalized on the growing auto trade, mailing a merchandise price list to every car owner in the province. They named their company Canadian Tire Corp Ltd in 1927. CTC was one of the first companies to introduce the concept of the dealer-owner, who would own his store and purchase merchandise from the parent. By 1940 there were 105 stores. In the 1950s the stores pioneered one-stop car-servicing and premium coupons. Today, Canadian Tire is represented in all provinces, and 91 gas stations operate through a subsidiary. In 1981 the company purchased most of the merchandise and assets of White Stores Inc of Texas, in an attempt to break into the US market. By the time it sold the chain in 1986, it had lost over $300 million. In 1986 it had sales of $2.3 billion and assets of $1.3

billion. J.W. Billes died in 1956, leaving his shares to 23 charities. In 1986-87 ownership of the company was contested as A.J. Billes's children unsuccessfully attempted to sell the company.

Canadian Transport Commission, established 19 Sept 1967 pursuant to the National Transportation Act to co-ordinate and harmonize the operation of all carriers engaged in transport, as well as to undertake programs of study and research towards the development of a national TRANSPORTATION policy. It replaced the Board of Transport Commissioners, the Air Transport Board and the Canadian Maritime Commission. Committees existed for air, rail and commodity pipeline; for extraprovincial transport of the CN-operated bus service in Newfoundland; for reviews and appeals and for consideration of international transport policy. A traffic and tariff branch monitored transport tolls and tariffs under a number of statutes. The Commission regulated fares and competition of commercial air carriers and approved their schedule integration. The Commission was disbanded in 1987 and a new organization, the National Transportation Agency of Canada, was scheduled to assume its duties.

Canadian Travellers Abroad When Hugh Allan and Samuel Cunard's steamship lines began to cross the Atlantic regularly in the 1850s, Canadians – who also took advantage of Thomas Cook's organized tours and of reduced return fares – began to travel abroad in increasing numbers. With few exceptions, travel abroad in the 19th century meant, above all, travel to Europe, following the traditional routes through Great Britain, France, Italy, Switzerland, the Rhine Valley and the Lowlands, with some travellers venturing off the beaten track into Spain, eastern Europe or Scandinavia. Mostly a prerogative of the elite, who mingled with the fashionable set in the new grand hotels, attended theatre and opera performances, consulted eminent physicians, or sent their offspring on a *grand tour*, travel was also accessible to those whose expenses were covered by their employers: clergymen frequented the sermons of the great London preachers to derive inspiration for their own work at home; educators visited schools and libraries, attended conferences and shopped for scientific apparatus, plaster casts and copied paintings; and journalists were dispatched to cover special events or simply report on the as-yet novel experience of transatlantic travel. Written travel records, both published and unpublished, survive in great numbers. They are important cultural documents which not only chart the intimate connections between Canadian and European culture but also chronicle a greater awareness of the world at large and a dawning sense of independent identity.

From early writings onwards, such as Joseph HOWE's letters to the *Novascotian* on the occasion of his journey to Queen Victoria's coronation in 1838, to Caniff Haight's *Here and There in the Homeland: England, Scotland and Ireland, as Seen by a Canadian* (1895), republished in 1904 as *A United Empire Loyalist in Great Britain*, travel to Britain was frequently understood in the sense of both a family reunion and a religious pilgrimage. "I would have every colonist look to Old England as the Hindoo to his Ganges," Moses Harvey, famous expert on Newfoundland's history and resources, wrote in 1871 in one of his many travel essays for the periodical press, and he advocated travel as a means to nurture "that reverential attachment that most resembles the love of child for parent." In a similar vein, Sir Sandford FLEMING, in *England and Canada: A Summer Tour Between Old and New Westminster* (1884), celebrated developments in transport as equalling the discovery of America, the Gutenberg Bible and the Reforma-

tion in importance, a view shared in J.J. Miller's *Vancouver to the Coronation: A Four Months' Holiday Trip* (1912). Other tourists began to criticize such unconditional devotion. The Scottish-born, Montréal schoolteacher Andrew Spedon lamented Canada's self-representation as that of "an affrighted child ... crouching behind the forest shadows of the savage age," when he described his country's exhibit at the 1867 Paris exposition in *Sketches of a Tour from Canada to Paris, by Way of the British Isles, During the Summer of 1867* (1868). A dissenting voice also emerges from the highly popular writing of Kathleen "Kit" Coleman, a native of Ireland whose enthusiastic letters to the *Mail and Empire* on the occasion of the Diamond Jubilee, and later collected in *To London for the Jubilee* (1897), gently criticized imperialist self-display in times of social duress. Shunning the conventional routes and sights, Grace E. Denison travelled through the Continent before she began her column as "Lady Gay" in *Saturday Night*, airing her feminist views before recalcitrant Europeans and recording her impressions in *A Happy Holiday* (1890).

Less concerned with social reform, their colleague Alice Jones of *The Week* and other contributors to that periodical wrote impressionist vignettes inspired by Ruskin, Pater, Browning and James, thus modifying literary pilgrimages such as the school principal James Elgin Wetherell's earnest visits to the "Land of Burns," Walter Scott country, Stratford-upon-Avon and "Tennyson Land" described in *Over the Sea: A Summer Trip to England* (1892). *The Week* documented Canadian responses to fin-de-siècle aestheticism, which contrast strongly with the attitudes of clergymen such as William Withrow and Hugh Johnston who, in *A Canadian in Europe* (1881) and *Toward the Sunrise: Being Sketches of Travel in Europe and the East* (1881), respectively, gave vent to their Methodist displeasure at the sensual statuary of the Roman Catholic Church, "the livid Christs stained with gore."

Views of the natives of the countries visited rarely transcended clichés and caricatures, and descriptions such as Thomas Stinson Jarvis's *Letters from East Longitudes* (1875), about his expedition to the Holy Land, or Chester Glass's *The World: Round It and Over It* (1881), anticipate some of the difficulties Canada was to face as a multicultural society. Canadians had to defend themselves against stereotyping as well when they were treated as colonial ingénus or mistaken for Americans, an experience that gave rise to Sara Jeannette DUNCAN's many semi-fictional parodies of contemporary travel reports such as *A Social Departure: How Orthodocia and I Went Around the World By Ourselves* (1890) and *A Voyage of Consolation* (1898). After the 1890s, travel literature began to deteriorate as photographic albums made detailed descriptions superfluous. More importantly, the 2 world wars brought significant changes: a mainstay of the periodical press so far, travel writing about Europe was now, for practical or patriotic reasons, largely replaced by essays about Canada's own tourist attractions, particularly the Prairies and BC. Writings about foreign places in the *Canadian Magazine*, *Maclean's* or *Saturday Night* now tended toward analysis of wartime effort and morale or hostile caricature, depending on the country covered, or else were nostalgic escapism. Postwar travel writings, such as Charles Lanphier's *Our Trip to Rome* (1953) and C.H. Blakeny's *"Fragments": Impressions of Holland, Belgium, Germany, Austria, Luxembourg, France, Italy, Scotland and England* (1956), inferior descendants of the Victorian travel book, often seem like ghoulish pilgrimages through the ruins of previously admired civilizations. However, a new generation of travel writers appears to have

emerged, blending the observant impressionism and astute journalism of earlier writings and widening their scope to include the world: among them are Charles RITCHIE, George WOODCOCK, Bharati MUKHERJEE, Clark BLAISE, Gwendolyn MACEWEN and others. EVA-MARIE KRÖLLER

Reading: Eva-Marie Kröller, *Canadian Travellers in Europe, 1851-1900* (1987); Kildare Dobbs, *Away from Home: Canadian Writers in Exotic Places* (1985).

Canadian Union of Public Employees, fd 1963 with 86 000 members, a merger of the National Union of Public Employees and the National Union of Public Service Employees. CUPE members are employed mainly in municipal and provincial governments, and in schools, universities, hospitals, nursing homes, electrical utilities, libraries, social service agencies, broadcasting and airlines. CUPE's main function has been to bargain collectively for improved working conditions and to press for progressive labour and social legislation. It is Canada's largest labour union with 330 000 members (1986), of whom 50% are women. GILBERT LEVINE

Canadian Unity, Task Force on, est 1977 by the federal government in response to the election of a sovereignty-oriented Québec government. It was co-chaired by Jean-Luc PEPIN, former federal Liberal minister, and John ROBARTS, former Conservative premier of Ontario. Its purpose was to gather opinions about the problems of unity in the country, to publicize efforts being made to solve those problems and to advise the government on how to strengthen national unity. In its report (1979) it recommended that language rights be left to provincial jurisdiction rather than being entrenched in the CONSTITUTION (contrary to federal Liberal government strategy from 1969-79); that federal power be reduced (except in the area of economic management); that changes be made in the federal election system to introduce some proportional representation; that the Senate be replaced with a Council of the Federation appointed by provincial governments; and that the provinces be given power to rule on federal appointments to the Supreme Court of Canada and certain major regulatory bodies. The Québec delegation alone invoked these recommendations during the 1980 constitutional discussions. The report stirred much discussion and its recommendations were given serious attention before the constitutional developments. However, the accord reached between the federal government and the other 9 provinces (1981) revealed how little influence the task force had ultimately had. R. HUDON

Canadian Wheat Board, established in 1935 as an AGRICULTURAL MARKETING BOARD charged with the orderly marketing of western grains. The CWB is the sole marketing agency for prairie WHEAT, BARLEY and OATS destined for export or for human consumption in Canada. Throughout its history the CWB has been a major agent of government policy for western grains. Temporary forerunners of the board operated from 1917 to 1920. The CWB was established as a voluntary marketing agency for prairie wheat, but the sale of wheat through the board became compulsory in 1943 and, in 1949, CWB powers were extended to include prairie oats and barley. The CWB administers the government-guaranteed initial prices paid to producers and operates a system of annual averaging (pooling) of producers' prices. It regulates producers' deliveries of major prairie grains from country elevators to export ports. The board generally does not own or operate physical marketing facilities but uses various GRAIN HANDLING AND MARKETING companies as agents to buy, handle and, sometimes, sell grain on its behalf.

The board directly sells export grain; many of its sales are made to state trading agencies of importing countries (eg, sales to the USSR and the People's Republic of China). It also sells to international grain companies. Following changes in feed-grain policy in 1974 and 1976, the CWB no longer holds exclusive marketing rights over interprovincial sale of prairie grain fed to animals in Canada, but acts as a residual supplier of feed grains to the domestic market. The CWB is a self-financing CROWN CORPORATION with 3-5 federally appointed commissioners and an 11-member advisory committee elected by prairie grain farmers. Board headquarters are in Winnipeg.

M.M. AND T.S. VEEMAN

Canadian Wildlife Federation, national, nonprofit, nongovernmental CONSERVATION organization founded in 1961 and chartered in 1962. CWF was created to promote an understanding of Canada's wildlife resources and ensure that stocks of all species would be preserved for the use and enjoyment of all Canadians. Originally, membership included the 10 provincial wildlife federations; in the early 1970s, individual Canadians were allowed to become direct members. CWF now represents over 500 000 members and supporters across Canada and has a wildlife affiliate in the YT. The federation is affiliated with the International Bird Preservation Society and is a voting member of the International Union for the Conservation of Nature and Natural Resources and the Committee on the Status of Endangered Wildlife in Canada. It is administered by a 40-member voluntary board of directors, elected at each annual convention. Staff, located at CWF offices in Ottawa, carry out policies and directives established by the board. Resource-action programs range from studying long-term environmental implications of development projects to recommending legislative changes to protect wildlife resources and their habitat (including ENDANGERED species and migratory species). The federation conducts public-education campaigns and sponsors research to heighten public awareness. Schoolteachers receive posters, classroom lessons, manuals, etc, during National Wildlife Week and throughout the year. Resource materials, career guidance, scholarships, awards and financial-assistance information are available for students. The federation has received various awards, including the Ernest Thompson Seton Award of the International Association of Fish and Wildlife Agencies, for outstanding contributions to conservation education in Canada.

LUBA MYCIO

Canadian Wildlife Service In 1917 the Migratory Birds Convention Act gave the federal government responsibility for protecting and managing migratory birds in Canada. In 1947 the small unit within the Department of the Interior given responsibility for this area was expanded into the Canadian Wildlife Service. The CWS is now part of Environment Canada. In consultation with provincial wildlife agencies, it recommends and helps enforce annual revisions of hunting regulations. Over 40 national wildlife areas have been established under the Canada Wildlife Act to protect wildlife habitat and over 80 nesting areas for migratory birds have been declared sanctuaries. CWS conducts surveys of waterfowl hunters and studies crop damage and waterfowl populations and habitat conditions in western Canada. CWS headquarters in Ottawa keeps continental bird-banding records and controls activities of banders. Other areas where the CWS is active include the following: in the North, studies of caribou and polar bear populations; research into the impacts of the long-range transport of air pollutants (ACID RAIN) on wildlife; along the coastal waters studies

into seabird and shorebird numbers and distributions. Special attention is given to species greatly reduced in number or in danger of extinction, such as the WHOOPING CRANE. CWS is responsible in Canada for the administration of the Convention on International Trade in Endangered Species. In 1987-88 the budget of CWS was $23.4 million and it employed a staff of 306.

Canadian Women's Army Corps, est 13 Aug 1941 to answer the Canadian Army's need for manpower and the demand of volunteer women's paramilitary groups to render official uniformed service. Except for nursing sisters, women had not previously been admitted into the Canadian ARMED FORCES. CWAC was separate from and supplementary to the Canadian Militia until 1 Mar 1942, when it became an integral part of the defence forces. CWAC officers thereafter could hold commissions and use military titles and badges. Initially the army needed women in uniform as clerks. All occupations open to CWAC women were noncombatant, although their diversity and number increased to include technical trades. Nonetheless, in 1945 as in 1941, the clerk or secretary in uniform was the typical CWAC. In 1941 basic pay was set at two-thirds that of servicemen of equivalent rank. Trades pay was substantially lower than that for servicemen, and servicewomen could not claim dependants' allowances. These inequalities were cause for complaint from both uniformed and civilian women. In July 1943 the government raised basic pay to four-fifths that of men of the same rank, equalized trades pay and granted allowances for dependent parents and siblings, but not for dependent husbands or children. Although inequalities remained, the services were ahead of most private industry in narrowing the gap between men's and women's pay and benefits.

A 1943 public opinion survey revealed that only 7% of Canadians regarded joining the women's forces as the best way for women to serve Canada's war effort. This attitude accompanied widespread resistance to the breaking down of sexual divisions of labour and authority. Braving the opposition, 21 624 women served in CWAC before its dissolution in 1946. Almost 3000 were stationed in the UK; starting May 1944, select groups of these were dispatched to operational areas in Europe to serve as support staff for Canadian invasion forces. When Germany surrendered in May 1945, the CWAC constituted 2.8% of the total strength of the Canadian Army. Col Margaret Eaton headed the corps Apr 1944-Oct 1945 in the position of Director General, CWAC. Thereafter, this position was gradually downgraded in preparation for the disbanding of the corps. Servicemen as well as women proposed inclusion of women's corps in postwar RESERVE FORCES, but Cabinet did not give approval. Only in 1951, during the KOREAN WAR, was the decision taken to enlist women again in the regular forces.

RUTH ROACH PIERSON

Canadian Women's Press Club was founded in June 1904 in a CPR pullman car when 13 Canadian women journalists were returning home after covering the St Louis World's Fair. The first president was Kathleen "Kit" Blake Coleman of the Toronto *Mail and Empire,* one of the first female war correspondents covering the Spanish-American War. Other early members were Nellie MCCLUNG, Emily MURPHY and Helen MCGILL, who campaigned successfully for women's enfranchisement, had careers in politics and law, and used JOURNALISM as a means of promoting social reform to gain legal rights for women and children.

The CWPC included novelists, short-story writers, newspaper and magazine editors, re-

porters, playwrights, poets, historians and freelancers in print, radio, television and film. In June 1971 members voted to change the name to the Media Club of Canada, to permit membership by any qualified person active in media communications. The Media Club is an independent national corporation with a head office in Ottawa.

DONNA JAMES

Canals and Inland Waterways Canada is unique in having almost 800 000 km² of freshwater within its boundaries. The lakes which make up most of this vast area are interconnected by river systems. The Mackenzie R, draining an area of 1 870 000 km², is the seventh-largest river system of the world. Better known is the St Lawrence R-Great Lakes Waterway extending halfway across the continent. Using Canada's inland waterways, it is possible to travel on water, by canoe, from tide water near Québec to the Arctic coast in the far northwest, and even across the mountains to the Pacific coast. These 2 great journeys were first made just before the end of the 18th century, and by the same man. Alexander MACKENZIE reached the mouth of the river which now bears his name in 1789, and was the first European to cross the N American continent (to Bella Coola) in 1793. He was one of the almost legendary fur trader-explorers of those days. Banded together in the North West Company, these men, with Indian and Métis guides and translators, pioneered the exploration of the main water routes of the West and the Mid-West. One of the barriers they had to pass was the rough water of the St Marys R as it leaves Lk Superior. Here the NWC constructed one of the first navigation locks in Canada (1819), a small affair indeed, as were the even earlier tiny locks at rapids in the Soulanges section of the St Lawrence, started by the Royal Engineers (1779) under the direction of Governor Haldimand. With a depth over sills of less than 0.5 m, these primitive locks were the beginnings of Canada's notable group of canals, some still in use in their original form, others enlarged and improved (*see* FUR TRADE ROUTES).

The Lachine Canal, bypassing the rapids on the St Lawrence upstream from Montréal, was the first real canal to be finished, built between 1821 and 1825. Planned by Montréal merchants, it required substantial investment of public funds before completion. The other canals of this early period, the 3 Ottawa R canals (1819-34) and the RIDEAU CANAL (1826-32), were planned and built to provide an alternative military waterway between Montréal and Kingston, following the War of 1812. They were therefore paid for by government, even though they were used for commerce rather than military traffic. The Ottawa R canals were in use until 1961 when they were submerged by the Carillon hydroelectric dam of Hydro-Québec. Navigation remains possible via a new lock adjacent to the Carillon powerhouse. The Rideau Canal is still in regular use, essentially as built over 150 years ago. Rapids on the Richelieu R, upstream from St-Jean, Qué, were bypassed by the Chambly Canal (1833-43). With a lock at St-Ours, near Sorel, vessels had access from the St Lawrence to Lk Champlain and so to the Champlain Canal (US) and the Hudson R. But the narrow locks on the Chambly Canal (only 7.1 m wide) were, and still are, a bottleneck in this international waterway.

Great plans for canals were developed in the Maritime provinces. The Shubenacadie Canal, linking Halifax with the Bay of Fundy, was started in 1826 but completed only in 1861, being lightly used for a mere 10 years. The little St Peter's Canal, linking Bras d'Or Lake with the ocean, was built between 1854 and 1869; enlarged, it is still in use. The greatest dream of all, from as early as

Lachine Canal, from *Life of Lord Sydenham* (1843). The Lachine Canal, bypassing the St Lawrence rapids upstream from Montréal, was the first real canal built in Canada, 1821-25 (*courtesy National Archives of Canada/C-5955*).

1686, was for a canal across the Isthmus of Chignecto. Studied more than any other canal project in Canada, it has not yet been built, although a massive marine railway, as an alternative, was started in 1882, only to be abandoned in 1891 before completion.

All of these early canals, as well as the TRENT CANAL system, which follows old Indian routes through the Kawartha Lakes, were intended to facilitate the movement of small steamboats. The Chambly Canal and the Grenville Canal (one of the Ottawa R canals) were alone in their resemblance to the familiar canals of Europe with towpaths for horse-haulage of barges. In the second half of the 19th century, as the population of Canada became more mobile, and in the absence of improved roads, steamboat services proliferated on all the country's major rivers and lakes. For many years, Sir John A. Macdonald had a cabin reserved on the fine daily boat service between Ottawa and Montréal. Some of the services lasted well into the 20th century. The Montréal-Québec-Saguenay service, for example, stopped in 1965; that on the Mackenzie R still operates, although now with diesel-powered vessels.

The greatest success in the improvement of Canada's waterways has been the development of the St Lawrence R into the ST LAWRENCE SEAWAY of today. The Lachine Canal (1825) was the real start, closely followed by the completion in 1829 of the first WELLAND CANAL. Forty small timber locks were required to raise vessels the 100 m from Lk Ontario to Lk Erie, most of them necessary for the steep climb up the Niagara escarpment. Initially built with private funds, the Welland Canal was later taken over by government (as was the Lachine Canal). In effect, all improvements to the waterways of Canada have been publicly financed, and the facilities operated by government. The Welland Canal was rebuilt (1845) with larger locks, now of masonry, as one of the first major operations of the new Board of Works of the United Province of Canada. The Board also completed the several small canals necessary for overcoming the rapids on the St Lawrence between Lk St Louis and Lk Ontario – the Beauharnois (later Soulanges), Cornwall and Williamsburg canals. Only at mid-century was this group of canals complete and in regular use. From 1834 to 1850 the Ottawa R canals and the Rideau Canal, with the rivers they served, constituted the Seaway.

Following Confederation in 1867, inland transportation in Canada was given high priority by the new government. The 1870s and 1880s were years of active canal rebuilding and improvement. The bottleneck locks on the Grenville, the third of the Ottawa R canals, were finally rebuilt; a new Carillon Canal replaced the original canal and the Chute à Blondeau single-lock canal. All the locks on the Lachine and St Lawrence R canals were rebuilt in this period to standard dimensions, each 84 m long and 14 m wide with a depth over sills of 4.2 m (14 feet). The third Welland Canal, a major rebuilding of the second, was finished by 1887. To serve the new St Lawrence system, a fleet of almost 200 stubby, inelegant but efficient freight steamers was gradually developed, achieving fame as "the fourteen-footers" and serving faithfully for 75 years.

After 1909, control of the St Lawrence R came under the INTERNATIONAL JOINT COMMISSION, a Canadian-US tribunal. Discussion of a much enlarged canal system intensified almost immediately. The Ottawa R provided a 483 km shorter route for a seaway to the Great Lakes, but the general election of 1911 put an end to the dream of the Georgian Bay Ship Canal. Construction of the fourth Welland Canal, as part of the alternative St Lawrence route, started in 1913. A wholly Canadian venture, this world-famous canal, with only 8 locks, was officially opened in 1932. Its locks, 260 m long by 24 m wide, enabled a fleet of "upper lakers" to be developed for bulk freight service; they later dictated the size of the St Lawrence Seaway locks when the Seaway was built (1954-59) (*see* LAKE CARRIERS).

Today, the St Lawrence Seaway, incorporating the fourth Welland Canal, is one of the few great ship canals of the world, carrying freight from and to the rest of the world and to and from the heart of the N American continent. The great passenger ship services of earlier years have almost all disappeared, their place now taken (especially on the smaller canals) by ubiquitous private pleasure craft. Once away from these main routes, the lakes and streams remain as one of the delights of Canada. Still used today as they have been for centuries, they illustrate how appropriate the designation "Dominion" is for Canada – "from sea to sea, and from the river unto the ends of the Earth." R.F. LEGGET

Reading: R.F. Legget, Canals of Canada (1976).

Cancer is a term describing more than 100 different diseases characterized by the common property of abnormal cell growth. Cancer is the second leading cause of death in Canada and second only to accidents as a cause of death in children under 15 years of age. With no change in our current methods of prevention, diagnosis and treatment, one of every 3 N American babies born in 1985 will eventually develop some form of cancer during their lifetime. Slightly more men are cancer victims. One of 4 men and one of 5 women will die of cancer, half of these under age 65.

Some cancers (for instance, lung cancer) have become more common since the 1940s; some (eg, breast cancer in women) have maintained a steady incidence; and others (for instance, cancers of the stomach and uterus, of the bladder and rectum in women) have become less frequent. Lung cancer is the leading cause of death among all cancer patients. Because of SMOKING, its incidence is rising rapidly in young women and may soon exceed that of breast cancer. Cancer of the bowel and rectum is the second leading cause of death from cancer; breast cancer is the third leading cause of cancer deaths and the most common cause in women. In order of mortality rates, other forms of cancers are prostatic, uterine, urologic, oral and pancreatic, followed by leukemia and cancers of the ovary and skin (skin cancer is actually the most common cancer by incidence, but the usual forms are readily treatable and are not fatal).

Causes of Cancer The body is made of billions of different types of cells which normally multiply at a rate just sufficient to compensate for cell losses. When they multiply uncontrollably a tumour (also called a neoplasm) results. There are 2 basic tumour types. *Benign* are those in which cells multiply but remain tightly together; adjacent tissues often develop a fibrous tissue ("capsule") between themselves and the tumour. Benign tumours can be treated successfully by surgery. Malignant tumours can be *locally invasive*, ie, cells spread into adjacent tissues by sending out finger-like probes. These potentially damaging tumours are often on the skin and can therefore often be treated successfully with surgery or radiation. Malignant tumours can also be *metastatic*. These tumours are the most devastating, because they "seed" themselves via the blood and other body fluids. These seeds, or metastases, create a new tumour. It was once believed that seeding occurred only when a tumour had reached a certain size, and that if the tumour could be eliminated before it reached this size, it could be cured. Unfortunately, it is now known that metastatic tumours may seed long before they are detected.

The basis of malignant transformation remains unknown, but the recent discovery of oncogenes (cancer genes) is an important development in understanding cancer. In their inactive form these widespread genes are part of the normal genetic complement. Their structure has been carefully conserved during evolution, indicating that they have an important function in aiding the growth of normal cells. They may be activated and transformed by specific viruses, or through minor mutations which may be induced by radiation and some kinds of chemicals. They can also be activated by duplication into multiple copies, or by being transported to different chromosomes. Multiple (at least 2) genetic events appear to be needed for transformation (*see* GENETICS; VIRUS). Oncogenes appear to code for a number of small molecules called growth factors. These substances play a key role in directing the growth and differentiation of normal cells. As oncogene products they provide abnormal growth stimulation; thus cancer can be thought of as a disorder of cellular growth and development.

Although the cause of human cancer cannot yet be explained fully at the molecular level, epidemiological studies have revealed the practical clinical significance of environmental hazards, social habits and genetic factors. Because of the prolonged period generally required for the development of cancer, it is difficult to analyse the exact roles of such factors, but some 80% of all human cancers are now thought to be related in some way to environmental factors and to be preventable. Two-thirds are preventable alone by not smoking and by dietary modifications. Hundreds of chemicals including those used in foods as additives and preservatives have been implicated, as have various drugs and radiation. About 40% of all cancers are thought to be related directly or indirectly to cigarette smoking. Viruses produce cancer in several animal species, including mammals, chickens, fish and frogs, but cause only about 5% of human cancers.

Clinical Manifestations of Cancer Particularly for the more common cancers, early detection and diagnosis are important for cure and prolonged survival. The Papanicolaou (Pap) smear has reduced the incidence and mortality of invasive cervical cancer. The National Cancer Institute of Canada (which along with the Medical Research Council funds cancer research in Canada), in co-operation with cancer agencies across Canada, is studying the effectiveness of screening programs for breast cancer using breast self-examination and mammography (over 90% of new breast cancers are discovered each year by patients). The "7 early-warning signals of cancer" (American Cancer Society) are designed to encourage people to seek medical help for the early detection of cancers of the skin, breast, larynx, lung and genitourinary and gastrointestinal tracts. The signals are change in bowel or bladder habits; a sore that does not heal; unusual bleeding or discharge; a thickening or a lump in the breast or elsewhere; indigestion or difficulty in swallowing; obvious change in a wart or mole; and nagging cough or hoarseness. Since cancer can affect any tissue and any bodily part, its clinical manifestations are very diverse and may often be silent for a long period before detection. Examination of tissues or cells by the pathologist remains the essential method of diagnosis.

Principles of Therapy In treating cancer it is assumed that all malignant cells should be destroyed, removed or neutralized. It is not known, however, whether successful treatment must eradicate all malignant cells or merely reduce the cell number to a level where the patient's own defences can gain control. Five kinds of therapy exist today: surgery, radiotherapy, hormone therapy, chemotherapy and immunotherapy. Because cancer is not one but many different diseases, a combination of therapies is sometimes needed and will differ widely for each type of tumour. For solid tumours, surgery and radiotherapy are used to treat the local disease. Metastatic disease requires a systemic therapy such as chemotherapy (use of anti-cancer drugs) which may be used initially or for secondary treatment. With malignancies involving the blood, chemotherapy may be the initial treatment. Chemotherapy often dramatically reduces the size of the tumour. Over 30 drugs, which may be used singly or in various combinations, exist for the chemical management of cancer. Their mechanisms of action on the cancer cell are varied. Although their selective action is on tumour cells, normal tissues which are rapidly growing may also be damaged, leading to side effects such as reduced circulatory blood cells, loss of hair and bowel upset.

Tumours arising from the breast, prostate and uterine lining may respond to hormonal therapy. Certain hormones (eg, estrogens) may act by binding to specific receptors in the tumour cell. Breast and prostate cancers may be treated by removing sources of circulating hormones that could stimulate or support tumour growth or by the administration of estrogens, androgens, progesterones, glucocorticoids or various pituitary peptides to suppress tumour growth. The use of immunotherapy as an adjuvant to surgery, chemotherapy and radiotherapy can control only small numbers of cells, and it is still used experimentally. There is great interest currently in the use of biologicals such as interferons or interleukins for cancer therapy. These are substances produced by cells of the immune system, and have been made available to investigators as a re-

sult of recent advances in genetic engineering. They may be used alone or in combination with immune cells (LAK or lymphokine activated killer cells) from the patient which have been activated in the laboratory and then readministered. Monoclonal antibodies are also products of immune cells which are being studied for use in diagnosis, imaging and therapy of cancer. Surgical excision is still the current principal curative therapy, especially for those cancers that can be diagnosed early and removed completely. The surgeon is limited by the location and extent of the tumour rather than by its type.

Ionizing radiations of various types and energies are also used to destroy localized populations of cancer cells. As with surgery, results are best with relatively small tumours detected before they are locally or systemically widespread. The tolerance of adjacent normal tissues limits the amount of radiation that can be given. Although exact mechanisms are undefined, radiation appears to kill cells by interfering with their genetic apparatus through ionization of water molecules. Cobalt irradiation units and more recently computerized linear (electron) accelerators are being used, and research is being conducted on neutrons and atomic particles. Drugs are sometimes used to sensitize tumour tissues to radiation. Patients are generally informed of both the benefits and hazards of treatment.

Cancer Services During the past decade cancer services have been organized into regional comprehensive cancer centres in which are integrated the sophisticated technology needed for diagnosis and treatment, educational and consultative resources to surrounding communities, and clinical and basic research programs. In some provinces, including BC, Alberta, Saskatchewan, Manitoba, Ontario and the Maritimes, cancer services are centrally organized and in many provinces registration of cancer patients is mandatory.

Cancer patients are managed largely as outpatients, often even in the terminal phase of illness. The early referral of cancer patients for multidisciplinary assessment by specialists is important; often the only chance for cure is the first attempt at treatment.

Psychosocial Aspects of Cancer Much has been written regarding the psychosocial dimensions of terminal cancer, but cancer patients who survive also face severe psychological adjustments to accepting the diagnosis of a chronic and potentially fatal disease. Life with cancer still implies social unacceptability, including fear of painful sufferings, disability, disfigurement, impaired bodily function, and loss of sexual attractiveness and self-esteem. It is commonly believed that once cancer has been diagnosed, a patient is helpless before the relentless onslaught of the disease. This misconception fuels the excessive sense of hopelessness and despair that characterizes the word "cancer." Current research is evolving a biology of host cell resistance to cancer, identifying mechanisms that are similar to those that operate to resist infections. Age, sex, immunity, hormones, nutrition, and psychological and probably other as yet undefined factors appear to influence resistance and help determine favourable or unfavourable outcomes, responses to treatment, and occasionally periods of long remission or even spontaneous regression. *See also* CANADIAN CANCER SOCIETY. L. MARTIN JERRY

Reading: Samuel S. Epstein, *Politics of Cancer* (1978); C.F. McKhann, *The Facts About Cancer* (1981).

CANDU, *see* NUCLEAR POWER PLANTS.

Caniapiscau, Rivière, *see* KOKSOAK, RIVIÈRE.

Canmore, Alta, Town, pop 4182 (1986c). In 1883 Canmore, named after King Malcolm Can-

more, Scotland, became the first divisional point for the CPR west of Calgary. The railway and the coal mines first developed in 1886 were the mainstays of the local economy. By 1891 Canmore was flourishing. The mines were, however, closed by serious labour unrest in the 1920s and were affected by failing markets in the 1930s and again in the late 1960s and early 1970s. The first Presbyterian Church in Canmore (now a provincial historic resource) was built by the Rev Charles GORDON (aka Ralph Connor). The Canmore Mines closed down their operation in 1979. Today Canmore is a growing recreation and tourism centre. The Canmore Nordic Centre, a state-of-the-art winter sports facility, was developed for the 1988 Calgary Olympics by the province of Alberta. FRITS PANNEKOEK

Canniff, William, physician, amateur historian (b at Thurlow, Upper Canada 20 June 1830; d at Belleville, Ont 18 Oct 1910). A noted doctor, medical educator, public-health advocate and Canadian nationalist, Canniff is best known as author of *History of the Settlement of Upper Canada* (1869) and *The Medical Profession in Upper Canada* (1894). Educated in Canada, the US, Great Britain and Europe, he practised surgery in Toronto and Belleville, taught pathology and surgery at Victoria Coll Medical School, and produced the first Canadian textbook in pathology (1866). He was a founding member of the Canadian Medical Assn in 1867 and the Ontario Medical Assn in 1880. He served as the president of the CMA (1880) and as Toronto's first permanent medical health officer (1883-90). As a member of the CANADA FIRST movement in the 1870s and through his historical writings, Canniff expressed his ardent Canadian nationalism.

HEATHER MacDOUGALL

Canning, NS, UP, pop 819 (1986c), 763 (1981c), located 100 km NW of Halifax. Once part of the Acadian district of Minas (Les Mines), in the 1760s Canning was resettled by New Englanders as part of Cornwallis Township. Although it was known as Apple Tree Landing and later as Habitant Corner, the residents changed the name to Canning in 1830 to honour the British PM George Canning. Situated on the Habitant R, Canning was one of the many Bay of Fundy communities to take part in the prosperous shipbuilding era of the mid-19th century. Because of its location in the Annapolis Valley agricultural region, farming has always been important to the community. Troubled by devastating fires throughout its history, Canning received national attention in 1986 when a warehouse agricultural chemical fire on the community's main street caused the evacuation of 750 residents. The disaster raised questions regarding the contamination of air, soil and water and the appropriateness of chemical storage in residential areas.

DEBRA McNABB

Cannington Manor, est 1882 when an Englishman, Capt Edward Michell Pierce, claimed 5 townships 65 km S of Whitewood, NWT (now in SE Saskatchewan), the nearest point on the CPR. Cannington was the name of an English town; "Manor" was added later to avoid confusion with an Ontario town. Knowing little about farming, Pierce nevertheless established an agricultural college for the sons of wealthy Englishmen. The "pups," as his students were known, refused to mingle with Canadian settlers. Three pups built a 26-room house which boasted a ballroom, billiard room and servants' quarters. In the ma-

hogany-lined stable each racehorse had a brass nameplate above its stall. By 1890 Cannington Manor included an Anglican church, a flour mill, hotel, smithy, carpentry shop, carriage shop and general store. But the rich English were not serious agriculturalists, playing tennis, cricket and rugby, and spending a week during harvest hunting and playing polo. Failure to adjust to life in Canada quickly brought business and farm bankruptcies. In 1901-02, when a new CPR line bypassed the village, the remaining businesses moved and Cannington Manor gradually disappeared. The site is now a provincial historic park, and a number of the original buildings have been reconstructed.   JANE MCCRACKEN

Canoe, Birchbark, principal means of water transportation of the woodlands Indians and the VOYAGEURS. Light and maneuverable, they were perfectly adapted to summer travel through the network of shallow streams, ponds, lakes and swift rivers of the Canadian SHIELD. Canoes were a necessity for the nomadic northern Indians, such as the Montagnais-Naskapi, and were used by the voyageurs in exploiting the fur country. Birchbark was an ideal material, being smooth, hard, light, resilient and waterproof. BIRCH trees were found almost everywhere across Canada, but not always in sufficient number or size – some 8 to 12 trees were required for 1 canoe – and spruce bark had to be substituted in some areas, particularly the western Subarctic. The skills required to build the canoes were passed on through generations of master builders. The joints were sewn with white pine roots, which were pulled up, split and boiled by Indian women. The frames were usually of cedar, soaked in water and bent to the shape of the canoe. The seams were made waterproof with spruce or pine resin gathered and applied with a hot stick. As the FUR TRADE grew, the Indians could no longer supply all the canoes needed, and around 1750 the French set up a factory at Trois-Rivières.

The famous *canot du maître*, on which the fur trade depended, was up to 12 m long and carried 6 to 12 crew and a load of 2300 kg over the route from Montréal to Lk Superior. The smaller *canot du nord* carried a crew of 5 or 6 and a cargo of 1360 kg over the smaller lakes, rivers and streams of the North-West. The canoes were propelled by narrow paddles with quick, continuous strokes, averaging 45 per minute. The *avant* (bowsman) carried a larger paddle for maneuvering in rapids and the *gouvernail* (helmsman) stood in the stern. A canoe could manage 7 to 9 km per hour, and a special express canoe, carrying a large crew and little freight, could achieve up to 140 km in an 18-hour day. Most of inland Canada was first explored in birchbark canoes, and they were used for inland transportation until around 1820 when they began to be replaced by boats. *See also* YORK BOATS.   JAMES MARSH

Canoe, Dugout, a common type of canoe used by Indians and early settlers wherever the size of tree growth made construction possible. Dugouts used by forest Indians were crudely constructed from softwoods – cedar, basswood, balsam, etc – using controlled burning techniques and bone and stone chipping tools. Settlers using iron tools created smoothly crafted dugouts prior to the advent of the plank-built canoe.

The dugout canoe reached its zenith of construction along the West Coast where waters, teeming with sea life – whales, seals, sea lions, salmon, halibut, herring, ouchalon and shellfish – sustained a complex, maritime culture. Although there was considerable variation in size and shape of West Coast dugouts, 2 basic designs dominated the large, 10 to 15 m, sea-going canoes. The Northern style used by TLINGIT, TSIMSHI-

The Esquimalt, by Paul Kane, depicts the Northwest Coast dugout canoes (*courtesy Royal Ontario Museum/Department of Ethnology*).

AN, BELLA COOLA and KWAKIUTL was perfected by the HAIDA of the Queen Charlotte Is. It had a rounded hull, flaring sides and a strong sheer along the gunwales rising to high stem and stern projections. The extended prow culminated in a near vertical cutwater. The intrepid Haida seamen dominated coastal trade and their canoe was the most prized object of trade with the mainland Indians. A Southern or Chinook canoe form was dictated by the Nootka of western Vancouver I. Their canoe, much in demand by Salish and Makah Indians on the mainland, was V-shaped with flared-out sides and a low, vertical stem post with a small capped platform. There was a graceful arc to the sheerline as it approached the bow, culminating in a projecting prow which resembled a deer or doglike snout. These massive ocean canoes, designed for trade, whaling and sealing, were mistakenly referred to as "war canoes" by settlers. Early maritime explorers did record their observation of authentic war canoes, up to 24 m long, with the tell-tale, protective prow which was both high and wide to shield the paddlers from enemy missiles. Such craft were quite rare by the 1860s.

The gigantic red cedar was the preferred wood used by the highly esteemed canoe builders. Drift logs were desirable but, if unavailable, trees were felled using a stone maul with bone, antler or stone chisels and controlled burning. Hand adzes were used to shape the exterior form, followed by hollowing out of the interior. Hot water was used to render the canoe pliable; wooden spreaders were then inserted between the gunwales to extend the beam of the canoe beyond the natural width of the log. High end pieces were carved separately and attached to the bow or stern using a sewing technique. Canoes were colourfully decorated with animal designs using red ochre, black char and assorted animal teeth and shells. Propulsion was achieved using leaf-shaped or lanceolated single-blade paddles and square, cedar mat sails.

West Coast dugouts all but disappeared with the advent of 20th century power boats. A specialized, Nootka-style dugout is still used by West Coast Indians for canoe racing.

C. FRED JOHNSTON

Canoeing, an aquatic activity using a small boat, sharp at both ends, paddle-propelled by one or more persons who face the direction in which the craft is heading. There are 2 types of canoe: the open, propelled by a single-blade paddle and known internationally as a "Canadian" or C-boat, and the closed (decked), with a double-blade paddle and known as a kayak or K-boat. Contemporary canoes come in a variety of shapes and materials suited to the variety of water conditions and to recreational or competitive purposes. Most popular is the open canoe used for recreation, hunting and fishing. It is about 5 m long and constructed of wood, canvas, aluminum, fibreglass or plastic. The best-known forms of competitive canoeing are sprint racing, held over 500, 1000 and 10 000 m, with various numbers of paddlers – the only canoe discipline in the Olympic program; "white water" racing with one or 2 paddlers on downriver and slalom courses; and marathon racing over lake and river water and across portages.

Contemporary canoeing has 2 distinct lines of development. One originated with the native peoples of Canada and continued with the early explorers, fur traders, lumbermen and settlers. Canoeing in open and decked canoes is an indigenous activity of Canadian Indians and Inuit, who designed an amazing variety of water craft, each suited to local materials, the physical environment and tribal customs. Principal classes are the skin boat (KAYAK), the bark boat (particularly the birchbark CANOE) and the log dugout (some up to 15 m long). European explorers, beginning with Jacques CARTIER, readily adopted the light and maneuverable birchbark canoe in place of the heavy, cumbersome rowboats from their ships. In these craft the early explorers and fur traders reached the farthest frontiers of the country. The birchbark canoe was the foundation of a supply route spanning 6500 km from Montréal to the Pacific Ocean and the Mackenzie R, and continued in use for far northern travel to the end of the 19th century. Early settlers along the water routes of central Canada used birchbark canoes for local travel, hunting and fishing. With metal tools they also constructed finely shaped dugout canoes and eventually plank canoes, still fashioned along the lines of the Indian craft. The classic open Canadian canoe – 5 m long, 81 cm beam and 30 cm deep – constructed from cedar planks and elm ribs was developed during the late 1850s along the Otonabee R near Peterborough, Ont. The manufacture of the board-and-batten open canoe, more durable and long lasting than the birch canoe, came in time to serve the needs of cottagers, hunters and fishermen. During the last 3 decades of the 19th century the canoe from the Peterborough region was exported throughout the world.

Shooting the Rapids, oil painting by Frances Ann Hopkins. The bark canoe was the means of transport of most of the native peoples, and the great *canot du maître* was the means of transport of the fur trade between Montréal and Lake Superior (*courtesy National Archives of Canada/C-2774*).

The second line of development was strongly influenced by British military personnel stationed in British N America who frequently sponsored competitive aquatic events. Rowing and sailing races were of great interest, but more spectator enthusiasm was generated by Indian canoe races, which were incorporated in regattas from the early 1800s. General boating clubs were started in such places as Kingston, Halifax, Montréal, Peterborough and Toronto. During the 1870s canoe races for gentlemen were added to aquatic events. The formation and the first regatta of the American Canoe Assn at Lake George, NY, in 1880, launched an upsurge in organized canoeing throughout N America. At the ACA's first meet in 1880, Canadian T.H. Wallace from Rice Lake, Ont, won 2 races in his open Rice Lake canoe. In response to the ACA, the Toronto Canoe Club was formed in Dec 1880, and thereafter canoe clubs emerged across the country. In 1887 all Canadian clubs banded together as the northern division of the ACA. A national association was founded at Brockville, Ont, in 1900, and that August the first Canadian championships were held there. National championships have been held annually since that time, except during WWI and WWII. In 1924 Canadian and US teams demonstrated canoe racing at the Paris Olympics and an international organization, the IRK, was founded. Since 1936, when canoeing was accepted as an Olympic sport, Canadian paddlers have fared well, especially in the Canadian canoe events. Francis AMYOT won a gold medal in the 1000 m singles in 1936 and Larry CAIN a gold and silver in the C-1 canoe at Los Angeles in 1984. In 1986 Cain went on to win golds in the 1000 m and 500 m C-1s in the Commonwealth championships.

After WWII, the infusion of Europeans to Canada helped popularize white-water canoeing. A national organization, the Canadian White Water Affiliation, was formed in 1964. In 1967 the first National Slalom and Wild Water Championships were held at the Elora Gorge, Ont. After 1945 professional long-distance paddling was popular in western Canada, Northern Ontario and Québec, but only in April 1980, at Ottawa, was an organization (Canadian Marathon Canoe Racing Assn) established to oversee long-distance racing. The CMCRA held its first national championships in Ottawa in 1981. The Canadian Recreational Canoeing Assn was founded in May 1972, and it works to develop noncompetitive programs to improve paddling skills, instruction and safety in recreational canoeing.   C. FRED JOHNSTON

Reading: E.T. Adney and H.I. Chapelle, *The Bark Canoes and Skin Boats of North America* (1964); Bill Durham, *Canoes and Kayaks of Western America* (1960); C.E.S. Franks, *The Canoe and White Water* (1977); Fred Heese, *Canoe Racing* (1979); Bill Mason, *Path of the Paddle* (1980); Wolf Ruck, *Canoeing and Kayaking* (1974).

Canol Pipeline, a 10 cm oil PIPELINE built from 1942 to 1944 from Norman Wells, NWT, 1000 km to a refinery at Whitehorse, Yukon. The American armed forces, which urged the project on a reluctant Canadian government, wanted a secure supply of oil products to fuel defence efforts in the Northwest. The refinery was to produce 3000 barrels a day. The pipeline was a fiasco, costing over 5 times its $24-million estimate, and it was plagued by shoddy workmanship. Its deficiencies, exposed by a United States Senate committee chaired by Harry Truman, embarrassed the American military. When the pipeline was abandoned in Mar 1945 after 13 months' operation, it left a festering scar across the Canadian Northwest – a "junkyard monument to military stupidity."   KENNETH S. COATES

Canola, common name for the oil, meal and seed of Canadian-developed rape plant varieties with bred-in, superior nutritional qualities. Canola plants are varieties of turnip rape (*Brassica campestris*) and rape (*B. napus*) of the Cruciferae family. TURNIPS (*B. rapa* or, more properly, *B. campestris rapifera*) are very closely related; hence, the name "rape" [from Lat *rapum*, "turnip"]. RUTABAGAS (*B. napus*), CABBAGE and CAULIFLOWER (*B. oleracea*) are also closely related. *B. campestris* originated in the foothills of the Himalayan Mountains; *B. napus* probably originated in the Mediterranean region as the result of natural crosses between *B. campestris* and *B. oleracea* plants.

Rapeseed has been an important source of edible vegetable oil in Asia for almost 4000 years. It was first grown in Canada during WWII as a source of high-quality lubricant for marine engines. After the war, Canadian plant-breeding programs, combined with changes in processing techniques, led to a reduction of erucic acid (very high consumption of which has been associated with heart lesions in laboratory animals) and glucosinolates (which cause enlarged thyroids and poor feed conversion in livestock). As a consequence, canola has become established as a major Canadian and European source of cooking oil, margarine, salad dressing and shortening. The meal remaining after oil extraction is a high-protein feed for livestock.

As with most scientific developments, the evolution of canola was a broadly co-operative venture. Early warnings of potential problems with erucic acid were given by K. Carrol and J. Beare-Rogers and provided the motivation for changing the fatty acid composition of the oil. Baldur STEFANSSON and R.K. DOWNEY jointly identified the first low erucic plants in rape (*Brassica napus*). Downey selected the first low erucic plant of turnip rape (*B. campestris*) and developed the first low erucic varieties in both species (Oro and Span). J. Krzymanski, a postdoctoral fellow from Poland, and Downey found the first low glucosinolate *B. napus* plants; Stefansson produced the first low erucic low glucosinolate variety, Tower. Downey and his colleagues bred the first low glucosinolate *B. campestris* plants and the first canola quality variety of this species, Candle. J.M. Bell and D.R. Clandinin did much of the early feeding studies to establish the nutritional superiority of canola meal; B.M. Craig, C. Youngs, and R.L. Wetter developed the analytical techniques which permitted the breeding for canola quality, and J.K.G. Kramer and F. Saurer established the nutritional superiority of the low erucic acid oil. Stefansson and Downey were both awarded the Royal Bank Award in recognition of their contributions to developing canola.

Canola is grown on some 2.6 million ha of the prairies. The winter form, popular in Europe, is grown to a limited extent in Ontario. About half of Canadian production is processed domestically; the remainder, exported as seed. Sowing and harvesting methods are similar to those of spring CEREALS. *B. napus* canola varieties mature at the same time as wheat and grow 1-1.5 m tall. Although *B. campestris* matures 10-14 days earlier than *B. napus*, less is grown because varieties have a lower potential yield. Flowers have 4 bright yellow petals and, following fertilization by wind or insects, each develops a pod with 15-40 small, round seeds (1.5-2 mm diameter) arranged in 2 rows. Mature seeds contain 40-44% oil and have thin black, brown or yellow seed coats.   R.K. DOWNEY AND B.R. STEFANSSON

Canora, Sask, Town, pop 2602 (1986c), inc 1910, is located 50 km N of Yorkton. The community was a creation of the CANADIAN NORTHERN RY which laid steel through the site in 1904. The town's name is a combination of the first 2 letters of each word in "Canadian Northern Railway." The town established itself as the trading centre for the surrounding district and has maintained this role. The district is typical parkland and is suited to mixed farming as well as providing good recreational areas to inhabitants and visitors.   DON HERPERGER

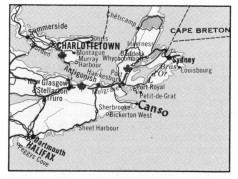

Canso, NS, Town, pop 1285 (1986c), 1255 (1981c), inc 1901, is located on Chedabucto Bay, on the NE shore of mainland NS. Its name derives from the Micmac *Kamsok* ("the place beyond the cliffs"). As early as 1604 the French used Canso as a summer fishing base. During the 1700s the settlement was destroyed several times by natives,

French-English conflicts and Revolutionary privateers. Successful settlement did not occur until 1812. Shipbuilding, trading and fishing became major industries. Between 1881 and 1894 transatlantic cables were landed here, making Canso a major communications link between N America and Europe. In 1955 the completion of the Canso Causeway, linking CAPE BRETON I with nearby Pt Hawksbury on mainland NS, created one of the finest ice-free harbours in the world. Twentieth-century Canso has enjoyed a burst of industrial development. HEATHER MACDONALD

Canso, Strait of, 27 km long, 3 km wide, 60 m deep, is a deep, narrow channel separating the Nova Scotian mainland and CAPE BRETON I. Formerly this waterway provided free communication between the waters of St Georges Bay in the Gulf of St Lawrence and the Atlantic Ocean. However, in the early 1950s, the Canso Causeway was built to carry rail and highway traffic between the mainland and the Island. The completion of the causeway in 1955 created a year-round ice-free port for the major towns along the strait, Port Hawkesbury and Mulgrave, and helped establish the area as an important pulpwood centre. But the closing of the strait has also cut off the supply of gulf-spawned lobster larvae to the Atlantic side. This is thought to be one of the major factors responsible for the precipitous decline of the lobster fishery on the southeastern Atlantic coast since the late 1950s. P.C. SMITH

Cantley, Thomas, businessman, politician (b at New Glasgow, NS 19 Apr 1857; d there 24 Feb 1945). Entering the iron-forging business as a youth when his province was rapidly industrializing, Cantley rose quickly and helped develop a modern steel complex in Pictou County. By 1915 he was president of the Nova Scotia Steel and Coal Corp and a member of the government's Shell Committee, which administered munitions contracts. His firm was the first in Canada to develop steel suitable for shell manufacture, a major contribution. He later served overseas and in 1925 was elected to the House of Commons for Pictou as a Conservative, remaining there until his appointment to the Senate in 1935. P.E. RIDER

Caouette, Joseph-David-Réal, politician, leader of the Social Credit Party (b at Amos, Abitibi, Qué 26 Sept 1917; d at Ottawa, 16 Dec 1976). Rising in the 1962 general election from virtual obscurity, Réal Caouette became a national political force as leader of the Québec SOCIAL CREDIT movement. Caouette joined the movement in 1939. He was elected to the Commons in a 1946 by-election as a member of the Union des électeurs. Unsuccessful in subsequent efforts to re-enter either the federal or the Québec Houses, Caouette allied his Ralliement des CRÉDITISTES with the national Social Credit Party in 1961 and ran for the post of national leader. Defeated by Robert THOMPSON, he was appointed Thompson's deputy and Québec's leader. In the 1962 general election, which resulted in a Conservative minority government, 26 of the 30 Social Credit MPs elected were Caouette's followers. Caouette's and Social Credit's appeal in Québec was primarily to voters in rural and small-town ridings, and Caouette's dramatic and exciting oratory, both in person and on his 15-minute TV shows, raised him to the status of a major political figure in Québec. He was a devoted federalist, though many of his economic views, loosely drawn from more orthodox Social Credit positions, represented a radical revolt against large power structures, especially the banks. In September 1963 he broke with Thompson, to become leader of his own Ralliement des créditistes, joined by 12 Québec MPs. His party's strength remained relatively stable in subsequent elections. In 1971 he reunited his Québec national party and became national leader, a post he held until ill health forced him to yield it to André Fortin in 1976. WILLIAM CHRISTIAN

Cap aux Meules, Île du, Qué, 50 km², one of the Îles de la MADELEINE (Magdalen Islands) in the middle of the Gulf of ST LAWRENCE, is named after the mountain that supplies the stone used to make grindstones for flour mills. Historically linked to the Magdalens, its inhabitants are French-speaking and of Acadian descent. The sandstone island is round and quite mountainous; Butte du Vent (165 m) is surrounded by undulating plains that were once farmland stretching to the sea. Half the population on the Magdalens is concentrated in 3 main areas: Capaux Meules, Fatima and Étang-du-Nord. Cap aux Meules's industrial and commercial activity includes fish plants, herring smokehouses, fishing ports, a seaport and lobster grounds. A thriving tourist industry has also developed because of the spectacular view from Butte du Vent, the unusual coastal relief, and the sand dunes extending as far as the eye can see.

JEAN-MARIE DUBOIS AND PIERRE MAILHOT

Cap-de-la-Madeleine, Qué, City, pop 32 800 (1986c), 32 626 (1981c), inc 1923, is located on the N shore of the ST LAWRENCE R at its confluence with the Rivière ST-MAURICE, opposite TROIS-RIVIÈRES. Originally the site of a seigneury (1636) and a Jesuit mission (1640), by 1900 "the Cap" had 300 families who lived from agriculture and lumbering. The arrival of electricity, a railway and a quay set the stage for an industrial boom that began in 1909 with the Grès Falls Co, followed in 1912 by the Wayagamack Pulp and Paper Co (later integrated into Consolidated Corp). Industrialization brought major residential construction. A second development phase began in 1938 with the opening of International Foils Ltd (Reynolds), which still operates. Despite the arrival of Lupel Amiante, a subsidiary of the Cascades Group, industrial activities have slowed since the 1970s and the Cap is increasingly a residential suburb of Trois-Rivières. The sanctuary, Notre-Dame du Cap, built in 1714, is a national pilgrimage site. Construction of the octagonal basilica, renowned for its stained-glass windows, dates from 1974.

CLAUDINE PIERRE-DESCHÊNES

Aerial view of a national pilgrimage site, Notre-Dame-du-Cap Shrine in Cap-de-la-Madeleine (*courtesy SSC Photocentre/photo by Michel Gagné*).

Cap des Rosiers, Anse du [Fr, "cove of the cape of rosebushes"]. Named for the many wild rosebushes found there, this steep and shrub-covered promontory is located at the eastern extremity of the GASPÉ Peninsula. A line drawn from the N shore to Cap des Rosiers, according to the ROYAL PROCLAMATION OF 1763, marks where the ST LAWRENCE R ends and the Gulf of ST LAWRENCE begins. It boasts the highest lighthouse in the Gaspé area (33 m, completed 1858) and borders on the eastern edge of FORILLON NATIONAL PARK (est 1970). A strategic contact point for shipping approaching the St Lawrence R, the cape was named by Samuel de CHAMPLAIN and appears on his map of 1632. It was here, in 1759, that the French first observed the approach of the British fleet sent to capture Québec City. DAVID EVANS

Cape Blomidon lies along the SE shore of the Bay of FUNDY at the mouth of MINAS BASIN, the site of some of the world's highest tides. A provincial park, high on the cape's red sandstone headland, is the home of the legendary GLOOSCAP, powerful man-god leader of the MICMAC, who, as the story goes, scattered agate and amethyst over this region. These semiprecious stones are avidly sought by modern rock hounds. Extending W from the cape is a fingerlike promontory called Cape Split, which divides Minas Channel on the N from Scots Bay and helps to create intense tidal rip currents near the tip. Strong tidal streams are also responsible for the continual erosion of the Blomidon headlands. The name is likely a contraction of the nautical phrase "blow me down." P.C. SMITH

Cape Bonavista, elev 15-30 m, is the bare, rocky extremity of the Bonavista Pen, N of BONAVISTA in eastern Newfoundland. Traditionally the landfall (1497) of John CABOT (who is said to have named it), it was from 1713 to 1783 the southern terminus of the FRENCH SHORE. One of Newfoundland's earliest lighthouses was built here 1843 and declared a provincial historic site in 1970. It was subsequently restored and opened as a museum. ROBERT D. PITT

Cape Breton Highlands National Park (est 1936) stretches across the northern tip of CAPE BRETON I, occupying 950 km² of a high plateau covered with bogs and forest and dotted with ponds. Around the seaward edge of the park are 300 m cliffs, sheltered coves and rocky beaches, all under constant attack from the Atlantic Ocean. Vegetation is varied: hardwood forests of maple, beech and yellow birch contrast with muskeg and heath barrens. Wildlife species include moose, white-tailed deer, black bear, snowshoe hare, bobcat, lynx and, possibly, cougar. Over 230 species of birds have been recorded. This is one of the places claimed as the site of John CABOT's landfall in 1497. MICMAC were living in the area at the time. Portuguese fishermen were the first Europeans to settle, followed by French and Scottish immigrants. Tradition is strong in fishing villages near the park. French is the first language of many residents, while the use of Gaelic reflects a Highland heritage. The 298 km Cabot Trail, a modern scenic highway, is one way to experience the park's beauty. LILLIAN STEWART

Cape Breton Island, NS, 10 311 km², a rugged and irregularly shaped island, approximately 175 km long by 135 km at its widest, is located at the eastern extremity of the Gulf of ST LAWRENCE. Its land mass slopes upward from S to N, culminating in the massive highlands of its northern cape, the highest elevation in the Atlantic region. A saltwater lake (the BRAS D'OR) forms the island's core and has provided the only significant access to its interior for purposes of settlement. Divided politically into 4 counties — Cape Breton, Inverness, Richmond and Victoria — it is separated from mainland NS by the narrow Str of CANSO (bridged by a 2 km causeway in 1955), and from neighbouring Newfoundland by the 110 km wide CABOT STR. Its name likely derives from the Basque Cap Breton, a location near Bayonne, France.

Its population of 166 116 (1986c) is one-fifth of NS's total, but over 70% live in industrialized Cape Breton County, which has been steadily declining in numbers since WWII. Its principal city is SYDNEY, a large industrial, commercial and administrative centre, which is surrounded by a group of declining coal-mining towns, the largest of which is GLACE BAY. More recently, there has been a surge of urbanization in the SE corner of the island, where a substantial oil-refining and pulp- and paper-making industry has emerged at Port Hawkesbury, taking advantage of the large harbour created by construction of the causeway to the mainland.

History The island was probably known to BASQUE fishermen as early as the 15th century and was sighted and identified by John CABOT (1497) and Jacques CARTIER (1534). Claimed by the French as part of Acadia, it remained largely undeveloped and unsettled, apart from a minor role as a fur-trading and fishing outpost. When the Treaty of UTRECHT, 1713, ceded most of Acadia to the British, the French retained Cape Breton, which they renamed Île Royale. Shortly thereafter, they began construction of the fortress of LOUISBOURG at a small harbour along the SE coast. For its time, it was the most imposing European-style fortress in N America. When Louisbourg and the rest of New France fell to the British during the SEVEN YEARS' WAR, the fortress was destroyed; the Treaty of PARIS, 1763, ceded the island and France's remaining possessions in the area to the British.

Cape Breton became part of the colony of Nova Scotia in 1763, but it remained largely undeveloped until 1784, when it became a separate colony, as one of several separate jurisdictions created for the LOYALIST refugees. The Loyalists, who made Sydney the capital of their new colony, were soon overwhelmed by successive waves of Scottish immigrants. They occupied most of the available arable land along the seacoasts and around Bras d'Or Lake, and with a few hundred returning Acadians made up the bulk of the island's largely rural population, which subsisted mostly on farming and the inshore fishery. In 1820 the island was reunited to the jurisdiction of NS following almost 40 years of tempestuous separate status.

Economy The emergence of a vital and expansive coal-mining industry from the 1830s on completely transformed the island economy. The mines surrounding Sydney harbour attracted the excess population of the already overpopulated rural areas and weighted the island towards the industrial base emerging in Cape Breton County. While the area was the most dynamic growth zone in the Atlantic region up to WWI, its boom was short-lived. When the coal mines were depleted and the steel mill became obsolete, the central Canadian capitalists who had come to dominate the industrial advance abandoned the area for greener fields, leaving the industrial sector to survive on a succession of inadequate subventions from federal and provincial governments. The result was a heritage of industrial decline, labour unrest and a massive out-migration.

Today the island is recovering somewhat. New coal seams are being exploited and the industry has rebounded somewhat from its post-WWII collapse. Smaller industries have taken root to some extent, and the rebirth of the fishery and an expanding pulp and paper industry has combined with the oil refineries and the promise of offshore petroleum resources in pointing to a better future. Despite continuing high unemployment (15.1% in July 1987), investment in Cape Breton doubled between 1980 and 1986 (to more than $95 million).

Institutions Cape Breton has a proud Scottish heritage that finds expression in lively performing arts and a commitment to maintaining traditional crafts. In addition, there are several important educational and cultural institutions: the University College of Cape Breton in Sydney, the Miners' Memorial Museum in Glace Bay, the Alexander Graham Bell Museum in BADDECK and Fortress Louisbourg (a magnificent reconstruction of the

18th-century site). CAPE BRETON HIGHLANDS NATIONAL PARK preserves the rugged beauty of the island's northern cape, around which curves the scenic Cabot Trail.   D.A. MUISE

Cape Breton Strikes, 1920s The CAPE BRETON labour wars of the early 1920s represented an intense local episode of class conflict, similar to the WINNIPEG GENERAL STRIKE (1919). In such conflicts militant unions, often led by radical leaders, were attempting to change the balance of power in Canadian industry by insisting on union recognition and improved living standards for the workers. In Cape Breton, despite an earlier defeat in 1909-10, the coal miners had won recognition of District 26, United Mine Workers of America, in 1919. Their main antagonist was the Montréal-based British Empire Steel Corp, which dominated the coal and steel industry in the Maritimes after 1920. Unfortunately, this company faced problems in maintaining traditional markets in central Canada and in surviving its own financial mismanagement. Determined to save costs by reducing wages, the company met strenuous resistance from its employees. In the closely knit, single-industry towns of Cape Breton, the unions benefited from a network of local loyalties, such as the widely shared Scottish background of the coal miners and their support for labour parties, co-operatives and workers' control in industry. Dramatic confrontations followed, and 3 major strikes accounted for more than 2 million striker-days. There were also a large number of short, local strikes, often over work-discipline and managerial authority in the mines. At the company's request, provincial police and federal troops were ordered into the coal and steel towns. The labour wars lasted 4 years. In 1922, when the company introduced a one-third reduction in wages, the coal miners responded by restricting output at the pits and reducing production by one-third. When the SYDNEY steelworkers went on strike in 1923, seeking union recognition, the provincial police turned out in force and charged through the streets of Whitney Pier. The coal miners came out in a sympathetic strike, but this ended in the arrest of 2 union leaders, Dan Livingstone and J.B. MCLACHLAN, on charges of seditious libel, and the temporary suspension of District 26 by the international office of the UMWA. In 1925 the coal miners continued to face short time and wage reductions at the mines. When the company cut off credit at the company stores, local communities threw their resources behind the coal miners and the desperate conditions in the coalfield began to attract headlines and sympathy across the country. The 1925 strike lasted 5 months and culminated in a bloody battle at Waterford Lake, where coal miner William Davis was killed by company police on 11 June 1925.

In the end the British Empire Steel Corp was chastised by a royal commission in 1926 for its unenlightened labour policies and subsequently collapsed into bankruptcy. The use of the armed forces had been a highly unpopular aspect of the strikes, and the federal government took steps to restrict the ease with which the troops could be called out in labour disputes. In their epic battle for union recognition, the coal miners had succeeded in preserving their union and partly protecting their living standards. In the case of the

steelworkers, union recognition was achieved in the 1930s, when Premier Angus L. MACDONALD, remembering the earlier conflict, introduced the first Nova Scotia Trade Union Act (1937), protecting the right to collective bargaining. The unions' aim of public ownership for the coal and steel industries, which they believed would bring about a more responsible form of economic development for the area, was not achieved, however, until the final withdrawal of private enterprise in 1967. The Cape Breton labour wars marked the growth of a persistent tradition of working-class consciousness, which is often reflected in local culture and politics. The death of William Davis in 1925 is still remembered on June 11 each year, which is marked as a Miners' Memorial Day. *See also* WORKING-CLASS HISTORY and various entries under LABOUR.   DAVID FRANK

Cape Dorset, NWT, Hamlet, pop 872 (1986c), 784 (1981c), is situated on Dorset I, SW of BAFFIN ISLAND, 1891 air km NE of YELLOWKNIFE. The rolling tundra surrounding the community is actually part of the Kingnait Mtn range. It is the entry point to the nesting grounds of the blue goose at the Dewey Soper Bird Sanctuary, NE of the community. While the traditional economy is based on hunting and sealing, many of the majority Inuit population are artists. The famous Dorset printmaking shop is located there.   ANNELIES POOL

Cape Kildare extends eastward into the Gulf of St Lawrence, at the northern end of PEI. Named by Samuel Holland in 1765 after James, 20th earl of Kildare, it is part of a series of capes in the area known as the Kildare Capes. The harvesting and sale of Irish moss, a seaweed used as a stabilizer in food processing, is an important local industry.   P.C. SMITH

Cape North is the northern promontory on CAPE BRETON I. Its bald, rocky headland rises abruptly from the shoreline to heights of over 300 m. Nearby Sugarloaf Mtn is one of the sites claimed to have been John CABOT's landfall in 1497. The currents around the cape are generally directed out of the Gulf of St Lawrence as part of the Cape Breton Current. However, violent local storms with sustained easterly winds can create opposing flow near the coast and strong current rips. Cape North has long been an important centre for communications. The first undersea telegraph cable from Newfoundland came ashore here in 1856 and was used until 1867 when it was replaced by the N Sydney-Placentia line.   P.C. SMITH

Cape Race, elev 30-40 m, is the southeastern extremity of Newfoundland's AVALON PENINSULA. Named for its flat-topped (Portuguese, *raso*) cliffs, it has a barren appearance that creates a stark impression for transatlantic passengers arriving in Canada by sea. It is the site of a powerful transmitter for the Loran C navigation system, an important aid to mariners. Icebergs may be seen in the waters off the cape from March to July. In 1977 Cape Race became a national historic site.   P.C. SMITH

Cape Sable is the southernmost point of land on CAPE SABLE I, which lies off the southwestern tip of Nova Scotia. It is composed of shifting sand dunes (French, *sable*) up to 9 m high and is nearly joined to the island by a sandy beach transversed by Hawk Channel. Hawk Inlet, on the E side of the channel, dries at low tide. Cape Sable Light, a white octagonal tower on the cape, houses a radar-transponding beacon in addition to a light and foghorn, important navigational aids to mariners in the often fogbound coastal waters.   P.C. SMITH

Cape Sable Island is a flat, wooded island off the southwestern tip of Nova Scotia. Connected to

Cape St Mary's, Nfld, located on the Avalon Peninsula. The cape and an adjacent rock island became a provincial seabird sanctuary in 1964 (*photo by John deVisser*).

the mainland by a causeway on the N side, it shelters the waters of Barrington Bay to the E. The main settlement on the island is CLARK'S HARBOUR, which has been incorporated as a town since 1919. The primary industry is fishing, with major landings of ground fish (cod, haddock), lobster and scallops. There is also a strong tradition of boatbuilding here: the first Cape Island boat, the familiar craft of Atlantic inshore fishermen, was launched in 1905. In summer the island is often shrouded in fog, produced when warm, moist continental air encounters the unusually cold surface waters off CAPE SABLE. The low sea surface temperatures are caused by intense tidal mixing that blends cold deep water with the warmer surface layer. These conditions also support a highly productive ecosystem and are, in part, responsible for the valuable fisheries.   P.C. SMITH

Cape St Mary forms the southern boundary of St Mary's Bay in an area of Nova Scotia's northwestern coast known as the French Shore. Fishing is the principal activity in this region; the cape was once the site of the International Tuna Cup matches. Below the cape lies Mavillette Beach, a long stretch of sand that has been developed into a provincial park. The marsh behind the dunes is ideal for bird watching.   P.C. SMITH

Cape St Mary's, elev 105 m, on Newfoundland's AVALON PENINSULA, is the steep and spectacular terminus of the land separating ST MARY'S BAY and PLACENTIA BAY near rich fishing grounds. The site of a lighthouse since 1860, the cape and an adjacent rock island have been a provincial seabird sanctuary since 1964. It is home to large populations of birds, including one of N America's largest gannet colonies.   ROBERT D. PITT

Cape Scott Provincial Park (est 1973, 50 km²), on the NW tip of VANCOUVER I, BC, includes 64 km of coast, with 23 km of sandy beaches interspersed by rocky headlands. The land rises inland to Mt St Patrick (415 m) and there is a 44 ha body of freshwater, Eric Lk. The park has a rigorous climate with storms and heavy rainfalls; annual precipitation is 375-500 cm. Forests include cedar, pine, hemlock and fir, with a dense undergrowth of salal, salmonberry, huckleberry and fern. Animals include deer, elk, bears, otters, cou-

gars and wolves, with seals, sea lions and gulls along the shore, and migrating Canada geese at Hansen Lagoon. Coastal Indians first occupied and exploited the area. Cape Scott was named in 1786 after David Scott, a Bombay merchant who backed a trading voyage along the coast under Captains Guise and Lowrie. In 1897 and 1910 Danish pioneers made unsuccessful attempts to settle, leaving only place-names and abandoned buildings as evidence. Trails provide the only access, the trailhead being reached by public highway and logging road from Port Hardy, some 60 km East. There are few facilities except primitive, often muddy trails that run from the trailhead to Cape Scott, a distance of 27 km.   JOHN S. MARSH

Cape Spear, Nfld, the most easterly point of the N American mainland. It has long been a prime landfall for transatlantic navigators (*photo by Jim Merrithew*).

Cape Spear, elev 75 m, most easterly point in N America (excluding Greenland), is located 6.7 km SE of the entrance to St John's harbour, Nfld. A rocky, windswept promontory of Precambrian formation, with a thin, sporadic cover of till and bog, it was first named by the Portuguese (*spera,* "hope"). It has been a prime landfall for transatlantic navigators, and since 1836 has been the site of an important lighthouse, continuously in use until 1955, when a modern structure was built. During WWII gun emplacements, now largely demolished, were built on the cape. In 1962 Cape Spear was declared a National Historic Park, and the original lighthouse has been restored to its 1840 condition.   MICHAEL STAVELEY

Cape Traverse is a small peninsula along the southwestern shore of PEI on NORTHUMBERLAND

STRAIT. Bells Point on the cape was used by the French as the terminus for crossing from the mainland. Present-day traffic aboard the CN ferry lands at Borden, 5 km to the West.
   P.C. SMITH

Cape Wolstenholme, 384 m high, imposing headland marking the western limit of HUDSON STR. The western side of the peninsula is a perpendicular rampart, which in summer provides a nesting place for swarms of Brunneck's guillemots, or murres.   JAMES MARSH

Capilano Review (1972) is a magazine of literature and the arts, founded at Capilano College, N Vancouver, as an offshoot of the creative-writing program. The magazine publishes poetry, fiction, reviews and also drama. It has made something of a speciality of interviews with writers, and explores those points of contact between the arts offered by experimental movements such as concrete and visual poetry. Most contributors are West Coast Canadian writers, but *Capilano Review* has published many translations of works by foreign experimental writers.   GEORGE WOODCOCK

Capital Cities are the designated centres of formal political power and administrative authority in their respective territories. They are also very often the chief focus of economic power and thereby of real political power, particularly in the form of head offices of business corporations and nongovernmental institutions of all kinds. They may as a consequence attract a considerable proportion of a nation's intellectuals and creative individuals. In short, capitals are usually the seats of the power elites which dominate public decision making. Through their control over the transportation and communications networks, capital elites have been able increasingly to dominate their dependent territories both politically and commercially.

Capitals also serve as symbols of political identity and legitimacy. Public buildings (and commercial head offices too) are usually designed to impress the populace with the dignity of power, the majesty of law, and an implied assurance of personal security. Most legislatures and court buildings are constructed in styles strongly influenced by some great kingdom, republic or empire of the past – to hint as it were that authority flows from a grand historical tradition and has therefore deep and legitimate historical roots. The "capitol" of the Roman Republic is one such archetype, the medieval "Parlement" of the common people is another.

Canada's capital cities can be classed into 2 groups, according to whether the territory they now control politically was defined so as to reflect and enhance their political and commercial interests, or whether the territory had been delimited already before the capital site was chosen. Cities of the first group are more likely to be totally dominant within their respective territories, having the advantage of prior communications routes; those in the other are more likely to share dominance with some other city in the same territory or elsewhere.

The first group includes St John's, Halifax, Charlottetown, Québec, Toronto, Winnipeg, Victoria and Dawson. All were originally founded at strategic locations as outposts of a European empire and, except for Winnipeg and Dawson, were located under the constraints of sailing ship technology. St John's (fd 1583), Halifax (fd 1749) and Victoria (fd 1843) were all harbours of refuge for the large ships of the Royal Navy and of oceanic trade. Québec (fd 1608) stands at a defensible location as far up the St Lawrence R as these large sailing vessels could safely proceed. Toronto (fd as York 1793) was selected largely for its protected anchorage on the inland sea of Lake Ontario. Because they are gateways to some sort of resources, for land, forests, mines or fisheries, all of these capitals have developed important commercial functions. Even Winnipeg (fd 1812) is a gateway – to the great plains – though its "shores" are defined by topography and the US boundary. Charlottetown, the smallest provincial capital, has been the chief point of access to its small island territory since 1769, while Dawson, the heart of the KLONDIKE GOLD RUSH, gained capital status in the Yukon Territory in 1898.

All of this group have dominated their official territories from the first, and except for Québec and Victoria, still do. Québec's rival for real power is Montréal, which though founded as an outpost upriver in 1642 remained in economic dependency until after the American Revolution. Its growth and financial power really "took off" after the introduction of steam boats, canals and railways in the 19th century enabled entrepreneurs to take good advantage of its much better access to the interior of N America. The same is true of Vancouver, founded in 1886 at the terminus of the Canadian Pacific Ry as Canada's gateway to the steam-powered trade of the Pacific basin, a role the senior city of Victoria could not well fulfil from its island location.

The other group of capitals includes Fredericton, Regina, Edmonton, Yellowknife and, indeed, Ottawa. Each has a rival for real power – in the case of Ottawa, at least 2 – and has had from its inception a political focus. Fredericton (fd 1784) was placed well up the Saint John R in the new colony of New Brunswick, both for defence and to stimulate inland settlement; but as the Saint John R is not accessible to ocean shipping, New Brunswick's gateway has been the port of Saint John (fd 1785), the largest city in the province.

The capitals of Saskatchewan and Alberta were chosen by 1905 from among numerous claimants for the honour (and the perquisites) of accommodating the governments of the 2 new provinces. Even today Regina (fd 1882) shares real power with Saskatoon (fd 1882), and Edmonton (fd 1796) with Calgary (fd 1875); all 4 are on major national transcontinental routes. Yellowknife (fd 1789) is the newest capital, designated in 1967; but the economic core of the Northwest is predominantly Edmonton.

The timing of the choice of Ottawa places it in the second group. Though it became the capital of the Canadian Confederation in 1867, Ottawa had only just begun to function as a political capital after a long struggle to decide the seat of government of the Province of Canada (today forming the southern parts of Ontario and Québec). This united province was proclaimed in 1841, but because of political wrangling among supporters of Toronto, Kingston, Montréal, Québec and eventually Ottawa (then called Bytown) the functions of capital were moved among the first 4 places for over 20 years. Finally, the choice being left with Queen Victoria and her advisers, in 1858 she selected the newly incorporated city of Ottawa; but it took another 6 years before the PARLIAMENT BUILDINGS were ready for occupancy.

Meanwhile, CONFEDERATION had been agreed upon, with a view to incorporating into one policy both Atlantic and Pacific shores of British N America. At the time, Ottawa was seen as more easily defended than Toronto or Montréal (the security issue was acute because of the American Civil War), was already a thriving city from the lumber trade, was equally accessible to both the major cultural communities of the time, and was well placed on the Ottawa Valley routeway to the western interior territories. It was also conveniently close to Montréal and the transatlantic communications routes, and thus Ottawa has not

Provincial legislative building, Regina, Sask. Capital buildings are usually constructed in styles strongly influenced by some great kingdom or empire of the past (*photo by John deVisser*).

been able to garner real power at national scale to match its formal constitutional power. Montréal and increasingly Toronto continue to share the real power, though western cities in Alberta and BC have been gaining in this respect.

The iconic or symbolic role of Ottawa is evident in almost every national news telecast. The austere grey stones of the Gothic-style buildings on Parliament Hill (emphatically not the "Capitol Hill" of a republic) cling to the land with a timeless gravity, while the thrusting central tower draws attention to higher themes, emphasizing Canadian commitment to "peace, order, and good government." *See also* GOVERNMENT BUILDING.
C.F.J. WHEBELL

Capital Formation The "capital stock" is one of the basic determinants of an economy's ability to produce income for its members. Composed of equipment, buildings and intermediate goods not themselves directly consumed, the capital stock produces a flow of services which, when combined with labour, yield "value-added," the sum of which is the value of all goods and services produced in the economy. This, in turn, is the NATIONAL INCOME received in the economy. "Capital formation" is simply the enlargement of the capital stock. The higher the rate of capital formation, the more rapid is the growth of the economy's productive capacity and, hence, the more rapid the growth of aggregate income.

Capital formation may be viewed in several ways. First, since part of the capital stock wears out or loses some of its economic potential each year ("depreciation"), provision must be made for its replacement. A certain amount of capital formation must be allocated to depreciation in order for the economy's capital stock to remain constant. Second, after depreciation charges, additions to the capital stock are known as "net investment" or "net capital formation." Third, since capital formation may be financed by both domestic savings and foreign savings, and because Canadians can invest their savings abroad, a distinction is made similar to that found in Canada's national accounts: Gross National Capital Formation (GNCF) measures the flow of real new capital created by Canadians, whereas Gross Do-

mestic Capital Formation (GDCF) measures new capital created in Canada by Canadians and foreigners alike. The aggregate income flows to which these correspond are, respectively, Gross National Product (GNP) and Gross Domestic Product (GDP); the former is the income received by Canadians from all sources and the latter is the aggregate income received by all individuals from the Canadian domestic economy.

The composition of real capital formation has changed spectacularly in modern history. The important broad categories of investment are construction of both industrial plant and residential buildings; producers' equipment; and inventory adjustment. In a simple trading economy such as early 19th-century Canada, inventories of export goods such as cereal grains and timber constituted a major portion of capital formation alone. As the economy grew in size and took on more industrial characteristics, the importance of inventories declined while the relative importance of construction and producers' equipment increased. Also, more producers' equipment came to be located in the manufacturing sector as agriculture and primary resource harvesting declined in relative importance. In contemporary Canada, construction accounts for about two-thirds of all capital formation, machinery and equipment are about 30% of investment, and inventories are less than 5%. The creation of real capital is financed through the use of savings. Since savings represent a supply of funds that can be loaned, mechanisms were evolved to marshal and channel savings to the particular types of capital formation. This process of capital mobilization generally required specialized financial intermediaries which of course make a profit from the act of financial arbitrage.
DONALD G. PATERSON

Reading: K.A.H. Buckley, *Capital Formation in Canada, 1896-1930* (1955); O.J. Firestone, *Canada's Economic Development, 1867-1953* (1958); W.L. Marr and D.G. Paterson, *Canada: An Economic History* (1980).

Capital Punishment Under British law prevailing in Canada until 1859 some 230 offences, including stealing turnips and being found disguised in a forest were punishable by death. By 1865 only murder, TREASON and RAPE were capital offences. The drive either to limit or abolish capital punishment began in 1914, when Robert Bickerdike presented a private member's bill calling for its abolition, but the law remained unchanged despite frequent submissions to Parliament. In 1967, a government bill to apply mandatory life imprisonment in all murder cases, except when the victim was an on-duty police officer or prison guard, was passed by a vote of 105 to 70 for a 5-year trial period. This legislation was again sustained in 1973, supported by a 13-vote majority. By a majority of 6 votes, the House of Commons abolished hanging in 1976 (although under the National Defence Act capital punishment can still be used for cowardice, desertion, unlawful surrender and spying for the enemy). The last execution in Canada occurred in 1962.

Recently there has been a vigorous public debate over whether capital punishment should be reinstated. Although those in favour claim it is an effective deterrent to HOMICIDE, among other reasons, the majority of studies in Western societies conclude that murder rates have remained stable or declined with the decreasing use of capital punishment. Neither abolition nor reintroduction of capital punishment have been shown to affect homicide rates significantly. In a historic vote, 30 June 1987, Parliament voted 148-127 not to restore the death penalty, effectively quashing any attempt to restore the death penalty in the near future. Subsequently, a Commons justice committee was struck to shape a decent and practical alternative that keeps dangerous offenders in prison and allows for a more efficacious use of parole that better protects society.

PAUL GENDREAU

Caplan, Gerald Lewis, political administrator, historian (b at Toronto 1938). Educated at U of T and London U in history, Caplan wrote one of the best books to have appeared on the CCF Party, *The Dilemma of Canadian Socialism* (1973), a study that sprang from his university friendship with Stephen LEWIS. He taught history at the Ontario Institute for Studies in Education from 1967 to 1977, worked as a close adviser to Lewis in Ontario politics, and served as CUSO's director in Nigeria from 1977 to 1979. Caplan returned to Canada and worked for Toronto's Health Advocacy Unit, and then became national director of the NDP in 1982 and campaign director in 1984. In 1985 the Mulroney government named him to co-chair the Task Force on Broadcasting Policy which reported the next year with a strongly nationalist series of recommendations.

J.L. GRANATSTEIN

Capote, a hooded greatcoat rather like a parka, usually worn with a sash around the waist, popular with habitants of New France and French Canadian traders and trappers. The word is derived from the French word for "cape." *See also* CLOTHING.

JOHN ROBERT COLOMBO

Capper, Stewart Henbest, architect, educator, army officer (b at London, Eng Dec 1859; d at Cairo, Egypt 8 Jan 1925). He graduated in classics from Edinburgh U 1880 and in 1884 entered the École des beaux-arts, Paris. Returning to Edinburgh 1887, he soon set up his own practice. Through William Peterson, principal of McGill in Montréal, and G. Baldwin Brown, former colleagues at Edinburgh, Capper became the first Macdonald Professor of Architecture at McGill 1896-1903. He initiated practical and theoretical training based on his knowledge of European architecture and encouraged the study of architectural history and the development of national architectural styles. He held a similar position at Victoria U in Manchester until his resignation in 1912 for health reasons. He continued a military career, begun in Montréal, as a major in the Manchester Volunteers, and went to Egypt in 1914. Declared unfit for active duty, he became a military censor because of his extensive knowledge of languages. After demobilization he continued similar work in Cairo. ROBERT LEMIRE

Capricieuse, La The first French naval vessel to visit Canada after the CONQUEST, *La Capricieuse* received a tumultuous welcome at Québec on 14 July 1855. Commander Paul-Henry de Belvèze proceeded by steamer and train to Montréal, Toronto and Ottawa before leaving Québec for France on Aug 25. His mission was to report on the prospects of trade with Canada, made possible by Britain's proclamation of free trade and by the Anglo-French alliance of 1854. The result was the opening of a French consulate at Québec in 1859, followed by mutual, short-lived tariff concessions and the development of a modest trade. However, the visit is remembered chiefly as the official endorsement of the Franco-Canadian cultural rapprochement that had been gathering impetus since the 1830s. DALE MIQUELON

Caraquet, NB, Town, pop 4493 (1986c), 4315 (1981c), inc 1961, is located 68 km NE of Bathurst. Its houses line the Baie de Caraquet, a rocky section of CHALEUR BAY's southern coast, offering magnificent views of the sea and the GASPÉ PENINSULA. Attracted by the rich fishing grounds, the first French settlers arrived about 1750. ACADIAN refugees, Québec fishermen and English-

speaking traders followed, and from 1837 to 1939, the Jersey-based Robin fishing company dominated the economy. Local industry still depends on the excellent harbour and on fishing and boatbuilding, despite government-subsidized efforts to attract other industries.

A centre of Acadian religion and culture, Caraquet saw riots in 1875 when the government threatened to stop funding the convent school. The Sacré Coeur Coll, operating here 1899-1915, hosted the Acadian Convention of 1905. The Acadian Federation of Caisses Populaires headquarters and the Acadian Museum are in Caraquet, and the Acadian Historical Village is just outside. The Caraquet Festival attracts the best Acadian composers and performers.

SHEILA ANDREW

Carbonear, Nfld, Town, pop 5337 (1986c), 5335 (1981c), inc 1948, is located on the W shore of CONCEPTION BAY. The name may come from the Spanish *Carbonera* ("a seller of charcoal"), or the French family name *Carbonnier* or place-name *La Carbonnière*. Near excellent fishing grounds, Carbonear was first fished in the early 1600s and in 1631 Nicholas Guy from the CUPIDS colony was fishing and farming there. It was settled in the late 1600s by English West Country fishermen and Channel Islanders. Nearby Carbonear I was fortified in the 1680s and was the only Newfoundland site to resist French attacks in 1696 and 1697, although Carbonear itself was razed. The town again fell to the French in 1704 and 1705, and was the object of numerous other attacks by French and American privateers until the early 1800s. With the rise of the seal hunt and the Labrador cod fishery, Carbonear became a major commercial centre in the 1800s. Violent political riots here in the early and mid-1800s led to the dissolution of the Newfoundland Legislature 1840 and the suspension of the constitution. In the 1900s the economy diversified; Carbonear

has become a regional service, transportation, government and fish-processing centre.

JANET E.M. PITT AND ROBERT D. PITT

Carcross, YT, Settlement, pop 209 (1986c), 216 (1981c), is located at the N end of Bennett Lk, 70 km S of Whitehorse. The WHITE PASS AND YUKON RY pre-empted the townsite in 1898 and made it a stopping point on the line to Whitehorse. Originally Caribou Crossing, the name was changed (1904) to end confusion with places of the same name in Alaska and BC. William C. BOMPAS, who established a boarding school for native children here (1901) is buried at Carcross, as are Kate Carmack, "Skookum" Jim Mason and Tagish Charlie, who were associated with the KLONDIKE gold discovery. H. GUEST

Cardigan, PEI, Village, pop 346 (1986c), situated 54 km NE of Charlottetown. A fishing and farming community and the site of a major shipbuilding industry in the 19th century, Cardigan is located at the head of the Cardigan R. Really a long inlet, the river is salt water and it finds its mouth in the Northumberland Str. Settled originally by ACADIANS and then by SCOTS and IRISH immigrants, most Cardiganites claim a mixture of French and British descent. The majority of the population speaks only English. W. S. KEIZER

Cardinal, Douglas Joseph, architect (b at Red Deer, Alta 7 Mar 1934). Cardinal was the eldest of 8 children. His father, half Blackfoot, was a provincial wildlife warden and his mother a nurse. Educated at St Joseph's Convent School and at high school in Red Deer, he enrolled in the School of Architecture at UBC in 1953 but was asked to withdraw in his second year, partly because his designs were considered too radical and partly because his background was not considered appropriate. After work and travel in Mexico, Cardinal enrolled at U of Texas in 1956, graduating with honours in 1963 and returning to Red Deer to apprentice with Bissell and Holman. His first commission was the round Guloien House at Sylvan Lake, followed by ST MARY'S CHURCH at Red Deer, generally considered his masterpiece. Structural calculations for St Mary's complex shape had to be made by computer, and Cardinal later became the first western Canadian architect

St Mary's Church at Red Deer, Alta, generally considered architect Douglas Cardinal's masterpiece (*photo by J.A. Kraulis*).

to convert to electronic drawings. In the 1970s Cardinal produced an erratic but innovative body of work and established his reputation for designing curving brick buildings. In 1983 he was awarded the commission to design the $93-million CANADIAN MUSEUM OF CIVILIZATION in Hull, Qué, an achievement hinting at future recognition. In 1985 he established an office in Ottawa, where he now lives. In the early 1970s Cardinal studied native religion and became involved in numerous Indian and Métis issues. He is a rare synthesis of native sensibility with Western technology, a Métis thriving in the professional world.

Cardinal, Harold, Indian leader, author (b at High Prairie, Alta 27 Jan 1945). Member of the Sucker Creek Reserve, he became in 1968 the youngest elected president of the Indian Assn of Alberta. During his 9 terms in office 1968-77, he initiated many programs to affirm Indian culture, religion and traditions. He helped draft the "Red Paper" of 1970, titled *Citizens Plus*, and authored 2 strongly critical statements on Canadian Indian policy, *The Unjust Society* (1969) and *The Rebirth of Canada's Indians* (1977). Leaving provincial native politics, he was the first Indian appointed regional director general of Indian affairs in Alberta, where he undertook several innovative reforms. After a controversial 7-month term, he left the public service and subsequently worked as a consultant to Indian bands in northern Alberta. He was elected chief of the Sucker Creek band in 1982-83 and briefly returned to national Indian politics in 1983 when he was appointed vice-chief for the prairie region under the ASSEMBLY OF FIRST NATIONS. IAN A.L. GETTY

Cardston, Alta, Town, pop 3497 (1986c), 3267 (1981c), inc 1901, is located 75 km SW of Lethbridge. It was named for Charles Ora Card (1839-1906), a son-in-law of Brigham Young. In order to escape American anti-polygamy laws, Card led the first 10 Mormon families there from Utah in 1887. The Mormon settlers and their church were the focus of economic and agricultural activity. Church-based co-operatives started in 1888 and included, among other enterprises, a store, a sawmill, a cheese factory and a flour mill. In 1898 the church built the first irrigation works on the St Mary's R, and in 1913 started construction of Canada's only Mormon temple, finished in 1923. Today Cardston is an important farming and ranching centre, home of the Remington carriage collection, and the famous Cobblestone Manor, a provincial historic site. *See also* MORMON CHURCH. FRITS PANNEKOEK

Career Counselling One of the major responsibilities of schools is to prepare students for employment and one of the ways they achieve this is through career counselling. Guidance counsellors are specialized teachers hired by schools to aid students in making educational and personal decisions regarding career opportunities. Counsellors sometimes use guidance courses, which introduce students to issues in the work world, and sometimes administer tests or provide other means of assisting students in matching their skills to job requirements. They may organize work experience for students or provide career-education materials for classroom use. The motivation to provide career counselling developed from early 20th-century educational reforms. Provision for the appointment of guidance counsellors was first made in 1921 in the Ontario Vocational Education Act. The number and role of counsellors gradually increased in all the provinces, but it was not until the 1960s that specialized guidance personnel were well established in Canadian schools.

Vocational guidance has been controversial since its inception. Many have challenged the need for schools to play a vocational, rather than an academic, role. As youth UNEMPLOYMENT has increased, counsellors have been criticized for lacking sufficient information about the job market and for being unable to match students to jobs. Some efforts have been made to shift career counselling to outside the schools, eg, into employment information centres. As new forms of testing and of work-related curriculum have been introduced, the biases in the materials have been questioned.

The objective of counselling is to increase opportunities for all students to achieve satisfaction and rewards from work, but all students do not have equal access to jobs. Because many jobs require post-secondary degrees, students counselled to discontinue schooling are denied access to employment opportunities. The research evidence reveals that male students, students from higher social-class backgrounds, and students from white, Anglo-Saxon families occupy the better paid, interesting jobs – often because they have better education. Counsellors are more likely to encourage middle-class rather than working-class students to pursue academic work. Girls are often urged to take traditional "women's" courses and jobs, and are discouraged from unconventional career paths or from studying courses in mathematics and sciences. To overcome these discriminatory practices, new materials, encouraging all students to think carefully about their options and interests, have been developed and career counsellors are being urged to use them. M. LAZERSON AND JANE GASKELL

Reading: Al Herman, *Guidance in Canadian Schools* (1981).

Careless, James Maurice Stockford, historian (b at Toronto 17 Feb 1919). A graduate of U of T (1940) and Harvard (1950), Careless began his teaching career at U of T as lecturer in history in 1945; he was chairman of the history department for 8 years and was named professor in 1972. The analytical framework he developed for studying the rise of Canadian cities incorporated ideas from the FRONTIER THESIS and the STAPLE THESIS. He is perhaps best known for his elaboration of the METROPOLITAN-HINTERLAND THESIS. He has been honoured for his historical writing (Tyrrell Medal, 1962; Gov Gen's Awards for *Canada: A Story of Challenge*, 1953, and *Brown of The Globe*, 1963), and has served on the boards of various historical societies and as mentor to a generation of urban historians. He was elected a fellow of the ROYAL SOCIETY OF CANADA (1962) and appointed University Professor at U of T (1977). He was made Officer of the Order of Canada in 1981 and received an honorary doctorate from U Calgary in 1986. MARGARET E. McCALLUM

Cariboo Gold Rush BC's most famous GOLD RUSH to the remote, isolated Cariboo Mts region occurred between 1860, when prospectors drawn from the Fraser Gold Rush discovered free gold on the Horsefly R, and 1863, when international publicity given to news of the rich payload found near bedrock at BARKERVILLE in 1862 drew a large and diverse mix of miners, goldseekers and adventurers into the former fur-trading territory. The most promising discoveries of free gold were made at Williams, Lightning and Lowhee creeks, but the former proved the richest; hence it became the centre of mining operations for the district. Here (125 km SE of Prince George), in a canyon with a narrow, steep-sided and isolated creek bed, a trio of supply, service and administrative towns – Richfield, Camerontown and, the only one to outlast the mining boom days, Bark-

Cariboo Road above Yale, BC, 1867-68. Much of the road had to be blasted from solid rock along the treacherous Fraser Canyon (*courtesy National Archives of Canada/C-8077*).

erville – were established. Barkerville's deep placers and rich hillside deposits were worked from 1864 to the 1930s. This required the use of expensive and complex technology, including hydraulic monitors which directed jets of water to wash the gold-bearing hillsides into sluice boxes, and the development of a more permanent mining community. Placer gold production in the Cariboo approximated $50 million, about one-half the BC total since 1858. DIANNE NEWELL

Reading: M. McNaughton, *Overland to Cariboo* (1898, repr 1973).

Cariboo Mountains are located between the Fraser R to the N and the North Thompson R to the S. They lie between the Columbia Mts to the E with the Fraser Plateau to the W. The highest peak is Mt Spranger at 3024 m. Wells Gray and Bowron Lakes provincial parks are located within the range. The area is noted for its canoe routes and helicopter skiing. In 1858, during a 3-month period between May and July, 30 000 miners came to the area from the California goldfields (*see* CARIBOO GOLD RUSH). The most productive area for gold was from the quartz intrusions in the NE corner of the range. MARGIE JAMIESON

Cariboo Road, running some 650 km along the FRASER RIVER CANYON between Yale and Barkerville, BC, was begun in 1862 to provide a wagon route to the goldfields of the Cariboo region of S-central BC. By 1860 gold returns from the area convinced Governor James DOUGLAS that a system of communication was necessary. A road to the interior would relieve the plight of the miners forced to pay exorbitant rates for supplies and would make the Fraser R the great commercial highway of BC. A contingent of Royal Engineers was brought from Britain to survey the route from Yale, at the head of navigation on the Fraser R, along extremely treacherous terrain to the administrative centre of the Cariboo. The work was begun by the army engineers who completed the 2 most difficult stretches – 10 km from Yale to Boston Bar and 15 km from Cook's Ferry along the Thompson R. Much of the road had to be blasted from solid rock. The rest of the construction was let out to private contractors, and the road was opened in 1864. The TRANS-CANADA HIGHWAY follows much of the route of this early road along the Fraser Canyon. C.J. TAYLOR

Caribou, Canada's symbol of the North, represented on the 25-cent piece, belong to the DEER family (Cervidae). All caribou herds throughout Scandinavia, USSR, Alaska and Canada belong to the species *Rangifer tarandus*. In Canada, one subspecies, *R. t. pearyi*, lives on the arctic islands. A second group, barren-ground caribou, are found N of the treeline in the NWT in summer, migrating S to northern Sask and Man in winter. The third group, woodland caribou, inhabit

Yukon bull caribou (*Rangifer tarandus*) (*photo by Stephen J. Krasemann/DRK Photo*).

mountains and forests from BC to Nfld. Bulls have palmate antlers, as do barren-ground cows; not all woodland cows have antlers. Males use antlers for fighting during the breeding season in Oct, shedding them in early winter. Females shed their antlers at about the time they give birth to a single calf, at the end of May or beginning of June. Newborns weigh 5-9 kg, and follow their dams within an hour of birth. Adult bulls weigh 125-275 kg; females 91-136 kg. Caribou range from forest to tundra habitats, feeding heavily on ground lichens. They also eat mushrooms, leaves and plants, including grasses and sedges. Formerly, biologists believed caribou required lichens and that loss of lichens by fire had caused population declines. It is now recognized that fires are a natural aspect of northern ecosystems and that caribou are adapted to cope with the loss of lichen habitats. Before settlement, some 3-5 million caribou lived in N America; today, there are about one million. Caribou are extinct in NB, NS and large parts of Ont and BC. On the arctic islands, large numbers of Peary caribou starve in some years. Southern woodland caribou are susceptible to brain-worm disease transmitted from white-tail deer, and cannot co-exist with high numbers of infected deer. Wolves have been the most constant threat, and much herding and migratory behaviour has evolved to minimize the impact of predation. Wolves often kill enough calves and adults to prevent population increase. If HUNTING is added to these losses, populations commonly decline. Even today, native peoples harvest thousands of caribou, waiting each year for the long line of migrating caribou that trek in single file down trails followed for millennia. In Oct 1984 some 10 000 migrating caribou were drowned while attempting to cross the swollen Caniapiscau R.   A.T. BERGERUD

Caribou Inuit, so named because of their almost total reliance on CARIBOU for food, clothing and shelter. During the 19th and early 20th centuries they occupied the Barren Grounds region to the W of Hudson Bay. The population of some 500 people was divided into 4 regional groups. They differed greatly from other Inuit in their dependence on inland resources, making only occa-

sional visits to the coast to obtain sea mammal products either through hunting or by trading with coastal Inuit. When first studied by anthropologists during the 1920s, they were thought to be a remnant of an ancient way of life that existed before most Inuit groups descended to the coasts and became marine hunters. This view was based on their unique adaptation to the interior, and on the meagre and primitive character of their aboriginal material culture. It has since become apparent that the Caribou Inuit way of life was a recent phenomenon, originating after indirect (and, later, direct) involvement with European traders and whalers. Until the late 18th century, CHIPEWYAN Indians had occupied most of the Barren Grounds area. A few decades later, the Inuit of the W coast of Hudson Bay began to receive firearms which allowed them to hunt caribou more efficiently, and involvement in the FUR TRADE gave them an incentive to move to the interior. The meagreness of their aboriginal material culture came from the fact that, by the time they were studied by anthropologists, they had used and relied upon European technology for over a century.

The traditional social organization of the Caribou Inuit was based on family relationships and partnerships, and families frequently moved from one regional group to another. Religion was based on Shamanism, and most of their language and beliefs were similar to those of other central Arctic INUIT groups. Their traditional seasonal round of activities involved primarily fishing, and hunting caribou during the spring and fall migrations. During the fall hunt, populations gathered at a few good hunting spots and attempted to obtain enough food for the winter, when the majority of the caribou had moved S into the forests. Caribou skin tents were used during the summer months, and snow houses during the winter. The descendants of the Caribou Inuit, numbering perhaps about 1000 people, now occupy the villages of Eskimo Point, Rankin Inlet, BAKER LAKE and Whale Cove. *See also* NATIVE PEOPLE: ARCTIC.

ROBERT MCGHEE

Carignan, Jean, "Ti-Jean," fiddler (b at Lévis, Qué 7 Dec 1916). The leading exponent of the Celtic tradition in French Canadian fiddling, he played the violin from age 4. He first played on street corners and later with various dance bands in the Montréal area. In 1956 he decided to perform only at concerts and folk festivals in N America and Europe. He premiered in 1976 a concerto written for him by André GAGNON and in 1979 was featured with Yehudi Menuhin on the TV series "The Music of Man." He was awarded the 1977 Prix de Musique Calixa-Lavallée. But the most memorable tribute to this fiddler who combines rare technical expertise with a true passion for music came in 1973 when 400 fiddlers from across N America gathered near Montréal to pay tribute to him.   RICHARD GREEN

Carignan-Salières Regiment, of some 1100 strong, sent from France in June 1665 to curb the devastating attacks of the IROQUOIS on Canadian settlements. By November a chain of forts had been built along the RICHELIEU R, blocking that main invasion route. When peace negotiations proved futile, a foolhardy midwinter expedition was mounted: approximately 600 of the troops and 70 Canadians invaded the Mohawk canton in Feb 1666. Some of them were ambushed, but no harm was done to the enemy. Some 60 more of the French perished during the retreat to Canada. In September the regiment again invaded the Mohawk country, found the villages deserted, and burned them and the surrounding cornfields. In July 1667 the Iroquois finally came to terms. The regiment was recalled to France in 1668 but some

400 officers and men chose to remain and settle on seigneuries along the Richelieu R, greatly strengthening the colony's defences, military ethos, and economy.   W.J. ECCLES

Carle, Gilles, director, screenwriter (b at Maniwaki, Qué 31 July 1929). A prolific filmmaker, Carle is regarded as one of the most important talents in the Canadian film industry. During the 1940s and 1950s he was a graphic artist. He joined the NFB in 1960 when the French production unit was expanding. In 1965 he made his first feature film, *La Vie heureuse de Léopold Z*, a comedy. When the NFB subsequently rejected several projects, Carle began working independently. Supporting himself by producing TV commercials, he directed 3 feature films in 3 years, *Le Viol d'une jeune fille douce* (1968), *Red* (1969) and *Les Mâles* (1970). These films, combining Carle's commentary on Québec society with scenes of sex and violence, generated a large popular following. In 1972 he produced his greatest commercial success, *La Vraie Nature de Bernadette;* this film earned him recognition in Europe where audiences were captivated by the quality of his direction and fresh approach. He immediately planned 2 films with his new star Carole LAURE, *La Mort d'un bûcheron* (1973) and *Les Corps célestes* (1973). The Carole Laure cycle was to last a little less than 10 years. An immensely skilled director, Carle blends eroticism, romanticism and fantasy to create films as fresh and original as *La Tête de Normande St-Onge* (1975). Despite his popular success in Québec and his international reputation, Carle has had financial difficulties. *L'Ange et la femme* (1977), which he produced himself on a small budget, defied the conventions of commercial cinema and had a mixed reception. In 1980 he tried his hand at musical comedy with *Fantastica*. In the following year, however, his production of *Les Plouffe*, adapted from Roger LEMELIN's TV series, was enthusiastically received, and provided in 1984 a follow-up, *Le Crime d'Ovide Plouffe*. After a dramatized documentary on chess players, *Jouer sa vie* (1982), Carle tackled another Québec literary classic, Louis HÉMON's *Maria Chapdelaine* (1983). In 1985 he directed a dramatized documentary on the 25th anniversary of French production at the NFB (*Cinéma, cinéma*), then another on Picasso (*Ô Picasso*, 1985). His most recent thriller is entitled *Laguêpe* (1986).

PIERRE VÉRONNEAU

Carleton, Guy, 1st Baron Dorchester, army officer, twice governor at Québec, 1768-78 and 1785-95, British commander in chief at New York, 1782-83 (b at Strabane, Ire 3 Sept 1724; d near Maidenhead, Eng 10 Nov 1808). A colonel at the capture of Québec in 1759, he was made lieutenant-governor at Québec 7 April 1766, reaching the province 23 Sept 1766, and succeeded James MURRAY as governor in April 1768. He advised the passing of the QUEBEC ACT in 1774 and administered it so as to support the Roman Catholic Church and to retain French civil law. He overestimated the importance of the seigneurs, however, and was disappointed by Canadian passivity during the AMERICAN REVOLUTION. He repelled the American invasion of 1775-76, but he was criticized for his slow pursuit of the retreating invaders. He resigned after quarrels with his councillors, especially Chief Justice Peter Livius, leaving July 1778. In 1782-83 he was commander in chief at New York, which he refused to evacuate until the LOYALIST refugees had been sent to safety and urged their reception in Québec and Nova Scotia. Influenced by William SMITH, he unsuccessfully proposed while in England a single governor general for BNA. He was commissioned again as governor at Québec on 12 Sept 1791, but did not arrive in Lower Canada until 24 Sept

Guy Carleton, 1st Baron Dorchester. Becoming governor of Québec in 1768, he sought to support the traditional bases of French Canadian society and opposed the elected assemblies provided for in the Constitutional Act, 1791 (*courtesy National Archives of Canada/C-2833*).

1793. Anxious to encourage commerce with the American West, he interpreted the imperial ban on American imports to apply only to seaports. He opposed the division of the Province of Québec into Upper and Lower Canada and the elected assemblies provided for by the CONSTITUTIONAL ACT, 1791, but advised the retention of Montréal in the lower province. Expecting war with the US just before the signing of JAY'S TREATY in 1794, he made an inflammatory speech to Indians and ordered the reoccupation of Fort Miamis (Maumee, Ohio). Given a gentle reprimand, he asked leave to resign on 4 Sept 1794 and was granted it July 1795. He left the province 9 July 1796.

S.R. MEALING

Reading: A.L. Burt, *Guy Carleton, Lord Dorchester, 1724-1808* (1955).

Carleton, Thomas, British army officer, lieutenant-governor of NB (b in Ire *c*1735; d at Ramsgate, Eng 2 Feb 1817), brother of Guy CARLETON, Baron Dorchester. After military service in Europe and America, Carleton was appointed first lieutenant-governor of the newly created colony of New Brunswick on 28 July 1784. He held this position until his death in 1817, although he resided in England from 1803 on. Because of his Anglo-Irish and military background he sympathized with the LOYALIST elite's aspirations. Hence the early development of NB was shaped by Carleton and the Loyalist leaders, with the choice of capital, appointments, religious, political, educa-

Carleton Place, Ont, located on Ontario's Mississippi R, 45km SW of Ottawa (*photo by Richard Vroom*).

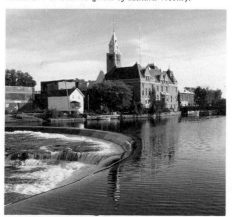

tional and even economic decisions reflecting this alliance. Carleton had originally hoped his New Brunswick posting would lead to a more substantial military command. Disappointed in this and in the slow growth of the colony, along with an increasingly assertive Assembly-rights party by 1795, Carleton tired of his office. He took a leave of absence, destined to be permanent, in 1803. After 1807 there is little evidence that he played any role in NB affairs and no evidence that he intended to take up residence in the province again. Carleton had many critics during his lifetime and among historical observers but he deserves to be acknowledged as a founding father of New Brunswick.

WILLIAM G. GODFREY

Carleton Place, Ont, Town, pop 6520 (1986c), 5626 (1981c), inc 1890, located on the Mississippi R, 45 km SW of Ottawa at the junction of 2 CPR lines; it was founded (1818) by William Morphy and his sons. The name is a corruption of Carlton Place, a famous square in Glasgow, Scotland. Lumber mills and manufacturing, especially of textiles and stoves, drew power from nearby falls in the past. Now electronics and tourism dominate the economy. A plaque in Memorial Pk honours native son A. Roy BROWN, WWI flying ace.

K.L. MORRISON

Carleton University, Ottawa, Ont, founded in 1942 as Carleton College to provide elementary university courses in the evening for government employees. The return of WWII veterans led to day courses and in 1946 the college acquired a building on First Avenue. Degree programs were established in arts, science, public administration and journalism, although the college did not receive a provincial charter until 1952. Officially it became a university in 1957 and moved to its present site on the Rideau R in 1959. It is governed by a president, a board of governors and a senate. A. Davidson DUNTON presided over the phenomenal growth between 1958 and 1972, with enrolment rising from 1000 to 7000 full-time students. By the end of the 1960s Carleton was offering degrees in engineering, architecture, industrial design and social work. The 1970s was a decade of consolidation, with steady growth in enrolment despite financial constraints. It now has faculties of arts, science, social sciences, engineering, and graduate studies, and it offers a graduate degree in Canadian studies. Carleton is a publicly supported institution.

H. BLAIR NEATBY

Enrolment: Carleton University, 1985-86 (Source: Statistics Canada)			
Full-time Undergrad	Full-time Graduate	Part-time Undergrad	Part-time Graduate
10 256	1117	4526	850

Carlin, Robert Hugh, trade unionist (b at Buckingham, Qué 10 Feb 1901). In 1916 he moved to COBALT, Ont, to work in the mines. He joined the miners' local union in the Western Federation of Miners (WFM), participated in the 1919 strike and belonged to the WFM's successor, the International Union of Mine Mill and Smelter Workers (Mine Mill). A founding member of Kirkland Lake Local 240, he was fired for union activity in 1940 but appointed a union organizer. In 1941 he led the historic Kirkland Lake gold miners' strike for union recognition. In 1942 he was elected to the union's international board to represent the Canadian District. An advocate of political action by labour, Carlin was elected CCF MPP in Ontario in 1943 and 1945. He was defeated in 1948 after a disagreement with his party, which viewed him as pro-communist. As an executive member of the CCL, he served on the Congress's Political Action

Committee. In 1962, after the Steelworkers' Union defeated Mine Mill and became the bargaining agent at Inco, Carlin became a Steelworkers' representative until his retirement in the 1970s.

LAUREL SEFTON MACDOWELL

Carling, Sir John, brewer, politician (b in London Twp, Upper Canada 23 Jan 1828; d at London, Ont 6 Nov 1911). His father, Thomas C. Carling, a Methodist agricultural labourer, had emigrated from Yorkshire in 1818. At age 21 John joined the brewing and malting business which his father had established in 1843 near Victoria Barracks, London. He inherited the business in 1849 and continued as president, but he left its operation to his brother William and entered politics. He represented London as a Conservative in the assembly of the Province of Canada 1857-67 and in the Ontario Assembly 1867-73. After Confederation, Carling also sat in the House of Commons 1867-74, 1878-91 and 1892-95. He held several Cabinet posts, most notably as postmaster general, under John A. Macdonald 1882-85, and minister of agriculture 1885-92. In 1893 he was created KCMG; he sat in the Senate 1891-92 and 1896 to his death. The incorporation of the Carling Brewing and Malting Co in 1883 helped to finance his political career.

ALBERT TUCKER

Carmacks, YT, Village, pop 280 (1986c), 256 (1981c), is located on the YUKON R at the mouth of the Nordenskiold R, 175 km downstream from Whitehorse. It was named for George Washington Carmack, who built a cabin at the forks (1893), from which he traded for furs. Carmack found coal at the site and in 1896 was one of 3 prospectors who staked the claim on Bonanza Cr that touched off the KLONDIKE GOLD RUSH. Carmacks grew during the rush as a supply point and fuel stop for riverboats. Now a local improvement district, it remains a service centre for travellers on the Klondike and Campbell highways.

H. GUEST

Carman, Man, Town, pop 2500 (1986c), inc 1905, located 80 km SW of Winnipeg on the Boyne R in the Pembina Triangle, is one of the most prosperous agricultural districts in Manitoba. Carman was first settled in the 1870s and named after Rev Albert CARMAN, an episcopal bishop, who dedicated the first church built in the community in 1882. With the arrival of the railway in 1888, the town built on its agricultural base, providing a variety of farming supply services and food processing plants. Along with fertilizers and farm equipment sales, the town processes a number of special crops as well as horticultural products. Nurseries and greenhouses are of increasing importance. The Dufferin Agricultural Society's annual fair is one of the region's longest established events.

JOHN SELWOOD

Carman, Albert, Methodist clergyman, teacher (b at Iroquois, Upper Canada 27 June 1833; d at Toronto 3 Nov 1917). Dr Carman was a skilled administrator and preacher, firmly committed to the warm, personal piety of traditional Methodism. Although he had spent 2 decades as a mathematics teacher and school administrator before becoming a clergyman, he opposed those who advocated the "higher criticism" or scientific study of the Bible, charging that they were undermining Christian faith. He was bishop of the Methodist Episcopal Church before the 1884 union of all Canadian Methodist churches. Though a genial man, he took his personal authority seriously. As general superintendent after union until retirement, he successfully encouraged missions to prairie settlers. His last decade in office was marked by spectacular clashes with more liberal Methodists. He retired in 1915.

TOM SINCLAIR-FAULKNER

Carman, Bliss, poet, editor, journalist (b at Fredericton 15 Apr 1861; d at New Canaan, Conn 8 June 1929). Of Puritan New England and LOYAL-IST descent, he attended University of New Brunswick and Edinburgh and Harvard universities. In 1890 he joined the editorial staff of the New York *Independent,* introducing Canadian poets to its readers, and later worked on *Cosmopolitan, Atlantic Monthly, Chap Book* and other literary journals. With *Low Tide on Grand Pré* (1893) and the 3 volumes of "Vagabondia" poems (1894-1900), Carman won international recognition. Some of his best-known work appeared in *The Pipes of Pan* (5 vols, 1902-05). His collected *Poems* (2 vols, 1904) and *Sappho* (1905) contain almost all his best lyrical output.

Carman conducted a syndicated newspaper column, essays from which were reprinted in 3 volumes, notably *The Kinship of Nature* (1903). With Mary Perry King, he collaborated on *The Making of Personality* (1908) and in that year moved to New Canaan. With Mrs King he wrote *Daughters of Dawn* (1913) and *Earth Deities and Other Masques* (1914). Suffering from tuberculosis, he spent many months during 1919 and 1920 in sanitaria. Upon recovery, he embarked on reading and lecture tours of Canada and the US which brought renewed popularity. In 1928 he was awarded the Lorne Pierce Gold Medal by the Royal Society of Canada. Carman's prose works reflect his wide interests but are otherwise undistinguished. As an inveterate letter writer, however, he did develop a lively, epistolary style, and he achieved in his best verse a few finely wrought lyrics of enduring quality. H.P. GUNDY

Carmichael, Franklin, painter (b at Orillia, Ont 4 May 1890; d at Toronto 24 Oct 1945). A founding member of the GROUP OF SEVEN, Carmichael was active as a painter, industrial designer and teacher. In 1911 he apprenticed with the Toronto commercial-art firm Grip Ltd, where he met several artists who later formed the Group. He studied in Antwerp 1913-14, and then worked as a designer in Toronto, at the same time painting watercolours and oils of northern Ontario landscape. Such paintings as *Jackfish Village* (1926) exhibit elegant compositional structures and lyric charm, gentler in feeling than many paintings by other Group of Seven members. Carmichael was a founding member 1925 and president 1932-34 of the Canadian Society of Painters in Water Colour and a founding member in 1933 of the Canadian Group of Painters. He taught at the Ontario College of Art 1932-45. DOROTHY FARR

Snow Clouds (1938), oil on canvas, by Franklin Carmichael, a founding member of the Group of Seven (*courtesy National Gallery of Canada*).

Carmichael, Harry John, industrialist (b at New Haven, Conn 29 Sept 1891; d at Toronto 28 Oct 1979). Born in the US of Canadian parents, Carmichael came to Canada and became president and general manager of McKinnon Indus-

tries, St Catharines, Ont, in 1929. In 1936 he became VP and general manager of General Motors of Canada at Oshawa. In WWII Carmichael's familiarity with mass-production techniques proved invaluable to the Canadian economic war effort, and his appointment to head C.D. HOWE's war production was no surprise. In 1944 and 1945 Carmichael turned to the reconversion of industry to meet peacetime requirements, and at the end of 1945 he left Ottawa. Later, Carmichael served on the Industrial Defence Board (1948-51) and held many corporate directorships, including that of ARGUS CORPORATION LTD. ROBERT BOTHWELL

Carmichael, James William, shipbuilder-owner, merchant, politician (b at New Glasgow, NS 16 Dec 1819; d there 1 May 1903). Carmichael, son of New Glasgow's founder, James Carmichael, became its most prominent merchant, shipbuilder and shipowner. He supported the transition to manufacturing and in 1882 invested in Canada's first steel company, Nova Scotia Steel. A Liberal and federal MP 1867-71 and 1874-78, Carmichael's strong views against Confederation and in support of free trade brought electoral defeat in 1872, 1878, 1882 and 1896. Appointed to the Senate in 1899, he resigned in 1903. L.D. McCANN

Reading: J.M. Cameron, *Political Pictonians* (1967).

Carnarvon, Henry Howard Molyneux Herbert, 4th Earl of, politician (b at London, Eng 24 June 1831; d there 28 June 1890). As secretary of state for the colonies 1866-67, Carnarvon supervised the drafting of the BRITISH NORTH AMERICA ACT and steered it through the British Parliament. A Conservative and imperialist, Carnarvon believed that Canadian CONFEDERATION would strengthen the political integrity of the empire. As chairman of the Royal Commission on the Defence of British Possessions and Commerce Abroad, 1879-82, he was instrumental in the reform of Britain's defence policy and urged that Canada increase its role in imperial defence. ROGER SARTY

Carney, Patricia, economist, journalist, politician (b at Shanghai, China 26 May 1935). In 1939 her parents brought her to Canada. While working as a journalist she studied economics at UBC and graduated in 1960. She was a successful business columnist, writing principally for the Vancouver *Sun* and *Province*. In 1970 she started her own consulting firm on northern Canadian matters and prepared studies on subjects such as pipelines, satellite communications and labour relations. After returning to Vancouver from Yellowknife she ran as a Progressive Conservative candidate in Vancouver Centre in the 1979 federal election but was narrowly defeated. The next year she was elected and, in opposition, served as energy critic. She was re-elected in 1984 and was appointed minister of energy, mines and resources, with primary responsibility for working out a new energy deal with the Western provinces. In a June 1986 Cabinet shuffle she became minister of international trade. She was deeply involved in the SOFTWOOD LUMBER DISPUTE and the FREE TRADE negotiations with the US. PATRICIA ROY

Carnivora, order of flesh-eating mammals which includes terrestrial and aquatic families. Terrestrial carnivores include Canidae (dogs, wolves, jackals, foxes); Ursidae (bears, giant panda); Procyonidae (raccoons, lesser panda); Mustelidae (skunks, weasels, badgers, otters, martens, wolverine); Viverridae (civets, mongooses); Hyaenidae (hyenas, aard wolves); and Felidae (cats). Marine carnivores include Otari-

idae (eared seals); Phocidae (earless seals); Odobenidae (walruses). In Canada, 8 families are represented with 25 genera and 38 species. Only Felidae and the marine carnivores are almost exclusively meat-eaters; the remainder can eat other foods. Many are partly herbivorous; some have become, secondarily, wholly herbivorous. Carnivores arose from primitive Insectivora in the Paleocene epoch (66.4-57.8 million years ago). Their great variety shows how well adapted carnivores are to the prey available on land and sea. Solitary carnivores usually take prey smaller than themselves, eg, foxes eat mice; pack hunters take game as large as or larger than themselves, as wolves take caribou. Some (eg, bears and raccoons) are specialized omnivores, eating any plant or animal food; others (eg, mongooses) eat only insects. Giant pandas eat only bamboo shoots and polar bears eat mainly seals.

A carnivore's tools are its teeth and feet. Cursorial (running) forms have nonretractile claws, eg, dogs and cheetahs; springing or stalking forms have retractile claws, eg, most cats. Carnivores depend on strong incisors, large, prominent canines and crushing or shearing cheek-teeth, and damaged teeth can bring death as surely as a broken leg. Female terrestrial carnivores also use their large canines to protect helpless young. Terrestrial females usually bear their multiple young in dens or lairs, and rejoin their social group when the young are mobile. Seals bear their single young on land, usually in a harem dominated by a breeding bull. Successful Carnivora have to outwit prey and, thus, are highly intelligent. They hunt cautiously, avoiding injury. Many co-operate in hunting, live in social groups, follow a leader, and share resources to ensure the group's survival. Not all carnivorous animals are Carnivora, since many animals eat other animals. Other carnivorous vertebrates include whales, marsupial native cats, lizards, crocodiles, newts, frogs and many fish. *See also* separate entries under species names, eg, WOLVES, OTTERS, SEALS. C.S. CHURCHER

Reading: R.F. Ewer, *The Carnivores* (1973).

Carnivorous Plants are flowering plants with leaves adapted for trapping small animals. Pitcher plants (genera *Nepenthes, Sarracenia, Darlingtonia, Cephalotus*) have open, water-filled traps that act as pitfalls for insects attracted by nectar around the rim of the pitchers. In butterworts (*Pinguicula*), sticky leaf surfaces act as flypaper to trap prey; in sundews (*Drosera*), sticky, long-stalked glands serve the same function, then bend inwards to enfold the victim. In aquatic bladderworts (*Utricularia*), each of numerous submerged bladders has a trap door that springs open when trigger hairs around it are touched. The minute animal is then carried inside by the rush of water. Once trapped, the animal is digested by enzyme secretions or decomposed by micro-organisms. Its remains release soluble organic molecules (eg, amino acids) which supplement nutrients in short supply in the plant's habitat. Worldwide, about 500 species have been described and classified; 18 species occur in Canada, among them a single species of PITCHER PLANT (*Sarracenia purpurea*), common to eastern N American bogs. The best-known carnivorous plant, the Venus flytrap, does not occur in Canada. ERICH HABER

Reading: D.E. Schnell, *Carnivorous Plants of the US and Canada* (1976).

Caroline After the abortive 1837 Upper Canadian Rebellion, its leader, William Lyon MACKENZIE, retreated with some 200 followers to Navy I in the Niagara R. There the *Caroline,* an American-owned ship based in Ft Schlosser, NY, was employed carrying supplies to the rebels. On 29 Dec 1837 a force of UC militia, led by Commander

Andrew Drew, Royal Navy, found her moored at Schlosser. A brief encounter ensued, in which one American was killed. The *Caroline*, set ablaze and then adrift, foundered above the falls and sank. The incident exacerbated the already strained relations between Britain and America.

J.E. REA

Caron, Sir Joseph-Philippe-René-Adolphe, politician (b at Québec C 24 Dec 1843; d at Montréal 20 Apr 1908). Seminary educated, trained as a lawyer and something of a *bon vivant*, Caron was a Conservative MP, 1873-1900, serving as the minister of militia and defence, 1880-92, and postmaster-general, 1892-96. Caron oversaw the expansion of the tiny Canadian permanent force in 1883, but he put his party's political interests over the military reforms urged by the British government. A master of patronage but generally a weak minister, he was surprisingly effective in mobilizing a force to counter the North-West Rebellion. Afterwards Caron stood by John A. MACDONALD in his determination to deal harshly with Louis RIEL. Caron was left out of the Cabinet formed in 1896 by Sir Charles TUPPER.

NORMAN HILLMER

Caron, Louis, journalist, writer (b at Sorel, Qué 21 July 1942). He quit his classical studies to try several trades before becoming a journalist, 1960-76, with Radio-Canada, *Le Nouvelliste* of Trois-Rivières and the Québec government. After 1976 he devoted himself to writing. After his first works, *L'Illusionniste* and *Le Guetteur* (1978), came 4 novels, *L'Emmitouflé* (1977), Prix Hermès and Prix France-Canada; *Le Bonhomme sept-heures*; and the first 2 volumes of *Fils de la Liberté – Le Canard de bois* (1981), Prix France-Québec, produced as a TV serial, and *La Corne de brume* (1982). In general, Caron takes his subjects from history but without ever writing so-called historical novels: the conscription crisis of 1917 (*L'Emmitouflé*), a 1955 earthquake in Nicolet (*Le Bonhomme sept-heures*), the Rebellions of 1837-38 (*Le Canard de bois, La Corne de brume*). Yet Caron is essentially a raconteur, with a vivid, graphic style. In 1986 he and journalist Réjean Tremblay co-wrote the TV series *Lance et compte*.

GILLES DORION

Carpmael, Charles, meteorologist (b at Streatham Hall, Eng 19 Sept 1846; d in Eng 21 Oct 1894). Carpmael directed the development and extension of the Canadian storm-warning and weather-forecasting services for more than a decade. Following graduation from Cambridge, he came to Canada in 1872 as deputy director of the national meteorological service and succeeded G.T. KINGSTON as director in 1880. Director until 1894, Carpmael expanded the activities of the service in astronomy and became responsible for a national time service in 1883. He was a charter fellow and officer of the RSC and an officer of the Royal Canadian Institute.

MORLEY THOMAS

Carr, Emily, painter, writer (b at Victoria 13 Dec 1871; d there 2 Mar 1945). Her English parents had settled in Victoria where her father was a successful businessman. With her brother and 4 older sisters, Emily, a child of independent spirit, grew up in a disciplined, orderly household in the restricted social and intellectual climate of the small, island city. Orphaned in her teens she went in 1891 to study art at California School of Design in San Francisco, pursuing an interest that had little opportunity of serious development in Victoria. On her return home 2 years later, she set up a studio and started art classes for children. A study trip to England in 1899 did little to advance her art, and a lengthy illness extended the stay into 1904. More signif-

Emily Carr, *Big Raven* (1931), oil on canvas. Carr's work was deeply influenced by the art of the Northwest Coast Indians (*courtesy Vancouver Art Gallery*).

icant was a visit to France in 1910, for she returned in the autumn of 1911 with a vigorous, colourful, postimpressionist style of painting that marked the end of her earlier anachronistic English watercolour mode. Back in BC she continued a program begun in 1908 to visit Indian sites, many in remote areas, and paint a record of the vanishing villages, houses and totem poles. By 1913 she had produced a large body of work on the Indian theme but, unable to live from her art, she built a small apartment house in Victoria for income and spent most of the next 15 dispiriting years in its management.

The period of mature and original production on which her reputation rests commenced when Carr was 57 and was stimulated by a trip to eastern Canada where she was included in a national exhibition, and met Lawren HARRIS and other members of the GROUP OF SEVEN. Their work, friendliness, and encouragement renewed her ambition and brought fresh direction to her art. Slowly, from 1928 on, critical recognition, exposure in exhibitions other than regional, and occasional purchases began to diminish her sense of neglect and artistic isolation, though she experienced only the most modest practical success during her lifetime. After 1932, nature themes replaced Indian subjects, and her work became less designed and more freely expressive of the large rhythms of western forests, beaches and skies.

A severe heart attack in 1937 signalled the start of declining health, and she began devoting more time to writing, an activity begun in the 1920s. In 1941 KLEE WYCK was published and received a Governor General's Award. *The Book of Small* was published in 1942, her last year of substantial painting, and *The House of All Sorts* in 1944. *Growing Pains*, *The Heart of a Peacock*, *Pause*, and *Hundreds and Thousands*, her journals, were published posthumously.

DORIS SHADBOLT

Reading: Edythe Hembroff-Schleicher, *Emily Carr: The Untold Story* (1978); Doris Shadbolt, *The Art of Emily Carr* (1979); Maria Tippett, *Emily Carr: A Biography* (1979).

Carr, Shirley, union officer (b at Niagara Falls, Ont). In 1960 she became a union activist, serving in several executive positions in Local 133, Canadian Union of Public Employees (CUPE). In 1970 she was instrumental in the formation of a CUPE local representing employees of the Regional Municipality of Niagara and was the local's president until 1974. From 1967 she was an active officer of the Ontario Division of CUPE and at the national level she was elected regional and then general vice-president of the union. She was elected an executive vice-president of the Canadian Labour Congress in 1974. She replaced Dennis McDermott as president after being elected unanimously 1 May 1986, the first woman and the first candidate with a public service background to hold the position.

LAUREL SEFTON MACDOWELL

Carrier are an Athapaskan, or DENE, group of about 5000 in north-central BC. Their name (Carrier, *Porteur*) derives from the custom of widows carrying the ashes of a deceased husband in a bag for about a year, at which time a ceremonial distribution of goods released her of the obligation. The Carrier also call themselves Dakelh. There are 3 major subgroupings, based on dialect and culture: Upper Carrier, or Babine, located along Bulkley R and Babine Lk; Central Carrier in the Stuart Lk and Fraser Lk basins; and Lower Carrier in the Blackwater R region.

In the 18th century the Carrier relied upon hunting and fishing. Lower Carrier social organization was based on the extended family, consisting of brothers, their wives and children and married sons' wives and children. Each group (or *sadeku*) was associated with a hunting territory and with fishing sites, but individual ownership of land was not developed. Upper and Central Carrier had matrilineal descent groups (clans). Inheritance of property and use rights was matrilineal for Upper and Central Carrier, and bilateral elsewhere.

Trade and other interaction with Gitksan and BELLA COOLA peoples resulted in Carrier adoption of POTLATCH and ranking systems. Fur-trade posts were established at Ft McLeod (1805), Stuart Lk and Fraser Lk (1806) and at the confluence of the Nechako and Fraser rivers (Ft George, 1807). The Stuart Lk post (Ft St James) was headquarters for the entire New Caledonia fur trading district. The fur trade not only brought technological changes with the influx of European goods, but extensive changes in living patterns and resource allocations as well. After 1860, settlement and mining on the upper Fraser R also broke the relative isolation of the native people in the area. The Oblates established a mission at Ft St James (1873) and pressured the Carrier to end potlatching and other customs. Because of the mission and trading post, Ft St James became an important centre for seasonal gatherings of Carrier from throughout the region. After the completion of a railway in the area (1914), the Carrier became involved in the logging industry as seasonal labourers, though maintaining hunting, trapping and fishing activities – an economic pattern that continues today. Diseases such as smallpox, measles and influenza reduced the Carrier populations, which reached a low point in the late 1920s.

The Carrier, numbering 6591, are divided into 14 administrative bands, each with several small reserves (est in the 1890s). Members of each community are connected by extensive kinship ties, which act as a framework for the inheritance of traplines and the exchange of goods and services. Extensive industrial operations in the region in the past decades have highlighted Carrier dependence on traditional bush resources.

DOUGLAS HUDSON

Carrier, Roch, poet, storywriter, novelist, playwright, essayist (b in the Beauce, Qué 13 May 1937). After publishing 2 collections of poetry, *Les Jeux incompris* (1956) and *Cherche tes mots, cherche tes pas* (1958), Carrier offered critics *Jolis deuils* (1964), a group of bizarre stories that won him a province of Québec award, Les Concours littéraires du Québec (1965). *La* GUERRE, YES SIR! (1968) made his reputation in Québec and abroad. His extraordinary talent as a storyteller was confirmed with *Floralie, où est-tu?* (1969) and *Il est par là le soleil* (1970), which brought back some of the characters from *La Guerre,* as well as themes of war, sexual repression, exploitation of the little guys, French Canadians' distrust of the "Anglais" and the hold of a religion that borders on superstition. This trilogy presents a search for meaning in life and death, a search that permeates all Carrier's work. *De l'Amour dans la feraille* (1984; tr *Heartbreaks Along the Road,* 1987) focused on the Duplessis era and was his largest and most ambitious novel. Carrier has also written a film script, a collection of short stories, a children's story and 2 plays. Individually and collectively, these works bear eloquent witness to Roch Carrier's rich imagination and desire to keep developing his narrative technique and themes, even though he continues to stress certain cherished topics.

JACQUES COTNAM

Carrot (*Daucus carota*), cool-climate plant belonging to the Umbelliferae family and grown as a ROOT CROP in Canada. Carrots are biennials, but are grown as annuals. They are native to central Asia and were used as medicinal herbs in Afghanistan before their introduction to Europe in medieval times. Carrots have been improved by selection and hybridization: those destined for processing have large, thick, conical roots; those for the fresh market are rather long and cylindrical. The root is a reservoir for sugars manufactured by the leaves. Leafstalks and leaves, which are used to pull the carrot from the soil during mechanical harvesting, must be protected from leaf diseases. Carrots require 70-100 days to produce a harvest of approximately 30 t/ha for the fresh market and 60 t/ha for the processing industry. Principal insect pests are weevils and flies; common plant diseases, *Alternaria* and *Cercospora* blights. Carrots are a source of ascorbic acid and are consumed fresh, cooked or as juice. They are grown in every province; nearly 8000 ha (over 4000 ha in Québec alone) are devoted to commercial production.

PIERRE SAURIOL

Carse, Margaret Ruth Pringle, dancer, choreographer, teacher, director (b at Edmonton 7 Dec 1916). A woman of courage and optimism, Ruth Carse founded the ALBERTA BALLET CO and nurtured it to professional status. She performed with Boris VOLKOFF's Canadian Ballet and as a member of the Radio City Music Hall's ballet corps in New York C before injury forced her retirement in 1954. She returned to teach in Edmonton and formed small amateur companies; Dance Interlude became the Edmonton Ballet in 1960 and the Alberta Ballet Company in 1966. Carse founded the Alberta Ballet School in 1971 and resigned as director of the company to teach. She has choreographed more than 50 works for TV, opera and musical theatre, and for the Alberta Ballet. In 1986 she was inducted into Canada's Cultural Hall of Fame. In 1987 she was on the advisory board of Calgary's Mount Royal School of Dance.

MICHAEL CRABB

Carson, William, physician, reformer, politician (b at Kirkcudbright, Scotland 1770; d at St John's, Nfld 26 Feb 1843). After arriving in St John's in 1808 he was connected to the local garrison until the opening in 1814 of a public hospital he helped to found. After 1811, through pamphlet writing and direct petition to Britain, Carson began a long and sometimes vituperative campaign to improve social conditions in Newfoundland, to repeal certain restrictive colonial laws and ultimately to establish some form of local popular representation. Carson, Patrick Morris and other associates finally achieved a partial victory in 1832 when the British Parliament granted Newfoundland a bicameral representative legislature comprising an appointed council and an elected assembly. Carson was defeated when he ran for election in 1832 but was returned in a by-election the next year. Both within and outside the assembly he maintained his struggle for reform in agriculture, education, health care and government. He continued to be elected to the assembly and was elected its speaker in 1837; he was appointed to the executive council in 1842 just before his death. *See also* NEWFOUNDLAND: HISTORY.

ROBERT D. PITT

Carter, Sir Frederick Bowker Terrington, politician, judge, prime minister of Newfoundland 1865-78 (b at St John's 12 Feb 1819; d there 1 Mar 1900). Born into one of Newfoundland's most distinguished families, Carter was educated in St John's and in London, Eng, and was called to the Newfoundland Bar in 1842. He was elected to the House of Assembly as a Conservative in 1855. One of leader Hugh HOYLES's most trusted advisers, he became Speaker of the House when the Conservatives won the 1861 election. A Newfoundland representative at the 1864 Québec Conference, Carter returned home a convinced Confederate. Upon Hoyles's retirement (1865), he became prime minister. His government was the first to include both Protestants and Roman Catholics, and thus significantly eased the sectarian tensions that had plagued Newfoundland. Carter's government ran for reelection in 1869 on a platform that promised to bring Newfoundland into Canadian CONFEDERATION and was badly defeated. Although he again became prime minister in 1874, he made no effort to raise the contentious Confederation issue. Carter retired as prime minister in 1878 and was appointed to the Newfoundland Supreme Court. In 1880 he became chief justice.

GEOFF BUDDEN

Carter, Sidney Robert, art and antique dealer, photographer (b at Toronto 18 Feb 1880; d at Montréal 27 Mar 1956). Carter was an early advocate of pictorialism in photography, and by 1901-02 was exhibiting in London, the US and Canada. In 1904 he became an associate of Alfred Stieglitz's Photo-Secession in New York C, and 3 years later in Montréal he prepared an exhibition promoting pictorialism. Largely between about 1917 and 1928 Carter accepted portrait commissions; his style, however, slowly lost the haunting quality evident in his portrait of Rudyard Kipling (1907), favouring graphic effect and a firmer outline. His photographs from the 1930s are conservative, and he seemed to lose interest in the medium that had won him prominence.

LILLY KOLTUN

Carter, Wilfred Arthur Charles, Wilf, singer, songwriter (b at Port Hilford, NS 18 Dec 1904). He left the Maritimes in the 1920s and reached Alberta, becoming a cowboy and part-time entertainer. In 1930 he made his radio debut in Calgary. In Montréal, a few years later, he recorded, for RCA Victor, "My Swiss Moonlight Lullaby" and "The Capture of Albert Johnson," which were hits. His popularity grew with subsequent recordings and radio shows on the CBC and on CBS and NBC in the US, where his stage name was "Montana Slim." In 1940 he was seriously hurt in a car crash, and though still able to record, was unable to perform until 1949. Throughout the 1950s Carter's touring show was one of Canada's most popular attractions. In the 1980s he was still performing, writing songs and recording for RCA, which in 1983 released a 2-record 50th-anniversary salute to him, one of the fathers of Canadian COUNTRY AND WESTERN MUSIC. In 1985 he was inducted into the Juno Hall of Fame.

RICHARD GREEN

Cartier, Sir George-Étienne, lawyer, railway promoter, politician, prime minister of the Province of Canada (b at St-Antoine, Lower Canada 6 Sept 1814; d at London, Eng 20 May 1873). From a wealthy family of grain exporters and millers, and supposedly a descendant of Jacques CARTIER, he was a FATHER OF CONFEDERATION and dominated the politics of Québec for a generation. A graduate of the Sulpician Collège de Montréal and called to the bar in 1835, Cartier joined the radical FILS DE LA LIBERTÉ (Sons of Liberty), composed the patriotic song, "O Canada, mon pays, mes amours" – perhaps the model for

Sir George-Étienne Cartier, lawyer, railway promoter, and Father of Confederation. His great accomplishment was reconciling French Canadians to Confederation (*courtesy National Archives of Canada /C-8007*).

the later national anthem – and was secretary of the reorganized ST-JEAN-BAPTISTE SOCIETY in 1843.

In 1837, at SAINT-DENIS, Cartier fought bravely alongside Wolfred NELSON and the rebels as they successfully routed Col Charles Gore's Waterloo veterans. After a narrow escape and exile in Vermont, he successfully petitioned in 1838 to return and practise law in Montréal. Specializing in property and railway promotion, Cartier was active in politics and became Louis-Hippolyte LAFONTAINE's campaign manager and right-hand man. With responsible government won, he agreed to run as a Liberal Reformer in Verchères in 1848. He moved to Montréal E in 1861 after the coalition with the Upper Canadian Conservatives, and as Bleu chief, served as co-premier with John A. MACDONALD in the Union parliaments of 1857-58 and 1858-62, in which ministry he set in motion the movement toward CONFEDERATION.

Cartier involved himself heavily in the development of the GRAND TRUNK RY, becoming its solicitor. After his election, despite government assistance to the line he served, he became chairman of the Railway Committee of Parliament. He was a driving force in the early promotion of the CPR, with the goal of making Montréal the terminus of a transcontinental trading network. Rival railway promoters funded his defeat in Montréal E by Louis-Amable Jetté of the short-lived Parti national in 1872 and engineered the release in Apr 1873 of election fund-raising telegrams – the so-called PACIFIC SCANDAL. Cartier, whose letters had promised Sir Hugh ALLAN the railway contract, was already mortally ill with Bright's disease. He died soon after seeking treatment in London and the CPR languished for almost a decade.

Cartier's accomplishments included ensuring the choice of Ottawa as the national capital and reconciling the majority of French Canada to Confederation on the grounds that it made possible the re-establishment of the old Province of Québec. He negotiated in London for the transfer of the HBC territory of RUPERT'S LAND to the Dominion. While acting PM during Macdonald's illnesses and after personal meetings with provincial delegations, he played the primary role in drafting the Manitoba and British Columbia Acts. He probably met with RIEL, who idolized him, and after passage of the Manitoba Act, sent many of his own handpicked men to administer the new province. A former rebel against the Crown, this great patriot served as Canada's first minister of militia and defence. ALASTAIR SWEENY

Reading: J. Boyd, *Sir George Étienne Cartier* (1914); Alastair Sweeny, *George-Étienne Cartier* (1976); B. Young, *Sir George-Étienne Cartier* (1981).

Cartier, Jacques, navigator (b at St-Malo, France, between 7 June and 23 Dec 1491; d there 1 Sept 1557). Cartier led 3 voyages of exploration to the St Lawrence region in 1534, 1535-36 and 1541-42. He is usually credited with discovering Canada, meaning the small region of Québec he named Canada during his 1535 voyage. He was the first explorer of the Gulf of St Lawrence and certainly the first to chart the ST LAWRENCE R – the discovery of which in 1535 enabled France to occupy the interior of N America. From remarks in the travel accounts credited to him, it would seem that Cartier's career began with voyages to Brazil. He probably accompanied Giovanni da VERRAZZANO to America in 1524 and 1528, and certainly came to Newfoundland before 1534, since the stated destination of his first official voyage was the "Baie des Châteaux" (Str of Belle Isle), and he sailed there directly as if it were familiar to him.

Charged by François I to look for gold in the New World and a passage to Asia, Cartier set off from St-Malo 20 Apr 1534 with 2 ships and 61 men. He arrived off Newfoundland 20 days later.

The N American portion of a 1546 world map by Pierre Desceliers is one of the earliest maps to show Jacques Cartier's exploration of the St Lawrence River. Labrador is at lower left, Mexico is at the upper right (*courtesy John Ryland's Library, Manchester, 11546/ copy in National Archives of Canada/NMC-40461*).

Searching for a passage through the continent, he explored areas that were already known, freely assigning names to the N coast of the Gulf of ST LAWRENCE. He sailed along the W coast of Newfoundland and reached Cabot Str. On June 26 he reached the Îles de la Madeleine and on June 29 discovered Prince Edward Island. He searched vainly for a passage, entering Baie de Chaleur and Baie de Gaspé, where he made contact with a group of Iroquois who had come there to hunt seal. He raised a cross on July 24, bearing the arms of France. The meaning was clear to the Iroquois chief DONNACONA, who protested but later relented and allowed Cartier to leave with 2 of his sons. Cartier sailed N to Anticosti I (missing the opening to the river), thence to Newfoundland, and on Aug 15 headed home, arriving at St-Malo 5 Sept 1534.

The larger 1535 expedition had 3 ships, *Grande Hermine, Petite Hermine* and *Émérillon,* and a crew of 110. Cartier left St-Malo 19 May 1535 and reached the Gulf after a long 50-day crossing and on Aug 13, led by his 2 Indian guides, entered the river which was called Rivière du Canada, and which was renamed St Lawrence early in the 1600s. He sailed upriver to STADACONA [Québec], which he reached on Sept 7. Against Donnacona's wishes, Cartier set out Sept 19 to explore the river farther, reaching HOCHELAGA [Montréal] on Oct 2. On his return to Stadacona he found that relations with the natives were strained. The effect of a severe winter was made more tragic by SCURVY, which claimed 25 lives among the French. On 6 May 1536 he left for France with some captured Iroquois, including Donnacona, arriving July 16. Cartier's reports, supported by Donnacona, of a golden "Kingdom of Saguenay," led to a third voyage.

Cartier made ready, but on 15 Jan 1541 Jean-François de la Rocque, sieur de ROBERVAL received a commission placing him, not Cartier, at the head of the expedition to colonize the St

Lawrence. Cartier put to sea first, on May 23, with 5 ships and a crew of some 1500. He reappeared before Stadacona on 23 Aug 1541, announced Donnacona's death, and set up at the western tip of Cap Diamant [Cap Rouge]. He made another trip to Hochelaga and again found himself at odds with the inhabitants of Stadacona, who kept the French under constant siege. Convinced that he had found diamonds and gold among the rocks, Cartier struck camp in June 1542. He met Roberval in the harbour of St John's, Nfld, and was ordered to return to Stadacona, but slipped away under cover of darkness and headed for France. The "gold" proved to be only iron pyrite and the "diamonds," worthless quartz. It is not known if Cartier was reprimanded but he was not entrusted with another long-range expedition. He retired to his manor at Limoilu and died at age 66. Cartier deserves mention among the great explorers of the 16th century. He discovered one of the world's great rivers, which was to become the axis of French power in N America. MARCEL TRUDEL

Reading: Marcel Trudel, *The Beginnings of New France, 1524-1663* (1973).

Cartography, History of Cartography is the art, science and technology of making maps, plans, charts and globes representing the Earth or any celestial body at any scale. Cartographic documents have been used as vehicles of communication by different cultures for many millennia; the earliest map to survive, drawn about 2300 BC on a clay tablet, was found in the Middle East. Centuries before Christ, Greek philosophers and mathematicians such as Pythagoras and Aristotle advanced the concept that the Earth was a sphere, and Eratosthenes (*c*276-196 BC) made a reasonable calculation of the Earth's circumference. In the 2nd century AD Claudius Ptolemy compiled and systematized the geographical knowledge of the day and encouraged the scientific study of geography. He suggested, for example, that maps be drawn strictly to scale (at that time not a common practice), that general world maps should be supplemented with a series of regional maps drawn at appropriate scales, and that maps should be drawn with co-ordinates.

Ptolemy's works were ignored until early in the 15th century, when an avid interest in the classical

New information about the Great Lakes not found on Champlain's 1632 map appears on Sanson's map of New France (*courtesy National Archives of Canada/NMC-21100*).

period had been revived by the Renaissance. His writings, translated from the Byzantine Greek, were copied in manuscript and later published. In a 1507-08 edition of his *Geographia*, a map showing a portion of eastern Canada appeared, and during the next century the Ptolemaic atlases became a major instrument of the diffusion of geographical knowledge of Canada.

In the following centuries the mapping of Canada evolved with the advance of cartographic techniques around the world and with continued EXPLORATION along the coasts and into the heart of the country. The development of instruments and techniques also changed the nature of the data gathered and the maps produced. The maps of the 16th century were rough and often conjectural; maps of the French period became more accurate in the better-known areas; and after 1800, with the widespread use of the sextant and advanced astronomical techniques for determining longitude (for example, using the marine chronometer), the major gaps in the map of Canada were filled. The 20th century has seen great refinement of mapping skills in Canada.

EDWARD H. DAHL

Native Mapmaking

Mapmaking was a widespread and well-developed art among the Indians and Inuit, although this fact has been largely ignored in the history of cartography. Most common were navigational maps, because the more nomadic hunting and gathering bands depended upon effective navigation over great expanses of wilderness. Maps were also drawn to facilitate trade and warfare over long distances. Military maps were used especially by the equestrian plains Indians, whose war parties sometimes ventured into unfamiliar regions of the grasslands.

Inuit and Indian navigational maps were usually drawn on the ground or in the snow. Sketched from memory, these stationary maps were accompanied by verbal descriptions of the country in question. They were thus ephemeral and, in contrast to the European use of maps,

required the successful traveller to rely entirely upon memory, a task for which Indians and Inuit were trained from childhood.

When a map was committed to media which affected its size, such as skins or bark, no attempt was made to fill in the entire space. Instead, detail was elaborated only where necessary. Shape was accurately portrayed on most native maps, and in this respect they differ little from modern survey maps. Scale, however, was often measured by the day's journey, and hence varied according to factors affecting travel time. Scale was also varied to exaggerate or clarify significant features for navigation, and in some maps reflected the cartographer's relative familiarity with different areas. Although Europeans frequently found these maps overly simple and of-

All of the Great Lakes are finally shown in the 1688 map of Vincenzo Coronelli (*courtesy National Archives of Canada/NMC-6411*).

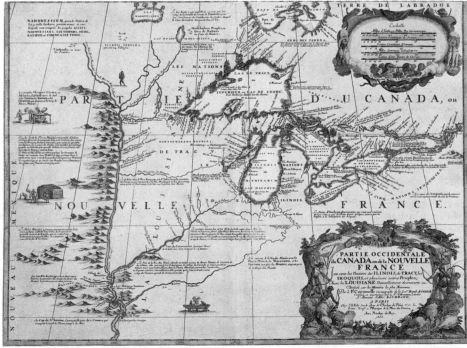

ten confusing, they were eminently suited to the overriding objective of most native cartography: to accentuate the environmental information salient to successful wilderness navigation.

Native maps were also used as general media of communication and as repositories of cultural life and lore. SHAWNANDITHIT, for example, drew a series of maps to illustrate the history of her tribe in the years leading up to its extinction. Maps also recalled historical events such as battles, and the OJIBWA elaborated charts to record their earlier migrations and past sacred events. Combined with PICTOGRAPHS, maps were used for general communication, most commonly in the form of notices of direction and of trips, and in missives that might properly be called "map letters." Just as native people in these ways communicated crucial geographical information to their fellows, so they afforded the early European explorers, traders and missionaries much of the geographical information that eventually carried them and their supporting enterprises from the Atlantic to the Pacific.

D.W. MOODIE

Early Explorers' Mapping

Most 16th-century maps relating to Canada are manuscript compilations, often undated and anonymous, prepared by European cartographers rather than by explorers. Since cartographers had to work with available material, these maps are at times a perplexing mixture of new information and old, copied from unspecified sources. Any review of the sequence in which Canada was first mapped is therefore somewhat conjectural. Until 1974 a map known as the "Vinland Map," acquired by Yale University almost a decade earlier and showing the NE coast of N America, was thought to be the earliest cartographic representation of Canada. It is now generally believed to be a forgery. The earliest known maps of Canada date from about 1502 to 1506. They depict the E coast of Newfoundland as that of an island in the N Atlantic. None of the land between Greenland and the Caribbean was known to Europeans. The most significant early configurations are those known as the "Cantino," "Canerio," "King-Hamy" (in Huntington Library, San Marino, Calif), "Oliveriana" (at Pesaro, Italy) and "Kunstmann II" charts. The earliest of these is probably the "Cantino" chart (*c*1502) which appears to have originated with the voyages of Gaspar CORTE-REAL (1500-01). No maps from John CABOT's voyage (1497) appear to have survived. Some scholars have interpreted the La Cosa chart, dated 1500, as a confused copy of a Cabot map, whereas others have pointed out that it contains information available only as late as 1508. In any case, none of the geographical features of the map that some scholars have interpreted as showing the eastern coast of Canada can be identified in such a way as to achieve scholarly consensus. The first printed maps to show parts of the New World, such as the Contarini (1506) and Ruysch (1507-08) maps, show the E coast of Newfoundland joined to Greenland as an extension of Asia. These configurations were probably based on the guess that Greenland and Newfoundland were connected (Corte-Real) and were all part of Asia (Cabot). In 1507 a map by Waldseemüller was the first to separate the New World from Asia, a concept that gained popularity during the next decade.

During the 1520s the E and S shores of Newfoundland as well as the E shore of Nova Scotia became better known, and maps of this period portray geographical features less ambiguously than those of the previous 20 years. Better maps, such as the "Miller I" (c1516-22), the Pedro Reinel (1516-20) and the map attributed to Diogo Ribeiro (the "Weimar" map, 1527), even hint at openings S and N of Newfoundland where later the Cabot Str and the Str of Belle Isle were explored by Jacques CARTIER. At least some of the features on these maps appear to be based on the exploration of João Alvares FAGUNDES (c1519-26). The first maps showing the entire coastline from Florida to Newfoundland were based on the explorations of Esteban Gómez (1525) and Giovanni da VERRAZZANO (1524). Although Gómez had hinted at an opening where the Bay of Fundy should be, all the maps of this period show an unbroken coastline. Later maps, such as the ones by Santa Cruz (1542), Lopo Homem (1554) and Diogo Homem (1558), drawn from data produced in the 1520s, demonstrate that Gómez actually suspected Nova Scotia to be an island, while some Portuguese more or less knew its true configuration. After Cartier's explorations (1534-42) the entire cartography of Canada underwent revision. None of Cartier's maps have survived. Those believed to be closest to his originals are a chart by John Rotz (1542) depicting the results of Cartier's first voyage (1534), the Desceliers map of 1546 and the "Harleian" world map (c1547). The last 2 depict Cartier's explorations to 1536. The outstanding contribution of these maps is that they add the gulf and river of St Lawrence to the shape of N America. A second group of maps, based apparently on French and Portuguese mapping, depicts the St Lawrence along with more realistic shapes for Newfoundland and Nova Scotia. The best example of these maps is the so-called "Vallard map" (1547). Few printed maps of this period deserve consideration, but one of significance is the famous 1569 world chart by Gerard Mercator which introduced the map projection bearing his name.

Arctic mapping began with Martin FROBISHER's first voyage (1576), although the southern tip of Greenland had appeared on maps since 1502. Frobisher's map of his bay on southeastern Baffin I has survived but, since he did not place his explorations in the context of the rest of N America, cartographers were uncertain where to place it. On the maps of George Best (1578) and Michael Lok (1582), Frobisher's Bay appears as NORTHWEST PASSAGE across N America. Following the less ambiguous maps that emanated from John DAVIS's voyages (1585-1587), Frobisher's "strait" was moved to the southern tip of Greenland, where it remained through much of the 17th century. Only a few cartographers made any attempt to link the northern discoveries with those on the St Lawrence and E coast. Probably the best attempt is a world map by Edward Wright printed in 1599.

C.E. HEIDENREICH

Mapping to 1763

Scientific mapping began with Samuel de CHAMPLAIN in 1603. In 1613 he published the first modern-looking map of eastern Canada, combining in it his own explorations with those of Henry HUDSON. By 1616 he had explored and mapped as far W as Georgian Bay. For other areas he used native maps and verbal accounts. His observations were made from compass and latitude readings as well as estimates of distance. Besides his 6 small-scale maps, of which that of 1632 is the most comprehensive, Champlain also produced 23 large-scale maps and picture plans of places between Cape Cod and Montréal.

From the time of Champlain's death in 1635 to the 1670s, the major explorers furnishing geographical information to European cartographers were Jesuit missionaries. By 1649 they had explored the eastern Great Lakes; the maps of Sanson (1650, 1656), and Fathers Bressani (1657) and Du Creux (1660) have survived in printed form. On these the Great Lakes are recognizable for the first time. Further Jesuit mapping led to the first good map of Lk Superior and northern Lk Michigan (1672) by Fathers Allouez and Dablon; the first delineation of the Mississippi R by Father MARQUETTE and Louis JOLLIET (1673); and a series of maps of the Iroquois country in upper New York state by Father Raffeix and others. One of the few non-Jesuit maps of the period was by the Sulpician Galinée, detailing his journey with Dollier from Montréal through the lower Great Lakes to Sault Ste Marie (1670). The necessary observations used to construct all these maps were similar to those used for Champlain's. In 1632 the Jesuits

---

Delisle's 1703 map of New France is the first to depict latitude and longitude more or less correctly (*courtesy National Archives of Canada/NMC-24722*).

began to observe and, later, to time lunar eclipses to establish longitude W of Paris or Rome.

From the 1670s to the end of the century the mapping of Canada is primarily associated with Jolliet and Jean-Baptiste-Louis FRANQUELIN, the latter being the more talented draftsman. He was Hydrographe du Roy at Québec 1686-97 and 1701-03, teaching hydrography and keeping the maps of NEW FRANCE up to date. The manuscript maps of explorers such as LA SALLE, Jolliet and a number of military surveyors were incorporated in large compilations sent to France, where professional mapmakers had access to them. The chief cartographers to the French court, such as Vincenzo Coronelli and Guillaume Delisle, based their printed maps in part on the information furnished by Franquelin. The maps of Coronelli (1688-89) and Delisle (1703) best sum up the late 17th-century cartography of Canada. The Delisle map also has the distinction of being the first with a fairly modern grid of longitude based on a lunar eclipse recorded at Québec in 1685 by Jean Deshayes.

Large-scale mapping during the 17th century was understandably confined to the St Lawrence R valley. Cadastral mapping (ie, mapping of property boundaries, building locations, etc) commenced with Jean Bourdon's mapping of seigneuries (1641); Bourdon also produced an early plan of Québec (1660). The St Lawrence R was charted by Jolliet and Franquelin (1685), but much more competently by Jean Deshayes (1685-86). Although the printed results of Deshayes's survey (1702) became the standard chart of the river, more accurate surveys were undertaken in the mid-18th century by Testu de la Richardière (1730-41), Gabriel Pellegrin (1734-55) and others. Cadastral maps also continued to be produced during the 18th century, one of the most notable being by Jean-Baptiste Decouagne in 1709. These maps and charts were all constructed by competent surveyors and military engineers using up-to-date instruments and surveying principles.

Increasingly strained relations with England made the activities of the French military engi-

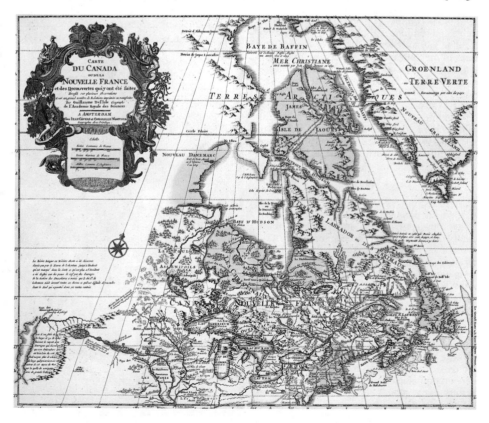

neers more important in the 18th century. The lower Great Lakes frontier was charted with some accuracy by the engineer Gaspard-Joseph CHAUSSEGROS DE LÉRY and his son of the same name. They also prepared maps of Québec and major fortifications from LOUISBOURG to Detroit. On the E Coast one of the first accurate hydrographic surveys was made by Joseph Bernard de Chabert (1750-51). In 1750 he built Canada's first observatory at Louisbourg for astronomical observation and longitude calculation.

While the settled and strategic areas of New France were being charted by trained engineers and surveyors, the interior was still being mapped by amateurs with little training and no instruments more sophisticated than a compass. The first maps of the region W of Lk Superior resulted from the LA VÉRENDRYE expeditions after 1731, while the northern interior of Québec was being mapped by the Jesuit Father Laure. These maps portray a recognizable lake and river system based on untrained observations and native information.

Very little 18th-century manuscript mapping found its way to printed maps until Jacques-Nicolas Bellin became chief engineer and geographer of the Dépôt des cartes, plans et journaux of the French MINISTÈRE DE LA MARINE. In 1744 he published 28 maps in Father P.F.X. CHARLEVOIX's combined *Histoire* and *Journal* (1744). These were the first printed maps of Canada based on new material since Delisle's of 40 years earlier. In succeeding years Bellin regularly updated his maps. Another important cartographer, Jean-Baptiste Bourguignon D'Anville, like Bellin, had access to original material, and he produced a series of fine maps between 1746 and 1755. Both cartographers published pamphlets explaining their source material and the reliability of their maps.

Primary English mapping of Canada before 1763 was confined entirely to the Arctic and the shores of Hudson Bay. Hudson's 1612 map of the bay's E shore and the straits was quickly replaced by maps of the entire bay by Thomas JAMES (1633) and Luke FOX. John Thornton produced a more accurate chart for the HUDSON'S BAY COMPANY (1685). The HBC did no more mapping until Arthur Dobbs criticized the company for its dismal record in exploration; beginning in 1741, expeditions resulted in a series of excellent charts by Christopher Middleton (1743), John Wigate (1746) and Henry Ellis (1748) as far N as Repulse Bay.

In 1756 the SEVEN YEARS' WAR interrupted mapping activities in New France. The last French map of N America, summarizing the latest geographical information available on Canada before it passed into British hands, was Bellin's "Carte de l'Amérique septentrionale" (1755). It shows that Canada had been mapped, roughly but recognizably, to about 102° W in present-day Manitoba and along the W shore of Hudson Bay to the Arctic Circle.   C.E. HEIDENREICH

Explorers' Maps after 1763

Although Québec fell in 1760, the Treaty of PARIS was not signed until Feb 1763. During the truce the British army under Gen MURRAY made the first detailed survey of this area, from a point above Montréal downstream to below Québec City. The "Murray Map," of which at least 5 hand-drawn copies were made, was drawn at a scale of 2000 feet to the inch (1:24 000) and showed much information of military importance, such as the population of villages and the positions of houses, churches and mills. Two originals of this map are held in the National Map Collection, Ottawa.

Britain's vast colonial empire in N America now stretched from the High Arctic to the Gulf of Mexico. Huge areas were essentially unknown to Europeans, with only sketchily charted coasts and a largely unmapped hinterland. For the development of resources and the expansion of trade, better charts of the harbours and coastal waters and more accurate maps of the interior were required. There were 3 excellent surveyors serving with the British forces in Canada. Samuel HOLLAND and Joseph DESBARRES were army officers; James COOK was the master of a ship in the British fleet. The work was divided among them: Cook was commissioned to chart the island of Newfoundland and the adjacent Labrador coast; Holland, appointed surveyor general of the Northern District of N America (which included all British holdings N of the Potomac R), concentrated on the Gulf of St Lawrence, including Prince Edward and Cape Breton islands and the New England coast; and DesBarres turned his attention to Nova Scotia, which at that time included present-day New Brunswick.

Many valuable maps and charts resulted. Cook's charts were of such high quality that his reputation was assured. DesBarres's major publication was *The Atlantic Neptune*, a navigational atlas of the E coast of N America containing charts at various scales, coastal views, tide tables and sailing directions. He was allowed to publish the *Neptune* privately under his own name, although Holland and Cook had been responsible for some of its charts. Holland's publications concentrated on landward mapping, but of course he used the data produced by the surveys of his colleagues. His map, "A General Map of the Northern British Colonies in America," drawn at 60 miles to the inch (1:3 801 600), is one of the most important of this period.

Meanwhile, other surveyors were carrying out the necessary property surveys so that farmsteads could be established. This work increased greatly after LOYALISTS began arriving in 1783. Settlement in Nova Scotia was handicapped by the lack of a comprehensive land-granting procedure. In the Province of Quebec (which included much of present-day southern Ontario), by contrast, the settlement of the Loyalists was carried out with military efficiency. Gov Gen Frederick HALDIMAND and Holland devised a system, comprising townships and lots, for each settler to get a measured portion of land, surveyed at minimal cost and marked on the ground. An important requirement was the preparation of a map of each township showing the layout of farm lots and the major topographic features.

According to Hocquart, the Domaine du Roi extended "from Île aux Coudres to two leagues below Sept-Îles, in which area were the posts of Tadoussac, Chicoutimi, Lac Saint-Jean, Sept-Îles and the Moisie River" among other places (*courtesy Service historique de la Marine, Vincennes, France: Service hydrographique, recueil 67, 0° 10*).

A second type of 19th-century cartographic survey that equalled the township surveys in importance was the hydrographic survey of the Great Lakes carried out originally by the British Admiralty, but after 1884 by Canadian hydrographers. The work was started in 1815 by Capt William F. Owen and was turned over to Lt Henry BAYFIELD the following year. During the next 40 years Bayfield supervised the surveying of the Great Lakes, the St Lawrence and the Nova Scotia coast, and was personally responsible for the high quality of the charts produced.

Throughout the 19th century and into the 20th, there were hundreds of maps drawn of parts of eastern Canada that were simply compilations and redraftings of the information available from township plans and hydrographic charts. When such maps were extended to cover an area not reached by the township surveyors, the sketch maps of geologists, foresters and even fur traders were used. The "office compiled maps" were poor substitutes for true topographic maps, but they were inexpensive to produce and they were the only large- and medium-scale mapping that Canada could afford.

"County maps" and "county atlases" were very popular. These had a semiofficial status because the basic survey data were supplied without charge to private publishers who then added a certain amount of current information. The roads and trails opened by the settlers were shown, as were stores, mills, wharves, churches and, in many cases, individual houses. The scales ranged from 40 chains to 128 chains to the inch (1:31 680 to 1:101 376) depending on the size of the county. To increase sales the publisher inscribed the name of the owner on each occupied farm lot.

Government agencies also compiled maps from existing survey data. When Holland died in 1801, Joseph Bouchette became acting surveyor general of Lower Canada and, in 1804, surveyor general. He produced 2 remarkable maps of his province, the first in 1815 at 2.66 miles to the inch (1:168 500) and a revised version in 1831 at 2.8 miles to the inch (1:177 400). William MacKay's map of Nova Scotia, published in 1834 at 6 miles to the inch (1:380 160), is a fine example of medium-scale mapping.

The British army produced military route-marching maps and larger-scale "reconnoitering plans" from township surveys by adding details such as the strength of bridges and the billeting capacity of villages. Examples are Col John Oldfield's "Map of the Province of Canada" (1843), drawn at 6 miles to the inch, and "Map of the Principal Communications in Canada West," drawn at 2 miles to the inch (1:126 720) in 1850 under the direction of Maj George Baron de Rottenburg.

During the 1850s Bayfield made another significant contribution to Canadian mapping, instituting telegraph longitude observations at a number of eastern Canadian cities. By using the commercial telegraph companies' lines for the exchange of time signals, he was able to determine very accurately the geographical position of an observatory or a public building in each of the cities. This "known position" was then used to correct the mapping of the surrounding area.

The Western Interior In 1760 the land W of the Great Lakes was poorly mapped. HBC explorers such as Henry KELSEY, Anthony HENDAY and Samuel HEARNE had been sent out on early exploratory journeys, and the La Vérendryes had been able to view only a fraction of the great land. Since none of them could make astronomic observations to fix their positions, they were able to produce only rough sketch maps or route descriptions. In 1778 the HBC hired Philip TURNOR, a trained inland surveyor. Turnor mapped the river routes across the company's vast holdings, and trained junior surveyors such as David THOMPSON and Peter FIDLER in the art of field astronomy for position-fixing, and track-surveying for filling in map detail between the "peg points" provided by the astro-fixes.

By this time the HBC was in competition with the NORTH WEST COMPANY, which also had surveyors. Shortly after 1778 one of these surveyors, Peter POND, discovered a practical canoe route from the prairie rivers over the height of land into the Athabasca and Mackenzie rivers (*see* PORTAGE LA LOCHE). His 1785 map showing the route led other explorers such as Alexander MACKENZIE and John FRANKLIN into the central Arctic. London map publishers made good use of the information flowing out of the fur-trade lands. By examining the resulting maps in their various editions one can almost see the unfolding of Canada. One in particular stands out: "A Map Exhibiting All the New Discoveries in the Interior Parts of North America," published by Aaron Arrowsmith in 1795 and updated 19 times until after 1850.

In 1857, 2 scientific expeditions, one Canadian and the other British, were sent to the Canadian prairies. The British party under Capt John PALLISER spent 3 years in the West. The Canadian expedition concentrated on the country between Lk Superior and the Red R. Both expeditions gathered topographical and geographical data which were subsequently published on maps and in reports. These were influential in the negotiations preceding the purchase of RUPERT'S LAND.

The West Coast In 1774 Capt Juan PÉREZ HERNÁNDEZ and his men aboard the Spanish ship *Santiago* were the first Europeans to view the NORTHWEST COAST. Pérez had been dispatched there to counter the threat to Spanish sovereignty presented by the Russian expeditions of Bering and Chirikov along the Alaska coastline in 1741. He made several coastal sightings as far N as Dixon Entrance (54° N), but submitted no maps or detailed reports. The following year Spanish hydrographer Juan Francisco de la BODEGA Y QUADRA drew the first chart to show a portion of Canada's West Coast (*see* SPANISH EXPLORATION). James Cook arrived in 1778 to search for the western end of any channel that might connect with the Arctic

Ocean, seen 7 years before by Samuel Hearne at the mouth of the Coppermine R, but he found no Northwest Passage.

The sovereignty of the W Coast was to remain in dispute for many years. While diplomatic negotiations were being conducted in Europe during the NOOTKA SOUND CONTROVERSY, both Spain and Britain were allowed to make charts of the coast to support their claims. The British work was done 1791-92 under Capt George VANCOUVER, and the Spanish hydrographers worked under Dionisio Alcalá-Galiano and Cayetano Valdés. There was no animosity between these groups, and on several occasions they exchanged data to improve the work on both sides.

In 1793 Alexander Mackenzie, a NWC explorer, travelled from Lk Athabasca to Pacific tidewater at the mouth of the Bella Coola R. During the next half century fur-trade employees such as Thompson, Simon FRASER, Samuel Black and John McLeod made reconnaissance surveys into what is now central BC, increasing the knowledge of this rugged land and producing, in many cases, significant maps recording the topography of the area. Land surveying began when HBC surveyor Joseph Pemberton arrived in Victoria in 1851. In 1858 he completed a map of Victoria. Gold had been found in the Fraser R, and before the year ended a full-fledged GOLD RUSH was in progress. One section of a detachment of Royal Engineers consisting of 20 surveyors carried out a variety of tasks, including townsite surveys and topographic mapping. By Confederation much of the BC northern interior was still unknown. The coastline had been surveyed, several routes through the mountains to the prairies were known, and military surveyors had mapped small areas in the south.

The Arctic The truly remarkable accomplishments in the Arctic were 2 overland journeys: in 1771 Hearne reached the mouth of the Coppermine R at 67° N, and in 1789 Mackenzie descended the river that today bears his name to tidewater at about 68°N. As well, British navigators still sought the Northwest Passage by sea. Their fascination with this navigational will-o'-the-wisp culminated in the ill-fated FRANKLIN EXPEDITION of 1845. During the ensuing attempts to find Franklin and his men, the searchers undertook further explorations. The resulting maps revealed the outline of Canada's mainland coast and disclosed the positions and shorelines of the major islands lying S of Lancaster and Melville sounds. Admiralty charts compiled from the navigational records of these voyages provided the most reliable geographical information about the region until after WWII. In fact, some of the aeronautical charts of northern Canada used during WWII showed little more than this information.

L.M. SEBERT

Official Surveys

Hydrographic Surveys The British North America Act assigned responsibility for safe navigation in Canadian waters to the federal government. This initially involved the erection and maintenance of navigational aids such as lighthouses and buoys. The charting of Canadian waters started in 1883 in GEORGIAN BAY. Canada had hitherto relied on British Admiralty charts for navigation on the East and West coasts, and on the Bayfield charts of the Great Lakes. During the late 19th century, navigation on Georgian Bay became very important in national development: its ports were serving agricultural areas and mining and lumbering industries, and many of these ports were developing industries to supply the westward expansion of railways and the new prairie settlements. Navigation on Georgian Bay was of

little interest to the US or Britain, so the Georgian Bay Survey was set up within Canada's Dept of Marine and Fisheries.

In 1891 a party from Georgian Bay was sent to Vancouver to survey Burrard Inlet. This survey was the first undertaken by Canada in salt water. In 1904 the Dept of Marine and Fisheries began officially charting Canadian coastal waters. The Hydrographic Survey Branch was formed, and the Great Lakes Survey amalgamated with a unit in Public Works that had been doing harbour surveys and a unit in Railways and Canals that had been working on the St Lawrence and Ottawa rivers. In 1928 it was renamed the Canadian Hydrographic Service (*see* HYDROGRAPHY).

Canada has the longest national coastline in the world, much of it the scene of either active shipping or resource development. The towing in 1981 of a barge-mounted ore-concentration plant, 138 m long, from Sorel on the St Lawrence R to Little Cornwallis I in the central Arctic could not have been done if good charts had not been available. The voyage of the US supertanker *Manhattan*, accompanied by Canadian ICEBREAKER *John A. Macdonald*, through the Northwest Passage in 1969 also illustrates the vast responsibility of the Canadian Hydrographic Service.

Cadastral Surveying "Cadastre" is a technical term used in Europe for the registration of land in a given municipal area such as a city or a county. A "cadastral survey" is the measuring, marking and description of parcels of land sufficient for their correct entry into the public land register; or, conversely, the marking on the ground of parcels in accordance with a description in the register. In the latter instance this could be either an original survey or a retracement when the position of the original boundary is not clear. Within provincial boundaries in Canada, land ownership and all fiscal matters pertaining to land are under provincial jurisdiction. The provinces set the rules and procedures for the cadastral surveys of their lands, including the licensing of surveyors. In the Yukon, the NWT and federal lands in the provinces, such as INDIAN RESERVES and national PARKS, the federal government has this responsibility.

An essential part of any cadastral survey is the legal description, which must give the size, shape and location of the parcel being surveyed. It may be in writing, in writing with a plan, or entirely on a registered plan. The traditional written description is by "metes and bounds": the parcel's boundary lines are described in succession by stating the direction and length of each line, and by describing the survey markers or natural features that identify the boundary lines on the ground. A registered plan is used when a parcel is being subdivided and a number of lots are being established simultaneously. Such a plan must show the dimensions, boundary line bearings, areas and survey markers of each lot, and each lot must be numbered or otherwise identified. It can then be identified in a deed or other document by plan and lot number and the office where the plan is registered.

In many parts of Canada the original subdivision of crown land was done by township surveys, essential to orderly settlement. Different sizes of townships have been used (eg, Québec's irregularly shaped cantons and Ontario's concession townships), but all were designed to provide rectangular farm lots within a defined rural community. The survey of a township was essentially a subdivision survey, because the plan of the township was registered and the lots (sometimes called sections) were numbered. The description of a whole lot for legal purposes is complete in the identification of the township and the lot within the township. If only part of a lot is in question, a metes and bounds description, or some other method such as fractional parts, must be used (eg, "the north half of Lot 24, Concession II, in the Township of North Burgess"). As cities and towns extend into rural areas, it is common to find a township farm lot being subdivided into a number of city lots.

Urban Mapping All cities and large towns must have maps for tax assessment, for the location and planning of public utilities, for traffic planning and for many other purposes. Most cities have a survey office, but towns generally have a municipal engineer. Both are responsible for the maintenance of survey records and the custody of maps, but the actual mapping is done by contract with Canada's air-survey industry.

Cities use map scales ranging from 1:500 for plans of sewage systems to 1:50 000 for tourist maps showing complete street layouts. Cities are 3-dimensional structures, and the utility mapping must show surface construction underlain by sewers which themselves may be built over power conduits, subways, service tunnels, etc. City maps must be kept up to date; many disastrous delays in municipal works have been caused by unexpected encounters with vital utility lines. Fortunately, most Canadian cities can take pride in the completeness of their maps and survey records.

Boundary Surveys In the "township provinces," the townships are the building blocks of counties and rural and regional municipalities. The district ("land district" in BC) is the equivalent of a county in a sparsely populated wilderness area, and any townships surveyed within its BOUNDARIES form only a small proportion of its total area. Since counties and rural municipalities are composed of townships, their boundaries are surveyed during the opening of the township lines forming their boundaries. District boundaries are rarely surveyed except where they coincide with a provincial or county boundary. Provincial and territorial boundaries, except between Québec and Labrador and between the Yukon and the NWT, have all been surveyed. Canada's international boundary has been surveyed and marked on the ground, and the boundary markers are under continual inspection by the joint US-Canadian INTERNATIONAL BOUNDARY COMMISSION. L.M. SEBERT

Modernization

Because of Canada's size, maps have always been important in the planning and execution of major development projects. The successful settlement of the PRAIRIE WEST between 1872 and the 1930s was the result of good planning, police supervision, and having each farm lot surveyed and marked on the ground before the arrival of most of the homesteaders. Surveyors employed by the Department of the Interior marked on the ground the perimeters of the 6-mile (10 km) square townships and then the sidelines of each of the 36 sections within the township. They also recorded the positions of major topographic features such as rivers, streams, trails and sloughs. From these notes, draftsmen in Ottawa were able to compile the sheets of Canada's first extensive map series, the Three-Mile Sectional Maps of the Canadian Prairies drawn at 3 miles to the inch (1:190 080).

Series mapping provides detailed mapping at medium or large scale, yet the individual sheets are kept to a manageable size. Because the sheet boundaries conform to a predetermined grid, a number of sheets can be joined together to provide a large map of an extensive area such as a drainage basin, a forest-protection area, a county or even a whole province. Ideally a country should first be covered by a large-scale topographic series that displays the complete face of the land, including man-made features, relief, drainage pattern and forest cover. In the early days Canada could afford only the rather simple maps that could be drawn from the field notes sent in by surveyors whose main employment was staking farm lots, not surveying for maps.

The first sheets of the Three-Mile Series appeared in 1892. In all, 134 sheets were published, covering approximately 1.4 million km². Each sheet covered 8 townships N-S and from 13 to 15 townships (depending on the latitude) E-W. From 1920 to 1946, 51 of these simple outline maps were converted into true topographic maps through the addition of contours and other details. The series was abandoned in 1956 in favour of the 1:250 000 series (originally drawn at 1:253 440, or 4 miles to the inch) of the National Topographic System (NTS).

Simple straight-line surveys were ideal on the flat prairies, but impractical in the Rocky Mts. When township surveys reached the mountains in 1886, a system was developed using panoramic photographs taken from mountain peaks. A small but important series of mountain maps resulted. The maps themselves were useful, but the technique of mapping from photographs was even more useful because it was adapted to mapping from oblique aerial photographs when these became available after 1925.

The success of the Three-Mile Series encouraged the Dept of the Interior to begin similar medium-scale office-compiled mapping for eastern Canada. The department's chief geographer gathered the information from the many land surveys that had been made and compiled it into maps of a standard design. The maps were published at 2 scales (1:250 000 and 1:500 000), and were known as the Chief Geographer's Series. The first sheet was published in 1904, and by 1948, when work was stopped, 33 sheets at 1:250 000 and another 25 at 1:500 000 had been published. For many years they were the most detailed maps available for the settled parts of eastern Canada.

The original Three-Mile Series and the Chief Geographer's Series were not contoured, and because contoured maps were a military requirement, the Dept of Militia and Defence started its own series of true topographic maps in 1904. These were drawn at one mile to the inch (1:63 360), and were modelled on the British Ordnance Survey maps at the same scale. This design, with a few modifications to accommodate the Canadian landscape, proved so successful that it was eventually adopted for the basic topographic mapping of Canada at the 1:50 000 scale.

Since its inception in 1842, the GEOLOGICAL SURVEY OF CANADA had been hampered by the lack of good base maps on which to display the results of field investigations. In many cases geologists had to do their own topographic mapping. This was poor use of geologists, so in 1908 a Topographical Survey Division was formed within the GSC. It was to provide topographic maps that could be used both as bases for geological maps and as general-purpose topographic maps.

In 1920 the Dept of the Interior joined the military and the geologists in the separate production of topographic maps. In 1922 senior officers in the 3 agencies began to unite their efforts into a single topographic system. After study and experimentation, by 1927 what became the NTS had been developed. It was designed as a series of map scales of 1, 2, 4, 8 and 16 miles to the inch. Such a system makes topographic maps available for all requirements, ranging from military and geological use at the one-mile scale to aeronautical chart use at 8 and 16 miles to the inch. In 1950 the basic scales were converted to their metric equivalents of 1:50 000, 1:125 000, 1:250 000, 1:500 000 and 1:1 000 000, and in 1952 a larger scale, 1:25 000, was added to the system for military and urban use. The smallest scale, 1:1 000 000, provides the basic grid that covers the whole country. This grid is quartered successively to provide the sheet boundaries of each larger scale until the largest (1:25 000) is reached. The numbering of each sheet indicates both the scale and the position of the sheet in the grid.

Two NTS scales were subsequently dropped: the 1:125 000 scale because it had few uses that could not be fulfilled by the other scales and the 1:25 000 scale because it competed with provincial programs started in the 1970s at the 1:20 000 scale. The resources previously devoted to these scales are now being used to hasten the completion of the 1:50 000 series and to produce a National Digital Topographical Data Base. Complete coverage of Canada at the 1:50 000 scale will require about 12 922 sheets. As of Aug 1987 there were 10 634 sheets of the series in print and completion is expected in the mid-1990s.

By virtue of having their topographic mapping well in hand, Canadians enjoy the availability of a wide range of thematic maps: geological, forestry, pipeline and power transmission, tourist, etc. Many are produced by federal agencies, but the provinces, responsible for the development of their own natural resources, have become active in producing thematic maps.

L.M. SEBERT

Mapping Since WWII

WWII can be considered a turning point in Canadian topographic mapping. Before the war topographers used plane tables and sketched out small sections of the terrain which were subsequently joined together into a map. This method was slow, not very accurate and unusable in forested areas. Aerial photographs were used, but in the whole country only one instrument plotted map detail directly from air photos. During the war the staff of Canada's military mapping units became familiar with European photomapping equipment, and they became a postwar source of trained technicians available for the modernization of Canada's mapping agencies. The introduction of photogrammetry (the drawing of maps from aerial photographs) was only one of many technological innovations that have transformed every phase of topographic mapping in Canada.

In remote areas, large tracts of country are normally mapped in a single operation. For example, a block 100 km N-S and 300 km E-W is mapped on 32 sheets (4 rows of 8) in the NTS. Aerial photography is done with certain features predetermined· scale, direction of the flight lines (normally E-W), forward overlap of the photos (normally 60%) and the side overlap of the flight lines (normally 30%). About 850 photos are needed. Overlap is necessary to provide areas on the photos for "tie-points" (points of ground detail selected in the overlapping areas) used to "pin" the photos of the block together. Tie-points are marked by tiny holes drilled in the emulsion on film positives of the air photos, and are measured precisely on a grid co-ordinate system provided for each photo. Each tie-point falls on 3 or more photos, allowing individual photo grids to be combined into a master system covering the whole photogrammetric block. This extension of the grid system is done by computer.

Although photogrammetric techniques have reduced the amount of field surveying required, some surveyed points must still be placed at strategic positions in the photogrammetric block. These are "control points" because they "control" the scale, the orientation, and the position of the lines and symbols on the map. There are 2 types of control points: horizontal (precisely known latitude and longitude) and vertical (precisely known elevation). The horizontal control points must be situated around the perimeter of the photogrammetric block where, in effect, they hold the block in position. It must be remembered that all mapping that covers an appreciable area must be drawn according to the mathematical rules of the chosen map projection. In Canadian topographic mapping this is generally the Universal Transverse Mercator (UTM) projection, which means that the latitude and longitude values of all horizontal control points must be converted to the equivalent grid co-ordinates of the UTM projection. The grid of the photogrammetric block is then adjusted in scale and orientation to fit the UTM grid. This in turn gives UTM-grid values to all the tie-points. The vertical control is set out in lines spaced across the block at right angles to the flight lines. This allows computation of tie-point elevations above sea level.

The overlapping portion of 2 adjoining aerial photographs forms a rectangle that is about half a photo wide and a photo long. A tie-point falls in each corner of this rectangle. Such rectangles are "photogrammetric models" because when viewed through a stereoscopic instrument they appear to be 3-dimensional models of the ground. They are the mapping units of a photogrammetric block. The models are set up, one by one, in photogrammetric plotting instruments, which are adjusted to the known values of the tie-points. The map detail is then traced from the model by the operator, who moves an optical aiming mark, visible in the eyepiece of the instrument, along the roads and streams, around the lakes, etc, of the model. As the aiming mark moves, a pencil recording every move of the mark moves over a drafting table attached to the plotter. This is the process of drawing the linework of the map. In modern systems the movement of the mark is recorded digitally on magnetic tapes or discs so that the map can be drawn automatically after the plotting is complete.

Each phase of the mapping process has its own instrumentation, almost all of which has been developed since the early 1960s. The most dramatic advances have been made in horizontal control, which is simply establishing points of known latitude and longitude. The positions of such points were formerly found by measuring the sides and angles of a series of triangles set out over the surface of the earth. Today it is more usual to obtain the position directly by using a Satellite Doppler System (SDS). This instrument resembles a radio receiver, and is set up with its antenna at the point to be surveyed. Signals are received from US Navy navigation satellites which pass through the sky several times daily. The SDS takes the satellite information and, by measuring the change in frequency of these signals as the satellite approaches and departs, it computes the position of the antenna of the set. If readings are taken over 2 days and compared with readings taken somewhere in the region by a second SDS at a previously surveyed station, the location of the new station can be calculated to about 1.2 m accuracy. The SDS is used extensively to establish the fundamental stations of the Canadian primary horizontal survey net (*see* REMOTE SENSING).

Additional points can be surveyed between Doppler stations by using an Inertial Survey System (ISS), consisting of delicate sensors which record with remarkable accuracy any movement of the set. It can be mounted in a car or helicopter, and by starting from a known position (a Doppler station or an older triangulation station), it measures the vehicle's movement along a preselected route, and stopping points where accurate positions are needed. Such a traverse is checked by stopping at known positions to confirm the accuracy of the readings taken along the way. Perimeter control around a photogrammetric block is greatly facilitated by an ISS survey, which is accurate within about 1 m.

Vertical control is traditionally placed by running lines of levels from bench marks (points of known elevation) to the point where an elevation is needed. In northern Canada this method would be prohibitively slow and expensive. Shortly after WWII a Canadian invention, the AIR PROFILE RECORDER (APR), revolutionized vertical control surveys in wilderness areas. It is a RADAR device that measures vertical distance from an airplane flying at a constant altitude above the line where elevations are needed. The absolute value of the survey line is established by flying over a lake or broad river of which the elevation is known. The ISS can also be used to establish elevations, since it records changes in elevation as well as in direction. Thus if the ISS starts off from a bench mark it can provide accurate elevations along a survey line, such as the lines of elevations across a photogrammetric block. An APR elevation is correct within 3 to 5 m, whereas an ISS elevation is correct within 1.2 to 1 m.

Photogrammetric plotters and plotting systems have undergone improvements over the last 20 years. The optics now give a sharper view of the model, and the measuring systems allow photogrid measurements of control points and tie-points to be made with much greater accuracy. But since the early 1970s the actual plotting of map detail has taken a dramatic step forward. Lines and symbols of the map are now recorded, not on a manuscript, but on magnetic tapes or discs. This information, including colour coding, can subsequently be read from the tapes or discs by computer-controlled drafting machines that can work rapidly around the clock. The many advantages of such a system include the ease with which the original lines can be drawn and adjusted electronically, as well as the efficiency with which the whole map can be revised when changes in the terrain, made by man and nature, necessitate the drawing of a new edition of the map. *See also* GEOGRAPHICAL INFORMATION SYSTEMS.

L.M. SEBERT

Reading: W.P. Cumming et al, *The Discovery of North America* (1971) and *The Exploration of North America, 1630-1776* (1974); Energy, Mines and Resources, *The National Atlas of Canada* (5th ed, 1985); J.B. Harley and D. Woodward, eds, *History of Cartography* (5 vols projected, 1985-); R. Cole Harris, ed, *Historical Atlas of Canada* (vol 1, 1987); C.E. Heidenreich, "Mapping the Great Lakes...1603-1700," *Cartographica* 17.3 (1980) and "Mapping the Great Lakes...1700-1760," *Cartographica* 18.3 (1981); G.M. Lewis, "The Indigenous Maps and Mapping of North American Indians," *The Map Collector*, 9 (1979); N.L. Nicholson and L.M. Sebert, *The Maps of Canada* (1981); D.W. Thomson, *Men and Meridians* (3 vols, 1966-69).

Cartoons, Humorous, designed primarily for amusement rather than to transmit a political or moral message, date from the mid-19th century when technological changes in the PRINT INDUSTRY made possible their publication in humour magazines such as J.W. BENGOUGH's *Grip* (1873-94) and *Le Canard* (1877-99) founded by Hector Berthelot (1842-95). After 1900, humorous cartoons in panel or strip form became an indispensable part of all successful daily newspapers. Some editorial cartoonists such as the Montréal *Star*'s Arthur Racey (1870-1941) drew occasional humorous cartoons, but almost all of the humorous cartoons or "comics" which appeared in Canadian newspapers were purchased from American newspaper features syndicates.

Comic Strips Only the rival Montréal journals *La Presse* and *La Patrie* regularly featured original Canadian-drawn material in addition to syndicated US cartoons. The first Canadian comic strip was "Pour un dîner de Noël," (1902) drawn for *La Presse* by Raoul Barré (1874-1932). Albérique Bourgeois (1876-1962) created "Les Aventures de Toinon" (1905-08) and "Les Fables du Parc Lafontaine" (1906-08) for *La Presse* but had his greatest success with "Le Père Ladébauche," a French Canadian folk character he inherited from Berthelot and developed into a staple figure of Québec's popular culture. *La Patrie*'s comics included Barré's "Les Contes du Père Rhault" (1906-08), "Les Aventures de Timothée" (1920-25) by Arthur Lemay (1900-44), and "La Vie en images" (1944-56) by Jacques Gagnier (1917-78) and Paul Leduc (1930-).

Other than those who drew political cartoons, Canadians who sought careers as cartoonists found it necessary to move to the US, as did Raoul Barré and Harold FOSTER. Arch Dale (1882-1962), for example, developed his "Doo Dads" (1921-27) at the *Grain Growers' Guide* in Winnipeg, but emigrated to Chicago to market the cartoon through Universal Features.

The simple sight gags of the early humorous cartoons were supplemented in the 1920s and 1930s by detective stories such as "Dick Tracy," science fiction with "Buck Rogers," jungle adventure with "Tarzan" and historical romance with "Prince Valiant" (the former drawn and the latter created by Harold Foster). These new strips won cartoons a broader audience: millionaire businessman J.W. Flavelle never missed "Little Orphan Annie" and PM Mackenzie King was a faithful follower of "Tillie the Toiler." With the exception of the small number of Québec strips, however, Canadian comic pages continued to originate in the US.

The popularity of American cartoons with English Canadian readers was demonstrated by the success of the *Toronto Star*, which purchased "Bringing Up Father," "Barney Google," "Mutt and Jeff" and 5 other strips in 1923, and copied American newspapers by adding a 4-colour comic section to its Saturday edition. The new comics helped the *Star* to double its readership and its subsidiary, the *Toronto Star Weekly*, to build a national circulation which reached 1 million in the 1950s.

"Well, if you knows of a better 'ole, go for it!" (*courtesy National Archives of Canada/MISA/ #12747*).

The first English Canadian cartoons to reach a wide audience were James SIMPKIN's "Jasper" which began a 24-year run in *Maclean's* in 1948 and "Nipper" by Doug Wright (1917-) in *Weekend* and later in *The Canadian*, magazine supplements distributed with Saturday newspapers. These magazines also regularly published gag cartoons by Peter Whalley (1921-) and George Feyer (1921-67). The comic strip in Canada has yet to establish the strong tradition of political cartooning, but at present there are 3 syndicated strips by Canadians which enjoy international circulation: Jim UNGER's "Herman," Ben WICKS's "The Outcasts," and "For Better or For Worse," by Lynn JOHNSTON.

Comic Books, which evolved in the US in the 1930s, were simply collections of newspaper strips until *Superman* came to life in *Action Comics* in 1938. The prototype for every other "superhero," the "Man of Steel" – drawn by expatriate Toronto artist Joe SHUSTER – was an instantly profitable success and inspired many imitations. By 1940, millions of garishly coloured 10-cent comic books were sold every month. All were produced in the US, but Canadian youngsters absorbed them as avidly as did their US counterparts: between 1937 and 1940, the value of magazines imported from the US increased from $2.25 million to $6.5 million.

In 1941 comics were included among "nonessential" imports from the US banned by the War Exchange Conservation Act, and to prevent US publishers from evading the embargo, the Act made it illegal to ship the "mats" north to print the comics in Canada. The restriction on American comic books quickly gave birth to a domestic Canadian comic industry. *"Wow" Comics #1* reached the newsstands in the summer of 1941, and by 1945, 4 companies – Anglo-American Publishing, Superior Publishing and Bell Features in Toronto, and Maple Leaf Publishing in Vancouver – were printing comic books on a significant scale. Bell Features employed 60 artists to turn out 7 books each month. *Wow, Triumph, Active, Dime* and *Commando* were adventure comics; *Joke* and *Dizzy Don* were comedy titles. Canadian comic publishers saved time and money by printing in black and white; only the covers were coloured.

These "Canadian whites" were miniature replicas of the familiar American comic panorama of detectives, super-heroes, cowboys and secret agents, and some of the characters were transparent "swipes" from the US. But despite obvious imitations, the wartime comics were in important respects distinctively Canadian. As patriotic propaganda for the war effort, they outdid the efforts of the government's Wartime Information Board. In the adventure titles, gallant Canadian servicemen (and in one case a servicewoman) dealt crushing blows to crude German and Japanese stereotypes. The most popular of these was "Johnny Canuck," "Canada's answer to Nazi oppression," intended by his creator Leo Bachle to "typify the Canadian character." Unlike the super-heroes in the US comics, Johnny had no special powers but carried on his one-person war with Hitler with only the human muscle given to any "fine fighting Canuck." The most original character to appear in the Canadian whites was "Nelvana of the Northern Lights," an arctic superheroine in a miniskirt who defended the Inuit from the evil Kablunets. Although Nelvana shows occasional similarities to "Wonder Woman," artist Adrian Dingle claimed that his inspiration was an Inuit legend passed on to him by Franz JOHNSTON of the Group of Seven.

The production of Canadian comics ended in 1946 when wartime exchange controls were eased to allow printing "mats" to be imported

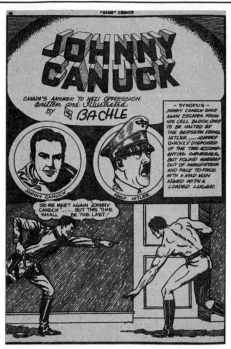

Johnny Canuck – Canada's answer to Nazi oppression. Written and illustrated by Leo Bachle in *Dime Comics*, *c*1943 *(courtesy National Archives of Canada/C-99610)*.

from the US. Canadian publishers laid off their artists and became branch plants which reprinted American comics. French-language translations were prepared of some titles by simply lettering in French text in the word balloons. Nationalist intellectuals had long worried about the effects of "cruel, simean and unclean American cartoons" upon Canadian children, and in 1949 E. Davie FULTON introduced a private member's bill to ban so-called "crime" and "horror" comics, which he argued contributed to juvenile delinquency. After receiving petitions from churches, the YMCA, YWCA and parent-teacher associations, the St. Laurent government amended the Criminal Code to ban the importation or domestic production of about half the American comic books then being published. Canadian police departments generally ignored anti-comic book legislation, but in the US the law was held up as a shining example to Congress. Anti-comic crusaders achieved their goal when fear of Congressional regulation led US comic book publishers to adopt a rigorous "Comics Code" of self-censorship. Paradoxically the Canadian debate ignored newspaper strips such as "Steve Canyon," "Terry and the Pirates" or "Little Orphan Annie" which, in addition to their violence, were transparent American cold-war propaganda.

Canadian comic books reappeared in the 1960s and 1970s; as with the earlier period of the humorous cartoon, there was much more activity in Québec than in English Canada (*see* POPULAR LITERATURE IN FRENCH). The most interesting new titles in English are Dave Sim's "Cerebus the Aardvark" and Richard Comely's "Captain Canuck," a nationalist super-hero outfitted in red and white with maple leaves emblazoned on his belt buckle and mask. *See also* CARTOONS, POLITICAL.

JOHN HERD THOMPSON

Reading: M. Hirsch and P. Loubert, *The Great Canadian Comic Books* (1971); M. Horn, ed, *World Encyclopedia of Cartoons* (1978); D. Theaker, *An Introduction to Canadian Comic Books* (1986).

Cartoons, Political The term cartoon originally meant an artist's preliminary sketch for a painting, fresco or tapestry. Although it retains this

technical meaning for artists, cartoon now commonly designates a drawing produced to amuse, and perhaps to inform, a mass audience. The cartoonist's art ranges from the comic slapstick of TV cartoons to the social and political satires published in newspapers and magazines. Caricature is a common but not essential element of cartooning, using exaggeration to ridicule a subject, sometimes gently, sometimes with destructive intent. The oldest surviving example of the caricaturist's art may be a sketch of Ikhnaton, drawn in Egypt about 1360 BC. (Or it may be that Ikhnaton really was ugly – the experts still disagree.) Primitive art sometimes verges on caricature. Among the artifacts traditionally produced by the Salish Indians of BC, for instance, are small carvings that bear uncanny resemblance to the little clay effigies of the great French caricaturist of the 19th century, Honoré Daumier.

It was less than 400 years ago that caricature as a consciously developed art first flowered in Italy. Modern political cartooning began at roughly the same time as the political beginnings of Confederation. With the founding of *Punch and London Charivari* (England, 1841), the satirical magazine became the main vehicle for political cartoons in Europe, and soon after in N America. In the 1890s in Canada and the US, somewhat later in Europe, political cartoons became regular features of daily newspapers.

The political cartoon as we know it today, a product of art and journalism, came of age in our own century. More than in many older countries, Canada's image of itself has been shaped by political cartoonists communicating with mass audiences in the years when illustrated magazines and newspapers were at their most influential. Recent decades have seen a "golden age" of political cartooning in Canada, but the future of the art seems to depend on the future of newspapers. Attempts to adapt political cartooning to TV have been unsuccessful so far.

The first recognized and feared cartoonist to work in Canada was Brigadier-General George TOWNSHEND, third in command of the British forces that conquered Québec in 1759. The satirical drawings of Townshend already were the talk of London when this witty aristocrat joined General James WOLFE. His caricatures of his commander infuriated Wolfe, who threatened revenge after the siege, but when Wolfe died on the battlefield, it was Townshend who accepted the surrender of the French. For a brief moment of history, the entire colony was at the mercy of an amateur cartoonist.

The start of cartooning as a profession in Canada followed the appearance of *Punch* and other early comic journals in London. *Punch in Canada*, launched in Montréal (1849) by J.B. Walker, an 18-year-old designer and wood engraver, was the first comic journal to publish political cartoons regularly in Canada. Starting in 1869, political and social cartoons were used extensively in Canada's first illustrated national news magazine, the *Canadian Illustrated News*, and its French-language edition, *L'Opinion publique*. Edward Jump, an itinerant French-born artist who worked for the *Canadian Illustrated News* from 1871 to 1873, was the most accomplished caricaturist in Canada up to that time. J.W. "Johnny" BENGOUGH was the first memorable Canadian cartoonist. Starting his career as a compositor and occasional journalist for the *Whitby Gazette*, and later as a reporter for the *Globe*, he was strongly influenced by the work of Thomas Nast, the celebrated American cartoonist whose work appeared in *Harper's Weekly*. Bengough started his own magazine in 1873; for the next 21 years, he was editor and chief illustrator of *Grip*, working under his own name and pseudonyms. His cartoons about Québec, for in-

"Confederation! The Much-Fathered Youngster" by J.W. Bengough, from *A Caricature History of Canadian Politics*, Toronto, 1886 (*courtesy National Archives of Canada/C-78676*).

stance, were done in a "slashing French style" and signed L. Côté, as he later confessed. Bengough once called Sir John A. Macdonald "my chief stock in trade," and his cartoons of Canada's first prime minister are engraved on the memories of Canadians who have seen them. Bengough's cartoons have survived because of their lively portrayal of Canadian politics, but his draftsmanship often was rough, almost childish. The first native-born caricaturist of the first rank to appear in Canada was Henri JULIEN, the son of a Québec printer. Effective but crude cartoons had appeared in French-language comic journals in the 1860s but Julien's experience as an engraver and his technical skill as an artist enabled him to inaugurate a new era in Québec cartooning when his work first started to appear in 1873 in *L'Opinion publique* and the *Canadian Illustrated News*. In 1888, he became chief cartoonist and illustrator for the *Montreal Star*. Among his notable caricatures were the "Bytown Coons" series, which depicted Ottawa politicians as members of a blackface minstrel troupe. Most of the important contemporary Canadian attitudes were sketched in the cartoons of the 19th century; the rivalry between regions and language groups, for instance, and resentment of interference in Canadian affairs, particularly by the United States. In Canadian cartoons of the last century, Uncle Sam or Brother Jonathan were often shown as a crafty and disreputable Yankee carpetbagger trying to take

Untitled cartoon by Duncan Macpherson, 16 Dec 1978 (*courtesy National Archives of Canada/C-112673/Toronto Star Syndicate*).

advantage of a brawny, virtuous, but naive Jack Canuck.

In the first half of this century, Canadian cartoonists were influenced strongly by British and American models. Cartoonists were prized for "punch" rather than artistic ability. Above all, they were expected to entertain newspaper readers. Among the best in these years were Arch Dale, who started to draw for the Winnipeg *Free Press* in 1913 and produced his last cartoon in 1954; Arthur Racey, who succeeded Julien at the *Montreal Star* in 1899 and remained there for 42 years; and C.W. JEFFERYS, who started as a cartoonist with *Grip* (1901) and later became an illustrator with the *Moon* (1902) and the *Toronto Star* (1903). He went on to become Canada's best-known historical illustrator.

A new style and era of political cartooning in newspapers began in the 1950s when Robert LaPalme reached his peak at *Le Devoir* in Montréal. A self-taught Québec artist who had worked briefly in New York as a free-lance magazine illustrator in the 1930s, LaPalme shocked the readers of *Le Devoir* with vicious, avant-garde drawings of Québec Premier Maurice Duplessis, portraying him as a pimp selling Québec to the Americans or as a corrupt priest attended by his acolyte ministers. LaPalme organized an exhibition of caricatures in Montréal (1963) that developed into the International Salon of Caricature and Cartoon, a permanent museum reputed to be the largest and most important of its kind in the world. Contemporary with LaPalme, Len Norris for more than 30 years has been consistently the funniest cartoonist in the country and among the most popular. Since 1950, when he joined the Vancouver *Sun,* he has delighted Canadians with whimsical, detailed drawings of post-Victorian existence in BC.

Duncan MACPHERSON is generally regarded as the best political cartoonist that Canada has produced. Writing in the *New Yorker* (1964), critic Edmund Wilson credited Macpherson with creating "a phantasmagoria for which the mediocre subjects themselves seem hardly adequate." Within a few months of joining the *Toronto Star* in 1958, Macpherson's caricatures of PM John Diefenbaker brought him wide recognition. He was given a solo exhibition of his work by the Public Archives (now National Archives) in Ottawa (1980), where most of his original drawings are stored. Macpherson not only raised the artistic level of cartooning in Canada but forged a new editorial role for himself at the *Star*. He refused to become merely an illustrator of the newspaper's editorials, as his predecessors had been, claiming for himself the freedom enjoyed by columnists who signed their own names to their articles and who often disagreed with the newspaper's editorial writers. This new approach has influenced many Canadian cartoonists since.

Among younger cartoonists, Terry Mosher, working under the name "Aislin" at the *Gazette* in Montréal, has achieved a national reputation that rivals the fame of Macpherson and Norris. Aislin has won the Canadian National Newspaper Award for Political Cartooning several times, as has Roy Peterson, Norris's successor at the Vancouver *Sun*. In Québec, LaPalme's place has been claimed by Jean-Pierre Girerd, of *La Presse*, who left Algeria in 1961 and arrived in Montréal 3 years later. At present, there are about 25 cartoonists in Canada who support themselves by working for newspapers. Within this group, there is a consensus that rapid political and social changes in Canada, the rise of such charismatic political leaders as Pierre Trudeau and René Lévesque, and the existence of a relatively stable and prosperous newspaper industry, have created unprecedented and unparalleled opportunities for cartoonists. As a result, it is widely be-

lieved that the standard of political cartooning in Canada has never been higher. *See also* CARTOONS, HUMOROUS.   PETER DESBARATS

Reading: Art Gallery of Ontario, *Canadian Cartoon and Caricature* (1969); Peter Desbarats and T. Mosher, *The Hecklers* (1979).

Cartwright, Nfld, Community, inc 1956, pop 674 (1986c), is located at the mouth of Sandwich Bay on the S coast of Labrador. It is named for George CARTWRIGHT who established a fishing and fur-trading post in the area in the 1770s. In 1815 the business was sold and eventually acquired by the Hudson's Bay Co in the 1870s. Settlement grew in association with the company and other trading and lumbering firms which were established at or near Cartwright. Independent fishermen settled there because of the availability of other amenities, such as medical services provided by a Grenfell Assn hospital. Today with medical facilities, an airstrip, a sizable fish plant and other businesses it is a local service centre. Because it is ice-bound during the winter and not connected by road, for half the year it is accessible only by air.   ROBERT D. PITT

Cartwright, George, soldier, diarist, entrepreneur (b at Marnham, Eng 12 Feb 1739 or 1740; d at Mansfield, Eng 19 May 1819). Cartwright entered the British army at 16, serving in India, Ireland, Minorca and Germany, and in 1769 he went on half pay. His interest in Newfoundland having been aroused by an earlier voyage, he turned Labrador trader, operating coastal posts between Cape Charles and Hamilton Inlet from 1770 to 1786. With his wide-ranging curiosity, Cartwright was a careful student of the native people and natural history of the region. The voluminous *Journal of Transactions and Events, During a Residence of Nearly Sixteen Years on the Coast of Labrador* (3 vols, 1792) is a singular record of his experiences and observations.   G.M. STORY

Cartwright, Richard, businessman, officeholder, judge, militia officer, author (b at Albany, NY 2 Feb 1759; d at Montréal, 27 July 1815). A committed LOYALIST, Cartwright was expelled from New York in Oct 1777. After serving until 1780 as secretary for John Butler's Rangers based at Niagara, he became a merchant involved in the provisioning trade. By 1785 Cartwright had moved to the Kingston area where he soon became an influential commercial, legal, political and religious leader. Cartwright was, because of his influence on John STRACHAN, a critically important link in the ideological chain that connects the American Loyalist thought of the 1770s with the English-speaking, Upper Canadian Tory conceptual framework of the post-War-of-1812 period. Though Cartwright vigorously opposed, in the early 1790s, many of Lieutenant-Governor SIMCOE's anglophile policies, he had become by 1800 an ardent supporter of the Upper Canadian Conservative status quo.   GEORGE A. RAWLYK

Cartwright, Sir Richard John, politician (b at Kingston, Upper Canada 4 Dec 1835; d there 24 Sept 1912), grandson of Richard CARTWRIGHT. The scion of a rich, powerful, conservative and LOYALIST family, he was educated at Trinity College, Dublin, which he attended 1851-56 although he took no degree. Using family money, he became a businessman-investor with extensive interests in finance, transportation, real estate, mining and manufacturing. Cartwright represented various Ontario constituencies in Parliament 1863-1904, then entered the Senate where he remained until he died. Initially a Tory, he broke with Sir John A. Macdonald in 1869 and was an Independent until 1873 when he joined the Liberal Party. He was a powerful Liberal leader, serving as minister of finance 1873-78 and minister of trade and commerce 1896-1911. From 1887 until after the 1891 general election he was the effective leader of the Ontario wing of the Liberal Party and also led the faction within the party that wanted free trade with the US. He was knighted in 1879.

DONALD SWAINSON

Carver, Humphrey Stephen Mumford, architect, community planner, author (b at Birmingham, Eng 29 Nov 1902). Educated in England, he arrived in Canada in 1930. He practised landscape architecture with Carl Borgstrum (1931-37), taught at U of T's School of Architecture (1938-41) and Social Work (1946-48), and pioneered the Regent Park N public-housing project. He was active in the LEAGUE FOR SOCIAL RECONSTRUCTION, outlining in the 1930s the social policy basis for a national housing program. He organized the landmark 1939 Housing Conference and was at the centre of virtually all institutional developments in community planning and housing after 1940. He chaired the Research Committee of Canada Mortgage and Housing Corporation (1948-55) and its Advisory Group (1955-67). In his book *Cities in the Suburbs* (1962), Carver advocated that the planning of suburbs be integrated with the wider social community. Under Carver's leadership of the CMHC Advisory Group, Canada's research and programs in housing policy, housing design and community planning attained an international reputation for innovation and progressive development standards.

WILLIAM PERKS

Casavant frères ltée, the largest and most famous Canadian organ-making company. It was founded in St-Hyacinthe in 1879 by brothers Joseph-Claver and Samuel-Marie Casavant, who were sons of Joseph Casavant, the first Canadian-born organ-maker of any significance. Having learned the rudiments of their art from Eusébe Brodeur, the 2 brothers perfected their skills in Europe. Their first organ was installed in Montréal in the Notre-Dame-de-Lourdes chapel in 1880. The firm has several worldwide innovations to its credit: pedals with adjustable combinations (1880), the use of tubular traction (1884) and the first satisfactory results from electrified traction (1892). The instruments of this firm, whose chairman has been Bertin Nadeau since 1976, are found in all 3 Americas, Europe, Africa, India, Japan and Australia. In June 1986 total output reached an impressive 3636 organs.

HÉLÈNE PLOUFFE

Cascade Mountains, BC, are the N end of mountain ranges extending to California, 180-260 km E of the Pacific Ocean. The BC Cascades show a transition from the wet coastal forest of the rugged Skagit Range to the drier interior vegetation of the Okanagan Range and of the ridge E of the Fraser R and S of LYTTON. Eastward they merge with the Thompson Plateau. (There are no active volcanoes in BC as in the US Cascades' Mt St Helens and others.) Near the US border are popular recreation and outdoor areas: Cultus Lk, Skagit Valley, Manning and Cathedral provincial parks. A gold-silver mine opened near HOPE in 1978.

PETER GRANT

Casgrain, Henri-Raymond, historian, literary critic (b at Rivière-Ouelle, Qué 16 Dec 1831; d at Québec City 12 Jan 1904). Casgrain was ordained a priest in 1856. After teaching at his former college, Ste-Anne-de-la-Pocatière, he was named vicar at Beauport and then at Notre-Dame de Québec. In Québec City he was a leading figure in the literary movement of 1860, being a founder of its 2 literary magazines, *Les Soirées canadiennes* (1861-65) and *Le Foyer canadien* (1863-66), and author of *Légendes canadiennes* (1861). Casgrain specialized in biography. Despite his poor health and failing eyesight, he published lives of MARIE DE

L'INCARNATION (1864), François-Xavier GARNEAU (1866), Philippe-Joseph AUBERT DE GASPÉ (1871), Francis Parkman (1872) and Antoine GÉRIN-LAJOIE (1886), as well as numerous historical studies. His scholarship was sometimes questioned, as was his lack of scruples in copyright matters, but his energy and exuberant style ensured his reputation. A founding fellow of the RSC (1882), he became its president in 1889 and was an honorary doctor of Université Laval. DAVID M. HAYNE

Casgrain, Thérèse, née Forget, reformer (b at Montréal 10 July 1896; d there 2 Nov 1981). Best remembered for her leadership of the campaign for women's suffrage in Québec before WWII, she was a leading 20th-century Canadian reformer. Born to a wealthy family, she married Pierre-François Casgrain, Liberal lawyer and politician, and raised 4 children. A founding member of the Provincial Franchise Committee for women's suffrage in 1921, she campaigned ceaselessly for women's rights in Québec and hosted a popular Radio Canada program in the 1930s, "Fémina." During WWII she was one of 2 presidents of the Women's Surveillance Committee for the WARTIME PRICES AND TRADE BOARD. In 1946 she joined the CO-OPERATIVE COMMONWEALTH FEDERATION, becoming provincial leader 1951-57. She worked within the party, strengthening international socialist links, and in Québec helped mobilize opposition to Premier DUPLESSIS. In 1961 she founded the Québec branch of the VOICE OF WOMEN to protest the nuclear threat. She was a founder of the League for Human Rights (1960) and of the Fédération des femmes du Québec (1966). In 1970 she was appointed to the Senate. In her autobiography, *A Woman in a Man's World* (1972), she characterized herself as a humanist.

JENNIFER STODDART

Cashin, Peter J., politician, businessman, soldier (b at Cape Broyle, Nfld 8 Mar 1890; d at St John's 21 May 1977). He joined the Nfld Regiment in 1915, served overseas and in Mar 1918 was promoted major in command of the British Machine Gun Corp. After the war he joined the family business. In 1923 he first won election to the Assembly as a Liberal-Labour-Progressive. Crossing to the Liberals in 1925, he was re-elected in 1928 and was minister of finance 1928-32. A consistent opponent of the COMMISSION OF GOVERNMENT, Cashin was elected as one of the 3 delegates for St John's W in the National Convention Vote in 1946. Subsequently, he emerged as strongly anti-Confederate and the leader of the Responsible Government advocates at the convention. After Newfoundland joined Canada in 1949, Cashin ran provincially and was elected as an Independent. He was later recruited by the Progressive Conservative Party and served as leader of the PC Opposition until 1953 when he retired from active politics. He was director of civil defence for Newfoundland from 1954 until his retirement in the mid-1960s. JOHN PARSONS

Reading: Peter Cashin, *My Life and Times, 1890-1919* (1976).

Cashin, Richard, lawyer, politician, union leader (b at St John's 5 Jan 1937). He was a grandson of Sir Michael Cashin, sometimes known as "King of the Robbers" for his S shore salvage operations, who was frequent Cabinet minister and prime minister of Newfoundland, and he was the nephew of Peter J. CASHIN. Cashin was himself elected Liberal MP for St John's West in 1962, 1963 and 1965. After his defeat in 1968 he practised law and won a significant settlement for Placentia Bay fishermen who were suing the Electric Reduction Co for phosphorus-based destruction of their fish. In 1970 he joined with Father Desmond McGrath, a former St Francis

Xavier U classmate, to help organize the Fishermen's Union. After major victories over the fishing companies at Burgeo in 1972 and in the trawlermen's strike of 1975, the union fully established itself. Now the biggest union in Newfoundland by far, the Newfoundland Fishermen, Food and Allied Workers' Union is a major political force. Cashin supported NDP candidates in the mid-1970s but joined the National Unity Task Force and the board of Petro-Canada in 1977. In the 1980s, however, he has led the NFFAWU into full support of the NDP and is himself a party vice-president. The union has also been very active in the Coalition for Equality, a broad coalition of labour and other progressive groups. In spring 1987 he led the union out of the United Food and Commercial Workers International Union into the new Canadian Auto Workers.

GREGORY S. KEALEY

Reading: Gordon Inglis, *More Than Just a Union: The Story of the NFFAWU* (1985).

Cassiar District, lies in the province's NW corner S of the lake district; it historically encompasses the Stikine and Dease River watersheds and that of the upper Taku, Nass and Keichika. Most of it is the traditional territory of the TAHLTAN Indians. It reputedly derived its name from the Indian word, *Caseah(r)*, for McDame Creek. Hudson's Bay Co traders made exploratory trips into the area in the 1830s and 1840s. GOLD RUSHES in 1862 and 1873-74 brought thousands of people to the Cassiar, and some stayed to develop the fur trade. Placer mining and trapping continue along with hardrock gold, asbestos and jade mining, outfitting big-game hunters and lately, logging and coal mining. The Cassiar is known for its spectacular scenery, particularly the magnificent STIKINE RIVER valley, with its glaciers, grand canyon, lava beds and volcanic cones nearby. The major settlements are Cassiar, Dease Lake, Telegraph Creek and Iskut Lake.

GEORGIANA BALL

Reading: R.M. Patterson, *Trail to the Interior* (1966).

Cassiar Mountains extend from the Yukon Territory 440 km SE to the confluence of the Finlay and Fox rivers in N-central BC. The name is thought to derive from a Nahanni word, *kaska,* or *kasha* ("creek" or "small river"). The Stikine Ranges, with a central ridge of granite, rise to 2760 m. Peaks lower than 2000 m were rounded by glacial action. They have low relief and extensive tundra, owing to the area's severe boreal climate. The Dease R attracted gold prospectors in the 1870s, and mineral exploration continues, especially in the Toodoggone R area, but the mountains remain a remote part of BC. The one community, Cassiar, where an asbestos mine opened in 1952, is company owned. An all-weather highway through the mountains opened in 1972.

PETER GRANT

Casson, Alfred Joseph, painter (b at Toronto 17 May 1898). After study at Hamilton (1913-15) and Toronto (1915-17), A.J. Casson got his first real job in 1919 at a Toronto commercial art firm as Franklin CARMICHAEL's apprentice. Carmichael had the greatest influence on Casson as an artist, taking him sketching and camping, and introducing him to members of the GROUP OF SEVEN, including Lawren HARRIS and J.E.H. MACDONALD. Along with Carmichael and F.H. Brigden, Casson revived and championed the watercolour medium. In 1926 Casson was invited to join the Group to replace Franz JOHNSTON who had shown only in the group's first exhibition (1920). He also bought his first car and began exploring villages near Toronto. Ontario small towns, particularly places such as Elora and Alton, were to become his preferred subjects.

Casson's style always retained what Harris had talked to him about – simplification and the elimination of all nonessentials. This quality in his work culminated in *Country Store* (1945), the start of his so-called period of abstraction. In later years, besides painting, Casson has helped detect forgeries, particularly of Group of Seven works, for the Ontario Provincial Police. In 1987 250 silkscreen reproductions of his watercolour *The Entrance to Baie Furie* were prepared, to be sold for $800 each by the North Channel Preservation Society to help finance the group's fight against a long-range plan to open a strip mine in the quartzite hills that are the subject of the painting.   JOAN MURRAY

Reading: Paul Duval, *A.J. Casson* (1980).

Castlegar, BC, City, pop 6385 (1986c), 6902 (1981c), inc (with Kinnaird) 1974, is located on the W bank of the COLUMBIA R at its junction with the Kootenay, midway between Calgary and Vancouver, and about 35 km N of the US border. The Lakes Band of Interior SALISH dominated this vital transportation and fishing site until the mid-18th century. Edgar DEWDNEY pre-empted the site 1865 while building the Dewdney Trail. A trail linked it with Nelson (43 km NE) in 1889; the first railway followed in 1892. In 1908 DOUKHOBORS took up land in the area, and thrived until 1924 when their spiritual leader, Peter "The Lordly" VERIGIN, was assassinated. Since the 1940s Castlegar has been a bedroom town for Cominco employees, a centre for dam construction workers on the Kootenay and Columbia projects and the Revelstoke Canyon Dam, and a home for pulpmill employees. BC Timber Pulp Mill and Saw Mill, and Selkirk College, with a variety of university courses and technological training, are important employers. Having excellent transportation facilities, the city is a trade centre with a substantial service area.   WILLIAM A. SLOAN

Castors ("Beavers"), a group of ultramontane dissident Conservatives (*see* ULTRAMONTANISM), established in 1882. Members opposed Québec Conservative premiers J.A. CHAPLEAU and J.A. MOUSSEAU, whom they accused of ousting them from power in order to ally themselves with the moderate Liberals. The group opposed the government's lax administration, its co-operation with unscrupulous businessmen and its favouring Québec City over Montréal, especially in university matters. François-Xavier-Anselme Trudel gave the group its name by signing the pseudonym "Castor" to his pamphlet, *Le Pays, le parti et le grand homme* (1882). The group lacked structure and remained a fringe group until its demise in the late 19th century.   NIVE VOISINE

Cat The domestic cat, a species of flesh-eating mammal belonging to family Felidae, order CARNIVORA, is a small, lithe, intelligent, soft-furred animal. About 4.1 million domestic cats inhabit Canada, averaging 1.6 per cat-owning household (just over 1 in every 2 households).

The origin of the domesticated cat is shrouded in mystery. Scientists speculate that a long-extinct animal, the small arboreal miacis, existed 40-50 million years ago and was probably ancestral to the bear, weasel, fox, coyote, raccoon, dog and cat. Another very agile animal which more closely resembled today's cat, the dinictis, is thought to have appeared 10 million years later. It is now generally accepted that house cats originated in the African wildcat, *Felis catus lybica,* which later interbred with the European wildcat, *Felis c. silvestris.* The earliest evidence of domesticated cats can be traced to ancient Egypt about 2500 BC. Egyptians held the cat in great esteem, worshipped it and protected it from injury. Phoenician trading ships are thought to have

brought the first domesticated cats to Europe around 900 BC. Romans are believed to have introduced the cat to England. It was not until settlers arrived from Europe with their domesticated cats that cats were kept as PETS in North America.

Physiology Feline structure is mammalian and, in many respects, similar to that of humans, physiologically and anatomically. The cat's skeleton has about 244 bones (nearly 40 more than the human adult). This extremely flexible skeleton, controlled by more than 500 skeletal muscles, gives the cat its ability and fluid motion. This superb mechanism is geared for enormous bursts of power, but the cat has little sustaining vigour. Unlike most animals, which move the left front leg with the right hind leg, the cat walks or runs by moving the front and hind legs on one side, then those on the other. The cat walks or runs on its toes with the heels up. Movement is silent because the paws are thickly cushioned. A cat's main defensive weapon is its claws (normally 5 in front, 4 in the back) which are extended or retracted by means of flexor tendons. Curved and very sharp, they are well adapted for grasping prey. The cat's 30 teeth (16, upper jaw; 14, lower) are the most specialized teeth among carnivores. Cats cannot chew; their food is cut and torn, not crushed or ground. Their teeth are also used for grasping and holding. Cats' skin is exceptionally quick to regenerate and to fight off infection entering through a wound. Coat hairs are shed continuously, but, to a greater degree, seasonally.

Sensory Functions Cats' eyes have very swift accommodation (the power of adjusting focus to distance) and can function equally well in almost complete darkness and in bright daylight. A cat has supersensitive hearing and can perceive ultrasonic sounds far higher in pitch than humans can detect. It can respond to sounds as high as 65 kilohertz. A cat's sense of touch can be compared with that of an insect. Every hair is sensitive, eyebrows, whiskers, cheek hair, ear tufts; as is the tip of the nose and the paw pads. The sense of taste and smell are closely allied. Cats select and find their food through olfaction. The cat's tongue has several functions associated with grooming and eating, and is the primary organ of taste.

Breeds The 36 recognized breeds have developed gradually, either naturally or by deliberate selective breeding. Cats are of 2 types: the very popular house cat, product of chance mating of different breeds; and the purebreed, belonging to a breed with recognized characteristics maintained through generations of unmixed descent. Generally, purebreds are divided into longhaired and short-haired breeds. Cats have diverse coat colours and patterns. They can be one solid colour or can have more than one colour arranged in a pattern as in tabbies, tortoiseshells and calicos. They can also be point coloured as in Siamese, Birman, Balinese and Himalayan.

Associations Cat fancy in Canada developed gradually. The first recorded show, a 2-day show with one officiating judge, was held in 1906 in Toronto. Most of the original purebred stock was imported from England. During the war years (1939-45), cat breeding and showing was greatly curtailed. After WWII interest revived and in 1960 the Canadian Cat Association (CCA) was founded. Today there are active clubs in most major cities and they hold at least one show annually. The Canadian National Cat Club, one of the oldest active clubs, sponsored cat shows at the annual CANADIAN NATIONAL EXHIBITION (CNE). In 1968 CNCC disbanded and sponsorship of CNE was passed to the Royal Canadian Cat Club, an affiliate of CCA. Many clubs in Canada are

affiliated with other associations, such as Cat Fanciers Assn (CFA), American Cat Fanciers Assn (ACFA) and American Cat Assn (ACA). Winnipeg's Manitoba Cat Club, the largest and most active club in Canada, averaging approximately 150 members, was organized in 1962 and became affiliated with ACFA.   JOHN M. BODNER

Reading: G. Pong, *The Complete Cat Encyclopedia* (1972); M. Wright and S. Walter, *The Book of the Cat* (1980).

Catfish, small to large, primarily freshwater FISHES of order Siluriformes (about 2000 species worldwide). In southern Canada, 10 species of genera *Ictalurus, Noturus* and *Pylodictis* of the N American family Ictaluridae (40 species in all) are known. They are characterized by having a scaleless body, several pairs of barbels (elongate, fleshy projections around the mouth region), adipose (fatty) dorsal fin in front of the tail, and dorsal and pectoral fin spines that can inflict painful wounds. In some smaller madtoms, the spines have a groove and venom sac. The barbels and much of the skin are covered with taste buds for locating food at night, when catfish are most active. Catfish eat aquatic insects, molluscs, crustaceans, plant material, and other fishes. Ictalurid catfish provide parental care, excavating a nest and guarding eggs and young. The reproductive pair engages in a head-to-tail clasping behaviour before deposition of eggs. Most catfish are not used by humans, but the brown bullhead and the channel catfish are fished for sport and commercially in Canada.   BRIAN W. COAD

Cathcart, Charles Murray, 2nd Earl, general, governor general of BNA (b at Walton, Eng 21 Dec 1783; d at St Leonard's-on-Sea, Eng 16 July 1859). One of Wellington's staff officers in the Napoleonic wars, Cathcart was also an amateur scientist of some reputation. In 1841 he discovered the mineral greenockite, a sulphate of cadmium. He served as commander of British forces in N America, 15 June 1845 to 13 May 1847, and added the responsibility of administrator, 26 Nov 1845 to 24 Apr 1846, and gov gen 24 Apr 1846 to 30 Jan 1847. The highest civil and military executive powers were thus briefly united because of a severe crisis in Anglo-American relations during the Oregon boundary dispute. Cathcart was inexperienced in politics but an effective interim governor. He became dispensable with the signing of the OREGON TREATY.

OWEN COOKE AND NORMAN HILLMER

Catherwood, Ethel, track and field athlete (b in Haldimand County, Ont 1909). She is the only Canadian woman ever to win an individual gold medal in Olympic track and field competition. Raised in Saskatoon, she emerged as a high jumper in 1926 when she equalled the Canadian record at a city meet; later that year she broke the world record with a jump of 1.58 m. Followers dubbed her "The Saskatoon Lily" in Toronto, where philanthropist Teddy Oke took her under his wing. At the 1928 Canadian championships in Halifax, she set a new record of 1.6 m. On the final day of the 1928 Amsterdam Olympics, Catherwood cleared 1.59 m in the women's "running high jump" for the gold medal. After a hero's welcome, she turned down motion-picture offers in favour of a business course and piano study; she married and moved to California, never to compete again.   TED BARRIS

Catholic Action Faithful to the Vatican's teachings and following the example of the church in France, elements of the Roman Catholic Church in Québec established Catholic Action groups to associate laymen of various ages and professions with the church's social work, particularly in urban areas. The Association catholique de la jeunesse canadienne-française was founded in 1903-04 by Fathers Lionel GROULX and Émile Chartier. Other groups comprised farmers and workers, and the youth movement included Jeunesse ouvrière catholique (JOC), Jeunesse étudiante catholique and Jeunesse rurale catholique, which were formed in the 1930s following the papal encyclical *Urbi Arcano* (1922) and the subsequent formation of JOC groups in Belgium. The influence of these associations, which were criticized by the conservative clergy as being too activist, is difficult to measure. They declined rapidly in the 1950s. *See also* CATHOLICISM; SOCIAL DOCTRINE. RICHARD JONES

Catholic Women's League of Canada, The, with 128 000 members in 1987, represents the largest organized body of Catholic women in Canada. Formed nationally in 1920, the league is committed to the upholding of Christian values and education in the modern world, the understanding and growth of religious freedom, social justice, peace and harmony, and the recognition of the human dignity of all people everywhere. It has been at the forefront of the anti-ABORTION lobby in Canada. Structured to enable members to make their views known at parish, diocesan and provincial levels, the CWL, through its National Council, actively translates the objectives of the organization into statements and briefs to the government on a broad spectrum of concerns. VALERIE J. FALL

Catholicism The word [Gk *katholikos*, "general" or "universal"] refers most commonly to that CHRISTIANITY which is in communion with the pope and the Church of Rome, although the modern ecumenical movement sees all Christians as sharing in the church's catholicism, which is derived from the universal headship and reign of Christ. (Many Protestant denominations include the word "catholic" in their creeds, referring thereby to the Christian Church as a whole.) The term is not biblical: St Ignatius of Antioch (d about 110 AD) was the first person known to have referred to the "Catholic Church." St Vincent of Lerins (5th century) later defined the catholic faith as "that which has been believed everywhere, always, and by all." In the church's belief God the creator is father of all, and God the son (Christ) has a universal kingdom, the church. The earliest Christian churches, established amid great linguistic, cultural and ethnic diversity, regarded themselves as constituting one holy, catholic church of Christ.

The Roman Catholic Church recognizes 7 religious acts, or sacraments: baptism, normally of infants; confirmation; the Eucharist (communion), celebrated centrally in the mass (public worship) and offered only to the baptized; confession, which involves the petitioner's penance and absolution by a priest; ordination (admission to one of 7 clerical ranks); marriage; and unction (anointing), normally administered only if the recipient is seriously ill or death is imminent. Government of the church is by a hierarchy of bishops, priests and deacons under the authority of the pope, who is bishop of Rome. The doctrine of apostolic succession holds that the spiritual authority vested in the apostles by Christ has descended in unbroken succession to the present pope, bishops and priests, who possess this authority in varying degrees. All clergy must be male. The church has numerous CHRISTIAN RELIGIOUS COMMUNITIES of both sexes; members commit themselves to chastity, as do priests and bishops of the Western rite.

Since the early centuries of Christianity, Easter, which commemorates Christ's Resurrection, has been the central feast of the liturgical calendar. In the course of time other seasonal and thematic

St-Pierre, the Church of Sts Pierre et Paul, *c*1718-34. Roman Catholicism came to Canada in the 16th century with French explorers, chaplains and missionaries. By the 17th century the parish was the backbone of religious life (© *Hartill Art Associates, London, Ont*).

feasts have been added; in contemporary Catholicism, Christmas (feast of the birth of Jesus) and Epiphany (feast of the early manifestations of Christ's divinity) have been highlighted along with Easter as the central feasts of the year (*see* RELIGIOUS FESTIVALS).

Adherents to Eastern rite Catholic churches are not numerous in Canada: in 1981 (the last year for which figures are available) the census showed a total of 190 585 Ukrainian Catholics (the largest Eastern rite denomination in Canada). The Western rite, or Roman Catholic, church is much more strongly represented: close to one-half of Canada's population declared itself to be Roman Catholic in 1981. (Census data must be treated with care; identification with the church does not necessarily imply active membership.) This proportion increased from 38.7% in 1921, largely as a result of immigration by great numbers of Roman Catholics. Canada's more than 11.2 million Roman Catholics are unevenly distributed across the country, with 50.0% of them in Québec, 26.6% in Ontario, 14.7% west of Ontario and 8.4% east of Québec.

Roman Catholic Church

Roman Catholicism came to what is now Canada with the first European explorers but was slow to establish itself: whether or not Jacques CARTIER really was accompanied by chaplains in 1535, it took Samuel de CHAMPLAIN and his pro-settlement propaganda to persuade the French church to plant a branch in the St Lawrence Valley. Circumstances then favoured the missionary spirit that led to a Canadian Catholic church; these included the interest of the papacy and the religious orders in the New World; the end of the religious wars in France; the reforms following the Council of Trent, which regenerated the French church; and the enthusiasm of the devout for missions abroad. Supported by noble benefactors and the French clergy, members of the Récollet order established themselves in Québec in 1615, followed in 1625 by the Jesuits. The missionaries went home to France during the English occupation, 1629-32, but then re-

turned in force (although, by order of Cardinal Richelieu, only the Jesuits were permitted to resume their work).

This young Canadian church was devoted almost entirely to evangelizing the Indians. Without neglecting the increasing number of settlers in NEW FRANCE, the Jesuits (and later the Sulpicians) concentrated on living with the Indians. The accounts of their labours, published in the JESUIT RELATIONS, helped them to hold the interest of Catholics in France. Generous donations funded the Jesuit college (1635); the SILLERY reserve (1637); the URSULINE Convent school (1639) run by MARIE DE L'INCARNATION; the HÔTEL-DIEU (1639); and VILLE-MARIE (1642), where the same institutions as those in Québec were established. The church supported the colony and was dominant even in politics, with the Jesuit superior often supplanting the governor.

Everything had changed by the 1650s. In 1648-50 the Iroquois destroyed HURONIA, and with it the Jesuits' most promising mission, STE-MARIE AMONG THE HURONS. Thereafter the Jesuits worked in scattered missions among the native peoples, but they had to devote increasing attention to the growing French population. The church received its first prelate in 1659. Though François de LAVAL was only vicar apostolic (ie, acting bishop where no hierarchy exists), he had sufficient jurisdiction to co-ordinate the establishment of the necessary institutions, including the SÉMINAIRE DE QUÉBEC. After New France's reorganization in 1663 as a royal colony, the church had to accept state intervention in joint questions (eg, establishment of parishes) and even in purely religious ones (eg, regulation of religious communities); in return, it could count on state support, which included money. Harmony was sometimes hard to maintain.

Gradually a distinctive Christianity developed. It was homogeneous, for Protestants were allowed into the colony only for brief visits (*see* HUGUENOTS). Most members of the population practised their faith, following the severe Catholicism developed primarily by Mgr de SAINT-VALLIER (*see* JANSENISM). The parish, backbone of religious life, was financially administered by churchwardens (the only elected officials in New France), who were usually influenced by the parish priest. In 1760 Canada had about 100 parishes, most of them run by diocesan clergy (84 members), of whom four-fifths were Canadian-born. The priests were assisted by 30 Sulpicians, 25 Jesuits and 24 Récollets, and over 200 nuns belonging to 6 communities who were responsible for educational and welfare activities. These communities of men and women could offer their services free because the king had granted them lands and financial support. This equilibrium, which characterized church-state relations 1660-1760, was vulnerable to any change in the balance between the forces that composed it.

After the CONQUEST of 1759-60, the Catholic Church of Québec, already weakened by the effects of war, had also to deal with new British – and Protestant – masters. The new authorities were expected to favour the Church of England (*see* ANGLICANISM) and attempt to convert their new Catholic subjects. However, the free exercise of the Catholic rite had been guaranteed in the terms of surrender, though under British limits of toleration, and greater freedom for Roman Catholics soon evolved. Nevertheless, the British interfered in the nomination of bishops and sometimes priests, and required the clergy to communicate certain government documents to their parishioners. The QUEBEC ACT of 1774 further guaranteed free exercise of Roman Catholicism and made it easier for Catholics to enter public office. To protect the newly won freedoms the bishops preached obedience (in varying degrees), led their people in opposition to the American invaders of 1775 and sang hymns of thanksgiving for British victories over the French in the AMERICAN REVOLUTION.

In other parts of present-day Canada, the French church had established missions in the Maritimes by the early 17th century and in Newfoundland by mid-century, but there was soon settlement by nonfrancophone Roman Catholics as well in these areas. Late in the 17th century Irish Catholics began to arrive in Newfoundland, which was under Québec's jurisdiction until 1713; that year France ceded Newfoundland to Britain by the Treaty of UTRECHT, and ecclesiastical jurisdiction over the island passed to the vicar apostolic of London. In 1796 Newfoundland became a separate diocese under Bishop J.L. O'Donel.

In the late 18th century significant numbers of Scottish Roman Catholics settled on Prince Edward Island and in Nova Scotia. For various personal, political and ecclesiastical reasons, however, the church there and in the other settled parts of present-day Canada, excepting Newfoundland, remained under the jurisdiction of the bishop of Québec until 1817; that year Nova Scotia was made a separate vicariate apostolic under Bishop Edmund Burke. Thereafter, new vicariates and dioceses appeared as settlement spread. The growth of the church in anglophone Canada was spurred especially by the arrival in the 19th century of large numbers of Irish immigrants.

Meanwhile, in LOWER CANADA [Québec], by the early 19th century numerous Catholics, especially the rising professional class, had distanced themselves from their church. The priests could not direct the populace as they had done before, and the people tended to neglect religious practices. Church authorities warded off efforts at secular domination, won official recognition from the bishop and encouraged education (including religious vocations), and revived the Catholic faith. But the 323 priests could not meet the needs of Québec's 500 000 inhabitants and could no longer count on the support of male religious communities, which (apart from the Sulpicians) had disappeared, or of female ones, which were in difficulties. The Parti PATRI-OTE (fd 1826), which had mass support, proposed a liberal program that alarmed the clergy and began a Protestant-style proselytism, primarily around Montréal. The beleaguered bishop of Québec won the nomination of a Montréal auxiliary, Mgr Jean-Jacques Lartigue, who became bishop of Montréal in 1836. Lartigue condemned the REBELLIONS OF 1837 but, by siding with the government, temporarily alienated himself from his people.

The church was as badly shaken as the rest of society by the insurrection's aftereffects, but it was the first to recover. Under the dynamic new bishop of Montréal, Mgr Ignace BOURGET (installed in 1840), the clergy assumed increasing power. Bourget set out to "Christianize" and "regenerate" society, applying the ideas of his predecessor and using the populist sermons of the French Mgr Charles de Forbin-Janson (see EVAN-GELISM) to advantage. Bourget made full use of the religious press, run with passion and skill by laymen; he headed fund drives in the city and made begging trips to Europe. He worked for the people's advancement, allying his church with Rome on liturgy, theological studies and devotions. He supported campaigns for public morality (eg, TEM-PERANCE campaigns and the fight against "evil" literature led by the Oeuvre des bons livres and the Cabinets de lecture paroissiaux), ran a social-as-sistance program for the poor, the sick, the orphaned and the handicapped, and preached social mutual assistance. The Montréal example was followed throughout Québec, though often to a lesser degree.

During the same period a sharp increase in religious vocations led to more and better-served parishes; the number of dioceses (10 in 1900) rose with the birthrate. The priests, now more numerous, often involved themselves in secular activities and seemed to run everything in Québec. Parishes periodically called in specialists (Jesuits, Oblates, Redemptorists, Dominicans and Franciscans) to preach at spiritual-renewal missions. The lay response seemed satisfactory: most were now practising and an elite could even be called devoted.

Catholicism in both English and French Canada was aligned with international Catholicism, whose leadership was becoming progressively more defensive and fearful of postrevolutionary (American and French) Western society. During the early 19th century sectarian violence grew, as demonstrated by the brawling of Irish Catholics with Irish Protestants (see ORANGE ORDER) on several occasions in Upper Canada, and by the fighting involved in the so-called SHINERS' WAR of the 1840s. Catholic churchmen saw the social upheaval resulting from industrialization and urbanization as the work of the devil, the French Revolution, Freemasonry, socialism and laissez-faire capitalism, and they urged the faithful to return to a stable Christian social order such as that prevailing in the Middle Ages.

One social area in which the church was always active was education. Catholic clergy throughout Canada had been pioneers in early 19th-century education, establishing small local schools with teachers whose primary concern was the moral education of their charges. But toward mid-century the state began to provide schooling, thus moving into an area of social concern that had been a church responsibility for centuries. The first school Act (1841) of the PROVINCE OF CANADA was aimed at the establishment of a Christian but nondenominational school system. However, political realities ensured that Canada East [Québec] soon developed a dual confessional school system (Catholic and Protestant), whereas Canada West [Ontario] allowed the creation of a divided, state-supported school system, one section being nondenominational (public), the other confessional (SEPARATE SCHOOLS). The latter soon became largely Roman Catholic. In subsequent decades other provinces frequently modelled their school systems on that of either Québec or Ontario. As the state took over the schooling of Canadians, therefore, confessional and Catholic schools obtained recognition in law. During the second half of the 19th century, the Canadian Catholic hierarchy was determined to strengthen its Catholic schools, while public school promoters considered that their "public" schools alone should enjoy the support of the state. There ensued lengthy and virulent controversies, such as the NEW BRUNSWICK SCHOOL QUESTION of 1871, the MANITOBA SCHOOLS QUESTION of the 1890s and the NORTH-WEST SCHOOLS QUESTION at the turn of the century; the ONTARIO SCHOOLS QUESTION of 1912-27 was not only a fight between English Protestants and French Catholics, but also the result of a power struggle between French Canadian and Irish Canadian clerics within the church. Other parts of Canada experienced similar quarrels as ethnic groups struggled for church control, but in the process some clerics learned to value diversity and to respect and love one another. Meanwhile, the church had founded numerous denominational institutions of higher learning. A number of Canadian UNIVERSITIES originated in this way, including UNIVERSITY OF OT-TAWA and U of St Michael's College (Toronto). In most cases, their administration has passed gradually into secular hands.

As the church increased its influence on society, especially in French Canada, some clergy were tempted by politics. Imbued with ultramontane principles (see ULTRAMONTANISM), and fearing reforms being suggested by the Liberal Party, the Québec clergy accused that party's supporters of Catholic liberalism and denounced them at election time. In 1871, laymen supported by Bourget and Mgr Louis-François LAFLÈCHE published an election manifesto, the *Programme catholique,* which could have led to religious control of the provincial Conservative Party. The strong reaction of 3 bishops (Archbishop Elzéar-Alexandre TASCHEREAU, Mgr Charles LaRocque and Mgr Jean Langevin) and of politicians doomed the project and made public the split between moderate and intransigent ultramontanists ("Programmists"). In 1875 the groups united in a virulent denunciation of Catholic liberalism; in 1876 the election results in 2 provincial ridings were annulled because of "undue influence" by the clergy. Tension grew between church and state. Rome was consulted, and it sent an apostolic delegate, Mgr George Conroy, to re-establish harmony between the prelates and force them to declare that their condemnation of Catholic liberalism had not been directed against the Liberal Party. Clerical intervention in politics was thereafter more discreet.

During the latter 19th century Québec Catholicism discovered a missionary vocation that persists today. Nuns, priests and brothers first established missions in English Canada (including the present-day Prairie provinces and Northwest Territories) and the US, and then throughout the world. (*See also* MISSIONS AND MISSIONARIES.)

The church was active in broader social concerns as well. Various 19th-century sociologists had recognized that new forms of society, with new needs, were being created by growing industrialization and urbanization. Protestants responded to the new "social question" with the SOCIAL GOSPEL movement late in the century. By the 20th century, Québec Catholicism was preoccupied with social concerns. Aware of the problems created by the new technology and the migration to the cities, and challenged by Pope Leo XIII's 1891 encyclical, *Rerum Novarum,* the clergy developed a SOCIAL DOCTRINE to guide the new society. In Québec the Jesuits were particularly active through the École sociale populaire. Their Programme de restauration sociale (fd 1933) was the main inspiration for the political movements ACTION LIBÉRALE NATIONALE, BLOC POPULAIRE CANADI-EN and, to a lesser degree, UNION NATIONALE. They supported and directed Catholic trade unions, formed 1907-20, and credit unions, co-operatives and every kind of league, each of which had Roman Catholicism as its main characteristic. Moreover, the church in Québec continued to control education. Secular activities left only about 45% of the clergy for parish duties. This disequilibrium posed few problems, since the province's clergy kept growing: 2091 in 1890, 3263 in 1920, 5000 in 1940 (a ratio of 567, 578 and 539 parishioners to each priest), exclusive of religious communities. The faithful were guided by their priests and in their religious practice emphasized parish missions, pilgrimages and provincial, regional and local conferences. CATHOLIC ACTION helped to form "new" Catholics, whose methods disturbed traditionalists and sometimes led to conflict with clergy.

In Canadian Catholicism's commitment to sociopolitical activity, doctrine and moral teaching were stringent, and political and social involve-

The dome of St Mary's Ukrainian Catholic Church in Yorkton displays one of the major religious frescoes of N America. In the centre, Mary is crowned in Heaven, attended by the Father, the Son and the Holy Spirit; 157 angels adorn the perimeter (*photo by John deVisser*).

ment was uncompromising. The GREAT DEPRESSION of the 1930s again tested the readiness of Catholics to deal with major social problems. The hard times that gave birth to the CO-OPERATIVE COMMONWEALTH FEDERATION also saw the beginnings of the Catholic ANTIGONISH MOVEMENT. Many Catholic bishops condemned the CCF because it was socialist. True to its tradition the church was generally conservative, supporting the status quo and uneasy with change. But WWII brought with it an increasing awareness of the outside world among Canadian Catholics, and made the church appear to many of them to be too self-sufficient and complacent.

During the century of highly centralized and disciplined Catholicism (1850-1950), while regular worship had become habitual for most Canadian Catholics, it had done so in the form of an increasing number of devotions set in a framework of intense and colourful piety. Devotion to the papacy had intensified after 1850, culminating in 1870 when the dogma of papal infallibility was defined, and successive popes strongly encouraged special devotions, eg, to the Sacred Heart of Jesus, the Virgin Mary or Saint Joseph. The Catholic Church built upon centuries-old customs in nurturing various forms of piety, such as the Rosary, the scapular, adoration of the Blessed Sacrament, and the Forty Hours; pilgrimages became popular, both to the shrines in Europe and the Holy Land and to various shrines in Canada. The crucifix adorned most Canadian Catholic homes, and wayside crosses and shrines were erected in massively Catholic areas. This intense piety would dissipate only after 1960.

Canadian Catholicism emerged from WWII as a church triumphant, as is suggested by the pageantry surrounding the 1947 Marian Congress in Ottawa and the installation ceremonies of Archbishop Paul-Émile LÉGER in Montréal in 1950. But the conservative administrations of Pope Pius XII and US Pres Eisenhower ended in the late 1950s, and the new liberal spirit emerging in the Western world began to affect the church in anglophone Canada. In Québec the changes were more extreme and jarring than they were elsewhere in Canada. WWII and the postwar period were a time

of profound transformation for all Québec. Traditional values, even religious ones, were challenged by people wanting an expansion of missionary and community values, an increased lay role in the church and a warmer welcome for the positive values of the modern world. Some groups, eg, the Faculté des sciences sociales of U Laval and the Commission sacerdotale d'études sociales, made a new reading of the church's social doctrine and proposed modern solutions to social problems. They were in the forefront of opposition to the Duplessis government during the 1949 ASBESTOS STRIKE and inspired a collective pastoral letter of 1950 which expressed a new sensitivity to labour and to women.

Until 1959, however, Catholicism in Québec still wore the face of a triumphalist, conservative institution. Then the QUIET REVOLUTION of the 1960s forced the church to face some weaknesses. In just a few years, a wind of change produced both the declericalization of society (welfare, health and education passed from church to state control) and the secularization of institutions (eg, Catholic trade unions shed their confessionality to become the CONFEDERATION OF NATIONAL TRADE UNIONS), and associations, social clubs, universities and the state all adopted religious pluralism. At the same time, much of the population ceased practising, and there was a break with traditional morality, especially in sexual matters; a major exodus of members of the clergy and of religious orders; and a sharp drop in religious vocations. The hierarchy and the clergy as a whole seemed overwhelmed, and kept prudent silence.

In 1959 Pope John XXIII announced the convening of an ecumenical council, and the Catholic faith throughout the world began to seek new forms of expression and witness. In Vatican Council II (1962-65) international Catholicism was caught up in a whirlwind of change and challenge that sought to revitalize all areas of Christian concern, from theology to political action, from spirituality to administration, from ecumenism to moral codes. A number of Canadians (eg, Cardinal Léger, theologian Bernard LONERGAN and humanitarian Jean VANIER) emerged as leaders of the *aggiornamento* (modernization movement) in various spheres of activity. The church in Canada could no longer rely on social custom and constraint, as it had done in the past, to ensure church attendance or to influence government decision making. The effects were particularly marked in Québec, where the Quiet Rev-

olution coincided with the church's international renewal. The loosening of these ties to society led to a decade or more of generalized confusion for many Canadian Catholics. Those who had attended mass every Sunday fearing the pain of sin learned the importance of personal responsibility in attendance at worship. Those who saw the cleric as "another Christ" discovered that he was also human. Those who were concerned over sexual sin as "the only sin" discovered the importance of loving God and one's neighbour. Churchmen learned to share some authority and Catholics were called upon to take some responsibility.

One sign of Catholic renewal was a softening of the teaching on marriage. Before 1960 a Roman Catholic needed special permission to marry a non-Catholic, and the non-Catholic partner needed to agree in writing to the education of his children in the Catholic faith. After Vatican II the church discovered the primacy of conscience and the real Christian faith of many non-Catholic Christians. This led to less stringent disciplinary dictums, many Catholic pastors now acknowledging that the children born of a mixed marriage are best raised in the church of the more committed Christian partner. The ecumenical campaign has been strengthened in the process.

Indeed, Vatican II and the papal documents that followed in its wake constitute a milestone in the history of the Roman Catholic Church. New bridgeheads were established on the shores of a postmodern world whose links with the Christian church had been deteriorating since the 17th century. The fear of the world that characterized so much of previous spirituality became an openhearted reaching out towards contemporary humanity. There was greater emphasis on the church as a people of God, and less on the dominant hierarchy; the laity made some advances (although in the early 1980s Canadian women were lobbying for access to the hierarchy through women's ordination); Protestants were promoted in the eyes of the Roman Catholic Church from the rank of heretics to that of "separated brethren"; the Third World was given its due as an area of major concern to the church; the scarecrow of socialism became acceptable ideology under certain circumstances; and the treatment reserved for linguistic, cultural and political minorities was recognized as a valid test of the quality of governments.

Forms of worship changed as well after Vatican II, and many of the changes centered on the renewed emphasis on the people as the principal constituent of the church. Although communion remains the focal point of the mass, partaking of it is not linked as closely to individual confession as it formerly was. Priests now conduct mass facing the people, and the Latin of the Tridentine rite has given way to vernacular languages. The practice of preaching and interpretation of scripture has been revived, and lay members of the congregation participate more fully in the various aspects of the worship service. There is also a resurgence of congregational singing and popular hymnology. At the same time, certain features of popular piety (eg, benedictions, stations of the cross) have virtually disappeared (*see also* CHARISMATIC RENEWAL).

In the wake of Vatican II the Canadian Catholic church reassessed its attitude toward "other" linguistic and cultural groups. In early Ontario and English Canada, for instance, the leadership of various Catholic churches had been largely French or French Canadian (there was no francophone bishop in the Maritimes before 1912). As an English-speaking (largely Irish) hierarchy came to the fore in these areas, ethnolinguistic polarization developed simultaneously in the ranks of the hierarchy and in Canada generally. The result was a Canadian Catholic Church that pretended to be united, but was in fact separated on English-French lines. While Rome preached bilingualism for the Canadian church, Canada's bishops indulged in their own peculiar brand of ethnocultural warfare.

The new spirit that prevailed after 1960 led Canada's Catholic churchmen to reassess their attitudes. At the centennial of Confederation (1967) as well as on several other occasions ranging from the adoption of Québec's charter of the French language (1977) to Canada's constitutional debate (to 1982), the bishops of Canada, Québec and Ontario issued a series of statements on the question of minority language rights and the status of French and English in Canada. For the first time in a century, the leaders of Canada's Catholic Church were constructively coming to grips with an issue that had long divided them. The Canadian Catholic Church had practised bilingualism before Confederation, a policy that had served it well in evangelizing much of Canada. It is now returning to such a policy, realizing along with others that it is the *sine qua non* of successful policy in Canada. Given the church's numbers and geographic distribution, it can contribute immensely to French-English understanding in Canada.

The turbulence of the 1960s and 1970s, with its catastrophic effects on the ecclesiastical institution, nevertheless left a solid core: a significant number of practicants; a virtually intact network of parishes; an organization of religious communities of men and women who had rethought their objectives; confessional schools and some private colleges; a new plan for parish action and greater lay participation in religious activities. The episcopacy more frequently joined in ECUMENICAL SOCIAL ACTION, taking positions on such topics as BIRTH CONTROL and ABORTION (1977, 1981) and the economic crisis (1982). But it is perhaps at the level of popular religion that the continuity and the hopes are most visible, given (among other things) a new interest in Scripture, the continued popularity of pilgrimage and the growth of the Charismatic movement.

The rapidly changing Canadian church experienced in Sept 1984 a climactic event in the visit to Canada of Pope John Paul II. This pilgrim pontiff, who has been seen by more people than all other popes together, was the first reigning pope to set foot in Canada. He visited many regions, preaching a gospel of peace, reconciliation and disciplined belief. To fulfil a promise made to the residents of Fort Simpson, NWT, where he was unable to land because of fog, he returned in Sept 1987.

NIVE VOISINE AND ROBERT CHOQUETTE

Eastern Rite Catholic Churches

Eastern Catholicism is a federation of particular and semiautonomous churches in communion with Rome. The history of the Eastern Catholic churches has been a struggle to remain faithful to unity with Rome without Latinization or absorption into the Latin (ie, Western or Roman) rite church, and to preserve particularity – ie, local and cultural autonomy – of both material and formal elements. The material elements are a group of faithful (the people of God); an indigenous hierarchy with apostolic succession; a particular discipline of general norms and canons embodied in liturgical practice; and a spiritual tradition. This tradition entails history, language(s), culture and mentality rooted in a specific world view, connections with particular ethnic communities and a distinct theological orientation; monastic life; religious instruction rooted in the liturgy; and a tradition of religious art imbued with spiritual meaning.

The formal elements of local autonomy consist of recognition (expressed or tacit) of the church's self-governing nature by ecumenical councils and individuals in the church hierarchy, including the pope, and by the faithful themselves; exclusive membership in one's own rite; and the formal exercise of autonomy or particularity.

Eastern and Western Christianity have suffered a long process of drifting apart. In the first 7 centuries of the Christian era, philosophic-minded people began to question their beliefs, especially the mystery of Christ. It took 7 ecumenical councils to resolve such questions to the satisfaction of the church hierarchy. Meanwhile, Monophysites and Nestorians seceded from the unity of the church. Political problems further complicated the matter (eg, in 330 AD Emperor Constantine moved the capital of the Roman Empire from Rome to "New Rome": Byzantium, or Constantinople). For centuries there were rivalries and tensions between the patriarchs of Rome, Constantinople, Alexandria, Antioch and Jerusalem concerning their authority. The church-state relationship was complicated by the "caesaropapism" of the Byzantine emperors and the "papocaesarism" of Pope Leo I and his successors. In 1054 in Constantinople, Patriarch Cerularius and papal representative Cardinal Humbertus de Silva Candida excommunicated each other. In 1204 the knights of the Fourth Crusade sacked Constantinople and established their empire and Latin rite patriarchate. These were the final events that brought about the schism which has lasted to the present time.

The Eastern Catholic churches came into being as a result of a series of reunions with Rome: Maronites in 1181; Italo-Albanians in Sicily and Calabria during the 15th century; Chaldeans in 1553; Ruthenians (Ukrainians and Byelorussians) in 1596; Ethiopians in 1626; Chaldeo-Malabars (St Thomas Christians) in 1699; the Eparchy of Priashiv in 1646; Syrians of Antioch in 1663; Ruthenians of Valachia and Moldavia (today Romanians) in 1697; Melkites in 1724; Armenians in 1742; the Eparchy of Krizhevci in Yugoslavia (Ukrainians, Ruthenians, Croatians, Macedonians and Romanians) in 1777; Bulgarians in 1860; Copts in 1739; and the Syro-Malankarese in 1930.

The Eastern Catholic churches are grouped according to 5 rites, the Alexandrian, Antiochian, Byzantine, Chaldean and Armenian. Eastern rite Catholics in Canada are almost exclusively within the Antiochian, Byzantine and Armenian rites. Ukrainian Catholics, the largest group in Canada, adhere to the Byzantine rite; while in communion with Rome, they share with much of the ORTHODOX CHURCH the Liturgy of St John Chrysostom. The denomination was brought to Canada by UKRAINIAN immigrants around the turn of the century, and the first bishop for Canada was Niceta Budka, appointed by Pope Pius X in 1912. Canadian Ukrainian Catholics are organized in a metropolitan province under the leadership of His Grace Maxim Hermaniuk, Archbishop of Winnipeg and Metropolitan of All Canada; the province is divided into 5 eparchies: Winnipeg, Edmonton, Toronto, Saskatoon and New Westminster. Church statistics show some 229 000 members, although the 1981 Canadian census registered less than 200 000. The faithful, distributed through about 200 parishes, are served by over 260 clergy. Religious orders include BASILIAN FATHERS (OSBM), Redemptorist Fathers (CSsR), Studites, Sisters Servants of Mary Immaculate (SSMI), Missionary Sisters of Christian Charity (MSCC), Basilian Sisters (OSBM), Sisters of St Joseph and Studite nuns. Future priests are educated at the Seminary of the Holy Spirit in Ottawa and at U of Ottawa. The Ukrainian Catholic

community has an active press, which publishes the weeklies *Nasha Meta* (Toronto, fd 1948), *Postup-Progress* (bilingual, Winnipeg, 1959), and *Ukrainski Visti* and its English version, *The Ukrainian Record* (Edmonton, 1961); the scholarly theological journal, *Logos;* and the popular religious journals *Redeemer's Voice, Svitlo* and *Beacon.* Two religious presses, the Basilian Press (Toronto) and Redeemer's Voice (Yorkton, Sask), have distinguished themselves through the publication of books and pamphlets.

Slovaks of the Byzantine Rite in Canada are organized in 6 parishes in the Eparchy of Saints Cyril and Methodius (Toronto, est 1980). The approximately 5000 faithful are served by 10 missions and 6 priests under Bishop Michael Rusnak. Their official publication is the monthly journal *Maria.* Armenians in Canada have 2 parishes (Québec and Toronto). The approximately 8000 faithful are served in the Armenian rite by 2 priests and 2 sisters, and are under Bishop Nerses M. Sétian, exarch since 1981 for Armenians in the US and Canada.

The small number of Melkites in Canada, who come from the Middle East, follow the Byzantine rite. They are under Archbishop Michael Hakim, apostolic exarch for the Melkite Greek Catholics in Canada (Outremont, Qué), who was appointed in 1980. Maronites, also from the Middle East but adherents to the Antiochian rite, are under Mgr Elias Shaheen, eparch for the Maronite Catholics in Canada (Montréal), who was appointed in 1982. All other Eastern Catholics are under the jurisdiction of the local Latin-rite ordinaries and do not have their own organizational structures. Their numbers are unknown.

PETRO B.T. BILANIUK

Reading: D. Attwater, *Eastern Churches in Communion with Rome,* (2 vols, rev ed 1961-62); Gregory Baum, *Catholics and Canadian Socialism* (1980); J.W. Grant, *The Church in the Canadian Era* (1972); J.S. Moir, *The Church in the British Era* (1972); Nive Voisine, *Histoire de l'Église catholique au Québec (1608-1970)* (1971); H.H. Walsh, *The Church in the French Era* (1966).

Cattail, common name for herbaceous, perennial plants (genus *Typha*) of the cattail family (Typhaceae) which grow in marshes and waterways. The name derives from the cylindrical, brown fruiting spikes. At least 8 species exist worldwide;

Cattails grow across Canada in marshes and along waterways (*photo by Tim Fitzharris*).

2 in Canada (narrow leaved cattail, *T. angustifolia*, and common cattail, *T. latifolia*). Clusters of stiff, ribbonlike leaves, up to 3 m (or more) tall, grow from a thick, horizontal rootstock. The rootstock is a rich source of starch; the succulent, young shoots and green flower spikes·are also edible; and the pollen and oil-rich seeds have livestock feed potential. The leaves are tough and pithy, and were used by native peoples to make mats, bags, baskets and clothing. Stems and leaves are suitable for making paper and cloth. Formerly, the cottony fluff attached to fruits was used to stuff bedding. Cattails also provide food and shelter for wildlife. These plants are also called bulrushes, a name which sometimes refers to plants of genus *Scirpus* of the SEDGE family. *See also* PLANTS, NATIVE USES.   NANCY J. TURNER

Caven, William, Presbyterian minister, educator (b at Kirkcolm, Scot 26 Dec 1830, d at Toronto 1 Dec 1904). Immigrating to Canada in 1847, Caven studied at United Presbyterian Seminary at London, Canada W, and entered the ministry in 1852. In 1865 he was called to the Chair of Exegetical Theology in Knox College, Toronto, became principal in 1873, and led the college into full affiliation with U of T. He remained as principal until his death.

In 1875, as moderator of the General Assembly of the Canada Presbyterian Church, he was involved in the negotiations which united the Free Church and Kirk in the Presbyterian Church in Canada. Later, he was also a strong advocate of interdenomination Protestant union, in part because of the seeming threat of Roman Catholicism. Caven's ecumenicism in the late 1880s and 1890s must be seen in the context of his strong opposition to the JESUITS' ESTATES ACT of 1888 and to denominational schools in Manitoba in the 1890s.   A.B. MCKILLOP

Cavendish, PEI, UP, pop 94 (1986c), 93 (1981c), is situated 38 km NW of Charlottetown, approximately in the middle of the province's N shore. It was named for Field Marshal Lord Frederick Cavendish, patron of a local landholder. During the summer months the year-round population is submerged by tourists and seasonal residents who flock to PEI National Pk, Canada's second-most-popular such park. Established in 1790 by Scottish immigrants, Cavendish was originally a farming community. With the 1930s' establishment of the national park, tourism has become the community's principal employer. It was in Cavendish that novelist and native Lucy Maud MONTGOMERY wrote ANNE OF GREEN GABLES.   W.S. KEIZER

Cayuga, when first encountered by Europeans, occupied several villages near the lake bearing their name in NY state. As a member of the IROQUOIS Confederacy, they are represented by 10 chiefs on the confederacy council. During the 17th century, population losses to disease and warfare were offset by large-scale adoption of captives and refugees. War with the Susquehannock to the S led some Cayuga to settle briefly on the N shore of Lk Ontario in the 1660s. For the most part neutral during the French-English conflicts of the 18th century, they fought on the British side during the American Revolution. An American army under Gen John Sullivan burned their villages in 1779. After the war, almost half the Cayuga chose to settle in Canada. In population they are second only to the MOHAWK among the peoples of the Six Nations Reserve near Brantford, Ont. Cayuga there number over 3400, but fewer than 400 still speak their native language. *See also* NATIVE PEOPLE: EASTERN WOODLANDS and general articles under NATIVE PEOPLE.
                    THOMAS S. ABLER

Reading: B.G. Trigger, ed, *Handbook of North American Indians*, vol 15: *Northeast* (1978).

Cedar, in Canada, refers to evergreen CONIFERS (genus *Thuja*) of cypress family (Cupressaceae). They are also called arbor vitae [Lat, "tree of life"]. The true cedars belong to the coniferous genus *Cedrus* (pine family) and are found from the Mediterranean to the Himalayas. Six species of *Thuja* are recognized: 2 in N America; 4 in eastern Asia. Western red cedar (*T. plicata*), found along the BC coast and western slopes of the Rocky Mts, may attain 60 m in height, 3 m in diameter. Eastern white cedar (*T. occidentalis*), growing to 25 m, occurs in the Great Lakes-St Lawrence forest region. Asiatic species, *T. orientalis*, is often planted as an ORNAMENTAL. Small, scalelike leaves cover flat, spraylike branches. Oval cones are 1-2 cm long. Bracts (modified leaves) and scales (ovule-bearing structures) are fused. POLLINATION occurs in spring; seeds (small, with 2 lateral wings) are shed in fall. Soft, light, aromatic, decay-resistant wood is used for ornament and finishing. West Coast Indians used cedar for totem poles, canoes and lodges.   JOHN N. OWENS

Eastern white cedar (*Thuja occidentalis*), with male flowers (dark red) and female flowers (brownish yellow) and cones (*artwork by Claire Tremblay*).

Cedar Lake Reservoir, 1353 km², 62.5 km long, elev 253 m, is located in W-central Manitoba, N of Lk WINNIPEGOSIS. The lake draws most of its waters from the huge SASKATCHEWAN R drainage basin. Construction of an earthfill dam and 25.6 km of dikes in 1961-64 caused lake levels to rise 3.65 m, creating Cedar Lk Reservoir and assuring a mean annual flow of 688 m³/s at the associated Grand Rapids hydroelectric generating station.   R.A. MCGINN

CEGEP, *see* COLLÈGE D'ENSEIGNEMENT GÉNÉRAL ET PROFESSIONNEL.

Celery (*Apium graveolens* var. *dulce*), biennial plant of the Umbelliferae family, widely grown as an annual for its nutritious leafstalks. Rape celery or celeriac (*A. graveolens* var. *rapaceum*) is grown on a more limited basis for its thick, edible root. Celery originated in the Mediterranean basin, was first grown as a medicinal plant, and was possibly first cultivated as a condiment in Italy in the 16th century. Celery has a well-developed root system, a short, fleshy crown (modified stem) and a rosette of leaves. Celery's characteristic taste and odour is produced by volatile oils in its stalk, leaves and seeds. It is rich in ascorbic acid. Preferring a cool climate, celery is sown in spring and transplanted after about 60 days, needing another 90 days to reach maturity. It also requires fertil-

izer and regular irrigation to produce approximately 90 t/ha. Mechanical harvest is increasing; harvested celery is peeled, measured, chilled in iced water and crated. Principal diseases are *Septoria* blight and black heart. In Canada, over 700 ha are devoted to celery production, mainly in Québec and Ontario. In 1985 Canadian production was valued at about $8.9 million and imports, almost all of which came from the US, were valued at $39.8 million.   PIERRE SAURIOL

Celtic Languages belong to the family of languages known as Indo-European and as such are related to most of the languages of Europe and many others found east of Europe as far as India. Linguists recognize 2 main divisions of Celtic: Continental Celtic and Insular Celtic. By about 300 BC Continental Celtic was spoken over a vast area of Europe, stretching, in modern terms, from western France eastwards into Turkey. However, with the expansion of the Roman Empire from the 3rd century BC, Latin (mainly) gradually replaced Celtic, with the process being complete almost everywhere by the 2nd century AD (although some Celtic may have lingered on in the Swiss mountains as late as the 5th century AD). Insular Celtic was spoken in Ireland and the British Isles from the arrival of the Celts there about the 4th century BC. It also includes Breton which was introduced to Brittany from SW Britain during the 4th-6th centuries AD. Insular Celtic divides into 2 main branches, which are conveniently known as Q-Celtic and P-Celtic (a distinction also appearing in Continental Celtic). Insular Q-Celtic takes in Scottish Gaelic, Irish Gaelic and Manx Gaelic, while Insular P-Celtic includes Welsh, Cornish, Breton and Pictish (at least Celtic Pictish, since the ancient Picts of northern Scotland appear to have spoken more than one language). This terminology was inspired by the fact that Q-Celtic preserved an older *kw* sound (written as *q* in the ancient Gaelic Ogham script and *c* in modern Gaelic) where P-Celtic developed a *p* sound, for instance Gaelic *mac* ("son") corresponds to Old Welsh *map*, and Old Gaelic *cenn* ("head") to Welsh *pen*. Cornish died out by the 18th century and Manx in this century, although in both Cornwall and the Isle of Man there has been a revival and a number of enthusiasts can now speak these languages. The other languages are still spoken, and although exact figures are not available, one·can estimate, for native speakers, about 80 000 Gaelic-speakers in Scotland, about 60 000 in Ireland (supplemented by over 750 000 non-native-speakers who claim to know Irish Gaelic, although their degree of fluency is unknown). Welsh is in better numerical shape with *c*500 000 native-speakers. No reliable statistics exist for Breton and estimates vary wildly from 20 000 to 700 000.

In Canada only the Highland SCOTS and the WELSH managed to establish colonies where their native language survived late into this century. Scottish Gaelic colonies established themselves in Cape Breton and 3 eastern counties of Nova Scotia (Guysborough, Pictou and Antigonish), in Prince Edward Island, in the Codroy Valley in SW Newfoundland, in Compton County, Québec, in southern Ontario (Stormont, Dundas and Glengarry counties SE of Ottawa, and in Middlesex County W of London), and on each side of the Manitoba-Saskatchewan border.

Gaelic-speakers have been recorded in all of these areas in recent years although only in CAPE BRETON is there any real vigour left in the culture, which, even there, is confined to little more than a thousand of the middle-aged and the old. Two Welsh colonies had less than 100 elderly (mainly) and middle-aged Welsh-speakers between them according to a survey done in 1974:

Ponoka in Alberta and Bangor in Saskatchewan. People speaking one or other of the 4 main Celtic languages can be found in many Canadian cities and towns, with Montréal being the centre for an unknown number (probably small) of Breton-speakers. Recent keen interest in Celtic culture has manifested itself by the establishment of a Chair of Celtic Studies at U of Ottawa; a Chair of Gaelic Studies at St Francis Xavier U, Antigonish, NS; a Chair of Irish Studies at St Mary's U, Halifax; and a program of Celtic studies at St Michael's Coll at U of T. *See also* LANGUAGE.

GORDON W. MACLENNAN

Reading: Gordon W. MacLennan, ed, *Proceedings of the First North American Congress of Celtic Studies* (1987).

Celtic Music References in ancient sagas, medieval texts, even in the works of Dante and Shakespeare, all attest the importance of music, both vocal and instrumental, in Celtic realms. Celtic music, in Canada as elsewhere, is derivative of a genre whose antecedents are rooted in Continental and Insular CELTIC LANGUAGES. During the last 2 centuries, collectors and musicologists have retrieved, edited and analysed an impressive corpus of Irish, Scottish, Welsh, Breton, Manx and Cornish folk-songs. All of them have emphasized the importance of folk music as the prime medium through which the musical style of a nation can develop as a distinctive art form.

Celtic folk song is for the most part pentatonic in origin. The 5-scale note forms the basis of the 6-note (hexatonic) and 7-note (heptatonic) scales, respectively. It is this gapped scale system that distinguishes the music of the Celts from the more widely used major-minor system. To avoid monotony, folk singers exercise their creative instincts through the use of melodic and ornamental variants.

The principal instruments identified with Celtic music are the harp, the bagpipe and the fiddle. The harp is common to all Celtic areas. Harpers, many of them blind, flourished in Ireland, Wales and Scotland until the 18th century when political, religious and social changes threatened the extinction of their language and their culture. The harp was used both for accompaniment and as a solo instrument. It was the instrument which incited Highlanders to battle until it ceded that role to the bagpipe after the Battle of Harlaw in 1411. Harpers disdained the adaptations of their music to the pipes at that time, and later to the fiddle which they regarded as an inferior instrument.

The bagpipe has a long history in Celtic society. The war-pipes and small pipes of Scotland, the Uilleanann pipes of Ireland, and the biniou, a smaller instrument played in Brittany only in accompaniment with the bombard, all had their own music, and all are still very much part of the music in their respective areas. The fiddle tradition is a more recent development. Although well known in Scotland prior to 1680, it was enhanced and enriched by the great upsurge of dancing in the 19th century. Scores of folk tunes were adapted as dance music and transmitted in writing, not orally as with other forms of folk culture. Ireland, too, has a strong fiddle tradition. In both countries, as in Canada, the fiddle has experienced phenomenal popularity during the past 2 decades.

In Canada the preservation and development of authentic Celtic music has occurred wherever Celtic languages have been retained. Highland SCOTS, in particular, for generations continued to sing the songs of their forebears, to which they added their own compositions reflecting their fortunes in the New World. Their piping and fiddling remained strong too. This is not to say that other Celts neglected their traditional music. WELSH, IRISH and Breton tunes can be heard in choral, or-

chestral, solo and folk-group renditions in many parts of the country today. Local dance groups stimulate and perpetuate music essential to their art. Whatever the form, their music remains for Celts a distinctive and treasured part of their cultural heritage. *See also* FOLK MUSIC, ANGLO-CANADIAN; FOLK MUSIC, FRANCO-CANADIAN.

Cement Industry comprises establishments engaged in producing hydraulic cements, ie, cements which set and harden to a stonelike mass by reacting with water. The principal hydraulic cement is portland cement, a finely ground, usually grey, manufactured mineral product. Cement by itself has limited application, but when mixed with water and SAND, gravel, crushed stone or other aggregates, it forms concrete, a rocklike substance that is the most widely used CONSTRUCTION material in Canada and the world. Concrete is used to pave highways, sidewalks and airport runways; in the construction of virtually all types of buildings, bridges, dams, dry docks, harbours, irrigation structures, water resources, sewage disposal systems, piping and storage silos; and in a multitude of other major and minor construction projects, including "do-it-yourself" projects.

Joseph Aspdin, an English mason, is generally credited with the invention of portland cement. In 1824 he obtained a patent for his product, which he named portland cement because it produced a concrete the colour of limestone quarried on the Isle of Portland. The name is used worldwide, with many manufacturers adding their own trade or brand names. Canadian production began in Hull, Qué, in 1889. Before that time portland cement was imported from England in wooden barrels. Plants were soon established at Napanee and Shallow Lake, Ont, and on Montréal Island. The first plant in the western provinces was built in Vancouver in 1893.

Materials used in MANUFACTURING portland cement must contain appropriate proportions of lime, silica alumina and iron components. During manufacture, frequent analyses are made to ensure a uniformly high-quality product. The raw materials are pulverized and mixed in the desired proportions. After blending, the prepared mix is fed into the upper end of a rotary kiln where it is burned or fired at temperatures of 1400-1650°C and changed into portland cement clinker. The clinker is then cooled and pulverized. During this operation, a small amount of GYPSUM is added to regulate the initial chemical reaction of the cement. This pulverized product is finished portland cement, ready for use in making concrete. Different types of portland cement are manufactured in Canada to meet physical and chemical requirements for specific purposes. The Canadian Standards Association provides for 5 types of portland cement for specific purposes, ie, normal, moderate and high early strength, low heat of hydration, and sulphate resisting. Normal portland cement is the type most commonly manufactured; high early strength and sulphate resisting types are usually available. Like moderate and low heat of hydration forms of portland cement, other special cements (masonry, oil well, expansive, regulated set) may not always be readily available from manufacturers because of low demand.

In 1986, 12 Canadian cement companies operated 22 plants. The oldest cement kiln was built in the 1950s but most are around 15 years old. Total clinker capacity was 16.6 million t and finish grinding capacity, 17 million t. Regionally Ont and Qué combine to have the majority of capacity – over 60% of clinker and over 50% of finish grinding capacity. Canada Cement Lafarge was Canada's largest cement company, with slightly over one-third of the nation's capacity. The next 2

Cement plant at Exshaw, Alta (*photo by Jim Merrithew*).

largest producers, St Lawrence Cement Inc and Inland Cement Ltd, combine to account for an additional 40% of Canada's capacity. Moreover, they have other N American affiliates which contribute to the size of the Canadian producers. Canadian cement plants tend to be modern and larger than other N American facilities and rely more heavily on oil and natural gas as kiln fuels. Slightly over half of Canadian capacity is coal fired; initiatives to conserve energy should continue to increase this proportion. Over 72% of Canadian kiln capacity now uses the dry-process technology that contributed to a sustained 9-12% reduction in overall energy consumption achieved during the latter half of the 1970s. The Canadian industry is strongly regionalized, with most plants located in high-population areas. High transportation and energy costs strongly influence plant location and economic viability.

Cement consumption in Canada (producers' shipments plus imports less exports) has been slowly increasing to 7.7 million t annually from 1982-86. At this level, the value of production was estimated at about $610 million. Primary sources of demand are from Qué and, particularly, Ont. Total Canadian consumption dropped to 6 million t during the 1982-84 period but by 1986 had increased to 7.5 million t. Canada ranks behind 18 other countries in apparent consumption of cement by the leading producers but, ranked per capita, is approximately tenth, with an apparent consumption of 390 kg per capita.

Although individual companies do research on cement production, much experimentation on the use and application of cement and concrete is done through the Canadian Portland Cement Assn, an industry-supported, nonprofit organization, the purpose of which is to improve and extend the uses of cement and concrete through scientific research and engineering fieldwork. The association is active throughout Canada and offers detailed information on concrete use, design and construction.

R.A. SERNE

Cemeteries are designated and usually consecrated places in which the dead are deposited. The word comes from the Greek *koimeterion* or the Latin *coemeterium,* meaning "to lie down to rest" or "to sleep." This usage alludes to the Christian belief in resurrection which robbed death and burial of many of their previously perceived terrors, but burial is not only a Christian practice. In Canada, people of all faiths generally locate their dead in a cemetery, whether in a grave or mausoleum or in an urn stored in a special structure, although some people have their cremated remains strewn or stored elsewhere, as in a church's columbarium.

Purpose and Location of Cemeteries Cemeteries are both the accepted places for the dead and for symbols of remembrance, usually gravemarkers. They also serve a psychologically important role for surviving relatives and friends who can visit gravesides. Cemeteries are often located on hill tops or slopes. Drainage is important, but the notion of hill sites as spiritual locations is deeply rooted in Judeo-Christian tradition.

Cemetery operations come under provincial jurisdiction. Cemeteries are owned by private corporations, nonprofit trust companies, churches, synagogues and municipalities. Plots range in price from $200 to over $10 000, with $600-$1600 being common. A percentage of plot prices covers perpetual care. The urban land value of cemeteries ranks extremely high, at times even higher than values at the primary intersections in central business districts. Some urban cemeteries preserve open spaces and locations for leisure activities (including bird watching).

Types of Cemeteries Viewed historically, there are several types of burial places. First, undifferentiated, which include burial sites of early explorers and voyageurs along river routes. Remains may be invisible today because of decayed wooden markers or flood-damaged rock piles; some remain, as on the Madawaska R, Ontario. Second, now usually abandoned small family plots dot the agricultural landscape, ranging in size from 5 to perhaps 20 burials. Early farmers who had difficulty reaching community cemeteries buried family members on their farms. The plots became disused and overgrown as children moved away or when farms were sold. Third, some rural activity foci (churches and small villages) have cemeteries serving the surrounding communities. Like small rural schools and churches, many such sites are now rarely used or are abandoned. Fourth, most burials today are in large population centre cemeteries, in towns and cities. Some have grown from small predecessors, others are new; some are relatively small, others are huge; some are surrounded by urban developments, others are peripheral to built-up areas.

Design of Cemeteries Older cemeteries were rectangular in form, reflecting a sense of order also found in town and rural surveying schemes. Most post-1920s cemeteries have meandering crescents and driveways similar to new residential subdivisions. Recent design changes reflect a move from "cemeteries" or "burial grounds" to pleasantly landscaped "memorial parks" and "gardens," a trend that may have resulted from secular attitudes and a need to soften the finality of death. The word "garden" also has special significance for Christians: in Old Testament tradition, man was shut out of the Garden of Eden and cannot return by his volition; in New Testament tradition, Jesus was betrayed in a garden and buried in a garden, so that what man lost by sin and disobedience may now be recovered in a garden by obedience unto death, with Paradise regained. While such religious symbolism is important to many Christians, to most Canadians "garden" cemeteries are simply aesthetically pleasing places for burial. New and some old cemeteries have "gardens of memories" which include mausoleums and columbaria. Holding vaults are seldom used today since excavation technicians – "gravediggers" of old – increasingly use mechanical means to penetrate frozen ground. High-rise mausoleums (some holding 65 000 remains), as found in Japan, Italy and the US, probably will not be built in Canada because

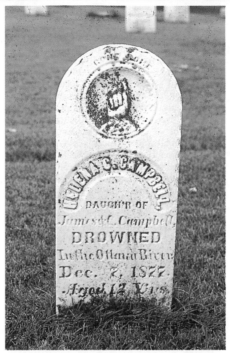

Gravestone at Cassburn Cemetery, Ont. A great deal of social and demographic information can be gained from early gravestones (*photo by David B. Knight*).

of tradition and, especially, investment constraints.

Religious preference leads people to be buried in different cemeteries, eg, Catholic, Jewish, Protestant (of various varieties), interfaith or nondenominational. In the past, people of minority races and of "disapproved" ethnic origins were forced to be buried apart from others. Distributional patterns within cemeteries reflect societal characteristics, eg, socially prominent families clustered in higher priced lots.

Grave Markers Stone markers generally indicate graves with, at minimum, names and dates of birth and death inscribed. Markers record past life but also provide a means by which a private family experience with death is made a public one to be shared. In some instances, markers may indicate more about the surviving families' wealth and self-perceived status than about the departed. Some large urban cemetery monuments are extremely grand. Other Canadians shy away from elaborate markers, including the Doukhobors who do not glorify their dead by erecting monuments.

Gravestone styles have changed. In the 18th century stones were severely simple; then Victorian grandeur and fussiness (1880s to early 1900s) gave way to a more severe modern style. Forms have included tablet shapes, obelisks (symbols of eternity), Celtic crosses, scrolls, blocks and pulpits. Heights have decreased through time. Some cemeteries now permit only lawn-height markers that help to create a parklike atmosphere.

Markers may have engraved symbols, including the open Bible, symbolizing the Word through which one gains salvation and revelation; urns, symbolic of the body's death from which rises the soul to heaven; a dove, for the Holy Spirit, peace and Christian constancy and devotion; Star of David, symbolizing Jewish faith; flowers, symbolizing both beauty and brevity of life; grapevines, symbolizing Christ as "the true vine"; carved portraits or photographs embedded in the stone; or symbols of fraternal societies. Epitaphs were commonly inscribed on stones in the past but today more than "in memoriam" is rare.

Cemeteries as Research Tools Cemeteries are im-

portant for tracing genealogy. Other facts can be gained and inferences made about settlement patterns and the history of surrounding communities, including ethnic origins, disease and death relationships, attitudes (from epitaphs) about death, societal standing (from relative locations and style of markers) and gravestone styles as reflections of culture change. *See also* DEATH AND DYING; FUNERAL PRACTICES; TOMBSTONES.　　　DAVID B. KNIGHT

Reading: C. Hanks, *Early Ontario Gravestones* (1974); D.B. Knight, *Cemeteries as Living Landscapes* (1982); P.E. Roy, *Les cimetières de Québec* (1941).

Censorship is the exercise of prior governmental control over what can be printed, published, represented or broadcast. Soon after the invention of the printing press, the English CROWN resorted to various censorship controls. Printing was allowed only under special licences, and this was reinforced by press offences and given a statutory basis with the Licensing Act of 1662. In 1695, when the House of Commons refused to renew the Licensing Act (not so much out of concern for freedom of expression as for a number of reasons related to commercial restrictions, house searches, etc), prior censorship of the press ended, except during wartime. Freedom of the press has since consisted "in laying no previous restraints upon publication, and not in freedom from censure for criminal matter when published."

However, censorship can be practised in covert ways. One of the earliest attempts to restrict publication was the use of deliberate taxation to inhibit circulation. A Stamp Tax introduced in England in 1712 (and not removed until 1855) required newspapers to affix stamps so that by raising the price of stamps newspaper prices could be raised beyond the purchasing power of all but wealthy readers. Censorship can also be practised through harassment and intimidation. During the "McCarthy era" in the US, the American Supreme Court, in *US* v *Rumely*, warned, "Through the harassment of hearings, investigations, reports, and subpoenas, government will hold a club over speech and over the press." Censorship can also be exercised through the pressure of advertisers and decisions by newspapers themselves, particularly in circumstances where no competitive or alternative source of news is available. R.M. MacIvor, writing after WWII, observed that "one of the major difficulties lies in the extension of large-scale enterprise to the media of opinion. In certain areas modern technology gives an economic advantage to the greater opinion-promulgating units and to the combination of small local units under the control of one syndicate or capitalist owner.... In consequence the number of independently owned newspapers continually decreases and many editors become the agents of one owner."

The Canadian CRIMINAL CODE makes it an offence to mail "obscene, indecent, immoral or scurrilous" matter (*see* OBSCENITY), and the Post Office Act provides for interruption of such service. Similarly, the Customs Tariff Act prohibits the importation of "treasonable, seditious, immoral or indecent" literature.

The best-known attempts by provinces to impose censorship are the various provincial FILM CENSORSHIP Acts. In *Nova Scotia Board of Censors* v *McNeil* the Supreme Court of Canada held that provincial legislation establishing a board of censors with powers to prohibit the exhibition of films was within the jurisdiction of the provinces, despite the federal jurisdiction in the Criminal Code over determination of what is "obscene." On the other hand, in *Ontario Film and Video Appreciation Society* (1984), the Ontario Court of Appeal has held that s1 of the Canadian Charter, which requires that limitations on Charter rights and freedoms must be "prescribed by law," requires censorship powers to be specifically prescribed. Other censorship attempts by the provinces have been less successful. Under the 1937 Alberta Press Act, to Ensure the Publication of Accurate News and Information, newspapers would be compelled to disclose the source of their news information and to print government statements to correct previous articles. Three of the 6 Supreme Court justices hearing the case held that the bill was an invasion of liberty of the press and the right of public discussion, which could only be limited by Parliament under its CRIMINAL LAW power. In *Switzman v Elbling* (the PADLOCK ACT case), which dealt with the 1937 Québec Act Respecting Communistic Propaganda, under which it was illegal to use a house for the propagation of communism, the Supreme Court declared this was legislation with respect to criminal law and therefore within federal jurisdiction.

Censorship can take many forms. To persons or groups who cannot afford to print newspapers, or to advertise, or who might not be given the opportunity to do so, supervision of the distribution of handbills or posters is a form of censorship. This supervision has been effected through municipal bylaws regulating the use of streets, sidewalks and parks, and requiring the prior approval of the police or some civic official before printed materials can be distributed (*see* SAUMUR V CITY OF QUÉBEC). In *Attorney General of Canada v Dupond*, the Supreme Court of Canada held that a city ordinance that prohibited "the holding of any assembly, parade or gathering on the public domain of the City of Montréal for a time-period of 30 days" was valid, being of a "merely local character."

The censorship practised under the OFFICIAL SECRETS ACT (1970) essentially covers 2 distinct, if somewhat similar, activities: spying and wrongful communication of government information, or leakage (s4.3). The latter provides: "Every person who receives any...information, knowing, or having reasonable ground to believe, at the time when he receives it, that the...information is communicated to him in contravention of this Act, is guilty of an offence under this Act unless he proves that the communication to him of the...information was contrary to his desire." In Canada since WWII, this section has been the basis of prosecution only twice. However, a recent example in the UK illustrates the extent of possible censorship under the Official Secrets Act. In 1987 the House of Lords upheld a banning of the book *Spycatcher* by Peter Wright on the ground that he had breached his oath under the Act when he tried to publish the book which was based on his experience in the British Security Service known as MI5 (*Attorney-General v Guardian Newspapers Ltd*). WALTER S. TARNOPOLSKY

Census Metropolitan Area (CMA), a geographical area created by Statistics Canada for the purposes of collecting and organizing data. CMAs define the main labour market of an urbanized core or of built-up areas, and have a population of 100 000 or more. They contain municipalities completely or partly inside the urbanized core and other municipalities if 1) at least 40% of the employed work force living in the municipality works in the core, or 2) at least 25% of the employed labour force working in the municipality lives in the urbanized core. CMAs may differ from metropolitan areas designated by local governments. They are usually known by the name of the urban area forming their core, eg, Halifax or Winnipeg.

Centaur Theatre Co was founded in 1969 by Maurice Podbrey (current artistic director) and

Herbert C. Auerbach (founding chairman) and has become a prominent English-language theatre in Québec. The Centaur is housed in the Old Exchange Arts Centre (formerly the Montreal Stock Exchange) in Montréal, originally having one 255-seat theatre, then expanding to a second 440-seat theatre in 1974. Drawing from the energy of the Québec theatre scene, the theatre company has met the challenge of presenting innovative international programming with such authors as David Mamet, Tom Stoppard, Bertolt Brecht and S African playwright Athol Fugard. It has also placed emphasis on English Canadian authors (David FENNARIO, John GRAY, David FRENCH, Paul Ledoux and David Young, among others), with some experimentation in bilingual productions such as Fennario's *Balconville* and the first English-language production of the French Canadian hit *Broue*. The Centaur enjoys continued success and in 1983 won the Vantage Arts Academy Award for outstanding contribution to Canadian theatre. *See also* THEATRE, ENGLISH-LANGUAGE.

MARILYN BASZCZYNSKI

Centennial Year, 1967, was Canada's enthusiastic celebration of the 100th anniversary of CONFEDERATION, 1867. The festivities were launched at midnight on 31 Dec 1966 on Parliament Hill, when Prime Minister Lester PEARSON, Secretary of State Judy LAMARSH (the minister responsible for Centennial), Opposition Leader John DIEFENBAKER, and thousands of others participated in a ceremony that culminated in the lighting of the Centennial Flame.

A committee of businessmen, chaired by C.M. DRURY, was originally instrumental in convincing Diefenbaker, then prime minister, that Canada's 100th anniversary should be a memorable occasion. One of the country's best-known publicists, John FISHER, "Mr Canada," was appointed centennial commissioner. Fisher, whose tenure continued under Pearson, was ably assisted by Georges E. Gauthier and then by Gilles Bergeron (both associate commissioners).

The year's events fell into 2 categories: those that were monumental and those that were active. In a desire to leave behind a literally concrete memory of the year, the federal and provincial governments financed a wide variety of building projects. Each province acquired a centennial memorial building, and each $1 that was spent on a centennial edifice by a municipality was matched by an equal amount from both the federal government and the respective provincial government. Such largesse encouraged the construction of facilities such as libraries, art galleries, theatres and sport complexes. The most lavish concrete monument was the NATIONAL ARTS CENTRE in Ottawa, paid for entirely by the federal government.

The Centennial Train and Caravans, which graphically depicted Canadian history and the contributions made by many different cultures, were visited by over 10 million people. Local histories were compiled and historic sites were restored. The performing arts flourished as Festival Canada commissioned plays, musicals, operas and ballets.

In a lighter vein, there were bathtub races, parades and period costume parties. One town even built a landing pad for flying saucers. As the year progressed, it became evident that the country's most spectacular event, EXPO 67, was a national and international success. The year ended, as it had begun, on Parliament Hill. But the Centennial Flame that was originally to have been extinguished was left alight by popular consent. It was to become a symbol for a year that was not merely significant in and for itself,

Lester Pearson lighting the Centennial Flame, Parliament Hill, 31 Dec 1966 (*courtesy National Archives of Canada/C-26964*).

but one that marked the emergence of Canada as a mature and self-confident nation.

ROBERT BOTHWELL

Centipede (class Chilopoda), elongate, flattened terrestrial arthropod. The head bears antennae. The adult is composed of 18-180 segments, plus a tail-plate. Almost all body segments, except the last, have a pair of appendages totalling, in adults, from 15 (as in the most familiar Canadian species) to 179 pairs. The first pair is modified to form large, poisonous claws; the last pair, less strongly modified, has a reproductive function; others are walking legs. About 2500 species are known worldwide, mostly from the tropics. About 70 species occur in Canada and Alaska; a dozen of these have been introduced from Europe. The latter species are largely eastern. Some tropical species are very large, one reaches nearly 30 cm long. The largest Canadian species seldom reaches 8 cm; most familiar centipedes are less than 2.5 cm long. Centipedes are chiefly nocturnal, living under stones, bark, leaf-litter or in soil. One or 2 species live in crevices and under seaweed in marine, intertidal zones. Virtually all centipedes prey on smaller animals (eg, insects) captured with poisonous claws. Some large species may inflict poisonous "bites" on humans if taken unawares, but they are aggressive only toward prey. In Canada, only the introduced house centipede (*Scutigera coleoptrata*) can inflict a painful (not dangerous) nip to humans. The introduced garden or "greenhouse centipede" (*Scutigerella immaculata*), sometimes a horticultural pest, especially in southern Ontario, is not a true centipede but belongs to a small, distantly related, noncarnivorous class (Symphyla), with only 2-3 species in Canada.

D.K. McEWAN KEVAN

Central Agency may refer to a departmental central agency in government finance and administration or, generally, to any group whose terms of reference extend across all policy areas. The Department of Finance, for example, is responsible on behalf of all ministers for preparing the budget. The TREASURY BOARD Secretariat (TBS) develops, approves and subsequently monitors the spending plans of departments and agencies. The PUBLIC SERVICE COMMISSION, in conjunction with the TBS, is important in personnel management. The PRIVY COUNCIL OFFICE provides the secretariats for CABINET and its committees, and is involved in wide-ranging liaison, co-ordinating and advisory functions stemming from its links with the Cabinet and prime minister. More intimately associated with the party and political responsibilities of the prime minister is the PRIME MINISTER'S OFFICE. Recent candidates as central agencies include the ministries of State for Social Development and for Regional Economic Development for their role in co-ordinating sectors of the budgetary "envelope" into which the total budget is currently divided. The growth of central agencies reflects the increasing size and interrelatedness of government activities; their presence has led to controls that compel regular ("line") departments to provide programs and services effectively and efficiently.   J.E. HODGETTS

Central Coast Salish share the same culture but speak 4 distinct languages of the Coast Salish language family. They occupied contiguous territories in and adjacent to the Lower Fraser Valley, on SE Vancouver I, and on intervening San Juan and Gulf Islands. Three of these groups are known by indigenous names: Halkomelem, the largest group, and Squamish bear the names for their respective languages; Nooksack, now entirely in Washington state, is an anglicization of the native name by which other Coast Salish groups knew them. The fourth group, living in both BC and Washington state, has no all-encompassing name for itself and is best known as Straits Salish.

The Central Coast Salish area, with a mild and relatively dry climate, had rich and varied resources. Paramount were tremendous annual runs of salmon which ascended the Fraser and Squamish rivers from May through November. Members of all 4 groups fished the Fraser, but most favourably situated were Halkomelem, who fished with dip nets and large trawl nets towed between CANOES. Straits Salish perfected the reef net, a unique trap set between pairs of canoes at owned locations in the sea where Fraser-bound salmon were known to pass. Most salmon were caught in summer when surplus quantities could be dried on open-air racks.

Large shed-roofed houses were built in villages, from which trips were made to gather seasonal resources. Life centered around the household groups, consisting of extended families with a core or lineage of people linked through male or female lines of descent. Marriage with blood kin was not allowed; thus spouses usually came from different villages and networks of kinship linked people throughout Central Coast Salish territory. Special resource sites and ritual privileges were owned by lineages or kin groups, whose members worked co-operatively under the direction of esteemed leaders. There was a class structure with high and low classes as well as slaves. Class position was imprecise, without ranked lineages or titled positions, but people strove to maintain class standing by hard work, selective marriages and proper behaviour.

Summer and autumn were times for potlatches, when people from neighbouring villages were invited to feast and acclaim the hosts' social position (*see* POTLATCH).

Religious activity focused on spirit helpers who conferred personal powers for hunting, doctoring or other human endeavours. These individual powers were celebrated during winter in rituals referred to as spirit dances. Some spirit powers took the form of hereditary cleansing rituals, performed with masks, effigies or decorated rattles. Sculptural art found additional expression in tombs, house posts and implements (*see* NORTHWEST COAST INDIAN ART).

The early maritime fur trade, concentrated on the outer coast, did not directly affect Central Coast Salish, whose territory was first explored by Spanish and British ships in the early 1790s. In 1827 the HUDSON'S BAY CO established FT LANGLEY in the centre of Halkomelem territory. In the late 19th century, as settlers were attracted to south Vancouver I and the Fraser Valley, Central Coast Salish territory became the most heavily populated part of BC.

There are more than 11 500 registered Central Coast Salish listed in 49 bands in BC, and about 2000 tribal members in Washington. Despite great changes of culture, distinctive rituals and religious expression survive, uniting small, dispersed villages and permitting the maintenance of a vigorous sense of Indian identity. *See also* NATIVE PEOPLE: NORTHWEST COAST and general articles under NATIVE PEOPLE.   MICHAEL KEW

Reading: H. Barnett, *The Coast Salish of British Columbia* (1975); P. Amoss, *Coast Salish Spirit Dancing* (1978).

Centre de recherche industrielle du Québec (CRIQ) In 1966, 2 bills to establish a scientific advisory agency in Québec were lost when the government changed; CRIQ was finally established as a CROWN CORPORATION in 1969. Until laboratories were completed at Ste-Foy (1975), facilities were rented at Québec City, Sherbrooke and Dorval. That same year, a branch specializing in microelectronics was established in Montréal, and the functions of CRIQ were reassessed to re-emphasize its advisory role to small business. In 1985 a new laboratory facility was opened in Montréal. It has since served to stimulate development through technical and scientific research and advice. In 1979 the government expanded the centre's role to include provision of advice on licensing requirements and advising or collaborating with business on patenting inventions. CRIQ's aid to business allayed early opposition by the scientific community, but some economists criticized the emphasis on small companies. The centre is headed by a president-director general, with a board of 16, who have been responsible to various government ministries at different stages. CRIQ employs over 400 people. Although much of its advice to small business is free, over 60% of CRIQ's income was derived from the industrial sector through contracts and shares of patents. CRIQ is best known for innovations in FURNITURE design and FOOD processing. Co-operative research is under way with various Québec universities and colleges for research in ROBOTICS (eg, computer-aided design, computer-assisted MANUFACTURING), microelectronics, BIOMASS, BIOTECHNOLOGY and PLASTICS.   MARTIN K. McNICHOLL

Centre for Research on French Canadian Culture/Le Centre de recherche en civilization canadienne-française, fd 2 Oct 1958 at the U of Ottawa by 4 professors of literature: Fr Bernard Julien, OMI; Jean Ménard; Réjean Robidoux; and Paul Wyczynski, who was its director for 15 years. The first task was to organize the methodical teaching and study of LITERATURE IN FRENCH at the university level. The scope broadened in 1963 to include history and the fine arts. In 1977 the centre became a multidisciplinary research body, with a council of 16 members chosen from a wide range of the human sciences. From its start, the centre has encouraged research into the culture of French Canada, primarily in Québec and Ontario, but without ignoring the other francophone minorities in N America. Its contribution is made through the acquisition of archival documents, the development of a specialized library, the publication of scientific papers and the organization of seminars, conferences and exhibitions. The centre encourages research projects through grants from its budget and supplies administrative support for long-term projects which have received funding elsewhere, such as *Le Dictionnaire des auteurs de langue française en Amérique du nord*, *Le Dictionnaire de l'Amérique française*, *L'Édition critique des oeuvres complètes de François-Xavier Garneau*, etc. Moreover, it oversees 4 collections of papers and publishes an annual multidisciplinary review, *Cultures du Canada français*. As well as manuscripts, the archives service makes available to researchers and the public more than 18 000 photographs, 1350 audiotapes, cassettes and videocassettes, 950 museum pieces, 3300 brochures, 2340 reference works, 822 periodicals and 253 newspapers. A favoured meeting ground,

Watercooler of salt-glazed stoneware attributed to R.G. Goold, 1864-67 (*courtesy Royal Ontario Museum*).

the centre has numerous connections with Canadian and foreign institutions. In 1985 it welcomed 1100 researchers.   YOLANDE GRISE

Ceramics are products made from a nonmetallic mineral compound (especially CLAY) and fired to set the shape. The principal types of ceramic wares are porcelain, which is usually translucent, and earthenware, which is opaque. Both porcelains and earthenware may be glazed or unglazed; unglazed wares are known as biscuit. Unglazed earthenware is porous and needs glazing to make it waterproof.

Canadian-made Ceramics

Earthenware utility pottery has been produced by Europeans in Canada since the mid-17th century (and by the native peoples long before). Utility pottery was the most widely used form of container ware since, being made of local clay, it was inexpensive and readily replaceable. Handblown glass, cast or soldered metalwares and barrels or firkins were considerably more expensive and had fewer uses.

Earthenware, produced from indigenous, red firing clays, was formed into various types of vessel. Earthenware production required raw natural clay, which was liquefied, screened to eliminate grit or other intrusions and redried to a more plastic consistency. To assure uniformity between pieces, clay for the wheel was often measured by weight. As the potter produced each vessel on the wheel, it was taken out for air drying to evaporate all possible water (potters had to watch the weather while drying finished pots). Dried pots were stacked into a wood-fired kiln for firing. The process required care, for a kiln load could represent a month's production. Firing was done with dry wood (to minimize effects from smoke) in fireplaces surrounding the kiln. It lasted 2-3 days, after which the kiln temperature was reduced gradually, as the pottery could crack from too-rapid cooling. Pottery was then glazed by dipping in the glaze mixture; for interiors, glaze was poured in, swirled around and poured off. The glazing mixture (usually a lead-oxide and silica mixture in water) was allowed to dry, and the pots were again kiln-stacked and refired to fuse the dried glaze. A lower temperature was used than for the initial biscuit firing.

Stoneware was first produced in Canada in 1849 using clays imported from Amboy, New Jersey. In form and fabrication technique, Canadian stoneware was identical to American stoneware of the same period, and many of the early producers had come from American potteries. The expensive New Jersey clay was fired at a temperature of about 1200°C. In Canada it was often "bulked up" with local earthenware clay, which reduced its effective firing temperature to about 850-1000°C. Stoneware clays have a high SILICA content. A Canadian source was not discovered until the late 19th century, when a deposit was located along the Shubenacadie R, NS. The clay was used by the Enfield pottery. The only other source of stoneware clay in Canada was that used by Medalta Pottery, Medicine Hat, Alta.

Production of stoneware required a more sophisticated technology than earthenware. Stoneware, fired at much higher temperatures than earthenware, is a vitrified pottery, ie, waterproof in an unglazed state. Glazing is done by throwing salt into the kiln at maximum firing temperature. The salt (sodium chloride) gasifies; the sodium combines chemically with the silica to form a sodium silicate glaze (ie, a form of glass). The chlorine is either given off as deadly chlorine gas or, if the kiln is cooling, recondenses as hydrochloric acid. Because of its vitrified structure, glazed stoneware is less fragile than red earthenware. The sodium silicate glaze, in chemical combination with the pottery body (rather than an overlaid layer as the glazes on earthenware), is insoluble and impervious to acids or alkalis.

Once formed into vessels, stoneware was typically stamped (using printer's type) with either the maker's name or that of a commercial purchaser. The pottery was dried and often decorated before firing, with designs in cobalt-oxide blue, referred to as powder-blue in potters' glaze recipes. COBALT was the only glazing oxide used for decoration, as it alone could withstand the firing temperatures. The designs ranged from simple brushed-on floral motifs to elaborate incised or glaze-trailed figures or scenes.

Because of its durable body and impervious glaze, stoneware was preferred to cheaper, lead-glazed earthenware for food preparation and storage, especially pickling or salting. However, by the last quarter of the 19th century, a gradual shift of food preparation, from the home to the processing plant, began, and refrigeration, commercial canning and dairy processing began to erode the market for the utility pottery necessary for home processing. In the 1880s, mass-produced, inexpensive GLASS provided the advantage of visible contents and further reduced the pottery market. By the late 1880s the number of pottery operations in Canada was declining and, because of accelerating changes in food preparation and marketing, most potteries closed between 1890 and 1910.

Archaeological investigations of early potteries indicate that firing accidents were common: great quantities of "waster" pottery were discarded. Before the 20th century, potters had little knowledge of the components of their clays and only rudimentary means of measuring kiln temperatures. In small local potteries, an average loss of some 50% of production seems a realistic estimate. Prior to the 20th century, Canadian earthenware pottery followed 4 basic regional forms.

Québec Pottery, the earliest type, was produced from the mid-17th century to the early 20th century. Although the earliest Québec pottery was established in 1655, New France imported French earthenware until 1760. These imports consisted primarily of basic bowls, pitchers and jugs glazed with a green, copper-oxide glaze. Québec potters emulated the forms but not the colour of French ware. Their pottery usually had a transparent lead-oxide glaze, sometimes over a brown slip coating which covered the pottery body. Québec pottery was not decorated in the

18th century; in the 19th century, a simple American decoration of spatterings of brown slip was adopted.

Maritime Pottery, particularly that of NS and PEI, was basically northern English and Scottish in design derivation. Earthenware was not produced in the Maritimes before the early 19th century and, with rare exceptions, was produced in limited variety. Maritime earthenware was based on the dense iron-rich clays of the area and fired to a dark red. The interior lining of vessels and the sparse decoration made use of white slip, made of fine white clay from the Magdalen Is. The most common items are crocks and large bowls with deep-red bodies, interiors coated in white slip, and transparent lead-oxide glazes.

Upper Canada Pottery shows various ethnic influences, the strongest being that of the Pennsylvania GERMANS who had migrated into the region. Ontario Germanic pottery is characterized by a wide variety of forms and shapes and, often, by imaginative and colourful uses of coloured clay slips and different metallic-oxide glazes (eg, copper, iron and manganese, as well as lead). Glaze colour, pattern and variation are infinite, as are vessel forms. Most potters produced primarily basic utility and container vessels, but they also made slipcast wares, molded figures, miniatures, toys, and gift and presentation pieces. The earliest pottery in the region was established in 1794; unlike the situation in Québec and the Maritimes, potteries proliferated because of isolation and the difficulty of receiving British imports.

Generic North American Pottery, eg, slip-cast tablewares, canning vacuum jars and short-term fashions like the "rustic" wares of the 1880s, appeared and became universally popular after regional distinctions began to disappear about 1870. The influence of widespread advertising and the appearance of mail-order catalogues very quickly outweighed regional tradition, not only in pottery but in all decorative art forms. The age of the individual craftsman was effectively giving way to the age of the machine and the factory.

Little early pottery is known from W of Ontario because, by the time European settlement began in the late 19th century, the domestic use of hand-made earthenware was declining. A pottery was established in Winnipeg in the 1880s. Evidence provided by industrial ARCHAEOLOGY studies indicates that it produced only utility wares. Later, the Medalta Pottery was established at Medicine Hat, producing stoneware from local clay discovered about 1910.   D.B. WEBSTER

British-made Ceramics

After the British CONQUEST, 1760, the ceramic wares most generally used in Canada came from Great Britain. Three factors accounted for this situation: Britain regarded its colonies as natural markets for British goods; developments were occurring in the British pottery industry; and British potters promoted their wares aggressively. Canada came under British rule just as British potters were on the verge of making a determined bid for world prominence. By the mid-19th century, when changes in trade and navigation laws permitted freer entry of foreign goods, the range and variety of British ceramic products was so great and their position so entrenched that Canadians continued to buy them in substantial quantities. In early days, ships' captains were recruited to take out samples and make contacts for future sales; Canadian agents were appointed; some potters journeyed to Canada to assess the market; others opened warehouses in cities such as Québec and Toronto. In 1836, William Taylor Copeland, a prominent Staffordshire potter, became the supplier of ceramic wares to HUDSON'S

Red earthenware jug and washbasin, c1870 (*courtesy Royal Ontario Museum*).

BAY COMPANY posts and shops throughout the North-West.

Earthenware Although, over the years, everything from pickling pots to ornaments was imported, certain types of British ware predominated in the Canadian market. The first of these popular items was an 18th-century lead-glazed earthenware for the table. Ranging from deep to pale cream in colour, it was called creamware or, after Josiah Wedgwood gained Queen Charlotte's patronage for it in the 1760s, Queensware. Creamware is known to have been used in French Canadian farmhouses, city merchants' homes and government residences.

Early in the 19th century, creamware, its decoration usually hand-painted on glaze, was displaced as the chief tableware by an earthenware of whiter appearance, decorated by a semi-mechanical process called underglaze transfer printing. The technique involved transferring impressions from engraved copperplates to paper and then to the earthenware. It permitted an endless variety of designs (including Canadian scenes) to be printed on tableware at relatively low cost. The glaze over the decoration protected it and gave it brilliance. Hailed as the coming ware by a Halifax importer in 1811, underglaze transfer-printed earthenware became, and remained, the most widely used tableware in Canada.

Another British development important in the Canadian trade had to do with the earthenware body, as distinct from its decoration. In 1813 Charles James Mason, a Staffordshire potter, patented a tough, high-fired earthenware called ironstone china. Scores of British potters copied Mason's product, marketing it under many names (stone china, opaque china, etc) and offering it painted, printed or plain. Its durability, and the cheapness of the undecorated variety, ensured sales in a pioneer country such as Canada.

Porcelain was never imported in the same quantities as earthenware, although there had always been some supplies of this more expensive ceramic product. In 1793, for example, Worcester porcelain was being offered in Saint John, NB, in exchange for furs if cash was not available. Eighteenth-century English porcelains were apt to be capricious in the kiln. The invention, towards the end of the century, of what is now called English bone china (basically, a composition of china clay, china stone and a high proportion of bone ash) cut kiln losses and ensured wider sales of British porcelain in Canada. By Victorian times, virtually every British porcelain manufacturer had switched to a bone formula.

Victorian times also brought an unprecedented taste for what a Toronto importer called "articles to fill a space and gratify the eye." Of the ceramic ornaments that poured from Britain's potteries into Canadian homes, none had a greater appeal than those in Parian, a porcelain invented in Staffordshire in the 1840s and named after marble from the Greek island, Paros. Its avowed object was to simulate marble. Busts, eg, of Sir John A. MACDONALD and Edward HANLAN (the Toronto oarsman who became world champion in 1880), were produced in Parian.

Canada never developed a pottery industry that seriously challenged imported tablewares or ornaments. As Canadian potters turned out more and more of the common, dark-bodied earthenwares and stonewares for kitchen or storage use, in the second half of the 19th century, imports of these wares dwindled. However, by that time Canada's population was expanding rapidly and the demand for finer wares was increasing in proportion. British potters continued to have a market that saw at least some of their products in every home in Canada.   ELIZABETH COLLARD

Reading: Elizabeth Collard, Nineteenth-Century Pottery and Porcelain in Canada (1984).

Ceramics, Contemporary

A study conducted in 1975 indicated that 10 000-12 000 people were employed full time in crafts in Canada and over 4 million people attended a crafts fair or exhibition. Pottery has been estimated to constitute nearly one-third of all craft activity; it is relatively more popular in the western provinces.

Before 1950 Canadian ceramists often learned their craft abroad and brought back with them current styles. Thus, their work generally shared the interests of the decorative arts of the time. A lack of focus in Canada led many potters to look to the annual, competitive ceramic National Exhibition in Syracuse, NY, where they repeatedly made a strong showing. Exhibitors included Kjeld and Erica Deichmann from NB, Bailey Leslie from Ontario and Konrad and Krystyna Sadowska from the Ontario College of Art. No typical Canadian style emerged during the period, although excellent individual pieces were created in various idioms. Diversity and growth characterize the post-1950 period. Ceramists added oriental to earlier American and European influences. These 3 influences are to be found in most late Canadian work, mixed and remixed in differing relationships.

The work and writings of British potter Bernard Leach (*A Potter's Book*, 1940) were influential in disseminating technical information and a regard for disciplined experience, mixed with spontaneity and sturdy practicality and combining the standards of Oriental and traditional English ware. Canadian John Reeve, who worked with Leach, left a mark in his brief but influential sojourns on both Canadian coasts and in his workshops across the country. The example of Leach and his followers contrasted with an American antitraditionalist movement, based principally in the art schools, which investigated the abstract possibilities of material and conventional forms. Beginning in the 1960s, controversy raged between sculptors (nonfunctional) and potters (functional). Many ceramic teachers emigrated from the US to Canada in this period. Acceptance of the use of clay for purely artistic purposes led to the proliferation of various low-fire technologies, eg, raku, a free-form pottery derived from Japanese methods, and over-glazes. Canadians such as Wayne Ngan and Walter Dexter are notable exponents of raku. "Funk" was the most controversial form of nonfunctional clay use in the early 1970s and made various technologies acceptable in the service of artistic intent. The work of David Gilhooly, based at York University, became the most notable example. Members of both the functional and nonfunctional schools explored new materials and processes, for example, low-fire glazes (eg, lead, overglaze lustre, majolica), high-temperature processes (eg, salt glazing, wood firing) and, above all, the controlled chances of re-

Contemporary ceramic by Robin Hopper (*courtesy Canadian Crafts Council/Robin Hopper*).

duction firing. Ruth Gowdy McKinley was an investigator of the exquisite balance between accident and control.

By the 1970s Canadian tendencies began to be perceptible, epitomized by a restrained interpretation of current international preoccupations. French Canadians, such as Maurice Savoie, Enid Le Gros and Joe FAFARD, maintained connections with their heritage. Louise Doucet-Saito and Satashi Saito combined European, pre-Columbian and Oriental interests. Many other Canadians, such as Jack Sures, Les Manning, John Chalke and Robin Hopper (the first Bronfman Award for Excellence recipient) pointed towards a style – cool, well designed, sometimes rich in detail yet severe overall – bearing the mark of its northern origins.

Reliable statistics on the economic significance of ceramics are difficult to obtain. Like any craft, ceramics creates employment in areas where there otherwise might be none: relatively little capital is involved, local materials are used and tourism is attracted. In addition to the revenues derived from sales, these factors comprise the economic significance of ceramics. Ceramics has established itself as a minor but real factor in local and provincial economies.

Many organizations designed to give individuals collective strength and services have been established since 1955, often partly funded by government grants. In many provinces, ceramic organizations parallel, affiliate with or have their functions fulfilled by provincial or territorial umbrella organizations, which in turn are affiliated with the Canadian Crafts Council. Of the purely ceramic organizations, Ontario Potters Assn (est 1948) is the largest. A national organization called Ceramic Masters was founded in 1975. Earlier, the Canadian Guild of Potters attempted to establish a national focus. A tradition of native work in clay was not strongly established, as cookware, ceremonial items, and containers were supplied mostly by other means. Significant native involvement in the contemporary period is naturally limited. An important but isolated case is the work from the Rankin Inlet Pottery which operated from 1965-76. Workshops, providing students with exposure to methods over one or more days, are run by schools and organizations and have been very influential in the maturation of ceramics in Canada. They have also offered the opportunity to view most of the world's major practitioners at work. Formal education in ceramics has occurred entirely as part of the general development in crafts; an APPRENTICESHIP SYSTEM has not existed. Periodicals (except for *Tactile,* which ceased publication in Aug 1976) have been few or foreign in origin or provincial in scope. Adequate galleries are rare; however, an international symposium held in Oct

1985 in Toronto included exhibitions in 49 major public and private galleries and did much to stimulate exposure.   CHRISTOPHER D. TYLER

Cereal Crops

Cereal Crops are members of the grass family grown for their edible starchy seeds. The important cereal crops produced in Canada are WHEAT, BARLEY, OATS, RYE and CORN; small hectarages of TRITICALE and grain MILLETS are grown. The cool, short growing seasons prevent commercial production of rice and grain sorghum.

Cereal crops may be divided into spring-sown types, which complete their life cycle in one season (summer annuals), and fall-sown types, which require an overwintering period (winter annuals). Among the fall-sown types, winter rye is the most winter hardy, followed by winter triticale and winter wheat, then winter barley; winter oats are least hardy. No winter forms of grain millets or corn exist. Spring-sown cereals are grown in all provinces except Newfoundland. In 1986 approximately 97% of the 14.2 million ha of wheat, 90% of the 4.8 million ha of barley and 81% of the 1.2 million ha of oats produced were grown in the Prairie provinces. Saskatchewan is the leading producer of spring wheat; Alberta, of barley and oats. Significant quantities of oats and barley are also produced in Ontario and Québec. In 1986, 379 115 ha of mixed grain (usually oats and barley grown together) are produced, mainly in Ontario. Production of spring rye is negligible. Of almost one million hectares of grain corn produced, about 75% is grown in southern Ontario; smaller hectarages, in Québec and Manitoba. Winter rye can be grown in many areas of Canada but, of the 273 486 ha, 89% is produced on the Prairies. Significant winter-wheat production is limited to southern Ontario and southern Alberta. Small hectarages of winter triticale and winter barley are produced in southern Ontario, but winter conditions in Canada are too severe for winter oats.

Wheat, oats, barley, rye and triticale are considered cool-season crops. Their spring forms are normally seeded between mid-Apr and mid-May, completing their life cycles in 80-100 days under Canadian conditions. The winter forms, seeded in Sept, overwinter as seedling plants and mature the following July. The other cereals are warm-season crops. Corn is seeded during the first 3 weeks of May and requires the full growing season to reach maturity. Grain millets may be seeded in May or June and mature in about 90 days. Rye, corn and sorghum are cross-pollinated species; the other cereal crops are self-pollinated.

Corn Grain corn is normally planted in rows 70-90 cm apart, with populations of 50 000-60 000 plants per hectare. Silage corn is more productive at slightly higher populations. Grain corn is harvested (with ear-pickers or picker-sheller combines) when the kernel moisture content is 25-30%. The stalks are left in the field and plowed under. Picked whole-ear corn may be stored outside in slatted cribs, which permit air circulation and low-energy, natural drying. Shelled corn may be dried artificially to 15% moisture content to permit inside storage in open containers, or it may be stored as high-moisture corn without drying, either in airtight containers or in open bins, following treatment with an organic acid to prevent spoilage. Grain yield in corn varies from 5 to 10 tonnes per hectare (t/ha), depending on the length of the growing season, temperature, moisture availability and soil fertility. Whole-plant silage corn yields range from 10 to over 20 t of dry matter per ha.

Small Grain Cereals and millets are seeded in rows 15-20 cm apart, at rates of 60-120 kg of seed per hectare. Small grain cereals are normally harvested with combine threshers, with or without prior cutting and swathing. Moisture content at harvest is usually below 15%, allowing storage of the grain without artificial drying. The remaining straw may be left in the field and incorporated with the soil, or removed and used as feed or bedding for livestock. Grain yields from spring-sown small-grain cereals range from less than 2 t/ha, under dry prairie conditions, to over 4 t/ha, under ideal growing conditions in eastern Canada. Where they survive the winter, fall-sown cereals yield 15-25% more than spring-sown types. Straw yields range from 2 t/ha to 4 t/ha.

Usage

The use made of a cereal crop depends on the chemical composition and quality of its seeds. Over 75% of the spring-wheat crop is used to produce bread flour; much of it is exported for this purpose. Smaller quantities of spring (durum) wheats go into the manufacture of pasta products. Winter wheat is used extensively for cake and pastry flour. All wheats are used to some extent for livestock feed. About 20% of the barley produced in Canada is processed by the malting and BREWING INDUSTRIES, domestic and foreign. Most of the remainder goes for livestock feed. Oats are grown primarily for livestock feed but small quantities are used in oatmeal and other food products. Rye and corn grains are also fed to livestock, although significant quantities are used in the DISTILLING INDUSTRY. Small amounts of corn are milled for starch, oil, syrup and other products. Triticale seed is used mainly for feeding livestock but small quantities are milled for flour. Grain millets are used in N America for animal feed and in the bird-seed industry. In some cases, the entire cereal plant (excluding roots) is used; for example, the entire oat plant, harvested well before the grain is ripe, may be used as hay or silage (feed preserved by the acid-forming action of bacteria); whole-plant corn is also preserved as silage. The total annual value of Canadian cereal crops is estimated at $3.7 billion, ie, about 1% of the Gross Domestic Product (see FOOD AND BEVERAGE INDUSTRY).   HAROLD R. KLINCK

CESAR The 1983 Canadian Expedition to Study the Alpha Ridge was among the most important scientific expeditions ever mounted in Canada. Discovered in 1963, the Alpha Ridge is a submerged mountain chain traversing the Arctic from off ELLESMERE ISLAND to the Siberian Continental Shelf. The range rises 2.7 km above the seafloor, is 200-450 km wide, and is the most westerly of the 3 ranges dividing the Arctic Basin (the others being the Nansen-Gakkel and Lomonosov ridges). The expedition involved over 40 researchers, working from March to May. The cost of the operation ($1.7 million) was defrayed by the federal government, and the expedition's activities were led by Dr Hans Weber of the Earth Physics Branch, Dept of ENERGY, MINES AND RESOURCES. Canadian Armed Forces aircraft transported the 300 000 kg of equipment, which included kitchen and mess structures, dormitory tents, prefabricated plywood buildings for use as offices and laboratories, scientific equipment, food, etc.

The main objective of the multidisciplinary expedition was to carry out a geological survey of the ridge. Researchers, therefore, brought a veritable geotechnical arsenal to bear on the polar ice to gather seismic, gravimetric, bathymetric and other data. They also made observations regarding the origin of the ridge. The question of origin is very important because the answer may determine whether or not Canada has RESOURCE RIGHTS in the region. It is important to determine if the ridge is a genuine oceanic ridge born in a volcanic upheaval, a prolongation of the N American Continental Shelf or a fragment, possibly from the

Russian side of the shelf. Under the LAW OF THE SEA countries have exclusive rights to the resources of their continental shelves. If it is found that the ridge is an extension of the continent from Ellesmere I, Canada could lay claim to part of the ridge itself and to 322 km on either side. The issue is the more crucial because, in the Canadian Arctic, the continental shelves offer the best prospects for PETROLEUM EXPLORATION, as is witnessed by soundings in the Beaufort Sea. Much study, analysis of data, and discussion among researchers will be needed to settle the question of origin definitively.

Like its earlier counterpart LOREX (Lomonosov Ridge Experiment, 1979), CESAR ended when the seasonal ice on which the camp was built began to melt. In the fall of 1984 scientists built a more permanent station on an ice "island," an ICEBERG that calved from the Ward Hunt ice shelf, off Ellesmere I, in 1982. Since then the station has collected geological and geophysical data while drifting in Canadian waters. It is expected to drift into international waters by 1990.

LUC CHARTRAND

Cetacea, order of mammals consisting of WHALES, DOLPHINS and porpoises. It includes about 80 living species, with worldwide distribution. Highly specialized anatomy and physiology allow cetaceans to maintain a fully aquatic existence while breathing air. Anatomical modifications of modern cetaceans include short neck with vertebrae sometimes fused; fusiform (cigar-shaped) body; body hair generally absent or reduced to isolated whiskers on the jaws, chin and rostrum (part of skull in front of eyes); horizontal caudal (tail) flukes supported by cartilage; hindlimbs reduced to small bones embedded in the flank musculature; and forelimbs flattened to flippers with bony digits enclosed in a common integument. Most modern species have a single fin on the back. Immediately below the epidermis is a blubber layer, developed in many modern species to provide thermal insulation and storage for lipids (fats). The cetacean skull is "telescoped," ie, the bones of the rostrum extend over and under the braincase. Except in the sperm whale (*Physeter catodon*), the external nasal opening is positioned on the upper rear of the skull and allows quick, efficient breathing at the air-water interface. Concealment of genital, mammary and excretory organs within the body outline contributes to streamlining. There is no external ear; a pinhole opening leads to a pinched-off ear canal. Nevertheless, hearing is well developed; sound plays a key role in communication, navigation and object detection.

Cetaceans are classified in 3 suborders: Archaeoceti, Mysticeti and Odontoceti. Archaeocetes, now extinct, were comparatively primitive: their skull bones were not telescoped; they had milk teeth, shed and replaced by permanent teeth; they had reduced hindlimbs, probably protruding externally. They were serpentlike animals up to 20 m long, with a full battery of teeth which made them formidable predators. Their descendants are the mysticetes (baleen whales) and odontocetes (toothed whales). Living mysticetes comprise 3 families, 6 genera and 10 species (in Canada, 3 families, 5 genera, 8 species); living odontocetes, 7 families, 31 genera and about 70 species (in Canada, 5 families, 19 genera, about 25 species). Their paired, external fleshy nostrils (blowholes) distinguish the mysticetes from the odontocetes, which have a single blowhole. Feeding adaptations also differ. The vestigial teeth of mysticetes are lost before birth, and replaced by baleen (whalebone), hornlike modified skin tissue rooted in and suspended from the palate. Baleen consists of many fibrous tubules packed together to form plates, arranged in a row

on either side of the mouth. The ends of the plates become frayed and interwoven, creating an efficient sieve for trapping small fish and ZOOPLANKTON. Most odontocetes have undifferentiated, functional teeth. Food passes unchewed through the esophagus and into a specialized, multichambered stomach where digestion occurs. The kidney is divided into many small lobules or renules (300-3000 per side). Cetaceans usually pass normal mammalian urine, but there is some evidence that dolphins can, for short periods, excrete urine with an unusually high salt concentration.

Most cetaceans are seasonal breeders; the timing of peak breeding varies according to a species' or population's ecology. Most mysticetes migrate annually between summer feeding grounds and winter breeding and calving grounds; some odontocete populations are relatively more sedentary. Gestation lasts for a little less than one year in most species. Sperm whales have a 16-month gestation period and in some other odontocetes it exceeds one year. Cetacean females rarely carry more than one fetus to term; energy requirements make it difficult for a female to rear more than one calf in the same season. Calves are born tail first and are well developed at birth. Birth and nursing take place underwater. Mysticetes wean calves after 7-10 or more months; some odontocetes, much later at 18 or more months. Thus, except for a few smaller species, the interbirth interval is at least 2 years.

Maximum swimming speeds range from at least 30 km/h in some porpoises to 37 km/h or faster in the large rorquals (eg, sei whale). Diving capabilities vary greatly by species. Sperm whales and certain beaked whales often submerge for over an hour. Cases of entanglement in submarine cables show that sperm whales reach depths of at least 1100 m; other evidence points to even deeper dives. Baleen whales generally do not dive for longer than 20-30 min, although the ice-adapted bowhead (*Balaena mysticetus*) is known to dive for over 30 min. Dolphins and porpoises normally surface at intervals of 5-7 min or less.

The only serious, nonhuman predators of cetaceans are large SHARKS and killer whales (*Orcinus orca*). The latter are known to attack virtually all species of marine mammal, including the blue whale (*Balaenoptera musculus*), the largest cetacean. Strong, lasting social cohesion within killer whale pods (extended family units) facilitates group hunting. Odontocetes are observably gregarious, and many are thought to have complex social structures. Most mysticetes are thought to be only moderately gregarious, although their long-range communication signals may permit more co-ordinated activity than is evident from casual observation. Only odontocetes have been proven capable of echolocation. The 2 major types of sounds made by cetaceans are low-pitched moans, screams, whistles and grunts, probably used for social communication, and high-intensity clicks, with frequencies ranging up to 200 kHz (about 13 times the upper frequency of human hearing capability), used for discrimination and navigation. Excellent vision has been demonstrated experimentally in some small odontocetes; however, several kinds of freshwater dolphins (platanistids) have reduced eyes—Ganges and Indus dolphins (*Platanista gangetica, P. minor*, respectively) are nearly blind. Cetaceans have well-developed taste buds, but chemoreceptor organs are reduced (Jacobson's organ of mysticetes) or absent (odontocetes).

The many important anatomical differences between the 2 suborders have been sometimes interpreted to reflect different terrestrial ancestries. However, an increasingly well-documented FOSSIL record of Archaeoceti shows this group to be sufficiently diverse to have given rise to both squalodonts (early odontocetes) and agorophiids (early mysticetes). *See also* WHALING.

E.D. MITCHELL AND R. REEVES

Reading: D.E. Gaskin, *The Ecology of Whales and Dolphins* (1982).

Chaleur Bay, which lies between the Gaspé Peninsula, Qué, and northern New Brunswick, is the largest bay in the Gulf of St Lawrence. It is divided into 2 basins: the outer or eastern basin, with water depths mostly 70-90 m, and the inner or western basin, with depths generally less than 50 m. The RESTIGOUCHE R enters the western end of the bay to produce an estuary roughly 160 km long. In ancient times the western basin and Chaleur Trough to the E were part of the Restigouche Channel, providing a natural preglacial drainage system for the surrounding area.

Near the mouth of the bay, cold, fresh surface water from the Gaspé Current enters on the N side, while flow on the S shore is directed outward into the Gulf to create a counterclockwise gyre in the surface circulation. The Gaspé water is rich in nutrients and promotes a high and sustained level of primary production throughout the summer months. The bay is a famous fishing ground for salmon and also supports important scallop and clam fisheries. As the name bestowed on the bay by Jacques CARTIER suggests, the climate of the bay is unusually warm compared to adjacent areas of the Gulf, making it a favoured location for summer resorts. Cartier explored the bay in July 1534 and traded for furs with the natives, likely MICMAC. DALHOUSIE, at the mouth of the Restigouche estuary, is a major port for northern NB.

P.C. SMITH

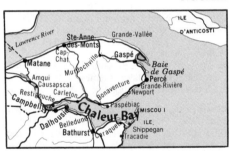

Chalk River, Ont, Village, pop 923 (1986c), 1010 (1981c), inc 1954, located on Chalk R, a tributary of Ottawa R, 210 km NW of Ottawa. Origin of the name is unknown; it may refer to the colour of the river or to the practice of charring local poplar and alder trees and using them to mark square timbers during the heyday of the logging industry in the 19th century. Prior to WWII, Chalk River was a small bush settlement. In 1944 it was chosen as the site for a heavy-water reactor to produce plutonium from uranium – the first reactor built outside the US. Subsequently the Chalk River Nuclear Laboratories developed into a complex of 5 nuclear reactors owned by Atomic Energy of Canada, Ltd, a crown corporation. Most employees live in nearby DEEP RIVER.

DANIEL FRANCIS

Chalk River Nuclear Laboratories, *see* NUCLEAR RESEARCH ESTABLISHMENTS.

Challenger Expedition, the first worldwide oceanographic expedition, voyaged 127 663 km in the Atlantic, Southern, Indian and Pacific oceans between Dec 1872 and May 1876. The voyage of HMS *Challenger*, a 69 m corvette specially modified for research in OCEANOGRAPHY, was intended to investigate the distribution of animals in the deep sea (particularly representatives of ancient groups) and to solve the problem of how the OCEANS circulate. The voyage was organized by

Charles Wyville Thomson and W.B. Carpenter, with the financial support of the British government and the patronage of the Royal Society. The scientific work of *Challenger* was directed by Thomson aided by a small staff, notably John MURRAY, a Scot born in Cobourg, Ont, who later completed the 50-volume report of the expedition. *Challenger*'s captain was George S. NARES, later famed for arctic exploration.

The Challenger Expedition provided large amounts of new information about the oceans. Hundreds of previously unknown animal species were described. But although animals were found at the greatest depths sampled (5500 m), showing that the oceans were inhabited at all depths, there were no "living fossils" as Wyville Thomson had expected. Carpenter's hope that the mechanism by which the oceans circulated could be discovered was not realized, although abundant information on the temperature, salinity and specific gravity of seawater was collected during the $3\frac{1}{2}$-year cruise. The composition of seawater was well established by William Dittmar of Glasgow University; and Murray and Alphonse Renard mapped ocean sediments, which proved to be quite different from terrestrial ones. The lengthy reports of the expedition contain information still useful to oceanographers.

Challenger visited Halifax for 10 days in May 1873 before leaving for Africa and S America. Its visit was celebrated by the Nova Scotian Institute of Science and aroused a brief interest in deep-sea animals, particularly on the part of the institute's secretary, Provincial Geologist David Honeyman. A small collection of animals from the voyage is found in the Nova Scotia Museum of Science, and some original volumes of the results are in Dalhousie University Library. The Challenger Expedition's effect on Canadian SCIENCE was short-lived, but the voyage stimulated worldwide explorations by many western European nations later in the century. *See also* SEASHELL.

ERIC L. MILLS

Reading: E. Linklater, *The Voyage of the Challenger* (1972).

Chalmers, Floyd Sherman, editor, publisher, arts patron (b at Chicago, Ill 14 Sept 1898). Brought to Canada by his Canadian father, Chalmers grew up in Orillia, Ont, and Toronto. After WWI service overseas he joined the *Financial Post*, becoming editor in chief at 27. He was president of MACLEAN HUNTER from 1952 to 1964 and then chairman of the board of directors until 1969. He and his wife Jean were volunteers or board members of many cultural organizations and established numerous prizes and awards. In 1964 Chalmers established the Floyd S. Chalmers Foundation to assist young artists and to support innovative projects. It has also commissioned such important compositions as the opera *Louis Riel* by Harry SOMERS. One of his most important contributions was his original sponsorship and ongoing financial support of the manuscript preparation of the ENCYCLOPEDIA OF MUSIC IN CANADA. In 1983 Chalmers completed his autobiography, *Both Sides of the Street*. A Companion of the Order of Canada (1985), he received the Diplôme d'honneur, honorary degrees, and was chancellor of York U 1968-73. In 1984, through a bequest of $1 million, Chalmers and his wife established the Jean A. Chalmers Chair in Canadian Music and the Institute for Canadian Music at the Faculty of Music, University of Toronto. The first director of the institute and Jean A. Chalmers Professor of Canadian Music was John BECKWITH, composer and teacher.

MABEL H. LAINE

Chamber Music refers to that body of composition for up to about 12 parts in which there is little

or no doubling and in which each part is of equal importance. During Canada's formative years, from the 18th century, Haydn, Mozart and Beethoven were establishing the forms and typical groupings of instruments that have become standard, such as the string trio (violin, viola, 'cello), piano trio (violin, 'cello, piano), and especially the string quartet (2 violins, viola, 'cello).

The earliest known activity of classical chamber music performance in Canada, at the opening of the 19th century, centered on Judge Jonathan SEWELL of Québec City, an amateur violinist. Unfortunately, there is little evidence of composition in Canada of chamber music at this time. A contemporary of Sewell's, Joseph QUESNEL from Montréal, is said to have written duos and quartets, although none has survived.

While European composers, from Beethoven to Brahms, were developing the genre in which both the musical language and the classical forms were much extended, Canadians turned scant attention to the medium until the last quarter of the 19th century. There were a number of marches, dances and character pieces for flute, violin and cornet, with piano accompaniment, but few examples of concert chamber music. Such composers as J.P. CLARKE and Calixa LAVALLÉE supposedly wrote for the genre, but these works too seem not to have survived. One of the earliest extant chamber works is *Fantaisie sonate* (1858) for flute and string quartet by Antoine DESSANE, a Québec City composer, organist and cellist.

From the 1870s several conservatories opened their doors, providing their string, woodwind and brass faculty with the opportunity to form chamber ensembles. Chamber music performance has flourished up to the present day in such teaching institutions. From Québec City's Septuor Haydn (founded in 1871 with string quintet, flute and piano), through several prominent string quartets, including the Toronto String Quartette Club (1884-87), Dubois (1910-38), (Toronto) Conservatory (1929-46), HART HOUSE (1923-46), Parlow (1943-58), ORFORD (fd 1965), Vághy (est in Canada 1968) and PURCELL (fd 1968) string quartets, many of Canada's leading performers have added their expertise to the performance of works by the European masters as well as by Canadian composers.

With the opportunity for performance by the late 19th century, a few composers turned their attention to the genre, including Guillaume COUTURE (*String Quartet*, 1875), W.O. Forsyth (*Quintette*, 1886), Edward Manning (*Trio*, about 1900), Alexis Contant (*Trio*, 1907), and Sir Ernest MACMILLAN (*String Quartet*, 1914). Though these works exhibit a certain cautiousness in expression, lacking elements of current musical ideas from Europe such as in the work of Scriabin, Debussy and Schoenberg, they indicate nevertheless that Canadian composition had reached a high level of craft and expression within its conservative idiom.

A correlation exists between the growth in popularity of the genre among Canadian composers and the growth in experimentation of 20th-century techniques, owing to the flexibility of chamber music as a vehicle for experimentation. The evolution towards greater experimentation began with Rodolphe MATHIEU, whose chromaticism stems from Debussy and early Schoenberg and is most apparent in his work from the 1920s (*Quatuor no. 1*, 1920, and *Trio*, 1921). Unfortunately, his work was not well received in Canada.

It was the next generation of composers (those born in the early 20th century) whose experimentation was a more successful attempt to break with the past. John WEINZWEIG, Barbara PENTLAND and Jean PAPINEAU-COUTURE are among the first

Canadian composers to have devoted a large part of their output to chamber music. Whether serialism, in the case of Weinzweig and Pentland, or chromaticism generally, in the case of Papineau-Couture, their musical language showed an awareness of current musical thought, which they then imparted to their students. They produced a number of string quartets, in addition to Weinzweig's *Woodwind Quintet* (1964) and Papineau-Couture's *Églogues* (1942), with voice, and *Sextuor* (1967). The influence of Bartók and Hindemith is evident in Violet ARCHER's *Trio no. 2* (1957), and Boulez's rigorous serialism is reflected in Serge GARANT's *Offrande I* (1969) and *III* (1971) and *Circuits I & II* (1972) and *III* (1973). Harry SOMERS's 3 string quartets (1943, 1950, 1959) show the influence of his primary teacher, Weinzweig, while his *Twelve Miniatures* (1964), which includes voice, indicates the independent road his style had taken. One of Canada's most widely known composers, R. Murray SCHAFER, contributed much to the genre, including *Requiems for the Party Girl* (1966), which reflects his predilection for vocal lines sung to his own texts, and *String Quartet No. 2* (1976), which shows his interest in the sound environment. Gilles TREMBLAY's interest in timbre is evident in such works as *Champs I* (1965), *II* (*Souffles*, 1968) and *III* (*Vers*, 1969) and *Solstices* (1971). Among the works of younger composers, John Hawkins's *Remembrances* (1969) and Claude Vivier's *Prolifération* (1969) are of particular interest for their incorporation of elements of theatre, which became a prominent preoccupation of many composers in the 1970s. Recent developments such as the influences of minimalism, mysticism and eastern music have also played important roles in the eclectic style of Canadian composition.

The flourishing of chamber music composition would not have been possible without the establishment of ensembles after WWII. Besides the string quartets already mentioned, brass and woodwind ensembles were formed, including the York Winds, the CANADIAN BRASS, and the Montreal Brass Quintet, as well as several ensembles of nontraditional groupings. Perhaps most important for composition in the genre was the establishment of several societies devoted to avant-garde chamber music, including the Société de musique contemporaine du Québec (Montréal), New Music Concerts (Toronto), Array Music (Toronto), and the Vancouver New Music Society. CLIFFORD FORD

Reading: J. Beckwith and K. MacMillan, eds, *Contemporary Canadian Composers* (1975); *Encyclopedia of Music in Canada* (1981); Clifford Ford, *Canada's Music: An Historical Survey* (1982); H. Kallmann, *A History of Music in Canada 1534-1914* (1960).

Chamber of Commerce, a nonprofit organization of business people and corporations established to promote economic development and collectively represent their concerns to government on public policy. Chambers of commerce, or boards of trade as they are sometimes known, operate at all 3 levels of government – community, provincial and national. The Canadian Chamber of Commerce (est 1929) is a member of the International Chamber of Commerce. The first chamber in N America was founded in Halifax in 1750. Today, there are local chambers of commerce or boards of trade in about 600 communities across Canada, with about 170 000 individual and corporate memberships. The Board of Trade of Metropolitan Toronto, with about 16 000 members, is the largest in N America. Community chambers or boards exist principally to promote industrial development or other economic activities such as tourism or resource development, although the larger chambers also conduct salary and other economic surveys for their members.

There are 7 provincial chambers of commerce in Canada that date to the early part of this century. The local chambers of New Brunswick, Nova Scotia, PEI and Newfoundland are organized in one body: the Atlantic Provinces Chamber of Commerce. There are also loosely assembled associations in the Yukon and the Northwest Territories. The Canadian chamber's head office was located in Montréal until 1982, when it was moved to Ottawa; it has a full-time president and elected chairman. The chamber has offices in Toronto and Montréal, as well as Ottawa, and has a full-time staff of about 50. In addition to corporate and community chambers, its membership includes about 90 trade associations. All provincial chamber presidents are on the board of the Canadian Chamber of Commerce. DAVID CRANE

Chamberland, Paul, poet (b at Longueuil, Qué 16 May 1939). Chamberland was the most iconoclastic Québec poet of the 1960s and one of the most innovative essayists of the 1970s. His first collections of poetry, *Genèses* (1962), *Le Pays* (a 1963 collaboration), *Terre Québec* (1964), *L'Afficheur hurle* (1965) and *L'Inavouable* (1968) cried out "the savage need for liberation." He rejected "unidimensional" politics after 1968, and as prophet and mystic he announced the arrival of "the Kingdom" and named the "Agents of the Future" – the Hommenfandieux and Essaimour. Some of his books were written as manifestos, such as *Éclats de la pierre noire d'où rejaillit ma vie* (1972), *Demain les dieux naîtront* (1974). He was the writer-animator of the Fabrike d'ékriture and a contributor to the magazines *Mainmise* and *Hobo-Québec*. Chamberland's books of the 1980s continued to explore the "resolutely lucid delirium" of his earlier works: *Terre souveraine* (1980), *Le Courage de la poésie* (1981), *L'Enfant doré* (1981) and *Émergence de l'adultenfant* (1981). *Un Parti pris anthropologique* (1983) is a collection of Chamberland's work published in the magazine *Parti pris*. In 1983 he published *Aléatoire instantané & Midsummer 82* and the essay *Le Recommencement du monde*. RICHARD GIGUÈRE

Chambers, Jack, painter (b at London, Ont 25 Mar 1931; d there 13 Apr 1978). After studying at a technical school in his home town, Chambers spent the years 1953-61 in Europe, travelling and studying at the San Fernando Academia de Bellas Artes in Madrid. He returned to London in 1961. Chambers's paintings through the 1960s contained dreamlike images, combining his immediate personal experience and memory. In 1969, the year he was diagnosed as having leukemia, he published the essay he called "Perceptual Realism," developed on a range of philosophical and theological sources, in particular the French existential phenomenologist Maurice Merleau-Ponty. From this date a striking change took place in his art. The visionary character of his work through the 1960s gave way to an intense and precise representation of reality. Throughout Chambers's artistic life, his work was developed around subjects of great importance to him: his family, his home, the city of London and the surrounding landscape. He expressed a notion of regionalism not based on a nostalgic and sentimental restrictiveness but on a celebration of the reality of living and working in a particular place. He also worked as a filmmaker, producing 8 films between 1964 and 1970.

In 1967, following a dispute with the National Gallery of Canada over reproduction rights, he founded Canadian Artists Representation (CAR) to try to establish fee scales for reproduction rights and rental fees for works in public exhibitions. Under his presidency (1967-75) CAR became a national organization with local bodies across the country. DAVID BURNETT

Chambly, Qué, City, pop 12 869 (1986c), 12 190 (1981c), inc 1951, is situated within the south-shore satellite area SE of Montréal. The community fans out around Bassin de Chambly, a widening in the RICHELIEU R. FORT CHAMBLY was erected nearby in 1665 as one of several outposts defending the French colony against Iroquois, and later American, raids. It was named for a soldier who held the first seigneury here. Millet flour and textile mills dominated the Chambly economy 1806-1911. The Chambly Canal, completed 1843, was a key shipping link to the US-Lac CHAMPLAIN region until 1901. Today, shoe, clothing and seasonal canning industries are important employers. PAULA KESTELMAN

Champagne, Claude, composer, teacher (b at Montréal 27 May 1891; d there 21 Dec 1965). He studied piano and theory with Orpha Deveaux and Romain-Octave Pelletier, and then the violin with Albert Chamberland. Alfred La Liberté had faith in Champagne's ability as a composer and helped him go to Paris to study (1921-28), where *Hercule et Omphale* and the *Suite canadienne* were created. After returning to Canada, Champagne devoted himself to teaching, composition and administration. Director of musical instruction for Montréal's Catholic School Commission (1934-42), he was also author of 5 volumes of solfeggio for primary-school teachers and taught at McGill 1932-41. As the result of a report he prepared, the Conservatoire de musique du Québec à Montréal was created in 1942 and he became its assistant director. He trained an impressive number of composers, including François BRASSARD, Serge GARANT, Pierre MERCURE, François MOREL, Clermont PÉPIN, Gilles TREMBLAY and Jean VALLERAND. From 1949 to 1965 he was editor in chief for BMI Canada, responsible for the publication of Canadian works. The Canada Council awarded him its medal in 1963 and he was honoured with a "Claude Champagne Year" in 1964, which included a NFB film and a CBC production. French lyricism and Québec folklore themes are important elements in his compositions. HÉLÈNE PLOUFFE

Champigny, Jean Bochart de chevalier, INTENDANT of New France 1686-1702 (b after 1645; d at Hâvre-de-Grâce, France Dec 1720). A competent and conscientious intendant, Champigny worked to sustain military preparedness during 13 years of war with the Iroquois nations and the British. He participated in the treaty negotiations with Iroquois, signed at Montréal in 1701. Champigny encouraged the cultivation of flax and hemp and the fishing and forestry industries. He instituted reforms in military supply as well as social reforms such as a system of poor relief. After his return to France in 1702, he often acted as an adviser to the minister in charge of Canadian affairs.

JEANNETTE LAROUCHE

Champlain, Lake, 1269 km², of which only the northernmost tip lies in Canada. Together with the RICHELIEU R, which drains the lake northward to the St Lawrence R, Lk Champlain provided a convenient invasion route through the Adirondack and Green Mts, which otherwise isolate the ST LAWRENCE LOWLAND. The lake is long (201 km) and narrow (0.8 to 23 km wide) and interspersed with numerous islands.

The lake route was used by war parties of contesting native groups. Samuel de CHAMPLAIN discovered it (and named it for himself) in 1609 accompanying a Montagnais war party against the Iroquois. Little settlement took place in the area in the time of New France, but French FORTIFICATIONS were established at Ft St-Frédéric (later Crown Point) in 1725-26 and Ft Carillon (later Ft Ticonderoga) in 1755. The British suffered some 2000 casualties in an ill-conceived assault on Carillon (1758), but MONTCALM evacuated the forts and the British pressed northward into Canada (*see* SEVEN YEARS' WAR). The same invasion route was followed by the Americans during the AMERICAN REVOLUTION and in a British counterattack southward. During the WAR OF 1812 a British strike against the US was thwarted when the British

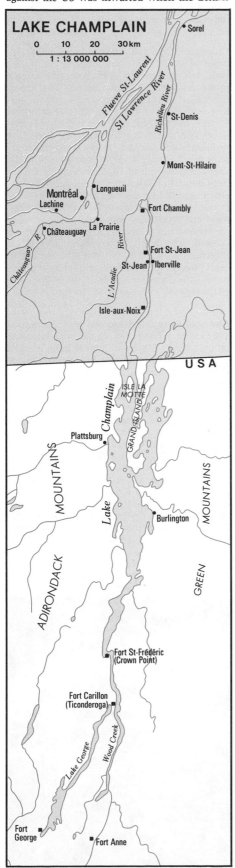

LAKE CHAMPLAIN

Champlain's 1632 map of New France records his contribution to the geographic knowledge of eastern Canada (*courtesy National Archives of Canada/NMC-15661*).

fleet was destroyed at PLATTSBURG, NY.

In more peaceful times, the lake was used as a transportation route. When frozen it made for fast travel by sleigh in winter. Steamboats were plying the lake by 1810. Canada's first railway, the CHAMPLAIN AND ST LAWRENCE RAILROAD was built to connect Montréal with the lake (1836), which in turn was linked to the Hudson R, providing a connection to New York.   JAMES MARSH

Champlain, Samuel de, cartographer, explorer, governor of New France (b at Brouage, France *c*1570; d at Québec City 25 Dec 1635). The major role Champlain played in the St Lawrence R area earned him the title of "father of New France." There is no authentic portrait of Champlain and little is known about his family background or youth. He may have been baptized a Protestant, but as of 1603 he was a Catholic. He probably made a voyage to the West Indies around 1600; though the account of these voyages, *Brief Discours*, is attributed to him, he himself never referred to it. When his career in Canada began in 1603, on a voyage up the St Lawrence with François Gravé Du Pont, he still had no official position. He published an account of this voyage, the first detailed description of the St Lawrence since Jacques CARTIER's explorations. By this time the Algonquins had taken over the area from the Iroquois, but nothing in this account suggested a program of colonization at any place in the valley. In 1604 Champlain sailed to Acadia with the Sieur de MONTS, who planned to establish a French colony there. Champlain had no position of command at either of the Acadian settlements at Ste-Croix or

PORT-ROYAL (Annapolis Royal, NS). As a cartographer, he was given responsibility for investigating the coast in search of an ideal location for settlement. Twice, in 1605 and 1606, he explored the coastline of what is now New England, going as far S as Cape Cod. Still the leaders of Acadia chose no location. Finally deciding on the St Lawrence instead, de Monts in 1608 sent Champlain to establish a settlement at QUÉBEC, where the fur trade with native peoples in the interior could be controlled more easily.

Champlain established and developed a vast trade network by forming alliances with the Montagnais of the St Lawrence, the nations on the Ottawa R and the Hurons of the Great Lks. This system obliged him to support his allies in their traditional wars against the Iroquois, whose territory was to the S of Lk Ontario; he participated in military campaigns (one in 1609 on Lk Champlain and one in 1615 in Iroquois territory); he spent the winter of 1615-16 in HURONIA. Despite opposition from the various merchant companies that employed him and found it more profitable to be involved only in the fur trade, Champlain vowed to make Québec the centre of a powerful colony. In a 1618 report, he outlined its commercial, industrial and agricultural opportunities. His dream seemed about to come true in 1627 when the COMPAGNIE DES CENTS-ASSOCIÉS was founded. But then war broke out and Québec was taken by the KIRKE brothers

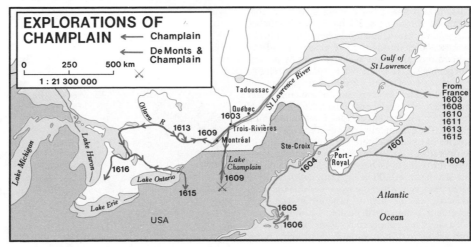

EXPLORATIONS OF CHAMPLAIN

and occupied by the English 1629-32. Appointed governor by Cardinal Richelieu, Champlain returned in 1633 to Québec, where he had time to see the promising beginnings of the colony he had planned. Paralyzed in the fall of 1635, he died the following Dec. His remains, buried under the Champlain chapel which adjoined Notre-Dame-de-la-Recouvrance, may today lie under Notre-Dame-de-Québec, though they have not been identified. In 1610 he had married a young Protestant woman, Hélène Boullé, who was not yet 12 years old but who brought him a useful dowry. This marriage was to prove disappointing for Champlain. His young wife deserted him, returned reluctantly and was not with him in Canada except 1620-24.

Champlain left behind a considerable body of writing, largely relating to his voyages. The most important editions of his work are the ones prepared by C.H. Laverdière (1870) and the bilingual edition of H.P. BIGGAR (*The Works of Samuel de Champlain*, 1922-36). Champlain's works are the only account of the Laurentian colony during the first quarter of the 17th century. As a geographer and "artist" (as a factum states), he illustrated his accounts with numerous maps, of which the most important and the last was that of 1632. It includes a list of place names not found on the map as well as unpublished explanations and it presents everything known about N America at that time. MARCEL TRUDEL

Reading: Marcel Trudel, *Le Comptoir* (1966); S.E. Morison, *Samuel de Champlain* (1972).

Champlain and Saint Lawrence Railroad

(incorporated 1832), Canada's first railway, ran between LA PRAIRIE on the St Lawrence R and St Johns [ST-JEAN] on the Richelieu. In effect, it served as a portage over the most troublesome part of the journey from Montréal to New York, which continued by steamer via Lk Champlain and the Hudson R. Construction began in 1835 with financing from Montréal brewer John MOLSON. The rails consisted of 6" (14 cm)-wide pine timbers joined by iron plates and bolts. Iron straps were then spiked to the upper surface. The railway officially opened 21 July 1836 and began regular operations July 25. The locomotive, the wood-burning *Dorchester* built in Newcastle-upon-Tyne, Eng, could reach up to 48 km/h. The railway was extended to Rouses Point, NY, in 1851 and to St Lambert, Qué, in 1852. In 1857 it amalgamated with the Montréal and New York Railroad (formerly MONTREAL AND LACHINE RAILROAD) under the name Montreal and Champlain Railroad Company. It was leased to the GRAND TRUNK RAILWAY in 1864, and purchased by GTR in 1872. *See also* LOCOMOTIVES AND ROLLING STOCK; RAILWAY HISTORY. JAMES MARSH

Champlain Sea,

a body of brackish water that occupied the depressed land between Québec City and Cornwall, Ont, and extended up the Ottawa R Valley during the late glacial period (*see* GLACIATION). The name was first used by American geologist C.H. Hitchcock in 1906. The relative rise of sea level about 12 800 years ago was as much the result of depression of the land under the weight of glacial ice as of the rise of water level caused by meltwater released from the waning glacier. The Champlain Sea was cold initially, but studies of its invertebrate fauna indicate that its temperature rose. Its maximum depth, in the centre of the basin, must have been about 200 m. The sea lasted some 2000 years, until approximately 9800 years ago, when the water became too fresh to accommodate marine organisms. The most abundant sediments deposited by the sea, the Leda clays, are mainly rock "flour" incorporated into glacier ice. Their mineralogy principally reflects the composition of the Precambrian rocks from which they are derived, ie, they contain quartz, amphiboles and pyroxenes (*see* GEOLOGICAL REGIONS). Many landslides and earthflows have occurred in the clays, sometimes with loss of life and considerable material damage. When disturbed the clays become fluid; therefore, landslides result when a bank is undermined by erosion, overloaded by a new building or when the clays are disturbed and their internal structure is destroyed. The Champlain Sea area has gradually become an erosional environment. When properly drained, its marine clays constitute the best agricultural land in Québec. PIERRE LaSALLE

Champlain Society,

fd 1905 in Toronto to publish manuscripts and new editions of rare books relating to Canada's history. Membership, limited at first to 250, now exceeds 1000. Many early volumes related to New France, including a 6-volume edition of Champlain's works in French and in English translation. The society soon became interested in the fur trade and published the first dozen volumes prepared by the HUDSON'S BAY RECORD SOCIETY. In recent years, volumes have been devoted to later material, some of a political nature. At the Ontario government's request and expense the society sponsors the Ontario Series, devoted to the province's history. The society has published over 80 volumes in all, more than 60 in the main series. In 1980 it published a sketch of its own history in observance of its 75th anniversary. W. KAYE LAMB

Chanak Affair,

1922, PM Mackenzie KING's first major foreign policy test. Britain and Canada signed the Treaty of Sèvres with defeated Turkey after WWI, but the treaty was soon in shreds; by Sept 1922 nationalist forces controlled most of Turkey. British occupation troops were pinned down at Chanak (now Canakkale), a small seaport on the Dardanelles. On Sept 15 Britain sent a telegram calling upon the Dominions to contribute soldiers in a demonstration of the Empire's solidarity against the Turks. The next day the request was made public, a breach of imperial etiquette and political good sense. To make matters worse, King heard from a Toronto *Star* reporter about the developing danger before he received the official British dispatch. King was

Extent of the Champlain Sea, about 12 000 years ago. As the glaciers melted, sea levels rose everywhere and water surged into the St Lawrence Valley. This short-lived extension of the Atlantic Ocean is called the Champlain Sea (*courtesy National Capital Commission/artwork by Kiyomi Shoyama*).

noncommittal until Sept 18, when Cabinet agreed that only Parliament could decide such matters. The crisis quickly passed. King's detached attitude gave notice of his desire to disengage Canadian external policy from that of the British. Chanak, however, was not a revolution in Canadian affairs: prime ministers since Macdonald had been reluctant to involve Canada in imperial skirmishes which did not threaten Britain itself. NORMAN HILLMER

Chandler, Edward Barron,

judge, politician, lt-gov of NB 1878-80 (b at Amherst, NS 22 Aug 1800; d at Fredericton 6 Feb 1880). Born into a prominent LOYALIST family, he was admitted to the NB Bar in 1823 and appointed judge of probate and clerk of the peace for Westmorland County. In 1827 he was elected to the NB Assembly, where he was regarded as a spokesman of the people and as a cautious reformer, opposed to RESPONSIBLE GOVERNMENT. He was appointed to the Legislative Council in 1836. Joining the Executive Council in 1843, he became leader of the government in 1848 and served until its defeat in the House in 1854. He supported railway development and reciprocity with the US. He attended the conferences on the union of BNA and was a constant supporter of CONFEDERATION, despite his objections to John A. Macdonald's version of centralized government. He refused an appointment to the Canadian Senate, but in 1878 accepted the position of lt-gov of NB. He died in office. J.M. BUMSTED

Channel-Port aux Basques,

Nfld, Town, pop 5901 (1986c), 5988 (1981c), inc 1945, is located on the Island's SW coast. It is the main western port of entry for the province, the eastern terminal for the CN Marine Gulf Ferry Service to N Sydney, NS, connecting the Trans-Canada Hwy. The modern town comprises the former settlements of Channel, Port aux Basques, Grand Bay E, Grand Bay W and Mouse I. Port aux Basques was named for BASQUE whalers who skirted the southwestern tip of Newfoundland en route to Labrador in the 1500s. Until the 1890s, when Port aux Basques became a railway centre, the settlements were mainly fishing communities settled by the French and later by Channel Islanders and the English. The community expanded as a trade centre, especially later when Port aux Basques was chosen as the terminus of the trans-insular Newfoundland Ry in the 1890s. In 1893 the railway was linked by the gulf steamer service to the Canadian railways. A number of fish plants were built by the 1950s, and one large firm continued to the 1980s. Since incorporation, Channel-Port aux Basques has been the administrative centre for the Burgeo-La Poile region.   JANET E.M. PITT

Chant, Clarence Augustus, professor of astrophysics (b at Hagerman's Corners, Ont 31 May 1865; d at Observatory House, Richmond Hill, Ont 18 Nov 1956). He is often called the "father of Canadian astronomy" because he trained so many young astronomers. Educated at U of T and Harvard, he taught at U of T from 1891 until retirement in 1935. Chant was notable for his early work on X-ray photographs, but especially for his development of Canadian ASTRONOMY. He organized the department at U of T and built up the Royal Astronomical Soc of Canada (established 1890) into one of the world's most successful organizations of its kind. From 1907 through 1956 he edited its *Journal* (published monthly or bimonthly) and its annual *Observer's Handbook* as well as writing many of the articles. He participated in 5 total solar-eclipse expeditions, the most important being the one he led to Australia 1922 to test Einstein's theory of the deflection of starlight by a massive body. Through his efforts the dream of a great observatory near Toronto came to fruition in 1933 when Mrs David Dunlap presented to U of T an observatory with a 74-inch (1.88 m) telescope (still the largest optical telescope in Canada). Chant was coauthor of 2 widely used textbooks. His popular *Our Wonderful Universe* (1928, new ed 1940) has been translated into 5 other languages, and he described the early days in *Astronomy in the University of Toronto* (1954). In Sept 1987 Minor Planet No 3314 was named for him.

HELEN S. HOGG

Chant, Donald Alfred, scientist, educator, environmental advocate, businessman (b at Toronto 30 Sept 1928). Chant's early university research at UBC and University of London led him to the forefront of nonchemical pest-control research in Canada, the US and England. A U of T professor of zoology from 1967 with a respected scientific record, Chant was the rare academic who turned his attention to informing the public on environmental issues in the 1970s – pesticides, pollution, wildlife preservation and arctic ecosystems. Eminent, eloquent and outspoken, he was welcomed by the media. In 1980, after 5 years as U of T vice-president and provost and after founding the Joint Guelph-Toronto Centre for Toxicology, Chant became first chairman and president of the Ontario Waste Management Corp, a position he still holds. His mandate was to solve one of the complex problems he had helped bring to public debate: the treatment of toxic industrial waste. He has remained a U of T zoology professor, directing a research program on the use of predators for insect control.   TONY BARRETT

Chapais, Jean-Charles, businessman, politician (b at Rivière-Ouelle, Qué 2 Dec 1811; d at Ottawa 17 July 1885). He was a prosperous merchant and dealer in St-Denis de Kamouraska and member for Kamouraska in the Legislative Assembly of the Province of Canada 1851-67. In 1867 he was elected to represent Kamouraska both provincially and federally but lost both seats because of electoral irregularities. Chapais took refuge in Champlain which he won by acclamation. In Jan 1868, while serving as federal minister of agriculture (1867-69) for the Conservative government, he was appointed to the Senate; he was receiver general 1869-73. Chapais was a FATHER OF CONFEDERATION and one of those politicians who monopolized power in Québec C and Ottawa after the formation of Canada.

ANDRÉE DÉSILETS

Chapleau, Ont, Township, Sudbury District, pop 3184 (1986c), is located on the Kapuskasing

R in NE Ontario, 272 km NW of Sudbury. A divisional point on the CANADIAN PACIFIC RY, the community was named after Sir J.-A. CHAPLEAU, the secretary of state in the Conservative government of Sir John A. Macdonald during the railway's construction in the 1880s. Over a century before, in 1777, the HUDSON'S BAY CO had established the first of a series of fur-trading posts in the area, which served the native Cree and Ojibwa populations until WWI. Since its inception in 1885, Chapleau has acted as a home terminal for the CPR, as well as a distribution and administrative centre for mining, lumbering and pulpwood operations, Indian affairs and provincial government forest management activities in the region.

MATT BRAY

Chapleau, Sir Joseph-Adolphe, lawyer, journalist, businessman, politician, premier of Québec 1879-82 (b at St-Thérèse-de-Blainville, Lower Canada 7 Nov 1840; d at Montréal 13 June 1898). He was admitted to the bar in 1861 and taught criminal law at U Laval in Montréal from 1878 to 1885. One of the owners of *Le Colonisateur* 1862-63 and *La Presse* in 1889, he was also a director of the Laurentides and the Pontiac and Pacific railway companies. He was elected to the Québec legislature in 1867, re-elected in 1871, and he was attorney general 1873-74 and provincial secretary 1876-78. He then led the Conservative Party to become premier in 1879. He left provincial politics in 1882, winning a federal by-election in Terrebonne. He was secretary of state until 1892, when he became minister of customs. He became lieutenant-governor of Québec in Nov 1892, retiring on 1 Feb 1898.   ANDRÉE DÉSILETS

Chapman, John Herbert, physicist, space scientist, administrator, architect of the Canadian space program (b at London, Ont 28 Aug 1921; d at Vancouver 28 Sept 1979). In Ottawa, he was scientist, superintendent and deputy chief superintendent in the Defence Research Telecommunications Establishment 1949-68 and then assistant deputy minister for research 1968-74 and for the space program 1974-79 in the Dept of Communications.

From 1958-71 Chapman played a key role in initiating and directing the spectacularly successful Alouette/ISIS scientific Earth SATELLITE program. With the launch of Alouette 1 in Sept 1962 Canada became the third country to design and build an Earth satellite. In 1966 he was appointed chairman of a government study group to examine the upper atmosphere and space programs in Canada. The resulting report was a landmark contribution to space policies and plans in Canada and led to the redirection of Canada's space program from scientific to applications satellites. The formation of Telesat in 1969 and the launching of its first satellite (Anik A-1) in Nov 1972 made Canada the first country to have a domestic geostationary communications satellite system. He was also the prime mover behind Canada's co-operative program with NASA and the European Space Agency to design, build and demonstrate the Hermes Communications Technology Satellite. Launched in 1976, the Hermes was a forerunner of the direct-to-home TV broadcast satellite. Chapman was a tireless advocate of the Canadian space industry and of the use of space technology to serve the needs of the Canadian people.   C.A. FRANKLIN

Chaput-Rolland, Solange, writer, editor, broadcaster (b at Montréal 14 May 1919). Chaput-Rolland is a Québecoise federalist, best known in English Canada for her book *Dear Enemies* (1963), a collection of letters exchanged with coauthor Gwethalyn Graham on French-English

relations. Her other books include *Mon pays, Québec ou Canada* (1966), *Québec année zéro* (1968) and *Face to Face* (1972) with Gertrude Laing. Chaput-Rolland served on the federal Task Force on CANADIAN UNITY. In 1979 she won a seat for the Liberals in the Québec National Assembly in a by-election, losing it to the PQ in 1981. In 1984 she received an honorary LLD from Queen's.

MARGARET E. McCALLUM

Char, common name for several species of fish of genus *Salvelinus* of the SALMON family (Salmonidae). Approximately 11 char species occur worldwide. Five are native to Canada: arctic char (*S. alpinus*), Dolly Varden (*S. malma*), bull trout (*S. confluentus*), brook trout (*S. fontinalis*) and lake trout (*S. namaycush*). Chars are distinguished from other salmonids by light-coloured spots (red, pink, orange, yellow or grey) on their dark backs, and the number of anal fin rays (7-12). They spawn in fresh water in fall: arctic char in lakes or rivers; Dolly Varden, bull trout and brook trout usually in rivers; lake trout primarily in lakes. All char, except lake and bull trout, have both freshwater and sea-run populations.

Arctic char, the most northern salmonid, has circumpolar distribution. In Canada, it is found in the Yukon, northern Northwest Territories, along Hudson Bay, Ungava, Newfoundland and the St Lawrence. It is important to Inuit and northern Indians as a source of food and income, and supports a small sports fishery.

Dolly Varden is restricted to north Pacific Rim countries; in Canada, to southern YT and coastal BC. The species was considered destructive to salmon and TROUT, and a bounty was paid in Alaska. Generally, it is not a popular sport fish where other salmonids are available; however, increasing pressure on all sport fish has prompted a steady increase in its use.

Bull trout has only recently been recognized as a separate species closely related to Dolly Varden. In Canada it occurs in northern and eastern BC and western Alberta.

Brook or speckled trout, naturally ranging eastwards from Ontario, is now distributed throughout all provinces. Until the mid-1900s, it was highly prized as a sport fish, and has been introduced as far afield as New Zealand and the Falkland Is. However, like brown trout, it has been replaced by rainbow trout transplants. It is the smallest char (25-30 cm long) and is often found in small, spring-fed, headwater streams.

Lake trout is the largest char; in 1961 a 46.3 kg fish was taken in Lk Athabasca. It has the widest native range of all salmonids in Canada, including all provinces and territories, and some low-latitude arctic islands, and has been widely transplanted. It is the most valuable char in commercial and sport fisheries; however, catches have declined since the early 1960s.

Splake or wendigo, a fertile hybrid of lake and brook trout has been developed and introduced to many parts of N America, primarily Ontario, where a breeding and stocking program has existed for some time.   E.D. LANE

Charbonneau, Robert, journalist, writer (b at Montréal 3 Feb 1911; d at St-Jovite, Qué 26 June 1967). Because of Charbonneau's work, French Canadian literature, particularly the novel, underwent a profound transformation. Considered the leader of the 1940s and postwar generation, he gave literature this new direction through his literary output (particularly his novels and a literary essay), his articles, and his work as an editor (*La* RELÈVE, which became *La Nouvelle Relève*, 1934-48; Éditions de l'Arbre, 1940-48). He was also a founding member of the Académie canadienne-française and president of the Société des écrivains canadiens 1966-67. Because of Charbonneau, Québec literature broke with literary convention and its idealized and stereotyped characters, as well as with the literature of France. Charbonneau's creative spirit, critical acumen and originality were recognized in his lifetime. He won the Québec Literary Competition in 1942, the Prix Duvernay in 1946 and the RSC's Médaille Chauveau in 1965. His works include the essays *Connaissance du personnage* (1944) and *La France et nous* (1947); novels *Ils posséderont la terre* (1941), *Fontile* (1945), *Les Désirs et les jours* (1948), *Aucune créature* (1961), *Chronique de l'âge amer* (1967); and poetry *Petits poèmes retrouvés* (1945).

MADELEINE DUCROCQ-POIRIER

Charbonneau, Yvon, teacher, president of the Centrale de l'enseignement du Québec (CEQ) (b at Mont-Laurier, Qué 11 July 1940). After studying at U de M, Charbonneau taught French and the humanities in Québec and Tunisia 1961-69. His election to the CEQ in 1970 marked the union's abandonment of corporatism as advocated by Roman Catholic social doctrine. Under Charbonneau the CEQ became a genuine union, renouncing its corporate charter, changing its name and opening its ranks to other education workers. The union took a harder line in negotiations with the government and in 1972 formed a Common Front with other unions. This Common Front led to the imprisonment of Charbonneau, Louis LABERGE, president of the Fédération des travailleurs du Québec, and Marcel PEPIN, president of the Confédération des syndicats nationaux, for urging their members to ignore a no-strike injunction. Defeated as CEQ president in 1978, Charbonneau was kept on as a special adviser and later, director of communications. He resumed presidency of the CEQ in 1982 and was re-elected in 1984 and 1986.

JACQUES ROUILLARD

Charbonnel, Armand-François-Marie de, Roman Catholic bishop of Toronto (b near Monistrol-sur-Loire, France 1 Dec 1802; d at Crest, France 29 Mar 1891). Of noble birth, Charbonnel entered the priesthood in the Society of St-Sulpice. Coming to N America in 1839, he served as priest in Montréal until 1847. He was consecrated bishop of Toronto in 1850. As bishop, he pressured the Famine Irish laity and politicians to gain separate education for Catholics. The Basilian Fathers, the Christian Brothers and the Sisters of St Joseph were brought to Toronto to assist with education and social work. He established St Michael's College, the House of Providence to shelter the sick, aged and orphaned, and instituted the St Vincent de Paul Soc, the Toronto Savings Bank and other charitable associations. Utilizing his paternal estate, Charbonnel eradicated the diocesan debt, including that of St Michael's Cathedral. He succeeded in having the large diocese of Toronto divided into 3 sees (Toronto, Hamilton, London) in 1856. Living an exemplary life of a beggar among the Irish poor, Charbonnel resigned his see in 1860, entering the Capuchin Order in France and later becoming the archbishop of Sozopolis.   MURRAY WILLIAM NICOLSON

Charcoal, or Si'k-okskitsis, meaning Black Wood Ashes, outlaw (b 1856?; d at Ft Macleod, Alta 16 Mar 1897). A renowned warrior of the BLOOD tribe, Charcoal, in 1896, killed Medicine Pipe Stem, his wife's lover. In the course of a vendetta he shot and wounded a white farm instructor, fired on a police post, and threatened the lives of Blood leaders. Pursued by police, Charcoal evaded capture for several weeks, during which time he killed Sgt W.B. Wilde of the NWMP. The police exerted pressure on Char-

coal's family to help trap him. When Charcoal visited their cabin looking for food and shelter, 2 of his brothers overpowered him and turned him over to the NWMP. He was convicted on 2 counts of murder and hanged.   EDWARD BUTTS

Reading: Hugh A. Dempsey, *Charcoal's World* (1978).

Charismatic Renewal, a transdenominational Christian movement, theologically diverse and ecumenical, characterizing significant segments of the church in the 1960s and 1970s, and frequently referred to as neo-Pentecostal. The principal similarity with the classical PENTECOSTAL MOVEMENTS is the importance of experiential religion, particularly of experiencing the presence of God, along with appropriate manifestations of the encounter. Like the old Pentecostals, charismatics emphasize the baptism of the Holy Spirit or the reception of the Spirit's power. The external manifestations of that power are charisms (gifts), such as speaking in tongues (glossolalia, or ecstatic speech), healing and prophesying. Although such evidences of the supernatural are not seen as being essential to designating someone as spirit-filled, they are nevertheless frequently sought. The experience of the Holy Spirit should not be confused with conversion, but is rather a second "blessing" to be sought by all Christians.

Perhaps the most significant difference from the old Pentecostals is that most charismatics have chosen to stay within existing churches. They form a movement rather than a sectarian group or distinct denomination, although occasionally individual churches with charismatic tendencies may sever ties with a denomination. Charismatics do not share the anti-intellectualism, fundamentalism and dispensational theology of the Pentecostals, nor is the primacy of ecstatic spiritual experience seen as necessarily antithetical to the development of a social conscience.

The movement's distribution among established denominations makes it impossible to obtain meaningful statistics. Since there is not a separate organization, there is no formal membership. Nevertheless the renewal has influenced LUTHERAN, PRESBYTERIAN, ANGLICAN, UNITED, MENNONITE, BAPTIST, ORTHODOX and Roman CATHOLIC churches across the country. Its message appears to be a call to the church to be what it is meant to be: catholic in its commitment to the body of Christ, charismatic in being open to the power of the resurrected Christ, and evangelical in its obedience to mission. Charismatics therefore stress the total work of the church based on the experience of God's power. Although individuals may define themselves as charismatics by speaking in tongues or belonging to identifiable prayer and praise groups, the accent tends to be on participation in the church in order to call the church to its true mission.   RONALD NEUFELDT

Over 50 000 Roman Catholics attended a charismatic mass held in Montréal's Olympic Stadium in 1979 (*courtesy Canapress Photo Service*).

Charlebois, Robert, singer, actor, author-composer, guitarist, pianist (b at Montréal 25 June 1945). As well as studying music (6 years of piano), Charlebois studied dramatic arts at the National Theatre School in Montréal from 1962 to 1965. A pioneer among *chansonniers*, both in his use of *joual* and in the theatrical way in which he presented his music, Charlebois received the Prix Félix-Leclerc in 1969 at the Festival du disque with "Lindberg," the same song that in 1968 had won him the grand prize at the Festival international de la chanson française in Spa, Belgium. Another success was "Ordinaire," which took first prize at the International Festival in Sopot, Poland, in 1970. Louise Forestier and Mouffe (Claudine Monfette) have often appeared with him. As an actor, Charlebois appeared in the films, *Un Génie, deux associés, une cloche* and *Entre la mer et l'eau douce*.   HÉLÈNE PLOUFFE

Charlesworth, Hector Willoughby, editor, critic, memoirist (b at Hamilton 28 Sept 1872; d at Toronto 30 Dec 1945). He was a Toronto newspaperman and arts commentator, particularly on music and drama, and editor of *Saturday Night* magazine 1926-32, leaving to become first head of Canadian Radio Broadcasting Commission, precursor of the CBC. His autobiography, in 3 volumes, is a splendid source of literary, political, journalistic and theatrical anecdote. Among those only casually acquainted with his work, this honest and productive journalist is best known for having once viciously attacked the GROUP OF SEVEN and also for the uncanny resemblance he bore to Edward VII.   DOUG FETHERLING

Charlevoix, Pierre-François-Xavier de, Jesuit historian (b at Saint-Quentin, France 24 or 29 Oct 1682; d at La Flèche, France 1 Feb 1761). Author of the first comprehensive history of NEW FRANCE, Charlevoix taught at the Jesuit Coll at Québec (1705-09) and in 1720 was again in New France, charged with reporting on the boundaries of Acadia and on the existence of the "Western Sea." In 1721-22 he travelled by canoe in the Great Lks basin and down the Mississippi to New Orleans before returning to France. His 2½ years in N America were marked by frustration and illness, but his detailed notes and scientific observations furnished the material for a travel narrative published in 1744 as part of his 3-vol *Histoire et description générale de la Nouvelle France*. He also published a biography of MARIE DE L'INCARNATION (1724), a history of Christianity in Japan (1715, new ed 1736) and histories of Santo Domingo (1730-31) and Paraguay (1756). Unusually accurate and well documented for their time, Charlevoix's elegantly written histories became erudite obituaries for the French regime in N America and the Jesuit empires in Japan and Paraguay.   DAVID M. HAYNE

Charlo, NB, Village, pop 1602 (1986c), inc 1969, located 8 km SE of Dalhousie on CHALEUR BAY. The first settlers, who arrived in 1755, were ACADIAN refugees who had travelled north from Nova Scotia to escape the deportation. The village was incorporated, from 1966 to 1969, as Colborne, in honour of Sir John COLBORNE, governor general in 1839, the year it was legally established as a civil parish. It was renamed in 1969 for an early resident and founder of Petit Rocher, Charles Doucet. There are no major manufacturing industries in the village; 40% of the work force is engaged in fishing, forestry and agriculture. Charlo airport serves northeastern New Brunswick, with regularly scheduled flights connecting that area to Montréal. Nearby is picturesque Charlo Falls and a summer resort on Chaleur Bay.

BURTON GLENDENNING

Charlottetown, pop 15 776 (1986c), capital of Prince Edward Island and seat of the province's

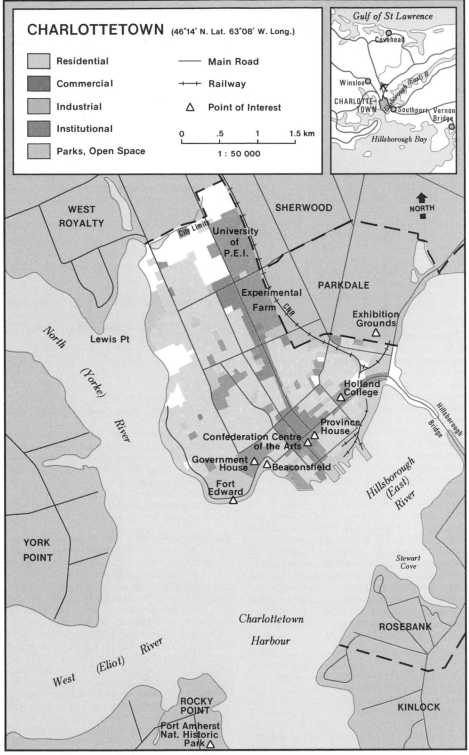

CHARLOTTETOWN (46°14′ N. Lat. 63°08′ W. Long.)

▢ Residential	—— Main Road
▢ Commercial	+—+ Railway
▢ Industrial	△ Point of Interest
▢ Institutional	
▢ Parks, Open Space	

0   .5   1   1.5 km

1 : 50 000

Gulf of St Lawrence

Covehead

Winsloe

CHARLOTTE-TOWN

Southport   Vernon Bridge

Hillsborough Bay

Population: 15 776 (1986c), 15 282 (1981c); 53 868
    (1986, CA), 50 995 (1981, ACA)
Rate of Increase (1981-86): (City) +3.2%; (CA) +5.6%
    (1976-86) City -0.7%*
Rank in Canada: Forty-eighth (by CA)
Date of Incorporation: 1855
Land Area: (City) 6.99 km²; (CA) 991.99 km²
Elevation: 55 m (Charlottetown Airport)
Climate: Average daily temp, July 18.3°C, Jan -7.1°C;
    Yearly precip 1169.4 mm; Hours of sunshine
    1818.4 per year
*1976 pop is 15 893; dropped to 15 282 for 1981; and
    increased to 15 776 for 1986

the community was christened Charlottetown, after Charlotte, wife of King George III. While the area was distant from the lucrative fisheries, it offered excellent transportation corridors to the interior via the rivers and was close to Nova Scotia and a road to Halifax.

The original town plan provided for broad streets on a grid pattern, with the main axis running N from the Hillsborough R, a common for future expansion and a royalty for pasturage and gardening. Sites were designated for a market house, church, courthouse and jail, but it was some time before all of these facilities were provided. Meanwhile, defence works were begun and, after American privateers ransacked the settlement in 1775, strengthened. By then the town's status had been enhanced by a decision of the British government in 1769 to separate the Island, renamed Prince Edward Island in 1799, from Nova Scotia and to make the little community the capital of the new colony. The first governor, Walter PATTERSON, began establishing essential administrative services, but just as significantly commenced work on roads to more distant parts of the colony. As settlement of agricultural areas progressed, Charlottetown became a market town as well as a communications and administrative centre. These functions remain essential elements in the city's economy.

Throughout the 19th century Charlottetown's population averaged about 9% of the Island's total and grew as the Island grew. Most settlers were of English, Scottish or Irish origin, with a sizable Acadian element and smaller numbers of other ethnic groups, but by 1848 over half of the population were native-born Islanders. When PEI entered Confederation in 1873, Charlottetown was the eleventh-largest city in Canada.

Shipbuilding and ship-owning, plus small-scale manufacturing such as tanning, brewing and shoe production, had diversified the economy somewhat. The prosperity, however, was sufficiently limited to ensure thrift in the provision of community services. Vigorous opposition to taxes meant that improvements to counter fire and disease tended to follow disasters such as the Great Fire of 1866 or the smallpox epidemic of 1887. Nevertheless, by the end of the century, Charlottetown possessed modern water and sewer services, electric street lighting, proper hospitals and schools and a varied cultural life. Communications links, including coastal steamship service, the railway, and the telephone and telegraph, allowed the city to expand its influence over more distant parts of the Island, although communications difficulties with mainland centres of commerce highlighted Charlottetown's relative isolation.

Economy In the 20th century the population of Charlottetown and its environs has grown steadily as part of the Island's total, but has failed to keep pace with massive urban growth in the rest of Canada. The city's population decreased 0.7% from 1976 to 1986, but in the same period the metropolitan area population grew by 5.6%.

middle county of Queens, is situated on a broad harbour opening into the NORTHUMBERLAND STR. Three rivers conjoin there, with the city located on a low-rising point of land between the Hillsborough (East) and North (Yorke) rivers just opposite the harbour's mouth. Some suburban development has also occurred across the Hillsborough at Southport and Bunbury, and between the North and West (Eliot) rivers at Cornwall. Besides its administrative functions, Charlottetown services a considerable agricultural hinterland and is the focus of Island communications. Its favourable climate and nearby beaches have made it a major tourist centre.

History and Development Although the city was incorporated 1855, settlement in the region dates

back to 1720, when an expedition sent by the Comte de Saint-Pierre established itself W of the harbour's entrance at a site named Port La Joie. After the assumption of direct control of Île Saint-Jean (the Island's former name) by the French government in 1730, Port La Joie was retained as the administrative centre, even though other Island locales showed more commercial promise. This decision was confirmed by the British when they finally achieved mastery in the region following the capitulation of Louisbourg (1758). Port La Joie, which never had a population much over 100, was renamed Fort Amherst, and its defences were strengthened. In 1768, however, Charles Morris, chief surveyor of Nova Scotia, laid out a new townsite across the harbour, and

Many 19th-century industries, including ship-building, have disappeared. In their stead are plants processing fish, seafood, meat and dairy products and manufacturing knitwear, clothing, farm and marine equipment, metal products and building supplies. Through the port pass outbound agricultural produce and imported petroleum products. While all these activities contribute significantly to the local economy, they have been overshadowed by tourism. First encouraged by the erection of a major railway hotel in 1931, the tourist trade was expanded by motel construction in the 1950s and 1960s and by the completion of an extensive network of paved roads radiating from Charlottetown. In 1964 the Confederation Centre, a large performing-arts and museum complex, was opened to commemorate the CHARLOTTETOWN CONFERENCE of 1864, an event that gave the city the title "The Cradle of Confederation," though largely ignored by the citizens of that era. The centre now houses the very successful Charlottetown Summer Festival of music and light entertainment. A new convention facility has further enhanced the city's tourist appeal. Another recent development has been the transfer of the Department of Veterans Affairs from Ottawa, a move that brought many newcomers and heightened the significance of the administrative sector.

Cityscape Charlottetown today is a city of contrasts. A market-town atmosphere exists beside extensive cultural facilities, large government offices and 2 institutions of higher education—Holland College, a community college, and UPEI. Expansive suburbs with modern shopping malls are strikingly dissimilar to "Old Charlottetown," which features the classic revival legislature known as Province House, stately old mansions, and refurbished shops and commercial buildings dating from the last century. A new harbour-front complex of homes and offices echoes the old and helps to emphasize the importance of the city's core. Thus, though declining in the order of Canadian municipalities in size, Charlottetown offers a quality of life far richer than its small population would suggest. PETER E. RIDER

Reading: Benjamin Bremmer, *Memories of Long Ago* (1930); A.H. Clark, *Three Centuries and the Island* (1969); I.L. Rogers, *Charlottetown: The Life in Its Buildings* (1983); A.B. Warburton, *A History of Prince Edward Island* (1923).

Charlottetown Conference, 1-9 Sept 1864 in Charlottetown, PEI, set CONFEDERATION in motion. Maritime union had long been talked of in NS, NB and PEI. In Mar-Apr 1864 all 3 legislatures passed resolutions to have a conference to discuss it. Nothing happened until after the June 1864 constitutional crisis in the PROVINCE OF CANADA, when the Canadians asked to attend the conference to propose a union of all BRITISH NORTH AMERICA. This request rather staggered the Maritime governments, but through the action of NS Lt-Gov Richard MacDonnell the place and date of meeting were selected. At the conference Maritime union was virtually dropped, and the delegates agreed on the outline of a scheme for more general union. It was decided to have a more comprehensive meeting at Québec in Oct. External circumstances, such as the AMERICAN CIVIL WAR, Britain's desire to divest itself of financial and administrative colonial obligations, and the political condition of the Province of Canada, combined to create an ambience at Charlottetown which produced the momentum that was so obvious at the QUÉBEC CONFERENCE and that was so necessary to carry Confederation. P.B. WAITE

Charlottetown Summer Festival The Confederation Centre of the Arts in Charlottetown is a national memorial to the founding of Canada,

an event which was set in motion at the CHARLOTTETOWN CONFERENCE of 1864. The centre, whose construction was financed by the federal and provincial governments, has its operating expenses still partly borne by subventions from Ottawa and 8 of the 10 provinces.

The Charlottetown Festival held in the auditorium of the centre every summer, has as its mandate therefore the celebration of Canada by Canadian artists of Canadian themes. To achieve this, the Charlottetown Festival has produced a succession of original Canadian musical plays. ANNE OF GREEN GABLES, with words by Donald Harron and music by Norman Campbell, has been produced every season since the festival's opening in 1965. It has also toured Canada on several occasions, and been seen in London and New York. *Johnny Belinda, Sunshine Town* (based on Stephen Leacock's *Sketches*), *Private Turvey's War* and *Rowdyman* have all been successful adaptations of Canadian books for summer musicals. Some 50 original musical presentations were produced at Charlottetown in its first 20 years.

The festival runs from June to September and, by the 1970s, it had replaced beaches and lobster as the main tourist attraction of Prince Edward Island. ARNOLD EDINBOROUGH

Charney, Melvin, architect, artist, educator (b at Montréal 28 Aug 1935). Educated at McGill and Yale, Charney was for some time best known for his Corridart project, a construction commissioned by the 1976 Olympics' Arts and Culture Program, and erected along a 9 km stretch of Sherbrooke St, only to be demolished by the Montréal city fathers on the eve of the opening ceremonies on the grounds that it was obscene. His major works, consisting of experiments with built forms usually constructed of wood, have been exhibited in museums, installed on streets, on select city sites and, more recently, as extensions of the museum buildings themselves (The Museum of Contemporary Art, Chicago, Ill, 1982; Agnes Etherington Art Centre, Kingston, Ont, 1983). Professor of architecture at U de M 1984, Charney has worked successfully apart from the mainstream of traditional architectural activity and has distinguished himself on an international scale. In 1986 he won the Canadian Human Rights Tribute to Human Rights design competition (a monument to be constructed on Elgin St in Ottawa) and in Oct 1987 the Canadian Centre for Architecture commissioned him to design a sculpture garden in Montréal. SUSAN FORD

Charpentier, Alfred, labour leader (b at Montréal 25 Nov 1888; d there 13 Nov 1982). Working as a bricklayer 1905-15, he became president of the International Union of Bricklayers in 1911. In 1916 he turned towards the Catholic union movement, which was slowly being created by several clerics led by Fathers Joseph-Papin Archambault and Maxime Fortin during and after WWI. Charpentier's union experience helped define the primary role of Catholic unions as one of defending the professional interests of the workers. Several thousand French Canadian workers belonging to national unions subsequently reorganized themselves as Catholic unions. With their constitution largely written by Charpentier, 80 Catholic unions created the Confédération des travailleurs catholiques du Canada (CTCC) in 1921. Charpentier was its president 1935-46. A tireless advocate of Catholic social thought, he fought for improvements to Québec's antiquated labour legislation and for the creation of a Conseil supérieur du travail and a system of courts to resolve labour disputes. After stepping down in 1946, he wrote extensively on labour issues and published his memoirs, *Cinquante ans d'action ouvrière* (1971). M.D. BEHIELS

Charpentier, Gabriel, composer, poet, artistic adviser (b at Richmond, Qué 13 Sept 1925). Having studied piano with, among others, Jean PAPINEAU-COUTURE, he stayed with the Benedictines at St-Benoît-du-Lac, where he studied Gregorian chant. He continued his studies in Paris (1947-53), notably with Norbert Dufourcq and Nadia Boulanger. Fascinated by the theatre, for which most of his compositions were intended, Charpentier realized that music written for a theatrical production had to be integral to that production. One of his operas, *Orphée I*, was commissioned for the inauguration of the National Arts Centre in Ottawa (1969). He is a member of the artistic committee for a performing artists' centre in Brussels and a member of the administrative council of the Comus Music Theatre Foundation of Canada, Toronto. He has also been artistic director of the Pro Musica Society (1979-81). HÉLÈNE PLOUFFE

Chartered Bank is an institution whose primary business is financial intermediation, meaning the bringing together of borrowers and lenders. Chartered banks offer a range of other financial services to their customers as well, such as cheque clearing, credit cards and safekeeping. Banks' profits come from the spread between interest paid to depositors by the bank and the interest paid to the bank by borrowers.

Banks receive their charters from the federal government under the BANK ACT. Formerly, banks required a special Act of Parliament in order to receive their charter. However, since 1980 banks have been chartered by letters patent which is a legal requirement not requiring special approval by Parliament.

Banks are named under 2 different schedules in the Act. Schedule A banks are widely held (no single person or corporation may control more than 10% of the voting stock); Schedule B banks are closely held (ownership is more concentrated). Most Schedule B banks are foreign owned and the size of Schedule B banks is controlled by the federal government. *See also* BANKING. PAUL BOOTHE

Chartrand, Michel, labour and political activist (b at Outremont, Qué 20 Dec 1913). After a classical education and 2 years as an Oblate monk, he joined the Jeunesses patriotes. After becoming a typographer, he took part in the anti-conscriptionist League for the Defence of Canada and the Bloc populaire canadien. During the 1950s he worked for the Fédération nationale des travailleurs du vêtement and the Syndicat des Métallos, in charge of education. A member and leader of the Parti sociale démocratique (CCF), he helped found the NEW DEMOCRATIC PARTY, but broke with it on the question of Québec's independence. In 1963 he helped found the Parti socialiste du Québec, becoming its first president 1964-65. Critical of Québec's organized labour for its refusal to back a working-class political party, he became an ardent supporter of the PARTI QUÉBÉCOIS. As president of the Conseil central des syndicats nationaux de Montréal 1968-78 he helped advance the rapidly growing movement within organized labour for an independent, socialist Québec. M.D. BEHIELS

Chasse-Galerie French Canadian variant of the Wild Hunt, a legend which interprets strange noises in the air as relating to a hunter condemned to hunt throughout eternity. In Chasse-Galerie, one or several persons together are able, with the help of the devil, to travel in a canoe through the air at tremendous speed. They must take care not to have any blessed object on their person or to pronounce the name of God, lest the canoe crash. The name appears to be derived from the French *chasse*, "hunt"; *galerie*, Sire de Gallery, a condemned hunter. NANCY SCHMITZ

Château Clique, nickname given to the small group of officials, usually members of the anglophone merchant community including John MOLSON and James MCGILL, who dominated the executive and legislative councils, the judiciary and senior bureaucratic positions of LOWER CANADA until the 1830s. Appointed by the governor, members of the councils advised him on local matters, helped shape public policy, and controlled revenues, patronage and land grants. The term referred to the governor's residence and the location of government offices, Château St-Louis.

The clique aggressively pursued canal building, the establishment of banking institutions, and the abolition of the SEIGNEURIAL SYSTEM and French CIVIL LAW. By 1810 mercantile influence in the government was limited to the appointed councils, for not only did imperial authorities tend to grant concessions to the French-speaking majority, but anglophone merchants had been squeezed out of the elected assembly by French Canadian professionals. Before 1810 the appointed councils resisted Pierre BÉDARD's attempts to institute ministerial responsibility; in the 1820s they opposed efforts by the assembly to control public revenues and continued their efforts aimed at the assimilation of French Canadians; in 1822 the clique supported a scheme to reunite Upper and Lower Canada; and in the 1830s it blocked Louis-Joseph PAPINEAU's resolutions demanding RESPONSIBLE GOVERNMENT in the form of an elected legislative council. By 1834 ethnic and class tensions had so polarized politics that only 9 English-speaking assemblymen supported the appointed councils, and thereafter the influence of the Château Clique steadily declined.   DAVID MILLS

Châteauguay, Battle of, fought 26 Oct 1813 between the leading elements of an American army of invasion and a smaller Canadian force consisting principally of the VOLTIGEURS, a French Canadian fencible corps under Lt-Col Charles de SALABERRY. The field of battle was along the Châteauguay R about 50 km S of Montréal. Through innovative devices and scare tactics, including the blowing of horns in the woods to suggest a large force of defenders, the Canadians confused the Americans, who became overly cautious and soon retreated. Montréal was not seriously threatened for the remainder of the WAR OF 1812.   ROBERT S. ALLEN

Chatelaine, a Canadian women's magazine, was started by MACLEAN HUNTER LTD in 1928 with a circulation of 57 053. The first editor was Anne Elizabeth Wilson, followed by Byrne Hope Sanders. During the 1930s and 1940s, like most N American MAGAZINES, *Chatelaine* ran a heavy content of fiction, recipes, beauty, fashion, child care and etiquette, with emphasis on the role of woman as homemaker. In 1951 Lotta Dempsey became editor, followed by John Clare and, in 1957, Doris McCubbin Anderson. By the 1960s *Chatelaine* was the sole remaining women's magazine in Canada. A dozen other magazines had died owing to the domination of US magazines on newsstands (1961) and to over 50% of Canadian advertising dollars flowing into *Time* and *Readers' Digest*. *Chatelaine* survived by responding more rapidly than its US competitors to the concerns of women joining the work force and the beginning of the WOMEN'S MOVEMENT, with articles on equal pay, child abuse, abortion, the poverty of women, as well as traditional service articles geared to the working woman's life. It became the biggest paid-circulation magazine in Canada and in 1976 Bill C-58 effectively stemmed the US competition. Mildred Istona has been editor since 1978. The average total paid circulation in 1986 was 1 089 496. CHÂTELAINE is a separate French-language magazine.   DORIS ANDERSON

Châtelaine, fd Oct 1960 and published in Montréal by Maclean Hunter Ltée, is one of the largest French-language women's magazines in the world, with a total paid circulation of 294 116 (1986). Launched by its first director general, Lloyd M. Hodgkinson, *Châtelaine* grew rapidly from its original run of 111 905 copies. Three editors in chief have directed it over its 25 years: Fernande Saint-Martin until 1973, Francine Montpetit until 1984, and Martine Thornton since 1985. The publisher and director general in 1987 was Jean Paré.

The magazine has played an important role in Québec for the last quarter century. Virtually alone in the field when it first appeared, at a time when TV though still in its infancy had virtually wiped out francophone magazines, it decided that its mandate would be to inform Québec women of the huge changes in society and in their family or personal roles. From its first issues, it has tackled controversial questions such as contraception, equal rights for women, divorce, child care and the role of women in politics. The publication has also offered its readers fiction by the country's best writers, including Gabrielle ROY, Anne HÉBERT and Yves THÉRIAULT. Over the years, major sections on fashion, food and consumerism have been added.

Chatham, NB, Town, pop 6219 (1986c), 6780 (1981c), inc 1896, is located near the mouth of the MIRAMICHI R. The settlement was named about 1800 by its founder Francis Peabody for William Pitt, earl of Chatham and PM of England. The town's early political and business life was dominated by Joseph CUNARD, of the world-famous shipping family, who controlled most lumbering and shipbuilding interests until his bankruptcy in 1847. Livelihood has long been dependent on the fluctuating timber economy. The removal of the Roman Catholic St Thomas College (est 1910) to Fredericton in 1964 was a severe blow to the area. Since 1941 CFB Chatham and St Margarets nearby have been crucial to the local economy. Chatham boasts a fine collection of artifacts at its natural history museum. WILLIAM R. MACKINNON

Chatham, Ont, City, pop 42 211 (1986c), 40 952 (1981c), fd 1794, inc 1895, located on Thames R, 73 km E of Windsor. One of the oldest communities in western Ontario, it was planned originally as a military settlement by John Graves SIMCOE, lt-gov of UC. The military function did not develop, however, and settlement lagged until the 1830s. The name, given by Simcoe, refers to Chatham, Eng. Prior to the American Civil War, Chatham was a centre of antislavery activity and one of the northern terminuses for the UNDERGROUND RAILROAD which brought fugitive slaves to Canada, and descendants of thousands of these former slaves are an integral part of the local population. The county town and geographic centre of Kent County, it developed as a marketing centre for the rich, surrounding agricultural area. The local economy now depends on diversified light industry. A campus of St Clair College of Applied Arts and Technology is located here.   DANIEL FRANCIS

Chauchetière, Claude, Jesuit missionary, painter (b at St-Porchaire-de-Poitiers, France 7 Sept 1645; d at Québec C 17 Apr 1709). A number of Jesuits used illustrations in their evangelization work with the Indians, but the only authentic pieces to survive – bound in book form – are by

Chauchetière. He arrived in Canada in 1677 and went in 1678 to the Iroquois mission of St-François-Xavier at Sault-St-Louis [Caughnawaga, Qué]. Most of his time as a missionary was spent in this village of converted Indians. His *Narration annuelle de la Mission du Sault depuis la fondation jusqu'à l'an 1686* relates and illustrates the main events of his mission. The full-length portrait of Kateri TEKAKWITHA in the church at Caughnawaga is attributed to him, even though the chapel in the tableau appears more recent than any he could have known. The work may be an old copy of his painting.   FRANÇOIS-MARC GAGNON

Chaudière, Rivière, 193 km long, basin 6603 km², located in southern Québec, is named after the waters that "boil" from its falls. The ABENAKI called it *Kikonteku,* meaning "cornfields river." It flows NE from Lac MÉGANTIC to the foot of the Montagnes Frontalières, passes through the rapids of the Appalachian Plateau, and arrives at the lowlands of the St Lawrence R downstream from Ste-Marie, where it flows into the river almost opposite QUÉBEC CITY. It has a 40 m waterfall, "Le Saut de la Chaudière," 6 km from its mouth. The winding river with its pebbly bed is known for its flooding and for the fertile land of its floodplain, Les Beaucerons. As early as 1640, the Abenaki used the Chaudière to travel from Québec City to Maine. In 1776, during the American Revolution, the troops of Col Benedict ARNOLD set out from Boston and used the route for their attack on Québec City.   JEAN-MARIE DUBOIS AND PIERRE MAILHOT

Chaussé, Joseph-Alcide, architect, author (b at St-Sulpice, Qué 7 Jan 1868; d at Montréal 7 Oct 1944). After working in private practice in Montréal, Chaussé was building inspector for the city 1900-18. He wrote articles on fire prevention and handbooks on building laws for Montréal and the province of Québec. Chaussé was the chief promoter of the Royal Architectural Inst of Canada and served as honorary secretary from its formation in 1907 until 1942. Throughout his career he sought the improvement of architectural standards. His most famous work is the Empress Theatre on Sherbrooke St W, a design in the Egyptian manner inspired by the excitement of the discovery of Tutankhamen's tomb in 1922.
                                        ROBERT LEMIRE

Chaussegros de Léry, Gaspard-Joseph, military engineer (b at Toulon, France 3 Oct 1682; d at Québec City 23 Mar 1756). After over 10 years' combat service in Europe, Chaussegros de Léry came to Canada in 1716. Subsequently appointed chief military engineer, he served as such until his death in 1756. He was responsible for 40 years for the design and construction of fortifications, town plans and public buildings at Québec and Montréal as well as of such forts as Chambly and Niagara. Through his marriage into a prominent Canadian family, Chaussegros de Léry established a dynasty that distinguished itself in both Canada and France.   F.J. THORPE

Chautauqua, a travelling institution begun on Chautauqua Lk, NY, and with Canadian roots in Methodist Temperance rallies, which carried education, inspiration and entertainment across N America. John M. Erickson brought the idea from the US to Alberta in 1917. He established Dominion Chautauquas (Canadian Chautauquas after 1926) with headquarters in Calgary, and with the help of his wife, Nola, operated successfully until 1935. They spread a network of tent circuits across Canada from the Pacific into Ontario, edging into Québec, and pushing into the northern fringes of settlement across the prairies.

Chautauqua programs consisted of 4 to 6 days of musical numbers, lectures, dramatic productions and magic or puppet shows. A different performance was presented daily, and performers then moved on to the next town on the circuit. Keeping workers, artists, tents and equipment moving smoothly along the circuits required careful organization and many employees. A total of some 50 young men handled the tents and approximately 80 young women helped organize local committees and directed the operation. These people, mainly university students, developed initiative, self-confidence and skills that gave them an excellent foundation for success in life.

Chautauqua was good family entertainment and the people loved it. To many it provided their only opportunity for a cultural experience. It broadened horizons and brought colour and beauty into many lives. Its end can be attributed to changes in popular taste, the increasing availability of movies and the spread of radio, as well as to an easing of Depression conditions.

SHEILAGH S. JAMESON

Reading: Sheilagh S. Jameson, *Chautauqua in Canada* (1979).

Chauveau, Pierre-Joseph-Olivier, lawyer, educator, politician, premier of Québec 1867-73 (b at Charlesbourg, LC 30 May 1820; d at Québec 4 Apr 1890). Elected to the Assembly of the Province of Canada in 1844, he later held several Cabinet posts. He resigned from the Assembly in 1855 to become superintendent of education, a post he held until 1867, during which time the 15-member Council of Public Instruction was set up to supervise the school system. Conservatives John A. MACDONALD and George-Étienne CARTIER chose him to become the first premier of Québec, replacing J.É. CAUCHON in 1867, and Chauveau sat in both the provincial and federal houses. He was not a memorable premier and was persuaded to resign in 1873 to sit in the Senate. The following year, however, he unsuccessfully sought reelection to the Commons. In 1878 he began to teach in Laval's law faculty in Montréal and was its dean 1884-90. A man of letters, Chauveau was in demand as a lecturer, wrote extensively on education and other subjects, and wrote a novel, *Charles Guérin, roman de moeurs canadiennes* (1853, serialized 1846-47). DANIEL LATOUCHE

Chee Chee, Benjamin, artist (b Kenneth Thomas Benjamin at Temagami, Ont 26 Mar 1944; d at Ottawa 14 Mar 1977). After an unstable youth, Chee Chee, of Ojibwa descent, moved to Montréal in 1965 and was encouraged to develop his love of drawing. His first exhibition, held after his move to Ottawa in 1973, featured colourful abstract compositions of block-stamped geometric motifs. By 1976 his work had dramatically changed to spare, linear representations of birds and animals of great clarity and elegance, animated by a lively sense of humour and movement. Unlike other native artists, Chee Chee denied that his images had symbolic meaning; they were rather "creatures of the present" whose forms expressed aesthetic concerns. At the height of his success, after a renewal of a long-term problem with alcoholism, he committed suicide in an Ottawa jail. RUTH B. PHILLIPS

Cheese and Cheesemaking In Canada 327 730 t of cheese were produced in 1986; per capita consumption was 11.02 kg, consisting of 2.64 kg of Cheddar, 1.28 kg of Cottage and 7.10 kg of other cheeses. Consumption has increased more than threefold since 1950, aided by a wider selection of cheese varieties and better merchandising, transportation, refrigeration and packaging. Cheese, a valuable source of protein, energy, vitamins and minerals, is a useful alternative to meat in the diet: eg, Cheddar is composed of approximately 26% protein, 33% fat and 36% wa-

ter; creamed Cottage cheese, 12.5%, 4.5% and 79%, respectively.

Cheese was made for thousands of years as a means of preserving the valuable nutrients of milk. The first cheese was probably made from naturally soured milk, simply by allowing whey to drain from a bag, a procedure that can be used now for Cottage-type cheeses. Eventually, it was found that an enzyme from the fourth stomach of calves, kids or goats could coagulate milk. This enzyme, rennet, has been used for centuries for making most of the cheeses that we know today. Canadian settlers made cheese for their own use or for sale at markets. The first factory in Canada specializing in making cheese from milk from surrounding farms was opened by Harvey Farrington in Oxford County, CW [Ont], in 1864. A prototype of the early cheese factory operates at UPPER CANADA VILLAGE, Morrisburg, Ont. Factories proliferated quickly, reaching a peak of 2300 cheese factories and 570 combined cheese and butter factories at the turn of the century; about 10 000 t were exported annually to England at that time. Today, most cheese is made in large, automated factories; the largest was built in 1973 at Notre Dame du Bon Conseil, Qué, making 100 t daily. "Mammoth cheeses" were used for promotion, and aged Canadian Cheddar gained a reputation for top quality and fine flavour which it retains today. The largest cheese, the "Canadian Mite," weighed 10 t and was made in Perth, Ont. It was displayed at the World's Columbian Exposition in Chicago in 1893 and then in London, England, where eventually it was cut up and sold.

In cheesemaking, "starter" bacteria are added to milk to grow and convert the milk sugar (lactose) to lactic acid; rennet is added to coagulate the milk. The bacteria and rennet also aid in ripening and in the development of flavours typical of the variety. The curd is cut and usually cooked to 30-60°C. Whey comes out of the curd and is drained away; the curd is pressed in molds. Salt is added either before pressing or to the surface of the pressed cheese.

Cheese varieties differ because of variations in the making process. Differences in water, fat and salt contents of the cheese result in different firmness and taste. Differences in length and temperature of storage, and type of bacteria, YEAST OR MOLD also affect flavour and appearance. For example, the white mold, *Penicillium camemberti* or *P. candidum*, is used for Camembert cheese; the blue-green mold, *P. roqueforti*, is used for Blue cheese. The bacterium *Propionibacterium shermanii* gives the holes in Swiss-type cheeses. Most cheeses are ripened for periods of 2 weeks to 2 years to develop their distinctive flavour; eg, mild Cheddar is 1-2 months old, medium Cheddar, 5-8 months old and aged Cheddar, 10-24 months old. A few cheeses are not ripened and are consumed fresh, eg, Cottage, Cream and Ricotta cheeses. Processed cheese is made by grinding natural cheese, heating it to 70-80°C and cooling; added emulsifiers (eg, citrates, phosphates) give the typical smooth consistency.

Hundreds of varieties of cheese are made around the world. Canadian production includes Cheddar, Mozzarella, Cottage, Pizza, Ricotta, Brick, Brie, Caciocavallo, Camembert, Colby, Cream, Edam, Feta, Furlano, Gouda, Marble, Monterey Jack, Munster, Parmesan, Provolone, Romano, Scamorza, Trecca, Spiced, Swiss and Emmental. One of the earliest cheeses made in Canada by French settlers was "Isle d'Orleans" cheese. Probably Canada's best-known distinctive cheese other than Cheddar is Oka, originally developed and made by monks at the Trappist monastery in Oka, near Montréal. *See also* DAIRY INDUSTRY. D.B. EMMONS

Chemical Engineering is the technology of scaling up to commercial size chemical reactions which have been demonstrated in the laboratory. The sciences of CHEMISTRY, PHYSICS, BIOLOGY and MATHEMATICS underlie the ENGINEERING disciplines brought to bear on the design of safe and profitable chemical plants. An important objective of chemical engineering is to design the chemical reactors and physical processing equipment so that reactions proceed continuously, rather than occurring in batch operations. Because chemical engineers have become so adept at continuous processing, the CHEMICAL INDUSTRIES are skill and capital intensive, the ratio of employees to dollar revenue being low and the proportion of highly skilled employees being high. For the same reason, the chemical industries are quite scale-intensive, ie, the unit price of chemical products depends upon the size of the producing unit and the length of the production run.

The genesis of chemical engineering education in Canada was the formation in 1878 of a diploma program in Analytical and Applied Chemistry in the School of Practical Science, University of Toronto. In 1904 a course in chemical engineering was offered and in 1906 the School of Practical Science became the Faculty of Applied Science and Engineering. Twenty Canadian universities now offer undergraduate and graduate programs in chemical engineering. Details of the special research interests are published annually in the *Directory of Graduate Programs in Chemical Engineering in Canadian Universities.*

Canada's economy is still highly dependent on the RESOURCE industries, ie, FORESTRY, MINING, METALLURGY and ENERGY. The role of chemical engineering in these industries underlines the breadth of the profession. The PULP AND PAPER INDUSTRY involves the separation of lignin from cellulose and the formation, at very high speeds, of sheets which are amenable to a multitude of applications, the most important being in communications. Chemical engineers are involved in every phase: reactors for the digestion process, the behaviour of fibre suspensions, the application of surfactants and coatings, large-scale filtration and drying. Because the paper industry is so energy intensive, striking advances have been made in energy economy. Adhesive development has been crucial to the huge plywood industry.

In the metals industry, the flotation process depends upon knowledge of surface chemistry and the design of machines to exploit this knowledge in the concentration of ores. The revolution in the steel industry, the basic oxygen process, depended upon the development of plants for producing oxygen in tonnage quantities. The hydrometallurgical processes used for COBALT and NICKEL recovery at Sherritt Gordon depend upon research in reaction rates, diffusion, and heat and mass transfer.

The stability of modern life depends upon a sufficiency of energy and food. Because of the availability of hydroelectricity, Canada has an important world role in electrochemistry for metal refining and for the production of hydrogen, as a possible candidate for energy storage and transportation power. The technologies of PETROLEUM processing and of PETROCHEMICAL production (the basis of Canada's PLASTICS-PROCESSING INDUSTRY) are chemical engineering developments which have resulted in refineries throughout Canada and in a concentration of petrochemical industries in Ontario and Alberta. The Canadian NUCLEAR industry involves uranium extraction and concentration and the evolution of the CANDU reactor, made possible through extensive chemical engineering in the production of heavy water and purified uranium oxide, and in the transfer of heat under extreme conditions.

Responsibility for the productivity of the FOOD AND BEVERAGE INDUSTRIES is shared among agriculturalists, mechanical engineers and chemical engineers. The latter have made their contribution through the technology of the fertilizer industry, crucial to the continuity of current patterns of food consumption. In future, provision of protein and carbohydrate will provide a chemical engineering challenge as food processing increasingly employs the techniques of cryogenics, radiation preservation and high-vacuum technology. Here a bridge is forming to the emerging BIOTECHNOLOGIES, with their promising techniques of gene splicing, enzyme technology and new paths to chemical synthesis.

In addition to the foregoing examples, the chemical engineer makes large contributions to PHARMACEUTICAL, paint, TEXTILE, adhesive, health care and environmental technologies, as the bridge between the laboratory and the production-scale plant.

Societies The Canadian Society for Chemical Engineering is the principal technical organization of professional chemical engineers in Canada. It is a constituent society of the Chemical Institute of Canada, with a membership of over 2000 in 1987. In the same year, it was estimated that there were 10 000 chemical engineers in Canada. The society publishes the *Canadian Journal of Chemical Engineering* (est 1957) and organizes 2 conferences annually, a chemical engineering exhibition and professional development programs. In 1981, together with the Interamerican Congress of Chemical Engineering, the society hosted the Second World Congress of Chemical Engineering, held in Montréal and attended by 6500 chemical engineers from all over the world. In 1987 the society participated, along with other engineering societies, in the Engineering Centennial Conference in Montréal.

J.W. HODGINS

Chemical Industries Chemical MANUFACTURING entails the conversion of one material to another by a chemical reaction on a commercial scale. The starting material (feedstock) can be a natural substance or a relatively pure chemical used as an "intermediate" for subsequent upgrading. Hydrocarbons (ie, carbon-containing compounds) separated from natural gas or PETROLEUM are the most commonly used raw materials for PETROCHEMICALS, which range from relatively simple gases (eg, ethylene) to more complex solid compounds (eg, polyethylene). Other "organic" chemicals are also based on hydrogen and carbon and may be derived from COAL, sugar or similar nonpetroleum materials. Coexisting with thousands of organic compounds are inorganic chemicals, ie, chemicals normally obtained by processing various nonpetroleum MINERALS (eg, common SALT, LIMESTONE, POTASH, metallic ores) or atmospheric gases. Such classifications, historically evolved, are less precise than they might be. For example, inorganic nitrogen fertilizers, which embody atmospheric nitrogen in chemical combination, are not generally manufactured without burning natural gas for its hydrogen content.

History in Canada

At the turn of the century, the electrolytic production of chemicals was hailed as one of the modern marvels. Canada, having what then was estimated as 40% of the world's unharnessed HYDROELECTRIC potential, gained a modicum of attention as a home of large-scale chemical plants. Thomas WILLSON, a native of Princeton, Ont, built the first successful electric furnace to make calcium carbide from coke and lime and, in 1896, set up a manufacturing plant at Merritton, close to Niagara hydraulic power. He participated in the

establishment of Shawinigan Carbide Inc on the St-Maurice R in Québec, which began production in 1904. Meanwhile, 2 German chemists discovered that the nitrogen extracted from the atmosphere could be combined with the calcium carbide in a furnace to produce calcium cyanamide. The ability to "fix" atmospheric nitrogen in solid form meant that world AGRICULTURE no longer had to rely so heavily on Chilean sodium-nitrate deposits as the source of nitrogenous fertilizers. The N American licensee chose to exploit this new technology in a plant established on the Canadian side of Niagara Falls. By 1907 the electrochemistry that gave birth to 2 chemical multinationals (Union Carbide and American Cyanamid Co) had become a prominent part of Canada's nascent chemical-manufacturing industry. Along the Ottawa R, another furnace installation gave the country a local source of elemental phosphorus. William T. Gibbs used the since-depleted phosphate deposits along the Lièvre R in Québec as the raw material. He finally sold the Buckingham plant to a British firm in 1902 because the courts declared he was contravening the latter's patent.

Public awareness of chemical manufacturing rose sharply after 1914, when Canada was suddenly deprived of her main sources of potash, cyanide, dyestuffs and certain PHARMACEUTICALS. One response to the exigencies of war was a concerted effort to commercialize organic syntheses based on acetylene, the flammable gas generated from calcium carbide. Shawinigan Water & Power undertook the task of manufacturing key chemical intermediates (acetaldehyde, acetic acid and acetone) from acetylene in a separate manufacturing facility. Shawinigan was the chemical centre of Canada for the next few generations, producing vinyl resins and plasticizers as well as the organic intermediates. Other chemical firms located near the falls to make hydrogen peroxide, cellulose film, chlorinated solvents, chlorine and caustic soda.

WWII hurried the transition from electricity to OIL AND NATURAL GAS as the wellspring for chemical products. Shawinigan plants played a role in building up a munitions industry in Canada from 1939 to 1945. But this was the era of continuous processing of petroleum-refinery and other hydrocarbon products. Ammonia plants were built with government funds in Calgary, Alta, Trail, BC, and Niagara Falls, Ont, so that the operators could manufacture nitric acid and ammonium nitrate, the latter an effective blasting agent. Other wartime plants emerged, the most ambitious being along the western shore of the St Clair R in Ontario. Japanese occupation of the Far East RUBBER plantations prompted the Canadian government to pool the resources of 4 rubber-tire manufacturers, a Michigan styrene producer and a Sarnia petroleum refiner. The crown-owned Polymer Corp (known today as Polysar) was launched as an integrated supplier of several synthetic rubbers.

Once hostilities ceased, the direction of postwar chemical manufacture was dictated by the fact that Sarnia had a network of petrochemical plants. Discovery of oil at LEDUC, Alta, and completion of a PIPELINE from Alberta to Sarnia confirmed the St Clair R area as Canada's "chemical valley" during the next quarter century. A comparable buildup of petrochemical activities took place near Montréal, where a concentration of 6 petroleum refineries at the east end of the island provided an ample supply of both gaseous hydrocarbon by-products and relatively low-cost naphtha. Shawinigan's manufacture of organic chemicals was gradually transferred from the St-Maurice R location to the St Lawrence Valley (particularly Varennes on the south shore), but

others in the Montréal complex invested in thermoplastics (polyethylene and polypropylene) manufacturing.

Most of the installations in Montréal and Sarnia were modest by world standards and Canada still was not in a position to compete effectively in export markets. The US Gulf Coast states had come to dominate international trade in petrochemicals (including the major thermoplastics and man-made fibres) because producers there had access to low-cost natural-gas liquids. By the late 1970s, the dramatic rise in world oil prices, coupled with the increase in known natural-gas reserves in western Canada, altered the global economics of petrochemical manufacture. Several rounds of tariff reductions negotiated through the General Agreement on Tariffs and Trade also changed market patterns.

The result has been a pronounced preference by the larger chemical producers for investments predicated on natural-gas or associated liquids surplus to Canada's fuel requirements. Alberta has been home to several petrochemical works ever since the wartime ammonia plants were built. Two Edmonton-area developments of the 1950s presaged this migration to the West, although the construction of several pipelines to central Canada improved the viability of projects centered in Ontario. But the prospect is that Alberta will host most of the new world-scale manufacturing plants and that an increasingly important aspect of the chemical industry in Canada will be the efficient movement of large volumes of synthetic resins, organic intermediates and fertilizer materials to the US and to tidewater points. Chemical manufacturers stepped up capital spending rapidly, beginning in 1976. In the earlier part of that decade, they were collectively investing less than $200 million a year on plants and equipment. By the early 1980s, petrochemical producers alone had committed about $1.2 billion annually. Two large ammonia-based fertilizer projects were also completed during this time. Many projects were conceived when rising world oil prices and specific ENERGY POLICIES within Canada created a favourable climate for these investment decisions. The onset of the recession in 1981 and a downturn in petroleum prices led to the postponement of several ventures.

The Modern Industry

Chemical manufacturing is a diverse industry. In 1985 the shipment of manufactured chemicals (ie, industrial and fertilizer chemicals, and plastics and synthetics resins) amounted to $10.2 billion or 4.2% of all shipments of manufactured goods. The chemical industry ranked fifth in the manufacturing sector in Canada.

Location of Plants A handful of chemical companies produce a wide range of products, grossing over $1 billion each, but there are dozens of smaller companies as well. Almost 200 separate manufacturing plants in Canada produce at least one chemical for general sale. Most are located in central Canada because of the proximity of large cities, but every province, except PEI, has at least one chemical manufacturing operation. Some are associated with other processing activities: Trail, BC, for example, has for many years produced sulphuric acid, ammonia and fertilizer using the fumes from the zinc and lead smelters.

Ownership The large commodity chemicals can be successfully produced in Canada only with adequate economies of scale. This worldwide trend to higher levels of minimum scale has increased the influence of large multinationals endowed with sizable technological and financial resources and with global marketing skills (*see* FOREIGN INVESTMENT). Several major Canadian-owned corporations, however, have moved into the chemical business because they were already working in related areas. Cominco, NORANDA MINES and Sherritt Gordon Mines branched out into fertilizer manufacture. NOVA Corporation invested in petrochemicals as a corollary to its position in natural gas and associated liquids. Polysar, which had been set up to produce a few key petrochemicals during WWII, evolved almost logically into an international purveyor of synthetic rubbers and polystyrene.

In the late 1970s, various government agencies committed funds to chemical manufacture. The Société générale de financement established Ethylec Inc to participate in the Petromont consortium, operating 2 petrochemical plants in the Montréal area. The Potash Corporation of Saskatchewan acquired several operating potash mines in the province and has been studying the feasibility of investing further in fertilizer manufacturing. PETRO-CANADA is now a vendor of certain aromatic chemicals (benzene, toluene, xylenes) as a result of its purchase of the Petrofina interests in Montréal.

Technology The chemical industry is not built around any single technology. There are almost as many processes as there are establishments; the same product is often synthesized using different CHEMICAL ENGINEERING practices. Most processes have originated outside Canada. Yet Canadian chemical producers have consistently spent a significant percentage of gross income on INDUSTRIAL RESEARCH AND DEVELOPMENT. A membership survey by the Canadian Chemical Producers' Assn confirmed that chemical companies spend an average of about 1% of sales on R&D ($100 million or more annually); the average for all manufacturing industries was about 0.6% in the 1970s. In 1980 indirect expenditures on technical services, engineering, production support and other activities (indirectly related to improving technological excellence) came to $77.8 million.

Work Force In 1985, 24 318 people were employed in 3 major areas in the chemical industry. These figures are down from their 1980-81 peak as a result of the effect of the recession in the early 1980s. About half were in the petrochemical sector, 3181 were in the organic and specialty chemicals sector and 6750 were in the inorganic chemical sector. CHEMISTRY and engineering are common disciplines within the chemical industry and educational levels are high. In the petrochemical sector in 1985, for example, 2669 (18.5%) employees had a university degree. Canadian chemical workers do not belong to a single union. In Sarnia, Ont, the most active union is the Energy and Chemical Workers Union; in Montréal the Confederation of National Trade Unions is most prominent. There are independent unions in several locations. Unionization is least evident in newer companies in western Canada.

Energy Consumption The chemical industry accounts for 24% of energy used by all manufacturing industries in Canada. By most standards, the chemical industry is energy intensive, but not more so than certain other industries such as the pulp and paper industry or the primary iron and steel industry. Through the Canadian Industry Program for Energy Conservation, the chemical industry has been striving to use energy more efficiently, if only to be more competitive in world markets. The chemical industry has reduced its energy usage per unit of production some 31.2% since the base year of 1972, and it is involved in CIPEC's continuing program to reduce energy consumption by Canadian industries.

Export Status Chemical manufacturing relies heavily on exports. Fertilizers, generally not subject to custom duties, have long been shipped to external markets. In 1986, exports totalled $333.4 million (excluding potash, which is a mineral rather than a chemical-manufacture product). Exports of industrial inorganic chemicals in 1986 were worth $1.5 billion and industrial organic chemical exports were worth $1.1 billion. Industrial organic chemicals were in fact in a deficit situation in 1986, since imports amounted to $406.4 million more than exports. A dramatic shift in trading patterns has occurred in petrochemicals. In the past, Canadian chemical companies turned to foreign suppliers for products at the best possible prices. In the late 1970s the emergence of world-scale petrochemical facilities in Canada shifted the balance of trade toward net export, a trend that, with the exception of 1984, has continued. In 1985 petrochemical exports reached $1.94 billion, $209 million more than imports.

Government Control For many years there was no coherent government policy governing chemical manufacturing. It received about the same general tariff protection as other manufacturing sectors and Petrosar received some indirect federal support when the crown-owned CANADA DEVELOPMENT CORP acted as one of the principals. Ottawa has accepted the concept of 3 petrochemical centres in the country (Montréal, Sarnia and Alberta). The 1980 National Energy Program had a bearing on the fate of these centres in that it established different pricing regimes for petroleum and natural gas. For many years, a significant 10-20% tariff applied to chemicals not manufactured in Canada, but GATT negotiations have eroded this protection. In any event, Canadian export industries and agriculture have had access to duty-free imports through end-use drawbacks or other exemptions from the general tariff policy adopted by successive federal administrations.

Since chemicals are often toxic and have other adverse characteristics, they must be handled carefully during both manufacturing and transport (*see* HAZARDOUS WASTES). Thus, antipollution devices have been introduced into plants, and occupational health and safety considerations receive great emphasis (*see* OCCUPATIONAL DISEASE). Adverse effects on the environment and on the health of specific communities have been documented. MERCURY was released into waterways from certain chloralkali plants until it was shown in the 1970s that this heavy metal was being dissolved and incorporated into food chains. Mercury electrolyzers have since been shut down, fitted with special cleanup devices or replaced with electrolytic cells using a different technology. In other cases the production of chemical products believed to cause environmental problems has been affected. Fluorocarbons, used as aerosol propellants, provide a good example; their production in Canada was reduced after scientific studies indicated that they rise to the stratosphere and may destroy ozone, which protects life on Earth from the sun's ultraviolet radiation. Many aerosol producers now use other propellants.

Associations The chemical industry's commercial interests are most often handled through the Ottawa-based Canadian Chemical Producers' Assn (fd 1962). Many employees of the chemical companies are professional chemical engineers or chemists and are therefore usually members of the Canadian Society for Chemical Engineering (CSCE) or the Chemical Institute of Canada (CIC). CHARLES LAW

Chemistry, the science concerned primarily with the structure and properties of matter and with the transformation of one form of matter into another. Now one of the most theoretically and methodologically sophisticated sciences, chemistry had its beginnings in medieval alchemy. Because chemistry studies matter at a basic level, it is concerned with the physical sciences (eg, PHYSICS), the life sciences (eg, BIOCHEMISTRY, MEDICINE) and the earth sciences (eg, GEOLOGY, GEOCHEMISTRY). Not only do chemical studies result in an understanding of all natural processes, they also underpin production of many of the goods essential to daily living, ranging from food and drugs through the many substances used in the visual and plastic arts to heat and electricity. Chemical engineers specialize in the transfer of knowledge from the academic sphere to that of industry.

History and Training in Canada

Chemistry was first taught in Canada (1720) at the SÉMINAIRE DE QUÉBEC (in 1852, a sponsor of Université Laval). The first Canadian author of a chemistry textbook was J.B. Meilleur whose *Cours abrégé de leçons de chymie* was printed in Montréal in 1833. Perhaps the earliest academic recognition of the chemistry discipline was in 1837 when James Robb MD became professor of chemistry and natural science (botany and biology), King's College, Fredericton, now U of New Brunswick. By 1900 all universities in eastern Canada had chemistry departments, offered honours science degrees and had diversified into chemical physics and organic (ie, carbon-containing compounds) and inorganic chemistry. However, the rate of graduation of chemists was not high. By the end of WWI, a research focus had appeared and universities in the 4 western provinces had chemistry departments. Educational facilities expanded greatly after WWII, a trend that continued into the early 1970s. In later years, honours chemistry courses became more flexible, more interdisciplinary options were introduced and instrumental techniques played a much larger role in laboratory instruction. By the late 1970s and early 1980s, expansions of chemistry departments had stabilized as a result of budget restrictions, as had the number of chemists entering graduate studies. Some schools and faculties were combining facilities and personnel with neighbouring institutions to form chemical-research institutes.

Students are introduced to chemistry primarily at the high-school level. To become practising chemists, students require a university education. University course work involves classroom instruction and laboratory experience. After 3-4 years, the bachelor degree is awarded. Graduates may pursue graduate study or find employment, eg, in product and process control, analysis, science teaching, environmental planning and monitoring, technical sales, market research, scientific writing and management. Those with advanced degrees undertake research and teaching in post-secondary educational institutions or research institutes. The allied subjects of biochemistry and CHEMICAL ENGINEERING are taught in universities; chemical technology in community colleges.

The principles of chemistry are applied in most industries at one time or another because of the need for chemical analysis of raw materials and finished products. Major employers include various industries: chemical, pulp and paper, metallurgical, food and beverages, rubber, plastics, pharmaceuticals, petroleum, protective coatings, textiles, explosives and nuclear energy. During WWI the former Shawinigan Chemicals Ltd initiated industrial chemical research in Canada. The company's chemists developed a commercial process to make acetone required for explosives manufacturing. Today, most progressive companies carry out SCIENTIFIC RESEARCH AND DEVELOPMENT. Federal, provincial and a few municipal governments employ chemists in their control laboratories and research institutes.

The federal government's NATIONAL RESEARCH COUNCIL OF CANADA was established in 1916. Laboratory divisions, including a Division of Chemistry, were set up in 1928. One of NRC's scientists, Gerhard HERZBERG, won the Nobel Prize for Chemistry in 1971 for work in SPECTROSCOPY. A co-winner of the Nobel Prize for Chemistry in 1986 was John C. POLANYI, Dept of Chemistry, U of T, for his work on infrared chemiluminescence. The 7 provincial research councils conduct major programs in chemical research, the pioneer being the ALBERTA RESEARCH COUNCIL (est 1921). In Canada the universities are the major locations for fundamental chemical research. The earliest noteworthy work was done by physicist Ernest RUTHERFORD and chemist Frederick Soddy at McGill University at the turn of the century. They propounded the general theory of atomic disintegration, which was to earn Rutherford a Nobel Prize for Chemistry in 1908.

Chemistry in Use

The principles of chemistry are at work everyday all around us. In fact, our bodies are miniature chemical factories, producing a myriad of chemicals ranging from digestive acids to such esoteric organic chemicals as norepinephrine in the brain. We use the same principles to extract chemicals and chemical products from their natural environments (ie, the earth we walk on and the air we breathe) and transform them to enhance our daily lives. We mine or quarry the earth for inorganic chemicals (eg, salt, potash) and inorganic MINERALS (eg, limestone, gypsum) and nonferrous metallic ores, and for the source of organic (ie, carbon-containing) chemicals, petroleum, natural gas and other inorganics are extracted from the air, eg, nitrogen, oxygen, argon and neon. Chemicals are produced by the chemical industries and as by-products of smelting and petroleum refining.

Inorganic Chemicals The general public is largely unaware of the importance of inorganic chemicals to Canada's industrial health. We are all familiar with use of common salt as a condiment in the food industry, in restaurants and in homes. Few know, however, that salt is the starting material for producing chlorine, caustic soda and sodium chlorate. One or other of these chemicals is vital to the production of wood pulp, plastics, pharmaceuticals, disinfectants, pesticides, bleaches, ceramics, cosmetics, glass, rayon, detergents and aluminum. About 130 years ago, Canada was the world's largest exporter of potassium compounds, leached from wood ashes and used in soapmaking. Today, Canada is again a large exporter of potassium compounds in the form of potash (used in fertilizer) from large deposits in Saskatchewan. Limestone is another important chemical raw material. When heated in kilns, it forms lime, used as a flux to smelt iron ore and nonferrous ores, and to make wood-pulp cooking liquor. Until the advent of the petrochemical industry in Canada during WWII, inorganic limestone had been the basis of Canada's organic chemical industry, centered in Shawinigan, Qué. Limestone and coke from coal were allowed to react to produce calcium carbide, then to produce acetylene, the starting point for a variety of organic chemicals, synthetic resins and plastics. Acetylene was also used in welding. Cyanamide was the precursor of melamine-formaldehyde resins, used in the plastics industry to make tablewares. The cyanamide-based process was discontinued in the 1950s. When calcined, gypsum rock loses its water and can be used to make plaster wallboard or, in powdered form, to make molds

for medical or artistic purposes. Gypsum also slows the hardening time of portland cement, which itself is made by heating limestone with clay in large rotary kilns. Ammonia, another useful inorganic, is derived by combining nitrogen with hydrogen. Ammonia and its derivatives are used as fertilizers and also to make drugs, cosmetics, detergents, dyes and pesticides.

The metallurgical industries are also major sources of various inorganic chemicals produced as by-products during smelting operations. For example, since the 1920s, sulphur and sulphuric acid have been recovered from waste fumes resulting from the smelting of ores in Canada. These fumes continue to be a major source of this important acid, used in a vast number of chemical products and processes ranging from fertilizers and detergents to refining of nonferrous metals and petroleum. The other major source of sulphur is the sour natural gas found in Alberta. Recovery of sulphur from smelter fumes and sour natural gas reduces the ACID RAIN problem in Canada. Large volumes of the industrial gases nitrogen and oxygen are used in welding, food freezing and in medicine. Specialty gases (eg, argon, neon) are used for illuminated signs and for welding where inert atmospheres are required.

Organic Chemicals are created from crude oil and natural gas and, in smaller volume, from animal fats and vegetable oils. They are important ingredients in many consumer products. Canada's crude-oil deposits led to the start of the petrochemical industry, the products of which include alcohols, antifreeze, plastic resins, solvents, synthetic rubber, synthetic textile fibres and carbon black. Alberta's natural gas is used to produce chemicals such as benzene, toluene and methyl alcohol as well as elemental sulphur. Before the advent of petrochemicals, Canada's IRON AND STEEL INDUSTRY was the sole source for benzene, toluene and other "coal chemicals." With fears of a petroleum shortage, coal recently has become more interesting as a future source of organic chemicals; work on COAL GASIFICATION and liquefaction is under way at several Canadian research centres.

Specialty and Fine Chemicals contrast with "heavy chemicals" sold in tonnage quantities and used in various industrial processes. Specialty chemicals include such items as aerosols, detergents and water-treatment chemicals; flame retardants; food colorants and ingredients; pest-control agents; sanitary chemicals; waxes and polishes. Fine chemicals, including medicinals and pharmaceuticals, are specialized products that were first manufactured in local drugstores as early as the late 19th century. For example, only 4 months after the first use of chloroform in obstetrics in 1847, the chemical was made by an enterprising druggist-chemist in Pictou, NS. During WWI, manufacture of fine chemicals began to assume a substantial volume and Canadian manufacture of acetylsalicylic acid (ie, Aspirin) was begun. The manufacture of medicinal chemicals has since grown to include a range of products such as vitamins, hormones, antibiotics, etc. Other fine chemicals made in Canada include synthetic vanillin for flavours; citric acid for food and soft drinks; silver salts and iodines for the photographic industry; stearic acid and metal stearates for paints, lubricants, waterproofers and plastics; disinfectants for soapmakers and householders; silver chemicals for electroplating; cobalt salts to speed drying time of paints; and potassium iodide to add to table salt to prevent goitre. It is interesting to note that vanillin in Canada is produced as a by-product of the pulp and paper industry and that another by-product, lignin, is used as an ingredient in drilling muds for oil exploration.

In contrast with chemical-products industries

that produce chemicals, chemical-process industries use chemicals in making their products. Major examples of these "chemical-user" industries include pulp and paper (using sulphur, acids, alkalis, bleaches, starches, sizes, dyes and pigments); rubber tires and rubber goods (using synthetic rubber, carbon black, fillers, antioxidants, lubricants, antiozonants, detergents); plastics processing (using synthetic resins, carbon black, fillers and colours); and textiles (using synthetic fibres, soaps, detergents, dyes). Other areas such as agriculture and food use chemical fertilizers, herbicides, fungicides, insecticides and other crop-protection products; sulphur dioxide to produce starch; and oil from potatoes and corn.

Chemistry is closely linked with other science and engineering disciplines, as is shown by the following examples. In Vancouver, BC, the UBC Coal Research Centre was established in 1980. Its activities included coal geology and properties; mining and processing; use in coking, combustion and metallurgical processing; and conversion to gaseous and liquid fuels. The centre is made up of members of the departments of geological science, mining and mineral process engineering, metallurgical engineering, chemical and mechanical engineering and chemistry.

In the 1960s Merck Frosst Ltd scientists in Montréal began research on new drugs to control high blood pressure. A team of chemists, drawing on studies of their colleagues in biology and pharmacology, began synthesizing new organic chemicals to seek candidates and, by the late 1960s, developed a new chemical entity, called timolol maleate, which appeared to be a most promising new drug. Chemical engineering studies were carried out to develop a commercial production process and the drug was evaluated through pharmacy research and development. According to the Pharmaceutical Manufacturers Assn of Canada the process can take as long as 15 years. Timolol maleate passed the federal drug regulatory agency evaluation process in the late 1970s and enjoys a reputation for providing significantly effective therapy in several areas of medicine. Development and production required co-operation among chemists, biologists, toxicologists, pharmacologists, chemical engineers, physicians and pharmacists.

Societies and Journals

Chemical societies first appeared in Canada in 1902 with the McGill Chemical Society, Montréal, and the Canadian section of the Society of Chemical Industry (UK), Toronto. Over 100 people attended the first national conference in Ottawa in 1918, which led to formation of the first national society, the Canadian Institute of Chemistry (1920). The institute amalgamated with other groups in 1945 to form a new national scientific society, the Chemical Institute of Canada. By 1987 the CIC embraced 5600 chemists, 2400 chemical engineers, 1250 chemical technologists. The CIC is an umbrella organization for constituent societies: the Canadian Society for Chemical Engineering (est 1966), the Canadian Society for Chemical Technology (est 1970), and the Canadian Society for Chemistry (est 1985). Two separate societies in Ontario and Québec represent the nonscientific interests of chemists in provincial matters. Canadian chemists are also well served professionally by a number of journals. The *Canadian Journal of Research* was founded by the NRC in 1929 to publish original work in all sciences. Later, it was succeeded by several journals serving different disciplines, eg, the *Canadian Journal of Chemistry, Canadian Journal of Biochemistry and Cell Biology* and *The Canadian Journal of Technology*.

The latter was transferred to the CIC (and subsequently to the SCLE) in 1956 and renamed the *Canadian Journal of Chemical Engineering*. The CIC publishes a journal for general chemical news, *Chemistry in Canada*, which was founded in 1949 and renamed *Canadian Chemical News* in 1984. *See also* CHEMISTRY SUBDISCIPLINES.

DONALD W. EMMERSON

Chemistry Subdisciplines Early chemistry was principally analytical in nature; only as the body of experimental data increased did the present-day specialties evolve. The principal chemical subdisciplines are analytical, inorganic, organic and physical chemistry.

Analytical Chemistry

Analytical chemistry is the science of recognizing different substances and determining their constituents. Satisfactory methods are available for analysis of most of the major components of a material. The main problems arise in analysing for traces or for particular forms that may be present in a sample. Classical methods such as those using weight and volume (gravimetric and volumetric methods, respectively) are still used in analysis for major components and for standardization; however, measurement techniques have become increasingly sophisticated as desired detection limits continue to be lowered. For example, although all elements in Earth's crust are found in the ocean, only a dozen or so have concentrations above one part per million; most are at the part-per-billion level or less. Methods are being sought for nanogram (10^{-9}) to picogram (10^{-12}) quantities in a wide range of materials. Analysis at these levels requires more sensitive techniques and reduction of background effects; losses and contamination during sampling and storage become highly significant. As a result, considerable attention is being devoted to new preconcentration procedures that selectively concentrate and separate species of interest. Analytical procedures have been developed that use almost all the known chemical and physical properties of both atomic and molecular species. Procedures based on solution reactions, absorption and emission of radiation, thermal properties, optical properties, magnetic-field effects and electroanalytical behaviour are in common use. Computers have become commonplace for automation and handling of data.

Analytical chemistry contributes to daily living through the identification and monitoring of toxic substances in the environment and through the range of laboratory work required in industry (eg, food and beverages), the biological sciences (eg, medicine) and the physical sciences (eg, geology). Most screening programs and routine quality-control analyses are performed by automated equipment operated by technicians; analytical chemists advise on the selection of equipment, produce and develop new units, and ensure that procedures are scientifically sound.

Many unsolved analytical problems are retarding progress in all branches of science and the need for persons trained in analytical chemistry far exceeds the supply. It is therefore unfortunate that analytical chemistry has been largely neglected in Canada in the 20th century. Before WWII analytical chemistry research was done only at the universities of Alberta and Toronto. The Science Council of Canada's report, *Chemistry and Chemical Engineering in Canada* (1969), noted that there was a serious lack of university-trained personnel to carry out analytical chemistry research. A report on chemistry research personnel in Canadian universities (*Chemistry in Canada*, Nov 1978) pointed out that, of 25 universities with 15 or more chemists on the academic staff, only 2 (Alberta and Dalhousie) had a presence (group of 5 staff members) in analytical chemistry. By 1987, most chemistry departments in the major universities had only one or 2 analytical chemists in the faculty. Alberta and Dalhousie, with 6 staff members each, remained the major analytical schools in Canada. However, British Columbia, Saskatchewan (Saskatoon), McGill and Montréal were all actively expanding and developing their analytical chemistry departments. Of the older generation of analytical chemists, W.E. HARRIS (U of A) pioneered work in programmed temperature gas chromatography and D.E. Ryan (Dalhousie) established an institute for trace-analysis studies. Important contemporary research includes that of Walter Aue (Dalhousie) on gas chromatography, S. Berman (NATIONAL RESEARCH COUNCIL) on marine analytical chemistry, F.F. Cantwell (U of A) on liquid chromatography, C.L. Chakrabarti (Carleton) on atomic absorption, A. Chatt (Dalhousie) on nuclear analytical chemistry, N.J. Dovichi (U of A) on ultrasensitive laser based analytical instrumentation, D.J. Harrison (U of A) on chemical sensors, Gary Horlick (U of A) on instrumentation, electronics and spectroscopy, J. Hubert (U de M) on optical emission spectrometry and gas and liquid chromatography, Robert Jervis (University of Toronto), who pioneered Canadian research on identification of very low levels of mercury, B. Kratochvil (U of A) on sampling for chemical analysis, William Purdy (McGill) on studies in medical analytical chemistry, E.D. Salin (McGill) on atomic spectroscopy, R. Stephens (Dalhousie) on atomic spectroscopy, magneto-optic and electro-optic behaviour, and J. Van Loon (U of T) on environmental analysis.

D.E. RYAN

Inorganic Chemistry

Inorganic chemistry traditionally was concerned with the behaviour of chemical elements excluding carbon. Compounds based largely on carbon provided the basis for organic chemistry, but the boundary between inorganic and organic chemistry has become blurred. For example, a rapidly expanding field is organometallic chemistry which, being concerned with compounds containing metal atoms bound to one or several carbon atoms, bridges the 2 disciplines. In the early development of chemistry, inorganic chemistry included characterization of elements and the measurement of their physical properties (eg, boiling point, density); however, the main current concern of inorganic chemists is the chemical reactions that elements in combination undergo, and the identification and study of new compounds. In the early 20th century, the development of atomic theory made possible the organization of most information about the more common elements. From 1915 to 1940 inorganic chemistry developed more slowly. During WWII, however, it underwent a remarkable renaissance as a result of the need to understand the chemistry of uranium and other heavy elements, to separate the rare lanthanide elements (atomic numbers 57-71) and to determine their chemical behaviour (since these elements are formed in nuclear fission processes); to develop fully the chemistry of fluorine (since its high reactivity had previously limited its study), and to extend the chemistry of many other elements associated with the development of nuclear weaponry. Facilities at Chalk River, Ont, played a part in those developments and Canadian NUCLEAR RESEARCH ESTABLISHMENTS have continued this research.

In its present form, inorganic chemistry aims to understand the importance of reaction conditions (eg, reaction temperature), and thus find means to prepare new combinations of elements. For example, many inorganic reactions may be greatly modified by the solvent medium; therefore, much research involves inorganic reactions in different solvents, both organic (eg, benzene, alcohol) and inorganic (eg, liquefied ammonia, liquid sulphur dioxide). A second aim is to understand the detailed pathways by which reactions occur; a third, to determine the structure at the atomic level of the products of each reaction. Such structural information allows discussion of the binding forces that hold each molecule together.

In the 1970s and 1980s, considerable emphasis has been placed on aspects of inorganic chemistry related to the solid state and to compounds of the transition metals (eg, cobalt, platinum). Study of solid states has led to preparation of many new materials and to attempts to comprehend the electrical and mechanical properties of solids (relevant to the ELECTRONICS INDUSTRY and to the current interest in preparing new superconducting materials). Transition metals form numerous organometallic derivatives, many of which catalyze other chemical reactions, eg, syntheses of important chemical fuels, such as methanol.

Inorganic chemistry is particularly important to Canada's economy because of the significance of MINERAL RESOURCES. The development of Canada's extraction industries (eg, nickel, potash, lead, zinc, uranium) has involved the application of inorganic chemistry; however, Canada has been a significant contributor to the field mainly since the 1950s. Significant work in the field includes pioneering studies on acids by R.J. Gillespie (McMaster), work on organometallic chemistry by H.C. Clark and W.A.G. Graham, and X-ray diffraction studies of inorganic materials by J. Trotter (UBC). In 1962 N. Bartlett (UBC) showed that the so-called inert gases (now called noble gases) are not, in fact, inert but are capable of forming stable chemical compounds (eg, xenon tetrafluoride). In 1965 A.D. Allen and C.V. Senoff, at U of T, showed that molecular nitrogen can be bound chemically to a metal atom, thus laying the foundation for much of the present intensive search for alternative economical routes to nitrogen fixation (which is of enormous significance to Canadian crop production).

H.C. CLARK

Organic Chemistry

The isolation of products from animal and plant fluids and tissues has interested humans since antiquity. Few pure substances were identified before the 19th century. Then, as now, animal and plant products were extremely complex mixtures of largely nonvolatile molecules. Because these substances were derived from living organisms, those involved in investigating them were called organic chemists. The different materials that could be isolated all contained the element carbon. During the 19th century, the inventory grew rapidly of organic compounds that could be isolated in high purity, either directly (as naturally occurring products) or as derivatives (of their thermal or chemical degradation). The carbon content was found to vary greatly among them, and the most common other elements were hydrogen, nitrogen and oxygen. Sulphur and phosphorus also were often present but other elements occurred rarely. As both organic and inorganic (ie, mineral) reagents became available, the theory of organic chemistry developed rapidly. It became apparent that products from natural sources and related new substances could be synthesized from nonliving sources, using increasingly well-understood reaction pathways. These developments made possible an understanding of the molecular structures of organic compounds and their reaction properties.

Complex organic molecules owe their existence to a strong tendency for carbon atoms to share their electrons with other atoms, in strong, direct covalent bonds. This property is the source of the molecular structures that comprise the largest part of dry living matter, and of the over one million man-made synthetic compounds developed over the past century. The chemical manipulation of hydrocarbon molecules, derived mainly from petroleum, has given rise to such indispensable items as synthetic plastics, resins, fibres, rubbers, adhesives, paints, detergents, pesticides and explosives. The wide range of prescription drugs of the modern pharmaceuticals industry owe their existence to the knowledge and skills of organic chemists. Organic chemistry has also made major contributions to human pleasure, eg, through dyes, colour photography, perfumes, flavours and sweetening agents.

As a result of the continually increasing and widespread use of its basic principles, organic chemistry in the 20th century has become a mainstay of other scientific disciplines, both within and outside the field of chemistry. Indeed the processing of animal and plant tissues and studies of biological transformations have passed to new disciplines including BIOCHEMISTRY, PHARMACOLOGY, DIETETICS and MOLECULAR BIOLOGY. Nevertheless, although the field has become only marginally concerned with living matter, the term lives on to describe activities that concentrate on the chemistry of carbon-containing compounds. The term "bioorganic chemistry" refers to efforts to use the theory of organic chemistry to imitate living processes. The power of modern synthetic organic chemistry is illustrated by the completion (1973) of the chemical synthesis of vitamin B_{12}. Similar challenges continue to be met in laboratories throughout the world. The technologies behind the space program have also had a revolutionary effect on organic chemistry. In recent decades, developments in computer science, electronics, detectors and materials have placed at the disposal of organic chemists an array of sophisticated instruments for separation, identification and structural analysis of matter. In the case of living matter, such analysis raises moral issues which society, rather than organic chemists, biochemists, geneticists and microbiologists, will have to explore (*see* BIOETHICS, GENETIC ENGINEERING).

Much notable work in Canada has been carried out on naturally occurring compounds. Perhaps the most significant discovery was that of INSULIN by F.G. BANTING, C.H. BEST, and J.B. COLLIP at U of T (1922). The early work on alkaloids by L.E. MARION and R.H.F. MANSKE at the National Research Council in Ottawa, the first laboratory synthesis of sucrose by R.U. LEMIEUX at the Prairie Regional Laboratory of NRC in Saskatoon (1953), the first synthesis of ABO and other human blood group determinant, also by Lemieux, at the U of A (1975) and the brilliant syntheses of many natural products by K. WIESNER at the University of New Brunswick, all have received worldwide attention. Gobind KHORANA, who won the Nobel Prize for medicine in 1968 for his work on the genetic code, carried out his early work at the BRITISH COLUMBIA RESEARCH COUNCIL, Vancouver.   R.U. LEMIEUX

Physical Chemistry

Physical chemistry begins with the measurement and calculation of the physical properties of atoms and molecules in the gaseous, liquid and solid states (phases). Physical chemists use these results to characterize systems in chemical equilibrium; to study the energy, rate and direction of chemical transformations; and to understand the atomic and molecular structure of matter. In contemporary physical chemistry these goals are met through the study of chemical thermodynamics, SPECTROSCOPY, kinetics and theoretical chemistry.

Chemical Thermodynamics involves the calculation of energy (measured as heat and work) and the evaluation of entropy (degree of randomness). When energy, entropy and chemical potential are known, physical chemists can characterize equilibria in reactions, in solutions and between phases. Electrolysis, the formation of emulsions, the mechanism of transport through membranes and the description of adsorption on surfaces are a few examples of contemporary chemical problems that are treated using thermodynamics and statistical mechanics. The extension of thermodynamic principles to far-from-equilibrium systems (eg, biological systems with their highly ordered structures) has been successfully undertaken by physical chemists.

Spectroscopy The energy of atoms and molecules is available in small packets called quanta, which are characteristic of the energy of electronic, vibrational and rotational motions. Each quantum is associated with a particular wavelength of electromagnetic radiation and appears as a distinct line in a spectrum. Analysis of spectral lines in the visible and ultraviolet range has clarified the electronic structure of atoms and molecules; that of infrared spectra gives bond stretching and bending characteristics and, for simple molecules, bond lengths. X-ray crystallography permits the determination of nuclear positions even in very large molecules.

Chemical Kinetics involves measurement and interpretation of the rates at which molecules, atoms, ions and radicals react to form new products. The effect of pressure, temperature, concentration of reactants and radiation allows kineticists to specify how reactions occur in terms of collisions, transition complexes, intermediates and reaction paths. The study of gas-phase reactions has provided insight about how energy is redistributed as the reaction progresses; indeed the role of the electronic, vibrational and rotational states involved can be examined.

Theoretical Chemistry involves using fundamental principles of PHYSICS and MATHEMATICS to create models for chemical processes. It is best known for its role in explaining chemical bonding. The laws of quantum physics are essential in interpreting and directing spectroscopic measurements. Similar contributions have been made in the evolution of models for kinetic studies, particularly for the redistribution of energy in elementary reactions. With the aid of statistical mechanics, thermodynamic quantities (eg, specific heat) and transport properties (eg, viscosity) have yielded to theoretical interpretation. Computational chemistry began in the 1960s when large-capacity computers became available. Contemporary programs in quantum chemistry not only produce molecular orbitals and electronic energy levels but also provide a wide variety of molecular properties. Complex reaction schemes can be modelled, synthetic spectra can be produced, and even properties of fluids can be calculated by computer programs.

Physical chemistry began to take shape in the 1870s when Willard Gibbs's thermodynamics treatise appeared. By the 1890s, electrochemistry was a major preoccupation of physical chemists, especially for industrial applications (*see* METALLURGY), and by the early 1900s physical chemists were deeply involved in the study of radioactivity. The assimilation of results of work in other fields has continued and some ideas (eg, quantum theory) have changed the course of physical chemistry. Other ideas, such as nuclear-magnetic resonance and infrared spectroscopy, were nurtured and perfected by physical chemists and have emerged as essential tools in all chemical subdisciplines.

The past century has seen major Canadian contributions to this development of physical chemistry, from the thermodynamic work of William Lash MILLER in the 1890s to the spectroscopic stud-

ies of Gerhard HERZBERG in the 1980s. The electrochemical innovations of T.L. WILLSON (calcium carbide production patent, 1893) and A.E. LeSueur (chlorine production for bleaching paper pulp, 1888) received worldwide application and provided the impetus for Canadian hydroelectric development and the pulp and paper industries. This early interest in classical thermodynamics was furthered by Andrew GORDON (U of T), who carried out the first calculation of thermodynamic properties of triatomic molecules (1932), by the careful measurements of Otto MAASS on critical phenomena (1930s) and by the phase rule analyses of A.N. CAMPBELL (University of Manitoba, 1930s-60s). The work of R. Scheissler and J.H. Ross in developing explosives, during WWII, and the more recent development of improved recovery processes for copper-nickel mining and for extraction of BITUMEN from oil sands are examples of Canadian applications of classical thermodynamics to industrial problems. The modern experiments and analysis of S.G. Mason (Pulp and Paper Institute, Montréal) for fluid and particle flow have received worldwide recognition. Studies of radioactivity and atomic and nuclear structures came early to Canada, and the work of physical chemists, such as Ernest RUTHERFORD (on the atom) and Frederick Soddy (radioactivity) at McGill, led to Nobel prizes (in 1908 and 1921, respectively). This interest evolved into contemporary expertise in radiation chemistry (the use of cobalt-60 gamma radiation in cancer therapy was developed first in Canada by Harold JOHNS), to isotope separation (by H.G. THODE) and isotope-labelling techniques in tracer work (by J.W.T. SPINKS) and into the nuclear power reactor CANDU. The pioneering contributions of E.W.R. STEACIE (NRC), Carl Winkler (McGill) and M. Polanyi (U of T) to gas phase and solution kinetics placed Canada in a position to develop a polymer industry (wartime products, such as synthetic rubber, were manufactured at Polysar, Sarnia). This Canadian prominence in free radical chemistry and photochemistry has been carried forward by the conceptual contributions of J. POLANYI (U of T) and by experiments with photosensitized mercury carried out by H.E. GUNNING (U of A). Indeed, John Polanyi's observation of infrared chemiluminescence and its significance for chemical lasers was recognized by a Nobel prize in 1986. Another outstanding contribution of a Canadian to physical chemistry is the work of Herzberg, whose exhaustive investigation of the spectroscopy of small molecules culminated in a Nobel Prize in 1971.

In looking to the future the clearest trend in physical chemistry is the resurgence of interest in the complex chemistry of the liquid and solid phases. Certainly physical chemistry will also turn more and more to the study of biological processes. Computational chemistry must surely continue to expand and with it will come the opportunity to develop and test theoretical models, to do computer experiments.   W.G. LAIDLAW

Chenier, Georges, snooker player (b at Hull, Qué 1907; d at Toronto 16 Nov 1970). Chenier was the outstanding Canadian snooker player for a generation. He was N American champion 1947-70, even after suffering strokes in 1966 that reduced his stamina and caused partial paralysis. He was a leading challenger for the world championship. In 1950 he briefly held the world record high run with a break of 144. Chenier was also a leading pool player. In the 1963 world championships he became the first to run 150 and out. *See* BILLIARDS.   GRAHAM DUNCAN

Chénier, Jean-Olivier, medical doctor and PATRIOTE (b at Lachine or Montréal 9 Dec 1806; d at St-Eustache, LC 14 Dec 1837). Admitted to the practice of medicine in 1828, Chénier set up his offices in the village of St-Benoît [Mirabel] and quickly became involved in politics with the Patriote leaders of the Deux-Montagnes region. He moved his practice to St-Eustache in 1836. He played a very active role in the popular assemblies of 1836 and 1837, which called for the boycott of British goods and which, in the fall of 1837, suggested replacing justices of the peace and militia officers named by the government with people chosen in popular elections. Chénier was the main organizer of the St-Eustache camp during the armed resistance of the "Patriotes du Nord." He was killed in combat when, under the command of John COLBORNE, the regular army and volunteers overcame the fortified positions being defended by Chénier and his men at ST-EUSTACHE. *See also* REBELLIONS OF 1837.   JEAN-PAUL BERNARD

Cherry, common name for certain members of genus *Prunus* of the ROSE family, which produce small, fleshy single-stoned fruits (drupes). Two species, sweet cherry (*P. avium*) and sour cherry (*P. cerasus*) are grown for fruit. The mahaleb cherry (*P. mahaleb*) is used as a rootstock. Sweet cherries are native to Europe and western Asia; sour cherries, to Asia Minor. Cherry trees are tall, with reddish brown bark, large tapered leaves, white blossoms and black, red or yellow, round or heart-shaped fruit. Sweet cherries are grown in southern BC and southern Ontario, where cultivation hazards are minimal. Sweet cherry trees and fruit buds are sensitive to winter frosts; blossoms, to spring frosts; and the fruit is susceptible to cracking and to rot in rain. Sweet cherry trees are very large and are difficult to handle; until recently all cultivars were self-sterile and required selected pollenizers (ie, another plant source of pollen). Lately, self-fertile cultivars (eg, Stella) and dwarf mutants (eg, Compact Lambert, Compact Stella) have been grown. The main sweet cherry cultivars are Lambert, Bing, Van, Hedelfingen; sour cherry, Montmorency. Canadian plantings of cherries total 3000 ha. Cherry fruit is flavourful and rich in minerals, organic acids, riboflavin and niacin. Sweet cherries are consumed mostly fresh; sour cherries, as preserves. In 1985, 8690 t of sweet cherries were produced in Canada with a farm value of $8.9 million; 7349 t of sour cherries, valued at $6.2 million. In 1986, 4203 t of sweet cherries and 4549 t of sour cherries were produced.   K.O. LAPINS

Chesapeake During the NAPOLEONIC WARS, Britain insisted on the right to search neutral ships on the high seas for Royal Navy deserters. On 22 June 1807 HMS *Leopard* forcibly took 4 seamen from the American frigate *Chesapeake*. Despite apologizing to the US government and returning the 2 seamen who were Americans, the British continued to claim the right of inspection. This angered the American public, and the incident contributed to the tension leading to the WAR OF 1812. Britain gained a symbolic victory during the war when HMS *Shannon* captured the *Chesapeake* off Boston on 1 June 1813 and later towed her triumphantly into Halifax harbour.

CARL A. CHRISTIE

Chesapeake Affair On 7 Dec 1863, during the AMERICAN CIVIL WAR, 16 Confederates seized American coastal steamer *Chesapeake* off Cape Cod and diverted it to Saint John, NB. After refueling, it moved into Nova Scotian waters, where local residents co-operated with the hijackers. An American naval vessel then seized the ship within British waters, capturing with her 2 Nova Scotians. USS *Dacotah* towed the recaptured steamer into Halifax harbour, where in a melee one of the Nova Scotians escaped. The American vice-consul charged the Haligonians with violation of the ASHBURTON-WEBSTER TREATY. The inci-

dent, though ultimately harmless, vividly illustrated the hostility Maritimers felt towards the Northern States.   ROBIN W. WINKS

Chess About 20% of adult Canadians play at least one game of chess a year. These games are mostly played for fun in backyards and basements, but for several thousand tournament players chess is a serious game. In 1987 there were 3069 active players in Canada who had been "rated" according to their results in tournaments. Organized chess began in Canada in 1844 in Montréal with the establishment of the first chess club. The Canadian Chess Association was established in Hamilton in 1872 for the purpose of organizing Canadian championships. The modern descendant of this organization, the Chess Federation of Canada (CFC), has an office in Ottawa and sponsors a bimonthly magazine, *En Passant*. The CFC is affiliated with the World Chess Federation (FIDE) and the Canadian champion automatically qualifies for the Interzonals, the international preliminary events to determine world-title challengers.

As of 1987 there have been 65 Canadian Closed championships, played as round robins with entry restricted to provincial champions or top-rated players. Canadian Open championships, open to anyone, have been held since 1956 and usually involve 10 rounds of Swiss pairings in which players with the same scores are matched. The first Canadian Open in 1956 drew a field of 88, including a young Bobby Fischer. Kingston, 1966, was the first Open to draw over 100 players. The record entry was 648 in 1974 at Montréal. The Canadian women's championship was first held in 1975 in Ottawa, with Smilja Vujošević of Toronto winning the title. In 1978 in Vancouver and 1981 in Toronto the finals were won by Nava Shterenberg, a Soviet émigrée residing in Toronto. Junior championships of Canada have been held since 1970, with 12 players since 1978 in round-robin competition.

Canada has 7 women who possess the title of International Woman Master. They are Vujošević, Shterenberg, Angela Day, Diane Mongeau, Céline Roos, Vesma Baltgailif and Urmila Das. On the men's lists Canada has 3 international grandmasters (D.A. ("Abe") YANOFSKY, Duncan SUTTLES and Kevin Spraggett) and 11 international masters (George Kuprejanov, Geza Fuster, Laszlo Witt, Leon Piasetski, Bruce Amos, Zvonko Vranešić, Camille Coudari, Lawrence Day, Jean Hébert, Bryon Nickoloff and Igor Ivanov).

Canada has been the site of some important international matches. Montréal was one of the sponsors of the 1894 world championship match where Wilhelm Steinitz lost the title to Emanuel Lasker. Bobby Fischer's path to the world championship included a candidates match in 1971 at Vancouver, where he eliminated Soviet grandmaster Mark Taimanov by winning 6 straight games. Toronto hosted the 1957 world junior championship (won by American Bill Lombardy) and a Grandmaster Invitational was held in Winnipeg in 1967, to celebrate Canada's Centennial. Bent Larsen of Denmark and Klaus Darga of West Germany were joint winners. In 1979 one of the strongest grandmaster events ever held anywhere took place in Montréal. This "Tournament of Stars" was won jointly by world champion Anatoly Karpov and former champion Mikhail Tal.

Canada has competed in the World Team championships (Olympiad) 12 times since 1939, when the Canadian team at Buenos Aires placed 17th among 27 teams. In Olympiads up to 6 players comprise a team, although only 4 boards are played in a match. Canada's 1939 team had 5-time Canadian champion J.S. Morrison on first board and 14-year-old Winnipeg prodigy D.A.

Yanofsky on second. Yanofsky was the sensation of the tournament and won the prize for the best percentage on second board. Unfortunately, this Olympiad was interrupted by WWII, and it was not until 1946 at Groningen that Yanofsky had a chance to play in Europe. He had his best individual result there, defeating soon-to-be world champion Mikhail Botvinnik. After the war, a number of chess masters arrived from Eastern Europe, including Fyodor Bohatirchuk from Ukraine, ex-champion of Lithuania Paul Vaitonis and ex-champion of Hungary Geza Fuster. In 1954 Canada competed in the 11th Olympiad at Amsterdam, finishing 14th among 26 teams. Yanofsky played top board followed by Frank Anderson of Toronto, and by Vaitonis and Bohatirchuk. Anderson had been bedridden most of his youth and learned chess during this period. He won the second-board prize at Amsterdam and repeated the feat in the 1958 Olympiad at Munich, where Canada finished 15th among 36 teams. Had Anderson's ill health not kept him from an active chess career, he would have become a grandmaster.

At Tel Aviv in 1964 Canada had its best result yet, finishing 12th among 50 countries. The team was Yanofsky, Anderson, Zvonko Vranešić of Toronto, who had defected from a Yugoslavian soccer team in Paris, Elod Macskasy of Vancouver and Laszlo Witt of Montréal (both Hungarian émigrés) and prodigy Duncan Suttles of Vancouver. Yanofsky had his best result ever and received the Grandmaster title. Havana 1966 was a disappointment as Canada missed the finals (finishing 23rd among 52). But Canada rebounded at Lugano 1968, taking 13th among 53 countries, and it did even better at Siegen, 1970, ending 11th among 60 countries. The powerhouse of the 1968 team was Suttles, while in 1970 Vranešić had the best score.

In the late 1960s young Canadians were rising to challenge the immigrant masters. Lawrence Day first appeared on the team in 1968 and Bruce Amos in 1970. In the 1969 Canadian championship, Suttles took the title by a narrow $2\frac{1}{2}$-$1\frac{1}{2}$ margin in a playoff with Vranešić. In 1971 Canada played for the first time in the World Student Team championship, held in Puerto Rico, and was very successful, winning the bronze medal and missing the silver by only one-half point. The USSR won with future world champion Karpov on third board. Canada's team was Suttles, Amos, Day, Camille Coudari, Denis Allan and Peter BIYIASAS. Biyiasas advanced rapidly, winning the 1972 Closed at Toronto and the 1975 Closed at Calgary. At the 1972 Olympiad at Skopje, Canada was passed in the preliminaries by Sweden and finished a disappointing 19th among 62 countries. Later in the year Suttles became Canada's second grandmaster with a tremendous result at San Antonio. The 1974 Nice Olympiad was Canada's worst result ever, its team finishing 24th among 73 teams, but in 1976 at Haifa Canada rebounded to take 8th place in a field of only 48 teams (the event was boycotted by the Soviet Bloc). Biyiasas led the Haifa team and picked up the first third of his Grandmaster title. Good results at Lone Pine, 1978, and New York, 1978, confirmed his title just before the 1978 Closed in Toronto, where Jean Hébert of Québec City was the winner. Biyiasas represented Canada in the 1978 Olympiad at Buenos Aires, where he had a prizewinning score on second board, powering the team to a tie for 7th to 11th in a field of 66 countries. In 1979 Biyiasas immigrated to the US.

In 1980 at Malta, Canada finished by sharing 8th to 9th in a record field of 82. The team was Hébert, Day, Yanofsky, Yugoslav émigré Milan Vukadinov, Vranešić and Allan. At Malta Canada also played in the women's Olympiad, finishing

17th to 24th in a field of 42 countries. The team was Nava Shterenberg, Céline Roos (a French émigrée residing in Montréal), Urmila Das (a Czech émigrée residing in Calgary) and Angela Day. The 1982 Olympiad was held in Lucerne, Switzerland. Canada's men's team shared 15th to 20th in a field of 92 countries and the women's team finished 17th to 22nd in a field of 45. In 1984 in Thessaloniki, Greece, Canada's men's team shared 17th to 20th in a field of 91 countries and the women's team finished 17th in a field of 51. That year, Céline Roos won a gold medal for second board. In the 1986 Olympiad, held in Dubai, United Arab Emirates, 108 men's teams competed. Canada shared 18th to 23rd and no women's team was sent that year. The next Olympiad is scheduled for 1988 in Greece.

In July 1980 Igor Ivanov took advantage of the Gander stopover on the Havana to Moscow air route to defect to Canada. Within a year the Russian had firmly established himself as Canada's top player. At the 1981 Closed in Montréal he won easily ahead of Kevin Spraggett and Hébert.

In 1981 Suttles became Canada's first postal grandmaster. After an absence of 6 years from over-the-board play, Suttles shared first place with English grandmaster Tony Miles in an international Swiss at Vancouver in 1981. Suttles has an international reputation as one of the pioneers of modern chess strategy, and many of his novel ideas have been adopted by modern masters. Because of Canada's geographical remoteness from the European mainstream of chess theory, Canadians have often adopted openings unusual for their time. N.A. MacLeod, who represented Canada in the great 1889 New York tournament (the de facto Candidates of its day), specialized in what later became known as the Hippopotamus Defence; W.H. Pollack at Hastings 1895 played the Modern Benoni Defence, then quite unexplored. Canadian style in chess involves noncommital preservation of options often connected with a slow development of the pieces.

LAWRENCE DAY

Reading: Chess Canada, July/Aug 1972; *Chess Canada Echecs*, July 1977; and B. Kažić, *International Championship Chess* (1974).

Chester, NS, UP, pop 1170 (1986c), 1131 (1981c), 72 km W of Halifax, is situated on a point of land bounded by a harbour, at the N end of MAHONE BAY. In 19th-century NS coastal commerce Chester was important as a site of shipping, shipbuilding, lumbering and fishing. Its sheltered bay, favourable climate and natural beauty encouraged its gradual change to a popular summer retreat. Part of the Municipality of Chester from 1879, the village (first called Shoreham) of Chester was colonized in 1761, when New Englanders arrived and were greeted by about 30 well-established families; 2 sawmills were already in operation. Chester grew little through the 19th century; no direct roadway was built between Halifax and Chester until 1848. Today some light industry is carried on, the summer tourist industry flourishes and most of the labour force is engaged in support or professional services. The village's varied architectural composition includes several 18th-century buildings as well as many from the 19th century; the summer homes reflect this diversity. G.B. HALIBURTON

Chesterfield Inlet is a narrow, fjordlike arm of the NW coast of HUDSON BAY that stretches 160 km inland to the THELON R. It marks a physiographic divide along the bay, separating a narrow, rocky coastal plain backing onto a plain and hilly area to the N, from an enormous area of low relief, with poorly developed drainage farther S. Its climate is noteworthy for its windiness, since the inlet is aligned with the prevailing winds from the NW,

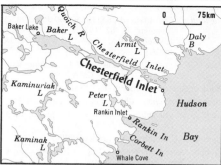

which are remarkably strong in winter (mean velocity 8.7 m/s, reaching 36 m/s) and constant, blowing on average 20% of the time. The area was first explored 1761-62 by Capt Christopher, an officer in the HBC. The inlet was named for the earl of Chesterfield. DOUG FINLAYSON

Chestnut (*Castanea*), genus of trees of BEECH family (Fagaceae). Of 10 known species, one, American chestnut (*C. dentata*), is indigenous to Canada. Its distribution is limited to N of Lk Erie. This species is on the verge of disappearing in N America because of the ravages of a blight caused by a fungus which appeared at the end of the 19th century. The few surviving trees barely reach 10 m in height; formerly specimens reached more than 30 m in height and 1 m in diameter. Leaves are alternate and spear shaped, with coarsely toothed margins. European sweet chestnut (*C. sativa*) is occasionally planted as an ORNAMENTAL. Horse chestnut (*Aesculus hippocastanum*), also an ornamental, is not related, although it can be mistaken for *Castanea* species. Chestnuts normally grow in sandy or gravelly, well-drained soils. The fruit is edible. The light, soft, decay-resistant wood was once used for posts and poles.

ESTELLE LACOURSIÈRE

American chestnut (*Castanea dentata*) (*artwork by Claire Tremblay*).

Chéticamp, Inverness Co, NS, UP, pop 979 (1986c), 3009 (1981c), is located on the Gulf of St Lawrence, 48 km NE of Inverness. The origin of the name is uncertain. Denys knew it as Chadye (1672), but the fishing station that started in 1752 was called Chéticamp. Cheticamp I, joined by a small isthmus to the mainland, became headquarters for the Jersey merchant, Robin, whose fishing business dominated the economy after 1776. His first employees, 14 Acadian fishermen, were seasonal residents only. In 1782 the Bois and Richard families settled. Eight years later, 26 Acadian families were living here, and by 1820 the population was 784. Early industries included fish plants and lobster canner-

ies, cod liver oil extraction, and mining for gold and galena. On the Cabot Trail, 4.8 km SW of Cape Breton Highlands Park, Cheticamp depends on fishing, farming, tourism and its longtime cottage crafts of tapestry and rug making.

JUDITH HOEGG RYAN

Chetwynd, BC, District Municipality, pop 2774 (1986c), located in the Pine R valley in the northeast corner of BC, 310 km N of Prince George, at the junctions of highways 97 and 29. Originally called Little Prairie, the community was renamed Chetwynd in the 1950s after Ralph Chetwynd, a BC pioneer and minister of railways in the Social Credit government. There was little development in the region until after WWII. With the extension of highways and BC Rail (formerly Pacific Great Eastern), Chetwynd has become a service centre for forestry, oil and gas fields and the northeastern coalfields. Two sawmills are the major employers in the community. Chetwynd was incorporated as a village in 1962 but changed its status to a district municipality in 1983. JOHN STEWART

Chibougamau, Québec, pop 9922 (1986c), inc 8 Nov 1952, is situated in Nouvelle Québec 60 km S of Lk Mistassini and 240 km NW of Lac Saint-Jean. Chibougamau and the small city of Chapais together form a mining enclave straddling the Abitibi and Lac Saint-Jean regions. Rich deposits of copper were identified in the first decade of the 20th century but the area's isolation prevented their exploitation. After a first effort in the 1930s, extraction really began in 1949 and the city was founded 3 years later. Chibougamau has gold, silver and zinc as well as copper. Forestry (cutting and sawmill operations) and commercial activities are also important. The city takes advantage of its northern location each year by organizing a "Folies frettes" festival and an international snowmobile rally. MARC ST-HILAIRE

Chickadee (Paridae), family of birds comprising 43 species of true tits (titmice), of which 6 species occur in Canada. Chickadees are tiny, vocal birds of scrub and forest, with stout, conical bills. Most species have striking black and white head markings; some have a conspicuous crest. Black-capped and boreal chickadees (*Parus atricapillus* and *P. hudsonicus*) are widely distributed in Canada. The black-capped favours deciduous woods and gardens; the boreal prefers coniferous forests. Species with restricted ranges are mountain, Siberian and chestnut-backed chickadees (*P. gambeli, P. cinctus, P. rufescens*, respectively) and tufted titmouse (*P. bicolor*). Chickadees are nonmigratory. They eat insects (especially caterpillars) and spiders in summer, and also seeds in winter. Chickadees often hang upside down to pick prey from undersides of leaves and twigs.

Black-capped chickadee (*Parus atricapillus*) close to its nest (*artwork by Claire Tremblay*).

Prey are held underfoot and hammered with the bill or beaten on branches. Chickadees nest in natural cavities in trees or stumps, raising one large brood (5-13 young) annually. Males feed their mates during courtship and incubation. The protected nest site allows a long incubation period (17-21 days). Chickadee groups often form a nucleus for mixed-species feeding flocks. Bushtits, formerly included in the Paridae, are now classified as family Aegithalidae. Common bushtit (*Psaltriparus minimus*), a very small, brownish grey bird with stubby bill and long tail, occurs in southwestern BC. JAMES N.M. SMITH

Chickliset, the northernmost tribe of NOOTKA on the W coast of Vancouver I, BC. Their traditional territory includes the S and E shores of the Brooks Peninsula, Checleset Bay, Nasparti Inlet, Ououkinsh Inlet and Malksope Inlet. Their tribal villages were Acous and Upsowis. In the 20th century the Chickliset intermarried extensively with the KYUQUOT, and by 1950 most Chickliset had settled in Kyuquot villages. The Chickliset Band has since officially amalgamated with the Kyuquot Band (pop 291, 1986). The Chickliset, however, still maintain their identity as a separate tribe. JOHN DEWHIRST

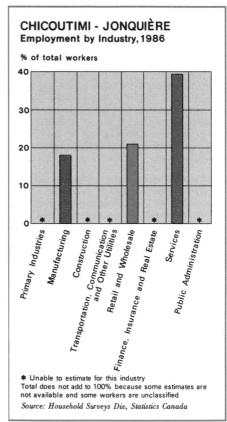

CHICOUTIMI - JONQUIÈRE
Employment by Industry, 1986

% of total workers

* Unable to estimate for this industry
Total does not add to 100% because some estimates are not available and some workers are unclassified
Source: Household Surveys Div, Statistics Canada

Chicoutimi, Qué, City, pop 61 083 (1986c), 60 064 (1981c), inc 1976, is located at the confluence of the Chicoutimi and SAGUENAY rivers between JONQUIÈRE and LA BAIE, 200 km N of Québec City. In the Montagnais language, Chicoutimi means "the end of the deep waters" – a reference to the tides reaching that point.

Regional capital of Saguenay-Lac St-Jean, county seat of Chicoutimi and headquarters of the judicial district of the same name, the city has been a diocesan centre since 1878 and has a major hospital (1884) and a university (Université du Québec à Chicoutimi, 1969). The present city is the amalgamation of the municipalities of Chicoutimi, Chicoutimi-Nord, Rivière-du-Moulin and the parish of Chicoutimi. It was an important staging point on the route that 17th-century Indian hunters took to sell their furs in

Population: Chicoutimi 61 083 (1986c), 60 064 (1981c); Jonquière 58 467 (1986c), 60 354 (1981c); 158 468 (CMA, 1986), 158 229 (CMA, 1981A)

Rate of Increase (1981-86): Chicoutimi 1.5%; Jonquière -3.1%; CMA 2.0%

Rank in Canada: Twentieth (by CMA)

Date of Incorporation: Chicoutimi 1976; Jonquière 1975

Land Area: Chicoutimi 156.66 km²; Jonquière 209.63 km²; (CMA) 1723.31 km²

Elevation: Chicoutimi 15 m; Jonquière 137 m

Climate: Average daily temp, July 19.1°C, Jan -14.6°C; Yearly precip 954.3 mm

Tadoussac, and in 1676 New France authorities built a trading post here. Peter McLeod, Jr, founder of the present city, built sawmills on the du Moulin and Chicoutimi rivers (1842-43), which were acquired by William PRICE in 1852 and operated until the early 20th century. The town's wholesale and retail trade expanded because of its role as a maritime (1875) and railway (1893) terminal. In 1898 the Compagnie de Pulpe de Chicoutimi opened its first pulp mill here, which grew rapidly until the paper industry crisis of the 1920s and the economic collapse of 1929 forced its closure. Prosperity returned with WWII, when many unemployed found work in the Arvida aluminum works. The service sector experienced rapid growth, making Chicoutimi a tertiary centre.

While developing its future, the city remains attached to its past. It houses the Société historique du Saguenay (1934), one of the major private historical societies of N America, and the Musée du Saguenay-Lac St-Jean (1959). As well, the Corporation de la vieille pulperie has restored the remains of the wood-pulp factories, a significant item in Canada's industrial heritage. Chicoutimi hosts, each February, the Carnaval-Souvenir which recalls the ancestral days of 100 years ago. Finally the city is the departure point for cruises through the majestic fjord of the Saguenay. MARC ST-HILAIRE

Chief Electoral Officer, Office of, est 1920, now operates under the Canada Elections Act. It was designated a department for the purposes of administration. The office ensures that eligible Canadians are able to vote for members of Parliament and that the election-expenses provisions of the Act are respected. The chief electoral officer, who is also responsible for the election process of the councils of the Yukon and NWT, examines the decennial census data and provides relevant data to the federal electoral boundaries commissions in each province, who redraw the boundaries. The Chief Electoral Officer is appointed by resolution of the House of Commons. *See also* FRANCHISE; ELECTORAL SYSTEMS.

Chignecto Bay, northeastern arm of the Bay of FUNDY. The name comes from an Indian word *sigunikt,* usually said to mean "foot cloth," perhaps from a MICMAC legend. The area around present-day SACKVILLE, NB, was first settled by ACADIANS in 1671 and by Yorkshire Methodists about 100 years later. The Petitcodiac R flows into the northwestern fork of the bay. A canal across the narrow (27 km) Chignecto Isthmus between the bay and Northumberland Strait was proposed as early as 1686. Henry Ketchum, a Fredericton engineer, built part of a proposed railway across the isthmus

in the 1890s and interest in a canal was revived by a feasibility study in 1958. FUNDY NATIONAL PARK is located on the northern (NB) coast of the bay. *See also* TANTRAMAR MARSH.

Chilcotin live between the Fraser R and the Coast Mts in west-central BC. Their territory includes most of the drainage of the Chilcotin R and the headwaters of several other rivers flowing westward through the Coast range. It is thought they may have entered this region from the north in fairly recent times. In 1986 there were 2018 registered Chilcotin.

The Chilcotin speak a Northern Athapaskan or Dene language and are closely related in language and culture to their CARRIER neighbours to the north. They served as intermediaries in trade between the Homalco and BELLA COOLA on the coast and the Shuswap in the interior, and had limited contact with the Lillooet to the south (*see* SALISH, INTERIOR).

Traditionally the Chilcotin were organized into autonomous bands. However, families might move from one band to another and there was a strong sense of overall Chilcotin identity. There were leaders, some of whom were forceful, but the society was basically egalitarian. The Chilcotin were nomadic most of the year, taking game and fish at traditional hunting and fishing locations. The major big game species now are deer and moose but earlier caribou and elk were available. In the late summer most families gathered along the rivers to fish the salmon runs. In midwinter the Chilcotin moved to sheltered campsites near lakes suitable for ice fishing, where they lived in shed-roofed houses or pit houses covered with bark and earth.

In 1808 Simon FRASER was the first European to encounter Chilcotin. The HUDSON'S BAY CO operated an outpost in Chilcotin territory, 1829-44, but the Chilcotin had little contact with gold miners of the Fraser R Gold Rush who had moved upriver (1859-60). In 1861 a pack-train trail was established from the Bella Coola Valley through Chilcotin territory and work was begun on a wagon road from Blue Inlet to the interior. Several labourers on this road were killed in the Chilcotin Uprising in 1864, and the 5 Chilcotin responsible were eventually tried and executed for these killings.

The Chilcotin have since lived quietly, following traditional ways as much as possible while striving to adjust to the modern world. INDIAN RESERVES were allotted between 1887 and 1904. Many men became cowboys and ranch hands. Some Chilcotin developed small ranches. By the 1960s game and fisheries resources had declined seriously and non-Indian settlement was making the maintenance of traditional Chilcotin life increasingly more difficult. The bands have attempted to develop community projects, such as irrigated farming and sawmilling, with limited success. Despite limited local economic opportunity, most Chilcotin prefer to live in their traditional territory. *See also* NATIVE PEOPLE: SUBARCTIC and general articles under NATIVE PEOPLE.

ROBERT LANE

Reading: J. Helm, ed, *Handbook of North American Indians,* vol 6: *Subarctic* (1981).

Child, Arthur James Edward, business executive (b at Guildford, Eng 19 May 1910). He was educated at Queen's, Harvard Business School and U of T. He is credited with saving Burns Foods from bankruptcy and making it into the second-largest meat packer in the country. He was president and chief executive officer for Burns 1966-86 and is now chairman and CEO. He owns 60% of the company's shares. He is a founder and chairman of the Canada West Foundation and author of *Economics and Politics in US Banking* (1965). Child, with Ronald Jackson, bought a group of meat packing companies in 1986 for $52.5 million, with Child being the majority shareholder.

Child, Philip Albert, writer, academic (b at Hamilton, Ont 19 Jan 1898; d at Toronto 6 Feb 1978). Child's fiction and poetry reflect a period in Canadian literature when traditional forms and subjects were being affected by radical social and cultural change. Novels such as *The Village of Souls* (1933) and *God's Sparrows* (1937) use near-contemporary and historic settings to depict heroes torn between opposing forces. A long poem, *The Victorian House* (1951), deals with the choice between refurbishing a tradition and discarding it. Chancellor's Professor of English Literature at Trinity College, Toronto, Child served as president of the CANADIAN AUTHORS ASSN in 1946. His novel *Mr. Ames against Time* (1949) won the Gov Gen's Award. DENNIS DUFFY

Child Abuse Child abuse is any form of physical harm, sexual exploitation, emotional maltreatment or neglect which results from acts of commission or omission on the part of the child's parent or caregiver. As child welfare is a provincial matter (*see* CHILD WELFARE), all Canadian provinces have legislation defining a "child in need of protection," but only some (eg, Ont, Man, PEI, NS), define the term "child abuse" by statute.

"Battered child syndrome" was a term coined in the early 1960s by Henry Kempe, MD, to characterize the clinical condition of young children who suffered serious physical abuse. Although neglect and abuse of children was occurring long before the 1960s, and child welfare specialists, public health nurses and other helping professionals were well aware of the fact, it was not until Dr Kempe and his associates labelled the phenomenon that people began to recognize child abuse as a leading cause of serious injury and death. Since that time, there has been the recognition that other forms of child abuse, such as sexual exploitation and emotional maltreatment, are as widespread as physical abuse, and can be as damaging. Indeed, emotional maltreatment, a relatively new category, is recognized as being at the core of all types of abuse.

Criminal Charges Although child welfare falls within provincial jurisdiction and matters relating to child protection are covered by provincial statute, cases of abuse can result in criminal charges under the Criminal Code of Canada. Recent amendments to that code clearly reflect the growing awareness that sexual exploitation of children is a serious problem which will not be tolerated by society (*see* SEXUAL ABUSE OF CHILDREN). As well, important amendments to the Canada Evidence Act, which will allow the evidence of a child under 14 to be heard, illustrates society's growing belief that children can be credible witnesses where their victimization is alleged.

Mandatory Reporting Identifying a child as being "in need of protection" and reporting that suspicion to the appropriate agency are necessary if children are to be protected from abuse. Each province has an agency which is mandated, by law, to take protective action if a child is found to be at risk for abuse or neglect. In all provinces, the public is required, by law, to report suspicions of abuse/neglect to the designated agency, but not all provincial legislation carries penalties for nonreporting. Some legislation, such as the Family and Children's Services Act of Ontario, puts a special onus on professionals to report abuse, and carries a penalty for the professional's failure to report.

Incidence Because of the wide range of definitions, reporting procedures and data collection, and because not all abuse is reported, it is impossible to determine the true incidence of child abuse and neglect in Canada. However, it is believed, by professionals, to be much more pervasive than any statistics indicate (see the Badgley Report of the Committee on Sexual Offences Against Children and Youths, 1984). Prevention services, including support systems for families under stress, parenting education, improved social conditions and strong social sanctions against violence, are recognized as being important and, in the long run, more effective than treating the results of abuse and neglect. PATRICIA SIBBALD

Child Labour Attitudes toward child labour (the regular employment of boys and girls under the age of 15 or 16) have altered dramatically since the late 18th century, when it was generally assumed that from about age 7 children should contribute to the family economy (*see* CHILDHOOD, HISTORY OF). In most cases, this meant assisting parents, but it could also entail paid employment outside the home. Such activity might include the acquisition of skills useful in adulthood, possibly even a formal apprenticeship. Child labour made an important contribution to native Indian culture and to the societies of New France and early English Canada.

During the 19th and early 20th centuries most Canadian children, formerly economic assets, became economic liabilities to their families. Boys' and girls' time was increasingly taken up in securing a formal education. By 1911 about 85% of all children 10-12 years old in Canada were in school. Proportions of 13-, 14- and 15-year-olds enrolled stood at 78%, 63% and 42%. The proportion of boys aged 10-14 who were gainfully employed had dropped from 25% in 1891 to 5% in 1911, although that of girls remained steady at 2%. (An important indicator of the decline in child labour is the steady increase in the percentage of children attending school.)

Opportunities for paid employment probably broadened for the minority of children not in school. From the mid-19th century Canada began to undergo industrialization and urbanization. As the proportion of urban residents grew from about 17% at Confederation, 1867, to over one-third by 1901 and almost one-half by 1921, new jobs for children became available in Montréal textile mills, Hamilton businesses, Cape Breton and BC mines and small manufacturing enterprises in the Maritimes. While the number of children 10-14 years old employed in agriculture dropped from 62 700 in 1891 to 5400 in 1911, the total otherwise gainfully employed, primarily in business and industry, actually expanded from 13 000 to about 20 000.

Several conditions combined to end child labour in Canada. Many jobs were "dead end": poorly paid, menial positions without any opportunity for advancement. Some positions, such as those of messenger boy and newspaper vendor, did not lead to adult employment. Moreover, most children holding jobs came from working-class backgrounds and were of special concern to middle-class reformers intent on improving Canadian society. As well as supporting compulsory schooling and measures to combat juvenile delinquency, reformers sought to ban child labour. Although the first provincial legislation regulating child labour in factories and mines had been passed in the 1870s and 1880s, the prohibition of child labour came only in the new century. By 1929 children under 14 had been legally excluded from factory and mine employment in most provinces. Then came the GREAT DEPRESSION, when many adults sought jobs formerly done largely by children. By 1931, 96-97% of children 9-12 years old were in school, with proportions of those 13, 14 and 15 years old having risen dramatically over the previous 2 decades to 93%, 83% and 67%. During

WWII many children probably entered the work force, defying school-attendance legislation. Since the war, it has been argued, women came to replace children as part-time contributors to family income.

Child labour did persist into the 20th century in less visible forms. Between Confederation and the mid-1920s about 80 000 British children, most under 14, were brought to Canada by humanitarians wishing to give them a new start away from their working-class backgrounds. Almost all were apprenticed to rural families and in general became child labourers rather than adopted children. Growing sensitivity to their fate led to the prohibition of child immigration in 1925. *See also* IMMIGRANT CHILDREN. JEAN BARMAN

Reading: K. Bagnell, *The Little Immigrants* (1980); G.S. Kealey, ed, *Canada Investigates Industrialism* (1973); Joy Parr, *Labouring Children* (1980) and ed, *Childhood and Family in Canadian History* (1982); Neil Sutherland, *Children in English Canadian Society* (1976).

Child Welfare in Canada refers to a system of services established by provincial and territorial governments, at times in partnership with private organizations called children's aid societies, to provide services that supplement or substitute for parental care and supervision. Each province now has a well-established system of child welfare services (*see* FAMILY LAW) to prevent or help remedy problems that may result in the neglect, abuse, exploitation or delinquency of children (*see* CHILD ABUSE; JUVENILE DELINQUENCY); to protect and care for homeless, dependent or neglected children; to protect the welfare of children of working mothers; to provide care, including foster care, group homes and residential centres and ADOPTION services for children removed from their homes; and to provide services for single mothers. Child welfare services are primarily concerned with parental behaviour and they pay little or no attention to other conditions that may jeopardize a child's development.

Historical Development The tendency of the state to intervene in the care of children is recent. Under the *patria potestas* of Roman law, wide powers of life and death were allotted to the head of the family. These powers were not part of European feudal law systems, although the latter reflected Roman civil law in stressing the family's importance. Under the English common law, over several centuries, guardianship, whether by the natural parent or by another guardian, was slowly recognized as including the right of custody, control over a child's education and religious training, consent to his or her marriage, right of chastisement, right of enjoyment of his or her services, etc. Between an Act of 1660 and one of 1886 (Guardianship of Infants Act), mothers were unable to interfere with the father's appointment of a guardian, although they could be designated guardian or co-guardian by him. Within a century, however, the mothers enjoyed equal if not superior claims to custody. The Court of Chancery assumed wardship if rights were abused, and the courts gradually, through various Acts, eg, Custody of Children Act (1891), Offenders Against the Person Act (1861), Poor Law Amendment Act (1868), etc, acquired control over abuse of the power of chastisement. If a child were to die as a consequence of punishment, the charge was for murder or manslaughter, whether the person charged be parent, guardian, teacher or employer.

In Upper and Lower Canada before Confederation, children were primarily the responsibility of the family. Any other assistance came from the church or from the local community. Provincial governments provided institutions, eg, jails, reformatories, industrial schools and support to orphanages run by churches and private organizations. They also established a system of indenture whereby a child could be assigned to an employer in exchange for room and board and sometimes wages. At that time most people in Canada lived on farms and family survival relied heavily on the work of children. CHILD LABOUR as a social problem is associated, however, with the rise of industrialism and capitalism. It first appeared with the development of the domestic system, which was replaced by the factory system. In Canada child labour did not become as serious a problem as it did in England or Europe because Canada was predominantly agricultural until well into the 20th century. However, when poverty and destitution, increased by industrialization and urbanization, took their toll, little public health or relief was available (*see* SOCIAL SECURITY). Growing numbers of homeless, destitute children in urban centres, greater juvenile crime and changes in child-labour practice pressured governments to respond to the plight of children. At the same time (1870-1925) large numbers of children were brought from Britain to Canada to serve as agricultural labourers and domestic servants, in effect the first large system of foster placement, which often did not serve the best interests of the child (*see* IMMIGRANT CHILDREN).

In the late 1800s the middle- and upper-class men and women who formed the Child Saving Movement sought to rescue children from undesirable circumstances. They blamed the parents of the children for the problem, but at the same time they ideologically reinforced the moral and social value of the family. With the enactment of child protection legislation in various provinces and the establishment and growth of the children's aid societies and child-welfare departments, the state began to regulate and finance a system of child-welfare services. The first Children's Aid Society was established in Toronto in 1891 and the first Child Protection Act was passed in Ontario in 1893. This Act for the Prevention of Cruelty to and Better Protection of Children made the abuse of children an indictable offence for the first time, promoted foster care and children's aid societies, gave the societies guardianship power, and established the office of the superintendent of neglected children. The rapid expansion of services in most provinces over the next 20 years bureaucratized and professionalized the services, greatly influencing the subsequent development of child-welfare services. Changes in child welfare were also affected by changing attitudes toward the participation of children in the labour market. Social workers were hired as the main professional workers in child welfare and they tended to reinforce the earlier approach of focusing on the family and its problems rather than on detrimental social conditions.

Simultaneously the increased bureaucratization led to the departmentalization of services (eg, infant care, protection, adoption, child care) and removed decision making farther from the frontline workers. The services developed at the turn of the century focused primarily on child protection and child control; major legislation for the adoption of children was not passed until the 1920s. Earlier child-welfare reformers preferred indenture to adoption, correctly believing it provided more protection for the child because the placement of children in new families was primarily a means of exploiting the child's labour.

Neglect and Abuse Each province's legislation now defines those situations in which state intervention is required to protect a child, eg, those who have been orphaned, deserted, physically or emotionally neglected or abused by the persons who are caring for the child, or whose guardians cannot provide adequate care, or a child whose behaviour is unacceptable to the authorities. Un-

der this legislation the responsibility for investigation and intervention lies with a provincial childwelfare officer or an organization designated for that purpose (eg, a children's aid society). Such offices must investigate any complaint of neglect or abuse and take whatever action is necessary to protect the child. Apparent neglect or abuse of a child can be reported by anyone in the community and in many provinces there is now legislation requiring certain professionals to report any suspected abuse of a child. If the child is removed from the home by the court, the child-welfare authority must arrange appropriate care (usually a temporary placement), and a social worker is assigned to work with the family so that the child can return to the home as soon as possible. Children permanently removed from their homes will usually remain in care until the age of majority, and in most cases the natural parents will be able to maintain contact except where their child is placed for adoption.

In recent years nonward or voluntary admissions, in which the parents request or agree with the temporary placement of the child, have increased. The child-welfare services provide counselling and supervision for children in their own homes and care of children in alternate settings such as foster homes, group homes and residential settings. The main support services offered to children in their own homes are designed to improve the parents' ability to care for the child and are not concerned with many of the broader social and economic problems that families face. The children of unmarried mothers once represented a large proportion of those admitted to care, and many were subsequently adopted, but this is no longer true and a higher proportion of women are deciding to keep their children.

Alternate Care The child admitted into the care of a child-welfare authority is usually placed in a foster family recruited by the local child-welfare office or by the children's aid society, and supervised by social-work staff. Foster parents are given considerable responsibility for the daily care of the child placed in their home. The fostercare allowance is the least expensive form of alternate care, utilizing the low-paid in-home labour of women as substitute mothers. There is difficulty in obtaining adequate foster homes for older children and for those with special needs. Some children are placed in state-financed group homes operated by the child-welfare authority or run privately, where group parents or child-care staff are employed. Some of these group homes simply provide an alternative home setting for a child while others provide specialized treatment for children and youths with special needs. Children are also placed in larger residential centres, some of which provide general custodian child care, while others provide services for children with special needs. The latter, frequently called treatment centres, are usually private and staffed by various professionals but are financed primarily by the state.

Adoption, which transfers rights and responsibilities for the care of a child from the natural parent(s) or the state to another person or persons, is regulated by the Child Welfare Act in each province. Traditionally, children available for adoption were primarily those of unmarried mothers, and abandoned, orphaned, neglected and abused children. Because fewer healthy infants are now available, many older or handicapped children are being adopted. Children are also adopted by the new spouse in many remarriages. Prospective adoptive parents are processed by the child-welfare authority and the child will be placed initially in their home for a probationary period before the final adoption order is granted by the court. In the past there was

little contact between the adoptive child and the natural parents, but recently the efforts of adoptive children and their natural parents to locate each other have increased and some provinces have set up systems to facilitate such contacts.

Native Child Welfare Proportionately more native children end up in care than non-native children. There are difficulties finding native foster homes, partly because of the severe poverty many native families endure, both on and off reserve, and partly because of the standards used by nonnative, middle-class staff to assess foster homes. Most adopted native children go to non-native homes, losing not only their families but also their culture. Because it is unclear which level of government is responsible for native child welfare, frequently neither government will assume responsibility. No federal legislation concerning native child welfare exists, resulting in less adequate services for native children than for nonnative children. JIM ALBERT

Childhood, History of Biology and the laws and customs of human culture together govern the nature of human childhood. The ways in which biology and culture come together in children change over time; the story of these changes forms the history of childhood. Human infants are born helpless and only gradually learn to care for themselves. In infancy and childhood they are vulnerable to a host of diseases; it is probable that until the 20th century at least one in 7 children born alive in Canada died during the first year. It is also probable that another one in 7 succumbed to disease during the vulnerable years from 1 to 7.

Children inherit possible patterns of growth from their parents, but these are realized in large part as a function of material conditions. Improved nutrition and living conditions have brought Canada closer than ever before to the optimal conditions for the physical growth of its children. In the mid-19th century, for example, some working-class boys did not reach their relatively short full growth until they were in their mid-20s. Today, Canadian children grow up faster, arrive at puberty earlier, pass through it more quickly, and achieve a greater final size than any preceding generation did.

Whereas biology makes all childhoods in some way similar, the customs and laws of each society make childhoods very different from each other in different places and in the same place at different times. The first child born in what is now Canada likely was born to people moving eastward along the shore of the Arctic Ocean over 30 000 years ago. Although we know nothing about childhood among these anonymous early settlers we do know something about it among the native peoples who were their eventual successors. The children of Canada's native peoples had to learn the ways of complex societies. These ways differed from one language group or native nation to another at least as much as child-rearing practices differ between modern nations. An important dimension of native childhood was framed by the ways in which tribes sustained themselves; whether they were primarily hunters like the Blackfoot, farmers like the Huron or fishermen like the Kwakiutl, or whether they lived by a combination of fishing, gathering and hunting, like the Micmac.

On the central West Coast, for example, Kwakiutl lived in *numaym*, extended households of up to 100 people. Midwives assisted at births. Four days after birth the infant was given its first name, and it spent its first year in a cradle carried by its mother. At about a year the child acquired a new name, and boys had their hair singed and holes pierced in their ears and nose. High-status children were later given other names, owned by the family, which parents saw as appropriate to their developing character. Families marked each new name with a POTLATCH, a gift-giving ceremony. Each *numaym* moved several times a year to one of the 5-7 resource sites owned by the chief. In a society highly conscious of property rights children learned the precise locations of fishing and food-gathering sites and winter village locations. By observation and practice, children gradually mastered some of the skills employed at each site: making wood, stone, bone and metal tools; constructing longhouses, canoes and watertight wooden boxes; preserving and storing food; carving poles and masks; and weaving aprons, capes and blankets. The children of a SHAMAN (medicine man) submitted themselves to rigorous schedules, as they mastered the rituals, spells and dances owned by their families. The children of wealthy and well-born Kwakiutl learned the complex protocol of the potlatch and privately owned songs and dances, and learned to recite their family trees. All children learned the religious notions, mythology and taboos, and the workaday names and winter titles of those in their own *numaym* and neighbouring ones. At puberty, a boy secluded himself and fasted before a ceremony at which he was given a name appropriate to his personal ability. A girl embarked on a complex regimen, governed by taboos and involving seclusion and periods of fasting.

Childhood among native peoples did not repeat itself exactly from generation to generation. When the Blackfoot acquired horses after about 1730, their way of life changed dramatically. Boys in particular had to learn new skills, rituals and taboos associated with caring for horses, and hunting and fighting bareback. Childhood in the various native nations changed again as various groups came into contact with European traders and settlers.

In New France mothers bore their children at home, assisted by a *sage femme* (midwife). Most infants were breast-fed by their mother or a wet nurse until about 14 months. Three or 4 days after birth the parents and godparents took the child to the nearest priest to be baptized. Children began their *enfance* swaddled or tightly bound. They slept in wooden cradles and were given rattles to play with. The average family in New France had 6 children. Some time before they were 7, children were thought to have begun to reason and therefore entered a stage known as *tendre jeunesse*. At about the same time they began to contribute to their family's welfare, at first through such tasks as looking after younger brothers and sisters, frightening birds from ripening crops and herding cows. As they got older their parents added to their responsibilities. In a day that was usually full from daylight to dark, children rose to light the fires in the morning, emptied the chamber pots into the outdoor privy, brought in wood and water, swept floors and cleaned muddy boots. They cleaned stables and tended the stock. They helped seed and weed the garden, and in the late summer and fall they joined the whole family in the arduous task of harvesting. By adolescence most boys and girls had learned the household and farm skills. This competence was reflected in the fact that, theoretically, those who reached puberty (legally 12 for girls and 14 for boys) could be married. In practice, very few youngsters took this step. Growing maturity was recognized by all taking on increased responsibilities, and by boys being enrolled in the militia at 16 and beginning their indentures at about the same time. Although most waited till age 25 for marriage (the mean age of marriage between 1700 and 1730 was 22.4 for women and 26.9 for men), a person became a functional adult in New France at about age 20. The push to maturity was probably has-

tened by high mortality rates, which ensured that half the adolescents in the colony had only one living parent.

In the late 18th and early 19th centuries childhood among the Loyalists and later anglophone settlers was very similar to that described for New France; children were needed and highly valued for the work they did. Since they could be easily fed and clothed from the produce of the household, they were soon an economic asset rather than a liability. Travellers commented that Canadian children of both French and British background tended to be more independent and self-reliant than their European counterparts.

In the 19th century schooling became a dominant childhood experience. Around 1800 only a small number, mostly boys, had much formal education. By 1900, most children attended publicly supported schools for a few years, and many attended consistently between about 5 and 16 years of age. One reason for this change was that Canadian children became the beneficiaries of new attitudes emerging in western Europe and N America, which saw childhood as a stage of life in which greater protection, sheltering, training and education were necessary. Although this change in attitude affected all children, we see evidence of it first in the care of dependent children. Canadians began to build special institutions to care for orphans and for children whose parents could not care for them. Changing economic conditions accompanied changing attitudes to children. Thus children attended school because maturity and compactness of settlement, improved roads, etc, made it easier for them to meet for schooling; because mature farms could more easily spare youngsters for at least part of the year to go to school; and because parents came to see that education was increasingly useful in a society in which commerce and then industry became important. Parents recognized that, for many jobs, literacy was becoming a practical necessity rather than an ornament.

The growth of cities and industries changed the rhythm of the seasonal cycles of farming, fishing, lumbering and trapping. The home ceased to be the primary place of production. A rising standard of living permitted families to devote more of their incomes to improving the quality of their lives. They moved to larger houses, they ate better food and lengthened the period of time that they kept their children out of the paid workforce. With fathers now away for the customary 60-hour work week, mothers who stayed at home had to assume most of the responsibility for raising the youngsters over this longer period of dependency.

Improved child rearing and child care became public concerns. By the 1920s in anglophone Canada (perhaps a little later in francophone Canada) new social policies and programs had been created for children. Social activists tried first to bolster families who were already doing a reasonable job of raising their youngsters. In their public health work they tried to increase the chances of survival of all children. They strove for an educational system which, in addition to teaching the traditional three Rs, would also prepare girls to be better housekeepers and mothers, and boys to be sober, honest, well-trained and industrious breadwinners and fathers. Reformers tried to improve the physical and social environment of homes and schools; they set aside and began to supervise playing-fields and parks, and supported such new organizations as the Boy SCOUTS and GIRL GUIDES.

The social reformers also tried to help children and families with special problems. So that reluctant families and young people would take advantage of the school system, they pressed for the regulation of CHILD LABOUR, compulsory school attendance and the appointment of truant officers. To prevent families from breaking up as a result of

the death or incapacitation of the father, they campaigned for workers' compensation and mothers' pensions. Factory Acts and anti-sweating legislation were introduced to protect the health of working-class mothers and their children, and a few DAY CARE operations were started. At some schools milk or hot lunches were provided, and "fresh air" funds were begun to take poor children and their parents out of their environment once a year.

Social reformers also tried new ways to salvage youngsters whose families would not or could not rear them. They began to question the merits of children staying for long periods of time in the institutions built in the 19th century. Canadians gradually ended the grim practice of "baby farming." They began ADOPTION services to place illegitimate babies in family homes rather than in foundling institutions and to legitimize children whose parents subsequently married. Socially conscious legislators shifted the care of vagrant, orphaned, neglected, dependent, "incorrigible" and delinquent children from institutions to families (*see* JUVENILE DELINQUENCY). They passed the Federal Juvenile Delinquents Act and set up a system of juvenile courts, detention homes, and probation officers to deflect youthful delinquents from crime. Between the 1920s and the 1970s Canadians strove to put all of these programs into effect and to bring them to bear on the lives of all children in the country. *See also* CHILD ABUSE; CHILD WELFARE.

NEIL SUTHERLAND

Reading: K. Bagnell, *The Little Immigrants* (1980); Joy Parr, ed, *Childhood and Family in Canadian History* (1982); Neil Sutherland, *Children in English-Canadian Society* (1976).

Children's Literature in English, literature for children up to early adolescence, has been written since the mid-19th century. It can be characterized as a literature in which portrayals of life in the new country – confrontations with and adaptations to the landscape and the native peoples, colonizing the territories and then creating and developing a nation – were in search of appropriate vehicles of expression. During the 19th and early 20th centuries the vehicles were generally those fashionable in Great Britain. At the turn of the century the animal story, the first distinctively Canadian genre, appeared.

Although animals had been mentioned in earlier literature, the works of Sir Charles G.D. ROBERTS and Ernest Thompson SETON gave the animal story its distinctive form. Seton's highly popular *Wild Animals I Have Known* (1898) influenced Roberts, whose *The Kindred of the Wild* appeared in 1902 and *Red Fox* in 1905. Drawing on their observations of wildlife and their study of Darwinistic theories of natural selection, both writers focused on the lives of superior members of various species. In *Red Fox*, Roberts combined exceptional strength and intelligence in an individual fox, making him the novel's hero. To Seton, the important fact of animal life was death, often at the hands of man and always tragic. Among later wild-animal stories which end with death are Roderick HAIG-BROWN's *Ki-yu: A Story of Panthers* (1934) and Fred Bodsworth's *Last of the Curlews* (1955).

Pets have also provided the focus for many children's books. One of the best-known early children's novels, Margaret Marshall Saunders's *Beautiful Joe* (1894), is the "autobiography" of a "cur" who, having been rescued from a cruel master, lives a long and happy life. Farley MOWAT's *The Dog Who Wouldn't Be* (1957) is the humorous story of Mutt, a pet who "at some early moment of his existence...concluded there was no future in being a dog." Sheila BURNFORD's *The Incredible Journey* (1960) is the account of a 400 km trek across northern Ontario undertaken by 2 dogs and a cat.

The adventure story, a major form of Victorian children's literature, influenced Canadian books in the 19th century and, to a lesser degree, the 20th. Emphasizing the goodness of the British Empire, Christianity and physical courage, such British novels as Frederick Marryat's *The Settlers in Canada* (1844) and G.A. Henty's *With Wolfe in Canada* (1886) were immensely popular in Britain and the colonies, and shaped many young Canadians' views of their country. R.M. Ballantyne's firsthand account of the fur trade, *Hudson's Bay* (1848), was followed by his novels *Snowflakes and Sunbeams* (1856) and *Ungava* (1858). The vast landscape, populated by fierce wild animals and heathen savages, was supposedly won for civilization by people such as the young white heroes and heroines of the novels of these authors.

Of 19th-century stories one of the most interesting is Catharine Parr TRAILL's *The Canadian Crusoes* (1852), which combines a knowledge of the wilderness N of Lk Ontario with elements of the survival story made popular by Daniel Defoe's *Robinson Crusoe*. In addition to describing how the 3 central figures, all teenagers, secure the basic necessities, the book portrays their strong belief in divine protection, and their rescue of a native girl to whom they teach the tenets of Christianity. The popularity of the traditional adventure story during the early 20th century (eg, Seton's *Two Little Savages*, 1906; Alan Sullivan's *Brother Eskimo*, 1921, and *Brother Blackfoot*, 1937) may account for the appearance of many of its traits in such novels as Haig-Brown's *Starbuck Valley Winter* (1943), Mowat's *Lost in the Barrens* (1956) and James HOUSTON's *Frozen Fire* (1977); in each story the male hero grows to maturity, drawing on lessons learned through meeting native people and coping with the harsh wilderness. Tony German's *Tom Penny* (1977) and Bill Freeman's *Shantymen of Cache Lake* (1975) combine historical backgrounds and foregrounds of danger and suspense as youthful heroes confront the elements and evil characters.

There is no self-conscious tradition in Canadian fiction of mythologizing major historical characters and events, as there is in American children's literature. Thus, in historical fiction, Canadian authors cannot relate their narratives with the confidence that their young readers will have a general familiarity with major eras or events. Certain periods of Canadian history, eg, the War of 1812 and the North-West Rebellion, seem to be favourites in novels. The former has been treated in Barbara and Heather Bramwell's *Adventure at the Mill* (1963) and John F. Hayes's *Treason at York* (1949); the latter in W.T Cutt's *On the Trail of Long Tom* (1970) and Jan Truss's *A Very Small Rebellion* (1977). The Royal Canadian Mounted Police are treated in J.W. Chalmers's *Horseman in Scarlet* (1961), the LOYALISTS' escape to Canada in Mary Alice and John Downie's *Honor Bound* (1971) and the Cariboo Gold Rush in Christie Harris's *Cariboo Trail* (1957). In *Underground to Canada* (1977), Barbara Smucker describes the dangerous journey to Ontario of 3 slaves who have escaped from a Southern plantation. Many contemporary authors have created historical novels about the first half of this century. Barbara Smucker's *Days of Terror* (1979) is an account of the struggles of Mennonites who have fled their Ukrainian village and come to Canada during WWI. Jean Little, in *Listen for the Singing* (1977), details the tensions of a German-Canadian family during WWII. Myra Paperny's family story, *The Wooden People* (1976) is set in Alberta in the 1920s, and Brian Doyle's *Up From Low* (1982) is based on the author's 1940s boyhood.

Perhaps the most distinguished historical fiction for children is found in books dealing with the native peoples, both before and after European con-tact. Often these stories centre on the rites of passage, as in Haig-Brown's *The Whale People* (1962) in which a Nootka youth is thrust into a position of authority after the death of his father. In Edith Sharp's *Nkwala* (1958), a Salish boy searches for a vision to guide him into adulthood. Cliff Faulknor's trilogy, *The White Calf* (1965), *The White Peril* (1966) and *The Smoke Horse* (1968), is set on the prairies just before and during the arrival of Europeans. Stories dealing with contacts between native and European cultures include J.F. Hayes's *Buckskin Colonist* (1947), Doris Andersen's *Blood Brothers* (1967) and Harris's *Forbidden Frontier* (1968). Jan Hudson's *Sweetgrass* (1984) combines historical research and a feminist viewpoint in detailing the life of a young Blackfoot woman in the early 19th century.

Writers of biography and historical nonfiction have always had to avoid the pitfalls of accurate but dry scholarship, and exciting but inaccurate fictionalization. Among those biographies which have avoided the dangers are Haig-Brown's *Captain of the Discovery: The Story of Captain George Vancouver* (1956), Kay Hill's *And Tomorrow the Stars: The Story of John Cabot* (1968), and Roy DANIELLS's *Alexander Mackenzie and the North West* (1969). Accurate and lively histories for young readers include Pierre BERTON's *The Golden Trail* (1954), T.M. Longstreth's *The Scarlet Force* (1953) and William Toye's *The St. Lawrence* (1959). Although native peoples have been sensitively treated in fiction and in adaptations of folklore, they have not, with the exception of Harris's *Raven's Cry* (1966), been the subject of major biographies or histories for children.

Domestic and school stories and the problem novel have not been as popular in Canada as in Britain and the US, but there are important works in this area. Ralph Connor (Charles W. GORDON), in *Glengarry School Days* (1902), and Nellie MC-CLUNG, in *Sowing Seeds in Danny* (1908), described the lives of young people growing up in small Canadian towns. Now criticized for their sentimentality and excessive moral earnestness, these books nonetheless reflect the daily activities, cultural climate and reading tastes of the period. L.M. MONTGOMERY's *Anne of Green Gables*, considered by many critics to be the only classic of Canadian children's literature, appeared in 1908. Although it too has been criticized for its sentimentality, in the lively presentation of an ebullient heroine and the difficult process of her socialization it remains one of the most widely read Canadian children's books.

The genre of social realism has grown rapidly since 1970. Jean Little, who has a severe visual handicap, has chronicled the lives of young people with physical problems, eg, in *Mine for Keeps* (1962), and *From Anna* (1972), and, in *Mama's Going to Buy You a Mockingbird* (1985), has vividly portrayed a boy's reaction to his father's death. Kevin Major's *Hold Fast* (1978) and *Far From Shore* (1980) deal with troubled adolescent boys who are in conflict with themselves and their Newfoundland society. The relationship between native peoples and other Canadians is considered in John Craig's *No Word for Good-bye* (1969). Native author Beatrice Culleton powerfully presents the life of a contemporary Metis woman in *In Search of April Raintree* (1983). Bryan Doyle's *Hey, Dad* (1978) and *You Can Pick Me Up at Peggy's Cove* (1979) focus on the troubled relationships between parents and children, while in Cora Taylor's *Julie* (1985), a mother must learn to accept her daughter's psychic powers.

Most of the POPULAR LITERATURE read by Canadian children has been written in Britain or the US. There are exceptions. Mary Grannan's *Just Mary Stories* (1942) and *Maggie Muggins and Mr. McGar-rity* (1952) are collections of humorous fantasy stories based on her long-running CBC radio series. Two recent authors are also significant. In such books as *Murder on the Canadian* (1976), *Terror in Winnipeg* (1979) and *The Ghost of Lunenburg Manor* (1981), Eric Wilson mixes Canadian settings and current social problems into the adventures of Tom Austen, a boy detective. Gordon Korman, who began publishing in his early teens, has created humorous stories about teenagers in *This Can't Be Happening at Macdonald Hall!* (1978), *Go Jump in the Pool* (1979) and *The War with Mr. Wizzle* (1982).

In the development of Canadian fantasy since WWII, many of the best writers have turned to the wilderness and to the native people's spiritual beliefs, as in Catherine Anthony Clark's fantasies, including *The Golden Pine Cone* (1950), *The Sun Horse* (1951) and *The Diamond Feather* (1962). Christie Harris links modern science and old beliefs in *Secret in the Stlalakum Wild* (1972) and *Sky Man on the Totem Pole?* (1975). Monica Hughes emphasizes the native reverence for both nature and the past in *Beyond the Dark River* (1979). Set in the 21st century after Edmonton has been devastated, presumably by nuclear war, the novel treats the relationship between a young Hutterite and a native healer. Hughes has also written science fiction, including *The Keeper of the Isis Light* (1980), *The Guardian of Isis* (1981) and *The Isis Pedlar* (1982), set on a planet inhabited by fugitives from an overcrowded, polluted Earth, who have degenerated into fearful and superstitious beings. Ruth Nichols has used rugged Canadian landscapes in *A Walk Out of the World* (1969) and *The Marrow of the World* (1972), in both of which children undertake arduous journeys from Earth to the alternate universes in which they were born.

Other works of fantasy include Pierre Berton's *The Secret World of Og* (1961), which portrays the adventures of children who travel down a tunnel found in the floor of their playhouse and enter a strange land. Mordecai RICHLER's *Jacob Two-Two Meets the Hooded Fang* (1975) describes the dream of an insecure child who becomes a hero after he is sent to the children's prison. Janet Lunn's *Double Spell* (1968, published in paperback as *Twin Spell*) and *The Root Cellar* (1981) are time-travel fantasies. Welwyn Wilton Katz, in *Witchery Hill* (1984) and *Sun God, Moon Witch* (1986), sends her young heroes and heroines to the Channel Islands and western England respectively, where they develop inner strengths while confronting supernatural powers. Donn Kushner's *The Violin-Maker's Gift* (1980) is about a magical bird who can predict the future.

Canadian folktales for children can be divided into European tales adapted by Canadian writers, indigenous folktales of European settlers, and reworkings of Indian and Inuit myths, legends and folktales. Two early collections, Cyrus Macmillan's *Canadian Wonder Tales* (1918) and *Canadian Fairy Tales* (1922), contain stories from each of the 3 categories, although most are derived from French Canadian and native tales. The tales reflect early 20th-century tastes, often written in the romantic manner that was popular in late 19th-century England. Legends of the Maritime provinces were collected by Helen CREIGHTON in *Bluenose Ghosts* (1957). Marius Barbeau's *The Golden Phoenix* (tr 1958), is a collection of French Canadian tales, one of which, *The Princess of Tomboso* (1960), was illustrated by Frank Newfeld. Newfeld also adapted and illustrated the Nova Scotia tale *Simon and the Golden Sword* (1976). Traditional European tales retold and illustrated by Canadians include *The Miraculous Hind* (1975) and *Petrouchka* (1980) by Elizabeth Cleaver; *Cinderella* (1969) by Alan Suddon; and *The Twelve Dancing Princesses* by Lunn, illustrated by Lazlo Gal (1979).

The collection of Indian and Inuit oral material began shortly after initial European contact. However, because of the strong Christian emphasis in children's literature well into the 20th century, adaptations of native folktales for children were relatively few. During the late 20th century, in part because of a general increase in awareness of minority cultures, there has been an outpouring of retold native legends. The most significant writers in this trend are Christie Harris and James Houston. Beginning with *Once Upon a Totem* (1963), Harris has written several collections of stories based on the legends of Northwest Coast Indians. Though much longer and containing far greater character development than her sources, the tales reflect her familiarity with the rugged landscape and the cultural beliefs of the peoples. Houston's stories, including *Tikta'liktak* (1965) and *The White Archer* (1967), draw on local legends heard during his 12 years in the Arctic. Other notable collections of native tales are Frances Fraser's retelling of Blackfoot legends in *The Bear Who Stole the Chinook* (1959); Dorothy Reid's *Tales of Nanabozho* (1963), a recasting of Ojibwa myths; and K.L. Hill's *Glooscap and His Magic* (1963), accounts of the Wabanaki hero-god. William Toye has retold and Elizabeth Cleaver illustrated several native tales, including *The Mountain Goats of Temlaham* (1969) and *The Fire Stealer* (1979). Cleaver has also retold and illustrated the Inuit legend *The Enchanted Caribou* (1985).

In recent years a growing number of native writers have retold the tales of their own people, hoping to preserve elements of a past that is rapidly becoming forgotten. In *Son of Raven, Son of Deer* (1967) George CLUTESI has adapted Vancouver Island stories and, in *Tales the Elders Told* (1981) by Basil Johnston, Ojibwa legends are retold. Maria CAMPBELL, in *Little Badger and the Fire Spirit* (1977), has created her own version of a plains *pourquoi* legend.

Although there is a long tradition of Canadian children's fiction, there are few widely known Canadian children's poets or poems. Poetic works written for adults by Thomas D'Arcy MCGEE, Pauline JOHNSON, Bliss CARMAN, Robert SERVICE and others were frequently memorized by children. Two popular anthologies, *The Wind Has Wings* (1968, rev 1984), edited by M.A. Downie and Barbara Robertson, and *All Kinds of Everything* (1973), edited by Louis DUDEK, contained poems by well-known adult Canadian poets. However, it was not until 1974, with the appearance of Dennis LEE's *Alligator Pie* and *Nicholas Knock and Other People*, that a group of poems written specifically for Canadian children achieved a wide audience. The humour and nonsense in these volumes and in Lee's *Garbage Delight* (1977) and *Jelly Belly* (1983) is also characteristic of much other Canadian children's poetry, including Susan Musgrave's *Gullband* (1974), Sue Ann Alderson's *Bonnie McSmithers (You're Driving Me Dithers)* (1974) and Al Pittman's *Down by Jim Long's Stage* (1976). Outstanding recent collections include Lois Simmie's *Auntie's Knitting a Baby* (1984), Robert Heidbreder's *Don't Eat Spiders* (1985), and Tim Wynne-Jones's *Mischief City* (1986). Ron Berg has illustrated Eugene Field's lullaby, *Wynken, Blynken, and Nod* (1985), and Ted HARRISON has illustrated the Robert Service Yukon favourite, *The Cremation of Sam McGee* (1986).

Because of high production costs and a relatively small market, there have been few picture books published in Canada. However, during the 1970s distinguished picture books appeared, many from Montréal's Tundra Books. Ann BLADES's *Mary of Mile 18* (1971) and William KURELEK's *A Prairie Boy's Winter* (1973) and *A Prairie Boy's Summer* (1975) are the best known.

Illustration from *Chin Chiang and the Dragon's Dance*, written and illustrated by Jan Wallace (*courtesy Douglas & McIntyre/Groundwood Books*).

Others include Shizuye Takashima's *A Child in Prison Camp* (1971) and Ted Harrison's *Children of the Yukon* (1977). Blades has also written *A Boy of Taché* (1973) and has illustrated several other books, including Michael Macklem's *Jacques the Woodcutter* (1977) and Betty Waterton's *A Salmon for Simon* (1978). During the 1980s a larger number of fine Canadian picture books have been published. Two outstanding newer artists are Jan Wallace (*Chin Chiang and the Dragon's Dance*, 1984; and *Very Last First Time*, 1985), and Ken Nutt, pseudonym for Eric Beddows, who provided illustrations for Tim Wynne-Jones's award winning *Zoom at Sea* (1983) and *Zoom Away* (1985). Michael Martchenko has supplied illustrations for the books of popular storyteller Robert Munsch, including *The Paperbag Princess* (1980) and *50 Below Zero*. Since the mid-1970s a number of good Canadian plays have been published. In 1975 Rolf Kalman edited *A Collection of Canadian Plays: Volume 4*, a gathering of 10 dramas for children, including Eric NICOL's "The Clam Made a Face," Carol BOLT's "Cyclone Jack" and Leonard PETERSON's "Billy Bishop & the Red Baron." Native people are the subject of Henry Beissel's *Inook and the Sun* (1974) and Dennis Foon's *The Windigo* (1978).

Although most books bought in Canada are still by English and American authors, Canadian writers are becoming more widely read. This is due in part to the increasing national consciousness manifested since the centennial of Confederation in 1967. However, many reasons for the growth of Canadian children's literature are to be found within the field itself. The CANADA COUNCIL has encouraged writers through a series of grants and the sponsorship of reading tours. In addition a number of LITERARY PRIZES recognizing meritorious works and authors have been established. These include the Canadian Assn of Children's Librarians' Book of the Year for Children (since 1947) and the Amelia Frances Howard-Gibbon Medal for outstanding illustration (1971), the Canada Council Children's Literature Prizes (1975), the Canadian Authors Assn's Award (1963) and the Canadian Booksellers' Assn's Ruth Schwartz Children's Book Award (1975).

In recent years, several SMALL PRESSES have published extensive lines of children's books. Among these are Tree Frog Press (Edmonton), Annick Press (Toronto), Kids Can Press (Toronto), Scholastic-TAB (Toronto), and Groundwood Books (Toronto). The 1970s also saw the beginning of the children's magazines *Owl* (1976-) and *Chickadee* (1979-) and of the *Canadian Children's Annual* (1975-).

Serious academic study of Canadian children's literature has also developed since 1967. Sheila Egoff's *The Republic of Childhood* (1967) appeared

in its second edition in 1975. The journal *In Review: Canadian Books for Children* was published 1967-82, and *Canadian Children's Literature* began publication in 1975. Canadian books are regularly studied in children's literature classes in Canadian universities, and the Children's Book Center was established in 1976 to publicize Canadian children's books and co-ordinate the annual Children's Book Festival. *See also* FOLKLORE; LITERATURE IN ENGLISH; CHILDREN'S LITERATURE IN FRENCH.

JON C. STOTT

Children's Literature in French does not have a long tradition, and scholarly research in the field is relatively new. If "children's literature" includes books read by children, but not written especially for them, then French Canadian children's literature had its start in the 19th century. One early book popular because of its subject matter was *L'Enfant perdu et retrouvé* (1887) by J.B. Proulx, an adventure story in which 3 kidnapped children are sold as cabin boys. Only the eldest survives to tell of his adventures. Several books devoted to traditional tales and legends were enjoyed by children because of the familiar background and speech patterns (more easily understood than those in the books imported from France), eg, Frederick Marryat's *The Settlers in Canada* (tr *Les Colons du Canada*, 1852), *Contes populaires* (1867) by Paul Stevens, *Légendes canadiennes* (1861) by H.R. CASGRAIN, *Le Tomahawk et l'épée* (1877) by Joseph Marmette, *La Terre paternelle* (1871) by Patrice Lacombe, *Une de perdue, deux de trouvées* (1874) by P.G. Boucher de Boucherville and *Christmas in French Canada* (1899, tr *La Noël au Canada*, 1900) by L.H. FRÉCHETTE. These books were often distributed as school prizes in Québec. The policy to circulate the books in the schools began in 1876 and continued through the early part of the 20th century, in the hope that a sound basis for the development of children's literature could be established.

In 1891 Laure Conan (Félicité ANGERS) published *A l'oeuvre et à l'épreuve*, the romanticized story of Jesuit martyr Charles Garnier, which was popular among young people until the 1950s. Her *L'Oublié* (1900), even more popular, is a historical novel about Lambert Closse who participated in the founding of Ville-Marie. Conan wrote numerous articles on Canadian personalities and collected several of them in *Silhouettes canadiennes* (1917). *Contes et légendes* (1915) by Adèle Lacerte was dedicated to Canadian children, for whom, she claimed, no one had previously made a particular effort to write. Four years later, *Récits laurentiens* (1919) by Frère MARIE-VICTORIN (Conrad Kirouac) was published. His *Croquis laurentiens* followed the next year.

In 1920 Arthur Saint-Pierre, managing editor of the magazine *L'Oiseau bleu* (published by the ST-JEAN-BAPTISTE SOCIETY) asked Marie-Claire Daveluy to contribute a pioneer story whose principal characters would be children. Her story about 2 French orphans who settle in New France was serialized in *L'Oiseau bleu*. Published as a book, *Les Aventures de Perrine et de Charlot* (1923), it received the Prix David and became very popular. Although Daveluy also wrote modern fairy tales, she is best known for her historical novels on the early French settlers. Other budding writers of the period, such as Marie-Louise d'Auteuil (*Mémoires d'une souris canadienne*, 1932), contributed to the success of *L'Oiseau bleu*, which ceased publication in 1940.

Others who began to write in the 1920s were Maxine (pseudonym of M.C.A. Taschereau-Fortier) and Eugène Achard. Maxine wrote many fanciful historical novels and short biographies, eg, *Le Marin de Saint-Malo, Jacques Cartier* (1946). She is fondly remembered for *Le Petit Page de Fron-*

"A little boy with green eyes in a green field with three green frogs and a green kite" (*courtesy* Blanc Comme Neige, *Éditions Ovale, 1984, Marie-Louise Gay*).

tenac (1930), a novel set in 17th-century New France. Achard, who immigrated to Canada from France, began his prolific writing career with *Aux quatre coins des routes canadiennes* (1921) and ended it with *Sur les sentiers de la Côte Nord* (1960). His books included retellings of traditional tales (*L'Oiseau vert et la princesse fortunée*, 1956) and biographies (*Les Grands Noms de l'histoire canadienne*, 1940), but are mostly fiction (*Sous les plis du drapeau blanc*, 1935) and collections of modern fairy tales with a Canadian or Québec setting (*Les Contes de la claire fontaine*, 1943). During this period there was an interest in publishing natural-science books, which included *L'ABC du petit naturaliste canadien* (9 vols, 1936) by Harry Bernard, *A travers les champs et les bois* by Louis-Jean Gagnon (1931), *Les Confidences de la nature* by Adolphe Brassard (1936), *Nos animaux domestiques* by Odette Oligny (1933) and *Oiseaux de mon pays* by Alice Duchesnay (1939). The trend was continued in the 1940s by Marcelle Gauvreau who wrote *Plantes curieuses de mon pays* (1943) and Claude Melançon who wrote several books, including one on Québec's birds (*Charmants voisins*, 1940) and one on Canadian animals (*Mon alphabet des animaux*, 1944). Besides these 2 books, Melançon wrote his popular *Légendes indiennes du Canada* (1967) and other informational books on a variety of subjects, eg, *Mon alphabet des villes du Québec* (1944) and *Les Poissons de nos eaux* (1936).

During WWII there were few children's books available from Europe, and publishers at home attempted to fill the gap. The ever-popular genres, fairy tale and legend, were represented by Achard's *Les Deux Bossus de l'Île d'Orléans et autres contes* (1944); Marius Barbeau's *Les Contes du grand-père sept-heures* (12 vols, 1950-53: parts tr in *The Golden Phoenix*, 1958) and *Les Rêves des chasseurs* (1942); and the successful trilogy of fables and poems *Adagio* (1943), *Allegro* (1944) and *Andante* (1944) by Félix Leclerc. Guy Boulizon (who also emigrated from France) and Ambroise Lafortune wrote adventure stories in which some of the principal characters were Boy Scouts. A typical book by Lafortune (himself a Scout leader) is *Le Secret de la rivière perdue* (1946). Boulizon's *Prisonniers des cavernes* (1950) was rewritten and published in 1979 as *Alexandre et les prisonniers des cavernes*. A few other notable books published during this period were Claude Aubry's *La Vengeance des hommes de bonne volonté* (1944), reprinted twice as *Le Loup de Noël*, and Andrée Maillet's *Le Marquiset têtu et le mulot réprobateur* (1944) and her picture book *Ristontac* (1945), illustrated by Robert LaPalme.

Public interest in children's books, however, was waning. To remedy the situation, author Beatrice Clément founded the Association des écrivains pour la jeunesse in 1948 to encourage excellence in writing and to arouse support for French Canadian children's books. The association lasted only 6 years, but it was active in creating the children's book firm Éditions Jeunesse. It was also largely responsible for persuading established firms such as Fides to renew their commitment to publishing children's books. Children's literature had reached a stage where changes were needed to reflect new social attitudes and to provide children with more books that responded to their needs and interests. Although books of the past still brought joy and excitement to countless children, stereotypes of whites and native peoples had developed, and as minor writers entered the field, there evolved a sameness of pattern in the themes and their treatment. Eventually, the literature was marked by lack of originality and often by mediocrity in writing style.

Children's books began to achieve new distinction in the late 1950s, with Paule Daveluy's *L'Été enchanté* (1958; tr *Summer in Ville-Marie*, 1962), Yves Thériault's *Alerte au camp 29* (1959), Claudine Vallerand's (pseudonym "Maman Fonfon") *Chante et joue* (1957) and Monique Corriveau's *Le Secret de Vanille* (1959). Corriveau develops atmosphere that becomes an essential component of the story, as in *Les Saisons de la mer* (1975), about an Irish family in Newfoundland in the 1920s. Another interesting writer of this period is Suzanne Martel, whose *Quatre montréalais en l'an 3000* (1963; repr *Surréal 3000*, 1980; tr *The City Underground*, 1982) shows her lively ability to introduce humour into inventive science fiction novels, which include *Nos amis robots* (1981, tr *Robot Alert*, 1985). Claude Aubry's *Agouhanna*, 1974, tr 1973), written in a simple, even poetic, manner, has also worn well. Informational books, eg, *Chevalier du roi; vie de saint Ignace de Loyola* (1956) by Beatrice Clément were not as appealing to young readers as were mysteries and adventures.

A slump occurred in children's literature between 1965 and 1970: books were no longer given as school prizes, and French and Belgian imports increased. Although some excellent books were available, they were poorly promoted. Retail trade declined while textbook publishing increased to meet the demands of the newly laicized educational system. Between 1965 and 1968 only about 70 titles appeared, and in 1969 and 1970, fewer than 10 – a mere trifle compared to the 1000 French titles appearing annually overseas. In the 1970s, efforts were made to revitalize children's literature. The founding of Com-

munication-Jeunesse in Québec in 1971 inspired authors, illustrators, publishers, booksellers, librarians and teachers to work together, and the organization became a key factor in the promotion of children's book publishing.

Several newcomers responded to the need for a specifically Québecois children's literature. Bertrand Gauthier produced inventive, droll stories filled with puns, such as *Hébert Luée* (1980) which, critical of contemporary society without being preachy, is illustrated with colourful, often outlandish, pictures by Marie-Louise Gay. Gay also wrote and illustrated a counting book, *De zéro à minuit* (1981). Ginette Anfousse wrote and illustrated a series of books about a little girl and her toy anteater, all translated into English. The first 2, *La Cachette* (tr *Hide and Seek*) and *Mon ami Pichou* (tr *My Friend Pichou*), were published in 1976. Tibo (Gilles Thibault) created the colour pictures for *Le Tour de l'île* (1980) by Félix Leclerc and excellent black-and-white drawings for *Je te laisse une caresse* and *Mon petit lutin s'endort*, (repr 1979), 2 small books of verse by André Cailloux (1976). *Une Fenêtre dans ma tête* (2 vols, 1979) by Raymond Plante, which describes a young child's fantasy world, is illustrated with lively drawings by Roger Paré. A charming fantasy story is *Le Voyage à la recherche du temps* (1981) by Lucie Ledoux, illustrated in black and white by Philippe Béha.

In 1974 Fides inaugurated its series "Du Goéland," whose titles include *Le Garçon au cerf-volant* (1974, tr *A Perfect Day for Kites*) by Monique Corriveau, illustrated by Louise Méthé; *Le Ru d'Ikoué* (1977) by Yves Thériault, illustrated by Michelle Poirier; *Le Chat de l'Oratoire* (1978, repr 1983 and tr *The Cat in the Cathedral*) by Bernadette Renaud, illustrated by Josette Michaud and *Chansons pour un ordinateur* (1980) by Francine Loranger, illustrated by Laurent Bouchard. Les Editions Héritage, which publishes the magazines *Hibou* and *Coulicou* (adaptations of the English-language magazines *Owl* and *Chickadee*), launched several series of children's books, among them "Pour lire avec toi" (1976), designed for young readers in transition between the picture book and the book for the older reader. Fantasy and reality intermingle in 3 books in this series: *Fend-le-vent et le visiteur mystérieux* (1980) by Serge Wilson, illustrated by Claude Poirier; *Emilie, la baignoire à pattes* (1976) by Bernadette Renaud, illustrated by France Bédard; and *Alfred dans le métro* (1980), written and illustrated by Cécile Gagnon. *La Révolte de la courtepointe* (1979), written by Bernadette Renaud and illustrated by Lucie Ledoux, also combines the real and the fantastic. Another Héritage series, Katimavik, includes Suzanne Martel's *Pi-Oui* (1974, repr 1979 and tr *Peewee*) and *Contes de mon pays* (1976, repr 1980) by Germain Lemieux. The series "Jeunesse-Pop" by Les Éditions Paulines includes Louis Landry's *Glausgab, créateur du monde* (1981) and *Glausgab, le protecteur* (1981), 2 novels that create a new mythological hero, an Algonquian Indian who lands in France in 1489 and tells his story to the French court.

Young francophone readers have been introduced to good texts from English Canada by Les Éditions Pierre Tisseyre. The works include stories about the art of growing up, eg, *Luke Baldwin's Vow* (tr *La Promesse de Luke Baldwin*, 1980) by Morley CALLAGHAN and *You Can Pick Me Up at Peggy's Cove* (tr *Je t'attends à Peggy's Cove*, 1982) by Brian Doyle; about handicapped children, eg, *Listen for the Singing* (tr *Écoute l'oiseau chantera*, 1980) by Jean Little; about animals, eg, *Owls in the Family* (tr *Deux Grands Ducs dans la famille*, 1980) by Farley MOWAT; about Russian Mennonites who settle in Manitoba, *Days of Terror* (tr *Jours de terreur*, 1981) by Barbara Smucker; and about a heroine in a well-loved Canadian classic, *Emily of*

New Moon (tr *Emilie de la Nouvelle Lune*, 1983) by Lucy Maud MONTGOMERY.

Some books offer children a chance to discover authors appreciated by their elders, eg, Gilles VI-GNEAULT's *Les Quatre Saisons de Piquot* (1979), illustrated by Hugh John Barrett, and *Quelques pas dans l'univers d'Eva* (1981), illustrated by Claude Fleury; Roch CARRIER's *Les Voyageurs de l'arc-en-ciel* (1980), illustrated by François Olivier, and *Les Contes du sommet bleu* (1980), written and illustrated by Claude Jasmin. For older readers Suzanne Martel has written several novels with historical settings, such as *Jeanne, fille du roy* (1974, tr *The King's Daughter*, 1980), an adventure story with an authentic 17th-century setting. Martel's stories of Les Montcorbier (*L'Apprentissage d'Arahé* and *Premières Armes*, both 1979) and of Menfou Carcajou (*Ville-Marie* and *La Baie du Nord*, 1980) are written for adults, although they can appeal to mature young readers. Another book for older readers is the farcical and fanciful, almost surreal, *La Planète guenille* (1980) by Gilles Rivard and Jean Clouâtre. A series by Éditions Ovale is called "Légendes du Québec," although the stories are not necessarily authentic. It includes *La Grange aux lutins* (1980), adapted by Robert Piette and illustrated by Josée Dombrowski; *La Chasse-galerie* (1980), adapted by Madeleine Chénard and illustrated by France Lebon; and *Les Feux follets* (1981), adapted by Johanne Bussières and illustrated by Josée Dombrowski. There are also mysteries set in Musée des beaux-arts de Montréal (*Le Visiteur du soir*, 1980) by Robert Soulières and in a manor house at the start of the colonial period (*L'Épée arhapal*, 1981) by Daniel Sernine.

Fantasy, humour and wordplay have become increasingly prevalent with such works as *Un Jour d'été à Fleurdepeau* (1981), written by Bertrand Gauthier and illustrated by Daniel Sylvestre; *Crapauds et autres animaux* (1981), a book of original verse by Yvan Adam in collaboration with several other authors and illustrators; *Monsieur Genou* (1981) by Raymond Plante, and *Une Journée dans la vie de Craquelin 1er, roi de soupe-au-lait* (1981) by J.M. Poupart.

In other regions of Canada where francophone communities exist, there are efforts to publish French books for children. Les Éditions d'Acadie in New Brunswick publishes picture books, eg, *Caprice à la campagne* (1982) by Melvin Gallant; Les Éditions des Plaines in Manitoba published *Le Petit dinosaure d'Alberta* (1980) by Nadine Mac-Kenzie; and Les Éditions Prise de Parole in Ontario has published a beautiful modern version of an Ojibwa legend, *Nanna Bijou, le géant endormi* (1981) by Jocelyne Villeneuve (tr *Nanna Bijou: The Sleeping Giant*, 1981). Other Ontario publishers are presenting French translations of Canadian or foreign titles, eg, *The Paper Bag Princess* (1980) by Robert Munsch (tr *La Princesse à la robe de papier*, 1981) and *Harold Greenhouse to the Rescue*, (1982; tr *Jérôme Lafeuille part à la rescousse*, 1982) by Michael Wilkins.

The momentum engendered by Communication-Jeunesse has supported steady growth in the number and quality of children's books, especially picture books, beginning readers, translations and books for young adults published in the series Conquêtes (eg, *Aller retour* by Yves Beauchesne and David Schinkel, 1986). Illustrators are exploring new techniques, and are making more effective use of design and increasingly integrating their pictures with the text (eg, the Drôle d'école series of 4 books written and illustrated by Marie-Louise Gay, 1984). Two major features of beginners' readers are diversity of themes and excellence of texts, eg, in *Le Bal des chenilles* (1979) by Robert Soulières and *Emilie, la baignoire à pattes* (1976) by Bernadette Renaud. By publishing

translations, publishers hope to promote better understanding of the principal Canadian cultures and provide a broader scope of material for readers. Apart from those mentioned above, there are excellent translations published by Les Éditions Héritage, eg, Erik Munsterhjelm's animal story *Canilou* (1979) and James HOUSTON's modern Inuit tale *L'Archer blanc* (1978), both beautifully translated by Maryse Côté. Nonfiction and novels with contemporary settings are still very much needed to provide Canadian children with themes close to home. Nevertheless, impressive strides in the development and promotion of French Canadian children's literature have been made, leading to the spread of that literature to many corners of Canada, and even across international borders.   IRENE E. AUBREY

Reading: Louise Lemieux, *Pleins feux sur la littérature de jeunesse au Canada français* (1972).

Chilkat Blanket, associated with the Chilkat (a northern tribe of Tlingit), was traded along the Northwest Coast. The blanket was made of mountain goat wool, spun over a core of cedar-bark string. The men hunted the goat, constructed the frame on which the weaving was done and painted the design board from which the women, who did the weaving, took the design. The design often represents an animal (such as a bear), but is reordered and modified through complex principles. Representing the high point of weaving in NORTHWEST COAST INDIAN ART, these blankets are almost always black, white, yellow and blue.

RENÉ R. GADACZ

Chilkoot Pass, elev 1067 m, is situated on the BC-Alaska border. It was used by the Chilkat Indians, a tribe of the TLINGIT, expert weavers who traded with the Nahani along the Yukon R to the N and later with HBC employees. In 1883 the US government, unknown to Canada, sent an expedition to the Yukon via the pass to study the terrain and the Indian situation. Irritated by this action, the Canadian government sent William Ogilvie via Chilcoot in 1887 to establish the 141st meridian at the Yukon R. During the KLONDIKE GOLD RUSH, an estimated 20 000 to 30 000 people crossed the pass 1897-98. The NWMP established a post here to stop lawlessness, collect duty and ensure that each person had supplies for 1 year. Several tramways were built over the pass to Crater Lk 1897-98, but the trams and pass fell into disuse with construction of the railway over WHITE PASS, completed in 1900. A hiking trail, "Trail of 98," over Chilkoot was rebuilt in the 1960s, complete with shelters, as a joint venture by the Yukon government and US National Pk Service.

GLEN BOLES

Chilkoot Trail, alternatively known as the Klondike Gold Rush Trail, is one of the most rugged and demanding long-distance trails in Canada. It extends about 53 km from Skagway, on the Alaska Panhandle, over the Coastal Mt range to Bennett, BC. Historically the trail dates to the 1897-98 KLONDIKE GOLD RUSH, when an estimated 30 000 gold seekers and traders fought their way over the tortuous route, braving a wild terrain, high altitudes and frequent severe weather changes. Today the trail has been somewhat improved and restored by US and Canadian park officials and offers designated campsites and other amenities. However, for the some 2000 people yearly who seek its adventure, it still represents a challenging 4-5 day hike.   BART F. DEEG

Chilliwack, Vancouver rock band, began as The Classics (fl 1964-67), and went through an experimental, psychedelic period (1967-70) as The Collectors before adopting the name and bright melodic style that brought international popularity in the late 1970s. Most popular songs include

"Lonesome Mary," "Baby Blue," and "Fly at Night." Singer and guitarist Bill Henderson has been the only constant through many personnel changes.   MARK MILLER

Chilliwack, BC, pop 41 337 (1986c), area 264 km², inc as city 1908 and District Municipality 1980, is 100 km E of Vancouver on the S shore of the FRASER R. The name derives from an Indian tribe and likely means "going back up" (ie, home from the Fraser). The district is governed by a mayor and 8 aldermen elected for 2-year terms. Agriculture is the leading resource sector; much of the milk and dairy products consumed in the Lower Mainland originates here. Manufacturing is focused on farm products or inputs and, in the eastern half of the district, on extensive logging. A Canadian Forces base at Vedder Crossing (10 km south) has a large military and civilian payroll. The recreation industry, particularly in the Cultus Lake area to the S, also supports the local economy. Although too far from Vancouver for most commuters, the area's reasonably priced land has prompted considerable residential development.

ALAN F.J. ARTIBISE

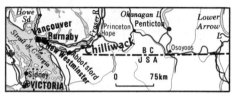

Chimaera, ratfish, or ghost shark, strange-looking marine fish belonging to the subclass Holocephali, class Chondrichthyes and thus related to SHARKS and RAYS. There are about 25 species (mostly in the family Chimaeridae), which occur in deep or cool waters of most seas. In Canada, 3 species in 3 genera (*Hydrolagus, Harriotta* and *Rhinochimaera*) occur in Atlantic waters and one species (*Hydrolagus colliei*) occurs in Pacific waters. Chimaeras are elongate and scaleless and range from 0.5 to 2.0 m in length. The ventral mouth is overhung by a projecting snout which is sometimes lancelike. At the front of the dorsal fin is a strong spine with a poison gland at its base. The pectoral fins are large and winglike. Males have a clasperlike organ on the front of the head in addition to pelvic claspers. All species deposit eggs, each in an elongate, horny capsule. Chimaeras eat bottom molluscs and crustaceans, crushing them with their strong, grinding teeth. They have no commercial importance.   W.B. SCOTT

Chinese immigrants first arrived in Canada from San Francisco in 1858, at the beginning of the Fraser R gold rush in BC. In BARKERVILLE, BC, the first Chinese community in Canada was founded. By 1860 it was estimated that the Chinese population of Vancouver I and British Columbia was about 7000. The first Chinese migrants were young peasants from South China; they were followed, in the 1870s and 1880s, by other young peasants who laboured under appalling conditions to build the CANADIAN PACIFIC RY. Chinese communities later spread to other parts of Canada. By 1987 (the preliminary figures from the 1986 census), through immigration and natural increase, the Chinese Canadian population was about 360 000.

Origins Both rural poverty and political upheavals have stimulated Chinese emigration. Historically, the majority came from the 4 districts (*sze-yap*) or counties in the Pearl R Delta of Guangdong province, between Canton and Hong Kong. A tradition existed in that locality of seeking opportunity overseas, sending money back to support relatives in China, and eventually returning, if possible.

Chinese work gang on the CPR tracks near Summit, BC, 1889. Between 1881 and 1885, more than 15 000 Chinese arrived to work on the CPR (*courtesy Glenbow Archives, Calgary*).

Migration The major periods of Chinese immigration (from 1858 to 1923 and since 1947) reflected changes in Canadian government IMMIGRATION POLICY. From 1885 Chinese migrants had been obliged to pay an "entry" or "head" tax before being admitted into Canada. By 1900, in response to agitation in BC, the Liberal government increasingly restricted Asian immigration by raising the head tax to $100. After this was greeted with the angry derision of BC politicians, who had demanded it be increased to $500, the government appointed a Royal Commission on Chinese and Japanese Immigration (1902) which concluded that the Asians were "unfit for full citizenship...obnoxious to a free community and dangerous to the state." The 1903 session of Parliament passed legislation raising the head tax to $500; the number of Chinese who paid the fee in the first fiscal year dropped from 4719 to 8. Soon afterwards, however, Chinese immigration increased again and on 1 July 1923 (known to the Canadian Chinese as "Humiliation Day") the Chinese Immigration Act was replaced by legislation which virtually suspended Chinese immigration, as it was intended to do. In 1947 the discriminatory legislation was repealed, although the restrictions on Chinese immigration were not entirely removed until 1967. Chinese and East Indian Canadians gained the vote federally and provincially in 1947.

Before 1947 Chinese immigration was either arranged by contractors or was individual and voluntary. Typically, and largely as a consequence of the head tax, which made the cost of bringing a wife or aged parents to Canada prohibitive, men came alone and lived as bachelors in Canada. In 1931, out of a total Chinese population of 46 519, only 3648 were women. In the late 1920s it has been estimated that there were only 5 married Chinese women in Calgary and 6 in Edmonton. Since 1947 immigration of families has been the rule. From 1950 onwards, the majority of immigrants have emigrated from Hong Kong (others have come from Southeast Asia, South Africa, the West Indies and Peru); these Chinese often speak English fluently, are well educated and frequently possess financial resources and professional skills. There is some tension between new and old immigrants, but the web of kinship is still strong.

Settlement Patterns Since 1900 Chinese Canadians have chosen to settle in urban areas and are now concentrated in the largest cities. The "Chinatowns" which grew up in the 19th and 20th centuries were originally classic ghettos – overcrowded and squalid – but they tended to crumble or change as the migrants experienced some upward social mobility. In Vancouver, restrictive covenants prevented the Chinese from buying property outside the Chinatown area until the 1930s. Until the 1880s almost all Chinese lived in BC, and until the 1940s almost 50% of their population still resided there, but Chinese communities have developed rapidly in other urban centres as well, particularly Toronto; 66% of Chinese Canadians now live in Toronto and Vancouver. Small groups or individual Chinese have also settled in towns across the Prairies, in BC and Ontario and in the Atlantic provinces.

Economic Life When they first arrived in BC the Chinese were involved in various kinds of work. Some were gleaners in the goldfields, often working abandoned claims; others became labourers, cooks, laundrymen, teamsters and merchants, providing auxiliary services to mining communities. Many worked as domestic servants in towns and villages. Between 1881 and 1885 more than 15 000 Chinese arrived to work the CPR and during the next 40 years became involved in the rough work of a pioneer industrial economy. Skilled or semiskilled Chinese worked in the BC sawmills and canneries; others became market gardeners or grocers, pedlars, shopkeepers and restaurateurs.

The work of Chinese industrial labourers was often organized under contract. Under the "credit-ticket" system, Chinese lenders in North America or China agreed to pay the travel expenses of a migrant who was then bound to the lender until the debt was repaid, although none of these contracts were legally enforceable in Canada. The other form of contract labour involved Chinese work gangs. At the turn of the century, Chinese cannery bosses were almost invariably hired on contract. They then recruited workers and assumed the financial risk of low production. From the 1880s this practice was employed in railway construction as well. Chinese labour was characterized by low wages (Chinese workers usually received less than 50% paid to white workers for the same work), high levels of transience and a strong work discipline.

The earliest Chinese professionals tended to serve primarily the Chinese community. In BC the Chinese were barred for years from many professions, eg, law, pharmacy and accountancy. The first Chinese Canadian lawyers were called to the bar only in the 1940s, but since then, as discriminatory laws have been repealed and the character of immigration has changed, many more Chinese professionals, serving a mixed clientele, have migrated. Nevertheless, even in the 1980s, Chinese are still heavily involved in service occupations.

Social Life and Community Chinese communities in Canada reflected their cultural traditions, particularly the kinship system (based on ancestral descent), the "joss house" or temple and the Chinese theatre, but they developed their own unique N American characteristics as well. For example, the community in Canada generated its own elite, that of the merchants, and their own "voluntary" associations adapted from models in China to provide personal and community welfare services, social contact and a base for political activity. Typically, rural Chinese who immigrated to Canada had to adapt to urban conditions, and these associations helped migrants adjust to a new culture and to racial PREJUDICE AND DISCRIMINATION. During the "bachelor" phase, when the men in Chinese communities far outnumbered the women, associations developed to provide services to single men who lived primarily in *fang-k'ou* – formally organized households of Chinese "bachelors" which still exist in the backstreets of Vancouver, Victoria, Toronto and Montréal. Certain principles – territory, dialect, surname – constituted the criteria for membership and recruitment. Older members who had never married or who were too poor to return to China lived in retirement in association halls.

Bachelor organizations have declined as the tendency of the Chinese to migrate as families increased. Associations open to everyone have included, notably, the Kuomintang (KMT) and the Freemasons, fraternal-political associations interested in Chinese and Chinatown politics and community issues. Larger Chinese communities have had Chinese Benevolent Associations at the apex of their organizational structures which have adjudicated disputes within the community and speak for the community to the outside world. None of these organizations, however, have been effective national voices. More recently, such typically Canadian organizations as the Lions, Elks and Veterans have appeared.

The original Chinese communities were isolated from the white culture for several reasons. The Chinese tended to consider themselves as "sojourners," in Canada temporarily to secure some financial security for relatives in China. This mentality was reinforced by legislation in Canada which prevented easy immigration of Chinese families and precluded their participation professionally, socially or politically in the dominant society. The white society of BC perceived the Chinese as unassimilable under any circumstances, and certain aspects of Chinese life in Canada reinforced the racial stereotype of the Chinese as a threat to white society. Fears of disease, eg, cholera and leprosy, white reaction to overcrowded living conditions in Chinatown, the introduction of opium and consequently of a drug trade, and an obsessive concern with Chinese gambling habits, all helped maintain the almost universally held conviction that the Chinese, as one senator speaking for white residents of BC explained, "are not of our race and cannot become part of ourselves."

By the 1970s, Chinese society in Canada had been transformed, although traditional, familiar values are still continued in some respects. For example, the majority of young, working Chinese

Chinatown, Dundas Street, Toronto (*courtesy SSC Photocentre/photo by David Lee*).

continue to commit resources to the support of their parents, and many grandparents live with their children.

Newspapers are an important form of community expression. Although Chinese-language papers have long been published in Vancouver and Toronto, they are now in some danger of being eclipsed by American editions of Hong Kong Chinese papers.

Religion and Cultural Life Chinese religion (eg, ancestor worship) in Canada has commonly been expressed in private but is declining in importance. The proportion of Christians in the Chinese population rose from 10% in 1921 to 60% in 1961. Chinese Christian churches (especially the UNITED CHURCH) are an important focal point of family activity and usually the centre of organized social activities for women. The major Chinese festival is the Lunar New Year (February or late January), celebrated in Chinatowns with firecrackers and lion and dragon dancers. Other important festive days are "Bright-Clear," a springtime sweeping of graves of ancestors, and "Mid-Autumn," a late summer occasion for moon watching.

Education Chinese schools date from the 1890s. By the 1930s, at their peak, there were 26 of them across the country. They were particularly important during periods in BC when attempts were made to segregate Chinese children. Chinese schools, however, have generally provided supplementary after-school classes in Chinese language, history and culture. The Chinese have never been legally prohibited by law from attending universities, even when professional fields were closed to them after graduation. With the growth of family life in the 1950s and the increasing affluence and professional character of the Chinese communities in the 1960s, much larger numbers of Chinese students have sought higher education.

Politics Until 1950, Chinese depended upon their leaders and other intermediaries who had amiable relations with Canadian politicians to speak on their behalf in Canadian affairs. They have since become more active in Canadian politics, particularly for the Liberal Party, probably because of its identification with relaxed immigration regulations. In 1957 Douglas Jung be-

came the first Chinese Canadian MP, and in various places mayors and aldermen of Chinese origin have been elected.

Group Maintenance In large Chinese Canadian communities professionals tend to sponsor cultural exchanges with China, Hong Kong and Taiwan to encourage the preservation of Chinese culture and then promote fair presentation of Chinese Canadians in the media and other issues. Canada-based Cantonese opera groups exist and martial arts organizations have flourished. The Hong Kong version of modern Chinese culture is very strongly reflected in Chinese Canadian society.

Language maintenance was essential before 1947, when only jobs in Chinatown, requiring knowledge of Chinese, were open to young Chinese Canadians. More recently, the use of written Chinese has declined. Spoken Chinese ranges from specific, very local dialects to Hong Kong Cantonese.

From their own perspective, the Chinese completed the CPR with great hardship and were then abandoned by those who hired them; only they were forced to pay a humiliating head tax, and only they were excluded from immigration. Chinese Canadian military service for Canada in WWII did help change white attitudes, but traces of nativism against Chinese Canadians still exist, exacerbated by economic recession and increased immigration.   E.B. WICKBERG

Reading: E.B. Wickberg et al, *From China to Canada* (1982); W. Peter Ward, *White Canada Forever* (1978); Anthony B. Chan, *Gold Mountain* (1983).

Chiniquy, Charles-Paschal-Télesphore, Roman Catholic priest turned Presbyterian minister (b at Kamouraska, LC 30 July 1809; d at Montréal 16 Jan 1899). He travelled throughout Lower Canada 1839-51, preaching temperance, and his fame was such that he was called "Father Matthew of Lower Canada." But he was so arrogant and undisciplined that in 1851 Mgr Ignace BOURGET asked him to leave the diocese. He settled in the parish Ste-Anne-de-Kankakee (Ill) where, in 1856, he was excommunicated by the bishop of Chicago for a grave infraction of ecclesiastical discipline. He then began a new career there, first as founder of the Catholic Christian Church and then as a Presbyterian minister. When he ran into difficulties with the Presbytery of Chicago, he applied in 1863 for admission with his Ste-Anne's congregation to the Synod of the Canada Presbyterian Church and was accepted. The bishops of Québec waged unrelenting war on him, worried by his oratorical talents and endless, outrageous attacks on the Catholic Church. Protestants, for the same reasons, welcomed him enthusiastically. He died after a ministry that had taken him throughout the US, to Europe, Australia and New Zealand. Almost a century later, his career is still highly controversial.
                                                                    YVES ROBY

Chinook, warm, dry, gusty, westerly WIND experienced in a shallow belt extending some 300-400 km E from the eastern slopes of the Rocky Mts. The wind was named after the Chinook tribe which occupied the mouth of the Columbia R in Oregon, the territory from which the wind seemed to originate. In Canada the highest frequency of chinooks occurs in southern Alberta. Pincher Creek and Calgary receive an average of 30-35 chinook days each winter. Chinooks occur in summer but are not always noticeable. They can raise air temperature by over 25°C in one hour. In winter they occur when a cold arctic air mass is replaced at ground level by warm Pacific air. When moist Pacific air is lifted over the Rockies, heat is added to it as the water vapour it carries condenses (thereby giving up latent heat) and falls as precipitation. The air then arrives on the eastern slopes as a warm, dry wind (foehn-type wind). The chinook is further

Chinook arch, southern Alberta. In winter chinooks, which can raise temperatures by over 25°C in one hour, occur when a cold arctic air mass is replaced at ground level by warm Pacific air (*Elliott and Nicole Bernshaw/ Bernshaw Photography*).

warmed by subsidence of the Pacific air down the eastern slopes of the Rockies; descending air is subject to warming at the rate of 1°C per 100 m of height.   L.C. NKEMDIRIM

Chinook Jargon, a trade language used along the West Coast from the 1830s until the early 20th century. Sometimes inaccurately referred to simply as "Chinook" (the Chinook Indians of the lower Columbia R area have their own language), this lingua franca was used for intercommunication between Indians and traders, officials, settlers and other Indians. It is not certain whether Chinook Jargon is based upon a previous trade language, employing words of the languages of the most enterprising aboriginal trading groups, such as the Nootka. It probably arose as an aspect of the fur trade in post-contact times. Like other pidgin languages, Chinook Jargon has a restricted grammar and small vocabulary of approximately 700 words, which derive from Chinook (approximately 30%), Nootka (20%), English (20%), French (20%), other Indian tongues (8%) and new coinages (2%). It is estimated that more than 100 000 people could use Chinook Jargon in 1900, and it was employed widely in court testimony, newspaper advertising, missionary activity among Indians, and everyday conversation from Central BC to northern California. A Chinook Jargon periodical, *The Kamloops Wawa*, was published 1891-1904, much of it written in a special shorthand script. Although entrenched in West Coast native Indian life at the turn of the century (by which time Chinook Jargon was the first language of a growing number of children), it was supplanted by English and has now gone out of use except in a few songs of the Indian Shaker Church and some aspects of old-timer slang in BC, eg, the *salt chuck*, "the ocean, salt water"; *skookum*, "strong"; *tillikums*, "friends"; *high muckamucks*, "the powerful and well-off" (literally "the ones with lots of grub"); *in the sticks*, "in the woods, trees"; *cheechako*, "newcomer"; *potlatch*, "ceremony where goods are distributed" (literally "giving"); and *klahowya*, "greetings." Various plants and sea life have names derived from Jargon: *tyee* ("chief"), *chum* ("painted"), and *chinook* salmon; *gooeyduck* clams, *camas* and *salal*. Chinook Jargon words were used in place-names throughout BC (as well as Washington and Oregon), including the noted Siwash Rock (from French *sauvage*, "Indian," a place-name used despite the current derogative implication attached to use of the term siwash). Other place-names derived from Jargon are Cultus ("worthless") Lake as well as Canim ("canoe"), Nanitch ("see"), Kikwillie ("deep"), Eena ("beaver"), Siam ("grizzly"), Mesachie ("bad"), and Wahpeeto ("potato") lakes. Also, Tsee ("sweet"), Memalose ("dead"), Snass ("rainy"), Sitkum ("half"), Ipsoot ("black bear"), Moosmoos ("cow") and Alki ("by-and-by") creeks, and Lolo ("rise, carry"), Lakit ("sixth"), Moloch ("elk") and Chee ("new") mountains are among many other names of Chinook Jargon origin. A successful CBC show called Klahanie ("out of doors"), Vancouver's Kumtux ("to learn") School and Tamahnous ("spirit") Theatre all took their names from Jargon, just as did Tillicum, the mascot of Vancouver's centennial celebrations. Numerous dictionaries of Chinook Jargon are available, including those of George Gibbs, Frederick Long and George Shaw.

J.V. POWELL

Chipewyan is a term of Cree derivation, meaning "pointed skins," but Chipewyan call themselves DENE or "people." They originally occupied the northern fringe of the boreal forest and adjacent tundra from the Seal R to near the mouth of the Coppermine R. By the 19th century their lands included northern portions of Manitoba, Saskatchewan, Alberta and the southern part of the NWT. The Chipewyan are the most numerous and most widely distributed of the northern Athapaskans. In 1749 the population was estimated at approximately 4000 individuals. Epidemics of European diseases decimated the population, but it has since recovered and in 1986 about 8400 persons were enrolled in Chipewyan bands.

Chipewyan is a branch of the northeastern Athapaskan language family, closely related to neighbouring DOGRIB and SLAVEY. The CREE, their southern neighbours, are known as *ena,* or "enemy," although peaceful relations were established between 1716 and 1760. The INUIT are known as *hotél ena,* or "enemies of the flat area," but peace was general by the early 19th century. The YELLOWKNIFE, the northwesternmost group of Chipewyan, were devastated by disease and warfare in the early 19th century. Chipewyan socio-territorial organization was based on hunting the migratory and nomadic herds of Barren Ground caribou. Hunting groups consisted of 2 or more related nuclear families, which joined with other such groups to form larger local and regional bands, coalescing or dispersing with the herds. Leaders had limited authority, which was based upon their ability, wisdom and generosity. Spiritual power was received in dream visions; some men had great powers for curing and some for doing harm.

In 1717 the HUDSON'S BAY CO founded Ft Churchill for the Chipewyan FUR TRADE. An attempt had been made to establish a post there in summer 1689, but it was abandoned Aug of that year. In the late 18th century the HBC and NORTH WEST CO established competitive posts in the western hinterland of Hudson Bay and, following the great smallpox epidemic of 1781-82, many Chipewyan began to hunt in the full boreal forest, where fur-bearing animals were more abundant. A few individuals are remembered for their aid to white explorers in the North. Thanadelther, also known as Slave Woman, guided the first English explorer from Cree country into Chipewyan territory in 1715-16. MATONABBEE guided Samuel HEARNE from Churchill to the Coppermine R 1770-72.

In the 1960s the Chipewyan way of life was threatened by a number of government policies that were meant to improve housing, education and health services. In order to receive these services, and the cash payments for family allowance and old-age pensions, many Chipewyan relocated to permanent settlements. The influence of a cash economy and the disruption of social and subsistence patterns often had harmful effects. Many Chipewyan have returned to a traditional relationship with the car-

Chipewyan woman's costume (*courtesy Provincial Museum of Alberta*).

ibou and their lands. *See also* NATIVE PEOPLE: SUBARCTIC and general articles under NATIVE PEOPLE.

JAMES G.E. SMITH

Reading: J. Helm, ed, *Handbook of North American Indians,* vol 6: *Subarctic* (1981).

Chipman, Ward, lawyer, public servant, politician (b at Marblehead, Mass 30 July 1754; d at Fredericton 9 Feb 1824). As a graduate of Harvard College (1770) who assisted the LOYALIST forces during the American Revolution, he helped organize the agitation which led to the creation of New Brunswick in 1784. He became the colony's solicitor general, drafted the charter for the city of Saint John, and as clerk of the Crown acted as crown prosecutor in most criminal cases for some 25 years. His law office was a Mecca for students. Chipman's arguments in defence of a black slave in 1800 contributed to the gradual disappearance of legal slavery in NB. An MLA, 1785-95, he was appointed to the council in 1806 and became a judge of the Supreme Court in 1809. As British agent to 2 commissions established to determine the boundary with Maine, he successfully upheld NB's claim to much of the disputed territory. Before his death, he briefly administered the government of the colony. He was arguably the most influential of NB's founding fathers.

P.A. BUCKNER

Chipman, Ward, politician, judge (b at Saint John, NB 10 July 1787; d there 26 Nov 1852), son of Ward CHIPMAN, Sr. Educated at Harvard and in London, Chipman succeeded to his father's extensive law practice and acted with him during the abortive commission established to settle the northeastern boundary dispute in 1817-21. He became a Saint John MLA in 1820, solicitor-general in 1823, Speaker of the Assembly in 1824 and in 1825 was appointed a judge and member of the council. Between 1828 and 1830 he assisted in preparing the British boundary submission for arbitration and was instrumental in convincing the British government of the validity of NB's claim. In 1834 he became chief justice of NB and president of the council.

Conservative in his political and religious views, he trained a large number of lawyers, drafted the amendments to the criminal code in 1831, chaired a special inquiry into the administration of justice in 1832 and supervised the preparation of the first compendium of New Brunswick's laws, thus imposing his conservative approach on the colony's legal system.

P.A. BUCKNER

Chipmunk, diminutive member of the SQUIRREL family belonging to genus *Tamias* or *Eutamias. Tamias* is restricted to eastern N America. A single species, eastern chipmunk (*T. striatus*), occurs in the Maritimes and southern Qué, Ont and Man. *Eutamias* species occur in N America and Eurasia. Four are found in Canada, from Ont to parts of BC, southern YT and southern NWT: least, yellow pine, Townsend's and red-tailed chipmunks (*E. minimus, E. amoenus, E. townsendii, E. ruficaudus,* respectively). Eastern chipmunks weigh about 100 g; *Eutamias* species are smaller – ranging from 35 g for least chipmunk to 85 g for Townsend's chipmunk. Alert, sprightly animals, chipmunks run with tails erect. All have 5 dark stripes down the back; eastern chipmunks also have 2 lateral stripes on each side ending at the rump. Chipmunks hibernate in subterranean nests, feeding on stored foodstuffs during frequent arousals. Most *Eutamias* species bear one litter (5-6 young) each summer; eastern chipmunks, 2 (3-4 young). Chipmunks are omnivorous, eating seeds, nuts, invertebrates and occasionally small eggs. They are too scarce to be economically significant, but being diurnal, attractive and almost constantly busy, they afford pleasure to all who watch them.

W.A. FULLER

Chipmunk (*Eutamias minimus*), diminutive member of the squirrel family (*artwork by Claire Tremblay*).

Chiriaeff, Ludmilla, née Otzoup-Gorny, dancer, choreographer, teacher, director (b at Riga, Latvia 10 Jan 1924). As founding director of Les GRANDS BALLETS CANADIENS, she has helped establish BALLET in Québec. She trained in Berlin and studied ballet with many distinguished teachers. Choreographer Michael Fokine was a family friend and powerful influence on her artistic development. After WWII, having settled in Switzerland, she danced and choreographed for various companies and directed her own Ballets des Arts in Geneva 1949-51.

Chiriaeff immigrated to Canada in 1952. She opened a school in Montréal and began to choreograph for the nascent French TV service in Québec. Her new company, Les Ballets Chiriaeff, in which she continued to dance, evolved into Les Grands Ballets Canadiens in 1958. She remained its artistic director until 1974. She has since devoted herself to the company's schools. Among the many ballets choreographed by Chiriaeff are *Suite canadienne* (1957; music by Michel Perrault), *Cendrillon* (1962) and *Pierrot de la lune* (1963).

MICHAEL CRABB

Chiropractic is the manipulation of the spinal column as a means of curing disease. The word comes from the Greek *chiro* ("hands") and *practic* ("to practice"). The theory of chiropractic originated with D.D. Palmer, who was born in Port Perry (Ont) in 1845. Palmer became a charismatic healer in Iowa and accidentally discovered chiropractic by adjusting a bump on the neck of his stone-deaf janitor. The janitor's hearing was restored immediately. Palmer began to look to the spine for solving further health problems and began to teach his theories and practices. The Palmer College of Chiropractic was established and promoted by Palmer's son, B.J. Palmer, who continued to research and develop the new healing art.

Chiropractors employ neither drugs nor surgery; they base their treatment on the assumption that good health requires a properly functioning nervous system, beginning with the brain and including the spinal cord. Chiropractors believe that, because no part of the body escapes the dominance of the nervous system, spinal biomechanical dysfunction (ie, improper joint function at a specific point or points in the spinal column) may therefore result in poor health generally – even in areas of the body that have no obvious connection with the spine. The lightest pressure by a vertebra may interrupt regular transmission of nerve impulses, preventing that portion of the body from responding fully. A chiropractic spinal adjustment, the application of a precise force to the specific part of the spinal segment, is thought to correct a vertebral problem, permitting normal nerve transmission and recuperative capabilities. Medical doctors reject the theory but accept that spinal adjustment treatments are beneficial for some patients.

The Canadian Memorial Chiropractic College in Toronto offers a 4-year academic program with a prerequisite of 2 years of university education in a science field with a background in chemistry and physics. M.L. WHITE

Reading: B. Inglis, *Fringe Medicine* (1964).

Chisholm, George Brock, psychiatrist, medical administrator (b at Oakville, Ont 18 May 1896; d at Victoria 2 Feb 1971). Chisholm enlisted as a private in WWI, was commissioned in the field, wounded and twice decorated. After the war he rose to senior ranks in the militia. He graduated in medicine from U of T in 1924 and after some years of general practice studied psychiatry in the US and England, practising in Toronto from 1934 to 1940. During WWII he became director of personnel selection and then director general of medical services for the Canadian Army. At the end of the war he was appointed federal deputy minister of health and was active in many national and international health commissions. In 1948 he was appointed first director general of the World Health Organization, a position he held until 1953.

He received many awards and honours and also his share of criticism for his attacks on superstitions, myths and methods of indoctrinating children. His attack on teaching children to believe in Santa Claus received national comment. Nevertheless, he remained tolerant, wise, realistic and logically persuasive. He was one of the first to emphasize the danger of pollution, overpopulation and the nuclear arms race. His published works range from pamphlets on army morale to books on world survival, and his last publication (1958) was prophetically titled *Can People Learn to Learn?* J.D.M. GRIFFIN

Chitty, Dennis Hubert, zoologist (b at Bristol, Eng 18 Sept 1912). Educated at U of T and Oxford, he studied rodent populations as a research officer at the Bureau of Animal Population, Oxford, 1935-61. His pioneering studies on population fluctuations in small rodents and snowshoe hares culminated in the Chitty Hypothesis of pop-

ulation regulation that population growth is stopped by behavioural interactions that lead to the genetic selection of highly aggressive animals. Moving, as professor, to UBC in 1961, Chitty taught ecology and the history and philosophy of biology. He was elected to the Royal Soc of Canada in 1969, and he retired from active teaching in 1978 to devote his time to ecological research on rodent populations. CHARLES J. KREBS

Cholera, acute infectious disease of the intestines, resulting from water contaminated by the bacterium *Vibrio comma*. It first reached Canada in 1832, brought by immigrants from Britain. Epidemics occurred in 1832, 1834, 1849, 1851, 1852 and 1854. There were cases in Halifax in 1881. The epidemics killed at least 20 000 people in Canada. Cholera was feared because it was deadly and no one understood how it spread or how to treat it. The death rate for untreated cases is extremely high. Grosse Île, near Québec, was opened in 1832 as a quarantine station and all ships stopped there for inspection. During epidemics, individual towns attempted to quarantine themselves against the disease. When quarantine failed to stop the disease, public-health measures were taken by towns and provincial and colonial governments. The response to cholera encouraged governments to act to protect the health of Canadians and to provide for the sick. Not all the actions were popular and there were riots in some towns. Crowds burned the cholera hospitals. Anger over cholera contributed to the antigovernment agitation in Lower Canada in the 1830s. Familiarity with the disease reduced the fear in later epidemics and a better understanding of how it spread made more effective prevention possible. *See also* EPIDEMIC.

GEOFFREY BILSON

Reading: Geoffrey Bilson, *A Darkened House: Cholera in Nineteenth Century Canada* (1980); C.M. Godfrey, *Cholera in Upper Canada 1832-1860* (1968).

Cholera hospital and immigrant sheds at Grosse Île (*courtesy National Archives of Canada/C-13630*).

Choquette, Robert, poet, novelist, playwright (b at Manchester, NH 22 Apr 1905). His family moved to Montréal in 1914 where he did his classical studies at Coll Saint-Laurent (1917-21) and Loyola Coll (1921-26). At 20, he published his first poetry collection, *A travers les vents*, winning the Prix David (1926). His first novel, *La Pension Leblanc*, appeared in 1927. After working a few months on the newspaper *The Gazette*, he became literary director of *La Revue moderne* (1928). Two years later, he became secretary-librarian for the École des beaux-arts de Montréal. The appearance of *Metropolitan Museum* (1931) won critical approval. That same year the poet began a career as a radio novelist, scriptwriter and producer which lasted more than 30 years. His greatest successes, *Le Curé de village* (1935-38), *La Pension Velder* (1938-42) and *Métropole* (1943-56), place him among Québec's most prolific radio writers. Several of his TV pieces (*Quatuor, La Pension Velder* and some TV plays) aired on the French

channel of Radio-Canada (1955-75). But he kept on writing: *Poésies nouvelles* (1933), *Suite marine* (1953) and *Oeuvres poétiques* (1956) won him the title (1961) "prince of poets" from the Société des poètes canadiens-français. In 1963, he became assistant commissioner of the Commission du centenaire canadien. The next year he was named Canadian consul-general to Bordeaux, then ambassador to Argentina (1968). Member of several literary societies, including the Académie canadienne-française from its founding, he has won many awards for his poetry and novels, including 3 Prix Davids (1926, 1932, 1956), the poetry prize of the Académie française (1954), the Prix Duvernay (1954), the Prix Edgar Poe (1956) and the Prix international des amitiés françaises (1962). KENNETH LANDRY

Choral Music is performed by groups of singers, called a choir or chorus, in which there is more than one voice to a part. A group with only one voice to a part is called an ensemble. A choir may consist of women only, men only (or boys and men) or may be mixed, with both women and men. The voice parts in a mixed choir are usually soprano, alto, tenor and bass. There is choral music for 8-part (or more) mixed choirs where the sections are subdivided into first and second soprano, first and second alto, first and second tenor, baritone and bass. The voices with the higher tessitura are designated by the term "first." Sometimes a descant (an ornamental line usually higher than the soprano) is added, most often to the harmony to enhance the sound but not to cover the voices. Choral music is commonly written on an open score with one of the staves for each voice part. Choral music may be written to be performed *a cappella* (unaccompanied) or it may be accompanied by piano, organ, instrumental ensembles of varying combinations or orchestra. The chorus or choir is often combined with solo singers as in operas or oratorios. Choral compositions exist in various styles and forms, often indicated by the term applied to them, such as anthem, hymn, chorale, psalm, motet, cantata, madrigal, mass, passion, requiem, oratorio or all manner of settings of secular texts. The performance of choral music requires that the director develop a unified sound from the singers. This is dependent on correctly produced tone, uniform in quality; good intonation which is dependent on correct tone production; and blend and balance, in turn dependent on intonation and on the number of singers in each voice part.

The first example of choral music known to have been written or arranged in Canada was "Great God Neptune" in the masque THÉATRE DE NEPTUNE EN LA NOUVELLE-FRANCE by Marc LESCARBOT, performed at Port-Royal (14 Nov 1606). Extant original writing or arranging of choral music by Canadian composers, in the 250 years following the Lescarbot composition, was published in church music collections, eg, J.P. Clarke's 6 hymn-tunes and 2 anthems in his *Canadian Church Psalmody* (1845). He also composed an 8-part anthem, "Arise, O Lord God, Forget Not the Poor" (1846). J.-C. Brauneis wrote a "Mass" (1835), for choir, violin, flute, bass viol, bassoon and organ. Born in Québec City, Brauneis was perhaps the first Canadian to receive additional music education outside Canada. Antoine DESSANE, who came to Canada from France (1849), composed a wealth of church music. Two other composers of the late 19th century were Joseph-Julien Perrault and Jean-Baptiste Labelle. In the first half of the 20th century, Canadian-born composers were among those writing choral music still directed to church performance. Noted for specific choral compositions are Guillaume COUTURE – the oratorio *Jean le Precurseur*

The Edmonton-based Pro Coro Canada performing in St Joseph's Basilica during the papal visit in Edmonton, 1984 (*photo by Victor Post*).

(1909) and a setting of the *Requiem Mass* – and William Reed and A.S. VOGT who wrote a number of short choral selections.

Contributions to choral composition by English composers living in Canada were made by Charles A.E. HARRISS, *Daniel before the King* (1890), *Festival Mass* (1901), *A Coronation Mass* (1902); Percival Illsley, a cantata, *Ruth* (1894); Albert Ham, cantatas, *The Solitude of the Passion* (1917) and *Advent Cantata*; and Edward Broome. W.H. Anderson came to Winnipeg (1910) and Alfred Whitehead came to NS (1912), later moving to Montréal. Both were prolific composers of sacred and secular music. Healey WILLAN, a well-established composer when he came to Canada (1913), left a legacy of outstanding choral music and was a strong influence on other composers. Claude CHAMPAGNE of Québec left the same type of influence on the young composers in his province, although he wrote few choral compositions.

By the middle of the 20th century, Canadian composers of choral music were composing for high-school and elementary school choruses, for secular choruses, as well as church choirs, and for a wide variety of choral societies. Catalogues of Canadian choral music, available through the CANADIAN MUSIC CENTRE, list published compositions as well as those available on loan from the CMC libraries. The composers listed in the catalogue who have written major choral works include Jean PAPINEAU-COUTURE, Pierre MERCURE, Roger Matton, Jacques HÉTU, Claude Vivier, Otto Joachim, Kelsey Jones, Godfrey RIDOUT, Robert FLEMING, Ben Steinberg, Keith Bissell, John BECK-WITH, Harry SOMERS, Harry FREEDMAN, Talivaldis Kenins, Oskar MORAWETZ, R. Murray SCHAFER, Clifford Ford, Violet ARCHER, Jean COULTHARD and Bernard Naylor. Choral composition, smaller in scope but of equally fine calibre, has been written by Hugh BANCROFT, Milton Barnes, Leslie Bell, Lorne Betts, Wolfgang Bottenberg, Alexander BROTT, Barrie Cabena, F.C. Clarke, Lionel Daunais, Richard Eaton, William France, James Gayfer, Graham George, Irving Glick, Frank Haworth, Derek Healey, Harry Hill, Derek Holman, Richard Johnston, Lothar Klein, Alfred Kunz, Quentin MacLean, Sir Ernest MACMILLAN, Michael Miller, David Ouchterlony, Welford Russell, Robert Turner and Charles Wilson.

It was in churches that choirs were organized and developed. Choirs often sponsored oratorio performances and sometimes concerts of both sacred and secular music. Various kinds of choral societies were formed by the middle of the 19th century. This growing interest in choral music

was coupled with an excellence in performance which reached a high standard by the beginning of WWI. This same interest, vigour and excellence was not to resume until early in the 1970s, with a few exceptions such as the TORONTO MENDELSSOHN CHOIR, the FESTIVAL SINGERS and the Montreal Bach Choir. In the 2 decades beginning in 1950, voluntary church choirs were no longer the main source of choral music. Many schools added choral music to the curriculum, and elementary and secondary schools and university music departments began to develop excellent choral groups. There is a great diversity in the groups that are spread across Canada. Examples are the Toronto Mendelssohn Choir, the Montagnards in Montréal, the Arion Male Voice Choir of Victoria, the Mennonite Children's Choir of Winnipeg, the Armdale Chorus of Halifax, the Montreal Bach Choir, the Elgar Choir of British Columbia, the Tudor Singers of Montreal, the Vancouver Chamber Choir and Pro Coro Canada in Edmonton. The CBC has provided opportunity for choirs to sing in radio competitions as well as on its network programs. By the late 1970s provincial choral federations were being formed, culminating in the foundation of the Assn of Canadian Choral Conductors in 1980. *See also* RELIGIOUS MUSIC.

ISABELLE MILLS

Reading: Helmut Kallmann, *A History of Music in Canada 1534-1914* (1960).

Chotem, Neil, pianist, composer, conductor, teacher (b at Saskatoon 9 Sept 1920). After the start of a promising career as a piano soloist was interrupted by WWII, Chotem forged a new career in Montréal as performer, conductor and composer. During appearances as soloist and guest conductor in concert halls and recording studios, he often supported fellow Canadian composers, notably in the CBC broadcast "Music from Montréal" (1955-60). Many of Chotem's own compositions are radio and TV scores. His style is conservative yet eclectic, exploring art and popular music as well as jazz. Since the 1960s he has worked with many Canadian performing artists, including Maureen FORRESTER and Renée CLAUDE. Some of his most acclaimed work has been recorded with the pop group Harmonium (*L'Heptade*). He has taught at McGill and U de M.

ANN SCHAU

Chown, Alice Amelia, feminist, suffragist, pacifist, socialist, writer (b at Kingston, Canada West 3 Feb 1866; d at Toronto 2 Mar 1949). She was educated at Queen's U. In 1912 she was a founding member of the Toronto Equal Franchise League. Her journal, *The Stairway* (1921), includes her views on many reforms: the settlement and co-operative movements, trade unionism, female suffrage, dress reform and sexual freedom. She also wrote about women's rights to higher

education, home economics education, urban improvement, universal brotherhood and world peace. Although she later denounced the church and, specifically, the wartime attitudes of her cousin, Samuel Dwight CHOWN, her unwavering belief in pacifism stemmed from her Methodist background. In 1930 she founded the Women's League of Nations Assn which was to provide innovative programs for peace education such as popular dramatic sketches written by Chown. Her life was concerned with changing those institutions and customs which she saw as suppressing the innate goodness of the (particularly female) individual.

DIANA CHOWN

Chown, Samuel Dwight, Methodist minister (b at Kingston, Canada W 11 Apr 1853; d at Toronto 30 Jan 1933). He was ordained 1879 and served several churches before his appointment 1902 as secretary of the newly created Dept of Temperance and Moral Reform, where he fought for social and political reform. In 1910 he was elected general superintendent of the Methodist Church and led that body into the UNITED CHURCH OF CANADA in 1925. His WWI experiences as chaplain led him to condemn war and actively support the League of Nations. Considered Canada's leading churchman, he continued work for world peace and social improvement after his retirement in 1926. Mount Chown in British Columbia commemorates his contribution to Canada's social development.

NEIL SEMPLE

Reading: S.D. Chown, *The Story of Church Union in Canada* (1930).

Chrétien, Joseph-Jacques-Jean, politician (b at Shawinigan, Qué 11 Jan 1934). Educated at Laval, Jean Chrétien practised law 1958-63, and won election to the House of Commons as a Liberal in 1963. He served in PM PEARSON's Cabinet as minister of state and then minister of national revenue; in 1968 he supported Mitchell SHARP for the party leadership. Under PM TRUDEAU, he occupied the portfolios of Indian affairs; treasury board; industry, trade and commerce; finance (the first French Canadian to do so); justice; and energy, mines and resources. A strong and emotional speaker, Chrétien enjoyed considerable popularity both inside and outside Québec. As minister of justice, 1980-82, he directed the federalist forces in the QUÉBEC REFERENDUM of May 1980

Jean Chrétien served as MP and Cabinet minister from 1963 until after his defeat by John Turner in the Liberal leadership race in 1984 (*courtesy* Globe and Mail, Toronto).

and then helped devise and implement the federal government's strategy for the patriation of the CONSTITUTION and the enactment of a charter of rights and freedoms. Using a folksy style in English and French, he was able to create an identification with his audiences. His forceful and engaging speaking style, strong identification with his audiences and skills as a political organizer were amply demonstrated when he ran second to John TURNER in the Liberal leadership campaign in 1984. Chrétien retained his seat in the subsequent election, but grew restive in opposition. With Turner's leadership confirmed at a party convention in 1986, Chrétien resigned his seat in the House of Commons and took up the private practice of law. His autobiography *Straight from the Heart* (1985) became a best-seller.　　　　　ROBERT BOTHWELL

Chrétien, Michel, physician, researcher, professor (b at Shawinigan, Qué 26 Mar 1936), brother of Jean CHRÉTIEN. Educated at Montréal, Boston and Berkeley, Chrétien is internationally recognized for his contribution to neuroendocrinology. In 1967 he was the first to propose that pituitary hormones were synthesized from larger precursors. Since then, he has concentrated his research efforts on this hypothesis, which he has proved to be of general application. His work has won him several awards including an honorary PhD from U of Liège (Belgium). Chrétien has spent all his professional career with the Clinical Research Inst of Montréal, of which he has been the scientific director since 1984. He is a member of numerous scientific societies and a strong advocate for increased basic medical research in Canada.　PHILIPPE CRINE

Christ Church Cathedral, Fredericton, was built 1846-53 to the neo-Gothic plans of British architects Frank Wills and William Butterfield, in collaboration with John MEDLEY, first Anglican bishop of Fredericton. In its cruciform plan, central tower, 3-sided porch and huge west window, it was the first Canadian building to follow closely the ideal of the Ecclesiological Society, a reformist movement of the Anglican Church which sought a return to the architecture of the Middle Ages. The cathedral is distinguished by its nave and side aisles oriented to the choir. Each part of the interior is visible from the exterior and has different roofing. *See also* RELIGIOUS BUILDING.　　NATHALIE CLERK

Christ Church Cathedral, Fredericton, NB, one of Canada's most impressive churches. It was built 1846-53 according to the ideals of a reformist group in the Anglican Church seeking a return to the architecture of the Middle Ages (*courtesy Environment Canada, Parks/Heritage Recording Services*).

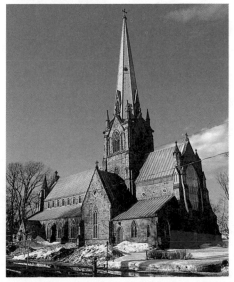

Christadelphians, Protestant movement fd 1844 by John Thomas in Richmond, Va. It grew out of the Campbellite movement (originally associated with the CHRISTIAN CHURCH), but its adherents are nontrinitarian, deny the immortal soul doctrine and do not believe in a personal devil. Organization is congregational, but there are several fellowships which differ somewhat doctrinally. Some hold that all having true knowledge of God's purposes will be resurrected either to eternal life or condemnation (annihilation). Others assert that only those who are justified at death will be resurrected. Small *ecclesias* (congregations) exist throughout Canada. Much attention is given to Bible study. Communion is held regularly on Sundays.　　M. JAMES PENTON

Christian Church (Disciples of Christ) in Canada, one of 35 regions of that denomination in N America. The Region of Canada, which has 38 churches and some 5000 members, is unique in that it functions as a national church and has full denominational status at national and international levels, eg, in the World Council of Churches, and in the CANADIAN COUNCIL OF CHURCHES, of which it is a charter member.

The Christian Church, fd 1804 in the US, joined with the Disciples of Christ in 1832. The first Canadian congregation was formed in 1810 near Charlottetown, PEI. Since restructuring, which culminated with publication of the Design, a constitutional document, in 1978, overall life of the church has been governed by the biennial General Assembly, whose decisions are referred to congregations and other church units for implementation. During non-Assembly years every region has its own convention. Local congregations, autonomously governed by elected boards, appoint voting members for the General Assembly and regional conventions.

Disciples hold nonsectarian views, working to unite all Christians under the restored authority of the New Testament. They are actively involved in social issues and cultural life, nationally and internationally. This participation, like the Disciples' sacramental life, which consists of believers' immersion baptism and weekly celebration of the Lord's Supper, is a response of obedience to the teachings, life and ministry, death and resurrection of Jesus. The Disciples distinguish between clergy and laypersons on functional rather than sacramental grounds. Congregations are led by elders and deacons who are neither ordained nor appointed for life. Lay elders, many of them women, often take charge of a Lord's Supper celebration. Regions ordain clergy to the ministry of the whole church and clergy are granted credentials by the regions.　　RUSSELL D. LEGGE

Reading: L.G. McAllister and W.E. Tucker, *Journey in Faith: A History of the Christian Church (Disciples of Christ)* (1975); K.L. Teegarden, *We Call Ourselves Disciples* (1976).

Christian Religious Communities are groups of religious (ie, men or women who have chosen to devote their lives to the work of their respective churches). In Canada, although some religious are within the various communions of the ORTHODOX CHURCH, more are Anglican and by far the greatest number are Roman Catholic.

Roman Catholic

Religious communities in the Roman Catholic Church are associations of men or women, approved by ecclesiastical authority as living out the love of God in a common life marked by vows or promises of poverty, chastity and obedience, according to the particular charism of their founder as specified in constitutional documents. According to their state of life, communities may be *clerical*, made up of priests and aspirants to the priest-

hood; or *lay*, whether of men or women. According to the force of their vows, communities may be divided into 4 categories: *orders*, with solemn vows, were usually founded before the 18th century and may be made up of monks or nuns, canons regular or canonesses, of mendicants or of regular clerics; *congregations*, with simple vows, include most modern communities of men or women; *secular institutes*, whose members normally take private vows or promises and do not live in community are a creation of this century; *societies of common life* are usually made up of priests who share a common work without special vows. According to their purpose, they may be *active*, taking on various types of charitable work; or *contemplative*, given primarily to prayer. With respect to ecclesiastical authority, they may be either *of pontifical right*, if the community has been approved by the Holy See, or *of diocesan right*, if approval has come only from the bishop of a diocese. All of these varieties are found in Canada.

NEW FRANCE was the place to which the first religious communities came. Two French Benedictine priests probably came with Jacques CARTIER on his second voyage (1535-36). The Récollets began missionary work with the Indians in 1615, at the invitation of Samuel de CHAMPLAIN, and in 1625 were joined by the Jesuits; but in 1629, with the capture of the colony by the KIRKE brothers, both communities were compelled to leave. In 1633, after the colony had been returned to France, only the Jesuits were permitted to resume their work. The Jesuit missionaries' work among the Huron (*see* BRÉBEUF; STE-MARIE AMONG THE HURON), culminating in the Jesuit martyrdom of the 1640s, was reported in the JESUIT RELATIONS and certainly became the best-known aspect of the colony. In 1657 the Sulpicians, a community of priests established in 1642 for the education of the diocesan clergy, came to Montréal.

By that time, religious communities of women had also been established. In 1639 two cloistered orders came to Québec: the AUGUSTINES DE LA MISÉRICORDE DE JÉSUS and the URSULINES. The Hospitalières were a community from Dieppe who founded the first HÔTEL-DIEU, or hospital; they had just recently adopted the Rule of St Augustine and the cloistered life of canonesses regular. The Ursulines, led by MARIE DE L'INCARNATION, came on the same ship to open a school for French and Indian girls. Another group, the Réligieuses hospitalières de Saint-Joseph (or Hospitallers of St-Joseph), was founded in France in 1636 by Jérôme Royer de La Dauversière specifically to establish a hospital in his projected settlement at Montréal, but it was unable to come until 1659 to take over the work begun by Jeanne MANCE. In 1658 Marguerite BOURGEOYS, who had come to Montréal 5 years before, gathered the first members of the Congrégation de Notre-Dame to begin their work of education. In the 1690s foundations were established by the Augustines for the care of the sick poor in Québec and by the Ursulines for both teaching and care of the sick in Trois-Rivières.

In 1737 Marguerite d'YOUVILLE founded what became known as the GREY NUNS to assume charge of the General Hospital of Montréal from the Frères Charon, a community of brothers founded for this work in 1694 but in the process of dissolution by 1737.

When the British conquered New France in 1760, there were 3 clerical communities there: Jesuits, Récollets (who had returned in 1670) and Sulpicians, for a total of 79 priests. There were also 7 communities of women, totalling 204 sisters. The British refused to allow the Jesuits and the Récollets to receive new members, but the Sulpicians, who could present themselves as diocesan clergy, were able to carry on. The women's communities, regarded by the British as less dangerous and as offering valuable social services, were allowed to continue. By 1837, although no new foundations had been made, there were over 300 professed sisters.

Meanwhile the structures of the church had been expanding, a process in which religious priests played some part. Capuchins were active in and around Halifax from 1785 to 1827 and a Trappist missionary in Nova Scotia founded a priory at Tracadie in 1815. But it was the establishment of the diocese of Montréal in 1836 that brought a dramatic change.

In 1837 Bishop LARTIGUE of Montréal invited the Brothers of the Christian Schools (Christian Brothers) to open a school, and by 1850 there were 107 brothers from Québec joined with 17 from France. When Bishop Ignace BOURGET succeeded Lartigue in 1840, developments came even more quickly. In 1841, on a visit to Europe, Bourget approached several French communities. The Oblates of Mary Immaculate, founded in 1816 by Eugène de Mazenod, were looking for a mission outside France. They came to Montréal in 1841 and soon moved on; they were in Ottawa and on James Bay by 1844, and in the following year they went to Red River [Winnipeg] to begin their work in the West. Their Canadian recruitment was slower than that of the Christian Brothers, but between 1841 and 1876 some 151 Oblates came to Canada from France. In 1842 the Jesuits, also at Bourget's invitation, sent 6 priests and 3 lay brothers to Montréal. The Viatorians (fd 1831 by Louis Querbes) hesitated, but in 1847 they sent 5 priests to open a college, school and novitiate in Joliette. Also in 1847 the Congregation of the Holy Cross, under its founder Basile Moreau, sent out a priest, 7 brothers and 4 sisters. For them, as for the Jesuits, this was part of a larger move to the US. Elsewhere, in 1850 Armand de Charbonnel, second bishop of Toronto, brought in the Basilian Fathers (fd 1822 in France).

If the influx of new communities of men in this period was remarkable, still more so was the founding of women's communities. Here too, the influence of Bishop Bourget was strong. In 1844 he approved Émilie Gamelin's founding the Sisters of Providence to care for the poor, and the establishment of the Sisters of the Holy Names of Jesus and Mary by Eulalie Durocher and her companions for the work of teaching. In 1848, to care for unwed mothers and their children, he called on Rosalie Jetté to found the Soeurs de miséricorde. In 1850 he approved the Sisters of Saint Anne, whose task, according to the inspiration of their foundress Marie-Esther Blondin, was to work in the public schools of the countryside. Elsewhere there were similar developments. In English-speaking Canada small contingents of sisters were brought from the US to found new communities. Thus the Sisters of Charity came to Halifax in 1849, the Sisters of Saint Joseph to Toronto in 1851 and to Hamilton in 1852, and the Ursulines to Chatham in the diocese of London in 1860. The Sisters of Providence were established in Kingston in 1861 as an independent foundation from the community of Montréal.

Even in these beginnings a striking difference can be seen in the development of men's and women's communities in Canada. Of some 118 men's communities which have had a presence in Canada, only 10 were founded here and only 4 of these still exist. These 4 are all societies of the common life, devoted mainly to missionary work, and they make up only 4% of the number of Canadian male religious today. On the other hand, of the 229 women's communities that have had a presence in Canada, some 75 were founded in this country, and of these only 6 no longer exist. Of the women in religious communities in Canada today over 70% belong to communities founded here.

The work of religious in education at every level, in care for the sick, the poor, orphans and aged, has been of great importance. Everywhere their schools and hospitals have been among the earliest institutions established. They went to the West and North as missionaries to the Indians and Inuit and, from the early 20th century, to missions overseas as well.

Increased government activity in education, health and welfare has greatly affected the work of religious. In Québec especially, the QUIET REVOLUTION of the 1960s led to the withdrawal of many responsibilities from their hands. The Second Vatican Council brought a profound process of internal renewal in almost all communities, but along with this has gone a crisis of withdrawals by individual members and a drop in vocations (joining by new members). In 1987 the 42 778 Roman Catholic religious in Canada included 4795 priests and seminarians, 3722 brothers and 34 261 sisters. Two-thirds (including 80% of the brothers) are in Québec. These figures show a reduction of 45% since 1967, when there were 78 269 religious in the country. There are fewer now, and they are older. By 1987, 56% of the women religious in Canada were over 65. In men's communities, only 6.3% of professed members were under 35, a proportion which points to problems in the future; women's communities, with only 1.4% under 35, face more immediate problems.

Despite such changes, however, the work of religious remains significant. In 1987 some 6927 were active in education, 2481 in hospitals and 1564 in social work. There were 5525 religious in parochial and diocesan functions. Contemplative communities had 1187 members, whose principal activity was prayer. The 3164 Canadian religious on missions in Latin America (1393), Africa (1157), Asia (495), Oceania (117) and Iceland (1) are not included in the figures for religious in Canada, but their work is an important aspect of the life and work of their communities. *See also* CATHOLICISM; CHRISTIANITY; RELIGION.

JAMES HANRAHAN

Anglican

Anglican religious orders provide an ordered life of prayer, study and community service, and generally advance the purposes of the whole church. Communities were re-established in the Church of England during the "catholic revival" sparked by the Oxford Movement in 1833. Monks and nuns live in communities. The basis of their life is the recitation of the daily offices (prayers), and mass. Activities outside the monastic environment range from teaching and the care of the sick to community social work and involvement in conferences.

There are 3 orders for women. The Sisterhood of St John the Divine (SSJD), founded in 1884 by Sister Hannah, is of entirely Canadian origin; in 1984 it had 52 members. The Community of the Sisters of the Church (CSC) was established in England in 1890. It has 15 sisters. The Society of St Margaret (SSM; 3 members), which has American roots, has been working in the diocese of Montréal since 1881.

The 2 communities for men which have been active in Canada are the Order of the Holy Cross (OHC), centered in Toronto, and the Society of St John the Evangelist (SSJE). OHC's 5 members provide alcohol and drug rehabilitation, programs for street people, and counselling. It supports the usual aims of developing and fostering spiritual life within the church. SSJE in Canada, a daughter community of the American congregation in Cambridge, Mass, associated with the Cowley Fathers of Oxford, Eng, was established

at Emsdale, Ont, in 1927. In 1984 this small community, at that time in Hamilton, ceased operation; the remaining brothers moved to the mother house in Cambridge. *See also* ANGLICANISM.

DONALD ANDREW DODMAN

Orthodox Church

Eastern Orthodox monasticism stems from the earliest Christian ideal of spiritual perfection and sanctity. It was animated by faith, eschatological hope, and love of God. Its foundations were poverty, virginity, obedience, and similarity to God or divinization. With St Anthony of Egypt (251-257) an ideal of anchorites (hermits) was reached. These "Desert Fathers" renounced the world to live in seclusion in total openness to God. A Coptic monk, St Pachomius, organized c320 the first monastic communities (cenobitic monasteries). Their spread culminated in the establishment of monasteries on Mount Athos.

In Canada there are 3 monasteries under the jurisdiction of the Russian Orthodox Church Outside of Russia: Monastery of the Protection of the Most Holy Mother of God (female), founded in 1950 at Bluffton, Alta, by Archbishop Iosif (Skorodumow); Holy Dormition Monastery (male), founded in 1955 at Northville, Alta; Holy Transfiguration Monastery (male), founded in 1960 at Masonville, Qué. Both male monasteries were established by Archbishop Vitaly (Oustinow). All of them follow the rule of St Basil the Great.

In 1979 the Orthodox Church of America founded the Holy Transfiguration Monastery at Rawdon, Qué, directed by Fr Gregory (Berdj Luc Papazian), and under the jurisdiction of Sylvester, Archbishop of Montréal and all Canada.

PETRO B.T. BILANIUK

Reading: Michel Theriault, *The Institutes of Consecrated Life in Canada*...(1980); J. Gribomont, et al, "Monasticism" in *New Catholic Encyclopedia* (1967), Vol IX, pp 1032-1048.

Christian Science, religion founded upon the principles of "primitive Christianity and its lost element of healing," and practised by the Church of Christ, Scientist. It was founded in Boston in 1879 by Mary Baker Eddy, whose teachings are set forth in *Science and Health, with Key to the Scriptures* (1875). The primary emphasis of the church is on moral and spiritual regeneration, although its most distinctive belief is that disease and injury can be healed by purely spiritual means. All Christian Science churches are self-governing branches of the Mother Church and accept the tenets of the *Church Manual*. There are no ordained clergy; services are conducted by 2 readers elected by the members. Among publications is the acclaimed newspaper *Christian Science Monitor*. The first services in Canada were held in Toronto in 1888. There are now 79 branch churches and societies in Canada, along with 11 organizations at universities and colleges.

Christianity, a major world religion, and the religion of some 90% of Canadians. Believers hold that the life, death and resurrection of Jesus in the first century AD, as presented in the Bible and in the Christian tradition, are central to their understanding of who they are and how they should live. As the Messiah, or the Christ (Gk *christos*, "the anointed one," or "the one chosen by God"), Jesus was to restore God's creation to the condition intended by its creator, and especially to restore order among God's chosen Jewish people, saving them from the deadly disorder into which sinful behaviour had brought them. Jesus' first followers included some fishermen, a rich woman, a tax collector and a rabbinical student — a diverse group of enthusiasts who scandalized their fellow Jews and puzzled their Greek neighbours. They claimed that Jesus had accomplished his redemptive mission by submitting himself to execution as a state criminal and later rising from the dead. They argued that he was thus revealed to be both human and divine, and they invited all, not just Jews, to join them in living as members of the Church [Gk *kuriakon*, "that which belongs to the Lord"]. Christianity gradually became interwoven with the histories of numerous nations, especially in Europe, and developed its own history, gaining and losing influence in both secular and spiritual worlds and surviving serious schisms within. Today the major divisions of Christianity, all well represented in Canada, are Roman CATHOLICISM (11.2 million adherents, 1981c), the Eastern ORTHODOX tradition (362 000 adherents) and Protestantism (9.9 million adherents). They have similar calendars of the church year, and all celebrate Christmas and Easter as the major feasts. Sacraments (religious acts regarded as outward signs of spiritual grace) are practised by most groups, although most Protestants view only baptism and communion (Eucharist) as sacramental, whereas the Roman Catholic and Orthodox churches include as sacraments baptism, confirmation (chrismation), Eucharist, penance, extreme unction, holy orders (ordination) and matrimony.

RELIGION is a response to ultimate questions, and it makes ultimate demands. What Christian in Canada can be said to be truly religious? Many Canadians are serious Christians, but although there is certainly a plurality of religious standpoints in modern Canada, there is no general acceptance of pluralism, even within the Christian community itself. All Christians look to the Bible, but Christians live different lives in the light of the Gospel, and Canadian Christians are far from a consensus that all ways are legitimate and worthy. Nor do all Canadian Christians commit themselves to the same degree. If there is disagreement about whether certain Canadians are properly called Christian, there is also dispute about whether Canada itself may be called Christian. Until the mid-20th century, public rhetoric and fundamental laws took it for granted that Canada was a Christian country, but since the 1950s there has been a significant shift away from Christian language in public life to more general affirmations that Canada is a country that recognizes "the supremacy of God," as the CONSTITUTION ACT 1982 puts it. Buddhists and other non-theists chafe at even this mild declaration. But such vague public theism may wither away by the end of the 20th century.

History in Canada Ville-Marie [Montréal], named in honour of Mary, the mother of Jesus, was founded 1642 as a mission station by Roman Catholics caught up in the great 17th-century religious revival in France. The island on which the mission stood had been named Montréal for the Italian home of a cardinal who helped sponsor Cartier's explorations of 1535. (The origin of the name was later ascribed to "Mont Réal" – mountain of the king – in honour of the king of France.) Although one should not romanticize such beginnings, it is true that many early settlers of NEW FRANCE were motivated in part by religious concerns. MARIE DE L'INCARNATION, the URSULINE nun who was a source of civil and spiritual strength to Québec, 1639-72, understood herself as a founder of a "New Church" rather than of a "New France." Later in the 17th century the colony passed effectively into the hands of the king, officially "His Most Christian Majesty." In practice, royal direction proved less Christian than secular. During the 18th century, both French and British governments took for granted the European tradition that political stability depends in part on the people's allegiance to one church, carefully established as an arm of the royal gov-

ernment. European kings were known as "vicars of Christ" long before the pope assumed that title, and many colonial administrators saw their own role in a religious light. But the notion of an "established church" was difficult to realize in Canada. In the first place, the established churches themselves, Roman Catholic and then Church of England (*see* ANGLICANISM), lacked the financial and human resources to bind together a scattered pioneer society. Secondly, Catholic and Anglican bishops often had agendas differing from those of the politicians. Thirdly, people often turned for inspiration to religious leaders such as the mystical revivalist Henry ALLINE, who shunned political involvement. Fourthly, from the common people's personal experience came religious responses and convictions only incidentally related to the rubrics laid down by church leaders, eg, the Acadians' "white mass" (mass without a priest), the curiously pagan healing practices of Scottish Highland settlers, and the home devotions and supernatural tales of French Canadian peasants.

Finally, the consolidation of Canada under the British Crown, effected by the Treaty of Paris, 1763, created a political entity comprising a highly diverse collection of Christians. To the existing Catholic population of Lower Canada [Québec] were added English-speaking immigrants of all kinds: sundry Protestant dissenters from England, northern Europe and the US; Catholics and Protestants from Ireland; Catholics and PRESBYTERIANS from Scotland. Clergy trained in the home country often accompanied the immigrants and, like the priests of LC, fought to hang on to their flocks and their distinctive traditions. During the early 19th century, independent religious revivals in LC, the Maritimes and Upper Canada [Ontario] greatly strengthened the hands of those churches that were opposing the feeble efforts of the Anglican establishment to reproduce in Canada the hegemony it had enjoyed in Britain.

By the middle of the 19th century, "public Christianity" was taking shape. Universities, founded by particular churches in order to train indigenous clergy, received public support and began to admit students from all religious backgrounds, even while retaining their peculiar denominational leanings. There developed public school systems officially committed to producing "Christian citizens"; outside Québec they were Protestant for all practical purposes, and English-speaking Catholics struggled to support private schools with little help from government (*see* SEPARATE SCHOOLS). There arose a public rhetoric that was often biblical (eg, Canada was called a "Dominion" because the term is found in Psalm 72:8) and laws pertaining to personal morality reflected popular Christian standards. The public calendar was marked by Christian holidays, particularly Christmas and Easter, and Sunday was traditionally a day of rest.

Within Québec the Catholic majority and Protestant minority came gradually to a workable living arrangement, perhaps because Catholic numbers were balanced by Protestant economic power. Elsewhere, mainstream Protestants such as Anglicans, METHODISTS, Presbyterians, BAPTISTS and CONGREGATIONALISTS came to an accommodation but frequently had acrimonious disputes with the Catholic minority. George-Étienne CARTIER's dream of a Canada stretching from sea to sea with provinces evenly balanced between Protestant and Catholic, as Upper and Lower Canada had been, foundered in the wave of westward migration from Protestant Ontario and the sad results of the RIEL rebellions. French Canadian society adopted a defensively nationalist outlook (*see* FRENCH CANADIAN NATIONALISM), turning inward to consolidate a Catholic homeland while leaving the rest of Canada to more Protestant imaginings.

By mid-19th century both Protestant and Catholic leaders began to realize that they faced a common adversary: cities were beginning to attract more and more Canadians. Small-town parish and congregational organization failed to sink roots in the modern city with its cosmopolitan morality, its anonymity, separation of home and workplace, specialization of tasks and complex economy. In response all the churches began to stress the importance of a well-trained, professional clergy and to develop special programs for children – in Québec the clergy gradually replaced lay people teaching in the schools, and elsewhere the SUNDAY SCHOOL movement took hold. The local congregation or parish remained the fundamental unit of organization, but church newspapers and lay organizations based on particular occupational groups or age ranges went beyond the parish. The YMCA, for example, transcended traditional Protestant church boundaries, and the ST-JEAN-BAPTISTE SOCIETY transcended traditional Catholic diocesan boundaries. Church buildings became imposing, permanent and expensive structures, funded largely by prosperous church members (*see* RELIGIOUS BUILDING). Working-class Canadians then came to be seen as the object of missionary activity, which was sometimes directed through downtown missions.

The urban threat to traditional Christian ways brought Protestant and Catholic leaders together in support of the Lord's Day Act of 1906 (proclaimed 1907; *see* LORD'S DAY ALLIANCE). Respect for Sunday, the "Lord's Day," was hallowed by custom in rural society, but in urban society it could only be maintained by law. Many of the furthest-reaching modifications to the Act, permitting more amusement and labour on Sunday, occurred during the 2 world wars. The changes were justified as necessary to the success of war efforts "to defend Christian civilization." Some responses to urbanization were even more defensive. For example, the Catholic Church encouraged its people to shun the "Protestant" cities and Protestant New England in order to transform the wilderness of northern Québec into a Catholic, rural civilization. This "colonization movement" was more successful in novels such as *Jean Rivard* and *Maria Chapdelaine* than it was in practice.

But there were often positive and unexpected results from such defensive responses, eg, the efforts of many Christian temperance organizations, Protestant and Catholic, which culminated in Canada-wide PROHIBITION during WWI. After the war the legislation withered away, but meanwhile the Protestants of the WOMAN'S CHRISTIAN TEMPERANCE UNION (WCTU) formed the core of a movement that finally won the vote for women in 1918 (*see* WOMEN'S SUFFRAGE). Protestants often began in the TEMPERANCE MOVEMENT, then moved on to broader concerns, ultimately forming part of the SOCIAL GOSPEL movement which spawned Protestant social activists ranging from those who stayed firmly within church structures, eg, Nellie MCCLUNG and novelist C.W. GORDON, to others, eg, J.S. WOODSWORTH and T.C. DOUGLAS, who found the left-wing CO-OPERATIVE COMMONWEALTH FEDERATION less inhibiting. Catholic social activists were more likely than their Protestant counterparts to stay within church-affiliated groups, such as the various CATHOLIC ACTION organizations and the ANTIGONISH MOVEMENT.

By mid-20th century Québec was so highly clericalized that nearly half its Catholic priests were engaged in full-time work outside the traditional parish: teaching, guiding Catholic labour unions (*see* CONFEDERATION OF NATIONAL TRADE UNIONS), administering social services, etc. Catholic lay people had a great respect for the clergy but they were not puppets of the priesthood, as many Protestants thought. The vitality of anticlerical jokes and songs, and the largely spontaneous generation of popular devotions such as PILGRIMAGE to Brother André's shrine, demonstrated considerable independence from the hierarchy. The lay elites that formed in the worlds of politics and journalism included Henri BOURASSA, Maurice DUPLESSIS and André LAURENDEAU – Catholics who could scarcely be described as "priest ridden."

The Christian communities of the early 20th century suffered many tensions. Among English-speaking Protestants the disputes that arose over the value of the Bible as history and over church involvement in social action sometimes created new institutional divisions (eg, the Baptist schisms of the 1920s and the student divisions of the 1930s leading to the Student Christian Movement and Inter-Varsity Christian Fellowship) and sometimes encouraged solutions that buried the disputes, unresolved, in silence. The Catholic consensus was rarely disturbed, but when it was, the results were briefly spectacular (eg, in the ostracism of Jean-Charles HARVEY).

Most Protestant tensions were obscured by a series of movements toward union, starting in the mid-19th century and climaxing in the 1925 foundation of the UNITED CHURCH OF CANADA. Jesus' call to unity (eg, in John 17:21), together with the practical advantages gained by pooling scarce resources in a vast land and together with the Canadian tradition that the churches have a public role, have made this trend toward unity a characteristic of Canadian church history. It is remarkable that, although Canada's population is based on immigration from many different lands and cultures, almost three-quarters of its citizens claim to belong to 3 churches: Roman Catholic, United and Anglican. Nevertheless, diversity has thrived, largely as a result of the influx of numerous cultural groups and of ideas from outside Canada. Ukrainians, Romanians and others have brought various Orthodox Church traditions with them. MENNONITES and others with ANABAPTIST roots immigrated, as did LUTHERANS, chiefly from Europe; MORMONS came from the US. JEHOVAH'S WITNESSES and SEVENTH-DAY ADVENTISTS are well established, and HOLINESS CHURCHES, such as the SALVATION ARMY, have a long history in this country. Transdenominational movements are active as well: in the early 20th century, PENTECOSTAL MOVEMENTS crossed Protestant denominational boundaries, and more recently CHARISMATIC RENEWAL has attracted both Protestants and Catholics. The CHRISTIAN CHURCH (DISCIPLES OF CHRIST), though considered a denomination, is committed to the ultimate unity of all Christians across denominational lines.

In the wake of WWII church leaders were confident in the strength of the churches: attendance at weekly services was high, and the resources that once went into war could now be devoted to building the peace. But in the 1960s, church attendance and vocations to the ordained ministry fell off sharply, most dramatically in Québec, but elsewhere as well. In the 1970s it became apparent that conservative EVANGELICAL AND FUNDAMENTALIST CHURCHES whose membership made up only a tiny slice of the population as a whole were attracting as many Sunday worshippers as all the mainstream Protestant giants combined. The reason may lie in the nature of modern society in which, generally speaking, public life is secularized and religious life has become private. To secularize is to treat something as belonging to the world, rather than to God, and to judge the worth of things according to their usefulness in human activity. For example, the Lord's Day Act is regarded as valuable because it gives workers a weekly rest and therefore increases productivity, not because it honours God; religious education is good because it produces well-behaved citizens, not because it cultivates a person's love of God. Christians have frequently adopted purely secular values in the course of defending public Christianity. Virtually every contemporary Canadian author who writes about the awe and wonder experienced in human life has only scorn for modern churches – an indication, perhaps, that few Canadians expect to find that which is "holy" in the churches.

People have come to think of themselves as "real" or "themselves" only in private. Elsewhere they take on roles dictated by the institution that sustains them: eg, the same person will behave in markedly different ways in school, at work, at a political rally or in a sports arena. Only in the privacy of the home does the individual think that the real self emerges. Within this private segment of modern life religion has become lodged. The movement of religion into the individual's private life helps to explain why religion in Canadian public life has gradually become secular or has simply eroded, why church attendance is seen to be less and less important, and why private religious practices (eg, watching evangelical TV programs, reading religious paperbacks or magazines) are more widespread than ever in Canadian life. The few public issues seen to be clearly religious are closely tied to this private world of home and family: ABORTION, the use of alcoholic beverages, OBSCENITY, MARRIAGE AND DIVORCE, sex education, etc. People who tell the census taker that they are "Christian" generally want to be married and buried in a church setting, but they often feel no urgent need to take a larger part in the life of the institution with its tradition of public responsibility.

Nevertheless, Christianity remains, its contours constantly changing. The Bible is still the basic reference point for all Christians, though they often differ widely as to how it is to be understood. International Christianity continues to influence what happens in Canada: leaders of the World Council of Churches and the pope have visited Canada, and Canadians follow their doings through the secular media; most religious broadcasting in Canada originates in the US; candidates for the ministry often journey abroad for their theological education. At the same time, Canadian scholars such as Northrop FRYE, Bernard LONERGAN and Wilfred Cantwell Smith are familiar in Christian circles around the world.

The local parish or congregation continues as the basic unit of Christian organization in modern Canada, but the variety of views within congregations is often as significant as the divisions between the denominations to which the congregations belong. The more liberal Christians often find support in the activities of their denominational leaders, particularly those working in central offices, and tend to view the conservatives as too private; the more conservative Christians tend to view the liberals as too secular. Between these groups lies the broad "middle" of church membership, perhaps less intensely involved in the churches' institutional life, but providing stability at the centre.

Co-operation among the churches is channelled through several Canada-wide coalitions devoted to ECUMENICAL SOCIAL ACTION, but members of local congregations often feel alienated from these coalitions with their relatively progressive stances. In addition, public prayer meetings frequently bring Christians together during urban crusades led by travelling EVANGELISTS, or on special occasions such as Good Friday and Remembrance Day when ceremonies are held with local clerical leadership. The Eucharist (Communion or Lord's Supper, the ritual sharing of bread and wine that commemorates Jesus' crucifixion) is seldom celebrated at such interdenominational gatherings, since the particular ways of celebrating that central and nearly universal rite remain closely linked with denominational identity. But modern Christians in Canada are much more likely than their ancestors were to take part in another denomination's Eucharist, drawn by friendship or marriage to members of that congregation, and there are few clergy who would deny them access. Furthermore, these Christians are now much more likely to be favourably aware of the doctrines and practices of JUDAISM, ISLAM, HINDUISM, BUDDHISM, SIKHISM or the BAHA'I FAITH, and possibly even of NEW RELIGIOUS MOVEMENTS, as practised by other Canadians.

To the extent that Canadian Christians have accepted the secularization of public life and the increasingly private nature of religious life, they have made a working accommodation to the peculiar nature of modern society. But the accommodation is inconsistent with a tradition whose favourite prayer asks, "Thy kingdom come," and takes for granted that a kingdom is no merely private matter. It is also inconsistent with the fundamental nature of religion itself, which aspires to knit everything together into one ultimately meaningful pattern, and which demands that things be holy as well as useful. Therefore it seems likely that Christianity will persist as a useful thing proper to the private lives of many Canadians, but challenged from time to time to be open to that which is holy and to be active in that which is public. *See also* BIBLE SCHOOLS; CANADIAN COUNCIL OF CHURCHES; EVANGELICAL FELLOWSHIP OF CANADA; CHRISTIAN RELIGIOUS COMMUNITIES; CANADIAN BIBLE SOCIETY; CALVINISM; MILLENARIANISM; PACIFISM.

TOM SINCLAIR-FAULKNER

Reading: J.W. Grant, *The Church in the Canadian Era* (1972); R.T. Handy, *A History of the Churches in the United States and Canada* (1977); J. Moir, *The Church in the British Era* (1972); Nive Voisine, et al, *Histoire de l'Église catholique au Québec (1608-1970)* (1971); H. H. Walsh, *The Church in the French Era* (1966).

Christians, Assemblies of, a universal low-profile fellowship of primitive orthodox Christians introduced into Canada *c*1904 from the British Isles, popularly known as Two-by-Twos and incorrectly styled Cooneyites (a 1928 Irish splinter group), which does not fit into common religious typologies. There are in Canada about 230 full-time ministers, all of whom have undertaken to live in apostolic poverty and celibacy, dedicated to pastoral care of approximately 25 000 adherents and to general evangelization. Over 50 Canadians serve as missionaries abroad, notably in the Orient and S America. The community is unincorporated, owns no property, maintains no temples, shrines or seminaries, publishes no literature, and conducts no sensational campaigns or advertising. Weekly observance of the eucharist, presided over by elders (presbyters) appointed by the apostolic ministry, is central to worship conducted in consecrated homes. All members participate in prayers and ministry of the word. In addition to private Bible studies and public missions, there are larger special meetings and 30 annual regional conventions. The hymnals, both English and French, contain a number of traditional hymns. Baptism is by submersion. The polity is primarily episcopal. Worldwide observance of the "apostles' doctrine and fellowship" is maintained while respecting cultural differences.

CORNELIUS J. JAENEN

Christie, Loring Cheney, lawyer, diplomat (b at Amherst, NS 21 Jan 1885; d at New York 8 Apr 1941). Educated at Acadia and Harvard, Christie practised law in New York, then worked in the US Department of Justice, serving as acting solicitor general. In 1913 he joined the Canadian Department of External Affairs as its first legal adviser, and was adviser on foreign policy to PMs Borden and Meighen. He helped draft Resolution IX of the 1917 Imperial War Conference, which established a relationship of equality between Great Britain and the Dominions, and he represented Canada at the 1919 Peace Conference. Mistrusted by PM Mackenzie King, Christie resigned from government in 1923 to join a London financial house. Returning to Canada, he worked for Ontario Hydro and Beauharnois Light, Heat and Power Company, then rejoined External Affairs in 1935. An isolationist during the 1930s, Christie resisted efforts to bring Canada into a European war. In 1939 he became Canadian minister to the US.   ROBERT BOTHWELL

Christie, William Mellis, biscuit manufacturer (b at Huntley, Aberdeenshire, Scot 5 Jan 1829; d at Toronto 14 June 1900). He apprenticed as a baker in Scotland, and at age 19 immigrated to Canada. In 1848 he began working as a baker's assistant in Toronto and by 1853 had become co-owner of a city bakery. Christie began to acquire a reputation for biscuits after winning a local prize in 1858. In 1868 he joined with Alexander Brown to produce biscuits mechanically for shipment across Canada. Christie, Brown and Co expanded rapidly and in 1879 Christie bought out his partner while retaining the firm's name. The operation was incorporated as a joint stock company in 1899, with Christie holding all shares, worth $500 000. Apart from much time given his Toronto factory, Christie was an inveterate traveller, having visited most of Europe, Britain and N America in his later years. He died at his Toronto mansion after a short bout with cancer. The family sold the company to a US-based firm in the 1920s, which retained the name and continues to sell Christie biscuits.

DEAN BEEBY

Chromium (Cr), hard, brittle, silver-white metal (melting point 1875°C), widely known for its use as decorative trim on home appliances and automobiles. Chromium has several industrial uses, the most important being the manufacture of stainless steel, which typically contains about 20% chromium. In its natural mineral form (chromite), chromium has heat-resistant properties which find application in various types of furnaces. Chromium readily forms various chemical compounds with a wide range of applications, such as pigments and tanning agents. Chromite is the only commercially important ore mineral of chromium. Although chromite has not been produced in Canada since 1949 when small high-grade deposits were mined, there are large low-grade chromite deposits in central Canada which could be exploited in the future. DON LAW-WEST

Chrysler Canada Ltd, with head offices in WINDSOR, Ont, is a major manufacturer and distributor of cars and trucks in Canada. The Chrysler Corporation of Canada was incorporated in 1925 as the successor to Maxwell-Chalmers Motor Company of Canada. In 1929 it completed its passenger-car assembly plant outside Windsor, which is the nucleus of the present Chrysler Centre complex, and the same year absorbed Dodge Brothers (Canada), car manufacturers, and Graham Brothers (Canada), truck manufacturers. Since the 1950s, major expansion has occurred as the company established regional parts depots and zone offices and purchased supplier firms to ensure sources of supply. The company adopted its present name in 1963. Chrysler Canada manufactures and distributes Plymouth, Dodge and Chrysler passenger cars and Dodge trucks through over 500 dealer-

ships across Canada. In 1982 it ranked 16th by sales and 110th by assets. By 1986 it had sales of $7.4 billion (ranking 7th in Canada), assets of $2 billion (ranking 50th) and 12 516 employees. The company is 100% owned by Chrysler of Detroit. *See also* AUTOMOTIVE INDUSTRY. DEBORAH C. SAWYER

Chuckwagon races at the Calgary Stampede (*courtesy The Calgary Exhibition and Stampede*).

Chuckwagon Races, a RODEO event first staged at the CALGARY STAMPEDE in 1923, based on the cowboy tradition of breaking camp after a cattle round-up and racing for home. The first races mimicked range practice. Every entry had a regulation food wagon with chuck box, water barrel and camp stove, all drawn by a 4-horse team and guided by 4 outriders. A pistol shot signalled the outriders to load stove and gear into the wagon; the rigs then raced around barrels in the centre of the arena, ran a half-mile circuit of the racetrack, and finished by unhitching the team and firing up the cook stove. The first outfit to make smoke won. Ranches sponsored rigs in the races; prominent winners have included Dick Cosgrave (1930s and 40s), Hank Willard (1950s), Hally Walgenbach (1960s), Kelly Sutherland (1970s) and Tom Glass (1980s).

Chuckwagon races have become modified horse races; since 1923, races concluded, not by firing up the stove, but by crossing the finish line in front of the grandstand and, instead of draft horse teams, entrants used thoroughbreds.

Wrecks or crashes were always part of the races. The deaths of 3 competitors and numerous horses since the 1950s prompted some calls to ban the races. In 1986 controversy over a crash involving the deaths of several horses led to proposed safety changes, including removal of stove racks at the rear of the wagons, use of collapsible starting barrels, and reducing the size of each heat. TED BARRIS

Reading: Ted Barris, *Rodeo Cowboys: The Last Heroes* (1986).

CHUM Ltd, controlled by Allan Waters, and headquartered in Toronto, is one of Canada's largest radio and television broadcasting holding companies. CHUM operates 15 radio stations located in Vancouver; Drumheller, Stettler and Brooks, Alta; Winnipeg; Peterborough, Toronto, Windsor and Ottawa, Ont; Montréal; Halifax; and St John's. Its television operations include CJCH-TV in Halifax, CKCW-TV in Moncton-Charlottetown, CKLT-TV in Saint John-Fredericton, CJCB-TV in Sydney, NS, CKVR-TV in Barrie, Ont, and CITY-TV, Canada's second-largest independent television station. Other CHUM interests include CHUM-SEEBURG franchises for Vancouver, Victoria, Calgary and Ontario; MuchMusic, an English music TV service and its French counterpart MusiquePlus; and is involved with the production of commercials. CHUM's total assets in 1986 were $111.5 million, with revenues of $135 million. PETER S. ANDERSON

Churchill, Gordon Minto, lawyer, teacher, politician (b at Coldwater, Ont 8 Nov 1898; d at

Vancouver 3 Aug 1985). One of John DIEFENBAKER's closest Cabinet confidants, Churchill was a knowledgeable and respected parliamentarian who served as Tory House leader in the Diefenbaker era. A veteran of both world wars, he was first elected to the House in 1951. In 1956 he organized and led caucus support for Diefenbaker's leadership bid and was his political adviser during the 1957 election. He was appointed minister of trade and commerce in 1957; in this capacity he led several Commonwealth trade delegations. He moved to the Dept of Veterans Affairs in 1960. After the Feb 1963 Cabinet resignations, Churchill served as defence minister until the election, and was a rallying point for Diefenbaker loyalists in the caucus until 1968.

PATRICIA WILLIAMS

Churchill, Man, Local Government District, pop 1217 (1986c), 1186 (1981c), is located at the mouth of the CHURCHILL R on the SW shore of HUDSON BAY. Although discovered by the Danish explorer Jens MUNK in 1619, the site was not "settled" until 1689, when the HBC attempted to establish a post a few kilometres upstream. The river was named for Lord Churchill (later the first duke of Marlborough) the post was permanently established near the coast in 1717. This structure was replaced by PRINCE OF WALES'S FORT, on the W bank of the estuary, which remained the centre of the FUR TRADE in the area until it was destroyed by the French in 1782. The HBC re-established Ft Churchill, which continued its role as a fur-trade post. The present town grew up on the E bank of the river after 1931 when the HUDSON BAY RY terminal and harbour facilities were completed. With WWII, the locality prospered as a northern supply centre and military base and continued as a research station and rocket launching site until the early 1960s, after which the district population declined from its peak of around 6000 as the federal government cut back its operations. Churchill is some 1600 km closer to Europe by sea than Montréal is, but its short 3-month shipping season and shallow waters have restricted its development as an ocean port. In 1987, in an attempt to lengthen the shipping season, the harbour was dredged and a tug was built to service the harbour. The upgrading of harbour facilities was part of a joint federal-provincial agreement, which also includes the improvement of rail and airport facilities by 1989. H. JOHN SELWOOD

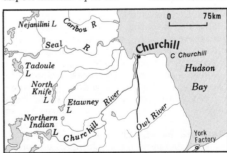

Churchill Falls, Labrador. The CHURCHILL R drops some 66 m before plummeting 75 m over the falls and a further 158 m through Bowdoin Canyon. The MONTAGNAIS-NASKAPI believed that to look on the awesome falls meant death. John MACLEAN was the first white man to see the falls (1839), but they were largely forgotten until Albert Peter LOW made a scientific excursion to the area in 1894. The massive hydroelectric potential of the falls was realized early on, but it was not until the completion of the QUEBEC, NORTH SHORE AND LABRADOR RY in 1954 and the development of long-distance electric-power transmission technology by HYDRO-QUÉBEC that exploitation became feasible. Complex negotiations between the governments of Newfoundland and

Churchill Falls, Labrador. A sight of the spectacular falls was thought by the Montagnais-Naskapi to bring death (*photo by J.A. Kraulis*).

Québec (through which the power would have to pass) were not completed until 1969. The contract provided for the sale of 5.2 million kW per year of power to Hydro-Québec for 40 years at a price of under 3 mills (three-tenths of one cent) per kWh. Hydro-Québec has the option to renew for another 25 years at only 2 mills per kWh.

The project was undertaken by a subsidiary of British Newfoundland Corp Ltd (Brinco), and was at the time the largest CIVIL ENGINEERING project ever undertaken in N America. Eighty strategically placed dikes pooled the vast waters of the Labrador Plateau in the Smallwood Reservoir. A massive underground powerhouse – until the JAMES BAY PROJECT, the largest in the world – was excavated. The project took 9 years to complete (1966-74), employed more than 30 000 people and cost $950 million. The first units began transmitting Dec 1971; the eleventh and final unit went into service in 1974.

With the dramatic rise in ENERGY costs in the 1980s, Hydro-Québec has reaped huge profits from the resale of the power from Churchill Falls, and the terms of the contract have been a source of acrimony between the governments of Newfoundland and Québec. In 1984 the Supreme Court of Canada ruled that a proposal by Newfoundland to divert water away from the falls was illegal. JAMES MARSH

Churchill River, Labrador, 856 km long (to head of Ashuanipi R), issues from Ashuanipi Lk, drops 75 m over CHURCHILL FALLS, broadens into Winokapau Lk and runs E through a deep glacial gorge past HAPPY VALLEY-GOOSE BAY into Lk Melville, Hamilton Inlet, entering the Atlantic near Rigolet (pop 317). It is the longest river in Labrador and has a DRAINAGE BASIN of 79 800 km² and a mean discharge of 1620 m³/s. The power development at Churchill Falls has backed up the river and created the enormous Smallwood Reservoir. Farther upstream, a hydroelectric plant at the outfall from Menihek Lakes provides power for the former iron-mining town of SCHEFFERVILLE, Qué. With a heavy flow and large drop from the Labrador Plateau, the river has probably the greatest hydroelectric potential of any in N America. Fort Smith (now North West River) was

an early HBC post at its mouth. John MCLEAN first reached the river from the interior 1839. It was named for Sir Charles Hamilton, governor of Newfoundland in 1821, but Premier Joseph SMALLWOOD renamed it in honour of Sir Winston Churchill (1965). The change has caused confusion since Canada already had a CHURCHILL R (in Manitoba and Saskatchewan). JAMES MARSH

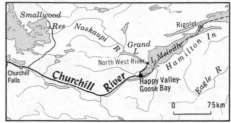

Churchill River, 1609 km long, issues from Lac La Loche in NW Saskatchewan and flows SE, E and NE across the lowlands of northern Saskatchewan and Manitoba to Hudson Bay at CHURCHILL, Man. Along the course are rapids, falls, narrow chutes, long placid stretches of smooth water, and – typical of rivers of the Canadian SHIELD – a chain of interconnected lakes. Largest of these are SOUTHERN INDIAN LK (2248 km²), Peter Pond Lk (777 km²), Churchill Lk (559 km²) and Lac Île-à-la-Crosse (391 km²) where the river takes in its main tributary, the Beaver R (491 km). The river was travelled by Cree and Chipewyan, and Jens MUNK wintered at its mouth 1619-20. The HBC built a post near its mouth in 1717; it was called Churchill River, Churchill, and Churchill Factory until 1719 when the name was changed to PRINCE OF WALES'S FORT. Samuel HEARNE re-established the fur trading post some 10 km upriver, calling it Churchill Factory and Prince of Wales Fort. The name, for John Churchill, first duke of Marlborough, governor of the HBC 1685-91 was applied to the river as early as 1686; its Indian name had been *Missinipi*, "big river." Joseph FROBISHER of the NWC established a trade link between the river and the Montréal route via the Saskatchewan and Sturgeon Weir rivers and Frog Portage. There are hydroelectric stations at Island Falls and Granville Falls, and at the N end of Southern Indian Lk an artificial diversion channel routes 75% to 85% of the river's flow to the Nelson R. This last project was completed in 1976 after much political wrangling; one result of the much reduced flow of the Churchill has been large-scale environmental impact to both the waterfowl and fish populations. JAMES MARSH

Chuvalo, George, boxer (b at Toronto 12 Sept 1937). Chuvalo became Canadian amateur heavyweight champion in 1955. He turned professional at 19, winning the Canadian heavyweight championship in 1956 when he defeated James J. Parker. Among the better-known of his vanquished opponents was Yvon Durelle. He lost the title to Bob Cleroux in 1960, regained it, then

Heavyweight champion Muhammad Ali lands a right against George Chuvalo in the third round of their Toronto bout, 29 Mar 1966 (*courtesy Canapress Photo Service*).

lost it to Cleroux again. He regained the title by beating Jean Claude Roy in 1968. He held the title this time for 11 years before giving it up in 1979. He is remembered internationally for his remarkable ability to stay with the world's highest ranked boxers, none of whom ever knocked him off his feet. His opponents included George Foreman, Ernie Terrell, Floyd Patterson, Joe Frazier and Muhammad Ali. Chuvalo finished with a lifetime professional record of 79-15-2; 70 of his 79 victories were by knockout.

A.J. "SANDY" YOUNG

Cineplex Odeon Corporation, an integrated entertainment company engaged in operating motion-picture theatres in Canada and the US. It also operates a film-distribution division, a production studio and Canada's largest film laboratory and post-production facility. Garth H. DRABINSKY is the chairman, president and CEO. The corporation opened its first multi-screen complex at EATON CENTRE, Toronto. Through acquisition of several theatre chains, including Canadian Odeon (1984), Plitt Theatres Inc (1985), Septum Theatres (1986) and RKO Century Warner (1986), the corporation is now one of the largest exhibitors in N America. It has over 1500 screens in some 500 locations and more than 12 500 employees.

The beginnings of the company's growth came in 1983 when, under pressure from the federal Dept of Communications, US film distributors allowed Cineplex Odeon access to first-run feature movies. In 1986, American-based MCA, Inc purchased a 50% equity in Cineplex Odeon, though in accordance with Canadian regulations MCA shares have restricted voting rights.

Cineplex Odeon Films (formerly Pan-Canadian Film Distributors) is a wholly owned division. It is the largest independent distributor of films in Canada. Cineplex Odeon also owns Toronto International Studios, Canada's largest studio facility and in 1986 it purchased The Film House Groups Inc, Canada's largest film laboratory and post-production facility. Cineplex's 1986 revenues were over $500 million and assets were nearly $900 million.

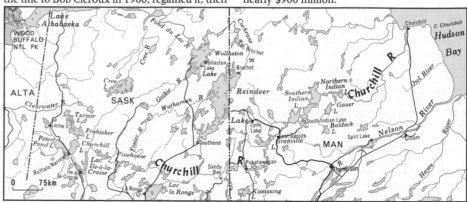

Cinq-Mars, Lionel, plant pathologist, vascular plant systematist (b at St-Coeur-de-Marie, Qué 12 June 1919; d at Québec C 6 Aug 1973). Trained in plant pathology, but interested in the taxonomy of vascular plants, Cinq-Mars initiated and encouraged continued development of floristic studies at Laval. During his early career as a phytopathologist, Cinq-Mars worked on apple diseases. In 1962 he was appointed professor of botany at Laval and remained there until his death. He became conservator of the Herbier Louis-Marie at Laval in 1968 and increased the holdings to over 10 000 specimens. His particular research interests were *Amelanchier* and *Viola*, especially in Québec. Cinq-Mars wrote more than 70 papers in plant pathology, vascular plant systematics and distribution, ornithology and natural history. He also established and edited 2 publications devoted to plant systematics, *Ludoviciana* and *Provanchera*. His name is commemorated by a species of saskatoon berry, *Amelanchier quinti-martii*. As a charter member and one of the first directors of the Canadian Botanical Assn, he is remembered by the Cinq-Mars Award for the outstanding student paper at the annual meeting. J.R. STEIN

Cipriani, André Joseph, biophysicist, avid sportsman, bon vivant (b at Port-of-Spain, Trinidad 2 Apr 1908; d at Deep River, Ont 23 Feb 1956). Educated in physics and medicine at McGill, he began his distinguished career with research in neurophysiology, cerebral blood flow, and acceleration and motion sickness at McGill and the Montreal Neurological Inst. Following biophysical medical research in the Royal Canadian Army Medical Corps, he joined Chalk River Nuclear Laboratories (CRNL) where he and W.V. Mayneord surveyed isotopes before selecting cobalt-60 as the most promising one for CANCER treatment. Further studies laid a sound basis for future cobalt therapy dose measurements. He pioneered the production of cobalt-60 for the first COBALT therapy machines used by H.E. JOHNS and others, and treatments began in Canada in fall 1951. His brilliant leadership in setting standards for radiation hazards control and safe reactor operation at CRNL led to outstanding success in both fields. JOAN MELVIN

Cisco, see WHITEFISH.

Citadel Theatre was founded in 1965 by Joseph H. SHOCTOR in the Salvation Army Citadel in Edmonton and rapidly outgrew its quarters. In 1976 the theatre was able to move into the striking building which now houses the Shoctor, Rice and Zeidler theatres in the heart of the city. One of Canada's theatrical showcases, it continues to grow and expand, offering the 350 000 patrons who attend each year world-class performances from international stars and directors. At least one major Canadian play is scheduled each season. The Citadel's travelling company, Citadel-On-Wheels/Wings, tours Alberta, the Arctic and the NWT; its in-house Theatre for Young Audi-

Exterior of Citadel Theatre, 1983 (*courtesy Provincial Archives of Alberta/A13324*).

ences, the School for the Performing Arts and the International Children's Festival make it one of the more comprehensive theatrical organizations in N America. In 1984 the Maclab, a 700-seat thrust theatre, and the Tucker, a 150-seat open-air amphitheatre, were completed. *See also* THE-ATRE, ENGLISH-LANGUAGE.

Cité libre, magazine fd 1950, bringing together Québec intellectuals who opposed Maurice DUPLESSIS. Inspired by Emmanuel Mounier's philosophic system that took man as its fundamental measure of value, the editorial board, which included Gérard PELLETIER and Pierre-Elliott TRUDEAU, assumed that universal man was to be defended from totalitarianism. This abstract philosophy was never translated into concrete social and political objectives. The journal was humanist, progressive and nondoctrinaire – Pierre VADEBONCOEUR and Pierre Vallières rubbed shoulders with Jean Le Moyne and Maurice Blain – and its content demonstrated the unease prevalent in Québec society. Secular and anticlericalist in orientation, *Cité libre* explored religious issues in depth. The journal met intellectual mediocrity and intolerance with a rationalism inspired by the great liberal thinkers. *Cité libre* sometimes took audacious stands on socioeconomic issues, yet never questioned basic social structures: it argued instead for gradual reform. It was antinationalist and, in politics, primarily concerned with the ethical issues of teaching democratic morality and fighting corruption. Its search for new values and an identity was more evident in its first series of issues (1950-59) than in its second (1960-66). In the interval, the QUIET REVOLUTION had begun. *See also* LITERARY PERIODICALS IN FRENCH.

BENOÎT MELANÇON

Citizen's Arrest originated in Medieval England when there was no police force and it was everyone's duty to assist in chasing criminals. These powers are now set out in the Criminal Code. First, anyone who owns or lawfully possesses property may arrest someone found committing a crime on or in relation to that property, eg, a farmer may arrest someone stealing his tractor. Secondly, anyone may arrest a person found in the act of committing a serious (indictable) offence or escaping from the police after committing a crime. In all cases, the arrested person must be delivered immediately to a police officer.

LEE PAIKIN

Citizenship The Citizenship Act, which is the current nationality legislation in force in Canada, came into effect on 15 Feb 1977. It defines "citizen" as "a Canadian citizen" and provides that both native-born and naturalized citizens are equally entitled to all the rights, powers and privileges and subject to all the obligations, duties and liabilities of a citizen, which are governed by numerous provincial and federal laws and the CONSTITUTION ACT. In all provinces and in the federal jurisdiction, citizens of the age of majority are guaranteed political rights including the right to vote and run for office.

Before 1947, Canada's Naturalization Acts conferred British subject status on immigrants being naturalized in Canada and on native-born alike. The Canadian Citizenship Act, the first nationality statute in Canada to define its people as Canadians, came into force on 1 Jan 1947. Among other things, the Act gave married women full authority over their nationality status. From 1947 onwards women have neither gained nor lost Canadian nationality status through marriage. Under nationality legislation in effect prior to 1947 a married woman's nationality status in Canada had, for the most part, been linked to that of her husband.

The Citizenship Act of 1976 recognized the equality of women in citizenship matters and as well removed the remaining differences between groups of people seeking to become citizens. All persons born in Canada are, with minor exceptions (eg, children of diplomats), Canadian citizens at birth.

Children born abroad on or after 15 Feb 1977 are automatically citizens if either parent was a citizen at the time of birth. However, children born abroad in the second and succeeding generations of children so born from that date are required before the age of 28 to apply to retain citizenship, to register as a citizen and either live in Canada for one year prior to making the application or have established a substantial connection with Canada. Children under the age of majority, one or both of whose parents have become citizens, are also eligible for citizenship provided an application for citizenship is made on their behalf and they have been admitted to Canada for permanent residence by the immigration authorities. Adult persons who have been admitted to Canada for permanent residence may qualify for citizenship after 3 or more years residence in Canada and the fulfilment of certain other conditions. The minister responsible for citizenship at present, the Secretary of State, has the discretion to waive some requirements for citizenship and the governor-in-council has the discretionary power to direct the grant of citizenship to any person to alleviate cases of special and unusual hardship or to reward services of an exceptional value to Canada. This latter power is rarely used but in a world community aware of human needs it could prove significant.

Under the 1976 Immigration Act (s4) Canadian citizens have the absolute right to enter and live in Canada. This right also pertains to Indians under the Indian Act whether or not they are citizens. Permanent residents and Convention REFUGEES who are allowed certain rights in Canada are also subject to certain restrictions. Only Canadian citizens are eligible to obtain Canadian passports, although permanent residents may be granted a travel document. Many Canadian professional associations, eg, law societies and medical associations, require practitioners of their profession to be citizens.

An application for the grant, retention, renunciation or resumption of citizenship (except for the grant of citizenship made on behalf of a minor) is initially considered by a citizenship judge. Both the minister and the person concerned have the right to appeal the judge's decision to the federal court, trial division. The governor-in-council may refuse an application for the grant, resumption, or renunciation of citizenship but the grounds for this are narrow. Both the grant of citizenship and the renunciation of citizenship can be revoked by the governor-in-council if obtained by fraud, misrepresentation or concealment of material circumstances. A person who was admitted to Canada for permanent residence under false pretenses is deemed to have obtained Canadian citizenship by false pretenses as well. The revocation is made by the governor-in-council following a report made by the minister which can only be made after the person has been notified of his or her right to have the case referred to the federal court, trial division.

The issue of revocation has acquired notoriety in recent years because of the controversy which surrounds the granting of citizenship to alleged Nazi war criminals. There could be doubt about the constitutionality of revocation, because the possibility creates a distinction between naturalized and native-born citizens which might run afoul of s15 of the Canadian Charter of Rights and Freedoms.

Citizens residing in Canada may not renounce their citizenship unless permitted to do so by the minister. Those who have ceased to be citizens may resume citizenship after being admitted to Canada for permanent residence and residing in Canada for at least one year following such admission and immediately preceding the date of application. Canadian citizens may hold any number of citizenships at the same time, providing the other country or countries concerned also recognize the concept of dual or plural nationality. Citizens of other Commonwealth countries and Ireland are recognized as Commonwealth citizens in Canada, a status which is viewed as symbolic.

In 1987 the government announced plans for a new citizenship act which would limit dual citizenship and tighten citizenship rules in general. No legislation has been introduced yet.

Noncitizens Noncitizens in Canada do not enjoy political rights but generally have all legal rights and are subject to the law in the same way as citizens. Permanent residents are entitled to work in Canada while visitors usually are not. *See also* IMMIGRATION.   JULIUS H. GREY

City In Canada "city" is a broad, generic term usually referring to an urbanized area. The size of this area, its economic base, social character and form of local government may be different in each province or territory because MUNICIPAL GOVERNMENT derives its authority from the provincial legislature, and in each province the conditions that must exist before an area may be classified as a city differ. As a result, it is simpler to examine the process of urbanization itself, defined as the generation and spread of characteristic features of urban life. The demographic trend toward urbanization in Canada began well before Confederation and still continues at a rapid pace. By 1987, over 80% of Canadians lived in urban areas, meaning cities, towns, villages or unincorporated settlements with populations greater than 1000 persons, or in built-up fringes of incorporated areas.

Historical Development to 1920 Great empires, with dynamic metropolitan centres such as Paris and London, expanded by establishing colonial outposts. Early Canadian colonial towns were part of this large-scale phenomenon and served as agents of the urban metropolitan centres. Economically, they exploited the colony's staples; culturally, they transmitted the metropolitan-centre style of life to a new frontier; militarily and administratively they were often the means of occupying and holding the colony. The colonial towns were generally entrepôts, collecting staples, eg, fur, fish, minerals or wheat, from the region for shipment to the metropolitan centre, where the final processing was done and from which the manufactured foods were, in turn, distributed. French and British colonial towns preceded the general settlement of a region and constituted an urban frontier, but the growth and prosperity of the colonial towns depended on the potential of their hinterlands. Initially the towns acted as a channel for a region's development and contained a high proportion of the colony's population. Decentralization began as the town's proportion of the total population dropped, even though the towns tended to grow rapidly. The new, smaller, secondary centres developed a degree of autonomy during this second phase because of their isolation in a pre-railway era and because the primary town of the region did not yet have the necessary facilities to dominate all aspects of life in the hinterland. This decentralization process was reversed when colonial towns such as Québec City, Montréal, Toronto and Halifax became major urban centres.

Colonial towns, primarily connected and concerned with the overseas metropolis, lacked significant connections with other colonial towns, even with those of their own region. The beginning of regional and inter-regional connections represented the end of the colonial phase and the beginning of the commercial era, as towns began to produce goods and services not only for themselves but for the entire region. By 1851, the 9 largest cities – MONTRÉAL, QUÉBEC CITY, SAINT JOHN, TORONTO, HALIFAX, HAMILTON, KINGSTON, OTTAWA and LONDON – had developed into dynamic commercial centres and had won considerable hegemony over sizable hinterlands.

The modern Canadian city emerged between 1851 and 1921, although in most respects the changes in the first 30 years after 1851 were relatively minor. Toronto replaced Québec City as Canada's second-largest city (after Montréal), and several manufacturing towns in southern Ontario increased their population to almost 10 000 (GUELPH, ST CATHARINES, BRANTFORD, BELLEVILLE), forming a second tier of cities. By the 1880s, however, Canada's 2 largest cities, Montréal and Toronto, began to outdistance their nearest rivals in importance. Equally dramatic was the rapid growth of western cities, led by WINNIPEG and VANCOUVER, followed by that of 2 other young giants, CALGARY and EDMONTON, developments which signalled the relative decline of Québec City and Kingston in central Canada and of Saint John and Halifax in the Atlantic provinces.

To some extent rapid urban growth and stagnation can be attributed to the aggressiveness of local ELITES. Winnipeg's business elite was crucial to that city's rise to metropolitan status, while the local leadership in many Atlantic cities faltered in critical periods; but more important were the vagaries of international markets in staples, and government and corporate decisions. These factors were beyond the control of individual cities. International political events stimulated the growth of Montréal's export trade and Toronto's successful competition with Montréal over the use of American trade routes. The policies of the federal government on tariffs and railways strengthened the growth of manufacturing in central cities and led to a simultaneous weakening of industry in the Maritimes. The CANADIAN PACIFIC RAILWAY decided to run its main line through Winnipeg and created a number of new communities, including Vancouver. Technological change was also important. The conversion from wood and sail to iron and steam undercut a major shipbuilding industry in Québec City and Saint John, and resulted in a shift from an Atlantic to a continental economy.

In their pursuit of metropolitan status, most Canadian cities passed through several stages of development: colonial entrepôt, commercial town, commercial-industrial city and diversified metropolis. Although all cities did not, of course, develop systematically in some deterministic fashion, Canada's urban development can nevertheless be distinguished by particular eras, and all cities and towns, regardless of scale, function and regional location, were shaped to a great extent by each era.

The Contemporary City Since 1920, Canadian cities have entered a phase dominated by the technology of the automobile and the truck, an economic orientation away from industry to service functions and to dramatic spatial decentralization of population and activities. City-building, however, is a cumulative process. The pre-1920 city is still the core of the modern, dispersed metropolis. The distinction between modern developments and those of earlier periods is usually very clear and can be identified on any

street map. The street systems of urban cores are set out on grids. Surrounding these urban cores are more recent suburban developments with curvilinear street systems. Many of the tensions in contemporary cities derive from the struggle for coexistence between parts of the city built before WWII and those built afterwards. As economic activity has shifted from industry to the service sector, the change has been reflected in building styles as office towers push factories to cheaper land at the urban fringe. Transportation facilities – streets, expressways and public transit lines – are crucial to the functioning of modern cities and often occupy 25% of urban land. Residential housing uses a slightly larger percentage of urban land, followed by industry and office buildings. These land uses represent outward expansion, as the city captures and incorporates more and more farmland, and upward expansion, as the downtown area expands with high-rise buildings that greatly intensify land use for both commercial and residential purposes. (*See* land-use maps accompanying entries on major cities.)

Suburbs The new portion of any city is usually known as the suburb. The suburbs of 1910 in Toronto, Vancouver, Montréal or Halifax are now considered to be part of the central city core, and the suburban additions of the 1920s are now integrated into the main area of the city proper. Shortly after 1945, however, the development of suburbs changed significantly. E.P. TAYLOR amassed 2000 acres (809.4 ha) of farmland on the outskirts of Toronto and developed a new town called Don Mills which, because of its scale, design and distinctive character, changed suburban development. Each of the 4 neighbourhoods into which it was divided centered or focused on a school. The curvilinear road system was used not only to discourage through traffic, but to allow roads to follow the topography. Houses of 1 1/2 storeys were set broadside to the street on large lots. Residential densities (at 25 units per ha) were half of standard densities. Land uses in each neighbourhood were deliberately separated. Space was allocated for a shopping centre, and single family dwellings were separated from apartment buildings, offices and industrial space. Don Mills was considered so successful, both financially and socially, that the model was repeated throughout Canada until the late 1970s.

Urban Renewal After 1945, urban renewal schemes were attempted by all levels of government (federal, provincial and municipal) to try to improve the housing conditions in city cores (*see* URBAN REFORM). Most politicians and planners believed that urban renewal – involving the expropriation of homes and businesses, the clearing of land and the building of new (often public) housing – would revitalize the edges of the downtown and make this housing more acceptable to those who were migrating to the suburbs. Massive urban renewal schemes met with stiff resistance from the displaced working-class families. Owners of expropriated property did not receive enough compensation to purchase a similar house elsewhere. Tenants complained that their lives were being uprooted and good housing was being demolished. Small businesses were destroyed. The basic objection to urban renewal came from people who had a different idea of their communities from that of the city planners and politicians. These residents argued strongly that the urban renewal program was wrongheaded because Canadian cities did not have the slums of American cities and that the 3 levels of government were replacing viable neighbourhoods with concrete jungles. The struggles over public urban renewal continued until the late 1960s, when after massive outcries in Vancouver, Winnipeg and Toronto, the federal government finally agreed to stop funding the public urban renewal program. Since then more modest attempts to revitalize the city have included improved street lighting, neighbourhood parks, decorative sidewalks and community centres.

Public authorities were not responsible for all urban renewal. The private development industry responded to the vastly increased housing needs of young Canadians by building large apartment buildings, usually where handsome 19th-century houses had been demolished as city councils had approved yet another rezoning. Neighbourhood groups were formed in reaction to the destruction of neighbourhoods, and in every Canadian city these groups had running battles with the developers and City Hall (see URBAN CITIZEN MOVEMENTS; CITY POLITICS). By the mid-1970s, as the apartment boom ended, mainly for economic reasons, cities began developing policies to strengthen downtown communities, rather than trying to obliterate them.

Cityscape The image of most Canadian cities is defined by the downtown, where tall office towers have now replaced smokestacks. Buildings are usually similar in design, reflecting the fact that development companies are among the largest of Canadian-owned corporations. The natural settings of most Canadian cities are now secondary in importance to the downtown, and in many cases even difficult to identify.

The explosive growth of cities since WWII has resulted in the destruction of much of Canada's urban heritage. Considerable political energy has been spent saving what remains of 19th-century buildings from the ravages of the latter half of the 20th century. By the end of the 1970s, city officials, developers and the public were ready to admit that more interesting buildings could be built and more attractive streetscapes could be designed, and most cities began to take steps to improve the downtown areas. These changes have certainly improved an otherwise bleak central city, but have done little to make the scale of cities human again.

City Life Since the introduction of federal government multicultural policies in the mid-1960s, the social participation by non-English-speaking cultures in Canadian cities has grown. Street signs exist in English, French, Chinese and Greek in various cities. Most cities take pride in ethnic celebrations and parades, and consciously try to encourage understanding and co-operation among different cultures seeking self-expression. City residents usually congregate because of professional sports events, although celebrations such as the CALGARY STAMPEDE and the Québec Winter Carnival have helped develop strong community feelings. While various mayors (notably Jean DRAPEAU of Montréal) have attempted to give their city a strong image, most such efforts have been interpreted as crass boosterism.

ALAN F.J. ARTIBISE AND JOHN SEWELL

Reading: Alan F.J. Artibise and G. Stelter, eds, *The Canadian City* (1974).

City Beautiful Movement was active in Canada from 1893 to 1930. It promoted the planned creation of civic beauty through architectural harmony, unified design and visual variety. The Canadian movement was highly influenced by writing and activities in the US. Projects ranged from creating magnificent civic centres, eg, Wascana Centre, Regina, to parkway systems (Ottawa; see NATIONAL CAPITAL COMMISSION). The amateur side of the movement was sustained by concerned citizens working through horticultural societies, newly formed civic improvement associations and even boards of trade. These smaller groups often effected greater change than the professionals: flower boxes on Main Street, street

tree plantings, landscaping of public buildings, school grounds beautification, neighbourhood clean-up campaigns and park creation. Worsening economic conditions, WWI and subsequent urban problems such as the need for affordable housing greatly diminished the larger projects while the smaller, amateur efforts continued on for a time. The movement's legacy is the persistence of certain ideals in the public mind: municipal parks, tree-lined streets, well-tended front lawns and public plantings.

EDWINNA VON BAEYER

City Politics The most obvious difference between city politics and federal or provincial politics in Canada is the absence of the major political parties. Although candidates often rely on partisan connections when building their electoral organizations, they generally present themselves to voters as independents. The spectacle of government and opposition, so familiar in Parliament and provincial legislatures, is usually missing in city politics. Mayors lack the powers that have enabled Cabinets to dominate Parliament and split them between supporters and opponents. Instead, city councils seem to work like the legislatures of the 18th century, with every member participating in the business of government and aligning with different people on different occasions. On most issues there is consensus, although this underlying agreement among the councillors is often clouded by heated disputes on particular matters. Since local politicians are free from party discipline, what surfaces are conflicts of personality, ambition, interest and only occasionally ideology. The complexity and apparent triviality of these conflicts obscure the structure and significance of local politics.

Most of the important conflicts in city politics concern real property – land and buildings. MUNICIPALITIES are primarily responsible for regulating the use of urban land and providing physical services, eg, streets and sewers. The city councils obtain most of their own revenues from taxing the land and buildings they are servicing and regulating. Legally, the municipalities are the creatures of the provinces and are subject to a host of legislative, judicial and administrative controls; recently, they have become heavily dependent on provincial and federal financial assistance. They have the most power and freedom of action in land development. Traditionally, they have been expected to promote development in the interests of economic growth. Most of the pressure for this has come from business, and businessmen and professionals with REAL-ESTATE interests have played a major role in Canadian city politics. On the other hand, business uses of municipal government have always met resistance from ratepayers concerned about rising taxes and homeowners worried about the effects of development on the value of their property and the quality of their lives. The clash between business and consumer interests is at the heart of city politics (see URBAN CITIZEN MOVEMENTS).

This clash became acute at the end of the long economic boom which followed WWII. Reform politicians, who identified with consumer interests, complained about the effects of rapid urban development that had been encouraged by traditional municipal politicians with close ties to local business (see URBAN REFORM). In a few cities – notably Winnipeg, Toronto and Ottawa – the New Democratic Party (NDP) has managed to establish itself as the main organization of the left in municipal politics, although generally the reformers have organized themselves into a coalition that is independent of any party. Some, like the Committee of Progressive Electors in Vancouver and the Montréal Citizens' Movement, are in

effect municipal parties, but they are loosely organized and weakly disciplined compared to their provincial counterparts. In this respect, the left has followed the example of the right. The most successful local parties have been loose electoral organizations established by conservatives to resist political incursions from the left. The oldest of these, like the Independent Citizens' Election Committee in Winnipeg (1921) and the Civic Non-Partisan Association in Vancouver (1934), originated between the wars. Ironically, one of their aims has been to keep "party politics" out of municipal government.

The only disciplined governing party in a Canadian city is the Montreal Citizens Movement, which follows the example of the Civic Party – the instrument of longtime mayor Jean DRAPEAU. It is unusual for a mayor to dominate a municipal council; power tends to be diffused among council committees, and executive functions are usually divided or assigned to a multimember board on which the mayor has only one vote. Incumbent city councillors normally can rely on their own reputations and organizations in seeking re-election and so remain independent of parties and political leaders. This is especially true of the traditional conservative politicians who hold most of the seats on virtually every municipal council. Reform politicians are perhaps more inclined to accept party discipline, but they are divided on issues of policy and rooted in community organizations with conflicting demands. In fact the concern of contemporary reformers with making city government more sensitive to the demands of people in particular neighbourhoods has contributed to the continuing fragmentation of city politics, in the face of efforts to organize the forces of the left and right.

About half as many voters turn out for municipal elections as for federal and provincial elections, perhaps because of the absence of the major parties, the relative lack of publicity and the seeming unimportance of the issues. Other forms of citizen participation, involving either direct contact between people and their representatives or popular input into public decisions or both, are more feasible and common at the municipal level. For many people, what counts is the sensitivity of councillors to citizen demands between elections. The low rate of voting in municipal elections may actually make politicians more responsive to the demands of small groups or individuals, because margins of victory are smaller. On the other hand, because city politics are focused on a relatively narrow range of issues, people are discouraged from taking part. Until fairly recently, this franchise was based on property qualifications. Recent upheavals in Canadian city politics have yet to broaden its scope sufficiently to encourage the mass commitment desired by proponents of local self-government.   WARREN MAGNUSSON

Reading: D.J.H. Higgins, *Local and Urban Politics in Canada* (1986); Warren Magnusson and A. Sancton, eds, *City Politics in Canada* (1983).

Civil Code, fundamental legislative enactment which contains a comprehensive and easily understood statement of a nation's private LAW. It is typically found in legal systems whose traditions are traceable to Roman law. In Canada, only Québec has a Civil Code. Unlike an Administrative Code, Criminal Code or Code of Civil Procedure, a Civil Code expounds only on matters of private law, eg, names, domicile, age of majority, filiation, marriage, property, successions, gifts, wills, trusts, contracts, delicts, sale, lease, mandate, partnership, pledge and hypothecs. It consolidates the fundamental concepts, rules, principles and ideals of a legal tradition in a clear nontechnical style and, as a codification, is intended to be comprehensive in scope. In codified legal systems, separate statutes covering private law matters are to be avoided. Further, by contrast with uncodified systems, judicial decisions are not conceived as setting down the law.

Today Québec has 2 partially overlapping Civil Codes, the 1866 Civil Code of Lower Canada, which still contains the bulk of the law, and the 1980 Civil Code of Québec, which covers only certain aspects of family law. The 1866 Code was the fruit of a Codification Commission created in 1857 to consolidate, in a bilingual statement, all civil laws in Canada East. For doctrine, the commissioners relied heavily on the works of the great French jurist, Pothier, to a lesser extent on various commentaries on the Code Napoléon and occasionally upon the text of the Louisiana Civil Code. They derived the majority of the Code's provisions from the Custom of Paris, brought to New France in 1663. The Code also includes rules drawn from several French royal ordinances and from the edicts and decisions of the Sovereign Council of New France prior to 1763. Various principles of common law, introduced either by the QUEBEC ACT of 1774 or by statutes of Lower Canada or the Province of Canada enacted between 1791 and 1866, were also included. For form, the commissioners adopted the model of the 1804 Code Napoléon, the 3 books of which were entitled Of Persons; Of Property and Ownership and its Different Modifications; and Of the Acquisition and Exercise of Rights of Property. To these they appended a fourth, dealing with commercial law. Despite its eclectic sources the Civil Code was a distinctive document closely reflecting the basic values of 19th-century Québec – moral authoritarianism, philosophical individualism and economic liberalism.

Québec society has undergone considerable change but until recently the Code remained largely unamended, principally because of its status as a reflection of Catholic and francophone culture and as a bulwark against the intrusions of English COMMON LAW. Consequently the 1866 Code lost many of its virtues as a codification. To overcome the growing chasm between the law of the Code and social reality, much noncodal special legislation has been enacted. Judicial interpretations often displaced Code provisions as the definitive statement of law. The language and organization of the Code became outdated. In 1955, the Québec legislature established the Civil Code Revision Office to revise the Code. In 1964, after completing, piecemeal, some of the more urgent reforms, the office embarked upon a comprehensive review of the Code and proposed, in a *Draft Civil Code and Commentaries,* fundamental alterations of many substantive, linguistic and organizational premises of the Code's predecessor. In 1981, a new Civil Code of Québec was promulgated but only certain recommendations relating to family law were enacted at that time. Since 1981 the legislature has also enacted reforms to the laws of persons, property, successions, trusts and administration of the property of another, although none of these has yet been proclaimed in force. Several other proposals will be considered and implemented over the next few years. It is now anticipated that the remaining titles of the 1981 Code will be proclaimed in force together in 1989 and that, as of that date, the 1866 Code will be entirely superseded.   R.A. MACDONALD

Civil Defence The problem of protecting civilian populations in wartime grew dramatically with the advent of mass air raids in WWII. Although the threat to N America was negligible, Canada introduced air-raid precautions which provided for active fighter defence, EARLY-WARNING RADAR, blackouts, and rescue and emergency relief orga-

nizations. The first peacetime civil defence co-ordinator was appointed Oct 1948 to supervise the work of federal, provincial, and municipal authorities in planning for public air-raid shelters, emergency food and medical supplies, and the evacuation of likely target areas. The development of nuclear weapons and the COLD WAR in the 1940s and 1950s forced Canadians to consider even more extensive measures. The Diefenbaker government in 1959 transferred responsibility for civil defence to the Emergency Measures Organization (Emergency Planning Canada 1974-86, Emergency Preparedness Canada since 1986) and then assigned all army units in Canada to post-atomic attack evacuation and survival operations. The next year the government launched a campaign in support of home fallout shelters. Public enthusiasm for such programs soon dwindled: costs were prohibitive, and the odds against survival mounted once the superpowers had more than enough missiles and warheads to destroy the world. Today the federal government maintains an attack warning system, and federal civil emergency planning for both war and peace is co-ordinated by Emergency Preparedness Canada.   STEPHEN HARRIS

Civil Engineering is a very broad field of ENGINEERING concerned with the planning, design, construction and operation of much of the infrastructure of civilization, such as buildings, transportation systems and sanitation systems, etc; with soil mechanics and water resources; with city planning; and with SURVEYING and mapping.

Before the multiplication of engineering disciplines in the late 19th and early 20th centuries, engineers were either military or civilian. Civilian engineers built nonmilitary structures; those in the military concentrated on FORTIFICATIONS. The early engineers in what is now Canada were almost exclusively military. In New France, military engineers were responsible for surveying, road building and fortification, and their work was taken over and further developed by British army sappers and miners (engineers) after the conquest. Civilian engineers became involved before the turn of the 19th century. For example, while CANAL building began as a military specialty, the first lock on the Sault Ste Marie canal was built in 1797-98 by the North West Company. Civil engineers were involved in such projects as the development of steamboats and railways and the construction of roads, public buildings, harbours, etc.

Early engineers received their training as apprentices to established professionals like Samuel KEEFER, his brother, Thomas KEEFER, leading hydraulic engineer of his time, or Sir Casimir GZOWSKI, engineer of the international bridge over the Niagara R. As the extent of Canada's mineral and other resource wealth became apparent, and as the railway boom developed, it became necessary to establish formal training programs to provide engineering expertise. The first such courses were offered at King's College (now University of New Brunswick) in 1854; however, the real expansion in training began in the 1870s, when, within the course of 5 years, programs were established at McGill, École Polytechnique de Montréal; School of Practical Sciences, Toronto; and Royal Military College, Kingston. The profession has continued to expand since that time; in 1987, 25 universities offered accredited programs in civil engineering to some 5000 students.

The Modern Profession

Today, the civil engineer's work tends to be highly specialized, covering every conceivable as-

pect of public and private construction.

Surveying is the delineation of the position and form of natural or man-made features on a tract of land. Land must be surveyed before building can start, to determine legal boundaries, slopes, potential hazards, etc.

Soil Mechanics or Geotechnical Engineering is the branch of civil engineering which deals with characteristics of the substrate (soil or rock) which influence the suitability of a site for a given form of construction (eg, shear stress on slopes, plasticity of soil, soil seepage) and the peripheral structures needed to make a site safe for a specific structure (eg, foundations, drainage structures). Soil mechanics is important not only to the safe and economical exploitation of familiar environments, but also to successful use of fragile or hostile environments (eg, PERMAFROST).

Structural Engineering, closely allied with architecture, deals with the design of buildings. Structural engineers translate architectural designs into precise instructions on building methods, materials, structural configurations (eg, column and beam designs), etc. Innovative buildings, such as Toronto's CN Tower, are lasting monuments to the structural engineer's skill.

Materials Engineering Practitioners of this branch set specifications for materials which are used in the construction industry (eg, asphalt used in road pavements, structural steels) and undertake research in order to improve such materials (*see* METALLURGY).

Transportation Engineering involves the planning, design and construction of transportation facilities, including roads, railways, airports and harbours, bus terminals, rapid transit and parking structures.

Hydrotechnical or Water Resource Engineering deals with irrigation, drainage, the control of water hazards (eg, floods), harbour and river development for transportation, the improvement of water availability and the protection of structures from attack by water (eg, ocean waves, normal river flow).

Environmental Engineering is concerned with minimizing the environmental impacts of proposed engineering schemes. It usually includes sanitary engineering, an important part of URBAN AND REGIONAL PLANNING, deals with the design of water distribution and waste disposal systems to ensure that people have clean, healthy water to drink and that sewage does not become a pollution hazard.

Before the turn of the century, a civil engineer would have designed many different structures; for example, Thomas Keefer began the survey of the Kingston to Toronto railway connection, and designed the waterworks for Hamilton, Ont (1859) and Ottawa (1874) and many other public works. Today, civil engineers must co-operate with specialists from many nonengineering disciplines and engineering subfields to complete a single project. For example, engineers who specialized in urban planning and transportation engineering assist architects and planners in the initial design of a shopping centre. Once the location and size of the centre is determined, a more detailed design is produced. Traffic engineers design entrances and exits and lay out parking lots; structural engineers work with the architect to design the buildings; other engineers design the heating and ventilation, plumbing and electrical systems and join in the design process, to produce a set of engineering drawings and specifications. These are the documents from which the construction engineer estimates the cost of erecting the centre. These drawings and specifications form part of a contract, specifying the rights and duties of the contractor, the engineer and the owner, drawn up with the aid of lawyers specializing in engineering law.

Training and Societies

Students studying to be civil engineers must complete a 4-5-year university program. Civil engineering programs are periodically reviewed and accredited by the Canadian Accreditation Board of the Canadian Council of Professional Engineers. After graduation the student may be required to write an exam on professional practice to be accepted into a provincial professional engineers association as an engineer in training. Two years later, the trainee may apply for full membership and, based on the recommendations of employers, will be accepted as a professional engineer.

The first engineering society in Canada, the Canadian Society of Civil Engineers, was established in 1887, becoming the Engineering Institute of Canada (EIC) in 1918 and an independent group, the Canadian Society for Civil Engineers, in 1986. Civil engineers are also represented by the Canadian Council of Professional Engineers (est 1936), and make up about one-quarter of its nearly 130 000 members in 1986. *See also* ENGINEERING HISTORY.   FRANK NAVIN

Civil Law, the system of LAW that evolved from the Roman law compilations of the Emperor Justinian. Today it is found in countries of continental Europe as well as their former colonies and, in Canada, in Québec. In many jurisdictions it is in force in the form of a CIVIL CODE.

JOHN E.C. BRIERLEY

Civil Liberties, generally, freedoms to do certain things without restraint from government although there can be some restraint from private individuals or agencies, eg, an individual may publish opinions without interference from government, but a newspaper or magazine is not obliged to publish them. In this respect civil liberties can be distinguished from civil rights. Civil rights may be protected by legislation prohibiting discrimination by public and private officials against persons because of such grounds as their race, colour, creed, sex, religion or national origin. Civil liberties reflect an essentially modern view of man and society but derive as well from older societies, such as those of Greece and Rome.

There is some overlap among the terms civil liberties, civil rights, HUMAN RIGHTS and fundamental freedoms and, in international law, civil and political rights. Traditionally those civil liberties which are called fundamental freedoms include the freedoms of religion, expression (speech and press), assembly and association. Those civil liberties known as due process of law or the principles of fundamental justice include prohibition of arbitrary arrest or detention, and unreasonable search or seizure; the rights to habeas corpus, retaining counsel, bail, presumption of innocence and a fair hearing; and the right not to be subjected to torture or to cruel and inhuman treatment or punishment. Until the enactment in the Constitution of the CANADIAN CHARTER OF RIGHTS AND FREEDOMS, civil liberties in Canada were recognized by the courts on the basis of the common law and such UK constitutional principles as the rule of law.   WALTER S. TARNOPOLSKY

Civil Procedure, the body of LAW concerning the prescribed methods of resolving disputes through litigation (*see* CIVIL LAW). "Civil" distinguishes this body of law from CRIMINAL PROCEDURE, which concerns the methods of prosecuting criminal offences. The subject matter of civil procedure includes the organization and jurisdiction of courts competent to dispose of civil suits, the conduct of actions from their institution through trial and to judgement, the conduct of appellate litigation, and the enforcement of judgements and judicial orders. The LAW OF EVIDENCE, which is germane to civil procedure, governs the admissibility and weight of proof adduced in the course of a trial. The study of civil procedure also extends to problems such as the advisability, cost of and alternatives to litigation, whether litigants are eligible for LEGAL AID, and the duties of the legal profession in the conduct of litigation. In the same way as rules of COMMERCIAL LAW by their configuration and soundness affect the course and volume of business, rules of civil procedure affect the administration and the quality of civil justice. They determine, among other important questions, when and how citizens can have their "day in court."

Legislative Authority Constitutionally, the primary responsibility for the administration of justice lies with the provinces and therefore most of the legislation pertaining to civil procedure emanates from provincial legislatures. However, under a special provision of the CONSTITUTION ACT, 1867, two of Canada's existing courts were created by Acts of Parliament: the SUPREME COURT OF CANADA (the highest appellate court in the country), created in 1875, and the FEDERAL COURT, a court created in 1971 for the better administration of federal law. The statutes establishing these courts also specify the main features of their procedure.

Sources and History In common-law provinces (ie, all provinces except Québec), the legal rules forming the core of civil procedure are contained in statutes, such as the Judicature Acts, or Rules of Practice, or Rules of Court. These Acts, inspired by English legislation, unified the courts of common law and the courts of equity. They made possible the collection into Rules of Practice of numerous and technical rules of procedure, most of which had been made by judges on a case-by-case basis. Today, judges still participate in making these rules. In the courts created by Parliament, detailed and often complex rules of practice also regulate most aspects of practice and procedure. In Québec the Code of Civil Procedure, an Act containing over 2000 articles, codifies most of the procedural rules and fulfils a similar function to rules of practice with which it shares many characteristics. Its origins can be traced to the French *Ordonnonce de la Procédure* of 1667. Judicial precedents are another important source of law in civil procedure, primarily in the common-law provinces.

The Process of Civil Litigation Throughout Canada the systems of civil procedure are adversarial in nature, designed to ensure opposing parties access to information necessary for the preparation of their case and to offer them an opportunity to argue against each other in court. Typically, individuals who believe they have suffered an infringement of their rights will consult a lawyer about the costs and risks of a suit. If it is decided to commence an action, the choice of the appropriate court will be the first procedural question considered by the lawyer. The answer depends on the nature of the case, the amount of the claim and on territorial considerations. There are several levels of trial courts in most provinces of Canada (*see* COURTS OF LAW), and within a province some of these courts are subdivided according to the territorial limits of counties or judicial districts. Once the choice is made, the lawyer representing the party who sues (the plaintiff) will attend the office of the court to have issued against the party being sued (the defendant) a document called a petition (or summons, statement of claim, writ of summons). In most cases the writ will be delivered (served) to the defendant in person by a bailiff. The document will inform the defendant of the nature of the claim against him and explain that if he does not appear and defend the action against him, the plaintiff may obtain judgement by default against the defendant. After service, each party in turn will give details of the claim or the defence or rebuttals of the opponent's claim in written pleadings (a statement of claim or declaration, sometimes already served with the original document, a statement of defence, an answer and a reply). The pleadings, served on the other party and filed with the court, will assist the plaintiff and defendant in determining the precise issues between them. The parties will also benefit from several "discovery procedures" (EXAMINATION FOR DISCOVERY, disclosure or discovery of documents, medical examination, etc) designed to facilitate the gathering of relevant information and the joining of issues.

If the parties cannot agree on a settlement out of court, they will proceed to trial. Because of the backlog of cases awaiting trial, months and sometimes years will elapse between the institution of the suit and the actual trial. The trial will take place either before a judge sitting alone or before a judge and a JURY. In Québec all civil trials are heard by judges sitting alone. At the trial each party will be entitled to lead (present) evidence, usually by live witnesses or by documents. Every witness called and examined by a party can be cross-examined by the other party. At this stage of the case, the rules of evidence are crucial. The parties then, through their lawyers, present closing arguments on the facts and the law of the case. The judge commonly renders judgement after preparing written reasons. Where there is a jury, however, the jury delivers a verdict on the issues of fact at the end of the trial and the judge renders judgement accordingly. When the defendant has failed to appear or to defend the action or where the plaintiff has failed to proceed with the action, judgement can be obtained summarily, without a trial. After judgement, the losing party may choose to APPEAL. Depending on the nature of the case and the amount in dispute, he may do so as of right or with the permission (leave) of the court of appeal.

There is a court of appeal for each Canadian jurisdiction, provincial or federal. Appellate litigation is usually confined to questions of law. No new evidence is led by the parties, who must rely on a record of the evidence presented at trial. With written arguments ("factums") and later orally, the appellant and the respondent will respectively argue against and in favour of the judgement appealed. The court of appeal may confirm, vary or reverse the trial judgement, or order a new trial. In some cases the party who loses on appeal will bring a second appeal to the Supreme Court of Canada, the judgement of which is not subject to a further appeal. The final judgement in the case (either by an appellate court or by the trial court if no appeal is brought) will dismiss the action, or maintain it in whole or in part. The costs of the action will usually be awarded to the winning party, who will recover them from the losing party. These costs usually amount to a mere fraction of the total expenses and normally do not include all the lawyers' professional fees.

The rules of civil procedure also provide for the compulsory enforcement of judgements in the event that the party against whom judgement was rendered fails to comply with the order of the court. The seizure and sale of property and the garnishment of moneys owed are among the measures available for this purpose. Sometimes a disobedient party may even be jailed.

The Reform and Future of Civil Procedure In the last 20 years efforts have been made in most provinces to modernize and improve the law of civil procedure. A growing concern with the costs and delays of civil litigation and with the poor accessibility of the courts led to the creation and improvement of legal-aid schemes, SMALL CLAIMS COURTS, class-action procedures, and methods of alternative dispute resolution such as mediation in family law. During the same period, the need for the simplification and rationalization of civil procedure led to the appearance of reforming bodies in many provinces – some of which extensively revised local rules of practice. Procedural reforms must strike a delicate balance between form and substance. On the one hand, PROCEDURAL LAW should be the servant of SUBSTANTIVE LAW: parties to litigation ought to be heard expeditiously on the merits of their claims and should not be forced into a debate on the manner in which their claims must be presented or heard. On the other hand, a body of procedural rules, the enforcement of which inevitably generates side issues, is essential to the achievement of justice: in a process of adjudication that defines itself as adversarial, what a court decides depends very much on how it is presented with the issues, which in turn depend on how procedural rules assist the parties in preparing their case.

YVES-MARIE MORISSETTE

Clair, Frank, football coach (b at Hamilton, Ohio 12 May 1917). His coaching record is unparalleled in Canadian FOOTBALL history. His teams made the playoffs in 17 of his 19 seasons, advanced to the conference final 12 times and appeared in 6 GREY CUP games, winning 5 times. He began his career as coach of the TORONTO ARGONAUTS from 1950 to 1954, winning Grey Cups in 1960 and in his final 2 seasons in 1968 and 1969. He became the Ottawa Rough Riders' general manager in 1970 and held that position until 1978. In 1982 he became the chief scout for the Argos. His total of 174 coaching wins is the most of any CFL head coach and Clair was twice honoured with the Annis Stukus Trophy as the CFL Coach of the Year (1966 and 1969). Clair was inducted into the Canadian Football Hall of Fame in 1981.

PETER WONS

Claire, Lake, 1437 km², elev 213 km, max length 63 km, located in NE Alberta in the SE corner of WOOD BUFFALO NATIONAL PARK, is an isolated western extension of Lk ATHABASCA and the largest lake entirely within Alberta. Situated W of Ft Chipewyan (est 1788), it is fed by the PEACE, Birch and McIvor rivers and drains eastward via Mamawi Lk into Lk Athabasca. Originally one of the deepest lakes in the Athabasca Delta region, it was named Clear Water Lk by Alexander MACKENZIE (1792), and its clarity was remarked upon by David THOMPSON (map of 1814). Over the years it has become shallow through silt accumulation, but still has a commercially profitable goldeye fishery.

DAVID EVANS

Clam, common name for any bivalve (hinged shell) MOLLUSC, referring especially to those of economic significance burrowing in beaches or the seafloor. In Canada, numerous species are fished for human consumption. On the West Coast, butter and littleneck clams (*Saxidomus giganteus, Protothaca staminea,* respectively) are most important, but the accidentally introduced Manila clam (*Tapes philippinarum*) is also taken. Recently, an important fishery for the geoduck (*Panope abrupta,* formerly *P. generosa*) has developed. It is the largest clam of the N Pacific, with a body weight up to 5 kg, and a lifespan of up to 150 years. On the East Coast, the soft-shell clam (*Mya arenaria*) and the ocean quahog (*Arctica islandica*) are commercially important.   FRANK R. BERNARD

Clan has been used to designate social groups whose members trace descent from either male or female ancestors. For the native people of Canada, the term has been used most often to designate groups based on unilineal descent. This means

that a person belongs to the clan of either parent. Examples of matrilineal societies, those tracing descent from a female, are the IROQUOIS, HAIDA and TSIMSHIAN. Clans, named after birds, fish or deer, were important in regulating marriage (usually to forbid marriage with a fellow clan member). Certain rights, privileges and property were also associated with clans, and they functioned as ceremonial units that cut across geographical and even linguistic divisions.   RENÉ R. GADACZ

Clancy, Francis Michael, "King," hockey player (b at Ottawa 25 Feb 1903; d at Toronto 10 Nov 1986). He joined Ottawa Senators in 1921 where he was a leader and local favourite. He was sold to TORONTO MAPLE LEAFS in 1930-31 for an unprecedented price of $35 000 and 2 players. Though light, his speed and nerve earned him popularity among fans, and his gritty play inspired the successful Leaf clubs of the 1930s. He was an NHL referee, coach of Toronto 1953-56 and later VP of Maple Leaf Gardens. His wit and lively recollections made him a popular commentator on his sport.   JAMES MARSH

Clarenville, Nfld, Town, pop 2967 (1986c), inc 1951, is situated in a long, picturesque arm facing Random I on the W side of Trinity Bay. An amalgamation (*c*1890) of several small logging and sawmilling communities which had been settled in the mid-1800s, it was named Clarenceville in honour of the Duke of Clarence but its name evolved to Clarenville by 1901. Located at the base of the Bonavista Peninsula on the original route of the Newfoundland Ry and at the start (after 1911) of the Bonavista branch line, it soon became the railway and transportation centre for the region. Today the Cabot Highway to Bonavista joins the Trans-Canada Highway at Clarenville. Shipbuilding, asphalt and creosote manufacture, agriculture and tourism have all been significant aspects of the Clarenville economy.

ROBERT D. PITT

Clark, Andrew Hill, historical geographer (b at Fairford, Man 29 Apr 1911; d at Madison, Wisc 21 May 1975). Son of a Baptist medical missionary, Clark was educated at McMaster and U of T where he studied with geographer Griffith TAYLOR and economic historian Harold INNIS. In 1938 he moved to Berkeley to work with cultural geographer Carl Sauer. His doctoral thesis, a study of the colonization of NZ by people, plants and animals, introduced his lifelong interest in the migration of Europeans to mid-latitude environments overseas. Professor of geography at U of Wisc from 1951 until his death, Clark directed a vigorous graduate program, wrote numerous books and articles, and became one of the best-known and most influential geographers of his day. His research focused on the early settlement of Canada, particularly of the Maritimes, whence his people came. With former students and friends scattered throughout Canadian universities, he was a founder of Canadian historical geography. His principal books are *The Invasion of New Zealand by People, Plants, and Animals: The South Island* (1949), *Three Centuries and the Island: A Historical Geography of Settlement and Agriculture in Prince Edward Island, Canada* (1959), and *Acadia: The Geography of Early Nova Scotia to 1760* (1968).

COLE HARRIS

Clark, Charles Joseph, Joe, politician, prime minister of Canada 1979-80 (b at High River, Alta 5 June 1939). The son of a newspaper editor, he was educated at U of Alberta, received a BA (and later an MA in political science) and was national Progressive Conservative student president. After working as a director of organization for the Alberta PCs and serving on the Ottawa staffs of Davie FULTON and Robert STANFIELD in the late

**Charles Joseph Clark
Sixteenth Prime Minister of Canada**

Name: Charles Joseph Clark
Birth: 5 June 1939, High River, Alta
Father/Mother: Charles/Grace Welch
Father's Occupation: Publisher
Education: U of Alberta; Dalhousie
Religious Affiliation: Roman Catholic
First Occupation: Journalist
Political Party: Progressive Conservative
Period(s) as PM: 4 June 1979 - 2 Mar 1980
Ridings: Rocky Mountain, Alta, 1972-79; Yellowhead, Alta, 1979-
Other Ministries: External Affairs 1984-
Marriage: 30 June 1973 to Maureen McTeer (b 1952)
Children: 1 girl
Other Information: Youngest to take office as PM.

(photo by John deVisser)

1960s, he was elected MP for Rocky Mountain, Alta, in 1972, and has represented Yellowhead, Alta, since 1979. In 1973 he married Maureen McTeer.

Clark emerged from a divided PC convention in Ottawa in 1976 as the surprise winner beneficiary of a mostly "progressive" consensus. In May 1979 the Conservatives won a minority government and he became Canada's sixteenth PM, the youngest ever and first native westerner to hold the office. He believed that he could build public approval by governing as if he had a majority, but he failed to win support from the other parties, especially the NDP, for key parts of his program, eg, the "privatization" of PETRO-CANADA, a mortgage tax credit, and austerity financing, and the government fell that December on a vote of non-confidence in the House on John CROSBIE's budget. In the ensuing Feb 1980 election Pierre TRUDEAU's Liberals returned to power. As leader of the Opposition 1980-83, Clark delayed the Trudeau constitutional plan in 1981 until judicial review was achieved and federal-provincial compromise was reached. Even though Clark received support at 2 national party meetings and by Jan 1983 his party held a wide Gallup Poll lead, a sizable minority of Conservatives still considered him too "progressive" and an electoral liability. He chose to settle the question of his leadership at a convention, held in June 1983, but lost on the fourth ballot to Brian MULRONEY. After the convention, Clark worked to avoid the divisions that had long plagued the Conservatives and he played a major role in drafting PC policies on international arms control. His unique position in the party, as a still young, bilingual and active former PM who had won the respect of many Canadians, was recognized when he was named secretary of state for external affairs in the Mulroney government.   RICHARD CLIPPINGDALE

Clark, Clifford, civil servant (b at Martintown, Ont 18 Apr 1889; d at Chicago 27 Dec 1952). Clark attended Queen's and Harvard before returning to Queen's as a lecturer in 1915, where he helped establish banking and commerce courses. In 1923 he joined the American investment firm of S.W. Strauss as an economic adviser. The Depression ended this career, however, and he returned to Queen's. In 1932 PM R.B. BENNETT made Clark an adviser during the Imperial Economic Conference, and subsequently offered him deputy ministership of the Dept of Finance. Clark helped make Finance a powerful government department by encouraging bright young economists to enter the public service and by taking their advice. Though initially cautious, he began to see an expanded role for the state in economic planning. The man who condemned wage controls at the end of WWI helped implement them in WWII.

As deputy minister, Clark supported the establishment of the BANK OF CANADA and a series of mortgage-assistance measures. During WWII he chaired the Economic Advisory Committee and helped convince PM Mackenzie KING to adopt, among other measures, the 1944 Family Allowance Bill. His ideas and influence made him important in the development of a more active government role in economic planning.

D.R. OWRAM

Clark, Greg, newspaperman, soldier, outdoorsman, humorist (b at Toronto 25 Sept 1892; d there 3 Feb 1977). In WWI he went overseas with the 4th Canadian Mounted Rifles and won the Military Cross as an infantry lieutenant at Vimy Ridge. He returned to the *Toronto Star* as a reporter and for the next 30 years he covered major news events, including the Great Haileybury Fire of 1922, the Lindbergh Kidnap Trial and many others. He began to write humour stories for the *Star's* companion publication, the *Toronto Star Weekly.* The most popular of these featured the comic misadventures of Clark and his hunting and fishing companion, cartoonist Jimmie Frise. In WWII Clark went overseas again as a war correspondent, reporting from the UK, Sicily, Italy and France. For this he was named an Officer of the Order of the British Empire and awarded the Service Medal of the Order of Canada. In 1947 Clark and Frise switched their work to the *Montreal Standard,* which became *Weekend Magazine.* After the death of Frise, Clark's stories were illustrated by Duncan MACPHERSON. Clark's zest for life was reflected in his 19 books, one of which won the Leacock Award For Humour.

JOCK CARROLL

Reading: Jock Carroll, *The Life & Times of Greg Clark* (1981).

Clark, Howard Charles, chemist, university administrator (b at Auckland, NZ 4 Sept 1929). Educated at U of Auckland and Cambridge, he came to BC in 1957 and rapidly established a reputation for original work in organo-metallic, co-ordination and fluorine chemistry. From 1965 he continued this research as professor of inorganic chemistry at Western, receiving the Noranda Award of the Chemical Institute of Canada, the ScD degree from Cambridge and fellowship in the RSC. He served as head of Western's chemistry department 1967-76, then moved to U of Guelph as VP Academic and professor of chemistry. In 1986 he was appointed president of Dalhousie U, Halifax.

CHRISTOPHER WILLIS

Clark, Karl Adolf, chemist (b at Georgetown, Ont 20 Oct 1888; d at Saanichton, BC 8 Dec 1966). A pioneer of the hot-water recovery process for extracting oil from tar sands, Clark devel-

oped an interest in tar during his first job after leaving university, as chief of the federal Mines Branch's Road Materials Division (1916-20). He then joined the ALBERTA RESEARCH COUNCIL, founded in 1919 by H.M. Tory and J.L. Côté expressly to apply science to local resources; the ARC functioned in its early years as part of U of A, where Clark worked until retirement (1954). The first tar-sands plants were built in the 1920s but were uneconomic. Clark's process was installed in the first successful plant, Great Canadian Oil Sands (later Suncor Ltd), opened in 1967 at Ft McMurray, Alta, and the later Syncrude plant. *See also* BITUMEN.

DONALD J.C. PHILLIPSON

Clark, Paraskeva, née Plistik, painter (b at St Petersburg [Leningrad], USSR 28 Oct 1898; d at Toronto 10 Aug 1986). Clark added a bright piquante flavour to the Toronto circle of painters in the 1930s and 1940s. Traces of Cubism in her paintings learned in Soviet Free Studios (1917-21) contrasted with the prevailing GROUP OF SEVEN, finding more affinity with the Montréal painters. Clark left Russia for Paris with her baby son on the death of her first husband (1923). There she met Canadian Philip Clark whom she married, moving to Toronto in 1931. She continued to paint, revealing Leftist concern in pictures like *Petrouschka* (1937). She developed solid form and an individualistic flair, gradually painting the Canadian scene, as well as flower studies, still life and self-portraits. She is the subject of an NFB film, *Portrait of the Artist as an Old Lady* (1982).

ANNE McDOUGALL

Self-Portrait (1933), by Paraskeva Clark, oil on canvas (*courtesy National Gallery of Canada*).

Clark, Samuel Delbert, sociologist (b at Lloydminster, Alta 24 Feb 1910). Trained in history and sociology at U of Sask, London School of Economics, McGill and U of T, he joined the political economy department at U of T in 1938 and became known for studies interpreting Canadian social development as a process of disorganization and reorganization on a series of economic frontiers. His scholarship won him acceptance when Canadian academics were still skeptical of the fledgling discipline of SOCIOLOGY. Under his direction, a series on the SOCIAL CREDIT movement produced 10 monographs by Canadian scholars. In the 1960s his interest shifted to contemporary consequences of economic change, especially suburban living and urban poverty. His publications include *The Canadian Manufacturers' Association* (1939), *The Social Development of Canada* (1942), *Church and Sect*

in Canada (1948), *Movements of Political Protest in Canada* (1959), *The Developing Canadian Community* (1962, 2nd ed 1968), *The Suburban Society* (1966), *Canadian Society in Historical Perspective* (1976) and *The New Urban Poor* (1978). A former president of the RSC, he became professor emeritus of U of T in 1976.

P.J. GIFFEN

Clark, Thomas, merchant and officeholder (b probably in Dumfrieshire, Scot *c*1770; d at Niagara Falls Oct 1835). Clark arrived in Upper Canada in 1791 and engaged in portaging and merchandizing under the patronage of his cousin, Robert Hamilton. Around 1808 he entered into partnership with Samuel Street to run 2 large-scale milling, processing and manufacturing complexes on the Niagara R. He acted as an agent and adviser to Lord SELKIRK on his settlements at Baldoon and Red River. He expanded into land speculation and large-scale money lending, including to the government. An early supporter of Robert GOURLAY, he later opposed him. As a legislative councillor, Clark was a powerful opponent of land reforms and a promoter of communication improvements. He was the richest and one of the most important entrepreneurs in Upper Canada at his death.

BRUCE WILSON

Clarke, Austin Chesterfield, novelist (b at St James, Barbados 26 July 1934). Clarke came to Canada as a student in 1955 and eventually became a journalist in Toronto. After the success of his short stories, published in *The Survivors of the Crossing* (1964), he taught and served as writer in residence in a number of N American universities. He went on to write the humorous yet socially critical trilogy of Caribbean immigrant life in Toronto for which he is best known, *The Meeting Point* (1967), *Storm of Fortune* (1973) and *The Bigger Light* (1975). He was vice-chairman of the Ontario Film Review Board 1984-87. Recent work includes *Amongst Thistles and Thorns* (1984), *When Women Rule* (1985) and *Nine Men Who Laughed* (1986).

TERRENCE CRAIG

Clarke, Charles Kirk, psychiatrist, educator (b at Elora, Canada W 16 Feb 1857; d at Toronto 20 Jan 1924). He received his MD from U of T 1879 but had already begun his career in PSYCHIATRY in 1874, serving as clinical assistant to Dr Joseph WORKMAN at the Provincial Lunatic Asylum in Toronto. He was assistant superintendent of the Hamilton asylum 1880-81, of the Rockwood asylum in Kingston 1881-85, and then superintendent at Rockwood, a position he retained until 1905. He was transferred to the Toronto asylum that year and resigned in 1911 to accept the superintendency of the Toronto General Hospital. At the same time he served as professor of psychiatry and dean of the Faculty of Medicine at U of T. In 1918 he founded (with Dr C.M. HINCKS) and became first medical director of the Canadian National Committee for Mental Hygiene, later the Canadian Mental Health Assn. The Clarke Institute of Psychiatry in Toronto is named after him.

THOMAS E. BROWN

Reading: C. Greenland, *Charles Kirk Clarke: A Pioneer of Canadian Psychiatry* (1966).

Clarke, George Johnson, lawyer, editor, premier of NB (b at St Andrews, NB 10 Oct 1857; d at St Stephen, NB 26 Feb 1917). Editor of the *St Croix Courier* and a prominent lawyer in St Stephen, Clarke became Speaker of the NB Legislature in 1909. He became premier in 1914 when James Kidd FLEMMING was forced to resign over fund-raising irregularities. He suffered poor health throughout most of his 3-year term and his administration accomplished little of lasting significance.

ARTHUR T. DOYLE

Clarke, Henry Joseph, lawyer, politician, premier of Manitoba 1872-74 (b in Donegal, Ire 7 July 1833; d on a train near Medicine Hat, Alta 13 Sept 1889). Admitted to the bar 1855, Clarke practised law in Montréal and spent several years in California and El Salvador. A bilingual Roman Catholic, Clarke came to Manitoba in Nov 1870 to assist Lt-Gov Adams G. ARCHIBALD establish the provincial government. Elected an MLA on 30 Dec 1870, he served as Manitoba's first attorney general from 3 Jan 1871 until 4 July 1874 and helped to found the province's legal system. After returning to California, where he divorced and remarried, Clarke resumed the practice of law in Winnipeg in 1877 and acted as counsel for 25 of Riel's followers after the NORTH-WEST REBELLION of 1885. A controversial figure, Clarke made many enemies but deserves credit for his support of the Métis.   LOVELL C. CLARK

Clarke, James Paton, composer, conductor, organist, teacher (b at Edinburgh? 1807 or 1808; d at Yorkville [Toronto], Ont 27 Aug 1877). An outstanding professional figure in early Toronto's musical development, as first conductor of the Toronto Philharmonic Soc, Clarke gave the city its earliest performances of several Mozart and Beethoven symphonies 1847-48. He taught singing, piano and guitar, and was organist of St James' Anglican Cathedral in 1848. Clarke composed songs – notably *Lays of the Maple Leaf or Songs of Canada* (1853) – and wrote and edited church music. Toronto's King's College granted him a bachelor of music degree – Canada's first – in 1846.   BARCLAY MCMILLAN

Clark's Harbour, NS, Town, pop 1098 (1986c), inc 1919, is situated on CAPE SABLE ISLAND in Shelburne County, about 95 km SE of Yarmouth. Lying adjacent to rich fishing grounds, it has always been an important fishing and fish-processing community. Both the inshore (lobster) and offshore (scallops, cod) fisheries are practised. It is the birthplace of the famed Cape Island boat, a style perfected by Ephraim Atkinson in the early 20th century with distinctive high bows and a long, broad, open workspace, low to the sea. Cape Islanders of various sizes (typically 12-15 m) are found everywhere on the Atlantic coast of the province. The residents, with family names like Swim, Nickerson and Smith, are chiefly descendants of the PLANTERS from Nantucket, Massachusetts who in 1760 replaced the Acadians expelled in 1755. Largely Baptist in faith, the town's population remains roughly the same number, as many youth migrate to urban areas.   L.D. MCCANN

Clarkson, Adrienne Louise, television personality, journalist and novelist, public servant, publisher (b at Hong Kong 10 Feb 1939). The daughter of a prominent businessman, William Poy, who lost his property after the Japanese invasion of HONG KONG in 1941, she came to Canada with her parents in 1942. After attending school in Ottawa, Clarkson received an MA at the U of T in 1961. From 1961-63 she studied at the Sorbonne, Paris, and in 1965 she began an award-winning, 18-year-long career as TV host-interviewer for the CBC programs "Take Thirty", "Adrienne at Large" and "the fifth estate", gaining a unique reputation for her incisiveness, charm and poise. Between 1968 and 1971 MCCLELLAND AND STEWART published her 2 novels, *A Lover More Condoling* and *Hunger Trace*, and New Press the interviews titled *True to You In My Fashion*. In 1982 she was appointed Ontario's agent-general in Paris, and in Mar 1987 she became president and publisher of M&S.
      ERIC KOCH

Classics, the study of Greek and Roman antiquity, revered for centuries as a quintessential element in a liberal education, gained its foothold in Canada during the 17th century when Latin entered the curriculum of the Jesuit College in Québec. The benevolent "tyranny" of Classics in French-speaking Canada, inaugurated in 1636, ended in 1960 when the collèges classiques ceased being the sole source of the BA degree and when it became acceptable to obtain a BA without Greek or Latin as background study. Elsewhere in Canada, particularly after Confederation, Latin and Greek, tenacious factors in secondary-school class offerings until WWII, were taught along Victorian and Edwardian disciplinarian lines favoured in English and Scottish universities and schools. Literary, historical and philosophical elements were reserved for university programs. Inroads and advances by scientific studies, engineering, medicine, law and business administration, and the effects of technological and social changes during the 1950s, shattered the security of Classics as a discipline. Greek and Latin, one-time haven of university scholarship holders and aspiring intellectuals, damaged by dispiriting teaching founded on grammatical exegesis and prose composition and on literal translation as training in exactitude of expression, were faced with plunging enrolments and with accusations of being outmoded and fossilized.

Classicists responded by devising and adopting new methodologies and livelier textbooks to present the ancient languages in the post-Sputnik era. The Cambridge Latin Course in particular won widespread adoption in the 1970s and helped save Latin from extinction in the high schools. Contemporary linguistic theory applied to Latin teaching engendered fresh notions of what a language-learning course should be. In particular, secondary-school students were encouraged to study material that merited both literary and sociological discussion and criticism. Greek, which was moribund or extinct in secondary schools by the 1960s, found renewed life with the McGill University Course, patterned after the successful structuralist Latin courses and employing practices familiar in the language laboratory. Both languages continue to attract registration in the universities, and Latin studies find slender but continuing commitment in secondary schools where administrators countenance small enrolments.

The universities, faced with deteriorating registration in Classics and in combined Honours courses including Latin or Greek, resorted to patterns pronounced successful in the US; courses in translation and in classical civilization or classical studies, introduced tentatively during the 1950s, multiplied rapidly. Nowadays, hundreds of students from different backgrounds and course affiliations attend classes in Greek and Roman drama, epic, biography and historiography, religion and mythology. Mounting interest in Mediterranean archaeology and in art history has also helped revive the Classics, and the incorporation of archaeological material into civilization courses has contributed greatly to their popularity. Ancient History, taught under the aegis of either Classics or History departments, supports classical studies in appropriate ways. Classics, by reason of its composite nature, and by choice, has also collaborated with programs in COMPARATIVE LITERATURE, hermeneutics and modern Greek.

Diminishing enrolment in Latin and the demise of secondary-school Greek failed to thwart the development of advanced study in Classics. MA programs exist at most major universities and doctoral studies have been developed at Dalhousie, Laval, McGill, U de Montréal, U of Ottawa, McMaster (Roman Studies), U of Alberta and UBC. The U of Toronto program has the most course offerings and largest enrolment. Degree programs and doctoral dissertations are generally conditioned by the particular scholarly expertise of professors involved and by the universities' research collections. Research and teaching are the primary functions of classicists in universities. Support for their programs derives from federal agencies, university resources and foundations and organizations outside Canada. Prime support comes from the SOCIAL SCIENCES AND HUMANITIES RESEARCH COUNCIL OF CANADA, the Killam Senior Research Fellowship Program, the American Council of Learned Societies, the Institute for Advanced Study at Princeton, NJ, and the Nuffield Foundation (England). Grants-in-aid of publication derive largely from Canadian federal agencies. The quality of teaching and research in the Classics has been recognized not only in national and international awards for excellence, but also in the rich diversity of journals and publishers who by publishing have promoted Canadian classical scholarship.

Several major scholarly projects are in progress: *Lexicon Iconographicum Mythologiae Classicae*, an international iconographical dictionary of classical mythology as depicted in the complete range of art works from the ancient world, and including material in Canadian museums and galleries, with support from the CANADIAN FEDERATION FOR THE HUMANITIES; the Dio Cassius project (U of Calgary); *Catalogus Translationum et Commentariorum* (Pontifical Institute of Mediaeval Studies, Toronto); Vergilian Bibliography (McMaster); and The Collected Works of Erasmus (U of Toronto).

Fresh incentive to classical scholarship and to archaeological and historical study is provided by 3 Mediterranean centres nestling under the aegis of the Canadian Mediterranean Institute since 1980: the Canadian Archaeological Institute at Athens (fd in 1974), the Canadian Academic Centre in Italy (Rome, fd in 1978) and the Canadian Institute in Egypt (Cairo, fd in 1980). These overseas headquarters enjoy amiable and hospitable links with the American Academy in Rome, the British Schools in Athens and Rome, the American School of Classical Studies in Athens and the Vergilian Society in Italy (at Cumae, near Naples).

The Classical Association of Canada (fd in 1946), although an outgrowth of the Ontario Classical Assn, was able to claim national identity by its membership *a mari usque ad mare*. Its annual meetings, in conjunction with those of the Royal Society of Canada and other LEARNED SOCIETIES, cater to anglophone and francophone audiences, and feature colloquia on material and issues of general interest. The association's journal, *Phoenix*, launched 1947, has attained international status as a scholarly quarterly. Canadian classicists have been numbered among presidents, editors and executive members of the various international classical organizations. Presidents of the CAC are recognized as vice-presidents of the Classical Association (UK).

The abolition of the Latin requirement at Oxford and Cambridge universities in the 1960s, and the restriction of the use of Latin in the Roman Catholic mass were but visible symbols of the dwindling capital and overstrained credit of the Classics. But new teaching techniques, vigorous research programs and interdisciplinary engagements by classical scholars mark a "Copernican revolution" in the discipline. Degree courses in classical studies for undergraduates who come to university with little or no experience with the classical languages would have been inconceivable to earlier generations. The continuing presence of Classics in the universities indicates that the ability of the Classics to sustain and fortify society in the face of life's problems and predicaments remains durable and intact. *See also* ARCHAEOLOGY, MEDITERRANEAN.   ALEXANDER G. MCKAY

Reading: W.H. Alexander, *The Amiable Tyranny of Pisistratus* (1931); M. Lebel, *Les Humanités classiques au Québec* (1967); Alexander G. McKay, "Latin Studies in Canada," *Romanitas* 4 (1962); J.E. Sharwood Smith, *On Teaching Classics* (1977).

Claude, Renée, stage name of Renée Bélanger, singer (b at Montréal 3 July 1939). While her early repertoire consisted of French songs, Claude soon became known for her interpretation of songs by Québec writers such as Jean-Pierre Ferland, Stéphane Venne, Clémence Desrochers and Luc Plamondon. In 1960 she made her first appearance on CBC television. In 1968 she was awarded the trophy for best performer in Montréal's Gala des Artistes. Two years later she performed with the Montreal Symphony Orchestra at Place des Arts. She has also appeared in the US, France, Belgium, Poland, the USSR, Japan, Greece and Venezuela. Her biggest hits include "C'est notre fête aujourd'hui," "Le Tour de la terre," "C'est le début d'un temps nouveau" and "Ce soir je fais l'amour avec toi." HÉLÈNE PLOUFFE

Claxton, Brian Brooke, lawyer, politician (b at Montréal 23 Aug 1898; d at Ottawa 13 June 1960). He attended Lower Canada College and McGill, graduating with an LLB in 1921, the year he began to practise law. During WWI he had served overseas with the 10th Siege Battery. He was active in many organizations, including the Canadian Clubs, the Canadian Radio League, the League of Nations Society, and the Canadian Institute of International Affairs, and he taught insurance law at McGill. Claxton was elected as a Liberal to represent St Lawrence/St George in 1940 and was soon appointed parliamentary secretary to PM King. While minister of health and welfare he was responsible for the introduction of family allowances and as minister of defence he supervised the rebuilding of the Canadian armed forces during and after the Korean War. He also helped negotiate Newfoundland's entry into Confederation in 1949. In 1954 he retired from politics to become general manager of Metropolitan Life and in 1957 was appointed first chairman of the Canada Council, a recognition of his major role in bringing the government more broadly into support for the arts. DAVID J. BERCUSON

Clay, common name for complex group of industrial MINERALS, each characterized by different mineralogy, occurrence and uses. All are natural, earthy, fine-grained minerals composed mainly of water-containing aluminum silicates; they may contain iron, alkalis and alkaline earths (*see* SAND AND GRAVEL). The commercial value of clays and of claylike shales depends on proximity to centres where clay products are used, and on physical properties, eg, plasticity, strength, shrinkage or heat resistance. Common clays and shales are the principal raw materials available from Canadian deposits for the manufacture of clay products, eg, common and facing brick and structural, partition, quarry and drain tiles. Fireclays are used principally for the manufacture of medium- and high-duty firebrick and for crucibles. Known Canadian fireclays are insufficiently refractory (heat resistant) without the addition of some very heat-resistant material, eg, alumina. Stoneware clays are similar to low-grade plastic clays and range from commercially inferior material through semirefractory to firebrick clays. Stoneware clays are used for sewer pipe, flue liners, facing brick, pottery, stoneware crocks and jugs and chemical stoneware. Ball clays are extremely heat resistant and are composed mainly of fine-particle kaolinite, quartz, illite and mica. However, widespread use of these clays in Canada has been hampered by distance from markets and lack of proven reserves. Known deposits of china clay (composed mainly of kaolinitic minerals), a high-quality clay with more alumina and less silica than ball clays, have not been developed in Canada, primarily because of their small size. Almost all clays produced in Canada are used for domestic requirements; however, exports of clay products and refractories were worth about $78 million in 1985.

Common clays and shales are found throughout Canada, but new deposits with improved drying and firing characteristics are sought. Fireclays occur in the Whitemud Formation of southern Saskatchewan and southeastern Alberta and at Sumas Mtn, BC. In NS some clays at Shubenacadie are sufficiently heat resistant for medium-duty refractories, and clays from Musquodoboit have been used by foundries in the Atlantic provinces. The principal source of stoneware clay in Canada is the Whitemud Formation. Common clays and shales are mined from open pits using modern, surface MINING equipment. Processing involves crushing, screening, blending and conditioning with water, extruding, firing and drying. Processing of fireclays and of bentonite (an absorptive clay) is more specialized and may involve calcining, in the former case, and acid activation, in the latter. MICHEL A. BOUCHER

Clayoquot, a NOOTKA tribe on the W coast of Vancouver I, BC. Prior to European contact, the Clayoquot, originally a small tribe on Kennedy Lk, allied with neighbouring groups and conquered the Esowistaht and other tribes whose territories included Tofino Inlet, most of Meares I and the Esowista Pen. The conquering chief later became the famous WICKANANISH, who controlled the sea-otter trade at Clayoquot Sd in the late 18th century. In 1811 the Clayoquot seized the TONQUIN, a trading ship of the Pacific Fur Co. This incident effectively ended the maritime fur trade at Clayoquot Sd. The Clayoquot were renowned for their fine canoes, and traded them to other Indian peoples. The main Clayoquot villages were Opitsat, Echachist and Okeamin. Today the Clayoquot occupy their villages of Opitsat and Esowista. JOHN DEWHIRST

Clayton-Thomas, David, pop singer, songwriter (b in Surrey, Eng 13 Sept 1941). An aggressive yet sensitive singer, he was raised in Toronto and led several local bands, including Fabulous Shays and Bossmen, before joining the New York jazz-rock ensemble Blood, Sweat and Tears in 1968. He fronted BS&T during its most successful years (1968-72), returned to it in 1974 and assumed leadership in 1976. He sang on its hit recordings of "Spinning Wheel," "Lucretia MacEvil" (his own songs), "You Make Me So Very Happy" and others. Largely a Canadian band in its last incarnation, BS&T broke up in 1980. MARK MILLER

Clear Grits, Upper Canadian Reformers who became discontented with the conservatism of the BALDWIN-LAFONTAINE ministry after 1849. The group was composed of Old Radicals, such as Peter Perry, who attempted to revive the agrarian republicanism of the prerebellion period, and young entrepreneurs such as William McDougall from the Toronto area, who advocated elective institutions, universal manhood suffrage, free trade with the US, secularization of the CLERGY RESERVES, and representation by population to overcome perceived French Canadian domination. As well, they attracted support in rural areas west of Toronto. After the Old Radicals were accommodated in the Hincks-Morin ministry (1851-54), the young Grits fell in behind George BROWN, who replaced their republicanism with British liberalism. The Brownite Liberals, advocating REP BY POP and annexation of the North-West, became the dominant party in Canada West by the mid-1850s and formed the basis of the LIBERAL PARTY after Confederation. DAVID MILLS

Clearwater River, 280 km long, rises in Patterson, Forest and Lloyd lakes in NW Saskatchewan, flows SE to Careen Lk and abruptly turns W to join the ATHABASCA R at Fort McMurray, Alta. It has cut spectacular gorges and waterfalls into the sandstone and limestone; the forest along its banks is still wild and is home to moose, deer, bear, wolf, lynx, geese, fox and beaver. The only westward-flowing river between Winnipeg and the Rockies, it was an important link in the FUR TRADE ROUTE, connected to the CHURCHILL R via Methye Portage. The river is "clear" only in relation to others in the area. JAMES MARSH

Cleaver, Elizabeth Ann, née Mrazik, illustrator, author (b at Montréal 19 Nov 1939; d there 27 July 1985). Cleaver, who studied art at various Montréal institutions including Concordia U (MFA 1980), won international recognition and election to the Royal Canadian Academy of Arts (1974). Most concerned with myths and legends of transformation, she developed distinctive, stylized collages presenting a symbolic world. She assembled her colourful, carefully researched illustrations from torn and cut monoprints (textured paper), linocuts and such natural and manufactured objects as leaves and lace. She received major awards for *The Wind Has Wings: Poems from Canada* (1968), *The Miraculous Hind: A Hungarian Legend* (1973), *The Loon's Necklace* (1977), an Indian myth and *Petrouchka* (1980), a retelling of Stravinsky's ballet. Study of shadow puppetry in Europe, Iran and Turkey in 1971 and with children at Baker Lake, NWT, in 1972 led to *The Enchanted Caribou* (1985), an Inuit legend illustrated with shadow puppets. RAYMOND E. JONES

Clergue, Francis Hector, financier and industrial promoter (b at Brewer, Maine 28 May 1856; d at Montréal 19 Sept 1939). Born of Huguenot parents, Clergue studied law at Maine State Coll. After a brief legal career, he gravitated into industrial promotion, pursuing tourist, railway, public utility and shipbuilding ventures in Maine, Alabama and Persia, all characterized by flamboyant promotion and poor execution. Central to Clergue's schemes was "the principle of correlation," the grouping of related industries around a common power source. Early in the 1890s he introduced this principle to somnolent SAULT STE MARIE. Generously supported by local and provincial politicians eager to develop "New Ontario" and by Philadelphia capital, Clergue built a complex of mining, forestry, railway, steel and power companies at the Soo which at its height employed 7000. In 1903 the "empire" collapsed under the strain of financial abuse and managerial incompetence. Clergue was pushed out of the reorganized Lake Superior Corp and turned to a series of ill-starred business ventures in Canada, the US, Russia and the Far East. Elements of Clergue's empire have survived, most notably the ALGOMA CENTRAL RAILWAY, ALGOMA STEEL CORP and Great Lakes Power. DUNCAN McDOWALL

Reading: D. McDowall, *Steel at the Sault: Francis H. Clerque, Sir James H. Dunn and the Algoma Steel Corporation, 1901-56* (1984); Alan Sullivan, *The Rapids* (1922).

Clergy Reserves, one-seventh of the public lands of Upper and Lower Canada, reserved by the 1791 CONSTITUTIONAL ACT for the maintenance of a "Protestant clergy," a phrase intended to apply to the Church of England alone. The reserves excited controversy, especially in UC, although for many years they brought no income since settlers could obtain other lands free. When free land grants ceased in the 1820s, Bishop John STRACHAN decided the C of E should sell rather than lease its lands as it had done since 1819. In 1827, having blocked a transfer to the CANADA COMPANY, he persuaded Britain to authorize sales of one-quarter of the reserves, but not to exceed 100 000 acres (40 468 ha) per year.

An increasingly powerful reform movement, including many denominational rivals, opposed Strachan's plans. In 1824 the legislature upheld the claim of the Church of Scotland to a share of the reserves. Later the debate over "co-establishment" of the C of S became an assault on the idea of establishment itself (*see* ANGLICANISM). In 1828 a Select Committee of the Assembly and the CANADA COMMITTEE of the British Commons criticized church establishment and recommended dividing profits from reserves among the Protestant denominations. In 1840 the Assembly accepted a bill dividing half the proceeds between the C of E and the C of S, leaving the remainder to other denominations. Still, by the early 1850s secularization of the reserves was being widely demanded. In late 1854 the MacNab-Morin coalition of UC conservatives and LC reformers passed a bill to transfer reserve-sale proceeds to the Municipalities Funds of UC and LC; to pay present clerical incumbents their stipends for life; and to allow them to cede their life claims to their respective churches, which could commute the total into 6% annuities. Commutation was attacked, but most wished to settle the controversy that had bedevilled religious and political life for 3 decades. The clergy reserves were secularized not because they were obstacles to settlement, but because the policy of church establishment they represented was unacceptable in religiously heterogeneous UC.　　　　　　　　　　　　CURTIS FAHEY

Clerics of Saint-Viateur A religious congregation founded in 1831 in Vourles (near Lyons), France, by Father Louis-Marie Querbes, to educate boys and to help in the general parish ministry. Following a request from Mgr Ignace BOURGET, bishop of Montréal, the congregation came to L'Industrie [Joliette], Canada East in 1847 and spread throughout Canada and into the US. The congregation is known for its invaluable contribution to the education of those with special needs (the blind, deaf mute) and for its modern teaching methods (which have sparked a great deal of controversy among teaching congregations). In 1986 there were 240 fathers and 349 brothers (60% of the world total) in Canada, divided into 4 religious provinces.

MICHEL THÉRIAULT

Clermont, Yves Wilfrid, anatomist (b at Montréal 14 Aug 1926). Clermont received a classical French education, but obtained his PhD at McGill Medical School. Less than 3 years after he joined its anatomy department, he became a teaching fellow in histology. He rose to full professorship and was chairman 1975-85. An outstanding teacher of histology, he is best known as a specialist in male reproduction. Over the years he has clarified the confusing structure of the human testis. Using both the light and electron microscopes with skill, he has described the full sequence of events that give rise to mature sperm cells. In recent years, he has devoted much of his activity to the analysis of an important cell organelle, the Golgi apparatus, not only in male reproductive cells but in many other systems. The resulting articles on Golgi morphology are probably the best on the subject. In 1986 he received the J.C.B. Brant Award from the Canadian Association of Anatomists.　　　CHARLES P. LEBLOND

Cliche, Robert C.R., judge (b at St-Joseph-de-Beauce 12 Apr 1921; d at Québec City 15 Sept 1978). Cliche did his classical studies (rhetoric) at the Petit Séminaire de Québec and philosophy at the Coll de Lévis (BA). He studied law at Laval (1941-44), received his degree and was admitted to the bar. He joined (1944) the Royal Marines as a sailor and left as an officer (1946). He established a general practice, taught at Laval (1962-65) and was named (1972) assistant chief justice to the provincial court. He published, with his wife Madeleine Ferron, *Quand le peuple fait la loi* (1972) and *Les Beaucerons ces insoumis* (1974). He

was elected assistant chairman of the NDP (1963) and the next year became leader of the provincial wing. Despite his magnetism and exceptional skills as an orator, he was defeated in 1965 and 1968, and returned to private practice. In 1974, he became chairman of a provincial commission of inquiry into the exercise of trade-union freedoms. Chairman and administrator of many cultural and social associations, he undertook with passion a huge legal practice and demanding political responsibilities. Posthumously, he received the Order de la Pleiade, an international distinction of the francophone world (1978). The Foundation Robert-Cliche is devoted to the conservation of the Beauce heritage.　　MARTHE LEGAULT

Clifford, Betsy, alpine skier (b at Old Chelsea, Qué 15 Oct 1953). Practically raised on the slopes of her father's Camp Fortune ski area, she began skiing at age 5. At 12 she was national junior champion and at 13 Canadian senior slalom champion (1967). She became the youngest ever world ski champion with her 1970 victory in the giant slalom championships in Val Gardena, but was most pleased with her silver medal in the 1974 World Downhill Championship.

MURRAY SHAW

Climate is often defined as average WEATHER, when weather means the current state of the atmosphere. For the scientist, climates are the result of the exchanges of heat and moisture at the Earth's surface. Here, climate will be used to describe the temperature and moisture conditions of the layer of air near the Earth's surface, ie, the air in which man lives.

Canada is a very large country with many different climates. It extends 4500 km, from 42° N lat (at Pelee I, Lk Erie) to 83° N (the tip of Ellesmere I). Thus, there are great differences in length of day from S to N: in Dec southern Canada receives 8 hours of daylight; Canada's northern tip, none.

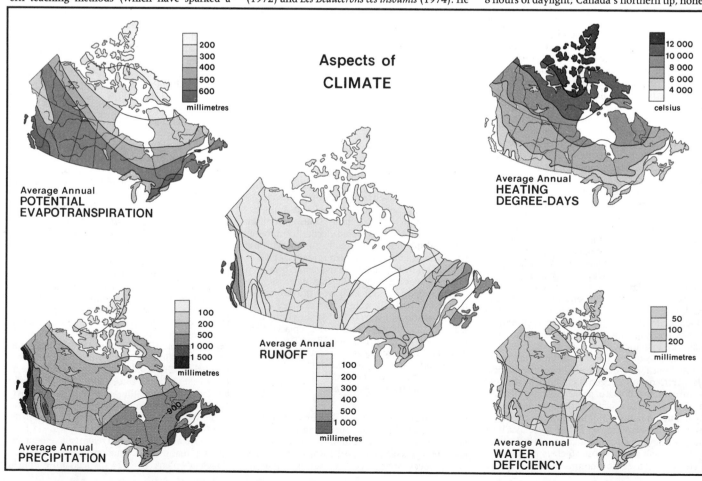

Aspects of **CLIMATE**

Average Annual **POTENTIAL EVAPOTRANSPIRATION**
200 300 400 500 600 millimetres

Average Annual **HEATING DEGREE-DAYS**
12 000 10 000 8 000 6 000 4 000 celsius

Average Annual **PRECIPITATION**
100 200 500 1 000 1 500 millimetres

Average Annual **RUNOFF**
100 200 300 400 500 1 000 millimetres

Average Annual **WATER DEFICIENCY**
50 100 200 millimetres

Latitude is also responsible for the generally westerly air flow in Canada. Southern Canada is often the battle zone between cold air from arctic regions and warm, moist air from the south; hence, airflow is channelled E-W. Latitude is not the only geographic factor significant to climate; position on the continent, especially distance from the OCEANS, also plays a part. Therefore, places with roughly the same latitude, eg, Victoria and Winnipeg, have very different climates since Victoria's climate is modified by the warm Pacific Ocean and Winnipeg's is not.

Temperature is the degree of warmness or coldness. Air temperatures have been measured in some places in southern Canada for over 100 years, but in the Arctic for a much shorter time. Climate statistics are usually expressed as 30-year averages, the most recently published being those for 1951-80. In winter, when northern Canada receives very little solar radiation, temperature differences from N to S are great. The average maximum Jan temperature of Alert, at the N tip of Ellesmere I, is -28.1°C, that of Windsor, Ont, -0.7°C, a difference of 27.4°C. In summer the long days in northern Canada result in smaller N-S differences, with maximum temperatures in July of 6.8°C for Alert and 27.8°C for Windsor.

Monthly air temperatures give an indication of the hotness or coldness of a place at a particular time of year, and monthly temperature maps can be drawn for Canada. However, it is also desirable to have a single map which expresses the total amount of heat received by a given place. To express this total, climatologists have formulated an index of potential evapotranspiration (PE), derived from monthly temperatures above 0°C. Potential evapotranspiration is the amount of water that potentially would evaporate and transpire from a vegetated surface; therefore, PE is an index of heat, but expressed in terms of depth of water at the Earth's surface. The high arctic islands, with a PE of under 200 mm, receive very little heat; the warmest areas in southern Ontario, Québec and BC receive 3 times as much. Canada is obviously not a warm country since tropical areas have an annual PE of over 1500 mm.

The coldness of a place is also of interest, especially in these days of expensive energy, when coldness can be equated with the cost of heating homes. A parameter which summarizes coldness is the heating degree day (HDD), a unit which sums the temperatures below 18°C, the point at which household furnaces must be turned on. Southern Ontario has 4000 HDD annually while the high arctic islands have 12 000 HDD.

Moisture The most important climatic parameter after temperature is precipitation, ie, moisture that falls to the Earth's surface as RAIN, snow, HAIL, etc. Because of Canada's size, there are great differences in the amounts of precipitation received. Since warm air can hold a great deal more moisture than cold, southern parts of Canada have more precipitation than northern parts. Because WINDS usually blow from W to E, West Coast areas receive the most precipitation. There are other complicating factors: the N-S trend of the western mountains greatly complicates the precipitation regime there, and the Great Lakes in central Canada affect precipitation in that region.

Usually, measurements of average annual precipitation are made where people live; therefore, the precipitation map is most accurate for southern Canada. The isohyets (lines of equal precipitation) are very generalized in mountainous regions and refer to valley conditions; precipitation totals at higher altitudes are not well known. Annual precipitation ranges from 100 mm in the High Arctic to over 1500 mm on the windward side of BC's mountains. Areas of anomalously high precipitation caused by increased winter snowfall appear E of the Great Lakes.

Climatic Regions

Defining climatic regions for any country is difficult; usually, climatologists discuss the various climatic parameters (eg, temperature, precipitation) and conclude by using vegetation as an index. Within a geographical area, climates gradually change from one type to another. There are 5 main climatic regions in the southern populated area of Canada: East Coast, Great Lakes, Prairies, Cordilleran and West Coast. The vast, mostly uninhabited area of northern Canada contains several different climatic regions but for the present purposes will be subdivided into Arctic and Subarctic. The stations described below are examples of the above regions, with the exception of the Cordilleran. The Cordilleran, or Rocky Mountain, region is a composite of many climatic types. The southern BC valleys have climates that are the driest in Canada, while some of the higher elevations, especially in the YT area, contain permanent ice caps. No one station is typical of its province.

Climate types result from the relationship between monthly potential evapotranspiration and precipitation. By comparing the PE or need for water with the supply for each month, graphs of the water balance can be obtained. In the settled parts of Canada, water need is usually zero during the winter months, rising to an average of 130 mm in July. Only Pacific Coast regions have temperatures high enough to cause a need for water in every month of the year. Monthly precipitation varies widely throughout Canada, and nowhere does it coincide with monthly PE. Most localities receive too much moisture in winter, when the PE is zero, and too little in summer, when maximum need occurs.

East Coast climates are represented by Halifax, NS. Precipitation is fairly uniform throughout the year and only in July does water need exceed supply. The vegetation does not suffer immediately since a moisture reserve is stored in the soil (*see* GROUNDWATER). For most soils the reserve is approximately 100 mm. In Halifax, this reserve is not exhausted before precipitation rises above need and the stored moisture is again built up to its maximum. Thus, for Halifax the actual amount of water loss is almost equal to the potential water loss. After soil moisture has reached its maximum, surface or subsurface runoff occurs; in Halifax, total annual runoff is 773 mm.

Great Lakes Southern Ontario climates are typified by Windsor. Precipitation is rather uniform throughout the year (although less so than at Halifax), but Windsor's summer PE is greater than that of the East Coast, reflecting the higher summer temperatures in the interior of the country. In May PE rises above precipitation; by mid-July, in an average year, the stored soil moisture is exhausted. From then until precipitation is again sufficient to build up the stored soil moisture, vegetation must depend solely on current precipitation. In Windsor this is insufficient and a water deficiency of 86 mm occurs in an average year.

Prairie climates are exemplified by Edmonton. Here, the annual precipitation of 447 mm is inadequate to meet the PE of 555 mm and deficits, averaging 120 mm, are common in the summer months. With low winter precipitation, soil moisture is not always restored to capacity in an average year and water surplus averages only 7 mm (*see* DROUGHT).

Subarctic and Arctic At Inuvik, N of the Arctic Circle, the monthly PE and precipitation resemble those of stations in the Prairies, but the growing season is shorter. Thus, there is a small amount of runoff as well as a deficiency of 100 mm. Alert, in the High Arctic, has a more severe arctic climate, with a growing season of one month and low precipitation. It too experiences water deficiency but has an annual runoff of 76 mm.

West Coast climates are characterized by a winter maximum and summer minimum precipitation regime. Victoria is a typical station. Mean monthly temperatures are usually above 0°C and water is needed in every month. In an average winter, 130 mm of rain falls every month and the PE is only 14 mm; therefore, large amounts of runoff occur in winter. In summer, precipitation is least when need is greatest and large water deficiencies occur.

The moisture map shows the distribution of moisture deficiency and runoff in Canada. The lines showing average annual water deficiency indicate the areas where precipitation is inadequate for vegetation needs and moisture is a problem. Even in southern Ontario, deficiencies occur regularly in summer. West Coast and East Coast areas rarely suffer moisture deficiencies. Much of the precipitation that falls in Canada evaporates again into the atmosphere (evapotranspiration); the water that does not evaporate runs off into the rivers and lakes and eventually to the ocean. The lines showing average annual runoff are almost the reverse of those showing average water deficiency. Canada's interior has little or no runoff. Eastern and western areas have large amounts; these are the areas which have major hydroelectric developments.

The above description of Canada's climatic types refers to average conditions; however, climate is very variable. For example, half the time the precipitation is less than the amounts shown and half the time it is greater. Consequently, climate involves more than average weather, and another series of maps showing the "expectation of weather" could be drawn. *See also* CLIMATE CHANGE; CLIMATE SEVERITY; CLIMATOLOGY; ICE; METEOROLOGY; URBAN EFFECT ON CLIMATE; WEATHER FORECASTING.   MARIE SANDERSON

Reading: F.K. Hare and M.K. Thomas, *Climate Canada* (1979).

Climate and Man Over millions of years, different climates have shaped landforms, laying down carbon deposits, feeding glaciers, sustaining rivers and producing soils. In addition, there is scarcely one aspect of society that is not affected, in some way, by climate variability. Foremost, climate provides life's essentials: heat, moisture and light. Climate influences dress, what we eat, how we feel and behave, the cost of heating or cooling our homes, and our vacation plans. By influencing market supply and demand, it can create inflation, financial crises and social unrest, sometimes global in scope. Climate can increase personal satisfaction and be a matter of great civic pride. It is essential to the production of trees and crops, to the success of fisheries and the management of water resources. Because it restricts agriculture, fisheries and forestry to specific geographical areas, climate has influenced human migration and settlement. Through DROUGHT and FLOOD, climate can destroy and debilitate life, damage property and isolate entire communities.

CLIMATE INFORMATION is of enormous economic worth in such activities as farming, recreation, energy and transportation, providing answers to such questions as, How much should be budgeted for snow removal? Are there sufficient hours of WIND blow to sustain a wind-driven generator? Which climates are best for people suffering from asthma or arthritis? Will peaches grow in Kapuskasing or cabbages in Whitehorse? Is there enough snowfall for a successful ski resort? What impact will the effects of carbon-dioxide warming have on the arctic ice pack?

Agriculture and Forestry Climate affects mankind most closely in farming. Crops that are economically viable in Canada include fruit trees in the Okanagan, wheat and oilseeds on the prairies, corn and grapes in southern Ontario and Québec, and potatoes and grain in the Maritimes. Only tropical and equatorial crops cannot be grown commercially. To be successful, a farmer must minimize risk from climate hazards by avoiding the risk in the first place or by protecting against the hazard when it threatens. All agricultural areas in Canada are subject to drought, frost, winterkill, wind, heavy precipitation, HAIL and flooding, and to climatically influenced diseases and insect infestations. Crop zonation is only one of many ways in which climate information can influence farming decisions. Seeding, irrigating, spraying, harvesting and labour and machinery management depend on the application of climate knowledge in agriculture. Post-harvest concerns of storage and transportation are also sensitive to climatic factors. Livestock performance is affected by temperature, radiation and wind. Climate is no less a controlling agent in tree production. Foresters seek information on how climate affects the growth and reproduction of forests, and they use climate data in protecting against hazards such as drought, excess water, fire, frost, blow down and air pollution.

Water Resources Precipitation is the source of all the Earth's fresh water and evaporation is the primary moisture input into the atmosphere. Canada contains no large areas where annual evaporation greatly exceeds precipitation, producing permanent DESERTS, or where precipitation exceeds evaporation, resulting in frequent flooding. Canada has more usable fresh water than any other country in the world; however, the water demand is so great that climate variations are of concern to those involved in securing water supplies. Climatologists work with hydrologists to manage effectively Canada's water resources. On the prairies, farmers anxious about water for irrigation and municipal officials worried about spring flooding regularly seek information about the winter's snowpack. Engineers on the Great Lakes make daily assessments of the basin's water balance in order to predict lake level changes. In eastern Canada where the export of hydroelectricity is big business, electric utilities count on ample winter precipitation to fill reservoirs. In moist regions with a reliable streamflow, engineers develop schemes for diverting surpluses to water-starved regions.

Energy Consumption Canada consumes more energy per capita than any other nation, the equivalent of 9 t of oil annually. This thirst for energy is caused largely by Canada's vast distances and its climate extremes. About a third of the energy now used in Canada is expended to offset the cold, ICE and snow of winter, and the heat and humidity of summer. In the 1970s and 1980s severe winters and uncertainty of foreign oil supplies focused attention on Canada's vulnerability to climate variations. Further cooling or increased snow would cost the Canadian economy dearly; on the other hand a warming of 2-3°C would decrease winter heating needs by about 15%, the equivalent of 45 million barrels of oil, an annual saving of $1.5 billion. The safe and economic exploitation of energy reserves, be they offshore in the Arctic, high on a mountain slope or inland in the oil sands, demands good climate information. Furthermore, climate-related applications are not restricted to energy exploration and development: electric-

power transmission lines are sensitive to icing, LIGHTNING and TORNADOES; and construction and operation of pipelines in permafrost depend on changes of temperature and soil moisture.

Another issue is how much of Canada's energy needs can be met by renewable sources. Passive solar heating could reduce energy bills. Inexhaustible, pollution-free wind energy, once very popular, could again supply much of the energy needs of small, remote communities.

Building and Construction Architects and builders are often guilty of placing structures suitable for one climate in a very different one, eg, California-style homes in Edmonton. Climate information is useful in determining the orientation of buildings so that there is minimum energy loss and reduced snow drifting, and in designing buildings that have comfortable, healthy, safe and economical indoor climates. Such information can also help in the choice of safe, economical materials that will withstand damage by strong winds, driving rain or frequent freeze-thaw temperature changes. Homeowners can realize greater comfort and reduced energy costs by considering such questions as where to plant trees in order to provide shelter from winter winds and to keep driveways free of snow; what sort of curtains to choose in order to keep out unwanted summer heat; or which wall of the house should contain a large area of glass to let in winter sun.

Transportation Transportation by water, land or air is influenced by climate variability or extremes. Route planning and scheduling and cargo handling and storage all depend upon sound climate information. In marine areas, SEA ICE, poor visibility and storm occurrence are significant problems and affect the design and operation of ships and port facilities. Design must incorporate information about storms, eg, that which sank the OCEAN RANGER oil rig off Newfoundland, drowning 84 men (15 Feb 1982), in order to defend against such hazards. Freezing and thawing, precipitation and snow cover are very important to land transportation by road, rail or pipeline. Annual snow removal costs may exceed $1 billion in Canada. Indirect costs are even greater, eg, 1 cm of snow increases vehicular fuel consumption by about 50% and causes average commuter delays of 30 minutes. Air transportation has always been concerned with wind, ceiling, visibility and turbulence, whether for airport siting, timing of favourable takeoffs and landings or en route aircraft operations.

Other Sectors One of the most interesting and challenging areas of modern CLIMATOLOGY deals with the effects of climate on human health. Climate-related health problems include the common cold, hypothermia, hay fever, asthma, frostbite and migraine complaints. Even more common are subtle climate-induced or climate-intensified sickness, fatigue, pain, depression and insomnia, all of which ultimately diminish alertness, learning ability, performance and productivity. Climatic factors are also pervasive in the field of recreation. The economic well-being of vacation areas depends upon the occurrence of expected weather. For example, downhill skiing is particularly sensitive to the variability of snowfall. The absence of snow generally keeps people from skiing despite snow-making equipment, and a lack of snow between Christmas and New Year's Day can spell disaster for resort operators. Climate information has been used in siting and design of trails and the design of equipment and facilities; in assessment of competing sites for sporting events; and in the scheduling of games and contests. *See also* CLIMATE SEVERITY.   D.W. PHILLIPS

Reading: W.W. Kellogg and R. Schware, *Climate Change and Society* (1981).

Mummified stump of a dawn redwood, Axel Heiberg I in the Canadian Arctic, about 45 million years old. High latitude fossil forests dramatically illustrate global climatic change (*courtesy James Basinger*).

Climate Change Climate is average or integrated WEATHER, where weather is defined as the current state of the atmosphere. Climate is often regarded, in fact, as the expectation of future weather. It is specified by average values of the main elements (eg, temperature, humidity) and of their variability, usually over a 30-year period. Climates vary: recent changes show in weather records; longer-term changes can be identified by studies of tree rings, deep-ocean sediments, glacial ICE and the pollen content of lake and bog sediments. These sources show that liquid water has been present at all times throughout the history of the Earth; hence, that the world-average surface-air temperature has always been above 0°C. In fact, this temperature was usually higher than the present 15°C. During the past 30 million years a cooling of the air and the oceans has taken place, culminating in repeated glacial episodes during the past 2 million years. The last cold episode peaked about 16 000 BC, when ice sheets covered N America as far S as the Ohio and Missouri valleys and the plateaus of Washington. Parts of the YT, NWT and Alaska, however, escaped GLACIATION.

Canada's climate appears to have rebounded to conditions much like those of today after about 9000 BC. The ice sheets melted slowly, vanishing over Labrador-Ungava and Keewatin about 4000 years ago. Forests and prairies re-colonized the country and with them came animals and human populations (*see* BIOGEOGRAPHY). Conditions were warmer than at present until about 2000 BC, then cooled slightly. Since then, the climate has fluctuated without major change. Data from the Northern Hemisphere show that temperatures have varied somewhat in the past century. The 1880s were cold, but temperatures rose about 0.6°C until the late 1930s. A cooling of about 0.4°C ensued but, since 1965, the hemisphere has become slightly warmer. Conditions in Canada were similar, although the warmest conditions here were delayed until the 1950s in some areas. Precipitation has also varied, eg, the 1930s and 1960s had many dry years, especially over the prairies.

In the 1980s few marked trends have been visible to indicate what will happen next; however, changes can be expected. For example, carbon dioxide (CO_2) is accumulating in the atmosphere, mainly from the burning of fuels and from forest clearance and soil losses. CO_2 tends to raise surface temperatures, as do various other pollutants (*see* AIR POLLUTION). Although not universally accepted, mathematical modelling suggests that a doubling of CO_2 (possible by mid- or late 21st century) could raise world temperatures by 2-3°C, the effects being strongest in high latitudes, especially in winter. This trend might lead to a longer growing season for Canada (1-3 weeks), earlier spring ice melt and lower soil-moisture availability in the growing season. Forestry and farming practices and the use of rivers for generating hydroelectricity may have to be altered. Navigation may also be affected, as the Arctic Ocean and the channels of the Canadian ARCTIC ARCHIPELAGO should have easier ice conditions. This warming trend should be detectable by 2000 AD. Canada is in an excellent position to monitor the trend and to develop necessary adaptations. Warming may affect sea level, which has risen by 10 cm since 1885, partly because the world's land ice has been melting. A further increase of 40-60 cm may occur by 2050 AD. Part of the antarctic glaciers may break up in the next few centuries, raising sea level by a further 5-6 m. But sudden effects are unlikely: a decrease in SEA ICE will result in heavier snowfall on glaciers, which will tend to offset the melting. *See also* PALYNOLOGY. F.K. HARE

Climate Information Climatological data are measurements of climate elements (eg, rainfall, wind speed) and are obtained hourly, daily and at other time intervals from observers at over 100 000 locations around the world. For many purposes, climatological data are simply information; in other cases, data must be processed or interpreted into values that are meaningful to planners, engineers and other decision makers. For example, temperature data are transformed by fuel companies into indices of fuel consumption (heating degree-days) used to schedule deliveries.

Observing climate has long been a human preoccupation, but the orderly measurement and assembly of climate records is relatively new, made possible by scientific developments of the past few centuries, eg, the invention of the thermometer and barometer in 17th-century Italy and the telegraph in 19th-century US. The telegraph permitted the transmission of weather observations taken simultaneously over large areas (ie, synoptic observations), paving the way for modern WEATHER FORECASTING. More recently, satellites and automatic weather stations have greatly expanded our ability to monitor the Earth's climate and to communicate information. Computers have enabled climatologists to acquire, record, process and retrieve the millions of pieces of information needed to describe the Earth's climate. Canadian climatological archives alone place at the disposal of all Canadians over 2 billion observations on the country's climate.

Early explorers such as Jacques Cartier and Henry Kelsey directly or indirectly described aspects of climate in their logbooks and journals. The first regular observations at a specific site in Canada were taken in the 1740s by J.F. GAULTIER in Montréal. Official observations began in 1839 at a magnetic and meteorological observatory on the grounds of University of Toronto, but the national program awaited the formation of the Meteorological Service of Canada in 1871. This institution was renamed the Atmospheric Environment Service (AES) in 1970. Development of the CPR and western agriculture provided the opportunity and further impetus for the development of a nationwide climate data-gathering system. In 1987, Canada's official climate archives received measurements from 3043 observing sites and held historic records for approximately 3000 more locations. Daily measurements of precipitation and temperature are the most commonly taken observations but much fuller programs exist at 350 locations. Hourly observations are taken at 411 (including 126 automated stations). These programs allow for the description of rates and types of precipitation, solar radiation, evaporation, brightness of sunshine, soil temperature, snow cover, cloud cover, humidity, wind, etc. In addition, there are upper air observations measuring temperature, humidity and winds at many levels. Measurements of precipitation and temperature are also taken by corporations, provincial governments and private citizens. Attempts are being made to reconstruct historical climate data. Diaries and indirect evidence, eg, tree rings, ice cores and sediment cores, reveal many aspects of climates that existed before settlement, and they are being analysed to obtain "proxy" climate data. RADAR and satellite weather observations present new opportunities for gathering data and new challenges in interpreting these data. The radio messages used to create a picture of Canada from a polar-orbiting weather satellite contain 186 million bits of information; a geostationary satellite can produce 7-8 million bits in 30 minutes.

Canada has approximately 1990 voluntary weather observers who record information daily. They mail their reports monthly to the regional office of the AES (1690) or to the Québec Meterological Service (300). Data from full-time weather stations are transmitted by teletype as are data from remote areas, after being relayed by satellite. Data from upper air stations, satellites, radar and special networks are received on magnetic or punched tape or as charts from recording instruments. On receipt, the data are documented and, when necessary, digitized for processing by computer. The digital archive is maintained on magnetic tapes or in other computer-acceptable form. Other parts of the archive contain printed records, summary tabulations on microfiche, maps and pictures of documents on microfilm. As of 1986 the "paper" section of the national climate archive contained over 15 million original observer reports from about 6500 climate stations, as well as serial publications, both dating back to the 19th century. The archive also contains limited data from around the world. Information is published on all official observations, in detailed and summary forms, for periods which include weeks, months, years, decades and 30-year "normal" periods. Data-oriented publications in 1986 included *Climatic Perspectives* (weekly and monthly), *Monthly Meteorological Summaries, Monthly Record-Meteorological Observations, Monthly Radiation Summary, Annual Meteorological Summaries, Snow Cover Data, Supplementary Precipitation Data* and *Climatic Normals, 1951-80* (for elements such as temperature, precipitation, frost, wind, radiation and degree-days). *See also* CLIMATE AND MAN; CLIMATE SEVERITY.

G.A. McKAY

Climate Severity There is scarcely an aspect of Canadian society and economy that is not in some way affected by CLIMATE. Icebergs crowding in the bays and inlets of Newfoundland prevent fishermen from leaving harbours and threaten their boats and fishing gear. Each year residents of southern Ontario endure steam-bath heat and humidity in summer and blinding whiteouts and bitter cold in winter, even if only infrequently or for short periods of time. Weeks of fog and drizzle depress coastal British Columbians, longing for Hawaii vacations, and Arctic inhabitants feel fortunate when it doesn't snow in July. Canada is a vast territory, and, not surprisingly, has a wide range of climates, from polar ice-cap, semi-desert, maritime and Mediterranean to dry and humid continental. Fortunately, each climate has its own season of tranquillity.

There are many excellent studies of the effects of climate on man's survival and comfort in Canada (*see* CLIMATE AND MAN) and several attempts to classify climate stress. W.H. Terjung employs a scheme to estimate human thermal sensations according to a simple temperature scale, but ignoring solar radiation and wind. In his world classification, he describes the Canadian winter as either very cold or extremely cold. A. Auliciems and F.K. HARE classify the cold stress during the winter

Climate Severity Index, Selected Places

Station	Severity Index (100)
British Columbia	
Kamloops	20
Penticton	16
Prince George	38
Vancouver	19
Victoria	15
Yukon	
Dawson	54
Whitehorse	46
Northwest Territories	
Alert	84
Inuvik	63
Isachsen	99
Yellowknife	57
Alberta	
Calgary	35
Edmonton	37
Fort McMurray	46
Lethbridge	33
Red Deer	41
Saskatchewan	
Regina	49
Saskatoon	42
Manitoba	
Churchill	82
Flin Flon	49
Winnipeg	51
Ontario	
London	41
Moosonee	56
Ottawa	44
Sudbury	54
Toronto	36
Windsor	37
Québec	
Fort Chimo	64
Montréal	43
Québec	52
Sherbrooke	43
New Brunswick	
Fredericton	41
Moncton	47
Saint John	48
Nova Scotia	
Halifax	47
Sydney	50
Yarmouth	40
Prince Edward Island	
Charlottetown	48
Newfoundland	
Gander	56
St John's	59

with the objective of predicting clothing requirements for comfort. C.C. Boughner and M.K. Thomas quantified the unfavourable aspects of the Canadian winter by weighting 4 factors (in order of decreasing weight): length of darkness, January wind chill, annual snowfall and heating degree-days. The inadequacy of their "climatological index" classification is readily apparent, eg, very disparate areas such as Whitehorse and Toronto, or Calgary and Victoria are considered to be homogeneous. B.M. Burns and others use 11 factors to describe the relative remoteness, or NORDICITY, of Canadian locations. Six parameters are climate-related and all are weighted equally. In developing an index for renumerating workers in the Canadian NORTH, L.E. Hamelin weights temperature, precipitation and ice to account for 40% of the index. None of these studies, however, produces a numerical means of assessing all of the year-round climate factors that make living in certain areas difficult and at times hazardous.

The "Climate Severity Index" takes into account 4 major factors most directly related to environmental stress: the comfort of individuals, their psychological state, safety and mobility. Comfort in our daily lives influences what we wear, how we feel, if and how we travel and how effective we work and play, and so this factor was considered the most important in the climate severity index. Psychological state and hazardousness are complementary factors but were judged to be of lesser importance than comfort because they are generally associated with less frequent and more ephemeral factors. Although weather restricts mobility, especially in winter, it is less significant as a year-round disruptive force than the other 3 factors. Without any further adjustments, a maximum value of 500 weighted points for discomfort, 200 each for psychological state and hazardousness and 100 for outdoor mobility would result in a total possible severity index of 100 points.

Discomfort Factor Winter is the most stressful time of the year in Canada. According to Statistics Canada, an average of 108 persons die each year from exposure to extreme cold temperatures, whereas 17 die from all other natural events, such as lightning, storms, floods, heat waves, earthquakes and tidal waves. The largest temperature contrasts occur during winter in Canada, while little contrast occurs during summer south of the Arctic Circle.

Three elements are considered essential to assess the discomfort of winter. These are the degree of coldness (wind chill) and the duration and severity of winter. Wind chill is a recognized index of heat loss and cold injury for humans, combining the effects of low temperature and strong WINDS.

The duration of summer is indicated by the number of months with a mean daily temperature of 10°C or more, and a measure of the warmth by the mean daily maximum temperature of the warmest month. Low values for these subfactors are stressful. On the other hand, extended periods of high temperature and high humidity have been responsible for many deaths, especially in crowded areas. Humidex is an accepted index of summer discomfort. The mean percentage of days with a Humidex value of 30°C for one hour or more at the height of summer was used as an indicator of heat. At a humidex value of 30°C some people become uncomfortable (below this value almost everyone is comfortable). A fourth summer discomfort factor is dampness, and it can be measured by the mean wet-bulb depression in July. The smaller this difference the more close is the weather.

Psychological State A wide variety of psychological complaints have been blamed upon weather. Symptoms include tiredness, depression, irritability, loss of sleep, lack of concentration, headaches, general nervousness, forgetfulness, photophobia, chest and joint pain, etc. Weather has frequently been blamed for spells of "cabin fever" or general monotony among isolated meteorological personnel. The climate elements that best represent psychological state and yet could be easily tabulated from the primary data were the length of the winter day, annual number of hours of sunshine, annual number of days with measurable precipitation, and the frequency of hours with FOG.

Long periods of darkness characteristic of high latitude winters are known to be especially detrimental—adversely affecting moods, attitudes and behaviour. Most meteorological personnel and others who have lived for extended periods in the Canadian Arctic quickly refer to the 24 hours of total darkness as being particularly debilitating.

Sunshine has important physiological and psychological implications. One beneficial aspect of sunshine is its action in converting pro-vitamin D in human skin to vitamin D. Clear, sunny weather, occurring especially at the end of a long spell of overcast, can be mentally uplifting.

Hazardousness Elements of climate either singly or together can produce widespread injury and death and bring about considerable damage to property and the environment. Obvious examples are FLOODS and BLIZZARDS, which may seriously disrupt entire communities. Extreme wind chill in winter and excessive heat and humidity in summer are also hazardous. The general hazardousness of a locality could be measured by considering the mean winter snowfall and the frequencies of 3 other elements: strong winds, thunderstorms and blowing snow. These phenomena can cause a whole host of personal hardship, including possible death, injuries, missed social and business events, delayed services and other privations.

Outdoor Mobility Snowfall must be taken into account for assessing the ease of outdoor movement on foot and by vehicle. Freezing precipitation restricts all forms of transportation from walking to flying. In addition, it frequently plays havoc with communication owing to downed telephone and hydro wires.

Climate Severity Index The climate severity index is designed so that values approaching 100 indicate the highest severity. In Canada, much of the northern Queen Elizabeth Islands, except for some sheltered locations, have the highest severity, with all 4 factors showing high values. Only slightly less severity exists in the remainder of the Arctic Islands, the Beaufort Sea coast, the District of Keewatin, northern Manitoba, the Hudson Bay coast of Ontario, the Ungava Peninsula and Hudson Strait shores of Québec and northern Labrador. Over the remainder of Canada, the factor values are much lower. Victoria (15) and Penticton (16) are among the most pleasant climates of Canada's populated places. Medicine Hat (29) and Lethbridge (33) are relatively benign. Among major cities Toronto (35) and Calgary (34) have only moderately stressful climates, whereas Winnipeg (51) and Montréal (44) are considerably more uncomfortable. St John's has the highest index value (56) among major cities.

The climate severity index is an indicator of the year-round rigours created by climate. It is not an absolute measure, since any such measure would involve subjective value judgements that cannot be precisely quantified.

D.W. PHILLIPS AND R.B. CROWE

Climatology, a division of METEOROLOGY concerned with the study over extended periods of time of CLIMATE, ie, of both average and extreme WEATHER conditions. Weather may be defined as the current state of the atmosphere, especially its temperature, humidity and movement. The 2 main theoretical branches of climatology are physical climatology, which seeks to understand the principles of mass and energy exchanges between the Earth and its atmosphere, and dynamic climatology, which examines the factors influencing climate according to the laws of physics. Other divisions include descriptive climatology (climatography); synoptic climatology, which deals with the correlation and analysis of weather observations taken simultaneously at widely distant points; and applied climatology, which makes CLIMATE INFORMATION available to engineers, planners, vacationers, etc (*see* CLIMATE AND MAN). The possibility that man can deliberately or inadvertently influence climate on a large scale is also of interest to climatologists but remains largely theoretical at present.

Physical Climatology

Physical climatology examines the processes, magnitudes and directions of energy and mass exchanges within the atmosphere at, and immediately below, the Earth's surface. These are important in determining all scales of climate, from local to global. Solar radiation drives the Earth-atmosphere system, which absorbs about 65% of the solar radiation that it receives and emits annually an identical amount of infrared radiation to space. This equilibrium may change, and with it the world's climate, with changes in solar emission, sun-Earth distance, reflectivity of the planet, etc. The effect of variations in the sun-Earth distance is negligible in the short term, but on geological time scales, orbital variation may have produced substantial radiation changes resulting in ICE AGES. The portion of the system between 40° N and S is an energy source, since radiant energy gains exceed losses here; poleward of these latitudes the system is an energy sink, where losses exceed gains. WINDS and ocean currents transport energy poleward to rectify this latitudinal imbalance, thereby preventing systematic warming or cooling. The planetary surface also has an annual surplus of energy, since radiant energy gains exceed losses; the atmosphere has an energy deficit. Convective transport of heat from the surface prevents systematic surface warming and atmospheric cooling.

An energy budget or balance can be drawn up for any volume or surface within the Earth-atmosphere system. The radiation balance in this budget is mainly governed by seasonal control of incoming solar radiation and the fraction reflected by the ground. In Canada during winter, low solar radiation and high surface reflectivity of snow produce a negative radiation balance (with inputs less than outputs) everywhere. In midsummer, the radiation balance is positive everywhere because solar radiation is greater and snow is less or absent. The midsummer budget is remarkably uniform between the US border and the High Arctic. Long daylight periods in the North compensate for a weak SUN which is low in the sky. Mean annual radiation balance increases gradually from zero in the Arctic Archipelago to about 17 MJ/m²/day (megajoules per square metre per day) in southern Canada.

The magnitudes and seasonal and geographical variations of the other energy-budget components are poorly known for Canada. Sensible and latent heat transfers are the major components, except in spring, when snowmelt uses a significant amount of energy (up to 1.25 MJ/m²/day). Sensible heat is the energy of the movements of the molecules that make up a mass and is perceived as the temperature of the substance. Latent heat is the energy required to change the phase of matter, ie, to rearrange the molecules (as from liquid to gas in evaporating moisture) whether the temperature of the mass changes or not. Latent heat transfer is always large (about 80-90% of the radiation balance) from open water, wetlands and transpiring vegetation and crops. In drier areas, or as wet surfaces become drier, sensible heat transfer becomes more important. Surface modifications may radically alter the relative magnitudes of energy-budget components, eg, in many cities replacement of vegetation with concrete and brick has reduced latent energy transfer and increased the transfer of sensible heat. Land management also has its effects, eg, in dry areas irrigation produces moist, cooler oases as a result of increased latent heat transfer.

J.A. DAVIES

Dynamic Climatology

Dynamic climatology is the study of climate as a branch of physics. The climate system is a physical system governed by reasonably well-known physical laws (fluid dynamics, thermodynamics, radiative transfer, etc). There are 5 major components of the climate system: atmosphere, hydrosphere (ie, oceans, lakes), land surface, cryosphere (sea ice, permanent ice caps, snow) and biosphere. The global system is interrelated in many complex ways, and the study of dynamic climatology requires expertise from many branches of science and data from all parts of the globe.

Some major aspects of the climate system may be appreciated by considering simpler, idealized systems. A nonrotating Earth with no topography or oceans would have a climate far different from that observed. If the atmosphere were not permitted to move in this idealized case, the resulting climate would not vary with longitude, but only with latitude, eg, temperatures would be high at equatorial latitudes, low at poleward latitudes. The resulting temperature structure at the surface, at various levels in the atmosphere and at various latitudes could be calculated using the equations of thermodynamics and radiative transfer. If the atmosphere were allowed to move on this nonrotating Earth, the warm air in equatorial regions would rise, flow polewards, cool, sink and flow equatorwards once more, giving rise to a Hadley circulation. The temperature difference from pole to equator provides the driving force for the motions and would be reduced as a consequence of the flow. If the planet now began to rotate, the nature of the flow (hence, the climate) would differ remarkably. A simple Hadley circulation would no longer be found but rather a flow from W to E at middle latitudes and a flow from E to W at lower latitudes. Superimposed on this general flow would be large ripples and eddies. Without the oceans, winter cold and summer warmth would be extreme and the coldest and warmest times of the year would occur at the solstices. If moisture were introduced into the system, as oceans and water vapour in the air, the resulting climate would again change dramatically; changes would include the appearance of major E-W asymmetries in the climate. The oceans have a profound effect on climate through storage and transport of heat. Topography, ICE and snow, etc, add further degrees of complexity to the system.

This complicated, 3-dimensional global system is studied observationally and numerically. Observational or diagnostic approaches proceed by the collection and study of many millions of observations of the atmosphere and oceans, not only at the surface but with height and depth. Such studies attempt to understand how the physical system operates and what the dominant mechanisms are. They also include attempts to understand past variations in climate and to detect and understand variations in the current climate. Numerical models of the climate system attempt to solve the mathematical equations which govern the physical system. These equations are so complex that they must be solved using computers. The more comprehensive of these general circulation models of the atmosphere, of the oceans, or both, require billions of computations to simulate the climate even approximately. In addition to providing an understanding of the current climate, these models may be used to investigate possible causes of CLIMATE CHANGE.

The climate system has undergone profound changes in the distant past and real but less extreme variations in historical times. Such changes are caused by natural phenomena (VOLCANOES, changes in the sun, etc) and human-induced factors (increased carbon dioxide, deforestation, etc). The physics-based investigations of dynamic climatology are designed to shed light on these and other climatic questions. The climate system must be studied from a global perspective. To this end, the World Meteorological Organization, an agency of the United Nations, has established the World Climate Program. In Canada, research in dynamic climatology is undertaken in the Canadian Climate Centre, which is part of the Atmospheric Environment Service, and in a number of universities and government laboratories. GEORGE J. BOER

Man's Effect on Climate

Human activities can change some aspects of the climate on a local scale. Some changes are deliberate, eg, use of trees or hedges as windbreaks, to prevent frost hollows or to control snow drifting. Others are incidental, eg, the warming of the downtown cores of expanding cities, or the increase in rainfall downstream from cities caused by increased release of heat and of pollutants which promote condensation (see AIR POLLUTION; URBAN EFFECT ON CLIMATE). There is no evidence that human activities have, as yet, had any detectable effect on the large-scale climate. Nevertheless, as the scale of human activities grows, and as the by-products of these activities increase, the potential for large-scale effects on climate becomes very real.

One such by-product is the carbon dioxide (CO_2) produced by the burning of coal, oil and gas to heat homes, operate equipment and generate electric power. Since 1880 the levels of CO_2 have increased by about 17%, more than half of that increase coming in the past 20 years. Although CO_2 represents less than 1% of the total volume of the atmosphere, it is very important because it interferes with the flow of heat radiated from the Earth into space (see GREENHOUSE EFFECT). Experiments using computer models of climate indicate that, if the volume of atmospheric CO_2 were double its preindustrial level, the average temperature of the air at ground level would increase by about 2-3°C. Such a change would be larger than any climate change in recorded history and would be accompanied by much larger regional shifts in climate. It has been discovered that the atmosphere concentration of greenhouse gases, other than CO_2 (such as chloroflorocarbons and methane), are also on the rise. Should present trends continue, the total effect of such gases is projected to be comparable to CO_2 effect. This implies that a climate warming will take place more rapidly than previously thought.

The possibility of deliberately modifying the large-scale climate is intriguing, but cursory examination of the question indicates that energies involved in the climate system are so large that a direct approach would be impossible. For example, the energy converted in a single one-hour THUNDERSTORM would supply Canada's entire electrical energy needs for one day. The energy converted in a single low-pressure system in one day is 10 000 times greater than that of a thunderstorm. It has taken 2 generations of burning fuels to produce a 17% change in CO_2 levels which has not yet produced any detectable effect. Thus, it is improbable that any direct action could be taken to modify our climates, even if methods of doing so were known. One possibility would be to influence the climate by depositing long-lived dust clouds in the high atmosphere: there is some evidence that volcanoes affect the climate by injecting large amounts of material at high altitudes. It is not known what effects such a deliberate modification would have on the climate at the surface. P.E. MERILEES

Reading: J.F. Griffiths and D.M. Driscoll, *Survey of Climatology* (1982).

Clockmaker; or The Sayings and Doings of Sam Slick of Slickville, The,

by Thomas Chandler HALIBURTON, originally appeared as newspaper sketches. Sam Slick's colloquial, vernacular, Yankee voice, peddling clocks as well as his views on "human natur," first beguiled Haligonians in 1835 in Joseph HOWE's newspaper, *The Novascotian.* The sketches were collected and published in Halifax, 1836; London and Philadelphia, 1837 (first series); Halifax, London and Philadelphia, 1838 (second series); and 1840 (third series). In 1923 the 3 series were combined in a single publication (ed Ray Palmer Baker, Toronto). Haliburton found in Sam Slick's Yankee idiom and wit the perfect voice for a running, wryly mocking commentary on Nova Scotia's social scene, its political life and its relations with the US and Britain. Before Charles Dickens achieved recognition, Haliburton was the unrivalled master and most popular writer of comic fiction in English. *The Clockmaker* was translated into German, 1840-42; it has run through almost countless editions to establish Haliburton as one of the founders of N American humour.

NEIL BESNER

Clocks and Watches The manufacture of clocks and watches in Canada may have begun as early as 1700; however, it is generally considered that the practising watch and clockmakers of that time did not make the entire mechanism. The watch or clock originated in England, continental Europe and, later, the US; it came to Canada as an *ebauche* (basic, unfinished movement) and was finished by the local horologist, and thus bears his initials or signature, or the stamp of his silversmith. From the beginning, retailers of clocks, and especially watches, were closely associated with silversmiths and jewellers. The arrangement was logical as the 2 groups were dependent on the same market and required one another's skills. Jean Filiot of Montréal and Thomas Gordon of Halifax were well-known watchmakers of the 18th century.

During the early part of the 19th century the pride of many homes was the grandfather or long-case clock, which would be passed from one generation to the next as a treasured heirloom. The movements of many of these clocks were imported from continental Europe and England; local merchants then ordered a pine case from the local cabinetmaker. Other clocks came from the US, eg, those of the Twiss brothers who operated from Montréal during the early 19th century, specializing in grandfather clocks which came in from the US. Their clocks are now sought by collectors.

Watch and clockmakers were frequently listed as having worked in several places, as they tended

Mahogany bracket clock with brass finials, feet and dial, from the late 18th century, Montréal (*courtesy Royal Ontario Museum*).

to try out several towns before settling down. In some cases, the second generation would set up shop in another town as an expansion of the family business. After the completion of the Canadian Pacific Railway, there was an extensive migration west, which undoubtedly included horologists to serve the growing population. Members of some communities (eg, the Hutterites) brought with them watches made entirely of wood by their own craftsmen. Wooden movements and cases continued to be made by such craftsmen; however, these artisans did not play an active part in the development of watch and clockmaking technology.

The first large-scale Canadian clock manufacturer on record was the Canada Clock Co of Whitby, Ont, which began production in 1872. The operation later moved to Hamilton, Ont, and continued to produce clocks until 1887. The largest and most successful clock company, that of Arthur Pequegnat, began in 1904 in Berlin (now Kitchener), Ont. Pequegnat's made many models of table, shelf, wall and standing clocks and sold throughout Canada until the company ceased production in 1941. Pequegnat clocks are desirable collectors' items; a nearly complete collection is exhibited at the NATIONAL MUSEUM OF SCIENCE AND TECHNOLOGY in Ottawa.

In 1891 the Canadian Horological Institute was established in Toronto by Henry Playtner of Preston, Ont. This excellent school of watchmaking and repairing produced many fine craftsmen. Playtner's book, *Canadian Horological Institute* (1904), contains a very interesting account of the early days of an apprentice. The school lasted until 1914 when Playtner moved to the United States to found the Elgin Watchmakers' College. From time to time "masterpieces" made by graduating students from the institute can be found. They represent a very high grade of horological craftsmanship.

An interesting, although fictional, account of the social aspects of clock marketing in the early 19th century is given by T.C. HALIBURTON in *The Clockmaker; or The Sayings and Doings of Sam Slick of Slickville*, a novel describing the travels of a somewhat disreputable person who sold clocks "door-to-door" in Canada and the US. *See also* JEWELLERY AND SILVERWARE INDUSTRY.

CAROL HAYTER AND PAUL LAVOIE

Reading: G.E. Burrows, *Canadian Clocks and Clockmakers* (1973); J.E. Langdon, *Clock and Watchmakers in Canada 1700-1900* (1976).

Closure, procedural provision allowing the Government to curtail debate in the HOUSE OF COMMONS and bring on a vote. A remedy for FILIBUSTERING, it entails 2 different decisions by the House: the vote to apply closure, and then the vote (or votes) on the business being closed. Closure takes 2 days; if the required oral notice is given on a Monday, closure will be moved and the closure vote taken (without debate) after routine proceedings on Tuesday; if the closure motion carries, the rest of that sitting is spent on the business to be closed, which is put to the vote at the end of the sitting. With closure on, the House sits late, with the vote (or votes) coming soon after 1:00 AM. The use of closure is highly controversial. The Opposition cries, "Dictatorship!"; the Government cries, "Filibuster!" Added to the Standing Orders in 1913, the rule was used 18 times before 1982, 4 times during the PIPELINE DEBATE in 1956. It was used to bring on the vote for concurrence in the flag committee report in 1964; and to add 3 new Standing Orders: SO 115, 116 and 117, which provide for limitation of debate at each stage of a bill's passage through the House (*see* ALLOTMENT OF TIME). Since 1982 closure has only been used once, in 1987 on the debate on CAPITAL PUNISHMENT.   JOHN B. STEWART

Men's 18th-century clothing. The velvet suit shown was semiformal attire in France and was worn in Montréal in the 1780s. The richly brocaded waistcoat was worn by Barthelemy Gugy, likely in Trois-Rivières, in the 1790s (*courtesy Royal Ontario Museum*).

Frock coat from Upper Canada. Frock coats were worn in rural areas on Sundays only. This example dates from the 1840s. It is of wool and may have been a local product (*courtesy Royal Ontario Museum/gift of Mr Sidney Holmes*).

Clothing The colonization of eastern Canada began with the French in the 17th century. For some years, these settlers depended for clothing on what they brought with them. New garb was expensive and the only clothing available was imported, ready-made clothing or garments made locally from imported cloth or, sometimes, from dressed skins. Weaving did not become widespread in the new settlement until early in the 18th century; some local manufacture of fashionable shoes and hats had begun by the late 17th century.

Fashionable Dress With the appearance of towns, well-to-do male and female inhabitants dressed in elegant clothing, similar to that worn in France. However, there was a time lag of at least a year between the initiation of a style in Europe and its appearance in Canada, since ships from the continent came only annually. In 17th-century Canada a fashionable male wore a periwig, rich fabrics and elegant lace. Portraits of Jean TALON, the first intendant of New France, show him stylishly attired in periwig, brocade dressing gown, shirt lavishly trimmed with lace at the wrists and lace cravat. In 1703 Madame Riverin, wife of a member of Québec City's Conseil Sou-

Women's homespun clothing. The green and pink check dress (left) is from Ontario (1860s). The petticoat (right) from Québec would have been worn as a skirt with a bodice or jacket or as a petticoat with a hitched-up skirt (*courtesy Royal Ontario Museum*).

Stylish silk dress worn in Montréal about 1882. The bodice is fitted, lined and boned, and the back section, supported by a bustle, extends into a fishtail (*courtesy McCord Museum/McGill University*).

verain, was painted in a stylish dress called a *mantua* and an elegant head-dress known as a *fontange*. Her daughters were dressed similarly and her son was garbed in miniature modish male clothing. Such imitation of adult clothing was customary in children's attire. When the province of Upper Canada was created in 1791, the newly formed governing class, as well as the other members of the elite, also attempted to maintain fashionable standards of dress. These standards, like those of English dress, were generally more conservative than the modish styles of Paris.

The first Canadian fashion plate, which appeared in Mar 1831 in the *Montreal Monthly Magazine*, probably was inspired by one in an English publication. With the improvement in overseas communication which took place in the mid-19th century, the time lag between new European fashions and their appearance in Canada was substantially reduced, becoming as short as 3 months.

Everyday Dress All but the wealthiest settlers wore clothing made in the home, often of cloth spun in the home and woven domestically or by professional local weavers. Styles tended to be conservative and to reflect rural French or, later, English styles. In the mid-19th century, as more

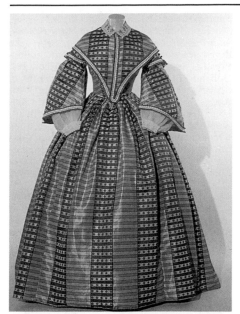

This ribbon silk dress was worn by a Toronto bride at her reception in 1859. The dress is completely hand sewn (*courtesy Royal Ontario Museum/gift of Mrs. J.D. Murray*).

Children's clothes, c1830-70 (*courtesy Royal Ontario Museum from left to right: gifts of Miss H.M. Armour, Miss Jean Robertson, Mr Norman MacDonald, and Miss Helen P. Lovesconte. Hats gift of Miss H.M. Armour*).

ready-made clothing became available, fashion slowly became more accessible to the masses; however, most working-class attire continued to be fashioned at home. Relatively small quantities of this clothing have survived because, as it wore out, it was recycled into QUILTS, RUGS, etc. In 1884 the first mail-order catalogue, the T. EATON COMPANY pamphlet, appeared, making recent styles more accessible to everyone, even in remote rural areas. This important development decreased the difference between conservative rural and up-to-date fashionable dress.

Men's Clothing In the early French colonial period, many of the garments worn by ordinary townsmen and male country dwellers (mostly farmers) were similar to those worn in France. In the 17th and 18th centuries these settlers would have worn a variety of garments, sometimes broadly echoing fashionable ones but of a simpler, more utilitarian cut and fabric. During the 19th century similar garments continued to be worn but variety was more limited; everyday clothes were principally reminiscent of fashionable garments. Breeches were replaced by trousers, and waist-length jackets were common. Beginning early in the 19th century, imported manufactured English cloth increasingly replaced homespun in everyday dress.

Certain types of nonfashionable attire for men, during both the French and English colonial periods (and sometimes persisting later), were different from their counterparts on the continent. Everyday clothing had been influenced by Indian garb, eg, the French Canadian's domestically manufactured leather attire, including footwear with a MOCCASIN shape (*bottes* or *souliers sauvages*) and leather or fabric leggings. These garments were especially common among country dwellers and those actively involved in the fur trade (eg, COUREURS DE BOIS). They were adopted as protection against harsh weather and rough countryside. The moccasin-type footwear (mandatory for snowshoes) was used by all HABITANTS. Also of interest were the decorative, high-crowned felt hats, trimmed with ostrich feathers, worn by the VOYAGEURS during the early 19th century. Voyageurs also frequently wore the *ceinture fléchée*, a woollen, finger-woven multicoloured sash with arrowhead motifs. This characteristic French Canadian accessory first appeared gener-

ally in the early 19th century and continued to be finger woven in Québec until late in the century. The *ceinture fléchée* was also worn by habitants, used as a trade item in the fur trade and, eventually, adopted for sports and leisure wear by the bourgeoisie, especially with the blanket *capot*. It has undergone a revival recently and is again produced in Québec.

The Québec *capot* (in the 17th century the term generally referred to a cloak and, later, to a greatcoat) developed slowly in response to the harsh winters. Beginning in the second quarter of the 18th century, it could also have a hood. Often, for country wear, it was made from thick grey homespun, *étoffe du pays*. From the 1770s hooded capots were made in Québec from Hudson's Bay Co blankets and became a typical costume for the rural Canadien. They were white, with blue bands from the blanket near the hemline and matching bands near the wrist. They had an upright collar and were closed in front by a series of ribbon ties in red, blue or both colours. A coat could be trimmed with ribbon rosettes in the aforementioned colour or colours. This picturesque dress was usually worn with a multicoloured wool sash, a red wool toque (lined in white) or fur cap, leggings (*mitasses*) and *bottes*.

In the 19th century, the blanket capot changed slightly to echo broadly the fashionable greatcoat of the time: buttons and epaulettes were added, ribbon decoration disappeared and different colour combinations in the TEXTILE appeared. During this period, the bourgeois adopted the capot for winter sports and leisure wear, and women began to wear a version of the garment. The attire, especially in white, remains a characteristic

---

Tweed suit showing "leg-o'-mutton" sleeve, made in the mid-1890s . As daytime wear, these suits were worn with a high-collared blouse and a bow tie (*courtesy Royal Ontario Museum/gift of Mr. Wood*).

one for Québec. Now known as the Hudson's Bay Co coat, it is manufactured in Canada for both sexes. FUR was also important to both men and women for combatting the winter cold. From the mid-19th century on, it was generally worn fur side out, creating a luxurious effect.

Women's Clothing For ordinary and rural wear during the 17th century, and through to the late 19th century in Québec, women generally wore separate tops and skirts. In the 17th century and until the second half of the 18th century, corset bodices (approximately waist length and usually sleeveless), chemises (knee-length undergarments which could function for the working classes as blouses), petticoats (ie, skirts), aprons and caps were worn. This costume resembled attire seen in France and western Europe. With the appearance of handweaving in New France, plain and checked or striped homespuns prevailed. Sometime during the mid-18th century, the corset bodice was replaced by a sleeveless one extending beyond the waist. With its possible stylistic variations, unknown today, it was referred to at the time as a short gown or jacket.

As our present century progressed, the dominant development was the gradual change in the supplier of clothing, ie, from the dressmaker to the department store. Yet, for wealthy clients, high-fashion dressmakers continued, for a time, to operate successfully in large cities. Such client were served in the post-WWII period, in Montréal, through couturiers (ie, stylish, high-quality dressmakers running expensive establishments), who modelled their operations on those of French couture salons. In Canada this type of operation persists, but in a very reduced form. The greatest difference in kinds of clothing in Canada, as elsewhere, relates less to an elite and nonelite mode than to trends towards fashion versus antifashion (attire which makes a point of going contrary to trends) and to an increasingly informal manner of dress.

Ethnic dress of relatively recent immigrants (eg, Lithuanians, Ukrainians) is generally worn on special occasions and has not blended into the mainstream of Canadian costume. Similarly, the plain, conservative everyday attire of the Doukhobors and Mennonites has remained independent. Religious, legal and academic dress, being of a conservative nature and mostly of medieval derivation, is familiar in Canada. The major development in this area has been the gradual disappearance of religious costume from the streets, especially in Québec, as a result of Vatican II (a gathering of the supreme authority of the Roman Catholic Church in Rome, 1962-65). Most provincial museums display some pioneer clothing, and excellent collections are held at the ROYAL ONTARIO MUSEUM and the NATIONAL MUSEUMS OF CANADA. *See also* FASHION DESIGN; UNIFORMS.

JACQUELINE BEAUDOIN-ROSS

Reading: K.B. Brett, *Modesty to Mod: Dress and Undress in Canada, 1780-1967* (1967).

Clothing Industries The Canadian clothing industries consist of companies that make consumer, industrial and institutional apparel. They cut and sew fabrics and knit yarns into garments and finish them for sale. The major subsectors include men's, women's and children's clothing, FUR goods, occupational clothing, foundation garments, gloves, hats and caps, hosiery and knitted goods.

Mechanization of clothing manufacture began with the invention of the sewing machine in 1775. Elias Howe obtained patents in the US in 1846. Mass production began during the American Civil War, when large numbers of blue and grey military uniforms were needed to distinguish friend from foe. The increasing sophistication of machines, combined with migration of skilled workers from the US, created a new production industry in Canada. Custom tailors and seamstresses had produced clothing in Canada from the time of Samuel de Champlain, but when volume production methods were developed in the US they were soon adopted in Canada and local craftsmen became entrepreneurial employers. Their factories were located in Montréal, Toronto and Winnipeg, where they could find IMMIGRANT LABOUR and young local women. The first apparel company in Canada that did all cutting and sewing on the premises was the men's fine clothing firm Livingstone and Johnston (est Toronto, 1868), later W.R. Johnston & Co. This company later became a subsidiary of Tip Top Tailors of Toronto, now part of Dylex Ltd, a Toronto-based conglomerate operating Canada-wide in both MANUFACTURING and RETAIL.

The union movement in the clothing business dates back to 1911 when the New York-based International Ladies' Garment Workers Union (ILGWU) started a local in Toronto. During the 1920s, as a result of the formation of unions in Toronto, much of the industry moved to Montréal, making that city a major apparel town. This distribution of production still prevails. In 1985 the clothing industry in Canada consisted of 2497 factories. Québec had 1628, mostly in Montréal, and Ontario had 632, mostly in Toronto, although a few were in Kitchener, Hamilton and Waterloo. 97 were in Manitoba, primarily in Winnipeg; 10 in Saskatchewan; 26 in Alberta, primarily in Edmonton; and 77 in BC, primarily in Vancouver. A few are found in the Atlantic provinces. Several factories are owned and operated by bands and councils of native people. Several manufacturers operate branch plants in Third World countries and the Pacific Rim.

Until 1983 there had not been a general strike in the apparel industry for 49 years because the ILGWU preferred mediation or arbitration. Other important unions active today are the Amalgamated Clothing Workers of America (men's clothing), the United Garment Workers of America (women's clothing) and the Allied Clothing and Textile Workers (mixed clothing production).

Canadians spent almost $9.6 billion on clothing in 1985, not including TEXTILES, FOOTWEAR and knitwear. The clothing industries employed almost 113 000 people in firms employing 20 or more workers. Thousands more work in smaller plants throughout Québec, Ontario and Manitoba. Almost all Canadian plants employ fewer than 50 people, although 281 have over 100

workers. In 1985 the average hourly wage in the industry was $6.63 but the average in Toronto was closer to $7.25. These averages can be misleading, however, because in Québec apprentices are treated differently in the statistics, but are lumped into the national averages. Today the national average is closing in on $7.00/hour, with Toronto still the highest.

The clothing industries are entering a new HIGH-TECHNOLOGY phase. Numerical- and computer-controlled equipment and ROBOTICS are being rapidly introduced into factories. The speed with which factories are modernizing is directly related to the supply of sewing-machine mechanics and technicians who are skilled in servicing the sophisticated equipment. A new program to train technicians has been started at George Brown College, Toronto. Today, alternatives to traditional cutting and sewing methods include LASER or computer-controlled waterjet cutting; and microchip-controlled, multiple-head sewing machines.

The industry in Canada is over 90% Canadian owned, but about 75 American firms and several British and Asian companies have subsidiary plants in Canada. Clothing plants use mostly electricity and are not large energy consumers. In 1985 the Canadian clothing industries produced nearly 337 million units with a work force of 113 000. They captured 80% of the market in dollars but only 58% in garments, not including the textile and knitting industries. The apparent Canadian market was about 581 million units. Imports accounted for 42.7% or $1.75 billion (before duties); exports for only 5 million units valued at $330 million.

The federal government is under constant pressure to limit imports and reduce quotas; at the same time, it must consider how exporting countries will react to Canadian quotas and exports and how this will affect the balance of payments. Protecting jobs within the country's second-largest employment sector is also a concern. Consequently the government formed the Canadian Industrial Renewal Board and its apparel section was given $250 million to assist the clothing industries to become more competitive in world markets, before tariff and other protection is reduced or eliminated under world trade agreements. The proposed FREE TRADE agreement, eg, would have a profound effect on the industry. Canadian clothing companies are expected to compete with Third World countries, but this is very difficult because industrial standards legislation in Canada's producing provinces establishes minimum wages, maximum hours and fringe benefits that are 2-10 times higher than standards in low-wage countries. Consequently, imported clothing, manufactured under conditions that are illegal in Canada, represents a real threat to the future of Canadian companies. The government attempts to control this problem by using a quota system and regulating imports, but $1.75 billion in clothing entered Canada in 1985, compared with exports of only $330 million.

The textile and clothing industries in Canada rank second to FOOD AND BEVERAGES in the number of employees. Some consider them expendable in a high-technology age. However, some European countries have regretted abandoning this sector and are now trying to restore an industry that is traditionally among the top 5 employers in many industrialized nations. For example, the clothing industries also support textile mills and retail stores that employ over 200 000 people.

Sectors of the industry are trying to meet the high-technology challenge with the aid of sophisticated trade associations (eg, the Dress and

Sportswear Guilds) and national magazines (eg, Maclean Hunter's *Style, Canadian Apparel Manufacturer*). Strong training programs have been developed that offer diploma courses in production and design at various community colleges: Holland, PEI; LaSalle, Montréal; George Brown, Seneca and Sheridan, Toronto; Red River, Winnipeg; Grant MacEwan, Edmonton; and Capilano, Vancouver. A new degree program in apparel-production management is offered by Ryerson Polytechnical Institute, Toronto. Continuing education courses are offered at Concordia and McGill universities, Montréal, and U of Manitoba, Winnipeg. SIDNEY S. SCHIPPER

Cloud, visible suspension in the atmosphere, composed of tiny water droplets or ice crystals from about one to a few hundred micrometres in diameter. Clouds occur when moist air cools to its saturation point as a result of loss of heat through vertical ascent, by radiation, or by mixing with cooler air. In Canada, mean cloud cover (fraction of the sky covered by clouds) varies from about 0.5 on the Prairies to 0.8 or more on the West and East coasts in winter. Clouds are named according to the nature of their motion, their composition and their height in the atmosphere. Two basic varieties are distinguished according to air motion. Heap clouds (cumulus family) result from local convection (overturning) in an unstable atmosphere; layer clouds (stratus family) from slow, widespread, vertical lifting. Nimbus signifies a precipitating cloud; cirrus, a high-level, ice-crystal cloud. A cloud that forms at the surface is called FOG; middle-level clouds (2-7 km above ground) are termed altus. Alone, in combination or with other adjectives, the terms stratus, cumulus, cirrus, nimbus and altus name the most frequently encountered cloud types. Viewed from a satellite, clouds are seen to be organized into bands, clusters and swirling patterns, reflecting large-scale motions of the atmosphere. Satellite images of cloud organization are helpful in WEATHER FORECASTING.

Cloud droplets form on hygroscopic (moisture-retaining) particles, about 0.1-1.0 μm in diameter, called cloud condensation nuclei. Cloud droplet concentrations may reach 1000/cm^3 and a liquid-water concentration of 0.1-10 g/m^3 of air is typical. Cloud droplets grow predominantly by condensation of water vapour when they are small and by collision and coalescence with each other when larger. In clouds with no ice (generally those warmer than -10°C to -15°C), RAIN occurs only if collision and coalescence produce millimetre-size raindrops before the cloud evaporates as a result of warming or mixing with its environment (the warm rain process). In clouds extending above the -15°C level, tiny ice nuclei cause some of the supercooled droplets to freeze. These grow rapidly into ice crystals by vapour deposition, while the nearby unfrozen droplets evaporate. The ice crystals may then aggregate into snowflakes, or grow into snow pellets by sweeping out supercooled cloud droplets as they fall. Depending upon season and cloud vigour, snowflakes and snow pellets may reach the ground intact, may melt and fall as rain, or may continue to grow into hailstones (*see* HAIL). This cold rain process is thought to be predominant in Canada.

Weather modification is an attempt to initiate the cold rain process in clouds deficient in ice crystals by seeding them with dry ice pellets or with silver iodide particles which act as ice nuclei (*see* RAINMAKING). In addition to producing precipitation, clouds play other important roles in the atmosphere. By reflecting solar radiation, they have a strong influence on the heat balance and therefore on the temperature of the atmo-

Altocumulus clouds. The clouds in the distance are a line of cumulus congestus formed by the merger of several towering cumulus elements. When organized into a line, as here, they often develop into cumulonimbus (*courtesy Arjen Verkaik, Skyart Productions, Islington, Ont*).

Cirrus cloud streaks. The clouds in this picture consist of falling ice crystals stretched out horizontally by the wind shear into long streaks known as mares' tails (*courtesy Arjen Verkaik, Skyart Productions, Islington, Ont*).

Cumulus clouds consist of individual detached elements that grow upwards as a result of convection. They may resemble small domes (fair weather cumulus) or towers with a cauliflower appearance as in this picture (towering cumulus) (*courtesy Arjen Verkaik, Skyart Productions, Islington, Ont*).

Altocumulus clouds. Wind shear has organized the convection (overturning) in this altocumulus layer into a corrugated pattern. Cumulus clouds result from local convection in an unstable atmosphere (*courtesy Arjen Verkaik, Skyart Productions, Islington, Ont*).

sphere. Cumulus cloud formation is important in the vertical mixing of atmospheric properties. Clouds and their precipitation also help cleanse the atmosphere of POLLUTION.   E.P. LOZOWSKI

Clover The "true" clovers (genus *Trifolium*) are herbaceous plants of the PEA family (Leguminosae or Fabaceae) and must be distinguished from bur clovers (*Medicago*) and sweet clovers (*Melilotus*) of the same family. They comprise about 300 species worldwide, occurring naturally in Eurasia (particularly the Mediterranean region), parts of Africa and western N and S America. White clover is found throughout most temperate regions. Some clovers are low and trailing, others grow to 1 m. Small, white, pink or red flowers are borne in dense clusters; leaves are trifoliolate. Nearly 20 European species are grown for FORAGE in America and Australia. In Canada, red clover (*Trifolium pratense*), white or Dutch clover (*T. repens*) and, to a lesser extent, alsike clover (*T. hybridum*) and crimson clover (*T. incarnatum*) are grown. Many short-lived, perennial cultivars of red clover exist. Most clovers are associated with nitrogen-fixing bacteria in the nitrogen cycle.   J.M. GILLETT

Clovis, or Llano culture (PALEOINDIAN), was widely distributed throughout a large part of prehistoric N America, though its duration was fairly short (9500-9000 BC). Major archaeological sites are located S of a line stretching from Arizona to NS, the most famous of which include Lehner and Naco in Arizona, Blackwater Draw and Clovis in New Mexico, and DEBERT in NS. The culture is characterized by a fluted or grooved lanceolate projectile point or knife called Clovis Fluted by archaeologists. Fluting was produced by removing long flakes from the flat surfaces along the complete length of the implement. The accompanying complex of stone tools included a variety of blades, burins, scrapers, knives and drills. These big-game hunters sought mammoths, mastodons, camels and horses that were native to N America at the time. Following the retreat of the Wisconsin glaciers, these animals became extinct, hastening the end of this stage of N American PREHISTORY.   RENÉ R. GADACZ

Club Moss, perennial, evergreen, coarsely mosslike plants belonging to the genus *Lycopodium* of the club moss family (Lycopodiaceae). Stems have forked branches, and are often prostrate and covered with scalelike leaves. Leaves are lanceolate to oblong or slender, tapering to linear in shape, entire or minutely toothed. Club mosses show alternation of generations, ie, an asexual phase alternates with a sexual one. Each stage is an independent plant. Reproduction is accomplished by spores produced in spore cases (sporangia) borne on the upper surfaces of modified leaves of plants of the asexual or sporophyte phase. In most Canadian species, these modified leaves are condensed to form a cone. Spores germinate, producing small underground plants (prothallia) on which are borne antheridia, which produce sperm, and archegonia, which produce eggs. Prothallia are the sexual generation. Fertilization of the egg and subsequent development produces the familiar club moss plant, the sporophyte generation. Some species reproduce by gemmae (asexual buds that detach from the parent plant), eg, in Canada, *L. selago*.

This diverse group dates at least to the Devonian period (408-360 million years ago). Tree-sized FOSSIL representatives (eg, *Lepidodendron* and *Sigillaria*) are abundant in coal beds of the Carboniferous period (360-286 million years old). About 100 living species are known. They are most abundant in tropical and subtropical regions, but 13 species occur in Canada, mainly in moist, wooded regions. *L. alpinum* and *L. selago* are alpine and arctic-alpine. Running pine (*L. complanatum* and *L. digitatum*) and ground pine (*L. obscurum*) make good Christmas decorations. The yellow spores were formerly used for coating pills and in

Alaskan club moss (*Lycopodium sitchense*) along Mt Edith Cavell Nature Trail, Jasper, Alta (*photo by Julie O. Hrapko*).

medicines; they are also explosive and were used in flash guns.   W.J. CODY

Cluny Earthlodge Village, archaeological site along the N bank of the BOW R in S-central Alberta, consists of a semicircular earth trench about 1 m deep and 2 to 2.5 m wide which, along with a natural terrace edge along one side, encloses an area 129 m long by 90 m wide. Paralleling and from 5 to 8 m inside the trench was a pole palisade. Between the trench and palisade was a spaced series of 10 roughly oval pits, 5 to 6.5 m in diameter and 0.75 to 1 m deep. Research indicates that these structures, similar to earthlodge villages found elsewhere in the region, served to fortify the area within for a small group of aboriginal inhabitants probably living in skin TIPIS. Cluny was apparently constructed and briefly occupied in the 1740s by Indian peoples related or ancestral to the historic Crow and Hidatsa. These inhabitants may have fled from their traditional territory along the Missouri R in what is now N and S Dakota to escape the ravages of a smallpox epidemic. *See also* ARCHAEOLOGY.

JOHN H. BRUMLEY

Clutesi, George Charles, artist, author, folklorist (b at Port Alberni, BC 1905), a member of a family of Nootka chiefs of Sheshaht, Vancouver I. His publications and public activities were among the first in the post-WWII period to gain recognition for Indian culture as interpreted by Indians themselves. A fisherman and pile driver for 21 years, Clutesi broke his back in the 1940s. During his convalescence, he began to record, reproduce and teach the stories, songs, dances and art of his people. Emily CARR left him her artist's materials at her death. His books, though conventional in language, are rich in engaging human and technical detail. Clutesi painted one of the murals of the Indians of Canada pavilion at Expo 67. He is the author of *Son of Raven, Son of Deer: Fables of the Tse-shaht People* (1967) and *Potlatch* (1969).

BENNETT McCARDLE

Clyde River, *see* KANGIRTUGAAPIK.

Clyne, John Valentine, lawyer, judge, business executive (b at Vancouver 14 Feb 1902). After graduating from UBC and articling in Vancouver and London, Eng, Clyne was called to the BC Bar in 1927. He developed a specialty in maritime law and in 1947 was appointed chairman of the new Canadian Maritime Commission. In 1950 he returned to BC as a judge of the Supreme Court but resigned in 1957 to become chief executive officer of MACMILLAN BLOEDEL LTD, the largest lumber producer in Canada. Following retirement in 1973 he remained active in public life in such capacities as chancellor of UBC, chairman of a federal Consultative Committee on the Implications of Telecommunications, and commentator on constitutional matters. In 1987 *Jack of All Trades: The Memoirs of J.V. Clyne* was published.

PATRICIA E. ROY

CN Tower, Toronto (architects John Andrews, International/Roger Du Toit, and the Webb Zerafa Menkes Housden Partnership; structural engineer R.R. Nicolet, 1973-76) is the world's tallest free-standing structure. Built at a cost of $52 million, it is topped off by a sophisticated communications antenna for transmission of both broadcast and microwave signals. Under the management of CN Hotels, the tower attracts thousands of tourists who ride the glassed-in elevators 342 m to the skypod which houses both wide observation decks and the world's highest revolving restaurant. The hexagonal post-tensioned concrete tower is braced by 3 wings to form a broad "Y" in plan at the ground. The tapering wings rise to 330 m, the concrete tower to 450 m. The tower is topped by a 100 m steel mast for a total height of 553 m. Of the world's observation and communications towers, the CN Tower is the most elegant.   MICHAEL MCMORDIE

Cnidaria, phylum of multicellular, radially symmetrical INVERTEBRATES (eg, hydroids, JELLYFISH, sea anemones, CORALS) dating to late Precambrian era (630-570 million years ago). Formerly, phylum Coelenterata included cnidarians and ctenophores (comb jellies). Today, these are considered separate phyla; Coelenterata is used synonymously with Cnidaria. Cnidaria [Gk *knide*, "nettle"] are characterized by their unusual stinging cells. They are found throughout the oceans; relatively few species have colonized fresh water. About 9700 species are known. Two body forms (polyp and medusa) are present, adapted for different life-styles. Polyps are attached to a surface (sessile); medusae are free-floating (planktonic).

The mouth, facing upward in polyps, downward in medusae, leads into a central gut cavity (coelenteron). The gut lining (gastrodermis) contains cells that secrete digestive enzymes; other cells absorb soluble nutrients. The other tissue layer (epidermis), covering the animal's exterior surface contains the highest concentration of stinging cells (cnidoblasts). They are particularly common on food-capturing surfaces (eg, tentacles). Each cnidoblast houses a flask-shaped nematocyst containing a coiled, hollow thread. The thread turns inside out as it is fired from the capsule by an influx of water that increases pressure inside the capsule. Nematocysts can be used once, then must be replaced. Apparently, a combination of touch and specific chemicals (probably amino acids) released from prey provides the discharge stimulus. Many types of nematocysts exist. One type, armed with spines, is capable of penetrating prey and injecting immobilizing toxins. Another, nontoxic type is sticky and wraps around prey, preventing its escape. Others provide adhesion to surfaces and defence from predators. The epidermis also contains muscle and nerve cells and ciliated cells (with hairlike appendages). A true nervous system probably evolved first in the Cnidaria. Anemones and corals perceive stimuli by sensory cells scattered throughout the epidermis. Medusae frequently have quite complex sense organs (simple eyes, ocelli; balance organs, statocysts). Between the tissue layers is a sheet of noncellular material (mesoglea) varying in thickness and consistency among species. In medusae, mesoglea is thick, watery and resembles jelly. In polyps, it is thin and resilient because of its high fibrous protein content.

The success of cnidarians, judged by species diversity and distribution, can probably be attributed to their efficiency as carnivores. Cnidarians usually present a large body area, covered with nematocysts, to the water; small animals are paralyzed and trapped when they touch this surface. Common prey include copepod crustaceans,

shrimps, worms and larvae. A few hydroids, anemones and medusae feed on decaying matter, collected by a combination of cilia and mucus. Several species of hydroids, anemones, corals and jellyfish, living in shallow water and receiving a lot of sunlight, harbour symbiotic ALGAE in their gut cells. The algae photosynthesize inside host cells, producing food for the host. In return, host cells provide a stable environment and ready access to nutrients and carbon dioxide. In freshwater hydras, these algae are called zoochlorellae; in marine species, zooxanthellae. Many cnidarians have complex life cycles in which body form alternates between polyp and medusa. Anemones and corals have no medusa stage. The 3 cnidarian classes are as follows.

Hydrozoa comprises hydroids and their medusae (hydromedusae). About 12 species of freshwater *Hydra* occur in Canadian lakes and streams. *Hydra* species are unusual in having no medusa stage. Hydroids are abundant on Canada's coasts: some 240 hydroid species and 84 hydromedusae species have been identified. Although some hydroids do not release medusae, many undescribed medusae must exist in Canadian waters. This is not surprising, since some are only 4 mm in diameter, with the largest about 12 cm across. Most hydroids have a treelike colonial form that develops by asexual budding of feeding individuals. As the colony grows, buds appear which develop into medusae that are released. Some planktonic hydrozoans, eg, *Velella*, *Nanomia* and *Physalia* (Portuguese man-of-war) are colonial, containing up to 7 types of individuals forming a co-operative whole. A group of hydrozoan corals, the Hydrocorallina, is common throughout tropical and subtropical seas. A few species which form pink encrustations on rocks in deep water occur in Canadian waters.

Anthozoa includes sea anemones, corals and sea pens. Anemones tend to be solitary. They are the largest cnidarian polyps; some species reach 1 m across the oral disc, eg, *Tealia columbiana* of the outer BC coast. Most anemones need a hard surface for attachment; a few species burrow in mud and sand, with tentacles showing above the surface. Several species prefer attaching themselves to snail shells occupied by hermit crabs. Eggs and sperm are released through the mouth; fertilization usually occurs externally. The resulting ciliated larva (planula) eventually settles to the bottom, attaches and transforms into a small polyp. A few anemones brood their young. Like tropical forms, the 65 species of Canadian anemones are often brightly coloured, eg, *Metridium senile* (white), *Anthopleura xanthogrammica* (green), and *Tealia lofotensis* (pink). The only true corals of Canadian waters are solitary, orange cup-corals (eg, *Balanophyllia*). Several species of treelike, horny corals (order Gorgonacea) are found in deep water. Feather-shaped sea pens are common along all Canadian coasts, wherever there is sand in which they can embed their fleshy anchors. Above the anchor is a stem from which numerous, retractable polyps are supported on side arms.

Scyphozoa (true jellyfish) are much larger than hydrozoan jellyfish. They exist throughout the oceans, particularly in coastal areas. Fourteen species commonly occur off Canadian coasts, including the conspicuous, golden orange *Cyanea capillata*, which may reach 1.5 m across. Scyphozoan polyps are small and difficult to find. Normally, a temporary larval form (ephyra) is budded off the polyp by repeated division, so that the polyp resembles a stack of plates. In some species, the medusa develops directly from the polyp; deep oceanic types (eg, *Periphylla*) have no polyp. The medusa stage is sexual, producing eggs or sperm. The planula larva, which develops after

fertilization, attaches to a hard surface; from it the polyp phase grows. One group, Stauromedusae, can be found permanently attached to seaweeds by stalks.   A.N. SPENCER

Coady, Moses Michael, "M.M.," priest, teacher (b at North East Margaree, NS 3 Jan 1882; d at Antigonish, NS 28 July 1959). First director of the extension department, St Francis Xavier U, Coady developed a program of ADULT EDUCATION involving economic self-help for the economically depressed Maritimes that by the time of his death had been adopted in many Third World countries. Coady organized the NS Teachers' Union, the United Maritime Fishermen and, as director of extension, launched the ANTIGONISH MOVEMENT. His *Masters of Their Own Destiny* (1939), the story of the movement, is still in print and has been translated into 7 languages. A volume of his speeches, *The Man From Margaree*, was published in 1971. Coady received numerous awards including 3 honorary degrees (Boston, Ottawa, Ohio). In 1959 the Coady International Institute was opened to continue his work in the Third World.   DOUGLAS F. CAMPBELL

Coaker, Sir William Ford, union leader, politician (b at St John's 19 Oct 1871; d at Boston 26 Oct 1938). Coaker began organizing the Fishermen's Protective Union during 1908-09. The Roman Catholic Church's hostility confined the union to the largely Protestant NE coast of Newfoundland; nevertheless it had 20 000 members by 1914. From the outset, Coaker had argued that the significant economic, social and political reforms needed to win justice for the working man could only be achieved if the union played a political role. The FPU did well in the 1913 election and joined the 1917 National Government. In 1919 Coaker entered Sir Richard SQUIRES's Cabinet and attempted but failed to impose order and regulation upon a fishing industry dislocated by postwar deflation and long characterized by inefficiency, particularly in marketing.   J.K. HILLER

Coal, combustible SEDIMENTARY ROCK formed from the remains of plant life, comprises the world's largest fossil energy resource. It is located primarily in the Northern Hemisphere. Coal is not a uniform substance; rather, it is a wide variety of minerals with different characteristics arising from the nature of its vegetation source and siltation history, and the time and geological forces involved in its formation (including temperature and pressure). Coal is classified according to 4 ranks or classes, each subdivided according to fixed carbon and volatile matter content and heating value. The anthracite class, the most valuable, is blended with bituminous coals to make coke for the iron and steel industry and is also used in the chemical industries. Bituminous coal, besides its use in steelmaking, is used as thermal coal for ELECTRIC-POWER GENERATION. Subbituminous coal supplies thermal-power fuel and steam for industry, and can be used in COAL GASIFICATION and COAL LIQUEFACTION. The lowest grade of coal, lignite, is used for the same purposes as subbituminous coal. Canada's only known body of anthracite was discovered in northwestern BC; bituminous coal is found in NS, NB, Alberta and BC; subbituminous, in Alberta; lignite in Saskatchewan and BC. With its usual perversity, nature did not distribute Canada's coal conveniently. In NS, most of it is under the seafloor; in western Canada, which has about 97% of the country's coal, almost all of it is located hundreds of kilometres from either the Pacific tidewater or the slowly growing and potentially larger markets of central Canada.

History in Canada Coal has been mined in Canada since 1639, when a small mine was opened at Grand Lk [NB]. In 1720 French soldiers began to mine at Cow Bay [Cape Breton, NS] to supply the fortress at LOUISBOURG. Cape Breton later supplied coal to Boston and other American ports, and to the militia in Halifax. By 1870, 21 collieries were operating in Cape Breton. These markets disappeared early in this century. Commercial coal mining in New Brunswick began in 1825 and, except for some early exports, most of the province's coal production has been used locally. In western Canada, coal was first mined on Vancouver I in the mid-19th century. The building of the transcontinental railways through Alberta and BC caused coal mines to be developed on the banks of the Oldman R near Lethbridge, at Drumheller and Edmonton.

By 1867 coal production had reached an annual total of 3 million t: over 2 million t in NS, most of the balance in western Canada and a small amount in NB. By 1911 western Canada had taken the lead and, despite serious downturns in the 1950s and 1960s, it now produces over 90% of the total. In 1947, the year that OIL AND NATURAL GAS were first produced commercially near Leduc, Alta, coal supplied one-half of Canada's ENERGY needs – Drumheller alone producing 2 million t of coal and employing 2000 men. The rapid conversion of coal's traditional markets to oil and gas caused the coal mining industry almost to disappear.

Beginning in about 1950, almost all coal used for domestic heating, industrial energy and transportation energy was replaced by petroleum products and natural gas. Coal now supplies less than 10% of Canada's energy needs. In the late 1960s and early 1970s it became clear that the coal-bearing provinces – Alberta, Saskatchewan, NB and NS – should rely increasingly on their coal deposits for the production of electricity, and that Ontario should consider adding Canadian sources of coal to the amounts historically supplied by nearby mines in the US. At about the same time, Japan's rapidly growing requirement for coking coal provided the opportunity for the rapid development of metallurgical coal production in BC, Alberta and NS. New mining companies were formed, modern coal-handling facilities were constructed, and a new and very efficient system of unit trains was designed and produced.

The Modern Industry The export demand for metallurgical coal has increased to include several other countries, but Canada's share of this demand will be affected by the world economic situation and by the development of competition from the few other metallurgical-coal exporting countries. Some of the factors that are causing a reduction in overall demand for metallurgical coal, such as a depressed world economy and policies of the Organization of Petroleum Exporting Countries, are bringing about a rising offshore demand for thermal coal. In the past dozen or more years these developments have created a Canadian coal industry that is vastly different from its predecessor. Over 400 small producers were in operation in the 1930s; today, Canada has only 11 large producers (plus a very few more under development) and a very small number of minor producers. Although no one is certain of the extent of the resource, Canada has at least 1% of the world's coal resources, and a very high resource and reserve/demand ratio compared to other countries. Estimates are constantly being revised upwards and may rise even more dramatically in the next few decades. Up to 2 trillion t are thought to lie deep under Alberta's plains, and there is serious speculation that one of the world's largest coal deposits lies between Cape Breton and Newfoundland.

The principal coal mines in Canada are located as follows.

Nova Scotia Lingan Mine, No 26 Colliery and the Prince Mine, all run by the Cape Breton Development Corp; Point Aconi Pit, Novaco Ltd; St Rose Mine, Evans Coal Mines Ltd; Drummond Mine, Drummond Coal Co.

New Brunswick Minto/Chipman area pits, NB Coal Ltd.

Saskatchewan Bienfait Mine, Bienfait Coal Co; Boundary Dam Mine, M&S Coal Co; Costello Mine (formerly Klimax Mine), Manalta Coal Ltd; Souris Valley Mine, Utility Valley Mine and Poplar River Mine, all owned by the Saskatchewan Power Corp (with Manalta operating the Utility Mine).

Alberta Montgomery Mine (formerly Roselyn Mine), Manalta Coal Ltd; Vesta Mine, Alberta Power Ltd, with Manalta as operator; Diplomat Mine, Paintearth Mine, Forestburg Collieries Ltd; Highvale Mine, Whitewood Mine, Transalta Utilities Corp, with Manalta as operator; Coal Valley Mine, Luscar Sterco Ltd; Luscar Mine, Cardinal River Coals Ltd; Gregg River Mine, Manalta Coal Ltd; Obed-Marsh Project, Union Oil Company of Canada Ltd; No 1765 Mine and No 1774 Mine, Smoky River Coals Ltd.

British Columbia Corbin Mine, Byron Creek Collieries Ltd; Harmer Surface Mine, Michel Underground Mine and Greenhills Mine, Westar Mining Ltd; Line Creek Mine, Crows Nest Resources Ltd; Fording River Mine, Fording Coal Ltd; Quintette Mine, Denison Mines Ltd and others; Bullmoose Mine, Teck Corp and others.

Some 25.9 million t of coal were exported in 1986, and 13.3 million t were imported; about 57 million t were produced and about 45 million t were consumed in Canada. One reason for the apparent anomalous situation of a major coal-producing country importing such a large quantity of coal is that most of Canada's higher-ranking coals are located about 2300 km from the industrial heartland of central Canada and about 1100 km from the Pacific coast. Transportation costs are high, and the steel mills and Ontario Hydro in Ontario have found it advantageous to import their coal supplies from nearby mines in the US. The other major reason is that the international demand for steel has slackened in the last few years, causing the planned expansion of several mines and the opening of a few others to be delayed.

Because of Canada's large size and the location of most of its coals far from large domestic markets in central Canada and from tidewater for export (except in NS and NB), transportation plays a critical role in the national and international coal trade. The 2 major railways that carry western coals to Pacific tidewater also carry potash, sulphur, grain, petrochemicals and forest products, and are approaching their maximum capacity to haul these bulk commodities. Huge capital investments are being made to increase rail capacity (including CP constructing a new tunnel and CN double tracking through much of the mountains), thus enabling the railways to meet projected offshore demand for these products.

Environmental Impact The production and use of coal creates certain environmental problems. In some countries regulatory processes imposed by governments restrict the expansion and use of coal, developments which are considered essential by the same governments. In fact, there is no way of obtaining and using all the energy needed now and in future without some adverse effects on the environment. What must be done is to make the best possible accommodation between energy, economics, and social needs and environmental concerns. In Canada, only relatively small areas in the West are being disturbed at any one time for the purpose of coal mining. Land disturbed annually by operating mines includes 182 ha in mountainous regions of BC, 174 ha in Alberta, and 130 ha in plains areas of Saskatchewan. Using technol-

ogy now available, coal can be mined, transported and used in most parts of the world in conformity with high standards of health, safety and environmental protection without unacceptable increases in cost.

Industry Organization Since the beginning of this century, the character and organization of Canada's coal-producing industry has reflected pressures from labour and external circumstances. In the fall of 1906, operators of steam-coal mines in southern Alberta and eastern BC formed the Western Coal Operators' Assn to make districtwide, collective labour and wage agreements. Coal mine employees in the area belonged to District 18 United Mine Workers of America. During WWI a director of coal operations was appointed to deal with labour relations and price adjustments in the absence of collective agreements. As a result, practically all of the larger operating companies in Alberta and eastern BC joined the Western Coal Operators' Assn. This directorate continued in operation until 18 May 1920. On that date, the name of the association was changed to the Western Canada Coal Operators' Association. That association entered into a collective agreement with District 18 United Mine Workers of America.

In 1925 the UMW of A became ineffective in western Canada, as rival labour organizations and various purely local unions designed to deal directly with specific employers were organized. This erosion of collective labour power led to a reduction in membership in the Western Canada Coal Operators' Assn and, in Nov 1925, the remaining members decided to disband it. By 1937 the UMW of A had again succeeded in bringing within its orbit most of the employees at the steam-coal mines and employers were again forced to consider districtwide agreements. As a result, the Western Canada Bituminous Coal Operators Association was organized and included almost all steam coal operators.

During WWII all concerned concentrated on producing as much coal as possible. At the end of the war, the association included in its 1945 membership almost all thermal coal operators in Alberta and eastern BC. On 27 Sept 1952 the Domestic Coal Operators Assn and the Western Canada Bituminous Coal Operators Assn amalgamated to form the Coal Operators' Assn of Western Canada, with power to deal with any matters affecting the industry as a whole, and exclusive power to make local and general agreements with labour, to settle disputes arising out of the agreements and to act upon legislation, federal or provincial, that might affect the membership.

In Apr 1971 the association became the Coal Association of Canada, which came to abandon its concern with labour and wage agreements and with the administration of welfare and retirement funds. On 24 Dec 1973 the federal government issued letters patent to this new association, with objectives appropriate to a national body representing the coal industry, ie, to project the views of the industry on the international, national and provincial levels, and to co-ordinate its efforts with those of government in policies affecting coal exploration, development and mining. Today the membership of the association includes all significant coal producers in Canada, mining companies which are seriously engaged in preparing to produce coal, and almost all petroleum companies with sizable coal holdings.   GARNET T. PAGE

Coal Demethanation, a process by which methane gas is removed from coal deposits. The principal objective of coal demethanation, since its introduction in 1943, has been to remove the safety hazard that the gas poses to miners; however, methane is the principal component of natural gas and can substitute for it. Methane is generated in coal during coalification, the process in which FOSSIL vegetation is gradually converted from low-rank to high-rank coal. As much as 1400 m³ of methane is produced per tonne of coal during coalification, but only about 2% is retained in the coal. The highest-recorded gas content of coal in Canada is 21 m³/t, measured in Canmore, Alta.

A relatively recent coal demethanation technique does not require the presence of a coal mine. The technique can be used to improve mine safety (by removing a major portion of the methane before the coal is mined) as well as to collect methane for use as a fuel. To gain access to the methane, a borehole is usually drilled from the ground surface or boreholes are drilled from a shaft. To start the gas desorbing, the conditions under which the methane is adsorbed on the coal must be changed, so that the coal can retain less gas. This is typically done by reducing the hydrostatic pressure on the coal by removing water. The permeability of coals is typically low; therefore, it is increased by techniques such as fracturing the seam (a technique borrowed from the oil industry). Sufficient pressure is generated in the system to move the methane to the well where it is collected; no suction needs to be applied to the borehole. With no suction applied, there is no air contamination of the methane. Unlike the gas produced in a methane drainage system in a mine, the gas produced by a virgin-coal demethanation system generally contains 95% or more methane. Such a gas has a heat value similar to that of natural gas (37 MJ/m³) and can be co-mingled with it. This gas can be used in all applications for which natural gas is used, except for some chemical processes. Research indicates that techniques are now sufficiently advanced to make a commercial project feasible. A. KAHIL

Coal Gasification, process by which coal is converted into a fuel gas rich in hydrogen and carbon monoxide. The process was first developed in about 1780 and was widely commercialized by the early 1900s. Before natural gas became widely available in the 1940s, many N American and European cities used a coal gas as a heating and lighting fuel. It was referred to variously as blue gas, producer gas, water gas, town gas or fuel gas. Often using the same low-pressure mains for distribution, natural gas replaced fuel gas in most uses by the 1950s because of its greater heating value and lack of contaminants. Recently, however, there has been renewed interest in coal gasification as a means of replacing or supplementing petroleum resources such as natural gas. In many parts of the world, including Canada, coal resources are so large that fuel gas could become a viable alternative fuel if natural-gas resources run low. A fuel gas is also produced as a by-product of coal mining, from COAL DEMETHANATION.

In recent years gasification has been attracting the attention as part of an integrated gasification-combined cycle (IGCC) technology. In this case, the gasifier products are purified to remove acidic compounds and particulates before entering turbines attached to power generators. Because the disposed flue gas is almost free of acidic species and particulates, the IGCC is being considered as the front-running technology to combat ACID RAIN. Interest in this technology is being shown in Alberta, where TransAlta Utilities together with the Alberta Office of Coal Research and Technology (AOCRT) have been evaluating the Kellog, Rust and Westinghouse (KRW) process for gasification of Highvale coal to produce electricity. Gasification R&D activities in Canada are being co-ordinated by the Gasification Technical Committee established on the initiative of AOCRT. The gasification pilot plant (fluidized or spouted

bed reactor) at UBC is being extensively used to test Canadian coals for gasification. The features of this reactor approach those of the KRW gasifier; therefore the test results can determine the coal suitability for this process. At the Canada Centre for Mineral and Energy Technology (CANMET) in Ottawa, the research has focused on gasification characteristics of Canadian coals under fixed and fluidized bed conditions. An entrained bed gasifier is now under construction at CANMET. Gasification research is also underway at the Alberta Research Council. R.W. GREGORY

Coal Liquefaction, process by which coal is converted from its solid state into liquid fuels, usually to provide substitutes for petroleum products. Coal liquefaction was first developed in the mid-19th century, but its exploitation was hindered by the relatively low price and wide availability of crude oil and natural gas. In only a few times and places (eg, Germany during WWII, S Africa since the 1960s) have the economics favoured development of coal liquefaction processes. However, since the oil-price increases of the 1970s and with the growing awareness that conventional supplies are being depleted, there was renewed interest in producing oil substitutes from the world's relatively abundant coal reserves. Owing to the close proximity of large reserves of coal and tar sand BITUMEN in Alberta, the simultaneous processing (co-processing) of these 2 abundant resources may be a viable alternative to direct coal liquefaction. Canadian Energy Developed Inc, a private Alberta company, is proposing to construct a demonstration plant to process Alberta sub-bituminous coal and tar sand bitumen in 1991.

The Alberta Research Council began research into coal liquefaction as early as 1934-35. Since 1980 the council's Coal and Hydrocarbon Processing Dept has had a coal liquefaction and co-processing program. The department shares facilities at a coal research centre, Devon, Alta, with the Western Regional Laboratories of the federal Dept of Energy, Mines and Resources and the federally and provincially funded Coal Mining Research Centre. A $1-million experimental coal liquefaction installation has been established at the Canada Centre for Mineral and Energy Technology at Bell's Corners, near Ottawa. SNC Inc, a Montréal engineering firm, is involved in testing the performance of Canadian coals in existing liquefaction processes. Coal-derived liquid fuels could be an economic proposition for Canada in the beginning of the next century.

Direct liquefaction, in which the coal is first converted into synthesis gas, was developed as a commercial process early in the 20th century. The chemist Friedrich Bergius constructed a pilot plant in Germany in 1922 to liquefy one tonne of coal per day. By 1932, 300 000 t of motor fuel was produced annually from coal in Germany. The direct liquefaction processes used in modern pilot plants are modifications of the original Bergius process. The coal is first ground into particles less than 1 mm in diameter and mixed in equal proportions with petroleum-type solvents, which typically are derived from coal as well. When the mixture is heated to about 475°C in a hydrogen atmosphere at a pressure of about 200 atmospheres, one tonne of coal yields about one-half tonne of liquids and tars. The rate of liquefaction reaction improves as the rank of the coal decreases: lignite gives the fastest reaction; bituminous coal is much slower; the reaction becomes impractically slow as the rank approaches semi-anthracite. The total yield of liquid remains surprisingly constant throughout the coal ranks.

Indirect liquefaction processes also were developed in oil-short Germany early in the 20th cen-

tury. In 1913 the chemical manufacturer BASF announced development of a process for producing a variety of organic chemicals. In the early 1920s, Franz Fischer and Hans Tropsch patented a process called Synthol to produce alcohols, aldehydes, fatty acids and other organic chemicals from a synthesis gas of hydrogen and carbon monoxide, which can be produced from coal gasification. This basic form of reaction has become known as the Fischer-Tropsch (F-T) process. Depending on the reaction conditions and the catalyst employed, the process can produce a variety of products with a wide range of molecular weights. This method was used to produce gasoline-type motor fuel during WWII and has been used by South Africa to produce motor fuels and petrochemical feedstocks since the 1960s.

More recent versions of the F-T process can produce gasoline, plus a few by-products, from methanol; work is also underway to produce diesel fuel from methanol. The main drawback to the F-T process is that it either produces too many by-products or too much water; research centers on new catalysts to improve its efficiency. For direct liquefaction, the key research objectives have been to lower the operating pressures of the processes and to improve the quality and quantity of the products. The goals have been partially met with some new mixtures of catalysts and changes in operating conditions, but no major breakthrough has occurred since WWII.

R.W. GREGORY

Coal Mining Although most of Canada's COAL lies at depths of 300 m or more, much of the coal now mined comes from surface mines. Strip mining is used where gently dipping seams lie close to the surface in relatively flat land; open-pit mining, where thick seams come near the surface in mountains or foothills. As the workings in a surface mine reach deeper, the amount of glacial debris and rock (overburden) that must be removed to expose the coal increases. The volume of overburden that must be moved to extract one tonne of coal, the "strip ratio," is an important factor in deciding the depth to which it is economically desirable to continue working. That depth is also influenced by technical considerations which take into account local geological factors and equipment limitations.

In areas suitable for strip mining, the rock strata above the coal bed are, as a rule, tectonically undisturbed (ie, not folded or faulted) and relatively soft; therefore, little, if any, blasting is needed before the dragline can dig the overburden. Overburden materials are deposited in spoil piles in a previously worked-out cut. Strip mining is widely employed in Alberta and Saskatchewan plains areas and in NB, to provide the coal that fuels nearby ("mine mouth") electric-power generation plants and other industrial installations. After exposure by the dragline, the coal is extracted by electric caterpillar-track shovels or rubber-tired, diesel-driven, front-end loaders, and transferred to bottom-dump trucks which haul it to its destination or to railcars for further transport. In open-pit mines, overburden rock normally requires drilling and blasting before it can be removed by shovels or backhoe excavators and loaded into trucks for disposal in dumps or worked-out pits. Open-pits are always worked down in a series of benches, but where the coal seam has been folded or displaced by a fault, open-pit operations may be severely limited.

In the Rocky Mts and their foothills, coal is mined in the East Kootenay and Peace R coalfields, with mining equipment very similar to that employed in plains strip mines. Rear-dump trucks are used for hauling blasted overburden and coal. The raw coal is taken to coal processing plants where it is prepared for export as metallurgical or high-grade steam coal. Preparation involves cleaning the coal, ie, removing inorganic rock material to meet market specifications, and normally is accomplished by processes using differences in specific gravity between coal and rock. Rock material is discarded and the cleaned coal is dried before loading into unit trains for transport. Typically the unit trains are composed of about 100 specially designed "gondola" cars, each of which can hold 100 t of coal.

Where the limits of surface mining have been reached or the coal is too deeply buried to be extracted in surface workings, underground mining methods are employed. Vertical shafts or inclined roadways, the latter known as "slopes" or "drifts," are driven into the coal seam or contiguous rock strata. How the seam is thereafter developed, and which of the several alternative mining techniques is used, depends on the geological "envelope" in which the coal lies and is also determined by detailed considerations of development costs, mine life, operating costs and operational flexibility.

In the Cape Breton I coalfields, which extend out under the Atlantic Ocean to depths of almost 1000 m and dip at approximately 12°, the shallower coals are only partially extracted. Coal pillars are left in place at predetermined intervals to support the overlying strata and avoid potential breaks from the mine workings through to the seabed. When development has reached sufficient depth, a longwall advance mining technique is employed, in which 200 m long panels are progressively cut, to up to 2 km from the dip slopes. Each panel can yield more than one million tonnes of coal. The coal-cutting machine, a longwall shearer, takes a slice up to one metre wide from the coal face, and a chain conveyor transports the cut coal along the face to a belt conveyor in the main roadway (gate) of the mine. To protect miners from roof falls, hydraulically operated shields and steel roadway arch supports are installed. Holes, drilled into the roof and floor, are connected to pipes to extract methane gas, also called firedamp, which might otherwise constitute an explosion hazard (*see* COAL DEMETHANATION). Water is automatically sprayed wherever coal is being cut or transferred, to eliminate risks of dust explosion and to protect miners against pneumoconiosis (black lung disease). This serious disease, which can result from inhalation of fine dust, used to be the scourge of coal-mining operations, but is now virtually stamped out.

In western Canada, adverse economic conditions forced abandonment of older underground mines in the 1950s and early 1960s, but a strong resurgence of the coal industry since the early 1970s has led to numerous new developments, mainly surface mines. Deep coal is also mined, with access by drifts and slopes. Coal seams in the Rockies are often up to 20 m thick and, in many places, have gradients as steep as 60°. In these circumstances, a variety of different mining methods, sometimes specially adapted to local conditions, must be used.

One operation in the CROWSNEST PASS region of southeastern BC has pioneered hydraulic mining for Canadian coal. The thick, pitching seams are cut by a high-pressure jet of water (monitor jet) and the broken coal, after further crushing at the coal face, is transported out of the mine in metal flumes which carry the coal in suspension in water. The water either flows down the mountainside or is pumped, from beneath the mountain, to a plant which recovers the coal and recycles the cleaned water to the monitor jet. The roof over the worked out part of the coal seam (the so-called "gob" area) is allowed to cave in.

In mines near Smoky R, Alta, with coal seams

2.5-7 m thick, caterpillar-track-mounted coal cutters (continuous miners) are used for room-and-pillar mining. In this system, the coal seam and surrounding rock is cut up into roughly 35 m by 25 m pillars which are removed, and the roof is allowed to collapse into the gob as operations retreat from the outer boundary of the working. During development, the rooms are secured against premature collapse by insertion of expanding roof bolts. The continuous miner cuts the coal and loads it into electric, rubber-tired shuttle cars which deliver it to the belt conveying system that takes it to the surface. This procedure has the flexibility needed for mining in disturbed mountain and foothill terrain but is less productive than longwall retreat mining in which the panels are driven to the far boundary and coal is cut back toward the entrance. It also demands greater skill and judgement of operating personnel.

Although production of underground coal presently represents less than 15% of Canada's total coal output, it is expected that future worldwide coal demand and further advances in mining technology (ie, automation and the introduction of computer-controlled mining operations) will promote increasing dependence on extraction of deep coal. *See also* DISASTERS.

N. BERKOWITZ AND N. DUNCAN

Open-pit coal mine, in Luscar, Alberta (*photo by Harry Savage*).

Coaldale, Alta, Town, pop 4796 (1986c), inc 1952. Shortly after the construction of the CPR line through southern Alberta in the mid-1890s, the railway company named its first rail siding 15 km E of Lethbridge Coaldale. The name came from Coaldale Home, the residence of Elliot T. Galt, a prominent figure in Lethbridge's early coal mining industry, rail interests and land development. However, irrigation farming on the shortgrass prairie, rather than coal mining, has been the dominant economic activity of the Coaldale area. An irrigation company owned by Galt brought water and promised rich grain yields to prospective settlers shortly after the turn of the century. While many of these first farmers came from the US, following WWI a veteran resettlement scheme drew former soldiers from many countries to the wheatlands. This settlement was followed by the Mennonites starting in the mid-1920s, uprooted Japanese Canadians from BC during WWII, and Dutch in the 1960s. The town today is a service centre for surrounding agriculture and a commuter community for Lethbridge.

MARK RASMUSSEN

Coalition Government includes members of different political parties and normally appears during crises such as war or political breakdown. The fluidity of party lines, the predominance of patronage, and the novelty of responsible government led to several experimental coalition arrangements in New Brunswick, Nova Scotia and Canada in the 1840s and 1850s. The best known were in 1854 and 1864 (the GREAT COALITION) in the Province of Canada. The former, which united moderate Reformers and Conservatives, was

the base for the post-Confederation CONSERVATIVE PARTY. The latter joined CLEAR GRIT Liberals, Conservatives and PARTI BLEU to bring about CONFEDERATION, although it had been dissolved by the 1872 election.

The strengthening of party affiliation and the development of the apparatus of a party system since Confederation have made coalitions more difficult to negotiate. At the national level, the only coalition has been Sir Robert BORDEN'S 1917 UNION GOVERNMENT. Faced with strong opposition to conscription and with other major difficulties during WWI, Borden sought to broaden his wartime political base by bringing several conscriptionist Liberals and other public figures into his government. In the Dec 1917 general election, this government won a decisive victory over Sir Wilfrid Laurier's Liberals. The Union coalition did not long survive its triumph: the end of the war brought many Liberals back to their old affiliation while other Unionists supported the new PROGRESSIVE PARTY. With Borden's resignation in 1920, even the pretense of coalition disappeared. The Union government illustrated the dangers of coalition: after 1917, French Canadians associated coalitions with conscription. Indeed, during WWII, proposals for coalitions or a "National Government" came from those who also called for a stronger war effort and conscription. Since WWII there have been few proposals for federal coalition governments.

At the provincial level coalitions have occurred in western Canada. Manitoba Liberals and Progressives combined in 1931, and in 1940 all the province's parties joined a nonpartisan administration formed to meet wartime demands. In BC a wartime coalition between the Liberals and Conservatives held off the challenge of the CO-OPERATIVE COMMONWEALTH FEDERATION. The coalition probably benefited the CCF; it certainly damaged the Liberals and Conservatives, soon supplanted by SOCIAL CREDIT. No coalition has been as successful as the "Great Coalition." Politicians have become so wary of the long-term results of coalitions that they are now most reluctant to introduce them. *See also* MINORITY GOVERNMENT.

JOHN ENGLISH

Coast Mountains are an unbroken mountain chain extending from the FRASER R LOWLANDS near Vancouver, BC, 1600 km N into the Yukon Territory. For most of their length they rise abruptly above a coastal strip, facing the Pacific Ocean with rugged slopes and tremendous relief, most extreme where glacial action cuts FJORDS up to 192 km long (one of only 4 such occurrences in the world). Some glaciers remain, notably around Mt WADDINGTON, highest point in the chain. Ice-age volcanic action created such features as Black Tusk in Garibaldi Provincial Park. Westerly winds drop upwards of 440 cm of precipitation a year on some exposed slopes of the mountains, nurturing rapid growth of coniferous forests. The rainiest spots in the mountains are likely the rainiest places in N America. Timber harvested from accessible areas is boomed or barged to tidewater mills. Copper-molybdenum mines operate intermittently in the Stewart area.   PETER GRANT

Coastal Landform The fundamental coastal landforms are the beach, a depositional feature, and the cliff, an erosional feature. A beach is an accumulation of wave-worked sediments above and below the waterline along the shore. Dynamically, it consists of 3 shore-parallel zones: backshore, only rarely affected by ocean waves; foreshore (beachface), continually subject to wave swash and backwash; and the shallow, subaqueous, nearshore (shoreface), where waves approaching from offshore move substantial quantities of sediment on the bottom. The foreshore on some tidal beaches may be hundreds of metres wide; the nearshore zone commonly extends offshore to depths exceeding 10 m. The overall profile of a beach depends on the size of the constituent material, but variations in wave conditions (daily and seasonal) may result in considerable short-term changes. Gravel and cobble beaches are usually steep; sand beaches are flatter and often exhibit a series of intertidal or subtidal bars or ridges. Beaches range from small, curved pocket beaches, contained between rock headlands, to straight, continuous beaches many kilometres long.

A coastal cliff is a steep, often vertical, face produced by wave EROSION of solid rock. The term bluff is often used for similar features developed in unconsolidated materials. The cliff base is frequently undercut by wave quarrying and abrasion, and may be fretted by caves. Weathering and slope failure are effective processes on the oversteepened coastal slopes above, and geological factors (eg, rock composition, bedding and jointing) are important controls on the rate of erosion and the form of the cliff. Intertidal shore platforms are developed as the cliffline retreats and these platforms are continually lowered by a combination of abrasion and rock weathering. Rock coastlines exhibiting a wide variety of cliff and shore platform morphologies dominate much of Canada's coastline (*see* PHYSIOGRAPHIC REGIONS). These features and the processes that produce them have been little studied.

Canada's mainland coastline, including the islands of Newfoundland, Cape Breton and PEI, is 71 261 km long and fronts on the North Pacific, Arctic and North Atlantic oceans. If all measurable islands are included, the saltwater coastline has been measured at 243 797 km long. There is an additional 3800 km of freshwater coastline along the Great Lakes. The character of any coast depends on a combination of factors, including the relief and geology of the land backing the coastline, the availability of coastal sediments, and the prevailing wave and tidal conditions. For example, deep, steep-walled FJORDS, characteristic of mountain coasts that are glaciated or have recently been glaciated, occur in BC and Baffin and Ellesmere islands. Estuaries, often the drowned lower sections of river valleys, are characteristic of lowland coasts; many small estuaries occur in the Atlantic provinces. In NB and PEI, where there is abundant sand in the shore zone, long, narrow spits and barrier beaches have developed across the mouths of the estuaries. The sand is derived from erosion of soft sandstone cliffs and sandy glacial deposits. Where rivers transporting large volumes of sediment reach the coast, DELTAS may develop.

A coastline is continually changing, not only as a result of short-term, readily observable effects of erosion and deposition, but also in the longer term in response to changes in the relative levels of land and sea. In the last 2 million years, several major fluctuations in world sea level have occurred as immense volumes of water were alternately stored in and released from the continental ice sheets during the Pleistocene glaciations. Coastline position has undergone dramatic shifts as a result of these changes. The most recent rise in sea level began about 18 000 years ago. Very rapid initially, it continues today at a very slow rate. This slow, continuing rise is one of the factors causing the erosion and retreat of sandy, depositional shorelines worldwide.

Large volumes of ice, which accumulated on the continents during periods of glaciation, not only lowered world sea level but also resulted in the depression of the land beneath the ice. With glacial retreat and release of the weight, rock material in and under the Earth's crust adjusted

to the decrease in gravitational stress (isostatic rebound). Coastal areas, initially inundated by the rapid rise of sea level during deglaciation, rebounded and beaches and other shoreline features were progressively elevated above the reach of marine action. Much of Canada's coastline was affected, and raised shorelines are characteristic of many areas, most notably the Hudson Bay Lowlands and Queen Elizabeth Is, where coastal evolution over the last 7000 years has been dominated by isostatic uplift.

The most important coastal processes are associated with water motions in the nearshore environment caused by TIDES and wind-generated waves. The energy contained in breaking waves can erode the strongest rocks, and the speed of wave-induced, longshore ocean currents in the nearshore zone can transport large quantities of sand along the shore. Tides cause a periodic, usually semidiurnal variation in sea level, thereby influencing the width of the zone in which wave processes are effective. Tidal currents transport mud in suspension and, at narrow inlets and in areas with large tidal ranges, attain sufficient velocities to transport large quantities of sand. The headward reaches of the Bay of FUNDY, with the largest tidal range in the world, are dominated by tidal processes as exemplified in the extensive intertidal sands of the Minas Basin. With larger tidal ranges, mud flats and salt marshes become key components of the coastal environment, particularly in protected estuaries and bays. Wind action is significant wherever abundant supplies of sand are available for the development of sand dunes (*see* AEOLIAN LANDFORMS). Salt marshes and dunes illustrate the role of vegetation in the development of coastal depositional landforms. SEA ICE is an important and sometimes overriding factor in zones around the Arctic, Subarctic and parts of the Atlantic coasts of Canada. The presence of sea ice restricts the operation of wave and tidal processes at the shore, and beach morphology may be dominated by the effects of ice push, ice scour and ice rafting.   S.B. McCANN

Reading: S.B. McCann, ed, *The Coastline of Canada* (1980).

Coastal Marine Flora, *see* VEGETATION REGIONS.

Coastal Waters Canada has the longest coastlines of any country in the world (58 509 km excluding islands, 243 797 including all measurable islands). Canadian coastal waters support valuable biological resources (eg, fish, crustaceans, molluscs, marine mammals, seaweeds) and are important for transportation, recreation and the mineral resources in the seafloor beneath them. The mountainous West Coast is characterized by deep FJORDS and large offshore islands which provide shelter for coastal waters (eg, in the Strait of Georgia). The moist, mild climate is influenced by an extension of the Kuroshio Current which moves warm water eastward across the Pacific Ocean. The most important fishes are the 5 species of PACIFIC SALMON, which breed in Canadian rivers but migrate to the sea where they live and grow for several years. For example, after hatching, pink salmon enter the Pacific and swim in the nutrient-rich gyre of the Alaska Current for about a year before returning to the rivers to breed.

North from BC, at the shores of the Arctic Ocean, lies the BEAUFORT SEA, into which flows one of Canada's major rivers, the Mackenzie. The fresh water discharged there forms heavy ice cover for much of the year. The Beaufort Sea has important petroleum deposits but extraction is rendered very expensive by the need

to contend with sea ice. Moreover, navigation is hazardous because of numerous submerged mounds of ice and sediment known as PINGOS.

Arctic surface water flows eastward to Baffin Bay through the Canadian Arctic Archipelago. This maze of waterways contains meagre fish resources, but parts of it (eg, Lancaster Sound) support large aggregations of SEABIRDS and mammals on which the native peoples have traditionally depended. Care must be taken to protect these resources during the extraction and transportation of oil and gas. Emerging through Jones and Lancaster sounds, the flow through the archipelago joins the southward-moving Baffin Current. At Hudson Str, large amounts of fresh water (derived primarily from ice melt and river discharge into Hudson Bay) are injected into the flow which continues S as the Labrador Current. This fresh water stimulates biological productivity in the coastal waters of Labrador, which become progressively more productive from N to S. The seasonal variation in river runoff (peaking in spring when the snow melts) may cause seasonal variation in fisheries production all the way to Newfoundland's GRAND BANKS. Hamilton Bank, offshore from Hamilton Inlet on the Labrador Shelf, is an important COD fishing area. In spring, the pack ice off Newfoundland and Labrador is an important breeding ground for harp and hooded seals.

The Grand Banks, with almost 250 000 km² of water shallower than 200 m, has been known for over 400 years as one of the world's great fishing banks. It is very rich in cod, haddock, redfish, flatfish (including halibut), mackerel and herring. There are substantial oil reserves beneath the seafloor, but their exploitation is made hazardous by the icebergs that drift S in the Labrador Current and by the prevalence of FOG, formed when warm air masses from the S and W encounter cold water from the N.

As the inshore branch of the Labrador Current continues around the S coast of Newfoundland, part of it enters the Gulf of St Lawrence where it joins an inflow from the Str of Belle Isle separating Newfoundland and Labrador. The outflow of the St Lawrence R tends to follow the S shore, producing an anticlockwise circulation in the gulf. Two main factors contribute to high biological productivity in the gulf: its warm summer temperatures and the mixing between surface and deep, nutrient-rich waters. The Gulf of St Lawrence is known particularly for its lobster, scallop, groundfish, mackerel and herring fisheries. Whales and other mammals are also abundant, especially near the N shore. There is important vessel traffic to the Great Lakes, but sea ice is a major impediment to shipping in winter.

The circulation on the SCOTIAN SHELF is dominated by a southwestward coastal current flowing from the Gulf of St Lawrence to the Gulf of Maine. The especially productive offshore edge of the shelf is influenced periodically by warm water masses which pinch off from the Gulf Stream to the S. At the southwestern end of the shelf, strong tidal currents cause a clockwise residual flow around shallow banks which is conducive to survival of larval fishes. Near the coast, tidal mixing and upwelling of nutrient-rich deep water ensures that production of finfish and lobsters is among the best in the province.

The Bay of FUNDY experiences some of the world's highest tides. To understand this phenomenon, the bay must be considered as part of a system encompassing the entire Gulf of Maine and having a natural period of oscillation of about 13 hours. Since the dominant, semidiurnal tidal period is 12.4 hours, tidal waves res-

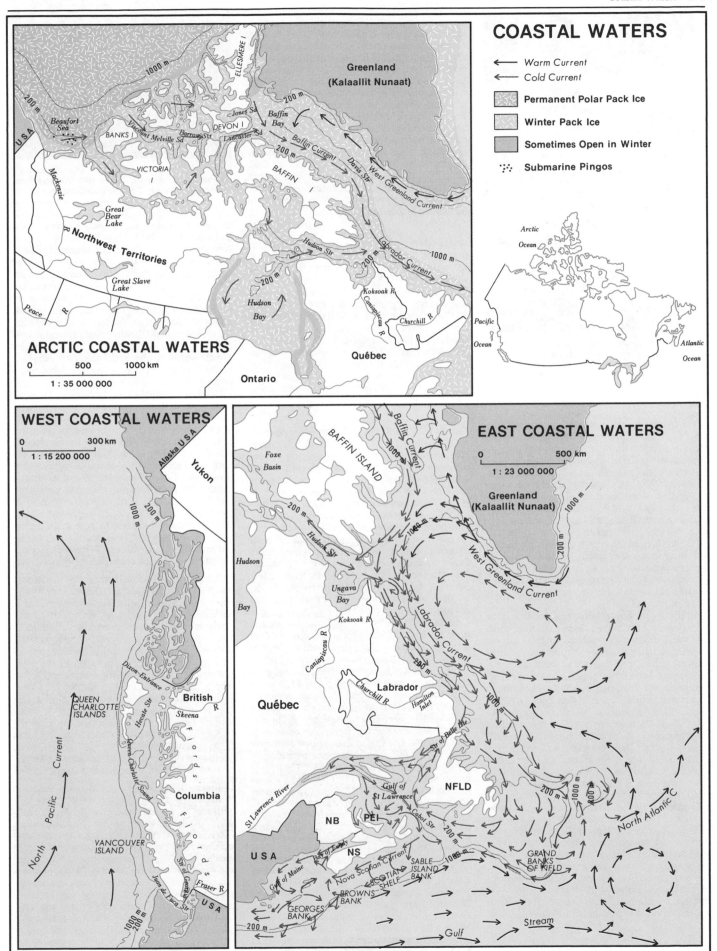

COASTAL WATERS

→ *Warm Current*

← *Cold Current*

Permanent Polar Pack Ice

Winter Pack Ice

Sometimes Open in Winter

⋯ Submarine Pingos

ARCTIC COASTAL WATERS

Greenland (Kalaallit Nunaat)

ELLESMERE I

Jones Sd

Baffin Bay

Beaufort Sea

BANKS I

Viscount Melville Sd

Barrow Str

DEVON I

Lancaster Sd

VICTORIA I

BAFFIN I

Baffin Current

Davis Str

West Greenland Current

1000 m

200 m

Mackenzie R

Great Bear Lake

Northwest Territories

Great Slave Lake

Peace R

Hudson Str

Hudson Bay

Labrador Current

200 m

1000 m

Koksoak R

Caniapiscau R

Churchill R

Québec

Ontario

Pacific Ocean

Arctic Ocean

Atlantic Ocean

0   500   1000 km

1 : 35 000 000

WEST COASTAL WATERS

0   300 km

1 : 15 200 000

Alaska USA

Yukon

Dixon Entrance

QUEEN CHARLOTTE ISLANDS

Hecate Str

Queen Charlotte Sound

Skeena R

Fiords

British Columbia

Fiords

VANCOUVER ISLAND

Strait of Georgia

Juan de Fuca Str

Fraser R

USA

North Pacific Current

1000 m

200 m

EAST COASTAL WATERS

0   500 km

1 : 23 000 000

Greenland (Kalaallit Nunaat)

BAFFIN ISLAND

Baffin Current

Foxe Basin

Hudson Str

Hudson Bay

Ungava Bay

Koksoak R

Caniapiscau R

Labrador

Churchill R

Hamilton Inlet

West Greenland Current

Labrador Current

Str of Belle Isle

Québec

NFLD

Gulf of St Lawrence

St Lawrence River

NB

PEI

Cabot Str

Bay of Fundy

NS

Gulf of Maine

Nova Scotian Current

SCOTIAN SHELF

SABLE ISLAND BANK

USA

BROWNS BANK

GEORGES BANK

GRAND BANKS OF NFLD

North Atlantic C

Gulf   Stream

200 m

1000 m

400 m

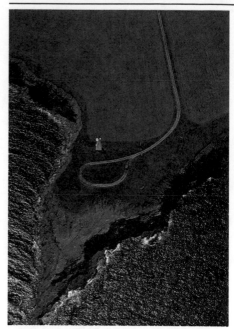

Canada has the longest coastline in the world. For the small portion of our coast which is regularly travelled, an extensive system of navigation aids is required. This unmanned light beacon marks Cape Tryon on the N coast of PEI (*photo by J.A. Kraulis*).

onate in this basin and build to a maximum height in the narrow bay. The vigorous water movement brings the deep, nutrient-rich water to the surface, but the heavy load of sediment stirred up into suspension limits the penetration of light. As a result, the bay's upper reaches have rather low productivity; they are used mainly by shorebirds and migrating shad, but the mouth of Fundy is an important fishing area for scallops and herring, and attracts whales and seabirds. Potentially, the bay's most important economic benefit is for TIDAL ENERGY. After intensive engineering and environmental studies, a pilot project has been constructed on the Annapolis R and the building of a tidal barrage in the upper reaches of the bay is being considered.

Straddling the border between Canada and the US is GEORGES BANK, which has outstandingly high biological productivity, related to tidal mixing and circulation. Bank waters support large stocks of herring, haddock, cod and scallops and it appears that lobster larvae produced there are carried to the southern part of NS, thus ensuring a continuing replenishment of that stock. A recent World Court decision has led to an adjustment of the Canada/US boundary and has resulted in a larger portion of the rich scallop ground in the NE peak of Georges Bank belonging to Canada.

Exploration for hydrocarbons has been active from the Beaufort Sea in the N to Georges Bank in the S (*see* PETROLEUM EXPLORATION AND PRODUCTION). The first field to be commercially exploited will probably be the Hibernia Field on the Newfoundland Grand Banks. In all these areas it will be necessary to strive to prevent exploration, production and transportation of oil and natural gas from harming the extremely valuable fisheries. PASSAMAQUODDY BAY, near the Canada/US border, has been the subject of international controversy because of a proposal to route supertankers through a relatively narrow channel in Canadian waters, en route to a refinery in Maine.

P.C. SMITH AND K.H. MANN

Coates, Wells Wintemute, architect, designer, writer (b at Tokyo, Japan 17 Dec 1895; d at Van-

couver 17 June 1958). Tutored in Japan, he studied engineering at UBC and in London, Eng, where he lived for most of his life. Coates worked there as a journalist before setting up a design practice in 1928. He invented the standard tubular D-handle for furniture, and his industrial design commissions included mass-produced furniture and electrical appliances. He produced a small number of buildings, interiors and exhibition stands in a plain modern style. Founder of the Modern Architecture Research Group, Coates published numerous essays promoting modern design. During WWII, he was awarded an OBE for service co-ordinating British fighter aircraft development. In 1955 he left Britain and taught at Harvard and then returned to Vancouver where he worked as a design consultant.

DAVID R. CONN

Coats Island, 5499 km², one of several islands that guard the northern entrance to HUDSON BAY. Known originally as Cary's Swan's Nest, a name still applied to its SE point, it received its modern name from William Coats, a sea captain who made many voyages into the bay for the HBC 1727-51. For the most part flat or gently rolling, it was believed by early mariners to be joined to the larger SOUTHAMPTON I. During the 1860s, American whalers began to visit the bay and discovered the straits that separate the islands. Uninhabited today, it was probably occupied seasonally by the SADLERMIUT of Southampton I who were annihilated by an epidemic after 1900.

DANIEL FRANCIS

Cobalt (Co), hard, greyish white magnetic metal which melts at 1495°C and which closely resembles iron and nickel. Cobalt is a minor constituent of many of the large copper ore bodies of Zaire and Zambia but its recovery as a by-product has made these ores the leading world source for over 50 years. Small quantities of cobalt are also recovered from copper-nickel sulphide ores. The latter, which are the source of most of the world's nickel, are extensively mined in Canada. Small amounts of cobalt occur in the deposits of oxidized nickel found in many countries, eg, New Caledonia, Zaire, Canada and the US. In Morocco and a few other countries small high-grade deposits of nickel-cobalt arsenides furnish significant quantities of cobalt. Arsenide ores from COBALT, Ont, gave Canada world leadership in production for the period 1905-25. A large potential source of cobalt is the manganese nodules on the ocean floor (*see* OCEAN MINING). The decorative qualities of cobalt compounds, which impart a blue colour to glass and ceramics, have been known for 4000 years. However, it was well into this century before cobalt's remarkable chemical and physical properties were recognized and exploited, eg, in permanent magnets and high-temperature superalloys. Cobalt is essential to livestock, and addition of its compounds to feedstuffs and pastures is widespread where deficiencies occur. The important radioisotope, cobalt-60, produced by neutron bombardment of cobalt metal in a fission reactor, is used as a radioactive tracer in chemical, biological or physical processes and as a source of gamma rays for treatment of cancer. Estimated production in 1986 was 2486 kg, valued at $56.2 million. Most of Canada's output is exported, especially to the US and Europe. R.S. YOUNG

Cobalt, Ont, Town, pop 1640 (1986c), 1759 (1981c), inc 1907, located about 480 km N of Toronto near the Québec border and Lk Timiskaming, lies between the clay belt to the N around New Liskeard and the heavily forested area of Temagami to the S. Extensive mining at the beginning of the 20th century so scarred the earth's surface that today Cobalt is surrounded

Street scene in Cobalt, Ont, around 1910. In the background can be seen the barren rock and slag heaps (*courtesy National Archives of Canada/C-44126*).

by barren rock and slag heaps, with deep craters and mine shafts dug into the hills. In 1903, work crews constructing the Temiskaming and Northern Ontario Ry (ONTARIO NORTHLAND) uncovered silver nuggets on the shore of Long Lk (Cobalt Lk), causing a stampede of prospectors. The town, named for the presence of cobalt in the ore, emerged on the W side of the lake to provide goods and services for the prospectors and mining companies which purchased the land around and under the townsite. The ethnic core of Cobalt was of British and French ancestry, but many people – primarily manual labourers – came from central and E Europe.

Its silver production, ranked 4th in the world in 1910, gave the impetus for exploring the Precambrian Shield. Many who had apprenticed in Cobalt went on to develop the mineral resources of the N. Similarly, the technique acquired to mill Cobalt's silver ore furthered the nation's scientific and technological skills. Cobalt was thus the cradle of Canadian mining, and its success spurred the growth of neighbouring HAILEYBURY and NEW LISKEARD. The silver began to run out in 1914, and today Cobalt is a depressed region, whose future would seem to depend on the development of tourism. The Cobalt Mining Museum and the annual Miners' Festival attract numerous visitors each summer. DOUG BALDWIN

Cobb, Andrew Randall, architect (b at Brooklyn, NY 13 June 1876; d at Halifax 2 June 1943). After studying at Acadia, Massachusetts Inst of Technology, and École des beaux-arts, Paris, Cobb travelled in Italy, returning to Halifax in 1909 and establishing his practice there in 1912. He was responsible for many of Halifax's important residential, commercial and institutional buildings, including the Dingle Memorial Tower with S.P. Dumaresq (1912); the Bank of Nova Scotia Headquarters Building with John M. LYLE (1931); and the Science Building (1913), MacDonald Library (1913), Law School, now the Faculty Club (1921), and Public Archives (1929), all at Dalhousie. In 1940 he was elected a fellow of the Royal Inst of British Architects.

GRANT WANZEL AND KAREN KALLWEIT

Cobham, Eric, pirate (*fl c*1740-60). Based in Newfoundland about 1740 to 1760, Cobham, a native of Poole, Eng, and his wife, Maria Lindsay, plundered shipping in the Gulf of St Lawrence, their crimes undetected because they sank nearly every vessel captured and murdered the crews. Cobham retired to an estate in France and was appointed a magistrate. Maria, reputedly a sadist who delighted in bizarre executions, eventually went insane and died by her own hand or Cobham's. Before his own death, Cobham dictated his life story, which was evidently published posthumously. His heirs tried to suppress the book, but a fragmentary copy survives in the Archives nationales, Paris. *See also* PIRACY.

EDWARD BUTTS

Cobourg, Ont, Town, inc 1837, pop 13 197 (1986c), 11 385 (1981c), located on N shore of Lk Ontario, 112 km E of Toronto. Founded as a LOYAL-IST settlement 1798 by Eluid Nickerson, Joseph Ash and Asa Burnham, it was originally called Amherst but was renamed Cobourg (1819), in honour of the marriage of Princess Charlotte to Prince Leopold of Saxe-Cobourg.

By 1817-18 more settlers began to arrive, many of them half-pay officers and retired North West Co traders. By the 1830s Cobourg emerged as an important regional centre possessing a fine harbour and a populated hinterland. It received a further boost (1842) when Victoria College, established in 1835 by the Wesleyan Conference, was granted powers to confer degrees; the college remained in Cobourg until 1892. Meanwhile, civic leaders hired a prominent architect, Kivas TULLY, to design an ornate town hall. Victoria Hall, completed 1860, survives as one of the most magnificent mid-Victorian structures in Ontario; a courtroom is a replica of London's Old Bailey.

In the 1850s, Cobourg citizens also financed construction of the Cobourg and Peterborough Ry, an ambitious enterprise designed to "capture" the hinterland. But the railway proved a failure, partly because of a tenuous bridge across Rice Lk, almost bankrupting the town in the 1860s. By the 1870s, however, wealthy Pittsburgh steel barons became interested in the railway and Marmora iron mines, which they later bought. Up to the stock market crash wealthy Americans built palatial summer homes in the area, making Cobourg one of the most fashionable summer colonies in the continent. After 1870, population showed little growth until after WWII. Today, it contains about 50 industrial firms and is also a tourist centre.

J. PETRYSHYN

Cobourg and Peterborough Railway One of the 2 earliest railway charters granted in Canada, the Cobourg Rail Road Co was incorporated in 1834 to build a railway from COBOURG northward to Peterborough across Rice Lk. The project was shelved until 1846, when it was revived as the Cobourg and Rice Lake Plank Road and Ferry Co. Samuel Gore built his plank road the 17 km to the lake, but it barely survived the first 2 winters. The Cobourg and Peterborough Railway, incorporated 1852, was similarly ill fated. Construction began in 1853 but a cholera epidemic ravaged the German immigrants who had signed on for $1 a day. The Rice Lk bridge – at nearly 5 km long the longest in N America – was largely completed by the end of 1853. It consisted of a long trestle set on piles, with 33 truss spans (24 m each) and a 36 m swing section in the navigation channel. The bridge could not survive the grinding and shifts of winter ice and extensive repairs were required every spring; in 1860 the visiting Prince of Wales was not allowed to cross the bridge for fear it would collapse. The following winter the bridge disintegrated entirely and with it faded Cobourg's hopes of becoming a thriving port. Its citizens had put up over $1 million for their 48 km railway. It was merged with the Marmora ironworks in 1866. The Peterborough to Rice Lk section eventually came under the control of the GRAND TRUNK RAILWAY.

JAMES MARSH

Coburn, Frederick Simpson, painter, illustrator (b at Upper Melbourne, Qué 18 Mar 1871; d there 25 May 1960). Coburn is known primarily as a painter of winter scenes of horses and sleighs emerging from a forest into a clearing, the majority executed after about 1916 in the Eastern Townships of Québec. From about 1890 until 1916, Coburn resided in Europe, where he enjoyed a lucrative career as an illustrator, his reputation having been established in 1897 with the highly successful illustrated publication of *The Habitant* by the Canadian poet W.H. DRUMMOND. In addition to 4 other volumes of Drummond's poetry, Coburn illustrated literature by such well-known authors as Louis-Honoré Fréchette, Washington Irving, Charles Dickens, Edgar Allan Poe, Alfred Lord Tennyson and Robert Browning. His later oils and etchings are bathed in a bright Canadian winter light in contrast to the heavy, sombre palette of his illustrations, which betray a European influence.

ELIZABETH H. KENNELL

Cochrane, Alta, Town, pop 4190 (1986c), 3544 (1981c), inc 1971, is located 35 km NW of Calgary, on the BOW R. It is named for Sen M.H. COCHRANE, who founded (1881) the Cochrane Ranch, which was declared a Prov Historic Site 1977. Cochrane became a CPR shipping point for cattle and is still a farming and ranching centre. Recently, it has become a dormitory town for Calgary. There is a weekly newspaper, the *Cochrane This Week.*

ERIC J. HOLMGREN

Cochrane, Ont, Town, pop 4662 (1986c), 4848 (1981c), inc 1910, located 375 km NW of North Bay. Named after the Hon Francis Cochrane, then Ontario minister of lands, forests and mines, the town was established 1908 at the point where the Temiskaming and Northern Ontario Ry (ONTARIO NORTHLAND) intersected with the NATIONAL TRANS-CONTINENTAL RAILWAY. Destroyed 3 times by fire during its first 8 years, Cochrane grew slowly as a railway-construction and repair centre, and in its early years also attracted a few farmers, lumbermen and merchants. More recently, it has become an important tourist centre, serving as departure point for the Polar Bear Express, Ontario Northland's train excursion to MOOSONEE on James Bay. Its single, largest year-round employer is Cochrane Enterprises Ltd, a plywood and planing mill. Cochrane is the judicial seat for the Cochrane District.

MATT BRAY

Cochrane, Charles Norris, historian, philosopher (b at Omenee, Ont 21 Aug 1889; d at Toronto 23 Nov 1945). He was educated at U of T (BA, 1911) and Corpus Christi Coll, Oxford, and was appointed to the Faculty of Ancient History at U of T in 1919. A classical historian by profession, but a deeply tragic thinker by heart, Cochrane devoted his life to an intellectual meditation on the failure of reason to secure a "permanent and enduring" basis for civilization. He was haunted by the insight that in the absence of a principle of "creative integration," Western civilization was doomed to oscillate between idealism (animal faith) and naturalism (the detritus of skepticism). Cochrane's principal book, *Christianity and Classical Culture* (1940), is a study of the emergence of Christian metaphysics from the ruins of (Roman) civilization. It argued that Augustine provided a coherent philosophy of civilization, overcoming the fatal deficiency of the classical experience: its absence of a principle of "creative integration." Among his other publications was *Thucydides and the Science of History* (1929). An unappreciated thinker, especially in his native Canada, Cochrane must be considered among the leading 20th-century philosophers of civilization.

ARTHUR KROKER

Cochrane, Matthew Henry, cattle breeder, businessman (b at Compton, Lower Canada 11 Nov 1823; d there 12 Aug 1903). Born of Irish immigrants, Cochrane went to Boston as a young man and prospered in the leather and shoe business, an enterprise he continued in Montréal after his return to Canada in 1864. Though his success brought a senatorship in 1872, his first interest was cattle breeding and by the 1870s his pedigreed Shorthorn herd was internationally renowned. Cochrane was largely responsible for the federal grazing-land policy upon which the western cattle-export industry was built (*see* DOMINION LANDS POLICY). The arrival in 1881 of the great Cochrane herd from Montana at the senator's vast grazing lease west of Calgary marked the beginning of the cattle company era in the Canadian West.

DAVID H. BREEN

Cockburn, Bruce, singer, songwriter (b at Ottawa 27 May 1945). After playing in Ottawa rock bands (The Children, Esquires, Three's A Crowd), he became a folksinger, with a humanist, poetic style combining elements of jazz, rock and reggae, emerging as an international artist by the end of the 1970s. His records include *Sunwheel Dance, In the Falling Dark* and *Dancing in the Dragon's Jaws.* He has written songs in English and French, including "Goin' to the Country," "Musical Friends," "Laughter" and "Prenons la mer"; some have been recorded by other artists (Anne MURRAY, Tom Rush). Songs such as "If I Had a Rocket Launcher" showed the increasing political content of his music after his experiences in El Salvador. In 1986 in 2 benefit concerts he raised $35 000 to help the Haida in their land claims struggle; that year as well he produced *World of Wonders. Waiting for a Miracle* (1987) is a retrospective double album of singles 1970-87.

MARK MILLER

Cockburn, James, politician, FATHER OF CONFEDERATION (b at Berwick-upon-Tweed, Eng 13 Feb 1819; d at Ottawa 14 Aug 1883). He was educated in Berwick and, after his family immigrated to Canada in 1832, at Upper Canada Coll. After admission to the bar of Upper Canada in 1846, he moved to Cobourg where, with little success, he practised law and participated in various business enterprises. He represented Northumberland W in Parliament 1861-74 and 1878-81. A Conservative after 1863, he was appointed solicitor general in Mar 1864. He retained his place in the GREAT COALITION and attended the QUEBEC CONFERENCE. In 1867 he was demoted and served as Speaker of the House of Commons until 1873. "An inferior man" according to Liberal Alexander MACKENZIE, Cockburn spent his last years in a genteel poverty that was relieved by occasional bits of Tory patronage.

DONALD SWAINSON

The Gate of the Citadel (c 1830), watercolour on paper by James P. Cockburn (*courtesy Musée du Québec/photo by Patrick Altman*).

Cockburn, James Patterson, soldier, topographic painter (b at Woolwich, Eng 1778-79; d there 1847). He learned painting from Paul Sandby at the Royal Military College, Woolwich, and had published numerous books before his arrival in Québec around 1826. He travelled widely throughout BNA and his precise depictions, particularly those of Québec City and Montréal, are treasured records of early Canada. He published *Quebec and Its Environs* in 1831 and brought out a folio of prints of Niagara and Québec 2 years later. *See also* TOPOGRAPHIC PAINTERS.

JAMES MARSH

Cockroach, swift-running, flattened, oval-shaped insect belonging to order Dictyoptera. Although in their native regions they live outdoors, several species are important domestic pests. Of the 3500 species known worldwide most are tropical and subtropical. Only 10 occur in Canada, of which 7 have been introduced through commerce and immigration. Most common are the 5 cm long American cockroach (*Periplaneta americana*), the 2-5 cm Oriental cockroach (*Blatta orientalis*), and the up to 2 cm German cockroach (*Blattella germanica*). The last is the most common urban species. All are general feeders, nocturnal in habit, guided by long antennae while scavenging in kitchens, bathrooms, cellars, restaurants and moist, warm places. Three or 4 species of wood cockroach (*Parcoblatta*) live in leaf litter and debris outdoors in Ontario and western Québec. After mating, the female produces 20-50 eggs that are retained in a leathery case (ootheca) projecting from the genital chamber. In some species, eggs hatch within this chamber, receive nourishment from the mother, and nymphs emerge alive. Nymphs grow slowly, molt as often as 13 times, and mature in 3-12 months. Adults live for several years. Cockroaches not only contaminate and destroy food but also carry disease-causing bacteria and secrete foul-smelling matter. A few have symbiotic protozoa or bacteria in the gut to help them digest wood and other vegetation.

P.W. RIEGERT

Cod, common name for fishes of class Osteichthyes, order Gadiformes, family Gadidae. This large family contains about 55 species of mostly bottom-living fishes, which, except for the Holarctic, freshwater burbot (*Lota lota*), are found in cool seas. In Canada, 21 species occur in Atlantic waters, 4 in Pacific. The family includes many important food fishes, eg, haddock (genus *Melanogrammus*), pollock (*Pollachius*), Pacific cod (*Gadus macrocephalus*), cusk (*Brosme*), hakes (*Urophycis* and *Antimora*), tomcods (*Microgadus*), whitings (*Merlangus*) and rocklings (*Motella*). Cods have elongate bodies, large heads with strong mouths and long dorsal and anal fins. Most species have a single, fleshy barbel (hairlike projection near the tip of the lower jaw).

The most important Canadian cod, the Atlantic cod (*Gadus morhua*), is heavy bodied, with a large head, 3 dorsal fins, 2 anal fins and an almost square caudal (tail) fin. Scales are small and smooth. The lateral line is pale. It may weigh up to 90 kg but usually averages 3-4 kg. Colour varies from grey or silvery green to brown or red, depending on bottom type and locality. The head and body are covered with many brown to reddish spots. Atlantic cod occurs on both sides of the N Atlantic. Off the N American coast, it ranges from Cape Hatteras to Hudson Str off W Greenland, but reaches greatest abundance off Newfoundland and Labrador. The closely related Pacific cod ranges from central California waters to the Bering Sea.

Spawning usually occurs during cool months, but exact time depends on water temperature and location of spawning grounds. On the GRAND BANKS, spawning occurs Apr-June, and on Nantucket Shoals, Oct-Feb. Atlantic cod are prolific: a 100 cm long female may produce about 5 million buoyant eggs. Hatching time depends on water temperature, and may take several weeks. Young cod grow at different rates in different areas: the colder the temperature, the slower the rate of growth. Young cod eat PLANKTON and bottom creatures, but adults are voracious and feed mainly on other fishes (eg, capelin, herring). Atlantic cod, one of the world's leading food fishes, has been fished on the Grand Banks for centuries. It is caught by vessels from many countries using otter, line or pair trawls, hand lines, jigs, Danish seines, traps and gill nets. The flesh is sold fresh, frozen, salted or smoked. Most of the catch is now frozen, but salted cod, once the most popular form, was esteemed in many countries. *See also* FISHERIES.

W.B. SCOTT

Cod Liver Oil was in the past a primary source of vitamin A, essential for bone growth, health of skin and mucous membranes, night vision, etc. Today, many other preparations containing vitamin A are available. Before the 1920s, most cod liver oil came from Norwegian COD. In 1924 William Harrison, Ontario sales manager of a Canadian drug company, became interested in a report that liver oil from cod caught off the Grand Banks of Newfoundland was a much richer source of vitamin A than the Norwegian oil. In Jan 1925 Harrison and associates, W.A.S. Ayerst, Hugh McPherson and W.J. McKenna, incorporated as Ayerst, McKenna and Harrison Ltd. Letters of patent not only granted the company rights to "produce, manufacture, purchase, sell, import, export chemicals, drugs and medicines of all kinds," but also some rights it never used, eg, "to sell snuff, spices, leaf tobacco, cheroots, shellacs, and crockery."

By Apr 1925 the company had 16 employees and immediately started researching the preparation of liver oil from Newfoundland cod. Its first department of biology consisted of a chicken-wire fence stretched from floor to ceiling. White rats were bought at $5 a head and were fed a normal diet fortified with cod liver oil. The experiment was a success. The white rats visibly thrived on the experimental supplementary diet. For the first time the potency of cod liver oil could be determined, regulated and assured. As soon as the new product became commercially available, Canadian physicians enthusiastically prescribed it; soon it was also sold in the US and worldwide. In 1929 Ayerst introduced the first cod liver oil concentrate in capsule form, under the brand name Alphamettes, a product still available in Canadian pharmacies.

ELVIRA STAHL

Cody, Henry John, clergyman, educator (b at Embro, Ont 6 Dec 1868; d at Toronto 27 Apr 1951). Educated at U of T, he was ordained a Church of England priest in 1894. He served at St Paul's Church, Toronto, for 40 years, the last 25 as rector. Appointed a canon of St Alban's Cathedral in 1903 and archdeacon of the diocese of York in 1909, he repeatedly turned down offers of a bishopric from a number of Canadian dioceses. During WWI Cody became a vocal supporter of PM BORDEN's government in Ottawa and the HEARST government in Toronto, while championing imperialism and a stronger war effort. He joined the Conservative Hearst administration as minister of education in 1918, resigning as MPP on its defeat in 1919. Cody was determined to use the schools in building a postwar society on the traditional foundations of Protestant Christianity, political conservatism and Anglo-Saxon racial superiority. While in office, he strengthened attendance requirements and promoted the cadet movement and patriotism in the schools.

Cody had a long connection with U of T. He was appointed to the provincial royal commission on the university in 1905 and chaired the 1922 commission on university finances. In 1917 he was appointed a member of the university's board of governors, and from 1923 to 1932 served as chairman. He was president of U of T 1932-44 and its chancellor 1944-47.

ROBERT M. STAMP

Cogswell, Fred, poet, editor, translator (b at East Centreville, NB 8 Nov 1917). In 1952 Cogswell joined the English dept at UNB, where he had been educated, and remained there 3 decades. He was long an important figure in maintaining the region's distinctive poetic tradition, both as a teacher and as editor of *The Fiddlehead* 1952-67. He also has national importance as founder and long-time proprietor of Fiddlehead Books, a series of poetry chapbooks especially hospitable to, but by no means limited to, young writers. Cogswell's early interest in Québecois verse, manifest in *One Hundred Poems of Modern Quebec* (1970) and other similar translations, has connected him to a larger movement. His own poetry, best represented in *Immortal Plowman* (1969) and *Pearls* (1983) but available in several selected and collected editions, is characterized by adherence to old conventions, a love of craftsmanship and an unhurried, lightly ironic tone. Recent work includes *Meditations* (1986). He has been professor emeritus, U of New Brunswick, since 1983 and is a Member of the Order of Canada. He is a man of letters in the best sense.

DOUG FETHERLING

Cohen, Jacob Laurence, lawyer (b at Manchester, Eng 1898; d at Toronto 24 May 1950). Immigrating with his family to Canada in 1908, Cohen supported his mother and 5 younger children after his father's death in 1911. He attended night school, worked as a law clerk and in 1918 graduated from law school. Associated with the ALL-CANADIAN CONGRESS OF LABOUR and the WORKERS' UNITY LEAGUE in the 1920s and 1930s, he turned to labour law and civil liberties, becoming the most influential labour lawyer in Canada. He was the union's counsel in the 1937 OSHAWA STRIKE and in major labour disputes during WWII. He sat on many conciliation boards and, as a member of the National War Labour Board, supported labour's right to organize and bargain collectively. Cohen was made a KC in 1937. Though disbarred in 1947 for assaulting his secretary and causing bodily harm, he was reinstated by the Law Society in 1950.

LAUREL SEFTON MACDOWELL

Cohen, Leonard, poet, novelist, songwriter (b at Montréal 21 Sept 1934). Cohen was one of the most influential and popular 1960s Canadian writers and his songs gained him an international reputation. He came from a wealthy Westmount family, and Montréal's atmosphere is pervasive in his writings, though he has also lived for extended periods in Greece and California. He attended McGill and Columbia but has spent most of his life as a full-time writer and performer. His first book of poetry, *Let us Compare Mythologies*, appeared in 1956. His major creative period was the early to mid-1960s, the highlights being, in poetry, *The Spice-Box of Earth* (1961) and *Flowers for Hitler* (1964), and in fiction, *The Favourite Game* (1963) and *Beautiful Losers* (1966). His first record, *The Songs of Leonard Cohen*, was issued in 1968 and there have been 7 subsequent albums. He won a Governor General's Award (1968) but declined it. His work in the 1970s was sporadic and hesitant: *The Energy of Slaves* (1972) is made up of "anti-poems," rejecting his own stance and stature as a poet; *Death of a Lady's Man* (1978) is diffuse and fragmentary. His recordings, however, have continued to be of a high quality, especially *New Skin for the Old Ceremony* (1974) and *Recent Songs* (1979). More recently, *Book of Mercy* (1984) and the record *Various Positions* (1985) reaffirmed the richness of his language, and reintroduced a tone of religious awe and veneration. Cohen's work has been widely translated; he is especially popular in France and Germany.

Leonard Cohen, one of Canada's most influential and popular poets and songwriters (*courtesy Ron Watts/First Light*).

Although the popular conception is of Cohen as a romantic love poet – author of the lovely lyrics of *The Spice-Box of Earth* – his imaginative vision is dark and despairing. As a Jew, Cohen has always been acutely aware of the Holocaust, and images of the Nazi genocide permeate and condition his work. Poetry, religion, sex, death, beauty and power form an interlocked pattern, heightened by the sensuousness of his language, and also emphasized by a wild, outrageous and black sense of humour. Cohen celebrates the destruction of the self and the abnegation of power. The harshness of this vision reaches its peak in *Beautiful Losers*, itself an extraordinary novel which is by turns historical and surreal, religious and obscene, comic and ecstatic; it remains the most radical (and beautiful) experimental novel ever published in Canada. The songs tend to be gentler, less absolute in their vision. If *Beautiful Losers* is Cohen's masterpiece, perhaps the most concise statement he has ever made of his central vision occurs in the last verse of his song "The Window," from *Recent Songs*:

Then lay your rose on the fire
The fire give up to the sun
The sun give over to splendour
In the arms of the High Holy One
For the Holy One dreams of a letter
Dreams of a letter's death
Oh bless the continuous stutter
Of the word being made into flesh
Only Leonard Cohen could conceive of the process of the Word being made Flesh as a stutter – and only Cohen could bless that insight.

STEPHEN SCOBIE

Reading: Stephen Scobie, *Leonard Cohen* (1978).

Cohen, Matt, author (b at Kingston, Ont 30 Dec 1942). Raised and educated in Ottawa before entering U of T (BA, 1964; MA in political science, 1965). Cohen has published 2 volumes of poetry, *Peach Melba* (1974) and *In Search of Leonardo*

(1986); and 4 collections of short fiction, *Columbus and the Fat Lady* (1972), *Night Flights* (1978), *Café Le Dog* (1983) and *The Expatriate: Collected Stories* (1982). These stories have secured him an international reputation as they have been translated into numerous languages. He has also published one children's book, *The Leaves of Louise* (1978), 2 novellas, *Korsoniloff* (1969) and *Johnny Crackles Sings* (1971) and 7 novels. The Salem Quartet, including *The Disinherited* (1974), *The Colours of War* (1977), *The Sweet Second Summer of Kitty Malone* (1979), and *Flowers of Darkness* (1981), is set in the fictional town of Salem, just north of Kingston, Ont. *Wooden Hunters* was published in 1975. The historical novel, *The Spanish Doctor* (1984), was his first attempt to deal with his Jewish heritage. The novel *Nadine* (1986) is also a coming to terms with his Jewish past. Both novels attempt to reconcile science with religion, a contemporary and universal imperative for Cohen.

SHARON DRACHE

Cohen, Maxwell, lawyer, scholar, jurist, public servant (b at Winnipeg 17 Mar 1910). After serving as a major in the Canadian Army, Cohen began his teaching career in 1946 at the Faculty of Law of McGill where he eventually became dean. There Cohen developed the National Programme which, in its day, uniquely combined the teaching of civil and common law. He also played an important role in reforming Canadian university government and he pioneered in the creation of specialized legal studies institutes. Nationally Cohen served as chairman of 5 royal commissions, notably the Special Committee on Hate Propaganda, and acted as a constitutional adviser to the New Brunswick government. Internationally, he has represented Canada as representative to the United Nations and Canadian chairman of the Canada-United States International Joint Commission. Cohen is currently judge ad hoc of the International Court of Justice in The Hague and scholar-in-residence at U of Ottawa.

WILLIAM KAPLAN

Cohen, Morris (Moishe) Abraham, "Two Gun," China hand and SOLDIER OF FORTUNE (b at London, Eng 3 Aug 1889; d at Salford, Eng 11 Sept 1970). An unruly youth, Cohen was sent to Canada, to a farm in Saskatchewan where he learned how to handle horses, guns and cards. He moved to Edmonton in 1912 where his skills as a gambler and as a real-estate promoter earned him a small fortune. In frequent contact with the law, Cohen was to change his life after a meeting with Dr Sun Yat-sen, father of the Chinese revolution. Cohen became a member of the Chinese National League and acted as its English-language secretary in Alberta. He represented Chinese interests to all levels of government, attempting, among other things, to combat the growing anti-Asian sentiment. He was invited to China in 1922 to serve as one of Sun Yat-sen's bodyguards and because of his habit of carrying more than one handgun was nicknamed "Two Gun." After Sun's death in 1925, Cohen was granted a pension and the rank of general. He remained close to Chinese politics for the next 2 decades, notably in Canton where he was involved in banking and in arranging arms deals with Western countries. Interned by the Japanese in Hong Kong in 1941, he was later repatriated to Canada. Following the communist victory in 1949, Cohen, persona grata in both Beijing and Taipei, made efforts at reconciliation – all of which failed. A man of great humanity and charm, Cohen in life came very close to matching the legends that flourished around him.

BRIAN L. EVANS

Reading: Charles Drage, *The Life and Times of General Two-Gun Cohen* (1954).

Cohen, Samuel Nathan, theatre critic, radio and TV broadcaster (b at Sydney, NS 16 Apr 1923; d at Toronto 26 Mar 1971). As Canada's only "national" theatre critic in the 1960s, travelling across the country for the Toronto *Star*, and as the only serious reviewer of drama in performance in Canada 1946-71, Cohen set the standards for Canadian theatre during its first quarter century of real growth following WWII. He entered Mt Allison U at 16; his erudition and radical editing of the university newspaper fascinated and enraged the authorities. After studying law briefly at U of T, he returned to the Maritimes to edit the mine union paper Glace Bay *Gazette* for 2 years. In the mid-1940s he wrote for communist newspapers in Toronto, began writing play reviews and attracted the attention of Mavor MOORE, who recommended him as a regular theatre critic for CBC Radio. Cohen broke with the effusive praise and uncritical approach that marked current criticism in Canada and forced the country to differentiate between amateur and professional performances for the first time. He enraged Canadians by mercilessly attacking plays, playwrights and performers, while cheering on promising new talents and theatres. Cohen also edited CBC radio scripts and was host of CBC TV's first successful discussion program, "Fighting Words." He was a colourful and controversial personality, both loved and hated for his profound integrity; his untimely death at the age of 47 was a blow to a Canadian theatre just entering its adolescence. The renaissance of alternative theatres and playwrights across Canada in the 1970s owed much to his critical acumen and standards.

ALLAN M. GOULD

Coinage Coins are small metal tokens issued, usually by governments, for use as MONEY. A quantity of coins issued at one time, or a series of coins issued under one authority, is called a coinage. Canada's complex political history has meant that Canadian numismatists (coin collectors) have an astonishing variety of coins and coinages to collect and study.

French Regime

The first coins struck for use anywhere in Canada were the famous "GLORIAM REGNI" silver coins of 1670, struck in Paris for use in all French colonies in the New World. Few specimens have been found in Canada; the piece of 15 sols is especially rare. In 1672 the value of these coins was raised by one-third in a vain attempt to keep them in local circulation. None were in use after 1680. In 1717 there was an attempt to produce a COPPER coinage for the French colonies but few were struck because of the poor quality of the available copper. In 1721 and 1722 an issue of copper coins of 9 deniers was struck for all French colonies and a large shipment was sent to Canada. There was considerable resistance to their circulation and, in 1726, most of the coins, which had lain unissued in the treasury at Québec City, were returned to France.

These coinages were inadequate for Canada's needs and French coins were shipped out annually. The treasure recovered from the wreck of the French supply ship *Le Chameau* (lost in a hurricane off Cape Breton I in 1725) was intended to supply the colonial governments at Québec and Louisbourg. The authorities at Québec also issued various kinds of paper money (*see* PLAYING CARD MONEY), eventually far too much of it, and at times had to permit the use of Spanish dollars and their subdivisions.

British Regime

For the first 50 years after the Conquest (1760), the British did almost nothing to provide coin,

Lower Canada halfpenny, 1837, reverse (left) and obverse (right) (*courtesy Currency Museum, Bank of Canada/Jas. Zagon*).

New Brunswick halfpenny, 1854, obverse (left) and reverse (right) (*courtesy Currency Museum, Bank of Canada/Jas. Zagon*).

One-penny token, Nova Scotia, 1856, obverse (left) and reverse (right) (*courtesy Currency Museum, Bank of Canada/Jas. Zagon*).

other than sending an occasional shipment of badly worn copper withdrawn from circulation in Britain. Gold coins consisted of British guineas and, later, sovereigns, some American eagles, French louis d'or, Spanish doubloons (and fractions thereof), and small quantities of Portuguese gold. Silver coins comprised mostly Spanish coins struck in Mexico and S America, some old French silver circulating in Lower Canada, and a sprinkling of English silver elsewhere. American silver appeared after 1815. Copper coins were an insufficient and dwindling supply of battered, worn-out, English and Irish halfpennies dating from the reign of George III, supplemented by locally issued and imported tokens and by small numbers of American cents and various foreign coins. Anything the size of a halfpenny would pass for one in Montréal between 1820 and 1837.

Prince Edward Island During this period, various tokens were in use. Large numbers of lightweight halfpenny tokens circulated from about 1830 till well after 1860. The most numerous were the "SHIPS COLONIES & COMMERCE" halfpennies and tokens inscribed "SUCCESS TO THE FISHERIES" or "SELF GOVERNMENT AND FREE TRADE."

Nova Scotia In 1813 certain Halifax businessmen began importing halfpennies into NS and, by 1816, a great variety was in circulation. The government ordered their withdrawal in 1817. Beginning in 1823, and again in 1824, 1832, 1840 and 1843, the government issued a copper coinage, without authority from England. In 1856 NS issued one of the most beautiful of the Canadian colonial coinages, with the permission of the British government.

New Brunswick An anonymous halfpenny appeared in Saint John about 1830. In 1843 the government issued copper pennies and halfpennies without authority from England. These were followed in 1854 with another coinage, this time

they were issued with the permission of the British authorities.

Lower Canada had the greatest number and variety of tokens in circulation. The Wellington tokens, a series of halfpenny and penny tokens with a bust of the duke of Wellington, appeared about 1814. They were popular and many varieties were issued locally after 1825. In 1825, a halfpenny of Irish design was imported; its popularity resulted in its being imitated in brass and these copies are very plentiful. In 1832 an anonymous halfpenny of English design appeared and was extensively imitated in brass. Then a Montréal blacksmith began to counterfeit the worn-out English and Irish George III copper and large numbers of these "Blacksmith tokens" circulated. This period ended in 1835 when the banks refused to accept such nondescript copper, except by weight.

The BANK OF MONTREAL circulated sous or halfpennies with a bouquet of heraldic flowers on one side and the value in French on the other. These sous were immediately popular and the government allowed the bank to supply Lower Canada with copper; however, the sous were very soon imitated anonymously. The imitations were accepted because they bore French inscriptions; but they became too numerous and, once again, the banks had to refuse them, except by weight. To replace them, the government authorized 4 banks, the Bank of Montreal, the Quebec Bank, the City Bank and La Banque du Peuple, to issue copper pennies and halfpennies with the arms of Montréal on one side and a standing habitant on the other. These coins arrived in Canada just as the Rebellion of 1837 began and were issued in 1838.

Upper Canada first used local tokens after 1812, when a series of lightweight halfpennies was issued in memory of Sir Isaac BROCK. These coins were superseded after 1825 by a series of tokens with a sloop on one side and various designs (eg, plow, keg, crossed shovels over an anvil) on the other. In 1822 a copper twopenny token was issued by Lesslie & Sons. The firm also issued halfpennies from 1824 to 1830. There were no government issues in Upper Canada.

When the 2 Canadas were reunited in 1841, the Bank of Montreal was allowed to coin copper; pennies and halfpennies appeared in 1842. Halfpennies were issued again in 1844. After 1849 the BANK OF UPPER CANADA received the right to coin copper and large issues of pennies and halfpennies appeared in 1850, 1852, 1854 and 1857. The Quebec Bank was allowed to issue pennies and halfpennies in 1852.

There was little need for coinage in the territories controlled by the Hudson's Bay Company; the fur trade depended primarily on barter, although brass tokens (*see* MADE BEAVER) served the purpose of coinage. In colonial BC, very few coins were in circulation. Copper was not used because prices were too high: nothing less than a dime was of any use. Small shipments of English silver and gold were sent to BC in 1861 and these coins, with American coins, were used until after Confederation. A proposed gold coinage was not made for fear of committing a breach of the Royal Prerogative, although a few patterns were struck.

The decimal system was first adopted by the Province of Canada (southern parts of today's Québec and Ontario) in 1858, based on a dollar equal in value to the American dollar. American silver had become very plentiful and trade with the US made it necessary to adopt a decimal system. NB and NS followed in 1860; Nfld, in 1863; PEI, in 1870. The coinage of the province of Canada consisted of silver 5-, 10- and 20-cent pieces and bronze cents. NS issued bronze cents and half cents in 1861 and 1864, cents alone in

One-cent decimal coin of Queen Victoria, 1882, obverse (left) and reverse (right) (*courtesy Currency Museum, Bank of Canada/Jas. Zagon*).

Upper Canada halfpenny, 1883, obverse (left) and reverse (right) (*courtesy Currency Museum, Bank of Canada/Jas. Zagon*).

Five-cent decimal coin of George VI, 1937, obverse (left) and reverse (right) (*courtesy Currency Museum, Bank of Canada/Jas. Zagon*).

Sterling silver $10 piece, struck to commemorate the 1976 Montréal Olympics reverse (left); $100 gold piece, reverse (right) (*courtesy Currency Museum, Bank of Canada/Jas. Zagon*).

1862; NB, cents in 1861 and 1864, and silver coins like the Canadian ones in 1862 and 1864; PEI issued a cent in 1871. Newfoundland's coinage began in 1865. All of these coins became legal tender in the Dominion of Canada after the various provinces entered Confederation.

1870 to Present

The first coins of the Dominion of Canada, issued in 1870, were silver 5-, 10-, 25- and 50-cent pieces. Bronze cents were added in 1876. All coins bore on the obverse the head of Queen Victoria. Silver coins bore the value and date in a crowned maple wreath on the reverse; the cent bore the value and date in a circle enclosed by a continuous maple vine. These coins were variously issued till 1901. In 1902 the crowned bust of Edward VII replaced the head of Queen Victoria. In 1911 the crowned bust of George V replaced that of Edward VII.

In 1920 the cent was reduced in size and, in 1922, the 5-cent piece was first coined in NICKEL. In 1942 and 1943 the 5-cent piece was coined in tombac, a copper-zinc alloy (the so-called "blackout" nickel) because of wartime nickel shortages. In 1935 the silver dollar was first coined to commemorate the silver jubilee of the reign of

George V. This dollar inaugurated a very popular series of Canadian coins. Except for the war years 1939 to 1944, silver dollars were coined every year until 1967. Special commemorative dollars were struck in 1939 for the royal visit to Canada; in 1949, for the entry of Newfoundland into Confederation; in 1958, for the centenary of the creation of the Crown Colony of British Columbia; in 1964, for the centenary of the Charlottetown Conference and the Quebec Conference; and, in 1967, for the centenary of Confederation.

In 1937 a completely new coinage was introduced after George VI ascended the throne. For the first time each denomination had its own pictorial reverse design. With some modifications, the same designs are on today's coinage. All denominations bore a splendid bare head of George VI. The reverse of the cent shows 2 maple leaves on a common twig; the nickel, a beaver chewing a log on a rock; the dime, a schooner closely resembling the famous *Bluenose;* the quarter, the head of a caribou; the 50-cent piece, the Canadian coat of arms; the dollar, 2 voyageurs in a canoe, with a wooded islet in the background.

There had never been a great need for gold in Canada, as American gold coins supplied domestic needs. Some sovereigns were struck at the Ottawa mint variously from 1908 to 1919. From 1912 to 1914 there was an attractive coinage of gold $5 and $10 pieces. The only other circulating gold coinage in Canada was the Newfoundland issue of $2 pieces, struck variously from 1865 to 1888. Plans to reissue gold coins in 1928 were stopped (*see* GOLD STANDARD). Special issue gold coins were struck in 1967, and annually since 1976, for sale to collectors.

In 1953 a bust of Elizabeth II replaced the head of George VI, and in 1965 was replaced by the portrait now in use, a draped bust of the Queen wearing a tiara. In 1967 a special coinage, commemorating the centenary of Confederation, was issued. Each coin bore the bust of the Queen on the obverse. The cent featured a dove in flight; the 5-cent piece, a hare; the 10-cent piece, a mackerel; the 25-cent piece, a bobcat; the 50-cent piece, a howling wolf; and the dollar, a Canada goose in flight. The motifs were created by artist Alexander COLVILLE. In the summer of 1967 the silver content of the dime and quarter were reduced from 80% to 50% and production of 50-cent pieces and dollars for general circulation was stopped. In 1968 the regular designs were resumed, the dime and quarter being in 50% silver. In Aug 1968 nickel replaced silver entirely for general circulation and a reduced 50-cent piece and dollar were coined in nickel. In 1987 a dollar coin was introduced to replace the dollar bill, which will be discontinued in 1989. The new coin is 11-sided and struck in nickel-plated tombac, and weighs 7 grams.

Beginning in 1950, special sets of coins for collectors were issued, ie, early strikings from the dies, handled with more care to ensure that they would not be marred. In 1953 the sets were mounted on a white card enclosed in cellophane. From 1961 they were heat-sealed in pliofilm. Silver dollars were also sold separately to collectors until 1965. Nickel dollars were sold separately, in special cases, beginning in 1970. In 1971 commemorative dollars were struck in 50% silver and sold in individual cases. Issued each year since, they commemorate special events. Special sets of sterling silver $5 and $10 pieces were struck from 1973 to 1976 to commemorate the 1976 Olympic Games, held in Montréal. The first gold $100 piece, struck in 1976 for the same event, is the first of a beautiful series of gold coins struck annually. From 1985 to 1987 a series of 10 sterling silver $20 pieces was struck to commemorate the 1988 Winter Olympic Games held in Calgary.

Canadian Rarities

The rarest Canadian decimal coins are the 50-cent piece of 1921, the 5-cent piece of 1921, the dotted 1936 cent and 10-cent pieces, the 10-cent piece of 1889, the 50-cent piece of 1890 and the 10-cent piece of 1893, with a round-topped 3. Most of the strikings of 1921 were never issued. After remaining in the vaults of the mint for some time, they were melted down. The dotted 1936 coinage was intended to be an extra issued from the 1936 dies to supply Canada's needs, pending the arrival of the 1937 dies. A hole punched into the bottom of the reverse dies produced the dot. Very few specimens are known. The other coins mentioned are rare because the coinages of those years were very small. *See also* MINTING.

R.C. WILLEY

Colas, Réjane L., née Laberge (b at Montréal 23 Oct 1923), m Emile Colas 1958. After studies at Villa Maria and Coll Marguerite-Bourgeois (BA), she received a law degree at U de Montréal. Member of the bar (1952-69) and of the Canadian Bar Association, she was part of the Geoffrion & Prud'homme legal study (1957-69) and named judge of the Superior Court. She became Queen's councillor in 1968. Among her many responsibilities, she was treasurer (1978-82) and president (1982-84) of the general committee of judges of the Québec Superior Court. She also served as chairman of the family law committee for the Québec section of the Canadian Bar Assn (1967-68) and was founding chairman of the Fédération des femmes du Québec (1966-67) and an active member of the Fondation Thérèse Casgrain.

MARTHE LEGAULT

Colborne, Sir John, 1st Baron Seaton, soldier, colonial administrator (b at Lyndhurst, Eng 16 Feb 1778; d at Torquay, Eng 17 Apr 1863). Colborne entered the British army in 1794 and distinguished himself at Waterloo (1815). From 1821 to 1828 he was lieutenant-governor of Guernsey and on 3 Nov 1828 assumed office as lieutenant-governor of Upper Canada. Colborne vigorously promoted public works and immigration and saw the colony's population increase by 50% between 1830 and 1833. Yet by showing considerable favouritism to the newer immigrants from Britain and diverting public funds in unpopular ways, he contributed to the popular unrest that culminated in the reform victory in the 1834 election and ultimately to the Upper Canadian REBELLION OF 1837. Early in 1836 Colborne was recalled as lt-gov but placed in command of the British forces in the Canadas. He personally led his troops in suppressing the 1837 insurrection in Lower Canada. He briefly acted as governor general from Nov 1838, until he was officially gazetted mid-Dec 1839. He crushed the second rebellion which erupted in Lower Canada in Nov 1838 with great severity. In Oct 1839 he returned to Britain and was elevated to the House of Lords, where he spoke against the Act uniting the Canadas. He was lord high commissioner of the Ionian Islands 1843-49 and commander of the forces in Ireland 1855-60. PHILLIP A. BUCKNER

Cold Lake, Alta, Town, pop 3195 (1986c) 2110 (1981c), inc 1955, is located on a lake of the same name, 290 km NE of Edmonton. The Cree named the lake for its deep, cold waters. Settlement commenced in 1910 and increased when a CPR branch line arrived (1928). A Canadian Forces base was established here in WWII and afterwards became a testing range as well as a training base for jet pilots. The base also houses a satellite tracking unit for NORAD. Cold Lake has been a centre of oil exploration, and in 1985 Esso Resources Canada Ltd began production of heavy oil nearby. Esso is only part of a heavy-oil megaproject which was shelved during the recession of the early 1980s and which has now been reinstated. The industry now employs several hundred personnel. The area is also a popular fishing resort and tourist centre with Saskatchewan's Meadow Lake Prov Pk nearby. ERIC J. HOLMGREN

Cold War, the term applied to the cool relations, roughly 1947-53, between the Western powers (including Canada and Britain, and led by the US) and communist countries dominated by the USSR. It was precipitated by the reluctance of the US and Britain to accept the extension of Soviet control and communist one-party systems over eastern Europe at the end of WWII. It now seems that each side was irrationally fearful of the other's apparent intentions. Canada's position was determined by its experience of Russian spying at the end of WWII (the GOUZENKO case); its detestation of the totalitarian Soviet regime; and its economic, cultural and strategic links to the US and Britain. For most of the Cold War both sides were convinced that ordinary diplomatic negotiations were pointless because there was no possibility of agreement or common interest on any important topic. The Cold War eased with the death of the Soviet dictator Joseph Stalin in 1953, and serious diplomatic discussions were then resumed.

ROBERT BOTHWELL

Coldstream, BC, District Municipality, pop 6872 (1986c), inc 1906, lies in the valley of Coldstream Creek, about 2 km SE of VERNON. Cpt Charles F. Houghton, the first settler in 1863, acquired his title through a military grant. His Coldstream Ranch, named for cold springs which rise on it, was transferred to Forbes G. and Charles A. Vernon and in 1891 was bought by the earl of ABERDEEN (gov gen, 1893-98). Aberdeen had large acreages of fruit trees and hops planted; by 1908 the estate had 800 acres of orchards. To encourage settlement Aberdeen subdivided part of the property which was sold in small parcels, but the Coldstream Ranch Ltd still owns 7675 acres, of which almost 2000 are under cultivation, including 108 acres in orchard. Agriculture, however, is no longer the main occupation in Coldstream; most residents work in nearby Vernon, although the Consumers Glass Co factory, with 500 workers, is the largest industrial employer in the northern OKANAGAN, and lumber mills provide local jobs. DUANE THOMSON

Coldwell, Major James William, "M.J.," teacher, politician (b at Seaton, Eng 2 Dec 1888; d at Ottawa 25 Aug 1974). One of the founders of the CO-OPERATIVE COMMONWEALTH FEDERATION, he succeeded J.S. WOODSWORTH as national CCF leader, 1942-60. Coldwell came to Canada as a teacher in 1910; he stayed briefly in Alberta and then moved to Regina. He first achieved national prominence as a leader in teachers' organizations, 1924-34. Also a popular alderman in Regina, he developed strong links with socialist labour and farm organizations. When the Great Depression came, he was a natural choice for leader of the new Saskatchewan Farmer-Labour Party in 1932 (which became a part of the CCF) and fought a strenuous campaign in the Saskatchewan general election of 1934, attracting enormous crowds; but the party sent only 5 members to the legislature against 47 Liberals. Himself defeated, Coldwell moved to the national scene.

As MP for Rosetown-Biggar (Sask) 1935-58, he was a polished performer in the House of Commons from the first. He disagreed with Woodsworth (who was a pacifist) on the war in 1939, and Coldwell and the majority of the CCF supported Canada's participation in WWII. His support of collective security was reinforced and he was a member of the Canadian delegation to the founding of the United Nations in 1945. He presided over both the peak of CCF support in the mid-1940s and its slow decline throughout the 1950s, leading the party in 5 general elections. His views seemed to moderate as more of the CCF's social welfare program was implemented by other governments, but he remained convinced of the need for a democratic socialist party. He was named to the Privy Council of Canada in 1964 and made Companion of the Order of Canada in 1967.   CARL WENAAS

Reading: M.J. Coldwell, *Left Turn, Canada* (1945).

Coleman, D'Alton Corey, railway executive (b at Carleton Place, Ont 9 July 1879; d at Montréal 17 Oct 1956). After acting as private secretary to Senator George Cox in 1897 and as editor of the Belleville *Intelligencer*, Coleman joined the CPR in 1899. He advanced rapidly and before turning 40 was put in charge of CPR's western lines. He presided over a great expansion in which 3520 km of track were added in branch lines. In 1934 Coleman became VP of the whole company and, as the health of president Sir Edward BEATTY deteriorated, increasingly took over his duties. Coleman was appointed president in 1942 and chairman in 1943. The company was then engaged not only in railway work but in war production, shipping and air traffic; under Coleman, Canadian Pacific Airlines was organized. He retired in 1947.
                                  ROBERT BOTHWELL

Coleman, James, journalist (b at Winnipeg 30 Oct 1911). Jim Coleman began his career in 1931 working at the *Winnipeg Tribune*. After a brief career with the *Edmonton Tribune* and the *Edmonton Bulletin*, he went to Toronto to write for the *Globe and Mail*. When his column was syndicated in 1950, he became the most widely read sports columnist in Canada. During his career he also wrote for Canadian Press and the Southam Press, retiring in 1983. His autobiography, *Hoofprints on My Heart* (1971), reflected his love for horse racing. *Hockey is Our Game* (1987) reflected on 50 years of avid hockey viewing. From 1952 to 1962 he was the publicity director for the Ontario Jockey Club. In retirement he held for 3 years the same position at Calgary's Stampede Park. His awards include the Order of Canada, Canadian News Hall of Fame, Canadian Horse Racing Hall of Fame and Canada's Sports Hall of Fame.
                                  J. THOMAS WEST

Coles, George, merchant, businessman, politician (b in PEI 20 Sept 1810; d at Charlottetown Royalty, PEI 21 Aug 1875). The son of a farmer, Coles began business as a merchant in 1833. He soon focused on brewing and distilling, although he was also active in other businesses in the Charlottetown area, and became a prominent capitalist in the colony. In 1842 he was elected to the House of Assembly as a Tory. By 1847 he had joined the Reformers, and by 1849 was leader of the struggle for RESPONSIBLE GOVERNMENT. He became the Island's first premier under that system, serving 3 times between 1851 and 1868. His first administration was his most successful, extending the franchise to virtually all adult males, abolishing tuition fees and local taxes for district schools, and enabling the government to purchase large landed estates and sell them to the occupying tenants and squatters. In 1868 Coles left the premiership because of the apparent onset of premature senility. He had been the outstanding Island parliamentarian of his era, dominating the Assembly with his quick native intelligence.
                                  IAN ROSS ROBERTSON

Colicos, John, actor (b at Toronto 10 Dec 1928). He has played classical and contemporary roles on the major stages of England, the US and Canada. His earliest professional work was with the Montreal Repertory Theatre. In 1951 he was selected best actor at the DOMINION DRAMA FESTIVAL. He acted in England as a member of the Old Vic Company, before beginning his career in the US in 1956. He joined the American Shakespeare Festival, Stratford, Conn, in 1957 for 2 seasons. Between 1961 and 1964, Colicos appeared at the STRATFORD FESTIVAL, playing the title roles in *King Lear, Timon of Athens* and *Cyrano de Bergerac*. Two roles on which Colicos has placed indelibly his intensity and strength as an actor are Musgrave in John Arden's *Serjeant Musgrave's Dance* and Winston Churchill in *Soldiers* by Rolf Hochhuth. He has appeared in numerous television and film dramas with much praise for his role of Lord Beaverbrook on CBC in 1976 and as Thomas Cromwell in the film *Anne of the Thousand Days* (1971). Other films include *Drum* (1976), *The Changeling* (1980) and *The Postman Always Rings Twice* (1981).   JAMES DEFELICE

Collected Works of Billy the Kid, The, by Michael ONDAATJE, won the 1970 Governor General's Literary Award for prose and poetry. Ondaatje's hauntingly disturbing evocation of the life and death of the 19th-century American outlaw placed him in the forefront of the new generation of Canadian poets emerging in the 1970s. *The Collected Works* commences with a list of 20 men killed by Billy the Kid and a foreshadowing of his own death. Using a highly visual, visceral poetic style, featuring violent surreal images of madness and men killed in gun fights, shifts in time and perspective, and impressionistic fragments of Billy's existence, Ondaatje traces his capture, escape and eventual death at the hands of Pat Garrett, the "ideal assassin." Following the publication of *The Collected Works* by HOUSE OF ANANSI in 1970, a stage adaptation received a dozen major productions across Canada.
                                  ANTON WAGNER

Collective Bargaining, a method of jointly determining working conditions, between one or more employers on one side and organized employees on the other. The normal outcome is a collective agreement outlining terms and conditions of employment as well as issues such as union recognition, grievance procedure and special committees. Each side tries to convince the other of the validity of its stand and uses whatever pressure and means of persuasion it can command within a closely prescribed legal framework, which may include recourse to STRIKES, LOCKOUTS and ARBITRATION. In N America a union must be certified as a bargaining unit, ie, prove it has the support of an absolute majority (50% + 1) of the employees before it may represent them in collective bargaining. Government administrative tribunals in all provinces have the power to verify the representative nature of the unions and may call for a vote to determine whether a majority of employees in a specifically defined bargaining unit wish to be represented by a union. In all provinces, an increasing number of aspects of the bargaining process are prescribed by legislation. The federal government has jurisdiction only over federally regulated industries, eg, transportation and broadcasting.

Collective bargaining is essentially a power struggle between 2 mutually dependent parties with very different interests. Historically, management has sought a greater degree of control over the workplace and employees have sought security, as reflected in the issues of wage rates, job security and working conditions. Anything not contrary to law may be written into a collective agreement, which can run 1-3 years. Union achievements at the bargaining table, often the result of a strike, commonly become part of legislation. After an autoworkers' strike in 1947, the basic principle of union recognition was established. Medical insurance in union contracts preceded national medicare, pensions preceded universal pension plans, safeguards against discrimination preceded human rights legislation.

Governments have decided that it is in the public interest to permit and even encourage collective bargaining, and they have legislated the format of the procedures and the requirements for workers who wish to use them. They have also sought to minimize the negative effects of these conflicts by providing the mechanisms of conciliation, or LABOUR MEDIATION, by regulating the use of the right to strike and of the lockout, and by demanding arbitration. The Industrial Disputes Investigations Act (1907), the first such formal intervention, resulted from an Alberta mineworkers' strike. Privy Council Act 1003 (1944), which established certification, bargaining, union recognition and final dispute settlement guidelines, has been a model for most subsequent provincial statutes. When 2 sides fail to reach an agreement, they may turn to a mediator from the Department of Labour to help them reconcile their positions. Some provinces require the 2 sides to submit to arbitration before resorting to a strike or lockout.

Although most unionized employees have a legally recognized right to strike, sometimes precisely defined waiting periods must be observed before a strike or lockout may begin. In numerous cases governments have suspended strikes, and occasionally lockouts. Certain groups, forbidden the right to strike, must submit their dispute to binding arbitration by a tribunal whose decision is final. In some provinces this restriction is imposed on "essential" services, eg, fire and police; in others (Alberta and Ontario) on employees of all crown agencies. The Québec government, upon request, can extend a collective agreement to cover all employers and employees in a given trade and area. The Loi des décrets de convention collective (SRQ 1964, c 143) authorizes the lieutenant-governor-in-council to do this when it thinks an agreement's terms have acquired major significance and importance for a whole trade or industry, the objective being to prevent unfair competition within an industry or trade between employers whose workers are unionized and those whose workers are not, and are therefore usually receiving lower wages.   JEAN BOIVIN

Collectivism, a group of ideologies, political, social and religious movements which argue that man is by nature co-operative, not competitive. Collectivism has taken many forms in Canadian history. The settlement process forced people in each stage of colonization to work together at building "bees" and road construction, and at overcoming adversities. The pioneer years were characterized, therefore, as much by mutual aid as by individualism. Intellectually, collectivism has many diverse roots. French Canadians, LOYALISTS and many 19th-century immigrants specifically rejected the 18th-century liberal, individualist philosophy common in the US. As the social evils of industrialization and urbanization unfolded in the later 19th century, many Canadians saw the basic problem as an excess of individualism. Early labour movements, farm organizations such as the Grange and Patrons of Industry, church reform groups (*see* SOCIAL GOSPEL) and even professional groups advocated collective protection against the changes of the age.

In politics, collectivist perspectives have been argued most vigorously by a series of socialist parties since the late 19th century. In the 20th, the

NEW DEMOCRATIC PARTY (successor to the CO-OPERATIVE COMMONWEALTH FEDERATION) and the COMMUNIST PARTY have been the main proponents of collectivism. The CO-OPERATIVE MOVEMENT, in its more idealistic institutions, has advocated an economic restructuring of society on a collectivist basis. Many religious and immigrant groups have also established their communities along collectivist lines. These include MENNONITES, HUTTERITES and DOUKHOBORS. English, Scottish and Finnish groups have also developed collectivist communities, particularly on the Prairies and the West Coast. During the 1960s, hundreds of young people organized communal settlements. Though seldom perceived as a major force in Canadian history, collectivism – instinctive or deliberately structured – has been a common response and remedy to contemporary problems.

IAN MACPHERSON

Collège classique Unique to French-speaking Canada, the *collège classique* (classical college) has over the centuries prepared Québec's social and intellectual elite for higher education. The first COLLÈGE DES JÉSUITES was established in New France by Jesuit missionaries in 1635. Though the Jesuit school did not survive the British Conquest in 1760, its legacy lived on. At the close of the 19th century, 24 classical colleges were in existence. In 1966-67 a record number of 98 colleges were in operation across the province. Yet a few years later these private, fee-paying institutions had all but disappeared, a casualty of a government policy that judged them ill-suited to a society committed to educational modernization.

Until its demise the classical college constituted the only avenue open to French Canadian boys and girls aspiring to university. Most colleges offered an 8-year program of academic studies divided into 2 stages of 4 years each: a secondary school course and a collegiate course, in effect the undergraduate program of the arts faculty of a French-language university. The BA was awarded upon completion of the program and permitted the holder to enrol in the university proper. Because the colleges were administered and staffed by the Roman Catholic clergy, their curriculum showed a pronounced religious and literary bent. Drawing from the example of early Jesuit traditions, students studied Latin, Greek and the writings of the ancients, and took courses in modern languages, philosophy, mathematics and religion. These disciplines were judged not only proper for the Christian but also essential for the development of his or her intellect.

ROGER MAGNUSON

Collège d'enseignement général et professionnel (CEGEP) Québec's first COMMUNITY COLLEGES of general and professional training [known in English and French by their acronym, "CEGEP"] opened their doors in 1967. Bill 21, which created the CEGEPs, also established the Commission of Collegiate Instruction within the Superior Council of Education. According to the legislature, this institution of post-secondary, pre-university education was established to provide interested secondary-school graduates with general training aimed at developing a critical sense and a spirit of analysis, synthesis and creativity, and with specialized training by concentration on studies of a limited number of disciplines or through preparation for a professional career.

The Royal Commission of Inquiry on Education in the Province of Québec (Parent Report) released in the 1960s, proposed the establishment of a level of studies beyond high school, 2 or 3 years in length and complete in itself, and clearly distinct from both secondary schooling and university education. The 2-year course would constitute a preparatory stage for university, and the 3-year course would lead to professional qualifications. These institutions, it was hoped, would raise the average level of scholarship, meet strong demands for education, raise the level of professional studies for technicians by integrating the studies into a multidisciplinary college, and remove from the university level all nonuniversity general or professional training.

The CEGEPs, as free and public institutions, were considered, along with the multidisciplinary secondary schools, to be a major part of the scholastic reforms of the 1960s. These reforms were inspired by the principles of democratization and equality of opportunity, of cultural pluralism and adaptation to the realities of an advanced industrial society.

The number of CEGEPs increased from 5 in 1967 to 46 in 1987 (4 of them anglophone). In 1985 some 137 000 students were enrolled in CEGEPs, which employ about 8900 teachers. Approximately 40% of students are from the lower socioeconomic levels of society.

Each college is administered by a board of administration consisting of teachers, parents, students, government representatives, local community representatives and college administrators.

Québec's CEGEPs offer 6 programs of general university preparation: health sciences, pure sciences, applied sciences, human sciences, administrative sciences, and arts and letters. They also offer 140 programs of professional training within 5 general categories: biological techniques, physical techniques, human techniques, administrative techniques and artistic techniques.

A training program consists of 12 obligatory courses (4 in language and literature, 4 in philosophy and 4 in physical education), 12 hours of concentration in a general-training program or specialization in a professional-training program, and 4 complementary courses. Those who succeed in these studies – most require a 60% average – receive a diploma of collegiate studies (DEC).

During the 1960s and 1970s post-secondary institutions in Québec, as elsewhere, were in ferment, shaken by challenges to authority and to traditional teaching. This ferment, accompanied by the demands of a radical teachers' union, created some dismay in certain parts of Québec's population.

The growth of CEGEPs has been accompanied by a continuing debate about (among other issues) their orientation, administrative structure and main pedagogic thrust. This debate led to the Rocquet Report on the pedagogic regime (1970), the Nadeau Report on student needs (1975), and the White Paper on collegiate training issued by the Québec Ministry of Education in 1980. The Rocquet Report recommended pedagogical changes according to which all students would be obliged to take courses in certain subject areas: mathematics, natural sciences, human sciences (philosophy, language, literature) technology, second language and physical education. In the White Paper the government announced its intention to render obligatory courses in the history and economy of Québec, as well as in philosophy, language, literature and physical education. The government has not implemented these changes, but in 1979 some of the aspects of Bill 21 were revised and the Council of Colleges was created.

The CEGEPs have maintained their original objectives and distinctive characteristics (generalized access to higher education for all levels of society, a diversified range of programs, the regionalization of educational resources, the establishment of organic ties with local communities and nonscholastic circles) and are now emphasizing the need for the rationalization of the collegiate network, the evaluation of each institution (eg, the administrative and pedagogic functioning and results) and an improved response to adult needs.

M. CLAUDE LESSARD

Collège des Jésuites During the Counter-Reformation, the Jesuits wished above all to attract Christian youth by creating colleges throughout Europe. Arriving in Canada in 1625, they received a gift from the marquis de Gamaches to establish a college in Québec City. The doors opened in 1635 and the course of study was complete 30 years later. In 1668, Mgr LAVAL, bishop of Québec, founded the SÉMINAIRE DE QUÉBEC to prepare future priests for his diocese and sent his students to study at this neighbouring Jesuit college. The Collège de Québec taught theology and the sciences as well as classical studies. As they had already done in several coastal cities in France, the Jesuits in 1708 opened a hydrography school where they taught mathematics, astronomy and physics to prepare young Canadians for jobs as navigators and surveyors.

An estimated 1700 students attended the Collège de Québec, more than half of them being students from the Petit Séminaire. These pupils were drawn much more from the Québec than from the Montréal region. Louis JOLLIET is one of the most famous alumni of the college. The professors all came from France. Scholastics, students of theology, came in their twenties to teach the grammar classes for 2 or 3 years before returning to France. The priests came in their thirties and spent at least a quarter century in New France, alternating between their roles as professor and missionary to the Indians. Some devoted themselves entirely to education. The college had among its professors Fr Pierre-François-Xavier de CHARLEVOIX, once Voltaire's master, whose *Histoire et description générale de la Nouvelle France* was published in Paris in 1744.

The college was built after 1640 in the style of such colleges in France, with 4 right-angled wings around an interior courtyard. An exterior chapel was added in the early 18th century. In 1759 the college became the barracks of the British army and was destroyed after their departure to make way for the present city hall.

CLAUDE GALARNEAU

Collège dominicain de philosophie et de théologie, Ottawa, was founded 1909 by the Order of Friars Preachers in Canada and recognized as a *studium generale* of the Order. In Mar 1967 it was granted a civil university charter by the province of Ontario, which conferred on the Academic Council the power to grant university degrees in theology and philosophy. There are 3 departments: pastoral studies (in Montréal) and philosophy and theology (both in Ottawa).

G.D. MAILHIOT

Collegiate, or collegiate institute, is a type of SECONDARY SCHOOL originally required to meet certain minimum standards regarding the number and qualifications of its teachers and its student enrolment in the classics. Within a decade of their introduction in the early 1870s, Ontario's collegiate institutes became markedly less classical, thereby becoming, in effect, high schools under another name. In general, the term no longer distinguishes one type of secondary school from another.

WILLARD BREHAUT

Collier, Ronald William, composer (b at Coleman, Alta 3 July 1930). An important participant as composer and trombonist in the Canadian third-stream movement, spearheaded by his teacher Gordon Delamont in Toronto, Collier subsequently wrote for radio, TV and film. His major compositions include *The City* (1960), *Hear Me Talkin' To Ya* (1964), *Carnaval* (1969) and *Humber Suite* (1973). His *Aurora Borealis* and *Silent Night, Lonely Night* were recorded in 1967 by Duke Ellington with a Toronto orchestra under Collier's direction; writing collaborations between Collier and Ellington followed. Collier began teaching at Humber Coll, Toronto, in 1974.   MARK MILLER

Collin, William Edwin, literary critic (b at Oakenshaw, Eng 9 May 1893; d at London, Ont 21 Dec 1984). His *The White Savannahs* (1936, repr 1975), a modernist study of 9 Canadian poets, established him as a major Canadian critic. Collin applied the ideas of such writers as T.S. Eliot, Sir James Frazer and the French Symbolists to Canadian poetry. A fine prose stylist, he also wrote a study of Paul-Jean Toulet and many articles and reviews, including from 1941 to 1956 the yearly review of French Canadian literature for the *U of T Quarterly*.   TRACY WARE

Collingwood, Ont, Town, pop 12 172 (1986c), 12 064 (1981c), inc 1858, located on Nottawasaga B at the southern end of GEORGIAN BAY, 55 km NW of Barrie. A battle site where the Huron tried to fight off invading Iroquois 1649-50, it was first settled by Europeans in 1835. The name commemorates Admiral Collingwood, Nelson's second-in-command at the Battle of Trafalgar. The Ontario, Simcoe and Huron Ry, later part of the CNR, arrived in 1855. The site of several scenic caves of limestone rock, it has an excellent harbour, surveyed by Sandford FLEMING, and has long been a shipbuilding centre for the Great Lks. Auto parts and home furnishings are also manufactured. It is now a popular winter ski resort and is famous for its Blue Mountain pottery, made from local red clay and originally manufactured after WWII by Jozo Weider, a Czechoslovakian refugee.

DANIEL FRANCIS

Collins, Enos, merchant, privateer, banker (b at Liverpool, NS 5 Sept 1774; d at Halifax 18 Nov 1871). Enos went to sea as a cabin boy on one of his father's fishing vessels, becoming master of a trading ship before he was 19. He sailed on privateers to the West Indies and in 1811 he bought the *Liverpool Packet,* one of the most famous privateers, which may have captured prizes worth a million dollars in the WAR OF 1812 (*see* PRIVATEERING). He sent ships loaded with provisions to Spain for Wellington's army during the Peninsular War and sold their cargoes at a handsome profit. In Halifax Collins bought ships and cargoes at auction; he stored the cargoes in a stone warehouse on the waterfront, one end of which became the Halifax Banking Company, a private bank nicknamed Collins's Bank, which still stands as part of Historic Properties. A shrewd businessman, he was reputedly "the wealthiest man in the Lower Provinces."

PHYLLIS R. BLAKELEY

Collins, Ralph Edgar, diplomat (b at Kunming, China 23 Nov 1914). An officer in the Dept of External Affairs, 1940-79, known for his brilliance in finding the right words to suit any occasion, Collins rose to be ambassador to S Africa and assistant undersecretary. He was an acknowledged China expert, having served there in WWII, and twice headed External Affairs' Far Eastern Division. Collins was Canada's first ambassador to the People's Republic of China, serving 1971-72.   ANNE HILLMER

Collins, Steve, ski jumper (b at Thunder Bay, Ont 13 Mar 1964). Trained in Thunder Bay, he burst into international prominence by winning the World Junior 70 m Championship in 1980 and went on to victories in a World Cup meet and an International Ski Flying Championship later the same year. Collins, who started skiing when age 4, has placed in the top 20 at several World Cup events. In 1985 he won his first national 90 m ski jumping title at the Export A Canadian Championships at Thunder Bay.   MURRAY SHAW

Collip, James Bertram, Bert, biochemist, educator, codiscoverer of INSULIN (b at Belleville, Ont 20 Nov 1892; d at London, Ont 19 June 1965). Collip received his PhD in biochemistry from U of T in 1916 and embarked on a long and extremely productive career as a medical researcher. In autumn 1921 he was working with J.J.R. MACLEOD in Toronto, during a sabbatical from U of A, when at Frederick BANTING's request Macleod asked him to join the team investigating the internal secretion of the pancreas. Collip's skills as a biochemist proved invaluable in the research, particularly in his Jan 1922 discovery of a method of producing a nontoxic, antidiabetic pancreatic extract. Collip produced the first insulin suitable for use on human beings. Serious quarrelling with Banting, however, as well as difficulties with insulin production in the laboratory, caused Collip to return to Alberta at the end of his sabbatical. With C.H. BEST and Banting he was one of the original patentees of insulin, and in 1923 received from Macleod a one-quarter share of the Nobel Prize money awarded to Banting and Macleod.

Collip plunged into endocrinological research and was one of the first to isolate the parathyroid hormone. In 1928 he succeeded A.B. MACALLUM as professor of biochemistry at McGill, where for the next decade he and his students were leaders in endocrinology, pioneering in the isolation and study of the ovarian and gonadotrophic hormones. A dominant figure in Canadian wartime medical research, Collip served as dean of medicine at Western 1947-61. A restless, driven man, Collip had been the best scientist on the insulin team, and afterwards made the most significant contributions to medical research. He did not court honours and seldom discussed the discovery of insulin. During the 1930s he became a good friend of Banting.   MICHAEL BLISS

Reading: Michael Bliss, *The Discovery of Insulin* (1982).

James Bertram Collip, biochemist and codiscoverer of insulin in 1922 (*courtesy National Archives of Canada/C-37756*).

Collishaw, Raymond, fighter pilot (b at Nanaimo, BC 22 Nov 1893; d at West Vancouver 29 Sept 1976). He was credited with 60 victories during WWI, placing him second on the roster of Canadian aces. He remained in the postwar RAF, leading British squadrons to southern Russia and Persia to fight against the "Reds" in 1919. At the beginning of WWII he commanded the RAF forces in Egypt, but his flair was for personal leadership, not office work. He was relieved in 1941, served briefly on the staff of Fighter Command in England, and retired with the rank of air vice-marshal in 1943.   BRERETON GREENHOUS

Colombo, John Robert, editor, anthologist, poet (b at Kitchener, Ont 24 Mar 1936). Colombo's career can be broken into 2 phases. The first involves him exclusively as a literary figure, particularly as an exponent and practitioner of "found poetry," with a vaguely European manner and a flair for causing literary activity to happen around him. This aspect became evident when he was at university in the 1950s and continued without challenge for 20 years, when it was joined by Colombo the bibliophile and creator of reference books. At their best, especially *Colombo's Canadian Quotations* (1974) and *Colombo's Canadian References* (1976) and in *Songs of the Indians* (2 vols, 1983), Colombo's compilations are examples of a kind of private-sector scholarship that is as admirable as it is rare. In all, Colombo has published well over 50 books, including translations. *New Canadian Quotations* was published in 1987.   DOUG FETHERLING

Colombo Plan (now known as the Asia Program) for Co-operative Economic Development in South and Southeast Asia was established following a Jan 1950 meeting of COMMONWEALTH foreign ministers in Colombo, Ceylon (now Sri Lanka), to attack the poverty upon which communist political movements in Asia were thought to feed. Initially confined to the Commonwealth countries of India, Pakistan, Ceylon, Australia, New Zealand, the UK and Canada, its membership soon widened to include most other S and SE Asian countries, along with the US as the largest donor. Specific development projects have always been arranged bilaterally by the governments concerned. Initial Canadian involvement was cautious, with a 1951-52 contribution of only $25 million. Ottawa's participation then grew rapidly, however, as its development-assistance programs expanded. India, Pakistan and Ceylon, together more recently with Bangladesh and Indonesia, have been the principal recipients. The Colombo Plan is now only one of a number of channels through which Canada supports Asian development; thus, in 1987 it accounted for only $145 000 of Canada's $9 billion aid programs.   DENIS STAIRS

Colonial and Imperial Conferences, 1887-1937, the principal means of high-level consultation between representatives from the United Kingdom, Canada and other self-governing parts of the British Empire – Commonwealth, helping to shape a framework of substantial economic and military co-operation, but consistently rejecting all forms of imperial centralization. Colonial Conferences took place in 1887, 1894, 1897, 1902 and 1907; Imperial Conferences were held in 1911, 1917, 1918, 1921, 1923, 1926, 1930, 1932 and 1937. Twice the conference was held in Ottawa (1894, 1932); all other meetings were in London, Eng. After 1937 the Imperial Conference was replaced by Prime Ministers' Meetings, theoretically without advisers or agendas, designed to produce more informal exchanges among COMMONWEALTH leaders. These met 17 times from 1944 to 1969. The designation was then changed to "Heads-of-Government Meetings," and these have been held every 2 years since 1971.

NORMAN HILLMER

Colonial Office, a department established by the British government to administer its colonial possessions, including British N America. It established forms of government and the church, appointed governors, approved local laws and made grants for particular purposes. It managed "imperial subjects," such as commerce and shipping, which gradually came under the exclusive control of the self-governing colonies.

Between the 1660s and 1768 British colonies had been governed by a combination of the secretary of state for the southern department and the Board of Trade and Plantations, a committee within the Privy Council. In 1768 the American or Colonial Department was established, but this office was abolished in 1782 after the loss of the American colonies. Jurisdiction over the remainder of British possessions was transferred to the home secretary's office until 1801, when colonial administration was moved to the secretary of state for war and the colonies. Colonial affairs expanded and became more important, and in 1825 a permanent undersecretary was appointed to deal with the colonies. This marks the beginning of the Colonial Office, although a separate secretary of state for the colonies was not created until 1854, after the Crimean War began. Further reorganization occurred as the range of powers claimed by the colonies expanded and as relations with these colonies became diplomatic rather than administrative.

A Dominion division within the Colonial Office dealt with the self-governing colonies between 1907 and 1 July 1925, when it became a separate ministry, the Secretary of State for Dominion Affairs. In 1947 this became the Commonwealth Relations Office, which in 1966 merged with the Colonial Office. Finally, in 1968, Britain combined the responsibility for all its external relations in the single Foreign and Commonwealth Office. *See also* COMMONWEALTH.

NANCY BROWN FOULDS

Reading: D.M.L. Farr, *The Colonial Office and Canada 1867-1887* (1955); J. Garner, *The Commonwealth Office 1925-68* (1978); D.M. Young, *The Colonial Office in the Nineteenth Century* (1961).

Colonization Companies, corporations designed to promote and co-ordinate immigration and settlement, employed at various times during Canada's history. Immigration and settlement were vital if the colony, and later the country, was to prosper. Colonization companies usually received blocks of land (eg, Huron Tract, Talbot Settlement) for reduced rates. They usually published brochures attracting potential settlers' attention, arranged for transportation to the block, helped settlers select land, provided (or helped them buy) equipment and seed for the first crop, and assisted with construction of homes. Once a group of settlers was established, the surrounding land would become more desirable to other settlers, and therefore more valuable to the company.

In 1627 the COMPAGNIE DES CENTS-ASSOCIÉS was founded to encourage permanent settlement in New France. It was granted a vast area in return for exclusive fur-trade rights, but was unsuccessful in its goals. The COMPAGNIE DES INDES OCCIDENTALES, fd 1664, assumed control of New France until 1674, when it reverted to the Crown. During the British regime, colonization companies such as the CANADA COMPANY in Upper Canada and the BRITISH AMERICAN LAND COMPANY in Lower Canada were formed to promote settlement.

By far the largest government-encouraged scheme, however, was the sale in the late 19th century of certain odd-numbered sections of land in the West to any business that demonstrated its goodwill and capabilities, and a sincere interest in promoting settlement. The measure was introduced by order-in-council 23 Dec 1881 as an amendment to the Dominion Lands Act of 1879 by John A. Macdonald's government, as an extension of its NATIONAL POLICY. The purchaser was required to locate 2 settlers upon each of the odd-and even-numbered sections of the tract within 5 years, although the Crown maintained exclusive ownership of the even-numbered sections. In return, the company was to receive a rebate of $160 for every newly established, bona fide settler within the colonization tract. Companies were expected to realize profits in proportion to the number of settlers they could induce onto their respective lands. With the maximum rebate, a company could pay as little as $1/acre for the odd-numbered sections. Once its even-numbered sections were fully occupied by HOMESTEADS or by pre-emptions, the company could demand $3-15/acre for odd-numbered sections.

The government wanted assistance in its DOMINION LANDS POLICY, and it hoped to sell 10 million acres (4.05 million ha) to private colonization corporations, to recover $10 million of the $25 million it had pledged to the CANADIAN PACIFIC RAILWAY syndicate, and simultaneously to secure the business community's assistance in developing the western frontier. Importunate politicians, church groups and prominent businessmen petitioned the government for land, convinced that the North-West would be invaded by hordes of settlers. Most of their applications were withdrawn after the 1881-82 speculative real-estate boom on the Prairies collapsed. Of 260 applicants, only 27 ratified contracts with the government, and the last of the companies involved was liquidated in 1891. After 1900, colonization companies, operating under the auspices of railway companies or the Dept of Immigration, were much more successful in the West because of the massive influx of settlers and a great demand for land which lasted until WWI. Most of Canada's colonization companies, however, languished; several took no initiative, whereas others were victimized by adverse economic or political conditions, successive crop failures and poor communication with settlers on their tracts.

ANDRÉ N. LALONDE

Columbia Icefield, a mass of ice covering a high plateau between Mt Columbia (3747 m) and Mt Athabasca (3491 m), located between Banff and Jasper national parks, along the BC-Alberta border. Astride the Great Divide, it lies at the hydrographic apex of N America. Called the "mother of rivers," its meltwaters nourish the North SASKATCHEWAN, COLUMBIA, ATHABASCA and FRASER river systems. It contains about 30 distinct glaciers, the largest being Saskatchewan and Athabasca. A vestige of the great ice shield that once lay over most of Canada, the Columbia Icefield is the largest accumulation of ice in the Rocky Mts, covering some 300 km² in depths from 100 to 365 m.

Columbia Icefield, located between Mt Columbia and Mt Athabasca, lies at the geographic and hydrographic apex of N America. It contains 30 distinct glaciers and its meltwaters feed the N Saskatchewan, Columbia, Athabasca and Fraser rivers (*photo by V. Claerhout*).

Tree-ring studies show that the icefield advances and recedes in cycles, the latest advance occurring around 1840. The icefield is a spectacular sight of undulating white, soaring rock peaks and deep ice caverns. At its S and N faces, it drops off into forested valleys. It can be reached from the Icefields Parkway, a scenic road connecting Lk Louise and Jasper, and can be climbed by experienced mountaineers to its crest, called Snow Dome, from which it is said waters melt into 3 oceans.

JAMES MARSH

Columbia Mountains are a block of mountains 608 km long and 256 km wide that dominate the landscape of southeastern BC. The MONASHEE, SELKIRK and Purcell mountains form parallel lines extending north-south from the US to the ROCKY MOUNTAIN TRENCH. Minerals in the Purcells, between the valley of KOOTENAY LK and the trench, have been exploited since the 1890s, notably silver-bearing lead-zinc ore from Cominco Ltd's huge Sullivan Mine in KIMBERLEY, BC. Alpine areas such as the Bugaboos are increasingly popular for skiing and hiking. To the NW, between the Quesnel-Shuswap Highlands and the trench, are the Cariboo Mts. They include Bowron Lk and most of Wells Gray Provincial Park, both noted for outstanding scenery and recreation.

PETER GRANT

Columbia River, 2000 km long (of which 748 km are in Canada), rises in Columbia Lk (elev 820 m) in SE British Columbia, flows NNW in a sharp detour around the Selkirk range and abruptly turns S past REVELSTOKE, through Arrow Lk and Lower Arrow Lk, past CASTLEGAR, and across the US border (at elev 390 m). This route was followed by the Big Bend Highway which opened in 1940 and provided the shortest route through the Rockies until the Rogers Pass section was opened. Just N of the border the river is joined by the Kootenay R, which also rises in the area of Columbia Lk, loops S into the US and N again into Kootenay Lk, before heading W to join the Columbia. The Columbia continues S across Washington state, but is forced off its natural course by lava flow and glacial debris into a second huge curve, also called the "Big Bend." At the top of the bend, it is joined by the Okanagan R (314 km), which drains the lakes of the OKANAGAN VALLEY. Just N of the Oregon border it is joined by the Snake R and makes a right-angled turn, flowing W to the Pacific below Portland, Oregon. The Columbia is a long, powerful river, which has cut deep gorges along much of its course, and it commands one of the greatest DRAINAGE BASINS in N America, totalling 155 000 km² (including 51 800 km² in the US). The average flow at the international boundary is 2800 m³/s.

Originally called Rio de San Roque by Spanish explorers, it was rediscovered by the Boston trader Capt Robert Gray, who named it after his ship, the *Columbia*. (The river may be unique in being named after a ship.) David THOMPSON of the NWC was the first to explore it from its headwaters to its mouth (1811), but American traders had preceded him overland, and were already at work on Ft Astoria. The HBC later built Ft Vancouver (1824-25) at its mouth, and as the only water route to the interior from the Pacific, the river served as the major transportation artery until the railways came. The Columbia became the de facto boundary between British and American territory, but by the 1840s American immigration to the area was ascendant, and the British agreed to set the border at the 49th parallel. Though its headwaters are in Canada, most of the river's development has been in the US. By the COLUMBIA RIVER TREATY (1961; ratified by Canada 1964), Canada agreed to build 3 storage dams: the Duncan (1967) N of Kootenay Lk, Hugh Keenleyside

The Columbia River commands one of the greatest drainage basins in N America; illustrated is Columbia Lake at the river's headwaters (*photo by Valerie J. May*).

(1968) on the Columbia, and Mica (1973) N of Revelstoke. The Mica project, which began generating 1976-77, has a nameplate capacity of 1736 MW, and the total potential of the river is estimated to be 4000 MW in Canada. The agreement has been controversial because of the environmental disruption of the dams and because the irrigation and hydroelectric power mostly benefit the US. However, Canada shares the power and revenue. Some of the world's largest hydroelectric generators are on the river, eg, at Grand Coulee. The dams have greatly impeded the salmon runs; the Columbia was one of the world's great spawning grounds.   JAMES MARSH

Columbia River Treaty, signed by Canada and the US on 17 Jan 1961 after 15 years of preliminary investigation by the INTERNATIONAL JOINT COMMISSION, and one year (1960) of direct international negotiation; dealt with the co-operative development of the Columbia River. Canada undertook to construct 3 dams for water storage projects in the Canadian portion of the COLUMBIA R basin and to operate them to produce maximum flood control and power downstream. In return, the US would pay Canada $US64.4 million (calculated to be half the worth, in 1961, of the flood protection the US would enjoy over the treaty's 60-year life); it would give Canada title to half the power produced; and would return this power to Canada. The treaty gave the US an option to build a transboundary project on the Kootenay R, and gave Canada the right at specified times to divert portions of the Kootenay's flow northward into the Columbia.

The treaty did not become effective until 16 Sept 1964, much of the delay resulting from a federal-provincial controversy over BC's 1961 decision to sell the power entitlement in the US. The province prevailed in Jan 1964, when the power benefit for the first 30 years was sold for a lump sum prepayment of $US254.4 million and the treaty was slightly modified by protocol. As the Canadian owner of the resource, BC was heavily involved in the negotiations, and in 1963 and 1964 it assumed Canada's obligations. Its agency, BC HYDRO, has constructed all the Canadian treaty projects, and, with an American counterpart, co-ordinates their storage releases to the advantage of both countries. Discussions will be held in 1994 when the downstream benefits revert to Canada.   NEIL SWAINSON

Columbine, herbaceous plant (genus *Aquilegia*) of buttercup family (Ranunculaceae). The generic name derives from Latin *aquila*, "eagle," common name from Latin *columba*, "dove." Nearly all of the 70 known species are native to the Northern Hemisphere, 5 to Canada. *A. brevistyla* ranges from western Canada to Ontario; *A. flavescens* (yellow columbine), *A. formosa* (Sitka columbine) and *A. jonesii* are native to the Rocky Mts; *A. canadensis* (wild columbine) extends east from Saskatchewan. Leaves are divided into 1-3 leaflets, each in 3 parts. The most distinctive feature of the nodding flower is the hornlike spur projecting backwards from each of the 5 petals. Columbines, a popular ORNAMENTAL cultivated for centuries, produce variable forms when grown from seed. Flowers (predominantly blue, lavender, red, yellow, white or a combination) were once used to garnish food and as medicine, until overdoses proved fatal. *A. canadensis* was used by N American Indians for intestinal disorders, to sweeten tobacco and as an aphrodisiac. *See also* PLANTS, NATIVE USES; POISONOUS PLANTS.   ROGER VICK

Five species of columbine are native to Canada (*photo by Tim Fitzharris*).

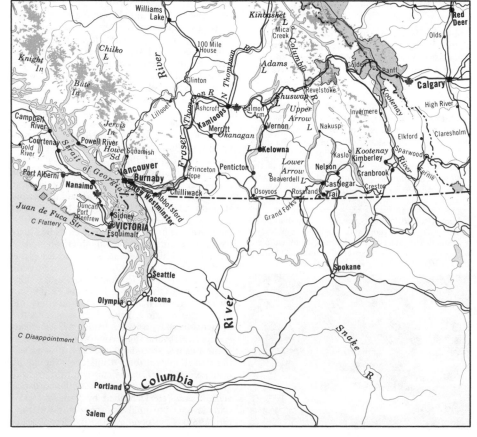

Columbium (Cb), or niobium, grey, ductile, tarnish-resistant and superconductive metal with a melting point of 2468°C. The name niobium (Nb) was officially adopted in 1951 by the International Union of Pure and Applied Chemistry, after 100

years of controversy. In N America many metal-lurgists and metal dealers still refer to the metal as columbium. Columbium is an important alloy in high-strength, low-alloy (HSLA) steels. High-purity columbium products are used in superalloys for the AEROSPACE INDUSTRY and in superconductor magnets for powerful generators. The main sources of columbium are the minerals pyrochlore and columbite; extensive reserves are found in Brazil, Canada, Nigeria and Zaire. In 1986 Niobec Inc, Canada's sole columbium source, produced 3346 t of Cb_2O_5 from a mine in southern Québec, about 16% of the world's output. Several large deposits, located mainly in Québec, could be developed in future. *See also* MINERAL RESOURCES.   D.G. FONG

Colvile, Eden, governor of Rupert's Land (b 1819; d in Devonshire, Eng 2 Apr 1893), son of the deputy governor of the HUDSON'S BAY CO. Educated at Eton and Trinity Coll, Cambridge, he was sent in 1844 by the London Land Co to manage the seigneury of Beauharnois, LC, apparently without much success. He also represented Beauharnois in the Legislative Assembly of the Province of Canada 1844-47. A pleasant enough patrician with business aspirations, he was made associate governor of Rupert's Land on 3 Jan 1849. Arriving at the RED RIVER COLONY on 11 Aug 1850, he provided a steadying influence in the settlement in a period of increasing racial, social and religious tension. After his departure in the fall of 1852 his connection with the HBC continued and in the 1860s when new interests took over he was one of the few that remained on its London Committee. In 1872 he became deputy governor and was governor from 1880 to 1889.
                                              FRITS PANNEKOEK

Colville, Alexander, painter (b at Toronto 24 Aug 1920). He moved with his family to Amherst, NS, in 1929 and studied at Mount Allison (1938-42). On graduating he joined the army and in 1944 was sent to Europe as a war artist. He returned to Canada late in 1945 and worked in Ottawa on paintings based on his European sketches and watercolours until his demobilization in 1946. Colville taught at Mount Allison 1946-63, when he resigned to devote himself to painting. Between 1952 and 1955 the Hewitt Gallery in New York gave Colville his earliest commercial exhibitions. The most substantial Canadian support for his work at this time came from the National Gallery of Canada, which acquired 7 of his paintings in the 1950s.

The 1950 painting *Nude and Dummy* marks the transition from the reportage of Colville's war pictures to a personal creative direction. His subject matter is invariably chosen from his immediate environment: his family, the animals he keeps, the landscape near his home. The representations, however, are never simply a recording of the everyday; they are highly representational reflections of a world which is at once filled with the joyful and the beautiful, the disturbing and the dangerous. Colville has changed his medium a number of times, from oil to tempera to oil and synthetic resin, and after 1963 to acrylic polymer emulsion. He follows a long, careful process for each composition, taking precise measurements and proportioning these to an underlying geometric scheme. He works on only one composition at a time, and since the 1950s has produced only 3 or 4 paintings or serigraphs a year. The first retrospective of his work was held at the Dalhousie Art Gallery in 1984.

In 1966 Colville represented Canada at the Venice Biennale. He was visiting professor at University of California at Santa Cruz in 1967, and in 1971 spent 6 months as a visiting artist in Berlin. He has served on numerous boards and commis-sions. He designed the Centennial coins, minted in 1967, and the Governor General's Medal, in 1978. In 1984 a film, *Alex Colville – The Splendour of Order* was produced by Minerva Films. In 1985 a very successful exhibition of Colville's work was held in Japan – the first by a Canadian artist in that country. He has lived in the small university town of Wolfville, NS, since 1971 and is chancellor of Acadia. In 1982 he was made a Companion of the Order of Canada.   MARILYN BURNETT

Reading: David Burnett, *Colville* (1983).

Come by Chance, Nfld, Town, pop 266 (1986c), 337 (1981c), inc 1969, is located at the head of PLACENTIA BAY on the Isthmus of Avalon. Originally called Passage Harbour by John GUY in 1612, the name "Comby Chance" was first recorded in 1706 – perhaps in reference to the discovery of the harbour "by chance." Despite the presence of a telegraph station in the early 1900s, the settlement was almost deserted by the late 1930s. It was then chosen as the site of a cottage hospital because of its central location in the TRIN-ITY BAY-Placentia Bay area. Come by Chance gained national importance in the 1970s with the building of a 16 350 m^3 per day oil refinery. The $120-million petroleum complex included two 99 000 m^3 crude-oil storage tanks, a CNR spur track, a deep-water oil terminal and the refinery itself, which produced its first oil in Dec 1973. However, after some malfunctions and the loss of its feedstock supply, the refinery went into receivership in 1976. The idle refinery was sold in July 1980 to PETRO-CANADA, which sold it for $1 to Newfoundland Energy Ltd in 1987. The Bermuda-based company reopened the refinery in Aug 1987.   JANET E.M. PITT

Comédie-Canadienne, La, *fl* 1958-69, was founded by Gratien GÉLINAS in 1957 to foster the production of plays by Canadian authors. After renovating the Radio-City cinema in Montréal, the company presented plays by authors such as Marcel DUBÉ, Jacques Bobet, Jacques Languirand and Gélinas. Seeking a wider audience, the Comédie-Canadienne offered innovations such as an earlier curtain time, a section of inexpensive seats, and acoustic subtitles for translation of plays. By 1961 Gélinas realized that Canadian plays alone could not sustain the 1200-seat theatre house, which was then made available to a variety of stage productions – theatre, dance and song. In the late 1960s an attempt was made to devote 43 weeks each year to Québécois music and theatre, but the company closed down in 1973 and its theatre became the permanent home of the THÉÂTRE DU NOUVEAU MONDE. *See also* THEATRE, FRENCH-LANGUAGE.   MARILYN BASZCZYNSKI

Comet, astronomical body orbiting the SUN, which appears for a few weeks as a faint, luminous patch moving slowly, from night to night, relative to the background of stars. The comet may also have a luminous tail pointing away from the sun. In recorded history about 750 comets have been observed well enough to allow an approximate determination of their orbits. Of these comets, about 140 have short periods (3-200 years) and have been observed more than once, so that about 1200 cometary apparitions have been observed in all. The remaining 600 or so long-period comets have been observed only once and their orbital periods are known roughly or not at all. Since a long-period comet is usually observed for only a small fraction of its orbital period, it is customary to represent its orbit by a parabola (an open curve). If the orbit of a comet were truly a parabola or a hyperbola, the comet would not be a permanent member of the solar system but would be passing from interstellar space. However, as far as we know, all comets that have been observed are probably solar-system objects, even if we cannot determine the periods of their orbits.

Upon its discovery (if a new comet) or recovery (if a short-period comet), the comet is assigned a temporary label consisting of the year of discovery plus a letter (a, b, c, etc) indicating the order of discovery (or recovery) in the year. Later, when all orbits have been worked out, it is assigned a permanent label consisting of the year plus a Roman numeral (I, II, III, etc) indicating the order of perihelion passage (ie, point in the orbit nearest the sun). The comet is also named after its discoverer(s). For example, Comet Van den Bergh – Comet 1974g-1974XII – discovered by Canadian astronomer Sidney VAN DEN BERGH, was the seventh comet to be discovered and the twelfth to pass through perihelion in 1974. A periodic comet may bear several numerical designations; eg, Comet Halley bears the designations 1835III and 1910II. One astronomer may have several comets named after him, eg, Canadian astronomer Rolf MEIER discovered comets 1978f, 1979i, 1980q and 1984o.

Most comets have rather eccentric orbits, spend most of their time far from both sun and Earth and are invisible, even through large telescopes. When a comet is far from the sun, it is a small, solid object, possibly not more than a few kilometres in diameter. The solid material probably consists partly of frozen volatile substances (eg, water, simple organic compounds) mixed with small particles of nonvolatile stony or metallic dust. The description "dirty ice" is often used.

Only when a comet comes close to the sun and Earth for a brief few weeks near perihelion can the familiar spectacular phenomena usually associated with comets be seen. The volatile substances evaporate and the organic molecules break up under the influence of sunlight and glow with an eerie fluorescence. Molecular fragments have been identified by analysing the fluorescence spectrographically (*see* SPECTROSCOPY). Some molecular fragments were observed in comets before being observed in any terrestrial laboratory and Canadian scientists have been prominent in subsequent identifications. Two cometary molecules were identified in the Ottawa laboratories of the NATIONAL RESEARCH COUNCIL: C_3 by Alex Douglas and H_2O^+ by Gerhard HERZBERG. Some of a comet's light is sunlight reflected from dust particles released when ice evaporates.

Although there is much variation in pattern, a fully developed comet typically has a head and 2 tails. The head consists of the central nucleus, the small (several-kilometre-sized) body from which gas and dust are evaporating, and the coma, the atmosphere of glowing gas surrounding the nucleus. One tail, known variously as the gas, ion or plasma tail, points directly away from the sun and consists of ionized gases being blown away from the sun. The second tail, the dust tail, is also directed away from the sun, but tends to be rather curved and is amorphous in appearance. Its spectrum (merely reflected sunlight) shows that it consists primarily of tiny solid particles. Because of geometrical circumstances, one tail is often behind the other as seen from Earth, leaving only one apparent.

Most comets are too faint to be seen with the naked eye and not all develop tails. However, occasionally, a large comet passing close to the Earth and sun produces a spectacular sight, eg, during the 1970s the newly discovered comets Bennett, Kohoutek and West. The most famous comet is Comet Halley. In late 17th-century England, Dr Edmond Halley investigated the orbits of several comets and showed that the bright comets of 1531, 1607 and 1682 were one and the same,

Image of Halley's Comet obtained by Canadian astronomer C.J. Pritchet in Mar 1986 with the Canada-France-Hawaii telescope. Jets of material are seen to be ejected from localized spots on the comet's nucleus. The jets are distorted into spirals by the clockwise rotation of the nucleus and are being swept towards the left by radiation and particle pressure issuing from the sun (*image by C.J. Pritchet and S. Van den Bergh*).

occurring at 76-year intervals. Subsequent investigations have shown that Comet Halley has been observed at every passage since 240 BC. It was last seen in 1985-86. It was visible faintly from Canada in Nov and Dec 1985; then it disappeared behind the sun while it passed perihelion in Feb 1986. It became a spectacular object for Southern Hemisphere observers in Mar and Apr before it was briefly and faintly seen from Canadian latitudes in May 1986. Its next perihelion passage will be in July 2061.

The years 1985 and 1986 saw enormous advances in cometary science. A worldwide organization called International Halley Watch was set up to plan and co-ordinate the tens of thousands of observations of many types that were made from ground-based observatories of Halley's Comet. But that was not all. For the first time in history, 2 comets – Halley's Comet and Comet Giacobini-Zinner – were met by a flotilla of spacecraft taking *in situ* measurements and transmitting them back to Earth.

The first of these encounters was between the International Cometary Explorer (ICE) spacecraft and Comet Giacobini-Zinner. ICE was originally launched in 1978 and was designed to orbit between the sun and Earth to measure the flow of charged particles ("solar wind") from the sun, and the interplanetary magnetic field. Later it was transferred to the Earth's geomagnetic tail to make similar measurements. Only in 1981, when these experiments were almost finished, was the brilliant idea conceived of making the spacecraft swing within 120 km of the moon's surface and using the moon's gravity to hurl the craft into an entirely new orbit towards Comet Giacobini-Zinner. This maneuvre was successfully carried out in Dec 1983, at which time the craft was christened ICE. It was an outstanding success, the craft passing through the tail of the comet in Sept 1985 only 7800 km from the nucleus. The ICE confirmed theoretical models that predicted that the magnetic field would be draped over the nucleus ("like limp spaghetti hanging over a fork") with the magnetic field lines in opposite directions on either side of the nucleus and a sheet of electric current in between. The craft also verified the presence of H_2O^+ (see above) and CO^+. An expected sharp "bow shock," where the outflow of cometary material interacts with the solar wind, was not confirmed.

Halley's Comet was met, in Mar 1986, by no fewer than 5 spacecraft specially launched for the event and crammed with numerous instruments for making many different sorts of measurements. Two of the craft, Vega I and Vega II, were from the USSR; 2 of them, Suisei and Sakigake, were from Japan; and Giotto was launched by the European Space Agency. The most spectacular results were probably the direct images of the nucleus of the comet obtained as Giotto passed only 540 km from the sunward side of it. It appears that the nucleus is exceedingly dark, with jets of material being ejected from highly localized active spots on the surface. Some of these jets were even detected from Earth in the remarkable accompanying image obtained by Canadian astronomers C.J. Pritchet and S. Van den Bergh with the Canada-France-Hawaii telescope in Mar 1986. Ejected from localized spots on the comet's nucleus, the jets are·distorted into lop-sided spirals by the clockwise rotation of the nucleus while they are simultaneously swept towards the left by radiation pressure issuing from the sun. If the nucleus is indeed a "dirty snowball," its surface is dirtier than we had imagined, and much of the dirt may be composed of a tarlike mixture of organic compounds.   JEREMY B. TATUM

Reading: J.C. Brandt and R.D. Chapman, *Introduction to Comets* (1981).

Comfort, Charles Fraser, painter (b at Edinburgh, Scot 22 July 1900). Comfort came to Winnipeg in 1912 and studied art there and at New York C (1922-23) with Robert Henri. His friendship with the GROUP OF SEVEN, his familiarity with the work of Paul Cézanne and other modernists, his interest in the history of art, and his work as a graphic designer in Winnipeg (1914-25) and Toronto (1925-36) were the major influences on his art. The expressive design and dramatic characterization of his large portraits of the 1920s and 1930s are also evident in his later landscapes as well as in his murals for the Toronto Stock Exchange (1937), the first modern interpretation of mural work in Canada. His numerous executive responsibilities in art societies (including president of the Royal Canadian Academy of Arts, 1957-60), and his record as a war artist (1943-46) resulted in his becoming the only artist to be appointed director of the National Gallery of Canada (1960-65). He was made an Officer of the Order of Canada in 1972.   CHARLES C. HILL

Commercial Empire of the St. Lawrence, 1760-1850, The, by D.G. CREIGHTON, was published in Toronto, New Haven and London, 1937 (reprinted 1956 as *The Empire of the St. Lawrence*). Reflecting the new emphasis on socioeconomic factors that dominated Canadian historical writing in the 1930s, this masterly and elegantly written work deals with the St Lawrence Valley's influence as a transportation system and a focus of economic activity up to 1850. Creighton argued that the geographic nature of the St Lawrence-Great Lakes system made it a rival of systems such as the Hudson-Mohawk route (NY). The natural advantages of the St Lawrence were, however, offset by political decisions, such as those made in 1783 regarding the international boundary, and by the animosity felt by agriculturally based Québec society toward the entrepreneurial class of Montréal.

Commercial Law, that branch of private law concerned primarily with the supply of goods or services by merchants and other businesses for profit. Textbooks on the subject frequently differ on the range of topics treated in them. Any serious exposition of commercial law, however, will include such topics as sale of goods, bailment and carriage of goods, documents of title and nego-

tiable instruments, banking, the various forms of secured credit, and BANKRUPTCY law.

These topics are often linked through an originating transaction. For example, a seller selling goods to a buyer at a distant location will often have to make arrangements for their shipment; this will involve a contract of carriage (by land or sea and, in overseas shipments, frequently both) with a carrier, who will issue the seller with a bill of lading (a "document of title"), which may be negotiable or non-negotiable. During their transit the goods will also usually be covered by a policy of insurance ("inland" or "marine" insurance) against loss or damage. In commercial transactions, the buyer will almost invariably make payment by means of a negotiable instrument, which in domestic transactions normally consists of a cheque drawn on the buyer's bank in the seller's favour. In international transactions payment will often be arranged through a banker's letter of credit.

If the buyer cannot or does not wish to make immediate payment, the seller may give him a short period of credit. Alternatively the seller may be willing to sell the goods on a "conditional sale" basis, involving an extension of medium- or long-term credit while reserving title until the goods have been paid for; or the buyer may arrange for a loan from a financial institution and give security to the lender to secure repayment of the loan. If the buyer becomes bankrupt before the goods have been paid for, the seller will want to know whether he can recover the goods and, if he cannot, how he will rank with other creditors who have claims against the bankrupt's estate.

In Canada, jurisdiction to regulate commercial transactions is divided between the federal and the provincial governments, so commercial lawyers must be familiar with federal as well as provincial laws. A further complication arises because the commercial law of Québec is derived from the CIVIL CODE of France while the commercial law of the English-speaking provinces is based on English law. At both the provincial and federal levels the relevant rules of many of the principal branches of commercial law have been reduced to statutory form. Thus, all English-speaking provinces have a substantially identical Sale of Goods Act while the Bills of Exchange Act, the Bank Act, the Carriage of Goods by Sea Act and the Bankruptcy Act codify all or a substantial part of the areas of commercial law under federal jurisdiction.

The function of sales law is primarily to determine the rights and duties of the seller and buyer where the contract itself does not contain a complete set of terms. The seller's obligations are generally the more onerous. The seller must not only deliver goods of the right quantity and description and at the agreed time; he must also supply goods that are of "merchantable quality" and reasonably fit for their intended purpose. The oft-quoted maxim *caveat emptor* ("let the buyer beware") has long ceased to represent the Canadian law. If the seller fails to live up to his obligations he may have to compensate the buyers for the losses suffered by them, and these could be very substantial. The buyer's primary obligations under the typical contract of sale are to accept the goods and to pay for them as agreed.

The federal Bills of Exchange Act deals with the following types of payment instrument: bills of exchange, cheques (ie, bills of exchange drawn on a bank or recognized near-bank) and promissory notes. An important function of the Act is to regulate the assignability (ie, negotiability) of rights obtained under one of these instruments and to determine when the transferee of an instrument can obtain better rights to payment than its original holder had. He is then said to be a "holder in due course." Similar principles of negotiability apply to "documents of title," ie, recognized types of documents (such as bills of lading and warehouse receipts) that indicate that the holder of them is entitled to the delivery of goods by the bailee who issued the document in the first place.

Canadian commercial law is changing rapidly in response to a variety of technological and other nonlegal factors. In the sales area, the courts and the legislatures are increasingly having to recognize that the typical retailer is only a conduit for the manufacturer, who produces the goods and creates a market for them through intensive advertising. There is strong pressure, therefore, to hold the manufacturer directly responsible to the ultimate buyer if the goods are defective, even though no formal contract exists between the parties.

Negotiable-instruments law is deeply affected by the use of electronic systems for the transfer of funds (including the use of automated tellers at the retail level) and the widespread substitution of cheques by CREDIT CARDS. In the foreseeable future debit cards will make a further inroad into the use of cheques, although the "cashless society" is still some distance away. Containerization of cargoes and intermodal methods of transport have radically altered the law of bills of lading and the traditional roles and duties of carriers.

The greatly increased importance of secured credit of all types is also contributing to changes in this branch of commercial law. In particular, 3 provinces (Ontario, Manitoba and Saskatchewan) and the Yukon Territory have now adopted a substantially similar Personal Property Security Act to replace the old provincial Conditional Sales, Chattel Mortgages, and Assignment of Book Debts Acts. The Uniform Law Conference of Canada and the Canadian Bar Association jointly sponsored the Uniform Personal Property Security Act, 1982, and urged its adoption by those provinces that are contemplating modernizing their chattel security law. JACOB S. ZIEGEL

Commission of Conservation, established 1909 to provide Canadian governments with the most up-to-date scientific advice on the CONSERVATION of human and natural resources. The wastefulness of the common methods of resource exploitation was widely admitted, and the conservation movement was beginning to offer alternative approaches, particularly in the US where the first national commission was struck in 1908. Canada was urged to follow suit, as a step towards a continental conservation policy. This plea won the support of 2 leading Canadian conservationists, Clifford SIFTON and PM Wilfrid LAURIER, by whose government the Canadian commission was created.

Sifton served as the commission's chairman until 1918 and was always its guiding spirit. To Sifton, conservation meant that resources should be used in ways that would generate the greatest benefit for all Canadians. The public interest demanded wise management, but wise management in turn demanded the best understanding of the resource base. The commission was expected to provide this knowledge.

The members of the commission included 3 federal Cabinet ministers, the 9 provincial ministers with responsibility for natural resources, and 20 members at large, including a professor from every province with a university. The commission was further organized into working committees which directed a diverse array of research in 7 topical fields: agricultural land, water and water power, fisheries, game and fur-bearing animals, forests, minerals, and public health. The results were published in some 200 books, reports and scientific papers that constituted the first large-scale survey of Canadian resources and resource problems. Achievements in public policy were not as great. Governments were slow to accept the commission's advice, and, as other agencies of the federal government became more active in resource management, the Commission of Conservation came to seem redundant. It was dissolved in 1921. P.J. SMITH

Commission of Government in Newfoundland was established in response to an extraordinary set of circumstances. The collapse of world trade during the GREAT DEPRESSION of the 1930s was particularly damaging to Newfoundland's economy, which depended on exporting large quantities of fish and forest products. In 1933, following several turbulent years of severe budget deficits and heavy foreign borrowing, the government of PM Frederick ALDERDICE asked the British government to establish a royal commission to investigate Newfoundland's financial difficulties. The commission's report blamed both political corruption and international conditions for Newfoundland's predicament, and advocated replacing RESPONSIBLE GOVERNMENT with a "Commission of Government" that would rule until Newfoundland was self-supporting again.

The commission government took office in Feb 1934 and remained in power until Newfoundland became a Canadian province in 1949. It was presided over by a governor who acted on the advice of 6 commissioners appointed by the British government. During its tenure the commission government introduced a number of reforms, including a land resettlement scheme, the reorganization of the civil service and the creation of the Newfoundland Fisheries Board. With the outbreak of WWII in 1939, however, large-scale reconstruction was postponed in favour of a total war effort.

Gradually much of the original goodwill toward the commission government dissipated, and after the war there was increasing agitation for the return of self-government. Consequently, in the first of 2 referendums held in 1948 to decide the island's future, commission government placed a distant third (behind the restoration of responsible government and Confederation), and when Newfoundland entered Confederation on 31 Mar 1949, few Newfoundlanders mourned the passing of the commission government.

DAVID CLARK MACKENZIE

Reading: S.J.R. Noel, *Politics in Newfoundland* (1971); F.W. Rowe, *A History of Newfoundland and Labrador* (1980).

Commissioner for Oaths is any person over 18 years of age commissioned by a lieutenant-governor to administer oaths and take affidavits. Oaths must be taken by the deponent in the presence of a commissioner, who satisfies himself of the signature's authenticity and administers the oath before signing the declaration. Members of Parliament, legislative assemblies, municipal councils, lawyers and many public officials are ex officio commissioners for oaths. K.G. MCSHANE

Committee for an Independent Canada (CIC) was conceived by Walter GORDON, Peter NEWMAN and Abraham Rotstein as a citizens' committee to promote Canadian economic and cultural independence. They recruited Jack MCCLELLAND and Claude RYAN as cochairmen and launched the CIC on 17 Sept 1970. By June 1971 the CIC had 170 000 signatures on a petition to Prime Minister Trudeau demanding limits to FOREIGN INVESTMENT and ownership. Many CIC ideas were eventually incorporated into law, eg, the establishment of the Canadian Development Corporation, PETRO-CANADA and the Foreign Invest- ment Review Agency; controls over land acquisition by nonresidents; tougher rules regarding Canadian content on radio and television; and the elimination of *Time's* and *Reader's Digest's* tax privileges.

The CIC's success can be attributed to the skilful use of media and effective persuasion by national chairmen (Edwin Goodman, Mel Hurtig, Robert Page, Dave Treleavan, Bruce Willson and Max Saltsman) and to local leaders who mobilized 10 000 members in 41 chapters. The organization was funded by private gifts, dues and chapter activities. Publications included the monthly *Independencer* and the books *Independence: The Canadian Challenge* (1972) and *Getting It Back* (1974) edited by Abraham Rotstein and Gary Lax. In 1981, the CIC was disbanded, many of its major goals achieved. *See also* COUNCIL OF CANADIANS; NATIONALISM; ECONOMIC NATIONALISM.

ROGER RICKWOOD

Committees Parliament has many committees which perform functions that cannot be adequately accomplished in debate or question period.

Committee of the Whole (Supply, Ways and Means), chaired by the Deputy Speaker, includes all members of the HOUSE OF COMMONS meeting in its normal chamber. Until 1969 the Commons met as a Committee of the Whole to consider legislation clause by clause after second reading of a bill, a task now delegated to the relevant standing committee (*see* PARLIAMENTARY PROCEDURE). Estimates were also considered in Committee of Supply and many members would like some estimates to be considered there again, because Committee of the Whole is a public forum attracting great media attention. The Committee of Ways and Means, another version of Committee of the Whole, which dealt with revenue, is now purely symbolic.

Standing Committees The 25 standing committees are the most important parliamentary committees. Usually chaired by government MPs (except for the Committee on Public Accounts), they have 7-11 members, party representation being proportionate to that in the House of Commons. They include specialist committees, corresponding roughly in concern to government departments, and other committees dealing with matters such as public accounts, miscellaneous estimates and private bills, procedures and organization, privileges and elections. In Parliament there are also joint standing committees of the House and SENATE. Ministers are not usually standing-committee members nor, since 1985, are parliamentary secretaries.

Legislative Committees were created in the reforms of 1985. They are established to examine legislation after it has passed second reading. A different one is created for each bill. The chairmen are selected from a panel, which contains backbench members from each party. They normally have 7 members. Committees exist to consider policy issues, to examine estimates and annual reports, and to scrutinize government legislation after second reading, including supply and ways-and-means legislation. They usually meet only in the capital city and their witnesses are therefore drawn chiefly from groups who can afford to travel or to maintain permanent representatives there. Many committees, however, make an effort to hold meetings across Canada. The committees choose witnesses and decide which recommendations to submit to the legislature, in the form of reports or amendments to bills. If they are reviewing legislation a minister is occasionally the first and last witness, and may review testimony. With supply bills the effectiveness of committees is limited, but the committee can serve as a forum for criticism of government programs and on occasion hold ministers accountable for estimated departmental expenditure. When the Committee on Public Accounts reviews government accounts and the AUDITOR GENERAL reports on them, this attracts important media attention – far more than when the committee submits its own report to the House.

Special committees (sometimes called select committees), eg, the Special Joint Committee of the Senate and of the House of Commons on the Constitution of Canada, are sometimes established by the House to study specific issues or to investigate public opinion on policy decisions. They are sometimes called task forces but should not be confused with government TASK FORCES. Both standing and special committees can be joint committees. The Senate also has standing committees, special committees and a committee of the whole. Their investigations on poverty, aging and science have been noteworthy.

Standing committees are too often partisan and government controlled; they suffer from amateurism because of high turnover in the House, they are inadequately staffed and cannot choose their own topics of study. In recent years they have overcome some of these weaknesses by creating subcommittees with small, stable membership and expert staff. An example was the Justice Committee's investigation of penitentiaries (1977). In 1982, as a result of reforms adopted for a trial period, the number of members and the number of membership changes on committees were reduced. Committees were given greater discretion to choose subjects for investigation. Following the report of the Special Committee on Reform of the House of Commons in 1985 the standing committees were given more autonomy and reduced in size. The system of legislative committees was also introduced at this time.

The increased use of committees has not altered the relationship between Parliament and government, which disappoints many critics and private MPs. But Parliament's role is not to govern but to examine, criticize and propose alternatives. On the other hand, committees have strengthened Parliament by increasing its ability to examine and publicize its activities.

Provincial Legislatures have committee systems similar to those of the federal government; but generally, partly because of the small size of the legislatures and greater government domination of the legislatures and the committees, they are less useful or active than their federal counterparts. C.E.S. FRANKS

Commodity Inspection and Grading Canada's AGRICULTURE AND FOOD inspection and grading system has 2 major goals: first, it endeavours to provide STANDARDS of quality and grades that are readily recognizable and acceptable in domestic and international commodity and food markets; second, it attempts to encourage concern for safety and nutrition in the processing, distribution and retailing of food products. Both of these objectives contribute to consumer protection. Commodity inspection and grading have a long history in Canada. Examples of commodity inspection legislation include the federal Act respecting contagious diseases of animals (1869), the Seed Control Act (1906), hog-grading regulations and grade standards for dressed poultry (1920s), the Canada Agricultural Products Standards Act (1955) and the Meat Inspection Act (1959). The list of federal and provincial government departments and agencies involved is very long, but the following examples illustrate the nature and scope of the system. The most important department, Agriculture Canada, conducts research into animal DISEASE and meat safety and

provides technical advisory services on biologics, PESTICIDES, FOOD ADDITIVES, chemical residues on food products, bacteriology and food-borne diseases. The Canadian Grain Commission provides a comprehensive grain-grading and inspection service and is responsible for licensing and for regulating grain-grading specifications. The Food and Drug Services Directorate of Health and Welfare Canada is responsible for the surveillance of food and drug quality. J.C. GILSON

Commodity Trading Commodity futures markets provide a means for the organized trading of contracts for the delivery of goods at a later date. Today, these include agricultural products, metals, forest products, petroleum products, interest rates and stocks. The first futures markets were developed to handle the problems created by the seasonal productions of grains. Grain is harvested in a short time period and needs to be stored for use throughout the rest of the year. This creates the potential for oversupply at harvest time and the threat of shortages before the next harvest is produced. At harvest, growers often faced a market glutted with supplies. As a result, prices could be severely depressed. Merchandisers, on the other hand, faced the problem of supplying their customers with a regular flow of grain despite the uncertainty about the amount of grain farmers would be selling and the timing of those sales. Futures markets give growers the ability to establish a price for their crop long before it is actually sold, and give merchandisers and processors assurance of both price and supplies throughout the crop year.

The first futures market was established in 1730 in Osaka, Japan. In the 1860s, futures trading began in Chicago to market the expanding production of the American plains, and in 1904 Canada's first futures market was established at what is now the Winnipeg Commodity Exchange. The Toronto Futures Exchange was established in 1980, sharing a trading floor with the Toronto Stock Exchange, and the Montreal Exchange established a futures market for lumber in 1984, but that contract has been dormant since 1986. In Toronto, futures contracts are traded for Canadian government bonds and Treasury bills and for a Canadian stock index. Trading volume in 1986 totalled 138 689 contracts. In Winnipeg, futures contracts are traded for canola, flaxseed and rye for international consumption, and for wheat, oats and barley for the domestic livestock feeding industry. In addition, the Winnipeg market also has future markets for gold and silver. The trading volume in 1986 totalled 1 995 185 contracts.

In the US, the world's largest futures markets are located in Chicago and New York, and there are also markets in Kansas City and Minneapolis. Important markets also exist in Europe, Asia, Australia and S America.

Commodity futures markets exist to provide a way to gain protection against the risk that prices will change. Commodity prices are determined by supply and demand. These, in turn, are affected by such unpredictable factors as weather, government policies, transportation and production and consumption decisions throughout the world. As a result, commodities are subject to large and unpredictable price changes. The commodity futures market gives commercial producers, merchandisers and processors the ability to protect themselves against the risk of price change through a process called hedging. Hedging makes it possible for risks to be managed and it reduces the cost of marketing commodities.

These commercial elements are the major users of futures markets. As examples, large borrowers, such as corporations, and large lenders, such as

pension funds, face the risk that interest rates will change before they are ready to sell bonds or to invest funds. They can guard against this risk by taking positions in the interest rates futures market. In the same way, farmers pay the cost of seeding a crop at least 4 months, and often as long as 15 months, before they will be able to sell their production. The futures market provides them with an opportunity to protect their selling price against the uncertainties of the international grain market.

In addition to the commercial producers and users of commodities, futures markets are also attractive to speculators, who attempt to profit by predicting the direction of commodity price movements. In the process, they provide the essential function of taking on the risk that commercial hedgers are trying to avoid. K.S. KEARNS

Common Front Strikes, a cartel of Québec public- and para-public-sector trade unions, formed in 1972 to negotiate with the provincial government. The cartel consisted primarily of unions affiliated to 3 UNION CENTRALS – the CNTU (CONFEDERATION OF NATIONAL TRADE UNIONS), the QFL (Québec Federation of Labour) and the QTC (Québec Teachers Corp) – plus some independent unions. The first Common Front was created during a round of bargaining in 1972. It united more than 210 000 employees, almost all of them working in government, in education and in social services (hospitals, etc). This round gave rise to several major events, including a 10-day general strike (Apr 11-12) which was ended with special legislation, a series of injunctions and the imprisonment of presidents of the 3 union centrals (Louis LABERGE, QFL; Marcel PÉPIN, CNTU; Yvon CHARBONNEAU, QTC) for having urged their members to defy the order to return to work. This round also saw the split in the CNTU which led to the creation of the CDTU (Central of Democratic Trade Unions). Similar common fronts were established during negotiations in 1976, 1979 and 1982. Each was marked by major clashes (strikes, injunctions and special laws). MAURICE LEMELIN

Common Law, the system of LAW that evolved from the decisions of the English royal courts of justice since the Norman Conquest (1066). Today the common law, considered more broadly to include statutes as well as decisions, applies in most English-speaking countries, including all Canadian provinces except Quebec.

JOHN E.C. BRIERLEY

Commonwealth, a loose, voluntary association of Great Britain and most of its former colonies; 49 independent nations – about one-quarter of the world's population – pledged (according to a 1971 declaration of principles) to consult and co-operate in furthering world peace, social understanding, racial equality and economic development. The Commonwealth Secretariat (est 1965) administers programs of co-operation, arranges meetings and provides specialist services to member countries. The British monarch is head of the Commonwealth, a purely symbolic role.

The roots of the Commonwealth are frequently traced back as far as the DURHAM REPORT (1839) and RESPONSIBLE GOVERNMENT in the 1840s. By 1867 the British North American provinces, as well as other British colonies in Newfoundland, Australia, New Zealand and South Africa, were self-governing with respect to internal affairs. With CONFEDERATION, 1867, Canada became the first federation in the British Empire; its size, economic strength and seniority enabled it to become a leader in the widening of colonial autonomy and the transformation of the empire into a commonwealth of equal nations.

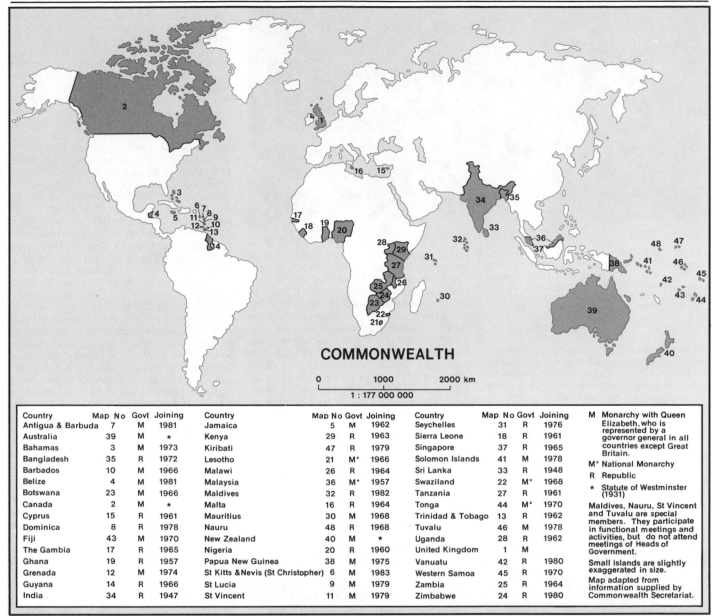

COMMONWEALTH

0   1000   2000 km

1 : 177 000 000

Country	Map No	Govt	Joining	Country	Map No	Govt	Joining	Country	Map No	Govt	Joining	
Antigua & Barbuda	7	M	1981	Jamaica	5	M	1962	Seychelles	31	R	1976	**M** Monarchy with Queen Elizabeth, who is represented by a governor general in all countries except Great Britain.
Australia	39	M	*	Kenya	29	R	1963	Sierra Leone	18	R	1961	
Bahamas	3	M	1973	Kiribati	47	R	1979	Singapore	37	R	1965	
Bangladesh	35	R	1972	Lesotho	21	M*	1966	Solomon Islands	41	M	1978	
Barbados	10	M	1966	Malawi	26	R	1964	Sri Lanka	33	R	1948	**M*** National Monarchy
Belize	4	M	1981	Malaysia	36	M*	1957	Swaziland	22	M*	1968	**R** Republic
Botswana	23	M	1966	Maldives	32	R	1982	Tanzania	27	R	1961	
Canada	2	M	*	Malta	16	R	1964	Tonga	44	M*	1970	***** Statute of Westminster (1931)
Cyprus	15	R	1961	Mauritius	30	M	1968	Trinidad & Tobago	13	R	1962	Maldives, Nauru, St Vincent and Tuvalu are special members. They participate in functional meetings and activities, but do not attend meetings of Heads of Government.
Dominica	8	R	1978	Nauru	48	R	1968	Tuvalu	46	M	1978	
Fiji	43	M	1970	New Zealand	40	M	*	Uganda	28	R	1962	
The Gambia	17	R	1965	Nigeria	20	R	1960	United Kingdom	1	M		
Ghana	19	R	1957	Papua New Guinea	38	M	1975	Vanuatu	42	R	1980	Small islands are slightly exaggerated in size.
Grenada	12	M	1974	St Kitts &Nevis (St Christopher)	6	M	1983	Western Samoa	45	R	1970	
Guyana	14	R	1966	St Lucia	9	M	1979	Zambia	25	R	1964	Map adapted from information supplied by Commonwealth Secretariat.
India	34	R	1947	St Vincent	11	M	1979	Zimbabwe	24	R	1980	

Contingents from all the self-governing colonies freely participated in the SOUTH AFRICAN WAR, 1899-1902. Canada sent only volunteers, and PM Sir Wilfrid LAURIER made it clear at Colonial and Imperial Conferences in 1902, 1907 and 1911 that participation in imperial defence would always be on Canadian terms. In 1914 the king declared war on behalf of the entire empire, but the Dominions (a term applied to Canada in 1867 and used in the first half of this century to describe the empire's other self-governing members) decided individually the nature and extent of their participation. They gave generously: over a million men from the Dominions and 1.5 million from India enlisted in the forces of the empire. There were also huge contributions of food, money and munitions. Although South African nationalists (Afrikaners) and many French Canadians opposed participation in a distant British war, the unity of the empire in WORLD WAR I was impressive.

Despite the extent of their WWI commitment, the Dominions at first played no part in the making of high policy. But Canadian PM Sir Robert BORDEN was especially critical when the war did not go well. When David Lloyd George became British prime minister in late 1916, he immediately convened an Imperial War Conference and created an Imperial War Cabinet, 2 separate bodies which met in 1917 and 1918. The former was remembered primarily for Resolution IX, which stated that the Dominions were "autonomous nations of an Imperial Commonwealth" with a "right...to an adequate voice in foreign policy and in foreign relations...." This was chiefly an initiative of PM Borden, carried at the conference with the help of Gen J.C. Smuts of South Africa, and it marked the first official use of the term "Commonwealth."

The Imperial War Cabinet gave leaders from the Dominions and India an opportunity to be informed, consulted and made to feel a part of the making of high-level policy. A similar body, the British Empire Delegation, was constructed at the Paris Peace Conference. Borden and Australian PM W.M. Hughes also successfully fought for separate Dominion representation at the conference and separate signatures on the Treaty of VERSAILLES. Constitutionally, however, the empire was still a single unit: Lloyd George's was the signature that counted. The Dominions, now members of the new LEAGUE OF NATIONS, remained ambiguous creatures – part nation, part colony, part imperial colleague.

The war pulled each Dominion in apparently opposite directions: widespread hopes for greater imperial unity clashed with intensified feelings of national pride and distinctiveness which resulted from wartime sacrifice and achievement. Borden, a nationalist who wished to enhance Canada's growing international status through commitment to a great empire-commonwealth, tried to reconcile the 2 impulses. He sought a closely knit commonwealth of equal nations that would consult and act together on the big issues of common concern. Resolution IX had called for a postwar conference to readjust constitutional relations along these lines. It was never held.

A nationalism quite different from Borden's took control of the Commonwealth in the 1920s. Canadian PM Mackenzie KING was the heir to Laurier's policy of "no commitments." The CHANAK AFFAIR and the HALIBUT TREATY set the tone, and King was a clear winner at the Imperial Conference of 1923. A trend away from imperial diplomatic unity and towards a devolved, autonomous relationship between Britain and the Dominions was established. King believed that the British connection could be maintained only if it allowed Canadians, particularly the substantial minority of non-British descent, to concentrate on developing a strong N American nation. He was not alone in wishing to emphasize diplomatic autonomy, although the reasons differed.

Imperial War Cabinet meeting 1 May 1917, remembered primarily for Resolution IX, which stated that the Dominions were "autonomous nations of an Imperial Commonwealth" – the first official use of the term Commonwealth. PM Robert Borden is 1st row, 3rd from right (*courtesy National Archives of Canada/C-6846*).

The British had little wish for a co-operative Anglo-Dominion foreign policy that would require the Foreign Office to engage in time-consuming consultation with much smaller powers. South Africa and the Irish Free State, which were granted Dominion status on the Canadian model in 1921, were even more radical than King in pushing for decentralization.

At the Imperial Conference of 1926, South African PM Gen J.B.M. Hertzog demanded a public declaration that the Dominions were independent states, equal in status to Britain and separately entitled to international recognition. King opposed the word "independent," which might conjure up unhappy visions of the American Revolution in pro-British parts of Canada, but he endorsed the thrust of Hertzog's demand. The conference adopted the BALFOUR REPORT, which led to the passage of the STATUTE OF WESTMINSTER, 1931, establishing the theoretical right of the Dominions to full legislative autonomy.

The Commonwealth of the 1930s was a study in contradiction, a mixture of the national and the imperial, and confusing to outsiders. To some extent Commonwealth countries conducted their own external affairs and managed their own defences. Yet a common head of state, common citizenship and substantial common legislation remained. Association with a vast and apparently powerful empire – then at its greatest extent, covering over 31 million km² – brought the Dominions prestige, prosperity and protection. The OTTAWA AGREEMENTS of 1932, although falling far short of creating the self-sufficient unit some had dreamed about, bound Commonwealth countries tighter in an interlocking series of bilateral trading agreements. There was also substantial military co-operation, of enormous benefit to the Dominions' fledgling ARMED FORCES. Newfoundland, proudly "Britain's oldest colony," had long had responsible government, was represented at Colonial and Imperial Conferences and had fought with distinction in WWI, but financial crisis brought about the return of British rule (*see* COMMISSION OF GOVERNMENT) from 1934 to 1949, at which time it became part of Canada.

Dependence and gratitude did not necessarily lead to commitment, and in peacetime the Dominions were wary of European entanglements. When Britain declared war on Germany in Sept 1939, Australia and New Zealand did not hesitate to become involved in WORLD WAR II. Canada waited one week before Parliament endorsed the King government's decision to fight. South Africans split on the issue and PM Hertzog resigned, but the final response was positive. Only Eire (as the Irish Free State became in 1937) stayed aloof. Immense contributions of men – over 2 million from the 4 Dominions and 2.5 million from India – and material were made. The BRITISH COMMONWEALTH AIR TRAINING PLAN, which trained 131 553 aircrew, was a major Canadian contribution. Such efforts were all the more important and valued because the Dominions alone fought at Britain's side from the first day to the last. But there was no Imperial War Cabinet this time, no Commonwealth consensus on the need to strengthen ties. British power was waning and Dominion confidence was on the rise, weakening traditional links. Britain's subject peoples in Africa and Asia also looked increasingly to themselves for solutions to their problems.

By 1949 the Commonwealth was completely transformed. Eire left in 1948. India, which had been lurching towards responsible government and Dominion status for decades, achieved independence in 1947, although at a price: it was divided on religious grounds into the Dominions of India and Pakistan. Neighbouring Ceylon (now Sri Lanka) and Burma achieved independence in 1947-48, the former obtaining Dominion status and choosing Commonwealth membership. In 1949 India was allowed to remain in the Commonwealth after declaring itself a republic. The British monarch was declared "the symbol of the free association of its member nations, and as such Head of the Commonwealth." The Commonwealth was no longer predominantly white and British; allegiance to a common crown was no longer a prerequisite of membership, and the concept of common citizenship was fading fast.

There were high hopes for the "multiracial" Commonwealth, which many believed could be a force and example for understanding among nations. A bigger grouping, however, was more difficult to keep together, particularly when members were moving more than ever before in different directions, partly in order to develop responses to a COLD WAR world dominated by hostility between the US and USSR. Britain began the long road to eventual membership (1973) in the European Economic Community, to the consternation of much of the older Commonwealth. Canada, Australia and New Zealand looked increasingly to the US as an ally and trading partner. India preached the doctrine of nonalignment with either of the superpowers. The SUEZ CRISIS of 1956, over which the Commonwealth was badly split, underlined the decline of Britain's power and gave rise to questions about its judgement and morality in the bargain.

But the Commonwealth did not die. As former British dependencies achieved self-government and took responsibility for their own external relations, it became customary to say that they had "achieved independence," and might or might not "join the Commonwealth" as monarchies or republics. Most did join. The decade after 1957 was one of dramatic growth: virtually all the colonies of British Africa, joined by 4 in the Caribbean, one in Asia and 2 in the Mediterranean, won their independence and became Commonwealth members. So did Bangladesh, on declaring independence from Pakistan in 1971; Pakistan then left the Commonwealth.

The multiracial composition of the postwar Commonwealth has affected both the politics and the policies of the UK. Pressure about its racial policies from Commonwealth colleagues (especially from Canada's PM John DIEFENBAKER) led to the withdrawal of South Africa in 1961. Until well into the 1960s, Britain was led by its Commonwealth connections to maintain an open-door policy towards immigrants from the Asian Commonwealth and the West Indies. When Rhodesia unilaterally declared independence in 1965 to continue white-settler supremacy, Commonwealth states exerted great pressure on Britain to ensure that international recognition would not be granted unless black majority rule was conceded. Only in 1980, when that condition had been satisfied, was the state's independence legalized; Rhodesia (as Zimbabwe) became a member of the Commonwealth.

The very idea of such an amorphous institution arouses an easy cynicism in Canada, when it is thought of at all. P.E. TRUDEAU was a cynic when he became prime minister in 1968, but he quickly became a believer. Trudeau played an important role in the 1971 heads-of-government meeting, when the future of the Commonwealth was in question because Britain wished to sell arms to South Africa. The Commonwealth in the 1980s has had its share of crises including the Falklands War (1982), the military takeover in Nigeria (1983) and the Grenada invasion (1983). S Africa continues to be a bone of contention, as shown by its importance at the Oct 1987 meeting of Commonwealth leaders in Vancouver. Canadian leaders and diplomats have played a prominent role throughout Commonwealth history (Arnold SMITH, for example, was the Commonwealth's first secretary general), not simply in helping to create an international institution, but in keeping it together in moments of stress. One of the Commonwealth's great attractions is that it gives members a forum for making themselves and their views known, and access to an expanding network of economic, social and educational programs – without demanding uniformity of outlook or purpose in return. The COLOMBO PLAN of 1950 was a pioneering effort in development assistance. The Commonwealth Fund for Technical Co-operation (fd 1971) is now the chief means of giving aid to developing countries, Canada providing more than 40% of the budget. The Commonwealth co-operates in ways which would never have been possible in the old days of empire. Today unofficial and official links are in the thousands – from regular meetings of the heads of government, and of their ministers and officials, to agencies such as the Commonwealth Youth Program, Commonwealth Scholarships and the COMMONWEALTH GAMES. *See also* EXTERNAL RELATIONS; CANADA AND AUSTRALIA; FRANCOPHONIE. NORMAN HILLMER

Reading: Norman Hillmer and P. Wigley, eds, *The First British Commonwealth* (1980); N. Mansergh, *The Commonwealth Experience* (2 vols, 1982); A. Smith, *Stitches in Time* (1981); P. Wigley, *Canada and the Transition to Commonwealth* (1977).

Commonwealth Games Since the first British Empire Games were held at Hamilton, Ont, in Aug 1930, attended by 400 competitors representing 11 countries, Canada has been a leading proponent and participant in this 4-yearly multisport festival. Succeeding Games were held at London (England), 1934; Sydney (Australia), 1938; Auckland (New Zealand), 1950; Vancouver, 1954 and renamed the British Empire and Commonwealth Games; Cardiff (Wales), 1958; Perth (Australia), 1962; Kingston (Jamaica), 1966 and renamed the British Commonwealth Games; Edinburgh (Scotland), 1970; Christchurch (New Zealand), 1974; and Edmonton, 1978 and renamed the Commonwealth Games, by which time nearly 1500 athletes from 46 countries competed. The 1982 Commonwealth Games took place in Brisbane, Australia, and in 1986 they were in Edinburgh, Scot. The 1990 Games will be in Auckland, NZ.

The Commonwealth Games have provided many memorable performances (10 world records were broken at Cardiff in 1958). "The Miracle Mile" at Vancouver, in 1954, when Roger Bannister of Great Britain defeated John Landy of Australia, was one of the most dramatic events in sport history. Canadian athletes have given outstanding performances at several Games – in swimming alone, Phyllis DEWAR (1934), Elaine TANNER (1966) and Graham Smith (1978) won 14 gold medals. At the XI Commonwealth Games (1978) in Edmonton, where 10 000 local volunteers assisted in the organization, Canada obtained an unprecedented 45 gold medals, 31 silver and 33 bronze, for a total of 109 (England was nearest with 27 gold and a total of 87). There were 11 sports at these Games: athletics (track and field), badminton, boxing, cycling, gymnastics, lawn bowling, shooting, swimming, weightlifting, wrestling and lacrosse (demonstration sport). Canada obtained a total of 115 medals (51 gold) at the 1986 Games, second only to England. The outstanding competitor in Canada's 380-member team was swimmer Jane Kerr who won 2 gold, 2 silver and 2 bronze medals.

GERALD REDMOND

Reading: History Committee of the XI Commonwealth Games, *A Historical Record of the Games Leading up to the Commonwealth Games of 1978* (1978); Gerald Redmond, ed, *Edmonton '78: The Official Pictorial Record of the XI Commonwealth Games* (1978).

Communal Properties Act Case *Walter v Attorney-General of Alberta* (1965-69) tested the constitutional validity of the Communal Properties Act (1955), which had the effect of restricting the territorial area of communal lands owned by religiously based groups such as the HUTTERITES and the DOUKHOBORS. Although it was argued that the Act dealt with religion and that only Parliament could pass legislation affecting religious freedom, the SUPREME COURT OF CANADA in a unanimous judgement upheld the validity of the statute, saying that it related to land ownership in Alberta and that the province had the constitutional competence to pass legislation dealing with "property in the province" even if it incidentally affected religious matters. The Act was repealed but the case is of historical interest because it tested the validity of what might be considered discriminatory legislation. The case also demonstrates how technical and superficial the Supreme Court of Canada was in protecting fundamental freedoms of Canadians. This may change as a result of the Canadian Charter of Rights and Freedoms. *See also* HUMAN RIGHTS.) M.M. LITMAN

Communauté des biens (community of property), term used in the legal codes of NEW FRANCE and Québec to describe the pooled assets of husband and wife. It began as part of the Coutume de Paris, introduced about 1640 and the sole legal code of the colony after 1664. The codes stipulated that all but the inherited immovable goods (essentially land and annuities) of the partners entered into this arrangement; that within certain limits the husband would be free to manage the communauté according to his lights; and that upon the death of one spouse, the survivor would receive half the communauté – debts and all – and the children the other half. Communauté des biens survived more than 3 centuries of social mutation; only in 1980 did the concept pass out of use. The Québec CIVIL CODE now refers to a *société des acquêts*, or "partnership of acquests."

THOMAS WIEN

Communauté des habitants (Compagnie des habitants), colonial merchants who held the FUR TRADE monopoly in NEW FRANCE, 1645-63. In principle the COMPAGNIE DES CENT-ASSOCIÉS ceded its monopoly to all inhabitants of the colony, but in practice only a few of the wealthiest benefited. The cost of the monopoly was the equivalent of the colony's administrative expenses plus an annual rent of 1000 livres' weight of beaver skins and the promise to import 20 colonists a year. The communauté was not a success: high interest rates, combined with a lack of experience in commerce, led to serious financial difficulties by 1652. The Conseil de Québec then declared the trade open to all HABITANTS, not just the original communauté members. This arrangement continued until the communauté's collapse in 1663.

Communication Studies explore the ways in which information is given meaning by those who produce, distribute and interpret it. Communication studies are a relatively new academic discipline, with departments or programs in 13 Canadian universities and many colleges; with 2 journals (*Communication et information*, Laval, and *Canadian Journal of Communication*, McGill U, Montréal); with national and Québec associations, and a number of organizations appealing to specialized interests and involving academics, representatives from industry and government and members of the public.

Research may focus on a variety of topics. Mass media are studied for the content of their programs, the way those programs are produced and the impact of various influences on programming. Media economic structure and the media's role in political life are also topics of research. Communication studies may also focus on how particular messages are presented in films, advertisements or school texts; in press statements made during election campaigns; in news reporting and in government documents; or in the way a group meeting or public inquiry is conducted. The purpose of communication analyses is to identify the full range of meanings, whether intended or not, to see how those meanings are structured into the final message that people receive, and to examine the impact of what is being communicated.

Some of the most important work in communication studies was done by Harold INNIS, the Canadian economic historian who turned his attention to communications in his later works. Innis argued that the way information is disseminated influences not only the impact of the message but also its content and the shape of social life as a whole. Although Innis died (1952) long before the computer or satellite age, his work on ancient writing systems and modern radio enabled him to predict many of the changes that were to occur in a society dependent upon rapid transmission of information. Research in communication studies today draws upon Innis's insights in examining, for example, the impact of literacy and TV on Inuit communities, the relationship between economic and communication development and the impact of new information technologies.

An important aspect of communication studies in Canada is the impact of government policies (*see* CULTURAL POLICY) and of agencies such as the CANADIAN RADIO-TELEVISION AND TELECOMMUNICATIONS COMMISSION.

Communication studies developed in the US as an amalgam of engineering, social psychology, advertising or propaganda rhetoric. The focus in the often highly empirical American work is on the dissemination of information. In Europe, communication studies are more often theoretical and include the study of ideology and consciousness. In Canada, communication studies drew their original impulse from the humanities – 2 of the better-known contributors being Marshall MCLUHAN and Northrop FRYE. Canadian communication studies also draw heavily from psychology, sociology, philosophy, political science and economics. This research can be distinguished from the American and European traditions by its synthesis of theoretical and empirical work and by the attention given by many writers to producing recommendations for government policy.

An underlying focus in much Canadian research, and certainly among the active francophone scholars, is "cultural" experience. Particular attention is given to COMMUNICATIONS IN QUÉBEC and among regional or native cultures; to problems associated with regional, francophone or national identity; and to centralist and decentralist strains in Canadian social development. Communication studies explore how, when and why cultural products such as film, music or literature become significant to some or all members of society. Communication studies may be taught in Canada in conjunction with journalism, business communication, cultural studies and educational or technical media programs. LIORA SALTER

Communications have been the key structural element in Canadian society since the time when canoes slipping down rivers were the connecting links between villages. Communications by water and land made Canadian federation possible; electronic communications today make possible the conduct of business, the political process and the sharing of culture and information. It is no accident that the most renowned commentator on communications in the world this century, Marshall MCLUHAN, was a Canadian. He spent his life in a country obsessed by communications. He was born in Edmonton, then an isolated prairie city connected by the railway, telephone and telegraph to the rest of Canada and the US; and he died in Toronto, the hub of English-language communications in Canada, where at the time of his death more TV channels were available than anywhere else in the world and where the social control of mass communications was a subject of comment in the daily press.

Communications influence all societies, but Canada in particular takes its shape and meaning from communications systems. Since Confederation, Canada has been a landmass much larger than most empires in history; governing its distant settlements and bringing them together in some form of political, social and cultural unity has been primarily a problem of communications management. A communications system is an attempt to offset distance between human beings, whether by railway, aircraft, telephone or post. The building of the CANADIAN PACIFIC RAILWAY in the 1880s, as part of the political arrangement that created Confederation, was an attempt to counteract the disintegrative effects of Canada's enormous space and to prevent the absorption of western Canada by the US. A similar impulse was behind the building of radio, television, TELEPHONE and TELECOMMUNICATIONS systems. Since Canada's inception governments have recognized the importance of communications in Canadian life, and communications systems usually have been developed under government sponsorship and always under government control. Since 1932 the federal government has been directly involved in BROADCASTING (see CANADIAN BROADCASTING CORPORATION), first radio and then TV. Since the late 1930s it has had its own filmmaking agency, the NATIONAL FILM BOARD, which produces and distributes films. Since the 1920s the government has regulated broadcasting and telephone systems; today it is a partner in SATELLITE COMMUNICATIONS. Private business has played an increasingly large role in broadcasting, particularly since the early 1960s. But many communities, especially in the North, would not be reached by mass communications without the active participation of the government (see COMMUNICATIONS IN THE NORTH).

ADVERTISING is a major component in almost all media and, within the business structure of Canada, consumer advertising is the main role of the media. The media have made the consumer society possible by providing fast, widespread dissemination of information or impressions about products and services. Experience has taught advertisers that TV is one of the most effective ways of selling products. Typically, a TV commercial sets out not to sell a product directly but to surround it with exciting or pleasing images and thereby to insert the product comfortably into the world view of the consumer. Thus, beer on TV is associated with good fellowship, long-distance telephone calls are associated with family feeling, clothing is associated with youth and beauty. A careful study of TV commercials provides a series of clues to the values held by most people at the time when the commercials were made.

The mass media constitute an elaborate and highly sensitive web, stretched over the country, the strands of which are individual NEWSPAPERS, MAGAZINES and radio and TV stations. The people who run these institutions are closely connected and their roles are often interchangeable. A magazine editor may write a book that is serialized in a newspaper, which he discusses at length on radio, and which he then helps to turn into a TV series. The media are also connected by the facts, themes and ideas they convey. Radio listeners will sometimes sense this interdependence when they realize that the news they hear at breakfast is a rewritten version of the news in the morning paper that was prepared the night before. News is a commodity that can be sold. The CANADIAN PRESS, the national newsgathering agency owned co-operatively by the newspapers, sells its service to broadcasters. Through that system, and also informally, news passes freely from one medium to another. A newspaper reporter's story or quotation will be selected by a TV reporter and combined with a fresh comment from a public official to become the basis for another story in another newspaper; a few hours later it may be the subject for a column of comment or a broadcast commentary by another journalist.

McLuhan – who based much of his work on the pioneering media studies of the economist Harold INNIS – believed that media reshape not only our perceptions but our actions. People seeking publicity often create "media events" that lend themselves to coverage by TV and to a lesser extent by newspapers and radio. Campaign tours by political leaders are arranged to provide interesting TV pictures; a visit to a steel plant, for instance, is not only an attempt to solicit the steelworkers' votes

but also a way of obtaining precious TV time by putting the candidate against an arresting background. A prime minister's press conference was a small, almost private affair in the years before TV; now it is normally a public performance. The most dramatic event of recent decades in Canada, the OCTOBER CRISIS of 1970 in Montréal, was a media event. The kidnappers set the tone by demanding that their separatist manifesto be read on TV and by regularly communicating with the police through dispatches sent to radio stations. In response, the WAR MEASURES ACT, imposed by the federal government, effectively blacked out the kidnappers' media activities and brought PUBLIC OPINION under the control of the authorities. One political scientist has remarked that the October Crisis could be seen as a battle for the temporary control of the communications systems in Québec.

Canadians receive most of their news from TV or radio, and, for both owners and journalists, broadcasting has become more profitable than newspaper and BOOK PUBLISHING. Newspapers, having lost much of their advertising revenue to the broadcasters, are increasingly subject to merger or elimination. Nevertheless, they remain at the centre of the communications web in most communities and in both national language groups because they employ more reporters than broadcasting networks and publish more news and comment. Newspapers provide broadcasting with information and a sense of what is important. Newspapers, not broadcasting networks, set the agenda for discussion of public affairs; in particular the GLOBE AND MAIL in English Canada and Le DEVOIR in French Canada play this role. Broadcasting, though it has drawn away much of the economic power of the newspapers, has magnified their role as shapers of opinion, a role the newspapers have played since colonial days.

One result of these media interconnections is the development of waves of opinion. A politician may be universally admired in the media one year, reviled the next, and then highly respected a few years later. Just such a series of transformations happened in the public career of Robert STANFIELD between his elevation to the leadership of the Progressive Conservatives in 1967 and his retirement in 1976. Public issues seem to rise and fall in the same way; for instance, abortion was held to be a crime in one decade and a human right in the next. In most cases the media reflect what they perceive to be public opinion and public interest, slightly and inevitably distorted by the people who staff the newspapers and broadcasting stations. The communications media sell fashions in thought and are themselves influenced by fashions. A popular broadcaster's intonation may be imitated by hundreds of newscasters, and a style of magazine writing may spread across the continent. There are times when the media seem dedicated to producing a pale sameness. But McLuhan has taught us to look at the technological development of the media for an understanding of their influence, and if we follow that course we see a process repeating itself throughout the communications media, an unexpected process of sophistication and refinement that works against the creation of a homogeneous mass society.

Each medium begins in a fairly basic way, with an attempt to appeal to everyone. The early promoters treat the medium almost as a toy. Later, as the techniques develop and potential audiences are explored by both entrepreneurs and imaginative public servants, it becomes possible to reach smaller, more select audiences and to appeal to specialized tastes. Thus, films began with a few studios in America and Europe trying to gain dominance; later, as the processes became widely

available, scores of countries and hundreds of companies developed the ability to make films, often great films. Phonograph records first became popular under the control of a few companies that dictated tastes everywhere; but with the rise of the economical LP record, beginning in 1948, the process of differentiation began and thousands of companies sprang up to serve disparate minority markets. Radio was born as a means of broadcasting popular music and later emerged as a way of conveying sophisticated documentaries, imaginative dramas and music on a specialized level. Something similar has happened to magazines recently: there are now perhaps 10 times as many magazines in Canada as there were in 1960, most of them catering to specialized tastes. In the late 1970s television began to fit into this historic pattern. With the rise of CABLE TELEVISION and PAY TELEVISION, "narrowcasting" (as opposed to broadcasting) became the object of many professionals searching for small, select, dedicated audiences. Only daily newspapers have moved in the opposite direction, growing fewer in number and broader in appeal despite their adoption of advanced techniques such as computerized typesetting. In the early 1980s it seemed that written JOURNALISM might find a new form through videotext systems of interactive TV. With videotext, the consumer calls up a text on a screen (sometimes with still pictures) by switching buttons. The text may be an advertisement, a weather report, an article from an encyclopedia, a news item or anything that can be reduced to words and pictures. This produces a new form of "publishing." Many countries are experimenting with various videotext systems, including TELIDON, the Canadian system created at the Dept of Communications in Ottawa during the 1970s.

As these media developed through the first 80 years of this century, Canada's experience was in some ways identical to that of other countries. Collecting hundreds of Mozart records was no more or less rewarding in Vancouver than in Melbourne or Vienna. But in many other ways Canada is a special case, because Canada exists next door to the most powerful and innovative communications system in the world. American mass culture dominates the Canadian imagination. Most countries regulate imported culture through quotas on FILM and broadcasting, but Canada has set up few barriers and even those have been ineffective. In 1932, when Prime Minister R.B. Bennett introduced legislation that created public broadcasting, he declared in Parliament: "This country must be assured of complete Canadian control of broadcasting from Canadian sources, free from foreign interference or influence. Without such control radio broadcasting can never become a great agency for the communication of matters of national concern and for the diffusion of national thought and ideals, and without such control it can never be the agency by which national consciousness may be fostered and sustained and national unity still further strengthened." Since then, most federal governments and several royal commissions have reaffirmed these views, but with only modest effect. News and public affairs programs on TV have focused the concern of all Canadians on national public issues, but in most other ways our media have lived wanly in the American shadow. As a result, mass communications have been the ground on which some of the most important battles of Canadian sovereignty have been fought. Only occasionally have the forces of national culture been triumphant, as in the creation of French and English TV and radio networks by the CBC or the 1975 legislation which prevented American magazines from establishing Canadian subsidiary

First wireless transmission across the Atlantic, 12 Dec 1901. Marconi and his instrument inside Cabot Tower, Signal Hill, St John's, Nfld (*courtesy National Archives of Canada/C-5945*).

editions. One major reason is cost. Canada provides a small market split into 2 language groups: in broadcasting, as with paperback books and magazines and many other fields, Canadians have found it cheaper and more convenient to import what they view or read. Another reason is the ongoing struggle between private and public interests. As a general rule, private interests have encouraged the cultural Americanization of Canada, on the grounds that it is more profitable to resell American films, TV shows and records than to make them in Canada.

The forces representing public interest (the CBC, the federal regulatory agencies and the provincial TV networks) have been sharply divided over the issue of regional interests versus national unity. The latter has implied increasing centralization, a Toronto-dominated system of production, similar to the growing power of federal agencies in Ottawa. Regionalists contend that national media will extinguish the centres of provincial vitality and expression. Centralists argue that Canada's population can support no more than 2 first-class production centres, in Toronto and Montréal, and will be lucky if these cities can produce material good enough to meet foreign competition.

Canadian nationalism became a more powerful force in the 1960s and the 1970s than at any point since the 1920s, and the appreciation and development of national and regional Canadian culture became a public issue. This interest has led to fundamental changes in publishing and the performing arts, but has made no great impression on TV because a more powerful counterforce was at work: cable TV. Bringing American stations to a majority of viewers, cable effectively put Canadian broadcasters in a minority in their own country, pushing Canadian TELEVISION DRAMA and entertainment out to the edge of the country's consciousness. In a period when mass communications in Canada might have flourished, they found themselves more overshadowed than ever. The effect of cable was marked even in Québec. The first 2 decades of TV had tended to strengthen Québec identity by producing a generation of French Canadian TV writers, stars and commentators – the most famous being René LÉVESQUE, a commentator on Radio-Canada in the 1950s who became provincial premier in 1976. But when cable made a broad spectrum of American stations available, French Canadians in considerable numbers began viewing them, and TV presented yet another threat to the survival of the French language. In mass communications, every fresh development brings social problems as well as benefits. **ROBERT FULFORD**

Reading: P. Hindley, G. Martin and J. McNulty, eds, *The Tangled Net* (1977); P. Rutherford, *The Making of the Canadian Media* (1978); B. Singer, ed, *Communications in Canadian Society* (1972).

Communications, Department of, was established by the Department of Communications Act in 1969. The minister is responsible for fostering the orderly operation and development of communications in Canada. The powers and functions of the minister extend to TELECOMMUNICATIONS, national communications policy, BROADCASTING policy, radio and radar research, and actions necessary to secure the international rights of Canada in communications. The Space Sector is responsible for SATELLITE COMMUNICATIONS and support of the Canadian space industry. The CANADIAN BROADCASTING CORPORATION, CANADIAN FILM DEVELOPMENT CORPORATION (formerly called Telefilm Canada), NATIONAL ARTS CENTRE Corporation, NATIONAL LIBRARY, NATIONAL MUSEUMS OF CANADA, SOCIAL SCIENCES AND HUMANITIES RESEARCH COUNCIL, CANADA COUNCIL, NATIONAL FILM BOARD, the Space Program, Teleglobe Canada, Telesat Canada and the CANADIAN RADIO-TELEVISION AND TELECOMMUNICATIONS COMMISSION report to Parliament through the minister. The department's 1986-87 budget was $270 million.

Communications in Québec What is distinctive about communications in Québec is the existence of 2, often competing, media serving different cultures and, above all, the ways in which francophone media have expressed or reinforced the character of French Canada. The development of communications in Québec is associated with an underlying constitutional conflict between Québec City and Ottawa. The government of Québec, basing its position on jurisdiction over language, education and culture, claims complete authority for communications in the province. The scope of the political battle can only be fully understood when viewed in terms of the linguistic and cultural situation of Québec in N America. The evolution of the media is intimately linked with the process of modernization that has been under way in Québec since WWII, particularly the political and cultural upheavals of the 1960s and 1970s.

The federal-provincial battle over communications began in 1929, the year in which the Aird Report was published, when the TASCHEREAU government adopted the first "law respecting broadcasting in this province." In 1931 subsequent Québec legislation concerning radio led to court action by the federal government, which won its case before the Supreme Court of Canada. Québec appealed to the Judicial Committee of the Privy Council in London, which in 1932 confirmed the verdict of the Supreme Court. The reasoning invoked in support of the federal position was based on an interpretation of paragraph 10 of s92 of the CONSTITUTION ACT, 1867, which makes reference to the telegraph, the only modern method of communication in existence at the time of Confederation. Radio communication was likened to the telegraph in that radio waves could not easily be contained within the borders of a province.

Because the media are major instruments for promoting and broadcasting information, successive Québec governments have claimed responsibility for matters relating to cultural development. In 1945 Maurice DUPLESSIS adopted an "Act authorizing the creation of a provincial broadcasting service," but it was not until 1968 that Radio-Québec was founded. In 1972 the educational network of Radio-Québec offered several hours of programming on cable and in 1975 began broadcasting on UHF.

The Daniel JOHNSON government created Québec's Dept of Communications in 1969, and in 1972 the Robert BOURASSA government broadened the mandate of the Régie des services publics (Public Service Board) to "the broadcasting,

transmission and reception of sounds, images, signs, signals, data or messages by wire, cable, waves, or any electrical, electronic, magnetic, electromagnetic or optical means." The major issue was control of CABLE TELEVISION broadcasting, as the CRTC and the Régie both claimed authority for granting licences. In 1977 the Supreme Court of Canada ruled in favour of the federal government, granting it exclusive jurisdiction.

The birth of broadcasting in Montréal took place in 1919 with the inauguration of station XWA (later to become CFCF). In 1932 CKAC became the first French-language radio station. The advent of television and its rapid development in the 1950s helped pave the way for the QUIET REVOLUTION, in particular the program "Point de Mire," with host René LÉVESQUE. Francophone NEWSPAPERS, MAGAZINES, novelists and singers also contributed to the revolution. The francophone advertising industry, once little more than a translation service, after 1960 broke free from Anglo control to embrace the French Canadian milieu. The media drew inspiration from and encouraged the creative turmoil that marked all aspects of culture at the end of the Duplessis regime; certain radio and television programs were very successful (*see* RADIO DRAMA, FRENCH-LANGUAGE; RADIO PROGRAMMING; TELEVISION PROGRAMMING). In the early 1970s open-line radio programs became popular to a degree rarely equalled elsewhere. Novels adapted for television – the typical Québec formula for dramatic series – experienced a popularity that has not declined over the years (*see* TELEVISION DRAMA, FRENCH-LANGUAGE). Variety shows involving audience participation were also successful.

In 1987 the CRTC had given licences to 71 AM and 82 FM stations in Québec and to 34 TV stations – 6 owned by and 6 affiliated with Radio-Canada (CBC) and others affiliated with Télédiffuseurs Associés, Radio-Québec and CTV Television Network Ltd. There were 2 independents (including Quatre Saisons), 1 educational channel, 1 community channel and 6 remote and native community stations. In addition there are 6 PAY-TV networks. The print media consisted of 12 dailies, 102 regional periodicals, 122 specialized periodicals and 120 miscellaneous ones.

Despite constant financing and distribution difficulties, Québec FILM directors have made significant contributions to the development of their art, particularly in what is known as *cinéma-vérité* or *cinéma-direct.* Several others are well known for their research in cinematography.

Since 1960 a series of original experiments have been made in Québec in which the media are used for educational, social and cultural purposes. Québec has earned an international reputation as a testing ground for social communications. In the early 1960s, as part of the work for the Bureau d'aménagement de l'est du Québec (BAEQ) and the Aménagement rural et développement agricole (ARDA), some film documentaries were produced for use in group discussions. The NATIONAL FILM BOARD, especially in its "Challenge for Change" ("Société nouvelle") program, was active in Québec and across Canada in the late 1960s and early 1970s. Over the past few years, Le Groupe de recherches sociales has brought together the pioneers in *cinéma d'intervention,* whose circle now includes video groups (*see* VIDEO ART). Their productions are used in various social movements.

In 1967-68 the Québec Dept of Education established a daring educational television pilot (TEVEC) in Saguenay-Lac Saint-Jean. Its success led to the introduction of an even larger and more ambitious program, Multi-Média, serving a number of regions in the province.

The 1970s saw the birth of several experiments

in community media, the first of which was community television, the broadcasting by cable of programs that varied greatly in quantity and quality. Financing, recruitment and organizational problems, as well as battles over ideology, resulted in many of these cable groups closing down after a short period of operation. In addition, the Supreme Court's 1977 decision on cable broadcasting cooled the ardour of the Ministry of Communications and its enthusiasm for giving financial support to these experiments through its community media assistance program.

Community radio started more slowly but is now growing rapidly. Nineteen such stations are in operation and every year new ones go on the air on the FM band. Less burdensome in financing and cost of operations, they fill gaps in local and regional information. The ARCQ, the Association des radio communautaires du Québec, organized the first world conference on community radio in Montréal in Aug 1983.

Québec is attempting to meet the challenges posed by the development of new communications technology. The multiplication of available television channels is but one symptom of the danger of American cultural influences. The rapid expansion of cable broadcasting, computers, office automation systems and telematics requires prompt action on the part of Québecois wishing to develop a domestic software and hardware industry. As in the past, the small size of Québec's domestic market makes this an even more difficult task.   GAËTAN TREMBLAY

Reading: CRTC Annual Report 1986-1987; Government of Québec, *Québec: Mastercraftsman of Its Own Communications Policy* (1973); J.P. LaFrance and C. Gousse, eds, *La Télévision payante: Jeux et enjeux* (1982); Ministère des Communications, Gouvernement du Québec, *Le Québec et les communications: Un futur simple?* (1983).

Communications in the North Communications have played a special role in the NORTH. Terrain, climate and distance made it difficult for northerners to communicate with each other or with southern Canada before the advent of electronic media. In traditional times, Inuit messages were passed through personal contact. Like other native peoples, Inuit had no written language when in the 16th century they encountered literate Europeans.

Early Interaction The early explorers travelled in ships and encountered Inuit only by chance. As whalers and traders entered the North in the 19th century, they brought trade goods and technology which were given to native people in exchange for hunting and trapping. This required Inuit-non-native interaction, but there was little real communication.

In the late 1800s missionaries developed systems for writing native languages (*see* CREE SYLLABICS). By 1910 probably 98% of the Inuit in the eastern Arctic could read and write their own language, but because 3 different systems were used for writing Inuktitut, the dialect and regional differences among Inuit in Canada were reinforced. Few books were translated into Inuktitut, and since most Inuit did not read or write English they could not participate in the economic and social changes southern agencies brought to the North. The military and economic significance of the North encouraged the introduction of electronic media.

Radio and Television Radio reached the North in the late 1920s. Messages to and from southern Canada no longer had to rely on annual supply ships. By the 1930s, agencies in the North used high frequency radio for medical emergencies and business, and broadcast radio kept them in contact with the South. Because programs were in English, early radio did little to encourage communication between Inuit and other Canadians. The first Inuit-language broadcast occurred in 1960 and, by 1972, only 17% of CBC Northern Service shortwave programming was in Inuktitut (*see* BROADCASTING, RADIO AND TELEVISION). Early television service in the North followed the same pattern.

In 1967 television programming was introduced to the first of 17 communities in the western Arctic through delayed transmission of videotapes in 4-hour packages. The Telesat Canada Act of 1969 supported satellite development in Canada to deliver TELEPHONE and CBC television service to remote areas of the country, including the North (*see* SATELLITE COMMUNICATIONS).

Videotape service was extended to the eastern Arctic community of Frobisher Bay [Iqaluit] in 1972. The same year, Canada launched the Anik A satellite, which in 1973 began to transmit telephone, radio and television services to the North. In 1974 CBC established the Accelerated Coverage Plan to bring broadcasting services to communities having 500 or more as funds became available.

Some Inuit were enthusiastic about television; others joined Canadians concerned about the impact this compelling new medium would have on their language and culture (*see* NATIVE PEOPLE, COMMUNICATIONS). The northern videotape service did not include native programs. In 1972 the NATIONAL FILM BOARD established the first of 2 film workshops in Baffin I. The Frobisher Bay [Iqaluit] workshop developed into Nunatsiakmiut Native Communications Society in 1975. Through this society, Inuit began to produce programs for CBC television. Before 1982, however, CBC carried less than one hour a week of Inuktitut programming, none of which could be broadcast live from the North.

It was clear that with electronic media, northerners could more readily communicate with each other and with the South, but native people were not benefiting fully from this potential. New projects encouraged their participation.

Northern Satellite Experiments In 1976 Canada launched the first of 2 experimental satellite programs to test the uses of new COMMUNICATIONS TECHNOLOGY. Interactive satellites brought tele-health and tele-education to remote northern communities. Inuit in northern Québec used the Hermes satellite and the earlier Anik A system to establish an interactive radio network among 8 communities. People in these communities could telephone their radio stations to have their questions or comments broadcast over the network. In 1978 the Anik B satellite was launched and was used by Inuit in northern Québec and the NWT for interactive experiments including television broadcasting. In each of these regions the Anik B satellite linked 6 communities to form a small television network. Television was transmitted from only one community in each region, but people in all 6 communities could speak with each other and their messages were broadcast over the network.

These experiments led to the formation of the Inuit Broadcasting Corporation in the summer of 1981. IBC broadcasts several hours of Inuit-language television each week, including "live" northern television programming.

Native initiatives in broadcasting were further encouraged by the 1980 CANADIAN RADIO-TELEVISION AND TELECOMMUNICATIONS COMMISSION report of the Committee on the Extension of Service to Northern and Remote Communities. The report established the first framework for northern communication policy in Canada, and it stressed native participation in northern broadcasting.

Recent Developments The 1980s have brought many new communication services to the North.

By 1981 all northern communities had satellite telephone service, and in 1983 the last of 57 Inuit communities received CBC television. All communities receive CBC radio and most have community radio stations through programs sponsored by CBC, by provincial or territorial governments, or by the northern native communications societies. At least 11 Inuit communities have facilities to produce community television and more use CBC equipment for community broadcasting. Broadcasting services other than CBC's are available in the North through Cancom, a package of southern television and radio channels which the CRTC approved in 1981. Many northern communities have receiver dishes and get television programming directly from American satellites, and video playback units are common in northern homes. Indians in the western Arctic and the Yukon have established native broadcasting networks, and in northern Saskatchewan and the Yukon native people have experimented with TELIDON, a new type of interactive technology.

Many native northerners still do not speak or read English. The Northern Native Broadcast Access Program, established in 1983, provides the facilities for native people to receive and send information in their own languages. With northern communication policy and programs, electronic media have brought northerners closer together, have assured their communication with other Canadians, and have encouraged native participation in changes taking place in the North.
                                        GAIL VALASKAKIS

Communications Law encompasses not only the actions of the courts in interpreting statutes governing COMMUNICATIONS but also those by federal and provincial authorities that regulate radio, television, CABLE TELEVISION, some telephone companies and some telecommunications services. In contrast with the US, administrative decisions by the agencies are usually the focus of study. Courts have ruled on questions of jurisdiction, eg, on whether federal or provincial authorities should license particular communication services. Courts have also acted to delimit the scope and powers of regulatory authorities, when licensed operators have contravened regulations, and in several appeals of CRTC decisions.

Both broadcasting and some TELECOMMUNICATIONS are regulated by the CANADIAN RADIO-TELEVISION AND TELECOMMUNICATIONS COMMISSION, although different legislative mandates govern the CRTC's actions in each sphere of activity. Some services and companies (Telesat Canada) have their own legislative mandates as well.

Broadcasting is defined as any service involving the transmission or reception of programs intended for a general audience and distributed, in part at least, by means of hertzian waves. Thus, although cable television is delivered by wire to homes, it is regulated as broadcasting because the signals delivered were originally broadcast and were received via hertzian waves by the cable company. Cable television is also regulated as broadcasting because broadcasting is regulated as a single system, with the effects of any action taken by a licensee or the agencies considered in terms of the system as a whole. Any new service might not be licensed if, for example, the CRTC believed that it would affect broadcast services negatively or cause serious disruption of existing programming. NEWSPAPERS are not regulated, although broadcast licensing decisions now take into account whether the applicant also owns a daily newspaper serving the same area (*see* MEDIA OWNERSHIP). FILMS are not regulated except by provincial authorities with respect to classification and possible CENSORSHIP of their content.

The mandate and powers of the CRTC, as laid down in the Broadcasting Act (1968), set the framework for the granting of broadcast licences, the supervision of cable rates and changes in ownership or control, and the quality of programming. The CRTC has also been empowered to "strengthen and enrich the social, cultural and economic fabric of Canada" and to ensure that the broadcasting system is predominantly Canadian. Thus, the CRTC issues, and periodically reviews, Canadian content regulations and, with the support of an order-in-council on ownership first promulgated in 1969, has ensured that the private broadcasting companies are effectively owned and controlled by Canadians.

The CRTC has power to investigate program content to ensure that high standards are met, but has no control over the content of individual programs. Instead, the Act calls for broadcasting to be "varied and comprehensive" and for programming to reflect a diversity of viewpoints. A number of policies are designed to facilitate this diversity, as, for example, the FM policy which calls for only noncompeting FM radio services to be licensed in an area. For many years the CRTC did not license religious stations and currently will only license those that reflect a diversity of religious viewpoints (see RADIO PROGRAMMING; TELEVISION PROGRAMMING).

Except in the case of political broadcasts before an election, Canada has no equivalent to an "equal time provision" or "first amendment right" of free speech, although the impact of the Charter of Rights and Freedoms on broadcasting is still to be determined. The CRTC has held several inquiries to ensure that the CBC provides reasonably balanced programming, that controversial issues are covered fairly, that hot-line programmers provide basic information to facilitate informed discussion among their listeners, and that abusive comment is not permitted in the name of free speech. Broadcasters are responsible for their promise of performance and for all the content of their programming. The CRTC may also attach conditions on licences, which are enforceable through the courts.

Individuals who feel wronged may appeal to the station, network or the CRTC, who may decide to review the situation in a special public hearing or when a licence is being renewed, or simply to act as mediator in a dispute. Broadcast media do not fall under the terms of reference of the federal Human Rights Commission. Rather, the CRTC and the public rely upon persuasion and industry self-regulation to curb abuses and correct problems.

The CRTC is generally master of its own procedures and need not follow courtlike rules or rely on precedents in making decisions. Notice of applications being considered and of policies or new regulations is given in the *Canada Gazette* and, often, in local newspapers or broadcasts. Unless the CRTC specifies otherwise, all information must be made available publicly by the applicant and through the CRTC's regional offices. Public hearings may be scheduled on the merits of a policy or applications. (Public hearings must be scheduled in broadcasting only when consideration is of licence revocation.) Members of the public are invited to intervene, to submit comments in writing and possibly discuss them at a hearing, in support, opposition or simply with regard to any application. Rules of procedure are available from any CRTC office. Groups may also comment on general matters by making a representation to the CRTC, after requesting permission to appear at least 3 days in advance of a hearing.

The CRTC publishes all its decisions, which may be appealed to the federal Cabinet within 60 days. The Cabinet can issue policy directives to the CRTC or request a re-examination of any CRTC decision. Cabinet decisions cannot be appealed and few CRTC decisions have been successfully appealed to the courts to date. However, questions of the CRTC's right to license particular services or facilities are increasingly being addressed by the courts when the CRTC has sought an injunction against an unlicensed operator or service.

Since 1976 the CRTC has regulated some telephone companies (though not, for example, the Prairie telephone companies or some in the Maritimes) and telecommunications services offered by those companies or operating interprovincially (see TELEPHONES). The Canadian Radio-television and Telecommunications Act incorporates sections of the Railway Act and the National Transportation Act and empowers the CRTC to hold hearings, issue orders, and make regulations. The CRTC must ensure that the rates charged for federally regulated telecommunication services are "just and reasonable" and that any paying user of these services is granted access without discrimination. Telecommunication carriers are not legally responsible for the content of messages carried over their services.

To ensure that the provisions of the Act are met, the CRTC has held a number of special inquiries in telecommunications; eg, the CRTC examined the methods by which costs are allocated within the operation of major telephone companies, as those costs are reflected in the rates charged for specific services. In general, the CRTC has sought to promote competitive opportunities for new providers of communication services, except for basic SATELLITE and telephone local and long-distance calling facilities. To the extent permitted by its mandate, the CRTC may consider the needs of specially affected groups within the population (eg, the disabled or residents in the North) when making telecommunication decisions.

The minister of communications issues technical construction-operating certificates for both broadcast and telecommunication services, although the CRTC receives comments on the quality of service and may consider them at a regional hearing or when an application for a change in rates is being decided. In telecommunications, public hearings are mandatory and those involved are often represented by legal counsel. Hearings are usually preceded by an exchange of questions ("interrogatories") and demands for information ("particulars"), and informal meetings may be scheduled. All information submitted by the applicants must be made public, unless the CRTC decides it is contrary to the public interest to do so. Participation by the public is welcomed and the CRTC may award costs against an applicant to the intervenors if their intervention is considered substantive in the decision.

Provincial governments regulate telephone companies whose operations are solely within their borders unless the charter of the companies involved specifies otherwise. Most provinces are active in EDUCATIONAL BROADCASTING, usually through an educational broadcasting authority, although educational broadcast stations are provided for but must also be licensed by the CRTC. Provincial governments have been seeking a more active role in communications for many years, through federal-provincial negotiations and agreements, the courts and, in some provinces, by promulgating and implementing legislation to establish regulatory authority over intraprovincial and nonbroadcast PAY TELEVISION (see COMMUNICATIONS IN QUÉBEC).

History Since 1919, radio stations have been licensed, but comprehensive government involvement in broadcasting began with the Canadian Radio Broadcasting Act in 1932. Before that, in 1929, the Aird Commission had recommended that Canada establish a single, national, publicly owned system. The commission was responding to the expansion of American networks into Canada through affiliation with Canadian stations, to reception problems, to the scarcity of available frequencies for Canadian stations, and to charges of influence peddling in licensing. As well, in 1932, the Privy Council awarded the federal government exclusive jurisdiction over broadcasting and a special parliamentary committee recommended that private stations be permitted to continue offering local services. Both the Canadian Radio Broadcasting Act and the Canadian Broadcasting Act (passed in 1936) permitted private broadcasting, but after 1936 the Canadian Radio Broadcasting Commission was disbanded and the CBC became both the national service and the regulator of the private sector.

Change came after 2 royal commissions, Massey (reporting in 1951) and Fowler (reporting in 1957), reiterated the concerns and principles of the Aird Report. In response to growing influence of the private sector and the election of a Conservative government in 1957, the Broadcasting Act in 1958 set up a separate regulatory agency for private stations. It was replaced by the Broadcasting Act of 1968, which brought all stations, public and private, under a single regulatory authority. In both the 1958 and 1968 Acts the public-system needs were granted priority, but, with serious underfunding of the CBC and the development of new services (eg, cable) by an increasingly powerful private sector, public broadcasting, once the cornerstone of Canadian broadcasting, has become one component in a mix of services all regulated by the CRTC.

New technological developments and communication services have thrown communication law and regulation into flux. Problems arise when these new services cannot be classified easily as either broadcasting or telecommunication, as intra- or interprovincial, or as legitimately subject to regulation or not. Pay television, satellite receiving stations ("dishes"), nonprogramming or broadcast-originated services on cable, and new data transmission or information services offered by telephone or cable companies' new interconnections have all been the subject of controversy and increasingly of actions by the courts with respect to jurisdiction or the licensing powers of the CRTC.   LIORA SALTER

Reading: R.E. Babe, *Canadian Television Broadcasting* (1979); C.C. Johnston, *The Canadian Radio-television and Telecommunications Commission* (1980).

Communications Technology refers to the variety of techniques, tools and methods that are used to facilitate communication. In its larger sense it includes language, gestures, dress, codes of behaviour and religious rituals, as well as artistic and cultural traditions. It encompasses developments such as eye-glasses, hearing aids and artificial limbs which have enhanced the ability of many individuals to communicate, and includes smoke and flag signals, paper, quill pens and lead pencils, all of which have profoundly influenced the evolution of societies. In technologically advanced countries, the term generally refers more narrowly to those electronic techniques that have permitted communication to overcome the constraints of time and distance.

General Characteristics The TELEGRAPH (1837) and telephone (1876) permitted communication by wire over long distances almost instantaneously, a vast improvement over the earlier methods of rail, ship and pony express (see TELEPHONES). Communication by the wireless telegraph (1895), shortwave radio (1926) and then more reliable high-frequency microwave radio (1946) overcame the physical constraint of connecting every point by wire or cable. Microwave provided larger capacity communication channels for transmitting television signals and set the stage for the development of satellites and space communication (1957). Now communication signals can be sent around the world instantaneously.

The thrust of communications technology in recent years has been to expand both the capabilities and the capacity of the facilities used to communicate. The communication system now can carry different types of messages, including not only telegraph, voice, and television signals, but also facsimile, video and computer data signals. Off-air broadcasting has been supplemented by CABLE TELEVISION and direct broadcast satellites as well as video cassettes and recorders.

Cellular radio is expanding the possibilities for mobile communication within cities. Telephone companies are upgrading their voice telephone systems with digital switching and fibre-optics cable to facilitate computer data processing over telecommunication networks with greatly expanded capacity. Some experts predict that by the year 2000 there will be more data than voice communication on the telecommunication system. Cable-television companies are upgrading their distribution cables to permit data transfer and even limited voice communication. Business and residential subscribers may now select from a wide variety of computer communication terminals that can be used to obtain access to computer databanks. In addition, the quality of equipment used to record and to transmit visual images (film, television) and sound (music, FM radio) continues to improve at a steady pace, as do the instruments that are employed by the artistic community.

Canada always has had a unique association with communications technology, perhaps because of its relatively small population distributed over a vast geographical area. Effective communications networks were soon recognized as essential to the establishment and maintenance of Canada as a nation. Alexander Graham BELL made the world's first long distance telephone call in Canada, and telephone systems spread from coast to coast. In the 1960s and 1970s, Canada established cable-television systems more rapidly than other nations. It was the first to establish a national digital data network for computer users and a commercial domestic satellite system (*see* SATELLITE, ARTIFICIAL). It has pioneered in the development of a videotex terminal, TELIDON, especially designed for COMPUTER COMMUNICATIONS, and in the field of telemedicine – the transmission of computerized images and data for long-distance diagnoses and treatment. In 1984 Canada was the only nation employing a direct broadcast satellite system (*see* SATELLITE COMMUNICATIONS). The federal government has promoted and subsidized the rapid introduction of new communication and information processing technologies, including OFFICE AUTOMATION, as a means of speeding Canada's entry to the INFORMATION SOCIETY.

Institutional Basis It has long been recognized that advanced communication techniques can provide enormous military, political and economic advantages. Information is power, and communication techniques have had an important influence on the distribution of power within societies, as well as the rise and fall of empires, as the studies of Canadian scholar Harold INNIS have shown. The major portion of research and development in communications technology has been financed by the military budgets of the major powers. Current military concerns include the encryption of data to protect against the interception of signals, techniques for more precise satellite surveillance, communication control over weapons in space, and techniques for jamming enemy communications.

Today, for Canada and other technologically developed nations, communications technology is the cornerstone of an industrial strategy seeking advantage in the competitive world economy. It is hoped that advanced communications technology not only will improve the efficiency of the Canadian economy generally, but also will provide Canada with substantial international sales of communication equipment, services, and management consulting, particularly in developing countries.

The development, application and use of modern communications technology (as well as other technologies) is the result of the expenditure of massive amounts of money on research and development, on the learning of specialized skills, on equipment manufacturing, on system installation and operation, and ultimately on the marketing of communication services. It reflects major resource allocation decisions, taken by leading government and industrial institutions in Canada and other countries, to give communications technology a high priority and a particular direction.

Promises and Problems for Canada The specific technologies adopted have significant influences on the way many Canadians live and work. Inevitably new opportunities are opened for some Canadians, but traditional ways of doing things are rendered impossible for others. Upgrading the TELECOMMUNICATIONS system to computer standards permits enhanced information service, but the increased costs may force low-income people to disconnect from the system, thereby losing basic telephone service. Computerized information banks provide access to more and better information for government agencies, large corporations and certain professions at a cost they are willing to pay. But with the availability of information banks, the collections and services of public LIBRARIES are already being reduced. Satellites have enabled telemedical services to save the lives of Canadians in the North; but they have also brought an endless flow of southern television that has contributed to the disruption of native life-styles (*see* COMMUNICATIONS IN THE NORTH). The automated office portends efficiency in information processing, but it also displaces skilled office workers, creates some dull, monotonous jobs, and for some workers contributes to health problems.

Unfortunately, all the effects of technology cannot be foreseen in advance, and in the competition to obtain the advantages of new technologies, the potential disadvantages and problems of adjustment are too often ignored and sometimes suppressed. It is already apparent that the transition to the information society will not be an easy one. A host of economic, social and political problems will have to be addressed with farsighted policies.

Pioneering in communications technology has been a mixed blessing for Canada. The introduction of cable television and direct broadcast satellite facilities has dramatically expanded the choice of US television programs available to Canadians, but it also has had detrimental financial effects on Canadian television and FILM production and has reduced opportunities for Canadian artistic and cultural expression through its own mass media. Several governmental commissions (eg, the Applebaum-Hébert Commission, 1983, and the Caplan-Sauvageau task force, 1985) have been created in an attempt to suggest government policies that will overcome these problems (*see* TELEVISION PROGRAMMING).

Similarly, promotion of the computer communications technologies in anticipation of the information society is creating a network of physical facilities over which Canadian information can be transmitted efficiently out of Canada, and Canadians can obtain ready access to information banks outside Canada. Credit, medical and tax information about Canadians is stored in computers outside Canada, as is specialized information about the location and value of Canada's national resources, and many other types of information – some trivial, some crucial.

This compilation has created a series of intergovernmental problems relating to the terms and conditions of trans-border data flow, including the applicability of national laws, rights of access and privacy, as well as implications for the Canadian economy and Canadian sovereignty. Canada has a large and growing balance-of-payments deficit in the communication/information sector. There is some concern that Canadian government policies may be promoting new communications technologies too rapidly and with an imbalanced emphasis on the physical facilities rather than the communication content that is transmitted over them.

Global Implications Historically, the distribution of benefits of communications technology throughout the world has been unbalanced. Most modern communications technology requires the use of the radio spectrum, and synchronous satellites require orbital slots 35 900 km over the equator. These are limited public resources, common to all nations. Yet the most desirable frequencies and orbital slots have been taken by the technologically advanced nations on a first come, first served basis. The vast majority of the world's population does not have access to a telephone, and 75% of the world's telephones are found in only 8 of the world's 175 countries. This is a far cry from the "global village" ideal envisioned by Marshall MCLUHAN.

By overcoming the limits of time and space, and expanding enormously the volume and variety of information that can be transmitted and processed, the new communications technologies provide substantial benefits and economies to very large users with substantial budgets for specialized computer communication equipment. The new technologies permit an extension of the bounds of administrative control that is possible and offer increased efficiency in large centralized organizations. Perhaps the principal beneficiaries will be transnational corporations that will be able to expand their scope, enlarge their markets, and transfer financial resources instantaneously around the world. In many countries, especially Third World countries, this development may be seen as a threat to domestic production and employment, to national sovereignty and local cultures. Inasmuch as 25% of the world's adult population (and 95% in some countries) has never had an opportunity to learn to read and write, the most important communications technology for many countries might well be pencil, paper and native-language books and teachers.

Communications technology opens new opportunities and inevitably creates new problems. The new techniques have the capability to help in making the world a safer place, in solving political and economic problems, and in permitting a more informed democratic participation in society. Alternatively, they can help create a fragmented and disoriented society of passive observers with access to an endless supply of facts but little knowledge or wisdom, and helplessly vulnerable to instant destruction. The balance will be struck by the political, military, economic and social policies that emanate from the dominant institutions that influence Canadian society and the larger world community. WILLIAM H. MELODY

Reading: Dept of Communications, "The Future of Communications Technology," Telecommission Study 4(a) (1971); Economic Council of Canada, *The Bottom Line: Technology, Trade and Income Growth* (1983); H.A. Innis, *The Bias of Communication* (1951); B. Maddox, "The Born-Again Technology," *The Economist*, 22 Aug 1981; W.H. Melody, "Development of the Communication and Information Industries: Impact on Social Structures," UNESCO (1983); Ministry of State for Science and Technology, *The Government of Canada's Support for Technology Development* (1983); D.W. Smythe, *Dependency Road: Communications, Capitalism, Consciousness and Canada* (1981).

Communist Party of Canada was founded in Guelph, Ont, in June 1921 as a secret organization with a public alter ego in the Workers' Party established Feb 1922. The Communist Party of Canada became an open party in 1924 by changing the name of the Workers' Party and eliminating the secret body. Banned in 1940 under the WAR MEASURES ACT, it re-formed for a time as the Labor-Progressive Party (LPP). At the outset the CP was brought together by those members of 3 Canadian Marxist socialist parties who were prepared to accept the strict rules and principles outlined as conditions for membership in the Communist International (CI), especially the one stating that all decisions taken by affiliated parties had to be approved by CI headquarters and that all CI decisions were binding on member units.

Throughout the 1920s and the 1930s the police, acting under a Criminal Code amendment (s98), later repealed, against "unlawful associations," harassed the party, broke up meetings, dispersed audiences, raided party offices, confiscated literature and arrested the main party leaders. Hundreds of foreign-born, suspected communists were deported. After the WINNIPEG GENERAL STRIKE, demands for COLLECTIVE BARGAINING rights were frequently denounced as communist inspired. The PADLOCK ACT (Québec, 1937) gave the attorney general of that province authority to padlock any house or other building and evict the occupants if he believed it was being used to propagate communism. The Act was declared ultra vires by the Supreme Court of Canada, 1957. Over a hundred communists were interned for opposing the war, but were released after the Soviet Union became an ally.

Many communists became leaders and organizers of important trade unions and were instrumental in creating the Congress of Industrial Organizations (CIO) in Canada. But in 1940 the CIO merged with the All-Canadian Congress of Labour (CCL) to form the CANADIAN CONGRESS OF LABOUR (CCL) and the communists were gradually expelled. During the 1930s the communists were responsible for initiating the ON TO OTTAWA TREK of the single unemployed; raising a Canadian contingent to the Spanish Civil War (MACKENZIE-PAPINEAU BATTALION); and forming the Canadian Youth Congress. The communists have elected a number of members to municipal bodies, but only 3 to provincial legislatures (Manitoba, 1936; Ontario, 1943) and one, Fred ROSE (later convicted of conspiracy in the GOUZENKO case), to the House of Commons. Since 1954 the party has retained only aldermanic and school trustee seats (Winnipeg, Vancouver).

Among the better known names of the Communist Party were Tim BUCK, its long time leader; Dr Norman BETHUNE who organized medical help to the Spanish government in its Civil War and became a hero in China for his assistance to the revolutionary army in 1939; Jacob PENNER and Joseph Zuken, who held municipal office in Winnipeg 1934-83; A.A. MacLeod and J.B. Salsberg, who were first elected to the Ontario Legislature

in 1943; W.A. Kardash, member of the Manitoba legislature, Rev A.E. Smith, who headed the movement for the release of the imprisoned communist leaders; Stewart Smith, who served 4 terms on the Toronto City Council, including one on its Board of Control; J.B. MCLACHLAN, fiery leader of the Cape Breton coal miners from 1909 until his death in 1937.

In the 1950s and 1960s revelations about Stalin, the Soviet Union's intervention in Hungary and Czechoslovakia, and the Sino-Soviet tensions split the party, and many members, including some of the top leaders, quit over what they considered continued uncritical support for the Soviet Union.

The Communist Party registered 3500 members at its first public convention (the Workers' Party) and until the mid-1930s its membership fluctuated around that figure. It shot up quickly from 1935 to 1939 and again from 1943 to 1945, when it claimed 20 000 dues-paying members. After the war it declined, and it now has about 4000 on its books. It is still very active in the trade-union movement, although its influence there is considerably less than it was in the late thirties and forties. It participates in many movements such as women's rights, peace, tenants, senior citizens. It considers as a most important role, the dissemination of news and features about life in the Soviet and socialist countries.

NORMAN PENNER

Reading: Ivan Avakumovic, *The Communist Party in Canada* (1975); Norman Penner, *The Canadian Left* (1977) and *Canadian Communism* (1987); Ian Angus, *Canadian Bolsheviks* (1981); Tim Buck, *Yours in the Struggle – Reminiscences* (1977).

Community There are 2 basic ideas embedded in the concept of "community." One is concerned with order and consensus, and the other with locale. The second report of the Task Force on Canadian Unity (1979) stated that "a community is a group of persons joined together by a consciousness of the characteristics they have in common ... and by a consciousness of the interests they share." Any given human group will exhibit such a consciousness to one degree or another, be it a local sports club, a group of scientists with a special interest, an ethnic group, or an age group. On the other hand, community studies as such usually focus on places – hamlets, villages, towns, cities – as the unit of analysis. Everett Hughes's *French Canada in Transition* (1943), John Bennett's *Northern Plainsmen* (1969) and John Jackson's *Community and Conflict* (1975), to name a few of the many studies of local settings in Canada, all deal with a particular locale. An American sociologist, Jessie Bernard, referred to these 2 concepts of community as "community" and "the community." The first denotes shared values and interests and a common sense of identity; the second denotes places and the activities therein, or locale. Indeed, it has been said that "the term settlement might serve as well as the term community."

Although the 2 concepts are easily distinguished from each other, a problem arises when the latter is defined in terms of the former. If "the community" is defined as shared values, interests and identity, as is often the case, then it would be difficult to find a locale or settlement that conformed to these criteria. Any given locale is as likely as not to exhibit within its boundaries harmony and disharmony, conflict and consensus, order and disorder, as various social groupings struggle over resources. The idea of "community" is therefore better retained as an empirical question in relation to particular communities as locale, or to "the community." K. Westhues and P.R. Sinclair's *Village in Crisis* (1974), a study of

conflict over development plans in an Ontario town, Gold's *St. Pascal*, a study of changing elites in a Québec town, and D.H. Clairmont and D.W. Magill's *Africville* (1974), a study of a land development crisis in Halifax, address the issue of conflict within a particular locale – conflicts which are rooted in differing, not common, values and interests.

The tendency to confuse the 2 ways of defining the concept has its origins in earlier sociological studies that stressed the broad historical changes occurring in Western societies as the growth of capitalism and its concomitant processes of rapid urbanization and industrialization gradually transformed human relations into commodity relations. The change from person-centered to commodity-centered human relations is part of the transformation of human labour into a commodity to be bought and sold in the marketplace (*see* WORK). This transformation was a classic theme in 19th- and early 20th-century sociology. Exemplary among those who wrote on this theme was Ferdinand Tönnies. His 1887 essay, *Gemeinschaft (Community) and Gesellschaft (Association): A Treatise on Communism and Socialism as Empirical Forms of Culture*, drew attention to this shift in the quality of human relations. Tönnies was writing about communities in the sense of a particular quality of human relations that permeated all activities and social groups, a quality that was disintegrating in the wake of capitalism. The confusion arose when sociologists later reduced this general historical thesis to a definition of communities as settlements, thereby associating a particular quality of human relations, which may or may not be present in any given group, with human settlements as such.

For the most part the confusion has been resolved or, at worst, put aside. Over the past 25 years, Canadian community studies have followed one of 2 routes: network analysis or continuing studies of locale. Regarding the first, the Centre for Urban and Community Studies and the sociology department at University of Toronto have developed network analysis into a highly sophisticated tool for describing and understanding human interaction at the local level by analysing the bonds among persons relative to the positions and roles they occupy in particular social settings. Their findings demonstrate that "community" is still very much part of the everyday experiences of people in urban centres.

In the continuing studies of locale, the emphasis is on the fate of particular settlements in relation to the political economy of regions and of Canada as a whole. Patricia Marchak's *Green Gold* (1983) studies the effects of decisions, made by multinational corporations in BC's forest industry, on the everyday lives of people in 2 resource-based settlements. C. Zimmerman and G. Moneo's *The Prairie Community System* (1970) examines different types of western settlement in relation to the overall organization of the West to meet the interests of central Canadian capital.

There is perhaps a third route, one that is as yet underdeveloped but is present in various studies. It is at the local level, in "the community," where most people live out their daily lives – go to school, raise families, work, join associations, attend religious ceremonies – forming networks with others based on common values and interests (communities in the first sense). In the formation of such networks, be they based on friendship, kinship or workplace, there exists a potential for collective action, for mounting resistance and opposition to the overwhelming forces of individualization. This kind of activity, which takes the form of self-determination and self-organization, is not new to Canadian life. Ralph Matthews considers this issue in his study of 3 settlements in Newfoundland, where he found resistance based on "community" to the plans of government policymakers. The potential to oppose the impositions of public and private corporations on local life has been referred to as "emancipatory practices" by Marcel Rioux, a University of Montréal sociologist. "The community" as a base for emancipatory practices is a relatively unexplored route in the field of community studies, but one which may be pursued.

JOHN D. JACKSON

Community College, a publicly funded, non-degree granting post-secondary educational institution which offers a variety of programs with both an academic and technical-vocational emphasis, while responding to needs of its community. Community colleges were first established in Canada in the 1960s, when it was believed that both formal and informal learning were necessary for economic growth and for steady employment.

Canadian community colleges are not an extension of secondary schools, or a dwarf species of UNIVERSITY, or junior colleges. A separate social invention, legitimate in their own right, their goals are responsiveness to community concerns; commitment to excellent teaching; emphasis on student counselling and placement services; open-admissions policy; and low tuition fees. They offer students a curriculum that typically provides vocational and technical programs preparatory to employment in the trades, industry, agriculture or the professions; APPRENTICESHIP training; university parallel courses (in Alberta and BC) providing first- and second-year credits toward a university degree; remedial courses; and programs for personal and community enrichment. To allow for part-time study, courses are offered during evenings and weekends as well as during the day. Most community colleges are located in population centres, but community college courses may be held in places convenient to learners, eg, church basements, community halls or high-rise buildings.

Administration Community colleges in Canada are the creation and ultimately the responsibility of provincial governments. In some provinces, community colleges and universities are included under a department or ministry independent of a general department of education; in others, they are incorporated in a ministry of education. In all provinces except New Brunswick and Manitoba a board of governors or trustees appointed by the provincial government administers the colleges. Boards vary in size, autonomy, range of representation and effectiveness. Some (eg, in Alberta) include a faculty member, a student representative and a representative from the support staff. Boards in Québec are large and tend to be representative of many groups, eg, faculty, students, administrators, noninstructional staff, parents and part-time students. In some provinces (eg, Ont and Qué) intermediary councils have been established on matters relating to college development. In most provinces, however, the appropriate ministry exercises direct control over the colleges.

Community college boards in Canada have tended to become politicized through the practice of direct appointment of their members by the government in power. The chief executive officers are styled variously as presidents, principals or directors general, and they are responsible for administering the policies established by the boards.

Federal Government Involvement Through a series of federal Acts, such as the Technical-Vocational Training Assistance Act (1960) and the National Training Act (1982), the federal government has financially supported job training and upgrading in the college sector. Recently, with the introduction of Canadian Job Strategy (1985), the federal government has directed a good deal of the funding to the private sector, which works with the community colleges in the provision of training opportunities.

Students of community colleges in Canada reflect a wider range in age, academic competency, career expectation and economic background than students in any other category. Community colleges provide "a second chance" for mature persons to return to the classroom for the purpose of enhancing marketable skills, or of preparing for a new vocation. In Québec, Alberta and BC, community colleges attract students headed towards university, as well as those preparing themselves for early employment. Community colleges in Ontario and elsewhere in Canada tend to serve students who will proceed directly to the labour market.

According to Statistics Canada, full-time enrolment in community colleges (including institutes of technology or short-term trade programs) reached 322 500 in 1986, of which 166 000 were females. Approximately 30% of these students were enrolled in academic programs, while the remainder were engaged in specific career preparation. While statistics on part-time students are not kept, part-time enrollees exceed the number of full-time students in colleges, a conservative estimate being in the vicinity of 1.5 million.

Teachers Community college teachers are expected to have had field experience in their subject area; ordinarily, they are not researchers. Most belong to a union. In some provinces, one civil-service union bargains collectively for all community colleges; in others college unions bargain individually with their respective boards.

In 1987, there were approximately 25 000 full-time and 150 000 part-time instructors in community colleges. More than one third of the college teaching staff are women. Support staff and administrative personnel number about 9000 and, while more than 1200 citizens serve on college boards, another 7000 representatives from business and industry are involved in advisory committees.

Provincial Community College System Colleges have been established to different degrees in all 10 provinces and the 2 territories of Canada. The outstanding characteristic is the diversity of the various systems which tend to reflect the educational, sociocultural, and economic differences which exist among the regions. In brief, community college systems in Canada may be described as follows.

BC colleges were established after intense community activity in the 1960s and 1970s. The 15 colleges are supplemented by the BC Institute of Technology and a number of specialized institutes, including the Open Learning Institute. BC colleges offer a wide range of programs including the first 2 years of university degrees. The Ministry of Advanced Education and Job Training is responsible for the entire post-secondary educational system.

Alberta has 11 community colleges, 2 institutes of technology and 4 vocational centres. There are 5 educational consortia distributed through the province which "broker" programs from other institutions. Alberta's colleges are part of the system under the Ministry of Advanced Education, and offer a wide range of programs, university equivalent, technical-vocational upgrading and community education. The college system is decentralized, each institution having its own board of governors.

In Saskatchewan a major reorganization occurred in 1987. The 3 community colleges in the north were amalgamated to form Northlands Career College, while the 4 technical institutes were combined under a single board. The original purpose of the community colleges to offer regionally based community education has been replaced by more academic and vocationally oriented missions. The 4 urban community colleges have also been amalgamated with the technical institutes.

In spite of their names, Manitoba's 3 community colleges are really technical-vocational institutes under the direct authority of the government. There are no boards of governors and faculty bargain through a civil service union.

Ontario's 22 Colleges of Applied Arts and Technology were all established following the passing of provincial legislation in 1965. Many were created from existing technical and vocational schools. Ontario's colleges offer a primarily vocationally oriented curriculum and provide a clear alternative to universities. In spite of the presence of governing boards, Ontario colleges are provincially oriented and the teaching and support staff are all within province-wide unions. Recent changes in Ontario include the addition of faculty and students to college boards and the creation of academic councils within each college to advise the president. In addition to the CAATS, Ontario has 9 specialized institutes.

Québec's 46 public colleges, which are called COLLÈGES D'ENSEIGNEMENT GÉNÉRAL ET PROFESSIONNEL (CEGEPs), were created in the mid-1960s from a wide variety of post-secondary institutions. The CEGEPs were designed as instruments of sociopolitical change in Québec following the Quiet Revolution. Their prime function is to provide a general education for Grade 11 graduates who plan to continue to university and the world of work. The colleges have continued to be exciting, volatile centres of educational reform. Québec also has 24 private colleges and 11 specialized institutes. Although the spirit of democratic governance prevails, the CEGEPs are very much under the direct control of the government in matters of curriculum and funding.

PEI has only one institution, Holland College, which offers a wide range of technological, vocational and upgrading programs, and is governed by a board with wide representation.

New Brunswick Community College has 9 campuses (5 English and 4 French speaking), and is the most highly centralized organization among Canada's colleges. The campuses are primarily concerned with career training and programs are assigned by the Ministry of Advanced Education and Training. There is no board. New Brunswick also has 8 specialized institutes including a Forest Ranger School.

Although Nova Scotia has no community colleges in the popular sense of the term, a recent government study (1987) is addressing the need to establish a system comparable to other provinces. However, Nova Scotia has a wide variety of post-secondary institutions, many of which are degree granting.

Up to 1987 Newfoundland has had only one community college, Bay St George, in Stephenville. However, an expansion plan for the future includes the creation of 5 regional community colleges and 3 technical institutes. At the same time a Department of Career Development and Advanced Studies will co-ordinate the post-secondary system.

Yukon Territory has one college in Whitehorse with a broad range of academic and technical-vocational courses.

While one comprehensive community college has been established in Yellowknife, NWT, a number of branch campuses are being developed in the territories. It is governed by a broadly representative board.

Finance The 200 community colleges and allied institutions in Canada spent approximately $3 billion in 1984-85, or 9% of the total educational expenditures in the nation. Of the total budget 8% was generated from tuition fees, which varied from 14% in BC to 0% in the NWT. Full-time students in Québec pay no tuition fees.

National Organization Leading educators in the 1960s felt there was enough common interest among colleges across Canada to warrant the creation of a national association. The Association of Canadian Community Colleges was formed in 1970; by the 1980s, it had 100 institutional members and has added a large international bureau.

Conclusion Canada's financial commitment – provincial and federal – to community colleges is proportionately higher than that of any other advanced industrial society, including the US. Although not united by national policies and overall goals, the network of Canada's community colleges ranks among the most comprehensive in the world. The strengths of the 200 community colleges include their accessibility to all citizens, old and young, and the attention given to the individual student. Their service to communities may be in jeopardy, however, because of increasing provincial centralization of control. The restrictive intervention of provincial governments and the burgeoning bureaucracies within the colleges themselves represent the greatest threat to the continuing and imaginative development of community colleges.

G. CAMPBELL AND JOHN D. DENNISON

Reading: John D. Dennison and P. Gallagher, *Canada's Community Colleges: A Critical Analysis* (1986).

Comox, BC, Town, pop 6873 (1986c), 6607 (1981c), inc 1967, is located on the E coast of Vancouver I, 223 km N of Victoria, overlooking Comox Harbour. The Beaufort Mtn Range and Comox Glacier enhance the town's natural beauty. The adjacent ski slopes of Mt Washington and Forbidden Plateau make it a popular winter sports centre. First inhabited by SALISH, and then by Europeans in the early 1860s, Comox slowly became a service centre and shipment point for the Comox Valley. It has recently become the centre of a rich agricultural area, producing potatoes, fruit and dairy products. (The name, of Indian origin, means "abundance.") The area's mild climate has made it popular with retired people. CFB Lazo, 5 km NE, is important for the local economy. There is a ferry service from the Comox peninsula to POWELL RIVER on the mainland.

ALAN F.J. ARTIBISE

Compact Theory of Confederation, *see* CONSTITUTIONAL HISTORY.

Compagnie des Cent-Associés (Compagnie de la Nouvelle France) was founded 29 Apr 1627 (royal approbation 6 May 1628) by Cardinal Richelieu, chief minister of Louis XIII, to establish the French empire in N America; it was granted NEW FRANCE from Florida to the Arctic and from the Atlantic to the unknown West, as well as extensive trading privileges. English rivals captured the company's fleet in 1628 and both the fleet and the colony in 1629; the colony was restored to France in Mar 1632, but the company never recovered. In 1645 it sublet its rights and obligations in Canada to the COMMUNAUTÉ DES HABITANTS; on 24 Feb 1663 the Cent-Associés' grant was revoked and Canada became a royal province.

DALE MIQUELON

Compagnie des Indes occidentales, which replaced the COMPAGNIE DES CENT-ASSOCIÉS, was established in May 1664 by Jean-Baptiste Colbert to drive Dutch traders from French colonies in the West Indies and the Americas, and to emulate Dutch and English commercial success. The company succeeded in the first aim, but failed in the second. It was essentially a state enterprise run by Colbert, and its impressive trade monopoly and seigneurial and governmental rights did not attract private capital. In Dec 1674 Colbert dissolved the ailing company and initiated the regime of direct governmental administration of colonies.

DALE MIQUELON

Compagnie du Nord (Compagnie de la Baie du Nord), fd 1682 by Canadian merchants, led by Charles Aubert de la Chesnaye, to trade into Hudson Bay by sea. The company upheld French claims on the bay by dispatching Pierre-Esprit RADISSON and Médard Chouart DES GROSEILLIERS there with 2 ships, and stabilized NEW FRANCE's Indian alliances N of the Great Lakes. In 1685 King Louis XIV granted the company a monopoly of the Hudson Bay FUR TRADE, but costly military expeditions against the HUDSON'S BAY COMPANY (*see* TROYES, Pierre de) and ruinous taxation (the *quart*) bankrupted the company. Its monopoly was revoked on 10 Jan 1700 and transferred to the Compagnie de la Colonie.

DALE MIQUELON

Company of Young Canadians, a short-lived voluntary agency of the government of Canada, established with a mandate to encourage social, economic and community development in Canada. Promised in 1965 and formally established in 1966, the Company of Young Canadians, or CYC, recruited young Canadians, trained them in "social animation" techniques and sent them out to work for a moderate salary on community programs across the country. The idea was to organize the downtrodden of society whom the political process had not touched, and to enable them to demand and bring about improvements in their own lives. Some of the CYC's initiatives were successful, but the volunteers and then the company became caught up in the political ferment that characterized the 1960s. Many of its members embarrassed the government with their separatist and Marxist views. Although the company was intended to operate with a high degree of autonomy, the government felt constrained to impose controls, resulting in friction between volunteers in the field and the head office in Ottawa, and between government-appointed councillors and radical volunteers. The company's autonomy was terminated in 1969, but the organization lingered until abolished during a government economy drive in 1976.

ROBERT BOTHWELL

Company Towns, important in Canada's capital formation and industrialization, urban development, and trade-union movement. Few survive in the sense used by sociologist Rex Lucas: "closed communities owned and administered by the industrial employer," with homes, stores and even the church owned by the firm. The decline of the small firm, the enhanced status of trade unions since WWII, and more liberal interpretations of property and civil rights have combined to render the institution largely obsolete. The paternalism of the traditional company town is no longer acceptable to Canadians, but single-industry communities, especially those on the resource frontier from Newfoundland to the Yukon, still bear similarities to earlier company towns.

Company towns emerged during the colonial period, for the purpose of ensuring a reserve of skilled workers for family-based firms. They were islands of stability in the chaotic preindustrial labour market. The thrust of industrial revolution between the 1850s and 1890s occurred in cities, not company towns. One exception was the cotton industry, which often created new communities such as Valleyfield, Qué, based on British or American paternalistic principles. Significantly, Valleyfield's cotton workers, many of them women, were among the minority in true factory settings who organized collectively before WWI and used strike and "riot" tactics to advance their claims.

The Canadian company town's development peaked in the post-1890s mining industry. Cape Breton I coal communities, Québec asbestos towns and Ontario gold, silver and nickel towns began as company towns. Often the dominant note of social relations was not paternalism but the hard edge of authoritarianism and naked exploitation. During the 1909-10 strike, members of the United Mine Workers in Cape Breton were thrown out of their homes and locked out of the company stores, where lines of credit formed part of a system of peonage. Clergymen sheltering workers in churches were ordered by the hierarchy to stop. Mine operators in Timmins, Ont, employed "gun thugs" to patrol the town during the 1912-13 gold-mine strike. Only after blood flowed did the provincial government order their removal.

Canadian company towns were generally less violent than their American counterparts, largely because Canadian opinion opposed the use of private armies. But there were exceptions, such as Cape Breton's coal-and-iron police. Once companies lost moral authority, as they almost invariably did, true discipline could be maintained only by force, which politicians often decided not to provide in crises. The Crow's Nest Pass Coal Co at Fernie, BC, for example, failed to evict striking tenants in 1906 because the provincial attorney general heeded local police and maintained a "neutral" stance.

There are examples of attempts to reassert traditional moral authority through "model" community building and social engineering. Coal companies at Brule and Nordegg, Alta, made such attempts during and after WWI. Their position was uniquely favourable, insofar as in NW Alberta companies operated on inalienable crown lands under long-term government leases. The usual challenges to the company town – acquisition of property by individuals, municipal incorporation and incursions by independent merchants – were closed off. But alongside the managers' claims regarding community progress must be placed the long list of residents' petitions and protests. Neither attempt achieved its primary object of avoiding unions and strikes.

Life in the company town could often be fulfilling, but never certain. The fruit of 40 years in Nordegg was destroyed in one day in 1955: Canadian National Railways, increasingly using diesel power, cancelled its Nordegg coal contract, effectively shutting down the mine and consequently the town. It is not the "pluck-me" store or the coal-and-iron police which defines the company town but the basic economic power wielded over the single-industry community by public and private interests that remain unaccountable for decreeing the life or death of the community. Few may remember that Dominion, NS, is a perpetual monument to long-departed DOSCO, or Cadomin, Alta, to Canada & Dominion Mining, but the phrase "company town" still flourishes in the Canadian language. *See also* RESOURCE TOWN.

ALLEN SEAGER

Reading: R.J. Bowles, *Little Communities and Big Industries* (1982); R. Lucas, *Minetown, Milltown, Railtown* (1971).

Comparative Literature is the international or multilingual study of literary history, ie, of broad currents of thought and style and of major schools; of literary genres, forms and modes; of motifs and themes; of the presence of a work of literature, an author, a whole literature or even a country, in another national literature; of authors writing in different languages, but linked with "influences" and typological affinities. Comparative literature includes literary criticism and theory, and sometimes folk or ORAL LITERATURE, as well as the interdisciplinary interrelationships of literature with the other arts and even with other expressions and studies of man, eg, philosophy and psychology. Although present in most countries with established universities and research centres in the humanities, the discipline has been traditionally strong in France, the US and eastern Europe. It varies from the "orthodox" or "French" school, with its rigorous search for historical evidence of contacts, imitations, translations and influences, to the N American insistence on methodology and theory, to the eastern European insertion of this approach into the vast study of the history, theory and criticism of world literature.

The term *"littérature comparée"* was probably first used in 1827-28 by the French scholar Ville-main and was popularized by the influential critic C.A. Sainte-Beuve. Its rendering in English as "comparative literature" by Matthew Arnold is somewhat misleading, for the discipline is defined less by comparisons (which occur in any inquiry in the humanities) than by studies based on the concept that literature, in addition to being the product of a nation and the expression of a language, is also – like music or painting – a universal human phenomenon. The discipline has been exposed to older methodological trends in scholarship, such as 19th-century positivism and philology, 20th-century history of ideas, Marxism, sociological perspectives and psychoanalysis. Recently it has been inspired increasingly by linguistic models, eg, in belated manifestations of formalism and particularly structuralism and communication theory (semiotics).

In Canada, comparative literature became an academic discipline only in the 1960s. Among the academics interested at an early point in comparative literature, the foremost place belongs to Northrop FRYE, who was the first chairman of U of T's Comparative Literature Programme. His various works, including *Anatomy of Criticism* (1957), *The Secular Scripture* (1976) and *The Great Code* (1982), have confirmed him as the prime Canadian literary historian and theoretician.

Although there was little systematic teaching of comparative literature until the end of the 1960s, Canadian universities granted, between 1921 and 1969, about 125 graduate degrees based on comparative topics; quite a few Canadians studied abroad (mainly in France, eastern Europe and the US).

The graduate program at University of Alberta, the first in Canada (est 1964), became a full-fledged department in 1969, with both undergraduate and postgraduate instruction. During this period other universities created graduate programs, sharing staff and facilities with English or French and departments of foreign languages. In the early 1980s graduate degrees were offered at Carleton, McGill, U de Montréal, U of T, UBC and U de Sherbrooke; experiments with undergraduate courses have taken place at Windsor, Dalhousie, Mount Saint Vincent, Saint Mary's, Athabasca and Calgary. Some preferences are visible in Canadian schools: eg, literary theory and methodology with an emphasis on structuralism and semiotics at U de Montréal; social theories and literature practice at McGill; theory and methodology with myth criticism, hermeneutics, phenomenology and structuralism at Toronto; methodological pluralism, translation theory and literary history at U of A; and comparative Canadian literature at Sherbrooke. Specialized research centres have been established at Carleton, McGill and Toronto, and a research institute has been established at U of A.

Comparative Literature in Canada, a bilingual newsletter started in 1968, publicizes Canadian programs and theses. It also acts as the "public archives" of the Canadian Comparative Literature Assn (fd 1969). The association, which organizes yearly scholarly meetings, founded the *Canadian Review of Comparative Literature/Revue canadienne de littérature comparée* in 1974, and embarked on a series of books and monographs in 1977. The association and its members have contributed markedly to the professional and scholarly life of the International Comparative Literature Assn, of which a Canadian, Eva Kushner, has been president. Canadian comparatists have participated at most international and many national meetings of the profession and have published widely at home and abroad. Comparative literature as a discipline in Canada has contributed to the methodological renewal of literary studies in the country and has facilitated research links with international scholarship. Nevertheless, it is financially, administratively and academically still in a precarious position, without a firm basis in the high-school curriculum or in the undergraduate liberal arts education. From the outside it is often perceived as elitist and cosmopolitan, whereas from the inside it appears to its practitioners as today's core of inquiries into literature. There is no doubt, however, that it corresponds to the very multicultural and multilingual nature of Canada, and to the character of international scholarship. MILAN V. DIMIĆ

Comparative Literature, Canadian The comparative study of the Canadian literatures (which normally means writing in English and French) is of recent origin, the best work dating from the late 1960s. The linguistic situation that obtains in Canada is not unlike that of other countries that practise bilingual policies (eg, Cameroon and Belgium). The problem with language is that it often establishes zones of territoriality, rather than opening lines of communication, and in Canada this situation has profoundly inhibited the comparative study of the country's literatures. Another reason for the slow pace of such studies in Canada is that the normal model for comparative studies has been between, rather than within, nations. Furthermore, since the rise of comparative studies in the 18th century, the assumption has been that the object of COMPARATIVE LITERATURE in general is to unify the literatures of the world and to examine them as part of a harmonious whole. Thus literatures that constitute the culture of a country already unified do not seem to require further unification. Finally the literatures of Canada, until recently, have usually been treated as colonial, and therefore more closely allied to the literature of their respective mother countries. The Official Languages Act, as well as the sense of national unity generated by the centennial of Confederation, tended to provide the impetus not only to overcome colonial attitudes but also to permit an examination of the 2 literatures as significant enough to be studied in their own right. A satisfactory model for comparison, however, has yet to be found. The most frequently cited image is that of the double staircase at the Château de Chambord, proposed over a century ago by P.J.O. CHAUVEAU. The image is apt, for it suggests 2 cultures that constantly spiral around each other without ever coming into direct contact.

The model is most often used by anglophone critics; francophone critics, by contrast, complain of too much contact. Not surprisingly, the majority of scholars who study the Canadian literatures comparatively are anglophone, for it is there that the ideology of comparative studies as conducive to unity is most strongly felt. It is felt, however, with paradoxical delicacy. As Philip Stratford has argued, the Canadian comparatist "must neither unify, nor divide."

The usual method of following, at least implicitly, such an injunction has been to include francophone literature in histories of Canadian literature in a special chapter. Archibald MacMechan's *Headwaters of Canadian Literature* (1924), a pioneering work, only includes francophone literature because it constitutes an exception to "Canadian" literature. That literature also merits a chapter in Lorne PIERCE's *An Outline of Canadian Literature* (1927), and the same position is given the writing of Québec in Margaret ATWOOD's widely read *Survival* (1972). Of studies exclusively devoted to probing how two literatures relate, Ronald Sutherland's *Second Image* (1971) must be considered the fundamental point of departure. While confirming that the two literatures cannot be compared as a result of mutual contact, Sutherland argues that on the basis of shared themes they possess sufficient likeness to merit mutual study. The same point is developed in *The New Hero* (1977). Margot Northey's *The Haunted Wilderness* (1976) follows a similar methodology with more attention paid to issues of form. The most significant Québec critic is Clément Moisan, whose first book, *L'Âge de la littérature canadienne* (1969), echoes the pioneering work of Edmond Lareau's *Histoire de la littérature canadienne* (1874); both examine the two cultures from broad, sociological perspectives. Moisan's second book, *Poésie des frontières* (1979; trans *A Poetry of Frontiers*, 1983), follows Sutherland's method in poetry rather than in the novel. The technique is one of "facing-off" thematically similar francophone and anglophone writers. E.D. Blodgett's *Configuration* (1982), more pluralistic in design, endeavours to overcome the impasse of shared francophone and anglophone themes, first, by examining Ukrainian and especially German texts and, second, by employing critical methods more various than thematic analysis. Nevertheless, the trend continues to examine similar patterns between the 2 founding literatures. The title of Philip Stratford's study, *All the Polarities* (1986), makes this manifest, and his method consists in pairing off anglophone and francophone novels to assess both similarity and dissimilarity. It might be observed that studies in English generally address prose, while those in French turn to poetry, which is the object of Richard Giguère's *Exil, Révolte et Dissidence* (1984), a study of French and English poetry from 1925 to 1955. The fundamental desideratum of the field, however, is a history of the Canadian literatures, both the founding literatures and those of lesser diffusion, and the kind of mosaic they continue to shape. E.D. BLODGETT

Reading: D.M. Hayne, "Comparative Canadian Literature...," *Canadian Review of Comparative Literature* III.2 (1976); Hayne and A. Sirois, "Preliminary Bibliography of Comparative Canadian Literature," *CRCL* (various issues 1975-83); D.G. Jones *Butterfly on Rock* (1970); A.J.M. Smith, "Introduction," *The Oxford Book of Canadian Verse* (1960); Philip Stratford, ed, *Comparative Canadian Literature*, a special issue of *CRCL* VI.2 (1979).

Competition Policy, legislation used by the federal government to eliminate privately imposed restraints on trade and to encourage competition. The statutory basis of federal competition policy is contained in the Competition Act and Competition Tribunal Act which came into force on 19 June 1986, replacing the Combines Investigation Act, whose history can be traced to 1889. The purpose of the legislation "is to maintain and encourage competition in Canada in order to promote the efficiency and adaptability of the Canadian economy...." The Act applies to all economic activities (both goods and services) except those specifically exempted, eg, COLLECTIVE BARGAINING, amateur sports, securities underwriting or activities subject to other legislation, eg, industries where price or output or both are regulated by federal or provincial governments. The Competition Act incorporates both criminal offences and civil reviewable matters. The director is authorized to make representations in respect to competition in the proceedings of federal regulatory tribunals and at the request of provincial regulatory bodies. An inquiry into alleged offences may be initiated by the director following an application by 6 adult Canadian citizens, at the direction of the minister of consumer and corporate affairs, or on the director's own initiative.

The majority of inquiries result from complaints by business people and consumers. While the director may apply to the Competition Tribunal for an order to prohibit the continuation of a civil reviewable trade practice, criminal prosecutions are conducted by the Dept of Justice before the courts. The principal criminal offences are as follows: first, agreements to lessen competition, although only those agreements concerning the supply, manufacture, production, etc, of a product to lessen competition *unduly* are prohibited. Second, agreements among banks, eg, to fix interest rates on loans or deposits, are illegal per se (new in 1986). Third, suppliers may not attempt to influence upwardly or discourage the reduction of the price at which another person supplies or advertises a product. It is also an offence to refuse to supply anyone because of that person's low-pricing policy. Fourth, it is an offence to discriminate against competitors of a purchaser of an article by granting a price discount or other advantage (eg, advertising allowances) to the purchase that is not also available to the competitors. It is also illegal to engage in a policy of predatory pricing policies, so that products are sold at lower prices in one area of the country than in others, or to sell at unreasonably low prices where the effect or tendency is to lessen competition substantially or eliminate a competitor. Fifth, all false or misleading advertising and representations are prohibited. Other sections of the Act prohibit double ticketing, "bait-and-switch" advertising, and pyramid and referral-selling schemes. Civil reviewable matters are adjudicated by the new Competition Tribunal rather than the courts. The Tribunal, which works in panels of 3, consists of both lay persons and 4 judges of the Federal Court of Canada. Decisions may be appealed to the Federal Court-Appeal Division. Civil reviewable matters include a variety of trade practices which may be anti-competitive in their effects, eg, delivered pricing (new in 1986), refusal to supply, consignment selling for the purpose of controlling dealer prices, tied selling and market restriction. However, the most important reviewable matters are 3 new ones: mergers, abuse of dominant position and specialization agreements.

To obtain an order by the Tribunal dissolving a previous merger or prohibiting a proposed one, the director must show, on the balance of probabilities, that the merger has or is likely to "prevent or lessen competition substantially." The new merger provisions, which deal with both horizontal and vertical mergers, replace the previous, totally ineffectual, criminal law provisions under which only a handful of cases were brought between 1910 and 1976, and only one conviction was obtained upon a plea of guilty. Mergers involving large firms (assets or sales exceeding $400 million) or large acquisitions (assets or sales exceeding $35 million) have been subject to advance notification rules since 15 July 1987.

The abuse of dominant position provisions replace the ineffectual criminal law monopoly provisions which resulted in few convictions in the 16 cases brought between 1910 and 1986. To obtain an order prohibiting the anti-competitive behaviour, the director must establish that the firm(s) involved i) substantially or completely control the market, ii) have engaged or are engaged in a "practice of anti-competitive acts," and iii) the practice has had, is having, or is likely to have the effect of "preventing or lessening competition substantially in a market." The Tribunal is required to consider whether a practice has had the effect of lessening competition substantially, "whether the practice is a result of superior competitive performance."

Unfortunately, none of the key words or phrases in either the merger or abuse of dominant position provisions are defined in the new Act. Although there has been a high volume of merger activity in 1986 and 1987 (over 1300 mergers, 80 of which had a transaction value exceeding $100 million), only 2 merger cases were brought to the Tribunal in the first 18 months the new legislation was in effect. No abuse of dominant position cases were filed. Hence, the effectiveness of the new legislation has yet to be determined.

In order to encourage efficiency, the Competition Act provides for the registration of specialization agreements under which 2 or more firms each agree to discontinue the production of certain articles or services and to buy that item exclusively from another party to the agreement. In this way, all of the firms involved can specialize to a greater degree and enjoy lower costs through longer production runs. If the agreement meets the conditions in the Act and is registered by the Competition Tribunal, it is then exempt from the conspiracy and exclusive dealing provisions.

The new Act contains other notable changes: i) the conspiracy provisions were amended to overcome recent adverse interpretations by the Supreme Court of Canada, ii) the commercial activities of federal and provincial Crown corporations were made subject to the Act, iii) the maximum fine for conspiracies to fix prices or allocate markets was increased from $1 million to $10 million, iv) applications for the use of formal investigatory powers, eg, search orders, written returns of information, examination of witnesses under oath, must now be made to the courts so as to be consistent with the charter provisions of the new constitution enacted in 1982.

The process of reforming competition legislation stretched over more than 2 decades, beginning in 1971 with Bill C-256 and its amendment in 1976. In 1977 the government introduced Bills C-42 and C-13, but neither was enacted, largely because of the opposition of business. In 1984 Bill C-29 was given first reading, but was not enacted due to the dissolution of Parliament, and the general election in September 1984. The Mulroney government circulated its own policy proposals in May 1985 and introduced Bill C-91 in December. After some amendments were made, the new Competition Act became law 6 months later.

W.T. STANBURY

Readings: B. Dunlop, D. McQueen and M. Trebilcock, *Canadian Competition Policy: A Legal and Economic Analysis* (1987); W.T. Stanbury, "The New Competition Act and Competition Tribunal Act: 'Not With a Bang, But a Whimper'," *Canadian Business Law Journal*, XII, 1 (1986), pp 2-42.

Computer-Assisted Learning (CAL) generally refers to 2 major uses of computers in education and training. The first is often called computer-assisted instruction (CAI) and can be described as "learning through a computer." In CAI, instructional sequence and questions must be prepro-grammed. These sequences may be called drill and practice, tutorial, socratic, simulation, gaming, testing and computer-managed instruction (CMI), ie, computer assistance in testing, diagnosing, prescribing, grading and record keeping. The emphasis in CAI is on having students learn new concepts or reinforce previously learned concepts by interacting with a CAI program. Unfortunately, because it takes many hours to develop even one hour of CAI, the cost of producing CAI programs can be expensive. The second major use of CAL is one in which students tend to write their own programs to solve problems; this is described as "learning with computers" or, more simply, using computers as tools. Various programming languages such as LISP, PILOT, APL, BASIC, LOGO and Pascal are being used by students to explore solutions to a variety of problems in a number of different areas.

Until 1977, when fully assembled, low-cost microcomputers became generally available, most CAL activities tended to be centered either in post-secondary institutions or in business and industry. The early uses of CAL in Canada were non-CAI in nature. As programming and problem-solving applications evolved and developed, many universities, colleges and technical institutes established academic computing centres and teaching departments of computing science. In the late 1960s, Ontario school boards took advantage of federal funding to acquire computing equipment and they have since established a strong computing program in many Ontario high schools. One of the first prominent Canadians in this field was Alberta-born K. Iverson. In 1962 he designed a language called APL (A Programming Language), which was later taken over by IBM and is now used worldwide on a wide variety of computers. The University of Waterloo is a leader in the design of student compilers and interpreters. Waterloo's compilers and interpreters run on many varieties of computers and are used by students at universities and colleges in many countries.

The first major CAI project in Canada was initiated by Dr Steve Hunka in the Faculty of Education at U of A. An experimental computer-based instructional system, one of about 20 developed by IBM (IBM 1500 System), was installed at the university in 1968. This system was used at U of A for research and development for 12 years and was replaced in 1980 by a Control Data Corporation PLATO System. Other major CAI projects in 1968 and 1969 were at Ontario Institute for Studies in Education (OISE), University of Calgary and the National Research Council (NRC). As a result of the work at these and other CAI centres, 2 major Canadian CAI authoring systems have evolved: CAN, which was originally developed at OISE and which is being used in Canada, the US and Europe, and NATAL-74, which was developed by NRC and Honeywell; both systems can run on a number of different microcomputers.

Large-scale CAI materials tend to be produced by development teams, which might include subject-matter experts, instructors, graphic artists, programmers, analysts and technical writers. The time required to develop CAI materials depends on the authoring system, the expertise of the team, and the complexity of the instructional application. Estimates of 100-300 hours of development time being required for each student hour of "on-line instruction" are quite common.

Most CAI programs tend to reinforce previously learned skills by asking questions, analysing the student's responses and presenting summaries of the student's performance; this is evident in many of the commercial mathematics, spelling and language-arts drill and practice programs that are available for microcomputers. As the programs become more sophisticated (eg, tutorial) students are presented with new material based on their performance both within the lessons and in end-of-unit quizzes. Some CAI courses are quite long (100 hours or more) and are primarily intended to be used without an instructor, whereas others may last only 10 or 15 minutes and are intended to supplement classroom work.

Since 1977, uses of CAL have spread rapidly throughout the Canadian educational system. Almost every provincial department (or ministry) of education has initiated projects to help cope with the rapid increase of computer use in the public school sector. In 1983 Ontario and Québec each announced unique microcomputer hardware specifications and they have made funds available for development on various lesson materials for use on these microcomputers. For example, Ontario provided support to the Canadian Education Microprocessor Corp (CEMCORP) to develop and manufacture an Ontario-based microcomputer called the ICON. Marketing of the ICON is being handled by UNISYS Canada. The Ontario Ministry of Education pays its school boards 75% of the cost of computer systems if the systems comply with Stage I approved provincial specifications. There are approximately 17 000 ICONs in Ontario schools. A second system, the IBM Ednet has also been ministry approved. Stage II specifications for the next generation of Ontario-approved educational microcomputers are now being finalized.

Although microcomputers have also had a significant impact upon post-secondary institutions, these institutions primarily use mainframe computers and occasionally local area networks to provide CAL to their students. There appears to be more CAL development activity in post-secondary institutions than in the elementary and secondary schools, partly because courses tend to be taught in shorter periods. On the other hand, most Canadian elementary and secondary schools operate on a system in which there is no positive incentive to use instructional techniques to decrease student learning time. This is a major reason for the emphasis upon learning *with* the computer rather than learning *through* the computer. So far, CAI has had little effect on classroom structures and practices, but as computers gain a foothold the curriculum is being modified to reflect their increasing importance.

Ontario and Québec seem to be making organized attempts at providing hardware and software to educational institutions at reasonable prices. The intent of both provinces is to develop their own software and thereby rely less upon American- or French-produced software. Because most commercial software is developed by Americans, attempts are being made to establish a Canadian "courseware" industry that could provide CAL materials with Canadian content for Canadian schools.　　　E.W. ROMANIUK

Computer Communications The COMPUTER INDUSTRY grew by developing faster and cheaper methods of processing and storing data. Computer communication occurs when computers are attached to communications lines. Data processing becomes teleprocessing, or, data processing at a distance. Teleprocessing has stimulated explosive growth both in the use of computer terminals and in the creation of central data or information banks to which the terminals have access via the TELECOMMUNICATIONS system. Users may have computer terminals anywhere within the range of the telecommunications system – at the office, at home, on the farm. They may obtain access to central computers and databanks located across town or in other countries. One of the earliest users was the airline industry with its computerized reservation systems.

Business and government offices are becoming more automated with increased use of computers (*see* OFFICE AUTOMATION). Even typewriters can be connected to a central computer via telecommunications lines. At home, personal computers and modern TV sets can be used to contact databanks over telephone or CABLE TELEVISION company lines. Computer communication networks may be designed for many different purposes. They can connect a company's plants located around the world. They can provide specialized information to an industry (eg, stock market information for brokers) or a profession (eg, court decisions for lawyers). They can provide specialized information to companies (eg, credit information) and commercial information to consumers (eg, theatre listings in an electronic yellow pages). They can provide access to special types of computer processing capability for handling voluminous data or highly technical scientific calculations. Computer communications also can be used to facilitate certain kinds of education and training as well as to provide a source of entertainment via access to computer games.

The extent to which computer communication spreads throughout Canadian society will depend heavily on its costs. The unit cost of all 3 major elements – the computer terminal, the information in the databank, and the communications – are expected to decline as a result of improved technology. The costs of transmitting data over the telecommunications system are declining because new technologies permit greater volumes of data to be transmitted at higher speeds, or, more bits of information per second. The telecommunications system, which was initially designed to provide communication to voice signals in analogue form, is now being upgraded to provide all types of communication – data, voice, facsimile and video – using the digital technique of computers.

New communications switching machines are really specialized digital computers. Some new kinds of TELEPHONES have the capabilities of computer terminals. Many new telecommunication local-distribution cables contain optical fibre, which has many times the capacity of the older copper wires and is technically much better for digital communications. New long-distance systems, including optical fibre, single-sideband microwave radio and satellites, can be designed for digital communications. In essence, the telecommunications system is being converted into a giant computer.

The costs of this conversion are substantial. Telephone companies have indicated a desire to introduce new usage charges for local service before 1990, as well as increased monthly flat-rate access charges. Thus the decline in communications costs may not continue. The costs may be a barrier to the use of computer communication services by a high proportion of residential subscribers, although business use is expected to grow at a high rate.

By providing access to more data, computer communication systems open possibilities for more informed decision-making and improved efficiency. Businesses will be able to extend their markets to larger geographical areas. Centralized control by large organizations will be facilitated. But this may lead to a loss of independence for smaller organizations and organizations outside central areas. The free flow of information over international computer communication systems may result in important information about Canada and Canadians being kept outside of Canada and of Canadian control. In order to get the full benefits of computer communication systems, Canadians must have access to these systems and consequently could become dependent on them and the organizations that control them.

If computer communication systems are vulnerable to the theft, misuse, destruction or unauthorized manipulation of data, enormous damage can be done (*see* COMPUTERS AND SOCIETY). The problem is made especially difficult because there is seldom any physical evidence of such activity. If a file of data is stolen by an unauthorized person, the data is still in the computer databank. Erroneous information in a credit or medical file could ruin reputations or lead to faulty diagnosis of illness. Information gathered in databanks may invade personal privacy. Specialized information may be used by some interests to gain unfair control over others.

Thus, although computer communication systems may provide increased freedom of information for some people, it may result in reduced freedom for others. The successful utilization of computer communication systems will require effective regulations to preserve the rights of individuals, regions and nations. It will require public policies to ensure that the evolving INFORMATION SOCIETY benefits all citizens and not simply a few at the expense of the many. *See also* COMMUNICATIONS TECHNOLOGY.　　　WILLIAM H. MELODY

Reading: M. Andrieu and S. Serafini, *The Information Revolution and Its Implications for Canada* (1980); R. Cruise O'Brien, ed, *Information, Economics and Power: The North-South Dimension* (1983); S. Nora and A. Minc, *The Computerization of Society* (1980).

Computer Industry, a subcomponent of the ELECTRONICS INDUSTRY that makes use of the same goods and services and relies on the same basic technologies. Goods include hardware and software. Hardware comprises central processors, memories and peripheral devices. Central processors are electronic systems and components capable of performing arithmetic operations at very high speeds. They range in size and complexity from a single semiconductor "chip," which can be held in the hand, to a large cabinet or series of cabinets each the size of a refrigerator. Memories are electronic devices capable of storing large amounts of data and transferring such data at high speed to the central processing unit or to external peripheral devices. The most common peripherals are page printers, keyboards, video display terminals, communications devices and mechanical bulk memory devices (eg, rotating magnetic discs), but modern computers are capable of interacting with almost any electronic device available on the market. Software comprises the programs necessary to make the central processor interact with the memory and the peripheral devices to carry out a specific function or series of functions. Software is usually written by the supplier of the hardware or by firms specializing in such activity and is supplied on a storage medium (eg, magnetic disc, magnetic tape).

Services include hardware maintenance, software consulting and maintenance, and computer service bureaus. Hardware maintenance is the servicing of the computer system after installation. Software consulting and maintenance provides programming expertise (by the original software supplier or a third party) and ensures the continual upgrading of the software to take advantage of new developments in hardware. Computer service bureaus are firms that sell computing power and services, much the same as common carriers sell communications and communications services.

Scope of the Industry In 1987 the information processing industry was expected to account for 2% of Canada's Gross Domestic Product. This figure is significant in that it is still growing and is still a young and small industry when compared with pulp and paper, agriculture, mining, etc. Also in

1987, Canadians are expected to spend about $10.5 billion on computer goods and services. Hardware and software will cost $7.5 billion and $1.5 billion, respectively. Professional services will cost $700 million and processing services will amount to $600 million.

The major suppliers of computing equipment are subsidiaries of foreign-owned multinational firms. These subsidiaries import most of the goods they supply, although in recent years a number of small domestic firms have carved out specialty "niches" in this sector for domestic and international markets. The distinction between computers and other devices that perform communications operations and specialized functions (eg, word processing, digital switching) is becoming increasingly blurred. Exports of such specialized systems (including software) by domestic firms, along with exports of subcomponents of computer systems manufactured in Canada by the multinational subsidiaries, have helped alleviate what would otherwise be an enormous trade deficit in this sector. The 1986 trade deficit was approximately $500 million resulting from imports of $1 billion and exports of $500 million. The deficit is expected to increase as imports increase and exports remain constant.

The heavy foreign domination of the supply sector by multinational corporations has caused several infrastructural problems in the Canadian industry. A report by Evans Research Corp (Toronto), which compared the economic benefits flowing to Canada with those flowing to the home country of the largest foreign computer and communications companies operating in Canada, reached 4 major conclusions. First, if the firms were putting as much investment into Canada, proportionally, as into their own countries, there would be 21 100 more jobs for Canadians in the computer and communications industries. Second, if these firms were putting proportional investment into INDUSTRIAL RESEARCH AND DEVELOPMENT in Canada, 2392 of those jobs would be in R&D – an area vital to Canada's technological future. For firms reporting such expenditures, R&D investment in Canada represented an average of 2% of revenue. This figure compares poorly with the overall proportion of 6% of revenue spent on R&D worldwide. Third, if these firms were manufacturing in Canada on a scale proportional to their manufacturing elsewhere, they would have invested at least $500 million more than the $224 million they already have in property, plants and equipment. The employment so generated would be in addition to the jobs mentioned above. Fourth, if these firms had paid taxes in Canada at a rate proportional to the US rate, the Canadian government would have obtained an additional $49 million, or 30% more than it actually received in 1980.

The $3-billion expenditure on computer personnel is nearly all spent in Canada, as is the $700 million for data-transmission services that goes to the telephone companies and other common carriers. Such carriers, along with the computer service bureaus, acquire hardware and software from the computer suppliers. These expenditures were estimated at about $200 million in 1985. If the 90% ratio of imports to exports exists in this sector, such expenditures will add a further $180 million to the trade deficit. It is in the fourth area of expenditure, purchased computer services, that the Canadian economic contribution is greatest. Canada's service bureaus are among the best in the world. They, along with computer consulting firms, have figured prominently in a number of Canadian firsts in computer technology, particularly in the merger of computer and communications technology.

Canadian Achievements In the mid-1960s, Interprovincial Pipe Line Ltd designed and implemented a network of minicomputers to monitor and control its entire pipeline system linking Edmonton to eastern Canada and the US. This network embodied concepts in software, communications and process control that were at least a decade ahead of their time. The system was conceptualized and designed by a Toronto consulting firm; the hardware was manufactured in Canada by one of the foreign-owned computer suppliers. Other Canadian firsts include the development of what could have been the prototype of the world's first minicomputer at University of Toronto in the late 1950s; invention of a nuclear instrument called a kicksorter, at Atomic Energy of Canada's Chalk River laboratories in the early 1960s, which could also have become a minicomputer with only minor modifications; and creation of a powerful time-sharing computer by Ferranti Packard Ltd of Toronto also in the early 1960s.

Growth Rate The annual growth rate of total expenditure in computer goods and services was as high as 20% during the 1970s, but in recent years it has been closer to 12%. This reduction is not the result of any slowdown in the use of computers: Canada ranks second only to the US in its yearly computer expenditure as a percentage of Gross Domestic Product. Rather, it reflects a dramatic reduction in computer hardware prices and improved operator and programming efficiencies brought about by more powerful and "user-friendly" software packages.

Research and Development Total Canadian expenditures on computer and communications research and development in Canada in 1985 was expected to be about $300 million, of which about 25% was to be spent in government laboratories, 25% in the universities and 50% in the private sector. Of private-sector R&D expenditures, about 75% or $100 million was to be spent by Canadian-owned firms; in contrast the world's 10 major computer companies were expected to spend over $8 billion. Canadian industrial expenditure will clearly be inadequate for anything other than the creation of very small, specialized niches in the world computer market.

A number of Canada's computer manufacturing and industrial research facilities are located in Ontario: firms such as Gandalf and Mitel in the Ottawa area; IBM and Xerox have establishments in the Toronto area. Some notable other facilities are Matrox in Montréal, Develcon in Saskatoon, Myrias Research in Edmonton, and LSI Logic with fabrication facilities in Calgary and design stations across the country. The country's major common carriers have their own research facilities and some also have manufacturing facilities. These establishments are dispersed throughout Canada and tend to specialize in computerlike communications control systems and intelligent terminals that incorporate microcomputers.

In 1987, 1 561 000 personal computers were installed in Canada, overshadowing by a considerable margin the 25 000 other computers. Of the total number 610 500 were used in business, 301 300 in education and 649 700 in the home. The importance of "mainframes" or large central systems has decreased considerably. The power and capability of the so-called "micro" has enabled the average user to perform 90% of the required computation on a "stand-alone" which can be interfaced to the mainframe for operations that either are too big to be handled locally or need access to large data bases. An examination of the 100 top computer companies in 1986 reflects this trend: IBM had a negative 7% growth which was reflected by a similar 7.1% decrease for all mainframe suppliers. Suppliers of small

and medium systems, on the other hand, grew by 18%. Computers and related devices are expected to change dramatically during the remainder of the 20th century and industries based on computer technology will become extremely important to the economic well-being of Canada. Some experts predict that the information industry (ie, the computer-communications industry) will rival the transportation industry as a contributor to Canada's Gross Domestic Product by the year 2000. *See also* HIGH TECHNOLOGY; MICROCHIPS AND TRANSISTORS; ROBOTICS.   D.J. DOYLE

Computer Science addresses the theory, design and application of information-processing machines. The field is very new: the first successful electronic computer ENIAC (Electronic Numerical Integrator and Computer) was developed in the 1940s at University of Pennsylvania. During the 1950s, 4 main areas of focus emerged. One area concentrated on "hardware," ie, the construction of reliable equipment with faster central-processing units (CPUs), larger memories and more input and output devices, to solve increasingly ambitious problems. Another area covered "software," ie, programming languages, logical techniques and structures needed to direct hardware and organize computational processes. These hardware and software systems rapidly expanded the range of applications, the third area of research and development. The initial applications were in MATHEMATICS, followed by science and engineering, then business, social science, and eventually almost every field of endeavour. As these 3 areas developed, theorists worked on algorithms (descriptions of how to solve a problem, expressed in a language understood by the computer). This fourth area of study questioned what it meant for an algorithm to be efficient, searched for efficient algorithms in a wide variety of contexts and sought to establish a theory of computation.

During the 1960s, as the body of literature in these areas accumulated, computer science emerged as a distinct discipline separated, in many universities, from mathematics and ELECTRICAL ENGINEERING departments and from the computing service bureaus with which they had been associated. Curricula were drawn up and formal computer-science programs initiated.

Relationship to Other Disciplines Of the 4 areas outlined, only part of one, ie, system software, belongs mainly in computer science and not in the domain of another discipline. Included in system software are such components as operating systems (for starting up and governing program execution, managing memory, recording use of resources, etc); input/output and other utilities (for reading, writing and copying data); monitor and debugging routines (for program development); and compilers and interpreters (for translating statements in a high-level language to the computer's assembly code).

Software in general, but system software in particular, must be clearly specified, well structured, carefully tested and documented and regularly maintained. The methodology for accomplishing this function is known as software engineering.

Computer science has a special relationship with mathematics, drawing heavily on the formalism of logic, algebraic structures, automata theory and graph theory. Subjects such as numerical analysis and computational complexity belong to both computer science and mathematics. The components of computers (registers, MICROCHIPS, memory devices) are products of electrical engineering. The study of communication systems is central both to electrical engineering and to the subject of computer-systems architecture. Computer and communication technologies appear to be merging as the variety and volume of services based on them grow.

Many disciplines interact with computer science. Together with industrial engineering, computer science addresses systems analysis, process design, modelling and simulation; with linguistics, it shares an interest in language syntax and semantics. The theories and techniques of information storage, retrieval and dissemination are important to both library information science and computing science. With management science, computer science studies data bases, query languages, decision systems and office information systems. Through ARTIFICIAL INTELLIGENCE studies, it shares with philosophy an interest in logic, understanding and knowledge formation. With psychology and neurological science, computer science is concerned with signal processing and the interpretation of sensory perception. Because computers are research tools in so many natural, engineering and biological sciences, control devices in industrial processes and machines central to the conduct of businesses, computer science interacts with many other disciplines.

Computer Science in Canada The work of the first Canadian group addressing the design and use of electronic computers led to the construction of UTEC (University of Toronto Model Electronic Computer) in 1948 and the acquisition of FERUT (Ferranti Computer at U of T) in 1951. Some hardware developments have taken place in Canadian universities, government laboratories (eg, Defence Research Telecommunications Establishment) and industries (Computing Devices of Canada, Ferranti-Packard). However, most computer science research has focused on software, numerical analysis and computer applications, eg, the water-level calculations for the St Lawrence Seaway Project, done on FERUT for the Hydro Electric Power Commission of Ontario.

Starting in the 1950s university courses in computer science became available at U of T, McGill, UBC, U of Alberta, Carleton and others, first as extension courses, then as undergraduate and graduate subjects. Much of the impetus for the establishment of university programs came from business and government. The Canadian Conference for Computing and Data Processing, held in 1958, attracted 400 participants and led in the same year to the formation of the Computing and Data Processing Society of Canada (now CIPS, the Canadian Information Processing Society). The WATFOR compiler, developed in the early 1960s by University of Waterloo for fast processing of student jobs, was the first Canadian program product to achieve international distribution. By 1964, computer science courses were being taught at 22 universities and technical schools across the country. Today almost all postsecondary institutions offer computer science programs, and programming courses are given in many high schools. Research laboratories can be found at the universities, the NATIONAL RESEARCH COUNCIL, Northern Telecom, IBM and other computer manufacturers. Many of the larger companies using computers are engaged in active research.

A significant Canadian computer industry has evolved from these developments in computer science. For complete systems US-based companies (IBM, Digital Equipment, UNISYS, Honeywell, NCR) are dominant. In computer service bureaus, communications and software, Canadian companies are important nationally and internationally (Canada Systems Group, Systemhouse, Northern Telecom, Gandalf, Mitel, I.P. Sharp, Cognos).   C.C. GOTLIEB

Programming Languages

Programming languages are formal notations for expressing algorithms and data so that they can be "understood" by computers. Popular programming languages include Ada, named after Lady Lovelace, Lord Byron's daughter, who worked on Charles Babbage's "analytical engine"; ALGOL, *Algo*rithmic *L*anguage; APL, *A Programming L*anguage; BASIC, *B*eginner's *A*ll-Purpose *S*ymbolic *I*nstruction *C*ode; COBOL, *Co*mmon *B*usiness-*O*riented *L*anguage; FORTRAN, *For*mula *Tran*slation; GPSS, *G*eneral Purpose *S*ystems *S*imulation; LISP, *Lis*t *P*rocessing; Pascal, named after the French mathematician Blaise Pascal, who in 1642 developed a calculating machine; SIMULA, *Simu*lation *La*nguage; SNOBOL, *Strin*g-*O*riented *Symbo*lic *L*anguage; SPSS, *S*tatistical *P*ackage for the *S*ocial *S*ciences. Unlike natural languages (eg, English, French), programming languages must have precise definitions of form (syntax) and meaning (semantics). General-purpose languages are used for problems in many areas; eg, Pascal can be used for information retrieval, numerical computation and system programming. Special-purpose languages are more limited in scope, being designed for specific application areas. For example, GPSS is used for simulation studies.

Programs contain definitions and computer-executable statements and expressions. A programmer can usually define names of data objects (variables) and executable objects (subroutines, functions) and, in some languages, types. A type is a set of values together with appropriate operations; for example, a queue of integers would have integer sequences as values and "insert" and "delete" as operations. Statements include assignment, input, output and invocation of subroutines, plus ways of constructing sequences of statements, selecting among statements and repeating statements.

Since a computer directly understands operations encoded as binary numbers, programs can be written in binary. A binary number is one expressed using only the numerals 0 and 1. In this lowest level, called machine language or executable code, each instruction and reference to a data object is a binary number. Assembly languages allow the use of symbolic names for instructions and data; these symbols must be transformed to numbers before the program can be executed. High-level languages (eg, COBOL) allow use of terminology and constructs more convenient for humans, and require more complex transformations to executable code. Very high-level languages allow expression of what is required, rather than how it is to be computed. For example, in some data-base query languages characteristics of required data are specified, not ways of finding them in the data base.

Program syntax is usually precisely defined using a notation called Backus-Naur Form (BNF). The structure of a program is described in terms of its components, which in turn are described in terms of their components, and so on, until everything has been defined in terms of words in the language. This situation is similar to the way sentences in a natural language are described. Once a machine-language program exists, it can be improved by being transformed to an equivalent program of fewer or faster instructions.

DAVID T. BARNARD

Hardware

When computers were first developed, the physical equipment was referred to as "hardware"; the computer industry soon coined the term "software" to describe the program components executed by the hardware. In overall terms, digital computer hardware, whether for small (microcomputer) or large (mainframe) computers, comprises processors, peripheral devices and memories. In describing the operation of the computer, it is convenient to consider that processors provide control and processing functions, and that peripheral devices provide input and output functions. Information that is read into the memory through the input unit, whether numbers or textual information, is encoded into blocks of binary digits or "bits." Each bit has the value 0 or 1 and common encoding techniques use a block of 8 bits (a "byte") to represent the letters A-Z, digits 0-9 and punctuation marks. The values of individual bits are physically represented by small electrical voltages and currents, or by the state of magnetization of very tiny areas on surfaces coated with magnetic material. The form of representation depends on whether the information is being processed, stored, or transmitted between functional units.

The numerical calculations or text processing to be done on the data in the memory is specified by a machine program. This program is also stored in the memory. It consists of a sequence of simple steps called instructions. Examples of typical instructions include "add 2 numbers and store the sum in a specific memory location"; "jump to a different section of the program if the value just computed is negative"; "send the contents of a particular memory location to an output device for printing." An instruction can usually be encoded in about 30 bits. The electrical networks that fetch individual instructions from the memory and execute them in the processor are composed of many thousands of transistors fabricated in integrated circuits. These circuits are encapsulated in small, flat plastic cases of a few square centimetres area, each containing up to tens of thousands of transistors. The time needed to fetch and to execute an instruction varies with the complexity of the instruction, but it is generally on the order of one-millionth of a second.

Input and Output Units provide communication with the external world (people or electronic and electromechanical devices). Typical input devices are keyboards, which resemble typewriters, graphical tablets that react to pointer positioning and communication signal converters that transform signal values into binary-coded numbers. Output devices include video displays for characters and graphical shapes, printers for recording output on paper, and converters that transform binary-coded numbers into electrical output signals to control motor drives, etc. The magnetic tapes and discs used to store data and programs outside of the processor and memory units are usually classified as input/output devices. They are capable of storing large amounts of data (hundreds of millions of bytes) and constitute the storage media used by business enterprises (eg, insurance companies, banks) for customer records and other business-data files.

Memory Unit Information, which is kept in the memory unit while processing is taking place, is organized into words of a few bytes each. The memory is physically implemented from integrated circuits, each typically containing tens or hundreds of thousands of bits. The complete memory of a medium-size computer might contain on the order of a few million words, which can be moved in or out of the memory at rates of a few million words per second.

Control and Processor Units Control networks, implemented from integrated circuits, are needed to perform the overall sequencing of operations that co-ordinate the activities of all units of the computer. The largest single concentration of controls is associated with the process that performs arithmetic operations on numbers and comparison/searching/sorting operations on text. These controls are needed during processing as well as during the fetch/store operations used to move data between the memory and the processor. Controls are also needed in the circuitry that connects input/output devices to the processor/ memory units. In many computer applications, multiple processors and memories must be employed to provide sufficient computing power. Such distributed processing situations lead to the need for synchronization control among the various processors, memories, and communication facilities. This area of computer systems design, including communication networks, represents the most difficult and challenging task for the hardware designer. V. CARL HAMACHER

Software

A digital computer stores data and performs various operations on that data (eg, addition, multiplication and comparison). A sequence of operations or instructions (the "program") is also stored in the computer and is interpreted sequentially by the computer's CPU (central-processing unit). A typical instruction might tell the CPU to perform an arithmetic operation using a special place in storage called an accumulator. The collection of operations, and their meaning, is called the computer's native or machine language. Writing a program using machine language is tedious and programs are usually written in a high-level language (eg, FORTRAN and COBOL). A single statement in a high-level language would require hundreds of instructions if written in machine language. Thus a translator (ie, compiler), which generates a machine-language program from the corresponding high-level-language program, is usually required, although some programs can be analysed and executed in one step.

An operating system is a special program that manages the computer system's resources. For example, when several people use the computer simultaneously, they must be prevented from conflicting with one another; there is usually only one processor, and people must be scheduled to use it in turn. An operating system also provides services for the user, such as facilities to input and store data in the computer. These services provide access to sequences of instructions which are required by most programs. The operating system is normally the first program loaded into the computer. Each user communicates with the operating system using a command language in order to request services. There are now hundreds of different operating systems in use; and many of them are tailored to a specific application area (eg, process control) or to particular, specialized hardware configurations.

A program that addresses a specialized requirement (eg, general ledger accounting) is called an application program. A payroll application program would accept information such as hours worked, and one output might be payroll cheques. Most application programs can be tailored to accommodate various circumstances; some (eg, engineering-design packages and systems for computer-assisted instruction) use special application-oriented languages. Properly designed programs are a good way for most people to use computer systems because they make it unnecessary for users to memorize the details of the computer system. Computer programs are often quite large and can take months or years to prepare. They may be used for years, with changes made to reflect new circumstances. Software methodology provides techniques for writing programs (including structured programming,

design and analysis) that are easily understood and modified by other programmers. Some of the tools used are flowcharts, structure diagrams, data-flow diagrams and decision tables. J.W. GRAHAM

Theoretical Computer Science

Theoretical computer science is the precise (ie, mathematical) study of particular problems and phenomena in computing, including treatment of the inherent limitations of computers, representations of programming languages and program correctness and efficiency. Disciplines in this area are distinguished by their approach and mathematical tools rather than by their subject matter.

Automata Theory is the study of models of computers and their inherent power. Key issues in determining what a computer can do are how much memory it has and how this memory is accessed. Even if time and memory are unlimited, there are tasks that computers cannot do. For example, it can be proved that no computer program can inspect another arbitrary program and determine whether or not it would ever stop running. The unsolvability of this "halting problem" is an important point in computability theory.

Formal Language Theory A program can be thought of as accepting (saying "yes") or rejecting (saying "no"). Hence, we may speak of the set of inputs or language accepted by the program. This formal language theory has been a productive way of studying possible forms and specifications of programming languages, among other computational issues.

Program Correctness Theory The task of writing a correct computer program is difficult; indeed, almost all large programs (including operating systems and compilers) contain errors which can be disastrous. One way to deal with this problem is to develop techniques that offer formal proof that a program does what it is supposed to do, perhaps as part of the process of writing the program. Several approaches have been taken, all based on mathematical logic. A general thread which runs through most approaches is that one must be able to write down assertions that must hold whenever particular lines in the program are to be executed. The theory of program correctness is at the basis of the study of the semantics (meaning) of programs.

Computational Complexity Theory Many problems are best handled by computers because of the large amounts of data involved (eg, income-tax records) or because there are numerous possibilities to explore, even with a moderate amount of data. For instance, to determine the most effective order in which to do 30 jobs, over 10^{32} possible orders could be explored. The fastest computer available today would take 10^8 times the age of the universe to count that high. Therefore, although computers are fast, it is still crucial that efficient methods, or algorithms, be used. The study of the efficiency of algorithms and data organization is a key area of computer science. Consider, for example, a computerized telephone book with a million names and numbers. If the algorithm for finding a number were simply to scan for a given name, a half-million names (on average) would have to be inspected for each search. Instead, a technique known as binary search can be applied. Because the list is sorted by name, the computer can look at the middle element of the name and decide whether to continue the search in the first or second half of the list. Continuing in this way, only about 20 names need be read to complete a search. It can be proved that, for this type of search, this is the best search technique. The study of algorithms has led

to many efficient methods, and also to an understanding of why no more efficient method may exist. J. IAN MUNRO

Reading: J. Bleakley and J. La Prarie, *Entering the Computer Age. The Computer Industry in Canada* (1982); Anthony Ralston, ed, *Encyclopedia of Computer Science* (1976, rev 1983).

Computer Systems Applications MATHEMATICS spawned the computer, gave it its name and was its first field of application (ie, in the computation of military ballistic tables). Although many early computers resembled their mechanical predecessors in that they could multiply or divide only by repeated add or subtract functions, their revolutionary speed and precision thrust them quickly into fields involving heavy multiplication. Thus, although computers were later to be emphasized as "information system" devices and applied to logical and sorting problems that did not involve multiplication, literal "computing" dominated the first decade of their use. Two technologies, those of atomic energy and missiles, relied heavily on computation and thus provided the critical demand for ever-better computers. The iterative calculation (ie, repeating to produce a more and more nearly accurate solution) required by atomic physics remains the principal stimulus to production of the biggest computers. The missile industry, which spawned the space industry, related more to data handling as multitudinous observations had to be processed to derive actual trajectories, to monitor performance via telemetry, and later to enhance RE-MOTE-SENSING data. The space industry spurred the miniaturization of computers through developments in microelectronic technology. Many observers believe that American space achievements were completely dependent on computers.

Even the earliest computers were useful in constructing mathematical tables; however, when computer processing resorted to fundamentals (ie, ascertaining trigonometric values from formulas, square roots by iterative approximation, etc), the value of such tables quickly diminished. This concentration on basic values stimulated reconsideration and refinement of classical numerical methods (including their use of rounding off) to make use of the power and reduce the limitations of the new tool.

Census tabulation, a field with heavy addition requirements that had influenced developments in punched-card technology, lent itself to computerization, especially in N America where computers were usually tied to card devices. The electronic computing of pay followed, particularly where hourly rates meant extensive multiplication. This step took the computer from the scientific world into that of commerce, and thus from the hands of the science graduate to those of the accountant and eventually the lay user. Computer functions soon moved from payroll into accounts receivable and other financial applications and into inventory control. Speed of processing was the motivator, allowing reduction of the size of inventory and of the delay in receiving payment, and hence decreasing tied-up funds. Energy utilities and insurance companies were among the pioneers in extending the use of computers beyond the payroll function. The addition of video display terminals gave the user immediate access to data. Among the first to capitalize on this now widely used feature was Air Canada (for reservations).

Given appropriate sensors, the computer can use its speed and stamina to provide vigilant monitoring (eg, of patients) and elaborate interpretation of events (eg, construction of 3-dimensional images from X-ray data). Given appropriate actuators, a computer can react and hence control events in ways specified by program and human input. Today, computers control pipeline flows, NUCLEAR POWER PLANTS, traffic signals, aircraft, refineries, telephone exchanges and, on a smaller scale, machine tools and car engines. Interprovincial Pipe Line Ltd of Edmonton, Alta, ATOMIC ENERGY OF CANADA LTD, and the city of Toronto have been notable pioneers, as has the TRANSCANADA TELEPHONE SYSTEM in its innovative Dataroute and Datapac digital transmission networks. Using early and cumbersome computers, the Canadian navy, with its DATARS Project, pioneered "Command Control" of warships. Small, inexpensive microprocessors today allow computer control to be so unobtrusive as to make the presence of a computer go unnoticed. Minuscule energy demands allow computers to be used in a wristwatch or implanted in the human body to control an aberrant heart.

Compared with numbers, textual data is expensive to enter and store (because of its great redundancy), and it lacks the notable profitability of automatic multiplication. While these relative disadvantages cannot be eliminated, vast improvements in hardware economics in the 1970s lessened them and, with improved algorithms (definitions of the means of solving a problem, expressed in a language which the device understands), allowed exploitation of electronic sorting. Textual indexes, notably of scientific literature abstracts, promoted growth in this field in the 1960s. Various forms of text editors have accommodated the computer's own source program material, plus an ever-growing array of documents. The need for speed in the NEWSPAPER industry led to the development of computer programs which took original draft articles and performed all editing and layout, including automatic typesetting. Related software served in the preparation of catalogues, books and, in the special form of word processing, simple correspondence. Tied to laser-beam xerographic printers, the computer has become an information machine, able to produce customized copies as required rather than blind facsimiles in bulk. Computers have become information storehouses, releasing their knowledge to remote callers by means of synthesized speech, data circuits or television images; Canada's TELIDON system is an example of this type of application.

Graphical data is yet more demanding, but the great improvement in electronic storage has accommodated applications with very sophisticated visual images, in multi-colour, with computer capacity to reshape and vary views. Function, style and efficiency can all be addressed by "computer-aided design," and then followed into the factory with "computer-aided manufacturing" (CAD/CAM). Animated and art films are related derivatives. Special forms of graphics include complex scripts and music; for the latter, the inclusion of sound synthesizers allows computer-assisted composition.

The ability to branch (ie, to take alternative paths according to conditions) is an essential computer operation. This characteristic makes the computer a logical device that, for example, can be made to play chess. The computer makes choices by trying alternatives: by internally playing several steps down each feasible path and assessing the consequent situations. The computer can use this form of simulation in many practical scenarios (eg, traffic flow, command/supply economics, patient care) to support decision making and for modelling, teaching and examination. A refinement allows the computer to remember the consequences of past choices and hence to improve its decision mak-

ing (see ARTIFICIAL INTELLIGENCE and COMPUTER-ASSISTED LEARNING).

From its rough laboratory beginnings the computer has come to embrace a myriad of applications. This extension has led to the development of various special-purpose computers and to a vast range of power and size, but the trend of application is now towards integration. A single network, if not a single computer, encompasses commercial and scientific applications, secretarial work, message communications and even speech communications. Refinement of the public telecommunications networks is allowing any computer to "talk" to any other computer, making the world one network. "Electronic mail" and "electronic bulletin boards" are widespread outcomes. Simultaneously the microcomputer has become also a toy, albeit an often useful and educational one, that increasingly absorbs the recreational time and money of Canadians.

DONALD FENNA

Computers and Society Computers are the centrepiece of a vast TECHNOLOGY by which goods and services are produced and nations are governed. A massive invasion of personal computers (PCs) into Canadian homes heralds the growth of a potential computer utility. Because this technology is so pervasive, it has and will continue to have profound effects on individuals and on the conduct of public and private organizations. Many of these impacts are beneficial; others exact a cost. The balance between costs and benefits cannot yet be anticipated for some areas.

Because computers can control other instruments, vast improvements have taken place in activities in which "smart" instruments play an important role. The actions of groups of machines and instruments can be co-ordinated by computers and these machines then function as robots, with uses ranging from the improvement of industrial processes and medical applications to the creation of more destructive instruments of warfare. Computers also influence the structure and functioning of governmental and private organizations. These technological and procedural advances in industry, government, science and medicine entail certain social and economic costs. In the past, technological advances have balanced lost employment opportunities by creating jobs through the opening of new fields of endeavour, the exploitation of new opportunities and the satisfaction of new demands. It is still unclear whether such a balance will emerge from labour savings made through computers. The automation of office and bureaucratic procedures will certainly lead to a sharply decreased need for office personnel and managers (see OFFICE AUTOMATION). This anticipated decline in white-collar employment is still masked by the need for white-collar workers to computerize the work of the larger organizations that now produce, distribute, provide services or govern. However, once computerization has been completed, white-collar employment will follow the patterns set in industrial work, where there has been a generally lower demand for semiskilled and unskilled labour.

It is in their effect on the management of large organizations that computers have the greatest social impact. Here they are more than machines; they become the focus of a new management technology, which includes not only the physical machine (called "hardware") but also the program packages, their descriptions and protocols ("software"). Computer technology has also encouraged reorganization of the way public and private bureaucracies conduct their business, the development of new and diverse skills, new organizational units to supply and maintain comput-

er-related services, and new attitudes about what computing is good for and how it may be used efficiently.

Computerization of large organizations has led to centralization and to increasingly hierarchical management structures, in part because vertically organized software for management systems is far less costly than software for distributed data processing, which would support diffusion of authority. The resulting shifts in administrative power in most public and private agencies are not subjected to the judgement of shareholders, voters or elected representatives, although some of these power shifts may significantly influence the future of such agencies.

Because computers support centralized organizational structure, it is becoming more difficult for individual citizens to obtain direct access to decision-making centres, which are often physically and organizationally distant from the individual with a problem. This distance is especially apparent when clients, customers or citizens attempt to correct errors in transactions, obtain necessary exemptions or act in any way that deviates from normal procedures. While computerization decreases the possibility of some errors in transactions between citizens and organizations, it increases the chance of others (eg, through flaws in programs) and simultaneously makes it more difficult to have such errors corrected.

The computerization of organizations may change the pattern of white-collar crime, making vandalism and theft take on much more serious proportions than in the past. Vandalism might involve destruction of the records of information systems on which large organizations depend. Opportunities for direct, physical theft are decreased because of the difficulty of gaining access to the financial networks; however, opportunities are available for embezzling very large sums of money by manipulating computer transactions. Other kinds of computer crime include the theft of computer time and the illegal manipulation or accession of confidential computer files.

A great deal of attention has been given to the possible loss of anonymity through the increasing access public and private organizations have to detailed personal records. The files of public and private organizations contain a great deal of information on the activities of individuals. Once these records become machine readable and records from different files can be linked, government and other agencies can obtain information which an individual may not wish them to have, resulting in a "loss of privacy." Some people believe that public agencies engaged in the control of those who abuse the system (eg, welfare cheaters or criminals) may perform their jobs better if they have access to detailed information. Their opponents argue that such agencies might be tempted to obtain records unrelated to their direct operation and thus conduct surveillance of a citizen's personal activities – eg, if Revenue Canada could catch income tax evaders by searching medical, real estate or other records. Of special importance to Canadians is the international flow of information among members of a large network that includes the US, the UK and Commonwealth nations, and Western Europe. Information about the transactions of Canadians flows freely across borders and is made available to authorities in other countries. The possible misuse of this data has not yet been addressed by legislative authorities.

Machine-readable membership lists of persons belonging to various interest groups have proved to be important in the formation of political coalitions (eg, in the US). This type of party coalition may be viewed as counteracting the distribution of powers within a democratic government. The ease with which such coalitions can be formed and manipulated and the effect of this phenomenon on the political process have yet to be seen. In Canada the creation of a national coalition might be valuable in counteracting the regionalism of Canadian politics.

In recent years there has been a spectacular growth of home computing, using personal computers. In 1981, Canadians spent $150 million on PCs out of a total computer market of $4.1 billion. Four years later (1985), Canadians spent $1.18 billion on PCs out of $7.3 billion spent on computers. In fact, in that year the cumulative processing power of PCs surpassed that of mainframes in Canada. (Not all of this growth is in home computing. Many PCs are far from small and IBM PCs and compatibles dominate the Canadian business market.)

Education was one of the first fields outside of business to embrace PCs. Canadian schoolboards began to buy PCs in 1979 and from then on market penetration was rapid. (For example, Alberta schools had 265 PCs in 1981 and 3535 in 1983. By 1985, BC and Ontario had PCs in over half their elementary schools, while the Atlantic provinces had 10% to 20% penetration. Québec allocated $150 million in 1983 to purchase 32 000 PCs by 1985.)

TELECOMMUNICATIONS is one area where the PC appears to become truly useful for the average consumer. The home computer owner with a telephone and a modem (a device that allows computer data to be sent over the phone) can purchase goods, receive stock quotations, participate in computer conference discussions, send messages to anywhere in North America, access data banks (over 2900 were available worldwide in 1985), and get software from so-called bulletin boards located in almost all North American cities. These services are still forming and mostly appeal to scientists, businessmen and computer hobbyists; but each year they cater to new interest groups. For example, Canadian poet George BOWERING organized a conferencing system which enabled fellow writers to read and criticize works in progress.

The social impact of the PC as an extension of the telephone can be seen from current uses. Many PC users own an inexpensive piece of software which turns their computer into a bulletin board and enables any owner of a telephone and a PC to take and leave messages – a sort of unbounded laundry message board. These bulletin boards link geographically dispersed interest communities. Such interest communities may be of computer hobbyists or of individuals pursuing other hobbies such as astronomy or environmental conservation. They may be of special interest or issue groups, pro or con certain social issues, such as abortion. There are also groups using bulletin boards for anti-social activities such as to disseminate hate literature or pornography. These latter groups present a special problem for Canada Customs Service, who are charged with controlling hate and pornographic literature at the border. This literature now crosses the US border via the telephone system. Transborder flow of information actually affirms constitutional provisions for free speech, even if its content is not welcomed by many Canadians.

Related to bulletin boards, but much more expanded, are conferencing systems. Numerous conferencing systems have been set up since the early 1970s. These differ from bulletin boards in that they allow users to review and respond to groups of messages linked by theme; in effect, people separated geographically are linked by topic. (Recently, an impromptu worldwide debate of the Libyan airstrike was held on *Byte* Magazine's conferencing system.) As usual, business-

men, scientists and technophiles were the first to embrace this technology. Existing, cheap, powerful machines could enable other groups of individuals to set up their own conferencing systems. Thus, for example, environmentalists will be able to have worldwide strategy sessions.

Computer utilities are, by their nature, transnational: they link cosmopolitan interest groups. But Canadians are a part of this development. For example, a major conferencing system was developed at Guelph University by an Englishman for an American company – in many ways, such developments are typically Canadian.

THEODOR D. STERLING

Conacher, Charles William, hockey player (b at Toronto 10 Dec 1909; d there 30 Dec 1967). Playing right wing on Toronto's potent "Kid Line," with Joe Primeau and Henry "Busher" Jackson, he was known for his rambunctious play and booming shot. He played 12 seasons in the NHL, mostly with TORONTO MAPLE LEAFS, winning the scoring title 1933-34 and 1934-35 and sharing it twice more. He was traded to Detroit 1938 and finished his career with New York Americans. He scored 225 goals, 173 assists in regular season play, adding 17 goals, 18 assists in playoffs.

JAMES MARSH

Conacher, Lionel Pretoria, all-round athlete, politician (b at Toronto 24 May 1902; d at Ottawa 26 May 1954). One of 10 children, he grew up in a tough working-class district of Toronto. He got his first taste of sports at Jesse Ketchum School, went on to excel at football, lacrosse, baseball, boxing, wrestling, hockey and track and field, and won the 125-lb wrestling championship of Ontario. In 1920, in his first boxing competition, he won the Canadian light-heavyweight championship. The following year he boxed a 3-round exhibition bout with Jack Dempsey, the world heavyweight champion. Conacher's power, stamina and speed (he ran 100 yards in under 10 seconds) were particularly suited to lacrosse and football. He helped Toronto to win the Ontario Lacrosse Assn senior title in 1922. In football he was a ferocious runner and perhaps the best punter in the game. In the 1921 GREY CUP game he led Toronto Argonauts to a 23-0 victory over Edmonton, scoring 15 points himself. He did not learn to skate until age 16, but his aggressive, determined play made him one of the best defencemen in hockey. He turned professional with Pittsburgh in

Lionel Conacher, "The Big Train," Canada's finest all-round athlete, shown here in the uniform of the New York Americans (*courtesy Canada's Sports Hall of Fame*).

1925 and played for New York Americans, Chicago Black Hawks and Montreal Maroons (1930-33 and 1934-37). Rugged and ready to brawl (even with his brother Charlie), he was NHL first all-star in 1934.

Conacher entered politics in 1937 and was Liberal MPP for Toronto Bracondale. He was Ontario athletic commissioner and worked to provide recreational facilities in city parks. In 1949 he was elected federal MP for Toronto Trinity. He died of a heart attack after hitting a triple in a charity softball game. Deserving of his nickname "The Big Train," Conacher was the greatest all-round athlete that Canada has produced.   JAMES MARSH

Conant, Gordon Daniel, lawyer, Liberal politician, premier of Ontario (b near Oshawa, Ont 11 Jan 1885; d at Oshawa 2 Jan 1953). From 1937 the capable, faithful attorney general in the Ontario government of Mitchell HEPBURN, he inherited the premiership from his leader in Oct 1942. But Hepburn's feud with PM KING was tearing apart Ontario Liberals and his arbitrary choice of successor deepened resentment. Despite a productive legislative session, Conant could not heal the rift and in Apr 1943 he resigned.

BARBARA A. McKENNA

Conception Bay is one of the principal bays of Newfoundland, formed by 2 N-reaching arms of the AVALON PENINSULA. Its name, one of the earliest recorded (1527), commemorates the Feast of the Immaculate Conception. Cape St Francis to the E and Split Point, 32 km NW, mark the mouth of the bay, which stretches 70 km S to Holyrood. Its shoreline, varying from rugged cliffs and fjordlike inlets to gentle sandy beaches and excellent harbours, was the province's earliest settled; its rich marine resources were utilized by Europeans from the early 1500s. In 1610 CUPIDS was the site of the first formal English colony in present-day Canada. The bay has always been Newfoundland's most populous. BELL ISLAND in the E, the bay's largest island, was the location of an important iron-ore mine.   ROBERT D. PITT

Conception Bay South, Nfld, Town, pop 15 531 (1986c), 10 856 (1981c), inc 1971, is located on the SE shore of CONCEPTION BAY on the AVALON PENINSULA. The town, 32 km long, 5 km wide, comprises a number of smaller former settlements that ring the shoreline: Topsail, Chamberlains, Codner, Long Pond, Manuels, Upper Gullies, Indian Pond and Seal Cove. Most of the constituent settlements were founded by fishermen before 1800. Crops were grown in the areas backing the fishing sites and sold in nearby ST JOHN'S. The area, dotted by numerous ponds and with good seafront beaches, has also been a popular summer resort for St John's residents. Since 1945 most of the labour force has commuted to St John's. Some small-scale fishing and truck farming is still carried on; but the local service industry makes up the balance of the community's employment.   JANET E.M. PITT AND ROBERT D. PITT

Concert Halls and Opera Houses When Canada was being settled in the 17th and 18th centuries, buildings for defence, accommodation and religious worship took priority. However, once these essential structures were completed and social order established, inhabitants could consider entertainment. In Québec and the Maritimes early concerts and theatrical presentations took place in what 18th-century newspapers advertised as a concert hall or theatre. In fact, performances generally were located in an assembly room of a hotel or inn, the upper floor of a tavern, or in the local mechanics' hall. During the last 2 decades of the 18th century and especially in the first half of the 19th century, concerts and dramas were regularly presented in Québec C (Thespian

Massey Hall, Toronto, the best example of its period of a concert hall designed for large orchestral performances. It opened in 1894 (*photo by J.A. Kraulis*).

Theatre, Marchant's Coffee House, Frank's Tavern), Montréal (THEATRE ROYAL, Dillon's Hotel, Salle de Spectacle), Halifax (British Tavern, Theatre Royal), Saint John (Mallard's Long Room), St John's, Nfld (Globe Tavern), and at the end of the 19th century, Toronto (St Lawrence Hall). Most 18th- and 19th-century structures have not survived fires and demolition. However, some travellers and residents left brief descriptions of

these early buildings. For example, William Dyott, a British army lieutenant stationed in Halifax, describes in his diary the first Maritime theatre built for dramas, operas and mixed entertainments: "February (1789) – the officers in garrison fitted up a new theatre....It was as complete a thing for the size as I ever saw. Boxes and a first and second pit." By the mid-19th century, touring performers could find some sort of facility in many towns of central Canada. "Our stay at Hamilton was marked with signal success in a professional light. We played at the Mechanics' Hall – fine one for singing in – well situated and tolerably cheap – 15 dols. a night....We played

also at the Templars' Hall, a charming little room well worthy of a trial by any one attempting Entertainments" (Horton Rhys, *A Theatrical Trip for a Wager*, 1861).

With the advent of touring theatrical and musical companies, between 1870 and 1900, a series of opera houses were constructed across Canada. These buildings formed one of the first important Canadian cultural links. With the completion of the railway from east to west, entertainers could travel economically and efficiently. By 1900, Montréal, Ottawa, Kingston, Winnipeg, Vancouver and many smaller cities had completed buildings. Even Dawson City and Barkerville had opera houses – monuments to the extravagance of the gold rush. The name opera house was somewhat misleading because dramas, mixed entertainments of acting and singing, and performances of feats of skill were the most common attractions.

Some early opera houses could seat between 1000 and 2000 people. Toronto's MASSEY HALL, opened in 1894 with a seating capacity of 4000, is the best period example of a concert hall primarily designed for large orchestral and choral performances. However, during the first half of the 20th century few cities had concert halls or opera houses for these specialized purposes. Most of the old so-called opera houses, if they were not destroyed, became movie theatres. Concerts and opera performances usually took place in high-school auditoriums, sports arenas or other makeshift venues. The second half of the 20th century witnessed a growth in the building and restoring of recital halls, opera houses and large multi-purpose performing complexes. PLACE DES ARTS (Montréal), Confederation Centre of the Arts (Charlottetown), NATIONAL ARTS CENTRE (Ottawa), Grand Théâtre de Québec (Québec City), Saskatchewan Centre of the Arts (Regina), Hamilton Place (Hamilton), Orpheum Theatre (Vancouver), Roy Thomson Hall (Toronto), and the companion Jubilee auditoriums (Calgary and Edmonton) are some examples. The 1800-seat Jack Singer Concert Hall, part of the Calgary Centre for Performing Arts, opened in Sept 1985. These structures are the homes for resident orchestras which present concert series to surrounding communities. In addition, concert halls present touring entertainers from North America and abroad, and extensive seasons of varied entertainment. FREDERICK HALL

Concession Line, a term used especially in Ontario to refer to the frontages of concessions, or property lots, which if extended would run from one end of a TOWNSHIP to the other. In practice a concession line is likely to be a road with a number ("First Concession," "Concession Road 10," etc). Concession lines are normally spaced at 1.25 mile (2 km) intervals. JOHN ROBERT COLOMBO

Concordia University, Montréal, was founded 1974 by merger of Sir George Williams University and Loyola College. Loyola, originally the English section of the Jesuit Collège Sainte-Marie (est 1848) had become a separate entity in 1899; SGWU had evolved from the formal educational work of the Montréal YMCA and had received its university charter in 1948. Concordia has 2 campuses, one in downtown Montréal (SGWU) and one in its west end (Loyola). It offers programs in 4 faculties: arts and science, commerce and administration, engineering and computer science, and fine arts. Bachelors' degrees are awarded in administration, arts, commerce, computer sci-

Roy Thomson Hall interior, Toronto, designed by Arthur Erickson/Mathers and Haldenby Assoc Architects (*courtesy Canapress Photo Service*).

Enrolment: Concordia University, 1985-86 (Source: Statistics Canada)			
Full-time Undergrad	*Full-time Graduate*	*Part-time Undergrad*	*Part-time Graduate*
11 572	1744	11 080	1703

ence, education, engineering, fine arts and science; undergraduate-level certificate programs are also offered in some areas, and graduate degrees and diploma programs are available in many disciplines. Most undergraduate and graduate programs are open to part-time students, and about half the total student population attends part time.

Condiment Crops grown on a commercial scale in Canada include ONIONS (*Allium cepa*), yellow or white mustard (*Brassica hirta*), brown mustard (*B. juncea*), horseradish (*Armoracia rusticana*), dill (*Anethum graveolens*), caraway (*Carum carvi*) and coriander (*Coriandrum sativum*). Basil (*Ocimum basilicum*), fennel (*Foeniculum vulgare*), garlic (*Allium sativum*), MINT (*Mentha piperita, M. spicata*), sage (*Salvia officinalis*) and savory (*Satureia hortensis*) are grown by small cottage industries. The common onion is a herbaceous biennial plant with a single large bulb; the numerous cultivars (commercial varieties) differ in size, colour, shape and flavour. Onions are used as seasoning in many foods (eg, sauces, soups, omelettes, meats, pickles). Onions are grown on some 4000 ha. Québec produces 35% of Canada's onions; Ontario, 55%; western Canada, 10%. Yellow and brown mustards are herbaceous annuals, brown mustard being more pungent. Mustard seed is used to prepare mustard pastes (used in flavouring hot dogs, cheeses, eggs, meats, salad dressing, etc) and as whole seeds (in pickling or boiled with vegetables). Mustards are grown in Manitoba (8%), Saskatchewan (77%) and Alberta (15%) on approximately 185 000 ha. The 250 000 t produced annually is valued at $68.75 million. Canada is the world's leading exporter of mustard seed. Horseradish is a hardy perennial of the mustard family. Its white, fleshy, cylindrical roots are used as a table relish with roast beef, raw oysters and fish, in pickling or in sauces or prepared mustards. Horseradish is grown in southern Ontario on approximately 200 ha, which produce 2400 t of fresh roots, valued at $1.5 million. Dill, an annual, is used to flavour soups, sauces and pickled cucumbers. It is grown in Manitoba for the production of dill-weed oil; each year the approximately 400 ha produce 32 000 kg of oil, valued at $0.5 million. Coriander, an annual, is used as whole seed in mixed pickling spice or in ground form in curry powder and flavouring for pastries, sausages and frankfurters. In Canada it is grown mainly on the prairies on approximately 150 ha, which produce 160 t of seed, valued at $0.1 million. Caraway, a biennial, is used to flavour rye bread, cakes, cheese, applesauce, cookies, etc. In Canada it is grown mainly on the prairies on approximately 500 ha, which yield 80 t of seed, valued at $0.2 million. B.B. CHUBEY

Condominium is a form of tenure that consists of a combination of ownership in fee simple in respect of a described and specific condominium unit, combined with an interest as a tenant in common in respect of the remaining (common) areas.

Condominiums are a creation of statute law. When they are created the developer must identify the "individual units" that are to be owned in fee simple, the remaining areas become the common property or common areas held as tenants in common. It is essential that potential buyers look at the particular provincial statute and the details of the condominium plans that create the particu-

lar project to determine what constitutes the privately owned portions.

Owners in a condominium project are responsible for all expenses relating to their own individual unit, but in addition the condominium owners must pay their share of the expenses relating to the common areas.

All provincial Condominium Acts provide for the creation of an administrative structure to supervise the day-to-day operation of the project and orchestrate effectively the collective interests of the owners. This administrative structure includes a condominium corporation and governing council.

To most people the term "condominium" implies the ownership of a suite in an apartment building or townhouse complex. While this is generally true it should be noted that many condominiums are not in apartments or townhouses. Condominiums can be vacant lands, non-residential space and recreational properties.

S.W. HAMILTON

Conductors and Conducting The musician who directs a group of singers or instrumentalists without participating in the actual singing or playing essentially is the creation of the early 19th century; the one who makes a full-time career of such leadership the product of the final decades of that century. Thus one may assume that the orchestral performances given in Québec City in the 1790s were still cued by the principal first violin or the harpsichord player, and that the hundreds of choir- and bandmasters of Victorian Canada made their living from music teaching, playing a church organ or running a music store, if entirely from music at all. Musicians of exceptional talent might gain prestige, though hardly a livelihood, as organizers and conductors of the philharmonic societies that specialized in oratorios and cantatas. Guillaume COUTURE and the English-born Frederick Herbert Torrington, in Montréal and Toronto, respectively, are late 19th-century examples. Conditions were not ripe for assembling and financing permanent orchestras and OPERA companies, but by the turn of the century choirs and bands flourished. Outstanding leaders were Augustus Stephen VOGT, founder (1894) of the Toronto Mendelssohn Choir and Joseph Vézina, organizer of many bands and first conductor of the Société symphonique de Québec (1903, now Orchestre symphonique de Québec), the oldest surviving orchestra in Canada. In the early 20th century, orchestras, partly or fully professional, became the leading musical ensembles of most large cities. The pioneer orchestra builders usually were immigrant orchestra players or church organists turned conductor by the Canadian opportunity, such as Joseph-Jean Goulet and Douglas CLARKE in Montréal, Donald Heins in Ottawa, and Luigi von Kunits in Toronto. Immigrants were also prominent in the choral field: Herbert Austin Fricker succeeded Vogt, Hugh BANCROFT was active in Winnipeg and Vancouver, Frederic Lord formed the Canadian Choir in Brantford, Ont, to mention but a few. At the same time, Canadians made a name as conductors in the US, Bruce Carey and Gena BRANSCOMBE in the choral field, and Wilfrid PELLETIER at the Metropolitan Opera in New York City. For many years a coach at the opera house, Pelletier became one of its conductors in 1922, specializing in the French repertoire. Beginning with the mid-1930s he also played an important role in organizing and conducting orchestras in Montréal and Québec. Pelletier was also a pioneer in designing concerts for young people. Pelletier was born in 1896, Sir Ernest MACMILLAN in 1893. Although close contemporaries and the most famous conductors Canada has produced so far, they came to conducting in different ways.

MacMillan had been an organist and music educator with only occasional conducting experience when in 1931, on the death of von Kunits and on the strength of his musicianship, he was appointed conductor of the Toronto Symphony orchestra. Over a 25-year period he led the orchestra to its first flourishing, excelling in the music of Bach but introducing a wide range of the repertoire. MacMillan guest-conducted in all parts of Canada and occasionally abroad, and in 1942 he assumed leadership also of the Toronto Mendelssohn Choir.

Both immigrants and native Canadian conductors have enriched concert life and raised performance standards in the mid-20th century. The Europeans brought experience in the standard orchestral and operatic repertoire while the Canadians have often became experts in the new field of studio conducting, a by-product of the developing broadcast and film technologies. The studio conductor rarely conducts to impress a watching audience, his concerns are with the microphone and the clock. The stylistic scope of broadcast programming is limitless, including concert, incidental and background music. Conductors heard mostly on CBC broadcasts, such as John AVISON, Jean-Marie BEAUDET, J.-J. Gagnier (better known as a band director), Roland Leduc or Geoffrey WADDINGTON, did indeed develop great adaptability and versatility. Related was the recording studio conducting of Rosario BOURDON and Percy FAITH, mainly for Victor and Columbia. Fame was also won by two conductors of light music, Guy LOMBARDO in the US and Robert FARNON in England. The varied contributions of immigrants ranged from developing orchestras, as in the case of Allard de Ridder and the Vancouver Symphony Society, to establishing opera, as in the case of Nicholas Goldschmidt or Ernesto Barbini and to specialization in certain branches of musical literature. Thus Ettore Mazzoleni introduced many English works, Boyd Neel cultivated baroque music and Heinz Unger broke ground for Bruckner and Mahler. Foreign-born musicians have occupied nearly all the major symphony orchestra positions and continue to do so, a policy that has received some criticism. World-class orchestras deserve first-rate conductors and often foreign musicians have the advantage of training and the benefit of old tradition; on the other hand some show little commitment to musical life in Canada as such and to the Canadian composer in particular. There is no doubt, however, that Canadian orchestras owe their excellence in large measure to men such as Zubin Mehta and Charles Dutoit (Montréal), Seiji Ozawa, Karel Ancerl and Andrew Davis (Toronto), Kazuyoshi Akiyama (Vancouver) and Piero Gamba (Winnipeg), to name but a few.

In the choral field, Canadian-born (or -educated) conductors occupy most leading positions. Charles Goulet was founder (1928) and conductor of the Montréal choir Les Disciples de Massenet, Leslie BELL's female voice choir achieved a nationwide reputation, and Elmer Iseler's Festival Singers, more recently replaced by the Elmer Iseler Singers, have received international praise. Elmer ISELER has also enhanced the reputation of the Toronto Mendelssohn Choir which he has led since 1964. Brian Law, Georges Little, Chantal Masson, Wayne Riddell and Jon Washburn are other outstanding choir leaders.

The fact that Canada has produced many singers, pianists and string players, but only very few conductors of world reputation, may be related to insufficiencies in the training system as well as the lack of opportunities. The older among the living Canadian conductors are often string players by training: Alexander BROTT, director of the McGill Chamber Orchestra, Eugene Kash, conductor of the Ottawa Philharmonic Orchestra in the 1950s, Ethel Stark, founder of the now defunct Montreal Women's Symphony Orchestra, and Victor FELDBRILL, for many years leader of the Winnipeg Symphony Orchestra and more recently active in Toronto and Tokyo. Feldbrill's great merit is his indefatigable championing of new Canadian works. Most conductors born since about 1930 appear to have the background of pianist. First to be named is Mario BERNARDI, whose conducting experience began with the Canadian Opera Co and led to the Sadler's Wells opera company in London, and in 1969 to his appointment as conductor of the new National Arts Centre Orchestra, followed by positions in Calgary and Vancouver. Similarly wide-ranging is the career of Boris BROTT who has been a regular conductor of orchestras from Regina to Halifax and Newcastle, Eng, but whose closest association has been, since 1969, with the Hamilton Philharmonic Orchestra. Pierre HÉTU was associated with the Edmonton Symphony Orchestra for many years; Françoys Bernier in the 1960s and Simon Streatfeild currently have conducted the Orchestre symphonique de Québec; and Raffi Armenian, who came to Canada after studies in Vienna, is active in Stratford and Kitchener and gives a conducting course at the Montreal Conservatoire. Armenian was a finalist at the Besançon (France) International Competition for Young Conductors, as have been Pierre Hétu and, more recently, Gilles Auger. Among several scholarships to young conductors in Canada is the Heinz Unger Award, issued annually.

HELMUT KALLMANN

Reading: Directory of Conductors in Canada/Annuaire des Chefs d'orchestre au Canada (1977); *Encyclopedia of Music in Canada* (1981).

Conestoga Wagon A large wagon, with broad wheels and a white hemp or canvas cover, used for the transportation of persons and goods across the N American continent prior to the introduction of the railway in the 1850s and 1860s. Named for the town in Pennsylvania where it was first built around 1725, the Conestoga wagon was drawn by up to 6 horses. It was the predecessor of the lighter wagon known as the prairie schooner which could be drawn by 2 to 4 horses or oxen. The prairie schooner was used extensively in wagon trains on the American plains, less so on the Canadian prairies. The Conestoga wagon was favoured by the Swiss and Amish Mennonites who rode in them from Pennsylvania, between the late 18th century and the middle of the 19th century, when they settled in the Niagara Peninsula and York and Waterloo counties of present-day Ontario.

JOHN ROBERT COLOMBO

Confectionery Industry, a manufacturing sector made up of companies primarily involved in processing candies, chocolate and cocoa products, chewing gum and other products such as salted nuts and popcorn. Confectionery manufacturing started to emerge as an important industry in the late 1800s. One of the earliest commercial operations, McCormick's Ltd, was established in London, Ont, in 1857. Robertson Brothers Ltd was in the candy business in Toronto by 1864, and Ganong Brothers opened in St Stephen, NB, in 1873. In 1873 Moirs Ltd, originally a bakery, commenced candy production in Halifax, NS. Robert Watson Co started in Toronto in 1874, and by 1879 Viau Ltée was in production in Montréal. In Toronto, Patterson Candy Co was established in 1888; the Cowan Co in 1890. Confectionery production greatly increased in Canada in the early 1900s with the establishment of several major producers, including William Neilson Ltd in Toronto in 1908, Willard's Chocolates Ltd, Toronto, 1914, and Fry-Cadbury Ltd, Mont-

réal, 1920. Walter M. Lowney Co of Montréal and Walter Baker Co of Canada, Toronto, also became established during this period. In these formative years the industry was concentrated in eastern Canada, a situation that prevails today, although in western Canada a number of smaller manufacturers emerged during this period and new companies are still appearing.

Confectionery packaging is controlled by regulations enforced by Consumer and Corporate Affairs Canada. Sanitation and related matters are controlled by the Health Protection Branch of Health and Welfare Canada. The industry is represented by the Confectionery Manufacturers Association of Canada, Toronto.

During the past 2 decades, a considerable amount of plant consolidation has taken place. In 1961 the industry had 194 plants in production. By 1984 Statistics Canada reported 94 plants in production: NS had 4; NB, 2; Qué, 29; Ont, 41; Man, 3; Sask, 0; Alta, 2; and BC, 13. As is the case in most other food sectors, the major cause of the reduction has been the steady phasing out of smaller, obsolete production facilities and their replacement with fewer, larger, highly efficient operations.

The confectionery industry is unique among segments of the Canadian FOOD AND BEVERAGE manufacturing system in that it is dependent on foreign supply for 2 of its primary ingredients: sugar and cocoa. Unfortunately, these commodities are subject to rapidly changing prices in spite of accords such as the International Sugar Agreement. This factor, in turn, can seriously affect the industry's sales volumes and profit margins. Any sharp increase in the international price of raw sugarcane or cocoa beans is quickly translated into increased production costs and higher consumer prices; a downturn in production volumes usually follows. Steadily increasing provincial sales taxes are another indirect cost that can have a negative effect on industry sales. However, over the long term, production volumes in most categories have shown slow, steady growth. For example, in 1973 the industry produced 68 895 t of all types of chocolate products, including chocolate bars, boxed chocolates, seasonal novelties and chocolate products sold in bulk and other forms. By 1984 the production of chocolate confectionery had increased to 90 003 t. Similarly, in 1971, 16 772 t of chewing-gum products came off the industry's production lines; by 1984 this amount had increased to 19 565 t. Trends in sugar confectionery, which includes hard candy, pan goods (hard and soft) and similar products, fluctuate. In 1971 the industry produced 49 114 t of sugar confectionery; in 1984 the volume was 52 264 t. Importation of hard-candy products affects the trend. The UK has always been a major Canadian supplier of high-quality candies, but imports are increasing from S American countries, notably Brazil and Argentina.

In 1984 the industry employed 9014 people and spent $386 million on materials and supplies. Statistics Canada reported that in 1984 the industry made shipments valued at $927.9 million.

ROBERT F. BARRATT

Confederation, the union of the British North American colonies of New Brunswick, Nova Scotia and Canada (Canada being an earlier, 1841, union of Lower Canada and Upper Canada), achieved 1 July 1867 under the new name, Dominion of Canada. It was soon expanded with the addition of Manitoba and the North-West Territory (15 July 1870), British Columbia (20 July 1871), Prince Edward Island (1 July 1873), and ultimately Newfoundland (31 March 1949). The Confederation movement followed Newton's first law of motion: all bodies continue in a state of

rest or of uniform motion unless compelled by some force to change their state. In the 1860s political union of BRITISH NORTH AMERICA was an idea, the subject of occasional dinner speeches when wine raised a man's sights, softened political asperities, and broadened his horizons. But only in 1864 did it become a serious question in the PROVINCE OF CANADA, and in the Atlantic colonies a great deal of pressure would be necessary to convert romantic ideas of a nation *a mari usque ad mare* into political reality.

A series of fortuitous events helped. Nova Scotia and New Brunswick had some interest in reuniting the 2 colonies separated since 1784; they were helped by the British COLONIAL OFFICE who felt that a political union of all 3 Maritime colonies was desirable, including Prince Edward Island. Maritime union would abolish 3 colonial legislatures and governments and replace them with one. In the spring of 1864 all 3 legislatures passed pious resolutions declaring a certain lukewarm interest in having a conference on the subject. But nothing was done; it was only when the Province of Canada positively announced its interest in being asked to attend such a conference that the Maritime governments woke up. If the Province of Canada was going to attend, then there had to be a conference for them to come to. The governor of Nova Scotia got busy; Charlottetown was appointed as the place – Prince Edward Island would not attend otherwise – and 1 Sept 1864 the time.

As the Province of Canada grew larger and more prosperous and developed politically, socially and industrially, so grew its internal rivalries and difficulties. Whereas the Conservative party believed the 1841 constitution had by no means outlived its usefulness, the Reform party insisted that change was essential. Canada West [Ont], wanting divorce more than Canada East [Qué], could make difficult all ministries that did not conform to its belief in "representation by population." In 1864, after 4 short-lived ministries had fought to stay in power, a coalition was formed, promising Confederation. The province's problems were to be solved by division of its 2 sections and the union of all BNA. With support from 3 of the province's 4 major political groups, the coalition gave Confederation a driving force that it never lost. Canada West's 2 major political groups were united on the issue; their leaders, John A. MACDONALD and George BROWN, were peculiar partners, but their alliance meant that Confederation proceeded with support from BNA's most populous province. In Canada East, although Confederation was opposed by A.A. DORION'S PARTI ROUGE, it was supported by the dominant political group, the Conservatives under George-Étienne CARTIER, Hector LANGEVIN and Alexander T. GALT. By 1867 they had the necessary support of the Catholic Church. Confederation was justified by the arguments that French Canadians would get back their provincial identity – the capital of their province would once more be Québec; the anglophone domination of Ottawa feared by French Canadians would be mitigated by the presence of strong French Canadian representation in the federal Cabinet; and Confederation was the least undesirable of the changes proposed.

So the "Canadians" sailed from Québec City on 29 Aug 1864, aboard the Canadian government steamer *Queen Victoria* for the CHARLOTTETOWN CONFERENCE. They were soon invited to join the conference, and open up their proposals, Maritime union not making very much headway. The "Canadian" ideas for a federal union of *all* the British North American provinces swept the board, and the glittering idea of a union *a mari usque ad mare* took over. The QUÉBEC CONFERENCE,

Reading the Confederation Proclamation, 1 July 1867, Market Square, Kingston, Ont (*courtesy Queen's University Archives*).

called a month later, made explicit, in the form of 72 Resolutions, fundamental decisions already taken at Charlottetown. The colonies were also joined in Québec by Newfoundland. The Atlantic colonies of Newfoundland, PEI, NS and NB each had aspirations, but none was as dissatisfied with the status quo as was Canada West. With the exception of Newfoundland, they felt comfortable as they were, and the bulk of the population, especially in NS and PEI, saw no reason to change their constitution just because Canada was finding it had outgrown its own. Even Newfoundland, after economic difficulties in the 1860s had made it susceptible to mainland blandishments, postponed decision in 1865, and in the 1869 Newfoundland general election decisively rejected Confederation. The more prosperous PEI resisted almost from the start. A small, dedicated group of Confederationists made little headway until, early in the 1870s, the railway adventures of successive Island governments forced PEI to have its railway, and its debt, taken over by the new Dominion. NS was more complicated. Along the axis of the railway that already ran from Halifax to Truro and was to continue to Québec, there was real support for Confederation. The manufacturing and coal-producing areas, Pictou County and to some extent Cape Breton, were also interested. But along the S shore and in the Annapolis Valley – the prosperous world of shipping, shipbuilding, potatoes and apples – Confederation appeared unattractive or even dangerous. Conservative Premier Charles TUPPER, ambitious, aggressive and confident, went ahead with Confederation, convinced that in the long run it would be best for NS, and perhaps also for himself. Fortunately for Confederation, Tupper did not test his electorate: elected in 1863, his government did not need to go to the polls until 1867, after Confederation. Then, too late, it was clear that 65% of Nova Scotians opposed Confederation (*see* REPEAL MOVEMENT). NB supported Confederation only slightly more than any other Atlantic province. In Feb 1865 the anti-Confederate government of A.J. SMITH was elected. Confederation could go nowhere until the Smith government collapsed, as it did in 1866 and a new pro-Confederate government was brought in, helped by the FENIAN invasions of Apr and June 1866, which badly weakened anti-Confederate positions.

External forces such as the American Civil War and the truculence of American foreign policy (symbolized in the 1866 abrogation of the RECIPROCITY Treaty and 1867 Alaska purchase) made the separate colonies of BNA uneasy about their future. Duty would compel Britain to respond to any military aggression against BNA, as the TRENT AFFAIR showed; but Britain had no taste for it. The best British defence against the US was a BNA federation. Confederation thus had powerful support from London, especially from Colonial Secretary Edward Cardwell. Cardwell instructed his BNA governors, in the strongest language possible, to support Confederation. They did. The LONDON CONFERENCE, Dec 1866 to Feb 1867, was the final stage of translating the 72 Resolutions of 1864 into legislation. The result was the British North America Act of 1867 (now called CONSTITUTION ACT, 1867) which passed through Parliament, the British House of Commons and House of Lords, and was signed by the Queen on 29 Mar 1867. It was proclaimed into law 1 July 1867.

British policy favouring the union of all of British North America continued under Cardwell's successors. The HBC sold RUPERT'S LAND to Canada in 1870, and BC was brought into Confederation in 1871. The only defeat British policy sustained was in Newfoundland in 1869; but 80 years later it finally made its contribution to Confederation.

Although the form of Confederation was the product of 3 conferences and delegates from both sides of politics from 5 colonies, the practical ideas of how it might actually be achieved came from John A. Macdonald, with help on the financial side from A.T. Galt, and with G.-E. Cartier's insistence on a certain essential minimum of provincial rights. Confederation had not been originally Macdonald's idea; but he was finally the one who took hold of it and made the running. Thus, it is to Macdonald and his ideas that Canadians should look to understand the character of that 1867 union. *See also* CONSTITUTIONAL HISTORY; FATHERS OF CONFEDERATION. P.B. WAITE

Reading: J.M.S. Careless, Brown of the Globe (1963); D.G. Creighton, The Road to Confederation (1964) and John A. Macdonald: The Young Politician (1952); W.L. Morton, The Critical Years (1964); P.B. Waite, The Confederation Debates in the Province of Canada (1963) and The Life and Times of Confederation (1962).

Confederation of Canadian Unions

Founded in 1969 on the initiative of veteran labour organizers Kent ROWLEY and Madeleine PARENT, the Confederation of Canadian Unions (originally the Council of Canadian Unions 1969-73) is dedicated to the establishment of an independent Canadian labour movement free of the influence of American-based international unions. In 1986 the CCU contained approximately 40 000 members in 20 affiliated unions, some of which had broken away from their international parents. The CCU draws on data provided by the Corporations and Labour Unions Returns Act to prove that Canadian members of international unions pay substantially more in dues to their American headquarters than they receive in services and benefits. Criticism of international unionism and competition for members frequently brings the CCU into conflict with Canada's major labour federation, the CANADIAN LABOUR CONGRESS. Although the CCU accounts for only a tiny percentage of organized labour in Canada, its appeals for independence and new members have influenced the creation of autonomy guidelines within many international unions and encouraged some independent breakaways. JOHN BULLEN

Confederation of National Trade Unions

(CNTU, or Confederation des syndicats nationaux, CSN) was called the Canadian Catholic Federation of Labour (CCFL) from its beginnings in 1921 until 1960, when the organization abandoned its religious identity. It was founded by 2 union groups: the national, nonconfessional unions which had emerged in Québec at the beginning of the century, and the Catholic unions founded by members of the clergy in some dioceses in Québec after 1907.

The national unions had refused to join the international unions because they hoped to establish a truly Canadian union movement. But they had little support from English Canadian workers and their movement, limited almost entirely to Québec, remained very small until it merged with the Catholic unions during WWI. The Catholic unions had been founded by priests who feared the "socialist" and anticlerical ideas of the international unions. These national and Catholic unions promoted the ideal of good understanding and co-operation between management and workers. However, this was quickly seen to be a utopian dream and some of these new unions witnessed a dramatic decline in membership.

The Catholic unions were reorganized at the end of WWI, stressing protection of members' professional rights and interests. Anxious to unite their forces, they jointly formed the Canadian Catholic Confederation of Labour in 1921 with about 17 600 members. Membership declined during the 1920s but increased again after 1934, especially after WWII (62 690 members in 1946). Support came primarily from the construction, leatherworking, textile and garment industries. After WWII the CCCL's ideology gradually lost its religious nature. A new leadership emerged who rejected corporation and who wanted the union to become more activist in nature. Major strikes during the 1950s and opposition from the government of Maurice DUPLESSIS increased union militancy. In 1960 the confederation dropped "Catholic" from its title (it became the Confederation of National Trade Unions) and dropped references to the SOCIAL DOCTRINE of the church from its statement of principles.

The CNTU, radicalized after 1964 by the influx of workers in the public and para-public sectors (*see* PUBLIC-SERVICE UNIONS), gradually became committed to the fight for a new social order. Convinced that the bourgeoisie dominated the state and that workers were inevitably in conflict with this economic power, the leaders argued for the replacement of capitalism by democratic socialism. This ideological swing caused much turmoil within the CNTU. During the 1972 COMMON

FRONT STRIKES some leaders, including 3 members of the executive committee, left the CNTU to form the Central of Democratic Trade Unions (CDTU). Some 30 000 CNTU members, especially in clothing, textiles, leather and mining industries, joined the breakaway organization.

Since 1964 the CNTU, with its many members in the civil service, hospitals and some education positions, has been at the centre of public sector employees' struggles for better working conditions. In 1972 the CNTU persuaded the Québec Teachers Corporation and the public sector workers of the Québec Federation of Labour to join it in a common front for negotiations with government. Then and in 1976 and 1979, the common front approach won valuable gains in minimum salary, job security and pensions. In 1986 the CNTU consisted of 1717 unions, divided into 9 federations and 22 central councils with a total membership of 218 865. *See also* UNION CENTRALS.

JACQUES ROUILLARD

Conference Board of Canada, officially incorporated as AERTC Inc, is a nonprofit economic research and analysis institution funded by business, government, unions and universities. It was established (1954) as a division of the American National Industrial Conference Board Inc, which itself was founded (1916) on the belief that many of industrial society's problems could be eased by discussion based on scientifically researched facts. The Conference Board acquired a separate legal identity in 1981. It publishes quarterly reports on the national and provincial economic outlook, and 2 quarterly surveys, one on business attitudes and investment-spending plans, the other on consumer-spending intentions. Its public affairs division publishes reports on business management issues such as the responsibilities of corporate directors.

DUNCAN McDOWALL

Conflict of Interest may be defined as a situation in which politicians and public servants have an actual or potential interest (usually financial) that may influence or appear to influence the conduct of their official duties (*see* PATRONAGE; CORRUPTION). Even when this conflict is not illegal, it may create doubts or suspicions concerning the integrity or fairness of decisions made by such officials, and over time recurring conflicts may increase the level of distrust and cynicism toward government. In Canada, conflicts of interest have arisen when, for example, the ownership of land by the family of a provincial Cabinet minister could have influenced the minister's decision to approve a new subdivision or influence other officials to do so; when a senator invested money in a firm that subsequently received a lucrative government contract; and when a former federal Cabinet minister had dealings with his department that may have resulted in favouritism in the government's decision to issue a grant to the minister's new company.

Except for bribery and FRAUD, which are covered under the Criminal Code, legislation on broader conflict of interest questions has been relatively uncommon in the past. However, in recent years there has been increasing use of statutes, as in the case of Newfoundland (1973), New Brunswick (1978) and Manitoba (1983, proclaimed 1985, and amended, 1986). Otherwise, guidelines on conflict of interest, like those originally issued by the federal government for civil servants (1973) and Cabinet ministers (1979), have apparently been preferred by public officials. Continued evidence of this preference is seen in the Mulroney government's new federal guidelines for ministers and other public office holders issued in 1985. As a rule, guidelines are more ambiguous than statutes. Further, they do not generally provide sufficient sanctions to deter

potential conflicts, or appropriate mechanisms to determine the existence of violations. When charges of conflict of interest fail to provoke disciplinary actions, however, they may cause such acute political embarrassment that a Cabinet minister may feel it necessary to resign to protect the government's integrity, which, although rare, happened in Ontario in 1972.

More recently, a federal inquiry was begun in July 1986 to examine allegations of conflict of interest regarding the business dealings of a federal Cabinet minister, Sinclair STEVENS. The inquiry was to cost more than $2.9 million, and the Mulroney government's popularity declined as a result, in part, of the negative publicity generated by the affair. In Dec 1987 the report concluded that Stevens had broken the conflict of interest guideline 14 times. Added to this political embarrassment was another Cabinet resignation, this time junior transport minister André Bissonnette, who was accused of improper land deals relating to a government defence contract with Swiss-based Oerlikon Aerospace Inc.

KENNETH GIBBONS

Reading: Canada, *Members of Parliament and Conflict of Interest* (1973).

Congdon, Dwayne Lyle, mountaineer and guide (b at Lethbridge, Alta 7 Aug 1956). From a love fostered by his parents on camping trips in the Rockies, Congdon decided in his early 20s to become an alpine guide. In 1981 he participated in 2 Himalayan climbs and earned a name for being a strong, effective high-altitude mountaineer, a reputation enhanced by his 1982 role in the Canadian MOUNT EVEREST EXPEDITION. His experience on that climb, and a subsequent attempt on another Himalayan giant, 8490 m Makalu, stood him in good stead for his success in the 1986 Canadian Everest Light Expedition. On May 20, Congdon and partner Sharon WOOD became the third and fourth Canadians to reach the 8848 m summit of the world's highest mountain.

BART ROBINSON

Congdon, Frederick Tennyson, lawyer, politician, commissioner of the Yukon Territory, MP (b at Annapolis, NS 16 Nov 1858; d at Ottawa 13 Mar 1932). Although Congdon was a dynamic speaker and shrewd organizer, his tenure as Yukon Commissioner was characterized by corruption and controversy. His unscrupulous manipulations led to the disincorporation of the city of Dawson in 1904.

After attending Yarmouth High School and U of T (BA 1879, LLB 1883), he studied law at the Inner Temple in London. He was an editorial writer for the *Halifax Morning Chronicle* (1885-87), then practised law and in 1896 lectured at the Dalhousie Law School. In 1898, he compiled *Congdon's Digest of Nova Scotia Reports*. A prominent Liberal, he moved to the Yukon where he served as crown prosecutor and legal advisor to the Yukon Council before being appointed commissioner of the territory in 1903. He resigned in 1904 in order to contest the Yukon seat in Parliament but was defeated. He won the seat in a 1909 by-election but lost it in 1911. He ran again in a deferred election in 1918, winning a majority in the Yukon but lost the seat when the soldier vote was apportioned to his opponent. He practised law in Toronto after another defeat in 1921.

H. GUEST

Congregational Churches, Protestant groups arising from Puritanism, and organized on the principle that each congregation should be autonomous. Congregations were established among New England settlers in NS from 1751 and later in NB. By 1800, because of the disruptive influence of Henry ALLINE's preaching (as a result of which many congregations became BAPTIST),

and because most of the ministers were identified with disloyalty during the American Revolution, only 2 churches survived. During the 19th century, receiving its main support up to 1861 from the British Congregational Union, the denomination's strength was among central Canada's urban middle class. With its extension into western Canada after 1879, it developed a strong commitment to missionary work, both at home among German and Swedish immigrants and abroad in Angola. In 1925 the Congregational Union of Canada, fd 1906, consisted of 17 churches in NS and NB, 20 in Québec, 50 in Ontario, 24 (including 14 student fields) in western Canada and 26 Russo-Swedish mission churches, with a combined total of 31 012 members. That year the Union voted 118 to 8 to form part of the UNITED CHURCH OF CANADA.

J.P.B. KENYON

Reading: E.B. Eddy, "The Congregational Tradition," in J.W. Grant (ed), *The Churches and the Canadian Experience* (1963).

Conifers, a large group of cone-bearing trees and shrubs with about 48 genera and over 500 species, comprise the order Coniferales of the gymnosperms (nonflowering, naked seed plants). The group contains the oldest (bristlecone pines, over 4000 years old) and largest (redwoods, over 100 m tall) living things. Some 34 conifers (eg, pine, spruce, hemlock, fir, larch, Douglas fir, cedar, juniper and yew) grow in Canada.

Seeds are borne on the surface of scales that form seed cones which are usually large and woody, occasionally small and fleshy. In some conifers, seeds are borne singly, occasionally with a berrylike covering. All conifers bear pollen in cones. Most conifers are evergreen but some (eg, larch) are deciduous. Leaves usually persist for several years and are needlelike, scalelike or, rarely, broad. A lateral growth zone (cambium) produces large amounts of wood in the stem and root. Wood is generally soft, consisting primarily of long, hollow cells (tracheids).

Families Conifers are a primitive plant group which evolved from ancient gymnosperms. All modern genera originated in the Mesozoic era (245-66.4 million years ago), and many have persisted relatively unchanged. Eight families are usually recognized. One, Lebachiaceae, is extinct. The oldest living family, Podocarpaceae, with 7 genera and 150 species, occurs in semitropical and southern temperate regions. Araucariaceae (monkey puzzle tree family), a small but ancient family of 2 genera and 40 species, is native to the Southern Hemisphere. Cupressaceae (cypress family) has 18 genera and over 100 species, found primarily in northern temperate regions. Taxodiaceae (redwood family) is native to northern temperate regions and has 10 genera and about 18 species. Pinaceae (pine family), the largest and most familiar family, containing 10 genera and about 240 species, is restricted primarily to north-

Mature, open cone of Scotch pine (*Pinus sylvestris*), shedding a seed (*courtesy National Museums of Canada/ National Museum of Natural Sciences/artwork by Marcel Jomphe*).

ern temperate regions. Cephalotaxaceae (plum-yew family) consists of one genus and about 5 species, native to China, Japan and Korea. Members of Taxaceae (yew family) are often considered not to be conifers, because they lack seed cones and bear individual seeds enclosed in a berrylike structure (aril).

Structure Mature stems and roots consist primarily of a central core of wood (xylem) produced by cambium (formative or "meristematic" layer). The xylem conducts water and minerals, and also supports the tree. Cambium also forms phloem to the outside, which conducts dissolved food up and down the tree. Outside the phloem, a cork cambium forms outer bark (periderm) that protects the stem and root. Growth rings are prominent in the xylem. Early or springwood consists of tracheids of large diameter; dark, late or summerwood of tracheids of smaller diameter with thicker walls. Some conifer wood contains resin ducts. Conifer leaves are adapted to prevent water loss: the waxy surface (cuticle) is thick and pores (stomata) are recessed. Usually, a single large vein (vascular bundle) and several resin ducts occur in each leaf. Most conifer leaves are arranged spirally, but both leaf arrangement and shape may vary during tree growth.

Reproduction Like other seed plants, conifers show alternation of generations, ie, a sexual stage alternates with an asexual stage. The dominant stage is the asexual sporophyte (spore-producing) generation. The sexual or gametophyte phase is reduced to a one-celled stage retained by and parasitic on the sporophyte. Sporophytes have separate male and female cones (strobili), usually on a single tree. Each cone produces one kind of spore that develops into a gametophyte (reproductive body). Male cones produce thousands of pollen grains (male gametophytes). Pollen may have 2 wings or lack wings entirely. Released in spring, it is carried by wind to a seed cone (female), consisting of a series of modified leaves (bracts), each with a broad, ovule-bearing scale. Bracts and scales may be separate or fused. Each scale usually has 2 ovules. Within each ovule, a female gametophyte develops, containing one to several eggs. Pollen enters the ovule through the micropyle (opening), and germinates, forming a pollen tube that grows into ovule tissue.

The pollen tube reaches a female gametophyte and releases 2 male gametes (sperm) into an egg cell. One sperm fertilizes the egg; the other degenerates. The fertilized egg nucleus divides, ultimately forming a massive embryo. Several eggs in the same ovule may be fertilized, and each may form an embryo (simple polyembryony). In some conifers each fertilized egg forms 4 embryos (cleavage polyembryony). In either case, only one embryo, the most vigorous, normally survives. Conifer embryos develop 2 or many embryonic leaves (cotyledons). The development of the embryo – the new individual of the sporophyte generation – completes the conifer life cycle. The mature ovule (containing female gametophyte and embryo) is a seed. In most conifers, seeds mature in the fall of the same year in which pollination occurs. In others (eg, pine) seeds mature after 2 growing seasons. Most conifer seeds have one or 2 wings. Seed cones open in fall and seeds are wind dispersed. Seeds of most temperate-zone conifers require a chilling period (stratification) before germination. At germination the primary root penetrates soil and branches. The young stem bears cotyledons, but soon forms juvenile leaves and lateral branches.

Uses The forest industry is the largest Canadian natural-resource industry, and conifers are its major component. Most lumber and pulp and paper is obtained from conifers, primarily from species of spruce, pine, fir, hemlock and Douglas fir. Conifer wood is classified as softwood, in contrast to the hardwoods of broadleaf trees (eg, maple, oak, birch and ash). Conifers also yield resin (pitch), turpentine and various oils. Tannin, for tanning leather, comes from bark of larches. Juniper "berries" are used for flavouring (eg, gin), and seeds (pine nuts) of some species are edible. Many conifers are used as ornamentals. Some Canadian conifers (eg, Douglas fir, lodgepole pine and spruce) are planted for timber in Great Britain, New Zealand and many European countries. *See also* individual species entries.

JOHN N. OWENS

Reading: R.C. Hosie, *Native Trees of Canada* (1979).

Conn Smythe Trophy is awarded annually to the player judged most valuable to his team in the NATIONAL HOCKEY LEAGUE playoffs. The player is selected by hockey writers. The trophy was first presented in 1964 in honour of Conn SMYTHE, former coach, manager and owner of Toronto Maple Leafs. The only 2-time winners are Bobby ORR (1970 and 1972) and Bernie Parent (1974 and 1975).

JAMES MARSH

Connaught and Strathearn, Arthur William Patrick Albert, 1st Duke of, governor general of Canada 1911-16 (b at Buckingham Palace 1 May 1850; d at Bagshot Park, Surrey, Eng 16 January 1942). The third and favourite son of Queen Victoria, Prince Arthur was educated privately before attending the Royal Military Academy, Woolwich. He spent a year with the first battalion of the Rifle Brigade in Montréal, where he turned out for a Fenian raid in 1870. After a military career which took him to Egypt, India, Ireland and S Africa, he was made a field marshal in 1902. Disappointed by his failure to succeed the duke of Cambridge as commander in chief of the British army in 1895, as governor general of Canada he took his nominal position as commander in chief of the Canadian Militia more seriously than he ought, particularly during WWI. His advice, opinions and insistence on being consulted about the details of war administration created considerable tension between him and the minister of militia, Sam HUGHES, and stretched his constitutional position and the patience of PM Robert L. BORDEN to the limit.

CARMAN MILLER

Connaught Laboratories Limited is a producer of BIOLOGICAL PRODUCTS, including bacterial vaccines (eg, pertussis), toxoids (eg, tetanus), viral vaccines (eg, polio, rabies), hormones (eg, INSULIN), blood fractions (eg, albumin, coagulation factor VIII), diagnostics (eg, for detection of hepatitis B). The company was established in 1914 in the Department of Hygiene of University of Toronto, largely through the efforts of John G. Fitzgerald, associate professor of hygiene. The laboratories functioned as a financially self-supporting organization and remained an integral part of U of T until 1972.

The first products included a live rabies vaccine and horse antitoxins for diphtheria. In Jan 1922 Frederick G. BANTING and Charles H. BEST demonstrated the effectiveness of insulin against DIABETES. In the same year, Connaught became the first laboratory to introduce insulin commercially. Connaught in the 1980s produced over 95% of the insulin used in Canada. During WWII, Connaught began preparation of fractions of human blood plasma (eg, albumin, immune serum globulin) collected by the Canadian RED CROSS. Clinical use of such fractions has permitted far greater use of each blood donation. Connaught was also one of the early producers of penicillin and, in fact, was the first to prepare the antibiotic in crystalline form. After the war, the tremendous scale of production in other countries and resulting low costs caused Connaught to drop the product. Another major advance was Raymond Parker's discovery, in the late 1940s, of a solution in which monkey kidney cells could be kept growing in glass bottles. This discovery enabled Connaught to prepare a large part of the inactivated polio vaccine (Salk) used in clinical trials in Canada and the United States.

In 1972 the Canada Development Corporation (CDC) purchased the laboratories from U of T, changing its name to Connaught Laboratories Ltd. Connaught is a wholly owned subsidiary of CDC Life Sciences, a widely held public company. In 1976 Connaught purchased a production facility in Pennsylvania, the main product of which is influenza vaccine. This facility, known as Connaught Laboratories, Inc, provides access to the US market. Connaught also has joint ventures with American and Japanese companies in the vaccine field.

A total of 750 employees work at the Toronto site. Of Connaught's total annual sales of about $150 million, 12-15% is spent on research. Current research is in the areas of improved human vaccines, GENETIC ENGINEERING of hormones, vaccines and blood products, fish vaccines, diabetes prevention and diagnostic test development.

A.A. MAGNIN

Connolly, Harold Joseph, newspaperman, politician, premier of NS (b at Sydney, NS 8 Sept 1901; d at Halifax 17 May 1980). Connolly worked with the Halifax *Chronicle* and was editor of the *Daily Star* when elected a Liberal MLA in 1936. He sat 20 years, first as an assemblyman and after 1941 as a Cabinet minister. Senior minister when Premier Angus L. MACDONALD died in 1954, he became interim Liberal leader and premier. He lost a leadership convention in 1954 when the Protestant delegates apparently united against the only Catholic candidate, the result being a disastrous religious rift within the party. He retired from provincial politics in 1955 to become a member of the Senate, from which he retired in 1979.

J. MURRAY BECK

Connor, Ralph, *see* GORDON, CHARLES WILLIAM.

Connors, "Stompin' Tom," singer-songwriter, guitarist (b at Saint John, 3 Feb 1936). He had been singing and writing verses since his childhood in Skinners Pond, PEI, but only began to sing for a living in 1964 when he found himself broke in Timmins, Ont. His success at the Maple Leaf Hotel led to radio and records. His trademark was his pounding foot, first inspired by the need to be heard above the din of a noisy tavern. He was the subject of 2 films, *This is Stompin' Tom* and *Across This Land With Stompin' Tom* (1973). In 1986 he released his first album in many years.

RICHARD GREEN

Conquest (La Conquête), the term used to designate the acquisition of Canada by Great Britain in the SEVEN YEARS' WAR and, by extension, the resulting changed conditions of life experienced by Canada's 60 000 to 70 000 French-speaking inhabitants and numerous Indian tribes. Québec surrendered to British forces on 18 Sept 1759, a few days after the crucial Battle of the PLAINS OF ABRAHAM. French resistance ended a year later with the capitulation of Montréal. By the terms signed 8 Sept 1760, the British guaranteed the people of New France immunity from deportation or maltreatment; the right to depart for France with all their possessions; continued enjoyment of property rights; the right to carry on the fur trade on an equal basis with the English; and freedom of worship. By the Treaty of PARIS, 10 Feb 1763, the French colony became a British possession.

After the French Revolution (1789) many Canadians came to see the Conquest as a providential rescue from revolutionary chaos – an idea that was long influential. Later generations, viewing the past through the prism of their own political and constitutional preoccupations, also tended to see the conquest positively – not without reason – as leading to religious toleration and REPRESENTATIVE GOVERNMENT. They were less welcoming of the ethnic dualism that was the inevitable result of the marriage of English government and immigration with an established French colony of settlement. Some modern historians, such as Michel Brunet, have seen the Conquest as a disaster, drawing attention to the monopolization of the higher levels of government and business by English-speaking newcomers as evidence that the Conquest made French Canadians second-class subjects and, ultimately, an ethnic proletariat. Others, such as Fernand OUELLET, downplay harmful effects, pointing to fairly continuous development of economic foundations, of institutions and of culture, little affected by the event. For the native people, the end of Anglo-French hostility meant a fateful decline in their value as allies and warriors, making them increasingly irrelevant to white society.

The Conquest must always remain a subject of debate, interwoven with and inseparable as it is from other influences on Canadian development. Its influence is also evident in the AMERICAN REVOLUTION, which was possible only when the American colonies no longer needed British protection from French forces in North America.

DALE MIQUELON

Reading: Dale Miquelon, *Society and Conquest* (1977).

Conroy, Pat, labour leader (b at Baillieston, Scot 1900). Conroy began to work as a miner at 13 and joined the British Mineworkers' Federation. In 1919 he immigrated to Canada, settling in Drumheller, Alta. He worked in the coal mines and joined the United Mine Workers of America. After a tour of the US, he returned to Alberta and from 1922 held several union positions until he became VP of the Western Canadian District 18. In 1940 when the CANADIAN CONGRESS OF LABOUR (CCL) was founded, he became its VP and the next year its full-time secretary-treasurer. In 1949 he helped found the International Confederation of Free Trade Unions. In 1951 he suddenly resigned from the CCL position because of differences with his colleagues on the executive. As a dynamic leader, he wished the Congress to play a larger role. In 1952 he was appointed labour attaché to the Canadian embassy in Washington, a post he held until his retirement in 1972.

LAUREL SEFTON MACDOWELL

Conscription, the compulsory enlistment of citizens for military service. Forms of conscription were adopted by the Canadian government in both world wars.

World War I

By late 1916 the terrible casualties at the front in France and Flanders were beginning to cause reinforcement problems for the Canadian commanders overseas. Recruitment at home was slowing, and the manpower and enlistment system was disorganized. For PM Sir Robert BORDEN, the first necessity was to assist the men in the trenches, and by May 1917, when he returned to Canada from the Imperial War Conference in London and from visits to the trenches, he had decided that compulsory service was necessary. He announced his decision in Parliament on May 18 and then offered a political coalition to Sir Wilfrid LAURIER, the Liberal leader. After consulting his supporters, Laurier refused. Québec would

Anti-conscription parade, Victoria Square, Montréal, *c*24 May 1917 (*courtesy National Archives of Canada/C-6859*).

never agree to conscription, he believed, and if he joined the pro-conscription coalition French Canada would be delivered into the hands of Henri BOURASSA and his *nationalistes.* The course was set for collision.

By the fall, after enormous difficulty, Borden had created his UNION GOVERNMENT, and the MILITARY SERVICE ACT became law on 29 Aug 1917. Virtually every French-speaking MP opposed conscription, and almost all the English-speaking MPs supported it. The election of 1917 was as racially divided, and English Canada gave Borden his mandate to put conscription into effect. In Jan 1918 the process of call-ups began, but out of the 401 882 men registered (and despite the lifting of farmers' exemptions in the spring of 1918) only 124 588 were added to the strength of the CANADIAN EXPEDITIONARY FORCE; 24 132 men made it to France by the war's end. As a military measure conscription was a failure; as a political measure it had largely been responsible for the re-election of the Borden government, but it left the Conservative Party with a heavy liability in Québec and in the agricultural West.

J.L. GRANATSTEIN

World War II

As the threat of a new war in Europe became acute, the question of military conscription again caused lively political debate in French Canada. The federal Liberals, sensitive to strong francophone feelings on this issue, repeatedly pledged not to resort to compulsory enlistment for overseas military service. War broke out in Sept 1939, and by the spring of 1940 the government had adopted the NATIONAL RESOURCES MOBILIZATION ACT providing for enlistment for home defence. Registration took place almost without incident, except for the public opposition of Montréal mayor Camillien HOUDE, who was later interned. In 1941, as recruitment slowly progressed, more voices were raised in favour of conscription, first within the Conservative Party and later among English Canadians in general. To appease the supporters of conscription, Prime Minister W.L. Mackenzie KING decided to hold a plebiscite asking Canadians to release the government from its anti-conscription promises. In Québec, the Ligue pour la défense du Canada campaigned for the "no" side, and on 27 Apr 1942, 72.9% of Québec residents voted "no," while in the other provinces the "yes" vote triumphed by 80%. The government then passed Bill 80, authorizing conscription for overseas service if it was deemed necessary. Québec's BLOC POPULAIRE continued to fight against conscription by presenting candidates for the Aug 1944 provincial elections and the June 1945 federal elections.

By the autumn of 1944 J.L. RALSTON, minister of national defence, was convinced of the need for conscription. Unexpectedly high casualties on the front, combined with a large commitment to

the RCAF and the RCN, left the Canadian Army short of manpower. King, who had hoped he would not have to invoke Bill 80, replaced Ralston with Gen A.G.L. MCNAUGHTON, a supporter of voluntary service. On Nov 22, however, the prime minister, acknowledging the open proconscriptionist sentiments of many of his anglophone ministers, reversed his decision in an effort to save his government and announced that conscripts would be sent overseas. Even though only 12 908 conscripted soldiers were actually sent abroad, this second conscription crisis again worsened relations between Anglophones and Francophones in Canada, though to a lesser extent than during WWI.

RICHARD JONES

Reading: J.L. Granatstein and J.M. Hitsman, *Broken Promises* (1977).

Conservation can be defined as the wise use of RESOURCES for industrial and nonconsumptive purposes (eg, recreation, research), in the spirit of responsible stewardship, and to preserve the productivity and diversity of the world's resources. Conservation parallels "environmentalism," but covers a wider spectrum. Conservation traditionally focused on natural resources but the concept has been expanded to include ENERGY, urban spaces, works of art, historical artifacts, heritage buildings, languages and cultures.

Conservation is a matter of trade-offs: deciding how much can be lost to achieve specific gains without losing productive potential and diversity of resources. Many people engaged in RESOURCE USE and management equate conservation exclusively with preservation and environmentalism and feel that its proponents obstruct economic and social progress. Conversely, some preservationists deplore any disturbance of natural conditions, forgetting that disturbances can be natural or man-made and that wildfires and even insect attack can play important roles in plant succession and biological evolution. While "wise use" may at times require unmodified preservation, it usually permits and sometimes requires carefully planned modifications. In fact, both sides have common interests: resource users and managers profit by maintaining resource productivity and a large number of options; and a sound economy, even if based on resource development, is essential if resource renewal, recycling and preservation programs are to be financed.

The modern concept of conservation has evolved since the beginning of the 20th century from a simple hoarding and slow use of resources to attempts to manage resources for sustained yield, minimal waste, recycling, controlling POLLUTION and maintaining the quality of the ENVIRONMENT. Early conservation activities in Canada, focused largely among the forestry community, were initiated in the late 19th century, when the national economy was largely based on natural resources. Economic growth has been the objective of escalating industrial activity over the past 50 years. The resulting wasteful energy use, diminution of high-grade resources and pollution of land, air and water have led to the questioning of the desirability of high levels of economic and population growth. People have begun to realize that maximum resource use for maximum economic gain is incompatible with society's longterm objectives. The idea that resource use for optimal sustainable economic gain permits wider social benefits is slowly gaining acceptance (*see* CONSERVER SOCIETY). The desirability of socioeconomic rather than purely economic goals is the subject of considerable debate, and there is a trend toward viewing resources as borrowed from future generations rather than as inherited from the past. Thus, support has grown for ecological reserves, restoration of endangered species and habitats, and careful environmental planning before new industrial developments.

Geographic Factors Various factors, including the diversity of rock formations, soils, climate, wildlife, vegetation and people, present special conservation problems. Canada's land area is vast, its human population relatively small, and people with limited funds can do relatively little to preserve and manage extensive resources. Canada encompasses an area of 9.98 million km² and has the longest coastline (71 261 km including major island coastlines) in the world. The land ascends from sea level on the shores of the Pacific, Atlantic and Arctic OCEANS TO MOUNTAINS as high as 5950 m in the CORDILLERA. The huge northern plains, E of the Cordillera, contain fertile agricultural soils and immense energy reserves in the form of coal and PETROLEUM resources. The Canadian Shield, a mass of mineral-rich Precambrian rocks, forms the core of central Canada, and glaciation has molded the landforms over large areas. The climate of Canada varies from harshly continental (cold dry winters, hot summers) to mildly oceanic; winter temperatures can be well below -40°C, summer days 33°C or more. Average annual temperatures range from -18°C to -12°C in the Arctic Archipelago to 10°C in southwestern BC. Nearly 48% of Canada's land surface is covered by forests, 28% by tundra, 12% by peatland, and about 3% by grassland, each with its own type of wildlife. Freshwater lakes, covering 7.6% of Canada's surface, account for 15% of the world's total volume of lake water, and Canada has 7.5% of the world's streamflow. The nation's resources extend onto the Continental Shelf, which is known to contain considerable quantities of minerals and oil and gas. The lakes, rivers and oceans also contain fish and mammals of considerable economic importance.

Renewable versus Nonrenewable Renewable and nonrenewable resources require different conservation approaches. To enable society to use rather than consume resources, renewable biomes such as forests, tundra and grasslands must be maintained. Such maintenance involves management of the genetic base (vegetation, animals) and the environment (water, air, light, soil) to preserve productivity, genetic diversity and renewal processes. Conservation of nonrenewable resources (eg, minerals, fossil fuels) requires development of policies to avoid waste (eg, by oil spills, gas flaring), to promote wise use and encourage recycling, to minimize adverse effects of mineral extraction on renewable resources and to develop renewable substitutes. Uses of renewable and nonrenewable resources are interdependent; neither can be exploited or managed in complete isolation. Excessive use ("mining") of renewable resources may transform them into unrenewable losses, as when forest depletion leads to desert formation or an endangered species is hunted to extinction.

Demographic Factors Canada's great regional disparity in economic development tends to focus attention on the short-term solution of economic problems rather than on the long-term consequences of resource use; hence, resource exploitation often takes priority over wise management and preservation (*see* REGIONAL ECONOMICS). During the past 25 years, Canadians have become more aware of the degradation of the nation's resources and the alarming long-term consequences of this continuing process. The need to conserve resources and develop conservation policies involving ecological, economic, social, ethical, political and legal factors are becoming increasingly apparent.

Human Factors Human activities are responsible for many conservation problems, although natural disturbances also have considerable impact. Technological innovations allow increasingly rapid and efficient harvesting of forests, agricultural crops, wildlife and fish. In forestry, chain saws, mechanical harvesters and on-site tree chippers allow the quick and efficient harvest of huge numbers of trees, including stems, branches and leaves. Forest renewal technology has developed much less rapidly. Forest-harvesting activities, forest fires, unsuccessful farming attempts and inadequate reforestation have resulted in a backlog of about 16.8 million ha of forest land that has failed to regenerate with commercially useful trees. This problem is even more acute in tropical areas, where forest destruction is threatening the entire ecosystem. Heavy harvesting and processing equipment has been developed for the proposed extraction of energy from Canada's peatlands, placing one of the world's major reserves of carbon under threat. Canada's natural grasslands have been nearly depleted through plowing for agriculture.

The development of electronic equipment for locating fish shoals has made fishing more efficient, and the pollution of freshwater lakes by industry has led to serious problems of eutrophication, thereby reducing fish populations and recreational values (*see* WATER POLLUTION). In spite of attempts to restock lakes and rivers, overfishing in many accessible areas has reduced fish populations. Wildlife sustains, at least partially, Canada's native peoples, and provide recreation for hunters as well as considerable revenues. In many cases, wildlife populations are seriously threatened by habitat destruction and by easier access to remote areas by snow vehicles and helicopters. Large mammals and sensitive species are particularly vulnerable. Migratory herds of CARIBOU in northern Canada are threatened by increasing industrial activity in their main habitats and along migration routes. Disturbance by visitors to bird colonies may inadvertently reduce nesting success.

Man's activities have provided new habitats, enabling some species to expand into areas where they were formerly scarce or absent. Extensive monoculture cropping practices have resulted in increases of some species (eg, red-winged blackbird) to the extent that they become pests, but have caused a marked decrease in species diversity. Exotic wildlife, vegetation and insects have been introduced to Canada. Some have been harmless or possibly beneficial, but many have had disastrous effects (eg, Dutch elm disease, balsam woolly aphid, winter moth).

SOIL CONSERVATION, the maintenance of soil stability and fertility, is vital if water quality and food, wood, fibre and other crops are to be sustained for future generations. Until recently, soil stability was seriously impaired in some areas (eg, mountainous areas of BC) by forest harvesting, forest road construction and slash burning. Provincial agencies, responsible for the management of natural resources, are now paying increased attention to environmental concerns. Delays in replacing trees after harvesting result in heavy losses of soil nitrogen caused by the accelerated mineralization of soil organic matter. The recent trend toward using high-yielding tree species and shorter rotations involves an inherent risk of accelerating nutrient removal and reducing soil fertility. The massive soil erosion and desert formation in farmlands of western N America in the 1930s illustrate the consequences of inadequate soil management (*see* DROUGHT; GREAT DEPRESSION). Intensive agricultural practices led to widespread reduction of vital organic matter in agricultural soils. There is evidence that, on Canada's northern Great Plains, as little as 34 years of agricultural cropping has resulted in a loss of 35% of the soil's organic matter and 41% of soil nitrogen. Large areas of fertile agricultural soils are destroyed each year by expansion of cities onto productive farmland. Considerable proportions of high-grade mineral ores and readily accessible fossil fuels, particularly oil, have been consumed in the last 50 years to meet the increasing demands of an industrial society and exports. Consequently, industry must now rely on lower-grade or relatively inaccessible mineral and fossil-fuel resources which are costly to locate, extract, transport and process.

Legislation and Political Activity Legislation in Canada, with its federal, provincial and municipal levels of government, is complex and traditionally oriented more towards consumptive resource use for economic purposes than to site preservation, but this is gradually changing. In the last 10 years there has been a great deal of conservation legislation (*see* ENVIRONMENTAL LAW). The federal government is responsible for national parks and for the management and use of large areas of land in the YT and the NWT, as well as for international aspects of control of pollution, migratory birds and import and export of plants and wildlife. Provincial governments are responsible for the use, management and conservation of most of Canada's natural resources. Consequently, conservation measures and associated legislation vary from province to province.

Conservation priorities in Canada have developed in the context of an industrialized nation with a rapidly expanding, mainly urban population, now over 25 million people. Heavy and often conflicting demands are being made on the nation's vast but limited resources. Conservation provides a philosophical and conceptual framework within which resources can be allocated in a manner in keeping with the needs, aspirations and desires of society.

J.S. MAINI AND J.A. CARLISLE

Reading: J.S. Maini and J.A. Carlisle, eds, *Conservation in Canada: A Conspectus* (1974).

Conservation of Movable Cultural Property Conservation is the technology by which preservation (one of the 4 classic museum functions: acquisition, preservation, research, presentation) is achieved. Its relatively recent evolution from the ancient art of restoration represents a fundamental reorientation of museology; while the need remains to restore damaged objects as a last resort, conservation seeks to prevent rather than repair deterioration. This development originated with the need of curators and restorers to have a better understanding of the nature of the materials in their care; but it was not until the 20th century that major institutions recognized that both the control and the repair of damage depends upon the correct diagnosis of its causes.

The first conservation research laboratory was established at the British Museum in 1919 and was followed by others in the US and Western Europe. In 1950 the International Institute for the Conservation of Historic and Artistic Works (IIC) was founded to disseminate the growing body of conservation knowledge among scientists and restorers, and by 1958 it was able to publish an integrated explanation of the general mechanisms of decay in museum materials. From that time both preventive and remedial techniques advanced rapidly and progressive institutions sought to control the deterioration caused by such environmental factors as temperature, humidity, light, airborne contaminants and biological activity, and by human errors in handling, cleaning, storage, exhibition and transportation. Conservation emerged as a profession based upon the chemistry and physics of materials and of the environment; on biology, history, anthropology, photography, radiography and engineering; and on the history and technology of art and architecture; which in turn influenced all the other disciplines of museology.

Some major institutions in Québec and Ontario had employed restorers intermittently since the 19th century, but by 1970 only the NATIONAL GALLERY OF CANADA (1956), the ROYAL ONTARIO MUSEUM (1956), the National Historic Sites Service (1966), the NATIONAL ARCHIVES OF CANADA (1966) and, in the West, the British Columbia Provincial Museum (1966) had established permanent units specifically devoted to the conservation of their collections. Nationwide, fewer than 20 persons were employed full-time in conservation. In 1971 this small nucleus founded the Canadian Association of Professional Conservators (CAPC) in order to accredit and register conservators, and the following year the Canadian Group of IIC (IIC-CG) was formed to spread technical and scientific information.

In 1972, as part of its National Cultural Policy, the federal government founded the Canadian Conservation Institute (CCI) to provide conservation treatment, research and training services to all public museums and galleries. In the same year Parks Canada amalgamated its conservation facilities into a single Conservation Division to serve its National Historic Parks and Sites. However, the development of all conservation agencies was severely handicapped during the early 1970s by the absence of training facilities, and later by the deteriorating economic situation.

The first academic credit course in conservation was offered by U Victoria from 1970 to 1977, but it was not until Queen's introduced an MA program in 1974 and Sir Sandford Fleming College at Peterborough introduced its diploma in conservation technology in 1976 that the supply of Canadian-trained conservators was assured. Career-development training became available in 1977, when the CCI commenced its conservation internships.

During the 1970s the BC Provincial Museum earned a national reputation for its advocacy of conservation and for its training and consultation services; in several other provinces facilities developed gradually throughout the decade. The GLENBOW MUSEUM, the Provincial Museum of Alberta, the Prince of Wales Northern Heritage Centre, (NWT), and archives in NB, Ontario, Manitoba, Saskatchewan and BC all established facilities, while in 1979 the Centre de conservation du Québec offered the first provincial government conservation service.

Meanwhile, the unique climatic and geographical challenges of conservation in Canada demanded research and innovation. New techniques, developed by the CCI and ranging from environmental control to the treatment of waterlogged wood and corroded iron, explored the use of light energy as a cleaning tool, analysed artifacts for authentication studies, responded to disasters and provided a nationwide mobile laboratory service. From the TOTEM POLE sites of the West Coast to the arctic islands and the BASQUE settlements of Labrador, conservators of provincial as well as federal agencies devised solutions to problems unknown elsewhere.

By 1980 fewer than 30 of the 1500 provincial custodial agencies employed conservators, and it was evident that financial as well as technical assistance was required. In 1981 the NATIONAL MUSEUMS OF CANADA introduced a Conservation Assistance Programme, by 1987 administered by the Museums Assistance Programs, to provide salary assistance to qualifying institutions wishing to establish new conservation positions, and the CCI's mandate was revised to meet the needs of a less centralized national conservation structure. De-

spite economic hardship, heritage agencies seized the opportunity to develop conservation capabilities to such effect that the nonfederal conservation work force doubled in just a few years.

PHILIP R. WARD

Reading: J. Des Gagniers, *La conservation du patrimoine museologique du Québec* (1981); A.M. Lambert, *Conservation in Canadian Museums* (1980); National Museums of Canada, *A National Museums Policy for the 80's* (1981); H.J. Plenderleith and A.E.A. Werner, *The Conservation of Antiquities and Works of Art* (1974, 1st ed 1958); M. Ruggles, "The History of Conservation in Canada: Developments to the Early 1970's," *Journal of the International Institute for Conservation – Canadian Group*; Philip R. Ward, *Keeping the Past Alive* (1974) and *The Nature of Conservation: A Race Against Time* (1986).

Conservatism Few political terms are more widely appropriated (some would say misappropriated) than conservatism. In Canada, those calling themselves conservative range from zealous proponents of free enterprise and limited government to so-called "RED TORIES," who support a significant role for the state in Canada's social and economic life.

Historically, Canadian conservatism was rooted in British Toryism of the preindustrial era. It was reinforced by the influx of United Empire LOYALISTS during and after the American Revolution. While the Loyalists did not comprise a solid Tory phalanx, most were MONARCHISTS who favoured an organic and hierarchical society with a due respect for law and order, ideals generally shared by immigrants from Britain who arrived in the first half of the 19th century. Conservative impulses had also long prevailed among French Canadians as a result of the dominance of the Roman Catholic Church and the determination of a conquered people to preserve their language and culture. Canadian political life was distinguished by an early "Tory touch," in contrast to the liberal republicanism of the US, which many Canadians saw as excessively lawless and POPULIST. Where the American Declaration of Independence espoused the right to "life, liberty and the pursuit of happiness," the BRITISH NORTH AMERICA ACT enshrined the imperatives of "peace, order and good government." Whatever else it may entail, conservatism is based on a respect for lawful authority, tradition and continuity in human affairs. This does not preclude necessary reforms, but conservatives have no use for reforms that are produced by abstract reason and not rooted in communal experience. Most Canadian conservatives, past and present, would agree with Edmund Burke's dictum, "A disposition to preserve, and an ability to improve, taken together, would be my standard of a statesman. Everything else is vulgar in conception, perilous in the execution."

Despite this hostility to rapid change, Canadian conservatism was suffused with liberal strains from the start, with consequent semantic and partisan confusion. The ideas of John Locke (1632-1704), the founder of British empirical philosophy and an advocate of civil and religious liberties, are the common heritage of both Canadian conservatives and Canadian liberals. From the time of Sir John A. MACDONALD conservatives have been prepared to change when the need for change was indisputable; however, as historian W.L. MORTON has written, "The essential principles of Canadian conservatism have not changed. It has remained traditional and constitutional, progressive and pragmatic. It has concerned itself with sound administration of existing laws rather than the forming of new laws, and with economic development rather than political reform."

To Canadian conservatives, tradition implied loyalty to the Crown and to British parliamentary procedures. In recent decades the British connection and even the COMMONWEALTH have faded as

issues in Canadian politics, and an excess of anglophilia would be a distinct electoral liability. But most Canadian conservatives (as well as many liberals and socialists) still regard parliamentary government under the monarchy as the best means of ensuring individual freedom, cultural diversity and social cohesion. Some Canadian conservatives have also tended to be staunch nationalists, partly because the US, not the UK, has posed the only serious threat to Canadian political, economic and cultural independence, but also because NATIONALISM is based on an appreciation of history and tradition and a conservative sense of a collective entity – dubious values to liberals, who generally respond in an accommodating and continentalist way to the US.

The Canadian conservative tradition has nothing to do with contemporary neo-conservatism, basically an offshoot of laissez-faire liberalism. To the true conservative, human society is an organic entity in which each member has duties as well as rights. For this reason, Canadian conservatives have favoured government initiatives to protect the disadvantaged and to further economic development. Although the Progressive CONSERVATIVE PARTY attracts its share of right-wing ideologues, Conservative governments since Macdonald's have launched social-welfare programs and many public enterprises in areas such as transportation, broadcasting, banking, grain marketing and hydroelectric power.

At its worst, Canadian conservatism has been conformist and authoritarian, insufficiently appreciating Canada's racial and regional diversities. Conservative dedication to peace, order and good government has evoked a popular impression of conservatives (and especially Progressive Conservatives) as a privileged elite – white, Protestant and largely affluent. At its best, however, Canadian conservatism has been compassionate and pragmatic, eschewing ideology in favour of a careful balance between the conflicting claims of social order and individual liberty.

CHARLES TAYLOR

Reading: W. Christian and C. Campbell, *Political Parties and Ideologies in Canada: Liberals, Conservatives, Socialists, Nationalists* (1974); G. Grant, *Lament for a Nation: The Defeat of Canadian Nationalism* (1965); Charles Taylor, *Radical Tories: The Conservative Tradition in Canada* (1982).

Conservative Party In 1844 in *Coningsby*, Benjamin Disraeli, future Conservative prime minister of Britain, described CONSERVATISM as "an unhappy cross-breed; the mule of politics that engenders nothing." He wrote this when "Conservative" was first appearing as a party designation, a shift intended to broaden the TORY Party's appeal. In Canada as in Britain, Toryism's mid-19th century anti-democratic values were difficult to maintain when the electoral franchise was continually expanding. The Conservative Party in Canada embraced British Tory traditions, but other strains flowed into it. Indeed, the ancestor of the modern Progressive Conservative Party can be discovered in the 1854 Liberal-Conservative COALITION GOVERNMENT of the PROVINCE OF CANADA. John A. MACDONALD entered the 1854 coalition as a moderate Conservative, and it was he who eventually shaped the Liberal-Conservative Party which was dominant at CONFEDERATION. As Canada's first prime minister, Macdonald constructed a party that emphasized the commitment to Confederation and a policy of national economic development. The party's name symbolized Macdonald's own commitment to equilibrium and moderation, to an emphasis on what Canadians held in common, and to an obscuring of those matters where they divided. He managed to combine ULTRAMONTANE

Campaign poster neatly summarizing the powerful appeal of John A. Macdonald's Conservative Party in the 19th century (*courtesy National Archives of Canada/C-6536*).

Roman Catholics from Québec, Tories, Orangemen and businessmen in all 4 founding provinces. Rejecting "abstract debate," he emphasized personality, patronage and compromise; but by 1872 the many parts of the expanding nation had become too different to patch together. In 1872 he won 103 seats to 97 for the Opposition Liberals. The majority did not hold; in Nov 1873 his government fell.

The PACIFIC SCANDAL which brought down Macdonald's government indicated the problems of his approach. The Pacific railway was essential to his nation-building dream; however, its construction and similar development policies linked the government too closely with private interests which did not always serve the public interest. In opposition Macdonald seems to have become convinced that his party should represent something more than simply support of Canada. By then the party had largely dropped the Liberal-Conservative label in favour of Conservative. In the 1878 election campaign Macdonald committed his party to the NATIONAL POLICY, which emphasized PROTECTIONISM, expansion in the West, and an assertive central government. This appealed to Ontario and Québec manufacturers and to those who feared the US following its rejection of free trade and RECIPROCITY. A strong pro-British message was added, its effectiveness proven by Macdonald's re-election in 1882, 1887 and 1891.

Macdonald complemented the National Policy with shrewd and lavish patronage and a willingness to compromise, although compromise evaded him in the case of Louis RIEL after the 1885 North-West Rebellion. Riel's execution, along with weak leadership among Québec Conservatives, led to a decline in support there from 48 seats in 1882 to 30 in 1891. Macdonald's reaction to Riel followed logically from his centralist perspective, which kept provinces and local interests in the background. The result was that the provinces became increasingly Liberal, and supported the provincial rights stand of Liberal leader Wilfrid LAURIER. After Macdonald's death in 1891, his party could not endure attacks on so

many fronts. The Conservative governments of John ABBOTT, John THOMPSON, Mackenzie BOWELL and Charles TUPPER struggled to maintain supremacy, but language and religious problems (*see* MANITOBA SCHOOLS QUESTION) and patronage problems in Québec were great obstacles. The Conservatives lost the 1896 election and for many years did not regain their pre-eminence.

Nova Scotia lawyer Robert BORDEN, Conservative leader 1901-20, sought to expand the Macdonald legacy. He experimented with a Québec lieutenant, flirted with American progressivism and advocated civil service reform and public ownership. He lost the elections of 1904 and 1908. To win in 1911 Borden emphasized the National Policy and the imperial connection, winning support in Ontario, BC and part of the Maritimes. In Québec the Conservatives allied themselves with anti-Laurier *nationalistes* who were seduced by Borden's promise of a referendum on naval assistance to Great Britain. The Conservatives won the election, but the imperialist-*nationaliste* coalition collapsed. By 1913 *nationalistes* in his caucus were bitterly disillusioned with Borden's siding with the more numerous imperialists. WWI extended Borden's mandate, but in 1917 an election could be postponed no longer. The Dec 1917 election was critical for Canadian conservatism. To ensure that his CONSCRIPTION policy was upheld, Borden made an alliance with conscriptionist Liberals. The resulting UNION GOVERNMENT triumphed, but the victory created lasting resentment among French Canadians and immigrants, especially German Canadians. Liberals soon deserted the coalition, leaving the Conservative party with a narrower base than ever before. Moreover, nationalization of the Grand Trunk and Canadian Northern railways caused the defection of the Montréal business community, probably the party's greatest source of funds.

Arthur MEIGHEN, Borden's successor, immediately tried to shape the remnants of Unionism into Conservatism. In the 1921 election the Conservatives finished third with 50 seats, behind the PROGRESSIVE PARTY with 65 and the Liberals with 116. Meighen's support of conscription meant the loss of francophone support. In western Canada Progressives identified more readily with Liberals since they associated Conservatives with the despised National Policy. Meighen served briefly as prime minister in 1926, but a Liberal majority soon returned (*see* KING-BYNG AFFAIR). Conservatives were too closely linked with Britain when Canada's Britishness was disappearing. Nor did Meighen manage to adapt the National Policy to postwar economic conditions.

In 1927 R.B. BENNETT, a wealthy Calgary businessman, succeeded him and in 1930 won a majority, taking 25 Québec seats. The GREAT DEPRESSION created the climate for Bennett's victory; it also assured his defeat 5 years later. Bennett's initial response to the depression was a characteristically Conservative attempt to protect industry and to obtain IMPERIAL PREFERENCE. It did not work. In 1935 Bennett called for many social reforms, but these proposals came too late to be convincing (*see* BENNETT'S NEW DEAL). Many Reformist Conservatives had already left to join the Reconstruction Party founded by former Bennett minister H.H. STEVENS. Moreover, 2 new parties, SOCIAL CREDIT and the CO-OPERATIVE COMMONWEALTH FEDERATION, appealed to areas of English Canada. The 1935 election witnessed the worst Conservative defeat; they took only 40 seats against the Liberals' 173.

Thereafter the Conservatives struggled to rebuild a successful coalition. The enmity of French Canada endured, even though in 1938 the party chose Robert J. MANION, who had opposed conscription, was Catholic and had married a French

Canadian. His attempts to conciliate Québec only angered numerous colleagues once WWII began. Party funds were depleted, and party organization had atrophied. In 1940 the Conservatives again won only 40 seats. Manion's defeat turned the party back towards Arthur Meighen, who shunned compromises and to many Conservatives appeared to be the Canadian Churchill. Canada, however, was not Britain, and Meighen lost a Feb 1942 by-election.

Encouraged by Meighen, Manitoba Premier John BRACKEN, a Progressive with no Conservative experience, sought and won the 1942 leadership, and the party's name was changed to Progressive Conservative Party. It was attempting to turn left to place itself on the path of wartime reform sentiment. But the CCF and the Liberals were also moving left. In 1944 the Conservatives were caught up again in the proconscription movement. Although the Liberals brought in conscription, the Conservatives' enthusiasm ensured that they would bear the blame. In the 1945 election, they could not even find candidates for most Québec ridings. Elsewhere conscription was largely forgotten when the war ended. The PCs came fourth on the Prairies, behind CCF, Liberals and Social Credit.

The Conservatives were becoming an Ontario party, as indicated by the 1948 choice of Ontario premier George DREW as leader. Drew was unable to escape the Ontario mantle. After 2 disastrous defeats, in 1949 and 1953, the party decided to gamble on John DIEFENBAKER, a westerner, a populist and a remarkable showman. Diefenbaker offered both fiery leadership and a visionary program. He excited Canadians, lulled by 2 decades of Liberal administration. In 1957 he won a minority; and in 1958 he astonished Canadians by winning 208 out of 265 seats, including 50 from Québec. For the first time since 1911 the Conservatives were truly a national party.

The Conservative platform appeared to have more substance than it had. Despite strong Québec support, Diefenbaker could not come to terms with Canada's bicultural nature. His policy initiatives seemed eclectic rather than parts of a larger vision. In 1962 Diefenbaker lost his majority, and in 1963 his government collapsed and the Liberals won the subsequent election. Diefenbaker's populism had lost much business support and now lacked urban support generally. French Canada once again shunned the Conservatives. Diefenbaker, however, retained strong support in the West and in pockets elsewhere. His removal as leader in Sept 1967 damaged party unity, and his successor, Nova Scotia Prem Robert STANFIELD, felt the wounds.

Diefenbaker's legacy was strong Conservative support in western Canada. Other successes in the 1960s and 1970s occurred provincially, especially in Ontario, where the Conservatives maintained a regime from 1943 to 1985. By 1979 Conservatives governed in Ontario, Manitoba, Alberta, Nova Scotia, Newfoundland, PEI and New Brunswick. But Stanfield was unable to lead the federal party to power, and in Feb 1976 Joe CLARK, an Albertan, became its leader. In May 1979 the Conservatives under Clark formed a minority government, but they were defeated in the House in Dec and lost the Feb 1980 election.

The defeat of the Conservatives in 1980 brought Joe Clark's leadership into question. In 1983 the party rejected Clark and chose the bilingual Quebecer Brian MULRONEY as its leader. Although Mulroney lacked any parliamentary experience, he possessed superb organizational skills and a deep knowledge of his native province. The party, so often fractious, united behind the new leader as he faced Pierre TRUDEAU's successor, John TURNER, in the federal election of

Sept 1984. Mulroney, backed by a phalanx of provincial premiers and assisted by a Liberal Party which could not decide whether it accepted its heritage, won an overwhelming victory. Despite the party's numerous federal losses since 1963, it had constructed a base from which it could move forward when the Liberal Party stumbled. The new government quickly showed its inexperience and despite major economic (*see* FREE TRADE) and constitutional (*see* MEECH LAKE ACCORD) initiatives was plagued by ministerial resignations and the plummeting popularity of its leader. The Conservative Party may have been the mule of Canadian politics, but it has stood the long haul well.

JOHN ENGLISH

Reading: John English, *The Decline of Politics* (1977); H. Macquarrie, *The Conservative Party* (1965); J.R. Williams, *The Conservative Party of Canada: 1920-1949* (1956).

Conservatoire de musique du Québec, network of 7 music-teaching institutions established in the province of Québec, beginning in 1942. It was founded by Wilfrid PELLETIER with the aim of co-ordinating the professional training of composers, singers, instrumentalists and actors. Provincial standardization of curricula and of criteria for the selection of teachers has produced a remarkable equality in the calibre of teaching and the availability of advanced musical training throughout Québec. The establishment of full-time staff appointments in 1961 and the opening of preparatory schools in Trois-Rivières, Sherbrooke and Arvida [Chicoutimi] in 1963-64 were important landmarks in the institution's development. The operation of the Conservatoire has been governed by 2 broad principles: admission to its courses by competition and the training of professional musicians through specialized cost-free instruction. Through an agreement between the Ministry of Education and certain CEGEPs, the Conservatoire is able to offer the Diplôme d'études collégiales (DEC) and the Diplôme d'études supérieures (DES), which qualify holders for admission to the faculties of education in the universities. The 7 branches are in Chicoutimi, Hull, Montréal, Québec, Rimouski, Trois-Rivières and Val-d'Or.

Conserver Society "Canadians as individuals, and their governments, institutions and industries [must] begin the transition from a consumer society preoccupied with resource exploitation to a conserver society engaged in more constructive endeavours." This statement, which includes the first use of the phrase "conserver society," appeared in the SCIENCE COUNCIL OF CANADA report *Natural Resource Policy Issues in Canada,* released in Jan 1973. It was intended to suggest that many environmental problems are symptoms of the larger problems of a society dedicated to turning resources into garbage as fast as possible in the interests of short-term economic growth; it suggested as well that most environmental problems cannot be resolved until the basic causes are corrected. The Canadian press gave unanticipated attention to the conserver society recommendation when the report was released. Public attention and interest led to a series of studies sponsored by the federal government and others. The use of the term also spread to the US, Australia and New Zealand.

According to the Science Council's brief definition, a conserver society uses 5 principal policy thrusts in making decisions affecting the ENVIRONMENT or its resources: concern for the future; economy of design; diversity, flexibility and responsibility; recognition of total costs; and respect for the biosphere and its capabilities. Ideas included in the concept have been expressed as "doing more with less," "living within the limits to growth," "using technology appropriate to the cultural context and resource base," etc. A conserver society would introduce social and environmental concerns at the very beginning of the design, planning and policy formulation processes and would make resource CONSERVATION and social and environmental impact assessments integral components of all projects. In an advanced conserver society, ENVIRONMENTAL LAW would diminish in importance as sound environmental planning and resource conservation became routine.

There have been a few significant government actions directed at bringing about a conserver society. Canadians still consume more energy, and N Americans produce more garbage per capita, than any other society. However, some progress has been made toward a conserver-society future emphasizing conservation of resources, environmental protection, and the development of a comfortable, safe society with long-term viability. Areas of significant advancement include improvements in environmental education; establishment of environmental legislation (eg, requirements for environmental impact assessments); increase in skills and knowledge in such areas as environmental and resource management; decreases in the importance of MEGAPROJECTS; changes in corporate attitudes; a relative decline in confrontation and increase in co-operation on environmental issues; and continuing development of the cultural foundations needed to make judgements about environmental issues. In 1987 the Brundtland commission emphasized the close relationship between a prosperous economy and a healthy environment.

A major difficulty in persuading Canadians of the desirability of a conserver society lies in the persistence of 2 misconceptions about Canada's resources and the economic benefits to be derived from them. The first misconception is that Canada has enormous, even infinite, resources. Confusion still occurs about the difference between our very large land area (about 10 million km^2) and our agricultural land (700 000 km^2 of arable land and about an equal amount of pasture). Until the 1980s government and industry thought that Canada's forest resources were so large that there was no pressing need for reforestation. Canadians are frequently told that we have more fresh water than any other nation, but are not reminded that our water is spread over a very large area, or that much of it is frozen for part of the year. These misconceptions of abundance have made it difficult to introduce conservation and the husbanding of resources.

The second misconception is derived loosely from economics. It is based on beliefs that resource conservation and recycling are inherently less economical than the exploitation of virgin resources; that environmental protection and sound environmental design and planning penalize industry; that all economic growth is good and accelerating economic growth is necessary for the well-being of Canadians; and that there is a direct correlation between energy and resource consumption and the quality of life. Failure to comprehend the dangers of continued population growth and the heightened environmental impact of each citizen in countries with HIGH TECHNOLOGY further slows acceptance of the conserver-society concept.

DIXON THOMPSON

Reading: L. Soloman, *The Conserver Solution* (1978).

Conspiracy, a difficult legal term to define, implies an agreement between 2 or more persons to commit an unlawful or criminal act, or an act which though lawful in itself becomes unlawful when done by the joint action of the agreeing parties, or for the purpose of using some unlawful means to commit what would otherwise be a lawful act, such as the breaking of a contract. Criminal conspiracy is condemned by the Canadian Criminal Code (s423) but sentences vary according to the intended crime. For example, a conspiracy to commit murder is punishable by 14 years' imprisonment, while a conspiracy to prosecute an innocent person is punishable by 5 to 10 years' imprisonment. A conspiracy to have a woman commit adultery or fornication is punishable by 2 years; the conspirators may also be guilty, in this case, of ABDUCTION. Any conspiracy to achieve an unlawful purpose or a lawful purpose by unlawful means, eg, the use of bribes, is criminal and punishable by 2 years' imprisonment. A mere intention to conspire or to commit an unlawful act is not sufficient to create criminal liability; there must be an actual agreement to act. The Code (s424) expressly provides that a conspiracy in restraint of trade (preventing another from carrying on his trade in a particular way or in a particular area) is not criminal when done by or on behalf of a trade union, which is therefore able to call its members out on strike regardless of any contract of service by which they may be bound, or is able to declare a sympathy strike on behalf of others engaged in a lawful strike.

L.C. GREEN

Constantine, Charles, mounted policeman (b at Bradford, Yorkshire 13 Nov 1849; d at Long Beach, Calif 5 May 1912). Immigrating to Canada as a young man, Constantine was a member of the RED RIVER EXPEDITION sent against Louis Riel and the Manitoba Métis in 1870. Later he was chief of the Manitoba Provincial Police and served in the NORTH-WEST REBELLION of 1885. Commissioned in the North-West Mounted Police as inspector, he was ordered to Yukon in 1894 to investigate reports of abuses by the miners. In 1895 he commanded a detachment of 20 members of the NWMP which went to Yukon to enforce Canadian law, and he was in command of the police there when gold was discovered in 1896. By tact and firmness he prevented challenges to Canadian sovereignty in the region. In 1903 he led the first police expedition to the western Arctic, establishing posts at Fort McPherson and Herschel I. He died on leave in California.

W.R. MORRISON

Constitution, the system of laws and conventions by which a state governs itself; the basic law of a country; the law of laws. A distinction is often made between a formal Constitution, a venerable document formally drawn up that can only be modified through specific procedures, and a material Constitution, a body of dispositions providing for the organization and functioning of the state. Canada's Constitution, though similar to the largely unwritten Constitution of Great Britain, is primarily written, notably the sections on the DISTRIBUTION OF POWERS.

The ROYAL PROCLAMATION OF 1763, the QUEBEC ACT (1774), the CONSTITUTIONAL ACT (1791) and the ACT OF UNION (1840) which preceded the BRITISH NORTH AMERICA ACT (1867), are all constitutional Acts concerning Canada. The STATUTE OF WESTMINSTER (1931) recognized the independence of Canada; the Canada Act, 1982 and the Constitution Act, 1982, patriated the Constitution and gave Canada a Charter of Rights and Freedoms and a general amending formula. Since 17 Apr 1982, the BNA Act has been styled the Constitution Act, 1867, while the Constitution Acts, 1867 to 1975 and the Constitution Act, 1982, have been collectively titled the Constitution Acts, 1867 to 1982. The Constitution of Canada also comprises other legislative documents and decrees, including the British Magna Carta (1215), Bill of Rights (1689), Petition of Right (1629) and Act of Settlement (1701). In its judgement of 28 Sept 1981, the

Supreme Court of Canada noted that the Constitution consists of legislative rules, rules of the common law and constitutional conventions. The first 2 comprise CONSTITUTIONAL LAW, the third, while part of the Constitution and recognized and commented upon by the courts, are not imposed by the courts and are not a source of constitutional law; when they are flouted the remedy is political, not legal. The Supreme Court declared that nothing in constitutional law precluded Parliament from presenting an Address to the British Parliament requesting amendment to the Constitution of Canada, but that a constitutional convention nonetheless required that Parliament enjoy substantial support from the provinces before doing so. The Supreme Court provided several examples of such conventions. One of the most important is that of RESPONSIBLE GOVERNMENT, eg, the Cabinet may only stay in power as long as it enjoys the confidence of the House of Commons. According to the Supreme Court, "a convention occupies a position somewhere in between usage or custom on the one hand and a constitutional law on the other," and its main purpose "is to ensure that the legal framework of the Constitution will be operated in accordance with the prevailing constitutional values or principles of the period."

GÉRALD-A. BEAUDOIN

Constitution, Patriation of For 18 long months – from the May 1980 QUÉBEC REFERENDUM ON SOVEREIGNTY-ASSOCIATION to the signing of the constitutional "accord" between the federal government and 9 provinces in Nov 1981 – the political battle to "patriate" and revise Canada's CONSTITUTION raged furiously, dominating headlines and the political agendas of every government and major institution in the country. The patriation (the term is uniquely Canadian) battle of 1980-81 originated in the failings of a half century of domestic diplomacy and the unexpected second chance offered to PM Pierre TRUDEAU when the Liberal Party was swept back to power in Feb 1980, after 9 months of aborted Tory rule. Constitutional reform became one of several major Liberal initiatives and, apparently by accident, the immediate response to the ongoing Québec referendum campaign, a political fight the federal Liberals had not expected to wage from the seat of power. While Jean CHRÉTIEN lobbied against sovereignty-association in the numerous small towns across Québec during the campaign, Trudeau gave 4 major speeches, promising, "We will immediately take action to renew the Constitution and we will not stop until we have done that" – a statement vague enough to defy definition yet inspiring enough to help swing the tide in favour of the federalist forces. Conceding defeat in the referendum on 20 May 1980, Québec Premier René LÉVESQUE immediately demanded that the PM fulfil his promise. Trudeau quickly despatched Chrétien to arrange a meeting with all the premiers.

In the weeks before the June 9 meeting Trudeau assembled a new cadre of aggressive constitutional advisers and a new set of federal demands. The concessions that Ottawa had been prepared to make in the failed round of constitutional talks in 1978 and 1979 were withdrawn; in their place the federal government, for the first time since the failed Victoria Conference in 1971 made significant demands of its own – for new, centralized powers over the economy – while at the same time insisting that the so-called "people's package" of patriation and enshrinement of a CANADIAN CHARTER OF RIGHTS AND FREEDOMS was not a matter for tawdry, political tradeoffs. The premiers responded angrily to the change of tactics but nevertheless agreed to set in motion a uniquely Canadian event – a summer

The constitution document (*courtesy National Archives of Canada*).

constitutional roadshow of ministers, senior officials and political aides to explore the 12 agreed-upon agenda items and to report to a FIRST MINISTERS CONFERENCE in early Sept.

However, by the time of the Sept 8 First Ministers Conference (the tenth round of negotiations to be held since 1927 on the reform of Canada's Constitution), the battle lines had already begun to harden. On the eve of the conference, Lévesque quietly circulated to the premiers a leaked copy of Ottawa's 64-page, top-secret negotiating strategy, known as the Kirby Memorandum after its chief compiler Michael KIRBY, secretary to the Cabinet for federal-provincial relations. The document was leaked to the press on the second day of the conference, helping to sour an already bitter mood of distrust. During 4 days under hot television lights, the premiers and the prime minister articulated, occasionally impressively, widely different visions of Canada, which were repeated backstage in private meetings. The intractable views of the participants led to the inevitable failure of the conference. On Oct 2, following consultations with his caucus and Cabinet, Trudeau announced, not unexpectedly, that Ottawa would make a unilateral request to the British Parliament. The government planned to recall Parliament early and press the resolution through by Christmas before significant opposition could be mounted.

The New Democratic Party, under leader Edward BROADBENT, gave tentative approval to the plan, though it split his caucus, essentially along east-west lines. The federal Conservatives, under besieged leader Joe CLARK, strongly opposed the plan and used every procedural device at their disposal to halt the resolution. The resolution finally went before the SUPREME COURT OF CANADA in late spring 1981. When the Liberals invoked CLOSURE to move the resolution into the COMMITTEE stage, a handful of Tories rushed the Speaker's chair with fists waving, demanding to be heard.

The Constitution fight offered Clark an explosive issue around which to consolidate his flagging leadership and an opportunity to advance his view of the country as a "community of communities." But his position underscored a rift be-

tween the federal Tories and their influential Ontario cousins; Ontario Premier William DAVIS and NB Premier Richard HATFIELD, both Conservatives and the only 2 to attend the aborted Victoria Conference in 1971, supported the prime minister's plan.

The constitutional resolution, with its centre-piece, the Charter, was offered to a special joint parliamentary committee for study, where it was harshly criticized. The first parliamentary committee to have its sittings televised, it was petitioned by 914 individuals and 294 groups. It sat a total of 267 hours over 65 days; and largely because of its deliberations the first charter was significantly redrafted 5 times. The revisions included the incorporation of provisions on aboriginal rights, sexual equality and equal rights for the handicapped. The Conservative Party advocated the entrenchment of "property rights," but the Liberals rejected this proposal because of opposition to it by their allies, the NDP.

The 6 dissident provinces (Québec, Alberta, Manitoba, PEI, Newfoundland and BC) most strongly opposed to the plan united to form a common front. Led largely by the strong-willed premiers of Québec, Alberta (Peter LOUGHEED) and Manitoba (Sterling LYON), they were joined eventually by those of Saskatchewan and Nova Scotia. The group, dubbed the "Gang of Eight," mounted court challenges against the resolution in provincial courts of appeal in Manitoba, Québec and Newfoundland, and launched a public-relations campaign against it both in Canada and in Great Britain where they lobbied MPs strenuously. These resulting pressures on the British government led to increased tensions between the 2 governments.

Meanwhile the CONSTITUTION REFERENCE case was weaving a tortuous path through the courts. In Feb 1981 the Manitoba Court of Appeal decided 3-2 in favour of Ottawa. In April the Québec Superior Court of Appeal, in a 4-1 decision, also supported Ottawa. However, just weeks earlier, the 3 justices of the Supreme Court of Newfoundland had condemned unanimously the federal procedure. The Newfoundland judgement was handed down as the Commons was tied in procedural knots by the Conservative opposition and while the 8 dissident premiers were preparing for their own conference to sign an alternative constitutional "Accord," one that would limit the request to Britain to simple patriation with a different amending formula, promoted largely by Premier Lougheed. Trudeau suddenly agreed to submit his resolution to the Supreme Court of Canada for judicial settlement but would not meet the dissident premiers when they arrived in Ottawa 16 April 1981, and he ridiculed their "April Accord" in which Québec's Lévesque had agreed to an amending formula that did not provide a specific veto for his province.

On Sept 28 the court brought down its judgement; it found that Ottawa was legally allowed to make this request of the British Parliament but that the resolution offended the constitutional "conventions" which had developed in Canada over the years, referring to practices which were important but not legally enforceable. The court held by a 7-2 majority that no *legal* limit "to the power of the Houses to pass resolutions" existed. By a 6-3 majority, however, the court also ruled that whenever amendments were proposed that would reduce provincial powers, the presentation of a joint resolution by Ottawa without a "consensus" of the provinces would be a breach of constitutional convention. Although such practice was a matter of convention rather than law, the court argued that such conventions are of great significance. In the words of the court, "Constitutional convention plus constitutional law equal the total constitution of the country." This split decision, interpreted as a messy win for both sides, soon sparked a final round of hurried negotiations and what the prime minister came to call "the one last time" conference of Nov 2.

On the first day of the 4-day conference, the federal side appeared to take the initiative when Premiers Davis and Hatfield offered compromise proposals: Davis to forego Ontario's traditional veto and Hatfield to postpone parts of the Charter of Rights for 2 years. After an opening round of public statements the first ministers and their key lieutenants continued their discussions in a private room on the top floor of the conference centre. The rancour returned on the second day and the formal conference broke up at noon. The Gang of Eight, sequestered in their suite across the street at the Château Laurier Hotel, debated a vague compromise plan put together by BC Premier William BENNETT. Eventually, Bennett, Lougheed and NS Premier John BUCHANAN took the scheme to Trudeau who rejected it in an angry confrontation. On the third day Saskatchewan Premier Allan BLAKENEY put forth his own proposal. Manitoba Premier Sterling Lyon was leaving at the end of the day for the campaign trail; Lévesque, too, planned to leave and accused Blakeney of breaking up the defensive alliance. The Blakeney proposal was given short shrift around the conference table, but an apparently off-the-cuff remark by Trudeau that perhaps only a referendum could resolve the conundrum was unexpectedly well received by Lévesque, to the annoyance of all the other premiers. Nearly all day was devoted to discussing a possible referendum, and Trudeau emerged in the afternoon to announce to the press somewhat facetiously that there was a new Québec-Ottawa alliance.

Various ministers from the different provinces had been meeting privately in the meantime to discuss other options. Three attorneys general – Chrétien, Saskatchewan's Roy ROMANOW and Ontario's Roy McMurtry – had traded notes earlier that morning. During the afternoon discussion of referendum procedures, Chrétien and Romanow slipped away to an unused kitchen pantry to continue with their talks. During the so-called "Kitchen Meeting," the scraps of paper exchanged formed the basis, along with similar notions from Newfoundland Premier Brian

Queen Elizabeth II signing the Canadian constitution document after patriation, as PM Pierre Elliott Trudeau (left), Michael Pitfield (centre) and Michael Kirby look on, Ottawa, 17 Apr 1982 (*courtesy SSC Photocentre*).

PECKFORD and Alberta Premier Lougheed, for an eventual compromise. That night, officials from Saskatchewan, BC, Alberta and Newfoundland worked out a one-page compromise, substituting their preferred amending formula (known at the time as the Alberta-Vancouver formula) and introducing a *non obstante* clause to limit the effect of the Charter of Rights. All the other participants were informed of their progress, except for Lyon, who was campaigning, and Lévesque, who was dining late with his top staff. The next morning the deal was presented to Lévesque at breakfast and formally to the prime minister at the conference table. With some minor adjustments, the deed was done. Lévesque complained bitterly, refused to sign the accord, and tried in vain to press Trudeau to embrace the referendum option.

By Nov 5 the constitutional fight was essentially over. In the next few weeks, native peoples and women's groups lobbied successfully to reinstate certain clauses that had been dropped in the late-night compromise; the resolution was sent to Britain for relatively quick approval and Queen Elizabeth II came to Canada to proclaim the new Constitution Act on Parliament Hill 17 Apr 1982. On that same day Lévesque left Ottawa prophesying dire consequences for Confederation. "The Canadian Way," he said, mocking the phrase his fellow premiers had used to trumpet their compromise, was "to abandon Québec at the moment of crisis." It was to be another 5 years before an agreement was reached to bring Québec into the constitutional accord. By then the players had changed, including Québec's premier, now Robert BOURASSA and Canada's PM, now Brian MULRONEY. *See also* MEECH LAKE ACCORD.

ROBERT SHEPPARD

Reading: K. Banting and R. Simeon, *And No One Cheered* (1983); Robert Sheppard and M. Valpy, *The National Deal* (1982).

Constitution Act, 1867, originally the BRITISH NORTH AMERICA ACT, statute enacted 29 Mar 1867 by the British Parliament, providing for CONFEDERATION of the PROVINCE OF CANADA (Ontario and Québec), Nova Scotia and New Brunswick into a federal state with a parliamentary system modelled on that of Britain. RUPERT'S LAND was acquired in 1870, and 6 provinces have been added to the original 4: Manitoba (1870), BC (1871), PEI (1873), Alberta and Saskatchewan (1905), and Newfoundland (1949). The Act does not contain the entire CONSTITUTION of Canada. Complementing its text are British and Canadian statutes having constitutional effect (eg, the Canada Elections Act), and certain unwritten principles known as "the conventions of the constitution." Conventions, such as the power vested in the Crown to dissolve Parliament and call a general election, are usually exercised on the advice of the prime minister.

The Act outlines the DISTRIBUTION OF POWERS between the central Parliament (s91, eg, over banking, interest, criminal law, the postal system and the armed forces) and the provincial legislatures (s92, eg, over property; most contracts and torts; local works, undertakings and businesses). Because of the breadth or generality of the legislative powers conferred, occasionally a direct conflict arises between provincial and federal laws regulating the same things (eg, security frauds). By paramountcy, federal law prevails. In the case of concurrent powers, exercisable by both jurisdictions, federal paramountcy prevails in matters involving agriculture and immigration (s95), but provincial in old-age pensions (s94A). Unallocated powers (eg, aeronautics, radio, official languages) go to the federal government rather than to the local units as in the US and Australia. The federal PEACE, ORDER AND GOOD GOVERNMENT power embraces these "residuary" areas and matters falling under "national dimensions" and "emergencies." "National dimensions" signifies that selected matters originally of a local nature and under provincial jurisdiction (eg, day-to-day health care) can, through altered circumstances, such as an epidemic, acquire a new

Constitution Act, 1982

Part 1
Canadian Charter of Rights and Freedoms

Whereas Canada is founded upon principles that recognize the supremacy of God and the rule of law:

Guarantee of Rights and Freedoms

1. The *Canadian Charter of Rights and Freedoms* guarantees the rights and freedoms set out in it subject only to such reasonable limits prescribed by law as can be demonstrably justified in a free and democratic society.

Fundamental Freedoms

2. Everyone has the following fundamental freedoms:
(a) freedom of conscience and religion;
(b) freedom of thought, belief, opinion and expression, including freedom of the press and other media of communication;
(c) freedom of peaceful assembly; and
(d) freedom of association.

Democratic Rights

3. Every citizen of Canada has the right to vote in an election of members of the House of Commons or of a legislative assembly and to be qualified for membership therein.

4. (1) No House of Commons and no legislative assembly shall continue for longer than five years from the date fixed for the return of the writs at a general election of its members.
(2) In time of real or apprehended war, invasion or insurrection, a House of Commons may be continued by Parliament and a legislative assembly may be continued by the legislature beyond five years if such continuation is not opposed by the votes of more than one-third of the members of the House of Commons or the legislative assembly, as the case may be.

5. There shall be a sitting of Parliament and of each legislature at least once every twelve months.

Mobility Rights

6. (1) Every citizen of Canada has the right to enter, remain in and leave Canada.
(2) Every citizen of Canada and every person who has the status of a permanent resident of Canada has the right
(a) to move to and take up residence in any province; and
(b) to pursue the gaining of a livelihood in any province.
(3) The rights specified in subsection (2) are subject to
(a) any laws or practices of general application in force in a province other than those that discriminate among persons primarily on the basis of province of present or previous residence; and
(b) any laws providing for reasonable residency requirements as a qualification for the receipt of publicly provided social services.
(4) Subsections (2) and (3) do not preclude any law, program or activity that has as its object the amelioration in a province of conditions of individuals in that province who are socially or economically disadvantaged if the rate of employment in that province is below the rate of employment in Canada.

Legal Rights

7. Everyone has the right to life, liberty and security of the person and the right not to be deprived thereof except in accordance with the principles of fundamental justice.

8. Everyone has the right to be secure against unreasonable search or seizure.

9. Everyone has the right not to be arbitrarily detained or imprisoned.

10. Everyone has the right on arrest or detention
(a) to be informed promptly of the reasons therefor;
(b) to retain and instruct counsel without delay and to be informed of that right; and
(c) to have the validity of the detention determined by way of *habeas corpus* and to be released if the detention is not lawful.

11. Any person charged with an offence has the right
(a) to be informed without unreasonable delay of the specific offence;
(b) to be tried within a reasonable time;
(c) not to be compelled to be a witness in proceedings against that person in respect of the offence;
(d) to be presumed innocent until proven guilty according to law in a fair and public hearing by an independent and impartial tribunal;
(e) not to be denied reasonable bail without just cause;
(f) except in the case of an offence under military law tried before a military tribunal, to the benefit of trial by jury where the maximum punishment for the offence is imprisonment for five years or a more severe punishment;
(g) not to be found guilty on account of any act or omission unless, at the time of the act or omission, it constituted an offence under Canadian or international law or was criminal according to the general principles of law recognized by the community of nations;
(h) if finally acquitted of the offence, not to be tried for it again and, if finally found guilty and punished for the offence, not to be tried or punished for it again; and
(i) if found guilty of the offence and if the punishment for the offence has been varied between the time of commission and the time of sentencing, to the benefit of the lesser punishment.

12. Everyone has the right not to be subjected to any cruel and unusual treatment or punishment.

13. A witness who testifies in any proceedings has the right not to have any incriminating evidence so given used to incriminate that witness in any other proceedings, except in a prosecution for perjury or for the giving of contradictory evidence.

14. A party or witness in any proceedings who does not understand or speak the language in which the proceedings are conducted or who is deaf has the right to the assistance of an interpreter.

Equality Rights

15. (1) Every individual is equal before and under the law and has the right to the equal protection and equal benefit of the law without discrimination and, in particular, without discrimination based on race, national or ethnic origin, colour, religion, sex, age or mental or physical disability.
(2) Subsection (1) does not preclude any law, program or activity that has as its object the amelioration of conditions of disadvantaged individuals or groups including those that are disadvantaged because of race, national or ethnic origin, colour, religion, sex, age or mental or physical disability.

Official Languages of Canada

16. (1) English and French are the official languages of Canada and have equality of status and equal rights and privileges as to their use in all institutions of the Parliament and government of Canada.
(2) English and French are the official languages of New Brunswick and have equality of status and equal rights and privileges as to their use in all institutions of the legislature and government of New Brunswick.

Schedule to the Constitution Act, 1982
Modernization of the Constitution

Item	Column I *Act Affected*	Column II *Amendment*	Column III *New Name*
1.	British North America Act, 1867, 30-31 Vict., c. 3 (U.K.)	(1) Section 1 is repealed and the following substituted therefor: "1. This Act may be cited as the *Constitution Act, 1867.*" (2) Section 20 is repealed. (3) Class 1 of section 91 is repealed. (4) Class 1 of section 92 is repealed.	Constitution Act, 1867
2.	An Act to amend and continue the Act 32-33 Victoria chapter 3; and to establish and provide for the Government of the Province of Manitoba, 1870, 33 Vict., c. 3 (Can.)	(1) The long title is repealed and the following substituted therefor: "*Manitoba Act, 1870.*" (2) Section 20 is repealed.	Manitoba Act, 1870
3.	Order of Her Majesty in Council admitting Rupert's Land and the North-Western Territory into the union, dated the 23rd day of June, 1870		Rupert's Land and North-Western Territory Order
4.	Order of Her Majesty in Council admitting British Columbia into the Union, dated the 16th day of May, 1871		British Columbia Terms of Union
5.	British North America Act, 1871, 34-35 Vict., c. 28 (U.K.)	Section 1 is repealed and the following substituted therefor: "1. This Act may be cited as the *Constitution Act, 1871.*"	Constitution Act, 1871
6.	Order of Her Majesty in Council admitting Prince Edward Island into the Union, dated the 26th day of June, 1873		Prince Edward Island Terms of Union
7.	Parliament of Canada Act, 1875, 38-39 Vict., c. 38 (U.K.)		Parliament of Canada Act, 1875
8.	Order of Her Majesty in Council admitting all British possessions and Territories in North America and islands adjacent thereto into the Union, dated the 31st day of July, 1880		Adjacent Territories Order
9.	British North America Act, 1886, 49-50 Vict., c. 35 (U.K.)	Section 3 is repealed and the following substituted therefor: "3. This Act may be cited as the *Constitution Act, 1886.*"	Constitution Act, 1886
10.	Canada (Ontario Boundary) Act, 1889, 52-53 Vict., c. 28 (U.K.)		Canada (Ontario Boundary) Act, 1889
11.	Canadian Speaker (Appointment of Deputy) Act, 1895, 2nd Sess., 59 Vict., c. 3 (U.K.)	The Act is repealed.	
12.	The Alberta Act, 1905, 4-5 Edw. VII, c. 3 (Can.)		Alberta Act
13.	The Saskatchewan Act, 1905, 4-5 Edw. VII, c. 42 (Can.)		Saskatchewan Act
14.	British North America Act, 1907, 7 Edw. VII, c. 11 (U.K.)	Section 2 is repealed and the following substituted therefor: "2. This Act may be cited as the *Constitution Act, 1907.*"	Constitution Act, 1907

No.	Act	Amendment	New Citation
15.	British North America Act, 1915, 5-6 Geo. V, c. 45 (U.K.)	Section 3 is repealed and the following substituted therefor: "3. This Act may be cited as the *Constitution Act, 1915.*"	Constitution Act, 1915
16.	British North America Act, 1930, 20-21 Geo. V, c. 26 (U.K.)	Section 3 is repealed and the following substituted therefor: "3. This Act may be cited as the *Constitution Act, 1930.*"	Constitution Act, 1930
17.	Statute of Westminster, 1931, 22 Geo. V. c. 4 (U.K.)	In so far as they apply to Canada, (a) section 4 is repealed; and (b) subsection 7(1) is repealed	Statute of Westminster, 1931
18.	British North America Act, 1940, 3-4 Geo. VI, c. 36 (U.K.)	Section 2 is repealed and the following substituted therefor: "2. This Act may be cited as the *Constitution Act, 1940.*"	Constitution Act, 1940
19.	British North America Act, 1943, 6-7 Geo. VI, c. 30 (U.K.)	The Act is repealed.	
20.	British North America Act, 1946, 9-10 Geo. VI, c. 63 (U.K.)	The Act is repealed.	
21.	British North America Act, 1949, 12-13 Geo. VI, c. 22 (U.K.)	Section 3 is repealed and the following substituted therefor: "3. This Act may be cited as the *Newfoundland Act.*"	Newfoundland Act
22.	British North America (No. 2) Act 1949, 13 Geo. VI, c. 81 (U.K.)	The Act is repealed.	
23.	British North America Act, 1951, 14-15 Geo. VI, c. 32 (U.K.)	The Act is repealed.	
24.	British North America Act, 1952, 1 Eliz. II, c. 15 (Can.)	The Act is repealed.	
25.	British North America Act, 1960, 9 Eliz. II, c. 2 (U.K.)	Section 2 is repealed and the following substituted therefor: "2. This Act may be cited as the *Constitution Act, 1960.*"	Constitution Act, 1960
26.	British North America Act, 1964, 12-13 Eliz. II, c. 73 (U.K.)	Section 2 is repealed and the following substituted therefor: "2. This Act may be cited as the *Constitution Act, 1964.*"	Constitution Act, 1964
27.	British North America Act, 1965, 14 Eliz. II, C. 4, Part I (Can.)	Section 2 is repealed and the following substituted therefor: "2. This Part may be cited as the *Constitution Act, 1965.*"	Constitution Act, 1965
28.	British North America Act, 1974, 23 Eliz. II, c. 13, Part I (Can.)	Section 3, as amended by 25-26 Eliz. II, c. 28, s. 38(1) (Can.), is repealed and the following substituted therefor: "3. This Part may be cited as the *Constitution Act, 1974.*"	Constitution Act, 1974
29.	British North America Act, 1975, 23-24 Eliz. II, c. 28, Part I (Can.)	Section 3, as amended by 25-26 Eliz. II, c. 28, s. 31 (Can.), is repealed and the following substituted therefor: "3. This Part may be cited as the *Constitution Act (No. 1), 1975.*"	Constitution Act (No. 1), 1975
30.	British North America Act (No. 2), 1975, 23-24 Eliz. II, c. 53 (Can.)	Section 3 is repealed and the following substituted therefor: "3. This Act may be cited as the *Constitution Act (No. 2), 1975.*"	Constitution Act (No. 2), 1975

(3) Nothing in this Charter limits the authority of Parliament or a legislature to advance the equality of status or use of English and French.

17. (1) Everyone has the right to use English or French in any debates and other proceedings of Parliament.

(2) Everyone has the right to use English or French in any debates and other proceedings of the legislature of New Brunswick.

18. (1) The statutes, records and journals of Parliament shall be printed and published in English and French and both language versions are equally authoritative.

(2) The statutes, records and journals of the legislature of New Brunswick shall be printed and published in English and French and both language versions are equally authoritative.

19. (1) Either English or French may be used by any person in, or in any pleading in or process issuing from, any court established by Parliament.

(2) Either English or French may be used by any person in, or in any pleading in or process issuing from, any court of New Brunswick.

20. (1) Any member of the public in Canada has the right to communicate with, and to receive available services from, any head or central office of an institution of the Parliament or government of Canada in English or French, and has the same right with respect to any other office of any such institution where (a) there is a significant demand for communications with and services from that office in such language; or

(b) due to the nature of the office, it is reasonable that communications with and services from that office be available in both English and French.

(2) Any member of the public in New Brunswick has the right to communicate with, and to receive available services from, any office of an institution of the legislature or government of New Brunswick in English or French.

21. Nothing in sections 16 to 20 abrogates or derogates from any right, privilege or obligation with respect to the English and French languages, or either of them, that exists or is continued by virtue of any other provision of the Constitution of Canada.

22. Nothing in sections 16 to 20 abrogates or derogates from any legal or customary right or privilege acquired or enjoyed either before or after the coming into force of this Charter with respect to any language that is not English or French.

Minority Language Educational Rights

23. (1) Citizens of Canada

(a) whose first language learned and still understood is that of the English or French linguistic minority population of the province in which they reside, or

(b) who have received their primary school instruction in Canada in English or French and reside in a province where the language in which they received that instruction is the language of the English or French linguistic minority population of the province, have the right to have their children receive primary and secondary school instruction in that language in that province.

(2) Citizens of Canada of whom any child has received or is receiving primary or secondary school instruction in English or French in Canada, have the right to have all their children receive primary and secondary school instruction in the same language.

(3) The right of citizens of Canada under subsections (1) and (2) to have their children receive primary and secondary school instruction in the language of the English or French linguistic minority population of a province

(a) applies wherever in the province the number of children of citizens who have such a right is sufficient to warrant the provision to them out of public funds of minority language instruction; and

(b) includes, where the number of those children so warrants, the right to have them receive that instruction in minority language educational facilities provided out of public funds.

Enforcement

24. (1) Anyone whose rights or freedoms, as guaranteed by this Charter, have been infringed or denied may apply to a court of competent jurisdiction to obtain such remedy as the court considers appropriate and just in the circumstances.

(2) Where, in proceedings under subsection (1), a court concludes that evidence was obtained in a manner that infringed or denied any rights or freedoms guaranteed by this Charter, the evidence shall be excluded if it is established that, having regard to all the circumstances, the admission of it in the proceedings would bring the administration of justice into disrepute.

General

25. The guarantee in this Charter of certain rights and freedoms shall not be construed so as to abrogate or derogate from any aboriginal, treaty or other rights or freedoms that pertain to the aboriginal peoples of Canada including (a) any rights or freedoms that have been recognized by the Royal Proclamation of October 7, 1763; and (b) any rights or freedoms that may be acquired by the aboriginal peoples of Canada by way of land claims settlement.

26. The guarantee in this Charter of certain rights and freedoms shall not be construed as denying the existence of any other rights or freedoms that exist in Canada.

27. This Charter shall be interpreted in a manner consistent with the preservation and enhancement of the multicultural heritage of Canadians.

28. Notwithstanding anything in this Charter, the rights and freedoms referred to in it are guaranteed equally to male and female persons.

29. Nothing in this Charter abrogates or derogates from any rights or privileges guaranteed by or under the Constitution of Canada in respect of denominational, separate or dissentient schools.

30. A reference in this Charter to a province or to the legislative assembly or legislature of a province shall be deemed to include a reference to the Yukon Territory and the Northwest Territories, or to the appropriate legislative authority thereof, as the case may be.

31. Nothing in this Charter extends the legislative powers of any body or authority.

Application of Charter

32. (1) This Charter applies

(a) to the Parliament and government of Canada in respect of all matters within the authority of Parliament including all matters relating to the Yukon Territory and Northwest Territories; and

(b) to the legislature and government of each province in respect of all matters within the authority of the legislature of each province.

(2) Notwithstanding subsection (1), section 15 shall not have effect until three years after this section comes into force.

33. (1) Parliament or the legislature of a province may expressly declare in an Act of Parliament or of the legislature, as the case may be, that the Act or a provision thereof shall operate notwithstanding a provision included in section 2 or sections 7 to 15 of this Charter.

(2) An Act or a provision of an Act in respect of which a declaration made under this section is in effect shall have such operation as it would have but for the provision of this Charter referred to in the declaration.

(3) A declaration made under subsection (1) shall cease to have effect five years after it comes into force or on such earlier date as may be specified in the declaration.

(4) Parliament or the legislature of a province may re-enact a declaration made under subsection (1).

(5) Subsection (3) applies in respect of a re-enactment made under subsection (4).

34. This Part may be cited as the *Canadian Charter of Rights and Freedoms.*

Part II
Rights of the Aboriginal Peoples of Canada

35. (1) The existing aboriginal and treaty rights of the aboriginal peoples of Canada are hereby recognized and affirmed.

(2) In this Act, "aboriginal peoples of Canada" includes the Indian, Inuit and Métis peoples of Canada.

Part III
Equalization and Regional Disparities

36. (1) Without altering the legislative authority of Parliament or of the provincial legislatures, or the rights of any of them with respect to the exercise of their legislative authority, Parliament and the legislatures, together with the government of Canada and the provincial governments, are committed to

(a) promoting equal opportunities for the well-being of Canadians;

(b) furthering economic development to reduce disparity in opportunities; and

(c) providing essential public services of reasonable quality to all Canadians.

(2) Parliament and the government of Canada are committed to the principle of making equalization payments to ensure that provincial governments have sufficient revenues to provide reasonably comparable levels of public services at reasonably comparable levels of taxation.

Part IV
Constitutional Conference

37. (1) A constitutional conference composed of the Prime Minister of Canada and the first ministers of the provinces shall be convened by the Prime Minister of Canada within one year after this Part comes into force.

(2) The conference convened under subsection (1) shall have included in its agenda an item respecting constitutional matters that directly affect the aboriginal peoples of Canada, including the identification and definition of the rights of those peoples to be included in the Constitution of Canada, and the Prime Minister of Canada shall invite representatives of those peoples to participate in the discussions on that item.

(3) The Prime Minister of Canada shall invite elected representatives of the governments of the Yukon Territory and the Northwest Territories to participate in the discussions on any item on the agenda of the conference convened under subsection (1) that, in the opinion of the Prime Minister, directly affects the Yukon Territory and the Northwest Territories.

Part V
Procedure for Amending Constitution of Canada

38. (1) An amendment to the Constitution of Canada may be made by proclamation issued by the Governor General under the Great Seal of Canada where so authorized by

(a) resolutions of the Senate and House of Commons; and

(b) resolutions of the legislative assemblies of at least two-thirds of the provinces that have, in the aggregate, according to the then latest general census, at least fifty per cent of the population of all the provinces.

(2) An amendment made under subsection (1) that derogates from the legislative powers, the proprietary rights or any other rights or privileges of the legislature or government of a province shall require a resolution supported by a majority of the members of each of the Senate, the House of Commons and the legislative assemblies required under subsection (1).

(3) An amendment referred to in subsection (2) shall not have effect in a province the legislative assembly of which has expressed its dissent thereto by resolution supported by a majority of its members prior to the issue of the proclamation to which the amendment relates unless that legislative assembly, subsequently, by resolution supported by a majority of its members, revokes its

dissent and authorizes the amendment.

(4) A resolution of dissent made for the purposes of subsection (3) may be revoked at any time before or after the issue of the proclamation to which it relates.

39. (1) A proclamation shall not be issued under subsection 38(1) before the expiration of one year from the adoption of the resolution initiating the amendment procedure thereunder, unless the legislative assembly of each province has previously adopted a resolution of assent or dissent.

(2) A proclamation shall not be issued under subsection 38(1) after the expiration of three years from the adoption of the resolution initiating the amendment procedure thereunder.

40. Where an amendment is made under subsection 38(1) that transfers provincial legislative powers relating to education or other cultural matters from provincial legislatures to Parliament, Canada shall provide reasonable compensation to any province to which the amendment does not apply.

41. An amendment to the Constitution of Canada in relation to the following matters may be made by proclamation issued by the Governor General under the Great Seal of Canada only where authorized by resolutions of the Senate and House of Commons and of the legislative assembly of each province:

(a) the office of the Queen, the Governor General and the Lieutenant Governor of a province;

(b) the right of a province to a number of members in the House of Commons not less than the number of Senators by which the province is entitled to be represented at the time this Part comes into force;

(c) subject to section 43, the use of the English or the French language;

(d) the composition of the Supreme Court of Canada; and

(e) an amendment to this Part.

42. (1) An amendment to the Constitution of Canada in relation to the following matters may be made only in accordance with subsection 38(1):

(a) the principle of proportionate representation of the provinces in the House of Commons prescribed by the Constitution of Canada;

(b) the powers of the Senate and the method of selecting Senators;

(c) the number of members by which a province is entitled to be represented in the Senate and the residence qualifications of Senators;

(d) subject to paragraph 41(d), the Supreme Court of Canada;

(e) the extension of existing provinces into the territories; and

(f) notwithstanding any other law or practice, the establishment of new provinces. (2) Subsections 38(2) to (4) do not apply in respect of amendments in relation to matters referred to in subsection (1).

43. An amendment to the Constitution of Canada in relation to any provision that applies to one or more, but not all, provinces, including

(a) any alteration to boundaries between provinces, and

(b) any amendment to any provision that relates to the use of the English or the French language within a province, may be made by proclamation issued by the Governor General under the Great Seal of Canada only where so authorized by resolutions of the Senate and House of Commons and of the legislative assembly of each province to which the amendment applies.

44. Subject to sections 41 and 42, Parliament may exclusively make laws amending the Constitution of Canada in relation to the executive government of Canada or the Senate and House of Commons.

45. Subject to section 41, the legislature of each province may exclusively make laws amending the constitution of the province.

46. (1) The procedures for amendment under sections 38, 41, 42 and 43 may be initiated either by the Senate or the House of Commons or by the legislative assembly of a province.

(2) A resolution of assent made for the purposes of this Part may be revoked at any time before the issue of a proclamation authorized by it.

47. (1) An amendment to the Constitution of Canada made by proclamation under section 38, 41, 42 or 43 may be made without a resolution of the Senate authorizing the issue of the proclamation if, within one hundred and eighty days after the adoption by the House of Commons of a resolution authorizing its issue, the Senate has not adopted such a resolution and if, at any time after the expiration of that period, the House of Commons again adopts the resolution.

(2) Any period when Parliament is prorogued or dissolved shall not be counted in computing the one hundred and eighty day period referred to in subsection (1).

48. The Queen's Privy Council for Canada shall advise the Governor General to issue a proclamation under this Part forthwith on the adoption of the resolutions required for an amendment made by proclamation under this Part.

49. A constitutional conference composed of the Prime Minister of Canada and the first ministers of the provinces shall be convened by the Prime Minister of Canada within fifteen years after this Part comes into force to review the provisions of this Part.

Part VI - Amendment to the Constitution Act, 1867

50. The *Constitution Act, 1867* (formerly named the *British North America Act, 1867*) is amended by adding thereto, immediately after section 92 thereof, the following heading and section:

"Non-Renewable Natural Resources, Forestry Resources and Electrical Energy

92A. (1) In each province, the legislature may exclusively make laws in relation to

(a) exploration for non-renewable natural resources in the province;

(b) development, conservation and management of non-renewable natural resources and forestry resources in the province, including laws in relation to the rate of primary production therefrom; and

(c) development, conservation and management of sites and facilities in the province for the generation and production of electrical energy.

(2) In each province, the legislature may make laws in relation to the export from the province to another part of Canada of the primary production from non-renewable natural resources and forestry resources in the province and the production from facilities in the province for the generation of electrical energy, but such laws may not authorize or provide for discrimination in prices or in supplies exported to another part of Canada.

(3) Nothing in subsection (2) derogates from the authority of Parliament to enact laws in relation to the matters referred to in that subsection and, where such a law of Parliament and a law of a province conflict, the law of Parliament prevails to the extent of the conflict.

(4) In each province, the legislature may make laws in relation to the raising of money by any mode or system of taxation in respect of

(a) non-renewable natural resources and forestry resources in the province and the primary production therefrom, and

(b) sites and facilities in the province for the generation of electrical energy and the production therefrom, whether or not such production is exported in whole or in part from the province, but such laws may not authorize or provide for taxation that differentiates between production exported to another part of Canada and production not exported from the province.

(5) The expression "primary production" has the meaning assigned by the Sixth Schedule.

(6) Nothing in subsections (1) to (5) derogates from any powers or rights that a legislature or government of a province had immediately before the coming into force of this section."

51. The said Act is further amended by adding thereto the following Schedule:

"THE SIXTH SCHEDULE - Primary Production from *Non-Renewable Natural Resources and Forestry Resources 1.* For the purposes of section 92A of this Act,

(a) production from a non-renewable natural resource is primary production therefrom if

(i) it is in the form in which it exists upon its recovery or severance from its natural state, or

(ii) it is a product resulting from processing or refining the resource, and is not a manufactured product or a product resulting from refining crude oil, refining upgraded heavy crude oil, refining gases or liquids derived from coal or refining a synthetic equivalent of crude oil; and

(b) production from a forestry resource is primary production therefrom if it consists of sawlogs, poles, lumber, wood chips, sawdust or any other primary wood product, or wood pulp, and is not a product manufactured from wood."

Part VII - General

52. (1) The Constitution of Canada is the supreme law of Canada, and any law that is inconsistent with the provisions of the Constitution is, to the extent of the inconsistency, of no force or effect.

(2) The Constitution of Canada includes
(a) the *Canada Act 1982*, including this Act;
(b) the Acts and orders referred to in the schedule; and
(c) any amendment to any Act or order referred to in paragraph (a) or (b).
(3) Amendments to the Constitution of Canada shall be made only in accordance with the authority contained in the Constitution of Canada.
53. (1) The enactments referred to in Column I of the schedule are hereby repealed or amended to the extent indicated in Column II thereof and, unless repealed, shall continue as law in Canada under the names set out in Column III thereof.
(2) Every enactment, except the *Canada Act 1982*, that refers to an enactment referred to in the schedule by the name in Column I thereof is hereby amended by substituting for that name the corresponding name in Column III thereof, and any British North America Act not referred to in the schedule may be cited as the *Constitution Act* followed by the year and number, if any, of its enactment.
54. Part IV is repealed on the day that is one year after this Part comes into force and this section may be repealed and this Act renumbered, consequentially upon the repeal of Part IV and this section, by proclamation issued by the Governor General under the Great Seal of Canada.
55. A French version of the portions of the Constitution of Canada referred to in the schedule shall be prepared by the Minister of Justice of Canada as expeditiously as possible and, when any portion thereof sufficient to warrant action being taken has been so prepared, it shall be put forward for enactment by proclamation issued by the Governor General under the Great Seal of Canada pursuant to the procedure then applicable to an amendment of the same provisions of the Constitution of Canada.
56. Where any portion of the Constitution of Canada has been or is enacted in English and French or where a French version of any portion of the Constitution is enacted pursuant to section 55, the English and French versions of that portion of the Constitution are equally authoritative.
57. The English and French versions of this Act are equally authoritative.
58. Subject to section 59, this Act shall come into force on a day to be fixed by proclamation issued by the Queen or the Governor General under the Great Seal of Canada.
59. (1) Paragraph 23(1)(a) shall come into force in respect of Quebec on a day to be fixed by proclamation issued by the Queen or the Governor General under the Great Seal of Canada.
(2) A proclamation under subsection (1) shall be issued only where authorized by the legislative assembly or government of Quebec.
(3) This section may be repealed on the day paragraph 23(1)(a) comes into force in respect of Quebec and this Act amended and renumbered, consequentially upon the repeal of this section, by proclamation issued by the Queen or the Governor General under the Great Seal of Canada.
60. This Act may be cited as the *Constitution Act, 1982*, and the Constitution Acts 1867 to 1975 (No 2) and this Act may be cited together as the *Constitution Acts, 1867 to 1982*.

---

aspect transcending provincial competence and thereby become subject to federal jurisdiction. In wartime virtually all provincial powers may come under central control. In 1976 the SUPREME COURT OF CANADA decided that Parliament also possessed what amounted to a peacetime emergency power to impose national wage and price controls to combat serious national inflation. Unlike the American constitution, the Constitution Act contains no postulate that all local units are constitutionally equal. The Prairie provinces, for example, unlike the original 4, did not possess their lands and minerals for 25 years after their acquisition of provincial status.

Judicial interpretation has had a substantial effect on the ambit of provincial and federal powers. Until appeals to Britain were abolished in 1949, influential judges on the JUDICIAL COMMITTEE OF THE PRIVY COUNCIL often expansively interpreted provincial powers, such as those over property and civil rights, when they came into conflict with federal powers over peace, order and good government or the regulation of trade and

commerce. They sought thereby to offset the excessive centralism they perceived in the BNA Act (eg, the federal veto over any provincial statute in s90) and to preserve a viable federal system. Since 1949 the Supreme Court has pursued a more centralist interpretation. In 1980, the omission of a domestic amending formula in the BNA Act led to a constitutional crisis when PM TRUDEAU attempted unilaterally to patriate the Constitution, by the "joint address" procedure, without provincial consent. When the Supreme Court decided in Sept 1981 that his proposal was unconstitutional in the conventional sense, Trudeau relented, with "patriation" finally being achieved in Apr 1982 by federal-provincial consensus. *See also* CONSTITUTIONAL HISTORY; CONSTITUTIONAL LAW; CONSTITUTION REFERENCE. **W.H. McCONNELL**

Reading: P.W. Hogg, *Constitutional Law in Canada* (1977); W.H. McConnell, *Commentary on the British North America Act* (1977).

Constitution Reference (1981), known as the Resolution to Amend the Constitution. As a prelude to patriation of the Canadian Constitution, the Supreme Court of Canada was asked to rule upon a resolution asking the Queen to place before the British Parliament a bill that included a Charter of Rights and Freedoms, an amending formula and certain amendments to the Constitution. The majority of the Court found that the resolution could be adopted by the federal Houses and the British Parliament without provincial consent. But the majority of the Court also declared that, according to a constitutional convention, the federal resolution should have "substantial" though not necessarily unanimous provincial consent. Approval by 2 provinces (as was the case) was insufficient. Judged by convention the Resolution was unconstitutional, but because the Court may declare the existence of conventions but may not enforce them, flouting a convention can give rise to a political rather than a juridical remedy. **GÉRALD-A. BEAUDOIN**

Constitutional Act, 1791, Act of the British Parliament creating UPPER CANADA and LOWER CANADA. It came into effect on Dec 26, having received royal assent the preceding June. This Act enshrined constitutional changes that were part of that reorganization of BRITISH NORTH AMERICA which took place under the pressure of thousands of LOYALISTS seeking refuge after the American Revolution. Modelled on the earlier creation of the provinces of New Brunswick and Cape Breton in 1784, a constitutional bill was prepared by William Wyndham Grenville to ensure the development of British parliamentary institutions in the territory governed by the QUEBEC ACT of 1774. According to its author, the bill's general purpose was to "assimilate" each colony's constitution to that of Britain.

The bill had 4 main objectives: to guarantee the same rights and privileges as were enjoyed by loyal subjects elsewhere in N America; to ease the burden on the imperial treasury by granting colonial assemblies the right to levy taxes with which to pay for local civil and legal administration; to justify the territorial division of the PROVINCE OF QUEBEC and the creation of separate provincial legislatures; and to maintain and strengthen the bonds of political dependency by remedying acknowledged constitutional weaknesses of previous colonial governments. This involved bolstering the authority and prestige of the governor by making him a true representative of the imperial power, and limiting the powers of the elected colonial assemblies by creating independent legislative councils whose appointed members comprised an aristocratic body modelled on the House of Lords and devoted to the interests of the Crown (*see* CHÂTEAU CLIQUE; FAMILY COMPACT). The Act

guaranteed continuity of ownership of lands held under the SEIGNEURIAL SYSTEM in Lower Canada and created the CLERGY RESERVES in Upper Canada.

By giving Upper Canada a provincial constitution and a separate existence, and by favouring British colonization there, Britain took the first steps on the path that led, ultimately, to the creation of the Canadian Confederation. Nevertheless, many historians have considered that the Act's failure to establish RESPONSIBLE GOVERNMENT and its distribution of financial powers in favour of the appointed councils were factors contributing to the political conflict of the early 19th century. *See also* REBELLIONS OF 1837. PIERRE TOUSIGNANT

Constitutional History The CONSTITUTION ACT, 1867 (formerly the BRITISH NORTH AMERICA ACT) with its authoritative division of powers between federal and provincial legislatures, is of central importance in the Canadian CONSTITUTION, but there are other sources of constitutional principles which also apply, among them unwritten custom or convention, and British and Canadian statutes and court decisions. The unwritten convention that in order to remain in power a person appointed PRIME MINISTER or PREMIER should retain the support of the elected branch of the legislature, or that seats on the 9-member SUPREME COURT OF CANADA should be allocated regionally, are nowhere expressed in statutory form. Although not "laws" enforceable in the courts, such principles are of the utmost importance to effective constitutional government. The Supreme Court stated in 1981 (*see* CONSTITUTION, PATRIATION OF) that "constitutional conventions plus constitutional law equal the total constitution of the country." Since the courts will not enforce conventions, they can be implemented only by the people or the CROWN. A government that violated convention would almost certainly face electoral defeat or, in the extreme case, revolution.

The Crown, moreover, has the reserve power to dismiss a premier or prime minister who has clearly lost the confidence of the elected legislature and refuses to resign or have an election called. Such unwritten principles can be more important than many laws. According to British and Canadian constitutional theory, settlers bring with them to new shores those of their former laws that are appropriate to local circumstances. Such English laws as the Bill of Rights (1689), with its concept of limited constitutional monarchy, and the Act of Settlement (1701), with its doctrine of an independent judiciary, are salient features of the Canadian Constitution. So too is the Canada Election Act. From France is derived Québec's CIVIL LAW system, and combination of the French heritage with the English has resulted in Canada's having 2 official languages. From Britain comes the principle of parliamentary supremacy, modified in Canada's federal structure by the division of powers and an entrenched rights Charter, which were suggested by the classical model of the US.

Historical Overview Prior to 1663, control of the French colonies in N America was vested in chartered companies which exercised extensive administrative, lawmaking and judicial powers. It is uncertain what system of law was in effect. In 1663 France's N American possessions came under direct royal rule and the uncodified Coutume de Paris became the civil law of NEW FRANCE.

In the period of absolute monarchy, Louis XIV acted through Jean-Baptiste Colbert, who supervised colonial affairs, and his 2 local officials, the GOUVERNEUR (governor) and the INTENDANT. The governor was military commander, negotiator with the Indians and emissary to other colonial outposts. The intendant was overseer of civil administration and was responsible for settlement, finance, public order, justice and the building of public works. Although under royal rule there were no elected representative institutions, a SOVEREIGN COUNCIL, consisting of the governor, the intendant, the bishop and 5 other councillors, met weekly. From 1663 to 1675 the councillors were nominated jointly by the bishop and governor; thereafter they were chosen by the king. The council dispensed justice swiftly and inexpensively, superintended spending and regulated the fur trade and other commercial activities. Limitations, or "servitudes," exempted civil officials from ecclesiastical discipline; no government official could be excommunicated for performing his duties, whatever they might entail. The church was also powerless to impose its taxes without the consent of the civil authorities.

During the 18th century France lost its N American territories to Britain. By the Treaty of UTRECHT (1713), ACADIA was ceded to Britain, although France retained control of Île Royale (Cape Breton), Île Saint-Jean (PEI) and part of modern New Brunswick. France interpreted in a restrictive sense the grant made under the treaty, arguing that the Acadians, who lived mostly on the western fringes of the territory, continued under French sovereignty. Caught between rival European powers, the Acadians were expelled by the British in 1755. The French fortress of LOUISBOURG on Cape Breton fell to the British for the last time in 1758, the same year that the Nova Scotia Legislative Assembly (English Canada's oldest representative body) was convened in Halifax. When the SEVEN YEARS' WAR ended with the Treaty of PARIS (1763), the northern Atlantic seaboard, with the sole exception of Saint-Pierre and Miquelon, came indisputably under British rule.

In accordance with the ROYAL PROCLAMATION OF 1763, Gov James MURRAY was to extend English laws and institutions to Québec. He was instructed to govern with the assistance of a council of 8. An elected assembly was planned but did not appear. Murray's instructions also prescribed a Test Oath for officeholders which, because of its doctrinal content, no Catholic could conscientiously take. This provision would have resulted in all public offices being occupied by English-speaking Protestants, of whom there were only about 200, to the exclusion of nearly 70 000 French-speaking Catholics. Murray interpreted his instructions in such a way that he could govern through a 12-member appointed council. English was the official language, but the government was conducted in French. Catholicism was tolerated; although the British at first refused to allow a bishop to be appointed to the vacant see, they made no difficulties when Jean-Olivier Briand was consecrated bishop in 1766. The Proclamation of 1763 also recognized Indian land title and provided that Indians could relinquish their land only to the Crown and only collectively.

The substitution of British courts and laws in Québec created difficulties. The new Court of King's Bench convened only twice a year, making justice more costly and less expeditious than it had been under the Sovereign Council. With the abolition of the Coutume de Paris, the *censitaires* (tenants) on seigneuries suffered because their rents could be raised arbitrarily according to English law. Because of the Test Oath, no Catholics could practise law in the new Court of King's Bench, although they could practise in some inferior courts.

The QUEBEC ACT (1774) introduced nonrepresentative government by a colonial governor and an appointed council of 17-23 members. The Act was silent on the use of French, but a new oath allowed Roman Catholics to accept office. The council was not empowered to impose taxes, a matter separately dealt with under the Quebec Revenue Act. The SEIGNEURIAL SYSTEM was retained and French civil law was restored, supplemented by English criminal law. Although Gov Sir Guy CARLETON was instructed to introduce English commercial law as well, he did not. The Act was unpopular with Americans because of its toleration of Catholicism and because it extended Québec's SW boundary to the junction of the Mississippi and Ohio rivers, thus impeding American expansion. The Quebec Act became one of the "intolerable acts" which prompted Americans to revolt, but many historians feel its concessions helped encourage Québecois support of continued British rule.

The influx of LOYALISTS after 1783 led to the creation in 1784 of the separate colonies New Brunswick and Cape Breton from parts of Nova Scotia. In 1791 UPPER CANADA [Ontario] was separated from LOWER CANADA [Québec], with the Ottawa R forming the boundary. In Canada, by the CONSTITUTIONAL ACT, 1791, each of the two constitutive provinces was given a bicameral legislature. The nominated executive council was appointed by the governor whose responsibility was to the British COLONIAL OFFICE rather than to the people or their elected representatives. Thus, there was REPRESENTATIVE GOVERNMENT, but without the executive council being responsible to the assembly.

In the early 19th century, the appointment to office of a few intimates of various governors led to charges of government by clique (*see* CHÂTEAU CLIQUE; FAMILY COMPACT; COUNCIL OF TWELVE). In 1837, unsuccessful rebellions broke out in both provinces of Canada. In the MARITIME PROVINCES executive power was enhanced and the assembly weakened by the division of Nova Scotia. Cape Breton, which remained separate until 1820, lacked an assembly altogether and Prince Edward Island, which had possessed its own legislature from 1769 (having been joined briefly to Nova Scotia, 1763-69), was at times in danger of losing it. Newfoundland had an appointed governor and acquired a representative assembly only in 1832.

Gov Gen Lord DURHAM, who came to Canada in 1838 after the recent insurrections, came to regard the French Canadians as unprogressive and lacking a history or culture. He feared that Québec would use any independent political powers it might acquire to frustrate the policies and objectives of the established government. Preferable, he argued, would be the "fusion" of Upper and Lower Canada in a legislative union with a single government dominated by the "more reliable" English-speaking elite. The governor's appointed executive council, moreover, must enjoy the support of a majority in the elected assembly. Under the new system, the responsibility of the council ("Cabinet") would be to the elected assembly and indirectly to the electors, rather than to the Crown. Local policy would be decided at home. Matters of "imperial interest," such as constitutional changes, EXTERNAL RELATIONS, trade and the management of public lands, would remain with Britain.

The DURHAM REPORT marked the watershed between the first and second British empires, as British holdings, including Canada, began to change status, from colonies to self-governing nations. The ACT OF UNION (1840; proclaimed 1841) established equality of representation between Canada East [Québec] and Canada West [Ontario] in the common legislature (although Canada East was much more populous) in order to ensure the political ascendancy of the "British" element throughout the reconstituted province. After some hesitation, RESPONSIBLE GOVERNMENT was introduced in 1848 in Nova Scotia and in the PROVINCE OF CANADA, and was soon in effect throughout BNA. In 1849 Gov Gen Lord ELGIN courageously signed the REBELLION LOSSES BILL on the advice of his ministers, thus affirming the principle of responsible government. Elgin was also instrumental in introducing French as a language of debate in the Canadian legislature, although English was the sole official language.

The equal representation of sections made government of the Province of Canada unwieldy by promoting deadlock. By 1851 the English-speaking population outnumbered the French, and agitation began for "representation by population" instead of sectional parity. With George Brown's Reform Party energetically advocating REP BY POP, and the Conservatives opposing it, a political stalemate lasted from 1858 to 1864. In 1864 the parties formed a GREAT COALITION with the federation of BNA as its object.

The imperial authorities were coincidentally relinquishing control over Canada. Unoccupied Crown lands were surrendered to the provinces, 1840-52; the British submitted to a Canadian tariff imposed on their imported goods in 1858. In 1865, the British Colonial Laws Validity Act affirmed that no colonial law could be challenged unless it was expressly in conflict with an imperial statute intended to apply to the colony. Politicians from Canada East and West, the Maritimes and Newfoundland met at the CHARLOTTETOWN CONFERENCE in 1864 to discuss union. The QUÉBEC CONFERENCE and LONDON CONFERENCE saw further discussion, and CONFEDERATION of the provinces of Canada, Nova Scotia and New Brunswick was achieved on 1 July 1867.

At Confederation, a PARLIAMENT of 2 chambers was established, with seats in the HOUSE OF COMMONS allocated on the basis of population, while each of the existing 3 regions (Ontario, Québec and the Maritime provinces) was given equal representation (24 seats) in the SENATE. In 1915 the 4 western provinces became a full-fledged region with 24 senators, and Newfoundland received 6 in 1949. The Senate was conceived as a guardian of regional or provincial interests, but it did not play that role very effectively, especially since a federal Cabinet, drawn largely from the lower house and appointed on a regional basis, assumed that function.

Historians sometimes debate whether the federal PEACE, ORDER AND GOOD GOVERNMENT power was designed to endow Ottawa with jurisdiction over all matters not defined as exclusively provincial. If it were, federal jurisdiction would probably be enhanced, since the "powers" enumerated in s91 of the British North America Act would be presented merely to illustrate a single broad power embracing everything not given to the provinces. Under the BNA Act those broad matters appropriately treated nationally (eg, defence, post office, trade and commerce, most communications, currency and coinage, weights and measures) were centralized, whereas powers over property, local works and undertakings, municipalities, and most private law matters (eg, contracts and torts) went to the provinces. Where a conflict occurs in "concurrent" areas such as agriculture and immigration, or in any subject matter (except old age pensions, where provincial paramountcy obtains), federal law prevails.

Under the Constitution (which contains, as constituent parts, all provincial constitutions), Canadian provinces, which were added or created at various times, are not all treated as equals. Saskatchewan, for example, was precluded in its founding statute from taxing the Canadian Pacific Railway, whereas Québec and Manitoba were required to publish their laws, and allow proceedings in their courts and legislature, in both English and French. The Prairie provinces, unlike the original 4, did not own their natural resources when they entered Confederation, and only received them by transfer from Ottawa in 1930. Federal retention of such assets was defended by Ottawa on the grounds that the resources were needed for railway building and the settlement of immigrants. The Northwest Territories and the Yukon Territory possess elected legislatures but still do not own their lands or minerals, and they retain a semi-colonial dependency on the federal government.

After Confederation, some provinces advanced the "compact theory," which likened the BNA Act to a treaty that could be changed only by the unanimous consent of Ottawa and the provinces. Opponents of the theory denied its constitutionality, arguing that the final terms of the BNA Act were never ratified, since the Act was not an agreement but a statute of a superior legislature.

With the centralist Macdonald for long at the helm of the national government, premiers Honoré MERCIER of Québec and Oliver MOWAT of Ontario met in Québec City on 20 Oct 1887 with representatives from New Brunswick, Nova Scotia and Manitoba (BC and PEI did not participate) to promote "provincial rights" against an encroaching federal government. The provinces censured the use of the federal power of DISALLOWANCE, which enabled Ottawa arbitrarily to nullify any provincial law; they called for appointment of senators by the provinces and affirmed the right of the provincial Crown to exercise prerogative powers such as the pardoning power over provincial offences. Macdonald chose to portray the "malcontents" as Liberals confronting their Conservative foes in Ottawa for political reasons.

Another sharp confrontation arose when Manitoba, in 1890, purported to make English the only official language in the province, substituting, as well, a single public school system for the former Roman Catholic and Protestant schools. In 1895 the JUDICIAL COMMITTEE OF THE PRIVY COUNCIL agreed that the educational rights of the religious minority had been adversely affected, and thus enabled the minority to appeal to the federal Cabinet for redress. When the Liberals assumed office in 1896, PM Laurier settled the matter by compromise. (In the 1979 *Forest* case, the Supreme Court of Canada held the 1890 Manitoba language law invalid, casting some doubt on the legal validity of 90 years of provincial legislation, and requiring all future laws to be bilingual.)

The early 20th century saw further advances toward full Canadian independence. When WORLD WAR I began in 1914, by constitutional convention Canada was automatically included in the British declaration of war. After WWI, Canada's separate signature at the Treaty of VERSAILLES and its membership in the LEAGUE OF NATIONS symbolized its developing independence. In 1923 Hon Ernest LAPOINTE signed the HALIBUT TREATY without British participation (as formerly required), despite British objections. In 1926 Gov Gen Lord BYNG's refusal to grant a dissolution of Parliament to PM Mackenzie KING was portrayed by the latter as imperial interference in Canada's domestic affairs, although Byng's refusal was constitutional (*see* KING-BYNG AFFAIR). At the Imperial Conference in the same year, the BALFOUR REPORT described the self-governing Dominions as autonomous and equal communities within the British Empire (*see* COMMONWEALTH). In 1931 the STATUTE OF WESTMINSTER stipulated that the imperial Parliament would no longer legislate for a Dominion unless the latter requested and consented to the law. Other provisions empowered local legislatures to enact laws even if repugnant to the Colonial Laws Validity Act, and allowed Canada to legislate extraterritorially, eg, establishing shipping laws applying to Canadian vessels on the high seas or applying criminal law to Canadian military personnel serving abroad. The statute

Prime Minister Brian Mulroney signs the constitutional accord, Langevin Block, 3 June 1987 (*photo by Andrew Clark, Prime Minister's Office*).

affirmed (at least according to the provinces) that provincial jurisdiction could not be unilaterally altered by the newly sovereign federal power.

After 1931, in constitutional theory, London was no more central politically than was Ottawa or Canberra, Australia. The Crown, formerly indivisible, now became divided. In 1939 Canada made a separate declaration of war. Treaties between Canadian Indian bands and the British Crown were now deemed to be the concern of the Canadian government. The monarch became king or queen of Canada, with the GOVERNOR GENERAL acceding to all the remaining prerogative powers in 1947. In 1952 Vincent MASSEY became the first native-born governor general, and he was succeeded in 1959 by Georges VANIER. Thereafter incumbents from English- and French-speaking Canada alternated.

In 1949 a constitutional amendment enabled Parliament to make amendments solely affecting the federal power (eg, redistribution of seats in the House of Commons), with designated exceptions in sensitive areas (eg, the requirement of holding annual sessions of Parliament). Other indications of sovereignty were the Canadian Citizenship Act (1947) and the adoption of the maple leaf flag in 1965 (*see* FLAG DEBATE).

Between 1934 and 1949 Newfoundland was governed by an appointed COMMISSION OF GOVERNMENT which had full lawmaking powers. After WWII, debate arose about Newfoundland's future. Peter CASHIN, a former Newfoundland finance minister, advocated a return to Dominion status, while Joseph R. SMALLWOOD led the pro-Confederation forces. Some Newfoundlanders supported the retention of commission government. In the second of 2 referenda held in 1948 the Confederation forces prevailed, and in 1949 Newfoundland became Canada's 10th province, with 6 senators and 7 members of Parliament.

Until 1949, when overseas appeals were abolished, the British Privy Council was Canada's ultimate court of appeal, overshadowing Canadian courts. Some important appeals had been made directly from provincial tribunals to Britain without any participation by the Supreme Court of Canada (est 1875). Lords Watson and Haldane, in particular, decentralized the centralist provisions of the BNA Act, demoting the federal peace, order and good government power and expanding

provincial jurisdiction over property and civil rights. In 1929 the Judicial Committee of the British Privy Council ruled that women were legal "persons" capable of being summoned to the Senate (*see* PERSONS CASE). In 1932 the JCPC granted power over aeronautics and radio to Ottawa. In 1937, however, it eviscerated PM R.B. Bennett's "New Deal" social program (*see* BENNETT'S NEW DEAL), gravely curtailing federal power over such matters. Judicial metaphors such as "living tree" and "watertight compartments" denoted alternate phases of centralist and provincialist interpretation. In 1937 Alberta Prem ABERHART attempted to enact a Social Credit legislative program that invaded federal jurisdiction, particularly the federal power over banking. When the provincial legislation was disallowed a bitter confrontation ensued, but the courts later upheld the federal position.

The Rowell-Sirois Commission, appointed by Mackenzie King's government in 1937, made far-reaching economic recommendations for restructuring the Canadian federation (*see* DOMINION-PROVINCIAL RELATIONS). The commissioners said that Ottawa should have the exclusive right to levy personal and corporate income taxes and succession duties (concurrent fields under the BNA Act). In return, the federal government would assume all provincial debt and certain responsibilities over relief and unemployment insurance (which the court had just consigned to the provinces), and would pay the less affluent provinces a "National Adjustment Grant" enabling them to maintain services at the average national level. Québec's Tremblay Commission (1953-56), established by Prem Maurice DUPLESSIS, saw this proposal as too centralist, arguing for the principle of "subsidiarity": likening FEDERALISM to a pyramid, he suggested that as many economic functions as possible should be carried out by local organizations at the base (eg, municipalities, co-operatives, churches) with the federal government at the apex performing only those limited economic functions beyond the capacities of local groups. This concept, of course, would powerfully reinforce provincial autonomy.

The Rowell-Sirois Commission's 1940 recommendations were never really implemented, although the EQUALIZATION PAYMENTS to the provinces, begun by PM Louis ST. LAURENT after the marked centralization of powers during WWII, achieved a similar purpose. In one form or another, federal equalization payments to less wealthy provinces have continued. Although unemployment insurance was centralized by a 1940 amendment, the richer provinces (Ont, Alta, BC) objected to subsidies to the poorer provinces which they would have had to fund. The federal "spending power" was used to fund FAMILY ALLOWANCES and shared-cost programs entered into jointly with the provinces, such as OLD AGE PENSIONS and medicare. These costly social programs placed an enormous strain on all governments in the late 1970s and early 1980s, leading some politicians to question the constitutionality of universal coverage.

With the proclamation of the WAR MEASURES ACT in both world wars and during the 1970 OCTOBER CRISIS the federal Cabinet acquired all legal powers essential to cope with the existing emergencies (whether or not such powers would ordinarily fall under provincial jurisdiction); constitutionally speaking, for the duration of and in relation to the emergency, under the Act it is almost as if the constitutional division of powers did not exist.

An important constitutional development in 1969 was the OFFICIAL LANGUAGES ACT, which declared English and French to be Canada's "official languages," and extended an array of government services in both tongues to all citizens. The election of the separatist PARTI QUÉBÉCOIS in Québec on 15 Nov 1976 emphasized that the threat of SEPARATISM was real, but in a referendum on 20 May 1980 Québec voters rejected the provincial government's SOVEREIGNTY-ASSOCIATION option by a margin of 60-40%.

PM Pierre E. TRUDEAU supported continued federalism by promising Québec constitutional renewal in the event of a negative vote. After a deadlocked federal-provincial conference, he announced on 2 Oct 1980 that Ottawa proposed to entrench unilaterally the core of a new Constitution embracing a domestic amending formula and a rights charter (*see* CANADIAN CHARTER OF RIGHTS AND FREEDOMS) which would replace PM DIEFENBAKER's 1960 CANADIAN BILL OF RIGHTS. Trudeau emphasized that an amending formula had eluded federal-provincial negotiators since 1927. The controversy in the 1980s ranged Ottawa and 2 provincial allies, Ontario and New Brunswick, against the other 8 provinces. Central to the debate was whether, by convention, provincial consent was required before an amendment could be obtained from Britain affecting provincial rights, privileges or powers. In Sept 1981 the Supreme Court held that although Ottawa had the legal power to present a joint address of the Senate and House of Commons to Westminster seeking an amendment, it was improper, by convention, to do so without a "consensus" (undefined, but at least a clear majority) of the provinces. Since neither Ottawa nor the dissentient provinces had won outright, compromise was essential, and all parties except Québec reached agreement on 5 Nov 1981. Spokesmen for Québec argued that according to the "duality" principle the concurrence of both English- and French-speaking Canada was required for basic constitutional change, and that the absence of one "national" will constituted a veto. All the other parties denied the existence of the "duality" principle in the form asserted by Québec. Left unresolved for future consideration were such knotty problems as constitutional revision of the division of powers and institutional reform of the Supreme Court, the Senate and the Crown.

Québec's concurrence to the constitution was secured in June 1987 when the first ministers completed the text of the MEECH LAKE ACCORD reached earlier in the year. Québec was recognized as a "distinct society" and its legislature and government was charged with preserving and protecting the province's distinct identity. English-speaking Canadians within Québec and French-speaking Canadians outside its borders were also constitutionally acknowledged. In future, provinces were empowered to submit names acceptable to the federal government for appointment by the latter as vacancies arose in the Senate and the Supreme Court of Canada. Only when the chief justice was appointed from among the sitting members of the Supreme Court was the appointment to be an exclusively federal responsibility. Three of the 9 members of the entrenched Supreme Court were to be Québec barristers trained in the provinces distinctive civil law system. Until unanimous federal-provincial agreement for change was secured, moreover, no change was to be made to the Senate or the Supreme Court. Some people considered that this meant the end of any realistic prospect of Senate reform, although annual conferences of first ministers were to be held to consider reform of the upper house.

Where new initiatives were established by Ottawa under the federal spending power, such as a national daycare program or a minimum guaranteed annual income, provided that their alternative programs "conformed to the national objectives," provinces could get out and would receive reasonable compensation from Ottawa to fund their own programs. The admission as provinces of the Yukon or the Northwest Territories was to require the consent of all federal and provincial legislative bodies, rather than just the agreement of Parliament and 7 provinces having half the total population, as in the Constitution Act, 1982, or the simple federal statute required before that date. All provinces were also given, in addition, a share in the immigration process. In order to be entrenched, Parliament and each provincial legislature had to accept the proposed Meech Lake text as it stood within 3 years after Parliament's enabling resolution was passed. Any change in the proposed text required unanimous agreement.

Some features of the accord elicited strong criticism. Former PM Trudeau described it as being excessively decentralizing in character and as undermining the prospect of strong federal leadership. The accord was criticized by territorial residents as an instrument which could indefinitely delay their accession to provincial status, since a single provincial or federal government could prevent their admission as provinces. Aboriginal peoples charged that the accord ignored their quest for self-government.   W.H. McCONNELL

Reading: W.J. Eccles, *France in America* (1972); D. Lindsay Keir, *The Constitutional History of Modern Britain 1485-1937* (1966); Arthur R.M. Lower, *Colony to Nation* (1977); W.H. McConnell, *Commentary on the British North America Act* (1977); G.F.G. Stanley, *A Short History of the Canadian Constitution* (1969).

Constitutional Law, a branch of public law, the body of rules regulating the functioning of the state. According to the patriation decision of the SUPREME COURT OF CANADA (*see also* CONSTITUTION, PATRIATION OF) on 28 Sept 1981, the CONSTITUTION, the supreme law of Canada, comprises statutory rules and rules of the COMMON LAW (which together make up constitutional law), and conventions (usually unwritten) derived from British constitutional history which have developed through the political and constitutional experience of Canada. The courts, which administer constitutional law, recognize the conventions but do not enforce them and the conventions are not, strictly speaking, part of constitutional law.

The primary sources of Canadian constitutional law are legislative rules. They include the Constitution Acts, 1867-1982, and other documents comprising the Constitution of Canada, eg, federal and provincial statutes related to constitutional matters, orders-in-council, letters patent and proclamations. Section 52 of the CONSTITUTION ACT, 1982, provides for the Constitution of Canada to include the Canada Act, 1982, and the Constitution Act, 1982, legislative texts and decrees included in Appendix I of the latter Act, and the modifications to these legislative texts and decrees. According to the preamble of the CONSTITUTION ACT, 1867, the Canadian Constitution is similar in principle to the Constitution of the UK; therefore, Canadians have inherited the Bill of Rights of 1689, the Act of Settlement of 1701 and various other British statutes and charters. Other sources of constitutional law include case law, ie, the interpretation of the Constitution by the courts, which is just as important as the Constitution itself, especially in Canada where statutes are subject to judicial review for their constitutionality. Section 52 of the Constitution Act, 1982, provides that the Constitution overrides any incompatible provision of any piece of legislation. The JUDICIAL COMMITTEE OF THE PRIVY COUNCIL has rendered some 120 judgements on the distribution of legislative powers alone; the Supreme Court has handed down even more. Among the more important cases that have affected the Canadian Constitution are the following: in the field of the distribution of powers, the Hodge Case (local order), FORT FRANCES CASE (emergency power), Aeronautics Reference (residual power), Labour Conventions Reference (treaties), OFFSHORE MINERAL RIGHTS (resources under the sea), JONES CASE (official languages), DIONNE CASE (cablevision), MONTCALM CONSTRUCTION CASE (labour relations), ANTI-INFLATION ACT REFERENCE (peacetime emergency powers) and CONSTITUTION REFERENCE (patriation); and in the field of civil liberties, the ALBERTA PRESS ACT REFERENCE (freedom of the press), DRYBONES CASE (equality before the law), DUPOND CASE (street manifestations), MILLER AND COCKRIELL CASE (death penalty), MCNEIL CASE (film regulation) and MACKAY CASE (military offences).

The character of the Canadian Constitution reflects Canada's position as a constitutional monarchy (*see* CROWN), a parliamentary democracy and a federation. As a constitutional monarch the Queen, who is SOVEREIGN in Canada, reigns but does not rule. Executive power is effectively wielded by the PRIME MINISTER and the CABINET. The Queen, because of Canada's federal system, is represented at both levels of GOVERNMENT, federally by the GOVERNOR GENERAL and in each province by a federally appointed LIEUTENANT-GOVERNOR. In the Jan 1982 judgement of the British Court of Appeal on the *Indians of Alberta,* Lord Denning stated that although in principle the Crown is indivisible, it has become separate and divisible through practice and usage.

The conventional rules of the Canadian Constitution accurately reflect the actual exercise of executive power. For example, although the Crown can refuse to assent to or reserve assent of legislation, under constitutional law this power will not likely be exercised in future. Nowadays it is very unlikely that a governor general or a lieutenant-governor would refuse to give royal assent to a bill duly passed by Parliament or a legislature. Although possible legally, it would constitute in practice a negation of the principle of RESPONSIBLE GOVERNMENT and, as stated by the Supreme Court in the patriation case, it would be contrary to a convention of the Constitution. The Imperial Conference of 1930 ended the governor general's power to reserve a federal bill that had been adopted by Parliament; it also ended the imperial power of DISALLOWANCE in relation to federal bills.

The power of reserve and disallowance of provincial bills is, in the words of Chief Justice LASKIN, "dormant if not entirely dead." The power of disallowance was last used in 1943; the power of reserve was used as recently as 1961 in Saskatchewan, but the bill was given royal assent by the governor general. The powers of the prime minister and government officials are not unlimited, however. According to the British constitutional expert A.V. Dicey, all officials, from the prime minister to a collector of taxes, are under the same responsibility for any act done without legal justification as every other citizen is, reflecting the principle of the RULE OF LAW, which is also part of Canadian constitutional law (*see* ADMINISTRATIVE LAW).

In Canada the distinction between legislative, executive and judicial powers is not as sharp as it is in the US. Judicial power is separate in Canada, but in the Canadian parliamentary system, although the Cabinet is responsible to the legislative branch of the government, it dominates both the executive and legislative powers. Parliament comprises the Queen, as head of Canada, a SENATE and a HOUSE OF COMMONS. A well-established constitutional convention requires that the government maintain the confidence of the Commons to remain in power. If such confidence is lost, the prime minister must either resign or seek dissolution of Parliament. The government is not responsible to the Senate. On matters of constitutional amendment, the Senate only has a delaying veto of 180 days; otherwise it has the same decision-making powers as the House of Commons, although money bills must originate in the Commons. The concept of parliamentary supremacy, ie, that Parliament's powers are unlimited, originates in British constitutional law. Canada has inherited this concept in its Constitution, but under its federal system the federal and provincial governments are only sovereign within the legislative limits outlined by the Constitution, and their powers are also limited by the CANADIAN CHARTER OF RIGHTS AND FREEDOMS.

In contrast to the American system of government, the Canadian system is a parliamentary democracy in which the offices of head of government (prime minister) and chief of state (Queen of Canada) are distinct; the government is responsible to the elected Commons. In the Canadian system, the legislative and executive branches of the state are not completely separate, since most ministers are members of the elected house. Under the US presidential system, the president is both the chief of state and the head of government; reflecting the American theory of checks and balances among the 3 powers, the executive and legislative branches are more separate than in Canada, and the executive (the president) is not responsible to the Congress. The majority in the Congress does not necessarily belong to the same party as the president. The president is elected for a fixed term of 4 years and may be re-elected once. A president's tenure may be shortened only by death, resignation or impeachment, but even in these cases an election is not held until the term is complete. In Canada the House can be dissolved before the 5-year term; usually it lasts 4 years. In both systems, however, the judicial power is separate, independent and strong. In both countries a charter or bill of rights is entrenched in the Constitution, and a supreme court determines the constitutionality of laws and statutes. Although both countries are democracies, the American republic is based on the principle of popular sovereignty. The preamble to the American Constitution states, "We, the people of the United States." By contrast, the Supreme Court of Canada stated, in its decision to patriate the constitution: "At law, the Government is in office by the pleasure of the Crown although by convention it is there by the will of the people."

Canada has been a federation since 1867. Legislative, executive and judicial powers are divided between the 2 levels of government. The Constitution Act, 1867, lists areas of federal jurisdiction (eg, the postal system, criminal law, banking, navigation, defence, bankruptcy) and areas of provincial jurisdiction (eg, property and civil rights, municipal institutions). Other articles or sections allocate special powers (eg, education) and concurrent jurisdictions (eg, agriculture and immigration, old-age pensions, supplementary benefits).

Theoretically the distribution of executive power resembles that of legislative power. Judicial power is also distributed in the Constitution Act, 1867. JURISPRUDENCE in constitutional law has established the principle that Parliament and the provincial legislatures may not delegate legislative powers to each other, but that a sovereign authority can delegate powers to a subordinate body which it has created – the classic example being the relationship of the municipality to the provincial legislature. Power can also be delegated from a sovereign body (eg, Parliament or a provincial legislature) to a subordinate body of the other government. For example, Parliament has delegated to provincial commissions the power to issue permits or make regulations in areas of federal jurisdiction, such as extraprovincial motor transport or marketing.

Under the Constitution Act, 1867, the provinces have exclusive jurisdiction over the creation of civil and criminal courts and in the administration of civil and criminal justice, but Parliament has exclusive jurisdiction in respect of criminal law and procedure. Criminal law generally includes matters under criminal jurisprudence contained in legislation promoting public peace, order, security and the protection of health and morality (in certain aspects). The provinces, however, can legislate in regulatory and quasi-criminal matters. Provincial quasi-criminal legislation may be enacted to suppress conditions that may foster the development of crime.

For the administration of federal laws, Parliament may establish ADMINISTRATIVE TRIBUNALS. Parliament has also created a FEDERAL COURT under s101, and under the same section the Supreme Court of Canada was established by statute in 1875. All judges in federal courts are federally appointed, as are those under s96 of the Constitution Act, 1867, of the higher provincial courts. The judges presiding over lower provincial courts are provincially appointed.

The role of the JUDICIARY is of cardinal importance because the interpretation of the Constitution is as important as the Constitution itself. Courts give life to a Constitution, which must endure, as it cannot be amended as often as a statute can. Courts must favour the evolution of a Constitution. In a federation a supreme court plays a crucial role in the distribution of legislative powers. For example, in the US the Supreme Court centralized the Constitution, but in Canada the Privy Council generally decentralized the Constitution, although the Supreme Court has in certain areas reversed this trend. The courts also play a major role in the interpretation of the Canadian Charter of Rights and Freedoms or, in the US, the Bill of Rights.

EXTERNAL RELATIONS fall under federal jurisdiction because of federal residuary power and royal PREROGATIVE POWERS. Under s132 Parliament and the federal government were given all the desired powers to fulfil, as part of the British Empire, the obligations of Canada or any of its provinces to foreign countries arising from treaties between the empire and those countries. This section has fallen into disuse since 1931. In the *Labour Convention Reference* (1937) the judiciary established that the central authority could conclude treaties in Canada's name but that such treaties would not modify internal law (*see* TREATY-MAKING POWER). If a treaty does require a change in internal law, this must be accomplished through the enactment of a statute. The implementation of a treaty must respect the distribution of legislative powers as defined by the Constitution. Parliament implements treaties relating to federal matters; if a treaty relates to provincial matters, the provincial legislatures are responsible for implementing legislation.

In addition to the 10 provinces, Canada has 2 federal territories – the Yukon and the Northwest Territories. Under the Constitution the territories fall under the legislative jurisdiction of Parliament. They have been delegated certain important powers by Parliament. The commissioners of the respective territories are Crown representatives, and the executive exercises substantial power, but the principle of responsible government does not apply because the delegated powers can be modified, extended or withdrawn. Prior to 17 Apr 1982 the territories could have gained provincial status by a simple Act of Parliament. Now, under the Constitution Act, 1982, it is necessary that both federal houses and 7 provinces (with an aggregate of 50% of the country's population) concur in such a move.

FEDERALISM in Canada rests on a trilogy of factors: the DISTRIBUTION OF POWERS; the interpretation of these powers by the courts, who must ensure that the distribution of powers in the Constitution is not violated and that all enacted legislation is constitutional; and the formula for constitutional amendment. The Constitution of 1867 had no general amending formula. Since 1867 the provincial legislatures have had the right to amend their internal constitutions (except where they concerned the role of the lieutenant-governor), but Parliament did not gain the right to amend its internal constitution until 1949. For changes to the most important part of the Constitution it had to address the Parliament at Westminster, which would legislate a constitutional amendment if requested to by both federal houses.

From 1927 to 1981, the federal and provincial governments tried unsuccessfully to agree on an amending formula, suggestions for which have included the Fulton Formula, the Fulton-Favreau Formula, the Turner-Trudeau Formula, and the Alberta-Vancouver Formula. Named after E. Davie FULTON, the Fulton Formula provided that the Constitution was to be amendable by federal law but that no law relating to the legislative powers of a province, the assets of a province, the privileges of a province, the use of the English and French languages, the determination of representation by province in the House of Commons and the amending formula itself, was to go into effect unless it was concurred in by all provinces; that no law affecting other provisions of the Constitution should come into effect unless it was concurred in by the legislatures of at least two-thirds of the provinces, representing at least 50% of the population; that no law in relation to one or more provinces (but not all provinces) should come into effect unless accepted by each province concerned; and that no law in relation to education should come into force unless concurred in by all provinces other than Newfoundland. (A law amending education in that province was not to come into effect except with the consent of that province.) The formula also included the delegation clause, permitting provinces to delegate powers to Parliament, and vice versa.

The Fulton-Favreau Formula of 1964 (named after 2 successive federal ministers of justice, E. Davie Fulton and Guy FAVREAU) was basically a modification of the Fulton Formula; the federal amending power under s91.1, as revised, and the provincial amending power under s92.1, which had not been covered in 1961, were included in the amending formula of 1964. Both powers were defined with greater accuracy and precision. This formula was finally rejected by Québec. The delegation clause was retained.

The Victoria Charter, 1971, was an agreement reached by Canadian heads of government (with the exception of Québec's Premier Robert Bourassa) concerning constitutional reform. The Turner-Trudeau Formula contained in the Victoria Charter provided that the Constitution could be amended by a resolution of the House of Commons and Senate and by at least a majority of the provinces, which would have included each province with a population of at least 25% of the national population, at least 2 Atlantic provinces, and at least 2 western provinces having a combined population of at least 50% of all western provinces. The delegation clause was dropped. Québec agreed with the Turner-Trudeau Formula but rejected the charter because it proposed paramount power in programs related to social security. Only in 1982 did the British Parliament divest itself of its power of amendment to the Canadian Constitution. By s2 of the Canada Act, 1982 (UK), no Act of Parliament of the UK passed after the Constitution Act, 1982, can extend to Canada as part of its law. The British renounced any legislative role for Canada after 17 Apr 1982. The Constitution Act, 1982, includes a general amending formula (the Alberta-Vancouver Formula) under which an amendment requires the agreement of the federal houses and two-thirds of the provinces comprising 50% of the population. A dissenting province may opt out (*see* OPTING-OUT) of an amendment concerning a transfer of power from a provincial to a federal jurisdiction, in which case, if the amendment is related to education, or other matters, the province will receive fair financial compensation. If the amendment concerns the composition of the Supreme Court, the role of the monarchy or the amending formula itself, all 11 authorities (the federal government and 10 provinces) must agree on its adoption. On the other hand, some amendments need only the agreement of the federal government and the particular provinces concerned. In principle both Parliament and the provincial legislatures may still amend their internal constitutions.

On 30 Apr 1987 at Meech Lake and on 3 June 1987 in Ottawa, Prime Minister Mulroney and the premiers of the 10 provinces agreed on a constitutional accord termed the MEECH LAKE ACCORD to allow Québec to give a "political" adhesion to the patriation of the Constitution in 1982 and the Constitution Act, 1982. The 5 points of the accord pertain 1) to the entrenchment in the Constitution of the linguistic duality of Canada and to the distinct society of Québec; 2) to the right of a province to opt-out with compensation in national share cost programs in exclusive provincial fields, established by the federal authority by virtue of its spending power; 3) to accrued powers of the provinces in immigration; 4) to the appointment by the federal government of Supreme Court judges and senators, from provincial lists; and, 5) to the amending formula of the Constitution, the unanimity rule being extended to cover central institutions, the establishment of new provinces and the extension of existing provinces into the territories. GÉRALD-A. BEAUDOIN

Reading: G. Favreau, *The Amendment of the Constitution of Canada* (1965); P.W. Hogg, *Constitutional Law of Canada* (1977).

Constitutional Problems, Royal Commission of Inquiry on (Tremblay Commission), appointed by the Québec government under chairman Mr Justice Thomas Tremblay to study the

distribution of taxes among the federal government, the provinces, the municipalities and the school boards; the "encroachments" of the federal government into the field of direct taxation, especially its taxes on revenue, corporations and inheritances; the consequences of these "encroachments" for the legislative and administrative system of Québec and for the collective, family and individual life of its population; and generally the constitutional problems of a fiscal character. The commission's 4-volume report (1956) supported the view that the federal government was a creation of the provinces and that the role of the political regime of 1867 was to establish a framework within which English and French communities could live in a federal state. It called for greater provincial autonomy, proposing that social programs be under provincial jurisdiction. It also proposed major fiscal reforms very different from those recommended by the Royal Commission on DOMINION-PROVINCIAL RELATIONS. The report is considered a classic in-depth analysis of Québec's nationalistic and traditional approach to the federal system.

GÉRALD-A. BEAUDOIN

Construction Industry, Canada's largest industry, executes most of the construction activity in the country. It provides a wide variety of buildings, ranging from houses to skyscrapers and from schools and hospitals to factories and shopping centres, and carries out an equally wide variety of ENGINEERING construction projects, ranging from highways to nuclear-power stations and from dams and dredging to petrochemical plants and PIPELINES. Members of the construction industry put in place most of the capital investment of all other industries, governments, business and individual citizens. Thus, construction is both a production industry, providing the physical means for shelter and industrial development, and a SERVICE INDUSTRY, most work being carried out in response to orders and investment decisions of others.

The construction process involves many different functions from concept to commissioning. Owners in most cases initiate construction projects, acquire necessary sites and arrange for project financing. A design team consists of the architect or consulting engineer and their specialist subconsultants who together prepare the detailed specifications and drawings for a project's design. General or prime contractors assume responsibility for the co-ordination of construction activities and project completion. Trades or specialty contractors perform work related to the various trades, eg, mechanical, electrical, carpentry, etc. Manufacturers and suppliers include importers, wholesalers and retailers engaged in the production and merchandising of thousands of construction items.

The Modern Industry After the decrease in construction that occurred during the Great Depression, WWII brought about a substantial resurgence in activity in Canada, and noteworthy achievements during this period included construction of the synthetic-rubber plant at SARNIA, Ont, and of numerous British Commonwealth Air Training Program aerodromes. This rapid increase in wartime construction and the ability of the industry to execute it quickly and efficiently marked the establishment of Canada's modern construction industry. Construction has continued to expand throughout the postwar period and there has been a striking increase in the size and complexity of many inuividual projects. For example, the postwar housing boom saw the development of "project housing," comprising hundreds of units, of high-rise apartment buildings and complexes and of entire communities. A new

construction market developed in northern Canada with the building of EARLY-WARNING RADAR defence installations, MINING and other resource developments and transportation facilities. In southern Canada the TRANS-CANADA HIGHWAY and the ST LAWRENCE SEAWAY were finally completed. Canada has long been famous for its large-scale hydroelectric power projects (eg, CHURCHILL FALLS; JAMES BAY PROJECT); this program was expanded and augmented by thermal and nuclear-power plants. Perhaps the most striking change wrought by the construction industry in this period was the creation of new skylines in Canada's cities and towns.

By 1987 the total annual construction program in Canada amounted to over $72.3 billion (16% of the gross domestic product). Roughly 7% of all the people employed in Canada are directly engaged in construction activity. An even greater number are engaged in producing, transporting and merchandising construction materials and equipment.

For many years after the war, the regional breakdown of construction activity showed one-third or more of the total located in Ontario; about one-quarter in Québec; and one-tenth in BC. Toronto and Montréal were the main centres of construction activity, accounting for perhaps 25% of the total. Similarly, there was a quite constant breakdown by main components: residential 30%; other building construction 30%; and engineering construction 40%. Significant shifts became evident in the 1970s in favour of western Canada and of engineering construction. By 1981 the value of Alberta's construction equalled that of Ontario (both 25%); residential construction's share fell to 25% and that of engineering construction rose to nearly 50%. In 1987, $72.3 billion was spent on construction in Canada: 40.5% ($29.3 billion) for residential construction, 26.8% ($19.4 billion) for nonresidential buildings and 32.7% ($23.6 billion) for engineering construction. The Atlantic provinces accounted for 7.5% ($5.4 billion) of construction; Qué, 22.3% ($16.1 billion); Ont, 36.4% ($26.3 billion); Man and Sask, 8.1% ($5.9 billion); BC, NWT and YT, 11.6% ($8.4 billion). Alberta's share was reduced to 14.0% ($10.1 billion) but it still ranked third. Material costs accounted for 38.3% of the total (ie, $27.1 billion); labour costs, 33.3% ($24.1 billion); and other factors, 28.4% ($20.5 billion). Construction contractors took 70% of this market ($50.5 billion); others, 30% ($21.8 billion).

Over one-quarter of the total program is financed directly by government departments or agencies at the federal, provincial or municipal level. In addition to construction carried out in Canada, members of the industry have also taken on an increasing volume of business in other countries.

Construction Cycles The seasonal and cyclical fluctuations in the volume of construction have a close relationship to the overall business cycle. Therefore, because of the "multiplier effect" of construction activity on other economic sectors, public-works programs are frequently advocated in times of serious unemployment. Conversely, when governments deem that the rate of economic development should be slowed down to avoid undue inflation, they often implement cuts in public-works programs and other measures designed to curb construction.

This use of the construction industry as a regulator of the general ECONOMY has tended to accentuate the swings in the construction cycle. This instability is the root cause of the industry's major problems. A detailed study on construction instability was launched under the direction of the ECONOMIC COUNCIL OF CANADA in 1972 and there is a growing appreciation that a more steady growth rate in the construction program would be of general benefit to the industry and the economy as a whole. Progress in implementing policy recommendations to this end has been slow and the industry continues to experience rapid changes in its work load, especially on a sector or regional basis or both.

Associations The construction industry's voluntary organizations are structured along specialized lines related to a trade, product, project type, service or interest and along co-ordinated, industry-wide or sector lines. Employers' associations, professional societies and labour unions are organized and operate on the national, regional or provincial and local levels.

The principal employers' group is the Canadian Construction Assn, which has maintained its head office in Ottawa since its incorporation in 1919. The CCA represents general building and engineering contractors, trade contractors, industrial contractors, manufacturers and suppliers of construction materials and equipment and professional and service firms allied to the industry. Its membership also includes a lengthy list of provincial construction and roadbuilders' associations, national specialty contractor associations, construction labour-relations associations and local construction associations. Virtually every major component of the industry has its own national body to deal with its special interests. The traditional nature of many of the building trades and familiarity with the European guild system led to the early establishment of labour unions in the Canadian construction industry. With certain notable exceptions, the building trades unions were organized along craft lines and were affiliated with unions operating in the US or in Great Britain. Local construction-employees' groups now operate mainly under charters received from international unions with head offices in the US. Of the Canadian-based labour organizations representing construction employees, the largest is the construction branch of the Québec Federation of Labour. Advisory committees and joint committees operate at the various levels to achieve closer liaison between the construction industry, governments and other groups. At the national level, the Canadian Construction Documents Committee develops standard forms for construction contracts and guides, relating to various aspects of tendering and contract administration.

Training and Education Organized vocational training for construction careers in Canada is carried out under the APPRENTICESHIP system. Trades instruction is also available at technical schools and through correspondence courses. Construction-technician courses are commonly given at institutes of technology and special courses are available for supervisory personnel. The increasing complexity of construction operations has led to a substantial increase in the number of professionally trained individuals in supervisory and managerial positions. A number of universities have established special centres for building studies and construction engineering.   S.D.C. CHUTTER

Construction Industry, History of The first permanent structures at PORT-ROYAL were erected in 1605 by French artisans using local materials. In 1607 the first water mill in N America was erected nearby (on the L'Equille R) to assist with the grinding of the first locally grown corn. Engineering construction therefore began at the same time as residential construction and agriculture. For almost 200 years, the limited settlements of New France and Acadia were served by simple wooden structures. Small water mills or windmills provided power. Simple trails had to suffice as ROADS. Masonry construction was used occasionally in the few better houses and some churches but was mainly confined to military FORTIFICATIONS, such as LOUISBOURG and PRINCE OF WALES'S FORT.

Military engineers constructed the first public works, tiny locks, at the rapids on the Soulanges section of the St Lawrence R. These locks were started in 1779 by a British regiment, the Royal Engineers, for Governor Haldimand. The first major public work to be started in Canada was the Grenville Canal on the Ottawa R begun in 1819 and ready for use in 1834. The canal was built by another British regiment, the Royal Staff Corps, as part of the alternative military route from Montréal to Kingston, Ont, demanded after the War of 1812. The main part of the alternate route was the RIDEAU CANAL, a 200 km waterway from Bytown [Ottawa] to Kingston with 47 locks and 50 dams. It was built by hand in just 5 working seasons (1826-32) by civilian contractors and 2 companies of the Royal Sappers and Miners (UK) working under the direction of the Royal Engineers. It is still used as originally constructed. The construction of the whole canal, but especially that of its great arched dam at Jones Falls, was a stupendous achievement for the time. It was also significant in that all major works were built under contract, employing essentially the same contracting system that is in use today. The Royal Engineers made great contributions to the development of Canada (the CARIBOO ROAD in BC is one of their most remarkable achievements), but as development increased with the coming of RAILWAYS civil (ie, civilian) engineers assumed responsibility for design and Canadian contractors steadily increased their capability.

The great era of railway building began in the 1850s. A leading British contractor worked on the GRAND TRUNK PACIFIC RAILWAY, but Canadian contractors were wholly responsible for building the INTERCOLONIAL RAILWAY (1868-76) from Halifax to Montréal and later the CANADIAN PACIFIC RAILWAY, finished in 1885. The skill of Canadian contractors is shown by the Hoosac Tunnel, Mass (built 1868-74), still the longest railway tunnel E of the Mississippi. The increasing maturity of the profession was indicated by the establishment of builders' associations in Halifax (1862) and Toronto (1867).

The opening in 1860 of the Victoria Bridge across the St Lawrence R at Montréal was a noteworthy event in Canadian construction. Steam pile drivers were used to build the piers; steam-operated rock drills replaced laborious hand drilling; and steam shovels effected great changes in excavation. Mass concrete started to replace masonry, at first as Canadian-made "natural cements," which were replaced before the end of the century by portland cement (also made in Canada). The wrought iron used for the first tubular superstructure of the Victoria Bridge was replaced by structural steel at the turn of the century. Thus the main modern building materials and construction equipment were in use by the turn of the century; further construction advances were in scale rather than in kind, except for the relatively recent switch from steam to internal combustion engines for motive power.

Canal construction inevitably looms large in the history of Canadian construction because of the importance of waterways in the national economy. The fourth WELLAND CANAL, opened in 1932 after a limited start in 1913, with locks of the same size as those of the modern ST LAWRENCE SEAWAY, was another outstanding achievement. The twin-flight locks at Thorold, Ont, have long been world famous. This gigantic structure of mass concrete, with its 6 locks, is almost a kilometre long, yet it was contracted for by one notable Canadian construction firm.

Canadian contractors have introduced major innovations in many fields. Canadian hydroelectric power plants are among the largest in the world and often were built in remote locations where logistics were of supreme importance (*see* CHURCHILL FALLS; JAMES BAY PROJECT). Canadians have made some major innovations in BRIDGE construction and have used special skills in constructing buildings in confined working areas within cities. The Canadian climate has provided its own challenges and winter construction practices in this country are known and respected around the world. Outstanding work has also been done in road construction, often in isolated areas (eg, ALASKA HIGHWAY). At the start of WWII, a unique contribution of the Royal Canadian Engineers was the building of a bypass road in Surrey, England, at a speed previously unknown in the UK. The wheel had turned full circle. *See also* ARCHITECTURE; ENGINEERING, HISTORY OF; MEGAPROJECTS; URBAN DESIGN.
                                                                R.F. LEGGET

Consumer and Corporate Affairs, Department of, was established in 1967 to bring together under one minister the administering of federal policies regulating the marketplace. Its responsibilities include consumer affairs; corporations and corporate securities; combines, mergers, monopolies and restraint of trade; bankruptcy and insolvency; patents, copyrights, trademarks and industrial design; and programs designed to promote the interests of Canadian consumers. The minister, as registrar general of Canada, is the custodian of the Great Seal of Canada, Privy Seal of the governor general and the seals of the administrator and registrar general of Canada. The department is composed of 4 bureaus and 2 functional services: the Bureau of Competition Policy, which includes the RESTRICTIVE TRADE PRACTICES COMMISSION; the Bureau of Consumer Affairs, which is concerned with the fair treatment of consumers in the marketplace; the Bureau of Corporate Affairs, which regulates much of the legal framework in which business operates; and the Bureau of Policy Co-ordination. Field Operations is responsible for the implementation of programs and the Legal Branch prepares and conducts legal cases. The department's 1986-87 expenditures were $149 million, down from a peak of $261 million in 1983-84.

Consumer Credit Canadian consumers obtain consumer credit whenever they purchase goods or services on account, or whenever they borrow funds to finance purchases already made. The most common type of consumer credit arrangements involve cash loans, whose purpose is usually to finance retail purchases on instalments. These loans are usually made by financial institutions; about 85% of outstanding consumer credit takes the form of cash loans while the remaining 15% is actually made by retail vendors at the time of a sale. The goods purchased on credit are usually large items such as household furnishings and cars. In addition, cash loans to consolidate existing debts and unpaid balances on CREDIT CARDS constitute important proportions of the total amount of consumer credit. By the late 1980s, consumer credit arrangements of this type accounted for about 25-30% of all the personal indebtedness in Canada.

Today the dominant suppliers of consumer credit in Canada are the banks, either through instalment loans carried directly on their own books or through the credit-card plans they operate. Mortgage and TRUST COMPANIES also provide consumer credit although they are relatively new entrants to the business and account for a much smaller proportion of the total consumer credit market. CREDIT UNIONS and CAISSES POPULAIRES are also major suppliers of consumer credit, but these institutions deal exclusively with their members and have traditionally offered loans at lower rates than those charged by other financial institutions.

Consumer loan and finance companies are financial intermediaries specializing in the provision of both consumer credit and the wholesale financing of consumer durable goods. Some firms of this type, known as acceptance companies, are owned by automobile or other manufacturers. Many large retailers also own and manage finance companies to serve the credit needs of their customers. Finance companies have declined in importance since 1955. At that time, they accounted for over 30% of the consumer credit market; now their share is approximately 7%. Life-insurance companies also provide consumer credit by means of policy loans – loans to policyholders secured by the cash value of their life-insurance policies.

Apart from credit unions and caisses populaires and some mutually owned life insurance companies, the suppliers of consumer credit are profit-oriented firms. These lenders will extend credit, if it is profitable, to any class of client, but are reluctant to extend credit to clients whom they regard as presenting either a low potential for profit or a higher than normal risk. Consequently, disadvantaged minorities sometimes find it difficult to obtain consumer credit because lenders regard these borrowers either as less profitable or more risky. Because credit unions and caisses populaires are co-operative organizations founded on a self-help principle, they will sometimes extend consumer credit in situations where the other lenders are unwilling. Also, within limits defined in their policies, life-insurance policy loans are made at the sole discretion of policyholders.

The principal advantage of credit is that it allows consumers to purchase and use an item before they have the funds to pay for it completely. Through consumer credit, goods or services can be obtained with someone else's money for a price, ie, INTEREST. Borrowers determine the size of monthly payments by choosing the terms of the loan. A second advantage of using consumer credit is that responsible borrowers have the opportunity to establish a good credit rating, making it easier for them to obtain credit for future dealings. The principal disadvantage of consumer credit is that some persons are tempted to borrow more than their earning power allows them to repay readily, with the result that they can become so heavily indebted that they have difficulty in meeting the instalment payments on their loans.

WILLIAM T. CANNON AND EDWIN H. NEAVE

Consumer Law, that branch of law concerned with the supply of goods and services in the most comprehensive sense for the personal use or consumption of individuals and their families. It differs from COMMERCIAL LAW in that in commercial transactions, the participants engage in such transactions for the purpose of profit or otherwise in the course of a business. Consumer law is barely 25 years old. Its growth reflects the tremendous changes in life-styles and in the products and services offered in the modern marketplace since WWII. Some of the important factors contributing to the rise of consumerism are the transition in N America from an agrarian to a predominantly urban life-style, mass production and the proliferation of new and often very complex products, a more affluent society with greater discretionary incomes, and the phenomenal growth of consumer credit.

Concerns about the vulnerability of consumers are not new; significant traces of it are found in the Bible (in the condemnation of usury, for example) and throughout medieval and modern European history. In Canada, both the Interest Act and the Food and Drugs Act, to give 2 important examples, originated in 19th-century concerns. Consumer problems today are more numerous and complex than those faced by consumers before WWII, and in most cases cannot be solved by an individual without governmental or other outside assistance.

At the federal and provincial levels, departments or ministries of consumer affairs and consumer-protection bureaus were rapidly established from about 1965 onwards. The federal Department of CONSUMER AND CORPORATE AFFAIRS was established in 1967. The institutional changes have been accompanied by the adoption of much new consumer-protection legislation and the revision of older legislation. Generally speaking, existing legislation is designed to promote one or more of the following objectives.

Protection Against Dangerous Products Federal examples of this type of legislation include the Food and Drugs Act, the Hazardous Products Act, the Motor Vehicle Safety Act and the Motor Vehicle Tire Safety Act. Consumer protection is achieved by a variety of means, such as prohibiting the sale of dangerous, unsafe or adulterated products, limiting sales to prescribed outlets and on prescription, or by setting standards of safety and purity.

Protection Against Fraudulent and Deceptive Practices The federal Weights and Measures Act is an early example of this type of legislation. More recent examples include the Competition Act with its important provisions concerning misleading advertising. From 1974 onwards a substantial number of the provinces also adopted "trade practices" or "business practices" Acts with the same objectives but employing different enforcement techniques.

Protection Against Unconscionable Contracts Many modern contracts are standardized and sometimes contain harsh or unreasonable terms. The average consumer would not know of their existence and would be powerless to change them even if he or she knew they were there (*see* CONTRACT LAW). Legislation directed against this and related types of abuse include the previously mentioned trade practice Acts, as well as warranty provisions in the provincial consumer-protection Acts and Part V of the federal Bills of Exchange Act. The latter provisions deal with the use of negotiable instruments in consumer credit sales.

Better Access to Information Modern consumers are not always given sufficient information to make an informed choice between competing products or services, or else the information is presented in a confusing form. The "truth in lending" provisions in the provincial consumer-protection Acts and the federal Banking Act are designed to provide the needed information in consumer-credit contracts. Important disclosure requirements with similar objectives are found in the federal Consumer Packaging and Labelling Act and the Textile Labelling Act.

Improved Sources of Advice and Access to Conflict Resolution Agencies Provincial consumer-protection bureaus have been created to provide general advice on consumer problems and to receive complaints. Community legal service clinics (now found in large cities across Canada) and, to a lesser extent, provincial legal aid plans provide legal advice and other forms of assistance to those who cannot afford a private lawyer. At the judicial level the jurisdiction of the SMALL CLAIMS COURTS has been substantially increased with respect to the size of claims; also noteworthy are the important procedural innovations introduced in the Québec Access to Justice Act of 1971 and the Class Actions Act (the first in Canada) adopted in 1978.

This description of postwar legislative developments may leave the impression that the modern Canadian consumer is well protected. The appearance is unfortunately misleading, and the picture is not as encouraging as a recitation of the legislation may suggest. The principal difficulty is that much of the legislation is only weakly enforced or not enforced at all. Some of the legislation is also poorly drafted. Most of the provincial consumer-protection agencies have always suffered from inadequate funding; since the early 1980s the inadequacy has become chronic and both the federal and provincial governments have reduced or eliminated important programs altogether.

This anticlimax to the postwar period of intense legislative activity is explained by some critics on the ground that much of the legislation was never really needed or that, in some cases, it went too far. A more persuasive explanation is that consumers are not politically a cohesive group and cannot match opposing interest groups in effectiveness and resources, particularly during periods of economic adversity. JACOB S. ZIEGEL

Consumer Price Index, a monthly measure of changes in the retail prices of goods and services purchased by Canadians in communities of 30 000 or more across the country. The index is based on the shopping "basket" of 375 goods and services (excluding commodities for personal benefit, eg, education or health care, which are financed by government) which, in 1967, families of 2-6 people with annual incomes of $4000-$6000 would buy. The index is also "weighted," emphasizing price changes in food and housing. The CPI is published monthly for Canada and for 15 major cities, using 1971 as a base year (1971=100). The base year changes about every 10 years. The CPI in Canada has risen dramatically but erratically since WWII – 50% from 1945 to 1951; 50% from 1951 to 1971; 137% from 1971 to 1981 and 136.4% from 1981 to 1986. Generally, the CPI is used in cost-of-living allowance clauses and in indexing of income taxes and social-security benefits.

Consumer Standards are documents describing acceptable characteristics or usage for products, materials and services used by individual consumers. They may specify dimensional, performance or safety requirements for household products. In Canada, standards are published by specialized private and government organizations grouped in the National Standards System, co-ordinated by the Standards Council of Canada. Standardization begins when public needs are recognized and involves field and laboratory research. The detailed work of writing a consumer standard is performed by volunteers representing a balance of all groups having an interest in the particular product, material or service. Such standards are known as consensus standards, as their final acceptance depends on substantial agreement among the participants. Standards are usually applied voluntarily. If governments pass laws making usage mandatory, they often simply refer to consensus standards, rather than specifying detailed technical requirements. The development of a consumer standard is one of the most difficult tasks of standardization. Part of the difficulty is identifying precisely the purpose of a standard for a particular product. For example, except for those regulating safety of operation, no Canadian standard yet exists for television sets because of the difficulty of agreeing on the requirements that the standard should cover.

Consumer groups (eg, the CONSUMERS' ASSOCIATION OF CANADA) are actively involved in the standardization process. Consumer representatives have been participating in standards-writing groups or committees since the 1950s. Standardization professionals generally agree on the necessity of having adequate consumer representation during the preparation of standards affecting consumer products. Because of the somewhat limited role consumer representatives have had in standards-writing committees, and because of consumers' ever-growing demands to be more involved in the standards-writing process, consumer advisory panels have been set up. Each panel consists of 30-40 individuals who meet regularly to study, comment and make recommendations regarding a particular consumer standard. Through the Standards Council of Canada, consumer representatives also participate in international standardization work. They are represented on the Committee on Consumer Policy (COPOLCO), a committee of the International Standards Organization (ISO).

In Canada one of the better-known series of consumer standards pertains to children's clothing sizes, prepared by the then Canadian Government Specifications Board (CGSB, now Canadian General Standards Board) at the request of the Consumers' Association of Canada. This series demanded one of the most exhaustive technical investigations ever carried out in Canada prior to the publication of a consumer standard. Research culminated in 1969 with the publication of 75 CGSB standards specifying "Canada Standards Sizes" for children's clothing. Use of these standards is entirely voluntary but the benefits are clear: they help reduce buyer frustration, facilitate ordering by mail or telephone and reduce the need to return clothing because of poor fit.

Many other far-reaching consumer standards are legislated by government. Legislation regulating WEIGHTS AND MEASURES has been in effect since 1872, when reference was made to British standards. Today's law stipulates that "all units of measurement in Canada shall be determined on the basis of the International System of Units determined by the General Conference on Weights and Measures," although provisions are made for use of the imperial system (*see* METRIC CONVERSION). The Packaging and Labelling Act specifies that packages for food and nonfood products intended for consumption must carry a label showing the name, nature, volume and weight of the product along with the name and address of the manufacturer. Federal departments of health and welfare, agriculture and CONSUMER AND CORPORATE AFFAIRS share responsibilities in administering food standards and FOOD LEGISLATION. Agriculture Canada is responsible for enforcing government standards affecting the quality and condition of agricultural food products and the wholesomeness of meats and meat products. Meats are graded into different classes, thereby indicating that standards have been met. Health and Welfare Canada is chiefly concerned with enforcing standards specifying the composition and wholesomeness of nonagricultural foods and food products. It also administers the Food and Drugs Act and Regulations, which set minimum standards for various products. The Act is intended to protect the public against health hazards and fraud in the sale and use of foods, drugs, cosmetics and medical devices (*see* SAFETY STANDARDS). Among other things, this exhaustive Act prohibits the sale of foods, drugs or cosmetics manufactured under unsanitary conditions; of any article of food that contains any poisonous or harmful substance; of drugs that do not perform according to prescribed standards; and of cosmetics that may cause injury to health. The Dept of Consumer and Corporate Affairs is responsible for investigating economic fraud concerning food and for administering the packaging, labelling and advertising of food products.   R.L. HENNESSY

Consumers' Association of Canada (CAC), a voluntary, nonsectarian, nonprofit, nongovernmental organization known until 1962 as the Canadian Association of Consumers. The CAC was formally est in 1947 as the outgrowth of successful efforts of the federal WARTIME PRICES and TRADE BOARD to enlist (1941) 56 various women's organizations to monitor prices in aid of wartime rationing. In 1961 the association expanded its membership to include men.

CAC volunteers serve their communities across Canada in over 70 local organizations affiliated with provincial organizations which are in turn affiliated with CAC National. CAC's policies are developed by its members and are administered by a board of directors elected annually from among the membership. The board maintains the National Office in Ottawa with its 4 directorates: association policy and activities; finance and administration; publications and testing (responsible for the magazine *Canadian Consumer/Le consommateur canadien*, CAC's testing laboratory, research and marketing); and regulated industries program (established 1973 to intervene before regulating tribunals and encourage responsiveness to consumer interests in industries under government regulatory supervision).

The CAC has helped achieve change in many areas, including the ban on use of DDT and other long-life pesticides; removal of federal tax on prescription drugs; development and use of safety closure for drugs; passage of the Packaging and Labelling Act; establishment of the Food Prices Review Board; many regulations under the Hazardous Products Act; lowered speed limits; safety standards for school buses; nonsmoking areas in public conveyances; warnings on tobacco products; elimination of sales tax on building materials; and decreases in proposed telephone rate increases. The association in 1987 was reluctant to endorse the Canada-US trade agreement since its specific content was unknown. The CAC wished to ensure that such an agreement would substantially benefit consumers.   MARILYN LISTER

Contact (1952-54) was a mimeographed "little magazine" of poetry, the third journal founded by Toronto poet Raymond SOUSTER. Its predecessors were *Direction* (1943-46) and *Enterprise* (1948). It came into existence as an alternative to John SUTHERLAND'S NORTHERN REVIEW, which assumed a traditional direction after Sutherland's conversion to Roman Catholicism; Souster, with his close associates Louis DUDEK and Irving LAYTON, felt that a more experimental magazine was needed. *Contact* was open to young Canadian writers, but also published American and European poets such as Charles Olson, Robert Creeley, Denise Levertov and Jean Cocteau. *Contact*'s influence was carried on by CONTACT PRESS (1952-67).   GEORGE WOODCOCK

Contact Press (1952-67), founded as a poets' co-operative by Louis DUDEK, Raymond SOUSTER and Irving LAYTON who were generally dissatisfied with the slight opportunities for publication available to Canadian poets. Contact went on, in the course of its 15-year history, to become the most important SMALL PRESS of its time. Launched at the mid-century, it published all the major Canadian poets of the period, and transformed literary life and small-press activity in Canada by its openness to a variety of poetic styles and its assertiveness of the poet's role in the production of his own work. Beginning before subsidies and government aid to Canadian BOOK PUBLISHING had become a mainstay of such activity, Contact was a self-financed act of faith on the part of its founders. While its main thrust was in publishing the new work of individual poets, it produced a milestone anthology, *Canadian Poems 1850-1952*, co-edited by Dudek and Layton in 1952, and an avant-garde manifesto in Souster's selection of young poets published as *New Wave Canada: The New Explosion in Canadian Poetry* (1966). This was a successor to Souster's *Poets 56* which had featured young poets in response to Dudek's query "Où sont les jeunes?" Essentially a "no-frills" press, Contact published handsome, workmanlike books with, on occasion, a mimeographed pamphlet. Its writers ranged from F.R. SCOTT, one of the early moderns, to the newest wave represented by Margaret ATWOOD, George BOWERING and John NEWLOVE.
      MICHAEL GNAROWSKI

Reading: Michael Gnarowski, *Contact Press 1952-1967* (1970).

Contemporary Arts Society (Société d'art contemporain) was formed Jan 1939 to promote public awareness of modern art in Montréal. Membership was open to all artists of "non-academic tendencies," and the initial 25 members included Paul-Émile BORDUAS, Fritz BRANDTNER, Stanley COSGROVE, Louis MUHLSTOCK, Goodridge ROBERTS, Jori Smith and Philip SURREY. John LYMAN, a prominent Montréal painter and critic, was the society's founder and first president. In May 1939 the CAS began to admit nonartist associate members, many of whom were francophone art teachers, critics and collectors. This transformation from an essentially anglophone group continued in 1943 when Alfred PELLAN and Borduas were allowed to bring their young followers into the society as exhibiting but nonvoting junior artists. These new members included Marcel BARBEAU, Léon Bellefleur, Pierre GAUVREAU, Fernand LEDUC and Jean-Paul RIOPELLE.

Lyman did not conceive of the CAS as an exhibiting organization, but many members realized that by banding together it would be easier to get exhibition space and to lobby for attention at the conservative Art Assn of Montreal (now the Musée des beaux-arts de Montréal). In May 1939 the Society sponsored "Art of Our Day," a survey of modern European art in Montréal collections. In Dec it held the first annual members' show at a commercial gallery in the city, though many subsequent shows were hung in the Art Assn itself. Most of the early anglophone members of the CAS could be broadly described as French-influenced post-impressionists. Roberts was one of the most respected painters within this group, but as Borduas and Pellan rose to prominence in the early 1940s, the society's exhibitions were increasingly dominated by abstraction. Borduas's personal influence also grew steadily, to the vexation of some conservative anglophone members and Pellan's circle of admirers. Although the CAS was a dynamic and forward-looking artists' organization in Canada during the 1940s, it received little attention outside of Montréal. Jack HUMPHREY and Miller BRITTAIN from Saint John were the only non-Québec artists to join. The National Gallery of Canada, which played an important role in promoting the GROUP OF SEVEN, gave it no support.

By 1945 the CAS included virtually every innovative and ambitious painter in Montréal. The size, diversity and growing divisions within the society made it increasingly difficult to govern or direct. In an effort to save the organization in 1948, Borduas was elected president, but he was met by a storm of protest from members who considered him too radical (he was circulating draft copies of REFUS GLOBAL at the time). Sensing he would be unable to govern, Borduas resigned from the presidency and the CAS the day after his election. Shortly thereafter, Pellan and several of his supporters left. Lyman's coalition of artists must be considered a success: many artists found mutual support and encouragement in the society, and through its lectures, exhibitions and lobbying, it greatly increased public awareness of modern art in Montréal. *See also* PAINTING.

CHRISTOPHER VARLEY

Reading: D. Burnett and M. Schiff, *Contemporary Canadian Art* (1983); J. Russell Harper, *Painting in Canada* (1977); J. Murray, *The Best Contemporary Canadian Art* (1987); D. Reid, *A Concise History of Canadian Painting* (1973); Christopher Varley, *Contemporary Arts Society* (1980).

Contemporary Verse (1940-52), poetry magazine founded by Alan Crawley in N Vancouver. It appeared when there were few literary magazines of any kind in Canada. Because Crawley was blind and all work submitted had to be read to him, editing was difficult, but he maintained a high standard while admitting a wide variety of poets; all he asked was that their work be "serious in thought and expression and contemporary in theme, treatment and technique." The writings of more than 120 poets were printed; contributors included leading figures of that vital, formative time in Canadian writing, but also new poets, some of whom later became distinguished. After 39 issues Crawley felt *Contemporary Verse* had fulfilled its role. More than 20 years after *Contemporary Verse*'s termination, *CV/II* was founded in 1975 as its successor; Dorothy LIVESAY, who had helped Crawley with *Contemporary Verse*, was one of its founders. GEORGE WOODCOCK

Continental Bank of Canada, with head offices in Toronto, began operations as a subsidiary of a finance company, IAC Limited (fd 1925 as Industrial Acceptance Corp Ltd). In 1981 it absorbed IAC and was chartered as a bank. In 1986 the company had revenues of over $650 million and assets of $5.5 billion (ranking 15th among financial institutions in Canada). In Nov of that year Lloyds Bank of Canada took over ownership of the Continental Bank, prompting a parliamentary debate because according to the Bank Act a Schedule A bank cannot be sold to a Schedule B bank. Lloyds finally purchased 90%; the remaining 10% included $18 million in loans to the energy sector, Continental's Latin American loan portfolio and its leasing operations.

DEBORAH C. SAWYER

Continental Divide, also known as the Great Divide, is the line following the HEIGHT OF LAND that separates areas drained by rivers that flow to opposite sides of the N American continent. In Canada, the water flowing in rivers eventually reaches the sea in either the Arctic, Atlantic or Pacific oceans. The line dividing rivers flowing W to the Pacific from drainage to the Arctic and Atlantic is easiest to visualize, since it lies along the main ranges of the ROCKY MTS. Often it is convenient to use such natural boundaries for human organization and the ALBERTA-BRITISH COLUMBIA border follows the divide for a considerable distance, as does the border between the YUKON and NORTHWEST TERRITORIES. The divide running across the interior of Canada is low and less obvious. This line starts from a point somewhere in the COLUMBIA ICEFIELD of the Rockies from which the 3 axes of the Continental Divide diverge. It follows a line through southern Alberta and SASKATCHEWAN, N of which drainage flows to the Arctic through the PEACE, ATHABASCA and MACKENZIE rivers, or to HUDSON BAY by the N and S SASKATCHEWAN and NELSON rivers. Rivers S of this line are part of the Missouri-Mississippi system. The divide swings into the US south of the RED R which flows N into MANITOBA. The divide continues into Canada, separating drainage going N and that entering N into GREAT LAKES-ST LAWRENCE R basin. Along the much-eroded SHIELD in QUÉBEC and Labrador the

divide is indistinct, permitting the diversion and transfer of water from rivers south of the divide to south-flowing rivers, as developed in the JAMES BAY PROJECT. Although the divide is used as the Québec-Labrador border, the low relief along which the line is presumed to lie makes it hard to demarcate on the ground. *See also* LABRADOR BOUNDARY DISPUTE. DOUG FINLAYSON

Continentalism is a term used to describe the theory of closer ties (eg, in the form of closer trade links, energy sharing or common water-use policies) with the US. An impressive number of the crucial turning points in Canadian political history have pitted the forces of NATIONALISM against those of continentalism. Washington's abrogation in 1866 of the RECIPROCITY Treaty of 1854 deprived Canadians of the considerable access they had enjoyed to the US market, and so contributed to the BNA colonies' decision to federate in order to solve their economic problems. The celebrated NATIONAL POLICY of 1879 was Sir John A. MACDONALD's response to his failure to achieve his preferred policy, a free-trade arrangement with the US. When the government of Sir Wilfrid LAURIER proposed signing a free-trade treaty with the US, it was decisively defeated in the 1911 election by the Conservatives, who exploited anti-American nationalism.

Much of Canadian development can be seen as the product of a dynamic interaction between forces pressing for national autonomy and those pushing for continental integration. Although the extreme form of Canadian continentalism advocates outright political absorption of Canada by the US, such positions have been argued only by fringe elements since the annexation movement died out as a significant political force in the 19th century. The best articulation of current continentalist thinking is in the writings of Canadian mainstream economists who have identified a goal and a program concerning Canada's relationship with the US. The goal is maximum continental integration. "I believe that closer integration of the two economies into one continental economy would be beneficial to both countries, and would involve no loss of any Canadian nationalist objectives worth pursuing," wrote the late Harry Johnson, Canada's pre-eminent economist, in 1965. The program consists essentially of opposition to policies that put obstacles in the way of FOREIGN INVESTMENT and strong advocacy of tariff reduction to the point of achieving continental free trade.

Unrestricted free trade is another important component of continentalism: "A totally free trade situation has to be seen as the best answer to Canada's industrial concerns," since "in a single step our living standards would be raised permanently to a new level," the ECONOMIC COUNCIL OF CANADA suggested in 1975.

Strong hostility to nationalism is a third characteristic of continentalism. Nationalism complicates CANADIAN-AMERICAN RELATIONS, in the opinion of the Canadian-American Committee, an active lobby for American and Canadian conglomerates. "With economic nationalism once again increasing in Western Europe and in other parts of the world, Canada and the United States can ill afford to indulge in measures which involve sacrificing the benefits of economic interdependence," the CAC wrote in 1971. Interdependence, the operative concept, is the natural economic state with which governmental policy should not interfere. A key mechanism for ensuring interdependence is the maintenance of a common market for capital without regard for which country controls the dominant corporations.

Continentalism is not merely an economic phenomenon. Culturally, the dissemination of

American values in Canada through the mass media plays a powerful role in instilling American values and attitudes in the Canadian psyche. Canada's integration into US defence planning and the American military-industrial complex was institutionalized by the North American Air Defence command (NORAD) of 1958 and the Defence Production Sharing Arrangement of 1959.

The politics of continentalism is a complex product of the interactions of the American and Canadian governments, corporate interests, public opinion and political parties. Following the 1971 blow to N American harmony provoked by Pres Richard Nixon's drastic program of PROTECTIONISM, Ottawa responded with a series of nationalist measures designed to protect Canadian interests, eg, the FOREIGN INVESTMENT REVIEW AGENCY, the CANADA DEVELOPMENT CORPORATION and PETRO-CANADA. The unveiling of the ambitious NATIONAL ENERGY PROGRAM in 1980 represented the farthest point to which the nationalism of the Trudeau period went (*see* ENERGY POLICY). By the late 1980s, the reactions to these policies from both American and Canadian interests had moved the Canadian pendulum back again toward continentalism.

Historically dramatic was the shift of the Conservatives beginning in the 1970s from the nationalist position, last espoused by John DIEFENBAKER, to one that is even more continentalist than that of the Liberals. Conservative PM Brian MULRONEY and his senior Cabinet members have adopted continentalist positions favouring virtually unrestricted American investment, furthering the continental military planning for space-age weaponry and, most notably, negotiating in 1987 a FREE TRADE agreement with the US intended to create a N American energy market, to abolish all tariffs and to accelerate the expansion of US capital throughout the Canadian services industry. In response to what he saw as a "sell out" that gave Canadian business few benefits, John TURNER, Trudeau's successor as Liberal leader, came out against Mulroney's deal with the Reagan administration, and so brought his party back to a position approximating the nationalism of the NDP.

While it has been subjected to far less academic analysis than its opposing ideology, nationalism, continentalism must be recognized as a force that continues to have a powerful impact on Canada's POLITICAL ECONOMY. *See also* ECONOMICS.

STEPHEN CLARKSON

Contraception, *see* BIRTH CONTROL.

Contract Law A contract is a legally binding agreement between 2 or more persons for a particular purpose. In general, contracts are always formed on the same pattern. A person offers to give another person something (eg, to deliver an item in return for a certain price); to provide a service (eg, to work for a certain salary); or to refrain from doing something (eg, not to compete for a certain time in return for compensation). If the offer is accepted, the contract is then valid in principle. A contract is, above all, an instrument for the economic exchange of goods and services. The most common types of contracts are the contract of sale, whereby a person acquires the ownership of property in return for payment of a certain price; lease and hire of services, whereby a person offers his services to another in return for remuneration; and lease and hire of things, whereby a person is temporarily granted the enjoyment of property (eg, an apartment), in return for a price (rent).

Unlike other agreements, a contract is considered to be a binding promise; if one of the parties fails or refuses to fulfil its promise, eg, to pay the agreed price, to provide the rented space, or pay the employee's salary, without a valid reason recognized by law, the party suffering the consequence of this breach of promise may call upon the courts either to force the defaulting party to carry out its promise (specific performance) or to demand compensation in the form of damages. Québec CIVIL LAW and Canadian COMMON LAW follow similar rules in this regard: a contract legally entered into represents a legal bond between the parties. Parties are free to contract whenever and for whatever reason they wish. The only limits to absolute contractual freedom are certain restrictions imposed by legislation and by accepted ethics. Contracts contrary to a statutory law such as the Canadian CRIMINAL CODE are null and void. The same is true for a contract, eg, a work contract for a professional killer or a prostitute, that goes against accepted ethics. CIVIL CODE regulations governing contracts in Québec are derived mainly from French civil law which is in turn derived from Roman law. These rules are written and codified in sections of the Québec Civil Code. In other provinces, regulations governing contracts are based on the jurisprudence of British common law. Many provinces, however, have adopted laws codifying the rules of certain contracts, particularly sales contracts. Although Canada's 2 major legal systems differ in certain respects, in contract law the practical solutions they provide are very similar.

Conditions To be valid and therefore legally binding, 5 conditions must be met. The first is the mutual consent of both parties. No one can be held to a promise involuntarily made. When consent is given by error, under physical or moral duress, or as a result of fraudulent practices, the contract may be declared null and void at the request of the innocent party. The second is contractual capacity – the ability to keep the promise one has made. A young child, a person suffering from a serious mental disorder and sometimes even a minor are all considered incapable of contracting. The third condition is that the contract should have a purpose; it must concern a specific and agreed-upon good or service. The fourth condition is "lawful cause" in civil law and "consideration" in common law. In this area technical differences arise between the 2 legal systems. Briefly, however, according to this fourth condition, the promise made must be serious and each promise made by one of the parties must find a corresponding, but not necessarily equivalent or equal, promise made by the other party. Thus a person may legally sell goods at a price that does not represent their actual market value. The fifth condition, which is not required in all cases, is the adherence in certain cases to formalities provided by law. In general, this condition holds for contracts that may have enormous consequences for the parties, or those that must be made public.

Sanctions Parties to a valid contract are always bound to carry out their promise. If they do not, the other party is free to go to court to force them to do so. At times, the court may order the defaulting party to do exactly what he has promised. Civil law provides more readily for the forced execution of promises than common law, in which specific performance is still an exception to the rule (*see* TORTS; DELICTS). Sometimes the courts award financial compensation in the form of damages equal in value to the loss suffered and profits lost as a result of the breach of promise, but this loss and profit must be directly related to the unfulfilled promise. Furthermore, the courts award only damages equal to those benefits that the parties might reasonably have expected to receive at the time the agreement was concluded.

Increasingly, provincial and federal legislatures are acting to protect citizens against certain contractual abuses. CONSUMER LAW, in which rules and standards are imposed to suppress FRAUD, to avoid forced sales and to protect the consumer against dishonest practices, is an example of this type of action. JEAN-LOUIS BAUDOUIN

Convention of 1818 (Convention of Commerce), 20 Oct 1818, describing the boundary between BNA and the US as a line from the farthest NW point of Lake of the Woods "north or south, as the case may be" to the 49th parallel and thence west along the parallel to the "Stony" [Rocky] Mts. The area west of the Rocky Mts was to be "free and open" to either Britain or the US for the next 10 years. In 1827 this period was indefinitely extended, but it was ultimately terminated by the 1846 OREGON TREATY. *See also* TERRITORIAL EVOLUTION. N.L. NICHOLSON

Convey, John, metallurgist (b at Craghead, Eng 29 Mar 1910). Having immigrated to Alberta in 1929, he later moved to Ontario, where he earned a PhD in atomic physics at U of T in 1940. After service in the navy during WWII and a spell of teaching at U of T, he went to Ottawa in 1948 to become chief metallurgist at the federal government's Mines Branch, later renamed the Canada Centre for Mineral and Energy Technology. He served as director 1951-73, and it was under his leadership that the extensive laboratories became an important scientific base for national research into mining, metallurgy and energy resources. A man of wide interests and a talented raconteur and public speaker, he has received many honours, including the Blaylock Medal of the Canadian Institute of Mining and Metallurgy, fellowship in the American Soc for Metals, the Jean P. Carriere Award of the Standards Council of Canada and the John Jenkins Award of the Canadian Standards Assn. He retired from the public service in 1974. W.M. WILLIAMS

Conway, Brian Evans, chemistry professor (b at Farnborough, Eng 26 Jan 1927). After obtaining his doctorate from U of London in 1949, Conway worked as a research associate at the Chester Beatty Cancer Research Inst in London. From 1955 until 1957 he was assistant professor at U of Penn and since then has been with the Dept of Chemistry, U of Ottawa. He has published over 260 scientific research articles, is a senior editor of 2 series, *Comprehensive Treatise of Electrochemistry* and *Modern Aspects of Electrochemistry*, and has written *Electrochemical Data*, *Electrode Processes* and *Ionic Hydration in Chemistry and Biophysics*. A fellow of the RSC, he can be called the dean of electrochemistry in Canada. R.G. BARRADAS

Cook, George Ramsay, historian (b at Alameda, Sask 28 Nov 1931). Educated at the U of Manitoba (BA), Queen's (MA) and U of T (PhD), he taught first at U of T and is currently at York U as a professor of history. One of Canada's best-known historians, Cook has written widely in the area of political and social history including such works as *John W. Dafoe and the Free Press* (1963), *Canada and the French Canadian Question* (1966), *The Maple Leaf Forever* (1971) and *The Regenerators* (1985). Concern for the nature of Canadian NATIONALISM dominates many of Cook's writings and is expressed in 2 major themes. The first is the importance of ideas in the shaping of the national identity, including the force of historical understanding. The second is the necessity of mutual understanding between French and English in Canada. Cook's writings have done much to contribute to English Canada's understanding of the complexities of Québec thought. D.R. OWRAM

Cook, James, explorer (b near Marton, Eng 27 Oct 1728; d at Kealakekua Bay, Sandwich Is

Portrait of Captain James Cook by Nathaniel Dance, 1776 (*courtesy National Maritime Museum, London, England*).

[Hawaii] 14 Feb 1779). The greatest navigator of his era, he served as master of the *Pembroke* at the siege of LOUISBOURG (1758) during the SEVEN YEARS' WAR. He charted part of Gaspé and helped prepare the map that enabled James WOLFE's armada to navigate the St Lawrence R. He was a painstaking surveyor, and was chiefly responsible 1763-67 for mapping the intricate and treacherous coast of Newfoundland, which England acquired at the end of the war; he had charted part of its E shore in 1762, including St John's harbour. Cook revolutionized Europe's knowledge of the S Pacific in his great circumnavigations 1768-71 and 1772-75. In July 1776 he began a third voyage, to search for a NORTHWEST PASSAGE. He sailed E across the Pacific and anchored in NOOTKA SOUND, on Vancouver I (29 Mar 1778). His men repaired his ships and carried on a lucrative trade with the Nootka for otter pelts. He departed 26 Apr 1778 and sailed into Bering Str in search of the passage, retreating in the face of a wall of ice. He was killed in the Sandwich Is in an altercation with the local people. Cook was not the first to explore the NORTHWEST COAST, but he and his men were the first to reveal its attractions, particularly the FUR TRADE. Among those who followed was George VANCOUVER, who had sailed with Cook on his second and third voyages. JAMES MARSH

Reading: J.C. Beaglehole, *The Life of Captain James Cook* (1974).

Cook, Michael, playwright (b at London, Eng 14 Feb 1933). Cook spent 12 years in the British army and earned a teaching degree at Nottingham U before immigrating to Newfoundland in 1966. First in St John's and later from the isolation of Random I he wrote a series of powerful plays about his adopted home, describing Newfoundlanders' struggles with history and environment and chronicling the disintegration of their unique language and culture. Among his historical dramas are *Colour the Flesh the Colour of Dust* (1971), *On the Rim of the Curve* (1977) and *The Gayden Chronicles* (1980). His major plays of contemporary Newfoundland, *The Head, Guts and Soundbone Dance* (1973) and *Jacob's Wake* (1974), offer jaundiced views of the fate of the traditional fishing and sealing economies under the pressures of the modern age. Cook is also a prolific radio dramatist and teaches English at

Memorial U. In 1987 he was playwright in residence at Stratford Festival. JERRY WASSERMAN

Cook, William Harrison, chemist (b at Alnwick, Eng 2 Sept 1903). Living on an Alberta homestead from age 8, Cook began his formal education at agricultural school at 17 – which led to U of A and Stanford (PhD 1931). From 1924 he assisted Robert NEWTON's research on drying damp wheat, joined the NATIONAL RESEARCH COUNCIL staff under Newton in 1932 and succeeded him as director of biology in 1941. A natural engineer, Cook worked as a young scientist on constant-condition chambers (ie, refrigerated greenhouses to simulate prairie farming conditions). This led to unusual war work such as the overnight conversion of freighters into refrigerated food ships. After 1945 he reorganized the NRC's food research laboratories and personally solved the structure of polysaccharide proteins in carrageenan, a seaweed used by the food industry. After nominal retirement in 1968 he continued to work as executive director of the NRC and director general of Canadian participation in the International Biological Program until 1976. In 1986 he was a titular member of the IUPAC Commission on Electrochemistry. He has written 2 books, *My Fifty Years with NRC, 1924-1974* and a memoir of his cowboy youth.

DONALD J.C. PHILLIPSON

Cook, William Osser, hockey player (b at Brantford, Ont 6 Oct 1896; d at Kingston 5 May 1986). He played 12 seasons with New York Rangers on an effective line with his brother Bun and Frank BOUCHER. One of the finest right wingers of his era, he scored 223 goals and 132 assists in regular-season play, and 13 goals, 12 assists in playoffs. He twice led the NHL in goals, and tied for the scoring title in 1927.

JAMES MARSH

Cooper, William, sea captain, land agent, land reform politician (b in Britain 1786?; d at Sailor's Hope, PEI 10 June 1867). During his lifetime, Cooper dwelt in controversy, a central mover in the century-long struggle of poor settlers to wrest Island land from the stranglehold of absentee proprietors. Although he and his followers flirted with violence, his agitation took the form of political pressure rather than armed uprising. As founder and leader of the Escheat Party, and speaker of the Legislative Assembly (1839-43), he advocated a radical confiscation of landlord property and its reallocation to those who farmed it. When reform did occur, culminating in the Land Purchase Acts of 1853 and 1875, it took the more moderate guise of purchase by the Island government and resale to tenants. Cooper's contribution was as a powerful focal point for tenant energy and frustration. After his death, he was largely forgotten. More recently, his name has been invoked by social critics from a working class perspective, and an adult education and research organization has been named, in his honour, the Cooper Institute. *See also* LAND QUESTION, PEI. HARRY BAGLOLE

Co-operative Commonwealth Federation (CCF), fd 1932 in Calgary as a political coalition of progressive, socialist and labour forces anxious to establish a political vehicle capable of bringing about economic reforms to improve the circumstances of those suffering the effects of the GREAT DEPRESSION. The main impetus for the formation of the new party came from farmers' organizations (including the UNITED FARMERS OF ALBERTA, which governed that province), a handful of academics in the LEAGUE FOR SOCIAL RECONSTRUCTION (LSR) and a GINGER GROUP of MPs in Ottawa allied with both farmer and trade-union organizations.

In 1933 the party met in Regina, where it chose J.S. WOODSWORTH as its first president. Woodsworth, an MP since 1921, was the acknowledged leader of the party both inside and outside Parliament. The party also adopted the Regina Manifesto, which set out its goals, including that of creating a mixed economy through the NATIONALIZATION of key industries and that of establishing a WELFARE STATE with universal pensions, health and welfare insurance, children's allowances, unemployment insurance, workers' compensation and similar programs.

The CCF quickly established itself in Canadian political life, electing members to Parliament and to several provincial legislatures. In 1935, 7 CCF MPs were returned and the party captured 8.9% of the popular vote. In 1940, 8 MPs were returned on 8.5% of the popular vote. At the beginning of WWII the CCF was split between supporters of Woodsworth's uncompromising pacifism and supporters of Canada's entry into the conflict. M.J. COLDWELL, who succeeded Woodsworth as leader during this period, favoured Canada's participation, and under his moderate guidance the party began to flourish electorally. It won the critical York South by-election in Feb 1942, in the process preventing the Conservative leader, former PM Arthur MEIGHEN, from entering the Commons; topped a Sept 1943 national Gallup poll; came second in that year's Ontario elections; and, under the leadership of T.C. DOUGLAS, took office in Saskatchewan in 1944. In the 1945 federal election the CCF returned 28 MPs, garnering 15.6% of the popular vote.

Although the CCF was well established, it gradually declined in popular appeal after the war. A socialist party, it was accused of being associated with communism, and during COLD WAR tension this image was damaging. An attempt in 1956 to soften the party's image by replacing the Regina Manifesto with a new, moderate document, the Winnipeg Declaration, could not reverse the trend, and in 1958 the party suffered a disastrous defeat: only 8 MPs were elected with a mere 9.5% of the popular vote. Both Coldwell and Deputy Leader Stanley KNOWLES were personally defeated.

Following this debacle an arrangement was negotiated by David LEWIS between the CCF and the CANADIAN LABOUR CONGRESS. The CLC, urged by Lewis to save democratic socialism in Canada, agreed to enter a formal alliance with the CCF to create a new party. In 1961 the CCF entered a new phase, and emerged from a founding convention as the NEW DEMOCRATIC PARTY. Although the CCF had never held power nationally, the adoption of many of its ideas by ruling parties contributed greatly to the development of the Canadian welfare state. J.T. MORLEY

Reading: W.D. Young, *The Anatomy of a Party* (1969).

Co-operative Movement, a social and economic movement which emerged in Europe as a reaction to early 19th-century industrialization. Co-operative organizations, enterprises owned by and operated for the benefit of their members, follow a set of principles best defined in 1844 by co-operators in Rochdale, England. The most important principles were that members in a co-operative each had one vote regardless of the investments made; anyone could join; surpluses or profits were distributed to members according to their levels of participation; and co-operatives would undertake educational activities for their members. Co-operative marketing organizations began to appear in British North America in the 1840s when British labourers attempted unsuccessfully to start stores similar to those common in Britain. The first stable store, or society, was developed in 1861 in Stellarton, NS. Others appeared briefly in industrial areas from Cape Breton to Victoria. In the 1880s another wave of stores appeared with the KNIGHTS OF LABOR, an early trade union. Most soon closed, the casualties of depression, recession, poor management or member indifference. A number of producer co-operatives, or worker co-partnerships, were also started, but all soon failed. In the 20th century many trade unionists have supported workers' and housing co-operatives, but they have generally shown a greater interest in issues of wages and working conditions or in political activity.

Co-operative principles were applied early to community experiments as well. During Canada's settlement period numerous utopian communities were established, but most, such as an Owenite community begun 1813 in Lambton County, UC, and the much later CANNINGTON MANOR in Saskatchewan, did not last long; others, such as the BARR COLONY and Sylvan Lake, Alta, survived, but at the expense of their comprehensive co-operative ideals.

Farmers were the first Canadian group which successfully developed co-operatives. Between 1860 and 1900 farmers in Ontario, Québec and Atlantic Canada developed over 1200 co-operative creameries and cheese factories to meet the needs of the rapidly growing DAIRY INDUSTRY. Mutual-insurance companies were organized to provide inexpensive protection against the ravages of fire, hail and early frost. Prairie farmers led by E.A. PARTRIDGE organized the Grain Growers' Grain Co in 1906 to market directly to millers and European buyers. In 1911 Saskatchewan farmers, aided by the provincial government, organized the Saskatchewan Co-operative Elevator Co. Two years later, Alberta farmers organized the Alberta Farmers' Co-operative Elevator Co.

Co-operative Commonwealth Federation (CCF), founding meeting at Calgary, 1932. Among those present was J.S. Woodsworth, first row, third from right (*courtesy National Archives of Canada/C-29313*).

Numerous other Canadian farm groups – fruit growers, livestock producers, tobacco growers – organized smaller but important supply-purchasing and marketing groups before WWI. Meanwhile, workers and farmers in industrial areas formed co-operative stores. A few from Ontario and Nova Scotia met in Hamilton in 1909 to form the Co-operative Union of Canada, a national representative body and educational institution. And in 1900 in Québec, Alphonse DESJARDINS developed co-operative banking in organizing his first CAISSE POPULAIRE.

During WWI co-operative organizations flourished, as more farmers became concerned about marketing, consumers sought cheaper food in an inflationary period, and hard-pressed Canadians explored co-operative ways to save and borrow money. Farm co-operatives expanded rapidly, including the new multipurpose Co-operative Fédérée (est 1910 in Québec), and United Farmers' Co-operative (est 1914 in Ontario).

By 1919 most farmers wished to gain greater control over the marketing of their produce. They were soon drawn to "co-operative pooling," a system whereby members contracted to sell all produce through their co-operative and in return would receive dividends based on the quality of the produce they supplied. In 1923 and 1924 prairie grain growers organized wheat pools according to these principles. Other producers organized similar pools, usually provincially.

Co-operative stores did not develop as rapidly as marketing co-operatives. To secure supplies as inexpensively as possible, to start manufacture of their own goods and to provide assistance to stores needing help, co-operatives in Alberta, Saskatchewan and Manitoba organized wholesales, an important step in creating an integrated co-operative system in the West.

During the GREAT DEPRESSION many co-operatives folded. The wheat pools survived only because of financial assistance from provincial and federal governments. But the movement itself generally found new strength. Surviving co-operatives devoted considerable attention to their memberships and educational programs. The co-operative press, including the *Canadian Co-operator*, the *UFA*, the *Western Producer* and numerous bulletins, flourished. Several co-operatives, particularly the Wheat Pool, also hired organizers to help start co-operatives of all kinds. The most innovative effort was developed by the Extension Dept of ST FRANCIS XAVIER UNIVERSITY in Antigo-

nish, NS. The ANTIGONISH MOVEMENT was particularly effective in developing study clubs which became the basis of CREDIT UNIONS, fishing and housing co-operatives, and co-operative stores. Other forms of co-operatives appearing during the 1930s included handicraft co-operatives in Atlantic Canada, fishing co-operatives on both coasts and on inland lakes, recreation co-operatives, co-operative health facilities, co-operative film clubs, and a petroleum co-operative and a farm-implement co-operative organized by prairie farmers.

During the 1940s, war and postwar prosperity allowed the movement to gain more power and influence. The co-operative financial sector gained significant new dimensions when insurance and TRUST COMPANIES were organized during the late 1940s and early 1950s in Québec, Ontario and Saskatchewan. The wholesalers began some manufacturing, and the influence of marketing co-operatives grew steadily. Since the 1950s the co-operative movement has continued to grow. Today, it consists of related organizations with significant influence in the agriculture, finance, insurance, fishing, retail and housing industries. The grain- and dairy-marketing co-operatives dominate their industries; and the retail co-operatives play significant roles on the Prairies and in Atlantic Canada. Since the mid-1970s, co-operatives have become particularly important in Québec – powerful forces in the provincial economy and important for the projected future of the province.

Despite these successes, co-operatives in the late 1980s face many problems. Their strengths lie largely in rural areas where declining populations will ultimately mean reduced total support. There is also a decrease in the number of larger co-operative organizations. As the organizations grow, it is very difficult to maintain the sense of ownership and the degree of commitment typical of smaller co-operatives. Perhaps most importantly, co-operators are challenged with deciding whether they want to create a distinctly different economic system, operating according to principles and goals different from private or government enterprise, or want merely to own a series of companies operating in those areas where, for historical and social reasons, they have happened to emerge.   IAN MACPHERSON

Reading: Ian MacPherson, *Each For All* (1979).

Coot, aquatic bird of the RAIL family. Ten species occur worldwide; only the American coot (*Fulica americana*) is found in N America. Although a marsh dweller, the coot is conspicuous because, except when molting, it swims, dives and feeds in

American coot (*Fulica americana*), the only one of 10 species of coot found in N America (*artwork by Claire Tremblay*).

open water rather than confining itself to dense marsh thickets. Its lobed toes are an adaptation to aquatic life. Its pugnacious behaviour helps ensure biological success. This white-billed, slaty black, chickenlike bird bobs its head as it swims, picking bits of vegetation and animal life from the surface, occasionally diving for food. Coots, often called mud hens, breed in pothole marshes and sloughs of southern Canada and as far N as Great Slave Lk. Coots lay 8-12 light brown eggs, speckled with dark brown, on a floating platform of marsh plants. Young are black with startling, orange-red heads and shoulders. Coots migrate in the evening and at night, wintering on lakes, brackish water and estuaries on the southern and eastern US coasts.   E. KUYT

Copper (Cu), tough, soft, ductile, reddish metal which melts at 1083°C. Only SILVER is a better thermal and electrical conductor. Copper slowly forms a greenish surface, called patina, in moist air. Copper is sometimes found in the native state, eg, near Lk Superior, but more commonly occurs in sulphide MINERALS (chalcopyrite, bornite, covelite, chalcocite), in tetrahedrite, enargite, cuprite, azurite, malachite, chrysocolla and others. It is readily extracted and easily worked. Chalcopyrite and, to a much lesser extent, bornite are the minerals most commonly found in Canadian copper mines. Copper ores often provide significant quantities of gold, silver, nickel, molybdenum, selenium and tellurium.

In Canada, native copper from the Coppermine R area of the NWT and from the southern shore of Lk Superior was used by native peoples to manufacture weapons and tools. Commercial production began at the Bruce Mine, which was discovered in 1846, E of SAULT STE MARIE, Ont. Mines were later developed in Québec's Eastern Townships and in the Precambrian SHIELD. In the 1960s the large copper ore bodies of the CORDILLERA were discovered and developed. In 1986 an estimated 768 million kg of copper were produced, with an estimated value of $1.7 billion. Canada ranks after the USSR, the US and Chile in world mine production. About 55% of copper concentrate from Canadian mines is converted to copper metal (99% pure) at smelters in Québec, Ontario and Manitoba. Refined copper is produced in Montréal (the world's largest copper refinery) and in TIMMINS and SUDBURY, Ont. BC is the leading mine producer; much BC copper is shipped as mineral concentrate to Japan for smelting and refining.

Copper was one of the first metals used by man; alloyed with tin it was widely used for weapons and tools during the Bronze Age. About half of today's copper consumption is for electrical uses, eg, electrical and telecommunications wire and cable, and electric motors. Other major uses are in industrial machinery, heat exchangers (such as refrigerators), turbines, locomotives and plumbing. Copper is alloyed with zinc to make brass,

Manitoba Wheat Pool tents at the Co-operative headquarters, Brandon Manitoba Fair, 1928 (*courtesy Western Canada Pictorial Index*).

with tin and zinc for bronze, and with zinc and nickel for German silver. Other significant uses are in copper chemicals, munitions, coinage and jewellery. Copper-nickel alloys have also been developed for use in both marine and desalination equipment. D. CRANSTONE

Copper Inuit, so named because of their extensive use of artifacts made from the native copper deposits of the region, aboriginally occupied BANKS and VICTORIA islands and the adjacent mainland region of the central Canadian Arctic. In the early 20th century, they numbered about 800 people, divided into numerous regional bands averaging about 50. Several bands would combine during the winter when engaged in hunting seals. At this season they lived in large snow-house communities on the sea ice, moving to new areas as the local seal population was hunted out. In the spring these communities broke up and the bands moved to specific areas on the coasts, from where they travelled into the interior in search of caribou, musk oxen and fish. Throughout the summer they moved about the interior within defined territories, in small groups of one or a few families, living in skin tents. Caribou hunting was intensified in late summer, and people began to gather at points along the coast where the women prepared winter clothing.

Social organization was based on kinship and on various types of formal partnership, and affiliation between individuals tended to be more a matter of personal choice than is usually found among other INUIT groups. Religion was based on shamanism, with the SHAMAN charged primarily with curing the sick and providing good hunting. Religion, language and most other aspects of the culture were similar to those of other central arctic Inuit groups, of whom the Copper Inuit were the most westerly.

Archaeology indicates that the Copper Inuit are descended from a group of THULE CULTURE people who moved into the area shortly after 1000 AD, and adapted their maritime way of life to seal and caribou resources. During the cooler climate of the Little Ice Age of the 17th to 19th centuries, these people abandoned the permanent winter houses and other elements of their Thule ancestors. Greater nomadism and increasing exposure and involvement with imported European technology gave rise to the distinctive culture of the historic Copper Inuit. Regular European contact began during the early 20th century, involving the Copper Inuit in a trapping economy. Most now live in the villages of Sachs Harbour, Holman, Coppermine, Bathurst Inlet and Cambridge Bay. *See also* NATIVE PEOPLE: ARCTIC.

ROBERT McGHEE

Reading: Diamond Jenness, *The People of the Twilight* (1959).

Coppermine, NWT, Hamlet, pop 888 (1986c), 809 (1981c), is situated W of the mouth of the COPPERMINE R on the mainland Arctic coast, 602 air km N of YELLOWKNIFE. The way of life for the INUIT living around this semipermanent fishing and sealing camp changed in 1916, when a trading post was established at the site. As more services became available, the COPPER INUIT began to settle permanently. In the late 1970s, oil and gas exploration in the BEAUFORT SEA has provided some economic diversity to this community, where the residents still subsist on hunting, trapping, sealing and craftwork. ANNELIES POOL

Coppermine River, 845 km long, rises in the Barren Lands of the NWT in Lac de Gras, flows NW through Point and Itchen lakes to Coronation Gulf on the Arctic Ocean. At Bloody Falls, 16 km S of the ocean, a series of rapids tumble through a narrow gorge of volcanic rock. The val-

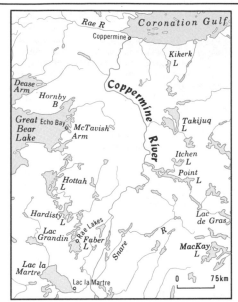

ley floor lies some 150-200 m below the surrounding plateau. Samuel HEARNE named the falls in 1771 after witnessing the killing of a party of Inuit by his Chipewyan guides. Sir John FRANKLIN and George BACK travelled the river 50 years later. The river is named for the COPPER INUIT.

JAMES MARSH

Coppers, pieces of copper hammered into the shape of a shield, were among the most valued items at Northwest Coast potlatches. They were often decorated with crests and designs. Each copper had a name, and its POTLATCH history determined its value. Among the KWAKIUTL, coppers increased in value each time they changed hands. In the late 19th and early 20th centuries, Hudson's Bay Co blankets were used to purchase them, and some coppers were worth thousands of these blankets. Coppers were sometimes broken and thrown into the sea or a fire as signs of the owner's wealth and status, but more frequently they were transferred between families at the time of marriage. RENÉ R. GADACZ

Copperware, usually of sheet COPPER, hand formed and soldered, was in common use for cooking vessels from the late 18th century. Most copperware of this period was imported from England or continental Europe, although so much has been imported in recent times by dealers that it is impossible to identify Canadian con-

Copper kettle marked "Made by W.J. Clouston NFLD," Newfoundland, 1930 (*courtesy Royal Ontario Museum*).

texts. Canadian sheet-metal workers who produced copperware in the early part of the 19th century did not mark their work. Most existing Canadian copperware dates from the manufacturing period, from 1880 to the 1930s. Cooking pots, measures and teakettles are found marked by McClary, GSW (General Steel Wares) and various other makers. Manufactured copperware was being produced in Canada as late as the middle 1930s. The metal was subject to tarnishing and contained corrosive salts that were toxic if mixed with food; therefore, use of copperware began to decline rapidly in the 1890s with the introduction of ALUMINUM cookware. By 1897 Sears Roebuck listed only copper teakettles and washtubs; as of 1901, the T. EATON COMPANY of Toronto no longer offered polished copperwares at all.

D.B. WEBSTER

Copway, George, or Kahgegagahbowh, meaning "He Who Stands Forever," Mississauga (Ojibwa) translator, Methodist minister, lecturer, author (b near present-day Trenton, Ont 1818; d at Oka, Lake of Two Mountains, Qué Jan 1869). At age 12 Copway converted to METHODISM, and later became an ordained minister. He helped translate into Ojibwa the Acts of the Apostles and the Gospel of St Luke. But when 2 Upper Canadian Indian bands accused him of embezzling their funds, the Methodists expelled him. In late 1846 Copway left for the US, where he became a successful lecturer and author. Between 1847 and 1851 he published 3 books: his autobiography, a history of the Ojibwa and an account of his European travels in 1850. He edited the weekly *Copway's American Indian* for several months in New York. Immediately before his death in 1869, he converted to Roman Catholicism.

DONALD B. SMITH

Copyright Law is included in what is commonly known as the law of intellectual and industrial property. This branch of law also includes PATENTS, TRADE MARKS and the law of industrial designs. In Canada, the CONSTITUTION ACT, 1867, gives exclusive jurisdiction over the law of copyright to the federal government. The current Copyright Act was enacted by Parliament in 1921.

Copyright is the right of an author to prevent unauthorized copying or use by others. Because s4(1) of the Copyright Act provides that copyright subsists in every "original literary, dramatic, musical and artistic work," copyright protection applies to books, poetry, plays, motion pictures, songs, phonograph records, paintings, drawings, sculptures and photographs. However, not every literary, dramatic, musical or artistic work is protected. A work must be "original" in the sense that it must not be a copy itself. Secondly, the work must be in fixed or written form capable of identification. Finally, for copyright to subsist in Canada the author must, at the date of creation, be a subject or citizen of a Commonwealth country or a foreign country that either is a member of an international agreement of which Canada is also a member or has arrived at an international agreement with Canada.

The specific rights underlying copyright that arise automatically with the creation of an original work are enumerated in s3(1) of the Copyright Act. The most important rights include the right "to produce or reproduce the work or any substantial part thereof in any material form whatever," "to perform the work or any substantial part thereof in public" and, "if the work is unpublished, to publish the work or any substantial part thereof." These rights continue, in most cases, for the life of the author and a period of 50 years after his or her death.

Section 12(1) of the Copyright Act provides that the author of the work is the first owner of the copyright. However, if a work is created by an employee in the course of employment, the employer is the first owner of the copyright. Owners can sell or assign their rights in return for a lump-sum payment or a royalty.

Any person who, without the consent of the copyright owner, does anything that only the copyright owner has the right to do or who sells, rents, distributes, exhibits by way of trade in public or imports into Canada any work that infringes copyright or, for private profit, permits a theatre to be used for a public performance without the owner's consent, has broken the law of copyright. However, where the similarity of the work and the alleged copy arises from mere coincidence or from resort to the same source, copyright has not been infringed upon. Further, under s17 of the Copyright Act, "fair dealing with any work for the purposes of private study, research, criticism, review or newspaper summary" does not constitute infringement.

Particulars of a copyright work and its owner, as well as assignments and licences, may be registered at the Copyright Office in the Department of Consumer and Corporate Affairs in Ottawa.

Canada has signed 2 major international copyright agreements: the 1928 Rome revision of the Berne Convention and the 1952 Universal Copyright Convention. The Berne Convention provides for automatic reciprocal copyright protection in Canada and other member countries. The Universal Copyright Convention, the only major international copyright agreement signed by the US, also provides for reciprocal copyright protection in Canada and member countries, but only upon compliance with certain formalities. The US and Canada also have a reciprocal arrangement.

Membership in the Berne Convention has an important bearing on the importation of foreign editions of Canadian books. Under the Copyright Act (s17), copyright in a work is infringed by a person who imports into Canada any work that infringes copyright. Indeed, under s27 of the Act, the copyright owner can appeal to customs officials to bar importation of such copies into Canada. However, s28 allows the importation of foreign editions of books by Canadian authors if those books have been printed in Great Britain or in a foreign country adhering to the Berne Convention. Unfortunately, there may be practical impediments to the protection guaranteed by the Copyright Act. For example, it may be difficult for customs officials to determine which books, among a large number imported into Canada from the US, are editions of a "Canadian" book.

New technology constantly challenges the law of copyright. In the 1950s a Canadian court held that the distribution of film telecasts by CABLE TELEVISION to individual subscribers at home does not constitute infringement of copyright in the film telecasts. In the US the practice of sound recording at home is not considered to be copyright infringement of the sound production; and the US Supreme Court ruled in 1984 that audio-video recording at home is not copyright infringement. Under Canadian law, both such practices would most likely be considered infringements of copyright. However, it is almost impossible in both cases for the copyright owners to detect infringement and enforce their rights. Similarly, reprography, the technology of reproduction that includes photocopying, is an infringement of copyright in literary work; however, the difficult problems of detection again arise. Computer software is more challenging; even if it is accepted that copyright protection can extend to software, which is not conventionally regarded as a literary work, there may be major problems in proving infringement when a copy is, for example, merely "reproduced" by storage in the memory of a computer.

In 1984 the Liberal government issued a white paper, *From Gutenberg to Telidon*, on revision of copyright law. In the spring of 1987, after much study, the Conservative government introduced new copyright legislation which, among other goals, would protect special works such as computer programs and data bases, choreography, photography and films; expand the protection of creators' moral rights; and increase penalties to deter piracy. As well, the Copyright Appeal Board would be reconstituted as the Copyright Board and its mandate would be expanded.
BRIAN A. CRANE

Reading: A.G. Blomquist and Chin Lim, *Copyright, Competition and Canadian Culture* (1981); P. Burn, *Guide to Patent, Trademark, Copyright Law in Canada* (1977); J. Palmer and R. Reesendes, *Copyright and the Computer* (1982).

Coquihalla Highway, through the BC CASCADE MOUNTAINS, is the largest (4 to 6 lanes) and newest (completed from Hope to Merritt 1986) of 3 routes connecting Pacific coast centres with eastern centres, built to enhance regional highway tourism and to lighten traffic on the busy trucking routes between Kamloops and Vancouver. The new route, following the earlier routes of cattle trails (1876), the Kettle Valley Ry (1913-59) and oil and gas industry pipelines (begun 1958), proceeds W along the Coldwater R, through the Coquihalla Pass (a Halkomelem Salish name meaning "stingy"). Costing two-thirds more than the budgeted $250 million, this 120 km section has 38 overpasses, extensive avalanche control installations, including a 300 m show shed, a steelhead fishery diversion installation and extensive highway park facilities. Completed, the 325 km highway will branch across the Thompson Plateau, N to KAMLOOPS and east to the OKANAGAN VALLEY.
PETER GRANT

Coquitlam, BC, District Municipality, pop 69 291 (1986c), 61 077 (1981c), inc 1891, is located on the N bank of the FRASER R between Burnaby and New Westminster (W) and Pitt Meadows (E). The name derives from a Salish tribal name meaning "small red salmon." NE Coquitlam includes the lower slopes of Mts Coquitlam, Eagle and Burke – with peaks up to 1600 m high. The district is mainly residential but has some large industries, including extraction (primarily gravel), wood products, wholesaling and warehousing, and transportation and trucking. There are 45 parks (about 748 ha) within the district, including Mundy Park (about 176 ha). French Canadians arrived from Québec 1909-10 to work in the logging trades at Fraser Mills, and Maillardville remains the largest French-speaking community in BC.

The district council consists of 6 aldermen and a mayor elected at large. The Town Centre area, in the NE section, is one of 4 such proposed areas in the Greater Vancouver Regional Dist. About one-third complete, it is expected to accommodate 27 000 residents. To the north, the province plans to develop the Westwood Plateau region for about 15 000 residents.
ALAN F.J. ARTIBISE

Coral, common name for various small, sessile, usually colonial, marine invertebrates of phylum CNIDARIA. The individual coral animal (polyp) secretes a cup-shaped exoskeleton around its saclike body. The mouth is surrounded by tentacles covered with specialized poison cells (nematocysts), used to immobilize prey. Colonial corals reproduce by budding and, in tropical areas, may form massive coral reefs composed of skeletal material. The cold, often turbid, Canadian waters support no coral reefs. There are, however, numerous solitary stony corals, none larger than 10 cm, in all Canadian oceans. Colonial forms develop in the soft corals (subclass Octocorallia). Some of these, the huge sea fans, grow slowly off Canadian coasts. In the deep waters off BC they reach 2 m high.
V. TUNNICLIFFE

Coral Harbour, NWT, Hamlet, pop 477 (1986c), is located at the head of South Bay on Southampton I in Hudson Bay, 1560 air km ENE of Yellowknife. Situated on bedrock ridges above the tidal flats, this was originally the home of the SADLERMIUT INUIT who ultimately perished from disease contracted from European whalers. The whalers subsequently brought in people from the Wager Bay-Repulse Bay area along with Inuit from Baffin Island and northern Québec.

The present community was established in 1924 with the establishment of a HBC trading post, previously located on Coats I to the S. The RCAF and USAF built an airfield here during WWII which was later taken over by the federal Dept of Transport. The Inuit saw a major transformation of their traditional hunting activities in the 1950s after the last caribou on the island was shot. More emphasis was subsequently placed on marine mammals and birds. This changed once again after a new caribou herd was introduced to the area in the 1960s. Today, the Inuit continue to live a traditional life-style although many are employed by the government.
EDWARD STRUZIK

Corbett, Edward Annand, adult educator (b at Truro, NS 12 Apr 1887; d at Toronto 28 Nov 1964). He did his BA, MA and 3 years in theology at McGill U, completing his studies in 1912. He fought in WWI and was invited in 1917 by Henry Marshall TORY, then president of KHAKI UNIVERSITY in England, to join the staff of the university. In 1921, Tory, now president of the U of Alberta, invited him to join the staff of the extension department. In 1925 he persuaded U of A of the need for its own radio station. As director of the U of A extension department, he organized the Banff School of Fine Arts (later BANFF CENTRE for Continuing Education) and was the first director, 1933-36. In 1936 he became the first director of the Canadian Association for Adult Education, a position he held until 1951. As director of the CAAE he proposed to the CBC a joint project to investigate the possibilities of setting up radio listening and discussion groups, resulting in the launching of the national FARM RADIO FORUM in 1941. In 1943 this led to the beginning of the Citizen's Forum, which was intended to heighten public concerns for the political, social and economic questions of the day. In 1944 the Wartime Information Board sent Corbett to England where he toured the country speaking to Canadian troops about the Rehabilitation Act and educational opportunities in Canada. In 1949, he headed the Canadian delegation to the first UNESCO World Conference on Adult Education, held in Denmark. He was noted for his leadership in ADULT EDUCATION in Canada and internationally, and for his innovative ideas, his wit and animated story-telling. Among his writings is a biography of Henry Marshall Tory.
JAMES A. DRAPER

Corbett, Percy Ellwood, international law scholar (b at Tyne Valley, PEI 20 Dec 1892; d at Derby Line, Vermont, 24 Oct 1983). Educated at McGill U (BA, 1913; MA, 1915) and Balliol College, Oxford (BA Jurisprudence, 1921; MA, 1925), he was twice wounded on the Western Front during WWI and was awarded the Military Cross. In 1943 he moved to Yale U as professor of government and jurisprudence, taking out American citizenship in 1948. In 1951 he joined the Centre of International Studies at Princeton, became emeritus professor, Yale, 1958 and lectured at The Hague, 1954, California, 1956, New Delhi, 1958-59.

Corbett was influential throughout Canada in improving legal education, redefining the university's role in the postwar world and in developing the science of international law in Canada. An activist, he joined others in attacking the injustices of the national as well as the international political and economic systems of the day. Corbett was widely recognized as perhaps Canada's greatest (and one of the world's leading) international law scholars, an innovative thinker whose opinions were both eagerly sought and frequently accepted. His motivation was "universal peace, always," and his objective, detailed in a long series of outstanding articles and books, notably *Law and Society in the Relations of States* (1951), *The Growth of World Law* (1971) and, with C.B. Joynt, *Theory and Reality in World Politics* (1978), was the creation of a new world order based more on a recognition of individuals and intergovernmental agencies than on sovereign states. His pioneering contributions were formally recognized in 1972 when the Canadian Council on International Law presented him with its John E. Read Medal. His intellectual brilliance was matched by a warm, gracious, and engaging personality.　　R. St. J. MACDONALD

Cordillera [Span, "mountains"], a term that is normally applied to groups of MOUNTAIN RANGES. Sierra [Span, "sawtooth"] is applied to individual ranges, eg, Sierra Nevada. In English, cordillera refers to a major mountain system and includes the plateaus, valleys and plains enclosed by the mountains. The various mountain ranges and plateaus of eastern N America are sometimes collectively referred to as the Eastern Cordillera. The name Western Cordillera is commonly applied to all mountains and intermontane plateaus of the western part of the continent. *See also* GEOLOGICAL REGIONS; PHYSIOGRAPHIC REGIONS; VEGETATION REGIONS.　　J.M. RYDER

Coriander, *see* CONDIMENT CROPS.

Cormack, William Eppes (Epps), merchant, explorer, naturalist (b at St John's 5 May 1796; d at New Westminster, BC 30 Apr 1868). During 2 expeditions to the Newfoundland interior he made important contributions to knowledge about the island's geography and collected information about the BEOTHUK Indians. Educated in Scotland, Cormack returned to St John's early in 1822 to run his family's business interests. A keen naturalist and explorer, he crossed Newfoundland on foot that year with an Indian guide, the first white man to do so. His account of the expedition is a classic of Newfoundland literature. Host for several years of SHAWNANDITHIT, Cormack founded the Beothic Institution in 1827 in a fruitless attempt to locate survivors of this tribe. He left Newfoundland about 1830, eventually settling in British Columbia.　　DANIEL FRANCIS

Cormier, Ernest, architect, engineer (b at Montréal 5 Dec 1885; d there 1 Jan 1980). A dominant figure in Québec ARCHITECTURE in the 20th century, Cormier is notable for his quest for high-quality building appropriate to its physical and historical context. He graduated in engineering from École Polytechnique, Montréal. Influenced by the École des beaux-arts in Paris, where he studied 1908-14 (Grand Prix de Rome, 1914), Cormier made many trips to France and incorporated into his projects many major trends in contemporary European architecture. The Palais de Justice, Montréal (1920), reflected Cormier's interest in art deco, as did his own house (1418 av des Pins, Montréal) built 1930-31. The UNIVERSITÉ DE MONTRÉAL (1924-50), his major work, incorporates both the ornamental art-deco style and the more refined international style which he later favoured, and illustrates the

complementary balance between Cormier's engineering knowledge and architectural talents. Other famous buildings include the Supreme Court building, Ottawa, and St Michael's College, Toronto. In 1975 he became an Officer of the Order of Canada.　　ODILE HÉNAULT

Cormorant (Phalacrocoracidae), family of predominantly black birds with hooked, laterally compressed bills and naked, coloured skin on the throat. Highly adapted to an aquatic environment (eg, all toes are connected by a web), cormorants are awkward on land. When standing or perching they assume an upright posture. Twenty-eight species occur worldwide; 4 in Canada, 3 restricted to marine environments. The great cormorant (*Phalacrocorax carbo*, 2.4-5.3 kg) breeds along the Gulf of St Lawrence and the East Coast. Brandt's cormorant (*P. penicillatus*) inhabits brackish to nearshore waters around Vancouver I. The pelagic cormorant (*P. pelagicus*, 1.6-2.7 kg), Canada's smallest, most marine species, nests on cliffs along the BC coast, often wintering on the open ocean. The double-crested cormorant (*P. auritus*) occurs across much of southern Canada, inhabiting freshwater lakes, brackish waters and marine islands. Nests are on the ground or in trees, on islands or cliffs. Cormorants are fish eaters. They forage gregariously and capture prey by diving from the surface. Frequently, swimming birds form a semicircle, driving their prey. Capable of diving up to 37 m, cormorants perhaps use wings as well as feet for underwater propulsion. They are susceptible to disturbance when nesting. Cormorants have been persecuted for presumed depletion of economic fish stocks, although they subsist mainly on coarse fish. Double-crested cormorant populations, greatly affected by habitat loss caused in part by the drought of the 1930s, have increased in recent years.
　　PHILIP H.R. STEPNEY

Great cormorant (*artwork by John Crosby*).

Cormorant Island is a small, wooded island fringed with rock beaches close to the NE coast of Vancouver I. ALERT BAY, a fishing port and commercial centre for nearby logging communities, is located on its S shore. The island boasts some of the finest TOTEM POLES on the BC coast. It is named after a British warship which was stationed in the area 1846-48.　　DANIEL FRANCIS

Corn, Field (*Zea mays*), spring-sown annual belonging to the grass family (Gramineae). Native to N America, Indian corn, or maize, has diverged so radically from its ancestral species that these forerunners cannot be identified with certainty. Maize is the tallest of the CEREAL CROPS (reaching over 4 m in height). The single, thick stalk is pithy and jointed; leaves are large. Each plant bears both male and female flowers: male flowers in a tassel at the top of the stalk, female flowers in a cluster (cob) enclosed in a leafy husk at the stalk joint. Corn silks, projecting beyond the husk, pick up pollen, which grows down the silk to reach the

egg cell. Field corn has become a major commercial crop in Canada only during the last 3 decades. Before 1960 most of the corn produced was used on the farm, primarily as fodder. World grain-corn production reached an all-time high of nearly 483.1 million t in 1985: 48% was produced in the US; about 1.5% in Canada. Between 1977 and 1982, Canadian production of grain corn increased 50% (4.2 million t - 6.3 million t). Since 1982 production has fluctuated from 5.9 million t in 1983 and 1986 to as much as 7.5 million t in 1985. Maize is produced in all provinces except Nfld; the 2 leading producers are Ont and Qué with a combined hectarage of 97% of the total hectarage of grain corn planted in 1987. Corn is relatively easy to grow, but the profit margin was low in the early 1980s.

"Corn breeding" was practised by native peoples and farmers before 1900. Scientific corn breeding, which depends on GENETICS and STATISTICS, was initiated in universities and RESEARCH STATIONS across N America by 1920, but has come to be largely the responsibility of seed companies. A company may have 10-15 research stations from Texas to Ontario, employing a large number of scientists and technicians, making up to a few million controlled pollinations and testing untold millions of plants each year. Breeders attempt to build up genetic resistance to PLANT DISEASES and to breed for maximum yield. Corn represents humanity's greatest plant breeding achievement: 50 years ago, yields averaged under 75 bushels/ha (2727 L); now, yields of 350 bushels/ha (12 726 L) are often attained. Similarly, 50 years ago, 100% of the corn crop was used for food or feed. Today, although over 10% of the 12 000 different items sold in a modern supermarket derive directly from corn, less than 50% of the total crop goes into the food system; the remainder constitutes the raw material for a vast array of industrial products, eg, paper, insulation.　　D.B. WALDEN

Corn, Sweet (*Zea mays* var. *saccharata* or *rugosa*), annual vegetable of the grass family. Sweet corn is the result of a gene mutation (in dent corn), which appeared in the US early in the 19th century. The genetic change prevents sugar in the kernels from being converted into starch; hence, the sweet taste. Otherwise, sweet corn is identical to field corn. In Canada and the US, sweet corn is an important vegetable, eaten fresh (on the cob) or stored canned or frozen (on or off the cob). Sweet corn requires at least 10°C for germination; its growth is progressively better up to 35°C. Sweet corn requires 60-100 days to reach maturity, depending on cultivar and locality. The newest hybrids have been bred for additional sugar and for slower conversion of sugar into starch (to prolong the period of high quality). Hybrids make it possible to grow sweet corn in regions where the temperatures at harvest time would otherwise be too high. Harvesting is done by hand for the fresh market, by mechanical harvesters for the canning industry. In 1985 Canada had 32 252 ha of sweet corn planted.　　ROGER BEDARD

Corn Laws, 1794-1846, set duties on grain imports into Britain to protect British agriculture from outside competition. (In Britain, "corn" is the name for CEREAL CROPS.) By the 1820s, increased food demands in Britain led to revisions giving preference (lower duties) to colonial over foreign imports, thereby promoting an imperial grain supply. Preferential rates offset the costs of transatlantic transport for BNA grain and built up a major colonial stake in wheat exporting. Shifts in the level of duties primarily to suit British harvests and prices could still trouble this commerce; yet in general it rose steadily, particularly after the CANADA CORN ACT was passed in 1843. Then in

1846 Britain repealed the Corn Laws as part of a movement towards free trade. The consequent loss of preferential duties seemed a hard blow to the Canadian grain trade; but it recovered in the prosperous 1850s. Moreover, the lifting of imperial economic controls also brought relief from political controls, and thus imperial recognition of RESPONSIBLE GOVERNMENT in British North America.
J.M.S. CARELESS

Corner Brook, Nfld, City, pop 22 719 (1986c), 24 339 (1981c), inc 1956, is located on Humber Arm of the Bay of Islands on Newfoundland's W coast. The province's second-largest city, it is the amalgamation of 4 towns: Curling, Corner Brook West and East and Townsite. Fishing, farming and lumbering attracted settlers to this hilly, heavily wooded area on fjordlike Humber Arm, which culminates in a deep-water port open year-round to oceangoing vessels. Curling, formerly Birchy Cove, was settled first and by 1864 Corner Brook had a sawmill. The subsequent growth of Corner Brook and Curling sparked the Newfoundland government's interest in its potential industrial development, and in 1923 the Newfoundland Power and Paper Co, in association with the British Armstrong, Whitworth and Co, was formed. By 1925 the company had constructed a wholly company-owned and planned townsite, a large pulp and newsprint paper mill, and a power plant at nearby DEER LAKE. In 1938 the mill became the property of the British Bowater-Lloyd firm. The Bowater pulp and paper mill made Corner Brook one of the most prosperous cities in Atlantic Canada. The announcement that the company was leaving Newfoundland at the end of 1984 left the city's future in grave doubt, but the mill was sold to Kruger Inc and became known as Corner Brook Pulp and Paper Ltd.

After Confederation (1949), a gypsum plant, a construction company, a cement plant and 3 fish plants were built, attracting new residents and leading to haphazard growth of the area beyond the townsite until amalgamation under one municipal government in 1956. The modern city of Corner Brook has attracted many other facilities, including Sir Wilfred Grenfell College (1975), the western branch of MEMORIAL UNIVERSITY and Western Memorial Regional Hospital.
JANET E.M. PITT AND ROBERT D. PITT

Corner Brook, Nfld, looking E from Crow Head, with the pulp and paper mill in the foreground. The mill, one of the world's largest, began production in 1925 (*photo by John deVisser/Masterfile*).

Cornwall, Ont, City, pop 46 425 (1986c), 46 144 (1981c), inc 1945, seat of the counties of Stormont, Dundas and Glengarry, is located on the ST LAWRENCE R, 110 km SW of Montréal. Founded in 1784 as a LOYALIST settlement by veterans of Sir John JOHNSON's regiment, it was called New Johnstown and renamed Cornwall for the Prince of Wales (also duke of Cornwall) by the 1790s. A regional administrative centre, it was also an important transshipment point until completion of the upper St Lawrence canals in the 1840s and the GRAND TRUNK RY in 1856. In the 1870s and 1880s several textile and paper mills located here, revitalizing the community and drawing a large French-speaking work force from Québec. Today about half of Cornwall's inhabitants are of French origin. Domtar Fine Papers is the main employer, augmented by petrochemical and textile industries. Construction of the ST LAWRENCE SEAWAY and of a hydroelectric generating station in the late 1950s brought temporary prosperity. The city is now trying to widen its industrial base and develop as a tourism centre. Cornwall has a campus of St Lawrence Coll of Applied Arts and Technology and a satellite campus of U of Ottawa. It has one of the oldest courthouses in the province (1833) and a restored "Regency Cottage" museum, "Inverarden" (1816).
ROBERT J. BURNS

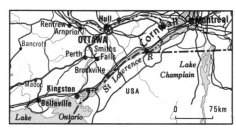

Cornwall, James Kennedy, known as "Peace River Jim," "Apostle of the North," "Lord of the Athabasca," adventurer, businessman, politician, soldier (b at Brantford, Ont 29 Oct 1869; d at Calgary 20 Nov 1955). For 60 years Cornwall was the northland's most effective ambassador. By the time he arrived in Alberta in 1896, he had crisscrossed the Atlantic and hiked across Europe, Russia and Asia. In 1897 he settled at Athabasca Landing where he founded several businesses, including the Northern Transportation Co. He was Liberal MLA for Peace River, 1908-12. Cornwall served overseas in WWI as lt-col of the 218th Battalion of the CEF, a railway unit he founded and financed. He was awarded the Croix de Guerre by the French and the DSO by King George V. He was the champion promoter of his beloved north country, and through his efforts capital was raised, telegraph lines and railways built and settlement encouraged.
J.B. CZYPIONKA

Cornwall Island, 2258 km², located in the northern ARCTIC ARCHIPELAGO, some 100 km W of Ellesmere I. It is generally low, rising to a 375 m summit towards the W. The island was discovered in 1852 by Sir Edward BELCHER and named North Cornwall.
JAMES MARSH

Cornwallis, Canadian Forces Base, Naval Training Centre, 1358 personnel, is located at Deep Brook, NS, on the Fundy Shore, 17 km E of DIGBY. Established 1942, it became the site of naval training 1943. In 1951 the first regular-force female training began here. Designated a CFB in 1966, the base covers 250 ha and is essentially a self-contained town with its own post office, bank, hospital, gymnasium, theatre, library and weekly newspaper. The training centre for all English-speaking recruits, it takes semi-trained personnel from basic-training establishments and turns out practised seamen with sea experience, able to operate and maintain complicated naval equipment. The base provides an economic support for the farming-fishing community of Deep Brook.
JANICE MILTON AND JEAN PETERSON

Cornwallis, Edward, soldier, administrator (b at London, Eng 22 Feb 1712/13; d at Gibraltar 14 Jan 1776). He served 17 years in the British army until retiring (1748) with the rank of lt-col. In 1749 he was appointed governor of Nova Scotia. Arriving in the summer of that year with about 2500 English settlers, Cornwallis founded the new townsite of Chebucto (later renamed HALIFAX). Despite the British government's determination to combat the French presence at LOUISBOURG and to exploit the area's cod fishery, the settlers' lot was a difficult one and many soon became discouraged by the continued Micmac raids. When Cornwallis returned to England in 1752, the future of the settlement was far from secure. After resuming his military career, he was eventually given the governorship of Gibraltar in 1762, and held this post until his death.
DAVID EVANS

Edward Cornwallis, founder of Halifax (1749), governor of Nova Scotia and later of Gibraltar (*courtesy National Archives of Canada/C-11070*).

Cornwallis Island, 6996 km², located between Bathurst I and Devon I in the ARCTIC ARCHIPELAGO. It is separated from Somerset I to the S by Barrow Str. The island is generally flat, though there are prominent (400 m) cliffs along the E coast. The land surface is strewn with rock debris, cemented by PERMAFROST. Traces of ancient INUIT camps are common along the S coast. It was discovered by Sir William PARRY in 1819 and named for Sir William Cornwallis. An airstrip was established at Resolute on the S coast in 1947 – it is now the major communications centre of the Arctic Archipelago and also a weather station and transshipment point to stations on the icebound outer islands.
JAMES MARSH

Coronation Gulf, a broad indentation in the arctic shore of the NWT, roughly the shape of the S coast of VICTORIA I, which lies directly N. The gulf receives the COPPERMINE R, Tree R, Rae R and others and merges with BATHURST INLET to the E. The small settlement of Coppermine lies at the mouth of the Coppermine R. The gulf was named by Sir John FRANKLIN in 1821, in honour of the coronation of King George IV. The environment and native culture of the area were studied by R.M. Anderson and Diamond JENNESS in 1916, as part of the CANADIAN ARCTIC EXPEDITION.   JAMES MARSH

Coroner, public servant responsible for carrying out investigations to determine how and why deaths other than those by natural causes occurred. The investigation is in the form of an inquest; the coroner listens to evidence of the circumstances surrounding the death and is entitled to question all witnesses during the proceedings. Inquests are governed by different rules in different provinces. In some, a jury will also be selected to hear the evidence; in others, the coroner, who may be a judge, magistrate or ordinary citizen, presides alone.   B. WINDWICK

Corporate Concentration, Royal Commission on (Bryce Commission), appointed in Apr 1975 under R.B. BRYCE, and reported 1978. It was convened in response to POWER CORPORATION OF CANADA's bid to take control of ARGUS CORPORATION, to study and report upon "the nature and role of major concentrations of corporate power in Canada; the economic and social implications for the public interest of such concentrations; and whether safeguards exist or may be required to protect the public interest in the presence of such concentrations." The resignation of Bryce, due to illness (1977), as chairman greatly influenced the commission's conclusions, summarized as, "While we have recommended a number of improvements (in public policy), we conclude that no radical changes in the laws governing corporate activity are necessary at this time to protect the public interest." However, changes in COMPETITION POLICY legislation were passed in 1986.   THOMAS K. SHOYAMA

Corporation Law is a term used to describe the immense and varied body of law concerning corporations. In Canada the phrase "corporation law" is generally synonymous with "company law." (In England, corporation law is invariably referred to as "company law"; in the US, as "corporation law.") Modern Canadian law in this area is a combination of English and American law with some purely Canadian innovations. Throughout the remainder of this article the phrase "corporation law" and the word "corporation" will be used, and unless the text draws a particular distinction, these terms will include "company law" and "company."

A corporation is considered a separate legal person, ie, it has the legal status to enter into contracts, to sue and to be sued and to do everything that a natural person can do with a few exceptions that are obvious and some that are not so obvious. For example, a corporation cannot swear an affidavit because it has no conscience to bind it, from which fact probably derives the phrase "the soulless corporation." A corporation can be convicted of a crime under the CRIMINAL CODE or any of the vast number of other regulatory statutes, but only if the penalizing section provides for a fine in lieu of imprisonment. When a statute in Canada uses the word "person" it includes a corporation; when a statute uses the word "individual" it generally refers only to natural persons.

The corporate form of conducting any particular activity has 4 main advantages. First, the corporation continues to exist until it is liquidated or dissolved; the death of a shareholder, even if there is only one shareholder, does not affect the life of the corporation. In law, this is referred to as the right of perpetual succession. Second, because the corporation is a separate juristic personality apart from its shareholders, any liability it incurs in carrying on its activities redounds to the corporation alone; the shareholders or members are not responsible for the corporation's debts unless they have personally guaranteed their payment. In law this concept is referred to as "limited liability." Third, the corporation provides a mechanism for the accumulation of blocks of capital with which large projects can be financed and developed. The public can participate in these projects through the ownership of shares. Fourth, for both large and particularly small corporations the structure provides a unique and convenient method of financing day-to-day operations through the mechanism of the "floating charge debenture." A partnership, unless the partnership agreement is carefully drawn, or a sole proprietorship, have neither of the first 2 advantages and neither the sole proprietorship nor the partnership, no matter how carefully drawn the partnership agreement, have the last 2 advantages.

The structure of a corporation consists of the shareholders or members, the directors and the officers. The directors are responsible for the management of the corporation, for the appointment of the officers and for broad policy decisions. The officers are responsible for the day-to-day operation of the corporation's business. Ultimate power rests with the voting shareholders or members who, in theory, can at least elect a new and different board of directors. In the one-person corporation all of these functions may be carried on by the single shareholder and director who is also the president of the organization.

The bewildering array of corporate forms in modern Canadian society can be divided by function into 3 main categories: municipal corporations, nonprofit (or charitable) corporations, and commercial corporations (including some CROWN CORPORATIONS).

Municipal Corporations include cities, towns, villages, COUNTIES and municipal districts, each of which is governed by an elected board (*see* MUNICIPAL GOVERNMENT). Municipal corporations have all of the features of any other corporation except shares. They are separate legal persons having perpetual succession and their liabilities are the liabilities of the corporation, not the residents of the area. The Crown in the right of Canada and in the right of each province is a corporation and has the same attributes, although many statutes exempt the Crown or its servants from being sued.

Charitable Corporations Medieval charitable corporations, created by crown charter or as part of the medieval church, predate commercial corporations. The early universities of Oxford and Cambridge were created by crown grant. Hospitals and almshouses were separate entities under various orders or dioceses of the church. Following the Reformation and Henry VIII's confiscation of church property, charity became a secular activity. While the Crown occasionally granted charters for charitable organizations, charitable activity was overwhelmingly accomplished with the mechanism of the charitable trust. It was not until approximately 100 years ago that English company law made any provision for nonprofit corporations by means of special provisions in the Companies Act of England.

Nonprofit or charitable corporations, despite their nomenclature, can make a profit, but any profit must be used to further an activity that is charitable or beneficial to the community. For example, a symphony society that profits from an auction must use those profits to support the orchestra and may not distribute them among members of the society.

Since Confederation, 1867, Québec's CIVIL CODE has differed from the CIVIL LAW of the remaining 9 common-law provinces, although each regime has influenced the other. The laws governing the formation and the conduct of nonprofit corporations testify to the different attitudes prevailing in various provinces. Alberta permits incorporation under either a Societies Act or a Companies Act, and Saskatchewan does the same under the Not-for-Profit Corporations Act. Manitoba, Ontario, New Brunswick, Newfoundland, Québec and the federal jurisdiction of Canada have no General Societies Act. Incorporation must be achieved, as in England, under special sections of each respective Corporation Act. In BC, Nova Scotia and PEI, incorporation can only be accomplished under the provisions of a general Societies Act.

The Income Tax Act imposes different rules for their own classification of nonprofit corporations. A corporation whose objects are charitable (the legal definition of "charitable" is neither simple nor precise but organizations such as the Red Cross, various health societies and foundations and cultural societies fall in this category) or for whom special provision is made in the Income Tax Act, is exempt from income tax and may issue receipts that are deductible from the donor's income tax if the organization has been approved and issued a number by the minister of national revenue. Before the minister will issue a number he must be satisfied that the corporation falls within the exempt classification, that its constitution prohibits any distribution of assets or profits to the members during the life of the organization, and that upon liquidation or dissolution any funds left over following payment of all creditors will not be distributed among the members but will be donated to another charitable corporation whose objects are most similar to those of the dissolved corporation. Mutual benefit corporations (eg, trade associations, clubs organized for various sports) are exempt from tax on their income but cannot issue deductible receipts. They only need to provide for an exempt object and a prohibition against distribution during their existence. Upon dissolution they may distribute any remaining surplus to their members. A golf club, for example, is not taxable on the dues that it receives from members to operate the golf course; it is, however, taxable on any income from investments or from any profit it earns in renting out facilities for meetings or receptions.

There are, in addition to the commercial and nonprofit corporations, a wide variety of specialized corporations in each province. All provinces provide for the incorporation of co-operatives. All provinces have enacted CONDOMINIUM laws and all, except Québec, provide for condominium corporations whose shareholders are the unit holders in the building. Each province has a number of specialized nonprofit corporations Acts. For example, Alberta provides for agricultural societies under the Agricultural Societies Act, for the ownership of church lands under the Religious Societies Lands Act, and for ownership of cemeteries under the Cemetery Companies Act.

Over and above all of these are the corporations incorporated by private Act of the legislature of each province, the vast majority of which are nonprofit corporations. They run the spectrum from private clubs to hospital boards and hospitals operated by various religious orders, and include incorporated charitable trusts, FOUNDATIONS, and several religious and educational organizations.

Commercial Corporations, which may vary in size from the corner store to national corporations such as Alcan, constitute by far the majority of corporations in Canada. They are created with the intention of engaging in business, of making a profit and of distributing that profit among their shareholders.

Before 1970, Canadian corporation law, with one main exception, was based on English company law. English company law embraces both pure company law and that area of law referred to in N America as securities law. Securities legislation in Canada, as distinct from corporation law, has since its inception relied more on the model of American law and the concepts developed by the US Securities Exchange Commission. Canada differs from the US in that it has no federal securities Act. On the other hand Canada, unlike the US, provides for federally incorporated corporations.

Under the Constitution Act, 1867, the provinces were given the power to incorporate companies with provincial objects. The Act contains no reference to the power of the federal government to incorporate or regulate companies, but the power to do so has been determined by judicial interpretation to be included in s91(2), the trade and commerce section, or as part of the implicit jurisdiction of any sovereign state to grant incorporation.

Before 1970 there were 2 basic forms used by the various jurisdictions in Canada for the creation of companies. Both derived from English law. The first is by a grant of letters patent from the Crown as represented by the particular provincial government. This form is the direct descendant of the great monopolistic Crown charter companies of the 16th and 17th centuries in England, eg, "The Governor and Company of Adventurers Trading into Hudsons Bay" (HUDSON'S BAY CO), whose charter was granted by Charles II in 1670. Three hundred years later it became a Canadian corporation under the jurisdiction of the Canada Corporations Act. Whether or not a Crown will grant letters patent for a particular corporation is still, in theory though seldom in practice, entirely dependent on the Crown's discretion. Until 1970 Manitoba, Ontario, Québec, PEI, New Brunswick and the federal government used this form. Once incorporated under this form, the incorporators prepare bylaws to govern the internal management of the corporation.

The second form of incorporation is by registration of memorandum and articles of association, and so long as the documents are properly prepared incorporation is a matter of right. This form derives from the English Companies Act of 1862 which in turn derived from an earlier form known as the Deed of Settlement Company, basically a use of the TRUST devised by English lawyers. Under this system the incorporators prepare a memorandum of association setting out the name of the company, the objects for which it is to be incorporated, and the proposed capitalization of the company. They also prepare articles of association which set out procedural rules for the calling of meetings of shareholders and directors, the procedure to be followed at these meetings, and such other matters as the ingenuity of legal draftsmen can devise. Alberta and Saskatchewan used this form until recently. BC, Nova Scotia and Newfoundland still do. The provisions of the memorandum and articles of association are deemed to represent a contract among all of the shareholders and as such the provisions are enforceable by any one or more shareholders as a party to the contract.

The 1970s saw a wave of law reform in corporation law in Canada. In 1970 Ontario enacted the Ontario Business Corporations Act modelled primarily on the corporate law of New York state together with some concepts taken from the US Uniform Commercial Code. The form of incorporation may be described as a halfway house between the letters patent form and the articles and memorandum form. Under this system the corporation is created by one or more incorporators filing a statutory form called "articles of incorporation," together with a notice of registered office and a notice of directors, with the Registrar of Corporations. Following the issuance of a certificate of incorporation by the registrar, the corporation comes into existence. The directors named in the notice of directors then hold an organizational meeting, issue the shares of the corporation and adopt bylaws to govern procedural matters and internal management. In 1975 the federal government enacted the Canada Business Corporations Act, a modified form of which has now been enacted in Alberta, Saskatchewan, Manitoba and New Brunswick.

Commercial corporations are either private or nondistributing corporations, or public or distributing corporations. The private or nondistributing corporation has a limited number of shareholders, restricts the transferability of its shares and is prohibited from soliciting public purchase of its securities. Unless such a corporation is a subsidiary of a public or distributing corporation, it does not come under the jurisdiction of the provincial securities acts. American law generally refers to such corporations as "close corporations", but English law tends to use the phrase "incorporated partnership."

Public or distributing corporations can have an unlimited number of shareholders whose shares are freely transferable and are usually traded on a stock exchange. It actively solicits the public to buy its securities and is subject to regulation by the Securities Act of each province in which its securities are traded, and by the regulations of each stock exchange upon which its stock is traded.

Basically, corporation law attempts to balance 2 conflicting interests; the external conflict between the corporation and its creditors or others with whom the corporation has dealings, and the internal conflict between the majority or control group of shareholders and the minority group. Corporation law does not by itself attempt to deal with the duties and responsibilities of a manufacturing corporation to produce a safe and usable product nor does it deal with such matters as pollution or SAFETY STANDARDS in the workplace of the employees. All of these and similar matters are the subject of separate legislation.

Given the fact that the corporation is a separate person in law and that the shareholders are not personally liable for the corporation's debts, the questions arise of how employees and creditors who supply goods or services to the corporation can ensure that they will be paid, and how lenders who have financed the corporation's operations can ensure that their loans will be repaid. Practice or legislation has sought to protect employees and lenders; normal trade creditors who supply goods or services to creditors are more or less left to their own devices to protect themselves as best they can and in the event of BANKRUPTCY of the corporation usually end up the last in line, receiving very little, if any, of their claim.

Originally, the expectation was that the fund to which all of the creditors could look to payment was the basic capital of the company raised through the issue of shares. Historically, and except for the modern business corporations statutes in Canada, this amount was called "paid-up capital." Under the modern corporations status it is referred to as "stated capital." No dividend can be paid out of this sum; dividends can only be paid out of profits. There is no minimum amount that a private or nondistributing corporation must raise as stated capital before it commences business. The paid-in or stated capital may amount to no more than $10 and in some cases even less. Slightly over 97% of the companies incorporated in Alberta fall within this class and the percentage does not vary greatly from province to province. The original concept of the fund has therefore become almost totally meaningless for the vast majority of corporations. Historically a British or Canadian corporation could not buy back its own shares, because by doing so it would reduce its capital. However, the ability to do so has long been part of American corporation law and the modern Canadian Acts all make provision, subject to certain safeguards, for the repurchase by a corporation of its own shares.

A share in a corporation confers 3 basic rights, although all may not be included in any one class of shares. These rights are the right to vote at a meeting of the shareholders, a right to share in the profits of the corporation by the receipt of dividends, and the right to receive a share of the capital of the corporation upon its liquidation or dissolution. If there is only one class of shares these rights are equal among all shareholders. They may however be divided among different classes of shares, and this division can be very complex, depending upon the particular purpose for which each class of share is issued and the ingenuity of the lawyer who drafted the provisions regarding the rights, privileges and restrictions attaching to each class. Shares that confer some preference in payment of dividends or upon repayment of capital upon liquidation or dissolution are generally referred to as preference shares or preferred shares. Common or equity shares are those that carry a right to vote and a right to share in the assets of a corporation remaining after payment of all creditors and preferred shares upon liquidation or dissolution.

Generally, only the large public or distributing corporations have a substantial amount of share capital. Institutional lenders therefore protect themselves by taking additional forms of security when lending money to the private or nondistributing corporations that have no large share capital base. The forms of additional security usually demanded by lenders are a personal guarantee by the shareholders and directors that they will repay the loan if the corporation does not; a general assignment of the corporation's accounts receivable; and a mortgage on any real property owned by the corporation together with an assignment of loss payable under a policy of fire insurance insuring the real property. If the corporation's success depends on the efforts of the principals, the lender will often insist that the corporation take out a policy of life insurance on the life of the principals with an assignment of the proceeds to the lender in the event of the death of one or any of them.

Over and above all of these forms of additional security is the "floating charge debenture" granted by the corporation in favour of the lender. It is a unique and expeditious form of security that is available only to corporations. From the time it is granted and registered it creates an equitable charge over all of the corporation's assets, but the corporation can still deal with its assets in the normal day-to-day course of its business. The debenture contains a provision that in the event of default in payment of the loan or in other circumstances that create an event of default, the lender can appoint a receiver who will take control and management of the corporation and can sell off whatever assets he chooses in order to repay the debt. A floating charge debenture has been described as a great black cloud hanging over the assets of the corporation that crystallizes into hail when the receiver is appointed. Receivership does not preclude bankruptcy proceedings, which may be commenced by any other creditor. Employees are given a priority for wage claims under the provisions of the various labour Acts in each province and under federal bankruptcy legislation. Over and above this, they have the right to sue the directors for up to 6 months' wages if they have been unable to collect what is due to them from the corporation.

The most intractable practical problem facing any person desiring to incorporate a corporation today is the problem of obtaining clearance for the name of the proposed corporation. A corporate name must be unique and distinct from the name of all other existing corporations in the province of incorporation and may not conflict with the name of a federally incorporated company. If the organizers plan to carry on business in more than one province they must be sure that the name will not conflict with that of a corporation existing in that other province. In addition there are a large number of prohibitions on corporate names. Words such as "government," "university" or "bank" may not be used as part of an ordinary corporation name, nor may any name that is obscene in the opinion of the registrar of corporations. Obtaining clearance for the name of a proposed incorporation can involve long and substantial delays. It is for this reason and to enable speedy incorporation that every Canadian jurisdiction now permits the incorporation of number companies with the addition of the name of the province or, in the case of a federal corporation, the word "Canada" (*see* TRADE MARK).

Until the 1950s, the lot of minority shareholders was not a happy one. A group that controlled over 50% of the voting shares had the power to elect themselves as directors of the corporation. The concept of the directors' fiduciary duty did evolve in the courts, but it was a limited concept and often of little avail. A director must act in good faith when exercising the powers of his office, but there is no similar duty upon him to act in good faith when he is voting as a shareholder at a shareholders' meeting. It is a breach of the directors' fiduciary duty if they issue more shares in the company to themselves to obtain or regain voting control. A director who finds himself in a conflict-of-interest situation acts at his peril because he can be held accountable for any profit he might make in such circumstances. These shadowy controls over the conduct of directors were often defeated by the principle of ratification, ie, directors holding voting control of a corporation could convene a meeting of the shareholders at any time and ratify any questionable acts they had done. Courts were loath to interfere and to substitute their judgement for that of the corporation's controllers unless they could be shown that the conduct in question amounted to fraud.

Modern corporate law seeks to protect the interest of minority shareholders by 3 divergent but interlocking concepts. The first is to define more precisely the directors' duties and liabilities within the corporate statute; the second is to give minority shareholders specific remedies and easy access to the courts to redress their grievances; and the third has been described as "the glaring searchlight" of full disclosure.

Under the modern corporation statutes, a director has a statutory duty to act with the highest good faith in his relations to the corporation, with diligence and with a reasonable degree of skill and prudence. Directors are personally liable if they vote for the declaration of a dividend or for other matters affecting the capital of the corporation and the corporation is unable to meet the statutory requirement for the proposed action. Directors are liable if they use information not generally known to the public to profit from the sale or purchase of the corporation's shares, an activity known as "insider trading."

Minority shareholders have the right to dissent from any fundamental change in the constitution of the corporation, such as an amalgamation or the alteration of the share structure. They can also compel the corporation to buy back their shares at fair value. A shareholder can apply to the court for an order that an investigation be conducted of the corporation's affairs and has the right to apply to the court for leave to commence or defend an action in the name of the corporation in the event that the directors have failed to do so because of a personal interest in the matter. Finally, minority shareholders have the broad general right to commence an action against the corporation and its directors if they feel that the conduct of the latter has been oppressive or unfairly prejudicial to the shareholders' interests.

These remedies are of little use to shareholders who do not know what is going on. The primary source of information about the affairs of a large corporation is the annual report, which must contain the audited financial statements with their accompanying notes. ACCOUNTING has been described as an art, not a science; the format of presentation of financial statements has now been generally standardized in Canada to comply with the recommendations set out in the handbook of the Canadian Institute of Chartered Accountants. The auditor of a corporation has been called the watchdog of the shareholder. To supervise the auditor's work, to act as a channel of communication between the auditor and the directors and management, and to ensure the independence of the auditor, distributing corporations must now have an audit committee of the directors, the majority of whom cannot be full-time employees of the corporation.

Notice of the annual meeting of the shareholders of any distributing corporation must include an annual report and a proxy circular containing information about the corporation and the proposed slate of directors. A copy of the information circular must be filed with the securities commission in each province in which the corporation has distributed its securities. Directors and officers must notify the provincial securities commission in writing of any purchase or sale of shares of their corporation within 10 days of the purchase or sale. In the event of any proposed major change in the corporation, the directors must include an information circular along with the notice of the meeting of the shareholders convened to approve the change. The circular must contain sufficient information to enable a reasonably intelligent shareholder to assess the proposed changes and to determine whether it is or is not in his interest. Full disclosure is presumed therefore to have a dual effect: it gives the shareholders the information they may need to commence some remedial action, and it encourages directors not to do anything that they would not wish to be disclosed.   G. FIELD

Corporatism was originally a 19th-century doctrine which arose in reaction to the competition and class conflict of capitalist society. In opposition to the trend towards both mass suffrage and independent trade unionism, it promoted a form of functional representation – everyone would be organized into vocational or industrial associations integrated with the state through representation and administration. The contention was that if these groups (especially capital and labour) could be imbued with a sense of mutual rights and obligations, such as presumably united the medieval estates, a stable order based on "organic unity" could be established. Although the notion of industrial parliaments was commonly raised in liberal democracies after WWI, the only states that explicitly adopted a corporative form of representation were the fascist regimes of Italy, Germany, Spain, Portugal, Vichy France and various S American dictatorships. In all these cases, corporatist structures were primarily a decorative façade for authoritarian rule, state repression of independent trade unionism being the main motive and consequence. Given this experience, corporatist ideology has not been popular in Western liberal democratic societies, but it has become increasingly common for social scientists to discern that certain political arrangements have developed within these frameworks, which in operative premise and institutional form bear resemblance to the functional-representation notions of corporatism. This has been particularly true in many W European countries, where the central trade-union and business federations have joined government representatives in national economic and incomes policy planning. These arrangements conform to the concept of the Keynesian welfare state, in which governments seek to stem inflationary tendencies in the economy and encourage productivity. Central to all such arrangements has been the effort to persuade unions to accept national wage-restraint policies in exchange for representation in economic decision making.

Corporatism is now seen by many social scientists as either a new economic system, successor to capitalism, where the state controls and directs a highly concentrated, but still privately owned economy; or a new form of state, where the important representation, decision making and administration take place not in the parties, parliaments and ministerial bureaucracies, but in the tripartite structures where business, labour and governments are joined; or a new form of interest-group politics, where instead of the competitive, lobbying activities of many pressure groups, there is a monopoly of access to the state by one group from each sector of society, with the state exercising reciprocal influence over the groups. While each of these scenarios captures some aspects of modern corporatist developments, they are all too expansive and grandiose. Corporatist structures may take supplemental parliamentary forms in certain countries, but they have hardly become the centre of the liberal democratic state. They have been confined primarily to the relations among big business, organized labour and government. Above all, corporatist arrangements do not challenge capitalism as the economic system of these societies. Important key investment decisions, although influenced by the state partly through corporatist structures, remain with private corporations. Indeed, far from emerging as the new dominant institutions, corporatist structures have displayed an inherent instability, reflecting the asymmetry of the relative power of capital and labour and the tendency of trade unions to withdraw their co-operation in wage-restraint policies when members insist that their leaders represent their demands rather than act as junior partners in managing the modern capitalist economy.

Corporatist ideologies were popular in Canada in the first half of this century. The Québec Catholic Church was heavily influenced by corporatist doctrine and this had a direct impact on French Canadian trade unionism, through the Confédération des travailleurs catholiques du Canada (CTCC), and on political parties such as the UNION NATIONALE. Corporatist influences were also at work in the doctrine of "group government" espoused by the Prairie farmers' parties between the wars. Mackenzie KING explicitly espoused a corporatist ideology in his book *Industry and Humanity* (1918). However, political and economic conditions have not been propitious for corporatist developments; both the decentralized nature of the movement and the absence of a governing social-democratic party at the national level have been critical in precluding them. Additionally, the heavy pro-business bias of the Canadian state and the difficulty of planning an economy as open as Canada's to FOREIGN INVESTMENT led the state, even in the post-1945 era, to rely much more on unemployment and on legislative restriction of the right to strike than on the incorporation of union leaders into national decision making. Various attempts, ranging from the establishment of the Economic Council of Canada to the discussions with business and labour around prices and incomes policy in 1969-70 and 1975-78, were made in the 1960s and 1970s to create national corporatist structures, but these developments have either remained exceedingly minor or have come to nothing because business and unions have refused to engage in the necessary compromises to institutionalize corporatism. The government itself, while increasingly vocal in calling for voluntary co-operation between capital and labour in restraining inflation, has tended to impose statutory wage controls and restrictions on the right to strike rather than creating a groundwork for integrating the union leadership into economic decision-making structures. While particular examples of corporatism exist in federal and provincial labour-relations boards, in various government-sponsored "quality of working life" programs and in occasional task forces on economic development, they are modest.   LEO PANITCH

Reading: R. Schultz et al, eds, *The Canadian Political Process* (1979).

Corriveau, La, popular designation of Marie-Josephte Corriveau (b at St-Vallier, Qué 14 May 1733; d at Québec City 18 Apr 1763). In Apr 1763 a controversial court martial, based largely on rumour and hearsay, convicted Joseph Corriveau of the murder of his son-in-law, Louis Dodier. His daughter, Marie-Josephte, was convicted as an accessory and a servant, Isabelle Sylvain, was convicted for perjury. After being sentenced to hang, Corriveau confessed that he was merely an accessory to his daughter's crime. In a second trial she confessed and was sentenced to be hanged and then gibbeted in an iron cage at Pointe-Lévy – an unusual punishment unknown during the French regime and reserved in England for persons found guilty of particularly heinous crimes. This treatment fired the popular imagination and gave rise to many legends and myths. Following the discovery about 1850 of an iron cage near the Lauzon cemetery, the oral traditions concerning the incident were transferred into literature by Philippe AUBERT DE GASPÉ in *Les* ANCIENS CANADIENS (1863). Several other authors, notably Louis FRÉCHETTE, Sir James MacPherson LEMOINE and William KIRBY, elaborated on the legend by adding imaginary crimes and gruesome details. Other embellishments include the number of husbands killed (2 to 7), her dissolute life and her haunting various places. In 1981 Andrée LeBel published the historical novel *La Corriveau*.   JOHN A. DICKINSON

Corruption Political corruption may be defined as behaviour by public officials, elected or appointed, which violates social or legal norms regarding what is or is not legitimate private gain at public expense. For example, the direct profiting by an official or his family from the use of his official position to secure contracts for the family business is a violation of social and, increasingly, of legal norms, although these norms may change. Political corruption exists in a variety of forms. Some are almost universally condemned. Others are frequently held to be corrupt, but

members of the public or political decision makers may disagree as to the ethicality of the behaviour. Finally, there are those behaviours that may be mildly corrupt for many, but which are widely tolerated. Some might argue that behaviour in the latter category is not really corrupt. Rather, it may be socially acceptable, even though it may not be actively encouraged. However, this behaviour is often considered ethically dubious, but it is too difficult to uproot. These forms are sometimes referred to as "black," "grey," and "white" corruption, respectively.

CONFLICT OF INTEREST is a form of political corruption which is quickly becoming universally condemned. Although all corruption constitutes a type of conflict of interest, the term refers to corruption arising from the conflict between the actions of an individual officeholder and the public interest. Examples include having a financial interest which may benefit from an official's decision or vote and in some cases, taking a job in the private sector, with a firm with which one had dealt as a public official. Certain forms of conflict of interest are illegal in Newfoundland (since 1973), NB (since 1978) and Manitoba (since 1986). In other jurisdictions, conflict of interest, although not illegal, may violate guidelines and be penalized by resignation from office or temporary suspension. Guidelines, however, lack the force of law, and their implementation often rests on the goodwill and fairness of the government rather than upon the independent judiciary. Such is the case with the Mulroney government's Conflict of Interest and Post-Employment Code for Public Office Holders (1985).

Vote buying, illegal and proscribed by the Canada Elections Act, is a form of corruption which is almost universally condemned, although some campaign workers and candidates may feel it is simply a pragmatic form of campaigning. As recently as 1975, the then premier of NS admitted publicly that it was still practised in his province. Other illicit electoral practices, eg, forging of ballot papers, voting twice or impersonating another voter, are also proscribed by the Act. Bribery, by which an official is offered, and may even accept, money or other valuable considerations in exchange for doing or not doing what he is expected to do in fulfilment of his official duties, is almost universally condemned as corrupt. Bribery is apparently less common in Canada than in countries where public servants and politicians are poorly paid. Illegal under the Criminal Code, it carries a maximum sentence of 14 years in prison for the official, the person guilty of bribing the official, or both. Graft is much like bribery except that the official initiates the exchange, and demands money or other considerations from the public in return for carrying out (or not carrying out) his official duty. Bribery and graft both fall under the same section of the Criminal Code and it is sometimes difficult to distinguish between them, even analytically. For example, in 1873 Prime Minister John A. MACDONALD was directly implicated in the PACIFIC SCANDAL when he was charged by the Opposition spokesman and by newspapers with accepting $10 000, during the previous years, in return for his support in Parliament of a group bidding for the railway contract. The evidence took the form of one of the most famous telegrams in Canadian history; on 26 Aug 1872, Macdonald had wired railway lawyer and politician J.J.C. ABBOTT, "I must have another ten thousand." Bribery and graft are also occasionally linked with government licensing or government contracts. Robert Summers, forestry minister for the BC government (1958), became the first Cabinet minister in the Commonwealth to be jailed for corruption in office when he was convicted of accepting bribes.

Influence peddling, which occurs when someone, not necessarily a government official, offers to use his presumed influence over other officials to secure a benefit for another in exchange for a reward, is a somewhat grey form of corruption, not because there is disagreement on the principle but because it is difficult to decide, in practice, what is legitimate influence. Attempts to influence Parliament by means of a petition or by appearing before a legislative committee during a hearing are examples of legitimate tactics, as is an attempt to influence Parliament or a city council by a public demonstration, although this is usually more controversial (*see* PRESSURE GROUPS). But if a Cabinet minister were to promote mining legislation that would benefit an old friend's company or taxation policies that would help a manufacturer who was also a friend, there would be cause for concern, even if the minister did not benefit personally. These are examples of the "old-boy" network, where political decisions are made not for personal profit but to benefit those who share the same social and economic values as the minister. The study of ELITE politics is frequently concerned with political decisions that are based on the needs and desires of political, administrative and economic elites. Nevertheless, convictions have occurred under section 110 of the Criminal Code, despite the rather subtle nature of the offences. In May 1983, 2 prominent Nova Scotians were convicted of influence peddling and fined $25 000 each. One was a senator in danger of losing his seat. A third individual had been fined $75 000 in the same case one year earlier. The 3 men were prosecuted for charging a fee from distillers in exchange for their influence in securing the distiller's products a place on government liquor-store shelves.

Corrupt campaign financing provides an excellent illustration of changing social and legal norms. Prior to recent federal and provincial statutory innovations, there was no consensus about the degree of corruption involved in excessive campaign contributions and spending. With laws such as Alberta's Election Finances and Contributions Disclosures Act of 1977, which made certain contributions illegal, this has changed. For example, contributions of more than $10 000 to any single political party by an individual, group or company may result in a fine of up to $10 000. Québec, more stringent than other jurisdictions, even prohibits any contributions to parties or candidates by companies. Only electors may contribute. The purpose of such laws is to avoid the possibility that wealthy contributors to party campaigns might buy political favours in return. No one would suggest, however, that the laws are foolproof (*see* PARTY FINANCING).

PATRONAGE and nepotism are frequently, but not universally, condemned as corrupt. Patronage, the practice of hiring and promoting civil servants and other government officials on the basis of their party affiliation rather than merit or ability to do the job, is common in Canada. Patronage can become a major political issue, as it did during the 1984 federal election. During June and July 1984, outgoing PM Pierre Trudeau and incoming PM John Turner appointed at least 225 people, the vast majority of whom were said to be Liberal Party supporters, to senior level government positions as senators, judges, ambassadors, commission members, crown corporation executives and civil servants. Some of these appointments created a great deal of public criticism as an abuse of public office, and at least one member of Trudeau's Cabinet publicly criticized Trudeau for ignoring competence in some of the appointments. Interestingly, Turner's Progressive Conservative opponent, Brian Mulroney, was also criticized for indicating that he too would engage in such activities if he were in a position to do so. Nepotism refers to the hiring and promoting of relatives or friends who are not necessarily qualified. These terms are also applied to the letting of government contracts for the same reasons. Patronage has been defended as a method for ensuring the vitality of the Canadian party system by providing sufficient incentive to recruit prospective party members and even possible candidates for public office. For example, a defeated candidate may, if his party is victorious, be appointed to a government post as a reward for running, but it may be asked whether this is a proper use of public money. A second rationale for patronage is that unless new governments can replace civil servants and other government officials, the permanent administrative personnel may effectively block new programs. This rationale is more difficult to criticize. Critics do argue that patronage is inefficient because employees are not chosen on the basis of their ability to perform a task, and that it is unfair because it discriminates against those who do not support the "right party." The debate over this issue has continued since the 1830s, the time of Jacksonian democracy in the US, when patronage became a popular political tool. In Canada, in the 1970s and 1980s, 2 successive Manitoba governments attacked each other with repeated allegations of patronage. The federal and all provincial governments have established PUBLIC SERVICE commissions designed to preclude the practice of patronage or nepotism, but they have not been completely effective because governing parties often consider government jobs the spoils of electoral wars and their followers often demand jobs as a just reward. In recent years, patronage has apparently declined for the lower-level civil service positions but has increased for the higher levels.

Finally, pork-barrelling, the offer of a public-works project to a constituency in exchange for its electoral support, is frequently decried by journalists, academics and reform-minded politicians, but continues unabated. Opponents condemn it because rational planning and national or provincial priorities are overridden for local voter support, eg, a road is built in a constituency not because it is needed but as a reward for voting the "right" way. Others claim it is the duty of those who represent constituencies to look after their interests and that all parties dispense such rewards. Examples of pork-barrelling are rampant at almost every election and it is not likely to become illegal, since it would be extremely difficult to decide fairly which campaign promises were pork-barrelling and which were not.

Causes of Corruption Political corruption, according to functional theories, arises in response to societal needs. For example, it has been argued that political machines practise certain forms of corruption in order to provide necessary social services or to provide a less impersonal form of government. Unfortunately, this does not explain why corruption is the only response or why it continues long after the need has evaporated. Another explanation is that corruption is a consequence of greed and the desire for power. Many forms of corruption provide new and illicit avenues to wealth for public officials willing to use them, an explanation frequently advanced to explain corruption in developing nations, where civil servants are comparatively much less well paid than in developed nations. The desire for power, on the other hand, explains why individuals and parties, some of whom are capable of much higher earnings outside government, are still willing to pursue public office through corrupt means. The notion that power is the cause of corruption is frequently noted in political science literature. According to the theory of patron-client relations, corruption is an exchange mechanism which frequently reflects the unequal distribution of wealth and power in society; the relatively powerless can exchange votes or campaign work for something else. Other theories contend that corruption is a persistent but necessary feature of capitalist economics, but this does not account for the chronic corruption found in noncapitalist systems, although it could be argued that in these societies power is also unequally distributed.

The consequences of corruption are somewhat clearer and are most noticeable perhaps in the increase in public cynicism and distrust of government and politicians, which may lead to alienation from the political system and a resulting decline in the legitimacy of the state. Corruption creates a major problem for public policy, because public money is being diverted to satisfy the needs of a few. It also affects a nation's image abroad. Canadian governments, relatively virtuous by international standards, are still troubled by corruption despite new legislation and regulations which attempt to control it. Ultimately it is up to the public, however, to demand honest and less self-serving government officials. KENNETH M. GIBBONS

Reading: Kenneth M. Gibbons and Donald C. Rowat, *Political Corruption in Canada* (1976); Canada, Task Force on Conflict of Interest, *Ethical Conduct in the Public Sector* (1984).

Corte-Real, Gaspar, explorer (b 1450?; d 1501). A native of the Azores, he initiated Portuguese claims in the N Atlantic. It is thought that he reached Greenland and worked his way S to Newfoundland in 1500, and that he returned in 1501 with 3 caravels and explored the Labrador coast and Hamilton Inlet. Two of the vessels returned with native captives, but his vessel disappeared. His brother Miguel searched for him the following year but was lost as well. A third brother was refused permission to follow. JAMES MARSH

Corvée, required labour. Labour demanded of HABITANTS in NEW FRANCE by seigneurs in addition to rent or for pasture rights was illegal and was suppressed by the INTENDANTS. As militiamen, all habitants were required to work on roads, bridges, fortifications and transport; this enforcement of labour was legal and of indeterminate duration and, though resented, it continued after the French regime. By mid-19th century the term had come to mean voluntary help from the community for building a church, erecting a barn, etc. DALE MIQUELON

Cosentino, Frank, football player, educator (b at Hamilton, Ont 22 May 1937). He played 10 years in the Canadian Football League after a stellar university career at the University of Western Ontario where he quarterbacked and captained the first Canadian Intercollegiate Athletic Union football champion in 1959. His CFL career began in 1960 with the HAMILTON TIGER-CATS, and he played there until 1966, participating on 2 GREY CUP championship squads in 1963 and 1965. He was traded to Edmonton in 1967 and again to Toronto in 1969 where he finished his career that year. An able pro quarterback, Cosentino is best known for his several books on the CFL and the history of football in Canada. He is currently head of the department of physical education and athletics at York University in Toronto. PETER WONS

Cosgrove, Stanley Morel, painter (b at Montréal 23 Dec 1911). Of Irish and French Canadian descent, Cosgrove studied at Montréal's École des beaux-arts and at the Art Assn of Montreal under Charles Maillard and Edwin HOLGATE. With a provincial scholarship in 1939, he pursued his studies in New York C and Mexico. He returned to Montréal in 1944 and taught decorative composition, painting and fresco painting at the École. In 1953 he was awarded a one-year Canadian government fellowship to visit museums in France. Since 1958 he has devoted himself to his own work, figuring in numerous group and solo exhibitions. Cosgrove, a member of the Royal Canadian Academy of Arts (1951), is a superb draftsman and fine colourist. His landscapes, still lifes, figures and portraits are characterized by a subtle combination of form and colour. JULES BAZIN

Reading: Jules Bazin, *Cosgrove* (1980).

Cosmology, the branch of ASTRONOMY that studies the cosmos, ie, the universe (in the astronomical sense): its origin, evolution, structure, etc. Since cosmological experiments cannot be performed in a laboratory, the interpretation of observational data is often in dispute. Canadian work has tended to focus on obtaining and interpreting observational data. Although speculation about the universe has occurred since the earliest civilizations, modern cosmology dates from 1917, when Albert Einstein applied his newly developed General Theory of Relativity to produce a geometrical model of the universe. Most cosmological models are now based on General Relativity, the best existing theory of gravity. Such models predict that the expansion of the universe (first observed in the 1920s) began with an explosive origin, a "Big Bang," 10-18 billion years ago.

Modern cosmological theory is predicated on the Cosmological Principle, which assumes that the universe is homogeneous and isotropic (ie, distribution of matter and motion is the same in all directions). In 1922 A. Friedmann, a Russian mathematician, proposed 3 models of the universe: "open," in which the universe expands without limit; "closed," in which the universe expands to a finite size and recollapses; and "flat," in which the universe expands without limit but the rate of expansion of its parts tends towards zero in the infinite future. Significant work in this area is being done by Paul Hickson at University of British Columbia.

American astronomers Edwin Hubble and M.L. Humason, as a result of studies of the spectral lines of galaxies, noted that the galaxies are moving away from each other at great speeds and that the universe is therefore expanding. The Hubble Constant (H_0) relates the radial velocity of a GALAXY to its distance from Earth. Sidney VAN DEN BERGH of the Dominion Astrophysical Observatory, Victoria, and astronomers in the US suggest that the value of the Hubble Constant is in the range 75-100 km per second per megaparsec; Allan Sandage (Mt Wilson Observatory, California) and his colleagues, however, favour 50-60 km/s/Mpc. The age of the universe, ie, the time since the Big Bang, is inversely proportional to Hubble's Constant.

The lumpy structure of the universe, galaxies and clusters of galaxies has become an important area of theoretical research, since simple cosmological models assume a homogeneous distribution of matter. Canadian work in this area includes that of Charles Dyer and Robert Roeder (U of T, the latter now in Texas) on deviations from the "classical" Hubble Law; Charles Hellaby and Kayll Lake (Queen's U, the former now at U of Capetown, S Africa) on possibilities of galaxy formation; and Paul Wesson (U of Alberta, now at U of Waterloo) on clusters of galaxies. In addition, the formation of the Canadian Institute for Theoretical Astrophysics, located at the U of T, has resulted in an additional research group in cosmology, including J.R. Bond and N. Kaiser.

In the mid-1980s, a development of interest to observational cosmology has been the discovery of a number of convincing candidates for the gravitational lensing of a distant quasar by an intervening galaxy. This lensing is made observable by the existence of 2 or more nearly identical images of the distant quasar. The study of such systems can yield independent estimates for the Hubble constant as well as provide a basis for the study of the mass distribution in the lensing galaxy. This subject has been pursued for a number of years by Dyer and Roeder at Toronto. As more data become available, it is hoped that this lensing phenomenon will become an important tool in determining the structure of the universe and especially the distribution of dark matter in the universe. ROBERT ROEDER

Reading: J. Silk, *The Big Bang* (1980).

Costain, Thomas Bertram, editor, novelist (b at Brantford, Ont 8 May 1885; d at New York, NY 8 Oct 1965). Costain worked as an editor and reporter with several newspapers and magazines and was editor of *Maclean's* from 1914 until 1920 when he emigrated to the US to be associate editor of *Saturday Evening Post.* From 1934 to 1936 he was a story editor at Twentieth-Century Fox, returning to publishing as advisory editor at Doubleday in 1939. His writing career began in 1942 with publication of *For My Great Folly,* a best-seller. His fast-paced historical fiction was extremely popular and sold in the millions. *The Black Rose* (1945) sold more than 2 million copies. His novels with Canadian settings are *High Towers* (1949), dealing with the LE MOYNE family of New France; and *Son of a Hundred Kings* (1950). He also wrote a history of New France, *The White and the Gold* (1954). DAVID EVANS

Côté, Gérard, runner (b at Saint-Barnabé, Qué 1913). A Canadian sports pioneer in an age when training facilities were rare, he first distinguished himself in the sport of his forefathers: snowshoeing. Then he switched to foot races, running 40 km 3 times a week. Hardened by this training, he set a record of 2 hr 28 min 28 sec for the Boston Marathon of 1940. He quickly became a popular figure in that city, winning again in 1943, 1944 and 1948. He was 3 times marathon champion of the Athletic Amateur Union of the US and won the Lou Marsh Trophy as best Canadian athlete of 1940. He is a member of the Canadian Sports Hall of Fame. YVON DORE

Côté, Jean-Léon, surveyor, legislator (b at Les Éboulements, Qué 26 May 1867; d there 24 Sept 1924). After studies at Montmagny and Ottawa, Côté became a land surveyor with the Department of the Interior in 1890; he settled in Edmonton in 1903. Between 1893 and 1895 he was on the ALASKA BOUNDARY COMMISSION doing the preliminary survey (completed after WWI). Mt Côté, near Ketchikan, Alaska, was named after him. In Dawson, YT, during the KLONDIKE GOLD RUSH, he was associated with the Cautley Bros. Elected MLA for Athabasca/Grouard in 1909, his interests focused on Alberta's natural resources, including the McMurray tar sands. Côté was appointed to the provincial Cabinet in 1918 as provincial secretary, eventually becoming minister of mines, and minister of railways and telephones. In 1919 he was instrumental in the establishment of what became the ALBERTA RESEARCH COUNCIL. Named to the federal Senate in mid-1923, he succumbed to an attack of peritonitis in 1924. JEAN G. CÔTÉ

Coté, Jean-Pierre, MP, minister, senator and lt-gov of Qué (b at Montréal 9 Jan 1926). He studied at the School of Dental Technology, and was first elected to the House of Commons for Longueil riding in 1963. He was named to the Privy Council and served as postmaster general (1965), minister of national revenue (1968) and again post-master general (1970). He was named to the Senate in 1972 but left it in 1978 to become lt-gov of Québec, a position he held until 1984. Admired and consulted because of his good judgement, discretion and public spirit, he sits on several administrative bodies. In the last few years, he has taken up painting. MARTHE LEGAULT

Cottnam, Deborah, née How, teacher, poet (b probably at Grassy Island, Canso, NS 1728; d at Windsor, NS 31 Dec 1806). Polished and literarily inclined, Cottnam met the vicissitudes of the French-English wars and the American Revolution with an initiative rare in 18th-century women and established a high standard of female private education in the Maritimes. Cottnam and her family were displaced after the fall of Canso (1744), and again displaced in the mid-1770s when their Tory sympathies forced them to leave their merchant life in Salem, Mass, although she tried to return briefly to open a school. From 1777 to 1786 Cottnam directed an academy for women in Halifax, moving by invitation to Saint John from 1786 to 1793, where she continued to instruct the daughters of the LOYALIST elite. After the death of her husband, Capt Samuel Cottnam, in 1780, both her settlement of 405 ha of land on Minor Basin in NS in 1785 and her government pension in 1793 reflected her widowed state and the service of her family to the Crown. Although retiring to Windsor later in the 1790s, she wrote from Halifax in 1794 that she had just opened a day school. A poet of classical control (pseudonym "Portia"), she was a literary inspiration for her students and for her great-granddaughter, poet Griselda Tonge. GWENDOLYN DAVIES

Couchiching Conference is the usual name for the annual conference held at Geneva Park on Lake Couchiching, near Orillia, Ont, by the Canadian Institute on Public Affairs (fd in 1932 by the YMCA National Council as an educational body for the critical discussion of national and international issues). The conferences, ordinarily held in August, quickly became a gathering place for those interested in the intelligent discussion of Canadian concerns. During the GREAT DEPRESSION the focus was on such issues as social reform, the state of the economy and the darkening world scene, and during WWII much attention was paid

---

Cougar (*Felis concolor*), the most gracile of the American wild cats, is found in forested areas across Canada (*photo by Lyn Hancock*).

to reconstruction planning. In 1947 the possibility of a military alliance of N Atlantic nations (later NATO) was first raised in an address there by Escott REID of the Dept of External Affairs. More recently, Couchiching's topics have ranged widely through politics and international affairs, technology and other subjects. J.L. GRANATSTEIN

Coudres, Île aux, 30 km², 11 km long, 4.3 km wide, 92 m high, is situated 60 km downstream from Québec City in the ST LAWRENCE R estuary. The island consists of 2 Appalachian ridges joined by an embankment. Their rocky upstream end forms the coves of L'Église and du Havre. A broad sandbank surrounds the island. Earth tremors are frequent. In 1535 Jacques CARTIER named the island in recognition of its many hazel trees (*coudriers*). The island was given as a fief to Étienne de Lessard in 1677, then to the SÉMINAIRE DE QUÉBEC in 1687, and received its first colonists around 1720. In 1759 it provided moorage to the Durell flotilla. Fishing for porpoise took place here. SERGE OCCHIETTI

Cougar, puma or mountain lion (*Felis concolor,* family Felidae), is the most gracile of the New World wild CATS. It has long legs and tail and a small head. Colour varies from grizzled grey or light brown to cinnamon or reddish brown; underparts are dull white. The backs of the ears and the last 5-8 cm of the tail are black. Cougars are swift, skilful, solitary hunters that run down their prey. They hunt wapiti, deer, hares and other small game. Their range was northern BC, across southern Alberta, Saskatchewan, Ontario and Québec to NB and NS, as well as S America — in fact, wherever their chief prey, deer, was present. Because they were believed to take domestic stock, they have been exterminated in settled N America, but populations still survive in forested mountainous regions. Females breed at 2-3 years and at any time of the year, although 1-6 (usually 2) kittens are born in the spring, after 90-97 days gestation. Newborn kittens are spotted and weigh 250-500 g. At 3 months, after weaning, the mother teaches them to climb trees and hunt. Cougars may purr, hiss, growl or scream. C.S. CHURCHER

Coughlan, Laurence, missionary (b at Drummersnave, Ire; d in London, Eng 1784?). Ordained a Church of England priest in 1765, Coughlan sailed to Newfoundland that same year under the auspices of the Society for the Propagation of the Gospel. A Methodist in doctrine and discipline, his evangelical labours in the Harbour Grace area were the origin of METHODISM in Newfoundland. He aroused great hostility during his mission, partly because of his abrasive tongue. In 1773, Coughlan left Conception Bay because of ill health. He returned to Great Britain and 3 years later published *An Account of the Work of God in Newfoundland*. J. ROGERS

Coughtry, Graham, painter (b at St-Lambert, Qué 8 June 1931). Coughtry studied at the Ontario Coll of Art 1949-53. His first exhibition was with Michael SNOW at Hart House, U of T, in 1955, and his first one-man show was held the following year at Avrom Isaacs's Greenwich Gallery in Toronto. He became, along with Snow, Joyce WIELAND, Dennis BURTON, Gordon RAYNER, John MEREDITH and others, part of the "Isaacs Group," artists joined by the radicalism of their art and by their interests in dadaism and jazz. Coughtry became a member of the Artists' Jazz Band formed about 1962. Coughtry's work is almost exclusively concerned with the abstracted human figure and is characterized by rich colour and powerful impasto surfaces. Through his teaching at the ONTARIO COLLEGE OF ART, the New School of Art, and York University, and by the example of his work, he has had a substantial influence on a younger generation of painters in Toronto. DAVID BURNETT

Reading: B. Hale, *Graham Coughtry Retrospective* (1976).

Coulter, John William, writer (b at Belfast, Ire 12 Feb 1888; d at Toronto 1 Dec 1980). Coulter is best known for his historical trilogy *Riel* (written and produced 1950; publ 1962), *The Crime of Louis Riel* (1968) and *The Trial of Louis Riel* (1968). Most of his other plays are on Irish subjects. Among them, *The House in the Quiet Glen* (1937) won the Dominion Drama Festival Bessborough Trophy and *The Drums Are Out* was premiered at the Abbey Theatre, Dublin, Ire, in 1948. With composer Healey WILLAN he created the first 2 operas commissioned and broadcast by the CBC: *Transit through Fire* (1942) and *Deirdre of the Sorrows* (1944). His nondramatic works include a biography of Winston Churchill and a record of his courtship, *Prelude to a Marriage* (1979).
ROTA HERZBERG LISTER

Coulthard, Jean, composer, educator (b at Vancouver 10 Feb 1908). The creator of music remarkable for its integrity, purity of expression and deeply emotional language, Coulthard was

Jean Coulthard's music is remarkable for its integrity and deeply emotional expression (*photo by Andreas Poulsson*).

the first of Canada's West Coast composers to receive wide recognition. She began to compose as a child while studying with her mother, Jean Blake Coulthard (née Robinson). English composer Ralph Vaughan Williams was prominent among Coulthard's later teachers. She also received critical assessments from Arnold Schoenberg, Bela Bartok and Darius Milhaud. The *Variations on B-A-C-H* (1951), *Spring Rhapsody* (for Maureen FORRESTER, 1958), *Choral Symphony "This Land"* (1966-67), *The Pines of Emily Carr* (1969) and the *Lyric Sonatinas* (1969, 1971, 1976) are representative of more than 100 compositions for a wide variety of vocal and instrumental media, many of them commissions and award winners. From 1947 until her retirement in 1973, Coulthard taught at UBC. She was named an Officer of the Order of Canada in 1979.
BARCLAY MCMILLAN

Council of Canadians, public-interest group, founded by Edmonton publisher Mel Hurtig in 1985, dedicated to the development of policies that will encourage economic, political, social and cultural sovereignty for Canada. Among fundamental goals of the council are greater Canadian ownership of business and resources, stronger support for public enterprises such as the CBC, NFB and NRC and foreign and defence policies which reflect "the independence of Canada as a sovereign nation." The catalyst in the formation of the council was the FREE TRADE initiative undertaken by the Conservative government of Brian MULRONEY and the government's "open for business" policy on FOREIGN INVESTMENT. The council has appeared before numerous government bodies, held public conferences across Canada and dropped the Canadian flag on the US icebreaker *Polar Sea*. In Nov 1986 a conference on defence policy held in Edmonton attracted over 5000 people from across Canada. In 1987 the COC formed the Pro-Canada network of some 30 national organizations. 1987 membership was over 7000. *See also* COMMITTEE FOR AN INDEPENDENT CANADA.

Council of Ministers of Education, Canada (CMEC), modelled on the West German Kultursministerkonferenz, was established in 1967 to provide a collective provincial voice on educational matters to federal government offices and agencies and to facilitate interprovincial consultation and co-operation. One of the council's outstanding accomplishments was that of co-ordinating the Organization for Economic Co-operation and Development (OECD) review of national policies for education in Canada, which was completed in 1975. It has also administered federally supported official-languages programs in the provinces, the preparation of the metric style manual, and a guide for the equivalency assessment of transfer students. Its concerns include multi-media school programs, computer education, curriculum surveys and the preparation of reports on manpower research, financing of education, women's issues in education and multicultural education policies in Canada. Since 1977 the CMEC has increased its efforts to conduct conferences with representatives of nongovernmental national educational organizations, such as those representing second-language teachers, school trustees, teachers, colleges and university associations.

The council also provides for representation at international meetings, such as those of UNESCO and OECD, and arranges for the hosting of visiting international scholars. The council has no constitutional powers; although council decisions are not binding on any minister of education, decisions of the council generally reflect consensus positions of the provinces. There is unfortunately a continuing turnover in council

membership because of the relatively brief tenure of provincial education ministers.
JOHN J. BERGEN

Council of Twelve, est 1719 in Nova Scotia to advise the governor, deliberate on bills in the legislature's upper house, and act as a civil court of appeal. Councillors were appointed by the governor and served for life. Until the 1750s the council was dominated by military officers. After the introduction in 1758 of REPRESENTATIVE GOVERNMENT, the council, now including a growing Halifax merchant elite, began to perform both executive and legislative functions, controlling local patronage and land grants and ensuring Halifax's domination over the colony. LOYALISTS were added after Sir John Wentworth, a Loyalist, became governor in 1792. By 1830 the council consisted of an anglophone, Anglican merchant elite linked by family connection, and including Bishop John Inglis, R.J. UNIACKE and Samual CUNARD.

Growing opposition to the council's domination came from the middle class, non-Anglicans and a number of young professionals, including Joseph HOWE. In 1836 Howe was elected to the Assembly and demanded an elected council. In 1837 the old council was divided into an appointed legislative council of 19 members and an executive council of 12 which remained dominated by the old elite. The agitation for RESPONSIBLE GOVERNMENT continued, however, and by the 1840s the power of the Halifax elite was broken and its bastion, the legislative council, had collapsed. The executive became the focus of political conflict as reformers continued the struggle until 1848, when responsible government was granted.
DAVID MILLS

Countertrade, *see* BARTER.

Country and Western Music roots lie in the British folk tradition, particularly as preserved in the rural mountain areas of the southern US. Pop music, black music and the demands of commercial recording and radio have also influenced C and W music.

The Maritimes, parts of Ontario and BC shared a strong folk tradition similar to that of the Appalachian region, and country music found ready acceptance in Canada. Country music was first popularized by fiddlers such as Don MESSER and George Wade, who started their careers on radio in the late 1920s. Canadian Victor Record Co signed Wilf CARTER in 1932, and his success prompted Victor to sign Wade (1933), Hank SNOW (1936) and Hank LaRiviere (1941). Carter, Snow, and later Earl Heywood started a unique style of country music that uses a lower, less nasal-sounding voice with clearer enunciation and fewer of the blues-like slurs and high whining sounds that dominate much American country music. Canadian singers have continued to rely more on the traditional ballad and story songs than on the "cheating" and barroom songs often preferred in the US.

The Great Depression, WWII, a more mobile population, the success of the "singing cowboy" movies, the number of US radio stations with access to Canada, the increasing number of pop adaptations in country music, and national radio shows and tours all increased the popularity of country music throughout the 1930s, 1940s and into the 1950s. Canadian artists have been hampered by the sparse population and the regional nature of the country. Until the mid-1950s country artists relied on live radio shows, extensive regional touring in clubs, and barndances and local TV appearances to earn a living. With a shortage of places to perform and the absence of good recording studios numerous artists, including Ray Griff, Stu Phillips, Lucille Starr and Ronnie

Prophet, followed the lead of Hank Snow and moved to the US.

In the 1960s the instrumentation and singing style on country records became more pop oriented. Artists such as Anne MURRAY, R. Harlan Smith and Shirley Eikhardt received airplay on commercial radio, while rock music reflected in the Good Brothers, Danny Hooper and Colleen Peterson gained a wider audience. The urban folk boom of the 1960s fostered artists such as IAN AND SYLVIA Tyson, Gordon LIGHTFOOT, Murray MCLAUCHLAN and Bob Ruzicka, who have both a strong urban and a strong country appeal. The folk-music boom also introduced bluegrass, the jazz of country music, and traditional Canadian fiddle music to a much larger audience. In 1986 the CRTC released a comprehensive study *The Country Music Industry in Canada* in response to the Canadian Broadcasters Assn's request to lessen the restrictions on Canadian content. Based on the reports and findings, the CRTC ruled the regulations should remain in place.

Canadian-content regulations for commercial radio in 1970 gave valuable airplay to artists such as Dick Damron, Stompin' Tom CONNORS, Carroll BAKER, Gary BUCK and the Family Brown. More radio stations were licensed and more began to program for specialized markets. In 1960 there was one radio station, CFCW in Alberta, featuring country music entirely. By 1987 there were 85 originating stations programming some country music during their broadcast day. In the 1980s, there has been a revival of interest in the older styles of country music of Ian Tyson, k.d. Lang and groups such as Blue Rodeo and Spirit of the West. The more mainstream music of Eddie Eastman, Terry Sumsion, Terry Carisee, etc, remains popular. The Academy of Country Music Entertainment (formed 1975) has sponsored an annual country-music week in different cities across Canada. Country Music Week and the Big Country Awards have brought artists and industry people together and have become major events in the promotion and development of country music.

RICHARD GREEN

Country Life Movement This movement of loose alliances flourished in the 1900-20 period, a response to the drift to cities and to the perceived loss of rural values. It was fed by the exuberance of the settlement of the Prairie West and by the importance that the Great War lent to farmers. At its base was an ideology that adulated rural life. Promoted by agricultural colleges, university extension departments, land dealers, women's groups, "new" education reformers, and the farm press, the movement resurrected ancient idealizations of agriculture. *The Farm and Ranch Review* (Calgary) relayed Socrates' pronouncement that agriculture was the employment most suitable to man's nature. It was "the source of health, strength, plenty, riches and of a thousand sober delights and honest pleasures"; it taught "sobriety, temperance, justice, religion, in short all virtues." Country life plainly was closer to God than city life. Advocates included J.B. Reynolds, president of the Manitoba and later Ontario Agricultural College; S.E. Greenway, Saskatchewan director of extension; J.W. Gibson, BC director of elementary agricultural instruction, and James W. Robertson, chairman of the Royal Commission on Technical Education (1909-13).

The country life ideology underlay many reform crusades – the pure food and health drives, the TEMPERANCE and moral reform leagues, the CITY BEAUTIFUL and conservation campaigns, school gardening and agricultural clubs. It permeated Canadian literature of the times and motivated virtually every educational strategy designed in the era to elevate life on the farm.

DAVID C. JONES

County is the principal division of land subordinate to the province in Nova Scotia, PEI, New Brunswick, Québec and Ontario. Counties were first established in these provinces, after the English model, for a variety of purposes, principally property registration, local judicial courts, local MUNICIPAL ADMINISTRATION and provincial electoral districts. In PEI, New Brunswick and Québec, the historic county structure is now used only in property description, with the remaining functions being administered through reorganized provincial and municipal structures. In Nova Scotia the county remains a rural administrative unit, with some of the counties divided into districts for municipal purposes. Ontario has retained many of its counties as municipal and judicial units, with some of them united for these purposes although maintaining separate registry offices. Wellington represents the typical county structure in Ontario. There are 22 municipalities united in the county: one city, 4 towns, 5 villages and 12 TOWNSHIPS. The county's functions embrace a variety of services including roads, building inspection and social services, SCHOOL BOARDS and senior-citizen homes. Ontario, north of Muskoka and Algonquin Provincial Park, is organized into districts for judicial and administrative purposes. Québec completely reorganized its municipal county administration in 1979, resulting in new units known as "regional county municipalities" (MRC). The 71 former municipal counties are now components of the 95 MRCs, 2 urban communities, one regional community and one regional administration. Within this new municipal structure are over 1500 cities, towns, villages and other rural municipalities. The only western province using the county structure is Alberta, where 30 municipal counties and 20 municipal districts have a combination of administrative and educational functions. In BC the word county is used in terms of the county court divisions. Elsewhere in Canada the land division comparable to "county" is usually called a district or rural municipality.

ALAN RAYBURN

Reading: C.R. Tindal, *Local Government in Canada* (1979).

Courcelle, Daniel de Rémy de, governor of New France 1665-72 (b in France 1626; d there 24 Oct 1698). Courcelle, a nobleman and a military officer, arrived at Québec "breathing nothing but war" and determined to defeat the powerful Iroquois Confederacy. In the winter of 1666, he led an ill-fated expedition into the Mohawk country, losing many men to cold and hunger but failing to engage the enemy. A second attack later that year established the French for the first time as the principal power in the Great Lakes area. In civil matters, Courcelle quarrelled frequently with the INTENDANT, Jean TALON.

ALLAN GREER

Coureurs de bois, itinerant, unlicensed fur traders of NEW FRANCE, known as "wood-runners" to the English on Hudson Bay and "bush-lopers" to the Anglo-Dutch of Albany (NY). Few French colonists had ventured W of the Ottawa R until the mid-1660s, when a sudden drop in the price of beaver, the arrival of some 3000 indentured servants and soldiers, and peace with the Iroquois made the change both necessary and feasible. By 1680, despite repeated prohibitions from both the church and colonial authorities, some 500 coureurs de bois were in the Lk Superior country attempting to outdistance the Indian middlemen. As a result, fewer Indians brought furs to trade at Montréal and Trois-Rivières, inducing colonial merchants to hire some coureurs de bois in order to remain in business. Licensing was eventually introduced by the authorities to control the seasonal exodus into the hinterland. Thus professional, "respectable" VOYAGEURS, usually associated with particular interior posts, came into being. Renegade traders persisted, becoming the primary bearers of the designation "coureur de bois" after the emergence of New Orleans as an alternative focus of the trade in the 18th century. The independent coureurs de bois played an important role in the European exploration of the continent and in establishing trading contacts with the Indians.

TOM WIEN

Coureurs des côtes, itinerant traders of 18th-century rural French Canada, who emerged in significant numbers when LOUISBOURG and the West Indies began to furnish an irregular market for the colony's surplus wheat. Since the countryside was not populous enough to support periodic markets, the travelling agents of export merchants increased in number, constituting a formidable competition for sedentary merchants both in the towns and in the *côtes* (one of the merchants referred to these itinerant buyers as "strolling imps"). Yet presumably the peasants, at least those who were not tied by debt to a resident merchant, appreciated the agents, who offered higher prices and, in many cases, cash advances as well.

TOM WIEN

Courtenay, BC, City, pop 9631 (1986c), 8992 (1981c), inc 1915, is located on the E coast of Vancouver I, 219 km by road N of Victoria. The city is situated on a narrow plain, with mountains to the W rising to 1830 m. An abundance of fish, game and berries brought a large Comox Indian community to the area. The first white explorers were Spanish navigators in 1791. Rear-Adm George William Courtenay (RN) surveyed the area 1846-49. An HBC store was established in the 1850s and white settlement began in the 1860s. Reginald Pidcock, who owned the site and built a mill, and Nova Scotian Joseph McPhee, who started the first store and later bought most of Pidcock's land, helped develop the community. Completion of a road from Victoria 1910 and the arrival 4 years later of the Esquimalt and Nanaimo Ry spurred Courtenay's growth. Immigration from England, Scotland and the Maritimes followed WWI. Courtenay has become a service centre for the surrounding fishing, logging and farming region of 35 000 people. CFB Comox and tourism are also important economic features of this region. An annual event of increasing importance is the 9-day winter carnival, which attracts many visitors to the region's excellent skiing facilities. A special summer attraction is the Courtenay Youth Music Centre, known throughout N America as Canada's summer community of musicians.

ALAN F.J. ARTIBISE

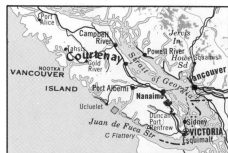

Courts of Law The Constitution Act, 1867, provides for provincial superior courts of general jurisdiction to be established by the provinces, with federally appointed judges. These courts are charged with administering all laws in force in Canada, whether enacted by Parliament, provincial legislatures or municipalities. This essentially unitary aspect of Canadian courts is fundamental to the Canadian judicial system. The provinces constitute, maintain and organize superior, county and district courts, of both civil and criminal jurisdiction, and the federal government appoints the judges (*see* JUDICIARY) and pays their salaries. The remaining provincial courts are courts of inferior jurisdiction whose presiding officers are appointed by the province in which they sit. In addition, section 101 of the Act gives Parliament power to "provide for the Constitution, Maintenance and Organization of a General Court of Appeal for Canada, and for the establishment of any additional Courts for the better Administration of the Laws of Canada." All of the courts constituted and appointed solely by the federal government owe their existence to this power. Finally, all courts, except those in Québec, enforce the common LAW. In Québec the source of the civil or noncriminal law is the CIVIL LAW.

Federally Constituted Courts

The Supreme Court of Canada was established in 1875 by the SUPREME COURT Act as a general court of appeal for Canada. The court comprises 9 judges, appointed by the governor-in-council, 3 of whom must come from the Bench or Bar of Québec. The composition of the court can now only be amended by resolutions of Parliament and each province. An amendment relating to the court in other respects can, however, be effected with a parliamentary resolution concurred in by the legislatures of two-thirds of the provinces comprising at least 50% of the population of all of the provinces. Changes to the appointment procedure to the court may occur as a result of the MEECH LAKE ACCORD (1987). The court has, since 1949, been the ultimate court of appeal for Canada. Prior to 1949 the final appellate tribunal was the JUDICIAL COMMITTEE OF THE PRIVY COUNCIL. In 1975, the role and function of the court changed again when the automatic right to appeal to it in civil matters, previously based on a purely monetary criterion, was abolished. Appeals may now only be taken to the Supreme Court with leave of the Supreme Court or of the lower court whose decision is being challenged. There remains a right of appeal in criminal cases in circumstances where one judge of a provincial court of appeal has dissented on a question of law, where an acquittal of an indictable offence by the trial court has been set aside by the court of appeal or where the accused has been found not guilty by reason of insanity.

In civil matters, the court now only hears cases which, in its opinion or in the opinion of the court of appeal, are of importance to the country as a whole or involve some important question of law; these include a large number of cases involving the constitutional validity of federal or provincial statutes, the application of the Canadian Charter of Rights and Freedoms and the authority for decisions of government officials and tribunals. Fewer cases involving purely private law issues now are heard by the court. The court must also adjudicate upon questions referred to it by the governor-in-council or appeals from questions referred to provincial courts of appeal by the executive governments of the provinces. These cases, known as references, almost always deal with the constitutional validity of legislation, proposed or existing. References are peculiar to the Canadian legal system. They enable governments to know, expeditiously, whether legislation on which their actions depend is lawful.

The Federal Court of Canada was established by Parliament in 1971. Prior to that time, its predecessor, the Exchequer Court of Canada, established by parliamentary statute, existed principally to judge claims by or against the federal government or matters relating to maritime law (*see* LAW OF THE SEA), COPYRIGHT, patent and trademark law and federal taxation statutes. The FEDERAL COURT of Canada has the same jurisdiction, but also has a supervisory jurisdiction in relation to decisions of tribunals and inferior bodies established by federal law. It is divided into a Trial Division and a Court of Appeal. Generally, matters originate in the Trial Division, but some appeals from interior tribunals and some actions to set aside decisions of inferior tribunals proceed directly to the Federal Court of Appeal. An appeal lies from the Court of Appeal to the Supreme Court of Canada with leave of either court. The main office of the court is in Ottawa, but it regularly sits throughout Canada according to the circumstances of the action and to suit the convenience of the parties. In 1983 several new positions were added to its Trial Division because of its increasing case load.

Other Federal Courts The Court Martial Appeal Court, established under the National Defence Act, is composed of judges of the Federal Court and provincial superior courts named by the governor-in-council. The Court Martial Appeal Court hears appeals from decisions of the service tribunals of the Canadian ARMED FORCES and its decisions can be appealed to the Supreme Court of Canada in a procedure similar to appeals in ordinary criminal matters. The Tax Court of Canada was created in 1983 as a continuation of the Tax Review Board. This court hears and determines appeals on matters arising under the various statutes relating to taxation, eg, the Income Tax Act. Its decisions are subject to review by the Federal Court.

Because they conduct some judicial and quasi-judicial functions, certain federal administrative boards and tribunals are designated courts of record. These include the CANADIAN TRANSPORT COMMISSION, the NATIONAL ENERGY BOARD and the Tariff Board. The decisions of such boards are subject to review by the Federal Court (*see* ADMINISTRATIVE TRIBUNALS).

Courts Established by the Provinces or Territories

Superior Courts Provincial and territorial superior courts can hear and determine any civil cause of action brought before them, with the exception of suits within the exclusive jurisdiction of courts established by Parliament. In criminal matters, superior courts have jurisdiction to hear trials of any serious offences and have exclusive jurisdiction to hear cases involving particularly serious crimes, such as murder, treason and piracy. For a number of other crimes, eg, serious sexual assault, manslaughter and attempted murder, accused persons can demand that their trial be heard by a superior court.

In every province except Alberta JURIES are mandatory in criminal trials for charges over which superior courts have exclusive jurisdiction, and a jury can be demanded by either the prosecution or the accused in every other trial of an indictable offence over which the superior court has jurisdiction. Twelve persons comprise juries in criminal cases, except in the Yukon and NWT, where there are 6 jury members. The constitution of juries for civil cases is now rare. It can be requested by either side when permitted by provincial law, and it is within the discretion of the trial court whether to allow the request. Civil juries have 6 members. In all trials in which a judge and jury are involved, it is the judge's duty to determine questions of law and instruct the jury and it is the jury's duty to determine the questions of fact.

Superior courts are usually divided into trial and appeal divisions. The appellate division is, in most provinces, called the Court of Appeal; it hears appeals from the trial division and lower courts, and its decisions can, subject to certain restrictions, be appealed to the Supreme Court of Canada. In most provinces the Court of Appeal has no original jurisdiction; all cases come to it as appeals from the trial division or from lower courts, the principal exception being the reference procedure whereby the provincial Cabinet may refer questions to the Court of Appeal.

In NS, Ontario and BC, where the amount of money involved in a civil action surpasses the limit for SMALL-CLAIMS COURT (and is less than a specified amount), county or district courts have jurisdiction to hear civil trials. The trial division of the superior court hears all other civil trials in those provinces and all civil trials in other provinces, without regard to monetary limit. Similarly, in criminal cases in all provinces except NS, Ontario, BC and Québec, the trial division will hear all trials of indictable offences except those where the accused has elected to be tried by a provincial court judge or where the offence is one over which the provincial court judge has absolute jurisdiction. The superior-court trial division is referred to as the Court of Queen's Bench in NB, Manitoba, Saskatchewan and Alberta. In Newfoundland and BC it is called the Supreme Court of the province. Nova Scotia's is entitled the Supreme Court of Nova Scotia Trial Division; Québec's, the Superior Court of Québec. In Ontario the trial division is called the High Court of Justice, which for the purposes of reviewing the actions of administrative tribunals is constituted as the Divisional Court. PEI is unique in that its Supreme Court is the only court (other than provincial criminal courts) in the province, the General Division of which fulfils the function of other provinces' superior trial courts. The Supreme Court of the Yukon exercises superior-court jurisdiction in the YT; in the NWT it is the Supreme Court of the NWT.

County or District Courts At one time all provinces had a system of county or district courts with local jurisdiction within the provinces to hear criminal trials of serious offences that were not within the exclusive jurisdiction of a superior court or within the absolute jurisdiction of a magistrate, and to hear civil cases involving specified amounts of money. Only NS, Ontario and BC have retained these courts. As well as civil and criminal trials, these courts hear appeals from magistrates' courts or provincial judges' courts in less serious criminal cases. In all other provinces the jurisdiction of county and district courts now belongs to the superior courts.

Provincial Courts All provinces have courts staffed by judges appointed by the province to deal with lesser criminal matters, including trials of minor or summary conviction offences, trials of serious (indictable) offences where the accused elects to be so tried, and preliminary inquiries of indictable offences – a procedure whereby the MAGISTRATE determines whether there is sufficient evidence against the accused to warrant a trial. In some provinces, eg, Newfoundland, Ontario and Manitoba, the provincial court (criminal division) handles the matters assigned to provincial court judges under the Criminal Code, while other divisions handle small claims and such matters as FAMILY LAW. In Québec, similar functions are performed by the Courts of the Sessions of the Peace, and in some cities, by municipal courts. The YT has a magistrate's court, but in the NWT the Territorial Court now performs these functions. Most provinces also have a court, presided over by Justices of the Peace, for minor offences, such as infractions of the provincial and municipal laws. In Québec, this is referred to as the Court of Justices of the Peace; in Ontario, as the Provincial Offences Court.

Family Court While divorces and their results fall under the jurisdiction of a superior court, family courts, which are provincially constituted and appointed, are responsible for custody of and access to children, support obligations and adoption. In most provinces the family court is part of the provincial court. In PEI the provincial court only deals with criminal matters and there is a Family Division of the Supreme Court. In Saskatchewan and in parts of Newfoundland and Ontario, the Unified Family Court, with judges appointed jointly by the federal and provincial governments, can adjudicate all family-law matters, including divorce and division of property.

Juvenile Court Children charged with offences contrary to federal, provincial or municipal laws appear before juvenile court. By 1985 everyone under 18 charged with an offence came under the jurisdiction of juvenile or youth courts (*see* JUVENILE DELINQUENCY). In most provinces such cases are heard by the family division of the provincial court. In PEI it is the Family Division of the Supreme Court, in Québec the Social Welfare Court, and in Saskatchewan the Unified Family Court that has jurisdiction.

Small-Claims Court is responsible for civil cases involving sums less than a set amount. In Québec this limit is $10 000, but in the other provinces it is $1000, $2000 or $3000. Most provinces have a small-claims or civil division of the provincial court to hear these cases. There are some variations, eg, in Halifax the municipal court can hear cases of less than $500.

Probate or Surrogate Court, established in most provinces and usually presided over by judges of county or superior courts, adjudicates matters involving estates of deceased persons.

P.K. DOODY AND T.B. SMITH

Coutts, James Allan, politician, businessman (b at High River, Alta 16 May 1938). Educated at U of A and Harvard, Coutts took an interest in politics at university. After being defeated as a Liberal candidate in 1962, he worked as PM PEARSON's appointments secretary 1963-66. After a period as a private consultant, Coutts returned to Ottawa in 1975 as Pierre TRUDEAU's principal secretary 1975-81. He ran unsuccessfully for Parliament in a by-election in 1981 and in the 1984 general election. Coutts was identified with the reform wing of the Liberal Party and was known for his interest in social-welfare causes. In 1985 he and Toronto developer Dan Casey formed Canadian Investment Capital Ltd, of which Coutts is chairman. In 1987 CIC bought the N American explosives interests of DuPont Inc.

ROBERT BOTHWELL

Coutume de Paris, the customary law of the *Prévoté et Vicomté de Paris* (written 1510; revised 1580), was a code of law first introduced to what is now Canada by the COMPAGNIE DES CENT-ASSOCIÉS in 1627. In 1664, under the royal Act creating the COMPAGNIE DES INDES OCCIDENTALES, it officially became NEW FRANCE's only legal code. *See also* CIVIL CODE.

Couture, Guillaume, teacher, choirmaster, composer (b at Montréal 23 Oct 1851; d there 15 Jan 1915), grandfather of Jean PAPINEAU-COUTURE. One of Canada's music pioneers, Couture studied in Paris with Romain Bussine and Théodore Dubois and in 1875 his *Rêverie* opus 2 was performed in concert, along with works by Duparc, Fauré and Franck. On his return to Montréal that year, he began teaching and also became a music critic for *La Minerve.* Léo-Paul MORIN and Rodolphe PLAMONDON were among his pupils. Renowned for his teaching skill, Couture returned to Paris in 1876 and became choirmaster at Ste-Clotilde church with organists César

Franck and Charles Bordes. Late in 1877 he returned to Canada and in 1894 founded the Montréal Symphony Orchestra and was its director 1894-96. Between 1907 and 1909 he composed his major work, the oratorio *Jean le Précurseur.*

HÉLÈNE PLOUFFE

Couture, Joseph-Alphonse, veterinarian (b at Ste-Claire, Qué 15 Dec 1850; d at Québec C 12 Mar 1922). He served in the Canadian militia 1866-68 against the FENIANS and then in the Papal ZOUAVES in Italy, 1868-70. Bilingual, he entered the anglophone Montreal Veterinary College in 1870 and was granted a veterinary degree from McGill in 1873, becoming one of Canada's first francophone veterinarians. He lectured and gave demonstrations in animal anatomy to French-speaking students at Montreal Veterinary Coll 1876-78. Posted to Québec C as a federal veterinary inspector in 1878, he was superintendent of the Animal Quarantine Station at Lévis 1879-1922. He organized this major gateway for pure-bred livestock imported into Canada to prevent the introduction of epidemic infectious diseases and protect exports of Canadian live animals and animal products. Couture produced the first Canadian textbook on breeding and livestock diseases in 1882. A gifted communicator, he wrote in agricultural journals and spoke at farmer's meetings to support and defend Canadian livestock breeds. Under the pseudonym of Jérôme Aubry he also contributed fiery columns on current religious and sociopolitical issues of the early 1900s in *La Vérité*, an influential weekly owned by J.P. TARDIVEL.   LOUIS-PHILIPPE PHANEUF

Covington, Arthur Edwin, radio scientist, astronomer (b at Regina 21 Sept 1913). In 1946 near Ottawa, Covington made the first radio astronomical observations in Canada using surplus equipment from the wartime development of radar at the National Research Council Laboratories. His discovery, during the partial solar eclipse on Nov 23 of that year, that microwave emission was by far weaker from the bright undisturbed surface of the sun than from dark, relatively cooler sunspots was startling. His subsequent pioneering observations on the variability and polarization of sunspot-associated microwave emission stimulated study of how the solar corona is energized above sunspots. In Feb 1947 Covington inaugurated at NRC daily measurements of the total flux from the entire solar surface. The program, which he supervised for 31 years, now provides the longest accurate record of solar radio emission anywhere, precise data often supplanting the sunspot numbers traditionally used as an index of solar activity.   V. GAIZAUSKAS

Cowan, Gary, golfer (b at Kitchener, Ont 28 Oct 1938). One of Canada's finest amateur golfers, Cowan learned his craft under teaching professional Lloyd Tucker in Kitchener. He represented Canada in many international competitions, including the World Amateur and Commonwealth team matches. He was the only Canadian to win 2 US Amateur championships (1966, 1971). He won the 1961 Canadian Amateur championship and between 1964 and 1984 took 9 Ontario Amateurs. Cowan resisted the temptation to turn professional.   LORNE RUBENSTEIN

Cowansville, Qué, Town, pop 11 643 (1986c), 12 240 (1981c), inc 1931, is located on the S fork of the Yamaska R in the EASTERN TOWNSHIPS of Québec. Named after Peter Cowan, its first postmaster and storekeeper, it was originally settled by LOYALISTS from the US. Its present population is predominantly French Canadian, with a substantial English Canadian presence. Cowansville was an agricultural and textile centre until 1940, when it underwent industrial diversification. Sit-

uated about 20 km from the US border and 85 km SE of Montréal, it has attracted several large companies based in the northern states and Ontario. Major industrial employers include producers of consumer and industrial textiles and plastics, printed paper, skis and hockey sticks. Smaller firms supply the construction and transportation sectors of the province. Social services – including the Institut de Cowansville, a federal penitentiary – employ a large professional work force. The town's preserved Victorian architecture and proximity to Mount Brome are enduring tourist attractions.   PAULA KESTELMAN

Cowboy The Spanish conquistadors who ruled Mexico in the 16th century recruited native herdsmen on horseback to tend wild cattle on open rangeland. These "vaqueros" wore buckskin clothes, wide-brimmed hats, tall boots and spurs, and chaperajos (shaggy protective leggings), and carried la reata (rope). From that tradition came the itinerant cowpunchers, or cowhands, who drove Texas longhorn cattle to pasture and to market across the American southwest in the 1830s, and who established cattle ranches in the Canadian West in the 1880s. The term encompassed all cattle-handlers from simple livestock growers to moneyed English lords, REMITTANCE MEN and North-West Mounted Police ranchers. The cowboy has been mythologized and popularized by entertainers who exhibited the cowboy skills of riding and roping at early "wild west" shows, later in RODEOS and stampedes, and eventually in Hollywood movie westerns. Legendary cowboys in Canada include Guy Weadick, creator of the CALGARY STAMPEDE; John WARE, former black slave who ranched in southern Alberta; and rodeo competitors Pete Knight and Herman LINDER. *See also* RANCHING HISTORY.

TED BARRIS

Cox, George Albertus, financier, senator, philanthropist (b at Colborne, Upper Canada 7 May 1840; d at Toronto 16 Jan 1914). A telegraph operator, Cox became prominent in Peterborough, Ont, as mayor, TEMPERANCE leader and president of the Midland Ry and the Central Canada Loan and Savings Co. In 1888 he moved to Toronto and by 1900 had become one of Canada's most influential businessmen as president of the Bank of Commerce and the Canada Life Assurance Co and founder, president, VP or director of over 40 other firms. Although colleagues found his individualistic business methods and efforts to create a family dynasty inappropriate, Cox symbolized Toronto's aggressive challenge to Montréal's financial leadership in the prewar period. In 1896 Sir Wilfrid LAURIER appointed him to the Senate. A Methodist, Cox helped many needy individuals and contributed generously to that church, Toronto General Hospital and U of Toronto.

J. LINDSEY

Coyne, James Elliott, banker, businessman (b at Winnipeg 17 July 1910). Coyne became the highly controversial governor of the BANK OF CANADA in 1955 after 17 years with the bank. He warned against the dangers of FOREIGN INVESTMENT and spoke out on economic matters despite the divergence of his views from government policy. His outspokenness caused friction with the DIEFENBAKER government, which already distrusted him because of his close links with prominent Liberals. Ultimately, Coyne's refusal to adopt the government's expansionist MONETARY POLICY irritated not only Finance Minister Donald FLEMING but many leading economists, who signed an open letter calling for his resignation. Coyne initially refused but, confronted with a bill firing him, he stepped down 13 July 1961.

JOHN ENGLISH

Coyote (*Canis latrans*, family Canidae), often called prairie wolf or brush wolf, is intermediate in size between WOLF and FOX. It resembles a lightly built German shepherd dog with erect, pointed ears, pointed muzzle, flat forehead, bushy tail (usually held rather low), and coat of long, grey, russet or yellowish brown hair. Coyotes are restricted to the N American prairies and to open mixed hardwood and coniferous habitats. In Canada they are found in BC, YT and western NWT, Alta, central and southern Sask and Man, and E to the Maritimes. Coyotes usually breed in Feb; litters of 5-7 pups (maximum 19) are born 60-63 days later (Apr-early May) in a den. Breeding begins at one year, and coyotes mate for life. They co-operate in hunting, denning and raising young. Coyotes can howl, singly or in unison, and reply to howls of other coyotes, wolves or dogs, and even to car horns or sirens. They are primarily carnivorous, preying chiefly on rabbits and rodents, but they also consume insects and fruits. Coyotes are mistakenly considered a threat to livestock.   C.S. CHURCHER

Crab, common name for 2 groups of decapod ("ten-footed") CRUSTACEANS. The Anomura, including hermit, mole and lithoid crabs, have relatively normal abdomens. In true crabs, infraorder Brachyura, including genera *Cancer* and *Carcinus*, the abdomen is greatly reduced in size and is flexed beneath the thorax. Worldwide there are 4500 species inhabiting marine, freshwater and terrestrial environments. Crabs comprise one of the largest groups of the subphylum Crustacea; as individuals, they are among the largest of arthropods. Giant Japanese and Australian spider crabs, larger in size than the largest lobsters but weighing somewhat less, may have a claw span of over 3 m and weigh up to 14 kg. In Canada, crabs are found in marine deep-water and in intertidal and estuarine environments on both coasts. Some, eg, East Coast snow or queen crab (*Chionoecetes opilio*) and West Coast Dungeness crab (*Cancer magister*), are of considerable economic value. *See also* CRUSTACEAN RESOURCES.   D.E. AIKEN

Crab Apple (genus *Malus*), deciduous tree that differs from the orchard APPLE in bearing smaller, often acid, fruits. It is grown for its special ORNAMENTAL attributes (eg, tree form, showy blossoms, colour of fruit) and climatic adaptability. The fruits are valued for their superior jelly-making properties and as preserves. The numerous ancestral wild species probably include *M. sylvestris*, *M. prunifolia* and *M. pumila*. Considerable efforts have been made in Canada to improve hardiness with *M. baccata*, the Siberian crab apple, as a major source for hardiness. Recently, a number of species have been used as sources of disease resistance; *M. floribunda*, the Japanese flowering crab, has been a major source for resistance to apple scab (*Venturia inaequalis*). Several local forms of *M. fusca* have been collected at University of British Columbia.   A.D. CROWE

Cradle Board, or papoose carrier, served (and in some areas still serves) as home to an Indian infant. Securely bound to the thin rectangular board, the baby could be carried on its mother's back or placed out of the way while she worked. The design of the board prevented injury to the child even if the board were to fall over (in many types a hoop or bow at the top of the cradle board served to protect the infant's head). The exact form varied from group to group throughout the continent, but almost invariably considerable energy was spent decorating the cradle board and its fittings.   RENÉ R. GADACZ

Craft Unionism, a form of labour organization developed to promote and defend the interests of skilled workers (variously known as artisans, me-

The coyote (*Canis latrans*) is found in Canada's prairies and in open mixed hardwood and coniferous habitats (*photo by Stephen J. Krasemann/DRK Photo*).

chanics, craftsmen and tradesmen). Craft skills have always involved both manual dexterity and conceptual abilities; their value and scarcity have given such workers considerable power in the workplace. Craft unions sought to maintain that power by controlling training, regulating the work process, and insisting that only members should practise any particular trade. Pride and independence bred a spirit of solidarity and led to Canada's first labour movement.

A full-fledged guild system protecting traditional crafts on the British and European model never developed in BNA. Men were generally expected to serve lengthy apprenticeships before becoming fully qualified practitioners or journeymen. Craft unions first appeared early in the 19th century when some journeymen began to recognize their common interests. By the 1830s journeymen shipwrights, printers, tailors, stonecutters, carpenters and others had formed unions and had even launched a few strikes for higher wages and improved working conditions. Many of these unions also established mutual-benefit funds to help their members cope with sickness, accident or death.

The first craft unions united skilled workers in single communities but, beginning in the 1850s, craftsmen began to affiliate with larger organizations. At first, British workers established local branches of the unions they had left behind, like the Amalgamated Society of Engineers or the Amalgamated Society of Carpenters and Joiners. But skilled workers in Canada increasingly linked their local unions to such new American craft unions as the Iron Molders' Union and the National Typographical Union, which were organizing workers across the continent – a development that reflected the growing tendency of workers to "tramp" around N America in search of work. This "international unionism" was intended to establish common standards of employment across the continent. Many craft unions in Québec, however, refused to join the internationals because of their insensitivity to French language and culture.

When Canada's INDUSTRIALIZATION began after 1850, many employers attempted to erode craft skills by subdividing tasks among less-skilled workers and by introducing new machinery. By

WWI these changes had brought mass production and "scientific" management. Craftsmen used their unions to resist any changes they believed would disrupt work routines, lower wages or threaten unemployment. For the practice of each craft the unions developed much tighter rules and regulations, which employers were expected to accept as a condition of hiring skilled workmen. These new rules governed such matters as apprenticeship, daily workload, hours of labour and tools of the trade.

Many employers resisted these restrictions on their unbridled control, and craft unionists fought hundreds of bitter strikes in the half century before 1920. Craftsmen were often the most vigorous and articulate critics of industrialization, which they believed was degrading the worker and his job. By the 1920s industrialists had driven craft unions out of most workplaces and had transformed work processes so thoroughly that they no longer relied on many scarce handicraft skills. It was only in the printing and construction industries that craft unionism survived with any vitality.

Craft unions had a long history of uniting across occupational lines to form labour councils in individual communities, at the national level in the TRADES AND LABOR CONGRESS of Canada, and across the continent in the American Federation of Labor. Many craftsmen became uneasy, however, about the rise of INDUSTRIAL UNIONISM, which would unite all workers in a single industry regardless of skill and might dilute the skilled workers' power. In 1919 they opposed the ONE BIG UNION, which promoted the new form of industrial organization, and in the 1930s set themselves against the American-based Congress of Industrial Organizations. In 1939 the TLC succumbed to AFL pressure and ousted CIO unions from its ranks. Some craft unions (eg, machinists' and carpenters' unions) nonetheless broadened their membership base gradually to include workers in mass production and related industries.

In Québec, craft and industrial unions had co-existed inside the Canadian Catholic Confederation of Labour since 1921. Elsewhere, these 2 streams were reunited in the new CANADIAN LABOUR CONGRESS. The friction did not disappear, however, and during the 1970s disputes over craft-union jurisdictions and autonomy of Canadian unions from international headquarters prompted several construction unions to withhold their CLC dues. Suspended in 1981, the following year these craft unions formed a new national organization, the CANADIAN FEDERATION OF LABOUR. Thus craft unionism once again had a distinct identity. *See also* WORKING-CLASS HISTORY. CRAIG HERON

Reading: Eugene Forsey, *Trade Unions in Canada, 1812-1902* (1982); Desmond Morton with Terry Copp, *Working People* (1980); Bryan D. Palmer, *Working-Class Experience* (1983); H. Clare Pentland, *Labour and Capital in Canada, 1650-1860* (1981).

Crafts An accurate and useful definition of contemporary crafts is unattainable, partly because the concepts underlying crafts are changing and partly because the word is used in 2 different senses. The root meaning [Ger *kraft*, "strength"] is the skilful application of force, yet, in ordinary speech, the words "art" and "craft" are sometimes used interchangeably to mean a highly skilled occupation, as in the art of cookery or the craft of poetry. As a term for objects, crafts is largely a 20th-century usage; in the 19th century such artifacts were called applied, decorative or ornamental arts, terms which usually meant utilitarian objects that were a pleasure to the senses and showed high skill in execution. Unfortunately, the Victorians' love of excessive decoration brought the decorative arts and their producers into disrepute. It was not always so: many of the greatest artists of the Renaissance were trained as goldsmiths and applied their skills equally well to the design of tapestries, goblets, stage sets and more.

By the beginning of the 20th century, crafts had become "handicrafts," ie, products of cottage or home industry. This definition still applies in the Third World where crafts are still a matter of tradition, handed down from parent to child. Side by side with the large demand for utilitarian objects (eg, baskets, pots, boxes) there has always existed a luxury market, ie, objects required for religious or ceremonial purposes or used by the wealthy. This division still exists everywhere. In Europe, N America and Australasia the luxury market often involves objects of "art," ie, unique objects serving a purely aesthetic function, which are made in traditional craft media (eg, clay, fibres, wood, GLASS, metal, LEATHER).

Contemporary Crafts in Canada The 1950s and 1960s saw an upsurge in the number of people producing crafts for a livelihood. In part, this growth was an extension of the self-sufficiency movement of those years. However, the trend (called voluntary simplicity) continues today, partly as a result of high unemployment. Concurrently the number of hobbyists and "do-it-yourselfers" has increased. Various surveys in Canada indicate that over 1.5 million people spend more than 7 hours per week on a craft; about 12 000 earn their living from making and selling craft items. The retail value of domestically produced crafts in Canada is about $375 million per year. The market for well-made, well-designed things, which express the individuality of the purchaser as well as the producer, has also expanded.

In Canada most raw materials used in crafts (eg, cotton, silk, jute) are imported; the growing of hemp (the source of marijuana and hashish) was banned half a century ago. Recently, concern has arisen about the use of materials from endangered species (eg, various skins, ivory) but most craft materials are still the traditional ones. Newer substances have given rise to health concerns: craftspeople and hobbyists have unknowingly been put at risk by using solvents, varnishes, glazes, pigments, plastics and additives that have been found to be dangerous. However, craftwork also has considerable therapeutic value. Occupational therapists have long recognized the value of handiwork in rehabilitation, and millions of people all over the world simply derive satisfaction and pleasure from working with their hands.

Traditionally, crafts were taught by APPRENTICESHIP or by transmission of skills from parents to children. Various new movements in education led to the use of traditional craft materials (eg, clay) in primary education, but as a means of self-expression, not to instil basic training in the medium. Formal education in craft techniques hardly existed in Canada before the boom in the construction of COMMUNITY COLLEGES in the late 1960s. For example, in Ontario a school of crafts and design was founded and attached to Sheridan College, although the school was residential and intended to teach crafts and design to all Ontario students. There is also considerable demand for evening classes and summer courses teaching the basic skills. In times of economic hardship, schools of crafts and design that are not autonomous are finding their programs being cut and suspended, sometimes whole departments, and, in one case in BC, an entire college.

Modern communications have largely destroyed the distinctive provincial or regional craft styles that once prevailed in Canada. Québec and Newfoundland probably have the greatest claim to distinction, as certain traditional styles have not yet been widely copied, eg, *ceinture fléché* weaving and hooked rugs, respectively. Some provinces have established a particular name, eg, Nova Scotia is well known in Canada and the US for QUILTING. But CERAMICS are extensively produced in every province, WEAVING and surface printing are taught everywhere and there is little distinction between one region and another. Even less common crafts (eg, glassblowing) still share an international style. In Canada as a whole, the most advanced work internationally is probably being done in glass and leather, but these media are not the prerogative of any particular province, although Québec and Ontario, being the largest provinces, also have the greatest number of craftspeople.

Associations Because the basic skills of many crafts are quickly learned, many amateurs attempt to sell what they make. The consequences are an undercutting of the professional market and a deterioration of standards. Craft organizations have long played an important role in maintaining standards of quality in design and production. In 1902, in part as a result of the general interest in handicrafts aroused by the art nouveau movement, the Women's Art Association succeeded in setting up a shop in Montréal. The group was chartered in 1906 as the Canadian Handicrafts Guild (later renamed the Canadian Guild of Crafts). The objectives of the guild are to encourage, revive and develop crafts; to aid craftsmen in marketing; to undertake and participate in exhibitions; to provide craft instruction; and to educate the public in the value of crafts and good handiwork. At the request of Sir Wilfred GRENFELL the guild set up craft centres in Labrador. In Newfoundland, the Outport Nursing Committee (fd in 1920) established a service whereby local women could help pay for nursing and medical care by knitting and weaving goods which were later sold. The trademark for the goods produced later became "NONIA" to reflect the group's new name (Newfoundland Outport Nurses' Industrial Assn).

From its beginning, the guild was interested in native crafts. In 1930 they held a major exhibition of Inuit work in Montréal. In 1933, they formed an Indian Committee to help renew INDIAN ARTS; in 1940, they were asked to include INUIT ART as well. In 1948-49 they appointed James HOUSTON as their Arctic representative and it was largely his work that led to a renaissance of Inuit art.

Every province and territory has a major craft organization. For example, in 1986, the Corporation des métiers d'art du Québec brought together more than 500 members (professional craftspeople or apprentices), in such varied disciplines as

wood, ceramics, textile printing and soft sculpture, metal jewellery, leather, skins and engravings. Each year the Corporation du salon des métiers d'art du Québec chooses some of these works for an exhibition. There is one national body, the Canadian Crafts Council. If these organizations are still devoted to the aims that stimulated the Canadian Handicrafts Guild in 1906, it is not because they have failed to learn from history but rather because the problems of that time are still with us today. PETER H. WEINRICH

Reading: U. Abrahamson, *Crafts Canada: The Useful Arts* (1974); J. Flanders, *The Craftsman's Way: Canadian Expression* (1981); H. Gordon Green, *A Heritage of Canadian Handicrafts* (1967).

Craig, Sir James Henry, officer, colonial administrator (b at Gibraltar 1748; d at London, Eng 12 Jan 1812). Governor general of the Canadas and administrator of LOWER CANADA from 1807 to 1811, Craig tried to influence the elections of 1809 and 1810, imprisoning without trial leaders of the Parti canadien in Mar 1810 in what has been called a "reign of terror." Craig, his senior administrators and leading British merchants advocated a variety of ways to eradicate what they viewed as the menaces of democracy and FRENCH CANADIAN NATIONALISM, suggesting union of the Canadas and creation of English counties in the Townships or replacing the Assembly by a primarily British and aristocratic council, abolishing the seigneurial regime, and encouraging immigration from Great Britain and the US, church submission to royal prerogative and control of education. Thus they heightened French Canadian nationalism. Under the threat of war between England and the US, Craig strengthened ties with the Indians and reinforced the fortifications of Québec City and the surrounding district.

JEAN-PIERRE WALLOT

Craigellachie, BC, located at the W entrance to EAGLE PASS, was the place where Donald SMITH drove the symbolic "last spike" in a ceremony marking the completion of the CANADIAN PACIFIC RY, 7 Nov 1885. It was named for a rocky crag in Morayshire, Scotland, where Smith grew up.

Craigflower Manor and Schoolhouse was built in 1856 by the Puget's Sound Agricultural Co, a subsidiary of the HUDSON'S BAY COMPANY. The manor was to house the manager of Craigflower Farm (developed to provide fresh farm produce to the nearby Hudson's Bay post at Ft Victoria) and to form the basis of a permanent agricultural settlement in the area. Craigflower Schoolhouse was built in 1855 to encourage settlers into the community. Both buildings are modest 2-storey wood-frame structures. The combination of classical and Gothic details on the manor was an unusual design feature, but both buildings, with their compact rectangular plans and regularly spaced windows, were typical of vernacular building within a British classical tradition. The buildings are owned by the province of BC and have been restored. JANET WRIGHT

Craigie, John Hubert, plant pathologist (b at Merigomish, NS 8 Dec 1887). Craigie discovered the sexual process in rust diseases of wheat. After military service (1914-20), Craigie joined the Dominion Rust Research Laboratory at Winnipeg in 1925 as its specialist in plant diseases. The laboratory was created that year to apply science to crop epidemics that threatened the whole prairie economy, based as it was on Marquis wheat. Earlier scientists assumed that wheat rust (named for its visible red spores) was a single disease that could be controlled by a single chemical or by breeding a naturally rust-resistant wheat. By 1916 it was discovered that rust comprised a whole family of diseases, which affected different wheat varieties differently. In 1927 Craigie made a fundamental discovery, that the rust organism reproduced sexually. It could hybridize – and thus produce new strains of the disease – every season. This breakthrough provided the intellectual basis for research that continues to this day. Wheat crops have to be monitored constantly to detect new strains of rust as early as possible, and the task of breeding new wheats that resist new rusts is never ending (*see* C.H. GOULDEN). Craigie received many honours and awards for his discovery, notably fellowship in the Royal Soc of London. He was director of the Rust Laboratory 1928-45 and subsequently Dominion botanist.

DONALD J.C. PHILLIPSON

Cramp, John Mockett, Baptist minister, writer, educator (b at St Peter's, Isle of Thanet, Eng 25 July 1796; d at Wolfville, NS 6 Dec 1881). Although a well-known writer and theologian, Cramp made his important contribution in higher education. After an unsuccessful period at the Canada Baptist Coll, Montréal, Cramp was appointed president of Acadia Coll, Wolfville. He was president 1850-53 and 1860-69, principal of its theological institute 1853-69, and "chairman of faculty" 1856-60. Over these years, he built that small Baptist college into a flourishing institution. He taught a vast array of courses, established an endowment fund, increased the number of students and professors significantly, and still found time for writing, editing and preaching. More than anyone else, Cramp shaped the early development of ACADIA UNIVERSITY, at a time when most institutions of higher learning in the Maritimes were experiencing severe difficulties. In the process he influenced several generations of Baptist ministers, educators and leaders.

BARRY M. MOODY

Cranberry, *see* BERRIES, CULTIVATED; BERRIES, WILD.

Cranbrook , BC, City, pop 15 893 (1986c), 15 915 (1981c), lies near the western edge of the ROCKY MTN TRENCH, in the Kootenay region, 870 km E of Vancouver. Located at the apex of 3 large valleys, the Elk to the E, the Central and the Valley of Moyie to the W, it is scenically situated between prominent Mt Baker (7244 m) and Cranbrook Mtn (6711 m) on the S and W and the massive Kootenay Ranges to the E. It lies near the prehistoric population centre of the Upper KOOTENAY Indians. The city site was known by Indians and early Europeans as Joseph's Prairie. James Baker, an early settler, named his lands Cranbrook Farm after his English birthplace. Railway development in the late 1890s and lumbering at nearby Lumberton were the impetus for Cranbrook's growth. Cattle raising developed also to serve railway construction workers. It later became a CPR divisional point as shops, roundhouse and accommodation were centered there. The first urban centre of the region, Cranbrook today is East Kootenay's main service and commercial centre. Recent expansion of coal mining and the forest industry has increased its role in warehousing and distribution. To some extent it is integrated commercially with the city of KIMBERLEY, 26 km to the N. WILLIAM A. SLOAN

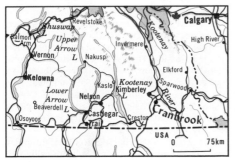

Crane (Gruidae), family of large, long-necked birds with sturdy bills and long, powerful legs. They nest in marshes, bogs, sedge meadows and upland tundra. Of the 14 species found worldwide, at least 5 have become rare, partly because of loss of nesting habitat. In Canada, 2 species occur: sandhill crane (*Grus canadensis*) is common, although the greater sandhill subspecies is considered threatened in BC; WHOOPING CRANE (*G. americana*) is endangered. The sandhill crane nests as far N as Banks and Devon islands. Nests are large mounds of dry plant material. Usually 2 brown or buff eggs with dark brown or purplish spots and blotches are laid, hatching after about 30 days. Parents share incubation. During MIGRATION, sandhill cranes favour uplands and agricultural areas and may be seen in spectacular concentrations in south-central Saskatchewan, where they feed in grainfields. Large numbers winter in southern US and Mexico. Limited hunting is allowed in portions of Saskatchewan and in several states of the US. Cranes may live as long as 20 years. E. KUYT

Cranston, Toller, figure skater (b at Hamilton, Ont 20 Apr 1949). A creative and controversial skater and artist, Cranston is widely known for his unique free-skating style. Although never a world champion, he gained more attention in the early 1970s than many who did win gold medals. With his highly individualistic approach, he is credited with opening men's FIGURE SKATING to a more artistic style of bodily movement. Cranston was Canadian senior men's champion from 1971 to 1976. He won the free-skate segment of the world championship 4 times and in 1976 was the bronze medallist at the Olympic Games in Innsbruck. Turning professional that year, he formed his own ice show, and toured with it for 2 years. He subsequently starred in the Ice Capades show, in several television ice shows, and in the professional competition, Pro Skate. Cranston is also an accomplished artist and author; his most recent work is *The Nutcracker* (1985). BARBARA SCHRODT

Crawford, Isabella Valancy, author, poet (b at Dublin, Ire 25 Dec 1850; d at Toronto, 12 Feb 1887). The daughter of a rather unsuccessful physician, Crawford immigrated with her family to Canada (1857?) and lived in a succession of Ontario settlements before moving to Peterborough in 1869. There she began to write and publish the poems and stories that became her family's chief source of income following her father's death in 1875. To further her writing career, she moved with her family to Toronto, where they lived in a succession of boarding houses (1883-87). During this productive period she contributed numerous serialized novels and novellas to New York and Toronto publications and wrote much popular verse. The one book of poetry published during her lifetime, *Old Spookses' Pass, Malcolm's Katie, and other poems* (1884), was privately printed and sold few copies, and it was only with J.W. Garvin's *The Collected Poems of Isabella Valancy Crawford* (1905) and Katherine Hale's *Isabella Valancy Crawford* (1923) that she began to be recognized as a serious writer. In the early 1970s renewed interest in Crawford resulted in the publication of forgotten manuscripts and critical articles. Her long narrative poems have received particular attention, but generally she is admired for her unique response to a distinctly Canadian landscape. C.J. TAYLOR

Crawley, Frank Radford, "Budge," film producer (b at Ottawa 14 Nov 1911; d at Toronto 13 May 1987). Through his company Crawley Films, he produced hundreds of films over his 40-year career. His vitality and enthusiasm combined with his enterprising nature enabled him to

F.R. "Budge" Crawley, filmmaker, receiving an Academy Award (1976) for *The Man Who Skied Down Everest* (*courtesy Canapress Photo Service*).

turn his filmmaking hobby into a career. *Île d'Orléans* (1938), a film he made on his honeymoon, won the Hiram Percy Maxim Award for best amateur film in 1939. With the outbreak of war there was a pressing need for training films; John GRIERSON hired Crawley's fledgling company to make many of them. After the war Crawley Films survived by making films for government and corporate sponsors. *The Loon's Necklace* (1948) won Film of the Year honours at the first Canadian Film Awards, 1949. *Newfoundland Scene* (1950), *The Power Within* (1953), *The Legend of the Raven* (1958) and *The Entertainers* (1967) were all award winners. In the late 1950s Crawley moved his company into TV production and developed an animation studio. Crawley's interest increasingly turned to feature films. *Amanita Pestilens* (1963) was quickly followed by the acclaimed *The Luck of Ginger Coffey* (1964). Crawley also produced the popular *The Rowdyman* (1972), starring Gordon PINSENT. He also worked closely with his wife Judith CRAWLEY, and their best-known film, *The Man Who Skied Down Everest* (1975), won the Academy Award for feature-length documentary. PIERS HANDLING

Crawley, Judith, "Judy," film producer, director, scriptwriter (b at Ottawa 21 Apr 1914; d there 15 Sept 1986). She was close collaborator and wife of Frank "Budge" CRAWLEY and her contribution to their company was extensive throughout its history. They made their first film, *Île d'Orleans* (1938), on their honeymoon, and shortly thereafter formed Crawley Films, which became one of Canada's foremost independent production companies. She directed a number of documentaries in the 1940s and 1950s, many of which dealt with child care, most notably the *Ages and Stages* series (1949-57). After 1961 she gave up directing and concentrated her energies on producing and writing. These activities culminated in the Academy Award for best documentary film the couple won for producing *The Man Who Skied Down Everest* (1975). While "Budge" turned his energies to producing feature films, she continued to produce educational documentaries. From 1979 to 1982 she was president of the Canadian Film Institute.

PIERS HANDLING

Crayfish, moderately sized freshwater CRUS-TACEAN of order Decapoda, similar in appearance to the American LOBSTER. The term is also applied occasionally to marine spiny lobsters, although there have been attempts to discourage this usage. In southern US, the preferred spelling is "crawfish." Crayfish are the *écrevisses* of French cuisine. Freshwater crayfish, found on all continents except Africa, number about 300 species worldwide. Distribution spans both hemispheres except for a narrow tropical belt approximately 15-20° on either side of the equator. In Canada, there are 11 species in 2 distinct subfamilies separated by the Rocky Mts. The Pacific watershed of BC contains 2 subspecies of *Pacifastacus leniusculus*. East of the Rockies, there are 9 species in 2 genera: *Orconectes* and *Cambarus*. They are found from Alberta (*Orconectes virilis*) to NB (*Cambarus bartonii*), but the most diverse population appears to be in Ontario, where all 9 species have been recorded. D.E. AIKEN

Cream, Thomas Neill, doctor, murderer (b at Glasgow, Scot 1850; d at London, Eng 15 Nov 1892). Educated in medicine at McGill, Cream was responsible for a string of murders in Canada, the US and Britain. He was also a thief, arsonist, blackmailer and illegal abortionist. Two possible Canadian victims were his wife, probably poisoned in England, and a mistress, whose body was found near Cream's London, Ont, office. In Chicago, 1881, Cream was sentenced to life imprisonment for poisoning the husband of another mistress, and his licence to practise medicine was revoked by McGill. He was released in 1891, returned briefly to Canada, then went to England where he embarked on a murder spree, poisoning at least 5 London prostitutes before he was arrested. Just before he was hanged in Newgate prison, he allegedly confessed to being Jack the Ripper. There has been speculation that Cream could have been responsible for some of the "Ripper" murders, though he was in an American prison in 1888 when most of the mysterious killings took place. EDWARD BUTTS

Credit Bureau provides a credit profile of consumers based on their repayment record of outstanding debts. A credit bureau monitors, with constantly updated information provided by credit card and other lenders, not only whether consumers repay loans but whether they do so regularly and on time. Credit bureaus, unlike investigative agencies, do not assemble information on the life-style or character of individuals, or determine whether or not an individual is credit worthy; that is decided by lenders. Credit bureaus merely provide information to help lenders make decisions. Many of Canada's early credit bureaus were organized by merchants in the 1920s as a more efficient means of maintaining information on the credit history of individuals than the prevailing practice of contacting each other to conduct a credit check. There are about 125 credit bureaus in Canada. A national association, the Associated Credit Bureaus of Canada (est 1939) is based in Toronto. There are also provincial associations. The activities of credit bureaus fall under provincial jurisdiction, and legislation in each province allows individuals to know the contents of their credit files and requires credit-granting bodies to advise individuals seeking a loan, a credit card or other financing that their credit history will be checked. DAVID CRANE

Credit Card, a card authorizing the holder to make purchases on credit. Cards are issued by department stores, banks, credit-card companies, airlines, car-rental agencies, gasoline companies and other businesses. Billings are usually monthly, and interest is generally charged only on the balance outstanding at the end of 30 days or less. Credit-card companies and banks issuing cards usually charge businesses a percentage of the bill as a handling charge, and charge the card user a fee. Payments by credit card are settled between banks and participating institutions through a system administered by the Canadian Payments Association. According to a 1984 study, in 1981 about 23 million credit cards had been issued by 40 institutions. Major changes in credit card numbers and use are expected in the late 1980s, as "SMART" cards and debit cards come into use. Only 5%-7% of total consumer debt results from credit-card use because most Canadians pay off the balance owing within the interest-free period. With the computerization of banking operations, however, a client's bank balance will probably be debited instantaneously for the amount of purchases, and if clients wish to postpone payment they will likely incur a true debt. HENRI-PAUL ROUSSEAU

Credit Unions, financial co-operatives that provide deposit, chequing and lending services to the member owners. Owned locally and operated under provincial jurisdiction, they jointly own provincial central organizations. Robert Owen began a consumer co-operative among unemployed weavers of Rochdale, England, in 1844, and co-operative principles for buying and selling were applied to borrowing and lending in an experiment in Germany. The original credit unions were not only mutual self-help societies but a strong moral and spiritual force.

The first successful credit union in Canada, a CAISSE POPULAIRE, was started at Lévis, Qué, in 1900 by Alphonse DESJARDINS. Attempts in the 1920s to establish credit unions in English-speaking areas in Ontario and the West did not succeed. In the 1930s the organizers of the ANTIGONISH MOVEMENT associated themselves with the (American) Credit Union National Association and established a credit union in Broad Cove (1932). Credit unions grew rapidly in Atlantic Canada during the GREAT DEPRESSION, and by the early 1940s they were being established across English Canada. The CCF government in Saskatchewan specifically encouraged their formation. To facilitate the exchange of savings and to help local credit unions become more efficient, credit-union leaders in all the English-speaking provinces organized provincial centrals (called co-operative credit societies or credit-union leagues), which distinguished them in name if not in substance from caisses populaires. In 1953 some of the centrals, along with other nonfinancial co-operatives, organized the Canadian Co-operative Credit Society, a national organization used primarily to transfer funds among the centrals. During the 1950s and 1960s credit unions, which are generally smaller than caisses populaires, grew rapidly, largely through using member savings to provide mortgages and short-term loans. They were able to compete effectively with banks because of low administrative costs, inexpensive premises, and convenient service hours. In the same period, they gradually acquired the legal right to offer most of the financial services, such as chequing, provided by banks. In many areas, particularly on the Prairies and in BC, anyone in a geographic area could join – not just members of a specific trades union or of specific professional or church organizations. Growth continued through to the early 1980s, largely because of the demand for mortgages (caisses populaires have, on the other hand, reduced the proportion of their funds invested in securities and mortgages).

The recession of the early 1980s was particularly hard on all western credit-granting institutions, and the credit unions were no exception. The general collapse in property values, attendant upon the recession, meant that asset values of credit unions declined correspondingly. The inevitable liquidity crisis meant that provincial government assistance was necessary in order to maintain solvency.

After the recession had reached its worst stages, the growth of the credit union movements continued. In 1986, credit unions served over 4.2 million members and had more than $47 billion in assets. Vancouver City Savings Credit Union had more than 164 000 members and $1.5 billion in assets in 1986; several others had over $100 million in assets. IAN MACPHERSON

Créditistes, Québec party involved in federal politics. For nearly 2 decades before its 1958 formation into a political party, the Ralliement des créditistes had operated a mass sociopolitical movement known as the union des électeurs. With Réal CAOUETTE as their fiery leader, Créditistes burst upon Canadian politics in the 1962 federal election, capturing 26 seats and 26% of the popular vote in Québec. The Québec wing was then affiliated with the national SOCIAL CREDIT Party. With a handful of western Social Credit MPs, the party held the balance of power in the House of Commons until the federal election of 1963. Soon after, a majority of its remaining MPs and most of its rank and file supporters split with the national party and formed an independent parliamentary grouping under its own name. The party continued to operate separately as the Ralliement des créditistes in the federal Parliament until the end of the decade. In 1970 the party entered Québec provincial politics and won 12 seats in the National Assembly, led by a colourful Caouette protégé, Camil Samson. But like the federal party, the provincial party was weakened by internal splits, and it was wiped out in the 1973 provincial sweep of Liberal Premier Robert Bourassa. In 1971 Caouette reunited the federal party with the national Social Credit Party, and became the national Social Credit leader. Despite his spirited leadership over the next few years, the party experienced a steady decline in popular support. Its parliamentary representation disappeared entirely in 1980, 4 years after Caouette's death.

The party's ideology reflected the traditional right-of-centre attitudes of Québec's rural and small urban population, and embraced Major C.H. Douglas's monetary reform ideas. In its early years in Parliament, it also supported the expansion of the French language in the federal Parliament and public service, and flirted briefly with the idea of "special status" for Québec. But by the late 1960s, under Caouette's firm policy guidance, it embraced the concepts of official bilingualism and multiculturalism, and strongly opposed Québec's independence. MICHAEL STEIN

Reading: Michael Stein, *The Dynamics of Right-wing Protest* (1973).

Cree The tribal name originated from a group of Indians near James Bay, recorded by the French as *Kiristinon* and later contracted to Cri, spelled Cree in English. Most Cree use this name only when speaking or writing in English and have other, more localized names for themselves. Cree live in areas from Alberta to Québec, a geographic distribution larger than that of any other native group in Canada. The major divisions of environment and dialect are the Plains Cree (Alberta and Saskatchewan), Woods Cree (Saskatchewan and Manitoba) and Swampy Cree (Manitoba, Ontario and Québec). Their population in the 1600s is estimated to have been 30 000 and in 1986 was roughly 122 000.

The Cree language belongs to the Algonquian language family, and the people historically had

Cree Indians in blanket costume (*courtesy Provincial Archives of Alberta/E. Brown Coll/B766*).

relations with other Algonquian-speaking tribes, most directly with the MONTAGNAIS-NASKAPI, ALGONQUIN and OJIBWA. For perhaps 7000 years the ancestors of the Cree were thinly spread over much of the woodland area that they still occupy. Following contact with the HUDSON'S BAY CO, some Cree moved westward to trap in the new territories. Those who remained on the plains became the Plains Cree. During the late 1700s and the 1800s, they changed with rapid, dramatic success from trappers and hunters of the forest to horse-mounted warriors and bison hunters. Smallpox, destruction of the bison herds, and INDIAN TREATIES brought the Plains Cree and other "horse-culture" tribes to ruin by the 1880s. Obliged to live on INDIAN RESERVES, they existed by farming, ranching and casual labour, yet the majority preserved their native language and religion.

During this time, many Cree remained in the boreal forest and the tundra area to the north, where a remarkably stable culture persisted. In aboriginal times their living came from hunting moose, caribou, smaller game, geese, ducks and fish, which they preserved by drying over fire. They travelled by CANOE in summer and by SNOWSHOES and TOBOGGAN in winter, living in conical or dome-shaped lodges, clothed in animal skins and making tools from wood, bone, hide and stone. Later, they traded meat, furs and other goods in exchange for metal tools, twine and European goods.

The Cree lived in small BANDS or hunting groups for most of the year, and gathered into larger groups in the summer for socializing, exchanges and ceremonies. Religious life was based on belief in animal and other spirits which revealed themselves in dreams. People tried to show respect for each other by an ideal ethic of noninterference, in which each individual was responsible for his actions and the consequences of his actions. Leaders in group hunts, raids and trading were granted authority in directing such tasks, but otherwise the ideal was to lead by means of exemplary action and discreet suggestion.

The European traders were new authority figures, but only while the Cree were at trading posts, since few white men went into the bush. For many years the traders depended on the Indians for fresh meat. Gradually an increasing number of Cree remained near the posts, hunting and doing odd jobs and becoming involved in the church, schools and nursing stations. Today, many Cree are townsmen for much of the year; others have migrated to cities, though often for only a temporary stay. Self-government and economic development are major contemporary goals of the Cree. *See also* NATIVE PEOPLE: PLAINS; NATIVE PEOPLE: SUBARCTIC and general articles under NATIVE PEOPLE. RICHARD J. PRESTON

Reading: D. Ahenakew, *Voices of the Plains Cree* (1977); J. Helm, ed, *Handbook of North American Indians*, vol 6: *Subarctic* (1981); D. Mandelbaum, *The Plains Cree* (1979).

Cree Lake, 1435 km², elev 487 m, max length 81 km, max width 57 km, located in northern Saskatchewan W of REINDEER LK and S of Lk ATHABASCA, is the fourth-largest lake in Saskatchewan. Containing many islands, one of which has the settlement of Cree Lake, it drains in a northerly direction into the Lk Athabasca system, via Cree R and Black Lk, and eventually into the DUBAWNT R. A trading post was established there as early as the 1870s, and the present name (from a French corruption – *Kiristinon* – of an Indian name of unknown origin) was suggested by J.C. Sproule, a geologist with the Dept of Mines and Resources. DAVID EVANS

Cree Syllabics The CREE language is traditionally written not in the Roman alphabet but in syllabics, symbols representing a combination of consonant and vowel. This system is appropriate for Cree because the language is syllabic in its structure, ie, words are composed of consonant-vowel, consonant-vowel sequences. Syllabics work less well for the Athapaskan and Inuktitut (Inuit) languages, for which they were later adapted.

Syllabics are widely known among Canadian Cree, especially older people who learned the system in mission schools (*see* NATIVE PEOPLE, EDUCATION). Moreover, syllabics are currently taught in many reserve schools. Although Cree usually consider the syllabic alphabet to be uniquely Indian (as opposed to the white man's alphabet), it was actually devised by the Rev James EVANS at Norway House [in present-day Man] in 1840. He

ᐅᐱᑲᐃᑎᕐ

ᐅᐱᑲᐃᑎᕐ ᖃᖅᑲᐃᑦ ᖁᖄᖃᑲᐊᕝ
ᐱᐅᐊᖃᔪᖅᑦ᙮
ᑕᑯᓄᖔ ᑕᑯᖅᑲᕋᐊᑦ ᑕᑯᐊᕋᑦᔪᑎᑦ
ᓄᑦᒐᖅᑐᒦᑦ ᓄᐊᒥᕝᑦ, ᐊᓕᖃᖅ
ᔨᑎᓇᔪ ᔨᖅᐱᓕᓇᔪ ᐅᒥᐊᑦᔪᖄᖅᑦᑐᑦ,
ᐊᓐᖃᔪᕋᑦ ... ᐊᓐᖃᑦᔪᑎᑦ ... ᐊᓐᖃᔪᑎᑦ,
ᖅᑐᐊᐊᑦ ᓇᖃᖅᑐᐊᑦ,
ᐱᔅᕑᖅᑐᐃᑦ ᓇᑕᕐᑦ ᐊᐃᓄᔪᑎᑦ
ᐊᐊᕑᔪᔪᑦᖃᑦ᙮
ᑕᐊᐦᐱ ᐱᖃᖅᑕᑦᖅᑐᑦ ᐅᐱᑲᐃᑎᕐ᙮

Syllabic version of a poem about winter's exodus (*from* Inuktitut, *May 1972*).

had designed a similar alphabet for Ojibwa, a closely related language, in 1836. Evans produced considerable printed material in syllabics, largely hymnals and prayer books.

Evans's system has been modified slightly to adapt to local dialect variation and to increase its phonetic accuracy (correspondence of sound to alphabet symbol). Nine geometric forms, each associated with a consonant (m, p, k, n, y, s, ch, r, ø), are rotated through 4 geometric positions (representing the vowels a, i, e, o) to produce 36 syllabic characters. A system of final diacritics allows for syllables of consonant-vowel-consonant structure and for diphthongs (which are rare in Cree). A diacritic is also used for /h/.

The system provides a consistent and reliable orthography for Cree and shows no signs of dying out. Rather, it is closely associated with Cree cultural identity. *See also* NATIVE PEOPLE, LANGUAGES. REGNA DARNELL

Reading: Regna Darnell and A.L. Vanek, "The Psychological Reality of Cree Syllabics" in Regna Darnell, ed, *Canadian Languages in their Social Context* (1973); N. Shipley, *The James Evans Story* (1966).

Creeper (family Certhiidae), small, brown-backed bird with stiff tail and thin, downward-curved bill. Of the 5 species known worldwide, only the brown creeper (*Certhia americana*) is native, found throughout southern Canada. Creepers forage in a distinctive way, alighting low on a tree trunk, spiralling upwards and probing in crevices for insects and spiders. They nest in crevices, often behind loose bark, laying 5-7 eggs. Creepers are common in Canada but are easily overlooked because of their inconspicuous habits and colour. In winter they often associate with other birds in mixed-species feeding flocks. JAMES N.M. SMITH

Creighton, Donald Grant, historian (b at Toronto 15 July 1902; d at Brooklin, Ont 19 Dec 1979). Creighton studied at Victoria College, U of T and Balliol College, Oxford. In 1927 he was hired as a lecturer in U of T's Dept of History, becoming professor in 1945, chairman 1954-59 and professor emeritus in 1971. The first of his many books, *The COMMERCIAL EMPIRE OF THE ST. LAWRENCE* (1937), established him as the foremost English Canadian historian of his generation. Under the influence of Harold INNIS, Creighton adopted as a first principle the idea of the St Lawrence as the basis of a transcontinental economic and political system: the LAURENTIAN THESIS. He was also committed to history as a literary art, and his 2-volume biography of John A. MACDONALD won the Gov Gen's Award (1952, 1955). As a nationalist with a centralist bias, Creighton in later years spoke out against the threats of continentalism and regionalism. His histories became increasingly didactic and he frequently turned to journal-

Cree Indians from Big Bear's band trading furs inside Fort Pitt, NWT, just before the North-West Rebellion (*courtesy National Archives of Canada/C-14154*).

Donald Grant Creighton, a historian committed to history as a literary art. His increasingly didactic works warned against the threats of continentalism and regionalism (*courtesy National Archives of Canada/PA-123984/Robert Lansdale*).

ism, where unfortunately his views were open to caricature and exploitation.   M. BROOK TAYLOR

Reading: Carl Berger, *The Writing of Canadian History* (1976).

Creighton, Mary Helen, song collector, folklorist, writer (b at Dartmouth, NS 5 Sept 1899). A pioneer collector of FOLK MUSIC of the Maritimes, Creighton first travelled throughout NS, often on foot, with a melodeon in a wheelbarrow, listening to and transcribing the songs she heard. Short-term teaching jobs provided minimal finances, but she gradually received academic recognition and won 3 Rockefeller Foundation fellowships. After collecting for the Library of Congress she joined the National Museum of Canada and remained for 20 years, ultimately bringing to light over 4000 songs in English, French, Gaelic, Micmac and German. Creighton lectured throughout N America, helped to organize folk choirs, and assisted in CBC presentations of folk music. She is a member of the Order of Canada, has received 5 honorary doctorates and the Canadian Music Council Medal. In 1986 she published a children's book, *With a Heigh-Heigh-Ho*. A half-hour film, *The Nova Scotia Story* (1987), produced by the NFB, consists of interviews with and about her.   MABEL H. LAINE

Reading: H. Creighton, *Bluenose Ghosts* (1957); *Bluenose Magic* (1968) and *A Life in Folklore* (1975).

Crémazie, Octave, bap Claude-Joseph-Olivier, poet, bookseller (b at Québec, Lower Canada 16 Apr 1827; d at Le Havre, France 16 Jan 1879). Known as the father of French Canadian poetry, Crémazie on finishing his studies in 1844 was one of those French Canadians determined to preserve their identity within the United Province of Canada through economic and cultural development. He opened a French bookstore in Québec City, which prospered. He was a founder at Québec of the traditionalist IN-STITUT CANADIEN and was its president 1857-58. But it was his poetry which made him famous. His nostalgic evocation of the happiness that preceded the Conquest and the miseries that followed roused his compatriots' fervour. "Le vieux soldat canadien" (1855) and *Le Drapeau de*

Carillon (1858) were enthusiastically received and won Crémazie his title as "national bard." He tackled other lyrical subjects as his range of interests broadened, and seemed destined to play a major role in the 1860s literary movement. But after his bookstore's 1862 bankruptcy he fled to France and abandoned poetry. His writings consist of his youthful poetry, his correspondence and a "Journal du siège de Paris." His letters to Henri-Raymond CASGRAIN offer pertinent thoughts on poetry and criticism and his own literary beliefs. Crémazie loved romanticism; realism and fantasy attracted him. This poet who celebrated the glories of his ancestors received extraordinary posthumous acclaim.
ODETTE CONDEMINE

Crerar, Henry Duncan Graham, army officer (b at Hamilton, Ont 28 Apr 1888; d at Ottawa 1 Apr 1965). A graduate of RMC he was commissioned into the artillery in 1910 and was counter battery staff officer of the Canadian Corps at the end of WWI. Between the wars he held various staff appointments and attended the British Staff College and the Imperial Defence College. He became chief of the general staff in 1940 and must bear much of the responsibility for the dispatch of Canadian troops to HONG KONG in Nov 1941. A month later Crerar was appointed to command of I Canadian Corps in the UK; he took that formation to Italy in Nov 1943. He was brought back to England to lead the First Canadian Army in the invasion of France. Promoted full general on 21 Nov 1944, he commanded the field army throughout the NW Europe campaign. He retired in Oct 1946. Although Crerar was an excellent staff officer, he was a mediocre commander, and Field Marshal Montgomery, under whose command First Canadian Army served, had little confidence in him.
BRERETON GREENHOUS

Crerar, Thomas Alexander, businessman, politician (b at Molesworth, Ont 17 June 1876; d at Victoria 11 Apr 1975). He taught school, farmed and managed a Farmers' Elevator Co-op in Manitoba. President-manager of the Grain Growers' Grain Co (United Grain Growers), Winnipeg 1907-30, he was a Mill-Gladstonian Liberal and agrarian-reform activist, endorsing the Single Tax and Free Trade and farmers' economic ventures, though skeptical of the wheat pools of the 1920s. Appointed minister of agriculture and privy councillor in the UNION GOVERN-MENT in 1917, he resigned in 1919 when agrarian discontent heightened. He reluctantly accepted the formation of a farmers' party and became leader of the PROGRESSIVE PARTY in 1920. Though the Progressives won 65 seats in the 1921 election, Crerar refused official opposition status, hoping for an accommodation with the Liberals. Unable to achieve it, he resigned in 1922, and the Progressives fragmented. Leaving politics in 1925, he resurfaced as minister of railways and canals in 1929 in PM KING's Cabinet. Defeated in 1930, he returned with the Liberals in 1935 as minister of mines and resources. In 1945 he was appointed to the Senate; he resigned in 1966. His business connections were maintained by various directorships, and he was the first politician to be named Companion of the Order of Canada (1974).   F.J.K. GRIEZIC

Reading: F.J.K. Griezic, "The Honourable Thomas Alexander Crerar," in S.M. Trofimenkoff, ed, *The Twenties in Western Canada* (1972).

Creston, BC, Town, pop 4098 (1986), inc 1924, is located in the W Kootenay region of SE British Columbia. The focal point of the Creston Valley, the town is situated on Highway 3, the Crowsnest Highway (southern Trans-Canada)

109 km W of Cranbrook and 119 km E of Castlegar. Originally it had been known as Seventh Siding, when the CPR was under construction and later as Fisher. In 1898 the CPR officially recognized the name Creston, after a town in Iowa, on the insistence of one of Creston's founders. In the late 1890s the townsite was laid out on the land between the Canadian Pacific and the Great Northern railway lines, although settlers soon began to occupy the land to the N and E.

David THOMPSON was probably the first white man in the area, in the year 1809. A band of the KOOTENAY originally populated the area, living mainly by fishing the Kootenay R and Kootenay Lk. In the 1860s the DEWDNEY TRAIL, which traversed the valley, was cut from Hope, at the N end of the Fraser Valley, to the Wild Horse gold diggings near FORT STEELE. Few ventured this way after the gold fields were abandoned a short time later, until the discovery of silver in the West Kootenays, when sternwheelers were introduced on the Kootenay R and Lk to ferry miners and supplies into Ainsworth, Kaslo and other Lake points, and to carry out the ore. In 1890 the Alice Mine was staked, although work did not begin until later. Activity began to shift to logging in the valley, but by 1908, when the provincial government broke up the Crown lands for sale, it was recognized that it was fruit growing that showed long-range potential. William A. Baillie-Grohman proposed the reclamation of the alluvial flood plain of the Kootenay R west of the town by a diversion of the Kootenay into the Columbia R at Canal Flats – named after the canal dug at that point. The unusually high water in 1894 ruined the dikes and his company failed, and it was not until the early 1930s that the federal government began reclaiming bottomlands on a vast scale (eventually 8100 ha). The Creston Valley Wildlife Management Area, extending S from Lk Kootenay to the US border, is a stopover point for migrating waterfowl, notably swans.   WILLIAM. A. SLOAN

Cricket is a game played with a ball and solid wood bat by 2 sides of 11 players on a grassy field centering on 2 wickets, each defended in turn by a batsman. The name may come from the Saxon word *cryce* or the French word *criquet*, both meaning stick. It was probably the first of the major games played in Canada, being popular among the garrisons in the late 18th century. An early contest between the 68th Regiment and the Montreal Cricket Club was reported in 1829. The first regular club formed was probably the St John's Cricket Club (1828).

The first international match in cricket history took place between teams from Canada and the US in Toronto in 1844. Some 5000 spectators watched the Canadian team win. The match began a series that has continued, with interruptions, and is likely the oldest of its kind in the world. On the Canadian side was G.A. Barber, of Upper Canada College, sometimes called the "Father of Canadian Cricket." The game was nurtured in other private schools as well, and in 1847 UCC defeated a provincial team. In 1858, *The Canadian Cricketer's Guide* noted 81 matches played the previous season. The first visit by a team from another continent for sports competition came in 1859, when an English team played in Montréal and Hamilton. International matches continued with visits by English teams (which included the famous Dr W.G. Grace) in 1868 and 1872 and a West Indian side in 1886. A Canadian team toured England in 1887, obtaining the creditable record of 5 wins, 5 losses and 9 draws. Aided by the patronage of the governor general, Lord Lansdowne, by advertising, reporting and the spread of railways, the game was nationwide

Cricket at Trinity College School, Port Hope, Ont. The sport was probably the first of the major games played in Canada (*photo by John deVisser*).

by the 1890s. The Canadian Cricket Assn was formed in 1892 and is still the governing cricket body, with 8 member provincial associations.

By 1911-12, when the John Ross Robertson Trophy was first offered for the national championship, there were leagues and associations across Canada. Participation declined in the 1920s but was revived in 1932 by a tour of an Australian team, featuring the famous Don Bradman. In 1936, a strong Canadian team toured England and defeated Marylebone Cricket Club (the traditional name of the English national side) at Lords. The first interprovincial senior tournament took place in 1947. The sport was well served by the untiring administrative efforts of Donald King during the 1960s and 1970s, when teams from several countries toured Canada. A highlight was the victory of eastern Canada over the Australians in 1975. Since 1979, the Canada senior team has been a strong contender in the quadrennial International Cricket Conference Associate Member's World Cup competition (the team reached the event final that year). Frequent senior and youth international and national events and training camps are now staged. Active youth development, coaching and umpiring programs have spurred a rapid growth in numbers of participants in most regions throughout Canada.

GERALD REDMOND

Reading: R. Bowen, *Cricket: A History of its Growth and Development throughout the World* (1970); *Canadian Cricketer* magazine; J. Hall and R. McCulloch, *Sixty Years of Canadian Cricket* (1895).

Cricket Over 2000 species of true crickets (superfamily Grylloidea) are known worldwide. Closely related species include the long-horned grasshoppers, basement-inhabiting camel crickets and katydids. These species resemble GRASSHOPPERS with long antennae. All belong to order Grylloptera, with 96 representatives in Canada. Crickets are frequently wingless. All have hind legs fitted for leaping. Their front wings, when present, lie flat on the back; the ovipositor is needlelike or spear-shaped. Most species are nocturnal and feed on plant and animal matter. Eggs are laid singly in the ground, or in twigs by some species. These eggs overwinter,

producing one generation annually in northern areas. Crops and gardens can be severely damaged by black field crickets (genus *Gryllus*), which can also invade dwellings in autumn. Twigs and berry canes are damaged by pale green tree crickets (*Oecanthus*). The chirping songs of true crickets, often high-pitched, pulsating or buzzing, are very familiar. P.W. RIEGERT

Criddle Family, naturalists known for detailed and long-term records of fauna and flora at Aweme (near Treesbank), Man, starting with Percy's diaries kept since their arrival from England in 1882. Of the 8 children, Norman (b at Addleton, Eng 14 May 1875; d at Brandon, Man 4 May 1933) and Stuart (b at Addleton, Eng 4 Dec 1877; d at Surrey, BC 23 Oct 1971) were best known, publishing about 150 papers. Norman became the dean of western Canadian ENTOMOLOGY, recognized for development of the "Criddle mixture" for grasshopper control and for his early application of biological observations to insect control. Their studies included long-term weather records for which Maida received a government award, one of the first breeding-bird censuses and one of the longest migration chronologies in N America, and a detailed floral calendar. Norman attempted to forecast the grasshopper plagues based on sunspot cycles, and with Stuart he was active in many organizations and influenced the work of colleagues.

MARTIN K. McNICHOLL

Reading: A. Criddle, *Criddle-de-diddle-ensis* (1973)

Crime, in modern societies, can be defined officially as acts or omissions prohibited by law and punishable by sanctions. Although crime is sometimes viewed broadly as the equivalent of antisocial, immoral and sinful behaviour or as a violation of any important group standard, no act is legally a crime unless prohibited by law. Conceptions of crime vary widely from culture to culture; only treason (disloyalty to the group) and incest are condemned virtually universally, but they were not always treated as crimes. Societies tend to prohibit acts they fear will harm their structure, eg, heresy is labelled criminal by theocracies and other states where civil and religious codes of behaviour are not clearly distinguished from each other; totalitarian regimes make political dissent criminal, and capitalist societies proliferate statutes to protect private property (*see* PROPERTY LAW). Even within one culture the definition

of crime will vary over time. Adultery, fornication, PROSTITUTION, HOMOSEXUALITY and other disapproved forms of sexual activity sometimes fall under the CRIMINAL CODE of various contemporary societies and sometimes do not. The killing of a human being, a crime in all civilized societies, may in primitive societies be considered a private matter to be settled within kin groups. On the other hand, if crime is defined as violation of criminal codes enforced by the state, it cannot be said to exist in societies where political and legal institutions are not codified, and where conduct is largely controlled by customs and standards shared by all members. Generally, in primitive societies infractions of social norms are treated as private wrongs rather than crimes, there is less concern with the state of mind or intention of the offender (*see* MENS REA), and guilt is usually collectively assessed. The criminal codes of modern nations, however, are complicated, growing bodies of written rules.

History of Crime The earliest comprehensive laws extant, the Babylonian Code of Hammurabi (1900 BC), are apparently based on retribution, eg, "an eye for an eye, a tooth for a tooth," but most early laws allow compensation of the value of an eye or a tooth or any other thing, including life. All codes reflect social class differences. Under Mosaic law the 10 commandments have no punishment attached as such, but severe punishment is threatened for the breaking of all kinds of rules, many of them ritual in nature. Their application, however, was limited by rules of procedure and evidence which were almost insurmountable as far as establishing a crime was concerned. The Greeks, too, allowed compensation; the word "punishment" in Greek meant *harm money*. After Solon, in the 6th century BC, all Athenian citizens had the right to initiate prosecutions. In Rome, civil law developed into a coherent system but CRIMINAL LAW remained largely a matter of local custom.

In medieval England, crime was not at first distinguished from what are now known as civil wrongs (tort), and even killing could be compensated by "wergilt" (man-money). Only the body of the king was excepted, and this exception is now the rule as "the King's peace," and a crime is still charged as having been committed against the Crown. A distinctive body of criminal law developed only after the Norman conquest. Under the influence of Christianity, concepts such as guilt ("guilt" derives from geld-money paid for a fine) and sentence (first used in conjunction with excommunication) entered the law. Torture was used for extracting confessions and punishments were harsh, but their application varied. Criminal prohibitions were increasingly used as a means of social control, as they are now.

In Canada offences are set out in the Criminal Code, numerous other federal statutes, provincial statutes and municipal bylaws. The Law Reform Commission of Canada has estimated that there are about 40 000 offences, not counting those in municipal bylaws, for which Canadian citizens can be prosecuted. Ignorance of these offences is no defence. In addition, most of the more recent offences are ones of "strict liability," meaning that commission of the act (*actus rea*) alone constitutes guilt, without necessary proof of a mental element such as intent, recklessness or negligence (*see* TORTS).

Measurement and Statistics Information about crime is generally derived from official agencies. Additional information is supplied by research projects and surveys, eg, those on self-reported crimes, victim surveys and special offence groups, that attempt to shed light on the "dark" or unreported crime figures. Even some violent crimes, such as assaults between family members, are rarely reported, and it is difficult to establish whether incidents such as wife beating and CHILD ABUSE are increasing or whether they are more frequently detected, reported and prosecuted. Serious problems have plagued the collecting and processing of national data. As a result, the Canadian Centre for Justice Statistics (Juristat) was established in 1981, and it is beginning to yield more reliable and useful data, although a consistent national reporting system will still take years to develop. Many provinces have now begun to develop their own data systems.

Crime statistics have to be viewed with reservation. While the national figure for offences reported to the police was nearly 3 million in 1986, charges laid in Ontario alone during the same period were reported to be almost 390 000. Statistics based on offences, offenders or charges yield very different counts. Figures also change in the process from complaint to conviction. Nevertheless, crime figures are constantly quoted. Increases in crime are widely publicized but little notice is taken of decreases. For example, violent crimes have constantly increased, but the most serious and most reliably measured crime, HOMICIDE, has tended to decrease in Canada.

Causes and Explanations of Crime Contemporary literature on causes of crime is linked with literature in anthropology, psychiatry, social psychology and sociology. Criminologists have studied how people become criminals and the relation of crime rates to culture and social organization. Little systematic theoretical research on crime was conducted until the 20th century; before that this subject was generally treated by theologians, physicians and reformers. During the past 100 years crime has been blamed on the biological constitution and heredity of offenders, their psychological makeup, and social conditions. It has also been seen as an expression of political power. Offenders are a selected group identified by official agencies, but many other people actually commit crimes. Also, crime involves so many different situations and acts that it is difficult to generalize. The definition of crime is not static but contextual, eg, the overrepresentation of native people in Canadian prisons reveals more about cultural differences and social deprivation than about criminal behaviour as such. The 2 territories have consistently a much higher crime rate and rate of imprisonment than that of any of the provinces.

It is now generally agreed that what is defined and measured as crime reflects the values and judgements of a society. Changes in crime patterns express social stresses, social change and uncertainties. One of the recent crime waves, the use of prohibited drugs, is a case in point (*see* DRUG USE, NON-MEDICAL).

Classification of Offences Offences and offenders can be classified in many ways. The most common, but not necessarily the most helpful, are groupings of charges according to the various statutes, eg, Criminal Code offences, which include offences against the person (now more frequently referred to as offences of violence, although actual violence may or may not have occurred); offences against property; sex offences and others. Property offences are by far the most common in criminal statistics although, judging from the business of the courts, offences involving motor vehicles are even more common and no less serious, as there is more loss of life, limb and property damage caused by motor vehicles than by traditional street crimes. Social scientists now classify criminal activity according to the discernible behaviour systems of those who practise it (although such classification does not necessarily correlate with crime statistics): violent personal crime, eg, murder, sexual assault, child mo-

lesting; property crime, eg, shoplifting, cheque forgery; occupational crime (*see* WHITE-COLLAR CRIME); political crime, eg, treason, sedition, espionage; public-order crime, eg, drunkenness, vagrancy, gambling, drug addiction; conventional crime, eg, ROBBERY, larceny; ORGANIZED CRIME, eg, racketeering; and professional crime, eg, confidence games, forgery, counterfeiting.

General offence classifications, however, tell us little about when and where crime occurs and who is involved. It is often assumed that violence takes place mainly in public places and is committed by strangers, but the opposite is true. With an offence such as theft, which is classified by whether the value of the stolen article(s) was under or over $200, there is no way of knowing whether the thief picked pockets, shoplifted, stole cars or stole from cars, or was involved in corporate or white-collar crimes. Almost every legitimate activity has its criminal counterpart and there are "grey" areas in between which are often the most profitable (*see* UNDERGROUND ECONOMY). It is important that the bewildering variety of crimes be appreciated if we are to avoid simplistic solutions – the greatest problem with anti-crime measures.

Control of Crime "Keeping the peace" has become the "war against crime." Veritable armies of LAW ENFORCEMENT and correctional officers have grown phenomenally since the 1960s, not only in manpower but in programs and technical sophistication. For example, in 1985-86 there were over 68 688 POLICE and 25 000 correctional personnel in Canada. Expenditures for correctional services (*see* PRISON) alone were $1.367 billion in 1985-86, a 62% increase over 1980-81. The private security industry is larger in many places than the official police force. More attention is paid to housing design, street lighting and security installations, measures that unfortunately also encourage the creation of a fortress mentality.

Punishment, however, is still the basic response to crime. The threat of punishment is supposed to deter the population from committing crime (general deterrence) and accordingly the imposition of punishment is supposed to deter offenders (specific deterrence). There is no conclusive evidence that punishment does deter crime, a fact recognized long before actual studies threw doubts on its effectiveness. Measures such as penitence, work, education and treatment have also been discredited as deterrents. Crime is now seen predominantly as a social and political problem, but class differences and POVERTY cannot be solved by anti-crime agencies. The growing recognition that crime is an expression of human conflict is reflected in new approaches to its solution which attempt at least to reduce the vicious circles of accusation, conviction and punishment. Demands are being made to decriminalize certain forms of behaviour, especially victimless crimes. Diversion programs are being instituted to provide alternative options for offenders (*see* PROBATION AND PAROLE). The basis of victim assistance and compensation programs is that the victim, and not the state, is the hurt party. In sentencing, more stress is laid on restitution and community service orders to try and make offenders responsible for their acts. It is now recognized that even large expenditures on crime control are not likely to reduce crime substantially, and communities and citizens have to recognize their responsibility in crime control. J.W. MOHR

Crimean War, 1854-56, interrupted a half-century of peace between the European great powers. What began as a diplomatic tussle for influence between Britain, France and Russia over the weakening Ottoman Empire soon turned into a bitter and drawn-out war in the Near East, focused on the Crimean peninsula.

Canada played no direct role in the Crimean War, but even this distant eruption of battle had some notable results in the country. One was that Canada was stripped of its garrison of British troops to supply the needs of the Crimean Expeditionary Force. This led in turn to the establishment of a permanent Canadian militia in 1855, including provisions for volunteer troops. So popular was the militia idea, in the wake of Canadian enthusiasm for the spectacle of the Crimean war, that recruiting far outstripped demand and helped convince the government that universal military service (or conscription) was unnecessary to sustain the defence of Canada. While no Canadian units fought in the Crimean War, individuals did enlist and reach the battlefront. In fact, the first Canadian to win the VICTORIA CROSS, Lt Alexander DUNN of the 11th Hussars, gained this coveted honour for his participation in the ill-fated charge of the Light Brigade at Balaclava on 25 Oct 1854, certainly the most famous single action of the war. WESLEY K. WARK

Criminal Code, a federal statute enacted by Parliament pursuant to s91(27) of the CONSTITUTION ACT, 1867, which provides the federal government exclusive jurisdiction to legislate criminal offences in Canada. The Criminal Code contains most of the Criminal offences that have been created by Parliament; however, some other criminal offences (for instance, narcotics offences) have been incorporated into other federal statutes. The Code not only defines types of conduct that constitute criminal offences but also establishes the kind and degree of punishment that may be imposed when an individual is convicted of an offence and the procedures to be followed throughout the criminal process (*see* CRIMINAL PROCEDURE).

Based on a proposed codification of English CRIMINAL LAW (which was never enacted in England), the Criminal Code was originally enacted in 1892. It has never been fundamentally revised, although there were consolidations in 1906, 1927 and 1953. The 1953 consolidation was an attempt to reorganize, clarify and reconcile internal inconsistencies. More significantly, this consolidation abolished all COMMON-LAW offences (ie, those created by case law rather than by a statute) while preserving common-law defences, justifications and excuses.

Amendments to the Code have been made almost yearly, to keep abreast of technological, social and economic changes in society (eg, new offences being created such as theft of telecommunications, use of credit cards and hijacking of aircraft, and changes with respect to existing offences such as those that have recently occurred with respect to sexual assaults and impaired driving offences).

The first portion of the Code consists of enactments of general principles followed by parts (several sections each) creating offences that are grouped under different categories such as offences against the person, offences against property, offences against the administration of law and justice, sexual offences, currency offences, and conspiracies. The rest of the Code is concerned with procedure and sentencing. It is estimated that 40% of the Criminal Code deals with criminal law procedure and the remaining 60% with the definition of criminal law offences, the codification of some of the defences that are available to criminal charges, and finally sentencing options available to judges.

The Code has been severely criticized, however, for failing to reflect the attitudes of the majority of Canadians. The Law Reform Commission of Canada in November 1986, produced a completely revised draft of the Code which will now be the subject of public hearings. The Law Reform Commission apparently feels that its proposed revision of the Code sets out more realistically the essential aims and principles of criminal law in the context of modern Canadian society. Also, this revised Code contains some major revisions which would allow the Code to be more consistent with the values and principles set out in the Canadian Charter of Rights and Freedoms. Mr Justice Allan Linden, the president of the LAW REFORM COMMISSION, stated when unveiling this draft Code that the Commission hopes that Parliament will see fit to enact this revised Code, with suitable amendments, so that it will be in force by the 100th anniversary of the original 1892 Criminal Code of Canada. A. PRINGLE

Criminal Investigation involves the investigation of violations of CRIMINAL LAW. In a criminal investigation, the state is responsible for the expense of investigating a case and presenting it in court. This responsibility includes ensuring that all witnesses (prosecution and defence alike) appear at the trial. The victim (if there is one) of the criminal act is considered a witness; the complainant can be compelled to testify in almost all cases. It is the state that decides whether a matter will proceed through the COURTS, and in making this determination it is not bound by the wishes of the victim or complainant. In contrast, in civil court, the person who considers himself wronged must launch the action, secure his own witnesses, serve all processes and be responsible for the costs of the hearing. The 2 processes differ also in the type of penalty handed down. In a criminal matter, convicted individuals either serve a term of imprisonment or pay a fine to the state; in the civil process, there can be no imprisonment and the disputants may be ordered to pay to the offended party certain sums of money.

Constitutionally, the federal government is responsible for legislating in all areas that relate to criminal matters, while the various provinces are responsible for legislating in the areas of POLICING and the administration of justice within their boundaries. Each province has passed a Police Act to meet these responsibilities.

Types of Crime Historically, all CRIMES have devolved either from a trespass against a person or a trespass against a person's property. Today the distinction is less clear because of the growth of numerous so-called victimless crimes. The particular crime being investigated will, to a large degree, dictate the course that an investigation will follow. For example, some crimes are planned and deliberate while others happen spontaneously; some are motivated by revenge, gain, pride or greed; some are committed by people suffering psychological abnormalities.

Evidence A criminal investigation is conducted to identify, gather and preserve evidence. Almost anything can constitute evidence, according to the particular circumstances of a case. The legal definition of evidence, "all means by which a fact may be proved or disproved in a court of law," is of necessity very broad (*see* LAW OF EVIDENCE). Evidence must be factual or based upon factual grounds; opinion evidence is sometimes admissible, usually with the prerequisite that it is an opinion given by an expert on a specific matter. Evidence can also be categorized by the forms it takes (eg, real, documentary or testimonial) and the purpose it serves. Real evidence includes physical objects that are either used in the commission of a crime, are found at the scene of a crime, or will in some way help to prove or disprove evidence that is relevant to a crime. Documentary evidence is any type of document entered as evidence. Testimonial evidence is that given by witnesses under oath at a trial. All evidence will eventually become testimonial because a witness will be required to explain the relevance of a real object or a document. Historically, it was relevance that determined whether evidence was admissible, but with the entrenchment of the CANADIAN CHARTER OF RIGHTS AND FREEDOMS admissibility also depends on how the evidence was gathered. At present the law does not prescribe any procedural rules for the conduct of investigations. Some indirect regulation has been provided by a rule of evidence, according to which a statement by a suspect will only be admitted as evidence if a prosecutor can prove the statement was not induced by fear or hope held out to the suspect by an authority, ie, if the statement was "voluntary." Nothing in the law requires that the police issue a warning about the rights of a suspect to remain silent before he or she is interrogated. Nor does the law oblige the police to prepare a thorough and reliable record of an interrogation, although both these issues are addressed in a recent working paper by the LAW REFORM COMMISSION OF CANADA. If, in a judge's view, a suspect's rights have been violated in the process of gathering evidence, the admission of such evidence must be disallowed.

Evidence is also categorized by purpose: direct and circumstantial. Direct evidence denotes testimony of eyewitnesses to the actual crime. Circumstantial evidence supports one of the circumstances that form part of the overall picture of the crime. For example, B is poisoned and dies and there are no witnesses to the murder, but the investigation reveals that A was being blackmailed by B, that A purchased an amount of the same type of poison found in the victim's body and that A's vehicle was seen in the area around B's home on the night of the murder. None of these facts, in isolation, would be sufficient to convict A of the murder, but their cumulative effect might be sufficient.

Ingredients of Crimes All crimes have essential "ingredients," each of which must be proven beyond any reasonable doubt before an individual can be convicted. For example, the crime of possession of stolen property is composed of 4 essential ingredients: that the property was stolen by someone; that the accused had possession of it; that the accused knew that someone had stolen it; and that the identity of the accused is known. The investigator must be aware of the ingredients of a crime before an investigation commences so that he or she can gather evidence to support each one.

Investigation of a Crime A criminal investigation is a search for facts and information which can be supplied by witnesses, articles or documents. A criminal investigation may be initiated when a peace officer witnesses the crime or when it is reported, in which case an officer will be dispatched to investigate. The type and severity of the crime will dictate the rank of the investigating peace officer.

When a crime (regardless of its nature) is reported to the police, a constable will almost always be the first peace officer to respond. Depending upon the crime and the circumstances upon his arrival at the scene of the crime, the constable may do no more than protect the scene to preserve it in its original state; or he may arrest a suspect and conduct the entire investigation himself. A constable is trained to attend to various tasks in a specific order: care for any person in need; arrest the suspect; identify and locate witnesses; and secure whatever physical evidence is available at the scene. For example, if a call is received concerning the robbery of a corner grocery store and if the constable arrives in time to see the culprit fleeing the store and manages to catch him, and if the culprit is still in possession of the stolen money, the circumstances are such that there is no need for specialized assistance from detectives or officers; there is abundant direct and circumstantial evidence.

In another situation, a constable may be dispatched to a stabbing in a restaurant. Upon his arrival, he finds the victim dead. The assailant has fled but 2 people witnessed the stabbing. The constable will order all doors to the restaurant locked, will ensure that nothing is disturbed, and will call for specialized help immediately. He will endeavour to keep the witnesses at the scene until the homicide detectives and identification officers arrive. He will also summon his immediate supervisor. Upon the arrival of the detectives, the constable will be relegated to the role of assistant.

Detectives are trained to investigate crimes, such as homicide, sex crimes, fraud and arson, which may require protracted work or specialized knowledge. Where possible, detectives will seek from the victim(s) an exact description of the culprit, with emphasis on unique identifying marks such as scars, tattoos or deformities, and will want to know about weapons used, money or property stolen, mode and direction of flight, and any accessories who might have been involved. In many crimes, the culprit is acquainted with the victim; in others, the knowledge possessed by the culprit, eg, the place where the money is hidden in a restaurant, is known only to a few. If the culprit is identified at this stage, all efforts will be made to apprehend him, leaving him less time to create an alibi or dispose of the property or weapons.

Witnesses are critical to the successful apprehension of a criminal, but individuals cannot be compelled to help police or to provide them with information about a crime. However, if witnesses have been identified, they can be compelled to testify in court, although the prosecution generally tries to discover, before calling them to the stand, what they will say.

Physical evidence (eg, anything transferred from the victim or the scene to the assailant; anything transferred from the assailant to the victim or the scene), opportunity and motive are also crucial to a criminal investigation. An experienced detective will seek to understand the culprit's method of operation ("MO"); he will also want to know who is in or out of prison at that time and who has used similar MOs in the past.

Some crimes are insoluble without the help of informants. An informant is often a member of the criminal strata of society who may sell information or who may owe a favour to a particular peace officer. Informants, however, include anyone who can provide information; detectives will therefore often try to cultivate friendships with taxi drivers, hotel desk clerks, apartment-building managers, etc.

Many police departments in Canada have advertised call-in telephone numbers whereby people who wish to remain anonymous can provide information about crimes in return for cash. For example, the TIPS operation of the Edmonton police is funded by the business community but manned by police personnel. Each week, they re-enact an unsolved crime and air it on local television and solicit telephone calls with information. Most informants are reluctant to testify at trial and generally will not be compelled to do so unless to prove the accused innocent.

Preservation of Evidence Investigators must record and preserve evidence to ensure that it is available at trial and to prove that the articles produced at trial are those that were seized at the time of the investigation. For example, in a narcotics trial, if continuity of possession by the investigator cannot be proved, the defence could allege that between the investigation and the trial there was a switch of substance, creating a reasonable doubt about what exactly was taken from the accused. It is critical that any victims' or witnesses' statements be written down as soon after the incident as possible, so that people may refresh their memories from these recorded statements prior to testifying. The investigator also records an account of the investigation as soon as possible.

Investigative Aids Criminal investigation has been greatly influenced by technological developments in fields such as forensic science and pathology. For example, in *R* v *Workman and Huculak*, the 2 accused were convicted of murder, although the body of the deceased was never found. There was sufficient circumstantial evidence, much of it of a medical nature, to prove that not only had the deceased been murdered but that he was murdered by the 2 accused. Technology used in criminal investigation includes breathalyzers, polygraphs, listening devices and surveillance cameras.

Identification Officers Most police departments have Identification Sections staffed by personnel (often civilian) trained in the various methods of evidence gathering, eg, fingerprints and photography. Generally, these specialists are called upon by an investigator either when there are no good witnesses and the investigator has been unable to find sufficient evidence, or if the crime is serious. It has been estimated that latent evidence, eg, fingerprints or other identifying evidence, can be found at the scene of the crime in 50% of cases.

Search Warrants, as a general rule, will be issued by a judge if reasonable grounds exist to believe that the described articles will be found in a described place involving a particular crime. Search warrants empower police to enter private dwellings or other places for the purpose of searching for the articles named in the warrants. In some instances, searches of persons found on the premises are allowed. If evidence is found, it may be seized and held until the trial date.

Conclusion It can be said that successful criminal investigators are fashioned not so much by training and education as by personal traits, eg, qualities such as curiosity, intuition, patience, affability and the ability to judge people's characters and to analyse evidence. The successful investigator may find that these qualities, rather than technical or legal skills learned in training, are crucial to criminal investigation. CHRIS BRAIDEN

Reading: M. Campbell, *A Century of Crime* (1970); R. Ericson, *Making Crime* (1981); Law Reform Commission of Canada, *Police Powers* (1983).

Criminal Law, in its widest sense, includes substantive criminal law, the operation of penal institutions, CRIMINAL PROCEDURE and evidence, and POLICE investigations (*see* CRIMINAL INVESTIGATION). More precisely, the term refers to substantive criminal law – a body of law that prohibits certain kinds of conduct and imposes sanctions for unlawful behaviour. In general, the prohibitions contained in criminal offences are concerned with protecting the public at large and maintaining the accepted values of society. These values include the preservation of morality (through such laws as the OBSCENITY and PROSTITUTION offences); protection of the person (eg, murder and assault offences); protection of property (eg, theft and fraud offences); preservation of the public peace (eg, incitement to RIOT and causing a disturbance offences); and preservation of the STATE (eg, TREASON offences).

Underlying the various theories explaining the purpose of criminal law is the basic premise that criminal law is a means by which society reaffirms its values and denounces violators. A change in values entails a change in the types of conduct society wishes to prohibit. Amendments to the CRIMINAL CODE in areas such as sexual offences, ABORTION, pornography and punishment for mur-

der demonstrate that Canadian criminal laws develop, at least to some extent, in response to changing social values. Criminal law has also changed in response to technical advances, eg, recent amendments to the Criminal Code concerning theft of telecommunications, and CREDIT CARD fraud and provisions regulating the use of wiretap surveillance.

The sources of substantive criminal law in Canada are limited. Most offences are created by the Criminal Code, which prohibits conviction of an offence at COMMON LAW (except for the offence of contempt of court). Criminal offences are also contained in other related federal statutes, such as the Narcotic Control Act, the Food and Drugs Act, and the Young Offenders Act.

A number of federal offences and offences under provincial statutes (eg, liquor and highway control offences) and municipal bylaws (eg, parking tickets, pet control) are not criminal offences in the true sense, but are generally processed through the courts in the same general manner as criminal offences. These offences are often called "regulatory offences."

Origin of Criminal Law

According to the CONSTITUTION ACT, 1867, Parliament was granted legislative jurisdiction with respect to "the criminal law, except for the Constitution of the Courts of Criminal Jurisdiction but including the Procedure in Criminal Matters." This particular constitutional provision gives the federal government power to pass laws concerning criminal law and procedure. The provinces can pass legislation dealing with subjects in which provinces have constitutional power and can enforce these laws (under s92 of the Constitution Act, 1867) by imposing "punishment by fine, penalty, or imprisonment." It is therefore possible to have "provincial offences" enacted by the province, but if these offences conflict with a statute passed under the federal government's criminal-law power, the federal law is generally paramount. The provinces were also granted legislative competence concerning "the administration of justice in the Province, including the Constitution, Maintenance and Organization of Provincial Courts, both of Civil and of Criminal Jurisdiction." Therefore, POLICING, appointment of prosecutors, administration of the COURTS and appointment of lower-court judges are provincial responsibilities. The appointment of county and supreme court judges is a federal responsibility under s96 of the Constitution Act (*see* JUDICIARY).

Criminal law and procedures are subject to provisions of the CANADIAN CHARTER OF RIGHTS AND FREEDOMS. The Charter is part of the Constitution of Canada. The CONSTITUTION ACT, 1982, holds that "the Constitution of Canada is the Supreme Law of Canada, and any law that is inconsistent with the provisions of the Constitution is, to the extent of the inconsistency, of no force or effect." The courts must therefore measure all legislation, including the Criminal Code and related statutes, against the Charter's provisions. The Charter may directly affect criminal-law procedure and may have an impact on the definition of certain crimes and the resulting punishment.

It is a cardinal principle of Canadian criminal law that there can be no crime or punishment except in accordance with fixed, predetermined LAW. To this end, the courts have concluded that a criminal prohibition must be in existence at the time of the alleged crime and that the offence created by such prohibition must be clearly ascertainable. If the provision providing for the criminal offence is ambiguous, then it will be interpreted by the courts in favour of the accused.

The application of the criminal law by police, prosecutors, judges and juries depends very much upon the facts of each case. Courts seek to apply the law consistently. Judges, when determining the law applicable to a case, are influenced greatly by previous court decisions, ie, "precedents" involving similar situations. The fact that judges tend to follow precedents creates consistency in the interpretation of the statutory law and helps to indicate how the law will be interpreted in the future. An appeal system exists in the criminal courts not only to correct injustices but also to avoid inconsistencies in the application of the law itself. Previous legal precedents, upon which the judge hearing the case feels bound, can be overruled by higher courts if it can be demonstrated that the precedent is either wrongly decided or out of date.

There are many legal wrongs that are not crimes. They fall in the field of CIVIL LAW and are the basis of private law suits. A civil action is a private legal proceeding brought to court by one person against another. A civil court can compensate the aggrieved party by providing monetary damages or, in some cases, can cause the defendant to rectify the wrong caused. In criminal law a crime is a wrong against the community as a whole rather than against the individual victim; consequently a criminal prosecution is launched by the state and the victim is merely a voluntary (and sometimes reluctant) witness for the prosecution. Recently, more attention has been paid to victims, including such measures as restitution and compensation.

Constituents of a Crime

A crime may be divided into 2 elements: the prohibited conduct or act (*actus rea*) and the required mental element (MENS REA). Generally, before an act can become a crime it must fall precisely within the definition of the offence. It may be an act of omission as well as commission. It is a general rule that individuals cannot be found guilty of an offence for only hoping or thinking that they had committed it.

Mens rea ("guilty mind") is a difficult concept. It is not defined in the Criminal Code and in Canada, depending upon the particular offence, the prosecution may be required to prove a state of mind that may include either intention (the most common state of mind required to be proven in criminal cases), advertent negligence, knowledge, recklessness, wilful blindness or more specific states of mind contemplated by such words as "maliciously" or "fraudulently." Nevertheless, there is still an overriding principle in the criminal law that there is no criminal responsibility unless the guilty mind required by the offence can be proven. Most criminal trials are in fact contested on the basis of whether the accused had the requisite state of mind rather than whether he actually performed the prohibited act. This state of mind has to be proven with the same certainty as the other ingredients of a crime, and the prosecution must therefore present a clear picture of what was in the individual's mind at the time the offence was committed. In order to ease this difficulty, some criminal law statutes create or recognize a presumption or inference regarding the required mental element; however, many of these "reverse onus clauses" have recently been declared unconstitutional as various courts have ruled the provisions conflict with the rights of an accused as set out in the Charter.

In regulatory offences, the law distinguishes 3 different forms of the mental element. If the legislation uses words such as "wilfully" or "intentionally," the legislature is presumed to have intended that the mental element required is an intent to commit the prohibited act. For the second class of regulatory offences, eg, those relating to PUBLIC HEALTH, highway traffic, ENVIRONMENTAL LAW, and safety in the workplace, it is only necessary that the accused knows that his acts or omissions may result in the offence being committed. The final category of regulatory offences (strict liability offences) requires no mental element whatsoever and there is consequently no necessity of proving any fault on the part of the accused; the Crown need only prove that the accused was responsible for the prohibited act.

Under Canadian law, criminal responsibility may be placed on parties other than the actual perpetrator. Persons who aid, assist or counsel the commission of an offence can be found guilty of the same offence as the perpetrator. Also, attempting or conspiring to commit a crime or counselling an offence that is not actually committed are all criminal offences. However, courts have held that mere preparation to commit a crime is not sufficient to constitute an attempt.

In any criminal trial, one of the most important principles of all is the presumption of innocence. According to this principle, the Crown must prove the guilt of the accused, and it is not for the accused to establish innocence. Furthermore, the Crown must establish guilt beyond a reasonable doubt. This principle has been enshrined in the Charter and is considered by many to be one of the most important protections for the individual against the state.

Defences

Both the Criminal Code and the COMMON LAW recognize a number of defences to criminal charges.

Defence of Capacity In certain cases individuals will be found not guilty, even though the prohibited act and the intention to commit this act are proven, because the individuals are deemed incapable by law of committing the offence in question. For example, any child under the age of 12 years cannot commit a criminal offence. As well, any boy or girl under the age of 18 must be tried in the juvenile courts under the Young Offenders Act unless he or she is ordered to stand trial in the adult court by a juvenile court judge (*see* JUVENILE JUSTICE SYSTEM).

Insane persons are also considered to be incapable of committing criminal offences. Section 16 of the Criminal Code presumes that everyone is sane but permits defendants to establish that they were insane at the time of the commission of an offence. If insanity is established, then the person is found to be not guilty by reason of insanity and is detained indeterminately for treatment until a government-appointed board of review determines that the individual may return to society. In addition, an individual cannot be found guilty of a crime if he or she is unfit to stand trial because of mental illness. These individuals are held in mental hospitals until they recover sufficiently to understand the legal proceedings against them.

Defences that Negate Proof of the Prohibited Act To prove that someone has committed a prohibited act, it must be demonstrated that the act or omission was consciously and voluntarily committed. Defences that fall into this category include accident, duress (ie, a person has been compelled to commit an offence because his or his family's life or safety have been threatened), and automatism, which may be generally defined as involuntary, unconscious behaviour where the physical movements are performed without volition or without exercise of the will (eg, a person, as a result of an external blow to the head, commits a prohibited act while in an unconscious or

semiconscious state, or a person who commits an offence while sleepwalking).

Defences that Negate Proof of Mens Rea In most "true" criminal offences, the Crown must prove that, before committing the act, the accused actually intended to achieve the unlawful result. The law recognizes that certain factors raise a reasonable doubt that the person intended to achieve the unlawful consequence. The defences usually mentioned in this context include intoxication (which is commonly used to reduce a murder charge to the lesser offence of manslaughter), honest mistake of fact, and, in some very limited circumstances, mistake of law. However, in the vast majority of factual situations, ignorance of the law provides no defence.

Defences of Excuse or Justification With these defences the law recognizes human frailty and weaknesses and will hold that the accused was either justified in committing the unlawful act or is at least partially excused for the conduct. Examples of defences of justification are self-defence and defence of property. Defences of excuse include obedience to authority (eg, a soldier who believes he is simply obeying lawful orders), provocation (which only applies in murder cases and involves a killing committed in the heat of passion, which has been caused suddenly by a wrongful act or insult sufficient to deprive an ordinary person of his self-control), and entrapment (in which the person has committed the offence under pressure by police authorities).

Sanctions

If an individual is convicted of a criminal offence, the presiding judge must impose a sentence. In Canada, judges have a great deal of discretion in sentencing. There are few mandatory minimum sentences and the maximum sentences given in the Criminal Code are generally set quite high. A judge may choose an absolute discharge, conditional discharge, probation, suspended sentence, fines or imprisonment.

In determining an appropriate sentence, judges must consider a multitude of factors and remind themselves that each sentencing is unique because the individual characteristics of each crime and offender are never the same. Some of the more important factors that they take into consideration when imposing sentence are the degree of premeditation, whether the accused has a previous criminal record, the gravity of the crime committed, the degree of participation of the offender in the crime, the incidence of this particular crime in the jurisdiction, past sentences imposed for the same or similar offences, and the age, life-style and personality of the offender.

In 1987, a federal commission (the Canadian Sentencing Commission, chaired by Judge J.R.O. Archambault) issued a report recommending some drastic revisions to the current system of sentencing offenders. In particular, this commission suggested that legislation should be passed restricting considerably the wide discretion currently exercised by judges in sentencing offenders. Parliament is now studying these recommendations and some legislative changes to the sentencing process are expected.   A. PRINGLE

Criminal Procedure is an integral but distinct part of CRIMINAL LAW in Canada. It is distinct from the substance of criminal law in that it does not define the type of conduct that constitutes a criminal offence or establishes punishment, but rather determines by whom and in what circumstances prosecutions against accused offenders may be initiated, conducted, terminated and appealed. Criminal procedure is a set of rules according to which the substantive law is administered. The principal objective of criminal law procedure is to

ensure a fair and just process in the determination of guilt or innocence. This determination is made in accord with those principles that Canadians have accepted as reflecting the proper balance between the value of protection of society and the value of individual freedom (*see* LAW AND SOCIETY).

Criminal procedure commences long before an accused person appears in court, as detailed laws cover how police may investigate a crime (*see* CRIMINAL INVESTIGATION). For example, there are many procedural rules in the CRIMINAL CODE or in the COMMON LAW that define how and when police may interrogate witnesses or suspects, search persons and places, arrest suspects, seize evidence, and use telephone wiretaps. Criminal procedure then sets out the rules as to how a charge is laid, when accused persons will obtain bail, and in what court they will eventually have their trial. The actual court process is set in motion by the swearing of an Information (popularly known as a charge) before a justice of the peace or MAGISTRATE (provincial court judge). An Information is an allegation by a citizen (usually a police officer) that reasonable and probable grounds exist to believe another person (the accused) has committed a crime.

All offences in Canada may be classified as indictable (the more serious) or summary conviction (the less serious). Some offences may, at the discretion of the Crown, be prosecuted either by indictment or by summary conviction. The trial of summary conviction offences is either before a magistrate or a justice of the peace, and generally they carry a maximum punishment of $2000 or 6 months in prison. Summary conviction proceedings generally have a limitation period of 6 months from the date of the offence.

Procedure with respect to indictable offences is more complicated and varies from province to province. Depending upon the type of indictable offence, the Criminal Code will determine whether the trial can be heard by a magistrate, a high-court judge (County Court, District Court, Supreme Court or Queen's Bench judges appointed by the federal government), or by a court composed of a high court sitting with a JURY. Generally, when an accused is going to have a trial by a high-court judge or by a court composed of a judge and jury, he has the right to a preliminary hearing. There are several procedural provisions in the Criminal Code that deal with how the preliminary hearing should be conducted and what rights the accused has at this stage of the criminal prosecution. The preliminary hearing is held by a magistrate and the crown prosecutor presents the witnesses that he will rely upon at the trial. The accused through his counsel is allowed to cross-examine these witnesses. The public is allowed to attend, but often the press are not able to report the evidence heard. The issue at the preliminary hearing is not to determine innocence or guilt but to determine whether there is sufficient evidence to justify a trial. If it is decided sufficient evidence exists, the accused will be ordered to stand trial in the higher court by the magistrate.

There is no specific time limitation regarding when the accused must be charged with an indictable offence, although the CANADIAN CHARTER OF RIGHTS AND FREEDOMS indicates that an accused must have a trial within a reasonable time. The maximum punishment for each indictable offence is set out in the Criminal Code and varies from offence to offence.

Whether an accused is charged with a summary conviction offence or an indictable offence, he is eventually called upon to state in open court whether he pleads guilty or not guilty. If the plea is not guilty, the case will proceed to trial; if guilty, then a sentencing will take place before the judge who received the plea. There are several procedural rules as to how guilty pleas may be entered and how a judge may sentence an accused. In all criminal cases, both the accused and the Crown may have statutory rights of appeal against the determination of guilt or innocence, as well as sentence. Once again, there are many procedural rules governing appeals.

There are different theories concerning the best method of achieving a balance between the control of crime and the protection of individual rights. In Canada, England and the US, an adversarial or accusatorial system is used, in contrast to the inquisitorial system practised in France and other European countries. Canadian procedural rules are therefore designed to support the adversarial system in which the proceeding is a dispute between the state or Crown and the defendant or accused. As has been indicated above, the parties appear before an independent arbitrator, either a judge or jury, who must determine whether the accused is guilty or not guilty. Both parties are responsible for gathering and presenting evidence. The arbitrator is expected to play a relatively passive role, maintaining an impression of independence and impartiality, and ensuring that the rules of procedure are observed. In contrast, the inquisitorial system is a judicial inquiry. The responsibility for investigating and bringing out the facts rests upon the decision maker. The parties' roles are restricted to ensuring that their interests are properly represented during the trial.

The adversarial system and the procedural rules which comprise that system unquestionably favour the accused to a greater degree than the inquisitorial system. The Crown generally has the burden of adducing evidence to prove the guilt of the accused, who is almost always entitled to a presumption of innocence until the Crown has proven otherwise beyond a reasonable doubt. The accused is not required to give evidence and the court must acquit him if the Crown has not proven its case. If the accused elects not to give evidence or call witnesses, he (through his counsel) is still actively involved in the trial through cross-examinations of crown witnesses. This is very different from the inquisitorial system in which the accused is generally subjected, without election on his part, to extensive questioning but is otherwise inactive in the process.

Nevertheless, certain principles are common to both systems, including the requirements that trials be public, that determinations be based on evidence presented in open court, and that the accused is presumed innocent until proven guilty. However, even though both systems share these fundamental principles, there are differences in the manner in which they are applied.

The Constitution Act, 1867, gave the federal government jurisdiction to legislate with respect to "the criminal law, except the constitution of Courts of criminal jurisdiction, but including the procedure in criminal matters." Pursuant to this authority, Parliament has incorporated most Canadian procedural rules in the Criminal Code. Also, related statutes, such as the Narcotic Control Act, include their own specific procedures. One must remember that much criminal procedure is established by the Courts, as the various legislative provisions dealing with procedure often require interpretation.

A very important development in Canadian criminal procedure (as in most, if not all, areas of criminal law) is the inclusion of the Canadian Charter of Rights and Freedoms into the Constitution Act, 1982. Although the Charter does not set out any procedural rules, it does provide many of the principles that procedural rules must follow. Legislative procedures, such as the reverse onus requirement (in which the accused must prove his innocence) under the "possession for the purpose of trafficking" offence found in the Narcotic Control Act, have been struck down as contrary to the Charter.

Judicial interpretation of procedural rules has also been affected by the Charter. For instance, the police now have to be much more careful, when questioning suspects, to ensure that they are aware that they have the right to consult with a lawyer without delay as is guaranteed by s10(B) of the Charter. If the police do not allow an accused to exercise this right, then there is an excellent chance that any confession or other evidence subsequently obtained will be declared inadmissable. Formerly, a violation of this nature did not generally result in the exclusion of evidence.

A. PRINGLE

Criminology At the beginning of the 20th century criminology was primarily limited to explaining the behaviour of those who committed crimes. Since then criminologists have examined the characteristics of societies, the clash between cultural values, family characteristics, and a variety of social factors. Studies of prisons initially focused on individual inmates but the "culture" of inmate society was being looked at by the 1930s. For most criminologists, criminal behaviour is now viewed as something integral to a complex society, rather than as something inherent in individuals. Recently, criminologists have studied the POLICE, the courts and other aspects of the social-control system, as well as WHITE-COLLAR CRIMES and crimes without victims, eg, DRUG USE and PROSTITUTION.

The Université de Montréal established Canada's first School of Criminology, with Denis Szabo in 1960. In the 1980s the school had approximately 20 professors and 400 students, and offered 60 courses in criminology. The approach is interdisciplinary and includes academic programs leading to BA, MA and PhD degrees. While much of the work is theoretical, some courses provide training for workers in the field, eg, correctional services. In 1970 the Centre international de criminologie comparée was established.

The Centre of Criminology at University of Toronto was established by J.Ll.J. Edwards initially (1963) as a research organization. Although much early research was oriented towards law, the centre later reflected the influence of informal links with the Clarke Institute of Psychiatry and has conducted research on the police, the courts and other agencies of control in Canada.

Criminology at University of Alberta is under the auspices of the Department of Sociology. By the early 1970s, 1000 students were enrolled in 5 courses of introductory criminology; and 1000 others in deviance courses, advanced criminology and graduate seminars. Gwynn Nettler influenced criminology in Canada by supervising the doctoral dissertations of many professors who are now teaching and writing in criminology. His textbook, *Explaining Crime*, has been popular both in the US and in Canada. The Centre for Criminological Research at U of A was established in 1977 and currently sponsors seminars, research and other activities.

The Department of Criminology at University of Ottawa was created under Tadeusz Grygier in 1967 to offer an MA program. The interdisciplinary program in both French and English stresses applied criminology. The Department of Criminology at Simon Fraser University was established in 1973 and grew to 20 members by the 1980s. Extensive financial support from the BC government made this possible. MA and PhD programs are in place. The Human Justice Program established at the University of Regina in 1977, with a grant from the federal SOLICITOR GENERAL, offers an undergraduate degree in criminal justice and conducts contract research within Saskatchewan.

Other criminology programs have been developed at Carleton University, the University of Manitoba and University of Windsor. A police administration program was introduced at St Mary's University in Halifax, and the Atlantic Institute of Criminology was established at Dalhousie University.

The training of criminologists in Canada reflects 2 distinct strategies. Université de Montréal, Simon Fraser, and U of O offer programs that emphasize specialization in criminology, while U of A and U of T offer less course work in criminology itself and more background in the established social sciences.

Criminologists in Canada approach their field from different perspectives. Traditional theories locate the source of deviant behaviour in factors such as personality, family structures, CULTURE, social disorganization and differences in opportunity. This "consensus" perspective argues that rules for living are shared by all; therefore it is the behaviour of those who violate the rules that deserves attention. "Conflict" criminologists hold that deviant behaviour cannot be studied apart from particular historical forms of political and economic organization and that it is important to study the powerful groups in society and the way they exert control over others (*see* SOCIAL CLASS).

Regardless of the perspective employed, there is little evidence that Canadian criminologists have had much impact on legislation or on the criminal justice system. For example, although criminological research suggests that laws regarding marijuana are unrealistically harsh, that the numbers of inmates incarcerated and the length of time they serve does little to reduce crime, that the preponderance of persons from lower socioeconomic groups in prison creates cynicism about social justice, and that the offences of those in higher socioeconomic brackets are much more damaging to society than those committed by persons in lower socioeconomic brackets, this research has had little influence on government policy. When political pressures do lead to new legislation, research that is compatible with the winds of political change may be acknowledged. For example, changes in policy regarding wife beating and CHILD ABUSE which are politically important may be based on or may reflect criminological research. But generally such research has little impact on reform, at least in the short term.

The Social Sciences and Humanities Research Council supports criminological research. The ministry of the solicitor-general of Canada focuses on research related to policy issues and provides specific research contracts and sustaining grants to 7 university centres. These sustaining grants, called contribution grants, are unique and provide modest but flexible funding for research training and small-scale research.

Canadian criminologists participate in organizations representing the social sciences and the law in Canada, the US and internationally. These include the American Society of Criminology, the Society for the Study of Social Problems, and the Law and Society Association. Canadian criminologists may also be involved with the Canadian Criminal Justice Assn. The biennial congress emphasizes corrections and prevention, but the *Canadian Journal of Criminology*, produced by the association, is mainly research oriented.

JIM HACKLER

Croatians The first Croatians to arrive in Canada may have been 2 sailors from Dalmatia serving as crew on the third voyage of Jacques Cartier (1541-42) and a miner who accompanied Samuel de Champlain (1604-06). Later, Croatians served in Austrian military units sent by the French government to help defend NEW FRANCE (1758-59) and were involved in the early salmon fisheries of BC, the Cariboo Gold Rush of the 1860s and the Klondike Gold Rush of the late 1890s. Over the main period of migration, which spans the 20th century, approximately 75 000 Croatians have immigrated to Canada.

Origins Calculating numbers of Croatian immigrants has been difficult because Croatia has since the 10th and 11th centuries been variously a part of the Hungarian dynasty, the Holy Roman Empire, the Austro-Hungarian Empire (to WWI), the Kingdom of the Serbs, Croats and Slovenes (1918-29), the Kingdom of Yugoslavia (1929-41) and the Independent State of Croatia (1941-45); since 1945, it has constituted one of the republics of the Socialist Federal Republic of Yugoslavia. Croatians were classified with Austrians and Hungarians before 1918, and as Yugoslavs after the formal establishment of Yugoslavia in 1929. It has been estimated that 65% of the emigrants from what is now Yugoslavia have been Croatian. Because only 32 210 of the Croatians and their descendants now in Canada identified themselves in the 1981 census (the most recent figures available) as Croatian by mother tongue, it is assumed that many in the second and third generation classified themselves as English Canadians or were described by census takers as Yugoslav.

The Croatians were predominantly Roman Catholic peasants in the 19th and early 20th centuries, particularly those from the inland regions of Slavonia, Zumberak and Zagorje. The population of the Croatian littoral (Istria, Primorje and Dalmatia) on the Adriatic was somewhat more diverse, comprising some people of Muslim faith and a social mix of traders, sailors, fishermen, woodsmen and herders. Most of the immigration to Canada has been from this coastal region inland to the capital of Zagreb.

Migration and Settlement Prior to WWI, about 4 000 Croatians immigrated to Canada. Between 1928 and 1939 some 12 000 arrived. The third major group of post-WWII immigrants came in a wave of over 100 000 emigrants from Yugoslavia, the majority of whom were from Croatia. The main motive for immigration has been the search for a better life, but in the 1920s and after WWII many Croatians emigrated in protest against political conditions in their homeland. Many recent immigrants have been from an urban and professional class from the larger Croatian towns and cities, eg, Zagreb, Rijeka, Karlovac, Split and Zadar.

Of the 29 Croatian settlements established before WWI, 14 were in BC. Other Croatians settled in Saskatchewan, Alberta and northern and southern Ontario. During the 1920s some 171 settlements were established in the mining towns and mill towns across Canada's mining, forest and agricultural frontier and in Windsor, Toronto and Montréal. The postwar immigrants have largely settled in major cities, particularly Toronto and Montréal. The majority of postwar foreign-born immigrants were part of the industrial labour force, while the majority of the Canadian-born have been employed in the professional, clerical and service sectors of the economy.

Social Life and Community For the first and second group of immigrants, group life centered about kinship circles reminiscent of the familial and communal peasant *zadruga*. Fraternal and self-help organizations were established, eg, the American-based Croatian Fraternal Union, which opened its first Canadian lodge in Nanaimo in 1903 and which had 10 000 members by 1971. Other networks were sponsored by po-

litical parties such as the Croatian Peasant Party of the 1920s, which founded the Croatian Peasant Society in 1930. Other social, cultural and political activities were promoted by the Communist Party and also by the monarchist Yugoslav organizations in the 1930s. Since the war, organizations have proliferated, eg, the United Croats of Canada, the Federation of Croatian Societies in Canada and the Croatian Cultural Societies. More recently, Croatian folklore and dance groups have enjoyed a certain prominence within the multicultural folklore festivals of urban ethnic communities.

Religion and Cultural Life and Education The Roman Catholic Church, while unable to serve the isolated frontier communities of the 1920s and 1930s, has played a prominent role in Croatian Canadian life since 1950, the year the first Croatian Catholic parish was established in Windsor. Currently there are parishes and churches in all of the major urban communities, in addition to the community halls and cultural centres sponsored by political and fraternal organizations. Croatians have also enjoyed an active ethnic press, broadly representative of political factions from far left to right. *Hrvatski Glas* (*The Croatian Voice*), est 1929 and sponsored by the Croatian Peasant Society, and the Communist Party's *Borba* (*The Struggle*), est 1930, are both still published, the latter more recently as *Jedinstvo* (*Unity*) and then as *Naše Novine* (*Our News*). Other nationalist newspapers include *Naš Put* (*Our Way*), *Hrvatski Put* (*The Croatian Way*) and *Nezavisna Država Hrvatska* (*The Independent State of Croatia*). Several writers have also emerged from the émigré community, such as the poet Alan Horić, who won recognition for his works *L'Aube assassiné* and *Blessure au flanc du ciel*. Others in the fields of ballet, classical music and the fine arts have also won acclaim. Chess and soccer are very popular among postwar immigrants. Croatian chess clubs have won at least 2 provincial chess championships and the Metros-Croatia soccer team (later the Toronto Blizzard) won the North American Soccer League Championship in 1976.

The Croatian language was maintained by the family until the 1950s, when informal extracurricular schools were organized by community leaders and organizations. In the 1970s a network of Croatian-language schools established in the US spread into Canada, and a few courses on Croatian language and culture at the university level have been introduced as well. Language skills and cultural traditions have been somewhat lost through assimilation, particularly in the small isolated communities of the 1920s and 1930s, but because of the more recent and greater concentration of Croatians in larger cities, cultural maintenance has been more consciously pursued by community leaders.   A.W. RASPORICH

Reading: A.W. Rasporich, *For a Better Life: A History of the Croatians in Canada* (1982); N. Paveskovic, "Croatians in Canada," in *Slavs in Canada* (1968).

Crocus, Prairie, *see* ANEMONE.

Croft, Henry Holmes, educator, scientist (b at London, Eng 6 Mar 1820; d near San Diego, Tex 1 Mar 1883). For 37 years Croft was professor of chemistry (the first) at U of T and its antecedent, King's College. His special interests included toxicology and forensic science, which led to his frequent service as a consultant and expert witness in the courts. He also supplied scientific advice to the early refiners of Ontario petroleum. Having a keen interest in biology, Croft contributed to the formation and activities of the Entomological Soc of Canada. Inspired to disseminate scientific knowledge, he participated in the work of the MECHANICS' INSTITUTE and the Canadian Institute

(now Royal Canadian Institute) in Toronto.
W.A.E. McBRYDE

Croil, George Mitchell, airman (b at Milwaukee, Wis 5 June 1893; d at Vancouver 8 Apr 1959). Croil flew with the Royal Flying Corps in Salonika and trained pilots in the Middle East in WWI. In 1919 he joined the Canadian Air Board and was one of 62 officers granted RCAF commissions in 1924. After graduating from RAF Staff College and the Imperial Defence College, Croil became first chief of the air staff in 1938. A reserved, straighforward and meticulous officer, he directed the RCAF's prewar expansion. He retired as RCAF inspector general in 1944.
W.J. McANDREW

Croix de Saint Louis The Ordre royal et militaire de Saint Louis, fd 1693, was the only military order awarded in NEW FRANCE. The insignia, which had to be returned to the king when the owner died, was a golden cross edged with golden fleurs-de-lis, with 8 points enamelled in white. Commanders of the order wore it on a sash and chevaliers wore it on a small red ribbon. To qualify one had to be an officer in the regular army and serve the king of France. In Canada Louis-Hector de CALLIÈRE (1694) was the first to receive the decoration; Louis de Buade de FRONTENAC received it in 1697. The first Canadian chevalier was Pierre Le Moyne d'IBERVILLE (1699). By 1760 some 145 men had been decorated in Canada. The Croix de Saint Louis rapidly lost its value in France because it was too easily obtained, but in Canada it was rare and therefore retained its value. *See also* HONOURS; DECORATIONS.

Croke, John Bernard, soldier (b at Little Bay, Nfld 18 May 1892; d near Amiens, France 9 Aug 1918). At an early age, Croke moved with his family to Glace Bay, NS, where he later worked in the coal mines. During WWI he served with the 13th Infantry Btn, Quebec Reg, CEF, and was recognized and honoured for valour, 8 Aug 1918, during the opening stage of the Battle of AMIENS. Croke was the posthumous recipient of the first Victoria Cross awarded a Newfoundlander. Single-handedly, he. bombed a machine-gun nest and captured the crew and gun. Despite a severe wound, he rejoined his platoon and led a charge into a trench line, capturing 3 guns and the garrison. Again he was severely wounded, and died shortly after.   JOHN PARSONS

Croll, David Arnold, lawyer, politician (b at Moscow, Russia 12 Mar 1900). Elected a Liberal MLA in 1934, he became the first Jewish Cabinet minister but resigned in Apr 1937 over Prem HEPBURN's opposition to industrial unionism. Croll served in the Canadian Army 1939-45 and was MP for Toronto-Spadina 1945-55. Appointed the first Jewish senator in 1955, he was responsible for several studies on poverty and aging.
ROBERT BOTHWELL

Crombie, David, teacher, politician (b at Toronto 24 Apr 1936). Educated at Western and U of T, he was appointed lecturer in political science and urban affairs at Ryerson Polytechnical Inst. From 1966 to 1971, Crombie was director of student affairs at Ryerson. A central figure in the civic reform movement of the late 1960s in Toronto, Crombie was a co-founder of the short-lived Civic Action Party (CIVAC). He was unsuccessful in aldermanic elections for 1966, but sat for Ward 11, 1970-72. In 1973 he won the mayoralty, following a well-orchestrated personal campaign. Crombie's success within City Hall and increasing public popularity made the "Tiny Perfect Mayor" unbeatable at the polls; he was easily re-elected in 1975 and 1977. In Aug 1978 he resigned as mayor and won the federal by-election in Rosedale

David Cronenberg, Canadian director of horror and science-fiction films (*courtesy David Cronenberg Productions*).

riding for the Progressive Conservatives. He held the seat for the PCs in the general elections of 1979, 1980 and 1984 in spite of strong challenges and was minister of health and welfare in the Joe CLARK government and minister of Indian and northern affairs in the MULRONEY Cabinet in 1984. He was made secretary of state and minister responsible for multiculturalism on 30 June 1986.

VICTOR RUSSELL

Cronenberg, David, filmmaker (b at Toronto 15 Mar 1943). Cronenberg studied literature at U of T and while there made several short films. His first 2 feature films, *Stereo* (1969) and *Crimes of the Future* (1970), were abstract and ironic commentaries on contemporary life. *Shivers* (1976) launched his career as an original and inventive writer and director of horror and science-fiction films. In *Rabid* (1977), *The Brood* (1979), *Scanners* (1980) and *Videodrome* (1983), Cronenberg explored large philosophical questions, demonstrating that even within the constraints of commercial genres a personal vision could be conveyed. Cronenberg has made films for the CBC. His features *The Dead Zone* (1983) and *The Fly* (1986) marked his emergence as a filmmaker of international status. PIERS HANDLING

Cronyn, Benjamin, first Anglican bishop of Huron (b at Kilkenny, Ire 11 July 1802; d at London, Ont 22 Sept 1871), father-in-law of Edward BLAKE. Cronyn enjoyed a first-rate education at Kilkenny College and Trinity College, Dublin, earning the divinity prize and eventually 4 degrees at the latter. During his formative years, he came under the indelible influence of the Reverend Peter Roe, a leading Irish evangelical. Cronyn moved to Upper Canada late in 1832 as a missionary under the Society for the Propagation of the Gospel. He was soon licensed to St Paul's Church, London, and from the outset he figured formidably in that largely Irish Protestant community. A man of extraordinary physical stamina, he laboured assiduously among his backwoods parishioners and the garrison. Around him, Cronyn systematically constructed an "Irish Compact," a phalanx of aggressive low-church evangelicalism, which harassed the

high-church stronghold of Bishop John STRACHAN of Toronto.

In 1857, Dr Cronyn (as he had become in 1855) was elected first Bishop of Huron and consecrated at Lambeth Palace. His elevation to the episcopate established 2 important precedents in Canadian church government: he was the first bishop in the British Empire to be elected by a diocesan synod of lay and clerical representatives (previously colonial bishops had been appointed from England); and consequently he was "the last Canadian bishop required to go to England for consecration." Benjamin Huron further augmented his position in 1863 by establishing a low-church theological school in his see-city of London, Ont; Huron College served not only as Cronyn's counterplot to the "unsound and un-Protestant" teachings of Strachan's Trinity College in Toronto, but also as the founding college of the University of Western Ontario. So vigorously and solidly did Bishop Cronyn promote his form of "extreme Protestant" ANGLICANISM that its stamp remains evident on the church in southwestern Ontario and indeed elsewhere. A churchman of unflinching fundamentalist convictions, the ambitious Irish cobbler's son also proved a skilful steward of those 2 keys to worldly success — politics and business. His descendants include the distinguished actor, Hume CRONYN. JOHN D. BLACKWELL

Cronyn, Hume, actor, director (b at London, Ont 18 July 1911). He is a skilled farceur and character player who often teamed with his wife Jessica TANDY. Educated at Ridley Coll, St Catharines, Ont, and McGill, Cronyn was an active amateur with the Montreal Repertory Theatre before training in Austria and New York. His professional career began in 1931 in Washington, DC, and from 1934 on he established his Broadway reputation in productions of *Three Men on a Horse, High Tor, Room Service* and *The Three Sisters*. He won his first Tony Award opposite Tandy in *The Fourposter* (1951-53). They were also together in *A Day by the Sea* (1955), the London production of *Big Fish, Little Fish* (1962), the inaugural season of the Guthrie Theatre in Minneapolis (1963), *A Delicate Balance* (1966), *Happy Days* (1972), and *The Merchant of Venice* as well as *A Midsummer Night's Dream* (1976), *The Gin Game* (1978) and *Foxfire* (1980) at Canada's STRATFORD FESTIVAL. The pair toured the USSR with *The Gin Game* in 1979-80 and took *Foxfire*, which Cronyn co-authored, to Minneapolis and then to New York (1985). Their appearance in the film *Cocoon* (1985) was followed by the Broadway play, *The Petition.* Cronyn's famous stage roles have included Polonius (Tony Award 1964), Shylock, Richard III, Willy Loman in *Death of a Salesman*, and Hadrian VII, the last again for Stratford. DAVID GARDNER

Crop Insurance An all-risk crop-insurance program is available to Canadian farmers under the authority of the federal Crop Insurance Act (1959) and through concurrent and complementary legislation enacted by each province. This federal-provincial cost-shared program is designed to stabilize farm income by minimizing, at the individual farm level, the detrimental effects of crop losses caused by uncontrollable natural hazards. More than 100 000 farmers participate voluntarily. Most major commercial crops in Canada are now insurable under the program. When crop yields fall below some actuarially determined level, the insured farmer is given an indemnity payment to make up the difference.

J.C. GILSON

Crop Research may be defined as activity directed to making the growing and marketing of commercial crops more efficient and profitable. Hence, crop research may comprise any or all of

the following: PLANT BREEDING, plant physiology and BIOCHEMISTRY, crop protection studies, cultural management studies, storage methods research, and processing and products studies. The importance of plant breeding in the adaptation of crop plants to Canadian conditions is treated in a separate article. Well-known successes include MARQUIS WHEAT, TRITICALE and CANOLA.

Plant Physiology and Biochemistry

Canadian plant physiologists and biochemists have contributed to both on-farm research and basic research conducted under carefully controlled conditions at the laboratories of the NATIONAL RESEARCH COUNCIL, research stations and the universities. Important work has been done in tissue culture, weed control, host-parasite relationships and PESTICIDE research.

Tissue Culture is the growing of complete plants from individual cells, small groups of cells, tissue explants, and isolated apical or axillary buds. Since many new plants can be produced from a small amount of starting material it is possible to produce large numbers of cloned plants (ie, all individuals are genetically identical). Clonal lowbush blueberry plants and apple seedlings have been produced by tissue culture at the Kentville, NS, Research Station. Methods for *in vitro* propagation of a number of ornamental plants have been developed at UNB, Fredericton, and U of Guelph. Similarly, grapes and kiwi fruit have been propagated at Saanichton's BC research station.

In addition there are several Canadian laboratories in which tissue culture of conifers is being studied. These include the Canadian Forest Service laboratories at Fredericton, NB, and Chalk River, Ont, and the research labs at Queen's in Kingston and at the U of Calgary. Also a vigorous program in tissue culture of conifers is in operation at the National Research Council's Plant Biotechnology Institute at Saskatoon, Sask.

Weed-Control Research by Agriculture Canada researchers has centered at Regina, but other research station and university laboratories have also contributed.

Host-parasite Relationships Canadian research into the relationship between the wheat plant and the stem and leaf rust organisms began in earnest with the establishment of the Dominion Rust Research Laboratory at Winnipeg in 1925. Major contributions were made by J.H. CRAIGIE, Margaret NEWTON, Thorvaldur JOHNSON, C.H. GOULDEN and others. Professor M. Shaw and his students at the U of Saskatchewan, Saskatoon, began a very productive research program on the plant physiological and biochemical aspects of the wheat rust problem in 1950. Shortly afterwards research programs were begun at the Winnipeg Rust Research Laboratory by F.R. Forsyth and at the Botany Department of the U of Manitoba by P.K. Isaac. The Winnipeg Research Station still maintains an active program on all aspects of preventing and controlling the harmful effects of the rusts of wheat, oats, sunflower, etc. Although some progress was made in the use of fungicides to control stem and leaf rust of wheat, the main importance of this work was a better understanding of the physiological and biochemical interactions of the rust fungus and the wheat plant. The simultaneous studies on the genetics of the wheat and the rusts have resulted in a steady production, by the plant breeders, of rust-resistant varieties. This has essentially prevented the possible serious economic effects of the wheat rusts from occurring.

Other noteworthy achievements include the outstanding work on the physiology and biochemistry of lignin (a substance related to cellulose), fungal by-products and edible seaweeds, at

Spraying seed potatoes, Saint Quentin, NB (*photo by Richard Vroom*).

the NRC laboratories at Ottawa, Saskatoon and Halifax, respectively; and the pionering work in GENETIC ENGINEERING done by O. Gamborg at NRC's Prairie Regional Laboratory in the 1960s and 1970s.

Crop Protection

Although weed competition, insects, fungi and bacteria were serious problems from the beginning of agricultural practice in Canada, weed-control chemicals, broad-spectrum organic insecticides and fungicides did not become available until after WWII. Most new pesticides were discovered outside Canada, and Canadian research dealing with such chemicals has centered on determining the proper amounts to use and the most effective means and time for application. The notable exception to the above restriction is a program on the chemical basis of the activity of many of the pesticides currently in use, carried on at Agriculture Canada's Research Institute at London, Ont.

The preferred means of protecting plants against diseases and insects is to find or produce resistant varieties. Excellent research to this end has been accomplished in Canada, eg, plant breeders have consistently been able to provide new varieties of hard red spring wheat resistant to stem rust and oat varieties resistant to crown rust. Resistance to wheat stem sawfly has been incorporated into winter wheat. In the control of wheat stem rust, the campaign to eradicate barberry plants, the parasite's alternative host, was as important as the development of resistant wheat varieties. Similarly, the campaign to eradicate buckthorn, the alternate host of oat crown rust, was important in crown rust control. In eastern Canada, the removal of wild apple trees has been a key in the fight against the apple maggot.

The integrated method of pest control involves using the smallest possible amount of chemicals and encouraging natural predators to assist in insect control. The method received its impetus from the increased cost of pesticides, the development of plant and insect resistance to chemicals and the uneasiness of the general public about the use of toxic substances in food production. A.D. Pickett of the Kentville, NS, research station was a leader in the development of the method (*see* INSECT, BENEFICIAL).

Cultural Management

When large-scale agriculture was introduced to Canada, the thrust was to clear all unwanted trees, plants or sod from the SOIL so that monoculture (cultivation of one type of plant) could be practised. After the disastrous loss of topsoil during drought years in western Canada and similar losses during excessively wet years in denuded rolling land elsewhere, the trend has been towards the use of more responsible AGRICULTURAL SOIL PRACTICES. Attempts have been made to control wind erosion by maintaining sufficient straw in or on the soil and by avoiding exposure of fine-

ly divided soil to wind action (*see* SOIL CONSERVATION). To minimize disturbance of soil, no-till methods have been developed for many crops: the annual crop may be seeded into rye or clover which is then removed by chemical weed control before the annual crop has sprouted. The practice of grassing down apple and pear orchards once they approach bearing age also helps protect soil from washing or blowing away. Perhaps the most significant addition to Canadian soil management has been the promotion of the liming of the acidic soils of eastern Canada. Once soil acidity has been substantially reduced, plants can use added nutrients more effectively. The NS government subsidizes the cost of lime used for agricultural purposes.

Storage

The native people stored grains (eg, corn), fruits (eg, cranberries) and vegetables (eg, beans, squash) for winter use. European settlers introduced other fruits (eg, apples, pears) and vegetables (eg, potatoes, cabbage, celery, turnips, onions, carrots) which required new methods of long-term storage. The first storages were of a type known as common, air or ventilated storage. Many are still in use in Canada because, after fall harvest, ambient nighttime temperatures are usually suitable for preserving potatoes, dry onions, cabbage and mature carrots. Earlier storages were underground, but the modern trend is to locate most of the building above ground and use automatic control of louvres and fans to draw in cool, outside air when required. A few cool stores used ice to lower temperatures inside a storage room. For many years after ice-cooled stores were abandoned, ice was used to cool railway cars carrying perishable products. Mechanically refrigerated storage was a major advance, allowing many fruits and vegetables to be maintained for up to 6 months in good condition. Fruits and vegetables not adapted to long-term storage could benefit from refrigeration for short terms, allowing orderly marketing. Canadian government and university research laboratories have made noteworthy advances in the science of food storage; the more recent improvements are described below.

Jacketed Storage rooms are built so that cooling air circulates around the room in a sealed envelope. Jacketed storage is especially effective for maintaining high relative humidities and is used for storing carrots, cabbage and celery.

Controlled-atmosphere Storage is a system for holding produce in an atmosphere that differs substantially from air in the proportion of nitrogen, oxygen or carbon dioxide present. The research has been done mainly at Agriculture Canada laboratories at Kentville (NS), Ottawa and Summerland (BC), at NRC laboratories in Ottawa and at U of Guelph. Over a period of many years, valuable information about the optimum conditions for storing fruits and vegetables has been passed along to commercial interests. The term "controlled atmosphere storage," first suggested by W.P. Phillips of Agriculture Canada, is now used around the world.

Low-pressure Storage involves holding products in a partial vacuum, with controlled oxygen levels. The system is still largely experimental, although prototype vans are available. Pioneering work in the use of LPS for fruits and vegetables has been conducted at U of Guelph.

Ultra-low-oxygen Storage is the most successful development in McIntosh apple marketing since controlled-atmosphere storage began. It reduces oxygen from 5% to a range of 0.5-1.5% and also lowers carbon dioxide levels. The altered composition of the atmosphere slows the ripening pro-

cess; thus, the system allows marketing over a year after harvest, with little loss of original flavour and texture. Canadian experiments on ultra-low-oxygen storage began in Kentville in 1976, following initial work conducted in the UK.

Processing and Products

Raw agricultural products produced in Canada are valued annually at some $20 billion. Processing adds greatly to the final value and provides thousands of jobs. The FOOD AND BEVERAGE INDUSTRIES have been very innovative in creating new products (eg, new breakfast cereals). In addition, the provincial research laboratories at Vineland, Ont, and the federal laboratories at Summerland and Kentville have searched for new means of processing fruits and vegetables, mainly with a view to reducing costs. For example, the steam blancher developed at Kentville to replace hot-water treatment saves energy as well as conserving the vitamin content by using a shorter blanching period. Another example is the rotated can method (roll cooker) of heat-processing tinned fruit, developed at Summerland to provide more rapid and effective heat treatment and thus to preserve the product's quality.

The Canadian WINE INDUSTRY improved rapidly following WWII with the influx of European wine-making experts and hybrid grapes from France. The research stations at Summerland and Kentville have been active in testing newly introduced grape varieties because of the desire to maintain and expand wine-making facilities in BC and NS. Government research has also assisted the MAPLE SUGAR INDUSTRY by testing pilot plant models of a method of concentration known as reverse osmosis. In reverse osmosis a liquid under pressure is restrained by a membrane through which water molecules will pass but the molecule to be concentrated (eg, the sugar in maple sap) will not.

The Kentville research station acquired a small flexible-retortable-pouch processor from France in 1977. The laminated plastic and foil pouches are able to withstand heat and pressure in cooking and to resist puncture during commercial handling. The advantages of processing food products in the pouch include transportation and storage savings on empty and filled containers, energy conservation during processing, and better nutritional, flavour and textural properties. The new container is likely to replace cans and bottles. Finally, by-products of the agricultural industry are being studied as possible raw products for single-cell-protein production, at first for animal feed, but eventually for human consumption as well. *See also* AGRICULTURAL RESEARCH AND DEVELOPMENT.   F.R. FORSYTH

Crops are plant species grown for human or animal consumption or for special purposes (eg, FLAX, TOBACCO). In Canada, most major crops grown are used for food and feed. Crops can be classified in several ways. By growth habit they are annual, biennial or perennial, depending on whether they complete their life cycle in one or 2 years, or persist for over 2 years. The special term "winter annuals" is used for crops that are planted and germinate in fall, overwinter in a dormant state, renew growth in spring and are harvested in July or Aug. A more useful classification of crops, based on the general trade use, divides them into CEREAL CROPS, FORAGES, OILSEEDS, orchard crops, BERRIES, VEGETABLES and special crops. Cereals are plants grown for the mature seeds they produce (eg, WHEAT, OATS, BARLEY, RYE, CORN). Forage crops are grown for animal fodder. They may be harvested and stored until used, or grazed as a pasture or range crop (eg, GRASSES such as timothy and bromegrass, LEGUMES such as CLOVER and AL-

FALFA). When cereal crops (especially corn) are harvested as whole plants, chopped and fed to animals, the crop is classed as a forage or fodder crop. Oilseed crops are grown for their oil-bearing seeds (eg, soybeans, sunflowers, flax, canola). Orchard crops are edible FRUITS or nuts (eg, apples, peaches, pears, walnuts). Berries are small, fleshy fruits grown on a vine or small shrub (eg, strawberries, raspberries, currants, blueberries, grapes). Vegetables are herbaceous plants of which all or a part is eaten, raw or cooked (eg, carrots, onions, tomatoes, lettuce). Potatoes are classed as a trade vegetable but also considered a field crop when hectarages are large. The term "special crops" designates crops that do not fit neatly into other categories (eg, tobacco, buckwheat) or vegetable crops traded in a manner different from the normal one, such as peas, beans or lentils, which are raised as field crops and sold like grain through the elevator system.

Canadian Constraints While the total land area of Canada is nearly one billion hectares, only about 45 or 46 million ha (5%) is improved farmland. An additional 24 million ha of rangeland and wild pasture, mostly in the Prairie provinces and BC, is used by ranchers. The northern sections of the Prairies and the northern clay belt of Ontario and Québec include some 15 million ha that could be used for agricultural production, but the soils are marginally developed and a very short growing season makes the potential much less than that of the land now farmed. The most productive land is the 40 million ha in crop and summer fallow. Summer fallowing, the practice of leaving land unplanted to a crop, is a moisture-conserving measure, forming part of the sequence of crop rotation on the prairies. About 80% of Canada's farmland is located in the Prairie provinces of Alberta, Saskatchewan and Manitoba; about 10%, in Ontario; the remainder, in the other provinces.

Canada lies in the North Temperate Zone; all its prairie farmland is N of the 49th parallel of latitude. Productive farming, therefore, depends upon crops that ripen early, if they are spring sown, or are winter hardy, if they are winter annuals, biennial or perennial. Unlike many producers in tropical and subtropical areas where 2 or more crops per year are possible, Canadians can rely on only one crop. The vastness of Canada and the variations in climate preclude accuracy in any general statement but, with the exception of the lower mainland of BC and southern Ontario (where less hardy crops survive), crop growth, other than for forage or for range, is secure only from May to Sept. Victoria Day, around May 24, is a safe date for gardeners from coast to coast to transplant ORNAMENTAL and garden plants that have been started in GREENHOUSES. Late spring frosts may occur after that date, but the probability is not great. Early fall frosts occur in Sept; thus, the frost-free period is 100-120 days. Canadian summers are usually quite warm, with temperatures often reaching over 30°C. These temperatures, coupled with adequate sunshine, make crop growth rapid. However, as the climate is continental, much of the farmland of Canada (especially the Prairie provinces) suffers from lack of moisture. Some grain crops are produced with as little as 375 mm of rain, but the moisture usually comes when needed for fast summer growth. 559 954 ha of land are irrigated in the Prairie provinces.

Canada's soils developed under regimes of varying amounts of rainfall and are dependent upon the inherent properties of the material from which they formed; thus, they may be either alkaline or acidic. In general, western soils are alkaline; eastern ones, acidic. Acid soils can be limed to alter the acidity, but the practice is costly and must be done annually. Liming is subsidized by some provincial governments. In eastern Canada, higher water tables and poor drainage reduce the capacity of soils to produce some crops. In spring, flooding can occur in some areas of all parts of Canada.

When settlers first opened up the country, many different crops were grown on each farm to provide subsistence. The practice is still followed in some remote regions or on isolated farms but, in general, crop production has been specialized to provide economic returns. As land prices increase, greater returns per hectare are needed, and producers have had to specialize. The choice of a crop is dictated by geographic region, latitude and moisture; therefore, there is a strong regional bias in the production of most crops. Most wheat, oats, barley, rye, flax, canola, mustard and sunflowers are grown on the prairies. Wheat and summer fallow occupy about one-third of the total hectarage. Soybeans, tobacco and beans are grown mostly in Ontario; fodder and grain corn, in Ontario and Québec; fruit, in BC, Ontario and NS. Potatoes are grown in all provinces; sugar beets, in Manitoba and Québec and, under irrigation, in Alberta.

Handling In 1986 there were 293 089 farms in Canada, down from 318 000 in 1981. The size of individual farms varies greatly: by census definition, farms can be as small as one acre with produce of only $250, or they can be extensive, highly capitalized holdings with sales in the thousands of dollars. The latter group comprises only about 20% of all producers but accounts for over 70% of total farm production. A wide variety of crops can be grown in all regions of Canada, and the handling of crops will vary with the size of the farm and the type of production carried out. The major producers of cereal crops, oilseeds and some special crops aim their production for cash sales. The standard practice for such crops in the Prairie provinces is for farmers to have on-farm storage for a quantity of produce and to deliver the remainder to grain elevators, where it is graded, stored or shipped to terminal elevators for sale domestically or abroad. The price is established by grade and quantity. Grading factors include purity of type, soundness, maturity and test weight. Because weather at harvest can greatly affect the quality of grain crops, grades obtained by farmers will vary by year, district and cultivar (commercial variety) grown. In Ontario, where quantities of winter wheat, soybeans, corn and field beans are grown, there is very little farm storage, and producers rely on feed and grain companies to purchase quantities of produce harvested in fall. Many farmers produce cereal and forage crops for their own use as feed for livestock. Some farmers produce hay for cash sales; most, for home use. Other forage crops make up pasture and rangeland used for cattle production.

Many Canadian gardeners produce a mixture of vegetables, berries or orchard crops for their own use. With more extensive holdings, some off-farm sales are made, eg, "U-pick" strawberries or roadside stands for fruits and vegetables. A subsistence farmer normally plans to live off his farm but may supplement his income with some off-farm sales. Market-garden operations grow vegetables for local markets or shipment into large urban areas. Orchard crops, potatoes, tobacco, sugar beets and vegetables grown for off-farm sales are marketed through special systems. Canada is a net exporter of agricultural products, the chief exports being grains and oilseeds. Our chief imports are fruits, vegetables and specialty items (eg, sugar). The pattern of net exports has long been a part of Canada's normal trade pattern and will likely remain so. *J.W. MORRISON*

Crosbie, John Carnell, lawyer, politician (b at St John's 30 Jan 1931). He was elected to the St John's City Council in Nov 1965 and appointed deputy mayor on 1 Jan 1966. He resigned that July to join the Cabinet of Liberal Premier Joey SMALLWOOD and won election to the Assembly in Sept. In 1969 he unsuccessfully challenged Smallwood in a party leadership convention. He joined the Progressive Conservatives led by Frank MOORES in June 1971 and his support helped Moores win the 1972 election. Crosbie held several senior Cabinet portfolios and was the main advocate of the government's policy of greater local control and management of Newfoundland's resources. Elected to the House of Commons in 1976, he was minister of finance in the brief 1979 minority government of Joe CLARK, which on Dec 13 lost a nonconfidence vote when Crosbie's budget was defeated. In 1983 he contested the leadership of the PC Party, finishing third behind Brian MULRONEY; he was appointed minister of justice in the new Conservative government in 1984 and was shifted to the ministry of transport in 1986. *MELVIN BAKER*

Crosbie, Sir John Chalker, merchant, politician (b at Brigus, Nfld 11 Sept 1876; d at St John's 5 Oct 1932). An aggressive and energetic entrepreneur, he created a fortune (which he lost) and started the Crosbie dynasty, which continues to flourish. Crosbie founded Crosbie and Co in 1900 and by 1920 was one of the leading fish exporters in Newfoundland. He entered politics as MHA for Bay de Verde in 1908. He was minister of shipping 1918-19 and minister of finance and customs under PM MONROE from 1924 until 1928, when he retired from politics. *KEITH MATTHEWS*

Cross, Alfred Ernest, rancher, brewer (b at Montréal 26 June 1861; d there 10 Mar 1932). A graduate of Ontario Agricultural Coll and Montreal Veterinary Coll, Cross came to Calgary in 1884 as veterinarian and assistant manager of the British-American Horse Ranch Co. In 1885 he started his own ranch, the A7, becoming one of the West's most prominent cattlemen and one of the "Big Four" founders of the CALGARY STAMPEDE. The A7 is still owned by the Cross family and remains one of the largest ranches in the West. In 1892 he founded the Calgary Brewing and Malting Co and in 1899 he was elected Conservative MLA for the NWT. *DAVID H. BREEN*

Reading: David H. Breen, *The Canadian Prairie West* (1983).

Cross-Country Skiing From its origins over 5000 years ago in Scandinavia up to the early 1900s, SKIING was mainly a form of winter transport. Although a few daring athletes intentionally challenged their skills by SKI JUMPING or racing down hills, most of the early ski pioneers simply toured "cross country" over relatively flat routes. In 1905, for example, the Montreal Ski Club built on a long-established snowshoe club tradition by introducing largely social ski tours into the LAURENTIAN HIGHLANDS.

In the early 1900s, most skiers carried a single pole and wore long (2.5 to 4 m), wide (over 80 mm), unlaminated wooden skis that were so heavy (several kg each) and awkwardly fastened that skiers usually removed them and carried them up steep hills. In 1915 the Norwegian Thorleaf Haug invented screw-on steel toe-plates which eliminated the need to carve slots through the middle of the skis to hold toe-straps. This made skis much stronger and permitted the adoption of shorter (under 2.5 m), narrower (less than 60 mm) and lighter (under 1 kg each) skis. Used with a pair of bamboo poles, such skis remained the standard for all forms of skiing for the next 20 years.

In order to ski efficiently over a variety of snow types, ski-base preparation became an inconvenient but highly aromatic art. Pine tar was carefully heated into the bases and then covered with various complex and often secret "dopes." In the West, where there were long steep slopes to be climbed, stronger grip was obtained by fastening sealskin under the skis, with the hairs pointed backward.

In 1927 the CPR introduced Laurentian ski trains, which led to the wide use of an extensive trail network blazed by "Jackrabbit" JOHANNSEN and the resorts opened by early developers such as Louis Cochand and the Wheeler brothers. By 1935 similar developments were to be found all across N America, where skiers enthusiastically adopted the use of ski lifts, from the rope tow, invented in Shawbridge, Qué, in 1932, to the chairlift, introduced into Canada at Mont Tremblant in 1938. Skis were quickly adapted for use on large hills through the introduction of steel edges for stability on ice (about 1930) and cable bindings that held the heels down for greater control. Within a decade, cross-country skiing became a sport requiring special equipment, and practised by only a small core of devotees.

During the 1970s people caught up in the FITNESS boom or rebelling against the expense and congestion of alpine skiing took up cross country in great numbers. The CANADIAN SKI MARATHON, for example, grew from 400 to over 4000 participants during that decade, and scores of other tours and races for the general public sprang up across the country. Although Canadian national cross-country championships have been held since 1921, only within the last few years has increased interest in the sport produced internationally competitive athletes such as Sharon and Shirley Firth and Pierre HARVEY.

During the 1970s and 1980s, technological innovation has changed the sport. Simple waxing systems and no-wax skis have reduced the complexity of ski preparation. Synthetic materials have allowed the manufacture of extremely light, strong skis and poles. New boot-binding systems improve control at high speeds. Since the new skis glide much faster, skating and double-poling techniques have assumed increasing dominance of international competition. In the mid-1980s, in fact, a separate "classical" racing category was created to preserve the traditional techniques apart from the faster "freestyle" skating. The skating technique is also popular with recreational skiers using prepared trails, since it is relatively simple to learn and requires no gripping waxes, only gliders.

Despite the increasing cost and sophistication of the competitive sport, cross-country skiing remains extremely popular with its almost 4 million Canadian participants. More than half of them set forth at least once a week to rediscover the age-old joys of the sport. MURRAY SHAW

Crow (Corvidae), large family of birds that includes JAYS, MAGPIES and nutcrackers as well as crows and RAVENS. The family is thought to have originated during the middle Miocene period (23.7-5.3 million years ago) in the Old World. Jays are believed to be the most primitive Corvidae. From this group, magpies and, later, ravens and typical crows evolved. At present, 103 species of Corvidae are recognized. Crows, largest members of the order Passeriformes (perching birds), range in length from 17.5 to 70 cm. The typical crow (genus *Corvus*) is either wholly black (including bill and legs) or black with white, grey and brown. Of the 3 species of *Corvus* native to Canada, only the northwestern crow (*C. caurinus*) has a limited range. It inhabits the coast and islands of BC, where it forages along shores, beaches and tidal flats. The highly adaptable American crow (*C. brachyrhynchos*) occupies

many habitats and feeds on both animal and vegetable matter. It breeds from north-central BC to Newfoundland. Similarly, the common raven (*C. corax*) is found in most of Canada. Both northwestern and American crows tend to forage in open areas but prefer wooded regions for nesting and roosting. The northwestern crow nests mainly in coniferous trees; the American crow, in deciduous and coniferous trees and, occasionally, in low bushes. The male American crow helps incubate the clutches of 4-6 eggs. The crow family represents one of the most advanced stages of avian evolution, showing, for example, a highly developed intelligence and a complex social organization. In places, crows have proven more harmful than helpful to humans, since although they kill a large number of insects, they also damage CROPS, particularly corn. They also prey on eggs and young of many desirable birds.

LORRAINE G. D'AGINCOURT

Crow, John William, economist and governor of the BANK OF CANADA (b at London, Eng 22 Jan 1937). He succeeded Gerald BOUEY in 1987 as the Bank of Canada's fifth governor. After service with the Royal Air Force (1956-58), Crow attended Oxford, where he studied philosophy, politics and economics. In 1961 he joined the staff of the International Monetary Fund in Washington, where he served in a variety of positions in its Western Hemisphere Division. After joining the Bank of Canada in 1973, he became chief of its research department in 1974. Appointed an adviser to the governor in 1979 and a deputy governor in 1981, Crow became senior deputy governor in 1984. As the crucial instrument of Canada's MONETARY POLICY, the bank under Crow is generally believed to be inclined to pursue Bouey's dedication to the suppression of inflation, even at the cost of high interest rates.

DUNCAN MCDOWALL

Crowfoot, Blackfoot chief (b near Belly R, Alta c1830; d near Blackfoot Crossing, Alta 25 Apr 1890). Born a BLOOD, he grew up among the BLACKFOOT. As a teenager, he showed great bravery in a battle by advancing and striking a painted tipi in the hostile Crow camp. For this deed he was given an ancestor's name, *Isapo-muxika*, meaning "Crow Indian's Big Foot," shortened by interpreters to Crowfoot. He went to war 19 times and was wounded 6 times. His most heroic deed was to attack and kill a grizzly bear with a lance in

Crowfoot, head chief of the Blackfoot, 1887 (*courtesy Glenbow Archives, Calgary*).

sight of the whole camp. Shortly after, in 1865, he became chief of the Big Pipes band, and in 1870 became one of the 3 head chiefs of the tribe.

Crowfoot was perceptive, farseeing and a diplomat. He established good relations with fur traders and peace with the CREE. He adopted a Cree named POUNDMAKER, who became a leader of his own people, and rescued missionary Albert LACOMBE during a Cree raid. In 1874 Crowfoot welcomed the NWMP when they came W to stamp out the whisky trade. He was recognized as an ally and was given a prominent role in Treaty No 7 negotiations in 1877.

After the Blackfoot settled on their reserve in 1881, Crowfoot became disillusioned with the Canadian government, but he refused to allow his people to join the 1885 NORTH-WEST REBELLION, less out of loyalty to the government than from the belief that it was a losing fight. Sick during his last decade, he constantly mourned the loss of his children, of whom only one blind son and 3 daughters reached maturity. HUGH A. DEMPSEY

Reading: Hugh A. Dempsey, *Crowfoot* (1972).

Crown, the collectivity of executive powers exercised, in a monarchy, by or in the name of the SOVEREIGN. These powers flow from the historic rights and privileges known as Crown or PREROGATIVE POWERS of the English Crown. In Canada, a monarchy since its founding, the Fathers of Confederation created a parliamentary democracy through a unique partnership between a federal STATE and a monarchy. Through the Crown, power is held in a nonpartisan office. Federally the Crown is represented by the GOVERNOR GENERAL and provincially by the LIEUTENANT-GOVERNORS, although both are federal offices. The statutory responsibilities of Crown representatives are outlined in the CONSTITUTION ACT, 1867, and delineated further in the Letters Patent (1947), which allow the governor general to exercise royal prerogatives at his discretion. *See also* ADMINISTRATIVE LAW.

JACQUES MONET, S.J.

Crown Attorney Criminal prosecutions are the responsibility of the ATTORNEYS GENERAL but are normally conducted by their agents, crown attorneys, who prepare and conduct prosecutions of all indictable offences. In criminal proceedings, the prosecuting counsel is frequently referred to as the Crown, short for crown attorney.

K.G. MCSHANE

Crown Corporation, wholly owned federal or provincial organization, structured like private or independent enterprises. Established to carry out regulatory, advisory, administrative, financial or other services or to provide goods and services, crown corporations generally enjoy greater freedom from direct political control than government departments. Although the 1951 federal Financial Administration Act (FAA) declared that crown corporations are "ultimately accountable, through a minister, to Parliament, for the conduct of (their) affairs," they are not subject to budgetary systems or direct control of a minister in the same way as government departments.

The first crown corporation, the Board of Works, was established in 1841 to construct a canal system in the Province of Canada. Crown corporations such as CANADIAN NATIONAL RAILWAYS, PETRO-CANADA and several provincial hydro firms now rank among Canada's largest enterprises. They have been created by various governments, including NDP, Liberal, Progressive Conservative and Social Credit governments. The establishment of important crown corporations in the fields of transportation (AIR CANADA, CNR, ST LAWRENCE SEAWAY) and communications (CANADIAN BROADCASTING CORPORATION) attests to the unwillingness or inability of private firms to provide important services in a vast, sparsely populated country, rather than to a preference for PUBLIC OWNERSHIP *per se*. Since WWII other federal crown corporations have emerged as important providers of loans and related financial services to farmers (Farm Credit Corporation), small businesses (Federal Business Development Bank) and exporters (Export Development Corporation), interests whose needs were not always met by private financial institutions. The federal government also owns and operates coal mines (Cape Breton Development Corp) and Petro-Canada, a major integrated oil and gas company. For many observers this major role for crown corporations constitutes the essence of this country's "mixed" economy and a central difference between the industrial organization of Canada and the US.

Provincial crown corporations are also significant, although differences exist in their roles, economic importance and administration. In most provinces crown corporations are responsible for the generation and transmission of electricity and the retail distribution of liquor. In the Prairie provinces, telephone service is usually provided by crown corporations (*see* UTILITIES). Recently, provincial crown corporations as diverse as the Potash Corp of Saskatchewan, the Sydney Steel Corp of NS and provincial energy companies in Saskatchewan, Ontario and Québec have been formed. In BC, Saskatchewan, Manitoba and Québec, crown corporations sell automobile insurance, while the Alberta, BC and Ontario governments own railways.

Crown corporations assume special prominence in Québec and Saskatchewan. In Saskatchewan, crown corporations were extended deep into the provincial economy after the CCF's landmark electoral victory in 1944. In that province, crown corporations were conceived as a key element in Saskatchewan's efforts to establish a more diversified economy through the creation of secondary industry. And since the early 1960s, successive Québec governments have employed crown corporations to diversify the provincial economy, to preserve and create jobs, and to nurture francophone managers. HYDRO-QUÉBEC is a major example but crown corporations were also established in the steel, oil and gas, forestry, and asbestos industries to name a few.

A central rationale of crown corporations is that the commercial activities of government, to be performed successfully, must be shielded from constant government intervention and legislative oversight. Hence, crown corporations enjoy greater administrative freedom than government departments. As government enterprises, however, their autonomy cannot be absolute and must be tempered by some public control over policy-making. The Canadian experience suggests that the imperatives of corporate autonomy, government control, and legislative oversight are often conflicting and difficult to reconcile.

The range of controls and influences over federal crown corporations has developed piecemeal. But a key element was section VIII of the FAA which in 1951 established a regime of financial controls over most crown corporations. It did so by organizing them into 3 "schedules" or types – departmental, agency, and proprietary – each of which performed different functions and enjoyed a different relationship with the state. Departmental corporations, such as the Economic Council of Canada, performed no obvious commercial functions and were treated the same as government departments. Agency corporations, such as Atomic Energy of Canada Ltd, were accorded greater freedom while the proprietary corporations such as Air Canada, CNR and Petro-Canada, enjoyed even greater autonomy in financial matters.

The FAA's provisions required agency and proprietary corporations to submit annual capital budgets to the responsible minister, the minister of finance and the president of the Treasury Board. The budgets needed the approval of these 3 ministers, Cabinet and ultimately Parliament. Agency corporations also submitted operating budgets for approval to the responsible minister and the president of the Treasury Board. Cabinet also controls the appointments, remuneration and dismissal of crown corporation's boards of directors and senior officers. Theoretically, boards provide the key link between the government and corporate management, but their effectiveness may be undermined by a lack of precise definitions of the powers, duties and responsibilities of boards, political PATRONAGE in the selection of members and, finally, the federal government's unorthodox and controversial practice of appointing senior civil servants to the boards. Ineffective boards may not be able to withstand government intervention. The Acts of some federal crown corporations, notably Petro-Canada, empower the Cabinet and sometimes the minister responsible to issue directives allowing the government to order a crown corporation to implement particular government policies. The use of directives remains controversial as does the question of whether crown corporations should be compensated by the government for the costs incurred in implementing directives.

Parliament passes the legislation establishing federal crown corporations and must approve any subsequent amendments. It approves the tabled budgets of crown corporations and any government-requested appropriations to cover operating deficits. Parliament also reviews the annual reports of crown corporations, queries ministers during question period and discusses corporate performance with ministers and senior management in the forum of parliamentary committees. In federal politics, however, no standing committee specializes in the scrutiny of crown corporations, although such a committee operates in Saskatchewan.

Such formal controls on crown corporations are buttressed by a range of informal processes and influences. In fact, the relationships between governments and crown corporations, like most political relationships, are sometimes fractious and often characterized by bargaining, negotiations, and compromise.

The traditionally quiet environment of federal crown corporations was shattered in the 1970s when a major debate emerged about their roles and effectiveness. At the heart of the debate was the view that the scope and economic importance of crown corporations had outdistanced Ottawa's capacity to control them and that crown corporations had become too prominent in the economy. This debate continues unabated. To many observers, the FAA was antiquated and some felt that major crown corporations, particularly the CNR, had escaped political control. Successive auditors-general criticized the financial management of crown corporations and controversy surrounded the activities of Atomic Energy of Canada Ltd and Air Canada. Petro-Canada's rapid expansion and Via Rail's chronic problems fuelled the discontent. The role of crown corporations is also a problem in several provinces including British Columbia, Saskatchewan, Manitoba and Québec.

In Canada, the reform of crown corporations is proceeding along 2 different courses – the establishment of revised regimes of control and accountability and more controversially, "privatization." In 1984 with the passage of Bill C-24, the federal government replaced the 1951 provisions of the FAA with a new legislative framework. Among other things, the law establishes new schedules, extends the Cabinet's capacity to issue directives, and stresses the notion that crown corporations can neither establish nor dispose of subsidiaries without Cabinet approval. It also clarifies processes of budgetary approval, and provides for the submission of corporate plans to the Cabinet for its approval and to Parliament for discussion.

The passage of such reforms, although politically difficult and slow, has not brought about major changes in the relationships between crown corporations and governments. Indeed, observers note that Bill C-24 generally codifies existing procedures and policies, breaks little new ground, and leaves major problems unsolved. To a degree, the continuing stalemate reflects the diversity, complexity and the rapidly changing nature of the crown corporation sector. But a deeper problem is disagreement about the role, nature and purposes of crown corporations in the Canadian ECONOMY. Should crown corporations use the same criteria as private firms in their decision making? What rules should govern competition between public and private firms? What balance should crown corporations strike between commercial considerations and the accomplishment of political and social goals? And in a general sense, is an effective crown corporation one whose behaviour is similar to or different from a comparable private firm? Comprehensive reform of crown corporations awaits resolution of perennially controversial questions about the economic role of government.

In "privatization," Canadians are presented with a more radical prescription. Proponents of privatization maintain that Canada's political and economic well-being will be enhanced if the assets or shares of crown corporations are sold to private investors, however defined, in whole or in part. The appeal of privatization, bolstered by the example of the British government's policy, is rooted in the contemporary enthusiasm for more "market driven" policies and a reduced economic role for government. Advocates believe that crown corporations are inefficient, too sheltered from market forces, and simply too numerous. A related proposition is that many crown corporations have outlived their usefulness as policy instruments and ought to be sold to the private sector. The government of Brian MULRONEY has raised the concept to new prominence by appointing a minister of state for privatization, by selling de Havilland Aircraft Co and Canadair, and by proposing the sale of several other crown firms.

Privatization also has critics, some of whom see it as an ideological crusade and as a short-sighted policy. Critics of the sale of de Havilland Aircraft to Boeing Corporation of Seattle question the wisdom of selling a potentially dynamic Canadian firm to a foreign company. Others worry about the terms and conditions of proposed sales and the possible loss of government control over the economy. Another line of reasoning asserts that ownership may ultimately be less important than the exposure of firms to competitive forces. Finally, other critics maintain that a partially "privatized" enterprise, embracing a mixture of public as well as private ownership, will be an unwieldy organization.

For these reasons, questions about the role of crown corporations will remain controversial for the foreseeable future. ALLAN TUPPER

Reading: M. Gordon, *Government in Business* (1981); Allan Tupper and G.B. Doern, eds, *Public Corporations and Public Policy in Canada* (1981).

Crown Land, the term used to describe land owned by the federal or provincial governments. Authority for control of these public lands rests with the Crown, hence their name. Less than 11% of Canada's land is in private hands; 41% is federal crown land and 48% is provincial crown land. The YUKON TERRITORY and NORTHWEST TERRITORIES are administered on behalf of Canada by the Department of Indian and Northern Affairs (Territorial Lands Act and Public Lands Grants Act). About 4% (17 million ha) of federally administered land is found in the provinces, ranging from 10.6% in Alberta to only 0.2% in Québec. Provincial crown land ownership varies, too, from a high of 95% in Newfoundland to less than 2% in PEI. Surface and subsurface rights to the mineral, energy, forest and water resources may be leased to private enterprise – a very important source of government income in Canada. National and provincial PARKS, Indian reserves, federal military bases and provincial forests are the largest and most visible allocations of crown land.

V.P. NEIMANIS

Reading: I. Marshall, *Canada's Federal Lands* (1986).

Crown Point, a large peninsula strategically commanding the narrow passage of the southwestern portion of Lake CHAMPLAIN in upper New York state. It was initially the site of Fort Saint-Frédéric, built by the French in 1731 to gain advantages of trade and empire against the British settlements in colonial America. The fort was destroyed by the retreating French in 1759 during the SEVEN YEARS' WAR. Between 1759 and 1761 the British began the construction of the more impressive Fort Crown Point. In 1773, the fort, incomplete, neglected and in disrepair, was largely destroyed by accidental fire. Occupied during the AMERICAN REVOLUTION by colonial rebels in 1775, Crown Point was retaken by royal forces during the Gen John BURGOYNE campaign of 1777, and was used until 1781 as a base for Loyalist raiding parties. Crown Point is a New York State Historic Site.

ROBERT S. ALLEN

Crow's Nest Pass Agreement In the 1890s, when rich mineral deposits were discovered in the Kootenay region of southern BC, American developers began to move into the region and extend rail lines northward from their transcontinentals. The CANADIAN PACIFIC RAILWAY, determined to retain control of southwestern Canada, asked the federal government for assistance to extend its own line over the CROWSNEST PASS into BC. At the same time, Prairie farmers were complaining about high freight rates charged by the CPR, and further federal assistance to that company would be unpopular unless something was done about the freight rates.

The Crow's Nest Pass Agreement, dated 6 Sept 1897, was an agreement between the CPR and the Canadian government. The CPR was given a cash subsidy of $3.3 million and title to pass into BC, in exchange for reducing, in perpetuity, eastbound rates on grain and flour and westbound ones on a specified list of "settlers' effects" (total rate reduction about 15%). The CPR obtained access to the valuable mining and smelting activities in the BC interior, and the government was able to allay western concerns over national transportation policies. The rate reduction coincided almost exactly with the beginning of the settlement boom, and quickly became enshrined in the public mind as a key part of the economic strategy of the day.

The suspension of the agreement in response to wartime inflation created consternation among western farmers. The CPR resisted attempts by the Board of Railway Commissioners to reimpose the terms after 1922, and there followed a period of complicated political and legal maneuvering. In 1925 the 1897 rates on grain and flour traffic were reinstated, applicable to all such traffic on all rail lines to Ft William, and the "settlers' effects" provision was cancelled. This solution was not satisfactory to anyone, and further negotiations produced in 1927 the agreement that the rates would be applied to all the company's lines but only on grain and unprocessed grain products.

Over time the Crow rate represented an ever-smaller fraction of what it cost the railways to transport grain, and there began a lengthy search for a more equitable rate. For farmers the Crow rate was an important factor in reducing costs enough to attract and keep export markets. But the railways were unable to afford the improvements and expansion to their lines made necessary by increased traffic and demanded by the farmers. After much heated discussion and disagreement by government, railway, farmers and farmers' organizations, the Western Grain Transportation Act was passed 17 Nov 1983 (effective 1 Jan 1984). It allowed grain-shipping costs to increase gradually, but never to exceed 10% of the world price for grain. The federal government agreed to pay the rest of grain-transportation costs, $675 million in 1987. The railways agreed to spend $16.5 billion on new equipment and expansion of service by 1992. An alternative proposal to pay the subsidy directly to farmers and to let rail rates rise to cover full costs of operation was rejected in 1983, although the idea retains considerable support today.

T.D. REGEHR AND KEN NORRIE

Crowsnest Pass Strike, 1932 This 7-month strike, involving all but one mine in Alberta's CROWSNEST PASS, was the most bitter strike in the region's turbulent history. It began in Coleman in Jan 1932 with demands that companies divide available work in the depressed coalmining industry equally among miners rather than playing favourites. Coal companies refused to deal with the workers' militant union, the Mine Workers' Union of Canada, and showdown between the coal operators and the MWUC caused the strike to spread through the Pass. The poor market for coal enabled sufficient labour to be hired to match output to demand. But the RCMP were required to separate strikers and "scabs" and numerous confrontations marked the strike. While the strikers' demands were not met, the strike left a left-wing legacy in the Pass because of resentment against the companies, the RCMP and provincial authorities. From 1933 to 1939, Blairmore elected a "Red" town council.

ALVIN FINKEL

Crowsnest Pass, elev 1357 m, is situated in the ROCKY MTS, on the BC-Alberta border, 40 km N of the US border. The name possibly came from a story in which Crow Indians "nested" after a battle with another tribe. The area was explored extensively by the PALLISER EXPEDITION 1857-60. Extensive geological work was carried out by G.M. DAWSON of the Geological Survey of Canada in 1882 and 1883, possibly in search of a railway route. A railway was built in 1898 as part of the CPR system to develop the coal potential of the area and mineral deposits of the East Kootenays of BC. From the E portal at Burmis to Fernie, 30 km SW of the pass, are many towns and villages famous for their coal production, particularly between 1910 and 1950, when there was great demand. The most southerly of the important railway passes crossing the CONTINENTAL DIVIDE, the pass is also crossed by Hwy No 3 and a pipeline.

GLEN BOLES

Crozier, Leif Newry Fitzroy, soldier, policeman (b at Newry, Ire 11 June 1846; d in Oklahoma, US 25 Feb 1901). He was appointed an inspector in the NWMP in 1873. Prominent in earlier Indian-police relations, Crozier's career was blighted in Mar 1885 when, ignoring approaching reinforcements, he bravely but impetuously led a party of Mounted Police and volunteers against a superior force of Métis at DUCK LAKE. The retreat of the government troops under heavy fire in the opening engagement of the NORTH-WEST REBELLION gave encouragement to the Métis, but tarnished the reputation of the NWMP. Crozier resigned in 1886 after John A. Macdonald passed him over to appoint a civilian NWMP commissioner.

S.W. HORRALL

CRTC, *see* CANADIAN RADIO-TELEVISION AND TELECOMMUNICATIONS COMMISSION.

Cruise Missile Case (1985) A group of organizations went to court to argue that the decision of the Canadian government to allow the US to test Cruise missiles in Canada was contrary to s7 of the CANADIAN CHARTER OF RIGHTS AND FREEDOMS, which states "Everyone has the right to life, liberty and security of the person and the right not to

Downtown Coleman, in SW Alberta, one of the old coal mining towns of the Crowsnest Pass. Visible are the coal piles behind the town and the coaltipple in the middle of the town (*courtesy Elliott and Nicole Bernshaw/Bernshaw Photography*).

be deprived thereof except in accordance with the principles of fundamental justice." The Supreme Court of Canada declared on 9 May 1985 that federal Cabinet decisions are subject to judicial control by virtue of s32(1) of the Charter. The appeal to the Supreme Court was rejected. In fact, there was no violation of s7 of the Charter. The possible consequences of the authorization given by the Cabinet are conjectural. One cannot establish the causal relationship between the permission that was given and an increase in the threat of nuclear conflict.   GÉRALD-A. BEAUDOIN

Crum, George, conductor (b at Providence, RI 26 Oct 1926). A student at Toronto's Royal Conservatory of Music, Crum made his professional debut as a pianist at age 16 and soon joined the faculty of the Conservatory's OPERA department. In 1951 he became the first conductor and music director of the NATIONAL BALLET OF CANADA, building its orchestra and repertoire while conducting operas throughout Canada and the US, leading Prom concerts in Toronto and conducting for the CBC. With the National Ballet, Crum conducted award-winning performances of *Cinderella* and *The Sleeping Beauty* (Emmys in 1970 and 1973) and of *Romeo and Juliet* (Prix René Barthélemy, 1966); in 1972 he won the Celia Award. He retired from the National Ballet in 1984. He still works occasionally as a guest conductor in Canada and the US.   PENELOPE DOOB

Crump, Norris Roy, railway executive (b at Revelstoke, BC 30 July 1904). Born into a railway family, Crump began with the CANADIAN PACIFIC RAILWAY as a labourer in 1920, taking time off to study science at Purdue U. He graduated in 1929 and in 1936 received a master's degree. Crump was especially interested in the new diesel electric engines and it was becoming clear that the railway would have to confront "dieselization." Crump was promoted through the CPR's engineering departments and, as a senior executive, was responsible for the transcontinental flagship train, the "Canadian." He became president in 1955 and chairman in 1961. Under him Canadian ownership of company stock rose from 15% in 1955 to 55% in 1965 and 63% in 1972. In 1962 Crump diversified the company by forming Canadian Pacific Investments to handle nontransport investments. The CPR named a railway car "Norris Crump," but it burned. He retired as president in 1964 and as chairman in 1972. In 1971 he became a Companion of the Order of Canada.
                                          ROBERT BOTHWELL

Crustacean, shelled INVERTEBRATE with segmented body and limbs at some stage of its life, an exoskeleton and 2 pairs of antennae. The exoskeleton, a protective and supportive framework located outside the body, is periodically molted to allow for growth. Crustaceans, with over 31 300 living species, comprise a subphylum of the phylum Arthropoda. They occupy terrestrial and fresh and saltwater habitats, and range in size from the Japanese spider crab, with a 3.65 m claw-span, to microscopic WATER FLEAS. The well-known SHRIMP, CRAB and LOBSTER belong to the Malacostraca, one of 8 classes. Various reductions and fusions notwithstanding, the crustacean body is essentially composed of a head with 5 pairs of appendages, and a trunk with numerous segments and appendages. The Cephalocarida, first discovered near New York (1955), are reminiscent of the primitive crustacean condition: many segments and trunk limbs are very similar, one after another (serial homology). Diversification and specialization of the appendages has occurred through evolutionary time: the modern crab bears little superficial resemblance to the BARNACLE or wood louse.

The filter-feeding habit is common and many bottom-dwelling forms are detritus feeders. Anterior appendages (often 7 pairs) catch and handle food. In some Malacostracans, food maceration is aided by chitinous (horny) teeth in the muscular stomach. Gas exchange takes place in gills attached to the bases of the trunk appendages. A copper-based respiratory pigment in some crustaceans causes blue-tinged blood. Sexes are separate in some species; others change sexes in mid-life, are hermaphroditic, or are born pregnant (making males unnecessary most of the time). Many brood their eggs until larvae emerge. Numerous molts follow while the larva is free swimming. The presence of a rigid exoskeleton necessitates a molting process initiated by hormones, following which the naked crustacean rapidly swells with water. The outer cuticle (tough covering) hardens again while the animal remains in hiding.

Ancestral crustaceans were probably swimmers. Through appendage modification, walking, crawling, burrowing, sessile and parasitic life-styles have also been adopted. The ZOOPLANKTON link in the ocean's food chain is composed primarily of tiny crustaceans. Many of Canada's great whales, the fin, grey, sei, blue and humpback, feed almost exclusively on these small animals. Some crustaceans are common pests (eg, terrestrial amphipods in greenhouses, isopods boring into wood and barnacles fouling ships); however, the group makes a major contribution to Canadian FISHERIES. A brief discussion of the 8 crustacean classes follows.   V. TUNNICLIFFE

Cephalocarida, tiny (2-4 mm long), hermaphroditic, shrimplike crustaceans; 9 species and 4 genera are known. Inadequate collection probably accounts for absence of Canadian records. The body consists of a shield-shaped head, elongated thorax and abdomen. The head has 5 pairs of appendages; the thorax, 8 segments, each possessing a similar pair of legs, the last pair reduced or absent; the abdomen, 11 ringlike, limbless body segments (somites) and an anal segment bearing a pair of appendages (uropods). These most primitive living crustaceans inhabit soft, muddy bottoms, silty sands or algal beds and occur in the Atlantic and Pacific oceans between 40° N and S latitudes, usually from intertidal zones to 300 m depths.   C.T. SHIH

Branchiopoda, crustacean class comprising 3 orders: Anostraca (fairy shrimps), Notostraca (tadpole shrimps) and Diplostraca (clam shrimps and water fleas). Branchiopods are nearly all restricted to fresh water. Although most are microscopic, they represent an important element in the planktonic food chain. The name derives from structures on the legs that function as gills; the multiple appendages are used for swimming and filter feeding. Branchiopods are characteristic of waters that frequently dry or freeze. Many branchiopods are parthenogenetic (males are rare; females are born pregnant). Thus, they can quickly take advantage of the reconstitution of their habitat. Most branchiopods are pale and transparent; hemoglobin in the body gives some a rosy colour.
                                          V. TUNNICLIFFE

Ostracoda, seed shrimp, are microscopic, bean-shaped, bivalved crustaceans living at the bottom of fresh or marine bodies of water. Over 2000 living species have been described worldwide; about 150 freshwater species and many more marine forms are known from Canada. Habitats range from temporary pools in semiarid southern Saskatchewan to large lakes and streams transcontinentally, including the Arctic. Ostracodes molt about 8 times before adulthood; shells lack growth lines. Ostracodes serve as food for bottom-dwelling fish. They are important indicators of habitat changes. Their FOSSIL record is

continuous and contains the largest number of fossil species (about 10 000) among crustaceans.
                                          L.D. DELORME

Mystacocarida, a small class of minute crustaceans, usually less than 0.5 mm long. The elongated, cylindrical body is divided into head, bearing 5 pairs of appendages, and 11-segmented trunk. Each of the first 5 trunk segments bears a pair of appendages. The telson possesses a pair of clawlike tail branches. Sexes are separate. These marine, benthic animals live between fine sand grains in intertidal and subtidal zones of the Atlantic and SW Indian oceans. There are 10 known species in 2 genera. Inadequate collection probably accounts for the absence of any Canadian records.   C.T. SHIH

Copepoda, small crustaceans, from 0.1-300 mm long (usually 0.5-5.0 mm), some free-living, others parasitic during part of their lives. The body is divided into cephalothorax, bearing up to 11 pairs of appendages, and limbless abdomen. Parasitic copepods may deviate from the basic form. Copepods inhabit all aquatic environments (including the High Arctic), from deep oceans to temporary freshwater ponds, and may be PLANKTONIC, benthic or periphytonic (living attached to underwater surfaces). Some are symbionts with other marine invertebrates. Parasitic species attach themselves externally or internally to fishes, marine mammals and marine invertebrates. About 8000 species are known. In Canada the most common species belong to the following genera: *Calanus*, *Oithona* (marine); *Diaptomus*, *Cyclops* (freshwater); and *Caligus* (parasitic).
                                          C.T. SHIH

Branchiura, fish lice, are crustaceans with a depressed body (up to 3 cm long) divided into head, 4-segmented thorax and unsegmented abdomen. A shield-shaped carapace covers head and part of thorax. The head and its 5 pairs of appendages are adapted for locomotion. Each thoracic segment bears a pair of legs modified to form a grasping organ in the male. The reduced, fin-shaped abdomen bears a pair of minute tail branches. Sexes are separate. Fertilized eggs are laid on hard substrata. Young hatch as modified larvae or juveniles and soon attach to a host. Branchiura are external parasites of marine and freshwater fishes, but frequently leave the host to swim or crawl. About 130 species and 4 genera are known. Ten species of genus *Argulus* are recorded from Canadian Atlantic and Pacific coastal waters and freshwater lakes.   C.T. SHIH

Cirripedia, a group of crustaceans with over 900 species, including sessile and parasitic forms. They live from intertidal zones to the deep sea. Familiarly known as barnacles, most cirripedes cement themselves to hard surfaces and secrete protective calcareous plates. A goose barnacle has its plates perched on a flexible stalk. Fine setae (bristles) filter out food particles from water currents generated by leg movements. Parasitic barnacles can be found on organisms ranging from jellyfish to whales. There are at least 20 species of acorn and goose barnacles on the rocks of Canada's West Coast. One species grows to 15 cm.   V. TUNNICLIFFE

Malacostraca Ancestral malacostracans lived in the oceans some 200 million years before DINOSAURS roamed the earth. Today, they constitute nearly 75% of all crustacean species and include lobsters, crabs, CRAYFISH and shrimp, some of the largest and most economically valuable invertebrate species. Most are still found in the marine environment, although a significant number of species have become established in fresh water, and the pill bugs (wood lice) are a fairly large terrestrial group. A typical malacostracan has stalked eyes, 19 segments plus a telson (18 according to some experts, who do not

Purple crab. Crabs comprise one of the largest groups of crustaceans. In Canada, they are found in marine environments on both coasts (*photo by Tim Fitzharris*).

consider the antennules to be associated with a true segment), a cylindrical body in which the thorax is partially fused with the head and covered with a carapace, and one or more pairs of anterior thoracic appendages modified for handling food. However, the malacostracans are a diverse group, with as many exceptions to this basic plan as followers of it. In 2 of the largest orders, the Isopoda and Amphipoda, there is no carapace and the eyes are sessile (immovable) rather than stalked. In the isopods the body is generally flattened from back to belly (dorsoventrally); in the amphipods it is more commonly compressed laterally. Variations on the generalized plan seem limited only by the number of species and the variety of ecological niches occupied.

The various classification systems divide Malacostraca into 10-12 orders, of which only 4 have freshwater representatives in N America. Two-thirds of all malacostracans are in 3 major orders: Isopoda, Amphipoda and Decapoda. The remainder are mainly small, little-known species, but many are important parts of aquatic food chains for economically valuable animals. Mysids (opossum shrimp) are almost exclusively marine, but in the Great Lakes a freshwater mysid occasionally constitutes 80% of the diet of trout. Another lesser-known group, the pelagic euphausiids (krill) often occur in large numbers in the marine environment; some species form a major part of the diet of large whales. It has been estimated that a blue whale can consume 2-3 t of euphausiids in a single feeding. The euphausiids are also unusual in being bioluminescent, ie, capable of producing their own light from organs (photophores) located at several points on the body.

The order Isopoda includes some 4000 species, most of which are marine and have dorsoventrally flattened bodies, sessile eyes and no carapace. The order also includes parasitic forms, freshwater species and the only large group of terrestrial crustaceans, the pill bugs, sow bugs or wood lice. The name pill bug comes from the animal's tendency to roll into a pill-shaped sphere for protection from physical danger or dehydration. The various species of pill bugs can be found beneath stones, matted vegetation and fallen trees, where they feed on algae, moss, bark and decaying organic matter.

The order Amphipoda comprises about 3600 species, typically with sessile eyes, no carapace and a humpbacked, laterally compressed body. Most are marine but there are a significant number of freshwater species, and even a few that might be considered terrestrial. Although some live in the ocean depths, amphipods are most common in shallow water and in the intertidal zone, where they are known as sand-hoppers or beach fleas. In the freshwater habitat they serve as transmitters of acanthocephalan parasites (intestinal worms) of ducks, and as an important food for aquatic birds and fish.

The order Decapoda contains 8500 species, including the shrimp, crayfish, crabs and lobsters, and is by far the largest crustacean group. Most decapods are marine, but crayfish, some shrimp and a few other species are found in fresh water. In decapods, the first 3 pairs of thoracic appendages are modified as maxillipeds for the handling of food, leaving 5 pairs as walking legs (hence the name Decapoda, "ten feet"). Decapoda are divided into 2 major groups: the Natantia (swimmers), encompassing the shrimp; and the Reptantia (crawlers), including lobsters, crayfish and crabs. Decapods are among the most interesting invertebrates and, as a group, are certainly the most economically valuable in Canada.

D.E. AIKEN

Reading: R.D. Barnes, *Invertebrate Zoology* (1980).

Crustacean Resources In Canada, all crustacean species with significant economic value are in the order Decapoda. The decapods constitute a major portion of the dollar value of various Canadian FISHERIES, and in some areas, particularly in the East, the local economy is almost completely dependent on them. The American lobster (*Homarus americanus*) is the most valuable of these resources. Freshly caught LOBSTER may be shipped live immediately to points in N America, Europe and Asia, or held in pounds until demand and price are more favourable. A much smaller percentage is cooked and canned. Some areas in the Gulf of St Lawrence have special fisheries for "canner" lobsters, which are slightly smaller than the "market" sizes shipped live. In 1985, almost 33 000 t were landed along the Atlantic coast, valued at over $193 million — more than twice the combined value of the CRAB and SHRIMP industries. On the East Coast, snow or queen crab (*Chionoecetes opilio*) is the most valuable crab species (over $47 million), a distinction that goes to Dungeness crab (*Cancer magister*) on the West Coast (nearly $5 million in 1985). In BC waters the principal commercial species is the prawn (*Pandalus platyceros*) which, with the smooth pink shrimp (*Pandalus jordani*), was worth about $4.6 million in 1985, considerably less than the nearly $19 million commanded by *Pandalus borealis* on the East Coast. Because of the seasonality and unpredictability of traditional fishing, AQUACULTURE of valuable species is an attractive prospect. Of all decapods in Canada with potential for culture, the American lobster has received the most attention. Most of the technological and biological problems have been overcome, but the high cost of rearing from egg to market size remains a constraint.

D.E. AIKEN

Cryptozoology is the scientific study of unknown animals (cryptids, from the Greek *kryptos* meaning "hidden"), about which only circumstantial, or at best insufficient, material evidence is available. Cryptids are reported from many parts of the world in local folklore and explorers' reports. Widely known examples include still-mysterious creatures such as the Loch Ness "monster" in Scotland and the "Abominable Snowman" of the Himalayas; giant varieties of known animals (squids, octopus); and creatures normally thought to be extinct, such as the Mokele-Mbembe, a dinosaur-like animal reported from equatorial Africa.

In Canada, there have been numerous reports of land, lake and sea cryptids. Giant hairy wild men appear in native folklore under a variety of names: Windigo among the Cree and Ojibwa of the Hudson Bay area, Chenoo to the Micmacs of Nova Scotia, Tornit to the Inuits of Labrador and the Northwest Territories. Best known through its giant footprints, recent visual sightings and even a movie film, is the SASQUATCH, which roams the mountainous areas of BC and Alberta as well as those of the western US, where it is called "Bigfoot."

Unidentified lake creatures are claimed to hide in many Canadian lakes. OGOPOGO in Lake Okanagan, BC, and Champ in Lake Champlain are most often reported. Similar, often horse-headed and serpentine creatures, have been reported from Lake Utopia, NB, Pohenegamook, Qué, and Manitoba, among others.

Strandings of giant squids (up to 15 m) in Newfoundland, particularly on the shores of the Bonavista Pen, provided essential material evidence to remove the giant squid from the realm of marine folklore and the ranks of cryptids and elevated it to the accepted zoological genus Architeuthis. Other unidentified marine creatures seen in Canadian waters include the "Cheval de Mer" described by early explorers of Atlantic shores, a long-necked horse-headed creature very similar to that seen more frequently in recent years in BC waters and known under the name of "Caddy" (for Cadboro Bay, near Victoria, BC). A large serpentine creature, up to 30 m in length and fitting the description of the great sea serpent seen by hundreds of witnesses in Massachusetts Bay in the 19th century, has also been spotted occasionally off the Atlantic coast.

Cryptozoologists seek and interpret evidence either to confirm the existence of cryptids or to relegate them definitively to the realm of fantasy or erroneous interpretation. The field attracts natural scientists, anthropologists and folklorists as well as anyone interested in the mysteries of the animal world.

PAUL H. LEBLOND

Reading: B. Heuvelmans, *On the Track of Unknown Animals* (1972); R. Mackal, *Searching for Hidden Animals* (1980).

Crysler's Farm, site of a battle fought 11 Nov 1813 between 4000 American troops and a combined force of about 800 British regulars, Canadian militia and a few of His Majesty's Indian allies. The location was along the upper St Lawrence R near present-day Morrisburg, Ont. Led by Lt-Col Joseph Wanton Morrison of the 89th Regiment of Foot and elements of the 49th Foot, the British won a resounding victory over the American invasion force, which was attempting to capture Montréal and thus isolate UPPER CANADA. This was one of the most decisive battles of the WAR OF 1812. A monument commemorating the Battle of Crysler's Farm is at UPPER CANADA VILLAGE.

ROBERT S. ALLEN

Cuban Missile Crisis began 22 Oct 1962. Following intelligence reports that the USSR was installing ballistic missiles in Cuba capable of hitting US and Canadian targets, Pres John Kennedy announced an American naval blockade of the island, threatening further action if preparation of the sites continued. The issue for the Canadian government, informed of Kennedy's intentions only one-and-a-half hours in advance, was whether to comply with an American request to move Canadian forces to an alert status known as "Defcon 3." With the approval of Minister of National Defence Douglas Harkness, the units concerned quietly did so, but formal authorization was delayed while Cabinet debated, Oct 23-24. Harkness argued that the nature of the crisis, combined with existing arrangements for defence co-operation, made the alert necessary. Fearing a Canadian alert would provoke the USSR, believing the Americans' Cuban policy to be generally unbalanced, angered by the lack of advance consultation and concerned about implications for Canadian policy on nuclear weapons, PM John Diefenbaker and Secretary of State for External Affairs Howard Green were reluctant to acquiesce. About half the ministers were undecided, but, as Soviet ships approached the quarantine zone later in the week, the Harkness position gained support. On Oct 24 Diefenbaker authorized the alert, and the decision was announced Oct 25 in the Commons.

The hesitant Canadian response reflected in part the desire of the prime minister and others to preserve the independence of Canadian foreign policy and to maintain a balanced posture in crisis conditions. The delay, however, was widely criticized and contributed to a growing perception of indecisiveness in the Diefenbaker government. It also exacerbated already difficult relations with the Kennedy administration and fuelled further controversy over nuclear weapons. The crisis itself ended Oct 27-28 when Soviet Premier Nikita Khrushchev agreed to dismantle and remove the missiles. DENIS STAIRS

Cuckoo (Cuculidae), family of birds with 125-127 species, including common cuckoo, anis, couas, coucals and roadrunners, distributed almost worldwide. Cuckoos are long and slim with long tails, longish wings and stout to long, usually slightly downcurved bills. Legs are short except in ground-dwelling species with zygodactylous feet (2 toes forward, 2 back). The loud, unmusical call of the commonest European species gives the family its name. A false belief that cuckoos call only before rain accounts for a colloquial name, rain crow. Several species are brood parasites, laying their eggs in nests of other birds. The hosts raise the young cuckoos, often at the expense of their own young. Most cuckoos establish exclusive breeding territories, but the tropical anis build large communal nests in which each pair occupies a compartment. Two species occur in Canada, the black-billed cuckoo (*Coccyzus erythropthalmus*) breeding from the Maritimes to central Alberta, and the yellow-billed cuckoo (*C. americanus*) primarily in SE Ontario and adjacent Québec, with smaller populations in southwest NB and S coastal BC, rarely also in Manitoba. They are similar in appearance: plain brown above, white below. Both species lay 2-5 eggs in frail nests in trees of open woodland, with both species incubating, although both occasionally lay eggs in other birds' nests, including each others'. Larger species eat lizards, snakes and occasionally birds, but most are insectivorous. The fondness of the 2 Canadian species for tent caterpillars makes them economically valuable.

MARTIN K. McNICHOLL

Cucumber (*Cucumis sativus*), herbaceous annual vegetable of the Cucurbitaceae family. Only 3 wild plants belonging to this family occur in Canada, the most common being the climbing cucumber, a distant relative of the cultivated cucumber. Cultivated in China 3000 years ago, the cucumber spread to Europe in the 14th century. Christopher Columbus introduced it to Haiti. Generally, each plant bears both male and female flowers; however, female and seedless varieties also exist. The cucumber develops long stems with tendrils. Some plants have small, short fruits called gherkins; others produce long fruit, either American (field) type or European (greenhouse) type. Cucumber is usually sown in fields but can be cultivated out of season in GREENHOUSES. Few insects attack cucumbers and modern strains are becoming increasingly disease resistant. Although low in vitamins and minerals, cucumbers are rich in water and have practically no calories. In 1985, 3330 ha were cultivated in Canada, producing 54 387 t valued at over $17 million.

ROGER DOUCET

Cullen, Maurice Galbraith, painter (b at St John's 6 June 1866; d at Chambly, Qué 28 Mar 1934). Cullen moved to Montréal with his family in 1870. There he began his art training as a sculptor at the Conseil des arts et manufactures and with sculptor Louis-Philippe HÉBERT. Like other artists of his generation, he went to Paris for additional training. He arrived there in 1889 and decided to become a painter; he attended the École des beaux-arts, studying, like Paul PEEL, with Jean-Léon Gérôme, then with Élie Delaunay. By 1895, when Cullen returned to Montréal, he had darkened the tonality of the impressionist style learned abroad. In time he became the true interpreter of Montréal's cityscape, particularly of night or dusk scenes, invariably with shimmering lights. He was also one of Canada's great painters of snow. Like his colleague and friend James Wilson MORRICE, Cullen was a major figure in Canadian art. His gift was that of a romantic – an ability to capture light and mood. Some of his work was influenced by William Blair Bruce, whom Cullen often visited in Gréz 1892-94. Cullen in turn influenced many by teaching for years at the Art Assn of Montreal. He showed in the first exhibition of the Canadian Art Club, an advanced group of the period, and was made a member in 1910. JOAN MURRAY

Cultural Dualism is both a term that describes some characteristics of Canadian society and, in many people's view, an ideology according to which the social and political systems of Canada should be organized. It is based on the historical fact that Canada was colonized by both the French and the English, and that both groups are therefore the "founding peoples" of Canada. This fact is used to justify the privileges accorded these 2 groups in comparison to those accorded other ethnic groups, and to justify the equality of the 2 groups.

Although the notion of cultural dualism has been translated into legislation and into policies of schooling, religion, language and the institutional rights of provinces, its origins are difficult to determine. Some legislation, eg, constitutional laws of Canada, can be interpreted as a defence of cultural dualism. For example, the 1774 QUE-

Old Houses, Montreal (c 1908) by Maurice Cullen, oil on canvas. In his impressionist style, Cullen was the true interpreter of Montréal's cityscape and one of Canada's great painters of snow (*courtesy the Montreal Museum of Fine Arts*).

BEC ACT legally recognized the Catholic religion, the seigneurial system and French CIVIL LAW in Québec. The ACT OF UNION proclaimed in 1841 recognized that the 2 colonizing groups coexisted, and the CONSTITUTION ACT, 1867, formalized some of the principles of cultural dualism. First, it determined the powers of the federal state and of the provinces (thus recognizing some of the specificities of Québec, where French Canadians formed the majority); second, legislation in regard to civil law was confirmed; third, in education, a provincial domain, a clause allowed for public funds to subsidize confessional schools and protected religious minorities in Québec. Ironically, this clause was demanded by Québec English Protestants, who feared they would be outnumbered and overpowered by French Catholics in Québec. French Catholics in the rest of Canada later attempted, with little success, to use the same clause to defend themselves against similar fears with regard to the English Canadians. Under Québec language legislation (BILL 22 and BILL 101), children of some groups, particularly immigrants, have been obliged to attend French schools, but the legislation has not altered the denominational structure of education in Montréal or the public funding of private, religious or ethnic schools in Québec.

It has often been said that Canada was created as a state by mercantile capitalists and railway owners who needed a central administration from which to settle and exploit the country. Others, especially many French Canadians, believed that CONFEDERATION was a step towards a new state, one that was independent of England. It was understood that the 2 founding groups were to coexist, but the rights and privileges of Catholic French Canadians outside Québec were either not specified or were denied or ignored (*see* NEW BRUNSWICK SCHOOL QUESTION; ONTARIO SCHOOLS QUESTION; MANITOBA SCHOOLS QUESTION); Catholic schools (often French) were not subsidized by public funds; French was forbidden in the public schools (as were all languages other than English); and a general assimilation into the "Anglo-Saxon," "British" or Anglo-Canadian world was seen as the only future for both French Canadians and immigrants.

In the 1960s, the Royal Commission on BILINGUALISM AND BICULTURALISM brought to light some of the difficulties encountered by French speakers and other groups in Canada. In 1969 the OFFICIAL LANGUAGES ACT made Canada, at least symbolically, an officially bilingual country and measures were taken to allow for service in French in the federal administration. In 1971 the government adopted the policy of MULTICULTURALISM in a bilingual framework. Finally the CONSTITUTION ACT, 1982, affirmed some of the principles of cultural dualism; the CANADIAN CHARTER OF RIGHTS AND FREEDOMS stresses the right to equality and forbids discrimination. French and English are described as "the official languages of Canada" with equality in status in all parliamentary institutions and in the Government of Canada. The Charter also protects the rights of French and English minorities to be educated in their own languages, and allows for minority schools to be funded by public funds, and confirms that it does not modify "any rights or privileges guaranteed by or under the Constitution of Canada in respect of denominational, separate or dissentient schools." French and English are also official languages in New Brunswick, the only officially bilingual province.

There have been various interpretations of how the ideology of cultural dualism should actually manifest itself. It has been argued that French and English should be equally represented by bilingual public servants at all levels of the federal system (or that every federal government unit should have 2 components, one French, one English) and that there should be equality of opportunity at all levels of society, eg, political, economic, educational and social.

Many French Canadians believe that cultural dualism recognizes their specificity and their rights, while others believe that it has never been applied in practice and that Canada, originally a British colony, is now a US colony. Part of the French Canadian population has also been in favour of a unilingual Québec as a "refuge" for francophones, and some believe that Québec should secede from Confederation. But cultural dualism has been opposed most vociferously by English-speaking groups. Many British colonialists wanted Canada to be primarily an English-speaking, Anglo-Saxon dependency of Britain. Today, several groups (particularly, but not exclusively in the West) consider that Canada should be unilingually English and that CANADIAN-AMERICAN RELATIONS should be fostered because of a common general culture and because of the economic power of the US.

Other groups have very much resented the ideology of cultural dualism, believing that it excludes them from Canadian life. The native people stress that they were the first inhabitants of Canada and that the French and English have eliminated them from the political and social life of the country. Ethnic groups who have immigrated during the last 2 centuries believe that cultural dualism effectively excludes them as well from social and political life. On the other hand, many French Canadians do not support the policy of multiculturalism, because they consider that it does not recognize their special status. The MEECH LAKE ACCORD, if accepted by the 10 provincial legislative assemblies and the House of Commons, may be considered as a further step toward cultural dualism.   MICHEL LAFERRIÈRE

Cultural Policy, in general refers to government measures taken to encourage or to protect activities in areas defined as cultural. Much of the confusion over the objectives of cultural policy has derived from the term CULTURE itself, an omnibus word with distant origins in the Latin word *cultura*, referring to cultivation of the soil. At one level, culture refers primarily to excellence in the arts, and in this sense cultural policy is largely concerned with ARTS FUNDING. All societies have recognized the power of art and most have honoured and supported artists. In our century, governments have come to fill the role played in previous times by the church, by royalty or by wealthy patrons. At another level, culture is associated with COMMUNICATIONS and "mass culture" through broadcasting, film, book publishing, video, sound recording, etc. Cultural expression is more and more bound up with the development of cultural industries, which play a key role not only in disseminating works, but in forming the way in which the culture itself is perceived. The idea of culture has an even broader usage, developed from philosophy but given its greatest currency in the social sciences. These definitions of culture encompass nothing less than "that complex whole which includes knowledge, belief, art, law, morals, custom and any other capabilities and habits acquired by man as a member of society." In this domain, cultural policies emphasize the need to preserve or to invigorate cultural identity, or at least to create an environment in which a distinctive culture can emerge. Such policies are often developed as an antidote to external pressures. In the case of Canada, this pressure has traditionally come from the overwhelming presence of the United States. While Canadians are often chided, not least by themselves, for their inability to provide a simple description of their "identity," it is not possible to define any cultural identity by reducing it to a few immutable traits. Culture is inherently diverse and varied; it cannot be characterized by a few national idiosyncracies. A dilemma in any cultural policy is defending what cannot be specifically defined; remaining open to external stimuli while not being overwhelmed by them.

Those who support a vigorous cultural policy in Canada point out that while Canadians are avid consumers of culture, most of what they consume comes from elsewhere. The vast majority of books, films and records bought here is produced outside Canada for foreign markets. Most of the revenues from the sale of these products in Canada flow outside Canada and not to Canadians who would be inclined to help finance the development of Canadian talent. In film, for example, foreign-controlled firms generate 90% of the $1 billion in Canadian box-office revenues. In book publishing, foreign subsidiaries earn 61% of the revenues but publish only 22% of Canadian titles. In sound recording, foreign firms earn 89% of the revenues but produce only 28% of Canadian albums. In short, Canadian producers have very limited access to their own market while foreign firms, with formidable advantages of scale and cost, profit greatly from their Canadian operations.

Virtually all Western nations support artists and arts organizations as well as domestic production in the cultural industries. A recent study of 13 European countries documented some 400 measures that favour the production of domestic cultural products. Many of these countries have much larger domestic markets than Canada, as well as the protection of a national language. In France, for example, television networks are allowed to purchase programming only from domestically owned distributors; foreign investment in publishing is limited to 20% in a joint venture. Most EEC nations operate public-broadcasting networks. European nations began limiting film imports as early as the mid-1920s. In view of foreign takeovers in their industry, American book publishers are lobbying the US government for protective action. While comparisons are difficult, it is clear that Canada maintains a far more open market for foreign culture than most nations.

History of Cultural Policy The earliest form of government support for culture in Canada came in the 19th century with the tentative funding of archives, museums and art galleries that came with an awakening interest in the past. The archival tradition dates back to New France, although the NATIONAL ARCHIVES OF CANADA was not formed until 1903. The National Museum of Canada began with a grant of £1500 from Queen Victoria in 1841. These measures were acknowledgement of the worth of preserving heritage through documents and cultural artifacts, but serious government involvement in the arts in Canada did not really begin until after WWII, as part of the general growth of state involvement in social life that accelerated after the Great Depression. The power of communications had been acknowledged in WWI as government attempted to control how the war was perceived through widespread censorship and propaganda. WAR ARTISTS were hired to depict Canada's participation in the war. But it was the advent of radio in the 1920s that opened official eyes to the need for a domestic policy. In 1928 when Canadian radio technology was still rudimentary, American stations were beaming freely across an open border. As a result, the Royal Commission on Radio Broadcasting (Aird Commission) was struck. In its report (1929), it recommended a state-owned system capable of "fostering a national spirit and interpreting national citizenship." In turn, film, television and other technologies raised the same concerns.

The lobbying of the Canadian Radio League (fd 1930) had a major influence on the realization of the Aird Commission's recommendations, and the establishment of the publicly funded CANADIAN BROADCASTING CORPORATION in 1936. Other voluntary groups emerged in the 1930s and 1940s. Among these, the Federation of Canadian Artists was among the first to apply for government support for the arts. The Turgeon Committee on Reconstruction and Re-establishment (1944) was lobbied by arts groups to set up a board to promote culture. These activities helped to create an awareness of cultural issues and an environment in which later developments could take place.

The most comprehensive and influential document in the development of Canadian cultural policy was the report (1951) of the Royal Commission on NATIONAL DEVELOPMENT IN THE ARTS, LETTERS AND SCIENCES (Massey Commission). The report focused on the extreme vulnerability of Canada to American influences and drew attention to the American newspapers, books and magazines, etc, flooding across the border. Furthermore, the commission noted with embarrassment that whatever support there had been in Canada for the arts had come primarily from American foundations, $7.3 million alone from the Carnegie Foundation and another $11.8 million from the Rockefeller Foundation. Canada had paid a heavy price for this easy dependence, stated the report, in loss of talent, the impoverishment of our universities, and "an uncritical acceptance of ideas and assumptions which are alien to our tradition." In a typical example, the report noted that in a grade 8 class of 34 Canadian children, 19 knew the significance of July 4; only 7 could explain that of July 1. Among the concrete results of the report were the founding of the NATIONAL LIBRARY (1953) and the CANADA COUNCIL (1957). But the report also eloquently raised fundamental questions about the meaning of SOVEREIGNTY, the role of government in fostering the creativity of its citizenry and of the peculiar problems Canada faced if it is to survive the cultural barrage from the United States.

Similar sentiments were expressed by the Royal Commission on BROADCASTING (report 1957), which emphasized the "need for a broadcasting system to help establish a Canadian cultural identity, particularly in the face of American encroachments." The Royal Commission on PUB-

LICATIONS (report 1961), was convened to investigate a troubled magazine industry, which it stated is "a part of our national heritage, reflecting something else than our concern for the market place." The Royal Commission on Book Publishing (Ontario, 1972) recognized that "the cultural implications of book publishing far outweigh the economic implications to society." Further support came from the Special Senate Committee on Mass Media (1970), the Royal Commission on Newspapers (1981) and the report of the FEDERAL CULTURAL POLICY REVIEW COMMITTEE (1982).

A number of themes recur throughout these examinations. First among these is that Canadian culture must be fostered with public money and protected by government regulation. In fact, cultural expenditures did rise dramatically to a total by all governments of over $4.5 billion in 1985-86. There is recognition that Canadian cultural industries are at a severe disadvantage because they lack the large market required for economies of scale, and because so much income from the distribution of cultural products is drained from the country. Secondly, most of these reports argued that cultural support should be given without political influence and that key cultural agencies should be at "arms length" from the political process. Finally, there is the assumption in these investigations that cultural activity is of great significance to the character and value of our very way of life and to the survival of a distinctive Canadian society. Needless to say, these principles have been contested, and the measures taken to implement them have often created controversy, not the least of which has been disputes over DISTRIBUTION OF POWERS.

"Culture" was not specifically assigned under the terms of the BNA Act in 1867, except for EDUCATION, which was assigned to the provinces. In 1932 Québec and Ontario contested the federal government's right to control broadcasting. Federal jurisdiction was upheld in the courts, but other challenges have arisen as each new technology has made an impact.

Québec has always interpreted provincial powers, particularly those referring to education, as including those necessary for the preservation of a French Canadian culture. With the efflorescence of Québec in the 1960s, the issue of culture was increasingly politicized. Federal institutions, such as the Canada Council, NATIONAL FILM BOARD and CBC, were often seen as intruders in Québec, eroding indigenous culture. As a result, Société Radio-Canada became virtually an autonomous broadcasting system in Québec and the NFB set up a French-language unit in Montréal. Prem Jean Lesage created the Department of Cultural Affairs in 1961; it began with a budget of $3 million, which grew to $57 million by 1977. It became the Ministry of State for Cultural Development under the PQ and its responsibilities grew to include language and immigration. During the UN government of Prem Daniel Johnson, Jean-Noël Tremblay, as minister of cultural affairs, set about establishing "instruments de la culture," such as the National Library of Québec. He launched the Grande Théâtre de Québec and the magazine Culture Vivante. Successive reports by Marcel Rioux (1968) and Jean-Paul Allier (1975) argued for support of policies that would "create an environment." Critical to all these efforts was the assumption that Québec culture could flourish only under conditions of sovereignty and under direction of a strengthened provincial, or independent, Québec government. Under the PQ government after 1976 a massive study prepared under the direction of Fernand DUMONT extended the meaning of culture beyond education and the arts to take in almost every aspect of society. The 1987 MEECH LAKE ACCORD, with its recognition of Québec as a "distinct society," could have pro-

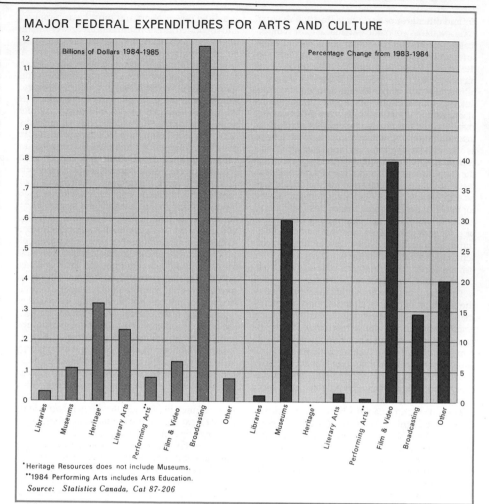

MAJOR FEDERAL EXPENDITURES FOR ARTS AND CULTURE

Billions of Dollars 1984-1985   Percentage Change from 1983-1984

(Categories: Libraries, Museums, Heritage*, Literary Arts, Performing Arts**, Film & Video, Broadcasting, Other)

*Heritage Resources does not include Museums.
**1984 Performing Arts includes Arts Education.
Source: Statistics Canada, Cat 87-206

found long-term effects on jurisdiction in cultural matters.

While the provinces now spend over $1 billion per year on culture ($1.26 billion in 1985-86), very little of this is spent in clearly articulated policies. About 40% goes to libraries and another 30% to heritage resources and parks, leaving little for the visual, performing or literary arts. In 1984-85 the provinces spent only $12.3 million on literary arts and $99.6 million on performing arts. Most provinces have a ministry of culture, although these do not always have parallel functions, nor do all ministers have the power of Québec's minister of culture. For example, cultural matters are under the ministry of tourism in New

Brunswick and the provincial secretary in BC. Much of the thrust of provincial cultural policies has been motivated by a recognition that the cultural fields are important sources of employment, revenue and tourism; in BC the film industry now ranks second only to forestry in revenues. The number of films being produced in Toronto by 1987 was causing consternation in the American film industry. Municipalities have also become more involved; in 1985-86 they spent $625 million; $497 million of which went to libraries.

A second contentious issue has been that of political interference in the disbursement of funds. Politicization of federal policy grew with such events as CENTENNIAL and the heating up of "national" goals as a response to separatist sentiments in Québec. For example, in 1977 the Canada Council was offered special funds, on condition that they be earmarked for national unity. Once the Canada Council began receiving government grants, it came under scrutiny; in 1977 for example, questions were raised about grants given to separatists. In 1978 complaints were expressed over grants given to writers considered pornographic. The federal Dept of Communications (DOC), created in 1969 to deal with the technical aspects of communications, assumed control of many cultural agencies in the 1980-84 period. The creation of many parallel programs, such as Opportunities for Youth 1971, Local Initiatives, Explorations (CC) SOCIAL SCIENCES AND HUMANITIES RESEARCH COUNCIL (SSHRC) 1977 and the Art Bank 1972, created confusion and some consternation over political motivation. In fact, some political influence is inevitable because of budget controls and because all senior appointments are made by Cabinet ministers or the prime minister.

Provincial Government Total Expenditures on Culture by Function, 1985-86
(thousands of dollars)

1	Libraries	483 629
2	Heritage Resources	
	Museums	123 323
	Archives	14 702
	Historic Parks and Sites	71 468
	Nature/Provincial Parks	64 466
	Other Heritage	25 133
	Total	299 092
3	Arts Education	40 179
4	Literary Arts	12 363
5	Performing Arts	99 626
6	Visual Arts and Crafts	21 187
7	Film and Video	17 086
8	Broadcasting	147 770
9	Sound Recording	1 584
10	Multiculturalism	21 755
11	Multidisciplinary Activities	61 471
12	Other	57 133
	Total	1 262 875

Instruments of Culture A great deal of Canada's cultural policy has been carried out by cultural agencies, most of them created over the past 50 years. In 1936 the CBC began to provide Canada with a state-owned broadcasting system, but the corporation has had a confused and sweeping mandate which it has struggled to fulfil particularly on television. The Canada Council soon became the central granting agency for the arts, although some politicians have had difficulty dealing with the independence that is essential to the Council's granting process. Many of the programs administered by the Council were transferred to the SSHRC, which was created to fund research and scholarship in the social sciences and humanities. In Ottawa the NATIONAL CAPITAL COMMISSION was created in 1958 with a mandate to maintain a capital region in accord with its national significance. The NATIONAL ARTS CENTRE was built to be a showcase of Canadian performance, but it has lacked the financial support to carry out its objectives. The NFB was established in 1939 and by 1945 was under fire for supposed left-wing tendencies, but it survived to provide a unique focus for Canadian film. As each of these agencies has gained in influence, it has become vulnerable to funding cuts which in turn threaten the individuals and organizations that it supports – indeed may have created. Each agency was formed as an "arms length" body, responsible for operating independent of political interference. As such, each pursues its own "policy," generally of supporting excellence as judged by peers.

The federal DOC, meanwhile, has steadily expanded its role not only through regulation but through its own programs. The DOC has responsibility for such matters as COPYRIGHT, licensing, etc, through which it can pursue ministerial policies. However, the minister of communications can easily end up in conflict with other, more powerful departments; for example, in 1986 the DOC was unable to prevent the sale of Prentice-Hall despite the book-publishing policy of then-minister Marcel MASSE, which was committed to Canadian ownership. The DOC's proposed policies, such as that making a special case of culture under the Investment Canada Act, were strongly contested by the Dept of External Affairs during FREE TRADE negotiations with the US in 1986-87. The view that cultural industries must be "off the table" was challenged not only by the Americans, who wanted free access to the Canadian "market," but also by many inside the government itself.

Specific Policies Despite shifting mandates and jurisdictional disputes, the federal and provincial governments have been increasingly involved in cultural matters. Government has been involved in broadcasting since the 1920s and the formation of the CBC in 1936. Canadian-content regulations somewhat limit the play of foreign programs on television. Canadian stations are permitted to substitute their own signals on CABLE TELEVISION when showing the same program as an American station. Only Canadians are allowed to own cable systems or radio or television stations and Canadian cable companies are not obliged to pay for US signals they retransmit – a major irritant to American broadcasters. In 1976 amendments to the Income Tax Act diverted Canadian advertising revenues from American border stations to Canada. In 1983 the Canadian Broadcasting Program Development Fund was set up to increase the production of Canadian programs.

In book publishing, the federal government began giving aid to Canadian publishers in 1972 after Ryerson and Gage were sold to foreign interest and MCCLELLAND AND STEWART neared collapse. In 1979 the Book Publishing Development Program was introduced, providing up to $9.7 million an-

nually. Postal subsidies to Canadian publishers amount to some $60 million per year in indirect subsidies. In 1986 the DOC announced a new Book Publishing Industry Development Program with a budget of $8.2 million per year. Beginning in 1988-89, $4.8 million per year will be allocated to the Canada Council to support important new books. Postal subsidies also greatly aid the magazine industry, which was virtually transformed by legislation. Bill C-58, introduced in 1965 and amended in 1976, channelled advertising money into Canadian-owned magazines. As a result, Canadian titles increased their share of total circulation from 30% in 1971 to about 40% in 1981. The Canada Council spends some $2 million per year assisting literary, artistic and children's periodicals. The SSHRC awards the same amount to scholarly journals. NSERC grants $500 000 to scientific journals.

In sound recording, Canadian-content regulations adopted by the CRTC in 1971 require that 30% of all music played on AM radio in prime time be Canadian. On FM, however, regulations vary from 30% Canadian content for classical music to 70% for popular music. In 1986 the federal government announced a Sound Recording Development Program to encourage Canadian recordings.

Government involvement in FILM increased in 1968 with the creation of the CANADIAN FILM DEVELOPMENT CORPORATION (later Telefilm Canada), whose purpose is to assist the financing of feature films. During its first decade the CFDC pumped $26 million into the industry. In 1974 a 100% tax deduction for investment in Canadian film produced a boom in production, but resulted in numerous "tax-shelter films" of dubious worth. The Canadian Broadcasting Program Development Fund was created at Telefilm Canada and in 1986 the DOC announced a Feature-Film Fund of $165 million over 5 years. In the 1980s, Québec, Ontario, Alberta and Manitoba have established their own feature-film funds. Other programs in BC, Ontario and Québec concentrate on attracting foreign production. As a result of these measures, a favourable exchange rate and other factors, some 25% of American production was based in Canada in 1987. In Québec, a decline in the film industry led in 1983 to the passage of Bill 109, which regulates distributors of films and videos.

Preserving Culture in Mass Society In rejecting the revolutionary traditions of the American and French Revolutions, as well as its own republican outbursts of the 1830s, and in the unique compromise of region and nation inherent in Confederation, Canada emerged from its colonial past with a distinctive political culture.

Ironically, at the time when Canadians have the most confidence to make a virtue of their diversity, their cultural environment is rapidly becoming a fragment of the American "entertainment" market. The order-in-council through which the Massey Commission was formed stated that "it is in the national interest to give encouragement to institutions which express national feeling, promote common understanding and add to the variety and richness of Canadian life." The communications technology which has offered a great opportunity to achieve such goals has as often been used to subject Canadians to the myths, anxieties and manufactured values of a foreign society.

The ultimate goal of cultural policy is the creation of conditions which will encourage all forms of creativity. The values of the "free-market" economy, those of profit seeking and competition for gain, which most economists and businessmen claim should govern culture as much as any consumer product, are often anathema to art,

which values challenge, risk, experiment and criticism. For those who believe that artistic expression is critically important to society and for those who acknowledge that the potential of communications technology lies beyond expanding the market for consumer goods, it is unacceptable to leave culture to a "free market" that is overwhelmingly dominated by a few foreign corporations. The disparities between the production, distribution and marketing capacities between the US and Canada would, in a "free market," quickly reduce the smaller nation to passive consumers.

Any attempt to limit the flow of cultural products or ideas can appear to be narrow minded. But the purpose of cultural policy is to promote tolerance of all forms of artistic expression, while ensuring that a creative community will have access to its own audience. Modern consumer society has brought a high material standard of living, but undoubted anxiety as well. The creative spirit, which probes the ethical and aesthetic meanings of life, is as crucial now as much as ever. In referring to our society's commitments to expend large sums of money on defence, the Massey Commission commented "what we may ask ourselves, are we defending? We are defending civilization, our share of it, our contribution to it. The things with which our inquiry deals are the elements which give civilization its character and its meaning. It would be paradoxical to defend something which we are unwilling to strengthen and enrich, and which we even would allow to decline."

JAMES MARSH

Culture, a term used by social scientists, is also widely used in popular speech. It apparently arose first in the Old French of the Middle Ages to indicate a religious cult, or religious worship or ceremony. The verb *culturer* meant "working the soil." In the 17th century, people referred to the "wheat culture," "legume culture," and, by analogy, to the "culture of letters" and "culture of sciences." In the 18th century the word was used alone to mean "formation of the spirit." Eighteenth-century German philosophers and historians borrowed the term from the French, but *Kultur*, as it was written, had for the Germans both social and historical dimensions. Some writers used it to mean progress, the improvement of the human spirit, a step towards the perfection of humanity. Others used it to mean "civilization," that is, the refinement of mores, customs and knowledge. For German (and some French) authors of the day, the terms "culture" and "civilization" referred to the progress of Reason, that is, of science, knowledge and a new moral conscience which had been liberated from religions and mythologies.

It was in English, however, that the term "culture" took on the modern meaning (culture signifying "husbandry" appeared in English as early as 1420). Anthropologists used the term to denote the mores, customs and beliefs of the "primitive" people they were studying. By the early 20th century, culture had become a central concept of the SOCIAL SCIENCES; it is a term now used in all the social sciences and in all languages. The technical use of the term in ANTHROPOLOGY was introduced by the English anthropologist E.B. Tylor (1871): "Culture or civilization, taken in its wide enthnographic sense, is that complex whole which includes knowledge, belief, art, law, morals, custom and any other capabilities and habits acquired by man as a member of society."

In *Culture: A Critical Review of Concepts and Definitions* (1952) A.L. Kroeber and C. Kluckhohn analysed 160 English definitions of culture used by anthropologists, sociologists, psychologists, psychiatrists and others, and classified them according to their principal emphasis. Drawing on all these definitions and on others more recent, culture may be defined as an ensemble, formalized in varying degrees, of ways of thinking, feeling and behaving which once learned give people a particular and distinct collectivity.

Canadian Culture Given the diversity of Canadian society it is easier to describe Canadian culture as a group of cultures interrelated with and juxtaposed to the 2 dominant cultural groups.

It is not surprising, given its size, that Canada should have several regional subcultures (*see* REGIONALISM). No exhaustive study has yet been made of these subcultures, yet it is possible to assert that West Coast Canadians have a different way of thinking and a different spirit from central or East Coast Canadians. Canadians who live on the Prairies are distinct from those in Ontario, as are Quebeckers or Newfoundlanders. Further divisions exist within the subcultures: northern Ontarians distinguish themselves from southern ones; Quebeckers in Abitibi, the Beauce or Lac St-Jean are different from those in Montréal or Québec City. Differences in spirit, ways of thinking and attitude exist between Edmonton and Calgary, Victoria and Vancouver, Montréal and Québec City.

But the expression "Canadian mosaic" refers to the ethnic and cultural diversity of the country. Four constituent cultural groupings are usually distinguished in Canada. The first 2 are the cultures of the "founding peoples," the Anglo-Saxon culture and French culture (*see* ETHNIC AND RACE RELATIONS). The former subdivides into cultures of different origin – ENGLISH, SCOTS, IRISH, WELSH. French culture is more homogenous. Though French Canadians originally emigrated from different provinces of France, under the French regime they quickly merged into one "Canadian" culture, although those French Canadians living in Ontario or Manitoba are quite different from those in Québec (*see* FRENCH IN THE WEST).

With the exception of the native peoples, the remaining non-British and non-French cultural groups comprise all the other ethnic groups that have immigrated to Canada since the beginning of the 19th century. The vitality of these cultural communities has grown in recent years. This composite of cultural groups includes cultures from Europe, the Near East, Asia, Central and S America, and Africa. The members of these communities usually adopt English as their working language and finally as their mother tongue, but many still speak their former national language and teach it to their children (*see* LANGUAGES IN USE) and many devotedly maintain the customs and traditions of the old country. Canadian television and (especially) radio offer programs in a wide variety of languages.

The fourth Canadian cultural group consists of the native peoples. This group includes many subdivisions. When the first Europeans arrived in N America at least 6 cultural groups apparently inhabited what is now Canada. Each of these cultural and linguistic groups contained a certain number of tribes. These differences still exist to some extent; the greatest distinguishing factor among native peoples now is the degree to which they maintain ancestral ways or have integrated into the structures and adopted the culture of industrial society. The MÉTIS and mixed blood are the most highly integrated into urban and industrial life, but they have always fought and still fight for the preservation and recognition of their own cultural identity and for political rights (*see* NATIVE-WHITE RELATIONS and various entries under NATIVE PEOPLE).

Cultural Conflicts Canada has experienced many cultural conflicts. In the 17th century, the French vainly tried to convert the Indians to a non-nomadic, Christian and French way of life. After the British Conquest (1759-60) of NEW FRANCE, the conflict between the English and French moved from the military to the political battlefield. Many British colonists, merchants and administrators thought it simpler to anglicize the 70 000 French colonists and to impose on them British political, legal and religious institutions than to live peacefully with them. Nevertheless, the 2 groups have had to accept coexistence. The coexistence has, however, suffered many stumbling blocks; eg, the battles are still being fought for the recognition of French outside Québec and of English inside Québec (*see* FRANCOPHONE-ANGLOPHONE RELATIONS).

In the 20th century, and particularly since WWII, the massive arrival of new cultural minorities has posed other problems. Sociologists have identified the various forms that characterize the relations of the English and French to cultural minorities as assimilation, integration and accommodation (*see* MULTICULTURALISM). In Canada there has been a certain amount of assimilation of native people and of French Canadians (outside Québec) into the dominant anglophone culture. Other cultural communities have been both assimilated and integrated. On their arrival in Québec, members of these communities choose for themselves or their children one of Canada's 2 official languages. Simultaneously, many have fought to have the culture of their countries of origin recognized as constituent elements of the Canadian mosaic.

Finally, the reality of both conflict and complementarity has led each cultural group within the Canadian ensemble to seek out some form of accommodation. GUY ROCHER

Cumberland, BC, Village, pop 1853 (1986c), 1947 (1981c), inc as a town 1898 but reclassified as a village 1958, is located on the E coast of Vancouver I about 6 km S of Courtenay and 100 km NW of Nanaimo. Robert Dunsmuir became involved in COAL mining here in the 1880s and by 1891 a townsite was planned. In 1898 it was named after Cumberland, Eng. At its height the town had a population of 10 000 and its "Chinatown" was the largest N of San Francisco. From the 1940s on the community declined rapidly and logging replaced mining as the main industry. Agriculture has also developed in the region, and Cumberland has become a tourist destination. ALAN F.J. ARTIBISE

Cumberland, Frederick William, engineer, architect, railway manager, legislator (b at London, Eng 10 Apr 1821; d at Toronto 5 August 1881). Educated in England and Ireland, Cumberland served as an assistant engineer under the great Isambard Brunel on docks and railways in England, giving him not only a solid engineering background but also a special touch in design. He arrived in Toronto in 1847 and, after the city suffered its first great fire in Aug 1849, he won the competition for the rebuilding of St James' Cathedral. But his engineering training became known and he was appointed engineer for the first railway in Upper Canada; he selected Sandford FLEMING as one of his assistants. His architectural practice grew concurrently. In partnership he designed UNIVERSITY COLLEGE, Toronto, but his main task was the building of the Northern Ry, of which he was made general manager in 1858. A man of many parts, he was elected a member of the first Ontario legislature in 1867 and of the House of Commons in 1871. R.F. LEGGET

Cumberland House, Sask, the oldest continuously occupied site in Saskatchewan and the first inland post built by the HUDSON'S BAY COMPANY. It was named for Prince Rupert, duke of Cumber-

land. The site, at the SE corner of Cumberland Lk on the route from Hudson Bay to the Saskatchewan R and Churchill R fur-trading areas, was selected in 1774 by Samuel HEARNE after competitors began to intercept furs from the area's Indians. The construction of Cumberland House in 1774 marked a change in HBC policy, which had hitherto expected Indians to bring their furs to the bay posts to trade. It also marked the beginning of intense rivalry between the HBC and Montréal traders, later the NORTH WEST COMPANY, which lasted until 1821. Cumberland House became less important to the FUR TRADE in the mid-19th century when more direct trade routes to the interior were developed. The HBC still operates a trading post at Cumberland House. The iron keel of the sternwheeler *Northcote*, burned by Gabriel Dumont's men at the siege of Batoche in 1885, lies on the S bank of the Saskatchewan R nearby.

Cumberland Sound is a major inlet, 300 km long, with an average width of 65 km, in the E coast of BAFFIN I. Its steep sides rise over 2125 m to glacier-covered uplands. Past continental glaciation, followed by modification of the upland margins by local alpine glaciation, has created a shoreline deeply indented with FJORDS. Outwash deposits at the head of fjords during deglaciation have been elevated as raised deltas and are markedly terraced. The head of the sound is backed by a hilly lowland with valleys leading to interior plains. The structural alignment and parallel sides of Cumberland Sound suggest it originated through large-scale faulting.

DOUG FINLAYSON

Cummings, Burton, singer, songwriter, musician (b at Winnipeg, Man 31 Dec 1947). Vocalist for the leading Canadian rock group GUESS WHO from 1968-75, Cummings began a solo career in 1976. The singer soared onto the charts with a self-titled debut album which included hit singles "I'm Scared" and "Stand Tall." Follow-up albums provided a stream of hit singles through the late 1970s and into the early 1980s. Cummings has won a number of important music awards, including Juno Awards for Male Vocalist of the Year in 1976 and 1979. Television appearances as host of the Juno Awards ceremony and several TV specials received critical acclaim and led to an acting role in the feature film, *Melanie*. Cummings also provided vocals for "Tears Are Not Enough," a song recorded in 1985 to aid African famine relief. In 1987 he and Randy Bachman participated in a national tour and were working on an album of new material. JOHN GEIGER

Cunard, Joseph, businessman, politician (b at Halifax 1799; d at Liverpool, Eng 16 Jan 1865), brother of Samuel CUNARD. He left Halifax around 1820 and established a branch of his father's firm at Chatham, NB, where he was soon involved in lumbering, milling and shipbuilding. In 1832 he was described as one of the wealthiest men in the province. He expanded into Kent and Gloucester counties and became involved in a bitter rivalry with Alexander Rankin, head of the largest commercial firm in northern NB. Having entered politics in 1828 as an MLA, he was appointed to the Legislative Council 1833 and sat on the Executive Council 1838-46. His bankruptcy in 1847 left hundreds out of work. He moved to Liverpool where he entered the commission business, purchasing supplies for colonial merchants and selling their ships and lumber. WILLIAM A. SPRAY

Cunard, Sir Samuel, merchant, shipowner (b at Halifax 21 Nov 1787; d at London, Eng 28 Apr 1865). Cunard joined his father in the timber business and with interests that expanded into whaling, lumber, coal and iron as well as shipping, he amassed a large personal fortune by the 1830s. His shipping activities largely encompassed SAILING SHIPS although he had some experience in early steam navigation as a shareholder in the wooden paddle wheeler, the ROYAL WILLIAM, which in 1833 made an historic crossing of the Atlantic, mainly under steam power. Among his business interests, Cunard was a founder of the Halifax Banking Company in 1825 along with Enos COLLINS. A Tory supporter, he was a member of the COUNCIL OF TWELVE 1830-38 and of the NS Executive Council 1838-40, although he was active in council meetings only for the first 3 years.

In 1839 he submitted a bid to the British government to undertake a regular mail service, by steamship, across the N Atlantic from Liverpool to Halifax, Québec and Boston, for £55 000 annually for 10 years. The bid was successful and in the same year Cunard, with associates in Glasgow and Liverpool, established the British and North American Royal Mail Steam Packet Company, the ancestor of the Cunard Line. The first Cunard sailing was made in May 1840, but the paddle steamer *Britannia* began regular mail service by steam that July by crossing from Liverpool to Halifax and then Boston in 14 days and 8 hours. Although Cunard had severe financial difficulties in his NS and NB businesses in the early 1840s, his shipping operation, well managed and technically innovative, prospered. It relied on iron ships after 1855 and on screws rather than paddles by the early 1860s. It was forced, by stiff competition from the US, to drop Halifax as a regular port of call and send its vessels directly to New York. There were no Cunard sailings to Canada until just before WWI but thereafter service was maintained from Montréal until air transportation brought about its demise.

Cunard moved to England to supervise his shipping interests, was made a baronet in 1859 for the services of his vessels in the Crimean War and died in London. He left an estate estimated by some at £350 000, by others at considerably more. He was the largest of PEI's absentee land proprietors by 1860 (*see* LAND QUESTION, PEI), and

Sir Samuel Cunard, from J.C. Dent's *The Canadian Portrait Gallery* (1881) (*courtesy National Archives of Canada/ C-7044*).

his holdings there were sold in 1866 for some $258 000. D.M.L. FARR

Cunard Company, conceived and built by the Haligonian shipowner and entrepreneur Samuel CUNARD. With several British partners Cunard formed the British and North American Royal Mail Steam Packet Company in 1839, winning the British government contract and subsidy to carry mail to Canada and the US. Cunard and his Scots engineer Robert Napier built 4 side-wheelers for the N American service; the first, the *Britannia*, left Liverpool 4 July 1840 and arrived at Halifax 12 days later. (It then went on to Boston, the entire trip taking 14 days, 8 hours.) Thus was established a regular, fast steam packet service which eventually led to the decline of N American shipping and the disappearance of transatlantic commercial sailing ships. In 1867 Cunard ships ceased making regular stops at Halifax. The Cunard group became a public company in 1878, adopting the name Cunard Steamship Company Limited. It ultimately absorbed Canadian Northern Steamships Ltd and its competitor, the White Star Line. Cunard dominated the Atlantic passenger trade with liners such as the *Lusitania* and *Mauretania*, and later the legendary *Queen* ships (including the still-active *Queen Elizabeth 2*), almost to the end of the era of the superliners. *See also* SHIPBUILDING; MARITIME SHIPPING HISTORY TO 1900. PETER HOPWOOD

Reading: F.E. Hyde, *Cunard and the North Atlantic 1840-1973* (1975).

Cupids, Nfld, Town, pop 789 (1986c), 706 (1981c), inc 1965, is located in SW CONCEPTION B on the AVALON PENINSULA. Originally known as Cupers Cove (1612), and later as Cuperts, Coopers and Copers Cove (possibly variants of an English surname), it was the site of the Sea Forest Plantation, established by John GUY in Aug 1610, the first attempted colonization by the LONDON AND BRISTOL CO and one of the earliest English settlements in the New World. The colony, governed by Guy under the terms of the company's first charter, was effectively the seat of the first attempt to colonize Newfoundland, and the site of the earliest known English birth in Newfoundland (27 Mar 1613). Between 1621 and 1631 the formal colony collapsed, although the site was later used by migratory fishermen and had evolved as a year-round site by the early 1700s. A prosperous inshore cod fishery and the annual seal hunt were the main sources of employment in the settlement. Today the fishing community is the site of numerous plaques and monuments commemorating its history. In 1978 archaeologists excavated a sawpit, a cesspit, 2 building sites and a possible palisade and wharf believed to correspond roughly to descriptions of the site left by Guy. ROBERT D. PITT

Reading: G.T. Cell, *English Enterprise in Newfoundland 1577-1660* (1969).

Curley, Tagak, Inuk politician, administrator (b at Coral Harbour, NWT 1944). A strong advocate of Inuit concerns, Curley was a founding member and first president of the INUIT TAPIRISAT OF CANADA (1971). From 1979 to 1983 he was president of Nunasi Corp, an Inuit development corporation responsible for the investment of the proceeds of future Inuit LAND CLAIMS settlements. Curley was first elected to the NWT Assembly in 1979, representing Keewatin S. He led the Inuit "shadow" caucus, which formed the largest single block of votes within the legislature. In 1983 he was reelected for the newly renamed riding of Aivilik and was appointed to the NWT Executive Council in 1984, becoming minister of economic development until early 1987. He was defeated in the Oct 1987 territorial elections. HARRIET GORHAM

Curling, sport in which 2 teams of 4 players each send stones over an ice surface toward a target circle in an attempt to place nearest the centre. Although there is some artistic and etymological evidence from the 16th century in the Low Countries of Europe for a similar ice game, most authorities agree that curling as we know it today was codified in Scotland and exported from there in organized form. Certainly the origins and early evolution of this sport in Canada were due to a consistent, enthusiastic and ubiquitous presence of the SCOTS. Undoubtedly, too, curling has thrived to a prodigious and unparalleled extent here. Factors contributing to its contemporary popularity in Canada include the wintry climate, the traditions of the game, certain technological advances and the active patronage of influential persons (many of them Scottish). From their influential position in Canadian society, many Scots were comfortably situated to indulge in and promote the traditions of their native land, including curling.

Some historians have suggested, without documentation, that curling began on the N American continent among Scottish soldiers during the Seven Years' War of 1756-63. Curling certainly occurred informally before 1800, until a group of Scots who were identified chiefly with the fur trade formed the Montreal Curling Club in 1807, described as the first sports club in Canada. Other Scots formed clubs in Kingston (1820), Québec (1821) and Halifax (1824-25). These pioneering enthusiasts experimented with local "stones" made of iron or maple, besides importing them from Scotland. By 1839 when more clubs had been formed, locally made granite curling stones were being advertised in Toronto at $8 a pair. A year later the first book on curling in Canada was published – James Bicket's *The Canadian Curler's Manual.* Intercity matches began in 1835, interprovincial ones in 1858, and in 1865 the first international bonspiel was held between American and Canadian clubs at Buffalo, NY. Much of this progress was aided by the long, cold winters and the availability of innumerable lakes and rivers, ensuring abundant and safe ice on which to enjoy curling. Indeed, these conditions surpassed even those in Scotland, an unusual occurrence for a transplanted sport. In fact it was often too cold to participate outdoors, and curling fanatics took their sport indoors; members of the Montreal Curling Club were likely the first to do this in 1837. The neighbouring Thistle Club constructed an enclosed rink 7 years later. By 1859 Toronto had its first indoor facility, and soon indoor curling rinks became common across Canada. During the 1880s and 1890s, until ice HOCKEY arenas were created, these rinks were being used by many fledgling ice-hockey teams. By 1910 almost every town in the West had an arena, and Winnipeg was the acknowledged curling centre of Canada. In 1950 it had more curling clubs than Montréal and Toronto combined; and Manitoba had more clubs than Ontario and Québec. The Flin Flon club was the largest in the world, with more than 50 rinks.

Despite the dominating Scottish influence, other nationalities participated from an early date. Because a Canadian-born curler, William Reynolds, had won the Denham Medal in 1843, a Toronto newspaper claimed: "Curling may now be considered in this Province a Canadian rather than a Scottish game." Similar sentiments were expressed in Québec in 1861 when a French Canadian (Benjamin Rousseau) won a gold medal in curling competition. And the progress of non-Scottish teams (often called "barbarians") against Scottish-born teams was keenly reported. Perhaps on occasion the native-born were motivated towards success against the socially superior and influential Scots. But sporting rivalries were usually well controlled by the etiquette and code of conduct expected of curlers and the democratic traditions associated with the sport.

Since the earl of DALHOUSIE was reported as a member of the Quebec City Curling Club in 1828, the sport has never lacked for famous figures within its ranks. Naturally, many of these powerful men – such as Sir John A. Macdonald, Lord Aberdeen and Lord Strathcona – were Scots pursuing an ethnic interest. The vice-regal support of the governors general was especially significant. Lord DUFFERIN (1872-78) was an ardent exponent and had a rink built at his own expense at his official residence, Rideau Hall. In 1775 he instituted the Governor General's Prize, one of Canada's coveted curling trophies. His successors also sponsored the sport, adding to its prestige. Another stimulus to the sport was provided when at last a Scottish curling team toured Canada (1902-3), captained by Reverend Kerr. The team played matches in 11 cities from Halifax to Winnipeg, then visited 6 American cities. The Scots lost more matches than they won and returned home tremendously impressed with the status and progress of curling in the Dominion. When a Canadian team first toured Scotland in 1908, it won 23 of 26 matches, including 3 international contests for the Strathcona Cup.

The copious quantities of whisky said to be consumed at bonspiels apparently delayed the participation of women in curling, but in 1894 the first ladies' curling club was formed in Montréal. Before 1900 there were several women's clubs in eastern and western Canada, and curling was soon established as a sport for both sexes and almost all ages.

A Dominion championship competition was inaugurated in 1927, sponsored by the W.D. Macdonald Co, for a trophy known as the BRIER. This annual event gave curling a significant impetus and became one of the most prestigious trophies in Canadian sport. The Dominion Curling Assn (renamed the Canadian Curling Assn in 1968) was formed in 1935. During the 1940s, outdoor curling with cement-filled jam tins became a craze across the Prairie provinces; the first "Carspiel" was held at Nipawin, Sask, in 1947, with 4 Hudson sedans valued at $2200 each as prizes; and in 1949, Ken WATSON of Manitoba became the first curler to win the Brier 3 times. Ten years later Ernie RICHARDSON from Stoughton, Sask, formed the famous Richardson Rink in Regina, Sask, which went on to win 4 Briers in 5 years, together with many other titles, trophies and "cash bonspiels." Two other curlers, both from Alberta, also were 3-time Brier winners: Matt Baldwin (1954, 1957 and 1958) and Ron NORTHCOTT (1966, 1968 and 1969). In 1980, under the new sponsorship of Labatts, the format of Brier competition was changed to include semifinals and a final after the round robin.

Other curling competitions which are held in Canada include championships for Canadian Schoolboys (first held in 1950); Canadian Ladies (first Nationals in 1961, after formation of the Canadian Ladies Curling Assn in 1960); National Mixed (2 men and 2 women, est 1964); National Seniors (1965); Canadian Junior Girls (1971); and the Canadian Senior Ladies (55 and over, in 1973).

The winner of the Brier traditionally represents Canada in international competition for the World Curling Championship. The Scotch Cup competition began in 1959 between Canada and Scotland, sponsored by the Scotch Whiskey Assn, and this grew to a world championship among 10 nations. In 1968, Air Canada took over this sponsorship for a trophy known as the Silver Broom, and the first new world curling championship

took place that year in Montréal. This was won by the Ron Northcott Rink from Canada, which won it again the following year at Perth, Scotland. In fact, Canada was victorious at the first 5 Air Canada Silver Broom World Curling Championships: the Don Duguid Rink won in 1970 at Utica, NY, and repeated its success at Megeve, France in 1971; the Orest Meleschuk Rink came first at Garmisch-Partenkirchen, West Germany, in 1972.

Canada did not win again for 7 years. The US won 3 times in this period, Sweden twice, and other victories were gained by Switzerland and Norway. However, Canadian dominance has been restored in the 1980s with 6 victories: Rick Folk at Moncton, NB, in 1980; Al Hackner in 1982 and 1985 at Garmisch-Partenkirchen, West Germany, and Glasgow, Scotland, respectively; Ed Werenich at Regina, Sask, in 1983; Ed Lukowich at Toronto in 1986; and Russ Howard at Vancouver in 1987.

Several Canadians have also won the World Junior Curling Championship, including two-time winner Paul Gowsell of Alberta, who was the first Canadian to use the push broom (instead of the traditional "corn" broom) in international competition. Since then more and more Canadians have followed suit and the push broom is replacing the former favourite.

Although Canadian successes in world competition have been harder won in recent years, owing to the improvement in the calibre of curling in other nations, Canada still remains the major home of the sport. Curling, not surprisingly, was the sport chosen to be a demonstration sport at the 1988 Winter Olympic Games in Calgary. The Scottish bagpipes always heard at any one of the hundreds of curling bonspiels held across the country are the most obvious symbolic reminder of its illustrious heritage. *See also* F.L. STOREY.

GERALD REDMOND

Reading: W.A. Creelman, *Curling: Past and Present* (1950); Gerald Redmond, *The Sporting Scots of Nineteenth-Century Canada* (1982); D.B. Smith, *Curling: An Illustrated History* (1981).

Curnoe, Gregory Richard, artist (b at London, Ont 19 Nov 1936). After studies in Ontario at London (1954-56), Doon (1956) and Toronto (1956-60), Curnoe settled in London to start his career as a painter. He has since made the chronicle of his life there the source of all his works as a painter, as well as a writer in *20 Cents Magazine* and as a musician, with the Nihilist Spasm Band.

Curnoe's friends, family and surroundings have been the subject of countless paintings, watercolours, drawings and prints – the most important of these being the encyclopedic *The View of Victoria Hospital Second Series (10 February 1969-10 March 1971*), the 194 drawings illustrating David McFadden's *The Great Canadian Sonnet* (1970), the watercolour *Homage to Van Dongen No 1 (Sheila)* (1979-80) and the silk screen on Plexiglas, *Mariposa T.T.* (1978-79). In 1981 Curnoe had a major retrospective at the National Gallery of Canada and in 1985 La Galerie Esperansa in Montréal held a Curnoe exhibition; important work of his is also at the Art Gallery of Ontario and the London Regional Art Gallery.

PIERRE THÉBERGE

Reading: Pierre Théberge, *Greg Curnoe* (1982).

Currant, *see* BERRIES, WILD.

Curriculum Development can be defined as the systematic planning of what is taught and learned in schools as reflected in courses of study and the school programs that are embodied in official documents and made mandatory by provincial and territorial departments of education. Typically, programs are accompanied by text-

books for pupils and curriculum "guides" for teachers. Textbooks have often constituted the content of the curriculum, thus giving publishers a powerful role in curriculum development which they still retain.

Although "curriculum" as a term seems to have been rarely used in Canada before Confederation, the Jesuit *Ratio Studiorum* ("plan of studies"), arguably the most systematic course of study ever devised, was introduced in New France in the 1630s. This established a classical tradition based on centralized control and ensured that the Canadian curriculum would develop in an international context.

Early French Canadian education was expected to "render children good servants of the King ... and of God." Later, in Nova Scotia and Upper Canada, anglophone education had similar goals, expressed in the teaching of Judeo-Christian morality and British patriotism. As a result, when education came under provincial jurisdiction after Confederation, the curriculum was based on common conservative social values. As such, it served (and still serves) an imperative of cultural survival that resulted from the efforts of various groups in the Canadian mosaic to maintain their distinctive identities through the agency of the school. Political, linguistic and religious conflicts in Canada have often arisen from the objectives, content and materials of the school curriculum.

Prior to 1840 schooling in Canada was an informal and intermittent experience, not yet sharply separated from work. It took place in a parent- and church-controlled "system" aimed at teaching basic literacy and religious precepts. In New France, a formal curriculum was available to only an elite minority who were trained for religious and other high-status vocations. Following the British Conquest in 1759-60, church-controlled schooling in Québec was a primary agent of cultural survival and remained so until 1964, serving to maintain the French language and the Catholic religion.

In anglophone Canada, survival was linked to fears of Americanization. American textbooks, widely used in Canada, described the US population as "the most free and enlightened under heaven." Fears were exacerbated, especially in Upper Canada, by the arrival during the 1840s of the "famine IRISH" and other dispossessed immigrants. School promoters such as Egerton RYERSON, the founding father of Canadian curriculum development, saw state-controlled schooling as the primary means of assimilating these "alien" elements. Over the next half-century school promoters elsewhere in Canada followed Ryerson's lead by establishing administrative structures that enabled them to sort children into classes and grades, to create a trained, hierarchically organized teaching force, and to devise a common curriculum for a whole province. This curriculum was implemented through uniform textbooks and was policed through inspection and examinations in a system that ensured that all children were taught to believe, to think and to behave in the same way (*see also* EDUCATION, HISTORY OF).

Over several decades following 1900, this system produced a *de facto* national curriculum across anglophone Canada. Curriculum change occurred by accretion during a period of urbanization and industrialization as traditional education was called into question in all Western nations. Herbert Spencer's question, "What knowledge is of most worth?" posed earlier in England, became an international rallying cry for a more systematic, deliberate process of curriculum development to meet pressing social needs. In Canada, typically cautious adaptation took the form of the "New Education" whereby such innovations as KINDERGARTEN, manual training, domestic science (HOME ECONOMICS), agriculture and "nature study," temperance and health education, PHYSICAL EDUCATION and commercial education were introduced with mixed success. Nevertheless, the schools were given credit for the sharp decline in illiteracy by the 1920s. They were a prime agent of assimilation of the huge numbers of non-English-speaking "new Canadians" who thronged into the eastern cities and the Prairies. Anglo-Saxon values infused the curriculum; bilingual education in all "second languages," including French, was virtually eliminated.

During the interwar years further progressive (mainly American) ideas were adopted, including new notions of scientific testing, mental health, and administrative structures based on business management models, while the cultural content of the anglophone curriculum remained British. However, serious deficiencies in Canadian schooling were revealed during WWII and various studies during the 1940s proposed new efforts to broaden the curriculum and keep pupils in school. Postwar affluence, the BABY BOOM and unprecedented public demands led to an expansion of schooling at the same time that conservative criticism of the supposed excesses of progressive education created a shift to a more subject-centered curriculum (see SCHOOL SYSTEMS). This shift has been reinforced by 1960 as Canadians followed their American neighbours in demanding a more rigorous curriculum, especially in science and mathematics, in order to "catch up with the Russians." This was to be achieved by teaching the "structure" (basic concepts) of each subject by means of inquiry "discovery" methods, which ironically owed much to the despised progressive theories. These ideas gained cautious approval in Canada where, typically, a lack of resources forced curriculum developers to rely on British and American innovations.

After 1965 a new permissiveness in the school curriculum was manifested by a relaxation of centralized control, fragmentation of courses of study, a new child-centered thrust in elementary education. New knowledge, new demands for more practical schooling, a larger and more diverse school population, and new tensions in society resulting from a breakdown of the old social consensus and from a questioning of traditional values led to demands for innovation. With renewed fears of Americanization, with the rise of Québec separatism, and in response to the demands of the native peoples and other minority groups for equality, curriculum developers moved to establish bilingual, multicultural and native studies programs, while also seeking to counter RACISM and sexism through more balanced and accurate treatment of minorities and women in textbooks. Special curricula were designed for the estimated 1 million exceptional children (see EDUCATION, SPECIAL). Ontario's master list of approved classroom materials increased from 61 titles (1950) to 1648 (1972). New advocacy groups included not only liberal proponents of "values education" but conservative advocates of "values schools." The latter group demanded the inclusion of traditional Christian beliefs, the censorship of curriculum materials, and stricter discipline. Other advocacy groups – federal agencies, human rights, environmental and consumer organizations, foundations, labour and business groups and others who saw the school as a proselytizing agency – directed a steady stream of teaching materials at classrooms. What was most striking about the efforts of all those who sought to influence the curriculum was their immense faith in the power of schooling to redress social and economic inequities.

As the curriculum development process became apparently more open, policymakers were frequently forced to respond in an ad hoc fashion to broad but often fleeting public concerns. Sometimes demands led to immediate action for which teachers, in the absence of adequate support, training and materials, were often ill-prepared. The result was that curriculum development was less rational than it appeared to be. By 1980 ministries of education were reverting to centralization as demands for "accountability" led to a restoration, in most provinces, of previously abandoned province-wide testing. This new interest in "evaluation" was accompanied by a concern for curriculum "implementation," as developers sought to ensure that programs were taught as prescribed. Implementation was promoted by "guidelines" in the form of detailed suggestions that tacitly acknowledged the teacher's central role in curriculum change.

These and other trends revealed a new interest in "scientific" curriculum development, entailing precise statements of "objectives" and the assessment of pupil "behaviours" measured by skill performance in the traditional "three r's." This emphasis on the "basics" belied the lack of consensus on what constituted basics and on the extent to which emphasis on them had declined in schools. Ironically, in 1976 a unique external study of Canadian education by the Paris-based Organization for Economic Cooperation and Development (OECD) praised the remarkable growth and the high standards of schooling in Canada but criticized the limited place in curricula of such "frills" as music and art.

Demands for greater uniformity of curricula across Canada ignored the fact that a considerable degree of communality in goals, subject matter, textbooks and teaching methods already existed. By 1980 the interprovincial Council of Ministers of Education (CMEC) was consciously attempting to align curricula across Canada more closely. After 1960 Québec and Newfoundland, by creating their first truly public high-school systems, by adopting "scientific" ideas of school administration and by modernizing their programs, brought their curricula into line with those of other provinces. The increased availability of resources and facilities across Canada reduced educational disparities between rural and urban areas and between have and have-not provinces, with the result that curricula were enriched everywhere. Students shared more common learning experiences even as those experiences became more diverse. In this respect, their school lives paralleled the general social life of Canadians, whose life-styles had become at once more homogeneous and more diverse and culturally enriched since 1950. National studies of science teaching, the educational work of many national organizations and growing university-based research indicated that despite provincial differences, the concept of a Canadian curriculum was very much alive. Although controversy over curriculum revealed sharp differences among Canadians regarding what knowledge was of most worth, it also obscured the fact that in accommodating, however imperfectly, conflicting demands, the schools were reflecting a new social consensus based on a new ethic of respect for cultural diversity. *G.S. TOMKINS*

Reading: A. Chaiton and N. McDonald, eds, *Canadian Schools among Canadian Identity* (1976); H.A. Stevenson and J.D. Wilson, eds, *Precepts, Policy and Process* (1977); G.S. Tomkins, *A Common Continuance* (1986).

Currie, Sir Arthur William (changed from Curry in 1887), soldier, educator (b at Strathroy, Ont 5 Dec 1875; d at Montréal, Qué 30 Nov 1933). He was the first Canadian appointed commander of the Canadian Corps during WWI. He began the war with no professional military experience but several years of service in the Canadian

Inspector-General Sir A.W. Currie with Muggins. Currie was acknowledged as perhaps the ablest corps commander of WWI (*by permission of the British Library*).

Militia. He was appointed commander of the 2nd Canadian Infantry Brigade on 29 Sept 1914, commander of the 1st Canadian Division on 13 Sept 1915 and commander of the Canadian Corps on 9 June 1917. He participated in all major actions of the Canadian forces, including PASSCHENDAELE, during the war but is best known for his planning and leadership during the last 100 days, beginning Aug 8 and lasting until 11 Nov 1918, perhaps the most successful of all Allied offensives during the war (see VIMY RIDGE). Criticism of this campaign by Sir Sam HUGHES in Parliament resulted in postwar controversy and a libel action in 1928 which completely vindicated Currie. Fighting off bankruptcy, Currie diverted $11 000 of his regiment's money to cover his personal debts. The affair came to the attention of PM Borden, who refused to consider court-martialling Canada's best soldier. British wartime PM Lloyd George called Currie a "brilliant military commander," and might have appointed him commander of all British forces had the war continued.

Currie served as inspector general of the militia forces in Canada, 23 Aug 1919 to 30 July 1920, and in Aug 1920 became principal and vice-chancellor of McGill, a position he held until his death. Without benefit of post-secondary education himself, he was extraordinarily successful as a university administrator, and at a time of particular importance in McGill's development.

A.M.J. HYATT

Reading: D.G. Dancocks, *Legacy of Valour: The Canadians at Passchendaele* (1986); A.M.J. Hyatt, *General Sir Arthur Currie* (1987); H.M. Urquhart, *Arthur Currie* (1950).

Currie, Walter, teacher, administrator (b at Chatham, Ont 1 Oct 1922). He was among the earliest activists in Indian educational reform during the period after WWII. A nonstatus Indian born of Potawatomi and Ojibwa parents, Currie was a schoolteacher in Kitchener and principal in Toronto (1953-68) before becoming assistant superintendent for supervision with the Ontario Dept of Education, with responsibility for native and northern schools (1968-71). He was concurrently president of the Indian-Eskimo Assn and first chairman of the Toronto Indian Friendship Centre (1969-71). He was first chairman of

Trent's Dept of Native Studies (1971-75) and one of the first 2 members of Ontario's Human Rights Commission (1972-74). He has advocated improving standards of government-funded Indian schools and fitting them more closely to native needs.   BENNETT MCCARDLE

Curtin, Walter Anthony, photographer (b at Vienna, Austria 16 Aug 1911). He left Vienna in 1939 for England and served in the British army. He turned to photography in 1946, setting up his own shop in London (1948), and moved to near Toronto in 1952. He became an outstanding photojournalist, using a fast-handling rangefinder camera. His photo essays have appeared in *Life, Time, Maclean's, Star Weekly, Fortune, Chatelaine* and *Saturday Night,* among others. Since 1974 he has concentrated on photographing Canadian musicians. In 1982, the NFB Still Photography Division produced an exhibition of his work, entitled "The Musicians." In 1985 the Canadian Museum of Contemporary Photography in co-operation with the National Photography Collection of the National Archives of Canada produced a retrospective exhibition and catalogue of his photographs. A member of the Royal Canadian Academy, Curtin has been honoured with medals, certificates of merit and other awards, such as the Max Sauer Memorial Award.

LOUISE ABBOTT

Curtis, Wilfred Austin, air marshal (b at Havelock, Ont 21 Aug 1893; d at Nassau, Bahamas 7 Aug 1977). As chief of the air staff 1947-53, Curtis presided over unprecedented peacetime growth in the RCAF. He flew with the Royal Naval Air Service on the Western Front 1917-18, being credited with downing 13 enemy aircraft. In the interwar years, he had his own insurance business while helping to start the Toronto Flying Club and assisting as a RCAF reservist. He was called back to active service in 1939 and was deputy air officer commanding, RCAF Overseas Headquarters in London 1941-44. He became a member of the Air Council in 1944 and then succeeded Robert LECKIE as chief of the air staff. His appointment, after only 8 years of full-time RCAF service, was controversial. Astute and businesslike, he successfully pushed for the acquisition of the AVRO CF-100 and other modern aircraft. Upon his retirement he became vice-chairman of A.V. Roe (Canada) Ltd and subsequently of Hawker Siddeley (Canada) Ltd. Understandably, he lamented the cancellation of the AVRO ARROW. He was one of the founders of York U in Toronto and was its first chancellor.   NORMAN HILLMER

Curtola, Robert Allen, "Boby," singer (b at Port Arthur, Ont 17 Apr 1943). He was discovered singing at a high school dance in his home town of Thunder Bay. His first recording, "Hand in Hand With You," released in 1960, became a hit and established Curtola as Canada's leading teen idol. A string of minor hits on Tartan Records followed, including "Fortune Teller." As with other teen idols from the early 1960s, Curtola's career suffered a setback in the late 1960s but he has continued performing on the nightclub circuit, including appearances in Las Vegas, telethons and TV commercials. Currently based in Edmonton, Curtola was presented with a CASBY Award in 1986 for his contributions to Canadian POPULAR MUSIC.   JOHN GEIGER

CUSO (formerly Canadian University Services Overseas), is a nongovernment international development organization best known for placing skilled Canadians in 2-year postings to provide technical assistance in the Third World. The organization also funds Third World projects and is involved in development education in Canada. Founded on 6 June 1961 by representatives of 21 universities and 22 organizations from across Canada, it has remained independent of government control although the greater part of its administrative budget comes from the CANADIAN INTERNATIONAL DEVELOPMENT AGENCY. Canadian donors contribute some $1 million a year to its projects.

Since its founding, CUSO has placed 9000 skilled Canadians in Third World postings. In the early years, the majority were recent university graduates who were placed mainly in teaching positions. In the last decade, the need for formal teachers has declined as Third World countries have trained enough of their own. Instead, CUSO is filling requests for tradespeople, agriculturalists, foresters, fisheries workers, those skilled in small business, co-operatives and community development as well as the more traditional fields of health and education. Because of the declining number of placements requiring a university background, CUSO dropped the university affiliation from its title in 1981 and since then has been known simply as CUSO. At that time it also became a separate entity from its francophone counterpart, SUCO (Service universitaire canadien outremer).

The number of workers placed peaked in the late 1960s at 1000, and there are now 400-500 in the field at any one time. They are no longer known as volunteers but as "co-operants" because co-operation and partnership is imperative to the give and take of working in another culture.

Volunteer placement agencies from most other countries pay their own workers. CUSO has adopted a different policy: the overseas government or agency requesting the services pays the CUSO worker at local rates of pay. Therefore, when a CUSO worker is requested, it is usually because there is not a skilled local person available. The fact that CUSO workers receive the same salary as their colleagues also eases their integration into the local workplace. Supplements can be provided by CUSO where local salaries are low, and terms can be extended beyond the initial 2-year contract.

Much of CUSO's work is community-based and it is becoming increasingly involved in large development projects. In the past decade, it has been engaged in a literacy project involving 56 villages in Sierra Leone, a community project in Bangladesh, technical assistance to mining co-operatives in Bolivia, an education and crop-and-craft production project among the Guaymi Indians, a potato production program in Nicaragua, and a wells project in Togo. CUSO also administers overseas projects for other international development organizations and has been active in helping to establish local nongovernment organizations – NGOs – in developing countries which can eventually manage their own affairs without external assistance. Because of its base of returned co-operants, the organization is in a unique position to assist community groups across Canada in developing awareness and action programs.   RICHARD STUART

Customs and Excise, taxes on goods, are one of the world's oldest sources of government revenue. Customs duties are applied on imported products while excise duties and taxes are generally applied on goods of domestic manufacture, notably liquor and tobacco. The word "customs" derives from custom, a habit. Customs and excise have played a vital role in Canada's development. They were at the centre of the dispute, especially in Nova Scotia, between Crown and legislature for the right to impose and dispose of customs duties; they were the key element in the NATIONAL POLICY, which endured for nearly a century; and they were central to the achievement of national independence through government use of tariff negotiations with other countries.

Customs duties were already here when the Europeans brought rum and religion to N America: some Indian tribes exacted tribute from members of other tribes passing through their territories. The French regime helped to support New France through an export duty on furs and did not rely on import duties until its dying years. The British did not use customs as much for revenue as for enforcement of their NAVIGATION ACTS, which required that British goods be carried in British ships. After Britain turned to free trade in the 1840s, customs and excise in Canada became almost exclusively a revenue producer until after Confederation.

When BNA representatives met in 1864, they discussed a "common commercial policy." Until then their only common policy had been for each to tax the manufactured goods of the others as readily as those of other nations. In 1867 responsibility for the tariff was given to the national government. The Province of Canada's Customs Act of 1866 was adopted, and in 1868 the average tariff was set at 15%, a compromise between protectionist Canada's 20% and free-trading Nova Scotia's and New Brunswick's 10-12%. A higher tariff to nourish and protect domestic manufacture was not introduced until 1879 under PM Sir John A. MACDONALD. By 1883, annual revenue had risen to $23.2 million. Until WWI, when income and sales taxes were first imposed in Canada, customs and excise revenue comprised about 75% of the federal government's revenue.

In the Province of Canada (1841-67) customs was administered by the Finance Dept. Customs and Inland Revenue, established in 1867 as separate ministries, were united in 1918 and in 1921 became Customs and Excise. In 1925, income tax collection was moved from Finance to Customs and Excise, resulting in another name change, to National Revenue, in 1927. The unofficial motto of Customs and Excise was "The Revenue [always spelled with a capital R] must be protected." Early collectors had to swear on the Bible before a judge 4 times a year that they had turned in all of their quarterly collections. On the Klondike Trail in 1897, the customs officer set up a tent beside Tagish Lake and waded out to the passing prospectors' boats to collect duty on any American goods. Sometimes the revenue was not properly protected. During PROHIBITION, the golden age of liquor SMUGGLING and bootlegging, a 1926 customs scandal temporarily brought down the government (*see* KING-BYNG AFFAIR).

A political battle has long raged in Canada between protectionists and free traders. In 1854 Canada and the US signed a RECIPROCITY treaty (free trade in 50 items). The US abrogated the agreement in 1866, and it was not until 1935 that the 2 countries extended most-favoured-nation treatment to each other in tariff matters. During that time, Canadian voters were occasionally presented with the clear issue of protection versus free trade and every time free trade lost. High tariff walls were not breached until after WWII through the GENERAL AGREEMENT ON TARIFFS AND TRADE, signed 18 Nov 1947. By the 1980s the tariff, with some major exceptions, was generally at the level it held at Confederation. Even the British trade preference, which had been established in 1769, had vanished.

Most customs work used to be conducted at seaports and on the 8893 km frontier with the US. But rail, motor and plane travel has changed that. A staff of some 10 000 operates 650 Customs and Excise locations in Canada, 140 of them on the border, some so remote (eg, Little Gold Creek, YT) that they are abandoned in winter. The cost of collecting the revenue is less than 2% of collections which, in 1985-86, amounted to $19.7 billion. The Finance Dept sets taxing laws, including the tariff, while Customs and Excise administers them. These include narcotics, pornographic materials, firearms, diseased plants and "dumped" foreign goods that injure Canadian industry and employment. DAVE MCINTOSH

Reading: G. Blake, *Customs Administration in Canada* (1957); Dave McIntosh, *The Collectors* (1985).

Cut Knife, Battle of On 2 May 1885, during the NORTH-WEST REBELLION, Cree and Assiniboine Indians defeated 300 soldiers commanded by Lt-Col William OTTER. Using a limited number of men, war chief Fine Day virtually surrounded and pinned down Otter's force on an exposed plain. After 6 hours of fighting, Otter retreated as Cree Chief POUNDMAKER held the warriors back. Eight of Otter's force died; 5 or 6 Indians were killed. The battlefield is on the Poundmaker Reserve, about 40 km W of Battleford, Sask, just N of Cut Knife Hill, a feature named for a Sarcee warrior who died near there. A cairn sits near the middle of the battlefield, near Chief Poundmaker's grave. His body was moved to the site in 1967 from Blackfoot Crossing, Alta, where he died in 1886. BOB BEAL

Cutler, David Robert Stuart, football player (b at Biggar, Sask 17 Oct 1945). He joined the EDMONTON ESKIMOS in 1969 as a placement kicker and stayed there for 16 years until his retirement in 1984. He led the CANADIAN FOOTBALL LEAGUE in scoring 7 times and holds the CFL career marks for most converts (627), field goals (464), singles (218) and total points (2237). In 1983 he passed George Blanda to become the all-time points leader in professional football. PETER WONS

Cuttlefish, decapod ("ten-footed") MOLLUSC of class Cephalopoda. Cuttlefish comprise over 100 species in genera *Sepia* and *Spirula.* They are characterized by porous, calcareous, internal shells, best known as cuttlebones, which are given to caged birds as a source of lime salts. The pores are gas filled to adjust the animal's buoyancy, and even dead shells float. The closest Canadian relatives are 4 species of small *Rossia* of the same order, Sepioidea, but lacking cuttlebones. Cuttlefish have oval bodies up to 60 cm long and look rather like flattened SQUID. Thousands of nervously controlled chromatophores (pigment-bearing cells) give them capabilities for camouflage and pattern formation, eg, mating males display a revolving zebra-stripe pattern unequalled in nature. To escape predators, they darken, eject a gelatinous, cuttlefish-shaped, dark brown ink-blob decoy, turn pale instantly and swim away. Sepia ink, derived from and named for the organism, has been used as an artist's medium. R.K. O'DOR

Cuvillier, Augustin, soldier, banker, politician (b at Québec C 21 Aug 1779; d at Montréal 11 July 1849). He attended the Collège de Montréal and became a Montréal merchant and auctioneer, served in the militia during and after the War of 1812, and was promoted to major. One of the promoters of the Bank of Montreal, he served as a director from 1817 to 1826. He was president of the Montreal Committee of Trade in the 1830s and helped to form the Board of Trade in 1842. He served as a magistrate during the election riots of 1832. Cuvillier represented Huntingdon in Lower Canada's legislative assembly from 1812 to 1830, and Laprairie from 1830 to 1834. He was one of the 3-man delegation sent by the assembly in 1828 to advise the British on the political and economic problems of Lower Canada (*see* CANADA COMMITTEE). However, he withdrew from active political life in 1834 after being estranged from Louis-Joseph Papineau's PATRIOTES. Having re-

turned to politics in 1841 as the member for Huntingdon, he was elected speaker of the assembly but was defeated in the 1844 election.
GERALD TULCHINSKY

Cycling Bicycle racing comprises many events, from short-distance sprints on banked velodromes to road races covering distances of 30 to 3000 km. Although there is no reliable information on when the first bicycle reached Canada, the Toronto *Globe* of 6 Mar 1869 reports on a "Grand Riding Academy" with pupils instructed in the art of velocipede riding. The first "high wheel" was imported in 1876 by A.T. Lane. The mayor of Montréal was so impressed that he proclaimed a half-day holiday for the citizens to see Lane ride through the city. The Montreal Bicycle Club, the first in Canada, was formed in 1876. The Canadian Wheelmen's Assn, later renamed the Canadian Cycling Assn, was formed at St Thomas, Ont, in Sept 1882 to protect cyclists' rights, promote bicycling and control championships. It was a founding member of the Union cycliste internationale, the world governing body now listing 132 affiliations. The association launched a campaign to improve roads, a struggle that involved members in political activity at many levels, and produced a series of travel guides and road maps – the first of their kind in Canada. Bicycle ownership significantly affected the social mores of the day. It allowed the owner to travel farther, to socialize with greater ease, especially at the parks and places where cyclists congregated, and in the case of women, to travel unchaperoned. Mainly a Sunday activity, it suffered the wrath of many ministers of the church who attacked this freedom as a pastime of the devil, referring in particular to its adverse effect on women. They were further incensed by the "rational dress" adopted by those daring women who refused to cycle in the voluminous ankle length dresses then considered the appropriate costume. Despite persistent harassment, women continued to cycle.

The 1880s and 1890s were boom years. Racing on outdoor tracks attracted large crowds and produced many notable performers. The Dunlop Trophy Race, instituted in 1894, ran for 33 years and attracted the leading Canadian and American competitors. The World Cycling Championships were held in Montréal in 1899, and in 1912 the

first Canadian 6-day race was held at the Arena Gardens, Toronto. In the 1920s and 1930s, the 6-day race was a regular promotion throughout N America and lucrative contracts drew the best amateurs to the professional ranks, the most famous being W.J. "Torchy" PEDEN of Vancouver, who amassed a total of 38 wins, a record unbeaten until the mid-1960s.

Early in 1900, the arrival of the automobile diverted public interest from cycling with a consequent drop in attendance at meetings and in membership of the CWA. Much of the enthusiasm generated by cycling was transferred to AUTOMOBILE RACING, and innovations which appeared first on bicycles found their way to the automobile. Popularity waned, although competitors and crowds continued to be attracted to 6-day races. The cycling boom of the 1960s revived interest. Road racing, always strong in Québec, grew apace with the introduction of "tours" modelled on the Tour de France. In 1974 Montréal once again hosted the World Cycling Championships, which were attended by over 1000 riders and officials, amateurs and professionals. During the 1970s, Jocelyn Lovell of Toronto was virtually unbeatable in Canada. He won gold medals in Commonwealth and Pan-American Games and a silver in the 1978 World Championships. Lovell's career ended tragically when he was seriously injured in a collision with a truck near Toronto in 1983; he was paralysed from the shoulders down. Gordon Singleton of St Catharines, Ont, emerged as a world-class sprinter, placing 2nd in the 1979 World Amateur Championships and in the 1981 World Professional Sprint Championships. Women's cycling was in the ascendant with Karen Strong-Hearth, of St Catharines, winning a bronze medal in the 1976 World Championships and sweeping the women's events at the 1976 Canadian Cycling Championships. In the 1984 Olympic Games, Canadian competitive cycling achieved world recognition when Canada won its first 2 silver medals. Curt Harnett of Thunder Bay, Ont, captured the silver in the 1000 m time trial; and Stephen Bauer of Fenwick, Ont, narrowly missed taking the gold medal in the 190 km road race. Bauer then turned professional and, one month later, went on to win the bronze medal in the 250 km World Professional Road Race Championships.

In the 1987 Pan-American Games (Indianapolis, Ind), Canadian cyclists won gold, silver and bronze medals. Curt Harnett of Thunder Bay,

Jocelyn Lovell was virtually unbeatable in cycling in Canada during the 1970s (*courtesy Ron Watts/First Light*).

Ont, won a gold medal in the kilometre time-trial and a bronze in the sprint. Kelly-Ann Carter of Edmonton won a silver medal in women's individual pursuit, and Patrick Beauchemin of Montréal and Sara Neil of Vancouver won bronze medals in the men's individual pursuit and 57 km road race, respectively. KENNETH V. SMITH

Reading: *Canadian Cyclist* periodical (1973-76); Kenneth V. Smith, *The Canadian Bicycle Book* (1972).

Cypress, in Canada, common name for white cedars or false cypresses, evergreen CONIFERS of genus *Chamaecyparis* of the cypress family (Cupressaceae). Six species are recognized: one in western Canada, 2 in the US and 3 in eastern Asia, Japan and Taiwan. Alaska or yellow cypress (*C. nootkatensis*) occurs in a narrow band from Alaska, along the BC coast and in the Cascade Mts into northern California. It is medium-sized, up to 30 m in height and 1.5 m in diameter. Leaves are small and scalelike; cones are round (1 cm diameter), bracts (modified leaves) and scales (ovule-bearing structures) are fused. POLLINATION occurs in spring. The seeds are small with 2 lateral wings. They complete their development and are shed in the fall of the second year after pollination. The wood is light, hard, strong and decay resistant. True cypresses belong to the genus *Taxodium*, not native to Canada. JOHN N. OWENS

Nootka cypress (*Chamaecyparis nootkatensis*), with young cones (top), female flowers and older cones (right) and male flowers (*artwork by Claire Tremblay*).

Cypress Hills, about 2500 km², are situated in southeastern Alberta and southwestern Saskatchewan. With a maximum elevation of over 1460 m, they rise 600 m above the surrounding prairies, forming the highest point in mainland Canada between the Rocky Mts and Labrador. Their name probably derives from an early French Canadian explorers' term, *montagne de cyprès*, used to describe their pine-covered character. The word *cyprès* (cypress) was widely, though erroneously, used in reference to Canadian pine forests. The area is identified as the Cypress Hills on the PALLISER map of 1857-60. It was a centre of whisky trade in the late 1860s, and in 1873 a gang of American and Canadian wolf hunters massacred 36 Assiniboine there. The incident spurred PM John A. MACDONALD's government who sought to establish quick passage of the recently introduced bill to create the North-West Mounted Police. FORT WALSH was built in 1875 near the site of the massacre.

The hills form a rolling plateaulike upland, rising sharply to the north and in the south gradually dropping to meet the plains. Fed by numerous

The Cypress Hills: flat-topped uplands amid the great plains (*courtesy Alberta Recreation and Parks*).

springs that emerge along the hillsides, the slopes are covered by a mixed forest of lodgepole pine, white spruce, balsam poplar and aspen. The quick-draining open plateau supports drier grass and shrubs. The area is a humid island in the semiarid prairies, with many varieties of plants and animals representative of the Rocky Mts, over 200 km to the W. Some 200 bird species have been sighted here. Capped by a layer of stream-laid gravels up to 100 m thick (the Oligocene-aged Cypress Hills formation) derived from the Rockies, the Cypress Hills are an erosional remnant of a once-extensive higher-level plains surface that was largely removed by stream action during later Tertiary and early Quaternary times (*see* GEOLOGICAL HISTORY). The hills were high enough to have been one of the few areas in Canada not completely ice-covered during the Wisconsin glaciation. Their higher portions projected through the ice as NUNATAKS. Wind-blown loess, in places over 2 m thick, was deposited during this period. CYPRESS HILLS PROVINCIAL PK (Alberta) contains evidence of human habitation dating back over 7000 years, making the area of special archaeological interest in addition to its unique physical environment. IAN A. CAMPBELL

Cypress Hills Provincial Parks, located in the CYPRESS HILLS, consists of 2 blocks, one in Saskatchewan, located some 30 km S and SW of Maple Creek, Sask and comprising 182 km². Cypress Hills Provincial Park (Alberta) is located adjacent to the Sask park and is 65 km SE of Medicine Hat, Alta. At 204 km², it is Alberta's second largest provincial park.

Cyr, Louis, strongman (b at St-Cyprien-de-Napierville, Canada E 10 Oct 1863; d at St-Jean-de-Matha, Qué 10 Nov 1912). Cyr's family moved to Massachusetts and as a young man he was a lumberjack in New England before returning to Montréal in 1882 to take a job as a policeman. Though not unusually tall, Cyr weighed as much as 165 kg and was immensely strong. In days when feats of strongmen aroused intense interest, Cyr became a legend. There was no formal sport of WEIGHTLIFTING; competitions were held as challenge matches, and at these he was never defeated. He won the "weightlifting" championship of N America in 1885 and the "world championship" in 1892. Most of his feats were public demonstrations that drew great crowds, including royalty. He was fêted in London, Eng, where on 19 Jan 1889 he lifted in succession a 250 kg weight with one finger, 1860 kg on his back, and 124 kg above his head with one hand. He proudly returned to Canada with one of the marquis of Queensberry's horses after winning a bet that he could hold 2 driving horses to a standstill, one tied to each of his massive arms. In 1895 in Boston he lifted on his back a platform holding 18 fat men, weighing 1967 kg — believed the heaviest weight ever lifted by a man. From 1894 to 1899 he toured

with Ringling Brothers and Barnum and Bailey circuses and he later opened a tavern in Montréal. He died of Bright's disease, perhaps brought on by the amount of food he had to eat to fuel his enormous strength. JAMES MARSH

Czechs It is generally recognized that the Czechs and SLOVAKS comprise one ethnic group composed of 2 closely connected but still distinct Slavic units. Until the 19th century they shared a common literary language, that of the 16th-century Czech translation of the scriptures, the Králice Bible. The spoken languages are still very similar. In 1771 a lay religious community, the Moravian Brethren (which had emerged in Saxony in 1727 as a continuation of the old Hussite Fellowship of Brethren) arrived in Labrador to do missionary and social work among the Inuit. Not long afterwards a group of Moravian Brethren from the US led by David ZEISBERGER founded Fairfield, commonly known as Moraviantown, on the Thames R near present-day Thamesville, Ont. The colony was razed during the WAR OF 1812, but the mission, rebuilt across the river, continued until 1903.

Czech immigration into Canada started in the mid-1880s (*see* IMMIGRATION POLICY). The first recorded Czech immigrants settled in Kolin, Sask, in 1884. In Alberta Czechs founded Prague; in Manitoba Moravian Brethren settled in the Mennonite community. The early immigrants, farmers, miners, artisans and labourers came for economic reasons. After 1921, when the US introduced a quota system for immigration, many Czechs immigrated to Canada instead. The 1921 census reported 8840 people of Czech origin in Canada; this figure jumped to 30 401 (1931), 42 912 (1941) and 57 840 (1971). Emigration increased 1938-39 as a result of German occupation; and rose again in 1948 with the establishment of a communist regime and in 1968 because of the Soviet invasion. In 1981, the last census year for which figures are available, there were 67 695 persons of Czech and Slovak origin in Canada.

The Czechs and Slovaks have as a rule had little difficulty integrating themselves into Canadian life, but they have also been rather successful in maintaining their cultural heritage. Their first newspaper, the *Slovenské Slovo* (*Slovak Word*), started publication in the coal-mining town of Blairmore, Alta, in 1910. There are now several publications. The national association, the Czechoslovak National Alliance (est 1939 in Toronto), promotes Czech and Slovak cultural and educational activities and is also active in the social field. Politically, it supports the Council of Free Czechoslovakia, a group advocating the re-establishment of a democratic Czechoslovakia. Another Czech social and cultural organization is the Sokol ("Falcon") movement, patterned on an athletic and patriotic organization founded in the Czech lands in the 19th century. Although the majority of Czechs are Roman Catholic, it was not until larger Czech and Slovak communities were founded that Czech-language parishes were built. There are also numerous Baptist congregations. Czechs and Slovaks have made important contributions to Canadian economic development and Canadian cultural life. Well-known names include Thomas BATA, head of the world-wide Bata shoe-manufacturing and retailing enterprise; Stephen ROMAN, pioneer of uranium mining in Canada; the KOERNER brothers, leaders in BC's lumber industry; Oskar MORAWETZ, composer; Peter C. NEWMAN, author; the poet and novelist Pavel Javor; and writer Josef ŠKVORECKÝ. JOHN GELLNER

Reading: John Gellner and J. Smerek, *The Czechs and Slovaks in Canada* (1968).

Da Roza, Gustavo Uriel, architect (b at Hong Kong 24 Feb 1933). Of Chinese and Portuguese descent and one of the best-known architects practising in Winnipeg since WWII, da Roza received his architectural education in Asia. In 1958 he joined U of Calif, Berkeley, and in 1960 came to Winnipeg and University of Manitoba. While da Roza's principal commissions have been houses, a significant recent work is the Winnipeg Art Gallery (1971). As an educator, visiting critic and member of competition juries, da Roza has greatly influenced Canadian architecture.
WILLIAM P. THOMPSON

Dafoe, Allan Roy, physician (b at Madoc, Ont 29 Mar 1883; d at North Bay, Ont 2 June 1943). A shy recluse with an indifferent academic record, he achieved worldwide fame for his successful delivery on 28 May 1934 of the DIONNE QUINTUPLETS. Dafoe's commonsense approach, together with the advice of his brother William, a Toronto gynecologist, kept the babies alive. Placed in charge of their welfare (over the protests of their father, Oliva Dionne), Dafoe became a public figure, portrayed on films and radio by Hollywood actor Jean Hersholt. Created OBE, 1935, he was author of *Dr. Dafoe's Guidebook for Mothers* (1936) and *How To Raise Your Baby* (1941). PIERRE BERTON

Dafoe, John Wesley, journalist, liberal reformer (b at Combermere, Canada W 8 Mar 1866; d at Winnipeg 9 Jan 1944). As editor of the Manitoba, later Winnipeg *Free Press* from 1901 until his death, he was one of the most influential Canadian journalists in history, continuing the editor-as-public-man tradition of Joseph HOWE, W.L. MACKENZIE and others. Born and reared a Conservative, he shifted to liberalism in 1885-1900, when he worked variously in Ottawa (as premier editor of the *Journal*) and Montréal. A great admirer of LAURIER and his policies, he viewed the Liberal Party as the best means of social progress and greater national autonomy, but was not slavish in his devotion. He endorsed Sir Robert BORDEN for his nationalism and later, briefly, the Progressive Party for its concern with

Dr A.R. Dafoe, shown with the Dionne quintuplets, was placed in charge of the famous girls' welfare and became a well-known public figure himself (*courtesy National Archives of Canada/PA-26034*).

agriculture. A man of the centre, he always denounced extremes of the left and right, represented in his view by the CCF and Social Credit, respectively. He wrote several books, including *Laurier: A Study in Canadian Politics* (1922) and *Canada: An American Nation* (1935). Dafoe also founded an editorial dynasty. His son Edwin (1894-1981) became editor of the *Free Press*, and 2 nephews are now prominent in Canadian publishing: one as editor of the *The Beaver* and the other with the *Globe and Mail*. DOUGLAS FETHERLING

Reading: R. Cook, *The Politics of John W. Dafoe and the Free Press* (1963).

Dagger, Francis telephone expert (b at Liverpool, Eng 3 June 1865; d at Unionville, Ont 21 June 1945). He was an active participant in the movement for public ownership of Canadian telephones, and his efforts are reflected today in government ownership of telephone systems in the Prairies. After gaining experience with privately owned telephone companies in England 1881-99, he moved to Canada, joining the Bell Telephone Co for 11 months. By 1900 he was agitating for municipal ownership of telephones by Toronto. Retained by the federal government to report on telephones in Canada and England (1903), Dagger was then appointed technical adviser to the Select Committee on Telephone Systems, chaired by Sir William MULOCK (1905). He was hired both by Manitoba (1905) and Saskatchewan (1907) as a telephone expert to facilitate provincial takeover of Bell's operations in these provinces. He served as supervisor of telephone systems for the Ontario Railway and Municipal Board from 1910 until his retirement in 1931. ROBERT E. BABE

Dair, Carl, typographer, typographic designer, teacher, writer (b at Welland, Ont 14 Feb 1912; d on flight from New York C to Toronto 28 Sept 1967). Dair became interested in typesetting as a child and by age 18 was doing advertising and layouts for the *Stratford Beacon-Herald*. He moved to Montréal and opened a design studio in 1947. He also began to teach design and typography and to write on typographic design and its relationship to commerce, art and communication. There followed 10 years of commercial design, teaching and writing in Montréal and Toronto, during which he built an international reputation. In 1956 he was awarded an RSC fellowship to study type design and manufacture in Holland, where he began to design the typeface he called Cartier. He continued to work on this intermittently until 1967, when he published the *First Proof of Cartier Roman and Italic*, the first typeface for text composition designed in Canada. It is now widely used and appears to have achieved the status of an identifiable national type. Over 3 decades, he inspired a generation of graphic designers, not only with standards of excellence in design but with his personal philosophy which saw "inspired typography" as an important "means of visual communication." Among his many publications is *Design with Type* (1952; 2nd ed 1967), now a standard text on the subject. LAURIE LEWIS

Dairy Farming Dairy cattle (family Bovidae, genus *Bos)* are breeds of cattle raised for their ability to produce large quantities of high butterfat-content milk. In 1986 Canada had some 2.14 million milk cows and dairy heifers (1.46 million lactating cows), about 73% in Ontario and Québec. Between 1951 and 1981, the number of dairy farms declined from 451 000 to 67 890, and to 42 325 by 1986. At the same time, herd size and production per cow increased; hence, production output has been maintained. About 60% of the milk produced is processed into butter, cheese and skim milk powder; the remainder is consumed in liquid form. Canadian dairy products for domestic consumption or export must meet stringent quality regulations imposed by Agriculture Canada and Health and Welfare Canada.

Per capita consumption of milk, pure cream, butter and evaporated milk has gradually decreased, although consumption of products such as specialty cheeses and yogurt has increased. Milk marketing boards ensure stable, orderly production and marketing of milk, thus benefiting producer and consumer. Producers can plan in advance, adopting modern animal-management, ANIMAL-BREEDING and financial techniques; consumers are provided with a range of dairy products at stable prices year-round.

The Canadian DAIRY INDUSTRY uses 7 breeds of cattle: Holstein-Friesian, Ayrshire, Jersey, Guernsey, Canadian, Shorthorn and Brown Swiss. These dairy breeds are distinguished from BEEF CATTLE by their triangular, elongated, tall body form. In addition to their physical and performance characteristics, all breeds have distinctive behavioural traits. For example, heavy breeds (eg, Holstein, Brown Swiss) are quite calm and easy to manage.

Holstein-Friesian Cattle, which originated in Holland and were introduced to Canada in 1881, today comprise over 85% of Canadian dairy cattle. The breed is characterized by its colour (shiny black on a white background), large size and exceptional milk production. Mature bulls weigh up to 1090 kg; mature cows, up to 635 kg. A mature

Cecile
Dr A.R. Dafoe
Annette
Marie
Yvonne
Emelie

Brown Swiss cattle were developed in Europe, particularly in Switzerland, and were brought to Canada in 1888 (*photo by Walt Browarny, Browarny Photographics Ltd*).

cow annually produces an average of 6500 kg of 3.7% butterfat, 3.1% protein milk.

Ayrshire Cattle originated in Ayrshire, Scotland. They were introduced to Canada around 1821. The coat is light or dark red and white in varying proportions. Roughly one-half of Canada's Ayrshires are found in Québec. Bulls weigh up to 910 kg; cows, 570 kg. A cow annually produces about 5000 kg of 4.0% butterfat, 3.3% protein milk.

Jersey Cattle originated on Jersey I and were brought to Montréal in 1868. Jerseys are a fawn colour, except along the spine, around the muzzle and on the inside of the legs, where they are a paler shade. Bulls are darker than cows and some strains produce offspring with white markings. Bulls weigh up to 725 kg; cows, 500 kg. Each cow produces about 4200 kg of milk annually.

Guernsey Cattle, like Jerseys, were produced from Breton and Norman breeds. Developed on Guernsey I, they were brought to Canada in 1876. Guernseys are comparable in size to Ayrshires, buff in colour, with distinctive white spots. A mature cow produces about 4700 kg of 4.9% butterfat, 3.6% protein milk annually.

Canadian Cattle were developed in Québec from cows imported from Brittany and Normandy, by French settlers early in the history of New France. This breed is limited almost entirely to Québec. It is black or brown, although the back, muzzle and udder or scrotum are generally paler (sometimes yellow). Bulls weigh up to 770 kg; cows, 545 kg. A cow annually produces about 3800 kg of 4.4% butterfat, 3.6% protein milk.

Shorthorn Cattle originated in England and were first imported in 1832. They are considered a dual-purpose (milk and beef) breed; in Canada, all strains are registered in the same herd book. Shorthorns are red, white, roan or a mixture of red and white. Bulls weigh up to 1045 kg; cows, 770 kg. Cows annually produce about 4250 kg of 3.8% butterfat milk.

Brown Swiss Cattle originated in Asia, were developed in Europe, particularly Switzerland, and

Holstein-Friesian cattle today comprise more than 85% of Canadian dairy cattle (*photo by Walt Browarny, Browarny Photographics Ltd*).

were brought to Canada in 1888. These cattle mate well with beef breeds. Bulls weigh up to 1135 kg; cows, 635 kg. Mature cows will annually produce about 5900 kg of 4.0% butterfat, 3.5% protein milk.

Good nutrition, sound management and breeding are the major criteria of successful herd improvement and, in Canada, have led to an average increase of over 50 kg of milk per cow per year in the past decade. Generally, breeders select mainly for milk production, then, for body conformation characteristics associated with production and longevity. Federal and provincial governments offer record-of-performance services. Quantity, butterfat content and protein content of milk produced by each cow are periodically recorded, and compared to conformation standards established by various breeder associations. This information is officially recorded (in herd books) for each breed and used to judge quality of bulls and performance of cows. Since most milk producers use artificial insemination, evaluation of bulls is of critical importance. A detailed file on production and conformation is kept for each bull used in insemination centres. Artificial insemination has played a key role in improving the productivity of dairy cattle.

New developments in animal reproduction will have a further impact. Embryo transfer is already practised commercially; the best dairy cattle are superovulated (forced to produce exceptional numbers of eggs at one time) and impregnated with the semen from exceptional bulls; embryo freezing and the cloning of embryonic tissues are also practised. Canada has achieved an international reputation for the quality of its dairy cattle and now exports bull semen as well as livestock. In 1986, for example, 22 429 purebred dairy cattle were exported to 22 countries. Embryo freezing will facilitate our international cattle trade, and sperm and embryo sexing also offer enormous potential. Rapid developments in BIOTECHNOLOGY will make it possible to increase productivity still further, through production of vaccines, hormones and certain nutrients. For example, a growth hormone injected into a lactating cow increases milk production without changing food consumption.

Feed represents over half of the cost of milk production: in high-performance herds, nutrition and food management are the factors promoting highest production. Cattle are ruminants, ie, they have a 4-compartment stomach in which bacteria and protozoa break down fibrous plant material into usable nutrients. A high-performance dairy cow annually consumes roughly 75% of its nutrients as fibre-rich grasses. The Canadian climate imposes difficult conditions on feed production and storage, and optimal use of grasses is a challenge. Milk production is increasing in all regions which are suitable for livestock feed production.

Increased productivity has resulted in higher frequency of mammary, digestive and reproductive disorders. Infertility and sterility are the 2 major reasons for culling dairy cattle. The causes of these disorders are complex and a great deal of research is conducted into reproduction problems and mammary disorders. Detecting when the cow is in season continues to be a major concern for producers. It is reported that roughly 50% of N American cattle suffer from various forms of mastitis (an infection of the mammary gland).

GASTON J. ST-LAURENT

Dairy Industry Canada's dairy-products industry is made up of companies that process raw milk and cream. Primary products include pasteurized, packaged fluid milk and cream; cheese (natural, process, paste, spreads, curds); condensed, evaporated or powdered milk or cream; creamery butter, butter oil and whey butter; ice cream, ice-cream mix and ice-cream novelties; and frozen desserts (eg, sherbets, ices).

The first dairy product consumed by humans was fluid milk. While the cow is the major milk producer today, the milk of other mammals (eg, buffalo, reindeer, goat) is widely consumed in some parts of the world. Unquestionably, the first "processed" dairy product made from fluid milk was cheese. It was standard fare in ancient Egypt, Greece and Rome and was frequently used as field rations by ancient armies. In Europe, cheesemaking industries were run in monasteries, which produced varieties still made today. In Canada the popular Oka cheese was developed in a Québec monastery. Canada's modern, highly sophisticated, multi-billion-dollar dairy-processing industry began in the early 1600s, when French settlers brought in dairy cattle. For the next 250 years, dairy production remained a farm or cottage industry. As towns and villages were established, fluid milk, butter and cheese were provided by local farmers, a situation that did not change until the 1850s. The modern factory method of cheesemaking was introduced by Jesse Williams, who built the first cheese factory in Rome, NY, in 1851. The first cheese factories in Canada were built in Oxford County, Ont, in 1864 and at Dunham, Qué, in 1865. About 20 years later, the factory method of cheese production was introduced to Scotland where it was called the Canadian cheesemaking system.

By 1873 there were about 200 cheese factories in Canada. In 1873 a group of farmers established the first creamery in Canada at Athelstan, Qué, but it survived for only about 10 weeks. Another creamery, started in Helena, Qué, in the same year, remained in production for about 11 years before being converted to a cheese factory. The first Canadian company to produce condensed milk was established in Truro, NS, in 1883. Dried milk powder was manufactured for the first time by a company started in Brownsville, Ont, in 1904. In 1900 modern large-scale milk distribution began in Toronto, Montréal and Ottawa; in 1927 homogenized milk was sold in Oshawa, a N American first.

As is the case in a number of other Canadian FOOD AND BEVERAGE processing sectors, the dairy industry has experienced a substantial decrease in numbers of factories. Improvements in road and rail delivery systems, packaging methods and processing techniques permitted dairies to increase dramatically the distribution range of even their most perishable product, pasteurized fluid milk. Consequently, large, modern, centrally located production facilities have been constructed and many small, regional dairy companies phased out. In 1961 there were 1710 dairies; by 1985, 394. Retail distribution of most dairy products has also changed significantly. In the 1940s and 1950s many dairy products were delivered door-to-door; today, consumers buy most dairy products directly from a grocery store and home delivery has virtually disappeared.

Major changes have also occurred in the packaging of pasteurized fluid-milk products. Until fairly recently, most fluid dairy products were in returnable glass containers; now most are in plastic, heat-sealed bags or in rigid containers made from paper laminated with plastic film. Both packaging types have significantly increased the shelf life of liquid dairy products. The latest development in milk packaging is the so-called "aseptic" (sterile) packaging. A totally sterile container is filled with fully sterile milk and sealed in a sterile environment before going to an outside carton-handling line. Fluid dairy products so processed are shelf stable at room temperatures for 6 months or more. The first Canadian aseptically packaged fluid milk was produced by a Montréal dairy in the mid-1960s. After a slow start, aseptic packaging facilities were established in most provinces.

The Canadian dairy manufacturing industry is highly regulated (*see* FOOD LEGISLATION). It must comply with regulations set by the dairy division of Agriculture Canada, by the Health Protection Branch of Health and Welfare Canada, by Consumer and Corporate Affairs Canada and by provincial counterpart agencies. The dairy-processing sector is represented by the National Dairy Council of Canada in Ottawa. In 1985 there were 394 dairy manufacturing operations in Canada: Nfld had 4; PEI, 14; NS, 15; NB, 9; Qué, 109; Ont, 145; Man, 25; Sask, 14; Alta, 33; and BC, 26. In 1973, with 646 plants in production, the industry had shipments valued at nearly $1.7 billion. Materials and supplies that year cost $1.3 billion; fuel and electricity costs were $24.3 million; and the industry employed 27 819 people. In 1985 industry sales had increased to almost $6.4 billion. Materials and supplies costs increased to $4.7 billion; fuel and electricity costs increased to $104 million. Employment had declined to 25 445, undoubtedly as a result of the changing distribution patterns.   ROBERT F. BARRATT

Dakota (Sioux) Archaeological evidence indicates that the Dakota occupied what is now western Ontario and eastern Manitoba prior to 1200 AD, and western Manitoba and eastern Saskatchewan prior to 900 AD. These populations later withdrew to the drainage basins of the Red, Mississippi and Rainy rivers, where they were located when first contacted by Pierre RADISSON in 1659. By then the Siouan-speaking Dakota population had divided into 3 groups. Farthest E, along the Mississippi R and its tributaries, dwelt the Dakota (Santee Sioux), who practised horticulture, occupied semipermanent villages, harvested wild rice as a food staple and hunted buffalo (*see* BUFFALO HUNT). Between the Mississippi and the lower Missouri R were the Nakota (Yanktonai Sioux), speakers of the same dialect of Dakota as is spoken by the ASSINIBOINE and STONEY of Canada. This population wintered along the wooded tributaries of the Mississippi and summered on the plains, hunting big game. Farthest W, along the Missouri R, lived the Lakota (Teton Sioux), who were wholly mobile and largely dependent upon the buffalo. Even though different in many respects, all were politically united and referred to themselves collectively as *Dakota* (Nakota, Lakota) or "the allies."

After acquiring the HORSE in the early 1700s, the Dakota expanded their territory from the Mississippi R to the Yellowstone R, and from the Platte R to the Qu'Appelle R. HUDSON'S BAY CO records from Ft Qu'Appelle to Rainy Lake House (Ft Frances, Ont) commonly mention the Dakota occupying that territory from the late 1700s. During the WAR OF 1812, the Dakota pledged their alliance to Britain, in return for oaths of perpetual obligation. This alliance was betrayed at the Treaty of GHENT (1814), when Britain abandoned her Indian allies as a term of peace. The Dakota then drew closer to their lands in the US; however, though land use in Canada decreased, the northern territory was never abandoned.

The western expansion of the Americans ended Dakota territorial sovereignty when, in 1862, the US military, after the Minnesota Troubles, drove some of the eastern population into Canada, where they have since taken up reserve lands in Manitoba, Saskatchewan and Alberta. A few Lakota, including SITTING BULL, moved into southern Saskatchewan following the Battle of the Lit-

A Sioux (Dakota), oil on canvas by Paul Kane (*courtesy Royal Ontario Museum*).

tle Big Horn (1876). The Dakota have since been treated as political refugees by Canadian governments. They were never admitted to treaty, as were all other Plains Indian populations, and were expected to make their own future in Canada (*see* INDIAN TREATIES). The Dakota became commercial farmers, producers of specialty crops, woodworkers, cattle ranchers, small-scale resource exploiters and labourers, traditions that are carried on today. In 1986 the Dakota in Canada numbered about 2500 and occupied 12 INDIAN RESERVES. *See also* NATIVE PEOPLE: PLAINS and general articles under NATIVE PEOPLE.   PETER DOUGLAS ELIAS

Reading: G. MacEwan, *Sitting Bull: The Years in Canada* (1973); R.W. Meyer, *History of the Santee Sioux* (1967).

Dalhousie, NB, Town, pop 5363 (1986c), 4958 (1981c), inc 1905, shire town of Restigouche County, is located on NB's north shore, at the mouth of the Restigouche R. The population is primarily English and French speaking. Founded 1826 and named for Gov Gen the earl of Dalhousie, it developed as a shipbuilding and lumbering centre. Lumbering lost its pre-eminence in 1930 with the opening of the NBIP paper mill. Chemical plants constitute the other major industry. The town is a year-round seaport and site of a NBEPC 300 MW thermoelectric generating station. The Chaleur Area History Museum has displays on pioneer life and early industries.
                          BURTON GLENDENNING

Dalhousie, George Ramsay, 9th Earl of, soldier, administrator, governor-in-chief of British N America 1820-28 (b 23 Oct 1770; d at Dalhousie Castle, Scot 21 Mar 1838). He joined the British army in 1788 and saw service in both Spain and France 1812-14. After fighting at the Battle of Waterloo 1815, he began a career in administration. In 1816 he was appointed lieutenant-governor of Nova Scotia and, after the sudden death of the duke of RICHMOND, became governor-in-chief of Canada 1820. Known for his authoritarian views, Dalhousie clashed with the French Canadian majority led by Louis-Joseph PAPINEAU. He was recalled in 1828, and a British parliamentary committee was formed to deal with the Canadian situation. During his tenure he founded Dalhousie College (later DALHOUSIE UNIVERSITY) in 1818 and the Québec Literary and Historical Society. After leaving Canada, he was appointed commander in chief of the forces in India (1829-32).   DAVID EVANS

Dalhousie Review, fd 1921 at DALHOUSIE UNIVERSITY as "A Canadian Journal of Literature and Opinion," is one of those academic quarterlies that have largely taken the place in Canada of the journals of affairs that flourish in Britain and the US. The first editor, H.L. STEWART, declared, "We avow a nationalism that is not prejudice and a provincialism that is not narrowness." The *Review* has sustained this ideal, representing faithfully the intellectual life of the Maritimes while remaining open to scholars from elsewhere. *Dalhousie Review* also publishes the work of fiction writers and poets, many of them, like W.K. Valgardson, early in their careers. A large section is devoted to reviews of recent books and current affairs.   GEORGE WOODCOCK

Dalhousie University, Halifax, was founded in 1818 by Lt-Gov George Ramsay, 9th earl of DALHOUSIE. Dalhousie envisaged a liberal, nondenominational college, based on the educational standards of Edinburgh U and offering a progressive alternative to the Anglican UNIVERSITY OF KING'S COLLEGE at Windsor, NS. The institution's initial funding came from customs duties collected at Castine, Maine, during the British occupation, 1814-15. Its auspicious beginnings were soon marred by governmental indifference and sectarian rivalry. Both the colonial establishment and the college's board of governors were unenthusiastic, favouring instead the precedence of King's College. Religious guidelines excluded all but ANGLICANS from King's and, during the early years, effectively restricted faculty appointments at Dalhousie to Presbyterians. As a result, various denominational colleges were established throughout Nova Scotia, seriously impeding the growth of higher education for some 50 years. Attempts to unite with King's College failed in 1824 and 1832, with the Windsor group fearing a dilution of their Anglican exclusivity and Oxford standards. (Affiliation did not occur until 1923, when circumstances dictated that King's adopt a more pragmatic educational approach.) Dalhousie languished until 1838, when Thomas MCCULLOCH became the first president. University status was granted in 1841 but, after McCulloch's death in 1843, the institution again declined and in 1848 was reorganized as a high school. In 1863 Dalhousie was reconstituted as a university, primarily through co-operative Presbyterian efforts to improve higher education. The Presbyterians' willingness to renounce denominational control opened the way for expansion, and progress since then has been continuous.

An early emphasis on mathematics and the classics shifted to modern scientific studies, introduced during the latter 19th century. A medical faculty began in 1868; women were admitted in 1881; and the law school – the first to teach common law in the British Empire – was founded in 1883. Since 1879 the university has been financially assisted by such benefactors as George Munro, Sir William YOUNG and Dorothy Killam, enabling continual expansion of both the curriculum and the physical plant. In 1887 Dalhousie moved from its original downtown location to Forrest Hall, now part of a 24 ha campus. Today, Dalhousie provides over 100 degree and diploma programs in arts and science, management studies, the health professions, dentistry, law, medicine and graduate work. The university is world renowned for law, medical research and ocean studies. In 1985-86 it had 8143 full-time students.   LOIS KERNAGHAN

Dallaire, Jean-Philippe, painter, illustrator, professor (b at Hull, Qué 9 June 1916; d at Vence, France 27 Nov 1965). Raised in a working-class family of 15, he started drawing at age 11. Though he registered in various art classes, he was mostly self-taught. In Oct 1938, with the support of a Québec government grant, Dallaire went to Paris where he attended the Atelier d'art sacré, the Lhote studio and worked in his Montmartre studio. He became familiar with the work of Picasso and the surrealists and met Alfred PELLAN. Under the German Occupation (1940-44) he was prisoner at St-Denis. He taught painting at the Ecole des beaux-arts in Québec City 1946-52, worked for the NATIONAL FILM BOARD in Ottawa 1952-57, mostly illustrating animated films, then lived and painted in Montréal 1957-59. In 1959 he went to Europe to stay. He died of heart failure, thus ending prematurely a brilliant career. Dallaire's works show varied stylistic influences and are always recognized by their draftmanship and spontaneity in subject and use of colour.

MICHEL VINCENT CHEFF

Dally, Frederick, professional portrait and landscape photographer (b at Southwark, Eng 29 July 1838; d at Wolverhampton, Eng 28 July 1914). Educated at Christ's Hospital, London, Dally arrived in Victoria at the height of the Cariboo gold rush in 1862. He began business as a general merchant but in 1866 turned to photography. Prominent citizens, public buildings, local scenes and special events were all his subjects. In and around Victoria, he recorded the presence of the colonial government and the Royal Navy. A keen observer and amateur anthropologist, Dally photographed the coast and interior tribes and also collected Indian artifacts. Best known are his 1867-68 photographs of the CARIBOO ROAD and of the creeks and claims of the goldfields; many of these views were later used to produce engravings for the pictorial press. In Sept 1870 Dally sold his stock-in-trade and left Victoria. After studying at the Philadelphia Dental Coll, he returned to England to work in dental surgery.

JOAN M. SCHWARTZ

Daly, Kathleen Frances, painter (b at Napanee, Ont 28 May 1898). Daly studied in Toronto, Paris and New York. She travelled annually, 1924-30, on sketching trips to Europe. Her accomplished sense of line and rhythm, although closely associated with the work of the GROUP OF SEVEN, reveals an underlying confidence in her own stylistic interpretation and use of colour. She married George PEPPER in 1929 and they worked out of the Studio Building, Toronto, 1934-35. They painted together in all parts of Canada, and over a period of 25 years (1930-56) she showed work in all the major Canadian exhibitions, as well as in London, Eng.

ERIK J. PETERS

Daly, Thomas Cullen, filmmaker, film producer (b at Toronto 25 Apr 1918). Daly has been a key figure at the NATIONAL FILM BOARD since its inception. His influence on the NFB aesthetic has been considerable. After graduating from U of T, he went directly to the NFB in 1940, assisting Stuart Legg in the editing of *The World in Action* series. He was in charge of the famed Unit B 1950-64 and responsible for such classic films as *Corral* (1954), *City of Gold* (1957), *Universe* (1960) and *Lonely Boy* (1962), as well as the multi-screen *Labyrinth*, produced for EXPO 67. Since that time, he produced numerous NFB films, retiring in 1985.

PIERS HANDLING

Damselfly, thin-bodied, carnivorous insect with 2 pairs of long, membranous, narrow-based wings. Damselflies belong to order Odonata [Gk "toothed," referring to mouthparts], suborder Zygoptera. There are over 2800 known species worldwide, most in the tropics, 51 in Canada. Adults are brightly coloured, generally about 3 cm long, with mobile heads and large compound eyes. Larvae are aquatic, usually dark in colour, and characterized by 3 flat tail appendages, prob-

ably serving as gills. Larvae shoot out a peculiarly modified, toothed mouthpart (labium) to capture small aquatic insects and worms; adults sweep up small, flying insects with their legs. Adults usually occur near water. Eggs are placed in aquatic plants. Although some species may spend over 3 years as larvae, larval stages of Canadian species usually last only one year. Transformation to the adult occurs after the larva leaves the water. Adults live for a few weeks. *See also* DRAGONFLY.

G. PRITCHARD

Danby, Kenneth Edison, painter (b at Sault Ste Marie, Ont 6 Mar 1940). Ken Danby was at Toronto's Ontario College of Art 1958-60 and studied with J.W.G. MACDONALD. He began as an abstract painter, though a visit to an exhibition of Andrew Wyeth's work at Buffalo, NY, in 1962 confirmed his disenchantment with abstraction. He turned to painting carefully posed, snapshot-like views, often of rural Ontario seen in a strong light. Danby is best known for his study of anonymous sports figures: subjects from everyday life, which at the same time reveal his rare gift of creating unforgettable visual images. In *At the Crease* (1972) the masked ice-hockey goalie recalls knights of an earlier day; for many, the painting has become something of a national symbol. In 1983 and 1984 he prepared a series of watercolours on the Americas Cup and the Canadian athletes at the 1984 Sarajevo Olympics. In 1985 he was named to the governing board of the Canada Council.

JOAN MURRAY

Dance Education refers to education or training that leads to dancing, as opposed to "dance in education," which is limited to dance in elementary, secondary and post-secondary schools, where dance is considered to be a useful tool for physical and personality development. The distinction is not always clear. Some universities claim, for instance, that whether or not students emerge as dancers, they should be given the same intensity of training a dancer would be given; and conservatories are beginning to offer courses in dance notation, anatomy, music, and other related subjects not previously thought to be essential to dance training.

Dance, and consequently dance education, grew dramatically in Canada during the 1960s and 1970s. Dance as a performing art gained a large supportive audience, and thousands of young people now enrol in studios hoping to become professional dancers. Many more take dance classes for enjoyment or physical exercise. Ballroom dancing remains popular and franchised ballroom studios are still found in most Canadian cities. Ethnic, folk, and square dancing are encouraged through dance clubs and festivals of dance across the country. It was also during the 1960s and 1970s that the scope of dance expanded in educational institutions. Previously, university dance was limited to physical-education departments, with little emphasis on dance as an arts discipline. Taking the lead from the US, degree-granting programs have now been established in several Canadian universities, offering programs in dance notation, composition, analysis, history, criticism, pedagogy, and performance. YORK UNIVERSITY was the first to offer all these options, with an additional study stream in dance therapy. Its dance department was the first in the world to offer a graduate degree (MFA) in dance history and criticism. The UNIVERSITY OF WATERLOO offers a BA degree in dance, with a wide range of subject possibilities, including kinetic and historical dance research. SIMON FRASER UNIVERSITY grants a major degree to dancers and choreographers within an interdisciplinary framework. The UNIVERSITÉ DU QUÉBEC À MONTRÉAL awards a BA in dance, concentrating on the

training of teachers for primary and secondary levels of education. CONCORDIA UNIVERSITY emphasizes modern dance studies, leading to performance and choreography with a BA degree. Diplomas in dance are awarded at George Brown College/Lois Smith School of Dance, Ryerson Theatre Canadian College of Dance (both in Toronto), and Grant MacEwan Community College in Edmonton. The U de Montréal has a certificate program.

Dance in education is another important stream of dance study within Canadian universities. The Canadian Association of Health, Physical Education and Recreation (CAHPER), Dance Portfolio, has campaigned for the introduction of dance into primary and secondary schools. CAHPER is modelled after its American counterpart, AAHPER, but it is influenced by the teachings of Rudolf von Laban, who introduced dance into English schools shortly after WWII. The Dance and Child Conference, which was held in Edmonton in 1978, was a landmark contribution from this organization.

Almost every community in Canada has a studio where children and young adults may study ballet, tap, baton, jazz, ballroom and modern dance. But studio dance teaching has always existed without comprehensive controls on teaching standards. No licence is required to open a studio. The national Canadian Dance Teachers Association sets specific criteria for its own membership. The Dance in Canada Association, formed in 1973 to serve all aspects of professional dance, serves the large constituency of dance teachers through its information services.

Before the formation of Canada's 3 major ballet companies, excellent teachers in Canada helped provide the base for what has become a ballet tradition. Gerald Crevier and Elizabeth Leese of Montréal; Mildred Wickson, Bettina Byers and Boris VOLKOFF of Toronto; and June Roper and Mara McBirney in Vancouver trained dancers who joined the original companies of Les GRANDS BALLET CANADIENS, the NATIONAL BALLET OF CANADA and the ROYAL WINNIPEG BALLET. As these companies grew it was necessary to provide professional schools to ensure consistently well-trained dancers suitable to the repertory of each company. The NATIONAL BALLET SCHOOL, which has a resident day school, funded by government agencies and staffed by excellent teachers, has produced a number of very successful dancers for the National Ballet and for other companies throughout the world. Les Grands Ballets Canadiens provides an excellent training program through l'École supérieure de danse, and the professional program of the Royal Winnipeg Ballet produces well-trained dance personnel. Schools have also recently attached to modern-dance companies in Canada. The largest and first of these is the school of the TORONTO DANCE THEATRE. Others are affiliated with the ANNA WYMAN DANCE THEATRE, WINNIPEG'S CONTEMPORARY DANCERS and Le GROUPE DE LA PLACE ROYALE. There is also a school attached to Les BALLETS JAZZ DE MONTRÉAL, with satellite schools in Québec City and Toronto.

There are also professional schools not aligned with a specific company. The BANFF CENTRE FOR CONTINUING EDUCATION is a stimulating meeting ground for dancers and choreographers during summer months. The Canadian College of Dance is a teacher-training school emphasizing the Royal Academy of Dance syllabus and has been a part of the RYERSON POLYTECHNICAL INSTITUTE in Toronto for many years. The Lois Smith School of Dance joined George Brown College in Toronto to offer a 2-year professional curriculum. The National Choreographic Seminars brought choreographers, composers, musicians and dancers to creative heights in 1978 at York U, the Banff

Centre in 1980 and the Centre for the Arts at SFU in 1985. Summer sessions held annually at SFU and York attract professionals interested in intensive work in technique and dance composition.

Dance education has grown phenomenally, but a healthy future will depend on the development of choreographers, which has not kept stride with the increase of dance activity in Canada, as well as on more effective dance teaching in primary and secondary schools. Many educators are working to establish dance as an accepted study within schools, but little has been accomplished beyond the occasional inclusion of dance as a recreational activity in physical-education programs. A recognition of dance for its aesthetic and cultural potential within schools will ensure an informed, discriminating dance public for the future. GRANT STRATE

Dance History Dance has always been an integral part of Canadian Indian and Inuit life, giving ritual expression to the social and religious aspects of culture. A rich and complex dance heritage existed in Canada long before the arrival of the first explorers. The earliest written record of dancing in Canada is found in the diaries of explorer Jacques Cartier, who wrote in 1534 of being approached, along the shore of Chalem Bay, by 7 canoes bearing "wild men ... dancing and making many signs of joy and mirth." Explorers and settlers who followed him made frequent reference to Indian dance in their journals. However, the indigenous dance forms of Canada have had little influence on the country's theatre-dance traditions. Theatre dance has existed in Canada for more than 300 years, but the significant influences on its development have been largely external and closely linked with the influences most affecting the development of Canadian society as a whole: colonization by 2 invading cultures; the inhibiting force in Québec of a conservative church; massive immigration, particularly from Europe in the middle 19th and early 20th centuries; and, in the 20th century, the pervasive cultural influence of the US. However, the history of professional theatre dance in Canada dates from as recently as the 1930s, and 50 years later there still is not an identifiably Canadian dance character. Canadian dance is a mosaic of diverse traditions and influences.

The earliest imported dance influences were French. A masque, probably containing dance, was mounted in the harbour at PORT-ROYAL in 1606. Forty years later the Jesuit fathers were reporting the performance of a kind of ballet at the marriage of a soldier in Québec City, and the following Feb a ballet was given at the warehouse of the Compagnie des Cent-Associés. Ballet at this time was far closer to pageantry, blending movement with singing and acting, than to classical dance as it is known today. Audiences would have seen little intricate technical display or elevation. However, ballet technique and content evolved steadily throughout the 18th and early 19th centuries, and Canada was exposed to a variety of itinerant troupes, generally offering dance as a divertissement alongside plays. John Durang, one of the earliest professional dancers in the US, appeared with a circus company in Montréal and Québec City in the winter of 1797-98; comedy ballets were regularly given in Halifax in the same period; Jean Dauberval's *La Fille mal gardée*, first performed in Bordeaux in 1789, was seen in Canada for the first time in Québec City in 1816; the famous French dancer Mme Celeste (Keppler) visited Québec City and Montréal several times in the 1820s and 1830s; and in 1847 a highlight of the entertainment year in Canada East seems to have been a tour by the Petites Danseuses Viennoises, a troupe of 48 dancing children.

Canada continued to provide a fertile touring ground for foreign dancers in the late 19th and early 20th centuries. Loie Fuller performed her famous *Fire Dance* at the Vancouver Opera House in 1896; Anna Pavlova toured the country regularly from 1910; Ruth St Denis and Ted Shawn were frequent visitors between 1914 and 1924; the Diaghilev Ballet Russe company, with Vaslav Nijinsky, made its only Canadian appearance in Vancouver in 1917. Later, Martha Graham, Doris Humphrey and other pioneers of American modern dance made frequent tours; in the 1930s the itinerant Ballets Russes companies paid regular visits. Despite this frequent exposure to much of the best and most innovative theatre dance then available, professional dance in Canada was slow to develop, and until as late as the 1950s it was necessary for Canadians wishing to make a career in dancing to leave the country to do so.

The groundwork for professionalism in Canadian dance was laid in the 1930s by a handful of immigrant teachers, most of them women. In Vancouver, June Roper, from Rosebud, Texas, combined the theatrical flair of her Hollywood teacher, Ernest Belcher, and her experience as a star of supported adagio in Europe and the US to become, in the late 1930s, what *Dancemagazine* was later to call "North America's greatest starmaker." Over a 5-year period beginning late in 1934, she turned out over 60 dancers for the world's major professional companies, 8 of them for the Ballets Russes. In Ottawa at about the same time, the Boston-born Gwendolyn Osborne was doing the same thing on a smaller scale. Since this was a period in which Russian dance had captured the public imagination, many of the Canadians who went to the senior companies adopted Russianized names. Roper students Rosemary Deveson and Patricia Meyers, for instance, became Natasha Sobinova and Alexandra Denisova; Osborne student Betty Lowe became Ludmilla Lvova.

Boris VOLKOFF, born Boris Baskakoff in Tula, Russia, arrived in Toronto in 1929 from the US after a career as a character dancer in Russia and the Far East. He found work as a dancer and ballet master for live divertissements presented between films at a city movie theatre, and rapidly established himself as a teacher and choreographer. Among his pupils was young Mildred Herman, later to become, as Melissa Hayden, a star of the New York City Ballet. Volkoff's work as a choreographer of ice ballets for the Toronto Skating Club in the early 1930s first brought him to Canada in the noncompetitive dance section of the Berlin Olympiad. Three years later, in May 1939, he launched the Volkoff Canadian Ballet. It was Canada's first company by a matter of weeks. In June, the group that was to become the ROYAL WINNIPEG BALLET gave its first performance. The Winnipeg company was the creation of 2 immigrant English dance teachers, Gweneth LLOYD and Betty FARRALLY. Two of its first members were David Adams, later to become a soloist of Britain's Royal Ballet, and Paddy Stone, later to become a prominent variety choreographer in London. From the start, the company's founders opted to keep its membership small, dancing a repertoire designed to appeal to a broad audience.

The year 1948 was an important one in the development of dance in Canada. In Winnipeg, the Canadian Ballet Festival movement was launched; and in Montréal, REFUS GLOBAL was published. The festival was conceived by RWB manager David Yeddeau and Boris Volkoff as a means to give dancers in Canada a sense of what was happening in their art elsewhere in the country. The first festival was held in Winnipeg, and brought together 3 companies: the Winnipeg ballet, Volkoff's company, and a Montréal modern-

dance group led by the Polish-German immigrant Ruth Sorel. The following year, 10 companies met in Toronto. Over the 6 years of the movement's existence, the festivals became so popular, and so effective as vehicles of communication for the dance community, that Anatole Chujoy, editor of the NY publication *Dance News*, urged the adoption of the idea in the US, giving direct rise to the powerful and extensive regional ballet movement of today.

Refus Global was the title of a manifesto of cultural rebellion published in 1948 by a group of Québecois artists of various disciplines clustered around the automatiste painter Paul-Émile BORDUAS. The manifesto demanded an end to social, religious, and political restrictions on art in Québec. Its significance for dance lies in its influence on the thinking and artistic attitudes of 3 women who were to help shape modern dance in Québec: Françoise Sullivan (who both signed and contributed to the manifesto), Jeanne Renaud and Françoise Riopelle (both connected with the Borduas group). Sullivan spent several years in the late 1940s and early 1950s as a choreographer, turned to sculpture and painting, and returned to choreography in the late 1970s, establishing a company of her own and passing on the surrealist influence to a new generation of Québec choreographers. In 1962, Renaud and Riopelle, after each spending several years in Paris, founded a Montréal-based modern-dance group which, in 1966, under Renaud and Peter Boneham, a dancer from New York, became Le GROUPE DE LA PLACE ROYALE, a company that developed a reputation as one of the country's most audacious dance experimenters and a nursery of new dance thinking in Canada.

The success of the RWB in the late 1940s, and the first visit to Canada by the highly regarded Sadler's Wells company from London in 1949, convinced a group of Toronto dance enthusiasts that Toronto should have a professional company of its own. Acting on the advice of Sadler's Wells founder-director Ninette de Valois, the Torontonians invited the young English dancer-choreographer Celia FRANCA to observe the standard of Canadian dance at the 1950 festival, in Montréal. She was impressed by the enthusiasm she saw, returned to Canada the following year and, in the fall of 1951, launched the NATIONAL BALLET OF CANADA. From the start its structure and philosophy differed from those of the RWB; Franca set out to create a major ballet company in the European opera-house style, dancing a repertoire rooted firmly in the staples of the 19th-century classical ballet repertoire. Among the company's founder-members were David ADAMS and his wife Lois SMITH, who would become Canada's first nationally famous ballerina; Grant STRATE, who would later become immensely influential in the field of Canadian dance education; and Brian MACDONALD, whose active international career as a choreographer and artistic director would begin in 1953, following the abrupt curtailment of his dancing career because of an accident.

Canada's third major ballet company, Les GRANDS BALLETS CANADIENS, owes its origins to the launching of the French Canadian TV branch of the CBC in Montréal (1952). Ludmilla CHIRIAEFF, born into a Russian literary family in Riga, Latvia (1924), and raised in Berlin, arrived in Montréal with her family in 1952, after a dancing career in which she had performed with the de Basil Ballet Russe company and with various companies in Germany and Switzerland. She immediately found work choreographing short ballets for the French TV station's first music producer, Pierre MERCURE (*see* DANCE ON TELEVISION AND FILM). Soon she had created Les Ballets Chiriaeff, a performing ensemble that appeared many times on TV.

The company gave its first live performance in 1954, and after an enormous success with a Chiriaeff version of *Les Noces* (music: Stravinsky) at the Montréal Festival (1956) changed its name in 1958 to Les Grands Ballets Canadiens and concentrated on live performance. Like the early Lloyd works in Winnipeg, the ballets made for the Montréal company in its early years were carefully tailored to show the company to its best effect and to appeal to diverse audiences.

The launching of TV in Canada was one of the earliest responses of government to the Massey Commission (NATIONAL DEVELOPMENT IN THE ARTS, LETTERS AND SCIENCES), which had been appointed in 1949 and reported in 1951. A far more significant recommendation of the commission, for all the performing arts, was the establishment of the CANADA COUNCIL (1957). Implicit in its creation was a recognition, at the federal level, of the responsibility of government to provide state patronage of the arts, to establish and affirm a particularly Canadian culture, built from Canadian talents. All 3 of the ballet companies received grants in the council's first year – $100 000 to the National Ballet of Canada, $20 000 to the RWB and $10 000 to LGBC, out of a total for all the arts of $749 000. In the 1980-81 season, the council gave $5.6 million to dance alone, a 43-fold growth over 23 years and a reflection of the phenomenal explosion of dance activity that took place in the late 1960s and early 1970s. By 1986-87, $12.1 million was given to dance.

It was an explosion fostered in part by the very availability of funding for the arts. But it was also fostered by the new social climate of Canada. The 1960s, a time of social and intellectual liberalization in much of the Western world, had broken the tight bond between modern Canada and its prim past. The art form of the body attracted new audiences, new practitioners and new acceptability. At the same time, audiences broadened their receptiveness and increased their anticipation. Choreographers found a new freedom to create works in which form was content; the nonliteral and the abstract won a slowly widening respect. A series of modern-dance festivals was held in Toronto in the early 1960s, and by 1965 modern-dance companies existed in Winnipeg (Rachel Browne's WINNIPEG'S CONTEMPORARY DANCERS) and Vancouver (the PAULA ROSS DANCE CO). The beginnings of the TORONTO DANCE THEATRE, regarded today as one of the foremost modern-dance companies in Canada and the principal Canadian repository of the Martha Graham technique and tradition, can be traced to the establishment in 1966 of the New Dance Group of Canada by Patricia BEATTY, a Torontonian who had studied in the US with Graham and danced with Pearl Lang. In 1968 the NDGC was absorbed into the newly formed TDT, and Beatty joined 2 other Graham disciples, Canadian David EARLE and former Graham company member Peter RANDAZZO, an American, as co-director.

Lavish spending by government on the Centennial and Expo celebrations of 1967 gave an added boost to dance, as politicans realized the value of the arts in creating a national image. Federal make-work programs in the early 1970s gave further stimulus to the emergence of new, young dance-makers. In this period new modern-dance companies came to prominence, including ANNA WYMAN DANCE THEATRE, Regina Modern Dance Works, and a little later, the DANNY GROSSMAN DANCE CO; and Les BALLETS JAZZ DE MONTRÉAL, a lively hybrid, first made its mark. Alongside this burgeoning modern-dance scene, Canada's 3 senior ballet companies also experienced a period of unprecedented expansion and succcess. The Royal Winnipeg Ballet won medals in Paris and audience enthusiasm in the USSR; Les Grands Ballets Canadiens caught the pulse of the youth generation with Fernand Nault's setting of the rock opera *Tommy*; the National Ballet of Canada celebrated its coming-of-age by performing to great acclaim in London, Franca's hometown, and, a little later, acquired both Rudolf Nureyev (as a regular guest) and a sumptuous new Nureyev mounting of *The Sleeping Beauty*.

Inevitably, this growth, much of which had been stimulated by Canada Council funding, strained the council's resources, and as the world economy began to lose its buoyancy in the mid-1970s, economic cutbacks meant the council was unable to keep pace with the growth it had helped to foster. However, the council continues to play a major role in the 1980s in developing new programs and in answering the needs of modern dance companies and independent artists. In dance, the economic crisis of the 1970s split the community into 2 clear camps – those with adequate federal funding (the 3 major ballet companies, the 4 modern-dance companies, and the National Ballet School) and those without. In the late 1970s, conditions became tense. The Dance in Canada Assn, which had been created (1973) as a point of contact and a lobbying force for the Canadian dance community, had, by 1977, become the spokesman of the underprivileged groups, voicing outspoken criticism of the council's policies and priorities. Partly in protest against this, partly out of a desire to create a voice for professional dance, the 8 "senior" organizations broke away from DICA to form the Canadian Assn of Professional Dance Organizations. The rifts have since healed and the 2 groups act as lobbying and service agencies for further constituents. DICA is the grassroots service organization for the broad Canadian dance community, producing a quarterly magazine, *Dance in Canada*, a monthly newsletter and performance calendar. It organizes annual national conferences. In 1987 it collaborated with the National Arts Centre to organize the first Canadian Dance Festival. CAPDO concerns itself with professional companies and continues to address major issues concerning the dance community in Canada.

In the late 1970s and early 1980s, the most marked phenomenon of Canadian dance was the emergence of independent CHOREOGRAPHY, owing partly to new financial pressures, partly to the desire of young creators to make dance outside the confines of a company, and partly to the influence of the New York modernist movement. Some choreographers, Marie Chouinard, Julie West and Margie Gillis, have tried to make their way alone; some, such as members of the Toronto Independent Dance Enterprise or Terminal City Dance Research and Vancouver's (later Special Delivery Moving Theatre) and EDAM (Experimental Dance and Music), formed themselves into loose, exploratory ensembles. Others, such as Judith Marcuse, Karen Jamieson, and Lee Eisler and Neilson Gray, co-founders of Vancouver's Jumpstart, formed companies on which to base their work. In Québec, where the liberating influences of the 1970s were accentuated by a politico-cultural revolution uniquely French Canadian, the experimentalism of the 1980s had an enormous vitality, as young choreographers such as Paul-André Fortier, Édouard Lock, Daniel Leveillé and Jinette Laurin tested the limits of new freedoms of subject, style and approach.

The education of dancers and of choreographers began to take on a new significance at this time. Dance schools of varying quality have existed in Canada since at least the 18th century, but only since the establishment of the senior ballet companies in the 1950s was the training of professional dancers given serious attention. Even after the country's 3 companies had become es-tablished, it was still common for Canadian dancers of exceptional talent to go abroad. Lynn SEYMOUR and Jennifer Penney both left BC for distinguished careers with the Royal Ballet in London; Wayne Eagling, of Montréal, did the same; and Reid Anderson, from New Westminster, BC, joined Annette AV PAUL, upon his return to Canada in 1986, at the head of the newly formed Ballet BC and assumed sole artistic direction the following year. However, the development of professional dance schools (*see* DANCE EDUCATION)and the sudden expansion of interest and activity in dance in the 1970s lessened this trend.

The pre-eminent institution for ballet training in Canada is the NATIONAL BALLET SCHOOL, which has won international recognition for the thoroughness of its training and the quality of the dancers it produces. Graduates have frequently won awards in international competition: most notable have been Karen KAIN (silver prizewinner, women's solo, Moscow, 1973), her partner Frank AUGUSTYN (together they won first prize for the *pas de deux* the same year) and Kevin Pugh (silver medal, Moscow, 1981). Other important ballet training programs are attached to the Royal Winnipeg Ballet. One of its most distinguished graduates is Evelyn HART, who won the women's solo gold medal at the Varna competition in 1980. Les Grands Ballets Canadiens produced Sylvie Kinal-Chevalier, winner of the silver medal at Varna (1976) at the age of 17.

Though Canadian dancers have made considerable impact abroad, Canadian choreographers have made little impact internationally, and their development was given little serious attention until the late 1970s. In ballet, the emphasis on imported work and (in the case of the National Ballet of Canada) on remounted classics of the 19th century provided a clear reflection of the early tastes of the Canadian audience. The market for the home-made has never been large, and the reluctance of those in charge of the major companies to devote large amounts of time, space, and money to the development of choreographic talent is understandable. Without that commitment, however, it will be impossible for Canadian dance to establish itself as anything more than a branch plant, albeit a diverse one, of the choreographic creativity of other cultures.

Arnold SPOHR, who took control of the RWB in 1958 and directed it to international glories, was responsible for encouraging the early work of a number of choreographers, particularly Brian MACDONALD and Norbert VESAK. Les Grands Ballets Canadiens later came to give extensive regular display to the work of Macdonald and, to a lesser extent, other Canadian choreographers (primarily Fernand NAULT). The National Ballet of Canada has always had a policy of encouraging its own (in the company's first decade both David Adams and Grant Strate were given a number of opportunities to choreograph), and in the late 1970s an interesting group of choreographers (Ann Ditchburn, James Kudelka and Constantin PATSALAS) began to emerge from the company's sporadically held choreographic workshops. Even so, the lack of opportunity for young choreographers to learn their craft and experiment with technique within the country's major companies is a recurring complaint. It was not until the institution of the dance program at York University in the early 1970s and Grant Strate's introduction of the National Choreographic Seminars at York (1978) and at the BANFF CENTRE for Continuing Education (1980), that there was any concentrated or responsible attempt to develop Canada's indigenous choreographic talent. Giving extra stimulus to the emergence of new creators are 2 national choreographic awards, presented annually by the Chalmers Foundation (Toronto), and the Clifford

E. Lee Foundation (Calgary), and both the Canada Council and the Ontario Arts Council make regular grant awards to underwrite developing choreographers.

The growing achievements of Canadian choreographers, particularly in the field of modern dance, are marked by a series of new-work commissions, both at Expo 86 and at the Olympic Arts Festival in Calgary.   MAX WYMAN

Dance, Modern Unlike classical dance, with its adherence to academic principles of movement developed through past centuries, modern dance stresses individual expression and personal style. Canadian modern dance has derived from 2 powerful influences, European and American. Before the founding of TORONTO DANCE THEATRE (1968), virtually all modern dance in Canada owed its origin to central and eastern European traditions, particularly the work of Rudolf von Laban. Laban, an influential theorist, viewed dance as an enriching and ennobling art experience.

Elizabeth Leese was the first of several exiles from Europe's political turmoil to bring this seriousness of purpose to Canadian dance. Leese joined Boris VOLKOFF's Toronto-based ballet company in 1939 and then, in early 1940, moved to Montréal to open her own school. In 1944, Ruth Sorel also established a school in Montréal. She had studied and danced with Mary Wigman, herself a pupil of Laban and a leading figure in European modern dance. Leese and Sorel played important roles in the early years of the annual Canadian Ballet Festival (1948-54), which brought together dancers and choreographers from across the country. They created a vibrant atmosphere in Montréal in which a second generation of modern dancers could grow. Over 20 years after the arrival of Leese and Sorel in Montréal, Jeanne Renaud and ex-ballet dancer Peter Boneham founded Le GROUPE DE LA PLACE ROYALE. Le Groupe, which has made its home in Ottawa since 1977, keeps alive a fiercely cerebral approach to modern dance. The European tradition continues in the work of such Montréal choreographers as Paul-André FORTIER and Marie Chouinard.

The European influence also dominated early modern dance in Toronto. Its major practitioners, Bianca Rogge and Yone Kvietys, were both eastern European refugees, and with a former pupil of Leese's, Nancy Lima Dent, they mounted Canada's first modern-dance festivals (1960-62). Among Rogge's pupils was Judy Jarvis, who

The Stand, which premiered in 1987, was choreographed by Anna Wyman (*courtesy Anna Wyman Dance Theatre*).

Tango Accelerando (1987), choreographed by Ginette Laurin. Les Grands Ballets Canadiens was Canada's third major ballet company (*courtesy Les Grands Ballets Canadiens/photo by Andrew Oxenham*).

studied in Germany with Mary Wigman. On her return she established the Judy Jarvis Dance and Theatre Co, which, throughout the 1970s, presented the spare and haunting vision of human existence that was Wigman's trademark. Although her company eventually foundered, Jarvis remained an inspirational teacher until her death in 1986. Yone Kvietys, a less flamboyant figure than Rogge, gave classes to Donald Himes, Susan Macpherson, and David EARLE, and so could be called an indirect progenitor of Toronto Dance Theatre.

The TDT heralded the appearance of the more personal expression of American modern dance, which places less emphasis on formal training. Rachel Browne, a former soloist with the ROYAL WINNIPEG BALLET, left that company in 1964 and by the early 1970s had created the highly skilled and versatile company, WINNIPEG'S CONTEMPORARY DANCERS. WCD has helped develop the careers of freelance choreographers Anna Blewchamp and Judith Marcuse, both of whom are trained in classical and modern dance. Blewchamp's training in the technique of American modern dance pioneer Martha Graham is obvious in many of her works of which *Arrival of All Time* is an enduring example. Marcuse's style is more eclectic and continues to be seen in the work of her own Dance Repertory Company of Canada.

The Graham influence played an important part in the formation of Toronto Dance Theatre since its 3 co-founders, Patricia BEATTY, Peter RANDAZZO and David Earle were trained in the Graham technique.

More individualistic expressions of modern dance were introduced in Vancouver by Paula Ross and Anna Wyman. The company Ross established in the late 1960s had fallen into abeyance by 1987, but her strongly personal and emotional statements in dance, rooted in humanistic values, made a distinct impact. With a background in ballet and show-dancing, Ross has experimented freely with a variety of modern movement styles. Wyman turned to modern dance after a successful professional career in ballet. Settling in Canada in 1967 she soon began to present groups of dancers in her choreography, which ranges freely through a variety of contemporary movement styles.

The modern dance movement in Canada was significantly stimulated in the early 1970s by formation of a dance department at York U. Although its founding head, Grant STRATE, came from a ballet tradition his dance interests always tended toward experimentation and innovation. He proved a visionary and inspirational teacher at York, attracting distinguished artists to the faculty and encouraging the appearance, often for the first time in Canada, of notable American modern-dance artists. In a sense, 40 years of American dance history was compressed into

less than 10 in Toronto. Early graduates from York constituted a new generation of dancers and choreographers for Canadian modern dance. As early as 1974, York students Marcie Radler and Andrea Smith founded Dancemakers, a versatile modern dance repertory company that has provided an outlet for both merging and established choreographers.

The American influence was felt most keenly in Toronto, although it spread to other centres. Toronto-born Jennifer Mascall, a former participant in New Yorker Douglas Dunn's postmodernist experiments, took her interest in improvisation to Vancouver, where Iris Garland had been exposing her students at Simon Fraser to the work of a wide range of American modernist choreographers and where Helen Goodwin had been doing the same thing on a smaller scale at University of British Columbia. The Graham tradition turned up in Calgary with Elaine Bowman, formerly with TDT, at Dancers Studio West; in Edmonton with Brian Webb, who had studied extensively with Graham's first male partner, Erick Hawkins; and for several years in Halifax, where until 1987 Jeanne Robinson directed Nova Dance Theatre.

In the mid-1970s Danny Grossman who, under the name Danny Williams, had been a leading member of New York's acclaimed Paul Taylor Dance company, settled in Canada, began to choreograph and founded what quickly became one of Canada's busiest and most popular modern dance troupes.

In the 1980s a younger generation of choreographers was willing to draw from a wide range of styles and influences to evolve personal approaches to dance. Traditional distinctions between modern dance and classical ballet were often forgotten as dancers and choreographers from each school shared ideas and attempted to learn from each other. Classical ballet companies such as the NATIONAL BALLET OF CANADA and Les GRANDS BALLETS CANADIENS invited modern dance choreographers to work for them – Christopher HOUSE, Edouard LOCK and Ginette Laurin for Les GBC; Danny Grossman and Robert DESROSIERS for the National.

Modern dance in Canada, as in other countries, tends to be amorphous and turbulent. Companies come and go. Dancers and choreographers often work independently. Toronto's 15

Peter Ottmann and Ann Ditchburn dancing "Love's got to breathe and fly," from *A Moving Picture*, choreographed by Ann Ditchburn (*courtesy Rhombus Media Inc, photo by Anita Olanick*).

Dance Lab, opened in 1972 by former National Ballet dancers Lawrence and Miriam Adams, offered a forum for these independents. Similar venues opened up across Canada to provide a network of low-cost performing spaces for the growing number of free-lance choreographers and solo performers. Toronto's Danceworks and Montreal's Tangente became 2 of the most important of these venues. During the late 1970s Montréal became a noted centre for modern dance experimentation, following the path opened by companies such as Le Groupe de la Place Royale and Groupe Nouvelle Aire. Choreographers such as Daniel Leveillé, Ginette Laurin and Edouard Lock began to attract popular followings. Lock founded his own company, La La La Human Steps, as a vehicle for his gangling, loose-limbed, punk-influenced style. The vitality of the Montréal scene has led to the holding of international festivals of new dance in Montréal featuring local choreographers alongside those of their counterparts from across Canada and leading exponents from abroad. A notable development was the increased accessibility of the new dance to a broader audience. An increased emphasis on production values and an overt desire to entertain was aptly demonstrated by the Robert Desrosiers Dance Theatre which provides spectacular interpretations of Desrosiers's surrealistic theatrical vision. Under the artistic direction of Tedd Robinson, assisted by Murray Darroch, Winnipeg's Contemporary Dancers also moved in the late 1980s towards a flamboyantly whimsical and theatrical style. In Vancouver Karen Jamieson, who as Karen Rimmer had been a key figure in the experimental Terminal City Dance company, continued to produce emotionally charged work. Many of these creators have chosen to explore other media beyond movement. Toronto Independent Dance Enterprise, which often uses an improvisational creative approach, uses acting techniques and spoken text along with movement. Choreographer Conrad Alexandrowicz has also experimented with new ways of integrating words and movement. The rapid development of electronic technology has also been exploited by a number of experimental choreographers, by the use of video within the body of their work and by drawing live musicians directly into the centre of a performance as quasi-dancers. The wide variety of approaches now adopted by Canadian choreographers and their continuing urge to explore fresh territory testifies to the vitality of their art and to the development of distinctly personal forms of expression. From its heavy reliance on outside sources of creative stimulation Canadian modern dance has found its own multifaceted and self-confident identity.

GRAHAM JACKSON AND MICHAEL CRABB

Dance of the Happy Shades (Toronto, 1968), Alice MUNRO's first book of stories, established her as one of Canada's most accomplished contemporary writers. Her preferred settings, always painstakingly realized, are recognizably southwestern Ontarian; her themes include the gaps in communication within families and the pressures exerted by memory and the past. Munro's powerful realism, her precision of style and her eye for revelatory detail place her stories among the finest being written in English today. *Dance of the Happy Shades* was translated into French as *Danse des ombres* (Montréal, 1979).   NEIL BESNER

Dance on Television and Film offers an unsurpassed degree of public exposure to dance. Although the small two-dimensional image lacks the impact and viewer involvement of a live performance, television and film can offer visions impossible to duplicate on the theatrical stage. Recently, video has begun to play an important

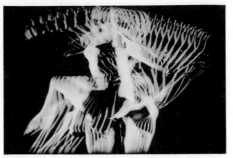

Still from Norman McLaren's film *Pas de Deux* (1968) (*courtesy National Film Board of Canada*).

role on a smaller local level, offering the opportunity to risk experimentation and to document lesser-known artists and dance companies.

Dance first became a regular feature on television in Québec in the 1950s, under the direction of producer-composer Pierre MERCURE, in series such as "L'Heure du concert." Les Grands Ballets Chiriaeff (later Les Grands Ballets Canadiens) appeared on TV more than 300 times between 1952 and 1958. CBC television was 2 years old when the NATIONAL BALLET OF CANADA made its TV debut, and series such as "Musicamera," "Festival" and "Spectrum" have helped secure a place for dance on TV.

The 2 great innovators were producer-director Norman CAMPBELL and Norman MCLAREN, who was best known for his film features created for the NATIONAL FILM BOARD. Campbell successfully combined dance and TV with smooth and mobile camerawork, well-placed close-ups and imaginative use of special effects. His 1965 *Romeo and Juliet*, featuring Earl Kraul and Veronica TENNANT, won the Prix René Barthelemy for artistic excellence at the International Television Festival of Monte Carlo. His 1970 Emmy-winning *Cinderella* (1968) used slow motion and trick photography to enhance the ethereal qualities of the fairies. Unlike these ballets, which were recorded in slightly remodelled studios, Rudolf Nureyev's Emmy-winning *The Sleeping Beauty* (1972) was a stage performance recorded by 6 cameras. Norman McLaren experimented boldly with the dancing figure. His remarkable *Pas de Deux* (1967) displayed dancers Margaret Mercier and Vincent Warren of Les Grands Ballets Canadiens in "memory images" – individual frames were exposed up to 11 times and overlapped. The dancers, dressed in white and lit from behind as silhouettes, were filmed against a black backdrop. In his *Ballet Adagio* (1972) McLaren filmed and projected the dancers 4 times more slowly than normal.

Other stage dances impressively mounted by CBC include James KUDELKA's *A Party* (1978); the 1982 presentation of Agnes de Mille's *Fall River Legend* (1980) with the ROYAL WINNIPEG BALLET; Ann Ditchburn's *Mad Shadows* (1979); an energetic dance through Canada's native and pioneer roots by Les FEUX FOLLETS and choreographed by Alan LUND; and Campbell's 3 *Swan Lakes*, 1956, 1961 and 1965, the first of which was the first full-length ballet on CBC. Two particularly important works in the development of dance on TV were *Dancin' Man* (1980) by dancer-choreographer Jeff Hyslop and director-producer Bernard Picard, and Brian Macdonald's *Catulli Carmina* (1981). *A Moving Picture* (1987) by Ann Ditchburn combined animation and dancing and included trick photography. A new CBC series scheduled for early 1988, called "Dance Makers," was also to have a cinematic release.

Among the many film documentaries are Grant Munro's *Tour en l'air*, a 1973 study of David and

Anne-Marie Holmes; *Gala*, the NFB's film of the historic 1981 Canadian Dance Spectacular at Ottawa's National Arts Centre, which gathered 8 of Canada's top professional companies; *For the Love of Dance*, an NFB film about the daily activities of those 8 companies; *Young and Just Beginning – Pierre*, a sentimental 1979 study of a young boy entering the National Ballet School; Norman Campbell's *The Looking Glass People*, a 1962 behind-the-scenes look at the National Ballet; and a 1965 CFTO special, *Inside the National Ballet*. The works of modern-dance companies, such as Entre-Six and the DANNY GROSSMAN DANCE COMPANY, receive a more documentary approach from the CBC. An inspired exception was a modern *L'Oiseau de Feu* by Hugo Romero, filmed in 1981 and produced for Radio Canada with dancers Claudia Moore, Louis Robitaille and Jean-Marc Lebeau and incorporating animation and electronic effects. It was awarded an International Emmy. CBC Vancouver director Keith Christie has made 2 nationally aired programs on the ANNA WYMAN DANCE THEATRE, *Klee Wyck: A Ballet for Emily* (1975) and *Anna in Graz* (1974). Recent films include *Onegin* by Norman Campbell (1986); and *Blue Snake* by Rhombus Media (1986) with the National Ballet.   PAT KAISER

Dandelion [Fr, *dent-de-lion*, "lion's tooth"], perennial, herbaceous plant of family Compositae or Asteraceae. Over 1000 species have been named. Because dandelions reproduce without fertilization, innumerable variants have arisen. Common dandelion (*Taraxacum officinale*) has many names including blowball, faceclock, dumble-dor (Newfoundland) and pissenlit (Québec). Each mature flowerhead produces approximately 180 wind-dispersed, seedlike achenes. Preferring moist, grassy places and disturbed sites, dandelions occur from sea level to subalpine elevations. This European native has become a tenacious farm and garden WEED. However, its golden yellow flowers provide nectar for innumerable pollinating insects; its achenes, food for many birds. Much of the plant is edible. Leaves are high in vitamin A, iron, phosphorus, calcium and potassium, and are among the best sources of copper known. Valued for its medicinal properties, the dandelion has been used to stimulate the kidneys and to combat liver disorders, weak digestion, anemia and eczema.

BERNARD S. JACKSON

The dandelion (*Taraxacum officinale*) is a tenacious weed (*artwork by Claire Tremblay*).

Danes The first Danish contact with Canada resulted from the voyage of Captain Jens MUNK, who had been dispatched by King Christian IV of Denmark in the early 17th century to find the NORTHWEST PASSAGE. On 7 Sept 1619 Munk landed at the mouth of the Churchill R, named it Munk's Bay and claimed the land for the Danish king, calling it "Nova Dania" — New Denmark. For many years thereafter, individual Danes, mainly sailors, migrated to N America. There are early accounts of Danes working as trappers in Canada but few traces of their experiences. In the 1860s, however, Danes in large numbers joined the massive European migration to N America. The 1961 census enumerated 85 473 Canadian residents of Danish origin, although by 1986 the estimated number had declined to 39 950. By 1987 fewer than 100 Danes immigrated to Canada.

Migration and Settlement From 1870 to WWI, of 20 000 Danish immigrants, some migrated directly from Denmark and others from the US. There was a large increase in the population of Denmark in the 19th century (as there was in all of Europe) and many Danes preferred to seek better opportunities overseas. Political and religious events also inspired many Danes to migrate. Danes have been the only Scandinavian group to settle in large numbers in the Maritimes.

In 1893 some Danes settled also in London, Ont; in 1924 Danish immigrants established the community of Pass Lake near Thunder Bay. Most of the first Danish settlers on the Canadian prairies arrived via the American midwest and northwest.

Between 1951 and 1960, thousands of Danes, attracted to Canada by the postwar economic opportunities, emigrated. The 1961 census enumerated more than double the number of Canadians of Danish origin to that listed in the 1951 census. Most headed directly for the cities of BC, Alberta and Ontario. According to the 1981 census (the last year for which figures are available), these 3 provinces each had 14 000 to 17 000 inhabitants of Danish origin. Many postwar Danish immigrants have returned to Denmark.

Social and Cultural Life Most of the Danish Canadian cultural activities in Canada have been at the local community level. In 1981 the Federation of Danish Associations in Canada was established to co-ordinate the activities of 30 member-organizations. Danish Lutheran congregations, direct offshoots of congregations established in the US, played a major role in the small Danish communities of the prairies. Most of these Danish Canadian congregations were affiliated with the United Danish Synod, which became a part of the American Lutheran Church in 1960. All have lost their original Danish-language identity. Danish immigrants arriving after WWII have established a number of Danish Lutheran congregations that are not affiliated with any N American Lutheran synod but maintain direct ties with the state Evangelical Lutheran Church of Denmark.

Four Danish-language periodicals have existed since 1893, 2 of which (*Modersmaalet* and the Federation of Danish Assn's *Newsletter*) still exist. Danish Canadians have established a number of organizations to serve their social and cultural interests, eg, choirs, sports clubs, and various kinds of social events.

Group Maintenance Although Danes have lived in Canada for over a century, their group identity is not as strong as other ethnic groups of the same size. Many of the early Danish immigrants to the prairies, and their children, had lived in the US and had generally acculturated into the N American way of life before arriving in Canada.

LENNARD SILLANPAA

Reading: F.M. Paulsen, *Danish Settlements on the Canadian Prairies* (1974).

Chemical fire resulting from the train derailment at Mississauga, Ont, Nov 1979 (*courtesy Canada Wide Feature Services Ltd*).

Dangerous Goods, Movement of Some materials and products that move by rail, ship, air or highway within Canada or across our national boundaries are classified as dangerous goods because they are flammable, explosive, toxic or potentially harmful to people or the environment. Until 1985 their movement was not well controlled. Several well-published incidents involving dangerous goods, which forced the evacuation of thousands of people or caused millions of dollars worth of environmental cleanup work, led the federal government to introduce the Transportation of Dangerous Goods Act, whose regulations became effective in Ontario 1 July 1985, and in the rest of Canada 1 Feb 1986. Because these regulations apply only to international or interprovincial movement of goods, parallel provincial and territorial regulations were introduced to control highway transport within individual provinces and territories.

Manufacturers, shippers and transporters of dangerous goods are responsible for proper packaging, labelling and handling. Documentation must be prepared to allow the movement of goods to be traced from the moment they are packaged until they arrive at their destination. Certain government authorities must be notified in advance of their movement. Violation of the regulations can result in fines of up to $100 000. R.C. MACKENZIE

Daniells, Roy, professor, poet, critic (b at London, Eng 6 Apr 1902; d at Vancouver 13 Apr 1979). Educated at UBC and U of T, Daniells taught for most of his career at UBC, retiring in 1974. He was one of the editors of the *Literary History of Canada* (1965), and he wrote numerous insightful articles on a wide range of Canadian poetry and fiction. His major critical work was on Milton (1963). His 2 books of poetry, *Deeper Into the Forest* (1948) and *The Chequered Shade* (1963), show his mastery of the sonnet form and his sophisticated technical skills. NEIL BESNER

Danny Grossman Dance Company, a Toronto-based modern dance troupe founded (1975) by Danny GROSSMAN, had grown from 2 members to a company of 14 by 1987. The company became fully professional in 1978 and since 1979 has made annual tours to the US, Europe, S America and Israel. All works performed by the company are choreographed by Grossman. One of his better known pieces is *Higher*, choreographed (1975) to music by Ray Charles, and originally performed by Grossman and Judith Hendin. In 1978, Danny Grossman was awarded the Jean A. Chalmers Award in Choreography. His works have been included in the repertoire of the National Ballet of Canada, Le Grande Ballet du Canada, Theatre Ballet of Canada and the Paris Opera Ballet. SUSAN PEDWELL

Dansereau, Mireille, filmmaker (b at Montréal 19 Sept 1943). Dansereau directed the first dramatic feature film made by a woman in Québec, *La Vie*

rêvée (1972). After studying at U de M, she obtained an MA in film and TV in London, Eng, where *Compromise* (1968) won first prize at the 1969 National Student Film Festival. Returning to Québec she helped form the Association coopérative des productions audio-visuelles, which produced *La Vie rêvée*. She worked for the NFB, directing 2 feature documentaries, *J'me marie, j'me marie pas* (1973) and *Famille et variations* (1977). She returned to the private sector to make *L'Arrache-Coeur* (1979), a bleak, uncompromising examination of a marriage in crisis, and *Le Sourd dans la ville* (1987), a dark, disturbing adaptation of Marie-Claire Blais's novel, centered on a rooming house full of marginal people.

PIERS HANDLING

Dansereau, Pierre, ecologist, educator (b at Montréal 5 Oct 1911). Educated at the Institut agricole d'Oka, Qué, and at Geneva (DSc 1939), Dansereau worked at the Montréal Botanical Garden 1939-50 and taught at U of Michigan before becoming dean of science at the U de M in 1955. He was professor of botany and geography at Columbia U 1961-68 (and, at the same time, was adjunct director of the New York Botanical Garden) and joined UQAM as professor of ecology in 1971. Dansereau's 1957 book *Biogeography, an Ecological Perspective* won him an international reputation, and he later popularized his theme in the influential CBC Massey lectures "Inscape and Landscape" (1972). He transmitted important scientific and humane values to his students and sought to combine the strengths of technical scholarship in English with the broader emphases of the French tradition, notably Teilhard de Chardin's concept of mind as part of the continuum of evolution. He is a member of the Royal Society, Companion of the Order of Canada and has received the Molson Prize (1975), the Killam Prize (1985), the Ordre national du Québec (1985) and the Lawson Medal from the Canadian Botanical Assn (1986). *See also* BIOGEOGRAPHY.

DONALD J.C. PHILLIPSON

Dark Harbour, located on the W side of GRAND MANAN I, NB, is the only suitable haven for fishing craft along the island's western shore, which is dominated by high cliffs. It is relatively isolated from the communities on the more hospitable eastern side facing the Bay of Fundy. In the 1840s Dark Harbour's potential as a natural deep-water port was recognized by marine surveyors, along with its commercial viability as a fishing centre; but except for sporadic seasonal fishing stations, it drew little attention until the close of the 19th century. A sizable smoked-fish operation was established on a natural break wall of Dark Harbour in the 1890s, and though lobster and herring fisheries have been an integral part of its history, the worldwide reputation of Dark Harbour rests on the presence along its rocky shoreline of dulse, a popular edible seaweed. Still relatively unpopulated, Dark Harbour offers a unique landscape and has become a popular draw to tourists because of its natural beauty. ROGER P. NASON

Dartmouth, NS, City, inc 1961, pop 65 243 (1986c), 63 667 (1981c), is located on the eastern side of Halifax Harbour. Founded in 1750, the community developed slowly, its early importance being to supply farm produce to HALIFAX. The agricultural base was later diversified, beginning in 1826 with construction of the Shubenacadie Canal system, intended to connect Halifax Harbour with the Bay of Fundy. The scheme subsequently failed, but the availability of waterpower led to the establishment of some light industry by mid-century.

Although a sugar refinery (1883) and an oil refinery (1916) were precursors, rapid development did not begin until after WWII. A ferry service crossing Halifax Harbour has operated

continually since 1752, but the completion of the first cross-harbour bridge in 1955 (a second was opened in 1970) greatly facilitated access from Halifax. This coincided with the expansion of several existing industries and resulted in a housing boom and new industrial development. Since then, Dartmouth has taken advantage of geographic and economic factors to become the light industrial and commercial centre of the Maritimes. Burnside Industrial Park, opened in 1968, is the largest such complex in Atlantic Canada, catering predominantly to sales and service industries. The BEDFORD INSTITUTE OF OCEANOGRAPHY is a world-renowned research facility, and the NOVA SCOTIA RESEARCH FOUNDATION CORP and the Nova Scotia Hospital are also located in Dartmouth. A modern highway network circumvents the revitalized downtown core and connects Dartmouth's growing residential and industrial districts. Excellent medical, educational, recreational and shopping facilities make the "City of Lakes" a popular place in which to live and work.
LOIS KERNAGHAN

Reading: J.P. Martin, *The Story of Dartmouth* (1957).

Dartmouth Lakes are 25 separate lakes located within the city of DARTMOUTH, NS, across the harbour from HALIFAX. Formed by Pleistocene glaciation about 15 000 years ago, they range in area from 1 to 140 ha.

Long before British settlement of Halifax in 1749, the principal lakes (Banook, Micmac and Charles) had been used for thousands of years by the seminomadic MICMAC as part of a transprovince canoe route from Chebucto (Halifax) to Cobequid (head of the Bay of Fundy). The same 3 lakes formed a critical part of the ill-fated Shubenacadie Canal, constructed 1826-61 but abandoned 1870 because of railway competition. Sections of the canal and deteriorating locks remain today. The lakes have been a water supply since settlement. Prior to 1950 an ice-cutting industry flourished and icehouses were common along the shores. The lakes have played an important recreational role for over a century. In the 19th century, residents from Halifax crossed the harbour by ferry to take part in skating, hockey, curling and iceboating. Dartmouth's Starr Manufacturing Co was world famous for its innovative metal skates. Around the turn of the century, canoeing and rowing became popular and regattas were started by newly formed boat clubs. Five boat clubs are active today and Lk Banook is the site of many regional, national and international competitive paddling events. Swimming, waterskiing and cross-country skiing, fishing and sailing have also become popular activities in more recent years.

Despite extensive urbanization in the city during the past 30 years, the Dartmouth Lks are relatively clean, and pollution only occasionally interferes with recreational use. Recognizing the tremendous value of the lakes to all residents, the city gives high priority to lake protection, and is assisted in this task by a unique volunteer organization known as the Dartmouth Lakes Advisory Board.
D.C. GORDON

Daudelin, Charles, sculptor (b at Granby, Qué 1 Oct 1920). He worked in Beaugrand's studio 1939-41, went to the École du meuble in Montréal, and made 2 stays in New York (1943, 1948), working with Fernand Léger and Henri Laurens. He taught at the École des beaux-arts in Montréal until 1967. The recipient of first prizes in the Concours artistiques du Québec for painting (1946) and sculpture (1964), Daudelin has created important pieces for the National Arts Centre (Ottawa), Palais de Justice (Montréal), parliamentary fountain in Charlottetown and the Church of St-Thomas d'Aquin in St-Lambert. He also created

the reredos in the Sacred Heart Chapel of Montréal's Église Notre-Dame and the visual conceptualization of Montréal's Mont-Royal metro station and a fountain on Québec Place in Paris. Daudelin has made marionettes, created stage sets and illustrated several books. His work is held in private and public collections at home and abroad. He received the Lynch-Staunton Award from the Canada Council (1972), the Prix Philippe-Hébert from the St-Jean-Baptiste Society of Montréal (1981) and the Prix Émile-Borduas Award from the Québec government (1985).
MICHEL CHAMPAGNE

Daudelin, Robert, archivist, producer (b at West Shefford, Qué 31 May 1939). In 1960 Daudelin and some other Québecois movie lovers repudiated the Catholic-morality approach which dominated movie criticism to found a magazine called *Objectif*; he was its editor in chief until it folded in 1967. In 1963 he also took on responsibility for the Canadian film section of the International Film Festival of Montreal. In 1965, he became assistant director of the festival. Daudelin published the first monograph on Québec cinema: *Vingt Ans de cinéma au Canada français* (1967). In 1969 Daudelin became the first director-general of the Conseil québécois pour la diffusion du cinéma. He established its policies and animation program and created its collection of monographs, "Cinéastes du Québec."
PIERRE VÉRONNEAU

Dauphin, Man, Town, pop 8875 (1986c), 8971 (1981c), inc as a village 1898, as a town 1910, is located in SW Manitoba, 310 km by road NW of Winnipeg, on the Vermilion R. It is a prosperous supply, distribution and transportation centre, serving a rich agricultural region stretching from the Saskatchewan border E to Lks Manitoba and Winnipeg and N to Swan R. It is also a government administration centre and has an active tourist trade. LA VÉRENDRYE first visited the area in the 1730s and gave the name Dauphin, for the eldest son of the king of France, to a post in the area (1741). Settlers from Ontario arrived in the 1880s, and the villages of Old Dauphin and Gartmore developed near the present townsite, which was established after the arrival of the Lk Manitoba Ry (1896). UKRAINIANS set up one of their earliest rural settlements in the area (1896-98) and still maintain a strong sense of their cultural past. Dauphin initiated Canada's annual National Ukrainian Festival in the early 1960s.
ALAN F.J. ARTIBISE

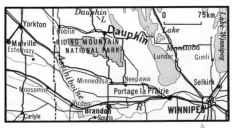

Davaugour, Pierre Dubois, Baron, governor of New France 1661-63 (d fighting the Turks on the border of Croatia 24 July 1664). Davaugour was the last governor to serve the COMPAGNIE DES CENT-ASSOCIÉS. He was enthusiastic about Canada's potential but insisted on the need for massive reinforcements to protect it from the Iroquois. When he removed restrictions on the brandy trade with the Indians, Davaugour became embroiled in bitter disputes with Bishop LAVAL and with MAISONNEUVE, the governor of Montréal, which led to his recall.
ALLAN GREER

Daveluy, Raymond, organist, composer, administrator, teacher (b at Victoriaville, Qué 23 Dec 1926). Having studied in Canada with his fa-

ther Lucien, he won the Prix d'Europe (1948) and studied organ with Hugh Giles in New York. First N American organist invited to the improvisation competition in Haarlem, Netherlands (1959), he went on to participate in many European festivals. In Montréal, Daveluy has been organist for the churches of Saint-Jean-Baptiste (1946-51), Immaculée-Conception (1951-54), Saint-Sixte (1954-59) and, as of 1960, the St Joseph Oratory. He has taught at the Québec Music Conservatory in Montréal (1957-60), (1978-) and in Trois-Rivières (1966-67), as well as occasionally at McGill U. Daveluy was director (1974-78) of the Montreal Conservatory and that of Trois-Rivières (1970-74). His main works are 3 sonatas for organ, a concerto for organ and orchestra and 2 masses. He was made a Member of the Order of Canada in 1980.
HÉLÈNE PLOUFFE

Davey, Frank, poet, critic, editor (b at Vancouver 19 Apr 1940). As a 1960s UBC student, Davey was a founding editor of the controversial poetry newsletter *Tish*. Since 1970 he has taught at York U in Toronto, and is the editor of *Open Letter*, the most important Canadian magazine for critical discussion of avant-garde literary works and theories. Davey has argued strongly against the thematic basis of much Canadian criticism and in favour of a more formalist approach. Through his work with Coach House Press, Davey has been in the forefront of the application of computer technology to small-press publishing. He has published 15 volumes of poetry, the most recent being *The Louis Riel Organ & Piano Co* (1985). Much of his best work is collected in *The Arches: Selected Poems* (1980). He has also published numerous articles on Canadian literature and several critical studies. Davey's poetry reveals a strong mistrust of metaphor: he bases his work on a direct emotional presentation of both public and private events.
STEPHEN SCOBIE

Davey, Keith, politician (b at Toronto 21 Apr 1926). After graduating from U of T's Victoria College, Davey worked in radio and held a number of positions in the Toronto-area Liberal Party. After Liberal defeats in the 1957 and 1958 general elections, Davey organized a small group, known as "Cell 13," to rejuvenate the party in Ontario. In 1961 Davey became the Liberal's national campaign director and helped to devise the strategy that defeated the Conservatives in 1963. His advice was less successful in 1965, when the Liberals sought a parliamentary majority. Made a senator by PM PEARSON in 1966, Davey chaired a Senate investigation of Canadian mass media. Following the Liberal Party's near-defeat in 1972, Davey was summoned by PM TRUDEAU to guide the party's electoral fortunes and was rewarded by a successful election in 1974. Although the Liberals were defeated in 1979, Davey returned the Liberals to power in 1980 as their national campaign co-chairman and was brought back in mid-campaign to try to revitalize John TURNER's flagging campaign in 1984. The experience was not a happy one, and in 1986 Davey took his doubts about Turner's leadership to the public in a book, *The Rainmaker*.
ROBERT BOTHWELL

David, Joe, Nuu-chah-nulth (Nootka or Westcoast) artist (b at Opitsat, BC 1946). A member of the Clayoquot Band, Joe David is a leading figure in modern NORTHWEST COAST INDIAN ART. Inspired by the arts of the Clayoquot people from childhood, and in particular by his father Hyacinth David, Sr, a carver and painter, he studied in Seattle and apprenticed with Duane Pasco. In later years his cousin Ron Hamilton (Hupquatchew) inspired him to take interest in all aspects of his culture. David's works are found in international public and private collections, including the

Canadian Museum of Civilization. Noted for his innovative silkscreen drum design prints he is also much sought after as a mask-maker.

CAROL SHEEHAN

David, Paul, founder of the Montreal Institute of Cardiology in 1954 (b at Montréal 25 Dec 1919). After his studies at Collège Stanislas de Paris before WWII, he did a doctorate in medicine at U de Montréal (1944). He specialized in cardiology at Massachusetts General Hospital (1946) and the Hôpital Lariboisière in Paris. It was at the cardiology institute of which he was director that the team led by Dr Pierre Grondin carried out the first heart transplant in Canada (31 May 1968). After 9 transplants, with the patient dying very soon after in each case, David ordered in 1969 a moratorium on transplants which lasted until 1983, when cyclosporine, a new anti-rejection drug, made its appearance. The first of the second-generation heart transplants took place at the institute (24 Apr 1983), giving the young Diane Larose a new heart. Since then, heart transplants have become a "routine" procedure. In 1984 David retired and left "his" institute. He was named the following year to the Senate.

FRANÇOISE CÔTÉ

David Dunlap Observatory, see OBSERVATORY.

Davidialuk, Alasua Amittuq, Inuk artist (b on a small island near Povungnituk, Qué c1910; d on an emergency evacuation flight near Povungnituk 1 Aug 1976). An indifferent hunter, he lived in poverty until he gained recognition as a folk artist near mid-life. Only then could he afford the hunter's indispensable dog team (and later snowmobile). Davidialuk entranced his countrymen with spellbinding "true stories" – legends, myths and his own inventions. These he later translated into stone carvings, prints and drawings, now collected because of their ingenuous revelations of a cultural mystique. His last creative outpouring suggests a precognitive need to broadcast his personal view of Inuit history and morals.

M.M. CRAIG

Davidson, Florence Edenshaw, or *Jadalloz/ g'ege∂ngaá,* "Story Maid," Haida elder, artist (b at Masset, Queen Charlotte Is, BC 1895), daughter of Charlie EDENSHAW. She began weaving Haida-style baskets and sewing ceremonial button blankets as a girl, but she put such works aside with marriage to Robert Davidson, Sr, and the subsequent birth of 13 children. In 1952 she began making button and appliqué blankets again, and since then she has made over 50, as well as traditional spruce-root and cedar-bark hats. She has willingly shared her knowledge of traditional Haida ways, and thus has been a key figure in the resurgence of Haida culture. Her son Claude Davidson and grandsons Robert DAVIDSON and Reggie are all accomplished artists.

CAROL SHEEHAN

Davidson, Joe, labour leader (b at Shotts, Scot 1915; d at Motherwell, Scot 23 Sept 1985). Always political, he described himself as an evolutionary socialist "with the proviso that evolution needed a shove at every opportunity." He came to Canada in 1957 and worked in iron foundries in Hamilton and Dundas, Ont, before he became a mail sorter in Toronto and a shop steward in the Canadian Postal Employees Assn (CPEA), transformed into the Canadian Union of Postal Workers (CUPW) in 1965. During the 1965 strike, he was active on the Toronto strike committee. He was elected president of the Toronto local 1967, became VP of CUPW in 1968 and was president 1974-77. His presidency encompassed 2 national postal strikes and dozens of smaller skirmishes over automation. He became the media's choice

as the most hated man in Canada and in 1983 he retired.

LAUREL SEFTON MACDOWELL

Reading: Joe Davidson and J. Deverall, *Joe Davidson* (1978).

Davidson, Robert Charles, Haida artist (b at Hydaburg, Alaska 4 Nov 1946). Master carver, printmaker and jeweller, Robert Davidson is greatgrandson and heir to the legacy of Charlie EDENSHAW. Robert first learned carving from his grandfather. In 1966 he apprenticed to Bill REID and the next year followed him to the Vancouver School of Art. While a student, Davidson became an able instructor at the Gitanmaax School of Northwest Coast Indian Art at KSAN, Hazelton, BC. He secured a grant to carve the 12 m Bear Mother pole, erected in Masset in 1969, the first TOTEM POLE to be raised in living memory of the Masset elders. Ever maturing and innovative, he has expanded the boundaries of Northwest Coast image and design in increasingly complex and unconventional serigraphs. Davidson's 3 monumental totem poles erected in 1984 in the Maclean Hunter Building, Toronto, reflect the artist's deep personal commitment to innovative art, and to the evolving culture of the Haida people. Three large poles were erected for Pepsico's Purchase, NY, sculpture garden in 1986 and later that year he was working on a large pole for a Toronto collector.

CAROL SHEEHAN

Davie, Alexander Edmund Batson, lawyer, politician, premier of BC 1887-89 (b at Wells, Eng 24 Nov 1847; d at Victoria 1 Aug 1889). He immigrated to Vancouver I in 1862 and was the first person to receive a complete legal education there, being called to the bar in 1873. He was clerk of the BC legislature 1872-74 and was elected in Cariboo, 1875, with the patronage of Premier WALKEM, but he gravitated to the Opposition. In 1877 he accepted office in the government of A.C. ELLIOTT but was defeated in the resulting by-election. Elected for Lillooet, 1882, he became attorney general in the new William SMITHE government (1883) and supervised an extensive revision of the province's statutes. Davie succeeded Smithe as premier (1887) but soon fell ill and died in office.

H. KEITH RALSTON

Davie, Theodore, lawyer, judge, politician, premier of BC 1892-95 (b at Brixton, Eng 22 Mar 1852; d at Victoria 7 Mar 1898). The brother of A.E.B. DAVIE, he was called to the bar in 1877 and elected to the BC legislature in 1882. In 1889, when John ROBSON became premier, he was chosen attorney general and in 1892 succeeded Robson as premier. In 1895 he resigned to become chief justice of BC. Davie was one of a succession of premiers who embodied the dominance of Victoria and Vancouver I in the political and economic life of late 19th-century BC. During his premiership a loan bill for new Parliament Buildings "anchored" the capital in Victoria.

H. KEITH RALSTON AND MAIRI DONALDSON

Davies, Sir Louis Henry, lawyer, politician, judge, premier of PEI (b at Charlottetown 4 May 1845; d at Ottawa 1 May 1924). Member of a family prominent in local business and politics, Davies was educated at Prince of Wales College, Charlottetown, before studying law in London. Upon returning to PEI he was active in politics and won a by-election to the Assembly in Nov 1872. An outstanding public speaker, he became PEI's youngest premier in 1876 as leader of a coalition committed to resolving the school question. In 1877 his government passed the Public Schools Act, making attendance compulsory and the educational system nonsectarian. Despite the Act's success, the coalition disintegrated and in 1879 left office. Davies was elected in 1882 to the House of Commons, where he was a leading

member of the Liberal caucus. He became Wilfrid LAURIER's minister of marine and fisheries in 1896, and was knighted in 1897. He left the Cabinet in 1901 for the Supreme Court of Canada, remaining a member until his death. He was appointed chief justice in 1918.

IAN ROSS ROBERTSON

Davies, Robertson William, writer, journalist, professor (b at Thamesville, Ont 28 Aug 1913). Davies is acknowledged as an outstanding essayist and brilliant novelist. Third son of Senator William Rupert Davies, Robertson Davies participated in stage productions as a child and developed a lifelong interest in drama. He attended Upper Canada Coll 1926-32 and went on to Queen's 1932-35 as a special student not working towards a degree. At Balliol Coll, Oxford, he received the BLit in 1938. His thesis, *Shakespeare's Boy Actors,* appeared in 1939, a year in which he pursued an acting career outside London. He spent 1940 playing minor roles and doing literary work for the director at the Old Vic Repertory Company in London. That year he married Brenda Mathews, a girl he had met at Oxford, who was then working as stage manager for the theatre. Davies returned to Canada in 1940 as literary editor of *Saturday Night.* Two years later, he became editor of the Peterborough *Examiner,* a position that afforded him unlimited material for many characters and situations which appeared in his novels and plays. While editing this paper 1940-55, and when he was publisher 1955-65, Davies published 18 books, produced several of his own plays and wrote numerous articles for various journals.

Davies moved from the theory of acting outlined in *Shakespeare for Young Players* (1947) to the writing of plays with *Eros at Breakfast,* a one-act play which won the 1948 Dominion Drama Festival Award for best Canadian play. *Eros at Breakfast and Other Plays* and award-winning *Fortune, My Foe* were published in 1949; *At My Heart's Core,* a 3-act play based on the Strickland sisters, appeared in 1950. Meanwhile, Davies collected some of his humorous essays (under the pseudonym Samuel Marchbanks) from the *Examiner* in *The Diary of Samuel Marchbanks* (1947), *The Table Talk of Samuel Marchbanks* (1949) and *Samuel Marchbanks' Almanack* (1967).

In 1960 Davies joined Trinity College at University of Toronto, where he taught literature courses for the next 21 years. The next year he published a collection of essays on literature, *A*

Robertson Davies, outstanding essayist and author of the Deptford Trilogy: *Fifth Business, The Manticore* and *World of Wonders* (photo by Peter Paterson).

Voice from the Attic, and was awarded the Lorne Pierce Medal for his literary achievements. In 1963 he became master of Massey Coll, the university's new graduate college. By 1967 he was made an RSC fellow, and soon began receiving honorary degrees from many Canadian universities. Some of his best essays and speeches appeared later in *One Half of Robertson Davies*, *The Enthusiasms of Robertson Davies* and *The Well-Tempered Critic*. In them, Davies explored his many esoteric interests with characteristic wit.

Davies found his metier neither in drama nor in occasional humorous essays, but in fiction. His first 3 novels, later known as the Salterton trilogy, were *Tempest-Tost* (1951), *Leaven of Malice* (1954), which won the Stephen Leacock Medal for Humour, and *A Mixture of Frailties* (1958). These novels explored the difficulty of sustaining a cultural life in Canada. During the 1950s, he played a major role in launching the STRATFORD FESTIVAL, serving on the board of governors and publishing with director Sir Tyrone Guthrie (1953-55). He also continued to produce plays, none of which ranked with his novels.

In 1970 Davies drew on Jungian psychology (a preoccupation which replaced his earlier interest in Freud) to produce his best novel to date, *Fifth Business*. The novel casts characters in roles that roughly correspond to Jungian archetypes to show Davies's belief that things of the spirit are more important than worldly concerns. He built on the success of *Fifth Business* with 2 sequel novels (the 3 later known as The Deptford Trilogy): *The Manticore* (1972), a novel cast in the form of Jungian psychoanalysis which won the Gov Gen's Award for fiction, and *World of Wonders* (1975). A seventh novel satirizing academic life, *The Rebel Angels* (1981), appeared at the close of Davies's academic career, and another, *Bred in the Bone* (1985), was published not long after. In 1983 Davies published *The Mirror of Nature*, an examination of 19th-century melodrama.

ELSPETH CAMERON

Reading: Elspeth Buitenhuis [Cameron], *Robertson Davies* (1972); P. Morley, *Robertson Davies* (1977).

Davin, Nicholas Flood, lawyer, journalist, politician (b at Kilfinane, Ire 13 Jan 1843; d at Winnipeg 18 Oct 1901). First MP for Assiniboia W, Davin was known as the voice of the North-West. Davin was a parliamentary and war correspondent in England before arriving in Toronto in 1872, where he wrote for the *Globe* and the *Mail*. Although a fully qualified lawyer, Davin practised little law. The highlight of his legal career was his 1880 defence of George Bennett, who murdered George BROWN.

A chance visit to the West in 1882 determined his future. He founded (1883) and edited the Regina *Leader*, the first newspaper in Assiniboia; the paper carried his detailed reports of the 1885 trial of Louis RIEL. A spell-binding speaker and Conservative MP for Assiniboia W, 1887-1900, Davin tried to gain provincial status for the territory, economic and property advantages for the new settlers, and even the franchise for women, but he never achieved his ambition to be a Cabinet minister. A mercurial personality, he became depressed by the decline of his political and personal fortunes and shot himself during a visit to Winnipeg. Davin wrote *The Irishman in Canada* (1877), as well as poetry and an unpublished novel.

LEE GIBSON

Davis, John, also spelled **Davys,** explorer (b near Dartmouth, Eng 1550?; d near Singapore 27 Dec 1605). His great ambition was to find the NORTHWEST PASSAGE, to which end he sailed from Dartmouth in June 1585. He rediscovered Green-

Davis quadrant or backstaff, of the early 18th century. Davis is credited with inventing this instrument for determining latitude (*courtesy Royal Ontario Museum*).

land, mostly forgotten from Norse times, and crossed the strait later named for him, making a landfall on the E coast of Baffin I, at about 66° 40'N. He returned to DAVIS STRAIT the following year and a third time in 1587 when he reached 72° 12'N along the Greenland coast (Hope Sanderson) and turned S down the Baffin coast, noting the entrances to Frobisher Bay and Hudson Strait and entering Davis Inlet and Hamilton Inlet along the Labrador coast. He had charted much of the unknown arctic coast and had made keen observations of weather, geology and vegetation as well as one of the most accurate and sympathetic accounts of the Inuit. He never returned to the Arctic but took part in a disastrous attempt to circumnavigate the globe (during which Davis was, however, credited with discovering the Falkland Is). He was chief pilot on the first successful expedition of the East India Co and on his third Indies voyage was killed by Japanese pirates off the coast of Malaya. Davis was an outstanding navigator and his exemplary character made him greatly admired by his colleagues. His *Seaman's secrets* (1599) was long the mariner's handbook and his *The worldes hydrographical description* (1595) provided a masterly summary of the geographical knowledge of the day. He was the inventor of the backstaff, a device for determining latitude.

JAMES MARSH

Victor Davis in action at the 1984 Los Angeles Olympics at which he won a gold medal (*courtesy Athlete Information Bureau/Service Information-Athlètes*).

Davis, Robert Atkinson, businessman, politician, premier of Manitoba 1874-78 (b at Dudswell, Qué 9 Mar 1841; d at Phoenix, Ariz 7 Jan 1903). Davis came to Winnipeg in May 1870 and bought a downtown hotel, which he named Davis House. Elected an MLA in Apr 1874, Davis was appointed provincial treasurer that July and succeeded Marc GIRARD as premier on 3 Dec 1874. Davis emphasized economy and retrenchment, negotiated better financial terms with Ottawa, and abolished the Legislative Council. Davis retired from politics after resigning the premiership 15 Oct 1878, sold his property in Winnipeg, and removed to Chicago where he became a wealthy businessman.

LOVELL C. CLARK

Davis, Victor, swimmer (b at Guelph, Ont 10 Feb 1964). He won the 100 m and 200 m breaststroke events at the Canada-USSR-W Germany Meet in July 1981, set a world record for the 200 m breaststroke at the world championships in Ecuador, Aug 1982, and won a gold medal and set a Commonwealth record at the 1982 Australia COMMONWEALTH GAMES in the 200 m breaststroke. He was incapacitated in 1983 by mononucleosis but at the 1984 Los Angeles Olympics won a gold medal in the 200 m breaststroke (world record, time 2:13.34) and silver medals in the 100 m breaststroke and 4x100 m medley relay. In 1986 he won gold medals in the 100 m breaststroke and 4x100 m medley relay at the Commonwealth Games and finished first (100 m breaststroke) and second (200 m breaststroke) at the world championships. Davis is known for his fiercely competitive approach to swimming.

JAMES MARSH

Davis, William Grenville lawyer, politician, premier of Ontario 1971-85 (b at Brampton, Ont 30 July 1929). Davis was leader of one of the most successful political parties in any democracy. He is a product of small-town Ontario. Brampton is now merely a bedroom suburb of Toronto, but when the future premier was born it was a separate, small community where people took their politics seriously. Educated in the local schools, Davis went to U of T (BA, 1951) and Osgoode Law School. He was called to the bar in 1955 and 4 years later won election as Conservative MPP for Brampton. In 1962 Premier John ROBARTS gave the novice the political "hot potato" of the Dept of Education, and as minister Davis presided over the most extraordinary period of change since Egerton RYERSON's day. Universities such as TRENT and BROCK were created. Rural schools were consolidated, forcing students to be bused long distances twice each day. And a new attitude, that schools should be co-operative not competitive, took root in public schools. Over this frenetic change, the calm, unflappable Davis presided, and by 1971 education in the province had been transformed.

Davis was the beneficiary of this process. He had begun to build a national reputation – in 1967 he was policy chairman at the Conservatives' national convention – and he seemed the logical heir to Robarts. At a convention in Feb 1971 Davis won the leadership on the fourth ballot, and the new premier, still only 42, came to power with a progressive (if rather undefined) image. This was crystallized 4 months later when Davis forced a halt to the Spadina Expressway, a roadway cutting through downtown Toronto, which had been vigorously opposed by neighborhood groups. That startling decision became almost typical. His cautious government was capable of rapid change, not least the decision in 1984 to give full financial support to SEPARATE SCHOOLS beginning in 1985.

Davis's calm style (and the "Big Blue Machine") won each election, as his government's moderate reformism struck a responsive chord

As premier of Ontario from 1971 to 1985, William Davis presided over extraordinary growth and change (*courtesy Canapress Photo Service*).

with the electorate. His record was good, but there were flaws. Education was allowed to starve from the mid-1970s as the public mood and economic situation altered, and despite his support of PM Pierre TRUDEAU in the negotiations leading to the CONSTITUTION ACT, 1982, Davis was unwilling to give Ontario's half million Francophones official bilingual status, although characteristically he had put the infrastructure in place. Although in 1984 he and his party were unchallenged, Davis surprisingly announced his resignation on 8 Oct 1984, yielding the premiership to Frank MILLER in Feb 1985. Under Miller, the long Conservative reign of Ontario came to an end. Davis himself joined a Toronto law firm as senior counsel and that year became a Companion of the Order of Canada. In 1987 he held directorships in a number of companies.

J.L. GRANATSTEIN

Davis Strait, situated between BAFFIN I and Greenland, is the entrance to BAFFIN BAY from the N Atlantic. It is a large stretch of water over 950 km across at its greatest width and never less than 300 km wide. At the narrowest point, its submarine topography consists of an undersea ridge, a continuation of the mid-Labrador ridge, extending from the coast of Baffin I to Greenland. The shallowest waters in the strait are found along this sill, from 350 to 550 m deep, before plunging down to abyssal basins on either side. Some of the greatest depths in the eastern Arctic are reached here (3660 m) in the southern end of the strait. The surface waters are strongly affected by counterclockwise-flowing currents. Along the W side, an outflow of cold water from the Arctic Basin moves S, at flow velocities of 8-20 km/day, to feed the Labrador current. On the E side the W Greenland countercurrent brings warmer water N. Ice conditions reflect this flow regime, with heavy ice movement and icebergs along the western shore, contrasting sharply with more open water along the Greenland side. The strait was first explored by John DAVIS, leader of 3 voyages 1585-87 organized by merchants of London, Eng.   DOUG FINLAYSON

d'Avray, Joseph Marshall de Brett Maréchal, 2nd Baron, educator, journalist (b at London, Eng 30 Nov 1811; d at Fredericton 26 Nov 1871). Educated at the French royal court, Marshall d'Avray (as he preferred to be known) established a normal school on Mauritius prior to his arrival in NB in 1848. As first master of the Fredericton Normal School (1848-50) and later

as superintendent of education (1854-58), d'Avray was frequently involved in political turmoil and debate. In 1854, as editor of the Fredericton *Headquarters*, he seized every opportunity to satirize opponents of his progressive views on teacher training, compulsory assessment and a "rounded" liberal education. From 1852 until his death, d'Avray was professor of modern languages at King's College (which became UNB in 1859). Removed from office as superintendent for "political reasons" in 1858, the Baron devoted the remainder of his life to teaching, leaving an indelible mark on his students.

WILLIAM B. HAMILTON

Dawes, Norman James, brewer, corporate director (b at Lachine, Qué 13 July 1874; d at Montréal 14 Apr 1967). Son of James P. Dawes, a third-generation Montréal brewer, he was educated at McGill and the US Brewers' Academy and entered the family brewing business in 1894. In 1909 he joined his father in forming National Breweries, the largest brewing merger in Canada to that date, involving 14 Québec companies. As managing director of National Breweries 1922-26 and president 1926-52, Dawes was one of the most powerful brewing figures in Canada. He remained chairman when National was bought by Canadian Breweries in 1952. ALBERT TUCKER

Reading: M. Denison, *The Barley and the Stream* (1955).

Dawson, YT, City, pop 896 (1986c), 697 (1981c), inc 1902, is located on the E bank of the YUKON R at the mouth of the Klondike R, 530 km N of Whitehorse. The Klondike was originally a salmon stream, and each summer the Indians dried their catch on the flat where it joined the Yukon. In Aug 1896 Joseph Ladue, a trader and prospector, staked the flat as a townsite, in anticipation of a rush into the KLONDIKE valley. The town was named after G.M. DAWSON, director of the GEOLOGICAL SURVEY OF CANADA and leader of the expedition that explored the region in 1887. Although Dawson became the Yukon capital in 1898, it lacked municipal institutions until after the turn of the century.

Economy At the axis of 2 transportation corridors, Dawson grew quickly as the transshipment point for men and materials destined for the Klondike goldfields. As a port, it developed service industries for the people who disembarked, and it became the mercantile and distribution centre of the Yukon. At the height of the gold rush in the summer of 1898, the Klondike region had a population of some 30 000, of whom some

Dawson, YT, nestles on the flats of the junction of the Klondike and Yukon rivers. It was founded as a transshipment point for men bound for the Klondike goldfields (*photo by Richard Harrington*).

16 000 could be found in Dawson. It declined throughout the following decade, however, and the introduction of sophisticated mining technology slowly drove people from its hinterland, thus reducing the need for its services. WWI curtailed mining activity, and the next 20 years saw little development in the Klondike. Dawson experienced some growth when the mining industry expanded in the 1930s, but WWII disrupted gold production again. The building of the ALASKA HWY enabled Whitehorse to supersede Dawson as the commercial and administrative centre of the territory, and the capital was transferred S in 1953. The opening of the Klondike Hwy in the same period put an end to commercial traffic on the Yukon R and rendered Dawson's port facilities obsolete. Another blow came in 1966, when the Yukon Consolidated Gold Corp shut down its last dredge in the Klondike valley. Since then, tourism has been the major industry for Dawson's permanent residents.

Townscape In 1960 Parks Canada rebuilt and reconstructed the Palace Grand Theatre and has continued to restore buildings over the past 25 years. Long-range plans to maintain Dawson as a national historic site have not materialized, however. The Klondike Visitors Association produces a theatrical revue at the Palace Grand Theatre each summer and operates Diamond Tooth Gertie's Gambling Casino in the old Arctic Brotherhood Hall. The Dawson Museum is housed in the former administration building (designed by Thomas Fuller and built 1901). People from throughout the Yukon flock to Dawson to celebrate Discovery Day, a territorial holiday commemorating George Carmack's discovery of gold on 17 Aug 1896.   H. GUEST

Reading: H.J. Woodside, "Dawson As It Is," *Canadian Magazine,* Sept 1901; Pierre Berton, *Klondike* (1958).

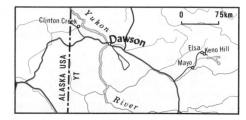

Dawson, George Mercer, geologist (b at Pictou, NS 1 Aug 1849; d at Ottawa 2 Mar 1901), son of Sir John William DAWSON. He studied at McGill, then at the Royal School of Mines, London. His superior mental and observational powers became widely known from his work as a geologist and botanist to the International Boundary Commission, which surveyed the FORTY-NINTH PARALLEL from Lk of the Woods to the Rockies 1873-75. He accurately reported on the geology, mineral resources, agriculture and climate, including locust invasions, of the western plains. In 1875 he joined the GEOLOGICAL SURVEY OF CANADA. His survey of BC strongly influenced government decisions on the proposed route of the CANADIAN PACIFIC RY. A charter ROYAL SOCIETY OF CANADA member (1882), Dawson by 1883 was assistant director of the GSC. In 1887 he surveyed the Alaska boundary at the Yukon R and investigated gold discoveries there. In 1892 he became British commissioner on Bering Sea natural resources and in 1896, a member of the Ethnological Survey of Canada. He was also GSC director 1895-1901.

Dawson's brilliance in systematic mapping provided a sound basis for understanding the geology and mineral resources of much of northern and western Canada, and offered reliable guidance to mining, ranching, agricultural and lumbering industries. He also encouraged investigation and development of western coal and petroleum resources. The first comprehensive work on Canada's physiography, *Descriptive Sketch of the Physical Geography and Geology of the Dominion of Canada* was published by Dawson and A.R.C. Selwyn (1884). SUZANNE ZELLER

Reading: Morris Zaslow, *Reading the Rocks* (1975).

Dawson, Sir John William, geologist, principal of McGill (b at Pictou, NS 13 Oct 1820; d at Montréal 19 Nov 1899). The first Canadian-born scientist of worldwide reputation, Dawson personally created most of the 19th-century foundations of the 20th-century Canadian scientific community.

Educated in Pictou, NS, and Edinburgh, Scot, as a geologist, then the most advanced branch of applied science, Dawson became superintendent of education for NS in 1850 and principal of McGill in 1855. Over the next 38 years, he built McGill into one of the world's leading universities; he taught 20 hours a week, published 20 books, formed the ROYAL SOCIETY OF CANADA, became the only individual ever to preside over both the American and the British Assns for the Advancement of Science, and was knighted in 1884 for his public services. His son, G.M. DAWSON, was director of the GEOLOGICAL SURVEY OF CANADA.

Principal Dawson's career spanned the transformation of science from a fixed curriculum of "natural philosophy" to an array of professional disciplines focused on research. Like his predecessors, he wrote on subjects from farming to philanthropy, but he also earned a solid reputation as a geologist, equally at home on a cliff, chipping out samples, or in his study, synthesizing and interpreting the processes of geological time. He was the leading expert of his day on early FOSSIL PLANTS and took special pride in his identification as a coral of Eozoon canadense, the oldest nonplant fossil known: always controversial, it was not for another 50 years that Eozoon was shown to be a rare crystal formation rather than a living animal.

As well as a modernist in science and education (eg, admitting women to McGill), Dawson was a devout Christian and the leading anti-Darwinist of the late Victorian period. As a geologist, he knew the Earth was very old (100 million years and perhaps older); but he could not see, from his direct knowledge of the fossil evidence, that new species had actually evolved out of earlier ones.

Sir John William Dawson (*courtesy National Archives of Canada/C-49822*).

Many of his books were technical criticisms of Darwinism and attempts to reconcile up-to-date science with the Christian scriptural tradition. Since the theory of EVOLUTION lacked any mechanical explanation until the science of GENETICS appeared in the 20th century, Dawson's being wrong does not diminish his historical importance. The remoteness of Canada and McGill's newness did not prevent Dawson's leading one faction in the greatest scientific controversy of his day. His international reputation added strength to his mission to establish in Canada the institutions of up-to-date science: higher degrees, lifelong research and publication of research results. DONALD J.C. PHILLIPSON

Reading: W.R. Shea, "Introduction" to J.W. Dawson, *Modern Ideas of Evolution* (repr 1977).

Dawson, Robert McGregor, political scientist (b at Bridgewater, NS 1 Mar 1895; d there 16 July 1958). He was a graduate of Dalhousie, Harvard and London School of Economics, and taught at Dalhousie, Rutgers and U Sask before going to U of T in 1937. He wrote major studies on the Canadian civil service, the constitution and on Dominion status, and his textbook, *The Government of Canada*, first published in 1947, was the standard introduction to the subject for a generation of students. The sixth edition of it was published in 1987. Many of his graduate students became prominent academics and public servants. He demanded high standards of scholarship and literary style, but with colleagues and students his arguments were leavened by a vital enthusiasm and a sense of humour. He left U of T in 1951 to write the official biography of Mackenzie KING, but completed only one volume before his death. H. BLAIR NEATBY

Dawson, Simon James, surveyor, engineer, legislator (b at Redhaven, Scot 1820; d at Ottawa 20 Nov 1902). After immigrating to Canada, Dawson was engaged initially on surveys in Québec but by Apr 1858 was surveying the rough country between Lk Superior and the Red R. In 1868 he was asked to construct the line of communication proposed in his 1859 report of that survey. Work on what came to be known as the DAWSON ROAD, which involved the use of lakes and portage trails, was well advanced when, in 1870, he was ordered to assist in transporting the RED RIVER EXPEDITION along the still incomplete "road." The route remained in use until the opening of the CPR. Dawson was elected to the Ontario legislature in 1874 and to the House of Commons in 1878, where he served until 1891. R.F. LEGGET

Dawson, William Bell, surveyor, engineer, civil servant (b at Pictou, NS 2 May 1854; d at Montréal 21 May 1944). Son of Sir John William DAWSON, he studied at McGill and the École des Ponts et Chaussées, Paris, France. After working several years as a surveyor and engineer, he joined the CANADIAN PACIFIC RY in 1884 and was involved in the arbitration between the Canadian government and the railway over the quality of construction of the western sections of the railway in BC. He is best known for his work as engineer and superintendent of the Tidal Survey, Canadian Dept of Marine and Fisheries, 1893-1924. Technically difficult and performed under arduous conditions, the work resulted in tide tables for all the principal harbours of Canada, invaluable for the fishing, lumber and coal industries. A member of the Royal Society of Canada, in retirement Dawson devoted much time to writing articles on the relationships between religion and science. M.J. KEEN

Dawson Creek, BC, City, pop 10 544 (1986c), 11 373 (1981c), inc 1958, is located near the BC-Alberta border, about 400 km NE of Prince

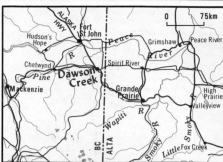

George and 580 km NW of Edmonton. It is the regional centre for northeastern BC. The region's economy is based on agriculture, forestry and mineral (oil and gas) exploration and development. The construction of the BC Ry, the massive Peace R hydroelectric project and, in the early 1980s, the development of Northeast Coal near Tumbler Ridge, have produced continual growth over the past 30 years. Dawson Creek's mile "0" on the ALASKA HWY has made tourism important (over 30 000 tourists in 1986), as all traffic over the highway must pass through the city. The area also boasts excellent hunting and fishing opportunities for sportsmen. As the terminus of the BC Railway and CN Railways, the city is an important grain-shipping centre. Its attractions include the Northern Alberta Ry Park and Museum, and numerous recreational facilities. ALAN F.J. ARTIBISE

Dawson Road, a trail running from the NW corner of LAKE OF THE WOODS to Fort Garry [Winnipeg], a distance of about 120 km, was the western end of the "Dawson Route," an all-Canadian route from Thunder Bay to the Red River district of southern Manitoba. Part land and part water, the route required a month of travel, and 70 loadings and unloadings of freight and baggage. It was surveyed in 1858 by S.J. DAWSON for the Canadian government, and work on it was begun in 1868 as a make-work project after a crop failure in Red River. Before it was completed, the RED RIVER EXPEDITION of 1870 used the road on its way to suppress the Red River Rebellion of that year. In 1873, 1600 travellers used it, but most preferred the faster and easier route via Duluth and the Red R steamers to Winnipeg. The road fell into disuse except for local traffic after the CPR was finished in 1885. WILLIAM R. MORRISON

Day, James, equestrian (b at Thornhill, Ont 7 July 1946). A specialist in show jumping, Day was a member – with James ELDER and Thomas GAYFORD – of the gold-medal Canadian team at the 1968 Mexico City Olympics. Day first entered international competition in 1964, winning the N American junior jumping championship; in 1966 he was senior champion. He won the individual jumping event at the Pan-American Games in Winnipeg and was on the team that won the Grand Prix events at the N American jumping championship and Royal Horse Show (1969) and the world championships (1970). Day also represented Canada in both the 1972 and 1976 Olympics. BARBARA SCHRODT

Day and Night, by Dorothy LIVESAY (Ryerson, 1944). This collection of poetry reflects the author's commitment to socialist concerns in the 1930s and her enduring faith in human potential. The narrative poems "The Outrider" and "Day and Night" document the oppression of farm and industrial labour, and envision a new social order. In "Lorca," a revolutionary hero transcends death. The inclusion of personal poems in the collection suggests the interdependence of public and private experience. Livesay's poetic innovation – her mixed verse forms, her sound effects and taut, economic language – and her ability to integrate form and meaning give the collection its striking power. *Day and Night* won the Governor General's Award in 1944.

CAROL W. FULLERTON

Day Care The licensed or approved care of young children, for all or part of the day, outside the children's own home. The 2 most common types of day care are centre care and family day care. The latter refers to the care of children (between a few weeks of age to about 12 years old) in private homes that have been assessed and are supervised by a social agency or governmental staff. The older children are cared for in after-school programs during their out-of-school hours. Major types of day care include private commercial; private nonprofit; and those under municipal welfare services.

The federal government, through the provisions of the Canada Assistance Plan, shares in the cost to provinces and municipalities of providing day care to families who are in need, or who may fall into this category if they do not receive the service. Health and Welfare Canada also provides consultation services on day care to the provinces and the public and operates a National Day Care Information Centre in Ottawa.

Because day care falls under provincial jurisdiction, the provinces are responsible for the licensing procedures, the establishment of standards, and the basic design of the day-care system. Day-care programs across Canada share some similarities, particularly regarding standards regulating health and safety, child-staff ratios and staff training; but there are some significant differences, because of differing provincial philosophies and perspectives. For example, Saskatchewan will only license day-care centres that are operated as parent co-operatives, while in Alberta about 75% of day-care centres are operated as commercial ventures. Ontario and Alberta are the only provinces where municipally owned and operated day-care centres exist, although they are not numerous. Some provinces will provide a partial subsidy to everyone using the service regardless of family income, while others restrict subsidization to families who pass a needs or income test.

Although some day-care centres date to WWII and before, the majority have been established since 1972 in direct response to the increasing number of working mothers with preschool children. In 1971 there were only 17 400 full-time day-care spaces in Canada; by Mar 1987 there were approximately 250 000 spaces, a 14-fold increase. The availability of service is different depending on the age of the child. In 1986 there were enough spaces to serve about 34% of children aged 3 to 6 whose parents worked at least 20 hours per week or who were enrolled in school. However, there were only sufficient spaces to meet about 7% of children under 18 months of age whose parents were in the same category. Part of the reason for the underdevelopment of infant day care is the high cost.

The cost of day-care services is directly related to almost all of the current day-care issues. Day-care staff, generally underpaid, are faced with the dilemma that because day care is so labour intensive (representing about 70-80% of day-care costs), an increase in salaries places its cost beyond the means of many low-income and middle-income earners. In fact, a 1985 report commissioned by the federal government found that day-care staff in Ont and BC earned 30% less than general labourers, farmhands and animal care workers in those provinces. In reviewing day care needs in Canada, the federal government has identified the main areas of concern to include quality of care, accessibility to care and affordability of care. In 1987 the federal Cabinet announced a new child-care policy with 2 components: a shared-cost program with the provinces and a tax-credit system designed to benefit parents seeking child care. Size of the program was estimated at between $3 and $7 billion over 7 years.

HOWARD CLIFFORD

Amor De Cosmos, 1874, eccentric politician who promoted Confederation in BC (*courtesy National Archives of Canada/PA-25397*).

De Cosmos, Amor, newspaper editor, politician, premier of BC (b William Alexander Smith at Windsor, NS 20 Aug 1825; d at Victoria, BC 4 July 1897). Smith left his job in a Halifax wholesale warehouse in 1851 to make his way to the California goldfields. A keen amateur photographer, when he reached the Pacific he set up a studio instead of digging for gold. Settling in Mud Springs, soon renamed El Dorado, Smith followed the town's example. In 1854, the California Senate passed a bill naming him Amor de Cosmos; the name, he said, "tells what I love most ... order, beauty, the world, the universe." When news of gold on the FRASER R reached California in 1858, De Cosmos trekked northward, but stayed in Victoria and founded the *British Colonist*. Highly critical of Governor James DOUGLAS, De Cosmos began a political career as well. He served in the Legislative Assembly of Vancouver I 1863-66, and in the Legislative Council of BC 1867-71. De Cosmos promoted CONFEDERATION with Canada, but organized a "Confederation League" to get RESPONSIBLE GOVERNMENT in the "Terms of Union." When both were achieved (1871), he was elected to the new provincial legislature as well as the House of Commons. From 1872 to 1874 he was both premier of BC and a federal MP. He proved as mediocre in power as he had been brilliant in Opposition, and his career ended in 1882, when Victoria voters rejected him for advocating Canadian independence. De Cosmos's last years were marked by growing eccentricity and finally, in 1895, madness.

GEORGE WOODCOCK

Reading: G. Woodcock, *Amor de Cosmos* (1975).

de Cotret, Robert-René, politician (b at Ottawa 20 Feb 1944). After an MBA at McGill and a doctorate in business economics at U of Mich, de Cotret served as a staff member of the President's Council of Economic Advisers in the US, 1970-71, and as an adviser to the Dept of Finance 1971-72. From 1972 to 1978 he was a director and then president of the CONFERENCE BOARD OF CANADA. He was elected Conservative MP for Ottawa Centre in a 1978 by-election, immediately becoming a trusted economic adviser of Opposition leader Joe CLARK. He was defeated in the 1979 election but was appointed senator so that he could serve in Clark's Cabinet as minister of industry, trade and commerce. He resigned from the Senate to run unsuccessfully in the 1980 election. He was VP of the National Bank of Canada to 1984, when he regained a seat in the Commons and became president of the Treasury Board in the MULRONEY Cabinet. In 1987 de Cotret took over what was to become the new Ministry of Industry, Science and Technology.

NORMAN HILLMER

de Havilland Aircraft of Canada Limited, with head offices in Toronto, is an aircraft manufacturer. Incorporated in Ontario in 1928, the company manufactures the DE HAVILLAND OTTER (now Twin Otter), the Buffalo (a military plane) and the DE HAVILLAND DASH 7 and Dash 8 aircraft. During the 1970s the company experienced difficulty when commuter airlines did not create the high demand for Dash 7s that de Havilland had expected. In 1974 the federal government purchased the company from its British owners, Hawker Siddeley Aviation, and invested in research and development. But it was not until 1978, as airlines began facing deregulation in the US and higher fuel costs, that sales of the Dash 7 started to climb. The Dash 8 Series 300, scheduled to appear in 1988, was an extended version of the Series 100. De Havilland is designing the Dash 9 to replace the Twin Otter in 1991. Continuing difficulties prompted government assistance in 1985 and in 1986 the company was sold to Boeing Commercial Aircraft Company of Seattle, Wash, for $155 million.

DEBORAH C. SAWYER

The de Havilland Beaver, outstanding STOL aircraft (*courtesy de Havilland Aircraft of Canada Ltd*).

de Havilland Beaver, DHC-2, successor to the NOORDUYN NORSEMAN as the all-purpose bush plane of the Canadian North. Its specifications were based on results of a questionnaire circulated by "Punch" DICKINS, and it first flew 16 Aug 1947. Generous power and a special wing/flap system designed by R.D. Hiscocks gave it excellent STOL capabilities; it could take off in 181 m. Carrying a pilot, 6 passengers and heavy loads, it saw service in both polar regions, in African deserts and in airfields high in the Andes. Service in Antarctica was so valuable that a lake, glacier and island were named after it. By 1965, some 1600 were operating in 63 countries, with the biggest customer being the US Army. There are 6 in museums, including one, the prototype, CF-FHB, in the National Aviation Museum, Ottawa.

JAMES MARSH

de Havilland Caribou, DHC-4, twin-engined STOL aircraft, capable of taking off in only 220 m. It was characterized by the sharp upward angle of the rear fuselage, providing access for large loads. It first flew July 1958, and was used mostly in a military role. In 1965, it was replaced by the similar but larger DHC-5 Buffalo, which was the first

The de Havilland Otter, versatile STOL aircraft which has provided dependable transport in the Canadian North since the 1950s (*courtesy de Havilland Aircraft of Canada Ltd*).

aircraft of its size to execute the steep takeoff and descent required for city-centre STOL operation.

JAMES MARSH

de Havilland Dash 7, DHC-7, STOL aircraft designed for efficient transport from city centres. It first flew Mar 1975 after a long development costing $120 million, four-fifths of which was paid by the federal government. Its outstanding STOL performance comes from highly specialized wings; it can take off in 914 m and seats 54 people. Its turbine engines and slowly revolving propellers make it the world's quietest airliner. It first went into operation in Colorado, later from Yellowknife to northern communities. The CANADIAN COAST GUARD uses the Dash 7 for monitoring offshore pollution and the 200-mile limit.

JAMES MARSH

de Havilland Otter, DHC-3, versatile bush aircraft with STOL capabilities designed to operate on wheels, floats or skis in extreme conditions. It first flew Dec 1951 and provided dependable transport in the Canadian North, Greenland, Norway, Antarctica, Nepal, China and numerous other countries. The Canadian forces used it for search and rescue, and commercial airlines for feedliner routes and air taxi. The Twin Otter, DHC-6, which first flew 1965, is powered by 2 Canadian-made Pratt and Whitney PT6 turbine engines, giving it 50% more speed. It was used for the first city-centre air service, from Ottawa to Montréal, July 1974, and has had more involvement with Canadian arctic development than any other aircraft.

JAMES MARSH

De Koninck, Charles, philosopher (b at Thourout, Belgium 29 July 1906; d at Rome, Italy 13 Feb 1965). When he arrived at Québec's Laval U, a graduate of Louvain U, Thomism was the established doctrine of PHILOSOPHY in Québec. Director of Laval's philosophy faculty 1939-56, he determined the course of philosophy there and in much of French Canada through his numerous publications and his connections with the Roman Catholic Church.

De Koninck's work, more than 150 papers and books, was devoted mainly to the philosophy of science. He published also in the philosophy of religion and metaphysics. Because of his willing-

ness to write in both English and French he became well known in English Canada and in the US, where he lectured frequently. His popular book *The Hollow Universe* (1960), published after a series of lectures at McMaster in Hamilton, attempted to reconcile philosophy, science and religion. De Koninck argued that, divorced from concrete experience, the scientific world was an empty shell. A controversial philosopher, he was influential for many years.

ELIZABETH A. TROTT

De la Roche, Mazo, writer (b at Newmarket, Ont 15 Jan 1879; d at Toronto 12 July 1961). Among the most prolific and widely read of Canadian authors, she wrote 23 novels, more than 50 short stories, 13 plays and many other works. Her Jalna novels have sold 9 million copies in 193 English- and 92 foreign-language editions. Mazo de la Roche began writing short stories before WWI and published 2 novels in the 1920s before winning international recognition with the publication of *Jalna* in 1927. This story of an Ontario family named Whiteoak and its home Jalna won the *Atlantic Monthly* award for the best novel of that year. Sequels depicted other episodes in the history of the Whiteoaks. *Young Renny* (1935) was several months on the New York *Herald* bestseller list. A play based on the Jalna stories was a hit in London, New York and Toronto and inspired a Hollywood film. Her books continued to sell well after WWII (20 of her books were still in print in 1960), although her novels of the 1950s do not compare well with her earlier work. In 1972 the CBC produced a TV series based on the Jalna stories.

Although still a best-selling author, Mazo de la Roche was not taken seriously by critics after WWII. Her later works too closely resembled formula romances and succumbed to sentimentality. This later criticism has been unfairly extended to the full body of her work, including her earlier novels, which are distinguished by well-defined characters, good dialogue and subtle imagery. Therefore, one of the greatest of 20th-century Canadian writers is also one of the most underrated.

C.J. TAYLOR

Reading: R. Hambleton, *Mazo de la Roche of Jalna* (1966).

De Meurons, Swiss infantry regiment raised 1781; transferred 1795 to the British army. It served in India until Oct 1806, then moved to England, and was sent to Lower Canada in Aug 1813. There it saw limited service in the WAR OF 1812 under Sir George PREVOST during the PLATTS-

BURGH câmpaign of Sept 1814. Remaining in the Canadas, it was disbanded in July 1816, more than half of the 640 other ranks electing to stay as settlers. Some were immediately recruited by Lord SELKIRK for his expedition to the RED RIVER COLONY. In 1821 some former officers helped recruit Swiss settlers for Red River.

STUART R.J. SUTHERLAND

De Mille, James, professor, novelist (b at Saint John 23 Aug 1833; d at Halifax 28 Jan 1880). He spent most of his life teaching history, rhetoric and literature at Dalhousie in Halifax. His reputation, however, rested on his writing; he was one of N America's most popular novelists of the late 19th century. He wrote historical romances, novels of manners and adventure with international settings, and tales of mystery and sensation. In addition, De Mille produced 2 notable series of books for boys, in which he avoided much of the trite moralizing found in such works during this period.

THOMAS B. VINCENT

de Pédery-Hunt, Dora, sculptor (b at Budapest, Hungary 16 Nov 1913). Dora de Pédery-Hunt completed her studies in sculpture and design in Budapest in 1943 and immigrated to Canada in 1948. Her first solo show of medals and small sculptures in Toronto established her reputation as a sensitive representational artist endowed with superb technical skills. She was instrumental in introducing the ancient art of medal sculpture to Canada and is the Canadian representative of the Fédération internationale de la médaille. A cast bronze medal she created for the Canada Council in 1961 and her design for the Canadian Olympic gold coin in 1976 are among her public commissions. Her work is in numerous public collections, including the National Gallery of Canada, the British Museum and the Smithsonian Institute.

CLARA HARGITTAY

Dora de Pédery-Hunt, *The Last Supper* (1979), bronze, 92 mm in diameter (*courtesy Dora de Pédery-Hunt/photo by Elizabeth Frey*).

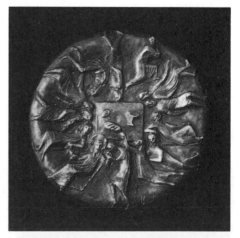

De Roo, Remi J., Roman Catholic bishop of Victoria (b at Swan Lake, Man 24 Feb 1924). Bishop De Roo has been president of the Bishops' Western Catholic Conference, founding member of the World Conference of Religions for Peace, chairman of the Human Rights Commission of British Columbia and an author. Ordained Bishop of Victoria on 14 Dec 1962, he has implemented the ecclesiology of Vatican II in his own diocese. Because of his outspoken attitude on such controversial issues as the Church and social action and liberation theology, together with his critique of the capitalist system, De Roo has received many labels including radical and liberal. His influence has reached far beyond the diocese of Victoria. As representative of the Canadian Conference of Catholic Bishops, he has championed the cause of Central and S American countries to develop their own form of democracy.

MARGARET WHITEHEAD

De Sola, Alexander Abraham, clergyman, professor, author, publisher (b at London, Eng 18 Sept 1825; d at New York, NY 5 June 1882). During his ministry to Montréal's Sephardic Jewish Congregation, Shearith Israel (1847-82), De Sola organized its educational, benevolent and fraternal life; taught Hebrew, rabbinical literature, oriental literature, Spanish and philology at McGill; and played an active part in the city's literary and scientific life. A prolific author, editor and translator, and concerned chiefly with the contemporary debate on religion and science, De Sola's own writings included studies on Jewish history, cosmography and medicine. In 1858 McGill made him an honorary doctor of laws, the first Jewish minister to receive this honour in England or N America; in 1872 De Sola became the first British subject to open the US House of Representatives with prayer, a privilege that brought him wide acclaim. CARMAN MILLER

de Wit, Willie, boxer (b at Grande Prairie, Alta 13 June 1961). One of Canada's most outstanding amateur boxers, de Wit's amateur record was 67-12 and included the N American amateur heavyweight championship (twice) and the world amateur heavyweight title (also twice). At the 1984 Los Angeles Olympics he lost the gold medal match to Henry Tilman of the US and had to settle for the Olympic silver. He turned professional immediately after the games and, persuaded by a contract offer reportedly worth $5 million, began to train and fight out of Burnet, Texas. Although he defeated Ken Lakusta to capture the Canadian heavyweight championship, he faced a number of undistinguished opponents before his professional career suffered a severe setback when he was knocked out by American Bert Cooper before successfully defending his title against Lakusta again in 1987.

Deacon, William Arthur, literary critic and editor (b at Pembroke, Ont 1890; d at Toronto Aug 1977). Trained as a lawyer in Winnipeg, Deacon was book review editor of, in turn, the *Manitoba Free Press* (1921), *Saturday Night* (1922-28), the Toronto *Mail and Empire* (1928-36) and the *Mail and Empire's* successor *The Globe and Mail* (1936-61). A pioneer literary nationalist, he was both a provoker of and a participant in the cultural ferment of the 1920s when he did his own best work: *Pens and Pirates* (1923), *Poteen and Other Essays* (1926) and especially *The Four Jameses* (1927), a satirical study of Canadian poetasters. But in the 1930s his reputation withered in the shade of modernist writing and radical politics. At length he came to appear as a retrograde force to a literary culture that did not give him the credit he deserved for his long years of tireless activity.

DOUGLAS FETHERLING

Reading: C. Thomas and J. Lennox, *William Arthur Deacon: A Canadian Literary Life* (1982).

Deafness, *see* AUDITORY IMPAIRMENT.

Dean River, 241 km long, world-famous steelhead- and salmon-fishing stream, rises in the Fraser Plateau of west-central BC, flows NW and W through the COAST MOUNTAINS and empties near the head of Dean Channel. The name was given by Capt George VANCOUVER in 1793, the same year Alexander MACKENZIE paddled the upper Dean R in his overland journey to the Pacific Ocean.

PETER GRANT

Dease, Peter Warren, fur trader, arctic explorer (b at Mackinac I, Mich 1 Jan 1788; d at Montréal 17 Jan 1863). From age 13 he was engaged in the FUR TRADE, first with the XY Co, then the NORTH WEST CO and finally the HUDSON'S BAY CO. He served principally in the Athabasca and Mackenzie districts, though he was in charge of the New Caledonia trade 1831-35. Dease assisted Sir John FRANKLIN on his second land expedition to the Arctic. Between 1837 and 1839 Dease and Thomas Simpson made 3 expeditions along the Arctic coast, leaving only a small part of the NORTHWEST PASSAGE unsurveyed. Dease retired to a farm near Montréal in 1841. DANIEL FRANCIS

Death For centuries the law has accepted the cessation of heartbeat and respiration as the determination of death, but now the heart can be removed, the breathing stopped and blood pumped by machines without preventing the individual's resumption of lucid consciousness. The Manitoba legislature, in its Vital Statistics Act (1975), has provided the only statutory definition of death in Canada: "For all purposes within the legislative competence of the Legislature of Manitoba the death of a person takes place at the time at which irreversible cessation of all that person's brain function occurs." In 1981 the Law Reform Commission of Canada recommended that Parliament enact this provision in the Interpretation Act: "For all purposes within the jurisdiction of the Parliament of Canada, a person is dead when an irreversible cessation of all that person's brain functions has occurred." Rules relating to the registration of death vary from province to province, but generally, when death occurs an appropriate person, eg, a relative, must complete an official form for the district registrar. At the same time a certificate of the cause of death must be completed and sent to the district registrar either by a doctor or, in suspicious circumstances, by a coroner. Morticians need certificates in order to bury a body. FRANCIS C. MULDOON

Death and Dying Death, the irreversible cessation of life, has always intrigued and frightened mankind. Every known culture has attempted to provide an explanation of its meaning; like birth or marriage it is universally considered an event of social significance, amplified by ritual and supported by institutions. Death has been studied by anthropologists, sociologists, philosophers, psychologists and biologists who have tried to understand its cultural, social or individual meanings. Death is also a matter of legal and political concern – the Law Reform Commission of Canada has published several working papers on euthanasia, cessation of treatment, the definition of death and related matters, while Health and Welfare Canada has published analyses and guidelines for establishing standards for hospital-based palliative care. Answers to problems caused by death have been addressed by RELIGION, PHILOSOPHY and political ideology (*see* BUDDHISM; CATHOLICISM; MORMON CHURCH).

Prior to the Industrial Revolution, mortality rates in Canada were high, extremely variable and dependent upon crop conditions, weather, EPIDEMICS, etc. The crude death rate (number of deaths per 1000 people per year) has declined from 22-25 deaths in the mid-1800s to 11.8 in 1923 to just 7.2 in 1985, while at the same time the infant death rate (deaths during the first year) has decreased dramatically by 79% between 1951 and 1985 (*see* POPULATION). Life expectancy at birth has reached 73 years for males and 80 years for females. Age-specific mortality rates for the native population are higher than those for the Canadian population in almost all age categories; as a result, life expectancy at birth for the native population is about 10 years less than for the population as a whole. Women have lower death rates than men at all ages and have actually increased their life-span advantage over men in the past several decades. Today, a woman who reaches the age of 65 has a 50% chance of living an additional 19 years, while a 65-year-old man has a similar chance of living another 15 years. About 68% of all deaths are of people over the age of 60, and death at an earlier age is frequently considered tragic. Health and Welfare Canada treats deaths occurring before the age of 70 as premature. Today it is difficult to appreciate that children a century ago could reasonably expect to be orphaned before reaching maturity, or that parents might expect to lose one or several children before the children reached adulthood.

Causes of death have also changed dramatically since 1867. Deaths from infectious diseases have declined, while those from chronic diseases, especially cardiovascular diseases, account for 32% of all deaths. About 25% of deaths are caused by neoplasms (cancer), and about 1 in 10 is caused by accident, poisoning or violence. Pneumonia used to be called "the old man's friend" because it brought a swift and relatively painless death to the elderly, but today it accounts for less than 3% of deaths.

Social institutions have generally evolved to facilitate life and prevent death. Some social scientists have postulated that death in societies with low mortality rates poses a greater threat to the personality than it does in societies with high mortality rates because such societies tend to proscribe social solutions to the problems of mortality. Studies of attitudes toward death have revealed the importance to the dying individual of a secure environment and close family ties. The fact that dying is now usually the termination of a long, chronic illness, most likely in advanced age, affects not only how people think about death and about their own dying, but the type of care provided to dying persons. The great majority of nonaccidental deaths occur in hospitals, but nursing homes have also become an important place where people, especially women, die. As a result, death is less familiar in the experience of most people and dying is largely a process managed by health-care professionals. Since the late 1960s, the increasingly technological nature of hospital death has aroused concern. A hospital is perceived as a cold and indifferent setting where existence is often prolonged by technology long after the individual has ceased to enjoy quality of life and where the needs of the dying person and his or her relatives or friends are less important than the smooth functioning of the hospital bureaucracy. Dr Cicely Saunders in England, Dr Elizabeth Kübler-Ross in the US and Dr Balfour Mount of the Royal Victoria Hospital in Montréal have pioneered palliative-care services or "hospice" units which specialize in caring for the terminally ill. St Christopher's Hospice in England, established by Dr Saunders, is a freestanding, 62-bed unit. Today, smaller units based within hospital settings are more common; often these are linked to community-based home-care services because, although palliative care began as an attempt to humanize dying in hospitals, it has increasingly emphasized community-based care and the use of nonprofessional volunteers. These services share a commitment to providing high-quality care, including an emphasis on adequate pain control; to ensuring emotional support to patients who realize they are dying; to allowing the staff to develop an emotional commitment to the patients; and to recognizing a concern for the relatives and others close to the patients. Some programs also provide counselling and support for staff. Hospice units, some integrated into hospitals, and palliative-care programs, which support the dying and those who care for them, have spread rapidly in Canada. In Toronto in 1981, the

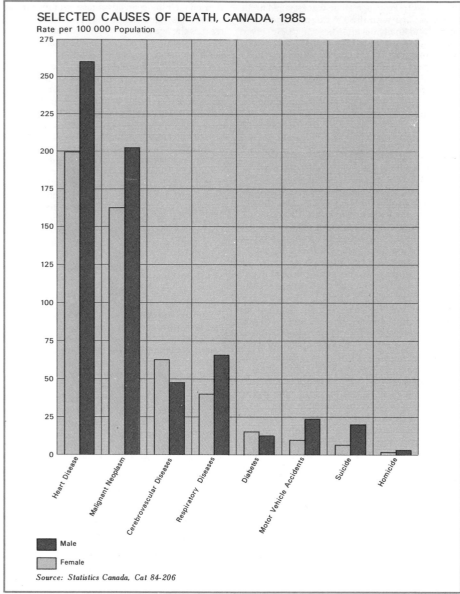

SELECTED CAUSES OF DEATH, CANADA, 1985
Rate per 100 000 Population

Male
Female

Source: Statistics Canada, Cat 84-206

Palliative Care Foundation conducted a survey which identified 109 palliative-care groups, organizations, programs or centres of activity in Canada, ranging from hospital-based programs and hospices to professional groups such as the Toronto Palliative Care Working Group and the Ontario Palliative Care Association.

Research and teaching about death and dying, particularly from social-science and health-care perspectives, has burgeoned in N America, perhaps because through science and technology we have gained much more control over the timing of death and are now confronted with the dilemma of determining to what extent and with what measures dying should be shortened or prolonged (*see* MEDICAL ETHICS). In 1969 there were about 6 university-level courses on death and dying, one of which was taught at U of Calgary. Today there are hundreds of such courses, as well as numerous in-service and continuing-education courses in health care. Curricula for such courses vary widely but may include attention to changing causes of death, clinical help for the dying, psychological impact of death and dying on those of various ages who are dying and on those around them, the processes of bereavement and grief, and ethical issues, eg, euthanasia and clinical decision making. Many courses also focus on philosophical or literary treatments of death and dying. In 1969, the journal *Omega*, a major re-

search journal in the area, was founded. *Essence: Issues in the Study of Aging, Dying and Death*, a York University journal, published international research until 1982.

Fear of death is the subject of extensive current psychological and sociological research. The anticipation of personal death apparently initiates preparatory processes in which people try to put their affairs in order and to make sense of their impending death and of their lives. Fear and other attitudes toward death appear to vary by age (ie, anticipated remaining years of life), by education levels and by belief systems. The fear of death can be mediated by a sense of continuity, eg, through biology, through works that will survive the creator, through a belief in a deep relationship with nature, etc.

Counsellors claim that compassion, honesty and reassurance help the seriously ill adapt to the approach of death. Dying persons are often abandoned psychologically by family, friends and doctors. Dr Kübler-Ross has claimed that psychological distress diminishes if the patient is not alone and is able to express feelings and concerns, but her theories that dying patients experience a predictable 5-stage sequence of adjustment after learning of their condition, although held by many health-care practitioners, are rejected by most reputable scholars in this field. Bereavement is now perceived as a normal psychological

and physiological reaction to death. Grief can be characterized by somatic distress, guilt, hostility, change in patterns of conduct, etc. In Western societies, individuals, after the initial shock, are typically left to grieve alone and there is no conclusive evidence that religious belief helps to alleviate bereavement.

The new character of death is associated with changes in the way it is experienced; eg, usually it follows a lengthy, chronic illness and occurs late in life. In modern Canadian society it is in many respects hidden, especially from the young, as few people die at home. Formal ritual to mark its occurrence has also changed. Mourning dress is now rare in Canada except among some ethnic communities, and FUNERAL PRACTICES are becoming less ornate, frequently reflecting the wishes and prior arrangements of the deceased.

VICTOR W. MARSHALL

Reading: C. Charmaz, *The Social Reality of Death* (1980); Victor W. Marshall, *Last Chapters* (1980); R. Kastenbaum and R. Aisenberg, *The Psychology of Death* (1972); J. Fruehling, ed, *Sourcebook on Death and Dying* (1982).

Debassige, Blake Randolph, artist (b at West Bay, Ont 22 June 1956). A leading member of the "second generation" of Ojibwa artists influenced by MORRISSEAU, Debassige has broadened the stylistic and thematic range of this school. In his teens he was deeply influenced by the legend painter Isidore Wadow and by a close study of rock art. From these sources he has developed a "visual language" to express both personal experiences and traditional values of continuing relevance. Debassige married the Cree painter Shirley CheeChoo in 1978. RUTH B. PHILLIPS

Debert, archaeological site located in north-central NS. It is the earliest dated archaeological site found in eastern Canada. Radiocarbon dating places its age at about 10 600 years. Among the many stone implements are distinctive fluted, lanceolate spearpoints of a type ultimately derived from the CLOVIS Big-Game Hunting tradition of western N America. Similar assemblages found at sites in the eastern US suggest a rapid spread of early man into the Maritimes region. Many of the stone tools found at Debert relate to hunting and butchering activities. Although no bone remains were preserved, it is believed that the site served as a hunting encampment, strategically located to intercept herds of Woodland caribou then abundant in the region. Paleoecological data indicate a forest-tundra environment prevailing at the time of site habitation. *See also* ARCHAEOLOGY.

DAVID L. KEENLYSIDE

Decentralization, in federal countries, occurs when there is a substantial sharing of power, authority, financial resources and political support among federal, provincial and local GOVERNMENTS. The less concentrated these resources are in the central government, the more decentralized the system. Decentralization may also mean a process of shifting power from the federal to provincial governments. It is often said that the provinces' strength may make Canada the world's most decentralized federal country, and that Canada has resisted economic and social forces which increased centralization elsewhere (*see* FEDERALISM). Decentralization also means power-sharing among any set of units; centralization within the federal or provincial governments can be gauged by assessing power in Cabinet as compared to that in legislatures, judiciaries or other bodies. RICHARD SIMEON

Decline of the American Empire, The (1986) film directed by Denys ARCAND, who also wrote the screenplay. The director of photography was Guy Dufaux; the editor, Monique Fortier, and co-production was by Corporation

Image M&M and the NFB. Four history professors (played by Daniel Brière, Rémy Girard, Pierre Curzi and Yves Jacques) prepare a gourmet dinner while their friends (played by Dominique Michel, Dorothée Berryman, Louise Portal and Geneviève Rioux) work out at a sports complex. The film also starred Gabriel Arcand. This study of manners, in the form of a social satire, is a cynical commentary on the decline of collective ideals in present-day society; its subjects are male-female relationships, private life, the search for sexual originality and the rejection of moralism. Unlike anonymous products aimed at the international market, this film emphasizes its regional and cultural identity. Yet *Decline* won unprecedented international acclaim – prizes in Chicago; Cannes and Sète, France; Rio, Brazil; and Taormina, Italy; acclaim in New York and Toronto and an Academy Award nomination. Simultaneous release was in French and in English. Produced for $1 775 000, it broke box-office records, earning $2 500 000 in 6 months in Québec. It was a huge success in English Canada, and had an unprecedented foreign commercial distribution (more than 30 countries). From every point of view, it was a phenomenon in the history of Canadian cinema.   PIERRE VÉRONNEAU

Decorations for Bravery Three decorations for bravery were instituted in 1972 to serve as a public expression of respect and admiration for persons who perform selfless acts of courage. The scale of awards reflects the degree of peril faced by the recipients.

The Cross of Valour, at the head of Canada's system of HONOURS, takes precedence before all orders and other decorations except the VICTORIA CROSS and GEORGE CROSS. It is a gold cross of 4 equal limbs, the obverse enamelled red with, at its centre, a maple leaf surrounded by a laurel wreath. On the reverse is the royal crown and cypher with the words "Valour-Vaillance." The decoration is worn at the neck on a red ribbon. The Star of Courage is a 4-pointed silver star with a maple leaf encircled by a laurel wreath at the centre and, on the reverse, the word "Courage." The ribbon is red with 2 blue stripes. The Medal of Bravery is a circular silver medal with a maple leaf centered within a laurel wreath on the obverse and the words "Bravery-Bravoure" on the reverse. The

Star of Courage (*courtesy National Archives of Canada*).

Medal of Bravery (*courtesy National Archives of Canada*).

ribbon is red with 3 blue stripes. Recipients of bravery decorations are entitled to have the relevant letters placed after their names: CV, SC or MB.

Awards are made by the governor general with the advice and assistance of the Canadian Decorations Advisory Committee and the investigative resources of the police services.   CARL LOCHNAN

Deep River, Ont, Town, pop 4602 (1986c), inc 1959, located in eastern Ontario, 208 km NW of Ottawa, on the section of the OTTAWA R referred to as La Rivière Creuse (the Deep River) by 17th-century French explorers and which later was at the heart of Canada's 19th-century TIMBER TRADE. In a beautiful natural setting with excellent year-round recreational facilities, Canada's first "atomic town" is a planned community where streets follow natural land contours and bear names reflecting the area's history: eg, Algonquin, Champlain, Spruce and Rutherford. Established by the federal government in 1944 to house employees of the Chalk River Nuclear Laboratories of Atomic Energy of Canada Ltd, it re-

mains a residential community whose economy is rooted in the Canadian nuclear industry.
                                              JOAN MELVIN

Deep Rover A one-man submersible capable of working 4-6 hours under water to a depth of 914 m at speeds up to 1.5 knots, Deep Rover was designed by Graham Hawkes at San Leandro, Calif, and built by Can-Dive Services Ltd of Vancouver and in Dartmouth, NS, in 1984 to work in the offshore oil industry. Weighing 3266 kg, its acrylic hull gives the operator a 360° field of view. A pair of specially designed manipulator arms enables the operator to move or service equipment and even to sense the texture of objects. Somewhat like a helicopter, the submersible can operate moving freely, or it can be tethered to a surface platform such as an oil rig supply vessel. After the decline of offshore exploration in Canada in the mid-1980s, it was used mainly for basic science studies in the US.   ERIC L. MILLS

Deer (Cervidae), family of antlered, hoofed ruminants containing about 40 species worldwide (5 in Canada: white-tailed and mule deer, CARIBOU, MOOSE, WAPITI). Deer are large-brained and adaptable. Antlers are found in males of all Canadian species, and in most female caribou. They consist of bone and grow rapidly (4 months in moose), and are shed annually. Velvet (hairy skin, well supplied with nerves and blood vessels) covers and nourishes the growing antlers. In autumn, when antlers are fully grown, the velvet dies and is rubbed off and males are ready to mate. Antlers are used as weapons against rival males and predators and as display organs to intimidate rivals and lure females. Increase in antler size, symmetry and complexity varies with age, health and diet. Deer began their evolutionary radiation as small-bodied, antlerless, tropical herbivores. For 30 million years they evolved slowly. As they invaded open parkland habitats and harsher climates, increases occurred in body size, antler size and complexity, and coat coloration and ornamentation. This evolution resulted in grotesque giants in subarctic, subalpine and glacial environments, eg, the extinct Irish elk (Old World), and the moose (New World). Both could exceed 600 kg. The Alaska bull moose may carry antlers ex-

White-tailed deer fawn. White-tailed deer (*O. virginianus*) are dispersed widely across Canada and live secretly in cities where green belts or large parks provide cover (*photo by V. Claerhout*).

ceeding 30 kg and 2 m in spread; those of Irish elk exceeded 38 kg and 3 m.

The 2 most common deer in Canada, white-tailed and mule deer, are closely related species of genus *Odocoileus*. Both occur in many subspecies including dwarf island forms. A Eurasian species, fallow deer (*Cervus dama*), has been successfully introduced to James I, BC. Fossils of white-tailed deer (*O. virginianus*) predate the Ice Age; the mule deer (*O. hemionus*) originated more recently. Its most primitive subspecies, black-tailed deer (*O. h. columbianus*), lives along the Pacific coastline from Alaska to California. Mule deer, characteristic of the mountains and foothills of western N America, sometimes occur as far E as Manitoba. White-tailed deer occur across southern Canada and as far N as the Peace R, Alta. If protected, both species thrive around human settlements; white-tails, being very secretive, may thrive with little protection. Both are adapted to feed on soft vegetation; however, they have different antipredator strategies. Mule deer throw obstacles in the path of pursuing predators; white-tails combine hiding with rapid getaway over unobstructed ground. Both can be gregarious on open terrain, secretive in dense forests. Females may become territorial when raising young; black-tailed deer may cluster into group territories. At northern latitudes, mating occurs in late Nov and early Dec; fawns are born in June. Males guard one female at a time and do not advertise their whereabouts to rivals. Both species have long sparring ceremonies, but few fights occur. Deer are economically significant mainly as game animals, although the reindeer is domesticated and the velveted antler has been used for pharmaceutical purposes. Deer have been widely introduced as game and park animals. They generally respond well to adequate habitat and protection from excessive HUNTING: moose have spread widely in Eurasia and N America; in America, white-tailed and mule deer have dispersed widely and live secretly in cities where green belts or large parks provide food and cover. In Canada, the caribou is economically and culturally significant to native people; moose and white-tailed deer have provided meat for many rural families. White-tails are the most important big-game animals in N America today. VALERIUS GEIST

Deer Island abuts the border with the US at the entrance to PASSAMAQUODDY BAY on the S coast of New Brunswick. Long in dispute with the US, sovereignty over the island passed to NB in 1817. The name is probably descriptive. Fishing is the most important economic activity. The island is the site of the world's 3 largest lobster pounds, natural inlets converted by fences and nets into corrals where lobsters are held while waiting shipment to market. The 2 largest communities are Fairhaven and Leonardville. Ferry service connects with Letete, NB, and Eastport, Maine. DANIEL FRANCIS

Deer Lake, Nfld, Town, pop 4233 (1986c), 4348 (1981c), inc 1950, is located at the N end of Deer Lk in western Newfoundland. The eastern shore of the lake was settled 1867 by a Cape Breton I family who began an operation to cut pine trees. The site was named Nicholsville and expanded with the building of the railway in the 1880s and 1890s. In 1923 Deer Lake was selected as the site of a power plant to support a pulp and paper mill at nearby CORNER BROOK. In 1957 the federal government built a large airstrip here. This, with the railway and highway connections to Bay of Islands, Humber Valley, Great Northern Pen and Baie Verte Pen, has made Deer Lk one of the main pulpwood, service and transportation centres of Newfoundland. JANET E.M. PITT AND ROBERT D. PITT

Deer Mouse (*Peromyscus maniculatus*), typical MOUSE with moderately long tail, large ears, prominent eyes and pointed nose well supplied with tactile hairs. Upperparts are grey or brown, depending on age and subspecies; underside, white. Even the tail is 2-toned. Deer mice occur in forests and grasslands throughout Canada, excluding Newfoundland, and down the Mackenzie Valley beyond the Arctic Circle. They are strongly nocturnal. In winter, northern deer mice (*P. m. borealis*) undergo bouts of light torpor, lasting for up to several days, in which body temperature may fall several degrees, but they do not actually hibernate. Deer mice breed only in summer. Females of northern populations never have more than 2 litters (of about 5 young). In southern Canada, females produce more, smaller litters; some may become sexually mature in the season of their birth. A few animals are known to have survived 2 winters. Deer mice may destroy stored food, but otherwise are of little direct economic importance. They provide food for carnivorous birds and mammals. The large, pale-grey Cascade deer mouse (*P. oreas*) of the Coast Range of BC may represent a distinct species. W.A. FULLER

Defamation law protects an individual's reputation and good name. Traditionally, libel included defamatory written words, pictures, statues, films and even conduct; whereas slander was a defamatory spoken word. With the advent of the electronic media, such as radio and television, the difference between the written and spoken word became less important than whether the defamation was in permanent or nonpermanent form. Some provinces have even eliminated any practical distinctions between libel and slander. A claimant must prove that the material was defamatory, that it referred to the claimant and that it was communicated to a third person. There are certain occasions of qualified privilege when a defamation can be published as long as this is not done maliciously. The defence of fair comment protects any opinion fairly made on a matter of public interest. In the COMMON LAW provinces, the truth of the material provides the defendant with a complete defence. (In Québec, truth is only a defence if the material was in the public interest and there was no malice.) If someone is liable, compensatory and punitive damages may be awarded. The court can also order that there be no further publications of the defamation. In certain forums, such as Parliament and courts, free speech is deemed so important that no defamation proceedings can be brought for statements made there. LEWIS N. KLAR

Reading: G.A. Flaherty, *Defamation Law in Canada* (1984).

Defence Counsel, lawyer who advises accused (defendants in civil cases) and presents their case to the court, ensuring that clients have a fair trial. If a client is convicted, the defence counsel speaks in respect of sentence. K.G. McSHANE

Defence Policy Canada, according to C.P. Stacey, is "an unmilitary community." This is no accident. Canadians have paid no price for unpreparedness. FORTIFICATIONS built at British or French expense serve crowds of tourists as monuments to folly. Capital which might have been lavished on defence was available for the Intercolonial and the Canadian Pacific railways and to finance the social programs of the 20th century.

Before 1870, the defence of Canada was a costly burden for France and then Great Britain, invariably against enemies to the south, be they Iroquois, English or the American invaders of 1775-76 (*see* AMERICAN REVOLUTION) or of 1812-14. The AMERICAN CIVIL WAR persuaded the British that there could be no successful replay of the WAR OF 1812. Confederation in 1867 became, in British eyes, a device to help their N American colonists accept the hopeless burden of their own defence. Withdrawal of British garrisons from central Canada in 1871 left the young Dominion to its own devices.

Canadians faced the paradox of being at once invulnerable and indefensible. Distance and the Royal Navy safeguarded both ocean frontiers from all but occasional raids. The North remained impassable until the advent of long-range aircraft in the 1930s. To the south, whatever George T. DENISON and other militia colonels might assert, defence was impossible without a level of preparedness that would, itself, be provocative. The answer, as A.-A. DORION warned in 1865, was "to keep quiet and give no cause for war." The Treaty of WASHINGTON, 1871 and the ALASKA BOUNDARY DISPUTE, 1903, removed threats to peace. So did the NORTH-WEST MOUNTED POLICE, created in 1873 to prevent the banditry and border violence that might draw US troops into "the Great Lone Land" as they did in Mexico, Nicaragua, Haiti and other countries to the south.

Canada's second line of defence was a British guarantee, offered in 1865, to defend every part of the empire "with all the forces at its command," in return for a Canadian pledge to "devote all her resources, both in men and money, to the maintenance of her connection with the Mother Country." The Venezuela crisis of 1895-96 showed that the British had given no thought to their commitment. Nor had Canada. A militia of 40 000 on paper, costing $1 million a year, was described by an American observer as "a kind of Military Tammany." Reformers were not welcome. Both Conservatives and Liberals promoted Canada as a refuge from conscription and a haven from what Sir Wilfrid LAURIER called "the vortex of European militarism."

When wars came in the 20th century, Canadians could answer the call of a noble cause or a half-remembered homeland because their own country was inviolable. Others, unmoved by the crusading fever, would grow resentful that fellow citizens would involve them in what Armand Laverge termed "a somewhat interesting adventure in a foreign country." In WWI, the external threat was sufficiently remote that the few thousand defenders of Halifax or the Welland Canal were denied the status of veterans. In WWII, somewhat a more real threat from German and Japanese submarines hardly justified the 3 army divisions or the large Home War Establishment of the RCAF. Even in the crisis of 1940, Canada was still, in the words of Senator Raoul Dandurand 16 years earlier, "a fireproof house, far from the sources of conflagration."

That status ended abruptly in 1945. Five years earlier, at Ogdensburg, NY, US President Franklin Delano Roosevelt had invited Canada into the American defence system largely to meet Washington's anxiety about potential hostile use of the North as a staging area for air attacks. Convinced that he was serving his linchpin role between the US and Britain, PM Mackenzie KING enthusiastically agreed. Canadians had largely ignored the military significance of the Arctic; Americans did not. Only belatedly did Ottawa recognize the threat to Canadian ARCTIC SOVEREIGNTY as Americans poured north to build the ALASKA HIGHWAY and northern air bases. In the postwar period, as Soviet-American hostility rapidly developed into a COLD WAR, Canada found itself between 2 belligerent superpowers. Canadian defence faced a new paradox: the Soviet Union was the ultimate enemy, but the US was the immediate threat. Washington would be sole judge of N America's security; Canadians could play their assigned role or Americans would do it for them.

By the 1950s, the USSR had thermonuclear weapons and a limited capacity to deliver them to US and Canadian cities. Canadians became partners in a continental air defence system with 3 northern radar lines and fighter-interceptor squadrons that operated largely on Canadian soil. NATO, Canada's "providential solution" to the dangers of a lopsided bilateral alliance, was rejected by Washington as an agency for N American defence. The North American Air Defence (NORAD) agreement, accepted by Ottawa in 1957, made military sense for a continent in danger; politically it gave Washington effective control over Canada's right to make war or peace. That fact, belatedly absorbed by the Diefenbaker government during the 1962 CUBAN MISSILE CRISIS, left a gap in NORAD defences and a political crisis. The ensuing 1963 election led to a change of governments – a rare intervention of defence issues in peacetime Canadian politics.

Technology temporarily rescued Canadians from domestic defence dilemmas. Nuclear warfare was transformed by the stratospheric trajectory of intercontinental ballistic missiles (ICBMs) and the abstractions of MAD (mutually-assured destruction). Nuclear-tipped rockets would pass far over Canada to fall on superpower soil. Defence priorities which, in 1949, 1959 and 1964, had formally listed NATO, NORAD and Canada's PEACEKEEPING contribution to the UNITED NATIONS at the top, were abruptly reversed by the Trudeau government. Defence "Priority One" became SOVEREIGNTY, whether defined as surveillance of Canada's frontiers or overawing opponents of national unity in the October Crisis of 1970. Fishery patrols, arctic overflights and a tiny Northern Command at Yellowknife were combined with drastic reductions in armed forces strength, largely at the expense of Canada's NATO commitment. Armed Forces strength, which had dropped from 120 000 to 100 000 in the Pearson years, was slashed by the Trudeau government to 78 000 men and women in the regular forces and less than 20 000 in the reserves. Re-equipment programs languished until the late 1970s when pressure from Washington and NATO allies forced the government to buy new fighter aircraft (the CF-18 Hornet) and long-range patrol aircraft.

By 1984, many Canadians were embarrassed by the weakness and obsolescence of their defences. The Anglo-Argentine conflict in the Falklands reminded Canadians that their own small fleet was utterly defenceless in modern war. The Mulroney government, elected in Sept 1984, pledged expansion and modernization, partly to restore national pride, partly to reassure the Reagan administration. In 1987, a long-awaited White Paper, issued by defence minister Perrin Beatty, reasserted Canada's alliance commitments, promised a "total force" concept with the reserves rebuilt to a strength of 90 000 and major capital funding to reverse the "rust-out" of weapons and equipment.

The most controversial feature of the policy was a greater concentration on defending Canadian sovereignty, most notably by the promised acquisition of 12 nuclear submarines, the only warships capable of operating in all 3 of Canada's ocean frontiers. The government was also committed to 60% of the cost of a new North Warning system and to developing 5 northern air bases for high-performance fighters.

Canada's defence policies since 1945 have reflected a slow realization that neither oceans nor empty landmasses will protect Canadians. The air-breathing Cruise missile has become an air-defence problem analogous to the manned bomber of the 1950s, requiring the same countermeasures of radar detection and fighter interception. Arctic waters, once ignored, could become

an under-ice battleground. Critics, represented most strongly in Canada's New Democratic Party, have argued that Canadian resources are fully needed to defend Canadian space without a distracting token commitment to defend Europe's Central Front. On the whole, Canadians supported NATO, partly because of memories of 2 world wars, partly because of alliance inertia and partly because of fears of being left in an unbalanced bilateral relationship with the US. "Twelve in the bed," said an early proponent of NATO, "means no rape."

Canadians have also sought their own security through a persistent postwar involvement in disarmament, with credentials established by Canada's early contribution to nuclear technology. Peacekeeping in the Sinai, Cyprus or the Golan Heights has also been a way of limiting and localizing conflicts that could draw the superpowers into conflict.

Canadian strategists will increasingly face the difficulties imposed by terrain, climate, resources and a limited population. They will also have to argue with experience. For 2 centuries, Canadian wars have happened somewhere else. The illusion of inviolability co-exists with a widespread belief in the futility and folly of military preparations. In a world more dangerous than Canadians have ever known, ideas shaped in an age of "fireproof houses" and victorious foreign wars may be obsolete. The problem is that new ideas must rest on imagination: in a nuclear age, learning from experience is far too horrible even to contemplate. DESMOND MORTON

Defence Research, initiation and development of weapons or technologies likely to be useful in national defence, is a comparatively recent phenomenon in Canada. Although there were some rudimentary efforts at developing new defence technologies during WWI, it was only with WWII that the Canadian government began to pay attention to innovations in equipment and techniques. Various research establishments were set up to investigate problems as diverse as ordnance, ballistics, radar, winter warfare, chemical warfare and aviation medicine.

At the end of the war, at the insistence of Chief of the General Staff Gen Charles FOULKES, Canada's defence research programs were consolidated and preserved as much as limited funds would allow. It was obvious that certain limitations obtained: only a few projects could be pursued at any time; research had to be co-ordinated with that of Canada's principal allies, Britain and the US, and the research program should be integrated as far as possible into other research enterprises. It was decided that the best means of securing a relatively independent and prestigious research enterprise was to set up a Defence Research Board under the Department of NATIONAL DEFENCE. In addition to members and staff of the board in Canada, liaison officers were appointed to work in London and Washington, and later also in Paris.

The work of the DRB has been extremely varied. Attention has been given to relatively conventional subjects such as explosives and propellants, but also to missile development (on a modest scale compared to the US or the USSR), northern or arctic research, and telecommunications, including research into exploring the ionosphere. At the Suffield Experimental Station at Ralston, Alta, chemical and other highly classified work has been carried on since WWII. In co-operation with the navy the DRB developed new antisubmarine technologies, such as the Variable Depth SONAR, and helped to adapt helicopters for antisubmarine work. The DRB also contributed heavily to siting and developing the EARLY-WARNING RADAR of the 1950s across the Canadian North (see NORAD).

More broadly, Canadian defence research has contributed technological expertise to Canadian industry, although there is some dispute as to whether the DRB is the appropriate organization to help guide industrial development. Defence research also presents the possibility of aiding in arms control as well as weapons research, but whether such a linkage will prove successful is not certain. ROBERT BOTHWELL

Deiter, Walter, politician, businessman (b at Peepeekesis Indian Reserve, Sask 31 May 1916). Deiter was active in the development of Indian political organizations in the 1960s. His first political position was as president of the Regina Indian and Métis Friendship Centre (1962-67). As chief (1967-68) of the newly reactivated Federation of Saskatchewan Indians (now informally the Federation of Saskatchewan Indian nations) he helped establish the National Indian Brotherhood (see ASSEMBLY OF FIRST NATIONS) and became its first president (1968-70). During his tenure the NIB became a working national organization and helped to oppose the 1969 White Paper. Deiter maintained a relatively conservative stand on such matters as Indian-government relations, education and community development. Opposition from local and more radical factions of the Indian movement led to his defeat by George MANUEL in 1970. Since that time he has worked with various Indian organizations in Saskatchewan and is a senator of the Federation of Saskatchewan Indian Nations. BENNETT McCARDLE

Dekanahwideh, "the Heavenly Messenger," reputed founder of the Five Nations Confederacy. He was said to have been born among the HURON of a virgin mother, destined to bring peace and power to his people. His first miracle was building a stone canoe, in which he travelled to the Onondaga, where he made his first convert – Hiawatha. He spoke his message of peace among the warring Mohawk, Oneida, Cayuga and Seneca. His power in defying death and darkening the sun converted sceptics; a Great Peace was achieved and the Confederacy of the Five (later Six) Nations was born. Dekanahwideh planted a great white pine, the Tree of Peace, appointed 50 chiefs and slipped into the Great Lakes in his stone canoe, promising to return if the peace were threatened. This majestic narrative fostered unity among the fiercely independent IROQUOIS, and homage is still paid to his memory among the Six Nations people. JAMES MARSH

Delamont, Gordon, music teacher, composer (b at Moose Jaw, Sask 27 Oct 1918; d at Toronto 16 Jan 1981). After failing health curtailed his career as a trumpeter in 1949, Delamont turned to teaching in Toronto and guided many prominent Canadian jazz and pop musicians, among them Ron COLLIER, Jimmy Dale, Hagood HARDY, Rob MC-CONNELL, Ben McPeek, Fred Stone and Norman SYMONDS. Delamont completed 6 volumes of composition-technique studies, published between 1965 and 1976 and used internationally. He also composed several works in the third-stream idiom that he, Collier and Symonds promoted in Canada during the 1950s and 1960s. His best-known composition was *Three Entertainments for Saxophone Quartet* (1969). MARK MILLER

Délégations du Québec In 1871 the Québec government opened an immigration office in London, Eng, and in 1882 it named the first commercial representative for trade and commerce to France. Since then, Québec has established 28 delegations abroad, under the jurisdiction of the ministère des relations internationales (Department of International Relations), and 4 Bureaux du Québec within Canada, administered by the Secrétariat aux affaires intergouvernementales.

The delegations and the bureaux organize industrial missions and exchanges of specialists, encourage investment in Québec and participate in or organize fairs and expositions. They also promote Québec artists, writers and publishers and their work. One of their foremost objectives abroad is to make known the French presence in N America. The dissemination of French as a modern language is also a priority. Since 1970 more than 5000 Quebeckers have participated in exchanges in a variety of fields under the auspices of Délégations.   GISÈLE VILLENEUVE

Delict, in Québec CIVIL LAW, is a civil wrong other than a breach of contract. The law of delicts covers approximately the same field as that of TORTS in COMMON LAW. Strictly speaking, a distinction should be made between delicts, ie, intentionally committed wrongs, and quasi-delicts, ie, unintentionally or negligently committed wrongs, although with some minor exceptions, the practical consequences of both are identical. The purpose of the law is not to punish but to provide compensation for damages (material and moral), compensation aimed at putting injured parties back into the situation they enjoyed before the delict or quasi-delict was committed. In a number of isolated instances Québec law now awards punitive or exemplary damages as well, particularly for wrongs committed under Article 49 of the Québec Human Rights Charter and Article 272 of the Consumer Protection Act.

The Québec law of delicts is part of the law of obligations. Traditionally, delicts did not govern breach of contract, but recently Québec courts and the SUPREME COURT OF CANADA have allowed plaintiffs to sue in delict even if there exists a contractual agreement with the defendant. Examples of delictual liabilities include those arising from traffic accidents, destruction of or damage to property, nuisance, medical and other professional MALPRACTICES, DEFAMATION and the manufacturing and distribution of defective or dangerous products.

The Québec law of delicts originated in the Napoleonic Code and the works of the French jurist Domat. Both the French and the Québec laws of delicts contain one general delictual principle and a number of subsidiary special rules. In that sense French and Québec law differ from both traditional Roman and traditional common law, which know a system of different nominate torts or delicts, each with its own rules and fields of application.

The Napoleonic Code and the Québec CIVIL CODE are extremely concise in their treatment of delicts, but although their basic notions are identical, drafting and substantive differences do exist. In both France and Québec JURISPRUDENCE (in the civil-law sense of case law) is extremely important to the law of delicts precisely because the codes' treatment of the subject matter is so concise and often very general. The law of delicts cannot be understood unless the text of the code is read in conjunction with the court cases that interpret and elaborate upon it. In Québec, common law has considerably influenced the cases governed by the law of delicts.

The fundamental principles and concepts of the Québec law of delicts are contained in Articles 1053-1056 of the Civil Code. Article 1053 states, "Every person capable of discerning right from wrong is responsible for the damage caused by his own fault to another, whether by positive act, imprudence, neglect or want of skill." On the basis of this provision, of case law and of doctrine, 4 characteristics of a delict or quasi-delict can be identified: fault, imputability, damage and causality. First, the wrongdoer must be at fault. Fault is an objective criterion; it can consist of commission,

eg, acting contrary to the standard of a reasonable person in similar circumstances, or of omission, eg, failure to act where the reasonable person would be under a legal duty to do so. Second, the wrongdoer must be imputable, ie, able to discern right from wrong. Imputability is a subjective criterion. Young children (generally under 6 years of age) and insane persons, for instance, are held unable to discern right from wrong. Third, the wrongdoer must cause damage. Damage may be material (injury, property damage, loss of profit) or immaterial (harm to reputation, pain and suffering, loss of enjoyment of life). Fourth, the fault must have caused the damage. Québec case law does not adhere to any particular causation theory, but generally the courts say that the fault must have been the determining cause of the damage. There is no compensation for so-called indirect or ricochet damage. Once a delict has been established, the victim is entitled to obtain payment of damages from the wrongdoer. Sometimes the victim can also obtain a court injunction against the wrongdoer under the provisions of the Code of CIVIL PROCEDURE.

Article 1053 covers liability for one's personal acts. Articles 1054 and 1055 deal with liability for the acts of others and liability for things under one's care. Article 1054 (s2-7) makes parents liable for the damage caused by their minor children; tutors for damage caused by their pupils; guardians for damage caused by insane persons under their care; teachers for damage caused by their students; and employers for damage caused by their employees. The main difference between Articles 1053 and 1054 (s2-7) is that generally the wrongdoer's fault under Article 1053 must be proven by the victim, but the fault of the responsible persons under article 1054 is legally presumed. They can exculpate themselves by proving absence of fault, eg, having adequately fulfilled their duties of supervision or upbringing or both. However, an employer's fault is irrefutably presumed; if an employee has through his fault caused damage during employment, the employer is automatically liable. Liability for things under one's care is based on Articles 1054(s1) and 1055. Owners and users of animals are liable for damage done by such animals unless they can prove the occurrence of a fortuitous event. The same applies to owners of buildings for total or partial ruin of a building due to construction defects or want of repairs. For things other than animals and buildings, there is a legal presumption that the guardian of a thing is responsible for damage caused by the autonomous act of the thing, although the guardian can rebut the presumption by proving absence of fault.

Although generally both direct and indirect victims (eg, relatives of the victim, or his employer) may sue for damages in delict, under Article 1056, which originated in the English Lord Campbell's Act, in death actions only the spouse, parents and children of the deceased victim are considered indirect victims.

Recently, delictual rules have also surfaced outside the Civil Code in special statutes. Besides the Human Rights Charter and the Consumer Protection Act, relevant statutes include the Automobile Insurance Act and the Crime Victims Compensation Act. Furthermore, a revision of the code articles on delicts has been proposed by the Civil Code Revision Office in its 1977 Draft Civil Code.   P. HAANAPPEL

Reading: M. Lancelin, *Théorie du droit des obligations* (1975); J. Pineau, Théorie des obligations (1979).

Delta, BC, District Municipality, pop 79 610 (1986c), 74 692 (1981c), area 17 600 ha, inc as the Corporation of Delta 1879, is located in the southern part of Greater VANCOUVER — S of the

Fraser R, W of the municipality of Surrey and touching the US border. Its 3 main communities are North Delta, Ladner and South Delta. Most of the district, as its name implies, is low-lying delta land, and much is farmland designated "Agricultural Land Reserve" by the province. By the early 1900s the community supported 40 businesses, but with the shift of marine traffic from the Lower Fraser to Burrard Inlet and the newly emerging port of Vancouver, Delta's importance declined and it became a rural farming area with limited fishing activity. The opening of Boundary Bay Air Force Station in 1941 significantly increased Ladner's population. Postwar growth was first felt in N Delta as the Vancouver metropolitan area spread S of the Fraser. Completion of the Massey Tunnel under the Fraser in 1959 increased suburban growth. Completion of a ferry terminal in 1960 on Roberts Bank in S Delta was followed by construction of the Roberts Bank Superport. The communities of Beach Grove, Boundary Bay and Tsawwassen offer beaches and other recreational facilities for tourists. Distinctive features and attractions include the recently opened Deas Island Regional Park, the Delta Museum and Archives, the Reifel Bird Sanctuary and Point Roberts (American territory not connected by land to the US). The municipality remains largely a suburban community, with a strong industrial base.

ALAN F.J. ARTIBISE

Delta (1957-66), poetry magazine established in Montréal by Louis DUDEK. Its 26 issues appeared irregularly. Dudek encouraged experimental POETRY and occasionally published essays of his own; these reflected his conviction that poetry should have clear relevance to its time and particularly to social issues. *Delta* strongly projected its editor's personality and spoke especially to those who shared his modernist views.

GEORGE WOODCOCK

Delta, deposit of sediment accumulating at the mouth of a river. By-products of continental EROSION, deltas form when rivers flow into standing bodies of water (eg, lakes, oceans) rapidly depositing their load of alluvial material (eg, gravel, sand, silt and clay). Deposition results from a loss of transporting capacity caused by deceleration of the current. Deltas vary enormously in scale and complexity, ranging from small lacustrine deltas with lobate shape and tripartite structure (topset, foreset and bottomset) to large, composite bird-foot deltas formed along ocean shorelines. The shape of large deltas, many of which have persisted over long periods of time, is controlled by stream HYDROLOGY, the nature of transported sediment, wave and tidal dynamics, sea-level changes, crustal movements and basin and coastline configuration. Depending on density differences between the sediment-laden river water and the lake or ocean water, the inflowing water may move down the prodelta slope as a gravity underflow (ie, below the surface), spread out over the surface of the standing body of water, or otherwise mix with it as an interflow. The kind of movement has a bearing on the mechanism of growth. Strong tidal currents and high WAVE ENERGY, which tend to disperse sediment, militate against delta formation. Large deltas (eg, Mississippi) are traversed by a network of distributory channels, and delta growth is accompanied by development of a low-lying delta plain associated with different depositional environments, eg, distributary, levee, backswamp and marsh (*see* SWAMP). Superposition of depositional environments over time may produce a favourable habitat for oil and gas accumulation, eg, the MACKENZIE RIVER delta region, NWT. Because of their rich soils, water supply and transportation access, deltas in temperate and tropical climates have played an important role in the history of civilization. However, FLOOD control, land reclamation and channel maintenance have posed problems for inhabitants. In Canada the Mackenzie and Fraser river deltas are outstanding examples of this RIVER LANDFORM. ALAN V. JOPLING

Demasduwit, Shendoreth, Waunathoake, Mary March, one of the last of the BEOTHUKS (b 1796; d at Bay of Exploits, Nfld 8 Jan 1820). An expedition sent to Red Indian Lk in Mar 1819 to recover stolen articles and establish friendly contact with the dwindling Beothuk tribe captured Demasduwit and killed her husband Nonosbawsut. Demasduwit was taken to Twillingate and put in the care of Anglican missionary John Leigh, who recorded from her a Beothuk vocabulary. She was later brought to St John's and an unsuccessful effort made to return her to her own tribe. Demasduwit succumbed to pulmonary consumption and her body was returned to Red Indian Lk in Feb 1820 by a party led by British naval officer David Buchan. In 1828 W.E. CORMACK saw her body, placed side by side with that of Nonosbawsut, in an elevated sepulchre erected by the last survivors of her people. G.M. STORY

Demers, Jérôme, priest, vicar general, architect, teacher (b at St-Nicolas, Qué 1 Aug 1774; d at Québec City, Canada E 17 May 1853). Demers taught literature, philosophy, architecture and science for over 50 years at the Séminaire de Québec and was also superior and bursar of the community. In 1835 he published *Institutiones philosophicae ad usum studiosae juventutis*, his course notes made over 30 years of teaching and the first Canadian PHILOSOPHY textbook. A master in communicating his knowledge and in stimulating appreciation of difficult philosophical problems and discoveries in physics and astronomy, Demers also respected his students and treated them with kindness and understanding. He took charge of building the new churches needed in the diocese and drew up plans for others and for the Collège de Nicolet. Demers's advice was also sought by politicians, such as his former pupil Louis-Joseph PAPINEAU. CLAUDE GALARNEAU

Demeter, Peter, real-estate developer (b at Budapest, Hungary 19 Apr 1933). The son of a wealthy family impoverished as a consequence of WWII, Demeter immigrated to Canada in 1956 and by 1962 had embarked on a successful career as a property developer in Toronto. In 1967 he married Christine Ferrari, an Austrian-born model. The marriage was not successful, and when in 1973 Christine was murdered he was charged with hiring an unidentified person to kill her. The trial, the longest in Canadian history, attracted international attention as it exposed bizarre elements of the Hungarian Canadian underworld as well as the possibility that husband and wife had been simultaneously plotting to kill each other in order to collect a $1-million insurance policy. Demeter was convicted, although the actual killer was never found. STANLEY GORDON

Reading: G. Jonas and B. Amiel, *By Persons Unknown* (1977).

Demographic Data Collection As civilization has developed, so have systems of counting and record keeping. Periodic population counts have been an essential activity of human societies throughout history, but modern industrialized nations are more dependent upon detailed knowledge of their populations than ever before. Representation in government, generation of revenue, mobilization of manpower, and effective economic and social planning require information about population characteristics, eg, numbers, distribution, education, language spoken, labour-force status and occupation, age, sex and marital status.

Historically, demographic data have been acquired by total enumerations (census), which are basically inventories of defined populations within specified areas at particular periods of time; by continuing registers which maintain a complete record of individuals throughout their lifetime; by registration systems which record births, deaths and marriages by place of occurrence; and by sample surveys that are used to collect data on part of the population (which are used to represent the whole). Census and registration systems were used as early as 1000 BC by the Chinese. Sporadic local and national censuses were relatively common prior to the 18th century, and by the mid-19th century most European countries were taking censuses of one kind or another. The first continuing periodic census was established by Sweden in 1749, and in 1787 the new American Constitution established the basis for the regular US decennial census. Canada did not commence its series of regular censuses until 1851 (provided for in the Statistical Act of 1848), but since then has conducted a census every 10 years. In 1886 it established a quinquennial census of the Prairie provinces, which was expanded to include the rest of Canada in 1956.

Early Data Collection in Canada The first modern population census was conducted by Jean Talon in N America in 1666 by order of Louis XIV. The names, ages, occupations, conjugal condition and the relationship of persons to the head of the family in which they lived were obtained for all persons then residing in NEW FRANCE. This was followed by the first agricultural census in 1667 of cattle, sheep, and of farmland under cultivation. Over the next 100 years no less than 45 complete or partial censuses were taken in New France, and during the latter part of the French regime as many as 78 complete or partial censuses were taken in ACADIA, Terre-Neuve [Newfoundland], Île Royale [Cape Breton I] and Île St-Jean [PEI].

When the British assumed control in 1763, both the quality and quantity of censuses declined. Only 3 (1765, 1784, 1790) were taken of the PROVINCE OF QUEBEC before the end of the century. UPPER CANADA had an annual census from 1824 to 1844. They were less frequent in Nova Scotia and New Brunswick, but censuses of Assiniboia and Red River District were taken, on average, every 3 years between 1814 and 1856. The Statistical Act of 1848 provided for the census of 1851-52 and the 1861 census, and reaffirmed the principle of a regular decennial census for Canada. The results of all censuses during more than 2 centuries preceding Confederation were made available in Volume IV of the 1871 Census of Canada.

Vital statistics on baptisms, burials and marriages within the French Catholic population were kept by ecclesiastical authorities from the beginning of the 17th century. The system of keeping vital statistics was extended to British North America and continued until it was replaced by provincial registration systems run by civil authorities.

Data Collection Activities Since Confederation According to the BRITISH NORTH AMERICA ACT, 1867, representation in the federal House of Commons was to be based on population. The Dominion was responsible for censuses and statistics, and provision was made for the registration of births and deaths in the provinces. In 1870 an Act provided for the census of 1871. Its provisions were later extended to the territory beyond the original 4 provinces and to any territory that might be added. An Act of 1879 provided for the census of 1881 and the "collection, abstraction, tabulation and publication of vital, agricultural, commercial, criminal and other statistics."

Continuing demand for population data led to the establishment of a permanent Census and Statistics Office in 1905 under the Ministry of Agriculture. Following recommendations of a review commission in 1912, the Office of Dominion Statistician was created in 1915. The Dominion Bureau of Statistics was created and given the mandate in 1918 to "collect, compile, analyse, abstract and publish statistical information relating to the commercial, industrial, financial, social, economic and general activities of the people of Canada." It was also instructed to "establish a system of co-ordination with provincial governments in order that statistics collected by provinces could be processed for inclusion in national summaries." The Dominion Bureau of Statistics was renamed STATISTICS CANADA in 1971.

Dominion censuses collected data on births and deaths prior to the 1911 census, but a Dominion-Provincial Conference on Vital Statistics in 1918 shifted the responsibility for collecting vital statistics to the provinces. Since 1921, according to legislation in every province except Québec and Newfoundland, the registration of births, stillbirths, marriages and deaths is compulsory. Québec entered the national registration system in 1926 and Newfoundland in 1949, when it joined Confederation. A nationwide conference in 1920 established nationwide statistics on education and shortly after arrangements were made with the Department of Immigration for securing more comprehensive data on the characteristics of immigrants that would be comparable to data collected during the regular decennial censuses. Canada's WWII mobilization effort and a review of its statistical activities in 1943 led to the establishment of a Research and Development Division and a sampling organization within the bureau. The former compiled a new series of economic statistics that have provided the basic statistical background for financial and fiscal policy in postwar Canada. The work of the sampling group led to a 1948 amendment of the Statistics Act authorizing the collection of statistics using more efficient sampling techniques. LABOUR-FORCE data from the census are now supplemented and updated through monthly labour-force surveys.

Scope of Demographic Data Collection Prior to 1851, censuses collected only names of heads of households and the total number of persons in each household, or in some cases reported only aggregate numbers without names. Most included censuses of agriculture, eg, livestock as well as population. Between 1871 and 1911, census coverage expanded considerably. Census schedules included questions on age, sex, marital status, religion, origin, birthplace, occupation, literacy and an assortment of infirmities. Information was also collected on housing, agricultural products, implements and livestock, as well as on industrial establishments, forest and mineral products, shipping and fisheries, and public institutions, eg, schools and churches.

Since 1921 the decennial census has been primarily a population and agriculture census, but censuses of RETAIL TRADE and WHOLESALE TRADE and services have also been taken since that time. In 1941 a sample survey of housing was included in the census and in 1961 additional questions of fertility, internal migration and income of persons not living on farms were asked of respondents selected in the 20% sample of households for the housing census. In the 1971 census, the number of questions asked and the number of topics covered were greater than in any previous Canadian census. In all but the more remote areas of Canada, data on all the population and household questions were collected from every third private household. In the census of 1981, most persons answered a basic questionnaire of only 12 questions on age, sex, marital status, language and housing. The more comprehensive data on housing expenses, education, ethnic origin, migration, income, employment and occupation were only obtained from those individuals selected in a 20% sample of private households. The 1986 census was similar in most respects to the 1981 census.

Many of the same questions have been included in every census since Confederation; some have changed over the years while new ones have been added and others dropped in response to altered social and economic conditions. Because of more efficient collecting and processing techniques and the use of sampling, an increase in the number of questions included in the census has been possible. Increasing population, periods of economic inflation and more complex census operations have contributed to a dramatic rise in the cost of censuses. In 1891 the census cost only $250 000. By 1971 the price tag had increased to $15 million, and by 1981 it had reached $143.3 million. Five years later, in 1986, using a format and procedures similar to those used for the 1981 census, the cost to enumerate the 25 354 054 residents of Canada was $150 million.

Improvements in Data Collecting and Processing Mechanical tabulation was first used in 1911 to increase the efficiency and accuracy of data processing, and unique innovations of tabulating equipment were introduced in both 1931 and 1941. The 1951 census employed "mark-sense" documents and the new IBM 101 (ESM) "electronic statistical machine." This was followed in 1961 by the use of an optical document reader that directly transferred information from the census schedules to magnetic computer tapes for processing by high-speed computers. Through improved computer technology, not only were large amounts of data more ably and speedily processed, but many sources of human error were eliminated.

Errors of coverage, concept, definition, reporting and enumerating are all potential errors of census taking. Experience and tests have shown that the largest source of error has been enumerator fallibility. To reduce enumerator-related errors, mail questionnaires and self-enumeration forms were introduced for the first time in 1971 and have continued to be used in subsequent censuses. The estimated census undercounts in 1971 and 1981 were in the neighbourhood of 2% compared to an undercount of between 2.5% and 3.0% in 1961. The accuracy of coverage tends to vary between regions and various subgroups within the population. Young and mobile adults are more difficult to locate and have been undercounted at more than twice the rate for the population as a whole. Divorced persons also tend to be more easily missed than those of other marital statuses, as are persons who rent or live in mobile homes.

Response errors also vary according to the kind and difficulty of the questions asked. In tests the greatest errors have been found in responses to questions about mother tongue, language use, ethnic origin and employment status. The ability to obtain answers varies according to the type of respondent as well as the type of question. Mathematical techniques have been devised for correcting certain types of errors in population aggregates, eg, misstatements of age; techniques for imputing information, in the case of missing data on the basis of observed levels of social and economic homogeneity of neighbourhoods and known correlations of individual and family characteristics. In the final analysis, the quality of timeliness of population data is directly related to the degree of literacy and educational attainment

levels of the population, the willingness of individuals to co-operate, their confidence in government, and the efficiency and dedication of those involved in the collection, processing and dissemination of data.

There are basic data needs of government and business that cannot entirely be met by the national census. The amount of time required to carry out an extensive national census operation, process the data and publish the results, minimizes the usefulness of some data where timeliness is important, eg, unemployment data. A number of factors, including considerations of cost and the limits of respondent co-operation argue against any significant expansion of census content beyond its present size to attempt to meet all possible needs at national, provincial and municipal levels. To solve the problem of timeliness, to fill in gaps in the national statistical information system, and to provide new types of data required to assess current socioeconomic trends, the government has turned to national sample surveys. Canada introduced a labour force survey in Nov 1945, first on a quarterly basis, and since Nov 1952 on a monthly basis. In addition, it has occasionally used its Labour Force Survey to "piggy back" other surveys on special topics. The government introduced an annual general social survey (GSS) in 1985 to collect data required to monitor long-term social trends and measure temporal changes related to living conditions and personal well-being, such as information on individual health, education, and social environment. The GSS is also used to obtain information on specific and timely policy issues and social problems, eg, social support networks, and youth unemployment (1985 GSS).

Technological, political, economic and social change will continue to create new demands for accurate, consistent, comparable and timely statistics. The government is likely to meet these requirements through continued use of national sample surveys and innovative "cost effective" interviewing techniques. Improvements in computer technology will improve the quality, quantity and accessibility of the national census, sample survey and vital statistics.

WARREN E. KALBACH

Reading: Warren E. Kalbach and W.W. McVey Jr, Demographic Bases of Canadian Society (1979); Statistics Canada, 1981 Census Dictionary.

Demography, the study of changes affecting human population, is concerned with the overall POPULATION, the immediate phenomena that alter it as a whole (births, deaths, migrations), or changes in its composition (sex, age, marital status, language, religion, education, income, etc). A population is usually defined as a group of individuals living in a particular area. However, studies are often conducted on subpopulations, eg, ethnic groups, the school-age population or the working population. This is the "narrow" concept of demography. Over the past 300 years, demographers have developed an impressive battery of methods for analysing all these phenomena and the ways in which they relate to one another. This set of facts, relationships and methods constitutes the heart of demography. When confined to this core area, demography is virtually the study of renewable resources in the mathematical sense of the term, and can also be applied to animal or plant populations.

Most demographers, however, devote themselves to studies that go beyond this core, eg, by questioning why purely demographic phenomena (fertility, mortality, nuptiality, age structure) vary and what social consequences may result from these variations. The resulting studies cover a large number of disciplines, in particular

sociology, economics, history, psychology and biology.

Strictly speaking, demography has no subdisciplines. Two types of demographic studies may, however, be defined: those confined to narrow demography (some of these studies use rather sophisticated mathematical models), and those concerned with relationships between purely demographic and social (or sometimes biological) phenomena.

Evolution of Demography in Canada Demography, a very empirical discipline, draws upon few theoretical models and many statistical findings. These findings were mostly supplied by censuses and vital statistics (ie, statistical information on births, marriages and deaths). In Canada, as in other industrialized countries, these information sources once constituted the very basis of demography (*see* DEMOGRAPHIC DATA COLLECTION).

With the 1871 census, a few elementary analyses of a historical nature were performed, but it was not until 60 years later that the Dominion Bureau of Statistics, the predecessor of Statistics Canada, once again began to conduct demographic analyses of its data. The 1931 census contained 10 very detailed monographs published in 2 volumes. There were 2 census monographs in 1941, none in 1951, 8 in 1961 and about 10 in 1971. The authors were primarily university researchers. Since 1961 more limited studies, always linked to censuses, have been conducted on various aspects of Canada's population. Since 1974 Statistics Canada has from time to time published population forecasts for all of Canada and for every province. Statistics Canada employs many, but certainly not all, demographers. The contributions of a few independent researchers are noteworthy, including *Histoire de la population canadienne-française*, the work of journalist Georges Langlois. During the 1950s several researchers, including 2 Canadian demographers who now work in American universities, Nathan Keyfitz and Norman B. Ryder, began to produce work in demography.

It was not until the 1960s that groups of professors specializing in population research and training students in demography established a few Canadian university programs designed specifically for this discipline. There is only one real department of demography (at the Université de Montréal), but at University of Alberta and University of Western Ontario, groups of professors, researchers and students interested mainly in population studies work within departments of sociology. Demography is also taught at a number of other universities, where there is no formal program. Outside of universities, most researchers in demography are employed in departments and certain para-public agencies of the federal and Québec governments.

Scope of Application In examining the work of the 200-300 Canadian demographers, it will be found that "applied" demographic studies relate mainly to the forecasting of housing, health and education needs, and services to the elderly; client forecasts concerning certain major public services; and the development of policies relating to economic planning, birth control, social welfare, manpower, immigration, language and the preservation of cultural minority groups. However, certain studies, eg, population forecasts, which are helpful to all sorts of users, and some research conducted in universities, which is oriented toward knowledge of the past and problems of Third World countries, are not as precisely defined.

Institutions In Canada there are 2 demography associations and a national federation. Founded in 1971, the Association des démographes du Québec has a membership of approximately 200 francophone demographers. It publishes the *Cahiers québécois de démographie* 3 times a year. The English counterpart is the Canadian Population Society, fd in 1974. It has approximately 160 members and publishes the annual journal, *Canadian Studies in Population*. The Federation of Canadian Demographers links the 2 associations.

JACQUES HENRIPIN

Dempster Highway runs from near Dawson, YT, 720 km across the northern Yukon through the Richardson Mts to Ft McPherson and Inuvik, in the MACKENZIE DELTA of the NWT. Begun in 1959, it was the first of the "Roads to Resources" of the government and PM John Diefenbaker. In Sept 1963 the highway was named after Inspector W.J.D. Dempster of the RCMP (b in Wales 21 Oct 1876, d at Vancouver 25 Oct 1964), who served with the Mounted Police from 1897 to 1934, all but one year at various posts in the Yukon. The route, opened to the public in the spring of 1979, cost $100 million, required major bridges across the Eagle and Ogilvie rivers, and crosses some of the most formidable and beautiful terrain in N America.   KENNETH S. COATES

Construction on the Dempster Hwy at North Fork Pass, Yukon (*courtesy SSC Photocentre/photo by Pat Morrow*).

Dene Nation (prior to 1978 the Indian Brotherhood of the Northwest Territories) is the political organization that represents the Dene, or northern Athapaskan-speaking peoples and their descendants, of the Mackenzie R valley and the Barren Grounds in the NWT. It has its headquarters in Yellowknife.

Incorporated in 1970, the organization evolved in response to long-standing concerns over the written terms found in the federal government's version of Treaties 8 and 11 signed with the Dene in 1899-1900 and 1921-22 respectively. This concern led, soon after incorporation, to the filing of a caveat (or legal warning to third parties) respecting continued Dene interests in lands described in these treaties. This caveat (the so-called *Paulette* caveat) was challenged, but in 1973 Mr Justice W. Morrow of the Supreme Court of the NWT found that certain native rights continued to exist. Although this judgement was subsequently overturned by the Appeal Court on technical grounds, it led the federal government to accept that further negotiations on the Dene interests were necessary.

The Dene Nation consistently held that ABORIGINAL RIGHTS negotiations were essentially over the establishment of a political relationship between the Dene and the Canadian state: a view that was underscored by the wording on self-determination in the Dene Declaration (1975), in the Preamble to a Proposed Agreement-in-Principle (1976), and in evidence led at the Berger hearings on a proposed MACKENZIE VALLEY PIPELINE (1975-77). Incompatibility between this position and that of the federal government of the time, to the effect that the negotiations were to deal with non-political matters alone, stalled progress on claims until 1981. Since then, progress on resolving the nonpolitical matters respecting the claim has

been considerable, although no final agreement has been reached as of 1987.

The Dene Nation is also engaged in programs concerning Dene health, education, community development, legal issues, land and resource development, and communications. The first president of the Dene Nation was Mona Jacobs of Ft Smith, NWT. Subsequently, Roy Daniells, Richard Nerysoo, Georges ERASMUS and Stephen Kakfwi have held the senior executive position. *See also* LAND CLAIMS, NATIVE PEOPLE, POLITICAL ORGANIZATION AND ACTIVISM.   MICHAEL I. ASCH

Reading: R. Fumoleau, *As Long as This Land Shall Last* (1977) and *Denendeh: A Dene Celebration* (1984); M. Watkins, *Dene Nation: The Colony Within* (1977).

Denison, Flora MacDonald, née Merrill, feminist, journalist, businesswoman (b in N Hastings County, Ont 20? Feb 1867; d at Toronto 23 May 1921). Denison, who combined running a successful Toronto dressmaking business with a writing career, was active in the suffrage movement in Toronto from 1906. Her views on religion, marriage, birth control and social class, expressed through her regular 1909-13 column in the *Toronto Sunday World*, were more radical than those of most Canadian suffragists. President of the Canadian Suffrage Assn 1911-14, she was forced to resign because of her support for the English militant suffragettes. At the outbreak of WWI, Denison initially opposed the conflict, and while she did not sustain an unequivocal anti-war position throughout the war years, WWI deepened her commitment to thoroughgoing social and spiritual reformation. She expressed this commitment first through the Canadian Whitmanite movement, a social and spiritual movement that owed its inspiration to the American poet Walt Whitman. At her country property, Bon Echo, she created a retreat dedicated to Whitmanite ideals and beginning in 1916 she published the Whitmanite magazine the *Sunset of Bon Echo*. Later she became a theosophist, and in the years just before her death she participated in the Theosophist Social Reconstruction League.

DEBORAH GORHAM

Denison, Francis Napier, weather forecaster, engineer, scientist (b at Toronto, Canada W 19 Apr 1866; d at Victoria 24 June 1946). An innovative scientist, Denison was known to thousands of Victorians as "our weatherman." Educated at Upper Canada Coll, he joined the Meteorological Service in 1882 and subsequently was appointed assistant observer at the Toronto Observatory (1884). He was transferred to Victoria as weather forecaster/observer in 1898. In Victoria, Denison became one of the best-known meteorological scientists in N America. His many contributions ranged from studies of weather cycles to research on seismic disturbances. Coincidentally, he developed several ingenious instruments to aid in daily weather prediction. He retired with honours in 1936, but even in retirement produced a seismograph, intended for use in mines as a safety device, and also a dust remover for hospital cabinets.   J.R. MATHIESON

Denison, George Taylor (3rd), lawyer, magistrate, soldier, author (b at Toronto 31 Aug 1839; d there 6 June 1925). The descendant of Loyalists, he enjoyed an international reputation as a military historian and analyst, foreseeing the tactical advantages of rapidly deployed mobilized infantry in modern warfare. As Toronto's senior police magistrate 1877-1921, he meted out justice in such a colourful fashion that his court became a tourist attraction. Commanding the Governor General's Body Guard, a cavalry troop established and supported by his family, he saw action in the 1866 FENIAN raid and during the 1885

NORTH-WEST REBELLION. Denison was an active supporter of the Confederacy's operations in Canada during the American Civil War. Afterward, he was a founder of the CANADA FIRST movement (1868) and the Canadian National Assn, a short-lived political organization (1874). As the most vocal Canadian spokesman for the idea of imperial unity 1880-1910, Denison portrayed the US as the chief threat to Canadian nationhood, and reasoned that a federation of the British Empire, with Canada as an equal partner, would provide the security, prestige and power essential to national greatness.   DAVID P. GAGAN

Reading: David P. Gagan, *The Denison Family of Toronto* (1974).

Denison, Merrill, playwright, journalist, writer, historian (b at Detroit, Mich 23 June 1893; d at San Diego, Calif 13 June 1975). English Canada's first important 20th-century playwright, he emerged from the Canadian Little Theatre movement in the 1920s. His satire *Brothers in Arms*, produced in 1921 at Hart House Theatre, U of T, became one of the most frequently produced English Canadian plays. Denison's literary reputation as a playwright of realistic dramas and satirical comedies is largely based on his 1923 anthology *The Unheroic North*, which contains his most important naturalistic social problem play, *Marsh Hay*, not produced until 1974. *Henry Hudson and Other Plays* (1931) was the first Canadian radio play anthology published. Denison also authored the novel *Klondike Mike* (1943) and corporate histories for Massey-Harris, Molson's, Ontario Hydro and the Bank of Montreal.   ANTON WAGNER

Dennis, Agnes, née Miller, teacher, feminist (b at Truro, NS 11 Apr 1859; d at Halifax 21 Apr 1947). Dennis succeeded Edith ARCHIBALD as president of the Halifax VICTORIAN ORDER OF NURSES, 1901-46, and of the Halifax Local Council of Women 1906-20. She mobilized women in WWI for the RED CROSS, of which she was provincial president 1914-20. They produced medical supplies, organized hospitals, looked after prisoners of war overseas, and sought to enter the jobs left by soldiers recruited for overseas service. Dennis also helped co-ordinate relief efforts for victims of the 1917 HALIFAX EXPLOSION. Her determined but self-effacing style of leadership proved highly effective in building and winning recognition for women's organizations. On the death of her husband, Senator William Dennis, in 1920, she became president of the Halifax *Herald* Ltd. She had 10 children.   ERNEST R. FORBES

Dennis, John Stoughton, surveyor, soldier (b at Kingston 19 Oct 1820; d at Kingsmere, Qué 7 July 1885). Of UE Loyalist stock, Dennis was commissioned a surveyor in the Department of Crown Lands in 1843. He joined the militia in 1855, becoming in 1862 Brigade Major of No 3 Military District, Toronto. He was exonerated by a court of inquiry concerning his leadership in a skirmish against FENIANS in 1866, but the episode seems to have ended his army career. In 1869 Dennis was placed in charge of surveying the North-West Territories, where his arrival helped precipitate the RED RIVER REBELLION. In 1871 he became surveyor-general of DOMINION LANDS, ie, the person chiefly responsible for mapping the Prairie West, and was deputy minister of the Interior Department 1887-81. His son, J.S. Dennis Jr, followed a similar career, as a surveyor in the West 1872, commander of a militia unit against Riel at BATOCHE in 1885, and inspector of surveys 1887-94. J.S. Dennis Jr wrote a history of the Dominion lands survey 1869-89 (when his father had proposed a better system than the US standard eventually adopted) and ended his career as chief of the CPR Department of Natural Resources, in charge of lands and irrigation.

DONALD J.C. PHILLIPSON

Reading: D.W. Thomson, *Men and Meridians,* Vol 2 (1967).

Denny, Sir Cecil Edward, 6th baronet of Tralee Castle, police officer, Indian agent, author (b in Hampshire, Eng 14 Dec 1850; d at Edmonton 24 Aug 1928). Denny is best known as the author of 2 colourful accounts of life with the NWMP – *The Riders of the Plains: A Reminiscence of the Early and Exciting Days in the North West* (1905) and *The Law Marches West* (1939). He joined the force in 1874 and served principally in the Whoop-Up country. Although able, he was undisciplined, and he resigned following a scandal involving a woman. He served as Indian agent at FT WALSH and in Treaty No 7. He was sympathetic to the Indians but resigned as a result of a number of factors, including disagreement with departmental policy (including reduction of rations to the Indians), staff cuts and the belief that his authority was being undercut. He served as a special Indian agent during the NORTH-WEST REBELLION. Subsequently, he ranched and worked as police scout, packer, guide and fire ranger until 1922 when he was appointed assistant archivist of Alberta; he was dismissed Aug 1927.

A.B. McCULLOUGH

Denonville, Jacques-René de Brisay, Marquis de, governor general of New France, 1685-89 (b at Denonville, France 10 Dec 1637; d there 22 Sept 1710). He arrived at Québec 1 Aug 1685 at a dangerous point in the colony's conflict with the IROQUOIS and English. Taking the initiative, he sent de TROYES overland to attack English posts on James Bay (1686), thereby removing the threat on the colony's northern flank. In 1687 he led a punitive campaign against the Seneca, systematically destroying their villages. Denonville did his best to strengthen the colony's defences, but it remained vulnerable. In Aug 1689 the Five Nations struck at Lachine with 1500 warriors, cutting off Ft Frontenac, which Denonville abandoned and destroyed. Although criticized for his caution and his compliance with orders to send Iroquois prisoners to France for service in galleys, Denonville was the first governor to show concern for social and health conditions in New France. He attempted to curb abuses in the fur trade and established a navigation school at Québec to train pilots. He was recalled to military service in Europe and sailed from Québec in Nov 1689.

JAMES MARSH

Dent, John Charles, journalist, historian (b at Kendal, Eng 8 Nov 1841; d at Toronto 27 Sept 1888). After a newspaper career abroad and in Toronto he became a free-lance writer. His most successful book was the illustrated 4-vol *Canadian Portrait Gallery* (1880-81); he wrote 185 of its 204 sketches. In *The Last Forty Years: Canada since the Union of 1841* (2 vols, 1881) and the more partisan *The Story of the Upper Canadian Rebellion* (2 vols, 1885) he sided with moderate reformers. John King, W.L. MACKENZIE's son-in-law, attacked him in *The Other Side of the "Story"* (1886). Later, however, Dent thought that RESPONSIBLE GOVERNMENT had made Canadian politics corrupt. A convinced free trader and lifelong admirer of John Bright, he insisted on economy and probity in government. In addition to history, Dent also wrote fiction, much of which was published posthumously.

S.R. MEALING

Dentistry is the art of the treatment of teeth and their supporting tissues. The Egyptians, in their papyri dating back to 3500 BC, described dental and gingival ("of the gums") maladies and their management, and evidence of teeth restoration has been found in Egyptian mummies. Docu-

ments from the Hebrews, Chinese, Greeks and Romans all refer to aspects of dentistry. In more recent times, the Frenchman Pierre Fauchard (1678-1761) author of the first classic treatise on dentistry, *Le Chirurgien dentiste* (1728), has been recognized as the founder of modern scientific dentistry. He was responsible for the separation of the science and art of dentistry from general medicine and surgery.

In N America, physicians and barber surgeons accompanied colonists to America. Although several people advertised that they could extract and replace teeth, they were not trained dentists. They included an ivory turner and umbrella maker, a wigmaker and hairdresser, and Paul Revere, a silversmith. During this colonial period dentistry in N America lagged far behind the advances being made in Europe. In the early 1800s "dentists" with some skills acquired through apprenticeship immigrated to Canada from the US. They included a Mr Hume, who advertised his profession in Halifax in the *Acadian Reporter* in 1814; and a Mr L.S. Parmly, who practised in Montréal in 1815 and published the first Canadian book on dentistry, *The Summum Bonum,* and who called himself a dentist and "medical electrician."

On 3 Jan 1867, 9 dentists met in Toronto to form the Ontario Dental Association, and in 1868 the Royal College of Dental Surgeons of Ontario was established. Also in that year, *The Canada Journal of Dental Science* began publication. After several attempts from 1867 to 1870 to establish a school, the first dental college in Canada was founded, in Toronto, in 1875 by the Royal College of Dental Surgeons of Ontario; it consisted of 2 full-time staff, 5 part-time staff and 11 students. Over the next 100 years dental schools were incorporated into Canadian universities. In 1888 the Royal College of Dental Surgeons of Ontario became affiliated with U of T and the university agreed to confer the degree of Doctor of Dental Surgery upon students completing the prescribed course of study. The first examination was held after 4 months' instruction, in 1889; 25 candidates were successful. These were the first doctorate degrees conferred on dental graduates outside the US.

McGill U Dental School dates from 1905, but its origins can be traced to 1892 when the Association of Dental Surgeons of the Province of Québec was founded in Montréal. A French-speaking school was established at Université de Montréal in 1905. A fourth dental school was opened in 1908 as part of Dalhousie U. In western Canada, the first dental school was not established until 1923, when a 4-year program was introduced at U of Alberta; it was followed by one at U of Manitoba (1958) and at UBC (1964). Three further dental schools were introduced during the 1960s and 1970s: at U of Western Ontario (1966), U of Saskatchewan (1968), and Laval (1971). Some 13 164 dentists were practising in Canada in 1986, a dentist to population ratio of 1:1926.

During the 20th century, dentistry evolved from a profession based on empirical methods, through one based on mechanics, to one based on sound research methodology supported by both basic science and clinical research. In 1983, at the annual meeting of the International Association of Dental Research, over 1200 research presentations were given.

Specialization in dentistry in N America began during the early 20th century. W.G. Beers of Montréal (1843-1900) confined his practice to exodontia (oral surgery) and is considered to be the first specialist in dentistry in Canada. The main specialties that subsequently developed were exodontia, periodontia and orthodontia. Several societies and graduate programs related to specializations were established; after many

controversial years the Royal College of Dentists of Canada was created in 1964 by federal statute to promote high standards of specialization, to determine qualifications, to establish training programs in Canadian dental schools, and to provide the recognition and designation of dentists who possessed special qualifications. This legislation was supported by all the provincial dental licensing boards, which are responsible for the licensing of dentists and the practice of dentistry in each province.

With the development of the profession of dentistry, it was proposed that a profession of auxiliary dental workers might be established, but the issue was hotly debated. In 1947 the Ontario laws governing dentistry were amended to cover dental hygienists. The first Canadian dental training school for dental hygienists was opened at the Toronto dental school in 1951, and by the mid-1960s most schools and provinces offered similar training programs. Dental hygienists are employed in private dental offices and dental public-health programs, and recently their duties have been extended in several provinces. Saskatchewan, for example, has instituted a program, based on the New Zealand Dental Nurse system, whereby certain operative procedures on children can be undertaken.

Dental mechanics, responsible for the manufacture of dental appliances for dentists, have been allowed in some provinces to work directly with the public to provide dentures. Dental assistants work closely with dentists in the chairside provision of dental care to patients.

Canada has a lower percentage of women dentists than many other countries. The first Canadian woman to graduate from a dental college was Mrs Caroline Louisa Josephine Wells, who completed her training at the Royal College of Dental Surgeons of Ontario in 1893.

Dental associations have been established in each province, but the national spokesman is the Canadian Dental Association. One of the association's objectives has been to ensure that dentistry is considered an autonomous healing art, ie, not part of medicine and therefore not covered by medicare programs. In many countries dental care falls under government health-care programs, but in Canada only selected groups, eg, children and the elderly, have benefited from subsidization for dental expenses, and then only in some provinces.

J.A. HARGREAVES

Reading: D.W. Gullett, *A History of Dentistry in Canada* (1971).

Denys, Nicolas, trader, colonial promoter (b at Tours, France 1598; d 1688). A young La Rochelle merchant, Denys sailed for Acadia in 1632 with Isaac de RAZILLY, and spent the next 40 years trying to develop the colony. Many of his ventures were unsuccessful, and he suffered heavy losses from such commercial failures as his fishing establishments at Port Rossignol (Liverpool, NS) in the 1630s and on Cape Breton I in the 1650s. Other enterprises provoked conflicts with rival traders and he made a powerful enemy of colonial governor Charles de MENOU D'AULNAY. In 1653 he acquired territory on the Gulf of St Lawrence from Canso to the Gaspé, including Cape Breton and the other gulf islands, with rights to land and government. Plans to bring settlers were never fulfilled, but he continued trading. About 1670, leaving his headquarters at Nipisiquit (Bathurst, NB) to his son Richard, Denys returned to France to publish his *Description and Natural History of the Coasts of North America* (1672; repr, ed W.F. Ganong, 1908). It is a vivid account of Acadia and a reminder that Denys, despite many reverses, promoted French colonial development there for 4 decades.

JOHN G. REID

Broadcaster Norman Depoe (*courtesy National Archives of Canada/MISA/CBC Coll/14597*).

DePoe, Norman Reade, broadcaster, journalist (b at Portland, Ore 4 May 1917; d at Toronto 13 Mar 1980). In his prime in the eventful 1960s, he was for 8 years CBC-TV's chief Ottawa correspondent and a household name as Canadian broadcasting's star reporter on national and international affairs. His colourful screen image was enhanced by rumpled features, raspy voice and a reputation as a hard-drinking, plain-spoken, go-for-broke newsman. He came to Canada at 6, took out citizenship in 1931, attended UBC, served as a signals corps captain in Italy and NW Europe during WWII, and studied French and Italian at U of T after the war. He joined the CBC news service in 1948 and helped create the TV news operation in the 1950s. Viewers applauded a reporter who was worldly yet caring, and not afraid to puncture official pomposity. Colleagues envied his extraordinary memory and his ability to boil a complicated story down to 90 seconds of clear, crisp English. At a time when electronic journalism was finding its feet, he set standards that proved enduring.   DOUGLAS MARSHALL

Depression, see GREAT DEPRESSION.

Deputy Minister, generally an officer of the public service appointed as managerial and administrative head of a department or ministry of the federal or provincial governments. A deputy minister is the official primarily responsible for the co-ordination and flow of policy and program advice and technical analysis to the minister or CABINET and for management of the department and program implementation. The appointment of deputy ministers, based in statute law and customary practice, is federally the prime minister's responsibility and provincially that of the premier, although at the provincial level ministers may exercise greater influence in the selection. Because tradition and convention have established that they should be politically nonpartisan in their work, deputy ministers are entitled to continue in office even with a change of government, although in recent years there have been demands for the politicization of such ORDER-IN-COUNCIL appointees, after the American model.
                THOMAS K. SHOYAMA

Derick, Carrie Matilda, natural scientist (b at Clarenceville, Qué 14 Jan 1862; d at Montréal 10 Nov 1941). A brilliant student at McGill (BA, 1890; MA, 1896), she also studied at Harvard, the Marine Biological Laboratory at Woods Hole,

Mass, the Royal Coll of Science in London and University of Bonn, Germany. She was appointed demonstrator in botany at McGill in 1891 – first woman on McGill's academic staff; in 1912 she became professor of morphological botany – the first woman in Canada to be made a full professor. Her courses introduced the teaching of genetics at McGill. A social activist, she championed such causes as compulsory school attendance, care for abnormal children, industrial and technical education, women's rights and birth control.
                MARGARET GILLETT

Reading: Margaret Gillett, *We Walked Very Warily: A History of Women at McGill* (1981).

Dernière Heure et la première, La (1970), a theoretical essay by Pierre VADEBONCOEUR arguing that the French Canadian people have paradoxically been excluded from history in their successful pursuit of "la survivance": entrenched language rights and a thriving culture are no substitute for genuine political power, the power of sovereignty. Focusing on the liberal philosophy of FEDERALISM articulated by the CITÉ LIBRE group in the 1950s and 1960s, Vadeboncoeur claims that Pierre TRUDEAU's view of Québec nationalism was merely an extension of traditional 19th-century nationalism, a palliative measure. According to Vadeboncoeur, only the neo-nationalism of the sovereignty movement, implicitly socialist, addresses the cultural and economic deprivation of the inner exile, a colonized being. "Intuitively" substituting a vision of universally recognized self-determination for the technocrat's "sterile" obsession with statistics, Vadeboncoeur aims to delineate the points of continuity and departure between traditional and radical nationalism. Vadeboncoeur's cultural depth, clarity of style and intellectual sophistication preclude any simplistic summary of his ideas and loyalties.   MICHÈLE LACOMBE

Des Groseilliers, Médard Chouart, explorer, fur trader (bap at Charly-sur-Marne, France 31 July 1618; d at New France 1696?). A man of courage who valued personal freedom and initiative, Des Groseilliers opened Lks Michigan and Superior to the fur trade and Jesuit missionaries. Resentful of perceived injustices at the hands of French officials, he joined the English and with Pierre-Esprit RADISSON helped found the HUDSON'S BAY CO. Des Groseilliers probably came to Canada in 1641. In 1645-46 he worked for the Jesuits at Ste Marie in Huronia. The latter phase of the IROQUOIS WARS (1648-53) cut the St Lawrence colonies off from their fur suppliers, but a peace made with the Iroquois early in 1654 and the arrival of a contingent of Ottawa-Huron gave Des Groseilliers the opportunity to explore W of Lk Huron. He left 6 Aug 1654 and returned Aug 1656 with 250 natives in 50 canoes from the Green Bay (Wis) area and the southwestern shore of Lk Superior, bearing a fortune in furs. During this trip he learned of the rich fur country N and NW of Lk Superior which, he was told, was only 7 days by canoe from Hudson Bay. In Aug 1659 Des Groseilliers, this time accompanied by his brother-in-law Radisson, undertook a second voyage to the S shore of Lk Superior to Chequamegon, Mille Lacs area of Wisconsin, and in the spring of 1660, to the N shore of Lk Superior near Pigeon R. Upon their return to Trois-Rivières on 24 Aug 1660, with 60 canoes and another fortune in furs, they were arrested for illegal trading and their furs were confiscated. Further frustrations with French officials took the pair to Boston in 1662 to solicit English help in a venture directly to Hudson Bay.

After an abortive New England expedition Des Groseilliers was persuaded to take his plans to

England (1665). Three years later (1668), with the backing of Prince Rupert and London merchants, Groseilliers sailed from London to the mouth of the Rupert R in the 45-ton ketch NONSUCH, commanded by Zachariah Gillam, where the crew wintered and traded for furs. The following year the NONSUCH returned to England, proving that it was possible, as Groseilliers had predicted, to exploit the fur trade from Hudson Bay. The successful conclusion of this voyage led to the founding of the HBC on 2 May 1670. Over the next 5 years he was busy setting up company posts on James Bay. Persuaded by Father ALBANEL to rejoin the French, he returned to Canada in 1676. In 1682 he entered the COMPAGNIE DU NORD and built a French post at the mouth of the Hayes R. English complaints of the destruction of their posts by Des Groseilliers and his companions as well as evasion of the French tax on furs again led him into trouble. After pleading his case in Paris (1684) he returned to New France and seems to have retired.   C.E. HEIDENREICH

Des Sauvages, ou, Voyage de Samuel Champlain (1603) records CHAMPLAIN's first voyage to Canada as François Gravé Du Pont's guest aboard *La Bonne Renommée,* searching for the NORTHWEST PASSAGE. The 1603 summer voyage took them up the St Lawrence to the present location of Montréal; Champlain describes the Gaspé coast, the Saguenay R and the Lachine Rapids. Cast as a diary, his first book of travels relates conversations with MICMAC and MONTAGNAIS, and includes useful impressions of the climate and topography. Gravé du Pont took a Micmac family back to France, and Champlain contributed to the European fascination with the Indian by recounting Indian legends and customs and telling of his attempt to convert natives to Christianity. *Des Sauvages* is included in the first Canadian edition of Champlain's complete works (*Oeuvres de Champlain,* 6 vols, 1870) and in the standard CHAMPLAIN SOCIETY edition (1922-35). A facsimile of *Des Sauvages* appeared in 1978.   MICHÈLE LACOMBE

Desbarats, Georges-Édouard, publisher, inventor of halftone photographic printing (b at Québec City 5 Apr 1838; d at Ottawa 18 Feb 1893). Desbarats briefly succeeded his father (d 1864) as queen's printer in Ottawa (a post held by his family since 1799), but resigned in 1869 to found the weekly *Canadian Illustrated News.* This was the first periodical in the world to carry halftone photographs, rather than engravings prepared by artists, using a process invented by Desbarats and his engraver, William Leggo. The two went to New York in 1873 to found the *Daily Graphic,* the first daily paper to use photographic illustrations. *Canadian Illustrated News* appeared weekly 1869-83. Other Canadian periodicals created by Desbarats included the *Dominion Illustrated, Canadian Patent Office Record* and *Mechanic's Magazine.*   DONALD J.C. PHILLIPSON

DesBarres, Joseph Frederick Wallet, military engineer, surveyor, governor of Cape Breton and of PEI (b probably at Basle, Switz Nov 1722; d at Halifax 27 Oct 1824). At age 31 he immigrated to Britain and attended the Royal Military Coll, Woolwich. In 1756 he was posted to N America as a lieutenant in the Royal American Regiment and saw action at LOUISBOURG in 1758, Québec in 1759 and in the expedition against the French at St John's, Nfld, in 1762. His skill in surveying and mapping had been noted, and in 1763 he was employed by the Admiralty to prepare charts of the coastline and offshore waters of NS, at the same time that James COOK was working in Newfoundland and Samuel HOLLAND in the Gulf of St Lawrence and New England. DesBarres published the first version of his navigational atlas,

West Shore of Richmond Isle, near the entrance of the Gut of Canso, c1779, aquatint, coloured by hand, by Joseph F.W. DesBarres (*courtesy National Archives of Canada/C-41564*).

Atlantic Neptune, in 1777, containing his charts and sketches from the previous 10 years along with some adaptations of Holland's work. The final version was published in 1781. In 1784, Des-Barres embarked on a new career when he was appointed the first lieutenant-governor of Cape Breton, and in 1785 he laid out the settlement that would become SYDNEY. He left the island in 1787. In May 1804 he became governor of PEI. He was finally recalled at age 90.

DesBarres possessed an abrasive personality. He was impatient and quarrelsome, but no one has ever denied his splendid talents and energy.

L.M. SEBERT

Reading: G.N.D. Evans, Uncommon Obdurate: The Several Public Careers of J.F.W. DesBarres (1969).

Desbiens, Jean-Paul, member of the Marist order of brothers, teacher, philosopher, writer, journalist (b at Métabetchouan, Qué 7 Mar 1927). His book describing the failure of the Québec educational system, *Les Insolences du Frère Untel* (publ in English as *The Insolences of Brother Anonymous*), had unprecedented success. His debut as a writer and pamphleteer coincided with the debut of the QUIET REVOLUTION, with which he was closely associated, although he was removed from the debate by his superiors and sent off to Europe (1961) where he studied theology and philosophy. Upon his return to Québec (1964), he joined the Ministry of Education and became one of its chief architects of reform. In 1970 he joined *La Presse* as chief editorial writer and in 1972 returned to education as a school principal. He continues to write for various publications with his characteristic sense of the sacred and deep respect for man. He has a weekly column in *La Presse*.

ROBERT BRISEBOIS

Deschamps, Yvon, actor, comedian (b at Montréal 1935). He left school early and worked at Radio-Canada as a messenger. He took private drama lessons from Paul Buissonneau, who offered him work in 1959 as an actor at the Roulotte, hired him as an assistant in 1963 and cofounded the Théâtre de Quat'sous with him in 1964. Deschamps played his first roles at the Théâtre universitaire canadien with Paul Hébert in 1958-59. In 1959 he also made his first TV appearance, on CBC. He appeared at La Poudrière and L'Égrégore in 1960 and, as of 1961, at Claude LÉVEILLEÉ concerts. He appeared in his first revues in 1963 and in his first film, *Délivrez-nous du mal*, in 1964. But Deschamps is above all known for his satirical, political monologues, which he began to perform in 1967 in restaurants and clubs such as the Boîte à Clémence. He became famous especially after his participation in *L'Osstidcho*, a revue that also brought Louise Forestier and Robert CHARLEBOIS into the limelight.

ANDRÉ G. BOURASSA

Deserontyon, John, "Captain John," Mohawk chief (b in the Mohawk Valley, NY 1740s; d at Bay of Quinte, Upper Canada 7 Jan 1811). As a young man Deserontyon aided the British in the SEVEN YEARS' WAR and later during the 1763 PONTIAC uprising. When the American Revolution broke out, by which time he had become a chief, he again sided with his old allies. With Joseph BRANT he participated in the Battle of Oriskany (1777), and on his own organized raids into enemy territory. After the American victory Deserontyon and Brant were angered to learn that the 1783 peace treaty made no provision for restoration of the Mohawks' ancestral lands in NY, and they heatedly made their position known to Gov HALDIMAND in Montréal. Eventually they were obliged to accept the situation and settled their followers on lands granted elsewhere. Brant opted for a "retreat" in the Grand R valley and urged Deserontyon to join him there in a unified community, but Deserontyon preferred a Bay of Quinte site far removed from the victorious "Yankees," where he could manage his own affairs. With government assistance Deserontyon built a church and a schoolhouse for his followers, most of whom were Christians. At times, his leadership proved controversial, and quarrels and factionalism disrupted the closing years of his life. The modern town of Deseronto, Ont, was named for him.

CHARLES M. JOHNSTON

Desert, region in which evaporation greatly exceeds precipitation, resulting in a water deficiency which only a few life forms can endure. Precipitation is under 200 mm annually, coming at very irregular intervals. Deserts cover 20% of the Earth's surface. Tropical deserts occur between 15° and 35° N and S latitudes in regions in which dry air masses allow intense solar radiation to reach the ground surface. Mid-latitude deserts are located in the centres of large continental masses, far beyond the reach of moisture-bearing oceanic air masses. Desert landforms are diverse, consisting of mountains and plains. The mountains are characteristic, angular forms and end abruptly at the edge of plains, where they are replaced by gently inclined, eroded bedrock surfaces (pediments). Desert regions have internal drainage, where runoff waters are directly evaporated.

Canada has no true deserts, although some regions exhibit desertlike features, such as this area of southern BC, near Osoyoos (*photo by Tim Fitzharris*).

Ephemeral streams carry the runoff in channels called *wadis* (N Africa) or *arroyos* (western US). The centre of desert basins may be occupied by a dry, flat area (playa) which occasionally receives runoff carrying fine silts and clays. Rarely, a playa lake may form, lasting only a few days. Relatively small portions of desert regions (20%) are occupied by sand dunes, which may be transverse, barchane, longitudinal (seif), star or dome shaped (*see* AEOLIAN LANDFORMS). Canada has no true deserts, only regions that exhibit some desertlike features, eg, the sandy expanse S of Lk Athabasca, which lies within a forested region with a humid CLIMATE. It formed on raised, coarse-grained, glacial deltaic deposits which retain insufficient surface moisture to allow vegetation to become established. Smaller areas in the Canadian Arctic, lacking vegetation and being exposed to strong winds, exhibit a desertlike appearance. In the driest parts of the prairies (eg, N and S of the CYPRESS HILLS) and the most southerly parts of the Fraser, Thompson, Nicola, Similkameen, Okanagan and Kootenay river valleys, precipitation can be as low as 250-300 mm and vegetation is of the semiarid type (eg, sagebrush, rabbitbrush).

P.P. DAVID

Desjardins, Alphonse, journalist, parliamentary reporter, founder of the CAISSE POPULAIRE (b at Lévis, Canada E 5 Nov 1854; d there 31 Oct 1920). Desjardins was 46 and French-language reporter for Hansard when on 6 Dec 1900 he founded the first Caisse populaire, or people's bank, in Lévis. In promoting the doctrine of co-operation, Desjardins's goals were to fight usury, to improve the lot of the working classes, to bring economic liberation to French Canadians and to slow their exodus to the US. The Caisse populaire was the fruit of 3 years' study, discussion and assiduous correspondence with the great advocates of mutualism and economic co-operation in Québec and Europe. His was an original synthesis, a true "plum pudding" composed of foreign elements but adapted to local conditions. Desjardins was responsible for everything. He ran the Caisse in Lévis, saw to the establishment of 205 other Caisses in Québec, the rest of Canada and the US and, with solid support from the clergy, assured their success.

After 1916, illness forced him to abandon the taxing work of promotion and expansion. He devoted the last 4 years of his life to considering how to protect and guarantee the survival of his life's work. Death prevented him from realizing his plans for a federation of Caisse populaire centrale. His success won Desjardins an international reputation. Honours and requests poured in from all over Europe, the US, Latin America and even from New Zealand. He acknowledged that the custom, which caught on after 1913, of calling the new institutions "Caisses populaires Desjardins" gave him the most pleasure of all.

YVES ROBY

Deskaheh, also known as **Levi General,** Cayuga chief and speaker of the Six Nations Hereditary Council (b on the Six Nations Reserve near Brantford, Ont 1873; d at the Tuscarora Reservation, NY 25 June 1925). A member of the Longhouse religion, Deskaheh insisted that the Six Nations retain their languages and distinctive culture. When the Canadian government tried in 1923 to unseat the Six Nations Hereditary Council and to institute an elected one, Deskaheh acted immediately. He worked to obtain international recognition of the Six Nations as a sovereign Indian nation ruled by a hereditary council of chiefs. Travelling on a passport issued by the council he went to the League of Nations in Geneva, Switz. But the League's secretariat refused to allow him to address the assembly, arguing that Canada had jurisdiction over the Six Nations. Exhausted, Deskaheh became ill shortly after returning to N America and died from pneumonia. Six months before his death the Canadian government ended the Confederacy's administrative functions on the reserve and organized a vote for an elected council. Both councils existed well into the 1980s, but only the elected body is recognized by the state. DONALD B. SMITH

Deslongchamps, Pierre, chemist, educator (b at St-Lin, Qué 8 May 1938). He is an international leader in the field of organic synthesis and his work on the stereo-electronic effects operative in many organic processes is widely acclaimed. After studies at Université de Montréal (BSc 1959) and UNB (PhD 1964), he became assistant professor at U de M in 1966 and the next year moved to U de Sherbrooke, where he was promoted professor of chemistry in 1972. Well-spoken in both national languages, he is a polished and popular lecturer and a stimulating teacher. His synthesis of the complex insecticide ryanodine stands as a landmark achievement in the field of organic synthesis. He was elected to the Royal Society of Canada in 1974 and in the same year awarded the E.W.R. STEACIE prize by the National Research Council. Twice honoured by the Assn canadienne-française pour l'avancement des sciences (Médaille Vincent, Médaille Pariseau), he won the Merck, Sharp and Dohme Award of the Chemical Institute of Canada in 1976. In 1983 he was elected to the Royal Soc (London). W.A. AYER

Desmarais, Paul, financier (b at Sudbury, Ont 4 Jan 1927). After studying at U of O and McGill, Desmarais worked for Courtois, Fredette et Cie, a Montréal accounting firm, 1945-51; he then returned to Sudbury to run his father's bus company. In 1961 he gained control of Provincial Transport, a sizable passenger-transport company. In 1965 he bought his first conglomerate, Trans-Canada Corp Fund, through which he gained control of the major French-language newspaper *La Presse* (Montréal), the major francophone radio station CKAC, a large assurance company (Imperial Life, Toronto) and several other daily and weekly newspapers. In 1968 he took control of POWER CORP OF CANADA; one of the major conglomerates in Canada, Power Corp now includes the principal mutual fund in Canada (Investors Group), one of the largest trust funds (Montreal Trust), the fourth-largest paper company in the country (Consolidated-Bathurst), the second-largest life-assurance company (Great-West Life Co, Winnipeg) and several other Canadian and European firms. In 1987 Desmarais sat on the boards of 15 companies other than Power Corp. He was made a Companion of the Order of Canada in 1987. JORGE NIOSI

Reading: D. Grebes, *Rising to Power* (1987).

Desmarteau, Étienne, strongman (b at Boucherville, Qué 4 Feb 1873; d at Montréal 29 Oct 1905). A Montréal policeman, Desmarteau excelled in tug-of-war and weight-throwing events and was the first Canadian to win an Olympic gold medal. He won the world heavy-weight and the junior world hammer-throwing championships in 1902, captured the gold medal in the 56-lb throw at the 1904 St Louis Olympics and set two 56-lb world records in 1905, but died of typhoid fever later that year. In 1972, Montréal dedicated a park to Desmarteau's memory. JEAN R. DUPERREAULT

DesRochers, Alfred, journalist, translator, poet, critic (b at Saint-Élie d'Orford, Qué 5 Aug 1901; d at Montréal 12 Oct 1978). As a poet and critic DesRochers was an important figure in Qué-

bec literature between the wars. *L'Offrande aux vierges folles* (1928) and, in particular, *À l'ombre del'Orford* (1929, Prix David 1932) reveal an innovative poet who went beyond the regionalism and land-based themes of his time. Inspired by French romanticism and by the vastness of N America, DesRochers adopted a realistic viewpoint as well as the verse and structures of traditional versification. *Paragraphes* (1931) is the work of an original critic who greatly influenced 1930s poets. Two other collections of his poetry appeared in the 1960s, *Le Retour de Titus* (1963) and *Elégies pour l'épouse en-allée* (1967). *Oeuvres poétiques* (1977) included some important poems that had appeared in magazines and newspapers. RICHARD GIGUÈRE

Desrosiers, Léo-Paul, writer, civil servant (b at Berthier-en-Haut, Qué 11 Apr 1896; d at Montréal 20 Apr 1967). Desrosiers, who lifted the genre of historical novel to a new level, is the least appreciated and most retiring writer of his generation. He came from a peasant family whose ancestors were among the first colonists of the St Lawrence Valley. After classical studies at the Séminaire de Joliette, he was influenced by the nationalism of Henri BOURASSA and Lionel GROULX. He was successively parliamentary correspondent in Ottawa for Le DEVOIR, editor of *Hansard* and chief librarian of the Montréal Municipal Library; he was a member of the Société des dix, the Royal Society of Canada and the Académie canadienne-française. Desrosiers's interest in history inspired biographies as well as his best novels. His greatest contribution to literature was without doubt *Les Engagés du Grand Portage* (1938), set in the fur-trade years of the early 19th century. Desrosiers's *L'Ampoule d'or* (1951) deserves rereading for the sobriety and poetry of its narration. RÉJEAN BEAUDOIN

Desrosiers, Robert Guy, dancer, choreographer, director (b at Montréal 10 Oct 1953). A brilliant dancer in his own right, Desrosiers has assumed national prominence as a choreographer of startling imagination and originality. He graduated from the NATIONAL BALLET SCHOOL in 1971 and danced briefly with the NATIONAL BALLET OF CANADA before continuing to dance and train in France, England and the US. He was never able to settle long in any one company, but instead began to develop his own choreographic ideas which found full expression in the creation of his own Robert Desrosiers Dance Co in 1980. He won the Jean A. Chalmers Award in Choreography in 1985, and that year the National Ballet premiered his *The Blue Snake*. In 1987 he created *Laundry Day* for the Contemporary Dancers of Winnipeg. MICHAEL CRABB

Dessailliant, dit Richeterre, Michel, painter (fl 1701-23). A victim of France's mercantile policy, he was not able to settle permanently in New France and practise his art. This fact is regrettable since the only work that may be attributed to him with certainty, the portrait of Mère Louise Soumande, *dite* de Saint-Augustin (1708), shows great skill and sensitivity. Archival documents record that he did other portraits, but there is no proof that he painted the ex-votos now in Ste-Anne Beaupré that are attributed to him. FRANÇOIS-MARC GAGNON

Dessane, Antoine, organist, pianist, cellist, teacher, composer (b at Forcalquier, near Aix-en-Provence, France 10 Dec 1826; d at Québec City 8 June 1873). Founder of the choral Société musicale Ste-Cécile (1869), Antoine Dessane was an active member of several Québec music clubs. He received his musical education from his older brother and his father until he enrolled in the Paris Conservatory at age 10. Life was difficult for

artists after the 1848 Revolution, and Dessane accepted a position as organist at Notre-Dame Basilica in Québec C (1849-60). He was subsequently an organist in New York, but returned to Québec C in 1869, this time to a position at St-Roch Church. Many of his works – over 50 sacred and secular pieces – reflect his adopted country; they include *La Québécoise* and *Souvenir de Kamouraska*. HÉLÈNE PLOUFFE

Désy, Jean, diplomat (b at Montréal 8 Jan 1893; d at Paris, France 19 Dec 1960). Educated at Laval and the Sorbonne, the highly intelligent Désy was called to the Québec Bar in 1915 and taught history and law at U de M, 1919-25. He joined the Dept of External Affairs in 1925, the year it came under the direction of O.D. SKELTON. Along with Laurent Beaudry and Pierre Dupuy, he was one of the pioneering Francophones in the department; like Dupuy, he avoided Ottawa, preferring to serve abroad. As minister to Belgium and the Netherlands, 1939-40, Désy was among the first career diplomats to head a Canadian post in a foreign country. Ambassadorships in Brazil, Italy and finally France followed. NORMAN HILLMER

Detroit River, 52 km long, flows S from Lk ST CLAIR to the W end of Lake ERIE, forming part of the boundary between Ontario and Michigan. Detroit, Mich, and WINDSOR, Ont, dominate its shores. Part of the ST LAWRENCE SEAWAY, it is heavily used by commercial traffic. The largest islands are Michigan's Belle I, a park, and Grosse I, site of an American naval base, and Ontario's Fighting I. The name comes from the French word for strait or narrows. DANIEL FRANCIS

Deutsch, John James, educator, public servant (b at Quinton, Sask 26 Feb 1911; d at Kingston, Ont Mar 1976). He was educated at Queen's (B Com), and spent over half his life in the federal public service: as a member of the research department of the Bank of Canada 1936-42, although often on loan to government departments and especially the Rowell-Sirois Royal Commission; as special assistant in External Affairs 1942-44; as director of the International Economic Relations Division of the Dept of Finance 1946-53; as secretary of the Treasury Board 1954-56; and finally, as first chairman of the Economic Council of Canada 1963-67. In addition, he was a member of several other royal commissions, commissions of inquiry and advisory commissions or committees. As an educator, he was head of the dept of economics at UBC 1956-59; vice-principal administration and professor of economics at Queen's 1959-63; principal designate 1967 and principal and vice-chancellor of Queen's, 1968-74; professor of economics, Queen's 1967 to his death. He was coauthor or coeditor of 3 books and author of many articles. Unassuming and warmly regarded, he had the ability to recognize the core of a problem at once, and his greatest achievements may be found in his influence on government economic policy over 40 years. A Companion of the Order of Canada, he received 17 honorary degrees. M.C. URQUHART

Development Industry Developers build and own all types of urban property, from high-rise apartments to industrial buildings and shopping centres.

Though most developers think of themselves as individualists opposed to government regulation, the land-development industry is in fact the creation of postwar industrial development policy. Ottawa set out to foster large construction companies that would provide employment while needed housing and other facilities were being built. A crown corporation, CANADA MORTGAGE AND HOUSING CORPORATION, was established to provide the necessary support. Ottawa helped ensure the availability of the necessary investment capital through financial institutions and investors, and provided the industry with special tax concessions so that developers paid little or no tax on their profits.

After 1945 entrepreneurs in every city saw opportunities in suburban house-building. Some entrepreneurs realized that land development was more profitable than construction. In the 1950s other entrepreneurs saw the potential of high-rise apartments. By the 1960s and 1970s developers were producing many commercial and retail projects along with housing.

The postwar city the developers built was a radical departure from the past. Five building types are particularly important: high-rise apartments in the central city and in the suburbs; new suburbs, featuring a new style of house on a larger lot, on streets laid out in a circular pattern rather than on the rectangular grid (the prototype was Don Mills, built next to Toronto in the 1950s by industrialist-promoter E.P. TAYLOR); suburban industrial parks, with single-storey buildings on large lots serviced by road rather than rail; downtown office-commercial complexes, combining huge amounts of office space with some shopping (the prototype was Montréal's PLACE VILLE MARIE, built 1956-65 by US developer William Zeckendorf); shopping centres, where a developer-owner provides all the retail facilities, renting space mainly to chain retailers (the prototype was Vancouver's Park Royal, built by the Guinness brewing family).

Developers of these projects are often embroiled in controversy. In the mid-1970s the industry was criticized for the rapidly increasing prices of the housing it produced. The focus was on land, because serviced building lots were selling at prices that had no relationship to the developers' costs. Some analysts suggested that the few large firms supplying a major share of serviced lots were taking advantage of their market power. Others argued that the high prices and profits resulted from artificial regulation on the supply of land, imposed by planners and municipalities (*see* ZONING). In 1980 the market reached a postwar peak when an ordinary 3-bedroom house in suburban Vancouver cost more than twice as much as the same house in suburban Montréal. Montréal was unusual in that building lots were produced by hundreds of small developers.

During Canada's urban boom, land-development companies grew quickly. More than a dozen firms with assets of $100 million or more had emerged, partly from internal expansion, partly from takeovers. Some were entrepreneur owned; others were owned by Canadian and foreign investors. One industry leader was Cadillac-Fairview Corporation Ltd (assets $3.7 billion, 1986), the result of a merger between a Toronto-based entrepreneur-owned firm and a Montréal-based company owned by one branch of the Bronfman family. Another was Olympia & York Developments Ltd, a private company owned by the REICHMANN FAMILY of Toronto.

As the boom slowed in the late 1970s many Canadian developers expanded into the US. The deep recession and high interest rates of 1980 only worsened their problems. Some firms had difficulty paying interest on money borrowed to finance this American expansion and had to sell valuable assets to generate cash. The same high interest rates caused the demand for housing to collapse in Canada. During the early 1980s many leading developers experienced severe problems, and some large firms went through receiverships and major asset sales. The greatest difficulties were faced by companies who operated in western Canada, particularly Alberta where the collapse of high land prices (and real-estate values generally) was most dramatic. The survivors of

this shakeout were often not the entrepreneurs but the largest firms such as Olympia & York and Cadillac-Fairview which focused on building and holding downtown office buildings, shopping centres and other rental projects.

As an industry, land development is a remarkable example of what can happen when entrepreneurs are combined with profit opportunities and large amounts of investment capital. Canadian financial institutions and other lenders provided $14 billion for real-estate financing in the 1960s, $90 billion in the 1970s and $140 billion in the 1980s. The developers earned very substantial profits, and paid little or no corporate tax. They provided much-needed accommodation in Canada's cities, though the standard building forms they used came to be questioned on social, economic and ecological grounds. The Canadian funds invested in property, which arguably could have gone to other, more productive uses, fueled a real-estate price boom and overexpansion by the developers. Ultimately, this led to the collapse of many of the large development firms and to severe problems for financial institutions, particularly those in western Canada, which lent mortgage money based on these inflated prices.   JAMES LORIMER

Reading: R.W. Collier, *Contemporary Cathedrals: Large-Scale Developments in Canadian Cities* (1974); Federal-Provincial Task Force on the Supply and Price of Serviced Residential Land, *Down to Earth,* 2 vols (1978); James Lorimer, *The Developers* (1978) and *The City Book* (1976); James Lorimer and C. MacGregor, eds, *After the Developers* (1981); L.B. Smith and M. Walker, eds, *Public Property? The Habitat Debate Continued* (1977); P. Spurr, *Land and Urban Development* (1976).

Deverell, Rex, playwright (b at Toronto 17 July 1941). With a degree in divinity from McMaster U, Deverell was pastor of a rural Ontario Baptist congregation before turning to playwriting in 1970. Two years later he began his association with Regina's Globe Theatre where he has been writer-in-residence since 1975. Deverell's numerous plays for children are distinguished by their concern with social issues. His best-known adult plays range from the gentle fantasy of *2 derelicts* in *Boiler Room Suite* (1977), winner of the Canadian Authors Assn Literary Award, to docu-dramas of Saskatchewan history, *Medicare!* (1979) and *Black Powder: Estevan 1931* (1981). Recent works include *Melody Meets the Baglady* (1985), *Fallout* (1985) and *Switching Places* (1986), all children's plays, as well as *Resuscitation of a Dying Mouse* (1986) and *Quartet for Three Actors* (1987), for adults.   JERRY WASSERMAN

Deville, Édouard-Gaston, surveyor (b at La Charité sur Noire, Nièvre, France 21 Feb 1849; d at Ottawa 21 Sept 1924). Educated at the naval school at Brest, Deville served in the French Navy and was in charge of its hydrographic surveys throughout the world. In 1875 he retired and came to Canada, becoming inspector of surveys in Québec. In 1881 he was appointed inspector of Dominion Land Surveys and in 1885 surveyor general of Canada. He experimented with photography in surveying in mountainous areas and in 1889 published *Photographic Surveying*. Regarded as the father of photogrammetry in Canada, he supervised many major surveys. He was a founding member of the Royal Society of Canada.   ERIC J. HOLMGREN

Devine, Donald Grant, agricultural economist, teacher, farmer, premier of Saskatchewan (b at Regina 5 July 1944). Raised on a farm near Lake Valley, Sask, Devine attended U of Sask (BSc 1967), U of A (M AgEc 1970) and Ohio State (PhD 1976). While continuing to farm near Moose Jaw he taught agricultural economics at U of Sask 1976-79. Though defeated in Nutana in

1978, he was elected leader of the Saskatchewan PC Party in Nov 1979. Defeated again in a by-election in Estevan in 1980 he was elected there in 1982 when he led his party to an overwhelming victory, bringing it to power in Saskatchewan for the first time since 1929. He was sworn in as premier on 8 May 1982. In 1986 with the support of the rural vote, Devine became the province's first PC premier to win re-election. D.H. BOCKING

Devoir, Le, Montréal NEWSPAPER started by Henri BOURASSA in 1910 as a pan-Canadian nationalist, pro-French Canadian, pro-Catholic, anti-British but independent newspaper. Its editors and publishers were Bourassa (1910-32), Georges Pelletier (1932-47), Gérard FILION (1947-63), Claude RYAN (1963-78), Michel Roy (interim editor, 1978-81), Jean-Louis Roy (1981-86) and Benoit Lauzière (1986-). From 1958 to 1968 André LAURENDEAU was the chief editorial writer. Daily circulation was 12 529 in 1910, 20 112 in 1940, 48 284 in 1965, and 27 714 in 1976. In 1986 *Le Devoir* had an estimated circulation of 30 000-35 000.

Le Devoir was well known as a newspaper of opinion. It campaigned against CONSCRIPTION in 1917 and 1942 and opposed Maurice DUPLESSIS and the patronage system. In the 1970s it remained federalist but continued to be a pan-Canadian and French Canadian nationalist paper. Its international coverage was excellent, based on the *Agence France Presse* (AFP) and *Le Monde*, but, in an attempt to increase its audience in the early 1980s, it expanded its economic and leisure content to the detriment of foreign news. However, in 1986 *Le Devoir* again began to use *Le Monde* for international coverage.

ANDRÉ DONNEUR AND ONNIG BEYLERIAN

Devon, Alta, Town, pop 3691 (1986), inc as a village in 1949 and as a town in 1950, located about 30 km SW of Edmonton. In 1947 the town site was a grain field, but with the discovery of oil at Leduc No 1 Wellsite, Imperial Oil established the town in the centre of the Leduc oil discovery to service the surrounding oil fields. The town was planned according to modern town-planning principles by the Edmonton District Planning Commission and CMHC. The town grew extremely quickly, but because of planning controls, its development was orderly. The town is located high on the banks of the N Saskatchewan R. Its economy is still based on the oil and gas industry; however, the addition of the Devon Coal Research Centre provides more employment. Many people from Devon commute to work in nearby Edmonton.   D.G. WETHERELL

Devon Island is the second-largest island (55 247 km²) among the QUEEN ELIZABETH ISLANDS, NWT. The island was first sighted by William Baffin in 1616 and was named North Devon by W.E. PARRY for Devon, Eng. Its eastern third is covered with an ice cap with a maximum thickness of 500-700 m. The rocks are very old, consisting of Precambrian, Cambrian and Ordovician in the E and Ordovician and Silurian siltstones and shales in the W. Because most of the island is a plateau, 300-500 m in elevation, it is a barren landscape, dominated by frost-shattered rocks and nearly devoid of plants and animals. The mean annual temperature averages about -16°C.

The Truelove Lowland area of the island has diverse vegetation and wildlife, an abundance of soil water in the summer owing to blocked drainage, and greater precipitation and higher summer temperatures (4° to 8°C), with more clear days than other parts of the island. The ground is snow free for only 45-50 days each summer. The poorly drained lowlands are characterized by a sedge-moss tundra in which

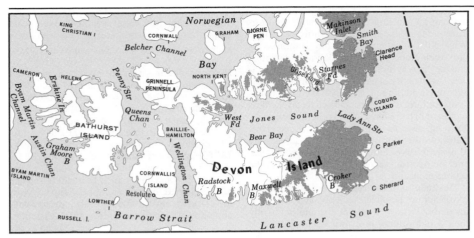

MUSKOXEN graze year-round. Most of the living organisms in this system (98.9%) are plants, with the remainder being herbivores and carnivores, soil bacteria, fungi and INVERTEBRATES that decompose the organic matter. The peaty soils are cold and wet all summer and have low levels of available nutrients. The island's raised beach ridges of coarse gravels and sands have higher summer air and soil temperatures and drier soils than elsewhere on the island. This system is characterized by a cushion plant (polar semidesert) vegetation on which collared LEMMING feed year-round. Of the living mass in this system, 98.7% are plants.

On both the beach ridges and wet sedge meadows, the soil invertebrates (worms, protozoa, midge and fly larvae, and collembola) are more productive and consume more organic matter (4.73%) than do the lemming, waterfowl and large muskox. Clearly the tiny insects and other soil organisms are more important in the functioning of this system than are the 15-25 muskoxen that graze in summer and 60-125 that graze in winter in this small oasis in the High Arctic. Because of the island's short growing season (40-55 days) and low daily summer temperatures (2° to 8°C), plants and animals grow slowly and have a long life cycle. Many invertebrates that take from a few weeks to 1 or 2 years to complete their life cycle in temperate regions require 2-9 years at these latitudes. While the same basic ecosystem components are found in a Saskatchewan grassland or an Ontario hardwood or coniferous forest as those that occur in the High Arctic, the diversity of species, rates of organismic growth and levels of ecosystem production are much reduced, owing to the limited solar-energy input into these cold and nutrient-deficient systems near the top of the world.   LAWRENCE BLISS

Devonshire, Victor Christian William Cavendish, 9th Duke of, governor general of Canada 1916-21 (b at London, Eng 31 May 1868; d at Chatsworth House, Devonshire, Eng 6 May 1938). The youngest member in the British House of Commons in 1891, he remained there until 1908, when he succeeded to the dukedom. Retiring, deliberate and a pedestrian speaker, he was easy to underestimate as governor general. But he travelled widely, was politically helpful and was the soul of constitutional propriety. There were none of the problems there had been with his predecessor, the duke of CONNAUGHT. As one of Britain's great landowners, he took a particular interest in Canadian agriculture. After returning home, he served briefly as secretary of state for the colonies. His wife was the daughter of the marquess of LANSDOWNE, governor general in the 1880s. Their son-in-law, Harold Macmillan, provides an affectionate portrait of Devonshire in the first volume of his memoirs, *Winds of Change* (1966).   NORMAN HILLMER

Dewar, Marion, née Bell, public-health nurse, feminist, politician (b at Montréal 17 Feb 1928). She was first elected Ottawa alderman in 1972, and later became deputy mayor. While defeated as provincial candidate in Ottawa West 1977, she was elected mayor of Ottawa from 1978 to 1985. Among the policy areas she emphasized were improved public access to municipal decision making, low-cost housing and child care. She co-hosted the Women's Constitutional Conference calling for gender equality provisions in the Canadian Charter of Rights. Under her mayoralty, Ottawa was declared a nuclear-free zone and provided homes to some 4000 Southeast Asian refugees. In 1985 Dewar was elected NDP federal president and urged the party to have more female candidates. In July 1987 she was a successful candidate for the NDP in the federal by-election in Hamilton West.   ALAN WHITEHORN

Dewar, Phyllis, swimmer (b at Moose Jaw, Sask 5 Mar 1916; d at Toronto 8 Apr 1961). Spurred from age 4 by a strong competitive instinct, Dewar was the best swimmer on the prairies by age 17. She became Canada's aquatic darling at the 1934 British Empire Games by winning gold medals in the 100- and 400-yd freestyle, the 300-yd medley and the 400-yd relay, and was crowned Canada's female athlete of the year. Weakened by flu, she performed poorly in the 1936 Berlin Olympics but regained top form to win another gold medal in the 1938 British Empire Games. After her husband's death in a 1954 car accident, the mother of 4 young children grew despondent; her health failed, and she died at 45.   BOB FERGUSON

Dewdney, Christopher, poet, artist (b at London, Ont 9 May 1951). Dewdney's poetry combines fabulous life forms and esoteric language with more readily accessible imagery, peppered with his own drawings. Since his first published collections, *Golders Green* (1972) and *A Paleozoic Geologic of London, Ontario* (1973), further volumes have followed at 2-3 year intervals ending, to date, with *The Immaculate Perception* (1986). Dewdney offers an introduction to his work via comments on his major ongoing poetic work *A Natural History of Southwestern Ontario*, ". . . the book is the voice of the land and the creatures themselves, speaking from the inviolate fortress of a primeval history uncorrupted by humans. It is a codex of the plants and animals whose technology is truly miraculous, and for whom I am merely a scribe." Dewdney teaches at York U, Toronto.   MARLENE ALT

Dewdney, Sir Edgar, surveyor, politician (b in Devonshire, Eng 1835; d at Victoria 8 Aug 1916). Dewdney came to BC in 1859 and built the DEWD-NEY TRAIL. In 1870 he was elected to the Legislative Council of BC as member for Kootenay. He was

elected to Parliament as Conservative member for Yale, BC, in 1872, 1874 and 1878. He was Indian commissioner for the North-West Territories 1879-88 and lieutenant-governor of the North-West Territories (1881-88). In 1888 and 1891 he was re-elected to the House of Commons as member for Assiniboia East. He was created privy councillor in 1888 and until 1892 was minister of the interior and supt general of Indian affairs. He was lt-gov of BC 1892-97, after which he retired from public life to become a mining broker and financial agent in Victoria.   ERIC J. HOLMGREN

Dewdney Trail The original Dewdney Trail was a 400 km trail route extending from Hope to Galbraith's Ferry on the Kootenay R. The trail was routed and constructed under the supervision of Edgar DEWDNEY, a civil engineer appointed by Frederick Seymour, the governor of the colony of BC, in Apr 1865. The purpose of the trail was to provide a route to the BC Interior in order for the British to maintain control over the growing gold-mining interests in the region. The trail was constructed in a 6-month period; however, many sections were in rough condition. With the advent of other roads and the shift in mining interests to the Columbia Valley, the Dewdney Trail soon lost its significance. By the 1880s the section through the West Kootenays was impassable.

Today, one of the better preserved sections of the trail is a 36 km segment extending from Christina Lake to Rossland. The BC government, working in co-operation with private landowners over whose property 50% of the trail crosses, have reopened the Dewdney Trail. It remains a scenic and historically significant tribute to the heritage of our country.   BART DEEG

Dewhurst, Colleen, actress (b at Montréal 3 June 1926). Her family moved to the US Midwest when she was 5. She made her professional debut in *The Royal Family* (NY 1946), while still a student at the American Academy of Dramatic Arts. Dubbed "The Matriarch of Broadway" by *Time* magazine for her portrayal of powerful women, she has been one of the notable stage actresses of her generation, and has won numerous awards. She has been closely identified with Eugene O'Neill's heroines, especially Josie Hogan in *A Moon For the Misbegotten*. In the one-woman show *My Gene* (NY 1987), she played O'Neill's widow Carlotta. She has starred in modern Broadway plays and several TV drama specials. Dewhurst has appeared in 3 CBC-TV dramas, *A Cheap Bunch of Nice Flowers* (1965), *Anne of Green Gables* (1986), and *Anne of Green Gables: The Sequel* (1987). Hollywood films include *The Nun's Story* (1959), *The Cowboys* (1972) and *The Dead Zone* (1983).   JOHN CHARLES

Dexter, Alexander Grant, journalist (b at St Andrews, Man 3 Feb 1896; d at Winnipeg 12 Dec 1961). Grant Dexter was the archetypal Canadian political reporter of the 1940s, a splendid journalist with access to the best governmental sources. After attending Brandon College, in 1912 he joined the *Manitoba Free Press*, where, with time out for war service, he was schooled in Liberal journalism by J.W. DAFOE. After serving in various posts, in 1938 he became Ottawa correspondent. Through links to T.A. CRERAR, in particular, and to key bureaucrats, Dexter learned of government decisions more quickly than most, and his coverage of politics was informed by this inside knowledge. Although he was editor of the *Free Press* 1948-54, he is remembered for his reportage and through his fine collection of papers at Queen's U.   J.L. GRANATSTEIN

Dextraze, Jacques Alfred, "Ja Dex," soldier (b at Montréal 15 Aug 1919). He served during WWII in Iceland, England, France, Germany and the Netherlands and was promoted from private to lt-col commanding the Fusiliers Mount-Royal. In the Korean War he commanded the 2nd Battalion, Royal 22e Régiment. Commandant of the Royal Canadian Infantry School at Camp Borden and commander at Camp Valcartier, he was chief of general staff in charge of UN operations in the Congo in 1963. In 1972 he was promoted general and became chief of defence staff. In 1977 he retired from the CAF to serve as chairman of the board of directors of CN until 1982. He is a Companion of the Order of Canada. JEAN PARISEAU

Di Cicco, Pier Giorgio, poet (b at Arezzo, Italy 5 July 1949; immigrated to Montréal 1953). Since U of Toronto (BA, 1973; BEd, 1976) Di Cicco has published 14 books, his major collections being *The Tough Romance* (1979), *Flying Deeper into the Century* (1982) and *Virgin Science* (1986). After editing the anthology *Roman Candles* (1978), he became a seminal figure in Italian Canadian writing, being anthologized in national and international collections. His poetry demonstrates the influence of Italian and Latin American writers and is characterized by a fusion of "deep image" and neo-surreal elements. In 1985 he entered an Augustinian monastery. *See also* ITALIAN WRITING. JOSEPH PIVATO

di Michele, Mary, writer (b at Lanciano, Italy 6 Aug 1949; immigrated to Canada 1955). After U of T (BA, 1972) and U of Windsor (MA, 1974), she contributed to *Toronto Life* and Canadian literary magazines. Her early books, *Bread and Chocolate* (1980) and *Mimosa and Other Poems* (1981), deal with conflicts in the immigrant family; her later books, *Necessary Sugar* (1984) and *Immune to Gravity* (1986) explore the universal issues of women. Her anthology of women poets, *Anything is Possible* (1984), her inclusion in major Canadian anthologies and several literary prizes attest to her exceptional gifts as a writer. After being writer-in-residence at U of T (1985-86), di Michele began to work in narrative prose. Her poetry has been translated into Italian and Spanish. *See also* ITALIAN WRITING. JOSEPH PIVATO

Diabetes Mellitus is a disease complex resulting from relative or absolute INSULIN deficiency, which may also be associated with altered effectiveness of insulin. Diabetes, which causes a disease of blood vessels most noticeably in the eyes and kidneys, is the most frequent cause of blindness and a common cause of kidney failures. Because of complications arising from diabetes, it is also ranked as the third most important cause of death in Canada.

Diabetes mellitus has been known for millennia. The familial nature of the disease has also been recognized for a long time, but the genetic determinants are still controversial. The characteristics and causes of a patient's illness may differ according to the type of diabetes. Effective treatment for diabetes became available only after the discovery and isolation of insulin, for which F.G. BANTING, J.J. R. MACLEOD and associates were awarded a Nobel Prize in 1923.

It has been estimated that 1 million Canadians have diabetes; 50% of them may be undiagnosed. No age group is immune, but people between the ages of 15 and 64 are the most prone to diabetes. The chances of developing diabetes double with every 20% of excess body weight.

The characteristics and causes of a patient's illness may differ according to the type of diabetes. Type I is insulin-dependent diabetes mellitus (IDDM). Autoimmunity is a major mechanism in the causation of IDDM. Antibodies develop to the pancreatic islets where insulin is made, and the islets are ultimately destroyed. A genetic susceptibility to viral infection may be another

mechanism causing IDDM. Type II is non-insulin-dependent diabetes mellitus (NIDDM). While NIDDM patients retain some insulin secretion, their blood glucose regulation is disturbed and they may exhibit other metabolic abnormalities. The majority of patients with NIDDM are diagnosed in adulthood. Obesity is common in patients with NIDDM. Secondary diabetes mellitus is present in patients in whom other health problems, eg, diseases of the pancreas or overactive states of other hormone-producing glands such as the adrenals or pituitary, have caused interference with insulin secretion or impairment of the actions of insulin.

Treatment of diabetes, designed to correct as completely as possible metabolic abnormalities, invariably includes a special diet and frequently the use of insulin or oral antidiabetic drugs. It is estimated that 50% of diabetics are treated by diet alone; 24% by oral hypoglycemic agents; and 26% by insulin injection. Because exercise can lower diabetic blood glucose levels, physical activity is also important as part of the treatment. The insulin treatment is intended to make up for the insulin deficiency. Usually insulin must be injected beneath the skin, because digestive enzymes make it unavailable from the gastrointestinal tract if taken orally. Oral antidiabetic drugs (principally sulfonylureas), promote insulin secretion. The safety of these drugs in diabetic (Type II) management has been questioned on the basis of large-scale but controversial studies. G.D. MOLNAR

Reading: J. Biermann and B. Tookey, *The Diabetic's Book* (1981); L.P. Krall and R.S. Beaser, eds, *Joslin Diabetes Manual* (12th ed, 1987).

Diamond, Billy, politician (b at Rupert House, Qué 17 May 1949). A leading figure in Indian politics of the James Bay region of Québec, Diamond was born and raised in the Cree community of Rupert House, becoming band manager there in the 1960s and chief of the band, 1970-76. As founding member and grand chief of the Grand Council of the Cree of Québec (1974-84) he was a prime mover and signator of the JAMES BAY AGREEMENT on behalf of his people, and chairman of the Cree Regional Authority (est 1975) which administers the implementation of the agreement in relation to land, economic development and social services. He has also been involved in a wide variety of local services (eg, as chairman of the James Bay Cree school board from 1976 and president of Air Creebec from 1980) and political activities. BENNETT McCARDLE

Diamonds of Canada, mined by Jacques CARTIER's men at the mouth of Rivière du Cap-Rouge in 1541. Cartier's "treasure" proved to be worthless quartz. The episode is remembered in the name of Québec's Cap aux Diamants and also in the French saying, "As false as Canadian diamonds."

Dick, Evelyn, née Maclean, murderer (b at Beamsville, Ont 13 Oct 1920). The Evelyn Dick case is one of the most grisly murder stories on record in Canada. On 16 Mar 1946, a male body minus head and limbs was found on Hamilton Mountain. The victim was identified as John Dick, and suspicion quickly fell on his wife, Evelyn. An eccentric woman, Evelyn had deserted Dick apparently because her parents did not approve of their marriage and because he could not support her expensive life-style. Weeks after the discovery of the torso, police found the body of Evelyn's infant son in a suitcase. Dick made statements implicating herself, her lover William Bohozuk and her father Donald Maclean in the murders. After 3 trials she was sentenced to life

imprisonment. Maclean was sentenced to 5 years and Bohozuk was acquitted. EDWARD BUTTS

Reading: Marjorie Freeman Campbell, *Torso* (1974).

Dickens, Francis Jeffrey, NWMP inspector (b at London, Eng 15 Jan 1844; d at Moline, Ill 11 June 1886), third son of Charles Dickens. In 1864, after numerous unsuccessful career starts, Dickens joined the Bengal Mounted Police in India. He returned to England in 1871 and eventually obtained a commission in the NWMP in 1874. His unspectacular career was marked by recklessness, laziness and heavy drinking. He retired in 1886 and died shortly thereafter. Dickens can be blamed for worsening relations between the Blackfoot and the NWMP and for the growing antipathy of the officer cadre toward Englishmen. DAVID EVANS

Dickie, Donalda James, educator, author (b at Hespeler, Ont 5 Oct 1883; d at Haney, BC 1972). Educated at Queen's, Columbia, Oxford and Toronto, Dickie was influential in Alberta education as a NORMAL SCHOOL instructor, curriculum reviser and textbook author. She advocated the "Enterprise," a progressive educational approach to teaching the elementary school curriculum. By offering courses at the normal schools, writing a reference book, *The Enterprise in Theory and Practice* (1940), and publishing a variety of textbooks that incorporated progressive philosophy, she passed her ideas on to the next generation of teachers and children. Besides textbooks in composition, reading, geography and history, she also wrote many children's stories, receiving the Governor General's Award for juvenile literature in 1950. NANCY M. SHEEHAN

Dickie, Lloyd Merlin, marine ecologist (b at Canning, NS 6 Mar 1926). After studying at Acadia, Yale and Toronto, Dickie became founding director of the Marine Ecology Laboratory as a component of the BEDFORD INSTITUTE OF OCEANOGRAPHY, NS, in 1965, establishing it as a major centre for the study of marine production systems for the Fisheries Research Board of Canada. He was chairman of the Department of Oceanography at Dalhousie from 1974 to 1977 and since 1978 has been senior research scientist at the Marine Ecology Laboratory. Dickie has an international reputation for his work on marine production systems, including fisheries bio-energetics, genetics, acoustics, theory of search, species interactions and population demography. He is also well known as a teacher and has been appointed to various academic, governmental and international agencies concerned with fisheries and biological OCEANOGRAPHY. S.R. KERR

Dickins, Clennell Haggerston, "Punch," aviation pioneer (b at Portage la Prairie, Man 12 Jan 1899). Dickins grew up and was educated in Edmonton, Alta. He was awarded the Distinguished Flying Cross for gallantry in the Royal Flying Corps in WWI. In 1927 he joined Western Canada Airways and dramatized the value of the bush plane, flying vast distances across northern Canada. He piloted the first aircraft on the prairie airmail circuit and as part of his surveying and mapping expedition of 1928-29 flew the first prospectors into the Great Bear Lk area. Operations manager of FERRY COMMAND in WWII, he managed 6 BRITISH COMMONWEALTH AIR TRAINING PLAN schools. He joined de Havilland Aircraft as director in 1947, and developed a successful worldwide sales organization. He was awarded the MCKEE TROPHY in 1928 and was named an officer of the Order of the British Empire in 1936 and Officer of the ORDER OF CANADA in 1968. JAMES MARSH

"Punch" Dickins, aviation pioneer who dramatized the value of the bush plane, flying vast distances across the North (*courtesy National Archives of Canada/C-57671*).

Dickson, Horatio Henry Lovat, publisher, writer (b at Victoria, Australia 30 June 1902; d at Toronto 2 Jan 1987). Of United Empire Loyalist descent and a member of the Royal Society of Canada, Lovat Dickson was educated at the U of Alberta (BA, 1927; MA, 1929) before becoming the first Canadian to achieve a commanding position in British publishing. From 1941 until his retirement in 1964, he was general editor and a director of Macmillan & Co, London, an experience recounted in part in his autobiography: *The Ante-Room* (1959) and *The House of Words* (1963). Author of 6 biographies, including *The Museum Makers: the Story of the Royal Ontario Museum* (1986), he is best remembered as publisher, promoter and biographer of Grey Owl [Archibald Stansfeld BELANEY], whom he defended against accusations of being an imposter in *Half-Breed: The Story of Grey Owl* (1939), an imbalanced portrait righted in his definitive life, *Wilderness Man: The Strange Story of Grey Owl* (1973). MARYLYNN SCOTT

Dickson, Robert George Brian, chief justice of Canada (b at Yorkton, Sask 25 May 1916). As chief justice of Canada from 1984, he has had an important role in the initial interpretation of the CANADIAN CHARTER OF RIGHTS AND FREEDOMS, which came into effect in 1982. After graduating from the U of Manitoba Law School with the gold medal in 1938, he was called to the Manitoba Bar in 1940. He served with distinction with the Royal Canadian Artillery 1940-45 and was seriously wounded during the invasion of Normandy. He practised corporate law in Winnipeg 1945-63, when he joined the Manitoba Court of Queen's Bench. In 1967 he was appointed to the Manitoba Court of Appeal, and in 1973 he became a member of the SUPREME COURT OF CANADA. In 1984 he became chief justice. He is well known for the clarity and thoughtfulness of his written judgements and his willingness to consider material beyond decided cases, including academic writing. In his tenure as chief justice, the Court has tried to make itself more accessible; eg, it has permitted argument on motions for leave to appeal from areas outside Ottawa through closed-circuit television, and it has increased press access to proceedings. With the implementation of the Charter, much of the Court's time has been spent on constitutional and criminal law cases – areas in which Dickson has written many influential judgements. KATHERINE SWINTON

Dictionary, broadly a reference book that explains items listed in alphabetical order; in Canada, for example, there are *The Dictionary of Canadian Quotations and Phrases,* by Robert M. Hamilton and Dorothy Shields (1979), and the multivolume DICTIONARY OF CANADIAN BIOGRAPHY (est 1966). Normally, however, the word "dictionary" refers to a book that lists the words of a language alphabetically and shows the spelling and meaning of each, along with such other information (eg, pronunciation, part of speech, examples of use, derived forms, origin and history) as the editors choose. From time to time "lexicon" has been used as a synonym for "dictionary," but it is now used mainly to refer to all the words in a language, as in "No dictionary covers the whole lexicon of English." Even so, a person who compiles dictionaries is still called a "lexicographer," and dictionary-making is called "lexicography."

The earliest dictionaries of English, beginning with Robert Cawdrey's *A Table Alphabeticall . . .* (1604), gave explanations of "hard words." The first book that sought to be a complete dictionary of English was Nathaniel Bailey's *Universal Etymological English Dictionary* (1721), which was a starting point for Samuel Johnson's *A Dictionary of the English Language* (1755). This in turn formed the basis for the 10-volume *Oxford English Dictionary* (1884-1928). The 12-volume 1933 reprint with *Supplement* contains over 400 000 definitions. The updated *Supplement to the Oxford English Dictionary* (ed R.W. Burchfield) is being published in 4 volumes (1972-) and includes many items from the US, Australia, Canada and other English-speaking countries. In 1984 U of Waterloo became involved in a project to place the OED on a computer data base in order to make it easy to update and accessible on-line. Among the best-known dictionaries of the French language are the *Dictionnaire de l'Académie Française* (first published in 1694), the Littré *Dictionnaire de la langue française* (5 vols, 1863-72) and the *Dictionnaire alphabétique et analogique de la langue française* (7 vols, 1965) by Paul Robert.

Dictionaries used in English-speaking Canada have too often been either British or American, few of them showing Canadian terms or even Canadian variant spellings and pronunciations. But even some dictionaries published in Canada have had little Canadian content. As early as 1937 there appeared *The Winston Dictionary for Canadian Schools,* which was simply an American work with a few Canadian additions and alterations. In recent years the desire of school authorities to purchase books of Canadian origin and manufacture has resulted in several publishers producing "Canadian" volumes that are reprintings of American dictionaries with some Canadian entries incorporated.

In the 1960s Gage Publishing produced the *Dictionary of Canadian English* series, 3 graded books covering the needs of students from Grade 3 or 4 through senior high school. These books were based on the American Thorndike-Barnhart series, but the text was thoroughly revised for Canadian use. The dictionaries are frequently updated and now exist in revised editions as the *Canadian Junior Dictionary* (1977), the *Canadian Intermediate Dictionary* (1979) and the *Gage Canadian Dictionary* (1983; now in use as a general desk dictionary).

Also fully edited for Canadian students was *The Winston Dictionary of Canadian English,* of which only the *Intermediate Edition* (1969) and the *Elementary Edition* (1975) were published, both edited by T.M. Paikeday and based on American models. They have not been kept up to date. *Funk and Wagnalls Standard College Dictionary, Canadian Edition* (1973), published by Fitzhenry and Whiteside, has since 1976 been revised and published independently of its American parent.

Distinct from these are dictionaries on historical principles, based on the tradition of the OED, which give dated citations to illustrate each meaning of every entry word. Such is *A Dictionary of Canadianisms on Historical Principles* (1967), published as part of the Dictionary of Canadian English program and prepared for the Lexicographical Centre for Canadian English by editors Walter S. Avis, Charles Crate, Patrick Drysdale, Douglas Leechman and M.H. Scargill. It presents over 10 000 words that originated in Canada, have meanings peculiar to Canada or have special significance in Canada. A shorter version, *A Concise Dictionary of Canadianisms,* was published in 1972. In the same historical tradition is the *Dictionary of Newfoundland English* (1982), edited by G.M. Story, W.J. Kirwin and J.D.A. Widdowson, which uses authenticated oral evidence as well as citations from Newfoundland literature and folklore. Rich material exists for other regional dictionaries if the personnel and the funds can be found.

Another scholarly project in the OED tradition is the *Dictionary of Old English,* which is being prepared under the auspices of the Centre for Medieval Studies, U of Toronto, with an international group of advisers. This project is interesting for its use of the computer in collating and editing material. The data base, from which entry words and citations are being drawn, consists of every word of every known text in Old English.

Speakers of Canadian French started in the late 19th century to produce dictionaries showing how their variety of French differed from the standard form of France. The first was *Dictionnaire canadien-français* by Sylva Clapin (1894), and in 1930 La Société du parler français au Canada published *Glossaire du parler français au Canada.* Louis-Alexandre Bélisle compiled and published *Dictionnaire général de la langue française au Canada* (1957), a significant work of scholarship which was revised in 1974 and then republished as *Dictionnaire nord-américain de la langue française* (1979). Several recent books have concentrated on the distinctiveness of current Québec French, often admitting variant forms and expressions, such as anglicisms and vulgarisms, that are frowned upon by traditionalists. An example is Léandre Bergeron's *Dictionnaire de la langue québécoise* (1980), which has been translated into English as *The Québécois Dictionary* (1982). Canadian Francophones, like Anglophones, have suffered from having a Canadian label placed on imported dictionaries that have been reprinted with little or no revision (eg, *Dictionnaire Beauchemin canadien,* 1968). But French Canadians will soon enjoy their own dictionary on historical principles, *Trésor de la langue française au Québec,* now being prepared at Laval.

A bilingual dictionary, *The Canadian Dictionary/Dictionnaire canadien* (ed Jean-Paul Vinay, 1962), is being revised and expanded under the Canadian Bilingual Dictionary Project at U of Victoria. Such dictionaries are not limited to French and English: interest in the cultures of Canada's native peoples has resulted in the publication of a number of bilingual dictionaries of indigenous languages, such as Anne Anderson's *Cree Dictionary in the "y" Dialect,* 1975.

Indigenous Canadian dictionaries have helped to define a Canadian identity and have provided valuable sources of reference for writers and scholars; lexicographers, for their part, have benefited from the surge of Canadian writing since the 1960s. The original research on which the dictionaries of the 1960s and 1970s were based is now over 20 years old, but the small size of the Canadian market makes it difficult for publishers to undertake anew the production of original dictionaries. No Canadian publisher has produced a college dictionary or a mass-market paperback dictionary from scratch, and only one English Canadian publisher maintains a dictionary department. Although the use of computers for editing, revision and typesetting is now making lexicography more efficient, outside funding will undoubtedly be needed to initiate new projects. PATRICK DRYSDALE

Reading: Walter S. Avis, "Introduction," *A Dictionary of Canadianisms* (1967), and "Canadian English," in *Gage Canadian Dictionary* (1983); Angus Cameron and Roberta Frank, *A Plan for the Dictionary of Old English* (1973); Patrick Drysdale, "Aspects of Canadian Lexicography," in *Papers on Lexicography in Honor of Warren N. Cordell* (1979).

Dictionary of Canadian Biography/Dictionnaire biographique du Canada is a multivolume, comprehensive reference work on the lives of people who have contributed to Canada's history in every field of endeavour. The volumes are arranged according to the death dates of subjects, so that each one gives a full picture of a period in Canadian history. Contributions to the DCB/DBC, which are based on the best scholarship and documentary sources available, are written by a wide variety of specialists. They are painstakingly edited and checked for accuracy by teams of editors in Toronto and Québec, who have worked under the direction of general editors George Brown (1959-63), David Hayne (1965-69) and Francess HALPENNY (1969-) and, in Québec, directeurs générals adjoints Marcel Trudel (1961-65), André Vachon (1965-71) and Jean Hamelin (1973-).

The project began with the bequest of Toronto businessman James Nicholson, who left most of his estate to U of Toronto for the preparation of a Canadian biographical reference work on the model of Britain's *Dictionary of National Biography.* Work began at U of T Press in 1959 on the English edition, and in 1961 a French edition was announced by Les Presses de l'université Laval. By 1987, 10 of the 12 volumes planned for the period 1000-1900, each containing 500-600 biographies, had been published in both languages. Since the mid-1960s the project has received additional funding from government sources; this practice was regularized through major operating grants from the CANADA COUNCIL and the SOCIAL SCIENCES AND HUMANITIES RESEARCH COUNCIL. JAMES A. OGILVY

Diefenbaker, John George, lawyer, politician, prime minister (b at Neustadt, Ont 18 Sept 1895; d at Ottawa 16 Aug 1979). Well known as a defence lawyer before his election to Parliament, Canada's 13th prime minister was an eloquent spokesman for "nonestablishment" Canada both as a lawyer and as a politician. He developed a distinctive speaking style that allowed him to talk directly to his audience; his speeches were both inspiring and popular.

He moved to the Fort Carlton region of the North-West Territories with his family in 1903 and attended schools in several prairie communities before moving to Saskatoon in 1910. He saw and was profoundly influenced by the transition of Saskatchewan from a frontier to a modern society. He attended U of Sask and, after serving in the army in WWI, completed his law degree and articles and was called to the Saskatchewan Bar in 1919. His first law office was in Wakaw, Sask, but the larger northern centre of Prince Albert attracted him and he moved there in 1924.

Diefenbaker's path to the prime minister's office was long. He ran federally for Prince Albert

John George Diefenbaker
Thirteenth Prime Minister of Canada

Birth: 18 Sept 1895, Neustadt, Ont
Father/Mother: William/Mary Bannerman
Father's Occupation: Teacher
Education: U of Saskatchewan, Saskatoon
Religious Affiliation: Baptist
First Occupation: Lawyer
Last Private Occupation: Lawyer
Political Party: Progressive Conservative
Period(s) as PM: 21 June 1957 - 22 Apr 1963
Ridings: Lake Centre, Sask, 1940-53 Prince Albert, Sask, 1953-79
Other Ministries: External Affairs 1957
Marriage: 29 June 1929 to Edna Brower (1901-51); 8 Dec 1953 to Olive Palmer (1902-76)
Children: 1) none 2) 1 stepdaughter
Died: 16 Aug 1979 in Ottawa
Cause of Death at Age: Heart failure at 83
Burial Place: Saskatoon
(photo courtesy Canapress Photo Service)

in 1925 and 1926; provincially in 1929 and 1938; and for mayor of Prince Albert in 1933. He lost each time. Despite a growing reputation as an able defence lawyer (named KC, 1929), he held firmly to the belief that his future lay in politics. He was given some encouragement when he became leader of the Saskatchewan Conservative Party in 1936, only to preside over the party's defeat in the 1938 election when they won no seats. He continued to preach his own brand of Conservative politics, visiting many Saskatchewan communities with his wife, Edna Mae Brower, building party organization and exhorting his colleagues to "keep the faith."

In June 1939 Diefenbaker was nominated for the federal riding of Lake Centre and in Mar 1940 he was elected an MP. The skills he had refined during his legal career served him well on the Opposition back benches. He gained a reputation as an astute questioner of government actions, a reputation that went far beyond the boundaries of his constituency. He was re-elected for Lake Centre in 1945 and 1949 but, when redistribution radically altered his constituency, he almost quit politics.

His legal career was flourishing, and *R* v *Atherton,* known as the Canoe River case, was one of his more famous trials during this period. He

successfully defended Jack Atherton, a railway telegrapher, accused of causing a crash at Canoe River, BC. Two trains had collided head on, killing a number of soldiers en route to Korea. He had not yet recovered from the death of his wife in Feb 1951, but Diefenbaker's friends in Prince Albert persuaded him to let his name stand as the PC candidate for Prince Albert in the 1953 election. The campaign and its slogan, "Not a partisan cry, but a national need," captured the imagination of Prince Albert voters and Diefenbaker was elected. That same year he married Olive Freeman Palmer, who gave up her own highly successful career in the Ontario Dept of Education. Olive Diefenbaker was closely associated with her husband's political career for the rest of her life.

In 1956 Diefenbaker was chosen to succeed George DREW who resigned as leader of the PC Party. In 1957 Diefenbaker led his party to an upset victory over the Liberals, who were led by Louis ST. LAURENT, and formed the first Tory government since that of R.B. BENNETT. Backed by a Cabinet that included Davie FULTON, Donald FLEMING, George HEES, G.R. PEARKES, Douglas HARKNESS, Ellen FAIRCLOUGH, Léon Balcer and Gordon CHURCHILL, Diefenbaker consolidated his position in Mar 1958 when the electorate returned his government with 208 seats – the highest number held by a single party in Canada to that time.

The Diefenbaker era featured the personality and the style of the "man from Prince Albert"; many things now taken for granted were initiated during his administration. Wheat sales to China and agricultural reform revitalized western agriculture. His determination to guarantee certain rights for all led to the CANADIAN BILL OF RIGHTS and to granting the federal franchise to Canada's native peoples; James GLADSTONE, a Blood from Alberta, was appointed to the Senate. Under the philosophical umbrella of "social justice" many programs were restructured to provide aid to those in need. The "northern vision" that figured so prominently in rhetoric of the 1957 and 1958 elections increased public awareness of the Far North and led to some economic development. A tour of the COMMONWEALTH in 1958 reinforced Diefenbaker's strong feelings about the value of that organization and other international bodies. It also helped to define his role as a supporter of the nonwhite Commonwealth; he played a key role in the 1961 anti-apartheid statement that contributed to South Africa's withdrawal from the Commonwealth.

During the 1962 election, the Liberals were able to exploit the crisis in the economy (the Canadian dollar had dropped to 92.5¢ US), the debate over nuclear weapons on Canadian soil (with charges against Diefenbaker of anti-Americanism) as well as the controversial 1959 cancellation of the AVRO ARROW; the PC government was reduced to a minority. The 1963 election returned the Liberals to power, but Diefenbaker, travelling the country by train, almost won the election for his party. It was possibly the most spectacular one-man political campaign in Canadian history. In the period following that election, Diefenbaker delighted in questioning PM PEARSON's government to such an extent that the House's business slowed considerably. He argued vigorously against Pearson's proposal for a new Canadian flag (*see* FLAG DEBATE) and led the attack on the Liberals during the scandals of 1965.

Despite the recent electoral setbacks and a party deeply split over the question of his continuing leadership, Diefenbaker refused to resign and put up a spirited defence at the 1967 LEADERSHIP CONVENTION, which chose Robert STANFIELD as the new leader. Diefenbaker remained in politics, however, and won a seat for the thirteenth time in May 1979. His state funeral in Ottawa, the final train journey across Canada, and his burial in Saskatoon beside the Right Honourable John G. Diefenbaker Centre at U of Sask – all planned by himself – is pageantry that few Canadians who witnessed it will forget. PATRICIA WILLIAMS

Diefenbaker Lake, a man-made reservoir lake S of Saskatoon, Sask. It was formed by the construction of 2 dams that created a widening in the S SASKATCHEWAN R as part of the S Saskatchewan R Development Project, inaugurated 1958. The reservoir has a live storage capacity of about 4 billion m³ of water that feeds a hydroelectric power plant and an irrigation project. It contributes to the water supply of Saskatoon and is a popular water recreation area. It was named in 1967 for John DIEFENBAKER, the first Saskatchewan resident to become prime minister of Canada; the larger of the 2 dams is named for J.G. GARDINER, Diefenbaker's arch-opponent. DANIEL FRANCIS

Dieppe, NB, Town, pop 9084 (1986c), inc 1952, located on the eastern boundary of MONCTON, between that city and the airport. Officially named Leger Corner as early as 1897, it was incorporated as a village in 1946 and renamed to honour the servicemen who took part in the DIEPPE RAID of WWII. The town is a dormitory community with most of the work force employed in Moncton. It is the site of regional shopping centres and Champlain Raceway, a harness racing track opened in 1984. Although the province is officially bilingual, most of the population is not and this town is remarkable in that 72% of the population speaks both languages. BURTON GLENDENNING

Dieppe Raid The raid across the English Channel (Operation *Jubilee,* 19 Aug 1942) on Dieppe, a small port on the French coast between Le Havre and Boulogne, was planned as a "reconnaissance in force" to test the defences of Hitler's continental fortress and the capability of the Western Allies to launch large-scale amphibious assaults against his *Festung Europa* (Fortress Europe). It was a major disaster; only the battle-hardened British commandos assigned to subdue the coast artillery batteries near Varengeville and Berneval enjoyed some success. Troops of the 2nd Canadian Infantry Division under Maj-Gen J.H. Roberts, landing on the Dieppe esplanade, at Puys, 1.6 km east, and Pourville, 3 km west, failed to achieve any of their objectives. The raid lasted only 9 hours, but among nearly 5000 Canadian soldiers involved more than

900 were killed and 1874 taken prisoner – more prisoners than the army lost in the 11 months of the 1944-45 NW Europe campaign. Two Canadians, Hon Capt J.W. Foote of the Royal Hamilton Light Infantry and Lt-Col C.C. Merritt, commanding officer of the South Saskatchewan Regiment, received the VICTORIA CROSS. In the air battle the Allies lost 106 aircraft and 81 airmen, the RCAF 13 machines and 10 pilots. German casualties were light, although they could ill afford the loss of 48 aircraft. For the Allies, the raid did provide valuable experience for subsequent amphibious assaults in N Africa, Italy and, most notably, NORMANDY on 6 June 1944.

Although it has been suggested that the Germans had prior knowledge of the raid, there is much evidence to the contrary. The enemy was alert but not forewarned, and failure was primarily caused by poor and overly complex planning, inadequate training, insufficient fire support, and the employment of troops undergoing their baptism of fire. BRERETON GREENHOUS

Dietetics Diet (from the Greek *diaita,* meaning "mode of life") has been implicated in the cause, cure and prevention of disease from earliest recorded history. The profession of dietetics, which is based on the philosophy that optimal nutrition is essential for the health and well-being of every person, is concerned with the science of human nutritional care; the practice of dietetics involves the application of knowledge about nutrition. Dietitians may specialize in various areas, including general practice, administration of dietetic services, clinical nutrition and nutrition education.

In Canada the origin of dietetics and the founding of the Canadian Dietetic Association are closely related to the history of household science at U of T where the first degree course of its kind was initiated in 1902. In 1908 the first qualified dietitian was appointed to the staff of the Hospital for Sick Children in Toronto. The American Dietetic Association then offered accredited courses for dietetic training at U of A Hospital in Edmonton and Vancouver General Hospital. Some 12 Canadian hospitals had developed similar training programs by the time the Canadian Dietetic Assocation was established in 1935, and provincial associations were already functioning in Ontario, Québec and BC.

In Canada professional competence in dietetics is determined and warranted by certification and registration by nationally affiliated provincial associations. Universities in all provinces now offer

academic programs in dietetics; but, in addition, to be a qualified dietitian one must serve an approved internship or have equivalent experience. M.T. CLANDININ

Reading: M. Long and E. Upton, eds, *The Dietetic Profession in Canada* (1983).

Digby, NS, Town, pop 2525 (1986c), 2558 (1981c), inc 1890, is located on the W side of the Annapolis Basin in western NS. Referred to as *Oositookum* ("ear") by the Micmac, it was called Conway by some early New England settlers, and was later named for Admiral Robert Digby, commander of the HMS *Atlanta,* which had conveyed LOYALISTS to the area in 1783. By the 1790s Digby was exporting lumber, fish and some farm produce. At the end of the 19th century, Digby and nearby Smiths Cove had been established as tourist resort areas. Today a major seaport, Digby is noted for having one of the world's largest SCALLOP fleets. It is a centre for distribution, shipping, fishing and general commerce. A ferry makes 3 trips daily to Saint John, NB. JEAN PETERSON

Dimakopoulos, Dimitri, architect, urban designer (b at Athens, Greece 14 Sept 1929). He came to Canada in 1948 to study architecture at McGill, and in 1957, with Fred LEBENSOLD, became a founding member of Arcop Associates, an acclaimed architectural firm with great influence upon contemporary Canadian design development. The firm has won numerous prizes in design competitions across Canada. The present partnership designed the UNIVERSITÉ DU QUÉBEC campus in Montréal and the provincial courthouse in Québec City, and other works in Greece, Italy, Saudi Arabia, Hong Kong and Algeria. NORBERT SCHOENAUER

Dinosaur [Gk *deinosauros,* "terrible lizard"] term used for 2 orders of large REPTILES, Saurischia (lizard-hipped) and Ornithischia (bird-hipped), that dominated Earth during the Mesozoic era (225-65 million years ago). The 2 lineages probably evolved independently from the same ancestral stock as pterosaurs (flying reptiles) and crocodiles. Saurischians can be subdivided into 2 major types: theropods (beast-footed) and sauropods (lizard-footed). Theropods, dominant carnivores of the Mesozoic, were bipedal and include some of the smallest (eg, genus *Compsognathus,* less than 3 kg) and largest known dinosaurs. Typical forms, *Albertosaurus* and *Tyrannosaurus,* have been found in Alberta, Saskatchewan, Montana and S Dakota. Although dinosaurs are legendary for their small brains, some smaller theropods had relatively large brains, comparable to those of primitive MAMMALS. Primitive sauropods, like *Plateosaurus* from the early Mesozoic, are best known from Europe and Africa, although footprints and isolated bones have been found in Nova Scotia and New England. *Apatosaurus,* or *"Brontosaurus",* and *Diplodocus* are 2 of the best known, but not largest, sauropods. Two forms found recently in Colorado, nicknamed *"Supersaurus"* and *"Ultrasaurus,"* would have weighed more than 50 t each. Sauropods were herbivorous.

Ornithischians (all herbivorous) can be assigned to at least 4 suborders: Ornithopoda, Stegosauria, Ankylosauria and Ceratopsia. Ornithopods are generally considered the least specialized; many were able to walk on their hind limbs. Duck-billed dinosaurs (hadrosaurs) are known from N and S America, Europe and Asia; approximately half of the known species have been found in Alberta. Hadrosaur nests, some with embryos, are known from Alberta and Montana. Stegosaurs had characteristic bony plates running down their backs. These may have protected them from large carnivores, or their pur-

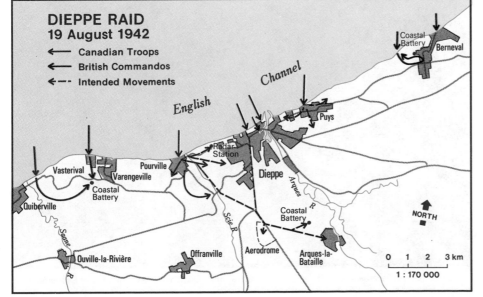

DIEPPE RAID
19 August 1942

← Canadian Troops
← British Commandos
←–· Intended Movements

English Channel

Coastal Battery
Berneval

Puys

Radar Station

Vasterival
Varengeville
Coastal Battery

Pourville

Quiberville

Dieppe

Arques R

Coastal Battery

Scie R

Saâne R

NORTH

Ouville-la-Rivière

Offranville

Aerodrome

Arques-la-Bataille

0   1   2   3 km

1 : 170 000

Waning supernova over the body of a dead *Ankylosaurus*. Among the innumerable theories for the abrupt extinction of the dinosaurs are cosmic catastrophies such as that pictured here *(courtesy Eleanor M. Kish, National Museums of Canada/National Museum of Natural Sciences)*.

Duckbilled dinosaur, *Hypacrosaurus*, pictured in a forest near Trochu, Alberta *(courtesy Eleanor M. Kish, National Museums of Canada/National Museum of Natural Sciences)*.

Duckbilled dinosaur, *Saurolophus*, along with a swimming plesiosaur, near Trochu, Alberta *(courtesy Eleanor M. Kish, National Museums of Canada/National Museum of Natural Sciences)*.

Duckbilled dinosaur, *Edmontosaurus*, pictured in a swamp setting near Drumheller, Alberta *(courtesy Eleanor M. Kish, National Museums of Canada/National Museum of Natural Science)*.

Dome-headed dinosaur, *Pachycephalosaurus*, in a leafy setting, with tree fern, screw pines and a large podocarp, near Wood Mountain, Saskatchewan *(courtesy Eleanor M. Kish, National Museums of Canada/National Museum of Natural Sciences)*.

Marine lizards, *Platecarpus*, feeding near Morden, Manitoba. The large background fish, *Protosphyraena*, are primeval swordfish and distant relatives of today's bowfins.

Tyrannosaur, *Daspletosaurus*, pictured with a swiftly moving *Champsosaurus* near the edge of a stream bordered by china firs, Katsura trees and dawn redwoods, near Dinosaur Provincial Park, northeast of Brooks, Alberta *(courtesy Eleanor M. Kish, National Museums of Canada/National Museum of Natural Sciences)*.

Ostrich dinosaur, *Dromiceiomimus*, in a grove of tall redwood trees, near Trochu, Alberta *(courtesy Eleanor M. Kish, National Museums of Canada/National Museum of Natural Sciences)*.

pose may have been to regulate body temperature by acting as radiators. Stegosaurs are best known from Jurassic deposits of the western US. Ankylosaurs were armoured dinosaurs, protected by thousands of bony plates covering the top of the head and body, even the eyelids and cheeks of some species. *Panoplosaurus, Euoplocephalus* and *Ankylosaurus* once lived in western Canada. Horned dinosaurs (ceratopsians) were one of the most successful groups. More than 10 genera, including *Triceratops, Centrosaurus* and *Styracosaurus*, are known from Alberta alone. Enormous diversity of form occurred in the horns projecting from over the nose and eyes, and in the frill extending backwards over the neck.

Even the earliest dinosaurs must have been well adapted to their environment. One of the best sites for early dinosaurs is near Parrsboro, NS, where small primitive dinosaur skeletons and footprints have been collected in recent years. A major find in 1986 has revealed 100 000 fossilized jaws, skulls and teeth of tiny dinosaurs, crocodiles, lizards, sharks and fishes. It is the largest find in the world from the Triassic and Jurassic periods (245-144 million years ago).

From their first appearance early in the Mesozoic, they rapidly evolved into many different forms, and competed so successfully with the mammallike reptiles that they became the dominant land animals. Mammals did not rise to prominence until almost 150 million years later, after dinosaurs became extinct. The success of dinosaurs has long been a source of wonder. It has only been since the 1970s that reasons for this success have been seriously examined. A breakthrough came when scientists realized that it might be more appropriate to compare dinosaurs with mammals and birds than with living reptiles. Debate continues on whether or not dinosaurs were warm-blooded; however, it is now generally accepted that they were not simply oversized crocodiles in their physiology, ecology, behaviour and other adaptations. Detailed examination of dinosaur bone cells shows that dinosaur bone is much closer to that of mammals and birds than to that of living reptiles. Other evidence, including limb structure and the presence of sophisticated feeding and breathing adaptations, has been used to support the hypothesis that dinosaurs were warm-blooded. However, most paleontologists feel that the evidence is inconclusive.

Although size range of dinosaurs is enormous, most species were over 100 kg at maturity. Because they hatched from eggs, baby dinosaurs would have been relatively small. Dinosaur eggs have been found at numerous localities worldwide, but embryos within eggs are currently only known from Alberta and Montana. Sauropod eggs, from France and Mongolia, have diameters of less than 20 cm, and eggs of most other dinosaurs are much smaller. The sauropod hatchling would have been less than 2 m long. Because dinosaurs could grow throughout their lives, this hatchling might have increased its size more than 15 times during its lifetime. Baby dinosaurs are rare. Perhaps they never made up a significant portion of the population, or, as seems more likely, these tasty little morsels would simply have been eaten whole when caught by predators. Occasionally, the bones of baby hadrosaurs and ceratopsians are found in Alberta, and footprints of baby hadrosaurs have been identified in BC's Peace River Canyon. A spectacular site at which about 75% of dinosaurs recovered are juveniles was found in Montana. Eighteen baby hadrosaurs were recovered from one nest alone. The fact that these babies had hatched several months before they died suggests that the juveniles were gregarious animals and that there may have been some form of parental care. In the summer of

1987, hadrosaur nests with eggs were discovered in S Alberta in rock strata correlative with those in Montana. The Alberta eggs have yielded well-preserved embryolic hadrosaurs, the full implications of which await study.

Study of dinosaurian anatomy has long been a fascinating subject because of its diversity. For example, hadrosaurs were born with relatively flat heads, but forms such as *Lambeosaurus* developed characteristic bony crests on the head as they increased in size. Crest size differed in males and females. Diversity of shape and size of hadrosaurian crests has been a source of speculation since the discovery of the first hooded form, but the key to their function lies in the pronounced development of crest, which came only at sexual maturity. It appears probable that crests were little more than display structures recognized visually for mating, protection of territory, dominance display, etc. A space inside the crest, connected to nasal passages, probably served as a resonating chamber. As each species had a crest of a different shape, each would have made different sounds, allowing members of the same species to recognize one another.

Most of our understanding of the ecology of late Mesozoic terrestrial faunas and floras is derived from DINOSAUR PROVINCIAL PARK, Alta, because of numerous specimens and other data collected there. In many ways, the world of dinosaurs was not as exotic as most people imagine. The environment superficially resembled that of northern Florida. Dinosaurs were greatly outnumbered by insects, fish, turtles, lizards, snakes, crocodilians and other animals, which were no larger than their living relatives and, in many cases, indistinguishable from them. Small mammals, including relatives of the modern opossum, would have been seen scurrying through the undergrowth, and BIRDS would have occupied many of the niches they do today. Our understanding of dinosaurian ecology is constantly being refined. Fragmentary specimens that would have been ignored before now provide information on previously unknown animals. Species have been identified in Alberta that were once known only from Mongolia, and scientists now realize that many of the differences between Asian and N American forms were related to differences in environment, not to simple geographic separation.

It is becoming apparent that dinosaurs were capable of more complex behavioural patterns than modern reptile species. Trackways can be particularly useful in showing what animals were doing when alive. Herding behaviour can be implied for hadrosaurian dinosaurs because of trackways found in Peace River Canyon. At one site, parallel trackways show a herd of 17 hadrosaurs walking in the same direction. At one point, 4 animals were walking so closely together that when one lurched sideways it bumped its neighbour, initiating a chain reaction that affected all 4. Other trackways suggest that juveniles stayed together after hatching. They may not have joined more mature herds until almost half-grown. Recent expeditions by the Dinosaur Project (TYRRELL MUSEUM OF PALAEONTOLOGY, Drumheller; Institute of Vertebrate Palaeontology and Palaeoanthropology, Beijing, China; and Ex Terra Foundation, Edmonton) have conducted fieldwork and research in Alberta, the Arctic and China, seeking supportive evidence for intercontinental migrations. The Dinosaur Project will end with a major international travelling exhibit in the early 1990s.

Bonebeds are accumulations of bones from many individuals concentrated by natural processes into a single area. A river in flood, for example, might pick up bones of animals that died along its banks. In most cases, it is impossible to know which bones came from which individuals,

although types of animals can be identified. There are probably thousands of Cretaceous bonebeds in western Canada, study of which is producing important anatomical, ecological and behavioural data. A small percentage of these bonebeds is dominated by single species of ceratopsian (eg, *Centrosaurus, Styracosaurus*, and *Pachyrhinosaurus*). Some sites appear to represent mass deaths of herds, occurring over a period of at least 10 million years.

A major question concerning dinosaurs is why they became extinct at the end of the Mesozoic (66.4 million years ago). Dinosaurs were not the only animals affected. Some evidence suggests that perhaps as many as 75% of all known types of animal species (INVERTEBRATES, AMPHIBIANS, reptiles, mammals) may have become extinct at the same time. PLANTS, on the other hand, seem to have had relatively few problems in crossing the boundary into the Cenozoic era (Age of Mammals). Innumerable theories have been proposed to explain the extinctions. They range from climatic changes and the collapse of ecosystems to a collision between Earth and an asteroid. Two related questions are critical if the answer is ever to be found. Did the extinctions take place over a period of several million years, or were they catastrophic? Did the extinctions occur worldwide at the same time on land and sea, or did dinosaurs live in some parts of the world for millions of years after they became extinct in N America? Paleontologists, geologists, physicists and even astronomers are working to answer these questions. Whatever the cause, it is remarkable that animals as diverse, adaptable and successful as dinosaurs could have died out completely. Completely, that is, with the exception of their descendants – the birds. PHILIP J. CURRIE

Reading: D.A. Russell, *A Vanished World: the Dinosaurs of Western Canada* (1977), W. Stout et al, *The Dinosaurs* (1981).

Dinosaur Hunting in Western Canada Dinosaurs were unknown to science until 1824, when FOSSIL teeth and bones were discovered in the late Jurassic and early Cretaceous rocks of southern England. Since then, their remains have been found on all continents and in rocks 200 million to 64 million years old. Most early discoveries were made in artificial excavations, eg, rock quarries or coal mines. With the opening of western N America to geological exploration, large areas were found where natural erosion had removed soil and rock, making possible the deliberate search for, and organized collection of, fossil skeletons. One such area is the Red Deer R valley in Alberta, the so-called BADLANDS. Here DINOSAUR fossils were first collected by a scientist over 100 years ago. Joseph B. TYRRELL, a young geologist with the Geological Survey of Canada (GSC), discovered the incomplete skull of a flesh-eating dinosaur, now known as *Albertosaurus sarcophagus*, the Alberta carcass eater. This was found in the valley of Kneehills Creek, about 5 km NW of DRUMHELLER. Five years later another skull of the same species was found by Thomas C. Weston, also a member of the GSC. This was in the Red Deer R valley near Rumsey. Weston also discovered the more southern area of fossil-bearing badlands, which now make up the DINOSAUR PROVINCIAL PARK.

A Canadian expedition specifically organized to collect dinosaur fossils was conducted in 1898 and again in 1901 by Lawrence M. Lambe of the GSC. In 1901 he published the first detailed account of Alberta dinosaurs . This was good by the standards of the time, but did not reveal fully the richness of the Alberta deposits. This was first done by an American paleontologist, Barnum Brown of the American Museum of Natural History in New York City. In 1909 a rancher named John L. Wegener, who lived near the site of present-day Drumheller, visited the New York museum and reported the occurrence of numerous fossil bones on his ranch. Brown, who was an experienced fossil collector, came to the Wegener ranch and verified the reported occurrence. In 1910 he went to the town of Red Deer with 3 trained assistants and had a barge built, on which he and his companions floated down the Red Deer R, prospecting and collecting from temporary camps along the way. This program was continued for 5 summers, resulting in the discovery and removal of some 16 dinosaur specimens, most of which were new to science.

Acquisition of these spectacular Canadian fossils by a foreign museum prompted the GSC to resume collecting in the Red Deer R badlands, but there were no Canadians who were skilled in the special techniques required to excavate and transport these large but fragile skeletons. So the services of the Sternberg family of Lawrence, Kansas, were engaged. The father, Charles H. Sternberg, had been a professional fossil collector for various museums since 1876. His 3 sons, George F. Sternberg, Charles M. STERNBERG and Levi Sternberg, all learned the techniques from their father, and became famous collectors in their own right. The first Sternberg expedition for the GSC was in 1912, to the area visited by Brown in his reconnaissance of 1909. They had some success, but in 1913 they moved to the more southern field, then known as the Stephenville badlands, now the Dinosaur Provincial Park. Here they collected many important specimens now housed in the National Museum of Natural Sciences in Ottawa, but in 1916 C.H. Sternberg and his son Levi left the GSC to work for other museums, to be followed in 1918 by the eldest son George. Charles M. Sternberg, the second son, remained with the GSC and the National Museum of Canada for the remainder of his career, and became a world-recognized authority on dinosaurs. In addition to the specimens housed in Ottawa, dinosaur skeletons collected by the Sternbergs in Alberta are preserved today in the Royal Ontario Museum in Toronto, the U of Alberta in Edmonton, the American Museum of Natural History in New York City, the Field Museum in Chicago, the San Diego Museum in California and the British Museum (Natural History) in London, Eng.

The government of Alberta in 1956 began a program of dinosaur display, first with the Dinosaur Provincial Park near Brooks, and culminating in 1985 with the opening of the TYRRELL MUSEUM OF PALAEONTOLOGY at Drumheller, a world-class institution for research and display of dinosaurs and other fossils.

Because dinosaur fossils are irreplaceable, Alberta and Saskatchewan have legislation to prevent indiscriminate removal of these historical resources. In Alberta, would-be collectors of fossils must have the written permission of the minister of culture.

Collecting dinosaur fossils in the field involves 2 distinct phases, discovery and excavation. No modern technique has yet superseded the old-fashioned method of prospecting, ie, just looking. This requires keen, experienced eyes and strong, nimble legs. The dinosaur hunter carries a digging tool, usually a light pick, which serves in making exploratory excavations and is useful in climbing steep slopes. A typical prospecting party might consist of 3 persons. Each would concentrate on a particular level of the exposure. In the Red Deer R badlands, exposures are mostly intricate ravines, often with clifflike sides. Keeping as much as possible to his own level, the fossil hunter works his way along these slopes, up one side of the ravine

Dinosaur Provincial Park, Alta, est 1955, located in the badlands and prairie along the Red Deer R. The park has been declared a UNESCO World Heritage Site for its valuable fossil record (*courtesy J.A. Walper/Alberta Recreation and Parks*).

and down the other. It is important that rock surfaces be examined thoroughly but, often, a steep interval forces the hunter to detour up or down, then climb back to his original level. The work is strenuous and tiring, but the fossil hunter is kept alert by the thought that just ahead may be the discovery of the year.

There is no way of detecting fossil bone unless it is exposed. It is brittle and easily broken and, as natural erosion proceeds, pieces fall off and are strewn down slopes and erosion channels. These are the fossil prospector's "float," and he follows their lead to where they either give out or reveal bones still in place and projecting from rock surfaces. Fossil bone is usually easy to recognize from its smooth outer surface or, in broken specimens, its layered or honeycombed interior structure. Complete bones are recognizable by their form and their unique sheen, which is most easily recognized in bright sunshine.

The importance of the find must be tested by carefully uncovering the bone, using the pick or a hand tool like an awl, with a whisk broom to clear away debris. If the bone looks promising, the second phase of collecting begins: the uncovering of bones for wrapping and removal. A kind of quarry is made by excavating overlying rock layers. The steeper the slope on which the find occurs, the higher the excavation must be to obtain a flat working surface over the bones. The basic principle in uncovering specimens is to expose only as much bone as is needed to determine extent and orientation in the rock. The excavation would follow the bones, with minimum exposure, laying bare a floor of rock with patches of bone showing through. From the time of discovery, fossil bone must be protected from further disintegration. Exposed surfaces are hardened and cracks sealed by applying thin, liquid cement, which penetrates well and sets quickly.

After the area occupied by the bones has been delineated by a floor, a trench is dug around the perimeter to a depth well below the bone-bearing level. This trench is expanded as an undercut, as far beneath the bone-bearing layer as hand tools and the stability of the matrix will allow. Excess rock from the upper surface may be removed at

this time. Depending on the hardness of the rock, the tools may be scrapers or hand-held chisels. Small pneumatic or electric chisels may be used where suitable. Debris is brushed or shovelled away, and all exposed bone thoroughly impregnated with cement. When the cement is dry, rice paper or facial tissue is placed over the exposed bone and wetted down with brush or spray. This serves to separate bone and plaster wrapping.

Burlap is cut into long strips about 12 cm wide, and liquid plaster is prepared. One strip of burlap at a time is rolled into the liquid to impregnate the fabric and form an easily handled roll. The plaster-soaked burlap is unrolled across the rock and bone surface, patted and squeezed to form a close contact. The strips are continued over the edge of the rock and tucked into the undercut. Successive strips of plaster-burlap are applied, each overlapping the preceding strip by about 2.5 cm, until the entire block or section has been bandaged. When the plaster bandage has hardened, possibly overnight, the block of matrix and bone is undercut more deeply, until the remaining pedestal is small enough to crack across with careful prying. The block is then turned over. The unwrapped lower surface, if sufficiently strong and not too large, will remain intact. When the block is turned over, excess rock may be removed, as with the upper side. Exposed bone is cemented and covered with paper, and the protruding edges of the upper bandage are trimmed flush with the matrix. Then the plaster bandage is applied to the inverted underside, with edges firmly lapped over the upper bandage. If the specimen is too large to be bandaged and transported in one block, it is divided into sections, each of which is bandaged separately. When each section has hardened and dried, it is labelled, and moved to the packing area. Sometimes this is difficult, owing to the inaccessibility of the quarry. In earlier years a small wooden sled (stone boat) was used, the section being roped to the sled and the load dragged out by a team of horses. Today, 4-wheel-drive vehicles and power winches have made movement somewhat easier, and helicopters have been used, in Saskatchewan and Alberta, to retrieve large specimens.

Early collectors had only man or horse power for quarry excavation and transportation of bandaged blocks. Automobiles were introduced to the Alberta fossil fields in 1921, and motor transport has improved progressively. Motor-driven jack hammers speed up excavation. Dynamite may be used to loosen overburden or break up hard rock layers. House trailers have replaced tents, and camp kitchen facilities now include naphtha stoves and propane refrigerators. But success in dinosaur hunting still depends on walking and climbing, on the ability to recognize a find from a few fragments and on knowing what to do about it. *See also* PALEONTOLOGY.

L.S. RUSSELL

Reading: L.S. Russell, *Dinosaur Hunting in Western Canada* (1966).

Dinosaur Provincial Park (est 1955, 90 km²) encompasses BADLANDS and PRAIRIE along the RED DEER RIVER in SE Alberta. The badlands, named because the land is not arable, possess an exotic beauty and contain layers of sandstone and mudstone deposited by rivers almost 75 million years ago. The sediments were carried by prehistoric rivers to the Mowry Sea, which covered the great plains region of N America. Each layer of sediment contains characteristic FOSSIL plant and animal species of the epoch in which it was transported. The HOODOOS, gullies, etc, characteristic of the region, were formed as a result of EROSION processes following the last ICE AGE. Vegetation is sparse and desertlike (eg, CACTUS). The fossilized remains of DINOSAURS and other REPTILES, AMPHIBIANS, BIRDS and primitive MAMMALS are abundant, allowing scientists a detailed glimpse into a chapter of Earth's history. No other area of comparable size has produced such a diverse record of dinosaurs and their contemporaries. Bus tours and hikes are organized in summer and certain areas are restricted. Exhibits at the field station of the TYRRELL MUSEUM OF PALAEONTOLOGY are open year-round. The park has been declared a UNITED NATIONS WORLD HERITAGE SITE.

PHILIP J. CURRIE

Reading: G. Reid, *Dinosaur Provincial Park* (1986).

Dion, Gérard, priest, sociologist, professor (b at Ste-Cécile de Frontenac, Qué 5 Dec 1912). After receiving his BA at the Collège de Lévis in 1935, Dion completed a degree in theology at Laval in 1939 and was ordained a priest. He continued his studies at Laval and in 1943 joined Laval's faculty of social sciences, becoming assistant director of the newly established department of industrial relations in 1946; he was director in 1957-63. He also edited *Relations industrielles/Industrial Relations.* During the late 1940s and early 1950s he was an active member of the Commission sacerdotales d'études sociales, a committee of clerics established in 1948 to advise the Québec Assembly of Bishops on the numerous socioeconomic problems facing Québec society after WWII. Of particular concern were the roles to be adopted by the Confédération des travailleurs catholiques du Canada and the Association professionnelle des industriels. During the 1950s he and his colleague Father Louis O'Neill became public figures when they published a scathing indictment of Québec politics entitled *L'Immoralité politique dans la province de Québec.* Father Dion published extensively on labour relations, especially on the evolution of the Catholic labour movement in the 1940s and 1950s. His most important publication is the *Dictionnaire canadien des relations du travail* (1976; 2nd ed 1986).

M.D. BEHIELS

Dion, Joseph Francis, political organizer, teacher (b near Onion Lake, Sask 2 July 1888; d at Bonnyville, Alta 21 Dec 1960). Dion was central to the shaping of today's Prairie native political organizations. Born to a status-Indian family of Kehiwin's Band on the Alberta-Saskatchewan border — followers and relatives of BIG BEAR — Dion as an adult abandoned Indian status and became a farmer (1903) and teacher on the Kehiwin reserve (1916-40). In the 1930s he worked with Jim BRADY and Malcolm NORRIS to found what are now

the Métis Assn of Alberta (1932; president, 1932-58) and the Indian Assn of Alberta (1944). Serving in the executives of Indian, Métis and Catholic Church organizations, he travelled, lectured, recorded living traditions (published as *My Tribe the Crees,* 1979) and managed a Métis dance troupe. A relatively conservative reformer, Dion promoted the idea of native self-help through local agricultural development and the preservation of traditional culture.

BENNETT MCCARDLE

Dionne, Charles-Eusèbe, ornithologist (b at St-Denis de Kamouraska, Qué 11 July 1845; d at Québec City 25 Jan 1925). The model of the self-taught man, Dionne was one of the most respected naturalists of French Canada. At 16, he became a servant at the Séminaire de Québec, where he distinguished himself by his intelligence and thirst for knowledge. Having been successively a laboratory assistant in the Faculty of Medicine at Laval U and an assistant librarian, in 1882 he became curator of the zoology museum there. Under his direction, the museum rapidly became one of the richest and best organized in Québec. Dionne was a master taxidermist and the college's major source of natural-history specimens. In correspondence with ornithologists around the world and as member of the American Ornithologists' Union and several other learned societies, Dionne did much to popularize natural history in Canada with his articles in *Naturaliste canadien* and many books.

RAYMOND DUCHESNE

Dionne, Marcel, hockey player (b at Drummondville, Qué 3 Aug 1951). After an eventful career as a junior at St Catharines, in which he was twice the top scorer in the OHL, he was first choice of the Detroit Red Wings in the amateur draft of 1971. After 4 seasons he went to the Kings in Los Angeles as a free agent, where he had 6 seasons with more than 50 goals, before being traded to the New York Rangers in 1987. He has won the ART ROSS TROPHY (leading scorer, 1980), the LADY BYNG TROPHY (1975, 1977) and the Pearson Trophy (1979, 1980) for his contribution to hockey in Canada, and was first all-star centre in 1977 and 1980. In 1980 he was named player of the 1979-80 season by *Sporting News.* As of 1987, only Gordie HOWE had more points than Dionne (693 goals and 990 assists) in the history of professional hockey.

YVON DORE

Dionne, René, bibliographer, historian of Québec literature (b at Saint-Philippe-de-Néri, Qué 29 Jan 1929). After classical studies at Sainte-Anne-de-La-Pocatière, he received his MA and L ès L at U de Montréal, a LPh at Immaculée-Conception and a D ès L at U de Sherbrooke. Having taught at various Québec colleges and universities, he became professor at the U of Ottawa (1970); he was chairman of the department of French letters 1975-78 and titular professor (1981). Author of several hundred articles, bibliographies and accounts of Québec and Franco-Ontarian letters, he has also published a biography of Antoine GÉRIN-LAJOIE and an annotated edition of the latter's novel, *Jean Rivard.* Co-compiler of the *Anthologie de la littérature québécoise* (1978-80) of Gilles Marcotte, Dionne is also the founder of the *Revue d'histoire littéraire du Québec et du Canada français* (1979). In collaboration with Pierre Cantin, he publishes each year an exhaustive bibliography of studies of LITERATURE IN FRENCH.

DAVID M. HAYNE

Dionne Case (1978), known as Re Public Service Board et al, Dionne et al, and Attorney General of Canada et al. When François Dionne, a cable-system operator, challenged the Québec Public Service Board's competence to give licences, the Supreme Court of Canada found that Parliament had exclusive jurisdiction over the

regulation of the technical aspects of CABLE TELEVISION stations and over their programming if it involves the interception of television signals and their rebroadcast to subscribers of a cable-television company. Nevertheless, according to the minority opinion of 3 judges, a cable system is different from radio broadcasting (a federal matter), just as a navigation company is different from navigation, because distribution by cable can be limited to a defined territory and a cable-broadcasting company operating within a single province would therefore fall within provincial jurisdiction.

GÉRALD-A. BEAUDOIN

Dionne Quintuplets Annette, Emilie, Yvonne, Cecile and Marie aroused worldwide attention after their birth at Corbeil, Ont, to Oliva and Elzire Dionne on 28 May 1934. A sport on the human species (only 2 previous cases are on record), they were the only quintuplets to survive for more than a few days. This miracle, plus their baby cuteness, the poverty of their French Canadian parents and the controversy over their guardianship, made them the sensation of the 1930s. Fearing private exploitation, the Ontario government removed them from their parents and placed them in a specially built hospital under the care of Dr Allan Roy DAFOE, who had delivered them. Oliva Dionne fought a 9-year battle to regain them. In the interval, they became the country's biggest tourist attraction and a $500 million asset to the province. Three million people trekked to "Quintland" to watch the babies at play behind a one-way screen. Hollywood fictionalized their story in 3 movies. Dozens of commercial endorsements swelled their trust fund to nearly $1 million. But the reunion with the family in Nov 1943 was not successful. Eventually the quintuplets moved to Montréal. Three, Annette, Cecile and Marie, took husbands but the marriages failed. Emilie, an epileptic, entered a convent and died in Aug 1954 during a seizure. The 4 survivors told their own, often bitter, story in *We Were Five,* published in 1965. Marie, the weakest, died in Feb 1970. The remaining 3 shared the final instalment of the much depleted trust fund in 1979. Not until Sept 1987 was another set of quints, this time 2 boys and 3 girls, born in Canada.

PIERRE BERTON

Diorama, museum exhibit which creates the illusion of a natural or historic scene. Typically, mounted animals and preserved plants blend imperceptibly into a realistic background painting, simulating a natural habitat (the name habitat group is sometimes used). Miniature dioramas recreate natural or historic scenes on a reduced scale. Dioramas are expensive to produce, but effectively convey atmosphere as well as information and are rightly popular with museum visitors. Large dioramas are produced by artists, taxidermists and modellers, using traditional materials and new plastics. Some new dioramas are being created using computerized enlargements of smaller paintings. American taxidermist Carl Akeley created the first modern diorama in 1889. His first Canadian imitator, Lester Lynne Snyder, created dioramas at the ROYAL ONTARIO MUSEUM from 1919. Today, dioramas in major museums showcase the work of fine nature artists. The Nova Scotia Museum shows groups by Azor Vienneau. Ontario features Terry SHORTT's world landscapes at the ROM, and representative scenes by Hugh Monahan, Clarence Tillenius and others at the NATIONAL MUSEUMS OF CANADA. At the Manitoba Museum of Man and Nature, Tillenius's spectacular *Red River Hunt* is complemented by several large ecological dioramas. The Saskatchewan Museum of Natural History devotes a floor to dioramas, mainly by Fred Lahrman and Robert Symons. The Provincial Museum of Alberta features a large gallery of groups (some of unusual depth), largely by Ralph Carson and Ludo Bogaert. The BC Provincial Museum presents, among others, a spectacular walk-through diorama of coastal forest and beach.   DAVID SPALDING

Dioxin, a term used to describe one or more of the 75 chlorinated derivatives of dibenzo-*p*-dioxin. Dioxins differ enormously from each other, especially in levels of toxicity: 2,3,7,8-TCDD (one of the tetrachloro isomers of dibenzo-*p*-dioxin) is the most toxic. As chemicals dioxins are all useless; they are simply pollutants without redeeming features. At the present time the largest single source of dioxins is low-temperature combustion (burning accompanied by dark smoke, eg, a campfire or forest fire, of which Canada has its share, or burning garbage dumps that contain discarded fireproof synthetics). 2,3,7,8-TCDD has, in the past, been an unwanted side product in the manufacture of materials such as herbicides in amounts that caused many hundreds of people to become seriously ill with chloracne (a severe form of acne). Dioxins can be destroyed by ultraviolet light (such as sunlight) and also by high-temperature incineration.

If the 75 dioxins differ enormously from each other in toxicity, so too do the effects of dioxins in different species. Guinea pigs, for example, are extraordinarily sensitive (few substances are more toxic to them than 2,3,7,8-TCDD), whereas chickens are highly sensitive and hamsters much less sensitive. Humans have some 5-10 parts per trillion of 2,3,7,8-TCDD in body fat, and an expert opinion is that our threshold is many times higher than this natural level. Dioxins exist only in trace amounts and only recently have techniques been available that recognize their widespread existence in practically everything. As a result, dioxins have become a political issue on which there is now a good deal of information.   W.E. HARRIS

Reading: M. Gough, *Dioxin, Agent Orange* (1986).

Dipper (Cinclidae), family comprising 4 species of birds known colloquially as water ouzel. The American dipper (*Cinclus mexicanus*) occurs along mountain streams from Alaska to Panama, in Canada straying from the mountains only rarely into Saskatchewan. Dippers are plain, chunky and wrenlike, with short wings and tails and slender, straight bills. They dive and swim well. Both sexes sing all year. The territorial grey-black American species moves downstream in winter only where streams freeze. Dippers bob up and down on their long legs (hence their name), blinking their white eyelids as they fly into and out of water, hunting aquatic insects and sometimes fish. They are usually monogamous, occasionally polygynous. The female incubates the 4-5 eggs; both sexes care for young after they leave the nest. Nests, usually domed and made of moss, are above water, often behind waterfalls or on bridges, occasionally in artificial boxes or swallows' nests.   MARTIN K. MCNICHOLL

Disability, according to the World Health Organization's (WHO) International Classification of Impairments, Disabilities and Handicaps, is the temporary, prolonged or permanent reduction or absence of the ability to perform certain commonplace activities or roles: impairment, which produces this disability, is an abnormality in an organ or in the physical or mental functions of the body; and handicap refers to the social and environmental consequences of an individual's impairment and his inability to assume his social roles. These 3 notions are interrelated, disability being the direct and inevitable consequence of an anatomical, physiological or mental impairment of the individual's daily functions; a handicap be-

ing the sociocultural consequence, in the sense that it leaves a negative impression and stigmatizes the person who is different.

According to *Obstacles*, the 1981 report of the Special Committee on the Disabled and Handicapped, over 2 million Canadians are physically or mentally disabled. WHO maintains that, worldwide (1980), one in 10 adults suffers from some kind of chronic disability. The estimated prevalence of disability varies because categories of impairment and degrees of disability are not always calculated in the same way from one study to the next. The 1981 Canadian census did not contain a section on disabilities, and the 1986 census identified disabled persons in order to conduct a detailed survey in the future. At present, the most reliable data for Canada are included in the 1981 Canada Health survey, which clearly distinguishes between short-term disability, calculated on the basis of days of inactivity, and long-term disability, which involves prolonged or chronic restriction in one or several activities.

The WHO definitions do not entirely resolve the problem of identifying those who suffer from a disability and thus from a handicap-producing impairment. Present death rates resulting from HEART DISEASE, CANCER, arthritic problems (*see* ARTHRITIS) and the rapid AGING of the Canadian population, together with accompanying degenerative illnesses, are producing a new and complex situation in which growing numbers of Canadians are impaired for at least a few years of their lives.

Scientific literature generally distinguishes between muscular-skeletal, sensory, organic, mental and psychic impairments. Muscular, skeletal and motor impairments are usually the result of the way we live (stress, lack of exercise, etc) and threaten every Canadian in the forms of, first, encephalopathies, or brain diseases produced in about 80% of cases by sudden cerebrovascular disturbances in adults (usually aged 50 years or more) and resulting in paralysis; second, myelopathies, or diseases of the spinal cord, which are caused generally by accidents and frequently result in permanent paraplegia or quadriplegia among young adults between the years of 15 and 40; third, arthropathies, or diseases of the joints resulting from arthritic or rheumatic illnesses, the incidence of which increases among Canadians over 40; fourth, myopathies, or diseases of the muscles, which are either acquired (poliomyelitis) or congenital (muscular dystrophy). To the brain and spinal cord impairments can be added hereditary diseases of the central nervous system, eg, ataxias (inco-ordination of voluntary movements) or contracted diseases such as multiple sclerosis and Parkinson's disease, whose symptoms are well known but whose causes are not. Finally, there are amputations, usually the result of an accident or of an evolutive disease such as diabetes. Results of the 1981 Health Canada survey reveal an increase in motor impairments among Canadians; restriction of activities is generally caused by pains in parts of the body and joints, heart disease, arthritis and lesions.

Sensory impairments are visual, auditory or communicative. According to the 1981 Health Canada survey 45% of Canadians wear glasses, and another 4% complain of sight problems. However, only those whose central vision is equal to or less than 20/200 for the better eye with corrective lenses and those whose peripheral vision is 20/100 or less are considered legally blind (*see* BLINDNESS AND VISUAL IMPAIRMENT). There are also degrees of AUDITORY IMPAIRMENT. Health Canada estimates that over 200 000 Canadians are profoundly deaf (but less than 1% wear a hearing aid) and an additional 1.8 million suffer hearing

problems. There is a major distinction between congenital deafness, which in most cases delays a child's growth in every respect, and deafness that occurs later as a result of working conditions or age. Speech and language impairments vary in nature and severity. They generally accompany congenital deafness, but also occur in severely brain-damaged victims of sudden cerebrovascular disturbances.

Organic impairments do not always lead to a significant restriction of activities, although some have a real stigma attached to them. The organic diseases of cancer, diabetes, epilepsy, cystic fibrosis, emphysema, obesity, etc, may be the result, again, of how we live.

All mental impairments cannot be classified because not enough is yet known of them, and what happens in the life of the embryo to produce a permanently impaired person still remains a mystery. Mongolism, or Down's Syndrome, is the most frequent and best-understood type of mental retardation (about 1 birth in 600 and almost 10% of cases of mental retardation). However, only 33% of severely mentally retarded people are accurately diagnosed. Chromosome disorders, metabolic disturbances and severe neurological problems explain some cases of mental retardation, but infection and toxic agents (mainly mercury and lead) are increasingly being linked with the abnormal development of the fetus. People with IQs under 70 are generally included in the mentally retarded category, but most of them are only slightly impaired. The Canadian Association for the Mentally Retarded estimates that about 3% of Canadians suffer from some degree of mental retardation. The deteriorating quality of the environment may also play a large part in this high rate.

In Canada, severe psychic problems are generally judged by the disability they cause and the stigma attached to those suffering from them. There is a danger, however, in the resulting temptation to pass legislation making it easy to place people in protected environments and encouraging the institutionalization of "insanity." Although all major mental problems have disabling consequences for individuals, they should not be considered as psychopathological impairments that are to the mind what spinal diseases are to the body.

Attitudes Towards Impaired People People with noticeable impairments are labelled different or "deviant." Following the work of Irving Goffman, deviance has been interpreted as divergence from the dominant norms that vary from society to society. Stigmatization has been defined as the social process of identifying an undesirable difference in an individual and of disqualifying the individual with that deviance. Victimization is the process by which the stigmatized individuals interiorize the very norms that disqualify them, thus contributing to their own stigmatization. This is the complex process within which attitudes towards the disabled and programs designed to change other people's negative attitudes must be understood. Some 60 research studies clearly established the relationship between attitudes towards the disabled and variables such as categories of impairment, the setting in which the interaction occurs, and socio-personal data on the disabled and nondisabled groups. These studies have generally confirmed not only that people do have negative attitudes towards disabled persons, but that it is difficult to specify what exactly could be considered a positive attitude. These studies also reveal that negative attitudes can be altered when disabled persons are encountered in a day-to-day context, but that in these same circumstances the desire to help disabled persons diminishes and assistance may be viewed as springing more from a negative than a positive attitude. Most of the people taking part in the studies were intensely anxious in the presence of a disabled person and their avoidance increased with the visual severity of the handicap. A number of observations reveal that children react more positively to physical than to other impairments.

According to researchers who have studied methods of changing negative attitudes, professionals who are supposedly helping the disabled to readapt may be among those most guilty of stigmatization. The evidence of one study suggests that the programs that succeed in fostering positive attitudes are those in which equal status exists between the subjects (same age or professional category); those that reduce the discomfort of the nondisabled person; and those that include meetings with disabled people who do not behave according to stereotypical patterns. The failure of most programs to change social attitudes illustrates how deeply rooted – psychologically, socially and culturally – are negative behaviour and stigmatizing attitudes.

Rehabilitation Philosophies The new "normalization" philosophies that have been recently advanced by groups of disabled persons take exception to the marginalization noted above. Normalization implies that the disabled should be able to live as similarly as possible to the nondisabled. The Autonomous Living Movement is more particularly concerned with battling for rights and emphasizes that such rights will not be attained until the disabled, like any other minority group, demand them. The battle will probably be long because employers are less inclined to hire disabled people than any other group, believing it to be less expensive to hire nondisabled people. Twenty years ago, the creation of large specialized institutions such as residential centres, specialized schools and sheltered workshops represented Canada's most progressive solution to the problems posed by most disabled persons. In the early 1970s, society began to accept the philosophy of normalization and recognition of the rights of the disabled. Personalized services have now been established and integration and direct political activity by disabled groups have increased, all of which is beginning to change the nature of the services offered to these people. However, these advances are not very significant considering that 70% to 95% of provincial budgets in 1982 were still allocated to covering the cost of direct services in rehabilitation institutions cut off from society, and that few resources were used for personalized and integrated services. Genuine changes appear to be coming more from disabled groups themselves, which are organizing ongoing, self-help groups, or from politically militant action groups. It is no longer a question of adapting behaviour to the dominant social norms, but of challenging definitions established by those who are "normal" and demanding the right to be different.

Theoretically, it seems obvious that rehabilitation must occur in a context that is as similar as possible to that of the nondisabled and that it must include medical and physiotherapeutic features. Despite this emphasis on the rehabilitative process, the importance of early detection of impairment and prevention must not be ignored.

GILLES BIBEAU

Disallowance The CONSTITUTION ACT, 1867, provides that any ACT of a provincial legislature must be promptly sent to the GOVERNOR GENERAL and that the governor general-in-council (federal CABINET) may disallow any such Act (wipe it off the statute book) within 1 year. One hundred and twelve provincial Acts have been disallowed, in every province except PEI and Newfoundland, for a variety of reasons: they were considered unconstitutional, "contrary to Dominion policy" or "Dominion interest," or "contrary to reason, justice and natural equity." The last disallowance was in 1943.   EUGENE A. FORSEY

Disarmament Since the 19th century, world powers have conferred in peacetime about disarmament, believing that to avoid war, weapons should be reduced in number or eliminated. A new era in warfare began when the bombing of cities and industry through WORLD WAR II climaxed with the atomic bombing of Hiroshima and Nagasaki, Japan. Many political and scientific leaders began to place disarmament at the head of problems to be solved in order for humanity to have a better future.

Negotiations to prevent nuclear war began in 1946, usually under the auspices of the UN. In 1959 Nikita Khrushchev proposed in the UN General Assembly that the nations should commit themselves to complete disarmament. Although this was not achieved by several UN disarmament committees, some measure of "arms control" was reached – eg, the 1963 partial ban on testing nuclear weapons and the 1968 Non-Proliferation Treaty. Meanwhile, since the race to build intercontinental missiles continued, the superpowers in 1969 decided to hold strategic arms limitation talks by themselves. A treaty, SALT I, came into force in 1972. A second, SALT II, was rejected by the US Senate.

NATO fears that the Warsaw Treaty nations (the USSR and its eastern European allies) have superiority in conventional weapons (guns, tanks, attack aircraft), which would allow them to invade western Europe, sweeping aside the defending conventional forces. Until the 1970s the US was believed to have superiority in intercontinental aircraft and missiles so that it could deter any conventional attack by the threat of nuclear destruction, which it could visit on the USSR and its allies without incurring corresponding damage. However, with a change through the 1970s in the balance of intercontinental armaments, the theory of graduated response was evolved. An invasion by conventional forces would be met by limited response with nuclear weapons of theatre range, the threat of escalation causing the combatants to cease hostilities.

Because Canada helped produce the atomic bomb, it has participated in disarmament talks since the beginning, advocating mutually balanced, verifiable disarmament. But Canada's freedom of expression has been limited by the need for solidarity within NATO. The government's concerns, shared by an increasing number of Canadians in the 1980s, include global destruction, the strategic implications of a nuclear war between the superpowers (because of Canada's geographical location) and damage to delicate environments such as the Arctic, Great Lakes and coasts, caused by the testing of nuclear weapons or war. International conferences on arms control continue into the late 1980s. As part of the ongoing negotiations between US Pres Reagan and Soviet leader Gorbachev, a treaty was signed 8 Dec 1987 providing for the eventual removal of intermediate-range missiles, the first agreement to eliminate an entire class of nuclear weapons. *See also* ARMAMENTS; PACIFISM; WOMEN'S INTERNATIONAL LEAGUE FOR PEACE AND FREEDOM; PEACE MOVEMENT.   E.L.M. BURNS

Disasters Catastrophic accidents or natural disasters may be spectacular or tragic, but they seldom have great historical significance. In the spring of 1914 Canada's worst mining and marine calamities and Newfoundland's worst sealing disasters did not affect the world as much as a single assassination in Sarajevo. Nevertheless, catastrophic events even with few fatalities may have implications beyond the personal tragedies suffered by the victims, their families and communities. A gold-mine disaster in Moose River, NS, 12-23 Apr 1936, involved only 3 trapped men, 2 of whom survived; but firsthand accounts by the CBC broke new ground in radio news reporting. In addition, numerous major accidents have led to improvements in the safety of equipment and work practices.

The very size and varied geography of Canada creates the potential for countless disasters. In the first half of 1986, for example, a train collision near Hinton left 23 dead, a blizzard immobilized much of Alberta, forest fires blazed throughout the Atlantic provinces and nuclear fallout from Chernobyl began to drift over Canada. Disasters are of great interest, not for their morbid aspects but for the causes that lie behind them and the responses they draw from society.

In Canada, the agency responsible for co-ordinating the federal response to emergencies is Emergency Preparedness Canada, est 1974 and given its present name in 1986. The organization has operated under various titles since 1948 when the federal government established a CIVIL DEFENCE organization aimed at countering the threat of nuclear attack. The following catalogue, listed alphabetically by type, contains descriptions of Canada's worst disasters.

Avalanches and Rockfalls The Lower Town in Québec C has been the site of major rockfalls. On 17 May 1841, boulders from Cap Diamant demolished 8 houses and killed 32 people but did not deter building in dangerous areas. On 19 Sept 1889 a massive ROCKSLIDE smashed much of Champlain St. killing 45; the disaster would have been worse if many families had not been absent, attending 2 wakes. The most disastrous rockfall in Canadian history was the FRANK SLIDE of 29 Apr 1903, which claimed at least 70 lives in Frank, NWT (Alberta).

Snowslides have always been a threat in the Rockies. Just before midnight on 5 Mar 1910 an AVALANCHE at Bear Creek in the ROGERS PASS engulfed a work crew that had been clearing snow from an earlier slide across the CPR main line. One man survived; 62 were killed.

On 4 May 1971, during a rainstorm, a 213 m hole appeared in the mud and clay of St-Jean-Vianney, Qué. The crater swallowed 36 homes, several cars and a bus, and claimed 31 lives.

Aviation The first death involving an airplane in Canada was at Victoria, BC, on 6 Aug 1913, when American barnstormer John M. Bryant was killed in the crash of his Curtiss seaplane. In subsequent fatal accidents the small load capacities of the aircraft minimized the number of deaths, but when aircraft became larger, and their commercial use became more common, crashes assumed horrendous proportions. Canada's first major air disaster occurred on 25 Aug 1928 when a Ford Trimotor flew into Puget Sd in bad weather; 7 persons were killed. The worst commercial airline accident in Canada involving Canadian aircraft was at Ste-Thérèse-de-Blainville, Qué, on 29 Nov 1963, when a TCA DC-8F crashed 4 minutes after takeoff from Montréal International (Dorval) Airport, killing all 118 persons aboard. The cause of the crash was never satisfactorily explained. At Toronto on 5 July 1970 an Air Canada DC-8 made a heavy landing, bounced and lost one starboard engine. In the pilot's attempt to take off and land again the other starboard engine fell off and the aircraft crashed, killing all 109 per-

Wreckage of the first Québec Bridge, which collapsed 29 Aug 1907, killing 75 men (*courtesy National Archives of Canada/PA-109481/Dominion Bridge Co Ltd*).

sons aboard. The worst air disaster associated with Canada and the third worst in history was the explosion, likely from a terrorist bomb, of Air India Flight 182 from Toronto 25 June 1985. The plane crashed into the N Atlantic off the coast of Ireland, killing all 329 on board, including 280 Canadians. The incident resulted in major increases in airport security. Later that year, which was the worst for accidents in aviation history, a chartered DC-8 carrying 256 passengers, 248 of them US soldiers, crashed after takeoff from Gander, Nfld. All were killed in the worst air disaster over Canadian soil. Disturbing rumours of the aircraft's previous record of mechanical difficulties followed the crash. A number of other commercial airline crashes have occurred, several of them claiming dozens of lives. They have involved faulty aircraft, collisions between aircraft, collisions with ground vehicles and undetermined causes.

Some disasters are notable for reasons other than casualty figures. The crash of a Pan-Arctic Oils Lockheed Electra (Rea Point, NWT, 30 Oct 1974) was the worst accident involving a non-commercial aircraft; 32 of the 34 persons aboard were lost. Twenty-three persons were killed on 9 Sept 1949 when a Québec Airways DC-3 was sabotaged with a bomb and exploded and crashed near St-Joachim, Qué. J.A. Guay and 2 accomplices were convicted and hanged. The worst crash in the history of the RCAF, apart from casualties sustained overseas, occurred on 19 Oct 1943 when a Liberator bomber crashed near St-Donat, Qué, killing 24; many of those aboard were on leave. The wreckage was not located until June 1946.

Bridges The QUÉBEC BRIDGE was involved in 2 major accidents during construction. On 29 Aug 1907, 75 workmen were killed, and on 11 Sept 1916, 13 men died. Of the several bridges that have been built to cross the harbour of Victoria, BC, at Point Ellice, a metal, 4-span structure built in 1885 was too weak for tramlines that were later built across it. On 26 May 1896, during celebrations for the queen's birthday, one span fell out, taking a loaded streetcar with it. Fifty-five persons died in this, the worst streetcar accident in N American history. On 17 June 1958, during construction of Vancouver's present Second Narrows Bridge, one span collapsed into Burrard Inlet, taking 18 men to their deaths. It was later concluded that design errors had been committed by 2 engineers who were among the dead.

HUGH A. HALLIDAY

Coal Mining involves deep tunnels, soft rock, dust, explosives and vulnerable ventilation systems. Major coal-mine disasters have occurred at various times across the country. The first was probably at Westville, Pictou County, NS, on 13 May 1873 after a fire broke out at the coal face. As

workers were leaving and a squad of firefighters entering, an explosion ripped through the tunnels; secondary explosions trapped many rescuers. The mine was sealed to starve the fire of oxygen, and 2 years passed before the last of 60 bodies were recovered. The men left 31 widows and 80 children.

From 1866 to 1987 there were 1321 fatalities reported in Cape Breton mines, including 65 in an explosion at Dominion (25 July 1917), and 16 in Sydney Mines (6 Dec 1938) when a cable broke, sending a riding rake plummeting. The most recent explosion (Glace Bay, 24 Feb 1979) took 12 lives.

The Pictou County coal field was particularly dangerous because the thick, gassy seams made them prone to spontaneous combustion and explosion. Of the 650 known mining deaths, 246 were from explosions. After Drummond, Stellarton's Foord Pit exploded (12 Nov 1880) taking 44 lives, and the MacGregor explosion (14 Jan 1952) killed 19. Experts considered the Allan Shaft the most dangerous coal mine in the world. In the explosion of 23 Jan 1918, 88 died, leaving barely a family in the community untouched by the disaster. The tragedy was not only in lives lost, but also in the destitute families left to support themselves in a society with little, if any, compensation, and no government-sponsored income security programs. Moreover, many were permanently injured in mine disasters, never to work again. The destruction of the mine left many miners unemployed, as in 1929, when a bad explosion destroyed the Allan Shaft so completely that it took 2 years to recover the workplace, although, fortunately, the mine was empty of miners when the blast occurred.

The worst coal-mine disaster in Canadian history occurred on 19 June 1914 at Hillcrest, Alta. It is believed that a fall of rock struck a spark, setting off dust explosions that crippled the ventilating fans and burned away half the oxygen in the mine. A total of 189 men died, leaving 130 widows and about 400 children.

In the SPRINGHILL, NS, mines alone, from 1881 to 1969, 424 persons lost their lives. On 21 Feb 1891, 125 miners were killed in an explosion. On 1 Nov 1956 an accident killing 39 men was notable for the rescue of 88 trapped survivors. On 23 Oct 1958, after the collapse of a tunnel in which 74 men died, 18 were rescued from levels as deep as 3960 m – the deepest rescues ever conducted in Canada. The other 185 died in another 167 separate accidents.

Rescue teams have been specially trained to save miners trapped in gas, fire, explosive, flood or other dangerous conditions. In 1906 the first self-contained breathing apparatus for mine rescue in N America was obtained by Glace Bay collieries. Rescue teams were responsible for saving many lives in colliery disasters, usually working under precarious conditions and at great risk to their own lives. *See also* MINING SAFETY.

HUGH A. HALLIDAY AND JUDITH HOEGG RYAN

Earthquakes Although parts of central and Atlantic Canada have been shaken by earth tremors, the only one causing extensive loss of life was centered on the Gulf of St Lawrence on 18 Nov 1929. A 4.6 m tidal wave struck Newfoundland's Burin Peninsula, sweeping away houses, boats and fish stages. Damage was estimated at $1 million; 27 people died.

Epidemics Before modern immunization programs and vaccines practically eliminated EPIDEMICS in Canada, thousands of deaths resulted from outbreaks of SMALLPOX, CHOLERA, typhus, INFLUENZA and other contagious diseases. In 1953 polio affected more than 8000 Canadians, killing 481; the next year, with Salk vaccine coming into

In 1949, Toronto's worst human disaster occurred when the cruise ship *Noronic* went up in flames, taking 118 lives (*courtesy City of Toronto Archives/James Coll/1518*).

use, the death toll fell to 157. Such progress has sometimes been difficult; compulsory vaccination for smallpox was bitterly opposed in Montréal until an 1885 outbreak claimed 5864 lives and made vaccination respectable.

Fires and Explosions The most deadly structural fire in what is now Canada consumed the Knights of Columbus hostel in St John's, Nfld, on 12 Dec 1942. An arsonist set fire to the building when it was packed with military personnel and their companions. The hostel was a firetrap: doors opened inward, exits were restricted and there was no emergency lighting system. Within 5 minutes, 99 persons had been burned to death and 100 seriously injured. The main fire station was only 180 metres away, but the building was doomed before the engines arrived.

The burning of the cruise ship NORONIC in Toronto Harbour, on the night of 17 Sept 1949, claimed 118 lives. The blaze, apparently due to spontaneous combustion in a closet, broke out at 2:30 AM when passengers were asleep and fewer than 20 crewmen were aboard; it was well advanced before discovery. Contributing factors included the absence of automatic alarms, a lack of direction by officers and panic among passengers.

On 9 Jan 1927 a small fire broke out in the Laurier Palace Theatre, Montréal. Firemen arrived within 2 minutes and the blaze was extinguished in 10, but in the panic to escape an overcrowded building, many children piled up at the bases of stairways; 12 were crushed to death and 64 were asphyxiated. The most deadly fire in recent years occurred at Chapais, Qué (31 Dec 1979), when a man playing with a lighter in a social club set a fire that killed 44 persons.

Several major forest fires have destroyed large stands of timber and taken many lives. The Miramichi fire, which began 5 Oct 1825 after a dry summer, devastated some 15 500 km² north of NB's MIRAMICHI R, and destroyed Douglastown and NEWCASTLE. Estimates of the death toll run from 200 to 500. The area's TIMBER TRADE was crippled for many years, but the fire actually spurred development of logging elsewhere in British North America.

Northern Ontario has been struck by several disastrous forest fires. The worst, the Matheson fire, resulted from small blazes started by lightning and locomotive sparks which combined into a firestorm on 29 July 1916. A wall of flames struck Cochrane, Matheson and environs, burning both towns and killing at least 228.

Numerous cities have had disastrous fires, particularly in the 19th century when crowded, flammable buildings were concentrated, and before the advent of modern watermains, pumps and professional fire brigades. In St John's, Nfld, 3 fires (12 Feb 1816, 7 Nov 1817 and 21 Nov 1817) drove 2600 people (of a total population of

10 000) from their homes. Another fire, on 9 June 1846, levelled most of what was still a tinderbox. The city was rebuilt with more stone and fire-breaks. Nevertheless, on 8-9 July 1892 a wind-swept blaze destroyed the city again. Québec City had 2 fires, 28 May and 28 June 1845, which killed at least 23 and left 15 000-18 000 home-less. The old walled section and lower town were spared, but the surviving city was smaller than that captured by James Wolfe 86 years before. The city was rebuilt with more stone and wider streets. However, to save money the city skimped on fire-fighting equipment and in 1866 reduced the size of the fire brigade. On 14 Oct 1866 a fire pushed by high winds took 5 lives, burned over 2000 homes and left 18 000-20 000 homeless. Again, the walled city and lower town were spared.

Saint John, NB, had major fires in 1837 and 1839. In spite of tighter building bylaws, a fire on 20 June 1877 destroyed two-thirds of the city, leaving 15 000 homeless.

The HALIFAX EXPLOSION of 6 Dec 1917 probably ranks as Canada's most famous disaster and, epidemics aside, the worst single one in our history. Property damage exceeded $35 million and over 1600 persons were killed.

Highway The worst single-vehicle accident in Canada (and the worst bus disaster in Canada or the US) occurred near Eastman, Qué, on 4 Aug 1978. The brakes of a chartered bus failed and it plunged into Lac d'Argent, killing 41 physically or mentally handicapped persons. This toll was more than double that of Canada's worst previous accident, that of 31 July 1953, when a bus plunged into a canal near Morrisburg, Ont, drowning 20.

Marine The earliest shipwreck may have involved John CABOT, who disappeared in 1498 on his second voyage; or Gaspar CORTE-REAL, who vanished in 1501 on a voyage to Newfoundland; or an anonymous BASQUE whaler. The wreck of the *Delight*, one of Sir Humphrey GILBERT's ships, on Sable I on 29 Aug 1583, when at least 85 men were drowned, is the first identifiable marine disaster.

On 23 Aug 1711 a British fleet under Rear Adm Sir Hovenden Walker, sailing to attack Québec, blundered onto the rocks of Île-aux-Oeufs. The 19 warships and 41 other ships carried over 11 000 men; 7 transports and a supply ship were lost with as many as 950 men. Poor charts, rugged and sparsely inhabited coastlines and inadequate marine aids (fog signals, lighthouses, lifesaving stations) combined to take a terrible toll of ships, which frequently lacked lifeboat capacity for all aboard. As with air disasters, the casualty figures were often relatively low simply because the carriers had limited space.

Three Canadian marine disasters are particularly noteworthy. On 29 May 1914, on her first night out on a voyage from Québec, the EMPRESS OF IRELAND, owned by the Canadian Pacific Steamship Co, was sailing in scattered fog near Father Point [Rimouski], Qué. She was struck broadside by the loaded Norwegian collier *Storstad*, which opened a large hole in the liner's hull. The *Empress* filled rapidly and passengers were trapped. Only 14 minutes elapsed from impact to sinking. Of 1057 passengers and 420 crew, 1014 died.

On 20 Mar 1873 the *Atlantic*, owned by White Star Line, sailed from Liverpool to New York with 811 passengers, 4 officers and a crew of 141. Its coal was consumed faster than was anticipated, and on Mar 31 the captain decided to make for Halifax. At 3:15 AM, Apr 1, the ship blundered onto Meagher's Rock (Prospect, NS) and listed so sharply that those below deck were trapped; many who reached the deck were washed over-

board. In spite of heroic rescue efforts by crew-men and local inhabitants, 534 men and one child died.

On 23 Oct 1918, sailing in a snowstorm from Skagway, Alaska, to Vancouver, the *Princess Sophia*, CP Steamships, ran onto Vanderbilt Reef, Lynn Canal. Smaller craft approached, but heavy seas prevented them from rescuing passengers. Two days of pounding by waves finally broke the ship's hull; on Oct 25 the ship sank with the loss of all 343 aboard.

Some wrecks have attained notoriety for particularly dramatic, tragic or unusual aspects. The *Montreal* (715-ton paddle steamer) burned near Québec on 26 June 1857 with the loss of 253. The crew was scandalously slow responding to the report of fire; the ship had caught fire on at least 3 previous occasions. On 24 May 1881, the over-loaded *Victoria* (27-ton paddle steamer) capsized in the Thames R near London, Ont. In spite of relatively shallow water, 182 perished. The tragic sinking of the offshore oil rig OCEAN RANGER, 265 km east of Newfoundland on 15 Feb 1982, was Canada's first disaster with this type of vessel; 84 men were lost.

Both fishing and sealing off the Atlantic coast have claimed many lives over the years. As recently as 20 June 1959 the fishing fleet of Escumi-nac, NB, was hit by a massive storm that sank 22 boats and drowned 35 men. It is estimated that between 1810 and 1870 the Newfoundland seal fishery lost some 400 vessels and 1000 men in the ice floes. Although most mishaps involved relatively few lives, the failure of the *Newfoundland* to recover her sealers during a storm, 31 Mar-2 Apr 1914, caused 77 to perish; and the sealer *Southern Cross* vanished with 173 aboard.

Railways Rail accidents illustrate the multiple causes of disasters. Particularly in early times, accidents could result from improper trackbeds, metal fatigue, fire, flawed rails, human error and frail bridges.

Within a month of the opening of the Great Western Ry in 1854, 6 passengers were killed near London and 7 near Thorold. On 27·Oct 1854 at Baptiste Creek, 24 km W of Chatham, Ont, a gravel train sent out to shore up rail beds was hit by an express that was running 7 hours late. The accident killed 52 and injured 48 others, the worst rail disaster in N America to that time. Canada's deadliest wreck occurred at St-Hilaire, Qué, at 1:10 AM, 29 June 1864. A Grand Trunk train with 458 passengers, most of them newly arrived German and Polish immigrants, was unable to stop for an open swing bridge over the Richelieu R. The train plunged into the gap and the coaches piled on top of one another. Estimates of the deaths ran as high as 99, with another 100 injuries. A broken rail caused derailment of a CPR passenger train W of Sudbury 21 Jan 1910, killing 43.

Sabotage may have played a part in the wreck near Yamaska, Qué, 28 Sept 1875 as a train was derailed by heavy timbers and 10 were killed. Several wrecks have resulted from crews not taking to sidings to let an oncoming train pass. On 1 Sept 1947, 31 were killed at Dugald, Man, and on 21 Nov 1950, 21 were killed at Canoe River, BC, in crashes caused by errors of this kind. A report after 23 people died in a head-on collision between a CN freight and a Via Rail passenger train at Hinton, Alta, in Feb 1986, suggested that human error played a major role.

Storms and Floods The RED R in southern Manitoba floods regularly. In May 1950 a flood inundated many valley towns and one-sixth of WINNIPEG; more than 100 000 persons had to be evacuated. The worst aspects of such floods have been alleviated by the construction of floodways to carry off spring overflow.

A TORNADO struck the core of Regina on 30 June 1912, killing 28 persons and causing $6 million in damages. The worst inland storm was Hurricane Hazel, which struck southern and central Ontario on 15 Oct 1954 and dumped over 100 mm of rain on Toronto in 12 hours. There were 81 deaths, most of them in the Toronto area, and extensive property damage.

On 31 May 1985 a tornado hit Barrie, Ont, in the worst inland storm since Hurricane Hazel. Some 300 houses were destroyed, at least 8 were killed and thousands were left homeless.

On 31 July 1987 a tornado swept through parts of SE and NE Edmonton, flattening residences and laying waste to an industrial park and a trailer park. Twenty-seven people, mostly in the trailer park, were killed; insurance companies estimated that they would pay more than $250 million for damages.   HUGH A. HALLIDAY

Discovery, famous ship belonging to the East India Company, which first sailed into the Arctic under the command of George Weymouth in 1602. The same ship was used by Henry HUDSON to explore Hudson Bay in 1610. Hudson was cut adrift, but his ship and 8 of his mutinous crew survived the passage home. James COOK and George VANCOUVER sailed different ships of the same name.   JAMES MARSH

Disease can be defined as an unhealthy condition of body or mind. Many diseases are exacerbated by malnutrition and infection (which are often the consequence of poverty, ignorance, bad sanitation, polluted water, contaminated food) and are influenced by, among other factors, geography, climate and excessive population growth. Modern man, who has created a physical and social environment often inimical to his health, is vulnerable as well to a wide range of GENETIC DISEASES and conditions that may affect the whole body or parts of the body. These congenital diseases and conditions include clubfeet, heart defects, various deformities of the nervous system, Down's syndrome (characterized by distinctive physical appearance and mental defect) and many biochemical defects and anomalies.

In Canada in 1986 the average age at death of males and females was 73 years and 80 years, respectively. The leading causes of death in Canada are HEART DISEASE, CANCER, accidents, INFLUENZA and other respiratory diseases, DIABETES MELLITUS and chronic liver disease including cirrhosis. Infectious diseases, which killed between 25-33% of Canada's population in 1867, now rarely cause death. *See also* SEXUALLY TRANSMITTED DISEASE; ALCO-HOLISM; MENTAL HEALTH; NATIVE PEOPLE, HEALTH.

Disease, Animal The tissues and body fluids of ANIMALS are subject to the same types of abnormal structural and functional changes as are those of humans. Causes and circumstances may differ but the disease processes are very similar. An inflammation or a cancer in a dog or a cow could be identical in appearance and development to that found in a human.

The science of anatomy studies normal tissue structure in other animals, as in humans, the science of physiology, normal function; that of pathology, disease processes (abnormal structure and function). Veterinarians diagnose, treat and prevent diseases in animals.

Types of Disease Processes in Animals

Degenerative Individual cells or groups of cells which are sick and function abnormally are called degenerate because of their reduced ability to function. They have abnormal organelles (specialized cell parts) and functional abnormalities and can often be identified by their appearance under the microscope. Dead cells and tissues have a characteristic appearance called necrosis which is a common abnormality in injured tissue.

Circulatory Blood flows through tissues, providing nutriment and oxygen. Blood flow may be abnormal because of tissue lesions or abnormalities in the general circulation. If increased amounts of arterial blood fill capillary beds, the lesion, called hyperemia, is bright red. Such lesions are commonly found in inflammation. If venous drainage is impaired through local or generalized obstruction to flow, congestion results, appearing dark red. If excess fluid collects in tissues outside blood vessels, the lesion is called edema and tissue is swollen. This lesion may be caused by local injury or by a generalized inefficiency in circulation (eg, a failing heart). If red blood cells are outside blood vessels, the lesion is a hemorrhage. If blood constituents clot within a vessel, the lesion is a thrombus; the process is thrombosis. Thrombi occur because of injury to vessel linings, turbulent flow or slow flow and often occur on the heart valves of animals during a generalized bacterial infection. An infarct, necrosis of a segment of tissue through obstruction of blood flow (thrombosis), often occurs in organs having limited collateral circulation (eg, heart, kidney).

Inflammation, the body's response to injury, involves tissue and blood cells. Injured tissues release chemicals which initiate inflammation and bring white blood cells to the site to overcome an invading agent or remove injured tissue. The white blood cells (leukocytes, including neutrophils and macrophages) are able to eat up (phagocytose) invading agents and debris, although many die in the process. The fluids and cells which accumulate are called exudate. Inflammatory exudates differ according to the cause and the tissue affected. Inflammations which occur rapidly are acute; those occurring gradually, subacute; those which are prolonged, chronic. Some exudates are mainly fluid (eg, a "running nose," serous exudate); some induce mucus (eg, in bronchi, catarrhal exudate); some induce fibrin formation in blood leaked from damaged vessels (fibrinous exudate). Pus results from a predominance of neutrophils in the exudate (purulent exudate) and, if confined in tissue, is called an abscess. A prolonged battle with a stubborn agent causes macrophages or, sometimes, giant cells to predominate and connective tissue to form, in an effort to confine the lesion. A scar may be the long-term evidence of an inflammation.

Growth Disturbances Cells may decrease in size and number in a tissue, a process called atrophy. Hypertrophy is enlargement of existing cells; hyperplasia is an increase in number. Defects in tissue and organ formation are called anomalies. Parts may be absent (agenesis), incomplete (hypoplasia) or present but too small. Cancer is a growth disturbance which allows groups of cells to proliferate, sometimes in an uncontrolled manner. It occurs in all tissues and organs in humans, in wild and domestic animals and lower species, and in individuals of all ages, including the unborn. Causes include irradiation, viruses, chemicals, genetic abnormalities, etc. Carcinogenic agents cause groups of cells to lose their growth-control mechanisms and to proliferate abnormally. Cancers may expand as a solitary mass, infiltrate a tissue or organ, spread in the blood to other organs or implant on internal body surfaces. Tumours are common in animals, particularly poultry, cats, cattle, mice, rats and dogs. Many are known to be caused by viruses and are used to study mechanisms of cancer development in humans.

Diseases in Various Species

Many animal diseases are related to intensive husbandry resulting in crowded, poorly ventilated conditions often combined with the mixing of susceptible animals from several sources. The major economically important diseases of cattle are neonatal diarrhea and viruses (eg, corona virus, rotavirus). Enzootic pneumonia (ie, always present at a low level) is a serious problem in calves 2-6 months old. The causes are viruses and viruslike micro-organisms, together with secondary bacterial infection, often leading to a persistent bronchopneumonia. Affected calves have a fever, grow poorly, cough and breathe rapidly. Before the discovery of antibiotics, many calves died of pulmonary abscesses but now most survive if treated properly. Feedlot cattle very often have a more severe, often fatal pneumonia shortly after arrival at the feedlot (*see* BEEF CATTLE FARMING). Transportation stress, mixing of groups and crowding predispose the animals to bacterial pneumonia, known as "shipping fever," which is so acute that it is difficult to detect affected animals soon enough to treat them. Mastitis is a major problem in dairy cows because chronic inflammation of the mammary gland reduces milk yield (*see* DAIRY FARMING).

Infertility, a major problem in cattle, arises through abortion or failure to conceive at the proper time (*see* ANIMAL BREEDING). Abortion is caused by many different infectious agents. It is economically important for a cow to calve annually; therefore, the cow must come in estrus and be bred at the proper time. Detection of estrus is a major problem to many farmers. Some of the great plagues which affected cattle of past centuries (eg, foot-and-mouth, rinderpest, contagious bovine pleuropneumonia) still exist in Africa and Asia and periodically spread to Europe and the Americas. The risk of such diseases results in strict importation regulations for meat, animal products and animals.

Hog cholera and African swine fever are highly infectious, fatal diseases causing lesions in many tissues. Both could be considered in the plague category. The most prevalent diseases of pigs now are diarrhea and pneumonia. That specific diarrheas tend to occur in different age groups helps in diagnosis. Most are fatal or may cause pigs to be stunted and therefore uneconomical. The main pneumonia is caused by mycoplasma, a bacterialike organism. Diarrheas and pneumonia often lead producers to place antibiotics or similar compounds in the feed at subtreatment levels until marketing (*see* HOG FARMING). Bacteria often become resistant to antibiotics given at preventive rather than treatment levels.

Sheep and goats have many diseases in common, of which parasites are very important. Lungworms are common in both and often lead to chronic lung disease. Constant prevention and treatment efforts are required to overcome them. Several kinds of gastrointestinal parasitic worms occur, especially in sheep. Stomach worms, *Haemonchus*, suck blood from the stomach lining, often causing fatal acute anemia. White muscle disease caused by vitamin E deficiency can be prevented by adequate diet supplements. The name comes from the pale colour of degenerate muscle lesions in the heart and limbs of affected animals (*see* GOAT FARMING; SHEEP FARMING).

Domestic turkeys and chickens are raised in very crowded conditions (often thousands in one pen); therefore, infections can spread very rapidly (*see* POULTRY FARMING). Many vaccines, often given in the drinking water, are routinely used; drugs are included in the feed to prevent bacterial and parasitic diseases. Coccidiosis is a very common protozoan parasite causing a potentially fatal enteritis. The parasite is easily treated or prevented by drugs but keeps changing its sensitivity to drugs and requires constant checking. Respiratory diseases (particularly of the air sacs and si-nuses) are also significant and require constant control measures. A widespread poultry disease is a cancer of lymphocytes in the blood and blood-forming tissues, caused by a highly infectious virus. Some of the viral strains pass by contact, others through eggs. A vaccine is now available for prevention. Intense research is ongoing to determine whether other cancers, possibly those of humans, are viral in origin.

The requirement of veterinary services for PETS, particularly DOGS and CATS, has expanded rapidly and is now highly sophisticated, requiring hospital care and facilities very similar to human hospitals. Dogs have many diseases resembling those of humans and are often studied as models of human diseases. "Comparative medicine" refers to such combined studies and includes many diseases of other animals, particularly certain strains of rats, mice and primates. Dogs have the highest rates of cancer among animals. These originate in many tissues but those of the skin and blood-forming organs are most numerous. Biopsy examination of surgically removed lumps is a common procedure. The main infectious diseases of dogs are distemper and infectious canine hepatitis but these are now well controlled by vaccination. The frequently fatal acute parvoviral enteritis, a rather new disease in dogs, apparently arose as a variant of a nonpathogenic strain and became rampant across N America in the late 1970s and early 1980s.

The most devastating disease in cats, infectious feline enteritis, or panleukopenia, has many similarities to canine viral enteritis and is often fatal. It is also fatal to members of the MINK family. Cats have a high incidence of lymphosarcoma, a cancer of white blood cells. It is caused by a highly infectious virus but causes cancer in a relatively few animals which appear to have a defect in their immune response. The disease is being studied to see if the mechanisms involved relate to those of any human cancers.

The use of RABBITS, rats, mice, guinea pigs and primates for research on human disease or for testing drugs and vaccines has resulted in rapid expansion of knowledge of their naturally occurring diseases, which are similar to others discussed above (eg, enteritis, pneumonia, parasitic diseases). Many specific models of human disease have been found in these animals and are studied in detail (*see* ANIMAL ISSUES).

Wildlife species of all types have diseases, some occurring in epidemics. These diseases are no different from those occurring in domestic species. Less is known about most wildlife diseases because of problems in securing sufficient numbers for study. Particular attention is given to species that carry diseases which could affect humans or domestic animals (eg, rabies). Efforts are being made to vaccinate wildlife species for rabies by means of oral vaccines in food left in their natural environment. Fortunately, there are veterinarians who specialize in diseases of wildlife (*see* WILDLIFE CONSERVATION AND MANAGEMENT).

Captive animals have many disease problems related to captivity, ie, to strange or unnatural climates, mixing with unnatural neighbours, eating unnatural foods, etc. They may contract diseases to which they have no resistance from humans or from animals native to other continents. Zoo veterinarians have a tremendous responsibility in caring for expensive animals. Many problems occur as a result of restraint while the animals are being moved or treated. Injuries are common. There are now enough zoo veterinarians to allow for sharing of knowledge and experience.

The requirement that animals slaughtered for meat be inspected under veterinary supervision is designed, in part, to protect the public from the many diseases transmissible from animals to humans (*see* FOOD LEGISLATION; FOOD SAFETY). These diseases include listeriosis, anthrax, salmonellosis (typhoid fever), brucellosis (contagious abortion), tuberculosis, leptospirosis, some pox viruses, rabies, equine encephalitis, etc. Pasteurization of milk, meat inspection and generally improved personal hygiene have effected major improvements in control of these transmissible diseases. Because of the importance of ANIMAL AGRICULTURE to the Canadian economy, VETERINARY MEDICINE in Canada is pioneering new technology and treatments for diseases of domestic food-producing animals. Guelph researchers are concentrating on reproductive biotechnology including sexing and splitting embryos, in-vitro fertilization, recombinant cloning of toxins to produce anti-toxins, and radiation therapy for cancer in animals. At the Western College of Veterinary Medicine in Saskatoon calf diarrhea and respiratory disease of cattle, in particular shipping fever, are the subjects of research. At the U of Montreal at St-Hyacinthe, reproductive physiology is being researched. In PEI, at the Atlantic Veterinary College, epidemiology and health management systems for farm animals are being researched.

R.G. THOMSON

Reading: J. Baker and W.J. Green, *Animal Health* (1979); O.H. Siegmund, ed, *The Merck Veterinary Manual*, 5th ed (1979).

Distance Learning commonly refers to learning that takes place in a situation where teacher and student are physically separated. The related terms "distance education" and "open education" are often used interchangeably, although the latter also indicates that the standards for entry are "open," which may not be true for all distance-education institutions.

Distance education is not new, but it has only recently become the subject of academic interest. In 1969 the Open University was founded in the UK. Established by Harold Wilson's Labour government, it is committed, like distance-education programs everywhere, to democratizing education by making it accessible to people unable or unwilling to attend traditional institutions. Postsecondary distance-learning institutes, all patterned to some degree on Britain's Open University, have sprung up throughout the world. Distance educators in both industrialized and nonindustrialized nations share a belief in the power of education to help individuals realize their own potential and to help them contribute more productively to the economy. They are also united by the awareness that among traditional educators and the general public, distance education, perhaps particularly at the post-secondary level, is considered second-rate. This opinion stems partly from unreliable correspondence schools, partly from the belief that there is no valid substitute for face-to-face interaction between student and teacher, and partly from the lack of entrance requirements. Distance educators, in reaction to these negative opinions, avoid the term "correspondence" in favour of "distance" and "open." They argue that they meet and often surpass the rigorous standards of conventional universities by presenting uniform courses and by strictly regulating controls over examinations; that students receive support through tutors who are often more accessible than most professors are; and that students are encouraged to improve their writing skills and realistically plan their education with the help of the universities' counselling staff.

Distance learning has proven suitable to the needs of both industrialized and Third World nations. In the former, it is increasingly useful for continuing education (in Canada, distance-education programs have reached native people in rural areas, prisoners, the handicapped, etc); in the Third World, it is gaining favour as an economical means of raising the levels of LITERACY and of teaching skills to people who are under enormous pressure to industrialize.

In Canada, all 10 provinces have correspondence programs, most of which are run by the correspondence branch of the Department of Education. These programs, which serve individuals wishing to complete the provincial public-school curriculum, account for the majority of enrolments in distance education, and most of those enrolled are adults.

Several private companies and business and professional associations run their own continuing-education divisions, which develop programs for the professional upgrading of their employees or members. In most cases this involves specific vocational and professional courses rather than academic subjects. Where academic subjects are required, associations usually involve a university in the program. For example, ATHABASCA UNIVERSITY and the Law Society of Alberta jointly produced a distance-education course, "Accounting in a Law Office," which Athabasca offers to students identified by the society. At U of Alberta, the Faculty of Extension develops and delivers distance-education courses for local government administrators throughout the province. The Local Government Studies Certificate program has an advisory committee representing the university, 3 government departments and several municipal associations.

Although several colleges and institutes of technology have developed excellent distance-learning materials, generally these institutions tend to be more interested in increasing access to education through adult extension programs. The increasing involvement of universities, however, is reflected in the establishment of departments or faculties of extension on most Canadian campuses. Many of these faculties, which have developed steadily since the 1960s, have shifted their emphasis from offering evening courses on campus to offering correspondence credit courses. Although no postgraduate-level distance-education programs are yet available in Canada as they are in countries such as England and Australia, nearly 25 universities now offer distance-learning programs leading to undergraduate degrees and 3 Canadian institutions serve distance students exclusively at the university level: the Télé-université in Québec (est 1972); Athabasca U in Alberta (est 1972); and the Open Learning Institute of BC (est 1978). These 3 institutions are distinguished by their emphasis on services to students and on course design. Until recently, university correspondence courses consisted of elaborated lecture notes mailed to students. Interaction between teacher and student was restricted to the marking of assignments and exams. These 3 institutions, however, offer much more extensive assistance, ranging from teleconferencing (telephone tutoring to remote learning centres, which are equipped with video playback machines, computer terminals, etc) to group tutorials and seminars. The augmented services reflect the recognition that distance learning is a lonely activity and that the motivation traditionally supplied through personal contact with the instructor in the classroom is not available; course materials must therefore be carefully designed to alleviate some of the impersonal aspects of what has been called "the most industrialized form of education." Courses are designed by editors and instructional designers, working with the course author.

While correspondence courses in the past consisted entirely of printed materials, there is a growing use of educational technology, eg, radio, television, teleconferencing, audio cassettes and, most recently, computers.

In Alberta, for example, U of Calgary and Athabasca U have successfully conducted experiments in teleconferencing with TELIDON, Canada's computer-graphics innovation, and the Alberta Correspondence School has used Telidon to teach a course in mechanics. The private sector has also made advances in the area of computerized instruction, eg, a videodisc program was launched by General Motors throughout N America.

JOHN R. THOMPSON

Reading: J.S. Daniel, M.A. Stroud and John R. Thompson, eds, *Learning at a Distance* (1982).

Distant Early Warning (DEW) Line, *see* EARLY-WARNING RADAR.

Distilling Industry, that part of the FOOD AND BEVERAGE INDUSTRIES engaged in clarifying, flavouring, blending and aging alcohol to make potable spirits (eg, brandies, grain spirits, rum) and establishments which manufacture ethyl alcohol, whether or not used in potable spirits. Manufacturers of methyl, butyl or isopropyl alcohol are considered part of the CHEMICAL INDUSTRIES. The distilling industry is a world-class multinational INDUSTRY; in fact, Canada's SEAGRAM CO LTD is ranked one of the largest in the world. Canadian distilled spirits products are internationally renowned for quality and consistency.

In 1985 Canada's 31 distilleries employed over 2500 production workers and were responsible for over 10 000 jobs in the supplying industries. In 1986 Canadians consumed approximately 127 million litres of domestically distilled beverages. This amount was substantially less than the 1980 total of 160 million litres, and the decrease can be attributed to the general economic recession and to higher taxes on alcoholic beverages. In 1985 whisky accounted for two-thirds of the total domestic production of 111 million litres. The distilling industry is one of Canada's largest exporters of finished goods: over 40% of domestic production is exported each year.

Distillers annually purchase over $200 million worth of Canadian grain (the raw material used in making spirits) and manufactured goods (eg, GLASS bottles, caps, other packaging materials). Part of the stillage or refuse from grain distilleries has been turned into useful by-products, eg, supplements in cattle, poultry and hog feeds.

History The earliest settlers in New France imported their alcoholic beverages from France, usually (because of high transportation costs) high-proof brandies and liqueurs. The first distillery in what is now Canada was probably established by Intendant Jean TALON: there is evidence that the brewery he ordered built in 1668 contained a still. As West Indian rums became available relatively cheaply, there was little incentive for settlers to establish a domestic distilling industry until the latter half of the 18th century, when heavy shipping duties began to make West Indian rum prohibitively expensive. Thus, the first recorded distillery was established at Québec City in 1769 to produce rum from imported molasses. After the arrival of the LOYALISTS, whisky from grain began to be produced throughout the grain-growing areas. At that time, millers received a tithe (one-tenth) of all the grain they milled in payment. Some operators turned their surplus into whisky, which was usually easily sold in the neighbourhood and enjoyed the added advantage of being cheaper to transport than grain or flour. Canadian spirits were in demand in the US at least as early as 1861. Some millers abandoned the flour milling industry and, by 1840, over 200 distilleries were operating in Upper and Lower Canada. Some of the leading distillers began operations in this early period; eg, Hiram Walker established his enterprise in 1858.

Distillers played a vital part in WWI, since alcohol was a necessary product for various war materials. Every distiller contributed to the war effort and one entire plant was converted to the manufacture of acetone, a component of the smokeless explosive cordite. The wartime need for alcohol led to the adoption of prohibition in all provinces except Québec (which, in 1919, briefly prohibited retail sale of distilled spirits). Prohibition was repealed at different dates in the other provinces, between 1921 and 1930. PEI was the exception, retaining prohibition until 1948. Liquor rationing was common in many areas during WWII, largely because alcohol was again required for wartime purposes. In 1942 all Canadian distilleries began production of war alcohol and, from 1943 to 1945, produced 68 million litres of high-proof alcohol annually.

Even before its development into an industry proper, distilling had been under regulation. For example, John Graves SIMCOE, first lieutenant-governor of UPPER CANADA, issued 51 still licences during his first year in office. Shortly after the turn of the 19th century, the first government distillery inspectors were appointed and, in 1846, a law was enacted regarding strength requirements. The federal government's power to pass laws relating to the import or manufacture of liquors in Canada was established under the CONSTITUTION ACT, 1867; the same Act gave the provinces control of the retail liquor trade. The Canadian government enacted its first "adulteration of food" legislation in 1874, prompted by the quantity of adulterated liquor being sold. Common additives were salt, tobacco, opium, Indian hemp, copper sulphate and salts of lead or zinc. The Food and Drugs Act, passed in 1954 and now administered by Health and Welfare Canada, includes careful definitions of standards for all types of spirits and specifies packaging and labelling requirements. The department maintains a staff of inspectors to ensure the observance of the regulations (see FOOD LEGISLATION; REGULATORY PROCESS). Also, the excise division of Revenue Canada has specially trained officers to carry out the rigid regulations governing distillers and their products in every phase of the distilling, bottling and packaging operations. The offices and equipment they use are provided by the distillers and were located on their premises. A label marked, for example, "distilled," "blended," "bottled in bond," "under Canadian Government supervision," guarantees that the regulations have been carried out.

Duties were levied on alcoholic beverages imported into Canada from earliest colonial times; however, the first tax (one shilling and 3 pence per gallon) was imposed on Canadian-produced spirits in 1794. Today's excise duty stands at $10.733 per litre of pure alcohol. To this is added a 15% sales tax on the duty-paid value of the goods. After each province repealed PROHIBITION, it introduced government-controlled liquor stores. Today distillers may sell only to provincial and territorial liquor boards which, in turn, sell distilled spirits products in government-run retail stores. The federal and provincial governments now extract over $2 billion of direct taxes from distilled spirits products with an FOB (free on board) value of approximately $375 million.

KAY KENDALL

Distribution of Powers, the legislative competences of the federal and provincial orders of government as outlined in the CONSTITUTION ACT, 1867, and interpreted by the JUDICIAL COMMITTEE OF THE PRIVY COUNCIL until 1949, and from then by the SUPREME COURT OF CANADA. The distribution of executive power is theoretically similar to the distribution of legislative power; judicial power is also divided to some extent, although most of it belongs to the federal government. The Constitution Act, 1867 (s91), grants broad powers to the federal government to legislate for "Peace, Order and good Government in Canada in relation to all Matters not coming within the classes of subjects by this Act assigned exclusively to the Legislatures of the Provinces." The Fathers of Confederation took as their guiding principle that jurisdiction over matters of national interest would be given to Parliament and those of particular interest to the provinces. Because Québec was governed by a CIVIL CODE, the provinces were granted jurisdiction over property and civil rights and Québec was excluded from s94, which allowed for the possible standardization of private law for the provinces. Parliament was also given greater residuary jurisdiction than the provincial legislatures. Areas of federal jurisdiction include trade and commerce, direct and indirect taxation, currency, the postal service, census taking and statistics, national defence, the federal civil service, navigation, fisheries, banking, copyright, Indians and Indian reserves, naturalization, marriage and divorce, criminal law, penitentiaries and interprovincial works and undertakings. By constitutional amendment, Parliament gained exclusive jurisdiction over unemployment insurance in 1940.

In 1949, by amendment (s91.1) to the Constitution Act, Parliament was granted the power to amend the Constitution of Canada except in matters affecting provincial jurisdictions and privileges. In a 1949 decision on the Senate, the Supreme Court of Canada restricted the interpretation of the expression "Constitution of Canada" by stating that this expression in s91.1 referred to the internal federal Constitution and not to the Constitution of all Canada. For example, Parliament could not abolish the Senate because it represents the provinces and is not exclusively a federal concern. The Constitution Act, 1982, repealed s91.1. Section 44 of the Act states that, subject to sections 41 and 42, "Parliament may exclusively make laws amending the Constitution of Canada in relation to the executive government of Canada or the Senate and House of Commons." The provinces have had the right to amend their internal constitutions (except as regards the office of the lieutenant-governor) since 1867. Through jurisprudence, federal residuary power has come to include (partly or wholly) the incorporation of businesses with federal objectives, aeronautics, radio, television, nuclear energy, responsibility for the national capital, offshore mineral rights along the BC coast, official languages within the federal sphere, citizenship, foreign affairs and the control of drugs. Again, through jurisprudence, the introductory clause to s91 now includes emergency powers in peace and war.

Provincial legislatures have jurisdiction, among other things, over their internal constitutions, direct taxation for provincial purposes, municipalities, school boards, hospitals, property and civil rights (their largest area of competence), administration of civil and criminal justice, penalties for infraction of provincial statutes, prisons, celebration of marriage, provincial civil service, local works and corporations with provincial objectives. The courts have restrictively interpreted federal power over commerce and liberally interpreted provincial power over property and civil rights. There are 4 concurrent jurisdictions: agriculture, immigration (s95), old-age pensions and supplementary benefits (s94A). In the case of dispute, federal legislation will prevail for areas under s95 and provincial legislation for those under s94A. Education is allocated to the provinces (s93), but is subject to certain religious guarantees. The conditional and supplementary powers allocated in s93 to Parliament have fallen into disuse. Even though each level of government is restricted to its own legislative sphere, frequently one or another has assumed responsibilities which did not clearly belong to it. The provinces, through a legal fiction recognized by the courts, have converted some originally indirect taxes, eg, sales and purchase taxes, into direct ones. The power to spend money remains an extremely vague and contentious area. Parliament assumes that it may do so where it does not necessarily have the power to enact legislation; such spending is well received by the provinces when it applies to EQUALIZATION PAYMENTS, but less so when it infringes on provincial fields such as health, social security and education.

Under the Constitution Act, 1982, the principle of equalization is enshrined (s36), but it is unclear how it can be implemented. Provincial jurisdiction over natural resources was enlarged, in 1982, to include concurrent power in interprovincial commerce and extraterritorial marketing (though with federal paramountcy). The provinces have also been granted power of indirect taxation of their natural resources (see also INTERGOVERNMENTAL FINANCE). The history of Canadian FEDERALISM is basically an account of disputes over the distribution of powers. From the 1880s until the 1930s federal powers waned relatively, largely because the Judicial Committee of the Privy Council ignored the centralist intentions of many (but not all) of its creators and favoured provincial autonomy in its interpretation of the Constitution Act, 1867; the Supreme Court of Canada, on the other hand, has in its judgements tended generally to strengthen the legislative powers of the federal government in some areas. Despite several conferences between the provinces and the federal government there have been few amendments to the division of powers. Other than expanding provincial power in the area of appointments to the Supreme Court and the Senate and a slight provincial enhancement in the shared jurisdiction of immigration, the MEECH LAKE ACCORD (1987) produced no significant changes to the distribution of powers. See also CONSTITUTIONAL LAW.   GÉRALD-A. BEAUDOIN

Ditidaht ("people of Ditida"), a NOOTKA Indian tribe of the W coast of Vancouver I, BC. The Ditidaht (also known as Nitinaht) formerly consisted of several independent groups who amalgamated into a tribe as a result of warfare and population decline from disease. According to legend, one of the groups migrated from Cape Flattery across the Juan de Fuca Str to the village of Ditida at Jordan R and became the Ditidaht. Warfare with Coast SALISH groups caused the Ditidaht to relocate on the coast near Nitinat Narrows, where they settled in several villages, most notably Whyac. The Ditidaht united with several groups, among them the Cloose and the Carmanah, to form a large tribe. The tribal territory includes the outer coast from Pacheena Point to Bonilla Point, Nitinat Lk, the Nitinat R valley and the western end of Cowichan Lk. Today, the Ditidaht occupy their villages of Malachan and Whyac.

JOHN DEWHIRST

Diving, the sport of plunging into water from a platform, can be traced back to 400 BC through pictures on Egyptian and Roman vases. Plain diving was practised from cliffs to the oceans during the 8th to 10th centuries by Vikings in Sweden and later in the 1770s by Indians in Acapulco, Mexico. Between 1800 and 1820 a new form developed in Germany and Sweden. Acrobatic gymnastics over water was the beginning of the fancy diving known today. Competitive diving began in the 1880s in Germany and in 1904 became an Olympic event, but it did not commence until the 1920s in Canada, under the auspices of the Canadian Amateur Swimming Assn. In 1969 Vaughn L. Baird incorporated the Canadian Amateur Diving Assn as a member of the Aquatic Federation of Canada, a development largely responsible for the continued growth of the sport which is now practised in 9 provinces. Competitive diving is separated into men's and women's springboard and platform events. Competitors perform a set number of dives, each of which is marked on a scale of one to 10 by a panel of 5 or 7 judges, leading to a final total score.

Alfie Phillips was the first nationally recognized Canadian diver, winning 10 straight national championships 1926-35 and finishing seventh in both the 1928 and 1932 Olympics. During the 1940s and 1950s, George Athans, Bill Patrick and Irene MacDonald competed internationally for Canada. Macdonald won a bronze medal in the springboard event at the 1956 Melbourne Olympics and finished sixth at Rome in 1960. Beverley Boys won 4 Commonwealth gold medals in diving and was seventh in the 1968 Olympics, fifth in 1972 in the springboard and fourth in 1968 in the platform. Cindy Shatto was fifth in the platform event at the 1976 Montréal Olympics. The crowning achievement of Canadian competitive diving was Sylvie BERNIER's gold medal in 1984 in Los Angeles. In Aug 1987 at the Pan-Am Games Canada won 3 medals: a silver in the 10 m tower, a bronze in the springboard and a bronze in tower diving.

JANICE WATERS AND MARK LOWRY

Diving, Underwater Probably the first large-scale diving efforts, beginning at least 6500 years ago, were directed to acquiring pearls and mother-of-pearl and involved divers trained from childhood for lung capacity and endurance. The first underwater mechanical devices, eg, wooden diving bells, may have been constructed as early as 332 BC and underwent significant modification even before the 19th century. The first workable diving suit was developed by Augustus Siebe of England about 1839. This waterproof suit had a detachable helmet connected to the surface by a hose through which air was pumped. This kind of tethered suit remained the only practicable diving dress until 1943, when 2 Frenchmen, renowned underwater explorer Jacques-Yves Cousteau and engineer Émile Gagnan, adapted a previously developed breathing apparatus to underwater use. Their improvement was named the "aqualung," or *s*elf-*c*ontained *u*nderwater *b*reathing *a*pparatus (SCUBA).

Commercial Diving Diving equipment is being continually improved in response to demands from the offshore PETROLEUM EXPLORATION industry for diver support to ever greater depths. In some deepwater work the dexterity of a diver is not required or the cost of diver compression and decompression is prohibitive. A pressure-resistant diving suit (one atmosphere suit), developed in Britain, allows a diver to work to depths of 460 m and return to the surface with none of the usual problems associated with breathing high-pressure gases. These suits are massive and awkward; lighter and more versatile versions are being developed by Can-Dive Services, a prominent Canadian diving contractor (*see* OCEAN INDUSTRIES; SUBMERSIBLES).

Recreational Diving Diving for recreation is popular along Canada's coasts and waterways. Equipment providing the reliability and freedom needed by sport divers was developed a century later than the first standard commercial equipment. Recreational equipment has evolved steadily to the point where divers now employ higher pressure air cylinders, single-hose regulators for easier breathing and drysuits for greater warmth. Submersible diving computers, developed first in Canada by Kybertec International Inc, give continuous digital readouts of depth, time, air consumption and decompression status.

Sport divers are trained by certified instructors who are registered with training agencies. The largest agency in Canada, the National Association of Underwater Instructors (NAUI), incorporated in 1971, has headquarters at Toronto. The American and Canadian Underwater Certification Inc (ACUC) has an office in Burlington, Ont. The Professional Association of Diving Instructors (PADI) maintains an office in Victoria, BC. Other agencies providing instruction in Canada are the National Association of Skin Diving Schools, Scuba Schools International and the Confédération mondiale des activités sub-aquatiques. Diving councils and clubs are active throughout Canada and local diving retailers have information on these groups. The Ontario Underwater Council (OUC), the world's largest noncertified association of divers, celebrated 30 years of operation in 1988. This group holds an internationally recognized divers' show in Toronto every spring.

Scientific Diving Scientists in such fields as ARCHAEOLOGY, BIOLOGY, CHEMISTRY, GEOLOGY, marine ecology, OCEANOGRAPHY and PHYSICS use diving to make observations and gather data. Canadian researchers are prominent in the Scientific Division of the CMAS, the world federation which was established to promote interest in underwater studies and to advance the techniques and safety of diving. Canadian scientists and technicians are gaining world recognition for underwater studies carried out in challenging circumstances. Canadian arctic oil development prompted increased research and technological advances in areas such as oil and ice interaction.

Various federal departments and agencies such as Environment Canada, the Environment Protection Service, Fisheries and Oceans, and Energy, Mines and Resources use divers in scientific research. Such divers install and recover recording instruments; help maintain study platforms, canals and locks; collect bottom samples, water samples, fish or invertebrates for analysis; and make surveillance dives in environmentally sensitive areas. One Environment Canada, Parks group has logged thousands of diving hours locating and excavating historic underwater sites. Noteworthy are *San Juan*, a BASQUE whaling galleon sunk in RED BAY, Lab, in 1565, and *Machault*, one of 3 French supply ships sunk in Baie des Chaleurs in 1763. The American WAR OF 1812 frigates, *Hamilton* and *Scourge*, and BREADALBANE, an arctic expedition supply ship sunk in the NORTHWEST PASSAGE in 1853, are being investigated by privately funded groups under observation by Environment Canada, Parks (*see* J.B. MACINNIS). Environment Canada, Parks maintains a support system that includes a 150-ton research barge equipped with low-pressure compressors to supply airlifts, with generators to supply underwater lights, a recompression chamber, and offices and workshop facilities. The ROYAL ONTARIO MUSEUM used divers to recover artifacts found along the voyageur fur-trading routes and, in 1971, commissioned the search for *Hamilton* and *Scourge*. Canada is becoming an internationally recognized leader in underwater archaeology as a result of these enterprises.

Military Diving The work of military divers ranges from being clearance divers on board government vessels to performing classified defence tasks. The Defence and Civil Institute of Environmental Medicine (DCIEM) is a multidisciplinary laboratory of the Dept of National Defence. It provides for testing and development of personal diving equipment, training of military personnel, and research and development into the problems associated with human underwater operations.

VALERIE I. MACDONALD

Reading: Reg Vallintine, *Divers and Diving* (1981).

Dixon, Frederick Augustus, playwright, journalist, civil servant (b at London, Eng 7 May 1843; d at Ottawa 12 Jan 1919). Educated at King's School, Canterbury, he came to Canada in the 1870s and worked as a journalist in Toronto. During the time of the Dufferins at RIDEAU HALL (1872-78) he was appointed tutor to their 4 sons. On their departure he joined the Dept of Public Works; at the time of his death he was chief clerk of correspondence in the Dept of Railways and Canals. At Rideau Hall he wrote children's plays of wit and imagination for 4 of the Dufferins' New Year's Day festivities. He also wrote a libretto for the popular *The Maire of St Brieux: An Operetta in One Act* (1875) with music by Frederick W. Mills, performed at Rideau Hall in 1875, and *A Masque entitled Canada's Welcome* (1879) for the arrival of the next gov gen, the marquis of Lorne, and his wife Princess Louise, with music by Arthur A. Clappé. He continued to write plays, contributed articles to Canadian and British magazines, and collaborated on travel books on Canada. He was instrumental in the formation of the Royal Academy of Art in Canada. JAMES NOONAN

Dixon Entrance is a strait between the QUEEN CHARLOTTE ISLANDS, on the N coast of BC, and Prince of Wales and Dall islands in Alaska. About 65 km wide, it connects the Pacific Ocean with HECATE STR and the inside coastal passages. It was named for George Dixon, whose exploration of the BC coast in the 1780s helped to initiate the maritime fur trade. DANIEL FRANCIS

Dobsonfly, large, soft-bodied, freshwater insect of order Megaloptera, family Corydalidae; smaller forms are called fishflies. Dobsonflies have 2 pairs of veined membranous wings, chewing mouthparts, long, many-segmented antennae and 3 simple eyes. Dobsonflies are primarily nocturnal; closely related ALDERFLIES are smaller and diurnal. Dobsonflies deposit 2000-3000 dark brown eggs in rows forming large masses on objects near rapidly flowing water. Larvae hatch in 10-14 days, make their way into water and usually settle under stones or other debris. While adults do not feed and are short-lived, larvae are predaceous and take 2-3 years to develop. Fully grown larvae leave the water to pupate in a cell in soil, moss, under stones, etc. Adults, appearing in early summer, are feeble fliers usually found near water. Six species occur in Canada: *Corydalis cornutus*, with wingspread of about 125 mm, is perhaps the best-known eastern species. Males have hornlike mandibles often 25 mm long. Larvae and adults are food for many fish and bait for anglers, particularly larvae of *C. cornutus* (sometimes called hellgrammite). J.E.H. MARTIN

Dock, herbaceous plant of genus *Rumex*, family Polygonaceae (BUCKWHEAT); most docks are perennial. Some species are called sorrels. About 150 species occur worldwide; of 22 in Canada, about half are native. In the Northern Hemisphere, most docks are common WEEDS. The greenish flowers, at the top of the plant, turn reddish brown at maturity. The seeds are smooth, brown and 3-sided. Curled dock (*R. crispus*), one of the 5 most widely distributed plants in the world, is a troublesome weed in disturbed land in all provinces. Its long, narrow leaves have crumpled, wavy margins. Broad-leaved dock (*R. obtusifolius*) occurs in damper, partly shaded sites in eastern Canada and BC. Across the prairies, field dock (*R. pseudonatronatus*) is more common than curled dock. Sheep sorrel (*R. acetosella*) occurs on impoverished lands in all provinces. This slender plant, 15-30 cm high, has sour, acid-tasting leaves, each with 2 basal lobes on a long stalk. The larger, "narrow-leaved" garden sorrel (*R. triangulivalvis*) is abundant along the lower St Lawrence. Leaves of sorrel species can be eaten like spinach. Indians valued leaves and taproots for medicinal properties. *See also* PLANTS, NATIVE USES. PAUL B. CAVERS

Documentary Film, see FILM, DOCUMENTARY.

Dofasco Inc, fd 1912 as Dominion Steel Castings, Ltd in Hamilton, Ont. It poured its first heat of steel in 1912 and cast locomotive frames, axle boxes and mud rings for the CPR. In 1920 the company diversified into flat rolled steel and 15 years later began production of the first tinplate in Canada. In 1954 the company pioneered in N America the use of the oxygen furnace. The company changed its name to Dominion Foundries and Steel, Ltd (Dofasco) in 1980. Present production is about 4.5 million ingot tons of steel per year. Products include hot rolled, cold rolled, galvanized, tinplate, electrical steels, chromium coated steel and steel castings. Dofasco produces mainly steel sheet for the AUTOMOTIVE INDUSTRY. The company's 12 800 Hamilton employees have enjoyed profit sharing since 1938, employee recreation programs since the early 1940s, and a comprehensive medical program and employee suggestion system since 1936. Subsidiaries include National Steel Car of Hamilton and Prudential Steel of Calgary. Mining interests include the Adams mine in Kirkland Lake, Sherman Mine in Temagami, Wabush Mines in Labrador and the IRON ORE COMPANY OF CANADA. In 1986, company revenues were $1.9 billion and assets amounted to $2.8 billion. *See also* IRON AND STEEL INDUSTRIES.

Dog (*Canis familiaris*), carnivorous MAMMAL, probably the first domesticated animal. Many separate domestications occurred in different places beginning 10 000 to 20 000 years ago. The main progenitor was the WOLF; the jackal may also have contributed. In N America, local dog stocks may have derived in part from the COYOTE. These wild species can interbreed with dogs and produce fertile progeny. Despite persistent folk stories, hybridization between dogs and foxes is not successful and foxes cannot be considered ancestral to any dog breed.

Dogs were kept by native peoples throughout Canada in the centuries before European exploration and settlement. They had various uses: for transportation and draft work, hunting, clothing materials and sometimes human food. Inuit dogs are still used to pull sleds and carry backpacks; they are also used in SEALING and to provide protection from polar bears. Canadian Plains Indians relied on dogs for transportation (eg, by dog travois) until they acquired horses in the early 1700s; their breeds are now extinct. On the West Coast, the Salish kept a small, woolly type of dog, using the hair for weaving; it became extinct by about 1860. Dogs were also important in religion; the White Dog Festival, observed by some eastern tribes, required the sacrifice of dogs of a special breed. Dogs have been an important domestic animal wherever people have settled. Hundreds of distinctive breeds developed over the centuries, partly through regional isolation and partly through conscious selection by humans. Several hundred breeds are currently named and recognized by various kennel clubs; some, eg, Poodles, German Shepherd Dogs and Irish Setters, have worldwide distribution. The

Canadian dog breeds: Eskimo Dog (upper left); Nova Scotia Duck Tolling Retriever (lower left); Tahltan Bear Dog (centre); Newfoundland (upper right) and Labrador Retriever (lower right) (*artwork by L. Shaw*).

Canadian Kennel Club (CKC), which maintains registration records for Canadian purebred dogs, officially recognizes 143 breeds. Several other breeds are present but are not formally registered. The recognized breeds are classified into groups generally indicating the purpose for which they were developed: sporting dogs, hounds, working dogs, terriers, toys, nonsporting dogs and herding dogs. A miscellaneous category is for breeds in the process of achieving full recognition.

Canadian Breeds

Five of the breeds recognized by the CKC can be claimed to be uniquely Canadian: the Tahltan Bear Dog, the Canadian Eskimo Dog, the Nova Scotia Duck Tolling Retriever, the Newfoundland and the Labrador Retriever. The last 2 have Canadian names but owe most of their development to breeders in Great Britain and Europe.

Tahltan Bear Dog, kept by the Tahltan Indians of northwestern BC, was a small dog, probably of the Spitz family, with a foxy head and erect bat ears. Its distinctive, medium-length tail was carried erect and ended in a wide brush. Most were white with black patches. They were used for hunting bear and lynx. The breed was recognized by the CKC in 1940, but only 9 dogs were ever registered. There are none left in Tahltan country, and those that were registered have long since died. Breeders continue to search for survivors, without much hope of success.

Canadian Eskimo Dog When SNOWMOBILES were introduced to the Arctic, the need for sled dogs rapidly diminished. It soon became evident that the Eskimo dogs which had been kept by people of the Thule culture for 1100-2000 years were facing extinction. The breed had been recognized by the CKC but registered stock had not persisted. The Eskimo Dog Research Foundation was formed to re-establish the breed. A few dogs of the original type were obtained from remote Inuit camps in Boothia Pen, Melville Pen and Baffin I. They were taken to Yellowknife to form the nucleus of a breeding colony. This stock has now been accepted for registration by the CKC under the revised name "Canadian Eskimo Dog." Many

have been returned to the Inuit. They are intermediate in speed and strength to the Siberian Husky and Alaskan Malamute. They are sled and backpack dogs and are useful in hunting.

Nova Scotia Duck Tolling Retriever, a small breed familiar to Canadians, is almost unknown in other countries. To "toll" means to entice game to approach by arousing curiosity. A tolling dog is trained to play along the shoreline, attracting inquisitive ducks to swim within gunshot range; the dog is then sent into the water to retrieve the birds. In the late 19th century, a breed with these characteristics was developed in Yarmouth County, NS. Several breeds and crosses were used in its development. The dogs are rather foxlike in colour and activity and are intermediate in size and conformation to spaniels and retrievers.

Newfoundlands may have originated in dogs kept by native peoples, or may be traced to dogs brought by the Vikings about 1000 AD. There probably was later admixture with dogs brought to the island by Basque and Portuguese fishing fleets. British visitors were attracted to the big black dogs and took some of them back to England, where they became very popular. The heavy, long-coated dogs are excellent swimmers and are renowned as family companions and guardians. A black and white variety was depicted by Sir Edwin Landseer in his famous painting *A Distinguished Member of the Humane Society* and the variety has since become known as the Landseer.

Labrador Retriever These dogs, probably from the same stock as the Newfoundland, were shaped into a distinctive breed by the English nobility, who selected them for smaller size, finer bone and a short coat. Other sporting breeds were crossed into the stock. The breed is one of the best gundogs in existence and is used as a "seeing-eye" dog. Most are black but other colours (yellow, chocolate and cream) have become popular.

Most dogs in Canada are kept as pets. Many purebred dogs provide recreation and employment for people participating in competitive events governed by the CKC. Such competitions include conformation shows, obedience trials, field trials for hounds and sporting breeds, tracking tests, and the new spectator sports, lure coursing and scent hurdle racing. Sportsmen use various specially bred and trained breeds for hunting upland GAME BIRDS, WATERFOWL and small mammals. Greyhounds and wolfhounds are used in western Canada to hunt coyotes and wolves.

Many kinds of dogs actively work for man. Sled dogs are useful in the North. Border Collies retain their superiority for sheepherding, and the Komondor breed is being used experimentally in western Canada to guard flocks. Australian Cattle Dogs, formerly known as Queensland Heelers, are gaining popularity with Canadian cattlemen for driving livestock. The German Shepherd Dog, Doberman Pinscher and Bouvier des Flandres are widely used in police and military work and as guard dogs. *Schutzhund* (protection dog) training is increasing in Canada. It involves intensive schooling in obedience, tracking and defence. The most remarkable dogs are those trained to guide the blind; several hundred, many from training schools in Ontario and Edmonton, are at work in Canada helping their blind owners to lead more normal lives. Several breeds are used, including German Shepherd Dogs, Labrador Retrievers, Boxers and Collies. R.D. CRAWFORD

Reading: Canadian Kennel Club, *The Canadian Kennel Club Book of Dogs* (1982).

Dog Sledding is a method of winter travel developed by northern native peoples and adopted by early European explorers and trappers as the most efficient way to haul goods across snow-covered terrain. Teams of 2 to 12 or more dogs are commonly tied in pairs to a single towline, or gangline. The gangline is attached to a sled, and the dogs pull the sled across the snow. When crossing trackless terrain in deep snow, dogs may be placed in single file to follow the driver breaking a narrow trail in snowshoes. In the Arctic where the snow pack is hard, Inuit often use the "fan" hitch where each dog is attached to the sled by its own towline.

The first 1 or 2 dogs of a team are the leaders and guide the team. They are controlled by voice commands from the driver who either rides the rear of the sled or walks ahead or behind. Early French Canadian drivers called "Marche!" to spur their teams. This was misinterpreted by English explorers as "mush" — henceforth drivers were called "mushers."

Sleds vary with the people who make them and the snow conditions. In the Arctic the Inuit developed the heavy "komatik" designed to carry loads over rough terrain. Farther south, Indians made the flat-bottomed TOBOGGAN to haul loads through deep snow. Europeans modified these designs and developed the basket sled with its load raised off the snow and supported by 2 narrow runners for hauling over packed trails.

Although the SNOWMOBILE ("mechanical dog" in Inuktitut) has replaced the dog team in many ways, dog sledding has become a popular winter sport enjoyed by sled dog enthusiasts. Races are held across Canada, usually in association with winter carnivals. The sport helps preserve many breeds of northern working dog.

DON H. MEREDITH

Reading: L. Coppinger, *The World of Sled Dogs* (1977).

Dogrib, Their name for themselves is *Doné*, meaning "the People." They fall within the broader designation of DENE, tribes of the widespread Athapaskan language family. To distinguish themselves from their Dene neighbours — CHIPEWYAN, SLAVEY, BEARLAKE and HARE — they have come to identify themselves as "dog's rib," although the epithet derives from a Cree term for Athapaskan speakers. Dogrib lands lie E of the Mackenzie R between Great Slave Lk and Great Bear Lk in the NWT. From a population of about 800 (mid-19th century), the Dogrib numbered some 1700 by 1970, and over 1900 in 1986.

From aboriginal times to the present, Dogrib have hunted the barren-ground CARIBOU in the boreal forest during winter and followed them to the edge of the barrens in spring, where they meet

Western flowering dogwood (*Cornus nuttallii*), with flowers and fruits (*artwork by Claire Tremblay*).

them again in the fall. Moose and hare of the forest, and fish, are also important food resources. Extended kinship ties have allowed easy movement of families from one BAND group to another. In earlier times, supernatural powers gained through the aid of animal-spiritual beings were experienced by many persons. Hunting prowess coupled with generous concern for the well-being of the group, wisdom, oratorical skills and "medicine" power led to authority and leadership.

Dogrib began to be drawn into the FUR TRADE around the beginning of the 19th century. However, Ft Rae (1852), on the North Arm of Great Slave Lk, was the first trading post established on their lands. Roman Catholic missionaries began the conversion of Dogrib in 1859. In the early 19th century, Dogrib were intimidated and attacked by Yellowknife. In 1823 the massacre by Dogrib of Long Leg's Yellowknife band broke the threat. Dogrib oral tradition tells that, a few years later, the Dogrib Edzo and a few companions met the great Yellowknife leader, Akaitcho, and his band, and by medicine power and oratorical force brought a lasting peace.

The establishment of day schools at all Dogrib settlements (late 1950s) has facilitated access to advanced schooling and preparation for nontraditional occupations. Ft Rae has been transformed into a year-round settlement (Rae-Edzo complex) for hundreds of Dogrib. Other, smaller settlements include Detah, near the city of Yellowknife, and

hamlets at Lac la Martre, Rae Lakes and Snare Lk. In the isolated hamlets the traditional reliance on hunting, fishing and fur trapping remains vital. *See also* NATIVE PEOPLE: SUBARCTIC and general entries under NATIVE PEOPLE. JUNE HELM

Reading: June Helm, ed *Handbook of North American Indians*, vol 6: Subarctic (1981).

Dogwood (Cornaceae), family of perennial herbaceous plants, trees and shrubs, represented in N America by about 15 members of the genus *Cornus*. The genus comprises approximately 45 species, found mainly in N temperate regions. Of the 10 species native to Canada, 2 are herbaceous, the most familiar and smallest species being Canadian dogwood or bunchberry (*C. canadensis*). It is very common in the boreal forest, but also occurs across southern Canada. This species has 4-6 large, white bracts resembling petals, which attract insects to the dense flowerhead composed of small, greenish flowers. Its red fruit is edible. Most dogwoods are shrubs or small trees; however, Pacific or western flowering dogwood (*C. nuttallii*), the PROVINCIAL FLORAL EMBLEM of BC since 1956, grows to 25 m. It flowers Apr-May, before the leaves appear; flowers form a head supported by 4-6 white or pinkish bracts measuring 10-12 cm across. This tree, which prefers shade, is covered with bunches of red fruit and brilliantly coloured foliage in autumn. The very hard wood can be used to make small items (eg, mallet heads, piano keys). Several dogwood shrubs are popular ORNAMENTALS, growing easily in well-drained soil.

CÉLINE ARSENEAULT

Doherty, Charles Joseph, lawyer, educator, judge, politician (b at Montreal 11 May 1855; d there 28 July 1931). Educated at McGill, he later taught civil and international law there for many years while practising law. He served as a judge of the Quebec Superior Court 1891-1906. He entered federal politics and was an MP 1908-21 and minister of justice and attorney general 1911-21 in the administrations of PMs BORDEN and MEIGHEN. He was Canadian representative at the Versailles Peace Conference 1918-19 and Canadian delegate to the League of Nations 1920-22. He is credited with initiating the CANADIAN BAR ASSN in 1912 and was its first honorary president in 1914. Doherty was appointed to the Imperial Privy Council in 1921.

JOHN E.C. BRIERLEY

Dolbeau, Qué, Town, pop 8554 (1986c), 8762 (1981c), inc 1927, is located at the confluence of the Mistassini and Mistassibi rivers (Lac SAINT-JEAN), opposite the city of MISTASSINI. Named after Jean Dolbeau, a priest who served the Montagnais mission at Tadoussac, Dolbeau was born when the Lake St John Pulp & Paper Co, an American firm later bought out by the Canadian company Domtar, decided to build a paper mill on the Rivière Mistassibi. The factory owners also built a city to house their employees, making Dolbeau a company town whose charter, modelled on that of Arvida, contained some deviations from the Québec law for cities and towns. After WWII, Dolbeau became the major service centre, including a hospital (1955) for the area N of Lac Saint-Jean. It is also home to one of the few astronomic observatories in the province, and the site each July of a province-wide western festival.

MARC ST-HILAIRE

Dollar, Canada's currency, or MONEY. As money, it is the measure of value in which all prices are expressed. However, the term "Canadian dollar" is also used to relate the value of our currency to another country's currency through the EXCHANGE RATE.

Under the current, flexible exchange rate system, the value of the Canadian dollar is continuously determined by trading in the foreign exchange market. Trading is mostly carried out by CHARTERED BANKS and large corporations and is centered in Toronto, Montréal and New York. From day to day, the value of the Canadian dollar is affected by news regarding important economic events, changes in expectations about Canada's economic prospects and government actions. Over longer periods, the dollar's value is related to the cost of Canadian goods relative to comparable foreign goods. When Canadian prices rise (INFLATION) faster than foreign prices, the dollar's value falls relative to foreign currencies. If Canadian prices rise more slowly than foreign prices, the dollar's value rises.

The value of the dollar is important to Canadians for 2 reasons. First, because Canada is a trading nation, changes in the value of our currency affect the prices of the goods we sell to foreigners as well as those we buy from them. As the value of the Canadian dollar rises, our exports become more expensive, reducing foreign demand and causing domestic UNEMPLOYMENT. The Canadian prices of imported goods are reduced, reducing the rate of inflation. When the value of the Canadian dollar falls, foreigners demand more of our exports, reducing unemployment. The prices of imported goods rise, raising the rate of inflation. The second reason is that changes in the value of the Canadian dollar affect Canadians' financial dealings (both as lenders and borrowers) with foreigners. A rise in the value of the Canadian dollar reduces the cost of paying foreign loans

and the return on Canadians' investments abroad. A fall in the dollar's value has the opposite effect.

The government affects the value of the Canadian dollar in 2 ways. By buying or selling Canadian dollars in the market (called foreign exchange market intervention) the government can change the value of the Canadian dollar over short periods. A more long-lasting effect can be achieved by using MONETARY POLICY. In this case the government changes Canadian interest rates, changing the attractiveness of investing in Canada. This, in turn, affects the demand for, and ultimately the value of, the Canadian dollar.

PAUL BOOTHE

Dollar-a-Year Man, a term used during WWII to describe those business executives who were brought to Ottawa to work in government, largely in the Department of MUNITIONS AND SUPPLY and in the WARTIME PRICES AND TRADE BOARD. Their salaries were paid by their companies, while Ottawa provided living expenses.

J.L. GRANATSTEIN

Dollard Des Ormeaux, Adam, soldier (b in France 1635; d at Long Sault May 1660). In late Apr 1660, 17 Frenchmen with Dollard in command left Montréal to ambush Iroquois hunters returning by the Ottawa R. They were joined by 44 Hurons and Algonquins. At the foot of Long Sault rapids, they were soon discovered by the advance guard of 300 Iroquois. The allies took refuge in a derelict enclosure, where they were besieged for a week while the Iroquois summoned reinforcements. The Hurons deserted, water failed and when a gunpowder keg exploded within the palisade, the defenders were overwhelmed. Nine survived to be ritually tortured and eaten. Nineteenth-century historians converted the battle into a religious and nationalistic epic in which zealous Roman Catholics deliberately sacrificed themselves to fend off an attack on New France. Revenge, trophies and captives were the traditional goals of Iroquoian warfare and the Iroquois probably returned home well satisfied.

PETER N. MOOGK

Dollier de Casson, François, explorer, superior of the Sulpicians in New France (1670-74, 1678-1701), seigneur of Montréal, vicar general, historian (b in the château of Casson-sur-l'Erdre in Lower Brittany 1636; d at Montréal 27 Sept 1701). After 3 years' military service, Dollier joined the Sulpicians in Paris and was sent to Canada in 1666. He became military chaplain and then parish priest at Trois-Rivières, and in 1669 he undertook a missionary trip south of the Great Lakes. In 1670 he was named superior of the Sulpicians and seigneur of Montréal. He devoted himself to organizing the city, constructing a church and completing his *Histoire du Montréal*, an important document in French Canada's historiography. Respected for his humanity, energy and understanding of the colony's problems, he competently fulfilled his religious duties and tried to improve education in Montréal. After 1680 Dollier helped with the Lachine Canal project, and established a conciliatory climate for relations between the colony's civil and religious authorities.

JACQUES MATHIEU

Dolphin and Porpoise, common names for small, toothed mammals of the order CETACEA which also includes WHALES. They are known from all oceans and many major river systems. In N America dolphins, with long snouts, are distinguished from porpoises, with blunt heads, but the terms are sometimes applied interchangeably to many small toothed whales, including members of the families Delphinidae, Phocoenidae, Ste-

nidae and Platanistidae. Five species are common in Canada. Harbour porpoise (*Phocoena phocoena*) is especially abundant in the lower Bay of Fundy and parts of the Gulf of St Lawrence. This, one of the smallest Northern Hemisphere cetaceans, has a relatively high metabolic rate and a short life span (about 13 years). Unlike some dolphins and porpoises, it does not live in large social aggregations, nor does it normally engage in aerial displays. Dall porpoise (*Phocoenoides dalli*), native to the N Pacific, occurs along the BC coast. Its colour pattern is reminiscent of the killer whale (*Orcinus orca*) which, at 9.5 m and 8000 kg, is the largest delphinid. Three species of temperate-region dolphins occur in Canadian waters; all are gregarious and sometimes acrobatic. White-beaked dolphins (*Lagenorhynchus albirostris*) and Atlantic white-sided dolphins (*L. acutus*), both endemic to the N Atlantic, have overlapping ranges between Cape Cod and Davis Str. Their N Pacific relative is the Pacific white-sided dolphin (*L. obliquidens*). The bottlenose dolphin (*Tursiops truncatus*), popular in animal exhibits, generally does not range into Canadian waters. Most captive specimens come from Florida or the Gulf of Mexico region.

R. REEVES AND E.D. MITCHELL

Dome Petroleum Limited was a Canadian energy company with head offices in Calgary. Started in 1950 as Dome Exploration (Western) Ltd, the company became Dome Petroleum Limited in 1958 and grew by making acquisitions in the energy industry. Most famous was the 1981 acquisition of Hudson's Bay Oil and Gas Company Limited: Dome acquired a 52.9% interest through its wholly owned subsidiary, Dome Energy Limited. However, with increasing debts from past takeovers and a changed economic situation, Dome made history in 1982-83 by receiving substantial loans from 4 Canadian chartered banks and by having the federal government intervene in its affairs. The company's activities were divided between 2 entities: Dome Petroleum explored for, developed, produced and marketed crude oil, natural gas and natural gas liquids in Canada and the US, and HBOG handled natural resource exploration and development. The company explored mainly in western Canada, the Beaufort Sea and the arctic islands. In 1983 its revenues were $2.6 billion, dropping to $1.6 billion in 1986; 1983 assets were $8.2 billion, dropping to almost $5 billion in 1986. The number of employees dropped from 6500 in 1983 to 3800 in 1986. Foreign ownership of the company, 42% in 1983, stood at 60% in 1986. Dome's problems worsened as a result of the 1986 drop in world oil prices. In Nov 1987, after months of negotiation, an agreement in principle was reached to enable Amoco Canada Petroleum Co Ltd to buy Dome for $5.5 billion.

DEBORAH C. SAWYER

Domestic Service, a predominantly female occupation, was the most common paid employment for Canadian women before 1900: in 1891 there were nearly 80 000 women servants in Canada. With the expansion in the 20th century of factory, office and shopwork for women, the proportion of the female work force in domestic service decreased (from 41% in 1891 to 18% in 1921). The decline was most pronounced after WWII and was accompanied by an increase in shifts from live-in to live-out and part-time work. Most live-in domestics were young women who did general work in one- or 2-servant households; a small minority had specialized positions as part of a large staff.

Employers hired domestic servants to confirm middle-class status as well as to obtain needed help. The private employment conditions and general devaluation of housework made domestic service unpopular. Objections to low social status, unregulated hours, isolation and lack of independence remained unchanged over time. A shortage of Canadian domestic servants led to the employment of immigrant women from Britain, Scandinavia, central Europe and, after WWII, the West Indies and the Philippines. In the 19th and early 20th centuries, British child-emigration societies as well as Canadian orphanages placed girls in service (*see* CHILD LABOUR). The policy of welcoming immigrant domestics as permanent residents and future wives changed in the 1970s when the government introduced temporary employment visas which allowed domestics to stay in Canada only for a limited period and only on condition that they retain domestic employment.

The vulnerability of immigrants augmented the difficulty of improving conditions for workers in isolated, usually temporary, employment. The domestic-science movement in the early 20th century unsuccessfully tried to professionalize domestic service by raising standards. Early domestic-servant organizations in Vancouver and Toronto were short-lived, but beginning in the 1970s union activity has achieved immigration reform and some legislative control of employment standards.   MARILYN BARBER

Reading: B.D. Palmer, *Working-Class Experience* (1983).

Domestic Utensils may be classified into those used in the preparation of food and those employed in the cleaning of clothing and household furnishings. For many years after the settlement of Canada, household utensils were made by local craftsmen and BLACKSMITHS. By the middle of the 19th century more sophisticated devices were in use, most of them imported from Britain or the US.

Kitchen Utensils Much of the preparation of food (eg, peeling and slicing of vegetables, cutting of meat) was done with simple knives. Sausages were popular because they could be preserved, but it was necessary that the sausage meat be well minced and thoroughly mixed with the spices and seasoning that provided flavour and preservation. Cutting and mixing could be done in a wooden bowl, using a knife with the handle behind the blade rather than at one end. Patented chopping knives appeared late in the 19th century, with multiple or removable blades.

Mechanical devices for chopping or grinding meat and vegetables were imported from about 1860. These implements were hollow iron cylinders containing rotary shafts with teeth. By the end of the century, they had evolved into the familiar food grinder, in which a screwlike revolving shaft cut the meat and forced it through a perforated end plate, with or without cutting edges. A grinder of this type, identical with those still in use, was patented in Canada by L.T. Snow in 1897.

The ground sausage meat was usually wrapped in cloth bags and stored in a cool place until needed. Settlers of German origin preferred to make sausages in the familiar "links" by forcing the ground meat into a case (length of washed intestine) with a "sausage gun," ie, a metal cylinder with a narrow spout at one end and a wooden plunger at the other. More elaborate stuffers used a piston and lever; some were of wood and were made locally, but cast-iron stuffers appeared about 1850, with either a lever or a screw for applying pressure. The full case was tied at intervals into the sausage links.

Slicers were used with vegetables, most commonly with cabbage used for sauerkraut. They included the shredding board, which had a diagonal slot over which a cutting blade was mounted. The cabbage head was pushed down the board, and slices were cut off by the knife and fell through the slot into a pan. Plastic slicers of this design are still in use.

Stove from the Forges Saint-Maurice at Trois-Rivières, Canada's first ironworks, which began production in the 1730s. The cooking stove was first introduced in the 1830s (*courtesy National Museums of Canada/Canadian Museum of Civilization*).

Apples were widely available in 19th century Canada and were commonly preserved as dried slices. This method of preservation required paring, ie, removal of the skin. Paring could be done by hand with a sharp knife, although this technique was slow and semi-mechanical parers came into use at an early stage. Such implements might consist of a fork (on which the apple was impaled) turned by a handle or pulley. The knife edge was held against the revolving apple. By 1803 an apple parer with a knife mounted on an arm with a universal joint had appeared. Parers of this type were being made and used in Canada about 1840. Beginning about 1849 a host of mechanical metal parers appeared in the US and were soon in use in Canada. The cutting blade was attached to a threaded shaft or a set of gears, which caused the tool to travel across the surface of the apple as it was rotated by a hand crank. These utensils were later elaborated with the addition of a coring attachment and an arm to push off the pared apple.

Until about 1830 cooking was almost always done in an open fireplace. One of the problems was providing stability for the cooking utensils. Pots for stews or tea water had curved handles by which they were suspended from a swinging bar called a crane. A more reliable means of support was the trivet, an iron ring large enough to hold the pot and having 3 vertical legs that could be set in the fire. The trivet could be combined with the frying pan or skillet by attaching legs directly to the pan bottom; this combination was called a spider. Cooking pots were also made with permanently attached legs.

Meat could be cooked on a grill, an arrangement of parallel iron bars, spaced close enough to support the meat but far enough apart to provide exposure to the flames. In some grills, the bars were little troughs along which juices from the cooking meat could flow to a collecting cup at one end of the grill. Grills were usually supported on their own 4 legs. Roasting meat over the open fire was usually done on a spit, a horizontally mounted iron rod, which was thrust through the meat and supported on each side of the fire. The spit had to be turned to ensure uniform cooking; hence, the rod projected at one end beyond the heat of the fire, terminating in a handle or a pulley wheel. Meat could also be roasted by being suspended over the fire on a hook from the crane. To ensure uniform cooking a clock jack, ie, a powerful clockwork motor housed in a brass cylinder, might be used. Meat suspended below the jack was rotated back and forth automatically.

Introduction of the cooking stove in the 1830s fundamentally changed culinary techniques and

utensils. Pots, pans and skillets now had a solid base on which to rest. Degree of heat could be controlled by the position of the vessel on the stove top. If open flames were required, the lid could be removed from one of the pot holes and the vessel placed directly over the fire. The skillet without legs, renamed the frying pan, needed only a solid handle. Handles were made for lifting rather than for suspension. Grills and toasters could be placed directly over an open hole. Kettles were adapted by having the perimeter of the base recessed, to fit into the pot-hole rim.

The most fundamental change was the replacement of the fireplace oven by the stove oven. To heat the former, a fire had to be built in the oven, then removed, and the food introduced. The stove oven derived its heat directly from the firebox, which allowed for shorter cooking time and better temperature control. Cakes, pies and biscuits could be baked as well as bread; special baking pans and plates came into use. Roasting of meat could also be done in the oven, in large covered roasting pans.

In early years cooked food was usually served on plates of PEWTER, which is an alloy of lead and tin. Pewter, as preserved today, has the dull grey tarnish of time, but in the days of its use it was kept highly polished by scouring with wood ashes. Pewter spoons were cast in iron molds. Knives and forks were made of steel, and they had firmly attached wooden handles. Table knives were wiped on an abrasive scouring brick (a block of baked clay) to keep them free of rust or tarnish.

Laundry Utensils The change from fireplace to stove also altered the methods and utensils used in washing clothes. The large amounts of wash water needed could be heated on the stove in a washboiler, ie, an oval tub of sheet metal with a removable lid. The soiled clothes and the soap were dropped into the boiling water and stirred with a wooden stick or tongs. The actual washing was done on a low table in a circular tub, usually made of sheet metal but possibly of the lower half of a barrel. The traditional washboard was used, a corrugated surface on which the wet clothes were rubbed vigorously. After washing, the clothes were rinsed in clear water in the same tub.

Such scrubbing was one of the more tiring operations in laundering clothes. It was easier to use a plunger, an inverted sheet-metal funnel at the end of a wooden rod. Working this plunger up and down in the submerged clothes forced the hot soapy water into and out of the fabric. Improved plungers, eg, the double model, were patented in the 1880s. An ingenious version was invented in 1890 by Isaac Shupe of Newmarket, Ont. In Shupe's plunger the conical head was extended upward as a tube, which contained a spring-loaded piston with a valve. Soap was placed in the tube and, when the plunger was pushed down, the valve closed and water was squeezed through the clothes. On the upstroke the valve opened, releasing soap.

More elaborate washing devices combined a tub and manipulator, eg, a swinging set of slats, as in the Raulston (Ontario) patent of 1884, or a reciprocating rotary agitator, as in the Cadran (Quebec) patent of 1885. The latter arrangement has been retained in the modern automatic washer.

Before drying, washed clothes were wrung out, ie, squeezed free of excess water. Early in the 19th century, the old method of twisting by hand was replaced by the use of a set of rollers between which the saturated clothes were squeezed. These wringers persisted well into the time of the electric washing machine.

Ironing underwent an interesting development during the 19th century. In the fireplace era, the irons could not be heated directly without soiling the contact surface; therefore, they were hollow, with a removable core that could be heated separately and then placed inside the iron. Irons heated on a stove top could be solid, but this raised the problem of a handle too hot to hold. The difficulty was resolved in 1871 by Mrs Florence Potts of Iowa, who had already invented the double-pointed iron. The handle of the Potts iron was of wood, semicircular in shape, with a metal device at the base which could be latched or released on the top of the iron by lifting a small knob. Potts irons were manufactured in various Canadian foundries. Other irons with detachable handles were patented in the late 19th century, but the Potts iron outlasted them all. L.S. RUSSELL

Dominion refers primarily to Dominion of Canada (CONSTITUTION ACT, 1867, preamble and s3). The FATHERS OF CONFEDERATION wanted to call "the new nation" the Kingdom of Canada. The British Government feared this would offend the Americans, whom, after the stresses of the American Civil War, it was most anxious not to antagonize. It insisted on a different title. Sir Leonard TILLEY suggested "dominion": "He shall have dominion also from sea to sea, and from the river unto the ends of the earth" (Psalm 72:8). The Fathers said it was intended to give dignity to the federation, and as a tribute to the monarchical principle. The word came to be applied to the federal government and Parliament, and under the CONSTITUTION ACT, 1982, "Dominion" remains Canada's official title. EUGENE A. FORSEY

Dominion Arsenal, the first government cartridge and shell factory and proofing facility, est 1882 at Québec to provide the Canadian Militia with ammunition. A second arsenal was built in LINDSAY, Ont, during WWI, and other plants were built or converted to small arms and artillery-shell production during WWII by the Department of MUNITIONS AND SUPPLY. In Sept 1945 these were brought together as Canadian Arsenals Limited, a crown corporation now reporting to the Department of Supply and Services. STEPHEN HARRIS

Dominion Drama Festival (1932-39, 1947-78) was a co-lingual amateur theatre competition that bridged the 1930s collapse of foreign touring and the postwar emergence of Canada's professional THEATRE. On 29 Oct 1932, 60 theatre representatives gathered in RIDEAU HALL to hear Gov Gen Bessborough's brainchild and vote the DDF into existence. After regional preliminaries adjudged by a single travelling bilingual adjudicator, winners came together for an annual week-long spring festival where a second British or French adjudicator awarded coveted trophies for acting, design, direction, original writing and best production. The initial 5 festivals (Apr 1933-37) were held in Ottawa and then rotated between different cities. At first only one-act plays were presented, but by 1950 the DDF had transformed into a full-length play festival. Recurring financial problems necessitated the controversial patronage of Calvert's Distillers (1952-60) and the Canadian Assn of Broadcasters (1961-65), which in turn allowed an Ottawa office and the hiring of a permanent director. From 1960 Canadians were engaged to adjudicate preliminary runoffs and, after 1965, the finals as well. Centennial year was celebrated with an all-Canadian festival (62 plays, 29 premieres), but deficits loomed in 1969 and 1970, and the Amateurs of Québec formed a splinter association (ACTA). The DDF changed its name to Theatre Canada (May 1970) and sponsored 2 non-competitive "Showcase" festivals 1971 and 1972. However, these innovations were cancelled in 1973 for financial reasons, the same year the DDF's wry history, *Love and Whiskey*, had been published. By 1978 the Ottawa office was closed.

During the Depression and beyond, the DDF had been Canada's national theatre, fostering the writing of original plays and providing coast-to-coast training for hundreds of career-oriented actors, directors and technicians. Through the inspiration of its often distinguished European adjudicators, the DDF achieved some remarkable standards, and attracted loyal and fashionable audiences. However, it has been accused of perpetuating social and colonial values, and retarding the evolution of the professional theatre that supplanted it. DAVID GARDNER

Dominion Lands Policy When the Canadian government acquired RUPERT'S LAND from the Hudson's Bay Co and granted provincial status to Manitoba in 1870, it intended to use western natural resources and lands to promote western settlement and RAILWAY construction. Specific HOMESTEAD policies were devised to encourage settlers intending to establish themselves. The Dominion Lands Act of 1872, modelled on American homestead legislation, provided the legal authority under which lands were to be given to intending settlers in return for the payment of a small $10 fee and the performance of specified settlement duties, eg, building a habitable residence and cultivating a certain area annually. A simple, effective survey system divided the arable prairie lands into square townships, each comprisng 36 sections of 640 acres (259 ha), with the basic homestead comprising one 160-acre (64.75 ha) quarter section. Two sections in each township were reserved for the support of education, and a variety of grazing, haying and quarrying leases were available for lands not yet claimed for homesteading.

The Pacific railway, regarded as a national necessity, was to be financed through an elaborate system of land subsidies. Since it could not be completed without additional cash subsidies, the federal government also provided for the sale of Dominion lands at reduced prices to various COLONIZATION COMPANIES to provide the needed funds. In the 3 decades after 1870, settlement on the prairies was slow, but early in the 20th century it advanced rapidly. Prairie politicians regarded federal control over western Dominion lands and resources as an unfair intrusion into areas clearly given to provincial jurisdiction in the BRITISH NORTH AMERICA ACT. Negotiations undertaken to transfer control of the remaining western lands and resources to the provincial governments were completed in 1930. Thus ended the 60-year existence of Dominion lands. *See also* PRAIRIE WEST. T.D. REGEHR

Reading: C. Martin, *"Dominion Lands" Policy* (1938).

Dominion Police was originally a small protective force organized by the federal government in 1868 to guard the Parliament Buildings in Ottawa following the assassination of Thomas D'Arcy MCGEE. It also provided bodyguards for government leaders and operated an intelligence service whose agents infiltrated the FENIAN Brotherhood. Later the Dominion Police assumed responsibility for protecting naval dockyards at Halifax and Esquimalt (1911), the national fingerprint bureau (1911), the parole service and the enforcement of laws relating to counterfeiting and white slavery. During WWI its duties were expanded to co-ordinate the efforts of police and security agencies in Canada to enforce the provisions of the WAR MEASURES ACT. On 1 Feb 1920 the Dominion Police was absorbed by the RCMP. S.W. HORRALL

Dominion-Provincial Relations, Royal Commission on (Rowell-Sirois Report) A landmark in the development of Canadian FEDERALISM, the commission was established (1937) unilaterally by the federal government to re-examine "the economic and financial basis of Confederation and the distribution of legislative powers in the light of the economic and social developments of the last 70 years." Commonly named after its successive chairmen, N.W. Rowell and Joseph Sirois, the 3-volume report (1940) recommended a transfer of functions and a shifting of TAXATION power to the federal government and the creation of grants to the provinces to equalize provincial tax revenues, a principle enshrined in the 1982 Constitution. The federal government was to assume responsibility for unemployment insurance and contributory pensions, and full control of personal and corporate income taxes and succession duties, while taking responsibility for provincial debts. A program of National Adjustment Grants was to make payments to poorer provinces. On the grounds of administrative complexity, provincial autonomy and the need for legislative accountability, the commission rejected greater use of the shared-cost programs, which were to become a central device of postwar "co-operative federalism." WWII and opposition by some provinces prevented the adoption of many recommendations; others were introduced piecemeal. *See also* CONSTITUTIONAL PROBLEMS. RICHARD SIMEON

Dominion Securities Inc has carried on business as an investment dealer since 1901. Commencing in the early 1970s expansion of its operations accelerated significantly, through both internal growth and mergers with several other prominent Canadian investment dealers. In 1973 it merged with Harris & Partners Ltd, in 1977 with Draper Dobie Ltd, in 1981 with A.E. Ames & Co Ltd and in 1984 with Pitfield Mackay Ross Ltd. The firm engages in a broad range of investment services, including equity sales, trading and research, investment advice, bond sales and trading, funds management, lease financing, money market securities, financial advisory services, merger and acquisition assistance as well as underwriting of corporate and government securities. Business is conducted from head office in Toronto and a network of 61 branches in 58 cities in Canada as well as offices in New York, London, Paris, Geneva, Lausanne, Hong Kong and Tokyo, with a staff of more than 2000 people. With a capital of nearly $275 billion in 1986, the company ranked first among Canadian investment dealers. In Dec 1987 the Royal Bank purchased 75% control of the firm. ARTHUR E. GREGG

Dominion Stores Limited/Les Supermarchés Dominion Ltée, with head offices in Toronto, is a Canadian food distributor and merchandiser incorporated in 1919. The company was so named from 1976 to 1986 when it adopted the name Domgroup Ltd. Dominion grew by various acquisitions until 1983, when it acquired ARGUS CORPORATION's share of Standard Broadcasting Corp. That year Argus Corp increased its holdings in Dominion to 40%, and a government investigation of trading activities resulted. Dominion operated 390 grocery stores in 7 provinces (all its assets in Québec were sold in 1981) and, through subsidiaries, also operated convenience stores, delicatessens, drugstores and gas bars. In 1986 the Supreme Court of Ontario ordered the company to return $38 million it had withdrawn from the union pension fund. Later that year, it had sold, closed or franchised 43 supermarkets and most of its assets were held for sale. By Feb 1987, the dismantling and sale of the company were complete, bringing more than $300 million to its former owners. A & P Canada, the largest corporate grocery chain in eastern Canada, continues to operate some of the stores. DEBORAH C. SAWYER

Domtar Inc is a Canadian manufacturer of paper products with headquarters in Montréal.

Founded in 1929 as the Dominion Tar and Chemical Company Ltd to acquire the assets of a former business of the same name, the company became Domtar Ltd in 1965 and adopted its present name in 1977. It operates through 4 main groups – pulp and paper, construction, chemicals and packaging – producing a wide variety of products ranging from fine papers, envelopes and newsprint to construction materials, salts and special chemicals, and kraft papers and corrugated containers. Domtar operates plants in Canada, the US and the UK. In 1986 its revenues amounted to $2.3 billion, assets were $2.3 billion and employees numbered 15 332. DoFor Inc holds 28% of the shares and the CAISSE DE DÉPÔT ET PLACEMENT DU QUÉBEC 15%; foreign ownership stood at 8%.

DEBORAH C. SAWYER

Donalda, Pauline, stage name of Pauline Lightstone, soprano, teacher, administrator (b at Montréal 5 Mar 1882; d there 22 Oct 1970). Known for her contribution to lyrical art in Montréal, she was a pupil of Clara Lichtenstein and travelled to Paris on a grant from arts patron Lord STRATHCONA. With Massenet's help she made her debut in Nice in 1904. Later she performed at Covent Garden, sang with Caruso and, in 1906, made her professional Canadian debut at the Montreal Arena. She pursued her career in New York, at the Opéra-Comique in Paris and in Russia. In 1922 she devoted herself entirely to teaching. She settled in Montréal in 1937, where she founded the Opera Guild in 1942.

HÉLÈNE PLOUFFE

Donnacona, St Lawrence Iroquois leader (d in France probably in 1539), headman of the village of STADACONA [near Québec C] during Jacques CARTIER's voyages of 1534-36, protested when Cartier raised his cross in Gaspé in July 1534. He was seized, then fêted by Cartier and agreed to let his sons Domagaya and Taignoagy return with Cartier to France. In 1535 Cartier reached Stadacona and despite Donnacona's entreaties, pushed on to HOCHELAGA [Montréal]. Feeling betrayed, Donnacona broke off relations, leaving the French to fend for themselves during the ensuing winter. As scurvy ravaged the French, Domagaya was prompted to reveal the cure. Cartier used a dispute between Donnacona and a rival as a ruse to draw Donnacona into a meeting, seized him, his sons – 10 captives in all – and carried them off to France. Donnacona was presented to King Francis I, to whom he repeated tales of a rich Kingdom of Saguenay. Donnacona's death in France further embittered relations between the French and the inhabitants of Stadacona.

Donnell, David, poet, writer (b at St Mary's, Ont 1939). Donnell published his first poetry collection, *Poems*, in 1961. His second volume, *The Blue Sky*, did not appear until 1977. Then in 1979, after years spent in different factory and office jobs, he turned to writing full time. Recognition soon followed. He received the Canadian Comic Poet Award in 1981, followed in 1984 by the Governor General's Award for *Settlements*. Donnell's poetry speaks in the vernacular. Refreshingly accessible, it pulses with the realities of home, street and working life. He has published poems and art reviews in magazines, as well as a prose work *Hemingway in Toronto* (1982) and a short-story collection, *The Blue Ontario Hemingway Boat Race* (1985).

MARLENE ALT

Donnellys, The Early in the morning of 4 Feb 1880, a party of armed men brutally murdered James Donnelly, a farmer living near the village of LUCAN, Ont, his wife Johannah, his sons Thomas and John, and his niece Bridget Donnelly. Two eyewitnesses, 11-year-old Johnny O'Connor, and James Donnelly's eldest son, William,

claimed to have identified 6 of the murderers, who were subsequently brought to trial in nearby London. The case aroused international interest as it became known that the killings were the result of a factional feud originating in County Tipperary, Ire. In Canada, over the preceding 3 decades, the vendetta had claimed a heavy toll in lives and property. There were 2 trials of the accused men. At the first, in Sept 1880, the jury disagreed. A second jury, in Jan 1881, returned a directed verdict of "not guilty." A century later the case continues to excite interest and controversy. More than 100 factual and fictional accounts have appeared in recent years, the best known being T.P. Kelley, *The Black Donnellys* (1954); Orlo Miller, *The Donnellys Must Die* (1962); Ray Fazakas, *The Donnelly Album* (1977); and playwright James REANEY's Donnelly trilogy (1974-77).

ORLO MILLER

Doric Club, fd 1836 in Montréal, a paramilitary political association of young anglophone Tories. It replaced an earlier organization which, because of its armed contribution to political tensions in Montréal in the 1830s, was disbanded by Gov Gosford. A violent clash between the Doric Club and the patriote organization, the FILS DE LA LIBERTÉ, on 6 Nov 1837 was a prelude to the Lower Canadian Rebellions of 1837. The Doric Club dissolved when many of its members were recruited by Gen Colborne to fight the rebels.

Dorion, Sir Antoine-Aimé, lawyer, politican, judge (b at Ste-Anne-de-la-Pérade, LC 17 Jan 1818; d at Montréal 31 May 1891). A member of the Assembly of the Province of Canada 1854-61 and 1861-67, Dorion became a well-known PARTI ROUGE leader in the 1850s, praising American political institutions, supporting liberal ideas, promoting tariff reform and the colonization of virgin lands, and attacking financial and business interests as well as certain aspects of the Roman Catholic Church's presence in society. In 1858, CLEAR GRIT leader George BROWN formed a short-lived government with Dorion as leader for Canada E. He was also attorney general (Canada E) in the John Sandfield MACDONALD-Dorion ministry of 1863-64. Vigorously opposed to the CONFEDERATION project, however, he refused to adhere to the GREAT COALITION of 1864 that united Brown and the Clear Grits from Canada W with the Conservatives from both halves of the province. In Nov 1864, following the QUEBEC CONFERENCE, he denounced the projected federation as a disguised legislative union that would accord virtually no autonomy to the provinces even in matters of local concern. He also insisted that the people should be consulted, since it was their interest and prosperity that were clearly at stake. For the next 2 years Dorion led Lower Canadian opposition to the proposals.

Following Confederation, Dorion sat in the House of Commons until 1874 and was briefly minister of justice and attorney general in the Liberal government of Alexander MACKENZIE. In 1874 he was named chief justice of the Court of Queen's Bench of Québec.

RICHARD JONES

Dorion, Jean-Baptiste-Éric, journalist, politician, pioneer settler (b at Ste-Anne-de-la-Pérade, LC 17 Sept 1826; d at L'Avenir, Canada E 1 Nov 1866), brother of A.A. DORION. From a family that strongly supported liberal principles, he defended liberalism with such passion that his political adversaries nicknamed him "enfant terrible." On 17 Dec 1844, he helped found the INSTITUT CANADIEN in Montréal; with George Batchelor, he established the newspaper *L'Avenir*, the first edition of which appeared on 16 July 1847. Dorion used these 2 forums to express his views which became so radical after 1848 on issues such as the separa-

tion of church and state, nondenominational education and annexation of Canada by the US that in Nov 1852 the opposition to his demands obliged him to stop publishing *L'Avenir*. He withdrew to a community near Drummondville which he called L'Avenir where he was elected MP for Drummond-Arthabaska in 1854 and 1861. He argued at length on the disadvantages of CONFEDERATION in his newspaper *Le Défricheur*, which he founded in 1862.

PHILIPPE SYLVAIN

Dorset Culture, 500 BC-1500 AD, is known archaeologically from most coastal regions of arctic Canada. The Dorset people were descended from Paleoeskimos of the PRE-DORSET CULTURE. Compared to their ancestors, the Dorset people had a more successful economy and lived in more permanent houses built of snow and turf, heated with soapstone oil lamps. They may also have used dogsleds and KAYAKS. They lived primarily by hunting sea mammals and were capable of taking animals as large as walrus and narwhal. About 500 BC they moved down the Labrador coast and occupied the island of Newfoundland for about 1000 years. About 1000 AD they were displaced from most arctic regions by an invasion of THULE Inuit from Alaska, but they continued to live in northern Québec and Labrador until approximately 1500 AD. See also PREHISTORY.

ROBERT McGHEE

Reading: Robert McGhee, *Canadian Arctic Prehistory* (1978).

Dosquet, Pierre-Herman, Sulpician missionary, 4th bishop of Québec (b at Liège, Belgium 4 Mar 1691; d at Paris, France 4 Mar 1777). After serving with the Sulpicians and priests of the Missions étrangères, Dosquet was named administrator of the diocese of Québec in 1729 and coadjutor bishop in 1730. In Canada he attempted to restore the tithe to its normal rate, eradicate the brandy trade, reform monastic life and increase episcopal revenues. Titular bishop after 1733, he urged the priests to offer Latin instruction. He forbade schoolmasters to teach girls, and priests to wear wigs or employ young women domestics. He found the colonists undisciplined and materialistic; they regarded him as a foreigner. Despairing of restoring to his office and the clergy the power and prestige they traditionally could expect, he returned to France in 1735. Louis XV obtained his resignation only in 1739.

CORNELIUS J. JAENEN

Double Hook, The, by Sheila WATSON (Toronto, 1959), is described by some as Canada's first modern novel. *The Double Hook* departs from traditional plot, character development, form and style to tell a poetic tale of human suffering and redemption that is at once fabular, allegorical and symbolic. When James Potter kills his mother in the opening scene, he sets in motion the Potter family's struggle against fear – symbolized most dramatically by the figure of Coyote – and with various forms of withdrawal from community into isolation. James must discover "that when you fish for glory you catch the darkness too. That if you hook twice the glory you hook twice the fear." His return to his isolated community in the Rockies after first fleeing to town represents the rebirth of hope and the confrontation with fear which might knit the Potters into a human community. Watson weaves Christian myth, native legend and natural symbol into a profound prose poem. *The Double Hook* has been translated into French, as *Sous l'oeil de coyote* (Montréal, 1976), and Swedish.

NEIL BESNER

Double Majority, *see* MACDONALD, JOHN SANDFIELD.

Double Shuffle After the George-Étienne CARTIER-John A. MACDONALD ministry in the

PROVINCE OF CANADA was forced to resign on 29 July 1858, a Reform ministry was formed under George BROWN and A.A. DORION. Under parliamentary rules, newly appointed ministers were obliged to resign their seats and face a by-election; but this rule did not apply to a minister who resigned one office and took another within a month. When the Reform ministry fell on Aug 4 and Gov Gen Sir Edmund HEAD called upon Cartier and Macdonald to form a second government, each minister took a new portfolio on Aug 6 and resumed his former office on Aug 7. The notorious "double shuffle" allowed the Macdonald-Cartier ministry to retain power without facing by-elections.
DAVID MILLS

Dougall, Lily, novelist, religious writer (b at Montréal 16 Apr 1858; d at Cumnor, Eng 9 Oct 1923). In 1880 she went to Britain, deciding on permanent residence there in 1900. Her first story was published in 1889. Her first novel, *Beggars All* (1891), received critical and popular acclaim, as did *What Necessity Knows* (1893), one of 4 novels set in Canada. Her novels are carefully structured, with unusual plot twists, lively dialogue and flashes of humour. The characters usually face moral and ethical dilemmas. Dougall turned to religious writing with the anonymous essay *Pro Christo et Ecclesia* (1900), the first of 8 books on religious and theological topics. Farsighted in her views, she was concerned with the relationship between physical, psychological and spiritual health, and stressed Christianity's responsibility to adapt to new knowledge and to take a stand on contemporary issues.
LORRAINE MCMULLEN

Doughty, Sir Arthur George, archivist (b at Maidenhead, Eng 22 March 1860, d at Ottawa 1 Dec 1936). After considering a career in the church, he immigrated to Canada in 1886. Beginning in business, he quickly became an active figure in Montréal literary circles, publishing several works on Tennyson together with handsome volumes of his own poetry and establishing himself as a drama critic. He joined the Québec public service in 1897 becoming joint legislative librarian in 1901. The controversy over the precise location of the Battle of the PLAINS OF ABRAHAM first drew Doughty's attention to the neglected state of Canada's documentary heritage. A review of the differing interpretations of Canada's past presented in French and English history texts reinforced his determination to establish a comprehensive documentary foundation for a less biased, scientific HISTORIOGRAPHY. His efforts made him the obvious choice for the newly combined federal position of Dominion Archivist and Keeper of the Records in 1904.

Over the ensuing 31 years, Doughty established the Public Archives of Canada (now NATIONAL ARCHIVES OF CANADA) as a dynamic cultural institution. He had a genius for searching out significant historical materials. Official government records, the private manuscripts of colonial administrators, the Northcliffe Collection, the Durham Papers, transcripts of key documents in British, French and Canadian archives, historical artifacts, works of art and even WWI trophies and posters formed part of the collection he amassed, outgrowing both the archives building (1907) and an addition (1926). Exhibits, a circulating library of lantern slides, authoritative publications of selected documents, and an enthusiasm in assisting researchers encouraged a broad public to learn from the documentary record. The volumes he edited with Adam SHORTT of constitutional documents and the monumental history CANADA AND ITS PROVINCES (23 vols, 1913-17) have retained their influence for decades. Following his retirement (1935), he was named Dominion Archivist Emeritus and created KBE. The official statue erected in his honour remains a singular distinction among federal deputy ministers.
IAN E. WILSON

Douglas, Alexander Edgar, physicist (b at Melfort, Sask 12 Apr 1916; d at Ottawa 26 July 1981). Educated at the U of Saskatchewan and Pennsylvania State U, he joined the NATIONAL RESEARCH COUNCIL's physics division in 1941. For most of the period from 1949 until his retirement in 1980 he headed the SPECTROSCOPY section, which he and the director of the division, Gerhard HERZBERG (who had been his MA research supervisor) built into one of the foremost research laboratories in the field. His research has included the discovery of many new molecules and the analysis of their spectra; the identification of important features in the spectra of COMETS and of the interstellar medium; and the clarification of an important effect now known as the Douglas Effect in the dynamics of many polyatomic molecules. He was himself director of the Division of Physics from 1969 until 1973. He was a fellow of the Royal Society of Canada and was awarded the society's Henry Marshall Tory Medal, and a fellow of the Royal Society of London. He was also awarded the Medal for Achievement in Physics by the Canadian Assn of Physicists in 1970, and in 1975-76 served as president of the association.

Douglas, Alice Vibert, astronomer (b at Montréal 1894). Douglas received her doctorate from McGill in 1926. During WWI she was engaged in war work in England and then studied at the Cambridge Observatory and the Cavendish Laboratory 1921-23. On the McGill faculty until 1939, she became dean of women and later professor of astronomy at Queen's. Because of her interest in the history of astronomy and her personal knowledge of the man, she was asked to write the biography of Arthur Stanley Eddington. Published in 1956, it is still the only biography of this outstanding astronomer. An MBE (1918), Douglas was president of the Royal Astronomical Soc of Canada 1943-45 and of the International Federation of University Women 1947-50, and received honorary doctorates from McGill, Queen's and Queensland universities.
A.H. BATTEN

Douglas, Campbell Mellis, surgeon, soldier, writer, inventor and sportsman (b at Grosse Île, Qué 5 Aug 1840; d at Wells, Somerset, Eng 31 Dec 1909). Son of Dr George Douglas, superintendent of the GROSSE ÎLE quarantine station (1836-64), he was educated at St John's and Laval and the Edinburgh School of Medicine (MD, 1861). He entered the medical corps of the British army in 1862 and saw service in Burma, India and Canada. As medical officer to the expedition to the Little Andaman Is in 1867, he was awarded the VICTORIA CROSS for piloting a gig through a raging sea to relieve 17 of his comrades who were under attack by hostile natives. Upon his retirement from the military in 1882, he settled in Lakefield, Ont. He served as a medical officer during the NORTH-WEST REBELLION in 1885. His posting to Saskatoon was reached after a 320 km trip down the South Saskatchewan R in a collapsible canoe of his own invention. In 1894 he returned to England and a retired pay posting in the British army. Douglas designed and collected small boats: dugouts, open Canadians, decked sailing canoes, fold boats and small gigs. By sail and paddle, he explored the inland and coastal waters of India, Great Britain, US and Canada. He had his own decked racing canoe, the *Harmony*, built in England in 1864 and raced it as a member of the Toronto Canoe Club. Douglas's passionate involvement in his avocation did much to promote and document the early years of modern CANOEING.
C. FRED JOHNSTON

Douglas, David, botanist (b at Scone near Perth, Scotland 25 July 1799; d in Hawaii 12 July 1834). Douglas became an apprentice gardener at age 11; at 20 he moved to the Botanic Gardens, Glasgow, and at 23 became a collector for the Horticultural Society of London in N America. He collected in Canada: near Amherstburg, Upper Canada, in 1823; along the Columbia, Saskatchewan and Hayes rivers to Hudson Bay in 1827; and along the Okanagan and Fraser rivers beyond Fort George [Prince George] in 1833. Douglas was the first white man known to have climbed Mt Brown in the Canadian Rockies. He described nearly 200 new species of plants and introduced more plants (254) to Europe from N America than any other man. About 50 plant species and one genus, *Douglasia*, are named for him, in addition to the DOUGLAS FIR, "the most important tree in the American lumber trade." He died when he accidentally fell into a pit used to trap wild bullocks and was trampled.
C. STUART HOUSTON

Douglas, Sir Howard, soldier, author, colonial administrator (b at Gosport, Eng 23 Jan 1776; d at Tunbridge Wells, Eng 9 Nov 1861). The son of a naval officer, Douglas finished military academy in time to see action in the French Revolutionary and Napoleonic wars in Canada, Spain and Holland. Promoted major-gen in 1821, he became lieutenant-governor and commander in chief of New Brunswick serving from 27 Mar 1823 to 19 Feb 1831. During those preradical years he ruled effectively, becoming the "most popular" of all imperial governors. He oversaw administrative, military and cultural changes in a period of rapid growth. As would be expected of an author and fellow of the Royal Society, his major achievement was in the improvement of King's College (UNB), of which he was chancellor. The Douglas Gold Medal is still awarded annually at UNB. Militarily the troubled New Brunswick-Maine border led him to encourage an active local militia, which numbered over 15 000 by 1831. He was less successful in his battles over the civil list and with crown lands commissioner Thomas BAILLIE. Douglas returned to England in 1831 as a strong supporter of the British N American colonies and their preferences in the British marketplace.
CARL M. WALLACE

Douglas, James, surgeon (b at Brechin, Scot 20 May 1800; d at New York C, NY 14 Apr 1886). Admitted to the Edinburgh School of Medicine after a 5-year apprenticeship with Dr Thomas Law in Penrith, Eng, Douglas was admitted to the Edinburgh College of Surgeons in 1819 and to the London College of Surgeons in 1820. After practising in India, he came to Québec C in 1826 and around 1837 was given charge of the Marine and Emigrant Hospital, practising and teaching there. In 1845 he acquired the first Québec asylum for the mentally ill, the Centre hospitalier Robert Giffard at Beauport. Because of respiratory problems, he spent winters in Italy, Palestine or Egypt and in 1875 moved to Phoenixville, Pa. He is buried at Mount Hermon Cemetery, Sillery, Qué. The mental asylum of Verdun is now called the Douglas Hospital.
SYLVIO LEBLOND

Douglas, Sir James, fur trader, governor of Vancouver I, 1851-63, and of BC, 1858-64 (b at Demerara, British Guiana 15? Aug 1803; d at Victoria 2 Aug 1877). A resourceful, energetic and intelligent man, Douglas helped the HUDSON'S BAY CO become a trading monopoly in the N Pacific. As colonial governor he initiated British rule W of the Rocky Mts, and as the founder of settlement, trade and industry, he is remembered as "the Father of BC."

A "Scotch West Indian," Douglas was the son of "a free coloured woman" and a Scottish mer-

Sir James Douglas, governor of Vancouver I, 1851-63, and first governor of British Columbia, 1858-64 (*courtesy National Archives of Canada/PA-61930*).

chant. He was taken to Lanark for schooling when he was 12. At age 16 he was apprenticed to the NORTH WEST CO, and entered the HBC's employ on the merger of the 2 companies in 1821. In 1826, while attached to Ft St James in the New Caledonia district, Douglas accompanied Chief Factor William Connolly on the first annual fur brigade to Ft Vancouver. On 27 Apr 1828, after the custom of the country, he married Amelia, Connolly's part-Indian daughter, confirming the marriage in 1837.

George SIMPSON, governor of Rupert's Land, who met Douglas at Ft St James in 1828, described him as "a stout, powerful active man of good conduct and respectable abilities," but one who became "furiously violent when aroused," a tendency which brought Douglas into conflicts with the CARRIER Indians and caused Connolly to obtain his transfer in 1830 to Ft Vancouver to serve under John MCLOUGHLIN. There Douglas became chief trader in 1835 and chief factor in 1839. In 1842 Douglas accompanied Simpson to Alaska to negotiate with the Russian American Co. In 1843 Douglas began constructing Ft Victoria on the southern tip of Vancouver I to replace the northern coastal forts. Anticipating the eventual withdrawal of the HBC from Ft Vancouver after the British accepted the FORTY-NINTH PARALLEL as boundary in 1846, he had a new brigade trail blazed on British territory from New Caledonia to Ft Langley on the lower Fraser R. Ft Victoria, where the furs from the interior were transshipped, became the main Pacific depot in 1849. The fear of American expansion northward caused Britain on 13 Jan 1849 to lease Vancouver I to the HBC for 10 years. Douglas, the supervisor of the fur trade since 1845, was appointed HBC agent on the island.

The British government selected for governor Richard Blanshard, a barrister willing to serve without salary. Blanshard arrived at Ft Victoria in Mar 1850 to find his residence not completed. Remaining on shipboard, he sailed northward. Blanshard was shocked by the HBC's harsh discipline of striking miners at the Ft Rupert mine and accepted local fears of an Indian attack. Douglas would brook no interference with his Indian policy which now was based on mutual confidence. Blanshard soon resigned and departed in Aug 1851. Without pleasure or satisfaction, Douglas learned on Oct 30 that he had been chosen Blanshard's successor. His worries were great; it

would be difficult to reconcile the conflicting interests of governor and company official; the only revenue available for public buildings, schools, a church and road was from liquor licences; and qualified men were in such short supply that he appointed his own brother-in-law, newly arrived from Demerara, as chief justice of the Supreme Court. Blanshard had appointed a Legislative Council in 1851 and in 1856 Douglas was instructed to establish an Assembly for the island. He was opposed to universal suffrage and believed that people really wanted "the ruling classes" to make their decisions. Property qualifications for the franchise and for membership in the Assembly were set so high that only a few landowners could qualify.

The first evidence of impending change on the Pacific seaboard came on Sunday 25 Apr 1858 when a boatload of boisterous miners from California, the first wave of 25 000 newcomers, arrived on their way to search for gold on the Fraser sandbars. Douglas had taken the precaution of claiming the land and the minerals for the Crown. Now he began to license the miners and, to stem an invasion, to stop foreign vessels entering the river. For this action, which seemed designed to protect the HBC monopoly, he was reprimanded.

With the gold discovery, Britain decided to cancel the special privileges granted the HBC until Mar 1859. A new colony on the mainland was created by parliamentary Act. Douglas was offered the governorship on condition that he sever his fur-trade connections. He would be given extensive political power since it seemed unwise to experiment with self-government among men "so wild, so miscellaneous, and perhaps so transitory." In Nov 1858, no longer a fur trader, and the rights of his old company W of the mountains having been extinguished, Douglas, who was still governor of Vancouver I, was inaugurated at Ft Langley as governor of BC.

Douglas expected that a location near Ft Langley would be chosen for the colony's capital. But for military reasons Col Richard Clement Moody, RE, in Jan 1859 selected a steep, heavily timbered site (New Westminster) on the N bank of the Fraser. Douglas was concerned about the cost involved in laying it out. He also preferred Victoria as an administrative centre and as his place of residence. His visits to New Westminster were rare, and despite the grant of municipal self-government in 1860, the citizens demanded a resident governor and political reform.

As governor of BC, Douglas was chiefly concerned with the welfare of the miners. He relied on his gold commissioners to lay out reserves for the Indians and thus eliminate the threat of warfare, to record mining and land claims, and to adjudicate mining disputes. For the gold colony he devised a land policy which included mineral and pre-emption rights. His water legislation met the needs of the miners who employed rockers and flumes.

During the winter of 1858 he had used voluntary labour to make a pack trail to the mining area above the Fraser gorge. By 1862 he was planning to finance by loans (about which London was not fully informed) a wagon road 640 km long following the Fraser to distant Cariboo where gold nuggets had been found (*see* CARIBOO ROAD). It was extended in 1865 to Barkerville, an ebullient mining community.

Perhaps because of sensitivity over his, and his wife's, background, Douglas had developed a singularly aloof manner. Some of his old friends complained about his pomposity. New associates complained about his despotism. New Westminster merchants complained about having to pay customs duties. The effect was cumulative. Douglas's term as governor of Vancouver I was up in

1863; since BC was about to be given a more liberal type of government, it seemed to London an opportune time to retire him. Praise for his work and his talents and the award of a KCB softened the blow. MARGARET A. ORMSBY

Reading: D. Blakey Smith, *James Douglas* (1971); Margaret A. Ormsby, *British Columbia: a History* (rev ed, 1971).

Douglas, Thomas Clement, Tommy, Baptist minister, politician, premier of Saskatchewan (b at Falkirk, Scot 20 Oct 1904; d at Ottawa 24 Feb 1986). Douglas led the first socialist government elected in Canada and is recognized as the father of socialized medicine. He also helped establish democratic socialism in the mainstream of Canadian politics. His proudly working-class and religious family provided a strong background for both his politics and his faith. His family settled in Canada in 1919 in Winnipeg and Douglas witnessed the WINNIPEG GENERAL STRIKE of that year. Leaving school at the age of 14, Douglas began a printer's apprenticeship. He became involved in church work and in 1924 decided to enter the ministry. He was at Brandon Coll for 6 years, and it was here that he was exposed to and embraced the SOCIAL GOSPEL, a belief that Christianity was above all a social religion, concerned as much with improving this world as with the life hereafter.

When Douglas moved to Weyburn, Sask, following his ordination in 1930, he found much suffering, for that province had been especially hard hit by economic depression and drought.

T.C. Douglas, who served as CCF/NDP premier of Saskatchewan for 17 years, speaking at the National Steel Car Co plant in Hamilton, Ont, 1949 (*courtesy National Archives of Canada/PA-120532/United Steelworkers of America*).

Douglas soon became involved in ministering to people's physical and spiritual needs, while he pursued further academic studies in Christian ethics. These studies, along with his experience of the GREAT DEPRESSION, led him to conclude that that political action was necessary to alleviate the suffering. In 1931 he established a local association of the Independent Labour Party, and 2 years later he attended the first national convention of the new, avowedly socialist CO-OPERATIVE COMMONWEALTH FEDERATION (CCF). Douglas ran unsuccessfully in the 1934 Saskatchewan election. He was then convinced by friends that he should be a CCF candidate in the federal election of 1935. This time he was successful, partly because he had learned to exploit a special talent – the ability to make people laugh. WWII further convinced Douglas that the socialist case was valid. Although he heard it repeatedly argued in Parliament that money could not be found to put people to work, money was forthcoming to finance a war. During his first 2 terms in Parliament, Douglas earned a reputation as a skilful and witty debater. He claimed as his constituency the underprivileged and exploited, and he took unpopular stands in defence of civil liberties.

In 1944 Douglas resigned his federal seat to contest the Saskatchewan general election. As premier of the province for the next 17 years, he became a symbol of what the socialist alternative promised. His government was innovative and efficient, and pioneered many programs that would later be implemented by others, notably in the field of social services. Douglas resigned as premier in 1961 to lead the federal NEW DEMOCRATIC PARTY (NDP), created as a formal alliance between the CCF and organized labour. Douglas was the new party's obvious choice, primarily because of his success in Saskatchewan but also because he was universally regarded as the left's most eloquent spokesman. He was able to inspire and motivate party workers and he could also explain democratic socialism in moral, ethical and religious terms. Despite these qualifications, Douglas was defeated in the federal election of 1962, largely because of the backlash against the Saskatchewan government's introduction of Medicare, which had culminated in a long and bitter strike by the province's doctors (see SASKATCHEWAN DOCTORS' STRIKE). Winning a seat in a by-election, Douglas went on to serve as leader of the NDP until 1971, when he became his party's energy critic until his retirement in 1979. He was made Companion of the Order of Canada in 1980.

Though Douglas did not realize his dream of a socialist Canada, he and his colleagues had considerable influence on government. Programs such as Medicare, a Canada-wide pension plan and bargaining rights for civil servants were first advocated by Douglas and his party, and these are now more or less firmly in place and universally accepted in Canada.   L.D. LOVICK

Reading: T.C. Douglas, *The Making of a Socialist*, ed, L.H. Thomas (1982); T.H. McLeod and I. McLeod, *Tommy Douglas: The Road to Jerusalem* (1987); Doris Shackleton, *Tommy Douglas* (1975).

Douglas Fir (*Pseudotsuga menziesii*), evergreen CONIFER of PINE family (Pinaceae). Six species of *Pseudotsuga* ("false hemlock") are recognized: 2 in western N America; 4 in China, Taiwan and Japan. Only *P. menziesii* occurs in Canada, along the West Coast, E into the Rocky Mts and extending S to central Mexico. A coastal variety (var *menziesii*) may attain heights of 100 m and diameters of 2 m; an interior variety (var *glauca*) is smaller. The leaves are evergreen, needlelike and 2-3 cm long. The cones are 5-10 cm long, have rounded scales and distinct, three-pronged bracts (modified leaves). Pollination occurs in early spring; seeds are shed in late summer or

fall. Douglas fir resembles true firs, hemlocks and spruces but is most closely related to the LARCH. One of the most important timber species in N America, it is now planted in many regions of Europe. *See also* David DOUGLAS.   JOHN N. OWENS

Doukhobors, a sect of Russian dissenters, many of whom now live in western Canada. Since they arose as a peasant group in southern Russia, with orally transmitted teachings and traditions, their origin is obscure. Their doctrines appear to have been at least partially derived from those of a 17th-century renegade preacher, Danilo Filipov, who dissented radically from the ORTHODOX CHURCH. The Doukhobors rejected church liturgy, believing that God dwells in each man and not in a church; they rejected secular governments; and they preached PACIFISM. They replaced the Bible with orally transmitted psalms and hymns, which they called the Living Book; these are sung to this day at the *sobranyas* (gatherings which serve as both religious services and community meetings). Doukhobors revere their chosen leaders, whom they regard as especially inspired by God.

During the late 18th century the group was persecuted for its heresy and pacifism. In 1785 an Orthodox archbishop called them Doukhobors, or "Spirit-Wrestlers." It was intended to mean "Wrestlers against the Holy Spirit," but the group adopted it, interpreting it as "Wrestlers for and with the Spirit." Under Tsar Alexander I persecu-

tion lapsed, and in 1802 the Doukhobors were gathered in settlements in the Crimea, which was then a frontier region. Forty years later, under the less sympathetic Nicholas I, they were resettled among the fierce tribesmen of the recently conquered Caucasus. There they overcame initial difficulties and eventually prospered, particularly under their woman leader, Lukeria Kalmikova.

Lukeria died in 1886, and the ensuing struggle for leadership split the sect. Peter VERIGIN emerged as the majority leader, but was immediately arrested and sent into exile. From afar Verigin was nevertheless able to exhort his followers to reaffirm their ideals. Persecuted again, many of the Doukhobors were allowed to emigrate to Canada, assisted by novelist Leo Tolstoy and British and American QUAKERS. More than 7400 sailed in 1898-99 and settled in what was to become Saskatchewan, where they lived as a community. Verigin joined them there in 1902.

Initially, Doukhobors were permitted to register for individual homesteads but to live communally, and they received concessions regarding education and military service. Frank Oliver, who succeeded Clifford Sifton as minister of the

Douglas fir (*Pseudotsuga menziesii*), with male flowers (bottom left), female flowers (top left) and cones (*artwork by Claire Tremblay*).

The Doukhobor Pilgrims entering Yorkton, Sask, 1899. More than 7400 Doukhobors settled in Saskatchewan in 1898-99 (*by permission of the British Library*).

interior in 1905, interpreted the Dominion Lands Act more strictly. When Doukhobors refused to swear an oath of allegiance – a condition for the final granting of homestead titles – their homestead entries were cancelled.

In 1908 Verigin led most of his followers to southern BC, where he bought land and established a self-contained community of 6000. Some Doukhobors split off to their own farms and became Independents. A tiny splinter, the radical Sons of Freedom (fd in 1902 in Saskatchewan), burnt several schools in a dispute with BC over education. Many in this group were later imprisoned for nude protest parades. During the 1930s the effects of the Depression, internal disenchantment and mismanagement, combined with the incendiarism of fanatics and the unsympathetic policies of finance companies and government, ruined the community, which had been one of the largest and most complex undertakings in communal living in N American history. In 1939 foreclosure took place and the land passed to the BC government, from which individual Doukhobors bought it back in the 1960s. After much Sons of Freedom unrest in the 1950s and 1960s, fanatical activism died down.

Members of the various Doukhobor groupings still struggle to forestall the effects of encroaching assimilation. Descendants of the original Doukhobor settlers number approximately 30 000 across Canada, with about half of that number remaining active in the culture, maintaining their religious customs, Russian language and pacifism. The majority group, known as the Orthodox Doukhobors, or Union of Spiritual Communities of Christ (USCC), has been most successful in integrating into the Canadian multicultural mosaic. The USCC is headed by Peter Verigin's great-grandson John J. Verigin.

GEORGE WOODCOCK

Reading: George Woodcock and Ivan Avakumovic, *The Doukhobors* (1977).

Doutre, Joseph, lawyer, editor, writer (b at Beauharnois, LC 11 Mar 1825; d at Montréal 3 Feb 1886). As the editor of *L'Avenir* and a charter member of the INSTITUT CANADIEN of Montréal, Doutre had a career in law and politics as an early liberal that has obscured his literary reputation until recently. He is known primarily as the author of the romantic novel *Les Fiancés de 1812* (1844), and his significance as a novelist has been obscured by the tradition of the *roman du terroir*, a genre which developed in reaction to novels such as *Les Fiancés*. Part of the novel's importance lies in its effort to adapt the works of the French novelist Eugène Sue to Canadian fiction, and part in its preface, which attacks the contemporary audience for its indifference to Canadian literature. Since the novel attacks religious intolerance, it was predictably condemned as immoral. Valued now largely because of the author's commentary on contemporary society, the novel is rare in its refusal of official ideologies of the day.

E.D. BLODGETT

Dove, name applied to certain species of the PIGEON family, especially to those of smaller size. No scientific distinction exists between doves and pigeons, and the names are interchangeable; eg, *Columba livia* is commonly known as domestic pigeon, rock dove or rock pigeon.

W. EARL GODFREY

Dower refers to a form of marital property right. In its ancient form dower entitled a widow to a life interest in a portion of the lands owned by her deceased husband. Widowers were accorded similar rights, known as "curtesy." Modified forms of these dower rights existed in all Canadian provinces except Québec and Newfoundland but now have been replaced by other rights found in succession and matrimonial property statutes.

In the western Canadian provinces and the Northwest Territories, there exists modern "homestead" protection legislation, which creates marital property rights, sometimes specifically referred to as "Dower." Generally, this form of statutory regime is designed to prevent the spouse who owns the matrimonial home from disposing of that property without the consent of the other spouse. In specified instances, the need for such a consent may be dispensed with by a court order or waived by agreement. Furthermore, similar to the ancient dower right, the widow (or widower) is entitled to a life interest in the homestead on the death of the spouse who owns the property. Other incidental rights also enure to the benefit of the widow or widower. If the spouses divorce, however, dower rights over the homestead are normally at an end and the rights of the spouses over their property is governed by other matrimonial property legislation. M.M. LITMAN AND B.H. ZIFF

Dowling, Thomas Joseph, Roman Catholic bishop of Peterborough, Ont 1887-89, Hamilton, Ont 1889-1926 (b in Shannagh County, Limerick, Ire 28 Feb 1890; d at Hamilton, Ont 6 Aug 1924). In 1851 Dowling migrated with his family to Hamilton where he was ordained at Saint Mary's Cathedral, 5 Oct 1864. He was stationed first in Paris, Ont, and quickly established himself as a gifted orator, an able financial administrator and a builder priest. He was vicar general of Hamilton in 1881 and was raised shortly thereafter to the monsignorate. In 1887 he became second bishop of Peterborough and in 1889 was installed as fourth bishop of Hamilton. During his bishopric, Dowling oversaw great physical expansion in churches, convents and hospitals. His gregarious personality won him a personal affection but it was his work in providing foreign-language services for non-English-speaking immigrants of the diocese which set him apart. The Resurrectionists at Saint Jerome's College, Berlin [Kitchener], trained German-speaking priests and Italian parishes were established in Guelph and Hamilton and Polish-speaking priests recruited for new congregations in Hamilton and Berlin. GERALD J. STORTZ

Downey, Richard Keith, scientist, plant breeder (b at Saskatoon 26 Jan 1927). Educated at U of Sask and Cornell, he has been employed at Agriculture Canada research stations at Lethbridge, Alta, 1951-57, and Saskatoon from 1957. Since 1958 he has been principal research scientist in charge of oilseed crop breeding at Saskatoon. Downey initiated and carried out a plan to transform rapeseed into an edible oilseed crop of superior quality. His most outstanding work to the present is the development of low-erucic-acid and low-glucosinolate rapeseed, now designated in the world trade as CANOLA. He has delineated the scientific basis of his work in numerous scientific journals, books and articles, and his work has stimulated quality plant breeding worldwide by showing how an old common species can be transformed into a high-quality crop. He received the Royal Bank Award in 1975.

J.E.R. GREENSHIELDS

Downs, Barry Vance, architect (b at Vancouver 19 June 1930). After graduating in architecture from U of Washington, Seattle, in 1954, Downs worked for THOMPSON, BERWICK, PRATT AND PARTNERS in Vancouver before joining Fred Thornton Hollingsworth in partnership from 1963 to 1967. After 2 years of independent practice, he formed Downs/Archambault Architects with Richard B. Archambault in 1969.

Examples of the firm's work are the North Vancouver Civic Centre and Britannia Community Services Centre, Vancouver; Lester Pearson College of the Pacific, Pedder Bay, Vancouver I (in collaboration with Ron THOM), 1977; and a rich variety of houses and housing developments. Downs is a leading exponent of the thoughtful, low-key, mostly undecorated but carefully detailed architecture characteristic of the Canadian West Coast and the American northwest. His materials and colours are direct and unadorned, and his buildings, informally organized, low and economical, harmonize with the existing setting.

MICHAEL MCMORDIE

Doyle, Brian, children's novelist (b at Ottawa 12 Aug 1935). After a journalism degree from Carleton U (1957), he worked briefly for the Toronto *Telegram*. He returned to Carleton for a BA in English and became a high-school teacher in Ottawa. Inspired by his children and by his own childhood, Doyle's first-person narratives usually present themes through repetitive episodes. Typically, a physical journey becomes a symbolic journey to maturity when the narrator confronts the mysteries of love and death. Some form of reconciliation also occurs. Comic episodes, eccentric characters and language designed for reading aloud make *Hey, Dad!* (1978), *You Can Pick Me Up at Peggy's Cove* (1979) and *Angel Square* (1984) entertaining. *Up to Low* (1982), Canadian Library Assn Medal winner, stands apart; blending tall tale, black humour, and religious symbolism, it is his best work.   RAYMOND E. JONES

Doyle, Richard J., "Dic," newspaper editor (b at Toronto 10 Mar 1923). Reared at Chatham, Ont, he worked on the *Daily News* there following RCAF service during WWII. He soon joined the Toronto GLOBE AND MAIL as a reporter, becoming editor of the *Globe Magazine* (1957) and managing editor of the daily (1959). Editor of the *Globe* 1963-83, he was Canada's most influential newspaper editor and the one most respected by working journalists. He was renowned for his love of good prose, his feisty independence and his peculiar ability to match apparently unlikely personnel to particular jobs. He continued as a columnist for the paper until 1985, when he was summoned to the Senate (the first journalist to be called to the Senate since George Brown in 1873).

Drabinsky, Garth Howard, lawyer, entrepreneur (b at Toronto 27 Oct 1948). Although his CINEPLEX ODEON CORP (est 1979) was almost bankrupt by 1983, Drabinsky was by 1987 one of the world's most powerful film exhibitors, controlling 1511 screens in 465 locations across N America. His tactics have been brash, blunt and innovative. He won the crucial right to bid for first-run American productions for his theatres by exposing exclusive arrangements between the major established exhibitors – Famous Players and Odeon – and the studios, provoking government regulation to break an effective monopoly. His strategy of renovating old movie houses, as well as building stylish new ones to accommodate his multiscreen theatres, has been credited with drawing people back to the movies. Producer as well as exhibitor, Drabinsky financed 6 Canadian feature films 1977-82, which won more than a dozen major awards and nominations, and he backed Paul Newman's film of *The Glass Menagerie* (1987).   STANLEY GORDON

Dragonfly, common name for robust, carnivorous insects of order Odonata [Gk, "toothed," referring to mouthparts]. Name may include closely related DAMSELFLIES (suborder Zygoptera), but properly refers only to members of suborder Anisoptera. About 2800 species of anisopterids are known worldwide, 143 from Canada. Dragonflies have large, compound eyes, well-developed mouthparts, and 2 pairs of membranous wings,

Dragonfly, a carnivorous insect of the order Odonata; 143 species exist in Canada, including the 10-spot dragonfly (*photo by Mary W. Ferguson*).

with hindwings wider at the base than forewings. Larvae are aquatic, but lack tail gills. They obtain oxygen by taking water into the hindgut; rapid expulsion of this water allows them to propel themselves. Eggs are usually deposited in water or in aquatic vegetation. Larval life may last 1-3 years or more. The transformation from drab, aquatic larva to brightly coloured, aerodynamically adept, terrestrial adult is dramatic. Larvae and adults may feed partly on mosquitoes; adults may prey on bees.   G. PRITCHARD

Drainage Basin, area of land that contributes the water it receives as precipitation (except for losses through evaporation, transpiration from plants, incorporation into the SOIL or GROUNDWATER, etc) to a RIVER or network of rivers. Drainage basins are defined by topographical features, called drainage divides, which determine the direction of flow of water. Canada has 6 major drainage basins, each of which are described below. Note that upward revisions in river flow volumes, especially for the northern and western basins, are warranted with the new data we now have available, but good current regional estimates are not yet available.

Arctic Drainage

This region, of 3.58 million km², receives streamflow from the northern two-thirds of Alberta, northern BC, northern Saskatchewan, the YT and the NWT, including the arctic islands. The estimated average annual discharge rate is 15 500 m³/s. The largest river of the region is the MACKENZIE. Its watershed, 1.787 million km², comprises about 50% of the arctic drainage area, about 20% of Canada's area and 60% of the drainage water of the arctic region. The most important tributaries, the PEACE, ATHABASCA, LIARD and SOUTH NAHANNI rivers, all rise on the eastern slopes of the Rocky Mts. The Mackenzie has an average discharge of 9910 m³/s into the Beaufort Sea. The annual streamflow is equivalent to a mean depth on the watershed of 170 mm. The longest flow route is 4241 km, from the head of the Finlay R in northern BC via the Peace R, Lk Athabasca, Great Slave Lk and the Mackenzie R to its mouth. This length exceeds by over 1000 km that of any other Canadian river system. The Mackenzie's peak flow occurs in June; otherwise it is quite uniform from May to Sept, when 70% of the annual discharge occurs. This uniformity is attributable to the influence of the relatively flat Barren Lands E of the river and to the many lakes, the largest of which, GREAT BEAR and GREAT SLAVE, each cover about 30 000 km².

ICE is significant to the HYDROLOGY of the region and much of the terrain is underlain by PERMAFROST. Lakes and rivers are open from about June 15 to Nov 1 in the more northerly part of the Mackenzie Basin, less in the arctic islands. The Mackenzie R valley has been the subject of intensive technical, social and cultural studies during the 1970s because of concern over the potential impact of proposed petroleum PIPELINES. The delicate ecological balance existing between native people and their natural environment has given rise to many questions about the effects of TRANSPORTATION corridors in the valley.

Pacific Drainage

The 1.08 million km² Cordilleran region, W of the Continental Divide and extending from the international border at the boundary of Alberta and BC into the YT near the Mackenzie Delta, sheds water into the Pacific Ocean at an average rate of 21 200 m³/s. This rate is equivalent to an annual depth of 620 mm over the area, the largest hypothetical average depth of any hydrologic region of Canada. The high average discharge is attributable to the large amounts of precipitation

received at higher elevations of the Rockies and coastal mountain ranges, caused by moist air masses moving off the Pacific Ocean. Stream water supply is, however, highly variable. In the dry interior valleys the equivalent annual depth of runoff is 100 mm or less; in the coastal zone it is 3200 mm.

The 1368 km FRASER R flows through spectacular canyons and rich agricultural land to provide drainage to more than 230 000 km² of interior BC. The mean discharge rate is about 3620 m³/s. Highest flows are experienced in June; lowest in March. The risk of flooding in the Fraser's lower reaches has long been a matter of concern.

The COLUMBIA R system in southeastern BC has an average flow at the international boundary of 2800 m³/s. A portion of this flow originates from 50 000 km² of drainage area in the US. Three large RESERVOIRS in the Columbia system provide significant FLOOD-control benefits to the US and will ultimately allow installation of 4000 MW of hydroelectric-generating capacity in Canada (*see* BC HYDRO). The Okanagan R, which flows to join the Columbia S of the international boundary, is of great benefit to fruit growers in the semiarid valleys.

Coastal rivers, including the Fraser, swarm with SALMON during the season when they return inland to their spawning grounds. The other large rivers, the SKEENA, NASS and STIKINE, discharge a combined average of 3800 m³/s into the Pacific. The Yukon, with a drainage area of 800 000 km², has an average discharge of 2300 m³/s where it crosses into Alaska. Only a small fraction of the potential hydroelectric-generating capacity has been installed on any of these streams. In addition to the benefits to fisheries and agriculture and for HYDROELECTRICITY, the waters of the Pacific drainage provide a valuable resource to the LUMBER, PULP AND PAPER and mineral processing industries and to municipalities.

Western Hudson Bay and Mississippi Drainage

This region of 2.64 million km² includes all of Manitoba, most of Saskatchewan, the southern third of Alberta, most of the District of Keewatin, a part of Ontario W of Lk Superior and about 150 000 km² immediately S of the international boundary. A 27 500 km² zone of southern Saskatchewan and southeastern Alberta drains into the Mississippi Basin and thence to the Gulf of Mexico. The major rivers discharging into western HUDSON BAY are the HAYES, NELSON, CHURCHILL, KAZAN and THELON. The estimated mean rate of discharge for the region is about 9400 m³/s.

The most important drainage basin is the 1 million km² drained by the Saskatchewan-Nelson river system. The BOW, OLDMAN and North and South SASKATCHEWAN RIVERS rise on the eastern slopes of the Rockies and flow E for 1900 km through the central plains. Extensive tracts in the plains region drain into interior depressions (sloughs). Many of these sloughs have no outlet and many others have outlets only in the wetter years to the principal streams which enter a chain of lakes in south-central Manitoba. Here the flow is joined with that of the RED R flowing in from the S and the WINNIPEG R from the E. The latter carries drainage from southeastern Manitoba, the Lake of the Woods region of Ontario, and Minnesota. The flow discharges from Lk Winnipeg (24 000 km²) into Hudson Bay via the Nelson R.

The mean flow of the Nelson at its outlet is 2370 m³/s, equivalent to a mean depth of about 125 mm annually over the watershed. The principal source areas of streamflow for the Nelson are the eastern slopes of the Rockies and the lake area of Manitoba, northwestern Ontario and the adjacent states. The latter region contributes over 50%

DRAINAGE BASINS

0   500   1000 km

1 : 30 000 000

Pacific Drainage
Arctic Drainage
Interior Drainage
Gulf of Mexico Drainage
Hudson Bay Drainage
Atlantic Drainage

of the total annual discharge. The several large lakes and hundreds of smaller ones, totalling over 50 000 km² in area, regulate the Nelson's flow, so that the mean flow rate in any month is seldom 30% greater or less than the annual average. Highest discharge occurs in July; lowest flows in Jan-Mar. The Nelson and Churchill rivers are sites of large hydroelectric-power generating facilities with significant potential for further development.

The North and South Saskatchewan river system is important to agriculture since it flows through a region of fertile soils, limited in their productivity by uncertain rainfall. The water supply from the Bow, Oldman, North and South Saskatchewan rivers and their tributaries is vital to cities, towns and industries of Alberta and Saskatchewan. The high variability of local tributary flow has necessitated construction of many dams to provide carry-over storage from years of abundant flow to years of low discharge.

South and East Hudson Bay Drainage

This region includes most of northern Ontario and western and northern Québec, an area of about 1.4 million km². There are at least 15 individual watersheds of 30 000 km² or more in area. The largest of these are the SEVERN, draining into Hudson Bay, the ALBANY (134 000 km²), the MOOSE (108 000 km²); LA GRANDE RIVIÈRE (98 000 km²) flowing into JAMES BAY; and the KOKSOAK (133 000 km²) draining into UNGAVA BAY. The region, part of the Canadian Shield, consists of massive ancient crystalline rocks. As a result of GLACIATION there are large areas of lakes, ponds and swamps. In some parts as much as 15% of the drainage area is covered by fresh water. The many lakes result in fairly uniform rates of river flow throughout the year. The waters are generally of good quality and very little influenced by human activities.

Although the rivers and lakes are ice covered annually for 6 months, water continues to flow under the ice. The lowest flows occur in Mar for the more southerly streams, Apr for those draining into Ungava Bay. The time of highest discharge is late May or June, following the breakup of the ice cover in mid-May. About 45% of the total annual flow occurs May-July, except for streams draining into Ungava Bay, where about 60% of the annual flow occurs June-Aug. The average annual rate of flow of all streams draining into Hudson, James and Ungava bays is estimated at 20 000 m³/s, which is equivalent to a mean annual water depth of 450 mm over the entire region and represents about 60% of precipitation received. There is considerable hydroelectric potential in the region. The JAMES BAY PROJECT is one of the largest in the world. The average flow in La Grande Rivière is to be increased from 1700-3300 m³/s and the eventual generating capacity will be 10 000 MW.

Great Lakes-St Lawrence Drainage

This basin, with an area of 1 million km² above Montréal, is dominated by the GREAT LAKES, covering 245 000 km². About one half the basin is Canadian, Lake Michigan is wholly within the US; the international boundary passes through Lakes Superior, Huron, Erie, Ontario and St Clair. Most of the land drainage from the Canadian portion is from the Canadian Shield; the ST LAWRENCE LOWLANDS make a small contribution. The lowlands include peninsular Ontario, bounded by Georgian Bay, Lakes Huron, St Clair, Erie and Ontario and the fringes of the St Lawrence R. The Great Lakes-St Lawrence system provides an important navigable waterway of nearly 4000 km from Île d'Anticosti to the head of Lk Superior (*see* ST LAWRENCE SEAWAY).

Most streams in the lowlands are less than 300 km long. They are important for industry,

agriculture and urban water supply, and provide recreational opportunities for the region's urban population. The intensive land use in the southern parts of the basin, coupled with variability of the glacial deposits, results in high variability of seasonal flows, localized flooding, periodic low summer flows and impaired WATER quality.

The average flow in the NIAGARA R at Queenston, between Lake Erie and Lake Ontario, is 5760 m³/s. By the time the St Lawrence R reaches Cornwall, downstream of the Great Lakes, the average flow is 6430 m³/s. After the river is joined by the OTTAWA R at Montréal and by other tributaries, its average flow is 9800 m³/s, equivalent to an annual average depth of 300 mm over the entire basin. The St Lawrence Basin is the most southerly in Canada. This factor, coupled with the lakes' relatively large areas of open water, results in significant evaporation losses. Streamflow is reduced to about 25-30% of received precipitation. Nevertheless, the large lakes maintain a steady rate of flow throughout the year, and from one year to the next.

Atlantic Drainage

The region includes that part of Canada draining to the St Lawrence R (from Montréal eastward), the Gulf of ST LAWRENCE and the Atlantic Ocean. It includes all of Nfld, NS, NB, PEI and part of Québec, an area of 1 million km².

The drainage from the north shore of the St Lawrence and Labrador is largely from the Canadian Shield, where 10-15% of the area is in freshwater lakes. The balance of the area is part of the Appalachian Region, consisting of a mixture of crystalline and sedimentary rocks, with thin surficial materials. The rivers are short and drainage is well developed as a result of long periods of erosion. About 9% of Newfoundland and 5% of NS are in lakes. There are few lakes in NB and PEI.

The largest watersheds discharging into the St Lawrence R are the Manicouagan (45 000 km²) and the Saguenay (88 000 km²). The Churchill R in Labrador drains 79 800 km² and discharges directly to the Atlantic Ocean. The SAINT JOHN R, in NB, draining 55 400 km², discharges into the Bay of FUNDY. Most of the large rivers of the basin have extensive hydroelectric installations.

The total discharge of the watersheds in the basin averages 21 000 m³/s, ie, an equivalent annual depth of 650 mm of water, or about 50% of the annual precipitation. The annual rate of runoff per-unit area is lowest (17 L/s/km²) for the St Maurice R in the most westerly part of the region; highest (45 L/s/km²) in southwestern Newfoundland.

The minimum daily rates of runoff from the larger watersheds range from 3 L/s/km² for the Churchill R to 1 L/s/km² for the Aux Outardes R. Many smaller streams dry up completely for a short period during summer or as a result of ice formation in winter. Local problems of water-quality impairment are encountered in regions of intensive agricultural, forestry and industrial activity. *See also* GEOLOGICAL REGIONS; PHYSIOGRAPHIC REGIONS.   H.D. AYERS

Drainie, John Robert Roy, actor (b at Vancouver 1 Apr 1916; d at Toronto 30 Oct 1966). An actor of extraordinary versatility, he was the most renowned and best loved of the first truly professional community of performing artists in English Canada. Starting in radio in the late 1930s, he quickly became the leading actor of a repertory company established by CBC Radio drama producer Andrew ALLAN, first in Vancouver, later in Toronto. Primarily on Allan's "Stage" series (1944-56), Drainie performed hundreds of leading roles in classical drama and original Canadian plays, most notably his wicked satire of the red-baiting US senator Joseph McCarthy in Reuben Ship's "The Investigator." His 5-year radio portrayal of Saskatchewan hired man Jake Trumper on W.O. MITCHELL's "Jake and the Kid" and his recreation of humorist Stephen LEACOCK on radio, television and the stage were major contributions to Canadian entertainment and mythmaking. Completely self-taught, he set a standard of professional excellence for Canadian acting that is emulated to this day. His memory is honoured annually by ACTRA's John Drainie Award for Distinguished Contribution to Broadcasting.
                                        BRONWYN DRAINIE

John Drainie in characteristic Leacock pose in sun gallery at Leacock House, Old Brewery Bay, Orillia, Ont, 1959 (*courtesy National Archives of Canada/C-31945*).

Drake, Sir Francis, one of history's great seamen and adventurers (b near Tavistock, Eng 1540?; d off Panama 28 Jan 1596). He likely sighted VANCOUVER I on his voyage around the world (1577-80). After plundering Spanish ships off Mexico, Drake tried to find a polar route back to England; the supposition that he sailed N to Vancouver I is based on a study of the winds and currents of the northwestern Pacific.   JAMES MARSH

Drake, Theodore George Gustavus Harwood, physician, historian, collector (b at Webbwood, Ont 16 Sept 1891; d at Toronto 28 Oct 1959). Drake graduated from U of T in 1914. He was a co-developer of the infant food Pablum and Sunwheat Biscuits, and the royalties of these products were given to the Hospital for Sick Children (Toronto). He was awarded the OBE after WWII for designing nutrition levels for RCAF meals and prisoner-of-war parcels. Drake wrote extensively on the history of pediatrics and was the author of many scientific articles. His collection of some 5000 antiques of pediatric interest, from Ancient Greece and Egypt to 19th-century Europe, was donated to the Museum of the History of Medicine, Academy of Medicine, Toronto, in 1960.   WILHELMINA M. DRAKE

Drama in English Traditionally, drama is a term referring to a literary genre which consists of texts written for staging in the theatre. Dramatic literature, however, includes many texts that have never been performed and many that, despite their form, were not intended for performance. Moreover, the history of the theatre has often seen the composition of performance pieces which have not been (nor could they be) written and preserved as conventional texts. This is especially true of drama in the second half of the 20th century. In light of these considerations, the history of Canadian drama can be expected to consist of a range of forms shaped by the conditions and nature of our theatres as well as by literary conventions. Among the other influences shaping our drama have been the Canadian colonial experience, the rise of nationalism and various social and political forces generally seen to affect the arts and literature.

The naturally small amount of early Canadian drama in English is shaped largely by foreign modes, as in the case of Lt Adam Allan's *The New Gentle Shepherd* (1798), which is Allan Ramsay's *The Gentle Shepherd* (1725), a pastoral drama in Scottish dialect, "reduced to English." Seventeenth-century English heroic tragedies, such as John Dryden's *The Conquest of Granada* (1670, 1671), were the obvious antecedents for George Cocking's verse drama *The Conquest of Canada* (1766), in which Gen WOLFE leads his greatly outnumbered British soldiers to victory. Even Robert ROGERS's *Ponteach* (1766), a sometimes-engaging verse drama depicting the defeat of the noble savage, PONTIAC, by evil European invaders, is Canadian only in that its American-born author resided briefly in Canada. The anonymous "Acadius," staged in Halifax in 1774 and extant as a 2-act extract in the *Nova Scotia Gazette and the Weekly Chronicle* (1774), dramatizes a wealthy Boston merchant's extramarital activities and his black servants' attempts to cope with their exploitation.

The 19th Century The common impression that closet poetic drama was the 19th century's dominant dramatic genre can be challenged, as more plays are found in other modes. Certainly, authors with literary pretensions did write poetic dramas and "dramatic sketches" not intended for the stage, many of them published in the *Literary Garland*. The anonymous "The Queen's Oak" (1850), which treats in conventional verse Elizabeth Woodville's meeting with Edward IV, is typical. Eliza Lanesford Cushing is the most notable of the *Garland* contributors; among her 10 plays is "The Fatal Ring" (1840), about a virtuous countess seduced by an alluring, womanizing king. The uneven quality of its blank verse and its moral tone are evident also in Cushing's biblical drama, "Esther" (*Lady's Book*, vols 16-17, 1838). One of the first plays printed in monograph, Charles HEAVYSEGE's *Saul* (1857), gained the respect of both John A. MACDONALD and Henry Wadsworth Longfellow, among others, but, like Heavysege's *Count Filippo* (1859), this bulky, sententious piece has fallen into a well-deserved obscurity. Thomas Bush's sprawling *Santiago* (1866), one of the most ambitious poetic dramas of the age, suffers from obscure allusions, passages of incomprehensible blank verse and melodramatic excess.

The end of the century saw poetic dramatists using indigenous subjects with greater frequency, but the quality of their expression improved only slightly. *Tecumseh* (1886) displays Charles MAIR's minor poetic talent and his fervent patriotism. Sarah Anne Curzon, whose poetic talent was more limited than Mair's, also follows a patriotic bent in *Laura Secord* (1887). John Hunter-Duvar in *De Roberval* (1888) tries to dramatize too many themes suggested by Sieur de ROBERVAL's adventures in early Canada. Foreign and indigenous elements often came together in poetic drama, a fact well illustrated by the range of William Wilfred CAMPBELL's works; eg, "Daulac" (1908) presents DOLLARD DES ORMEAUX's brave defence at the Long Sault, whereas "Mordred" (1895) centres melodramatic intrigue on King Arthur's bastard son. As is characteristic of the genre, Campbell's 5 plays suffer from ponderous "Shakespearean" verse and weighty philosophy which render them impractical to stage.

The practice of publishing political or social satire in newspapers created a lively topical drama early in the century, as illustrated by "The Charrivarri" (*The Scribbler* vols 3-4, 1823) by Samuel Hull Wilcocke (pseudonym Lewis Luke MacCulloh), "The Triumph of Intrigue" (anon, *New Brunswick Courier*, 1833) and the "Provincial Drama Called the Family Compact" (*British Colonist*, 1839), attributed to Hugh Scobie (pseudonym Chrononhotonthologos). Similarly biting sketches, such as William Henry Fuller's "The Unspecific Scandal" (*Canadian Illustrated News*, 1874), which deals with the PACIFIC SCANDAL, and Curzon's "The Sweet Girl Graduate" (*Grip-Sack*, 1882), which exposes sexual discrimination against women at University of Toronto, continued to appear to the end of the century. Topical satire appeared in monographs by mid-century. *The Female Consistory of Brockville* (1856) allowed its anonymous author, "Caroli Candidus," to attack hypocrisy in the Brockville Presbytery. "Sam Scribble" wrote both *Dolorsolatio* (1865), a burlesque in which Federation is the answer to Grandpapa Canada's *dolors*, and *King of the Beavers* (1865), in which FENIANS conspire to attack Beaverland. *The Fair Grit* (1876) by Nicholas Flood DAVIN is an enjoyable satire on party politics.

Government figures played a significant role in the development of Canadian drama. In Ottawa, Lady Dufferin organized dramatic entertainments between 1872 and 1878 in the theatre in the governor general's residence, Rideau Hall. Frederick A. DIXON, author of the comic operetta, *The Maire of St. Brieux* (1875), was one playwright whose work she encouraged. Dixon's masque, entitled "Canada's Welcome" (1879), which chronicled pioneer settlement in the Canadian wilderness, was presented for the marquess of Lorne and Princess Louise at Ottawa's Grand Opera House in 1879.

Musical dramas were important entertainment in the 19th century. *Leo, the Royal Cadet* (1889) by George Frederick Cameron (music by Oscar Telgmann) centres on Nellie's love for Leo, an army cadet who becomes a hero fighting the Zulus. *Nina* (1880s) by Thomas Herbert Chesnut is a "nautical comic operetta" influenced by Gilbert and Sullivan. Musical parodies and burlesques prevailed, the most famous being William Henry Fuller's *H.M.S. Parliament* (1880), which borrowed from *H.M.S. Pinafore* to satirize Canadian politics and political figures. Jean Newton McIlwraith showed more originality exploring Canadian identity in the context of the ANNEXATION issue in her comic *Ptarmigan* (1895, music by J.E.P. Aldous).

The century produced plays in a number of other genres. Catharine Nina Merritt's prose history *When George the Third Was King* (1897) celebrates LOYALISTS who settled in Canada. Stage melodramas are represented by pieces like John Louis Carleton's *More Sinned Against than Sinning* (1883), a meaningless formula play which became an annual treat in Saint John, NB, for several years. Like Harry Lindley's inferior *Chick* (1893) or W.P. Wood's sketchy scenario *Minnie Trail* (1871), these melodramas suffer from the genre's weaknesses without having its strengths.

The 20th Century Poetic dramas, such as the Rev Robert Norwood's *The Witch of Endor* (1916), continued to be written in the 20th century, as did melodramas and light comedies by W.A. Tremayne and other professional playwrights. *The Man Who Went* (1918), a wartime spy thriller, is typical of Tremayne's formulaic plays for the American commercial stage. Children's plays and scripts for educational, temperance or religious purposes were prevalent during the early 20th century, as were humorous dramatic sketches, eg, adaptations from Dickens, and Stephen LEACOCK's burlesques of outdated theatrical modes. After WWI Canadians wrote in the environment of the amateur movement that grew up across the country. In *Canadian Plays from Hart House Theatre* (2 vols, 1926-27) editor Vincent MASSEY gives us examples in various genres of this "little theatre" activity, including 3 short, ironic comedies, "Balm," "Brothers in Arms" and "The Weather Breeder" by Merrill DENISON, the first significant playwright of the century. His "Marsh Hay," a 4-act, realistic drama published in *The Unheroic North* (1923), treats important Canadian themes.

One-act plays in a variety of styles became the predominant form of the time. Poet Marjorie Pickthall's evocative verse drama, "The Woodcarver's Wife" (*University Magazine*, 1920) was performed at Hart House, University of Toronto, but Amy Campbell's "The Cradle" (1928), which echoes Synge's poetic style, never received production. *One Act Plays by Canadian Authors* (1926) collects 19 plays, of which only "Come True" and "Low Life" bear mention, these chiefly because they are by Mazo DE LA ROCHE; they antedate *Whiteoaks* (1936), the conventional drama, adapted from her novel, which ran for over 2 years in London, Eng, before the war. In the mid-1930s, Samuel French (Canada) Ltd launched a Canadian Playwrights Series offering a range of one-act plays, including Martha Allan's *Summer Solstice* (1935), shaped by G.B. Shaw's *Heartbreak House*; Lillian Thomas's amusing *Jim Barber's Spite Fence* (1936); and *The Lampshade*, an English murder story by W.S. Milne. In his 4 *Plays of the Pacific Coast* (1935), A.M.D. Fairbairn dramatizes West Coast Indian stories and the collision of white and Indian cultures; the Québec legend of Rose's dance with the devil is rendered into rhyming couplets in E.W. Devlin's *Rose Latulippe* (1935). The hardships of the GREAT DEPRESSION inspired Eric Harris's domestic drama *Twenty Five Cents* (Toronto 1936) and Lois Reynolds Kerr's *Open Doors* (1930).

The Depression also led to numerous "Worker's Plays." Dorothy LIVESAY, whose "Joe Derry" (*Masses*, 1933) is a narrated pantomime, was the most famous author involved; *Eight Men Speak* (1934) by Oscar Ryan, E. Cecil-Smith, H. Francis and Mildred Goldberg, was the most notable play. Its importance is both historical and as an example of the effective use of agit prop and

related presentational techniques. Aside from "Worker's Plays," the most daring experiment was Herman VOADEN's "symphonic expressionism." His ballet-music-dramas were described at the time as compelling on stage, but now may seem dated, their image-laden language stilted. If a single one-act play of the period stands out, it is Gwen RINGWOOD's "Still Stands the House" (*Carolina Playbook*, 1938), a moving, realistic portrayal of spiritual starvation and repression in hard times on the Prairies. Len PETERSON's radio play, *Burlap Bags* (1946, pub 1972), also bears citing for its portrayal of an alienated, absurd postwar world. It seems a transitional play between the expressionism of the 1930s and the existentialist drama of the 1950s and 1960s.

The leading playwright of the late 1940s and early 1950s was Robertson DAVIES, who dramatized in a witty, often eloquent style his satirical view of philistine Canadians. His early plays received amateur productions, but *A Jig for the Gypsy* (1954) and *Hunting Stuart* (1955, pub 1972) were staged by Toronto's professional Crest Theatre. The 1950s saw the establishment of modern Canadian professional theatre, highlighted by the founding of the STRATFORD FESTIVAL. From the 1930s radio had aided the professional evolution by employing playwrights. Among them was Lister SINCLAIR, author of "The Blood is Strong" (*A Play on Words*, 1948), who emerged in the late 1940s as a prolific radio dramatist. W.O. MITCHELL, in "The Devil's Instrument" (1949, pub 1973), showed a prairie Hutterite youth rebelling against his religion; in "The Black Bonspiel of Wullie MacCrimmon" (1951, pub 1965) Mitchell humorously pitted Wullie against the Devil, an avid curler. Earle BIRNEY wrote "Trial of a City" (1952), an inventive, witty indictment of Vancouver. *Teach Me How to Cry* (1955), Patricia JOUDRY's sentimental study of small-town prejudice, was first a radio and television play (1953), then received a professional production in New York (1955) and won the 1956 Dominion Drama Festival Best Play Award. It was retitled *Noon Has No Shadows* for staging in London's West End in 1958 by an all-Canadian cast, and it subsequently became a movie. In the manner of Dylan Thomas's *Under Milk Wood*, John REEVES fashioned *A Beach of Strangers* (1961), hitting out at Canadian puritanism. John COULTER, whose 1930s plays were popular with amateur groups, also wrote for the radio, then used a Canadian hero in the episodic and moving *Riel* (1950, pub 1962). Coulter's last dramatic work was *François Bigot* (1978), also a history play. The late 1960s saw an unprecedented increase in the quantity and quality of drama, a trend which continued through the 1970s. In 1967 James REANEY's imaginative and metaphorical *Colours in the Dark*, which explores growing up in a repressive southern Ontario, was staged at the Stratford Festival. That same year, the Manitoba Theatre Centre produced Ann Henry's *Lulu Street* (1972), a sensitive, critical look at the Winnipeg General Strike. John Herbert's prison drama, *Fortune and Men's Eyes* (1967), graphically depicting intellectual and sexual oppression, received its first full, professional staging also in 1967, ironically in New York, although it had been presented in a workshop at the Stratford Festival in 1965. Also in 1967, at the Vancouver Playhouse, George RYGA's *The Ecstasy of Rita Joe* (1970) made an emotionally provocative statement on native-white relations; this was followed by *Rita Joe's* travelling to Ottawa's National Arts Centre in 1969. In Vancouver, Ryga's multi-media and highly successful "hippie" play, *Grass and Wild Strawberries* (1971) caused controversy, but nothing compared to the fuss over his *Captives of the Faceless Drummer* (1971). British Columbia playwright Beverly SI-

MONS used absurdist techniques in *Crabdance* (1971) to present the plight of middle-aged Sadie Goldman trapped by the stress of modern life.

In the early 1970s, small professional theatres dedicated to new Canadian plays sprang up across the country. Some relied on scripts of a traditional nature. In *Leaving Home* (1972) and its sequel, *Of the Fields, Lately* (1973), David FRENCH used the conventions of realism to explore the psychological tensions within a Newfoundland family forced to move to Toronto. His *Jitters* (1979, pub 1980) is a more successful comedy of manners satirizing Canadian theatre. Joining French in ushering in a muscular Canadian realism was David Freeman, whose *Creeps* (1972) is a searing revelation of life among the physically or psychologically handicapped. Freeman's subsequent plays have not been as successful as *Creeps*, but were also part of the early 1970s' realism, which included French's poolroom drama, *One Crack Out* (1975), William Fruet's "Wedding in White" (1973) and Mary Humphry Baldridge's *The Photographic Moment* (1974). Using less realistic conventions, Herschel Hardin's Inuit drama, "Esker Mike and his Wife Agiluk" (*TDR*, 1969), received attention, as did Carol BOLT's documentary satire *Buffalo Jump* (1972), about the ON TO OTTAWA TREK, and her episodic portrait of anarchist, feminist Emma Goldman, *Red Emma* (1974). Bolt's more recent psychological thriller, *One Night Stand* (1977), with its melodramatic ending, and her lightweight satire, *Escape Entertainment* (1982), suggest that she has allowed popular appeal to replace depth of insight as a dramatic value.

In Newfoundland, Michael COOK wrote "Colour the Flesh the Colour of Dust" (1972), "The Gayden Chronicles" (*CTR* 13, 1977) and "On the Rim of the Curve" (1977), this last about the demise of the BEOTHUK Indians. These somewhat Brechtian dramas use incidents from Canadian history to comment on modern social and political injustices, and head a list of large-scale history plays including Stewart Boston's "Counsellor Extraordinary" (1971), Michael Bawtree's *The Last of the Tsars* (1973), James Nichol's *Sainte-Marie Among the Hurons* (1977) and Ron Chudley's *After Abraham* (1978). Cook's shorter plays, "Quiller" (1975) and "Tiln" (1973), and his 2-act plays, "The Head, Guts and Sound Bone Dance" (*CTR* 1, 1974) and *Jacob's Wake* (1975), take a philosophical attitude to modern Newfoundland life and express it in an image-laden language.

In western Canada, *Walsh* (1972, publ 1974), an episodic treatment of the NWMP officer's anguish over the injustice he helped perpetrate on Sitting Bull, was the first of 5 major plays establishing Sharon POLLOCK's reputation. Since *Walsh*, she has written *The Komagata Maru Incident* (1978), which uses a circus atmosphere to comment on Canada's handling of a 1914 shipload of SIKH immigrants; "One Tiger to a Hill" (1981), depicting the complex tensions in a prison hostage taking, and "Blood Relations" (1981), a skilful handling of the Lizzie Borden tale. "Generations" (1981) is Pollock's only play in a wholly realistic mode; the others demonstrate an imaginative restructuring of reality that forces the audience to concentrate on issues inherent in the actual events portrayed.

"Collective creation" describes the working process of many theatres in the early 1970s in preparing performance pieces, often "documentary dramas" improvised around a specific topic or theme. Among the best of the genre are scripts such as *The Farm Show* (1976) by Toronto's Theatre Passe Muraille, *Far as the Eye Can See* (1977), which it did with Rudy WIEBE, and "Paper Wheat" (*CTR* 17, 1977) by Saskatoon's 25TH STREET THEATRE. They gain strength from imagina-

Eric Peterson as Billy Bishop, from John Gray's "Billy Bishop Goes to War" (1981) (*photo by Glen E. Erikson, Vancouver East Cultural Centre*).

tive staging rather than deep insight into the topic; hence, they yield little to traditional modes of dramatic analysis. As a result, this complex, sophisticated form is often misjudged or ignored by critics. Sometimes the collective process involves a playwright, as in *Far as the Eye Can See* and the very popular "1837: The Farmers' Revolt" (*CTR* 6, 1975), which Rick SALUTIN scripted with Theatre Passe Muraille. Salutin's equally famous *Les Canadiens* (1977), written "with an assist from Ken Dryden," uses the rapid changes of time, place and action, the character doubling and vignette structure associated with collective works, but provides more analysis of its topic: social and political life in Québec. Rex DEVERELL scripted "No I Hard" (1978) from a collective creation process, but he is the playwright of *Boiler Room Suite* (1978), where 2 old winos find joy in each other's company, and *Black Powder* (1982), his documentary drama about the 1931 Estevan riots. Even English Canada's most acclaimed dramatist, James REANEY, has often exercised his manifest genius through improvisational collaboration with acting companies. Over the years, following amateur first productions of his more conventional early plays, Reaney has evolved a mythopoeic drama based on fragmented plots and resonant thematic imagery that echoes between rich dialogue and the stage action, characters or objects. His Donnelly trilogy ("Sticks and Stones," *CTR* 2, 1974; *St. Nicholas Hotel*, 1976; *Handcuffs* 1977) has been called the strongest drama yet written in English Canada.

Experimental work by many other playwrights has challenged the boundaries of traditional English Canadian theatre. Québec dramas in translation, notably the multilayered, resonant plays of Michel TREMBLAY, have helped extend conven-

tional modes. Especially in the 1960s, Wilfred WATSON offered audiences multi-media dramas which were often surrealistic, satirical and poetic. "Let's murder Clytemnestra according to the principles of Marshall McLuhan" (1969) took place in a laboratory-like setting on a stage whose proscenium was fitted with numerous televisions carrying the bizarre action from the stage. A more recent *Gramsci X3* (1983) explores the murder/martyrdom of Antonio Gramsci. Part of the play uses Watson's number grid verse which enables performers to experiment with various solo and choral techniques in handling the dialogue. The many successful productions of Michael ONDAATJE's *The Collected Works of Billy the Kid*, which he adapted for the stage from his brilliant poetic narrative (1970), created a dramatic form by juxtaposing short scenes in prose and verse. Rich imagery, in the manner of Reaney's Donnelly plays, transforms the chronicle of Billy the Kid into myth, then ironically questions the nature of that myth. In the early 1970s, Lawrence Russell used surrealistic techniques in the short pieces in *Penetration* (1972) and *The Mystery of the Pig Killer's Daughter* (1975). Michael Hollingsworth dabbled with bizarre events in *Clear Light* (1973) and *Strawberry Fields* (1973). "Mathematics" (1973), 190 seconds without dialogue during which 6 groups of carefully selected objects are thrown one by one upon the stage, indicates the ephemeral, yet daring experiments of Hrant Alianak. His "Western" (1973) finds a gunslinger and 2 beautiful women in humorous dialogue consisting of the titles and names of stars from western movies while they wait for the cavalry to rescue them from 500 attacking Indians. Ken Gass, the author of the cartoonlike, anti-fascist *Hurrah for Johnny Canuck!* (1975), raised controversy with his *Winter Offensive* (1978) in which Adolf Eichmann's wife hosts a kinky sex party for Nazi officials. Bryan Wade's *Blitzkrieg* (1974), about Hitler and Eva Braun, and many of his earlier shorter plays (eg, *Lifeguard*, 1973 and "Alias," 1974) have imaginative unconventional qualities, but have not been followed by anything substantial. A talking dog and exploding croquet mallets make Larry Fineberg's *Hope* (1972) slightly unusual, but his other work is mainstream. His undistinguished adaptation of Constance BERESFORD-HOWE's novel *Eve* (1977) was performed at the Stratford Festival, as was his dull rendition of Euripides' *Medea* (1978). George Walker's *Zastrozzi* (1977), *Theatre of the Film Noir* (1981) and *Science and Madness* (1982) abound in entertaining theatricality, usually in the service of making fun of traditional dramatic modes, but when they move beyond simple parody, his plays flounder intellectually. One of the most innovative scripts in recent years is John Krizanc's "Tamara" (unpublished), which won a Dora Mavor Moore Award in 1981. Its "environmental theatre" form allowed audience members to follow a chosen character through the large, old house in which it was staged. No individual saw all the 1920s' political and amorous action unravelling simultaneously in the many rooms, but playgoers gained enjoyment piecing the strands together from chats with others after the show. Many, however, seemed to have missed the play's serious exploration of the clash between politics and art.

There was special attention focused on women in the theatre during the 1970s and after. The plays of Sharon Pollock and Carol BOLT pursue feminist themes, and Margaret HOLLINGSWORTH has entered the forefront of Canadian dramatists. Her full-length *Ever Loving* (1981) traces the lives of 3 war brides who come to Canada to live with their husbands. *Ever Loving* joins "The Apple in the Eye" (1977), *Mother Country* (1978), "Operators" and *Bushed* (1973) in illustrating Hollings-

worth's skill at creating lively human characters and scenes loaded with humour and tension. Erika RITTER demonstrates a rapierlike wit and a perceptive reading of life in *Automatic Pilot* (1980), her most significant play to date, but too often allows an easy laugh to deflect us from probing the relationships among her characters.

The period since the mid-1970s has produced many talented writers who have as yet only one or 2 considerable plays, eg, Timothy FINDLEY and his resonant *Can You See Me Yet?* (1977) and American-born Sheldon Rosen with *Ned and Jack* (1979). David FENNARIO has written what may be the most "Canadian" of plays, *Balconville* (1980), a bilingual slice of life comically revealing the oppression of French and English slum dwellers in Montréal. Tom WALMSLEY's handling of sex and violence in *Something Red* (1978), *The Jones Boy* (1978) and *The Workingman* (1976) is forceful and graphically realistic, if sometimes overdone. In *Waiting for the Parade* (1980), John MURRELL creates nostalgia to link the vignettes of 5 women living out WWII in Calgary. His earlier *Memoir* (1978) lacks truly dramatic action, but it is a theatrical vehicle for the actress playing the aged Sarah Bernhardt.

Most of the recent plays mentioned combine box-office appeal with enough substance to engage the mind, but a current trend has also seen the proliferation of situation comedies like Allan Stratton's *Nurse Jane Goes to Hawaii* (1981) and Alden NOWLAN and Walter Learning's *The Incredible Murder of Cardinal Tosca* (1978). In fairness, one must note Stratton's subtle, thoughtful *Rexy* (1981) and Nowlan-Learning's engrossing history play, *The Dollar Woman* (1981). Financial restraint has also fostered one-person shows seemingly beyond count. Pierre Trudeau's notorious marriage and the novelty of Linda Griffiths playing all three roles in *Maggie and Pierre* (1979, publ 1980), which she created with Paul Thompson, made this play exceedingly popular despite a very thin script. John GRAY's *Billy Bishop Goes to War* (1981) has been equally popular and combines the solo performer with another recent trend towards musical theatre. Gray has also written "18 Wheels" (unpublished) and *Rock and Roll* (*CTR* 35, 1982), 2 small-cast musicals. This form has been used well by Ken MITCHELL in his "trucker's *Othello*," *Cruel Tears* (1976). Contemporary Canadian drama is highly promising, in part because of the high quality of first major works by a new group of young dramatists which includes Judith Thompson, Frank Moher, Charles Tidler, Anne Chislett, Lawrence Jeffery and Gordon Pengilly. *See also* THEATRE, ENGLISH LANGUAGE.

RICHARD PLANT

Reading: G. Anthony, ed, *Stage Voices* (1978); J. Ball and R. Plant, eds, *A Bibliography of Canadian Theatre History 1583-1975* (1976) and *Supplement 1975-1976* (1979); D. Rubin and A. Cranmer-Byng, eds, *Canada's Playwrights* (1980); R. Usmiani, *Second Stage: The Alternative Theatre Movement in Canada* (1983); A. Wagner, ed, *The Brock Bibliography of Published Canadian Plays in English 1766-1978* (1980); R. Wallace and C. Zimmerman, eds, *The Work* (1982). In addition, informative articles appear regularly in the journals *Canadian Theatre Review* (1974-), *Canadian Drama/L'Art dramatique canadien* (1975-) and *Theatre History in Canada/Histoire du théâtre au Canada* (1980-).

Drama in French Québec drama is often said to have started in 1948, even though Gratien GÉLINAS's 1948 play *Tit-Coq* had been preceded by other popular works. One was the melodrama by Léon Petitjean and Henri Rollin, *Aurore, l'enfant martyre,* which made all Québec weep from 1920 to 1950. Québec theatre did not begin with Tit-Coq, successor to Gélinas's earlier character, Fridolin, another beloved child of the stage, whose heyday was 1938-46. But the theatre was limited for the first half of the 20th century to burlesque and reviews (many of them imported), to melodrama and the eclectic repertoire of the Compagnons de Saint-Laurent; it became a "national" theatre with the Gélinas play. It was only after this "baptism" that Québec professionals and amateurs busied themselves with this new and beloved child martyr, the Québec theatre. Even so, theatre had been part of the cultural expression of French Canada since the early days of the colony.

The first dramatic presentation was *Théâtre de Neptune en la Nouvelle France* by Marc LESCARBOT in 1606. This author had written a few rhymes "to serve our history as well as to show that we live joyfully." But such diversions in latter-day New France came up against the clergy who, through condemnations and threats of reprisal, long managed to keep the dramatic expression of the country both subdued and sporadic in nature. In 1789, for example, Montréal's Théâtre de la société and its leader Joseph QUESNEL fought with the clergy because they wished to present, among other pieces, the "first Canadian opera," Quesnel's *Colas et Colinette*. But clerical threats ensured that, until the early 20th century, the bishops, often through the lower clergy, firmly controlled public morality which (in their eyes) was being dangerously threatened by an already unduly liberal theatrical expression.

The clergy's clear and sustained opposition was not aimed solely at theatre: the clergy rejected all cultural activities outside the religious context as rebellious by definition. Yet despite clerical vigilance, during the 18th and 19th centuries it was possible to see a number of dramatic presentations, either local amateur productions or plays mounted by touring groups of American, French and English actors. Montréal and Québec City were then part of the "American circuit."

Drama began to appear more and more regularly in Montréal after 1825, when the Théâtre royal (Molson Theatre) was founded. Whether English or French, theatre always found part of its public among the Francophones, including some of the most respected members of the religious flock.

It took a long time for women, who traditionally supported the clergy in its self-appointed role as social educator, to find a place in Québec theatre as spectators, actors or characters. It was not until the 20th century that theatre made room for feminist expression, not until 1970-80 that plays such as France Theoret's *La Nef des sorcières*, (1976), Denise Boucher's *Les fées ont soif* (1978) and the sustained and consistent work of the Théâtre expérimental des femmes (TEF) gave Québec women their own dramatic voice. Finally, thanks to scripts by authors like Marie Laberge and Jovette Marchessault, we now have believable characters, full of female aspirations and capable of expressing themselves. After long exclusion, the female voice and feminism have won a special place in Québec drama.

The post-1948 theatre faced a double challenge until 1965. It had to create both the habit of theatre-going and a body of plays reflecting Québec experience. The Compagnons de Saint-Laurent (1937-52) and other less enduring troupes such as Pierre Dagenais's L'Équipe (1943-48) and the Compagnie du masque of Charlotte Boisjoli and Fernand Doré (1946-51) were followed by other groups in the 1950s which through their professionalism gave a certain institutional status to Québec theatre. The development of a Québec repertoire was not their major concern, but they created the structures which made its growth possible. The companies they founded – the THÉÂTRE DU RIDEAU VERT (1948), the THÉÂTRE DU NOUVEAU MONDE (1951), Théâtre-Club (1954-64) and the Théâtre de Quat'Sous (1955) – mainly offered boulevard and classical (foreign) theatre. They

marked a new approach to theatrical reality and an explosion of styles and challenges, even though they did not manage to develop a recognizably Québecois dramaturgy. The early plays by Marcel DUBÉ showed the viability of a distinctive Québec dramaturgy, but it was only in the 1960s, in the atmosphere of the QUIET REVOLUTION, that people felt an urgent need to see their own reality, their hopes and their setbacks, on stage. The occasional previous efforts to mount Québec plays had seldom drawn large audiences and had won more suspicion than praise.

These first steps in the 1950s to institutionalize the theatre were matched by the birth of more avant-garde companies which devoted themselves to the development and establishment of theatre in Québec. By 1949, the Troupe des Treize at Université Laval, founded by Jacques Duchesne in Québec City, was already sparking theatrical activity in the capital. This was the age of the "théâtres de poche" which generally lasted only a short time, eg, l'Anjou (1954), founded by Paul Hébert, and l'Amphitryon (1955), by Patrick Antoine. Alongside these brave but doomed efforts some other, largely amateur, groups managed to make contact with a faithful theatre-going public. These troupes – les Apprentis-Sorciers (1956), led by Jean-Guy Sabourin; l'Estoc (1957), by Jean-Louis Tremblay in Québec City; and l'Égrégore (1959), founded by Françoise Berd and Claude Préfontaine – brought the European avant-garde to Québec spectators. Another such group was Saltimbanques, born of a split within the Apprentis-Sorciers and led, after 1962, by Rodrigue Mathieu. In 1963 Jacques Duchesne founded the Théâtre de la Place Ville-Marie, whose repertoire expanded to include Québec plays as well.

Although there were many companies and much theatre, there were few authors, scripts, institutions and structures to support the activity. In the early 1960s European plays still dominated Québec boards, but steps were being taken to create support structures for the infant dramaturgy. In 1958 Gratien GÉLINAS had bought the old Gaiety Theatre and founded the COMÉDIE-CANADIENNE, whose very name signalled its intentions. The Théâtre du Gesù, taken over in 1961 by Gilles Marsolais and several others, played an educational role with the student public by transforming itself in 1964 into the Nouvelle Compagnie théâtrale. By 1963 the Jeunes Comédiens of the Théâtre du nouveau monde were touring Québec schools. But the establishment of a solid theatrical apparatus outpaced both the repertoire and the public's readiness to be educated.

Official theatre schools were established to fill the gaps in Québec drama: in 1954 Jan Doat set up the Conservatoire d'art dramatique which in 1962 came under the ministry of cultural affairs; in 1960 Jean GASCON founded the National Theatre School; in 1958 Guy BEAULNE founded the Association canadienne du théâtre d'amateurs (ACTA) which in 1972 became the Association québécoise du jeune théâtre (AQJT). But the catalyst for the modern growth of Québec drama was undoubtedly the founding of the Centre d'essai des auteurs dramatiques (CEAD) in 1965. Through its readings and round-table discussions, the CEAD gave young authors a chance to receive critiques on their early efforts and provided them with opportunities to meet the public and other writers and to escape their isolation into a collective theatrical experience. Two good examples of the vitality of this period are the readings of Michel TREMBLAY's *Les Belles-Soeurs* (1968) and Yves Sauvageau's *Wouf Wouf* (1969) – both of them major works of the new Québec dramaturgy.

Also in 1965, Pierre LAPORTE, minister of cultural affairs, created the Commission de la pièce canadienne, whose mandate was to establish an official

repertoire of original Canadian plays. The project ended 2 years later. This was also a time when numerous arts centres were built (eg, Montréal's Places des Arts, Québec's Grand Théâtre). Despite a lack of comprehensive planning by government, the times encouraged the emergence of original plays.

It is easy enough to list the few authors and companies of the pre-1965 days; it grows successively harder thereafter. There was an average of 80 new Québec plays (including those for radio and television) per year, 1965-73; the average rose to 100 after 1975. This abundance grew out of the potential of 1965. From the beginning, CEAD had fostered the work of such authors as Michel Tremblay, Robert Gurik, Antonine MAILLET, Michel Garneau and Yves Sauvageau. Françoise LORANGER and Claude Levac travelled a more political path. The vogue for collective creation which emerged in 1969 signalled an awareness of a new social and cultural reality. The collective voice – often fleeting, often vulgar – became part of the general questioning of traditional values and the vehicles which articulated them. This movement was not limited to Québec, but there it fitted perfectly with the sociopolitical currents of the Quiet Revolution: a political awakening with an independence orientation, the affirmation of a Québec language (JOUAL), anticlericalism, etc. This challenge to the idea of the sacred single author and script was led by Maurice Demers's Théâtre d'environnement intégral (1968), by Jean-Claude Germain's Théâtre du même nom (1969) at Théâtre d'aujourd'hui, the Grand Cirque ordinaire (1969) and Théâtre Euh! (1969) in Québec City. Each company, according to its own ethical and aesthetic criteria, set about developing new theatrical forms in an effort to reach spectators in their own lives and reality.

This period of intense activity was followed by a period of near stagnation. Both the Grand Cirque ordinaire (1977) and Théâtre Euh! (1978) disappeared. Collective creation flagged. The lack of real policy, of adaptable playhouses and adequate financial backing, plus a general decline in public enthusiasm for culture, caused some discouragement. But in the late 1970s and early 1980s, new regional companies began to appear (eg, Théâtre Parminou, Victoriaville; Théâtre les Gens d'en bas, Rimouski; le Théâtre du sang neuf, Sherbrooke) and urban groups, drawing on different aesthetic and political currents, are now beginning to renew the Québec theatrical landscape (eg, La Commune à Marie and Théâtre de la Bordée in Québec; l'Eskabel, le Mime omnibus, le Nouveau Théâtre expérimental, Productions Germaine Larose, Groupe de la veillée, Carbone 14, Troupe les Pichous, la Rallonge, Théâtre de quartier and others in Montréal). Many companies now specialize in the long-neglected area of children's theatre, eg, Théâtre de la Marmaille, Théâtre carrousel, Centre le gyroscope, le Théâtre petit à petit. They have an increasing number of good texts to perform. Women's theatre has grown rapidly since 1976 and has become part of the theatre of protest which had previously been limited to political theatre or collective creation.

The supporters of collective creation and those of single-author scripts have now reached a modus vivendi. Whether the result of spontaneous creativity or the occasional commission, new scripts use and honour this double reality of the process of dramatic creation. A number of young authors have now produced solid, socially relevant works that receive both critical and popular success. These playwrights include Réjean DUCHARME, Serge Mercier, Jeanne-Mance Delisle, Marie Laberge, Pierre K. Malouf, Elizabeth Bourget, Serge Sirois, René-Daniel Dubois and Normand Chaurette.

Québec theatre since 1976 has been enriched by new forms of expression, apprenticeship, investigation and analysis. Theatrical publishing is so abundant as to suggest a certain lack of discrimination. Québec publishers offer an alluring range of theatrical collections. Theatre programs and departments in the universities and theatre options in the community colleges make theatre and production more accessible than ever. Two magazines devoted exclusively to the theatre – *Jeu* (1976) and *La Grande Réplique* (1977, renamed *Pratiques théâtrales* in 1981) – also help spread appreciation of the theatre.

The economic crisis of recent years has led to the creation of new theatrical forms: the one-person show, café theatre, reviews, cabaret, improvisation, etc. The popularity of the Ligue nationale d'improvisation (LNI) and of plays such as *Broue* and *Pied de poule* remind us of the escapist theatre that appealed to earlier generations in times of economic and social crisis. At the same time, Québec theatre is increasingly recognized elsewhere, as is shown by some European tours (eg, the LNI tours, 1981-83; the CEAD tour of 1982) and by European productions of Québec scripts such as Tremblay's *Les Belles-soeurs*, 1973, and Jean-Pierre Ronfard's *Vie et mort du Roi boiteux*, 1982.

Improved stagecraft has become important to dramatists in recent years, and has made possible the appearance of script/productions such as Ronfard's *Vie et mort du Roi boiteux* – which is, read or seen, the most significant and daring show in recent years. The script, a cycle of 6 plays, is in the form of separate tableaus, drawing on such diverse inspirations as the Bible, Shakespeare, oriental culture, world geography and the levels of Québec language. It has not broken entirely with the review tradition, though it respects more classical rules of composition. Ronfard and his colleagues at the (Nouveau) Théâtre expérimental de Montréal have been consistently exploring possibilities since 1975. Their accumulated research and sense of fantasy have resulted in a very accessible show willing to draw from any source that meets its needs.

Between 1948's *Tit-Coq* and 1982's *Vie et mort du Roi boiteux* the antihero, central character of Québec dramaturgy, has bestowed upon himself an enormous territory whose size befits his excesses and his ambitions. During the 1970s this territory seems to have been integrated or at least associated with the search for independence. Now it appears to have opened itself culturally so that it is no longer confined by the geographic boundaries of Québec itself. Since its first theatrical venture in 1606, but especially with the appearance of Tit-Coq the bastard and Richard the cripple, Québec has been creating its own national dramaturgy so as to make its theatre its own.

LORRAINE CAMERLAIN AND PIERRE LAVOIE

Theatre of Intervention

In the early 1970s there emerged in Québec a theatre movement that was a distant heir to the European *agitprop* and *proletkult*, and was closely related to contemporary troupes such as the San Francisco Mime Troupe and El Teatro Campesino and to progressive black American theatre. Political theatre emerged in Québec in the aftermath of the Quiet Revolution, and was to some extent heralded by the journal PARTI PRIS (1963-68) and the FLQ movement. In 1971, 2 articles from Théâtre Euh! (1970-78), the real founder of the movement, set forth the major issues on which cultural and political establishments were being challenged. Members of this group denounced the alienation or "colonization" of the Québécois and argued that theatre should be given back to the people. The group also attacked elitist forms of

theatre, which it contrasted with the theatrical practice of group, or collective, creation, perceiving the latter as nonauthoritarian and capable of associating new content with popular forms (songs, monologues, farce and satire) in the tradition of street theatre.

The advocates of committed theatre met with a variety of disappointments in their militant effort to reach "the voiceless," partly because they lacked sufficient knowledge of the working class and also because their sociopolitical objectives were too radical for a time when nationalist sentiments left little room for class-related issues. With its *Manifeste pour un théâtre au service du peuple* (1975), the major part of the movement broke away from the Association québécoise du jeune théâtre (which dissolved 1986), despite the fact that the association had been a supportive, dynamic component of the new theatre. Consequently the thrust of political theatre slowed down: a number of groups, among them the Théâtre Euh!, disappeared, swept away by their leftist ideology. Militant theatre groups were unable to revitalize, enrich and give depth to their themes because of their growing isolation and lack of resources.

However, less radical or less impatient groups took over and became more directly involved by using themes that were more community-based than communist-inspired. The actresses of the Théâtre des Cuisines (1973-81), for example, concentrated on feminist consciousness-raising work, while other (sometimes amateur) groups dealt with such issues as day-care, senior citizens, drug abuse, poverty, the competitive nature of schooling and juvenile delinquency.

Another characteristic of this second wave of interventionist theatre is that it stresses the principle of presenting plays in the very settings it is trying to reach. Théâtre Parminou (1973) and Théâtre de Quartier (1975), for example, allied themselves with unions and citizens' groups. Group production remains the main vehicle of intervention troupes, although some occasionally appoint a dramatist or, like Théâtre du 1ᵉʳ mai (1972) and Gens d'en Bas (1973), produce foreign plays by such authors as Bertolt Brecht and Dario Fo, whom they consider relevant to their interests. Lately there have also been efforts, influenced by Augusto Boal (Théâtre de l'Opprimé, France), to present "invisible theatre," "forum theatre" and "instant theatre."

The aesthetic dimension of this theatre, which is usually circumstantial and produced with a small budget, is not left out. For example, productions of the Théâtre à l'Ouvrage (1978-83) used increasingly diversified stage language, a fact that suggests a trend toward stricter and more effective theatre, particularly when plays are designed for long runs and a broadly based public. However, by the 1980s, only 2 or 3 intervention-theatre troupes had folded amid the upsurge of experimental theatres with more conventional objectives. *See also* THEATRE, FRENCH LANGUAGE.

GILBERT DAVID

Reading: Jean Béraud, *350 ans de théâtre au Canada français* (1958); Jean-Cléo Godin and Laurent Mailhot, *Le Théâtre québécois*, 2 vols (1970, 1980).

Drapeau, Jean, lawyer, politician, mayor of Montréal (b at Montréal 18 Feb 1916). Jean Drapeau was the most daring and successful mayor Canada has ever seen. His longevity as a politician was such that during the 29 years he ruled Montréal, 7 prime ministers and 9 Québec premiers crossed the stage. He gave the city its greatest moments: a 1967 World Exposition celebrating Canada's centennial which drew 50 million visits, and the 1976 Summer Olympic Games. But he presided over the decline of Montréal as Cana-

da's business capital and largest city. As rival Toronto grew in size and prestige, Drapeau declared: "Let Toronto become Milan. Montréal will always be Rome."

The only son of an insurance salesman and a grande dame of an opera singer, Drapeau was a protégé of the nationalist priest and historian Lionel Groulx. He defended his own belief in a Catholic, conservative Québec as a nationalist candidate in a 1942 federal by-election and a 1944 provincial election. He lost both, but his reputation grew as he joined the shakers of his generation to defend a Catholic union during a brutal strike at Asbestos, Qué in 1949. Drapeau then caught Montréal's imagination, leading a public inquiry into police corruption and, when Mayor Camillien HOUDE suddenly retired, Drapeau swept to power in the 28 Oct 1954 election. He was only 37. He began the slow transformation of Montréal from a riverport city infamous for its brothels and night life to a world metropolis of the first rank. Rightfully sensing Drapeau had larger ambitions, Québec Premier Maurice DUPLESSIS smashed the Drapeau-led Civic Action League in the 1957 vote. After 3 years of brooding and the old Québec now dead with Duplessis, Drapeau purged many of his old allies, formed a private political club, the Civic Party, and, promising Montréal a subway and clean government, won the 1960 election at the same time that all of Québec was launching into the QUIET REVOLUTION. Drapeau kept the subway promise, delivering a distinctive and expensive system, its stations florentined with stained glass and mosaics. He reformed the electoral system and modernized the police department but ignored or skirted issues such as public housing, city planning and pollution control. In 1987 Montréal was still dumping raw sewage into the St Lawrence, much the same as it had when the city was founded in 1642.

Drapeau preferred the big show. In 1969, his labour relations grew so bad all but 47 of his 3780-member police force struck. The army was summoned to quell the looting and nationalist street riots. Yet the same year he single-handedly brought Montréal a major league baseball team, the MONTREAL EXPOS. More circuses, said his critics. Said the mayor: "What the masses want are monuments." He declared they were his contribution to *La Survivance*, the survival of French Canadians. But the nationalism of his youth was so tempered he stayed neutral during the 1980 referendum on Québec independence. Internationally, he won the respect of leaders ranging from Charles De Gaulle to the royal family. Wrote former British PM Edward Heath: "I was privileged to hear privately mayor Drapeau's revelations on how to gain and keep power through the manipulation of friend and foe alike. It was one of the most hilarious and entertaining talks I have ever had with a politician." One opponent called him "a combination of Walt Disney and Al Capone."

Drapeau's ruthless and authoritarian side emerged during the 1970 Québec kidnapping crisis (*see* OCTOBER CRISIS). In a city election held while the draconian powers of the War Measures Act were in force, Drapeau smeared the opposition as a terrorist front. Amid hysteria, his principal opponent was locked up with 467 others, and on 25 Oct 1970, Drapeau's private party won all 52 council seats. He rang up 92.5% of the mayoralty vote. The absolute power Drapeau won in that election allowed him to ram through his plan for Olympics whose massive white concrete structures incarnated his politique de grandeur. Budgeted at $310 million, the final cost was $1.3 billion, not counting the Olympic stadium tower which stood unfinished until 1987. A provincial enquiry blamed the mayor for the cost and rampant corruption. But there was no evidence that he lined his own pockets. Montréalers re-elected him in 1978 and again in 1982, but it was the end of big projects. Over the decades he received many appeals, some tantalizing, to run in provincial or federal politics, but he sensed Montréal was his best platform and there he remained until the end of his 8th term.

On 20 June 1986, slowed by a stroke, Drapeau summoned the press to a site in the shadow of his pyramids, the Olympic installations, in the east end neighbourhood where he began his political career and where he still lived in a modest house with his wife of 41 years. Many Montréalers wept with him as he announced his resignation. His friend, PM Brian Mulroney, appointed Drapeau to finish his political career in Paris as Canadian ambassador to UNESCO. With Drapeau gone, his Civic Party was reduced to a single council seat as the Montréal Citizen's Movement under Jean Doré took power in the Nov 1986 election.

BRIAN McKENNA

Reading: B. McKenna and S. Purcell, *Drapeau* (1980).

Drapell, Joseph, artist (b at Humpolec, Czech 13 Mar 1940), one of the most important abstract painters in the generation after PAINTERS ELEVEN. He immigrated to Halifax in 1966 and studied at the Cranbrook Academy (Bloomfield Hills, Mich) 1968-70, where he met visiting artist Jack BUSH and American critic Clement Greenberg. He moved to Toronto and, inspired by Georgian Bay and influenced by Morris Louis, developed his own technique of applying paint with a broad spreading device attached to a movable support (1972-74). The resultant "Great Spirit" pictures rank among the most successful of all Canadian efforts to find spiritual values in the land. His abstract 1977 "Red" paintings found little interest in Canada until the Boston Museum purchased one in 1979.

KEN CARPENTER

Draper, Patrick Martin "Paddy," printer, trade-union leader (b at Aylmer, Qué 1868; d at Ottawa 23 Nov 1943). Apprenticed as a printer, Draper began work at the Government Printing Bureau in Ottawa in 1888, and eventually served as director of printing from 1921 until retirement in 1933. He was also an active trade unionist; he joined the Ottawa local of the International Typographical Union in 1888 and filled various posts in this union and in Ottawa's Allied Trades and Labor Assn. He moved into national prominence in 1900 when he was elected secretary of the TRADES AND LABOR CONGRESS of Canada. Thanks to his energy, administrative abilities and popularity, he held that important office until 1935, when he was chosen TLC president. In these positions, he attempted to maintain a measure of Canadian autonomy within the international labour movement. He stepped down in 1939 because of failing health. In his long career, Draper had frequently represented the Canadian labour movement on the national and international stages, including the Versailles Peace Conference in 1919.

CRAIG HERON

Draper, William Henry, politician, judge (b at London, Eng 11 Mar 1801; d at Toronto 3 Nov 1877). Draper was instrumental in founding the Conservative Party and was the first colonial politican to be styled "premier." Brought into politics as a young lawyer in 1836 by John Beverley ROBINSON, Draper strove to turn the old FAMILY COMPACT into a modern Conservative Party with wide appeal through accepting a measure of RESPONSIBLE GOVERNMENT, through educational and sectarian reforms and through forming an alliance with the French Canadians. He attained his greatest power, as attorney general, during the administrations of Sir Charles METCALFE and Lord CATHCART. Although forced out of office by the

right wing of his own party in 1847, Draper later saw most of his political ideas fulfilled by his former follower, John A. MACDONALD. Appointed to the judiciary in 1847, Draper eventually became chief justice of the Court of Error and Appeal in Ontario in 1869.

GEORGE METCALF

Reading: George Metcalf, "William Henry Draper," in J.M.S. Careless, ed, *The Pre-Confederation Premiers* (1980).

Drawing may be an autonomous art form or a preparatory step in establishing the design of another work of art. Though drawing is defined by its linear quality and has nothing to do with the medium used, the principal drawing media are ink, pastel, charcoal, metal point, graphite pencil, conté crayon and chalk. The history of drawing in Canada is marked by blank areas, periods when artists produced few drawings or when "working drawings" were regarded as mere notations for compositions in other art forms. Not until late in the 19th century were collectors or exhibition bodies interested in drawings as finished works of art. By the 20th century the situation had changed and drawings were more appreciated by the public.

Drawings that belong to the period of early exploration, to CARTOGRAPHY and to developments in NEW FRANCE were carried out by Europeans exclusively and were closely tied to European stylistic traditions: fact, fantasy and contrivance are not easy to distinguish in such drawings (*see also* PAINTING). Changes in approach are visible by the 18th century when precision became important, as, for example, in the noble drawings of buildings in Québec City by Charles Bécart de Granville and the panoramic view of Louisbourg (1731) by Étienne VERRIER. In contrast to the French colonial period, when engineering drawings and draughtsmen's plans for FORTIFICATIONS and buildings were produced, the English colonial period generated a wealth of pen and ink or watercolour views, by travellers, military men and their dependents, which record exploration, military and naval campaigns, immigration and settlement. During the SEVEN YEARS' WAR, several British officers made sketches of the siege of Québec City (1759) and the ruins after the battle; Wolfe's aide-de-camp, Hervey Smyth, showed troops scaling the cliffs to the Plains of Abraham and naval vessels operating in the St Lawrence. Many historic Québec buildings are known only through the detailed drawings executed by Richard Short. In the peace that followed, officers trained at the Woolwich Military Academy in England made accurate drawings of fortifications and the scenic landscape, many of which were later engraved and reproduced in popular travel books (*see* TOPOGRAPHIC PAINTERS). In their westward travels after 1845, Paul KANE and William HIND made hundreds of on-the-spot pencil, ink and watercolour sketches – portraits, landscapes, and artifact and figure studies. Art in Québec in the same period was mainly religious painting and sculpture, but some preparatory drawings of church murals by artists such as François BAILLAIRGÉ have survived. The other mainstay of Québec art was portraiture, and many lovely drawings by the leading artists (Antoine PLAMONDON, François Beaucourt and Louis DULONGPRÉ) were made for those people who could not afford oil portraits.

As well-trained artists immigrated to Canada and native-born artists increasingly spent a period in study abroad, Canadian art became exposed to influences from France, Holland, Germany and the US. The artists' societies of the period, particularly the ROYAL CANADIAN ACADEMY OF ARTS (fd 1880), did little to encourage drawing as an art form, which probably explains the dearth

End and Beginning (1973) by Ernest Lindner, pen and ink (*courtesy National Gallery of Canada/Ernest Lindner*).

of finished drawings in the last 2 decades of the century (*see* ARTISTS' ORGANIZATIONS). Drawings tended to be regarded by many artists solely as preparation for paintings, and thus good drawings often remained hidden in sketchbooks. Yet these preliminary sketches often possess a spontaneity absent in the worked-over exhibition pieces of the academicians. The sketchbooks of Robert HARRIS and William RAPHAEL, for example, contain vivid studies of figures later incorporated in well-known paintings, while Lucius O'BRIEN, John A. FRASER and T. Mower Martin made quick and sometimes detailed drawings of the Rockies and the West during the CPR-sponsored excursions in the 1880s and 1890s. Homer WATSON, Horatio WALKER and Marc-Aurèle de Foy SUZOR-CÔTÉ made lush and beautiful drawings in chalk, graphite and charcoal of peasants in the rural landscape, the subject of their often prolific and popular paintings. While the drawings of James Wilson MORRICE, Maurice CULLEN and Clarence GAGNON show some of the elusive touch of French Impressionism, these artists were interested primarily in colour and light and their few surviving sketches are essentially notations for future paintings. Morrice, however, was a brilliant draughtsman and, in his hundreds of tiny oil sketches, the under drawing is often visible beneath a thin surface of paint. Ozias LEDUC was perhaps the most prolific draughtsman, creating detailed pencil or charcoal drawings of compositions and figures, some of which were intended for church murals and paintings; his study for *L'Enfant au pain* (1892-99) is remarkably close to the finished painting in the National Gallery.

The Canadian artists who studied in London, Paris or Philadelphia in the late 19th century – William BRYMNER, George REID, Paul PEEL, Sidney Strickland Tully – were well trained in "correct" drawing, first from plaster casts, then in life classes (*see* ART EDUCATION). They perpetuated the practice of preliminary sketches for paintings; however, a drawing, such as Reid's *Hattie* (1880), was obviously intended as a finished work.

At the end of the 19th century the bulk of Canadian drawing was done for the utilitarian purpose of periodical illustration. The Toronto Art Students' League (1886-1904), a society of artists dedicated to the art of drawing, took as its motto "Nulla Dies Sine Linea" ("No day without a

Tales Over the Camp Fire (1862) by W.G.R. Hind, pencil and grey wash (*courtesy National Archives of Canada/C-33722*).

drawing"). The members, some of whom were former students at the Ontario School of Art (now ONTARIO COLLEGE OF ART), worked in print shops and engraving firms and included Charles MacDonald Manly, Robert Holmes, Frederick Henry Brigden, William Cruikshank and Charles William JEFFERYS. This group of artists met for study and sketching trips and published a calendar illustrated with pen-and-ink drawings between 1892 and 1904; Jefferys, fascinated with historical themes, produced *The Picture Gallery of Canadian History*. Another well-known illustrator was Henri JULIEN, who contributed vigorous figure drawings and caricatures to journals in Montréal and abroad. Some prominent painters also supplemented their income by illustration, as when Lucius O'Brien, Henry Sandham and John Fraser contributed drawings to *Picturesque Canada* (1882).

Although members of the GROUP OF SEVEN made rapid and skilful sketches in pencil, ink or oil wherever they travelled across Canada, most of their drawings were working plans for paintings, never intended to be displayed in public. The sketchbooks that survive, however, are a creative shorthand to their more famous paintings – notations that isolate the images most characteristic of the landscape they wished to portray. A.Y. JACKSON, Arthur LISMER and F.H. VARLEY were the most able and prolific in the medium, though Varley surpassed the others in talent, sensibility and range. His drawings, whether landscapes, portraits of women, or sketches done on site during his period as an official war artist, show brilliant skill. Lismer, a superb and quick draughtsman and caricaturist, created a large gallery of irreverent portraits of his friends. The drawings of

The drawings of F.H. Varley, such as *Catherine* (charcoal on paper), show the brilliant skill of the artist in many media (*courtesy Art Gallery of Greater Victoria/Gift of Harold Mortimer-Lamb/photo by Trevor Mills*).

Lawren HARRIS, never an end in themselves, reflect his progression from streetscape to landscape to abstraction, and are often linked to his philosophy of art. Lionel LeMoine FITZGERALD was only briefly a member of the Group, but drawing was ideally suited to his subtle art. Whether his subject was still life, nudes or the landscape, he was concerned to set form against form, edge against edge, fine line against stippled areas, in an orchestrated, delicate design in space; he produced a large body of ephemeral drawings, often in coloured pencil or chalk.

While David MILNE produced little that can be called drawing in the strictest sense, his watercolours and drypoint etchings reveal his command over basic drawing techniques. His paintings are such triumphs of economy and linear strength that they might be seen as drawings in oil. His contemporary, Emily CARR, produced a large number of charcoal and oil drawings on paper, which were often done on the spot. These drawings reveal her powerful expressionist vision of the forest and her basic respect for Indian life and, in their rapid, broad, economic yet almost calligraphic strokes and scumbles, they capture the essence of her understanding of West Coast living and her awe before a totem pole.

Goodridge ROBERTS occupies a secure position among Canadian landscape painters, but his restrained and sometimes sombre brush drawings are reminiscent of Chinese ink drawings in their balance and subtlety. John LYMAN, in works such as *Dancing Nude*, took a new approach to drawing, based on ideas put forward by the French artist Matisse, in which the vitality of the line took precedence over the depiction of the model. In the next decade, the AUTOMATISTES brought spontaneous, unpremeditated, nonobjective art to Québec. As their leader, Paul-Émile BORDUAS went on to produce a series of powerful abstract drawings that forecast the major developments in his brilliant progress in abstract art. Alfred PELLAN, who returned to Montréal in 1940 from Paris, set up a rival movement. His drawings and paintings are imbued with Surrealist imagery.

In 1953 a group of nonobjective painters in Toronto, inspired more by Abstract Expressionism in New York than their contemporaries in Montréal, formed PAINTERS ELEVEN as a means of exhibiting their work. Oscar CAHÉN made many drawings incorporating Abstract Expressionist and Surrealist elements, but the most talented and prolific figurative draughtsman was Harold TOWN, who continues to create thoroughly independent series of drawings.

After the 1960s the number of artists working in drawing expanded considerably. Their variety of styles usually reflect their work in other media. Alex COLVILLE, Christopher PRATT and Jack CHAMBERS are known as "realists" whose drawings show a high degree of technical skill, if not vitality and spontaneity. Ernest LINDNER produces microscopically detailed drawings of trees in decay as potent metaphors of death and renewal. There are drawings by Christiane Pflug, imbued with haunting, sombre imagery; vibrant, mixed-media abstracts by Gordon RAYNER; subtle, textural abstracts by Betty Goodwin; figure studies by Robert Markle and Graham COUGHTRY; harsh, monumental drawings by John Scott; domestic interiors by Mary PRATT; and landscape sketches by Ann Kipling, Dorothy KNOWLES, Takao TANABE and Gordon A. SMITH.

Drawing is a 2-dimensional form of art, even if used on modern devices such as the computer screen. Drawing will continue to change in style, technique and media; but its content will capture the more personal, often private, reactions of artists to the world around, not unlike a tenuous melody which awaits orchestration.

Reading: M. Allodi, *Canadian Watercolours and Drawings in the Royal Ontario Museum*, 2 vols (1974); P. Duval, *Canadian Drawings and Prints* (1952) and *Group of Seven Drawings* (1965); *Harold Town Drawings*, Introduction and text by R. Fulford (1969); P. Krauz, *Drawing: A Canadian Survey, 1977-82* (1983); J. Morris, *100 Years of Canadian Drawings* (1980); D. Shadbolt, *The Art of Emily Carr* (1979).

Dray, William Herbert, philosopher, professor (b at Montréal 23 June 1921). After serving as a navigator in the RCAF during WWII, he studied history at U of T, before proceeding to Oxford (D Phil, 1956). He taught at U of T from 1953 until 1968, when he became chairman of the philosophy dept at Trent U. Since 1976 he has taught at U of Ottawa. Dray's main contribution has been to the analytical philosophy of history and the social sciences, in which he has been a persistent critic of positivist tendencies, arguing that the model of explanation used in the natural sciences is inappropriate for the human sciences. He has also contributed to the study of the historiography of the English Civil War and has stimulated an interest in major philosophers of history such as R.G. Collingwood. His major works, which have been translated into many languages, include *Laws and Explanation in History* (1957), *Philosophy of History* (1964) and *Perspectives on History* (1980). He is fellow of the RSC, was a Killam fellow 1980-81 and in 1986 received the Molson Prize.

DAVID RAYNOR

Drayton Valley, Alta, Town, pop 5290 (1986c), located about 120 km SW of Edmonton, inc as a village 1955, as a new town 1956, and as a town 1957. The first European settlers arrived about 1907 and practised marginal mixed farming, lumbering and trapping. In 1953 huge reserves of oil were discovered in the Pembina oil field and Drayton Valley, because of its proximity, was chosen as the centre of the oil-field development. The town was planned as a model town by the provincial government, but growth was so rapid that severe crowding resulted. The town's population grew from 75 to over 3000 in 1953 alone. In 1954 the Drayton Valley Townsite Act was passed to control land sales. The town is located on high land overlooking the N Saskatchewan R. It has continued to rely upon the oil and gas industry, although its economic base has diversified to include forestry; a $55-million strandboard plant was constructed there in the mid-1980s.

D.G. WETHERELL

Dresden, Ont, Town, pop 2573 (1986c), 2550 (1981c), inc 1881, located in SW Ontario on Sydenham R, 80 km S of Sarnia. It was named after the German city. In 1841 Rev Josiah HENSON, a former slave from the US, helped to establish the British-American Institute, a vocational school and refuge for fugitive slaves. Henson is reputed to have been the model for Uncle Tom in Harriet Beecher Stowe's *Uncle Tom's Cabin* (1852). His 2-storey house, built around 1842, is now part of the Uncle Tom's Cabin Museum in Dresden. The town has an economy based on diversified light industry, mainly food processing.

DANIEL FRANCIS

Drew, George Alexander, lawyer, politician, premier of Ontario 1943-48 (b at Guelph, Ont 7 May 1894; d at Toronto 4 Jan 1973). After recovering from a serious wound suffered in WWI, he attended Osgoode Hall. Called to the bar in 1920, he practised law in Guelph, of which he was mayor in 1925. He was made master of the Ontario Supreme Court 1929 and became first chairman of the Ontario Securities Commission 1931. An ardent Conservative, he was elected leader of the Ontario party 1938, and led it to victory 1943. He served as both premier and minister of education, and founded the dynasty that ruled Ontario into the 1980s. In 1948 he entered national politics as party leader, but he failed in 2 elections to mount an effective challenge to the Liberal administration. He resigned as leader 1956 and was appointed Canadian high commissioner to London, Eng, 1957 – the last distinction in a noteworthy public career. Eloquent, combative and patrician in bearing, Drew was never wholly at ease in the hurly-burly of democratic politics. His opponents labelled him reactionary, a reputation largely belied by his record as premier.   ROGER GRAHAM

Reading: Jonathan Manthorpe, *The Power & the Tories* (1974).

Drought is the condition of critically low water supply caused by persistently below-normal precipitation. Drought begins with decreased soil moisture and surface and underground water supplies, and leads to decreased plant growth and restrictions in the use of surface and underground water supplies for domestic, municipal, agricultural and industrial purposes. Drought temporarily disturbs the ecological regime, creating conditions favourable to the spread of certain insect pests and plant and animal diseases. Drought-tolerant plants tend to displace conventional vegetation, and wild and domestic animals put stress on the reduced vegetation, thereby adversely affecting future plant growth. Drought also creates conditions favourable to forest fires. There is no universally accepted definition of drought; definitions depend on how people are affected. Therefore, criteria may include factors such as precipitation, stream flow, lake levels, groundwater levels, soil moisture, crop yields and economic hardship.

Droughts have occurred throughout the world for millions of years. Prehistoric droughts can be inferred from evidence left in tree rings, lake and ocean sediments and ice cores from glaciers. Evidence is also available from ancient writings and diaries. Recent major droughts have affected the Great Plains of N America in the 1930s; the Sahel, a semiarid region between Ethiopia and Senegal, in the 1970s and 1980s; Great Britain in 1975-76; California in 1976-77; and the southeastern US in 1986.

Meteorological Drought is measured by the deficiency in precipitation compared to the normal precipitation received. Evaluation of such a drought requires consideration of factors such as total precipitation over a given period (week, month, year) and length of time between significant RAINS, as well as when they occur.

Agricultural Drought is caused by meteorological drought, but its severity is increased by high evapotranspiration losses. The practice of summer fallowing lessens the severity of an agricultural drought by carrying over soil moisture from the previous year. In areas where irrigation water is available and stored water supplies ample, a meteorological drought may not lead to an agricultural drought.

Hydrological Drought is measured by the decrease in available water supply in flowing streams and in surface and underground storage. Hydrological drought is primarily caused by a deficiency in precipitation and further intensified by high evaporation, but factors such as demand for water, availability of surface-storage reservoirs and development of wells to use underground storage affect its impact.

Weather and Drought

Atmospheric circulation usually provides a progression of low- and high-pressure systems across a region. Low-pressure systems usually produce general rains and trigger the formation of convective storms, which result in locally heavy thundershowers. Occasionally a situation known

Dust storm in the Lethbridge area, Alta, spring 1942. Disastrous droughts have occurred on the prairies in the 1940s, 1960s and late 1970s *(courtesy Glenbow Archives, Calgary/NA-1831-1)*.

as blocking develops when a high-pressure system becomes anchored over a region, causing storm-producing low-pressure systems to be steered well to the S or N. Such blocking can prevent normal rainfall for weeks, months or even years. Drought of regional or subcontinental proportions can strike anywhere on Earth, although the mechanism described above is limited mainly to temperate latitudes, in which much of Canada is located. The cause of blocking is not yet understood; therefore efforts to provide long-range drought predictions have been unsuccessful. Research includes COMPUTER modelling of the atmosphere, studies of drought cycles, identification of physical predictors such as solar activity or sea-surface temperature anomalies, and the search for matching weather patterns or analogies from the past.

Canadian Droughts

Written accounts of past droughts (in newspaper articles and in diaries of settlers and explorers) refer to major droughts during the 1800s on the prairies. A more recent major drought was recorded for the region in the 1930s. Local droughts of shorter duration have occurred since the 1930s in parts of Canada, especially in the prairies (1940s, early 1960s, late 1970s) and in Ontario (1963). In Canada the effects of droughts have been felt most severely in areas where agricultural activities allow little margin of safety in the water supply. One such area was identified by explorer Capt John PALLISER as a result of his field work (1857-60). The dry area (later referred to as Palliser's Triangle) is an irregularly shaped area roughly defined by lines joining Cartwright, Man; Lloydminster, Sask; and Calgary and Cardston, Alta. Annual precipitation averages 38 cm, compared to 80 cm at Toronto and 140 cm at Vancouver and Halifax.

The drought of the 1930s is of special importance because of its areal extent and severity, and because of the government policies, programs and farming practices that resulted. The drought began in 1929 and continued, with some respites, until midsummer of 1937. Some 7.3 million ha, one-quarter of the arable land in Canada, was affected. Severe wind EROSION of the topsoil compounded the effects of the drought. Consequently, many farms were abandoned and farm families moved elsewhere *(see* AGRICULTURE HISTORY; GREAT DEPRESSION).

The drought of the 1930s brought into being federal and provincial government agencies to develop and manage drought-alleviation programs, the most notable being the creation of the

PRAIRIE FARM REHABILITATION ADMINISTRATION by an Act of Parliament in 1935. The PFRA was established to help prairie farmers cope with drought by providing financial and technical assistance in the building of water-storage reservoirs such as dugouts and small dams. Submarginal farming lands were taken over by PFRA, regrassed and turned into community pastures. The farmers were assisted in moving to more suitable areas, including areas on which farm IRRIGATION was being practised.

The Dominion experimental farm system was expanded to provide research and advice to farmers on cropping and cultivation practices more suitable to drought conditions. The federal Indian Head Tree Nursery provided trees, free of charge, to prairie farmers for shelterbelts to control soil drifting and to trap snow. New tillage machines were developed which disturbed the soil as little as possible and therefore decreased soil susceptibility to wind erosion. Alleviation programs developed during the 1930s have been modified and expanded on the basis of experience gained during subsequent dry periods. Agencies of the governments of Alberta, Saskatchewan and Manitoba developed programs, alone and in combination with federal agencies, to provide facilities enabling overland pumping of water to fill small reservoirs, cattle-feed assistance, and wells and irrigation projects.

Future Droughts

Based on recorded and inferred evidence, droughts have been a recurring phenomenon. Unless there is a drastic change in CLIMATE, droughts will continue to occur with essentially the same frequency. The difficulty of forecasting the timing, extent and severity should not deter the development of contingency plans. In many areas of Canada water uses for agricultural, municipal and industrial purposes are rapidly reaching the limits of natural supplies. Thus there is always the possibility that a severe drought could cause a serious disturbance to the Canadian economy. Study and planning could alleviate many of the hardships of a drought. One necessary prerequisite in planning for future droughts is the gathering of information. Precipitation, stream-flow and water-level data, gathered by Environment Canada at some 2700 climatological stations and

2500 hydrometric stations, country wide are supplemented by information collected by provincial agencies. Statistical analyses can be made to determine long-term average conditions, the possible start of a drought and the severity of an ongoing drought. Mechanisms to alleviate drought hardships can then be activated.

H. HILL

Reading: N. J. Rosenberg, *North American Droughts* (1978).

Drug Use, Non-medical Although drug use generally refers to the nonmedical use of psychotropic (mind-affecting) drugs, eg, cannabis (marijuana and hashish), opiate narcotics (eg, heroin and morphine), amphetamines, cocaine, hallucinogens (eg, LSD, psilocybin and mescaline) and volatile solvents (including certain fast-drying glues, fingernail-polish removers and petroleum products), most drug-related problems in Canada derive from use of alcohol and tobacco. While some of these drugs have legitimate medical uses, their social use is generally considered potentially physically or psychologically harmful. Volatile solvents, alcohol and tobacco are readily available, but the importation, production, sale and in most cases possession of the other drugs are criminally prohibited – except for very narrow medical functions.

Prior to this century, the use of psychotropic drugs was not considered a serious social problem and was not a criminal offence – even though more Canadians were dependent on opiates at the turn of the century than at any time before or since. Canada's decision in 1908 to prohibit under criminal law the importation, manufacture and sale of opium (it was the first Western nation to do so) was inspired more, as were related statutes, by racial prejudice (particularly against Asians) and moralistic fervour than by any scientific knowledge. Until the 1960s, addiction to opiates, particularly heroin, was the greatest social concern. While other nations, such as the UK, experimented with medical management and maintenance programs, Canada relied almost exclusively on increasingly punitive applications of the criminal law. As a result of zealous law-enforcement efforts and the elimination of licit sources of supply or avenues of therapeutic assistance, most narcotics dependants were forced into subcultural ghettos, where they became the very kind of criminally involved person who advocates of the criminal-law solution had always maintained they were. The situation has not changed. For at least 30 years they have represented the stereotypical horrors of drug abuse in the public imagination. In reality the plight of most heroin dependants derives very little from the chemical properties of the drug. It is the official response to this problem which forces dependants to commit property crimes to purchase drugs at grossly inflated prices.

In the 1960s concern about heroin was eclipsed by that about the consumption of cannabis, amphetamines and hallucinogens. The use of many of the hallucinogens, especially LSD, was relatively new, but small groups had been inconspicuously indulging in many of these drugs in most Canadian urban centres for at least a decade before the public noticed. While Parliament had incorporated most of these drugs into existing criminal statutes (and added the newer ones as soon as their chemical composition could be identified), the sudden public and media attention was undoubtedly caused by the ostentatious use of these drugs by middle-class youths who affected an apparently alien life-style associated with the hippie movement. Unlike heroin dependants, a largely invisible presence, marijuana, hashish and LSD users were increasingly vocal about their indul-gences. Many openly championed what they perceived to be the beneficial attributes of recreational drug use and crusaded for legislative reform. By 1969 the number of persons charged with cannabis offences, almost negligible at the beginning of that decade, had risen to 5000, and by 1977 the annual figure had swollen to a relatively constant 50 000.

In 1969 the federal government appointed a royal commission to investigate the problem of the NON-MEDICAL USE OF DRUGS. In a series of internationally respected reports published over 4 years, the commission recommended, among other things, a gradual withdrawal of the use of the criminal law against nonmedical users of drugs, the repeal of the offence of possession of cannabis, a general reduction of penalties for all other cannabis offences and no increase in the penalties for other drug offences, and for opiate dependants an emphasis on treatment and medical management rather than criminal sanctions. Although none of these recommendations have been implemented in Canada, they did contribute to the decriminalization of cannabis use and possession in several American states. The commission also helped Canadians to consider drug use in a more rational perspective.

While more Canadians experiment with nonmedical drug use each year, the incidence of regular use has generally stabilized since the mid-1970s. Over 5 million Canadians have tried marijuana at least once during their lives and about 2 million have done so during each of the past several years. This use, like all unprescribed drug consumption, tends to be concentrated among adolescents and adults under 30 years of age. National survey data for 1981 indicate that most current marijuana users are regular but relatively infrequent consumers; of the some 2.4 million Canadians who used marijuana at some time during the month prior to being surveyed, only 500 000 were weekly users, and only 120 000 used it daily.

Provincial surveys of high-school students have tended to indicate relatively constant or moderately declining levels of use of most drugs over the past decade. It would appear that, apart from cannabis, the adolescent consumption of illicit drugs is a generally infrequent phenomenon indulged in by a very small proportion of that population. Cocaine use has undoubtedly increased significantly among Canadian teenagers and adults in the past decade (eg, the adult "ever used" rate has doubled from 3% to 6% between 1984 and 1987 in Ont), but remains only about half of comparable American figures. The high cost, occasionally adverse effects and faddish nature of the drug are likely to prevent the use of cocaine from ever reaching the high levels of marijuana and hashish. Heroin use is the most difficult form of drug consumption to measure reliably. Heroin dependents are chiefly concentrated in BC; nationally about 10 000 to 15 000 are dependent on the drug.

Over 80% of Canadians drink alcohol, although only about 10% are daily imbibers. Stimulants (pep and diet pills) were consumed by 2% of the Canadian adult population in the year prior to a mid-1985 national survey. Sleeping pills and tranquilizers, chiefly prescribed, were used by 8% and 6%, respectively, of the 1985 national survey's respondents.

Apart from some insignificant hallucinogen manufacturing, a small amount of low-grade marijuana cultivation and the diversion of pharmaceuticals from their licit channels of distribution, Canada is not a source for illicit drugs. Only 5-10% of the drugs imported into Canada each year are intercepted. International efforts to stem the drug trade have proven equally ineffective but have contributed to a continual inflation of the price of drugs without any apparent abatement of demand. Financially the drug trade has become the most attractive and corruptive criminal enterprise in the world. Some policymakers have recommended a strategy specifically directed at the health and safety hazards associated with each drug, including alcohol and tobacco, based on a scientific appraisal of drug-related risks. The perennial national debates about cannabis reform and heroin maintenance are 2 examples of this possible reorientation.

MELVYN GREEN

Drumheller, Alta, City, pop 6366 (1986c), 6508 (1981c), inc 1930, is located on the RED DEER R in southern Alberta, 136 km NE of Calgary, and lies at the head of the famed 48 km "Dinosaur Trail" of the Alberta BADLANDS. Shortly after ranchers first settled there (1897), the townsite was bought by Col Samuel Drumheller (1910). He started COAL MINING operations (at sites around the townsite) in 1911, and the first post office was named after him. The railway arrived in 1912, and in quick succession Drumheller became a village (1913) and a town (1916). Today, although coal mining has all but disappeared from the city's economy, the Drumheller Exhibition and Stampede (held each July), the Red Deer River valley fossil remains, the Drumheller Dinosaur Fossil Museum, and Prehistoric Park still attract many tourists yearly. In Sept 1985 the Alberta government opened the TYRRELL MUSEUM OF PALAEONTOLOGY. The museum exhibits include 50 complete DINOSAUR skeletons (the largest display of complete dinosaur skeletons in the world) and the skulls and parts of many other animals.

DAVID EVANS

Drumheller Strike, 1925, ushered in a period of rival or "dual" unionism in Alberta's coalfields. The Drumheller miners, rejecting wage cuts negotiated by the United Mine Workers, struck in June 1925. The strike faltered because many miners continued to work and provincial police protected them. A violent police-striker confrontation on June 26 effectively ended the strike. But miners, angry with the UMW's collaboration with the coal operators regarding wage cuts, formed the rival Mine Workers' Union of Canada which battled the UMW for a decade before declaring a truce and rejoining the old union. The MWUC-UMW rivalry, though beginning in Alberta, spread to coal mines across western Canada. It also had political overtones because of the major role of communists in the MWUC.

ALVIN FINKEL

Drumlin, smooth, half egg-shaped or ellipsoidal hill which formed beneath Quaternary GLACIERS. Drumlins [Gaelic *druim,* "hill"] were first described in Ireland. They lie parallel to the direction of ice movement, the blunt (stoss) end facing up-glacier, the lee sloping down-glacier. Drumlins may be up to 50 m high and several kilometres long, with an average length/width ratio of 2 or 3 to 1. Highly elongated drumlins are often called drumlinoids. Drumlins occur in broad fields or swarms, up-glacier from major end MORAINES in Europe and N America. Swarms of several thousands occur in NS, southern Ontario and the Thelon Plain of Keewatin, NWT; smaller groups, in most other provinces. Drumlins may

Fertile farmland and deeply eroded river gullies near Drumheller, Alta (*courtesy Colour Library Books*).

be composed of layers of till (sediment deposited by a glacier), frequently clay rich, in which the pebbles are oriented subparallel to drumlin elongation and the direction of ice flow, although many drumlins have cores of stratified sand, boulders or bedrock. Rock drumlins are rock outcrops smoothed by ice to a drumlin shape. Scientists are not certain how drumlins originated. The "dilatancy" theory postulates that drumlins were initiated beneath ice of a critical thickness, downglacier from high basal pressure zones and upglacier from moraine deposition, where till expanded, forming hummocks. Other hypotheses suggest that subglacial crevasses, frost heave, helical ice motion or water loss from saturated till initiated hummocks. Drumlins with a core of stratified sediments are glaciofluvial in origin, formed by deposition in cavities which were cut in the base of the ice by a large discharge of subglacial melt water. All theories hold that the hummocks were subsequently enlarged by layers of till which were plastered on and streamlined by the ice sliding over. *See also* GLACIATION.

R.J. ROGERSON

Drummond, Robert, labour leader (b at Greenock, Scot 9 Oct 1840; d at New Glasgow, NS 26 Dec 1925). Drummond helped organize one of Canada's first coal miners' unions, the Provincial Workmen's Assn of NS, in 1879 and was its grand secretary 1879-98. Appointed to the NS Legislative Council by Prem W.S. FIELDING in 1891, he advised the government on the coal trade until retiring in 1924. He founded, edited and published the PWA's *Trades Journal*. Under Drummond, the union grew to include some 2000 members and fought several strikes, and he increasingly emphasized lobbying for legislative re-

form, for example, the arbitration bill that became law in 1889. He resigned in 1898 after the American Knights of Labor raided PWA locals and the union was almost destroyed. Drummond then began publishing the *Maritime Mining Record*. He also wrote *Minerals and Mining, Nova Scotia* (1918).

SHARON REILLY

Drummond, Thomas, botanist, (b in Scot *c*1780; d at Havana, Cuba early Mar 1835). Assistant naturalist to John Richardson on the second expedition led by Sir John FRANKLIN, Drummond did not accompany Richardson to the Arctic but instead botanized at Cumberland House on the Saskatchewan R, 1825, in the Rocky Mts near Jasper, 1826, and at Carlton House, 1827. In the mountains alone, Drummond collected 1500 specimens of plants, 150 birds and 500 mammals, some new to science. He had a narrow escape from the jaws of a grizzly bear, and once went 7 days without food. In 1828 he became curator of the botanical garden in Belfast and from 1830 to 1834 made important collections in the southern US, especially Texas. A number of plants, including those of the genus *Drummondia*, and the yellow mountain avens, *Dryas drummondii*, bear his name.

C. STUART HOUSTON

Drummond, William Henry, poet (b at Mohill, County Leitrim, Ire 13 Apr 1854; d at Cobalt, Ont 6 Apr 1907). Drummond arrived in Canada with his parents in 1864. He studied at Bishop's and practised as a general physician in Montréal and Brome County, Qué. Attracted by the folkways of rural Québec, he began writing narrative verse in the English idiom of the French Canadian farmer. His first book of poetry, *The Habitant* (1897), was extremely successful, establishing for him a reputation as a writer of dialect verse that has faded since his death.

C.J. TAYLOR

Drummondville, Qué, City, pop 36 020 (1986c), 36 567 (1981c), inc 1875, is located on

the Rivière ST-FRANÇOIS, a tributary of the St Lawrence R, in the Piedmont Appalachians, 100 km NE of Montréal. The town was founded in 1815 and named in honour of colonial administrator Sir Gordon Drummond. The Abenaki called the site "the big waterway." Originally settled by English soldiers and French settlers who had to clear land to survive, it became a focal point for people crossing the river at the foot of the falls. Potash was the town's first economic activity. Later, the post-Confederation era brought industrialization: sawmills, tanneries, forges, the railway, a hydroelectric plant and a cement factory. In 1915, during WWI, a firm manufacturing "smokeless gunpowder" opened and transformed the town's economy. However, real development began with the establishment of the textile industry in 1918. Its proximity to major roadways between Montréal and the US has made it a favoured location for numerous trucking companies. Drummondville now has a number of diversified industrial parks. Subcontracting makes up the largest part of industrial production, with General Motors, Bell Canada, Northern Telecom, Bombardier and others making parts and equipment. The textile industry still employs over 30% of the work force of 10 000. The Parc des Voltigeurs, a popular camping ground, is set on the river and the Village Québécois d'Antan, with some 50 historical buildings, recalls life in the 19th century and is host to the World Folklore Festival — the largest such event in N America — which draws some 500 000 visitors.

JEAN-MARIE DUBOIS AND PIERRE MAILHOT

Drury, Charles Mills, "Bud," public servant, politician (b at Montréal 17 May 1912). During WWII Drury attained the rank of brigadier, and then was chief of the UN Relief and Rehabilitation Administration in Poland. After a brief stint in External Affairs, Drury was deputy minister of national defence 1948-55. He spent 1955-62 in private business, but in 1962 entered politics as a Liberal. Elected MP for St Antoine-Westmount, he joined the 1963 PEARSON Cabinet. He held various posts in both the Pearson and TRUDEAU governments, including president of the treasury board. He left the Cabinet in 1977 and the House of Commons in 1978, subsequently becoming chairman of the National Capital Commission.

ROBERT BOTHWELL

Drury, Ernest Charles, farmer, politician, writer, local historian, premier of Ontario 1919-23 (b at Crown Hill, Ont 22 Jan 1878; d at Barrie, Ont 17 Feb 1968). A son of Charles Drury, Ontario's first minister of agriculture, and a graduate of Ontario Agricultural Coll, Drury was active in the farm movement, serving as secretary of the Canadian Council of Agriculture and master of the Dominion Grange and Farmers' Alliance. He was a cofounder and first president of the UNITED FARMERS OF ONTARIO, formed in 1914 to promote agrarian interests in the province. After WWI the UFO became a political force, but Drury was not a candidate when it challenged the Conservative government in the Ontario general election of 1919. With the support of labour it won enough seats to form a government, and it called on Drury to lead it. He became the province's eighth premier and won a seat in Halton in Feb 1920. His administration was noted for important social legislation and for the strict enforcement of the Ontario Temperance Act. Following the defeat of his government in 1923 Drury retired from provincial politics and ventured unsuccessfully into the federal field as an independent Liberal. In 1934 he was appointed sheriff and registrar of Simcoe County and devoted considerable time to writing on public affairs and preparing local histories: *Forts of Folly* (1932), an attack on the tariff, and *All for a Beaver Hat* (1959), a history of early Simcoe County. His memoirs, *Farmer Premier*, were published shortly before his death.

CHARLES M. JOHNSTON

Dry Fishery, that portion of the Newfoundland cod fishery in which the split and cleaned product was salted and dried on shore before being transported and sold. Compared with the GREEN FISHERY, the dry fishery required less salt but more time curing on land – on fishing "flakes" or beaches – near the fishing grounds. The dry fishery, particularly popular with early English fishermen who had limited access to salt, required the use of the land and eventually promoted settlement. Because of its dependence on the land, it tended to be a more localized near-shore fishery in areas where the weather was suitable for drying fish. The fishing gounds were within easy reach of the home base. *See also* FISHERIES HISTORY.

ROBERT D. PITT

Drybones Case (1970) In *R v Drybones* the Supreme Court of Canada, in a divided judgement called by certain persons the decision of the century, rendered inoperative a provision of the Indian Act, basing its judgement on the "equality before the law" clause of the Canadian Bill of Rights. The court ruled that if a federal statute cannot be reasonably interpreted and applied without abolishing, limiting or infringing upon one of the rights or liberties recognized in the Bill of Rights, it is inoperative unless Parliament expressly declares that it is to apply notwithstanding the Bill of Rights. The court concluded that J. Drybones, who had been found drunk off reserve land in a lobby of a Yellowknife hotel, had been punished because of his race under a law whose scope and penalty differs from that governing other Canadians.

GÉRALD-A. BEAUDOIN

Dryden, Ont, Town, Kenora District, pop 6462 (1986c), 6640 (1981c), inc 1910, is situated on Lk Wabigoon in NW Ontario, 355 km NW of Thunder Bay. Lumbering operations and gold prospecting began in the Wabigoon area in early 1880s with the construction of the Canadian Pacific Ry, but permanent settlement dates only from 1894 when the Ontario minister of agriculture, John Dryden, opened the region to agricultural settlement by establishing a provincial experimental farm at New Prospect. In 1897, the year the first sawmill was constructed, the name was changed to Dryden, and in the next 2 decades successive provincial governments advertised widely the farming potential of the area. The year 1913 saw the commencement of the predecessor

Logs in boom near Great Lakes Forest Products Ltd mill at Dryden, pushed to conveyor by tugboat (*photo by Jim Merrithew*).

company to the modern Great Lakes Forest Products, and quickly the PULP AND PAPER INDUSTRY became the economic mainstay of the community. Population growth was relatively slow until shortly after WWII when the town expanded rapidly from about 1700 to 4400 in 1955. Because of its air, road and railway links to Winnipeg and Thunder Bay, Dryden today serves as a central distribution point not only for Wabigoon area but also for the entire Patricia Development Region.

MATT BRAY

Dryden, Kenneth Wayne, hockey player, lawyer (b at Hamilton, Ont 8 Aug 1947). He played at Cornell U and turned professional with Montreal Voyageurs of the AHL in 1970. After only 6 regular-season games in the NHL, he played the entire 1970-71 playoffs with the Montreal Canadiens. His outstanding play brought the Canadiens an unexpected Stanley Cup and won him the CONN SMYTHE TROPHY. His record over 8 NHL seasons to his retirement in 1978-79 (he sat out 1973-74 in a contract dispute) was the most consistent of any modern goalie. He recorded a 2.24 goals-against average and 46 shutouts in regular season play and a 2.40 average and 10 shutouts in 112 playoff games. He won the CALDER TROPHY (1972) and the VÉZINA TROPHY (1973 and 1976, and shared 1977, 1978 and 1979) and was first all-star goalie 5 times. He is now a lawyer in Toronto. Dryden was Ontario's first Youth Commissioner, 1984-86, and in 1986 issued a report recommending improved job training for youth. In 1985 a bronze statue of the former goalie was unveiled in St-Laurent, showing him in his familiar pose, leaning on his stick. In 1983 he published *The Game*, unique among books on his sport for its literate reflectiveness.

JAMES MARSH

Du Val, Mountenay William, (b at Île Bonaventure, Qué 30 Jan 1883; d at Mont-Joli, Qué 22 Feb 1960) and **Matilda Clara Du Val**, née Mauger (b at Île Bonaventure, Qué 4 Oct 1884; d at Montréal 13 Dec 1954). The Du Vals were both of Channel Island and Irish background and were raised at ÎLE BONAVENTURE. Matilda was educated in New York and was deeply influenced by CHRISTIAN SCIENCE and wildlife conservation movements. On a visit to her birthplace in July 1911, she became engaged to William Du Val; they married 23 Jan 1912.

William Du Val began looking after the island's many varieties of birds on his own in 1912. By 1920, he and his wife were "looking after" some 7000 birds. On 23 Mar 1920 William began as honorary warden; he was later a game warden, on a part-time salary. "Looking after the birds" consisted of counting and banding gannets, providing occasional veterinarian first aid and nurture, discouraging poaching, and educating the public. Visitors and publicists became aware of the hardships of this courageous couple during a time when wildlife preservation was in its infancy. William Du Val supported his family by a water tour of the bird colonies in a craft he built, piloted while giving lectures to his passengers. In 1947 the post of game officer was created for Du Val; he retired within 2 years of the death of his wife.

ALDO BROCHET

Dubawnt Lake, 3833 km², elev 236 m, is situated on the border of Mackenzie and Keewatin districts, NWT, 350 km S of the Arctic Circle. Within the Precambrian SHIELD, the lake has irregular shorelines and numerous islands. It is drained northward by DUBAWNT R into ABERDEEN LK, then eastward by THELON R into HUDSON BAY. Its water is clear and deep. Lake trout, lake and round whitefish and arctic grayling are common in the lake. The surrounding slopes consist of glacial till, fes-

tooned by the abandoned beaches of a proglacial lake up to 73 m above the present water level. The vegetation is low arctic tundra with heath and lichens, although scattered groves of stunted spruce occur at the south end. The lake is on the migration route of the Kaminuriak caribou herd, consisting of over 100 000 animals. Muskoxen occur in the area, especially to the W, within the Thelon Game Sanctuary. Wolves, foxes and grizzly bears are the main predators. The lake is at the contact point between the Chipewyan and inland Inuit, but there are no permanent settlements here. The lake was discovered by Samuel HEARNE in 1770, but remained virtually unknown until explored by J.B. TYRRELL in 1893.

S.C. ZOLTAI

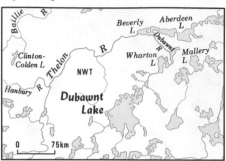

Dubawnt River, 842 km long, rises in a web of lakes in the NWT, 120 km NE of Lk Athabasca, flows NE, gathering the waters of Wholdaia, Boyd, Barlow, Nicholson, Dubawnt, Wharton and Marjorie lakes, and turns abruptly NW to join the THELON R at Beverly Lk. The Thelon flows on to Hudson Bay. The river was discovered by Samuel HEARNE 1770 and traversed by Joseph B. TYRRELL in 1893. DUBAWNT LK, icebound most of the summer, is just N of the treeline in the Barren Lands. The name Dubawnt is from the Chipewyan word "tobotua," meaning "water shore," possibly in reference to water between the shore and ice in late spring.

JAMES MARSH

Dubé, Marcel, writer (b at Montréal 3 Jan 1930). In 1950 Dubé helped found a troupe called La Jeune Scène. The 1951 production of *Le Bal triste* at L'Ermitage in Montréal was the first of a collection that is the most extensive, significant and representative body of Québec and Canadian plays of the 1950s and first half of the 1960s. Other plays of his, such as *De l'autre côté du mur* (1952) and *Zone* (1953), have won many awards and distinctions. Dubé's usual theme is the tragedy of human destiny. Dubé lived in France 1953-55. NFB scenarist, journalist, producer and author for both stage and TV, Dubé has received many grants and won the St-Jean-Baptiste Society's Prix Morin (1966), Québec's Prix David (1973) for his work as a whole, the Molson Prize for contribution to the arts in Canada (1984) and the medal of the Académie canadienne-française (1987).

PIERRE LAVOIE

Ducharme, Réjean, novelist, playwright, scriptwriter, songwriter (b at St-Félix-de-Valois, Qué 13 Aug 1942). Ducharme was one of the first Québec novelists to be published in France. A prolific writer, he is also one of the most original and innovative authors of French Canada. His first novel, *L'Avalée des avalés*, 1966 (trans *The Swallower Swallowed*, 1968), was published at the height of the QUIET REVOLUTION, and won a Governor General's Award. This book, like the next 2 (*Le Nez qui voque*, 1967, and *L'Océantume*, 1968) caused an uproar known as the "Ducharme Affair." His works (7 novels, 4 plays, 2 film scenarios) are marked by unfettered imagination, a characteristic language style approaching "verbal frenzy," antiheroes and heroines searching for freedom, and unexpected, hilarious plot developments. The counterpoint to this game-playing and carefree side of his writing are themes of love and death, the conflicts of child/adult, nature/culture, affirmation/negation, portrayed with lucidity and insight. Although Ducharme's works deal with universal themes such as religion and marriage, they are rooted in Québec and America. Two of his plays are parodies, but the other 2 and his film scripts present situations and characters similar to those in his novels. He has also written words for several songs by Robert CHARLEBOIS. *See also* NOVEL IN FRENCH.　　RENÉE LEDUC-PARK

Duchesneau de La Doussinière et d'Ambault, Jacques, chevalier, INTENDANT of New France 1675-82 (d at Ambrant, France 1696). Despite his experience and the high hopes of his protector, the French minister Colbert, Duchesneau did not live up to his illustrious predecessor, Jean TALON, largely because of his difficult relations with Governor FRONTENAC. Duchesneau denounced the illegal trafficking of many of the COUREURS DE BOIS and suggested that the governor's attitude was so permissive as to smack of desire for personal gain. When he backed Bishop LAVAL in his fight against the sale of alcohol to the Amerindians, Frontenac accused him of being the clergy's tool. The 2 antagonists were recalled to France simultaneously: their disputes had injured the colony and angered the minister.　　FRANCE BEAUREGARD

Duck, WATERFOWL with short legs, webbed feet and narrow, pointed wings. A few island species are flightless but most are strong fliers and migratory (*see* MIGRATION). Ducks, geese and swans comprise a family (Anatidae) with 142 to 148 living or recently extinct species. Ducks have worldwide distribution, except for polar regions. Canada's 29 breeding species belong to 4 tribes in one subfamily; 8 other species from this subfamily have occurred in Canada, as have one species of whistling duck and the Labrador duck (*Camptorhynchus labradorius*), last seen in 1878.

Bills of mergansers are long and tubular with deeply toothed edges. All other ducks have a flat, wide bill with fine serrations. The bill is swollen into a spoon shape in northern shovelers (*Anas clypeata*). Male breeding and winter plumage is distinct from that of females and post-breeding males. Plumage is often highly coloured in males, especially in the wood duck (*Aix sponsa*). An unusual feature of ducks is that all primaries (flight feathers) are moulted together, making the birds temporarily flightless. Legs of dabbling ducks are centrally placed, allowing easy takeoff and walking; those of diving ducks are placed far back, aiding in diving but impeding walking and necessitating "pattering" along the water surface prior to takeoff.

Most ducks are gregarious, gathering in large feeding, moulting and wintering flocks. At early stages of nesting, males in several species are territorial, but pair bonds are temporary and females

Wood duck (*Aix sponsa*) male shown in its highly coloured plumage (*photo by Stephen J. Krasemann/DRK Photo*).

There are 29 breeding species of ducks in Canada, including the mallard shown above (*Anas platyrhynchos*), which is widely domesticated for food (*photo by Tim Fitzharris*).

undertake all incubation and care of young. Female Barrow's goldeneye (*Bucephala islandica*) are also territorial. Nests of most species are of grasses and on the ground, often under shrubbery and usually near water. Wood duck, common goldeneye (*Bucephala clangula*), bufflehead (*B. albeola*) and the hooded merganser (*Lophdytes cucullatus*) nest in holes in trees; common and red-breasted mergansers (*Mergus merganser* and *M. serrator*, respectively) often nest in crevices underground. Mallards (*Anas platyrhynchos*) some times nest in trees or inside buildings. Several marsh-dwelling species have floating nests. The blackheaded duck (*Heteronetta atricapilla*) of S America always lays its eggs in nests of other species; such brood parasitism is frequent but less developed in redhead ducks (*Aythya americana*) and infrequent in ruddy ducks (*Oxyura jamaicensis*). Clutches are usually large, 4-16 eggs in Canadian species. Downy young are active at hatching, swimming within hours. Hens guard and brood ducklings but do not feed them.

Ducks nest in aquatic habitats ranging from marshes and tundra ponds to fast-flowing mountain streams and large lakes across Canada. Dabbling ducks are most common on the prairies; seaducks range far into the Arctic. The American black duck (*Anas rubripes*) is centered in the Maritimes and Québec; most other species are widespread or primarily western. Barrow's goldeneye and harlequin ducks (*Histrionicus histrionicus*) breed in disjunct populations on both coasts. The cinnamon teal (*Anas cyaoptera*), primarily of interior BC and extreme SW Alberta, has the most localized range in Canada. Most species gather along the coasts and Great Lakes in winter or fly S. Thermally maintained RESERVOIRS have resulted in increasing numbers of wintering ducks, even on the prairies. Two Eurasian species, Eurasian widgeon (*Anas penelope*) and tufted duck (*Aythya fuligula*), are increasingly wintering in coastal BC. Mallards and Muscovy ducks (*Cairina moschata*) are widely domesticated for food; the common eider (*Somateria mollissima*) is semidomesticated in Iceland for down. Most ducks eat a mixture of vegetation and invertebrates; several dabblers

sometimes feed on grain crops. Mergansers eat mostly fish. Ducks are a favourite object of HUNTING. *See also* GAME BIRD.　　MARTIN K. McNICHOLL

Duck Lake, Battle of On 26 Mar 1885, the NORTH-WEST REBELLION began W of the settlement of Duck Lake on the old Carlton Trail, N of modern Rosthern, Sask. Duck Lake was at the junction of the Carlton and Prince Albert trails, midway between Métis headquarters at BATOCHE and the NWMP at Fort Carlton. The battle began at about noon when a Cree emissary and a police interpreter scuffled during a parley. The police and volunteers retreated about half-an-hour later. Twelve of their force of 100 were killed. Six of the slightly larger rebel force died. Métis military commander Gabriel DUMONT was wounded; his brother, Isidore, was the first to die. A cairn now marks the eastern edge of the battlefield on Highway 212.　　BOB BEAL

Ducks Unlimited Canada is a private, nonprofit organization dedicated to the conservation of the wetland habitats of N America's WATERFOWL, some 70% of which breed in Canada's prairie provinces. DUC was founded in 1937, the same year as Ducks Unlimited Inc in the US, to collect money from waterfowl hunters and spend it on wetland development. From its first project in 1938, Big Grass Marsh, 120 km NW of Winnipeg, it has spent over $265 million to develop 2900 wetland projects. Concern over declining waterfowl populations in the early decades of the 20th century reached a crisis during the prairie drought of the 1930s. In recent years threats to waterfowl habitats have come from commercial land use. DUC has 35 offices in Canada and focuses its efforts on designing, building and operating dikes, channels, dams, nesting islands and water-level controls to provide waterfowl with nesting, feeding and brood-rearing habitats. *See also* SWAMP, MARSH AND BOG.

Dudek, Louis, poet, critic, professor and literary activist (b at Montréal 6 Feb 1918). He was educated in Montréal and went to McGill (BA), where he wrote for the *McGill Daily*. His early poems began to appear in 1941-42 in the *McGill Daily*, and at about this time he became involved with *First Statement*, the first of a series of *engagé* acts in the little press and little magazine movement in Canada. In 1944 Dudek moved to New York where he entered graduate school at Columbia; his doctoral dissertation was published as *Literature and the Press* (1960). In 1951 Dudek returned to Montréal to take up an appointment at McGill. While in New York, he had continued to contribute poems, reviews and articles to NORTHERN REVIEW. In 1952, together with Irving LAYTON and Raymond SOUSTER he established Contact Press, a venture which published most of the important Canadian poets of the fifties and sixties, with *Cerebus* (1952), the first title, being a jointly authored collection of poetry. With Layton and Aileen Collins, whom he later married, he founded, in 1954, an avant-garde magazine, *CIV/n*, and, in 1956, established The McGill Poetry Series, launching the careers of Leonard COHEN and Daryl Hine. In 1957 Dudek founded his own little magazine, *Delta* (1957-66), a vehicle for his poetry and ideas, and in which he featured the work of many promising new poets. His own writing had been evolving steadily out of the lyricism and social concern of *East of the City* (1946) into the longer, meditative statement of *Europe* (1954, *The Transparent Sea*, 1956, and *En Mexico*, 1958). He had become (not unlike his friend and correspondent, Ezra Pound) less a poet of the everyday and more a critic of civilization. He had also developed a distinctive poetic voice: thoughtful and undramatic. At odds with the literary histrionics and the cultural currents of the 1960s, Dudek withdrew into his teaching and the writing of his long poem *Atlantis* (1967).

In 1963 he joined with others to found a little press, Delta Canada (1963-71), which published his *Collected Poetry* (1971). Between 1965 and 1969 Dudek wrote a regular column on books, film and the arts for the *Montreal Gazette*. This activity together with his reviews, articles and radio talks has remained fundamental to Dudek's perception of the poet's and the critic's role in society. In 1967 he published *The First Person in Literature*, and in 1974 *Dk/Some Letters of Ezra Pound*. His *Selected Essays and Criticism* appeared in 1978 to be followed by *Technology & Culture: Six Lectures* in 1979. The later poetry, typified by the collection *Continuation 1* (1981), harks back to an earlier book, *Epigrams* (1975), and is an experiment in recording the fragmentary, poetic moment. A selection of his poetry, entitled *Cross-Section: Poems 1940-1980* was published in 1981, and *Zembla's Rocks* in 1986.

An anthologist of note (*Canadian Poems 1850-1952*, 1952, with Irving Layton; *Poetry of our Time*, 1965; *The Making of Modern Poetry in Canada*, 1967, with M. Gnarowski; and *All Kinds of Everything*, 1973), and frequent speaker, Dudek has influenced the teaching of poetry in Canadian schools and universities. Prior to his retirement he was Greenshields Professor of English. He is a Member of the Order of Canada.

MICHAEL GNAROWSKI

Reading: F. Davey, *Louis Dudek & Raymond Souster* (1980); F. Davey and bp Nichol, eds, *Louis Dudek: Texts & Essays* (*Open Letter*, Spring & Summer 1981. Fourth Series, Nos 8-9); S. Stromberg-Stein, *Louis Dudek: A Biographical Introduction to his Poetry* (1983).

Duel, formal armed combat between 2 people in the presence of witnesses, to settle differences or a point of honour. Duels were recorded in NEW FRANCE as early as 1646; the last known duel in what is now Canada occurred in 1873 at St John's, Nfld (a hilarious shoot-out for which the seconds had loaded the pistols with blanks). Duels in the French regime were fought exclusively with swords; after the Conquest almost all were with pistols. Most incidents ended without injury, but there were some fatal encounters: at least 9 died in New France, 2 in Lower Canada, 5 in Upper Canada, 2 each in Nova Scotia and New Brunswick and 1 in Newfoundland. The last fatal duel occurred 22 May 1838 at Verdun, Lower Canada, when lawyer Robert Sweeny shot and killed Maj Henry Warde, who had sent a love letter to Mrs Sweeny. The last fatal duel in Upper Canada [Ontario] took place in Perth 13 June 1833. Defending his honour, John Wilson shot and killed Robert Lyon who had called him a liar and had beaten him up. Wilson and his second were charged with murder, but were acquitted.

Several famous Canadians fought duels: James DOUGLAS duelled at Île-à-la-Crosse in 1820 during a fur-trade dispute; Joseph HOWE fought in 1840 to prove his courage and gain the opportunity to decline further challenges; George-Étienne CARTIER duelled in 1848 to refute accusations of cowardice 11 years earlier at the Battle of ST-DENIS; and in 1849 John A. MACDONALD had to be prevented from fighting a political opponent.

Duels were fought in a variety of places: in locked rooms, in open fields or across tables. Causes also varied, and were often trivial. In 1800 at York [Toronto], John Small shot and killed John White after the latter spread gossip that Mrs Small was the former mistress of an English lord. A quarrel over card-game winnings led to a fatal duel in St John's, Nfld, in Mar 1826. Sharp political disputes in Lower Canada resulted in a spate of challenges and meetings, 1834-37.

Authorities considered duelling a crime, and to kill in a duel was tantamount to murder. However, the laws were irregularly enforced. In New France, several duellists were imprisoned, banished or executed; even the bodies of men killed in duels were desecrated. Under English rule, juries consistently refused to convict duellists if they felt that the encounters had somehow been conducted fairly and honourably. HUGH A. HALLIDAY

Duff, Sir Lyman Poore, chief justice of Canada 1933-44 (b at Meaford, Ont 7 Jan 1865; d at Ottawa 26 Apr 1955). Educated and called to the bar in Ontario, he moved to Victoria in 1894 where he soon established himself as a skilled and busy counsel. After 2 years on the BC Supreme Court he went to the Supreme Court of Canada in 1906 where he served for nearly 38 years. He was the leading figure on the court while Canada was making the transition from an agrarian society to a modern industrial state. In constitutional law his decisions were, and still are, pre-eminent. Perhaps his greatest contribution to Canadian nationhood was his decision in 1940 upholding the power of the Dominion government to abolish appeals to the Privy Council in London unilaterally; the Privy Council agreed with Duff, though the legislation for that purpose did not become effective until 1 Jan 1949. He thereby can be credited with establishing a wholly indigenous court system. DAVID RICARDO WILLIAMS

Reading: David Ricardo Williams, *Duff: A Life in the Law* (1984).

Duff, Wilson, anthropologist, museologist (b at Vancouver 1925; d there 8 Aug 1976). Duff's entire professional career centered on the study of the Northwest Coast Indians. Educated at UBC (BA 1949) and U of Washington (MA 1951), Duff was curator of anthropology at the BC Provincial Museum 1950-65. He then moved to Vancouver to teach and do research at UBC's dept of anthropology and sociology and the Museum of Anthropology. He was a founding member of the BC Museums Assn, chaired the provincial government's Archaeological Sites Advisory Board (1960-66), and served on the province's Indian Advisory Committee (1963-76). He is perhaps best known for his work in helping preserve the last remaining TOTEM POLES from Kitwancool and the abandoned villages of the Queen Charlotte Is in the 1950s. Later in life, his interests changed from the empirically oriented ethnography reflected in such publications as *The Indian History of British Columbia*, vol 1 (1964) and *Arts of the Raven: Masterworks by the Northwest Coast Indians* (1967) to an analysis of the visual logic in Northwest Coast art forms, reflected in the catalogue *Images Stone: B.C.* (1975). CAROL SHEEHAN

Dufferin and Ava, Frederick Temple Blackwood, 1st Marquess of, governor general of Canada 1872-78, viceroy of India 1884-88 (b at Florence, Italy 21 June 1826; d at Clandeboye, Ire 12 Feb 1902). Frederick Temple Blackwood was educated at Eton and Christ Church, Oxford, but did not graduate. He served as lord-in-waiting to Queen Victoria 1849-52 and again 1854-58. Dufferin sat in the Lords as a Liberal and in 1868 entered Gladstone's ministry as chancellor of the duchy of Lancaster. He came to Canada in 1872 as governor general. Although initially he possessed an exalted view of his powers, this polished, articulate diplomat displayed great tact and judgement during the PACIFIC SCANDAL that forced John A. MACDONALD to resign and brought Alexander MACKENZIE in as prime minister. Dufferin's attempts to reconcile BC to CONFEDERATION annoyed the Mackenzie government. He supported the Supreme Court of Canada Bill, however, and his amnesty to those in the RED RIVER REBELLION saved the government considerable embarrassment. The first governor general to make the QUÉBEC CITADEL a vice-regal residence, Dufferin persuaded the city fathers to save the old French walls from destruction: Dufferin Terrace was named in his honour. After leaving Canada Dufferin was British ambassador to Russia, Turkey, Italy and France. CARMAN MILLER

Duffus, Romans, Kundzins, Rounsefell Ltd, architects, Halifax, was founded in 1949 and has executed a variety of important commissions, including the Nova Scotia Museum in Halifax, the Izaak Walton Killam Hospital for Children in Halifax and the BEDFORD INSTITUTE OF OCEANOGRAPHY in Dartmouth, NS. Its projects have received a number of design awards, including an Award of Excellence from the Canadian Architect Yearbook in 1972. The firm's directors have always been active in their professional associations and one of its founders, Allan Ferguson Duffus (b 16 June 1915), was elected a fellow of the Royal Architectural Inst of Canada in 1956, and served as dean of the College of Fellows 1969-72 and president 1973-74. GRANT WANZEL AND KAREN KALLWEIT

Dufresne, Diane, singer, actress (b at Montréal 30 Sept 1944). She first studied in Montréal, with Simone Quesnel (1957), and then in Paris (1965-67). In 1972 she had enormous success with the song "J'ai rencontré l'homme de ma vie." She had a reasonably successful début at the Olympia in Paris (1973) and a smash triumph there in 1978. The previous year she won the Prix jeune chanson from the Association française des échanges musicaux. Her most popular songs are composed by François Cousineau (music) and Luc Plamondon (music). She played the role of Stelle Spotlight in the rock opera *Starmania* by Michel Berger and Plamondon (Paris, 1979). With her dramatic ways and her distinctive vocal style (sometimes described as hysterical), Dufresne has been able to make herself a celebrity and rank herself among the artists identified with Québec. By 1986 she had released 14 albums and a few rock operas. HÉLÈNE PLOUFFE

Dufresne, Guy, playwright, scriptwriter (b at Montréal 17 Apr 1915). He studied at the Jesuit colleges of Ste-Marie and Jean-de-Brébeuf (BA 1939). Health problems caused him to abandon his studies and settle in Frelighsburg, Qué, to raise apples. Dufresne wrote for radio, TV and theatre; his scripts made him famous, either for the quality of his historic and ethnographic research (as in *Le*

Ciel par-dessus les toits, 1947-55; *Cap-aux-sorciers* 1955-58; and *Les Forges de St-Maurice*, 1972-76), or for his sensitive psychological analyses. The son and brother of physicians, he provided the public with his well-crafted observations about the hospital milieu in a TV series entitled "Septième-nord" (1963-67), which appeared well before most American series on this subject. He was awarded the Prix Anik in 1978 for his play *Johanne et ses vieux*. In 1980 he became visiting professor of drama at UQAM. He has published 5 plays and a remarkable TV adaptation of the John Steinbeck novel *Of Mice and Men*.

ANDRÉ G. BOURASSA

Duggan, Alphonsus Gregory, labour leader (b at Holyrood, Nfld 21 Sept 1884; d at Grand Falls, Nfld 26 July 1970). In 1913 Duggan helped organize Local 63 of the International Pulp, Sulphite and Papermill Workers Union and became its first president. He believed that social justice for the working class could best be achieved by means of one Newfoundland body for all unions. He organized the Newfoundland Trades and Labor Council in 1937, becoming its first president. In 1939 the council became the Newfoundland Federation of Labor, and Duggan became president emeritus. That same year King George VI made him a Member of the British Empire. Duggan was also active in the Grand Falls co-operative movement and was the first president of the Newfoundland Co-operative Union (1950).

BILL GILLESPIE AND MELVIN BAKER

Duggan, George Herrick, engineer (b at Toronto 6 Sept 1862; d near St-Jerome, Qué 8 Oct 1946). He was educated at Upper Canada Coll and U of T (DSc). He was an engineer with the CPR (1884-85) and the Dominion Bridge Co (1891-1903), where he was chief engineer and assistant to the president. He was second vice-president and general manager of Dominion Steel and Coal Co (1904-10), and chief engineer (1910-20), general manager (1913-19), president (1919-36) and chairman of the board (1936-46) of Dominion Bridge Co Ltd. He was simultaneously director and chief engineer of the St Lawrence Bridge Co when the QUÉBEC BRIDGE (world's longest cantilever span) was completed in 1917. In 1920 he organized Dominion Engineering Works Ltd to take over the former St Lawrence Bridge Works to manufacture paper machines and hydraulic turbines. Because of their innovative design and manufacture, these paper machines rapidly achieved record-breaking performance. Another of Duggan's contributions was the application of electric welding of steel members instead of costly riveting and forging. Duggan was an active yachtsman and designed and sailed the *Seawanhaka*, winner in the International Cup 1896-1901. He was president of the Canadian Society of Civil Engineers and was awarded the Royal Human Society Bronze Medal and Certificate 1893. ERIC A. SPRENGER

Duguay, Rodolphe, artist, engraver (b at Nicolet, Qué 1891; d there 1973). Duguay's work expresses a profound religious message based on goodness, innocence, purity and suffering. From a poor, rural environment, he began his studies at Montréal's Monument National only in 1911, and became familiar with the tradition established in French Canada by artists such as Joseph SAINT-CHARLES, Alfred LALIBERTÉ and Ozias LEDUC, as well as SUZOR-COTÉ with whom he worked 1918-20. From 1920 until 1927, he stayed in Paris, travelled around Europe, studied at the Académie Julian and learned in 1925 the techniques of wood engraving. It was in this medium that Duguay achieved his most original expression, in illustrating the texts of his wife, Jeanne

L'Archevêque-Duguay (*Écrin*, 1934; *Cantilènes*, 1936; *Offrande*, 1942), as well as those of many other writers, including Clément Marchand (*Courrier des villages*, 1941). Encouraged by Bishop Albert Tessier of Trois-Rivières, he began the publication in 1935 of two series of wood engravings that made his work more widely known. His *Carnets intimes*, covering his activities in Europe, were published in 1978. Two exhibitions at the National Gallery of Canada (1975) and the Musée du Québec (1977) showed his engravings and paintings as part of the slow movement toward modern art expression in Québec.

LAURIER LACROIX

Duley, Margaret Iris, writer (b at St John's 27 Sept 1894; d there 22 Mar 1968). Duley won international recognition with 4 novels: *The Eyes of the Gull* (1936), *Cold Pastoral* (1939), *Highway to Valour* (1941) and *Novelty on Earth* (1942). *The Caribou Hut* (1949), a brief history of a St John's hostel during WWII, is a local classic. Duley's work is regional. She depicts vividly the seasons, landscapes, folk customs, moody waters and winds of Newfoundland. Outport characters are unsophisticated and idiomatic, city characters cerebral and witty. The novels focus on the female psyche. Male protagonists are usually less courageous and less intellectual than the fine-grained heroines. Duley's ideas mark her as feminist in advance of her place and time. A poetic prose style, skilful use of animals and children and a ghoulish humour enhance her books.

ALISON FEDER

Dulhut, Daniel Greysolon, COUREUR DE BOIS, fur trader, explorer (b at St-Germain-Laval, France *c*1639; d at Montréal 25 Feb 1710). Dulhut helped extend the French trading empire around the Upper Great Lakes (*see* FUR TRADE). After military service in France, Dulhut immigrated to New France in 1675. In 1678-79 with a small party he travelled to the country of the Sioux (headwaters of the Mississippi) where he formally claimed the area for France, persuaded the Sioux [DAKOTA] and their neighbours to accept a tentative peace agreement, and began a profitable trade in furs. He returned to Montréal in 1681. In 1683 he was commissioned by GOV LA BARRE to return to the Lk Superior area, and he spent the next 3 years there trading and working to keep peace among the Indians. Stationed at Michilimackinac, he built posts at Lk Nipigon and at Kaministiquia on Lk Superior to facilitate the trade, as well as one at Detroit. Dulhut took part in the campaigns of the IROQUOIS WARS in 1687, 1689 and 1696, when he was left in command at FT FRONTENAC. The city of Duluth, Minn, at the head of Lk Superior, is named for him.

MARY MCDOUGALL MAUDE

Dumaresq, James Charles Philip, architect (b at Sydney, NS 18 Dec 1840; d at Halifax 20 Dec 1906). Educated at Acadia, Dumaresq began a practice 1870 that eventually extended throughout the Maritime provinces, Newfoundland, Ontario and Québec and from the eastern US to the W Indies. His work includes the Forrest Building at Dalhousie, the Pine Hill Library in Halifax, St Mary's Girls' School in Halifax and, most important, the Legislative Buildings in Fredericton.

GRANT WANZEL AND KAREN KALLWEIT

Dumbells One of several Canadian Army concert parties in France during WWI, the Dumbells were performers drawn from the Third Division who entertained front-line soldiers with collectively conceived skits about army life, popular songs and "torch" songs by Ross "Marjorie" Hamilton. They also played 4 weeks at various locations in London in 1918. Amalgamated with other top army performers in 1918-19, and re-

formed as civilians, the Dumbells, managed by "Capt" Merton Plunkett, undertook 12 cross-country tours in vaudeville revues between 1919 and 1932, including 12 weeks at the Ambassador, New York, with *Biff, Bing, Bang* in 1921. Members included Hamilton, Al Plunkett, "Red" Newman, Jack Ayre and Jack McLaren.

PATRICK B. O'NEILL

Dumbfounding, The, by Margaret AVISON (New York, 1966), is a major document of the new POETRY in English Canada. Avison is a master of organic form, and in this influential collection, she explored with linguistic and rhythmic daring a deeply held and highly personal Christian vision. Some critics rightly compared these poems to those of such 17th-century "Metaphysicals" as Herbert and Vaughan, but this was to miss their formal affinities with the work of such poets as Louis Zukofsky, Robert Creeley, Denise Levertov and others. Many younger poets have celebrated Avison's poetic integrity and her influence (eg, George BOWERING's "Avison's Imitation of Christ the Artist" in his *A Way with Words*, 1982). The poems stand as marvelous examples of commitment to and engagement with language and life.

DOUGLAS BARBOUR

Dumoine, Rivière, 129 km long, rises in Lac Dumoine in SW Québec and flows off the S edge of the LAURENTIAN HIGHLANDS through a series of waterfalls, wild rapids and long chutes into the OTTAWA R. It was an important route in the early fur trade, being used by the Huron to avoid tolls charged by the Allumette or Iroquois raids on southerly routes. Later, superb white pines were floated down the river, and decayed log chutes are still visible. Still in a wild state, the Dumoine is a popular canoe route. JAMES MARSH

Dumont, Fernand, sociologist, academic, poet (b at Montmorency, Qué 24 June 1927). Dumont is primarily a sensitive, dedicated and influential observer of Québec culture and society. He is also very much a poet, with 2 published volumes, *L'Ange du Matin* (1952) and *Parler de Septembre* (1970). His nonfiction publications encompass highly generalized yet sophisticated studies in the social sciences, to which he has devoted himself. His works consistently demonstrate a deep commitment to Catholicism. For his academic volumes he has received substantial acclaim. One of the studies, *L'Analyse des structures sociales régionales* (1963) earned the Prix du Concours littéraire de Québec and the Grand Prix de la Ville de Montréal. In 1975 he was honoured with the Prix David, for sustained contribution to literature. Dumont teaches sociology at U Laval, Québec City. In 1985 with Jacques Dufresne and Yves Martin, he published *Traité d'anthropologie médicale*, a study of attitudes toward health and health-care treatment in Québec. MARLENE ALT

Dumont, Gabriel, Métis leader (b at Red River Dec 1837; d near Batoche, Sask 19 May 1906). Gabriel Dumont, son of Métis hunter Isidore Dumont and grandson of French Canadian voyageur Jean-Baptiste Dumont, was brought up to the free prairie life of the age before government entered the West. Though he could not read or write, he knew 6 languages; he was a good shot with bow and rifle, a splendid horseman and canoeist and an unrivalled guide. Dumont was introduced early to plains warfare when, aged 13, he took part at Grand Coteau in the defence of a Métis encampment against a large Sioux war party. Yet in 1862, with his father, he concluded a treaty between the Métis and the Sioux, and later one with the Blackfoot, that helped ensure pacification of the Canadian prairie. Dumont's skill as a buffalo hunter led to his election in the summer of 1863, when he was still 25, as permanent chief of

As adjutant general of the Métis army during the 1885 North-West Rebellion, Gabriel Dumont showed himself to be a remarkable guerrilla leader (*courtesy Glenbow Archives, Calgary*).

the Métis hunters on the Saskatchewan. Until the virtual elimination of the buffalo he led the Métis on the hunt; the last time was in 1881.

Dumont took no direct part in the Red River rising of 1870, though he made an offer – rejected by Louis RIEL – to bring Métis to resist WOLSELEY'S expeditionary force. He recognized that great changes were coming to the prairie, with the decline of the buffalo and spread of Canadian influence. In 1873 he became president of the commune of St Laurent, the first local government between Manitoba and the Rockies. Modelled on the organization of the buffalo hunt, the commune tried to establish a system of landholding, since Dumont recognized that when hunting ended, his people would have to turn to farming. In 1875 the commune confronted the newly arrived NWMP and the attempt at local government ended; concern over land did not, however, for government surveyors and land speculators began to flood the West and Dumont led the Métis in agitating for recognition of their rights. When the campaign made no progress, Dumont was one of the delegates who sought Louis Riel's assistance. Negotiations with the government foundered, and when Riel declared a provisional government at Batoche, Dumont became "adjutant general" in charge of the tiny Métis army of 300 men formed at the beginning of the rebellion. During the subsequent NORTH-WEST REBELLION he was a remarkable guerrilla leader. He won the first battle against the NWMP at DUCK LK in Mar 1885; he halted Gen MIDDLETON'S army at Fish Creek on Apr 24. But Riel did not allow Dumont to continue his successful guerrilla campaign, and Batoche was besieged and captured, despite the resistance Dumont organized, on May 12. Hearing Riel had surrendered, Dumont fled to the US. He plotted to rescue Riel, but the latter was too carefully guarded; following Riel's execution Dumont joined Buffalo Bill's Wild West Show as a crack marksman. After the amnesty for rebels, he returned to Canada in 1888 and to Batoche in 1893. He hunted and traded a little, and dictated 2 vivid oral memoirs of the rebellion. He died suddenly of heart failure in 1906. Gabriel Dumont was a man of great chivalry, superbly adapted to the pre-settlement prairie life; in the world that followed, his skills lost their relevance, and so his

qualities of intelligence and personality were ultimately wasted. GEORGE WOODCOCK

Dumouchel, Albert, printmaker, teacher (b at Bellerive, Qué 15 Apr 1916; d at Montréal 11 Jan 1971). He studied etching and lithography in Paris. In Montréal in 1945, he participated in the "cadavres exquis" experiments with Léon Bellefleur, Jean BENOÎT, Jean Léonard, Mimi Parent and Alfred PELLAN, and, in 1947 and 1949, published 2 famous issues of *Les Ateliers d'arts graphiques*, the review of Montréal's École des arts graphiques. In 1948 he joined the free-art "Prisme d'yeux" group and later made contributions to the first publications of Roland GIGUÈRE's Éditions Erta. Between 1949 and 1954, his lithographs illustrated Giguère's *Faire naître*, *Les Nuits abat-jour* and *Les Armes blanches*. Giguère interested Dumouchel in the Cobra movement, and his work appeared in the *Revue internationale de l'art expérimental - Cobra* (1954), and in *Phases de l'art contemporain* (1955), the review published by poet and surrealist critic, Édouard Jaguer. His work as an art teacher at the École des arts graphiques and the École des beaux-arts in Montréal until his death influenced several generations of artists. The Montréal Musée d'art contemporain held an exhibition of his engravings in 1974.
ANDRÉ G. BOURASSA

Dunbar, Isobel Moira, public servant, ice research scientist (b at Edinburgh, Scot 3 Feb 1918). In 1947 Moira Dunbar, an Oxford graduate, immigrated to Canada after 7 years in professional theatre. She joined the Arctic Section of the Defence Research Board at a period when scientific work in the North was opening up. Collaborating with K.R. Greenaway, she produced the standard work *Arctic Canada from the Air* (1956), which led to her interest in ARCTIC EXPLORATION. She later specialized in SEA-ICE research, particularly the climatological aspects, and was the first woman to be taken on summer cruises in Canadian government icebreakers. Observations on these cruises and on reconnaissance flights over the arctic islands led to analytical studies of ice conditions and work on the standardization of ice terminology. She was active in evaluating remote sensors for collecting ice data and pioneered sideways-looking RADAR for airborne reconnaissance. She also visited the USSR and Finland in 1964 to look into icebreaking practices, worked as ice adviser on the hovercraft trials, 1966-69, and observed the cruise of the *Manhattan* in 1969 to test supertankers in ice. Author of many scientific articles, she is a Member of the Order of Canada, a fellow of the RSC, and has received the Massey Medal in 1972. DIANA ROWLEY

Dunbar, Maxwell John, oceanographer (b at Edinburgh, Scot 19 Sept 1914). Dunbar received his BA and MA from Oxford and his PhD from McGill. He was acting Canadian consul to Greenland between 1941 and 1946 and joined the McGill faculty in 1946. He is a fellow of the RSC, the Arctic Inst of N America, the Royal Geographical Soc and the Linnean Soc of London. Active in research in ARCTIC OCEANOGRAPHY all his professional life, he has published numerous works on marine biology in Canadian arctic waters. During the 1930s and 1940s he participated in numerous expeditions to Greenland and the Canadian Arctic. In 1947 he was appointed Director of the Eastern Arctic Investigations of the Fisheries Research Board, for which he played a decisive part in the design of the Arctic Research Vessel M/V *Calanus*. Emeritus professor in the Institute of Oceanography at McGill in 1982, Dunbar was professor of zoology and director of the Marine Sciences Centre. He was responsible for the training of a large group of oceanographers at work in the Canadian

North. He was awarded the Bruce Medal for Polar Research by the Royal Society of Edinburgh, the Fry Medal of the Canadian Society of Zoologists and the North Slope Borough (Alaska) Arctic Sciences prize (1986). JOHN B. LEWIS

Duncan, BC, City, pop 4039 (1986c), 4228 (1981c), inc 1912, is located on Vancouver I midway between Victoria and Nanaimo, in the Cowichan Valley, surrounded by scenic, rugged mountains. The area was first inhabited by the Cowichan ("Land Warmed by the Sun") nation, encompassing all the independent bands in the valley. The colonial government did not allow white settlement in the area until 1862, and although there were 18 200 ha of good agricultural land available, growth was slow until the valley was reached by the Esquimalt and Nanaimo Ry in 1886. William Duncan, a farmer, led a petition for a station, which was built on his land in 1887. His son, Kenneth, was the city's first mayor. Duncan became the service centre for the valley's main industries, lumbering and agriculture. Several trace deposits of gold were found and mined 1898-1908. More recently, Duncan's mild climate has attracted retired people.
ALAN F.J. ARTIBISE

Duncan, Douglas Moerdyke, art dealer (b at Kalamazoo, Mich 1902; d at Toronto 26 June 1968). Educated at U of T, Duncan lived in Paris 1925-28 where he studied fine bookbinding. He returned to Toronto in 1928 to establish himself as a bookbinder, earning a reputation as a skilled craftsman. He founded the Picture Loan Soc in 1936 with others and became sole sponsor and director, a position he held until his death. During this time Duncan was responsible for the first exhibitions of many distinguished artists, among them Carl SCHAEFER, Will OGILVIE, and Kazuo NAKAMURA. Many artists left the Picture Loan Soc because of its limited space and the difficulty of acquiring a financial accounting from Duncan. Nevertheless, he must be considered a significant force in the art market in the 1930s to 1950s, and as a confidant and adviser to the rich he was able to sustain the career of David MILNE, among others. HAROLD B. TOWN

Duncan, James Stuart, businessman (b at Paris 2 May 1893; d at Paget, Bermuda 20 Dec 1986). Duncan joined MASSEY-HARRIS in Berlin, Germany, in 1909 and transferred to Canada in 1911. He served in the British army in WWI, returning to Massey-Harris afterwards. He was appointed general manager in 1936 and president in 1941, a position he held until 1956. In 1940 Duncan declined PM Mackenzie KING's invitation to join his Cabinet, but agreed to serve as acting deputy minister of national defence for air. His work proved invaluable and was instrumental in the success of the BRITISH COMMONWEALTH AIR TRAINING PLAN. At the end of the war Duncan returned to Massey-Harris to find that the company was being reorganized out from under him. He left the firm in 1956 and later wrote a number of books, including his autobiography, *Not a One-Way Street* (1971). ROBERT BOTHWELL

Duncan, Norman, journalist, writer, professor (b in Oxford County, Ont 2 July 1871; d at Buffalo, NY 18 Oct 1916). Remembered today for his fiction, Duncan was also a successful journalist and travel writer. He was raised in small-town Ontario and reflects in his writing his love of different places and cultures. After working for the *New York Evening Post* (1897-1900), he travelled as a *McClure's Magazine* correspondent to Newfoundland and Labrador, where he met Sir Wilfred GRENFELL and gathered materials for his fictional best-sellers, *Doctor Luke of the Labrador*

(1904) and *The Cruise of the Shining Light* (1907). Of over 20 published volumes (short stories, novels, travel pieces), a number are suitable for younger readers, particularly the Billy Topsail series. After 1900 he lived primarily in the US, writing about his travels and teaching in universities.

MARY RUBIO

Duncan, Sara Jeannette, journalist, novelist (b at Brantford, Canada W 22 Dec 1861; d at Ashstead, Eng 22 July 1922). Duncan's notable career as a journalist in the 1880s testifies to her determination and ability. The first woman employed full time by the Toronto *Globe* 1886-87, she also worked for the Montreal *Star* 1887-88. In the fall of 1888, Duncan embarked upon a round-the-world tour which resulted in her first novel *A Social Departure* (1890). While in Calcutta, Duncan met her future husband, Everard Cotes. After her marriage, Duncan lived in India for the next 25 years, subsequently moving to England. Only 2 of Duncan's 22 books have Canada as their focus. The IMPERIALIST (1904) is a brilliant study of a small Ontario town in which an idealistic young man is thwarted in politics and love. *Cousin Cinderella* (1908) deals with the disillusionment that a similarly idealistic Canadian brother and sister experience in English aristocratic circles. One of the most penetrating observers of Canadian society in her time, Duncan combined shrewd analysis with a vivid, personal style.

THOMAS E. TAUSKY

Sara Jeannette Duncan, one of the most penetrating observers of Canadian society of her time (*courtesy National Archives of Canada/C-46447*).

Duncan, William, lay missionary to the TSIMSHIAN (b at Bishop Burton, Eng 1832; d in Alaska 30 Aug 1918). Trained as a schoolmaster by the Church Missionary Society, Duncan came in 1858 to Fort Simpson, BC. In 1862, during a devastating smallpox epidemic, he led several hundred Indians to METLAKATLA PASS SITES, an ancestral Tsimshian village. Following in part the native church policy of Henry Venn, Secretary of CMS, he created a utopian Christian Indian settlement whose success and material prosperity attracted the Northwest Coast Indians. Duncan's ideas and methods were widely imitated and he received international recognition. But the division within the Anglican Church at Victoria brought a new bishop to Metlakatla who challenged Duncan's authority, his reluctance to offer communion to converts and his emphasis on secular progress. A bitter schism divided the village and in 1887 Duncan and many Tsimshian created a second and independent Christian utopia at New Metlakatla, Annette Island, Alaska.

JEAN FRIESEN

Reading: P. Murray, *The Devil and Mr. Duncan* (1985); J. Usher, *William Duncan of Metlakatla* (1976).

Duncombe, Charles, doctor, politician, rebel (b at Stratford, Conn 28 July 1792; d at Hicksville, Calif 1 Oct 1867). Duncombe came to Upper Canada in 1819, finally settling in Burford Twp where he had a large medical practice. Elected to the assembly in 1830 as an independent, he gradually aligned himself with the Reformers, becoming a leading radical spokesman on social issues by the mid-1830s. He travelled to England to protest the corrupt election of 1836 but was disillusioned by the British government's disinterest. This blow and personal tragedy caused him to withdraw from politics until word came of the Toronto rising of 1837. In response, Duncombe hurriedly organized his area to fight, but the arrival of government forces caused him to disperse his forces and flee to the US. *See also* REBELLIONS OF 1837.

RONALD STAGG

Reading: C. Read, *The Rising in Western Upper Canada* (1982).

Dunkin, Christopher, lawyer, politician, judge (b at Walworth, Eng 25 Sept 1812; d at Knowlton, Qué 6 Jan 1881). Admitted to the bar in 1846, he gained renown defending the legal rights of the seigneurs in 1854. He was a Québec MLA 1858-71 and MP 1867-71, provincial treasurer 1867-69 and federal minister of agriculture 1869-71. A philosophical conservative, known for the pro-temperance Dunkin Act of 1864, he represented English Protestant and Eastern Townships interests in Québec and Ottawa. He was a brilliantly lucid opponent of CONFEDERATION in the debates of 1865.

PIERRE CORBEIL

Dunlap, Clarence Rupert, "Larry," air marshal (b at Sydney Mines, NS 1 Jan 1908). As a youngster in Cape Breton, Dunlap's imagination was fired by a nearby seaplane base and by memories of Baddeck, where the SILVER DART had flown. He joined the RCAF in 1928, specializing in aerial photography and then in air armament. Posted overseas in 1942, he commanded No 331 Wing in 1943, carrying out operations from Tunisia. He was the first RCAF officer to command a British operational bomber wing: his No 139 Wing participated in daylight raids from England against V-1 launching sites in Germany 1943-44, and Dunlap himself flew 35 operational sorties. A trim, competent, principled officer with a pleasant personality, he rose steadily after the war, serving as commandant, National Defence Coll 1951-54, and vice-chief of the air staff 1954-58, before becoming chief of the air staff 1962-64, and deputy commander in chief of NORAD 1964-67. He retired in 1968.

NORMAN HILLMER

Dunlap, David Alexander, lawyer, mine executive (b at Pembroke, Canada W 13 Oct 1863; d near Toronto 29 Oct 1924). Dunlap was a lawyer in Mattawa when he and his associates, Henry and Noah TIMMINS and the McMartin brothers, acquired the LaRose silver mine near COBALT, Ont. They also acquired properties in the Porcupine district that formed the basis of Hollinger Consolidated Gold Mines Ltd, of which Dunlap was secretary treasurer 1911-19, and VP and treasurer 1919-24. A Liberal and Methodist, Dunlap was honorary treasurer of the Social Services Council of Ontario and the Missionary Soc of the Methodist Church, trustee of the Art Gallery of Toronto (later Art Gallery of Ontario) and the Toronto General Hospital, and member of the Board of Regents of Victoria U. He bequeathed $250 000 to Victoria U and $100 000 to University of Toronto – to which his family presented the David Dunlap Observatory in 1935.

J. LINDSEY

Dunlop, William, "Tiger," journalist, politiian (b at Greenock, Scot 1792; d at Lachine, Canada E 1848). Dunlop was one of the most colourful figures of the 1820s and 1830s in UPPER CANADA. He first came to Canada in 1813 as a military physician, but a few years later went to India, where he edited a Bombay newspaper, and then back to England. In 1826 he re-emerged as a bureaucrat of the CANADA COMPANY, resigning some years later, after charging the company with neglect of settlers' rights. But while still in its employ he wrote *Statistical Sketches of Upper Canada* (1832) to try to lure more immigrants. He also wrote *Recollections of the American War, 1812-14. Two and Twenty Years Ago* (1859), a novel about the 1837 uprising, has sometimes been attributed to him as well. At the time of his death, he was superintendent of the Lachine Canal. He has often caught the sustained attention of Canadian historians and there are several biographies.

DOUGLAS FETHERLING

Dunn, Alexander Roberts, army officer (b at York, Upper Canada 15 Sept 1833; d near Senufe, Abyssinia 25 Jan 1868). Dunn was the first Canadian recipient of the VICTORIA CROSS, won as a lieutenant in the 11th (Prince Albert's Own) Regiment of Hussars at the charge of the Light Brigade at Balaklava in 1856. He helped to organize the 100th (Prince of Wales' Royal Canadian) Regiment of Foot, a British unit raised in Canada, and later became its commanding officer in Gibraltar. He was killed on an expedition to Abyssinia when his hunting rifle accidentally discharged.

O.A. COOKE

Dunn, Sir James Hamet, financier, industrialist (b at Bathurst, NB 29 Oct 1874; d at St Andrews, NB 1 Jan 1956). Dunn attended Dalhousie Law School 1895-98 and, after stints as a lawyer in Edmonton and Montréal, turned to investment banking. From the Montréal Stock Exchange, he graduated to the city of London, Eng, in 1905 and prospered in the arbitrage trade and in underwriting Canadian utilities and industries. In 1921 he was knighted for wartime services. In 1935 he gained control of the bankrupt Algoma Steel Corp, Sault Ste Marie, Ont. As principal and unchallenged owner, and assisted by his friend C.D. HOWE, Dunn used his position to control the value of the Algoma stock on the market and oversaw Algoma's emergence as a profitable company.

DUNCAN McDOWALL

Dunn, John Henry, officeholder, politician, businessman (bap at St Helena 26 Feb 1792; d at London, Eng 21 Apr 1854). His 23-year career as receiver general of Upper Canada was critical to the success of a number of early Canadian transportation projects, including the WELLAND CANAL and the St Lawrence canals, and had a lasting impact on public finance in Canada. Shortly after his appointment in 1820, he realized that the government revenues available from local sources, such as customs duties and the sales of CLERGY RESERVES, were insufficient to meet the province's immediate need for road, bridge and canal construction. During the 1820s and 1830s, Dunn began the practice of having the provincial government borrow large sums of private money, particularly from large British financial houses such as the Baring Bros, to finance its transportation projects. Although Dunn's social and political situation made him a suitable candidate for the FAMILY COMPACT, he was a moderate reformer who supported the union of the Canadas and the political ideals of both Robert BALDWIN and Louis-Hippolyte LAFONTAINE.

KEN CRUIKSHANK

Dunn, William Lawrence, Willie, or Roha'tiio, meaning "his voice is beautiful," musician, filmmaker (b at Montréal 14 Aug 1941). A folk musician of Micmac-Scottish origin, he served in the army 1960-63 (UN Congo medal) before joining the Newport, RI, folk-music festival. Since then he has developed his own quietly powerful style. He has made 6 albums in Canada, the US and Germany, and worked in the Company of Young Canadians with Ernie Benedict at the National Film Board. There he made the *Ballad of Crowfoot* (1968) and *The Other Side of the Ledger* (1972) with Martin Defalco. He has written and performed music for film and radio and has published several poems and song texts.

ROY WRIGHT

Dunning, Charles Avery, businessman, politician, premier of Saskatchewan (b at Croft, Eng 31 July 1885; d at Montréal 2 Oct 1958). General manager of the Saskatchewan Co-operative Elevator Company, Dunning entered provincial politics in 1916 when opposition to both national parties was spreading. He remained loyal to the Liberal Party, however, and his adroit political maneuvering as premier 1922-26 saved it from defeat. Dunning was elected MP in 1926, serving as minister of railways and canals and then minister of finance under Mackenzie KING, 1926-30 and 1935-39. Ill health forced his retirement in 1939 and he returned to business. He was named chancellor of Queen's University in 1940.

J. WILLIAM BRENNAN

Reading: J. William Brennan, "C.A. Dunning, 1916-1930," in J.E. Foster, ed, *The Developing West* (1983).

Dunnville, Ont, Town, pop 11 589 (1986c), established 1974 as a town in the Regional Municipality of Haldimand-Norfolk. Located on the Lower Grand R, SW of the Niagara Region, Dunnville was initiated in 1829 when a dam was built across the Grand R to supply water for the WELLAND CANAL. It grew with the construction of the feeder canal, mills and a port on the Grand River-Welland Canal system. It was incorporated as a village in 1860 and a town in 1900. It is a local centre for a rural mixed farming area which also has a number of gas wells. Port Maitland, a subsidiary centre at the entrance to the Grand R, was a naval base in the early 1800s, considered the best natural harbour on the N shore of Lk Erie, and was a former railway-ferry link to Ohio, and a former commercial fishing port. It is now important for chemical industries and boatbuilding.

JOHN N. JACKSON

Dunsmuir, James, industrialist, politician, premier of BC (b at Ft Vancouver, Wash 8 July 1851; d at Cowichan, BC 6 June 1920), son of Robert DUNSMUIR. Main heir to his family's coal fortune and spokesman for capital over labour, Dunsmuir dominated BC's economy until 1900. From 1876 to 1910 he managed the family coal operations on Vancouver I, increasing annual output tenfold by opening new fields and improving mining methods. He invested widely in transport, agriculture, manufacturing and other resource industries. Dunsmuir withstood all attempts at unionizing his operations, becoming labour's chief target in western Canada. In 1905 he sold the Esquimalt and Nanaimo Ry to the CPR and in 1910 he sold his collieries to William MACKENZIE and Donald MANN for $10 million.

Dunsmuir was elected MPP for Yale in 1898; he was premier of BC from 1900 to 1902, leading a Conservative administration concerned chiefly with oriental immigration, railway construction and BC's position within Confederation. A less prestigious figure would have had problems redistributing the legislature to reflect the now dominant mainland, and a more partisan politician would have remained longer in office. Dunsmuir disliked politics and served more from

a sense of public duty than a desire for power. He reluctantly agreed in 1906 to be the province's lt-gov, but resigned in 1909, relieved to be free to enjoy his lands and yacht. DANIEL T. GALLACHER

Reading: S. Jackman, *Portraits of the Premiers* (1969).

Dunsmuir, Robert, industrialist, politician (b at Hurlford, Scot 31 Aug 1825; d at Victoria 12 Apr 1889). Dunsmuir was best known as the coal king of BC. He came to Vancouver I in 1851 and worked as a coal miner for the HBC. After discovering a rich coal seam N of NANAIMO, he established his own mine and his own company town at Wellington. His disregard for safety, and his employment of cheap oriental labour and disallowance of unions made him unpopular with labour. Dunsmuir sat on Nanaimo's first school board and was elected MLA for Nanaimo in 1882 and 1886. In 1883 Dunsmuir and his son James DUNSMUIR contracted to build the Esquimalt and Nanaimo Ry, payment for which included $750 000 and about one-quarter of the land on Vancouver I. In 1888 he became president of the Executive Council of BC. Dunsmuir retired in Victoria, where his elaborate mansion, Craigdarroch Castle, was unfinished at his death.

DAVID R. ELLIOTT

Dunton, Arnold Davidson, public servant, educator (b at Montréal 4 July 1912; d at Ottawa 7 Feb 1987). He was educated at Lower Canada College, Montréal, and at universities in Canada, France, Britain and Germany. He worked as a reporter on the Montréal *Star* 1935-37 and as associate editor 1937-38 and was editor of the Montréal *Standard* in 1938. He joined the WARTIME INFORMATION BOARD in 1942 and was general manager 1944-45. In late 1945, at age 33, he was appointed the first full-time chairman of the CANADIAN BROADCASTING CORPORATION.

Throughout the controversies that arose over the funding and regulation of the new medium of television, Dunton was a persuasive defender of the corporation's independence and a strong advocate of the need to fund publicly a television system that would be of great national benefit. Shortly after the CBC completed its network from coast to coast in July 1958 he resigned and became president of CARLETON UNIVERSITY. Dunton was widely commended for the tact and intelligence with which he had overseen the development of the CBC.

He was appointed co-chairman of the Royal Commission on BILINGUALISM AND BICULTURALISM in 1963, which has profoundly influenced federal government language policies. He stepped down as Carleton's president in 1972 to become director of the Institute of Canadian Studies at Carleton 1973-78 and later fellow of the Institute. He was a Companion of the Order of Canada and received honorary diplomas from 7 Canadian universities.

JAMES MARSH

Duplessis, Maurice Le Noblet, prime minister and attorney general of Québec, 1936-39 and 1944-59 (b at Trois-Rivières, Qué 20 Apr 1890; d at Schefferville, Qué 7 Sept 1959). Duplessis's father, Nérée Le Noblet Duplessis, was a fervently Catholic and Conservative MLA for Trois-Rivières, 1886-1900, and an unsuccessful federal Conservative candidate before being named a superior court judge by Sir Robert L. BORDEN in 1915. Duplessis's mother was of part Scottish and Irish descent. After studying at Collège Notre-Dame in Montréal (where he became something of a protégé of Brother ANDRÉ) and the Séminaire de Trois-Rivières, he graduated from Laval's Montréal law faculty in 1913, spending WWI in the local militia. He developed a successful popular law practice in Trois-Rivières, was narrowly defeated there in the 1923 provincial election, but

Maurice Duplessis, known as "le Chef" in recognition of his strong though controversial leadership of Québec; 1930s photo (*courtesy National Archives of Canada/C-9338*).

won the first of 9 consecutive elections there in 1927.

He helped mayor Camillien HOUDE of Montréal ease out Arthur Sauvé as leader of the provincial Conservatives in 1929 and Duplessis deposed Houde after the electoral débâcle of 1931, in which the Conservative Party, led by Houde, was routed. Confirmed as leader of the Québec Conservative Party in 1933, Duplessis wooed disgruntled reform Liberals and Nationalists who had become disillusioned with the arch-conservative Liberal government of Louis-Alexandre TASCHEREAU and had formed a movement styled ACTION LIBÉRALE NATIONALE, and 2 weeks before the 1935 election he united with them to form the UNION NATIONALE, with the rather unworldly Paul GOUIN as ostensible co-leader. Taschereau was returned in 1935 but Duplessis forced him out in June 1936 with a sensational performance before the Public Accounts Committee exposing corruption and profligacy in the regime, accompanied by a filibuster in the Assembly. He also dispensed with Gouin and outmaneuvred his other Action libérale nationale allies, defeated the hapless Joseph-Adélard GODBOUT, and won a landslide victory in Aug 1936, ending 39 years of Liberal rule.

Duplessis's first term was a disappointment. Except for his successful farm credit scheme, his Fair Wages Commission (effectively minimum wages) and provisions for destitute mothers and the blind, there was little significant legislation. The administration was prodigal. Duplessis himself lived riotously (he was a lusty and somewhat alcoholic bachelor in these times, and never did marry), and he blundered disastrously in Sept 1939 by calling a snap election on the issue of participation in the war effort. The Québec federal ministers, including Ernest LAPOINTE, Arthur Cardin and C.G. POWER, threatened to resign, leaving Québec defenceless against a conscriptionist English Canada if Duplessis was re-elected, and pledged that they would prevent CONSCRIPTION if Duplessis was defeated.

Though he was personally re-elected, his government lost badly to Godbout. In opposition Duplessis's health collapsed, and, after months in hospital in 1941-42 fighting pneumonia and diabetes, he never drank again, campaigned strenuously for 2 years, and was narrowly re-elected in 1944 over Godbout, the nationalist BLOC POPULAIRE CANADIEN led by André LAURENDEAU and Jean DRAPEAU and supported by Henri BOURASSA. The Union nationale was re-elected in 1948, 1952 and 1956 and successfully intervened in other elections, especially the defeat of Mayor Drapeau in Montréal in 1957 and the election of 50 DIEFENBAKER Conservatives in Québec in 1958. His 15-year second term saw Duplessis assert the authority of the Québec state over that of the Church; wrestle part of the concurrent jurisdiction over direct taxes back from the federal government after WWII; and introduce social legislation, including Canada's most generous minimum wage and home ownership assistance Acts. His government produced enormous public works, highway, hospital, school and university construction projects and ambitious hydroelectric power schemes, extending electrification throughout rural Québec.

Duplessis became equally known for dealing harshly with striking unions, especially at Noranda, ASBESTOS, Louiseville and Murdochville; and for disdaining most contemporary concepts of civil liberties, particularly in litigation over the anticommunist PADLOCK ACT, overruled by the Supreme Court of Canada in 1957, and the RONCARELLI case in which Duplessis was personally ordered to pay damages of $46 132 by the Supreme Court in 1959. Apart from his jurisdictional gains, Duplessis presented a number of symbolic nationalist measures, such as the adoption of the Québec flag. Duplessis developed a very powerful political machine. The patronage system reached legendary proportions, yet Duplessis presided over a period of unprecedented prosperity, economic growth and investment in which Québec was for the first time by almost any social or economic yardstick gaining on Ontario.

A modernizer except in political methodology, Duplessis perfected the techniques of the past in exalting the Québec state to an unprecedented position of strength in relation to the church, the federal government and the Anglo-Saxon Montréal business establishment. His system depended upon employing the clergy at bargain wages to do what was really secular work in schools and hospitals, while reducing the episcopate to financial dependence; reducing taxes, balancing budgets and persuading the conservatives and nationalists to vote together (for "Autonomy" as he called it). His system crumbled after his death with the demise of his successors Paul SAUVÉ and Daniel JOHNSON and the triumph of the QUIET REVOLUTION. Maurice Duplessis was an enigmatic and picturesque character, the public demagogue at some variance with his urbane, elegant and witty private personality. For much of his career he was almost universally known as "le Chef" in recognition of his strong, though controversial leadership of Québec. CONRAD M. BLACK

Dupond Case (1978) In a case testing the scope of provincial interest in the area of public order, the Supreme Court ruled as valid a Montréal ordinance forbidding for 30 days any public assembly, parade or riotous gathering, on the grounds that it was a case, as in the HODGE CASE, of local public order in the province, and therefore authorized by the Constitution Act, 1867 (s92). The legislative measures were preventive and not punitive. A majority of the judges held that fundamental liberties fall under the concurrent legislative jurisdiction of the 2 orders of government. The holding of assemblies, parades or riots in the public domain falls within either federal or provincial jurisdiction, depending on the aspect in question. GÉRALD-A. BEAUDOIN

Dupuy, Claude-Thomas, lawyer, intendant of NEW FRANCE 1725-28 (b at Paris, France 10 Dec 1678; d near Rennes, France 15 Sept 1738). From a bourgeois family Dupuy became a lawyer in the *parlement* of Paris and in 1720 purchased the office of *maître des requêtes*. In 1725 he was appointed INTENDANT of New France and he took up the position in Sept 1726. Stubborn, inflexible and preoccupied by his status, by late 1726 he had already begun the quarrels with Governor BEAUHARNOIS that continued until his departure. Dupuy was recalled in 1728 when his precipitate actions in challenging the colony's ecclesiastical authorities over Bishop SAINT-VALLIER's death and funeral became known in France.
MARY McDOUGALL MAUDE

Duquesne, Ange Duquesne de Menneville, Marquis, naval officer, governor general of NEW FRANCE 1752-55 (b at Toulon, France *c*1700; d at Antony, France 17 Sept 1778). He joined the navy as a boy and saw action in the War of the Austrian Succession. Former governor LA GALISSONIERE put his name forward to succeed LA JONQUIERE in New France in 1752. Duquesne was instructed to secure the Ohio Valley where French sovereignty was being threatened by English traders, and to this end in 1753-54 he sent an expedition south under Paul Marin de La Malgue (also La Marque) to establish a series of forts. A second expedition in 1754 completed the occupation of the area with the building of Fort Duquesne [Pittsburgh, Pa].
MARY McDOUGALL MAUDE

Durham, John George Lambton, 1st Earl of, politician, diplomat, colonial administrator (b at London, Eng 12 Apr 1792; d at Cowes, Eng 28 July 1840). Scion of a wealthy Northumberland family, Durham was educated at Eton, briefly held an army commission, was elected to the Commons in 1813 and raised to the Lords in 1828. Affiliated with the liberal wing of the Whig party, "Radical Jack" was lord privy seal in 1830 in the Cabinet of his father-in-law, Lord Grey, and played a significant part in drafting the great Reform Bill of 1832. He was a difficult colleague and, suffering from poor health, he resigned in 1833 but was ambassador to Russia 1835-37.

Primarily to appease the radicals, PM Lord Melbourne persuaded him to become governor general and high commissioner to British N America with responsibility for preparing a report on the Canadian REBELLIONS OF 1837. On 29 May 1838 Durham landed in LOWER CANADA. His administration was warmly endorsed by the English minority in Lower Canada, the moderate reformers in Upper Canada and the American government, as well as the authorities at home. But when the British government refused to sanction an illegal ordinance exiling a handful of political prisoners to Bermuda, Durham submitted his letter of resignation 29 Sept 1838 and sailed from Québec 1 Nov 1838 to England where in Jan 1839 he completed his famous *Report on the Affairs of British North America*. His major recommendation was to reunite the Canadas in order to accelerate the assimilation of the French Canadians, whom he characterized as a people without a history or a culture; the union was brought into effect in 1841. He also recommended a reorganization of the system of colonial government, but the British government refused to accept the principle of RESPONSIBLE GOVERNMENT (a term for which Durham refused to accept paternity because of its ambiguity) because it was not prepared to accept the inevitability of a form of party government in the colonies. Although Lord Sydenham and his successors in the United Province of Canada and Lord Falkland in Nova Scotia in practice did ac-

Lord Durham issued his famous *Report* after only 6 months in Canada (*courtesy National Archives of Canada/C-121846*).

cept the necessity of governing through a majority in the assembly, the principle of responsible government was not formally recognized by the British government until 1847, and the first avowedly party governments were admitted to power in 1848, in Nova Scotia by Sir John Harvey and then in Canada by Durham's son-in-law Lord ELGIN. Recent historiography has tended to be more critical of Durham's behaviour and skeptical of his accomplishments, and he remains a hated figure in French Canada, but he was preeminent among the founders of the modern COMMONWEALTH. P. A. BUCKNER

Durham Report, completed Jan 1839 and officially presented to the Colonial Office 4 Feb 1839 by John George Lambton, the earl of DURHAM. A known reformer, Durham had been appointed governor general to investigate colonial grievances after the REBELLIONS OF 1837. His *Report on the Affairs of British North America* proposed such reforms as the creation of municipal governments and a supreme court, and resolution of the LAND QUESTION in Prince Edward Island. His plan for a union of all the British North American colonies was dropped because of objections in the Maritime provinces.

Durham's 2 main recommendations – RESPONSIBLE GOVERNMENT and union of Upper and Lower Canada – emerged from an analysis of the causes of the rebellions. He criticized the defective constitutional system in Upper Canada, where power was monopolized by "a petty, corrupt, insolent Tory clique." This FAMILY COMPACT blocked economic and social development in a potentially wealthy colony, thereby causing the discontent which led to the rebellion. His solution, based on advice from colonial reformers, was a system in which the executive would be drawn from the majority party in the assembly. It would stimulate colonial expansion, strengthen the imperial connection and minimize American influences. In Lower Canada, Durham described the problems as racially, not politically, based. He found "two nations warring in the bosom of a single state...." To ensure harmony and progress, he recommended assimilating the French Canadians, whom he called "a people with no literature and no history," through a legislative union of the Canadas, in which an English-speaking majority would dominate.

Durham's report was condemned by Upper Canada's Tory elite, but Reformers in UC and NS hailed the idea of responsible government. Montréal Tories supported the union largely because they saw it as a way to overcome French Canadian opposition to their plans for economic development. French Canadians were opposed to the union and reaffirmed their determination to defend their nationality. The British government accepted the recommendation for a union of the Canadas (*see* ACT OF UNION). However, responsible government was not formally implemented until 1847 and Durham's recommendation for a division of powers between imperial and colonial responsibilities was rejected. Although controversial in its direct influence in the creation of the Province of Canada, the emergence of a party system and the strengthening of local self-government, the Durham Report is generally regarded to have played an important role in the development of Canadian autonomy. DAVID MILLS

Reading: J.M.S. Careless, *The Union of the Canadas (1967)*; G.M. Craig, ed, *Lord Durham's Report* (1963); Chester New, *Lord Durham's Mission to Canada* (1963); J.M. Ward, *Colonial Self-Government* (1976).

Durkin, Douglas Leader, author (b at Parry Sound, Ont 9 July 1884; d at Seattle, Wash 4 June 1967). Raised to be a missionary, Durkin instead developed a literary interest and an appreciation for a profane life-style. A sense of justice and belief in spiritual redemption were retained, though, and these sentiments are found in his early publications, written during WWI while he was a lecturer at Brandon Coll and U of Manitoba. In 1921 Durkin moved to the US, abandoning his family and career, and completed *The Magpie*, a novel focusing on postwar unrest in Winnipeg. He was joined in 1923 by Martha OSTENSO, and the 2 collaborated on *Wild Geese*, published under her name in 1925. Thereafter Durkin issued only one novel under his own name, producing short pieces and working with Ostenso on various novels. Although long neglected by scholars and the public, Durkin's work is of enduring quality. P.E. RIDER

Durnan, William Arnold, hockey player (b at Toronto 22 Jan 1915; d there 31 Oct 1972). He was the greatest goaltender of his day. Tall but quick, he had a rare ability to catch and block shots with either hand. He joined MONTREAL CANADIENS 1943, age 29, and in only 7 seasons won the VEZINA TROPHY 6 times. Among his amazing records was a period of 309 min 21 sec (over 5 games) in which he did not allow a goal. His career record was 2.35 goals allowed per game and 34 shutouts in regular season play, and 2.20 goals per game and 2 shutouts in playoffs. He was a victim of the pressures of his profession, suffering from nausea and insomnia, and quit abruptly during the playoffs in 1950. JAMES MARSH

Dutch Although the Dutch arrived in N America in the 17th century, it was not until the American Revolution that an indeterminate number of Dutch American LOYALISTS entered the British N American colonies. Already considerably anglicized, this group was quickly assimilated into the welter of immigrants who flooded into the colonies after 1815. Because of economic pressures, emigration from the Netherlands grew rapidly at mid-century and in the following decades, but it was directed to the rapidly developing American frontier. When cheap arable land became scarce in the US, the Dutch and Dutch Americans turned to the Canadian "Last Best West." Since that time, about 200 000 immigrants of Dutch origin have settled in Canada; and today, numbering 400 000, they comprise the sixth-largest ethnic group. The Dutch quickly adopted Canadian culture and traditions, and they have been assimilated almost to the point of invisibility.

Migration and Settlement The Dutch have set-

tled in Canada in 3 main periods. During the first, 1890-1914, Dutch immigrants joined the migration to the Canadian West to take up homestead lands, helping to open the PRAIRIES and establishing ethnic settlements such as New Nijverdal (now Monarch, Alta), Neerlandia (Alta) and Edam (Sask). The majority of the immigrants were scattered across the West either as farmhands or farm owners. Some concentrations did occur, however, particularly in and around Calgary, Edmonton and Winnipeg. Indeed, Winnipeg probably had the largest Dutch community in Canada prior to WWI. The second period of immigration developed in the 1920s. Cheap, accessible arable land was in shorter supply, but the demand for farm, construction and industrial labour was high, particularly after 1925. Dutch immigrants spread across Canada to take up these opportunities, particularly in Ontario and the western provinces. During this period significant concentrations of Dutch immigrants settled in southern and southwestern Ontario, especially in Toronto. It is estimated that between 1890 and 1930 approximately 25 000 Dutch or Dutch American immigrants entered Canada. The Great Depression and WWII curtailed Dutch immigration until 1947, when 150 000 new immigrants fled from a war-devastated and economically ruined homeland. Initially the immigrants, as in the past, were agriculturalists, but by the mid-1950s they included many skilled and professional workers. Ontario became a particularly important destination, followed by Alberta, BC and the Maritimes. By the late 1960s these Dutch immigrants were well settled in all provinces, but particularly in Ontario and the urban areas of the western provinces. These communities served as beacons of welcome for other Dutch immigrants.

Social and Cultural Life The majority of Dutch immigrants have been of lower- or lower-middle-class and working-class origin. This common background has meant that social stratification within the community has not been a serious problem. Religion, however, has cut broad divisions across the Dutch Canadian community. While Dutch Roman Catholics formed the largest single religious entity, they have been outnumbered by the combined population of Dutch Protestant groups, many of whom have continued their religious traditions in Canada. The majority of Dutch Canadian Catholics and Protestants belong to "Canadian" churches and thus the only visible Dutch entity on the Canadian religious scene is the Dutch Calvinist or "reformed" tradition. The various churches unanimously encouraged integration and the adoption of those things Canadian that were not antithetical to social or religious practices. As a result, the Dutch language has largely been discarded, as have "old country" practices that could have blocked the attainment of economic security. This fact, combined with a strong work ethic and minimal past involvement in the cultural life of the native land, has meant that "ethnicity" has only a very personal, familiar or religious connotation to the Dutch, all of which helps to explain why Dutch Canadian clubs represent no more than a minority of the Dutch community. Only recently have the children of immigrants begun to examine the history of their parents' migration and struggle, and to give their discoveries academic or literary attention.

Group Maintenance The Dutch in Canada have until recently expressed little interest in maintaining or continuing their cultural traditions, the major exception being the Dutch Calvinists who have sought to make their religious ideas relevant to Canadian society by involving themselves in "Christian" schools. The rate of assimilation has been high and in most Canadian-born Dutch it is almost complete. While family ties remain strong,

intermarriage with other Canadians is not regarded as a problem by the majority. The Dutch church, the Dutch Credit Union and the Dutch Canadian clubs, which represent only a minority of Dutch Canadians, are the only remaining visible landmarks of an ethnic culture which is rapidly and willingly disappearing into the Canadian multicultural state. HERMAN GANZEVOORT

Reading: Herman Ganzevoort and M. Bockelman, *Dutch Immigration to North America* (1983); T.E. Hofman, *The Strength of Their Years* (1983).

Duvernay, Ludger, publisher, newspaperman, politician, patriote (b at Verchères, Qué 22 Jan 1799; d at Montréal 28 Nov 1852). Duvernay started his career at the age of 14 as a printer's apprentice. He launched 3 short-lived newspapers in Trois-Rivières, and then on 18 Jan 1827 he agreed to publish the *Canadian Spectator* of Montréal. On that same day, he purchased *La Minerve*, which became one of the most influential newspapers of Lower Canada, and a voice for the Patriote Party. He took part in the REBELLIONS OF 1837, and was forced into exile in the US until 1842, when he returned to Montréal and resumed publication of *La Minerve*. In 1843 he helped found the Association Saint-Jean-Baptiste and remained its president until his death. GISÈLE VILLENEUVE

Dye, Cecil Henry, "Babe," hockey player (b at Hamilton, Ont 13 May 1898; d 2 Jan 1962). His learning the skills of hockey from his mother on a backyard rink in Toronto became part of hockey lore. He joined Toronto St Pats in 1919, and in a brief, meteoric career led the NHL in scoring 4 times (1920-21, 1921-22, 1922-23 and 1924-25), scoring 5 goals in a game twice, 38 goals in 29 games 1924-25 and a total of 200 goals in 271 games. He played for Chicago 1926-28, for New York Americans 1928-29 and 6 games for Toronto Maple Leafs 1930-31. JAMES MARSH

Dyonnet, Edmond, painter, teacher (b at Crest, France 25 June 1859; d at Montréal 6 July 1954). Dyonnet studied in Turin with Gilardi and in Naples with Morelli. He came to Canada with his parents 1875. By 1891 he was teaching art at the Monument national and he was elected associate of the Royal Canadian Academy of Arts in 1893 and academician in 1903, also serving as the Academy's secretary 1910-49. A professor at and director of the design school at the Conseil des arts et manufactures in Montréal for 31 years, he also taught at the École polytechnique in Montréal 1907-22. Dyonnet helped found Montréal's École des beaux-arts in 1922 and was a professor there until 1924. He taught at McGill 1920-36. In 1910 France made him an officer of the Académie. He won silver medals at the exhibitions in Buffalo (1910) and in St Louis, Mo (1904). In 1968 U of Ottawa published his *Mémoires d'un artiste canadien*. MICHEL CHAMPAGNE

Dysart, A. Allison, lawyer, politician, judge, premier of NB (b at Cocagne, NB 22 Mar 1880; d at Moncton, NB 8 Dec 1962). Educated at Ont Agricultural Coll, St Joseph's U and Dalhousie, he practised law in Buctouche. He was elected MLA in 1917 for Kent County, was Speaker 1921-25 and minister of lands and mines 1925. Following the Liberal defeat, Dysart succeeded P.J. VENIOT in 1926 as leader of the Opposition. In 1935 he led his party to victory, defeating every member of the Cabinet of L.P.D. TILLEY. His government introduced the first Landlord and Tenants Act 1938, modernized the Labour Relations Act and worked to restore economic health following the Depression. Re-elected in 1939, Dysart resigned in 1940 as premier to become county court judge for Kent and Westmorland. He retired in 1957. DELLA M.M. STANLEY

Eagle (family Accipitridae), large BIRD OF PREY with exceptionally keen vision, long, powerful wings, hooked bill and strong feet with sharp curved talons. They are fierce predators, spotting their animal prey as they soar or from their perches, and then swooping to kill. The more than 50 species of eagles are found on all continents and are divided into 4 major groups: the mainly tropical snake eagles and harpy eagles, not found in Canada; fish eagles, represented in Canada by the bald eagle (*Haliaeetus leucocephalus*); and booted eagles, including the golden eagle (*Aquila chrysaetos*), which breeds in mountain regions of western and northwestern Canada. Bald and golden eagles are immediately recognizable by their large size and 1.8 m wingspan. As adults, the 2 are easily distinguished: the bald eagle has a white head (not truly bald) and tail, contrasting with the solid brown of the golden eagle, and the golden eagle has legs feathered to the talons. Bald and golden eagles nest in treetops or cliff ledges. Nests are made of sticks lined with grasses, weeds, etc. Because nests can be used for years, they can become enormous. Usually, 2 eggs are laid (range 1-3). Golden eagles incubate eggs for 43 days; bald eagles, 35 days. Young are down covered and remain helpless in the nest for 50-100 days. The feathers of an eagle were of great symbolic value to the Plains Indians, signifying bravery or holding the power of spirits.

R.W. FYFE

Eagle Pass, elev about 550 m, provides a corridor through the Gold Range in the MONASHEE MTS between Shuswap Lk and the Columbia R, 12 km SW of Revelstoke, BC. In 1865 Walter MOBERLY, BC's assistant surveyor general, set out to explore the interior for possible railway passes through the mountain barrier E of Shuswap Lk, and discovered and named the pass after he had shot up a nest of eagles that flew away through it. Eagle Pass was chosen as the CANADIAN PACIFIC RY route through the Monashees; there the western railway portion from Port Moody met the eastern rail crews, and on 7 Nov 1885 the last spike was driven at CRAIGELLACHIE, W of the pass. The Trans-Canada Hwy also traverses the pass. GLEN BOLES

Eagleson, Robert Alan, lawyer (b at St Catharines, Ont 24 Apr 1933). In 1966, as hockey's first player agent, he negotiated Bobby ORR's first contract with the Boston Bruins, a

$70 000 deal that made the 18-year-old rookie the highest-paid player in professional hockey. Eagleson ultimately built a practice with 150 athlete clients. He was dedicated to the idea of N American professionals playing Europe's best hockey teams, and his work was important to the success of the 1972 CANADA-SOVIET HOCKEY SERIES. He has remained the most important figure in the organization of hockey matches between European teams and the NHL. He was the organizer for the 1976, 1981, 1984 and 1987 CANADA CUP tournaments, and is the chief negotiator for Hockey Canada. He is also the executive director of the NHL Players Association and maintains an active law practice.

J. THOMAS WEST

Earle, David, dancer, choreographer (b at Toronto 17 Sept 1939). He trained in Toronto at the NATIONAL BALLET SCHOOL and studied in New York with Martha Graham. After a season in the José Limón Dance Company, he helped set up the London Contemporary Dance Theatre (Eng). In 1968 he returned to Toronto as co-director with Peter RANDAZZO and Patricia BEATTY of the TORONTO DANCE THEATRE. His dances are highly theatrical, reflecting perhaps his years with the Toronto Children's Players, and very lyrical. He has also shown an interest in the rituals of ancient cultures. His most popular

The bald eagle (*Haliaeetus leucocephalus*) is immediately recognizable by its large size, white (not bald) head and tail, and broad wingspan (*photo by Tim Fitzharris*).

work remains the *Baroque Suite,* a tribute to his late mentor, José Limón. His *Sacra Conversazione* premiered Mar 1986. GRAHAM JACKSON

Early-Warning Radar Air-defence RADAR stations were first established in Canada along the Atlantic and Pacific coasts in 1942, but were dismantled following the defeat of Germany and Japan in 1945. Although the USSR's military capabilities did not yet extend to launching a massive air bombardment on N America, in 1946 Canadian authorities began to consider the problem of building a radar chain in the Far North to guard against the possibility of Soviet attack. However, existing technology could not guarantee complete coverage of the northern frontier and would not permit accurate tracking of hostile aircraft once they had passed over the Arctic coast on their way to potential targets in southern Canada. Since this would leave the air force's fighter units without reliable information, it seemed unwise to spend vast sums on an ineffective early-warning system. The idea was shelved in 1947.

Conditions had changed by 1949. The USSR had developed its own atomic bomb and was in the process of creating a long-range bomber force. This, coupled with increased East-West tensions in Europe, convinced the Canadian government that it should construct a radar line, this time farther south, to provide early warning of an attack. The US decided to build a similar chain on its northern border that same year. Joint discussion eventually led to a co-operative effort, the Pinetree Line. Completed in 1954 for $450 million (of which Canada paid $150 million), it was a network of 33 stations running from Vancouver I through Alberta, northern Ontario and Québec to the Labrador coast. Eleven stations were financed and manned by Canada, and a further 5 were staffed by Canadians but paid for by the US.

Interest in improving N American radar coverage grew as the USSR upgraded its bomber force in the early 1950s. In Feb 1953 Defence Minister Brooke Claxton discussed the construction of an arctic chain with the Eisenhower administration, but no decisions were made. When the Soviets exploded their first hydrogen (thermonuclear) bomb in Aug 1953 the question became more urgent. Instead of an arctic chain, however, Canadian defence-research scientists recommended the construction of a mostly unmanned radar warning system (the McGill Fence) at 55° N to complement Pinetree. Louis St. Laurent's government accepted the advice in June 1954 and proceeded with this all-Canadian Mid-Canada Line project because technology was available in Canada, the line was cheaper than an arctic chain, and the plan avoided the troublesome issue of American presence on Canadian soil. Ninety-eight Mid-Canada stations were built by 1957 at a total cost of $250 million.

The idea of an arctic early-warning chain was not dropped. In June 1954 the Canada-US Military Studies Group — a bilateral advisory body under the aegis of the PERMANENT JOINT BOARD ON DEFENCE — urged that such a network be built because the USSR could outflank both the Pinetree and Mid-Canada lines. Under pressure from the US, and receiving similar advice from the RCAF, the federal government ultimately accepted the need for a radar chain in the Far North, and in Nov 1954 Canada and the US agreed to the construction of the Distant Early Warning (DEW) Line along the Arctic coast from Alaska to Baffin I. The US would bear the full cost of construction but had to employ Canadian firms and native labour. Canada also retained ownership of the sites located in Canada, and the

Dew Line site at Hall Beach, NWT (*courtesy Canadian Forces/photo by Sgt Jim Smith/ISC 86-753/National Defence Headquarters*).

major stations were to be commanded by Canadians. Stretching 8046 km (5944 in Canada), the 22-station DEW Line was completed in 1957 after a massive construction engineering job that employed over 25 000 people. Such extensive co-operation between Canada and the US to solve the common problem of N American air defence was an important first step in the creation of the bilateral North American Air Defence Command (NORAD) in 1958, which integrated all Canadian air-defence radars and fighter forces.

The importance of these radar lines decreased substantially almost as soon as they had been completed. Intercontinental and submarine-launched missiles, against which all 3 early-warning lines were useless, began to replace the manned bomber as the main Soviet threat in the early 1960s and a Ballistic Missile Early Warning System (BMEWS) was constructed in Alaska and Greenland. Satellites and BMEWS took over as the primary attack early-warning system. As a result the Mid-Canada Line was phased out of service in 1965, and in subsequent years 9 Pinetree stations were closed. By 1983, 21 modernized DEW Line stations and 24 Pinetree stations remained in operation to maintain sovereignty over Canada's airspace and to detect any Soviet aircraft undertaking a bombing raid on N America in conjunction with or following a ballistic missile attack.

The development of the Cruise missile, a low-flying weapon that could avoid detection by the DEW and Pinetree lines, reawakened interest in arctic air defence in the early 1980s. In the spring of 1985, following the Shamrock Summit between PM Mulroney and US Pres Reagan, the 2 countries agreed to complete by 1992 a modern radar line, the North Warning System, to replace the DEW and Pinetree chains, along Canada's Arctic coast at about 70° N. Consisting of 52 stations (47 in Canada, of which 11 would be manned), and expected to cost $1.5 billion (of which Canada's share would be $600 million), the new chain was designed to detect low-flying aircraft and missiles, and to pass information direct by satellite to NORAD headquarters. Additional detection capabilities would be provided by radar warning and control aircraft (AWACS), and long-range over-the-horizon radars on the eastern and western perimeters of N America. To facilitate interception and identification of unidentified objects, it was announced that 5 airfields in Canada's Far North would be upgraded to permit operations by Canadian CF-18 fighters.
STEPHEN HARRIS

Earnscliffe, built in 1857 for Thomas MacKinnon, a successful businessman, was one of Ottawa's most impressive mansions of the mid-19th century. Designed in a Gothic revival style, its asymmetrical plan, medieval window moldings, and multi-gabled roof accented by an ornately carved bargeboard provide an unusually elaborate interpretation of this style. Its picturesque quality is enhanced by its spectacular site on top of the limestone cliffs overlooking the Ottawa R. Earnscliffe has seen a succession of distinguished residents. Between 1871 and 1891 it was the home of Sir John A. MACDONALD, and since 1930 it has served as the official residence of the British high commissioner to Canada.   JANET WRIGHT

Earthquake, vibratory motion generated in the Earth by the rupture of subterranean rock subjected to elastic stresses greater than its breaking strength. The rupture gives rise to seismic waves which propagate outward from its initiation point or focus. Immediately above the focus at the surface, the epicentral region experiences the strongest shaking. At greater distances, the seismic ground motion is detectable only by sensitive instruments (eg, seismographs). There are many measures of an earthquake's size, the most commonly used being that devised by Charles Richter in 1935. Recognizing the need to quantify earthquake size, Richter created a scale (calibrated against seismograph records) that takes into account the attenuation of seismic waves with distance from the earthquake focus. On the Richter magnitude scale (M), earthquakes below M2 are generally not felt, even when occurring at shallow depth. Shallow M5 events cause damage only when the epicentral region supports structures built on loose soils or unconsolidated sediments. M6 earthquakes in populated areas frequently cause considerable damage. The great earthquakes of this century have had magnitudes of about 8.5. Approximately 100 earthquakes each year are of M6 strength or greater; fortunately, most occur offshore or in unpopulated areas.

The severity of surface ground shaking at a particular distance from the source is described by its intensity at that location. The Modified Mercalli Intensity Scale, used in N America to quantify the degree of surface effects, ranges from MMI (barely perceptible ground motion) to MMXII (total destruction). MMVI is the threshold of damage. The depth of an earthquake focus varies from near surface to 700 km. Most continental earthquakes occur in the crust at depths less than 40 km. Deep-focus earthquakes (below 300 km) are restricted to parts of very active seismic belts.

In Canada earthquakes occur in the Cordillera, along the West Coast and offshore, in the Yukon and the High Arctic, in eastern Canada and along the eastern seaboard. Elsewhere in Canada, earthquakes are rare and of small magnitude. In the Cordillera, moderate earthquakes occur in the crust at minor to moderate levels of activity throughout, in a generally compressive regime. A large earthquake (M7) occurred in the vicinity of Hope, BC, or farther S in northern Washington State, in 1872. This is the largest known event in the region; all others have been M6 or less.

Along the West Coast and beneath Vancouver I and the Str of Georgia, earthquakes are the product of active plate subduction (*see* PLATE TECTONICS; GEOLOGICAL HISTORY). The small Juan de Fuca Plate is at present being thrust beneath the Olympic Mts and southern Vancouver I. The result is a zone of earthquakes beneath Puget Sound at depths of 70-100 km, overlain by a zone of shallower, generally smaller events. The regime extends N to Canadian territory and the southern Str of Georgia. The smaller Explorer Plate is no longer being thrust beneath northern Vancouver I; thus the junction of the 2 plates is a shear zone marked in the offshore by the Nootka Fault and extending deep beneath the islands. The shallower crust is occasionally subjected to large earthquakes (eg, the M7 event on Vancouver I near Courtenay, 1946), presumably in response to the shearing stresses below.

Offshore, a transform-spreading ridge system separates the Explorer and Juan de Fuca plates from the Pacific Plate. None of the many earthquakes occurring there each year is felt onshore. Further N the transform system intersects the Continental Shelf and extends N along the shelf as a transcurrent fault. Canada's greatest known earthquakes have occurred along this feature. In 1949 a 200 km long segment of the fault ruptured in an M8 earthquake that caused chandeliers to sway in Jasper. The thrusting of the Pacific Plate beneath Alaska generates many severe (M8) earthquakes that may affect Canadian territory. The Good Friday, 1964, M8.6 earthquake generated a TSUNAMI or seismic sea wave that caused considerable damage in Port Alberni, Vancouver I.

There are active seismic zones in the Richardson and Mackenzie mountains, YT, and a relatively limited seismic zone in the Beaufort Sea. Numerous earthquake zones occur in the arctic islands, one extending S through the Boothia Pen, across the mouth of Hudson Bay and northern Québec to the Labrador Sea. Baffin Bay was the site of an M7 earthquake in 1933. An event of similar magnitude occurred in the Laurentian Channel S of Newfoundland in 1929, generating a tsunami that caused considerable damage and drowned 27 people on the Burin Pen.

In eastern Canada seismicity is diffuse throughout the northern Appalachians, the series of M5 events in the Miramichi region of NB in 1982 being the most recent example. More concentrated zones occur at the mouth of the St Lawrence, in the St Lawrence Valley near La Malbaie in Charlevoix County, and in western Québec. The Charlevoix zone is the site of most of the larger events in eastern Canada. One of the largest occurred in 1534-35 between the voyages of Jacques Cartier, and was reported to him by the Indians of the area on his return. More recently, an M7 earthquake in 1925 was felt throughout eastern Canada and the northeastern US. In the western Québec zone, damaging earthquakes have occurred at Témiscaming (1935) and Cornwall (1944). Both events were approximately M6.

Earthquakes in Canada are monitored by the National Seismograph Network operated by the Geological Survey, Dept of Energy, Mines and Resources. Approximately 100 seismographs are distributed from St John's to Vancouver I and from Alert in the High Arctic to the Niagara Pen. The network is capable of detecting all earthquakes greater than M3.5 anywhere in Canada and those greater than M2 in more densely populated regions. Approximately 300 events greater than M3 are located annually. Probability estimates of seismic ground motion resulting from Canadian earthquakes are incorporated into the National Building Code of Canada; structures designed according to its provisions can resist moderate earthquakes without significant damage and major earthquakes without collapse.   MICHAEL J. BERRY

Reading: Bruce A. Bolt, *Earthquakes: A Primer* (1978).

Earthworm, segmented worm of phylum ANNELIDA, class Oligochaeta. The class comprises some 14 families, including Lumbricidae to which the common earthworm (*Lumbricus terrestris*) belongs. Canadian species are all of familiar backyard size. Aquatic relatives may be microscopic; some Australian and Brazilian species may reach 3 m long and weigh 500 g. Earthworms are vital as soil mixers. Darwin estimated that 63 000 earthworms can shift, annually, 7.5-18 t of soil per acre (0.4 ha). In fact, there may be up to 32 million specimens per hectare in some places. Worms eat plant pieces and some animal remains in soil. They are reared and harvested for fishing bait (eg, night crawlers) and classroom specimens. Although hermaphroditic (of both sexes simultaneously), worms mate inside a mucus sheath secreted by the saddle-shaped thickening (clitellum) on the body of mature earthworms. The mucus sheath binds mating pairs and produces the egg-containing cocoon. Eggs and sperm fuse in the sheath, and fertilized eggs develop in the cocoons until tiny earthworms hatch. Many species are capable of self-fertilization, or eggs may develop without being fertilized. Very little work has been done on Canadian earthworms; only 19 species are recorded, 18 of which are primarily European, and one, *Bismastos parvus*, primarily N American. There are more than 150 related aquatic species. The ice ages are thought to have destroyed native earthworms wherever glaciers covered land; hence, all species in Canada are probably introduced (from Europe, often by humans) or reintroduced from southern US. Earthworms are separated from other oligochaetes by a combination of characteristics, including 8 setae per segment; multicellular clitellum; small eggs without yolks; 2 pairs of testes and one pair of ovaries; male pores opening behind female; and relatively large size, compared to aquatic species.   R.O. BRINKHURST

East India Company, trading company chartered 1600 by Elizabeth I of England with a monopoly over the Eastern Hemisphere. Schemes for promoting the British FUR TRADE between the Pacific coast and China, including those of Alexander Dalrymple and Alexander MACKENZIE, necessitated inclusion of the East India Company, whose privileges deterred such commerce. Except during the period 1814-16, when the EIC licensed the NORTH WEST COMPANY to use its own ships to carry furs to China, the NWC found EIC regulations sufficiently restrictive that it used American ships for this trade. The EIC's monopoly ended by 1833, and the company was dissolved in 1874.   JEAN MORRISON

Eastern Temperate Forests, *see* VEGETATION REGIONS.

Eastern Townships Region located in S-central Québec, between Montréal and Québec City. The townships extend from GRANBY to Lac MÉGANTIC and from DRUMMONDVILLE to the US border. The first inhabitants were the ABENAKI, who used the region for hunting and fishing. The only settlement during the French regime was a trading post at Grandes-Fourches [SHERBROOKE]. Early in the English regime (from 1760), the area was called Buckinghamshire. Shortly after the American Revolution a large number of English LOYALISTS left the US for Canada and settled on 259 km² in southern Québec. In 1791 the British government granted them land in the form of townships. The 93 townships formed thereafter became known as the "Eastern Townships" (as opposed to the "Western Townships" of Upper Canada). The English-speaking settlers were mainly American, English and Irish.

After 1840 a wave of French colonization swept into the region, and by 1871 Francophones constituted the majority in most of the townships. Anglophones now account for less than 10% of the region's population.

Equipped with an excellent road system since 1815, the region underwent considerable growth following construction of the GRAND TRUNK RY, which linked Montréal and Portland, Maine. The road and rail networks encouraged the exploitation and development of natural resources such as timber, asbestos, granite, copper and limestone. Hydroelectric power generated by the numerous waterfalls of the Rivière ST-FRANÇOIS and its tributaries resulted in the establishment of sawmills and flour mills, and the development of

textile plants, foundries and the pulp and paper industry. The 20th century brought heavy industry to Sherbrooke, and it gradually became the "Queen of the Eastern Townships." The snowmobile industry flourished in Valcourt after its foundation by J. Armand BOMBARDIER. Most of Canada's commercially important ASBESTOS comes from the Eastern Townships; in fact, mines in THETFORD-MINES and ASBESTOS produce a major portion of the world's asbestos. University research and the arrival of high technology in the field of microprocessors have resulted in the establishment of a microelectronics industry. The region has 2 universities – U Sherbrooke (francophone), and Bishop's (anglophone) in LENNOXVILLE. One of the region's curiosities is its round barns, designed – because of the legend that "the devil hides in the corners of barns" – to protect their owners from the devil. The MAGOG-Orford area has become a major international tourist centre.

JEAN-MARIE DUBOIS AND PIERRE MAILHOT

Eastmain (or East Main) refers to the E shore of Hudson Bay, although in the 1680s the term was restricted to the vicinity of the EASTMAIN R. The corresponding reference to the W shore of Hudson Bay is the Westmain (West Main). Both terms were used in the early FUR TRADE when the region was well travelled by trappers and traders.

JOHN ROBERT COLOMBO

Eastmain, Rivière, 756 km long, rises in the central part of Québec on the side of a low drainage divide from which streams flow W to JAMES BAY. The river's drainage basin is situated in an area of heavy snowfall, resulting in an impressive mean discharge and considerable potential for hydro development. The river encounters a sharp break of slope coming off the Canadian SHIELD peneplain as it meets the narrow coastal plain of James Bay, and in its final 65 km descends 125 m in a series of rapids and falls. *See also* JAMES BAY PROJECT.   DOUG FINLAYSON

Easton, Peter, pirate (*fl* 1602-15). He was a privateer in Elizabeth I's navy who lost his commission on the accession of James I in 1603 and turned to piracy. He looted shipping in the English Channel until 1610, when he withdrew rather than fight Sir Henry MAINWARING. He arrived in Newfoundland in 1610, built a fort at HARBOUR GRACE, and for several years plundered fishing fleets and settlements and recruited Newfoundland sailors into his private navy. He destroyed a Basque fleet intent upon capturing Harbour Grace, attacked Spanish shipping in the Caribbean, raided Puerto Rico, and captured the Spanish plate fleet in 1614. Pardoned by King James, Easton abandoned his Newfoundland base and settled in Savoy. He bought a castle at Villefranche, became "Marquis of Savoy," and lived the rest of his life in luxury. There is a monument to this Newfoundland folk hero at Harbour Grace.   EDWARD BUTTS

Eaton, Cyrus Stephen, financier, philanthropist (b at Pugwash, NS 27 Dec 1883; d at Cleveland, Ohio 9 May 1979). Educated at McMaster, Eaton moved to the US in 1900. He became involved in public utilities and after 1925 in steel, eventually forming Republic Steel. He also had investments in Canada, including Steep Rock Iron Ore. In 1950 Eaton and C.D. HOWE quarrelled over administration of the company. They became estranged and Eaton later helped Howe's political opponents in Port Arthur [Thunder Bay]. Eaton became best known for his sponsorship of a series of conferences at his birthplace, PUGWASH, at which he attempted to bring together scientists and public figures from East and West to foster international concilia-

tion. For his efforts he received the Lenin Peace Prize in 1960.   ROBERT BOTHWELL

Eaton, Fredrik Stefan, merchant (b at Toronto 26 June 1938), great-grandson of Timothy EATON and grandson of John Craig EATON; president of The T. EATON CO. At the conclusion of his university education in 1962, Eaton, following family tradition, gained on-the-job experience within the organization in numerous capacities in both Canada and England. Since 1977 he has presided over the continued expansion and consolidation of his great-grandfather's business and assisted in the development of Toronto's EATON CENTRE. In 1987 the company had 108 stores across Canada employing 35 000.   JOY L. SANTINK

Eaton, Sir John Craig, merchant, philanthropist (b at Toronto 28 Apr 1876; d there 30 Mar 1922). Third son of Timothy EATON, he worked in numerous capacities within The T. Eaton Co before becoming president 1907. Recognizing the opportunities for development in the West, he was largely responsible for establishing the Eaton store in Winnipeg 1905. He also opened buying offices in Great Britain, the US, Europe and the Orient. By 1919 he had established Saturday holidays and evening closing at 5 PM in his stores, factories and mail-order offices. The Eaton Boys and Girls clubs also provided educational and recreational facilities for company employees. Eaton employees on active war service continued to receive full pay for the duration of WWI – ultimately more than $2 million. He was knighted in 1915 for his philanthropic activities.   JOY L. SANTINK

Eaton, John David, merchant (b at Toronto 4 Oct 1909; d there 4 Aug 1973), second son of Sir John Craig EATON. He left Cambridge at age 21 to begin his apprenticeship with The T. EATON CO LTD in the men's wear dept of the Toronto store. He learned the firm's various operations, became a director in 1934, a VP in 1937, and president in 1942. During his presidency the business expanded in the North and West, and contributory medical insurance and a retirement plan for employees were introduced. Eaton personally contributed $50 million to the latter when it began in 1948, fuelling speculation that he was the richest man in the country. A shy man, he lived quietly.

Eaton, Timothy, merchant, founder of Canada's largest privately owned department store, The T. EATON CO (b near Ballymena, Ire 1834; d at Toronto 31 Jan 1907). After apprenticing in a general store in Ireland, Eaton followed 2 older brothers to Canada 1854 and worked for a time at a store in UC. In 1856 with his brother James, he opened a small store in the Huron Tract at Kirkton, which they moved in 1860 to St Mary's, near Stratford. Convinced that change was in the air, Eaton in 1869 opened his own store at 178 Yonge St, Toronto, and introduced Canadians to the idea of cash sales and one fixed price, in contrast to the older credit, bargain and barter method. He displayed a sympathetic attitude towards his employees, having by the late 1880s instituted evening closing at 6 PM and the summer Saturday afternoon holiday. He also vastly improved their working environment by creating light, airy workplaces. The introduction of the Eaton catalogue in 1884 gave Canadians, particularly those in pioneer farming communities, access to a variety of merchandise. At his death in 1907 at age 72, Eaton employed over 9000 people in his Toronto and Winnipeg stores, in factories in Toronto and Oshawa, and in offices in London, Eng, and Paris.   JOY L. SANTINK

Reading: J.W. Ferry, *A History of the Department Store* (1960); G.G. Nasmith, *Timothy Eaton* (1923); J.E. Middleton, *The Municipality of Toronto* I (1923).

Timothy Eaton introduced Canadians to the idea of cash sales and a fixed priced for goods. He built his small store into a thriving department store network employing over 9000 people at the time of his death in 1907 (*courtesy Archives/Eaton's of Canada Ltd*).

Eaton, Wyatt, portrait, genre and landscape painter, illustrator (b at Philipsburg, Qué 6 May 1849; d at Newport, RI 7 June 1896). Eaton left Canada for New York around 1867 and studied at the National Academy of Design, and then for 5 years under Joseph Oriel Eaton. He went to London, then Paris where he studied at the École des beaux-arts (1872-76) and became a disciple of Millet and several other Barbizon painters. On his return to New York (1876), he taught at the Cooper Union and executed a series of pen-and-ink portraits of American poets for *Century Magazine*. In France again, 1883-84, he painted his most famous canvas, *Harvest Field*. His portraits of George STEPHEN, Sir Donald SMITH and William VAN HORNE, painted in Montréal, 1892-93, were so well received that orders for portraits of Sir William DAWSON, William C. MACDONALD and others followed. His last working days were spent in Ottawa. He was a founding member and president of the American Art Assn (later Soc of American Artists), and founding member of the Soc of Canadian Artists (1867).   ROBERT STACEY

Eaton Centre, Toronto (designed by the ZEIDLER Partnership and BREGMAN AND HAMANN, phase 1 opening in 1977, phase 2 in 1979) is the epitome of those vast multistorey interior "atrium" spaces for which Canadian ARCHITECTURE became known internationally in the 1970s. The centre comprises The T. EATON CO LTD department store, 2 office buildings and a 274 m glass-covered shopping galleria flanked by 3 levels of shops and restaurants and 4 levels of parking. The architecture plays with the simple technological themes of traditional modern design, unadorned concrete and steel structure, metal pipe handrails, transparent and mirror glass, together with the decoration provided by plants and fountains, shop signs and banners to create a lively and varied gathering place that is well integrated with the existing downtown.   MICHAEL McMORDIE

Eaton Company Limited, The T., with head offices in Toronto, is a major Canadian retailer founded in Toronto in 1869 by Timothy EATON. Eaton revolutionized the commercial practice of the day by selling items for cash at a fixed price and offering satisfaction or money refunded. His store became one of the largest department stores in N America. Eaton's son John Craig EATON assumed the presidency on the death of his father in 1907; he was later knighted. His cousin, Robert Young Eaton, took over in 1922, followed by Sir John's son, John David EATON, in 1942. The current president, Fredrik S. EATON, is Timothy Eaton's great-grandson.

A cornerstone of the Eaton empire was its catalogue business, established in 1884 along with mail-order facilities to reach pioneer farm communities. The discontinuation of this business in 1976 spurred internal reorganization and revitalization. Other early innovations are still thriving: the Product Research Bureau was established in 1916 by John Craig Eaton, who was inspired by his father's insistence that customers should always know what was in their merchandise; it was the first developed in Canada by a retailer. Eaton's is still the only retailer in the country with its own complete research facilities. The company's sales revenues and assets are undisclosed, in 1987 it had an estimated 35 000 employees and 108 outlets. All shares are held by the Eaton family.   DEBORAH C. SAWYER

Eau Claire, Lac à l', 1383 km², elev 241 m, max length 68 km, is located in northwestern Québec about 133 km E of the southeastern shore of Hudson Bay. Probably formed by the impact of a meteorite, the lake drains W via the Clearwater R into Lac GUILLAUME-DELISLE (Richmond Gulf). After joining with the flow from the Rivière de Troyes, it empties into Hudson Bay. The lake's name is purely representative, and it is often called Clearwater Lk.   DAVID EVANS

Eayrs, James George, political scientist, educator (b at London, Eng 13 Oct 1926). Educated at U of T, Columbia and London School of Economics, Eayrs is Eric Dennis Memorial Professor of Political Science and Government at Dalhousie. He taught at U of T 1952-80 and was editor of *International Journal*, 1959-84. A superb stylist and an influential pioneer in the study of 20th-century Canadian foreign and defence policy, his major scholarly publications include *The Art of the Possible* (1961) and *In Defence of Canada* (5 vols, 1964-83). Eayrs's reputation outside the university world rests upon his controversial journalism and public commentary on Canadian and international affairs, selections of which are collected in *Northern Approaches* (1961), *Minutes of the Sixties* (1968) and *Greenpeace and her Enemies* (1973). His early journalism displays a pro-NATO, Cold War liberal sympathetic to the US. The 1960s and 1970s saw him an opponent of NATO, an advocate of Canadian neutrality and a harsh critic of diplomats and diplomacy. He received the MOLSON PRIZE in 1984.   NORMAN HILLMER

Eccles, William John, historian (b at Thirsk, Yorkshire, Eng 17 July 1917). A graduate of McGill U, Eccles taught at the universities of Manitoba (1953-57) and Alberta (1957-63), before being appointed professor of history at the U of T where he taught until 1983. Eccles was primarily responsible for reviving English Canadian interest in early Canadian history. His first book, *Frontenac: The Courtier Governor* (1959), established him as a major revisionist, and in subsequent works, *Canada Under Louis XIV, 1663-1701* (1964), *The Canadian Frontier, 1534-1763* (1969), *France in America* (1972) and *Essays on New France* (1987), he developed his unique vision of early Canadian society. According to Eccles, early French Canada was formed chiefly by the values of the 17th-century French nobility which sustained by its membership in the seigneurial class and military establishment. Each successive work developed his theme of the uniqueness of Canadian society on an ever-larger canvas. Despite the fact that he had refused to allow his name to stand for election to the ROYAL SOCIETY OF CANADA, in 1979 that body awarded him the Tyrrell Medal in recognition of his contribution to Canadian history writing.   JAMES PRITCHARD

Echinodermata [Gk, "spiny skin"], phylum of exclusively marine invertebrate animals. The 6000 known species occur from shores to greatest depths of all oceans. None are found in fresh water; very few are capable of coping with diluted seawater of estuaries. The name is derived from the characteristic internal skeleton of calcium carbonate formed into numerous small, bony structures (ossicles). Ossicles are embedded in the skin, often giving it a rough or spiny texture. There are 5 classes of living echinoderms: crinoids (sea lilies and feather stars); asteroids (STARFISH); ophiuroids (brittle stars); echinoids (SEA URCHINS, etc); and holothuroids (sea cucumbers). Echinoderms have been well preserved as FOSSILS; all existing classes and several others now extinct were present in the Ordovician (505-438 million years ago). They may have originated in the Precambrian (over 570 million years ago).

Living classes differ principally in body plan. All show radial symmetry (symmetry about an axis) but there are many variations. In general, the axis of symmetry runs between the oral and aboral surfaces (sides bearing mouth and anus, respectively). Crinoids, asteroids and ophiuroids are basically star shaped; the axis of symmetry is vertical. In asteroids and ophiuroids, the oral surface is usually directed downwards, in crinoids, upwards. Sea urchins are spherical, with the oral surface downwards. Holothuroids are sausage shaped and, typically, lie on one side; oral and aboral surfaces are at either end. Fundamentally, echinoderms are composed of 5 radially arranged parts. This configuration, most apparent in the star-shaped asteroids and ophiuroids, also occurs in echinoids and holothuroids, which typically have body parts in some multiple of 5.

Another characteristic is the water-vascular system, an arrangement of tubes and canals employing hydrostatic pressure to operate tube feet. Water within ampullae (small sacs resembling medicine-dropper bulbs) is squeezed out by muscular contraction, causing the tube feet to elongate. Contraction of muscles in the tube feet walls causes retraction of feet and return of water to the ampullae. Tube feet usually occur in rows radiating out from the oral surface. They function in locomotion, feeding and respiration.

Crinoids are the oldest and most primitive living class of echinoderms. Their common name, sea lilies, derives from the fact that some species are attached to the sea bottom by a stalk. Long, feathery arms surrounding the mouth give the appearance of a lilylike flower. Crinoids that have lost this sessile lifestyle and no longer have a stalk are commonly called feather stars. Crinoids usually feed on suspended particles that fall on their oral surface. Some feather stars swim by thrashing arms up and down. In a comical, unco-ordinated manner, they can lift themselves off the bottom and avoid predators.

Asteroids (starfish or sea stars) are common seashore animals. Starfish are voracious carnivores. Those that feed on clams and mussels pull open the hinged shell with their tube feet, evert their stomach into the slightly gaping MOLLUSC and secrete digestive juices that dissolve the victim in its shell. The remarkable regenerative powers of starfish enable them to regrow a lost body part. For most species, only a piece of central disc need be present for missing parts to grow back.

Ophiuroids (brittle stars) are named for their habit of casting off arms when threatened. The arms are not really brittle; the ophiuroid is using one of its remarkable capacities, autotomy or self-cutting. The ability to regrow missing parts is exceptionally well developed in ophiuroids. They are usually filter feeders, using tube feet to catch particles suspended in seawater.

Echinoids include sea urchins, sand dollars and heart urchins. Ossicles of the body wall have fused into a rigid, solid, internal skeleton (test). All members of the class have external surfaces covered with spines. In sand dollars, these are reduced to a fine, feltlike covering. The elaborate chewing apparatus just inside the mouth is called Aristotle's lantern, a name that originated with Aristotle, who thought the structure resembled lanterns of the day.

Holothuroids are called sea cucumbers because of their elongate bodies and habit of lying on their side. They frequently have numerous branched tentacles surrounding the mouth which serve to filter food. Other forms lack tentacles and sweep the bottom like vacuum cleaners, extracting nutrition from bottom sediments. In many parts of Asia holothuroids are considered a delicacy and are extensively fished.

Many echinoderms reproduce by releasing eggs and sperm into seawater, where fertilization occurs. The embryo develops into a small planktonic or swimming larva. Larvae of each class have their own characteristic forms and names. They differ dramatically from adult forms. Larvae may drift and feed in the PLANKTON for many weeks before they finally settle and metamorphose into adults. Each class contains many species that have a specialized brood pouch within the mother and, therefore, do not form larvae. There are also some species that reproduce asexually by dividing their bodies in half and regrowing missing parts. R.D. BURKE

Eckhardt-Gramatté, Sophie-Carmen, "Sonia," née Friedman, composer, pianist, violinist, teacher (b at Moscow? 6 Jan 1899; d at Stuttgart, West Germany 2 Dec 1974). Although most of her professional career was spent in Europe, she became a strong force in Canadian music from the time of her arrival in 1953 (with her husband, Dr Ferdinand Eckhardt, who had become director of the Winnipeg Art Gallery) until her death. As an 11-year-old prodigy she gave recitals on the violin and piano in Paris, Geneva and Berlin, and by age 13 had several small pieces published in Paris. Her concert career peaked in 1929 with performances in America where she was championed by Leopold Stokowski. She next concentrated on composition, her style gradually evolving through the conservative influence of her instructor, Max Trapp, and through her 1939 move from Berlin to Vienna (neoclassicism and a modest bow to serialism). Works written in Canada show an increasing emphasis on intervallic relationships (Bartok), metric organization and "basic note groups" (Webern). Many were commissioned: *Woodwind Quintet, Piano Trio, Duo Concertante* for cello and piano, *String Quartet No. 3, Symphony-Concerto* for piano and orchestra and the *Manitoba Symphony.* Her name is memorialized in the Eckhardt-Gramatté National Competition for the Performance of Canadian Music held annually at Brandon, Man. LORNE WATSON

ECOLOG, acoustic instrumentation system developed at the BEDFORD INSTITUTE OF OCEANOGRAPHY, Dartmouth, NS, for research on and survey of fish populations. A dual-beam, vertical echo sounder is towed from a ship, transmitting sound and receiving echoes at a frequency of 50 or 120 kHz (echoes from swim bladders of fish are strongest in the 30-120 kHz range). Echoes are received simultaneously on narrow- and wide-beam acoustic receivers. Echo signals are digitized and recorded on magnetic tape. Computer programs on board ship, or later in the laboratory, give position, depth, number and size of fish encountered, allowing estimates of local abundance. L.M. DICKIE

Economic and Regional Development Agreements (ERDAs) are bilateral agreements covering the period from 1984-94 which the federal government has signed with each of the 10 provinces. The ERDA system is an important instrument in federal regional economic policy. Each ERDA is essentially an "umbrella" agreement which sets out general objectives and priorities for action and a co-ordinating structure (including planning and annual meetings of ministers). A subsidiary agreement commits both governments to do certain things and usually requires cost-sharing. As of 1987, $4.44 billion had been committed by both levels of government by means of 93 ERDA subsidiary agreements. Nineteen memoranda of understanding also had been signed expressing intent. The ERDAs are the shared responsibility of the federal minister of regional industrial expansion and his counterpart in each province.

Economic Council of Canada, est 1963 to assess medium- and long-term prospects of the economy; to consider ways of strengthening Canada's international financial and trade position; to study the effects of economic growth and technical change on employment and income; to explore policies to foster regional development; and to study means of increasing Canadian participation in the ownership, control and management of industries in Canada. A federally funded crown corporation, it reports directly to the prime minister. It maintains a large staff in Ottawa and publishes not only its own consensus recommendations but research projects of individual economists as well. The Council publishes an *Annual Review* of the economy and a quarterly bulletin *Au Courant,* with 40 000 subscribers. Net cost of operations in 1987 was $9.7 million. WILLIAM F. FORWARD

Economic Forecasting is a projection or estimation of the future economic or technological performance of a country, group of countries, firm, industry or community. Economic forecasts may be short, medium or long term, and are published by banks, investment dealers, the CONFERENCE BOARD and economic-research organizations. The ECONOMIC COUNCIL OF CANADA publishes forecasts (also called, in this instance, 5-to-10-year economic and social goals), as do some provincial governments. Twice a year the Organization for Economic Cooperation and Development publishes forecasts, including those for individual members such as Canada.

The financial community pays close attention to forecasts. Companies, such as manufacturing businesses, use them to help plan for employment, production, inventories and costs. Large utilities such as telephone companies, electric-power suppliers and pipelines depend upon longer-term economic forecasts for help in planning the construction of new facilities.

Forecasters rely on various techniques, including an analysis of leading indicators (ie, statistical information on certain factors, such as steel production, which provide advance warning of changes in economic activity) and econometric computer models. In these models forecasters attempt to create mathematically, through equations, a picture of how the economy (or market, industry, etc) functions. These equations may identify relationships such as those between prices and wages, or between consumer spending and investment or production. Forecasts are very rarely completely correct and are often quite wrong, but the growing speed of computer processing may improve their accuracy. W. EMPEY

Economic History, the study of the evolution of the economy and economic institutions. The subject grew out of history and economics in the 19th century and arrived in Canada when an English economic historian was appointed professor of political economy in Toronto (1888). It uses material and ideas from economics, history, geography and political science, supplying information to these subjects; it must not be confused with the history of economic ideas or with the interpretation of general history using economic forces. Distinctive contributions to Canada's economic history came in the 1920s and 1930s both from economists such as H.A. INNIS and from historians such as D.G. CREIGHTON, who stressed the importance of what they called "staple products" – fur, fish, timber, wheat, metals – whose markets were abroad. Emphasizing the importance of Canada's distinctive geography – the Canadian Shield and the Great Lakes-St Lawrence system – they traced interactions between geography, resources, foreign markets and the inflow of people and funds from abroad. They treated regional growth in relation to the staple products. More recent approaches have supplemented the old with modern economics and statistics. Work has been done in areas, including WORKING-CLASS HISTORY, urban growth, BUSINESS HISTORY and the industrial development of central Canada, that fitted rather poorly into the STAPLE THESIS. Meanwhile, historical geographers produce invaluable material on settlement patterns and on the growth of towns, while regional studies, which staple theorists treated as components of nation-building, have become routes to regional self-confidence, especially in Québec and Atlantic Canada. Marxist scholars share business and labour history and other fields with scholars whose ideologies are very different.

Although the following sections describe Canadian economic history by region, the country is historically a single economic unit. The FUR TRADE

Portaging around Smith Rapids, Slave R. The fur trade was crucial to early economic development (*courtesy Provincial Archives of Alberta/E. Brown Coll/B2909*).

first created a single transcontinental trading economy; since Confederation, 1867, labour and finance have moved freely among the regions. The improvement of transportation – the railways between 1867 and 1915 (see RAILWAY HISTORY), and the highway and pipeline systems after 1945 – has helped. The provinces have become important markets and suppliers for one another, so that an investment boom in one region such as the Prairie West could create a nationwide boom, while a slump in Ontario manufacturing becomes a nationwide slump.

Central Canada

Most of the native peoples lived by hunting and gathering; only among the Iroquoian groups (Huron, Iroquois, Petun, Neutral) was agriculture established. Furbearing animals were trapped to provide clothing, and silver and copper were used to make ornaments. Trading among native groups, for a wide variety of items, was common, but there does not seem to have been any specialized merchant class. In the 16th century French and British traders began to buy furs, for which they offered iron tools, weapons and alcohol, all of which the Indians valued highly. The result was profound economic and cultural changes among the native peoples, who were to play a critical role in the early fur trade.

Permanent European settlers first came to Canada to exploit the FISHERY and the fur trade. Until the end of the 17th century, because the climate and soil were not encouraging, agricultural progress was slow (see AGRICULTURE HISTORY). Like the French, English-speaking merchants engaged in the fur trade; after the Conquest (1759-60), when many British businessmen began to control a large portion of the fur trade from Montréal, they also quickly extended their interests throughout commerce and finance. The population grew through natural increase and through immigration from Britain. By the 1820s the good agricultural land in the St Lawrence Valley had almost all been taken up. After the North West Company merged with the Hudson's Bay Company in 1821 the transcontinental fur trade was no longer managed from Montréal. But by that time Upper and Lower Canada had developed an immense trade in timber, which went first to Britain and then, after mid-century, to the US and domestic buyers (see TIMBER TRADE HISTORY).

Until the 1780s there was no significant European population in present-day Ontario, although its waterways were used by the fur traders. Settlement began with the arrival of the United Empire LOYALISTS, British and American settlers, and British troops and officials. Forest land was gradually cleared, and export trades in wheat, potash and timber developed. A few roads and canals were built, of which the most important were the Welland Canal and St Lawrence R canals. By 1867 most good land in the province had been claimed, although not all of it was under cultivation.

At the Conquest, present-day Québec contained 3 towns, Montréal, Québec and Trois-Rivières. Ontario contained none. Thereafter, towns appeared along with settlement and with the development of commerce and government. But even in 1871, much of central Canada's industry, including the 2 great industries, milling and lumbering, was dispersed through the countryside or in small villages. After Confederation, however, rapid industrialization and urbanization occurred in both provinces, so that by 1911 half of Ontario's population lived in cities and towns.

From 1870 to 1900 some established industries such as tailoring and shoemaking were becoming factory activities, and provincial governments be-

Square-rigged ships loading timber at Sinclair's Mill, Newcastle, NB, c1900. The timber trade was the basis for the early economies of New Brunswick, the Canadas and BC (*courtesy Provincial Archives of New Brunswick*).

gan to regulate working conditions. MINIMUM WAGE legislation came much later: Ontario adopted it partially in the 1920s. Some unions had begun in the 1830s, and in the 1880s, with the rise and decline of the American-based KNIGHTS OF LABOR, union activity increased. But relative to the nonfarm work force, union membership remained small until the 1940s, when federal and provincial protection was extended to unions.

Central Canada's industrial advance was especially rapid between 1896 and 1914, when the whole nation experienced investment and export booms. After 1900 a few industries such as carriage-making and blacksmithing declined. But new industries appeared: electrical equipment and chemicals in the 1890s, cars and aluminum after 1900, pulp and paper 1890-1914, radio and home appliances in the 1920s and aircraft in the 1940s. Cheap hydroelectric power during this period helped accelerate industrial change, as did both world wars and nuclear power in the 1970s (at least in Ontario). In both provinces labour was drawn from natural population increase and immigration.

There were cyclical downturns in the mid-1870s, the early 1890s, the early 1920s and especially between 1929 and 1933; the GREAT DEPRESSION lasted until the war began. Thereafter, economic expansion continued substantially uninterrupted until another cyclical downturn of the early 1980s (see BUSINESS CYCLES).

Because so many of the newer industries were concentrated in Ontario, during the 1920s Québec's economic advance was less spectacular; although it shared fully in the development of pulp, paper and nonferrous metals, it took no part in the automotive industry, and little part in the electrical appliance industries. Also, because a higher proportion of Québec industries were low-productivity activities which could not pay high wages, Ontario workers earned more on the average than Québec workers. After 1945, and especially after the 1960s, these gaps closed. Both federal and provincial authorities spent lavishly to attract factories into Québec; indeed, the Québec government owned plants in such industries as steel-making and auto assembly. Québec's birth rate became the lowest in Canada, and average REAL WAGES rose. Although the national financial centre had shifted from Montréal to Toronto by the beginning of WWII, Québec's financial sys-

tem became more sophisticated and more francophone in its attitudes. In the 1970s and early 1980s, as anglophone business and professional people left a province in which they no longer felt at home, there was increasing scope for francophone expertise. Much more serious than the uncertainty among investors were the troubles of Québec's established textile and clothing industries, increasingly threatened by cheaper goods from the Third World. The federal authorities provided advice, new kinds of PROTECTIONISM and adjustment finance. Furthermore, thanks to the presence of Northern Telecom and Bombardier, for example, Québec has become an important player in the game of "high-tech industry."

Agriculture in central Canada began as a battle against forest and climate, passed through an export phase, and by 1900 depended chiefly on the local urban markets which it was not able to supply fully. Around 1800 the farmers of the lower St Lawrence produced an exportable grain surplus, but for most of the 19th century Québec residents depended on grain from Ontario. In turn, for most of the century Ontario regularly exported grain not only to Québec, but overseas. However, after 1880, as Ontario's population rose while its wheat acreage declined, the province gradually imported more wheat from western Canada while increasing its output of oats and other fodder crops. Both Ontario and Québec, between 1871 and 1914, specialized increasingly in meat and dairy products. From the 1860s until the 20th century, much cheese, butter and Ontario bacon were sold abroad; thereafter, more of these goods were consumed within central Canada. After WWI, with the decline of the horse and the concomitant fall in oats acreage, the shift to other fodder crops became even more pronounced and some land began to fall out of cultivation. Meanwhile, city growth encroached on farmland.

From Confederation to 1929, spasmodic efforts were made to extend the frontier of agricultural settlement in Ontario and Québec. These efforts were not very successful, but by 1929 there were pockets of farmland around Lac Saint-Jean, the Ontario Clay Belt, Rainy River and Thunder Bay. More important for northern development were mining, and pulp and paper. These activities scattered small communities throughout northern Ontario and Québec between 1886 (when the Sudbury nickel deposits were first exploited) and 1929.

By 1867 the great cities of central Canada were Montréal and Toronto. The former began as a port and commercial centre. By mid-19th century it was a place of industry, and by 1900 it was producing large amounts of clothing and textile products, electrical equipment, railway rolling stock and many light industrial products. It was also an important financial centre. Toronto, after a slow and inauspicious beginning, developed after 1867 on similar lines, much of its early prosperity being based on Great Lakes shipping. By 1900 both cities had energetic banks and insurance companies and active stock exchanges. Both cities had begun to attract immigrants from central Europe and Italy. It was largely natural increase and migration from Britain that built the cities of central Canada between Confederation and 1914, or even 1939. Indeed, before 1900 many Québécois and Ontarians went to the US, where prospects were better: the nation was not managing to retain the natural increase of its own population (*see* FRANCO-AMERICANS). However, between 1900 and 1929, and again after 1939, the economic prospects were so much better that emigration was no longer a problem. Really large-scale immigration from Italy and central Europe occurred only after WWII.

In Québec and Ontario, as elsewhere in Canada, urbanization and industrialization were assisted by the thrift and diligence of the population, whose members were also willing to borrow funds and skills from abroad and, at least until the 1970s, to receive immigrants during times of prosperity. Educational arrangements helped, first by providing for general literacy; next, by arranging for higher liberal and professional education; and then, starting in the 1870s, by offering various sorts of specialized secondary and tertiary technological studies in, for example, engineering and agriculture.

By 1987 both economies had become very urbanized, and the "service" industries and occupations were much more important than manufacturing, which in turn was more important than agriculture, forestry or mining. The earnings from the service industries helped to balance central Canada's accounts with the rest of the country, a process to which the sale of manufactures also contributed. This pattern of regional specialization had established itself between Confederation and 1900; Ontario and Québec industrialization was not created at the expense of other regions. Most of the 2 provinces' markets have always been in central Canada because that is where most Canadians live. Also, since the 19th century there have been export markets for many Québec and Ontario manufactures – cheese, sawn lumber, cars, agricultural implements, pulp and paper, refined nickel and aluminum. Developments elsewhere in Canada, especially in the West, helped accelerate central Canada's industrialization, but they did not cause it. Economic evolution had been similar on the southern side of the Great Lakes, where there is a similar pool of raw materials, capital, labour and skills. Indeed, because on the Canadian side there was more hydroelectric potential, plus nickel, gold, silver, uranium and plenty of pulpwood, in some respects circumstances were more favourable. Since 1878-79 Canada's tariff has protected manufacturing industries, but locational advantages, not the tariff itself, ensured that most of that protected manufacturing would locate in central Canada.

Atlantic Canada

Although there was some early fur trading, serious economic development in the Atlantic provinces really began with the sea fisheries, whose markets were in Europe and later in the West Indies. Much of the 16th-century fishing was conducted from British and European bases. Settlement was slow, especially in Newfoundland. On the mainland some francophone settlers arrived during the 17th century (*see* ACADIA), and

Dories towed astern the schooner *Dorothy M. Smart*, 1911. Economic development in the Atlantic region long depended upon the fishery (*courtesy Maritime Museum of the Atlantic*).

some anglophone migrants from Britain and New England in the 18th, but the European population was small until the arrival of the Loyalists partly because there was little good agricultural land. Early in the 19th century Scots settled on Cape Breton. Prosperity came from the fisheries, forests and maritime carrying trades. Colonial lumber enjoyed preferential treatment in Britain (*see* TIMBER DUTIES), while the carrying trades served the whole Atlantic basin. By mid-19th century lumber preferences ended and, in shipping, iron and steam began to edge out wood and sail. Cape Breton coal found a market in Boston; other favourable developments were hard to find. Although there were efforts at manufacturing, local markets were small and communications among the colonies were bad. The Intercolonial Railway to Canada created some new markets for local industry, but the line did not eliminate the locational disadvantages. When the Dominion tariff was raised in 1879 (*see* NATIONAL POLICY) many Maritime capitalists built factories, only to find that markets were smaller than they had expected and that new managerial skills were needed. Nor could Maritime coal compete in Ontario with Pennsylvania coal. Bankruptcies and takeovers were numerous. However, iron and steel production in Nova Scotia was stimulated by the tariff, by the Dominion's iron and steel bounties and by the post-1900 railway-building boom. By 1900 Halifax had become a local financial centre whose capitalists were raising money not only for local industry, but for utilities in Latin America. But Maritime banks tended to fail, merge or move their executive offices to central Canada (*see* BANK OF NOVA SCOTIA; ROYAL BANK).

During the 19th century Newfoundland acquired a settled population largely by immigration from Britain. The rest of the region attracted few migrants, at least after 1867, and the population grew slowly: much of the natural increase flowed to the US or to other Canadian regions. The 1920s and 1930s were unhappy decades in the Atlantic region. The iron, steel, coal and machinery industries were in chronic difficulty and, like the fishery, they suffered severely in the Great Depression. Nor did new manufacturers make much headway, in spite of continuing federal subsidies for rail transport. The few rays of hope included new pulp and paper plants and new protected markets for apples and lumber in Britain. WWII brought hectic prosperity to those communities which served the naval and air bases, and after 1945 the situation improved. New hydroelectric plants and new governmental initiatives attracted new industry, but these programs had some successes and many failures. More useful to economic growth, perhaps, was the new army base in New Brunswick. By the mid-1980s offshore oil had been discovered in commercial quantities, and there were good

prospects for natural gas; but the old heavy industries and the fisheries were in chronic trouble and were kept alive by government subsidy (under various names) and government ownership.

Western Canada

Economic development in western Canada began with the fur trade. By the end of the 18th century the traders' activities on the prairies had produced a small population of Métis who, like the Indians, depended on the trade. Fur-trade posts were scattered throughout the region, and on Vancouver I, the city of Victoria began as an HBC trading post.

Settled agriculture began in 1812 with Lord Selkirk's RED RIVER COLONY. However, the building of the Canadian Pacific Railway in the 1880s gave Manitoba a wheat economy. Winnipeg became a centre for commerce and railways, and soon acquired a few factories. In the late 1890s, the prospects for development brightened as world prices rose, transport costs fell, methods of dryland farming improved, and more appropriate varieties of wheat became available. Until 1929 the Prairie provinces enjoyed an immense expansion of the wheat economy, onto which was grafted, before 1914, a very much larger rail system, a network of cities and towns, coal mining and ranching. By 1914 the frontier of settlement had been pushed well toward the northwest, attracting migrants from many lands. The result was a regional economy which depended almost entirely upon the world price of a single crop and on local yields, both of which fluctuated greatly. There was little diversification except in Alberta, which began to produce small quantities of oil and gas.

BC's economic evolution before 1929 was very different. There was little agricultural land, and most farm products were locally consumed. There were few European residents except fur traders until the Fraser R GOLD RUSH of the 1850s. After the gold rush, coal mining on Vancouver I was no substitute, and until well after Confederation the population grew very slowly. However, with the construction of the CPR and that of the Canadian Northern Railway and Grand Trunk Pacific Railway between 1900 and 1914, much more rapid development and urbanization occurred. Important activities were lumbering, the fisheries, and copper, silver, coal and base metal mining in the south. Ranching and fruit-growing were also established. Some industries, especially shipbuilding and repairing, were set up, and the great smelter at Trail came into operation in 1920. With regular transpacific sailings to the Far East and Australasia, Vancouver became an important port, not only for the province's own goods but for prairie grain. After the Panama Canal opened in 1914, trade with Britain became faster and much cheaper. Coastal shipping also developed, partly to serve the lumber trade. Thanks to urban growth, there was rapid development of hydroelectricity. There was very large immigration, not only from elsewhere in Canada but from Britain and Asia. Oriental immigration was much feared and rigidly controlled, although a small Oriental community did develop.

From 1914 to the late 1940s, especially during the Great Depression, conditions were often difficult. All 4 provinces felt themselves to be the victims of Canada's tariff policy, which raised the price of the manufactured goods that came from elsewhere but did nothing for the price of the primary products and simple processed goods which they had to sell. Prairie drought, adverse price movements and foreign protective tendencies, as in the 1920-22 recession and the slump of 1929-33, were serious matters. Ottawa provided relief money, protected the provincial governments from bankruptcy, and tried through trade negotiations to improve the conditions for western exports (*see* OTTAWA AGREEMENTS). After the collapse of the co-operative wheat pools in 1929-30, Ottawa also supported the marketing of prairie wheat, although until the middle of WWII the farmers could market their wheat through private channels if they wished. Wartime prosperity helped western farmers pay off their debts. In BC, meanwhile, co-operative marketing increased for such goods as apples and peaches. But new manufacturing plants were slow to appear. By 1939 a Ford assembly plant near Vancouver supplied export markets in India and the Pacific, but when these markets vanished after 1939 the plant vanished too. WWII saw a rapid development of shipbuilding and aircraft construction on the West Coast, but after the war these industries dwindled or vanished.

The years after 1945 saw new resource-based development, rapid urbanization and dramatic increases in standards of living. The most striking new projects were in oil, gas, pipeline-building and potash, which transformed the economies of Alberta and Saskatchewan. BC began to produce oil and gas; BC and Manitoba acquired immense new hydroelectric plants, and aluminum smelting began at Kitimat, BC, in 1951. There were new export markets, as oil and gas moved to Ontario and the US and as BC coal and lumber products moved to Japan. Prairie wheat, which gradually lost its old markets in Britain and Europe, eventually found new markets in the USSR, China and the Third World. Federal policy was helpful: Ottawa began to make EQUALIZATION PAYMENTS to Manitoba and Saskatchewan, and it provided a protected Ontario market for expensive Alberta oil 1960-73, although thereafter it held oil prices below world levels. It also reduced or removed many tariffs. Lumbering and pulp and paper expanded, and most of the time did well because of the N American construction and communication booms. In 1967 the exploitation of Alberta's tar sands (*see* BITUMEN) began. By 1987 Alberta had developed a petrochemical industry and Manitoba was producing buses and light aircraft. Yet the western provinces remained heavily dependent on the export of a few primary products and on the investment activity which the primary industries could generate. The West remained "development-minded" as it had been between 1896 and 1914.

By the 1980s most Canadians had become city dwellers and the majority of workers were in white-collar jobs, generally in the service-producing industries. Disparities in earnings, living standards and ways of life had been much reduced, especially after 1945. Nevertheless the various regional economies were still very different. Manufacturing remained largely a matter for Ontario and Québec, while the 4 western provinces still generated immense surpluses of natural products. In the Atlantic provinces, living standards remained comparatively low and prospects were much less bright. Partly for this reason, interregional subsidies have become deeply entrenched in Canada's way of life.   IAN M. DRUMMOND

Reading: W.T. Easterbrook and Hugh Aitken, *Canadian Economic History* (1956); W.L. Marr and D.G. Paterson, *Canada: An Economic History* (1980); R. Pomfret, *The Economic Development of Canada* (1981).

Economic Nationalism, in Canada, is a movement aimed at achieving greater control by Canadians of their own economy. In recent years it arose in response to the high degree of foreign (especially American) control of the Canadian economy. Two separate strands of economic nationalism can be distinguished. The first, protectionism

in trade – the establishment of a system of tariffs to favour domestic production of goods and to discourage imports – dates at least to the NATIONAL POLICY of 1879. The policy was partly intended to encourage the creation of an industrial base in Canada by protecting so-called "infant industries" against the competition of larger and more established firms abroad. The second strand is concerned with the ownership of Canadian businesses by foreigners and is largely a post-WWII phenomenon, although some foreign direct investment did exist prior to 1940 as a classic 1936 study, *Canadian-American Industry,* revealed.

The rapid increase of FOREIGN OWNERSHIP in the Canadian economy after WWII was linked to the rise of the MULTINATIONAL CORPORATION. Various multinationals realized they could bypass tariff restrictions by building and operating their own branch plants (or subsidiaries) inside Canada. As these foreign-owned corporations proliferated, economic nationalists became concerned with the special problems created by this type of investment, particularly the stunted and distorted pattern of economic development. Such investment also tended to shift control over economic decision making outside Canada to the head offices of these foreign corporations. Economic nationalists began to demand legislation to monitor the activities and to restrain the growth of foreign ownership in the Canadian economy.

Anti-nationalists generally responded to both strands of economic nationalism by emphasizing the benefits of a "free and unhampered" trade with all nations according to the doctrine of economics known as the law of comparative advantage. Economic growth will be maximized when government restraint, eg, tariffs on trade flows, is minimized and all countries specialize in the goods they produce best and trade freely with each other. Although this argument is only relevant to trade protectionism, it was extended to cover foreign direct investment – foreign-owned firms would succeed in establishing themselves in Canada only to the extent that they could produce their goods more cheaply than local firms, thus benefiting Canadian consumers and the Canadian economy; therefore foreign investment ought to be freely permitted for the same reason as FREE TRADE. This argument depends implicitly upon the assumption of a competitive economic environment with free markets where flexible prices prevail for flows of both goods and of capital. It is this very assumption that economic nationalists questioned by indicating the peculiar economic and political features of the extension of multinationals and of the American presence in the Canadian economy.

The concerns of economic nationalists were articulated in a series of 4 government-sponsored reports drawn up over the past several decades. The first, on Canada's Economic Prospects (1955-57), known as the Gordon Commission after its chairman, Walter L. GORDON, was established in response to the growing tide of foreign ownership in the Canadian economy, estimated at that time to be about 40%. The Gordon report was moderate; it noted the growth of foreign direct investment, concluded that perhaps "legitimate Canadian interests" were being compromised in the process, and recommended that Canadians be permitted at least part ownership in foreign-owned subsidiaries operating in Canada.

The governments of that period did not pay much attention to the report. Throughout the early 1960s the anti-nationalists, best represented by Professor Harry JOHNSON, dominated the debate. Johnson argued that nationalism "has been diverting Canada into a narrow and garbage-cluttered cul-de-sac" and that economic nationalism was an emotional reaction founded upon selfish,

middle-class interests. Canada and Canadian workers in particular, he argued, would benefit by the removal of all restrictions to trade and foreign direct investment, for nothing would raise the level of economic activity and boost incomes more rapidly.

However, a new current of economic nationalism emerged in the 1960s, best exemplified by some of the essays published by the University League for Social Reform in *Nationalism in Canada* (1966). The book was followed by 3 more government-sponsored reports in the late 1960s and early 1970s which described various problems created by foreign-owned subsidiaries operating in Canada. For example, Canadian branch plants generally did not conduct research and development and lacked the facilities to do so. They also lacked full-fledged marketing and purchasing departments because these functions would often be managed by the parent firm in the US or Europe. Consequently, Canadian initiatives in developing new technology and in the design and marketing of products were retarded. Because the companies were directed from abroad, Canadian managers and management were not able to develop to their full potential. A dependence on various US capabilities was slowly being built into the structure of Canadian industry, leaving it less able to adapt to change and international competition. There were other problems also, including the lack of Canadian directors on the boards of foreign-owned subsidiaries, and the tendency of branch plants to purchase their production inputs from the parent firm's suppliers abroad, thereby reducing the number of orders for Canadian companies. The ability of the head office to establish prices for both inputs and outputs ("transfer prices") of their subsidiaries made it possible to manipulate balance sheets to reduce taxes payable to the Canadian government.

Extraterritoriality – the tendency of the American government to assert legal jurisdiction over the branch plants of US-based firms operating in other countries – is a major political problem. Under the Foreign Assets Control Regulations (Trading with the Enemy Act), the Sherman Act and s7 of the Clayton Anti-Trust Act, the American government retained for itself the primary jurisdiction in deciding which countries its foreign subsidiaries could or could not trade with, when they might or might not discuss mergers, and various other functions. Canadian sovereignty in this regard has been compromised, for despite various negotiated administrative accommodations the US has successfully retained primary jurisdiction over its subsidiaries abroad.

In response to these various problems, a number of policies were recommended in 3 government studies. The Watkins Task Force, in its 1968 report FOREIGN OWNERSHIP AND THE STRUCTURE OF CANADIAN INDUSTRY, recommended the creation of a special agency to co-ordinate government policies and programs dealing with multinational corporations. One of its tasks would be the gathering of more information on their activities in Canada, enabling the government to better monitor their behaviour. The Wahn Report, published in 1970 (*The Eleventh Report of the Standing Committee on External Affairs and National Defence Respecting Canada-US Relations*), reiterated this recommendation, suggested that Canadians attempt to secure 51% ownership in foreign firms, and recommended, as the Watkins Report had done, stringent laws to countervail American extraterritorial jurisdiction. These laws would effectively make it illegal for corporations operating in Canada to refuse legitimate export orders from any country, regardless of the nature of that country's diplomatic relations with the US. It also proposed that any future takeovers of Canadian businesses by foreign-owned firms should require the consent of a control bureau such as the one outlined by the Watkins Report, and that certain "key sectors" of the economy should be identified "where no further takeovers would be allowed." The 1972 *Foreign Direct Investment in Canada*, known as the Gray Report after its chairman, Herb GRAY, again recommended the creation of a "screening agency," but also specified the particular areas that should be considered·in the decision to permit or forbid a foreign direct investment proposal. For example, a foreign firm contemplating the purchase or erection of a plant in Canada might be questioned about the need for its particular products (would it only duplicate products already available in Canada?); about the nature of the technology to be employed in comparison with technology available in Canada; about employment possibilities; and about its plans for research and development, its product innovation in Canada, and its plans for purchasing materials, components and services in Canada. On the basis of these reports, nationalist sentiment crystallized in Canada in various ways in the 1970s. Several organizations and lobby groups arose, eg, the COMMITTEE FOR AN INDEPENDENT CANADA (CIC), which was formed in 1970. Its members, from a broad array of professions and geographic locations and from all 3 major political parties, wanted to involve concerned citizens in a campaign to influence governments across Canada to adopt the "legislative policies that will significantly diminish the influence presently exerted by outside powers . . . on Canadian life." The CIC produced a number of books on economic nationalism and provided an important forum for nationalist policy proposals.

As a result of recommendations in the Watkins, Wahn and Gray reports, the FOREIGN INVESTMENT REVIEW AGENCY (FIRA) in 1974 began to review all proposals for foreign takeovers of existing businesses or the creation of new foreign-owned businesses in Canada, for the purpose of ensuring maximum benefits to Canadians from these enterprises. FIRA was structured very closely upon the recommendations of the Gray Report, and Herb Gray became its first chairman. However, because Canadian and foreign businesses complained that FIRA's lengthy review procedures effectively impeded new foreign direct investment, its procedures were revised in 1982. The shorter and less complicated "small business" review procedure applied to all proposals involving businesses with less than $5 million in gross assets and less than 200 employees (in contrast with the previous ceiling of $2 million and 100 employees).

The NATIONAL ENERGY PROGRAM (NEP), established by the Liberal government in 1980, also emerged from the movement for economic nationalism. It was created to guarantee the security of Canada's energy supply (in particular, to end Canadian dependence on world oil and gas supplies) and to provide Canadians with the opportunity to increase their ownership of the energy industry. The original goal was 50% ownership of Canadian oil and gas production by 1990. With the revenues from a new tax imposed upon all oil and gas producers in Canada the government funded the Petroleum Incentives Program, under which monies were redistributed to Canadian companies investing in the energy industry. Canadian control of the energy sector increased from 22.3% to 33.1% in the first 2 years.

The NEP was heavily censured by critics of the Liberal government, who claimed that the purchase of foreign assets under the NEP was made at inflated prices and extremely high interest rates. They also asserted that the NEP financially crippled Canadian energy companies by overextending their investment capabilities and that it was itself nothing more than a gigantic "revenue grab" on the part of the federal government. Advocates of the program conceded that bad luck and high interest rates dogged the NEP, but insisted the program itself was necessary in order to allow Canadians to share in the tens of billions of dollars of profits that would otherwise have flowed almost exclusively into foreign hands. This program was dismantled by the Conservative government of Brian Mulroney, which launched a new initiative for FREE TRADE with the United States.

Economic nationalism, it is important to realize, can best be understood in the broader context of Canadian dependence on the US. In entertainment, publishing, magazines, education, defence, the media, etc, American influences have threatened to become overwhelming, adding impetus to the arguments of economic nationalists who understood themselves to be fighting for the survival of a Canadian way of life. What was seen by anti-nationalists as self-interested protectionism at the expense of the economic welfare of the Canadian public, could better be regarded as a countermovement for the protection of Canadian society and sovereignty. ABRAHAM ROTSTEIN

Reading: H.G.J. Aitken, *American Capital and Canadian Resources* (1961); *Foreign Direct Investment in Canada* (1972); *Foreign Ownership and the Structure of Canadian Industry* (1968); H.G. Johnson, *The Canadian Quandary* (1963, repr 1970); A. Rotstein and G. Lax, eds, *Getting It Back: A Program for Canadian Independence* (1974) and *Independence: The Canadian Challenge* (1972).

Economic Regulation, a form of government intervention designed to influence the behaviour of firms and individuals in the private sector. Other forms include public expenditures, taxes, government ownership, loans and loan guarantees, tax expenditures, equity interests in private companies and moral suasion. Defined as the "imposition of rules by a government, backed by the use of penalties, that are intended specifically to modify the economic behavior of individuals and firms in the private sector," regulation in general is aimed at narrowing choices in certain areas, including prices (airline fares, minimum wages, certain agricultural products, telephone rates), supply (broadcasting licences, occupational licensing, agricultural production quotas, pipeline certificates "of public convenience and necessity"), rate of return (public utilities, pipelines), disclosure of information (securities prospectuses, content labelling), methods of production (effluent standards, worker health and safety standards), standards for products or services (safety of children's toys, quality of food products, Canadian-content requirements in broadcasting) and conditions of service (requirements to act as a common carrier or not to discriminate in hiring or selling goods and services).

Governments use economic regulation to improve the efficiency with which society's resources are allocated, to alter the distribution of income and to achieve broad social or cultural goals. Improving economic efficiency may involve the regulation of monopolies, which by restricting output and raising prices may restrict the production of the socially optimal amount of goods or services. Regulation may be used in situations in which costs are not paid by those responsible, eg, the social costs of extensive pollution caused by private firms. Because of interdependencies in the utilization of collectively owned resources, government management is necessary to prevent the overexploitation of such renewable resources as fish, whales and forests; and to prevent overcrowding of the broadcasting spectrum.

Government also imposes regulations to alter the distribution of income partly to prevent monopoly profits and certain kinds of price discrimination, which were the justification offered for the regulation of both the railways in the 19th century and the UTILITIES early in the 20th century. Regulation was an attempt to prevent unjust discrimination and to ensure that consumers were charged "fair and reasonable" rates, terms still used in regulatory statutes. Regulation may also be used to reduce the speed of economic change and the redistribution of income through administrative processes, a justification based on the notion that the public is generally averse to risk and that the marketplace, with its sometimes abrupt changes, unfairly distributes income. Finally, regulation may be used to confer benefits on certain customers at the expense of others.

Regulation has been used extensively in Canada in the pursuit of social and cultural goals, including nation building through the provision of transportation infrastructure (*see* TRANSPORTATION POLICY) and the promotion of national unity and cultural identification (broadcasting and Canadian-content regulations; *see* CANADIAN RADIO-TELEVISION AND TELECOMMUNICATIONS COMMISSION). There have also been attempts to increase domestic ownership of business enterprises by restricting foreign ownership in certain sectors, eg, broadcasting and banking (*see* ECONOMIC NATIONALISM). Direct and social regulation are conventionally distinguished from each other. Through the former, the price structure (rates, tariffs, fees, etc), the conditions of entry and exit or the level of output are altered. A specific regime of direct regulation is confined to a single industry, although quite a number of industries are subject to direct regulation, eg, airlines, railways, telecommunications, certain agricultural products, pipelines, taxicabs (in most cities) and broadcasting. Social regulation, on the other hand, is usually concerned with methods of production, attributes of a product or service, or disclosure of information. It typically affects a wide range of industries although its impact on different industries will vary enormously. It includes government rule making on environmental protection, health and safety, fairness (human rights, protection against fraud, deception or inaccuracy), culture (content, language), land use and building codes. Both the federal and provincial governments exercise significant regulatory responsibilities with respect to environmental protection, natural resources, the marketing of farm products, occupational health and safety, human rights, consumer protection, human health protection, employment standards and financial institutions. As a result, the complexity of economic regulation in Canada is increased. It should be emphasized that the cost of direct and social regulation in expenditures by federal, provincial or local governments is only a fraction of the cost of such regulations to the economy as a whole. The bulk of the costs are incurred by individuals and firms (and their customers) in complying with regulations.

The amount of government regulation has been measured in a variety of ways. For example, researchers have estimated that in Canada 29% of Gross Domestic Product at factor costs was subject to direct regulation in 1978. The comparable figure for the US was 26%, although these measures do not reflect the stringency of the controls, which varies enormously. Another estimate for 1980 described 34% of the private-sector economy as "government supervised or regulated." However, both estimates were done before the liberalization of regulation or deregulation occurred in transportation (airlines, rail freight, trucking), financial services and energy (oil and natural gas prices and exports) in the period 1985-88.

In the 1970s, federal regulation increased in both Canada and the US. Of the 140 federal economic regulatory statutes enacted in Canada at the end of 1978, 25 were enacted between 1970 and 1978. An additional 11 had been passed earlier but were re-enacted in the 1970s. More new federal regulatory statutes were passed in that period than were passed between 1940 and 1969. The new statutes were enacted primarily in the areas of environmental protection, health and safety, and consumer protection. However, after 1978 the growth of new regulatory provisions fell sharply as pressures for regulatory reform grew.

Two different kinds of efforts to reform regulation in Canada have occurred in the last decade. The first consists of studies, conducted largely by the federal government or its agencies, focusing on the REGULATORY PROCESS, eg, those conducted for the LAW REFORM COMMISSION, the Institute for Research on Public Policy, the ECONOMIC COUNCIL OF CANADA and the Canadian Consumer Council. Official inquiries include those of the Regulation Reference of the Economic Council of Canada; the Parliamentary Task Force on Regulatory Reform (Peterson Committee); and the Royal Commission on Financial Management and Accountability (the Lambert Commission). Generally, all the studies have recommended the requirement of an *ex ante* review of proposed regulations using cost-benefit analysis, earlier and more extensive consultation, the establishment of a regulatory agenda, the institutionalization of periodic *ex post* review of existing regulatory programs, the replacement of appeals to Cabinet by government policy directives, clearer definition of regulatory mandates in statutes and regulation, closer scrutiny of proposed new regulations and evaluation of existing ones by the legislature, and the improvement of the access and funding of public-interest groups. In the 1980s, the federal government adopted measures to more carefully scrutinize new regulatory initiatives, including the use of a regulatory calendar. The second kind of effort, which has been largely independent of the first, consists of a series of decisions by regulatory agencies or changes in government policy which have liberalized direct regulation in a number of industries.

The loosening of regulatory constraints and the increase of competition in the airline industry was accomplished first by a series of steps between 1977 and 1979 to remove the capacity restrictions on CP Air, allowing them to compete more effectively with Air Canada; second, under the 1978 Air Canada Act, the crown corporation became subject to the same statutory provisions and regulations as other carriers (until 1959 Air Canada had a monopoly on all transcontinental traffic); third, beginning in 1973, but particularly in the late 1970s, regulations governing both international and domestic charter flights were seriously altered, resulting in rapid growth of charter services; fourth, beginning in 1978 the Canadian Transport Commission permitted Canadian airlines to introduce a variety of discount fares. Fifth, in May 1984 the CTC gave airlines more freedom in setting fares, and reduced the restrictions on entry by new carriers and existing carriers into new routes. Finally, in 1988 new legislation went into effect that virtually eliminated economic regulation of air travel in southern Canada and modified the regulations applied to travel to and from and within the North. Following hearings requested by the minister of transport, the CTC decided in mid-1984 to give airlines more freedom in setting fares, and to reduce the restrictions on entry by new carriers and existing carriers into new routes.

Regulatory and policy decisions that have resulted in a loosening of regulatory restrictions and increased competition in the telecommunications industry stemmed, in part, from technological change. For example, technology has undermined the natural-monopoly rationale for government regulation of the telephone industry. In the 1970s the CRTC began to distinguish between the monopoly provision of transmission services from the supply of terminal equipment, eg, the basic black telephone, data terminals, etc. Following the terminal attachment decisions concerning Bell Canada and BC Tel in the early 1980s, subscribers were able to own their own equipment. As a result, there has been high degree of competition for the supply and maintenance of such equipment. Increased competition has also been greatly facilitated by the CRTC's decision in May 1979 regarding system interconnection. Customers of CNCP Telecommunications can now enjoy dial access to CNCP's data networks and private-line services. While CNCP cannot offer direct competition with unit-toll, voice long-distance or WATS services, it does offer strong competition for data transmission, private lines and telex services. The greatest barrier to increased competition for long-distance voice transmission is the high fraction of fixed common costs recovered from long-distance rates relative to local rates. In Aug 1985, the CRTC decided that competition should not be permitted in unit-toll, voice long-distance service, although such competition exists in the US.

While Canada has not experienced as much outright deregulation as has occurred in the US, in recent years a number of significant changes have occurred: grain freight rates were deregulated in Nov 1983, but some regulation was reintroduced in 1985; oil prices were deregulated and controls over short-term export contracts were removed 1 June 1985; airlines in southern Canada were deregulated in 1988. In addition, there have been some notable liberalizations of a number of types of direct regulation, eg, the Foreign Investment Review Act was replaced by the Investment Canada Act in June 1985; Canadian content requirements for pay-TV were reduced in 1986. At the same time, there are some situations where the scope of regulation has been extended, eg, more stringent Canadian content regulations in broadcasting were implemented in 1983.

W.T. STANBURY

Reading: Economic Council of Canada, *Reforming Regulation* (1981); W.T. Stanbury "Reforming Direct Regulation in Canada" in K.J. Button & N. Swann, eds, *The Age of Regulatory Reform* (1988).

Economic Union and Development Prospects for Canada, Royal Commission on the (Macdonald Commission), was appointed in 1982 to examine the future economic prospects of the country and the effectiveness of its political institutions. The commission, the largest in Canadian history, was chaired by Donald S. MACDONALD, a former minister of finance, and included 12 other commissioners who represented diverse elements of Canadian society. In addition to the normal representation of regional and linguistic interests, the commission included members from business, labour, the co-operative movement, the legal and academic communities, the public service and all 3 national political parties. In effect, many of the basic economic and ideological conflicts of the country were built into the commission from the outset, and the process of writing a report inevitably became an effort at consensus building.

The appointment of the commission by PM Trudeau came as a surprise, even to senior members of his government. The immediate catalyst was the recession of 1981-82, but the creation of the commission also reflected pervasive concern both about the performance of the ECONOMY, which had been marked by inflation, unemployment, low-productivity growth and difficult labour relations, and about the nation's political process, which seemed increasingly incapable of generating effective policy responses to economic and social problems.

Despite the commission's immense mandate, it was given only 3 years to complete its task. Styling themselves "A Commission of Canada's Future," the commissioners held 2 rounds of public hearings across the country, and launched a major research program. The 3-volume report was released in Sept 1985, and was supported by 72 research volumes. The commission's recommendations reflected 3 underlying themes. First, the report emphasized that Canada should maintain an adaptive economy, capable of adjusting rapidly to international economic changes and new technologies. Greater reliance on market mechanisms, as opposed to government intervention, and a FREE TRADE agreement with the US were the hallmarks of this theme. Second, while the commission agreed that the overall scope of the WELFARE STATE should be maintained, the report recommended reforms to important income security programs to ensure greater economic efficiency and social equity. Third, the commission reaffirmed the traditional model of parliamentary government, but recommended the adoption of an elected Senate to sensitize the federal government more fully to the aspirations of Canada's diverse regions. In the end, complete consensus eluded the commission. Several commissioners dissented from particular recommendations, with the politically most important dissent being that of the representative of organized labour. Similarly, while the report received substantial support after its publication from the business community, governments and the media, its emphasis on market mechanisms was often criticized by the labour movement, nationalist groups and social activists.

The most immediate impact of the commission was to give greater legitimacy and momentum to the argument for free trade with the US, and the new prime minister, Brian Mulroney, initiated trade negotiations with the American administration shortly after receiving the report. There was never any co-ordinated government response to the other recommendations, although the commission's thinking was undoubtedly absorbed in the ongoing debate in many policy sectors.

KEITH G. BANTING

Economics involves the study of 3 interrelated issues: the allocation of RESOURCES used for the satisfaction of human wants; the INCOME DISTRIBUTION among individuals and groups; and the determination of the level of national output and employment. Economists investigate these issues either from the perspective of microeconomics, an analysis of the behaviour of the individual units in the national economy, including business firms, workers and consumers; or from the perspective of macroeconomics, the study of the larger aggregates in the economy, such as total investment and consumption, the average levels of INTEREST rates and price indexes, and total employment and UNEMPLOYMENT.

Economic research consists primarily of the formulation of theories that seek to explain observable events (such as variations in Canadian exports of pulp and paper or Canadian purchases of computers), and the testing of theories by comparing their implications or predictions with actual events. Theories and tests may be formal and mathematical, or informal and based on nonmathematical discourse. The formulation and testing of both kinds of theories in Canada has been greatly aided by the growth of a reliable body of national statistical data on economic phenomena which followed the founding of the Dominion Bureau of Statistics in 1918.

The trend of economic research over the past 50 years has been toward reliance on increasingly sophisticated mathematical models and formal statistical tests, to the despair of some critics in the profession who argue that the discipline tends to ignore or distort human behaviour and institutional complexity, which are not easily amenable to such analysis. Mathematical models often focus on the concept of equilibrium, a situation in which producers and consumers of a good are assumed to be maximizing their incomes and utility subject to their initial wealth and to market prices, and have in the course of their trading found a consistent or equilibrium price that maintains the outputs and purchases of all parties. The models allow comparisons of equilibrium positions after a change in a particular parameter; for example, with a formal mathematical model of production in the plastics industry, the impact of a substantial increase in the price of oil on equilibrium output, employment and oil consumption in the industry can be determined, on the assumption that the industry seeks to minimize its costs of production.

Such "state" equilibrium analysis has often been criticized for its lack of attention to the dynamic elements of adjustment to changes such as resource discovery, population change, technical innovation, managerial initiative and investment undertaken when future market conditions are uncertain. Critics also charge that such an analysis does not deal adequately with either sustained long-term national growth or the so-called BUSINESS CYCLE of successive peaks and troughs in macroeconomic variables. Among the critics are the post-Keynesian economists (see KEYNESIAN ECONOMICS), who stress the dynamic analysis and emphasis on uncertainty in the work of John Maynard Keynes, a British economist who founded modern macroeconomics with his book, *The General Theory of Employment, Interest and Money* (1936). Other critics of formal mathematical equilibrium models stress the role of politics and institutions in economic affairs, often focusing on the inequality and dependency among persons, groups and nations which they see as characteristic of advanced industrial societies. There are many such schools of thought, including MARXISM, institutionalism, POLITICAL ECONOMY and radical economics (see ECONOMICS, RADICAL). For years many economics programs at Canadian universities were formally associated with POLITICAL SCIENCE in departments of political economy or economics and politics. To the dismay of many institutionalist economists, most of such joint departments have by now been formally split.

Econometrics, the branch of economics that deals with statistical tests of economic theories, has become an essential part of economic analysis over the past 2 decades, through its use in evaluating alternative policy decisions and theoretical models. Econometrics has been subject to criticism in recent years, primarily for the unfortunate practice of presenting statistical results from nonexperimental data as definitive, when in fact they are at best suggestive. There is concern about the advancement of economics as a scientific discipline, because of the fact that statistical tests are often inadequate for distinguishing among competing theories.

Canadian economics and economists are in constant interaction with economics and economists in the UK, Europe, the US and elsewhere, and it is thus no more possible to define "Canadian" economics today than it would be to define Canadian chemistry. Nonetheless the practice of economics in Canada has been strongly influenced by the distinctive demography and geography of the country – its large land base and relatively small population, and its proximity to a country with a national economy 10 times larger than its own. Professional economists generally specialize in one or more fields of the discipline, and Canadian economists have been particularly drawn to fields such as the economics of INTERNATIONAL TRADE and investment, resource economics and transportation economics. However, there is important work being done in Canada in all major fields of economics, including ECONOMIC HISTORY, economic growth of underdeveloped economies, mathematical economics, industrial organization, labour economics, money and BANKING, public finance, urban and REGIONAL ECONOMICS and econometrics.

Until the 1920s most writing on economics in Canada was done by government officials, businessmen, and citizens in other occupations concerned with certain issues of public policy, eg, the best methods of settlement on new lands, the relative advantages of free trade and tariff protection, and government control of currency and banking. Of the many pioneers of economics in Canada, 3 names stand out: Adam SHORTT and W.A. MACKINTOSH, both of Queen's University, and Harold INNIS of U of T. Shortt, appointed lecturer in political economy at Queen's, edited several volumes of documents on currency, finance and constitutional issues in Canada, and organized the remarkable 23-volume study, *Canada and Its Provinces* (1913-17), containing a wealth of material on Canadian economic development and public policy. W.A. Mackintosh edited volumes on western settlement and historical statistics but is best known as the author of *The Economic Background of Dominion-Provincial Relations* (1939), a classic economic history of post-Confederation Canada written as a background study for the Rowell-Sirois Royal Commission. In 1930 Innis published *The Fur Trade in Canada: An Introduction to Canadian Economic History*, a masterly survey of the importance of the trade in beaver furs in the 17th and 18th centuries and its decline in the face of the expanding settlement. His subsequent volume *The Cod Fisheries* (1940) and *Empire and Communications* (1950) and his many essays established him as Canada's most influential economic historian. Innis emphasized the role of staple exports – fur, fish, timber and wheat – in Canada's economic, political and social development, establishing what came to be known as the STAPLE THESIS.

International trade and investment has long been an important area of research for Canadian economists. This area was surveyed in 1924 by Jacob Viner, a Montréal-born economist who taught at University of Chicago and Princeton University, in his classic volume, *Canada's Balance of International Indebtedness, 1900-1913*. Canada's foremost trade economist was Harry G. JOHNSON, author of *The Canadian Quandary* (1977), who also wrote scores of articles on the pure theory of international trade, the BALANCE OF PAYMENTS and Canadian economic policy with regard to international trade and investment. Johnson, who published over 500 scientific papers and 19 books from 1947 to 1977, also made important contributions to macroeconomics, particularly in the areas of domestic and international monetary economics. Johnson's outspoken commitment to free trade and the free movement of international investment was not without its critics among Canadian nationalists, including Abraham Rotstein and Mel Watkins of U of T, who argued that Canadian economic dependence on the US necessarily implied political and cultural dependence and led ultimately to a lowering of the Canadian standard of living.

Economic research in French Canada in the 20th century has been centered at École des hautes études commerciales (HEC), founded in Montréal in 1970; Université de Montréal, which began its École des sciences sociales in 1921; and Université Laval, whose Faculté des sciences sociales was founded in 1938. HEC began publication of an economics journal, *L'Actualité économique*, in 1925, 10 years before the inauguration of the *Canadian Journal of Economics and Political Science* in 1935, and 4 decades before that of the *Canadian Journal of Economics* in 1968. Leading French Canadian economists from 1900 to 1945 included Robert Errol Bouchette, a civil servant, and Édouard Montpetit of HEC, both of whom wrote on the importance to French Canadian development of a knowledge of economics and participation in business affairs; Henry Laureys of HEC, who wrote on Canadian exports; and E. Minville, who wrote on social aspects of economic development in Québec. Important research after 1945 included that of Maurice LAMONTAGNE and Albert Faucher, whose 1953 paper on the "History of Industrial Development" in Québec explained the province's lag in industrialization in terms of geographical and technological factors, rather than cultural differences, an analysis developed at length in Faucher's *Québec en Amérique au XIXᵉ siècle* (1973); that of André Raynauld, who wrote a classic study of *Croissance et structure économiques de la province du Québec* (1961); and that of Roger Dehem, who published widely in the field of economic theory.

There has been a virtual explosion of economic research in Canada over the last 2 decades, fueled by a rapid expansion of graduate programs and a seemingly insatiable demand in the public and private sectors.

A taste of the wide variety of topics treated by Canadian economists is reflected in the annual Harold A. Innis Memorial Lecture, an invited public address by a distinguished economist to the Canadian Economics Association, which meets each spring. The lecture is published in the Nov issue of the *Canadian Journal of Economics* and generally contains an excellent bibliography of Canadian and foreign research on the topic in question. Some of the issues dealt with include the growth of government legislation designed to increase economic security for individuals and groups; the rise of marginalist economics in the 1870s in Europe, and its relation to the work of earlier British economists such as David Ricardo and John Stuart Mill; the role of property rights to land in the use and management of such resources as ground and inland water supplies, fisheries, forests, minerals and oil pools; and the issue of tax incidence, the study of who actually pays a given tax.

Unemployment and Inflation Perhaps the major reason for the growth of economics as a field of study over the past 2 decades has been its increasing importance in public-policy formation in areas such as TAXATION, income security, resource development, and federal-provincial financial relations. The issues of unemployment and inflation illustrate the interaction between economics and public policy.

The Canadian economy in the 1970s·was plagued by STAGFLATION, ie, sharp increases in unemployment and inflation, and a sustained slowdown in the rate of growth of real output and productivity. Both problems led to a remarkable volume of theoretical and applied work in Canada. The most disconcerting aspect of the increases in unemployment and inflation was their temporal coincidence. Economists had been accustomed to thinking of unemployment and inflation as alternative evils to be avoided. It was not easy to explain the concurrent increase in both problems during the 1970s or to suggest how government policy should respond to the new economic development.

The dominant view of inflation and unemployment until the mid-1970s was summarized in the "Phillips Curve," which showed a negative relation between inflation and unemployment, with more of one implying less of the other. Periods of high unemployment in Canada, such as the 1930s, and the recession years of 1958 to 1962, tended to have low inflation, while inflation tended to accelerate in boom years with low unemployment, as in the period 1947 to 1951 and in the late 1960s. Much of the statistical work by Canadian economists was devoted to estimating the coefficients of the Phillips Curve, with a view to understanding how much inflation was necessary to lower the unemployment rate by one percent. The Phillips Curve literature in Canada is reviewed in S.F. Kaliski, *The Trade-off Between Inflation and Unemployment: Some Explorations of the Recent Evidence for Canada* (1972); among the best-known estimates in the 1960s were those of R.G. Bodkin et al in *Price Stability and High Employment: The Options for Canadian Economic Policy* (1966).

In the 1970s the simple trade-off between unemployment and inflation implied in the Phillips Curve broke down. The generally difficult conditions in Western economies since 1973 have had important effects on economic policy, by encouraging governments to experiment with innovative policies designed to return economies to growth and unemployment rates closer to those which prevailed in the 1950s and 1960s. In Canada, the rate of growth of real gross national product fell from 5.5%, 1956-73, to 2.2%, 1973-86. The international oil price increases of 1972-73 and 1979-80 contributed greatly to the growth slowdown, as did the high nominal and real interest rates in Canada after 1977. The annual unemployment rate has been above 7% since 1976, averaging 11.3% from 1982 to 1985, and remaining as high as 9% in 1987. Business capital spending fell by some 20% from 1981 to 1983, and was still 10% below the 1981 level 6 years later in 1987. Economists differed greatly in their interpretation of these new trends. The Keynesians tended to focus on particular institutional and demographic events to explain the inflation of the 1970s, with special emphasis on the sharp increases in oil and other commodity prices in 1973-74 and 1979-80. They stressed the dangers of fighting such inflation with restrictive MONETARY POLICY and FISCAL POLICY, which would result in unacceptable increases in the unemployment rate. Unemployment had risen in part because of the large increases in the LABOUR FORCE as the BABY BOOM generation entered the LABOUR MARKET, and as the participation of WOMEN IN THE LABOUR FORCE increased in an unprecedented manner. Some Keynesians therefore argued for a reimposition in the 1980s of the federal government's WAGE AND PRICE CONTROLS of 1975 to 1978, which they credited with slowing the inflation caused by the oil price shock of 1973-74. The Keynesian case is set out in Clarence Barber and J. McCallum, *Unemployment and Inflation: The Canadian Experience* (1980).

Monetarist economists had a very different view of inflation and unemployment, as explained in a volume by Thomas J. Courchene, *Money, Inflation, and the Bank of Canada* (1976). The monetarists argued that inflation was caused by excessive expansion of the Canadian MONEY supply by the BANK OF CANADA, and that the bank should be charged with responsibility for fighting inflation by reducing the rate of growth of the money supply. In 1975 the governor of the Bank of Canada, Gerald BOUEY, announced the adoption of monetarist principles in future bank policy, which would be directed at a gradual reduction in the growth of the money supply until inflation was eliminated. This was easier said than done: the annual rate of growth of the money supply (defined here as currency and demand chequing deposits) was reduced from 13.8% in 1975 to 8.0% in 1976, but then increased to 10% in 1978. From Nov 1981 to Nov 1982, the money supply actually fell by 6.2% as the economy dived into the worst recession since the 1930s. By Oct 1982 the money supply was no higher than its level of 2 years earlier, but then it rebounded, growing by 13.3% to Sept 1983, when Bouey announced that the monetarist experiment was over.

Tax Policy and Income Security There is one area in which the monetarist and Keynesian schools have found much common ground, and that is on the importance of appropriate tax policies for optimal economic performance. Supply side economics, popularized in such books as George Gilder's *Wealth and Poverty* (1981), has laid special stress on the notion that high taxes reduce private incentives, and that tax cuts will stimulate effort and output. In an extreme case, illustrated in the Laffer curve by the American economist Arthur Laffer, output and taxable income may be so stimulated by a tax cut that tax revenues actually *rise*. In a similar manner, government policies designed to produce income security – such as unemployment insurance and welfare payments – may, if set too generously, produce an unwanted decline in the incentive to work. A common problem is the reduction of welfare payments by the amount of any earned income – such a 100% tax on productive effort is a major disincentive to even part-time work in welfare families (*see* WELFARE STATE).

In Canada during the 1980s, both the federal government and the provinces have been interested in using tax reform to produce better incentives for productive employment. A 1976 study, *People and Jobs*, by the Economic Council of Canada argued for better co-ordination between tax and transfer policies and our goal of high employment. In 1984 the Québec government issued a White Paper on the Personal Tax and Transfer System, with the goal of increasing work incentives while protecting those unable to work. While simulations tabled with the White Paper showed tax cuts producing impressive increases in employment, investment and output, the proposals were never put into law. In June 1987, federal Finance Minister Michael Wilson introduced a White Paper on Tax Reform, designed to produce greater equity and simplicity in the tax system by removing many of the exemptions and deductions previously allowed on personal and corporate incomes, while at the same time reducing the tax rates in order to stimulate economic activity; overall tax collections were to remain unchanged (the proposed reforms were thus "revenue neutral"). The political problem faced by such reforms in that while in the abstract removing exemptions seems equitable, those industries and companies which stand to suffer real capital losses if the reforms are introduced will cry foul, and loudly. Immediately after the release of the White Paper, it was clear that the mining and petroleum industries would launch a sustained attack against it. By the fall of 1987, the future of Wilson's proposals seemed uncertain. Similarly, innovative tax policies proposed by Alan MacEachen in his budget speech of Nov 1981, created such opposition that the reforms were quickly withdrawn and MacEachen was transferred out of the finance portfolio.

Free Trade and Industrial Policy The issues of FREE TRADE and industrial policy are good examples of the regional and political problems of formulating national economic policy. The period of slow growth and high unemployment has in general seemed to strengthen the case in Canada for freer trade with the US, but the hard economic times also increases the fears of those concerned about job and income loss during the transition to freer trade. Proponents of free trade, including the Macdonald Commission, which issued its report in 1985, see it as a necessary first step to returning the economy to higher growth rates of output, productivity and real incomes (*see* ECONOMIC UNION AND DEVELOPMENT PROSPECTS FOR CANADA). Critics of free trade argue that with an unemployment rate already above 8% for the last decade, Canada can ill afford the additional unemployment likely to follow free trade with the US.

During 1986 and 1987, the provinces proclaimed their positions with regard to free trade. Both Alberta and BC were strong proponents, in the belief that more secure access to the US market for their energy and forestry products would help them to reverse the economic slowdown of the early 1980s. Concerned about the competitiveness of its manufacturing base, Ontario expressed doubts about the benefits of general free trade with the US, and called instead for a sector by sector approach to tariff reductions. PEI and Manitoba declared opposition to a free trade agreement. The new premier of NB expressed preliminary doubts before giving his support. All provinces were worried by the apparent US refusal to exempt Canada, after a free trade agreement, from US legislation on "unfair" trade practices. Nevertheless, the Mulroney government signed a comprehensive agreement, in Oct 1987, which still required ratification in both countries.

Future Trends The economic context of the 1990s for advanced industrial countries such as Canada will almost certainly include continued growth in the degree of international competition and the importance of international technological exchanges. As a relatively small country in economic terms, Canada needs to design economic policies which allow it to reap the greatest benefits from international competition and technology advances, while maintaining those social, political, cultural and regional institutions deemed vital to the identity of the country. The opportunities and dangers offered by the international economy will make future policymaking in Canada especially challenging. PAUL DAVENPORT

Economics, Radical Originally the word "radical" meant relentlessly seeking the root of a problem and not shrinking from the action that follows as a logical consequence of its findings. More popularly, it denotes a sharp departure from conventional, orthodox interpretations of reality. The term "radical economics" is used to label the work and ideas of those (usually political economists) who take a so-called left-wing perspective on the discipline of ECONOMICS. There are orthodox and radical streams of economic thought. The specific contents of orthodoxy and radicalism shift from one generation to another as new problems arise in the economy. There are also variants of orthodoxy and radicalism. The presence of so many contending schools of thought produces a persistent tension within economics that mirrors, within the sphere of ideas, persistent conflicts between economic classes and groups in the real world.

During periods of economic stability (eg, the 1950s and early 1960s), a wide consensus develops around the prevailing orthodoxy, and radical economics is relegated to the fringe; but when existing economic arrangements fail to generate the kind of economic growth that ensures widespread prosperity and relative harmony among SOCIAL CLASSES, and when prevailing economic theories and conventional government economic policy fail to explain or to solve the persistence of social and economic problems, consensus among economists breaks down. In these circumstances some economists will search for an alternative economic analysis. Such a process of disillusion and reconstruction occurred in Canada in the mid-1970s with the beginning of the most severe economic crisis since the GREAT DEPRESSION. Economic thought shifted abruptly to both the right (eg, in the form of monetarism) and to the left (eg, in the form of MARXISM).

Modern radicalism originated with Karl Marx, author of *Capital,* but a wide variety of economic theories and policies, viewed as radical in their time, have also been developed, and some have been absorbed into orthodox economic thought and adopted by governments.

Orthodox Economics holds that the substance, manner and distribution of production are determined by individual preferences, technology and personal endowments, ie, consumers determine what is produced, technology prescribes how goods are made, transported and exchanged, and endowments of talent, skills and material wealth determine to whom goods are distributed. The economy cannot be changed unless these foundations are changed, but none of these foundations can be changed without violating what orthodox economists regard as "human nature" and "natural liberty." Because orthodox economists argue that disturbing INCOME DISTRIBUTION would destroy incentives (based on the assumption that all human effort is closely related to material reward), that technology is irremediably determined by science or history, and that ignoring consumer preferences violates freedom, they reject any role for the STATE that disturbs this "natural" economic order.

In 1848 John Stuart Mill, an orthodox but liberal and reform-minded critic, wrote in *Principles of Political Economy* that, while "laws of production" were "natural" and universal, those of distribution were "partly of human institution" and subject to alteration by legislation. Income redistribution via TAXATION was not perceived as a violation of any natural law, and a progressive tax structure was gradually accepted by economic orthodoxy. Canada introduced such a system in 1917. In the wake of the Great Depression, John Maynard Keynes, in *General Theory of Employment, Interest and Money* (1936), demonstrated that left to itself the mature capitalist economy tends to break down and stagnate, a process that was not, contrary to orthodox thought, self-correcting. Keynes advocated state regulation of the overall level of economic activity by means of what he called "socialization of investment," but he was satisfied to leave the composition of that output to the free market. By the end of WWII a modified version of his thought was being adopted and many governments accepted responsibility for maintaining high levels of output and employment. In Canada KEYNESIAN ECONOMICS was accepted in the highest levels of the civil service, and in the 1945 White Paper on EMPLOYMENT AND INCOME, the federal government pledged to maintain economic stability. In practice, this involved varying the money supply and the size of government deficits and surpluses to moderate the business cycle, as well as introducing UNEMPLOYMENT INSURANCE and WELFARE STATE measures to stabilize incomes. In 1958 traditional theories were further challenged in *The Affluent Society* by John Kenneth GALBRAITH, who wrote that consumer tastes are shaped by advertising, packaging and frequent style changes, and that the corporate sector rather than the sovereign consumer is to be held responsible for production priorities, including frivolous, wasteful and ecologically unsound consumption patterns. In particular, the massive effort devoted to advertising inevitably produces a bias in favour of private consumption as opposed to collective, community services. The result is private affluence on the one hand and public squalor on the other; as a corrective, Galbraith advocated greater state expenditures on social services and public infrastructures.

Generally, liberal critics of traditional economics have demonstrated that the free-market system can only function ideally if unrealistic circumstances exist, ie, perfect competition between large numbers of powerless buyers and sellers in the market for goods and services and for labour and capital; perfect mobility of human and physical resources; and perfect information on all alternatives available to buyers and sellers. The violation of even one condition may distort the system and justify extensive state intervention, including regulation and subsidization. These critiques have formed the basis for modified versions of traditional economics which in turn have provided the theoretical basis for the mixed ECONOMY.

From 1945 to 1970 a broad consensus developed among economists around the "neo-classical" synthesis, which in Canada was founded materially on the export of resources to the US. Resource extraction was largely financed by US-based MULTINATIONAL CORPORATIONS. The creation of US-owned branch plants and the resulting economic structure in manufacturing and economic growth was large enough to generate high profits and rising wages and to finance the welfare state and other state expenditures.

The consensus (1945-70) over the economy was shared by the major political parties and by labour and capital. The New Democratic Party and the affiliated trade-union movement accepted the basic economic institutions of the capitalist economy and the profit system, while emphasizing the need to pursue full employment policies, control giant corporations more stringently and expand the welfare state. Their demands have embodied in policy form what may be considered the "left wing" of the consensus (*see* SOCIAL DEMOCRACY). The Liberal Party, responsible for introducing modified versions of many of the social democratic reforms demanded by the labour movement and popularized by the NDP, has tended to occupy the centre of the spectrum.

The consensus among supporters of orthodox economics and its variations broke down in the 1970s and 1980s. Traditional orthodoxy was resurrected and refined under the name of monetarism and was adopted, in various degrees, by the federal and provincial governments. Another response has taken the form of post-Keynesian economics, which advocates, among other things, state supervision of wages and state guidance and subsidization of private investment. Both responses reveal that the size of government has little to do with "left" or "right" economic policy. The responses represent alternative policy options for meeting the economic crisis, the one calling for a dismantling of state regulation and a return to the free market, the other for the expansion of state regulation and assistance for private industry.

Radical Economics According to this school of thought, the process of production – ie, producers and their skills, materials and tools; the general level of technology; and the social relations among people in production – governs the economy and influences the shape and role of other institutions, eg, the family, state, education. Radical economics is concerned with how economic surplus (margin of output beyond that required for the maintenance of direct producers and the replacement of outworn capital equipment) is used and to whose benefit. Under capitalism, workers surrender, for wages, all rights of ownership to the product they produce and agree to submit to the control of the capitalist or his representative during the production process. A surplus or profit is extracted when the capitalist pockets the difference between what is paid to the workers and the value of the things produced. The surplus supports the capitalist but is also used to increase the productive capacity of the economy, from which more surplus can be extracted. In capitalist economies labour is necessarily treated as a commodity, from which stems many of the fundamental conflicts in industry, eg, because improvement in wages and conditions of work cut into profits, employers will naturally resist pressures for improving the workers' lot. Workers' jobs are always at the mercy of changing economic and technological circumstances; if the demand for goods and services slumps, or if new technology lessens the costs of production, workers will find themselves unemployed. Radical economists contend that mainstream thought, which has minutely analysed the laws of supply and demand, ignores the sphere of production. It leaves out the fact that once the ownership of the major means of production is confined to a small class of owners, the freedom of most workers is restricted to choosing from among those means of livelihood that do not require possession of land or capital. Workers can only gain a livelihood by selling their labour power on whatever terms and under whatever conditions they can negotiate, individually or collectively.

In disagreement with J.S. Mill and the reform school, radical economists believe that modifying the distribution of income through welfare, UNEMPLOYMENT INSURANCE and tax reforms is heavily constrained by the capitalist system's need for an incentives structure that does not interfere with the LABOUR MARKET or discourage private investment. While accepting Galbraith's critique of the mainstream assertion of consumer sovereignty, they reject his belief that the consumers' subordinate role results from the gullibility of consumers or the power of advertising. Radical economists also reject the liberal and social-democratic theory of a pluralistic society where power is distributed among different groups, with the state acting as arbitrator in cases of disagreement. Instead, they argue that because the prosperity of the nation ultimately depends on the willingness of capital to produce, the state cannot develop policies that severely impinge on their profits. In short, radicals believe that within a capitalist economy based on private ownership of the means of production the possibility of reform is necessarily limited, even if a benevolent state wants to introduce progessive measures.

Radical economists dispute the alleged efficiency of the capitalist economy. They see it as a highly wasteful system, laying off large numbers of workers and idling capital equipment during long stretches of stagnation and depression, and unable to tap the reservoir of creative abilities of an alienated, indifferent work force. Economic democracy at the workplace is the radicals' alternative to private enterprise.

While orthodox economists are viewed as working for the stabilization or reform of capitalism, radical economists work for the establishment of a new society that includes public ownership of all large enterprises; the elimination of production for profit; economy-wide planning to eliminate unemployment; and an egalitarian redistribution of income and wealth. However, the lessons of Soviet-style communism have convinced most radicals that changing the economic system cannot simply mean nationalizing industry and imposing centralized planning. It must involve worker control at the point of production and community control over investment decisions such as which goods and services are produced, in what amounts and in what locations. The most widely embraced vision of contemporary western Marxism is best expressed by the solidarity principle: keeping economic differences to a minimum while recognizing the variability in aptitude, taste and psychological temperament among individuals. Individuals advance as part of the general economic advancement rather than in competition one with the other, with the winnings of the few trickling down to meet the needs of the many.

The difference between the radical and the orthodox vision of good society stems from their divergent views of human nature. The rock upon which most orthodox thinking rests is that human beings are "naturally" acquisitive and are motivated primarily by self-gain. Radicals insist that human values and behaviour are socially determined and that survival and sustenance in capitalist societies require that people heed their own self-interest. Implicit in the radical vision is the belief that with a democratic and egalitarian social structure devoid of class denomination, human values and human behaviour can evolve towards a greater social consciousness and communal identity.

Introduced to Canada by small socialist groups early in the 20th century, the radical perspective has never informed the politics of any major Canadian party. It has always been part of the perspective of the Canadian working class and elements of it are apparent in the women's movement, the ecology movement, and the churches, eg, it was reflected in the *Ethical Reflections on the Economic Crisis* produced by the Canadian Conference of Catholic Bishops in 1983. The radical system of analysis has also made important inroads into various academic disciplines, including sociology, economics, political science, history and anthropology. In Canada radical economists include, among many others, Errol Black, Robert Chernomas, Sam Gindin, Michael Lebowitz, Kari Levitt, Jean-Guy Loranger, John Loxley, Martha Macdonald, Riel Miller, Tom Naylor, Ian Parker, Paul Phillips, Ed Shaffer, Andrew Sharpe, George Warskett and Mel Watkins.

In modern times, radical economics first re-emerged from the failure of mainstream economics to explain the perceived deterioration of the quality of life and the resulting social upheaval in prosperous western countries, the inability of much of the developing nations to wrestle themselves out of their state of economic dependence and subordination and the role of US imperialism in Vietnam. While remaining a minority paradigm, it gained some academic popularity with its views on the economic crisis of the 1970s and 1980s.   CY GONICK

Reading: I. Adams et al, *The Real Poverty Report* (1971); W. Clement, *Class, Power and Property* (1983); Clement and D. Drache, *A Practical Guide to Canadian Political Economy* (1978); Cy Gonick, *Out of Work* (1978).

Economy Most modern economists think of ECONOMICS as the study of choice, so that, strictly, an "economy" consists of human beings – in this case Canadians – making choices, which obviously includes just about all of Canadian experience. As much as this sweeping definition might please economists, however, it is probably more useful to think of economic activity – as most laymen do – as taking place when people produce and exchange goods and services. This definition has the advantage of according more or less closely with what the national accounts statisticians count when they try to measure economic activity. On the other hand, the overlap between "the economy" and the economic statistics the government collects is not perfect. Some goods and

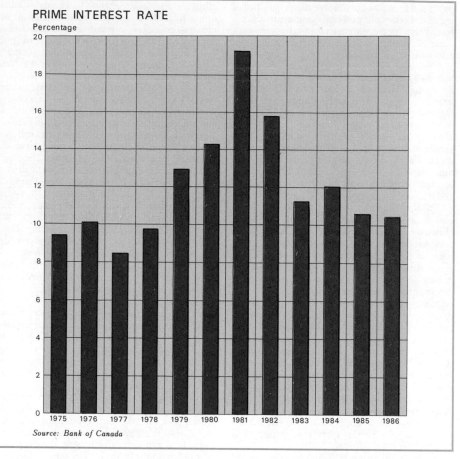

PRIME INTEREST RATE
Percentage

Source: Bank of Canada

services – such as prostitution and drugs –are produced and exchanged as far outside the government's ken as possible, while more and more otherwise legitimate economic activity now goes on clandestinely, so as to avoid taxation. Estimates of this UNDERGROUND ECONOMY currently run as high as 22% of overall economic activity. And, of course, many other quite legitimate goods and services – cleaning, maintenance, preparation of food, and the like – are produced in the home, without being exchanged (or therefore included in "Gross National Product"). If "above-ground" production and exchange are the definitive economic activities, then the Canadian economy can be described by examining what kinds of goods and services Canadians produce and consume, what sort of jobs they do, how much they earn, and whom they work for and trade with.

Industrial Structure Canadians have long been famous to themselves (if not to others) as "hewers of wood and drawers of water," and it is true that the European development of Canada was motivated mainly by a desire to exploit the country's natural RESOURCES, both renewable and nonrenewable (*see* ECONOMIC HISTORY; FISHERIES HISTORY; TIMBER TRADE HISTORY; FUR TRADE; STAPLE THESIS). Moreover, we still account for an impressive share of the world's output of resources. In minerals, for instance, in 1983 we produced over 20% of the world's potash and asbestos; over 15% of its nickel, zinc, molybdenum, sulphur and uranium; and over 5% of its copper, lead, gold, silver and aluminum; and in none of these did we rank lower than fifth in our share of world output. But while the resource industries still account for a significant share of overall economic activity – and also in part determine what goes on in the rest of the economy – the reality behind our self-image is that in Canada, as in all other developed countries, most output is produced in the manufacturing and service sectors. In 1985 manufac-

turing accounted for 18.8% of overall Canadian output, while agriculture and the resource industries – forestry, fishing and trapping, mining and petroleum, and electric power, gas and water – together accounted for only a little over 12.9%. By far the lion's share of output – 68.5% – was from the service industries, especially community, business and personal services (which include much of the "para-public" sector, education and health care, mainly), and public administration and defence. Other important service industries are construction, trade, and transportation and communication (the last 2 of which are crucial in a country as large as Canada). While Canada tends, if anything, to have a somewhat larger service sector and smaller manufacturing sector than other industrial countries, our sectoral balance is by no means unusual for an advanced economy. Nor, interestingly, is the current importance of manufacturing and services all that new. Agriculture did account for 37.1% of output in 1870, but natural resources, at 4.1%, were hardly dominant, and manufacturing and services, at 22.4% and 36%, respectively, were already well established. In fact, a rough summary of the last century's economic development is that the decline in the share (but not, of course, the level) of agricultural output has been matched by the growth of services, while natural resources and manufacturing have more or less held their own.

The current dominance of the service sector is even more dramatic when measured in terms of employees by industry (*see* SERVICE INDUSTRIES). In 1985 fully 74.5% of workers were employed in the service sector, with 17.5% in manufacturing, and only 8.1% in agriculture and natural resources. This compares with 68.5%, 18.9% and 12.9%, respectively, when output shares are calculated. That nonservice industries typically account for a larger share of output than employment is common in industrialized countries. The

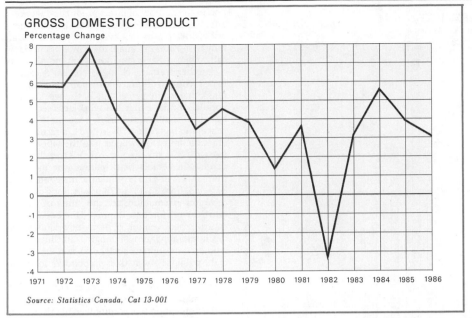

GROSS DOMESTIC PRODUCT
Percentage Change

Source: Statistics Canada, Cat 13-001

main reason is that in the postwar period, increases in productivity (output per worker) generally have been greater in manufacturing, agriculture and natural resources than in services, so that while over time virtually all industries have been able to produce the same output with fewer workers, these 3 very capital-intensive sectors have required even fewer workers than the service sector. But despite widespread concern in the 1980s about "de-industrialization," in most Western countries it is only manufacturing's share of employment – not output – that has declined. In fact, in the post-1973 period, Canada was one of the few industrialized countries in which the absolute number of manufacturing jobs increased (though as elsewhere manufacturing accounted for a declining share of employment).

Canadian Manufacturing That Canada seems not to have as large or competitive a manufacturing sector as some other advanced countries has long been a worry for those Canadian policymakers and economists who regard a resource-driven economy as being excessively prone to regional and cyclical variations in income and insufficiently dedicated to innovation and industrial research. Many others argue, on the contrary, that manufacturing-based economies are not immune to instability and that if resource development is the most profitable use for Canadian manpower and capital, and if the relatively high domestic wage levels to which such development leads make it difficult for Canadian manufacturers to compete internationally, then forcing growth in manufacturing by means of direct or indirect subsidies will mean lower incomes for Canadians.

In fact, Canada has a large and varied manufacturing sector. Between 1960 and 1982 it employed 23.3% of the work force, on average – which is only 1.5 percentage points less than the US average in this period and not far from the Organization for Economic Cooperation and Development average of 26.1%. It is true that roughly 40% of Canadian manufacturing involves processing of raw materials; on the other hand, a substantial proportion is now given over to the production of end products. Moreover, in the postwar period, Canada's manufacturing competitiveness improved dramatically; the historically large productivity gap between Canadian and US manufacturers closed substantially, and by 1985 manufactured exports represented fully 75% of overall exports. The increase has been es-

pecially dramatic for end products, whose share of exports has risen from 8.6% in 1954 to 43.1% in 1985. The CANADA-US AUTOMOTIVE PRODUCTS AGREEMENT of 1965, which created free trade in automobiles and automotive parts for producers (but not for consumers), is the largest single reason for this increase in manufactured exports, but, more generally, widespread reductions in tariff barriers, particularly between Canada and the US, have allowed many other Canadian manufacturers to enter the American market and take advantage of the benefits of large-scale production, which often were not available when producers were confined to the small Canadian market by the generally high tariffs of the 1879-1945 period.

International Payments Though Canadians do produce lots of services and manufactures for

each other, our "comparative advantage" (ie, what we do best of all) is still mainly in resource-related activities, a fact that is reflected in our trade statistics. After motor vehicles and parts (at 28.6% of merchandise exports) our biggest exports are crude oil, newsprint, lumber, natural gas, wheat, other food products, machinery and wood pulp. (In fact, our net exports – ie, our exports after our imports are subtracted – of oil, food products and machinery are either negative or not very large: though we export a lot, we also import a lot). Our most important imports are – by far – manufactured end products.

For most of the postwar period Canada has run a surplus on the "merchandise trade account," ie, we have exported substantially more commodities than we have imported. On the "service account," however, we have usually run an even larger deficit. The 2 most important components of the service account are travel and interest and dividend payments. The main reason for our large and growing deficit on the travel account is that, as Canadians have become richer, more and more of us have become accustomed to the luxury of a sun-seeking winter holiday. Our traditional deficit in interest and dividend payments results from the fact that through most of our history we have imported capital from other countries – in loans, in takeovers and in new investment. In our first 50 years capital inflows ran as high as 10% of GNP per year, and despite a postwar rise in Canadian savings rates, had risen substantially, we have remained a net importer of capital, which means we must continue to pay interest and dividends to our foreign creditors.

Together, the merchandise and service accounts make up the "current account" of the BALANCE OF PAYMENTS. Traditionally, Canada has run a deficit on the current account. Because the balance of payments is nothing more than a record of all purchases and sales of Canadian dollars – whether for trade, travel, interest, lending or borrowing – and because for every buyer of a Canadian dollar there must be a seller, the balance of

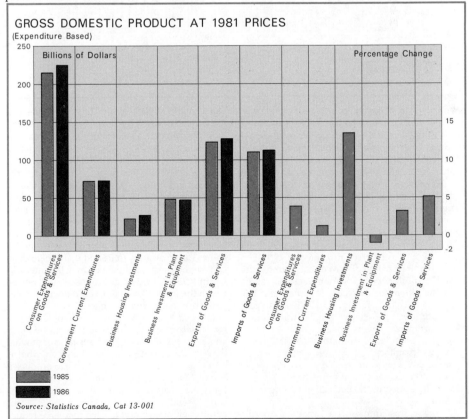

GROSS DOMESTIC PRODUCT AT 1981 PRICES
(Expenditure Based)

Billions of Dollars | Percentage Change

- Consumer Expenditures on Goods & Services
- Government Current Expenditures
- Business Housing Investments
- Business Investment in Plant & Equipment
- Exports of Goods & Services
- Imports of Goods & Services

1985
1986

Source: Statistics Canada, Cat 13-001

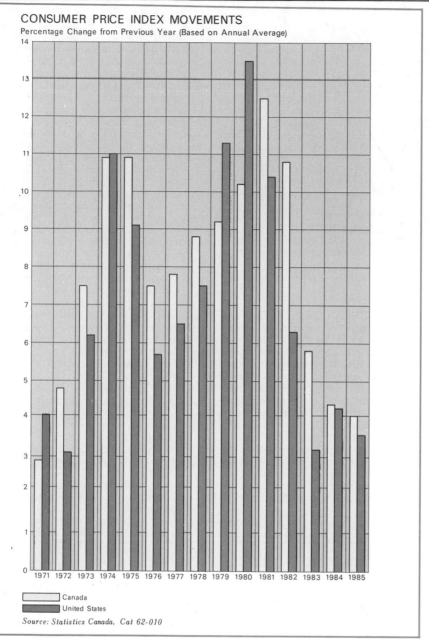

CONSUMER PRICE INDEX MOVEMENTS
Percentage Change from Previous Year (Based on Annual Average)

Canada
United States

Source: Statistics Canada, Cat 62-010

payments always balances. Thus our customary deficit on the current account has been offset by inflows on the capital account, ie, we have usually borrowed more from foreigners than they have borrowed from us. This only makes sense: money could not continue to flow out of Canada to cover our net current account obligations for interest and travel unless it also flowed back to us in the form of loans or investments from foreigners. In the early 1980s, our reliance on foreign investment declined sharply; in fact we invested more abroad than foreigners were investing here until the situation was reversed in 1986 and 1987.

In general the balance between the current and capital accounts depends on many factors, among them the difference between Canadian and US interest rates (which affects capital flows between the 2 countries), the relative value of the 2 countries' currencies, the relative growth of their GNPs, and the relative strength of protectionism (all of which affect trade flows). Since each of these variables depends in large part on the 2 countries' economic policies, it is hard to know what will happen to the balance of payments in the future.

Of course, this emphasis on Canadian-Ameri-

can economic relations (*see* CANADIAN-AMERICAN RELATIONS, ECONOMY) is not strictly correct: the balance of payments also depends on our relations with other countries. But by far the largest part of our INTERNATIONAL TRADE is with the US, and despite attempts in the early 1970s (under the Trudeau government's THIRD OPTION) to increase trade with non-US, non-European countries, our economic ties with the US have become even closer. While some economists worry that this makes us too dependent on swings in the US economy, others argue that trading with the US comes most naturally to us and that the possibly considerable expense involved in deliberately diverting trade in other directions would not be worth the (quite likely minimal) reduction in dependence that it would bring.

Jobs and Workers Another way to describe Canadian economic activity is to look at the kinds and amounts of work Canadians do, not at what they produce. The distinction between what is produced and the type of work done to produce it is often forgotten but, of course, is crucial. Not everyone working in the forest industry is a lumberjack, and in fact in most industries in recent decades mechanization has led to a large reduc-

tion in the number of direct production workers. The number of Canadians who actually hew, draw, drill or farm for a living is minuscule, while fully two-thirds of Canadians now work in classically white-collar occupations (*see* LABOUR FORCE).

Another dramatic change in recent decades is in just who is working. The overall "participation rate," that is, the percentage of the working-age population that either has work or is seeking it, has risen significantly, from 55% in 1946 to a peacetime high of 64.7% in 1981, a result of the dramatic influx of women into the labour force (*see* WOMEN IN THE LABOUR FORCE). Over the same period, the female participation rate increased from 24.7% to 51.6%, while the male rate in fact declined, from 85.1% to 78.3%. Among the most common explanations for the influx of women into the work force are improved methods of birth control, the invention of many new labour-saving home appliances, changing attitudes about women's appropriate social role, and the growth of the public sector, with its preponderance of service-type jobs.

One of the great puzzles of recent Canadian economic experience is that while the proportion of the population that is employed has risen more or less steadily, the UNEMPLOYMENT rate has also risen, though less steadily. Record increases in the creation of new jobs have been outstripped by even greater increases in the number of people seeking work. As a result, the national unemployment rate has risen from an average of 5.2% in the 1960s, to 6.7% in the 1970s, to 9.9% between 1980 and 1986 (though it was on a downward trend in the mid-1980s). Two common explanations for this phenomenon are that the unemployment insurance program has become much more generous than it used to be, so that people are more inclined to undergo periodic spells of unemployment, and that there are many more "secondary workers" – women and young people, mainly – who presumably are not as desperate for employment as was that archetypical worker of the 1950s, the male head of a household in which no one else earned income. On the other hand, the unemployment rate for prime-age males has also been creeping up over the last 2 decades. The relatively poor economic performance of the 1970s and 1980s also helps explain this, although even in the face of sustained economic expansion in the mid-1980s unemployment proved discouragingly resistant to rapid reduction. There is growing suspicion that more and more people simply are not qualified for employment in an increasingly technological economy. Many economists also point to high minimum wages, union wage policies, and restrictive LABOUR MARKET practices on the part of both unions and governments as reducing the labour market's ability to absorb the marginally employable.

Ownership Patterns More and more in the postwar period, Canadians went to work for their governments, both directly and through the intervention of CROWN CORPORATIONS. This growth in public employment took place at all levels of government but was most dramatic at the provincial and municipal levels, where employment in education and health care, especially, grew rapidly in the 1950s and 1960s. In 1960 only 8.6% of the work force was employed by provincial and local government, but by 1981 this had risen to 12.0%. On the other hand, the increase in public employment in the last 3 decades is nothing like the increase in PUBLIC EXPENDITURES (which have risen from 29.6% of GNP to 46.1%). This is because less than half the increase in spending was for the purchase or production of goods and services. Most went instead for transfers to individuals and interest payments on the PUBLIC DEBT.

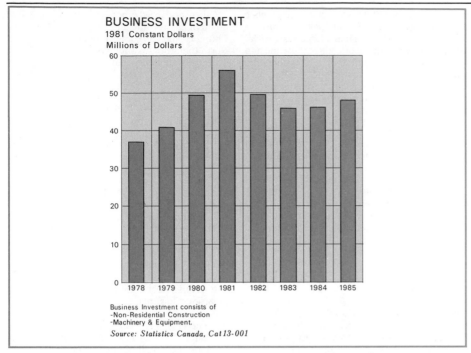

BUSINESS INVESTMENT
1981 Constant Dollars
Millions of Dollars

Business Investment consists of
-Non-Residential Construction
-Machinery & Equipment.

Source: Statistics Canada, Cat 13-001

While employment data for crown corporations are harder to come by, estimates suggest that nowadays upward of 3% of Canadians earn their living by working for such agencies, of which there are more than 230 at all levels of government in Canada.

Perhaps the best-known characteristic of Canadian economic life is that many Canadians who work in the private sector of the economy are employed by foreign-owned corporations. The level of foreign ownership – first mainly British and then, following WWII, largely American – has always been very high in Canada. By 1968, when the Watkins Task Force on FOREIGN OWNERSHIP reported to the federal government, foreign control of Canadian manufacturing had reached 57%, while foreigners owned even more – over 70% and 80%, respectively – of our mining and petroleum and gas industries. By the early 1970s, foreign ownership had become a contentious political issue and as a result the Trudeau government founded PETROCANADA, the state-owned oil company, set up the FOREIGN INVESTMENT REVIEW AGENCY, which was supposed to screen proposed foreign investments to assure they provided net benefits and, in 1980 after the second OPEC episode, introduced the NATIONAL ENERGY PROGRAM which included special incentives for Canadian-owned oil and gas companies.

Critics of these measures argued that the "Canadianization" they brought came at too high a cost both in damaged relations, especially with the US, and in discouraged investment in general. But, together with the turnaround in direct investment mentioned earlier, they helped reduce overall foreign ownership to 44% in manufacturing (in 1984), to 35% in mining, and to 39% in petroleum and gas. Although the Mulroney government replaced FIRA with Investment Canada in 1985, it retained general, if more relaxed, FOREIGN INVESTMENT restrictions and introduced special restrictions in publishing and other "cultural industries."

Economic Growth The customary measure of a country's economic well-being is the amount of goods and services it produces – its GNP – per capita. Man does not live by Gross National Product alone, of course, and as an index of happiness, GNP suffers several well-known deficiencies. Among the most obvious are that it does not take account of such things as pollution, urban crowding, health, security of person and property, and

the like. On the other hand, picking fault with GNP as a measure of well-being is much less fashionable now than it was before 1973, when economic growth began to slow in most industrial countries.

There is no question that Canadians enjoy a high standard of living, and that this has been true for the entire postwar period. The usual estimates place Canadian GNP per capita 5% to 15% below the US level and roughly equal to that in the north European democracies. Of course, many Canadians would argue that other aspects of Canadian life make up for the economic gap with the US, though it is still true that many of us choose to emigrate to the US each year.

Though average Canadian living standards remain high, in recent years there has been widespread concern both here and in the US that other countries, particularly Japan and W Germany, are catching up with – indeed, in the case of W Germany, may already have caught up with – N American living standards, and this has prompted a vigorous debate about which policies are most likely to rekindle N American economic growth. In part, the problem is statistical. The way living standards usually are compared across countries is to add up respective countries' GNPs, each measured in terms of their own currency, and then to translate across countries by using the current rates of exchange between currencies.

Though common, this procedure is fundamentally flawed: when our dollar falls by 30% vis-à-vis the Japanese yen this does not mean our living standards have fallen by 30% in comparison to Japan's. True, any Canadian who lives exclusively on Japanese goods, as some diplomatic personnel may do, will suffer a 30% decline in income, but everyone else loses only in proportion to their consumption of Japanese goods.

But even when statistical problems rising from movements in exchange rates are taken into account the Japanese and European economies have posted better per capita growth rates than either Canada or the US. Explaining this has become one of N America's growth industries. Both the Germans and Japanese began the postwar period at a significant disadvantage. Given their low initial base, it was not difficult for them to grow rapidly, and since a good part of their capital stock was destroyed during WWII, by the late 1950s they had a much newer industrial plant than most

of their competitors.

On the other hand, while advantages of this sort are temporary by definition, both West Germany and Japan have continued to grow more quickly than North America for fully 4 decades now. Momentum cannot be their only advantage, and other explanations point to significant organizational differences, especially between the Japanese and North American economies.

Unfortunately, for those seeking a clear understanding of Japanese success, the problem is too many explanations, not too few. Differences between our 2 societies abound. Does the Japanese advantage come from the more apparently collegial nature of worker-management relations in Japan? From the fact that their government seems to do more long-term industrial planning? From the very high Japanese savings rate and very low strike rate? From the practice of charging higher prices at home than in export markets? From the apparently unforgiving system of weeding out industrial managers? From the lower share of GNP that is funneled through the public sector? From the underdeveloped social security system? From the much greater prevalence of profit-sharing?

Many Canadian observers, notably the Science Council of Canada, argue that in fact the crucial difference is that Japan has a better worked-out set of "industrial policies," and they propose that Canada formally adopt a system of sectoral economic planning (*see* INDUSTRIAL STRATEGY). Critics of this view argue that planning probably is not the crucial Japanese advantage, that several of Japan's greatest industrial successes have been developed despite planners' wishes, and that in any case it would be very hard to transplant Japanese economic institutions to a society not well designed to accept them.

Regional Problems Another aspect of Canada's economic performance that has caused policymakers much concern through the years is that the country's different regions seem to share unequally in its economic fortunes. In part, this is because Canada consists not of a single economy but of several. The 5 traditional regions have significantly different industrial structures, with manufacturing being most important in Ontario and Québec, agriculture, petroleum and mining in the Prairies, fishing and agriculture in the Maritimes, and forestry and fishing in British Columbia (*see* REGIONAL ECONOMICS).

Regional differences in per capita income – usually termed regional "disparities" (with a strong negative connotation) – have narrowed slightly since the data were first kept. Though the Prairies' fortunes have swung widely over the last 50 years, and Alberta, at least, has recently vied with Ontario for the country's highest per capita income, the general rule is that earned incomes are higher in Ontario and in British Columbia than in the rest of the country. That these disparities have remained more or less constant, with only very gradual movement toward greater equality, suggests to many economists that in fact they represent "equilibrium" income differences. In this view, since mobility across the country is relatively easy – many millions of Canadians have moved between regions in the last 50 years – any persistent interregional differences in income are best interpreted as representing the nonpecuniary value of living in the outlying regions of the country. Thus people who live in the Maritimes may consider the social, cultural or environmental features of their region adequate compensation for income differences between themselves and, say, Toronto residents. In addition, many federal programs, most notably EQUALIZATION PAYMENTS to the "have-not" provinces, make it possible for people to stay where they are and receive comparable government services even though their own earned income is on average lower than it would be in central Canada.

More radical critics argue, however, that regional economic growth feeds on itself, in a process of "cumulative causation," especially when the best and brightest of the poorer regions' young people decide to take up roots and move to central Canada and Alberta or BC to seek their fortunes. If so, then the outlying regions of the country can be expected to become still poorer as the centre (ie, the Québec-Windsor corridor) continues to grow. Policymakers must then decide whether to sacrifice the greater private wealth that efficient urban agglomerations can produce and try instead to use subsidies of one kind or other to divert growth to the outlying regions – assuming subsidies of a manageable scale would be sufficient to do the job. Though the federal government has been trying since the mid-1960s to promote growth in the low-income regions of Canada, it is hard to discern any significant effect of these programs in the regional income data. However, federal programs such as equalization and the "Established Programs" do bring public services in the poorer provinces closer to the national average. And the fact that regional disparities have closed slightly in the last 50 years suggests that the more alarming versions of the "cumulative causation" story may not be that realistic.

Individual Inequality Though regional inequality has often had more dramatic effects on Canadian political life, inequalities among the incomes of individual Canadians are in fact much greater. There are, despite the stereotypes, rich Maritimers and poor Ontarians, and the differences in incomes in any given province are and always have been much greater than the differences in average incomes across provinces. Before taxes and government expenditure programs have their effect, there is a great deal of inequality in Canada, and there has not been much change in this inequality in the last 40 years. The top 10% of income earners accounted for 42.8% of earned income in 1951 and 41.8% in 1981, while the bottom 10% accounted for only 4.4% and 4.6%, respectively. It must be kept in mind, however, that there have been many changes in the composition of the work force and the pattern of employment between 1951 and 1981. There are now many more part-time workers than there used to be, and they naturally fall closer to the bottom of the distribution than full-time workers do. Similarly, relatively more generous social programs now enable workers to work full-time for some parts of the year and then take more or less voluntary spells of unemployment during others. It is therefore hard to draw meaningful conclusions about changes in the inequality of earned incomes. What is certain is that both taxes and government expenditures cause significant reductions in the degree of inequality. Still, while government programs do reduce inequality, they only redistribute 5% to 6% of GNP across income groups, despite the fact that in total government expenditures amount to over 45% of GNP. Clearly, a great deal of government activity involves "horizontal" redistribution among the members of the same income class, rather than "vertical" redistribution from higher income classes to lower. This is all but inevitable in a system in which many social programs are universal, rather than income-tested. In 1981, while 61.0% of social assistance and 41.0% of old age security/guaranteed income supplement monies went to people in the lowest fifth of the INCOME DISTRIBUTION, only 11.6% of unemployment in-

surance benefits, 23.3% of Canada and Québec Pension plan payments, and 7.8% of family allowances did. So long as many large-scale social programs are not aimed directly at those most in need, gross redistribution will inevitably be much greater than net redistribution. There may be some comfort in the fact that Canadian practice is not much different from that in the other industrialized countries. WILLIAM WATSON

Ecosystem, a limited space within which living beings interact with nonliving matter at a high level of interdependence to form an environmental unit. At a large scale, ecosystems have been defined on the basis of geographical extent alone, eg, "arctic," "tall-grass prairie" or "hardwood forest." These very large areas are often called biomes. At a smaller scale, for example, "dune ecosystem" and "bog ecosystem" refer to spatial dimensions and to precise soil conditions within which interactions among components take place.

Reading: Pierre Dansereau, *Harmony and Disorder in the Canadian Environment* (1975).

Ecumenical Social Action Church life in Canada since the late 1960s has been characterized by a reawakening of the SOCIAL GOSPEL passion for justice and a new level of co-operation between Protestants and Roman CATHOLICS. Following the Second Vatican Council (1962-65), Roman Catholics joined the Religion-Labour Council and the Women's Inter-Church Council and worked more closely with the CANADIAN COUNCIL OF CHURCHES. New organizations such as the National Committee on the Church and Industrial Society, the Inter-Church Consultative Committee on Development and Relief, and a number of jointly sponsored groups were designed to facilitate Protestant-Catholic collaboration. The war against domestic poverty provided an initial focus for ecumenical social action. The 1968 national conference, "Christian Conscience and Poverty," led to the creation of the Coalition for Development. This ambitious attempt to co-ordinate the antipoverty struggles of a wide range of organizations did not survive, but the desire to work together remained strong.

International emergencies such as the Biafran and Bangladesh crises of the late 1960s and early 1970s, and the growing gap between rich and poor nations, heightened the churches' desire to co-ordinate relief and development activities. The Inter-Church Campaign Committee produces shared materials for each denomination's annual appeal for relief and development funds; Ten Days for World Development co-ordinates a development education program; and CAFEA (Church Action for Emergency Aid) and ICFID (the Inter-Church Fund for International Development) co-ordinate emergency assistance and administer jointly sponsored development projects.

The churches' responses to domestic and Third World poverty reflected the social gospel conviction that justice, not charity, was required. The need for carefully targeted research was recognized as a starting point for combining compassion for victims with a sophisticated understanding of existing policies. For example, the experience of church observers at UNCTAD (United Nations Conference on Trade and Development) III (the poor nations' organization) strengthened the conviction that the churches should examine Canada's role as a member of the rich nations' club – the General Agreement on Tariffs and Trade (GATT). The GATT-Fly Project was created to help the churches to be more effective gadflies in criticizing Canada's trade and aid policies.

Other specialized groups created in response to different issues include the Task Force on Churches and Corporate Responsibility, Project North (native rights and northern development), the Inter-Church Committee on Human Rights in Latin America, the Church Council on Justice and Corrections, Project Ploughshares (defence policy and DISARMAMENT) and the Inter-Church Committee for Refugees. Each group has a small specialized staff and an administrative committee consisting of denominational representatives. PLURA (named after its Presbyterian, Lutheran, United, Roman Catholic and Anglican sponsors) works through regional committees to assist local antipoverty organizations.

Although participation in such activities has generally been more strongly supported by denominational headquarters than by ordinary church members, these organizational innovations have nevertheless been accompanied by a developing tradition of ecumenical social thought. The central conviction that the transformation of unjust social structures is an integral part of mission and ministry has been expressed in various documents. Statements typical of the ecumenical consensus can be found in briefs to the federal government, such as "Development Demands Justice" (1973), the "Inter-Church Brief on Economic Outlook" (1978) and the "Statement of Canadian Church Leaders on Canada's Nuclear Weapons Policies" (1982).

ROGER HUTCHINSON

Reading: J.R. Williams, ed, *Canadian Churches and Social Justice* (1984); E.F. Sheridan, S.J., *Do Justice: The Social Teaching of the Canadian Catholic Bishops* (1987).

Eddy, Ezra Butler, manufacturer (b near Bristol, Vt 22 Aug 1827; d at Hull, Qué 12 Feb 1906). Part of the influx of American manufacturers to the Ottawa Valley in the 1850s, Eddy moved his small friction-match factory from Burlington, Vt, to Hull in 1851 and developed markets from Winnipeg to Halifax. Overcoming a series of disastrous fires, notably in 1883 and 1900, Eddy expanded, modernized and diversified to produce a wide range of wood and paper products. At his death his business was estimated to be worth more than $4 million. Elected mayor of Hull 6 times, he represented Ottawa County in the Québec Assembly 1871-75. An opponent of "racialism," he supported Catholic and Protestant institutions alike. A vocal promoter of the British Empire, he was buried in Bristol, beneath the impressive monument which he had built in his honour. RICHARD REID

Edel, Leon, biographer, editor, critic (b at Pittsburgh, Pa 9 Sept 1907). Edel's 5-volume life of Henry James, which appeared between 1953 and 1972, is one of the major literary biographies of its time. Raised in Yorkton, Sask, Edel was educated at McGill and the Sorbonne and taught at New York U from 1953 to 1971 and the U of Hawaii from 1971 to 1978. Edel's celebrated biography draws on his encyclopedic knowledge of James's life and art, his keen psychological insight, and a supple narrative style. Edel has also written books on literary biography, literary psychology and the psychological novel; on James Joyce, Willa Cather (with E.K. BROWN) and Thoreau; and on Canadian writers John GLASSCO, Leo KENNEDY, A.M. KLEIN, A.J.M. SMITH, Morley CALLAGHAN and F.R. SCOTT. Edel has won numerous awards, including the Pulitzer Prize for Biography (1963). His most recent works are *Henry James: A Life* (1985) and ed, *Henry James: Selected Letters* (1987). NEIL BESNER

Edenshaw, Charlie, or Tahaygen, "Noise in the Housepit," and Nngkwigetklals, "They Gave Ten Potlatches for Him," Haida chief, artist (b at

Skidegate, Queen Charlotte Is, BC *c* 1839; d there 1920). Charlie Edenshaw was among the first professional Haida artists and is noted for his flawless execution of dynamic flowing forms in an otherwise strict and disciplined art tradition. Much of his early life was spent in the villages of Kiusta and Yatze, and in 1882 his Eagle clan moved to Masset. He was tutored in Haida traditions by his uncle, the chief of the Stastas Eagles, Albert Edward Edenshaw. Charlie Edenshaw frequently met museum anthropologists and collectors at Masset and Prince Rupert. His contributions to world art are therefore not only marked by exquisite works in gold, silver, ivory, argillite and wood, but are also found in the recording and documentation of Haida language and culture. Art historians and anthropologists continue to study his vast corpus of works.   CAROL SHEEHAN

Edith Cavell, Mount, elev 3363 m, highest mountain in the environs of JASPER, Alta, is situated W of the ATHABASCA R, 24 km S of Jasper. A prominent landmark, it was called "La Montagne de la Grande Traverse" by voyageurs during the days when ATHABASCA PASS was used as a fur-trade route across the Rockies. It was named in 1916 after the English matron of the Red Cross Hospital in Brussels. Its first ascent was made in 1915. Mountaineers consider the N face to be one of the great climbs in N America.   GLEN BOLES

Edmonton, capital of Alberta and largest city in the province (by CMA), is located on the N SASKATCHEWAN R, near the geographical centre of the province. Commonly known as the "Gateway to the North," it is strategically situated on an economic divide between the highly productive farmlands of central Alberta and a vast, resource-rich northern hinterland.

Settlement Edmonton's valley setting, with its abundance of water, timber and wildlife, has attracted settlement for several thousand years. The archaeological record is scanty, but in 1976 a large campsite containing stone tools from the Middle Prehistoric period (between 3000 and 500 BC) was discovered on a high bluff overlooking the N Saskatchewan R, likely a place where bands of seminomadic hunters and gatherers met regularly. Europeans began to penetrate the western plains in the 18th century. Settlement followed in 1795, when the Hudson's Bay Company and the North West Company built the first of a series of fortified trading posts. After the 2 companies merged (1821), FORT EDMONTON became the dominant centre of the western fur trade. The fort was reputedly named for Edmonton, now part of London, Eng, the birthplace of a clerk of the HBC. In 1830 the fort was rebuilt for the last time, on the present site of the Alberta Legislature Building. It gradually fell into disuse after the HBC surrendered its rights to RUPERT'S LAND (1870).

Development Permanent settlement outside the fort did not begin until the 1870s, and even then was slow to develop. The construction of the CPR through Calgary (1883) did not help. A branch railway came N in 1891, but it terminated at Strathcona, a community on the S bank of the N Saskatchewan R. Edmonton did not receive its

Population: 573 982 (1986c); 541 992 (1981cA); 785 465 (CMA, 1986c), 740 882 (ACMA, 1981c)

Rate of Increase (1981-86): City 5.9%; CMA 6.0%

Rank in Canada: Fifth (by CMA)

Date of Incorporation: Town 1892; City 1904

Land Area: City, 669.95 km²; CMA 11 396.68 km²

Elevation: 671 m

Climate: Average daily temp, July 17.4°C, Jan -15.0°C; Yearly precip 466.1 mm; Hours of sunshine 2263.7 per year

Jasper Avenue looking east, 1903. Within 2 years the city was made capital of the new province of Alberta (*courtesy Provincial Archives of Alberta/E. Brown Coll/ B5573*).

own transcontinental connection (Canadian Northern Ry) until 1905, by which time it was the designated capital of the newly created province of Alberta and the natural service centre for a huge agricultural region then coming under intensive development. With Strathcona, Edmonton entered a frantic boom period. When the 2 cities amalgamated (1912), their combined population was over 40 000 and may have reached 70 000 soon after, only to drop to 50 000 in WWI. For the next 25 years Edmonton's fortunes were closely linked with those of its agricultural hinterland. It grew in the good times, stagnated or declined in the bad. By 1941 it was still a small city (92 409), only the ninth largest in Canada. Its economy was built around local wholesale trade, transportation and the processing of agricultural produce, notably meat packing.

During WWII Edmonton began a sustained period of growth and assumed a distinctive new character: first as a strategic centre for northern military operations, including the construction of the ALASKA HIGHWAY, and later as a servicing and processing centre for the petroleum industry. It has since become the major location of oil refining and the petrochemical industry in western Canada, and has become prominent politically as well as economically. Edmonton's modern development, together with that of Calgary, has completely overshadowed Winnipeg, the historic commercial centre of the Prairie region. Today, Edmonton and Calgary compete more with each other for industrial investment and related services. Edmonton also has to compete more directly with Vancouver, as it tries to expand its influence in Pacific Rim countries while Vancouver intrudes upon Edmonton's traditional sphere of influence in the Mackenzie Valley and western Arctic.

Cityscape In the process of growth, the city of 1941 has been engulfed. The central area, in particular, has been continually rebuilt since the 1950s. A few noteworthy buildings have survived and several have been restored to fashionable use, but they are dwarfed by the clustered

towers that now dominate the Edmonton skyline. Only a few older buildings on open riverbank sites (the Legislature Building, Government House and the Macdonald Hotel) have retained some prominence. The river valley, which is Edmonton's outstanding natural feature, has had a profound influence. It is both a barrier, crossed by many bridges, and a magnificent amenity. High-rise apartments and elite residential areas compete along both banks for views of the river, and parks, golf courses and woodland trails stretch through the valley. Modern architecture, typified in the descending terraces of the Convention Centre, complements the valley setting. Downstream (NE) to Fort Saskatchewan and beyond, the valley has developed over the past 30 years into the largest industrial complex in Alberta. Fort Saskatchewan's industrial base makes it unusual; most of Edmonton's other satellites are bedroom communities for people working throughout the widespread metropolitan region. Metropolitan development came with postwar growth and led in 1950 to the establishment of the first regional planning organization in Canada. A city planning department was created at the same time and has been especially successful in keeping control over Edmonton's expansion. Development has been well regulated, though Edmonton has not been spared the problems of urban sprawl that beset other Canadian cities. In 1941 the city's territory covered 110 km²; in the 1980s it has reached 669.95 km², making it the largest major Canadian city in area. Unfortunately, Edmonton's area includes some of Alberta's richest farmland.

Photo of the first train over the bridge, Edmonton, 1902 (*by permission of the British Library*).

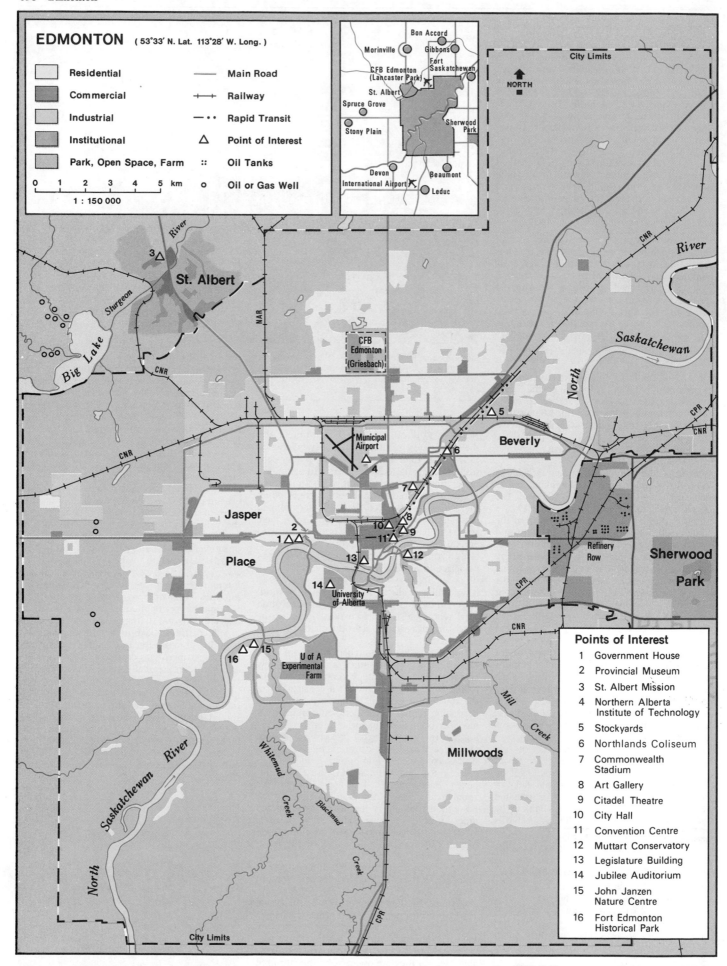

EDMONTON (53°33′ N. Lat. 113°28′ W. Long.)

Residential

Commercial

Industrial

Institutional

Park, Open Space, Farm

Main Road

Railway

Rapid Transit

Point of Interest

Oil Tanks

Oil or Gas Well

0 1 2 3 4 5 km

1 : 150 000

Morinville

Bon Accord

Gibbons

Fort
Saskatchewan

CFB Edmonton
(Lancaster Park)

St. Albert

Spruce Grove

Stony Plain

Sherwood
Park

Devon

International Airport

Beaumont

Leduc

City Limits

NORTH

River

Saskatchewan

CNR

North

CPR

CNR

St. Albert

3

Sturgeon

River

NAR

CFB
Edmonton
(Griesbach)

Big Lake

CNR

CNR

5

Beverly

Municipal
Airport

4

6

Jasper

7

Place

2

1

10

8

11

9

12

13

Refinery
Row

Sherwood
Park

14

University
of Alberta

CPR

CNR

16

15

U of A
Experimental
Farm

North

Saskatchewan

River

Whitemud

Creek

Blackmud

Creek

Mill

Creek

Millwoods

City Limits

CPR

Points of Interest

1 Government House
2 Provincial Museum
3 St. Albert Mission
4 Northern Alberta
   Institute of Technology
5 Stockyards
6 Northlands Coliseum
7 Commonwealth
   Stadium
8 Art Gallery
9 Citadel Theatre
10 City Hall
11 Convention Centre
12 Muttart Conservatory
13 Legislature Building
14 Jubilee Auditorium
15 John Janzen
   Nature Centre
16 Fort Edmonton
   Historical Park

Population Since the 1940s Edmonton has consistently been one of the 2 or 3 fastest-growing cities in Canada. Until about 1961, natural increase was high, but migration was the chief factor in the city's growth, as rural-urban migration from within Alberta and migration from Europe were both at a peak. Over the next decade, foreign migration dropped sharply and natural increase became more important, a fact reflected in the youthfulness of Edmonton's population. The pattern changed again in the 1970s, as birthrates fell and migration increased, though the majority of migrants now came from other Canadian provinces. Between 1941 and 1987, Edmonton's population increased more than sixfold, and its boundaries have been extended many times to accommodate anticipated growth.

Economy and Labour Force Edmonton's booming economy and normally low unemployment were extremely attractive to entrepreneurs and investors. Because of the high pace of development, the construction and service industries continued to prosper until 1982-83; the latter have accounted for the greatest increases in Edmonton's employment base since 1951. Traditional trade and transportation functions continue to be represented strongly, but the effect of the petroleum industry on employment is not easy to gauge because exploration and production generate relatively few jobs directly in Edmonton. The refining and manufacturing of petrochemical products are not labour intensive either. Like all facets of the oil and natural-gas industries, they generate growth in all other sectors of Edmonton's economy, but Edmonton does not have large numbers of industry-related office jobs in the way Calgary has, and it has comparatively few head offices of petroleum firms. Edmonton's employment is based more on government and administration.

Transportation Since the 1830s Edmonton has been a major hub in the transportation network of western Canada. As a modern rail centre, it occupies a key position in the transcontinental freight system of the CNR, and has strong links the CP Rail system as well. It

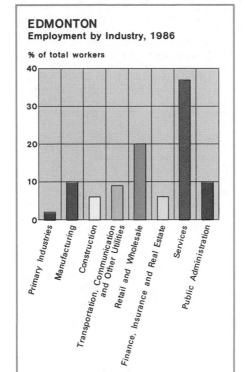

EDMONTON
Employment by Industry, 1986

% of total workers

Total does not add to 100% because some estimates are not available and some workers are unclassified
Source: Household Surveys Div, Statistics Canada

also dominates the transmission system for petroleum products of all kinds, a pattern that arose from the proximity of the Leduc, Redwater and Pembina oil fields, where exploitation began. LEDUC is also the location of the Edmonton International Airport, opened in 1957. It caters to main-line service to Canadian, American and European cities; the original airport, near the city centre, handles northern traffic and regular flights to Calgary. In intra-urban transportation, Edmonton was the first medium-sized Canadian city to construct a Light Rapid Transit (LRT) system (1978).

Government and Politics Until 1984 Edmonton had a council-commission board form of MUNICIPAL GOVERNMENT, with each council serving a 3-year term. The commission board has now

been replaced by an executive committee. The mayor is elected at large, while 12 aldermen represent 6 wards. Although most stand as Independents, the nomination of party slates of candidates is gaining popularity, and possible electoral reforms are frequently debated. So too are relations between city council and the only other elected bodies in Edmonton, the public (Protestant) and separate (Catholic) school boards. Half the annual property tax is raised for the school systems, yet city council has no control over the school boards' levies. Relations with the provincial government are typically ambivalent. Pleas for more financial assistance and a share of natural-resource revenues are tempered by the awareness that existing grants-in-aid, although generous, reduce the council's freedom of action. Indeed the principle of local autonomy is held to be so important for all municipalities in the Edmonton area that the province has so far rejected the implementation of REGIONAL GOVERNMENT or the unification of the metropolitan area under Edmonton's jurisdiction, despite the conflicts arising from the city's expansion. Instead, in 1982, the province proposed to create a regional service authority for the metropolitan communities, and reorganized the regional planning system to give stronger representation to Edmonton.

Cultural Life The Edmonton Symphony Society, the Edmonton Opera Assn and the Citadel Theatre are 3 of the largest performing-arts organizations in Canada, but they are merely the most visible elements in a prolific arts scene in Edmonton. There are musical and theatrical performances for every taste, and numerous talented painters, potters, actors, directors, writers, poets, filmmakers and artists are based in the city. In Aug 1987 the Fringe Theatre Event, a 9-day showcase for local, regional and international performing artists, attracted 175 000 people, making it the largest annual festival of its kind in Canada and the third-largest theatre festival in the world. The many different ethnic groups also contribute a lively folk culture, and artistic and ethnic festivals are increasingly popular. The chief facilities for artistic performances and displays are the Jubilee Auditorium, the Edmonton Art Gallery, the Edmonton Public Library, the Citadel Theatre and UNIVERSITY OF ALBERTA, now one of Canada's leading universities. Other major educational institutions are the Northern Alberta Institute of Technology and Grant MacEwan Community College. These are complemented by a range of popular facilities, including the Provincial Museum and Archives, Strathcona Science Pk, Muttart Conservatory, John Janzen Nature Centre, Fort Edmonton Historical Pk and the Space Sciences Centre. In sports, Edmonton holds 4 professional franchises, the EDMONTON ESKIMOS of the CFL, the EDMONTON OILERS of the NHL, the Edmonton Trappers of the Pacific Coast Baseball League and the Edmonton Brickmen of the Canadian Soccer League. The main facilities are Commonwealth Stadium (built for the 1978 COMMONWEALTH GAMES and expanded to 60 000 seats for the WORLD UNIVERSITY GAMES 1983), the Kinsmen Aquatic Centre (also built for the Commonwealth Games) and the Edmonton Northlands complex of hockey arena, racetrack and exhibition space.   P.J. SMITH

Reading: J.G. MacGregor, *Edmonton: A History* (1967); P.J. Smith, ed, *Edmonton: The Emerging Metropolitan Pattern* (1978).

Edmonton Eskimos, FOOTBALL team. They began play in 1910 and participated in the first 2 East-West GREY CUP games, losing to Toronto in 1921 and Queen's the following year. The Eski-

View of Edmonton from the east. The Convention Centre, built into the bank of the North Saskatchewan R, is seen in the foreground, with Canada Place to its right (*photo by James Marsh*).

mos competed on and off throughout the 1920s and 1930s and were reborn as a publicly owned enterprise in 1948, after which they recorded more Grey Cup appearances and victories than any other team in Canadian football's modern era. In 1952 they lost to Toronto in the Dominion final, but 2 years later, led by Jackie PARKER, Johnny BRIGHT and Normie KWONG, they defeated Montreal Alouettes in 3 straight Grey Cups (1954, 1955, 1956). The remnants of this fine squad lost to Ottawa in the 1960 Grey Cup and the club faded during the ensuing decade. Coach Ray Jauch helped return the Eskimos to power in the early 1970s, winning 3 straight Western Conference titles (1973, 1974, 1975) and one Grey Cup (1975). Under his successor, Hugh Campbell, the Eskimos made the 1978 move into Commonwealth Stadium (eventually expanded to hold over 60 000) and became one of the great dynasties of Canadian sport, winning a Western Conference title for each year of Campbell's tenure (1977-82) and an unprecedented 5 consecutive Grey Cups (1978-82). Jackie Parker was head coach 1983-87, when Joe Faragalli took over, and in 1986 Campbell returned as general manager. The Eskimos defeated Toronto in the 1987 Grey Cup game, by many accounts the most exciting ever played.   DEREK DRAGER

Edmonton Grads The Commercial Graduates Basketball Club was the formal name of the team, coached by Percy PAGE, based at McDougall Commercial High School in Edmonton. Beginning as a high-school team, the Grads ruled women's BASKETBALL from 1915 to 1940, winning 93% of their games and 49 out of a possible 51 domestic titles. They did not lose a series in the Underwood International Championships, winning 23 times. After losing the first N American Championship series (1933), the Grads came back to win the next 3 (1934, 1935, 1936). In 1924 they played 6 games in conjunction with the Women's Olympics and also in Paris at the invitation of Fédération Sportive Feminine Internationale, who declared the Grads world champions. In 1928 they won the French and European championships and they played 9 games in conjunction with the Berlin Olympics (1936). In their 3 European tours the Grads won all 24 games they played. At the time of their retirement, the Grads held 108 titles at local, provincial, western, national, international and world levels.

During the Grads' 25-year career, there were only 48 players listed in the official game reports. Allowing for an original core of 5 players, the average turnover was fewer than 2 players a year.

All but 2 of these came from the school at which Page taught. The Grads' competitive success was accompanied by the respect they earned in Canada and abroad. Edmontonians regarded them proudly as representatives of the city, while eastern sportswriters hailed them as a national institution. Perhaps the finest compliment came from the inventor of basketball, Dr James NAISMITH, who called them "the finest basketball team that ever stepped out on a floor."   CATHY MACDONALD

Edmonton Journal was founded as the *Evening Journal* 11 Nov 1903 by John Macpherson, John W. Cunningham and Arthur Moore, all of Portage La Prairie. The first issue of 1000 was produced on a hand-fed press and marked Edmonton's first telegraphic news service, but by 1908 the NEWSPAPER's position was precarious. In 1909, J.P. McConnell, publisher of *Vancouver Sunset* and founding editor of *Vancouver Sun*, had an option on *The Journal* and turned it over to J.H. Woods, also owner of the *Lethbridge News*. Woods declared political independence for the formerly Conservative paper and hired Milton Robbins Jennings as manager and editor. A former advertising manager of the Washington (DC) *Times*, Jennings' career included the *Montreal Herald, Toronto Mail and Empire* and *Toronto Telegram*. Under Jenning's, *Journal* readership soared. William SOUTHAM and Sons acquired a controlling interest in 1912, the year Jennings hired A. Balmer Watt, editor and owner of the financially troubled *Edmonton Capital,* as associate editor. Watt and Jennings launched a vigorous editorial campaign championing women's rights. Jennings died suddenly in 1921 of ailments contracted as a Spanish American War correspondent in Cuba. John Mills Imrie became managing director and appointed Watt editor-in-chief. Their battle against the Press Act of William Aberhart's SOCIAL CREDIT government won a special Pulitzer Award in 1938, the first ever bestowed outside the US. The *Journal* continues its editorial tradition and has won several national awards and citations for coverage of human rights issues. It has a strong interest in northern affairs and staffs a permanent bureau in the NWT. The *Journal* is one of Canada's most technologically advanced newspapers, publishing on 27 full-colour, computerized, automated Goss Metroliner presses. In 1984 the *Journal* became the first Canadian newspaper to

employ direct satellite links in transmission of colour photographs and in 1987 implemented advanced design and composition technology. Largest newspaper in Alberta, *The Journal*'s circulation district extends from Innisfail in the south, into Saskatchewan and British Columbia, and as far north as Inuvik on the Beaufort Sea. In 1987 the newspaper's average paid circulation Mon-Thurs and Sat was 160 934; Fri 195 438; and Sun 142 466, with a total readership of 498 838.   STEPHEN HUME

Edmonton Oilers, HOCKEY team. One of the World Hockey Association's (WHA) original franchises, they were known as the Alberta Oilers in the league's first season (1972-73), representing Edmonton and Calgary. Thereafter solely Edmonton's team, they moved into the new Northlands Coliseum in 1974 (since expanded to 17 308 seats) and into respectability as a hockey power in 1978 when the club's third owner, Peter Pocklington, acquired Wayne GRETZKY from erstwhile partner Nelson Skalbania. After losing to the Winnipeg Jets in the last WHA championship series (1979), they joined the NHL's Smythe Division and became the most rapidly successful expansion franchise in league history. Under coach, general manager and president Glen Sather, they captured the STANLEY CUP in only their fifth NHL season (1983-84), repeating the feat the following season and again in 1987, with outstanding performances by Gretzky, Mark Messier, Jari Kurri, Glenn Anderson and Grant Fuhr. In this period, the team has shattered practically every NHL point- and goal-scoring record.

DEREK DRAGER

Edmonton Symphony Orchestra, the successor to several previous orchestras in the city, was established in 1952 under conductor Lee Hepner. Thomas Rolston served as acting conductor, 1960-64, until Brian Priestman became conductor and music director. He was succeeded by Lawrence Leonard in 1968, Pierre HÉTU in 1973 and Uri Mayer since 1981. In addition to its subscription series and special concerts, the ESO performs for the ALBERTA BALLET COMPANY and Edmonton Opera Assn productions. It regularly travels in Alberta and has toured to the Yukon, the NWT and BC.   BARBARA NOVAK

Edmundston, NB, City, pop 11 497 (1986c), 12 044 (1981c), inc 1952, is nestled on the eastern bank of the SAINT JOHN R, opposite Madawaska, Maine, and 285 km above FREDERICTON. Initially called Little Falls (as contrasted with GRAND FALLS, 57 km downriver), it was renamed in 1848 in honour of Lt-Gov Sir Edmund Head. It was first settled as early as 1790 by ACADIANS who relocated from St Anne's Point (Fredericton) at the time of the LOYALIST influx. During the 19th century the community's population was supplemented by small numbers of English-speaking immigrants and by a protracted immigration of French-speaking settlers from Québec. For many years now, Edmundston has been the ski resort for much of western NB and the centre of francophone awareness, as embodied in the mythical "république du Madawaska." Since establishing a division in Edmundston in 1911, Fraser Inc has expanded from a sawmill operation to a pulp mill and has grown to be the city's primary employer. Collège St-Louis, an affiliate of U DE MONCTON, is situated here.   FRED FARRELL

Edmonton Grads, photo taken in 1923 after the Grads won the Underwood International Trophy (*courtesy Provincial Archives of Alberta/A-11413*).

Edson, Alta, Town, pop 7323 (1986c), 5835 (1981c), inc 1911, distribution centre for a mining, timber and oil area 200 km due W of Edmonton. Named for Edson J. Chamberlain, president of the GRAND TRUNK RY 1912-17, it was founded in 1910 as a divisional point, some 100 km from the mountains. It served as a point of departure to the PEACE RIVER country, via a trail to GRANDE PRAIRIE, until 1916.   ERIC J. HOLMGREN

Edson, Aaron Allan, landscape painter (b at Standbridge, Qué 18 Dec 1846; d at Glen-Sutton, Qué 1 May 1888). His first teacher (around 1863) was likely Robert Duncanson, an American artist living in Montréal, and later he studied in London, Eng. A founding member of the Soc of Canadian Artists, he exhibited in their first exhibition (1868). By the 1870s he was considered one of Canada's foremost landscape painters. He lived in Cernay-la-Ville, France, in the early 1880s, becoming a student of Barbizon painter Léon Pelouse, and in London in 1886-87. In 1887 he settled in the Eastern Townships, Qué. His early paintings (eg, *Sheep in Landscape,* 1869) show a quietude of mood, a strong interest in the effect of light and observation of detail, and warm, rich colour. His later work (*The Coming Storm, Lake Memphremagog,* 1880) is more dramatic. His best Canadian work synthesizes the influence of current American, British and French painting in a distinctive personal style.   JOYCE ZEMANS

Education is a basic activity of human association in any social group or community, regardless of size. It is a part of the regular interaction within a family, business or nation. The process whereby people gain knowledge, acquire understanding, master skills or internalize values is referred to as education. This same term is used to describe the outcomes of educational experiences. In other words, we may speak of education to refer to what school, television or recreational activity offer people or we may use the same term to indicate what the participants or viewers have received from their involvement in these educational experiences.

In human societies the maintenance and enhancement of the knowledge, skills and values of the group depend on instruction and learning. Failure to share and to pass on its social heritage leads to the eventual extinction of the group. For example, at the level of the FAMILY, our most basic social group, unless the members of the unit find ways to identify, preserve, communicate and share the beliefs, traditions, values and essential characteristics of the group, in time, the cohesiveness of the family will be lost, individual members will not identify with the unit or the name and new relationships with different norms and interests will replace it.

People in all of the varying roles and responsibilities of society share and acquire information, skills, attitudes and values. Whether raising a family, earning a living, administering a large corporation or conversing with friends, education occurs and is received. In its broadest sense education includes the total range and variety of processes evident in a social group or community by which the social heredity of the unit is maintained. The less knowledgeable and less experienced members of the group depend on educational experiences which will help them build on the established learning and practice of their predecessors. If this function was not performed, progress would be limited and slow. In more primitive or simple societies, the function of education is, relatively speaking, not as obvious: the more meagre the social life of a group, the less complex its knowledge and traditions and the less demanding and essential is the task of sharing and acquiring its social heritage. In groups of limited

sophistication, the less knowledgeable and less experienced members learn acceptable behaviour by imitating their elders, by obeying injunctions, by following suggestions and responding to prohibitions. As the complexity of the society increases and as the store of knowledge, traditions and values expand, the difference between those who possess the heritage and those who do not is more pronounced. Whereas in simple society no particular agency is charged with the responsibility of educating, in the more advanced social groups an institutionalized system emerges with specific agencies being charged with this responsibility. The emergence of schools, colleges and universities and other related institutions does not obviate the educational function of other social agencies. Instead it leads to the distinction between formal and informal education.

Formal education is the effort to do systematically and explicitly by means of specialist roles and functions what formerly transpired in the casual intercourse of family and community living. The differentiated system of education known as schooling has been charged with ever expanding duties and responsibilities. Initially the invention of letters that required specialist training for mastery and use gave rise to the role of teacher and the emergence of schools. Over time, this learning was not restricted to a privileged elite, but came to be regarded as the legitimate possession of all who had the ability to master it. Schooling has come to be regarded as a right of citizenship. An equally compelling reason for its growth and popularity is the belief that industrial and economic expansion depend on education. Leading industrial nations look to their schools to provide the training essential to continued economic and political prominence.

As important as formal SCHOOL SYSTEMS have become in modern society the influence and interplay of all educational influences should not be overlooked. The Royal Commission on National Development in the Arts, Letters and Sciences, 1949-51, defined education as "the progressive development of the individual in all his faculties, physical and intellectual, aesthetic and moral." The result of such disciplined growth, according to the commission, was the educated person who has fully realized his or her human possibilities. Three means or instruments for achieving this end were identified: common life experiences; various sources of popular culture and information such as television, radio, newspapers, magazines and books; and formal education in schools, colleges and universities. Development in each of these areas is essential to an understanding of education in Canada.

Common life experiences, according to the commission, were seen to be available through socializing agencies such as the family, the church, the government and the community. Traditionally, the family has been the most powerful of all educational institutions. Changing social conditions have had a noticeable effect on the influence of this agency within Canadian society. As an increasing number of married women are being employed outside the home, as the number of marriage dissolutions and single parents increases, and as nontraditional forms of marriage arrangements expand, the impact of the traditional family is lessened and other agencies such as the school are being expected to fill the educational void. Topics such as sex education, consumer spending and life skills are being turned over to the school along with extensive counselling responsibilities. As cohesion and solidarity of the contemporary Canadian family decline, so too does the effectiveness and influence of this educational agency.

The church, another social institution that once enjoyed a prominent role in the socializing of societal members, is also experiencing a diminished effect in the lives of Canadians. Until the mid-20th century, the 3 major churches in Canada — the Roman Catholic Church, the United Church of Canada and the Anglican Church — exerted significant influences on Canadian ethics and morals and provided obvious support to the maintenance of prevailing economic, social and political views. Membership and affiliation for many Canadians now is nominal in nature. Harmony of belief is less characteristic among Canadians as the authority of churches and clerics has been challenged, as religious views are less popular in a more materialistic society and as new religions within the Christian tradition and from outside gain in prominence.

Tensions and conflicts accompanying marked demographic changes in society also contribute to the increasing pluralism of Canadian life and the related difficulty of identifying and providing common socializing experiences. When the majority of Canadians were rural dwellers, their communities were perceived to be relatively homogeneous, closely knit and supportive of similar ideals and values. There was greater compatibility of the educational efforts and goals of the various socializing agencies. But in the 70-year period between 1901 and 1971 the percentage of Canada's rural population declined from roughly 62% to 24%, and the values associated with a rural economy and life-style were undermined and replaced. Impersonal relations and anonymity challenged feelings of closeness and mutual support. New social agencies and roles emerged and traditional institutions such as schools and churches took on modified responsibilities in an attempt to cope with social change and an obviously growing divergence of perspective. Another significant contributor to the mounting diversity in beliefs, practices and values in Canada was the introduction of large numbers of immigrants into Canada in the late 19th and early 20th centuries. Particularly since 1901 the proportion of the population composed of ethno-religious groups other than the founding French and English elements has increased from approximately 12% to nearly 27%. The declaration in Oct 1971 of an official Canadian policy of "multiculturalism within a bilingual framework" gave recognition to a cultural reality. Pluralism was an acknowledged condition and latitude was extended to those who wished to preserve their unique ethnic and linguistic roots. One effect of growing pluralism in Canada has been to expect more of schools in building a common culture and to compensate for diminishing contributions of families, churches and communities.

The Massey Commission also expressed concern over the effects of living in such close proximity to the US. The commission members recognized the importance of the mass media as a vital element of education particularly as American popular culture became more pervasive within Canada (see CULTURAL POLICY). While the influence of the traditional socializing agencies has been waning in Canada, the power of the mass media has been increasing significantly. From their earliest years children are subject to the influence of the media. Television, especially, has become the purveyor of values, beliefs and knowledge. Time formerly spent in discussing, playing or reading is now more commonly associated with television viewing as children are often left to watch unattended. The average Canadian watches 26.6 hours of television per week and cable and satellite broadcast facilities afford viewers wide choice in program selection with extensive exposure to American programs. Recognizing the educative influence of TV, the Canadian Radio-Television Commission stated in 1986 that it was working to "safeguard, enrich and strengthen the cultural, political, social and economic fabric of Canada."

One effect of all forms of mass media is that peoples' perspectives are broadened. The result in countries where information access is valued and sustained, is that the educational power of the media is pronounced, and leads to greater openness, pluralism and relatavism. The media, in testing public attitudes, also serve to influence and to shape them. Published sources, including books and newspapers, are important instruments of education (see LITERACY).

Film also contributes to the education of Canadians. The film viewing of Canadians is dominated by access to films produced in the US. Canadians, by an Act of Parliament established the NATIONAL FILM BOARD in 1939, charging it with the mandate "to initiate and promote the production of films in the national interest." Produced in Canada's 2 official languages, the films of the NFB depict events that shaped history and show the diversity of Canadian concerns and achievement. The efforts of the NFB are recognition of the value of this medium as an educational agent in providing a common Canadian viewpoint. However, the rapid expansion and popularity of television is overshadowing that of film in Canada, as videotape production now exceeds that of film production.

As prominent and important as are the socializing agencies and informal educational means of the mass media in Canada, the formal educational system is recognized as being central to the experience of the large majority of Canadians. Within Canada, residents of all ages and circumstances have come to seek and gain access to schools, universities and colleges. Relatively early in Canada's history, attention was directed to making some provision for schooling. The first teachers in Canada, 4 priests, came with Champlain in 1616. As settlements were established, *petites écoles* under the direction of parish priests became relatively common. The foundations of the present-day Canadian educational system were laid in the 19th century, with Egerton RYERSON playing an important role. Through his work in Canada West (present-day Ontario), a free, universal, nonsectarian and compulsory school system was established.

Provision of schooling has not been easy or inexpensive for Canadians, in part because of the vastness of the country and the sparsity of population. However, efforts have been made through the proliferation of one-room country schools which dotted the countryside even up to the outbreak of WWII and through novel arrangements such as railway and correspondence schools to extend schooling to as many children as possible. The importance assigned to education by Canadians over the years is evident

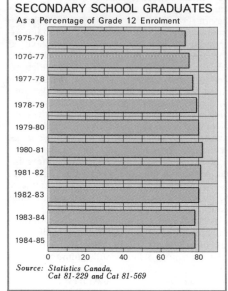

SECONDARY SCHOOL GRADUATES
As a Percentage of Grade 12 Enrolment

1975-76
1976-77
1977-78
1978-79
1979-80
1980-81
1981-82
1982-83
1983-84
1984-85

0 20 40 60 80

Source: Statistics Canada, Cat 81-229 and Cat 81-569

in the financial commitment made to provide it. Canada tends to spend a higher proportion of its Gross Domestic Product on education than other Western developed countries. In 1985-86 educational expenditures represented 7.6% of Canada's Gross Domestic Product.

Formal education within Canada has been subject to and influenced by American developments. As progressive education and the ideas of American educators such as John Dewey, W.H. Kilpatrick and George Counts found acceptance in the US between WWI and WWII, these same practices and ideas attracted attention in Canada. School curricula and methods were altered in all provinces to give place to learning by doing, integration of subject areas, individualized learning and instruction of the whole child. While the popularity of the movement subsided in the post-WWII era, the impact of the reform carried on. Schools have come to provide for a wider range of students, to offer a highly diversified curriculum, to be less authoritarian and to be willing to assume responsibility for an ever-increasing number of duties and responsibilities, many of which have resulted from the declining effectiveness of other social agencies such as the family.

The value and importance of education in Canada is seen in the increasing numbers who are pursuing post-secondary learning experiences. Lower birthrates and lower immigration help to account for the steady decline in elementary and secondary enrolment over the last 2 decades. In this same period, when elementary and secondary enrolment dropped 16%, full-time post-secondary numbers increased 4%. UNIVERSITY enrolment in 1986 made up 59% of the total, but the rate of increase over the last 2 decades was lower in universities than in community colleges where

full-time enrolment increased 48% from 1970-71 to 1985-86. Traditionally, there have been social and economic reasons for acquiring higher educational standards. Higher status occupations are generally awarded to people who hold college or university degrees. And on the economic side, better education appears to have raised labour earnings per worker by about 30% from 1911-61, according to one estimate.

Although the growth in provision of formal education reflects a continuing faith in the advantages of formal education, there is no longer an assurance that more education will result in employment or better-paying jobs. Many highly educated people are unemployed or underemployed, and some futurists predict that an increasing number of people will never be engaged in work as it is known in the 1980s. However, educational reforms and reviews undertaken across Canada continue to emphasize the need for schools to concentrate, more than they have in the recent past, on the preparation of students for useful work.

So inclusive has the mandate for schooling become that it is difficult to determine what themes or topics can or should be legitimately excluded. Relatively little attention seems to be paid to matters relating to ecology, world peace and imbalances in food, wealth and educational opportunity. UNESCO has identified the following as some of the important global issues deserving attention through education: the grievous inequalities among nations and peoples; the risk of growing dehumanization affecting both privileged and oppressed alike; the need for people to understand the global consequences of individual behaviour, of conceiving priorities and sharing of the joint responsibility in determining the destiny of the human race; and the need to give strong support to democracy as the only way to avoid becoming enslaved to machines, and as the only condition compatible with the dignity of the human race.

UNESCO recognized the lifelong nature of education as well as the fact that education occurs in many contexts within society. A multiplicity of out-of-school forms of learning must be used in providing instruction and education for pupils of all ages, adults included. However organized education provides systems of knowledge and methods which help and enable individuals to form their own personal interpretation of the tremendous information flow and to assimilate it in a useful way, it remains an essential element of society. The direction of education for the future is captured in the following observation, also from the UNESCO publication *Learning to Be:* "if learning involves all of one's life, in the sense of both timespan and diversity, and all of society, including its social and economic as well as its educational resources, then we must go even farther than the necessary overhaul of educational systems until we reach the stage of a learning society."

R.S. PATTERSON AND N. KACH

Artist's rendition of Canada as seen from far
above the Arctic Archipelago. Courtesy
Northern Transportation Company Limited.